Need an eleven-letter word meaning "fear of crowds"?

EASY.

Just look up **fear** (of)" in the alphabetical listing. Go down the list of alphabetized subcategories to *crowds*. And there it is—"ochlophobia."

The unique, convenient arrangement and design of this wonderful new dictionary makes it fast and easy to find just the word you need to fill in those baffling spaces. The words you want are listed by number of letters. You'll also find variant spellings and subcategories, and it's all arranged alphabetically under clue words.

Make puzzle solving more fun—and the results letter-perfect—with the newest and best crossword dictionary you can buy!

Webster's New World

Crossword
Puzzle
Dictionary

**COMPILED BY
JANE SHAW WHITFIELD**

PUBLISHED BY POCKET BOOKS NEW YORK

POCKET BOOKS, a division of Simon & Schuster, Inc.
1230 Avenue of the Americas, New York, N.Y. 10020

Copyright © 1975 by Jane Shaw Whitfield

Published by arrangement with William Collins + World
Publishing Company, Inc.
Library of Congress Card Number: 75-926

ISBN: 0-671-53268-5

First Pocket Books printing May, 1977

22 21 20 19 18 17 16 15 14 13

Webster's New World

Crossword Puzzle Dictionary

FOREWORD

This reference work has been compiled especially for the millions who enjoy solving crossword puzzles and for those who construct them. But because of its comprehensive coverage of rare, arcane, technical, and dialectal terms, as well as of many proper names from geography, literature, the Bible, and the like, it is also an invaluable aid to those who enjoy solving other kinds of word puzzles or playing word games. And its listings of synonyms and of identifying facts about persons, places, and things make it as well a useful thesaurus and general reference book for the home library.

Unlike some other puzzle dictionaries on the market, this one is not merely a mechanical listing of words of six letters or fewer, offering no clue as to meanings. This list contains answers actually found in a survey of thousands of puzzles, and so you will discover here words of from two to fourteen or more letters, as well as phrases and compounds of two or more words, of the kind frequently encountered in puzzles today, such as "in a trice" for "instantly" or "black eye" for "contusion."

A special feature of this book is the arrangement of the materials. All clue words are in bold-face type, alphabetically arranged, with subcategories, where these exist, in italic type, also in alphabetical order. The answer terms for each clue are arranged by the count of letters in each word (or phrase), in numerical order. Each group of answers with the same letter count are then arranged alphabetically to help you find quickly the solution to your problem fill-in.

For example: you need the six-letter name of a Greek sun god. You turn to **Greek god of,** find the subcategory *sun,* and discover after the numeral **6** the two names "Apollo" and "Helios." If you have even one letter of the answer already filled in, you know immediately which is the correct name.

In general, words are shown with their prevailing spellings, but certain rarer variants that commonly appear in puzzles are also given. Although upper-case and lower-case distinctions, and accents on foreign words, are insignificant in crossword puzzle practice, the other uses to which this book will undoubtedly be put made it desirable to observe these orthographic conventions.

So to all enthusiasts of crossword puzzles and to their creators, I hereby dedicate this *Webster's New World Crossword Puzzle Dictionary*.

Jane Shaw Whitfield

ABBREVIATIONS USED IN THIS WORK

Abbr	Abbreviation
abdom	abdominal
aborig	aboriginal
Acad	Academy
adj	adjective
adm	admitted
Afr	African
Agric	Agriculture
Alex	Alexander
Am Ind	American Indian
Anat	Anatomy
anc	ancient
Anglo-Ir	Anglo-Irish
Anthrop	Anthropology
Antiq	Antiquity
Arab	Arabian
Arch	Architecture
Archaeol	Archaeology
Astrol	Astrology
Astron	Astronomy
Austral	Australia(n)
Babyl	Babylonia
Belg	Belgium
Bib	Bible, Biblical
Biol	Biology
Bot	Botany
Braz	Brazil(ian)
Brit	Britain, British
Brit Col	British Columbia
Buddh	Buddhism
Bus	Business
Can	Canada, Canadian
Capt	Captain

Caucas	Caucasian
Celt	Celtic
Cent	Central, Century
Cent Am	Central America
Chem	Chemistry
Chin	Chinese
Chr	Christian
coll	colloquialism
comb form	combining form
Confed	Confederation
Constell	Constellation
contemp	contemporary
Criminol	Criminology
Dan	Danish
Dept	Department
derog	derogatory
dial	dialectal
div	division
Du	Dutch
E	East
East Ch	Eastern Church
Eccl	Ecclesiastical
Educ	Education
Egypt	Egyptian
Elec	Electricity
Eng	England, English
Episcop	Episcopal
equiv	equivalent
Esk	Eskimo
est	established
Eur	Europe(an)

exclam	exclamation
ext	extinct
FDR	Franklin D. Roosevelt
Fem	Feminine
Finan	Finance, Financial
Flem	Flemish
Fr	France, French
Gen	General
Geog	Geography
Geol	Geology
Geom	Geometry
Ger	German
Gov	Governor
Govt	Government
Gr	Greek
Gram	Grammar
Gr Brit	Great Britain
Haw	Hawaiian
Heb	Hebrew
Hem	Hemisphere
Her	Heraldry
Hind	Hinduism
Hindu	Hindustani
Hist	Historical
Holl	Holland
Horol	Horology
Hung	Hungarian
illeg	illegal
Ind	India, Indian
Indo-Chin	Indo-China
Ins	Insurance
Internat	International
Ir	Irish
irreg	irregular
Isl(s)	Island(s)
It	Italian
Jap	Japanese
Jew	Jewish
L	Latin
Legislat	Legislature
Lit	Literature
Log	Logic
Maced	Macedonia
Malay	Malayan
Math	Mathematics
MD	Doctor of Medicine
Med	Medical
Mex	Mexican
Mil	Military

Mohamm	Mohammedan
Mt(s)	Mountain(s)
Mus	Music
Myth	Mythology
Nat'l	National
Naut	Nautical
Nav	Naval, Navy
neg	negative
New Test	New Testament
NZ	New Zealand
No	North
No Am	North American
obs	obsolete
Old Test	Old Testament
opp	opposite
Orient	Oriental
Oxf Univ	Oxford University
Penol	Penology
Pers	Persian
pert	pertaining
Petrol	Petrology
Pg	Portuguese
Pharm	Pharmaceutical
Philat	Philately
Phil I	Philippine Islands
Philol	Philology
Philos	Philosophy
Phonet	Phonetics
Phys	Physical
pl	plural
PO	Post Office
poet	poetic
Polit	Politics, Political
Polyn	Polynesian
ppty	property
pref	prefix
P Rico	Puerto Rico
Pros	Prosody
R	Roman
RCCh	Roman Catholic Church
Rd	Road
ref	referring
Relig	Religion
R Estate	Real Estate
Rev War	Revolutionary War
Rhet	Rhetoric
Riv	River
Rom	Roman
rr	railroad
Rum	Rumania
Russ	Russian

S	South
Scot	Scotland, Scottish
Scand	Scandinavian
Shakesp	Shakespeare
sing	singular
sl	slang
Slav	Slavonic
So Afr	South Africa
So Am	South America
Sp	Spanish
Surg	Surgical
sym	symbol
Tag	Tagalog
Tahit	Tahiti
Terat	Teratology
terr	territory
Teut	Teutonic
Theat	Theatrical
Theol	Theology
Theos	Theosophy
triang	triangular
TID	Ter in die

Trop	Tropical
Turk	Turkish
TV	Television
U	Union
Univ	University
USS	United States Ship
USSR	Union of Soviet Socialist Republics
Vet	Veterinary
W	West
WAC	Women's Army Corps
W Indies	West Indies
WWI	World War I
Yidd	Yiddish
YMCA	Young Men's Christian Association
yr	year
Zool	Zoology

Webster's New World
Crossword Puzzle Dictionary

A

A... 5. alpha, first 7. article
A 1... 5. prime 6. symbol 8. superior 10. first–class
aa (Haw)... 4. lava
aal... 8. morindin (dye), mulberry
aam (Du)... 7. measure (liquid) 11. water bucket
Aani (Egypt)... 3. ape (sacred) 6. baboon 12. cynocephalus
aardvark... 3. pig 6. farrow 8. anteater
aardwolf... 5. hyena 8. Proteles
Aaron (pert to)...
  ally (Bib).. 3. Hur
  brother.. 5. Moses
  burial place.. 3. Hor
  leader (Jew).. 9. Levitical 10. High Priest
  rod.. 4. wand (magic) 7. molding, mullein
  sister.. 6. Miriam
  son.. 5. Abihu, Nadab
Aaru (Egypt Relig)... 12. fields of Aaru 14. abode of the dead
aasvogel... 7. vulture
abaca... 4. hemp 5. lupis 6. linaga
abacus... 4. slab 8. cupboard 10. calculator 11. compartment
Abaddon... 3. pit (bottomless) 4. Hell 5. Sheol 8. Apollyon (angel) 11. destruction
abaft... 3. aft 5. after 6. astern, behind
abalone... 5. awabi, ormer, uhllo (ullo) 6. sea ear 8. ear shell
abandon... 4. quit 5. cease, leave, remit, waive, yield 6. abjure, depart, desert, disuse, give up, maroon, reject, resign, vacate 7. cast off, discard, forsake, freedom, neglect 8. abdicate, forswear, renounce 9. surrender, turpitude 10. relinquish 11. abandonment, discontinue, unrestraint 12. carelessness, heedlessness
abandoned... 4. left, lost 7. disused, forlorn, given up 8. derelict, deserted, forsaken 9. desolated, discarded, neglected 11. surrendered 12. relinquished, unredeemable, unrestrained
abase... 5. lower, shame 6. bemean, depose, humble, reduce 7. degrade, mortify 8. cast down, disgrace 9. humiliate 10. depreciate
abash... 5. shame 6. appall, dismay 7. astound, confuse, disturb, mortify 8. bewilder, confound 9. discomfit, embarrass, humiliate 10. disconcert, put to shame
abate... 3. ebb 4. lull, wane 5. let up, relax, remit 6. deduct, lessen,

reduce 7. abolish, nullify, qualify, slacken, subside 8. decrease, diminish, discount, moderate
abatement... 5. letup 6. myosis (miosis), rebate 8. decrease 9. lessening, reduction 10. diminution, mitigation, moderation
abb... 4. wool, yarn 6. fleece (pert to)
Abba... 5. abbot, title 6. Father
abbe... 4. monk 6. cleric, curate, priest
abbess... 4. amma 15. spiritual mother
abbreviate... 5. brief, curtail, shorten 8. compress, condense, contract, simplify 9. epitomize 11. make briefer
abbreviation... 5. brief, lapse 6. digest 8. abstract 9. reduction 10. abridgment, compendium, shortening 11. contraction 12. condensation
abdicate... 4. cede, quit 5. demit, leave 6. depose, disown, resign, retire 7. lay down 8. disclaim, renounce, withdraw 9. surrender 10. disinherit, relinquish
Abdiel (Heb)... 5. angel 12. servant of God
abdomen... 3. pot (sl) 4. wame 5. belly, tharm (obs) 6. paunch, venter 7. stomach 8. potbelly 12. pelvic cavity
abdominal... 7. coeliac, gastric, ventral 11. ventricular
abdominal limb (crustacean)... 7. pleopod
Abel's brother... 4. Cain, Seth
aberration... 5. mania, wrong 6. lunacy, oddity 7. errancy, madness 9. dementia, insanity 9. departure, deviation, variation, wandering 10. alienation, digression, divergence 11. abnormality, derangement, distraction, peculiarity 12. eccentricity, irregularity 14. disorientation
abet... 3. aid, egg 4. back, help 5. egg on 6. assist, foment, incite, second, succor, uphold 7. connive, endorse, support, sustain 8. advocate 9. encourage, instigate 11. countenance
abeyance... 4. rest, stay 5. lapse, pause 7. waiting 9. inertness 10. expectancy, suspension
abhor... 2. ug 4. hate, shun 6. detest, loathe 7. despise, dislike 8. execrate 9. abominate
abhorrence... 5. odium 6. hatred, horror 7. dislike 8. aversion, loathing 9. antipathy, disliking, repulsion

1

10. repugnance

abide... 4. bide, live, stay, wait
5. await, dwell, pause, tarry
6. endure, remain, reside 7. sojourn
8. continue, submit to, tolerate
9. acquiesce, withstand

abide by... 3. own 4. avow, heed
5. admit, allow, yield 6. accept,
follow, regard 7. concede, respect
8. adhere to 9. conform to
11. acknowledge

abiding... 7. durable, lasting
8. constant, enduring 9. permanent,
steadfast 10. continuing, indwelling,
persisting

Abies... 4. firs 5. pines 8. conifers
10. evergreens

abigail... 4. ayah, maid 5. bonne
7. servant 9. soubrette

Abijah's son (Bib)... 3. Asa

ability... 4. gift 5. force, might,
power, skill 6. genius, talent
7. caliber, faculty, fitness, potency
8. aptitude, capacity, strength
10. capability, competence, efficiency
11. proficiency, sufficiency
13. qualification

abiosis... 11. without life

abject... 3. low 4. base, mean, meek,
vile 6. humble, menial, supine
7. hangdog, ignoble, servile, slavish
8. beggarly, contrite, cringing,
degraded, wretched 9. groveling,
miserable 10. despicable, obsequious

abjuration... 6. denial 8. palinode
(song), yielding 9. disavowal,
rejection, surrender 10. abjurement,
retraction, withdrawal
11. abandonment, forswearing,
recantation, repudiation
12. disclamation 14. relinquishment

abjure... 4. deny, wave 6. disown,
recant, reject, revoke 7. abandon,
disavow 8. disclaim, forswear,
renounce 9. disaffirm, repudiate

able... 3. can, fit 5. adept, smart
6. clever, fitted, suited 7. adapted,
capable, learned, solvent 8. adjusted,
literate, powerful, skillful (skilful),
vigorous 9. competent, effective,
efficient, qualified 10. omnipotent,
proficient

able (pert to)...
suffix.. 7. capable, fitness
to pay.. 7. moneyed, solvent
8. affluent 10. prosperous
to read and write.. 8. lettered, literate
10. book taught

ablepsia... 9. blindness

ably... 7. capably 11. competently,
effectively, efficiently

abnormal... 6. albino 7. erratic,
unusual 8. aberrant 9. deviative,
eccentric, irregular, unnatural
11. exceptional 13. extraordinary

aboard... 4. onto 6. across 7. athwart
9. alongside

abode... 3. dar, hut 4. cell, cote,
Eden, home 5. delay, house, lodge
7. habitat, Olympus, sojourn
8. dwelling, tenement 9. apartment,
residence 10. habitation

abode of the dead... 3. Dar 4. Aalu,
Aaru, Hell 5. Aralu, Hades, limbo,
Orcus, Sheol 6. Asgard, heaven,
Naraka 7. Abaddon, Elysium, Nirvana
8. paradise, Valhalla 9. perdition,
purgatory 11. Pandemonium

abolish... 4. undo 5. annul, quash
6. cancel, recall, repeal, revoke,
vacate 7. destroy, nullify, rescind,
retract, reverse 8. abrogate, withdraw
10. annihilate, invalidate
11. countermand

abominable... 4. base, dire, foul, vile
5. awful, gross 6. odious, wicked,
woeful 7. beastly, hateful 8. dreadful,
grievous, infamous, shocking, terrible,
wretched 9. execrable, loathsome,
obnoxious 10. despicable, detestable,
outrageous, unpleasant
12. disagreeable, disreputable

Abominable Snowman... 4. Yeti

abominate... 4. hate 5. abhor
6. detest, loathe 8. execrate

abomination... 3. woe 4. evil
5. odium, wrong 6. hatred, horror,
plague 7. disgust, outrage
8. aversion, loathing, vexation
9. grievance 10. abhorrence,
defilement, odiousness, repugnance

aboriginal... 5. first, natal 6. binghi,
native 7. ancient 8. original
9. beginning, primitive
10. autochthon, indigenous

aborigines... 4. Ainu (Aino), Toda
5. lubra, Sakai, Vedda 7. cave men,
Indians, natives, savages
9. indigenes, old–timers
10. Dravidians 11. preadamites

abortion... 6. arrest 7. failure
11. embryoctomy, miscarriage,
miscreation 13. misconception

abound... 4. flow, teem 5. swarm
8. overflow 9. exuberate, plentiful

abounding... 4. rife 5. ample, flush
7. copious, teeming 8. abundant
9. exuberant, luxuriant, plentiful

abounding in...
blossoms.. 7. flowery
forests.. 6. sylvan
grass.. 6. cressy
snow.. 6. nival

about... 2. of, on, re 3. amb (pref)
5. anent, astir, circa 6. almost,
around, nearly 8. circiter
10. concerning 13. approximately

about to happen... 8. imminent

above... 2. on, up 3. o'er, sur (pref)
4. atop, over, upon 5. aloft, super,
supra (pref)

abrade... 3. rub 4. file, fret, gall
5. chafe, grate 6. scrape
9. excoriate

Abraham (pert to)...
birthplace.. 2. Ur
concubine.. 5. Hagar
father.. 5. Terah
grandfather.. 5. Nahor
grandson.. 4. Esau
nephew.. 3. Lot
son.. 4. Shua (Shuah) 5. Isaac,
Medan 7. Ishmael
wife.. 5. Sarah (Sara, Sarai)

    7. Keturah

abrasion... 4. flaw, gall, hurt 5. scuff
    6. lesion, scrape 8. limation
    9. attrition

abrasive... 4. file, sand 5. emery
    6. garnet, polish, pumice 7. erodent
    8. abradant, corundum 9. attritive,
    sandpaper

abraxas... 3. gem 5. charm, stone

Abraxas (pert to)...
    god (anc Gnostic).. 12. Supreme
    Deity
    source of mind.. 4. Nous
    the Word.. 5. Logos

abreast... 4. even (with) 6. beside
    8. opposite 9. alongside

abrege... 7. epitome 10. abridgment

abri... 4. shed 6. cavity, dugout
    7. shelter

abridge... 5. brief, razee (rasee)
    7. curtail, shorten 8. abstract,
    condense, diminish, retrench
    9. epitomize 10. abbreviate

abridgment... 6. digest 7. compend,
    epitome, summary 8. abstract,
    syllabus, synopsis 9. lessening,
    reduction 10. compendium,
    diminution 11. deprivation

abroad... 4. away 5. forth 6. astray,
    widely 7. at large, broadly, distant
    8. away from 9. spread out
    11. widely apart

abrogate... 5. annul, quash 6. cancel,
    repeal, revoke 7. abolish, rescind
    8. set aside 10. put an end to

abrogation... 8. quashing 9. annulling,
    cessation 10. rescinding, rescission
    11. dissolution

abrupt... 4. curt, rude 5. blunt, hasty,
    quick, sharp, sheer, steep, terse
    6. broken, craggy, sudden
    7. brusque 8. headlong, vertical
    9. broken off, impetuous
    10. unexpected 11. precipitous
    12. disconnected 13. perpendicular,
    unceremonious

abruptly... 7. briefly, in brief
    8. suddenly

Absalom (pert to)...
    father.. 5. David (King)
    host's captain.. 5. Amasa
    sister.. 5. Tamar
    slayer.. 4. Joab

abscond... 3. run 4. bolt, flee, hide
    5. elope 6. decamp, desert, eloine,
    levant 8. steal off

absence... 4. AWOL, lack, void, want
    5. exeat, leave 6. vacuum 7. silence
    10. deficiency, withdrawal
    13. nonappearance, nonattendance

absence of... (see also *without*)
    animal, plant.. 8. lipotype
    hair.. 6. acomia
    pain.. 8. anodynia
    pigment.. 8. alphosis
    self–worth.. 7. modesty
    taste.. 7. ageusia

absent... 3. off, out 4. away, gone,
    lost 6. dreamy, musing, truant
    7. lacking 8. absorbed 9. engrossed
    10. abstracted 11. preoccupied
    12. nonattendant

absinthe... 5. green (color) 6. ajenjo,
    liquor

absolute... 4. alod, dead, pure, real,
    true, very 5. freed, sheer, total,
    utter, whole 6. empery, simple
    7. certain, elative, perfect, plenary
    8. absolved, complete, positive
    9. arbitrary, downright, unlimited
    10. autocratic, disengaged,
    peremptory 11. categorical,
    independent 13. unconditional
    15. plenipotentiary

absolute (pert to)...
    dominion.. 6. empery
    property.. 4. alod 7. alodium
    sovereign.. 8. autocrat
    superlative.. 7. elative
    time.. 9. Greenwich, universal

absolutely... 3. yes, yes 5. stark
    6. wholly 7. utterly 8. entirely
    10. altogether, positively, thoroughly
    13. unequivocally 15. unconditionally

absolution... 6. pardon, shrive
    7. penance 9. acquittal, remission
    11. exculpation, forgiveness

absolve... 4. free 5. remit 6. acquit,
    finish, pardon 9. discharge, exonerate
    10. accomplish

absonant... 8. contrary 10. discordant
    12. unreasonable

absorb... 3. eat 4. soak, suck
    5. drink, eat up, learn, use up
    6. corner, digest, engulf, imbibe,
    soak up, sponge 7. consume,
    swallow 10. assimilate, monopolize,
    understand 11. incorporate

absorbed... 4. deep, lost, rapt, sunk
    6. buried, intent, lost in
    7. bemused, devoted, engaged
    8. occupied 9. engrossed
    11. monopolized, preoccupied

absorbent... 5. fomes 6. spongy
    7. blotter 9. adsorbent
    10. imbibitory

absorption... 10. imbibition

abstain... 4. deny, fast, hold, shun
    5. avoid, cease, waive
    6. eschew 7. forbear, refrain
    8. restrain, teetotal, withhold

abstemious... 5. sober 7. sparing
    8. moderate 9. abstinent, temperate
    11. abstentious

abstinence... 6. disuse 7. encraty
    8. sobriety 9. restraint, sacrifice
    10. abstention, continence,
    desistance, moderation, self–denial,
    temperance 11. abandonment,
    forbearance, self–control
    13. self–restraint
    14. abstemiousness, discontinuance

abstract... 4. deed, part, take 5. brief,
    steal 6. deduct, noetic (purely),
    remove 7. abridge, epitome, shorten,
    summary 8. argument, condense,
    syllabus, withdraw 9. capsulize,
    statement 10. abridgment,
    compendium 12. nonobjective

abstract being... 3. ens 6. entity

abstruse... 4. deep 6. hidden
    7. obscure 8. esoteric, profound
    9. concealed, recondite
    10. acroamatic (acroatic)

16. incomprehensible

absurd... 4. wild 5. droll, inept, silly
6. stupid 7. asinine, foolish
8. fabulous 9. ludicrous
10. impossible, irrational, ridiculous
11. incongruous, nonsensical
12. inconsistent, unbelievable,
unreasonable

absurdity... 7. twaddle 8. nonsense
10. absurdness 11. foolishness
13. contradiction, impossibility
14. ridiculousness 16. inconceivability

abundance... 4. mass, much, rife
5. ample 6. galore, plenty, riches,
volume 8. fullness (fulness),
opulence, overflow, quantity
9. affluence 10. exuberance
11. copiousness, superfluity
12. extravagance, generousness
13. plenteousness

abundant... 4. lush, much, rich, rife,
teem 5. ample 6. galore, plenty
7. copious, profuse 9. abounding,
exuberant, luxuriant, plentiful
10. sufficient

abundant, not... 5. spare 6. lenten,
meager (meagre)

abuse... 4. gall, harm, hurt, maul, rail,
rape 5. crime, curse, scold, snash
6. berate, ill use, injure, insult,
malign, misuse, ravish, revile
7. calumny, deceive, obloquy,
offense, pervert, traduce, upbraid
8. dishonor, maltreat, misapply,
reproach 9. contumely, disparage,
invective, violation 10. opprobrium,
revilement, scurrility
11. debauchment, malediction,
objurgation 12. mistreatment,
vituperation

abusive... 3. mud (throw)
10. scurrilous 12. catachrestic

abut... 4. butt, join 5. touch
6. adjoin, appose, border, rest on
7. conjoin, connect 8. adjacent,
neighbor

abutment... 4. arch, pier, wall
6. alette 7. abuttal, sea wall
8. buttress, shoulder 13. fortification

abysmal... 4. deep 7. yawning
8. profound, unending 9. plumbless
10. bottomless, fathomless

abyss... 3. pit 4. Absu, gulf, hell,
hole, void, well 5. abysm, chaos,
chasm, cleft, shaft 6. cavity, vorago
8. infernal regions

Abyssinia, Ethiopia...
capital.. 10. Addis Ababa
city.. 5. Aduwa, Aksum (Axum)
6. Gondar 7. Ankober, Gambela,
Magdala
dialect.. 4. Geez
Empire (old).. 7. Axumite
Hamite.. 4. Afar
King.. 13. Haile Selassie
kingdom (former).. 4. Shoa 5. Tigre
6. Amhara
population.. 7. Hamites, Semites
8. Negroids
river (famed).. 5. Abdai (Blue Nile)
sea.. 3. Red
title (anc).. 12. Negusa Nagast

Abyssinian (pert to)...
fly.. 4. zimb
gold (artificial).. 5. talmi
lyre.. 6. kissar
tea leaves.. 3. kat
wolf.. 6. kaberu

Academe, The... 14. Academy of Plato
(Athens)

academic... 5. ideal, rigid 6. formal
7. classic, attain, comply, concur,
pedantic, Platonic 9. scholarly
10. Ciceronian, scholastic
11. educational, impractical,
speculative, theoretical
12. conventional, hypothetical
13. institutional

academy... 5. école 6. lyceum,
manège, school, Schule 7. college,
escuela, society 8. academie,
seminary 9. accademia, institute
10. university 11. institution

Acadia... 6. Acadie 10. Nova Scotia

acarpous... 7. sterile 9. fruitless

acaudal... 7. anurous 8. tailless

accede... 5. agree, enter, grant, yield
6. assent, attain, comply, concur,
relent, submit 7. conform, consent
9. acquiesce 11. acknowledge

accelerate... 4. rush 5. speed
6. hasten, step up 7. advance,
forward, further, quicken 8. activate,
dispatch, expedite

acceleration... 5. haste 6. pickup
8. velocity 9. catalysis, hastening
10. expedition, quickening
11. advancement

accelerator... 6. muscle 7. speeder
8. throttle 9. quickener

accent... 4. beat, mark, tone 5. breve,
ictus, pitch, twang 6. brogue, stress
7. cadence, dialect 8. emphasis
9. emphasize 10. accentuate,
expression, inflection, modulation
12. accentuation

accent (pert to)...
Irish.. 4. blas 6. brogue
on last syllable.. 7. oxytone
Scot.. 4. birr
unaccented syllable.. 5. arsis

accept... 2. OK 3. buy, own 4. avow,
fang, take 5. admit, adopt, agree,
allow, grant, trust, yield 6. assent,
comply, credit, expect, ratify
7. approve, believe, certify, condone,
confess, consent, embrace, receive,
swallow (coll) 8. accredit, tolerate,
validate 9. undertake
11. countenance

accept (as one's own)...
12. nostrificate (of foreign degrees)

acceptable... 2. OK 6. worthy
7. welcome 8. eligible, passable,
pleasant, pleasing, suitable
9. agreeable, allowable, desirable,
expedient, qualified, tolerable
10. admissible 11. comfortable
12. satisfactory

accepted... 6. chosen, deemed
7. adopted, assumed, popular,
reputed, trusted 8. admitted,
approved, believed, credited,
embraced, espoused, inferred,

orthodox, received, standard,
supposed 9. customary, prevalent
10. accredited, understood,
undertaken 11. traditional
12. conventional, unquestioned
13. authoritative

access... 3. way 4. adit, door, gain
5. entry 6. avenue, entree, ingate,
tunnel 7. ingress 8. approach,
entrance, entryway, increase
9. accession, accretion, admission
10. admittance 11. entranceway
13. accessibility, attainability
15. approachability

accessible... 4. open 5. handy
6. open to, public 7. getable
8. amenable, pervious 9. admissive,
available, permeable, reachable,
receptive 10. attainable, obtainable,
open-minded, penetrable, procurable
11. persuasible 12. approachable
13. communicative

accession... 6. access, assent, attack,
growth 7. adjunct, consent, joining,
uniting 8. addition, increase
9. accretion, agreement, increment
10. acceptance, affixation,
annexation, attainment, compliance,
concession, coronation
12. acquiescence 13. reinforcement
14. aggrandizement

accessory, accessary... 5. extra, party
7. abettor 8. addition, litigant
9. adjective, appendage, assistant,
attendant, auxiliary, obbligato
10. accomplish, additional, collateral,
subsidiary 11. appurtenant,
concomitant, participant
12. accompanying, appurtenance,
contributory, nonessential, participator
13. accompaniment, supplementary

accident... 3. hap 4. luck 6. chance,
hazard, mishap 8. calamity, casualty,
disaster 9. adventure, befalling,
mischance 10. misfortune
11. catastrophe

accidental... 6. casual, chance
9. unwitting 10. contingent,
unforeseen, unintended

acclaim... 4. hail, laud 6. praise
7. applaud 8. applause
11. acclamation, approbation

acclamation... 3. cry, joy 5. shout
7. acclaim, ovation, plaudit
8. applause, approval 9. unanimity

acclimate... 5. adapt, inure 6. adjust,
season 8. accustom 9. condition,
habituate 10. naturalize
11. acclimatize, familiarize

acclivity... 4. bank, brow, hill, rise
5. climb, slope, talus 6. ascent
7. upgrade 9. ascendant (ascendent)
11. inclination

accolade... 4. fold, rite 5. award,
brace, clasp, Oscar 6. praise, reward
7. embrace, tribute 8. encomium
9. panegyric 10. enfoldment

accommodate... 3. fit 4. help, lend,
meet, suit 5. adapt, favor, lodge,
shape, yield 6. adjust, afford,
comply, invest, oblige, orient, settle,
supply 7. conform, furnish

9. reconcile 10. correspond

accommodation... 3. aid 4. loan,
room 5. limit, space, terms
6. giving, volume 7. advance,
lodging, service 8. capacity
9. advantage, provision
10. adaptation, adjustment,
attunement, conformity, settlement
11. convenience, integration,
orientation, subsistence
12. coordination 13. harmonization
14. reconciliation

accompaniment... 7. adjunct, descant,
support 8. ornament 9. attendant,
obbligato 11. concurrence
12. concomitance

accompany... 4. join 6. attend,
convoy, escort, follow, squire
7. conduct 10. synchronize
12. contemporize

accomplice... 3. pal 4. aide, ally,
chum 6. stooge 7. abettor
9. accessory, assistant, associate
11. confederate, conspirator

accomplish... 2. do 3. win 4. make,
work 5. enact, equip 6. attain, effect
7. achieve, compass, execute,
furnish, operate, perfect, produce,
realize, succeed 8. contrive, engineer
9. negotiate 10. consummate,
effectuate

accomplishment... 4. deed, feat
5. skill 8. dispatch 9. discharge,
execution 10. attainment, completion
11. achievement, acquirement,
fulfillment, performance, proficiency,
transaction 12. effectuation

accord... 5. award, grant, unity
6. accede, unison 7. comport,
concede, concert, concord, harmony,
rapport 8. diapason, symphony
9. agreement, harmonize, reconcile,
unanimity 10. accordance, conformity,
uniformity 11. concurrence

accordant... 7. attuned 8. agreeing,
suitable 9. agreeable, assenting,
consonant 10. concordant,
concurrent, consenting, consilient,
consistent 11. conformable,
homogeneous 13. corresponding

accordingly... 2. so 4. then, thus
9. therefore 12. consequently

according to... 3. a la, aux 4. alla,
fact, true 5. datal 7. a la mode
8. pursuant

accost... 4. hail, meet 5. greet, speak
6. halloo, salute 7. address
8. approach

accoucheuse... 7. midwife

account... 3. sum, tab 4. bill, cast,
sake, tale, word 5. debit, honor,
score, tally 6. assign, credit, esteem,
profit, reckon, regard, report
7. compute, memoirs, recital
9. narration, reckoning, rehearsal,
statement, summation
10. numeration, recitation
11. description, explanation,
information 13. communication

accountable... 6. liable 8. amenable,
knowable 9. divinable, traceable
10. answerable, ascribable,

assignable, calculable, explicable, fathomable 11. explainable, predictable, responsible 12. attributable, intelligible 13. apprehensible 14. comprehensible

accountant... 5. clerk 7. actuary, auditor 8. reckoner 9. defendant, registrar 10. bookkeeper, calculator

accouter, accoutre... 3. fit, rig 4. deck, gird, suit 5. array, dress, equip, habit 6. attire, fettle, outfit 7. appoint, costume, furnish, provide

accouterment, accoutrement... 5. dress, sword 6. attire 8. trapping 9. equipment, haversack

accoy... 4. tame 5. daunt 6. soothe, subdue

accredit... 5. trust 6. accept, affirm, credit, depute, ratify 7. approve, ascribe, believe, certify, confirm, empower, endorse 8. deputize, sanction, validate 9. authorize 10. commission

accrete... 3. add 6. attach

accretion... 4. gain 6. growth 8. addition, adhesion, increase 9. coherence, increment 10. concretion 11. coagulation, enlargement 12. accumulation, augmentation 13. amplification

accrue... 4. grow 5. arise, ensue, issue 6. mature, result 7. acquire, collect, redound 8. accresce 10. accumulate

accumulate... 4. grow, heap, mass, save 5. amass, hoard, store 6. accrue, garner, gather, muster 7. advance, collect, store up 8. increase 9. aggregate

accumulation... 4. fund, gain, mass 5. hoard, store 7. accrual 8. gleaning, increase, treasure 9. accession, accretion, extension, gathering 10. acervation, assemblage, collection 11. acquisition, serendipity 12. augmentation 13. amplification 14. aggrandizement

accuracy... 6. nicety 9. exactness, fussiness, precision, rightness 11. correctness 14. meticulousness, scrupulousness

accurate... 4. just, nice, prim 5. close, exact, right 6. proper, strict 7. correct, perfect, precise 8. faithful 9. syntactic 10. meticulous, particular 11. grammatical

accursed... 6. cursed, damned, doomed 8. execrable, execrated 10. detestable 13. anathematized

accusation... 5. blame 6. attack, charge, taxing 7. calumny 8. reproach 9. complaint 10. imputation, indictment 11. impeachment 12. denunciation

accuse... 3. tax 5. blame 6. attack, charge, delate, indict 7. arraign, censure, impeach 8. denounce 9. criminate 11. incriminate, recriminate

accuser... 7. delator 8. accusant, libelant (libellant) 9. plaintiff

10. prosecutor 11. complainant 12. incriminator

accustom... 3. use 4. wont 5. enure, habit, inure, train 6. addict 7. educate, toughen 9. habituate 11. familiarize

accustomed... 4. used, wont 5. usual 6. enured, inured 8. familiar 9. customary, sedentary (to sit)

ace... 3. jot, one, pip, tib 4. atom, card, dole, dram, unit, whit 5. monad, pilot, point, shark (sl) 7. aviator 8. particle, pittance, superior 10. crackajack (sl), proficient 11. crackerjack (sl)

ace (pert to)...
ace–queen.. 6. tenace
of clubs.. 5. basto

acedia (Gr)... 5. sloth 6. torpor

acedia (Sp)... 8. flatfish

Aceldama, Akeldama (Bib)... 12. Field of Blood, potter's field

acemila... 8. pack mule

acephalous... 8. headless 10. leaderless

acephalus... 15. headless monster

acerb... 4. sour 5. harsh, sharp 6. bitter, unripe 7. acerbic, austere, pungent

acerbity... 7. acidity 8. acridity, acrimony, asperity, mordancy, pungency, severity 9. harshness 10. bitterness, causticity 11. astringency

acetic acid... 7. vinegar 8. vesicant 9. corrosive

Achaean, Achaian... 5. Greek (a) 6. Greece

ache... 4. burn, long, pain, pang 5. throb 6. grieve, sorrow, twinge 7. agonize, longing 10. suffer pain

achieve... 2. do 3. get, win 4. gain, kill 6. arrive, attain, effect, finish 7. compass, execute, fulfill, perform, produce, realize, succeed 8. complete, conclude, contrive 10. accomplish, consummate, effectuate

achievement... 3. act 4. deed, feat 5. doing, stunt 6. action, record 7. arrival, exploit 8. dispatch 9. adventure 10. attainment, escutcheon (Her) 11. fulfillment, performance, transaction 12. effectuation 14. accomplishment, implementation

Achilles (pert to)...
advisor.. 6. Nestor
dipped into.. 9. River Styx
father.. 6. Peleus
friend.. 9. Patroclus
horse.. 7. Xanthus
mother.. 6. Thetis
slayer.. 5. Paris
slayer of.. 6. Hector
son.. 7. Pyrrhus 11. Neoptolemus
vulnerable spot.. 4. heel

achromatic... 4. gray 8. achromic 9. achromous, colorless, uncolored 13. free from color

achropsia... 14. color blindness

acid... 4. keen, sour, tart 5. acrid,

amino, boric, malic, mucic, pyrol
6. acetic, arabic, biting, bromic,
nitric, oxalic, tannic 7. acetose,
caustic, chloric, racemic, stearic,
terebic, vinegar 9. corrosive
11. acrimonious

acid, removing... 12. edulcoration

acidity... 4. acor, sour 8. acrimony,
mordancy, sourness, tartness, verjuice
9. sharpness 10. bitterness
13. acidulousness

acknowledge... 3. nod, own, pay, say
4. avow, sign 5. admit, allow, grant,
own up, reply, swear, thank, vouch,
yield 6. accede, accept, answer,
assent, attest, redeem 7. certify,
concede, confess, testify 8. disclose
9. recognize

acknowledgment... 5. favor, reply
6. answer, avowal, avowry, shrift,
thanks 7. apology, epistle, receipt,
voucher, warrant 8. rescript
9. admission 10. acceptance,
concession, confession, disclosure,
owning up to 11. recognition
12. thanksgiving

acme... 3. top 4. apex 5. limit
6. apogee, climax, crisis, heyday,
summit, tip–top, vertex, zenith
7. ceiling, maximum 11. culmination
12. consummation

acology, science of... 8. remedies

acolyte... 7. patener 8. altar boy
9. assistant

acomia... 8. alopecia, baldness
12. hairlessness

aconite... 8. Cammarum, Eranthis
9. monkshood

acorn... 3. nut 4. duck 5. camata
10. meadowlark (color)

acosmic... 11. unorganized

acquaint... 4. tell 6. advise, impart,
inform 7. apprise 9. enlighten,
introduce 11. familiarize

acquaintance... 3. ken 5. amigo
6. friend 7. privity 8. familiar,
intimacy, intimate 9. companion,
knowledge 10. fellowship
11. familiarity, information,
sympathizer 15. familiarization

acquainted... 6. au fait 7. versant
8. familiar 9. cognizant
10. conversant

acquiesce... 3. bow 5. abide, agree,
chime, yield 6. accede, assent,
comply, concur, relent, resign, submit
7. conform, consent, succumb

acquire... 3. buy, get, win 4. earn,
gain, reap 5. adopt, catch, incur,
learn, steal 6. attain, effect, obtain,
secure 7. procure, receive
8. contract 9. cultivate

acquire (pert to)...
    beforehand.. 7. pre–empt
    feathers.. 6. fledge
    immunity.. 14. serum injection
    knowledge.. 5. clear, study
    9. ascertain

acquit... 4. free 5. clear 6. excuse,
pardon, pay off 7. absolve, fulfill,
release, requite 9. exculpate,
exonerate

acquittal... 7. freeing, payment, release
8. clearing, requital 9. clearance,
discharge 10. observance
11. exculpation, fulfillment
12. satisfaction

acquittance... 7. payment, quietus,
receipt 9. discharge, quittance

acre... 5. field 6. arpent 7. measure
8. farmhold

acre (pert to)...
    half.. 3. erf (S Afr)
    hundred.. 7. hectare (metric)
    quarter.. 4. rood (Brit)

acres... 5. lands 6. estate, ground

acrid... 4. acid, bask (dial), keen, sour,
tart 5. harsh, rough, sharp 6. acetic,
biting, bitter 7. acetose, caustic,
mordant, pungent, reeking
8. unsavory, virulent 9. acidulous,
corrosive 10. escharotic, irritating
11. acrimonious

acrimonious... 4. acid, keen 5. acrid,
angry, gruff, harsh, irate, sharp
6. bitter 7. caustic, stinging
9. rancorous, resentful

acrimony... 5. venom 6. rancor 7. ill
will, vitriol 8. acerbity, acridity,
asperity, mordancy, pungency,
rudeness, severity, sourness, tartness
9. animosity, virulence 10. bitterness,
causticity, resentment
11. astringency, crabbedness

acroamatic... 4. oral 5. parol
6. arcane, occult, secret, verbal
8. abstract, abstruse, anagogic,
esoteric, profound 9. recondite,
unwritten 11. nuncupative

acrobat... 7. gymnast, tumbler
8. balancer 10. ropedancer,
ropewalker 11. funambulist
13. contortionist, schoenobatist

acrochordon... 4. wart (small)

Acrocorinth, Acrocorinthus...
9. acropolis (Corinth) 12. Pirene
Spring (site)

acromegaly... 7. disease
11. enlargement (head, hands, feet)

**acronical, acronichal (opp of
cosmical)**... 10. rising star
11. setting star

acronyx... 13. ingrowing nail

acrophobia... fear of 7. heights

acropolis... 7. refuge 7. citadel

Acropolis (pert to)...
    Argos.. 7. Larissa
    Corinth.. 11. Acrocorinth
    Thebes.. 6. Cadmea

across... 4. over, span 5. cross
6. thwart 7. athwart 8. crossway,
traverse 9. crossways, crosswise
10. crisscross, transverse

across (pref)... 3. dia 4. tran 5. trans

acrostic... 4. agla, game, poem
6. puzzle 7. erratic 8. wordplay
9. crosswise, jeu de mots, telestich

act... 2. do 3. jus, law, lex 4. deed,
feat, play, task, turn, work 5. actus,
emote, favor, of God, stunt
6. action, behave, demean, motion
7. comport, measure, perform,
pretend, process 8. function,
kindness, simulate 9. enactment,

represent 10. enterprise, exert power, theatrical 11. impersonate, legislation, performance, transaction

act (pert to)...
a part.. 8. simulate 9. dissemble
causing ruin.. 11. Kiss of Death
criminal.. 8. villainy
detestable.. 11. abomination
formal.. 10. instrument
game.. 7. charade
illegal.. 4. tort 5. crime 6. delict
nonsense.. 10. tomfoolery
planned.. 12. premeditated
pompously.. 11. pontificate
suffix.. 3. ure

acting... 5. doing 6. action, posing 7. playing, serving 8. pretense 9. dramatics, execution, operating 10. masquerade, performing, simulating 11. make–believe 13. impersonating, impersonation

acting with force... 8. vehement

action... 2. re 3. act, res 4. deed, feat, play, stir, suit, work 5. award, doing, order, works 6. battle, decree, motion, praxis, ruling 7. conduct, contest, lawsuit, verdict, working 8. activity, behavior, demeanor, exercise, movement, sentence 9. mechanism, operation 10. automation, enterprise 11. performance 13. pronouncement

active... 4. spry 5. acute, agile, alert, brisk, quick, ready, smart, yauld 6. breezy, dapper, lively, nimble, prompt, strong 7. dynamic, intense, kinetic, vibrant 8. animated, forceful, spirited, vigorous 9. assiduous, effective, effectual, energetic, energized, operating, pragmatic, sprightly, vivacious 11. industrious

active, not... 6. static 7. dormant 11. inoperative

activity... 3. ado, gog, pep, vir 4. stir, work 5. vigor 6. action, energy 7. agility, bristle 8. business, movement 9. athletics, briskness, operation, quickness 10. activeness, employment, nimbleness, occupation

act of...
cutting.. 4. kerf 8. shearing
endearment.. 4. kiss 6. caress
God.. 8. accident
kindness.. 5. favor
leaving.. 6. congee, egress
respect.. 6. curtsy, homage
ruling.. 5. regle
self–examination.. 13. introspection
sharing.. 13. participation
witnessing.. 11. attestation
working together.. 13. collaboration
worship.. 6. prayer 8. devotion

actor... 3. ham 4. doer, hero, mime, star, supe 5. agent 6. mummer, player, worker 7. Roscius, trooper 8. aisteoir, comedian, histrion, Thespian 9. performer, portrayer, pretender, tragedian 10. comedienne, dramatizer, pantomimic, personator 11. barnstormer, entertainer, pantomimist, protagonist, tragedienne 12. impersonator

actor (personage)... 4. Lunt, Ward 5. Booth 7. Skinner 8. Warfield 9. Faversham

actors' group... 4. cast 6. troupe

actor's hint... 3. cue 12. teleprompter

actress (personage)... 5. Adams, Bates, Hayes, Terry 6. Robson, Scheff 7. Marlowe, Russell 8. Fontanne, Modjeska 9. Bernhardt

actual... 4. real, true 5. posit 7. factual, genuine, present 8. absolute, positive, tangible 9. practical, veritable 11. substantial

actual being... 4. esse

actuality... 4. fact 6. verity 7. reality 8. realness 9. existence 10. factuality 14. substantiality

actually... 5. quite, truly 6. indeed, really, verily 8. actively 9. assuredly, certainly

actuary... 5. clerk 9. registrar 10. accountant, bookkeeper, calculator 13. arithmetician, mathematician

actuate... 3. egg 4. move 5. force, impel, rouse 6. arouse, induce, prompt, propel 7. animate 8. motivate 9. stimulate

acuate... 7. sharpen 12. needle–shaped, sharp–pointed

acumen... 7. insight 8. gumption, keenness, sagacity 9. acuteness, sharpness 10. astuteness, perception, shrewdness 11. discernment 12. perspicacity 14. discrimination

acute... 4. high, keen, tart, thin 5. canny, sharp, smart, vivid 6. accent, biting, crafty, fierce, severe, shrewd, shrill, subtle 7. crucial, cutting, dynamic, intense, knowing, painful, pointed, violent 8. critical, deep–felt, forceful, incisive, piercing, poignant, rigorous, stabbing, stinging, vigorous 9. energetic, ingenious, sensitive 11. sharp–witted 13. perspicacious 14. discriminating

acuteness of...
sight.. 7. oxyopia 10. oxyblepsia
taste.. 9. oxygeusia
touch.. 8. oxyaphia

Adam (pert to)...
grandson.. 4. Enos
son.. 4. Abel, Cain, Seth
wife.. 3. Eve 6. Lilith (legend)

Adam's...
ale.. 5. water
apple.. 6. larynx 10. pomum Adami
herb.. 7. mullein
needle.. 5. yucca

adapt... 3. fit, set 4. suit 6. adjust, attune, comply, modify, orient, season 7. arrange, conform, prepare, qualify 8. accustom, regulate 9. acclimate, condition, habituate, harmonize, reconcile 11. accommodate

adaptable... 7. elastic, pliable 9. tractable, versatile 10. adjustable, responsive 11. conformable 13. accommodative

adaptation... 7. fitting 10. adjustment, attunement, conformity, regulation

11. arrangement, habituation, orientation 12. conditioning, coordination, modification 13. accommodation, harmonization, orchestration, qualification 15. familiarization

add... 5. eke, tot 4. foot, give, join, plus, tote 5. affix, annex, sum up, total, unite 6. append, attach, reckon 7. accrete, augment, compile, compute, put with, subjoin 8. increase 9. calculate 10. supplement

adda... 5. skink (scink) 6. lizard 7. reptile

addax... 6. pygarg (Bib) 8. antelope

added... 3. and 4. plus 5. extra 6. joined, united 7. affixed, annexed 8. appended, attached 9. appendant 13. supplementary

adder... 3. asp 5. Bitis, krait, snake, viper 6. nedder 7. machine, serpent 13. mathematician

addict... 4. buff 5. fiend 7. adjudge, devotee, hophead 9. habituate 15. apply habitually

addicted... 4. wont 5. prone 8. attached, disposed, inclined 9. devoted to 10. accustomed, habituated 11. given over to

addiction... 5. habit 9. surrender 10. attachment 11. enslavement

Addison's signature... 4. Clio (The Spectator) 7. Atticus (by the Pope)

addition... 3. and, ell, too 4. also, gain, plus, wing 5. farse (Relig), rider 6. addend, augend, lean—to 7. additum, adjunct, joining, uniting 8. addendum, additory, increase 9. accession, accretion, amendment, appendage, extension, reckoning 10. annexation 11. calculation, computation, enlargement 12. augmentation

additional... 3. new 4. else, more 5. added, extra, fresh, spare 7. besides, further 9. auxiliary, extrinsic 12. supervenient, supplemental 13. supplementary

additional (pert to)... *explanation*.. 10. epexegesis 11. elucidation *grant*.. 3. ann 5. bonus *specimen*.. 6. cotype

address... 3. air, wit, woo 4. call, hail, mien, pray, tact, talk 5. abode, court, grace, greet, guise, place, skill, speak 6. accost, direct, eulogy, salute, sermon, speech 7. arrange, conduct, consign, declaim, finesse, lecture, manners, oration, prepare, prowess, request 8. behavior, demeanor, greeting, harangue, inscribe, perorate, petition, presence 9. dexterity, diplomacy, direction, discourse, ingenuity, readiness 11. comportment, destination, inscription, savoir—faire 14. sophistication, superscription

addressee... 8. occupant 10. inhabitant 12. communicator 13. correspondent

adduce... 4. cite, name 5. argue,

infer, offer, plead, quote 6. allege, assign 7. advance, mention, present, produce

Adelphi... 7. theater (Strand, London) 13. London Quarter

adeps... 4. lard 9. animal fat

adept... 3. ace, apt 4. whiz (coll) 6. adroit, artist, expert, versed 7. capable, dabster, mahatma, skilled 8. skillful (skilful) 9. alchemist (formerly), occultist 10. conversant, proficient 11. crackerjack

adequate... 3. due, fit 4. able, full 5. ample, digne, equal 6. enough 7. capable 8. all right, equalize, suitable 9. competent, effective, effectual, sufficing, tolerable 10. sufficient 12. commensurate, satisfactory 13. proportionate

adhere... 4. cleg, glue, hold 5. cling, stick 6. cleave, cohere 7. accrete, observe, persist

adherent... 4. ally 6. adnate, sticky, votary 7. dangler, sequela 8. adhesive, clinging, disciple, faithful, follower, hanger—on, partisan, sticking, upholder 9. appendage, dependent, supporter

adherent to the Crown... 4. Tory

adhesive... 3. gum, wax 4. glue 5. paste 6. cement, mastic, sticky 8. adherent, mucilage 9. tenacious

adhesiveness... 4. stay 8. tenacity 12. cohesiveness 13. tenaciousness 16. stick—itiveness

adhibit... 3. use 5. admit, affix, apply 6. attach, devote 7. bring in 10. administer

adieu... 4. vale 5. adios, aloha 6. good—by, so long (sl) 7. cheerio, good—bye, good day 8. au revoir, farewell 11. leave—taking

adipose... 3. fat 4. oily 5. fatty, plump, pursy, squab 9. sebaceous

edit... 3. way 4. duct 5. entry, stulm 6. access, ingate, intake, tunnel 7. channel, conduit, haulage, ingress, passage 8. approach, drainage, entrance 9. admission 11. entranceway, ventilation

adjacent... 4. abut, near, nigh 5. close, handy 6. next to 7. meeting, nearest 8. abutting, touching 9. adjoining, bordering 10. contiguous, juxtaposed 11. neighboring 12. conterminous

adject... 3. add 4. join 5. annex

adjective... 3. the 6. adnoun 7. epithet (significant) 8. modifier 9. accessory, dependent

adjective (pert to)... *demonstrative*.. 4. that, this 5. these, those *suffix*.. 2. ic, il 3. ent, ial, ian, ile, ish, ist, ite, ive, ous *verbal*.. 9. gerundive

adjoin... 3. add 4. abut, butt, join 5. unite 6. attach, border 7. conjoin 8. neighbor

adjourn... 3. end 5. close, defer, delay 6. recess 7. suspend 8. dissolve, postpone, prorogue 11. discontinue

adjudge, adjudicate... 3. try 4. deem, doom, find, hold, pass 5. award, judge, order 6. assign, decree, esteem, ordain, reckon, regard, settle 7. condemn 8. consider, sentence 9. determine

adjunct... 4. ally, word 5. added 6. device 7. additum, annexed, consort 8. addition, appanage (apanage) 9. appendant, associate, auxiliary, colleague, companion, component, qualifier 11. confederate 12. appurtenance, nonessential

adjuration... 4. oath, plea 6. appeal, avowal, charge 8. entreaty, swearing, vouching 10. deposition 11. beseechment, obsecration, obtestation

adjure... 3. ask, beg, bid 4. bind, pray 5. plead 6. appeal, charge 7. beseech, command, entreat, implore, swear in

adjust... 3. fit, fix, set 4. meet, size, suit, trim, true 5. adapt, align, amend, frame, group, match, right, shape 6. accord, attune, orient, remedy, settle, square 7. arrange, conform, correct, justify, mediate, rectify, redress 8. accustom, organize, regulate 9. condition, habituate, harmonize, reconcile 10. compromise, coordinate, straighten 11. accommodate, systematize

adjuster, adjustor... 6. fitter 8. arranger 11. coordinator

adjustment... 4. gear 5. means, terms 7. fitting, suiting 8. bearings, disposal 9. bundobust 10. adaptation, attunement, compromise, concession, conclusion, conformity, regulation, settlement 11. arrangement, disposition, habituation, orientation 12. assimilation, coordination, organization 13. harmonization, methodization, rectification 14. naturalization, reconciliation

adjutant... 4. aide, ally 6. helper 7. officer 9. assistant, auxiliary

adjutant bird... 5. stork 6. argala 7. hurgila, marabou

ad lib, ad libit, ad libitum... 6. make up 7. cadenza 9. extempore, impromptu, improvise 10. at pleasure 11. play it by ear 13. accompaniment

administer... 4. give 5. apply, issue 6. bestow, direct, govern, manage, supply, tender 7. adhibit, conduct, dispose, execute, fulfill, furnish, give out, husband, perform 8. dispatch, dispense, transact 9. discharge 10. distribute 12. administrate

administer extreme unction... 5. anele 6. anoint

administration... 3. use 4. rule 6. employ, giving, policy 7. conduct, regimen 8. bestowal, disposal, issuance, ministry 9. direction, execution 10. employment, government, management, regulation 11. application, directorate, disposition 12. dispensation, ministration 13. apportionment

administration of justice... 10. judicatory, judicature

administrator... 2. fu 5. dewan 7. alcalde, manager, provost, trustee 8. director, executor 9. dispenser, executive 12. entrepreneur

admirable... 5. sweet 6. worthy 7. likable (likeable), winning, winsome 8. adorable, laudable 9. estimable, excellent, marvelous, wonderful 10. creditable 11. commendable, meritorious 12. praiseworthy

admiration... 6. esteem, liking, regard, wonder 7. respect 8. surprise 9. adoration, amazement, reverence 10. wonderment 11. astoundment, idolization 12. appreciation, confoundment

admire... 4. like, love 5. adore, honor 6. esteem, regard, revere 7. approve, idolize, respect 8. venerate

admissible... 3. fit 4. just, sane 5. sound 6. worthy 7. apropos, germane, logical 8. apposite, eligible, rational, relevant, suitable 9. admissory, agreeable, allowable, desirable, pertinent, qualified, receptive, tolerable 10. acceptable, applicable, legitimate, reasonable 11. justifiable, permissible, warrantable 12. satisfactory

admission... 4. adit 5. entry 6. access, assent, avowal, entree, shrift 8. entrance 9. agreement, allowance, inclusion, letting in, receiving, reception, testimony 10. accordance, admittance, allegation, avouchment, compliance, concession, confession, initiation, permission 11. affiliation, affirmation, declaration 12. acquiescence, assimilation 14. acknowledgment, naturalization 15. enfranchisement

Admission Day holiday... 6. Nevada (Oct 31) 7. Arizona (Feb 14) 10. California (Sept 9)

admit... 3. own 4. avow 5. adopt, allow, enter, grant, let in, own up, trust, yield 6. accept, credit, embody, permit 7. adhibit, believe, concede, confess, embrace, include, profess, receive 8. initiate 9. affiliate 10. naturalize 11. acknowledge, incorporate

admittance... 6. access 8. entrance, sanction 9. admission, letting in 10. initiation

admitted... 6. indeed 8. believed, conceded 12. acknowledged

admixture... 5. alloy, blend 6. fusion 7. mixture 8. compound, infusion 10. minglement 11. combination, composition

admonish... 4. warn 5. chide, scold 6. advise, enjoin, exhort, preach, rebuke, remind 7. caution, monitor, reprove, upbraid 8. dissuade 9. reprimand 11. expostulate,

remonstrate, give warning
admonition... 6. advice 7. caution,
censure, reproof, warning 8. reminder
10. counseling (counselling),
dissuasion 11. exhortation
12. remonstrance, reprehension
ado... 4. fuss, stir 5. doing, hurry
6. bustle, flurry, hubbub, pother,
rumpus, tumult 7. trouble, turmoil
9. commotion 10. excitement
11. disturbance
adobe... 4. clay, silt 5. brick, house
(clay)
adolescent... 3. lad 5. minor, youth
6. nonage 9. pubescent, youngster
10. developing
Adonis (pert to)...
  beloved by.. 9. Aphrodite
  festival.. 6. Adonia
  modern youth.. 6. a dandy
  mother.. 5. Myrrh
  slain by.. 8. wild boar
adopt... 4. take 5. admit, usurp
6. accept, assume, borrow, choose,
father, mother, select 7. embrace,
espouse, receive, welcome 9. affiliate
10. assimilate, naturalize
11. appropriate
adoption... 6. choice 8. espousal
9. admission, borrowing, reception
10. acceptance, assumption,
conversion, redemption, usurpation
11. embracement 13. appropriation
14. naturalization
adore... 4. love 5. enjoy, honor
6. esteem, regard, revere 7. idolize,
worship 8. venerate
adorn... 4. clad, deck 5. array, begem,
drape, grace, primp, prink 6. attire,
bedeck, clothe, enrich 7. bedight,
bejewel, dignify, garnish 8. beautify,
decorate 9. embellish
adorn (with)...
  color.. 4. gild 5. paint 7. emblaze
  feathers.. 7. implume
  needlework.. 9. embroider
  ornaments.. 6. tinsel 7. imagery
adorned... 4. clad 6. ornate
7. clothed, prinked 9. decorated
16. chryselephantine
adornment... 5. decor, frill 6. frills,
tinsel 10. decoration, embroidery
13. embellishment 14. beautification
ad patres... 4. dead 12. to his
Fathers
Adriatic (pert to)...
  city.. 5. Fiume 6. Venice 7. Lagosta,
    Trieste 8. Brandisi
  island.. 7. Lagosta
  peninsula.. 6. Istria
  wind (cold).. 4. bora
adrift... 4. asea, free, lost 5. at sea,
loose 6. afloat, astray, aweigh,
undone 7. aimless, unfixed
8. aberrant, derelict, floating,
insecure, straying, unmoored,
unstable 9. erroneous
10. bewildered, unanchored,
unfastened, without aim
adroit... 4. neat 5. quick, ready, smart
6. clever, expert, habile, nimble
7. cunning 8. skillful (skilful)

9. dexterous, ingenious
adroitness... 4. tact 5. knack, skill
7. address 9. dexterity, ingenuity,
readiness, smartness
adsorbent, absorbent... 6. spongy
7. osmotic, soaking 8. blotting
12. assimilative
adulation... 6. praise 8. flattery
9. adoration 10. compliment
adulterate... 3. mix 5. alter, taint
6. debase, defile 7. corrupt
8. denature 11. contaminate
adulterated... 6. impure 7. debased
8. spurious 9. denatured
11. counterfeit 12. contaminated
adust... 3. tan (color) 4. burn
5. burnt, dried, fiery 6. singed
7. parched 8. scorched 9. blistered
advance... 2. go 3. aid 4. gain, inch,
loan, move, near, nose, pass, push,
rise (in price) 5. ahead, boost, creep,
march, raise 6. better, stride
7. elevate, process, promote,
propose 8. approach, heighten,
increase, progress 9. aforehand,
elevation, promotion, upgrading
10. accelerate, beforehand,
preferment 11. advancement,
development, furtherance,
improvement, progression
advanced... 3. old 5. aged 6. modern
7. elderly, forward 8. bettered,
enhanced, enriched, foremost,
unproved 9. venerable 10. in the
front, precocious, senectuous
11. enlightened, progressive
advanced (pert to)...
  equally.. 7. abreast
  study.. 7. seminar
  time.. 6. modern 8. up–to–date
    12. contemporary
advantage... 3. use 4. boot, bote
(bot), edge, gain, good, hold, odds
5. avail, favor, start, stead 6. behalf,
behoof, profit 7. benefit, further,
promote, service, vantage 8. facility,
interest, purchase 9. appliance
10. expedience 11. convenience,
superiority 13. accommodation,
vantage ground
advantageous... 5. handy 6. aidful,
useful 7. helpful 8. edifying, salutary
9. expedient, favorable
10. auspicious, beneficial, convenient,
profitable, propitious, worthwhile
11. encouraging
advent... 6. coming 7. arrival
8. approach 11. forthcoming
Advent (Eccl)... 14. Coming of Christ
adventitious... 4. rale 6. casual
8. acquired 9. extrinsic
10. accidental, incidental
12. nonessential
adventure... 3. act (heroic), hap
4. bout, dare, deed, feat, gest, risk
5. event, quest, stunt 6. action,
hazard 7. episode, exploit, fortune,
venture 8. escapade, incident (novel),
maneuver, occasion 9. happening
10. enterprise, experience, occurrence
11. performance, undertaking
12. happenstance 13. striking event

14. accomplishment

adventurer... 4. goer 5. sport
7. bounder, gambler, Hessian,
parvenu, soldier, upstart 8. gamester,
hazarder, merchant, traveler
9. sportsman 10. speculator
16. soldier of fortune

adventuress... 7. demirep 10. gold
digger

adventurous... 4. rash 5. risky
6. daring 8. reckless 9. dangerous,
foolhardy, hazardous, venturous
11. venturesome 12. enterprising,
presumptuous

adversary... 3. foe 5. enemy, Satan
6. foeman 7. opponent 9. archfiend,
assailant 10. antagonist, competitor,
Philistine

adverse... 3. ill 4. anti 5. loath
7. opposed 8. contrary, converse,
opposing, sinister, untoward
9. reluctant, unwilling 10. afflictive,
calamitous, indisposed 11. conflicting,
disinclined, unfavorable
12. antagonistic, unpropitious

adversity... 6. misery 7. trouble
8. calamity, distress, hardship
9. suffering 10. affliction, misfortune,
opposition 11. destitution

advert... 5. recur, refer 6. allude,
return

advertent... 7. heedful 9. attentive

advertise... 4. plug, warn 5. boast,
boost 6. notify 7. promote, publish
8. announce, ballyhoo, proclaim
9. publicize 10. promulgate

advertisement... 2. ad 4. bill, copy,
Neon, plug, sign 6. notice, poster,
spread 7. placard 10. commercial
(TV)

advice... 4. rede 5. aviso 6. caveat,
wisdom 7. counsel, opinion, warning
8. prudence, reminder 9. knowledge
10. admonition, suggestion
11. exhortation, information,
instruction 12. consultation,
deliberation, intelligence
13. consideration
14. recommendation

advice, containing... 9. mentorial

advisable... 6. proper 7. prudent
9. befitting, desirable, expedient
11. commendable
13. recommendable

advise... 4. rede, tell, warn 5. coach
6. exhort, impart, inform, remind
7. apprise, bethink, caution, counsel,
suggest 8. acquaint, admonish,
advocate 9. enlighten, recommend
11. communicate, familiarize, take
counsel

adviser, advisor... 5. guide 6. Egeria,
nestor 7. monitor 8. appriser, kibitzer
(sl) 9. counselor (counsellor),
informant 10. admonisher

advisers, advisors... 7. Cabinet,
Council 10. councilors, counselors,
informants

advocate... 3. pro 4. urge 5. advise,
backer, defend, deputy, lawyer
7. endorse, espouse, pleader,
support 8. attorney, champion,

defender, exponent, plead for
9. barrister, counselor, justifier,
paraclete, proponent, recommend,
solicitor, supporter 11. protagonist

advocate of the simple life...
14. simplicitarian

adytum... 6. shrine 7. chamber (inner),
sanctum 9. sanctuary

Aeetes (pert to)...
daughter... 5. Medea
keeper of.. 12. Golden Fleece
king of.. 7. Colchis

Aegean Island group...
10. Dodecanese (including twelve)

aegis, egis... 4. care 5. guard
6. screen, shield, symbol (anc)
7. backing, defense 8. guidance
9. fosterage, patronage
10. protection

Aello (Gr)... 5. Harpy 7. monster

Aeneid... 4. poem (Vergil)

aerage... 11. ventilation

aerate... 6. aerify 7. freshen, inflate,
refresh 9. ventilate

aerial... 3. ear 4. aery, airy, mast
5. aeric, lofty 6. unreal 7. airlike,
antenna 8. ethereal, fanciful,
vaporous 9. pneumatic 10. chimerical
12. aeronautical 13. unsubstantial

aerie, eyrie... 4. nest 5. brood (birds)
6. family 9. penthouse

aeriform... 6. unreal 7. gaseous

aeroplane... 8. airplane

Aesir, Norse Gods... 3. Tyr (Tiu), Ull
4. Odin (Woden), Thor (Donar), Vali
5. Bragi 6. Balder, Hoenir 7. Forseti
8. Heimdall

Aeson's son... 5. Jason (Gr Myth)

affability... 6. comity 8. civility,
courtesy, urbanity 9. geniality
10. amiability, cordiality, politeness
11. sociability 12. conviviality
14. gregariousness
16. companionability
17. communicativeness

affable... 4. mild 5. civil, suave
6. benign, fluent, social 7. amiable
8. gracious, sociable 9. convivial,
courteous 10. accessible, gregarious
11. complaisant 13. communicative

affair... 4. duel, love 5. fight, issue,
thing, topic 6. action, gadget,
matter, object, soiree 7. concern,
problem 8. business, interest,
question, sociable 9. gathering,
reception, something 10. proceeding
11. get-together, transaction
12. circumstance

affect... 4. melt, move, stir 5. feign,
grate, haunt, touch 6. assume,
excite, regale, relate, soften, thrill
7. concern, involve, operate, pretend,
qualify 8. frequent, interest, simulate
9. influence 11. counterfeit,
hypothecate

affectation... 3. air 4. pose, sham
7. display, foppery, pietism
8. elegance, pretense 9. mannerism
12. affectedness 13. artificiality
14. grandiloquence
15. pretentiousness

affected... 4. airy, sham 5. faked,

moved, posey, put–on 6. fal–lal,
formal 7. assumed, beloved, elegant,
feigned, gushing, stilted 8. disposed,
mannered 9. impressed, pretended,
unnatural 10. artificial, euphuistic
11. pretentious 12. ostentatious
13. counterfeited, grandiloquent

affected by...
age.. 6. senile
love.. 4. smit 7. smitten
pain.. 4. pang 6. twinge
paralysis.. 7. paretic
wonder.. 6. marvel 9. convulsed
affectedly languid... 13. lackadaisical
affectedly shy... 3. coy, mim 4. prim
6. demure 10. coquettish
affection... 4. amor, love 6. animus,
defect, storge (animal) 7. disease,
emotion, feeling, illness, leaning,
passion 8. devotion, fondness,
tendency 9. attribute, infirmity,
sentiment 10. affliction, attachment,
disability, proclivity, propensity,
tenderness 11. disposition,
inclination, temperament
affectionate... 4. fond, soft, warm
6. ardent, loving, tender 7. adoring,
devoted, earnest, zealous
8. attached, friendly, parental,
romantic 10. headstrong
13. demonstrative
afferent... 8. esodic (nerves), inward
7. sensory 11. centripetal
affiance... 5. faith, troth, trust
6. belief, pledge, plight 7. betroth,
promise 8. credence, reliance
9. assurance, betrothal
10. confidence, engagement
affiche... 6. poster 7. placard
affidavit... 4. oath 9. statement
10. deposition 11. affirmation,
certificate, declaration
affiliation... 4. body, sect 5. group,
union 6. church, fusion, hookup,
league 7. faction, lineage
8. adoption, alliance, espousal,
relation 9. admission, alignment,
coalition 10. connection, federation,
fellowship, persuasion
11. association, cooperation
12. denomination, organization
13. confederation, consanguinity
14. naturalization
affinity... 3. kin 6. accord, family,
liking 7. kinship, rapport 8. relation,
soul mate 9. agreement
10. attraction, connection, similarity
11. propinquity, resemblance
12. congeniality, relationship
13. compatibility, rapprochement
affirm... 3. say 4. aver, avow 5. posit,
state, swear, vouch 6. allege, assert,
attest, avouch, ratify 7. asserver,
certify, confirm, declare, endorse,
profess, testify, warrant 8. sanction,
validate 9. predicate, pronounce
10. asseverate 12. authenticate,
substantiate
affirmation... 3. vow 4. amen, oath,
word 5. basis 6. ground 7. premise
8. averment 9. admission, assertion,
statement, testimony 10. affirmance,

allegation, avouchment, deposition,
foundation, profession
11. declaration, proposition
12. confirmation, ratification
affirmative... 3. aye (ay), nod, yea,
yes 8. dogmatic, positive, thumbs up
(coll) 10. cataphatic (rare)
11. affirmation, declarative,
predicative
affirmatory... 9. assertive
11. affirmative, assertional
affix... 3. add, fix, pen, tag 4. seal
5. annex, stamp 6. anchor, append,
attach, fasten, impose 7. connect,
subjoin 9. increment
11. superimpose
afflict... 3. ail, try, vex 4. hurt, pain
5. upset, wound 6. grieve, harass,
sicken 7. agitate, chasten, derange,
disturb, oppress, torment, trouble
8. disorder, distress, lacerate
9. overthrow, persecute
afflicted... 3. sad 5. ailed 6. pained
7. smitten, wounded 8. troubled
9. depressed, suffering 10. distressed
affliction... 3. woe 4. airs, bane, evil,
pain, pest 5. curse, grief 6. misery,
plague 7. illness, scourge, torment,
trouble 8. calamity, distress, hardship
9. adversity 10. misfortune, visitation
12. wretchedness
afflictive... 6. severe 11. causing pain,
distressing
affluence... 4. ease, flow 6. afflux,
influx, plenty, riches, wealth
8. opulence, richness 9. abundance,
concourse, plenitude, profusion
10. prosperity
affluent... 4. rich 5. flush 6. fluent
7. copious, moneyed, opulent,
wealthy 8. abundant, well–to–do
9. luxuriant, pecunious, plenteous
10. prosperous
afford... 4. bear, cost, give, lend
5. allow, endow, grant, spare, stand,
yield 6. accord, confer, invest, supply
7. furnish, provide, support, undergo
affray... 3. war 4. feud, fray, riot
5. brawl, fight, melee, scrap (sl),
set–to (coll) 6. battle, combat, tumult
7. assault, contest, quarrel, scuffle
9. encounter 11. disturbance
affright... 5. alarm, scare 6. appall
(appal), dismay 7. confuse, startle,
terrify 8. frighten
affront... 4. defy, face, meet, slap
5. abuse 6. harass, insult, offend,
oppose 7. offense, outrage, provoke
8. confront, dishonor, envisage,
ill–treat, irritate 9. encounter,
humiliate, indignity 11. provocation
afghan (pert to)...
fox.. 6. corsac
language.. 11. Afghanistan
prince.. 4. amir (ameer), emir (emeer)
rug.. 5. Herat 6. carpet
stitch.. 7. crochet
wrap.. 7. blanket (woolen)
Afghanistan...
capital.. 5. Kabul
city.. 5. Herat 8. Kandahar
language.. 6. Pushtu 7. Persian

mountain.. 9. Hindu Kush
Pass (famed).. 6. Khyber
people.. 6. Durani 7. Sistani
pony.. 4. yabu (yaboo)
religion.. 5. Islam
river.. 5. Indus
tribe.. 4. Safi, Ulus
Africa... see also *African*
desert.. 6. Libyan, Sahara 8. Kalahari
gulf.. 4. Aden 5. Gabes, Sidra
island (largest).. 10. Madagascar
lake.. 8. Nyassa 9. Victoria
10. Tanganyika
Mt.. 5. Kenya, Natal 8. Cameroon
9. Ruwenzori 11. Kilimanjaro
river.. 4. Nile 5. Congo, Niger
7. Senegal, Zambezi
size (in world).. 6. second
African (pert to)...
charm, fetish.. 4. juju 6. grigri
drum.. 8. bamboula
enclosure.. 4. boma 5. kraal
garment.. 4. haik, tobe 6. kaross
grass.. 7. esparto
grassland.. 4. veld (veldt) 8. bushveld
harp (Nubian).. 5. nanga
hemp.. 3. ife
herb.. 4. ocra
instrument.. 4. gora (gorah) 5. nanga,
rebab 6. balafo
language.. 3. Ibo 4. Zulu 5. Bantu,
Sotho, Tonga 6. Somali, Yoruba
7. Ashanti (Ashantee)
palm.. 6. ronier 7. palmyra
secret society.. 4. Egbo (Negro)
8. Bachichi (cannibal)
soldier.. 5. spahi 6. askari
sorcery.. 5. obeah
spiritual power.. 4. ngai
thong (rawhide).. 4. riem
tree.. 3. oak 4. akee, baku, cola,
etua, shea 5. artar, sassy, siris
6. baobab
African people (pert to)...
Islamitic sect.. 9. Almohades
Natal.. 4. Zulu 6. kaffir 7. Amazulu
Negro society.. 4. Egbo 6. Ogboni
pygmy.. 4. Akka, Doko 5. Afifi, Batwa
7. Bambute
race, tribe.. 4. Arab, Boer, Copt, Kafa
(Kaffa), Zulu 5. Bantu, Fulah, Negro
6. Berber, Kabyle, Kaffir, Nubian,
Semite, Somali 7. Ashanti (Ashantee),
Bushman, Swahili 8. Bechuana
9. Hottentot
African wildlife (pert to)...
antelope.. 3. gnu 4. oryx 5. addax,
eland, oribi 6. impala, rhebok
7. blaubok (small), blesbok, gemsbok
10. duikerbuck, hartebeest
bird.. 4. lory, taha 6. weaver
8. umbretti 9. beefeater, hammerkop
fly.. 4. kivu 6. tsetse
goat.. 5. Capra
horse disease.. 6. surra
mammal.. 8. anteater, pangolin
monkey.. 4. mona, waag 6. baboon,
grivet, guenon 7. guereza 8. talapoin
peacock.. 5. paauw
rhinoceros.. 6. borele 7. keitloa
rodent.. 4. jird 5. ratel
sheep.. 4. zenu 5. oudad (udad)

squirrel.. 5. xerus
stork.. 6. simbil 7. marabou
toad.. 7. Xenopus
worm.. 3. loa
aft, after.. 4. anon, past, rear
5. abaft, later, since 6. astern,
behind 9. posterior 10. subsequent,
succeeding
after (pert to)...
all.. 11. considering 12. nevertheless
awhile.. 4. anon 5. later
breast (Zool).. 10. metathorax
date.. 8. postdate
dinner.. 7. postprandial
dinner coffee.. 9. demitasse
prefix.. 4. meta, post
aftermath.. 4. crop 5. rowen
9. afterglow 12. consequences
aftermost.. 4. last 7. aftmost
8. hindmost, rearmost
afterpiece.. 3. act 4. coda 5. epode
exode 8. postlude 9. aftercome,
afterpart, tailpiece
after song.. 5. epode
afterthought.. 6. regret, sequel
10. reflection 13. arrière-pensée,
second thought
afterward, afterwards.. 4. next
5. after, later, since 6. ensues 7. by
and by 9. afterhand 10. thereafter
11. in the future 12. subsequently
aga, agha.. 5. chief, title
9. commander
agacant, agacante... 8. exciting
11. provocative
agacella (Her)... 8. antelope
again.. 2. re (pref) 3. yet 4. anew,
anon, back, over, then 5. ditto,
newly, often, recur 6. afresh, de
novo, encore, rather 7. freshly
8. eftsoons (eftsoon), likewise,
moreover, once more 9. twice over
10. repeatedly, second time
11. furthermore
against... 2. on, to, vs 3. con, non
4. agin (dial), anti, upon 6. contra,
versus 7. counter, opposed, towards
8. averse to, converse, opposite
against the...
clock.. 4. race, time 7. in haste
grain.. 6. across 7. oblique
9. backwards 10. contrarily
11. unwillingly
law.. 7. illegal, illicit 8. wrongful
12. illegitimate
sun.. 16. counterclockwise
agal... 4. cord (Bedouin head wrap)
agalloch... 4. agar 5. aloes 7. linalon
8. calambac 9. eaglewood, lignaloes
agama, agamoid.. 6. iguana, lizard
Agamemnon (pert to)...
brother.. 8. Menelaus
daughter.. 7. Electra 9. Iphigenia
father.. 6. Atreus
king of.. 7. Mycenae
rival.. 9. Aegisthus
son.. 7. Orestes
wife.. 12. Clytemnestra
wife's paramour.. 9. Aegisthus
agape.. 4. agog, ajar 6. aghast,
gaping 7. curious, yawning
8. open-eyed 9. expectant, love

feast (Chr) 10. astonished,
bewildered, breathless

agate... 3. taw 4. onyx, ruby, type
5. color 6. achate, marble (game),
pebble, quartz 10. birthstone,
chalcedony

agave... 4. aloe 5. datil 6. maguey,
mescal, pulque 8. henequen

age... 3. eon, era, old 4. aeon, date,
eral, eval, time 5. cycle, epoch,
major, minor, older, ripen 6. junior,
mature, mellow, modern, period,
remote, senior 7. century, grow old
8. eternity, lifetime, maturity
9. antiquate, senectude
10. generation

Age... 3. Air, Ice, Jet 4. Iron, Jazz,
Yuga 5. Azoic, Kalpa, Space, Steel,
Stone 6. Atomic, Bronze, Copper,
Eocene, Gilded, Golden, Heroic, Silver
7. Glacial, Homeric, Miocene
8. Cambrian, Cenozoic, Mesozoic
10. Geological, Supersonic
11. Elizabethan

aged... 3. eld, old 5. anile, hoary,
olden 6. feeble, infirm, senile
7. ancient, elderly, Ogygian
8. gerontic 9. Nestorian
10. senectuous

agency... 5. means 6. action, medium,
office 8. function 9. operation
10. collection, commission, efficiency,
management 14. intermediation
15. instrumentality

Agency, News... 2. AP, UP 3. DNB,
INS, UPI 4. Tass 5. Domei
7. Reuters 13. International

agenda... 5. slate 7. agendum (sing),
program 9. memoranda
14. memorandum book, things to be
done

agent... 3. spy 4. doer, test, tool
5. actor, buyer, envoy 6. author,
broker, deputy, factor, medium
7. creator, proctor, reagent, scalper
8. aumildar, emissary, operator,
salesman 9. canvasser, comprador,
consignee, go—between, operative
10. instrument, originator
11. facilitator 12. intermediary
14. representative

Ages... 4. Dark 6. Middle

aggrandize... 5. add to, exalt
6. extend 7. advance, enhance,
enlarge, glorify, magnify, promote
8. increase 10. exaggerate

aggravate... 3. irk, nag, vex 4. miff,
rile, twit 5. anger, annoy, chafe,
pique, sting, taunt, tease, worry
6. nettle, pester, ruffle, worsen
7. bedevil, disturb, incense, magnify,
provoke 8. heighten, increase, irritate
9. infuriate, intensify 10. exasperate

aggravation... 6. bother 7. anguish,
torment, trouble 8. vexation
9. annoyance, worsening
10. affliction, excitement, irritation,
resentment 11. displeasure,
provocation 12. exasperation
15. intensification

aggregate... 3. all, sum 4. mass
5. total, whole 6. amount, volume

8. compound, ensemble 9. accretion
10. collection 11. combination
12. accumulation

aggregate (pert to)...
definable member... 4. unit
fruit... 7. etaerio
in the... 7. en masse, totally
8. together 12. collectively
of plants... 5. flock, flora 7. cluster

aggregation... 4. heap 5. group, union
9. congeries 10. assemblage,
collection 11. combination
12. accumulation, amalgamation
13. consolidation

aggression... 6. attack, injury
7. assault, offense 8. invasion
9. hostility, intrusion, offensive
10. enterprise, initiative
11. provocation 12. encroachment
14. aggressiveness

aggressive... 7. hostile, pushing
9. assertive, attacking, bellicose,
combative, offensive 10. assaulting,
pugnacious 11. belligerent,
contentious, provocative
12. enterprising

aggrieve... 4. pain 6. grieve 7. afflict,
oppress, trouble 9. displease,
persecute, tyrannize

aggrieved... 6. pained, woeful
7. doleful 8. mournful 9. sorrowful
10. displeased

aghast... 4. agog 5. agape 6. afraid
8. appalled, dismayed 9. astounded,
horrified, terrified 10. astonished

agile... 4. fast, spry 5. alert, brisk,
quick, ready, swift 6. active, lively,
nimble, prompt, supple 7. lissome,
springe 11. expeditious

aging... 6. doting, fading 8. maturing,
ripening 9. mellowing, senescent
10. senescence

agio... 7. premium 8. discount,
exchange 9. brokerage 13. money
changing

agitate... 3. fan, jar, wey 4. fret,
move, plot, rile, stir 5. alarm, churn,
rouse, shake, upset 6. debate,
devise, excite, foment, incite, ruffle
7. canvass, perturb, revolve, trouble
8. disquiet, distract, distress
10. discompose

agitated... 7. anxious, excited, ruffled
8. alarming, troubled 9. disturbed,
perturbed, turbulent 10. distressed
11. discomposed, overwrought

agitation... 4. fury, rage, stir 5. alarm,
storm 6. debate, dither, foment,
frenzy, furore, hubbub, tumult, unrest,
uproar 7. anxiety, flutter, shaking,
turmoil 8. disorder, distress,
upheaval, vexation 9. commotion,
trepidity 10. discussion, excitement,
incitement, turbulence
11. disturbance, fomentation,
trepidation 12. deliberation,
perturbation, restlessness

agnate... 3. sib 4. akin 6. allied
7. connate, kindred, related (father's
side) 10. equiparent 11. correlative
14. consanguineous

agnomen... 4. name 5. alias, nomen

7. epithet, surname 8. nickname
agnus castus (Eccl)... 4. lamb
6. chaste 14. tree of chastity
Agnus Dei, Lamb of God... 4. disk
6. anthem, prayer 7. the Mass (part)
ago, agone... 2. by 4. erst, gone,
over, past, yore 5. since 6. bygone,
passed 7. extinct
agog... 4. avid, keen 5. agape, astir,
eager 6. lively, wonder 7. all eyes,
curious, excited, zestful
8. open–eyed, vigilant 9. expectant,
impatient 10. astonished, breathless
agonize... 4. pain, rack 6. grieve,
harrow, strive 7. crucify, torture
8. struggle 10. excruciate
agony... 4. pain, pang, rack 5. grief,
gripe, panic, throe 7. anguish,
torment, torture 8. distress
9. suffering 11. crucifixion
agrarian... 5. rural 6. rustic, sylvan
(silvan) 7. bucolic, hoosier
8. agrestic, Arcadian, frontier,
pastoral 10. campestral, hinterland,
provincial 11. countrified
12. agricultural
agree... 3. fit 4. give, jive, make,
rime, side 5. chime, ditto, grant,
match, rhyme, tally 6. accede,
accord, assent, commit, comply,
concur, engage, submit 7. bargain,
comport, concede, conform, consent,
promise 8. coincide, contract
9. acquiesce, harmonize, stipulate
10. coordinate, correspond
agreeable... 4. nice 5. amene, sapid,
suave 6. comely, dulcet, savory
7. amiable, likable, welcome, willing
8. charming, friendly, obliging,
pleasant, pleasing 9. accordant,
compliant, desirable, indulgent
10. acceptable, compatible,
concordant, consenting, euphonious,
harmonious 11. conformable,
considerate 12. reconcilable,
satisfactory
agreement... 4. mise, pact 5. terms
6. accord, assent, cartel, parity,
treaty, unison 7. bargain, compact,
concord, consent, entente, promise,
rapport 8. contract, covenant, identity
9. accession, consensus
10. accordment, comparison,
compliance, conformity, similarity
11. coincidence, concurrence,
parallelism, stipulation
agrestic... 5. rural 6. rustic 7. bucolic
8. pastoral 9. provincial
agriculture... 7. culture, farming, tillage
8. agrology, agronomy 9. husbandry
10. agrotechny 11. cultivation
13. sharecropping
agriculture (pert to)...
goddess of.. 3. Ops 4. Gaea (Gaia)
5. Ceres, Flora 6. Pomona, Vacuna
7. Demeter
god of.. 4. Nabu, Nebo 6. Faunus
8. Dionysus
means of.. 3. hoe 4. plow (plough)
6. harrow, header, reaper, seeder
7. combine, planter, tractor
8. thrasher 10. cultivator

11. caterpillar
ref to.. 7. georgic
science, crop growing.. 11. arviculture
terms.. 5. arado, grove, ranch, thorp
6. garden, hamlet 7. cropper,
orchard 8. haymaker, vineyard
9. homestead
agriculturist... 6. farmer 7. planter
10. agricolist, husbandman
Agrippina's son... 4. Nero
agrise... 5. abhor, dread 6. loathe
7. shudder, terrify, tremble 8. affright
agronomy, study of... 11. agriculture
aground... 5. stuck 6. ashore
7. swamped, wrecked 8. grounded,
stranded 10. high and dry
agrypnia... 5. vigil 8. insomnia
13. sleeplessness
agua... 4. toad 5. water
aguacate... 7. avocado
ague... 5. chill, fever 7. disease,
malaria, shaking, shivers 9. shivering
ague tree... 9. sassafras
agueweed... 7. boneset, gentian
Ahab (pert to)...
daughter.. 7. Athalie
king of.. 6. Israel
wife.. 7. Jezebel
ahead... 2. on 3. pre (pref) 4. fore
5. afore, early 6. before, onward
7. advance, forward, leading
10. successful, surpassing
ahoy... 4. hail, yo–ho 5. hello 8. ship
ahoy 9. attention
ahu... 5. mound 7. gazelle
8. memorial
ai... 5. sloth 11. exclamation
aid... 4. abet, aide, help, pony
5. allay, devil (printer's), favor, serve
6. assist, helper, incite, relief,
remedy, succor 7. benefit, service,
stipend, subsidy, support 8. befriend,
ministry 9. alleviate, allowance,
assistant 10. assistance, benefactor
11. countenance 13. accommodation
aim... 3. end, fix, way 4. bent, goal,
plan 5. point, scope 6. aspire,
direct, intend, intent, object, strive
7. bearing, current, meaning,
purpose 8. endeavor 9. direction,
intention, objective 11. destination
aimful... 8. aspiring 10. purposeful
aimless... 4. idle 5. blind, loose
6. chance, random 8. drifting
9. desultory, orderless, senseless
10. designless, unarranged,
undirected 11. meaningless,
purposeless, unorganized
aine... 5. elder 6. senior
air... 3. gas, oam, sky 4. aria, aura,
mien, tune, wind 5. draft, ether,
ozone, vapor 6. aerate, aerial,
aspect, breath, breeze, bubble,
manner, melody, oxygen 7. aerator,
bearing, climate, display, hyaline,
posture, publish, refresh 8. attitude,
aviation, behavior, buoyance,
demeanor, hydrogen, presence
9. lightness, publicize, ventilate
10. appearance, atmosphere,
deportment, navigation
11. haughtiness 12. stratosphere

air (pert to)...
disease.. 5. bends 7. caisson
  12. aeroembolism
music.. 4. aria, lilt, solo, tune
  6. melody 7. arietta, sortita
  8. postlude
passage.. 4. duct, flue, vent
  7. pharynx 9. ventiduct
pressure unit.. 8. millebar
ref to.. 9. catabatic
stone.. 8. aerolite 9. meteorite
term.. 5. aural 6. flight, flying
  11. aeronautics
tight.. 5. close, proof 6. sealed
  7. compact 8. hermetic 9. resistant
  11. impermeable
aircraft.. 3. jet 4. kite, link 5. avion,
  blimp 6. bomber, glider 7. airship,
  aviette, balloon, biplane, carrier,
  clipper, flattop 8. airplane, triplane,
  turbojet, zeppelin 9. amphibian,
  dirigible, monoplane, orthopter,
  spaceship, transport 10. helicopter,
  hydroplane, whirlybird
aircraft (pert to)...
designer.. 8. Sikorsky
formation.. 5. fleet 7. echelon
inventor.. 6. Wright (Brothers)
motorless.. 6. glider
part.. 3. fin 4. keel, tail, wing
  6. cabane 7. aileron, cockpit, nacelle
  8. fusilage 9. empennage (tail)
airfield (pert to)... 4. beam, dock,
  shed 5. apron, pylon, tower
  6. hangar, runway 7. airpost, fairway,
  taxiway 8. airstrip, heliport
  9. aerodrome (airdrome), helidrome
airily.. 5. gaily 6. thinly 7. lightly,
  loftily 8. jauntily 10. delicately
  13. pretentiously 14. ostentatiously
airiness.. 6. rarity 7. tenuity
  8. delicacy 9. gauziness, gustiness,
  lightness, loftiness, unreality,
  windiness 10. breeziness, jauntiness
  12. vaporousness
  16. lightheartedness, unsubstantiality
airing.. 4. walk 6. pasear 8. exposure
airy... 3. gay 4. aery, cool, rare, thin
  5. foamy, light, lofty, merry, windy
  6. aerial, breezy, drafty, frothy,
  jaunty, lively 7. gaseous, haughty,
  soaring 8. animated, aspiring,
  delicate, ethereal, fanciful, feathery,
  flippant, towering, volatile
  9. gossamery, vivacious
  10. chimerical, phantasmal
  11. atmospheric 12. lighthearted,
  ostentatious
aiseweed... 8. goutweed
aisle... 4. lane, nave 5. alley 6. artery,
  avenue 7. passage 8. corridor
  10. passageway
aisteori... 5. actor
ait, eyot... 3. oat 4. holm, isle, reef
  5. atoll, islet 10. island
aitu... 3. god 5. demon 6. spirit
Aix... 4. duck
aizle... 4. soot 5. ember, spark
Ajax (pert to)...
called... 11. Ajax the Less (next
  swiftest to Achilles)
father... 7. Telamon

hero of.. 8. The Iliad (Homer)
ajenjo... 8. absinthe
ajonjoli... 6. sesame
akimbo... 4. bent 6. angled, hooked
  7. angular, crooked
akin... 3. sib 4. like, near 5. close
  6. agnate, allied 7. cognate,
  germane, kindred, related, similar
  9. connected 10. correlated
  14. consanguineous
ala... 4. wing 8. winglike
a la... 2. so 4. thus 11. identically
  13. in the manner of
Alabama...
capital.. 10. Montgomery
Capitol, Confederate (2 months)..
  10. White House (1st, 1861,
  so–named)
carnival.. 11. Azalea Trail
city.. 6. Mobile 7. Gadsden
  10. Birmingham, Huntsville
flower.. 9. goldenrod
monument.. 11. Russell Cave
museum.. 22. George Washington
  Carver
native woman (famed).. 11. Helen
  Keller
President, Confederate.. 5. Davis
  (Jefferson)
State admission.. 12. Twenty–second
State motto.. 21. We Dare Defend
  Our Rights
State nickname.. 12. Heart of Dixie,
  Yellowhammer
statue (huge).. 6. Vulcan
alabaster... 6. gypsum, marble
  7. mineral
alacrity... 4. zest 7. avidity
  9. briskness, eagerness, immediacy,
  quickness, readiness, swiftness
  10. promptness 11. promptitude,
  punctuality, willingness
  13. sprightliness
Aladdin (pert to)...
possessor (of magic).. 4. lamp, ring
spirit (of magic).. 4. jinn
window.. 4. task (impossible)
youth (character).. 13. Arabian Nights
á la diable... 7. deviled (devilled)
  8. seasoned
alameda... 4. mall, walk 5. prado
  9. esplanade, promenade
Alamo... 6. poplar (tree) 7. Mission
  (San Antonio, Tex)
a la mode... 4. mode 5. smart
  6. modish, spruce 7. fashion, stylish,
  voguish 8. up–to–date 9. stylishly
  11. fashionably 12. with ice cream
alan... 3. dog (Her)
alar (pert to)... 4. wing 6. pteric
  8. axillary, shoulder
alarm... 3. din 4. call, fear, flap
  5. alert, broil, clock, daunt, panic,
  scare 6. alarum, arouse, dismay,
  fright, terror, tocsin 7. startle, terrify,
  warning 8. affright, frighten
  11. trepidation 12. apprehension
  13. consternation
alarmist... 6. scarer 9. pessimist,
  terrorist 10. frightener
  11. scaremonger
alas... 2. ah, ay, oh 3. ach, heu, och

4. oime 5. alack, ohone 7. woe is
me 8. lackaday

Alaska . . . see also *Alaskan*
  capital . . 6. Juneau
  city . . 4. Nome 5. Sitka 7. Skagway
    9. Anchorage, Fairbanks, Ketchikan
  discoverer . . 11. Vitus Bering
  fish . . 6. salmon, wachna 7. inconnu
  flower . . 11. forget—me—not
  glacier . . 4. Muir
  governor . . 4. Egan 6. Hickel
  highway . . 5. Alcan
  island . . 6. Kodiak, Unimak
    7. Diomede (Little), Nunivak
    9. Aleutians, Probilofs
  mountain . . 3. Ada 7. Foraker
    8. McKinley (highest in N Am),
    Wrangell
  northernmost point . . 11. Point Barrow
  peninsula . . 5. Kenai 6. Seward
  rapids . . 10. Whitehorse
  river . . 5. Yukon 9. Kuskokwim
  State admission . . 10. Forty–ninth
  State symbol . . 9. bald eagle
  strait . . 6. Bering
  volcano . . 6. Katmai 8. Wrangell
Alaskan (pert to) . . .
  boat . . 5. kayak, umiak 7. bidarka
    (bidarkee)
  codfish . . 6. wachna
  liquor . . 9. hoochinoo
  native . . 5. Aleut 6. Eskimo 7. Tlingit
    8. Aleutian
albacore . . 4. tuna 5. tunny 6. bonito,
  germon
Albania . . .
  capital . . 6. Tirana
  city . . 5. Berat 6. Durres, Valona
    7. Scutari 8. Elbasani
  dialect . . 4. Gheg, Tosk
  king . . 3. Zog
  lake . . 6. Prespa 7. Scutari
  mountain . . 5. Koreb 6. Pindus
  river . . 4. Drin 6. Bojana
  soldier . . 7. palikar
  tribe . . 4. Cham
albatross . . 5. nelly (sooty) 7. pelican
  9. mallemuck
albe (anc) . . 5. album
albert (pert to) . . .
  biscuit . . 6. pastry 7. dariole
  jewelry . . 10. watch chain
  medal . . 4. gold (for bravery)
  paper . . 4. size
  pottery . . 10. terra–cotta
Albion . . 7. England (Poet)
albumin . . 5. glair 7. protein
  9. endosperm
alcazar . . 6. palace 8. fortress
alchemy . . . 5. magic 6. change
  7. sorcery 10. change–over,
  conversion
alcohol . . 5. drink 6. liquor 7. ethanol,
  spirits, talitol, terpene 8. beverage
  9. aqua vitae, firewater 10. intoxicant
alcoholic beverage . . . 3. gin, rum
  4. beer, brew, grog, malt, mead,
  wine 5. booze, hooch, negus, punch,
  vodka 6. brandy, whisky (whiskey)
  7. bourbon, cordial, liqueur, tequila
  8. cocktail, highball 9. applejack,
  moonshine

alcoholism . . . 9. addiction, oenomania
  10. dipsomania 11. drunkenness
  12. intoxication
Alcott character . . . 2. Jo 3. Amy,
  Meg 4. Beth
alcove . . . 3. bay 4. cove, nook
  5. arbor, bower, kiosk, niche, oriel
  6. recess 7. cubicle, dinette, pergola
  8. alhacena
alder (pert to) . . .
  chief . . 5. ruler 6. prince
  fishing . . 3. fly (artificial)
  tree . . 8. sagerose (yellow)
ale . . . 3. mum 4. beer, flip 5. stout
  6. alegar, liquor (malt) 8. festival
alee . . . 7. leeward (opp of windward)
Aleppo (pert to) . . .
  city . . 5. Syria
  grass . . 7. Johnson
  stone . . 3. gem 5. agate 8. eye agate
alert . . . 4. keen, warn, wary 5. agile,
  alarm, alive, aware, brisk, peart
  (pert), quick, ready, sharp 6. active,
  bright, lively, nimble, prompt
  8. vigilant, watchful 9. attentive,
  observant, sprightly, wide–awake
  11. circumspect
Aleut . . . 4. Atka 6. Eskimo 7. Unungun
  8. Unalaska
Aleutians . . .
  islands (chain) . . 8. volcanic
  native of . . 5. Aleut
  site . . 5. Alaska 9. Bering Sea
alewife . . 4. fish 7. herring, pompano,
  walleye 9. gaspereau
Alexander the Great (pert to) . . .
  birthplace . . 5. Pella (Macedonia)
  conqueror of . . 6. Persia
  expedition . . 10. Hellespont
  horse . . 10. Bucephalus
Alexandria, Egypt . . .
  bishop . . 5. Arius 10. Athanasius
    12. Eratosthenes
  island . . 6. Pharos
  obelisks . . 17. Cleopatra's Needles
    (now in NY City & London)
  ruler . . 7. Ptolemy
  world wonder . . 10. Lighthouse
    (Pharos)
alfa . . 5. grass 7. esparto
alfalfa . . . 3. hay 5. medic 6. clover,
  fodder 7. lucerne (lucern)
alforja . . . 3. bag 5. pouch 6. wallet
  9. saddlebag
alfresco . . 4. airy 7. open–air, outside
alga, algae . . . 4. cell, moss, nori
  5. Dasya, fungi 6. Alaria, diatom,
  fungus, Padiva 7. seaweed
  8. plankton 9. stonewort
Algeria . . .
  capital . . 7. Algiers
  Mohammedan saint . . 8. Marabout
  monastery . . 5. ribat
  mountain . . 5. Atlas (Range)
  native . . 5. Arabs 7. Berbers, Kabyles
  ruler . . 3. bey, day
  ship . . 5. xebec
  soldier . . 5. spahi (spahee) 6. Zouave
algid . . . 3. icy 4. cold 5. brisk, crisp,
  nippy 6. frigid, wintry 7. ice–cold
algodon . . 6. cotton
algology, study of . . . 5. algae

8. seaweeds
Algonquian spirit... 6. manito
(manitou)
Algonquian tribe... 4. Cree, Sauk
5. Miami 6. Ottawa 7. Arapaho,
Ojibway, Shawnee 8. Cheyenne,
Delaware 9. Blackfoot
Alhambra (pert to)...
architecture.. 7. Moorish
palace, alcazar of.. 12. Moorish Kings
site.. 7. Granada (Spain)
alias... 6. anonym 7. epithet
8. cognomen, nickname 9. otherwise,
pseudonym, sobriquet
Ali Baba (pert to)...
adventurer.. 4. cave (Forty Thieves)
password to cave.. 6. Sesame
tale.. 13. Arabian Nights
alien... 3. ger 5. fremd 6. exotic,
remote 7. adverse, foreign, hostile,
opposed, strange 8. outsider,
stranger 9. foreigner, peregrine,
unrelated 10. extraneous, unfriendly
11. incongruous
alienate... 4. part, wean 6. demise,
detach, devest, divest, divide
8. disunite, estrange, separate
alienation... 4. outs 5. split 6. breach
8. disfavor 10. conveyance,
falling-out, withdrawal
12. amortization, disaffection,
estrangement
alienist... 12. psychiatrist
aliform... 8. winglike 10. wing-shaped
alight... 4. land, rest, stop 5. ditch,
lodge, perch 6. settle 7. burning,
descend, lighted 8. dismount
align, aline... 4. true 5. level, match
6. equate, line up 7. arrange,
marshal 9. collineate, straighten
11. parallelize
alike... 3. iso (comb form) 4. akin,
like, same, twin 7. similar, uniform
8. selfsame 9. duplicate, identical
10. homonymous
17. indistinguishable
aliment... 4. food, keep 5. broma,
manna 7. nurture, pabulum, support
9. nutriment, nutrition, refection
10. sustenance 11. nourishment,
refreshment
alimentary canal, part... 5. mouth
7. pharynx, stomach 9. esophagus,
intestine
alimony... 7. stipend 8. estovers
9. allotment
aline... see *align*
alipin... 5. slave (Phil)
alipod... 3. bat 10. wing-footed
aliquid... 6. somewhat 9. something
aliquot... 4. part 5. prime 7. decimal,
digital, divisor, partial 10. fractional,
reciprocal 11. submultiple (opp of
aliquant)
alive... 3. vif 4. keen 5. alert, awake,
brisk, vital 6. extant, lively, loving,
zoetic 7. animate, current, topical
8. animated, existent 9. breathing,
conscious, sensitive, sprightly
11. clear-witted, unforgotten
alkali... 3. lye 6. salt, soda
8. saltwort

alkaline... 3. reh 4. usar 6. alkali
7. antacid, nonacid
alkaline forming... 10. kaligenous
alkaloid... 6. codein, conine, eserin
7. aricine, caffein, cocaine, codeine
8. atropine, morphine 10. strychnine
13. physostigmine
alkaloid (pert to)...
bark.. 7. aricine
bean.. 13. physostigmine
beverage.. 8. caffeine (caffein)
drug.. 7. cocaine, codeine
8. morphine 10. strychnine
extract.. 6. curare (curari) 11. arrow
poison
hemlock.. 7. coniine
ipecac.. 7. emetine
lupine.. 8. lupinine
mustard seed.. 7. sinapin
all... 3. pan (pref), sum 4. omni (pref),
only, toto 5. alone, every, sum of,
total, tutti, whole 6. entire, wholly
7. perfect 8. ensemble, entirely,
totality 9. aggregate, everybody
10. altogether, completely,
everything, thoroughly 11. exclusively
all (pert to)...
absorbing.. 4. main 5. chief, prime
6. ruling 7. capital, leading, primary
8. foremost 9. paramount, principal
11. controlling
around.. 5. handy 9. versatile
devouring.. 6. greedy 9. rapacious
10. gluttonous
in all.. 9. generally 10. on the whole
inclusive.. 6. global 7. omneity
8. catholic, ecumenic, pandemic
9. universal 12. cosmopolitan
knowing.. 4. wise 6. divine
10. omniscient
powerful.. 6. divine 7. all-wise,
supreme 8. absolute, almighty
9. all-seeing 10. all-knowing,
omnipotent, omniscient, ubiquitous
the same.. 9. identical 10. equivalent
12. nevertheless
Allah... 3. God 5. deity 12. Supreme
Being
allay... 4. cool, ease 5. abate, check,
slake 6. pacify, soothe, subdue
7. appease, assuage, compose,
relieve, repress, satisfy 8. moderate
9. alleviate
allée... 4. mall, walk 5. aisle
6. avenue 7. passage
allege... 4. aver, cite 5. offer, plead,
quote, state 6. adduce, affirm,
assert, assign 7. advance, ascribe,
declare, present, pretend, profess,
propose 8. maintain 9. attribute
allegiance... 3. tie 4. bond 5. faith,
liege 6. fealty, homage 7. loyalty
8. devotion, fidelity, firmness
9. adherence, constancy
12. faithfulness 13. steadfastness
allegory... 5. fable, story 6. emblem
7. parable 8. apologue
alleviate... 4. ease 5. abate, allay,
erase, quiet, salve, slake 6. lessen,
pacify, reduce, soften, solace, soothe
7. assuage, compose, lighten, relieve
8. mitigate, moderate, palliate

9. extenuate 11. tranquilize

alley... 3. mig (marble), way 4. lane, mall, path, slum 5. aisle, byway, tewer 6. arcade, artery, byroad 8. cul-de-sac

alliance... 4. pact 5. union 6. fusion, league, treaty 7. compact, entente 8. affinity, agnation, covenant 9. coalition 10. federation 11. association, combination, confederacy 13. confederation

allied... 4. akin 6. agnate, linked, united 7. cognate, germane, kindred, leagued, related, similar 10. associated, correlated

alligator... 5. gator, niger 6. Caiman, cayman, jacare (yacare) 7. lagarto 9. crocodile

alligator pear... 7. avocado 8. aguacate

alliteration... 4. rime 5. rhyme 6. jingle 9. assonance 10. repetition

allocate... 4. deal, mete 5. allot 6. assign, locate, ordain 7. appoint, arrange, consign, reserve 9. apportion 10. distribute

allocation... 8. disposal 9. billeting 11. collocation, disposition 12. distribution

allot... 3. fix 4. cast, dole, mete 5. grant 6. assign, billet, design, intend, ordain, ration, specify 7. appoint, destine, specify 9. apportion, attribute, prescribe 11. appropriate

allotment... 5. cavel, share 6. ration 7. subsidy 10. allocation, assignment, ordainment 13. apportionment

allow... 3. let 4. bear, give 5. admit, think 6. endure, permit, rebate, suffer 7. approve, concede, suppose 8. consider, discount, tolerate 9. authorize 11. acknowledge

allowance... 3. fee 4. tare, tret 5. arras, grant 6. ration 7. pension, scalage, stipend 8. appenage (prince's), discount, granting, sanction 9. admitting, allotment, conceding, tolerance 10. permission 11. scholarship 13. authorization

allowing for... 2. if 8. provided

allow to pass... 5. lapse 6. expire, revert

alloy... 3. mix 4. asem 5. blend, mokum 6. billon, fusion, oroide 7. amalgam, bullion, corrupt, mixture 8. compound 9. composite 10. adulterate, amalgamate

alloys...
copper, aluminum.. 9. duralumin
copper, sulphur.. 6. niello
copper, tin.. 6. bronze
copper, white metal.. 6. oroide
copper, zinc.. 5. brass 6. tombac
copper, zinc, iron.. 4. Aich (Chin)
copper, zinc, nickel.. 4. iron 7. paktong (packtong)
copper, zinc, nickel, iron.. 7. rheotan
German silver.. 6. albata
gold, silver.. 4. asem

iron, carbon.. 5. steel
iron, nickel.. 6. Calite (trademark)
lead, tin.. 6. pewter, solder
nickel, steel.. 5. Invar

allspice tree... 7. pimento

alltud... 5. alien, slave 9. foreigner

allude... 4. hint 5. imply, point, refer 6. relate 7. mention, suggest 8. indicate, intimate 9. insinuate

allure... 3. win 4. bait, draw, lead, lure, tice, tole 5. charm, decoy, snare, tempt 6. entice, entrap, invite, seduce 7. attract, prevail 8. inveigle, persuade 9. captivate, fascinate, influence

allurement... 4. bait, lure 5. bride 7. glamour (glamor) 8. agacerie, coquetry 10. attraction, enticement, inducement, temptation 12. inveiglement

allusion... 4. clue, hint 7. inkling 8. innuendo, instance 9. reference 11. implication

alluvial deposit... 3. mud 4. silt 5. delta, geest 6. placer

ally... 3. pal 4. aide, join 5. union 6. fellow, friend, league 7. comrade, consort, kinsman, partner 8. adherent, relative 9. associate, attendant, colleague 10. accomplice 11. confederate 12. collaborator

Alma (It)... 4. soul 6. spirit 10. cherishing, nourishing

alma... 6. fabric (silk)

almacen... 4. shop 8. magazine 9. warehouse

Alma Mater... 6. school 7. college 9. goddesses 10. university

almanac... 5. fasti 6. record 7. calends (kalends) 8. calendar, register 9. ephemeris (obs)

almighty... 5. great 6. divine 10. omnipotent 11. all-powerful 12. irresistible

almost... 4. most, nigh 5. anear, close 6. all but, nearly 8. well-nigh 9. nearabout 13. approximately

alms... 4. dole, mite 6. aumous, bounty, corban, relief 7. charity, handout 8. donation, gratuity, pittance 12. contribution, philanthropy

alms (pert to)...
box.. 4. arca 5. chest
giver.. 5. donor 7. almoner 11. contributor 14. philanthropist
man.. 5. donee 6. pauper 7. feoffee 9. pensioner

alodium... 4. land 6. tenure 8. freehold 10. real estate

aloe, aloes... 4. drug 5. agave, plant 6. tambac 7. incense 8. agalloch

aloft... 2. up 4. high, over 5. aloof 7. skyward 8. overhead

aloha... 4. hail, love 7. good-bye 9. affection, greetings 11. salutations

Aloha State... 6. Hawaii

aloin... 4. drug 5. aloes 8. nataloin 9. barbaloin (Barbados) 12. isobarbaloin

alone... 4. solo 5. apart, solus 6. single, singly, solely, unique 8. desolate, homeless, isolated,

separate, solitary 9. exclusive,
matchless 10. unassisted
12. single–handed
13. companionless, independently,
unaccompanied

along... 2. on 3. via 4. with
6. beside, onward 7. forward
8. together

alongside... 2. by 4. near 6. beside
7. abreast 8. parallel

aloof... 6. offish, remote 7. distant,
haughty 8. reserved 10. unsociable
11. indifferent, standoffish
15. uncommunicative

aloofness... 7. reserve 10. offishness,
remoteness 11. haughtiness
12. indifference 13. unsociability

alopecia... 6. acomia 8. baldness
12. hairlessness

aloud... 4. oral 6. loudly 7. audibly,
plainly

alp... 3. tor 4. peak, pico, pike
6. summit 8. mountain 9. bullfinch

alp (Teut Folklore)... 5. demon, witch
9. nightmare

alpaca... 4. coat, paco 5. llama
7. garment

Alph... 11. sacred river (Kubla Khan)

alpha... 3. star 5. prime 6. letter
7. initial, numeral 9. beginning

alphabet... 4. ABC's 6. Sarada
(Kashmir) 9. abecedary
10. Davanagari (Sanskrit)

alphabet characters (Teut)... 4. ogam,
rune

alphabetize... 4. file 5. group, index
6. codify, letter 8. classify, tabulate
9. catalogue (catalog) 10. categorize

alpha test (Army)... 12. intelligence

alpine... 5. alpen, hilly 6. knobby
10. alpestrine 11. mountainous

Alpine (pert to)...
climber.. 10. alpestrian
dance.. 7. gavotte (gavot)
dress.. 6. dirndl
dwelling.. 6. chalet
goat.. 4. ibex
herdsman.. 4. senn
peak.. 5. Blanc 9. Monte Rosa
10. Matterhorn
plant.. 9. edelweiss
province.. 5. Tyrol
shelter.. 7. hospice
snowfield.. 4. firn, neve
tunnel.. 7. Simplon 10. St Gotthard
wind.. 4. bise 5. foehn

Alps... 5. Blanc, Tirol (Tyrol) 6. Julian
7. Dinaric 8. Jungfrau 9. Dolomites,
Monte Rosa (peak) 10. Matterhorn

already... 3. ere, yet 5. afore
6. before 7. earlier 8. hitherto
10. heretofore 11. theretofore

also... 2. as, et, so 3. and, too, yet
4. more, plus 5. besides, further
8. likewise, moreover 9. similarly
11. furthermore

altar (pert to)...
boy.. 7. acolyte
cloth.. 6. dossal (dossel) 7. haploma
9. ependytes
constellation.. 3. Ara
curtain.. 6. riddel

end of church.. 4. apse 7. chancel
Greek.. 5. bomos 6. hestia
7. eschara
Latin.. 7. scrobis
ledge.. 7. retable
platform.. 8. predella
screen.. 7. reredos
shelf, table.. 6. gradin 7. retable
8. credence
step.. 8. predella
top slab.. 5. mensa

alter... 4. geld, vary, veer 5. amend,
emend, reset, shift 6. adjust,
change, immute, modify, mutate,
revise 7. falsify 8. castrate
9. transform

alteration... 6. change 9. diversity,
variation 10. castration, correction
12. modification 13. interpolation
15. diversification

altercation... 3. row 4. feud, spat, tiff
5. fight, snarl 6. fracas, strife
7. dispute, quarrel, wrangle
8. squabble, vendetta 7. imbroglio
10. contention 11. controversy

alter ego... 4. mate, self, twin
7. oneself 10. complement
11. counterpart

alternate... 4. vary 5. proxy
6. change, deputy, rotate, seesaw
7. reverse, stand–in 8. delegate
9. oscillate 10. substitute
11. alternative, interchange,
reciprocate

alternate writing mode (anc)...
13. boustrophedon

alternative... 2. or 3. nor 5. other
6. choice, either, option, switch
7. dilemma 8. election, loophole
9. secondary 10. nip–and–tuck,
preference, substitute
11. replacement

although, altho... 4. even, when
5. while 6. albeit, though 7. despite,
whereas 15. notwithstanding

altimetry... 6. height 10. hypsometry
11. measurement

altitude... 6. height (highth) 7. heroics,
stature 8. eminence, highness,
tallness 9. elevation, loftiness

altogether... 5. fully, quite 6. bodily,
wholly 7. utterly 8. entirely, outright
9. generally 10. completely,
thoroughly 12. collectively

alto horn... 7. althorn, saxhorn
10. mellophone

altruism... 7. charity, concern
8. kindness 11. beneficence,
benevolence 12. philanthropy

alumnus (alumni)... 4. grad 5. pupil
6. alumna (alumnae) 8. graduate,
postgrad 12. postgraduate

alveary... 4. hive 6. apiary 7. beehive

alveola... 3. dip, pit 4. pore, sink
6. crater, pocket

alveolar... 6. pitted, pocked
7. notched 8. indented 10. depressed

always... 2. ay 3. aye, e'er 4. ever
6. anyway, semper 7. forever
8. evermore 9. eternally, uniformly
10. constantly, invariably
11. continually, everlasting,

perpetually, universally

ama... 4. tree 5. amula (Bib) 6. vessel

amabile... 6. gentle, tender
9. agreeable

Amadis de Gaul (Arthurian)... 4. hero
5. lover

amadou... 5. punk 6. tinder 7. styptic

amah... 5. nurse 7. servant
9. nursemaid 11. maidservant

amain... 5. apace 7. hastily, quickly,
swiftly 9. posthaste

amalgamate... 3. mix 4. fuse, join,
weld 5. blend, merge, unite
6. commix 7. combine 8. coalesce,
compound, intermix 11. consolidate

amalgamation... 6. fusion, merger
7. mixture 11. combination

Amalkite... 4. Agag (King) 5. nomad
7. Bedouin

amant... 5. lover 6. amante

amaryllis... 4. bulb, lily 5. agave, plant
6. flower 8. mistress 10. sweetheart
11. shepherdess

amass... 4. save 5. hoard, stack, store
6. gather 7. collect 8. assemble
10. accumulate

amate... 5. daunt 6. subdue
10. dishearten

amateur... 3. ham 4. tyro 6. novice
7. dabbler, fancier 8. beginner,
virtuoso 10. aficionado, apprentice,
dilettante 15. nonprofessional

amateurish... 5. inapt 9. unskilled,
untrained, untutored 10. unfinished
15. nonprofessional

Amati... 6. family, violin

amatory... 4. fond 6. ardent, erotic,
loving, tender 7. amorous, philter
9. loverlike 10. passionate

amaze... 4. awe 4. stun 7. astound,
perplex, stagger, startle, stupefy
8. astonish, bewilder, confound,
surprise 9. dumbfound, overwhelm

amazement... 3. awe 5. alarm
6. wonder 8. surprise 10. perplexity
12. bewilderment 13. consternation

Amazon... 5. Queen (Myth), river
6. virago 9. androgyne
10. warrioress 11. Penthesilea

Amazon river (pert to)...
cetacean.. 4. Inia
discoverer.. 6. Pinzon (1500)
mouth.. 4. Para
rain forest.. 5. selva
tributary.. 3. Apa 4. Napo

ambary... 2. da 4. hemp 5. fiber
6. Nolita

ambassador... 5. envoy 6. legate,
nuncio 8. diplomat, emissary,
minister 9. messenger
12. intermediary 14. representative
15. plenipotentiary

amber... 6. yellow 8. electrum

ambidextrous... 7. capable
8. two-faced 9. two-handed,
versatile 11. ambidextral, treacherous
13. double-dealing

ambiguous... 6. double 7. dubious
9. equivocal, uncertain, unsettled
10. indefinite, indistinct, mistakable
12. questionable 13. indeterminate

ambit... 5. orbit, scope 6. extent,

sphere 7. circuit 8. precinct

ambition... 4. goal, spur 6. desire
10. aspiration

amble... 4. pace, rack, trot 7. piaffer

ambrosia... 4. food 5. honey, manna
6. nectar 7. perfume 8. delicacy,
libation

ambulate... 4. hike, move, walk

ambush... 4. trap 5. snare 6. hiding,
waylay 7. mantrap 9. ambuscade
10. subterfuge 11. concealment

ameliorate... 4. ease, mend 5. emend
6. better 7. improve 8. progress
9. meliorate

amelioration... 10. betterment
11. improvement, restoration

amenable... 6. liable, pliant
7. movable 9. receptive
10. answerable, open-minded,
responsive 11. accountable,
persuadable, responsible

amend... 4. beat (dial), beet (beete)
5. alter, atone, emend 6. reform,
repeal 7. convert, correct, improve,
rectify, redress, restore

amendment... 5. rider 8. addition
10. conversion, correction
11. improvement, reformation

amends... 7. redress 8. reprisal
9. atonement 10. recompense,
reparation 11. restitution

amenities... 5. mores 7. decorum,
manners 8. etiquette 10. civilities,
courtesies 11. formalities, gentilities,
proprieties

ament... 6. catkin 7. cattail

American (pert to)...
bear.. 7. musquaw (black)
buffalo.. 5. bison
cactus.. 4. bleo 7. saguaro
carnivore.. 4. puma
cataract.. 7. Niagara (Falls)
cedar (red).. 5. savin
elk.. 6. wapiti
Japanese.. 5. Nisei 6. Kibbei
leopard.. 6. ocelot
marsupial.. 7. opossum
merganser.. 4. duck (fish-eating)
Mexican.. 6. gringo
mink.. 5. vison
moth.. 2. io
nickname.. 6. Yankee (Yank)
ostrich.. 4. rhea
palm.. 5. Sabal 8. palmetto
quail.. 5. colin
rail.. 4. sora
squirrel.. 9. chickaree (red)
vulture.. 5. urubu 6. condor

American, famed...
artist.. 5. Flagg, Peale 6. Stuart
7. Sargent 8. Rockwell, The Eight
astronomer.. 11. Rittenhouse
chemist.. 6. Carver (G Washington)
crusader (Temperance).. 12. Carrie
Nation
discoverer.. 4. Eric (The Red)
5. Cabot, Votan 8. Columbus
doctor, surgeon.. 4. Mayo 6. Schick
7. Cushing
educator.. 4. Hume, Mann 5. Eliot
10. Washington (Booker T)
explorer.. 4. Byrd 5. Boone, Clark,

Lewis, Peary 6. Carson (Kit)
9. Ellsworth

musician.. 6. Foster 8. Damrosch,
Gershwin 9. Bernstein, MacDowell,
Stokowski

naturalist.. 4. Muir 5. Beebe
7. Audubon, Burbank

patriot.. 4. Clay, Hale, Otis 5. Dawes,
Henry (Patrick), Paine (Thomas)
6. Revere

physicist.. 6. Teller (H–bomb)

pianist.. 6. Duchin, Levant
8. Horowitz, Liberace, Williams
(Roger) 10. Van Cliburn

pirate.. 4. Kidd (Capt)

poet.. 4. Nash 5. Benet, Eliot, Frost
6. Kilmer, Lowell, Millay 8. Sandburg
10. Longfellow

Red Cross organizer.. 6. Barton (Clara)

Scouts (Girl) organizer.. 3. Low
(Juliette)

sculptor.. 6. Calder 7. Borglum

singer.. 4. Pons 5. Jones, Moore
6. Farrar, Peerce 7. Kirsten, Merrill,
Tibbett 8. Anderson (Marian)

statesman.. 4. Clay, Root 6. Baruch,
Dulles 8. Harriman

suffragette.. 4. Catt (Carrie Chapman)

violinist.. 7. Menuhin

writer, novelist.. 6. Ferber 8. Faulkner
9. Hemingway

American Indian (pert to)...
chief.. 5. brave 6. sachem
child.. 7. papoose
conference.. 6. powwow
girl.. 7. Nokomis (Myth)
9. Minnehaha, Sacagawea
(Sakajawea) 10. Pocahontas
hero (Myth).. 8. Hiawatha
magician.. 6. shaman, wabeno
(Ojibway)
shelter.. 4. tent 5. hogan, tepee
(teepee) 6. wigwam 7. wickiup
(wikiup)

American Indian tribe... see also
Indian 3. Fox, Oto (Otoe), Ree, Sac,
Ute 4. Cree, Crow, Erie, Hopi, Iowa,
Pima 5. Creek, Kansa, Osage, Piute,
Sioux 6. Cayuga, Dakota, Mohawk,
Oneida, Pueblo, Seneca 7. Arapaho,
Choctaw, Mohican, Ojibway, Siksika
8. Cherokee, Chippewa, Iroquois,
Onondaga, Seminole 9. Algonquin,
Blackfoot, Chickasaw 10. Athapascan
Muskhogean

ami... 5. lover 6. friend (law)

amiable... 6. kindly 7. lovable
8. charming, friendly, pleasant,
pleasing 9. agreeable, indulgent
10. hospitable

amicable... 4. kind 8. friendly, sociable
9. congenial, peaceable
10. harmonious

amicus curiae... 5. judge 6. deputy,
lawyer 16. friend of the court

amid, amidst... 2. in 5. among
7. amongst, between

amigo... 6. friend 8. neighbor

amiss... 3. ill 5. badly, fault, wrong
6. astray, sinful 8. faultily, improper
10. disorderly 11. erroneously

amity... 4. love 5. peace 7. harmony
10. friendship 11. sociability
12. congeniality, friendliness

amma... 6. abbess, mother (spiritual)

ammonia... 9. hartshorn 10. fertilizer
11. refrigerant

ammoniac plant... 2. oshac

ammunition (pert to)...
box.. 9. bandoleer
chest.. 7. caisson
type.. 4. arms, bomb, shot 7. bullets
8. grenades, missiles, munition,
shrapnel 10. explosives
wagon.. 7. caisson

amnesty... 6. pardon 8. oblivion
9. acquittal 13. forgetfulness

amoeba, ameba... 3. olm 4. cell
7. proteus 10. protoplasm
13. microorganism

among, amongst... 2. in 3. mid
4. amid, with 5. midst 6. amidst,
imelle 7. between

among nations... 13. international

Amor... 4. Eros 5. Cupid

AMORC... 11. Rosicrucian

amorous... 4. fond 6. ardent, erotic,
loving, tender 7. adoring, devoted
8. enamored 10. passionate
12. affectionate

amorous looks... 4. ogle 5. stare
8. coquetry 10. come–hither,
flirtation

amorphous... 8. abnormal, formless
9. deviative, shapeless, subnormal
14. uncrystallized

amorphous mineral... 4. opal

amort... 8. dejected, lifeless
9. inanimate 10. spiritless

amortize... 5. clear 6. convey, payoff,
settle 9. discharge, negotiate

amount... 3. lot, sum 4. cost, rate,
rise, unit 5. chunk, price, ratal,
store, total 6. ascend, degree
7. quantum, signify 8. quantity

amount (pert to)...
due.. 5. price 6. arrear 7. default,
deficit
mean.. 7. average
realized.. 4. take 6. intake
8. proceeds
small.. 6. morsel 7. modicum
smallest.. 5. least
to.. 3. all 4. even 5. equal, match,
total 10. correspond

amour... 6. affair 7. liaison, romance
8. intrigue, triangle 10. flirtation

ampere... 3. amp 4. unit 6. ohmage
7. current, voltage

ampersand... 3. and 4. also

Amphibia... 5. Anura, frogs, toads
7. Aglossa 8. tadpoles 9. Salientia
11. salamanders

amphibious... 5. mixed 9. adaptable
10. fifty–fifty 11. half–and–half, mixed
nature (land and water)

amphibole... 7. edenite, mineral, uralite
8. aluminum, nephrite

amphigory, amphigouri... 5. rhyme
6. jingle, poetry 10. doggerel
9. rigmarole

amphilogism, amphilogy...
9. ambiguity, duplexity (meaning)

10. equivocacy

Amphion (pert to)...
capturer of.. 6. Thebes
husband of.. 5. Niobe
son of.. 4. Zeus
twin of.. 6. Zethus

amphitheater... 4. bowl 5. arena,
cavea, scene, stage 6. circus, cirque
7. stadium 8. coliseum, platform
10. hippodrome

amphora... 3. jar, urn 4. vase
5. diota, prize 7. measure
8. ornament

ample... 4. full, rich, wide 5. broad,
large, roomy 6. enough, plenty
7. liberal 8. abundant 9. bountiful,
capacious, extensive, plenteous,
plentiful, unstinted 10. munificent
12. satisfactory

ampliation... 5. flare 9. expansion,
extension 11. enlargement
12. postponement 13. amplification
14. aggrandizement

amplify... 3. pad 5. widen 6. dilate,
extend 7. develop, enlarge
8. increase 9. aggravate, expatiate
10. exaggerate, overstress

amplitude... 4. size 6. amount
7. breadth 8. fullness 9. greatness,
plenitude 12. spaciousness

amputate... 4. trim 5. prune, sever
6. cut off 8. mutilate, retrench,
truncate

amuck, amok... 3. fit 4. rage
6. attack, frenzy, malady
12. corybantiasm

amulet... 3. gem 5. charm 6. fetish,
scarab, voodoo 7. periapt
8. ornament, talisman 10. protection

amuse... 3. wow 6. divert, please,
regale, tickle 7. beguile, gratify
8. recreate 9. entertain, titillate
10. exhilarate

amusement... 3. fun 4. play 5. farce,
mirth, sport 7. pastime 9. avocation,
diversion 10. recreation, relaxation
13. divertisement, entertainment

amusement place... 4. club, park
6. casino, midway 7. cabaret, theater

ana... 5. books 6. events 8. analecta,
excerpts 9. Americana 10. collection
11. collectanea, compilation,
memorabilia

anachronous... 8. misdated, mistimed
10. beforehand, behindhand

anaglyph... 5. cameo, carve 6. chisel,
plaque, relief 10. embossment

Anak (Eccl)... 5. giant (Canaan)
6. Anakim

analogous... 4. like 7. similar
8. parallel 10. comparable, equivalent
11. correlative

analogue... 8. parallel 11. resemblance
13. correspondent
14. correspondence

analogy... 8. likeness, sameness
9. agreement 10. accordance,
comparison, similarity
14. correspondence

analysis... 5. assay, logic 6. biopsy,
theory 9. breakdown, diagnosis
10. compendium, discussion,

dissection 11. examination
14. classification

analyze... 5. assay, parse, study
7. discuss, dissect, examine
8. classify, describe, diagnose,
separate

Ananias (Bib)... 4. liar 8. disciple
(Damascus), Shadrack (Sidrack)
10. high priest 12. prevaricator

anarch, anarchist... 3. red 7. radical
8. nihilist 9. socialist, terrorist
13. revolutionist

anarchy... 4. riot 5. chaos 6. acracy
7. license, misrule 8. disorder
9. confusion, mobocracy, rebellion
10. ochlocracy

anathema... 3. ban 5. curse
9. damnation 11. abomination,
imprecation, malediction

Anatolian rug... 4. Kurd 5. Tuzla

anatomy... 4. body 5. build, frame
7. carcass 8. analysis, skeleton
9. formation, structure
11. arrangement

anatomy of animals... 7. zootomy

ancestor... 4. Adam, sire 5. elder,
stock 6. atavus, family, parent
8. forebear 9. patriarch, precursor
10. antecedent, forefather,
forerunner, progenitor
11. grandfather, predecessor

ancestral... 4. aval 6. avital, lineal
7. atavism 8. maternal, paternal
9. atavistic, primitive 10. hereditary
11. patrimonial

ancestral spirits... 5. lares, manes
7. lemures, penates

ancestry... 4. race, rank 5. birth,
blood 7. descent, lineage
11. antecedents 14. progenitorship

anchor... 3. fix, tie 4. hook, moor,
rest, stop 5. affix, clamp, kedge
6. attach, batten, fasten, secure
7. grapnel, killick

anchor (pert to)... 3. arm, cat, pee
4. cast, palm, tore (ring) 5. fluke
7. capstan

anchorite, anchoret... 6. hermit,
shut-in 7. ascetic, eremite, recluse,
stylite 8. homebody

anchor-shaped... 8. ankyroid
10. hook-shaped

anchovy... 4. alec 5. sauce, sprat
7. herring

ancienne noblesse... 5. elect, elite
7. royalty 8. nobility 11. aristocracy

ancient... 3. eld, old 4. aged, auld,
wise 5. adept, early, hoary, olden
7. antique 8. historic, obsolete,
outdated, primeval, pristine
9. grandeval, primitive, venerable
10. aboriginal, antiquated, preadamite
12. antediluvian

ancient (pert to)...
chariot.. 5. essed
city.. 4. Elis, Tyre 5. Argos, Sedon
6. Athens, Sparta, Thebes
drink.. 5. morat
empire.. 4. Gaul 5. Roman 6. Lydian
7. Persian 8. Assyrian, Athenian,
Chaldean, Hellenic 10. Babylonian,
Phoenician

god.. 4. Esus (Gaulish)
isles.. 5. Chios, Crete, Samos
6. Aegina, Ionian, Ithaca, Lemnos,
Lesbos, Rhodes 7. Salamis
8. Cyclades
language.. 4. Pali 5. Latin 6. Celtic,
Gaelic 7. Cornish, Gaulish
mariner.. 4. Rime (of) 5. rover
6. roamer, sailor, seaman
8. seafarer, wanderer 9. navigator
soldier.. 7. peltast
theater.. 7. odeum
and... 2. et 4. also, plus 8. et cetera
9. ampersand, including
12. additionally
andante.. 5. largo, tempo 6. slowly
Andean (pert to)...
camel.. 5. llama
deer.. 4. pudu
region, wind.. 4. puna
term.. 5. grand, lofty
andiron... 3. dog 7. firedog, Hessian
andrenid... 3. bee 10. Andrenidae
androgyny... 9. sissiness
10. effeminacy 11. unmanliness
15. hermaphroditism
android.∴. 5. robot 9. automaton
anecdote... 4. tale, yarn 5. story
7. account 9. chronicle, narrative
anecdotes... 3. ana 7. sayings, stories
anemone... 7. actinia 10. windflower
anent... 2. of, on, re 4. upon, with
5. about 8. opposite 10. concerning
anesthesia, anaesthesia...
8. deadness, numbness
13. insensibility
anesthetic... 3. gas 5. ether
8. freezing, Novocain, procaine
9. pentothal 10. chloroform
13. refrigeration
anesthetize... 4. dull, numb, stun
6. benumb, deaden, freeze 7. stupefy
8. etherize, paralyze 9. narcotize
10. chloroform 11. desensitize
anew... 5. again, newly 6. afresh, de
novo 8. recently
angel... 6. cherub, genius, seraph
(seraf) 7. Madonna, prophet
angel (pert to)...
Arab (apostate).. 5. Eblis
archangel.. 5. Uriel 7. Gabriel,
Michael, Raphael
Biblical.. 6. bishop, pastor
Fallen.. 6. Belial, Mammon
financial.. 6. backer, patron
7. sponsor 8. promoter
fish.. 5. shark 9. spadefish
Hebrew.. 6. Abdiel 8. cherubim,
seraphim
Jewish.. 6. Azrael (of death)
7. Zadkiel (of planet Jupiter)
8. Metatron
Mohammedan (Mus).. 7. Israfil
(Israfeel)
Moslem.. 5. Nakir (Repudiating)
6. Munkar (Unknown)
angelic... 5. godly 7. lovable, saintly
8. cherubic, heavenly, seraphic,
virtuous 9. celestial 10. beneficent
angelica... 4. herb 6. lovely 7. liqueur
Angelus... 4. bell, call 6. prayer
8. devotion

anger... 3. ire, vex 4. fume, rage, rile
5. annoy, chafe, wrath 6. choler,
dander, enrage, nettle, offend,
temper 7. dudgeon, emotion,
inflame, madness, passion, trouble
8. vexation 9. infuriate 10. affliction,
enragement, irritation, resentment
11. displeasure, indignation
12. exasperation
angered... 3. mad 5. irate, wroth
8. incensed, wrathful 9. indignant,
irascible
angle... 3. ell, tee, zig 4. axil, coin,
fish, fork, hade, nook 5. acute,
ancon, arris, right, slant, story
6. akimbo, distal, epaule, obtuse,
octant 7. bastion, outlook, ravelin,
salient 8. attitude 9. incidence,
rectangle, viewpoint
angler... 6. fisher 7. dibbler, trawler,
troller 8. piscator 9. fisherman,
Waltonian
angler's basket... 5. creel
Anglican... 7. English
Anglo-Celtic... 7. British
10. Anglo-Saxon
Anglo-Indian (pert to)...
Empire founder.. 5. Clive
measure.. 3. ser 4. tola
pageant.. 7. tamasha
peasant.. 4. ryot
princess.. 5. begum
wealthy.. 5. nabob
Anglo-Saxon (pert to)...
armor.. 7. hauberk
assembly.. 4. moot 5. gemot
(gemote)
attendant.. 5. thane
consonant.. 3. edh, eth
council.. 9. heptarchy
councilman.. 5. witan
epic (heroic).. 7. Beowulf
native.. 7. English 11. Anglo-Celtic
prince (heir apparent).. 8. atheling
slave.. 4. esne
tenant.. 6. geneat
warrior.. 5. thane
Angora...
capital of.. 6. Turkey
garment.. 5. shawl
goat.. 6. chamal
wool fabric.. 6. mohair
angry... 3. hot, mad 4. sore 5. cross,
grame, irate, irked, vexed 6. ireful,
stormy 7. enraged, painful
8. inflamed, wrathful 9. indignant,
irascible, resentful, turbulent
10. passionate
anguish... 3. woe 4. bale, pain, pang
5. agony, dolor, grief, throe
6. misery 7. remorse, sadness,
torment, torture 8. distress
9. heartache 10. desolation
11. lamentation
angular... 4. bent, bony, edgy
5. gaunt, sharp 6. abrupt, akimbo,
forked 7. crooked, pointed, scrawny
8. cornered, crotched
ani... 8. keelbill (keelbird) 9. blackbird
animadversion... 7. censure, comment,
obloquy 8. judgment, reproach
9. aspersion, criticism

10. imputation, reflection
12. condemnation

animadvert... 4. note 5. watch
6. notice, regard, remark 7. censure,
comment, observe 9. criticize
(criticise)

anima humana... 4. mind, self, soul
5. heart, human 6. psyche, spirit

animal (pert to)...
anatomy.. 7. zootomy
back, spine.. 4. nota 5. chine
body.. 4. soma
castrated.. 3. seg (segg)
coat.. 6. pelage
cud.. 5. rumen
disease.. 8. enzootic
enclosure.. 3. pen, sty 4. cage, coop,
cote, reem, yard 5. hutch, kraal, stall
6. corral 7. pasture
fabulous.. 7. griffin
group.. 3. gam, pod 4. herd
5. drove, flock, pride 9. menagerie
hairless.. 5. pelon
hindleg part.. 4. crus
hornless.. 7. pollard
hybrid.. 4. mule 5. hinny
hypnosis.. 9. cataplexy
male.. 3. tom 4. bull, jack, stag
5. steer 8. stallion
many–egged.. 5. zooid
many–footed.. 7. polyped
molt.. 8. exuviate
mother.. 3. dam
no feet.. 4. apod
nose.. 5. snout
oar–footed.. 7. remiped
one–egged.. 4. zoon
one–footed.. 6. uniped
pet.. 4. cade
reference to.. 4. wild 6. carnal
7. bestial, fleshly, kingdom
8. domestic 12. ferae naturae
14. domitae naturae
regional.. 5. fauna
small.. 10. animalcule
symbolic.. 5. totem
track, trail.. 4. rack 5. piste, spoor
web–footed.. 8. pinniped
wing–footed.. 6. aliped
worship.. 8. zoolatry
young.. 3. cub, kid, pup 4. calf, colt,
fawn, foal, lamb· 5. filly, puppy
6. kitten

animal family...
bear.. 6. ursine
cat.. 6. feline
cow.. 6. bovine
deer.. 7. cervine
dog.. 6. canine
fox.. 7. vulpine
horse.. 6. equine
pig.. 7. porcine
sheep.. 5. ovine
wolf.. 6. lupine

animal stomach...
1st.. 5. rumen 6. paunch
2nd.. 5. tripe 9. honeycomb,
reticulum
3rd.. 6. omasum 9. manyplies
4th.. 4. read (reed) 8. abomasum

animate... 3. act 4. fire, live, move
5. alive, cheer, imbue, impel, liven

6. arouse, ensoul, spirit, vivify
7. enliven, inspire, organic, refresh
8. energize, vitalize 9. stimulate
10. exhilarate

animated... 3. gay 5. alive, brisk
6. active, lively, living, minded
8. disposed (in mind), prompted
9. energetic, refreshed

animated spirit... 6. animus

animation... 3. pep 4. brio, dash, life
5. ardor 6. energy, gaiety, spirit
8. airiness, buoyancy, vivacity
10. excitement, liveliness, motivation
11. earnestness, inspiration
12. invigoration, vivification
13. sprightliness

animation suspended... 6. apathy,
torpor 8. dormancy, lethargy

animé... 6. bright 8. animated

animosity... 5. clash, spite 6. enmity,
hatred, rancor 7. ill will 8. conflict
9. antipathy, hostility
10. antagonism, opposition,
repugnance

animoso... 6. lively 8. animated
9. energetic

animous... 3. hot 8. resolute,
vehement

animus... 4. mind, will 6. desire,
spirit, temper 8. attitude, volition
9. intention 10. discretion
11. disposition, inclination

ankh (Egypt)... 3. tau 4. life 5. cross
6. emblem, symbol

ankle... 4. tali (pl) 5. joint, pivot, talus
6. tarsus 8. astragal 9. ginglymus
10. astragalus 11. diarthrosis

ankle cover... 4. spat 6. gaiter

ankylostoma... 7. lockjaw

annalist... 6. writer 8. recorder
9. historian 10. chronicler
11. memorialist 12. chronologist

annals... 5. diary 6. record 7. history,
journal 8. register 9. chronicle
11. publication

Annam... 5. Hanoi 6. Tonkin
(Tongking)

Annamese... 7. Chinese 8. Buddhist
9. Mongolian

anneal... 4. fuse, heat 6. harden,
temper 7. inflame, toughen
8. indurate

Anne Hathaway's home... 8. Shattery

annelid... 3. lug 4. lurg, naid, worm
6. phylum 7. lugworm

annex... 3. add, ell 4. join, wing
5. affix 6. append, attach, fasten
7. acquire, subjoin 8. addition
9. extension

annexation... 7. adjunct 8. addition
9. accession 10. affixation
13. appropriation

Annie Oakley... 4. pass 6. ticket
(free)

annihilate... 4. undo, void 5. erase,
wreck 6. quench, reduce, stifle
7. abolish, destroy, expunge, nullify,
smother 8. decimate 9. extirpate
10. extinguish, obliterate
11. exterminate

annihilation... 5. death 6. demise
7. passing 10. extinction

11. destruction, dissolution
13. extermination 14. extinguishment
anniversary... 5. cycle 6. course
7. jubilee, wedding 8. birthday
10. centennial, regularity
13. commemoration
annotation... 4. note 5. gloss
7. apostil, comment 8. exegesis,
notation, rescript, scholium
9. reference 10. commentary
annotator... 6. critic 7. analyst
8. expositor, expounder, publicist,
scholiast 10. glossarist
11. commentator
announce... 3. bid 4. call, tell 5. bruit
6. affirm, assert, herald, notify
7. declare, forerun, gazette, presage
8. proclaim 9. advertise, broadcast,
pronounce 10. annunciate,
promulgate
announcement... 4. fiat 5. blurb, edict
6. decree, notice 8. bulletin
9. manifesto 10. commercial
11. affirmation, declaration
12. notification, proclamation
13. advertisement
announcer... 4. page 5. crier, emcee
6. nuncio 9. harbinger, informant
10. newscaster, proclaimer
11. broadcaster
annoy... 3. irk, nag, try, vex 4. bore,
rile 5. anger, devil, harry, peeve,
spite, tease 6. bother, harass,
molest, offend, pester, ruffle
7. disturb, trouble 8. irritate
9. displease 13. inconvenience
annoyance... 4. bore, pest
8. nuisance, vexation 10. resentment
11. molestation 13. inconvenience
annoying... 4. sore 7. galling
9. vexatious 11. distressing
annual... 4. book 5. plant 6. yearly
7. etesian 10. periodical
11. publication
annuity... 5. rente, trust 6. income
(life) 7. pension, subsidy, tontine
9. allotment 10. investment, life
income
annul... 4. cass, undo, void 5. avoid,
blank, quash 6. cancel, repeal,
revoke 7. abolish, nullify, rescind
8. abrogate, derogate, overrule,
withdraw 9. disaffirm 10. invalidate,
neutralize, obliterate 11. countermand
annular... 6. banded, cyclic, ringed
8. cingular, circular
annulet... 4. ring (Her) 6. fillet
7. circlet, ringlet
annulment... 6. repeal 7. erasure,
vacatur 9. abolition 10. abrogation,
defeasance, revocation
12. invalidation 14. neutralization
annunciate... 6. affirm, assert
8. announce, proclaim
annunciation... 11. affirmation
12. announcement, proclamation
13. pronouncement
anoa... 2. ox (wild) 8. sapiutan
anode... 8. terminal (positive)
9. electrode (opp of cathode)
anodic... 12. turned toward
anodyne... 4. balm 6. opiate

7. soother 8. antalgic, narcotic,
pacifier, sedative 9. analgesic
10. depressant, palliative
anoesia... 6. idiocy
anoint... 3. oil 4. balm, cere, nard
5. anele, bribe, smear 6. chrism,
grease, spread 7. moisten
8. medicate 9. embrocate, lubricate
10. consecrate
anoli, anole... 6. lizard
anomalous... 3. odd 7. erratic,
strange, unusual 8. aberrant,
abnormal, peculiar 9. eccentric,
irregular 10. dissimilar
11. exceptional 13. unconformable
anomaly... 6. oddity, rarity
11. abnormality, nondescript
12. irregularity
anomy... 7. miracle
anon... 4. soon 5. again, later
6. mañana, thence 7. by-and-by
8. tomorrow 9. eventually
11. straightway
anonymous (opp of onomatous)...
7. unknown 8. nameless, unavowed
9. undefined
anoöpsia... 10. strabismus (upward)
Anopheles... 10. mosquitoes
anophthalmia... 13. absence of eyes
(congenital)
anopia... 15. defective vision
anorak... 12. hooded jacket (Arctic)
anorexia... 10. no appetite
anorthopia... 15. distorted vision
anosmia... 11. loss of smell
another... 3. new 4. more 5. alias,
extra, other 6. second 7. further
10. additional
another time... 5. again
10. otherwhile
ansa... 4. loop 6. handle
anserine... 6. stupid 9. gooselike
answer... 2. do 3. say 4. echo
5. avail, reply, sauce, serve
6. oracle, retort 7. defense, epistle,
respond, riposte 8. conclude,
reaction, repartee, response, solution
9. rejoinder 10. correspond,
responsory 11. acknowledge
16. counterstatement
answerable... 6. liable 8. amenable,
solvable 11. responsible
12. commensurate 13. proportionate
answer the purpose... 2. so 3. fit
4. suit 5. avail, serve 6. become
7. benefit, satisfy, suffice
ant (pert to)...
family.. 10. Formicidae, Myrmicidae
11. Formicoidea (super),
Hymenoptera
feeding on.. 13. formicivorous
genus.. 6. Eciton, Termes 7. Formica
killer.. 9. formicide
male.. 8. macraner (large), micraner
(small)
nest.. 9. formicary
ref to.. 6. formic
type.. 5. emmet 7. formica, pismire
white.. 4. anay (anai) 7. termite
wingless.. 9. ergatoid
worker.. 6. ergate 9. harvester
antacid... 6. alkali, remedy 8. medicine

9. absorbent 11. neutralizer
12. counteragent 13. counteractant

Antaeus, Antaios (Gr) ... 5. giant
6. Libyan 8. wrestler

antagonism ... 3. war 5. clash
8. conflict 9. antipathy, hostility
10. opposition, repugnance
11. contrariety 12. disagreement
13. counteraction

antagonist ... 3. foe 5. enemy, rival
6. foeman 8. opponent 9. adversary

antagonistic ... 7. hostile, opposed
8. contrary, converse, inimical,
opposite 9. repugnant 10. unfriendly
11. belligerent, disagreeing
13. counteractive

Antarctic ...
Circle .. 4. Pole 6. region
continent .. 10. Antarctica
explorer .. 4. Byrd, Ross
islands .. 11. Archipelago
rel to .. 8. subpolar 9. antipodal,
South Pole
sea .. 4. Ross 7. Weddell
seal (brown) discoverer .. 7. Weddell
volcano .. 6. Erebus

ante ... 3. pay, pot 4. bank, fund, pool
5. kitty, stake 7. jackpot

anteater ... 6. Manis 7. echidna
8. aardvark, edentate, pangolin,
tamandua

antecede ... 4. head 5. front 6. prefix
7. outrank, precede, preface

antecedent ... 4. fore 5. prior, scout
6. former 7. pioneer 8. ancestor,
previous 9. foregoing, precedent,
preceding, precursor 10. forerunner,
precedence 11. voortrekker (Dutch)
12. avant–courier

antecedents ... 7. fathers 9. ancestors,
forebears 10. ascendants
(ascendents) 11. forefathers
12. predecessors 13. prerequisites

antechamber ... 4. hall 5. lobby
6. lounge 7. chamber 8. anteroom
9. vestibule

antedate ... 7. precede, predate
8. datemark, pre–exist 10. anticipate

antelope ... 3. gau, gnu, kob, nil
4. guib, koba, oryx, roan 5. addax,
bovid, eland, goral, oribi, peele,
saiga, serow 6. cabree, dzeren,
impala, nilgai, pygarg 7. blaubok,
blesbok, bubalia, chamois, gazella,
gazelle, gemsbok, sassaby
8. agacella, bontebok, steinbok
9. duikerbok, pronghorn
10. hartebeest

antenna ... 4. horn, mast, palp
5. clava (Zool), tower 6. aerial, feeler
7. scanner

antepast ... 6. canape, repast
8. aperitif 9. antipasto, appetizer,
foretaste 11. hors d'oeuvre,
prelibation

anteroom ... 4. hall 5. lobby 6. lounge
7. chamber 9. vestibule
11. antechamber

anthem ... 3. lay 4. hymn, song
5. motet, music, psalm 7. chorale
8. doxology 9. antiphony, offertory
10. responsory

anthill ... 5. mound 9. formicary

anthology ... 3. ana 5. album
6. corpus 7. omnibus, prayers
8. analects 9. potpourri
10. collection 11. collectanea,
compilation

Anthozoa ... 6. corals, polyps
8. anemones

anthropoid ... 3. ape, lar, man
6. gibbon 7. gorilla, primate,
siamang 9. orangutan (orangoutang)
10. chimpanzee, troglodyte
12. Anthropoidea (suborder)

anthropophagi ... 9. cannibals,
man–eaters

anti ... 6. contra 7. adverse, counter,
opposed 8. contrary, converse
13. contradictory

antiaircraft artillery ... 4. guns
6. ack–ack, Archie, cannon
7. weapons 8. cannonry, ordnance
10. skysweeper

antibiotics ... 5. drugs 7. vaccine
10. penicillin 12. streptomycin

antic ... 4. dido 5. caper, prank, stunt
6. frolic, gambol 7. bizarre, buffoon,
gambado 8. grotesque
11. merry–andrew, monkeyshine

anticipate ... 4. hope 5. await, dread
6. expect 7. foresee, obviate,
portend, prevent 8. preclude
9. forestall, foretaste, forethink
11. contemplate

anticipation ... 4. hope 9. foresight,
foretaste, intuition, prolepsis
10. foreboding 11. expectation,
forethought 12. presentiment
13. preoccupation

anticlimax ... 6. bathos 8. comedown,
decrease

antidote ... 6. remedy 10. corrective,
preventive 11. neutralizer
12. counteragent, prophylactic
13. counteractant

Antioch ... 7. capital (Syria)

antipathy ... 6. hatred, nausea
7. dislike 8. aversion, loathing
9. disrelish, hostility 10. abhorrence,
antagonism, opposition, reluctance,
repugnance 11. contrariety,
detestation, inimicality
13. counteraction 14. disinclination

antipodal ... 5. polar 7. counter (global)
8. contrary, opposite
14. contrapositive

antiquated ... 4. aged 5. passé
6. bygone, voided 7. antique,
archaic, elderly 8. absolute, medieval
9. Victorian 10. fossilized
12. old–fashioned 13. superannuated

antique ... 3. old 5. hoary, relic
7. ageless, ancient 8. dateless,
outmoded 9. venerable
12. old–fashioned

antiquities ... 5. codex, ruins 6. relics
7. fossils, papyrus, remains, tablets
9. archaisms, artifacts, monuments
11. manuscripts, palimpsests

antiquity ... 3. ago, eld 4. past, yore
7. oldness 9. paleology
11. ancientness, elderliness
13. aboriginality, primitiveness

antisepsis... 7. asepsis 11. prophylaxis
12. disinfection, immunization
13. sterilization
antiseptic... 5. Salol 6. cresol, iodine
(iodin), phenol 7. alcohol, aristol,
aseptic 8. creosote, peroxide
9. germicide 12. disinfectant,
formaldehyde, prophylactic
antispasmodic... 7. anodyne
8. sedative 8. asadulcis (deadly
carrot), asafetida (asafoetida)
10. depressant 12. tranquilizer
antithesis (opp of thesis)... 8. contrast,
opposite 9. antipodes 10. opposition
11. contrariety 14. contraposition
antitoxin... 5. serum 8. antibody
9. antivenin (antivenene)
10. antibiotic 11. antipyretic,
immunotoxin
antler... 3. dag 4. horn, snag, tine
5. dague, point, prong, spike
6. bosset, rights 8. advancer
10. caducicorn
Antony & Cleopatra characters...
4. Eris, Iras 6. Caesar 7. Octavia
9. Demetrius
antonym (opp of synonym)... 7. reverse
8. contrary, opposite
antrum... 3. pit 5. sinus 6. cavern,
cavity, hollow 10. depression
Anu... 3. god (sky, heavens)
Anubis... 3. god (Necropolis)
6. Hermes
Anura... 4. Rana 5. frogs, toads
9. Salientia 10. amphibians
anvil... 5. block, incus, teest 6. stithy
7. bickern, incudes (pl) 8. beakiron
(horned)
anxiety... 4. care, fear 5. dread, worry
7. concern, trouble 8. disquiet,
distress, neurosis, suspense
9. eagerness, misgiving
10. foreboding, perplexity, solicitude,
uneasiness 12. apprehension,
restlessness
anxious... 4. cark 5. eager 6. uneasy
7. fearful, unquiet 8. watchful
9. concerned, disturbed, expectant,
impatient 10. disquieted
any... 3. all, ary (dial), one, oni (dial)
4. some, that, this 5. aught, every
8. quantity 9. unlimited
10. unmeasured 12. undetermined
anybody... 3. any, one 5. aught
6. anyone 7. someone, whoever
15. no-account person
anything... 3. any 4. some 5. at all,
aught 7. anywise 8. no choice,
whatever 9. something
14. choicelessness
anything (pert to)...
existing.. 6. entity
of value.. 5. asset
of value, least.. 5. plack
puzzling.. 4. crux
remote.. 6. forane
small.. 3. tot 5. minim
spiral.. 5. helix
terrifying.. 5. ghost 9. scarecrow
true.. 4. fact
worthless.. 4. mean 7. useless
9. valueless

aoudad... 5. sheep 7. chamois
apa... 7. wallaba
Apache (pert to)...
French.. 4. thug 8. assassin
Indian.. 5. nomad
Indian Chief (famed).. 8. Geronimo
Indian jacket (deerskin).. 6. bietle
State.. 7. Arizona
apart... 3. dis (pref) 4. away 5. alone,
aloof, aside, solus, split 6. singly
7. asunder, distant 8. secluded,
separate, unjoined 9. severally,
unrelated 10. separately
apartheid... 4. bias 5. twist 7. bigotry
9. prejudice 11. segregation
13. provincialism 14. discrimination
apartment... 4. flat 5. suite
7. chamber 8. tenement
11. compartment, condominium
apathetic... 4. dull 5. inert 6. torpid
7. passive 8. listless, sluggish
10. insouciant, phlegmatic
11. indifferent, unconcerned
apathy... 6. acedia (in a monastery),
torpor 7. languor 8. neurosis
9. lassitude, unconcern
12. indifference, sluggishness
13. insensibility, unfeelingness
ape... 4. copy, dupe, fool, mime
5. mimic 6. alalus, mocker, parrot
7. barbary, copycat, emulate, imitate,
portray 8. imitator, mimicker,
simulate 10. anthropoid
11. impersonate
ape (pert to)...
anthropoid.. 10. chimpanzee,
troglodyte
Egypt Relig.. 4. Aani
genus.. 5. Cebus, Simia
India.. 3. kra
kind.. 6. simian 7. macaque
largest.. 6. baboon 7. gorilla
Malay.. 3. lar 5. orang 6. gibbon
9. orangutan (orangoutang)
nocturnal.. 5. lemur
aperitif... 5. drink 6. canape
8. antepast 9. antipasto, appetizer
11. hors d'oeuvre
aperture... 3. gap, vue 4. hole, leak,
pore, rift, rima, slit, slot, vent
5. chasm, chink, cleft, inlet, mouth,
stoma 6. hiatus, window 7. fissure,
foramen, opening, orifice, osteole
8. fenestra 10. passageway
apex... 3. tip, top 4. acme, cone,
cusp, noon 5. point, spire
6. apogee, height, macron, summit,
tittle, vertex, zenith 7. cacumen
8. pinnacle 11. culmination
apex ornament... 6. finial
aphid... 5. Aphis, louse 6. insect
7. puceron
aphorism... 3. saw 5. adage, axiom,
gnome, maxim, moral 6. dictum,
saying 7. proverb 8. apothegm
Aphrodite (pert to)...
consort.. 4. Ares 10. Hephaestus
father.. Zeus
goddess of.. 4. love 6. beauty
mother.. 5. Dione
Roman equivalent.. 5. Venus
sacred birds.. 5. doves 8. sparrows

statue.. 17. Aphrodite of Cnidus (by
  Praxiteles)
zoology.. 9. butterfly
Apis... 4. bull (sacred)
aplomb... 5. poise 6. surety
  7. balance 8. fastness, firmness,
  security, solidity 9. assurance,
  erectness, plumbness, restraint,
  soundness, stability 10. confidence,
  equanimity 11. equilibrium
apocalypse... 8. prophecy, teaching
  9. discovery, scripture
  10. revealment, revelation
a poco... 6. little, slowly 9. gradually
apocryphal... 4. mock, sham
  5. bogus, false 6. mythic, unreal
  8. doubtful, mythical, spurious
  9. imitative 10. fictitious, unorthodox
  11. counterfeit 15. unauthoritative
apod... 8. footless
Apodes... 4. eels 6. morays
apogee (opp of perigee)... 4. acme,
  apex, peak 6. climax, summit, zenith
  11. culmination
apograph... 4. copy 5. tenor
  7. tracing 8. transfer 9. recording
  10. transcript 13. transcription
Apoidea... 4. Apis, bees 9. honeybees
  11. Hymenoptera
Apollo (pert to)...
  birthplace.. 5. Delos
  father.. 4. Zeus
  festival.. 5. Delia
  god.. 3. sun (personified)
  mother.. 6. Leto 6. Larona
  oracle.. 6. Delphi
  sage follower.. 6. Abaris
  sister (twin).. 5. Diana (Rom)
  7. Artemis
  son.. 3. Ion 5. Hymen, Linos
apologetic... 5. sorry 7. apology
  8. excusing 10. excusatory, justifying,
  remorseful 11. vindicative
  12. propitiatory 13. justification
apologue... 4. myth 5. fable, story
  6. legend 7. fantasy, parable
  8. allegory
apology... 4. plea 6. excuse
  7. pretext, regrets 9. makeshift
  11. explanation, vindication
  13. justification 14. acknowledgment
aport... 8. larboard, leftward
  9. sinistrad
apostasy... 5. lapse 9. desertion,
  recreancy 11. backsliding
apostate... 6. bolter 7. pervert,
  runaway, seceder 8. deserter,
  recreant, renegade, turncoat, turntail
  10. unfaithful
apostle... 5. saint 8. disciple, follower
  10. evangelist
Apostle (Bib)... 4. John, Jude, Paul
  5. James, Judas, Peter, Silas, Simon
  6. Andrew, Philip, Thomas
  7. Matthew 8. Barnabas, Matthias
  11. Bartholomew
Apostle of...
  France (Gauls).. 5. Denis
  Franks.. 4. Remi
  Gentiles.. 4. Paul
  Germany.. 8. Boniface
  Goths.. 7. Ulfilas

Indies.. 6. Xavier
Ireland.. 7. Patrick
Rome.. 4. Neri
Apostle to the Indians... 5. Eliot
apostolic... 5. faith, papal 6. gospel
  8. Biblical 9. evangelic 10. pontifical,
  scriptural
apostrophe... 8. squiggle 9. soliloquy
apothecary... 8. druggist, gallipot
  9. dispenser 10. pharmacist,
  posologist 13. pharmaceutist
  14. pharmacologist
apothecary measure... 4. dram, pint
  5. minim, ounce
apothecary weight... 4. dram
  5. grain, ounce, pound 7. scruple
apothegm... 3. saw 4. dict 5. adage,
  axiom, gnome, maxim 6. dictum,
  saying 7. precept 8. aphorism
apotheosis... 5. ideal 10. exaltation
  11. deification, ennoblement,
  idolization 12. resurrection
  13. dignification, glorification,
  magnification 14. aggrandizement
apotheosize... 5. deify, exalt
  7. ennoble, glorify, idolize 8. enshrine
  11. immortalize
appall, appal... 3. awe 5. shock
  6. dismay
appalling... 4. grim 5. awful
  7. awesome, fearful 8. dreadful,
  shocking, terrible, terrific 9. frightful
  10. remarkable
appalto... 8. monopoly
appanage... 7. adjunct, pendant
  8. property 9. appendage,
  endowment 10. perquisite
  11. prerogative 12. appurtenance
apparatus... 4. gear, tool 6. outfit
  7. machine, rigging, trapeze
  8. recorder 9. appliance, equipment,
  mechanism, trappings 10. instrument
  13. paraphernalia
apparatus (pert to)...
  distillation.. 7. alembic
  dyeing.. 4. ager
  heating.. 4. etna 5. stove 6. boiler
  7. furnace 8. radiator
  hoisting.. 3. pry 4. jack 5. davit,
  lever, lewis 7. capstan, derrick
  planetarium.. 6. orrery
  steering.. 4. helm 5. wheel 6. rudder,
  tiller
  water.. 4. pump 5. noria 6. faucet,
  siphon, tremie
apparel... 3. alb 4. deck, duds, garb,
  gear, togs, wear 5. dress, equip,
  habit 6. attire 7. clothes, costume,
  garment, raiment, toggery, vesture
  8. clothing, fatigues 10. garmenture
  11. habiliments
apparent... 4. open 5. clear, overt,
  plain 6. patent, visual 7. certain,
  evident, obvious, seeable, seeming,
  visible 8. distinct, illusory, manifest,
  specious 9. notorious, plausible
  10. ostensible 11. discernible,
  indubitable, perceivable, superficial
  12. recognizable
apparently... 7. visibly 9. evidently,
  obviously, seemingly 10. manifestly,
  presumably, speciously

11. perceptibly

apparition... 4. bogy, form 5. ghost, shade, spook 6. shadow, spirit, sprite, vision, wraith 7. eidolon, fantasy, phantom, specter (spectre) 8. illusion, phantasm, revenant 9. hobgoblin 10. appearance, phenomenon, revelation

appassionato... 9. emotional 11. impassioned

appeal... 3. beg, cry 4. call, cite, plea, pray, suit 5. charm, plead 6. avouch, invoke, prayer 7. address, beseech, entreat, implore, request, solicit 8. entreaty, petition 9. importune 10. lovability, loveliness, supplicate 11. winsomeness 12. supplication

appealing... 4. nice 7. winsome 8. alluring, charming, engaging, pleasant 9. agreeable, glamorous, imploring 10. attractive, beseeching, bewitching, delightful, enchanting, entreating 11. fascinating, interesting

appear... 4. loom, seem 5. occur 6. arrive, attend, emerge 11. materialize

appearance... 3. air 4. form, look, mien 5. front, guise, looks, phase 6. aspect, format, manner, ostent 7. arrival, feature, specter (spectre) 8. illusion, presence, pretense 9. emergence, semblance 10. apparition, disclosure, revelation 11. resemblance 13. manifestation

appearance (pert to)...
book.. 6. format
false.. 8. disguise
first.. 4. dawn 5. debut 8. premiere
frontal.. 6. facade
surface.. 6. patina
truth (appearance of)..
    14. verisimilitude
white.. 6. pallid

appease... 4. calm 5. allay, atone, mease, quiet, salve 6. pacify, soothe 7. content, placate, relieve, satisfy 8. mitigate 10. conciliate 11. tranquilize

appeasement... 6. relief 7. salving 8. easement 10. compromise, mitigation, palliation 12. pacification

appellation... 3. tag 4. name 5. label, style, title 7. calling, epithet 8. cognomen, nickname 9. sobriquet 11. designation 12. denomination, nomenclature 14. identification

append... 3. add 4. hang 5. affix, annex 6. adjoin, attach 7. subjoin 11. superimpose

appendage... 3. arm, awn, cue, tab, tag 4. barb, flap, lobe, tail 5. cauda, queue 6. ligule (Bot), palpus 7. adjunct, pigtail 8. addition, hanger–on, pendicle 9. accessory, tailpiece 10. dependency 12. appurtenance 13. accompaniment

appendix... 6. sequel 7. codicil, process 8. addendum, addition 9. accessory, appendage 10. dependency 12. augmentation

appertain... 4. bear 5. apply 6. affect, belong, regard, relate 7. involve, pertain

appetite... 4. zest 5. taste 6. desire, hunger, orexis, thirst 7. longing, passion 8. cupidity 9. appetency 10. hungriness, propensity

appetizer... 4. fish (sauce) 6. canape 8. antepast, aperitif 9. antipasto, foretaste 11. hors d'oeuvre

appetizing... 6. savory 7. piquant 8. tempting 9. appealing, desirable 10. attractive 11. captivating, provocative, tantalizing

applaud... 4. clap, hail, laud, root, yell 5. cheer, extol, shout 6. hurrah, praise 7. acclaim, approve, commend, endorse 10. compliment

applauders (paid)... 6. claque 8. clappers 9. claqueurs

applause... 4. clap, hand 5. bravo, éclat, huzza 6. encore, praise 7. acclaim, ovation 8. plaudits 11. acclamation 12. commendation

apple... 3. May, Spy 4. crab, pome 6. annona, pippin, rennet, russet 7. Baldwin, codling (codlin), costard, Newtown, Roxbury, winesap 8. Greening, Jonathan, Mandrake, McIntosh, queening 9. astrachan, Delicious 10. bellflower, Rome Beauty 11. Gravenstein, Northern Spy

apple (pert to)...
acid.. 5. malic
crushed.. 6. pomace
dessert.. 10. brown betty
disease.. 7. stippen
genus.. 5. Malus
juice.. 6. cider 9. applejack
love.. 6. tomato
seed.. 3. pip
shaped.. 8. pomiform

Apple of Discord (Gr Myth)... 4. Eris

apple of one's eye... 3. pet 4. idol 5. jewel, pupil 7. darling, desired 8. favorite 10. preference

applesauce... 4. bunk, pooh 5. tripe 6. phooey 7. baloney, hogwash 8. malarkey, nonsense, tommyrot 12. fiddlesticks 13. horsefeathers

appliance... 3. dam (dental) 4. tool 6. device, gadget 7. utensil 8. facility 9. commodity, implement 10. instrument 11. application, contraption, convenience

applicable... 3. apt, fit 6. usable 7. pliable 8. apposite, relative, relevant 9. compliant, pertinent 11. appropriate

application... 3. use 6. appeal, effort 7. bearing, concern, request 8. petition, recourse 9. attention, constancy, diligence, relevance, relevancy 10. connection, employment, pertinence 11. attribution, disposition, engrossment, persistence, requisition 12. perseverance 14. administration

application (body)... 4. balm 5. salve, stupe (hot) 7. plaster 8. cosmetic, poultice

apply... 3. use 4. suit 6. appose,

bestow, comply, devote, employ, relate 7. solicit, utilize 9. associate, attribute 10. administer 11. appropriate

appoggiature... 9. grace note 13. embellishment

appoint... 3. fix 4. name 5. equip 6. assign, decree, depute, detail, ordain 7. destine, prepare 8. delegate, deputize 9. designate, establish, prescribe 10. constitute

appointment... 4. date 5. order, tryst 7. command 8. position 9. direction, equipment, ordinance 10. engagement 11. designation 13. establishment

appointments... 6. things 8. fittings, fixtures 9. equipment, furniture 10. belongings, upholstery 11. acquirement, furnishings 12. accumulation, conveniences 13. accouterments, paraphernalia

apportion... 3. fix, lot 4. deal, dele, mete, part 5. allot, carve, share 6. assign, budget, divide 7. arrange, dispose 8. allocate 9. collocate, partition 10. distribute

appose... 4. abut 5. audit, liken, place 6. adjoin 7. compare, examine 9. juxtapose

apposite... 3. apt 4. like 5. close, match 6. timely 7. fitting, germane 8. position, relative, relevant 9. pertinent 11. appropriate

appraise... 4. mark, rank, rate 5. assay, gauge, judge, price, value 6. assess, evalue, praise 7. apprise, commend, measure 8. consider, estimate, evaluate 10. adjudicate, appreciate

appraiser (tax)... 5. rater 6. lister 8. assessor

appreciable... 3. any 8. tangible 9. estimable 11. perceptible

appreciate... 4. feel, grow, know 5. enjoy, prize, savor, value 6. admire, esteem 7. advance, amplify, approve, augment, realize, respect 8. estimate, increase, treasure

appreciation... 7. respect 9. appraisal, awareness, gratitude 10. estimation 11. realization, recognition, sensibility 12. gratefulness, thankfulness

apprehend... 3. ken, see 4. know, take 5. dread, grasp, pinch (sl), savvy, sense 6. arrest 7. capture, imagine, realize 8. conceive, perceive 10. anticipate, comprehend, understand

apprehensible... 8. knowable 9. scrutable 10. explicable, fathomable 11. accountable 12. discoverable, intelligible 14. comprehensible, understandable

apprehension... 4. fear, idea 5. alarm, doubt, dread, qualm 6. arrest 7. anxiety, capture, concern, opinion, seizure 8. distress, distrust, suspense 9. misgiving, suspicion 10. foreboding, solicitude, uneasiness 11. fearfulness, premonition

12. intelligence 13. understanding

apprehensive... 5. smart 6. uneasy 7. alarmed, fearful, knowing, nervous, worried 8. troubled 9. cognizant, concerned, conscious, perturbed 10. perceptive, solicitous

apprentice... 4. tyro 5. novice 7. amateur, trainee 8. beginner

apprize, apprise... 4. rate, tell 5. price, value 6. advise, assess, impart, inform, reckon 8. acquaint, appraise 9. enlighten 11. communicate

apprized... 5. aware 8. informed 9. cognizant

approach... 3. way 4. adit, come, near, road 5. stalk, verge 6. access, accost, advent, impend 7. arrival, nearing, sea gate 8. entryway, likeness, nearness, overture, resemble 11. approximate, entranceway

approachable... 4. open 8. gettable, passable 9. reachable 10. accessible, attainable 13. communicative

approbation... 5. favor, proof 6. praise 7. plaudit 8. applause, approval, sanction 10. acceptance, admiration 12. commendation, confirmation

appropriate... 3. apt, fit 4. akin, meet, take 5. allot, steal, usurp 6. borrow, pirate, proper, timely, worthy 7. condign, germane, related, special 8. deserved, relevant, suitable 9. befitting, expedient, favorable, opportune, pertinent 10. assimilate, monopolize, plagiarize 11. conformable

appropriately... 4. duly 5. aptly 6. timely

appropriation... 5. theft 6. corner, taking 8. monopoly 9. allotment 10. assignment, possession, usurpation

approval... 6. assent 7. consent, support 8. sanction 10. admiration 11. approbation, endorsement 12. ratification

approve... 2. OK 4. like, okay, pass, sign, test 6. attest, ratify 7. applaud, betoken, certify, confirm, endorse (indorse), signify 8. accredit, sanction, validate 9. authorize, undersign 10. appreciate 11. countenance 12. authenticate

approve of... 5. favor 6. accept 7. endorse (indorse) 8. sanction 11. countenance

approximate... 4. near 5. about, circa, match 6. approach, draw near, parallel, resemble 10. correspond

approximately... 5. about, circa 6. around, nearly 11. thereabouts

appui... 4. prop, stay 6. bridle (manège) 7. support

appulse... 6. syzygy 7. impinge 8. approach 9. collision 11. conjunction (Astron)

appurtenance... 4. gear 7. adjunct 8. addition 9. accessory, apparatus, appendage, belonging, component

appurtenant... 7. annexed 8. incident, relevant 9. appendant, belonging

11. appropriate
après... 5. after 10. afterwards
apricot (pert to)...
   African.. 6. meebos (dried)
   beverage.. 7. cordial, liqueur, persico
   color.. 9. red–yellow
   confection.. 6. meebos (mebos)
   Japanese.. 3. ume 4. ansu
   vine.. 6. maypop
a priori (opp of posteriori)...
   9. deductive 11. conditional,
   presumptive 12. hypothetical
   13. presumptively
apron... 3. bib 4. boot, brat, tier
   5. smock 6. barvel (barvell), runway
   7. garment, tablier 8. airstrip,
   lambskin (Masonic), pinafore
   9. appendage
apropos, a propos... 3. apt, pat
   7. germane, purpose 8. by the way,
   relevant, suitably 9. pertinent
   10. applicable, seasonable
   11. appurtenant, opportunely
   12. incidentally
apt... 3. fit, pat 4. deft 5. adept,
   prone, ready, smart 6. clever, expert,
   likely, prompt, suited 7. capable,
   elegant, subject 8. apposite,
   disposed, inclined, skillful, suitable
   9. competent, dexterous, ingenious,
   masterful, pertinent, qualified,
   teachable 10. proficient
   11. appropriate
apteral... 8. apterous, wingless
Apteryx... 3. moa (extinct) 4. kiwi
aptitude... 3. art 4. bent, gift, turn
   5. flair, skill 6. genius, talent
   7. ability, aptness, fitness, leaning
   8. penchant, tendency 9. liability
   10. likelihood, proclivity
   11. inclination 12. suitableness
   15. appropriateness
aptly... 7. exactly, readily 8. suitably
   11. pertinently
aptness... 5. skill 7. fitness
   8. tendency 9. smartness
   11. suitability 12. teachability
aqua... 3. eau 4. agua 5. water
aquatic... 6. natant, wading, watery
   8. natatory, swimming 12. grallatorial
   13. water–dwelling
Aquila... 5. eagles 13. constellation
   (Milky Way)
aquiline... 6. hanate, hooked
   7. curving 8. aduncous, unciform
   10. Roman–nosed
ara... 5. macaw 7. goddess
   (vengeance) 8. aracanga 9. screw
   pine 11. constellation
Arab... 4. waif 5. gamin, horse,
   nomad 6. Semite 7. Bedouin,
   Saracen 8. wanderer, Yemenite
   9. Caucasian
araba... 3. cab 5. coach 6. monkey
   (howling)
Arabia... see *Saudi–Arabia*
Arabian (pert to)...
   antelope.. 5. addax
   beverage.. 4. boza (bosa) 5. leban
   (lebban)
   bird.. 7. phoenix
   chief.. 5. sheik

cloth (shoulder).. 6. cabaan (caban)
demon.. 5. Eblis, jinni (jinnee)
   6. afreet
father.. 3. Abu (Ab, Abou) 4. Abba
garment.. 3. aba 4. haik 8. burnoose
gazelle.. 4. cora, oryx 5. ariel
horse.. 4. Kohl 8. kadischi, palomino
jasmine.. 4. bela
judge.. 4. cadi
juniper (*Bib*).. 5. retem
nomad.. 7. Saracen
peasant.. 6. fellah
physician.. 8. Avicenna
poet.. 5. Antar
prince.. 4. amir (ameer) 5. sheik
   6. sherif, sultan
romance.. 5. Antar (Antara)
ruler.. 6. caliph (calif)
Satan.. 5. Eblis 6. Azazel
scripture.. 7. Alcoran
seaport.. 4. Aden 5. Mocha
state of bliss.. 3. kef (kaif)
street urchin.. 5. gamin
tambourine.. 4. taar
tribe.. 3. Aus (anc)
vessel.. 4. dhow 6. boutre, sambuk
winds (hot).. 6. simoom (simoon)
arable land... 4. farm 5. arada, arado
   6. plowed, tilled 10. cultivated
arachnid... 4. mite, tick 6. spider
   8. scorpion 9. Arachnida
Aralu... 5. Hades
Aram (*Bib*)... 6. Rimmon (deity)
   7. Aramaic, Semitic language
araneous... 4. thin 7. weblike
   8. delicate 10. cobweblike
arapunga... 8. bellbird 9. campanero
Arawak... 5. Guana 6. Indian
arbeit... 4. work 8. research
arbiter... 3. ump 5. judge 6. umpire
   7. arbiter, referee 8. mediator
   9. moderator 10. arbitrator
arbitrary... 6. thetic 8. absolute,
   despotic, dogmatic 9. imperious,
   unlimited 10. autocratic, capricious,
   high–handed, peremptory, tyrannical
   11. determinate, dictatorial
   13. discretionary
arbitrate... 6. decide 7. bargain,
   mediate 9. determine, intervene,
   negotiate 12. intermediate
arbitrator... 5. judge 6. umpire
   7. arbiter, referee 8. mediator
   9. moderator 11. conciliator
arbor, arbour... 5. bower, kiosk
   6. alcove, garden, pandal 7. pergola,
   retreat, trellis 11. latticework,
   summerhouse
arboreal... 7. ramous 8. branched,
   treelike 10. arboriform
arboreal mammal... 2. ai 4. unau
   5. lemur, sloth 6. aye–aye, monkey
arc... 3. bow 5. curve 6. radian
   7. azimuth, rainbow
arca... 3. box 5. chest, paten
   9. reliquary
arcade... 3. orb 4. arch, hall
   6. arches, avenue 7. gallery, portico
   8. arcature, corridor 9. colonnade,
   peristyle 10. passageway
Arcadia...
   composition.. 4. poem 5. prose

7. romance
district.. 6. Greece
huntress.. 8. Atalanta
pert to.. 5. rural 8. pastoral
poetic.. 6. Arcady
priestess.. 4. Auge
woodland spirit.. 3. Pan
arcanum... 6. elixir, remedy, secret
7. mystery
arch... 3. arc, sly 4. ogee 5. chief,
hance (part), ogive, vault 6. fornix,
instep 7. cunning, eminent, roguish
8. greatest, memorial, monument
9. principal 11. mischievous
arch (pert to)...
enemy.. 5. devil, Satan 9. adversary
inner curve.. 5. intrados
memorial.. 6. pailou (pailoo)
stone.. 8. keystone
title.. 4. duke 6. bishop, deacon
7. duchess
archaic... 3. old 8. obsolete, old–world
10. antiquated 12. old–fashioned
archangel (celestial)... 5. Uriel
7. Gabriel, Michael, Raphael
archangel plant... 4. mint 8. angelica
archbishop... 6. bishop (chief), exarch
9. patriarch
arched... 6. curved 7. embowed
Archer (Astron)... 11. Sagittarius
archery... 3. bow 4. vane 5. arrow,
clout 5. fistmele, shooting
10. ballistics
archetype... 4. idea 5. model
7. pattern 8. standard 9. prototype
Archie (sl)... 3. gun 12. antiaircraft
Archipelago (pert to)...
Alaska.. 9. Alexander
Australia.. 8. Bismarck
Indonesia (largest).. 5. Malay
Italy.. 6. Aegean
architect... 6. artist, author 7. builder,
planner 8. designer 9. artificer,
draftsman 11. constructor, enterpriser
architectural (pert to)...
arch.. 8. keystone, voussoir
base.. 5. socle 6. plinth
construction.. 8. tectonic
ornament (part).. 5. gutta 6. bezant,
finial, frieze 8. acanthus, dosseret,
fretwork 10. chambranle
pier.. 4. anta
space (triang).. 8. pediment
style.. 5. Doric, Greek, Ionic, Tudor
6. Gothic 7. Baroque, Cape Cod,
Moorish, Spanish 8. Colonial,
Etruscan, Georgian 9. Byzantine,
Palladian 10. Corinthian, Romanesque
11. Renaissance 13. Mediterranean
archives... 6. annals 8. chancery,
registry 9. documents, registers
10. chronicles
arch traitor... 6. Arnold (Benedict),
Brutus 8. Quisling 13. Judas Iscariot
archway... 6. pailou (pailoo)
arctic... 6. polar 6. boreal, frigid,
galosh 7. Alaskan 8. hibernal,
Northern, Siberian 11. hyperborean
Arctic (pert to)...
base.. 4. Etah (Greenland)
bird.. 3. auk 4. xema 6. falcon
7. penguin

cetacean.. 7. narwhal
current.. 8. Labrador
dog.. 5. Husky (Siberian) 8. Malemute
jacket (hooded).. 5. parka (parkee)
6. anorak
native.. 5. Aleut 6. Eskimo, Indian
polar.. 6. Circle
sea.. 7. Barents 8. Beaufort
arctoid... 6. ursine 8. bearlike
Arctoidea... 4. bear 6. weasel
7. raccoon
ardent... 3. hot 4. avid, keen, warm
5. eager, fiery, rethe 6. fervid, fierce
7. amorous, cordial, fervent, flaming,
glowing, intense, shining, violent,
zealous 8. eloquent, vehement
10. passionate 12. affectionate,
enthusiastic
ardilla... 8. squirrel
ardor... 4. élan, fire, heat, love, zeal
5. estro, flame, gusto, verve
6. fervor, fougue, spirit 9. affection,
eagerness, eloquence 10. enthusiasm
11. impetuosity
arduous... 4. hard 5. steep 6. trying
7. onerous 8. toilsome 9. difficult,
laborious, strenuous, wearisome
10. burdensome, exhausting
area... 4. belt, loci (pl), size, zone
5. areal, basin, field, locus, range,
scope, space, tract 6. extent, locale,
region, sector, sphere 7. circuit,
compass, environ, expanse 8. vicinity
9. bailiwick, territory
12. neighborhood
Areca... 5. palm
arena... 4. bowl, oval, ring, rink
5. court, field 6. campus, circus
7. cockpit, stadium, theater
8. coliseum, platform 9. gymnasium
10. hippodrome 12. amphitheater
arenose... 5. sandy 6. grainy, gritty
8. sabulous
areola... 4. halo, ring 5. space
6. armlet, wreath 7. aureole, garland
10. interstice
Ares (pert to)...
consort.. 9. Aphrodite
father.. 4. Zeus
god.. 3. war
Roman equivalent.. 4. Mars
sister.. 4. Eris
argala... 7. marabou 8. adjutant (bird)
argent... 5. white 6. silver 7. shining,
silvery 9. whiteness
Argentina...
capital.. 11. Buenos Aires (1535)
city.. 5. Lanus 6. Paraná 7. Cordoba,
Mendoza, Rosario
Indian.. 4. Lule
mountain.. 5. Andes 9. Aconcagua
(peak) 10. Cordillera (Range)
native.. 7. Mestizo
Plains.. 6. Pampas 9. Gran Chaco
plateau.. 9. Patagonia
poet.. 7. Andrade 10. Echeverria
river.. 5. Plata 6. chubut, Paraná
8. Paraguay
Argentine (pert to)...
color.. 7. silvery 8. art brown
cowboy.. 6. gaucho
dance.. 5. tango

Argonauts (pert to)...
destination.. 7. Colchis (anc)
heroes (50).. 6. Jason's
objective.. 12. Golden Fleece
of '49.. 6. miners (gold)
ship.. 5. Argos

Argos... 3. dog (of Odysseus)

argosy... 4. ship 5. fleet 6. armada,
vessel 8. flotilla

argot... 4. cant, jive 5. lingo, slang
6. jargon, patois 7. dialect
10. vernacular

argue... 4. moot, spar 5. plead, prove
6. debate, evince, reason
7. contend, contest, discuss, dispute,
wrangle 8. indicate, maintain,
persuade 10. controvert
11. expostulate, ratiocinate,
remonstrate

argument... 4. case, plea, spar
5. cavil, lemma, proof, theme
6. debate, hassle 7. defense,
dispute, fallacy, polemic, premise,
sophism 8. dialectic
discourse, enthymeme, pro and con
10. discussion 11. altercation,
disputation 13. consideration,
ratiocination

argumentative... 7. eristic 8. forensic
10. indicative, rhetorical
11. belligerent, contentious,
presumptive, quarrelsome
12. disputatious 13. controversial

Argus (Gr Myth)... 7. monster (founder
of Argos)

Argus-eyed... 8. vigilant 9. observant
11. hundred-eyed 12. sharpsighted

argute... 5. acute, sharp 6. astute,
shrewd, shrill, subtle 9. sagacious

aria... 3. air, lay 4. solo, song, tune
5. canto 6. cantus, melody, strain
7. ariette, sortita

arid... 3. dry 4. dull 6. barren, jejune,
vacant 7. parched, sterile, thirsty
9. anhydrous, waterless
13. unimagination

Arid Austral zone... 7. Sonoran

Ariel... 5. angel, sylph 6. spirit
7. lioness 9. Jerusalem

ariel... 7. gazelle

Aries (Astron)... 3. ram 4. sign
6. meteor 13. constellation

aries... 12. battering-ram (anc)

aright... 4. fine, well 7. exactly
8. directly, straight 11. straightway

aril... 3. pod 7. arillus, coating
8. arillode (false), covering
9. appendage

Arion... 4. poet (of Lesbos) 5. horse
(talking)

arioso... 7. melodic, tuneful
9. melodious

arise... 4. lift, rise, soar, stem
5. begin, issue, mount, occur, rebel,
surge, tower, waken 6. appear,
ascend, emerge, revolt, spring
7. emanate, originate

Aristarch... 6. critic 10. grammarian

Aristides... 7. The Just 9. statesman
(Athens)

aristocracy... 5. elite 7. peerage,
royalty 8. nobility 10. government,

patriciate, upper class

aristocrat... 4. lord, peer 5. noble
7. aristos, Brahman, Brahmin,
grandee, parvenu 8. cavalier, eupatrid
(Athens), nobleman 9. blueblood,
patrician 12. silk-stocking

aristology, science of... 6. dining

Aristotle (pert to)...
birthplace.. 6. Thrace 7. Stagira
(Macedonia)
famed as.. 9. scientist
11. philosopher 12. The Stagirite
school.. 6. Athens
teacher.. 5. Plato
wife.. 7. Pythias

arithmetic... 4. sums 7. numbers
11. computation, enumeration,
mathematics

arithmetic terms... 6. result 7. divisor,
product 8. dividend, multiple,
quotient 9. remainder 10. multiplier
12. multiplicand

Arizona...
capital.. 7. Phoenix
city.. 4. Yuma 5. Tempe 6. Bisbee,
Tucson
famed site.. 9. Hoover Dam
11. Grand Canyon 13. Painted
Desert 15. Petrified Forest
flower (State).. 6. cactus 7. saguaro
Indian.. 4. Hopi, Pima 6. Apache,
Navaho (Navajo)
river.. 4. Gila 8. Colorado
State admission.. 11. Forty-eighth
State motto.. 9. Ditat Deus 11. God
Enriches
State nickname.. 11. Grand Canyon

ark... 3. vat 4. boat, ship 5. chest,
haven 6. asylum, refuge, vessel
8. flatboat 9. broadhorn, sanctuary
(Ararat)

Arkansas...
capital.. 10. Little Rock
city.. 8. El Dorado 9. Fort Smith
12. Fayetteville
famed for.. 8. diamonds (found in
Murfreesboro)
famed newspaper.. 7. Gazette (1819)
flower.. 12. apple blossom
mountain.. 6. Ozarks 9. Ouachitas
Park (Nat).. 10. Hot Springs
river.. 5. White 11. Mississippi
State admission.. 11. Twenty-fifth
State motto.. 13. Regnat Populus
16. Let the People Rule
State nickname.. 17. Land of
Opportunity

arm... 4. limb 5. equip, saber, sword
6. branch, member, pistol, tappet,
weapon 7. forearm, fortify, protect,
quillon (of sword), support 8. revolver
9. appendage 10. projection
12. ramification

arm (pert to)...
armpit.. 5. oxter 6. axilla
bone.. 4. ulna 6. radius 7. humerus
hole.. 4. scye (of sleeve)
muscle.. 6. biceps 7. triceps
projection.. 7. tappet
sea.. 4. gulf, mere 5. bayou, firth,
inlet 7. estuary
sundial.. 6. gnomon

walk arm in arm.. 5. oxter

armada... 5. fleet 6. argosy
8. armament, flotilla, squadron,
warships 10. escadrille

Armada (famed)... 7. Spanish (1588)
10. Invincible

armadillo... 4. apar, peba (peva)
5. apara, poyou, tatou (tatu)
6. mulita, peludo (giant) 7. tatouay
10. pichiciago, Tolypeutes
11. quirquincho (hairy)

Armageddon... 3. war 7. Megiddo
(Bib) 8. conflict, world war

armed... 6. fitted, rigged 7. clothed,
endowed 8. equipped, invested,
prepared, provided, supplied
9. furnished, outfitted 10. laquearian
(with noose)

armed (pert to)...
conflict.. 3. war 6. combat 7. warfare
11. hostilities
forces.. 4. army, host 5. ranks
6. troops 8. military 9. besiegers
vessel.. 3. HMS, sub, USS 5. U–boat
9. destroyer, submarine
10. battleship 11. battlewagon

Armenia...
anc name.. 9. Armenenak
capital.. 6. Erivan
founder.. 4. Haik
herb.. 5. cumin 7. caraway
highlanders.. 5. Gomer
mountain.. 6. Ararat, Taurus
river.. 3. Kur 5. Cyrus 6. Araxes,
Tigris 9. Euphrates
worshiper.. 7. Yesidio (Yesdi)
9. Gregorian

armistice... 5. peace, truce
9. cessation 12. pacification

armoire... 5. ambry 8. cupboard,
wardrobe 10. repository

armor... 4. arms, bard (barde), egis,
jamb, mail, tace 5. acton, aegis,
plate, seton, tasse 6. cuisse, gorget,
graith, greave, helmet, lorica, sconce,
shield, tasset, tuille 7. ailette,
cuirass, hauberk, jambeau, panoply
8. aventail, brassort, ordnance,
pallette, solleret 9. cubitiere,
epauliere, gardebras, mainferre,
rerebrace 10. cataphract

armor–bearer... 6. squire 7. armiger,
esquire

armored... 6. mailed 8. equipped,
ironclad, mailclad 9. cuirassed,
loricated, panoplied

armpit... 5. oxter 6. axilla

arms... 7. weapons 8. armament,
ordnance 9. munitions

arms depository... 5. depot 6. armory
7. arsenal

army... 3. mob 4. host, unit 5. array,
crowd, horde, posse 6. forces,
galaxy, legion, rabble, throng, troops
9. multitude, Salvation

army (pert to)...
brown.. 7. rosario
commission (special).. 6. brevet
trader.. 6. sutler

army unit... 4. ROTC 5. corps, guard
(Nat), squad 7. brigade, cavalry,
company, militia, platoon, Sabaoth

(Bib) 8. division, infantry, Landwehr,
regiment, reserves 9. artillery,
minutemen 10. volunteers

Arnold's co–conspirator... 5. Andre
(Maj)

aroma... 4. musk, odor, tang 5. attar,
balmy, nidor, savor, scent, smell,
spice 6. flavor 7. bouquet, feature,
incense, perfume 9. fragrance,
muskiness, redolence 11. peculiarity,
singularity

aromatic... 5. spicy 6. savory
7. odorous, pungent 8. fragrant,
redolent 11. fluorescent

aromatic (pert to)...
gum.. 5. myrrh 12. frankincense
herb.. 4. mint 5. clary, nondo
oil.. 4. balm 6. balsam 9. sassafras
seed.. 4. anis 6. nutmeg 7. aniseed
tree.. 5. aromo 6. balsam
7. champac 8. huisache

around... 4. near, peri (pref) 5. about,
circa 6. bordering, somewhere
11. thereabouts 13. approximately

arouse... 4. fire, stir, wake 5. alarm,
anger, evoke, raise, rally, roust
6. awaken, elicit, excite, incite,
kindle, summon 7. animate

arpa... 4. harp

arpeggio... 5. chord 7. roulade
8. division, flourish

arraign... 4. cite 6. accuse, charge,
indict 7. impeach 8. denounce,
reproach 9. prosecute

arrange... 3. fix 4. cast, cite, file,
plan, plot, sort 5. adapt, aline,
besee, drape, ettle, frame, grade,
preen, range, stack 6. adjust, deploy,
design, devise 7. dispose, mediate,
prepare, provide, seriate 8. classify,
contract, contrive, laminate, organize,
tabulate 9. catalogue (catalog),
negotiate 10. distribute, paniculate
11. alphabetize, systematize

arranged... 5. fixed, timed 6. ranked,
sorted 7. aligned, grouped, ordered,
orderly, planned, settled, uniform
9. regulated 10. contracted

arranged in...
fives.. 7. quinate
fours.. 11. tetramerous
hours.. 9. staggered
rays.. 6. radial
threes.. 7. ternate

arrangement... 3. art, rig (sails)
4. plan, rank 5. order, setup
6. series, syntax, system 7. echelon
(troops), musical 8. disposal,
neatness, trimness 9. agreement,
condition, structure 10. adaptation,
engagement, settlement
11. collocation, combination,
permutation, preparation
12. distribution

arrant... 3. bad 6. wicked 8. rascally
9. confirmed, shameless
11. unmitigated 12. disreputable

array... 3. don 4. deci, robe 5. adorn,
align, dress, order 6. clothe, muster,
series, throng 7. arrange, dispose,
envelop, marshal 8. clothing,
garments 9. adornment

11. arrangement

arrears... 3. due 4. debt 5. short
7. wanting 9. arrearage, deficient
10. behindhand, defaulting

arrest... 4. halt, hold, stop 5. check,
delay, seize 6. detain, hinder,
impede, retard 7. custody, seizure
8. obstruct, restrain, stoppage
9. apprehend, hindrance, intercept,
restraint 11. retardation

arrested... 6. behind 7. checked,
delayed, impeded, stopped
8. detained, retarded 10. restrained
11. intercepted

arrested development... 6. simple
7. dwarfed, idiotic, moronic
8. backward, retarded 10. half–witted
13. unintelligent

arrival... 5. comer (anc) 6. advent,
coming 8. landing 9. approach,
reaching 10. attainment, homecoming
11. achievement

arrive... 4. come 5. debus, reach
6. alight, debark, happen 7. detrain
9. disembark

arrogance... 5. pride 7. conceit,
disdain, hauteur 8. audacity,
rudeness, snobbery 9. brashness,
insolence, loftiness 10. effrontery
11. haughtiness 12. impertinence

arrogant... 4. bold, pert 5. cocky,
lofty, proud 6. lordly, uppish
7. forward 8. impudent, insolent
9. audacious, insulting, masterful,
presuming 10. disdainful
11. domineering, high–falutin,
impertinent, overbearing
12. contemptuous, contumelious,
presumptuous, supercilious

arrogate... 5. seize, usurp, wrest
6. assume 11. appropriate

arrow... 4. barb, dart, reed, vire
(feathered) 5. guide, shaft 6. finger
7. missile, pointer 10. guideboard

arrow (pert to)...
astronomy.. 7. Sagitta
bows.. 6. bowyer (maker, seller)
case.. 6. quiver
end.. 4. nock 9. arrowhead
feather (to).. 6. fletch
handle.. 6. stele
head.. 4. dart
poison.. 4. inee, upas 5. urali
6. curare, uzarin
poisoned.. 6. sumpit 8. sumpitan
propeller.. 3. bow
shape.. 6. beloid 8. cuneiform,
sagittate
stone.. 9. belemnite
variety.. 4. self 6. footed 7. chested
9. bobtailed

arrowroot... 3. pia 5. araru 6. ararao,
starch 7. Maranta

arroyo... 5. brook, creek 6. ravine,
stream 11. watercourse

arroz... 4. rice

arse... 4. butt, rump (vulgar)
8. buttocks 9. posterior

arsenal... 4. dump 5. depot, plant
6. armory 7. factory 8. magazine
10. depository, storehouse

arsis... 5. ictus 6. accent, stress (opp

of thesis), upbeat

arson... 7. burning, cautery
9. pyromania 12. incendiarism

art... 4. wile 5. cameo, craft, knack,
skill, taste, trade 6. design
7. calling, cartoon, cunning, drawing,
science 8. aptitude, artifice, artistry,
business, ceramics, drafting, intaglio,
painting, vocation 9. dexterity,
duplicate, engraving, ingenuity,
readiness, sculpture, sketching
10. adroitness, decoration, profession
11. contrivance, photography,
portraiture 12. architecture

art (pert to)...
addict.. 8. aesthete (esthete)
decoration.. 9. sgraffito
design.. 7. graphic
fancier.. 9. dilettante
gallery.. 5. salon
grotesque.. 11. incongruous
mystic.. 6. cabala
of assaying.. 8. docimasy
of discourse.. 8. rhetoric
of embossing.. 9. toreutics
of government.. 8. politics
of horsemanship.. 6. manège
of imitation.. 7. mimicry
of manual craft.. 5. sloyd
of memory.. 10. mneumonics
of metal inlay.. 8. niello
primitive.. 9. artifacts
realistic.. 5. genre
rhyming.. 5. poesy 6. poetry
self–defense.. 6. boxing 7. fencing,
jujitsu (jiujitsu)
style.. 6. cubism, purism 7. baroque,
Dadaism, Fauvism 8. futurism
9. modernism 10. surrealism
13. impressionism
theme.. 5. motif
tooling.. 10. diesinking
transmutation.. 7. alchemy

Artemis (pert to)...
brother (twin).. 6. Apollo
epithet (Homeric).. 6. Phoebe
father.. 4. Zeus
goddess of.. 4. moon 6. nature
7. the Hunt 8. Olympian
Mother.. 4. Leto
religion.. 4. Upis
Roman equivalent.. 5. Diana

artery... 4. tube, vein 6. avenue,
street, vessel 7. channel, highway,
passage 8. ligament 10. passageway

artery (Anat)... 4. tube, vein 5. aorta
6. vessel 7. anonyma, carotid,
trachea 9. capillary, pulmonary
10. innominate

artery pulsation... 4. beat 5. ictus

artful... 3. sly 4. foxy, wily 5. cagey
6. adroit, clever, crafty, shrewd,
subtle, tricky 7. crooked, cunning,
knowing, politic 8. skillful, stealthy
9. deceitful, deceptive, designing,
dexterous, imitative 10. artificial

Artful Dodger... 3. fox 6. rascal
7. slicker 8. deceiver 11. John
Dawkins (Dickens tale) 12. crafty
person

artfulness... 5. skill 7. finesse
8. artifice, subtlety, wiliness

9. stratagem 10. cleverness, refinement, shrewdness
arthron... 5. hinge, joint, pivot 12. articulation
Arthurian abode... 6. Avalon 9. Lyonnesse (Leonnoys)
Arthurian character... 6. Arthur (King), Elaine, Merlin 7. Geraint 8. Lancelot 9. Percivale
artichoke... 6. canada, Cynara 7. chorogi, thistle 9. Jerusalem
article... 3. mat 4. item, news, term 5. scoop, story, thing 6. belief, clause, detail, gadget, object, treaty 7. camelot, feature (news), grammar, integer 8. treatise 9. commodity, editorial 10. particular 11. composition, stipulation
article (Gram)...
  English.. 1. a 2. an 3. the
  French.. 2. la, le, un 3. les, une
  Spanish.. 2. el, un 3. las, los, una
article (of)...
  agreement.. 8. contract
  apparel.. 5. smock, tunic 6. duster, gaiter, mantle 8. pinafore
  faith.. 5. canon, creed, dogma, tenet 6. belief 7. precept
  property.. 7. chattel
  virtu.. 5. curio, relic 6. rarity 7. antique
articulation... 4. tone 5. hinge, joint, sound, voice 7. voicing 8. locution, sonation 9. phonation, utterance 11. enunciation 12. vocalization 13. pronunciation
artifact... 5. curio, relic, virtu 6. fossil 7. antique, remains 8. archaism
artifice... 4. plot, ruse, wile 5. blind, chest, craft, dodge, fraud, guile, shift, trick 6. deceit 7. cunning, evasion, finesse, knavery, sleight 8. intrigue, maneuver, trickery 9. chicanery, collusion, deception, expedient, imposture, stratagem 10. connivance, imposition, subterfuge 11. contrivance, machination, skulduggery
artificer... 5. smith 6. artist, framer 7. artisan, creator, deviser, workman 8. Daedalus, inventor, mechanic 9. architect, carpenter, craftsman, goldsmith 11. coppersmith, silversmith
artificial... 4. fake, mock, sham 5. bogus, dummy, false, phony 6. ersatz, forged, unreal 7. assumed, bastard, elegant, feigned 8. affected, fabulous, spurious 9. imaginary, imitation, pretended, unnatural 11. adulterated, counterfeit, unauthentic 12. suppositious
artificial (pert to)...
  butter.. 4. oleo 13. oleomargarine
  channel.. 3. gat 4. leat 5. canal, flume 6. sluice
  gum.. 7. dextrin
  language.. 2. ro 3. Ido 5. Arulo 7. Volapuk 9. Esperanto 10. Occidental
  silk.. 5. nylon, rayon
  surface.. 4. rink

  voice.. 8. falsetto
artillery... 4. army, guns 5. bombs 6. cannon, slings 7. cavalry, gunners, gunnery, mortars 8. ordnance 9. arbalests, catapults 10. ballistics
artillery (pert to)...
  emplacement.. 7. battery
  fire.. 5. salvo 6. rafale
  man.. 6. gunner 8. rifleman, topechee 9. cannoneer, musketeer 11. artillarist
  wagon.. 7. battery
artiodactyl... (opp of perissodactyl) 2. ox 3. pig 4. deer, goat 5. camel, sheep 6. artiad 7. giraffe 12. hippopotamus
artisan... 6. artist, limner 7. painter, workman 8. mechanic, virtuoso 9. artificer, craftsman
artist... 5. rapin (Fr pupil) 6. etcher, limner, potter 7. artisan, painter 8. designer, sculptor 9. architect, decorator 10. cartoonist, ceramacist 11. illustrator 12. photographer
artist (pert to)...
  equipment.. 5. easel 7. palette 8. maquette
  sleight of hand.. 4. mage 5. Magus 8. magician 9. alchemist
artiste... 5. actor, adept 6. dancer, singer 7. artisan 8. musician 9. performer
artistic... 4. pure 6. ornate 7. classic 8. graceful, skillful, tasteful 9. aesthetic (esthetic), art-minded, beautiful, exquisite
artistic (pert to)...
  ardor.. 5. verve 6. spirit
  dance.. 6. ballet
  quality.. 6. virtue
  symbol of the dead.. 5. orant
  temperament.. 7. caprice, emotion
artless... 4. naif, open, rude 5. frank, naive 6. candid, simple 7. natural, sincere 8. ignorant 9. guileless, ingenuous, unskilled 10. inartistic, unaffected, uncultured 11. undesigning 15. unsophisticated
artlessness... 6. candor 7. naiveté 9. frankness, innocence 11. naturalness 13. ungenuousness
arts (pert to)...
  liberal.. 7. trivium 10. quadrivium
  quadrivium.. 5. music 8. geometry 9. astronomy 10. arithmetic
  trivium.. 5. logic 7. grammar 8. rhetoric
aru... 6. indeed, really
arui... 5. ouadad, sheep 7. chamois (Bib)
arum... 4. taro 5. calla (lily) 6. starch 9. arrowroot
arx... 7. citadel
Aryan (pert to)...
  God of Fire.. 4. Agni
  invader.. 4. Pict
  people.. 4. Mede 5. Hindu 9. Caucasian 11. Indo-Iranian
as... 3. qua 4. como, than, thus 5. since, while 7. because, equally, similar 9. similarly

Asa... 11. King of Judah
asafetida... 8. medicine
   13. antispasmodic
Asa's son... 11. Jehoshaphat
ascend... 3. fly 4. rise, soar, upgo
   5. arise, climb, mount, scale, tower
   6. aspire, uprise 7. clamber, upsurge
ascendancy... 4. sway 7. control,
   mastery 8. dominion, prestige,
   priority 9. authority, influence,
   supremacy 10. domination
   11. sovereignty, superiority
   12. predominance 13. preponderance
ascendant, ascendent... 5. elder
   6. father 7. supreme 8. ancestor,
   forebear, superior 9. governing,
   patriarch 10. antecedent, decoration
   (Arch)
ascended... 4. rose 5. arose, risen
   6. uprose
ascending... 6. anodic, rising
   7. scaling, sloping 8. mounting,
   racemose 9. emanating
ascending signs... 5. Aries 6. Gemini,
   Pisces, Taurus 8. Aquarius
   9. Capricorn
ascenseur... 8. elevator
Ascension Day... 8. Thursday (Holy),
   (40 days after Easter)
Ascension lily... 7. Madonna
ascertain... 4. find 5. learn, prove,
   solve 6. decide 7. certify
   9. determine
ascetic... 4. yati, yoga, yogi 5. fakir,
   stoic 6. Essene, hermit, strict
   7. austere, eremite, puritan, recluse
   8. anchoret, Diogenes, solitary
   9. abstainer, anchorite, mendicant
   10. abstemious
asceticism... 4. Yoga 9. austerity,
   nephalism 10. abstention, abstinence,
   puritanism 11. anchoritism,
   teetotalism
ascribable... 3. due 9. traceable
   10. assignable 11. attributive
   12. attributable
ascribe... 5. count, refer 6. assign,
   attach, credit, impute, reckon
   7. ascribe 8. accredit 9. attribute
ascus fruit... 8. truffles
asepsis... 6. purity 7. clarity 9. sterility
   13. taintlessness
ash... 4. sorb, tree 5. rowan
   6. samara (true) 8. Fraxinus
ashes... 4. dust, lava, lees, slag
   5. dregs, ruins 6. embers
   7. cinders, residue
ash tree symbol (Norse Myth)...
   10. Yggdrasill (horse of Yggr)
Asia... 4. East 6. Orient, region 7. Far
   East 8. Old World 9. continent
Asia Minor...
  city (anc).. 4. Myra, Teos, Troy
   5. Ilium, Issus, Lydia 6. Nicaea,
   Sardes 7. Ephesus
  district.. 4. Aria 5. Ionia, Troad (The
   Troad) 6. Aeolis
  island.. 6. Lesbos
  language (anc).. 6. Lycian, Lydian
   8. Etruscan
  mountain.. 3. Ida
  old name.. 8. Anatolia

sea.. 5. Black 6. Aegean 7. Marmosa
   13. Mediterranean
Asiatic (pert to)...
  barbarian (anc).. 3. Hun 6. Vandal
  desert.. 4. Gobi
  gulf.. 4. Aden, Oman, Siam 6. Tonkin
   7. Persian
  island.. 4. Java 5. Luzon, Malay
   7. Celebes, Diomede (Big), Formosa,
   Sumatra 8. Japanese, Mindanao,
   Sakhalin 11. Philippines
  mountain.. 4. Ural 5. Altai, Sayan
   7. Everest 8. Caucasus, Himalaya
   9. Hindu Kush
  native.. 4. Arab, Turk, Yuit 5. Tatar
   6. Indian, Innuit (Esk), Syrian
   7. Chinese, Malayan 8. Annamese,
   Japanese 9. Mongolian
  nomad.. 4. Arab
  river.. 2. Ob 4. Amur, Lena
   5. Hwang, Indus 6. Ganges
   7. Yangtze, Yenisei 9. Euphrates,
   Irrawaddy 11. Brahmaputra
  sea.. 4. Azov (Azof) 5. Black, China,
   Japan 6. Bering, Yellow 7. Caspian,
   Okhotsk
Asiatic animal...
  antelope.. 5. goral
  ass.. 6. onager
  camel.. 8. Bactrian 9. dromedary
  carnivore.. 5. panda, tiger
  cattle.. 4. zobo
  deer.. 4. axis 10. chevrotain
  elephant.. 7. Elephas
  fox.. 6. corsac
  gazelle.. 3. ahu
  goat.. 5. serow
  lemur.. 5. loris 6. macaco
  lynx.. 7. caracal
  mongoose.. 4. urva
  monkey.. 6. langur (long–tailed)
  ox.. 3. yak
  rodent.. 4. pika
  sheep.. 3. sha 5. uriel 6. argali
  squirrel.. 8. jelerang 10. polatouche
Asiatic bird...
  finch.. 9. brambling
  jay.. 7. sirgang
  owl.. 4. utum
  partridge.. 6. seesee
  plover.. 8. dotterel
  songless.. 5. Pitta
  talking.. 4. myna (mynah)
Asiatic snake... 3. asp 5. cobra
   8. ringhals
Asiatic storm (pert to)...
  sand.. 6. simoom (simoon) 7. tebbard
  snow.. 5. buran
  wind.. 7. buran 7. monsoon
aside... 4. away 5. apart, hence
   6. aslant, astray, beside 7. whisper
   8. sidewise 9. alongside, privately,
   sotto voce 12. interjection
asinine... 4. dumb 5. inane, inept, silly
   6. mulish, stupid 7. doltish, foolish,
   idiotic 9. obstinate
ask... 3. beg 4. quiz 5. claim, exact,
   query, speer 6. assess, demand,
   invite 7. beseech, entreat, implore,
   inquire, request, require, solicit
   8. petition, question 9. catechize,
   obsecrate (Relig) 11. interrogate

askance... 4. awry 5. askew
7. asquint, crooked 8. sideways
9. obliquely

askew... 4. agee, alop, awry 5. agley,
amiss 6. faulty 7. askance, asquint,
crooked 8. deranged 9. distorted,
obliquely 10. catawampus, disorderly

aslant... 4. atilt 6. tilted, tipped
7. athwart, leaning, listing, pitched,
sloping 8. inclined 9. careening,
obliquely

asleep... 4. dead, dull, numb
7. dormant, unaware 8. deadened,
sleeping, unarisen 9. oblivious,
senseless, unruffled 10. motionless
11. inattentive, insensitive,
unconscious

Asoka's Empire (anc Ind)... 5. Patna

asp... 5. cobra, snake, viper 6. uraeus
(sacred sym)

aspect... 3. air 4. look, mien, pose,
side, view 5. angle, decil, facet,
guise, phase, shape, sight, state
6. decile, facies, status, visage
7. bearing, posture, scenery
8. attitude 9. astrology, component,
influence, seaminess, situation
10. appearance 11. countenance

aspen... 4. tree, wood 6. poplar
7. quaking 9. quivering, shivering,
trembling, tremulous, vibrating

asperge... 3. wet 4. damp 5. spray,
water 7. baptize 8. humidify, sprinkle

asperge... 9. asparagus

Asperges... 4. rite 6. anthem
10. sprinkling (altar)

aspergillum... 5. brush 7. sprayer
8. baptizer 9. sprinkler

asperity... 5. rigor 7. raucity
8. acerbity, acrimony, hardship,
severity, tartness 9. bleakness,
roughness 10. causticity, difficulty,
inclemency, moroseness, resentment

asperse... 4. slur 5. abuse, decry, libel
6. defame, malign, revile, vilify
7. blacken, slander, traduce
8. besmirch 9. bespatter, discredit
10. calumniate

aspersion... 4. rite, slur 6. insult
7. affront, baptism, calumny, outrage,
wetting 8. innuendo 9. indignity
10. defamation, sprinkling
12. calumniating, calumniation
13. disparagement

asphalt... 4. pave 5. pitch 7. bitumen,
mineral 8. blacktop, pavement,
uintaite 9. gilsonite 10. macadamize

asphyxia... 5. apnea (apnoea)
7. choking 11. suffocation
12. smotheration

aspic... 3. asp (poet) 4. jelly
6. cannon 8. lavender 9. galantine

aspiration... 3. aim 4. hope, wish
5. ideal 6. breath, desire
7. pumping, sucking, suction
8. ambition, staccato 9. breathing
10. exhalation 11. inspiration

aspire... 4. long, plan, rise, soar
5. tower 6. attain, desire, expect,
intend 7. breathe, propose

ass... 3. ono (comb form) 4. dolt,
dope, fool, jack 5. burro, jenny

assail... 4. pelt 5. beset, stone
6. attack 7. assault 9. implicate
11. incriminate

assailant... 3. foe 5. enemy 7. invader
8. assailer, attacker, opponent
9. adversary, aggressor
10. antagonist, challenger

Assam...
capital.. 8. Shillong
native.. 4. Ahom 8. Assamite
11. Indo–Chinese
province of.. 5. India
river.. 11. Brahmaputra
tribe.. 2. Ao 3. Aka 4. Garo, Naga

assassin... 4. Cain, thug 5. bravo
6. apache, cuttle, gunman, killer,
slayer 7. gorilla, ruffian 8. murderer,
sicarian 9. manslayer 11. slaughterer

assassination... 5. purge 6. murder
7. killing 8. regicide 11. liquidation
12. manslaughter

Assassin Order... 8. Ismalian
10. Mohammedan

assault... 5. onset, storm 6. assail,
attack, charge 7. descent, seizure
8. invasion 9. incursion
13. incrimination

assay... 3. try 4. test 5. prove, trial
6. accost 7. attempt 8. analysis,
docimasy (art), endeavor
10. experiment 12. verification

assay cup... 5. cupel

assemblage... 3. all 4. herd 6. throng
8. assembly, entirety 9. gathering
12. congregation

assemblage (pert to)...
cattle.. 5. drove, rodeo 7. roundup
fashionable.. 5. salon
mob.. 4. rout 6. rabble
splendid.. 6. galaxy
tents.. 4. camp 10. encampment

assemble... 3. pod 4. mass, meet
5. amass, piece, rally, unite
6. couple, gather, muster 7. cluster,
collect, convene, convoke, recruit
10. congregate

assembly... 4. bevy, diet, moot
5. agora, gemot, group, synod, troop
6. assize, sabbat 7. company,
council, landtag, meeting 8. auditory,
conclave (secret), folkmoot (Hist)
9. concourse, gathering
10. collection, convention
11. convocation 12. congregation

assent... 3. aye, nod, yea, yes
4. amen 5. admit, agree, grant
6. accede, accord, concur
7. consent 8. sanction 9. acquiesce,
agreement 10. compliance
12. acquiescence

assert... 3. say 4. aver, pose 5. claim,
plead, posit, state, voice 6. affirm,
allege, avouch, relate, uphold
7. contend, declare, profess, protest,
support 8. advocate 9. pronounce,
vindicate 10. asseverate

assertion... 5. claim 6. remark, thesis
7. premise 8. averment 9. statement
10. assumption, hypothesis
11. affirmation, declaration,
maintenance, proposition, vindication

assertiveness... 10. pragmatism

14. aggressiveness
assertor... 8. affirmer, defender
9. supporter 10. vindicator
assess... 3. ask, tax 4. cess, levy,
mise, rate 5. price, value 6. charge
7. measure 8. appraise, estimate
assessment... 3. fee, tax 4. levy, rate,
scot 5. ratal, stock, value 6. surtax
7. pricing, scutage 8. estimate
9. appraisal, valuation 10. evaluation
11. measurement
assets... 5. funds, means 6. wealth
7. capital 8. accounts, property
9. resources
asseverate... 3. say, vow 4. aver
5. state, swear 6. affirm, allege,
assert 7. contend, declare, profess,
protest 8. maintain 9. pronounce
asseveration... 3. vow 4. oath
(solemn) 8. averment 9. assertion
11. affirmation, declaration
13. pronouncement
assiduity... 8. industry 9. diligence
11. painstaking, persistence
12. perseverance
assiduous... 4. busy 6. active
7. intense, zealous 8. diligent,
sedulous 9. energetic, laborious,
unwearied 11. industrious,
perseverant 13. indefatigable,
unintermitted
assign... 3. fix, set 4. cast, cede, seal
5. allot, refer 6. allege, commit,
detail 7. address, adjudge, appoint,
ascribe, consign, empower
8. accredit, allocate, delegate,
nominate, transfer 9. attribute
10. commission 11. appropriate
assignment... 3. job 4. task 5. chore,
stint 6. lesson 7. mission
8. exercise, transfer 9. allotment
10. allocation, commission,
commitment 11. attribution
13. specification
assimilate... 5. adapt, learn, liken
6. absorb, digest, imbibe 7. convert
10. understand 11. approximate
assimilation... 8. imbibing, learning
9. anabolism, digestion, ingestion,
reduction 10. absorption, adaptation,
comparison, conversion
14. naturalization
assist... 3. aid 4. abet, back, help
5. avail, boost, favor 6. attend,
prompt, second, succor 7. benefit,
relieve, support, sustain 8. befriend
9. accompany, subsidize
assistance... 3. aid 4. help 5. grant
6. relief, succor 7. service, subsidy,
support 10. logrolling (Polit)
11. furtherance
assistant... 4. aide, ally 5. tutor
6. deputy, helper 7. abettor,
famulus, servant, teacher
9. associate, attendant, auxiliary
11. subordinate 12. right-hand man
assize... 3. fix 4. rate 5. edict, trial,
value 6. assess, decree 9. ordinance
10. regulation 11. instruction,
measurement
associate... 3. mix, pal 4. ally, chum,
mate 5. buddy, crony 6. fellow,

friend, hobnob, mingle 7. combine,
comrade, consort, partner
9. colleague, companion
10. accomplice 11. concomitant,
confederate
associated... 6. allied, banded, joined,
united 7. coupled, leagued, related
9. connected 10. affiliated
concurrent
associates... 4. crew 5. force, staff
7. retinue 9. personnel
12. constituency
association... 4. body, club 5. artel,
cabal, guild, hanse (Hist), union
6. league, lyceum, symbol
7. company, society 8. alliance,
relation, sodality, sorority 9. syndicate
10. fellowship, fraternity
11. affiliation, combination,
comradeship, concurrence, corporation
13. communication, interrelation
assonance... 3. pun 4. rime 5. rhyme
8. paragram 9. agreement
11. paronomasia, resemblance
12. alliteration
assort... 4. sort, suit 5. adapt, class,
grade, group 7. consort (with)
8. classify, separate 9. associate
(with) 10. categorize, distribute
assortment... 3. mix, set 4. hash,
mess, olio 5. class, group 6. jumble,
medley 7. mélange, mixture, sorting
9. potpourri 10. collection,
hodgepodge, miscellany
11. arrangement 14. conglomeration
assuage... 4. calm, ease 5. allay, slake
6. lessen, mellow, pacify, quench,
soften, solace, soothe 7. appease,
comfort, gratify, qualify, relieve,
satisfy 8. mitigate, palliate
9. alleviate
assuasive... 5. balmy 6. easing
8. remedial, soothing 9. relieving,
softening 10. mitigating, palliative
11. alleviative 13. tranquilizing
assume... 3. don 4. deem, sham, take
5. adopt, feign, guess, imply, infer,
judge, think, usurp 6. affect, allege,
betake, borrow, deduce 7. believe,
imagine, premise, presume, pretend,
suppose, surmise 8. arrogate,
conclude, simulate 9. undertake
11. appropriate, counterfeit
assume (pert to)...
character.. 11. impersonate
different forms.. 7. protean
unduly.. 5. usurp 8. arrogate
without proof.. 11. theoretical
12. hypothetical
assumed... 6. deemed 7. alleged,
implied, thought 8. affected, inferred,
presumed, supposed 9. fictional,
pretended 10. fictitious, understood,
undertaken 11. conjectured,
make-believe, presumptive,
presupposed, theoretical
12. appropriated, hypothetical,
suppositious
assuming... 5. lofty 8. arrogant,
superior 9. presuming
10. assumptive 11. overweening,
pretentious 12. presumptuous

assumption... 8. adoption
  9. arrogance, postulate, reception
  10. usurpation 11. implication,
  proposition, supposition
  13. appropriation, incorporation
  14. presupposition
assurance... 4. hope, oath 5. poise,
  trust 6. aplomb, belief, pledge,
  surety 7. comfort, courage, promise
  8. security, sureness 9. certainty,
  guarantee, impudence, insurance
  10. confidence, steadiness
  11. assuredness, intrepidity
  12. cocksureness 14. self-confidence
assure... 4. aver 5. vouch 6. assert,
  avouch, depose, ensure, insure,
  secure 7. confirm, declare, protest,
  satisfy 8. convince, embolden,
  persuade, reassure 9. encourage,
  guarantee 10. asseverate
Assyria...
  capital.. 7. Nineveh
  city.. 5. Calab (Bib) 9. Khorsabad
    (ruins)
  empire (anc).. 5. Assur (Ashur)
  language.. 6. Semite 9. cuneiform
    (written)
  people.. 6. Semite 7. Amorite (Bib)
Assyrian god...
  atmosphere.. 5. Hadad
  fire.. 7. Nusku
  hunt.. 7. Ninurta
  moon.. 3. Sin
  storm.. 2. Zu
  sun.. 7. Shamash
  war.. 6. Nergal 7. Ninurta
  winds.. 4. Adad 5. Hadad
Assyrian goddess... 5. Nanai
  6. Allatu, Ishtar 9. Sarpanitu
  (Zirbanit)
Assyriology, science of... 8. language
  11. antiquities
aster... 4. star 9. asterwort, karyaster
  10. Carduaceae
asterisk... 4. mark (reference), star
  6. accent, figure (star) 9. highlight
  10. asteriskos (Eccl)
astern... 3. aft 4. baft, rear 5. abaft,
  after 6. behind 8. hindward,
  rearward, tailward
asteroid... 5. Ceres (largest) 6. planet
  8. starlike 9. planetoid
Asteroidea... 8. starfish
astir... 2. up 5. about, afoot, eager
  6. active, moving 8. stirring
  9. forthcoming
as to... 7. apropos, suppose
  9. regarding 10. concerning,
  respecting
astonish... 4. stun 5. amaze, appal
  7. astound, stagger, startle
  8. bewilder, confound, surprise
  9. overwhelm
astonishing... 7. amazing 8. fabulous
  9. appalling, marvelous, wonderful
  10. incredible, remarkable
astound... 4. stun 5. abash, amaze,
  shock 6. appall (appal), dismay
  7. stagger, stupefy 8. astonish,
  surprise 10. disconcert
astounding... 8. horrible, shocking
  9. appalling, frightful 10. horrendous,

horrifying 11. astonishing
astraddle... 7. astride 9. horseback,
  pickaback (piggyback) 10. straddling
astral... 6. spirit, starry 7. stellar
  8. sidereal, starlike 9. celestial
  11. star-studded
astray... 4. lost 5. amiss, wrong
  6. adrift, afield, erring 8. aberrate,
  mistaken 9. erroneous 10. bewildered
astray, to go... 3. err, sin 4. mang,
  rove 5. drift, lapse, stray 6. wander
  7. deviate, digress 8. miscarry
  9. backslide 10. misbelieve
astriction... 4. bond 7. binding
  8. thirlage 9. fastening 10. litigation
  11. confinement, contraction
  12. constipation
astride... 8. straddle 9. astraddle,
  horseback, pickaback (piggyback)
astringent... 4. acid, alum, sloe, sour
  5. acerb, acrid, harsh, sapan, stern
  6. tannin 7. austere, bitters, caustic,
  pungent, rhatany (root), styptic
  9. vitriolic 10. antiseptic
  11. acrimonious, argentamine
  12. constrictive
astrologer... 8. Chaldean 9. stargazer
  11. astrologian, astromancer,
  Nostradamus
astrology (pert to)... 5. house, signs
  6. aspect, zodiac 7. mansion,
  mundane 8. siderism 9. horoscope,
  planetary 11. horoscopist
astronaut... 7. Martian 8. spaceman
  9. cosmonaut, rocketeer
astronomer... 9. stargazer
  11. uranologist 12. uranographer
  13. meteorologist, uranographist
astronomer, famed... 6. Kepler
  7. Galileo 12. Eratosthenes
astronomical... 4. huge, vast 5. large
  6. cosmic, uranic 7. immense,
  mammoth, Uranian 8. colossal,
  empyreal, heavenly 9. celestial
  10. prodigious, stupendous,
  tremendous
astronomy (pert to)... 4. coma (the)
  5. apsis, saros (Bab) 6. syzygy
  7. almanac, apsides, azimuth,
  gibbous 8. sidereal 9. idiometer,
  insulated 11. debilissima
astute... 3. sly 4. keen, wily 5. acute,
  canny, smart 6. artful, clever, crafty,
  shrewd 7. cunning, skilled
  9. insidious, sagacious 10. discerning
  14. discriminating
asunder... 5. apart, cleft, split
  6. atwain, halved 7. divided
  9. disjoined, separated
as yet... 8. hitherto
asylum... 3. ark 4. home, jail, port
  5. haven 6. harbor, refuge
  7. retreat, shelter 9. hospitium,
  infirmary, sanctuary 10. stronghold
  11. institution
asymmetrical... 6. uneven, warped
  7. twisted, unequal 9. contorted,
  distorted 11. zygomorphic
  16. disproportionate
at... 2. by, in 4. near, nigh 5. there
  8. location, position 9. direction,
  situation

at (pert to)...
  great length.. 7. on and on
    9. tediously
  home.. 2. in 4. here 9. en famille
  last.. 3. end 7. finally 9. extremely
    10. ultimately
  once.. 3. now 7. readily
  the same time.. 6. coeval
    10. coetaneous 12. contemporary
atabal... 4. drum 5. tabor
    10. kettledrum
atabeg... 5. title 6. vizier
Atalanta (pert to)...
  defeated in romantic race by..
    10. Hippomenes 17. three golden
    apples (Gr Myth)
  famed.. 8. huntress
  foe.. 9. Aphrodite
  husband.. 8. Milanion
  legend.. 8. Arcadian, Boeotian
atalaya... 10. watchtower
atap... 4. nipa, palm
atavism... 8. heredity 9. reversion
    10. regression
ate... 5. dined, fared 6. dieted,
    gnawed, supped
Ate... 7. goddess (of infatuation)
atelier... 5. easel 6. studio
    8. workshop
a tempo... 4. time
Aten (Egypt)... 9. solar disk
ates... 8. sweetsop
athanasia... 8. athanasy
    11. immortality 13. deathlessness
    16. imperishability
athanor (Fr)... 7. furnace (alchemist's)
Athapascan Indian... 5. Tinne
    6. Apache, Navaho (Navajo)
atheist... 5. pagan 7. heathen, infidel,
    nastika 8. agnostic 10. unbeliever
    11. disbeliever, unchristian
    13. antichristian
Athena (pert to)...
  attributes.. 3. owl 5. aegis 7. serpent
  festival.. 11. Panathenaea
  Rom equivalent.. 7. Minerva
  shrine.. 9. Parthenon (Athens)
Athena, goddess of...
  arts, crafts.. 6. Ergane
  health.. 6. Hygeia
  horses, tamer of.. 6. Hippia
  light.. 4. Alea
  maid of Athens.. 12. Pallas Athene
  poetry.. 6. Pallas
  victory.. 4. Nike
  wisdom.. 8. Palladis
Athenian (pert to)...
  assembly.. 4. Pnyx
  Bee.. 5. Plato
  general.. 8. Xenophon
  lawgiver.. 5. Draco, Solon
  sculptor.. 7. Phidias
  statesman.. 8. Pericles 9. Aristides
    (The Just) 10. Alcibiades
  temple.. 11. Nike Apteros
Athens...
  capital of.. 6. Attica (anc), Greece
  citadel.. 9. Acropolis
  magistrate.. 5. Draco, Solon
  rival.. 6. Sparta (anc)
  senate.. 5. boule
  temple.. 9. Parthenon

Athens of...
  America.. 6. Boston 9. Nashville (The
    South)
  Ireland.. 4. Cork 7. Belfast
  North.. 9. Edinburgh 10. Copenhagen
  Switzerland.. 6. Zurich
  West.. 7. Cordoba
athlete... 7. acrobat, gymnast, tumbler
    11. funambulist, palaestrian,
    pancratiast 13. contortionist
athlete (pert to)...
  foot disease.. 15. dermatophytosis
  of Christendom.. 10. Scanderbeg
  portico (Gr, Rom).. 6. xystus (xyst)
athletic... 5. lusty, thewy, yauld
    6. brawny, robust, sinewy, strong
    8. muscular, stalwart, vigorous
    9. acrobatic, agonistic, gymnastic
    10. palaestral (palestral)
    15. broad–shouldered
athwart... 6. across, aslant
    8. sideways, sidewise, traverse
    9. crosswise, obliquely
    10. crisscross, perversely
atimon... 9. muskmelon
Atlantean... 6. strong 7. titanic
    8. gigantic 9. Atlaslike
    10. Gargantuan
atlantes (opp of caryatids)...
    7. columns (carved men)
    9. telamones
Atlantic Sisters (Gr)... 8. Pleiades
    (stars)
Atlas (pert to)...
  converted into.. 7. Mt Atlas
  daughter.. 7. Calypso 8. Pleiades
  famed as a.. 5. giant, Titan
  king of.. 10. Mauretania
  mother.. 4. Asia 7. Clymene
  supporter of.. 5. earth 10. the
    heavens
Atman (Hind)... 3. ego 4. Self, Soul
    6. Brahma
atmosphere... 3. air 4. aura, mood
    5. ether, ozone 7. climate
    10. aerosphere, background
    11. environment, hydrosphere
atmosphere (pert to)...
  condition.. 9. epedaphic
  density.. 8. isostere, isoteric
  disturbance.. 5. storm 6. static
    9. tornadoes, whirlwind
  pressure.. 10. barometric
  shooting star.. 6. meteor
  spectrum.. 7. rainbow
atole... 5. gruel 8. porridge
atoll... 4. belt, reef (coral) 6. island
atom... 3. ace, bit, ion, jot 4. gram,
    iota, mite, whit 5. monad
    8. molecule, particle 9. corpuscle
atomic... 3. Age, ray 4. beam, bomb,
    tiny 5. power 6. energy, minute,
    number, radius, weight 7. nuclear
    9. atomistic, molecular, radiation
    10. intangible 11. microscopic
    13. infinitesimal
atomic submarine... 5. Skate 6. Triton
    8. Nautilus, Thresher 9. Sea Dragon
atomize... 4. fume 5. smash, spray
    6. aerate, gasify 7. fission, perfume,
    shatter 8. dissolve, fumigate, nucleize
    9. carbonate, decompose, evaporate,

micronize, pulverize 11. disorganize
12. disintegrate

atomy ... 4. atom, mote 5. dwarf,
pygmy 6. droich, midget 8. skeleton
10. micromorph

atonement ... 6. amends 7. apology,
penance, redress 8. requital
10. recompense, redemption,
reparation 11. reclamation, restitution
12. propitiation 15. indemnification

Atreus (pert to) ...
   brother .. 8. Thyestes
   father .. 6. Pelops
   king of .. 7. Mycenae
   mother .. 10. Hippodamia
   slayer of .. 12. Thyestes' sons
   son .. 8. Menelaus 9. Agamemnon
   wife .. 6. Aerope

atrium ... 4. hall, room 5. court (inner)
6. cavity (Anat) 7. chamber
9. peristyle

atrocious ... 4. rank, vile 5. awful,
cruel, grave 6. brutal, savage, sinful,
wicked 7. heinous, vicious, violent
8. dreadful, flagrant, horrible,
infamous, ruthless, shocking, terrible,
wretched 9. monstrous, nefarious
10. abominable, deplorable,
detestable, outrageous

atrociousness ... 8. baseness, vileness
12. dreadfulness, shamefulness
13. nefariousness 15. Schrecklichkeit

atrocity ... 4. evil, harm 5. abuse,
havoc, wrong 7. misdeed, outrage
8. enormity 9. indignity
12. mistreatment

atrophy ... 5. tabes 7. disease
8. marasmus 10. emaciation
11. attenuation

Atropos (Gr) ... 7. goddess (Fate)

attach ... 3. add, fix, pin, put, tag, tie
4. bind, glue, join, vest 5. affix,
annex, hitch, paste, seize, unite
6. append, assign, fasten 7. ascribe,
connect, postfix, subjoin 9. associate,
attribute 11. superimpose

attached ... 4. fond 6. adnate, welded
7. annexed, devoted, engaged,
sessile (Bot), smitten 8. cemented,
enamored

attachment ... 4. bond, love 5. fancy
6. liking, regard 7. adjunct, fixture
8. addition, devotion, fidelity,
fondness 9. accession, adherence,
affection, fastening, increment
10. annexation 11. attribution
12. augmentation

attack ... 3. fit 4. pang, raid 5. beset,
blitz, drive, feint, ictus, onset, sally,
siege, spasm 6. affret, assail, charge,
onrush, oppugn, sortie 7. aggress,
assault, bowling, descent, offense,
seizure 8. camisado (anc), paroxysm,
sickness 9. offensive, onslaught
10. aggression 11. enunciation
13. incrimination

attain ... 2. do 3. get, win 4. earn,
gain 5. enact, reach 6. accede,
arrive, effect, obtain 7. achieve,
acquire, compass, fulfill, perform,
realize 9. discharge 10. accomplish,
consummate

attainable ... 8. gettable 9. available
10. achievable

attainment ... 5. skill 7. arrival
8. learning 9. accession
11. acquirement, acquisition,
cultivation, edification, realization
14. accomplishment

attar ... 4. otto 5. scent 6. parfum
7. essence, perfume, rose oil

attempt ... 3. aim, jab (sl), try 4. dare,
seek, stab 5. assay, ensue, essay,
fling, offer, onset, siege, trial
6. attack, effort, result 7. venture
8. endeavor 9. undertake

attend ... 4. hark, heed, help, mind,
note, tend, wait 5. ensue, nurse,
serve, treat, visit 6. doctor, escort,
follow, foster, listen, result
7. conduct, hearken, nurture, observe
9. accompany

attendance ... 4. draw 5. court
7. service, turnout 8. presence,
tendance 9. following
13. accompaniment

attendant ... 4. maid, page 5. nurse,
staff, usher 6. caddie, escort, gillie,
porter, waiter 7. bellboy, orderly
8. follower 9. associate, attending,
companion 10. subsequent
11. concomitant, ministering

attendants, train of ... 5. suite
7. cortege, retinue 9. entourage

attention ... 3. ear 4. care, heed, hist,
note 6. notice, regard 7. concern,
hearing, respect, thought 8. courtesy
11. mindfulness 13. concentration,
consideration

attentive ... 5. alert, awake, eared
6. intent 7. careful, heedful, mindful
8. obedient, vigilant, watchful
9. courteous, listening, observant,
wide-awake 10. meticulous,
respectful 11. circumspect,
considerate, surveillant

attenuated ... 3. cut 4. fine, rare, slim,
thin 6. svelte, wasted 7. diluted,
gracile, reduced, slender, thinned,
watered 8. lessened, rarefied,
weakened 9. decreased, emaciated

attest ... 4. seal 5. vouch 6. adjure,
affirm, avouch, depose 7. certify,
testify, witness 8. evidence, indicate,
manifest 9. testimony 10. deposition
12. authenticate

attestation ... 4. oath (solemn) 5. proof
6. avowal 8. swearing 9. assertion
10. allegation 11. affirmation,
certificate, declaration, testimonial
13. testification 14. authentication

attic ... 3. top 4. dome, head, loft,
wall 6. belfry, garret 8. cockloft

Attic ... 5. salty, witty 6. simple
7. elegant, refined 8. academic,
Athenian, tasteful 9. classical
10. Ciceronian

Attic (pert to) ...
   Bee .. 9. Sophocles (poet)
   bird .. 11. nightingale (Milton)
   Muse .. 8. Xenophon
   native .. 8. Athenian
   school .. 9. sculpture

Attica (pert to) ...

capital of.. 6. Athens
state of.. 6. Greece (anc)
famed as.. 15. world's first city
Attila... 3. Hun (leader) 5. Etzel
(fabled) 12. Scourge of God
attitude... 3. air, set 4. pose, view
5. angle, slant, stand 7. bearing,
feeling, opinion, outlook, posture,
thought 8. position, reaction
9. arabesque (dance), sentiment,
viewpoint 10. estimation, impression
attitude (reverent)... 6. salaam
8. kneeling 9. obeisance
12. genuflection (genuflexion)
attorney... 6. lawyer 7. counsel,
pleader 9. barrister, counselor
(counsellor) 11. intercessor
attract... 4. bait, draw, lure, pull
5. charm, tempt 6. appeal, beckon,
enamor, engage, entice, invite
8. interest 9. captivate, fascinate,
influence, magnetize
attraction... 4. lure, pull, star
6. appeal 7. gravity 8. affinity,
headline, interest, penchant
9. magnetism, seduction
10. allurement 11. fascination
attractive... 4. cute 6. lovely, pretty,
taking 7. winsome 8. alluring,
engaging, fetching, graceful, magnetic
9. allicient, appealing, beauteous,
beautiful, desirable 10. attracting,
delightful 11. captivating, interesting
attractive and repellent...
10. ambivalent
attrahent... 6. magnet 7. drawing
8. sinapism (Med) 10. attracting
attribute... 3. owe 5. refer, trait
6. impute, nature, symbol 7. ascribe,
feature, quality 8. property
9. adjective, qualifier, specialty
attrition... 4. wear 5. grief (Theol)
7. massage 8. abrasion, friction,
limation 9. detrition 10. contrition
attune... 4. tune 5. chime 6. accord,
adjust 7. concord, harmony, syntony
9. melodious 10. symphonize
11. concordance
atwain... 7. asunder
atweel... 5. truly 6. surely
aubade (Fr)... 3. lay 4. poem, song
6. ballad 7. concert (morning)
8. serenade
auberge... 3. inn
aubergiste... 9. innkeeper
auction... 3. bid 4. cant, roup, sale
5. block 6. vendue 7. bidding
auction (game)... 4. pool 5. pitch
6. bridge, euchre, hearts 8. pinochle
audacious... 4. bold 5. saucy
6. brazen, daring 7. defiant
8. impudent, insolent, intrepid,
spirited 9. barefaced, foolhardy,
insulting 11. adventurous,
challenging, impertinent, presumptive,
venturesome
audacity... 5. cheek, crust, nerve
6. daring 7. courage 8. defiance,
temerity 9. assurance, hardihood,
impudence, insolence, sauciness
10. effrontery, enterprise
11. presumption 12. impertinence

13. audaciousness, foolhardiness,
shamelessness
audible... 5. aloud, clear 8. distinct,
hearable 10. articulate
audible respiration... 4. sigh
audience... 3. ear 5. house, trial
6. parley, tryout 7. hearing, theater
8. audition, auditory, congress
9. interview, listeners 10. conference
12. congregation
audit... 5. check 6. reckon, verify
7. certify, collate 10. accounting
11. examination
auditor... 5. clerk 6. censor, hearer
7. actuary, apposer 8. examiner,
listener 10. accountant, bookkeeper
11. comptroller
auditorium... 4. hall, nave (anc)
5. house 7. theater 8. auditory,
building 9. Guildhall
auditory... 4. otic 5. audio, aural
6. phonic 7. hearers 8. audience
9. accoustic, auricular
12. congregation
au fait... 4. able 6. expert 7. equal to
8. informed, skillful 9. qualified
10. conversant (with)
au fond... 9. basically, primarily
11. essentially 13. fundamentally
auger... 3. bit 4. bore, tool 5. borer,
drill 6. gimlet, wimble 10. perforator
aught... 3. any 4. none, some, zero
5. ought 6. cipher 7. nothing
8. anything
augment... 3. add, eke 5. affix, annex,
exalt, swell 6. expand, extend
7. amplify, broaden, develop,
enhance, enlarge 8. increase
9. reinforce
Augsburg Church... 8. Lutheran
augur... 4. bode, omen, seer 5. sibyl,
vates (Gauls) 6. oracle 7. betoken,
presage 8. forebode, forecast,
foretell, forewarn, haruspex (Rom),
indicate, prophesy 10. anticipate,
astrologer, conjecture, soothsayer
13. prognosticate 14. prognosticator
augury... 4. omen, rite 7. auspice,
portent 8. ceremony
august... 4. awful, grand, novel, regal
6. sedate, solemn 7. courtly,
eminent, stately 8. imposing, majestic
9. dignified, honorable, important,
venerable 11. magnificent, ritualistic
12. aristocratic
August... 6. Lammas 8. Sextilis
10. First month (Rom year)
August meteor (11th of month)...
7. Perseid
auk... 4. Alca, Alle, bird (sea), falk
5. murre, noddy 6. auklet, rotche
(rotch) 7. Alcidae, dovekie
9. guillemot, razorbill
Auk... 6. Indian 7. Alaskan, Tlingit
(tribe) 9. Koluschan
aula... 4. hall, room 5. court
6. emblic (E Ind tree) 9. ventricle
aulos... 5. flute 8. woodwind
9. woodwinds (collectively)
aura... 3. air 4. halo, ring 6. astral,
circle, fringe (Psychol), nimbus
7. aureola 9. effluvium, emanation

10. atmosphere, exhalation
aureole... 4. halo 5. glory 6. circle, nimbus
auricle... 3. ear 4. lobe 5. pinna 6. atrium (heart) 9. appendage
auricular... 4. otic 5. aural, eared 6. phonic 8. acoustic, auditory
aurifex... 9. goldsmith
aurochs... 3. tur 4. goat, urus 5. bison
aurora... 3. eos 4. dawn 5. sunup 7. sunrise 8. borealis, daybreak, daylight 9. australis 11. polar lights
aurora borealis... 14. northern lights
auroral... 4. dawn, eoan, rosy 7. eastern, radiant, roseate
auspices... 3. aid 4. care, sign, wing 5. aegis (egis) 6. charge 7. backing, custody 8. guidance 9. patronage 10. management, protection 11. sponsorship, supervision
auspicious... 4. good 6. timely 9. favorable, fortunate, opportune 10. convenient, propitious, prosperous, seasonable 12. advantageous
Aussie... 6. digger 10. Australian
Auster... 9. southland, south wind
austere... 4. dour, hard 5. acrid, harsh, rigid, rough, stern 6. bitter, severe, strict 7. ascetic, pungent 8. exacting 10. astringent
Australasia... 7. Oceania 15. South Sea Islands
Australasian bird... 8. lorikeet 9. pardalote
Australia... see also *Australian*
capital.. 8. Canberra
desert.. 10. Great Sandy 13. Great Victoria
First Englishman (1688).. 14. William Dampier
holiday.. 13. Foundation Day (Jan 26)
island.. 8. Tasmania
mountain peak.. 9. Kosciusko
ocean.. 6. Indian
river.. 6. Murray
sea.. 5. Coral 6. Tasman
Tropic (southern).. 9. Capricorn
Australian (pert to)...
bee.. 5. karbi
bedroll.. 6. bindle 7. matilda
candy.. 5. lolly
feast.. 10. corroboree
fish.. 4. mako (shark) 5. yabby
flag.. 13. Southern Cross
flower.. 7. waratah (tulip) 9. rhodanthe
hut.. 6. miamia
native.. 5. myall 6. Aussie, binghi 8. kangaroo, warragal 9. aborigine, Dravidian
reptile.. 6. elapid, goanna, lizard (barking, frilled)
soldier.. 5. Anzac 6. digger
Australian animal...
dog (wild).. 5. dingo
horse (wild).. 6. brumby
sheep dog.. 6. kelpie
mammal.. 7. daysure 8. duckbill, platypus 9. blind mole
marsupial.. 4. tait 5. koala 6. wombat

7. echidna 8. anteater, kangaroo 9. phalanger, teddy bear 10. kookaburra 14. Tasmanian Devil
Australian bird... 3. emu, owl 4. kiwi, lory, titi 5. arara, ariel, galah 6. leipoa, petrel 7. boobook, bustard corella (parrot), grinder, rosella (parakeet) 8. ganggang, lorikeet, lyrebird, morepork, nightjar, paradise 9. bowerbird, cassowary, pardalote 10. flycatcher, goatsucker 11. budgereegah (parakeet)
Australian State capitals... 5. Perth 6. Darwin, Hobart, Sydney 8. Adelaide, Brisbane, Canberra (chief) 9. Melbourne
Australian tree... 4. teak, toon 5. belah, penda 6. jarrah, mallee, marara, she–oak, wattle 7. gunnung (mahogany) 8. Alstonia (dogbane), ironbark (eucalypt) 9. boobyalla (willow)
Austria...
capital.. 6. Vienna
city.. 4. Graz, Linz 8. Salzburg 9. Innsbruck
forest belt.. 10. Wiener Wald
monarchy.. 14. Austria–Hungary
mountain.. 4. Alps 6. Otztal 9. Dolomites
mountain peak.. 10. Wildspitze 13. Gross–Glockner
Pass (famed).. 7. Brenner
river.. 3. Inn, Mur 4. Enns 6. Danube
Austrian (pert to)...
botanist.. 6. Mendel (Mendel's Law)
composer.. 6. Mozart 7. Strauss
inventor.. 8. Welsbach
pianist.. 8. Kreisler
ruler (former).. 6. Kaiser
scientist.. 5. Adler, Freud
soldier.. 5. jager
theaterman.. 9. Reinhardt (Max)
autarch... 6. despot, tyrant 8. autocrat
authentic... 4. pure, real, true 5. valid 6. native 7. certain, correct, genuine, natural 8. bona fide, credible, official, original, orthodox, reliable 9. firsthand 11. trustworthy 13. authoritative
authenticate... 6. affirm, attest, ratify 7. certify, confirm, warrant 8. validate 12. substantiate
authenticity... 11. genuineness, reliability 13. dependability 15. trustworthiness
author... 4. doer, poet 5. ghost, maker 6. parent, penman, writer 7. creator, inditer 8. annalist, begetter, compiler, composer, essayist, inventor, novelist, producer 9. dramatist, scribbler 10. originator 13. encyclopedist (encyclopaedist)
authoritative... 4. wise 5. valid 6. potent, ruling, strong 7. weighty 8. approved, forceful, official, oracular, orthodox, positive, powerful 9. authentic, imperious 10. commanding, peremptory 11. dictatorial, influential 13. determinative
authoritative (pert to)...

command.. 4. fiat 5. usage
6. decree, dictum 7. mandate
example.. 9. precedent
10. antecedent
letter.. 4. writ 5. breve
authority... 5. judge, power, right
6. critic, expert, oracle, regent
7. command, warrant, witness
8. dominion, validity 9. influence,
testimony 10. commission,
competency 11. connoisseur,
prerogative 12. jurisdiction
13. authorization
authorize... 6. accept, permit, ratify
7. certify, charter, empower, endorse,
entitle, justify, license, warrant
8. accredit, delegate, sanction,
validate 10. commission
11. enfranchise 12. legitimatize
authorless... 8. nameless
9. anonymous
autobiography... 7. journal, letters,
memoirs 11. memorabilia
autochton... 6. binghi, native
8. indigene 9. primitive
10. aboriginal
autocracy... 8. monarchy 9. despotism
10. absolutism 15. totalitarianism
autocrat... 4. czar (tsar) 5. mogul
6. despot 7. arbiter, monarch
8. dictator 9. sovereign
10. taskmaster
autodidactic... 8. self-made
10. self-taught 12. self-educated
autograph... 4. seal, sign 5. cross
9. signature 11. John Hancock
automatic... 7. machine
10. mechanical, self-acting
11. instinctive, involuntary,
spontaneous
automatic device... 3. gun 4. gear
5. drill, pilot, rifle, robot 6. pistol,
switch 8. computer, revolver
10. six-shooter
automaton... 5. golem, robot
6. puppet 7. android, machine
automobile... 3. cab, car 4. auto, taxi
5. coupe 6. jalopy 7. autocar,
flivver, machine, taxicab, vehicle
8. motorcar
autosuggestion... 7. therapy
8. hypnosis 9. hypnology, mesmerism
10. psychology 14. self-suggestion
autumn... 4. fall 6. mature, old age,
season (yearly) 7. equinox, harvest,
October 8. maturity, November
9. September
auxiliary... 4. ally, plus 5. extra
6. aiding, helper 7. adjunct, helping
9. accessory, ancillary, assistant,
attendant, coadjutor, colleague,
companion, secondary 10. additional,
subsidiary, supporting
11. confederate, cooperating,
subordinate, subservient
12. nonessential, supplemental
13. supplementary
auxiliary army... 6. relief 7. support
8. Landwehr, recruits, reserves
11. contingents 14. reinforcements
auxiliary verb... 3. can, had, has, may
4. hast, have, will 5. could, shall,

would 6. should
avail... 3. use 4. good, help 5. value
6. inform, profit 7. benefit, service,
utility 9. advantage, expedient
availability... 7. utility 9. usability
10. usefulness 13. acquirability,
attainability 14. serviceability
available... 4. free, open 5. handy,
ready, valid 6. on hand, usable,
vacant 8. unfilled 9. securable
10. accessible, attainable, convenient,
obtainable, unoccupied
avalanche... 5. slide 7. descent
(sudden) 8. slippage
avant-garde... 3. van 8. vanguard
avant-propos... 7. preface
12. introduction (remarks)
avarice... 4. lust 5. greed 7. avidity
8. avidness, cupidity, grasping,
rapacity, voracity 10. greediness
12. covetousness
avarice demon... 6. Mammon
avaricious... 5. close 6. grabby,
greedy 7. miserly 8. covetous,
grasping 9. niggardly, penurious,
rapacious, voracious 12. parsimonious
avatar... 8. epiphany 10. embodiment
11. incarnation 14. transmigration
avatars of Vishnu (Hind Relig)...
11. incarnation (deity to man)
avaunt... 4. away 5. allez, boast,
scram, vaunt 6. begone, depart
7. advance, vamoose
ave... 4. hail, viva, vive 8. farewell
Ave Maria... 4. bead (rosary), song
6. prayer 10. devotional
Avena... 4. oats 7. grasses
avenge... 7. requite 9. retaliate,
vindicate
Avenging Angels... 8. nickname (Polit
1858) 10. Danite Band (Mormons)
Avenging Spirit... 4. Fate, Fury
6. Erinys 7. Alastor, Atropos
avenue... 3. rue 4. land, pike, road,
vent 5. alley 6. arcade, artery, defile,
egress, outlet, street 7. ·channel,
freeway, highway, opening
8. corridor, turnpike 9. boulevard,
concourse 10. passageway
12. thoroughfare
aver... 3. say 5. state 6. affirm,
allege, assert 7. declare, profess,
protect 10. asseverate
average... 2. go 3. par, run 4. mean,
rule 6. common, medial, medium,
normal 7. balance 8. mediocre
10. generality
averment... 6. dictum, remark
7. witness 8. assertion, statement,
testimony, utterance 10. allegation
11. affirmation, attestation
12. verification 13. pronouncement
Avernus... 4. lake (poison vapors)
5. Hades
averse... 5. loath 7. adverse
9. reluctant, unwilling 11. disinclined
aversion... 4. hate 5. odium
6. hatred, horror 7. disgust, dislike
9. antipathy, repulsion
10. abhorrence, repugnance
11. abomination 12. estrangement
13. indisposition, unwillingness

aversion to... see also *fear of*
novelty.. 9. neophobia
society.. 14. anthropophobia
strangers.. 10. xenophobia
wine.. 10. oenophobia

avert... 4. fend, save 5. check, deter,
evade, repel 6. forbid, retard, switch,
thwart 7. deflect, prevent 8. alienate,
prohibit 9. forestall, sidetrack

aviary... 4. cage 5. house 7. dovecot
(dovecote) 8. ornithon 9. birdhouse,
columbary, enclosure
11. columbarium

aviation... 6. flight, flying 7. winging
9. skyriding 10. airplaning
11. aeronautics

aviation maneuver... 7. Immelmann
(Ger)

aviator... 3. Ace 5. flier (flyer), pilot
6. airman, Icarus (fabled first)
7. wingman 8. aeronaut, aviatrix,
operator 9. astronaut, birdwoman,
Immelmann

avichi (Buddh)... 4. Hell 5. Hades
9. depravity, perdition 10. underworld

avid... 4. agog, keen 5. eager
6. grabby, greedy 7. anxious,
craving, zestful 8. grasping
9. rapacious, voracious 10. avaricious

avidity... 4. lust 5. greed 7. avarice
8. cupidity, grasping 9. eagerness
10. greediness 12. covetousness

avion... 5. plane 8. airplane

avisa... 4. news 6. advice, caveat
7. tidings, warning 11. information

Avis Indica (Astron)... 4. Apus
13. constellation

avital... 9. ancestral

avoid... 4. shun, snub 5. annul,
dodge, elude, evade 6. escape,
eschew, repeal, revoke, vacate
7. abstain, forbear 10. invalidate

avoidance... 6. outlet 7. evasion,
removal 8. emptying, shunning,
vacating 9. annulment 10. withdrawal

avoirdupois... 4. beef 6. weight
7. gravity, tonnage 8. poundage
9. heaviness

avoirdupois weight... 3. ton 4. dram
5. grain, ounce, pound
13. hundred–weight

avow... 3. own, vow 5. admit, swear,
vouch 6. allege, assert, pledge
7. confess, declare, profess, promise
10. avouchment 11. acknowledge

avulsion... 7. removal 9. severance
10. extraction, separation (ppty),
withdrawal

awabi... 7. abalone

awaft... 6. adrift, afloat, wafted

await... 4. bide, come, heed, loom,
pend, wait 5. abide, tarry, watch
6. ambush, attend, expect, impend,
waylay 8. approach 9. forthcome

awake... 5. alert, alive, astir, rouse
6. arouse, excite, waking
8. open–eyed 9. attentive, conscious,
sleepless, wide–awake

awaken... 5. awake 6. arouse, excite,
stir up 8. roust out

award... 4. gift, give, meed, mete
5. allot, grant, medal, Oscar, prize

6. reward, trophy 7. adjudge,
present, verdict 8. accolade
9. medallion

aware... 3. hep 4. know 5. sense
7. mindful 8. apprized, sensible
9. cognizant, conscious
11. intelligent

awareness... 5. sense 7. feeling
9. sensation 10. impression,
perception 11. mindfulness, sensibility
13. consciousness

away... 2. on 3. awa, far, fro, off, out
4. gone 5. aside, hence 6. abroad,
absent, begone, onward, thence
7. escaped 8. vanished 9. elsewhere

away from...
body center.. 6. ectad 6. distal
mouth.. 6. aborad, aboral
wind.. 4. alee

awe... 3. cow 4. fear 5. dread
6. regard, terror, wonder 7. emotion,
respect 8. astonish, frighten, surprise
9. reverence 10. admiration,
veneration, wonderment
13. consideration

aweather (opp of alee) 8. windward
11. weatherward

awe–inspiring... 5. eerie (eery)
7. awesome, ghostly 8. glorious,
imposing, splendid, terrific
9. wonderful 10. impressive
11. magnificent

awe–struck... 4. awed 9. terrified
10. astonished, fear–struck,
spellbound 12. wonder–struck
13. thunderstruck

awful... 4. awed, ugly 5. dread, great,
gross 6. sacred, silent, solemn,
woeful 7. awesome, fearful, hideous
8. dreadful, infamous, reverent
shocking, terrible 9. appalling,
atrocious, deathlike, ludicrous,
venerable, wonderful 10. deplorable,
impressive, outrageous, unpleasant
11. exceedingly

awkward... 5. gawky, inapt, inept
6. clumsy, gauche 7. froward,
loutish, unhandy 8. bungling,
clownish, lubberly, perverse, ungainly,
unwieldy 9. graceless, inelegant,
lumbering, maladroit, ponderous
10. backhanded, blundering,
ungraceful 12. embarrassing,
incommodious, inconvenient

awkward age... 4. teen 5. teens

awkward fellow... 6. galoot
11. hobbledehoy

awless, aweless... 4. bald 6. brazen
8. fearless, unafraid 9. bold–faced,
dauntless 10. irreverent
11. unsurprised 12. unastonished

awn... 4. barb 5. beard (plant)
6. arista, papous 7. bristle

awning... 6. canopy, screen, shield
7. shelter 8. velarium (anc)

AWOL... 5. hooky 7. truancy
9. truantism 11. absenteeism

awry... 4. agee 5. agley, amiss, askew
6. faulty 7. askance, asquint,
crooked, oblique 9. distorted
10. disorderly 11. disarranged
12. disorganized

ax, axe... 3. adz (adze), ask (dial)
    4. tool 6. hammer, poleax (poleaxe)
    7. hatchet (small) 8. axhammer
    9. discharge, dismissal
ax (pert to)...
    ancient.. 4. celt 6. chisel
    blade.. 3. bit
    execution.. 10. guillotine
    handle.. 5. helve
axial... 7. central, midmost, pivotal
axilla... 3. ala 4. axil 5. oxter
    6. armpit 8. shoulder
axiom... 3. law, saw 4. rule 5. adage,
    maxim, motto, truth 6. byword,
    dictum, saying, truism 7. dictate,
    precept, proverb, theorem
    8. aphorism, apothegm 9. principle
    11. proposition
axiomatic... 10. aphoristic, proverbial
    11. self-evident, sententious
    12. epigrammatic
axis... 3. hub 4. axle, bloc, nave,
    stem 5. pivot, stalk 6. caulis, center,
    league 7. fulcrum 8. alliance,
    vertebra 9. coalition
axle... 3. pin 4. axis 5. pivot, shaft
    6. swivel 7. spindle 8. axletree
axle tooth... 5. molar
ayah... 4. amah, maid 5. mammy
    9. governess, nursemaid
    11. maidservant
aye... 2. ay 3. pro, yea, yes 4. ever,
    vote 5. voice 6. always, assent
    8. thumbs up, viva-voce

aye-aye... 5. lemur (Madagascar)
ayes... 10. all in favor
Azazel... 5. Eblis, Satan 9. scapegoat
Azerbaijanian... 4. Turk
    14. Transcaucasian
azimuth... 3. arc 4. dial 6. circle
    7. compass, horizon 8. distance,
    magnetic 10. North point
Azores...
    capital.. 5. Angra
    city.. 5. Horta
    group (islands).. 6. St Mary 8. St
    George 9. St Michael
    locale.. 8. Atlantic (Ocean)
    owner.. 8. Portugal
Aztec (pert to)...
    calendar.. 7. Mexican
    capital (anc).. 12. Tenochtitlan
    emperor.. 9. Montezuma
    god.. 4. Xipe (sowing)
    12. Quetzalcoatl (peace)
    hero.. 4. Nata (Myth) 6. Cortez
    language.. 7. Nahuatl
    locale (anc).. 6. Aztlan
    Noah (Mex).. 6. Coxcox
    stone.. 12. chalchihuitl
    temple.. 8. teocalli
    tribe.. 9. Nahuatlan
azure... 4. blue 7. celeste, sky-blue
    8. bice blue, cerulean 9. blue vault,
    cloudless 11. lapis lazuli
azygous... 3. odd 4. only, sole
    6. single, unique 8. singular
    10. unrepeated
azymous... 10. unleavened

B

B... 4. beta 6. letter (2nd)
ba (Egypt)... 3. khu 4. soul
baa... 5. bleet
baahling... 4. lamb
Baal... 4. idol 5. deity 6. Baalim (pl)
    7. Baalath 8. false god 9. fertility
baba (pert to)...
    India.. 4. baby 5. child
    Malaya.. 4. male
    Slavic.. 5. nurse 7. midwife 8. old
    woman
    Turkey.. 5. title (of respect)
babacoote... 5. lemur (Madagascar)
Babbar... 3. Utu (Utug) 6. sun god
babbo... 5. daddy 6. father
babel... 5. clang 6. jargon, tumult
    7. discord 9. confusion
    11. pandemonium
Babel (pert to)...
    Bible.. 5. Tower 8. ziggurat
    presently.. 14. Temple of Marduk
    site (ancient).. 6. Shinar (land of)
    site (present).. 7. Babylon
babirusa, babiroussa... 9. quadruped
    (hoglike)

Babism (Persia)... 4. sect
baboon... 3. ape 5. Papio 6. chacma
    7. babuina, monster 8. mandrill
babushka... 11. grandmother
baby... 4. babe, doll 6. coward, infant,
    puppet, weanie 7. bambino, chicken
    8. juvenile, weakling 9. miniature,
    youngling, youngster 10. diminutive
baby carriage... 4. pram 5. wagon
    6. go-cart 8. stroller
    12. perambulator
babyish... 6. simple 7. dollish, puerile
    8. childish 9. childlike, infantile
Babylon... see also *Babylonian*
    capital of.. 9. Babylonia
    kingdom.. 4. Elam 5. Akkad (Accad)
    meaning.. 9. Gate of God
    mountain.. 6. Ararat
    river.. 6. Tigris 9. Euphrates
    World Wonder.. 14. Hanging Gardens
Babylonian (pert to)...
    abode of the dead.. 5. Aralu
    chaos.. 4. Apsu
    deity.. 5. Alalu (Alala), Siris
    earth mother.. 6. Ishtar

god.. 2. Ea, Zu 3. Anu, Bel 4. Adad, Apsu, Irra 5. Dagan, Enlil 6. Nergal 7. Shamash
goddess.. 3. Aya 4. Nina 5. Belit (Beltis)
hero (Myth).. 5. Adapa, Etana 9. Tilgamesh
king.. 6. Sargon 9. Habonidus, Hammurabi 10. Nabonassar 14. Nebuchadnezzar (Nebuchadrezzar)
temple, tower.. 8. ziggurat
bacach... 6. beggar 7. cripple
bacalao... 7. codfish, grouper
bacalao bird... 3. auk 5. murre 9. guillemot
Bacardi... 3. rum
bacca... 5. berry
baccalaureate... 6. degree (college), sermon 8. bachelor
baccate... 5. pulpy 9. berrylike
bacchanal... 7. reveler 8. carouser
Bacchanalia... 4. orgy 5. feast 7. debauch 8. festival (Bacchus)
bacchante... 6. maenad 7. bacchae
Bacchus... 4. wine 5. god of wine
baccivorous... 11. berry-eating
bachelor... 4. male 6. degree (Acad), garçon 8. benedict, celibate 10. misogamist
bacillus... 9. bacterium
Bacis... 2. Ra 4. bull (sacred)
back... 3. aft, aid, fro 4. abet, hind, past, rear 5. stern 6. behind, second, uphold 7. finance, sponsor, support, sustain 8. extrados, intrados, resource 9. encourage, posterior 10. background
back (Anat)... 4. loin, nape 5. notum 6. dorsal, dorsum, lumbar, tergal, tergum 7. occiput 8. backbone, notalgia 10. opisthenar (hand)
backbone... 4. grit, guts 5. nerve, pluck, spunk 6. mettle, spirit 7. courage, stamina, support 8. firmness, gameness, mainstay 10. dependence
backbone (Anat)... 4. axis 5. brace, chine, spine 6. column, spinal 7. spinule, support 8. ossicles 9. vertebrae
backer... 5. angel 6. patron 7. abettor, sponsor 8. financer, promoter, upholder 9. supporter, sustainer 10. maintainer
background... (opp of foreground) 4. rear 5. stage 6. offing 7. horizon, setting 8. backdrop, distance, practice, training 9. education 10. experience 11. savoir-faire
backhanded... 6. clumsy 7. awkward, devious 9. insincere, insulting, sarcastic 10. circuitous
backslider... 8. apostate, deserter, recreant 10. unfaithful
back-to-back... 7. dos-à-dos
backward... 4. back, dull, late 5. arear, loath, tardy 6. averse, modest, stupid 7. bashful, belated, reverse 8. arrested, dilatory, perverse, rearward, retarded, reticent, retrorse, reversed 9. hindwards, recessive, reluctant, subnormal, unwilling

10. behindhand, hesitating, regressive, retrograde 11. unfavorable 13. retrogressive, retrospective
bacon... 4. lard, pork, side 5. prize 6. flitch, gammon, rasher 8. Canadian, sowbelly
Bacon's Rebellion... 6. revolt (Va 1676)
bacteria... 5. cocci, germs 7. aerobes, aerobia, bacilli 8. microbes, spirilla 9. organisms
bacteriologist culture... 4. agar
Bactrian camel... 9. two-humped
bad... 3. ill, mal (pref) 4. evil, fell, foul, poor, vile 5. drole, fetid, nasty, wrong 6. arrant, in pain, putrid, rotten, sinful, wanton, wicked 7. corrupt, hurtful, naughty, noxious, spoiled, tainted, unlucky, unmoral, unsound, vicious 8. annoying, criminal, improper, inferior, iniquity, sinister 9. dangerous, defective, offensive, perverted, worthless 10. iniquitous, malodorous, unsuitable 11. inexpedient, inopportune 12. disagreeable, inauspicious
bad (pert to)...
blood.. 4. feud 6. rancor 7. ill will 10. bitterness, resentment
custom.. 9. cacoethes
legislation.. 7. dysnomy
luck.. 5. deuce 7. ambsace
man's oatmeal.. 7. hemlock (poison) 11. wild chervil
badge... 3. pin 4. mark, sign, star 5. index, token 6. emblem, ensign, plaque, shield, symbol 7. earmark 8. insignia 14. identification
badger... 3. nag, rag 4. bait 5. harry, tease, worry 6. bother, extort, harass, hawker, heckle, hector, pester 8. huckster
badger (animal)... 5. Meles (anc), pahmi, ratel 6. bauson, mammal, teledu, wombat 9. bandicoot, mistonusk
Badger State... 9. Wisconsin
badinage... 4. fool 5. joker, sport 6. banter 8. raillery 9. badinerie, simpleton 10. persiflage, pleasantry
badly... 3. bad, ill 4. sick 5. amiss, wrong 6. poorly, unwell 8. faultily, wickedly 9. viciously 11. exceedingly, imperfectly 12. disagreeably, unskillfully 13. unfortunately
badly off... 3. sad 7. hapless, unblest, unhappy, unlucky 8. luckless 11. impecunious, unfortunate 12. unprosperous 14. unprovidential
baff... 4. beat, blow, thud 6. strike, stroke (golf)
baffle... 4. balk, foil 5. cheat, elude, evade, spike 6. defeat, delude, muffle, puzzle, thwart 7. mystify, nonplus 8. bewilder, confound 9. bamboozle, frustrate 10. disconcert
baffling... 7. elusive, evasive 8. puzzling 9. bothering, confusing, dismaying 10. mystifying, perplexing, perturbing 11. frustrating 13. disconcerting

baft... 3. aft 4. baff 5. abaff, cloth, shaft 6. astern
bag... 3. net, pac, pot, sac, sag 4. etui, grip, load, poke, sack, trap 5. ascus, belly, catch, droop, pouch, purse, seize, snare, steal 6. entrap, sachet, valise 7. bladder, capture, distend, handbag, pannier, satchel 8. reticule, suitcase 9. Gladstone, haversack, sac de nuit 10. pocketbook 11. portmanteau
bag and baggage... 10. completely 11. impedimenta
bagatelle... 3. toy 4. game 6. bauble, geegaw, trifle 7. trinket 10. knickknack, triviality 12. fiddle–faddle
Bagdad, Baghdad...
  capital of.. 4. Iraq
  character.. 6. Sinbad (The Sailor)
  city.. 6. Moslem
  founder (762).. 8. Almanzor
  kingdom (anc).. 11. Mesopotamia
  Oriental term.. 8. lambskin (raw)
  river.. 6. Tigris
  transportation (famed).. 7. Railway
bagpipe, bagpipes... 5. drone, pipes 7. musette 9. Dudelsack 10. doodlesack, sordellina
bagpipe (pert to)...
  music variations.. 7. pibroch
  parts.. 4. lill, oboe 5. drone 7. chanter 9. chalumeau
  player.. 5. piper
  tube.. 6. drones 7. chanter
  tune.. 4. port
Bahamas, Bahama Islands...
  capital.. 6. Nassau
  discoverer.. 8. Columbus
  native.. 5. conch
  naval base (US).. 9. Mayaguana
  San Salvador (now).. 14. Watlings Island (Watling Island)
bahan... 6. poplar, willow (Bib)
bahay... 5. house
bahi... 7. fortune (gypsy)
bail... 3. dip 4. bond, hoop, lade, lave, ring, rynd 5. court, ladle, throw 6. bucket, dipper, handle, pledge, secure, surety 8. replevin, security 9. guarantee
bailiff... 5. agent, bobby, reeve, staff 6. deputy, staves (pl) 7. marshal, officer, sheriff, shrieve, steward 8. bluecoat, gendarme, overseer 9. constable 12. understeward
bailiwick... 6. canton, county, domain 7. commune, diocese 8. precinct, province 12. municipality
bain... 4. near 5. lithe, ready, short 6. direct, limber, supple 7. forward, willing
bairn... 3. kid, tot 4. mite 5. child 6. urchin
bait... 3. fly 4. feed, hook, lure, trap 5. bribe, decoy, snare 6. badger, harass, hockle 7. fulcrum, torment 8. inveigle 9. persecute 10. enticement, exasperate, temptation
bait... 3. dap, dib 4. fish, hook 6. dibble

bakal (Orient)... 9. tradesman 10. shopkeeper
bake... 3. dry 4. cake, cook, fire, kiln 5. roast 6. anneal, harden 8. clambake 9. dehydrate
bakehead... 4. rail 5. guard, shack 6. stoker 7. fireman 8. trainman
baken... 4. buoy 6. beacon 8. landmark
baker's dozen... 4. long 6. devil's 7. inbread 8. thirteen
baksheesh... 3. sop, tip 5. bribe 7. largess (largesse) 8. gratuity 12. compensation
bal... 4. ball, mine, prom
balance... 4. even, rest, rule 5. poise, ratio, scale, weigh 6. adjust, aplomb, normal, offset, reason, rhythm, sanity 7. average, ballast, compare, euphony, measure, remains, surplus 8. equality, equalize, leftover, residual, saneness, serenity, symmetry 9. composure, equipoise, remainder, stability 10. equanimity, neutralize, proportion, symmetrize 11. equilibrium 12. counterpoise
balanced... 4. even, just 6. poised 7. equable 8. measured 9. equitable 10. euphonious 11. symmetrical 13. self-possessed
balancer... 7. acrobat, gymnast 10. ropedancer 11. equilibrist
balcony... 4. dais 5. stage 6. podium 7. estrade, gallery, rostrum 8. brattice, platform
bald... 4. bare, dull, mere, open 5. crude, naked, plain 6. simple 7. epilose 8. depilous, hairless 9. bald–pated 11. unconcealed
baldachin, baldaquin... 6. canopy (St Peter's, Rome), fabric
Balder (pert to)...
  father.. 4. Odin
  god of.. 5. light, peace
  mother.. 5. Frigg
  slain by.. 9. mistletoe (dart)
  wife.. 5. Nanna
balderdash... 3. rot 4. bosh 5. trash 6. bunkum, jargon 7. bombast 8. buncombe, falderal, nonsense, tommyrot 9. poppycock
baldness... 6. acomia 8. alopecia 11. phalacrosis 12. hairlessness
baldric... 4. belt (ornament) 6. zodiac 7. support (sword)
bale... 3. woe 4. bind, load, pack 5. truss 6. ballot, bundle, burden, misery, packet, seroon 7. anguish, package 11. encumbrance
Balearic Islands... 5. Iviza 7. Cabrera, Majorca, Minorca 10. Formentera
baleful... 3. bad, sad 4. dire 6. woeful 7. baneful, harmful, malific, noisome, noxious 8. damaging 9. ill–omened, malignant 10. pernicious 12. inauspicious
balk... 4. foil 5. check, ridge 6. baffle, defeat, fallow, rafter, signal (fishing), thwart 7. blunder, faux pas, stickle 9. frustrate, hindrance 10. bafflement, disappoint

14. disappointment
Balkan Peninsula...
native.. 4. Serb
river.. 3. Une 5. Saave 6. Danube
sea.. 3. Black 6. Aegean 7. Marmosa
8. Adriatic 13. Mediterranean
State.. 6. Greece, Serbia, Turkey (Eur)
7. Albania, Rumania 8. Bulgaria
balky... 7. restive 9. faltering,
obstinate, shrinking, stickling
ball... 3. bal, fly, hop, lob, orb
4. bead, clew (yarn), pill, shot
5. dance, globe, pearl, pinda (rice)
6. pellet, pelota, sphere 7. rissole
8. conglobe, snowball 9. eight ball
10. cannonball 12. medicine ball
ball (of games)... 4. golf, hand, polo,
soft 6. basket, tennis, volley
7. bowling, cricket, croquet, jai alai
8. baseball, billiard, ping-pong
ballad... 3. lay 4. lied, poem, song
5. derry, rhyme, verse 6. sonnet
7. ballade, canzone
ballast... 5. poise 6. aplomb, steady,
weight 7. balance 9. kentledge,
saburrate, stabilize 10. equanimity,
equivalent 14. counterbalance
balled up... 7. complex, mixed up,
muddled 8. confused, fouled up
9. befuddled, entangled, snarled up
10. disordered 11. complicated
ballet (pert to)...
arrangement.. 12. choreography
dance.. 6. adagio 9. pantomime
dancer.. 6. coryphee, danseuse
9. ballerina
jump.. 4. jeté 6. coupé
lover.. 11. balletomane
music.. 5. opera 6. comedy
7. d'action 14. divertissement
balloon... 3. bag 4. ball, tire 5. barge
(Siam), blimp, swell 6. aviate, ballon,
dilate, expand, gasbag 7. distend,
nacelle 8. aerostat, aircraft
9. dirigible
balloon (type)... 4. free, kite 5. pilot
7. captive 8. sounding
11. montgolfier, observation
ballot... 4. bale, poll, vote 5. elect,
slate, voice 6. select, ticket
8. suffrage
ballyhoo... 4. plug 5. boost, noise
6. fracas, hoopla, hubbub, ruckus,
rumpus 7. promote 9. advertise,
publicity 10. hullabaloo
balm... 3. oil 4. bito, calm 5. cream,
salve 6. balsam, elixir, lotion, pacify
7. anodyne, cushion, Melissa,
perfume, relieve, unction, unguent
8. liniment, mitigate, ointment
9. calmative, fragrance, mitigator
10. palliative
balm (pert to)... 5. Vicks 6. arnica,
zachun 7. camphor, lanolin, menthol
8. glycerin, ointment, vaseline
10. petrolatum
Balm of... 6. Gilead
balmy... 4. mild 5. batty, daffy, dippy,
drunk, goofy, moony, spicy, sweet
6. dreamy, insane, savory 7. healing
8. aromatic, fragrant, lenitive,
redolent, soothing 9. ambrosial,

assuaging, emollient 10. palliative,
refreshing 11. odoriferous
12. sweet-scented
balsam... 3. fir 4. riga, tolu 5. resin
6. embalm, poplar, storax
7. benzoin, perfume 8. bdellium
(Bib), medicine 9. oleoresin
12. Balsam of Peru, Balsam of Tolu
Baltimore...
Belle.. 4. rose
bird.. 6. oriole
butterfly.. 7. phaeton
city of.. 8. Maryland
hemp.. 4. flax
history of.. 18. Star Spangled Banner
(1814)
baluster... 4. post 7. support, upright
8. banister
bam... 4. fake, hoax, mock, sham
5. cheat, spoof, trick 6. deceit
7. wheedle 8. flimflam 9. deception,
imitation
bambino... 4. babe, baby, icon
5. child, Pietà 6. infant (Christ)
bamboo (pert to)...
curtain.. 8. frontier
English.. 10. Philippine
genus.. 7. Bambuss
sacred.. 6. nandin
sprouts (pickled).. 5. achar
stems.. 4. cane
sugar.. 6. silica 9. tabasheer
bamboozle... 4. dupe, hoax 5. trick
6. baffle, cajole, humbug 7. beguile,
deceive, mystify, perplex 9. victimize
ban... 4. coin, tabu, veto 5. curse,
edict, taboo, title (anc) 6. muslin,
outlaw 7. embargo, exclude, kokumin
8. anathema 9. interdict, ostracism,
ostracize 10. injunction, kokumingun
11. malediction, prohibition
12. proscription 15. excommunication
banal... 4. flat 5. corny, stale, trite
6. cliché, common, old hat
11. commonplace, stereotyped
13. platitudinous
banana... 4. Musa, saba 6. ensete
8. Musaceae, plantain
banana (pert to)...
Bananaland.. 10. Queensland
bananalike.. 8. plantain
bird.. 4. quit 6. oriole
boa.. 5. snake
color.. 7. sunbeam
fish.. 8. ladyfish
freckle.. 7. disease
leaf.. 5. frond
oil.. 7. lacquer
Philippine.. 7. saguing
shrub.. 9. evergreen
band... 3. bar, tie 4. belt, body, crew,
hoop, line, pack, ring, sash, zone
5. bunch, corps, group, patte, strap,
stria, strip, tribe, unite 6. cohort,
collar, fascia, fillet, girdle, ligula,
outfit, pledge, radula (Zool), tether
7. bandage, company 8. cincture,
encircle, ensemble, neckband, striping
9. frequency (radio), orchestra,
striation
bandage... 3. gag 4. bind, tape
5. sling, spica, truss 6. ligate,

swathe 7. wrapper 8. compress,
dressing, ligature 9. accipiter,
blindfold 10. tourniquet

bandicoot... 3. rat 9. Perameles

bandit... 4. thug 5. thief 6. dacoit,
outlaw, robber 7. bandido, brigand,
footpad, ladrone 8. marauder,
picaroon 9. bandolero
10. highwayman

bandmaster... 5. Sousa 6. leader
7. maestro 8. choragus, director
9. conductor 13. Kapellmeister

bandolero... 5. thief 6. robber
10. highwayman

bandy... 4. beat, cart, game 5. bowed
6. curved, strive, stroke (tennis)
7. contend, embowed 8. carriage
(Ind), exchange, to and fro
9. bowlegged 11. bandy-legged,
reciprocate

bandy words... 5. argue 6. bicker,
parley 7. contend, wrangle
8. converse

bane... 3. woe 4. evil, harm, kill, pest,
ruin 5. curse, venom 6. injury,
plague, poison, slayer 7. disease
(sheep), scourge 8. murderer,
vexation 9. grievance 10. affliction,
pestilence, visitation

baneful... 3. ill 4. vile 7. harmful,
noxious 9. injurious 10. pernicious
11. detrimental

bang... 3. hit, rap 4. beat, blow,
dash, drub, kick, lift, shut, slam
5. crack, knock, pound, punch,
smack, thump, verve, whack
6. energy, report, strike, thrash, thrill
7. collide 8. coiffure

bangle... 5. charm 7. circlet
8. bracelet

banish... 3. ban 4. oust 5. exile, expel
6. deport, dispel, outlaw, punish
7. condemn, dismiss, exclude
8. relegate 9. ostracize, proscribe
10. expatriate 11. excommunicate

banister... 4. post, rail 8. baluster
10. balustrade

banjo... 7. samisen

bank... 3. row 4. brae, edge, heap,
quay, ripa 5. brink, flock, hurst
(sandy), marge, shoal, shore, slope,
table 6. aviate, margin, quarry,
rivage, series, stakes, strand
7. anthill, barrier, deposit, incline
8. buttress, treasury 9. acclivity,
riverside 13. fortification

bank account... 5. funds, means
6. assets, moneys 8. finances
9. exchequer

banker... 4. game 6. broker, lender
9. financier 11. moneylender
12. money-changer

bankrupt... 4. bust, ruin 5. broke,
smash 6. failed, quisby (sl) 7. failure
9. destitute, insolvent, moneyless,
penniless 12. impoverished

banner... 4. fane, flag 6. ensign,
poster 7. leading, pennant, placard
8. foremost, headline, standard,
streamer 9. exemplary 10. surpassing

banns, marriage... 6. notice
7. sibrede 12. proclamation

banquet... 4. fete 5. diffa, feast, festa
6. fiesta, junket, regale, repast,
spread 8. festival, jamboree
10. regalement

Banquo... 9. character (Shak)

banshee, banshie... 4. shee 5. fairy,
Geist, sidhe 6. spirit, sprite

bantam (pert to)...
cock.. 3. fop 5. dandy, sport
7. peacock 8. strutter 9. swaggerer
12. swashbuckler
Java.. 4. duck, fowl 5. breed
6. Brahma, Cochin
slang.. 4. runt 6. peewee, shrimp
sports.. 6. weight

bantamweight... 5. boxer (118 lbs)
7. fighter 8. pugilist 9. contender
10. contestant

banter... 4. jest, josh, mock, twit
5. borak, chaff, sport, tease, trick
6. delude, deride, satire 7. asteism,
wheedle 8. badinage, raillery, ridicule
10. persiflage, pleasantry

Bantu, South Africa...
language.. 3. Ila 8. Kongoese
people.. 5. Duala 6. Basuto
tribe.. 4. Vili, Zulu 6. Damara, Kaffir
7. Negroid, Swahili 8. Bechuana

banzai... 4. hail 5. hello, hullo
6. attack, charge 9. greetings
11. salutations

baobab tree (pert to)...
bark.. 4. rope 5. cloth, paper
fruit.. 11. monkey bread
genus.. 9. Adansonia
pulp.. 8. beverage

baptism... 4. rite 6. naming 7. wetting
8. ablution 9. aspersion, immersion,
sacrament 10. initiation, sprinkling
11. christening 12. consecration,
purification, regeneration (spiritual)

baptism (pert to)...
cloth.. 7. chrisom
dead (RCCh).. 5. Blood 6. Desire
fire.. 9. fuertaufe
place.. 4. font 10. baptistery (anc)
receptacle.. 5. basin 7. piscina
water.. 5. laver

bar... 3. ban, dam, fid, pry, rod
4. bolt, deny, fess, joke, line, rack,
rail, sess, type 5. betty
(thieves'slang), block, court, deter,
easer, estop, ingot, lever, shoal,
space, staff 6. except, forbid, hinder,
ripper, saloon, stitch, stripe
7. barrier, barroom, bass-bar,
chevron, counter, crowbar, exclude,
prevent, railing, sandbar, trapeze
8. blockade, disallow, obstacle,
obstruct, preclude, prohibit
9. barricade, hindrance
10. impediment, profession,
singletree 11. obstruction,
whippletree 12. underscoring

barb... 3. jag 4. clip, flue, harl, herl,
seta 5. horse, point, ramus, scarf
(nun's), speed 6. setula, striga
7. bristle, feather, pinnula 8. kingfish
9. arrowhead 10. projection

Barbados Island...
capital.. 10. Bridgetown
drink.. 3. rum

government.. 7. British
location.. 8. Antilles (Lesser) 10. West
Indies
native.. 3. Bim (nickname)
barbarian... 3. hun 4. Goth, rude
5. beast, brute 6. savage, vandal
8. cannibal, man—eater 9. untutored,
vulgarian 10. extraneous, Philistine,
unlettered 11. uncivilized
15. anthropophagite
barbaric... 5. cruel 6. brutal, Gothic,
savage 7. foreign, inhuman, vicious
8. non—Greek, non—Latin, ruthless
9. barbarous, primitive
10. extraneous 11. uncivilized
12. non—Christian
barbarism... 6. ferity 8. rudeness,
solecism 9. barbarity, crudeness,
Gothicism, ignorance, vulgarism
10. coarseness, corruption,
foreignism 11. impropriety
Barbarossa... 7. emperor (Rom) 8. red
beard
Barbary ape... 5. magot
Barbary State (former)... 5. Tunis
7. Algiers, Morocco 12. Tripolitania
barbate... 7. bearded, stubbly
9. whiskered 11. barbigerous
barbecue... 5. feast, roast 6. animal
(whole), picnic 7. brazier, hibachi
9. Dutch oven 10. shish kebab
13. entertainment (out—of—doors)
barber... 5. shave 6. figaro, shaver,
tonsor 7. tonsure 10. haircutter
12. tonsorialist
Barber of Seville character...
6. Figaro, Rosina
Barcelona, Spain...
building (famed).. 6. palace (Kings of
Aragon) 9. Cathedral (Gothic)
port.. 13. Mediterranean
street (famed).. 6. Rambla
bard... 3. muse, poet, scop (Hist)
5. druid, runer, vates 8. minstrel,
musician (wandering) 10. Parnassian
Bard of...
Avon.. 11. Shakespeare
Ayrshire.. 5. Burns
Rydal Mount.. 10. Wordsworth
bare... 3. raw 4. bald, mere, nude,
open 5. alone, empty, naked, plain,
shear, sheer, stark, strip 6. barren,
denude, divest, expose, reveal,
simple, vacant 7. exposed, unarmed,
uncover 8. desolate, disclose,
stripped 9. destitute, unadorned,
uncovered 10. stark—naked,
threadbare 11. defenseless,
unconcealed
barefaced... 4. bare, bold 6. brassy,
brazen 8. impudent 9. audacious,
shameless 11. undisguised
barely... 4. jimp, only 5. faint
6. hardly, merely, nudely, poorly,
simply 7. nakedly 8. narrowly,
scantily, scarcely 14. insufficiently
bargain... 3. buy 4. deal, pact, prig,
sell 5. trade 6. barter, chisel, dicker,
haggle 7. chaffer, compact, mediate
8. contract, covenant, purchase
9. agreement, Bon Marché,
cheapness, negotiate 10. engagement

11. stipulation, transaction
barge... 3. ark, hoy 4. raft, scow, ship
5. ferry, float, praam, scold
6. berate, lumber, rebuke, tender
7. birlinn (birling) 9. transport
barge in... 5. enter 6. bungle, butt in,
invade, push in 7. blunder, intrude
barghest... 6. goblin
bargoose... 4. duck 9. merganser,
sheldrake
bark... 3. bay, yap, yip 4. bang, bast,
husk, peel, rind, ross, ship, skin,
tapa, yelp 5. cough, niepa, shout,
strip, youff 6. bowwow, clamor,
cortex, outcry, packet, scrape
7. canella 8. ballyhoo, periderm
9. sassafras
barker... 4. tout 6. pistol 7. spieler
9. solicitor 10. ballyhooer,
theaterman
barking... 7. latrant 8. hylactic
Barlaam and Josaphet (Joasaph)...
11. Buddha story (Christian version)
barley... 4. bigg, food, seed 5. grain
6. ptisan, tsamba 7. Hordeum
barley (pert to)...
bird.. 6. siskin 7. wagtail (yellow),
wryneck 11. nightingale
bree.. 3. ale 6. liquor
shaped.. 10. hordeiform
barlow... 9. jackknife (one—bladed)
barm... 5. froth, yeast 6. leaven
7. ferment
barn... 3. bay, mow 4. loft
barnacle... 4. bray (Her) 5. acorn,
goose, leech 6. animal, sucker
8. adherent, parasite 9. sycophant
10. Cirripedia, crustacean
barnstormer... 5. actor 7. aviator
11. entertainer
baron... 4. peer 5. mogul, noble
6. daimio, tycoon 7. freeman
8. nobleman, somebody 9. financier,
personage 10. capitalist
13. industrialist
baroque... 6. ornate, quaint, rococo
7. bizarre 9. irregular 11. extravagant
barracks... 4. camp, huts 6. casern,
laager 9. barracoon 10. encampment
barraclade... 7. blanket (homemade)
barracuda... 4. fish, spet 5. barry
(Bahamas) 6. sennet
barrage... 3. dam 4. weir 5. blitz
6. strafe 7. barrier, gunfire, milldaw
9. cannonade, roadblock
11. obstruction
barrage (military)... 3. box 5. mines
6. normal 7. balloon 8. creeping,
standing 9. emergency
12. anti—aircraft
barranca... 4. bank 5. bluff 6. ravine
barratry... 6. breach, simony 8. bad
faith, mala fide 10. infidelity
11. dereliction
barred... 6. cooped, fenced, grated,
ribbed 7. striped 8. confined,
debarred, excluded, streaked
barrel... 3. box, keg, tun 4. cade,
cask, drum, knag 5. quill, speed
6. runlet, tierce 7. calamus (Zool),
rundlet 8. cylinder 9. kilderkin
barrel (pert to)...

maker.. 6. cooper
miscellaneous.. 3. gun, pen 4. pipe
6. pencil
sling.. 9. parbuckle
stopper.. 4. bung
barren... 3. dry 4. arid, bare, dull
5. blank, empty, heath, inane
6. desert, effete, jejune, karroo,
meager, Sahara, stupid 7. sterile
8. desolate, impotent, unpoetic
9. infertile 10. unfruitful, unprolific
12. unproductive, unprofitable
barricade... 3. bar 4. bolt, rail, seal,
stop 5. block, close, fence 6. abatis
7. barrier, padlock 8. blockade,
obstacle, obstruct 11. obstruction
13. fortification
barrico... 3. keg 4. cask
barrier... 3. Alp, bar, dam 4. clog,
door, gate, wall, weir 5. block,
fence, hedge, panel 6. screen
7. parapet, railing 8. blockade,
boundary, fortress, obstacle, stockade,
stoppage 9. partition, restraint
10. impediment, portcullis
11. obstruction
barrikin (Eng sl)... 6. jargon
9. gibberish
barrister... 6. lawyer 7. adviser,
pleader 8. advocate, attorney
9. counselor (counsellor), solicitor
barroom... 3. bar, pub, tap 6. saloon,
tavern 7. cantina, taproom
8. alehouse 11. rathskeller
barrow... 3. hod, hog (male) 4. brae,
fell, hill, knap, moor 5. grave (anc),
mound 7. tumulus 8. mountain
11. wheelbarrow 12. Reihengräber
bartender... 5. mixer 6. barman, bistro
7. barkeep, tapster 8. publican
barter... 4. deal, sell, swap 5. trade,
truck 7. bargain, permute, traffic
8. commerce, exchange
Bartholomew (pert to)... 4. Fair, Play
(Shak) 5. Saint 6. martyr 7. Apostle
(one of 12) 8. Massacre
Bartimeus (Bib)... 6. beggar (blind)
barton... 4. farm 5. abode, manor
6. grange 7. demesne 8. farmyard,
hacienda 9. homestead
baru... 4. tree (fiber) 7. majagua
base... 3. bed, low 4. dado, evil, foot,
foul, mean, root, seat, site, sole
5. basis, basso, cause, petty, radix,
socle, voice 6. abject, bottom,
center, factor, patten, plinth, podium,
singer, sordid, vulgar, wicked
7. servile, station 8. basement,
cosmetic, degraded, infamous,
inferior, pedestal, shameful, standard
9. principle, worthless
10. despicable, foundation, villainous
12. contemptible, dishonorable,
headquarters
baseball (terms)... 3. bag, bat, box,
fan, fly, hit, lob, out, RBI, run
4. ball, base, bunt, deck, foul,
home, nine, pill, sack, save, walk,
wild 5. bench, clout, coach, count,
curve, drive, error, field, first, force,
glove, homer, liner, mound, pitch,
plate, pop-up, score, slide, sport,

swing, third 6. assist, batter, bungle,
double, dugout, fumble, ground,
putout, rubber, runner, screen,
second, series, single, sinker, stance,
strike, string, target, triple, windup
7. battery, bullpen, diamond, fielder,
floater, rhubarb (sl), squeeze, stretch
8. backstop, grounder, keystone,
knuckler, outfield, pinch-hit,
powdered, spit ball 9. sacrifice,
strikeout 10. ballplayer
baseborn... 3. low 4. mean 5. lowly,
plain 6. common, humble 7. bastard,
ignoble, lowborn 8. plebeian,
spurious 11. commonplace
12. illegitimate
based on...
evidence.. 7. damning 8. decisive
10. conclusive
experience.. 7. empiric 9. empirical
numbers.. 5. hexad 6. nonary, senary
7. tertial
baseness... 6. infamy 7. badness
9. servility, vulgarity 10. wickedness
11. inferiority 13. dastardliness,
subordination
bash... 3. bat, jab, lam 4. beat, belt,
biff, blow, conk, mash, slug, sock
5. clout, paste, punch, smack, whack
6. bruise, strike, wallop 7. clobber
Basham's King... 2. Og
bashful... 3. coy, shy 5. heloe, mousy,
timid 6. demure, modest
8. blushing, retiring, sheepish,
timorous, verecund 9. diffident
13. self-conscious
basic... 4. root 5. basal, basis
7. essence, primary 8. alkaline,
original 9. essential 10. underlying
11. fundamental
Basilian... 3. art 4. monk, rule
6. bishop 7. liturgy, St Basil (The
Great) 8. precepts 10. Cappadocia
basilica... 5. major, minor, title
6. canopy, church, shrine, temple
11. patriarchal
Basilican (pert to)...
books.. 5. sixty 6. Digest
century.. 5. Tenth
empire.. 9. Byzantine
laws.. 9. Justinian
basin... 3. bed (water), cup, pit, tub
4. bowl, cock, font, hole, sink, tank
5. laver, plain, playa, stoup 6. cavity,
chafer, coulee, ground, lavabo,
marine, valley, vessel 7. lowland,
piscina 8. curvette 9. washbasin
10. depression
basis... 4. base, fond, root 5. cause,
start 6. bottom, factor, motive,
reason, thesis 7. premise, warrant
9. assertion, principle 10. foundation,
groundwork 13. justification
bask... 3. sin, tub 4. warm 5. bathe,
revel 7. suffuse 8. apricate
9. luxuriate
basket... 3. bin, box, car (balloon),
net, ped, pod 4. caba, cage, kish,
skep, trug 5. cabas 6. dosser,
gabion, vessel, wisket 7. corbeil,
hanaper, pannier, scuttle, wattage
9. container

basket (pert to)...
  coal mine.. 3. tub 4. corf
  fig.. 5. frail 6. tapnet
  fire.. 5. grate 6. cresset
  fishing.. 3. pot 4. buck (eel), caul,
    weel 5. crail, crate, creel 6. hamper
  making.. 5. slath 6. slarth
  wicker.. 3. cob 5. cesta, osier
    6. hamper 7. hanaper 8. bassinet

Basque (pert to)...
  ancestors.. 8. Iberians
  cap.. 5. beret
  home.. 5. Spain 8. Pyrenees

bas–relief... 7. carving, relievo
  12. basso–relievo (basso–rilievo)

bass... 4. fish 5. fiber, voice (low)
  6. singer 8. weakfish 13. basso
  profundo

bassoon... 4. oboe 6. fagott 7. fagotto

bast... 4. bass 5. fiber

Bast (Egypt)... 4. Ptah 7. goddess
  10. lady of life

bastard... 3. odd 4. heel (sl), sham
  5. false, louse (sl) 7. batarde
  8. abnormal, bantling, spurious
  9. scoundrel 10. adulterate
  12. illegitimate 5. nullius filius

baste... 3. hit, sew 4. cook, lard, lash,
  tack, whip 6. stitch, thrash
  7. trounce 8. lambaste

bastion... 5. redan 7. fastness
  10. stronghold 13. fortification

bat... 3. hit, jag, lam, rap 4. belt,
  blow, clip, club, slug, sock, swat,
  wink 5. binge, clout, paste, smack,
  spree, stick, whack 6. bender,
  cudgel, racket, wallop 7. clobber

bat (mammal)... 6. aliped, fox bat,
  kalong 7. noctule, vampire
  8. serotine 9. flying fox, pipistrel
  (pipistrelle), reremouse 10. Chiroptera

batch... 3. lot 4. heap, lump, mess,
  slew 5. bunch, group, stack
  6. amount, baking 7. mixture
  8. quantity 10. collection

bath... 3. dip, tub 4. sitz 5. steam,
  sweat, vapor 6. plunge, shower,
  sponge 7. Finnish, mineral, sulphur

bath (pert to)...
  Eccl.. 8. ablution
  house.. 6. bagnic, cabana 8. balneary
    10. natatorium
  photography.. 5. toner 9. developer
  Roman.. 7. balneum 11. Warm
    Springs
  sitz.. 5. bidet
  warm.. 5. therm

bathe... 3. tub, wet 4. bask, lave,
  swim, wash 5. flush 6. drench
  7. immerse, moisten, pervade,
  suffuse 8. medicate, permeate

baton... 3. rod 4. mace, wand
  5. staff, stick 6. baston, cudgel,
  fasces 7. scepter, support
  9. truncheon

Batrachia... 5. Anura, frogs, toads
  7. Surinam 8. Salienta

Battalion of Death (Russ)...
  13. legion of women

batten... 3. close, gloat 6. fasten,
  fatten, secure, thrive, timber

battered... 6. beaten, pasted

  7. bruised 8. impaired 9. shattered,
  weathered

battery... 3. set 4. guns, pack
  6. cohort, series 7. assault, platoon
  8. baseball (term) 9. artillery

battery (Elec)... 4. cell, grid, pole
  5. anode, plate 6. Leyden
  7. storage, voltaic 9. electrode

battle... 3. war 4. fray, meet, tilt
  5. brush, fight, joust, scrap
  6. action, affray, barney, combat,
  tussle 7. contest, scuffle, warfare
  8. conflict, skirmish, struggle
  9. challenge, encounter
  10. engagement

Battle (pert to)...
  Bib.. 8. Aceldama 12. potter's field
  Civil War.. 7. Bull Run 15. Lookout
    Mountain
  formation.. 4. line 5. herse, order
  Great.. 10. Armageddon
  Hundred Years (1346).. 5. Crecy
  Revolution.. 10. Bunker Hill
  slogan.. 8. aux–armes 9. battle cry
  World War I.. 6. Verdun (1916)
  World War II.. 11. Pearl Harbor
    (1941)

battologize... 6. repeat 7. iterate,
  recount, restate 9. reiterate
  12. recapitulate

bauble... 3. toy 4. gaud 6. doodad,
  geegaw, trifle, trivia 7. bibelot, trinket
  8. falderal (folderol) 9. bagatelle,
  plaything 10. knickknack

Bavaria...
  capital.. 6. Munich
  city.. 8. Augsburg, Wurzburg
    9. Nuremburg 12. Ludwigshafen
  freeway.. 8. autobahn
  government.. 10. Third Reich
  king (former).. 10. Maximilian
  prince.. 6. Rupert
  river.. 4. Eger, Isar

bawdry... 6. filthy 8. ribaldry, salacity,
  unchaste 9. obscenity
  11. pornography

bawl... 3. cry, say, sob 4. bark, howl,
  roar, wail, weep, yell 5. blare, shout
  6. bellow, boohoo, plaint 8. proclaim
  10. vociferate

bay... 3. ria 4. cove, howl, roan, wail
  5. bight, horse, inlet, oriel, sinus
  6. recess, window 7. ululate

bay (pert to)...
  antler.. 9. stag's tine (2nd)
  bird.. 5. snipe 6. curlew, godwit,
    plover
  color.. 4. roan
  tree.. 6. laurel

Bayard... 5. horse, steed (Rinaldo's)

bayonet... 5. lance, saber, spear,
  sword 6. dagger, weapon 7. poniard

bayou... 5. creek, marsh 6. slough,
  stream 7. channel 11. watercourse

Bayou State... 11. Mississippi

Bay State... 13. Massachusetts

bazaar... 4. fair, shop 6. market
  7. canteen (army) 10. exposition

be... 2. am 3. are 4. live 5. exist
  7. prevail

beach... 5. coast, plage, playa, praya,
  sands, shore 6. shilla, strand

9. waterside

beachcomber... 4. wave 6. loafer
8. vagabond

beacon... 4. beam, flag, sign, vane
5. fanal, light, radar, radio
6. marker, pharos, signal 7. cresset,
lantern, seamark 10. lighthouse,
watchtower

bead... 4. ball, drop 5. bugle, pearl,
sight (firearm) 6. rondel 8. ornament

beads... 5. grain, sewan 6. rosary
7. chaplet, granose (antennae),
jewelry, prayers

beak... 3. neb, nib 4. bill, lora, nose,
peck, prow 5. judge, mouth, spout,
tutel 10. magistrate 11. stipendiary

beaker... 3. cup 6. vessel (Chem)

beakless... 9. erostrate

beam... 3. ray 4. emit, grin, sile, sill,
stud 5. caber, gleam, joist, shaft,
shine, smile, tonka, wand 6. girder,
mantel, rafter, timber 7. radiate,
support, trimmer 8. trabeate

bean... 4. buck, faba, gram, lima,
mung, navy, seed, soya 5. black,
coral, pinto, Sieva 6. adzuki, castor,
frijol (frijole), kidney, legume, lentil,
string 7. calabar 9. Phaseolus

bean (pert to)...
eye of.. 5. hilum
game.. 7. beanbag
licorice seed.. 9. jequirity
lima.. 4. haba
seed (string bean).. 7. haricot
shaped.. 8. fabiform
slang.. 4. buck, head 5. brain
6. dollar, noodle, trifle

bear... 3. aim, cub, lug 4. dubb, tote,
turn, ursa 5. bring, brown, bruin,
carry, clack, crank, koala, polar,
press, short, sloth, stand, ursus, yield
6. animal, endure, grouch, harbor,
Kodiak, stress, suffer, Syrian, uphold
7. Ephraim (nickname), furnish,
grizzly, incline, musquaw, produce,
support 8. cinnamon, fructify,
maintain, Melursus, sorehead, tolerate
10. speculator 11. short seller
(Finan)

bear (pert to)...
cat.. 5. panda 9. binturong
class.. 6. ursine 7. Ursidaw
color.. 6. yellow
constellation.. 9. Ursa Major, Ursa
Minor
flag.. 10. California (State)
head.. 4. hure
The.. 6. Russia

beard... 3. awn 6. arista, goatee
7. stubble, Vandyke 8. whiskers

bearded... 5. awned 7. barbate,
pappose 8. aristate 9. whiskered

beards, science of... 10. pogonology

bearer... 3. boy 5. macer, usher
6. porter, tender 7. carrier
8. cargador, conveyor, escudero
9. attendant 10. khidmatgar,
pallbearer

bearing... 3. air 4. mien, port
5. poise 6. bel air, regard
7. concern, conduct, dignity,
meaning, posture 8. behavior,

carriage, demeanor, relation, tendency
9. direction, influence, relevance
10. connection, deportment,
supporting 12. significance

bearing (Her)... 4. enté, orle 5. bevel,
pheon 6. billet

bear witness... 6. attest 7. testify

beast... 4. bête, game, lion, pard
5. brute, camel, demon, fiend, horse,
spado, tiger 6. animal, cattle,
dragon, savage 7. carrier, critter,
leopard, monster 8. behemoth,
creature 9. dromedary

beastly... 5. gross 6. animal, bloody,
carnal, odious 7. bestial, brutish,
hideous, inhuman, leonine, theroid,
ungodly 8. dreadful 9. execrable
10. abominable, disgusting

beat... 3. hit, lam, tan, taw, wap
4. bang, bash, best, cane, drub,
drum, flog, lace, lash, maul, pelt,
tund 5. baste, excel, pound, pulse,
route, scoop, throb, thump 6. bruise,
cudgel, defeat, larrup, pommel,
punish, rhythm, strike, stroke, swinge,
thrash, thresh 7. baffled, belabor,
cadence, clobber, conquer, flutter,
musical, pulsate, routine, surpass,
trounce 8. chastise, fatigued,
lambskin, overcome, vanquish
9. exhausted, pulsation

beat (pert to)...
back.. 7. repulse
black and blue.. 9. sugillate
down.. 6. haggle 7. cheapen
into plate.. 8. malleate
slang.. 4. blow 5. scoot, scram
6. beat it, skidoo 7. vamoose
traverse.. 6. patrol

beatify... 5. bless, cheer, saint
6. hallow 7. gladden, glorify
8. enshrine, sanctify

beatnik... 8. Bohemian, maverick,
sulphite 13. nonconformist

beau... 3. fop 5. blade, dandy, flame,
lover, spark, swain 6. escort, squire
7. admirer, courter 9. caballero,
inamorato 10. beau–garçon

beautiful... 4. fair, fine 5. bonny,
kalon (Gr) 6. comely, lovely, poetic,
pretty 7. elegant, Tempean
8. graceful, handsome, stunning
9. aesthetic (esthetic), exquisite
15. pulchritudinous

beautify... 4. deck, trim 5. adorn,
grace 6. bedeck, doll up, enrich
8. decorate, prettify 9. embellish,
glamorize

beauty... 5. belle, charm, glory, grace
8. elegance 10. loveliness, prettiness
11. pulchritude

beauty, famed...
Egypt.. 5. Cleopatra
Greek.. 4. Hebe 6. Graces
9. Aphrodite 11. Helen of Troy
Historical.. 4. Lais
Persian.. 4. peri 5. houri
Norse.. 5. Freya
Roman.. 5. Venus

Becken... 7. cymbals

beckon... 4. beck 5. court 6. invite,
summon 7. gesture 11. gesticulate

becloud... 5. bedim, cloud, shade, smoke 6. bemist, darken, opaque 7. conceal, encloud, obscure 8. nubilate, overcast 9. adumbrate

become... 2. go 3. fit, get, wax 4. grow, rise, suit 5. befit, grace 6. befall, beseem, mature, mellow 7. behoove, benefit 8. befuddle 9. originate

becoming... 3. fit 6. comely, decent, fitted, likely, proper, seemly, suited 7. decorum, suiting 8. decorous, pleasing, suitable, tasteful 9. befitting, expedient 11. appropriate

bec–scie... 4. duck 9. merganser

becuna... 9. barracuda

bed... 3. cot, kip, tye (feather) 4. bunk, crib, doss, lair, nest 5. basin, berth, couch 6. billet, bottom, flower, litter, pallet 7. channel, feather, stratum 8. bassinet 9. stretcher 10. foundation

bed (pert to)...
canopy.. 4. ceil 6. tester
coverlet.. 7. quilt 6. spread 7. blanket 9. comforter 11. counterpane
famed.. 15. bed of Procrustes

bedaub... 3. dab 4. blur, daub, soil 5. paint, smear, stain 6. belaud, smudge 7. bedizen, besmear 8. besmudge, ornament

bedazzle... 4. daze, stun 5. blind, shine 6. dazzle 7. astound, confuse 8. astonish, bewilder

bedeck... 3. gem 4. trim 5. adorn, array, grace, prink 6. clothe, rag out 7. bedrape 8. ornament

bedevil... 3. hex 4. foul, ride 5. abuse, tease 6. befoul, muddle, needle, pester, plague 7. bewitch, confuse, torment 8. demonize 9. diabolize, tantalize 10. complicate

bedight... 5. adorn, array, equip

bedikah... 6. ritual

bedim... 3. dim, fog 4. blur, fade 5. blear, cloud 6. bemist, darken 8. bedarken

bedlam... 3. din 6. clamor, tumult, uproar 8. madhouse 9. charivari 11. pandemonium

Bedlam (London)... 6. priory (1247) 8. Hospital St Mary of Bethlehem)

Bedouin... 4. Arab, Moor 5. gypsy, nomad 7. Saracen, vagrant

Bedouin head cord... 4. agal

bedroll... 6. bindle 7. matilda

bee... 3. dor 4. apis 5. drone, karbi, queen 6. insect, worker 8. andrenid, angelito, honeybee 9. bumblebee 12. carpenter bee

bee (pert to)...
fear of.. 9. apiphobia
glue.. 8. propolis
hive.. 4. butt, scap, skep (straw) 6. apiary 7. alveary 8. workshop
keeper.. 8. apiarist, skeppist
sociable.. 7. husking, raising 8. quilting, spelling
study.. 10. apiculture 11. melittology
wax.. 7. beeswax, ceresin, cerotic

9. cera flava

Beebe, William... 13. ichthyologist

beef... 4. heft, kine, thew 5. brawn, sinew, steer 6. buccan (dried), cattle, muscle 8. poundage 10. brawniness 11. muscularity

Beelzebub (pert to)...
Bible.. 5. deity 6. oracle 14. prince of demons
literature.. 5. demon (Prince), devil 11. fallen angel
zoology.. 6. monkey

beer... 3. ale 4. bock, flip, hops, suds 5. lager, weiss 6. liquor, porter, swipes

beer (pert to)...
cask.. 4. butt
inventor.. 9. Gambrinus (Myth king)
mug.. 4. toby 5. stein 8. schooner
vessel.. 6. tanker 9. blackjack

beet... 4. Beta 5. chard 6. mangel 8. beet root 9. sugar beet

Beethoven, Ludwig Van (pert to)...
birthplace.. 4. Bonn (Ger)
composed.. 7. Fidelio 10. symphonies
famed as.. 7. pianist 8. composer

beetle... 3. bat, bug, dor, jut, ram 4. June, rose 5. Amara, gogga, Hispa, meloe, snout 6. chafer, elater, golach, goloch, hammer, masher, sawyer, scarab, weevil 7. ladybug, prionid 8. circulio, sharnbud, skipjack 9. cockroach, dorbeetle 10. cockchafer, Elateridae

beetlehead... 5. stupe 6. plover (bird), stupid 8. bonehead 9. blockhead 10. loggerhead

befall... 3. hap 4. come 5. occur 6. betide, chance, happen 9. eventuate, transpire

befit... 4. suit 5. serve 6. become, beseem, please

befitting... 3. fit 4. meet 6. filial, proper, seemly, timely 7. ethical, fitting, suiting 8. becoming, decorous, suitable 9. expedient 10. seasonable 11. appropriate

befog... 3. dim, fog 5. blind, cloud 6. bemist 7. becloud, conceal, confuse, mystify, obscure

before... 3. ere 5. afore, ahead, avant, early, prior 6. anteal, facing, openly, sooner 7. already, earlier, forward, yestern 8. anterior, foremost, formerly, hitherto 9. foregoing, preceding 10. beforehand, face to face, heretofore, previously 11. theretofore

before (pert to)...
birth.. 8. prenatal
long.. 5. soon
mentioned.. 4. said, same, such 5. named 6. former 10. aforenamed
others.. 5. first
this.. 3. ere 5. prior 6. erenow

before (pref)... 3. pre, pro 4. ante, prae

befoul... 4. soil 5. taint 6. bemire, defile, muddle 7. bedevil 8. entangle 10. complicate 11. contaminate

befriend... 3. aid 4. abet, help 5. favor 6. assist, foster, succor

7. benefit, support, sustain
11. countenance

befuddle... 3. fog 5. addle, besot
6. fuddle, muddle 7. becloud,
confuse 9. inebriate 10. intoxicate

beg... 3. ask, sue, woo 4. pray, sorn
5. cadge, crave, mooch, plead,
touch (sl) 6. appeal 7. beseech,
entreat, implore, solicit 8. petition
9. importune 10. supplicate

beget... 3. ean 4. sire 5. breed,
hatch, spawn 6. father 7. develop
8. engender, generate 9. procreate,
reproduce

begetter... 4. sire 5. pater 6. author,
father, mother, parent 7. creator
10. procreator, progenitor

beggar... 3. bum 4. hobo, waif
5. fakir (Moslem), gamin, lazar, rogue
6. loafer, pauper, wretch
7. almsman, dervish, vagrant, wastral
8. indigent, vagabond 9. mendicant,
suppliant 10. panhandler, ragamuffin
14. tatterdemalion

beggarly... 3. low 4. base, mean,
poor, rank 5. petty 6. abject,
meanly, paltry, vulgar 7. hangdog,
ignoble 8. bankrupt, indigent,
infamous, wretched 9. miserable,
niggardly 10. despicably, obsequious
12. contemptible

Beggars, King of (Eng)... 5. Carew

beggary... 4. want 6. penury
9. indigence, mendicity, pauperism
10. mendicancy 11. destitution,
panhandling

begin... 4. open 5. enter, start
6. attack 8. commence, initiate, take
rise 9. institute, introduce, originate
10. inaugurate

begin again... 5. renew 6. resume
10. recommence

beginner... 3. dub 4. tyro (tiro)
5. chela 6. infant, novice
7. amateur, entrant, recruit
8. begetter, freshman, neophyte
9. debutante, fledgling, initiator,
novitiate 10. catechumen, originator,
tenderfoot 11. inaugurator

beginning... 4. head, rise, root
5. alpha, birth, debut, onset, start
6. origin, outset, source 7. genesis,
infancy, opening 8. entrance,
inchoate, nascency, outstart, starting
9. inception, threshold 10. derivation,
foundation, incomplete, initiation
12. commencement, introduction

begone... 3. out 4. away, scat, shoo
5. allez, scram 6. aroint, avaunt,
depart 7. vamoose

begrudge... 4. envy 5. covey, stint
6. grudge, refuse 7. grumble

beguile... 4. dupe, lure, vamp
5. amuse, charm, cozen, elude,
spend, trick 6. delude, divert, regale
7. bewitch, deceive, ensnare, mislead
8. enthrall, intrigue 9. bamboozle,
captivate, deception, entertain,
fascinate, victimize 11. double–cross
14. disappointment

begum (Hind)... 5. queen 7. heiress
8. princess

begunk... 4. jilt 5. trick

behalf... 4. gain, good, part, sake,
side 5. avail, stead 6. affair, matter,
profit 7. benefit, defense, service,
support, welfare 8. interest
9. advantage

behalf of... 3. for 6. lieu of, rather
7. defense (of), instead

behave... 2. do 3. act 4. bear
5. carry 6. demean, deport, manage
7. conduct 8. regulate, restrain

behavior, behaviour... 3. air 4. mien
6. action, manner 7. actions,
address, bearing, conduct, decorum,
manners 8. carriage, demeanor,
maintien 10. deportment
11. comportment

behavior (pert to)...
good.. 7. decorum, P's and Q's
riotous.. 7. rampage
wicked.. 10. wrongdoing

behead... 7. execute 9. decollate
10. decapitate, guillotine

Behemoth (Bib)... 5. beast
12. hippopotamus

behest... 3. vow 5. order 7. bidding,
command, mandate, promise
10. injunction 11. commandment

behind... 3. aft 4. late, past, rear,
rump (vulgar), slow, tail 5. abaff,
abaft, after, ahind, arear, later, tardy
6. astern 7. delayed, impeded
8. arrested, backward, retarded 9. in
the past, posterior, remaining

behindhand... 4. late 5. tardy
7. arrears, belated, overdue
8. backward, dilatory, misdated,
mistimed 10. defaulting, delinquent

behind the times... 5. passé

behold... 2. lo 3. see 4. ahoy, ecce,
ecco, espy, look, scan, view 5. voilà
6. descry, regard, retain 7. discern,
observe, witness 8. maintain,
perceive

beholden... 5. bound 6. bounden,
obliged 8. grateful, indebted, thankful
9. obligated

beholder... 5. gazer 7. watcher,
witness 8. looker–on, observer,
onlooker 9. spectator

beige... 4. ecru, hopi 5. grège
6. dorado 13. reddish–yellow

being... 3. ego, ens, man, one
4. bion, body, esse, home, life, self
5. entia, gnome, human, thing, wight
6. actual, animal, entity, extant,
mortal, person 7. Adamite, essence,
present, reality 8. creature, existent,
existing, organism, presence
9. actuality, existence, personage,
something 10. individual
11. subsistence

being (pert to)...
celestial.. 4. deva 5. angel 6. cherub,
seraph
imaginary.. 4. pixy (pixie) 5. fairy,
sylph
science of.. 8. ontology
supernatural.. 6. Garuda (Hind)
Supreme.. 3. God 7. Creator

belaud... 4. laud 5. extol 6. praise
7. glorify

belay... 4. halt, quit, stop 5. beset, cease, cover, halte 6. fasten, invest, waylay 7. besiege, silence 8. encircle

belch... 4. burp, emit, vent 5. eject, eruct, erupt, spout, vomit 7. gush out 8. disgorge, eructate 9. small beer (vulgar) 10. eructation

beldam, beldame... 3. cat, hag 4. fury 5. crone, frump, vixen, witch 6. virago 7. she–wolf, tigress 8. ancestor (fem) 9. termagant 11. grandmother

Belgian (pert to)... see also *Belgium*
  anthem.. 13. La Brabanconne
  hare.. 5. leporide
  horse.. 9. Brabancon
  marble.. 5. rance
  resort.. 6. Ostend
  sheep dog.. 8. Malinois 11. Groenendael
  tribe.. 8. Batetela 9. Bellovaci
  violinist.. 5. Ysaye

Belgian Congo (pert to)...
  capital.. 12. Leopoldville
  mandate.. 6. Ruanda, Rwanda (1962), Urundi (old) 7. Burundi (1962)
  river.. 4. Uele
  tribe.. 8. Batetela

Belgium...
  capital.. 8. Brussels
  city.. 5. Ghent, Liege 6. Bruges 7. Antwerp, Louvain 9. Charleroi
  commune.. 3. Ath
  forest.. 8. Ardennes
  king.. 6. Albert 7. Leopold 8. Baudouin
  native.. 7. Fleming (of Flanders), Flemish, Walloon
  nickname.. 15. cockpit of Europe
  World War II Battle of.. 8. The Bulge

Belgravia (London)... 8. district (fashion)

Belial... 5. devil, Satan (New Test) 10. wickedness (Old Test) 11. Fallen Angel

belie... 4. deny 6. belong, defame, oppose, oppugn 7. besiege, falsify, gainsay, pertain, slander 8. disclaim, disprove, surround 9. encompass 10. calumniate 12. misrepresent

belief... 3. fay (anc), ism 4. cult, rule, sect, view 5. credo, creed, dogma, faith, maxim, tenet 7. opinion, precept 8. credence, doctrine, reliance, religion, teaching 9. assurance, certainty, principle 10. confidence, conviction, persuasion 13. Apostles' Creed

believe... 3. buy 4. deem, feel, trow, ween 5. think, trust 6. accept, credit, reckon 7. suppose, swallow 8. conceive, consider

believer (pert to)...
  all religions.. 6. omnist
  facts.. 7. realist
  religion.. 5. deist 6. theist 9. Adventist, Calvinist 13. particularist

Belit (Bab)... 7. goddess (wife of Bel)

belittle... 5. decry, dwarf 6. debase

7. detract, run down 8. minimize 9. discredit, disparage, underrate 10. depreciate 13. underestimate

bell... 4. gong 5. codon, knell 6. curfew, tocsin 7. campana, cowbell 8. carillon, doorbell 9. ship's bell 10. dinnerbell, schoolbell 12. glockenspiel, tintinabulum

bell, bells (pert to)...
  bird.. 9. campanero 10. wood thrush
  botany.. 7. corolla
  evening.. 6. curfew
  flat.. 4. gong 6. tam–tam (Chin), tom–tom
  funeral.. 5. knell
  ringer.. 6. toller
  ringing.. 7. peeling 13. tintinabulism
  science of.. 11. campanology
  set of.. 6. chimes 8. carillon
  shaped.. 11. campaniform
  specialist.. 9. campanist 13. campanologist
  tongue.. 7. clapper
  tower.. 6. belfry 9. campanile
  warning.. 6. tocsin

belle... 4. lady (fine) 5. toast 6. beauty 7. charmer 8. handsome 10. grande dame

belles–lettres... 8. classics 10. Humanities (The), literature

bellflower... 8. daffodil

bellicose... see *belligerent*

belligerent... 7. hostile, scrappy, warlike 8. choleric, militant 9. bellicose, irascible, litigious, offensive, wrangling 10. aggressive, pugnacious 11. contentious, quarrelsome 12. disputatious

belligerent's right (Internat law)... 6. angary

bellow... 3. cry, low, moo, say 4. bawl, roar, wail, yawp 5. blare, shout 6. clamor 7. thunder 10. vociferate

bellows... 4. fish 5. gills, lungs 6. blower, lights (Zool), rotary 8. ctenidia (Zool)

bellwether... 5. sheep 6. leader, wether (with bell)

belly... 3. bag, pot 4. crap, wame 5. bulge, front, tummy 6. bottom, paunch, venter 7. abdomen, stomach 8. potbelly, swell out 9. ingluvies

belong (to)... 6. answer, inhere 7. pertain, related 9. appendant, ingrained, possessed (by) 10. correspond

belonging (to)...
  dean.. 7. decanal
  era.. 7. epochal
  Fall.. 8. autumnal
  pencil (a).. 6. desmic
  people.. 7. endemic
  present (the).. 7. current
  Spring.. 6. vernal
  Summer.. 7. estival
  Winter.. 6. hiemal

belongings... 4. duds 5. goods, traps 6. family, things 7. effects, kinsmen 8. chattels, property 9. homefolks, relations 11. connections, perquisites 13. appurtenances

beloved... 3. pet 4. dear 6. prized
7. darling 8. precious, truelove
9. cherished, inamorata
beloved physician... 6. St Luke
below... 4. alow, here, less 5. Hades,
neath, sotto, under 6. aneath, in hell
7. beneath, short of 10. downstairs
11. belowstairs
Belshazzar (Bib)... 11. crown prince
Bel's wife... 5. Belit (Beltis)
belt... 3. bar, bat, hit 4. area, band,
beat, blow, cest, mark, pelt, ring,
sash, sock, whip, zone 5. apron,
Libya, strap, whack, zonar 6. cestus,
cingle, cordon, fascia, fasten, fillet,
girdle, region, strait, streak, stripe
7. baldric, kurbash, sjambok,
stratum, terrain 8. cincture, encircle,
surround 9. encompass
10. cummerbund
Belteshazzar (Bib)... 6. Daniel
belt of heaven... 6. zodiac 7. circuit
beluga... 5. whale (white)
Belus (pert to)...
father of.. 4. Dido
king of.. 4. Tyre 7. Assyria
son of.. 5. Libya
sons.. 7. Cepheus, Phineus
8. Aegyptus
belvedere... 5. cigar 7. cypress (mock)
10. watchtower 11. summerhouse
bema... 8. platform 9. sanctuary
bemoan... 4. pity, wail 5. mourn
6. bewail, grieve, lament, regret,
repine 7. deplore 10. sympathize
bemuse... 4. daze 5. addle, besot
6. absorb, muddle 7. stupefy
8. befuddle, distract 10. intoxicate
ben... 2. in 3. oil, son 4. tree
(Moringa) 5. within
bench... 4. pew 5. banc (judge's),
seat 5. chair, court, siege, staff,
stand, stool, table 6. exedra, settee,
settle 7. terrace 8. platform,
woolsack 9. committee
bend... 3. bow, nod, ply, sag, sny
4. bias, flex, genu, kink, knot, sway,
turn, warp 5. crimp, crook, curve,
drink, kneel, prone, squat, stoop,
twist, yield 6. buckle, crouch, curtsy,
direct, divert, humble, inflex, kowtow,
pleach, relent, salaam, strain, swerve
7. bendlet (Her), chevron (Her),
incline, refract, retract 9. genuflect,
introvert, sinuosity 10. inflection
bend (pert to)...
an ear.. 4. hear, heed 5. listen
one's will.. 4. bias, move, sway
the elbow.. 5. drink
the knee.. 5. kneel 6. kowtow,
salaam 9. genuflect
the mind.. 5. think
bends... 7. caisson, disease
8. blackout (aeronaut)
beneath... 4. alow 5. below, lower
(than), 'neath, under 6. aneath,
nether 7. in Hades 11. underground
beneath one's dignity... 8. infradig
15. infra dignitatem
benedict... 7. husband
10. bridegroom, married man (newly)
benediction... 4. rite 6. praise, prayer,

thanks 7. benison 8. blessing
10. invocation 12. thanksgiving
benefaction... 4. alms, boon, gift,
good 5. favor 7. benefit, present
8. courtesy, donation, gratuity,
kindness 9. beau geste
11. beneficence, benevolence
benefactor... 5. angel, donor
6. backer, helper, patron 8. promoter
10. befriender
beneficence... 7. charity 8. goodness,
kindness 11. benefaction,
benevolence 12. philanthropy
beneficial... 4. good 6. benign, useful
7. helpful 8. edifying, salutary
9. favorable, healthful, lucrative,
wholesome 10. profitable, salubrious
11. serviceable 12. advantageous,
remunerative
beneficiary... 4. heir 5. donee
6. vassal 7. devisee, feoffee, grantee,
legatee 8. assignee 9. annuitant
benefit... 3. aid, use 4. boon, gift,
good, help, vail 5. avail, favor, trust
6. profit, relief, succor 7. advance,
concert, improve, service, welfare
8. blessing, kindness 9. advantage
11. benefaction, convenience,
performance
benevolence... 3. tax 4. gift, good
6. bounty, giving 7. charity
8. altruism, bestowal, blessing,
donation, kindness 10. generosity,
liberality 11. munificence
12. contribution, philanthropy
14. charitableness
benevolent... 4. free, good, king
6. benign 7. liberal 8. generous,
princely 9. benignant, bountiful
10. altruistic, charitable, munificent
11. magnanimous 13. philanthropic
Bengal, Indian State...
capital.. 8. Calcutta
gentleman.. 5. baboo (babu)
language.. 7. Bengali
native.. 3. Kol (Kohl) 6. banian
7. Bengali
negro.. 3. Ibo (Ebo)
river.. 6. Ganges 11. Brahmaputra
river boat.. 7. bauleah
benign... 4. mild 5. bland 6. genial,
humane, kindly 7. benefic (Astrol),
liberal 8. gracious, salutary
9. benignant, favorable, healthful,
wholesome 10. propitious, salubrious
benignity... 5. favor 7. benefit
8. blessing, goodness, mildness
9. salubrity 10. kindliness
11. benevolence 12. graciousness
benison... 4. boon 7. blessing 8. beatitude
10. invocation 11. benediction
benjamin... 6. jacket 7. benzoin
8. overcoat 9. spicebush
Benjamin (Bib), (pert to)...
father.. 5. Jacob
history.. 5. tribe
mother.. 6. Rachel
Benjamin's mess... 6. big end
10. lion's share
benjy (Brit sl)... 3. hat (straw)
9. waistcoat
benne... 6. sesame

bennet... 4. herb 5. daisy 7. hemlock
bent... 3. aim, way, wry 4. bias, turn,
warp 5. drift, grass, slant, tenor,
trend, twist 6. course, curved,
desire, minded, nature, swayed
7. angular, aptness, crooked,
heather, leaning, stooped 8. aptitude,
penchant, tendency 9. obliquity,
prejudice, proneness 10. propensity
11. disposition, inclination
12. idiosyncrasy, predilection
13. prepossession 14. predisposition
Benthamism... 9. welfarism
14. utilitarianism
benthonic... 7. benthal, deep sea
benthonic plant... 6. enalid
benthos... 5. deeps 6. depths
8. ocean bed 16. Davy Jones's
locker
benumb... 3. nip 4. drug, numb, stun
5. chill 6. deaden, freeze 7. stupefy
8. paralyze 11. anesthetize,
desensitize
Beowulf... 4. poem (oldest in Teutonic
language)
bequeath... 4. give, will 5. endow,
leave 6. bestow, demise, devise,
invest, will to 7. bequest 8. transmit
bequest... 4. will 6. devise, legacy
8. heritage 9. patrimony, testament
10. birthright 11. inheritance
berate... 3. jaw, nag 4. lash, rail
5. chide, scold, slate 7. censure,
reprove, upbraid
Berber... 4. Riff 6. Hamite, Kabyle,
Taureg
berceau... 4. walk (leaf–covered)
5. arbor, bower 6. cradle
berceuse... 10. cradlesong
11. composition
bereave... 3. die, rob 5. leave, strip
6. divest, orphan, sadden 7. deprive,
despoil 10. disentitle, dispossess
bereavement... 4. loss 5. death
9. privation 10. divestment
bereft... 4. lorn 7. denuded, fleeced,
shorn 8. witless 8. bereaved,
divested, orphaned, stripped
9. senseless 10. parentless,
pauperized
Bereshith (Jew)... 7. Genesis
9. Beginning
beret... 3. cap, tam 7. biretta
bergamot... 4. pear 5. snuff 6. orange
7. essence 9. fragrance
beriberi... 5. kakke 7. disease
Berkeleianism (pert to)...
founder.. 8. Berkeley (Bishop)
science.. 10. philosophy
system.. 8. idealism 13. immaterialism
Berlin, Germany...
avenue.. 14. Unter den Linden
capital.. 7. Germany
garden (Zool).. 10. Tiergarten
gate.. 11. Brandenburg
government.. 9. Reichstag
berm, berme... 4. mall, path 5. prado
6. runway 10. terrace 8. shoulder
(road)
Bermuda...
capital.. 8. Hamilton
color.. 12. geranium pink

discoverer.. 8. Bermudez
government... 7. British
grass.. 5. decil
ocean site.. 8. Atlantic
Bernardine Order... 11. Cistercians
Berne, Bern (Switz)... 7. capital
berry... 3. haw 4. buck, seed
5. bacca, cubeb, fruit, grain, money
6. acinus, kernel
berry, fruit... 5. grape, salal
6. banana, tomato 7. currant
8. bilberry, dewberry, hagberry,
mulberry 9. bearberry, blueberry,
cranberry, raspberry 10. blackberry,
elderberry, gooseberry, loganberry,
strawberry 11. boysenberry,
huckleberry 12. checkerberry,
whortleberry
berserk... 4. amok, bunk, dock, post,
room 5. house, roost 6. billet,
marina, office, reside 8. quarters
9. situation 11. appointment
bertha... 4. cape 6. cannon, collar
7. Perchta (goddess) 9. Big Bertha
(Ger gun)
beseech... 3. beg, sue 4. pray
5. crave, plead 6. obtest 7. entreat,
implore, solicit 9. obsecrate
10. supplicate
beset... 3. dun, ply, vex 4. stud
5. harry, haunt, hem in, siege, worry
6. attack, harass, infest, invade,
obsess, plague, ravage 7. besiege
8. blockade, surround 9. beleaguer,
importune, infatuate
beset with danger... 5. risky
6. chancy 8. perilous 9. dangerous
10. jeopardous
beset with hairs... 7. barbate,
bearded
beside, besides... 2. by 3. too, yet
4. also, else, near, nigh, para (pref)
5. about, along 6. nearby
8. likewise, moreover 9. other than
11. furthermore 12. over and above
beside oneself... 3. mad 4. wild
5. crazy, rabid 6. beserk, raging,
raving 7. frantic, ranting 8. frenzied
9. desperate, overjoyed
10. distracted, distraught
11. overwrought
besiege... 5. beset 6. attack, harass,
obsess, plague 7. torment
8. blockade, surround 9. beleaguer
besmear... 3. dab 4. coat, daub,
mark, soil, spot 5. paint, smear,
stain, taint 6. bedaub 7. tarnish
8. besmudge
besmirch... 4. blot, soil 5. smear, sully
6. defile, smirch, smudge, vilify
7. besmear, blacken, tarnish
8. discolor
besom... 5. broom, hussy
besotted... 4. dull 5. drunk
7. muddled, sottish 8. obsessed
9. senseless, stupefied 10. infatuated
11. intoxicated
bespangled... 5. aglow 7. lighted,
studded, trimmed 8. spangled
9. decorated, garnished
10. glittering, ornamented
11. embellished, illuminated

bespatter... 3. wet 4. blot, spot
5. dirty, slosh, smear, stain, sully
6. splash, vilify 7. asperse, scatter,
spatter, tarnish 8. besmirch, splatter,
sprinkle 9. denigrate 10. stigmatize

bespeak... 4. mean, show 5. imply
6. ask for, attest, engage, evince
7. address, betoken, connote, exhibit,
suggest, testify 8. foretell, indicate,
manifest 11. demonstrate

best... 4. aces, beat, most, tops
5. cream, elite, queen 6. choice,
finest 7. largest 8. champion,
outstrip 9. nonpareil, overmatch
11. superlative

bestial... 3. low 4. vile 5. cruel
6. brutal, filthy, savage 7. beastly,
brutish, inhuman, sensual
8. depraved, ruthless 9. barbarous

bestow... 4. deal, give 5. allot, apply,
award, grant, spend 6. accord,
confer, convey, demise, devote,
donate, impart, render, tender
7. deposit, present 8. transmit
10. administer

bestow honor upon... 5. adorn, exalt,
grace 7. dignify, ennoble, glorify
10. aggrandize 11. distinguish

bestride... 4. pass 5. mount 7. climb
on, protect, support 8. straddle
10. bestraddle

bet... 3. bas (roulette), pot 4. play
5. stake, wager 6. gamble, hazard,
pledge

beta test (army)... 12. intelligence

bête... 5. beast, silly 6. stupid
7. foolish

betel (pert to)...
  leaf... 3. pan 4. buyo, paun (pan)
  palm... 5. areca
  pepper... 4. itmo (ikmo)

bête noir... 4. ogre 7. bugbear
10. black beast, frightener,
mumbo-jumbo, Mumbo Jumbo

bethel... 4. kirk 6. chapel, church
8. Bethesda (Jerusalem)
12. meetinghouse

bethink... 5. think 6. recall 7. reflect
8. cogitate, remember 9. cerebrate,
recollect

betide... 3. hap 4. fall 5. occur
6. befall, happen 7. betoken,
presage 9. come about, eventuate,
transpire

betimes... 4. anon, soon 5. early
7. ere long, shortly 8. directly,
speedily 9. forthwith, presently
10. beforehand, seasonably
12. occasionally

betise... 5. folly 9. asininity, silliness,
stupidity 11. foolishness

betoken... 4. mark, mean, note
5. augur 6. denote, typify
7. bespeak, connote, express,
portend, presage, purport, signify
8. evidence, indicate 9. foretoken,
symbolize

betray... 4. blab, dupe, hoax, sell
5. bluff, peach, trick 6. reveal,
seduce, tattle 7. beguile, deceive,
divulge, mislead, sell out 8. disclose,

inform on 9. bamboozle, victimize
11. double-cross

betrayal... 4. ruse 5. trick 7. sellout,
treason 8. giveaway 9. Judas kiss,
seduction, treachery 10. disclosure

betrayer... 5. Judas 6. Arnold, Brutus
7. seducer, traitor 8. derelict,
informer, Quisling, turncoat
10. treasonist 13. double-crosser,
Judas Iscariot

betroth... 4. affy, earl 5. tryst
6. engage, pledge, plight
7. espouse, promise 8. affiance,
contract, espousal 10. engagement

better... 3. top 4. more 5. amend,
emend, excel, raise (poker), safer,
wiser 6. bigger, exceed, outwit,
reform 7. advance, choicer, greater,
improve, promote, surpass, victory
8. improved, superior 9. advantage,
meliorate 10. ameliorate, preferable
11. superiority

betting term... 4. ante, odds, tout
6. parlay 7. pyramid 10. parimutuel
11. sweepstakes

between... 5. among, mesne
6. atween 7. average, betwixt

bevel... 4. edge, ream 5. angle, bezel,
slant, slope, snape, splay 6. square
7. incline, oblique 9. obliquity

beverage... 3. ade, opo (comb form),
pop, tea 4. coke, malt, maté, mead,
milk, soda 5. cider, cocoa, drink,
leban, morat (anc), punch, water
6. coffee, eggnog, frappé, nectar
7. Seltzer 8. Adam's ale, Coca-Cola,
lemonade, root beer, sourdook
9. ginger ale, orangeade, phosphate
10. buttermilk, grape juice
12. sarsaparilla

beverage (alcoholic)... 3. ale, gin, rum
4. beer, brew, grog, kava, port, raki
5. booze, cider, hooch, julep, lager,
negus, punch, smash, vodka
6. arrack, bishop, brandy, cognac,
eggnog, kumiss, kummel, likker,
porter, posset, sherry, tiswin, whisky
(whiskey) 7. Bacardi, zythum (anc)
bootleg, bourbon, cordial, liqueur,
martini, tequila 8. absinthe, aleberry,
Burgundy, cocktail, highball, muscatel,
sauterne, vermouth 9. applejack,
aqua vitae, firewater, Manhattan
10. shandygaff, Tom Collins
11. Benedictine, boilermaker,
grasshopper, mountain dew

bevy... 4. bund, gang, herd, host
5. covey, flock, group, party, troop
6. galaxy, throng 7. company
8. assembly 10. collection

bewail... 4. rue 4. keen, mean
5. mourn 6. bemoan, grieve, lament,
regret, repine, sorrow 7. deplore

bewilder... 3. fog 4. daze 5. addle,
amaze 6. baffle, dazzle, puzzle
7. buffalo, confuse, fluster, mystify,
nonplus, perplex 8. astonish,
confound, distract 9. bamboozle,
embarrass

bewilderment... 3. awe, fog 4. maze
6. wonder 9. confusion
10. perplexity 11. distraction

12. perturbation 13. disconcertion, embarrassment

bewitch... 3. hex 5. charm, witch
6. enamor, entice, hoodoo, voodoo
7. beguile, delight, enchant
8. enthrall 9. captivate, enrapture, ensorcell, fascinate, infatuate

bewitching... 5. siren 6. hexing, lovely
7. magical 8. alluring, charming, enticing 10. enchanting
11. captivating, fascinating

bey (Turk)... 5. title 8. governor

beyond... 2. by 3. too, yet 4. meta (pref), past, plus, well 5. above, extra, ultra 6. yonder 7. besides, farther, further, yonside 8. moreover 9. exceeding, Hereafter (The)
11. furthermore 12. additionally, ultraliminal

beyond hope... 9. desperate

bezant (pert to)...
architecture.. 4. disc 8. ornament
coin (anc).. 7. solidus (gold)
heraldry.. 4. disc (gold)
offering (Eng king).. 4. gold

bezel... 4. edge 5. crown (gem), facet
6. chaton, flange 8. pavilion, template (templet) 9. obliquity

bezonian... 6. mucker, wretch
7. budmash, caitiff, recruit
8. blighter 9. pilgarlic, scoundrel

bhikshu... 6. gelong 7. ascetic
8. sannyasi 9. mendicant

bhut (Dravidian)... 5. demon, ghost
6. goblin

bias... 3. ply 4. awry, bent, turn, warp
5. amiss, slant, twist 6. desire
7. leaning, oblique 8. diagonal, slanting, tendency 9. obliquity, prejudice 10. favoritism, partiality, prepossess, transverse 11. disposition

biased... 4. bent 6. narrow, swayed
7. bigoted, partial 8. diagonal, partisan, slanting 10. prejudiced

bib... 3. sip, sup 4. swig 5. apron, drink, quaff 6. guzzle, imbibe, tipple, tucker 7. tablier 8. pinafore

bibacious... 6. toping 7. drunken, sottish 8. bibulous, drinking, tippling

Bible... 7. The Book, The Word, Vulgate 10. Scriptures, Testaments (Old, New)

Bible (pert to)...
battle site.. 10. Armageddon
city.. 2. Ur 5. Joppa, Sidon, Sodom
6. Hebron 9. Bethlehem, Jerusalem
coin.. 6. talent
Commandments.. 9. Decalogue
Holy Land.. 9. Palestine
interpretation.. 7. anagoge
introduction.. 9. Isagogics
kingdom.. 4. Elam 6. Basham, Canaan 9. Chaldea
land of plenty.. 6. Goshen
language.. 7. Aramaic
mountain.. 4. Ebol, Zion 5. Horeb, Sinai 6. Ararat, Gilead, Moriah, Olives (Olivet), Pisgah
pause.. 5. selah
pool.. 6. Siloam
precious stone.. 6. ligure (jacinth)
Promised Land.. 6. Canaan

sea.. 3. Red 4. Dead 7. Galilee
Sermon on the Mount..
10. Beatitudes
sheep.. 7. chamois
town.. 4. Edar 5. Babel
Wells of.. 5. Hagar, Jacob

Bible character...
archangel.. 7. Raphael
giant.. 4. Anak 7. Goliath
High Priest.. 3. Eli
hunter.. 6. Nimrod
liar.. 7. Ananias
patriarch.. 5. Jacob 6. Israel
prophet.. 4. Amos, Joel 5. Hosea, Jonah, Micah, Nahum 6. Daniel, Haggai, Isaiah, Joseph, Joshua, Samuel 7. Ezekiel, Malachi, Obadiah 8. Habakkuk, Jeremiah 9. Zachariah, Zephaniah

Bible version... 5. Douay, Reims
6. Geneva 7. Bishop's, Luther's, Revised, Targums, Vulgate
8. Cranmer's, Matthew's, Peshitta, Tyndale's, Wartburg, Wycliffe 9. King James, Maccabees 10. Great Bible, Septuagint 15. American Revised

bicker... 5. argue, cavil 6. hassle, quiver, strife 7. dispute, flicker, flutter, quarrel, quibble, rhubarb (sl), wrangle 8. argument, pettifog
9. scrimmage, tremulous
10. contention 11. altercation

bicuspid... 5. bifid, tooth, valve
6. cuspid 8. premolar
10. two-pointed 13. double-pointed

bid... 3. beg 4. pray 5. offer, order, utter 6. charge, direct, enjoin, invite, reveal, tender 7. command, declare, entreat, offered, summons
8. overture, proclaim 9. quotation
12. presentation

biddy... 3. hen 4. dame 5. skirt
6. female 7. chicken, Partlet
8. bedmaker 11. maidservant

bide... 4. bear, stay, wait 5. abide, await, tarry 6. endure, remain, suffer
8. continue, tolerate 9. encounter, withstand

bield... 3. den 4. cozy 7. comfort, courage, hearten, shelter 8. boldness, embolden 9. sheltered
10. confidence, habitation

bien... 4. fine, good, snug

bienseance... 7. decorum, manners
9. propriety 11. correctness, proprieties (the) 12. mannerliness
17. conventionality

bier... 6. coffin, litter 10. catafalque

Bier... 4. beer

biff... 4. bash, blow, slug, sock
5. paste, punch

bifold... 4. dual 5. duple 6. binary, binate, double 7. twofold

bifurcate... 3. wye (letter) 4. fork
7. forking, furcate 8. biforked, branched, forklike 9. two-forked

big... 4. huge 5. bulky, grand, great, grown, jumbo, large 6. august, famous, mighty 7. massive, pompous, teeming 8. boastful, powerful, pregnant, swelling
9. momentous 10. tremendous

11. magnanimous, pretentious
big (pert to)...
shot.. 3. VIP
stick.. 5. power (T Roosevelt)
toe.. 6. hallux
top.. 6. circus
wig.. 3. VIP (humorous)
Big (pert to)...
Ben.. 5. clock 13. Tower of London
Bend State.. 9. Tennessee
Bertha.. 3. gun 5. Krupp (factory)
Board.. 6. Bourse 8. Exchange
11. stock market 13. stock exchange
House.. 3. pen 6. prison (State)
12. penitentiary
Push (WWI).. 5. Somme
bight... 3. bay 4. bend, gulf, loop
5. angle, noose, point 6. corner,
hollow 7. estuary
bigot... 3. bug, nut 6. zealot
7. fanatic 8. dogmatist, hypocrite,
illiberal 10. enthusiast, opinionist,
positivist
bigoted... 5. petty 6. little, narrow
10. intolerant, prejudiced
12. narrow–minded
bijou... 5. jewel 7. trinket
bilbi, bilby... 8. kangaroo
bilbo.. 5. sword 6. rapier
bilingual... 6. diglot 12. linguistical
bilious... 3. ill 8. choleric, liverish
9. dyspectic, jaundiced
11. ill–tempered
bilk... 2. do 3. gyp 4. balk, hoax, sell
5. cheat, cozen, trick 6. delude,
fleece, illude 7. deceive, defraud,
swindle 8. flimflam 11. hornswoggle
bill... 3. dun, neb, nib, pee, tab, Vee
($5) 4. beak, deed, list, menu, sign
5. carte, money 6. docket, pickax,
poster, ticket 7. account, invoice,
mattock, placard, program, receipt,
statute, voucher 8. billhook, schedule
9. publicize, statement
10. prospectus 11. legislative
13. advertisement
billet... 3. bar, log 4. note, pass
5. berth, stick, strap 6. assign,
docket, letter, notice, ticket
7. bearing (Her), epistle, missive,
molding 8. dispatch, document,
insignia, position, quarters
11. appointment
billiard shot... 5. carom, masse
6. cannon
Billingsgate... 4. Gate (London)
10. fish market 12. vituperation
billow... 3. sea 4. roll, toss, wave
5. eagre, heave, surge, swell
6. dilate 7. distend 10. undulation
billowy... 4. wavy 5. surgy 7. surging
8. swelling 10. undulating
bin... 3. box 4. crib, loft, vina
5. frame, kench, pungi (Hind flute)
6. manger 8. elevator
binary... 4. dual 6. bifold, binate,
double, duplex 9. duplicate
bind... 3. jam, tie 4. ally, frap, gird,
gyve, hold, lace, lash, rope, tape
5. chain, leash, stick, truss, withe
6. engage, fasten, fetter, pinion,
pledge, secure 7. confine, shackle

8. obligate 10. constipate
binding... 4. tape 5. valid 6. binder,
edging 7. girding, joining, liaison
8. trimming, trussing, wrapping
9. bordering, fastening, stringent
10. astringent, compulsory, obligatory
11. restraining, restrictive
binding (agreement)... 4. bond, pact
7. bargain, promise 8. contract
binding (book)... 4. yapp 5. cover
6. jacket 10. bibliopegy
binge... 4. bout 5. spree 6. bender
8. carousal 11. celebration
bingo... 3. pop 4. bang, keno
5. lotto, socko 6. brandy
biographer... 8. annalist 9. historian
10. chronicler 11. biographist,
memorialist
biography... 4. life 6. memoir
7. history, memoire, recount
8. memorial 11. hagiography
biological... 4. gene 5. class, genus,
order, vital 6. biotic, family
7. animate, organic, paracme,
species
biology, science of... 6. botany
7. ecology, zoology 8. eugenics,
genetics 9. bionomics, organisms
10. embryology, morphology,
physiology
biopsy (Med)... 8. analysis (tissue)
9. diagnosis 11. examination
(microscopic)
biped... 3. man 9. two–legged
birch... 4. flog 5. stick 6. switch
birch tree (pert to)...
family.. 10. Betulaceae
genera.. 5. alder, birch, hazel
order.. 7. Fagales
product.. 16. oil of wintergreen
variety.. 5. paper, river, sweet, white
6. cherry, yellow
bird (pert to)...
best swimmer.. 4. loon 6. gannet
cage.. 6. aviary 7. paddock
8. dovecote
Class.. 4. Aves
crested.. 7. hoatzin 9. stinkbird
fabled, sacred.. 3. roc 4. ibis
fastest flyer.. 4. hawk 5. eagle, swift
6. falcon
fastest runner.. 7. ostrich
feathers.. 5. remix (sing) 7. remiges
first.. 13. archaeopteryx
footless.. 4. apod
greatest traveler.. 4. tern
greatest wingspread.. 9. albatross
halcyon.. 10. kingfisher
highest flyer.. 5. goose
immortal.. 7. phoenix
killing.. 7. avicide
largest.. 6. condor 7. ostrich
13. whooping crane
Latin.. 4. avis
life.. 5. ornis
longest–lived.. 5. macaw
lover.. 12. ornithophile
most dangerous.. 9. cassowary
naked hatched.. 11. gymnogenous
of prey (prized).. 6. falcon
oldest known.. 13. archaeopteryx
one year old.. 8. annotine

Order.. 7. Rasores 8. Raptores
smallest.. 14. bee hummingbird
smartest.. 4. crow
study.. 6. oology
young.. 4. eyas 8. birdikin, nestling
9. fledgling
bird, anatomy (pert to)...
beak.. 3. neb, nib 4. bill, lora
5. ceral.. 6. rostrum
eye process.. 6. pecten
head.. 4. lore 6. pileum
jaw.. 4. mala
leg (featherless).. 9. cnemidium
wing part.. 5. alula
bird, Arctic... 3. auk 4. gull, skua
5. brant 6. dunlin, fulmar, jaeger
7. penguin 9. ptarmigan
bird, colorful... 3. kea 5. egret,
macaw 6. magpie, parrot, trogon
7. peacock, quetzal (quezal)
8. lyrebird 10. kingfisher 14. bird of
paradise
bird, common... 3. ani, daw, owl
4. chat, dove, lark, pisk, wren
5. finch, pipit, robin, vireo 6. dunlin,
linnet, martin, oriole, phoebe, pigeon,
shrike, siskin, thrush, towhee 7. blue
jay, bunting, catbird, cowbird, flicker,
grackle, kinglet, sparrow, swallow,
tanager, warbler, waxwing
8. blackcap, bluebird, bobolink,
cardinal, grosbeak, kingbird, redstart,
starling, titmouse 9. chickadee,
goldfinch, nighthawk, sandpiper
10. flycatcher, meadowlark,
turtledove, woodpecker
11. hummingbird, mockingbird,
nightingale, pyrrhuloxia
12. whippoorwill, yellowhammer
14. scarlet tanager
bird, crow family... 4. crow, rook
5. crake, raven 6. chough, magpie
7. corvine, jackdaw
bird, duck family... 4. clee, coot,
lory, smew, teal, wood 5. eider,
goose 6. scoter 7. gadwall, mallard,
Muscovy, pintail, pochard
8. baldpate, redshank, shoveler
9. merganser 10. bufflehead,
canvasback
bird, flightless... 3. emu, moa
4. dodo (ext), kiwi, rhea, weka
7. apteryx, ostrich, peacock, penguin
8. Notornis 9. cassowary
bird, foreign...
Africa.. 4. taha 5. crane 6. cuckoo
7. ostrich 8. umbrette
10. weaverbird
Arctic.. 3. auk 4. gull, skua 5. brant
6. dunlin, falcon, jaeger 7. penguin
8. grayling 9. gyrfalcon, ptarmigan
Asia.. 4. myna 5. pitta 6. bulbul,
linnet 7. boobook, peacock, sirgang
8. dotterel, leaf bird 9. brambling,
muted swan
Australia.. 3. emu 4. kiwi, lory
5. lowan 6. leipoa 7. boobook,
grinder 8. ganggang, lorikeet,
lyrebird, morepork, parakeet, platypus
9. bowerbird, cassowary, pardalote
Central America.. 6. barbet, toucan
7. quetzal (quezal) 8. puffbird

Cuba.. 6. trogon 8. tocororo 14. bee
hummingbird
England.. 4. kite, rook 9. cormorant
11. carrion crow
Europe.. 4. merl 5. pipit, stilt
(3-toed), stork (white), swift, tarin
6. godwit, hoopoe, merlin, roller,
siskin 7. bittern, ortolan, skylark,
starnel 8. bee eater, dotterel,
garganey, nuthatch, redstart
9. brambling, chaffinch, gallinule,
sheldrake 10. lammergeir, turtledove
11. nightingale, wallcreeper
12. capercaillie (grouse)
Hawaii.. 2. io, o–o 3. ava, iwa, poe
4. iiwi, mamo 6. parson 7. frigate
India.. 5. shama 8. amadavat,
pheasant 11. red hornbill
Java.. 7. sparrow 8. rice bird 9. fruit
dove
New Guinea.. 9. cassowary 14. bird
of paradise
New Zealand.. 3. ihi, kea, moa, tui
4. kuku, weka
So America.. 4. guan 5. macaw
6. barbet, motmot, toucan
7. jacamar, tinamou, warrior
8. boatbill, caracara 9. trumpeter
11. scarlet ibis
bird, game... 4. teal 5. brant, goose,
quail, snipe 6. grouse, pigeon,
plover, turkey (wild) 7. bustard,
gadwall, mallard 8. bobwhite,
pheasant, woodcock 9. partridge,
ptarmigan 10. canvasback 14. prairie
chicken
bird, group...
partridge.. 5. covey
pheasant.. 3. nye 4. nide
quail.. 4. bevy
bird, long-legged... 4. ibis, rail, sora
5. crane, egret, heron, stilt, stork
6. avocet, curlew, jacana 7. seriema
8. flamingo 9. sandpiper
10. demoiselle
Bird of...
Freedom.. 9. bald eagle
Jove.. 6. eagle
June.. 7. peacock
Minerva.. 3. owl
Wonder.. 9. phoenix
bird, pet... 4. myna (mynah)
6. canary, parrot 8. cockatoo,
lovebird, parakeet
bird, poultry... 4. duck 5. goose
6. pigeon, turkey 7. chicken
8. pheasant
bird, shore... 4. swan 5. egret, heron,
stork 6. avocet, curlew, plover, willet
7. frigate, pelican 8. dotterel, killdeer
10. demoiselle
bird, sky... 4. erne (ern), gier (Bib),
hawk, kite 5. Buteo, eagle, saker
6. condor, falcon, gannet, jaeger,
merlin, osprey 7. buzzard, harrier,
kestral, vulture 8. caracara, ringtail
9. Accipiter 10. lammergeir
bird, water... 3. auk 4. coot, gull,
ibis, loon, rail, shag, skua, swan
5. cahow, crane, grebe, heron, stork
6. curlew, cygnet, gannet, jabiru,
jacana, petrel, plover 7. bittern,

bustard, dovekie, pelican, seriema,
skimmer 8. dabchick, flamingo,
umbrette 9. albatross, cormorant,
gallinule, guillemot, phalarope,
spoonbill 10. kingfisher, yellowlegs
biretta... 8. skullcap 9. headdress
birl... 4. spin 6. rattle 7. resolve
birth... 3. nee 4. line 5. blood, breed
6. origin 7. descent, genesis, lineage
8. heritage, nativity, nobility
9. beginning 10. derivation,
extraction, renascence
11. inheritance, Renaissance
birthday (pert to)...
  astrology.. 7. casting, lineage (the
  gods)
  nativities.. 9. genethlic 10. genethliac
  poems.. 12. genethliacon
birth flower (by months)...
  Jan.. 9. carnation
  Feb.. 8. primrose
  Mar.. 6. violet
  Apr.. 5. daisy
  May.. 15. lily of the valley
  June.. 4. rose
  July.. 8. sweet pea
  Aug.. 9. gladiolus
  Sept.. 5. aster
  Oct.. 6. dahlia
  Nov.. 13. chrysanthemum
  Dec.. 5. holly 10. poinsettia
birthmark... 4. mole 5. nevus (naevus)
birthright... 6. rights 8. heritage
9 privilege 10. possession
11. inheritance
birth seniority... 9. first–born
13. primogeniture
birthstone (by days)...
  Sun . 5. topaz 7. diamond
  Mon.. 5. pearl 7. crystal
  Tues.. 4. ruby 7. emerald
  Wed.. 8. amethyst 9. loadstone
  Thurs.. 8. sapphire 9. carnelian
  Fri.. 7. cat's eye, emerald
  Sat.. 7. diamond 9. turquoise
birthstone (by months)...
  Jan.. 6. garnet
  Feb.. 8. amethyst
  Mar.. 6. jasper
  Apr.. 7. diamond 8. sapphire
  May.. 5. agate 7. emerald
  June.. 7. emerald 11. alexandrite
  July.. 4. onyx, ruby
  Aug.. 8. sardonyx 9. carnelian
  Sept.. 8. sapphire 10. chrysolite
  Oct.. 4. opal 10. aquamarine
  Nov.. 5. topaz
  Dec.. 4. ruby 9. turquoise
bis... 5. again, ditto, twice 6. encore,
repeat 7. replica 8. repetend
9. duplicate 10. repetition
biscuit... 3. bun, doe 4. rusk
5. bread, cooky, scone, wafer
6. pommel 7. cracker 8. biscotin,
zwieback
bise... 4. wind (cold) 6. winter
7. Norther
bisect... 4. fork 5. cross, halve, split
6. cleave, divide
bishop... 4. Abba 7. pontiff, prelate
8. chessman, director, overseer
9. churchman, clergyman, inspector

14. superintendent
bishop (pert to)...
  Bible.. 10. Great Bible
  cap.. 4. hura 5. miter
  revenue.. 7. annates
  staff.. 7. baculus, crosier (crozier)
  throne.. 3. see 4. apse
  vestment.. 4. cope 5. stole 6. rochet
  7. gremial, pallium 8. dalmatic
  10. omophorion
bishopric... 3. see 4. seat 7. diocese
10. episcopacy, episcopate
bison... 2. ox 4. gaur, urus
7. aurochs, buffalo 9. quadruped
bisque (pert to)...
  ceramics (unglazed).. 7. biscuit
  color.. 9. red–yellow
  food.. 4. soup 8. ice cream
  term (sports).. 4. turn 5. point
  6. stroke
bissext (pert to)...
  calendar.. 6. Julian (Rom)
  day.. 5. sixth (intercalary)
  year.. 8. Leap Year
bistro... 6. tavern 7. barroom 8. wine
shop 10. restaurant
bit... 3. ace, jot, ort 4. bite, coin,
iota, mite, mote, part (acting), role,
snip, tool, tube, whit 5. check,
crumb, hitch, money, piece, scrap,
speck 6. morsel, smidge, tittle
7. portion, smidgen, traneen
8. somewhat 9. something
bit (harness)... 4. curb 6. bridle,
Pelham 7. snaffle 9. Liverpool
bit (money)...
  two bits.. 7. quarter 9. ninepence
  (Bahamas)
  four bits.. 10. half dollar
bitch... 6. female (animal) 8. slattern,
strumpet (vulgar)
bite... 3. cut, eat, nip, zip 4. food,
gnaw, grip, hold, knap, pang, tang,
zest 5. champ, smart, snack, sting,
taste 6. morsel, nibble, pierce
8. pungency
biting... 4. acid, tart 5. acerb, acrid,
sharp 6. bitter, rodent 7. caustic,
cutting, mordant, nipping, painful,
piquant, pungent 8. piercing,
poignant, scathing, stinging
9. sarcastic, trenchant, vitriolic,
withering 10. astringent, irritating
11. acrimonious, penetrating
biting nails... 12. phaneromania
bito (pert to)...
  bark.. 10. fish poison
  seeds.. 6. zachun (oil)
  tree.. 7. hajilij
bitter... 4. acid, cold, keen, sore, sour
5. acerb, acrid, irate, sharp
6. severe 7. cutting, hostile, pungent
8. grievous, stinging, virulent
9. rancorous, resentful
10. embittered, unpleasant
11. acrimonious, distressful,
reproachful
bitter (pert to)...
  apple (herb).. 9. colocynth
  chemical.. 4. alum
  earth.. 8. magnesia
  gentian.. 9. baldmoney

grass.. 9. colicroot
herb.. 3. rue 4. aloe 5. aloin
  8. centaury
plant.. 10. bitterroot 11. bittersweet
  (poisonous)
prefix.. 5. picro
salts.. 5. Epsom
suffix.. 6. picrin
vetch.. 8. ers
waters (Bib).. 5. Marah
wintergreen.. 10. pipsissewa
wormwood.. 8. de Gaulle (said of)
bitterness... 3. rue 5. venom
  6. rancor 7. remorse 8. acerbity,
  acrimony, tartness, wormwood
  9. animosity, poignancy, virulence
  10. causticity, resentment
bivalve... 4. clam, spat, Unio 5. pinna
  6. Anomia, mussel, oyster, Teredo
  7. mollusk, pandora, scallop
  10. brachiopod (fossil form)
bivocal... 9. diphthong (dipthong)
bivouac... 4. camp 6. encamp, laager
  7. camping, leaguer (Hist)
  10. encampment
biwa... 6. loquat
bizarre... 3. odd 5. dedal, outré, queer
  6. absurd, exotic, quaint, rococo
  7. baroque 8. fanciful 9. eccentric,
  fantastic, grotesque, highflown
  11. extravagant, sensational
Bizen... 7. pottery (unglazed)
Bizet... 8. composer (Carmen)
bizzarro (Mus)... 7. bizarre
  9. whimsical
blab... 6. gossip, reveal, snitch, tattle,
  tell on 7. blabber, chatter
  8. informer, squealer, telltale
  10. taleteller, tattletale 11. taletelling
blabber... 4. blab 6. babble, gabber,
  gossip, tattle 7. chatter, twaddle
  8. informer, nonsense
black... 3. ink, jet 4. ebon, evil, foul,
  inky, noir 5. color, cruel, ebony,
  murky, negro, niger, raven, sable,
  tarry 6. dismal, filthy, gloomy, pitchy,
  somber, sullen, wicked 7. hateful,
  melanic, nigrine, nigrous, ominous,
  unclean 8. atrament, menacing,
  mournful, sinister 9. atrocious,
  lightless, nigricant 10. calamitous,
  disastrous, forbidding
black (pert to)... see also *Black*
African.. 10. blackamoor
alloy.. 6. niello
and blue.. 5. livid 7. bruised
  10. discolored, ecchymosed,
  ecchymosis 11. bluish–black,
  lead–colored
art.. 5. magic 7. alchemy 8. wizardry
  10. black magic
ball.. 7. exclude 9. ostracize
bird.. 2. Zu (Myth) 3. ani, daw, pie
  4. crow, merl, rook 5. amsel, ouzel,
  raven 6. thrush 7. jackdaw
  10. Melanesian, Polynesian
bottom.. 9. clog dance
coffee.. 8. café noir
diamond.. 4. coal
duck.. 6. Cayuga
earth.. 4. mold 9. Chernozem (Russ)
face.. 4. type 5. sheep 8. minstrel

fish.. 6. tautog
garnet.. 8. melanite
gibbon.. 7. siamang
guard.. 5. drole, gamin, knave, rogue,
  scamp 6. rascal 7. vagrant, villain
  8. criminal, scalawag, scullion,
  vagabond 9. scoundrel
  11. rapscallion
Harry.. 7. sea bass
jack.. 4. flag (pirate) 6. coerce,
  cudgel, hijack 9. strong–arm
  10. Jolly Roger
partridge.. 9. francolin
rhinoceros.. 7. borelle
sheep.. 10. scapegrace
smith.. 5. smith 8. forger, smithy
  7. farrier
spruce.. 7. yewpine
strap.. 8. molasses
widow spider.. 6. pokomo
Black (pert to)...
Bess.. 4. mare (Dick Turpin's)
Current.. 5. Japan
Death.. 6. Plague (bubonic)
Foot.. 6. Indian (Siksika)
  10. Algonquian
Friar.. 4. monk 9. Dominican
  (mendicant Order)
Friday.. 10. Good Friday 14. public
  disaster (day)
Hand.. 7. anarchy, Camorra, Society
  (secret) 9. blackmail
Hawk.. 3. War (1831) 11. Indian
  Chief
Hole.. 8. Calcutta
Jack (General).. 5. Logan (Civil War)
  8. Pershing (WWI)
Maria.. 7. vehicle (prisoner's)
  14. explosive shell
Monday.. 12. Easter Monday (1630)
Monk.. 11. Benedictine
Plague.. 7. bubonic
Prince.. 6. Edward
Republic.. 5. Haiti
Rood.. 8. crucifix, Holy Rood (anc)
Sea (Asia).. 6. Euxine (anc)
Sea (Russia).. 11. Chernoe More
Shirt.. 7. Fascist 8. Fascisti
Watch.. 16. Royal Highlanders
Water State (nickname).. 8. Nebraska
blacken... 5. sully 6. defame
  9. denigrate
bladder... 3. bag, sac 4. sack
  5. pouch 6. bubble, pocket
  7. blister, globule
blade... 3. arm, bit, fop 4. beau,
  dude, edge, epee, foil, leaf, vane
  5. blood, dandy, frond, knife, spark,
  spear, spire, sport, sword 6. cutter,
  rafter (roof), runner, Toledo (sword)
  7. gallant, sabreur, scapula, traneen
  9. swordsman
blague... 6. humbug 8. claptrap
blah... 4. bunk 8. contempt, nonsense
blain... 4. bleb, sore 5. bulla
  7. blister, inflame, pustule
  8. swelling 9. chilblain
Blake's symbolic figure... 3. Zoa
blame... 5. chide, curse, shend
  6. accuse, charge, revile 7. accusal,
  censure, obloquy, reproof, reprove
  8. denounce, reproach 9. criticism,

damnation, reprehend 10. accusation, imputation 11. attribution, reprobation 12. condemnation, denunciation, reprehension 14. responsibility

blameless... 7. sinless 8. innocent 9. faultless, guiltless 12. sans reproche

blameworthy... 8. culpable 10. censurable, reprovable 11. impeachable 13. reprehensible

blanch... 4. fade, pale 5. gloss, scald 6. whiten 8. etiolate 9. whitewash

blanc mange... 7. dessert, pudding

bland... 4. glib, mild, oily, smug, soft, tame 5. suave 6. gentle, smooth 7. affable 8. soothing (manner), unctuous 9. temperate 10. flattering 12. hypocritical, ingratiating, mealy–mouthed, smooth–spoken

blandishment... 7. amenity, coaxing, palaver 8. cajolery, flattery 9. wheedling 10. allurement, inducement

blank... 4. arid, bare, dash, dull, form, nude, null, void 5. empty, naked, verse 6. closed, hollow, jejune, poetry, stupid, vacant, vacuum 8. bull's–eye, document, spotless (domino) 9. fruitless, unadorned, untrimmed 10. instrument (law), tabula rasa 11. empty–headed, thoughtless 13. unembellished, unintelligent 14. expressionless

blank book... 5. album 6. tablet 8. memo book, notebook 10. memorandum, pocketbook

blanket... 3. rug 4. robe 5. bluey, cloak, cotta, cover, manta, quilt, throw 6. afghan, shroud, spread 7. lap robe 8. covering, coverlet 10. barraclade (homespun)

blankness... 7. vacancy, vacuity 8. negation 9. emptiness

blare... 4. bawl, blow, bray, honk, peal, toot 5. blast, blaze, glare 6. bellow 7. fanfare, tantara 9. tantarara

blarney... 6. bunkum 7. wheedle 8. buncombe, cajolery, flattery, soft–soap 9. adulation

Blarney Stone site... 13. Blarney Castle (Cork, Ir)

blart... 4. blab, roar 5. bleat 6. bellow

blasé... 5. bored, sated 6. casual 9. easygoing, sans souci, surfeited 10. hard–boiled, nonchalant 11. indifferent, self–assured, unconcerned, worldly–wise 12. disenchanted 13. disillusioned, disinterested, lackadaisical

blaspheme... 4. damn 5. abuse, curse, swear 6. revile, vilify 10. calumniate

blasphemy... 7. cursing, impiety 8. anathema, swearing 9. profanity, sacrilege 10. execration 11. desecration, imprecation, irreverence, malediction

blast... 3. jet, pop 4. bang, blow, gust, ruin, shot, toot 5. curse, stunt 6. blight, flurry, onrush, wither 7. blowout, explode 9. discharge,

explosion, explosive, frustrate 10. detonation, propulsion 11. fulmination

blasted... 5. blown 6. blamed, cursed, danged (sl), darned, ruined 7. wrecked 8. blighted 10. confounded

blatant... 5. crude, noisy 6. garish, puling, vulgar 7. flaring, glaring, howling, ululant, wailing 8. brawling 9. clamorous, turbulent 10. blustering, uproarious, vociferous 12. obstreperous

blate... 4. blab, dull, slow 5. bleat, blunt, prate, timid 7. bashful 8. sheepish 9. diffident 10. spiritless

blaw... 4. blow, brag 5. boast

blaze... 4. fire, gash, mark (trail), sign 5. flame, flare 6. luster 7. bonfire, flare–up 8. eruption, outburst, radiance, splendor 9. explosion, firebrand 10. effulgence 11. resplendent

blazer... 6. jacket

blazon... 4. deck, show 5. adorn, blaze, grace, paint 6. enrich, shield 7. display, étalage, exhibit, furbish 8. proclaim 9. embellish 10. coat of arms, exhibition 11. publication

blazoning arms... 8. bearings, heraldry

bleach... 3. lye, sun 4. lime 6. blanch, purify, whiten 7. decolor, lighten 8. chemical, chlorine, etiolate, peroxide 9. whiteness 10. dealbation, decolorant 11. decolorizer

bleaching vat... 4. kier 5. kieve

bleak... 3. raw 4. arid, bare, cold, pale 5. gaunt, sharp 6. bitter, desert, dismal, dreary, frigid, pallid, severe 7. cutting, exposed 8. desolate, rigorous 9. cheerless, wind–blown, wind–swept 10. depressing

blear... 3. dim, fog 4. blur, dull, film 6. bleary 7. blurred 10. indistinct

bleat... 3. baa 4. blat 5. blate, whine 7. blather

bleb... 5. bulge, bulla 6. bubble 7. bladder, blister, globule, pustule, vesicle

bleed... 3. cup, tap 4. milk, soak 5. drain 6. fleece, grieve, let out, suffer 7. agonize, despoil, exploit, overtax 8. let blood, transude 9. surcharge 10. hemorrhage, overcharge

bleeding... 7. cupping 9. hemorrhea 10. hemorrhage, phlebotomy 11. venesection 12. bloodletting

blemish... 3. mar 4. blot, blue, dent, flaw, mole, mote, pock, rift, scar, spot, wart 5. crack, fault, nevus, sully, taint 6. breach, macula, macule, stigma 7. failing, fissure, freckle, lentigo 8. cicatrix, pockmark 9. birthmark, cicatrice, deformity, disfigure 10. defacement, deficiency 12. imperfection 13. disfigurement

blench... 4. duck, pale, wile 5. blink, dodge, quail, trick, wince 6. bleach, cringe, flinch, recoil, shrink, whiten 9. stratagem 10. disconcert

blend... 3. mix 4. fuse, melt
5. merge, shift, unite 6. fusion,
mingle 7. combine, mixture, scumble
8. coalesce, compound, tincture
9. commingle, composite, harmonize
10. amalgamate 11. combination,
incorporate
blended... 5. fondu, mixed 6. merged
7. mingled 9. confluent
blending... 6. crasis 11. inheritance
blessing... 4. boon, gift, good, luck,
rite 5. favor, grace 7. benefit,
benison, fortune, godsend, service,
welfare 8. good turn, kindness
9. advantage 10. benedicite, good
wishes 11. benediction, benevolence
12. felicitation 13. beatification
blight... 3. mar, nip 4. dash (hope),
ruin, rust, seer, smut 5. blast, crush,
spoil 6. freeze, mildew, wither
7. destroy, shatter 9. frustrate
10. disappoint
blighter... 4. chap 6. beggar (anc),
fellow
blimp... 6. ballon 7. airship, balloon
8. potbelly, zeppelin 9. dirigible
10. bureaucrat 12. Graf Zeppelin,
stuffed shirt
blind... 3. dim 4. ante (poker), mask,
peed, ruse, seel, slat, veil, wile
5. ciego, guise, trick 6. ambush,
scheme, screen 7. benight, conceal,
dim-eyed, eyeless, gimmick, obscure,
pretext, shutter 8. artifice, hoodwink,
jalousie, purblind, unseeing
9. dead-drunk, senseless, sightless
10. ableptical, dim-sighted,
subterfuge 11. inattentive
12. undiscerning 13. stalking-horse
blind (pert to)...
  alley.. 7. impasse 8. cul-de-sac
  fear.. 5. panic
  girl (of Pompeii).. 5. Nydia
  gut.. 6. caecum, window
  10. persiennes
  one eye.. 4. peed
  printing for.. 7. braille
blindness... 7. anopsia, meropia (part)
8. ablepsia 9. achropsia, amaurosis
10. bleariness, nyctalopia 11. gutta
serena, hemeralopia
13. achromatopsia
blink... 4. wink 5. light, quail, wince
6. cringe, flinch 7. flicker, glimmer,
glimpse, glitter, nictate, shimmer,
twinkle 9. nictitate 10. bat the eyes
blink at... 6. accept, ignore
7. condone 8. overlook, tolerate
9. be blind to, disregard
bliss... 3. joy 4. Eden 6. heaven
7. delight, harmony, rapture
8. felicity, gladness 9. beatitude,
happiness 11. blessedness
12. spirituality 14. blithesomeness
blissful... 4. holy 5. seely 6. Edenic
7. blessed, Elysian, Utopian
8. ecstatic 9. beatified, glorified
blister... 4. bleb, blob, burn, flay
5. blain, bulge, bulla, roast 6. beat
up, bubble, oyster, scorch (with
words), thrash 7. bladder, blemish,
pustule, trounce, vesicle 9. criticize

10. vesicatory
blistered... 6. seared, singed
7. parched 8. scorched 9. vesicated
blithe... 4. airy, glad 5. merry
6. cheery, joyous 7. jocular
8. cheerful 10. blithesome
blitz... 5. shell 6. strafe 7. bombard
10. blitzkrieg
blizzard... 4. blow, wind 5. purga
7. tornado 9. snowstorm 10. snow
squall 11. white squall
Blizzard State... 11. South Dakota
bloated... 5. cured (herring), proud,
tumid 6. sodden, turgid 7. dilated,
pompous, swollen 8. inflated, puffed
up, tumefied 9. distended, flatulent,
plethoric 10. incrassate
13. emphysematous
bloated plutocrat... 9. bourgeois
10. capitalist
blob... 3. wen 4. bleb, blot, daub,
drop, lump, mark 5. bulge
6. bubble, pimple 7. blister, globule,
pustule, splotch
bloc (political)... 4. axis 5. cabal, union
6. league 7. faction 8. alliance
9. coalition 11. combination
block... 3. bar, dam, set 4. cake,
clog, cube, mass, peck, plot, stop
5. check, parry, shape, solid
6. hamper, hinder, impede, oppose,
shares, stymie 7. auction, barrier,
outline 8. blockage, obstacle,
obstruct 9. barricade 10. impediment
11. obstruction
block (pert to)...
  architecture.. 5. socle 6. dentil,
    mutule, plinth 7. tessera
  blacksmith's.. 5. anvil
  coal (Eng).. 3. jud
  executioner's.. 10. guillotine
  falconry.. 5. perch
  finance.. 6. shares
  football.. 4. clip
  glacier.. 5. serac
  insulating.. 6. taplet
  land.. 4. city 5. tract 7. section
  medicine.. 10. anesthesia
  railroad.. 6. signal
  sandstone (Eng).. 6. sarsen
blockade... 3. bar, dam 5. hem in,
siege 6. shut in 7. closure, exclude,
fortify 8. obstacle, obstruct
9. exclusion 11. obstruction
blockhead... 3. oaf 4. dolt, fool,
mome (anc) 5. dunce, idiot
7. half-wit, tomfool 8. bonehead,
lunkhead 11. knucklehead
blockhouse... 4. fort 7. shelter 8. log
cabin 10. stronghold
bloke... 3. man 4. bird, chap, tuff
6. fellow 9. personage
blond, blonde... 4. fair 5. color, light
6. flaxen 10. goldilocks
blood... 4. cell, clot, type, vein
5. aorta, fluid, group, grume, hemad
(haemad), hemal, hemic, ichor
(gods'), lymph, serum 6. artery,
factor, fibrin, haemal, plasma, Rhesus
(type) 7. blister, carotid 8. platelet
9. corpuscle, hemamoeba, leucocyte
10. hemachrome, hemoglobin,

hemorrhage, phlebotomy
11. erythrocyte, transfusion
12. bloodletting

blood (pert to)...
clotted.. 4. gore 5. cruor
   8. thrombus
color.. 7. crimson, para red 8. blood
   red, sanguine 11. sanguineous
   13. sanguinaceous
feud.. 8. vendetta
flower.. 5. hippo 9. blood lily
horse.. 7. blooded 12. thoroughbred
hound.. 4. lyam (lyme)
mixed.. 6. mustee 7. mulatto
   8. octoroon 9. half–breed
money (anc).. 3. cro 4. eric
   7. galanas, wergild 9. bloodwite
particle (foreign).. 7. embolus
poisoning.. 6. pyemia (pyaemia)
pressure.. 12. hypertension
pudding.. 7. sausage
relationship.. 3. sib 6. agnate
   7. cognate, kinship, kinsman,
   progeny, sibship
shed.. 6. murder 7. killing, slaying
   9. slaughter
stone.. 10. chalcedony
sucker.. 5. leech 8. parasite
   10. sanguisuge
thirsty.. 5. cruel 8. sanguine
   9. ferocious, murderous
   10. sanguinary 11. ensanguined
vessel.. 3. vas 4. vein 6. artery
   9. capillary

blood, kinship... 4. race, ties 5. birth,
breed, stock 6. strain 7. descent,
kinsman, lineage, royalty, sibship
8. heredity, nobility, relation 9. blue
blood, lifeblood, life force
10. extraction 13. consanguinity

bloodless... 4. pale 5. ashen, faint
6. anemic (aenemic) 7. ghastly,
inhuman 8. lifeless, peaceful
9. unfeeling 11. cold of heart

bloody... 4. gory 5. cruel, wound
6. cruent (obs), cursed 7. smeared
8. infamous 9. murderous
10. sanguinary 11. ensanguined
12. bloodstained, bloodthirsty

Bloody (pert to)...
Angle.. 11. battlefield (Spotsylvania,
   1860)
Bill.. 14. law enforcement (US)
Mary.. 5. Queen (Eng) 8. cocktail
Shirts.. 8. Civil War

bloom... 3. dew 4. glow, posy
5. blush, youth 6. beauty,
flower, health, heyday, thrive
7. blossom 11. healthiness

bloomer... 5. boner, error 6. bobble,
boo–boo 7. blooper, blunder, failure,
faux pas, mistake, trouser

blossom... 4. bell, blow, grow, posy
5. bloom, ripen 6. floret, flower,
mature, thrive 7. develop, prosper
8. flourish, floweret, progress
10. effloresce 13. efflorescence

blossoming... 4. rise 6. growth
8. anthesis, blooming 9. flowerage,
flowering 10. florescent, unfoldment
11. development, florescence
flourishing, progressing

13. efflorescence, inflorescence

blot... 3. dry, mar 4. blur, soil, spot
5. erase, error, fleck, smear, speck,
stain, sully 6. absorb, blotch,
damage, impair, smutch, soak up,
sponge, stigma 7. blacken, blemish,
erasure, expunge 9. bespatter
10. obliterate, stigmatize
12. obliteration

blot (out)... 3. fix 4. dele, kill
5. purge 6. absorb, cancel, delete,
efface, excise, rub out 7. bump off,
destroy, expunge, obscure, wipe out
8. black out 10. obliterate

blotch... 4. bleb, mark, soil, spot
5. patch, stain 6. macula, mottle,
stigma 7. blemish

blotched... 4. pied 5. pinto 6. spotty
7. mottled 8. speckled

blouse... 3. blou, sark 5. bluey, middy,
shift, shirt, smock, tunic, waist
6. basque 7. casaque 15. shirtwaist

blow... 3. dab, hit, rap, tap 4. brag,
bump, coup, gust, pant, puff, slap,
toot, waft, wind 5. bloom, devel,
feint, impel, knock, shock, sound,
utter 6. expand, puff up 7. beating,
bluster, whiffle 8. calamity, disaster,
disclose, lambskin (obs)
14. disappointment

blow... 4. flee, over, rant, slog
5. boast, clout, scram 6. beat it,
betray, buffet, depart, wallop
8. squander 10. blow me down

blow (pert to)...
cement.. 6. kibosh
hard.. 6. blower 7. windbag
   8. braggart 11. braggadocio
hot and cold.. 4. vary 5. shift, waver
   6. seesaw 7. quibble 9. fluctuate,
   vacillate

blower... 4. blow, gale, wind 5. whale
6. puffer (fish), squall 7. bellows,
bloomer, blowgun, boaster, monsoon,
tornado 8. braggart 9. hurricane,
whirlwind, windstorm 11. braggadocio

blow up... 4. fail, rage 5. blast, bloat,
burst, fluff 6. berate, dilate, excite,
expand, forget, praise 7. blow out,
enlarge, explode, inflate 8. demolish,
detonate, disprove 9. fulminate

blowzy... 5. dowdy, ruddy, tacky
6. coarse, frowzy, sloppy, untidy
7. unkempt 8. careless, frumpish,
slovenly 10. disheveled, slatternly

blubber... 3. fat 4. weep 6. bubble
8. whale fat

blubbery... 3. fat 7. swollen
9. quivering 10. gelatinous
11. protuberant

bludgeon... 3. bat, hit 4. beat, club,
mace 5. billy, bully, stick 6. coerce,
cudgel, menace 8. browbeat,
bulldoze, threaten 10. intimidate,
shillelagh (shillalah)

blue... 4. baby, bice, bleu, navy
5. azure, beryl, Ching, email, king's,
merle, perse, royal, smalt 6. cobalt,
cyanic, French, indigo, powder
7. azarite, cesious, Dresden,
Dumont's, gobelin, lobelia, mesange,
peacock, Persian 8. caesious,

calamine, cerulean, Coventry, electric, lavender, midnight, pavonine, sapphire, wisteria 9. turquoise 10. aquamarine, cornflower

blue (pert to)... see also *Blue*
baby.. 8. cyanotic
bonnet.. 3. cap 4. Scot 6. flower (Texas State) 8. Scotsman, titmouse
china.. 7. Nanking
circle (archery).. 6. target
day.. 6. Monday
emblem of.. 6. Oxford 9. Cambridge
grass.. 3. poa
ground.. 10. kimberlite
hero.. 9. Bluebeard
melancholy.. 3. sad 6. gloomy 7. pensive, wistful 8. tristful 9. cheerless, depressed, penseroso 10. atrabiliar 11. atrabilious, melancholic 13. hypochondriac
nose.. 4. snob 5. prude 7. Puritan 10. goody-goody 11. Nova Scotian
pencil.. 4. dele, edit 6. delete, excise, revise
print.. 4. plan, plot 5. graph 6. layout 7. diagram, program 8. schedule 9. cyanotype 10. master plan, photograph, photoprint
ribbon.. 5. award, badge 10. cordon bleu, decoration
skin.. 5. livid
sky.. 5. ether, vault 6. caelum, heaven, welkin 7. the blue 8. empyrean 9. firmament 10. blue yonder, the heavens
stocking.. 4. blue 6. pedant 7. bas bleu 8. Gamaliel (Bib) 9. formalist, pedagogue 10. Parliament
Blue (pert to)...
Boy.. 8. painting (Gainsborough)
Grass State.. 8. Kentucky
Grotto site.. 5. Capri
Law State.. 11. Connecticut
Bluebeard's wife... 6. Fatima
blue-gray... 7. cesious (caesious)
blue-green... 8. calamine
bluff... 4. bank (steep), crag, curt, dupe, fool, rude, wall 5. brash, cliff, frank, gruff, krans, sheer, short 6. abrupt, crusty 7. beguile, blinder, blinker, bluffer, bluster, brusque, deceive, pretend, uncivil 8. impolite 9. bamboozle, blusterer, charlatan, falseness, four-flush, precipice 11. four-flusher 13. unceremonious
bluffer... 5. quack 9. blusterer, charlatan 10. mountebank 11. four-flusher
bluffness... 6. candor 9. bluntness 10. abruptness 11. brusqueness
blunder... 3. err, mix 4. bull, goof, slip 5. boner, botch, error, misdo 6. boo-boo, bungle, fumble 7. faux pas, mistake, stumble 8. flounder, solecism (speech) 9. mismanage
blunt... 4. curt, dull, open 5. bluff, frank, gruff, plain 6. benumb, candid, deaden, obtund, obtuse, snippy, stupid, weaken 7. artless, brusque, sincere 8. hebetate 9. ingenuous 13. unceremonious
blur... 3. bog, dim, hum 4. blob, blot,

film, mist, soil, spot 5. blear, cloud, smear, stain 6. blotch, darken, mackle 7. blemish, dimness, obscure, splotch 9. disfigure
blurb... 3. ad 4. plug 5. boost, brief 6. notice 7. write-up 8. ballyhoo 9. publicity 12. announcement, commendation 13. advertisement
blurt out... 4. blab, bolt 7. blunder 9. ejaculate
blush... 4. glow, look 5. bloom, color, flush 6. glance, mantle, redden 7. modesty, redness 9. suffusion
blushing... 4. meek 5. ruddy 6. modest 7. roseate 8. flushing, sheepish 9. reddening, rubescent 10. erubescent
bluster... 4. blow, bray, fume, rage, rant, roar 5. broil, bully, furor, noise 6. flurry, hoopla, hubbub, squall, tumult 7. roister, swagger, turmoil 8. boasting, bullying, threaten 9. agitation, confusion 10. swaggering, turbulence 11. rodomontade
blusterer... 5. bully 7. boaster 8. blowhard, braggart 9. roisterer, swaggerer 11. braggadocio 12. swashbuckler
bo... 4. hobo 5. buddy, tramp 9. sundowner 10. landlouper 11. bindle stiff
bo, boh (Burma)... 5. chief 6. leader 7. captain
boa... 5. aboma, scarf (feather), snake 8. anaconda
boar... 3. hog, sus 4. apex, hure (head) 5. swine 6. barrow, hogget (2-year) 9. hoggaster (3-year)
board... 4. deal, doll, feed, lath, side, slat, wood 5. curia (anc), enter, forum, meals, plank, table 6. border, lumber, timber 7. binding (book), council, lodging 8. approach, exchange (Finan), tribunal 9. committee, provision 11. accommodate, bed and board, directorate, refreshment 14. accommodations
boast... 4. brag, crow 5. extol, exult, glory, pride, vapor, vaunt 6. menace 7. bluster, swagger 8. braggart, flourish 9. gasconade
boastful... 4. vain 8. bragging 9. conceited, overproud, presuming 11. thrasonical 12. vainglorious 13. self-important
boat... 3. ark, bac, gig, tub, tug 4. brig, dhow, dory, junk, punt, saic, scow, ship, trow, yawl 5. aviso, balsa, barge, canoe, craft, dandy, dhoni, dingy, ferry, kayak, ketch, liner, oolak, praam, scull, skiff, U-boat, umiak, xebec, yacht 6. argosy, baidak, bateau, convoy, cutter, dinghy, dogger, launch, mistic, oomiac, packet, randan, sampan, settee, tanker, vessel, whaler 7. bidarka, caravel, coracle (anc), cruiser, gondola, masoola, piragua, pirogue, rowboat, scooter, shallop, trawler, tugboat, warship

8. dahabeah, man–of–war, palander, sailboat, seaplane 9. catamaran, destroyer, steamship, submarine 10. brigantine, windjammer 11. side–wheeler, treckschuyt

boat (pert to) . . .
boatswain . . 5. bosun 6. serang
captain . . 4. rais (reis) 6. master 7. skipper
deck . . 4. poop 6. flight 9. promenade
man . . 5. rower 6. bargee 7. ferrier, oarsman 9. gondolier, yachtsman
sail . . 3. jib 4. main, reef 6. lateen, mizzen
shaped . . 9. navicella, navicular
side . . 7. gunwale
song . . 7. chantey 9. barcarole
bob . . . 3. bow, cut, nod, rap, tap 4. bend, jeer, jerk, jest 5. cheat, filch, float, flout, plumb, shake, taunt, trick 6. bobble, curtsy, delude, hairdo, kowtow, sinker, weight 7. haircut 8. coiffure, greeting, shilling 9. obeisance, oscillate
bobac . . . 5. pahmi 6. marmot
bobber . . . 4. duck (ruddy) 5. float 6. bobfly 7. dropper 8. deadhead
bobbin . . . 3. pin 4. coil, cord, pirn, reel 5. braid, spool 7. spindle
bobble . . . 3. bob, dib (angling) 4. muff 5. shake 6. boggle, bungle, fumble 7. blunder 9. oscillate
bobby . . . 6. peeler 9. policeman
Boche . . . 6. German (a)
bodach . . . 5. churl, clown 7. bugaboo
bodacious . . . 4. bold 8. insolent, reckless 9. audacious, bumptious, insulting 12. contumelious
bode . . . 5. augur 6. divine 7. portend, presage 8. forebode, foreshow, foretell 13. prognosticate
bodhisattva . . . 8. Buddhism 13. Enlightenment
bodice . . . 4. belt 5. stays, waist 6. basque, girdle 7. corsage, garment
bodily . . . 6. carnal 7. fleshly, somatic 8. corporal, material, physical 9. corporeal 10. completely
boding . . . 7. ominous 10. foreboding, portentous, prediction, prognostic 12. apprehension
bodkin . . . 3. awl 6. dagger, needle 7. hairpin, poniard 8. stiletto 9. eyeleteer
body . . . 3. man 4. deha (Theos), homo, soma 5. being, human, trunk 6. corpse, entity, licham, mortal, person 7. carcass 8. creature, organism 9. substance 10. individual 13. corpus delicti 14. substantiality
body (pert to) . . .
armed . . 5. corps, posse
business . . 7. company 11. cooperation 12. organization
celestial . . 3. sun 4. luna, star 5. comet 6. meteor, planet
church . . 4. nave
dead . . 6. corpse 7. cadaver
division (mollusk) . . 7. prosoma
injury . . 6. mayhem, trauma
petrified . . 6. fossil

political . . 4. weal 6. senate 7. cabinet 11. legislature
small . . 6. nanoid 8. dwarfish
body of . . .
people . . 3. mob 4. band, bevy, gang, host 5. bunch, crowd, flock, group, horde 6. rabble, throng 9. multitude
singers . . 5. choir 6. chorus
soldiers . . 4. file 5. corps, squad, troop 7. brigade, company, platoon 8. division
water . . 3. bay, sea 4. lake, pond, pool 5. fiord (fjord), inlet, ocean 6. lagoon 9. reservoir
Boeotian (pert to) . . .
city . . 5. Ionia (Dist) 6. Thebes
figurine . . 7. Tanagra
king (Myth) . . 6. Ogyges
Boer (pert to) . . .
General, statesman . . 5. Botha
language . . 4. Taal 9. Afrikaans
War site . . 9. Ladysmith (S Afr)
bog . . . 3. bug, fen 4. blei, bold, holm, mire, moor, moss, ooze, quag, sink 5. jheel, marsh, saucy, swamp 6. morass, slough 8. quagmire 9. everglade
bogey, bogie, bogy . . . 3. par 5. Devil 6. goblin 7. bugaboo, bugbear
boggle . . . 3. shy 4. foil, quip 5. botch, cavil, demur, parry, pause, start 6. bicker, bungle, falter, object, shrink 7. dispute, quibble, scruple 8. hesitate, sidestep 9. dissemble, objection 10. difficulty, equivocate
bogglebo . . . 5. bogle 7. bugaboo, specter 9. hobgoblin, scarecrow
bogus . . . 4. fake, mock, sham 5. phony, queer 8. spurious 10. apocryphal, factitious, fictitious 11. counterfeit
bohawn . . . 3. hut 5. cabin 7. cottage
Bohemia . . .
capital . . 6. Prague
city . . 5. Praha 6. Aussig, Pilsen 7. Budweis, Teplitz 11. Reichenberg
dance . . 6. redowa
measure . . 5. stopa 6. merice
mineral . . 6. egeran
reformer . . 4. Huss
river . . 4. Elbe, Iser 6. Moldau
tribe (anc) . . 4. Boii
vagabond . . 5. gypsy (gipsy)
bohunk . . . 6. Slovak 7. laborer 8. Bohemian, Croatian (formerly)
boil . . . 3. sty (styr) 4. buck, cook, fume, stew 5. churn, steam 6. bubble, pimple, seethe 7. bristle 8. furuncle
boiling . . . 5. angry 7. cooking, flushed, stewing 8. seething, sizzling 9. agitating, ebullient 10. smoldering
bois (Fr) . . . 4. wood
boisterous . . . 4. loud 5. noisy, rough, rowdy 6. stormy 7. blatant, excited, furious, roaring, violent 8. brawling 9. clamorous, turbulent 10. blustering, roisterous, tumultuous, unyielding 12. obstreperous
Bokhara (pert to) . . .
fur . . 9. astrakhan, broadtail

rug .. 8. Turkoman
sheep .. 7. karakul (caracul)
site .. 4. Asia (Russ)
bola ... 4. tree (fiber) 6. weapon
bold ... 4. deep, pert, rash, rude, snug
5. steep, stout 6. abrupt, brazen,
daring, heroic, raised 7. dashing,
defiant, eminent, forward, salient,
valiant 8. fearless, immodest,
impudent, in relief, intrepid, powerful,
repoussé, stalwart 9. audacious,
confident, dauntless, shameless,
unabashed 10. courageous
11. lionhearted, outstanding,
precipitous 12. presumptuous,
stouthearted
boldness ... 5. valor 6. defial, virtue
7. bravery, courage 8. audacity,
defiance, salience, temerity
9. assurance, gallantry, hardihood,
immodesty, impudence
10. brazenness, confidence,
effrontery, prominence, resolution
11. forwardness, intrepidity,
obviousness 12. protuberance
13. dauntlessness
14. courageousness
bolero ... 5. dance, music, waist
6. jacket
boliche ... 3. inn 5. bowls
Bolivia ...
capital .. 5. La Paz (Polit), Oruro (anc),
Sucre (law)
hero .. 5. Sucre 7. Bolivar, Pizarro
Indian tribe .. 3. Uro 4. Iten, Moxo
lake .. 8. Titicaca (world's highest)
11. Desaguadero
mountain .. 5. Andes 6. Sorata
8. Illimani
product .. 3. tin
river .. 4. Beni
bolo ... 5. knife 7. machete 8. pacifist
(Bolo Pasha, traitor) 9. defeatist
Bolshevik, bolshevik ... 7. Marxian,
radical (Bolsheviki) 9. Communist
(1918), Socialist 13. revolutionist
14. Social Democrat 18. Third
International
Bolshevist (Communist) leader ...
5. Lenin 6. Stalin 7. Kosygin
8. Bulganin 10. Khrushchev
bolster ... 3. pad 4. bear, hold
6. pillow 7. cushion, support, sustain
8. maintain
bolt ... 3. bar 4. dart, flee, lock, roll,
sift 5. arrow, rivet, scram, screw,
shaft, speed 6. decamp, devour,
faster, flight, pintle, secede, staple,
toggle 7. missile, padlock 8. firebolt,
separate 10. projectile 11. eat
greedily, thunderbolt
bolus ... 4. bite, clay, clod, food
(chewed), mass, pill 6. tablet, troche
8. mouthful
bomb ... 3. dud, egg 5. shell 6. petard
7. grenade, missile 8. divebomb,
fireball, surprise 9. bombshell,
pineapple 10. projectile
bomb (type of) ... 4. time 5. stink
6. aerial, atomic, rocket 7. tear gas
8. hydrogen 10. demolition
bombard ... 5. blitz, shell 6. assail,

attack, strafe 7. atomize, barrage
9. cannonade
bombardier ... 5. jager 6. bomber,
gunner 9. cannoneer, musketeer
12. artilleryman
bombast ... 4. blow, brag, rage, rant,
rave 5. boast 7. fustian 8. boasting,
inflated, stuffing (Hist) 9. bombastic,
turgidity 11. rodomontade
12. magniloquent 13. grandiloquent
bombastic ... 5. tumid 7. orotund,
pompous, stilted 8. boastful, inflated
12. high-sounding 13. grandiloquent
Bombay ...
capital of .. 14. Bombay province
college .. 11. Elphinstone
duck .. 10. lizard fish
hemp .. 4. sunn 6. ambary
merchant .. 4. Arab
seaport of .. 5. India
bomber ... 5. stuka 10. bombardier
Bombyx ... 4. eria, moth 8. silkworm
bona fide ... 4. real 7. genuine
9. authentic 10. constantly, faithfully,
legitimate
bona mano ... 3. tip 8. gratuity
bon ami ... 5. lover 6. friend 10. good
friend, sweetheart
bonanza ... 6. riches 15. El Dorado
(Myth), gold mine (US)
Bonanza State ... 7. Montana
bond ... 3. tie, vow 4. duty, gyve, link,
mise, pact, yoke 5. chain, nexus,
rente 6. fetter, league 7. entente,
manacle, shackle 8. contract,
covenant, relation, security (Finan)
9. agreement, captivity
10. allegiance, connection
11. association, certificate
bondage ... 4. yoke 6. chains
7. serfdom, slavery 9. captivity,
restraint, servitude, thralldom
11. subjugation
bondman, bondsman ... 4. esne, serf
5. churl, helot, slave 6. thrall, vassal
7. servant 8. bailsman 9. guarantor
bone ... 2. os 4. chip 5. boner
6. dollar, osteon 7. blunder, counter
(game), ossicle 8. skeleton, wishbone
9. funny bone (humerus), pygostyle
(bird's)
bone (Anat) ... 3. rib 4. ulna 5. femur,
ilium, incus (ear), malar, skull, spine,
talus, tibia 6. carpus, coccyx, fibula,
tarsus 7. humerus, maxilla, patella,
scapula, sternum 8. astragal, clavicle,
mandible, phalange, vertebra
9. calcaneus, occipital
10. metacarpus, metatarsus
bone (pert to) ...
bonelike .. 6. osteal 7. osteoid
cell .. 10. osteoblast
china .. 7. English
curvature .. 8. lordosis
divination .. 10. osteomancy
fish .. 9. operculum
marrow .. 7. medulla
process .. 7. mastoid 9. apophysis
science .. 9. osteology
surgery .. 9. osteotomy 11. osteoclasis
12. osteoplastic
tissue .. 6. ossein

tumor.. 7. osteoma
bones... 4. body, dice, form, ossa
   5. cubes, frame, money, torso, trunk
   6. end man, refuse 7. carcass,
   ivories 8. skeleton 11. rattlebones
boneyard... 4. bank (game)
   8. golgotha 9. graveyard
   10. necropolis 11. polyandrium
bonhomie... 8. pleasant 9. good
   humor 10. affability, amiability
Bonhomme Richard... 4. ship
   8. man–of–war (1779), (opponent of
   Serapis)
bonito, bonita... 4. nice 6. pretty
   8. mackerel, skipjack
bon mot... 9. witticism 10. jeu
   d'esprit 11. smart saying
bonne... 5. mammy 9. nursemaid
   10. baby sitter 11. maidservant
bonnet... 3. cap, hat 4. coif, hood,
   poke 6. toque 7. chapeau
   9. headdress
bonnetman... 10. Highlander
bonny, bonnie... 3. bon 4. good
   5. plump 6. comely, lively, pretty
   7. healthy, très bon 8. handsome
   9. beautiful
Bontok... 7. Malayan (Luzon)
   10. Indonesian
bonus... 3. tip 4. cash, gift 5. batta,
   bribe, extra, share, stock (Finan)
   7. cumshaw, douceur, premium,
   rake–off, subsidy 8. dividend, gratuity
   9. Trinkgeld 10. honorarium
bon vivant... 7. epicure, gourmet
   8. gourmand, hedonist, sybarite
   10. boonfellow, good fellow,
   voluptuary 12. Heliogabalus (anc)
bony... 4. hard, thin 6. osteal, skinny
   7. osseous 8. rawboned, skeletal
bonze (Far East)... 2. bo 4. monk
boo... 4. hoot, jeer, razz 7. catcall,
   feather (ostrich) 9. raspberry
   10. Bronx cheer
boob... 4. dupe, fool, goon, jerk
   5. chump, dunce 6. nitwit
   7. fathead 9. schlemiel, simpleton
boobook... 3. owl 9. morepork
booby hatch... 3. can, jug 4. jail
   6. asylum, cooler, prison
   8. hoosegow, madhouse
   11. institution (mental)
boodle... 3. sop 4. loot, swag
   5. booty, bribe, bunch, crowd, graft,
   money (hush) 6. spoils 8. caboodle
   10. pork barrel 11. counterfeit
boohoo... 3. rob 4. bawl, hoot, weep
   5. shout 8. sailfish
book... 2. mo (abbr) 3. day 4. hire,
   opus, tome 5. album, atlas, Bible,
   canto, diary, folio, liber, novel
   6. agenda, engage, ledger, manual,
   missal, primer, record, sign up,
   volume 7. diurnal, journal, mystery
   8. brochure, libretto, register,
   schedule, songbook, whodunit
   9. paperback, storybook
   10. literature, memorandum
   11. publication
book (pert to)...
   announcement.. 5. blurb
   back.. 5. spine

binder.. 12. bibliopegist
binding devise.. 7. trindle
collector.. 10. bibliothec
   12. bibliomaniac 14. bibliothecaire
cover.. 5. recto 6. jacket
destroyer.. 11. biblioclast
division.. 7. chapter
lore.. 10. bibliology
lover.. 11. bibliophile
one versed in.. 11. bibliognost
page.. 5. folio
seller.. 10. bibliopole (rare books)
sheath.. 5. forel
size.. 6. quarto
stealer.. 11. biblioklept
style.. 6. Aldine 8. Etruscan
   9. Arabesque
treatise.. 8. isagogue
worshiper.. 11. bibliolater
writer.. 13. bibliographer
book (religious)... 4. Ordo 5. Bible,
   Kells, Tobit 6. Esdras, Mormon
   7. Psalter 8. Holy Writ
   9. Apocrypha, Catechism, Testament
   10. Pentateuch, Scriptures
Book of...
   award (Harvard).. 5. detur
   Concord.. 8. Lutheran
   Discipline.. 12. Presbyterian
   Hours.. 5. Horae
   Moses (Laws).. 10. Pentateuch
   Psalms.. 7. Psalter
   the Dead.. 12. Pyramid Texts
boom... 3. hum 4. gain, peal, raft,
   roar, spar, zoom 5. boost, cable,
   speed, sprit, withe 6. thrive, upturn
   7. pontoon, resound, thunder
   8. bowsprit, flourish, increase
   9. cannonade, Golden Age, outrigger
   10. navigation, prosperity
boomerang... 6. resile 7. rebound
   8. backfire, ricochet
Boomer State... 8. Oklahoma
boon... 3. gay 4. bene, gift, good,
   nice 5. favor, jolly 6. jovial, kindly
   7. benefit, gleeful, godsend, present
   8. blessing 9. convivial
   11. benefaction
boor... 3. cad, oaf 4. hick, lout
   5. churl, clown, yokel 6. rustic
   7. bumpkin, cauboge, peasant, ruffian
   9. roughneck, vulgarian
   10. clodhopper, husbandman
boorish... 4. rude 5. gawky, surly
   6. clumsy, rustic, sullen 7. awkward,
   crabbed, loutish, uncouth 8. churlish,
   inurbane, lubberly, ungainly
   9. farmerish, unrefined
   11. countrified
boost... 4. help, hike, lift, plug, push
   5. heist, raise, shove 6. assist,
   thrust 7. commend, hearten, inspire,
   promote, upswing 8. advocate,
   increase 9. promotion, publicize
   10. assistance 11. advancement
   12. commendation
boot... 3. pac 4. kick, pack, sack,
   shoe 5. armor, bonus, jemmy, kamik,
   wader 6. buskin, fumble, rookie,
   sheath 7. dismiss, recruit, trainee
   8. balmoral, enlistee, inductee,
   napoleon 9. discharge

booth... 3. hut, pew 4. crib, loge
5. stall, stand, store 6. manger
11. compartment

booty... 4. gain, loot, pelf, swag
5. graft, prize, spoil 6. spoils
7. pillage, plunder

booze... 4. bout 5. drink, spree
6. liquor 8. potation

boozer... 3. pub, sot 5. toper
6. barfly, bibber, saloon 7. guzzler,
reveler, tippler 8. drunkard
9. alcoholic, inebriate
11. dipsomaniac

Bordeaux, France...
capital.. 7. Gironde
entrance gate.. 16. Porte de
Bourgogne
Roman name.. 9. Burdigala
wine.. 5. Cotes, Medoc, Palus
6. claret (best–known), Graves

border... 3. hem, rim, tip 4. abut,
brow, dado, edge, line, rand, rund
5. bound, brink, flank, limit, marge,
shore, skirt, touch, verge, wings
6. adjoin, fringe, margin, ruffle
7. bordure, confine, flounce, selvage,
valance 8. boundary, frontier,
neighbor 9. periphery 10. borderland,
sidepieces

border (pert to)...
heraldry.. 4. orle 7. bordure
lace.. 5. picot 9. hemstitch
picture.. 3. mat 4. orle
stamps (PO).. 8. tressure
wall.. 4. dado

Border Country (Russ)... 6. Latvia,
Poland 7. Estonia, Finland, Romania
9. Lithuania

bordering... 4. near 6. edging
7. binding 8. abutting, adjacent,
marginal, skirting, trimming
9. adjoining, immediate
10. contiguous

Border State (Civil War Era)...
8. Arkansas, Delaware, Kentucky,
Maryland, Missouri, Virginia
9. Tennessee 13. North Carolina

bore... 3. irk, tap 4. drip, hole, pest,
pill, ream 5. auger, drill, eagre (tidal
wave), weary 6. bother, cavity, pierce
7. caliber, carried 8. diameter,
nuisance, ordnance (anc), puncture,
terebate 9. penetrate, perforate, tidal
wave, worriment 10. capability
11. perforation

boredom... 5. ennui 6. tedium

boring... 3. dry 5. yawny 6. tiring
7. irksome, tedious 8. piercing,
tiresome, wearying 11. penetrating

boring tool... 3. awl, bit 4. rime (Eng)
5. auger, drill 6. gimlet, reamer,
wimble

born... 3. ean, nee 4. bred, foal, lamb
5. calve, hatch, issue 7. hatched,
quicken 9. originate

born (pert to)...
after father's death.. 10. posthumous
again (Theos).. 7. renewed
high.. 8. imperial 11. to the purple
14. porphyrogenite
in the country.. 10. rurigenous
nature.. 6. inborn

well.. 7. eugenic

borne.. 4. held 6. eolian, upheld
7. aeolian, carried, endured
8. produced 9. cherished, supported
10. maintained

borné... 6. narrow 7. limited
12. narrow–minded

Borneo...
aborigine.. 4. Dyak (Dayak), Iban
5. Dusun, Malay
ape.. 9. orangutan (orangoutang)
island of.. 11. Archipelago (Malay)
mountain.. 8. Kinibalu
pirate tribe (anc).. 5. Bajau 9. Samal
Laut
protectorate.. 6. Brunei 7. Sarawak
river.. 7. Rejang
rubber.. 9. gutta susu
sea.. 4. Java, Sulu 10. South China
tree (antproof).. 7. billian

borough... 4. burg, town, ward
5. burgh, manor 6. suffix
8. precinct, township 10. municipium
11. corporation 12. municipality

borrow... 4. copy, take 5. adopt,
steal, touch 8. simulate
10. plagiarize, substitute
11. appropriate

borsch, borscht... 4. soup (beet juice)
6. ragout

borzoi... 9. wolfhound

Bos... 2. ox 3. cow 4. beef, calf, neat
6. cattle 8. ruminant 9. quadruped

bosh... 4. bull, bunk 5. trash
6. humbug, piffle 7. baloney
8. buncombe, falderal, nonsense
9. poppycock 10. balderdash

bosky... 5. braky, bushy, shady, tipsy,
woody 6. woodsy 7. fuddled,
shadowy 11. intoxicated (Eng)

Bosnia...
capital.. 8. Sarajevo
native.. 5. Croat 8. Adriatic, Croatian
race.. 4. tall 14. Slavic–speaking
republic (present).. 10. Yugoslavia
site.. 15. Balkan Peninsula

bosom... 4. bust 5. chest 6. breast,
dickey, spirit 7. cherish, embrace
8. inner man, interior 9. enclosure
(loving), innermost 10. affections
12. heartstrings

boss... 4. dean 6. manage, master
7. foreman 8. director 9. supervise
14. superintendent

boss (pert to)...
architecture.. 4. knob, stud
12. protuberance
politics.. 4. whip 6. leader 7. cacique
(W Indies) 8. dictator
sculpture.. 5. chase, raise 6. emboss,
relief 7. relievo 8. ornament
shield.. 4. umbo

bosthoon (Anglo–Ir)... 4. boor, dolt
5. clout

Boston...
building (Hist).. 11. Faneuil Hall
14. Old North Church
capital of.. 13. Massachusetts
famed names.. 6. Holmes, Lowell
7. Emerson 8. Whittier 9. Hawthorne
10. Longfellow
hero.. 10. Paul Revere

history.. 8. Massacre (1770), Tea
   Party (1773)
Puritan leader.. 8. Winthrop (Gov)
river.. 7. Charles
botany (pert to)...
   development (plant).. 7. peloria
      10. craticular
   research terms.. 7. ecology
      8. cytology, taxonomy 9. pathology
      10. morphology
   science.. 7. biology 9. plant life
Botany Bay...
   colony (original).. 5. penal
   discoverer.. 4. Cook (1770)
   settlers.. 8. convicts (Eng)
   site.. 9. Australia
botch... 3. fix, mar 4. hash, mend,
   mess, mull 5. patch, spoil 6. boggle,
   bungle, fiasco, goof up, muddle
   7. blunder, failure
both... 3. two 4. duad, pair 5. twain
   6. as well 7. equally
bother... 3. ado, ail, nag 4. fuss,
   to-do 5. annoy, tease 6. badger,
   bustle, harass, molest, pester, pother
   7. concern, confuse, fluster, torment,
   trouble 8. bewilder, distress, irritate,
   nuisance 9. commotion
   10. discommode, excitement,
   perplexity 11. botheration,
   disturbance 13. inconvenience
bothersome... 6. trying 7. galling,
   irksome, onerous 8. annoying
   9. difficult, worrisome 10. disturbing
   11. troublesome
both sexes... 7. epicene, sexless
   10. effeminate
bo tree (Buddh)... 5. pipal 6. sacred
   (at Buddh Gaya)
bottle... 3. pig 4. lota, vial 5. cruet,
   flask, gourd, phial 6. carafe, carboy,
   flagon, lagena, matara, vacuum
   7. ampoule (ampule), ampulla (anc),
   costrel, enclose 8. borachio,
   calabash, decanter, preserve
   9. aryballus (anc)
bottom... 3. bed (water) 4. base, glen,
   hulk, less, root, rump, vale, vlei
   5. basin, fanny, floor, marsh, nadir
   6. coulee, hopper (RR) 7. bedrock,
   channel 9. underside 10. nethermost
bottomless... 7. abysmal, abyssal
   8. baseless 9. plumbless, soundless
   10. fathomless 12. unfathomable
boudoir... 7. bedroom, cabinet,
   chamber 10. bedchamber
bouffant... 4. full 7. bulging 9. puffed
   out
bough... 4. fork, limb, spur, twig
   5. shoot, spray, sprig 6. branch
   8. offshoot
bought... 8. boughten (dial)
   9. purchased (see also *buy*)
bouillabaisse... 7. chowder (fish)
boulevard... 4. pike 7. highway
   8. highroad, turnpike
   12. thoroughfare
bounce... 3. hop 4. bang, brag,
   bump, jump, kick, leap, snap
   5. bound, burst, carom, eject, shake,
   thump, verve 6. levity, recoil, spring
   7. bluster, bravado, rebound

8. buoyancy, outburst, ricochet
   9. discharge, lightness 10. resilience
   11. fanfaronade, ostentation,
   springiness 16. lightheartedness
bouncer... 4. liar 5. bully 6. fibber,
   ouster 7. boaster, chucker, whopper
   8. braggart, fanfaron 9. falsehood
bound... 3. hop, run 4. jump, leap,
   skip, tied 5. ambit, limit, speed,
   taped, tiled (secrecy), vault, verge
   6. border, bounce, bourne, domain,
   hurdle, spring, sprint 7. barrier,
   certain, confine, cramped, limited,
   obliged, pledged, rebound, secured,
   trussed 8. beholden, boundary,
   confined, enclosed, frontier, precinct,
   promised, resolved, surround
   9. committed, duty-bound,
   encompass (incompass)
   10. borderland, determined,
   restrained, restricted 11. termination
   12. circumscribe
boundary... 3. end, rim 4. edge, mere
   (obs), mete, term, wall 5. ambit,
   bourn, fence, limit, march, verge
   7. barrier 8. terminus 9. perimeter
   11. conterminal, termination
   13. circumference
bounder... 3. cad 4. snob 6. rotter
   7. epicier, parvenu, upstart
bounding (Mus)... 8. saltando
boundless... 4. vast 7. endless
   8. infinite, termless 9. limitless,
   unlimited 10. unconfined
   11. illimitable 12. interminable,
   unfathomable
bounds... 4. pale 6. frames, limits,
   skirts 7. borders, margins
   8. confines, outlines 9. outskirts
   10. delineated 11. limitations
bounteous... 5. ample 6. freely, lavish
   7. liberal 8. generous, prodigal
   9. bountiful, plentiful 10. munificent
   11. extravagant
bountiful... 4. rich 7. copious, fertile,
   liberal, teeming, uberous
   8. abundant, fruitful, generous,
   prolific 9. bounteous, exuberant,
   luxuriant, plentiful
bounty... 3. fee 4. gift 5. bonus
   6. reward 7. largess, premium,
   subsidy 8. gratuity, solatium, sportula
   9. pourboire 10. generosity, liberality
   11. beneficence 12. compensation
bouquet... 4. odor, posy 5. aroma,
   cigar, spray 7. corsage, flowers,
   incense, nosegay, perfume
   9. fragrance, redolence
   10. compliment
Bourbon, bourbon...
   ancient.. 7. Reunion (Isl)
   dynasty.. 5. Spain 6. France, Naples
   famed personage.. 4. Duke
      13. French General
   famed ruins.. 7. castles (Dukes')
   liquor.. 6. whisky (whiskey)
   rose.. 9. Le Phoenix
bourd... 3. fun 4. jest 7. mockery
bourdon... 4. stop (organ) 5. baton,
   music (bagpipe), spear, staff
   6. burden (Fr), cudgel
bourgeois... 4. type (size)

8. commoner 9. common man,
plutocrat 10. capitalist
  11. middle–class, proletarian
bourn, bourne... 3. aim 4. goal, port
5. bound, brook, limit, realm
6. arroyo, stream 7. rivulet
8. boundary 11. destination
bourock... 3. hut 4. heap (stone)
5. crowd, mound 7. cluster
Bourse... 5. Board 8. Exchange
13. Stock Exchange
bouse... 3. cup 4. haul (Naut), swig,
tope 5. booze, drink, heave
6. beaker 7. carouse
bouser... 5. toper 6. boozer, bursar
7. fuddler, swigger
bout... 2. go 3. act, war 4. coup,
fray, game, spar, turn 5. cycle, fight,
match, revel, round, scrap, set–to,
spree, trial 6. fracas, inning, series,
stroke 7. attempt, circuit, contest,
exploit 8. conflict, maneuver, rotation
9. encounter 10. enterprise, prize
fight 11. celebration
boutade... 4. whim 5. dance, prank
7. caprice 8. outbreak
  11. composition (Mus)
boutonniere... 6. flower 7. bouquet,
nosegay 8. incision 10. buttonhole
bovine... 2. ox 3. Bos, cow, yak
4. bull, dull, goat, kine, neat
5. bison, dogie, steer, stirk, zebus
6. catalo, cattle, oxlike, stolid, stupid
7. bullock, cattalo, taurine, vaccine
8. maverick, sluggish 10. complacent
11. beef–brained
bow... 3. arc, bob, nod 4. arch, beak,
bend, knot, node, prow 5. bulge,
curve, debut, embow, kneel, stoop,
yield 6. assent, convex, curtsy,
encore, kowtow, salaam, submit,
weapon 7. curtain (Theat), incline,
rainbow 8. crossbow, greeting
9. obeisance 11. fiddlestick 12. bow
and scrape
bow (out)... 4. exit 6. depart
7. concede, dismiss
Bow Bells (pert to)...
  area.. 10. cockneydom
  bells of.. 9. Bow Church (St Mary le
   Bow)
  city.. 6. London
bowels... 3. pit 4. guts 5. abyss,
chasm, depth 7. innards, insides,
viscera 8. entrails, interior (earth)
10. compassion (Shak), tenderness
bower... 5. abode, arbor, cards
(game), kiosk 6. alcove, pandal
7. retreat, shelter 11. summerhouse
bowfin... 4. Amia 7. mudfish
bowhead (Arctic)... 10. Right whale
Bowie, bowie (pert to)...
  instrument.. 5. knife
  knife inventor.. 5. Bowie (James)
  Scottish.. 3. tub 4. cask 8. milk pail
  State nickname.. 8. Arkansas
bowkail... 4. kale (kail) 7. cabbage
bowl... 3. cup, jug 4. ball, roll, vase
5. arena, basin, kitty (poker), mazer,
rogan 6. cavity, crater, hollow, patina
(anc), vessel 7. stadium 8. washbowl
9. washbasin 10. hippodrome,

receptacle 12. amphitheater
Bowl (sports)...
  Abilene.. 5. Pecan
  Atlanta.. 5. Peach
  Dallas.. 6. Cotton
  El Paso.. 3. Sun
  Honolulu.. 4. Hula
  Houston.. 10. Bluebonnet
  Jacksonville.. 5. Gator
  Memphis.. 7. Liberty
  Miami.. 6. Orange
  Mobile.. 6. Senior
  New Orleans.. 5. Sugar
  Orlando.. 9. Tangerine
  Pasadena.. 4. Rose
  Sacramento.. 8. Camellia
bowlegged... 6. valgus
bowler... 3. hat 5. derby 6. kegler
7. trundle
bowling... 4. ball, rink 5. alley, green,
spare 6. strike 7. rolling, tenpins
8. ninepins 10. greensward,
playground
Bowling Green... 4. Park (Ky, NY)
bowsprit... 3. jib 4. boom 6. steeve
box... 2. ro (Jap) 3. bin, pew, pyx
4. arca (alms), cage, case, cist, cuff,
kist, kite, loge, safe, spar, tray
5. brace (faro), caddy (tea), cheat,
crate, stall, vault 6. buffet, carton,
casket, coffin, encase 7. confine,
enclose 8. bungalow 9. fisticuff
11. compartment
box (pert to)...
  alms.. 4. arca
  bed.. 7. springs
  cosmetic.. 4. inro
  floating.. 3. car (for fish)
  lifesaving.. 9. faking box
  railroad.. 6. boxcar 8. box wagon
  resistance.. 8. rheostat
  sewing.. 5. plait, pleat
  sleigh.. 4. pung
  sports.. 5. score
  tea.. 5. caddy 8. canister
  theater.. 4. loge, seat
  tree.. 8. Buxaceae
boxer... 3. dog, pug 5. champ
6. miller 7. bruiser, fighter, sparrer
8. derby hat, pugilist 11. fisticuffer
12. prizefighter 13. militia member
(Chin)
boxer weight... 3. fly 5. heavy, light
6. bantam, middle, welter 7. feather
10. light heavy
boxing... 4. bout 5. match, set–to
7. contest, crating 8. pugilism,
sparring 10. encasement, fisticuffs
12. shadowboxing
boy... 2. bo 3. bat, bus, lad, tad, tot
4. nino, page, puer 5. child, gamin,
knave, rogue, water, youth
6. garçon, laddie, master, rascal,
shaver, urchin, varlet 7. callant,
gossoon 8. muchacho
boy (pert to)...
  book author.. 5. Alger, Henty
  errand.. 4. page 9. messenger
  friend.. 4. beau 10. sweetheart
  interjection.. 5. Oh boy
  organization.. 6. Scouts
  Scout founder.. 11. Baden–Powell

street . . **4.** Arab **6.** urchin
boycott . . . **3.** ban **6.** oppose, strike
   9. blackball, ostracize
brace . . . **3.** leg, tie, two **4.** bind, cord,
   gird, pair, prop, span, stay, yoke
   5. spale, staff, stave, strut **6.** couple
   7. bandage, bracket, fulcrum, refresh,
   rigging, support **8.** encircle
   9. reinforce, stimulate **10.** invigorate,
   recuperate, strengthen
bracelet . . . **5.** armil, armor, chain
   6. sankha **7.** armilla **8.** handcuff,
   vambrace **10.** calombigas
bracer . . . **4.** prop **5.** tonic **7.** reviver,
   support **8.** pick–me–up, roborant
   9. stimulant
bracing . . . **5.** crisp, tonic **10.** salubrious
   11. stimulating **12.** invigorating
bracken . . . **4.** fern **5.** brake, plaid
bracket . . . **4.** mark **5.** ancon, angle,
   group, strut **6.** corbel, sconce
   7. fixture **11.** electrolier
brackish . . . **4.** foul **5.** salty **7.** saltish
   8. nauseous **11.** distasteful
bract . . . **4.** leaf **5.** glume, palea, palet
   6. spathe **8.** bractlet **9.** bracteole
brad . . . **3.** pin **4.** nail **5.** sprig
brae . . . **4.** bank, down, hill, moor
   5. slope **6.** valley **8.** hillside
brag . . . **4.** crow **5.** bluff, boast, vaunt
   6. flaunt **7.** blow off, bluster,
   deceive, roister, swagger **8.** braggart
   9. gasconade **11.** braggadocio
braggart . . . **4.** brag **6.** crower
   7. boaster **8.** boastful, fanfaron
   9. blusterer, swaggerer
   11. braggadocio **12.** swashbuckler
bragging . . . **11.** thrasonical
Brahma . . . **3.** God **4.** fowl **5.** Hindu
Brahman (pert to) . . .
   learned . . **6.** pundit
   precept . . **5.** sutra **8.** netineti
   sacred book . . **4.** Veda
   Sanskrit scholar . . **6.** pundit
   Supreme soul . . **6.** Brahma
   title . . **3.** Aya
   Trinity . . **4.** Siva **6.** Brahma, Vishnu
   woman created by . . **6.** Alalya
Brahmin . . . **4.** prig, snob **7.** egghead
   8. highbrow **10.** high–hatter
   12. intellectual
braid . . . **3.** cue **4.** cord, gimp, hair,
   plat, trim **5.** lacet, orris, plait, pleat,
   queue, tress, twist, weave **6.** oxreim,
   sennit **7.** entwine, outline, pigtail,
   topknot **8.** ornament, soutache
   9. interlace **10.** interweave
brain . . . **4.** head, mind, nous
   6. psyche, reason **9.** intellect,
   mentality **10.** encephalon, vital organ
brain (pert to) . . .
   canal . . **4.** iter
   case . . **3.** pan **5.** skull **7.** cranium
   division . . **8.** cerebrum **10.** cerebellum
   11. pons Varolii **16.** medulla
   oblongata
   matter . . **4.** alba, dura, tela
   operation . . **6.** trepan **8.** trephine
   term . . **4.** lobe, lura **6.** sulcus
   7. fissure **9.** ventricle
   11. convolution
   tumor . . **6.** glioma

X–ray . . **14.** encephalograph
brainless . . . **4.** dumb **5.** dizzy, giddy,
   silly **6.** unwise **7.** asinine, foolish,
   witless **9.** senseless **10.** unthinking
   11. thoughtless **14.** scatterbrained
brainy . . . **5.** smart **6.** bright, clever
   9. brilliant
brake . . . **4.** cage, curb, drag, fern, reef,
   skid, trap **5.** check, delay, snare
   6. bridle, retard **7.** dilemma, thicket
   9. canebrake **10.** decelerate
bramble . . . **4.** burr **5.** berry, brier,
   shrub (prickly), thorn **6.** nettle
   7. prickle, thicket **9.** brierbush
   10. blackberry **12.** brambleberry
branch . . . **3.** arm, set **4.** axil, fork,
   limb, rame, stem, twig, wing
   5. bough, class, frond, ramus, shoot,
   spray, sprig, vimen, withe **6.** divide,
   member, ramify, sprout, stolon,
   stream, switch **7.** descent, diverge,
   lineage **8.** category, division, offshoot
   9. affiliate, bloodline, filiation
   10. department, descendant,
   triskelion (three branches)
Branchiata (Group) . . . **6.** fishes
   9. Crustacea **10.** Amphibians
brand . . . **4.** burn, iron, kind, mark,
   sear, smit **5.** label, stamp, sword,
   torch **6.** smirch, stigma **7.** earmark,
   feature, hot iron, quality **8.** gridiron
   (Hist), hallmark **9.** trademark
   10. stigmatize
brandish . . . **5.** shake, swing, wield
   6. flaunt **7.** flutter, glitter **8.** flourish
brandy . . . **6.** cognac **7.** rosolio (cordial)
   8. rossolis **11.** aguardiente
brash . . . **4.** dash, rain, rash **5.** gruff,
   saucy, storm **6.** scurry **7.** brittle
   (lumber) **8.** impudent, tactless
   9. impetuous
brass . . . **4.** cash, gall **5.** alloy, braze,
   cheek, money, nerve, plate **6.** latten,
   ormolu, platen **8.** brass hat, officers,
   sisterce (anc coin) **9.** impudence
   10. instrument (wind)
brass (wind instrument) . . . **5.** bugle
   6. cornet, lituus (anc) **7.** althorn,
   brasses, clarion, saxhorn, trumpet
   8. trombone **9.** saxophone
   10. flügelhorn, French horn
brasserie . . . **6.** saloon **7.** brewery
   8. beer shop
brassy . . . **4.** bold **6.** aerose, brazen
   8. impudent
brat . . . **3.** bib, elf, imp **4.** film, minx,
   scum **5.** apron, bairn, child, cloak,
   minor **6.** mantle **7.** garment
   8. clothing **9.** offspring **14.** enfant
   terrible, whippersnapper
brattice . . . **7.** support **9.** partition
   (mining) **10.** breastwork
bravado . . . **6.** bounce, daring, defial
   7. bluster, bombast, bravery, bravura
   8. defiance **11.** braggadocio
brave . . . **4.** bold, buck, dare, game,
   hero, meet **5.** boast, bravo, bully,
   front, manly, showy, stout **6.** daring,
   endure, heroic, Indian **7.** Amerind,
   gallant, soldier, spartan, valiant,
   warrior **8.** confront, fearless, intrepid,
   valorous **10.** courageous, untimorous

12. stouthearted

bravery... 5. valor 7. bravado, bravura, courage

bravo... 3. mug 4. good, thug 5. rough, tough 6. bandit 7. gorilla, ruffian 8. assassin 9. blusterer, cutthroat, roisterer, roughneck, swaggerer 11. exclamation

bravura... 4. dash 6. daring 7. bravado, bravery 10. brilliance (Mus), confidence

brawl... 3. row 4. fray, fury, rage, riot 5. broil, fight, furor, scold 6. affray, clamor, fracas, hubbub, rumpus, shindy, tumult, uproar 7. dispute, quarrel, rampage, turmoil, wrangle 10. hullabaloo, turbulence 11. altercation, embroilment

brawny... 5. beefy, burly, lusty, thewy 6. fleshy, robust, sinewy, strong, sturdy 7. callous 8. muscular, powerful, stalwart 9. corpulent

bray... 4. beat, blare, bleat, grind, neigh 5. heehaw, powder, thrash, whinny 9. pulverize, triturate 12. disintegrate

braze... 4. weld 5. plate (with metal) 6. solder

brazen... 4. bold, pert 5. brass, brave, harsh 6. brassy, cheeky, harden 7. aweless, callous 8. immodest, impudent, indurate, insolent, metallic 9. bold–faced, shameless, unabashed 10. unblushing 13. bronze–colored, harsh–sounding

brazier... 6. brazer 7. hibachi 8. barbecue, gridiron 10. money chest (anc)

brazil... 3. red 4. wood (hard) 8. dyestuff

Brazil... see also *Brazilian*

capital.. 8. Brasilia 12. Rio de Janeiro (old)

city.. 5. Bahia, Belem, Goyaz 6. Recife, Santos 8. Sao Paulo 9. Horizonte 11. Porto Alegre, Sao Salvador

discoverer.. 6. Cabral (1500)

Falls (world Wonder).. 7. Iguassu

lake.. 12. Lago dos Patos

product.. 6. coffee

river.. 5. Negro 6. Amazon, Branco, Paranà 7. Madeira, Orinoco 8. Paraguay 9. Francisco, Tocantins

Brazilian (pert to)...

aborigine.. 5. Carib

ant (powerful).. 9. tucandera

bird.. 3. ani, ara 5. arara, macaw 6. cuckoo, darter, tiribo 7. maracan, sierema

crab (land).. 8. horseman

dance.. 6. maxixe

drink.. 5. assai

flycatcher.. 6. yetapa

Indian.. 4. Anta 5. Arara, Araua, Guana 6. Tupian 8. Araquayu, Arawakan (tribe)

mammal.. 5. tapir

nut.. 9. niggertoe

parrot.. 3. ara 5. macaw 6. tiriba

plant.. 4. yaje 5. caroa 7. ayapana (Med)

tree.. 3. apa 4. anda (oil), jara 5. assai (palm) 6. embuia, satiné 7. araroba, gomavel, seringa (rubber), wallaba 8. bakupari 10. barbatimao

weight.. 4. onza 5. libra 6. arroba 7. quintal

breach... 3. gap 4. rent, rift 5. break, burst, chasm, cleft, split 6. schism 7. caesura, dispute, quarrel, rupture 8. fracture, solecism 9. violation 10. disruption, falling–out, infraction, separation 12. infringement, interruption 16. misunderstanding

bread... 4. cush, food, gelt, loaf, pain (obs), pone, rusk 5. azyme, miche, panis, toady, toast, tommy 6. damper, panada, sippet 7. hoecake, matzoth 9. eucharist (part of), sourbread 10. livelihood

bread (pert to)...

basket.. 7. stomach

bread and butter.. 5. plate 6. letter (of thanks), pickle, staple 7. prosaic 8. juvenile

fruit.. 3. nut 4. tree 7. castana 8. chestnut

winner.. 6. earner, toiler, worker 7. workman 10. wage earner

break... 3. gap 4. dash, knap, luck, lull, rent, rift, ruin, rush, slip, snap, stop 5. blank, burst, cleft, lapse, letup, pause, smash, train 6. breach, chance, change, depose, escape, hiatus, injury, lacuna, market (Finan), recess, subdue, weaken 7. blunder, caesura (cesura), disrupt, getaway, respite, rupture, shatter, violate 8. bad break, bankrupt, breakage, breather, fracture, interval 9. interlude, jail break, violation 10. depreciate, falling–out, infraction, suspension 12. intermission, interruption

breakdown... 3. cry, sob 4. bawl, raze, weep 5. crush 6. boohoo, divide, master, reduce, revolt, subdue 7. analyze, crackup, debacle, dissect, failure, resolve, unnerve 8. analysis, classify, collapse, separate 9. cataclysm, decompose, diaeresis, overwhelm, subdivide 10. dissection, impairment, revolution

breakfast... 8. dejeuner 10. chota hazri

break in... 4. open, tame 5. enter, force, train 6. butt in, subdue 7. barge in, intrude, prepare 9. interrupt 10. housebreak

break up... 4. cure, rift, ruin 5. decay, leave, smash, spall, split, upset 7. adjourn, atomize, crumble, disband, relieve, scatter, shatter 8. disperse, dissolve, separate, unsettle 9. decompose 10. demobilize, dispersion, disruption 11. disorganize, dissolution 12. disintegrate

breakwater... 4. dike, mole, pier 5. jetty, jutty 6. refuge, riprap 7. sea wall 8. buttress 10. embankment 11. obstruction

bream... 4. fish, scup 5. clean (Naut)

breast... 4. bust, soul, teat 5. bosom,
cheat, gland (mammary), heart
6. spirit, thorax 8. inner man
9. encounter

breast (pert to)...
absence of.. 7. amastia
bone.. 6. ratite 7. sternum
breastlike.. 7. mastoid
plate.. 4. Urim 5. armor, ephod
6. gorget, lorica 7. poitrel
12. breastsummer
works.. 7. defense, parapet, railing
(Naut), ravelin 8. mantelet
9. banquette

breath... 3. air 4. fume, life, odor,
pant, puff, wind 5. draft, pause,
prana, scent, smell, touch, vapor,
whiff 6. breeze, caress, flatus,
pneuma, spirit 7. halitus, respite,
whisper 8. breather 9. emanation,
ozostomia, utterance 10. exhalation
11. respiration

breathe... 3. say, tip 4. gulp, live,
mean, pneo (comb form), rest, sigh,
tell 5. exist, imbue, imply, scent,
smell, snuff 6. evince, exhale, infuse,
inhale, let out, reveal 7. bespeak,
divulge, emanate, instill (instil),
pervade, respire, suspire, whisper
8. aspirate, indicate

breathe (pert to)...
comb form.. 4. pnea, pneo
convulsively.. 4. sigh
hard.. 4. pant
one's last.. 3. die 6. expire, perish
7. decease, succumb
vengeance.. 9. retaliate

breather... 4. lull, rest 5. break,
pause, truce 6. recess 7. interim,
respite 9. interlude 12. intermission

breathing... 5. alive, vital 6. living,
zoetic 7. animate, panting, respite
8. animated 9. conscious, phonation,
utterance 10. aspiration
11. respiration, respiratory, ventilation
12. articulation

breathing (pert to)...
apertures.. 5. stoma 8. spiracle
morbid.. 4. rale 7. stridor
8. rhonchus
painful.. 8. dyspnoea
pause.. 7. caesura
smooth.. 4. lene

breathless... 4. awed, dead, gone,
keen 5. eager 6. ardent, fervid,
winded 7. airless, demised, fervent
8. deceased, lifeless, windless,
wordless 9. impatient 10. astonished,
speechless, spellbound

bred... 4. hybrid, inbred, reared, tablet
(compressed) 7. lowbred, mongrel
8. exogamic, purebred 9. autogamic,
crossbred, endogamic, half-caste,
interbred 11. half-blooded,
impregnated, inseminated
12. thoroughbred

bree... 4. brow 5. broth, scare
6. liquor 7. eyebrow 9. commotion
11. disturbance

breech... 4. doup, rump, tall 5. fanny,
stern 6. bottom 8. buttocks
9. posterior, underside

breeches... 5. chaps, jeans, pants,
trews 8. britches, jodhpurs, trousers
10. pantaloons 12. galligaskins
(jocular)

breed... 3. ilk 4. kind, race, rear, sort
5. beget, brood, caste, class, mixed,
raise, stock, train, tribe 6. family
7. descent, educate, lineage,
mongrel, produce 8. engender,
generate, instruct 9. originate,
posterity, procreate, propagate
10. crossbreed

breeding... 6. polish 7. culture,
decorum, exogamy, manners, raising,
rearing 8. autogamy, endogamy,
hatching, training 9. education,
fostering, gentility 10. deportment,
upbringing 11. instruction,
procreation, propagation

breeding place... 4. nest 5. nidus
7. brooder 8. hatchery 9. incubator
10. birthplace

breeze... 3. air, row 4. aura, pirr,
snap, stir, wind 5. cinch, rumor
6. squall, zephyr 7. ill wind, whisper
8. duck soup, pushover
9. commotion 11. disturbance

breezy... 4. airy, spry 5. blowy, brisk,
gusty, windy 6. drafty, jaunty, lively
7. squally 8. animated, blustery,
spirited 9. vivaceous 12. lighthearted

Brehon Law... 4. eric (anc)
10. Senchus Mor 12. Book of Aicill

breve... 4. note (Mus), writ 5. brief,
order 7. compose

brevet... 4. fiat 5. ukase 6. decree
7. warrant 10. commission
11. certificate (teaching)

breveté... 8. patented

breviary... 6. manual, ritual
7. compend, epitome

brevity... 9. briefness, shortness,
terseness 11. conciseness,
transcience 12. succinctness

brew... 3. ale, mix 4. grog, plot
5. hatch, steep 6. cook up, foment,
gather, menace, scheme 7. concoct,
distill (distil) 8. contrive, threaten
9. aqua vitae

brewer's grain... 4. corn, malt
6. barley

brewer's yeast... 4. barm 6. leaven

bribe... 3. oil, sop 5. bonus
6. boodle, buy off, grease, suborn
9. hush money

bric-a-brac... 6. curios 7. artware
8. antiques, trinkets 9. artifacts,
objet d'art 11. knickknacks

bric-a-brac cabinet... 7. étagère,
whatnot

brick... 3. bat 4. dobe, tile 5. adobe,
stone 6. pament (pamment)
7. clinker 8. hardness

brick (pert to)...
color.. 3. red 7. Saravan
kiln.. 5. clamp
layer.. 4. cad (helper) 5. mason
laying.. 8. toothing
slang.. 3. pip 4. lulu 5. dilly, peach
6. corker, winner 8. jim-dandy
10. sweetheart 11. crackerjack
12. lollapaloosa

unburned.. 5. samel

brickbat... 4. rock 5. stone 7. affront, missile, offense 9. indignity

bridal (pert to)...
chest.. 9. trousseau
flower.. 13. orange blossom
ode, song.. 9. Brautlied
11. Epithalamon (anc)
portion.. 3. dot 5. dower, dowry (dowery)
rite.. 7. wedding 8. marriage, nuptials

bridge... 3. tie 4. arch, bond, link, pons, pont, span 5. unite 7. connect, passage (Mus), pontoon, viaduct 9. structure 13. steppingstone

bridge (pert to)... 4. deck, game, nose 5. magas, truss 6. phoebe (bird) 7. bascule, trestle 9. dentistry 10. ponticello (Mus)

bridge, historic...
Bridge of Boats.. 10. Hellespont
Bridge of Sighs.. 6. Venice (Doge's Palace) 7. Al Sirat (Moslem, over infernal fire)
Norse Myth.. 7. Bifrost (rainbow)
Old Bridge.. 12. Ponte Vecchio (Florence It 1345)

Bridge game... 3. bid 4. pass, ruff, slam 6. honors, points, renege, tenace 7. finesse 9. part–score

bridle... 3. bit 4. cord (kite), curb, rein 5. check, guide, smirk 6. fetter, govern, halter, master, simper, subdue 7. harness, manacle, repress, shackle, snaffle 8. cavesson, headgear, noseband, restrain, suppress 9. hackamore, headstall, restraint

brief... 4. curt, plan, writ 5. breve, charm, pithy, short, terse 6. report 7. compact, concise, laconic, summary 8. fleeting, instruct, succinct 9. condensed, ephemeral, summarize, transient 10. compendium, short-lived, transitory 11. compendious 14. inconsiderable

brier, briar... 4. burr, pipe 5. heath, shrub, spine, thorn 7. bramble, bruyère, clotbur, prickle, sticker, thistle 8. adherent 11. French brier

brig... 4. boat 6. vessel 10. guardhouse

brigade... 4. unit 6. troops 7. company 8. regiment

brigand... 5. rover, thief 6. bandit, dacoit, pirate, robber 7. bedouin, cateran, ladrone 8. picaroon 10. highwayman

bright... 3. apt, gay 4. naif, rosy 5. alert, beamy, fresh, lucid, nitid, palmy, sleek, smart, sunny, vivid, witty 6. brainy, clever, florid, garish, golden 7. halcyon, radiant, shining, unfaded 8. cheerful, colorful, flashing, gleaming, luminous, lustrous, splendid 9. brilliant, effulgent, refulgent, sparkling 10. auspicious, epiphanous, glistening, glittering, optimistic 11. intelligent, resplendent

brightness... 5. sheen 6. luster 7. sparkle 8. radiance, splendor 9. alertness, clearness, smartness 10. brilliance 12. cheerfulness, colorfulness, pleasantness

brilliance, brilliancy... 5. éclat, glory 6. luster 7. glitter, oriency, success 8. radiance, splendor 9. smartness, vividness 10. brightness, cleverness

brilliant... 5. smart, vivid, witty 6. bright 7. eminent, radiant, shining 8. gorgeous, meteoric, splendid 9. refulgent, sparkling 10. glittering 11. illustrious

brilliant group... 6. galaxy

brim... 3. hem, lip, rim 4. edge 5. brink, marge, verge 6. border, margin 7. selvage

brine... 3. sea 4. main, salt 5. brack, ocean, tears 6. pickle 7. the deep 12. preservative

bring... 3. get 4. bear, cost, haul, lead 5. carry, fetch, go get, yield 6. convey, entail, induce, obtain 7. contain, involve, require 8. comprise 9. transport

bring about... 2. do 4. make 5. cause 6. create, effect 7. achieve, produce 8. generate 9. instigate 10. accomplish, consummate, effectuate

bring around... 4. cure, heal, ween 5. renew, sober 6. revive 7. convert, restore, win over 8. persuade 10. rejuvenate

bring back... 5. fetch 6. recall, return, revive 7. restore 8. rekindle, remember, retrieve 9. recollect, resurrect

bring forth... 3. ean 4. bear, rise 5. beget, breed, cause, educe, hatch, spawn, yield 6. adduce, elicit, reveal 7. develop, produce 8. disclose, fructify, generate, manifest

bring forward... 4. cite 5. offer 6. adduce, broach, submit 7. advance, improve, promote, propose 8. manifest 9. introduce

bring into...
bondage.. 7. enslave
court.. 7. arraign
harmony.. 6. attune
position.. 5. align, aline
union.. 9. correlate

bring together... 5. amass, group 6. gather 7. cluster, compile, reunite 8. assemble 9. harmonize, reconcile 10. accumulate

bring to light... 4. find 5. trace 6. elicit, expose, reveal 7. uncover, unearth 8. disclose, discover

bring to mind... 6. recall, remind 8. look like, remember, resemble

bring to pass... 2. do 5. cause 6. author, father 9. originate 10. accomplish, effectuate

bring up... 4. rear, spew 5. drill, raise, train, vomit 6. foster, muster 7. advance, educate, nurture, propose 9. challenge, condition, cultivate 10. discipline 11. regurgitate

bring up to date... 4. post 6. update 9. modernize 10. streamline

brink... 3. lip, rim 4. bank, brow, edge, near 5. ditch, marge, skirt, verge 6. border, margin

briny... 3. sea 4. salt 5. salty 6. saline 8. brackish

Brisbane, capital of... 10. Queensland (Austral)

Brisbane tree... 3. box 8. quandong

brisk... 3. gay 4. cold, fast, keen, racy, spry, yern 5. agile, alert, alive, crisp, fresh, peart, quick, sharp, tangy, zippy 6. breezy, lively, nimble, snappy 7. caustic, pungent 8. animated, forceful, spirited, vigorous 9. energetic, sprightly, vivacious 11. stimulating

bristle... 4. barb, hair, seta 5. anger, seton 6. chaeta, palpus, ruffle, rumple, see red, setula, setule 7. acicula, prickle, stubble

bristling... 5. angry 6. horrid (anc) 7. horrent 9. offensive

bristly... 5. rough, setal 6. hispid, setose, thorny 7. prickly, scopate, unshorn 8. acicular, echinate 11. bristlelike

Bristol...
church (England's finest).. 15. St Mary Redcliffe
fashion.. 6. ataunt 9. shipshape
library.. 6. oldest (British Isles)
milk.. 6. sherry

Britain...
name, ancient.. 6. Albion
name, modern.. 12. British Isles, Commonwealth, Great Britain 13. United Kingdom
name, Roman.. 9. Brittania
native.. 5. Iceni (tribe), Jutes, Picts, Scots 6. Angles 7. Britons, Silures
native (sl).. 5. limey (limy), tommy 7. Blighty
sea.. 5. Irish, North 8. Atlantic, Hebrides

British (pert to)... see also *English*
battle.. 8. Hastings
boat (anc).. 7. coracle
cavalry.. 8. yeomanry
earldom (Egypt).. 7. Khartum (1898)
emblem.. 4. lion
fish.. 8. dragonet (gobylike)
oak.. 5. robur
Order of.. 9. The Garter
prison.. 4. gaol
pudding.. 4. suet 9. Yorkshire
tavern.. 3. pub 9. beerhouse, jerry shop
thief (wharf).. 6. tosher
Z (letter).. 3. Zed

British people...
author.. 6. Austen, Barrie, Jonson 7. Dickens
buccaneer.. 4. Kidd 6. Morgan
explorer.. 4. Cook, Ross 6. Baffin 7. Stanley 9. Vancouver 11. Livingstone
hero (sea).. 6. Nelson
king (legend, Myth).. 3. Lud 4. Beli, Bran, Brut 7. Belenus
painter.. 8. Rossetti

philosopher.. 7. Russell (Bertrand)
physicist.. 5. Boyle
poet.. 7. Chaucer 8. Browning, Tennyson 9. Masefield
soldier.. 7. Redcoat (Hist)

Brittany... 7. Armoric 8. Bretagne

brittle... 4. weak 5. brash, candy, crisp, frail 6. feeble, infirm, slight 7. fragile, friable 8. delicate, insecure 9. breakable, frangible 11. shatterable

broad... 4. free, girl, lake (Eng), wide 5. ample, large, roomy, thick, wench 7. breadth, diffuse, general, liberal 8. spacious, strumpet, sweeping, tabulate, tolerant 9. expansive, extensive 10. collective, commodious, indefinite, voluminous 13. comprehensive

broad (pert to)...
arrow.. 5. pheon (Her) 6. stigma 8. insignia
footed.. 8. platypod
hearted.. 8. generous 11. magnanimous
minded.. 7. liberal 8. tolerant 9. receptive

broaden... 5. swell, widen 6. dilate, expand, extend, spread 7. augment, enlarge, ennoble 8. increase

broadly... 3. far 6. widely 10. far and wide 11. extensively 12. indefinitely, right and left

broadside... 4. guns, side 6. folder 7. gunfire, quarter, surface 8. enfilade, sideways 10. broadsheet, floodlight 11. breadthwise

broadsword... 7. cutlass, Ferrara 8. claymore, scimitar

Brobdingnagian... 5. giant, titan 8. colossal, gigantic 10. gargantuan

brocade... 6. broché, fabric 8. baudekin 9. baldachin

brochan... 7. oatmeal 8. porridge

brochure... 5. tract 6. folder 7. booklet, leaflet 8. chapbook, pamphlet

brod... 3. awl 4. goad, pike, urge 5. thorn 6. sprout 9. incentive

brode, brodee... 11. embroidered

brodyaga... 7. vagrant 8. vagabond

brogan, brogue... 4. shoe

brogue... 4. burr 5. twang 6. accent 7. dialect

broil... 4. cook, fray, fume 5. brawl, grill, melee 6. affray, braise (braize), scorch 7. contest, discord, dispute, quarrel 8. conflict, grillade, scramble 10. contention, dissension, turbulence 11. altercation, embroilment

broke... 4. flat 6. busted, ruined 8. bankrupt, strapped 9. destitute, insolvent, penniless

broken... 4. tame 5. broke, bumpy, burst, rough, tamed 6. chined, ruined, shaken, uneven, zigzag 7. crushed, décousu, severed, subdued 8. bankrupt, detached, impaired, ruptured, sporadic, weakened 9. conquered, dispersed, irregular, shattered, unsettled 10. incoherent, incomplete

11. fragmentary, housebroken, interrupted 12. disconnected, domesticated, intermittent 13. discontinuous

broken pottery (anc)... 5. shard (sherd) 8. potsherd

broker... 5. agent 6. dealer, jobber 7. cambist, scalper (ticket) 8. marriage 9. go–between, insurance, middleman, schatchen 10. pawnbroker, real estate 11. internuncio, stockbroker 12. intermediary

brokerage... 3. fee 4. agio 6. charge 8. agiotage, business 9. exactment 10. commission

brolly... 5. chute 8. umbrella 9. brollyhop, parachute

bromide... 4. corn 5. trite 6. Babbit, cliché, halide, old hat 8. banality, sedative 9. conformer, criticism, platitude 10. conformist, Philistine 15. conventionalist

bronco, broncho... 4. pony 5. horse 6. cayuse 7. mustang 10. broomstick

bronco, bucking... 9. estrapade

broncobuster, bronchobuster... 6. cowboy 7. trainer, vaquero

Bronx cheer... 3. boo 4. hiss, razz 9. raspberry

bronze... 3. aes (anc), tan 5. alloy, color 6. ormolu, patina, suntan 9. sculpture

Bronze Age... 9. Neolithic 11. Aeneolithic

Bronze Plaques (pert to)...
called.. 14. Eugubine Tables (Iguvine Tables, 1444)
number.. 5. Seven
site.. 6. Gubbio (It)

brooch... 3. bar, pin 4. boss, ouch 5. cameo, clasp 6. fibula (anc), shield 8. pectoral 9. breastpin

brood... 3. fry, nye, set 4. kind, mope, mull, muse, nide, race 5. breed, covey, folks, hatch, pride (lions), young 6. clutch, family, farrow (pigs), litter, ménage, people, strain 7. lineage, progeny, reflect 8. cogitate, incubate, meditate, ruminate, soredium 9. household, offspring 11. contemplate

brood over... 4. fret, mope 5. hover 6. grieve, ponder 7. agonize 8. remember

brook... 3. run 4. bear, beck, burn, rill, sike 5. abide, bourn, creek, crick 6. arroyo, endure, rillet, runlet, suffer 7. freshet, rivulet 8. brooklet 9. arroyuelo, streamlet

broom... 5. besom, shrub, spart, sweep, whisk

broth... 4. soup 5. stock 6. brewis 8. bouillon, consommé

brother... 3. fra 4. mate, monk 5. friar, title 6. frater, friend, member, oblate 8. alter ego, relative 9. associate 11. counterpart

brotherhood... 5. lodge 7. kinship, society 8. sodality 10. fellowship, fraternity 11. association

12. fraternalism 13. confraternity

brotherly... 4. kind 6. tender 8. friendly 9. fraternal 11. sympathetic 12. affectionate

Brothers... 7. Danites (Mormon) 9. Christian (RCCh)

brothers and sisters (same family)... 8. siblings

brow... 3. cap, rim, tip, top 4. brae 5. brink, crest, crown 6. border, summit, tiptop, visage 7. eyebrow, feature 8. boldness, forehead 9. gangplank 10. effrontery 11. countenance

browbeat... 3. cow 5. bully 7. buffalo, henpeck 8. bulldoze, domineer 10. intimidate

brown... 4. dark 5. cheat, dusky 6. august, braise, tanned 9. red–yellow (class)

brown... 3. bay, dun, nut, tan 4. ecru, faon, fawn, roan, rust, seal 5. acorn, cocoa, hazel, henna, khaki, mocha, olive, otter, sepia, snuff, sumac, tawny, tenné, toast, topaz 6. auburn, bister, bronze, burnet, coffee, copper, loutre, oriole, russet, sienna, sorrel, titian, walnut 7. asphalt (smoke), gazelle, perique, rosario (army) 8. chestnut, cinnamon, mahogany 9. buckthorn, chocolate 10. café au lait, terra cotta

brown (pert to)...
Bess.. 6. musket
betty.. 5. daisy 7. pudding 10. coneflower
earth.. 6. umber
ebony.. 6. wamara 10. coffeewood

browned in deep fat... 7. rissole

Brownian movement (Bot)... 7. pedesis

brownie... 3. elf 4. cake 5. dwarf, gnome, nisse, pixie, Scout, urisk 6. camera, goblin 9. sandpiper

Brownism (Eng)... 17. Congregationalism

browze... 4. brut (obs), read, scan 5. graze 6. nibble

bruckle... 5. frail 7. brittle 9. breakable 10. changeable, inconstant

bruin... 4. bear

bruise... 4. bash, beat, hurt, maul 5. abuse, crush, dinge, pound, wound 6. batter, buffet, injury 7. contuse 8. abrasion, black eye 9. contusion, pulverize, triturate

bruiser... 3. mug, pug 5. boxer, bravo, tough 7. fighter, ruffian, sparrer 8. pugilist 11. fisticuffer

bruit, bruit about... 3. din 4. fame, hawk, tell 5. bandy, noise, rumor 6. clamor, report 9. advertise

brujo... 8. magician, sorcerer 11. witch doctor

brumal... 4. cold 6. hiemal, wintry 8. hibernal 10. winterlike

brune... 6. brunet (brunette) 11. Melanochroi

Brunhild... 5. Queen (wife of Siegfried) 8. Valkyrie (Myth)

brunt... 3. rub 4. crux 5. pinch, shock

6. stress 7. squeeze
brush... 3. art 4. bush, comb, tail
(fox), tuft 5. besom, briar, broom,
clash, graze, groom, sweep, touch
6. artist, forest, pappus, stroke,
teazel 7. painter, scuffle, thicket
8. conflict 9. brushwood, encounter
10. paintbrush 11. undergrowth
brush aside... 5. spurn 6. reject
7. dismiss 8. shrug off 9. disregard
brush wolf... 6. coyote
brusque... 4. curt 5. bluff, blunt,
brash, brusk, frank, gruff, rough,
sharp, short 6. abrupt, candid,
snippy
brutal... 5. cruel, gross 6. animal,
carnal, coarse, savage 7. bestial,
inhuman 8. ruthless 9. barbarous
brutality... 7. cruelty 9. barbarian,
carnality 12. ruthlessness
brute... 5. beast, gross, harsh, rough
6. animal 7. beastly, bestial, sensual,
varment 8. soulless 9. barbarian,
inanimate 10. unpolished
11. uncivilized
brutish... 4. rude 5. cruel, gross
6. brutal, carnal, fierce, savage,
stupid 7. bestial, inhuman, sensual,
vicious 8. barbarous, ferocious,
insensate, unfeeling 10. insensible,
irrational
Brutus... 3. wig 6. hairdo, peruke
7. traitor (Julius Caesar)
13. chrysanthemum
Bryan's speech (1896)... 11. Cross of
Gold 13. Crown of Thorns
bryology, science of... 6. mosses
10. bryophytes, liverworts
Brython... 4. Celt 6. Briton
8. Welshman
Brythonic god... 3. Ler 4. Bran
Brythonic goddess... 9. Arianrhod
bubble... 3. bead, bleb, blob, boil,
foam 5. bulge, empty, fancy, tumor
6. burble, gurgle, murmur, ripple,
scheme, trifle 7. chimera (chimaera),
globule, trickle 8. bubbling, delusive,
illusion 9. ephemeron, intumesce,
lightness 10. effervesce
16. unsubstantiality
buccal... 4. oral 5. cheek, mouth
buccaneer... 4. Kidd (Capt) 5. rover
6. Morgan, pirate, rifler, viking
7. corsair, Lafitte, spoiler
8. marooner, picaroon 9. privateer
10. Blackbeard (Capt Teach),
freebooter
Bucephalus... 5. horse, steed
7. charger 8. war horse (Alex the
Great)
buck... 3. man, ram, rat 4. bunt, butt,
deer, goat, hare, jump, male, sore
(4-yr deer) 5. fight, sasin 6. animal,
combat, dollar, Indian, oppose
7. contest, launder, pricket
8. antelope, sawhorse 10. fallow
deer
buckaroo... 6. cowboy 7. trainer,
vaquero 8. horseman
12. broncobuster (bronchobuster)
bucket... 3. tub 4. bail, bowk, pail,
ship 5. chest, cozen, scoop, skeel

6. bailer, bushel, drench, sityla
10. bucket shop
Buckeye State... 4. Ohio
Buckingham Palace... 9. residence
11. St James Park (London)
buckle... 3. bow 4. bend, curl, kink,
warp 5. tache 6. fasten 8. marriage
9. fastening
buckthorn... 4. tree 5. brown, shrub
7. cascara, Rhamnus
buckwheat... 4. cake, coal, herb,
seed, titi 5. flour
bucolic... 4. idyl, poem, poet 5. idyll,
local, rural 6. farmer, poetic, rustic
7. eclogue, georgic 8. agrestic,
pastoral 9. bucoliast
bud... 3. deb 4. bulb, cion, germ,
grow, knop, stem 5. brier, buddy,
gemma, graft, plant, shoat, youth
6. embryo, sprout 7. blossom,
brother, burgeon, develop
8. rudiment, soredium 9. debutante,
germinate
Buddha (Gautama)... 2. Fo 4. sage
(Shakya) 5. amita, deity 7. ascetic,
teacher 8. Daibutsu 10. Blessed One
Buddhism (pert to)...
  church.. 4. tera
  city (sacred).. 5. Lassa (Lhasa)
  evil spirit.. 4. Mara
  fate.. 5. Karma
  festival.. 3. Bon
  friar, monk.. 2. Bo 5. arbat, bonze
    6. bhikku, gelong 7. Mahatma
    8. poonghia 9. Dalai Lama
  goal.. 13. Enlightenment
  hell.. 6. Naraka
  language (sacred).. 4. Pali 5. sutra
    9. Tripitaka
  liberation.. 7. Nirvana
  mountain (sacred).. 4. Omei (Chin)
  paradise.. 4. Jodo 8. gokuraku
  sect.. 3. Zen
  shrine (Ind).. 4. tope 5. stupa
    6. dagoba
  temple.. 4. rath, Tera 6. vihara
  temple column.. 3. lat
  term.. 6. nidana
buddy... 3. pal 4. chum, mate
5. crony 7. brother, comrade
8. tentmate 9. bedfellow, companion
budge... 3. fur (lambskin) 4. grog,
move, stir 5. booze, brisk, stiff
6. guzzle, jocund, liquor, solemn,
tipple 7. austere, pompous
8. movement 11. nervousness
budget... 3. bag 4. bulk, plan, sack
5. funds, pouch, purse, store
6. agenda, assets, bundle, moneys,
packet, parcel, ration, wallet
7. program, stipend 8. finances,
quantity, schedule 9. allowance,
statement 12. accumulation
Buenos Aires (pert to)...
  avenue (famed).. 13. Avenida de
    Mayo
  bourse.. 5. Bolsa
  capital.. 9. Argentina
  river.. 7. La Plata
buff... 3. rub 4. hide (animal) 5. color,
scour 6. polish 7. burnish, leather
buffalo (animal)...

American.. 5. bison
Asian, African.. 2. ox 4. arna, Cape, gaur 8. seladang
European.. 7. aurochs
hybrid.. 7. cattalo (catalo)
Indian.. 4. arna
Philippines.. 7. carabao, timarau
buffalo (pert to)...
grass.. 5. grama 6. guinea 11. St. Augustine
pea.. 4. plum 5. vetch
10. bluebonnet
slang.. 3. cow 5. bully 7. perplex 8. bulldoze, confound
Buffalo Bill... 11. William Cody
buffer... 4. buff 5. guard, wheel 6. bumper 7. bulwark, cushion 8. backstop, polisher
buffet... 3. bar, box, hit 4. beat, blow, cuff, slap, toss, whip 5. abuse, smite, stool 6. bruise, oppose, strike 12. chastisement 14. disappointment
buffet... 6. supper 7. counter, hassock 8. cupboard 9. sideboard
buffo... 7. buffoon 10. bass singer (comic opera), buffo–basso
buffoon... 4. fool, mima (fem), mime, zany 5. actor, clown, mimer 6. jester, mummer 8. humorist, ridicule 9. Hanswurst, harlequin 12. Eulenspiegel (Tyll) 13. pickel–herring (pickle–herring)
buffoonery... 6. japery, pranks 7. fooling 8. clownery, drollery, trickery 9. slapstick 10. buffoonism 12. harlequinade
bug (insect)... 3. fly, sow 4. flea, gnat, moth, pill, tick 5. Anasa, aphid, Aphis, cimex, louse 6. beetle, cicada, earwig, locust, mantis, needle, scarab, slater, spider, weevil 7. firefly, hexapod, katydid, ladybug, Ranatra, termite 8. chilipod, diplopod, mosquito, myriapod 9. arthropod (jointed), centipede, cockroach, lightning, millipede, tarantula 10. silverfish 11. grasshopper
bug (slang)... 3. nut 4. bogy, flaw, rage 5. craze, fault, manis 6. defect, zealot 7. bugaboo, bugbear, fanatic, passion 9. energumen
bugaboo... 4. bogy, ogre, trap (golf)
bugan... 5. ghost 6. spirit (evil) 9. hobgoblin
bugger... 3. guy, rat 4. chap, heel 6. booger, jasper, wretch
buggy... 3. bus 4. ga–ga, shay 5. wagon 6. cuckoo 7. caboose, foolish, haywire, vehicle 8. carriage, demented, infested, stanhope 9. insectile 10. insectlike
bug juice... 6. liquor (strong), whisky (inferior)
bugle... 3. iva (ragweed) 4. bead, call (mating), honk, horn, nose, toot 7. clarion, trumpet 9. schnozzle 10. instrument
bugle call... 4. taps 6. alerte, sennet (Hist) 7. retreat, tantara 8. last post, reveille

build... 4. form, rear 5. edify, erect, found, frame, raise, shape 6. create, evolve, figure, nidify 7. fashion, stature 8. increase, physique 9. construct, establish
building... 4. barn, casa, crib, shed, wing 5. annex, tower 6. casino, castle, lean–to, making, museum 7. edifice, factory, forming, rookery, rotunda, theater 8. creation, dwelling, erecting, erection, tenement 9. apartment, structure 10. fashioning, production, skyscraper, storehouse 11. fabrication
build–up... 5. boost 9. promotion 11. advertising 12. commendation
built... 4. made 6. formed, shaped 7. crested, erected 9. fashioned 10. fabricated 11. constructed
bulb... 3. bud 4. corm, lily, root, sego, stem 5. onion, swell, tuber, tulip 6. bulbil, camass, crocus, dahlia 7. bulblet, globule, rhizome 8. earthnut
bulbous... 5. round 7. bulbose, bulging 8. swelling, tuberous
Bulgaria...
capital.. 5. Sofia
city.. 5. Varna 6. Plevna, Sliven 7. Ruschuk
native.. 6. Bulgar
origin.. 4. Slav 9. Mongolian
river.. 6. Danube, Marica (Maritsa), Struma
bulge... 3. bow 4. bump, edge, hump, jump, knob, odds 5. bilge, bloat, flash, pouch, swell 6. convex, wallet 7. vantage 8. advantage 10. projection 12. protuberance
bulk... 3. sum 4. loom, mass, most, size 6. extent, staple, volume 7. bigness, quantum 8. majority, quantity 9. dimension, largeness, substance, thickness 11. massiveness 12. accumulation 13. preponderance
bulky... 5. heavy, hulky, stout, thick 6. clumsy 7. awkward, lumpish, massive 8. unwieldy 9. corpulent, policemen (Eng sl), ponderous 10. cumbersome, unwielding 11. substantial
bull... 4. fiat, seal 5. edict, error, large, ukase 6. brevet, decree, firman, humbug, letter (papal), market (Finan), rising, Taurus 7. blunder 8. nonsense, solecism 9. Irish bull, policeman 10. speculator
bull (male animal)... 2. ox 3. cow 4. Apis (sacred), stot, toro, zebu 5. moose, steer, whale 6. walrus 7. bullock 8. elephant, Minotaur, terrapin
bull (slang)... 4. blah, bosh, bunk 5. hokum 6. hot air 7. baloney 8. buncombe, flimflam
bulla... 4. bleb, boss, case (leather), knob, seal (papal), stud 6. button 7. blister, globule, pendant, vesicle 8. ornament
bulldog... 3. ant 4. pipe 5. leech 6. courage, forceps 8. barnacle, stubborn, tenacity 9. newspaper

(early), tenacious

bulldoze... 3. cow 5. bully, grade, level 6. coerce, harass 7. buffalo 8. browbeat 10. intimidate

bullet... 4. ball (cannon), shot, slug 6. dumdum, pellet, sinker (angling), tracer 7. missile

bulletin... 5. brief, flash 6. notice, record 7. account, message 8. newsbill 9. statement 10. newsletter, periodical 11. publication 12. announcement

bullfighter... 6. torero 7. matador, picador 8. capeador, toreador

bullfinch... 3. alp 4. nope 5. hedge 11. pyrrhuloxia 12. gray grosbeak

Bull Moose... 16. Progressive Party

bullpen (pert to)...
   camp.. 8. barracks 9. enclosure
   ice hockey.. 5. bench (penalty)
   ring cell.. 5. toril
   Western US.. 6. corral

Bull Run (battle)... 8. Manassas

bully... 4. beef 6. hector, jovial 7. gleeful, ruffian 8. browbeat, bulldoze 9. bulldozer, tormentor 10. browbeater, intimidate

bulwark... 4. bank 6. buffer, sconce 7. barrier, parapet, rampart 8. abutment, buttress 10. protection 13. fortification

bum... 3. beg 5. idler, revel, rummy, souse, spree 6. beggar, loafer, tipple, wretch 7. budmash, moocher, wastrel 8. blighter, drunkard, vagabond 9. lazzarone, schnorrer 10. panhandler

bump... 3. hit, jog 4. bang, clop, jolt, lump, meet, push, thud 5. bulge, cahot, crash, crump, knock, lower, plunk, tumor 6. demote, impact, reduce, strike 7. collide 8. demotion, dilation, swelling 9. air pocket, collision, downgrade

bumpkin... 4. boor, clod, gawk, hick, lout, rube, tike 5. yokel 6. farmer, rustic 7. cauboge, hayseed, hoosier, lumpkin 9. chawbacon 10. clodhopper

bumptious... 8. insolent 9. audacious, insulting 12. contumelious

bunch... 3. bob, lot, mop, set 4. pack, tuft, wisp 5. batch, clump, covey, crowd, flock, grist, group 6. bundle 7. cluster, company 8. assemble, quantity 9. multitude 10. congregate

bundle... 3. lot, wad 4. bale, bolt, hank, pack, send 5. bluey, bunch, fagot, sheaf, shook 6. bindle, fardel, fascis, packet, parcel, seroon 7. fascine, package, rouleau 10. collection

bung... 3. tap 4. cork, plug, stop 5. spile 6. bruise 7. contuse, stopper, stopple, tampeon, tampoon 8. bankrupt, bunghole 9. falsehood

bungle... 3. err 4. muff 5. botch, fudge 6. bobble, foozle, fumble, tailor (hunting) 7. blunder

bungling... 5. fudgy 6. clumsy 7. awkward, unhandy 8. botchery

9. unskilled 10. blundering, unskillful

bunion... 12. hallux valgus

bunk... 3. bed, kip, rot 4. blah, brag 5. abide, berth, couch, dwell, hokum, hooey, sleep 6. humbug, kibosh 8. baloney, hogwash 8. nonsense, tommyrot 9. cross–beam (logging)

Bunker Hill (Mass)... 6. battle (1775)

bunkum... see *buncombe*

Bunsen... 4. cell, disk 5. flame, valve 6. burner 9. Professor (Ger)

bunt... 3. bat, dig, jab, jog, tap 4. blow, bump, butt, pike, push, tail (Scot) 5. knock, shove 7. bunting 10. propulsion

bunting... 4. flag, hood 5. flags 6. banner, pennon 7. pennant 8. streamer

bunting (bird)... 3. red 4. cirl, corn, crow, lark, pape (Creole) 5. finch 6. indigo, towhee 7. cowbird, ortolan 8. bobolink 12. yellowhammer

buoy... 3. dan 4. bell 5. float 6. marker 7. can buoy, nunbuoy 8. bell buoy, deadhead, life buoy, spar buoy 11. mooring buoy 12. breeches buoy 13. whistling buoy

buoyance, buoyancy... 4. hope, snap 5. verve 6. bounce 7. flotage 9. lightness 10. levitation, resilience 12. floatability 16. lightheartedness

buoyant... 5. light 7. elastic 8. cheerful, floating, levitate, volatile 11. supernatant 12. lighthearted, recuperative

bur, burr... 3. nut 5. thorn 8. adherent (see also *burr*)

burble... 6. muddle 7. confuse, trouble 8. disorder

burbot... 4. ling, Lota 7. eelpout

burden... 3. key, tax 4. birn, care, cark, clog, lade, load, note, onus, task, tone 5. cargo, cross, music, tenor, voice 6. charge, cumber, hamper, saddle, weight 7. bourdon, freight, oppress, payload, refrain 8. capacity, overload, pressure 10. impediment, imposition 11. encumbrance

burdensome... 5. heavy 7. arduous, massive, onerous, weighty 8. unwieldy 9. difficult, laborious, ponderous 10. cumbersome, oppressive 11. troublesome 12. impedimental

bureau... 4. desk, shop 6. office 7. dresser 8. chambers 10. chiffonier, department

bureaucracy... 10. government 11. directorate, officialdom, officialism

burgeon... 3. bud 4. grow 5. gemma, shoot, sprit 6. sprout

burglar... 4. yegg 5. thief 9. cracksman 11. safecracker 12. housebreaker

burglary... 5. theft 6. burgle 7. larceny, robbery 8. stealage 13. housebreaking

burgle... 3. rob 8. burglary 10. burglarize

burgomaster... 5. mayor 7. alcalde
10. magistrate 11. burghmaster
burgoo, burgout... 4. stew 5. gruel
7. pudding (oatmeal) 8. porridge
burial... 5. inurn 7. funeral
9. interment, sepulture
10. engulfment, inhumation,
submersion 11. concealment,
submergence
burial ground... 4. pyre 5. grave
6. barrow 7. tumulus 8. bone yard,
catacomb, cemetery, golgotha
9. graveyard 10. churchyard,
necropolis 11. polyandrium
12. potter's field
burlesque... 3. fun 4. jest 5. farce,
comic 6. parody, review, satire
7. mimicry, mockery, overact,
take–off 8. burletta, doggerel,
ridicule, travesty 9. charivari,
imitation, travestie 10. caricatura,
caricature 13. entertainment
Burlingame Treaty... 11. Immigration
(Chin 1868)
burly... 3. fat 5. bulky, large, noble,
obese, stout 6. brawny 7. stately
8. imposing, stalwart 9. corpulent,
excellent
Burma, Burmese...
alphabet.. 4. Pali
capital (anc).. 3. Ava 4. Pegu
capital, present.. 7. Rangoon
city.. 8. Mandalay
dagger.. 3. dah (dhao)
gibbon.. 3. lar
girl.. 4. mima
monk.. 2. bo
native.. 3. Lai
relation.. 5. Thais (Tais) 6. Malays
7. Chinese 8. Tibetans
10. Mongolians
religion.. 8. Buddhism
robber.. 6. dacoit
shed (public).. 5. zayat
tribe.. 3. Mon, Tai 4. Laos, Shan
7. Siamese
viol.. 4. turr (3–stringed)
Burma Road... 6. Lashio (to China,
1938–1942, replaced by Ledo Rd)
burn... 3. dry, tan 4. char, fire, glow,
hurt, pain, sear, sere 5. blaze,
brand, brook, cense, flame, scald,
singe 6. ignite, injury, scorch
7. cremate, encauma, flicker,
sunburn, swelter, torrefy 9. cauterize,
sacrifice 10. incandesce, incinerate
burner... 3. jet 4. lamp 5. torch
6. Bunsen, candle, censer (incense)
7. cresset 9. blowtorch
10. lucubrator 11. incinerator
burning... 3. hot 4. fire, pain, sore
5. afire, angry, ardor, arson, blaze,
fiery, flame 6. ablaze, ardent, fervid
7. blazing, cautery, excited, fervent,
flaming, glowing, shining, zealous
8. eloquent, feverish, inustion
9. cremating, cremation, execution
10. combustion, ustulation
13. conflagration
burning place... 4. ghat 9. crematory
10. cinerarium
burnish... 3. rub 4. buff 5. glaze,

gloss, shine 6. patina, polish
burnt... 3. red 5. dried 6. burned,
seared, singed 7. charred
8. hardened, scorched, sunburnt
9. blistered, sunburned
burnt (pert to)...
art.. 11. pygrography, pyrogravure
color.. 4. rose 5. ocher, topaz
6. almond, orange, russet, sienna
8. amethyst
sugar.. 7. caramel
burn with anger, excitement...
4. fume 5. smoke 6. seethe,
simmer, sizzle 7. smolder
burp... 5. belch, eruct 8. eructate
burr... 3. cut, hem 4. buzz, whir
5. brier, drone, gnarl, knurl, thorn
6. brogue, corona (moon), meatus
(ear) 7. bramble, clotbur, prickle,
silique, sticker 8. excavate, follicle
9. cocklebur, whetstone
burro... 3. ass 4. jack 5. cuddy,
neddy 6. dickey, donkey 7. jackass
burrow... 3. dig 4. abri, hide, hole,
lair, mine 5. couch (otter's), lodge
(beaver's) 6. search, tunnel 7. shelter
burrowing... 9. effodient, fossorial
11. lithodomous (in rock)
burrowing animal... 4. mole, peba
5. poyou 6. peludo 8. suricate
9. armadillo
burst... 3. pop 4. bang, rend 5. blast,
blaze, break, broke, erupt, flare,
flash, shots, spurt 6. volley
7. explode, flare–up, gunfire, implode
8. outbreak, outburst, ruptured
9. discharge, explosion, fractured
10. detonation 11. dissiliency
burst (forth)... 4. grow 5. erupt, sally
6. sprout
burst (pert to)...
applause.. 5. éclat, hands 7. ovation,
plaudit 8. clapping
cheers.. 5. salvo
gunfire.. 6. rafale
laughter.. 3. fit 4. peal, roar
10. convulsion
temper.. 4. rage 5. scene, storm
7. passion 9. explosion
bursting... 4. full 7. brimful, crammed,
excited, replete 8. overfull, thrilled,
volcanic 9. explosive, surfeited
10. detonating 11. impassioned,
overflowing, overwhelmed
bury... 4. hide, sink 5. cache, cover,
inter, inurn, plant, stash 6. engulf,
entomb, inhume 7. conceal,
embosom, repress, secrete
8. submerge 9. overwhelm, sepulture
bus... 6. jitney 7. omnibus 10. motor
coach
bush... 3. tod 4. shag (hair) 5. brush,
plain, shrub, wahoo, wilds 6. branch,
lining 7. boscage, bushing
8. bushveld, woodland 10. hinterland
bushed... 4. beat 5. all in 6. pooped
7. baffled 8. dog–tired 9. exhausted,
nonplused, perplexed, played out
10. nonplussed
bushel... 3. foo 4. full 6. basket,
vessel 7. measure (dry) 8. imperial,
standard 10. Winchester

Bushido (Jap)... **11**. code of honor
bushing... **4**. bush **6**. lining, sleeve
(mach) **7**. bearing, padding (piano)
Bushman... **3**. San **4**. Saan **5**. nomad,
pygmy **6**. Abatua, rustic
8. woodsman **9**. aborigine
bushmaster... **5**. snake
bushwhacker... **7**. pioneer **8**. guerilla
10. forerunner **11**. bushfighter,
voortrekker **12**. frontiersman
bushy... **5**. hairy, thick, woody
6. dumose, shaggy, woodsy
7. hirsute, scrubby, shrubby
business... **3**. job **4**. firm, game, line,
work **5**. craft, house, trade **6**. affair,
career, matter, racket **7**. calling,
company, concern, pursuit
8. commerce, industry, interest,
practice, vocation **10**. enterprise,
occupation, proceeding, profession
11. transaction **13**. establishment
business (pert to)...
agreement.. **6**. cartel
businesslike.. **11**. pragmatical
customer.. **6**. patron
cycle.. **9**. recession **10**. depression,
prosperity **11**. liquidation
deal.. **4**. turn **9**. operation
11. negotiation, transaction
Exchange.. **4**. bank **5**. Bolsa
6. Bourse **11**. stock market
man.. **7**. tycoon **8**. salesman
9. solicitor
place.. **4**. mart, shop **5**. store
6. office, shoppe **8**. Exchange
bust... **4**. bang, fail, hand (Bridge),
tame (bronco) **5**. burst, chest, crash,
flunk, spree **6**. breast, figure
7. degrade, explode, failure
8. collapse, demotion, fracture
9. sculpture **10**. bankruptcy
bustard... **4**. bird (Old World), kori,
Otis **5**. goose, paauw **6**. curlew
8. Otididae
busted... **4**. flat **5**. broke **6**. broken,
failed, ruined **7**. severed **8**. bankrupt,
ruptured, strapped **9**. insolvent,
penniless **10**. stone–broke
bustle... **3**. ado **4**. fuss, stir, to–do
5. haste, whirl **6**. flurry, hubbub,
hustle, pother, scurry, tumult
7. bluster, ferment, fluster, scamper,
turmoil **8**. activity **9**. agitation,
commotion **10**. excitement,
hurly–burly **11**. disturbance
bustling... **6**. active **7**. hurried, rushing
8. eventful, stirring
busy... **4**. nosy, work **5**. drive
6. active, devote, employ, engage,
occupy **7**. engaged, on the go,
operose **8**. diligent, employed,
meddling, occupied, on the run,
sedulous **9**. assiduous, attentive,
laborious, officious **10**. meddlesome
11. industrious, inquisitive,
persevering
busy... **4**. dick **6**. gossip **7**. gumshoe,
meddler **8**. busybody, flatfoot
9. detective
busybody... **6**. gossip **8**. quidnunc
9. pragmatic
but... **2**. ma **3**. yet **4**. even, just,

mere, save **5**. hence, outer, still
6. except **7**. however, without
10. regardless **12**. nevertheless
15. notwithstanding
butcher... **3**. fly (angling), mar **4**. kill,
slay **5**. botch, spoil **6**. killer, vendor
7. croaker, meatman **8**. merchant,
train–boy **9**. slaughter **11**. slaughterer
12. bloodshedder
butchery... **6**. murder **7**. carnage
8. business, massacre, shambles
9. slaughter **14**. slaughterhouse
butt... **3**. aim, end, jut, pit, ram, tun,
tup **4**. buck, bunt, cart, cask, goat,
rump, stub **5**. cigar, hinge, joint,
mound, piece, stump **6**. target
(archery), thrust (fencing) **7**. buttock,
parapet, project **8**. flatfish
9. cigarette **13**. laughingstock
butter... **3**. pat **4**. coat, ghee (ghi),
oleo **5**. smear **6**. bedaub, spread
7. butyric **8**. flattery **9**. margarine,
suaveness **10**. semiliquid
13. oleomargarine
butter–and–eggs... **8**. flaxweed,
ranstead, toadflax
buttercup fruit... **6**. achene
7. crowtoe
butterfingered... **6**. clumsy
7. awkward, unhandy **8**. bungling,
careless **9**. all thumbs **10**. blundering
butterflies (slang)... **6**. nerves
7. fidgets, jitters
butterfly (pert to)...
American.. **7**. viceroy
family.. **10**. Agapetidae
11. Rhopalocera
genus.. **7**. Lycaena **11**. Lepidoptera
large.. **7**. monarch
larva.. **11**. caterpillar
lily.. **4**. sego **8**. mariposa
peacock.. **2**. io **7**. buckeye
swallowtail.. **5**. black, tiger, zebra
type.. **4**. moth **5**. satyr **10**. fritillary,
silverspot
buttocks... **4**. butt (vulgar), hips, rear,
rump, seat **5**. fanny, podex
6. bottom **8**. haunches, maneuver
(wrestling) **10**. backsides, posterior
buttress... **4**. pier, pile, prop, stay
5. brace, tower **7**. shelter, support
8. abutment **10**. projection,
strengthen **11**. counterfort
13. fortification
buttress (Arch)... **4**. pier **6**. flying
7. hanging
buxom... **3**. gay **4**. boon, rosy **5**. jolly,
plump **6**. blithe, jocund, jovial
7. gleeful
buy... **5**. bribe **6**. accept, redeem
7. bargain, expiate **8**. purchase
buy back... **6**. redeem
Buyer Beware... **12**. Caveat Emptor
buzz... **3**. hum, saw **5**. rumor, snore
6. bustle, murmur, rumble
7. ferment, whisper **9**. fricative,
murmuring **10**. sibilation
buzzard... **4**. aura (turkey), hawk, pern
5. buteo **6**. osprey, stupid **7**. harrier
9. dorbeetle, senseless
10. cockchafer
buzz bomb... **9**. doodlebug

10. bumblebomb
14. Chase–Me–Charlie

bwana (Afr)... 4. boss 6. master

by... 2. at, in, on 3. ago, bei, par, per, via 4. away, gone, near, over, pass (bridge), past, with 5. after, aside 6. beside, beyond, nearby, toward 7. abreast, close by, through 9. in reserve

by–and–by... 4. anon, soon 5. later, sweet 6. mañana 7. betimes, bientôt, ere long, shortly 8. directly 9. presently 11. tout à l'heure

by birth... 3. nee

bygone... 3. ago 4. lost, over, past 6. buried, bypast, gone by, passed 7. elapsed, extinct 8. departed, preterit (preterite)

byname... 6. eponym 7. babyism, epithet, surname 8. cognomen, monicker, nickname 9. sobriquer 10. patronymic 11. appellation

bypass... 4. go by, miss 5. byway, elude 6. byroad, detour, escape 7. deviate, digress 8. side path

10. circumvent, roundabout

By the Grace of God... 9. Dei Gratia

byword... 3. mot, saw 5. adage, maxim 6. byname, phrase, saying, slogan 7. adagium, parable, proverb 8. aphorism, nickname, reproach 9. catchword, sobriquet 10. shibboleth

by word of mouth... 4. oral 5. parol (parole)

Byzantine Empire...
architecture.. 7. St Marks (Venice) 9. elaborate
bookbinding.. 9. unadorned (earlier) 10. bejewelled (later)
church.. 7. Eastern
city.. 14. Constantinople (Istanbul)
creator.. 11. Constantine (the Great)
historian.. 9. Procopius 11. Anna Comnena
poetry.. 5. hymns
scepter.. 6. ferula
writer.. 6. Prazes 7. Priscus, Romanus

Byzantium... 14. Constantinople (Istanbul)

C

C... 4. clef 7. cedilla, century, hundred, keynote

caama... 3. fox 4. asse 10. hartebeest

cab... 4. pony, taxi 7. measure, purloin, shelter, taxicab, vehicle 8. carriage (anc) 9. cabriolet 10. locomotive (part) 11. translation

cabal... 4. clan, plot 5. group, junta, party 7. chatter, complot, coterie, dispute, faction 8. intrigue 9. camarilla, collusion, Committee 10. complicity, conspiracy

cabala... 7. mystery 9. mystic art, occultism

cabalessou... 9. armadillo (giant)

cabalistic... 6. occult 7. cabalic 8. abstract, anagogic, esoteric, mystical 10. mysterious

caballeria... 7. measure (land) 8. chivalry 10. knighthood

caballero... 5. lover, rider 6. knight 8. cavalier, horseman 9. chevalier, gentleman 10. equestrian

caballo... 5. horse

cabaret... 3. inn 5. cafe 6. hostel, posado, tavern 7. barroom 9. night club, roadhouse 11. café dansant 13. entertainment

cabbage... 3. kos (cos) 4. cole, kale, palm 5. colza, savoy 7. collard 8. colewort, kohlrabi 11. cauliflower 15. Brussels sprouts

cabbage (pert to)...
curly leaf.. 5. savoy
daisy.. 11. globeflower

fermented.. 5. kraut
headless.. 4. kale
salad.. 4. slaw
seed.. 5. colza
slang.. 4. crib, fool 6. pilfer 7. fathead, purloin 9. numbskull 11. cabbagehead, knucklehead
species.. 8. Brassica
tree.. 4. palm 7. angelin 8. palmetto
white.. 9. butterfly
yellows.. 7. disease (destructive)

caber... 4. apar, beam, pole 6. rafter, timber

cabin... 3. hut 4. shed 5. booth, coach (Naut), house, hovel, lodge, shack 6. cabana, saloon 7. caboose 10. blockhouse

cabinet... 3. box, den 4. Body, buhl, case 5. bureau, closet, office 7. almirah, boudoir, council, étagère, whatnot 8. cellaret, cupboard, ministry 9. committee

cable... 4. boom, cord, rope, wire 5. chain, twine 6. fasten, hawser 7. coaxial, measure, molding, ropeway 8. telegram 9. cablegram

cable (pert to)...
car.. 7. telpher
holder (Naut).. 7. wildcat 10. cable wheel
post.. 4. bitt

cabling... 9. rudenture

cabochon... 5. jewel, stone (uncut), style (convex cut) 8. ornament

caboodle... 3. all, kit, lot 5. bunch,

whole 10. collection 14. kit and caboodle

caboose... 3. car (RR) 5. buggy 6. galley 7. kitchen 9. deckhouse

cabotin... 5. actor (strolling) 9. charlatan

cachaca... 3. rum (white)

cache... 4. hide, hole 5. stash, store 7. conceal, hide-out, retreat 8. hideaway 10. storehouse

cachet... 4. seal 5. sigil, stamp, wafer 6. signet 7. capsule

cachilla... 8. white man

cachot... 7. dungeon

cackle... 3. gab 4. cank, chat, crow, talk 5. clack, laugh, prate 6. babble, gabble, giggle, gossip, jabber 7. chatter, prattle 8. laughter

cacodemon... 4. deva 5. devil, fiend, Indra 10. evil spirit

cacology... 10. bad diction, corruption (speech) 16. mispronunciation

cacophonous... 7. raucous 8. jangling, strident 9. diaphonic, dissonant 10. discordant 11. unmelodious

cacophony... 5. clash 6. jangle 7. discord 8. diaphony (Mus) 9. harshness 10. dissodence

cactus... 4. bleo 5. agave 6. chaute, cholla, mescal 7. Opuntia, saguaro 8. fishhook 9. Turk's-head 11. prickly pear 12. Echinocactus

cad... 4. boor, chum, heel, hick 5. yokel 6. mucker 7. bounder, servant 8. townsman 9. scoundrel, vulgarian

cadaver... 4. body (dead) 5. stiff 6. corpse 7. carcass 8. skeleton

cadaverous... 4. pale 5. gaunt, lurid 6. sickly, wasted 7. ghastly, haggard 9. emaciated 10. attenuated, corpselike

caddis (pert to)...
bait.. 3. fly 4. worm 5. cadew
material.. 4. yarn 5. twill 6. crewel 7. worsted
worm.. 5. larva (aquatic)

caddle... 4. fuss 5. annoy, worry 6. gossip 7. confuse, trouble 8. disarray 9. confusion

cade... 3. keg, oil (Med), pet 4. cask, lamb (orphan) 6. barrel, coddle, petted

cadeau... 4. gift

cadence... 4. beat, lilt, tone 5. meter 6. rhythm 7. balance 9. free verse, vers libre 10. modulation

cadence... 4. half 5. trill 6. plagal 7. perfect 9. authentic, deceptive, imperfect, suspended 11. interrupted

cadency (Her)... 4. rose 5. label 6. mullet 7. annulet, martlet 8. crescent 10. fleur-de-lis 11. cross moline

cadenza... 7. cadence 8. flourish

cadet... 3. son 4. pleb 5. color (blue), youth 6. junior 10. midshipman

cadge... 3. beg 4. hawk 5. fakir, mooch 6. beggar, hawker, mumper, peddle, sponge, vendor 7. carrier, moocher, sponger 8. huckster, sannyasi

cadgy... 6. wanton 7. lustful 8. cheerful, mirthful

Cadmus (pert to)...
daughter.. 3. Ino 6. Semele
father.. 6. Agenor
founder of.. 6. Thebes (Boetia)
sister.. 6. Europa
wife.. 8. Harmonia

cadre... 4. list, unit 5. frame, panel 6. line-up, roster, scheme 8. cadastre, register, schedule, skeleton 9. framework

caduceus (Gr Antiq)... 4. wand (Hermes') 5. staff 6. symbol 8. insignia (Med Corps)

Caesar (pert to)...
betrayer.. 6. Brutus
colleague.. 7. Bibulus
death site.. 4. Nola
Emperor, Dictator of.. 4. Rome
fatal day.. 4. Ides (of March) 11. Ides of March
language.. 5. Latin
rival.. 6. Pompey
river.. 7. Rubicon
sister.. 4. Atia
uncle.. 11. Caius Marius
wife.. 8. Cornelia

caesura, cesura... 4. rest 5. break, colon, comma, pause 8. interval 12. interruption

cafard... 5. bigot, blues 6. humbug 9. hypocrite 10. depression

café... 5. coffe 6. coffee 10. restaurant 11. coffeehouse

café (pert to)...
au lait.. 5. brown 6. alesan 10. French nude
creme.. 5. suede (color)
noir.. 4. musk (color) 11. black coffee
parfait.. 8. beverage

cafetière... 9. coffeepot 10. percolator

caffeine... 6. coffee, theine (in tea) 8. alkaloid 9. stimulant

cafila... 7. caravan (camel)

cage... 3. mew, pen 4. coop 6. corral 7. confine, goal net, impound 8. goal post

cagey... 3. sly 4. foxy, wary, wily 5. canny, leery 6. artful, crafty, shifty, shrews 7. cunning, evasive, knowing

Cain (pert to)...
brother.. 4. Abel
founder of.. 5. Enoch (1st city)
Land of.. 3. Nod
slayer of.. 4. Abel
son.. 5. Enoch

cairn... 4. heap (stones) 6. menhir 8. catstone (catstane), landmark, memorial, monument

Cairo...
capital.. 5. Egypt
city gate (famed).. 9. Bab-el-Nasr
mosque.. 12. Sultan Hassan
resident.. 7. Cairene
river.. 4. Nile
seaport.. 10. Alexandria
tomb.. 10. Mehemet Ali
warrior.. 9. Rameses II

caisson... 3. box 4. case 5. chest, wagon 7. chamber

caitiff... 4. base, mean, vile
  6. coward, wicked, wretch
  7. budmash, captive 10. despicable
cajole... 4. coax, urge 5. cheat, jolly
  6. delude 7. flatter, palaver,
  sweeten, wheedle 8. blandish
  9. importune 10. honeyfogle
Cajun (pert to)...
  descent.. 6. French (Canadian)
  dialect.. 5. Cajun
  home (present).. 9. Louisiana
  native of.. 6. Acadia (Nova Scotia)
cake... 3. bun, wig 4. bake, food,
  lump, mass, wigg 5. batty, block,
  crust, solid, torte, wafer 6. gateau,
  harden 7. bannock, congeal, oatcake,
  pancake 8. corn pone, solidify
  9. charlotte, simpleton
  11. griddle–cake
cake (pert to)...
  almond paste.. 7. ratafia
  corn.. 4. pone
  flat.. 7. placent
  fried.. 7. cruller 8. doughnut
  Lenten.. 6. cimbal, simnel
  Scotch.. 4. farl (farle) 5. scone
  unleavened.. 8. tortilla
Cake Day (Scot)... 8. hogmanay (New
  Year's)
calabar bean... 6. myotic, ordeal
  7. eserine 8. alkaloid
  13. physostigmine
calabash... 5. gourd 6. baobab, bronze
  (color)
calaboose... 4. gaol, jail 5. choky,
  clink 6. bagnio, lockup, prison
  8. bastille, calabozo 9. Bridewell
calamitous... 3. sad 4. dire, evil
  5. black 6. tragic, woeful 7. adverse,
  baleful, ruinous, unhappy 8. grievous,
  tragical, wretched 10. afflictive,
  deplorable, disastrous
  11. cataclysmic, destructive,
  distressful, unfortunate
  12. catastrophic
calamity... 4. blow, evil, ruin 5. wrack
  6. mishap 7. tragedy 8. casualty,
  disaster, distress, fatality 9. adversity
  10. affliction, misfortune
  11. catastrophe, direfulness,
  unhappiness 12. wretchedness
calathiform... 9. cup–shaped
calcarea... 5. coral 7. sponges
calceiform... 10. orchidlike
  13. clipper–shaped
calcitrant... 8. stubborn
  12. recalcitrant
calcitrate... 4. boot, kick 6. oppose
calculate... 3. aim 4. deem, rate, tell
  5. allow, count, frame, judge, score,
  tally, think 6. cipher, deduce, figure,
  gather, number, reckon 7. average,
  compute, suppose 8. conclude,
  estimate 9. determine, enumerate
calculated... 7. advised, studied,
  weighed 8. measured
  10. considered, deliberate
  11. intentional 12. contemplated
calculating... 8. plotting, scheming
  9. computing, designing, judicious
  10. estimating, numerative, reflecting,
  thoughtful 11. circumspect,

  considerate 14. discriminative
calculator... 5. table 6. abacus
  7. suan pan (swan pan, Chin)
  8. computer 9. estimator, tabulator
  10. parimutuel 11. Comptometer,
  totalizator
caldron, cauldron... 3. pot, red
  (color), vat 6. boiler, kettle, mortar,
  retort 7. alembic 8. crucible
Caleb (pert to)...
  daughter.. 7. Achsaph
  literally.. 3. dog
  son.. 3. Hur, Iru
  spy of.. 6. Canaan
calèche... 7. vehicle (Quebec)
Caledonia (anc)... 8. Scotland
Caledonia bird... 4. kagu
Caledonian... 5. brown 6. Scotch
  8. Scotsman, Scottish
calefacient... 4. warm 6. remedy
  7. heating 11. calefactory
calendar... 4. list, Ordo 5. index, slate
  6. docket, line–up, record
  7. almanac, calends (kalends),
  program 8. register, schedule
  9. catalogue, ephemeris
  10. chronology, prospectus
calendar (type)... 5. Roman, Swiss
  6. Jewish, Julian 7. Chinese
  9. Cotsworth, Gregorian, perpetual
  13. International (fixed)
calenture... 4. glow 5. ardor, fever
  7. passion, pyrexia 9. febrility,
  sunstroke
calepin... 4. book (ref) 7. lexicon
  10. dictionary
calf... 3. leg (part) 4. dolt, fool, skin
  6. bovine, island, weaner 7. iceberg,
  leather 9. youngling
calf (pert to)...
  flesh.. 4. veal
  hide.. 3. kip
  leg (part).. 5. sural
  motherless.. 5. dogie 8. maverick
  sweetbread.. 9. ris de veau
  time.. 5. youth
Caliban (pert to)...
  character.. 5. brute, slave (The
  Tempest)
  deity.. 7. Setebos
  mother.. 7. Sycorax (witch)
caliber, calibre... 4. bore 7. ability
calico... 4. dame 5. cloth 6. salloo
  8. goldfish 12. multicolored
calico (pert to)...
  bird.. 9. turnstone
  bush.. 6. laurel
  horse, pony.. 5. pinto 7. piebald
  printing.. 4. teer 7. topical
calid... 3. hot 4. mild, warm 6. genial
  7. burning, thermal
California...
  bay.. 8. Monterey
  capital.. 10. Sacramento
  city.. 6. Fresno 7. Oakland 8. San
  Diego, Stockton 9. Long Beach
  10. Los Angeles 12. San Francisco,
  Santa Barbara
  desert.. 6. Mojave 8. Colorado
  discoverer.. 6. Cortez (1535)
  flower.. 5. poppy
  history.. 8. Gold Rush (1848),

Missions 11. Sutter's Mill
lake.. 5. Tahoe 8. Elsinore 9. Salton
Sea
lowest point.. 11. Death Valley
mountain.. 6. Lassen, Shasta
7. Whitney
oldest living thing.. 8. redwoods
14. General Sherman (tree)
15. bristlecone pine
river.. 4. Kern 7. Feather, Russian
10. Sacramento
pageant.. 10. Rose Parade
17. Tournament of Roses
State admission.. 11. thirty–first
State motto.. 6. Eureka
State nickname.. 6. Golden
caliph, calif... 3. Ali (4th) 4. Imam
(Imaum), Omar 6. Othman 7. Abu
Bekr 8. Islamite
Caliph Ali's descendants... 5. Alids
(Alides)
caliphate... 7. Omniads, Shiites
(Sectaries) 8. Idrisids 9. Fatimites
calk, caulk... 4. copy, plug, stop
5. close, sleep (Naut sl) 6. calque,
catnap, chinse, plug up, stop up
7. occlude
call... 3. bid, cry, dub, hip, nod
4. ahoy, beck, dial, name, plea, ring,
soho, sook (hog), taps, term, yell
5. alarm, basis, cause, clepe, rally,
rouse, shout, style, visit, waken
6. appeal, demand, ground, invoke,
motive, muster, option, reason,
sennet, signal, slogan, summon
7. appoint, bidding, collect, convoke,
fanfare, summons, trumpet
8. assemble, nominate, occasion,
reveille 9. battle cry, challenge,
designate, induction, telephone,
watchword 10. denominate, invitation
11. recruitment, requisition
12. conscription 13. justification
call (pert to)...
attention.. 6. direct, remind 8. point
out
back.. 6. recall, recant, repeal, revive,
revoke 7. retract 8. remember
9. recollect
down.. 6. invoke 7. bawl out,
reprove, tell off
evil upon.. 8. execrate
forth.. 5. evoke, rouse 6. elicit,
excite, induce, prompt, summon
names.. 4. cite 5. abuse, curse
6. insult, revile, vilify 8. besmirch
10. vituperate
together.. 6. muster, summon
7. convoke
to mind.. 4. cite 8. remember
9. visualize
callant, callan... 3. boy, lad 4. chap
5. youth 6. fellow, garçon, laddie
8. customer, muchacho
11. hobbledehoy
calle... 6. street
called... 5. named 6. dubbed, y–clept,
yermed 7. y–cleped
calling... 3. art, nod 4. beck, lure,
name, work 5. trade 6. career,
metier, naming, outcry 7. bidding,
mission, pursuit, styling, summons

8. biddance, business, labeling
(labelling), practice, vocation
9. condition, evocation
10. employment, invitation,
occupation, profession
13. circumstances
calling crab... 7. fiddler
calling hare... 4. pika
Calliope... 4. Muse (poet) 5. organ
8. asteroid
Calliope's son... 7. Orpheus
callous, calloused... 4. horn, sear
5. horny, inure 6. harden, seared
8. hardened 9. heartless, indurated,
unfeeling 10. impervious
11. hardhearted 12. thick–skinned
14. pachydermatous
callow... 5. crude, green 6. tender,
unripe, vernal 7. budding
8. immature, unformed 9. unfledged
10. unseasoned 11. undeveloped
15. unsophisticated
callus... 6. tyloma
calm... 3. lay 4. cool, dill, fair, lull,
mild 5. allay, balmy, peace, quiet,
sober, still 6. becalm, hushed, pacify,
placid, sedate, serene, smooth,
soothe, steady 7. appease, compose,
halcyon, orderly, pacific, placate,
restful, unmoved 8. peaceful, tranquil
9. quiescent, unruffled
10. phlegmatic 11. tranquilize,
undisturbed 13. dispassionate,
imperturbable
calmant, calmative... 7. anodyne,
soother 8. lenitive, pacifier, sedative,
soothing 10. depressant, palliative
11. alleviative 12. tranquilizer
calmato (Mus)... 4. calm 8. tranquil
calmness... 4. calm, lull 5. peace,
poise, quiet 6. repose 8. quietude,
serenity 9. composure, placidity
10. equanimity, quiescence
11. restfulness, self–control
calor... 4. heat 5. therm 7. thermal
calorifics... 4. heat 7. heating
calumniate... 4. slur 5. belie, libel
6. accuse, revile 7. asperse, slander,
traduce 9. blaspheme
calumnious... 7. abusive 8. derisive,
insolent, libelous 9. insulting
10. defamatory, derogatory,
slanderous 11. maledictory,
opprobrious
calumny... 5. abuse 7. lampoon,
slander 9. contumely 10. detraction,
scurrility 11. malediction
12. vilification
calvary... 8. crucifix
Calvary (Bib)... 8. Damascus, Golgotha
9. Jerusalem
Calvinism (pert to)...
author.. 6. Calvin
doctrine.. 5. Grace 9. Atonement,
Depravity (total) 12. Perseverance (of
Saints) 14. Predestination
site.. 6. Geneva
Calvinistic Methodist... 5. Welsh
10. Whitefield 14. Lady Huntingdon
Calypso... 6. Ogygia (home)
8. Cytherea, sea nymph (The
Odyssey)

calyx... 3. cup 4. husk 5. galea, sepal 6. corona 7. corolla 8. epicalyx, perianth
camarada... 7. comrade, partner 9. companion
camaraderie... 8. good will 11. familiarity 14. good–fellowship
camarilla... 5. cabal 6. clique 7. council
camata... 6. acorns 8. oak fruit
cambist... 6. banker, broker 9. financier 11. moneylender 12. money–changer
Cambodia...
  capital.. 6. Angkor 8. Pnom–Penh
  language.. 5. Khmer 9. Cambodian
  religion.. 8. Buddhism
  seaport.. 6. Kampot
Cambria... 5. Wales
Cambridge University (pert to)...
  English examination.. 6. tripos
  English student.. 5. sizar 6. optime (honor)
  Massachusetts.. 3. MIT 7. Harvard
camel... 4. oont 5. llama 6. deloul, mammal, vicuna 7. Camelus 8. Bactrian (2–humped) 9. Camelidae, dromedary
camel hair shawl... 8. cashmere
camelopard... 7. giraffe 13. constellation
Camelot... 6. legend 10. King Arthur, palace site, Round Table
cameo... 4. onyx 7. relievo 8. anaglyph
camera type... 5. Kodak 7. Brownie 10. Rollieflex
Cameroon...
  capital.. 7. Yaounde (Afr)
  native.. 4. Sara
  river.. 5. Shari
  seaport.. 6. Douala
  tribe.. 3. Abo 5. Bantu
Camino Real (Calif)... 9. Royal Road 12. El Camino Real, King's Highway
Camorra (It)... 12. organization (secret)
camouflage... 7. falsify 8. disguise 9. dissemble 10. false front 12. misrepresent
camp... 4. clan, tent 5. abode, etape, junto, tabor 6. campoo, clique, laager 7. bivouac, faction 10. encampment
campaign... 5. serve 7. crusade 9. operation
camphorated tincture of opium... 9. paregoric
campus... 4. quad 5. field (academic)
can... 3. jar, may, tin 6. hopper, vessel 7. capable 8. canister, conserve 9. competent 10. receptacle
can... 5. skill 7. ability 9. competent 10. receptacle
can (sl)... 3. jug, tin 4. boot, bump, fire, jail, john, kick 6. bounce, cooler, toilet 7. dismiss 9. discharge 11. give the gate
Canaan... 9. Palestine 12. Promised Land
Canada... see also *Canadian*
  capital (Federal).. 6. Ottawa
  city.. 7. Toronto 8. Hamilton, Montreal, Winnipeg 9. Vancouver
  discoverer.. 9. John Cabot (1497)
  Hudson's Bay Co.. 8. fur trade
  native.. 6. French 7. English
  nickname.. 6. Canuck
  park.. 6. Jasper
  peninsula.. 5. Gaspé
  police.. 8. Mounties 12. Royal Mounted (7,000)
  river.. 5. Peace, Slave 6. Fraser, Nelson, Ottawa 8. Gatineau 9. Athabasca, Churchill, Mackenzie 10. St Lawrence
Canadian (pert to)...
  flour.. 6. Shorts (milling) 8. canaille
  jay.. 9. moose bird 10. whisky jack
  lynx.. 5. pishu
  plum.. 6. cheney
  porcupine.. 5. urson 7. cawquaw
  squaw.. 6. mahala
canaille... 3. mob 4. ruck 6. rabble, ragtag, Shorts 8. riffraff 10. roughscuff
canal... 4. duct, iter (brain), pipe, tube 5. drain 6. meatus 7. acequia, channel 10. waterspout 11. watercourse
Canal... 4. Erie, Kiel, Suez 6. Panama 13. Sault Ste Marie (Soo)
Canal Zone Lock... 5. Gatun 10. Miraflores
canard... 4. duck, hoax 5. rumor 6. humbug 9. falsehood
canary... 6. yellow 8. song–bird, songster, weakling
Canary Islands...
  capital.. 9. Santa Cruz (Teneriffe)
  city.. 9. Las Palmas (Grand Canary)
  commune.. 4. Icod
  owner.. 5. Spain
cancel... 4. blot, dele, kill, omit, undo 5. annul, erase 6. delete, excise, recall, repeal, revoke 7. abolish, destroy, nullify, rescind, retract 8. write off 10. invalidate, neutralize, obliterate 11. countermand
cancellation... 6. repeal 7. erasure 8. deletion, write–off 10. moratorium 12. obliteration
cancer... 4. evil 5. tumor 6. canker, growth 7. sarcoma 8. neoplasm 9. carcinoma
Cancer... 4. crab 7. mansion (moon) 10. zodiac sign 13. constellation
cancion... 4. song 5. lyric
Candia... 5. Crete (Isl)
candid... 4. fair, just, open, pure 5. frank 6. direct, honest 7. sincere 9. guileless, impartial, ingenuous 10. impersonal 13. dispassionate 15. straightforward
candidate... 6. seeker 7. aspirer, electee, nominee 8. aspirant, selectee 9. applicant, appointee, postulant 10. solicitant
candidate list... 4. leet 5. slate 6. roster
Candide (pert to)...
  hero, title.. 5. novel
  novel, author.. 8. Voltaire
  philosophy.. 8. optimism

candied... 5. sweet 7. honeyed
    9. congealed, incrusted, preserved
    10. flattering, granulated
    12. crystallized
candied sea holly... 6. eryngo (eringo)
candle... 3. dip, wax 5. light, power,
    taper 6. bougie, cierge, tallow, votive
    7. paschal 8. bayberry 9. chandelle
candlestick (pert to)...
    Bib.. 6. lampad
    branched.. 9. girandole
    ornamental.. 10. candelabra
    Scot.. 6. crusie
    spike.. 7. pricket
    three–branched.. 9. tricerion
    torch type.. 8. flambeau
    wall.. 6. sconce
candlewood... 6. flower 8. ocotillo
candor... 8. fairness, openness
    9. frankness, sincerity, unreserve
    10. directness 11. artlessness,
    unrestraint 13. outspokenness
candy... 5. sweet 6. penide (pulled),
    sweets 7. sweeten 8. crystals
    9. granulate, sweetmeat
    10. confection 11. crystallize
    13. confectionary
candy (type)... 4. mint 5. fudge, taffy
    6. bonbon, nougat, toffee 7. brittle,
    caramel, fondant, panocha, penuche,
    praline 8. licorice, lollipop
    9. chocolate 11. marshmallow
candytuft... 6. iberis
cane... 3. rod 4. beat, club, reed,
    stem, whip 5. crook, sorgo, staff,
    stick, sugar 6. bamboo, rattan
    7. bagasse, bourdon, sorghum,
    sucrose 9. handstaff, truncheon
    12. swagger stick
canescent... 5. hoary, white 7. grizzly,
    silvery, whitish 9. snow–white
Canfield... 9. solitaire
canine... 3. cur, dog, fox, pug, pup
    4. lobo, mutt, tike 5. dingo, pooch,
    puppy, whelp 6. animal, coyote
    7. Canidae, doggish, laniary, mastiff,
    mongrel, reynard 8. dogtooth,
    eyetooth
canis... 3. dog
Canis Majoris... 13. Constellation (with
    Dog Star, Sirius)
cannibalism... 9. barbarity, endophagy
    10. perversion 11. blood thirst
    13. anthropophagy
cannon... 3. gun 5. crash 6. mortar
    7. firearm, robinet 8. dog of war,
    howitzer, ordnance 9. artillery,
    collision
cannon (pert to)...
    ball.. 6. pellet 7. missile
    bore.. 6. breech
    fire.. 7. barrage
    handle.. 4. anse
    nautical.. 5. chase
    part.. 8. cascabel
    pivot.. 8. trunnion
    platform.. 10. terreplein
    plug.. 7. tampion
    shot.. 5. grape
    shoulder part.. 7. rimbase
cannonade... 4. boom, peal, roar
    5. blitz, shell 6. rumble, strafe

    11. bombardment
canny... 3. sly 4. foxy, wary, wily
    6. artful, frugal, shrewd, subtle
    7. cunning, knowing, prudent, thrifty
    8. cautious 9. sagacious
canoe... 4. kiak, pahi, proa, waka
    5. bongo, bungo, kayak, umiak,
    waapa 6. corial, dugout, oomiak,
    pitpan 7. almadia, buckeye (bugeye),
    coracle, piragua, pirogue
    12. pambanmanche
canon... 3. law 4. code, list, rule,
    type 5. model, nodus (Mus)
    6. belief, clergy, decree, ritual
    7. measure, precept 8. decision
    9. catalogue, criterion 10. regulation
    11. composition 12. constitution
canonical... 4. None (hour), Sext
    (hour) 5. Lauds, Prime 6. Matins
    7. creedal 8. dogmatic, orthodox
    9. doctrinal 10. scriptural
    11. theological 14. ecclesiastical
canonization... 8. sainting
    10. ordainment, ordination
    12. consecration, enshrinement
canopy... 3. sky 4. ceil, cope, dais,
    tent 5. cover, shade, vault
    6. awning, tester 7. blanket,
    marquee, shelter 8. caponier
    (caponiere), ciborium, pavilion
    9. baldachin, firmament
canorous... 5. clear 8. sonorous
    9. melodious 10. euphonious
cant... 3. tip 4. lean, list, sing, song,
    sway, tack, tilt 5. angle, argot,
    chant, lingo, pitch, slang, slope,
    whine 6. careen, intone, jargon,
    patois, snivel 7. auction, incline,
    mummery 8. pretense 9. hypocrisy
    10. intonation, sanctimony
    17. sanctimoniousness
cantabank... 6. singer (ballad)
cantador... 6. singer (folk songs)
cantankerous... 8. perverse
    9. malicious 10. contention,
    ill–natured 11. cross–grained
cantata... 5. motet 8. serenata
    9. pastorale
canter... 4. gait, lope 6. gallop
    (Canterbury) 8. vagabond
Canterbury...
    archbishop.. 7. Cranmer, Primate
    13. Thomas à Becket (murdered)
    capital (Eng).. 14. ecclesiastical
    famed building.. 9. Cathedral
    gallop.. 5. aubin 6. canter
    Tales, author.. 7. Chaucer
canticle... 3. lay, ode 4. hymn, lied,
    song 5. carol, ditty 6. Te Deum
Canticle of Canticles (Bib)...
    11. Song of Songs 13. Song of
    Solomon
cantilena... 6. legato, melody
    8. graceful
cantina... 3. bag 6. pocket, saloon
    7. canteen
cantle... 4. nook, part 5. crown, slice
    6. corner, saddle (part) 7. segment
    11. cornerpiece
canto... 4. book, song 5. poems (div
    of), tenor, verse 6. cantus, melody,
    poetry 7. descort

canton... 3. Uri (Switz) 6. county
7. commune, quarter 8. district,
insignia (Her), mofussil (Ind)
9. bailiwick, partition
cantor... 6. leader, singer 7. soloist
8. melodist, vocalist 9. precentor
cantoria... 7. balcony, gallery (choir)
cantrip... 5. charm, magic, spell, trick
canty... 6. lively 7. chipper 8. cheerful
9. sprightly
Canuck... 8. Canadian
canvas... 4. sail, tent, tuke (tewke)
5. cloth 6. circus 7. picture, tentage
8. covering, likeness, pavilion
9. tarpaulin 14. representation
canvasback... 4. duck
canvass... 4. poll 5. study 6. survey
7. examine, inquiry, solicit
8. campaign, consider 10. scrutinize
11. electioneer 12. solicitation
13. questionnaire
canyon, cañon... 4. abra (mouth)
5. chasm, dalle (wall), gorge, gulch
6. arroyo, coulee, ravine, violet
7. couloir
canzone, canzonetta... 4. poem, song
6. ballad, melody 8. canzonet
madrigal
caoba... 8. mahogany, muskwood
caoutchouc... 3. ule 6. caucho, rubber
cap... 3. fez, hat, lid, taj, tam 4. atef,
coif, hood, kepi 5. beret, boina,
busby, shako, toque 6. barret,
biggin, bonnet, calpac, cloche, pileus,
turban 7. biretta (beretta), calotte,
calpack, chapeau 8. Balmoral,
havelock 9. headdress, headpiece,
shtreimal, sou'wester, zucchetto
10. cervelière 11. mortarboard,
tam-o'-shanter
cap (outer part)... 3. lid, tip, top
4. dome, fuze, peak, type 5. cover,
crown, excel, match, spire, trump
6. summit, top off 7. capital (Arch),
overlie, patella 8. complete
9. copestone, detonator
capa... 5. cloak 6. mantle 7. tobacco
capability... 5. power, skill 6. genius
7. ability, caliber, faculty, potency
8. ableness, adequacy, capacity
10. competence 13. qualification
capable... 3. apt, can, fit 4. able
5. adept 6. expert 7. equal to,
skilled 8. adequate 9. competent,
effective, efficient, qualified
10. proficient 12. accomplished
capable of...
boring.. 10. zylotomous
carrying.. 9. portative
flying.. 6. volant
growing.. 6. viable
living in harmony.. 10. compatible
penetration.. 8. pervious
suffering.. 8. passible 9. sensitive
capable of being...
ascertained.. 12. determinable
cultivated.. 6. arable
cut.. 7. sectile
defended.. 7. tenable
done.. 10. effectible
heard.. 7. audible
prevented.. 9. avertible

proved.. 8. testable 12. demonstrable
regulated.. 12. controllable
separated.. 9. divisible
spread.. 10. infectious
12. communicable
thrown.. 7. missile
uttered.. 7. effable
capacious... 4. full, much, wide
5. ample, broad, large, roomy
8. generous, spacious 9. expansive,
extensive 10. commodious,
voluminous 12. considerable
13. comprehensive
capacity... 4. role, room, size 5. limit,
power, skill, space 6. extent, spread,
status, talent, volume 7. caliber,
content, faculty, fitness, measure
8. adequacy, aptitude, function,
position, relation, strength
9. character 10. capability, efficiency
11. capacitance (Elec)
12. intelligence 13. accommodation
capacity for knowing... 9. intellect
cap and bells... 6. bauble, comedy
(symbol), motley 8. costume, marotti
9. headdress
caparison... 3. rig 4. tack 5. armor,
dress, get–up 6. livery 7. harness,
housing, panoply 10. horsecloth
12. horse blanket
cape... 3. ras 4. hood, mino, naze,
ness, spur 5. amice, cappa, cloak,
fichu, orale, point, sagum, talma
6. mantle, sontag, tippet 8. pelerine
(fur) 9. Inverness
cape (pert to)...
gooseberry.. 4. poha
hen.. 4. skua 6. petrel
pigeon.. 7. pintado
polecat.. 5. zoril
ruby.. 6. garnet, pyrope
sheep.. 9. albatross (Naut term)
Cape Cod turkey... 7. codfish (humor)
Cape Dutch... 9. Afrikaans (language)
Cape of Good Hope discoverer...
4. Diaz (1488)
caper... 3. tea 4. dido, leap, romp,
skip 5. antic, berry, dance, frisk,
prank 6. cavort, frolic, gambol,
prance 8. capriole, marigold
9. privateer (Hist)
capercaille... 6. grouse 13. cock of
the wood
caper herb family... 6. Cleome
8. Capparis 9. Polanisia
10. clammyweed 13. Capparidaceae
Cape Town... 7. capital (U of S Afr)
Cape Verde Island (Afr)... 3. Sal
Cape Verde negro... 5. Serer
capias... 4. writ 6. caveat 7. process,
warrant 8. mandamus 9. nisi prius
capillary... 4. fine, tube 6. minute,
vessel 7. slender 8. hairlike, trichoid
capilliform... 7. thready 8. hairlike
capillus... 4. hair
capistrate... 6. cowled, hooded
capital... 3. top 4. city, main, rare,
seat, type 5. chief, crest, crown,
funds, major, means, prime, vital
6. assets, letter, ruling, supply
7. leading, primary, serious, weighty
8. cardinal, dominant, foremost,

splendid 9. excellent, financial,
important, paramount, principal,
prominent 10. commanding,
preeminent, shoestring
capitalism... 8. politics
10. government 11. bourgeoisie
14. free enterprise
capitalist... 6. tycoon 7. rich man
8. investor 9. bourgeois, financier,
plutocrat
capital letter... 6. uncial 9. majuscule
capital punishment... 5. noose
7. gallows, hanging 8. shooting, the
chair 9. beheading, execution,
fusillade 10. guillotine
12. decapitation 13. electrocution
capitano... 5. chief 7. captain,
headman
capitate... 7. globose 8. enlarged,
headlike
Capitol (pert to)...
    County.. 10. Courthouse
    Federal.. 10. Washington (DC)
    State.. 10. Statehouse
capitulate... 4. cede, fall 9. surrender
capitulation... 6. resumé, review,
treaty 7. recount, summary
9. agreement, reckoning, rehearsal,
statement, summation, surrender
10. compendium 11. enumeration,
stipulation 14. relinquishment
capon... 3. hen 4. cock, fowl
6. pullet, rabbit (castrated)
7. chicken, poulard, poultry, rooster
caporal... 4. boss 7. foreman, tobacco
8. overseer
capote... 4. hood 6. cloak 6. bonnet,
mantle, piquet 8. overcoat
capped... 7. crested, pileata, pileate
Capri...
    beverage.. 4. wine (white)
    color.. 4. blue 5. blue–green
    island site.. 11. Bay of Naples
    ruins (famed).. 7. palaces (Tiberius)
    8. grottoes 10. Blue Grotto
caprice... 3. fad, toy 4. kink, mood,
whim 5. fancy, freak, humor, prank,
quirk 6. vagary 7. whimsey (whimsy)
8. crotchet, escapade, flimflam
capricious... 5. moody 6. fickle, fitful
7. erratic, wayward 8. fanciful,
freakish, humorous, notional,
sporadic, unsteady 9. arbitrary,
crotchety, eccentric, fantastic,
whimsical 10. inconstant
12. inconsistent 13. temperamental
Capricorn (Astrol)... 7. mansion (of
Saturn)
Capricorn (Astron)... 4. goat, sign
13. constellation
capriole... 4. leap 5. caper 6. cavort,
curvet, gambol
capsicum... 4. herb 5. chili 6. pepper
capsize... 5. spill, upset 7. subvert, tip
over 8. overturn 9. overthrow
10. turn turtle
capsule... 3. sac 4. pill 5. ascus,
brief, theca, wafer 6. précis, sheath
7. enclose, epitome 8. abstract,
envelope, pericarp, seedcase,
synopsis 10. compendium
capsulize... 5. brief 7. abridge, outline

8. abstract, condense 9. epitomize,
summarize
captain... 4. skip 5. chief, ruler
6. leader, master, patron, police
7. headman, officer, skipper
8. overlord 9. commander
10. shipmaster
Captain Kidd... 6. pirate
Captains Courageous (pert to)...
    author.. 7. Kipling
    setting.. 9. Grand Bank
    (Newfoundland)
    tale of.. 7. romance
captain's gratuity... 3. gig 7. primage
caption... 5. title 6. legend, rubric
7. capture, seizure 8. headline,
subtitle
captious... 6. severe 7. carping,
cynical, peevish 8. caviling, critical
9. bickering, paltering, quibbling
12. equivocatory, faultfinding
13. hypercritical
captivate... 4. vamp 5. charm
6. allure, enamor, ravish, seduce
7. attract, becharm, beguile, bewitch,
capture, delight, enchant 8. enthrall
9. enrapture, fascinate, infatuate,
transport
captive... 4. bond, serf 5. helot
6. détenu, thrall, unfree, vassal
8. conquest, enslaved, prisoner
10. subjugated
captivity... 6. duress 7. bondage,
serfdom, slavery 9. detention,
servitude, thralldom 10. internment,
subjection 11. confinement,
impoundment 12. imprisonment
13. incarceration
captor... 5. taker 7. catcher
8. capturer
capture... 3. beg, nab, net, win
4. gain, haul, take 5. catch, pinch,
raven 6. arrest, collar 7. caption,
seizure 8. apprehend, detention
12. apprehension
capuche (Eccl)... 4. cowl, hood
capuchin... 3. sai 5. Cebus
6. monkey, pigeon
caput... 3. cap, top 4. head 5. crest,
crown 7. chapter, section
9. paragraph
car... 4. auto, cart, jeep, tram
5. coupe, motor, sedan, truck,
wagon 6. jalopy 7. caboose, chariot,
flivver, machine, Pullman, vehicle
8. carriage 10. automobile
carabao... 5. mango 7. buffalo
carabinieri... 9. policeman
10. carabineer
caracal... 3. fur 4. lynx, pelt
caracara... 4. hawk 8. carancha
caracole... 5. caper (manège)
9. staircase
caract... 5. charm 6. symbol (magic)
carafe... 6. bottle
carafon... 8. decanter
carapace... 5. plate, shell (turtle)
6. chitin, lorica, shield 7. carapax
caravan... 3. van 5. wagon 6. cafila
(camel) 9. cavalcade, motorcade
10. expedition, procession
caravansary... 3. inn 4. khan (chan)

5. hotel, serai 6. hostel, imaret, posado 8. hostelry 9. resthouse, roadhouse

carbine... 5. rifle 6. musket 7. escopet

carbohydrate... 5. sugar 6. starch 7. dextrin, glucose, lactose, maltose, sucrose 8. dextrose, glycogen, nutrient 9. cellulose 10. saccharide, saccharose

carbon... 4. coke, copy, fuel, lead, soot 7. diamond, residue 8. graphite

carbonate... 3. ore 5. trona 6. aerate, natron 9. carbonize 11. chemicalize

carbon dioxide... 3. gas 6. dry ice 7. seeding (cloud) 11. refrigerant

Carborundum... 5. emery 8. abrasive 14. silicon carbide

carcass... 4. body 5. bones, kreng (whale) 6. corpse 7. cadaver, remains 8. skeleton

carcer... 5. stall (Rom circus) 6. prison

card... 4. map, tum 14. comb, menu, post, rove 6. docket, domino, oddity, postal, record, ticket 7. calling, program 8. calendar, schedule 9. character 13. communication

card game... 3. gin, hoc, loo, pan 4. bank, faro, keno, skat 5. cinch, comet, monte, pitch, poker, rummy, stuss, tarot, whist 6. bridge, casino, écarté, hearts, piquet, rounce 7. auction, bezique, canasta, cassino, cayenne 8. baccarat, contract, cribbage, pinochle 9. solitaire 10. panguingui

card game term... 3. ace 4. meld, pass, pone, slam, trey, vole 5. joker, pedro, tarot 6. cathop, misère, tenace, tricon 7. declare 9. mistigris

cardinal... 3. red 4. bird, fish, main 5. chief 6. bishop, deacon, number, priest, ruling 8. crowning, dominant, foremost 9. paramount, principal 10. preeminent

cardinal (pert to)...
astrology.. 5. nadir 6. zenith
astronomy.. 10. solstitial 11. equinoctial
biology.. 7. maximum, minimum, optimum
compass point.. 4. east, west 5. north, south
number.. 7. primary (one, two, three)
office.. 6. datary 7. dataria
virtues.. 7. justice 8. prudence 9. fortitude 10. temperance
virtues (Theol).. 4. hope 5. faith 7. charity

cardinal's hat... 3. red 4. rank 6. office

care... 4. duty, fret, heed, reck, task, tend, wish 5. aegis, worry 6. desire, regard 7. anxiety, caution, cherish, concern, custody, keeping 9. attention, patronage 10. carefulness, protection, solicitude 11. carefulness, heedfulness, supervision, thriftiness 12. jurisdiction 13. consideration

careen... 3. tip 4. cant, heel, keel, lean, list, tilt 5. slant, slope

career... 3. set 4. flow, flux, line, work 6. course, stream 7. calling, mission,

passage, pursuit 8. business, practice, progress, vocation 10. occupation, profession

care for... 4. help, like, love, mind, reck, tend 5. fancy, guard, nurse, prize, watch 6. attend, dote on, foster, mother, relish, wait on 7. nurture 10. appreciate

carefree... 5. happy 6. jaunty 8. debonair 10. insouciant 12. lighthearted

careful... 4. wary 5. canny, chary, exact 7. anxious, guarded, heedful, mindful, prudent, thrifty 8. cautious, discreet, gingerly, vigilant 9. advertent, attentive 10. meticulous, scrupulous, solicitous, thoughtful 11. circumspect, considerate, painstaking, punctilious

careless... 3. lax 5. loose 6. rakish, remiss, sloppy 8. heedless, mindless, reckless, slipshod, slovenly 9. impulsive, negligent, unheeding, unmindful 10. nonchalant, regardless, unthinking 11. inadvertent, thoughtless, unconcerned 13. inconsiderate

carelessness... 8. bungling, disorder 9. disregard, unconcern 10. blundering, negligence 11. nonchalance 12. heedlessness, indifference, recklessness 13. impulsiveness 15. inconsideration, thoughtlessness

caress... 3. pat, pet 4. bill, kiss 5. touch 6. coddle, cosset, dandle, fondle, pamper, stroke 10. endearment

caressing... 7. hugging, kissing 8. fondling 9. endearing

cargo... 4. load 5. goods 6. burden, charge, lading 7. carload, freight 8. boatload, shipload 9. truckload

cargo (pert to)...
afloat.. 7. flotsam
cast overboard.. 6. jetsam
loader, unloader.. 9. stevedore

Carib... 6. Indian

caribou... 4. deer 8. reindeer

caricature... 5. comic 6. overdo, parody 7. cartoon, picture 8. satirize, travesty 9. burlesque 10. caricatura, distortion 12. exaggeration

caricaturist... 6. artist 8. humorist, parodist 10. burlesquer

caries... 5. decay (Dent) 10. ulceration

carillon... 4. lyra 5. bells (fixed) 6. chimes 12. glockenspiel

cark... 3. vex 4. care, heed, load 5. pains, worry 6. burden, charge, harass 7. trouble 8. distress

carl, carlot... 4. boor 5. churl 6. rustic 7. peasant, villein 8. bondsman 10. husbandman, pinchpenny

Carmelite... 3. nun 4. monk 5. friar 8. White Nun 10. White Friar

carmen... 4. poem, song 11. incantation

Carmen... 5. gypsy, opera (1875) 7. heroine, romance

carmine... 3. red 5. color, stain

7. crimson, scarlet
carnage ... 8. butchery, massacre
  9. bloodshed, slaughter
  10. decimation
carnal ... 4. lewd 6. bodily, fleshy
  7. earthly, mundane, sensual, worldly
  9. corporeal 11. unspiritual
  12. bloodthirsty
carnation ... 3. red 4. pink, self
  7. bizarre, picotee 8. Dianthus
carnelian ... 4. sard 9. copper red
  10. chalcedony
carnival ... 4. fair, show 6. circus
  7. revelry 8. feasting, festival
  9. amusement, Mardi Gras
  11. merrymaking 12. masquerading
carnivore ... 3. cat, dog 4. bear, lion,
  puma, seal 5. civet, coati, genet,
  hyena, otter, panda, ratel, sable,
  tiger, ursus 6. badger, mammal,
  marten, weasel 7. meerkat, raccoon
  8. mongoose 9. ichneumon
  10. cacomistle
carnivorous ... 10. meat–eating,
  predaceous 11. omophageous
carol ... 3. lay 4. lied, lilt, noel, sing,
  song 5. dance (anc) 6. ballad,
  warble 7. rejoice
Caroline Islands (coral) ... 3. Yap
  5. Parao 6. Ponape
carom ... 4. bump 6. bounce, cannon,
  strike 8. ricochet
carousal ... 4. lark, orgy, romp
  5. binge, feast, fling, revel, spree
  6. frolic 7. banquet, carouse, revelry,
  wassail
carouse ... 4. birl 5. bouse, drink,
  spree, toast 9. dissipate
carpet ... 3. mat, rug 4. Agra, Kali,
  Kuba 5. Herat (Herati), namda, tapis
  6. nammad, Wilton 7. drugget
  8. Brussels, flooring, moquette
  9. Axminster, broadloom
  11. Baluchistan
carpetbagger ... 8. swindler
  10. politician
carriage ... 3. air 4. mien, pose
  7. bearing, posture 8. attitude,
  demeanor, presence 10. deportment
carriage (pert to) ...
  English .. 6. waggon 7. growler
    8. dormeuse, stanhope
  French .. 6. fiacre 7. caliche, voiture
  general .. 3. bus, cab, car, gig, rig,
    van 4. baby, hack, pram, shay, trap
    5. buggy, coach, wagon 6. calssh,
    chaise, cisium, dennet, go-cart,
    hansom, landau, surrey, tandem
    7. cariole, chariot, omnibus, phaeton,
    tallyho, vehicle 8. carryall, clarence,
    dearborn, rockaway, victoria
    9. kittereen, landaulet
    10. conveyance, shandrydan
    12. perambulator
  history .. 7. tumbrel, vis-à-vis, whiskey
    8. curricle
  Indian .. 4. okka 5. tonga 6. gharry
    7. hackery
  Italian .. 7. vettura
  one–horse .. 3. gig 4. shay 5. sulky
  Orient .. 4. sado 10. jinrikisha

Philippines .. 9. carromata
Russia .. 5. araba 6. troika 7. droshky
  9. tarantass
carried ... 5. borne, giddy, toted
  6. carted, lugged 8. conveyed,
  ravished 11. transported
carrier ... 3. boy 4. mail, mule, rail,
  ship, wave 5. crate 6. bearer, coolie,
  pigeon, porter, redcap, runner, vessel
  7. courier, drayman, express
  8. cargador, conveyor, teamster
  9. messenger, stevedore
carrier (pert to) ...
  disease .. 3. fly, rat 7. typhoid
    8. mosquito
  Indian .. 5. Tinne (Brit)
  staff .. 5. macer
carrion ... 4. vile 6. corpse, rotten
  7. carcass, corrupt 9. loathsome
carrion (pert to) ...
  bug .. 6. beetle
  buzzard .. 4. hawk 7. vulture
    8. caracara
  flower .. 5. morel
  fungus .. 9. stinkhorn
carrot ... 5. drias (deadly) 6. Daucus
  (Old World) 9. Ammiaceae
  10. nivernaise (glazed), umbellifer
carrousel ... 9. whirligig
  10. roundabout, tournament
  12. merry–go–round
carry ... 3. lug 4. bear, cart, hold,
  take, tote, wart 5. ferry 6. convey
  7. conduct, publish 8. transfer,
  transmit 9. transport
carry away, off ... 3. win 6. abduct,
  eloign, enamor, remove 7. succeed
  9. fascinate 10. accomplish
carry on ... 4. rage, wage 6. endure,
  frolic, manage 7. conduct, operate
  8. continue 9. misbehave, persevere
carry out, through ... 2. do 5. apply
  6. ravish 7. execute, perform, sustain
  8. complete, continue, transact
  10. accomplish
cart ... 4. dray, wain 5. carry, sulky,
  wagon 6. convey, reckla, telega
  7. morfrey (morphrey), tumbrel (anc),
  vehicle (2–wheeled)
carta, Charta ... 4. deed 5. Magna
  (Eng) 7. charter 9. parchment
cartage ... 7. drayage, portage
  8. carriage, teamster, truckage
  10. expressage 14. transportation
carte ... 3. map 4. card, list, menu
  5. chart 7. diagram 10. bill of fare
cartel ... 4. bloc (Polit), defy, pact, pool
  5. paper, truce, trust 6. letter
  7. compact, entente 8. covenant
  9. agreement, challenge, syndicate
  10. convention 11. arrangement
Carthage ... see also *Carthaginian*
  capital .. 13. Vandal Kingdom
  destroyer .. 6. Romans
  queen .. 4. Dido
  rebuilt by .. 8. Augustus
Carthaginian (pert to) ...
  apple .. 11. pomegranate
  foe .. 4. Cato
  general .. 6. Xerxes 8. Hannibal
  god .. 6. Moloch 8. Melkarth
  language .. 5. Punic

Lion.. 8. Hannibal
magistrate.. 7. suffete
name (later).. 15. Justinianopolis
wars (three).. 5. Punic
Carthusian Order (pert to)...
founder.. 7. St Bruno
monastery.. 7. Certosa (It, 1396)
site.. 8. Grenoble (Fr)
cartilage... 4. bone (ossified) 6. tissue
7. gristle
cartload... 6. fother
cartograph... 3. map 4. plat 5. chart
cartoon... 6. design, sketch 7. pattern,
picture 10. caricature
cartoonist... 4. Arno, Capp, Ding, Nast
6. Disney
cartouche... 5. shell 6. corbel, design,
shield (Her), tablet 7. console
8. cartridge 10. cantilever (Arch)
cartwheel... 4. coin 6. dollar
8. somerset 10. handspring,
somersault
carve... 3. cut, hew 4. form, make
5. chase, grave, sever, shape
6. chisel, cleave, furrow, incise
7. engrave, fashion 9. apportion,
fabricate, sculpture
carving... 5. cameo 8. diaglyph,
intaglio 9. anaglyphy, embossing,
sculpture 11. anaglyptics
caryatid... 6. column, figure (fem)
8. pilaster 11. priestesses (temple)
casa... 5. adobe, cabin, house
8. building
cascade... 4. fall, linn 5. Falls, Sault
7. Niagara 8. cataract 9. waterfall
case... 3. box 4. etui, file 5. cover,
crate, crush (sl), event, folio
6. carton, coffer, pillow, sheath,
victim 7. attaché, cabinet, example,
holster, lawsuit 8. argument,
covering, cupboard, instance
9. condition, portfolio 10. receptacle
12. circumstance
case (in any)... 3. yet 4. even
6. anyhow, anyway 7. anywise,
however 8. possibly, provided
10. regardless 15. notwithstanding
case (pert to)...
arrow.. 6. quiver
book.. 5. forel
bottle (liquor).. 8. cellaret
cigar.. 7. humidor
conscience (Sci).. 9. casuistry
grammar.. 8. dative 8. ablative,
genitive, vocative 10. nominative
history (disease).. 6. record
9. anamnesis
image (Bib).. 5. ephod
jewel, relics.. 3. tye 4. apse
spore.. 5. ascus
surgeon's.. 7. trousse
cash... 4. coin, dust (gold) 5. darby,
funds, money 6. silver, specie
7. capital, coinage, mintage
8. currency 9. spondulix
cashmere... 4. goat, wool 5. shawl
6. fabric
casino... 6. tavern 7. cabaret, cassino
(game) 8. ballroom, gambling
9. roadhouse 11. summerhouse
cask... 4. butt, case, drum, pipe

5. terce 6. bareca, barrel, casket,
firkin, tierce 8. puncheon 9. kilderkin
cask (pert to)...
amt when not filled.. 6. ullage
bulge.. 5. bilge
oil.. 4. rier
part.. 3. lag 4. hoop 5. stave
rim.. 5. chime (chimb)
support.. 8. stillage
casket... 3. box, pyx, tye (jewel)
4. cist, kist, tomb 5. chest
8. cassette 11. sarcophagus
casserole... 4. dish, mold 5. brown
(color) 6. vessel 8. saucepan
cassine... 4. game (card)
cast... 3. hue 4. form, hurl, kind, look,
mold, role, shed, tone, toss, type
5. eject, fling, heave, model, pitch,
sling, throw 6. glance, matrix, squint,
troupe 7. pattern 8. template
9. facsimile 10. impression,
strabismus 16. dramatis personae
cast (pert to)...
aside.. 4. jilt, junk, shed 5. scrap
6. reject 7. discard
away.. 5. eject, wreck 6. unmoor
9. shipwreck
blame.. 6. accuse 7. censure
8. reproach 9. reprehend
off.. 4. doff, knit, molt, shed 5. untie
6. unmoor 7. discard 9. eliminate
castaway... 6. pariah 7. outcast
8. derelict 9. reprobate
caste... 4. race, rank 5. breed, class,
stock 6. status 7. lineage, society
8. standing
caste (Ind)... 3. Dom, Meo 4. Ahir,
Jati, Koli, Magi, Mali, Pasi, Teli
5. Gaddi, Sudra, Varna 6. banian,
pariah, Vaisya 7. Brahman
9. Kshatriya
caster, castor... 4. vial 5. cruet, horse
(old), wheel 6. roller, vessel
(condiment)
castigate... 5. emend 6. punish,
revise, strafe 7. chasten, correct,
reprove 8. chastise, penalize
9. criticize 10. discipline
Castile... 4. soap 7. kingdom
Castilian... 7. Iberian, Spanish
castle... 4. fort, keep 5. house, tower,
villa 6. donjon 7. chateau, citadel
8. fortress 10. stronghold
13. fortification
Castor (pert to)...
brother (twin).. 6. Pollux
constellation.. 6. Gemini
mother.. 4. Leda
stars.. 6. Castor, Pollux
castrate... 4. geld, spay 5. alter,
prune 10. emasculate
castrated (pert to)...
bull.. 5. steer
cat.. 3. gib
horse.. 7. gelding
man.. 6. eunuch
rooster.. 5. capon
casual... 5. stray 6. chance, random
9. offhanded 10. contingent,
fortuitous, incidental, occasional,
unforeseen 11. indifferent
14. unpremeditated

casual observation... 6. remark

casualty... 6. chance, hazard, injury, mishap 7. payment, tragedy 8. accident, calamity, disaster, fatality 9. mischance 10. misfortune 11. contingency, contretemps 12. misadventure

casus (pert to)...
act of God.. 14. casus fortuitus
common law.. 12. casus omissus
conscience.. 17. casus conscientiae
Latin.. 4. case 5. event 8. occasion
treaty.. 13. casus foederis
war.. 10. casus belli

cat... 3. gib 4. balu, eyra, lynx, pard, puma 5. alley, civet, Felid, Felis, genet, hyena, manul, ounce, tabby, tiger 6. caffre, cougar, feline, jaguar, margay, ocelot, pajero, rasset, serval 7. cheetah, dasyure, leopard, panther, wildcat 9. catamount, grimalkin

cat (pert to)...
fear of.. 12. ailurophobia, aleurophobia
fish.. 4. pout, raad 6. hassar, tandan 7. eelpout
game.. 6. tipcat
gut.. 5. tharm 6. string (violin)
slang.. 6. hepcat
term.. 5. kitty, shrew, tabby, vixen 6. kitten 8. ailuroid 9. chessycat, Mehitabel (Mehetabel)

cat (species)... 4. Manx 5. Manul, Tibet 6. Angora, Caffre, Margay 7. Burmese, Maltese, Persian, Siamese, Turkish 8. Cheshire, Egyptian 10. Abyssinian, Chinchilla 13. tortoise-shell (black and yellow)

cataclysm... 4. ruin 6. deluge 7. debacle 8. calamity, disaster, The Flood, upheaval 10. convulsion, inundation, revolution 11. catastrophe

catacomb... 4. tomb 5. crypt, vault 6. grotto, locule 8. cemetery (underground) 9. Appian Way

catalepsy... 6. trance 8. hypnosis 9. cataplexy 10. thanatosis

catalogue... 4. book, file, list 5. index, tally 6. codify, digest, record 8. calendar, classify, pamphlet, register, schedule, tabulate 11. enumeration

catamaran... 4. boat, raft 5. balsa, float 6. vessel 7. jangada

catamount... 3. cat 6. cougar 12. catamountain

catapult... 4. hurl 5. shoot, sling 6. engine, onager 7. robinet 8. arbalest, ballista, scorpion 9. slingshot

cataract... 4. fall, linn 5. Falls, flood, sault (soo) 6. deluge 7. cascade, disease, Niagara, opacity (eye), torrent 8. downpour, Victoria 9. cachoeira, waterfall

cataria... 6. catnip

catasta... 5. stage (slave traffic) 6. stocks 7. scaffold

catastrophe... 4. doom, ruin 6. finale, mishap, payoff 7. tragedy 8. calamity, disaster 9. cataclysm

10. denouement, misfortune, revolution 11. termination

catastrophic... 4. dire 5. black 7. ruinous 10. calamitous, deplorable, disastrous

catawba... 4. wine 5. color (red), grape 6. Indian

catch... 3. get, nab 4. draw, hear, hold, hook, take, trap 5. fault, ketch, prize, reach, rondo, seize, snare, trick, troll 6. detent (clock), engage, entrap, ignite 7. attract, capture, seizure 8. overtake 9. intercept

catch (pert to)...
a likeness.. 4. draw 6. depict 7. portray
a ride.. 4. hook 5. hitch, thumb 9. hitchhike
sight of.. 3. see 4. espy 6. behold, descry 7. discern, glimpse

catchword... 3. cry, cue 6. byword, phrase, slogan 7. formula 10. shibboleth

cate... 4. food 5. viands 8. dainties 10. delicacies, provisions (bought)

catechism... 5. guide 6. belief, manual 9. questions (set of) 11. instruction (oral)

catechumen... 5. chela, pupil 6. layman, novice 7. convert 8. disciple, neophyte

categoric, categorical... 6. direct 7. crucial, logical 8. absolute, explicit, positive 9. arbitrary, pragmatic 10. convincing 11. dictatorial, unequivocal, unqualified

category... 4. head 5. class, genre, genus, group, order, state 6. branch, family, specie 7. bracket, species 8. division 12. denomination 14. classification

catena... 5. chain 6. series 8. sequence 10. continuity

catenary... 5. curve (Math) 9. chainlike

cater, cater to... 4. feed 5. favor, humor, serve, toady 6. oblige, pander, please, purvey 7. indulge, procure, provide, satisfy 10. minister to 11. diagonalize 13. cater-cornered

caterpillar... 4. grub, weri 5. aweto, eruca, larva 7. tractor

caterwaul... 3. woo (derog) 4. meow, wail 5. court, miaow 7. screech

cathedral... 3. dom 4. fane (anc) 5. duomo 6. church 8. official 10. ex cathedra 13. authoritative

Cathedral...
England.. 6. Durham 9. Salisbury
France.. 5. Reims (Rheims) 6. Amiens 9. Notre Dame
Istanbul (Constantinople).. 8. St Sophia
Italy.. 7. Lateran, St Mark's
Rome.. 8. St Peter's
Scotland.. 7. St Giles

cathedral (pert to)...
chair (Bishop's).. 8. cathedra
chapter member.. 10. capitulary
church.. 3. dom 7. Lateran (Rome)
city.. 3. Ely (Eng)
passage.. 5. slype

catholic... 4. wide 5. broad 6. church, global 7. general, liberal 8. orthodox, pandemic 9. Christian, universal 10. ecumenical 12. cosmopolitan

Catholic publication... 4. Ordo

catkin... 5. ament, spike 7. cattail

catlike... 5. catty 6. feline 8. stealthy 9. noiseless

catling... 3. cat (little) 6. kitten, string (violin)

Cato (pert to)...
author of.. 13. De Agri Cultura
famed as.. 7. General 9. statesman 10. ambassador (to Carthage)
nickname.. 8. The Elder 11. Cato of Utica

Catoism... 9. austerity, harshness

cats... 8. Kilkenny

cat's cradle... 3. hei 4. game 7. ribwort

cat's-paw... 4. dupe, gull, loof, pawn, tool 5. cully, hitch (knot) 6. breeze (Naut), puppet, stooge 10. instrument

cattail... 4. musk, reed, tule 5. ament, raupo, teree 6. catkin, totora 7. matreed 9. Typhaceae

cattle... 3. Bos 4. cows, kine, neat, oxen, stot, yaks 5. asses, goats, mules, sheep, stock, swine 6. bovine, camels, horses, llamas, niatas, rabble, Taurus 7. banteng, chattel 8. bullocks, property 9. livestock

cattle (breed)... 4. Zebu 5. Angus, Devon, Kerry, Niata, Welsh 6. Brahma, Durham, Jersey, Sussex 7. Dishley 8. Guernsey, Hereford, Holstein, Longhorn 9. Charolais, Leicester, Shorthorn 14. Santa Gertrudis

cattle (pert to)...
collection.. 4. herd 5. drove
disease.. 7. murrain 10. rinderpest
driver.. 6. drover
food.. 5. agist 6. forage
herder.. 6. cowboy, drover
hybrid.. 4. Zobo 7. cattalo 9. cattleyak
motherless.. 6. dogies
pen.. 4. crew 5. barth, reeve
shed.. 6. hemmel
stealer.. 7. abactor, abigeus, rustler
unbranded.. 9. mavericks

catty... 6. feline, weight 7. catlike, cattish 8. spiteful, stealthy 11. treacherous

cauboge... 4. boor 7. bumpkin

Caucasian... 4. race, Slav, Svan, Turk 5. gypsy, Latin, Norse, Osset, Pshav, white 6. Hebrew, Semite, Teuton, Viking 8. Armenian, Bohemian, Georgian, White Man 10. Anglo-Saxon 11. Xanthochroi

Caucasian (pert to)...
blond.. 6. Teuton 8. Estonian 11. Xanthochroi
brunette.. 7. Iberian 8. Armenian 11. Melanochroi
Chinese.. 4. Lolo, Nosu
dialect.. 4. Andi, Avar, Svan
European.. 8. Japhetic

goat (wild).. 3. tur
liquor.. 5. kefir
Moslem. . 3. Laz (Laze, Lazi) 7. Sunni᠎
mountain.. 8. Caucasus
peak.. 6. Elbrus (Elbruz), Kazbek

cauchemar... 9. nightmare

caucus... 7. meeting (Polit), primary 8. assembly

cauda... 4. scut, tail 9. appendage

caudata... 5. newts 8. Amphibia 11. salamanders

caught... see also *catch* 5. treed 7. latched 8. cornered

caught (pert to)...
napping.. 7. unready 8. unprimed 10. unprepared
sight of.. 3. saw 6. espied 8. descried
up in.. 4. tied 7. engaged, tangled 8. absorbed, intent on, involved 10. implicated

caul... 3. net 6. basket 7. netting, network, omentum 8. membrane

cause... 5. aetio (comb form), agent, basis, drive, greed 6. create, factor, ground, induce, motive, reason, source 7. crusade, produce, provoke 8. campaign, etiology, movement, occasion 9. originate 10. mainspring 13. justification

cause (pert to)...
approach.. 7. attract
be done.. 4. writ 11. fieri facias
bring about.. 6. effect
buy and sell.. 7. whipsaw
coagulate.. 4. curd 6. curdle 7. congeal, thicken
contract unevenly.. 6. pucker
face East.. 6. orient
harm.. 4. bane
irritate.. 6. rankle
raise in relief.. 6. emboss
remember.. 6. remind
roll.. 7. trundle
speed up.. 10. accelerate
take root.. 8. radicate

causerie... 4. chat, talk 6. parley 7. article 8. converse, treatise 9. paragraph 10. discussion 12. conversation

causes, science of... 8. etiology

causeuse... 4. sofa 9. tête-à-tête

causeway... 4. dike 7. highway 10. embankment

causing...
destiny.. 5. fatal
emotion.. 7. emotive
forgetfulness.. 8. nepenthe
laughter.. 8. risorial
motion.. 6. motile

caustic... 4. acid, tart 5. acrid, curve (optic), sharp 6. biting, bitter, severe 7. burning, cutting, erodent, mordant, pungent, pyrotic 8. snappish, stinging, virulent 9. corrosive, satirical, vitriolic 10. astringent, escharotic 11. acrimonious, penetrating

caustic agent... 3. lye 4. alum, lime 7. erodent 9. quicklime

causticity... 7. acidity 8. acerbity,

acrimony, asperity, pungency, tartness
9. mordacity 10. bitterness
11. astringency 13. corrosiveness

cautel... 5. trick 7. caution
8. prudence 9. direction (Eccl)
10. precaution

cauterize... 4. burn, char, sear
5. brand, singe 7. torrefy

cautery... 7. burning, searing
8. inustion 10. instrument
13. cauterization

caution.. 4. card (coll), care, heed,
warn 5. aviso 6. advice, caveat,
notice, oddity 7. anxiety, counsel,
precept, proviso, warning 8. forecast,
prudence, wariness 9. chariness,
vigilance 10. admonition, providence,
solicitude 11. exhortation,
forethought, mindfulness
12. cautiousness, notification,
watchfulness 14. circumspection

cautious... 4. wary 5. canny, chary
6. Fabian 7. careful, guarded,
heedful, mindful, prudent
11. circumspect

cautiously... 6. cagily, warily
7. cannily, charily 8. gingerly
9. carefully, guardedly, heedfully,
mindfully, prudently 10. discreetly
13. circumspectly

cavalcade... 4. raid, ride 5. march
6. parade, review 7. caravan,
pageant 9. motorcade 10. procession

cavalier... 3. gay 4. coin (Fr), curt
5. brave, frank, lover, rider 6. escort,
knight, squire 7. admirer, brusque,
esquire, gallant, haughty, soldier
8. horseman, Royalist 9. caballero,
cavaliere, chevalier, Roundhead
10. disdainful, equestrian
12. high-spirited, supercilious

cavalry... 4. army 6. horses, yellow
(color) 8. horsemen 10. knighthood
cavalry (pert to)...
horse.. 6. lancer
man.. 5. spahy, uhlan 6. Hussar,
lancer 7. dragoon, trooper
unit.. 5. troop
weapon.. 5. lance, saber 9. demilance

cave... 3. den, mew 4. abri, cove,
grot, hole, lair 5. antre, cover, lodge
(beaver), speos 6. antrum, cavern,
cellar, covert, dugout, grotto,
subway, tunnel 7. chamber, shelter,
spelunk 10. subterrane
cave (pert to)...
fish.. 9. blindfish
man.. 11. Paleolithic
nature of.. 9. speluncar
study of.. 10. speleology

cave canem... 11. Beware of Dog
cave dweller... 10. troglodyte
Cave of Adullam... 9. Seceeders
(1866)

caviar, caviare... 3. roe 5. garum
8. relish 8. delicacy, fish eggs

cavil... 4. cark, carp, marl, quip
5. dodge, evade, parry, shift
6. bicker, boggle, haggle, palter
7. quibble, shuffle 9. criticize,
pussyfoot 10. equivocate

caviler... 5. momus 6. critic, hedger

8. frondeur, quibbler 10. criticizer
11. equivocator, faultfinder

cavity... 3. dip, pit, sac, vug (voog)
4. aula, bore (gun), cava, hole, sink,
well 5. abyss, antra, atria, bursa,
chasm, fossa, fosse, geode, lumen,
shaft, sinus 6. antrum, areole,
atrium, caries, coelom, crater, hollow
7. cochlea, loculus 10. depression
11. compartment

cavort... 4. dido, romp, skip 5. antic,
caper, cut up, frisk, prank 6. curvet,
gambol, prance 7. flounce, gambade,
gambado

cavy... 3. pig 4. paca 5. stray
6. agouti, rodent 8. capybara
(capibara) 9. guinea pig

caw... 3. cry 5. croak, quark, quawk
11. exclamation

cay... 3. kay 5. islet

cease... 3. end 4. quit, rest (law),
stop 5. avast, pause, stint 6. desist,
perish 7. abandon, fade out, refrain
8. intermit, leave off, shutdown
9. disappear, pretermit
11. discontinue

ceaseless... 7. endless, nonstop
8. constant, unbroken, unending
9. continued, incessant, perennial,
perpetual, unceasing 10. continuous
12. interminable 13. round the
clock, uninterrupted

ceaselessness... 9. constancy
10. continuity, incessancy, perpetuity
11. endlessness 14. successiveness

cease to be... 3. die 6. expire, perish
8. dissolve 9. disappear

cease to please... 4. pall

Cebus... 3. sai 6. monkey 8. capuchin

cecils... 10. croquettes

cecity... 9. blindness

Cecrops (pert to)...
daughter.. 7. Herse 8. Aglauros
founder of (tradition).. 6. Athens
king of.. 6. Attica
symbol.. 7. half man 10. half dragon

cedar (pert to)...
bird.. 7. waxwing
class.. 7. conifer
fruit.. 6. cedron
genus.. 5. Thuja, Toona 6. Cedrus
9. Juniperus
green.. 5. cedre
moss.. 8. hornwort
type.. 5. savin 6. deodar, sabine
7. incense, juniper, Lebanon (Bib),
Spanish*10. arborvitae
11. cryptomeria

cede... 3. grant, waive, yield 6. assign,
confer 7. abandon 8. renounce
9. surrender 10. capitulate, relinquish

cedula... 3. tax 6. permit 8. schedule,
security (Finan) 10. obligation
11. certificate

ceil... 4. line 5. cover 7. overlay
8. wainscot

ceiling... 4. acme, roof 5. astel, limit,
price, trave 6. apogee, lining, screen,
utmost 7. curtain, lacunar, maximum,
plafond 8. covering 9. lacunaria
10. planchment, visibility
12. consummation

celebrant... 6. priest (Eucharist)
9. worshiper (worshipper)
11. communicant

celebrate... 4. keep, laud, sing
5. extol, honor, revel 6. herald,
praise 7. glorify, maffick, observe,
roister 8. emblazon, proclaim
9. solemnize 11. commemorate,
memorialize

celebrated... 5. famed, noted
6. famous 7. feasted, honored,
popular 8. far-famed, observed,
renowned 9. distingué, well-known
11. illustrious 13. distinguished

celebration... 4. bout, fete, rite
5. fling, revel, spree 6. bender
7. fanfare, jubilee 8. ceremony,
function 9. epinicion, festivity,
rejoicing 10. observance
13. commemoration

celebrity... 3. VIP 4. fame 5. éclat,
glory 6. notary 7. notable
8. luminary, somebody
10. famousness, popularity
11. recognition

celerity... 5. haste, speed 8. dispatch,
rapidity, velocity 9. swiftness
10. speediness

celery... 4. ache 8. smallage (wild)
9. Ammiacaea

celestial... 6. astral, divine, uranic
7. angelic, sky blue 8. ethereal,
heavenly 12. paradisaical

Celestial (pert to)...
being.. 5. angel 6. cherub, seraph
body.. 4. star 5. comet 6. nebula
city.. 6. heaven, utopia 9. Jerusalem
empire.. 7. Chinese, Tien Chu
equator.. 8. meridian
mind elevation.. 7. anagoge
teacher.. 6. Taoist

celibate... 4. monk 6. single
8. bachelor, monastic, Platonic,
spinster 9. abstinent, continent,
unmarried

cell... 3. egg, kil 4. cyst, germ, ovum
5. cnida, crypt 6. cytode, prison
7. alveola, cellule, dungeon
11. compartment

cell (pert to)...
animal.. 6. amoeba (ameba) 7. rotifer
8. protozoa
biology.. 7. energid, meiosis, mitosis,
nucleus, spireme
cell-like.. 9. celliform
division.. 5. linin 7. spireme
8. amitosis
eating.. 9. cytophagy
Egyptian (tomb).. 6. serdab
honeycomb.. 8. alveolus
Irish.. 3. kil (kill)
locomotive.. 5. sperm, zooid
Roman.. 4. alla, naos
study.. 8. cytology
substance.. 5. linin
walls.. 9. cellulose

cellaret... 4. case 8. tantalus
9. sideboard

Celt... 4. Erse, Gael, Manx, Scot
5. Welsh 6. Breton 7. Cornish

Celtic (pert to)...
abbot.. 5. coarb

bard.. 6. Ossian
cattle.. 2. ox
church.. 9. Christian
deity.. 7. Taranis
foot soldier.. 4. kern
horse.. 4. pony (Shetland)
Island.. 4. Manx
language.. 4. Erse
minstrel.. 4. bard
Mother of Gods.. 3. Ana (Anu)
mountain.. 3. ben
Neptune.. 3. Ler
nickname.. 10. Turtleback
Order.. 5. Druid
people.. 5. Gauls, Irish, Scots, Welsh
7. Bretons, Britons
perfume.. 4. nard 9. spikenard
sun god.. 3. Lug (Lugh)

cembalo... 8. dulcimer 11. harpsichord
12. clavicembalo

cement... 4. bind, fuse, glue, join,
paar, pave 5. putty, stick, unite
6. cohere, fasten, mastic, mortar,
solder 8. adhesive, concrete,
pavement, solidify

cemetery... 6. litten 7. Calvary
8. boneyard, catacomb, Golgotha,
lich gate (entrance), mortuary
9. graveyard, mausoleum
10. churchyard, necropolis
11. polyandrium 12. potter's field

cenobite... 4. Monk 5. Order (anc)
6. Essene 7. recluse

cenotaph... 4. tomb (empty)
7. memento 8. memorial, monument

censer bearer... 7. acolyte 8. altar
boy, thurifer

censor... 5. judge 6. critic 7. monitor
8. censurer, reviewer, superego
11. faultfinder

censure... 4. flay 5. blame, chide,
slate, targe 6. accuse 7. chasten,
condemn, impeach, inveigh, reprove,
slating 8. reproach 9. damnation,
expurgate, reprimand 11. reprobation
12. condemnation, denunciation,
reprehension

cent... 4. coin, game (old) 5. penny
6. copper, trifle 7. hundred, red cent

centaur (Myth)... 4. race (Thessaly)
6. Nessus 8. Lapithae, man-horse
(half man) 9. bucentaur, Centaurus
(Astron)

centennial... 4. game (dice)
9. hundredth, red-yellow
11. anniversary

Centennial State... 8. Colorado

center... 3. cor, hub 4. base, core,
nave 5. axial, focus, heart, midst
6. kernel, marrow, middle
7. midmost, nucleus, pivotal, seaport
8. emporium

center (pert to)...
away from.. 6. distal
bull's-eye.. 5. clout 6. target
line.. 6. axiate, cesura

center of...
attention.. 8. cynosure
earth.. 9. epicenter
gravity.. 6. kernel 7. centrum
nervous system.. 5. brain
sail.. 4. bunt

target.. 3. eye 8. bull's–eye
centerpiece... 7. epergne
centipede... 4. rope (Naut) 6. earwig,
  insect 8. chilipod, myriapod
central... 3. mid 4. arch, main
  5. axial, basic, chief, focal, prime
  6. master, middle 7. capital, centric,
  leading, midmost, pivotal, primary
  8. cardinal, dominant, foremost
  9. principal 11. equidistant
Central America...
  bird.. 7. jacamar 8. puffbird
  boat.. 6. cayuco, pitpan
  country.. 6. Panama 8. Honduras
  9. Costa Rica, Guatemala, Nicaragua
  10. El Salvador
  Indian.. 4. Maya 5. Carib
  monkey.. 4. mono
  rodent.. 4. paca
  snake.. 10. bushmaster
  tree.. 3. ebo, ule 5. amate
  9. sapodilla
Central Asia (pert to)...
  gazelle.. 3. ahu
  wild horse.. 6. tarpan
  wind storm.. 5. buran
Central State... 6. Kansas
centuries (ten)... 7. chiliad
century... 3. Age 4. aeon (eon)
  7. centred (anc), hundred 8. eternity
century plant... 4. aloe 5. agave
  6. maguey
ceorl (Eng Hist)... 5. churl, thane
  7. freeman, villein
cepa... 5. onion
cephalon... 5. head (Zool)
cephalopod... 3. ink (secretion)
  5. sepia 6. cuttle 7. octopus
  10. cuttlefish
ceramics... 4. tile 5. china, delft,
  Spode 7. pottery, Satsuma
  8. crockery, majolica 9. porcelain,
  Wedgwood
ceramics term... 4. clay, kiln, laun
  5. adobe, stove, wheel 6. sleeve
  (silk) 7. furnace 12. ceramography
ceratoid... 5. horny 8. hornlike
  10. horn–shaped
Cerberus (Myth)... 3. dog (3–headed)
  8. guardian
cere... 3. wax 6. wrap (dead body)
  6. anoint 12. protuberance (bird's)
cereal... 4. bran, mush, rice 5. gruel,
  wheat 6. hominy 7. oatmeal
  8. porridge
cereal grass... 3. oat, rye 4. ragi
  5. grain, maize, wheat 6. barley,
  raggee
cereal spike... 3. ear
cerebellum... 5. brain (part)
cerebral (pert to)... 4. lobe 5. brain
  6. speech 8. arteries, peduncle
  9. consonant (Phonet) 11. crus
  cerebri, hemispheres
cerebrum... 5. brain 10. encephalon
cere cloth... 7. wrapper (corpse)
  8. cerement, chrismal 12. grave
  clothes
ceremonial... 4. prim 5. stiff
  6. formal, ritual 7. precise, service,
  studied 8. ceremony, function, liturgic
  9. formality 11. punctilious

  12. conventional
ceremonial (pert to)...
  chamber.. 4. kiva
  departure.. 6. congee
  post, pole.. 5. totem
  splendor.. 9. pageantry
ceremonious... 6. formal, polite
  7. precise 8. gracious 9. attentive,
  courteous 10. ceremonial, respectful
  11. deferential, ritualistic
ceremony... 4. form, pomp, rite, show
  6. parade, review, ritual 8. function
  9. formality, solemnity
  10. observance 11. performance
ceremony, without... 6. humbly,
  meekly, simply 7. quietly 8. casually,
  modestly 9. sans façon
  10. informally
Ceres (pert to)...
  astronomy.. 8. asteroid (lst found)
  father.. 6. Saturn
  Feast.. 8. Cerialia (Apr 19)
  Goddess of.. 4. Corn 5. Grain
  9. Fertility 11. Agriculture
  Greek name.. 7. Demeter
  mother.. 3. Ops
Cereus... 6. cactus 7. saguaro
  13. night–blooming
cerise... 5. color 7. blue–red, fuchsia
  10. cherrylike
ceroplastics... 8. modeling, waxworks
certain... 3. one 4. sure 5. clear,
  exact, fixed, plain 7. assured,
  decided, insured, precise 8. absolute,
  definite, positive 9. certified,
  confident, exclusive, indubious,
  undoubted, warranted
  10. guaranteed, inevitable,
  undeniable, undoubting
  11. determinate, trustworthy
  14. unquestionable
  16. incontrovertible
certainly... 3. yea, yes 4. amen
  5. truly 6. indeed, really, surely,
  verily 7. clearly, in truth, utterly
  8. actually, of course 9. assuredly,
  precisely 10. absolutely, by all
  means, definitely, inevitably, positively
certainty... 6. pledge, surety
  8. sureness 9. assurance, certitude
  13. inevitability, infallibility
certificate... 5. check, money 6. ticket
  7. diploma, voucher 10. credential
  11. testimonial
certificate (pert to)...
  financial.. 3. IOU 5. draft, scrip
  9. debenture
  India.. 5. hundi
  medical (Eng college).. 8. aegrotat
certification... 2. OK 3. fix 5. proof
  8. sanction 10. validation
  11. affirmation, attestation, certificate,
  endorsement 12. confirmation,
  ratification 13. ascertainment,
  authorization 14. substantiation
certify... 5. prove, swear, vouch
  6. assure, attest, avouch, ratify, verify
  7. approve, confirm, endorse, witness
  8. accredit, validate 9. ascertain,
  determine, establish, guarantee
  11. acknowledge, corroborate
cerulean... 4. blue 5. azure

7. sky–blue
cerumen... 6. earwax
cervine... 8. deerlike
cess... 3. bag, tax 4. cede, duty, levy,
toll 5. yield 6. assess, impost, tariff
7. revenue 9. surrender
10. assessment
cessation... 3. end 4. lull, stay
5. letup, truce 7. respite
8. abeyance, desition 9. interlude
10. suspension 12. intermission,
interruption 14. discontinuance
cetacea, cetacean... 3. orc 4. apod,
orca, susu (blind) 5. whale 6. whales
7. cowfish, finback, grampus, narwhal
(narwal), rorqual
Cete... 5. whale 10. The Cetacea
Cetus... 8. The Whale 13. constellation
(Equator)
Ceylon...
  capital.. 7. Colombo
  city.. 5. Galle, Kandy (famed Buddhist
    Temple) 6. Jaffna
  mountain peak.. 14. Pidurutalagala
  ocean.. 6. Indian
  old name.. 9. Taprobane
  people.. 5. Tamil 6. Malays, Veddas
    8. Malabars 10. Singhalese
Ceylon (pert to)...
  boat.. 5. dhoni (doni)
  canoe.. 5. balsa
  Festival.. 8. Perahera
  garment.. 6. sarong
  hill dweller.. 4. Toda
  monkey.. 4. maha 6. langur, rillow
  moss.. 4. alga 6. Jaffna 7. gulaman
    8. agar–agar
  palm.. 7. talipot
  rat.. 9. bandicoot
  sand (sea bottom).. 4. paar
  tree.. 4. doon
chabouk, chabuk (Ind)... 4. whip
  9. horsewhip
chacma... 6. baboon
chafe... 3. cut, irk, rub, vex 4. fret,
fume, fuss, gall, heat, rage, skin,
warm 5. anger, annoy, grate, grind,
pique, scuff, worry, wound
6. abrade, banter, excite, harass,
injure, nettle, rankle 7. inflame
8. irritate
chaff... 3. hay 4. bran, husk, quiz,
twit 5. dregs, fluff, husks, palea,
straw, trash, waste 6. banter,
cobweb, glumes, refuse, scraps
7. remains, residue, tailing 8. raillery,
ridicule, riffraff
chaffer... 5. trade, wares 6. buying,
dicker, haggle, higgle, market
7. bargain, chaffer, chatter, selling
9. negotiate 11. merchandise
chafing dish... 7. cresset
chagrin... 7. anxiety, mortify
8. distress, troubles, vexation
13. mortification
chain... 3. bind, bond, boom, gyve,
reef, torc 5. cable, range 6. catena,
fasten, fetter, secure, series, tether,
torque 7. creeper, sorites
15. contravallation (fort series)
chair... 4. seat, sill 5. bench, sedan
6. rocker, throne 7. enchair, speaker

chair (pert to)...
  back.. 5. splat 7. upright
  collegiate.. 10. fellowship
    13. professorship
  cover.. 4. tidy 12. antimacassar
  India.. 6. musnud
  Japan.. 4. kago
  maker.. 5. caner 6. reeder
chair (type of)... 4. camp, deck, easy,
high, lawn, wing 6. lounge, Morris,
swivel 7. contour, folding, steamer,
Windsor 8. armchair, captain's,
electric, fauteuil, straight
10. ladder–back 11. overstuffed
chairman... 7. officer, speaker
8. director 9. moderator
chalcedony... 4. onyx, opal, sard
5. agate 6. jasper, quartz 7. opaline
9. carnelian 12. chrysoprase
Chaldean (pert to)... 2. Ur 4. seer
6. Semite 10. astrologer, soothsayer
13. Neo–Babylonian (language)
chalice... 3. ama, cup 5. amula (anc),
calix, grail 6. goblet 8. daffodil
chalice pall... 4. veil 8. animetta
chalk... 4. draw, mark, pale, tick
5. score 6. blanch, bleach, crayon,
credit, pastel, whiten 7. account,
drawing 9. limestone, reckoning
chalker... 7. milkman (Eng sl)
chalklike... 10. calcareous
chalky... 5. white 7. crumbly, friable,
powdery 10. cretaceous
challenge... 4. dare, defy, gage
5. claim, doubt, query 6. accost,
cartel, defial, demand, impugn
7. dispute, protest 8. question,
reproach 10. accusation, controvert
11. questioning
chamal... 4. goat (Angora)
chamber... 4. cave, hall, kiva, room
5. court 6. camera, cavity
7. bedroom, boudoir, cabinet,
chambre, cubicle 10. bedchamber
11. compartment
chamber (pert to)...
  harem.. 3. oda
  heart.. 7. auricle 9. ventricle
  King's.. 9. camarilla
  music.. 14. sonata da camera
chambers... 4. flat 5. suite 6. office
9. apartment, bicameral (Legis)
14. Inns of Chancery (Eng)
chameleon... 6. lizard 10. vacillator
13. changeability, constellation
chamfer (to)... 5. bevel, carve, flute,
score 6. chisel, groove
chamois... 5. Gemse, izard 8. antelope
champ... 4. bite, chew, mash
5. gnash 6. victor 7. trample
11. battlefield
champagne... 4. wine 9. red–yellow
13. chrysanthemum
champaign... 5. field, plain 7. expanse
11. battlefield
champion... 3. Ace 4. best, hero
5. champ 6. defend, expert, victor,
winner 7. espouse, fighter, titlist
8. advocate, defender 9. combatant,
conqueror 10. unexcelled
champion (pert to)...
  Christian (anc).. 3. Cid

constellation.. 7. Perseus
knight (legend).. 7. Paladin
Spanish.. 12. conquistador
chance... 3. die, hap, lot 4. fate, luck,
odds, risk, turn 6. casual, gamble,
happen, mishap, tossup 7. fortune,
lottery, tychism 8. fortuity, Lady
Luck, occasion 9. happening,
mischance 10. likelihood
11. opportunity, possibility, probability
12. happenstance
chancel (pert to)...
part.. 4. bema
screen.. 4. jube
seats.. 7. sedilia
change... 4. flux, move, turn, vary,
veer 5. alter, amend, break, coins,
money, shift 6. modify, mutate,
switch 7. caprice, convert, deviate,
variety 8. transfer 9. diversity,
transform, transmute, variation
10. alteration, fickleness, modulation
11. inconstancy, vicissitude
12. substitution 13. metamorphosis
14. transformation 15. diversification
change (pert to)...
color.. 3. dye, wan 4. fade, pale
5. blush 6. blanch, redden
medicine.. 11. heterotopia
mind.. 6. repent 12. tergiversate
music.. 4. muta
order of.. 9. metabolic, rearrange,
transpose
changeable... 6. fickle, fitful, mobile
7. erratic, flighty, mutable, protean
8. freakish, notional, unstable,
variable, volatile, weathery
9. alterable, chameleon, metabolic,
uncertain, unsettled, whimsical
10. capricious, inconstant
15. interchangeable
changeling... 3. oaf 4. dolt 5. idiot
7. waverer 8. imbecile, renegade,
turncoat 9. simpleton 10. substitute
(child)
channel... 3. bed, cut, gat, way
4. dike, duct, gate, gurt, leat,
pass, vein 5. basin, canal, ditch,
drain, flume, flute, fosse, radio, river,
sinus, stria 6. alveus, avenue, coulee,
groove, gutter, outlet, sluice, trench,
trough 7. conduit, tideway
8. aqueduct, tailrace 9. broadcast
10. passageway
Channel Islands... 4. Sark (Sercq)
6. Jersey 8. Alderney
chanson... 4. song 5. lyric 6. ballad
chant... 3. say 4. sing 6. intone,
melody, warble 7. introit, singing
8. canticle 10. intonation
11. composition
chanter... 6. cantor, singer 7. bagpipe
(part), intoner, sparrow (hedge)
8. songster, vocalist 9. chanteuse,
chorister
chanticleer... 4. cock 7. rooster
11. cock-a-doodle
14. cock-a-doodle-doo
chaos... 2. Nu (Egypt) 3. pie (type)
4. gulf, mess 5. abyss, babel, chasm
7. anarchy 8. disorder 9. confusion,
imbroglio 10. unruliness

13. orderlessness
Chaos (pert to)...
daughter.. 3. Nox, Nyx
parent of.. 5. earth 6. heaven
8. Creation
son.. 6. Erebus
chaotic... 6. muddle 8. confused,
formless 12. disorganized
chap... 3. boy, buy, guy, lad, man
4. kibe (sore) 5. buyer, chink, cleft,
crack, scout, split, youth 6. barter,
choose (Scot), fellow, galoot
7. chapman 8. customer
chapeau... 3. cap, hat, lid 5. beret
chapel... 4. cape, cope, cowl, hood
5. altar, choir 6. bethel 7. chantry,
galilee, oratory, service, Sistine
8. sacellum (anc) 9. reliquary
chaperon... 4. hood 6. attend,
duenna, escort 8. guardian
9. attendant 10. gooseberry
chaplet... 4. band 5. beads
6. anadem, wreath 7. garland,
prayers 8. beadroll, insignia, necklace
chappaul... 9. squawfish
chaps... 8. overalls 10. chaparajos
chapter... 4. Sura 5. topic 6. clause
7. council, meeting, passage,
section, Society 8. division
9. capitular 10. fraternity
12. organization
chaptrel... 6. impost
char... 4. burn 5. trout 6. scorch
8. charcoal, sandbank
character... 4. hero, kind, mark, role,
sign, star 5. trait 6. cipher, letter,
nature, repute, status, symbol
7. quality 8. function 9. reference
10. reputation 11. temperament
14. characteristic
character (pert to)...
giver.. 5. toner
Hebrew.. 3. Tav, Taw
Irish.. 5. Ogham
musical.. 3. bar 4. clef, rest
5. neume
of people.. 5. ethos
real.. 7. essence
science of.. 8. ethology
Teutonic.. 4. rune
characteristic... 4. mark 5. habit, trait
7. feature, impress, quality, typical
8. peculiar, symbolic 9. attribute,
character, idiopathy, lineament,
specialty 11. distinctive, peculiarity,
singularity, symptomatic
13. individualism
characteristic (pert to)...
descent.. 6. racial
peculiar.. 9. idiopathy
spirit.. 5. ethos
tone (Mus).. 7. seventh
characterization... 4. role 5. drama
9. depiction, portrayal
11. description, distinction
13. impersonation 14. identification,
representation
characterize... 4. mark, name 5. enact
7. engrave, imprint, portray
8. describe, inscribe 9. delineate,
designate, epitomize, represent
11. distinguish

characterized by...
abstinence.. 7. ascetic
bacteria exclusion.. 7. asepsis
cruelty.. 7. Neronic
exact thinking.. 13. ratiocinative
melody.. 6. ariose
poison (bloodstream).. 6. sepsis
pomposity.. 13. grandiloquent

characterless... 5. inane 9. colorless, pointless

charcoal... 4. coke, fuel, lave, peat 5. black, chark 6. carbon, fusain 7. drawing, residue 9. boneblack, briquette

charge... 4. bill, cost, dues, fill, load, onus, rate, task, toll, ward 5. blame, chore, debit, onset, order, price, trust 6. accuse, advice, advise, allege, amount, attack, client, commit, credit, demand, dictum, impute, indict 7. assault, command, concern, custody, expense, impeach, keeping, mandate, precept, primage, protégé 8. guidance, insignia, instruct, tutelage 9. dependent, electrify, exactment 10. accusation, commission, imposition, impregnate, injunction, management 11. arrangement, attribution, instruction, supervision 13. incrimination 14. responsibility

charge of affairs... 8. diplomat 15. chargé d'affaires

charge off... 5. debit 6. forget 7. dismiss, forgive 8. discount

charges (law)... 4. dues, fees 5. costs 9. retainers

charge with...
crime.. 6. indict 7. impeach 11. incriminate
debt.. 5. debit
gas.. 6. aerate
offense.. 6. accuse
to.. 5. blame 7. ascribe 9. attribute

charily... 6. cagily, warily 8. frugally 9. carefully, thriftily 10. cautiously 12. economically, suspiciously

chariness... 7. caution 8. caginess, distrust, wariness 9. frugality 11. heedfulness, thriftiness

chariot... 3. car 4. biga, cart, rath (ratha), wain 5. essed (anc), wagon 7. vehicle 8. quadriga

charioteer... 6. Auriga (Astron), Ben Hur

charitable... 3. big 4. kind 6. kindly 7. lenient, liberal 8. generous, tolerant 9. forgiving, indulgent 10. altruistic, benevolent, bighearted 11. beneficient 12. eleemosynary, humanitarian 13. compassionate, philanthropic

charity... 4. alms, dole 6. bounty, virtue 7. handout, largess 8. lenience, pittance 9. tolerance 10. almsgiving, liberality 11. benevolence 12. philanthropy

charity dispenser... 7. almoner

charivari... 5. babel 6. medley, uproar 8. serenade (mock) 9. callithump

charlatan... 5. faker, fraud, phony, quack 6. humbug 7. empiric

8. impostor 9. pretender
10. medicaster, mountebank

Charlemagne, Emperor (pert to)..
brother.. 8. Carloman
emperor of.. 7. The West
father.. 5. Pepin (the Short)
name also.. 15. Charles The Great
nephew.. 7. Orlando

charm... 3. obi 4. lure, mojo, play, song 5. grace, magic, oomph, spell 6. allure, amulet, appeal, beauty, enamor, entice, fetish, glamor, scarab 7. beguile, bewitch, cantrip, delight, enchant, glamour, periapt 8. breloque, elegance, entrance, ornament, talisman 9. captivate, fascinate, sex appeal, sweetness 10. allurement, attraction, brimborion (brimborium), lovability 11. captivation, conjuration, incantation, pulchritude, winsomeness 12. antinganting 14. attractiveness, delightfulness

charmer... 5. siren 6. beauty 7. enticer 8. exorcist, magician, sorcerer 9. bewitcher

charming... 7. winsome 8. alluring, pleasing 10. bewitching, delightful 11. captivating, fascinating

chart... 3. map 4. list, plat, plot 7. diagram

charter... 4. hire 5. carta, grant 6. charta, firman, treaty 7. license 9. privilege (special), purwannah

chartreuse... 4. mold (cookery) 5. color 7. liqueur

Chartreuse... 7. monastery 18. La Grande Chartreuse (Grenoble)

chary... 4. wary 5. cagey 6. frugal, skimpy 7. thrifty 8. cautious 10. suspicious 12. parsimonious

Charybdis... 6. Scylla 8. Galofaro 9. whirlpool (Messina)

chase (The), goddess of... 5. Diana

chasm... 3. gap, pit 4. gulf, hole, rift, well 5. abyss, cleft, shaft 6. breach, canyon, cavity, hiatus 7. fissure, opening 8. crevasse

chasma... 7. yawning

chasse... 4. step (dance) 6. shrine 9. reliquary

chaste... 4. pure 6. modest, simple 8. innocent, virtuous 9. continent, uncorrupt, undefiled, unmarried 10. immaculate

chasten... 4. rate 5. smote 6. punish, refine 7. correct 8. chastise, penalize, restrain 9. castigate 10. discipline

chastened... 4. meek 5. smote 7. subdued 8. punished, purified, tempered 10. restrained

chastise... 4. beat, slap, whip 5. amend, blame, scold, spank, taunt 6. punish, rebate, rebuke, swinge

7. correct, reprove 9. castigate
10. discipline

chastity . . . 6. purity, virtue 9. cleanness
10. chasteness 12. virtuousness
13. uncorruptness

chat . . . 3. gab 4. coze, jist, talk, tove
5. prate 6. babble, confab, gabble,
gibber, gossip, jabber 7. chatter,
prattle 8. causerie, chitchat, converse
12. conversation 14. chitter–chatter

chatelaine . . . 3. pin 4. etui, hook
5. clasp, purse, watch 6. brooch,
torque

chattels . . . 4. naam 5. goods, money,
wares 6. estate 7. effects
8. holdings, property 9. livestock,
principal 11. possessions

chatter . . . 3. gab, yap 5. clack, prate
7. clatter, prattle

chatterer . . . 3. jay, mag 4. bird, piet
6. magpie 10. chatterbox

chatty . . . 3. pot (earthen) 4. glib
5. gabby 6. affable 8. sociable
9. garrulous, prattling, talkative
14. conversational

Chaucer (pert to) . . .
author of . . 15. Canterbury Tales
Inn . . 6. (The) Tabard
pilgrimage city . . 10. Canterbury
style of work . . 7. novella

chauvinist . . . 5. jingo 6. Rajput
7. chauvin, patriot 8. jingoist
9. warmonger 10. militarist

cheap . . . 5. small, tinny, trade, value
6. paltry, plenty 7. abashed, bargain,
reduced 9. niggardly, plentiful
11. inexpensive

cheapen . . . 3. bid 6. haggle
7. bargain, chaffer 10. depreciate

cheat . . . 2. do 3. ban, con, fob, gyp
4. bilk, fake, flam, hoax, liar, rook,
sell, sham 5. cozen, elude, guile,
phony 6. deceit, fleece, humbug,
illude 7. deceive, finesse, sharpen,
swindle 8. artifice, impostor
9. bamboozle, overreach, stratagem,
victimize 10. thimblerig

check . . . 3. nip, tab 4. balk, curb,
damp, mark, rein, stem, stop, test
5. agree, brake, count, delay, limit,
money, plaid, repel, stunt, tally
6. bridle, cheque, detain, detent,
impede, oppose, rebuff, retard, ticket,
verify 7. counter, examine, inhibit,
measure, monitor, pattern, repress
9. hindrance, restraint 12. verification

check (pert to) . . .
in . . 3. die 6. arrive 8. register
out . . 3. die 5. croak, leave
8. withdraw
pattern . . 11. houndstooth
poison . . 8. antidote
game, term . . 5. chess 8. gambling

checkered . . . 4. vair 5. diced, plaid
6. mosaic, tartan, varied 7. checked
10. changeable, tesserated,
variegated 11. diversified

checkers, chequers . . . 4. game
8. draughts (Brit)

cheek . . . 4. gall, gena, jowl 5. brass,
bucca, crust, malar, nerve
8. audacity 9. impudence

10. buccinator

cheer . . . 3. rah 4. yell 5. bravo, elate,
huzza, liven, mirth, salvo 6. gaiety,
hurrah, regale, repast, salute, solace
7. animate, applaud, console,
gladden, hearten, jollity, refresh,
rejoice 8. applause, inspirit, pleasure,
vivacity 9. encourage, merriment
10. exhilarate 12. conviviality

cheerful . . . 3. gay 4. gleg (Scot), rosy
5. happy, peart, sunny 6. blithe,
cheery, genial, hearty, jocund, joyful
8. gladsome, homelike 9. contented,
lightsome 12. lighthearted

cheerfulness . . . 3. joy 4. glee
5. cheer, mirth 6. gaiety 7. jollity
8. gladness, hilarity 9. happiness,
merriment 12. exhilaration

cheerio . . . 5. adios, aloha, skoal, toast
6. hurrah, prosit 8. au revoir,
farewell, Godspeed 9. greetings

cheerless . . . 3. sad 4. cold, drab
5. drear 6. dismal, dreary, gloomy
7. forlorn, joyless, unhappy
8. dejected 9. unsmiling
10. depressing, melancholy
11. dispiriting 13. disconsolate

cheese . . . 3. pot 4. bleu, brie, edam,
jack 5. cream, Gouda, Swiss
6. barrie, Dunlop, mysost, Romano,
zieger 7. Cheddar, cottage, fromage,
sapsago 8. American, Parmesan
9. Camembert, Limburger, Roquefort
10. Gorgonsola, Neufchatel

cheese dish . . . 6. fondue, omelet
7. rarebit, soufflé

cheesy . . . 3. bad 6. paltry 8. inferior
9. worthless 12. disreputable

cheetah . . . 3. cat 5. youse (youze)
7. guepard (gueparde)

cheilos . . . 3. lip

chela . . . 4. claw 6. novice 8. disciple

Chelonia . . . 7. turtles 8. reptiles
9. tortoises

chemical (pert to) . . .
analysis . . 5. assay
cleanser . . 6. kryton
etching . . 11. chemigraphy
strength . . 5. titer (titre)
term . . 3. gas 4. acid, atom, base,
salt 6. alkali 7. hormone, nonacid,
organic, radical, valence 8. catalyst,
compound 10. bathoflore
11. bathochrome
vessel . . 4. etna 6. aludel, retort
7. alembic 8. crucible, reductor
washings . . 6. eluate

chemical suffix . . . 2. ac, el, yl 3. ane,
ene, ile, ine, ole, ose 4. enol, olic,
osan

chemin de fer . . . 7. railway
8. baccarat, railroad

chemist . . . 7. analyst 8. druggist
9. alchemist 10. apothecary,
biochemist 12. iatrochemist (anc)

cherish . . . 3. aid, hug, pet, woo
4. love 5. adore, cheer, nurse, prize
6. caress, faddle, fondle, foster
7. care for, comfort, nourish,
nurture, protect, support 8. enshrine,
remember, treasure 9. cultivate,
encourage, entertain

cherry... 3. pin 4. bird, gean, ming
5. black 6. egriot, Prunus 7. capulin,
marasca, mazzard, Morello, oxheart
8. Napoleon 9. amarelles, bigarreau
10. chokeberry 11. Montmorency

cherub... 5. angel, child, saint
6. seraph, spirit 7. darling, eudemon
8. cherubim, seraphim

chess (pert to)...
chessman.. 4. king, pawn, rook
5. piece, queen 6. bishop, castle,
knight
Italian.. 7. scacchi
term.. 4. dual, move 5. debut
6. chassé, fidate, gambit 7. end
game, opening, problem 9. en
passant, rook's tour, stalemate
10. fianchetto

chesslike... 8. scacchic

chest... 3. ark, box 4. arca, cist, kist
5. bahut 6. breast, cajeta, coffer,
coffin, locker 7. highboy, wanigan
(wangan) 10. chiffonier
11. gardeviance

chest (pert to)...
ammunition.. 7. caisson
animal.. 7. brisket
human.. 6. thorax 7. midriff
sound.. 4. rale
sepulchral.. 6. larnax

Chester (Eng), inhabitant... 8. Cestrian

chesterfield... 4. sofa 5. divan
8. overcoat 9. cigarette, davenport

chestnut... 4. ling, rata 5. horse,
water 6. marron 7. buckeye
8. Aesculus, Castanea 10. breadfruit,
chinquapin

chestnut... 4. joke 6. cliché
7. bromide 8. banality

chestnut color... 4. roan 5. brown
6. sorrel 12. reddish–brown

chevalier... 5. cadet (nobility), noble
6. knight 7. gallant 8. cavalier,
horseman 10. greenshank (bird)

chevron... 4. beam 5. glove 6. rafter,
stripe, zigzag 8. insignia
10. gravystain

chevrotain... 4. napu 7. deerlet,
kenchil, meminna 9. Tragulina

chevy... 3. cry (hunting) 4. game, hunt
5. chase 6. flight, harass, pursue
7. torment

chew... 3. cud 4. bite, chaw, gnaw,
quid 5. champ, chomp, grind, munch
6. chavel, ponder 8. meditate,
ruminate 9. masticate

chiasma... 11. decussation
12. intersection

chiasmus... 9. inversion (of words)

chib (Gypsy)... 6. tongue 8. language

chic... 4. trig, trim 5. natty, smart
6. modish, spruce 7. stylish

Chicago's nickname... 9. Windy City

chicanery... 4. ruse, wile 5. feint, trick
6. deceit 7. knavery 8. artifice,
trickery 9. stratagem 11. skulduggery

chickadee... 8. titmouse
10. Pebthestes

chicken... 3. hen 4. cock, fowl, girl
5. biddy, capon, chick, deedy, fryer,
poult, young 6. coward, pullet
7. broiler, rooster 8. cockerel,

weakling 9. youngling
11. chanticleer, milquetoast

chickenhearted... 5. timid 8. cowardly
12. fainthearted

chicory... 6. endive 7. succory
12. Cichoriaceae

chide... 4. rate 5. blame, scold
6. berate, rebuke 7. censure,
reprove, wrangle 8. admonish,
reproach 9. reprimand

chief... 3. dux, top 4. arch, head,
main, rais (reis) 5. first, forte, major,
mogul 6. leader, primal, staple,
syndic 7. kingpin, supreme
9. directing, governing, paramount,
potentate, principal, prominent
11. predominant

chief (pert to)...
African.. 3. bey 4. kaid 5. negus
6. induna
Am Indian.. 6. sachem 7. Osceola
8. sagamore
Arab.. 5. sheik
Chinook.. 4. tyee
Cossack.. 6. ataman, hetman
Egypt.. 3. Min (Panopolis)
Europe.. 6. syndic
Germany.. 6. Führer (Fuehrer), Kaiser
Italy.. 4. doge, duce
Japan.. 6. mikado, shogun
Mexico.. 7. cacique
Nepal.. 4. Rais
Oriental.. 4. kahn 6. sirdar
Persia.. 4. shah
Russia.. 4. czar (tsar)
Spain.. 7. alcalde
Tibet.. 9. Dalai Lama
Turkey.. 3. aga (agha) 6. vizier

chilblain... 6. pernio

child... 3. imp, tad, tot 4. babe, baby,
bata, brat, tike 5. bairn, cupid, elfin,
fetus 6. cherub, childe (anc), infant,
urchin 7. nestler, progeny
9. offspring 10. descendant

childish... 4. weak 5. naive, petty,
young 6. senile, simple 7. babyish,
kiddish, puerile, unmanly 8. immature
9. infantile, kittenish

children (pert to)...
doctor.. 12. pediatrician
mixed blood.. 6. mestee 8. quadroon
mythology.. 6. Titans
Patron Saint.. 5. Santa
rule by.. 9. paedarchy
slain by Herod.. 12. The Innocents
study of.. 8. pedology 10. pediatrics

Chile... see also *Chilean*
cape.. 4. Horn
capital.. 8. Santiago (1541)
city.. 4. Lota 5. Arica 6. Serena
8. Valdivia 10. Concepcion,
Valparaiso (1543) 11. Antofagasta
conqueror.. 7. Pizarro 8. Valdivia
desert.. 7. Atacama
explorer.. 8. Magellan (1520)
mountain.. 5. Andes 6. Juncal
river.. 3. Loa 5. Biobio
settlement (southernmost)..
8. Navarino (Isl) 14. Puerto Williams

Chilean (pert to)...
cocoanut.. 7. coquito
evergreen.. 6. pepino 10. arborvitae

shrub (poison).. **5**. lithi
wind.. **5**. sures **11**. sures pardos
workman.. **4**. rote
chiliad... **8**. thousand **9**. millenium
    13. thousand years
chill... **3**. ice, raw **4**. ague, cold,
    damp **5**. algor, frost, rigor
    6. damper, formal, shiver **7**. malaria
    8. coldness, coolness, dispirit
    10. depressing **11**. refrigerate
chilly... **3**. raw **4**. ague, cold **5**. gelid
    6. aguish, freeze, frosty
    12. refrigerated
chiloplasty... **10**. lip surgery
    12. mouth surgery
chime... **4**. bell, peal, ring, suit
    5. agree, bells, prate, rhyme
    6. accord, concur, cymbal, jingle
    7. harmony
chimera... **5**. dream, fancy, vapor
    6. bubble, utopia **7**. monster
    8. illusion, paradise (fool's)
chimerical... **4**. vain **7**. utopian
    6. delusive, fanciful, romantic
    9. fantastic, imaginary, unfounded
chimney... **3**. lum **4**. flue **5**. cleft,
    stack, tewel **10**. smokestack
chimpanzee... **6**. gibbon, nchega
    7. gorilla
chin... **4**. talk **5**. genio (comb form)
    6. mentum, weight (Chin)
    8. converse **10**. chew the rag
    11. genioplasty (Surg), mentoplasty
    (Surg)
china... **7**. Dresden, pottery
    8. crockery **9**. porcelain
    11. earthenware
China... see also *Chinese*
    Buddha.. **2**. Fo
    capital.. **7**. Nanking
    capital, former.. **7**. Peiping (Peking)
    city.. **4**. Amoy, Tsin, Wuhu **6**. Canton,
    Hankow, Ningpo **7**. Foochow,
    Nanking, Soochow **8**. Hangchow,
    Shanghai, Tientsin
    dynasty.. **3**. Han, Kin, Sui **4**. Chou,
    Hsia (BC), Ming, Tsin, Yuan **5**. Ching
    6. Mongol (Kublai Khan's)
    island.. **5**. Matsu **6**. Quemoy, Taiwan
    (Formosa)
    magistrate.. **5**. tupan **6**. tuchun
    8. mandarin
    Mainland.. **15**. People's Republic
    Military Academy.. **7**. Whompoa
    Mongol.. **3**. Hun
    mountain.. **7**. Kuen–lun **9**. Himalayas
    nickname.. **14**. Flowery Kingdom
    philosopher.. **6**. Laotse **9**. Confucius
    poet.. **4**. Li Po **7**. Li Tai Po
    race.. **9**. Mongoloid
    religion.. **7**. Taoism **8**. Buddhism
    9. Confucian **12**. Confucianism
    river.. **5**. Peibo **7**. Hwanglo, Yangtze
    sea.. **5**. China **6**. Yellow
    treaty port.. **4**. Amoy
Chinese (pert to)...
    antelope.. **6**. dzeren
    boat.. **4**. junk **5**. tanka **6**. sampan
    cabbage.. **7**. pakchoi
    card game.. **6**. fantan
    carpet.. **6**. Khotan **7**. Kashgar,
    Yarkand **9**. Samarkand, Turkestan

Catholic Church.. **11**. Tien Chu T'ang
    12. Tien Chu Chiao
chestnut.. **4**. ling
confection.. **8**. chowchow
deer.. **8**. elaphure
defense.. **4**. Wall (2,000 mi long)
desert.. **4**. Gobi **5**. Shamo
dragon.. **6**. chi–lin
fabric.. **3**. sha **7**. nankeen
festival (Spring).. **9**. Ch'ing Ming
flute.. **4**. tche (che)
fruit.. **6**. litchi (nut)
ginger.. **9**. galingale
God.. **4**. Shen (Chr) **7**. Shangti, Tien
    Chu (RCCh)
gong.. **6**. tam–tam, tom–tom
grass.. **5**. ramee
idol.. **4**. joss **6**. pagoda (pagod)
instrument.. **3**. che, kin **4**. tche
    5. sheng (cheng)
jade.. **2**. yu
jute.. **7**. chingma
laborer.. **6**. coolie
lily.. **9**. narcissus
liquor.. **6**. samshu (rice)
literary degree.. **8**. hsiu tsai
monkey.. **4**. douc
nurse.. **4**. amah
officer.. **4**. kwan
oil.. **4**. tung
ox.. **4**. zebu
pagoda.. **3**. taa
paradise (Buddh).. **4**. Jodo
    7. Ching–tu **8**. Gekuraku
philosophy.. **10**. Yang and Yin
religion.. **6**. Taoism **8**. Buddhism
    12. Confucianism
residence (official).. **5**. yamen
screen (folding).. **10**. Coromandel
silkworm.. **4**. sina **9**. ailanthus
sky.. **4**. tien
society (secret).. **3**. hui (hoey) **4**. tong
vessel.. **4**. junk **6**. lorcha
Chinese Wall, Great (pert to)...
    builder.. **15**. Ch'in Shih Huang Ti
    composition.. **7**. granite (blocks)
    length in miles.. **11**. two thousand
    time.. **2**. BC
chink... **4**. rent, rift, rima, rime, ring
    5. cleft, crack **6**. cranny, furrow
    7. bunting (bird), fissure
    10. interstice
chinook... **4**. herb, wind **6**. salmon
    7. quinnat
Chinook (pert to)...
    chief.. **4**. tyee
    tribe.. **8**. Flathead
    State (nickname of).. **10**. Washington
chinquapin... **3**. oak **6**. bonnet (water)
    8. chestnut
chip... **3**. cut, hew **4**. coin **5**. break,
    carve, flake, piece, scrap, token
    6. chisel, gallet (stone) **7**. counter
chipmunk... **6**. hackee
chipped stone (instrument)...
    9. paleolith
chipper... **5**. chirp **6**. babble, chisel,
    hammer, lively **7**. chirrup, twitter
    8. cheerful
chirognomy... **9**. palmistry
    10. chiromancy
chironomy... **7**. gesture (hands)

9. pantomime
chiropter... 3. bat 6. aliped
chirp... 3. pew (pue) 4. peep
5. cheep, chirl, tweet 7. chirrup,
twitter
chisel... 3. cut, gad, hew 4. celt
(anc), form, pare 5. bruzz, burin,
carve, cheat, drove, gouge, grave
6. furrow, jagger, mallet, peeker,
pommel 7. engrave, swindle
9. sculpture
chit... 4. note, runt, wisp 5. child,
shoot 6. sprout 10. memorandum
14. recommendation
chitarra, chitarrine... 6. guitar
chiton... 7. garment (anc), mollusk
chivalrous... 5. brave 6. gentle, heroic
7. gallant, valiant 8. knightly
9. courteous 11. magnanimous
chive... 4. stab 5. onion, plant
6. garlic
chloride... 3. ore 4. salt 5. ester
7. calomel
chlorine... 2. Cl 7. bromine, halogen,
radical 8. cyanogen, fluorine
chloroform... 4. dope, kill 6. poison
7. stupefy 9. narcotize
11. anesthetize
chlorophyll... 5. ester, green 7. etiolin
9. deodorant
chocolate... 5. brown, cacao, candy,
cocoa, color 6. pinole 8. beverage
13. Sterculiaceae
choice... 4. beat, rare, will 5. prime
6. dainty, option, select, tidbit
8. election, free will, uncommon
9. recherché, selection
10. preference, well-chosen
11. alternative
choir... 6. chorus 7. singers
choir leader... 6. cantor 9. precentor
choke... 3. gag, jam, ram 4. clog
5. burke, check 6. hinder, impede,
muffle, stifle 7. garrote, repress,
smother 8. obstruct, strangle, throttle
9. constrict, suffocate
choler... 3. ire 4. bile, foam, gall,
rage 5. anger, wrath 6. spleen
10. resentment 11. biliousness
12. irascibility
choleric... 5. angry, testy 7. bilious,
enraged, iracund 8. wrathful
9. dyspeptic, irascible 10. passionate
cholelith... 9. gallstone
choose... 3. opt 4. cull, like, list, pick,
want 5. elect 6. desire, optate,
prefer, select
choosing... 6. optant 8. eclectic,
elective 9. selecting
chop... 3. axe, cut, hew, jaw, lop
4. dice, fell, hack, jowl, meat, raze,
seal 5. cheek, mince, prune, sever,
stamp 7. griskin 8. noisette (eye of)
choppy... 5. bumpy, rough 6. uneven
7. jolting 8. unstable, variable
9. irregular 10. changeable,
incoherent 13. discontinuous
chord... 4. rope 5. radius, secant,
string, tendon 7. concord, harmony
8. arpeggio, concento, filament
chord (terms)... 5. major, minor, tonic,
triad 6. broken, common, tetrad

7. seventh 8. dominant, unbroken
10. enharmonic
chords... 4. tune 7. cadence, cantata
chore... 3. job (odd) 4. task, work
5. stint 10. assignment
chorography... 5. chart 7. diagram
10. topography 11. cartography,
description (region), ichnography
chortle... 5. laugh, snort 7. chuckle,
snortle
chorus... 4. echo 5. choir 6. accord,
outcry, unison 7. refrain, singers
8. chanters 9. unanimity
chorus (pert to)...
girl.. 7. chorine, chorist
leader.. 8. choragus 9. conductor
small.. 7. octette
Chosen (anc)... 5. Korea
Chosen People... 10. Israelites
chrism... 7. unction, unguent
10. anointment 12. confirmation
christen... 4. name 6. launch
7. baptize 10. denominate,
inaugurate 12. Christianize
Christian (pert to)...
Eastern.. 5. Uniat
feast.. 5. agape (anc) 8. Epiphany
9. Christmas
martyr (first).. 7. Stephen
philosopher (anc).. 6. Jesuit
9. Schoolman 10. Scholastic
sect.. 7. Docetae
symbol.. 9. orant (fem)
Christmas (pert to)...
bag.. 6. piñata
carol.. 4. Noel
decoration.. 6. crèche
feast.. 4. Yule
mummer.. 9. guiser
plant.. 5. holly 9. evergreen, mistletoe
term.. 4. Noel, Xmas 8. Nativity,
Yuletide 11. Weihnachten
Christ's-thorn... 4. nabk
chromosome... 2. id 5. idant
8. biophore, germ cell
chronic... 7. abiding 8. constant,
enduring, habitual 9. confirmed
10. continuous, inveterate, persistent
14. valetudinarian
chronicle... 4. sard 5. annal, diary
6. record 7. account, archive, history
8. register 9. narrative
10. chronology
chronicler... 6. writer 8. annalist,
compiler, recorder 9. historian
12. chronologist
chronology error... 9. prolepsis
chronometer... 5. clock, timer, watch
6. ghurry 7. sundial 9. hourglass,
metronome, timepiece
chrysolite... 5. green (color) 7. olivine,
peridot
chthonian... 4. gods (underworld)
7. hellish, worship 9. diabolist
11. demonolater
chub... 4. bass, dace, dolt, fool, lout
6. shiner, tautog 8. fallfish
9. hornyhead, squawfish
chubby... 3. fat 5. plump, pudgy,
round 6. stocky, stubby 9. corpulent
chuck... 4. beef, cast, food, hurl, jerk,
toss 5. fling, heave, pitch, throw

9. eliminate

chuckle . . . **5.** cluck, laugh **6.** cackle, wabble **7.** chortle

chuff . . . **3.** fat **4.** boor **5.** churl, clown, cross, proud, sulky, surly **6.** chubby, elated, rustic **9.** conceited **11.** ill-tempered

chum . . . **3.** pal **4.** bait, pard **5.** buddy, crony **6.** fellow, hobnob **7.** company, comrade, consort, partner **8.** playmate, roommate **9.** associate, classmate, colleague, companion

chump . . . **3.** ass **4.** dolt, dupe, fool, head **5.** block, booby **8.** endpiece

chunk . . . **3.** dab, gob, pat, wad **4.** hunk, junt, lump, slug (metal) **5.** stick, stump, throw **8.** fragment

chunky . . . **3.** fat **4.** game (Am Ind), junt **5.** lumpy, stout, tubby **6.** chubby, portly, stocky, stodgy, stubby **8.** thickset

church . . . **3.** dom **4.** fane (anc), kirk, sect **5.** abbey **6.** bethel, temple **7.** Lateran, minster, templet **8.** basilica, conclave **9.** cathedral **10.** House of God, worshipers **11.** Christendom **12.** denomination

church (pert to) . . .
assistant . . **5.** Elder
attendant . . **6.** sexton, verger
calendar . . **4.** Ordo
Court . . **10.** Consistory
dignitary . . **4.** dean **6.** bishop, priest **7.** prelate, primate **8.** benefice, minister
dissenter . . **7.** sectary **10.** anti-Nicean, anti-Nicene
doctrine (State, church) . . **8.** Erastian
dominion . . **10.** sacerdotum
doorkeeper . . **7.** ostiary
Elder . . **9.** Presbyter
feast . . **4.** utas (octave of) **6.** Easter
governing body . . **7.** classis
law . . **5.** canon, synod **7.** council
part . . **4.** apse, bema, nave **5.** altar, canon **7.** narthex **8.** transept **10.** clerestory
peace device . . **8.** irenicon
property . . **5.** glebe
Roman . . **7.** Lateran **8.** basilica
seats . . **4.** pews **7.** sedilla
service (part) . . **3.** pax **4.** Mass **5.** crede **7.** epistle, introit, sanctus **8.** Agnus Dei, blessing **9.** communion
stipend . . **7.** prebend
traffic (preferments) . . **6.** simony
vessel . . **3.** ama, pyx (pix) **6.** lavabo **8.** ciborium
vestry . . **8.** sacristy

churl . . . **3.** cad, oaf **4.** boor, carl, hind, lout, serf **5.** ceorl, knave **6.** rustic **7.** bondman, freeman, peasant, villain **9.** vulgarian **10.** countryman

churlish . . . **4.** mean **5.** gruff, rough, surly **6.** rustic, sordid, sullen, vulgar **7.** boorish, crabbed, knavish **9.** gruffness, niggardly **10.** ill-humored **11.** countrified

churn . . . **4.** beat, kirn, stir, whip **5.** mixer, shake **6.** beater, seethe, vessel **7.** agitate **8.** agitator, emulsify

chute . . . **4.** tube **5.** flume, scarp, slide **6.** trough **7.** channel, incline, passage **9.** parachute

cibel . . . **5.** chive, onion **7.** shallot

ciborium . . . **3.** pyx **6.** canopy, coffer, vessel

cicada . . . **6.** dog-day, locust **9.** Cicadidae

cicatrix . . . **4.** mark, scar **7.** blemish

Cid . . . **3.** Ruy **4.** hero, poem **5.** Chief **6.** leader (Christian) **7.** Rodrigo

cider (weak) . . . **6.** perkin

Cid's sword . . . **6.** colada

cienaga . . . **5.** marsh, swamp

cigar . . . **4.** rope, toby **5.** claro **6.** concha, corona, Havana, stogie **7.** cheroot, culebra, londres **8.** cigarite, colorado, panatela **9.** belvedere, cigarillo

cigarette . . . **3.** fag **4.** pill **5.** cubeb **6.** gasper, reefer **9.** cigarillo

cilium . . . **4.** hair, lash **7.** eyelash **8.** barbicel, ciliolum, filament **9.** eyewinker

cimarron . . . **6.** maroon **7.** bighorn, wild dog **8.** district (Okla)

cimex . . . **6.** bedbug

Cimmerian, Homer Myth . . . **4.** dark **5.** Nomad (anc) **6.** gloomy (abode) **8.** Cimmeria

cinch . . . **4.** game (cards), grip, sure **5.** girth **6.** fasten **7.** harness (part) **9.** certainty, sure thing

cinders . . . **3.** ash **4.** lava, slag **5.** ashes, dross **6.** embers **7.** residue **8.** clinkers

cinerarium . . . **8.** mortuary

cinerator . . . **7.** furnace **9.** crematory **11.** crematorium, incinerator

cingular . . . **7.** annular **8.** circular

cinnamon . . . **5.** brown, spice **6.** cassia **8.** ishpingo (S Am) **10.** Cinnamomum

cinque . . . **4.** dice, five

cipher . . . **3.** nil **4.** code, zero **5.** aught **6.** figure, nobody, number, symbol **7.** compute **9.** calculate, character, nonentity

circa . . . **5.** about **6.** around **13.** approximately

Circe (pert to) . . .
brother . . **6.** Aeetes
father . . **6.** Helios
Island abode . . **5.** Aeaea
role, Odyssey . . **5.** siren **7.** charmer **9.** sorceress, temptress
sister . . **5.** Medea

circle . . . **3.** orb **4.** halo, hoop, loop, ring **5.** ambit, orbit, rhomb, rigol, round, wheel **6.** clique, cordon, girdle, rotate, sphere **7.** annulus, aureole, circuit, compass, enclose, revolve **9.** circulate, encompass **13.** circumference

circle (pert to) . . .
astronomy . . **6.** tropic
celestial . . **6.** colure **10.** almucantar
Japan . . **4.** maru
luminous . . **6.** corona
of hell (8th) . . **9.** Malebolge
of monoliths . . **8.** cromlech **9.** cyclolith
part . . **3.** arc **6.** areola, octant, radius,

sector 7. sextant 8. diameter
circuit... 3. lap, orb 4. bout, gyre, loop, tour, zone 5. ambit, cycle, orbit, relay, round, route 6. circle, detour 7. compass 9. round trip 10. revolution
circuit court... 4. eyre
circuitous... 4. mazy 6. curved 7. crooked, devious, sinuous, twisted, vagrant, winding 8. circular, flexuous, indirect, tortuous 9. deceitful, deviating, underhand, wandering 10. roundabout, serpentine 12. disingenuous, labyrinthine 14. circumlocutory
circular... 5. round 6. ringed 7. annular, discoid, program 8. cingular, coronary, ringlike 9. crownlike, orbicular 10. circuitous, roundabout 13. advertisement
circular (pert to)...
enclosure.. 3. lis (liss)
indicator.. 4. dial
letter.. 10. encyclical
ornament.. 6. patera
circulate... 4. pass 5. issue 6. circle, rotate, spread 7. diffuse, publish 8. monetize 9. propagate 11. disseminate
circumference... 4. girt 5. ambit, bound, girth 6. bounds 7. circuit, compass 8. encircle, surround 9. outskirts, perimeter, periphery
circumscribe... 5. bound, fence, limit 6. define 7. enclose, environ 8. encircle, restrict 9. encompass
circumscribed... 6. finite, narrow 9. definable 10. restricted
circumspect... 4. wary 5. chary 7. careful, politic, prudent 8. cautious, discreet 9. judicious 10. thoughtful 11. considerate
circumstance... 4. fact, item, pomp 5. event, state 7. proviso 8. incident, occasion, position 9. condition, provision, situation 10. occurrence, particular 11. arrangement, opportunity, stipulation
circumstantial... 5. exact 6. minute 7. precise 8. detailed 10. evidential, incidental, particular 11. conditional 12. nonessential
circumvent... 5. cheat, evade 6. delude, entrap, outwit, thwart 7. capture, circuit, deceive 8. surround 9. encompass, frustrate
circus... 4. hawk, ring, show 5. arena 6. big top, circle, cirque 7. harrier, theater 8. carnival, side show 12. amphitheater
circus (pert to)...
concessionaire.. 7. grifter
hawk.. 15. circus assimilis
rider.. 8. desultor
Roman.. 13. Circus Maximus
sideshow.. 6. freaks
superintendent.. 10. ringmaster
cirque... 6. circle, corrie 7. circlet
cis (pref)...
cist... 3. box, pit 5. chest 7. chamber 8. cistvaen (kistvaen)

Cistercian... 4. monk, Rule (Benedictine) 5. Order 8. Trappist
cistern... 3. bac, sac, tub, vat 4. back, tank, well 7. cuvette, raintub 9. impluvium, reservoir
citadel... 3. arx 4. fort 5. Alamo, tower 6. castle 7. bastion, bulwark 8. fastness, fortress 9. acropolis 10. stronghold 13. fortification 14. propugnaculum
citation... 5. honor 6. eulogy, notice 7. mention, summons 8. subpoena 9. quotation 11. enumeration 12. verification
cite... 5. quote 6. adduce, allege, repeat, summon 7. extract 8. indicate
citizen... 3. cit 6. native 7. citoyen, denizen (of beasts), dweller 8. civilian, townsman 10. inhabitant
citizenship... 10. citizenism 15. enfranchisement
citron... 5. melon 6. cedrat (cedrate), citrus, yellow
citrus fruit... 4. lime 5. lemon 6. orange 7. kumquat 8. citrange, shaddock 9. grapefruit
cittern, cithern... 4. lute (anc) 6. zither 7. cithara, gittern
city... 4. town 8. township 10. metropolis 12. municipality
city (parts)... 4. ward 5. civic, urban 8. district, precinct
City of...
Bells.. 10. Strasbourg
Bridges.. 6. Bruges
Brotherly Love.. 12. Philadelphia
Churches.. 8. Brooklyn
David.. 9. Jerusalem
Dead (The).. 8. cemetery 10. Necropolis
Elms.. 8. New Haven
Gods.. 6. Asgard (Asgarth)
Golden Gate (The).. 12. San Francisco
Great King.. 9. Jerusalem
Hundred Towers.. 5. Pavia
Kings.. 4. Lira
Lilies.. 8. Florence
Magnificent Distances..
  10. Washington (DC)
Masts.. 6. London
Palms (Bib).. 7. Jericho
Prophet (The).. 6. Medina
Rams.. 6. Canton
Saints.. 8. Montreal
Seven Hills.. 4. Rome
Straits.. 7. Detroit
Sun (the).. 7. Baalbek 10. Heliopolis
Victory.. 5. Cairo
Violated Treaty.. 8. Limerick
Violet Crown.. 6. Athens
civet... 5. fossa, genet, rasse 6. foussa, musang 7. nandine 10. paradoxure
civic... 5. civil, urban 6. public 7. burghal, oppidan 9. municipal 12. metropolitan
civil... 4. hend (hende) 5. suave 6. decent, polite, public, urbane 7. affable, courtly, elegant, secular 8. discreet, gracious, obliging, polished, well-bred 9. courteous,

political 10. respectful
11. complaisant 13. condescending

civil (pert to)...
dress.. 5. mufti 7. civvies
fraud (Rom).. 11. stellionate
process.. 4. writ
strife.. 6. stasis
wrong.. 4. tort

civility... 6. comity 7. amenity
8. courtesy, urbanity 9. attention,
etiquette, gentility 10. affability,
politeness

civilization... 6. kultur, polish
7. culture 10. refinement
11. cultivation

civilize... 4. tame 6. polish
8. humanize, urbanize 9. cultivate
11. domesticate

clad... 5. robed 6. decked, garbed
7. arrayed, attired, clothed, dressed
9. appareled, garmented

claim... 3. hak (hakh) 4. case, lien,
name 5. right, title 6. assert,
demand 7. preempt, profess, require
8. arrogate, maintain, pretense
(pretence), proclaim 9. postulate
10. pretension

claimant... 7. claimer 9. applicant,
plaintiff, pretender 10. solicitant

clairvoyance... 3. ESP 7. insight
8. lucidity, sagacity 9. intuition
10. divination 11. penetration

clairvoyant... 4. seer 7. prophet,
seeress 9. sagacious 12. clearsighted

clam... 3. Mya 5. Chama, razor, Solen
6. gweduc, Mactra, quahog
7. mollusk 10. veneriform (shape)

clam destroyer... 6. winkle
10. periwinkle

clammy... 4. cool, damp, dank, soft
5. moist, mucid 6. sticky, sweaty

clamor... 3. cry, din, hue 4. roar, wail
5. decry, noise, vocal 6. hubbub,
outcry, racket, uproar 10. hullabaloo

clamorous... 4. loud 5. noisy
7. blatant, clamant, excited
8. brawling 9. demanding, insistent,
turbulent 10. blustering, uproarious,
vociferous

clamp... 4. vise 6. fasten 9. appliance

clan... 3. set 4. camp, club, cult,
gens, race, sept 5. group, party,
tribe 6. circle, clique, family
7. coterie, society

clan (quarrel)... 4. feud 8. vendetta

clandestine... 3. sly 5. privy 6. covert,
secret 7. furtive, illicit 8. stealthy
9. concealed, underhand
10. frandulent, undercover
11. unobtrusive 15. surreptitious

clang... 4. ding, ring 5. clank, sound
6. jangle 7. ringing

clang color... 6. timbre 8. tonality

clangor... 3. din 4. ring 5. clang,
noise 6. fracas, hubbub, jangle,
racket, ruckus, rumpus, tumult,
uproar 7. discord, ringing

clank... 4. ring 5. clang 7. ringing

clapper... 4. bell, clap 5. bones
(minstrel)

claque... 8. chaqueur, opera hat

9. applauder

clarify... 5. clear 6. filter, purify,
refine, render, strain 7. cleanse,
explain, rectify

clash... 3. jar 4. bang, bump 5. crash
6. impact, jangle, tussle 7. collide,
scuffle 8. conflict, disagree, skirmish
9. collision, encounter, hostility
10. dissonance

clasp... 3. hug 4. belt, grip, hasp,
hold, ouch (anc), tach 5. grasp,
morse (priest's), seize, stick, tache
(anc) 6. buckle, enwrap, fasten,
secure 7. agraffe (agrafe), embrace,
tendril 8. fastener 10. chatelaine

class... 3. ilk 4. rank, sect 5. caste,
genus, grade, order, tribe 6. brevet
(mil), status 7. station 8. category,
classify, division 9. catalogue
14. classification

class (learned)... 8. literate, literati
14. intelligentsia

classical... 4. pure 5. Attic 6. chaste
7. classis, elegant 8. academic,
literary, tasteful 10. Ciceronian

classification... 4. rank, sort 5. genus,
grade 6. rating, system 7. species
8. analysis, category, grouping
12. distribution

classify... 4. list, rank, rate, sort, type
5. grade, label, range 6. assort,
digest, ticket 7. aggroup, arrange
8. register 9. catalogue

clatter... 3. din, jar 5. noise, rumor
6. babble, gabble, hubbub, racket,
rattle, rumpus, tattle, uproar
7. chatter, prattle 9. commotion
11. disturbance

clause... 5. rider 6. phrase
7. passage, proviso, section

claustral... 9. cloistral 10. cloistered

claw... 4. hand, nail, unce 5. chela,
cloof, clufe, talon 6. nipper, unguis

claw... 3. dig 4. grab, grip, pull, tear
5. grasp, seize 6. clutch, scrape,
snatch 7. grapple, scratch

clay... 3. mud 4. marl, mire, soil
5. argil, earth 6. corpse, kaolin

clay (pert to)...
baked.. 4. tile 5. brick
box.. 6. sagger
covered.. 6. lutose
mix.. 3. pug
mold.. 3. dod
molded.. 7. fictile
nodule.. 10. eaglestone
pipe.. 2. TD 10. meerschaum
plug.. 4. bott
polish.. 5. rabat
softening.. 8. malaxage
variety.. 4. bole, loam, marl 5. gault,
ocher, tasco 8. petuntse

clayey... 4. soft 5. adobe, bolar
6. earthy 12. argillaceous

clean, cleanse... 4. dust, swab, wash,
wipe 5. brush, purge, rinse, scrub
6. kosher, purify, refine 7. cleanse,
deterge, launder 8. absterge,
depurate, renovate 9. disinfect,
elutriate, expurgate

cleanness... 6. purity (of life) 7. clarity
8. chastity, elegance, neatness,

pureness, tidiness 10. immaculacy
13. impeccability

clear... 3. net, rid 4. free, gain, over,
pure 5. clean, lucid, plain 6. acquit,
excuse, exempt, hurdle, limpid,
pardon, purify 7. absolve, concise,
crystal, evident, explain, graphic,
lighten, release 8. apparent, distinct,
incisive, luculent 9. cloudless,
exonerate, extricate, vindicate

clear land... 7. thwaite (Eng)

clearsighted... 4. keen 10. discerning
13. perspicacious

cleat... 4. bitt 5. level, strip, wedge
7. joinery

cleave... 3. cut 4. part, rend, rive,
tear 5. clave, cling, clove, crack,
sever, shear, split 6. adhere, bisect,
cohere, divide, pierce 7. dispart
8. separate

cleek... 5. marry, pluck, seize
6. clutch, snatch

clef... 1. C, F, G 4. alto, bass
6. treble 7. descant, soprano
9. character

cleft... 3. gap 4. reft, rent, rift, rima
5. chasm, chink, crack, notch, riven,
split 6. chappy, cranny, gaping,
recess 7. crevice, fissure 8. scissure

cleft palate operation...
13. staphyloraphy (staphylorrhaphy)

clemency... 5. favor, grace, mercy
6. lenity 7. quarter 8. kindness,
leniency, mildness 10. compassion,
indulgence 11. forbearance

Clemens (Samuel) pen name...
9. Mark Twain

clench... 4. fist, grip, grit, hold
5. grasp 6. clinch, clutch
8. purchase 9. interlock

Cleopatra (of)...
attendant.. 4. Iras
downfall.. 3. asp
lover.. 6. Antony (Marc), Caesar
obelisk (two).. 6. Needle
queen of.. 5. Egypt
river.. 4. Nile

clepe... 3. bid 4. call, name 6. invite,
invoke 7. address 8. christen

clergy... 5. cloth 6. pulpit
9. clergymen, clericals 10. priesthood

clergyman... 4. abbé, dean 5. canon,
vicar 6. cleric, curate, divine, parson,
pastor, priest, rector 7. dominie,
prelate 8. minister, preacher, sky
pilot 9. presbyter 12. ecclesiastic

clergywoman... 3. nun 8. minister
9. parsoness, priestess 10. religieuse

cleric, non... 4. laic

clerical... 7. scribal 11. ministerial

clerical (pert to)...
attire.. 3. alb 5. amice, cloth, fanon,
orale, stole
collar.. 5. rabat
hat.. 7. biretta

clerk... 3. nun 4. monk 5. write
6. cleric, hermit, layman, scribe
7. scholar (anc) 8. salesman
9. assistant, clergyman
12. ecclesiastic

cleronomy... 8. heritage
11. inheritancy

clever... 3. apt 4. able, cute, deft
5. handy, slick, smart, witty
6. adroit, astute, brainy, bright,
expert, habile, nimble 7. amiable,
cunning, parlous 8. pleasing, skillful,
talented 9. brilliant, dexterous,
ingenious 11. good-natured

cleverness... 4. tact, wits 5. skill
6. esprit 7. cunning 9. ingenuity,
smartness, wittiness 10. adroitness,
astuteness, shrewdness

clew, clue... 3. key 4. ball, loop
(Naut), rope 5. cloth 6. cocoon,
tackle (see also clue)

cliché... 4. joke 5. banal, trite 6. old
saw 7. bromide 8. banality, chestnut
9. Joe Miller, platitude

click... 3. rap 4. snap 5. clack 6. go
over 7. prosper, succeed

click beetle... 3. dor (dorr) 6. elater

cliff... 3. gat 4. crag, klip, rock, wall
5. bluff, cleve, crest, scarp, slope
6. rocher 7. clogwyn 8. palisade
9. precipice 10. escarpment

climax... 3. cap, epi (Arch) 4. acme,
near, peak, shut 5. tight 6. apogee,
result, summit 7. heights
11. culmination 12. consummation

climb... 3. fly, gad 4. shin 5. grimp,
scale, speel 6. ascend, ascent
7. clamber, upgrade 9. acclivity

climbing... 7. scaling 8. scandent
10. scansorial

climbing plant... 3. hop, ivy 4. bine,
nito, vine 5. betel, liana 6. bryony

clime... 4. zone 5. realm, tract
6. region 7. climate

clinch... 4. bind, grip, hold, seal
5. grasp, prove, seize 6. clutch,
fasten, secure 7. confirm, grapple
8. conclude, purchase 9. establish

cling... 4. hold 5. stick 6. adhere,
cohere

clingfish... 6. testar

clink... 4. rime, slap 5. rhyme
6. jingle, lockup, prison, strike
9. assonance

clinquant... 4. gold, sham 6. tinsel
8. frippery, tinseled 10. glittering

clip... 3. bob, lop, mow 4. barb,
blow, dock, gaff, snip, trim 5. clasp,
prune, shear 6. clutch, fasten
7. curtail, scissor, shorten
8. ornament 9. instrument

clique... 3. set 4. cell, clan, club, ring
5. group, Junta, junto 6. circle
(people) 7. coterie

Cloaca Maxima (anc Rome)...
5. sewer 10. repository

cloak... 3. aba 4. cape, mask, pall,
wrap 5. cover, grego, jelab, manta,
sagum 6. abolla, capote, dolman,
mantle, mantua, screen, serape,
shield 7. chlamys (anc), conceal,
galabia, manteau, paenula (anc),
paletot, pelisse, pretext, protect
8. disguise 9. dissemble, new-market
10. witzchoura

clobber... 3. hit 4. beat, conk, poke,
swat 5. clout, punch, whack
6. defeat, strike, wallop

clock... 3. nef (ship's) 4. dial, time

5. knock 6. record 8. recorder, sidereal 9. clepsydra, metronome, timepiece 10. isochronon 11. chronometer

clockwise... 6. deasil (dessil) 11. withershins 14. dextrorotation, dextrorotatory

clog... 4. stop 5. choke, dance 6. daggle, hamper, impede 8. encumber, obstruct, restrain

clog shoe... 4. geta 5. sabot 6. chopin, cobcab (Orient), patten 7. chopine

cloister... 4. stoa 5. abbey 6. arcade, friary, immure, priory 7. confine, convent, nunnery, retreat 9. anchorage, hermitage, monastery, peristyle 10. passageway

cloistered... 7. recluse 8. enclosed, monastic 11. sequestered

close... 3. at, by 3. end 4. near, nigh, seal, shut, slam 5. dense, finis, stivy 6. finale, finish, period, secret, stingy, sultry 7. airless, extreme, occlude, related 8. complete, conclude, familiar, imminent, intimate, stifling 9. extremity, secretive, terminate 11. approximate, termination 13. juxtaposition

close (pert to)...

eyes (the).. 4. seel
fasten.. 6. batten
of day.. 9. nightfall
poetic.. 5. anear
tightly.. 3. bar 4. bung, seal 6. clench, enseal

closely... 4. just 6. almost, barely, nearly 8. narrowly

closely allied... 6. chummy 7. germane 8. intimate

closeness... 7. density, secrecy 8. fidelity, intimacy, likeness, nearness, sameness 9. tightness 10. chumminess, narrowness, similarity, stinginess, strictness, sultriness 11. airlessness, compactness, conciseness, familiarity, resemblance 14. oppressiveness

closet... 5. ambry, cuddy, emery 6. locker, pantry 7. cabinet 8. cupboard, wardrobe 9. cloakroom, storeroom

closing device... 3. key 4. lock 6. zipper

closing measure (Mus)... 4. coda

clot... 3. lump, mass 5. grume 7. thicken 8. coagulum, concrete 9. coagulate 12. crassamentum

cloth... 3. net, tat 4. brin, crea, drap, felt, lamé, silk, tapa, wool 5. adati, baize, bezan, bluet, carda, crash, crepe, denim, khaki, linen, manta, nylon, orlon, rayon, satin, scrim, surat, tamis, terry, tulle, twill, voile 6. alpaca, burlap, calico, canvas, chintz, cotton, damask, dimity, dowlas, duffel, faille, jersey, madras, mohair, muslin, nankin, pongee, poplin, samite (gold), sateen, velour 7. acetate, baracan, brocade, bunting, cambric, challis, chiffon, drap d'or, flannel, foulard, gingham,

nankeen, organdy, organza, percale, sacking, taffeta, ticking, worsted 8. cashmere, chambray, corduroy, cretonne, drilling, nainsook, Shantung 9. crinoline, gabardine, sailcloth, tarpaulin, tricotine 10. broadcloth, seersucker 11. cheesecloth, drap d'argent (silver), marquisette

cloth (pert to)...

checkered.. 5. plaid
finisher.. 7. beetler
gold.. 7. drap d'or
piece.. 4. bolt
ridge.. 4. wale
selvage.. 4. roon 7. listing
silver.. 11. drap d'argent
twilled.. 5. denim, serge
weaving.. 4. warp, weft, woof

clothe... 3. tog 4. deck, garb, gird, robe, vest 5. array, drape, dress, endue, indue 6. afford, enrobe, invest 7. empower, provide, sheathe 8. accouter

clothes... 3. rig 4. duds, garb, togs 5. guise, habit 6. attire 7. apparel, costume, raiment, regalia 8. clothing, garments 9. dungarees 10. bedclothes, garmenture 11. habiliments, investiture

clothing spy... 4. keek

cloud... 3. fog, low 4. dust, film, haze, mist, rack, scud 5. nepho (comb form), nubia, stain, sully, taint, vapor 6. cirrus, damage, darken, defame, defect, nebule, nimbus, shadow, stigma 7. blacken, blemish, cumulus, nubilus, obscuræ, pea-soup, stratus, tarnish, tornado 8. cat's-tail, cocktail, overcast 10. horizontal

clouds (pert to)...

astronomy.. 4. coma 9. nubeculae
kind.. 6. cirrus, nimbus 7. cumulus, stratus 9. mare's-tail
luminous.. 5. nimbi
Magellanic.. 5. Major, Minor
photography.. 9. nephogram
science of.. 9. nephology
seeding.. 10. nucleation
vapory.. 4. rack

cloudy... 4. dark, hazy 5. filmy, foggy, misty, murky, shady, vague 6. gloomy, lowery, opaque 7. nebular, obscure 8. confused, overcast, vaporous 9. cloudlike 10. indistinct, lackluster

clout... 3. hit, jab, rag 4. blow, bump, clod, mend, nail, swat 5. patch, shred, sward 12. handkerchief

clove... see also *cleave* 5. brown, eagle (color), spice

clover... 3. red 4. bush 5. lotus, snail, white 6. alsike 7. crimson, melilot, prairie, spotted 9. Melilotus

clown... 3. oaf 4. boor, fool, lout, mime, mome, zany 5. comic, Kelly (Emmet), mimer, yahoo 6. jester, rustic 7. buffoon 9. harlequin 10. countryman 11. merry–andrew

clownish... 4. rude 5. gawky, rough 6. clumsy, coarse, rustic 7. awkward, boorish, ill–bred, loutish, uncivil 8. churlish, ungainly

9. untutored 10. buffoonish
11. countrified
cloy... 4. clog, glut, pall, sate
5. gorge, stuff 6. accloy 7. satiate,
satisfy, surfeit
club... 3. bat, hit 4. beat, join, mace
5. billy, clout, staff, unite, yokel
6. cudgel, league, weapon 7. society
8. bludgeon, spontoon
9. boomerang, espantoon
10. nulla-nulla, pogamoggan
11. association
club (pert to)...
actors.. 6. Friars
historic.. 5. Whigs 8. Jacobins
10. Cordeliers
Service.. 7. Kiwanis
Women's (first).. 7. Sorosis
clubfoot... 7. talipes 9. deformity, pes
valgus 13. talipes valgus
club-shaped... 7. clavate
clue, clew... 3. key, tip 4. data, hint
5. scent 6. thread 7. inkling
8. evidence 9. suspicion
11. fingerprint
clump... 3. tod 4. heap, lump, thud,
tuft 5. bunch, chunk, group, motte
(mott), patch, stamp 6. growth,
trudge 7. cluster, thicket
clumsy... 4. ugly 5. bulky, gawky,
inapt, inept, unfit 6. gauche, oafish
7. awkward, uncouth, unhandy
8. slipshod, ungainly, unwieldy
9. inelegant, lumbering, maladroit,
misshapen 10. blundering,
cumbersome, left-handed
13. inappropriate
clumsy person... 4. gawk 5. jumbo,
staup 7. bungler
clupeoid fish... 7. herring
cluster... 4. crop, cyme, gang, tuft
5. bunch, clump, group 6. huddle
8. fascicle 9. glomerule
cluster (pert to)...
bean.. 4. guar 6. legume
fibers.. 3. nep
flowers.. 6. raceme 7. rosette
8. anthemia, panticle
fruit.. 6. grapes
spores.. 5. sorus
stars.. 8. Globular, Pleiades (The)
clustery... 8. racemose
clutch... 3. nab 4. claw, grip, hold,
nest 5. brood, catch, clasp, grasp,
seize 6. clench, cletch, crisis
clyster... 5. enema 6. lavage
9. injection
Clytemnestra's mother... 4. Leda
cnemis... 4. shin 5. tibia
coach... 3. car, rig 5. prime, stage,
train, tutor 6. direct, fiacre, jarvey
7. adviser, prepare, tallyho, teacher
8. carriage, equipage, instruct,
preparer 9. charabanc 10. instructor
coach dog... 9. Dalmatian
coachman... 3. fly (angling) 4. fish,
jehu, whip 5. driver
coagulate... 3. gel, jel, set 4. cake,
clot, curd, lump 6. curdle, posset
7. congeal 9. solidify
coagulator... 6. enzyme, rennet
coagulum... 4. clot, curd 5. grume

7. clabber
coal... 4. fuel 5. black, ember
6. carbon, cinder 7. lignite, residue
coal (pert to)...
bin.. 6. bunker
car.. 3. dan 4. corf, tram 6. hopper
dust.. 4. coom (coomb), culm, smut
gas.. 7. Pintsch 9. acetylene
miner.. 7. collier
miner's disease.. 11. anthracosis
oil.. 8. kerosene
tar.. 5. lysol, pitch 6. cresol, decane,
phenol 7. toluene
tunnel.. 4. adit
type.. 3. egg, nut, pea 4. dant, hard,
peat, soft 6. broken, cannel
8. charcoal, chestnut 9. buckwheat
10. anthracite, bituminous
coalition... 5. trust, union 6. fusion,
hookup, league, merger 7. society
8. alliance 10. federation
11. affiliation, combination,
confederacy, conjunction
coalition advocate... 9. fusionist
coals... 5. gleed 6. embers 7. cinders
coarse... 3. fat, low 4. dank, lewd,
rude, vile 5. broad, crass, gross,
thick 6. carnal, earthy, impure,
ribald, rustic, vulgar 7. goatish,
obscene, sensual 8. granular,
immodest, indecent, inferior, unchaste
9. inelegant, offensive, unrefined
10. unfinished, unpolished
coarse (pert to)...
grain.. 4. meal
grass.. 4. reed 5. sedge 6. quitch
hominy.. 4. corn, samp
coast... 4. sail 5. beach, glide, shore,
slide 6. rivage 7. seaside
8. seaboard, seashore
coast (pert to)...
dweller.. 7. orarian
live oak.. 6. encina
projection.. 4. cape, ness
coat... 4. jupe 5. cloak, frock, parka,
tunic 6. blazer, capote, duster,
jacket, raglan, reefer, trench, tuxedo,
ulster 7. cassock, cutaway, paletot,
slicker 8. gossamer, Mackinaw,
tegument 9. newmarket, redingote
coat (pert to)...
fastener.. 4. frog 6. zipper
of animal.. 3. fur 4. pelt, wool
6. pelage 8. feathers
of arms.. 5. crest 8. blazonry
10. escutcheon
of mail.. 6. byrnia 7. hauberk
of the eye (inner).. 6. retina
coati... 5. Nasua 6. narica 7. raccoon
coating (pert to)...
cake.. 5. glacé, icing 8. frosting
copper, bronze.. 6. patina
grain.. 4. bran
medical.. 9. collodion
metal.. 5. plate
seed.. 5. testa 6. tegmen
10. endopleura
tin, lead.. 5. terne
vitreous.. 6. enamel
coax... 3. beg, ply 4. lure, urge
5. press, tease 6. cajole, entice,
exhort 7. beguile, flatter, implore,

wheedle 8. blandish, inveigle, persuade 9. importune 10. manipulate

cob... 4. axis, blow, gull, loaf, mole, pier, swan 5. block, chief, horse 6. basket, leader, muffin, spider 7. beating, corncob 8. dumpling 10. breakwater

cobbler... 3. pie 5. coler, sutor 6. bungle, repair, souter 7. botcher, crispin 9. fortescue (fortesque), shoemaker

cobbra... 4. head 5. skull

cobby... 5. stout 6. hearty, lively, stocky 10. headstrong

cobra... 3. asp 4. Naga (Myth), Naja 5. mamba, snake, viper 8. ringhals

cobweb... 3. net 4. trap 5. snare, wevet 7. fiction, network 8. filament, gossamer 9. intricacy

cobweblike... 8. araneous 9. arachnoid

cocaine... 4. coca, snow (sl) 8. narcotic 9. mydriatic 10. anesthetic

coccus... 4. cell 5. spore 9. bacterium, cochineal

cochleate... 6. spiral 11. shell-shaped

cock... 3. nab, tap 4. bird, heap, kora, pile, vane (weather) 5. strut, valve 6. faucet, grouse, leader, muckna 7. rooster, swagger

cockade... 4. knot 7. rosette

Cockade State... 8. Maryland

cockatoo... 3. ara 4. arara (palm), galah 6. parrot 8. ganggang

cockle... 4. boat, gith, kiln, oast 5. shell, stove 6. pucker 7. mollusk, wrinkle

cockpit... 3. pit 4. well 5. arena, cabin (airplane) 7. gallera

cockscomb (coxcomb)... 5. crest, plant

cocktail... 5. cloud, drink, horse 6. beetle 9. appetizer

cocky... 4. pert 5. saucy 6. jaunty 7. stuck-up 9. conceited

cocoa... 5. broma, cacao 8. beverage 9. chocolate 11. theobromine

coconut (pert to)...
fiber.. 4. coir, kyar
India.. 4. nargil (narghile)
meat.. 5. copra

cocoon... 3. pod 4. bave (silk), clew, kell, pupa 9. chrysalis

cod... 3. bib, cor 4. fish, ling 5. scrod, sprag 6. burbot, cultus, gadoid 7. bacalao

coddle... 3. pet 4. baby, cook 5. humor, spoil 6. caress, fondle, pamper 11. mollycoddle

code... 3. law 5. canon, codex, Morse, salic 6. digest, equity, signal, symbol 7. pandect, precept 12. Commandments

codfish (pert to)...
Alaska.. 6. wachna
genus.. 5. Gadus
ready for cooking.. 5. scrod
type.. 3. cod, ten 4. cusk, rock 6. Murray, tomcod 7. buffalo

codger... 5. crank, miser 6. oddity

codicil... 4. will 5. rider 6. sequel 8. addition, appendix 10. instrument

Cody (William)... 11. Buffalo Bill

coerce... 4. curb 5. force 6. compel 7. dragoon, enforce, repress 9. blackjack, strong-arm, terrorize 10. intimidate

coercion... 5. force 6. duress 8. violence 10. compulsion, constraint

coffee (pert to)...
bean.. 3. nib
container.. 8. canister
cup holder.. 4. zarf
extract.. 8. caffeine
kind.. 3. Rio 4. Java 5. Milds, Mocha 6. Bogota, Brazil, Santos 7. Sumatra, Turkish 8. Medellin 9. Maracaibo
mix.. 7. chicory
pot.. 6. biggin 10. percolator

coffin... 3. box, urn 4. bier, case, kist, mold 5. chest, crust 6. basket, casing, casket 11. sarcophagus

coffin (pert to)...
cloth.. 4. pall 5. cloak
litter.. 4. bier
nail.. 9. cigarette
prehistoric.. 4. cist 5. chest

cog... 3. cam 4. boat (fishing), gear 5. catch, cheat, cozen, tenon, tooth 7. ratchet, wheedle 8. sprocket 9. deception

cogent... 5. valid 6. potent, strong 7. telling 8. powerful 9. effective 10. compelling, conclusive, convincing, persuasive

cogitate... 4. mull, muse, plan 5. think 6. ponder 8. meditate 9. cerebrate

cognizance... 3. ken 4. heed, plea 5. badge (knight's) 9. knowledge 11. recognition 12. apprehension

cognizant... 5. aware 7. knowing 8. sensible 9. conscious 10. perceptive 11. intelligent

cognomen... 4. name 5. title 6. y-clept 7. surname 8. nickname 10. patronymic 11. appellation

coheir... 5. joint 8. parcener

cohere... 5. agree, cling, serry, stick, unite 6. adhere, cleave 9. glutinate

coherence... 5. cling 8. adhesion, cohesion, sticking 9. adherence, connected 11. consistency

coil... 4. ansa, clew, curl, loop, mesh, wind 5. querl, twine, twist 6. spiral 7. haycock 8. encircle 11. convolution

coiled... 7. tortile, twirled

coin... 3. rin, sou, yen 4. cash, cent 5. money, penny, stamp 6. specie

coin (pert to)...
Bib.. 6. talent
brass.. 13. Rosa Americana (1722)
gold.. 4. ryal (rial) 5. daric, eagle 6. guinea
minor.. 4. doit
parts of.. 4. flan 5. field, tails, verso 6. legend 7. exergue, obverse (front), reverse
silver.. 4. batz, obol, ryal (rial) 5. crown, ducat, sceat 6. tester
tester.. 6. shroff (saraf)

coincide... 5. agree, check, chime, match, tally 6. concur 7. consent 10. correspond 11. synchronize
coincident... 9. consonant 10. concurrent 12. contemporary
coiner... 8. inventor 9. neologist (words) 10. fabricator 13. counterfeiter
coins (pert to)...
roll of.. 7. rouleau
science of.. 11. numismatics
specialist.. 11. numismatist
colander... 5. sieve 6. filter, sorter 8. strainer
Colchis King... 6. Aeetes
cold... 3. icy, nip, raw 4. dank, dead, drow, dull, frio, sure 5. algid, bland, bleak, frore (anc), gelid 6. chilly, frigid, frosty 7. chilled, cinched 8. chilling, reserved, unheated 9. heartless 10. lackluster 11. indifferent, passionless, unconscious
cold (pert to)...
blooded.. 9. heartless, unfeeling 13. dispassionate, heterothermal 14. poikilothermal
feet.. 9. cowardice
infection.. 4. post 5. rheum 6. coryza 7. catarrh
sore.. 6. herpes 7. simplex, vesicle 14. herpes labialis
steel.. 5. sword 7. bayonet, weapons
term.. 8. frigoric
wind.. 4. bise
Coleoptera... 7. beetles, insects
Coleridge's sacred river... 4. Alph (Kubla Khan)
colewort... 5. kale 7. cabbage
colic... 4. pain 5. gripe, spasm 7. tormina 10. enteralgia 11. stomachache
coliseum... 4. bowl 5. arena 6. circus 7. stadium, theater 9. Colosseum 10. hippodrome 12. amphitheater
collaborate... 3. aid 6. co–work 8. coauthor 9. cooperate 10. fraternize
collage... 6. gluing 7. montage 8. abstract, adhesive 9. cyclorama
collapse... 4. cave, fail, fall 5. crash, slump 6. cave–in, defeat 7. crack–up, debacle, deflate, failure 8. downfall 9. breakdown, shrinking 10. bankruptcy, exhaustion 11. prostration
collar... 4. band, grab, ruff 5. chain, rabat, ruche 6. arrest, bertha, rabato, tackle, torque 7. barghan, capture, harness (part), shackle 8. carcanet, neckband 10. pickadilly
collate... 5. audit, check 6. verify 7. certify, compare, examine
collateral... 5. extra 6. margin 7. related 8. indirect, relation (folks), security 9. accessory, secondary 10. contingent, obligation, subsidiary 11. subordinate 12. nonessential
collation... 3. tea 4. meal 5. lunch 6. repast, sermon 7. address, reading 8. luncheon, treatise 10. collection, comparison,

conference 12. consultation, contribution
colleague... 6. fellow 7. compeer, comrade, consort, partner 8. camarada, confrere 9. associate, companion 11. confederate
collect... 3. bag, tax 4. levy, mass 5. amass, glean, raise, rally 6. deduce, forage, garner, gather, muster, prayer, sheave 7. compile, procure 8. assemble, mobilize 9. aggregate 10. accumulate, congregate
collection... 3. ana, bag, set 4. book, olio 5. group, hoard, store 6. rosary, sorite 8. assembly, donation, offering 9. aggregate, congeries, gathering, repertory 10. assemblage, repertoire 11. acquisition
collection (pert to)...
anecdotes.. 3. ana 4. data 8. analecta
animals (wild).. 3. zoo 9. menagerie
bubbles.. 4. foam
curiosities.. 6. museum
documents.. 4. Veda 6. corpus 7. dossier
fruit.. 7. syncarp
implements (Surg).. 7. trousse
of four.. 6. tetrad
of twenty–four.. 5. quire
poems.. 5. sylva 9. anthology
proper names.. 11. onomasticon
type.. 4. font
writing.. 10. literature
collector (pert to)...
bird eggs.. 8. oologist
books.. 10. bibliothec 11. bibliophile 12. bibliomaniac
coins.. 11. numismatist
rent.. 8. landlord
stamps.. 11. philatelist
colleen... 4. girl, lass, maid 6. damsel, maiden 7. girleen
college... 6. school 7. academy, society 9. Alma Mater, institute 10. université, university 11. corporation, institution
college (pert to)...
campus.. 4. lawn, quad 7. grounds
graduate.. 6. alumna 7. alumnus
license for absence.. 5. exeat
official.. 4. dean 5. prexy 6. beadle, bursar, regent 7. proctor
collegiate... 8. academic 9. collegian, scholarly 11. college–bred
collide with... 3. hit, ram 5. clash, crash 6. hurtle, strike 7. contend 8. conflict, disagree
collier... 5. miner 6. plover
collieshangie... 3. row 7. quarrel 8. squabble 11. disturbance (noisy)
collision... 4. bump 5. clash, crash 6. impact 7. smashup 8. accident 9. hostility 11. composition, impingement 12. interference
colloquial... 6. common 8. everyday, familiar, informal 9. unstudied 10. vernacular 11. undignified 14. conversational
colloquy... 4. chat, talk 6. parley 9. discourse 10. conference

12. conversation
Cologne Kings (legend)... **4.** Magi
  6. Gaspar **8.** Melchior **9.** Balthasar
Colombia...
  capital.. **6.** Bogota (1538)
  city.. **4.** Cali **5.** Pasto **8.** Medellin
  9. Cartagena **10.** Santa Marta
  12. Barranquilla
  Falls.. **10.** Tequendama
  Liberator.. **7.** Bolivar (Simon)
  mountain.. **5.** Andes **11.** Cordilleras
  river.. **6.** Yapuri **9.** Magdalena
colonize... **6.** gather, people, settle
  8. populate **9.** establish
colonizer... **3.** ant **6.** oecist **7.** planter,
  settler
colonnade... **3.** row (columns) **4.** stoa
  7. columns, portico **8.** cloister,
  corridor **9.** peristyle
colony... **4.** body **5.** group, swarm
  9. community **10.** dependency,
  settlement
colophon... **6.** emblem **9.** bookplate
  11. inscription (book)
color... **3.** dun, dye, hue **4.** tint, tone
  5. blush, paint, shade, stain, terne,
  tinge **6.** flaxen, nuance, pastel,
  sallow, timbre **7.** piebald, pigment
  8. tincture (Her) **10.** complexion
color (pert to)...
  application (paste).. **7.** impasto
  blending.. **4.** teer **5.** fondu
  9. scumbling
  blind.. **9.** achropsia **13.** achromatopsia
  clouded.. **9.** nebulated
  colorful.. **9.** chromatic
  colorless.. **4.** drab, dull, pale **6.** pallid
  7. whitish **8.** blanched
  10. achromatic
  irregularity.. **5.** fleck **6.** streak
  10. rivulation
  material.. **5.** eosin, morin, smalt
  7. pigment **11.** chlorophyll
  off color.. **8.** abnormal, improper
  organ.. **8.** clavilux
  paint, rouge.. **6.** ruddle
  science of.. **10.** chromatics
  11. spectrology
  variegated.. **7.** rainbow, The Flag,
  vibgyor **8.** spectrum **11.** iridescence
Colorado...
  canyon.. **5.** Black **10.** Royal Gorge
  capital.. **6.** Denver
  city.. **5.** Aspen, Lamar **6.** Pueblo
  7. Boulder, Manassa, Manitou
  9. Leadville **11.** Central City
  Indian.. **8.** Arapahoe
  lake (highest).. **10.** Frozen Lake
  Mt peak.. **6.** Elbert **9.** Pike's Peak
  park.. **5.** Estes **15.** Garden of the
  Gods
  river.. **4.** Gila **6.** Platte **8.** Arkansas,
  Colorado
  State admission.. **12.** Thirty–eighth
  State motto.. **13.** Nil Sine Numine
  (Nothing Without God)
  State nickname.. **10.** Centennial
colossal... **4.** huge **5.** great, large
  6. absurd, superb **7.** mammoth
  8. gigantic **9.** monstrous
colossal beast... **8.** behemoth (Bib)
colt... **3.** gun **4.** foal **5.** filly, horse

8. yearling
Columbus (pert to)...
  birthplace.. **5.** Genoa (It)
  companion.. **5.** Ojeda
  discoverer.. **7.** America (1492)
  landing site.. **11.** San Salvador
  sailing site.. **5.** Palos (Sp)
  vessel.. **4.** Nina **5.** Pinta **10.** Santa
  Maria
column... **3.** lat (Buddh) **4.** anta
  5. shaft, stele (stela) **6.** pillar
  7. telamon **8.** baluster, caryatid,
  pilaster
column (pert to)...
  base.. **5.** socle **6.** plinth **9.** stylobate
  military.. **4.** unit **9.** formation
  Order (Arch).. **5.** Doric, Ionic
  6. Tuscan **9.** Composite
  10. Corinthian
  ref to.. **5.** train **7.** cortege
  8. cylinder, memorial, monument
  10. procession
  shaft.. **4.** fust **5.** scape **8.** apophyge
  term.. **5.** bague, galbe, shank
  7. capital, entasis
coma... **4.** daze, tuft **5.** carus, sleep,
  sopor **6.** stupor, trance **9.** catalepsy
  12. sluggishness **13.** insensibility
  15. unconsciousness
comatose... **6.** drowsy, torpid
  9. apathetic, lethargic **10.** insensible
  11. unconscious
comb... **4.** card, wave **5.** cock's, crest,
  curry, groom, scour, tease **6.** search
  7. rummage **8.** caruncle
combat... **3.** war **4.** cope, duel, fray,
  tilt **5.** fight, joust (anc), repel
  6. action, battle, oppose, strife
  7. contest, scuffle **8.** argument,
  conflict **9.** withstand **10.** antagonize,
  contention, engagement
combat (pert to)...
  challenge.. **6.** cartel
  code.. **6.** duello
  scene.. **5.** arena
combatant... **6.** dueler **7.** battler,
  fighter **8.** disputer **9.** contender
  10. competitor, contestant
combative... **8.** militant **9.** agonistic,
  bellicose **10.** aggressive, pugnacious
  11. belligerent, contentious
combination... **4.** gang, pact, pool
  5. blend, combo, party, trust, union
  6. clique, fusion, hookup, league,
  merger **7.** amalgam, combine,
  faction, mixture **8.** alliance, coalesce,
  ensemble, junction **9.** camarilla,
  coalition, synthesis **10.** embodiment
  11. aggregation, association,
  confederacy, unification
  12. undergarment **13.** incorporation
combine... **3.** add, mix **4.** join, pool
  5. merge, unite **6.** concur, mingle
  7. machine
combining form...
  above, beyond.. **3.** sur **5.** ultra
  across.. **4.** tran **5.** trans
  bad.. **3.** dys, mal
  black.. **4.** mela
  earth.. **3.** geo
  equal.. **3.** iso **4.** pari
  far.. **3.** tel **4.** tele

good.. 2. eu
hundred.. 4. cent
inner, within.. 4. ento (ent)
kidney.. 4. reni
middle.. 4. medi 5. medio
mountain.. 3. oro
needle.. 3. acu
new.. 3. neo
not.. 2. un 3. non
old, ancient.. 5. paleo
one.. 3. uni 4. mono
outside, without.. 3. ect, ext 4. ecto
personal.. 4. idio
soft.. 4. leni
stone.. 4. lith
thought.. 4. ideo
thrice.. 3. ter
tooth.. 6. odonto
touch.. 3. tac
up, upward.. 3. ano
watery.. 4. sero

comblike... 7. ctenoid 8. pectinal
combustible... 5. fiery, quick
  7. piceous 8. volcanic 9. irascible
  10. accendible 11. hot-tempered,
  inflammable
combustion... 4. fire 6. tumult
  7. blazing, flaming 8. ignition
  9. agitation, confusion, cremation
  12. inflammation 13. conflagration
come... 3. hop 4. near 5. issue, occur
  6. appear, arrive, happen
  8. approach 9. transpire
come (pert to)...
  across.. 3. pay 4. meet 7. confess
    10. contribute
  back.. 6. answer, retort, return
    7. rebound, recover 8. remember,
    repartee
  before.. 4. lead 7. precede, prevene
    8. antecede
  between.. 8. estrange, interlie
    9. interpose, intervene
  by.. 3. get 4. gain 6. obtain
    7. acquire, inherit, receive
  forth.. 3. jet 4. gush, spew 5. hatch,
    issue, occur 6. appear, emerge,
    spring 7. emanate 9. originate
  together.. 4. join, knit, meet 5. clash
    7. collide, convene 8. assemble,
    converge
come (to)...
  light.. 7. develop
  maturity.. 5. ripen
  pass.. 5. occur 6. befall, betide,
    happen 9. eventuate
  rest.. 3. sit 5. light 6. settle
comedian, comedienne... 4. buff
  5. actor, comic 6. player 7. farcist
  8. funnyman 9. dramatist
comedy... 5. drama, farce, revue
  7. comedie 8. travesty 9. burlesque,
  slapstick
comestibles... 4. food 5. manna
  8. eatables, victuals
comfort... 4. ease 5. cheer, quilt
  6. relief, solace, soothe, succor
  7. confirm, console, enliven, fortify,
  refresh, relieve, support, sustain
  8. inspirit, nepenthe (drug)
  9. enjoyment 10. invigorate,

strengthen 11. consolation
  12. satisfaction
comfortable... 4. cozy, easy, snug
  5. scarf 8. adequate, cheerful,
  homelike, wristlet 9. contented,
  endemonic 10. complacent,
  prosperous 11. consolatory,
  encouraging
comforter... 5. quilt 6. tippet
  7. solacer 8. pacifier 9. Paraclete
comfortless... 7. forlorn 8. desolate
  9. cheerless, heartsick 10. despairing
  11. distressing 12. disconsolate,
  inconsolable
comic, comical... 3. odd 5. cutup,
  droll, funny, queer, witty 6. absurd,
  quaint 7. cartoon, risible
  8. comedian, farcical, humorous
  9. burlesque, laughable, ludicrous,
  quizzical, whimsical 10. capricious,
  outlandish
coming... 3. due 6. access, advent,
  future 7. arrival, forward, looming
  8. eventual, expected, imminent
  9. imminence 11. approaching,
  forthcoming
coming into being... 7. genesis,
  nascent
comity... 7. amenity, suavity 8. civility,
  courtesy, urbanity 10. affability
command... 3. bid, gee, haw, hup
  4. bade, beck, fiat, hest, rule, sway
  5. avast, check, edict, exact, grasp,
  order, power, ukase 6. behest,
  charge, compel, decree, direct,
  enjoin, govern 7. control, dictate,
  mandate, mastery 8. dominion,
  restrain 9. authority, prescribe
  10. domination 11. commandment
  12. jurisdiction
commander... 3. cid 5. chief, ruler
  6. leader 7. admiral, captain, skipper
  8. dictator, governor, myriarch,
  overlord
commander, Eastern... 3. ras 4. amir,
  emir, Imam, khan, rani 5. ameer,
  begum, dewan, emeer, nawab, Nizam
  6. caliph, regent, Sultan
commanding... 8. dominant
  9. imperious 10. imperative
  13. authoritative
commandments... 4. laws 6. orders,
  tables 8. mandates, precepts
  9. Decalogue (Ten)
comme il faut... 8. properly
  9. correctly 10. decorously 12. as it
  should be
commemoration... 7. service
  8. Encaenia (Oxford Univ)
  10. observance 11. anniversary,
  celebration, remembrance
  13. solemnization
commence... 4. open 5. arise, begin,
  start 6. spring 8. initiate 9. originate
commencement... 4. rite 6. source
  8. ceremony, nascency 9. beginning,
  formality, inception, novitiate
  10. initiation
commend... 4. plug 5. boost, extol,
  offer 6. assign, commit, praise,
  remand, resign 7. approve, deliver,
  entrust 8. advocate, delegate

9. recommend 10. compliment, ingratiate

commendation... 4. plug, puff
5. boost 8. approval 10. assignment, commitment, compliment, delegation
11. approbation, consignment, entrustment

comment... 4. note, talk 6. gossip, postil, remark, report 7. descant, discuss, explain, mention 8. annotate, critique 9. criticism, discourse

commentary... 5. gloss 6. memoir 7. remarks 8. treatise 9. memoranda 10. annotation 11. explanation

commerce... 5. trade 7. traffic 8. dealings 9. communion 11. interchange 13. communication

commis... 5. agent, clerk 6. deputy

commiserate... 4. pity 7. condole, console 10. sympathize

commiseration... 4. pity, ruth 5. mercy 6. sorrow 7. feeling 8. sympathy 10. compassion, condolence

commission... 4. duty, task 5. allot, board, share, trust 6. brevet, depute, office, ordain 7. empower, mandate, mission, payment, rake–off, warrant 8. delegate 9. authority 10. assignment, constitute, delegation, deputation 11. performance 12. perpetration

commissioned... 8. allotted, breveted 9. delegated 10. accredited, authorized

commissioner... 5. envoy 6. dubash, legate 7. steward 8. delegate, emissary, official 9. commissar

commissure... 4. seam 5. cleft, joint, mitre, raphe 6. stitch, suture 7. closure 8. juncture 10. interstice

commit... 2. do 3. con 4. game (cards) 5. refer 6. remand 7. confide, consign, entrust, promise 8. memorize, relegate 10. commission, perpetrate

commode... 3. cap 5. chest 8. fontange 9. washstand 10. chiffonier

commodious... 3. fit 5. ample, roomy 6. proper 8. suitable 9. capacious, expansive, opportune 10. convenient 11. comfortable, serviceable 13. accommodating

commodity, commodities... 5. goods, wares 6. profit 7. staples 9. appliance 10. appliances

common... 4. park 5. cheap, plain, stale, trite, usual 6. mutual, paltry, vulgar 7. average 8. familiar, frequent, mediocre, ordinary, plebeian 9. customary, household, universal 11. commonplace

common (pert to)...
ancestor.. 4. Adam
funds.. 4. pool
gender.. 7. epicene
informer.. 7. delator
people.. 5. demos, gente 6. vulgus 8. populace

commonly accepted... 7. vulgate

commonly thought... 8. putative

commonplace... 5. banal, daily, stale, theme, trite, usual 6. truism 7. humdrum, prosaic 8. ordinary 9. platitude

commonwealth... 5. group, State 7. society 8. Kentucky, Virginia 9. Australia, community 12. Pennsylvania 13. Massachusetts

commotion... 3. ado 4. fray, riot, to–do, whir 5. flare 6. flurry, fracas, rumpus, tumult, unrest 7. turmoil 8. uprising 9. agitation, confusion 10. concussion (Med), excitement, turbulence 12. perturbation

commune... 4. area, soil 5. realm, share 6. confer, impart 8. converse 9. communion 10. commonalty 11. intercourse (spiritual) 12. conversation

Commune of Paris (1871)... 10. government

communicate... 3. say 4. give, join 5. share 6. bestow, impart, inform 7. apprize 8. converse

communication... 4. word 5. radio 6. letter, report 7. account, epistle, message 9. statement 10. communiqué, connection 11. impartation, information, intercourse

communion... 5. share 6. church 7. concord 8. converse 9. agreement 11. intercourse 12. denomination 13. participation

Communion... 9. Eucharist, Sacrament 10. intinction, Last Supper 11. Lord's Supper

communion (pert to)...
bread (blessed).. 4. host 5. wafer 7. eulogia 9. antidoron
cloth.. 8. corporal, corporas
plate.. 5. paten
psalm.. 7. introit 12. processional
table.. 4. cena (of Last Supper) 5. altar
vessel.. 3. ama, pyx

communiqué... 4. word 7. message 8. dispatch 13. communication

comose... 5. hairy 6. tufted

compact... 4. etui, firm, pact, plot, snug, trim 5. brief, close, dense, pithy, press, solid, terse, tight 6. treaty, united, vanity 7. concise, crowded, entente, leagued, serried 8. alliance, compress, contract, covenant, succinct 9. agreement, condensed 10. compressed, conspiracy 11. compendious, sententious, stipulation

companion... 3. pal 4. ally, fare, mate, twin 5. amigo, crony 6. fellow, shadow 7. Achates, compeer, comrade, consort 8. alter ego 9. associate 11. confederate, counterpart

companionship... 7. society 10. fellowship, fraternity 11. comradeship, sociability 13. accompaniment

company... 3. set 4. band, bevy, body, crew, gang, ging, host 5. crowd, flock, group, party, troop

6. circle, cohort, throng, troupe
9. concourse, gathering

company (pert to)...
detachment.. 5. posse
people, players.. 4. bevy, crew, gang,
team 5. troop 6. galaxy, guests,
troupe 9. cavalcade
ships.. 5. fleet 6. armada
8. squadron
soldiers.. 5. corps, squad 7. brigade,
phalanx, platoon 9. battalion
travelers.. 7. caravan 8. pilgrims,
tourists 9. merchants

comparative... 5. equal, rival
8. relative 10. comparable, relational
compare... 4. even 5. liken 6. confer,
semble 7. collate, examine
8. contrast
comparison... 6. simile 7. parable
8. likening, metaphor
10. accordance, similarity
11. parallelism
compartment... 3. bin 4. cell, part
5. stall 6. alcove 7. cellule,
chamber, quarter 8. district, division
10. department
compass... 3. arc 4. area, plot, ring
5. guide, range (Mus), reach, solar,
sweep 6. attain, bounds, circle,
curved, degree, extent 7. circuit,
divider, enclose, imagine 8. circular,
distance, surround
compass (pert to)...
housing.. 8. binnacle
part.. 3. pen 6. needle
point.. 4. airt 5. rhumb 7. azimuth
sight.. 4. vane
suspender.. 6. gimbal
compassion... 4. pity, ruth (anc)
5. mercy 8. humanity, sympathy
10. condolence 13. commiseration
compassionate... 6. gentle, humane
7. clement, pitiful 8. merciful
11. sympathetic, warmhearted
12. sympathizing
compatible... 8. affinity, suitable
9. accordant, agreeable, congruous
10. consistent, harmonious
12. congeniality
compeer... 4. mate, peer 5. equal,
match, rival 7. comrade
9. companion
compel... 4. urge 5. drive, force,
impel, press 6. coerce, incite, oblige,
obsess 7. actuate, dragoon, require
9. constrain, influence, instigate
compelling... 6. urgent 7. driving
8. pressing 9. insistent, necessary,
obsessing 10. compulsory,
motivating, obligatory, persuasive
compelling assent... 6. cogent
compelling attention... 9. insistent
compendious... 5. brief, short, terse
7. compact, concise 8. abridged,
succinct 9. condensed
10. summarized
compendium... 5. brief 6. abrégé,
digest 7. capsule, epitome, medulla,
pandect, summary 8. abstract,
syllabus, synopsis 9. comprisal
10. abridgment 11. compilation,
contraction 12. abbreviation

compensate... 3. pay 5. atone, repay
6. reward 7. redress, requite
9. indemnify 10. recompense,
remunerate 14. counterbalance
compensation... 3. pay 4. hire
5. bonus, wages 6. manbot
(manbote), reward, salary 7. penalty,
stipend 8. gratuity, pittance, requital,
solatium 9. atonement, indemnity
10. reparation 12. remuneration,
satisfaction 15. indemnification
compete... 3. vie 4. cope 5. match
6. outvie, strive 7. contend, contest,
emulate
competence... 5. means, skill
7. ability, fitness 8. adequacy,
capacity, property 10. capability,
efficiency 11. proficiency, sufficiency,
suitability 13. effectiveness,
qualification
competent... 3. apt, can, fit 4. able
5. capax, smart 7. capable
8. adequate, suitable 9. effective,
effectual, efficient, qualified
10. catechumen, sufficient
12. appertaining (to)
competition... 5. match, trial 6. strife
7. contest, rivalry 8. ambition,
concours 9. emulation 10. corrivalry
compilation... 5. cento 6. digest
9. Americana 10. collection
compile... 3. add 4. edit 5. amass
6. gather 8. assemble
complacent... 4. smug 6. bovine
7. fatuous 9. contented, satisfied
11. considerate 13. self-satisfied
complain... 4. beef, carp, fret, kick,
pule, wail 5. gripe, growl, whine
6. accuse, bewail, grieve, grouse,
lament, murmur, mutter, repine,
squawk, yammer 7. deplore, grumble,
protest 9. bellyache
complaint... 6. charge, lament, malady
7. ailment, disease, illness, protest
8. disorder, repining, reproach
9. grievance, murmuring
10. accusation, imputation
11. declaration, lamentation
complaisance... 6. regard 7. amenity,
concern, suavity 8. civility, courtesy,
urbanity 10. indulgence, solicitude,
submission, toleration
13. consideration
complaisant... 4. easy, kind 5. civil
6. polite 7. lenient 8. gracious,
obliging 9. compliant, courteous
complement... 4. crew 7. adjunct
8. addition, complete
10. correspond, supplement
11. counterpart
complete... 3. all, end 4. dead, fill,
full, sole 5. stark, total, utter, whole
6. effect, entire, finish, intact, mature
7. achieve, execute, germane,
perfect, plenary, realize 8. absolute,
conclude, detailed, outright
9. terminate 10. accomplish,
complement, consummate
11. unqualified
completely... 3. all 5. fully, quite,
stark 7. solidly, totally, utterly
8. entirely

completeness... 9. entelechy, integrity
complex... 4. mazy 5. mixed 6. knotty
7. twisted 8. involute, involved
9. entangled, intricate, perplexed
10. interlaced 11. complicated
complexion... 4. blee, mode, tone
5. color, guise, tinge 10. appearance
compliance... 6. assent 7. consent
9. accession, obedience
10. concession, conformity,
observance, submission
11. willingness 12. acquiescence
compliant... 6. docile 7. duteous,
dutiful, willing 8. obedient
9. indulgent 10. submissive
11. acquiescent, complaisant,
conformable
complicated... 6. daedal 7. complex,
Gordian, snarled, tangled 8. involved
9. difficult, embroiled, intricate
11. embarrassed 12. labyrinthine
complication... 4. node (drama)
5. nodus 7. illness 9. complexus
10. complexity 11. combination
compliment... 6. praise 7. adulate,
commend, flatter 8. encomium,
flattery 9. adulation, servility
10. sycophancy 12. blandishment,
commendation 14. congratulation,
obsequiousness
comply... 4. obey 5. agree, yield
6. accede, accord, assent, submit
7. conform, observe 9. acquiesce
compone... 6. settle 7. arrange,
compose 8. compound
component... 3. ion 4. part 5. basis
6. factor 7. element 8. integral
10. ingredient 11. constituent
comport... 3. act 6. accord, behave
8. behavior, tolerant 10. correspond,
deportment
comportable... 8. suitable
10. consistent
compose... 3. pen 4. calm, form,
make 5. order, score, write
7. arrange, fashion, prepare
8. compound, melodize 9. reconcile
10. constitute 11. orchestrate,
tranquilize
composed... 4. calm, cool 5. quiet,
sober, wrote 6. sedate, serene
7. consist 8. arranged, tranquil
9. collected
composed of...
flat plates.. 9. lamellate
flowers.. 9. floscular
heaths.. 8. ericetal
lobes.. 6. lobate
rocks.. 10. rupestrian
composer... 6. author 7. idylist (idyllist)
10. compositor, typesetter
composer of...
Aida.. 5. Verdi
Carmen.. 5. Bizet
Faust.. 6. Gounod
La Boheme.. 7. Puccini
Merry Widow.. 5. Lehar
Mikado.. 8. Sullivan
Naughty Marietta.. 7. Herbert
Stars and Stripes Forever.. 5. Sousa
composition... 4. opus 5. piece,
theme 6. make-up 9. formation,

synthesis 12. constitution,
construction
composition (pert to)...
literature.. 5. cento, essay, poesy,
prose 6. poetry, satire, thesis
8. treatise
music.. 2. op 4. aria, glee, hymn,
opus 5. drama, étude, motet, nonet,
opera, rondo, suite 6. anthem, septet
(septuor), sextet (sestet), sonata
7. duetino, quartet 8. concerto,
oratorio, symphony
composure... 6. repose 8. calmness,
coolness, serenity 9. placidity
10. equanimity, quiescence,
sedateness 11. tranquility
14. imperturbation
compound... 3. mix 4. olio 5. agree,
amide, ester, oxide, pyran, unite
6. anisil, elixir, iodide, ketone
7. ammonia, combine, farrago,
metamer 8. tincture 9. composite
10. commixture, compromise
comprehend... 3. see 4. know
5. grasp, sense 6. embody, fathom
7. enclose, imagine, include, involve,
realize 8. comprise, conceive
10. understand
comprehensible... 8. exoteric, included,
knowable 9. comprised
11. conceivable, discernible,
perceptible 12. intelligible
comprehensive... 4. full, wide 5. large
7. generic, knowing 8. thorough
9. extensive, inclusive, universal
11. compendious
compress... 4. firm 5. cling, crowd,
pinch, press, stupe 7. compact,
densify, embrace, squeeze
8. astringe, condense, contract,
decrease 11. consolidate
comprise, comprize... 5. imply
6. number 7. contain, embrace,
inclose, include, involve 8. perceive
10. comprehend, constitute
compromise... 4. bind 6. adjust
8. compound, endanger
9. agreement, surrender
10. adjustment, concession,
settlement 11. appeasement,
arbitration
compt... 4. neat 6. spruce 8. polished
compulsion... 5. drive, force
6. duress, urging 7. impulse
8. coaction, coercion 9. necessity,
obsession 10. compelling
compulsory... 7. driving 9. mandatory,
necessary 10. compelling, imperative,
obligatory 11. involuntary
compunction... 3. rue 5. guilt, pangs
6. regret 7. remorse 8. pricking
9. penitence 11. impenitence
13. regretfulness
compute... 5. count, score, tally
6. cipher, figure, number, reckon
8. estimate 9. calculate, enumerate
comrade... 3. pal 4. ally, chum, mate,
peer 5. buddy, crony 6. fellow, frater
7. compeer 8. camarada, sidekick
9. associate, colleague, companion
con... 2. no 3. nay 4. know, read
5. cheat, learn, steer, study

6. peruse 7. convict, deceive, swindle 8. memorize, negative 10. understand 13. confidence man

conceal... 4. dern, hide, mask, palm, veil 5. cloak, cover, derne, eloin, feign 6. eloign, pocket, screen 7. secrete 8. bescreen, disguise, enshield

concealed... 5. doggo 6. covert, hidden, latent, perdue, secret, veiled, velate 7. covered, larvate, obscure, unknown, velated 9. disguised, incognito, insidious 11. clandestine

concede... 3. own 5. admit, agree, allow, grant, yield 6. accord 7. confess, consent 8. consider 9. surrender 11. acknowledge

conceit... 3. ego 4. idea 5. fancy, pride 6. vagary, vanity 7. caprice, egotism, foppery, tympany 8. priggery 12. boastfulness

conceited... 4. smug, vain 5. proud 7. foppish 8. arrogant, boastful, priggish 9. egotistic, pragmatic 11. egotistical, opinionated 12. stuffed shirt

conceivable... 7. tenable 8. credible 9. plausible 10. believable, imaginable 12. intelligible

conceive... 5. dream, fancy, think 6. create, devise, ideate 7. imagine, produce, realize, suppose, suspect 9. originate 10. understand

concentrate... 4. mass 5. focus 6. center 7. compact, densify, extract 8. condense, converge 9. intensify 10. centralize 11. consolidate

concept... 4. idea 5. image 7. opinion, thought 8. category

conception... 4. idea 5. image, savvy 6. notion 7. conceit, opinion 9. pregnancy 12. apprehension 13. comprehension, understanding

concern... 4. care, firm, sake 5. event, grief 6. affair, affect, import, matter 7. anxiety, pertain 8. business, interest, salience 9. relevance 10. importance 11. consequence 12. significance 13. consideration

concerning... 2. of, on, re 3. for 4. over, upon 5. about, anent 9. regarding 10. respecting

concert... 6. aubade 7. recital 9. agreement, unanimity 11. co-operation, performance

concert hall... 5. odeum (odeon) 6. lyceum 7. theater 9. music hall, playhouse

concession... 5. grant 6. market 7. consent 8. discount 10. compromise, confession 13. qualification

concierge... 6. porter, warden 7. ostiary 8. chokidar 10. doorkeeper

conciliate... 4. ease 6. pacify 7. appease, mollify, placate 9. reconcile 10. propitiate

conciliatory... 6. assent, irenic 8. irenical 9. appeasing, forgiving 10. mollifying

concise... 4. curt, neat 5. brief, crisp,

pithy, terse 6. précis 7. laconic, pointed, serried, summary 8. succinct 11. compendious, sententious 13. comprehensive

conclude... 3. end 4. rest 5. close, infer 6. deduce, endeth, finish, settle 7. arrange, presume, resolve, suppose 8. complete 9. determine, terminate

conclusion... 3. end 4. last 5. close, finis 6. finale, finish, result 8. decision, epilogue 9. deduction, diagnosis, inference 10. completion 13. determination

conclusive... 5. final, valid 8. decisive, ultimate 9. mandatory 10. convincing, evidential 11. irrefutable, sockdologer (answer) 12. unanswerable

concoct... 3. mix 4. brew, cook, make 6. devise, digest, invent, scheme 7. perfect, prepare 8. fabricate

concoction... 4. dish, plan, plot 6. device 7. mixture 8. compound 9. falsehood, invention 11. combination, fabrication, preparation

concomitant... 9. accessory, attendant, co-operant 10. coincident, concurrent 11. synchronous 12. accompanying, simultaneous

concord... 4. tune 5. chord, peace 6. accord, treaty, unison 7. concert, harmony, rapport 8. symphony 9. agreement, unanimity

concordant... 8. agreeing, harmonic, unisonal 9. consonant, unanimous 10. harmonious 11. conformable 13. correspondent

concrete... 4. hard, pave 5. béton, solid 6. cement 7. congeal, plaster 8. hardness, pavement, solidify 11. substantial

concur... 5. agree, chime, unite 6. accede, assent 7. approve, combine, consent 9. acquiesce, co-operate 11. synchronize

concurrence... 6. united 7. joining 9. adherence, concourse, unanimity 11. coincidence, conjunction, convergence, co-operation, parallelism

concurrent... 5. joint 6. united 7. meeting, uniting 8. parallel, syndrome 9. unanimous 10. associated, coincident, synergetic 11. co-operative, synchronous 12. accompanying, simultaneous

concussion... 5. clash, shock, smash, wound 6. injury, trauma 7. collision

condemn... 3. ban 4. doom 5. blame, decry 7. adjudge, censure, convict 8. penalize, sentence

condense... 3. mix 5. unite 6. absorb, decoct, deepen, harden, lessen, narrow, reduce 7. abridge, combine, compact, densify, enhance, shorten, squeeze, thicken 8. compress, contract, diminish, heighten, solidify 9. constrict, intensify 11. concentrate, consolidate

condensed... 7. compact, concise, cramped, tabloid 9. shortened

10. compressed, contracted
12. concentrated
condenser (anc)... 9. Leyden jar
condescend... 5. deign, stoop
6. submit, unbend 7. concede,
descend 9. patronize, vouchsafe
condign... 3. fit 4. just 6. severe,
worthy 7. fitting 8. adequate,
deserved, suitable
condiment... 3. soy 4. dill, mace,
mint, sage, salt 5. chili, clove, curry,
sauce, spice 6. catsup, garlic,
ginger, nutmeg, pepper, relish
7. cayenne, ketchup, mustard,
paprika, vinegar 9. seasoning
10. peppermint
condition... 2. if 4. case, haze, rank,
term 5. covin, limit, stage, state
6. estate, fettle, health, plight, status
7. posture, proviso, quality, station
8. capacity, position, standing
9. requisite, situation 10. limitation
11. predicament 12. circumstance
condition (pert to)...
  favorable.. 4. odds
  flushed.. 4. rosy
  habitual.. 5. tenor
  hypnotic.. 4. daze 6. stupor, trance
  7. narcose
  made.. 7. premise
  murk.. 3. fog 4. haze, mist 5. gloom
  proper.. 6. kilter
  stipulation.. 7. proviso
conditionally... 2. if 8. provided
11. tentatively 13. provisionally
condone... 5. remit 6. accept, excuse,
pardon 7. absolve, forgive 8. tolerate
11. countenance
condor... 6. falcon 7. vulture
conduce... 4. lend, tend 5. serve
6. effect 7. advance, dispose,
incline, redound 10. contribute
conducive... 6. useful 7. helpful
11. implemental, serviceable
12. instrumental
conduct... 3. act, run 4. lead, mien,
rule 5. guide, usage, usher
6. action, convey, convoy, direct,
escort, govern, manage 7. bearing,
comport, control, manners
8. behavior, demeanor, regulate
9. operation, supervise
10. deportment, management
11. comportment, superintend
conduct (pert to)...
  a cause.. 5. plead
  breach.. 6. guilty
  doctrine of.. 6. morals
  one's self.. 6. behave, demean
  7. comport
conducting inward... 9. afference
conductor... 5. guide 6. escort, leader
7. cathode, maestro, manager
8. cicerone, director, operator,
trainman
conduit... 3. way 4. adit, duct, pain,
pipe, tube 5. canal, sewer 6. course
7. channel 8. aqueduct
cone (pert to)...
  conelike.. 5. conic 6. pineal
  7. conical
  pine.. 8. strobile

silver.. 4. pina
tree.. 5. larch 7. conifer
confab, confabulation... 4. chat, talk
7. palaver, prattle 8. chinfest, talkfest
12. conversation
confection... 3. jam 5. candy, dulce,
icing, jelly 6. cimbal, comfit, nougat,
sweets 7. caramel, fondant, praline,
succade 8. preserve 9. sweetmeat
11. bittersweet, marshmallow
confederacy... 5. cabal, hanse, union
6. fusion, league 8. alliance,
covenant 9. coalition 10. complicity,
conspiracy, federation 11. affiliation,
association, combination
13. consolidation
confederate... 3. pal, reb 4. ally
5. stall 7. abettor 9. accessory,
assistant, associate, auxiliary
10. accomplice
confer... 4. give 6. advise, bestow,
invest, parley 7. collate, commune,
consign, consult, counsel 8. ordinate
(knighthood) 10. deliberate
conference... 5. trust 6. huddle,
parley, powwow 7. council, palaver
9. interview 10. discussion
12. consultation
conferring respect... 9. honorific
conferring title... 9. ennobling
confess... 3. own, rue 4. avow
5. admit, own up 6. regret, repent,
reveal, shrive 7. concede
11. acknowledge
confession... 5. credo (of faith), creed
6. avowal, shrift 9. admission,
communion 10. profession
14. acknowledgment
(acknowledgement)
confetti... 5. paper 6. ribbon
7. bonbons 9. cascarons (in
eggshells) 10. sweetmeats
11. confections
confidant... 6. friend 8. intimate
confide... 4. hope, rely 5. trust
6. commit, depend, repose
confidence... 5. faith, poise 6. belief,
morals, secret 7. courage
8. credence, sureness 9. assurance,
impudence 10. effrontery
12. impertinence
confident... 4. smug, sure 6. secure
7. assured, certain, hopeful, reliant
8. cocksure, positive, sanguine,
unafraid 9. convinced 10. determined
confidential... 5. privy 6. secret
7. private 8. esoteric, intimate
9. auricular 10. unquotable
11. trustworthy
confidentially... 7. sub rosa
configuration... 4. form 5. shape
6. figure 7. contour, Gestalt, pattern
8. asterism 13. constellation
confine... 3. dam, hem, mew, pen,
sty, tie 4. bind, cage, coop, jail,
lock 5. bound, limit, stint 6. border,
immure, intern, secure, strain
7. compass 8. imprison, restrain
9. enclosure 11. incarcerate,
restriction 12. circumscribe
confined... 4. pent 6. bound, caged
6. shut–in 7. cribbed, endemic,

limited 8. esoteric, impended,
interned 9. bedridden, impounded,
invalided, parochial
confinement... 7. durance, lying-in
9. restraint 10. childbirth
12. accouchement, imprisonment
13. incommunicado
15. circumscription
confirm... 4. seal 5. prove 6. assure,
attest, ratify, settle, verify 7. approve,
fortify, sustain 8. convince, sanction,
validate 9. establish 11. corroborate
12. substantiate
confirmed... 6. proved 7. chronic
8. habitual, ratified 10. encouraged,
inveterate 11. established
confiscate... 5. seize, usurp
7. impound 11. appropriate
conflagrant... 5. afire 6. ablaze, aflame
7. blazing, burning
conflagration... 4. fire 5. fever
12. inflammation
conflict... 3. war 4. bout, duel, fray
5. clash, fight 6. action, battle,
combat, oppose, strife 7. contend,
contest, discord 8. clashing, struggle
9. antipathy, collision, encounter,
hostility 10. contention, opposition
11. competition
confluence... 4. flow 5. crowd
6. stream 7. flowing (together),
meeting 8. junction 10. assemblage
11. concurrence, convergence
12. assimilation
conform... 2. go 3. fit 4. lean, obey,
suit 5. adapt, agree 6. adjust,
concur, settle 7. compose, consent,
observe 8. coincide 9. reconcile
11. accommodate
conformity... 6. dharma 8. legality,
symmetry 9. agreement, congruity
10. compliance 15. conventionality
confound... 3. mix 5. abash, amaze
6. baffle, dismay, puzzle, thwart
7. astound, buffalo, mystify, nonplus,
perplex 8. astonish, bewilder
9. dumbfound, embarrass, frustrate
10. complicate, disconcert
11. intermingle
confront... 4. face, meet 5. front
6. oppose 7. compare 8. encounter
confrontation... 8. showdown
10. opposition
confuse... 3. mix 4. maze 5. abash,
addle, upset 6. baffle, flurry, jumble,
muddle 7. derange, fluster
8. befuddle, bewilder, disorder,
distract, entangle 9. embrangle
10. complicate, disarrange,
discompose, disconcert
confused... 7. chaotic, jumbled, rattled
8. deranged 9. chagrined, flustered,
perplexed, uncertain 10. indistinct
confusion... 3. ado, din 4. mess, moll
5. babel, chaos 6. jumble, pother,
welter 7. anarchy, clutter, turmoil
8. disarray, disorder 9. abashment,
agitation 10. perplexity
11. derangement 12. bewilderment
13. embarrassment
confute... 4. deny 5. rebut 6. answer,
expose, refute 7. dismiss

8. confound, overcome, redargue
9. overwhelm (by argument)
congeal... 3. gel, ice, set 4. rime
6. freeze 7. pectize, thicken
congenial... 4. boon 7. kindred
8. friendly 9. accordant, agreeable
10. affinitive, compatible
11. sympathetic
congenital... 6. inborn, innate
7. connate, genetic, natural
14. constitutional
conger... 3. eel 8. cucumber
13. Leptocephalus
congeries... 4. heap 9. amassment
10. collection 11. aggregation
congestion... 3. jam 4. heap
8. fullness, stoppage 9. gathering
11. obstruction 12. accumulation
Congo
capital.. 12. Leopoldville
city.. 4. Boma 6. Matadi
12. Stanleyville
explorer.. 7. Stanley
highlands.. 4. Kivu 5. Ituri 7. Katanga
lake.. 5. Mweru 10. Tanganyika
mountain.. 9. Ruwenzori (Mountains of
the Moon)
river.. 5. Congo, Lulua
congratulate... 4. laud 5. bless
6. salute 7. rejoice 8. macarize
10. compliment, felicitate
congregate... 4. herd, mass, meet
5. group, troop 6. gather, muster
7. collect 8. assemble 9. forgather
congregation... 4. mass 5. house, laity
7. council 8. assembly, audience
9. gathering 10. collection
11. churchgoers
Congregation of Jesus and Mary...
6. Eudist
congress... 4. diet 5. synod 6. durbar,
indaba, soviet 7. council, meeting
8. assembly, conclave 9. Sanhedrin
10. convention, parliament
11. convergence, convocation,
legislature 12. congregation
congruous... 3. fit 4. meet 6. proper
7. fitting 8. agreeing, becoming,
suitable 9. consonant
conic, conical... 8. parabola
9. pyramidal 10. cone-shaped,
funnellike
conifers... 4. yews 5. pines 6. cedars
7. larches, Pinales, Sabines, Spruces,
Torreys 8. hemlocks, Soledads
9. Coniferae, Corsicans
10. evergreens
conjecture... 3. aim 5. ettle, guess,
opine, think 6. divine 7. conjoin,
imagine, presume, suppose, surmise,
suspect 8. supposal 9. inference
10. assumption 11. supposition
conjoin... 4. join 5. unite 6. adjoin,
concur 7. combine 8. corelate
9. correlate
conjoined parts... 6. adnexa
conjointly... 10. hand-in-hand
conjugal... 7. marital, nuptial
9. connubial 11. matrimonial
conjugate... 4. join 5. yoked
6. couple, united 7. coupled, related
8. bijugate, combined

10. paronymous 12. etymological

conjugation... 5. union 6. fusion
  7. duality, joining, uniting
  10. assemblage 11. combination
  13. juxtaposition

conjunct... 6. united 8. combined
  9. conjoined, corporate

conjunction... 2. as, et, if, or 3. and,
  but, nor 4. than, that 5. since,
  union 6. casual, though 7. whether
  10. connection 11. adversative,
  association, combination, concurrence,
  correlative

conjure... 4. pray 5. charm 6. adjure,
  enjoin, invoke, juggle, summon
  (magic) 7. beseech, enchant, entreat,
  implore 10. supplicate

conjure (up)... 5. raise 6. call up
  8. exorcise (exorcize), remember
  9. visualize

conjurer, conjuror... 4. mage
  6. voodoo, wizard 7. juggler
  8. exorcist, magician

conk... 4. head, nose 5. decay (tree)

conk out... 4. fade, fail 5. stall
  6. fizzle, perish, weaken

connate... 4. akin 6. allied 7. cognate,
  related, similar 9. congenial
  10. congenital

connect... 3. tie 4. ally, join, link,
  meet 5. unite 6. adjoin, attach,
  couple, enlink, fasten, relate
  7. bracket, succeed 9. associate,
  hyphenate

connected... 3. met 5. telic
  6. adnate, joined 7. serried, similar
  8. coherent, inlinked, syndetic
  10. continuous, correlated

Connecticut...
  capital.. 8. Hartford
  city.. 6. Darien, Mystic 7. Meriden
    8. Hartford, New Haven 9. Waterbury
    10. Bridgeport
  college (famed).. 4. Yale (1701)
  historic site.. 10. Charter Oak (1687,
    Hartford)
  museum.. 6. Barnum (P T)
  river.. 6. Thames 9. Naugatuck
    10. Housatonic 11. Connecticut
  State admission.. 5. Fifth
  State Motto.. 21. Qui Transtulit
    Sustinet (He Who Transplants
    Sustains)
  State nickname.. 6. Nutmeg
    12. Constitution

connecting link... 3. tie 4. bond
  6. connex 7. kiaison 8. ligament,
  vinculum 11. intermedium
  12. intermediary

connection... 4. bond 5. nexus, union
  6. clevis, family, series 7. kinship,
  passage 8. alliance, commerce,
  junction, relation 9. coherence,
  go–between, relevance 10. continuity
  11. association, intercourse
  12. intermediary, relationship
  13. communication, juxtaposition

conner... 5. pilot 6. balker, tester
  7. peruser 8. examiner 9. inspector

connive... 4. plot, wink 5. blink
  6. scheme 7. collude, complot,
  finagle 8. conspire, contrive,

  maneuver, overlook

conniving... 8. scheming 9. collusive,
  deceitful 10. conspiring
  11. calculating

connoisseur... 5. judge 6. expert
  7. epicure, gourmet 8. gourmand
  11. cognoscente, connaisseur

connotation... 5. sense 6. import,
  intent 7. meaning, purport
  10. denotation 11. implication
  12. significance 13. comprehension

connubial... 7. martial, nuptial
  8. conjugal 11. matrimonial
  12. epithalamium (song)

conquer... 3. win 4. beat, best
  5. crush 6. defeat, humble, master,
  reduce, subdue 7. subject
  8. overcome, overturn, surmount,
  vanquish 9. discomfit, overpower,
  overthrow, subjugate

conqueror... 4. hero 6. captor, Cortez,
  victor, winner 7. subduer
  10. subjugator 12. conquistador

conquest... 6. Norman (1066)
  7. mastery, triumph, victory

consanguinity... 5. nabob 7. kinship,
  sibship 8. affinity, relation (blood)
  12. relationship

conscience... 4. mind, self 6. psyche
  8. superego 9. casuistry

conscientious... 7. dutiful, servile
  8. faithful 10. fastidious, meticulous,
  scrupulous 11. punctilious

conscientious objection... 7. scruple

conscious... 4. keen 5. alive, awake,
  aware, vital 7. animate, feeling
  8. sensible, sentient 9. breathing,
  cognizant 13. self–conscious

consecrate... 4. sain 5. bless, exalt
  6. anoint, devote, hallow, ordain
  7. glorify 8. dedicate, sanctify

consecrated (pert to)...
  bread.. 4. host 5. wafer
  oil.. 6. chrism
  thing.. 6. sacrum

consent... 4. give 5. agree, grant,
  yield 6. accede, accord, assent,
  concur, permit 8. approval
  9. acquiesce 10. compliance,
  permission 11. concurrence
  13. understanding

consequence... 3. end 5. event
  6. course, effect, result, weight
  7. dignity, outcome 8. pursuant (in),
  sequence 9. aftermath, inference,
  influence, loftiness, outgrowth
  10. importance, notability
  11. distinction

consequential... 7. pompous
  8. eventual 9. important
  13. self–important

consequently... 2. do 4. ergo, then
  5. hence 9. as a result, therefore,
  wherefore 12. subsequently
  13. consecutively

conservative... 4. Tory 5. staid
  7. die–hard, fogyish, old–line
  8. moderate 10. long–haired
  11. reactionary 12. preservative
  13. unprogressive

conserve... 3. jam 4. save 5. guard,
  uvate 6. defend, secure, shield,

uphold 7. protect, sustain
8. maintain 9. preserves, sweetmeat
consider... 3. ain, see 4. care, deem,
heed, muse, rate 5. judge, think,
treat, weigh 6. esteem, intend,
ponder, regard 7. discuss, examine,
reflect, revolve 8. cogitate, meditate,
ruminate 10. deliberate
11. contemplate
considerable... 5. great, large
7. notable, several 8. numerous
9. important 10. noteworthy,
remarkable 13. authoritative
considerate... 4. kind 6. gentle
7. careful, heedful, prudent, serious
8. obliging 9. attentive, judicious
10. deliberate, reflective, solicitous,
thoughtful
consideration... 4. self 5. study
6. esteem, regard 7. respect,
thought 8. attention, deference,
incentive, influence 10. cogitation,
importance, meditation, reflection,
reputation, rumination
11. examination 12. compensation,
deliberation
considering... 2. if 5. since 8. after
all, inasmuch, in view of
consign... 5. allot 6. assign, commit,
devote, remand, resign 7. deliver,
entrust 8. transfer 11. subscribe to
consignee... 6. factor 7. awardee
8. assignee 9. committee
consign to...
a place.. 8. allocate
prison.. 6. commit, send up
ruin.. 4. doom
unimportance.. 8. relegate
consistent... 5. equal, solid, stiff
7. equable, logical, uniform
8. coherent 9. agreement,
consonant, steadfast 10. persisting
consisting of...
cavities.. 9. cellulose
layers (thin).. 8. laminate
names.. 8. onomatic
one word.. 7. monepic
pages.. 7. paginal
three measures.. 8. trimeter
three spots.. 5. trey
three styles (Bot).. 10. tristylous
two parts.. 6. binary
consist of... 5. imply 6. embody
7. contain, embrace, enclose, involve
8. comprise (comprize)
consolation... 6. solace 7. comfort
10. condolence
console... 4. desk 5. cheer, organ,
table 6. solace, soothe 7. bracket,
cabinet, comfort, support, sustain
9. alleviate, encourage
consolidate... 4. knit, mass 5. merge,
unify, unite 7. combine, densify
8. coalesce, compress, organize,
solidify 9. intensify 10. strengthen
consonant... 4. lene, surd 5. lenis,
nasal, velar 6. dental, labial
7. lingual, palatal, spirate 8. gutteral
9. accordant, congruous
10. compatible, concordant,
consistent
consonant (pert to)...

hissing.. 8. sibilant
rustling.. 9. fricative
voiceless (breathed).. 6. atonic
7. spirate
consort... 4. Devi (of Siva), mate, wife
5. group, Sakti 6. mingle, spouse
7. husband, partner 9. associate,
colleague, companion, harmonize
11. combination, confederate,
conjunction
conspicuous... 6. famous, signal
7. eminent, glaring, obvious, salient,
visible 8. distinct, lionized, manifest,
striking 9. important, prominent
10. celebrated, noticeable, remarkable
11. illustrious, outstanding
13. distinguished
conspiracy... 4. plot 5. cabal, unite
6. scheme 8. intrigue 9. collusion
10. connivance 11. confederacy,
machination
conspire... 4. plot 5. unite 6. concur,
scheme 7. collude, complot, finagle
9. fainaigue 11. confederate
constable... 3. cop 5. staff 6. beadle,
keeper, warden 7. bailiff 8. tipstaff
9. policeman
constabulary... 6. bureau (police)
10. constables
constancy... 4. zeal 5. ardor, faith,
truth 6. fealty, garnet (symbol)
7. honesty, loyalty 8. devotion,
fidelity 9. adherence, continual,
eagerness, integrity, stability
10. allegiance, attachment,
permanence, perpetuity, uniformity
11. devotedness, earnestness
12. faithfulness
constant... 4. firm, true 5. fixed
7. regular, uniform 8. faithful,
resolute 9. continual, invariant,
parameter (Math), perpetual, steadfast
10. continuous, invariable, persistent
12. unchangeable
constant desire... 4. itch 9. hankering
Constantine (pert to)...
birthplace.. 4. Nish (Nis) 7. Naissus
(now Yugoslavia)
known as.. 8. The Great
title.. 7. Emperor (Rome)
Constantinople...
official name.. 8. Istanbul
patriarch.. 9. Nestorius
site.. 6. Turkey (Eur)
constellation... 5. stars 6. galaxy
8. asterism 10. luminaries
13. configuration (stars)
Constellations (partial list)...
arrow.. 7. Sagitta
bears (Dipper).. 9. Ursa Major, Ursa
Minor
Bird of Paradise (S Pole).. 4. Apus
bull.. 6. Taurus
crab.. 6. Cancer
crane.. 4. Grus
dog.. 5. Canis
dragon.. 5. Draco
eagle.. 6. Aquila
fishes.. 6. Pisces
goat.. 9. Capricorn
goldfish.. 6. Dorado
hunter.. 5. Orion (most conspicuous)

lion.. 3. Leo
Noah's Ark.. 4. Argo
Northern Crown.. 14. Corona Borealis, Northern Lights
peacock.. 4. Pava
scorpion.. 7. Scorpio
serpent (sea).. 5. Hydra
Southern Cross.. 4. Crux
swan.. 6. Cygnus
Twins.. 6. Gemini
virgin.. 5. Virgo
water bearer.. 8. Aquarius
whale.. 6. Cestus
winged horse.. 7. Pegasus
wolf.. 5. Lupus

Constellations' brightest star...
3. Cor

Constellations of the Zodiac...
3. Leo 5. Aries, Libra, Virgo
6. Cancer, Gemini, Pisces, Taurus
7. Scorpio 8. Aquarius
11. Capricornus, Sagittarius

constituent... 5. voter 6. factor, matter 7. elector, element, essence 8. elective 9. component
10. ingredient 11. determinant (Math)

constituent of...
blood serum.. 7. opsonin
coal.. 6. carbon
coffee, tea.. 8. caffeine
hair, nails.. 7. keratin
oil of cloves.. 7. eugenol

constitute... 4. form 5. enact, found 6. create, depute 7. appoint, compose 8. legalize 9. determine, establish

constitution... 3. law 6. crasis, custom 7. passage 8. creation
9. enactment, essential, ordinance, structure 11. composition, institution 12. organization

Constitution (ship)... 12. Old Ironsides

constitutional... 5. legal, valid
6. innate 9. essential, healthful
12. governmental 13. dispositional

constitutional (pert to)...
health.. 4. walk 8. exercise
right.. 9. franchise
temperament.. 6. crasis
vigor.. 5. nerve

Constitution State... 11. Connecticut

constrain... 4. curb, urge 5. chain, check, drive, force, impel, press
6. compel, oblige 7. confine, repress 8. restrain 11. necessitate

constrained... 6. forced, modest
7. cramped 8. moderate, reserved 9. obligated

constraint... 4. bond, urge 5. force
6. duress, stress 7. modesty, reserve 8. coercion, pressure 9. restraint, stiffness 10. compulsion, moderation 11. confinement

constrict... 3. tie 4. bind 5. cramp
6. narrow, shrink 7. squeeze, tighten 8. astringe, condense, contract
10. constringe

constriction... 9. narrowing, stricture, tightness 11. contraction
13. strangulation

constrictor... 3. boa 5. snake

7. serpent, styptic 9. sphincter
10. compressor

construct... 4. make, rear 5. build, erect, frame 6. create 7. compose 9. establish, fabricate, originate

constructive... 7. virtual 8. creative, implicit 9. anabolism 10. suggestive
14. interpretation, interpretative

construe... 5. parse 6. deduce, render 7. explain 9. interpret, translate

consuetude... 5. habit, usage
6. custom

consuetudinary... 6. manual (customs), ritual 9. customary

consult (with)... 6. advise, confer, take up 7. discuss 10. deliberate

consultation... 7. counsel 8. audition, congress 9. interview 10. conference, discussion 12. deliberation

consume... 3. eat, use 4. burn
5. spend, waste 6. absorb, devour, expend 7. destroy (fire) 8. squander 9. dissipate 12. disintegrate

consumed... 3. pau

consummate... 3. end, top 4. ripe
5. ideal 6. finish, utmost 7. achieve, perfect 8. complete 10. accomplish

consumption... 3. use 4. loss
5. decay, waste 6. eating
7. disease, using up 8. phthisis
9. decrement 11. destruction
12. tuberculosis 13. deterioration

contact... 4. meet 5. touch, union
6. impact, syzygy (Astron)
7. meeting, oscnede (Math)
8. junction, tangency, touching
10. contiguity 13. communication

contain... 4. have, hold, keep 5. cover
6. embody, number, retain
7. embrace, enclose, include, involve, subsume 8. comprise, restrain
9. divisible (by) 10. comprehend

container... 3. bag, bin, box, can, cup, jug, lug, pan, pod, pot, tin, tub, urn, vat 4. case, crib, ewer, pail, sack, vase 5. crate, cruet, pouch 6. basket, bottle, carboy, carton, hamper, hatbox 7. capsule, hanaper 8. canister, decanter

containing...
air.. 9. pneumatic
antimony.. 8. stibiate
boron.. 7. boric 7. boracic
carbon.. 7. organic 13. carboniferous
copper.. 6. cupric
fire.. 7. igneous
gold.. 4. doré 5. auric
iron.. 6. ferric
silver.. 5. lunar
slag.. 6. drossy
ten.. 6. denary
tin.. 7. stannic

containing maxims... 6. gnomic

contaminate... 4. slur, soil 5. stain, sully, taint 6. befoul, defile, infect, poison 7. corrupt, debauch, degrade, pollute, vitiate 8. dishonor
9. desecrate 10. adulterate

contemn... 4. defy, hate 5. scorn, spurn 6. reject 7. despise, disdain

contemplate... 4. muse, plan, scan, view 5. study 6. design, expect, intend, ponder 7. examine, foresee, propose 8. consider, envision, meditate

contemplation... 5. study 6. musing 7. theoria, thought 8. scrutiny 9. foresight, intuition 10. expectancy, reflection 11. examination, expectation, speculation

contemplative... 6. sedate 7. pensive 10. meditative, reflective, ruminative, thoughtful 11. speculative 13. retrospective

contemporary... 6. coeval 7. present 10. coetaneous, coexistent, coincident 11. concomitant, synchronous 12. simultaneous 15. contemporaneous

contempt... 4. fico, geck 5. scorn, shame, sneer 7. despect, disdain 8. defiance, derision, ridicule 9. arrogance, contumely 10. disrespect 12. disobedience

contemptible... 3. low 4. base 5. cheap, petty, sorry 6. abject, paltry, sordid 7. pitiful 8. beggarly, inferior, unworthy 9. groveling, worthless 10. despicable 13. insignificant

contemptuous... 6. sneery 7. haughty 8. insolent, scornful 10. disdainful 12. contumelious, supercilious

contemptuous action... 9. indignity 10. incivility

contend... 3. vie, war 4. cope, deal, race 5. argue, fight 6. assert, bicker, insist, strive 7. compete, contest, grapple, quarrel, wrangle 8. contrive, maintain, militate

content, contents... 4. list, room 5. index, space 6. amount, please, volume 7. filling, gratify, makings, satisfy, suffice 8. capacity 9. contented, happiness, satisfied 10. components, dimensions 11. ingredients

contention... 3. war 4. feud 6. combat, debate, strife 7. quarrel, rivalry 8. argument, conflict, struggle, variance 9. emulation 10. dissension, litigation 11. altercation, competition, controversy 12. disagreement

contentious... 7. peevish 8. perverse 9. combative, litigious, wrangling 10. pugnacious 11. belligerent, dissentious, quarrelsome 13. argumentative

contentment... 4. ease 5. bliss 8. pleasure 11. peace of mind 12. satisfaction 13. contentedness, gratification

conterminous... 4. next 8. abutting, adjacent, proximal 9. adjoining

contest... 3. sue, vie 4. agon, bout, cope, deny, game, race, tilt 5. argue, set–to, trial 6. debate, oppose, strife, strive, tryout 7. contend, dispute, tourney, wrangle 8. argument, disclaim, litigate, skirmish, struggle 9. emulation 10. engagement 11. altercation, competition

contest (pert to)...

art of.. 10. agonistics

draw.. 9. stalemate

log hurling.. 5. roleo

prize.. 5. stake

undecided.. 4. draw

contestant... 5. rival 6. player 7. athlete, entrant 8. opponent 9. candidate, combatant, contender 10. competitor

contiguous... 4. near, next 8. adjacent, touching 9. adjoining, immediate, proximate 11. neighboring

Continent... 4. Asia 6. Africa, Europe 7. Eurasia, Lemuria 8. Atlantis (lost), Cascadia 9. Australia, Greenland 10. Antarctica 12. North America, South America

contingency... 4. case 5. event 6. chance 8. accident, casualty, exigency, juncture 9. emergency, liability 11. eventuality, possibility, uncertainty

contingent... 6. casual 8. eventual 9. dependent (law), provisory 10. accidental, fortuitous, incidental 11. conditional, provisional

continual... 7. endless, eternal, regular, undying, uniform 8. constant, enduring, frequent, unbroken 9. ceaseless, connected, continued, incessant, perennial, permanent, perpetual, unceasing 10. continuous, invariable 11. everlasting, intermitted, unremitting 12. imperishable 13. uninterrupted

continually... 3. aye 4. ever 5. often 7. eternal 8. eternally 10. constantly 11. perpetually, unceasingly 12. continuously

continuation... 6. sequel 8. addition, sequence 10. continuity 11. continuance, propagation, protraction 12. postponement, prolongation

continue... 3. run 4. go on, last, stay 5. abide 6. endure, extend, remain, resume 7. perdure, persist, proceed, sustain 8. protract 9. persevere, steadfast (be)

continuing... 5. still 7. chronic, durable, lasting 9. permanent 10. continuous 11. persevering

continuous... 7. chronic, endless, uniform 8. unbroken 9. continued, perpetual 13. uninterrupted

contorted... 3. wry 4. bent 6. coiled, warped 7. garbled, gnarled, twisted, wristed 8. deformed 9. perverted

contour... 4. form, line 5. curve, graph 6. figure 7. isobase, outline, profile 9. lineament, periphery 13. configuration

contra... 6. offset 7. against, counter, reverse 8. contrary, opposite 9. vice versa 10. conversely 12. contrariwise

contraband... 7. bootleg, illegal, illicit 8. unlawful 9. moonshine 10. prohibited

contract... 3. hale, knit, pact 5. incur, lease 6. cartel, engage, pledge, reduce, shrink 7. bargain, compact, promise, shorten, shrivel 8. covenant

9. agreement, constrict, indenture
10. convention, obligation, straighten
11. arrangement 13. understanding

contraction... 3. tic 4. coup, fist
5. spasm 7. elision, systole
8. decrease 9. reduction, short–hand,
stricture 11. compression

contrada... 3. way 4. ward 6. street
7. quarter

contradict... 4. deny 5. belie, rebut
6. impugn, negate, oppose, refute
7. gainsay 10. counteract

contradiction... 6. denial 7. paradox
10. opposition, refutation
11. contrariety 13. counteraction

contradictory... 7. denying 8. contrary,
opposite 10. refutatory
12. inconsistent

contrary... 7. adverse, counter,
froward, opposed, reverse
8. captious, inimical, opposite,
perverse, refutive 9. different,
repugnant 10. discordant, unorthodox
12. antagonistic

contrast... 7. compare 8. opposite
11. contrariety

contravene... 4. defy 6. hinder,
oppose, refute, thwart 7. violate
8. infringe 9. disregard

contravention... 6. denial 9. violation
10. opposition, refutation

contribute... 3. aid 4. give 6. donate
7. benefit, conduce, provide
9. subscribe

contribution... 3. tax, tip 4. boon,
gift, scot 6. tariff 7. payment, tribute
8. donation 12. subscription
13. participation

contrite... 6. abject, humble
8. penitent 9. repentant, sorrowful
10. remorseful 11. penitential

contrition... 7. remorse 9. attrition,
penitence 11. compunction

contrivance... 3. art 5. means, shift
6. design, devise 7. coinage,
machine, measure, project 8. artifice,
intrigue 9. expedient, invention,
makeshift 11. contraption

contrive... 4. plan, plot 5. frame,
hatch, weave 6. design, devise,
invent, manage, scheme 7. fashion,
project 9. fabricate

control... 4. hold, rein, rule, sway, test
5. check, gripe, guide, leash, power,
wield 6. direct, govern, manage,
subdue 7. conduct, mastery, preside,
regimen 8. dominate, dominion,
ironhand, regulate, restrain
9. direction, influence, regulator,
restraint 10. management, regulation
11. self–control, superintend

controller, comptroller... 7. auditor
8. governor 9. dominator, regulator

controversial... 7. eristic, polemic
9. eristical, polemical, pro and con
11. contentious 12. disputatious,
questionable 13. argumentative

controversy... 3. debate 7. dispute,
quarrel, wrangle 8. argument
10. contention 11. altercation
12. disagreement, disputatious

controvert... 4. deny, moot 5. argue

6. debate, oppose, refute 7. discuss,
dispute 10. contradict

contumacious... 6. unruly 7. riotous
8. mutinous, perverse 9. seditious
10. headstrong, rebellious, refractory,
unyielding 11. disobedient, intractable
12. ungovernable 13. insubordinate

contumelious... 7. haughty 8. insolent
9. insulting 10. derogatory,
despiteful, disdainful
12. contemptuous

contumely... 5. scorn 8. contempt
9. indignity, insolence 10. revilement
11. humiliation, malediction

contusion... 4. blow 6. bruise, injury
8. black eye 13. discoloration

conundrum... 5. rebus 6. enigma,
puzzle, riddle 7. charade

convalesce... 5. rally 7. recover,
recruit 10. recuperate

convene... 3. sit 4. come, meet
5. unite 6. summon 8. assemble
10. congregate, foregather

convenient... 5. handy, ready 6. fitted,
nearby, suited, timely 7. adapted
8. suitable 9. agreeable, available,
opportune 10. accessible,
commodious, seasonable
11. comfortable

convent... 4. meet 6. concur, friary,
priory 7. convene, nunnery
8. cloister, lamasery 9. monastery,
sanctuary

convention... 4. rule 5. usage
6. accord, custom 7. meeting
8. assembly 9. gathering, tradition
10. assemblage, compliance,
conformity

conventional... 5. fixed, nomic, usual
6. formal, modish 7. correct
8. accepted, orthodox 9. customary
10. ceremonial 11. established,
traditional

converge... 4. meet 5. focus, unite

conversant (with)... 5. adept 6. expert,
versed (in) 7. skilled 8. familiar
9. practiced 10. acquainted,
proficient

conversation... 3. chat, talk 7. trialog
8. causerie, converse, dialogue
9. communion, discourse
10. conference 11. association
13. conversazione, interlocution

conversationalist... 6. talker
9. converser 10. discourser
12. confabulator

convey... 4. cede, deed, pass, send
5. bring, carry, eloin, grant
6. assign, convoy, demise, devise,
impart, import 7. dispone 8. transfer,
transmit 9. transport 10. commission
11. communicate

conveyance... 3. bus, car, van
4. auto, sled, taxi, tram 5. plane,
train 6. demise, litter 7. cession,
norimon, trailer, vehicle 8. airplane,
carriage 10. automobile

conveyer, conveyor... 6. bearer,
coolie, pigeon (homing), porter
7. bheesty, carrier 8. cargador
9. stevedore

convict... 4. damn 5. felon, lifer

6. refute, termer, trusty 7. condemn, culprit 8. criminal, prisoner 10. malefactor

conviction... 4. hope 6. belief 7. opinion 10. persuasion 12. condemnation

convince... 6. assure, subdue 7. confute 8. overcome, persuade 9. overpower

convincing... 5. proof 6. cogent, potent 7. telling 8. assuring 10. conclusive, persuasive, satisfying

convivial... 3. gay 4. gala 5. jolly, merry 6. festal, jovial, joyful, joyous, social 7. festive, jocular 9. hilarious

convocation... 4. diet 5. synod 7. bidding, council, meeting, summons 8. assembly, congress 10. convention 12. congregation

convoke... 4. call 6. summon 7. convene 8. assemble

convoy... 5. guard, guide 6. attend, escort 7. conduct 8. navigate 9. accompany, conductor

convulse... 5. amuse, shake 6. regale 7. agitate, disturb, torture 9. entertain 10. discompose

convulsion... 5. cramp, spasm, throe 6. tumult, uproar 8. laughter, paroxysm 9. agitation, commotion 10. revolution 11. disturbance

cony, coney... 3. das, fur 4. hare, pika 5. daman, hyrax 6. burbot, rabbit

cony catcher... 5. cheat 7. sharper 8. swindler

coo... 4. bill (and), curr 5. chirr 6. murmur, mutter

cook... 4. bake, boil, chef, stew 5. broil, roast, sauté, spoil (chess), steam, trill 6. braise, seethe 7. parboil 8. barbecue, magirist 9. cuisinier

cooking (pert to)...
art.. 8. magirics
device.. 4. etna, olla 5. plate, stove 6. spider 7. griddle 9. autoclave
room.. 6. galley 7. cuisine, kitchen 9. scullery
scent.. 5. nidor

cooky... 5. scone 7. biscuit, brownie 8. macaroon 10. gingersnap, ladyfinger

cool... 3. fan, ice 4. calm 5. chill, fresh, nervy, sober, tepid 6. chilly, freeze, sedate, temper 7. unmoved 8. careless, composed, impudent, mitigate, reserved, tranquil 9. apathetic, collected, unruffled 10. nonchalant, unfriendly, unsociable 11. indifferent, levelheaded, unconcerned 13. imperturbable, self-possessed

cooler... 4. icer, jail 6. icebox, lockup, prison 7. chiller 10. ventilator 11. refrigerant 12. refrigerator

coolness... 4. cold 5. nerve 6. aplomb 7. reserve 12. indifference 14. unfriendliness

coop... 3. mew, pen 4. cage, cote, yard 5. court, hutch 6. confine 9. enclosure

cooper... 5. drink 6. vessel 8. grogshop (floating) 11. barrel maker 12. wine retailer

cooperate... 4. join, tend 5. agree, coact 6. concur 7. combine, conduce, connive 8. conspire 10. contribute 11. collaborate

coordinate... 5. talky 6. adjust 7. syntony (radio) 8. classify, equalize, organize, regulate 9. harmonize, integrate 10. proportion 11. systematize

copious... 4. full, rich 5. ample 7. diffuse, profuse 8. abundant 9. exuberant, plenteous, plentiful 11. overflowing

copper... 2. Cu 3. aes 4. cent, coin 5. metal, penny 6. cuprum 9. policeman 12. reddish–brown

copper (pert to)...
alloy.. 5. brass 6. bronze, oroide
brass.. 6. chalco
cup.. 3. dop
engraving.. 9. mezzotint
film.. 6. patina
kettle (anc).. 5. lebes
pewter.. 7. rheotan

Copperfield characters... 4. Dora 6. Dartle 8. Micawber 9. Uriah Heep 11. Little Emily

coppice... 4. bosk, holt 5. copse, grove 6. growth 7. boscage, thicket 9. brushwood, underwood

Coptic (pert to)...
church.. 8. Egyptian
color.. 7. oxblood
people.. 9. Egyptians
title.. 4. anba

copy... 3. ape 4. news 5. model 6. ectype, follow 7. edition, estreat, imitate, pattern, replica, reprint, tracing 8. protocol, revision 9. duplicate, imitation 10. transcribe, transcript 11. counterfeit 12. reproduction

coquet, coquette... 4. vamp 5. flirt 7. amorous 11. hummingbird

coquille... 5. shell 7. ruching

Coquille... 6. Indian 10. Athapascan 17. Mishikhwutmetunne (Oreg)

coquin... 5. knave, rogue 6. rascal

coral... 3. red 6. polyps, porite 8. Anthozoa 9. madrepore, millepore

coral (pert to)...
branch.. 7. ramicle
division.. 7. Aporosa
formation.. 5. palus
island.. 3. key 5. atoll
ridge.. 4. reef 5. shoal
snake.. 5. Elaps 6. garter 7. Micurus
worm.. 6. palolo

cord... 3. guy, rib 4. lace, line, rope, welt, wood 5. sinew, twine 6. lariat, sennet, spinal, string, tendon 7. measure (cubic), skirreh 8. corduroy, shoelace 9. hamstring 11. clothesline

cordage... 5. ropes 7. rigging 8. ropework

cordelle... 6. hauler 7. towline, towrope

cordial... 4. real, warm 6. ardent,

elixir, genial, hearty, liquor 7. fervent,
liqueur, sincere, zealous 8. friendly,
vigorous 9. unfeigned 10. hospitable
cordial (liqueur)... 5. shrub 6. kummel
8. anisette, periscot 9. Cointreau
11. Benedictine, crème de moka
13. crème de menthe
cordiality... 4. zeal 5. ardor 6. fervor
7. ardency 8. kindness, warmness
9. geniality 11. hospitality
12. empressement, friendliness
core... 3. ame, hub, nub, nut 4. gist,
nave, pith 5. heart, nowel 6. center,
kernel, matrix 7. nucleus
9. substance
Corinthian (pert to)...
Age.. 5. plush 11. extravagant
color.. 3. red 4. pink 6. purple
Epistles (Bib).. 12. New Testament
General (Rom).. 9. Flaminius
King.. 8. Polybius
Spring.. 14. Pirene Fountain
Temple.. 5. Doric 7. Minerva
cork... 3. ork 4. bark, bung, plug
5. float, shive, suber (oak)
7. blacken, stopgap, stopper, stopple
corm... 4. bulb (flower)
cormorant... 4. bird, shag 5. norie,
scart, urile 8. ravenous 9. snakebird,
voracious 13. Phalacrocorax
corn... 4. joke 5. grain, grist 6. cliché,
kaffir, kernel, liquor
corn (pert to)...
bread.. 4. pone 8. dumpling
10. corndodger
goddess.. 5. Ceres
hulled.. 4. samp 6. hominy
Indian.. 3. Zea 5. maize
lily.. 4. Ixia 8. bindweed
10. wandflower
liquor.. 6. whisky (whiskey)
meal.. 4. masa 7. hoecake
porridge.. 5. atole
salad.. 8. fetticus
Corn Belt... 4. Iowa, Ohio 6. Dakota,
Kansas 7. Indiana 8. Illinois,
Missouri, Nebraska 9. Minnesota
Corncracker State... 8. Kentucky
corner... 2. in 4. nook, pose, trap,
tree 5. angle, coign (coigne), herne,
ingle, niche, quoin
cornered... 5. cater (diagonal), sharp
7. angular, up a tree 10. cornerwise
cornerstone... 4. coin 5. quoin
8. keystone 10. foundation
Cornhusker State... 8. Nebraska
cornice... 4. drip, eave·7. antefix
8. astragal
Cornish... 3. elm 4. fowl 5. heath
7. dialect, diamond (Cornwall)
Cornwallis surrender site... 4. York
(Va)
corolla... 5. galea (Her), petal
8. perianth
corollary... 6. effect, porism, result
7. adjunct 8. addition 9. deduction
11. proposition
corona... 4. coin 5. cigar, crown
6. circle 7. aureole, circlet, garland,
scyphus 8. Borealis 11. corona lucis
Corona Australis... 13. Southern
Crown

Corona Borealis... 13. Northern Crown
coronet... 5. crown, tiara 6. anadem,
circle, diadem, wreath 8. insignia,
ornament
corporate... 5. joint 6. united
7. leagued 8. conjoint
10. associated
corporeal... 5. hylic, somal 6. bodily
7. fleshly, somatic 8. corporal,
material, physical, tangible
corpse... 4. body 7. cadaver, carcass
9. endowment (Eccl)
corpulent... 3. fat 5. bulky, obese,
stout 6. fleshy
corpuscle... 11. poikilocyte, schistocyte
12. erythroblast
corral... 3. mew, pen, sty 4. coop,
herd 5. atajo, pound, tambo
7. impound 8. stockade
9. enclosure, inclosure
correct... 2. OK 4. edit, okay, true
5. amend, emend, right 6. better,
proper, punish, reform, remedy,
revise, strict 7. chasten, improve,
perfect, rectify, regular, retouch
8. accurate, definite, orthodox,
rigorous 9. faultless 10. particular,
scrupulous 11. grammatical,
punctilious 12. conventional
correlative... 2. or 3. nor 6. mutual
7. similar 8. conjoint 10. reciprocal
11. conjunction, counterpart
13. corresponding
correspond... 3. fit 4. suit 5. agree,
equal, match, tally 6. accord
7. comport 8. assonate (sound),
coincide, parallel 9. analogous,
harmonize 11. parallelize
correspondence... 4. mail 8. homology
(Biol), identity, symmetry
10. conformity, epistolary, similarity
11. equivalence, intercourse
corresponding... 8. balanced
9. analogous, homologic, isometric
10. coinciding 11. paralleling
corridor... 4. hall 5. aisle 6. airway,
arcade 7. gallery 10. passageway
corrige (obs)... 6. punish 7. correct
corrigible... 8. amenable
10. submissive 11. rectifiable
corroborate... 5. prove 7. certify,
confirm, support 8. calidate, roborate
9. establish 12. adminiculate,
substantiate
corroborative... 11. adminicular
corrode... 3. eat 4. bite, etch, gnaw,
rust 5. erode, waste 11. deteriorate
12. disintegrate
corrosive... 4. acid 7. caustic,
erodent, erodine, mordant
9. corroding 10. escharotic
14. disintegrative
corrugate... 5. crimp 6. rugate
7. crumble, wrinkle 8. crumpled,
furrowed, wrinkled
corrupt... 3. rot 5. bribe, taint, venal
6. Augean, debase, putrid, rotten
7. attaint, crooked, defiled, deprave,
putrefy, vitiate 8. polluted
9. dishonest 11. adulterated
12. contaminated
corruption... 5. taint 6. pidgin

(language) 8. impurity 9. chicanery, pollution 10. debasement, defilement, distortion 11. depravation, putrescence 12. adulteration 13. contamination

corsage... 5. waist 6. bodice 7. bouquet (boquet), flowers

corsair... 5. rover 6. pirate 7. Saracen 8. picaroon, rockfish 9. buccaneer, privateer 10. freebooter

Corsica...
  capital.. 7. Ajaccio
  birthplace of.. 8. Napoleon
  feud (blood).. 8. vendetta
  seaport.. 7. Bastia

cortege... 5. train 6. parade 7. funeral, retinue 10. procession

Cortes palace site... 8. Coyoacan (Mexico)

cortex... 4. bark, peel, rind

corundum... 3. gem 5. emery 7. mineral 8. abrasive

corundum colors...
  blue.. 5. white 8. sapphire
  brown.. 14. adamantine spar
  green.. 7. emerald
  purple.. 8. amethyst
  red.. 4. ruby
  topaz.. 6. yellow

coruscate... 5. gleam, shine 7. glitter, radiate, sparkle 11. scintillate

cosmetic... 5. cream, henna, paint, rouge 6. enamel, lotion, make–up 7. mascara 8. lipstick, toiletry 11. beautifying

cosmic... 4. vast 5. great 7. orderly 8. catholic 9. grandiose, universal 10. harmonious

Cosmic Order... 4. Rita (Vedic law)

Cossack (pert to)...
  chief.. 6. ataman, hetman
  district.. 6. Voisko
  native.. 5. Tatar 7. Russian
  squadron.. 6. sotnia
  village.. 8. stanitsa (stanitza)
  whip (knotted).. 5. knout

cosset... 3. pet 4. lamb 6. caress, coddle, cuddle, fondle, pamper 8. favorite

cost... 4. loss, rate 5. price 6. amount, charge, figure, outlay, rental 7. expense 9. detriment, suffering 11. deprivation, expenditure

costa... 3. rib 4. vein (Bot) 6. border, midrib

Costa Rica...
  capital.. 7. San José
  crater (world's greatest).. 4. Poas
  discoverer.. 8. Columbus (4th visit)
  export.. 6. coffee 7. bananas
  port.. 5. Limon 10. Puntarenas

costate... 6. ribbed (Bot)

costermonger... 6. coster, hawker 7. peddler 9. costerman 11. apple seller

costly... 4. dear, rich 8. gorgeous, splendid 9. expensive, sumptuous 10. high–priced 11. extravagant

costume... 3. rig 4. garb, suit 5. dress, habit 6. attire, tights 7. apparel, raiment 8. clothing

cot... 3. bed, hut, pen, set 4. boat

(Ir), coop, cote 5. cabin, cover, house 6. cabana 7. charpoy, cottage, shelter 8. bedstead

cote... 3. hut, pen 4. coop 5. house 7. cottage, shelter 9. sheepfold

coterie... 3. set 4. clan, club, ring 5. cabal, group, junto 6. circle, clique 9. camarilla (secret)

cottage... 3. cot, hut 4. shed 5. cabin, house, villa 6. cabana 7. bungalo, shelter

cottager... 6. cottar (cotter) 7. cottier, laborer, peasant

cotton (pert to)...
  cloth.. 4. jean, lawn 5. denim, khaki, scrim, surat, terry 6. calico, dimity, madras, nettle 7. batiste, percale
  fiber.. 4. lint 6. staple 7. viscose
  gin inventor.. 7. Whitney (Eli)
  knot.. 3. nep
  medical.. 5. gauze 6. sponge
  raw.. 5. bayal
  roll.. 4. slub
  seed.. 4. bole, boll
  seed sugar.. 9. raffinose
  staple.. 6. upland (short) 8. Egyptian (long)
  twisted.. 5. lisle 6. thread
  waste.. 4. noil

Cotton State... 7. Alabama

couch... 3. bed, cot 4. lair, sofa 5. divan 6. canapé, canopy, litter, lounge, pallet, phrase 9. embroider (with gold), stretcher

cougar... 3. cat 4. lion, puma 7. panther 9. catamount

cough... 4. hack 6. tussis

council... 4. diet, rede 5. cabal, synod 6. senate 7. cabinet 8. assembly, conclave, tribunal 10. conference, parliament 12. consultation 15. League of Nations

council table cover... 5. tapis

counsel... 4. rede 6. advice, advise, confer, lawyer 8. guidance 9. recommend 10. suggestion 11. instruction 12. deliberation

counselor, counsellor... 4. sage 6. lawyer, mentor, nestor 7. adviser, advisor, counsel 8. attorney 9. barrister

count... 3. sum, tot 4. tale, tell 5. check, judge, relay, tally 6. number, reckon, rely on 7. compute, summary 8. nobleman 9. calculate, enumerate, reckoning, summation 12. capitulation

Count (pert to)...
  Mayence.. 3. Gan 7. Ganelon
  Monte Cristo.. 6. Dantes
  Rousillon.. 7. Bertram

countenance... 3. aid 4. abet, brow, face, mien 6. aspect, permit, visage 7. approve, endorse, support 8. approval, sanction, tolerate 9. composure 10. appearance, permission

counter... 4. chip 5. table, token 7. adverse 8. computer, contrary, opposite 9. retaliate 10. calculator

counteract... 6. offset, oppose, thwart 7. nullify 8. antidote 10. neutralize

11. countermand

counter current... 4. eddy 5. swirl
6. vortex 9. whirlpool
12. counterforce

counterfeit... 4. base, fake, mock,
sham 5. bogus, false, feign, forge,
phony, queer 6. assume, forged,
unreal 7. falsify, forgery, imitate
8. simulant, spurious 10. artificial,
fictitious 11. unauthentic

counterirritant... 4. moxa 5. seton
6. arnica, iodine, pepper 7. mustard

countermand... 5. annul 6. cancel,
forbid, recall, revoke 7. abolish,
reverse 8. prohibit 9. frustrate
10. counteract 12. counterorder

counterpane... 5. quilt 8. bedcover,
coverlet 9. comforter 10. counterpin
11. comfortable

counterpart... 4. copy, like, twin
5. image 6. double, eponym (name)
8. parallel 9. duplicate
10. complement, equivalent

counterpoise... 6. offset 8. equalize
10. compensate, counteract
12. counterforce 14. counterbalance

countersign... 4. sign 6. signal
7. tessera 8. password 9. signature,
watchword 10. mot de passé, open
sesame 12. counterstamp

countersink... 4. ream 5. bevel
6. deepen 7. chamfer

countertenor... 4. alto (male)
8. falsetto

counterthrust (fencing)... 7. riposte
(ripost) 12. return thrust

countless... 8. infinite 10. numberless,
unnumbered 11. innumerable
12. incalculable

countrified... 5. rural 7. boorish,
hickish, uncouth 8. inurbane
10. unpolished

country... 4. land, pais (law), vale
5. rurai, state, weald 6. nation,
region 9. territory 10. fatherland
12. commonwealth

country (pert to)...
alien.. 7. enclave, exclave
ancient.. 4. Aram, Elis, Gaul
bumpkin.. 4. clod, jake, rube
5. churl, yokel 9. greenhorn
gallant.. 9. swain
mythical.. 2. Oz
native (earliest).. 9. aborigine
Roman.. 8. campagna
term.. 5. rural, urban 6. rustic
8. agrestic, pastoral, praedial (predial)

countryman... 4. rube 5. yokel
6. rustic 7. hayseed, patriot, peasant
10. compatriot, home towner

county... 4. seat 5. shire 6. domain,
parish 8. district

coup... 3. buy 4. blow, move (games)
5. scoop, upset 6. barter, strike,
stroke (master) 8. overturn, strategy
9. trump card

coup de grâce... 9. deathblow

coup de main... 6. attack (sudden)
8. strategy 9. stratagem

coup d'état... 6. stroke (political)
8. strategy

couple... 3. duo, tie, two 4. bond,

dyad, join, link, mate, pair, span,
team, twin, yoke 5. brace, marry,
twain, unite 6. Gemini 7. bracket

coupled... 5. gemel, mated 6. braced,
joined, linked, paired, teamed, united
7. leagued, married

couplet... 3. two 4. pair 5. brace,
verse 7. distich, doublet

coupon... 5. scrip, stock, token
6. ticket 11. certificate (Finan)

courage... 4. grit, sand, will 5. heart,
metal, nerve, pluck, valor 7. bravery,
heroism, prowess 8. audacity,
boldness, firmness 9. fortitude,
gallantry, hardihood 11. intrepidity
12. fearlessness 13. dauntlessness

courageous... 4. bold, game 5. brave,
hardy, manly, stout 6. daring, heroic,
spunky 7. gallant, spartan, valiant
8. fearless, intrepid, knightly,
resolute, stalwart, valorous
11. adventurous 12. enterprising,
stouthearted

courant... 4. romp 5. caper 6. letter
7. gazette, running (Her)
9. messenger, newspaper

courier... 5. guide 8. dragoman,
horseman 9. attendant, messenger

course... 3. run 4. flow, line, mode,
path, road, rote, tack 5. route,
study, trend 6. career, manner,
method, policy, series, stream
8. progress 9. direction, procedure
10. succession

course (pert to)...
college.. 7. seminar
direct.. 7. beeline
regular.. 4. rote 6. regime 7. routine
roundabout.. 6. detour 11. indirection

course of...
action.. 5. habit 7. routine
9. procedure
eating.. 4. diet
instruction.. 6. lesson
procedure.. 4. rote
thought.. 5. tenor

courser... 5. horse, steed 6. hunter,
plover 7. charger 8. war horse

court... 3. see (papal), woo 4. area,
eyre, fawn (upon), rota 5. atria,
curia, dairi, gemot, patio, spark
6. palace, parvis, street 7. council,
tribune 8. tribunal 10. attendance,
curry favor, quadrangle

court (Eng)... 3. soc 4. eyre, leet
8. woodmate 10. court–baron

court (pert to)...
assistant.. 5. staff 6. elisor
crier, cry.. 4. hear, oyez (oyes)
6. beadle
criminal.. 6. assize
exemption, excuse.. 6. essoin
game.. 6. tennis 9. badminton
hearing.. 4. oyer
minutes.. 4. acta
order.. 4. writ 5. arret 6. capias
7. summons 8. subpoena
public.. 7. forum 8. forensic
sitting.. 7. session

courteous... 5. civil 6. gentle, polite,
urbane 7. affable, gallant
8. debonair, gracious 9. attentive

10. respectful

courtly... 4. hend (hende) 5. aulic,
civil 7. elegant, gallant, stately
9. dignified 10. obsequious
11. ceremonious

courtship... 4. suit 6. plight, wooing
7. romance 8. courting

covenant... 4. bond, pact 6. engage
7. bargain, compact, entente,
promise 8. contract 9. agreement,
stipulate, testament 11. undertaking

Covenant of God to Noah...
7. rainbow

cover... 3. cap, lap, lid 4. coat, cozy,
hide, mask, pale, pave, roof, span,
veil 5. blind, crust, drape, tapis
6. canopy, mantle, purdah, screen,
shield, thatch 8. elytron, overlay,
shelter 8. chrismal, coverlet
9. tarpaulin 10. overspread

cover (pert to)...
alloy.. 5. terne
cork.. 9. corticate
crumbs.. 5. bread
dots.. 7. stipple
figures (Her).. 4. seme
straw.. 6. thatch
turf.. 3. sod
up.. 4. bury 5. inter 7. conceal
8. submerge 10. camouflage
with wax.. 4. cere

covering... 3. mat, rug 4. caul, film,
hull, tile 5. apron, armor, shell, testa
6. awning, carpet, cestus, lorica,
pelage, screen, shroud 7. epeiric,
shelter, tegumen, wrapper
8. lineolum, pericarp 9. caparison
10. integument, protection
11. smoke screen

covering (head)... 3. cap, hat, wig
4. hood, beret, scarf, snood
6. bonnet, peruke, toupee
7. chapeau 10. fascinator

coverlet... 5. quilt 6. afghan, spread
7. blanket, lap robe 11. counterpane

covert... 3. den, lie 4. abri, lair
6. hidden, refuge, secret 7. covered,
private, thicket 9. concealed,
disguised, insidious, sheltered

covet... 4. envy 5. crave, yisse (obs)
6. aspire, desire, grudge, hanker
7. long for 8. begrudge

covetousness... 5. greed 7. avarice

covey... 4. bevy, pack 5. brood, flock,
hatch 6. flight 7. company
9. multitude

cow... 3. awe 5. abash, daunt
7. overawe, terrify 8. browbeat,
frighten 10. intimidate

cow (animal)... 3. Bos 4. calf, kine,
moil 5. Angus, bossy, brock (obs),
Kerry, vache 6. bovine, heifer
7. pollard 8. Ayrshire, maverick,
moulleen

cow (pert to)...
barn.. 4. byre, shed 5. reeve, stall
6. stable 7. vaccary, vachery
food (chewed).. 3. cud 5. rumen
hornless.. 6. mulley 7. pollard
8. moulleen
sea.. 6. dugong, walrus 7. manatee,
Sirenia 12. hippopotamus

tether.. 4. rope 6. baikie
unbranded.. 8. maverick
young.. 4. calf 6. heifer

coward, cowardly... 3. shy 5. sneak
6. afraid, craven, scared 7. caitiff,
chicken, dastard, milksop 8. poltroon,
recreant, weakling 9. dastardly,
fraidy–cat, jellyfish 12. uncourageous
13. pusillanimous

cowboy... 5. roper 6. herder
7. llamero, puncher, vaquero
8. jackaroo, neatherd
12. broncobuster (sl)

cowboy breeches... 5. chaps
8. jodhpurs

cower... 4. fawn 5. crawl, quail, stoop
6. cringe, crouch, grovel

cowfish... 3. ray 4. toto 7. dolphin,
grampus, manatee 8. porpoise

cowled... 9. cucullate

coxcomb... 3. fop 4. dude, fool
5. cleat (Naut) 6. dandy 8. popinjay

coy... 3. shy 4. arch 5. timid
6. demure, modest 7. bashful
10. coquettish 13. self–conscious

coyote... 4. wolf (prairie)

Coyote State... 11. South Dakota

coypu... 6. nutria, rodent

cozen... 5. cheat, trick 7. beguile,
deceive, defraud

cozy... 4. easy, snug 6. chatty
8. cheerful, familiar, homelike,
sociable 9. contented, talkative
11. comfortable

crab... 3. Uca 4. king, Maia (genus)
5. ayuyu (Guam) 6. partan, spider
7. fiddler, limulus, mollusk, Ocypode
8. Lithodes 9. horseshoe
10. crustacean

crabbed... 5. cross 6. bitter, crusty,
morose, trying 7. bilious, peevish
8. abstruse, liverish 9. difficult,
fractious, irascible, irregular
10. perplexing

crab claw... 5. chela 6. metope,
nipper

crab eater... 4. seal 5. heron
7. opossum, raccoon

crachoir... 8. cuspidor, spittoon

crack... 4. blow, chap, clap, flaw,
kibe, leak, quip, rift, rime, snap
5. brack, break, chink, craze, spang,
split 6. breach, cleave, cranny
7. crackle, crevice, fissure, rupture
8. fracture

Cracker State... 7. Georgia

crackle... 4. snap 5. craze (art), crink
9. crepitate

crackman... 5. yegg 7. burglar

cradle... 4. slee (ship's) 7. infancy,
nursery 8. bassinet, cunabula
10. beginnings, incunabula

cradle book... 11. incunabulum

Cradle of Liberty... 11. Faneuil Hall
(Boston)

cradle song... 7. lullaby 8. berceuse
13. Schlummerlied

craft... 3. art 4. boat 5. skill, trade
6. device, tender 7. cunning, finesse,
know–how, prowess 8. aptitude,
vocation 9. dexterity
10. employment, handicraft,

occupation, watercraft 12. skillfulness
craftsman ... 6. artist, writer 7. artisan, workman 9. artificer
crafty ... 3. sly 4. foxy, slim, wily, wise 6. artful, astute, shifty, shrewd, subtle, tricky 7. cunning 8. skillful (skilful) 9. deceitful, ingenious, underhand 10. fraudulent 13. Machiavellian 15. Mephistophelean
crag ... 3. tor 4. spur 5. arête, cliff 7. nunatak 9. precipice
craggy ... 5. rough 6. cliffy, clifty, knotty, rugged
cram ... 4. fill 5. choke, crowd, drive, force, gorge, press, study, stuff 9. overstuff 10. gluttonize
cramp ... 4. pain 5. stunt 6. hamper 7. confine, seizure 8. compress, restrict 9. hindrance, paralysis (muscle) 11. restriction
cranberry ... 3. red 9. Oxycoccus, sourberry
cranberry center of trade ... 10. Barnstable (Mass)
crane ... 3. gib, jib 5. davit, jenny, titan 7. derrick, machine
crane ... 4. Grus 5. heron, sarus 7. Gruidae 9. cormorant 10. Gruiformes 13. Constellation
cranial nerve ... 5. radix, vagus
cranium ... 5. skull 8. cerebrum
crank ... 3. wit 4. bear, crab 5. crook, winch 6. griper, grouch, handle 7. fanatic, growler, hothead 8. frondeur, grumbler, sorehead 9. eccentric 10. bellyacher, crosspatch, monomaniac
cranny ... 4. hole, nook 5. chink, cleft, crack 6. corner, furrow 7. crevice, fissure
crash ... 4. bank, fail 5. smash 7. debacle, failure, shatter 8. accident 9. collision 10. bankruptcy
crate ... 3. box 4. case 6. basket, cradle, encase, hamper 8. airplane 9. container 10. automobile
crater ... 3. pit 6. cavity 7. caldera 13. Constellation (The Cup)
cravat ... 3. tie 4. teck 5. ascot, stock 7. bandage, necktie 9. neckcloth 13. four-in-hand
crave ... 3. ask, beg 4. long, seek 5. covet, yearn 6. desire, hanker 8. beseech, entreat, implore, request, solicit 10. supplicate
craven ... 6. afraid, coward 7. caitiff, dastard 8. cowardly, poltroon, recreant 12. fainthearted 13. pusillanimous
craving ... 4. pica 6. desire, thirst 7. longing 8. appetite, yearning
craw ... 3. maw 4. crop 6. gebbie 7. gizzard, stomach 10. ingluvies
crawfish ... 5. yabby (yabbie) 7. back out, crawdad, lobster, retreat 8. crayfish
crawl ... 4. fawn, inch, shug 5. creep 6. cringe, grovel, recant
crayfish ... see *crawfish*

crayon ... 5. chalk 6. pastel, pencil 8. charcoal
craze ... 3. fad 4. flaw, maze 5. crack (ceramics), crush, furor, mania 6. defect, madden 7. crackle, fashion, whimsey 9. infirmity 11. infatuation
craze (for) ... see also *madness, mania*
foreign customs .. 9. xenomania
freedom .. 14. eleutheromania
love (erotic) .. 10. erotomania
music .. 9. melomania
religion .. 9. theomania
shopping .. 9. oniomania
stamps (postage) .. 11. timbromania
stealing .. 11. kleptomania
wandering .. 10. dromomania
wealth .. 10. plutomania
crazed ... 4. amok 5. insane, marked (with crazes) 7. severed 8. deranged 10. distraught
crazy ... 3. mad 4. amok, loco, luny 6. dottle, insane 7. damaged, foolish, unsound 9. deficient
cream ... 4. best, ream 5. elite 6. lotion 8. sillabub (with wine)
cream of tartar ... 5. argol
crease ... 4. fold, ruck 5. crimp 7. wrinkle
create ... 4. make 5. build, cause, hatch 6. invent 7. fashion, produce 8. generate 9. originate
creation ... 3. art 5. virtu, world 6. cosmos, making 7. classic, fantasy, forming, product 8. artifact, universe 9. objet d'art 10. providence 11. composition, fabrication, manufacture, masterpiece
creator ... 5. maker 6. author 8. designer, inventor, producer 10. originator
Creator ... 3. God 5. Maker 7. Jehovah 8. Almighty, Demiurge 11. King of Kings
creature (pert to) ...
civetlike .. 3. cat
elflike .. 4. peri
evil .. 7. hellcat 8. hellicat
fire .. 10. salamander
folklore .. 3. elf 5. dwarf, fairy, pixie
ghost .. 11. poltergeist
minute .. 10. animalcule
sentient .. 6. animal
timid .. 4. deer 5. sheep
underground .. 5. gnome
water .. 5. sylph 6. undine
winged (Myth) .. 6. wivern 10. cockatrice
credence ... 5. trust 6. belief, credit 8. affiance, reliance 10. acceptance, confidence, dependence 15. trustworthiness
credential ... 7. voucher 11. certificate, testimonial 14. recommendation
credible ... 6. likely 7. tenable 8. probable 9. plausible 10. believable
credit ... 5. faith, honor, trust 6. belief, esteem, impute 7. account, believe 8. accredit, credence 10. estimation, regulation 15. trustworthiness
creditor ... 5. agent (collection)

6. debtee, dunner, usurer 7. Shylock (greedy)

creed... 5. credo, dogma, tenet 6. belief, Nicene 8. Apostles' 9. Catechism 10. Athanasian, confession

creek... 3. rio 4. burn, slue, wick 6. arroyo, estero, slough, spruit, stream

creel... 4. rack, trap 6. basket (fish)

creep... 5. crawl, prowl, skulk, slink, sneak, steal (away) 6. grovel 8. scramble 9. pussyfoot

creeping... 4. slow 7. reptant 8. crawling 10. slithering 11. reptatorial

Cremona, famed names... 5. Amati 6. violin 10. Guarnerius 12. Stradivarius

crena... 4. gash, kerf, nick 5. cleft, notch 7. scallop 10. depression 11. indentation

creole... 6. French 7. mestizo 9. half-breed, janissary

Creole State... 9. Louisiana

crepitate... 4. snap 7. crackly 5. curve 8. meniscus

crescent... 4. cusp, horn, lune 5. curve 8. meniscus

crescent-shaped... 4. horn, lune 6. bicorn, lunate 7. lunular 8. lunulate 9. horseshoe, meniscate, semilunar

crest... 3. top 4. comb, peak, tuft 5. arête, crown, ridge 6. copple, crista, height, summit 7. panache, topknot, wave top 8. feathers, insignia, pinnacle 9. cockscomb 11. mountaintop

crested... 6. capped, topped, tufted 7. coppled, cristed, crowned, pileate

creta... 5. chalk

Crete...
capital.. 5. Canea
city.. 6. Candia, Khanis
civilization (anc).. 6. Aegean, Minoan
king (anc).. 5. Minos (Gr)
monster.. 8. Minotaur (man, bull)
mountain.. 3. Ida 9. Theodoros
priests.. 7. Curetes

cretin... 5. idiot 8. imbecile

crevice... 3. gap 4. rift 5. chink, cleft 6. cranny 7. fissure, opening 8. peephole 10. interstice

crew... 3. men 4. band, body, gang, pack 5. force, staff 7. company 9. employees, personnel

crib... 3. bed, bin, den (gambling) 5. cheat, stall, steal 6. Cratch (stars), manger, pilfer 7. brothel 8. Praesepe

cricket... 4. game, grig 6. acheta, cicada, locust 7. katydid 9. footstool 10. Orthoptera 11. grasshopper

cricket (pert to)...
game term.. 3. bye, run 6. yorker
noise.. 5. chirp 7. stridor
symbol (Myth).. 4. tice 5. ashes

cried... 4. wept 6. bawled, called, wailed, yelled 7. shouted, uttered 8. lamented, screamed, shrieked 9. exclaimed 10. proclaimed

crime... 3. sin 4. evil 5. guilt, wrong

6. delict, felony, mayhem 7. offense 8. delictum, iniquity 9. violation 10. illegality, wickedness, wrongdoing 11. malfeasance

crime (pert to)...
benefice (Eccl).. 6. simony
goddess (Myth).. 3. Ate
of 1873.. 12. Silver Dollar
scene.. 5. venue

Crimea...
city.. 5. Kerch, Yalta 10. Sevastopol
isthmus site.. 8. Black Sea
Russian.. 4. Krim
sea (Russ).. 4. Azof

criminal... 4. thug, yegg 5. crook, felon, thief 6. nocent 7. convict, yeggman 8. swindler 9. desperado, dishonest, felonious 10. malefactor, recidivist 11. blameworthy, disgraceful 13. reprehensible

criminal refuge... 7. Alsatia 11. Whitefriars (London)

criminology... 8. penology

crimp... 4. curl, fold 5. frizz, notch, plait 6. ruffle, thwart 7. crinkle, wrinkle 8. Shanghai

cringe... 4. fawn 5. cower, quail, sneak, wince 6. flinch, grovel, shrink, submit 7. truckle

crinkle... 4. curl, kink, turn, wind 5. twist 6. rustle 7. wrinkle

crinose... 5. hairy 7. hirsute 11. barbigerous

cripple... 4. halt, hock, lame, maim 6. injure, weaken 7. amputee, disable 8. handicap 9. hamstring 12. incapacitate

crisis... 5. cycle, peril 8. exigency, juncture 9. criterion, emergency 11. climacteric

crisp... 4. cold 5. curly, flaky, sharp, short, spalt 7. brittle, concise, crackle, crinkle, friable 8. clear-cut 9. frangible

criterion... 4. norm, rule, test, type 5. canon, model 7. measure 8. standard 9. yardstick

critic... 5. judge, Momus (Myth) 6. censor, slater, Zoilus 8. collator, reviewer 9. literator 11. connoisseur, criticaster, faultfinder

critical... 4. edgy 7. carping, crucial, cynical, Zoilean 8. captious, caviling, exacting 10. censorious, particular 12. faultfinding 13. hairsplitting 14. discriminating

Critical system of philosophy... 10. Kantianism

criticism... 3. rap 5. cavil, roast 6. report, review 7. censure, Zoilism 8. critique, judgment 9. aspersion 10. commentary

criticize, criticise... 3. pan 4. carp, flay 5. cavil, judge, knock, slate 6. review 7. censure, comment 9. castigate 10. animadvert

Croatian... 4. Slav 5. Croat 11. Yugoslavian

Croatian capital... 6. Zagreb

crock... 3. ewe (old), jug, pot, urn 4. smut, soil, soot 5. horse (old) 7. ceramic 8. potsherd

11. earthenware

crocodile... 3. goa 5. nakoo 6. gavial, mugger 7. reptile, sophism 9. Niloticus 10. Crocodilia, Crocodilus

crocus... 4. bulb, herb, iris 6. flower, yellow 7. saffron

croft... 5. crypt, field, vault 6. carafe, cavern 7. hillock

crone... 3. ewe (old), hag 5. witch 6. beldam (beldame)

Cronus (pert to)...
god of.. 8. Harvests
father.. 6. Uranus
son.. 4. Zeus
wife.. 4. Rhea

crony... 3. pal 4. chum 5. buddy 6. friend 9. companion 10. playfellow

crook... 4. bend, warp 5. angle, curve, staff, thief 6. akimbo 7. crosier 8. criminal, insignia 10. camshachle

crooked... 3. wry, zag 4. agee, awry, bent 5. agley, askew, false 6. aslant, curved, hooked, zigzag 7. angular, askance, asquint, oblique 8. deformed 9. dishonest, distorted 10. circuitous, fraudulent 12. dishonorable

crooked legs... 8. rhebosis (rhaebosis) 10. tortuosity

croon... 3. hum 4. boom, sing, wail 5. whine 6. bellow, lament, murmur 8. complain

crop... 3. lop, maw 4. clip, craw, dick, reap, whip 5. belly, shear, yield 6. gebbie, growth, sheave 7. harvest, produce, soilage, stomach 11. cultivation

cross... 2. go 3. tau 4. crux, ford, rood 5. bless, corse, irate, staff 6. oppose, thwart, touchy 7. athwart, fretful, oblique, peevish, pettish 8. crucifix, insignia, monument, obstruct, petulant, snappish, swastika (swastica), traverse 9. hybridize, intersect, irritable 10. disappoint, transverse 11. crucifixion

cross (pert to)...
archaeology.. 4. ankh
astronomy.. 13. Southern Cross
barred.. 11. trabeculate
beam.. 5. spale, trave 6. girder
bow.. 8. arbalest
breed.. 5. Husky (dog) 6. hybrid
British.. 6. Celtic
Egypt.. 10. life symbol
eye.. 9. esotropia 10. strabismus
heraldry.. 6. pattée 7. erminee, patonce
Latin.. 12. crux commissa
palm.. 5. bribe (gypsy)
St Anthony's.. 3. tau
stroke.. 5. serif
tau–shaped.. 10. crux ansata

crossing... 3. voyage 7. chiasma, fording, passage 8. cheating, opposing 9. hybridism 10. traversing 13. crossbreeding

crossing (famed)...
Alps.. 8. Hannibal, Napoleon
Hellespont.. 6. Xerxes

Pyrenees.. 8. Hannibal
Rubicon.. 6. Caesar

crouch... 4. bend, fawn 5. cower, squat, stoop 6. cringe, grovel, hunker

crow... 3. daw 4. brag, rook 5. aylet, boast, crake, raven, vaunt 6. chough, Corvus, Indian (Sioux) 7. corvine, jackdaw 8. laughter 13. constellation

crowbar... 5. jimmy, lever 7. gablock

crowberry... 5. shrub 6. bilberry 9. cranberry

crowd... 3. jam, mob 4. bike (Scot), cram, host, pack, push, ruck, urge 5. crush, drive, drove, horde, press, serry, swarm, three, wedge 6. galaxy, hasten, legion, masses, throng 7. squeeze 8. compress 9. multitude 10. assemblage

crowded... 6. packed 7. compact, crammed, serried, teeming 8. numerous, populous 9. congested, jampacked

crown... 3. cap, top 4. atef, coin, pate, peak, poll, tiar 5. crest, miter (mitre), tiara 6. anadem, circle, corona, diadem, fillet, reward, summit, trophy, wreath 7. chaplet, coronet, garland, glorify, install 8. coronate, enthrone, ornament, pinnacle, surmount

crowning glory... 8. last word

crucial... 5. final 6. severe, trying, urgent 7. crossed 8. critical, decisive 9. cruciform 13. demonstrative

crucible... 3. pot 4. etna, test 6. retort, vessel 10. conversion

crucifix... 3. pax 4. rood 5. cross 6. emblem

crucifixion... 5. death (on a cross) 7. torture 9. execution, suffering 11. persecution

crude... 3. raw 4. rude 5. crass, green, rough 6. callow, coarse, common, garish, savage, vulgar 8. unseemly 9. inelegant, rough–hewn, tasteless, uncourtly, unrefined 10. outlandish, unpolished 13. inexperienced

crudity... 7. rawness 9. crassness, harshness, roughness, vulgarity 10. immaturity

cruel... 4. fell, hard 5. harsh 6. brutal, savage, severe, unkind 7. inhuman, painful, unhuman 8. dreadful, fiendish, pitiless, ruthless, tyrannic 9. ferocious, heartless, merciless, murderous, truculent 11. remorseless

cruelty... 7. brutality 10. inclemency, inhumanity 12. ruthlessness 13. heartlessness 15. remorselessness

cruelty, lover of... 6. sadist 9. masochist

cruet... 3. ama 4. vial 6. bottle, caster (castor), vessel 7. ampulla, urceole

cruller... 7. olycook (olykoek) 8. doughnut 9. friedcake

crumb... 3. bit 5. break, piece 6. little 8. fragment

crumble... 5. decay 6. molder, powder

7. friable 9. pulverize
12. disintegrate
crumple... 4. ruck 6. crease, raffle, rumple 7. wrinkle 9. corrugate
cruor... 4. gore 5. blood, ichor
crusade... 5. cause, drive, issue, jihad (jehad) 7. crusado 8. campaign 10. expedition
Crusades... 8. Holy Land 9. Children's (1212)
crush... 3. jam 4. bray, mash, sink 5. crash, crowd, grind, press, smash 6. bruise, crunch 7. conquer, mortify, oppress, shatter, squeeze 8. compress, suppress 9. humiliate, pulverize 11. infatuation
crushed sugar cane... 7. bagasse
crust... 4. rind 5. shell 8. dumpling, exterior 9. impudence 11. lithosphere 14. aggressiveness
crustacean... 4. crab 5. prawn 6. huitre, isopod, limpet, mussel, oyster, shrimp 7. limulus, lobster, scallop 8. barnacle, crawfish, starfish 9. shellfish, trunkfish 10. coquillage, periwinkle
crustacean (pert to)...
extinct.. 5. Eryon
footless.. 4. apod, apus
fossil.. 9. trilobite
genus.. 5. Hippa 6. Triops 7. Caridea (Carida) 8. Copepoda, Decapoda 10. Notostraca
larva.. 5. alima
limb.. 6. endite, podite
crutch... 5. brace, staff, stave 6. crotch 7. support
cry... 3. baa, caw, cri, hue, mew, olé, sob 4. alas, barr, call, evoe, home, hoot, mewl, pish, pule, wail, weep, yell, yelp 5. alack, avast, bleat, crook, miaou, yoick 6. bellow, boohoo, clamor, outcry, scream, shriek, slogan, snivel, squawk 7. tantivy (hunting), trumpet, weeping 8. entreaty, jeremiad, lackaday, proclaim 10. shibboleth 11. lamentation
cry (out)... 5. crake, decry, shout 6. accuse, clamor, object, scream, suffer 7. censure, exclaim 8. complain, denounce 10. vociferate
crying... 6. puling, urgent 7. clamant, heinous, howling, sobbing, weeping 9. insistent, notorious
crying bird... 6. Aramus 7. courlan, limpkin 8. raillike
cryptic... 4. Rite (Freemasonry) 6. hidden, occult, secret 8. puzzling 9. concealed, enigmatic 10. mysterious 11. problematic 12. hieroglyphic
cryptogram... 4. code 5. agama 7. writing (secret) 8. symbolic
crystal... 4. dial 5. clear, glass, lucid 6. argent (Her), quartz 7. diamond 8. pellucid 9. glassware, snowflake 11. crystalline, transparent
crystal (pert to)...
diamond.. 7. glassie
gazer.. 4. seer 7. diviner 8. presager 10. soothsayer 13. fortuneteller

gazing.. 4. scry
twin.. 5. macle
crystalline... 4. pure 8. pellucid 11. transparent 12. crystal–clear
crystalline (pert to)...
colorless.. 7. orcinol
compound.. 5. oscin 6. anisil, dulcin
mineral.. 4. spar 7. apatite 8. elaterin, feldspar
rock.. 7. diorite, greisen
salt.. 8. borax 8. analgene (analgen)
cub... 3. bin, boy, fox, pen, pup 4. bear, coop, crib, lion, shed 5. shark, stall, tiger, whale, whelp 8. boy scout, cupboard 9. youngling
Cuba...
capital.. 6. Havana
castle.. 5. Morro
city.. 8. Santiago 10. Bahia Honda, Guantánamo
discoverer.. 8. Columbus (1492)
island.. 11. Isle of Pines (Isla de Pinos)
mountain.. 8. Camaguey 9. Las Villas 12. Pico Turquino
nickname.. 18. Pearl of the Antilles
province.. 7. Oriente
Cuban (pert to)...
asphalt.. 9. chapapote
bird.. 6. trogan 8. tocororo
dance.. 5. rumba
fish.. 4. bobo
rodent.. 5. hutia (jutia) 6. pilori
rum.. 7. Bacardi
cube... 3. die 4. dice 5. solid 6. triple 7. tessera (marble) 10. third power
cubic (pert to)...
body.. 3. die 4. dice
decimeter.. 5. litre
math.. 9. isometric
measure.. 4. cord
meter.. 5. stere
shape.. 6. cuboid 8. cubiform
cubicle... 4. cell, room, tomb 7. bedroom, chamber, roomlet 9. cubiculum
cuckoo... 5. mimic 8. imitator, songbird
cuckoo (pert to)...
ally.. 3. ani
American.. 8. Coccyzus
bees.. 9. Nomadidae
bird (Orient).. 4. coel (koel)
cap.. 9. monkshood
family.. 9. Cuculidae
fool.. 7. wryneck
pint.. 4. arum 10. cuckoo spit
cucumber... 4. cuke, pepo 6. pedata (sea), pepino
cucurbit... 5. flask, gourd 7. matrass
cud... 4. bite, quid 5. rumen 8. merycism
cuddle... 3. hug, pet 6. fondle, nestle 7. snuggle
cudgel... 3. bat, hit 4. beat, club, drub 5. baste, staff, stave, stick 6. alpeen 7. belabor 8. fustigate, shillalah (shillelagh)
cue... 3. nod, rod, tip 4. ball, clue, hint, role, tail 5. braid, queue, twist 6. prompt 8. billiard (term), function 9. catchword 10. intimation

cuerpo... 4. body, hulk 5. naked, torso 10. dishabille (in)

cuff... 3. hit 4. band, blow, slap 5. clout 6. strike 8. chastise, gauntlet, handcuff 12. chastisement

cuirass... 4. mail 5. armor 6. lorica 11. breastplate

cul-de-sac... 5. alley (blind) 7. impasse 14. pouch of Douglas

cull... 4. pick 6. assort, choose, select 8. separate

culmination... 3. end 4. acme, apex, auge, noon 6. ascent, climax, result, vertex, zenith 10. perfection 12. consummation

culpability... 5. blame, fault, guilt 11. criminality 15. blameworthiness

culpable... 6. faulty, guilty 7. immoral 8. criminal 9. accusable, imputable 10. censurable, indictable 11. blameworthy 12. reproachable 13. reprehensible

cultivate... 3. ear (dial), hoe 4. farm, grow, plow, teel, till 5. court, train 6. excite, foster, harrow, plough, refine 7. educate, improve 8. approach, civilize

cultivated... 4. grew, hoed 6. seeded, tilled, urbane 7. genteel, refined 8. cultured, polished, well-bred

cultivation... 5. tilth 7. culture, farming, tillage 9. husbandry 10. refinement 12. civilization

culver... 4. dove 5. pigeon 10. wood pigeon

cumbersome... 5. bulky 6. clumsy 8. cumbrous, unwieldy 10. burdensome

cummer... 4. lass 5. witch 6. friend (girl) 7. midwife 9. companion, godmother

cummerbund... 4. band, belt, sash 6. cestus, girdle

cumshaw... 3. tip 5. bonus 6. thanks 7. present 9. gratuity

cunning... 3. sly 4. cute, foxy, wile, wily 5. sharp, skill 6. artful, clever, crafty, dainty, shrewd, subtle, tricky 7. politic, shyness 8. dextrous, foxiness, skillful, stealthy, trickery 9. designing, dexterity, ingenious, ingenuity, insidious 13. Machiavellian

cunningly formed... 6. daedal (dedal)

cup... 3. ama, can, dop, mug, tyg 4. tass, teet, Toby 5. calyx, chark, cruse, cupel, cylix, grail, jorum, ladle, stein 6. beaker, goblet, noggin, trophy 7. chalice, tumbler

cupbearer... 4. Hebe, saki 8. Ganymede

cupboard... 3. kas 5. ambry (anc) 6. buffet, closet, larder, pantry 7. armoire, dresser 8. aparador 9. sideboard

Cupid... 3. boy, Dan 4. amor, Eros, Kama, love 5. Freya 7. Amorino, cupidon

Cupid (pert to)...
mother.. 5. Venus
sweetheart.. 6. Psyche
title.. 3. Dan

cupidity... 4. lust 5. greed 6. desire 7. avarice, avidity, longing 8. appetite, avidness, rapacity

cuplike (pert to)...
calyx.. 9. calicular
stone.. 5. geode
vessel.. 4. zarf

cupola... 4. dome, kiln 5. tower 6. concha (Arch) 7. ceiling, furnace (foundry)

cur... 3. dog 4. mutt 7. gurnard (fish), mongrel 9. goldeneye

curare, curari... 5. urali 7. extract 9. Strychnos 11. arrow poison

curate... 4. abbé 6. cleric, parson, pastor, priest 7. dominie 9. clergyman

curator... 5. keeper 7. manager, steward 8. guardian 9. custodian, librarian, treasurer

curb... 3. bit 4. rein 5. check, limit 6. arrest, border, bridle, market (Finan) 7. control, inhibit, repress 8. restrict 9. hindrance, restraint

curd... 4. crud 6. casein

curds and whey... 7. clabber

cure... 4. balm, heal, salt 5. smoke 6. elixir, remedy, rizzor 7. nostrum, panacea, restore, therapy 8. preserve 10. corrective

curio... 8. artifact 9. bric-a-brac, curiosity

curiosity... 5. curio 6. gabion (rare), oddity, prying, wonder 8. interest 9. exception, spectacle 14. meddlesomeness 15. inquisitiveness

curious... 3. odd 4. rare 5. nosey (nosy), outre, queer 6. prying, quaint 7. careful, strange, unusual 8. cautious, meddling, singular 9. inquiring, intrusive 10. meticulous 11. inquisitive

curl... 4. coil, kink, lock, roll 5. crimp, crisp, frizz, tress, twirl, twist 6. marcel, spiral 7. crinkle, frizzle, ringlet 8. curlicue 9. corkscrew 11. convolution

curled... 5. curly, spiry 6. coiled 7. crimped, savoyed, twisted 8. wrinkled (Bot)

curlew... 4. bird, fute 5. kioea, snipe, whaup 6. marlin 7. bustard 8. whimbrel

curlewlike... 6. godwit 9. sandpiper

curly... 4. wavy 5. kinky, oundy (obs) 6. crispy, frizzy, kinked 8. crinkled

curmudgeon... 4. crab 5. churl, miser 7. niggard 8. tightwad 9. skinflint

currant... 3. red 5. berry, Ribes 6. raisin, rizzar (rizzart)

currency... 5. money, scrip 6. dinero 9. publicity 10. greenbacks, popularity, prevalence 15. fashionableness

current... 3. eddy, flow, race (water), rife, tide 5. draft, going, rapid, trend, usual 6. course, stream 7. present, topical 8. existent 9. direction, prevalent 11. fashionable

current regulator...
electric.. 9. rheometer

12. galvanometer
physiology . . 11. hematometer
curriculum . . . 7. courses, studies, Three
R's 8. curricle
curry . . . 4. comb, cook, drub 5. dress,
groom 6. cajole 9. condiment
curry favor . . . 6. cajole 7. flatter,
smoodge (smooge), wheedle
curse . . . 3. ban 4. bane, damn, oath
5. swear 7. bewitch, malison
8. anathema, execrate 9. blaspheme
10. affliction 11. imprecation,
malediction 13. excommunicate
cursed . . . 6. damned, odious, wicked
7. hateful 8. damnable, shrewish
9. execrable 12. cantankerous
Cursores . . . 5. birds (long–legged)
7. spiders (wolf)
Cursoria . . . 6. mantes (mantis)
10. Orthoptera 11. cockroaches
cursory . . . 5. hasty 6. fitful, roving,
slight 7. passing 8. careless,
rambling 9. desultory, irregular
10. evanescent 12. disconnected,
unmethodical
curt . . . 4. buff 5. bluff, brief, brusk,
gruff, short, terse 6. abrupt
7. brusque, concise, curtate, laconic
9. condensed
curtail . . . 3. lop 4. crop, dock, pare,
slip 5. short 6. lessen, reduce
7. abridge, shorten 8. compress,
decrease, diminish, retrench
curtain . . . 4. mask, veil 5. drape,
shade 6. coster (altar), encore,
purdah, riddel, screen, shadow, shield
7. drapery, secrecy, shelter, vitrage
8. portiere
curtsy, curtsey . . . 3. bow, nod
4. bend 6. kowtow, salaam
12. genuflection
curvature . . . 3. arc, bow 4. arch, bend
5. plane, sinus 6. camber
7. arching, curving, evolute
8. aduncity, cyrtosis, lordosis,
vaulting 9. curvation 11. convolution
curve . . . 3. arc, bow, ess 4. arch,
bend, ogee, turn 5. crook, polar
6. spiral, toroid 7. cissoid, evolute,
flexure 8. extrados, parabola, sinusoid
9. curvature, sinuosity
curved (pert to) . . .
arch . . 8. arciform, arcuated
glass . . 4. lens
inward . . 5. adunc 8. aduncous
molding . . 4. ogee
planking (ship's) . . 3. sny
process . . 5. hamus (Zool)
roundabout . . 10. circuitous
staircase . . 8. caracole
wedge . . 3. cam
curvet . . . 4. leap 5. bound, caper,
frisk, prank 6. frolic, gambol
cush . . . 3. cow 5. money 7. cookery,
sorghum
Cush (pert to) . . .
father . . 3. Ham
land of . . 8. Ethiopia 10. land of Cush
son . . 4. Seba 6. Nimrod
cushion . . . 3. pad 4. mute, seat
6. ignore, pillow, sachet 7. brioche,
conceal, dashpot, muffler 8. plantula,

pulvinus, suppress, swelling (Queen
Mary's) 9. pulvillus 10. pincushion
cusk . . . 4. fish (codlike), tusk 5. torsk
6. burbot
cusp . . . 3. end, tip 4. apex, peak
5. crown, point 6. cantle, corner
8. paracone
custard . . . 4. flan 7. charlet, pudding
custard apple . . . 4. tree 5. papaw
8. sweetsop
custodian . . . 5. guard 6. bailee, jailer,
keeper, warden, warder 7. curator,
janitor 8. curatrix, guardian
custody . . . 4. care, keep 5. trust
6. charge 8. guidance 10. protection
12. guardianship, jurisdiction
custom . . . 3. fad, law, mos, use
4. mode, wont 5. habit, mores,
usage, vogue 7. fashion 8. practice
9. patronage, tradition
10. consuetude, consuetudo
customary . . . 5. usual 6. wonted
7. general, usitate 8. habitual,
orthodox 11. traditional
12. conventional
customs . . . 4. duty 5. mores, taxes
cut . . . 3. bob, lob, lop, mow, nip, rip
4. blow, chop, crop, dock, edit, fell,
gash, hack, make, mode, nick, open,
pain, pare, reap, slit, snee, snip,
snub, trim 5. canal, carve, cleft,
lance, notch, piece, plate, scarp,
sever, share, shear, shorn, slash,
slice, slish (Shak), snick, split, vogue
6. dilute, furrow, injury, mangle,
reduce, trench 7. affront, curtail,
engrave, offense, sectile, serrate,
truancy, whittle 8. discount, excision,
incision 9. engraving, indignity,
reduction 10. adulterate
cut (pert to) . . .
and furrow . . 7. chamfer
and polish . . 8. lapidate
and weave . . 5. plash
back . . 6. polled 7. shorten
capable of being . . 7. sectile
down . . 5. razee
fine . . 5. mince
in . . 7. intrude 9. interpose, interrupt,
introduce
in half . . 9. dimidiate
in squares . . 4. dice
into . . 6. incise
jaggedly . . 4. snag
out . . 6. excide, excise
up . . 6. frolic, grieve 9. apportion,
misbehave
vertically . . 5. scarp, slice
with shears . . 4. snip 5. shirl
cutaneous . . . 4. skin 6. dermal, dermic
cute . . . 4. keen 5. peart, sharp
6. brainy, clever, dainty, pretty,
shrewd 7. cunning 10. attractive
11. picturesque
cuticle . . . 4. skin 5. cutin, cutis
8. membrane, pellicle 9. epidermis,
scarfskin 10. integument
cut of beef . . . 4. loin, ribs, rump
5. chine, roast, steak 6. corned,
cutlet, rosbif, saddle 7. brisket,
icebone 8. shoulder 9. aitchbone,
roundbone

cut off... 3. bob 4. crop, dock, drib, snip 5. elide, pared, roach (Naut) 6. bereft, bobbed, divest, lopped, screen 7. abscind, abscise, clipped, deprive, severed 8. amputate 9. amputated, apocopate, intercept 10. disinherit

cut off (pert to)...
by bits.. 4. drib
edges (coins).. 3. nig
on slant.. 4. bias 5. bevel, miter
short.. 3. bob 4. crop
syllable.. 5. elide
with die.. 4. dink
wool.. 3. dod (dodd)

cut short... 3. bob, lop 4. crop, dock, halt, stop 5. check 6. arrest 7. clipped, cropped, curtail, shorten 9. terminate

cutter... 4. boat 5. knife, sloop, tooth 6. sleigh, vessel 7. incisor

cutting... 4. cold, slip, tart 5. piece, scion, sharp 6. biting, secant, severe 7. caustic, incisal, satiric, sectile 8. chilling, piercing 9. sarcastic, severance, trenchant 10. separating 11. penetrating 12. adulteration

cutting (pert to)...
diamonds (imperfect).. 4. bort
edge.. 5. blade
in two.. 6. secant
last letter of word.. 7. apocope
off.. 7. apocope 10. abscission, amputation
tool.. 3. axe (ax), bit 4. adze 5. razor 6. chisel
wit.. 6. satire

cuttle... 4. thug 5. knife 7. ruffian 8. assassin 9. swaggerer

cuttlebone... 7. osselet

cuttlefish... 5. Sepia, squid 7. mollusk, octopus

cuttlefish secretion... 3. ink (black)

cuttyhunk... 11. fishing line

Cyclades Islands (Gr)... (200 in all) 3. Ios 5. Delos (smallest), Melos, Naros, Paros, Tenos, Thera 6. Andros 7. Amorgos, Myconus

cycle... 3. Age, eon, era 4. aeon 5. orbit, recur, saros (Astron), wheel 6. course, period, series 7. bicycle, circuit 8. electric, tricycle 9. Arthurian 10. revolution 12. Carlovingian (Charlemagne)

cyclone... 5. storm 6. baguio 7. tornado, twister, typhoon 9. hurricane

cyclopean... 4. huge, vast 7. massive, one-eyed 8. gigantic

Cyclops (pert to)...
assistant to.. 6. Vulcan (Fire God)
father.. 6. Uranus
forger of.. 12. thunderbolts
home.. 6. Sicily (Mt Etna)
oddity.. 7. one-eyed
race (Myth).. 6. giants

cygneous... 8. swanlike

cygnet... 4. swan

cylinder... 4. drum, pipe, roll, tube 5. inker, stele 6. barrel, gabion,

platen, record, roller, rounce, terete 10. cylindroid

cylindrical... 5. conic 6. terete 7. tubular

cymbal, cymbals... 3. tal, zel 6. Becken, piatti 7. potlids 8. doughnut

Cymric... 5. Welsh 9. Brythonic

Cymric (pert to)...
bard.. 6. Merlin 7. Aneurin
god of the dead.. 5. Pwyll
god of the sky.. 7. Gwydion
god of the sun.. 4. Lleu
god of the waves.. 5. Dylan

cynic... 5. Timon 7. ascetic, doglike, egotist, snarler 9. pessimist 11. misanthrope

Cynic (pert to)...
pupil.. 8. Socrates
school.. 10. Philosophy
teacher.. 8. Diogenes
teaching.. 6. virtue

cynical... 7. currish 8. captious, snarling 9. sarcastic 11. pessimistic 12. misanthropic

cynosure... 5. guide 8. lodestar (loadstar), polestar 9. celebrity, North Star 13. constellation

cyprinoid (fish)... 2. id 3. ide, orf (orfe) 4. bass (black), carp, chub, dace 6. chevin, shiner 7. herring (lake) 8. fallfish 9. hornyhead, squawfish

Cyprus...
capital.. 7. Nicosia (Sicily)
colonizer (anc).. 11. Phoenicians
history.. 11. New Stone Age
mountain.. 7. Troodos
port.. 7. Lornaca 8. Limassol 9. Famagusto

Cyrenaic (pert to)...
city.. 6. Cyrene
country.. 9. Cyrenaica (Afr)
division of.. 5. Libya
harbor.. 6. Tobruk 7. Bengazi
philosophy.. 8. hedonism, pleasure

Cyrene... 4. city (anc) 5. nymph 7. goddess

cyrus... 5. crane, sarus

Cyrus the Elder (pert to)...
conqueror of.. 7. Babylon
founder of.. 6. Persia (Empire)
king of.. 5. Lydia, Media
subduer of.. 9. Palestine

cyst... 3. box, sac, wen 5. chest, pouch 7. vesicle

Czar... 4. Ivan, tsar, tzar 5. Peter 8. Nicholas

Czechoslovakia...
capital.. 6. Prague (Praha)
city.. 5. Praha 6. Pilsen 7. Ostrava 10. Bratislava
empire (anc).. 7. Bohemia, Moravia 8. Slovakia
forest.. 12. Great Bohemia
mountain, peak.. 3. Ore 6. Tatras 11. Carpathians
people.. 6. Czechs 7. Slovaks
river.. 4. Elbe (Labe), Iser, Oder 6. Vltava

czigany... 5. gypsy

D

D... 3. 500 6. letter (4th)
dab... 3. hit, tap 4. blow 5. paint, smear 6. expert, lizard, smooth 7. dabster 8. flatfish
dabble... 4. mass 5. dally 6. befoul, meddle, paddle, potter, splash, tamper, trifle 7. spatter 8. sprinkle
dabbler... 7. trifler 8. sciolist 10. dilettante
dabchick... 5. grebe 9. gallinule
dacha (Russ)... 5. villa 12. country house
dacoit... 6. bandit, robber
dacry, dacryo (comb form)... 5. tears
dactyl... 3. toe 4. foot 6. finger 8. dactylus
dactyliomancy... 17. divination by rings (finger)
dactylogram... 11. fingerprint
dactylology... 12. sign language
Dadaism... 4. cult 8. negation
daddy—longlegs... 5. stilt 6. curlew, spider, Tipula 7. spinner
daedal, dedal... 4. rich 6. varied 8. artistic, skillful (skilful) 9. ingenious, intricate 10. variegated
Daedalus (Gr Myth)... 9. artificer
daffodil... 6. yellow 9. narcissus 10. bellflower
daffy, daft... 3. gay, mad 4. wild 5. batty, crazy, giddy, goofy, loony 6. insane 7. foolish, idiotic
Dagda (pert to)...
    children.. 6. Aengus (Angus), Brigit
    famed as.. 7. harpist
    Gaelic name.. 7. Jupiter
    god of.. 10. pagan Irish
dagger... 4. dirk, kris, snee 5. kalar 6. anlace, bodkin, creese 7. bayonet, poniard 10. misericord
Daibutsu (pert to)...
    famed image.. 6. Buddha
    Japanese Bronze.. 11. Great Buddha
    site.. 8. Kamakura (near Tokyo)
daily... 4. a day 7. diurnal, journal 9. hodiurnal, newspaper, quotidian 11. day in day out
daily food... 4. fare 5. bread 10. livelihood 11. subsistence, substenance
dainties... 5. cates, estes 7. titbits (tidbits)
dainty... 4. fair, fine, rare 5. frail, small 6. choice, pretty, select 8. elegance 9. exquisite, toothsome 10. fastidious
dairy... 4. farm 8. creamery 9. lactarium
dairymen caste (Ind)... 4. Ahir

dais... 5. stage, table 7. estrade 8. platform
daisy... 5. gowan, oxeye 6. morgan, Shasta 7. Gerbera 9. Whiteweed
dale... 4. dell, dene, vale 5. spout 6. dingle, ravine, trough, valley
dalles... 5. dells 11. canyon walls
dalliance... 4. chat 5. delay 6. gossip, trifle 8. fondling, trifling 10. flirtation
dally... 3. toy 5. tarry 6. dawdle, linger 13. procrastinate
Dalmatia...
    capital.. 7. Spalato (Yugoslavia)
    cherry.. 7. marasca
    coast.. 8. Adriatic
    dog.. 5. coach 8. carriage
    home of.. 10. Diocletian
    people.. 5. Serbs 8. Adriatic 9. Yugoslavs
    product.. 4. lace
dam... 4. stay, stem, stop, weir 5. Aswan, block, check, choke, Gatun (CZ) 6. Hoover (Boulder), mother, Norris, parent 7. barrier 8. millpond, obstruct, Oroville, restrain 9. Roosevelt 10. Bull Shoals, Glen Canyon 11. Grand Coulee
damage... 3. mar 4. harm, hurt, loss, noxa 6. impair, injury, mayhem, scathe, strafe 8. disserve, sabotage 9. detriment, vandalism 10. impairment
daman... 4. cony (Bib) 5. Hyrax 6. mammal 8. Procavia
Damascus, Syria (pert to)...
    Bib scene.. 20. Street Called Straight
    division.. 6. Jewish, Moslem 9. Christian
    history.. 16. world's oldest city (inhabited)
    mosque (renowned).. 7. Ommiade
    river.. 5. Abana 6. Barada
damask... 3. red (color) 5. cloth, steel (Damascus) 8. to deface (the Great Seal, Eng)
dame... 4. lady, Miss 5. Madam, title 6. matron, Nature, parent
damn... 4. cuss, ruin 5. abuse, curse 6. shucks 7. accurse, condemn, swear at
damsel... 4. girl, lass 5. Rhoda (Bib), wench 7. colleen 10. damoiselle
dance... 4. jazz, prom, skip, trip 5. frisk, glide 6. cavort, frolic, gambol 7. flicker, flutter, rejoice, saltate 10. tripudiate
dance (pert to)...
    art.. 12. choreography
    clumsily.. 6. balter
    mimetic (Rom).. 5. Salii 7. Luperci

146

8. Curetics
movement.. 6. chassé, gestic
7. saltant 9. pirouette
step.. 3. pas 5. coupe 6. chassé
7. gambado (gambade), shuffle
8. glissade 9. arabesque, grapevine
10. pigeonwing
dance (type).. 3. bal, hop, jig, toe
4. ball, clog, haka, kolo, polo, reel,
shag 5. gavot (gavotte), pavan,
polka, tango, waltz 6. althea, apache,
ballet, bolero, cancan, corant, maxixe,
minuet, morris, redowa, rhumba
(rumba), shimmy, square, watusi
7. beguine, coranto (old), courant,
foxtrot, gavotte, hoedown, mazurka,
one-step, ridotto, tempete, two-step
8. bunny hug, cakewalk, courante,
fandango, halliard (anc), hornpipe,
lanciers, rigadoon 9. allemande (anc),
butterfly, farandole, polonaise,
quadrille 10. Charleston, tarantella
11. schottische (schottish)
dancer... 6. hoofer 7. danseur
8. coryphee, danseuse, stripper
9. ballerina, ecdysiast, jitterbug
11. terpsichore 13. choreographer
dancer (pert to)...
Bib.. 6. Salome
Egyptian.. 4. alme (almeh) 7. ghawazi
8. Baramika
Japanese.. 6. geisha (girl)
Oriental.. 4. hula 6. nautch
8. bayadere
dancing (pert to)...
arrangement.. 12. choreography
Muse of.. 11. Terpsichore
term.. 6. ballet, chassé, gestic
7. hoofing, saltant
dandelion... 4. herb 5. plant 6. yellow
9. Taraxacum
dandified... 7. foppish
dandify... 6. spruce 7. adonize,
smarten 8. titivate (tittivate)
dandy... 3. fop 4. beau, dude, good,
toff 5. daisy 6. Adonis 7. coxcomb
9. exquisite 11. Beau Brummel
dangerous... 3. bad 4. dire 5. feral,
risky 6. chancy 7. ominous, parlous
8. alarming, critical, insecure,
perilous 9. hazardous 10. jeopardous,
precarious
dangle... 3. lop 4. hang, loll, yawl
5. droop, swing 6. flaunt, mizzen
Daniel (pert to)...
Bib.. 4. Book (Old Test) 7. prophet
(Heb)
form of verse.. 7. lyrical, sestina
verse adopted by.. 5. Dante
8. Petrarch
Danish... see also *Denmark*
capital.. 10. Copenhagen
council (anc).. 8. Rigsraad
country.. 7. Denmark
doctor.. 6. Finsen
export.. 8. cryolite
fiord.. 3. Ise
flag.. 9. Dannebrog
island.. 3. Als (Alsen) 5. Faroe
9. Greenland
King (anc).. 6. Canute
native.. 4. Dane 12. Scandinavian

parliament.. 7. Rigsdag
prince (legend).. 6. Hamlet
settlers in Ireland.. 6. Ostmen
dank... 3. wet 4. damp 5. humid,
moist, muggy
Dan McGrew... 11. Hound of Hell
danseuse... 7. danseur 8. coryphee
9. ballerina
Dante (pert to)...
birthplace.. 8. Florence
famed as.. 4. poet 6. lyrist
famed poem.. 12. Divine Comedy
poem's companion.. 6. Vergil (Virgil)
poem's division.. 4. Hell 6. Heaven
9. Purgatory
poem's love.. 8. Beatrice
Danube River (pert to)...
end.. 8. Black Sea
source.. 11. Black Forest
tributary.. 4. Isar, Raab 5. Drava
6. Morava
Danubian (pert to)...
color.. 5. green
fish.. 6. huchen (huch)
goose.. 10. Sevastopol
Danzig...
Polish name.. 6. Gdansk
river site.. 7. Vistula
Sea.. 6. Baltic
territory of (now).. 6. Poland
dap... 3. bob, dab, dib, dip
6. bounce, dibble, guddle 7. rebound
Daphne (pert to)...
Bib.. 4. Park (Antioch, Syria)
father.. 5. Ladon 6. Peneus
lover.. 6. Apollo
transformation.. 10. laurel tree
dapper... 4. braw, neat, pert, trim
5. natty, sleek 6. jaunty, little, lively,
spruce 7. dashing, finical
dappled... 6. dotted 7. flecked,
piebald, spotted
dare... 4. daze, defy, face, osse, risk
5. brave 6. assume, dazzle
7. venture 8. confront, defiance,
paralyze 9. challenge, undertake
daring... 4. bold, rash 5. brave, manly
8. boldness, defiance 9. audacious,
foolhardy 11. adventurous,
venturesome 12. enterprising
dark... 3. dim, mum, sad 4. ebon
5. black, blind, dense, faint, mirky,
murky, night, unlit, vague 6. closed,
gloomy, occult, opaque, secret,
wicked 7. joyless, melanic, obscure,
stygian 8. abstruse, ignorant,
moonless 9. ambiguous, atrocious,
Cimmerian (realm), lightless, nightfall,
tenebrous, uncertain 10. foreboding,
indistinct
dark (pert to)...
Ages.. 6. Middle 8. Medieval
9. Neolithic
Continent.. 6. Africa (formerly)
10. unexplored
horse.. 7. unknown 9. candidate
hue.. 5. dusky, swart 6. somber
7. swarthy
moon area.. 4. mare
darken... 3. dim 4. dull 5. blind,
umber 6. darkle, sadden, shadow
7. becloud, blacken, confuse, eclipse,

enshade 8. bewilder 9. obfuscate

darkness... 4. dark, dusk, mirk, murk 5. shade 6. Erebus, shadow 7. dimness, tenebra 9. blackness, blindness, ignorance, obscurity 10. opaqueness

darling... 2. jo 3. pet 4. dear, idol, lief 5. cheri, sweet 6. minion 7. acushla, beloved 8. favorite 9. mavournin 10. mavourneen, sweetheart 13. cushlamochree (cushlamachree)

darnel... 4. tare, weed 5. grass 6. Lolium

dart... 4. barb, bolt, flit, leap, vire 5. arrow, bound, lance, scoot, shoot, start, throw 6. dartle, elance, glance, spring, weapon 7. javelin, missile, stinger 8. jaculate

Darwinism... 9. Evolution (theory, 1858) 12. Evolutionism

das, dasse... 6. badger

dash... 4. code, élan, gift, race, ruin, rush, slam 5. ardor, crash, haste, onset, plash, smash, speed, swash 6. energy, obelus (anc), spirit, sprint, strike, stroke 7. bravura, spatter, splurge 8. confound, gratuity 9. animation 11. punctuation

dashing... 3. gay 4. fast 5. showy 6. dapper, jaunty, sporty 7. stylish

dastardly... 4. base, foul 6. craven 8. cowardly

data... 5. facts, logic 7. grounds (for facts) 11. information

date... 3. age 4. line (newspaper), time 5. fruit, tryst 6. person 10. engagement 11. appointment

date (pert to)...
birth.. 7. natal
coin line.. 7. exergue
error.. 11. anachronism
fruit of.. 4. palm
plum.. 6. sapote

daub... 3. dab 4. blob, gaum, soil, teer 5. paint, smear, stain, sully 6. bedaub 7. besmear, picture (art), plaster 8. scribble

daughter... 5. child 7. cadette 9. offspring 10. descendant

daughter of...
Inachus (river god).. 2. Io
Night.. 7. Nemesis
the moon.. 7. Nokomis
the Spanish king.. 7. infanta

daunt... 3. awe, cow 4. faze 5. amate (anc) 6. dismay, subdue 7. overawe, repress 10. discourage, dishearten, intimidate

dauntless... 4. bold 7. aweless (awless) 8. fearless, intrepid, resolute 9. dreadless 11. unfaltering

davenport... 3. bed 4. desk, sofa 5. divan 12. Chesterfield

David (Bib)...
daughter.. 5. Tamar
father.. 5. Jesse
helpers.. 4. Igal 5. Abner 7. Shammah
king of.. 6. Israel (40 years)
slayer of.. 7. Goliath
son.. 7. Solomon

wife.. 7. Abigail

davit... 4. spar 5. crane

dawdle... 4. diddle, poke, toit 5. dally 6. linger, loiter, potter, trifle 9. vacillate 10. dillydally 13. procrastinate

dawn... 2. eo (comb form) 3. Eos (goddess), red 4. morn 5. sunup 6. appear, aurora, sink in 7. sunrise 8. daybreak 9. beginning, penetrate

day (pert to)...
Athenians, Jews.. 6. sunset
Babylonians.. 7. sunrise
blindness.. 10. nyctalopia 11. hemeralopia
divisions.. 5. lunar, solar 8. sidereal
dream.. 4. muse 5. fancy 7. fantasy, reverie 8. phantasy
Egyptians, Romans.. 8. midnight
god.. 5. Horus
nursery.. 6. crèche
scholar.. 7. externe

Day of...
Atonement.. 9. Yom Kippur
Brahma.. 9. Maha Yugas
doom.. 8. Judgment

day's march... 5. étape

day's work... 4. darg (dargue)

daze... 3. fog 4. asea, maze, stun 5. sopor, swoon 6. benumb, dazzle, stupid, trance 7. confuse, stupefy 8. bewilder 9. dumbfound 12. razzle-dazzle

dazzling... 6. bright, garish 7. glaring 8. blinding, gorgeous 9. beautiful, brilliant 11. bewildering

dead... 3. fey 4. flat, numb, obit 5. amort, blind, inert, napoo, passé 6. active, barren, lapsed 7. defunct, expired, insipid, tedious 8. ad patres, complete, deceased, inactive, lifeless, obsolete 9. apathetic, inanimate 10. lusterless, motionless, spiritless, unexciting 11. nonexistent

dead (pert to)...
Dead Sea apple.. 12. Apple of Sodom
Dead Sea country.. 4. Moab 5. Sodom 8. Gomorrah
language.. 5. Latin
rise from the.. 7. resurge 9. reanimate, resurrect
set (slang).. 8. full tilt, hell-bent
tree.. 7. rampike (rampick)

deaden... 4. damp, dull, mute, numb 6. muffle, obtund, opiate, weaken 7. relieve, repress 8. enfeeble 10. devitalize

deadly... 4. dire, mort 5. fatal 6. lethal, mortal 7. deathly 8. venomous 10. implacable, lifelessly 11. destructive, internecine

deaf... 4. surd 7. earless 10. intolerant 11. inattentive, preoccupied

deaf alphabet... 11. dactylology 12. sign language

deaf and dumb... 9. surdomute 10. deaf-mutism 11. surdimutism

deafness... 6. amusia (tone) 7. surdity 13. insensibility

deafness operation... 8. fenestra

deal . . . 3. lot 4. dole, give, mede,
mete, sale, sell 5. allot, share, trade,
treat 6. parcel 7. dispose, portion,
wrestle 8. business, dispense,
quantity 9. apportion, entertain
10. administer, distribute

dealer (pert to) . . .
  cattle . . 6. drover, herder
  cloth . . 6. draper, mercer
  drug . . 8. druggist 10. apothecary,
  pharmacist 14. pharmacopolist
  retail . . 6. grocer, monger 8. merchant
  9. tradesman
  stock exchange . . 6. broker, jobber,
  trader 11. stockbroker

dean, dene . . . 4. dell 6. valley

dean . . . 4. head, Inge 5. decan, doyen
6. fellow (Educ), master, senior,
verger 8. officer 9. churchman,
principal

dear . . . 5. chere, cheri, deary, lover,
sugar, sweet 7. beloved, darling
8. precious 9. expensive
10. sweetheart

dearth . . . 4. want 6. famine, rarity
7. paucity, poverty 8. rareness,
scarcity, sparsity

death . . . 4. doom, mort, obit 5. sleep
(eternal) 6. demise 7. decease,
passing, quietus, release
10. euthanasia (mercy), expiration
11. evanishment

death (pert to) . . .
  after . . 10. posthumous
  eternal . . 9. perdition
  foreboding . . 6. funest 7. doleful
  lawless . . 8. lynching
  notice . . 4. obit 5. orbit 8. obituary
  of a deity . . 4. Mors
  rattle . . 4. rale
  stoning (by) . . 8. lapidate

deathlessness . . . 9. athanasis
11. immortality 15. everlastingness

debacle . . . 4. rout 5. crash, flood
7. washout 8. collapse, stampede
9. breakdown, cataclysm
11. catastrophe, destruction

debar . . . 3. bar 4. deny 5. estop
6. forbid, hinder, refuse 7. exclude
8. obstruct, preclude, prohibit

debark . . . 4. land 8. go ashore
9. disembark

debase . . . 5. abase, alloy, lower
6. demean, demote, reduce
7. corrupt, degrade, deprave
8. disgrace 10. adulterate, depreciate
11. deteriorate

debasement . . . 8. demotion
9. abasement, abjection, reduction,
vitiation 11. degradation
13. deterioration

debatable . . . 4. moot 9. refutable
10. disputable 11. contestable
13. controversial

debate . . . 4. agon (anc), moot
5. argue, forum, plead, weigh
6. reason 7. analyze, closure,
cloture, dispute, wrangle
8. argument, consider, forensic,
militate 9. quodlibet 10. deliberate,
discussion 11. controversy
12. deliberation, dissertation

13. argumentation

debauch . . . 4. bout, orgy 5. broil,
spree, taint 6. defile, seduce, splore
7. mislead 8. carousal, escapade
9. disaffect, dissipate
11. contaminate

debauchee . . . 4. rake, roué 5. satyr
7. rounder 9. libertine 10. profligate

debenture (Finan) . . . 4. bond 5. claim
6. pledge 7. voucher 10. instrument
11. certificate

debilitated . . . 4. weak 5. seedy
6. feeble, infirm, sapped, sickly
7. languid 8. asthenic, impaired,
weakened 9. enfeebled, langorous
11. devitalized

debility . . . 5. atony 7. languor
8. adynamia, asthenia, cachexia,
weakness 9. infirmity, lassitude
10. feebleness, sickliness

debit . . . 4. debt 5. entry 6. charge

debonair, debonaire . . . 4. airy
5. suave 6. breezy, jaunty, urbane
7. affable, buoyant 8. carefree

debris . . . 4. junk 5. attle, ruins, scrap,
talus, trash 6. litter, refuse, rubble
7. deposit, remains, rubbish
8. detritus 10. clamjamfry

debt . . . 3. due, IOU, sin (Bib)
7. arrears, default 8. trespass
9. arrearage, liability 10. obligation

debut . . . 3. bow 8. entrance (formal)
9. coming out 12. introduction,
presentation

debutante . . . 3. bud, deb 6. subdeb
9. socialite

decade . . . 3. ten 9. decennium

decadence . . . 5. decay 7. decline
13. deterioration, retrogression

decamp . . . 4. flee 6. depart
7. abscond, vamoose
12. absquatulate

decanter . . . 4. ewer 5. croft 6. bottle,
carafe, vessel (liquors)

decapod . . . 4. crab 5. prawn 6. shrimp
7. Homarus, lobster 8. Decapoda
10. crustacean

decay . . . 3. rot 4. blet, doty 5. spoil,
waste 6. caries, wither 7. crumble,
mortify, putrefy 8. spoilage
9. decadence, decompose
11. deteriorate, dissolution
13. decomposition, deterioration

deceased . . . 4. dead, gone, late 6. at
rest 7. defunct, demised
8. decedent, departed

deceit . . . 5. covin, craft, fraud, guile,
guise 7. cunning 8. artifice,
cozenage, intrigue, subtlety, trickery,
wiliness 9. chicanery, deception,
duplicity, imposture, mendacity,
sophistry, treachery 10. craftiness,
sneakiness 13. deceitfulness,
dissimulation 14. tergiversation
15. treacherousness

deceitful . . . 4. wily 5. false 6. artful,
crafty, sneaky, tricky 8. guileful,
scheming, trickish 9. deceptive,
gnathonic, insincere 10. fraudulent
11. treacherous 13. Machiavellian

deceive . . . 3. cog, lie 4. bilk, dupe,
flam, fool, gull, hoax, sile 5. cheat,

cozen, elude, hocus, trick, troil
6. baffle, delude, illude, seduce
7. beguile, mislead 8. hoodwink

deceiver... 3. gay 5. cheat 6. hoaxer
trepan (trapan) 8. betrayer, impostor
9. trickster

decency... 7. decorum, fitness,
modesty 8. chastity, niceness
9. propriety 10. seemliness
12. tastefulness

decent... 4. kind 6. comely, kindly,
proper, seemly 7. clothed
8. adequate, gracious, suitable,
tasteful 9. tolerable

deception... 3. lie 4. hoax, wile
5. cheat, fraud, guile 6. deceit,
misled 7. fallacy 8. artifice, deceived,
flimflam, illusion 9. duplicity,
imposture

deceptive... 5. vague 8. illusive,
illusory 9. deceiving, sirenical (sirenic)
10. fallacious

decide (upon)... 3. opt 4. vote
5. adapt, elect, judge 6. choose,
settle 7. referee, resolve 9. arbitrate,
ascertain, determine, influence

decima... 4. stop (organ) 5. tenth,
tithe 8. interval

decimal... 3. ten 5. tenth 7. tenfold
8. repetend

decimate... 3. few 4. kill, slay
5. burke, tenth 6. divide 7. destroy
8. subtract 9. devastate, slaughter

decipher... 4. read 5. crack
6. decode, detect 7. unravel
8. discover 9. translate

decision... 4. grit 5. arret, nerve,
pluck 6. mettle, report 7. verdict
8. firmness 10. conclusion,
resolution, settlement
12. announcement 13. determination

decisive... 3. end 5. final 7. certain,
crucial 8. critical, resolute
9. mandatory 10. conclusive,
convincing

decisive moment... 6. crisis

deck (ship's)... 3. gun 4. main, poop
5. orlop, upper 6. bridge 7. scupper
(gutter) 8. hatchway, platform
9. promenade 10. forecastle

deck... 4. gild 5. adorn, array, cards
(playing), equip 6. blazon, clothe,
enrich 7. bedizen, dress up
8. emblazon

declaim... 4. rant, rave 5. orate, spiel,
spout 6. herald, recite 8. denounce,
harangue, perorate 9. discourse
11. declamation

declamation... 7. lecture 9. elocution
10. recitation

declaration... 3. vow 4. oath
6. avowal, decree, oracle 8. pleading
(law) 9. assertion, manifesto,
testimony 10. confession (of faith)
11. affirmation 12. proclamation
13. pronouncement

declare... 3. say 4. aver, avow, meld
5. bruit, state 6. affirm, allege,
assert, blazon, herald, spread
7. publish 8. announce, indicate,
maintain 9. advertise

declare (pert to)...

against.. 6. indict
as fact.. 5. posit
innocent.. 6. acquit

declension... 4. drop, fall 5. slope
7. decline, descent, refusal
10. inflection 13. deterioration

decline... 3. dip, ebb, sink 4. fade, fail,
fall, flag, sink, wane 5. droop, repel,
slope, slump, stoop 6. refuse, reject,
weaken 7. dwindle 8. decrease,
downhill 9. decadence, declivity,
repudiate 10. retrograde
12. depreciation

declivity... 3. dip 4. drop, hill
5. scarp, slope 7. descent
8. downgate 9. downgrade

decoction... 4. sapa (sape) 6. apozem,
cremor, tisane 7. boiling
10. extraction 11. preparation

decompose... 3. rot 4. frit 5. decay
7. resolve 10. photolysis
12. disintegrate

decorate... 4. deck, trim 5. adorn,
honor 6. emboss 7. bedizen,
brocade, miniate 8. beautify,
ornament 9. scrimshaw

decorated... 5. fancy 6. ornate
7. adorned 8. nielloed 9. sigillate
(pottery) 11. embellished

decoration... 4. buhl 5. gutta (anc),
medal 6. plaque, purfle, ribbon
7. epergne, festoon, garnish 8. gold
star, ornament, trimming
9. adornment, garniture, sgraffito
10. cordon bleu, emblazonry,
embroidery

decorous... 4. calm, prim 5. grave,
quiet, staid 6. decent, demure,
modest, proper, sedate, seemly,
serene 7. fitting, regular, settled
8. becoming, composed, suitable,
tasteful 9. unruffled 12. conventional

decorticate... 4. bark, flay, husk, pare,
peel, skin 5. strip 9. excoriate

decoy... 4. bait, lure, tole 6. capper,
entrap 8. by-bidder 9. come-on man
11. stool pigeon

decrease... 3. ebb 4. drop, sink, wane
5. abate, waste 6. decess, lessen,
reduce, shrink 7. decline, dwindle,
shorten, slacken, subside
8. compress, diminish, moderate
9. abatement, deduction, deflation,
lessening 10. diminution
11. contraction 12. depreciation

decree... 3. act, law 4. bull, fiat, rede
(anc), will 5. arret, canon, edict,
enact, irade, order, ukase 6. dictum,
ordain 7. command, mandate, verdict
8. decision, rescript 9. ordinance

decree beforehand... 7. destine

decree nisi... 7. divorce

decrepit... 3. old 4. aged, lame, weak
6. infirm, senile, wasted (with age)
7. worn out 8. unstable, unsturdy

decry... 3. boo 4. slur 5. lower
7. condemn, degrade, detract
8. belittle, denounce, derogate
9. discredit, disparage, underrate
10. depreciate, undervalue

dedal... see *daedal*

dedicate... 6. devote, hallow

7. address 8. inscribe
10. consecrate

deduce... 5. infer 6. deduct, derive, elicit, evolve 7. suppose

deduct... 4. bate, faik, take 6. remove 8. discount, retrench, separate, subtract

deduction... 6. rebate 7. reprise 8. discount, illation 9. allowance, corollary, induction, inference, reasoning, syllogism

deed... 3. act, ado 4. feat, fiat, gest (geste) 5. actum, actus, stunt, title 6. action, doings 7. exploit 8. contract, tenendum 11. achievement, malefaction, performance

deem... 5. judge, opine, think 6. esteem, regard 7. believe, presume, suppose 8. conclude, consider 10. adjudicate

deemed... 7. assumed, reputed 8. adjudged, inferred, presumed, supposed 10. considered

deep... 3. low, pit 4. rich, wide, wise 5. great 6. hidden, remote, solemn 7. learned, obscure, serious 8. immersed, involved, powerful, profound 9. engrossed, entangled, sagacious 10. deep-seated, mysterious

deep (pert to)...
dish pie.. 7. cobbler
sea.. 6. depths
seated.. 8. habitual 9. ingrained 11. established
sleep.. 5. sopor
sound.. 4. bell, gong

deepen... 5. lower 6. dredge 7. broaden, enhance 9. aggravate, intensify 10. strengthen

deer... 3. elk, red, roe 4. buck, fawn, hart, hind, maha, stag 5. eland, moose, ratwa 6. fallow, sambar, wapiti 7. caribou, deerlet, roebuck 8. reindeer, ruminant

deer (pert to)...
antler.. 3. dag 4. snag 8. tres-tine (royal)
Asiatic.. 6. sambar
barking.. 7. muntjac (muntjak)
deerlike.. 7. chevrotain
female.. 3. doe, roe 4. hind
genus.. 4. Dama 6. Cervus 8. Cervidae
Japanese.. 4. sika
Java.. 4. napu 7. muntjac (muntjak)
Lapland.. 8. reindeer
male.. 4. buck, hart, stag 6. havier 7. brocket (brok), pricket
meat.. 7. venison
mouse.. 7. plandok
Oriental.. 4. axis, Rusa 5. kakar 6. chital, rativa, sambar 7. kanchil, muntjac (muntjak)
Russian.. 4. olen
S American.. 4. pita 6. guemal (guemul) 7. brocket, spitter
Tibet.. 4. shou
tiger.. 6. cougar
tracks.. 3. run 4. slot
type.. 3. red, roe 4. mule 6. fallow

11. black-tailed, white-tailed

deface... 3. mar 4. ruin, scar 5. spoil 6. damage, injure 7. blemish, distort 9. discredit, disfigure

defamation... 5. libel 7. calumny, slander, spatter 8. disgrace, dishonor 9. aspersion 10. defilement, detraction

defame... 5. libel 6. accuse, charge, infamy, malign, vilify 7. asperse, blacken, detract, slander, traduce 8. dishonor 10. calumniate

default... 4. fail, lack, loss, mora 7. deficit, failure, neglect 9. deficient, denigrate, oversight 10. nonpayment 11. delinquency 14. nonfulfillment

defeat... 4. beat, best, lose, rout 5. worst 6. baffle, derout, master, refute 7. beating, clobber, confute, conquer, failure, mastery, repulse, triumph (over), undoing 8. Waterloo 9. frustrate, overthrow 10. disappoint 11. subjugation 12. discomfiture 14. disappointment

defeating... 7. beating, routing 10. anatreptic, conquering 11. vanquishing

defeatism... 6. malism 7. Boloism 10. retreatism

defect... 4. flaw, lisp, lock, quit, want 5. fault 7. blemish, forsake 8. withdraw 9. discredit 10. deficiency, inadequacy 12. imperfection, irregularity

defection... 4. loss 7. failing, failure 9. desertion 10. abjuration 11. abandonment

defective... 3. bad 4. lame 5. idiot 6. cretin, faulty 7. half-wit, lacking 8. crippled 9. deficient, imperfect, subnormal 10. incomplete

defective vision... 6. anopia, myopia

defend... 4. save, ward 5. guard, plead, shend, watch 6. screen, secure, shield, uphold 7. contest, justify, protect, shelter, support, sustain 8. enshield, preserve 10. controvert

defendant... 4. reus 7. accused, libelee, suspect 8. appellee 10. respondent

defender... 8. advocate, champion 9. justifier, protector 10. vindicator

defense... 4. boma, fort, plea 5. alibi, guard 6. abatis (abattis), glacis (slope) 7. bulwark, rampart, ravelin 8. estacade (dike), sepiment, stockade 10. protection 12. counterscarp 13. justification, machicolation

defenseless... 7. aidless, forlorn, unarmed 8. helpless 9. unarmored, unguarded 10. undefended, unshielded 11. unfortified, unprotected

defer... 3. bow 4. wait 5. delay 6. retard 7. adjourn, suspend 8. postpone, protract, stave off 13. procrastinate

defer (to)... 5. yield 6. admire, regard, submit 7. concede, respect

9. recognize 11. acknowledge

deference... 5. honor 6. esteem, fealty, homage, regard 7. respect 8. courtesy 9. reverence 10. politeness, submission 12. complaisance 13. consideration

deferential... 8. obeisant 9. attentive, courteous 10. respectful, submissive 11. ceremonious

defiance... 6. defial 7. audacity, boldness 9. challenge, disregard, insolence

deficiency... 4. lack, want 6. dearth, ullage 7. aneuria, deficit 8. scarcity, shortage 10. inadequacy 13. insufficiency 14. incompleteness

deficient... 5. minus, short 6. faulty, meager (meagre), scarce 7. lacking, missing, wanting 8. inferior 9. defective, imperfect 10. inadequate, incomplete 12. insufficient

defile... 4. file, pass (Mt), soil 5. dirty, gorge, notch, sully, taint 6. befoul, debase, ravine, vilify 7. corrupt, debauch, deprave, pollute, tarnish 8. dishonor 10. passageway

define... 3. fix 4. name 5. bound, limit 6. decide 7. delimit, explain, outline 8. boundary 9. delineate, determine, stipulate 11. distinguish 12. characterize, circumscribe

defined (sharply)... 8. clear-cut 9. trenchant

defined track... 3. rut 4. slot

definite... 4. sure 7. certain, limited, precise 8. absolute, distinct, explicit, manifest, positive 10. undeniable 11. determining, unqualified 12. unmistakable 14. unquestionable

definitely... 10. explicitly, positively 12. conclusively, unmistakably

definition... 6. naming 7. clarity, meaning 9. sharpness 11. description, explanation 12. delimitation, distinctness 14. interpretation

deflation... 7. decline 8. collapse 9. reduction 10. cheapening 11. devaluation, humiliation 12. depreciation

deflect... 4. bend, warp 5. avert 6. divert 7. deviate

deformed... 5. varus 7. taliped 8. formless 9. amorphous, distorted, grotesque, loathsome, malformed, misshapen, monstrous 10. clubfooted

defraud... 3. gyp, rob 4. bilk, gull 5. cheat, cozen 6. fleece 7. swindle

deft... 3. apt, fit, pat 4. meet, trim 5. adept, handy, quick 6. adroit, clever, expert 8. skillful (skilful) 9. dexterous, masterful

defunct... 3. die 4. dead, gone 6. depart, finish 7. extinct 8. deceased 11. nonexistent

defy... 4. dare 5. beard, brave, stump 6. cartel 7. disdain, disobey 9. challenge

degenerate... 6. debase, wicked, worsen 7. atrophy, corrupt, degrade, deprave 8. decadent 10. retrogress

11. deteriorate

degeneration... 7. decline 9. decadence, turpitude 10. degeneracy 11. degradation 13. deterioration, retrogression

degradation... 5. shame 7. censure, decline 8. demotion, disgrace, ignominy 9. reduction, turpitude 10. debasement, punishment 11. humiliation 13. deterioration

degrade... 5. abase, lower 6. debase, demean, demote, depose, humble 7. corrupt 8. disgrace, dishonor 9. humiliate 10. depreciate

degrade (socially)... 8. déclassé

degree... 4. rank, step, tate 5. class, grade, order, point, scope, shade, stage, stair 6. extent 7. station 8. capacity, relation 9. intensity

degree (pert to)...

academic.. 8. bachelor 9. doctorate, masterate 11. engineering 13. baccalaureate

highest.. 13. summa cum laude

slight.. 5. shade 9. gradation

to what.. 9. howsoever 10. howsomever

dehydrate... 3. dry 5. dry up 6. wither 8. preserve 9. anhydride, dessicate, evaporate, exsiccate

deify... 5. exalt 7. ennoble, glorify, idolize 8. enshrine 11. apotheosize, immortalize

deign... 7. consent 9. vouchsafe 10. condescend

deity... 2. El 3. Dea, God 4. Deus, deva 5. numen 6. Elohim 7. goddess, godhead, godhood 8. Almighty, Divinity, Immortal 12. Supreme Being

deity (aboriginal)... 4. mana, Zemi 5. huaca, wakan 6. manito (manitou), nagual, orenda, pokunt 8. tamanoas

deity (pert to)...

avenging.. 6. Erinys 7. Alastor, Anteros

destroying.. 4. Siva (Shiva)

evil.. 5. Sebek (crocodile-headed)

hearth.. 5. Vesta

household.. 3. Lar 7. Penates

human sacrifice.. 6. Moloch

judge of the dead.. 4. Yama

love.. 4. Amor, Eros 5. Cupid

mockery.. 5. Momus

music.. 6. Apollo

solar.. 5. Mentu (Ment, falcon-headed)

sun.. 2. Ra

supreme.. 6. Ormazd

two-faced.. 5. Janus

underworld.. 3. Dis 4. Gwyn 5. Pluto 6. Osiris

war.. 4. Ares

woodland.. 3. Pan 4. faun 5. satyr 7. silenus

dejected... 3. sad 5. amort 6. abased, droopy 8. à la mort, lowered 8. downcast 9. depressed, prostrate 10. despondent 11. downhearted, low-spirited

dejection... 7. lowness, sadness

10. depression, melancholy
11. despondency

Delaware...
beach.. 8. Rehoboth
capital.. 5. Dover
church (oldest Prot).. 9. Old Swedes
city.. 5. Lewes 9. New Castle
  10. Wilmington (Fort Christina, 1638)
corporation.. 6. DuPont
product.. 9. chemicals 13. Blue Hen chicks
river.. 8. Delaware 10. Brandywine
State admission.. 5. first
State motto.. 22. Liberty and Independence
State nickname.. 5. First 7. Diamond

delay... 3. lag 4. halt, mora, stay, wait 5. block, check, dally, defer, demur, pause, tarry 6. arrest, detain, hinder, impede, loiter, retard 7. confine, setback 8. lateness, obstruct, postpone, reprieve, slow–down 9. detention, hindrance 10. cunctation, moratorium 13. procrastinate 15. procrastination

delayed... 4. late, slow 5. tardy 7. belayed, overdue 10. behindhand

delectable... 6. savory 8. luscious, pleasing 9. ambrosial, delicious 10. delightful 11. scrumptious

delegate... 4. name, send 6. assign, commit, depute, deputy, legate 7. appoint, consign, entrust 8. deputize 9. authorize 10. commission 12. commissioner 14. representative

delete... 4. dele 5. erase 6. cut out, excise, remove 7. edit out, expunge 9. eradicate 10. obliterate

deleterious... 7. harmful, hurtful, noxious 9. injurious 10. pernicious, prejudiced 11. destructive, detrimental, prejudicial

deletion... 4. stet 7. apocope 8. excision 9. expunging

delf, delft... 3. pit 4. mine 6. quarry

Delhi... 7. capital (Ind)

deliberate... 4. cool, muse, pore, slow 5. study, think, weigh 6. ponder 7. discuss, reflect, studied 8. consider, measured, prepense 9. calculate, leisurely, speculate, unhurried, voluntary 11. contemplate, intentional, premeditate 12. premeditated 13. dispassionate

deliberately... 6. slowly 7. tardily 8. by design 9. expressly, purposely, willfully 13. intentionally

delicacy... 4. cate, tact 5. snack, taste 6. caviar, luxury, nicety, tidbit 7. finesse, frailty, tenuity 8. fineness, niceness, softness, subtlety 9. exactness, fragility, precision 10. daintiness, refinement, slightness 11. sensitivity

delicate... 3. sly 4. fine, lacy, nice, soft 5. frail, light 6. dainty, mignon, petite, pretty, queasy, subtle, tender 7. elegant, fragile, minikin, refined, tenuous 8. araneous, graceful, luscious, tasteful 9. exquisite,

sensitive 10. fastidious, meticulous, scrupulous 11. considerate

delicious... 5. tasty 8. luscious 9. ambrosial, nectarean 10. delightful, nectareous

delight... 3. joy 4. glee 5. amuse, bliss, charm, exult, mirth 6. divert, please, ravish, regale, relish 7. enchant, gratify, overjoy 8. pleasure 9. delectate, enrapture, happiness 13. gratification

delightful... 6. lovely, savory 7. amusing, winsome 8. charming, engaging, pleasant 9. appealing, delicious, enjoyable 10. enchanting 11. fascinating

delineate... 3. map 4. draw, limn, line 5. trace 6. define, depict 7. outline, picture, portray 8. describe 9. represent

delinquency... 7. default, failure 8. omission 9. violation 10. nonpayment 11. malfeasance, misdemeanor, misfeasance 13. nonobservance

deliquesce... 4. give, melt 6. ramify 7. liquefy 8. diminish, dissolve

delirious... 7. insane, raving 8. frenzied 9. wandering (mental) 14. disorientation

delirium... 4. fury, rage 6. frenzy, lunacy 7. madness, passion 8. insanity 9. phrenitis 10. aberration, excitement, unsaneness 11. derangement 13. hallucination

deliver... 4. free, give, save 5. speak 6. commit, impart, ransom, redeem, render, resign 7. consign, release, relieve 8. transfer 9. discharge, enunciate, extradite, surrender

deliver of evil spirits... 8. exorcise

deliver oration... 7. declaim

dell... 4. dale, dene, vale 5. slade 6. dalles (pl), dingle, ravine, valley

Delos...
famed for.. 5. ruins 10. Stone Lions
island group.. 8. Cyclades
sea.. 6. Aegean

Delphi, Delphoi (Gr)...
modern name.. 6. Kastri
oracle.. 7. Delphic 8. Delphian
priestess.. 6. Pythia

delude... 3. jig 4. dupe, flam, fool, hoax 5. elude, trick 6. befool 7. beguile, deceive, mislead 9. bamboozle, frustrate, victimize 11. double–cross

deluge... 5. flood 6. drench 7. freshet, Niagara, torrent 8. cataract, flooding, inundate, overflow, submerge, The Flood 9. cataclysm, overwhelm 10. oversupply 14. superabundance

delusion... 4. ruse 6. mirage 7. fallacy, fantasm 8. illusion, phantasm 9. deception 10. misleading 13. hallucination

delve... 3. dig 4. mine, till 5. gouge, scoop, spade 6. exhume 8. excavate

demand... 3. ask, COD, cry, dun, fee 4. call, need 5. claim, query 6. elicit 7. require 8. exaction, question

9. requisite, ultimatum
11. requirement, requisition

demeanor, demeanour... 4. mien
7. bearing, conduct, posture
8. behavior, carriage
11. comportment

demented... 3. mad 4. daft, loco, luny
5. crazy, loony 6. crazed, insane
7. cracked 8. deranged
10. unbalanced 11. disoriented

Demeter... 7. goddess (Agric)

demigod... 4. hero 5. satyr (sylvan)
6. Triton 7. godling, half–god
10. semidivine

demise... 5. death, lease 6. convey
7. decease 8. bequeath
10. alienation, conveyance

demit... 4. quit 5. leave 6. resign,
vacate 8. abdicate 10. relinquish
11. resignation

demiurgic... 8. creative 9. formative

demivolt... 4. jump 5. vault (half)
6. curvet 8. capriole

Democrat (Polit slang)... 6. Hunker

demoded... 5. passe 6. passed
10. out of style

demolish... 4. rase, raze, ruin, undo
5. wreck 7. destroy, shatter
9. devastate, dismantle, overthrow
11. disassemble

demon, daemon... 3. hag, imp, nat
4. atua, jinn, Mara, ogre, Rahu
5. asura, devil, Eolis, fiend, genie,
jinni (jinnee), lamia, Satan 6. afreet
7. Amaimon, villain 8. Asmodeus
9. cacodemon (cacodaemon)

demoniac... 8. devilish, fiendish

demons (pert to)...
adjurers.. 9. exorcists
assembly of.. 6. sabbat
charm against.. 10. demonifuge
possessed of.. 8. demoniac
theory of.. 10. demonology
worship of.. 11. demonolatry

demonstrate... 4. show 5. prove
6. evince, typify 7. display, explain,
portray 8. manifest 9. exemplify

demonstrative... 7. gushing 8. effusive
9. emotional 10. indicative
11. explanatory 12. affectionate,
illustrative

Demosthenes (Gr)... 6. orator
(greatest)

demur... 4. stay 5. delay, pause, tarry
6. linger, object (to) 7. scruple
8. demurrer, hesitate 9. objection
12. irresolution

demure... 3. coy, mim, shy 4. prim,
smug 5. grave, staid, timid
6. sedate, solemn, stuffy 7. bashful,
prudish, serious 8. decorous

den... 4. cave, dell, lair, nest, room
5. cavea (anc), group (scouts), haunt,
study 6. cavern, grotto, hollow,
ravine 7. retreat 8. hideaway

denial... 5. cross 7. refusal
8. demurrer, negation 9. disavowal,
disowning, rejection 10. refutation
11. deprivation 12. disallowance
13. disaffirmance

denizen... 3. cit 6. native 7. citizen,
dweller, hellion (of hell) 9. indweller

10. inhabitant 11. cosmopolite

Denmark... see also *Danish*
anc name.. 5. Thule
capital.. 10. Copenhagen
city.. 6. Nyborg (Fyn Isl), Odense
7. Aalborg 8. Elsinore
founder.. 7. Absalon (Axel)
Hamlet's grave.. 8. Elsinore
island possession.. 6. Faroes
9. Greenland
peninsula.. 7. Jutland
river.. 5. Guden
ruler (anc).. 6. Canute (Kanute)

denomination... 3. ism 4. cult, name,
sect 5. class, party, value 6. church,
number, school 7. society
8. category 10. persuasion
11. appellation, designation,
stipulation

denote... 4. mark, mean, note, show
5. imply 6. convey 7. bespeak,
betoken, connote, express, purport,
signify 8. indicate 10. denominate

denoting (pert to)...
equal pressure.. 8. isobaric
final end (Gram).. 5. telic
usual action.. 9. usitative

denouement... 3. end 5. issue
6. result 7. outcome (plot)
8. solution 10. revelation

denounce... 4. damn 6. accuse, assail,
scathe 7. arraign, censure, condemn,
upbraid 9. reprobate 10. denunciate,
stigmatize

de novo... 3. new 4. anew 5. fresh,
newly 6. afresh

dense... 4. dewy, firm 5. close, crass,
gross, heavy, solid, thick 6. opaque,
stupid 7. compact, crowded
8. populous, thickset 11. thickheaded

density... 4. dord (Chem) 8. dumbness
9. stupidity 11. compactness

dent... 3. pit 4. dint 5. dinge, notch,
tooth 6. batter, hollow, indent
7. imprint 10. depression, impression
11. indentation

dentagra... 7. forceps 9. dentalgia,
toothache

dental (pert to)...
appliance.. 3. dam 6. scaler
7. forceps
drill.. 8. cavitron
filling.. 5. inlay
measure.. 10. dentimeter
toothache.. 8. dentagra 9. dentalgia

dentate... 7. serried, toothed

dentine... 5. ivory

dentist... 10. exodontist
12. orthodontist 11. prosthodontist

denude... 4. bate 5. scalp, strip
6. divest, expose, unrobe 7. uncover

denunciation... 6. menace, threat
7. inveigh 8. reproach
10. accusation 11. arraignment

deny... 4. nego 5. debar 6. abjure,
impugn, negate, recant, refuse,
renege 7. confute, disavow, dispute,
gainsay 8. disclaim, forswear,
traverse 9. repudiate 10. contradict,
contravene, controvert

deodar (species)... 5. cedar

depart... 2. go 3. die 4. exit, quit

5. leave, mosey **6.** decamp, demise, egress, perish **7.** abscond, vamoose **8.** separate (Chem), withdraw

depraved... **4.** evil, vile **6.** shrewd, wicked **7.** corrupt, immoral, vicious **8.** vitiated **9.** debauched, dissolute, perverted **10.** degenerate

depravity... **8.** depraved **9.** turpitude **10.** corruption, wickedness **15.** incorrigibility

depreciate... **4.** fall **5.** lower, slump **6.** debase, lessen, reduce, shrink **7.** cheapen, deflate **8.** belittle, discount, pejorate, vilipend **9.** disparage **10.** undervalue

depreciation... **8.** decrease, discount **9.** deflation **10.** cheapening, pejoration **12.** belittlement **13.** disparagement **14.** undervaluation

depredator... **5.** thief **6.** looter, robber **7.** spoiler **8.** marauder, ravisher **9.** despoiler, plunderer

depress... **4.** dent, sink **5.** lower **6.** dampen, deepen, deject, indent, reduce, sadden **7.** flatten, imprint, oppress **8.** dispirit, enfeeble **10.** discourage

depressed... **3.** low, sad **4.** dire, sunk **6.** dismal, oblate **8.** dejected, downcast **9.** debruised (Her), flattened (vertically) **10.** dispirited **11.** downhearted **12.** disheartened

depressing... **5.** chill **6.** dismal, dreary, gloomy, somber **7.** joyless **9.** saddening **10.** melancholy

depression... **3.** col, dip, pit **4.** dent, fall **5.** blues, fossa (Anat), gloom, gully **6.** cavity, crater, ravine, trough, vapors **10.** melancholy **11.** despondency, humiliation

deprivation... **4.** loss, want **7.** deposal, ousting, removal **9.** privation, unseating **10.** divestment **11.** bereavement

deprive... **3.** rob **4.** take **5.** debar, mulct, strip **6.** divest, remove **7.** bereave, despoil **10.** dispossess

deprived of...
authority.. **9.** dethroned
life.. **5.** slain **6.** killed **12.** exterminated
limb.. **6.** maimed
natural qualities.. **9.** denatured
possessions.. **12.** expropriated
professional standing.. **8.** laicized
rank.. **7.** deposed
reason.. **8.** demented
vigor.. **6.** sapped **8.** deadened, unnerved **9.** enervated, enfeebled

depth... **5.** abyss, midst **6.** extent **9.** intensity **10.** profundity

depths... **3.** sea **5.** adyta (spiritual), ocean **6.** Davy Jones's locker

depute... **6.** assign, devote **7.** appoint **8.** delegate, deputize

deputy... **5.** agent, envoy, proxy, vicar **6.** legate **8.** alter ego **9.** alternate **10.** substitute

deracinate... **6.** evulse, unroot, uproot **7.** extract (forcibly)

deride... **3.** pan **4.** dupe, geck, gibe, jeer, mock, razz **5.** cheat, fleer, flout,

scoff, scorn, trick **6.** insult **8.** ridicule

derision... **5.** fleer, scorn **7.** asteism, mockery **8.** contempt, ridicule

derivation... **6.** effect, origin, source **7.** descent, lineage **9.** deduction, education, evolution **10.** derivative **12.** transmission

derivation of...
descent.. **7.** lineage **8.** pedigree **9.** genealogy
name (race, tribe).. **7.** eponymy
word.. **9.** etymology

derivative of...
bauxite.. **8.** aluminum
benzine.. **6.** phenol
coal tar.. **8.** creosote
flax.. **5.** linen
mercury.. **11.** quicksilver
milk.. **5.** lactic
morphine.. **6.** heroin
pitchblende.. **6.** radium **9.** uranium
sorrel.. **10.** oxalic acid

derogate... **5.** annul, decry **6.** repeal **7.** detract **8.** restrict, withdraw **9.** disparage

derogatory... **10.** detracting, detractory, pejorative **11.** deprecatory, disparaging **12.** depreciatory

derrick... **3.** rig **4.** spar **5.** crave, hoist, tower **6.** lifter, steeve, tackle **7.** hangman, staging

dervish... **4.** monk **5.** fakir, friar **6.** beggar, fakeer **7.** ascetic **11.** religionist

dervish cap... **3.** taj **4.** atef

dervishes...
howling.. **8.** Rufaiyah
wandering.. **12.** Kalandariyah
whirling, dancing.. **10.** Maulawiyah

descend... **4.** fall, sink **5.** deign, stoop **6.** alight, unbend **7.** decline **9.** gravitate **10.** condescend

descendant... **3.** son **5.** child, scion **8.** daughter, offshoot **9.** offspring

descendants... **5.** breed **7.** progeny **9.** posterity

descent... **4.** drop, fall, root **5.** birth, issue, scarp, slope, stock **7.** assault, decline, lineage **8.** ancestry, downfall, invasion (sea), pedigree **9.** declivity, incursion, posterity **10.** extraction **11.** degradation

describe... **4.** name **5.** paint, parse, state **6.** define, depict, relate **7.** explain, express, narrate, outline **9.** delineate, designate, represent **12.** characterize

description... **4.** idyl, kind, sort **5.** idyll **7.** account, version **8.** features, relation **9.** discourse, narration, narrative, portrayal **10.** definition **11.** delineation, explanation **14.** representation **18.** descriptio personae

descry... **3.** see **4.** espy, view **6.** behold, detect, reveal **7.** discern, observe, witness **8.** discover **9.** determine **11.** distinguish

Desdemona's husband... **7.** Othello

desecrate... **5.** abuse **6.** misuse **7.** profane, violate **8.** misapply

Deseret... **4.** Utah (1849)

desert... 3. due 4. bolt, fail 5. merit, oasis 6. defect, renege, reward 7. abandon, forsake 8. desolate 10. apostatize, relinquish, wilderness

desert (pert to)...
Africa.. 5. El Erg 6. Karroo
Algeria.. 3. Erg
Australia.. 10. Great Sandy 13. Great Victoria
beast.. 5. camel
dweller.. 4. Arab
Mongolia (Asia).. 4. Gobi
phenomenon.. 6. mirage
prospector.. 3. rat
ship.. 5. camel
shrub.. 5. ratem 6. Alhagi 7. juniper (Bib)
train, travelers.. 7. caravan
wind (hot).. 6. simoom (simoon) 7. sirocco

deserter... 3. rat 6. bolter 8. apostate, recreant, renegade, turncoat, turntail

deserved... 3. due 4. fair, just 5. rated 6. earned, worthy 7. condign, merited 8. rightful 9. justified, warranted 11. appropriate

deserving... 6. worthy 8. laudable 10. creditable, entitled to 11. commendable, meritorious 12. praiseworthy

desiccated... 3. dry 4. arid, sere 5. dried 6. seared 7. parched 9. preserved 10. dehydrated, exsiccated

design... 3. aim, art, end 4. draw, form, idea, mean, plan, plot 5. ettle 6. intent, layout, motive, object, scheme, sketch 7. destine, drawing, meaning, outline, pattern, propose 8. artifice, artistry, contrive 11. arrangement

design (pert to)...
carved.. 4. seme 5. cameo 8. intaglio
metal, glass.. 4. etch 6. niello
ornamental.. 9. medallion 10. needlework
pattern.. 5. batik 6. mosaic
skin.. 6. tattoo

designate... 3. fix, set 4. call, mark, name, show 5. state, style, title 6. select 7. appoint, entitle, specify 8. describe, indicate, nominate 9. determine, stipulate 10. denominate 11. distinguish 12. characterize

designation... 4. name 7. meaning 9. selection 10. indication 12. denomination 13. signification

desire... 3. yen 4. care, urge, want, wish 5. covet, crave, yearn 6. aspire, hunger, prefer, thirst 7. craving, longing, passion, request 8. appetite 9. appetency, eagerness 10. desiderium 11. inclination

desire (pert to)...
expectant.. 4. hope
greatly.. 6. aspire
liquid.. 6. thirst
ungovernable.. 5. mania

desirous... 4. avid 5. eager 6. ardent 7. envious, lustful, willing

8. covetous, spirited 9. ambitious 10. solicitous

desist... 2. ho 3. end 4. don't, halt, quit, stay, stop 5. cease 6. lay off 7. forbear, refrain 8. cut it out 11. discontinue

desk... 4. ambo, dais 5. board, table 6. pulpit 7. lectern, rostrum 8. kneehole 9. monocleid (monocleide), secretary 10. escritoire

desolate... 3. sad 4. arid, lorn, ruin 5. alone, bleak, drear, gaunt 6. barren, dismal, gloomy, lonely, ravage 7. forlorn 8. deserted, forsaken, solitary, wretched 9. destitute 10. depopulate 11. comfortless, uninhabited

desolation... 3. woe 4. ruin 5. gloom, grief, havoc, waste 6. ravage 7. sadness 10. gloominess, loneliness, melancholy 11. destitution, destruction, devastation, forlornness 12. depopulation, solitariness, wretchedness

despair... 11. desperation, despondency, forlornness 12. hopelessness

desperado... 5. brave 6. outlaw 7. ruffian 8. criminal 10. lawbreaker

desperate... 3. mad 4. rash, wild 7. frantic, furious 8. headlong, heedless, hopeless, reckless 10. despairing, desponding, distraught, infuriated 11. extravagant, precipitate 13. irretrievable

despicable... 4. base, vile 6. odious, shabby 8. terrible, unworthy, wretched 9. miserable 12. contemptible, contemptuous, disreputable, vilipendious

despise... 4. defy, hate 5. scorn, scout, spurn 6. detest, slight 7. contemn, disdain 8. vilipend 9. disregard

despised being... 6. pariah 7. outcast

despoil... 3. rip, rob 4. riot 5. reave, rifle, strip 6. divest, fleece, injure, ravage, ravish 7. bereave, debauch, deprive, disrobe, pillage, plunder 9. depredate

despondency... 7. despair 10. depression 11. desperation 13. heartlessness

despot... 4. czar (tsar), lord 6. master, satrap, tyrant 8. autocrat, dictator 9. patriarch

despotic... 8. arrogant 9. arbitrary, tyrannous 10. autocratic, tyrannical 11. dictatorial, patriarchal 12. governmental

dessert... 3. ice, pie 4. cake 5. fruit, glacé, sweet 6. mousse, pastry, sweets 7. parfait, pudding, sherbet, strudel 8. ice cream 10. shoofly pie

destination... 3. end 4. goal, port 5. bourn (bourne) 7. address, destiny 9. objective

destine... 4. doom, fate 5. allot 6. design, devote, intend, ordain 7. appoint 8. set apart 9. designate 10. foreordain, predestine 12. predetermine

destiny... 3. end, lot, ure (anc)
4. bahi, doom, eure, fate, goal
5. karma, stars 6. Kismet 7. fortune
11. destination
destitute... 4. void 5. needy 6. bereft,
devoid 7. forlorn, lacking
8. bankrupt, forsaken, homeless
9. abandoned, penniless
10. down-and-out
destitution... 6. penury 7. poverty
11. deprivation 12. helplessness
destroy... 3. end 4. kill, rase, raze,
root, ruin, sack, slay, undo 5. abash,
annul, erase 6. ravage 7. abolish,
consume, nullify, unbuild
8. decimate, demolish, overturn
9. dismantle, eradicate
10. annihilate, neutralize
11. exterminate
destroyer... 3. hun 6. ruiner, vandal
7. marplot, wrecker 8. nihilist,
saboteur 9. iconclast (of images)
11. torpedo boat
destroying angel... 6. Danite
7. Abaddon, Amanita (fungus)
8. Apollyon
destruction... 4. loss, ruin 5. havoc,
waste 7. killing 8. downfall,
genocide, ravaging, sabotage,
shambles 9. holocaust, overthrow,
perdition, ruination 10. decimation,
demolition, desolation, extinction,
subversion 11. devastation,
dissolution, extirpation
13. extermination
destructive... 5. fatal 6. deadly, mortal
7. baleful, fateful, ruinous 8. aneretic
(anaeretic), ravaging 10. calamitous,
catawampus, pernicious, subversive
desuetude... 6. disuse, nonuse
9. cessation 12. obsolescence
13. nonemployment
14. discontinuance
desultory... 4. idle 5. hasty 6. roving,
wanton 7. aimless, cursory, wayward
8. rambling, unsteady, wavering
9. deviative, orderless, unsettled
10. discursive, inconstant
detach... 4. part, wean 5. sever
7. disjoin, isolate 8. disunite,
separate, withdraw 9. disengage
detached... 4. free 5. alone, aloof,
scarp 7. detaché, retired, severed
8. isolated, secluded, separate,
solitary 9. unrelated, withdrawn
11. unconnected 12. disconnected
detachment... 8. disunion
9. aloneness, aloofness, isolation,
seclusion, unconcern 10. separation
11. disjunction 14. demobilization
detail... 4. item, unit 6. assign
7. appoint, itemize, minutia, narrate,
specify 9. enumerate, narrative
10. particular 12. technicality
details... 6. trivia 8. minutiae
11. particulars
detain... 4. hold, keep, stop 5. check,
delay 6. arrest, hinder, intern, retard
8. imprison, restrain, withhold
detect... 3. see, spy 4. show, spot,
tail 6. accuse, descry, reveal
7. discern, find out, uncover

8. discover, perceive 9. recognize
detective... 4. dick 6. beagle, sleuth,
tailer, tracer 7. gumshoe, spotter
8. exposing, flatfoot, Hawkshaw,
mouchard 9. operative
12. investigator
detent... 3. dog 4. pawl 5. catch,
click, fence 6. tongue 7. ratchet
detention... 5. delay 6. duress
7. detinue 9. captivity, hindrance
10. detainment, internment
11. restraining, retardation,
withholding 12. imprisonment
deter... 5. daunt, delay, repel
6. divert, hinder 7. prevent
8. restrain 10. discourage, disincline
deterge... 5. purge 6. purify
7. cleanse 8. depurate 9. elutriate
detergent... 4. soap 7. cleaner,
purging, saponin (saponine), smectic,
solvent 8. cleanser, medicine, purifier
9. cleansing 10. abstergent, lixiviator
deteriorate... 4. wear 6. impair,
weaken, worsen 10. degenerate,
retrogress
deterioration... 5. decay 7. decline
9. decadence 10. debasement,
declension, impairment, perversion
11. degradation 12. degeneration
13. retrogression
determinate... 5. fixed 6. cymose
7. certain, special 8. definite,
resolute, resolved, specific 9. arbitrary
10. definitive, invariable
11. established, unqualified
determination... 4. will 5. limit, proof
6. choice 7. purpose, resolve, verdict
8. decision, firmness, judgment
9. impulsion 10. conclusion,
definition, discussion, resolution,
settlement 11. disputation,
measurement, termination
12. decisiveness, dijudication,
resoluteness 13. specification
determine... 3. end 5. impel, learn,
prove, state 6. assess, choose,
decide, define, direct, ordain, settle
7. delimit, resolve, specify
8. conclude, discover 9. arbitrate,
ascertain, stipulate, terminate,
variously 10. dijudicate, foreordain
determined... 3. set 4. sure 5. fixed
6. mulish 7. assured, cinched,
decided, settled 8. foregone,
perverse, resolute, stubborn
9. obstinate, pigheaded
detest... 4. hate 5. abhor 8. execrate
9. abominate
detestable... 6. odious 7. hateful
8. accursed, terrible 9. abhorrent,
execrable, loathsome, obnoxious
10. abominable 12. contemptible
dethrone... 6. depose, disbar, divest
7. uncrown 8. disbench
detonation... 4. bang, boom 5. blast
7. blowout 8. backfire 9. discharge,
explosion 10. combustion
detract... 5. deduce, deduct, vilify
7. asperse, traduce 8. belittle,
derogate, distract, subtract, withdraw
9. disparage 10. depreciate
detraction... 5. delay 7. calumny,

slander 9. aspersion 10. belittling
11. distraction, subtraction
detriment... 4. hurt, loss 6. damage,
injury 8. mischief, weakness
10. impairment, impediment
12. disadvantage
detrimental... 7. baleful, baneful,
harmful, hurtful, noxious 9. injurious
10. pernicious 11. deleterious,
mischievous, prejudicial
15. disadvantageous
Deus Fidius... 7. Jupiter
Deus vobiscum... 12. God be with
you
Deus vult... 8. God wills (anc cry)
deuterogamy... 6. digamy
Deuteronomy (pert to)...
comprising.. 10. law of Moses
Fifth Book of.. 10. Pentateuch
meaning.. 11. repeated law (of
Moses)
devastate... 4. rape, ruin, sack
5. havoc, strip, waste 6. ravage
7. destroy, pillage, plunder, scourge
8. demolish, desolate 10. depopulate
devastation... 4. ruin 5. havoc, waste
6. ravage 7. scourge
develop... 4. grow 5. arise, ripen,
train 6. appear, detect, evolve,
expand, mature, reveal 7. advance,
convert, enlarge, expound, further,
improve, perfect, promote
8. discover, generate 9. elaborate
(details)
developed... 4. ripe, zoon 5. adult
6. mature, mellow 7. grownup
8. improved 9. perfected
10. precocious
development... 6. growth 7. changes,
endysis 8. increase, maturity
9. evolution, expansion, formation,
unfolding 10. maturation
11. elaboration, improvement,
ontogenesis 12. phylogenesis
devest... 5. strip 6. denude, divest
7. deprive, undress 8. alienate
Devi (Hind)... 3. Uma 4. Kali
5. Durga, Gauri 6. Chandi, Shakti
7. heroine, Parvati 8. divinity
9. Haimavati
deviate... 3. err, yaw 4. hade, miss,
slew, vary, veer 5. sheer, stray
6. change, depart, swerve, wander
7. deflect, digress, diverge
deviation... 3. yaw 5. lapse 6. change
7. circuit, synesis 8. aberrant
9. aberrance, deformity, departure,
diverging, obliquity, variation
10. deflection, difference, digressing,
digression, distortion, divergence
11. abnormality 12. eccentricity
device... 4. plan, tool 5. motto, shift,
trick 6. design, desire, gadget,
scheme 7. adjunct, compass, project,
purpose 8. artifice, insignia
9. appliance, expedient, implement,
invention, stratagem 10. instrument
11. contrivance
device (pert to)...
bark peeling.. 8. stripper
clamping.. 4. vise 7. pincers
distilling.. 7. alembic

fabric stretching.. 7. stenter
heating.. 4. etna 5. stove
hoisting.. 5. crane, davit, lewis
6. garnet 7. derrick 8. elevator
9. parbuckle
leveling.. 6. gimbal
measuring.. 4. gage, tape 5. chain,
gauge, meter, ruler 9. ergometer,
yardstick 10. micrometer
nautical.. 4. bitt 5. cleat, otter
6. becket 8. paravane
regulating.. 5. valve 9. remontoir
spraying.. 8. atomizer 9. sprinkler
steering.. 4. helm 5. wheel 6. rudder,
tiller
stopping.. 5. brake, sprag
devil... 3. imp 4. deil, deva, evil, haze
5. annoy, demon, error, fiend, grill,
ruler (of Hell), Satan, tease
7. hellion, serpent, tempter, torment
8. printer's 9. archenemy, daredevil,
dust devil
devil (pert to)...
dog.. 6. marine
bird.. 3. owl 5. swift 10. goatsucker
fish.. 3. ray 5. manta, whale (gray)
7. octopus
grass.. 7. Bermuda
lore.. 10. demonology
tree.. 4. dita
Devil, the... 5. Deuce, Eblis, Satan
6. Azazel, Belial, Diablo, Teufel
7. Ahriman, Amaimon (Amammion),
diavolo, Evil One, Lucifer, Old Nick,
Sammael, Shaitan (Sheitan)
8. Apollyon, Asmodeus, Diabolos
9. Archenemy, Archfiend, Beelzebub
11. Auld Clootie 14. Mephistopheles
devilish... 5. cruel 6. daring, rakish,
wicked 7. extreme, hellish, satanic
8. fiendish, infernal 9. chthonian
10. demoniacal 11. mischievous
deviltry... 6. malice 7. cruelty, devilry
8. mischief 9. diablerie, diabolism
10. black magic, wickedness
12. fiendishness
devious... 6. errant, erring, roving,
sinful 7. oblique, vagrant, winding
8. rambling, tortuous 9. deviative,
eccentric 10. circuitous
11. out-of-the-way
14. unconventional
devise... 3. aim 4. form, plan
5. array, build, frame 6. create,
divide, evolve, invent, scheme, will to
7. appoint, arrange, bequest,
concoct, fashion 8. bequeath,
contrive 9. fabricate 10. distribute,
excogitate 11. distinguish
deviser of IQ test... 5. Binet
devoid... 4. free, void 5. empty
6. faulty, vacant 7. without
9. destitute 11. nonexistent
devoid of...
feeling.. 9. apathetic, insensate
interest.. 6. jejune
devote... 3. use, vow 5. apply
6. employ, hallow, resign 7. address,
consign, destine 8. dedicate, set
apart 10. consecrate 11. appropriate
devoted... 5. loyal, pious, vowed
6. doomed, loving 7. zealous

8. addicted, constant, faithful, friendly, obedient 9. dedicated, engrossed, patriotic

devotee... 3. fan, ist, nun 4. monk 6. votary 7. epicure, fanatic, Pietist 8. aesthete (esthete), partisan

devotion... 4. love, zeal 5. ardor, piety 6. novena, prayer 7. pietism, worship 9. addiction, adoration, constancy 10. attachment, dedication, devoutness, friendship 11. devotedness, earnestness, engrossment 12. consecration 13. appropriation, religiousness

devour... 3. eat 4. bolt, gulp, wolf 5. gorge, use up, waste 6. absorb, engulf 7. consume, engorge, swallow (up) 8. prey upon 9. devastate 10. annihilate

devout... 4. holy, warm 5. godly, pious 6. hearty, solemn 7. cordial, devoted, saintly, sincere, zealous 8. reverent 9. religious, righteous 10. worshipful

dew... 4. rime 5. bedew, bloom, roris

dewy... 5. roral, roric

dexterity... 3. art 5. knack, magic, skill 7. ability, address, aptness, finesse, sleight 8. aptitude, deftness, facility 9. smartness 10. adroitness 15. right-handedness

dexterous... 3. apt 4. deft, yare 5. adept, handy, quick, ready 6. adroit, artful, clever 7. skilful 8. skilful 11. right-handed

dextral... 5. right (to the) 9. favorable

diabolical... 5. cruel 6. wicked 7. beastly, demonic, hellish, satanic, ungodly 8. damnable, demoniac, devilish, fiendish, infernal

diacritic... 4. mark 5. point 7. symptom 10. diagnostic 14. distinguishing

diacritical mark... 5. breve, tilde 6. tittle 9. diaeresis (dieresis)

diadem... 5. crown, tiara 6. anadem, circle, emblem, empire, fillet 7. coronet, headband, insignia, ornament 11. sovereignty

diaeresis, dieresis... 4. mark 5. break 8. division 10. resolution

diagnose... 7. analyze 8. construe 9. interpret

diagnosis... 8. analysis, decision, nosology 9. prognosis 14. interpretation

diagonal... 4. bias 7. oblique 8. bendwise (Her) 10. transverse 11. cater-corner 13. cater-cornered

diagram... 4. draw, icon, plan, plot, tree 5. chart, epure, gamut, graph 6. design 7. drawing 9. blueprint

dial... 4. disk 5. plate 8. horologe 9. indicator, timepiece 11. chronometer

dialect... 5. idiom, lingo 6. patois, speech 7. diction 8. language, locution, parlance 10. vernacular

dialect (pert to)...
Afrikaans.. 4. Taal
Aramaic.. 6. Syriac

Aryan.. 4. Pali
provincial.. 6. patois
Semitic.. 4. Geez

diameter... 2. pi (3.1416) 4. bore 5. width 6. module, radius 7. breadth, caliber (calibre) 9. thickness

diametric, diametrical... 6. averse 7. adverse 8. antipode, opposite 9. antipodal, diametral

diamond... 3. gem, ice 5. cards, field (baseball), jager, jewel, plane 6. carbon 7. adamant, infield, lozenge, rhombus 8. treasure

diamond (pert to)...
crystal.. 7. glassie
cutting.. 4. bort
cutting cups.. 3. dop
famed.. 4. Pitt 5. Sancy 6. Orloff 7. Lesotho (601 carat) 8. Cullinan, Koh-i-noor 10. Excelsior 10. Great Mogul 14. Star of the South
surface.. 5. facet
weight.. 5. carat (karat)

Diamond State... 8. Delaware

diaphanous... 4. fine, thin 5. filmy, gauzy, lucid, sheer 6. flimsy 9. gossamery 11. translucent, transparent

diaphragm... 4. wall 6. middle, septum 7. midriff 9. partition

diary... 3. log 6. record 7. journal 8. register 9. chronicle 13. autobiography

diaskeuast... 6. editor 7. reviser

diatribe... 6. screed, tirade 7. lecture 8. berating, harangue 9. invective, philippic 10. discussion (prolonged)

dice... 3. cog, die (sing) 4. cube, game, sice (6's) 5. bones, craps, cubes 7. ivories, tessera

Dickens characters... 3. Tim 4. Dora, Nell 5. Fagin, Miggs, Sikes 6. Cuttle 7. Barnaby 9. Pecksniff 10. Chuzzlewit 11. Oliver Twist

Dickens pseudonym... 3. Boz

dictate... 3. law 4. rule 5. maxim, order, utter 6. advise, dictum, enjoin, impose 7. command, deliver, require, suggest 9. prescribe 10. injunction

dictatorial... 5. bossy 6. lordly 7. pompous 8. absolute, arrogant, despotic, dogmatic, oracular, positive 9. imperious, masterful, pragmatic 10. autocratic, dogmatical, imperative, peremptory 11. categorical, domineering, magisterial, opinionated, overbearing 13. authoritative

diction... 5. style 8. language, parlance, phrasing 9. elocution 10. vocabulary 11. enunciation, phraseology 14. expressiveness

dictionary... 5. words 7. calepin, lexicon 8. wordbook 9. reference 10. vocabulary 11. terminology

dictionary compiler... 7. Webster (Noah) 13. lexicographer

dictum... 3. saw 5. adage, maxim 6. saying 7. opinion, precept, proverb 8. aphorism, apothegm 11. declaration

didactic... 8. teaching 9. mentorial 10. preceptive 11. instructive

dido... 5. antic, caper, prank, trick 6. frolic

Dido (also Elissa)... 5. Queen (of Carthage) 8. Princess (Tyrian)

die... see also *dice* 4. fade, mold, pass, seal, wane 5. stamp 6. expire, perish, recede, vanish, wither 7. decease, succumb 8. languish 12. extinguished (to be)

die–hard... 4. Tory 11. British Army 12. Conservative

dies... 3. day

dies atri... 9. black days

dies faustus... 13. favorable omen (day of)

diet... 4. fare 5. board 6. Hoftag, ration, viands 7. Council, Landtag, regimen 8. assembly, Kreistag 9. allowance, nutrition, Reichstag 10. Parliament

Diet (of)... 5. Worms (1521) 6. Speyer (1529), Spires 8. Augsburg (1530)

dietetics... 8. sitology 9. nutrition 12. biochemistry, dietotherapy

differ... 4. vary 5. clash 7. dispute, dissent, quarrel 8. disagree

difference... 3. sum 5. shade 6. nuance 8. variance 10. inequality, unlikeness 11. contrariety, distinction, distinguish 12. disagreement, discriminate 13. differentiate, dissimilarity

different... 4. many 5. novel, other 6. divers, sundry, unlike 7. diverse, several, unequal, unusual, variant 8. assorted, contrary, distinct, manifold, opposite, separate, variform 9. divergent, otherwise 10. dissimilar, variegated 11. diversified 13. heterogeneous

different place... 9. elsewhere 10. otherwhere

difficulty... 3. bar, rub 4. clog, crux, knot, snag 5. cavil, check, demur, nodus 6. plight, scrape, strait 7. barrier, problem, trouble 8. obstacle 9. hindrance 10. impediment, ruggedness 11. obstruction 12. disagreement

difficulty in swallowing... 9. dysphagia

diffidence... 5. doubt, qualm 7. anxiety, modesty 8. distrust, humility, timidity 10. hesitation 11. bashfulness 12. apprehension

diffident... 3. coy, shy 5. timid 6. modest 7. anxious 8. doubtful, reserved, retiring 9. shrinking, unwilling 11. distrustful 12. apprehensive

diffuse... 4. full, shed 5. strew 6. expand, extend, prolix 7. copious, perplex, pervade, publish, radiate, refract, verbose 8. disperse 9. redundant 10. widespread

diffused... 5. loose 6. sparse 7. flowing 9. dispersed

diffusion... 7. osmosis 9. pervasion, radiation 10. dispersion, refraction

dig... 3. jab 4. find, grub, mine, open, pion, prod, root 5. delve, dwell, spade 6. exhume, loosen, pierce, plunge, search, thrust 7. extract, unearth 8. excavate 10. understand

digamy... 11. deuterogamy 12. twice married (legally)

digest... 4. code 5. brief 6. abrégé, codify 7. epitome, Pandect 8. abstract, classify, synopsis 10. assimilate, compendium

digestion... 6. pepsis 8. eupepsia 9. dyspepsia, ingestion 10. absorption 12. alimentation, assimilation

digestive secretions... 4. bile, gall 6. pepsin, rennin 7. chalone, gastric, glucase, hormone, maltase 8. salivary, thyroxin 9. endocrine 10. intestinal, pancreatic

digestive tract... 7. enteron 15. alimentary canal

digger... 3. loy, pal 4. plow, wasp 5. spade 6. Indian, sapper 7. comrade, soldier 8. Levelers 9. excavator 12. New Zealander

digit... 3. toe 4. unit 5. thumb 6. finger, number (under 10) 7. dewclaw, integer, measure

digits repeated... 8. repetend

digitus... 6. finger, tarsus 8. dactylus

dignified... 5. grand, lofty, manly, sober, staid 6. august, graced, sedate 7. courtly, pompous, togated 8. decorous, ennobled, imposing, majestic 9. venerable 11. ceremonious 12. aristocratic

dignify... 5. exalt, grace, honor 7. elevate, ennoble 9. solemnize 11. distinguish

dignitary... 3. don 4. rank 5. mogul 6. priest, sachem 7. magnate, notable, prelate 9. clergyman

dignity... 4. rank 5. grace, honor 6. status 7. decorum, majesty 8. nobility, prestige, standing 9. loftiness, nobleness 10. excellence, sedateness

digraph... 8. ligature 9. diphthong

digress... 4. veer 5. shift 6. swerve, wander 7. deviate, diverge 8. divagate 9. turn aside 10. transgress

digression... 4. loop 6. ecbole 7. circuit, episode 8. excursus 9. deviation, excursion, obliquity 10. discussion

digressive... 8. rambling 9. deviative, excursive, wandering 10. circuitous, discursive

dike, dyke... 3. bar, dig, gap 4. bank, gulf, ha-ha, mole, pond, pool 5. ditch, levee, mound 7. barrier, channel 8. causeway, estacade 9. earthwork 10. embankment 11. watercourse 13. fortification

diked land... 6. polder

dike rock... 7. odinite

dilapidation... 4. ruin 5. decay, waste 7. breakup 8. disrepair 10. impairment 11. dissolution 13. decomposition 14. disintegration

dilate... 5. bulge, swell, widen
6. expand 7. distend, enlarge, inflate
9. expatiate

dilation... 7. ectasia, ectasis
8. swelling 9. expansion
10. dilatation, distension

dilatory... 3. lax 4. slow 5. slack,
tardy 6. fabian, remiss 8. backward,
delaying, inactive, sluggish
10. behindhand 13. lackadaisical
15. procrastinating

dilemma... 4. trap 5. brike (obs),
snare 8. argument, quandary
10. perplexity 11. alternative,
predicament

dilettante... 7. amateur, dabbler,
devotee, esthete (aesthete)

diligence... 4. care, heed 6. effort
7. caution 8. industry, sedulity
9. assiduity, attention, constancy
10. stagecoach 11. application,
earnestness, painstaking
12. heedlessness, perseverance,
sedulousness 15. industriousness

diligent... 4. busy 6. active 7. operose
8. sedulous 9. assiduous, attentive,
laborious 11. industrious, persevering

dill, dill seed... 4. anet, herb 5. anise
(Bib) 6. fennel

dillydally... 3. lag 6. linger, loiter,
trifle 9. vacillate 12. shilly–shally
13. procrastinate

dilute... 3. cut 4. thin 6. debase,
rarefy, reduce, weaken 8. lengthen
9. attenuate 10. adulterate
12. denaturalize

diluted... 4. thin, weak 7. reduced,
thinned, watered 10. attenuated

dim... 4. dull, fade, pale 5. bleak,
blear, faint 6. darken 7. darkish,
dimness, eclipse, obscure 8. overcast
10. caliginous, indistinct, mysterious

dimension... 4. size 6. extent, height,
length 7. breadth 8. magnitude,
thickness 11. measurement
13. circumference

diminish... 3. ebb 4. bate, fade, pare,
ploy, wane 5. abase, abate, lower,
peter, taper 6. lessen, recede,
reduce, weaken 7. curtail, dwindle
8. decrease, subtract 9. disparage

diminution... 5. abate, taper 7. litotes
8. decrease, lowering 9. decrement,
lessening, reduction 10. moderation

diminutive... 3. wee 4. runt, slip
5. minny, small 6. bantam, little,
peewee, petite 7. bendlet

diminutive suffix... 2. el, ie 3. ole,
ule 4. ette

dimmer... 8. rheostat

din... 4. ding 5. clang, noise
6. clamor, hubbub, racket, rattle,
tumult, uproar 7. clatter, turmoil
9. commotion

dingle... 4. dale, dell, glen, ring, vale
6. jingle, tingle, tinkle, valley
7. tremble 9. storm door

dining room... 4. hall 5. salon
6. spence 7. cenacle 8. mess hall
9. refectory 12. salle à manger

dining science... 10. aristology

dinosaur... 7. reptile 8. sauropod

9. Sauropoda 10. Diplodocus,
Morosaurus 11. Ornithopoda,
Stegosaurus 12. Brontosaurus,
Ceratosaurus, Megalosaurus,
Palaeosaurus 13. Atlantosaurus,
Tyrannosaurus

diocese... 3. see 6. parish 8. district,
province 9. bishopric 12. jurisdiction

Diocletian martyr (Rome)... 5. Agnes

Dionysus (pert to)...
birthplace.. 6. Thebes
father.. 4. Zeus
festival.. 8. Dionysia
god of (Gr).. 4. wine (Bacchus, later)
10. vegetation
lover.. 6. Selene
mother.. 6. Semele

Dioscuri, The (Gr Myth)... 4. cult
5. twins (Castor and Pollux)
8. Castores 10. Polydeuces

dip... 3. dap, dib, sop 4. bail, dunk,
lade 5. merge, merse, pitch, rinse,
scoop, slope, souse 6. candle,
plunge 7. baptize, immerse
9. declivity 10. pickpocket 11. hors
d'oeuvre

diphthong, dipthong... 5. sound
7. digraph 8. ligature

diploma... 8. testamur 9. sheepskin
10. credential 11. certificate,
testimonial

diplomacy... 4. tact 7. address,
cunning 9. dexterity 10. artfulness,
discretion 11. arbitration,
diplomatism, negotiation, savoir–faire

diplomat... 5. doyen (head), envoy
6. consul 7. attaché 8. emissary,
minister 10. ambassador, politician
15. chargé d'affaires, plenipotentiary

diplomatic... 6. crafty 7. cunning
8. consular 11. mediatorial

diplomatic corps, staff... 7. embassy
8. legation 17. corps diplomatique

dipsomania... 9. addiction, oenomania,
potomania 10. alcoholism
15. delirium tremens

dipthong... see *diphthong*

dire... 3. bad 4. base, evil, rank, want
5. awful, fatal, needy 6. deadly,
dismal, funest, odious 7. baneful,
doleful, fearful, ghastly 8. dreadful,
horrible, terrible, ultimate
10. oppressive 12. inauspicious,
overpowering

direct... 3. ain, bid, con 4. bend,
boss, head, lead, turn 5. order,
pilot, refer, steer, teach 6. govern,
manage 7. avigate, command,
conduct, marshal 8. instruct, straight
9. influence

direction... 3. way 4. airt, bent, care,
east, west 5. avast, belay, north,
route, south, trend 6. advice, course
7. address, command, pointer
8. guidance 10. management
11. instruction 15. superintendence

directly... 4. soon 6. pronto 7. shortly
8. as soon as, promptly 9. forthwith,
instantly, presently 11. immediately

directly opposite... 9. antipodal,
diametric 10. intipodean

director... 4. boss 5. aimer (gunner)

6. conner, leader 7. manager, teacher 8. governor, producer 14. superintendent

direful... 4. dire 6. woeful 8. dreadful, terrible 10. calamitous

dirge... 4. keen, Mass, song 5. psalm, rites 6. lament 7. requiem 8. coronach

dirigible... 4. Roma 5. blimp 7. balloon 10. Shenandoah 12. Graf Zeppelin

Dirigo... 5. I Lead 7. I Direct (Maine motto)

dirk... 4. snee, stab 5. knife, sword 6. dagger

dirt... 3. mud 4. dust, foul, land, muck, soil 5. earth, filth, grime, stain 6. gossip, refuse 7. scandal, slander 9. obscenity

dirty... 4. foul, mean 5. dingy, foggy, gusty, mucky, nasty 6. bemire, filthy, soiled, stormy, untidy 7. clouded, muddied, squalid, sullied

dis (pert to)...
    Greek.. 5. Pluto
    Norse.. 4. Freya 7. spirits 9. Valkyries 11. superhumans
    prefix.. 5. twice 6. double
    Roman.. 3. Dis 8. Dis pater 12. realm of Pluto

disable... 4. main 5. unfit 6. impair, weaken 7. cripple 9. disparage, hamstring 10. disqualify 12. incapacitate

disadvantage... 3. out 4. harm, hurt 6. damage, injury 7. penalty, trouble 8. drawback, handicap 9. detriment, liability, prejudice 12. inexpedience 13. inconvenience

disagreeable... 4. edgy 5. cross, nasty 7. fulsome 8. unsavory 9. dissonant, invidious, irritable, offensive, repugnant 10. ill–humored, unpleasant 11. displeasing, ill–tempered, incongruous 13. uncomfortable

disagreement... 5. clash 7. detente, discord, dispute, dissent, wrangle 8. variance 9. diversity 10. contention, difference, dissension, unlikeness 11. contrariety, controversy, discrepancy, incongruity 13. nonconformity 16. misunderstanding

disappear... 3. die 4. face, pass 5. cease 6. be lost, perish, vanish 7. dwindle 8. evanesce 9. evaporate

disappoint... 4. balk, bilk, fail, fall, foil 6. baffle, thwart 7. let down 9. frustrate 10. disenchant, dissatisfy 11. disillusion

disappointment... 3. rue 6. defeat 7. failure 10. bafflement 11. frustration 15. dissatisfaction

disapprobation... 5. odium 11. disapproval 12. condemnation 13. disparagement

disapproval... 3. boo 4. hiss, veto 7. censure, protest 9. objection, rejection 12. condemnation 14. disapprobation

disarrange... 4. muss 5. upset 6. foul

up, jumble 7. disturb 8. disorder, unsettle 10. discompose 11. disorganize

disarray... 5. strip 6. unrobe 7. despoil, undress, unkempt 8. disorder 9. confusion, ungarment 10. disarrange, dishabille 12. discomposure, dishevelment

disaster... 4. evil, ruin 6. mishap 8. accident, calamity, casualty, fatality 9. cataclysm, mischance 10. misfortune 11. catastrophe 12. misadventure

disastrous... 4. dire 7. unlucky 8. ill–fated 9. ill–boding 10. calamitous 11. destructive, unfortunate 12. unpropitious

disavow... 4. deny 6. abjure, disown, recant, refuse 7. decline, retract 8. disclaim, renounce 9. disaffirm, repudiate

disbeliever... 5. pagan 7. atheist, heathen, heretic, infidel 8. agnostic

disburse... 5. spend 6. defray, expend, pay out

disbursement... 5. outgo 6. outlay 7. payment 8. spending 11. expenditure

disc... see also *disk* 3. man 4. dial, puck 5. medal, plate, quoit, wheel 6. circle, record 7. discoid 8. artifact 9. gyroscope, medallion

discard... 4. drip, shed 5. scrap, sluff 6. disuse, reject, remove 7. abandon, cast off, dismiss, forsake 8. eliminate, eradicate, throw away

discern... 3. see, spy 4. espy, know, read, view 5. sight 6. behold, descry, detect 7. witness 8. discover, perceive 10. understand 11. distinguish 12. discriminate 13. differentiate

discernible... 7. evident, obvious, visible 8. apparent, distinct, knowable, manifest 11. conspicuous, perceptible 15. distinguishable

discerning... 4. sage 5. acute, sharp 6. astute, shrewd 9. sagacious 14. discriminating, discriminative

discernment... 4. tact 6. acumen 7. insight 8. sagacity 9. sharpness 10. astuteness, perception, shrewdness 12. perspicacity 14. discrimination

discharge... 2. do 4. bang, cass, fire, sack, shot 5. blast, egest, eject, erupt, expel, exude, flash, salvo, shoot, speed 6. acquit, bounce, defray, exempt, pay off, report, unload, volley 7. dismiss, execute, explode, payment, quietus, release 8. emission, eruption 9. acquittal, dismissal, excretion, execution, explosion, fusillade 10. accomplish, detonation, observance 11. performance

disciple... 5. chela, Judas, pupil 7. apostle, convert, learner, scholar, student 8. adherent, believer, follower

disciples (Bib)... 6. twelve (72, Vulgate) 10. Christians

disciplinarian... 7. Puritan, teacher,

trainer 8. martinet

discipline ... 4. rule, whip 6. govern, punish 7. chasten, control, culture, educate, penance, scourge 8. training 9. education, restraint 10. correction, punishment 11. castigation, instruction, self-control 12. chastisement 13. regimentation

disclaim ... 4. deny 6. abjure, cry out, disown, recant, refuse, reject 7. disavow 8. abnegate, disallow, renounce 9. repudiate

disclose ... 4. bare, open, show, tell 5. utter 6. expose, impart, reveal, unmask, unveil 7. divulge, uncloak, unclose 8. discover, indicate

disclosure ... 6. exposé 8. exposure 9. discovery, revealing, unmasking, unveiling 10. appearance, revealment, revelation

discolor ... 4. spot 5. stain 6. bruise 7. distain (anc) tarnish 9. ecchymose (by blood)

discolored ... 4. doty (by decay) 5. faded 7. altered 8. ustulate 10. variegated

discomfit ... 4. balk, rout 5. upset 6. baffle, defeat, dismay 7. confuse 9. embarrass, frustrate, overthrow 10. disconcert

discomfiture ... 4. rout 6. defeat, flurry 7. letdown 8. confusion, overthrow 10. bafflement 11. frustration 13. embarrassment, inconvenience 14. disappointment

discomfort ... 4. pain 6. sorrow 7. misease 8. distress 9. annoyance 10. uneasiness 11. displeasure 13. embarrassment, inconvenience

discommode ... 6. bother, molest, put out 7. trouble 8. incommode 13. inconvenience

discompose ... 4. fret 5. upset 6. excite, flurry, rubble 7. agitate, confuse, derange, disturb, fluster 8. unsettle 9. embarrass 10. disarrange, disconcert

disconcert ... 5. abash, alarm 6. rattle, thwart 7. confuse, disturb, fluster, nonplus 8. bewilder 9. discomfit, embarrass 10. disarrange

disconnect ... 5. sever 6. detach, unyoke 7. disjoin 8. disunite, separate, uncouple

disconnected ... 6. broken 8. detached, rambling 9. desultory, scattered 10. disjointed, incoherent 11. unconnected

disconsolate ... 3. sad 6. gloomy, woeful 7. forlorn 8. desolate, hopeless 9. sorrowful 10. despairing, despondent, melancholy 12. inconsolable

discontent ... 6. misery, unrest 8. disquiet 10. inquietude, uneasiness 11. displeasure, unhappiness 14. discontentment 15. dissatisfaction

discontinue ... 3. end 4. drop, quit, stop 5. cease 6. desist, give up 7. abandon, refrain 8. intermit 9. terminate

discord ... 3. din 5. noise 6. strife 7. dissent 8. disunity, variance 9. cacophony, Discordia, harshness 10. antagonism, contention, difference, discordant, disharmony, dissension, dissonance 11. altercation 12. disagreement

discord (goddess of) ... 3. Ate 4. Eris

discordant ... 5. harsh 7. grating, jarring 8. contrary, jangling 11. cacophonous, disagreeing, incongruous, quarrelsome, unmelodious 12. inconsistent, inharmonious 14. irreconcilable

discordant (pert to) ...
music .. 8. scordato
serenade .. 9. charivari 10. callithump
sound .. jangle

discount ... 3. cut 4. agio 6. rebate 9. abatement, allowance, reduction 10. concession, percentage

discourage ... 4. damp 5. check, daunt, deter 6. deject, dismay 7. oppose 8. depress 9. dispirit, dissuade 10. dishearten

discourse ... 4. talk, tell 5. essay, paper (written), prose, speak, spiel 6. homily, lesson, screed, sermon 7. account, address, article, declaim, discant, dissert, expound, lecture, narrate, oration 8. converse, treatise 9. expatiate, narrative 10. exposition, recitation 12. conversation, dissertation

discourteous ... 4. rude 7. uncivil 8. impolite, insolent 9. ungallant 10. ungracious 13. disrespectful

discover ... 3. see 4. espy, find 5. learn, descry, detect, expose 7. exhibit, find out, uncover, unearth 9. apprehend, ascertain

discoverer ... 3. spy 5. scout

discoverer of ...
America .. 4. Eric (the Red) 7. Vikings 8. Columbus (1492)
blood circulation .. 6. Harvey
electric light .. 6. Edison
North Pole .. 5. Peary (1909)
radium .. 5. Curie (Madame)
South Pole .. 8. Amundsen (1911)
telegraph .. 5. Morse (Samuel)
telephone .. 4. Bell (Alexander)
vaccination .. 6. Jenner

discovery, logic of ... 8. heuretic

discredit ... 5. doubt 7. asperse, falsify, scandal 8. disgrace, dishonor, disprove, distrust 9. disbelief, disparage, disrepute, misgiving, suspicion 10. invalidate 11. discredence

discreet ... 4. wary 5. civil 6. polite 7. careful, mindful, politic, prudent 8. cautious 9. judicious, selective 11. circumspect 12. noncommittal 13. discretionary

discrepancy ... 8. variance 9. disaccord, disparity, diversity 10. difference 11. contrariety 12. disagreement 13. inconsistency 15. incompatibility

discretion ... 4. tact, will 6. option 7. caution, reserve 8. judgment, prudence, wariness 11. disjunction

12. cautiousness, discreetness
13. discontinuity, judiciousness,
secretiveness 14. circumspection,
discrimination
discretionary... 7. politic, prudent
8. discreet 9. arbitrary, judicious,
voluntary 10. prudential
11. considerate 14. discriminating
discriminate... 6. divide, screen,
secern 8. separate, set apart
11. distinguish 13. differentiate
discrimination... 5. taste 6. acumen,
option 9. prejudice 10. discretion
11. discernment, distinction,
penetration, segregation
discursive... 6. roving 7. cursory
9. desultory, diffusive, wandering
10. circuitous, digressive
discus... 4. disk 5. plate, quoit
discuss... 3. air 4. moot 5. argue,
treat 6. debate, parley 7. bargain,
canvass, dispute, dissert, mention
9. discourse
discus thrower... 10. discobolus,
Discobolus (statue)
disdain... 5. pride, scorn 7. askance,
contemn, despise 8. contempt
9. arrogance 11. haughtiness
16. contemptuousness
disease... 6. malady 7. ailment, illness,
trouble 8. disorder, sickness
9. affection, infirmity 10. affliction,
disability 11. derangement
disease (of)...
animals (Afr).. 5. nenta
apoplexy.. 4. esca
apples.. 7. stippen 9. bitter pit
blood.. 6. anemia 8. leukemia
(leukaemia, leucemia)
cattle.. 5. hoose (hooze) 6. nagana,
wheeze 7. anthrax
chickens.. 3. pip 4. roup
diet.. 7. rickets 8. pellagra, rachitis
divers.. 5. bends 7. caisson
dog.. 5. lyssa 6. rabies
11. hydrophobia
eye.. 6. caligo 7. pinkeye 8. cataract,
glaucoma, trachoma 9. amaurosis
14. conjunctivitis
fungus.. 6. mildew 9. elm blight
horses.. 5. spavin
Oriental.. 8. beriberi
painful.. 7. lumbago 9. arthritis
parrot.. 11. psittacosis
plant.. 4. rust, smut 5. ergot, scald
7. erinose (grape)
potato, tomato.. 8. dartrose
sheep.. 3. coe, rot
skin.. 5. hives, psora 6. eczema,
herpes, tetter 7. scabies 8. impetigo,
shingles 9. psoriasis, urticaria
10. erysipelas
stonecutter's.. 9. silicosis
sugar cane.. 5. sereh
disease (pert to)...
classification.. 8. nosology
10. nosography
decline.. 9. catabasis
determination of.. 9. diagnosis
germ transfer.. 7. vection
native to.. 7. endemic
outlook.. 9. prognosis

science of.. 8. etiology, medicine
spread of.. 8. epidemic
suffix.. 4. itis
treatment (muscular).. 12. kinesiatrics
disembark... 4. land 6. alight, debark
7. detrain
disembowel... 3. gut 10. eviscerate
disengage... 5. clear 6. detach, loosen
7. release 8. liberate 9. extricate
11. disencumber, disentangle
12. disembarrass
disentangle... 4. card, comb 5. clear,
loose, ravel, solve 6. evolve, sleave,
sleeve 7. unravel, unsnare, untwine,
untwist 8. simplify 9. disengage,
extricate 10. disinvolve, unscramble
disfavor... 7. dislike 8. distaste
9. detriment, disrepute 10. alienation
11. disapproval, displeasure
14. discountenance
disfigure... 3. mar 4. scar 6. deface,
deform, injure, mangle 7. blemish
8. mutilate
disgorge... 4. spew, vent 5. eject,
eruct, erupt, expel, vomit 7. exhaust
9. discharge 10. relinquish
11. regurgitate
disgrace... 5. abase, odium, shame,
shend, sully 7. attaint, degrade,
distain, obloquy, upbraid 8. dishonor,
ignominy, reproach 9. discredit,
disesteem, disrepute, humiliate
10. opprobrium 11. abomination,
humiliation 13. disparagement
disguise... 3. mum (mumm) 4. mask,
veil 5. cloak, feign 6. covert, masque
7. conceal, costume, falsify, pretend
9. dissemble, incognito, inebriate
10. camouflage, masquerade
11. dissimulate 12. misrepresent
disgust... 6. nausea 7. offense, quarrel
8. aversion, loathing, nauseate
9. animosity, annoyance, antipathy
10. abhorrence, repugnance
11. abomination
disgusting... 5. nasty 6. filthy, odious
9. loathsome, obnoxious, offensive,
repellent, repugnant, revolting,
sickening
dish... 3. jar, pot 4. boat (gravy)
5. cruse, nappy, paten, plate
6. patera, saucer, tureen 7. charger
(anc), platter, ramekin 8. casserole
dish (food)... 5. pilau, salmi 6. hachis,
haslet, omelet, potage, ragout
7. chowder, pudding, soufflé
dishabille... 6. kimono 7. neglige,
undress 8. bathrobe, negligee,
peignoir
dishearten... 5. amate (anc), appal,
daunt, deter, unman 6. deject
7. depress 8. dispirit 10. discourage,
dissatisfy
disheveled... 5. tousy 6. mussed,
shaggy, untidy 7. ruffled, tousled,
tumbled, unkempt 8. deranged,
uncombed 10. disarrayed, disordered
11. disarranged
dishonest... 4. base 5. false 6. crafty,
unjust 7. corrupt, crooked, knavish
8. rascally, scheming 9. deceitful,
truthless 10. fraudulent, perfidious,

untruthful **12.** dishonorable
dishonor... **5.** shame **6.** defame,
infamy **7.** debauch, degrade, obloquy
8. disgrace, ignominy, reproach
9. desecrate, disrepute, improbity
10. disrespect, opprobrium
13. disparagement
dishonorable... **7.** ignoble **8.** infamous,
shameful **9.** dishonest **10.** inglorious
11. disesteemed, disgraceful
12. disreputable
disillusion... **10.** disquixote
disillusioned... **8.** thwarted
12. disappointed, disenchanted
disinclination... **7.** dislike **8.** aversion,
distaste **10.** reluctance, repugnance
12. disaffection **13.** indisposition
disinclined... **6.** averse **8.** indolent
9. reluctant, unwilling **10.** indisposed
disinfectant... **5.** Lysol **6.** cresol,
iodine, phenol **7.** alcohol
9. germicide **10.** antiseptic
12. formaldehyde
disintegrate... **5.** decay, erode
7. break up, corrode, crumble,
disband, resolve **8.** dissolve
9. decompose **11.** disorganize
disjoin... **4.** part, undo **5.** sever, untie
6. detach, sunder, unhook **7.** unhitch
8. disunite, separate, unbutton
9. disengage **10.** disconnect,
dissociate
disk, disc... **4.** puck **5.** medal, paten,
plate, quoit, wafer, wheel **6.** harrow,
record, sequin **7.** discoid, medalet
9. faceplate, gyroscope, medallion
dislike... **4.** mind **5.** odium **6.** detest
8. aversion, distaste **9.** antipathy,
disrelish **12.** disaffection
dislike of children... **9.** misopedia
dislike of home... **9.** ecophobia
disloyal... **5.** false **6.** fickle, untrue
9. faithless **10.** inconstant,
perfidious, unfaithful **11.** treacherous
dismal... **3.** sad, wan **4.** dark
5. black, bleak, drear, lurid
6. dreary, gloomy, somber **7.** doleful,
joyless, Stygian, unhappy, unlucky
8. dolorous, dreadful, funereal,
lonesome, mournful, overcast, sinister
9. ill-omened, sorrowful
10. calamitous, depressing,
lugubrious **11.** pessimistic,
unfortunate
dismantle... **4.** raze, undo **5.** strip
6. divest **7.** deprive, destroy, disrobe,
uncloak **8.** demolish **11.** disassemble
dismay... **4.** fear **5.** alarm, daunt
6. appall, fright, terror **8.** affright,
bewilder **9.** dejection **10.** depression,
disconcert **12.** apprehension
13. consternation
14. discouragement
dismiss... **4.** drip, fire **5.** amand,
amove, eject, exile, remue **6.** acquit,
bounce, depose, recall, refute, shelve
7. forgive, release **8.** relegate
9. discharge, disregard **10.** relinquish
dismount... **6.** alight **7.** descend,
unhorse, unmount **11.** disassemble
disobedient... **7.** forward, froward,
wayward **8.** mutinous **10.** rebellious,

refractory **11.** intractable
12. contumacious
disorder... **3.** tic **4.** mess, riot
5. chaos, deray, snarl **6.** malady,
tumult **7.** ailment, anarchy, derange,
illness, misdeed **8.** disarray, paranoia,
sickness **9.** confusion, craziness,
distemper, paranomia
10. discompose, revolution
11. lawlessness, misdemeanor
12. irregularity **13.** indisposition
14. disarrangement
15. disorganization
disorderly... **3.** bad **5.** mussy, rowdy
6. unruly **7.** chaotic, naughty, violent
8. confused, rowdyish, slipshod
9. irregular, offensive, turbulent
12. ungovernable, unmanageable
disorganization... **5.** decay **7.** anarchy,
breakup, split-up **8.** disorder
10. separation **11.** destruction,
dissolution **13.** disbandment
14. disarrangement, disintegration
disown... **4.** deny **5.** expel **6.** recant,
reject **7.** disavow **8.** disclaim,
renounce **9.** disaffirm, repudiate
10. disinherit
disparage... **4.** slur **5.** decry, lower (in
rank) **6.** slight **7.** degrade, detract
8. dishonor, minimize **10.** depreciate,
disapprove, discourage, undervalue
11. incongruity
disparagement... **7.** diasyrm
8. disgrace **9.** indignity
10. detraction **12.** depreciation
disparaging... **8.** decaying
10. defamatory, pejorative
11. unfavorable
dispart... **4.** open, rend, rive **5.** break,
sever, split **6.** cleave, divide
dispassionate... **4.** cool, fair **6.** serene
8. composed, moderate **9.** collected,
impartial, temperate, unruffled
11. unemotional **12.** unprejudiced
dispatch... **4.** kill, mail, post, send,
slay **5.** haste, speed **6.** hasten
7. message **8.** celerity, conclude,
expedite **9.** diligence **10.** accelerate,
accomplish, promptness
dispatch boat... **5.** aviso **6.** packet
Dis pater (Rom)... **3.** god (underworld)
5. Pluto (Gr) **12.** realm of Pluto
dispel... **6.** vanish **7.** scatter
8. disperse **9.** dissipate
dispensation... **6.** scheme **7.** economy
9. exemption, remission
10. dispersion, management,
misericord (misericorde)
11. arrangement **12.** distribution
13. apportionment **14.** administration
dispense... **4.** deal, dole, give, vend
6. effuse, excuse, exempt **7.** absolve
8. disperse **9.** apportion
10. administer
dispenser of alms... **7.** almoner
disperse... **3.** sow **4.** rout **5.** strew
6. branch, spread, vanish **7.** diffuse,
refract, scatter **9.** apportion, dissipate
10. distribute **11.** disseminate
dispirit... **3.** cow **4.** damp **5.** daunt
6. deject **7.** depress **10.** discourage,
dishearten, intimidate

displace... 6. depose, mislay, remove 8. misplace 9. discharge, dislocate, supersede 10. substitute

display... 3. air 4. pomp, show, wear 5. array 6. evince, flaunt, parade, set out 7. exhibit, pageant, splurge 8. emblazon 9. advertise 10. appearance 11. demonstrate, ostentation 13. manifestation

display (pert to)...
case.. 10. show window
in public.. 5. stage
of emotion.. 5. enthusiasm
of force (distant).. 9. telenergy
of temper.. 5. scene 9. spectacle

displease... 3. vex 4. miff 5. anger, annoy, pique 6. offend 7. provoke 8. irritate 10. dissatisfy

displeasure... 5. anger 7. disgust, dislike, offense, trouble 8. disfavor, distaste 10. resentment, uneasiness 11. indignation, unhappiness 14. disapprobation 15. dissatisfaction

dispose (of)... 3. set 4. give, mind, sell, tend 5. order, place 6. adjust, assign, bestow, settle 7. arrange, destroy, discard, testate 8. give away, regulate 9. eliminate 10. distribute, relinquish

disposed... 5. prone 7. settled, willing 8. arranged, assigned, inclined 11. distributed

disposed (pert to)...
favorably.. 7. propend
to cling together.. 8. clannish
to doubt.. 9. skeptical
to please.. 11. complaisant

disposition... 3. use 4. bent, bias, mood, turn 6. animus, giving, morale, nature, temper 7. control 8. tendency 9. character 10. management, settlement 11. arrangement, elimination, temperament 12. organization 13. apportionment

dispossess... 5. eject, evict 6. divest, refute 8. disseize

dispossessed... 6. bereft, ousted 7. ejected, evicted 8. deprived, divested

disproof... 6. answer, denial 8. negation, rebuttal 10. refutation 11. confutation 12. invalidation

disprove... 5. belie, rebut 6. refute 7. confute 9. discredit 10. invalidate

disputation... 6. debate 7. polemic 8. argument 10. contention 11. controversy 12. conversation

disputatious... 7. eristic, polemic 11. contentious, quarrelsome 13. argumentative, controversial

dispute... 4. deny, feud, moot, spar 5. brawl, broil 6. bicker, debate, haggle, higgle, naggle 7. contest, dissent, protest, quarrel, wrangle 8. argument, squabble 11. altercation, controversy

disqualify... 5. debar 9. indispose 10. invalidate 12. incapacitate

disquiet... 3. vix 4. fret 5. alarm 6. excite 7. agitate, concern, disturb 8. distress, frighten 12. apprehension

disquisition... 5. essay 10. discussion 12. dissertation

disregard... 4. snub 6. ignore, slight 7. neglect 8. defiance 9. unconcern 11. inattention

disreputable... 3. low 4. base 5. seamy 6. raffish 8. shameful, unworthy 13. discreditable 15. persona non grata

disrespect... 7. affront 9. disesteem, insolence 10. incivility 11. discourtesy

disrespectful... 7. uncivil 8. impudent, insolent 10. irreverent 12. discourteous

disrupt... 4. part (forcibly), rend, tear 5. upset 6. thwart 11. disorganize

dissatisfaction... 8. vexation 10. discontent 11. displeasure, unsatisfied

dissect... 3. cut 6. divide 7. analyze 8. separate 9. anatomize

disseize (law)... 4. oust 5. evict 6. depose 10. dispossess 11. expropriate

dissemble... 4. hide 5. cloak, feign 7. conceal 8. disguise 9. disregard 11. counterfeit

disseminate... 3. sow 6. effuse, spread 7. publish, scatter 8. disperse 9. circulate, propagate

dissension... 7. discord 8. brouille, friction 10. dissidence 12. disagreement

dissent... 3. nay 8. apostasy, disagree 10. separation 12. disagreement, nonagreement 13. nonconformity 14. nonconcurrence

dissenter... 7. heretic, Sectary 8. apostate, recusant 9. protester 10. Protestant 13. nonconformist

dissertation... 5. essay, tract 6. debate, thesis 7. article, lecture 8. treatise 9. discourse 10. discussion, exposition 12. disquisition

dissidence... 7. dissent 8. variance 9. cacophony 10. difference, dissension 12. disagreement

dissimilarity... 7. variety 9. disparity, diversity 10. difference, unlikeness, unsameness 13. dissimilation, heterogeneity 17. heterogeneousness

dissipate... 5. spend, waste 6. dispel, expend 7. consume, scatter, shatter 8. dispense, dissolve, squander 9. disappear

dissipation... 4. loss 9. decrement, diffusion 10. dispersion, profligacy 11. consumption, prodigality 12. intemperance 13. disappearance, dissoluteness 14. disintegration

dissolute... 3. lax 4. lewd, wild 5. loose 6. loosed, rakish, wanton, wicked 7. lawless, vicious 8. reckless, uncurbed 9. abandoned, debauched, unbridled 10. dissipated, licentious, profligate 11. demoralized 12. unrestrained

dissolve... 4. fuse, melt 5. solve 7. adjourn, liquefy 9. decompose, disappear 11. disorganize

12. disintegrate
dissolved... 6. solute 7. soluble
dissonant... 5. harsh 7. grating, jarring
8. jangling 9. deviative, different,
differing 10. discordant, discrepant
11. disagreeing, unmelodious
12. inconsistent, inharmonious
13. contradictory
dissuade... 5. deter 6. advise, dehort,
divert 8. admonish 10. discourage,
disincline 11. expostulate
distaff side... 5. women 6. female
distain... 5. stain, tinge 6. define
7. tarnish 8. discolor
distance... 4. step, yond 5. depth,
range, space 6. offing 7. mileage,
reserve, yardage 8. coldness, outstrip
9. aloofness, antiquity, dimension
10. remoteness
distant... 3. far, tel, yon 4. afar, cold,
tele (pref) 5. aloof 6. remote,
utmost, yonder 7. foreign 8. ulterior
distaste... 7. disgust 8. aversion
9. disrelish 10. repugnance
11. displeasure 14. disinclination
15. dissatisfaction
distasteful... 7. hateful 8. nauseous,
unsavory 9. loathsome, offensive
10. disgusting, unpleasant
11. displeasing, unpalatable
12. disagreeable
distemper... 3. vex 4. soak 5. anger,
color, steep 6. dilute, malady, ruffle
7. ailment, disease, disturb
8. painting (process), sickness
13. indisposition
distend... 4. grow 5. bulge, swell
6. dilate, expand, spread 7. enlarge,
inflate, stretch 8. lengthen
distended... 5. tumid 7. bloated,
swollen 8. inflated, patulous, puffed
up
distich... 7. couplet 8. two lines
distill, distil... 4. leak 6. decoct,
infuse 7. extract, squeeze, trickle
8. vaporize
distilling device... 5. flask 6. retort
7. alembic 10. distillery
distinct... 4. fair 5. clear 7. audible,
obvious, precise, several 8. explicit,
manifest 9. different 10. individual
13. distinguished
distinction... 4. rank 5. honor
6. repute 8. nobility 9. clearness,
greatness, variation 10. difference
14. discrimination 15. differentiation
distinctive... 7. typical 8. peculiar
9. prominent 14. characteristic,
discriminative
distinctive mark... 4. sign 5. badge
6. cachet, emblem, symbol
distinctive quality... 6. genius, talent
9. specialty
distinguish... 6. secern 7. discern
8. perceive, separate 9. recognize
12. discriminate 13. differentiate
distinguished... 5. great, noted
6. famous, marked 7. defined,
eminent, honored, special 8. laureate,
renowned, superior 9. different,
egregious, prominent 10. celebrated
11. conspicuous, illustrious

13. extraordinary 14. characteristic
distort... 4. warp 5. screw, twist,
wrest 8. deform 7. contort, falsify,
pervert 10. camshackle
12. misrepresent
distorted... 4. awry 6. rubato
7. twisted
distortion... 5. loxia 10. perversion
12. malformation
distract... 5. craze 6. divert, harass,
madden, puzzle 7. confuse, perplex
10. distraught
distracted... 3. mad 7. frantic
8. distrait, diverted, rambling
9. disturbed 10. distraught
11. overwrought
distraction... 6. frenzy, tumult
7. despair, madness 8. disorder
9. agitation, confusion, diversion
10. dissension, perplexity
11. derangement, disturbance,
inattention 12. perturbation
distress... 5. ail 4. pain 5. agony,
annoy, grief, worry 6. danger, grieve,
harrow, misery 7. anguish, anxiety,
perplex, poverty, trouble 8. distrain,
vexation 9. necessity 10. affliction,
discomfort
distress call... 3. SOS
distribute... 3. dot, sow 4. deal, dole,
mete 5. allot, share 6. assign,
assort, divide, spread 7. deal out,
prorate, scatter 8. allocate, classify,
dispense, disperse 9. apportion,
broadcast 10. administer
distribution... 8. disposal 9. allotment
10. dispersion 11. arrangement,
disposition 12. dispensation
13. apportionment 14. classification
distribution of favors... 9. patronage
11. benefaction
distributor... 5. agent 6. agency
8. merchant 11. broadcaster
district... 4. pale, slum, ward 5. realm
6. canton, domain, ghetto, region
7. circuit, demesne, quarter
8. province 9. bailiwick, territory
District of Columbia... see
Washington, DC
distrust... 5. doubt, qualm 8. jealousy,
mistrust, wariness 9. misgiving,
suspicion, treachery
disturb... 3. vex 4. riot, roil 5. alarm,
annoy, rouse, roust, upset 6. excite,
molest, ruffle 7. agitate, derange,
fluster, perturb, trouble 8. disorder,
distract 9. interrupt 10. discompose,
disconcert
disturbance... 5. alarm, brawl
6. hubbub, rumpus, static, tumult,
uproar 7. anxiety, clatter 8. stramash
9. agitation, annoyance, commotion,
confusion 10. excitement, turbulence
11. derangement 12. perturbation
disturbed... 6. uneasy 7. annoyed,
excited, inquiet, unquiet 8. agitated
10. bewildered 12. disconcerted
disunion... 9. severance 10. alienation,
detachment, dissension, separation
11. disjunction 13. disconnection
disunite... 3. rip 4. part 5. sever,
untie 6. divide, sunder, unteam,

unyoke 7. discerp, disjoin, unravel
8. alienate, separate 9. dismember

disuse... 6. misuse, nonuse
7. abandon, discard 8. disusage
9. desuetude 11. antiquation,
discontinue 10. obsolescence

ditch... 3. sap 4. dike, hole, moat,
rine 5. canal, evade, fossa, fosse,
rhine 6. escarp, furrow, relais, trench
7. abandon, acequia, channel

dithyramb... 3. ode 4. hymn 6. poetry
7. epithet (of Dionysus)

ditty... 3. lay 4. poem, sing, song
5. carol 6. saying 7. canzone
8. canticle

diurnal... 5. daily 8. everyday
9. quotidian

divan... 4. sofa 5. couch 6. leewan,
settee 9. davenport 12. Chesterfield

dive... 4. swim 6. plunge, resort,
saloon 7. brothel, descend, descent,
explore 8. submerge

divergence... 7. theorem 9. deviation,
obliquity 10. difference, separation
12. disagreement, divarication

divers... 5. cruel 6. sundry 7. several,
various 8. perverse 9. different

diver's disease... 5. bends 7. caisson

diverse... 6. sundry, unlike 7. several,
various 8. distinct, separate
9. different, multiform

diver's gear... 8. flippers
12. respirometer

diversify... 4. vary 6. change
7. variate 9. variegate 10. distribute
13. differentiate

diversion... 4. game, play 5. hobby,
sport 6. change 7. pastime
8. apostasy 9. amusement
10. deflection, recreation
11. distraction 13. entertainment

diversity... 7. variety 10. difference
11. variegation 12. multiformity

divert... 5. amuse, avert, parry
7. deflect, delight 8. dissuade,
distract, recreate 9. entertain
10. disincline

divest... 4. doff, reft, tirl 5. strip
6. debunk, depose 8. unclothe
10. dispossess

divide... 3. lot 4. fork, part 5. cleft,
halve, sever, share, slice, space, split
6. bisect, cleave, septum, sunder
7. prorate 8. alienate, classify,
separate 9. apportion, bifurcate,
calculate, dismember, partition,
segregate, watershed 11. distinguish

divide (pert to)...
areas (small).. 8. areolate
feet.. 4. scan
four parts.. 8. paly (Her) 7. quarter
many parts.. 8. fraction 9. multisect
seven parts.. 9. septimole
steps.. 8. graduate
transversely.. 12. cross-section
two parts.. 6. bisect

divided... 4. enté (Her), reft 5. bifid,
split, zoned 6. halved, parted
7. partial, partite, septate
8. aerolate, bifidate, unjoined
9. alienated, disunited 11. distributed

dividend... 5. bonus, share 6. number
7. payment

divination... 3. art (magic) 4. omen,
sors 6. augury, sortes 7. presage
9. intuition

divination by...
ashes (sacrificial).. 11. tephromancy
cards.. 10. cartomancy
dead spirits.. 10. necromancy
dreams.. 11. oneiromancy
eggs.. 7. oomancy
fig leaf.. 9. sycomancy
figures.. 8. geomancy
fire.. 9. pyromancy
footprints.. 10. ichnomancy
forehead.. 11. metapomancy
fountains.. 9. pegomancy
letters of a name.. 7. nomancy
   8. onomancy
mice.. 8. myomancy
moon.. 10. seleomancy
neighing horse.. 10. hippomancy
oracles.. 9. theomancy
palmistry.. 10. chiromancy
pebbles.. 9. thrioboly
romantic medium.. 5. daisy
salt.. 9. halomancy
serpents.. 10. ophiornancy
smoke (sacrificial).. 10. capromancy
stars.. 11. sideromancy
straws (burning).. 11. sideromancy
sword.. 13. machairomancy
verses.. 13. rhapsodomancy
wands, rods.. 11. rhabdomancy
water.. 10. hydromancy
weather.. 9. aeromancy
wild animals.. 11. theriomancy
wine.. 9. oenomancy

divine... 5. divus, guess, pious
6. priest, sacred, superb 7. foresee,
godlike, predict 8. forebode, foretell,
heavenly, minister, prophecy
9. beautiful, celestial, clergyman,
religious 10. anticipate, superhuman,
theologian 12. supernatural

divine (pert to)...
being.. 4. deva
breath.. 4. soul
force.. 5. deity, numen 6. spirit
gift.. 8. blessing
inspiration.. 8. afflatus
messenger.. 7. apostle
opinion.. 14. theologoumenon
power.. 7. entheos (obs)
utterance.. 8. prophecy
wisdom.. 8. theogamy
word.. 5. grace, logos
work.. 7. theurgy

divining rod... 4. wand 6. dowser
9. doodlebug

divinity... 3. God, Ler 4. Deus, Lord
5. Allah, deity, Khuda, Mazda
6. Brahma, Christ 7. Jehovah,
Saviour, Taranis, Trinity 8. Almighty

division... 4. part, sect, unit 5. share
6. schism, sector 7. faction, section
8. cleavage, disunion, variance
9. allotment, bisection, partition
10. alienation, department, separation
11. compartment, disjunction
12. distribution 13. apportionment,
disconnection, dismemberment
14. classification

division (pert to)...
center (Biol).. 9. centriole
city.. 4. ward 5. block 8. precinct
French.. 6. canton 7. Commune
    10. department 14. arrondissement
mankind.. 4. race
poem.. 5. canto, verse 8. stanza
time.. 3. Age, Eon (Aeon), Era
    6. Eugaea (Zool)
zone (earth).. 6. frigid, torrid, tropic
    9. temperate

divorce, Mohammedan law... 5. talak

divot... 3. sod 4. clod, turf

divulge... 4. tell 6. impart, reveal
    7. confide, publish, uncover
    8. disclose, discover, proclaim
    11. communicate

Dixie, Dixieland... 4. song 6. utopia
    8. The South (US)

dizziness... 5. whirl 7. vertigo
    9. giddiness 10. fickleness

dizzy... 5. crazy, giddy, tipsy 6. fickle,
    stupid 7. foolish 8. confused,
    swimming, unsteady 9. delirious
    10. capricious 11. vertiginous

do... 2. ut (Mus) 3. act, pay 4. dost,
    fare, make, suit, work 5. avoid,
    cause, cheat, exert, serve, solve
    6. answer, effect, finish 7. achieve,
    deceive, execute, perform, produce,
    prosper, suffice 8. transact
    9. discharge 10. administer

docile... 4. calm, tame 6. gentle
    7. duteous 9. compliant, teachable,
    tractable

dock... 4. clip, pier, slip 5. basin,
    jetty, plant, wharf 6. cut off, deduct,
    hangar 7. curtail, shorten
    8. waterway 9. anchorage
    12. witness stand

docket... 4. list, mark 6. record, ticket
    8. calendar, schedule 11. certificate

docking post... 7. bollard

dock worker... 6. loader 7. laborer
    9. stevedore 12. longshoreman

doctor... 3. cut, fly (angling) 4. dose
    5. spike, title, treat 6. degree, dilute,
    healer, intern (interne) 7. surgeon,
    teacher 9. physician 10. adulterate,
    veterinary 12. psychiatrist

doctrine... 3. ism, ist 4. rule
    5. credo, creed, dogma, logic,
    maxim, tenet 6. gospel 7. article,
    opinion, precept 8. position
    9. principle

doctrine (pert to)...
existence (Philos).. 6. henism
finality (Theol).. 11. eschatology
good.. 8. agathism
inevitability.. 8. fatalism
philosophy.. 10. pragmatism
secrecy.. 6. cabala 8. esoteric
selfishness.. 6. egoism

doctus... 7. learned

document... 4. deed, writ 5. paper,
    proof, scrip 6. escrow 7. archive
    11. corroborate

document (pert to)...
copy (true).. 7. estreat 8. syngraph
    9. duplicate, photostat
depository.. 8. archives
file, report.. 7. dossier

hamper.. 7. hanaper

dodecade... 5. dozen 6. twelve (series)

dodge... 4. duck, jouk, snub 5. avoid,
    cheat, elude, evade, parry, trick
    6. escape, palter 7. deceive
    8. artifice 9. expedient

dodger... 7. biscuit, shirker
    8. deceiver, handbill

dodo... 3. moa 4. bird (extinct)

doe... 3. tag, teg 4. deer, hind
    5. color

doer... 3. actor, agent, maker
    6. author, factor, worker 7. manager
    8. attorney, executor, producer
    9. performer

doff... 4. vail 5. strip 6. divest,
    remove 7. take off, undress

dog... 3. cur, pug 4. foot, lyam (lyme)
    5. canis, hound, pooch, whelp
    6. canine, fallow, shadow, wretch,
    yelper 7. mongrel 9. carnivore
    13. constellation

dog (breed)... 3. pom 4. chow, Dane
    5. boxer, husky 6. basset, beagle,
    collie, lucern, nootka, poodle, Saluki,
    setter, Sussex 7. bulldog, griffon,
    mastiff, pointer, Samoyed, spaniel,
    terrier, whippet 8. Airedale,
    Doberman, Keeshong, Labrador,
    Malemute, Pekinese, Sealyham,
    shepherd (shepard) 9. Chihuahua,
    dachshund, Dalmatian, greyhound,
    Pekingese (Pekinese), retriever,
    schnauzer, St Bernard, wolfhound
    10. bloodhound, Pomeranian,
    schipperke 12. gazelle hound
    13. Boston terrier

dog (pert to)...
Buster Brown.. 4. Tige
Cape (hunting).. 8. cynhyena
days.. 8. canicule
F D R's.. 4. Fala (Falla)
ferocious.. 7. agouara
fictional.. 4. Asta, Toby
house.. 6. kennel
howl.. 9. ululation
like.. 6. cynoid
mythical.. 7. Cerebus
part.. 5. flews 7. dewclaw
short–eared (Her).. 4. alan (aland)
star.. 4. Sept (Septi) 6. Sirius
    8. Canicula
Victor records.. 6. Nipper (His
    Master's Voice)
wild.. 5. dhole, dingo 6. bandog,
    kolsun 8. cimarron

Doge's barge... 9. Bucentaur

dogfish... 5. shark 6. burbot
    9. blackfish 10. nursehound

dogma... 4. code 5. tenet 6. belief,
    ritual 7. precept 8. doctrine
    9. Levitical, principle

dogmatic... 7. certain 8. absolute,
    positive 9. assertive, canonical,
    doctrinal, pragmatic 11. dictatorial,
    doctrinaire, magisterial, opinionated

dogmatic statement... 6. dictum

dogmatism... 10. pragmatism
    11. intolerance

dogwood... 6. osier 6. cornel
    7. boxwood

do it again... 5. itero

dole... 4. alms, mete 5. grief
6. sorrow 8. pittance 9. allotment
10. distribute, misfortune
12. distribution
doleful... 3. sad 4. dree 5. drear
6. dismal, dreary, rueful, woeful
8. doloroso, dolorous, grievous,
jeremiad, mournful 10. lugubrious,
melancholy
doll... 3. toy 4. baby (toy), girl
6. moppet, puppet 9. miniature,
plaything
dolphin... 4. fish, inia 5. bouto
6. dorado, dugong, sea pig
8. Cetacean, porpoise 9. goosebeak
10. bottlenose
dolt... 3. ass, oaf 4. clod, dope, loon,
lout, moke 5. dunce, idiot 7. dullard
8. clodpate, dumbbell, numskull
9. blockhead, dumb bunny
10. ignoramous
domain... 5. realm 6. empery, empire,
sphere 7. country, demesne
8. dominion
dome... 4. arch, head, roof (Astron)
5. spire, tower 6. cupola, turret
Domesday, doomsday... 4. Book (Eng
Hist) 11. Judgment Day 13. Great
Domesday 14. Little Domesday
17. Domesday of St Paul's
domestic... 4. tame 5. domal
7. servant 9. enchorial, home–grown,
intestine (not foreign)
domestic establishment... 6. ménage
9. household
domicile... 5. abode, house 7. habitat
8. dwelling 9. residence
10. habitation
dominant... 5. chief, chord 6. ruling
7. regnant, supreme 8. superior
9. ascendant, governing, imperious,
paramount, principal
10. pre–eminent, prevailing
11. influential, outweighing,
overtopping 12. preponderant
13. authoritative, overbalancing
dominate... 4. boss, rule, sway
5. reign 6. govern 7. command,
control, overtop, possess
11. predominate
domineering... 6. lordly 7. haughty
8. arrogant, blustery 9. imperious,
masterful 10. oppressive
11. overbearing
Dominican Republic...
capital.. 12. Santo Domingo
city.. 14. Ciudad Trujillo
discoverer.. 8. Columbus
island site.. 10. Hispaniola
oldest city (W Hem).. 12. Santo
Domingo (1496)
dominion... 4. rule, sway 5. realm
6. empery, empire, sphere 7. control
9. authority, hierarchy (celestial)
12. jurisdiction
domino... 3. pip (spot) 4. game (in
pl), hood, mask 5. amice, cloak,
ivory 7. costume
dominoes, galloping... 7. ivories
donate... 3. tip 4. give 6. bestow
7. present
done... 4. fini 5. baked, ended, finis

6. agreed, cooked 7. through
8. finished, tired out 9. completed,
concluded, exhausted
done (pert to)...
by stealth.. 13. surreptitious
by word of mouth.. 5. parol
for pay.. 9. mercenary
with effort.. 5. labor
Don Juan's girl (novel)... 6. Haidee
donkey... 3. ass 4. moke 5. burro,
neddy 6. onager
donna... 4. Dona, lady, wife
5. madam, woman 8. mistress
Don Quixote's steed... 9. Rosinante
doom... 3. fey, lot 4. fate, ruin
5. death 7. condemn, destine,
destiny 8. sentence 11. destruction
doomed... 3. fey 5. death, fated,
goner 9. sentenced
doomsday... 8. Ragnarok
11. Judgment Day (see *Domesday*)
door... 4. gate 6. portal 7. doorway,
opening, passage, postern
11. entranceway 12. porte–cochere
doorframe... 3. dar 4. jamb, rail,
sash, sill 5. janua, panel, stile
6. lintel 9. threshold
doorkeeper... 4. hasp 5. tiler 6. porter
7. durwaum, ostiary 8. chokidar
9. concierge
dope... 3. hop, LSD 4. hemp
5. mescal, opiate, peyoti (peyote)
6. fathead 8. narcotic 9. marijuana
Dorian Festival (Sparta)... 6. carnea
(carneia)
Dorian magistrates... 6. ephors
Doric Order (Gr Arch)...
capital.. 6. abacus
frieze fillet.. 6. taenia
frieze space.. 6. metope
history.. 6. oldest 8. simplest
dormant... 5. inert 6. asleep, latent,
torpid 7. resting 8. inactive, sleeping
9. quiescent
dormer window... 5. oriel 6. gablet
7. dormant (obs), lucarne
dormeuse... 5. couch 8. carriage
(sleeping), nightcap
dormouse... 4. Glis, loir 5. lerot
6. rodent
dorsal (pert to)...
back.. 5. notal, notum 6. dorsum,
lumbar, neural, tergal, tergum
column.. 6. spinal
dose... 5. bolus, draft, treat 6. potion
7. portion
dot... 3. jot 4. clot, code, lump
5. dowry, fleck, point, speck, telia
(fungus) 6. period 7. stipple
dote... 3. rot 5. decay, dowry
6. babble, dotage, dotard, drivel,
stupor 7. portion (marriage)
8. imbecile
dotted... 5. pinto 7. piebald, specked,
studded 8. stippled 9. sprinkled
11. diversified
Douay Bible... 4. Aree
double... 2. di (pref) 4. dual, fold,
twin 5. duple, plait, twice 6. binary,
binate, duplex, folded 7. twofold
8. artifice, two–faced 9. deceitful,
duplicate, insincere, intensify

11. counterpart
double (pert to)...
bars (Her).. 5. gemel
cross.. 7. deceive, two–time
dagger.. 6. diesis
edged.. 9. ancipital
ghost (live person).. 11. counterpart
12. Doppelgänger, doubleganger
meaning.. 9. equivocal
doubt... 5. demur, waver 8. hesitate,
mistrust, question 9. misgiving,
suspicion 10. Pyrrhonism, skepticism
11. uncertainty
doubter... 5. cynic 6. Humist
7. skeptic 10. Pyrrhonist
doubtful... 7. dubious 8. wavering
9. ambiguous, equivocal, uncertain,
undecided 10. hesitating, improbable,
precarious 11. distrustful, vacillating
12. questionable, unbelievable,
undetermined 13. problematical
doubtful authority... 6. mythic, unreal
10. apocryphal
dough... 4. cash, mash 5. money,
paste 6. leaven, noodle
doughnut... 6. sinker 7. cruller, simball
9. friedcake
dour... 5. harsh, stern 6. gloomy,
severe 9. obstinate 10. inflexible
dove... 3. nun 4. blue (color), Inca
5. color 6. culver, pigeon
7. Columba, tumbler
Dove, the... 6. symbol (Relig)
10. Holy Spirit
dovefoot... 8. geranium (wild)
dovekey, dovekie... 3. auk 4. Alle
6. rotche 9. guillemot
dowdy... 3. pie (deep–dish) 6. pastry,
shabby, untidy 7. pudding 8. slovenly
10. slatternly
dowel... 3. pin 4. coak 5. tenon
6. fasten, pintle
dower... 3. dos 5. dowry, endow,
grant 6. dotate 7. bequest
8. dotation, jointure
down... 2. de (pref) 3. nap 4. fuzz,
hair 5. adown, below, floor
7. descent 8. softness
downcast... 3. low, sad 7. lowered
8. dejected 9. bowed down,
depressed 10. despondent, dispirited
11. discouraged, downhearted
downright... 4. flat 5. blunt, plain,
sheer, stark, utter 6. arrant, candid
8. positive, thorough 10. absolutely,
forthright 11. unqualified
13. unceremonious
downy... 4. soft, wary 5. nappy, pilar,
quiet 6. placid 7. villous 8. feathery
10. flocculent, lanuginose, lanuginous
dowry... 3. dos, dot 4. gift 5. dower,
sulka 6. talent 7. endowment
dowser's tool... 4. wand 6. willow
Doxology... 4. hymn 6. praise
7. Kaddish
doze... 3. nap, nod 5. sleep
6. catnap, drowse, snooze 7. stupefy
(obs)
draft, draught... 3. map, nip 4. dose,
dram, draw, plan, pull, swig
5. drink, epure 6. current, diagram,
drawing, outline 8. protocol, recruits,

traction 9. conscript 10. money
order
drag... 3. lag, lug, tow, tug 4. clog,
draw, hale, haul, pull, sing, tump
5. drawl, scent (hunt), smoke, trail
6. drogue, harrow 7. grapnel
8. dragrope, linger on, obstacle
10. conveyance
dragoman... 11. interpreter (official)
dragon... 4. lung 5. drake, Rahab (Bib)
6. animal, duenna, lizard, musket
(anc), pigeon 7. dragoon, monster
(Her), serpent 10. earthdrake
14. Dragon of Komodo
drain... 3. gaw, sap 4. lade, loss,
sink, sump 5. ditch, dreen, empty,
rhine, sewer, siver 6. filter, trench
7. acequia, alberca, channel,
consume, exhaust, outflow
11. watercourse
dram... 4. mite, slug 5. draft,
drink 6. drachm 8. potation
11. indifferent
drama (pert to)...
beginning.. 8. Dyonysia (anc)
form.. 4. play 5. opera 6. comedy
7. tragedy 10. peripeteia
11. composition
parts.. 8. epitasis, protasis
12. introduction
scenery.. 7. diorama
dramatic... 4. wild 5. stagy, vivid,
vocal 6. poetic, scenic 8. thespian
10. histrionic, theatrical
11. pretentious, spectacular
12. melodramatic
dramatic piece... 4. skit
drastic... 5. stern 6. fierce, severe
7. intense, radical 8. rigorous
draught... see *draft*
Dravidian (pert to)...
country (anc).. 5. India
ghost.. 4. bhut
language.. 5. Tamil 8. Kanarese
12. Dravido–Munda
native.. 5. Croat 8. Croatian
people.. 4. Nair 6. Slavic
soldier.. 8. Croatian
draw... 3. lug, tie, tow, tug 4. drag,
etch, haul, limn, lure, plot, pull, tole
5. draft, smoke 6. allure, arroyo,
convey, entice 7. attract, conduct,
extract, lottery 9. delineate
10. attraction
draw (pert to)...
away.. 6. abduce, divert 7. detract
close.. 4. loom, near 5. hover
8. approach
forth.. 5. educe 6. elicit, ferret
7. extract
off.. 6. siphon 7. extract 8. abstract,
withdraw
through an eye.. 4. rove
together.. 4. coul, frap, lace, rake
8. assemble
drawback... 5. fault, wince 6. defect,
resile, retire 8. obstacle 9. objection
12. disadvantage
drawing... 3. art 5. draft 7. diagram,
hauling, picture, pulling 8. doodling
9. animation 10. attracting,
extracting

drawing back... 9. retrahent
drayage... 6. charge 7. cartage,
haulage 8. truckage
14. transportation
dread... 3. awe 4. fear 5. timor
6. dismay, horror, terror 7. anxiety
8. affright 9. reverence
12. apprehension
dreadful... 4. dire 6. horrid
7. awesome, fearful, hideous
8. horrible, terrible, terrific 9. frightful
10. formidable
dreadnaught, dreadnought... 5. cloth
7. garment 8. fearless
10. battleship, Battleship (Brit),
fearnought
dream... 4. muse, rêve 5. fancy
6. bubble, vision 7. imagine, reverie,
romance, suppose 8. illusion
11. contemplate
dream (pert to)...
    comb form.. 6. oneiro
    interpretation.. 10. oneirology
    interpreter.. 12. oneirocritic
    tranquility.. 3. kef (keef) 7. reverie
dreamer... 4. seer 7. fantast
8. idealist, puffbird 9. visionary
11. romanticist 13. castle-builder
dreamy... 3. kef (keef) 6. poetic
7. languid 8. soothing
11. imaginative
dreary... 3. sad 4. dull, gray 5. bleak,
ourie 6. dismal, elenge, gloomy,
remote 7. doleful, tedious
9. cheerless 10. depressing,
foreboding, monotonous
11. comfortless
dredge... 4. tong (for oysters) 5. scoop
6. burrow, deepen, grains, tunnel
8. excavate
dregs... 4. faex, lees, marc, silt
5. draff, dross, magma 6. refuse,
scoria, sludge 7. grounds, hogwash,
residue 8. riffraff, sediment
9. settlings 10. faex populi
drench... 4. hose, soak 5. douse,
draft, imbue, purge, scour, souse
6. potion 7. immerse 8. permeate,
saturate, submerge
drenched... 4. asop 5. asoak
6. doused, soaked 9. saturated
dress... 3. rig, tog 4. deck, garb,
gown, suit, trim 5. get-up, mufti,
preen 6. attire, clothe, enrobe, livery,
toilet 7. apparel 8. clothing,
decorate, negligee 10. habiliment
13. Mother Hubbard
dress (pert to)...
    flax.. 3. ted
    gaudily.. 5. prank 7. bedizen, spangle
    leather.. 3. taw, tew 5. curry
    of Mecca pilgrims.. 5. ihram
    riding.. 5. chaps, habit 8. jodhpurs
    10. chaparajos
    stone.. 3. dab, nig 5. nidge
    surgically.. 5. dight, panse
    7. bandage
    up.. 5. preen, primp 6. spruce
    8. titivate
dressed loosely... 8. discinct, ungirded
dressing... 4. lint 5. sauce
7. bandage, pledget, raiment, reproof

8. attiring, scolding 9. condiment,
neatsfoot (leather) 11. castigation
drew... see *draw*
dried... 4. sere 5. wiped 6. seared,
wasted 7. drained, parched, wizened
9. shriveled 10. dehydrated,
desiccated, exsiccated
dried meat... 7. biltong (biltongue),
charqui 8. pemmican 10. jerked beef
dried tubers (orchids)... 5. salep
drift... 3. aim, sag 4. idle, pile, sail,
soar, tide, tool 5. float, stray, tenor,
trend 6. course, intent 7. deposit,
impetus, meaning 8. crescent
(sidewise), movement, seaweeds,
tendency 9. deviation
drill... 3. gad, row (seeds), tap
4. bore 5. auger, borer, train
6. baboon, pierce 7. machine
8. excavate, exercise, practice,
rehearse 9. perforate
drilling... 5. denim 7. nurture
8. training
drink... 3. ade, ale, bib, lap, nip, pop,
rum, sip, tea, tot 4. flip, fram, grog,
mead, sake, shot, slug, soda, soma,
swig, tope 5. bouse, draft, julep,
negus, posca, quaff, skink, toast,
toddy, vodka, water 6. caudle,
coffee, imbibe, liquor, posset, potion,
ptisan, tipple 8. beverage, cocktail,
sangaree, sillabub 9. decoction
10. intoxicant
drink (pert to)...
    ancient.. 5. morat
    Arabian.. 4. boza
    English.. 7. wassail
    frozen.. 6. frappé
    gods (of the).. 6. nectar
    honey.. 5. morat
    hot.. 5. salep, toddy 6. posset,
    saloop
    Irish.. 10. shandygaff
    Japanese.. 4. sake 9. grenadine
    mix.. 9. grenadine
    rum.. 5. bumbo
    Russian.. 5. vodka 6. kumiss
    (koumiss)
    Spanish.. 7. tequila
    together.. 9. symposium
    tropical.. 8. sangaree
    Turkish.. 4. raki 5. airan
drinking salutation... 5. skoal, toast
6. prosit 7. propine
drinking vessel... 3. mug 4. bowl,
tass 5. cylix (anc), glass, gourd,
jorum, mazer, stein 6. goblet, rhyton
7. tankard 8. schooner 10. Vaphio
cups (gold)
drip... 4. bore, drop, leak 5. droop
7. dribble, falling, trickle
drive... 3. caa 4. herd, ride, slog,
urge 5. force, guide, impel, pilot,
press, rouse 6. attack, compel,
energy, propel, thrust 7. crusade,
operate 8. campaign 10. compulsion
drive (pert to)...
    away.. 4. rout 5. chase, exile, expel,
    repel 6. banish, dispel, rebuff
    7. repulse 8. disperse
    down.. 4. tamp
    frantic.. 4. loco 6. madden 7. bedevil

obliquely.. 3. toe 5. slice
stakes.. 4. camp, park 6. locate, settle
drivel... 4. dote 5. drool 6. slaver 7. slobber, twaddle 8. nonsense
driveler... 4. fool 5. doter, idiot 6. dotard, prater 8. jabberer 9. blatherer, chatterer
driver... 4. club (golf), jehu 6. drover, hammer, mahout, sarwan 7. speeder 8. coachman, engineer, motorist, operator, overseer, reinsman 9. propeller 10. charioteer, taskmaster
drizzle... 4. mist, rain, smur 6. mizzle (misle)
droll... 3. odd 4. zany 5. comic, merry, queer, witty 6. jester 7. amusing, buffoon, waggish 8. farcical, humorous 9. diverting, laughable, whimsical 10. ridiculous 11. merry-andrew
drollery... 3. wit 4. jest 5. farce, humor 6. puppet 9. absurdity 10. buffoonery
dromedary... 4. oont 5. camel (one–hump) 6. hageen 7. Camelus 8. Bactrian (two–hump)
drone... 3. bee, dor, hum 4. male (bee) 5. idler, snail 7. bagpipe, humming 8. sluggard 9. non–worker, slow mover
drool... 6. drivel, slaver 7. dribble, slabber, slobber
droop... 3. lop, sag 4. flag, hang, loll, pine, sink, tire, wilt 6. nutate, slouch 7. decline 8. languish
drooping... 4. alop, weak 5. loose 7. hanging, nodding, sinking 8. dejected, fatigued 11. languishing
drooping eyelids... 6. ptosis
drop... 4. bead, blob, dose, dram, drib, drip, fall, omit, shed, sink, slot, stop, tear 5. candy, dreep, droop, gutta, lower, minim, remit 6. letter, plunge 7. abandon, descent, distill (distil), earring, globule, pendant, trickle 8. ornament, trapdoor 9. declivity 10. relinquish
drop (pert to)...
anchor.. 4. moor
by drop.. 7. guttate 9. guttation
measure.. 7. pipette 11. stactometer
nautical.. 5. hance
serene.. 9. amaurosis (Med)
vowel.. 5. elide
dropsy... 5. edema 8. hydropsy, swelling
dross... 4. lees, scum, slag 5. chaff, dregs, scobs, sprue, waste 6. refuse, scoria, sinter (iron)
drove... 4. herd 5. crowd, drive, flock
drover... 4. boat 6. dealer (cattle), driver 8. herdsman
drowse... 3. nid, nod 4. doze 5. dover (Eng), sleep 6. snooze
drowsiness... 7. languor 8. dullness, lethargy 9. lassitude, oscitance 10. narcolepsy, sleepiness 12. listlessness, sluggishness
drowsy... 4. logy 6. sleepy 8. oscitant, soothing 9. somnolent, soporific

drudge... 3. fag 4. grub, hack, mail, plod, toil 5. labor, slave 6. toiler 7. plodder
drug... 4. alum, dope, dull, numb 6. opiate 7. stupefy 8. narcotic, sedative 10. medication 11. anesthetize
drug (pert to)...
action.. 7. synergy
addict.. 6. junkie
analgesic.. 6. Anacin 7. aspirin 10. acetanilid, phenacetin
anesthesia.. 3. gas 5. ether 8. Novocain 10. chloroform
dangerous.. 11. thalidomide
emetic.. 6. ipecac 11. ipecacuanha
eye.. 8. atropine 10. belladonna
forgetfulness.. 8. nepenthe
narcotic.. 3. hop, kif 4. hemp 5. bhang, daggo, opium 6. codein 7. cocaine 9. marijuana
sedative.. 7. bromide, Seconal, Veronal 8. barbital, Nembutal 11. scopolamine 13. phenobarbital
drugget... 3. mat, rug 5. cloth
druggist... 8. gallipot 10. apothecary, pharmacist
Druids (anc)... 5. Order (Relig) 9. conjurers 12. philosophers
drum... 4. beat 5. naker, snare, tabor, tombe 6. atabal, barrel, tambor (tambour), tom–tom, tympan 7. tabret, timbrel, timpany 8. cylinder, tympanum (ear)
drum (pert to)...
call.. 4. dian (diana) 6. rappel, tattoo 8. rataplan
Indian.. 6. nagara
nautical term.. 7. capstan
Oriental.. 6. tom–tom 7. anacara
drunkard... 3. sot 4. soak 5. souse, toper 6. addict, barfly, boozer 7. guzzler, tippler 9. alcoholic, inebriate 11. dipsomaniac
dry... 3. sec, ted 4. arid, blot, brut, dull, keen, seco, sere, wipe 5. drain, parch, vapid 6. aerify, barren, jejune, shrewd 7. insipid, sterile, thirsty, xerotic 8. solidify, tiresome 9. dehydrate, fruitless, pointless 12. unprofitable 13. uninteresting
dryad... 5. deity, Napea, nymph, oread
duck... 3. dip 4. flee, fowl 5. dodge, douse 6. plunge 7. bob down
duck (breed)... 8. Anas, coot, pato, skua, smee, smew, teal 5. Anser, eider, scaup 6. Aythya, Nyroca, Peking, scoter 7. mallard, Muscovy, pintail, pochard, Spatula, widgeon 8. Anatinae, bluebill, shoveler (shoveller) 9. harlequin, merganser, sheldrake 10. bufflehead, canvasback, ring–necked
duck (pert to)...
baby.. 8. duckling
class.. 3. sea 5. river 7. Muscovy
disabled.. 4. lame
ducklike.. 5. decoy 8. duckbill
fabric.. 5. cloth
flock (mallards).. 4. sord
flower.. 12. lady's slipper
game.. 6. tenter

hawk.. 6. falcon 7. harrier
litter.. 4. team
male.. 5. drake
ruddy.. 5. noddy
duct... 3. vas 4. main, pipe, race,
tube 5. canal 7. channel, passage,
trachea 8. aqueduct
ductile... 6. docile, facile, pliant
7. elastic, plastic, tensile 8. flexible,
tractile, yielding 9. compliant,
complying, malleable, tractable
10. manageable
dude... 4. fop 5. dandy 7. coxcomb,
Johnnie 10. tenderfoot
dudeen... 4. pipe (tobacco)
due... 4. debt, duty, just, meed, owed
5. owing 6. charge, lawful 7. exactly
8. adequate, directly, expected,
rightful 9. appointed 10. ascribable,
sufficient
duel... 4. tilt 5. fence 6. combat
7. contest 8. conflict 9. monomachy
12. satisfaction
duelist's aide... 6. second
duet... 3. duo 8. duettino
dug... see *dig*
dugong... 7. manatee, Sirenia
8. Halicore
dugout... 4. abri, cave, shed 5. canoe
6. cavity 7. pirogue, shelter
dulcet... 5. sweet 6. ariose 7. tuneful
8. pleasant, soothing 9. agreeable,
melodious 10. harmonious
dulcimer... 6. citole 7. bagpipe,
cembalo 8. psaltery 10. instrument
dull... 3. dim, dry, dun 4. dead, drab,
gray, logy, poky 6. barren, cloudy,
deaden, dismal, dreary, drowsy,
jejune, leaden, muffle, obtund,
obtuse, sleepy, somber, stupid
7. doltish, irksome, prosaic, tedious
8. lifeless, listless, overcast, sluggish,
stagnant, tiresome 9. apathetic,
inanimate, saturnine, unfeeling
10. insensible, lackluster, melancholy,
slow-witted 13. unimaginative
dull (pert to)...
finish.. 3. mat (matte)
heavy.. 4. logy 6. leady 6. stodgy
of cloth.. 6. starry (Eng)
statement.. 9. platitude
dullard... 3. oaf 4. dope, mope
5. dunce 8. dumbbell, numskull
9. dumb bunny
dumb... 4. mute 5. aphony, silent,
stupid 7. aphonia 8. ignorant,
taciturn 9. inanimate, irregular
10. speechless 12. inarticulate
dumbfounded... 6. amazed 7. crabbed
9. staggered, surprised
10. astonished, bewildered
11. overwhelmed 13. flabbergasted
dummy... 3. pel 4. copy, dolt, mort
(cards), sham 5. model 6. pontic,
silent 7. imitation, mannequin,
nonentity 10. figurehead, substitute
11. counterfeit
dump... 3. tip 4. bump, game (Eng)
jail, sell, thud, tune 5. empty, hovel
6. plunge, unload 7. discard
10. rendezvous

dumpling... 7. biscuit, gnocchi
10. appleberry
dupe... 3. fox 4. bilk, cull, tool
5. cheat, fraud, trick 6. delude,
sucker 7. cat's-paw, deceive, mislead
duplicate... 4. copy, game (cards),
twin 6. double, duplex 7. estreat,
mislead, replica, twofold 8. likeness
9. analogous, facsimile, identical,
replicate 10. transcript
11. counterpart 12. reproduction
duplicated... 7. dittoed 8. repeated
12. repetitive
duplicity... 5. fraud, guile 6. deceit
7. duality 9. deception, duplexity,
falsehood, treachery
13. dissimulation, double-dealing
durable... 4. firm 5. stout, tough
6. staple 7. lasting 8. constant,
enduring 9. permanent
10. continuing, persistent
11. everlasting, substantial
duration... 3. age 4. date, span, term,
time 6. period 8. eternity, lifetime
10. durability, permanence
11. continuance
during... 4. time 5. while 6. whilst
7. pending, through 10. throughout
dusk... 4. dark 5. dusky, gloom, slate
(color) 8. gloaming, twilight
dusky... 3. dim, sad 4. dark, dusk
5. murky, tawny, umbra 6. gloomy,
somber 7. swarthy 8. blackish
10. melancholy
dust... 4. cash, coom (coomb), dirt,
gold, pilm, soil 5. briss, brush, chaff,
clean, color, earth, money, stive,
stour (dial), trash 6. corpse, pollen,
powder 7. dryness, turmoil
9. commotion, confusion, sweepings
dust (pert to)...
flax.. 5. pouce
flour.. 5. stive
glacier.. 10. kryokonite
reduce to.. 4. mull
speck.. 4. mote
Dutch (pert to)... see also *Netherlands*
cheese.. 4. Edam 5. cottage
country. 7. Germany, Holland
11. Netherlands
man.. 10. Hogen-Mogen
news agency.. 5. Aneta
painter.. 4. Hals
poet.. 7. Da Costa
pottery.. 4. delf (delft) 9. delftware
river.. 3. Eem 4. Maas 5. Meuse
scholar.. 7. Erasmus (Humanist)
woman, wife.. 4. frow
uncle.. 3. eme (dial), oom
Dutch East Indies (Indonesia)...
capital.. 7. Batavia (former), Jakarta
(Djakarta)
islands (3,000), largest.. 4. Bali, Java
6. Borneo (part) 7. Celebes, Sumatra
8. Malaysia (part) 9. New Guinea
(part)
renamed.. 9. Indonesia
Dutch Guiana (Netherlands Antilles)...
capital.. 10. Paramaribo
mountain.. 10. Tumuc Humac
renamed.. 7. Surinam
dutiful... 6. devout, docile 7. deuteous

8. obedient, reverent 9. compliant
10. respectful, submissive
11. deferential, reverential

duty... 3. job, tax 4. care, onus, rite,
task, toll 5. chore, stint, trick
6. devoir, dharma, excise, heriot
(anc), impost, tariff 7. payment,
respect 9. reverence 10. imposition,
obligation

dwale... 5. sable (Her) 6. opiate,
potion 9. soporific 10. belladonna,
nightshade

dwarf... 3. elf, urf 4. grig, puny, runt
5. crile, gnome, midge, pygmy
(pigmy), small, stunt, troll 6. droich,
durgan, midget 7. manikin, Pacolet,
stunted 9. dandiprat, micrander
10. diminished, homunculus

dwarfish... 6. nanoid

dwarfishness... 6. nanism

Dwarfs, The Seven... 3. Doc
5. Dopey, Happy 6. Grumpy, Sleepy,
Sneezy 7. Bashful

dwell... 4. bide, harp, live, stay
5. abide, delay, lodge, pause, tarry
6. linger, remain, reside

dwelling... 3. hut 4. flat 5. abode,
hotel, house, hovel 6. duplex, shanty
7. trailer 8. abidance, domicile,
tenement 9. apartment, residence
10. habitation

dwelling (pert to)...
house (law).. 8. messuage
in field.. 10. arvicoline
in groves.. 10. nemoricole
of dead (Bab).. 5. Aralu
of souls (Polyn).. 2. Po
Oriental.. 3. dar

dwindle... 4. melt, wane 5. taper,
waste 6. lessen, shrink, sicken

8. decrease, diminish 10. degenerate

dyad... 3. two 4. duad, pair
6. couple, dyadic

Dyak, Dayak... 5. tribe (Borneo)
7. blowgun 8. sumpiter 9. aborigine

dye... 4. anil 5. color, imbue, stain,
tinge 7. pigment 8. colorant

dye stuff (pert to)...
blue.. 4. woad (wad, wade)
brown.. 5. erika, sumac
indigo.. 4. anil
mulberry.. 3. aal
red.. 4. chay 5. aurin, eosin, henna
6. isatin, madder, relbun 7. annatto,
magenta 8. morindin 9. rhodamine
10. orseilline
violet.. 5. murex 6. archil
yellow.. 7. xanthic 8. luteolin,
orpiment 10. quercitron

dyke... see *dike*

dynamic... 4. keen 5. acute, vivid
6. potent 7. intense, kinetic
8. forceful, forcible 9. energetic,
strenuous

dynamite inventor... 5. Nobel (1866)

dynamo (pert to)...
attachment.. 10. commutator
inventor.. 7. Faraday
machine.. 9. generator
part.. 5. rotor 8. armature

dynast... 5. ruler 6. prince 8. governor

dynasty... 4. race 8. dominion,
lordship 10. succession
11. sovereignty

dynasty (pert to)...
Chinese.. 2. Fo 3. Han, Yin 4. Isin,
Ming, Sung, Tang
Spanish.. 6. Ommiad

dysphoria... 7. illness 8. debility

dyvour... 6. beggar 8. bankrupt

dzeren... 8. antelope

E

E... 7. Epsilon (Gr)

Ea (Bab)... 3. God 5. deity

each... 3. all, per 5. alike, every
6. apiece, singly 10. separately
12. individually 14. distributively

eager... 3. apt 4. agog, avid, keen,
yare 5. agasp, sharp 6. ardent,
greedy, intent 7. anxious, burning,
excited, thirsty, willing, zealous
8. desirous, spirited 9. strenuous

eager beaver... 7. hustler 8. go-getter
10. enthusiast

eagerness... 4. élan, zeal 5. ardor
6. fervor 7. avidity 8. alacrity,
cupidity, fervency 9. alertness,
readiness 10. enthusiasm, impatience
13. impetuousness

eagle... 4. erne (ern), gier (Bib), seal
6. bergut, eaglet, emblem

8. standard (Rom) 13. constellation
(Milky Way)

eagle (pert to)...
American.. 4. bald
brood.. 5. aerie, eyrie
coin.. 4. gold
European.. 3. sea 5. harpy 6. golden
8. imperial
genus.. 6. Aquila
heraldry.. 8. allerion
male.. 6. tercil
sacred to Jupiter.. 9. Jove's bird
S America.. 9. eagle hawk
scout badge.. 5. merit

Eagles... 14. Fraternal Order

eagre (acker)... 4. bore, flow, wave
5. flood (tidal)

ear... 4. head 5. auris 7. auricle,
hearing 8. orillion 9. appendage,

attention, orecchion (obs)

ear (pert to)...
anvil.. 5. incus
bone.. 6. stapes, tegman 7. stirrup
canal.. 7. cochlea 9. labyrinth
10. Eustachian, scala media
external.. 6. concha
grain.. 3. epi 5. spica 6. mealie,
rizzom (ressum)
hammer.. 7. malleus
inflammation.. 6. otitis
middle.. 8. tympanum
part.. 5. helix, pinna 6. tragus
science.. 7. otology
shell.. 5. ormer 7. abalone
specialist.. 6. aurist 9. otologist
stone.. 7. otolith
term.. 5. otic 5. aural
wax.. 7. cerumen
earache... 6. otalgy 7. otalgia
early... 4. soon 7. ancient, betimes,
matinal 8. premature, primitive
10. beforehand, beforetime
early Greek... 5. Arius 6. oecist
early philosophy... 7. Eleatic (Gr)
earn... 3. get, win 4. gain 5. ettle,
merit 7. acquire, deserve
earnest... 5. arles (pledge), grave,
sober, staid 6. ardent, hearty,
pledge, sedate, solemn 7. handsel
(money), serious, sincere, zealous
8. resolute 9. heartfelt, important
10. thoughtful 12. wholehearted
earnestly... 8. solemnly 9. intensely,
zealously 10. resolutely
earphone... 7. trumpet (double)
8. otoscope 9. auriphone, topophone
(double) 11. stethoscope
earring... 6. erabob, pendle 7. pendant
9. girandole
earth... 3. erd 4. clay, clod, dirt, land,
marl, muck, sand, soil, vale 5. geest,
loess, sloam, terra 6. ground, planet,
rideau 7. topsoil 8. alluvium
earth (pert to)...
center.. 10. geocentric
12. centrosphere
comb form.. 3. geo
deformation.. 10. epeirogeny
formed beneath.. 8. hypogene,
plutonic
formed by ores.. 9. supergene
formed on surface.. 7. epigene
god (Egypt).. 3. Geb (Keb)
goddess.. 4. Erda, Tari 6. Semele
7. Demeter
produced by.. 6. mortal
11. terrigenous
satellite.. 4. Echo 5. Atlas
7. Mercury, Sputnik (Russ)
8. Explorer, Vanguard
volcanic.. 5. trass
earthdrake... 6. dragon
earthly... 7. mundane, secular, terrene,
worldly 8. temporal 11. terrestrial,
universally, unspiritual
13. materialistic
earth pig... 8. aardvark
earthquake... 5. quake, seism
7. temblor 12. diastrophism
earthstar... 6. fungus 7. Geaster
earthworm... 7. annelid, dew worm,

ipokoea 9. Lumbricus
earthy... 3. low 5. gross 6. coarse
7. worldly 8. material 9. unrefined
11. terrestrial, unspiritual
ease... 4. calm, rest 5. abate, allay,
peace, quiet, relax 6. pacify, relief,
repose, soothe 7. assuage, comfort,
content, leisure, relieve, slacken
8. facility, mitigate 9. alleviate,
disburden, enjoyment 10. prosperity,
relaxation, solicitude 11. informality,
tranquilize 11. tranquillity (tranquility)
easily... 4. eath (eith) 6. gently,
slowly, softly 7. readily 8. smoothly
11. comfortably, dexterously
12. effortlessly
easily (pert to)...
broken.. 6. shelly 7. fragile, friable
frightened.. 8. skittish
managed.. 6. docile
moved.. 6. mobile
offended.. 9. sensitive
split.. 8. schistic
understood.. 5. lucid
east... 4. Asia, dawn 6. Levant, Orient
7. sunrise 8. eastward
East Africa...
hartebeest.. 4. tora
house (mud).. 5. tembe
republic.. 5. Kenya 7. Somalia
sultanate, island.. 8. Zanzibar
terrorists.. 6. Mau Mau (Kenya)
vessel.. 4. dhow
East India... see also East Indian
drink.. 4. nipa
fan.. 6. punkah (punka)
garment.. 4. sari
gateway (temple).. 5. toran (torana)
hat, helmet.. 5. topee (topi)
language.. 4. Urdu
money of account.. 4. anna
mountain pass.. 4. ghat (ghaut)
musical instrument.. 4. vina 5. ruana,
saron
pipe (smoking).. 6. hookah
police station.. 5. thana (tanna)
sailing vessel.. 5. dhoni (doni)
7. patamar
sugar, molasses.. 3. gur
10. massecuite
water vessel (brass).. 4. lota (lotah)
East Indian animal...
antelope.. 5. bongo, takin 6. impala,
nilgai 8. axis deer
cattle.. 4. gaur, zebu 5. gayal, tsine
7. banteng
civet.. 5. musang 10. paradoxure
crocodile.. 6. mugger
goat (wild).. 4. tahr 7. markhor
lemurlike.. 7. tarsier
raccoonlike.. 3. wah 5. panda
rat.. 9. bandicoot
sheep (wild).. 5. urial
swine.. 8. babirusa (babiroussa)
East Indian bird...
broadbill.. 4. raya
bulbul.. 4. kala
falcon.. 5. besra
fruit pigeon.. 6. treron
thrush.. 5. shama
weaverbird.. 4. baya
East Indian people...

boatswain.. 6. serang
chief.. 6. sirdar
groom.. 4. syce
harem.. 6. zenana
native.. 6. Somali
native sailor, soldier.. 5. sepoy
  6. lascar
nurse.. 4. amah, ayah
peasant.. 4. ryot
poet.. 6. Tagore
princess.. 4. rani (ranee)
robber.. 6. dacoit
title.. 4. raja 5. rajah, sahib
warrior.. 5. singh
East Indian tree, plant...
bark.. 4. lodh 5. niepa
cedar.. 6. deodar
cotton.. 5. simal
fiber.. 4. jute
fruit.. 4. bel 6. lanseh (lansa)
gum.. 4. kino
herb.. 4. tikor 6. roselle
mahogany.. 4. toon
mulberry.. 4. tapa
palm.. 3. tal (fiber) 5. sural (juice),
  toddy 7. palmyra
pea.. 4. dhak 5. Butea
rubber.. 4. saj
shade.. 6. banyan
timber.. 3. saj, sal 4. poon, teak
  5. siris 6. sissoo
walnut.. 6. lebbek
east wind... 5. Eurus
easy... 4. calm, slow 5. loose, suave
  6. facile, gentle, simple 7. natural
  8. gullible, informal, moderate,
  tranquil, unforced 9. leisurely,
  unhurried 10. manageable,
  nonchalant, unaffected
  11. comfortable, complaisant,
  unconcerned
easy job... 8. sinecure
easy mark... 4. dupe, gull 6. sucker,
  victim 7. cat's-paw
eat... 3. sup 4. dine, etch, feed, gnaw
  5. board, erode 6. devour, ravage
  7. consume, corrode, destroy
eat (pert to)...
between meals.. 5. bever
by rule.. 4. diet
earth, clay.. 8. geophagy
  12. chthonophagy
flesh (raw).. 8. omophagy (anc)
greedily.. 3. lab 5. gorge 6. gobble
  7. edacity 8. voracity
eatable... 6. edible 8. esculent,
  gustable 10. comestible
eater... 5. diner 7. epicure, gourmet
  8. gourmand
eating (pert to)...
alone.. 9. monophagy
alone, fear of.. 10. monophobia
comb form.. 7. phagous
decay.. 12. saprophagous
fish.. 11. piscivorous
  13. icthyophagous
flesh, raw.. 8. omophagy
  9. omophagia 10. omophagous
flesh-eating.. 9. creophagy
  10. zoophagous 11. carnivorous,
  creophagous
horse.. 12. hippophagous

lizard.. 12. saurophagous
man–eating.. 12. androphagous
  13. anthropophagy
nuts.. 10. nucivorous 11. nuciphagous
plants, herbs.. 11. herbivorous
  12. phytophagous
roots.. 12. rhizophagous
eavesdrop... 4. drip 6. harken, listen
  10. stillicide 14. listen secretly
ebb... 3. low 4. neap, sink, tide, wane
  5. abate, decay 6. recede, reflux,
  retire 7. decline, shallow, subside
  8. decrease
ebb and flow... 5. surge 6. aestus
  (estus) 11. alternation
ebb tide... 8. low water
ebullition... 7. boiling, ferment
  8. bubbling 9. agitation, commotion
  12. fermentation 13. effervescence
eccentric... 3. cam (shaft), odd 4. tyke
  (tike) 7. erratic, strange 8. abnormal
  9. erratical, irregular
  13. nonconformist 15. idiosyncratical
eccentricity... 6. oddity 9. queerness
  10. aberration, erraticism
  11. abnormality, peculiarity,
  strangeness 12. idiosyncrasy,
  irregularity 13. nonconformity
  17. unconventionality
Ecclesiastes... 8. Koheleth (Gr)
echidna... 7. monster (Gr Myth)
  8. anteater
echinoderm... 8. starfish 9. sea urchin
echo... 4. mute, stop (organ)
  5. nymph (Myth), reply 6. repeat
  7. imitate, respond 8. resemble,
  response 9. duplicate 10. repetition
  13. reverberation
echoism... 12. onomatopoeia
Eciton... 4. ants (legionary)
eclipse... 5. cloud, sully 6. darken
  7. obscure, surpass 10. extinguish
ecliptic term... 5. lagna, orbit
  6. circle 9. penumbral
ecology, oecology... 6. botany
  7. biology 9. bionomics, sociology
  10. bioecology
economical... 5. canny, chary
  6. frugal, saving 7. careful, thrifty
  8. domestic 9. provident
  12. parsimonious
economics... 9. plutology
  10. production (wealth)
economize... 4. save 5. skimp, stint
  6. scrimp 7. husband, utilize
  8. retrench
economy... 4. care 6. saving, thrift
  7. cutback 8. prudence 9. canniness,
  husbandry 10. providence
ecstasy... 5. bliss 6. trance
  7. emotion, rapture 9. enrapture,
  transport
ecstatic... 4. rapt 7. rapture
  9. rapturous, rhapsodic
ectad... 7. outward
ecto (comb form)... 7. outside, without
  8. external
Ecuador (pert to)...
capital.. 5. Quito
export.. 7. bananas
hat.. 6. Panama 8. "Jipijapa"
island.. 9. Galapagos

mountain.. 5. Andes
reptile.. 6. iguana 8. tortoise
volcano.. 10. Chimborazo
ecumenical... 7. general, liberal
8. catholic, tolerant 9. universal,
world–wide 12. cosmopolitan
eczema... 6. herpes, tetter 8. eruption
9. salt rheum
edacity... 5. greed 7. avarice
8. appetite, gulosity, voracity
10. greediness
eddy... 4. bore, gulf 5. gurge, surge,
swirl, whirl 6. vortex 7. current,
wreathe 9. whirlpool
Edentate (Zool)... 6. sloths
7. mammals 9. aardvarks, anteaters
10. armadillos
edge... 3. hem, jag, lip, rim 4. brim,
brow, side 5. arris, brink, crest,
marge, sharp, sidle (to), splay, verge
6. border, flange, labrum, margin
7. ambitus, selvage 8. acrimony,
pungency, selvedge 9. advantage,
sharpness 10. escarpment
edged... 5. erose 7. crenate
8. bordered, invected (Her)
edging... 3. hem 4. lace, welt 5. frill,
ruche 6. border, fringe, ruffle
7. binding, bordure (Her), flounce,
tatting
edgy... 5. sharp 7. angular, nervous
8. critical, snappish 9. excitable,
impatient 13. sharp–cornered
edict... 3. act, ban 4. Bull (Pope's),
fiat 5. arret, dicta (pl), irade, order,
ukase 6. assize, decree, dictum,
firman 7. command, mandate
8. decretal 9. ordinance
12. proclamation
edification... 8. learning 9. knowledge
11. improvement, instruction
edifice... 5. house 6. church, palace,
temple 7. Capitol 8. building
9. structure 10. tabernacle
edify... 5. build, teach 7. educate,
improve 8. instruct, organize
9. construct, enlighten, establish
Edinburgh...
burgh.. 5. Leith
capital of.. 8. Scotland
county.. 10. Midlothian
famed street.. 9. Royal Mile
Gaelic name.. 7. Dun Edin (Dunedin)
nickname.. 16. Athens of the North
site.. 12. Firth of Forth
edit... 5. emend 6. direct, excise,
redact, revise, reword 7. arrange,
correct, prepare
edition... 4. copy 5. issue 6. number
7. version
editions (Bib)...
eight texts.. 7. octapla
four texts.. 8. tetrapla
six texts.. 7. hexapla
style and type.. 7. Elzevir (1583)
editor... 7. analyst, newsman, reviser
8. arranger, redactor 9. annotator,
gazetteer 10. journalist, supervisor
11. commentator 12. newspaperman
Edom... 5. Teman (Bib) 7. Idumaea
Edomite... 4. Esau 5. Isaac, Jacob
8. Idumaean

educate... 4. rear 5. teach, train
6. inform 7. develop 8. instruct
9. cultivate, enlighten 10. discipline
12. indoctrinate
educated... 6. taught 7. erudite,
learned, trained 8. cultured,
informed, lettered, literate
11. enlightened
education... 8. breeding, literacy,
training 9. opsimathy (late in life),
schooling 10. discipline
educe... 4. draw 6. deduce, elicit,
evolve, obtain, secure
eel (pert to)...
colorful.. 5. moray 7. Muraena
genus.. 8. Anguilla 13. Leptocephalus
marine.. 5. elver 6. conger
mud.. 5. siren
sand.. 4. grig
young.. 5. elver
eellike... 4. lant, ling 7. eelpout,
lamprey 8. Ophidion 10. anguilloid
11. Lepidosiren
eels, fishing for... 5. sniggle
eels, migration of... 7. eelfare
eelworm... 4. nema 8. Nematoda
9. roundworm 10. vinegar eel
eerie, eery... 5. scary, timid, weird
6. gloomy, spooky 7. awesome,
fearful, uncanny 9. deathlike,
unearthly 10. frightened
efface... 5. erase 6. cancel, delete
7. blot out, expunge 10. obliterate
effect... 4. does 5. close, éclat, force,
mneme 6. mirage, obtain, result
7. achieve, compass, conjure,
execute, fulfill, meaning, operate,
outcome, perform, reality, realize
8. complete 9. discharge, execution,
influence 10. accomplish,
appearance, consummate, impression
11. consequence, performance
effective... 4. able 6. active, actual,
cogent 7. capable, telling
8. adequate, eloquent, equipped,
striking 9. brilliant, competent,
effectual, efficient, operative,
trenchant 11. efficacious, influential
effects... 5. goods, wares 8. movables,
property
effeminate... 3. sop 5. sissy
6. female, tender 7. cockney,
epicene, womanly 8. feminine,
womanish 9. Sybaritic
11. mollycoddle 12. overdelicate
13. overemotional
effervescent... 5. fizzy 6. bubbly, lively
7. boiling, hissing 8. bubbling,
mousseux 9. ebullient, sparkling
10. boisterous
effete... 4. aged, idle 5. spent
6. barren 7. worn out 9. exhausted,
fruitless 11. ineffectual
efficacious... 4. able 5. valid
6. potent 9. effective, effectual,
operative 11. influential
efficacy... 4. dint 5. force, power
6. virtue 7. ability, potency
10. efficiency
efficiency... 5. power, skill 7. ability,
utility 8. efficacy 10. capability,
competence 11. proficiency

12. productivity 13. effectiveness
15. efficaciousness
efficient... 4. able 7. capable, operant
9. competent, effective, effectual,
operative 10. productive
12. businesslike
effigy... 4. copy, icon 5. image
8. likeness 9. facsimile, jackstraw,
semblance 11. resemblance
effluvium... 4. aura, fume, odor
9. ectoplasm, emanation
efflux... 3. end 6. expiry, runoff
7. outflow 8. effusion 9. effluence,
emanation
effodient... 9. burrowing, fossorial
effort... 3. try, tug 4. dint, jump, toil,
will, work 5. assay, burst, labor,
nisus, pains, trial 6. strain
7. attempt, conatus, trouble
8. endeavor, exertion, struggle
11. application
effrontery... 5. brass 8. audacity,
boldness 9. arrogance, impudence,
sauciness 11. presumption
effulgence... 5. aglow, glory 6. luster
8. radiance, rutilant, splendor
10. brightness, brilliance
effusive... 7. gushing 9. exuberant,
rhapsodic 13. demonstrative
eft... 4. evet, newt 6. lizard, triton
7. urodele 10. salamander
egest... 4. emit, void 7. excrete
9. discharge, ejaculate, eliminate
egg... 3. nit, ova (pl), ove 4. goad,
ovum, prod, urge 5. ovule 6. incite
9. instigate
egg (pert to)...
bird's.. 7. chalaza (white of), treadle
(embryo)
case.. 6. ovisac
comb form.. 2. oo 3. ovi
part.. 7. latebra
shaped.. 4. ooid, oval 5. ovate, ovoid
6. ooidal 9. ovaliform
shell.. 5. shard 6. ovisac
undeveloped.. 5. addle
white.. 5. glair 7. albumen
yolk, yelk.. 7. liaison 8. lecithin
eggplant... 9. melongena
eggs (pert to)...
feeding on.. 9. ovivorous
fish.. 3. roe 5. berry, spawn
preserved.. 5. pidan
tester of.. 7. candler
two at a time.. 8. ditokous
egis, aegis... 4. care 5. guard
6. shield, symbol (anc) 7. backing,
defense 8. advocacy, auspices,
guidance, tutelage 9. fosterage,
patronage 10. protection
11. sponsorship
ego... 3. man 4. self 5. atman (Hind)
6. psyche, spirit 7. conceit, jivatma
(Hind) 11. selfishness
egress... 4. exit 5. issue 6. outlet
8. issuance 9. departure
egret... 5. heron, plume 8. aigrette
Egypt, UAR... see also *Egypt*
capital.. 5. Cairo
Christian.. 4. Copt
city (ruined).. 5. Luxor, Tanis
6. Karnak, Thebes

dam.. 5. Aswan
desert.. 5. Dakla
gulf.. 4. Suez 5. Aqaba
language (anc).. 6. Coptic
lighthouse (anc).. 6. Pharos
mother.. 3. Mut
peninsula.. 5. Sinai
philosopher.. 8. Plotinus
port.. 4. Said, Suez 10. Alexandria
queen.. 9. Cleopatra
river.. 4. Nile
ruler.. 5. pasha 6. caliph 7. khedive
ruler.. 6. Farouk 7. Busiris (Myth),
Pharaoh, Ptolemy, Rameses
sea.. 3. Red 13. Mediterranean
Egyptian (pert to)...
abode of dead.. 4. Aaru (fields of)
6. Amenti
antelope.. 7. bubalis
ape (sacred).. 4. Aani
beetle.. 6. scarab
bird (crocodile).. 6. sicsac
bird (sacred).. 4. Benu, ibis
7. phoenix
bull.. 4. apis
cobra.. 4. haje
cross.. 3. tau 4. ankh (emblem of
life) 10. crux ansata
crown.. 4. atef
dancing girl.. 4. alma (alme, Almeh)
7. ghawazi 8. Baramika
dog.. 6. saluki (gazelle hound)
headdress of ruler.. 6. Uraeus
heaven.. 4. Aaru
lizard.. 4. adda 5. skink
lute.. 5. nable
paper.. 7. papyrus
solar disk.. 4. aten
soul.. 2. Ba 4. khet, sahu
stone (famed).. 7. Rosetta
symbol.. 3. asp 6. scarab (beetle)
tomb.. 6. serdab (cell) 7. mastaba
watchman.. 6. ghafir (ghaffir)
writing.. 13. hieroglyphics
Egyptian god of...
day.. 5. Horus
earth.. 3. Geb, Keb
life.. 4. Ptah
pleasure.. 3. Bes
primeval fluid.. 2. Nu
sea.. 5. Aegir
sun.. 2. Ra 3. Tem (Tum) 4. Atmu
5. Mentu (Ment) 7. Khepera
11. Harpocrates
supreme.. 4. Amen (Amon)
underworld.. 6. Osiris 7. Hershef
unknown.. 2. Ka
wisdom.. 5. Thoth 6. Dhouti
Egyptian goddess of...
arms.. 4. Anta
fertility.. 4. Isis
gods.. 4. Sati
motherhood.. 4. Apet
sea.. 3. Ran
truth.. 4. Maat
eidolon... 5. image 7. phantom
8. illusion 10. apparition
eight, eighth (pert to)...
day (every).. 5. octan
feast day.. 5. utas
group.. 5. octad, octet 6. octave
7. octette

heaven.. 5. stars (fixed)
number.. 4. ocho 6. ogdoad
philosophy.. 8. Diagrams
sided.. 9. octagonal
tone, note.. 4. unca 6. quaver (8th)
   8. diatonic
eighteen inches... 5. cubit
Eire... 4. Erin 7. Ireland
ejaculate... 4. emit, oust, void
   5. blurt, eject, evict, expel
   7. exclaim 8. dislodge
eject... 4. emit, oust, spew, void
   5. evict, expel, spout, spurt
   6. banish 7. extrude 9. discharge,
   eliminate
ejection... 6. ouster 8. eviction
   9. expulsion 11. elimination
eke (out)... 3. add, imp, tab 4. also,
   etch 8. addition, appendix (dial),
   increase, piece out 10. postscript
El... 3. God 5. deity
elaborate... 6. ornate, refine
   7. develop, improve, perfect, studied
   9. embellish, perfected, superfine
   11. complicated, high–wrought
Elam capital... 5. Susa (anc)
élan... 4. dash 5. ardor 6. spirit
   9. eagerness 10. enthusiasm
elapse... 2. go 3. die, fly, run 4. flit,
   pass, slip 5. lapse 6. expire
elastic... 6. pliant, rubber 7. buoyant,
   ductile, springy 8. flexible, stretchy
   9. expansive, resilient
   12. recuperative
elasticity... 4. give 6. elater, spring
   7. pliancy, rebound 9. ductility
   10. resilience
elated... 6. jovial 7. gleeful
   8. exultant, jubilant 9. overjoyed
Elbe tributary... 4. Eger, Iser
elbow... 5. ancon, joint, nudge
   6. jostle 8. chelidon (hollow of)
El Camino Real... 9. Royal Road
   12. King's Highway (Pac Hwy)
elder... 3. iva 4. ainé, blue (color)
   5. berry, judge, ruler 6. Mormon,
   senior 7. ancient 8. ancestor
   10. forefather
eldest... 5. eigne 6. oldest 8. earliest
   9. firstborn
eldritch... 4. wild 5. eerie (eery), weird
   9. frightful
elect... 3. ort 4. name 5. elite
   6. choose, select 9. designate
election... 6. choice 11. alternative
   13. determination 14. discrimination
electric (pert to)...
atom.. 3. electron
condenser (anc).. 9. Leyden jar
conductor.. 6. ohmage
current.. 2. AC, DC 7. circuit
force.. 4. elod
generator.. 6. dynamo
light.. 3. arc 4. neon
   12. incandescent
meter.. 7. ammeter 9. voltmeter,
   wattmeter
particle.. 3. ion 6. cation (kation)
power.. 7. wattage
safety device.. 4. fuse
unit.. 3. ohm, rel 4. volt, watt
   5. farad, henry, joule 6. ampere,

proton 7. coulomb, oersted
   8. kilowatt
electrical wonders... 6. Venus V
   9. Surveyor V 11. Oroville Dam
   12. nuclear plant
electricity... 5. juice, power
   10. illuminant
eleemosynary... 4. alms, free
   7. charity 10. almsgiving
elegance... 5. charm, grace, taste
   6. beauty, polish 9. propriety
   10. ornateness, politeness, refinement
   13. sumptuousness
elegant... 4. rich 6. dressy, ornate,
   soigné, urbane 7. courtly, genteel,
   refined 8. graceful, handsome,
   polished, tasteful 9. admirable,
   beautiful, excellent 10. fastidious
   11. fashionable 13. grandiloquent
element... 3. air 4. fire 5. earth,
   water
elementary... 5. basic 6. simple
   7. primary 8. inchoate, original
   9. beginning 11. fundamental
elephant... 3. cow 4. bull, calf
   5. hathi, rogue 6. tusker
   8. behemoth 10. pachyderm
elephant (pert to)...
apple.. 7. Feronia
boy.. 4. Sabu
call, cry.. 4. barr 7. trumpet
enclosure, trap.. 6. keddah
goad.. 5. ankus
keeper.. 6. mahout
seat.. 6. howdah
tusk.. 5. ivory 9. scrivello
young.. 4. calf
elevate... 4. lift, rear 5. elate, exalt,
   raise 6. refine, uplift 7. advance,
   dignify, ennoble, glorify, inspire,
   promote 10. exhilarate
elevated... 2. el 5. lofty, risen
   6. elated 7. exalted, sublime
   8. eminence
elevation... 4. hill 6. height (highth)
   9. promotion 10. exaltation
   11. composition (Eccl), distinction
   13. glorification
elevation of the mind... 7. anagoge
elevator... 3. bin 4. cage, lift, silo
   9. ascenseur
eleven... 7. hendeca (comb form)
elf... 3. fay, hob, imp, nix 4. peri
   5. fairy, gnome, ouphe, pixie
   6. goblin, sprite 7. brownie
elfish... 5. elfin 6. elvish, impish
   7. elflike, tricksy 8. eldritch
   11. mischievous
Elgin Marbles... 10. sculptures (by
   Phidias)
elicit... 3. get 4. draw, pump
   5. claim, educe, evoke, exact, wrest,
   wring 6. deduce, demand, entice,
   extort, induce, obtain 7. extract
elide... 4. dele, omit 5. annul
   6. ignore 7. destroy, nullify, shorten
   8. demolish, suppress 9. eliminate
eligible... 3. apt, fit 4. meet
   6. worthy 8. entitled, suitable
   9. competent, desirable, qualified
   10. acceptable, admissible
Elijah... 7. prophet 8. oratorio

14. John the Baptist (Bib)

eliminate... 3. rid 4. kill 5. erase, expel 6. detach, remove 7. discard, divulge, exclude, excrete, release 8. evacuate, separate 9. segregate 11. exterminate

Elisha... 7. prophet 8. disciple (of Elijah)

elision... 7. syncope 9. severance 10. abridgment, shortening 11. suppression (vowel)

elite... 5. stars 6. flower, galaxy 7. fashion, society 9. beau monde 10. upper crust

elixir... 6. remedy 7. cure-all, essence, extract, heal-all, panacea 8. medicine, tincture 10. catholicon 12. quintessence

elixir of life... 11. elixir vitae

Elixir of Love... 13. L'Elisir d'Amore

elk... 4. deer 5. Alces, eland, moose 6. sambar, wapiti

ellipse, elliptical... 5. curve, ovoid, ovule

elm (pert to)...
borer.. 6. beetle, lamiid
fruit.. 6. samara
genus.. 5. Ulmus
rock, wing (kinds).. 5. wahoo

Elm City... 8. New Haven

Elmo... 11. patron saint (sailors)

elocution... 7. oratory 8. rhetoric 9. eloquence 10. expression

elocutionist... 6. reader 7. reciter 11. elocutioner 13. recitationist

eloge... 6. eulogy 7. address, oration 8. encomium, eulogium

eloign... 6. convey, remove 7. conceal

elongate... 6. extend, remove 7. stretch 8. continue, lengthen, protract

elongated... 4. lank, long 6. linear, oblong 7. prolate, slender 8. extended 9. stretched 10. attenuated

elope... 6. decamp 7. abscond, skip out 8. slip away

eloquence... 7. fluency, oratory 9. discourse, elocution 14. expressiveness

eloquence, teacher of... 6. rhetor

eloquent... 5. vivid 10. Ciceronian, expressive, meaningful, oratorical 11. significant

else... 2. or 4. ense (ens) 5. if not, other 9. otherwise 10. additional 12. accompanying

elsewhere... 4. away 5. alibi (law)

elucidate... 5. clear, lucid 7. clarify, clear up 8. simplify 9. interpret 10. illustrate

elude... 4. flee, foil, mock, shun 5. avoid, dodge, evade 6. baffle, befool, escape 10. circumvent

elusive... 4. eely 6. subtle 7. elusory, evasive 8. baffling 9. equivocal 10. impalpable

elves... see elf

Elysium (Myth)... 8. paradise

em... 2. en (half) 4. unit (Elec)

emaciated... 4. lean 5. gaunt 6. peaked, wasted 7. pinched

10. attenuated, cadaverous

emanation... 4. aura, odor 5. light, niton (radium), vapor 7. outcome 8. creation, effluvia 9. ectoplasm, radiation 10. exhalation, generation 11. consequence

emancipation... 6. rescue 7. freedom, release 10. liberation 11. manumission 15. enfranchisement

emasculate... 4. geld, spay 5. unman 6. soften 8. castrate 9. expurgate, sterilize 10. effeminize

embalmer... 5. cerer 9. mortician, preserver 10. undertaker

embankment... 3. dam 4. bund, dike 5. levee, revet, shore 7. barrier, pilapil (rice field) 8. buttress 10. breakwater 13. fortification

embargo... 5. edict, order 7. exclude 8. blockade, prohibit, stoppage 9. exclusion 10. impediment 11. prohibition, requisition

embark... 4. sail, ship 6. depart, invest, unmoor 7. cast off, entrain

embarrass... 5. abash, shame 6. hamper, hinder, impede 7. confuse, fluster, involve, mortify, nonplus 8. bewilder, confound, encumber, handicap 9. discomfit, dumbfound 10. complicate, disconcert

embarrassment... 5. shame 9. abashment, confusion 11. involvement, predicament 12. discomfiture, entanglement 13. inconvenience, mortification

embellish... 3. gem 4. deck, gild 5. adorn, array, dress, gouge, grace 6. bedeck, enrich 7. bedrape, enhance, garnish 8. beautify, emblazon, furbelow, ornament 9. embroider 10. exaggerate

embellishment... 9. garniture 10. decoration, furbishing 12. exaggeration 13. ornamentation

ember... 3. ash 4. coal (live), izle 5. gleed 6. cinder 7. residue

embers... 5. ashes 8. emotions (past), memories

embezzle... 5. steal, swipe 6. lessen, thieve, weaken (obs) 7. purloin 8. peculate, squander 9. dissipate 11. appropriate

embitter... 4. sour 5. anger 7. envenom 8. acerbate 10. antagonize, exacerbate

emblazon... 4. laud 5. color, extol 6. praise 7. display, exhibit, glorify 9. celebrate, embellish

emblem... 3. rue 4. mace, sign, type 5. badge, crown, image, token, totem 6. device, figure, symbol 7. balance (justice), coronet, sceptor 9. prototype

emblematic... 5. typal 7. typical 8. symbolic 10. figurative 14. characteristic

embodiment... 4. Apis 6. avatar, matter 7. epitome 9. inclusion 10. enfoldment 11. combination, composition, incarnation

12. organization 13. incorporation
14. representative 15. personification

embolden... 5. nerve 6. assure
7. hearten 8. reassure 9. encourage

embosom... 6. foster 7. cherish,
embrace, enclose 8. surround

embrace... 3. hug 4. fold, gain, hold,
love, wrap 5. adopt, clasp, cling,
grasp, inarm, seize 6. accoll (obs),
caress, enfold 7. cherish, contain,
enclose, espouse, include, involve,
welcome 8. comprise, encircle,
greeting, surround 9. encompass

embroider... 7. falsify 8. decorate,
ornament 9. embellish
10. exaggerate

embroidery... 8. appliqué 9. hardanger

embroidery frame... 7. taboret
(tabouret)

embroil... 5. upset 6. jumble
7. agitate, disturb, perplex, trouble
8. convulse, disorder, distract
9. commingle, implicate
10. complicate, discompose

eme... 5. uncle 6. friend, gossip

emend... 4. edit, mend 5. amend,
right 6. better, remedy, revise
7. correct, improve, rectify

emerald... 5. beryl, color, green
7. smaragd

Emerald Isle... 4. Erin 7. Ireland

emerge... 3. dip 4. pend, rise
5. hatch, issue 6. appear
7. debouch, emanate
10. disembogue

emergency... 5. pinch 6. clutch, crisis,
strait 8. exigency, juncture
9. extremity, necessity 10. substitute

emery... 6. pumice 8. abradant,
abrasive, corundum 9. sandpaper

emesis... 6. puking 7. spewing
8. vomiting 12. disgorgement
13. regurgitation

emeute... 4. riot 6. Putsch
8. outbreak 10. insurgence
12. insurrection

emigrant... 4. emigré 7. migrant,
outgoer, settler 8. colonist, stranger
9. immigrant, migratory (of birds)

eminence... 4. hill 5. title 6. height,
rideau 7. dignity 9. authority,
elevation, greatness, loftiness
10. famousness, importance,
projection 11. superiority
13. transcendency

eminent... 4. arch, high 5. great,
lofty, noted 6. famous, marked,
signal 8. renowned, superior,
towering 9. important 10. celebrated,
protruding 11. illustrious
13. distinguished

emissary... 3. spy 5. agent, scout
8. delegate, diplomat

emit... 4. glow, reek, shed 5. eject,
eruct, exude, issue, pluff, voice
6. exhale 7. distill (distil), emanate,
publish, radiate 8. opalesce (colors),
transmit 9. discharge, irradiate

emmet... 3. ant 7. pismire 8. formicid

emollient... 4. balm 8. ointment,
soothing 9. lubricant, softening

emolument... 4. fees, gain 5. wages

6. profit, salary 7. stipend, tribute
9. allowance 12. compensation

emotion... 5. agony, stoic 6. pathos
7. feeling, passion 9. agitation,
gratitude, sensation, sentiment
10. excitement 11. disturbance,
sensibility

emotionless... 9. apathetic, impassive,
unfeeling 10. spiritless
11. unemotional 12. unresponsive

emperor... 4. czar, tsar 5. Mogul
7. monarch 9. commander,
imperator, sovereign

emphasis... 6. accent, stress
7. cadence 8. salience
10. insistence 14. impressiveness

emphasize... 6. accent, insist, stress
7. point up 9. punctuate
10. accentuate

emphatic... 7. earnest 8. forcible,
positive, striking 9. energetic,
insistent 10. expressive
11. significant

empire... 4. rule, sway 5. green
(color), reign, state 6. domain
7. control, country

Empire (pert to)...
of the Rising Sun.. 5. Japan
State.. 7. New York
State of the South.. 7. Georgia

empiric... 4. fake 5. cheat, quack
8. impostor 9. charlatan
10. mountebank

employ... 3. use 4. busy, coax, hire
5. apply, exert 6. devote, occupy
7. concern, entrust, service
10. occupation

employees... 4. crew, gang, help
5. force, hands, staff 9. personnel
10. associates

employer... 4. user 5. hirer 6. master
8. consumer 12. entrepreneur

employment... 3. use 4. work
5. trade 7. calling, purpose, service
8. business, vocation 10. occupation,
profession

emporium... 4. fair, mart 5. store
6. bazaar, market 10. exposition

empower... 6. enable 7. entitle
8. delegate, deputize 9. authorize
10. commission

empty... 4. idle, toom, vain, void
5. blank, clear, drain, inane
6. hollow, hungry, jejune, vacant,
vacate 7. deplete, foolish, vacuous
8. evacuate, unfilled 9. insincere
10. unburdened, unoccupied

empusa (Gr Myth)... 5. fungi
7. specter 9. hobgoblin

empyrean... 3. sky 5. ether 6. Caelus,
welkin 7. heavens, the blue

emulate... 5. equal, outdo, rival
7. compete, imitate, vie with
11. competition

emulsion... 9. demulcent
10. semiliquid, suspension

enable... 5. equip 6. clothe
7. empower, qualify 9. authorize
10. capacitate

enact... 4. pass, play 6. decree,
enjoin, ordain, record 7. actuate,
appoint, perform 9. legislate,

represent 10. constitute
11. impersonate

enactment... 3. law 4. veto 5. canon,
edict, usage 6. decree 7. statute
9. ordinance 11. legislation

encamp, encampment... 4. camp, tent
5. siege 6. bivouac, camping

enchant... 5. charm 6. delude
7. bewitch, delight 8. ensorcel
9. captivate, enrapture, fascinate

enchantment... 5. charm, magic, spell
7. sorcery 8. witchery
10. allurement, necromancy,
witchcraft 11. bewitchment,
fascination, incantation

enchantress... 5. Circe, Medea
7. charmer 9. bewitcher, sorceress,
temptress

encina... 7. live oak

encircle... 3. orb 4. gird, ring, zone
5. belay, inorb, twist 6. enfold
7. besiege, circuit, enclose, environ,
include, wreathe 8. surround
12. circumscribe

encircled... 4. girt 5. orbed, paled,
zoned 6. belted, forded, hooped,
ringed 7. enlaced 8. enclosed,
enfolded, wreathed 10. surrounded

enclose... 3. hem, mew 5. bound,
fence 6. corral, encase, engulf
7. enclave, envelop, harness, include
8. imprison, surround 9. encompass
12. circumscribe

enclosed... 4. pent, sept (area)
7. encased 8. confined
10. surrounded

enclosure... 3. pen 4. bawn, cage,
yair (yare), yard 5. carol (cloister),
kraal (craal), sekos 6. corral
8. contents, poundage, stockade

encomium... 4. hymn 5. eloge
6. eulogy, praise 7. tribute
8. accolade 9. panegyric

encompass... 4. ring 5. hem in
6. begird, effect 7. besiege, circuit,
compass, contain, enclose, environ,
include 8. encircle, surround
10. accomplish 12. circumscribe

encompassing... 7. ambient
13. circumambient

encore... 3. bis 4. echo, over 5. again
8. applause, once more

encounter... 4. bout, meet 5. brave,
brush, incur, onset 6. attack,
breast, oppose 7. collide, meeting
8. conflict 9. engagement,
experience

encourage... 4. abet, urge 5. boost,
cheer, impel, nerve, rally 6. assure,
exhort, foster, incite 7. advance,
comfort, console, hearten, inspire,
promote 8. embolden, inspirit
9. instigate, stimulate
11. countenance

encouragement... 3. aid 7. comfort
9. fosterage, incentive
10. inducement 11. emboldening

encroach upon... 5. poach 6. invade,
trench 7. impinge, intrude
8. infringe, overstep, trespass

encumber... 4. clog, load 5. check
6. burden, hamper, hinder, retard,

saddle 7. involve, oppress
8. entangle, handicap, obstruct,
overload 9. embarrass
10. overburden

encumbrance... 5. alien (law), claim
6. burden 9. dependent
10. impediment

encyclic... 6. letter 7. pandect
8. circular, treatise 10. encircling
13. comprehensive

encyclopedic learning, person of...
10. polyhistor 13. encyclopedist

end... 3. aim, neb, tip, toe 4. fate,
kill, ruin, tail 5. amend, close, death,
finis, limit, omega, point, telos,
upend 6. expire, finale, finish, result,
thirty 7. destroy, purpose
8. complete, conclude, dissolve
9. cessation, determine, extremity,
intention, objective, terminate
10. completion 11. termination

end (pert to)...
 arrow.. 4. nock
 boundary.. 5. bourn 7. abuttal
 cloth.. 7. remnant
 game.. 4. goal
 man.. 8. minstrel
 news.. 6. thirty
 timber.. 5. tenon

endanger... 4. risk 6. expose, hazard
7. imperil 10. compromise,
jeopardize

endeavor... 3. aim, try, vie 4. seek
5. essay, ettle, nisus, tempt
6. effort, strive 7. attempt
8. struggle

endemic... 6. native 10. indigenous
14. characteristic

ending... 5. death 6. result
9. cessation, desinence
10. completion, conclusion
11. destruction, termination

endless... 4. many 6. eterne
7. eternal, undying 8. eternity,
infinite, numerous, unending
9. boundless, continual, incessant,
perpetual, unceasing, unstinted
10. continuous 11. everlasting
12. interminable 13. uninterrupted

endorse, indorse... 4. sign 6. attest,
second 7. approve, support
8. sanction 9. authorize, guarantee

endorsement... 4. fiat, visa (vise)
8. approval, sanction 9. provision,
signature 10. acceptance, validation
12. ratification 14. authentication

endow... 3. dow, due 4. dote, vest
5. dower, endue, indue 6. bestow,
clothe, enrich, give to, invest
7. empower, furnish, provide

endowment... 4. gift 5. dower, grant
7. talents 8. appanage (apanage)
9. insurance, provision
11. empowerment, instruction
(Mormon)

endue... 5. endow, teach 6. clothe,
digest, invest, supply 7. empower

endurable... 7. bearable 9. tolerable
10. sufferable 11. supportable

endurance... 7. stamina 8. patience,
strength 9. fortitude, suffering
10. durability, permanence, sufferance

11. continuance, resignation
12. perseverance

endure... 4. bear, bide, dree, last, live, tide, wear 5. abide, allow, brook, stand 6. afford, remain, suffer 7. condone, persist, sustain, undergo 8. continue, tolerate 9. persevere, withstand

enduring... 7. durable, lasting, patient 9. permanent 11. persevering, substantial, unforgotten 13. long–suffering

enemy... 3. foe 5. devil, force, fremd (frenne), hater, rival, Satan 6. foeman 8. opponent 9. adversary 10. antagonist

energetic... 5. fresh 6. active 8. forceful, forcible, vigorous 9. strenuous 11. industrious

energy... 2. go 3. erg, pep, vim 4. bent 5. force, nerve, power, vigor 6. spirit 7. potency, sthenia 8. strength 9. animation

energy (pert to)...
lack of.. 5. atony 6. anergy 7. aneuria, inertia 8. asthenia
mental.. 9. psychurgy
personified.. 6. Shakti
potential.. 5. ergal
unit.. 3. erg 6. ergon

enervate... 3. sap 5. drain, unman 6. weaken 7. exhaust, unnerve 8. enfeeble 10. debilitate

enfeeble... 4. numb 6. sicken, soften, weaken 7. depress 8. enervate 9. attenuate 10. debilitate

enfilade... 4. rake 5. vista 7. barrage 9. broadside 11. arrangement (in rows)

enfold, infold... 4. fold, wrap 5. clasp, cover 6. infold 7. embrace, envelop 8. surround

enforce... 5. drive 6. assail, compel 7. execute, inspire 9. constrain, encourage, intensify, reinforce 10. invigorate

enfranchise... 4. free 5. admit 7. deliver, set free 8. liberate 10. emancipate

engage... 4. bind, draw, hire, rent 5. lease 6. absorb, embark, employ, enlist, induce, occupy, pledge 7. attract, betroth, engross, involve, promise 8. contract, entangle 9. interlock, intermesh

engaged... 4. busy 5. hired 6. bonded, meshed 7. earnest, entered, pledged, versant 8. embedded, employed, involved, occupied, promised 9. affianced, betrothed, engrossed 10. contracted

engaged in controversy.. 9. disputant

engagement.. 4. date 6. battle 7. promise 9. betrothal, encounter 10. attachment 11. appointment, involvement

engaging... 5. sapid 6. taking 8. alluring, duelling 10. attractive, delightful 11. interesting

engender... 3. sow (seeds) 5. beget, breed, cause 6. excite 7. develop, produce 8. generate, occasion 9. call

forth, procreate, propagate

engine... 3. gin, ram 5. mogul, motor 6. onager 7. machine, robinet, turbine 9. locomotive

engine (type).. 3. gas 5. motor, solar, steam 6. Diesel, rocket 8. gasoline 10. combustion

engineer... 4. plan 7. manager 8. computer, contrive, designer, inventor, maneuver, operator, therblig 9. construct 11. constructor, superintend

engineer (type)... 5. civil, corps, sales 6. driver, mining 7. planner 8. chemical, geodetic, military, railroad, research, sanitary 9. hydraulic 10. electrical, industrial, mechanical, structural 11. electronics 12. aeronautical, construction 14. administrative

engird... 6. begird, circle, girdle 7. envelop 8. encircle, ensphere

England.. see also *English*
called.. 6. Albion (anc) 7. Britain 9. Britannia
capital.. 6. London
city.. 3. Ely 4. Hull, York 5. Derby, Leeds 6. Exeter 7. Bristol, Croydon 8. Brighton, Coventry, Hastings, Plymouth 9. Liverpool, Sheffield 10. Birmingham, Epsom Downs, Manchester, Nottingham, Portsmouth 11. Southampton
college (famed).. 4. Eton 6. Harrow, Oxford 9. Cambridge, Sandhurst (military)
conqueror.. 5. Danes 6. Angles, Saxons 7. Normans
constitution.. 10. Magna Carta (1215) 12. Bill of Rights (1688)
county.. 4. Kent 5. Devon, Essex 6. Dorset, Sussex 9. Yorkshire
emblem.. 4. lion, rose
House of.. 4. York 5. Blois, Tudor 6. Stuart 7. Hanover, Windsor 8. Normandy 9. Lancaster 11. Plantagenet
island.. 5. Wight 6. Scilly, Virgin 7. Bahamas, Bermuda, Channel, Solomon 8. Falkland, Windward 9. Isle of Man
king (anc).. 6. Arthur (legend), Egbert 8. Ethelred 9. Ethelwulf
native (anc).. 4. Celt, Dane, Jute 5. Saxon 8. Anglican 9. Sassenach 10. Anglo–Saxon
river.. 3. Exe 4. Avon, Ouse 5. Trent 6. Thames
royal residence.. 7. Windsor
street (London).. 10. Piccadilly 12. Threadneedle

English (pert to)...
bride's gift.. 3. dos
court.. 4. eyre (circuit), leet (anc)
dislike of.. 11. Anglophobia
district.. 4. Soho
estate (feudal).. 4. fief
excuse (legal).. 6. essoin
festival (country).. 3. ale
field.. 5. croft
forest.. 5. Arden 8. Sherwood
freeman.. 5. ceorl, thane, thegn

hamlet.. 4. dorp
heather.. 4. ling
lawyer.. 9. barrister, solicitor
leave of absence (school).. 5. exeat
lover of.. 10. Anglophile
Marbles.. 6. Oxford 7. Arundel
money of account.. 3. ora
news agency.. 6. Reuter
Parliament process.. 7. Hansard
political party.. 4. Tory, Whig
　　8. Laborite
porcelain.. 5. Spode 9. Wedgwood
prehistoric site.. 8. Piltdown
race course.. 5. Ascot 10. Epsom
　　Downs
races (famed).. 5. Derby 7. The Oaks
sheep (blackface).. 4. Lonk
song (mock).. 12. lillibullero
stolen article (on thief).. 7. mainour
symbol.. 4. bull, lion, rose
thicket.. 7. spinney
tract (sandy).. 4. dene
trolley.. 4. tram
uplands.. 5. downs
wren.. 6. tomtit
English Channel... 8. La Manche
English, famed...
composer.. 6. Handel 7. Stainer
diarist.. 5. Pepys
engraver.. 3. Pye 7. Hogarth
essayist.. 4. Elia (Charles Lamb), Lang
　　6. Steele 7. Addison
explorer.. 4. Ross 5. Cabot 6. Baffin,
　　Beatty, Hudson 7. Raleigh
　　10. Shackleton
financier.. 7. Gresham
historian.. 4. Bede 7. Spelman,
　　Toynbee 8. Macaulay
humorist.. 4. Lear (Edward)
mathematician.. 5. Hooke 6. Gunter
murderer (famed).. 4. Aram
navigator.. 4. Cook 5. Drake
　　6. Nelson
painter.. 4. Lear 6. Turner
　　7. Hogarth, Lutyens, Millais
philosopher.. 7. Spencer
physicist.. 7. Faraday
poet.. 5. Noyes 8. Browning,
　　Tennyson 9. Masefield, Swinburne
printer.. 6. Caxton
reformer.. 4. Owen 6. Spence
saint.. 6. George (patron saint)
　　7. Alphege, Swithin
scientist.. 6. Newton
spy (in Am Rev).. 5. André
statesman.. 4. Peel, Pitt 7. Baldwin,
　　Balfour, Walpole 8. Cromwell, Disraeli
　　9. Churchill 11. Chamberlain, Lloyd
　　George
surgeon.. 5. Haden, Paget 6. Lister
theologian.. 5. Booth 6. Becket
　　7. Tyndall 8. Wycliffe 10. Whitefield
thesaurus compiler.. 5. Roget
engrave... 3. cut 4. etch, rist
　　5. carve, chase, infix 6. chisel, incise
　　7. enchase, impress, imprint, stipple
　　9. sculpture
engraver's tool... 5. burin
engraving... 3. cut 5. print
　　7. chasing, etching, tooling
　　8. celature, incising, intaglio
　　9. stippling 10. xylography (wood)

　　11. lithography 12. glyptography
engross... 6. absorb, engage
　　10. monopolize 11. concentrate
engrossed... 4. busy, rapt 6. intent
　　8. absorbed, employed 10. interested
engulf... 5. swamp 6. absorb
　　7. swallow 8. inundate, submerge
　　9. overwhelm
enhance... 4. lift 5. exalt, extol, raise
　　7. advance, augment, elevate,
　　enlarge, magnify 8. increase
　　9. aggravate 10. exaggerate
enigma... 3. why 5. rebus 6. puzzle,
　　riddle 7. charade, mystery
　　9. conundrum
enigmatic... 6. mystic 8. puzzling
　　12. inexplicable
enjoin... 3. bid 5. order 6. advise,
　　decree, direct, forbid 7. command
　　8. admonish, prohibit
enjoy... 4. bask, have 5. savor
　　6. relish
enjoyment... 4. ease, zest 6. relish
　　7. delight 8. felicity, fruition, pleasure
　　9. amusement, happiness
enlarge... 3. eke 4. ream 5. swell
　　6. dilate, expand, extend, spread
　　7. amplify, augment, develop
　　8. increase 9. expatiate
　　10. exaggerate
enlargement... 8. increase
　　9. expansion, extension
　　12. augmentation 13. amplification
enlighten... 5. teach 6. inform
　　7. educate, explain 8. enkindle,
　　instruct 10. illuminate 11. disillusion
enlightened person... 10. illuminate
enlist... 4. join, list 6. engage, enroll,
　　induce
enliven... 5. amuse, cheer, rouse
　　7. animate, comfort, inspire, refresh
　　8. brighten, energize, inspirit
　　9. encourage, stimulate
　　10. exhilarate, invigorate
enmity... 3. war 4. feud 6. hatred,
　　malice, rancor 7. discord 8. aversion
　　9. antipathy, disaccord, hostility
　　10. antagonism, repugnance
　　11. malevolence 14. unfriendliness
ennead... 4. gods (nine), nine
　　18. Ennead of Heliopolis (famed)
ennoble... 5. exalt, honor, raise
　　6. uplift 8. elevate, glorify, promote
ennui... 4. bore 5. bored 6. tedium
　　7. boredom, fatigue, languor
　　9. weariness 15. dissatisfaction
enormous... 4. huge, vast 5. great
　　6. wicked 7. immense, titanic
　　8. abnormal, colossal, gigantic,
　　infamous 9. atrocious, excessive,
　　monstrous 10. inordinate, prodigious,
　　stupendous
Enos' father... 4. Seth
enough... 4. enow 5. ample, basta,
　　fully, quite 6. plenty 8. adequate
　　9. tolerable 10. sufficient
　　12. satisfactory
enounce... 5. state, utter 9. enunciate,
　　pronounce
enow... 9. presently
enrage... 4. anger 6. madden
　　7. incense, inflame 9. infuriate

enraged... 5. irate 7. angered
8. maddened 10. infuriated

enraptured... 6. enrapt 8. ecstatic
9. delighted, entranced
10. enravished

enravished... 4. rapt 9. enchanted,
entranced, rapturous 10. enraptured

enrich... 4. lard 5. adorn, endow
6. fatten 7. improve 8. increase,
ornament 9. embellish, fertilize

enroll... 4. coil, join, list, roll 5. enter
6. enlist, induct, unfurl, wrap up
7. engross, impanel 8. initiate,
register 11. matriculate

ens... 5. being 6. entity 7. essence

ensconce... 4. hide 5. cover 6. settle
7. conceal, protect, shelter
9. establish

ensemble... 3. all 5. decor, group,
whole 7. costume

enshroud... 4. wrap 6. clothe, swathe
7. conceal, enclose 8. enshrine

ensiform... 12. xiphisternum

ensign... 4. flag 6. banner 7. officer
8. gonfalon, standard 9. oriflamme
(oriflamb, anc)

ensign of Othello... 4. Iago

enslave... 8. enthrall

ensnare... 3. web 4. trap 5. benet,
catch, innet, noose 6. allure,
enmesh, entrap, seduce 7. involve

ensorcell, ensorcel... 7. bewitch,
enchant

ensue... 6. follow, pursue, result
7. imitate, succeed 8. come next

ensuing... 4. next 9. resultant
10. subsequent, succeeding

ensure... 6. assure, insure, secure
7. protect, warrant 9. guarantee

entad... 6. inward (opp of ectad)

ental... 5. inner (opp of ectal)

entangle... 3. mat, web 4. mesh, mire
5. afoul, ravel, snarl, twist 6. enlace,
enmesh, involve, puzzle, raffle 7. confuse,
ensnare, involve, perplex 8. bewilder
9. embarrass 10. interweave

entanglement... 4. knot 5. snare, snarl
6. abatis 8. obstacle 9. barricade,
imbroglio 10. barbed wire, complexity
11. involvement

enter... 4. join, list 5. begin, start,
train 6. engage, enlist, enroll, insert,
record 7. initiate, inscribe, register
11. participate

enter (pert to)...
career.. 6. incept
legal objection.. 5. demur
with hostility.. 6. invade
without permission.. 7. intrude
8. encroach, infringe

enterprise... 4. firm 5. essay 6. daring
7. attempt, crusade, exploit, venture
10. initiative 11. undertaking

enterprising... 4. bold 6. daring
9. energetic 11. up-and-coming

entertain... 4. fete 5. amuse, treat
6. divert, regale 7. beguile, cherish
8. interest

entertainer... 5. actor 6. dancer,
singer 7. actress, speaker
8. magician 9. performer

11. pantomimist 12. impersonator

entertainment... 4. play 5. party,
revue, sport 6. kermis (kermess),
repast 7. pastime, ridotto, theater
8. entr'acte, musicale 9. amusement,
diversion, reception, wayzgoose
10. recreation 12. Roman holiday

enthusiasm... 4. élan, fire, zeal, zest
5. ardor, craze, estro, furor (furore),
mania, verve 6. fervor 7. ecstasy
8. interest 9. animation, eagerness,
transport 10. exaltation

enthusiast... 3. fan 5. bigot 6. rooter,
zealot 7. devotee, fanatic

enthusiastic... 5. eager, nutty, rabid
6. active, ardent 7. zealous
10. interested

entice... 4. bait, coax, lure, tole
5. decoy, tempt 6. allure, cajole,
incite, seduce 7. attract, wheedle
8. inveigle, persuade

enticement... 9. seduction
10. allurement, attraction, incitement,
inducement, persuasion, temptation
12. inveiglement

entire... 3. all 5. cover (Philat), sound,
total, utter, whole 6. intact
7. perfect, sincere, upright
8. complete, faithful, stallion
9. integrate, undivided
10. unimpaired 11. unqualified
12. undiminished

entirely... 3. all 5. clean, fully, stark
6. solely, wholly 7. totally 9. every
inch, perfectly, sincerely
10. completely

entitle... 3. dub 4. call, name, term
5. style 6. assign, enable, impute
7. empower, qualify 8. authorize,
designate 10. denominate

entity... 3. ens 4. soul, unit 5. being,
entia, thing 7. integer 8. infinity
(Math) 9. existence

entomb... 4. bury 5. inter, inurn
6. hearse, inhume 7. confine
9. sepulture

entourage... 5. suite, train 7. retinue
10. associates, attendants
12. surroundings

entr'acte... 3. act 5. dance, music
7. interim 9. interlude

entrails... 4. guts 6. bowels
7. insides, viscera 8. interior
10. intestines

entrance... 3. way 4. adit, door, gate
5. entry, inlet 6. access, portal
7. gateway, ingress, postern
9. admission, insertion, threshold,
vestibule 10. admittance

entrance (pert to)...
church (Eastern).. 5. Great 6. Little
formal.. 5. debut 12. introduction
hostile.. 9. incursion
temple (Buddh).. 5. toran (torana)

entranced... 4. rapt 8. dreaming
9. delighted, overjoyed
10. fascinated, hypnotized, spellbound
11. overpowered

entrap... 3. net 4. trap 5. catch,
decoy, noose, snare 6. tangle
7. beguile, ensnare 8. entangle,
inveigle

entreat... 3. ask, beg, woo 4. pray
5. crave, halse (obs), plead
6. adjure, appeal 7. beseech,
implore, solicit 8. petition
9. importune 10. supplicate

entreaty... 4. plea, suit 6. appeal,
prayer 7. request 8. petition
10. invitation 11. importunity
12. solicitation, supplication

entree, entrée... 4. dish 6. access
7. ingress, opening 8. admission
10. permission (to enter)

entrench... 6. invade 7. enter on,
fortify, intrude 8. encroach, trespass
9. establish

entrenchment... 7. defense, parapet
9. intrusion 10. protection
12. encroachment, infringement
13. establishment

entrepot... 5. depot, store
9. warehouse 10. depository

entrepreneur... 7. provost 8. executive
10. impresario 13. administrator

entrust... 6. commit 7. confide,
consign 8. delegate 10. commission

entry... 4. hall, item, lane, post
7. ingress 8. entrance, register
9. admission, vestibule
10. contestant, memorandum
12. introduction

entwine... 4. lace 5. clasp, twine,
twist, weave 6. enlace 7. wreathe
9. interknit

enumerate... 4. list, tell 5. count
6. detail, number, reckon, relate
7. compute 8. estimate, name over,
rehearse 9. calculate, catalogue
(catalog) 12. recapitulate
13. particularize

enumeration... 4. list 5. count
6. census 10. numeration
14. recapitulation

enunciate... 3. say 5. utter 6. affirm
7. declare 8. announce, proclaim
9. postulate, pronounce
10. articulate

enunciation... 9. statement, utterance
11. affirmation, attestation,
declaration 12. announcement
13. pronouncement, pronunciation

envelop... 4. case, wrap 5. cover
6. clothe, encase, enwrap, infold,
invest, sheath, shroud 7. conceal,
enclose, sheathe 8. encircle,
surround 9. encompass, enwreathe
10. integument

envelope... 3. bur (burr) 5. cover,
curve 6. jacket 7. conceal, rampart,
vesicle, wrapper 8. membrane
10. integument

enveloped... 6. amidst 7. covered
10. surrounded

envenom... 5. taint 6. poison
8. embitter

envious... 7. jealous 8. covetous,
grudging, spiteful 9. green-eyed
10. begrudging

environ... 3. hem 6. suburb
7. compass, envelop, hedge in,
involve, purlieu 8. encircle, outskirt,
surround 9. encompass

environment... 4. area 6. medium,

milieu 7. setting, suburbs, terrain
8. environs 10. background
12. neighborhood, surroundings
13. encompassment

envisage... 4. face 8. confront
9. visualize 11. contemplate
12. meet squarely

envision... 5. dream 7. picture
9. visualize 11. contemplate
12. meet squarely

envoy... 5. agent 6. legate, l'envoi,
stanza 7. refrain 8. ablegate,
delegate, diplomat 9. messenger
10. ambassador, postscript
12. commissioner

envy... 5. covet 6. grudge 8. jealousy
12. covetousness

enwrap, inwrap... 4. roll, wrap
6. clothe, enfold, infold 7. engross
8. surround

enzyme... 3. ase (suff) 5. bread (Eccl)
6. lotase, olease, pepsin, rennin,
urease 7. amylase, ferment, laccase,
ptyalin, trypsin 8. diastase, protease
9. digestant

enzyme activator... 11. biocatalyst

eoan... 7. auroral 8. daybreak, easterly

eon, aeon... 3. age, era 4. time
5. cycle 8. eternity 10. generation

ephemeral... 7. diurnal 9. chickweed,
deciduous, transient 10. short-lived

ephemeris... 5. diary 7. almanac,
journal 8. calendar 10. periodical
11. publication

Ephesus (pert to)...
city of.. 6. Greece (anc)
famed for.. 5. ruins 12. Christianity
site.. 7. Aegean Sea
temple.. 7. Artemis
visitor (early).. 6. St Paul

Ephraim... 4. bear (grizzly) 5. tribe
8. fruitful

epi... 6. finial

epic... 3. cid 4. epos, poem, saga
5. epode 6. Aeneid (by Vergil),
epopee, heroic 9. narrative

epicene... 7. neutral, sexless
10. effeminate

epicure... 6. friand (obs) 7. glutton,
gourmet 8. gourmand, Sybarite
10. voluptuary 11. connoisseur

epidemic... 4. pest 6. plague
8. pandemic 9. prevalent, spreading
10. contagious, pestilence

epidermis... 4. skin 7. cuticle
8. ectoderm 9. scarfskin

epigram... 3. mot, saw 4. poem, quip
5. adage, maxim 6. dictum, saying
7. distich 11. inscription (obs)

epigraph... 5. motto, title 9. quotation
11. inscription

Epiphany (Eccl)... 5. Feast (Jan 6)

Epirus, oracle of... 6. Dodona (Mt
Tomarus, Gr)

episode... 5. event, story 8. incident
10. digression (Mus), occurrence

epistle... 4. note, post 6. billet,
lesson, letter 7. message, missive,
writing 8. dispatch, rescript
13. communication

epitaph... 7. writing (monument) 8. hic
jacet 11. inscription

epithet... 4. name, term 5. label
6. byname 7. agnomen 9. sobriquet
11. appellation (significant)
epitome... 6. digest 7. summary
8. abstract 9. comprisal
10. abridgment, compendium
epitomize... 7. abridge, curtail
8. abstract, compress, condense,
contract, diminish 9. capsulize
epoch... 3. age, day, eon, era 4. date,
time 5. event 6. period
epopee... 4. epic, epos, poem
5. genre (epic) 6. poetry (epic)
epoptic... 6. mystic, secret
equable... 4. even 6. steady
7. uniform
equal... 3. iso (pref), par, tie 4. both,
even, fere (obs), just, pari (pref),
peer, same 5. match, rival
7. compeer, emulate, equable,
uniform 8. adequate, parallel
9. equitable, identical 10. coordinate,
equivalent, substitute 11. counterpart
12. commensurate 13. proportionate
equal day and night...
11. equidiurnal, equinoctial
equal density (atmospheric)...
8. isoteric
equality... 3. par, tie 6. equity, owelty
(payment), parity 7. egalite, isonomy
(law) 8. adequacy, evenness, fairness,
identity, sameness 10. uniformity
12. impartiality
Equality State... 7. Wyoming (first
with Woman Suffrage)
equalize... 4. even 5. equal, level,
match 6. equate, smooth 7. balance
10. symmetrize
equally... 2. as 4. equi (pref) 5. alike
6. evenly, justly 11. identically
15. correspondingly
equanimity... 5. poise 6. aplomb
7. balance 8. calmness, evenness,
serenity 9. assurance, composure
10. confidence, equability
11. tranquility 12. tranquillity
equilibrium... 5. poise 7. balance
8. equality 9. stability 10. equanimity
equine... 3. ass 4. colt, foal, mare
5. filly, horse, steed, zebra 6. donkey
equine cry... 5. neigh 6. whinny
equip... 3. arm, fit, imp, rig 4. deck,
gear, gird 5. dress, endow
7. costume, furnish, qualify
8. accouter
equipment... 4. gear 5. armor
6. outfit, tackle, traits (personal)
7. ability, panoply (warriors)
8. equipage 9. apparatus
11. preparation 12. accouterment,
accoutrement
equitable... 4. fair, just 5. right
6. honest 7. upright 9. impartial
10. bonitarian (Rom law), reasonable
equity... 4. laws 6. rights 7. honesty,
justice 8. fairness 9. rectitude
10. uprightness
equivalence... 3. par 7. valence
8. equality, sameness 10. relativity
11. correlation
equivalent... 5. alike, equal
9. identical 10. tantamount

equivocal... 7. dubious, obscure
8. doubtful, puzzling 9. ambiguous,
enigmatic, uncertain 10. amphibolic,
mysterious, perplexing
13. indeterminate, problematical
equivocate... 3. lie 5. dodge, evade,
fence, shift 6. palter, trifle
7. quibble, shuffle 11. prevaricate
12. tergiversate
era... 2. AD, BC 3. age, eon 4. date,
time 5. cycle, epoch 6. period
10. Anno Domini 12. Before Christ
eradicate... 4. dele, root, weed
5. annul, erase 6. remove, uproot
7. abolish, destroy, epilate, extract,
root out 9. eliminate, extirpate
10. annihilate 11. exterminate
erase... 4. dele, kill 5. arase (obs)
6. cancel, delete, efface, excise
7. expunge, relieve 10. obliterate
Erasmus (Dutch)... 6. lovely 7. scholar
Erastus (Swiss)... 9. physician
10. theologian
ere... 4. also, soon 5. early, prior
6. before, erenow, sooner 7. earlier,
ere long 8. erewhile, formerly
10. before long, previously, sooner
than
Erebus (pert to)...
brother.. 3. Nox
father of.. 3. Day 6. Aether
Greek myth.. 8. darkness (nether)
native of.. 5. Hades
son.. 5. Chaos
erect... 4. lift, rear, stay 5. build,
found, raise, stand, upend 6. raised
7. elevate, upright 8. uplifted
vertical 9. construct, establish,
institute 13. perpendicular
eremite... 6. hermit 7. recluse
8. anchoret, solitary 9. anchorite
erenow... 5. prior 8. erewhile, formerly
10. heretofore
ergo... 5. hence 9. therefore
Erin... 4. Eire 7. Ireland
Eritrea, Africa...
capital.. 6. Asmara
coastline of.. 8. Ethiopia
ruler.. 7. England (formerly It)
site.. 6. Red Sea
ermine... 3. fur 4. robe (emblem)
5. stoat (stot) 6. clothe, lasset,
weasel 7. ermelin
erode... 3. eat 4. gnaw, wear
7. corrode, decline, destroy
11. deteriorate 12. disintegrate
erotic... 6. loving, sexual 7. amative,
amatory, amorous 8. doctrine (of
love)
err... 3. sin 4. miss, slip 5. stray
6. bungle 7. blunder, deviate
10. transgress 12. miscalculate,
misinterpret
Er Rai... 5. stars 8. shepherd
errand... 4. task, trip 5. journey,
mission 8. business (special)
10. commission
errand boy... 4. page 7. bellboy,
bellhop, courier 9. messenger
errant... 6. erring, roving 7. peccant
8. fallible 9. deviating, erroneous,
itinerant, wandering 10. journeying

erratic... 5. queer, rogue 6. whacky
7. nomadic, strange 8. abnormal
9. eccentric, irregular, planetary,
wandering 10. capricious, changeable

erroneous... 5. false, wrong 6. untrue
7. peccant 8. illusory, mistaken
9. wandering

error... 3. sin 4. flub, muff, slip
5. boner, lapse 6. errata (pl), miscue
7. blunder, falsity, misstep, mistake
8. iniquity 11. anachronism,
misjudgment 14. miscalculation

ersatz... 5. proxy, token 9. vicarious
10. equivalent, substitute
11. alternative, replacement
12. substitution

Erse... 5. Irish 6. Celtic, Gaelic

erst, erstwhile... 4. also, once 5. first
6. former, sooner 8. earliest, formerly
10. heretofore, previously

erudite... 4. wise 7. learned
8. cultured, educated, literate
9. scholarly

erudition... 4. lore 6. finish, wisdom
7. letters 8. learning, pedantry
9. knowledge

eruption... 4. rash 6. geyser
7. volcano 8. ejection, outbreak,
outburst 9. commotion, exanthema
10. nettlerash 13. efflorescence

Esau (pert to)...
 Bible ref.. 7. Genesis
 brother.. 5. Jacob
 father.. 5. Isaac
 home.. 4. Seir
 mother.. 7. Rebekah
 name (later).. 4. Edom

escape... 4. flee 5. dodge, elope,
elude, evade, spill 7. evasion
9. avolation 13. circumvention

escargot... 5. snail

escarpment... 5. cliff, slope
9. precipice 13. fortification

eschar... 4. scab, sore 5. crust
6. slough

escharotic... 7. caustic, mordant
8. stinging 9. corrosive

escheat... 4. fall 5. lapse 6. revert
(land) 7. forfeit 9. reversion
10. forfeiture

eschew... 4. shun 5. avoid 7. abstain,
refrain

escolar... 4. fish 8. mackerel (like)

escort... 3. see 4. beau 5. guard
(honor), usher 6. attend, convoy,
gigolo, squire 7. conduct, retinue
8. chaperon 9. accompany
13. accompaniment

escritoire... 4. desk 6. bureau
7. dresser 9. secretary 10. secretaire

escrow... 4. bond, deed (deposit)
9. muniments

esculent... 6. edible 7. eatable
8. gustable 10. comestible

escutcheon... 4. fess (band), orle
(voided) 5. crest 6. shield

esker, eskar... 2. os 4. osar (pl)
5. drift, hills, mound, ridge

Eskimo... 3. Ita 4. Yuit 5. Aleut
6. Innuit 10. skraelling 11. Yikirgaulit
(Diomede Isles)

Eskimo (pert to)...

boat, canoe.. 5. kayak, umiak
(oomiac)

boot (sealskin).. 5. kamik

coat (bird skin).. 5. parka 6. temiak

color.. 5. brown (rustic)

dog.. 5. Husky 8. Malemute

family.. 9. Eskimauan

fish.. 4. Atka 8. mackerel

hut, house.. 5. igloo, tupek (tupik)

jacket.. 6. temiak

knife (woman's).. 3. ulu

memorial post.. 3. xat

settlement.. 4. Etah

totem.. 4. pole, post 6. symbol

esne... 4. serf 5. slave 8. hireling

esophagus, oesophagus... 4. crop,
gula 6. gullet, throat 7. pharynx

esoteric... 5. inner 6. occult, secret
7. private 8. abstruse, initiate,
personal 9. recondite 12. confidential

esoteric doctrine... 6. cabala

esoteric wisdom... 6. gnosis

espalier... 7. epaulet, railing, trellis

Español... 7. Spanish

especial... 5. chief 7. special
8. peculiar, uncommon

Esperanto... 3. Ido 8. language
(Internat)

espionage... 4. espy 6. spying
11. observation (secret)
14. reconnaissance

esplanade... 4. walk 5. drive, level,
Prado, praya 6. strand 7. walkway

espousal... 7. wedding 8. adoption,
ceremony 10. acceptance
11. embracement

espouse... 3. wed 4. bind, mate
5. adopt, marry 6. defend, pledge
7. betroth, embrace, support
8. maintain, plead for

esprit de corps... 3. wit 6. spirit
8. devotion 10. enthusiasm,
fellowship 11. partisanism

esprit fort (Relig)... 11. freethinker

espy... 3. see 5. watch 6. behold,
descry, detect 7. discern 8. discover
9. look about

esquire... 5. title 6. escort, gentry
7. armiger 8. escudero, nobleman
11. armor–bearer 12. shield–bearer

essay... 3. try 4. test 5. assay, chris
(Rhet), paper, theme, tract, trial
6. effort, thesis 7. attempt
8. endeavor, treatise 11. composition
12. disquisition, dissertation

esse... 5. being (real) 9. existence

essence... 3. ens 4. gist, odor, pith
5. attar, being, scent 6. nature
7. element, extract, perfume
9. principle, substance
12. quintessence

essential... 5. vital 6. mortal
7. needful 8. existent, inherent
9. necessary, necessity
13. indispensable

essential oil... 8. volatile 12. attar of
roses

essential part... 4. core, crux, gist,
pith 7. element 8. inherent
10. inwardness

establish... 3. fix 4. base, seat
5. build, enact, erect, found, plant,

prove, set up **6.** create, ground,
locate, ordain, settle **7.** confirm,
pre-empt **8.** ensconce, legalize,
radicate (rare) **9.** ascertain, originate
established... **5.** fixed **6.** proved,
rested, stable **11.** naturalized,
traditional **12.** conventional
established (pert to)...
  church.. **9.** Episcopal (Eng)
  rule.. **8.** standard
  thing.. **4.** fact
  truth.. **8.** verified
establishment... **4.** mill **5.** plant
6. custom, menage **7.** factory
9. structure **12.** organization
establishment of cordial relations...
13. rapprochement
establishment of new plant home...
6. ecesis
estate... **4.** alod, fief (feudal), rank
(social) **5.** manor, title **6.** assets,
equity **7.** alodium, demesne, fortune
8. interest, property **9.** situation
esteem... **4.** dear, love, honor,
judge, pride, value **6.** admire, regard,
repute, revere **7.** respect **8.** appraise,
venerate **10.** appreciate
13. consideration
ester of...
  silicic acid.. **8.** silicate
  stearic acid.. **7.** stearin **8.** stearate
  tropic acid.. **7.** tropate
  vinegar.. **7.** acetate
esthetic, aesthetic... **6.** essene
8. artistic, tasteful **9.** beautiful
estimable... **6.** worthy **8.** valuable
9. admirable, honorable, reputable,
venerable **10.** measurable
12. praiseworthy
estimate... **3.** aim, set **4.** gage, rank,
rate **5.** audit, gauge, guess, prize,
think **6.** assess, repute **7.** adjudge,
compute, measure, opinion
8. appraise, judgment **9.** calculate,
statement, valuation
Estonia...
  capital.. **5.** Revel **7.** Tallinn
  industry.. **3.** oil
  island.. **5.** Oesel
  peasant (rich).. **5.** kulak
  ruler.. **4.** USSR
estop... **3.** bar **4.** fill, halt, plug, stay
6. impede, stop up **7.** prevent
8. prohibit
estrange... **4.** part, wean **6.** divert,
divide **8.** alienate, disunite, separate
estreat... **4.** copy **6.** amerce, sconce
7. extract **9.** duplicate, penalties
(law)
estuary... **3.** bay **4.** Pará **5.** firth, frith,
Plata
etch... **3.** cut **4.** bite **5.** infix
7. corrode, engrave, impress (upon)
eternal... **6.** eonian **7.** aeonian,
ageless, endless, lasting **8.** enduring,
immortal, timeless **9.** boundless,
ceaseless, immutable, incessant,
unceasing **10.** unchanging
11. everlasting **12.** imperishable,
interminable, unchangeable
Eternal City... **4.** Rome
eternal death... **9.** perdition

eternal home... **6.** heaven **12.** The
Hereafter
eternity... **3.** eon **4.** aeon, ages, olam
8. Olam haba
etesian... **4.** wind (Aegean Sea)
6. annual **8.** seasonal **10.** periodical
ether... **3.** air, sky **5.** ester, space
6. anisol, heaven (anc) **8.** empyrean
10. anesthetic
ethereal... **4.** rare **5.** aerie (aery), light
7. fragile, slender, tenuous
8. delicate, heavenly, vaporous
9. celestial **10.** atmosphere (earth's),
spiritlike **11.** phantomlike
13. unsubstantial
ethereal (pert to)...
  being.. **5.** sylph
  color.. **7.** sky blue
  fluid.. **5.** ichor (icor)
  poetic.. **4.** aery
  salt.. **5.** ester
ethical... **5.** moral, right **7.** upright
8. virtuous
ethics... **6.** morals **8.** hedonics
10. principles (moral) **11.** highest
good, summum bonum **12.** Magna
Moralia (Aristotle)
Ethiopia (Abyssinia)...
  capital.. **10.** Addis Ababa
  city.. **5.** Adowa
  colony.. **7.** Eritrea
  empress.. **7.** Zauditu
  king (Myth).. **5.** Negus **6.** Memnon
  native.. **5.** Negro **6.** Hamite
    10. Abyssinian, black-a-moor
  river.. **3.** Omo **4.** Juba **5.** Abbai (Blue
    Nile)
  ruler.. **7.** Menelik **13.** Haile Selassie
  tribes (anc).. **5.** Bejas, Galla
    7. Hamites, Semites
Ethiopian (pert to)...
  ape.. **6.** gelada
  banana.. **6.** ensete
  dialect.. **4.** Geez
  lily.. **5.** calla
  Torah.. **5.** tetel
ethnic... **5.** pagan **6.** racial **7.** gentile,
heathen
ethnology... **5.** races (Man)
ethology... **7.** manners **9.** bionomics,
character
ethos (opp of pathos)... **9.** attitudes
(moral), esthetics
etiquette... **4.** form **5.** label, mores
6. ticket **7.** decorum, manners
9. amenities, propriety **10.** civilities
etiquette, breach of... **8.** solecism
Etruria, Italy... see *Etruscan*
Etruscan (pert to)...
  bookbinding (anc).. **9.** classical
  deity.. **3.** Lar, Uni
  pottery.. **8.** bucchero (black)
  race.. **7.** Rasenna **8.** Tursenoi,
    Tyrrheni
  soothsayer.. **8.** haruspex
  soothsayer's function.. **8.** extispex
ettle... **3.** try **4.** plan **6.** aspire,
design, intent **8.** consider, endeavor
etui, etwee... **4.** case **7.** trousse
etymology... **10.** word origin
eucalyptus... **4.** lerp (laap, juice)
7. gum tree **8.** eucalypt

Eucharist (pert to)...
  administer to.. 6. housel 8. viaticum
    (dying)
  plate.. 5. paten
  rite.. 9. Communion (Holy) 11. Lord's
    Supper
  wafer.. 4. host
  wafer vessel.. 8. ciborium
  wine.. 5. krama
  wine vessel.. 3. ama 5. amula
Euclid (Gr)... 8. geometer (BC)
eulogist... 9. encomiast 10. panegyrist
eulogize... 4. laud 5. boost, extol
    6. praise 7. commend, glorify
    9. celebrate 10. panegyrize
eulogy... 5. eloge 6. hesped (Heb),
    praise 7. oration 8. citation,
    encomium 9. laudation, panegyric
euphony... 5. meter 6. melody,
    rhythm, speech (ease of) 7. harmony
Eurafrica... 5. Egypt 6. Europe
    7. Algeria 9. Abyssinia (anc)
Eurasia... 4. Asia 6. Europe 7. Scythia
    (anc)
Eurasian (pert to)...
  herb.. 6. yarrow 7. gosmore
  mint.. 6. Nepeta
  people.. 5. Finns 7. Ugrians
    9. Armenians, Turanians
eureka... 11. exclamation 12. I Have
    Found It (Calif motto)
Euripides (Gr)... 4. poet (BC)
Europe... see also *European*
  basin (coal).. 4. Saar
  battlefield.. 5. Marne 6. Verdun
    8. Normandy, Waterloo 11. Belleau
    Wood
  capitals.. 4. Bonn, Oslo, Riga, Rome
    5. Berne, Paris, Sofia 6. Athens,
    Berlin, Lisbon, Madrid, Moscow,
    Prague, Warsaw 8. Belgrade,
    Budapest, Helsinki 9. Amsterdam,
    Bucharest, Stockholm
    10. Copenhagen, Monte Carlo
  country (anc).. 4. Elis (Gr) 7. Etruria
    (It)
  country (modern).. 5. Italy, Spain
    6. France, Greece, Latvia, Monaco,
    Norway, Poland, Russia, Sweden
    7. Denmark, Finland, Germany,
    Hungary, Rumania 8. Bulgaria,
    Portugal 10. Yugoslavia
    11. Netherlands, Switzerland
    14. Czechoslovakia
  gulf.. 4. Riga 7. Bothnia
  health resort.. 5. Baden 10. Baden
    Baden (Ger)
  invaders.. 4. Huns 5. Arabs, Turks
    7. Mongols
  kingdom (anc).. 5. Arles 6. Aragon
    8. Burgundy
  lake.. 9. Zuider Zee (Holland)
  lancer.. 4. uhlan 6. hussar
  mountain region.. 4. Alps 5. Tyrol
  race (anc).. 5. Goths 6. Teutons
    9. Visigoths 10. Ostrogoths
  river.. 4. Elbe, Isar 5. Loire, Meuse,
    Rhine, Rhone, Seine, Volga
    6. Danube 7. Dneiper, Moselle
  sea.. 4. Aral, Azov 5. North 6. Baltic
  strait.. 8. Bosporus
  valley.. 4. Ruhr

European (pert to)...
  antelope.. 7. chamois
  bat.. 8. serotine
  bird.. 3. ani, mew (gull) 4. kite, stag
    5. glede, mavis, ousel, serin
    6. godwit, linnet, marten, merlin
    (falcon) 7. bittern, ortolan, starnel
    8. dotterel, garganey 9. brambling,
    gallinule 10. turtledove
    11. lammergeier 12. capercaillie
  bison.. 7. aurochs
  clover.. 6. alsike
  dog.. 7. griffin
  fish.. 3. gar 4. dace, rudd, spet, tope
    (shark) 5. sprat 6. allice, barbel,
    brasse, morgay, turbot
  grape.. 6. muscat
  linden.. 4. teil
  mint.. 6. hyssop 9. horehound
  mouse.. 4. loir, vole 5. lerot
  polecat.. 7. fitchew
  rodent.. 3. erd 4. loir 5. stoat
    (ermine) 6. leriot 7. hamster
  sandpiper.. 4. ruff 5. terek
  squirrel.. 5. sisel 10. polatouche
  tree.. 4. cade (juniper), sorb (apple)
    5. carob 9. terebinth
  wheat.. 5. emmer (speltz) 7. einkorn
evacuant... 6. emetic 8. diuretic
    9. cathartic, purgative
evacuate... 4. void 5. empty, expel
    6. depart, vacate 7. deprive, exhaust
    8. withdraw 9. discharge
evade... 3. gee 4. foil, shun 5. avoid,
    dodge, elude, parry, shirk, shunt
    6. baffle, escape, illude 7. beguile,
    quibble 8. slip away 10. circumvent
evanescent... 8. fleeting 9. ephemeral,
    transient, vanishing 11. impermanent
    12. disappearing 13. infinitesimal
evangelical... 7. Gospels 8. orthodox
    10. Protestant, scriptural
Evangeline (pert to)...
  home.. 6. Acadia
  lover.. 7. Gabriel
  poem by.. 10. Longfellow (1847)
evangelist... 6. Graham, Sunday (Billy)
    7. apostle, Roberts 9. McPherson
evaporate... 3. dry 5. steam
    6. escape, exhale 7. avolate
    8. vaporize 9. cease to be,
    dehydrate, disappear
evasion... 5. dodge, shift 6. escape
    8. avoiding 9. avoidance, quibbling,
    shuffling 12. equivocation
    13. circumvention, secretiveness
evasive... 3. sly 4. eely 6. shifty
    7. elusive, elusory 9. deceitful,
    quibbling, secretive
eve... 3. iva (herb), wet 4. dusk, thaw
    6. sunset 12. on the brink of, on
    the verge of
even... 3. e'en, tie 4. just, tied
    5. equal, exact, level, match, plane
    6. placid, smooth, square, steady
    7. abreast, balance, equable, neutral,
    regular, uniform 8. directly, parallel
    9. impartial, precisely
    11. symmetrical
even (if)... 8. although
    12. nevertheless 15. notwithstanding
even (so)... 3. yes 12. nevertheless

evener... 9. equalizer 10. doubletree

evenglow... 3. red (color) 8. twilight

evening... 5. Abend 6. sunset

evening dress... 4. gown 6. jewels, tuxedo 8. slippers (high heel) 9. full dress, headdress 10. dinner coat 11. tie and tails 17. swallow−tailed coat

event... 4. fate (obs), game 5. drama, issue 6. result 7. contest, episode, scandal 8. incident 9. adventure, happening, milestone 10. conclusion, occurrence 11. consequence, termination 12. circumstance

event (pert to)...
extraordinary.. 10. phenomenon
supernatural.. 7. miracle
theater.. 6. opener 8. premiere
turning point.. 6. crisis 8. decision, landmark

eventide... 4. dusk 6. sunset, vesper 7. evening, sundown 8. twilight 9. nightfall

eventually... 3. yet 6. lastly 7. finally 10. ultimately

ever... 3. e'er 4. anon 5. at all 6. always 7. forever 10. constantly 11. perpetually

Everest peak... 6. Lhotse (28,100 ft)

evergreen shrub... 4. Ilex, moss, Olax, titi 5. heath, holly, savin, toyon 6. laurel 8. baretta, jasmine 9. perennial 12. rhododendron

evergreen tree... 3. fir, yew 4. pine 5. carob, cedar, larch, olive, Taxus 6. balsam, deodar, spruce, tarata 7. conifer, hemlock, madrona, redwood

everlasting... 6. eterne 7. aeonian, agelong, durable, endless, eternal, forever, lasting, tedious 8. enduring, evermore, immortal, infinite 9. continual, incessant, perpetual, unceasing, wearisome 10. immortelle, indefinite 11. never−ending, strawflower 12. Eternal Being, imperishable 13. unintermitted, uninterrupted

every... 3. all, any, ilk 4. each, ilka 6. entire 8. complete

every one, everyone... 3. all 4. each 9. everybody 10. individual

everything... 3. all, sum 5. total

evict... 4. oust 5. eject, expel, prove 6. remove 7. confute 8. force out

eviction... 6. ouster 9. ejectment 11. dislodgment 13. dispossession

evidence... 4. clue, sign 5. proof, token 8. attest, evince 7. constat (law), probate, support 8. argument, manifest, rebuttal 9. testimony 10. indication 15. circumstantiate

evident... 5. clear, plain 6. patent 7. obvious, visible 8. apparent, manifest, palpable 9. notorious 11. indubitable

evil... 3. bad, ill, mal (pref) 4. bane, vile 6. injury, sinful, wicked 7. adverse, baleful, corrupt, hurtful, immoral, malefic, misdeed, satanic, unsound, vicious 8. depraved, iniquity, sinister 9. injurious,

malignant, offensive 10. calamitous, malevolent, pernicious, wrongdoing 12. unpropitious

evil (pert to)...
child.. 3. imp
deed.. 3. sin 4. harm
devil (little).. 9. deevilick (Scot)
doer.. 5. cheat 9. miscreant, wrongdoer 10. malefactor
omen.. 5. knell
spirit.. 5. bugan, demon, devil, ghoul, Satan 6. Belial 7. Ahriman, Amaimon 8. Asmodeus 9. cacodemon, demonkind, lost souls

evils... 4. ills, mala

evince... 4. show 7. display, exhibit, express, provoke 8. convince, evidence, indicate, manifest

evoke... 4. call (out) 5. educe, voice 6. elicit, prompt, summon 7. conjure

evolution... 7. biogeny, cosmism 8. heredity, maneuver, movement 9. Darwinism, phylogeny, unfolding, unrolling 10. evolvement 11. development 13. manifestation, Spencerianism

evolve... 4. emit 5. educe 6. create, deduce, derive, unfold, unroll 7. develop, grow out 9. disengage, expatiate, extricate 11. disentangle

ewe... 3. keb 4. lamb 5. crone (old), sheep 6. theave

ewer... 3. jug 5. crock 7. pitcher

exacerbate... 5. anger 6. incite 8. embitter, irritate 9. aggravate

exact... 4. just, levy, nice 5. assess, demand, elicit, extort, formal, minute, oblige, strict 7. careful, correct, literal, precise, regular, require 8. accurate 10. methodical, meticulous

exact (pert to)...
opposite of.. 8. antipode 9. antipodal
penalty.. 4. fine 7. estreat
thinking.. 13. ratiocination
vengeance.. 6. avenge

exacting... 6. severe, strict 7. arduous 8. critical 9. demanding, elicitory 10. fastidious 12. extortionate

exacting devotion (exclusive)...
7. jealous

exactly... 3. due 5. spand 6. nicely 7. quite so 8. as you say 9. precisely 10. accurately

exaggerated... 8. outré 8. enhanced, enlarged, overdone, romanced 9. excessive, increased, magnified 10. overstated 11. exceptional 13. overestimated 14. misrepresented

exaggerated comedy... 5. farce

exalt... 5. elate, extol, raise 6. praise 7. elevate, ennoble, glorify, inspire, promote, worship 8. enthrone, increase, sanctify 10. aggrandize

exalted... 5. grand, noble, sheen 6. elated 7. refined, sublime 8. elevated, extolled 9. dignified 11. illustrious

examination... 4. test 5. audit, trial 7. inquiry 8. research, scrutiny, specimen 10. discussion, inspection 11. inquisition 13. investigation

examine... 3. pry, spy, try (law)
4. pore, scan, sift, test 5. audit,
probe, quest 6. censor, debate,
ponder 7. analyze, collate, discuss,
explore, inspect 8. consider
11. interrogate

examiner... 6. censor, conner, tester
7. auditor, officer (court) 9. inspector

example... 4. case, norm, type
5. bysen (obs), model 6. sample
7. pattern, warning 8. instance,
paradigm, specimen 9. exemplify,
precedent 12. illustration
15. exemplification

ex animo... 9. sincerely 12. from the
heart

excavate... 3. dig 4. cave, mine
5. dig up, scoop, stope 6. dredge,
exhume 9. hollow out

excavation... 3. pit 4. hole, mine
5. stope 6. cavity 7. digging
8. opencast

exceed... 3. top 4. pass 5. excel,
outdo 6. outvie, overdo 7. eclipse,
surpass 8. outstrip, overstep
9. overshoot, transcend
11. predominate

exceedingly... 4. many, very
9. extremely 13. extraordinary

excel... 3. cap, top 4. beat, best
5. outdo, outgo, rival 6. better,
exceed, precel 7. surpass 8. outshine
9. transcend

excellence... 4. meed 5. merit
6. desert, virtue 7. classic, probity
13. inimitability

excellent... 4. A-one, best, fine, good
5. bravo, prime, super 6. choice,
select, worthy 7. capital, corking
8. skillful (skilful), stunning, valuable
9. admirable, exquisite, first-rate
12. transcendent

except... 3. bar, but 4. omit, save
6. exempt, reject, unless 7. besides
9. eliminate, other than

exception... 4. plea 5. cavil, doubt
6. oddity 7. dissent 8. demurrer
9. condition, exclusion, exemption,
objection, rejection 11. restriction

exceptional... 4. rare 7. notable,
unusual 8. superior, uncommon
9. exclusive, wonderful
10. remarkable 11. outstanding
13. extraordinary

excerpt... 4. cite 5. quote, scrap
6. choice 7. extract, passage
(selected) 9. selection

excess... 3. too 4. over, plus 5. luxus
7. nimiety, overage, profuse, surplus
10. indulgence (undue), redundancy
11. superfluity 12. intemperance
14. immoderateness, superabundance

excess (solar over lunar month)...
5. epact

excessive... 3. too 5. undue 6. overly
7. extreme, profuse 8. overmuch
9. fanatical 10. exorbitant,
immoderate, inordinate, redundancy
11. exaggerated, extravagant
12. unreasonable

excessive (pert to)...
development.. 11. hypertrophy

fear.. 6. phobia
gushing.. 8. effusion
waste.. 12. extravagance

excessively... 3. too 5. enorm
6. unduly 12. exorbitantly,
inordinately 13. intemperately

exchange... 4. swap 5. bandy, trade
6. barter, resale, rialto 7. dealing,
traffic 9. transpose 10. substitute
11. interchange

exchange (pert to)...
discount.. 4. agio
for money.. 4. cash, sell
letters.. 10. correspond
place.. 4. mart 5. store 6. bourse,
market, shoppe
premium.. 4. agio
visits.. 3. gam

exchequer... 4. fisc (fisk) 5. funds,
purse 8. finances, treasury
11. possessions (money)

excise... 3. tax 4. toll 6. impost

exciseman... 5. gager 7. officer
8. revenuer

excision... 7. erasure, removal
10. cutting off, cutting out,
mutilation 11. destruction, extirpation

excite... 4. fire, roil, spur, stir, urge
5. elate, impel, rouse 6. arouse,
awaken, bestir, incite, kindle, prompt,
stir up 7. agitate, animate, inflame,
provoke 8. energize, interest
9. electrify, impassion, instigate,
stimulate

excited... 4. agog 6. hoopla
7. aroused, fevered 8. agitated,
startled 10. interested
11. impassioned

excited, not easily... 5. stoic
7. stoical

excitement... 3. ado 4. stir 5. fever
6. furore 7. emotion, ferment
9. agitation, commotion
10. incitement, irritation
11. disturbance, stimulation

exciting... 6. hectic 7. parlous
8. alluring 9. desirable, thrilling
10. delightful 11. interesting,
provocative

exciting compassion... 7. piteous

exclamation... 2. ah, lo, oh, so
3. aha, bah, boo, fie, hep, oho, tut,
ugh, yah 4. ahem, alas, drat, egad,
evoe, phew, pish, rats 5. bravo,
humph, pshaw 6. indeed 7. kerwham
9. alackaday 11. ejaculation
12. interjection

exclude... 3. bar 4. omit 5. debar,
eject, expel 6. banish 7. shut out
8. preclude, prohibit 9. eliminate
13. excommunicate

exclusive... 5. aloof 6. select
7. special 8. limiting, snobbish
9. seclusive 10. definitive, unsociable
11. prohibitive

exclusive right... 6. patent
10. concession 11. restriction

excoriate... 4. flay, gall, peel 5. strip
6. abrade 9. criticize

excrescence... 4. boss (Arch), lump
6. growth 8. appendage, outgrowth
10. protrusion

excrete... 5. egest 9. discharge, eliminate

excruciating... 7. painful, racking 9. agonizing, torturing 11. distressing

excursion... 3. row 4. ride, sail, tour, trek, trip 5. jaunt, sally 6. junket, outing, ramble 7. circuit, journey, outlope 8. circuity 9. deviation 10. digression, expedition

excusable... 6. venial 9. allowable, justified 10. defensible, exemptible, pardonable, remissible 11. justifiable

excuse... 4. plea 5. alibi, remit 6. acquit, essoin, pardon 7. absolve, apology, condone, forgive, pretext 8. overlook, exonerate, extenuate

execrable... 7. impious 9. nefandous

execute... 2. do 3. act 4. hang, vest 6. direct, effect, finish, manage 7. conduct, enforce, perform 8. carry out, complete, transact 10. accomplish, administer, put to death

execution... 4. writ 7. hanging 10. production, punishment 11. achievement, performance, transaction 14. accomplishment

exegate... 6. leader 7. adviser 8. dragoman 11. interpreter

exegesis... 7. explain 9. interpret 10. exposition, expounding 12. hermeneutics (Theol)

exemplar... 5. ideal, model 7. example, paragon, pattern 8. specimen 9. archetype

exemplary... 8. laudable, monitory 11. commendable 12. exemplifying, praiseworthy 14. representative

exemplify... 4. copy 6. typify 7. explain 10. illustrate, transcribe

exempt... 4. exon 5. clear 6. immune 7. absolve, release 8. excepted, excluded, released, set apart 10. privileged

exemption... 6. essoin 7. freedom 8. immunity, impunity, navicent 12. dispensation

exercise... 3. ply, ure (anc), use 4. task 5. drill, étude, exert, train 6. action, employ, lesson, praxis, school 7. display, problem 8. activity, ceremony, practice, training 9. athletics 10. exhibition, gymnastics

exertion... 5. essay, trial 6. effort 7. attempt 8. endeavor

exhalation... 4. aura, fume 5. steam 7. halitus 9. effluvium, emanation 10. expiration 11. evaporation 12. vaporization

exhale... 6. emit 8. vanish 7. exhaust, respite 9. transpire 10. breathe out

exhaust... 3. fag, sap 4. emit, jade, tire 5. drain, empty, spend, waste, weary 6. exhale, overdo, weaken 7. consume, deplete, fatigue 9. discharge 10. impoverish

exhausted... 4. done, worn 5. spent, tired 6. used up 7. emptied, petered (out) 8. forspent

exhaustion... 6. effete 7. fatigue 9. depletion, lassitude 11. prostration

14. impoverishment

exhibit... 3. air 4. fair, shew (anc), show, wear 5. stage, state 6. evince, expose, flaunt, parade, reveal 7. display 8. disclose, evidence, manifest 9. spectacle 11. demonstrate 15. circumstantiate

exhibit (pert to)...
colors (change of).. 8. iridesce, opalesce
pleasure.. 5. gloat
taste (refined).. 6. ostent 7. elegant

exhibition... 4. fair, show 9. spectacle 10. exposition 11. ostentation 13. manifestation

exhibition of learning... 8. pedantry

exhibition room... 10. panopticon

exhilaration... 6. gaiety 7. jollity 8. gladness, hilarity 9. animation, merriment 10. excitement, joyousness 11. refreshment 12. cheerfulness, invigoration

exhort... 4. urge, warn 6. advise, dehort, incite, preach 7. caution 9. encourage

exhume... 3. dig 5. delve 7. unearth 8. disinter, exhumate

exigeant... 8. exacting 11. importunate

exigency... 4. need, urge 6. crisis 7. demands, urgency 8. juncture, pressure 9. emergency, necessity 12. requirements

exigent... 4. writ 6. strict, urgent 8. critical, exacting, pressing 9. demanding, necessary 13. indispensable

exile... 6. banish, deport 7. outcast 8. outlawry, relegate 9. expulsion 10. banishment, expatriate 12. expatriation, proscription

exist... 2. am, be, is 3. are 4. live 5. alive 6. abound 9. be present

existence... 3. ens 4. esse, life 5. actus, being, entia 6. extant 7. essence, reality 8. presence 13. manifestation

existing (pert to)...
between States.. 10. interstate
fancifully.. 9. imaginary 10. transitory
name only (in).. 7. nominal, titular
now.. 6. extant 7. current, present 9. immediate
same time.. 15. contemporaneous

exit... 3. die 4. door, gate, vent 5. going, go out, issue 6. egress, outlet 7. passage (out) 9. departure

exitus... 5. death, issue 6. exodus, outlet 7. outcome

exlex... 6. outlaw

ex libris... 8. colophon 9. bookplate

exodus... 4. Book (Bib), exit 5. going 6. flight, hegira 9. departure

exonerate... 4. free 5. clear 6. acquit 7. absolve, release, relieve 9. disburden (obs), exculpate

exorbitant... 9. excessive 10. high-priced

exorbitant interest... 5. usury

exorcism... 5. spell 7. formula 9. expulsion (of evil spirits) 11. conjuration, incantation

exordium... 5. proem 7. preface,

prelude 8. overture 9. beginning
12. introduction

exoteric... 8. exterior, external, outsider
14. comprehensible

exotic... 5. alien 7. foreign, strange
8. colorful, ulterior 9. not native,
peregrine, unrelated 10. extraneous,
outlandish

expand... 4. grow, open 5. sheet,
splay, tract 6. dilate, spread
7. broaden, develop, distend, enlarge
9. expatiate, intumesce

expanse... 3. sea 4. main (broad)
5. ocean, plain, reach, tract
6. desert, extent, spread 7. stretch
8. eternity (time) 9. expansion

expansion... 4. size 6. extent, growth,
spread 8. dilation, increase
10. distention 11. development,
enlargement, expatiation

expansive... 4. wide 5. broad, large
7. elastic, liberal 8. effusive,
spacious 9. bombastic, grandiose
11. extensional, sympathetic
12. unrestrained 13. comprehensive

expatiate... 5. dwell 6. dilate
7. descant, enlarge 10. widespread

expatriate... 5. exile, expel 6. banish,
outlaw 7. exclude, outcast
9. ostracize 11. excommunicate

expect... 4. deem, hope, wait
5. await, think 6. intend 7. suppose
10. anticipate

expectation... 4. hope 9. imminence,
intention 12. anticipation

expedience... 6. wisdom 7. fitness
10. adaptation, timeliness
11. suitability

expedient... 4. wise 5. shift 6. timely
7. fitting, politic, ressort, stopgap
8. artifice, resource 9. advisable
10. profitable 12. advantageous

expedite... 3. hie 4. easy, free
5. hurry, light, speed 6. hasten
7. further, quicken 8. dispatch
10. accelerate, facilitate

expedition... 5. drave, foray, haste,
speed 6. safari 7. Crusade, entrada,
journey 8. Crusades 9. excursion,
hastening

expel... 4. oust, void 5. eject, evict,
exile 6. banish, exhale 7. extrude
9. discharge, eliminate
10. dispossess

expend... 3. pay, use 5. spend, waste
7. consume 8. disburse
10. distribute

expenditure... 5. outgo, price 6. outlay
7. expense, payment
11. consumption 12. disbursement

expense... 4. cost 5. price 6. outlay
9. allowance 11. consumption
12. disbursement

expensive... 4. dear, high 5. fancy,
steep 6. costly, lavish 7. liberal
10. high–priced 11. extravagant

experience... 3. see, try 4. feel, have,
know, test 5. maxim, sense, skill
6. ordeal, suffer, wisdom 7. emotion,
undergo 8. facility 9. knowledge,
sensation 10. occurrence

experience (pert to)...
pleasure.. 5. enjoy
regret.. 6. repent
suffering.. 7. calvary
worldly.. 14. sophistication

experiment... 3. try 4. test 5. essay,
proof, prove, trial 6. verify
11. observation

expert... 3. ace 4. deft 5. adept
6. adroit, clever, habile, master
7. casuist (in conscience) 8. artistic,
skillful 10. proficient 11. connoisseur,
experienced 12. professional

expiate... 5. atone, purge 6. purify,
shrive (anc)

expiation... 4. rite 6. amends
7. redress 8. piacular 9. atonement
10. redemption 12. compensation,
propitiation

expire... 3. die, end 4. pass 5. cease,
lapse 6. elapse, perish 7. breathe
(out) 9. terminate

explain... 5. clear, solve 6. define
7. expound, premise 8. describe
9. elucidate, interpret
11. demonstrate

explanation... 6. theory 7. meaning
8. exegesis, scholium, solution
10. exposition 11. description,
explication 13. clarification
14. interpretation 15. exemplification

explanatory description... 5. title
7. titulus

expletive... 3. gee 4. egad, gosh,
oath 5. curse, there, voilà 6. behold
8. addition 9. added word
11. exclamation

explicit... 4. open 5. exact, fixed
6. candid 7. express, precise
8. absolute, distinct, implicit,
manifest, positive 9. outspoken
11. unambiguous, unequivocal,
unqualified 13. unconditional
14. discriminating

explode... 3. pop 4. fail 5. blast,
burst 6. blow up 7. implode
8. backfire, detonate

exploit... 3. act (heroic) 4. dare, deed,
feat, gest, milk 5. bleed 7. heroism
9. advantage 10. overcharge
11. achievement

exploration, modern... 10. space
probe

explore... 4. look, view 5. probe
6. search 7. examine 8. discover
9. penetrate 11. investigate

explorer... 5. diver 7. pioneer
10. discoverer

explorer... 4. Byrd, Eric, Gama
7. Johnson (Osa), Wilkins (Hubert)
8. Amundsen, Magellan 9. Ellsworth

explosion... 3. pop 4. bank 5. blast,
noise 6. report 7. failure 8. outburst
10. detonation

explosive... 3. cap, TNT 4. mine
5. niter, shell 6. amatol, petard,
powder, tittle, tonite 7. cordite,
grenade, lyddite 8. dynamite
9. cartridge, cellulose, fulgurite,
guncotton, pyroxylin 11. firecracker
13. nitroglycerin 15. trinitrotoluene

exponent... 4. note 5. index

7. symptom 9. explainer, expounder
10. explaining 11. interpreter

expose... 3. air 4. bare, open
6. divest, reveal, unmask 7. exhibit,
unearth 8. disclose, discover,
endanger 9. ventilate 10. exposition

expose to danger... 11. periclitate

expose to scorn... 6. satire 7. pillory

exposition... 4. fair 6. bazaar, expose,
lesson 7. display 8. exposure,
treatise 9. discourse, spectacle
10. disclosure, exhibition
11. abandonment, explanation
12. dissertation 14. interpretation

expostulate... 5. orate 6. advise,
demand 7. call for, discuss, protest
8. complain, dissuade
11. remonstrate

exposure... 8. disproof, jeopardy,
openness, snapshot 9. liability
10. appearance, disclosure,
exposition, visibility

express... 3. say 4. mean, show
5. exude, speak, state, train, utter,
voice 6. depict, evince, extort,
phrase 7. betoken, carrier, declare,
exhibit, expound, extract, signify,
testify 8. describe, dispatch, indicate,
intimate, manifest 9. delineate,
messenger, posthaste, utterance
11. declaration

express (pert to)...
censure.. 10. animadvert
disapproval.. 9. deprecate
fervor.. 7. enthuse
gratitude.. 5. thank
indirectly.. 5. imply
in words.. 6. phrase
numerically.. 8. evaluate
regard.. 6. praise 10. compliment
regret.. 9. apologize
sympathy.. 7. condole, console
10. grieve with 11. commiserate

expressing...
doubt.. 10. dubitative
extra phrase (Gram).. 12. periphrastic
feeling.. 7. emotive
past tense.. 11. preteritive
pique.. 5. pouty
praise.. 9. laudatory

expression... 4. grin, show, term
5. scowl, smile 6. aspect, oracle,
phrase 7. diction, meaning
8. locution 9. statement, utterance
10. extraction, indication
11. delineation 13. manifestation
14. representation

expression (pert to)...
mathematics.. 8. equation
of approval.. 4. clap 7. ovation
8. applause
of contempt.. 3. fie 5. pshaw, sneer
of disapproval.. 6. rebuke
of ideas.. 4. mode 5. style 7. fashion
of politics.. 4. vote
of weariness.. 4. sigh
peculiar.. 5. idiom
without.. 7. deadpan

expressive motion... 7. gesture
13. gesticulation

expulsion... 5. exile 10. banishment,
expiration 11. elimination

expunction... 4. blot 7. erasure
10. effacement 12. obliteration

expunge... 4. dele 5. erase 6. cancel,
delete, efface, excise, rub out 7. blot
out, destroy 9. strike out
10. annihilate, obliterate

expurgate... 5. bathe, purge
6. censor, excise, purify 7. cleanse

exquisite... 4. fine, rare 6. dainty,
superb 7. perfect, refined 8. delicate
9. beautiful, delicious, matchless
10. delightful, fastidious

exsanguine... 6. anemic 9. bloodless

exsiccate... 3. dry 4. arid, sear 5. dry
up, parch 7. exhaust 9. evaporate

extant... 5. being 7. in vogue,
present, visible 8. existent, existing

extempore... 5. ad lib 7. offhand
9. impromptu 13. improvisation
14. unpremeditated

extend... 2. go 3. eke, jut, lie, run
4. give, span 5. bulge, reach,
renew, steal, widen 6. deepen,
deploy, expand, spread 7. amplify,
broaden, draw out, proffer, prolong,
radiate, stretch 8. continue, increase,
lengthen, postpone, protract, protrude
10. exaggerate, straighten

extended... 4. open 5. broad
6. valued 7. assured, diffuse
8. expanded, spacious
10. lengthened 12. outstretched

extended view... 8. panorama

extension... 4. area 5. range, scope
6. extent 8. addition, duration,
increase, sequence 9. expansion
10. denotation 11. continuance,
enlargement, lengthening
12. augmentation 13. extensiveness

extension of time... 4. stay 7. respite

extensive... 2. vast, wide 5. broad,
large 7. immense, titanic
8. expanded, spacious 9. expansive,
wholesale 10. widespread
11. far-reaching

extent... 4. area, bulk, room, side, writ
5. areal, range, reach, scope
6. amount, degree, length
7. breadth, compass, expanse
measure 8. distance, frontage
9. dimension 10. assessment (Hist),
denotation, proportion

extenuate... 4. thin 6. excuse, lessen,
reduce, sicken, weaken 7. justify
8. diminish, palliate 9. attenuate

extenuating... 10. justifying, qualifying

exterior... 5. ectad (toward), ectal,
outer 7. outside 8. external
10. extraneous

exterminate... 4. kill 5. expel
7. abolish, destroy 8. get rid of
9. eradicate, extirpate 10. annihilate

extermination... 9. expulsion
11. destruction, eradication

extern... 7. outward 8. exterior,
external 9. extrinsic

external... 4. ecto 5. outer, outre
6. nonego 7. outside 8. cortical
10. extraneous

external appearance... 5. guise,
image, looks 6. aspect 8. features
9. semblance

extinct ... 4. dead, past 5. passé
  7. defunct, died out, expired
  8. quenched 11. nonexistent
  12. extinguished
extinct bird ... 3. moa 4. dodo
extinction ... 5. death 9. quenching
  11. destruction 12. annihilation
extinct reptile ... 11. pterodactyl
extinguish ... 5. annul, choke, douse,
  quell 6. quench, stifle 7. destroy
  8. suppress
extirpate ... 4. dele, root, stub
  5. erase, expel 6. excise, uproot
  7. destroy 9. eradicate
  11. exterminate
extol ... 4. laud 5. exalt, kudos
  6. praise 7. applaud, commend,
  elevate, glorify 8. emblazon
  9. celebrate
extort ... 5. bleed, exact, steal, wrest,
  wring 6. compel, elicit, wrench
  7. extract 10. overcharge
extortion ... 7. robbery, seizure
  8. exaction, rapacity 10. extraction,
  oppression, overcharge
extortionist ... 5. harpy 7. vampire,
  vulture 9. profiteer 11. blackmailer
extra ... 3. bye 4. over 5. added,
  spare, super 7. surplus 8. superior
  9. accessory 10. additional
extra cache ... 5. stock, store
  7. reserve 9. reservoir
extract ... 4. cite, pull 6. deduce, elicit,
  select 7. essence, estreat, excerpt
  8. withdraw
extract (pert to) ...
  balsam .. 7. toluene
  Bible .. 7. passage 8. pericope
  forcibly .. 6. evulse
  newspaper .. 8. clipping
  orchid (climbing) .. 7. vanilla
extraction ... 5. birth, stock 6. origin
  7. essence, excerpt 8. tincture
  9. parentage 10. withdrawal
extraneous ... 5. outer 6. exotic
  7. foreign 9. extrinsic, separated,
  unrelated 11. unessential
extraordinary ... 3. odd 4. rare, unco
  5. great 7. notable, special, unusual
  8. singular 9. irregular, marvelous,
  wonderful 10. noteworthy, remarkable
  11. exceptional 13. distinguished
extravagance ... 5. waste 6. excess
  8. wildness 9. abundance
  10. fanaticism, lavishness
  11. exorbitance, prodigality
  12. exaggeration, intemperance,
  recklessness
extravagant ... 3. E la 4. ee la (Mus),
  high (priced) 5. outré 6. absurd
  7. baroque, bizarre, diffuse, fanatic
  8. boastful, prodigal, wasteful
  9. excessive, fanatical, fantastic,
  luxurious, plentiful 10. digressive
  11. intemperate 12. unrestrained
extreme ... 3. end 4. last, sore
  5. final, great, ultra 6. excess,
  severe, utmost 7. drastic, intense,
  outward, radical 8. farthest, greatest,
  ultimate 9. excessive, extremity,
  fanatical, outermost 10. conclusive,
  immoderate

extreme fear ... 5. panic 6. horror
extreme unction ... 5. anele 9. last
  rites, sacrament
extremist ... 7. radical 8. ultraist
extremity ... 3. end, tip 4. foot, limb
  (body), pole 5. verge 6. border,
  crisis, summit 8. terminal
  9. necessity 11. termination
extricate ... 4. free 5. loose 6. evolve,
  rescue, wangle 7. extract 8. liberate
  9. disengage 10. disembroil
  11. disentangle 12. disembarrass
extrinsic ... 7. foreign, outward
  8. external 9. objective
  10. accidental (Log), contingent,
  extraneous, incidental
  12. adventitious, nonessential
extrovert ... 11. personality (opp of
  introvert)
exuberance ... 6. excess, plenty
  8. overflow, rankness, vivacity
  9. abundance, animation, profusion
  10. friskiness, liveliness, luxuriance
  11. copiousness 14. superabundance
exuberant ... 6. frisky, lavish 7. fertile,
  profuse 8. effusive, fruitful, thriving
  9. luxuriant, plentiful 11. overflowing
  13. superabundant
exudation ... 3. gum, lac, tar 5. pitch,
  resin 6. oozing 8. emission, sweating
  9. discharge, excretion
exude ... 4. emit, ooze, reek 5. sweat
  7. excrete, give out 9. discharge
exult ... 3. joy 4. leap (obs), rave
  5. boast, elate, ovare, pride
  7. rejoice 8. jubilate
exultant ... 5. ovant 6. elated
exultation ... 3. joy 7. delight
  8. boasting 9. jubilance, rejoicing
  10. jubilation
exults ... 5. leaps 7. glories, springs
  9. jubilates
eye ... 2. ee 3. orb, see 4. auge, glim,
  hole, ogle 5. optic, organ (human),
  sight, watch 6. look at, peeper
  7. observe, witness 10. scrutinize
eye (pert to) ...
  absence of pupil .. 6. acorea
  black .. 5. mouse 6. shiner
  brow .. 4. arch 6. eebree
    11. supercilium
  cavity .. 5. orbit 6. hippus, socket
  disease .. 8. cataract, glaucoma,
    hypopyon, trachoma 9. amblyopia
    14. conjunctivitis
  disorder .. 6. squint 7. walleye
    9. exotropia 10. strabismus
  dropper .. 7. pipette
  glass .. 4. lens 7. lorgnon, monocle
    8. pince–nez 10. spectacles
  inflammation .. 6. ititis 7. uveitis
  lash, lashes .. 6. cilia (pl) 6. cilium
  lid .. 8. palpebra
  part .. 4. iris, uvea 5. pupil 6. cornea,
    retina
  to blind (falconry) .. 4. seel
eyelet ... 7. cringle, grommet, ocellus
  8. loophole, peephole
eyetooth ... 6. cuspid 8. dogtooth
eyot ... 3. ait 4. holm 5. islet
eyra ... 7. wildcat
eyrie, eyry ... 4. nest 5. aerie, nidus

F

F... 6. letter (6th)
fabes... 10. gooseberry
fabian... 7. caution 8. dilatory, inaction
  15. procrastination
Fabian... 7. General (Rom), Society
fable... 3. lie 4. myth 5. story
  6. legend 7. fabliau, fantasy, fiction,
  Marchen, parable 8. allegory,
  apologue, folk tale 9. falsehood
fable (pert to)...
  being.. 5. troll
  king.. 3. Log
  monster.. 4. ogre 7. centaur
  narrator.. 10. parabolist
  writer.. 5. Aesop
fabric... 5. build, cloth 6. tissue
  7. texture 8. erection, material
  9. framework 11. workmanship
  12. construction
fabric (types of)... 3. rep 4. alma,
  duck, felt, gros, jean, lawn, leno, silk
  5. baize, batik, beige, crash, crepe,
  denim, linen, nylon, pekin, rumal,
  satin, scrim, serge, suede, tulle,
  tweed, twill, voile, wigan 6. agaric,
  alpaca, burlap, calico, canvas, chintz,
  cotton, dimity, étoile, madras,
  mohair, moreen, muslin, penang,
  pongee, poplin, ratiné, sateen, tricot
  7. batiste, brocade, bunting, challis,
  chiffon, delaine, elastic, etamine,
  flannel, galatea, gingham, hernani,
  paisley, percale, satinet, ticking,
  worsted 8. cashmere, chambray,
  chenille, corduroy, cretonne, drilling,
  prunella, sarcenet, Shantung,
  sheeting, whipcord 9. crinoline,
  gabardine, grenadine, lansdowne,
  matelassé, paramatta 10. broadcloth,
  seersucker, terry cloth
fabric (pert to)...
  dealer.. 6. mercer
  ornamental.. 4. lace 8. fagoting
  silk, watered.. 5. moiré
  silk and gold.. 4. acca (anc)
    7. brocade
  twill.. 6. caddis (cadis)
  velvet.. 5. panne, terry 6. velure
    7. velours
  waste.. 5. mungo
  window shade.. 7. Holland
  woven.. 6. tricot
fabricate... 4. coin, form, make, mint
  5. build, frame, weave 6. create,
  devise, invent, scheme 7. falsify,
  fashion, produce, trump up
  9. construct 11. manufacture
fabrication... 3. lie, web 5. guile
  6. cogger, deceit, making 7. fiction,
  forging, untruth 9. falsehood,

invention 12. construction
fabulist... 4. liar 5. Aesop
  11. storyteller
fabulous... 6. absurd 7. feigned
  8. mythical 9. fictional, imaginary,
  legendary 10. fictitious, remarkable
  11. astonishing 12. mythological
fabulous (pert to)...
  animal.. 7. unicorn 9. rosmarine
    (walrus)
  beast.. 4. lung 6. dragon, wivern
    7. griffon, serpent 10. earthdrake
  being.. 6. Lapith, Nessus 7. centaur
  bird.. 3. moa, roc 4. rukh
facade... 4. face 5. facia, front
  7. frontal
face... 3. mug 4. dare, defy, dial, line,
  meet, moue, phiz 5. brave, cover,
  front 6. answer, obvert, oppose,
  phizog, visage 7. grimace
  8. boldness, confront, envisage,
  exterior, features, pretense
  9. encounter, impudence
  10. effrontery 11. countenance,
  physiognomy, self-respect
face (pert to)...
  bone.. 6. zygoma (cheek) 7. maxilla
    (jaw)
  east.. 9. orientate
  gem.. 5. facet
  lifting.. 13. rhytidoplasty
  masonry.. 5. revet
  nose.. 11. rhinoplasty
  pains.. 5. ague 10. tic douloureux
  surgery.. 14. blepharoplasty (eyelid)
  to face.. 6. afront 7. vis-à-vis
  value.. 3. par
faces (twelve)... 12. dodecahedron
facet... 4. face 5. bezel, culet
  6. aspect, collet 8. exterior
facetious... 5. droll, funny, witty
  6. facete, jocose 7. comical, jesting
  8. laughter 9. whimsical
facia... 5. plate 6. tablet
facial pain... 3. tic 4. ague
  9. neuralgia 13. tic douloureux
facient... 4. doer 5. agent
  10. multiplier
facile... 4. easy 5. quick, ready
  6. expert, fluent, gentle, pliant
  7. affable, lenient, pliable
  9. compliant, teachable
facilitate... 3. aid 4. ease, help
  6. assist
facility... 3. art 4. ease, help 5. éclat,
  means, skill 7. address, pliancy
  8. easiness 9. readiness
  10. adroitness, expertness, pliability
  11. convenience, furtherance
  13. accommodation

facing... 6. lining, veneer 7. coating, surface 8. opposite
facing (pert to)...
glacier direction.. 5. stoss
inward.. 7. introrse
outward.. 8. extrorse
facsimile... 4. copy 5. match 7. replica 9. duplicate 11. counterpart
fact, facts... 4. data, deed, feat, fiat 5. datum, event, posit, truth 6. really 7. keynote, lowdown, paradox 9. actuality
fact collector... 7. statist 12. statistician
faction... 4. bloc, camp, sect, side 5. cabal, junto, party 6. clique 7. machine (Polit) 11. combination, partisanism
factious... 9. demagogic, seditious, turbulent
factitious... 4. made (by art), mock, sham 5. phony 9. unnatural 10. artificial 11. make-believe
factor... 4. ager, gene 5. agent, cause 6. detail 9. component 11. constituent
factotum... 4. maid 5. do-all 7. servant 8. busybody
faculties... 4. wits 6. senses 7. talents 9. abilities, aptitudes 12. capabilities
faculty... 3. art 4. body, ease, gift 6. talent 7. ability, know-how 8. aptitude, teachers 9. endowment (mental) 12. professorate
fad... 4. rage, whim 5. craze, fancy, hobby 6. custom 7. caprice, fashion
faddist... 10. monomaniac
fade, fade out... 3. age, dim, dow, wan 4. flat, pale, wilt 5. daver, decay, peter 6. perish, vanish, weaken, wither 7. decline, insipid 8. discolor, dissolve, languish 9. disappear 11. deteriorate
faded... 3. dim 4. dull, pale 5. faint, passé 8. impaired
Faerie Queene (pert to)...
author.. 7. Spenser
character.. 3. Ate, Una 5. Guyon, Truth 7. Acrasia 8. Gloriana
theme.. 8. chivalry 10. knighthood
type work.. 4. poem 8. allegory
fag... 4. flag, hack, jade, tire, toil, work 5. droop, slave, weary 6. drudge, menial 7. exhaust, fatigue, untwist (rope end) 8. drudgery 9. cigarette
fag end... 3. end 4. tail 6. scraps, tag end 7. remnant 8. last part, leavings
Fagin... 3. Jew (Oliver Twist)
Fagin's pupil... 12. Artful Dodger (John Dawkins)
fagot, faggot... 4. bind 5. bunch 6. bundle, emblem (Her) 8. firewood, slattern
fail... 3. ebb, err 4. flop, lack, miss, sink 5. decay, flunk, lapse 6. defect, desert, weaken 7. decline, exhaust 8. unbetide 9. fall short 10. disappoint, go bankrupt

11. deteriorate
failed admission... 11. blackballed
failed to follow suit... 7. reneged
failure... 3. dud 4. flop, foil, lack, lose, miss 5. decay, fault, lapse 6. defeat, fiasco 7. default 10. bankruptcy, deficiency, insolvency, nonsuccess, suspension 11. delinquency
faint... 3. din, ill 4. pale, soft, weak 5. swelt, swoon, timid 6. feeble, sickly 7. languid 8. cowardly, fatigued, listless, timorous 10. indistinct, oppressive
faintness... 5. qualm (sudden) 7. dimness, syncope 8. paleness, weakness 10. feebleness
fair... 4. just, mart 6. bazaar, blonde, comely, honest, kermis 8. festival, mediocre, rainless, unbiased 9. impartial 10. auspicious, reasonable 12. unprejudiced 13. dispassionate
fairy, faery... 3. elf, fay 4. peri, pixy 5. genie, magic, nymph, ouphe, pixie 6. elfkin, sprite 7. brownie, gremlin 8. illusion
fairy (pert to)...
abode (Scot).. 4. shee (sidhe)
death spirit.. 7. banshee
evil.. 4. ogre, puck 8. hobgoblin
fort.. 3. lis (liss)
German.. 6. kobold
Irish.. 10. cluricaune, leprechaun
king.. 6. Oberon
Persian.. 4. peri
queen.. 3. Mab, Una 7. Titania
Scandinavian.. 5. nisse
tale.. 3. fib 7. Marchen 8. allegory 9. narrative
faith... 4. hope 5. creed, piety, troth, trust 6. belief, credit, verily, virtue 7. loyalty 8. credence, fidelity 9. assurance, authority, orthodoxy 10. confidence 11. credibility
faithful... 4. fast, feal, leal, true 5. liege, loyal, pious 6. devout, steady, trusty 7. devoted, sincere, staunch 8. constant, obedient, reliable 9. believers, steadfast, veracious
faithful friend... 7. Achates (Vergil's Aeneid)
faithless... 5. false, punic 6. fickle, untrue 8. apostate, disloyal, shifting 9. deceptive, mercurial, skeptical 10. perfidious, unfaithful 11. incredulous, irreligious, treacherous, unbelieving 12. falsehearted
fake... 3. rob 4. sham 5. cheat, fraud, trick 7. trump up 8. doctor up 9. deception, fabricate, imitation 11. counterfeit
faker... 5. cheat, fraud 7. bluffer 8. impostor 9. hypocrite, pretender
fakir... 4. sect (Moslem, Islam), yogi 7. dervish 9. mendicant
falcon... 4. hawk 5. besra, saker 6. laggar, lanner, luggar, merlin, shahin (shaheen), sorage, tercel 7. kestrel, sakeret 8. lanneret,

Raptores 9. gyrfalcon (gerfalcon),
peregrine

falcon, military... 8. ordnance

falconry term... 4. hood, jess, lure,
seel 6. rebate 7. hawking

fall... 3. ebb 4. bang, drop, plop,
ruin, sink, slip 5. crash, spill
6. autumn, defeat, perish, plunge,
tumble 7. descend, descent, devolve,
failure, plummet, relapse 8. collapse,
commence, downfall, rainfall
9. abatement, overthrow, surrender,
waterfall 10. depreciate, subversion
11. degradation, precipitate

fall (pert to)...
back.. 6. recede, recoil 7. relapse,
retreat 10. retrogress
behind.. 3. lag 4. lose 7. regress
guy.. 5. patsy
in.. 4. cave 5. agree, lapse
6. concur, line up 8. collapse
9. terminate
rhythmical.. 6. cadent
short.. 4. lack, want 10. disappoint

fallacious... 4. wily 5. false 6. crafty,
untrue 8. delusive, guileful
9. deceitful, deceptive, erroneous,
illogical, insidious 10. fraudulent,
misleading 13. disappointing

fallacy... 5. error 6. idolum
7. sophism 8. deception, falseness,
sophistry 13. deceitfulness

false... 4. sham, tale 5. bogus, paste
6. betray, impugn, pseudo, untrue
7. mislead 8. apostate, spurious
9. deceitful, deceptive, erroneous,
faithless, incorrect, insincere,
pretended, unfounded 10. fictitious,
mendacious, traitorous, unfaithful,
unreliable, untruthful 11. counterfeit
12. illegitimate

false (pert to)...
friend.. 5. Judas 7. traitor
front.. 8. disguise 11. affectation
fruit.. 10. pseudocarp
god.. 4. idol
hearted.. 9. deceitful 10. perfidious
11. treacherous
items.. 6. spuria
jewelry.. 5. paste 6. strass
reasoning.. 10. paralogism
report.. 5. rumor 6. canard 7. slander
show.. 6. tinsel
wing (bird's).. 5. alula

falsehood... 3. lie 4. tale 7. falsity,
fiction, perjury, untruth 9. imposture,
mendacity 11. counterfeit, fabrication
12. exaggeration

falseness... 5. error 8. illusion
9. deception, falsehood 10. infidelity

falsetto... 5. voice (false) 10. artificial
11. high-pitched

falsify... 3. lie 5. belie, forge
7. distort, pervert 8. disprove
10. adulterate 11. counterfeit
12. misrepresent

Falstaff... 5. opera (Verdi) 9. character
(Shak)

falter... 3. lag 4. fail 5. demur, pause,
waver 6. flinch, quaver, totter
7. stagger, stammer, stumble,
tremble 8. hesitate, lose hope

fame... 4. note 5. éclat, glory, kudos
6. renown, repute

famed... 7. eminent, honored, popular
8. renowned 9. notorious
10. celebrated

familiar... 4. easy 5. usual
6. common, versed 7. affable
8. domestic, frequent, friendly,
habitual, informal 9. companion,
customary, well-known
10. accustomed, colloquial,
conversant 12. domesticated,
presumptuous 13. unconstrained

familiarity... 8. intimacy 9. awareness,
knowledge, liberties 10. affability
12. acquaintance (close), friendliness

familiarize... 6. inform 8. accustom
9. habituate

family... 3. ilk, kin 4. clan, line, race
5. class, group, house, tribe
6. stirps 7. kindred, lineage
9. community, household, posterity
10. kith and kin

family (pert to)...
bees.. 5. apina 7. Apoidea
favoritism.. 8. nepotism
herbs.. 7. Ranales
Italians (famed).. 4. Este
kings.. 7. dynasty
name.. 7. surname

famous... 5. named, noted 7. eminent,
namable, notable 8. renowned
9. excellent, notorious
10. celebrated, remarkable
13. distinguished

famous murderer... 4. Aram, Cain
9. Bluebeard

famous pirate... 4. Kidd (Capt)

fan... 4. blow, cool, vane, whip
5. punka (punkah) 6. blower, foment,
incite, rooter, spread, thresh, winnow
7. admirer, devotee, refresh
9. stimulate, strike out (baseball),
ventilate 10. enthusiast

fanatic, fanatical... 3. mad 5. bigot,
crank, crazy, rabid 6. maniac, zealot
7. devotee, frantic, lunatic 8. frenzied
9. energumen, phrenetic
10. enthusiast, unbalanced
11. extravagant, overzealous
12. enthusiastic 13. nonconformist,
overreligious

fanatical partisan... 6. zealot

fancied... 6. unreal 7. dreamed,
ideated 8. favorite, imagined
9. well-liked 10. ornamental

fanciful... 3. odd 5. queer 7. bizarre,
strange 9. fantastic, grotesque,
visionary, whimsical 10. capricious,
chimerical 11. imaginative
13. grandiloquent

fancy... 3. fad 4. idea, like, love,
ween, whim 5. dream, freak
6. design, desire, devise, humour,
ideate, megrim, notion, ornate,
vagary 7. caprice, conceit, fantasy,
imagine, impulse, suppose, thought
8. illusion, phantasy, superior
9. expensive 10. conception,
impression 11. extravagant,
imagination, inclination
12. ostentatious

fandango... 3. hop 4. ball, prom
5. dance 7. cantico
fandango bird... 7. manakin
Faneuil Hall (1742)... 4. hall
6. market (Boston) 15. Cradle of
Liberty
fanion... 4. flag 6. guidon, marker
fanon... 4. cape (Pope's) 5. orale
6. banner 7. maniple
fan-shaped... 10. flabellate
fan sticks (radiating)... 4. brin
7. panache
fantastic... 3. odd 5. outré, queer
6. absurd, rococo, unreal
7. baroque, bizarre, caprice, foppish,
unusual 8. fanciful, freakish, illusory
9. eccentric, grotesque, visionary
10. capricious, chimerical, irrational
11. extravagant, imaginative
12. phantastical
fantastic imitation... 6. parody
8. travesty
fantasy... 5. dream, fancy, story
6. vision 7. caprice, phantom,
romance 8. illusion 10. apparition
13. hallucination
far... 3. tel (pref) 4. afar, long, tele
(pref) 6. marked, remote
9. separated 10. abstracted
farce... 4. mime, play 5. drama
(humorous), exode, humor, stuff
6. comedy 7. mockery 8. stuffing
9. burlesque, forcemeat
farceur... 5. joker 8. comedian
9. dramatist
fare... 3. eat 4. diet, food, rate
5. crowd, going, swarm, table
7. conduct, journey, passage,
prosper, succeed 9. passenger
10. expedition
farewell... 3. ave 4. vale 5. adieu,
adios, aloha, congé (formal)
7. good-bye, leaving, parting 8. au
revoir, Godspeed 9. bon voyage
11. leave-taking
farinaceous drink... 6. ptisan
farinaceous food... 4. sago 5. flour,
grain, salep, wheat 7. cereals
farm... 4. plot, till, torp 5. croft, ranch
6. grange, rancho 7. acreage,
cotland 9. cultivate
farm (pert to)...
  English.. 6. barton
  laborer.. 4. hind 6. farmer, tiller
  prefix.. 4. agro
  repairer.. 10. plowwright
  Spanish.. 8. hacienda
  steward.. 7. granger
  tenant.. 6. cotter
farmer... 4. ryot 5. kulak 6. grower,
tiller 7. cropper, metaver, peasant,
planter, rancher 10. agronomist,
cultivator 13. agriculturist
faro term... 4. bank 5. monte, stuss
6. cathop, layout
Faroe (Faeroe) Islands...
  called also.. 12. Sheep Islands
  capital.. 9. Thorshavn
  magistrate.. 4. foud
  rule.. 5. Norse (anc) 7. Denmark
  whirlwind.. 2. oe
far-reaching... 4. deep, long 5. scope

7. intense 9. extensive
farrow... 3. pig 6. litter
farsighted... 6. shrewd 9. provident,
sagacious 10. presbyopic
11. foresighted 12. clearsighted
farther, further... 4. also 7. thither
8. moreover 10. additional
farthest... 5. final 6. inmost, utmost
7. endmost, extreme, longest
fascia... 4. band, sash 6. fillet, ribbon
7. bandage
fascinate... 5. charm 6. allure,
enamor, thrill 7. bewitch, delight,
enchant 8. entrance, interest
9. captivate, enrapture
fascinating... 5. siren 8. alluring,
charming 10. attractive, bewitching,
delightful 11. interesting
Fascist (1919)... 6. Pareto
9. Mussolini 10. Black Shirt
fashion... 3. fad, fit, ton, way
4. make, mode, mold, rage
5. adapt, carve, craze, feign, forge,
frame, guise, model, shape, style,
vogue 6. create, custom, invent
7. compose 8. contrive 9. construct,
fabricate, smartness 10. appearance
fashionable... 5. smart 6. formal,
modish 7. a la mode, in vogue,
stylish 8. up-to-date 10. conforming
13. well-appearing
fast... 5. agile, fixed, fleet, hasty,
quick, rapid, sound, space, stuck,
swift 6. lively, speedy, staple
7. abiding, soundly 8. enduring,
securely 10. profligate, stationary,
unyielding 11. expeditious
fasten... 3. bar, pin, tie 4. bind, clip,
lace, lash, moor, nail, rope, seal,
tack, wire 5. affix, belay, chain,
clamp, clasp, latch, paste, rivet
6. attach, secure, solder, staple,
tether, toggle 7. padlock
fastening... 5. desmo (comb form)
fastest (pert to)...
  animals.. 6. coyote 7. cheetah
8. antelope
  birds.. 5. eagle, goose 7. ostrich
fast horse... 6. pelter
fastidious... 4. nice 6. dainty
7. elegant, finical, precise 8. critical,
delicate, exacting, overnice
9. squeamish 10. meticulous,
particular, scrupulous
fastness... 4. fort 6. fixity 7. citadel
8. celerity, firmness, velocity
9. stability 10. profligacy, stronghold
fat... 4. lard, oily, suet 5. adeps, fatty,
lipin, obese, olein, stout 6. axunge
(goose), grease, portly, steato (pref),
stocky, tallow 7. adipose, lanolin,
opulent, paunchy, stearin, wealthy
9. corpulent, plentiful 10. profitable
fatal... 5. fated 6. deadly, doomed,
lethal, mortal 7. fateful, ominous
8. destined 9. condemned, prophetic
10. calamitous, disastrous
11. destructive
fatality... 4. fate 5. death 8. disaster
10. deadliness
fatally... 8. mortally 9. ruinously
fate... 3. end, lot 4. doom, luck, ruin

5. karma 6. chance, kismet
7. destiny, fortune 8. disaster,
downfall 13. inevitability
fateful... 5. fated 6. deadly
9. momentous 10. inevitable,
portentous 11. destructive,
predestined
Fates (Gr)... 6. Clotho, Moirae (group
of Three) 7. Atropos 8. Lachesis
Fates (Norse)... 4. Urth 5. Norns
(group of three), Skuld 9. Verthandi
Fates (Rom)... 4. Fata, Mona 5. Morta
6. Decuma, Parcae (group of three)
father... 2. pa 3. Abu, dad 4. abba,
papa, père, sire 5. adopt, friar,
padre, pater, vater 6. priest, senior
7. creator 8. generate 9. confessor,
procreate 11. acknowledge
Father (of)...
Ajax.. 7. Telamon
Christmas.. 10. Santa Claus
English learning.. 4. Bede
engraving.. 3. Pye
Evil.. 5. Satan
his country.. 6. Cicero (Rom), Medici
(It) 10. Washington (US)
history.. 9. Herodotus
Mankind (Myth).. 7. Iapetus
New York.. 13. Knickerbocker
Ocean.. 7. Neptune
the Gods.. 6. Amen–Ra
Time.. 10. Methuselah
Waters.. 11. Mississippi
father (pert to)...
land.. 6. native
land, love of.. 10. philopater
term.. 6. agnate 8. paternal
wise.. 6. mentor
fatherless... 6. orbate 7. forlorn
8. helpless, orphaned
fathom... 3. try 4. test 5. delve,
plumb, solve, sound 7. measure,
plummet 8. encircle 9. penetrate
10. understand 13. take soundings
fatigued... 4. bored, faint, jaded,
spent, tired, weary 6. fagged
7. languid, wearied 9. exhausted
Fatima (pert to)...
character in.. 14. Arabian Nights
father.. 8. Mohammed
husband.. 9. Bluebeard
fatten... 4. feed 6. batten, enrich
7. improve, prosper 8. pinguefy
fatty... 5. suety 6. greasy 7. adipose
9. aliphatic
fatty (pert to)...
acid.. 6. adipic 7. valeric
degeneration.. 8. adiposis
substance, sheep.. 5. suint
tumor.. 6. lipoma
fatuous... 4. vain 5. inane, silly
6. vacant 7. foolish, idiotic, witless
8. demented, illusory, imbecile
9. insensate 11. thoughtless
faucet... 3. peg, tap 4. cock 6. spigot
7. fixture, hydrant, petcock
fault... 4. hade, lode, slip, vice
5. cavil, cleft, culpa (law), error,
lapse, tache (anc) 6. defect, foible
7. blemish, blunder, demerit, failing,
frailty, misdeed, offense 8. fracture
10. peccadillo 11. delinquency

12. imperfection
faultfinder... 6. carper, nagger
7. caviler 10. complainer, criticizer
faultfinding... 7. carping, nagging
8. captious, caviling, critical
9. censorial
faultless... 4. pure 5. right 7. correct,
paragon, perfect 8. flawless, innocent
9. blameless 10. impeccable
13. unimpeachable 14. irreproachable
faultlessness... 8. accuracy
9. innocence 10. perfection
11. preciseness
faulty... 3. ill 4. amiss, unfit 6. guilty
8. culpable 9. blemished, defective,
deficient, erroneous, imperfect
11. blameworthy
faun... 3. Pan 5. deity, satyr
6. Faunus 10. Praxiteles
Faust... 4. hero 5. drama (Goethe),
opera
faux pas... 5. error, gaffe 6. booboo
7. blunder, misstep, mistake
favor, favour... 3. aid 4. boon, gift,
help 5. bless, grace, token
6. esteem, letter, regard 8. good
will, kindness, leniency, resemble
9. patronage, patronize, privilege
10. assistance, concession,
favoritism, partiality, permission
11. approbation
favorable... 4. good, kind, rosy
6. benign, timely 7. helpful, hopeful,
popular 8. friendly, gracious, pleasing
9. approving, opportune
10. auspicious, beneficial, propitious
11. complaisant 12. advantageous
favorite... 3. pet 4. lamb (pet)
6. minion 7. darling 10. preference
favoritism... 4. bias 7. leaning
8. nepotism 10. partiality
12. predilection
fawn... 3. doe 4. buck, coax, deer,
faon (color) 5. color, cower, crawl,
creep, toady 6. cringe, grovel, shrink
7. truckle 10. ingratiate
fawning... 7. servile 8. toadyish
9. truckling 10. obsequious
11. bootlicking, sycophantic
fawnskin (classic art)... 6. nebris
fay... 3. elf 5. fairy 6. sprite
fealty... 4. duty 6. homage 7. loyalty,
respect 8. fidelity 9. constancy
10. allegiance, obligation
fear... 3. awe 5. alarm, dread, panic
6. dismay, fright, horror, phobia,
terror 7. anxiety 8. venerate
9. apprehend, cowardice, reverence
11. nervousness 13. consternation
fear (of)...
animals.. 9. zoophobia
bees.. 9. apiphobia
being alone.. 10. autophobia,
monophobia
blood.. 10. hemophobia
cats.. 12. aelurophobia
crossing streets.. 11. dromophobia
crowds.. 11. ochlophobia
darkness.. 11. nyctophobia,
scotophobia
death.. 11. necrophobia
disease.. 10. nosophobia

enclosures.. 14. claustrophobia
fire.. 10. pyrophobia
food.. 10. cibophobia
heights.. 10. acrophobia
　　11. hypsophobia
holy things.. 11. hagiophobia
men.. 11. androphobia
new things.. 9. neophobia
open spaces.. 11. agoraphobia
pain.. 10. algophobia
places (certain).. 10. topophobia
poison.. 10. toxiphobia
reptiles.. 13. herpetophobia
sea.. 14. thalassophobia
strangers.. 10. xenophobia
sunlight.. 11. heliophobia
thirteen.. 13. tridecaphobia
weeds.. 11. runcophobia
fearful... 4. dino (pref), dire 5. awful,
　　pavid, timid 6. afraid, craven
　　7. anxious, nervous 8. dreadful,
　　horrible, timorous 9. appealing,
　　frightful 11. distressing, frightening
　　12. apprehensive
fearless... 4. bold 5. brave 6. daring
　　7. impavid 8. harmless, intrepid
　　9. audacious, confident, dauntless,
　　undaunted 10. courageous
feast... 4. fete, meal 5. agape, epulo,
　　revel 6. junket, picnic, regale, repast
　　7. banquet, gratify 8. carousal,
　　festival 9. carrousel
Feast (of)...
　Lanterns (Jap).. 3. Bon
　Lots.. 5. Purim
　Nativity.. 9. Christmas
　Pentecost (weeks).. 8. Shabuoth
　Tabernacles.. 7. Succoth
feasting... 6. dining 9. epulation
feat... 3. act 4. deed 5. stunt
　　7. exploit 11. achievement,
　　performance 14. accomplishment
feather... 4. deck, flaw (jewel), tuft
　　5. adorn, penna, plume, quill
　　6. clothe, fletch, hackle, trifle
　　7. plumage 11. lightness
feather (pert to)...
　an arrow.. 6. fledge, fletch
　barb.. 7. pinnula 8. barbicel
　bird (area).. 7. pteryle
　featherlike.. 7. pinnate
　filament.. 4. dowl
　key (machine).. 6. spline
　molt.. 3. mew
　repair (falconry).. 3. imp
　shaft.. 5. scape
feathered... 5. swift 6. plumed,
　　winged 7. fledged 8. pennated,
　　plumaged 10. ornamented
feature... 4. face 5. motif, trait
　　6. aspect 7. special 8. headline,
　　resemble 9. component, lineament
　　10. appearance, comeliness
　　11. countenance 14. characteristic
features... 3. mug 4. face 5. looks
　　6. visage 7. outline 9. geography
February birthstone... 8. amethyst
federation... 5. union 6. league
　　8. alliance 10. government
　　11. affiliation 13. confederation
fed up... 5. bored, jaded 7. wearied
　　8. satiated 9. surfeited

fee... 3. feu, tip 4. fief, rate, wage
　　5. bribe 6. charge, estate (law)
　　8. gratuity, retainer 9. emolument
　　10. honorarium
feeble... 4. aged, lame, puny, weak
　　5. dotty 6. infirm 10. indistinct
　　11. debilitated
feeble–minded... 5. anile 9. infirmity
　　10. irresolute, weak–willed
　　11. vacillating
feed... 4. dine, meal, sate 5. stoke
　　6. fodder, gavage 7. engorge,
　　foldage, furnish, indulge, nourish,
　　nurture, pannage (swine)
　　9. encourage, provision
feel... 3. ail, air 4. palp 5. grope,
　　sense, touch 6. handle, suffer
　　7. examine, explore, quality, texture
　　8. perceive 10. atmosphere,
　　experience
feel (pert to)...
　compunction.. 6. repent
　dejection.. 6. repine
　fear.. 2. ug
　melancholy.. 6. grieve
　worth of.. 10. appreciate
feeler... 4. palp, test 6. barbal, palpus
　　7. antenna 8. question, tentacle
feeling... 4. feel, tact, view 5. hunch,
　　touch 7. emotion, opinion, passion
　　8. attitude 9. sensation, sentiment
　　10. atmosphere, experience,
　　perception 11. sensibility
　　13. consciousness
feeling (pert to)...
　capable of.. 5. emote 8. sentient
　　9. sensitive
　displeasure.. 9. resentful
　hostility.. 6. animus 9. animosity
　ill.. 7. malaise 10. discomfort
　impassive.. 8. stoicism
　joyful.. 6. jocund
　offense.. 5. pique
　superiority.. 9. arrogance
　without.. 6. apathy, steely 7. callous
　　8. numbness 9. unfeeling
　　13. insensibility
feet... see also *foot*
　designating.. 5. podal
　having.. 6. pedate
　number.. 7. footage
　two (Pros).. 6. dipody 7. dimeter
　　9. ditrochee
　without.. 4. apod 6. apodal
　　8. footless
feign... 3. act 4. sham 5. fable
　　6. affect, assume, gammon, garble,
　　invent 7. connive, imagine, pretend
　　8. malinger (illness), simulate
　　9. dissemble 11. counterfeit,
　　make–believe
feint... 5. appel (fencing), blind, shift,
　　trick 6. attack (mock), thrust
　　7. mislead, pretext 8. artifice,
　　pretense
Felicia... 7. thistle 9. happiness
felicitate... 4. laud 5. bless
　　8. macarize 10. compliment
　　12. congratulate
felicity... 5. bliss, grace 7. aptness,
　　success 8. aptitude 9. happiness,
　　well–being 11. achievement (happy),

blessedness 12. blissfulness

Felidae... 4. cats, lion, lynx, pard, puma 5. tiger 6. jaguar 7. cheetah, leopard, wildcat

feline... 3. sly 5. Felis 6. animal 7. catlike, furtive 8. stealthy 11. treacherous

Felis... 3. cat

fell... 3. cut, hem, hew 4. beat, hill, kill, pelt, ruin, skin 5. cruel, level 6. fierce, fleece, lay low, mighty, savage 7. brutish, tumbled 9. barbarous, ferocious, overthrow, prostrate

fellow... 3. lad, man 4. beau, chap, peer 5. equal 6. member, person 7. comrade 8. neighbor 9. associate, companion 10. sweetheart 11. confederate

fellow (pert to)...
accomplice.. 7. abettor 9. accessory 11. confederate
awkward.. 4. boor, gawk
clumsy.. 3. oaf 4. lout, pleb 5. yahoo 7. bumpkin
coward.. 3. cad, fop 4. drip 7. bounder 8. spalpeen
droll.. 3. wag 5. card
old.. 6. geezer 7. callant
small.. 6. shaver
smart.. 5. aleck
young.. 4. chap 5. blade, youth 7. younker 9. stripling

fellowman... 7. brother 11. fellow being

fellowship... 4. sect 5. guild, union 7. company 8. alliance, sodality 9. communion 10. membership 11. affiliation, comradeship, partnership, scholarship 12. friendliness 13. companionship

felon... 3. bum 4. wild 5. cruel 6. wicked 7. convict, culprit, outcast, villain, whitlow 8. criminal, disloyal 9. infection, malignant, murderous 10. malefactor, paronychia, traitorous

felony... 3. sin 5. crime, wrath 6. daring, deceit 8. baseness, burglary, outlawry 9. treachery 10. illegality, wickedness 11. misdemeanor

female... 4. bibi, dame, doña, girl, gyne, lady, miss 5. donna, femme, rhyme, squaw, woman 6. maiden, matron 7. distaff, dowager, fair sex, Sahibah 8. mistress 9. weaker sex

female (pert to)...
architecture.. 8. Caryatid
comb form.. 5. gyneo, thely
erudite.. 10. pedantress
fox.. 5. vixen
government.. 8. gynarchy
hormone.. 8. estrogen
monster.. 6. gorgon
prayerful.. 5. orant
spirit.. 7. banshee
suffix.. 4. ette
term.. 8. gynecoid
warrior.. 6. Amazon

feminine... 4. soft, weak 6. female, gender, tender 7. womanly 8. maidenly 10. effeminate

femme fatale... 4. vamp 5. siren 7. Lorelei, vampire

femur... 3. hip (bone) 4. bone (thigh), coxa

fen... 3. bog 4. moor, pool 5. marsh, swale 7. The Fens

fence... 3. aha 4. bank, duel, ha–ha, pale, rail, wall 5. close, ditch, fight, hedge, stile 6. paling, picket, secure 7. barrier, confine, enclose, fortify, protect, railing 8. palisade, prohibit 9. enclosure, swordplay 11. self–defense

fencing (pert to)...
breastplate.. 8. plastron
defense.. 5. carte, parry, prime, sixte 6. octave, quinte, tierce 7. seconds, septime
master.. 7. lanista
position.. 9. pronation 10. supination
sword.. 4. epee, foil, tuck 5. extoc 6. rapier
term.. 4. volt 7. corrida 8. estocado
thrust.. 6. remise 7. riposte

fend... 4. ward 5. avert, parry, shift 6. defend, resist 7. prevent, repulse, ward off

fender... 5. guard 6. buffer, bumper, shield, sluice 7. cushion 9. fireguard 10. firescreen 11. splashboard

fenestra... 6. window 7. foramen, opening, orifice

Fenian... 5. Irish 11. Brotherhood

fennel... 4. herb 6. Seseli 7. Azorian, Nigella

feral... 4. wild 6. deadly, ferine, savage 7. bestial, untamed 8. funereal, unbroken 9. malignant 12. uncultivated

feretory... 4. bier 6. chapel, shrine (saint's) 8. feretrum

ferment... 4. barm, brew, fret, sour, stum, zyme 5. anger, fever, yeast 6. enzyme, foment, leaven, rennin, seethe, uproar 7. glucase, maltase 8. diastase, disorder 9. agitation 10. effervesce, turbulence

fermentation... 6. unrest 9. agitation, chemistry, leavening 10. ebullition 13. effervescence

fermenting vat... 4. gyle

fern... 4. tara 5. brake, heath, holly 6. osmund, spider 7. bracken 8. polypody 10. maidenhair 11. elephant–ear

fern (pert to)...
family.. 12. pteridophyte
genus.. 6. Anemia
leaf.. 5. frond
scale.. 8. ramentum

ferocious... 4. grim, wild 5. cruel, feral 6. bloody, brutal, fierce, savage 7. acharne, inhuman 8. pitiless, ravenous, ruthless 9. barbarous, malignant, merciless, murderous, rapacious, truculent 10. implacable, malevolent, relentless, sanguinary 11. remorseless 12. bloodthirsty

ferret... 3. hob 4. hunt, jill, tape 5. worry 6. badger, harass, search, weasel 7. polecat

ferrotype... 7. tintype 10. photograph

ferrum... 2. Fe (sym) 4. iron

ferry... 7. traject 9. transport 10. sail across

ferryboat... 3. bac 4. pont 6. wherry

ferryman... 6. Charon (River Styx) 7. ferrier

fertile... 4. rank, rich 7. teeming 8. abundant, fruitful, prolific 9. exuberant, inventive, plenteous, plentiful 10. productive

fertilizer... 4. marl 5. guano 6. pollen 7. compost, nitrate 8. dressing 9. phosphate

ferule... 3. rod 5. ruler 6. fennel 10. punishment

fervency... 4. heat, keen, zeal 5. ardor, eager, fiery, gusto, verve 6. fervor, warmth 7. ardency, passion 9. eloquence, vehemence 12. empressement 15. impassionedness

fervent... 3. hot 4. keen, warm 5. eager, fiery 6. ardent, fervid 7. excited, intense, zealous 8. eloquent, vehement 10. passionate 11. impassioned

fervid... 3. hot 5. fiery 6. ardent, tropic 7. boiling, fervent, zealous 8. vehement 11. impassioned

fervor... 4. rage, zeal, zest 5. ardor 7. ecstasy, passion 11. earnestness

fester... 6. rankle 7. abscess, pustule, putrefy 9. suppurate

festival... 3. ale, bal 4. fete, gala 5. Delia (Apollo), feast, revel, Seder 6. Easter, Kermis 7. holiday, uphelya 8. apodosis (Church) 9. Christmas, Mardi gras 10. Parentalia, Saturnalia

festive... 3. gay 4. gala 5. merry 6. joyous 8. mirthful, sportive 9. convivial

festivity... 3. joy 4. fete, gala 5. mirth, revel 6. gaiety 7. jollity, whoopee 8. festival, jamboree 10. joyfulness 11. celebration, merrymaking 12. conviviality

fetch... 3. get 5. bring, reach 6. attain, deduce, revive 7. achieve 8. go and get, retrieve

fetching... 8. alluring, charming, pleasing 10. attractive, delightful 11. fascinating

fete... 4. gala 5. feast, party 6. fiesta 8. carnival, festival 10. Saturnalia 13. entertainment

fetid... 4. olid, rank 5. fusty 7. noisome 10. maladorous 11. ill-smelling

fetish... 3. obi 4. idol, joss, juju 5. charm, image, totem 6. amulet, avatar, mascot 7. Dahoman 8. talisman

fetter... 4. band, bond, gyve, iron 5. chain 6. hamper, hobble, hopple, thrall 7. enchain, manacle, shackle

feud... 4. fief, fray 5. broil 6. affray, estate, strife 7. contest, dispute, quarrel 8. vendetta 9. hostility

feudal (pert to)...
estate.. 3. fee 4. fief, soke
French.. 4. feod

lord.. 6. tenure 8. overlaid, suzerain
payment.. 6. socage
service.. 5. banal
tenant.. 4. leud 6. vassal
tribute.. 6. heriot

fever... 4. ague 5. ardor 6. frenzy 8. delirium, sickness 9. calenture 10. excitement

fever (pert to)...
heat.. 9. sunstroke
intermittent.. 5. octan 7. quartan
malarial.. 4. ague
marsh.. 6. elodes 7. helodes
subsidence.. 12. defervescent
term.. 7. febrile, pyretic
tropical.. 6. dengue 9. calenture

feverish... 5. hasty 7. excited, febrile, fervent, fevered 8. restless 9. delirious, overeager 10. disordered

fey... 4. dead 5. dying, elfin, fatal, spell 9. enfeebled, visionary 12. otherworldly

fez... 3. cap 5. busby, shako 8. tarboosh 9. headdress

fiat... 3. act 5. edict, order 6. decree 7. command 8. decision, sanction

fiber... 3. nap, nep, tal 4. bast, eruc, imbe, lint, pita, pile, silk, yarn 5. datil, istle, kapok, linen, nerve, rayon, sisal 6. fibril, raffia, staple, thread 7. filasse, texture 8. fibrilla, filament

fiber plant... 4. hemp, imbe, palm 5. abaca, agave 6. ambary, cotton, linaga

fibers... 5: hairs 7. strands 9. filaments

fibula... 4. bone (arm) 5. class 6. brooch (anc), buckle 9. safety pin

fickle... 5. false 6. mobile 7. mutable 8. unstable, unsteady, variable, wavering 9. deceptive, deceitful, faithless, unsettled 10. capricious, changeable, inconstant, irresolute, unfaithful 11. vacillating

fiction... 4. tale 5. false, fancy, novel, story 6. legend 7. coinage, figment, forgery, romance 9. falsehood, invention 11. fabrication

fictitious... 5. false 6. poetic, pseudo (pref) 7. assumed, feigned 8. chimeric 9. imaginary, imitative, pretended 10. artificial

fictitious name... 5. alias 6. anonym 7. pen name 8. nickname 9. pseudonym, stage name 10. nom de plume 11. nom de guerre

fidelity... 4. troth 5. topaz, troth, truth 6. fealty 7. honesty 8. accuracy, devotion, veracity 9. adherence, constancy, exactness 10. allegiance 12. faithfulness

fidget... 4. fuss 5. worry 6. twitch 9. dysphoria 10. uneasiness 12. restlessness

fidgety... 5. jerky 6. uneasy 7. nervous, restive, twitchy 8. bustling, restless 9. excitable, impatient

fiducial... 4. firm 5. solid, sound 6. secure, stable 7. trusted 8. trustful 9. confident

11. trustworthy

fiduciary... 4. held (in trust) 5. trust
7. founded, holding, in trust, trustee
12. confidential

fief... 3. fee 4. feud 6. estate

field... 3. lea, lot 4. acre, ager, land,
mead, rand 5. croft, glebe, range,
tract 6. campus, ground, meadow,
sphere 7. compass, diamond,
expanse, pasture, savanna (savannah),
terrain 8. clearing, gridiron
11. battlefield

field (pert to)...
  athletic.. 4. oval 5. arena, court, track
    6. course, sphere 7. diamond,
    stadium 8. gridiron
  bloodshed.. 8. Aceldama (Akeldama)
    13. Ager Sanguinis
  duck.. 7. bustard
  god of.. 4. Faun
  mouse.. 4. vole
  snow.. 4. neve
  stubble.. 5. rowen
  term.. 5. agral 8. agrarian
    10. campestral

fiend... 3. foe 5. demon, devil, enemy,
Satan 6. addict, wizard 7. Amaimon
(Amamon) 9. archfiend 10. evil spirit

fiendish... 5. cruel 6. wicked
7. Avernal, demonic 8. demoniac,
devilish, diabolic

fierce... 4. grim 5. cruel, eager
6. raging, savage 7. furious, racking,
violent 9. ferocious, impetuous,
truculent 10. catawampus, forbidding,
passionate 11. belligerent,
overwrought 12. overpowering

fierceness... 7. cruelty 8. violence
10. truculence

fiery... 3. hot, red 4. sore 5. angry
6. ardent 7. burning, excited,
fervent, flaming, glowing, igneous,
parched, violent 8. choleric, feverish,
inflamed, spirited, vehement
9. impetuous, irascible
10. mettlesome, passionate
11. hot-tempered, inflammable

fiery cross... 5. alarm 6. emblem,
signal, symbol 8. crantara 10. call to
arms

fiesta... 5. color 7. holiday 8. festival
9. festivity

fifish... 6. cranky 9. half crazy

Fifteenth Amendment... 16. Negro
Citizenship (1870)

fig... 3. fico 5. eleme, gruit 6. Carica,
Fiscus, Smyrna, trifle

fig basket... 5. cabas, seron

fight... 3. row, war 4. bout, duel, fray,
mell, tilt 5. brawl, melee, scrap
6. affray, attack, barney, battle,
combat, oppose, strife, strike, strive
7. contest, quarrel, warfare
8. conflict, struggle 9. pugnacity
13. combativeness

fighter... 7. battler, duelist, soldier,
warrior 8. champion, pugilist,
scrapper 9. combatant

fighting... 3. war 4. game 6. plucky
7. warlike 8. militant 10. contention,
pugnacious 11. belligerent

fig leaf... 6. symbol (modesty)

8. clothing (Bib), covering

figment... 5. fancy 7. fiction
9. falsehood, invention

figurative... 6. florid 7. flowery, typical
8. allusive 9. numerical
12. emblematical, metaphorical

figure... 4. body, dash, dope, form,
nude, rank, type 5. digit, image,
judge, price, shape, solve 6. aspect,
emblem, entail, number, symbol
7. diagram, numeral, outline, pattern
8. ornament, phantasm 9. calculate,
celebrity, character, personage
10. appearance, impression,
similitude 11. distinction

figure (pert to)...
  column.. 6. elamon 7. telamon
    8. Atlantes, Caryatid, pilaster
  geometric.. 4. cone, lune 5. prism,
    rhomb 6. isagon, isogen, isogon
    (rare) 7. ellipse, rhombus
    8. pentagon, triangle
    13. parallelogram, quadrilateral
    16. parallelepipedon
  praying.. 5. orant
  repeated digits.. 8. repetend
  speech.. 5. trope 6. aporia, simile
    8. metaphor
  star-shaped.. 8. pentacle

figured... 4. rich 6. ornate 7. façonné
10. ornamented

figurine... 4. doll 7. carving, tanagra
9. sculpture, statuette

Fiji Island, Viti Levu...
  capital.. 4. Suva
  export.. 5. sugar
  mountain.. 8. Victoria
  natives.. 9. cannibals (ang)
    11. Melanesians
  ruler.. 7. British

filament... 4. barb, dowl (dowle), hair
5. fiber (fibre), harle 6. strand,
thread

filament lamp... 12. incandescent

filbert... 3. nut 5. brown, hazel
7. Corylus 8. hazelnut

filch... 3. nim, rob 4. beat 5. steal,
theft 6. pilfer 7. purloin

file... 3. row 4. list, rasp, rate
5. enter, march, store 6. abrade,
smooth 7. sharpen 8. classify
9. catalogue 10. pickpocket
11. triggerfish (filefish)

file (combmaking)... 5. grail (graille)
6. carlet 7. quannet

filibeg... 4. kilt 5. skirt

filibuster... 6. pirate 7. impeder
8. thwarter 9. legislate
10. freebooter, obstructer
14. obstructionist

filicide... 6. murder (child by parent)

filigree... 4. lace 5. adorn (with)
7. pattern 8. fanciful 10. decorative
13. unsubstantial

Filipino, Filipina (pert to)...
  homeland (mostly).. 5. Luzon
  native of.. 11. Philippines
  tribe.. 5. Bikol (Bicol) 7. Malayan
    (Christian), Tagalog (Tagal), Visayan
    (see also *Philippine*)

fill... 3. pad 4. calk, feed, glut, hold,
plug 5. block, close, gorge, stuff

6. occupy, stop up 7. execute, fulfill, pervade, satiate, satisfy, suffuse 8. complete, compound, permeate 10. accomplish 11. superabound

fille... 4. girl 8. daughter

filled... 5. dated 7. replete 8. suffused 9. saturated

filled with crevices... 7. areolar

fillet... 4. band, orle, ring, tape 5. snood, tiara 6. anadem, border, ribbon, taenia 7. bandage 8. headband, insignia 9. lemniscus, scantling 10. tenderloin

fillet (Arch)... 5. stria 6. cimbia, listel, reglet, regula, taenia 7. chaplet, molding (part)

filly... 4. colt, foal, girl, mare

film... 4. brat, haze, scum, skin, veil 5. cover, layer 6. lamina, patina 7. coating 8. pellicle 10. photograph

filmy... 3. dim 4. fine 5. gauzy, misty 6. cloudy, opaque 7. clouded 9. laminated 10. indistinct

fils... 3. son

filter... 4. ooze 5. clean, drain 6. purify, strain 7. trickle 8. colature 9. percolate

filth... 4. dirt, muck, slut 5. lucre 6. vermin 7. squalor 9. excrement, obscenity, scoundrel

filthiness... 8. cenosity 9. fetidness, obscenity 10. odiousness

filthy... 3. low 4. foul, vile 5. dirty, fetid, gross 6. impure, odious, putrid 7. obscene, squalid, unclean 8. polluting 10. licentious

filthy lucre... 4. gain (shameful) 5. money

fimbriated... 5. edged 7. fringed 8. bordered (Her), margined

fin... 3. arm 4. five, keel

fin (pert to fish)...
median.. 4. anal 6. caudal, dorsal
paired.. 6. pelvic 7. ventral 8. pectoral

final... 3. end 4. last 5. be-all, telic 7. dernier 8. decisive, definite, eventual, ultimate 9. mandatory, ultimatum 10. conclusive, definitive 11. unqualified 13. determinating

final argument... 11. ultima ratio

finale... 3. end 4. coda 5. close 6. result 8. swan song 10. completion, conclusion 11. termination

finality... 5. finis 6. finale, finish, windup 10. conclusion 11. termination 12. decisiveness 14. conclusiveness

finally... 10. eventually, ultimately 12. conclusively

final outcome... 5. issue 6. upshot 10. denouement

financial... 6. fiscal 8. monetary 9. pecuniary

finch... 4. moro 5. Junco, serin, spink, tarin 6. burion, linnet, siskin, towhee 7. chewink, redpoll 9. brambling, chaffinch, Fringilla

find... 3. get 4. gain 5. learn 6. detect, locate, summon, supply

7. procure, provide 8. discover, meet with, perceive 9. determine, discovery, good thing 10. experience 11. acquisition

find fault... 4. beef, carp 5. cavil 8. complain 9. criticize

finding... 7. verdict 8. solution 9. discovery 11. serendipity

find out... 5. learn, solve 6. detect 8. discover 9. ascertain

fine... 3. fit 4. good, lacy, pure, rare, thin 5. dandy, filmy, frail, gaudy, noble, sharp, sheer 6. ornate, slight, smooth 7. elegant, fragile, healthy, perfect, powdery, precise, slender 8. absolute, ethereal, handsome, polished, skillful, superior 9. beautiful, excellent, sensitive 10. fastidious, pulverized, surpassing

finery... 6. beauty 7. clothes, gaudery, gewgaws 8. elegance, fineness, frippery, ornament 10. decoration, lavishness 11. refinements

finesse... 5. skill 6. purity, serene 7. cunning 8. artifice, card play, subtlety, thinness 9. clearness, good taste, stratagem 10. refinement 14. discrimination (subtle)

finger... 3. toy (with) 4. hook 5. digit, touch 6. dactyl, handle, pilfer 7. measure, purloin

finger (pert to)...
alphabet.. 11. dactylology
cymbal.. 8. castanet
fish.. 8. starfish
flower.. 8. foxglove
fore.. 5. index 7. pointer
little.. 6. pinkie 7. minimus 9. auricular
middle.. 6. medius
ring.. 7. annular
stall.. 3. cot
term.. 7. digital

fingernail moon... 6. lunule

fingernail overgrowth...
10. onychauxis

fingerprint (term)... 4. arch, loop 5. whorl 9. composite 11. dactylogram 12. dactyloscopy

finial... 3. epi, tee

finical... 4. nice 5. fussy 6. dainty, dapper, jaunty, spruce 7. finicky, foppish, mincing, prudish 8. delicate 9. finicking, squeamish 10. fastidious, meticulous 11. overprecise 14. overscrupulous

finis... 3. end 4. goal 6. finale 8. finality 10. conclusion 11. culmination

finish... 3. end 4. kill 5. chare, close, matte (mat), style 6. enamel, polish 7. destroy, perfect, surface, texture 8. complete, conclude 9. terminate 10. completion, consummate, perfection

finished... 3. o'er 4. done, fine, over, ripe 5. ended 6. closed 7. refined, stopped 8. climaxed, complete, lustered, polished 9. completed, concluded, perfected 10. terminated

finite... 7. fleshly, limited 9. definable 10. restricted, terminable

11. conditional

fink... 3. spy 4. scab 5. finch
8. informer 13. strikebreaker
Finland... see also *Finnish*
capital.. 8. Helsinki (Helsingfors)
Finnish for Finland.. 5. Suomi
government.. 8. republic
island.. 5. Aland
language.. 6. Magyar 7. Swedish
8. Estonian
legislature.. 9. Eduskunta
port.. 3. Abo 5. Turku 9. Mariehamn
Finnish (pert to)...
bath.. 5. sauna
dramatist.. 4. Kivi 7. Waltari
people.. 5. Finns, Suomi 9. Karelians
10. Tavastians
fire... 4. heat, zeal 5. blaze, fever,
flame 6. excite, fervor, igneus, ignite,
incite, kindle 7. barrage, explode,
inspire 8. detonate, illumine
9. discharge, eloquence
11. inspiration 12. inflammation
13. conflagration
fire (pert to)...
basket.. 5. grate 7. cresset
comb form.. 4. igni
cracker.. 6. petard
dog.. 7. andiron
fear of.. 10. pyrophobia
god.. 6. Vulcan
opal.. 7. girasol (girasole)
power over.. 10. ignipotent
worshiper.. 5. Parsi 9. pyrolater
10. ignicolist
firearm... 3. gat, gun 5. piece, rifle
6. musket 7. demihag, rimbase (part)
8. ordnance, revolver 9. harquebus
(arquebus)
firearms discharge... 9. fusillade
fired... 3. lit 4. shot 5. baked 6. on
fire (Her) 7. excited 8. inspired
10. discharged
fireman... 4. vamp 6. fueler, stoker
8. trainman 9. fire–eater
11. firefighter
fireplace... 5. fogon, forge, ingle
6. hearth 9. inglenook 13. Franklin
stove
fireside (home)... 11. hearthstone
firewood... 6. billet
fireworks... 4. caps, gerb 6. flares
7. fizgigs, gunfire, rip–raps, rockets
8. serpents 9. pinwheels, sparklers,
torpedoes 10. girandoles
12. firecrackers, Roman candles
firm... 4. fast, hard, safe, sure, trig
5. dense, fixed, rigid, solid, sound,
stout, tight 6. secure, stable, stanch,
steady, strict, strong 7. compact,
company, decided, devoted, staunch
8. faithful 9. immovable, steadfast
10. determined, unslipping, unyielding
11. substantial
firmament... 3. sky 5. vault 6. Caelus,
welkin 7. heavens 8. empyrean
firmly set... 5. fixed, solid 6. rooted
10. inveterate
firmness... 8. fidelity, rigidity, solidity,
strength, tenacity 9. constancy,
stability 10. immobility, steadiness
11. reliability 13. indissolubility

firmness, want of... 5. loose 6. laxity
8. weakness 11. instability, vacillation
firn... 3. ice 4. neve, snow
firs... 5. Abies, pines
first... 5. chief, front, prime 6. maiden,
primal, primus 7. highest, initial,
leading, primary 8. earliest, foremost,
original 9. beginning, elemental,
principal 10. primordial
first (pert to)...
appearance.. 5. debut 8. premiere
born.. 5. eigne 6. eldest
Christian martyr.. 7. Stephen
coin (silver).. 8. sesterce
days of Rom month.. 7. calends
(kalends)
fruits (Eccl).. 7. annates
letter.. 4. Alif 5. Aleph
stages.. 8. inchoate 9. rudiments
world navigator.. 8. Magellan
fish... 3. dib 4. food 5. angle, drail,
seine, troll 6. Pisces
13. constellation
fish (types of)... 2. id 3. cat, cod, gar,
ray 4. bass, carp, char, chub, cusk,
dace, goby, hake, ling, opah, parr,
peto, pike, ruff, scup, shad, sisi,
sole, tuna, ulua 5. bream, cisco,
fluke, guppy, perch, porgy, shark,
skate, smelt, snook, sprat, trout,
tunny, wahoo 6. barbel, bonito,
bowfin, burbot, conger, darter,
marlin, minnow, puffer, redfin,
salmon, shiner, sucker, tarpon,
tautog, turbot 7. alewife, anchovy,
catfish, crappie, croaker, dogfish,
garfish, grouper, haddock, halibut,
herring, hogfish, jewfish, lamprey,
mudfish, oquassa, pollack, pompano,
redfish, sardine, sawfish, sunfish,
torpedo, walleye 8. albacore, blue
fish, bluegill, bonefish, bullhead,
chimaera, filefish, flatfish, flounder,
goldfish, grayling, kingfish, lumpfish,
mackerel, menhaden, pickerel,
pilchard, sailfish, sergeant, sting ray,
sturgeon, toadfish, weakfish
9. barracuda, cigarfish, devilfish,
jellyfish, namaycush, sheatfish,
whitefish 10. barramunda, butterfish,
candlefish, hammerhead, yellowtail
11. muskellunge (see also *mammal*)
fish (pert to)...
adhering.. 4. pega 6. remora
ascending rivers.. 7. anadrom
10. anadromous
bait.. 4. chum 5. chack 6. minnow
9. killifish (killy)
basket.. 4. caul 5. creel, slath (slarth)
bivalve, mollusk.. 4. clam, slug
5. snail, whelk 6. limpet, mussel,
oyster 7. abalone, Ocypode (crab),
scallop
caviar–yielding.. 7. sterlet
climbing, jumping.. 5. saury
6. anabas 7. skipper
club.. 6. muckle
codfish.. 4. cusk 5. torsk 7. bacalao,
buffalo
comb form.. 7. ichthyo
crustacean.. 3. Uca 4. crab 6. shrimp
7. lobster 8. Decapoda

devil.. 3. ray 5. manta
eaters.. 12. ichthyophagi
eating.. 11. piscivorous
14. ichthyophagous
fabled (Pers).. 4. Mahi (Mah)
gaff (through ice).. 5. ching
game.. 4. tuna 5. chiro, sword, trout
6. marlin, salmon, tarpon 8. grayling
11. muskellunge
genus.. 4. Amia (bowfin), Mola
(sunfish) 5. Elops (tarpon), Perca
(perch) 8. Haliotis (abalone),
Octopoda (octopus)
hook.. 5. Kirby, snell (part)
8. Aberdeen, barbless, Carlisle,
Limerick
largest (freshwater).. 8. arapaima
like.. 8. ichthyic
line.. 6. nossel (norsel) 7. spillet
living by.. 9. piscatory
living on.. 12. ichthyophagy
man–eating.. 6. caribe 7. piranha
mollusk.. see bivalve
nest building.. 5. acara
net.. 4. fyke 5. seine, snell, trawl
7. boulter, spiller
pond.. 7. piscina 8. aquarium
roe.. 6. caviar
salmon.. 3. fog 4. masu, parr
5. sprod 6. alevin 7. gilling
sauce.. 4. alec
spear.. 3. gig
taboo.. 13. ichthyophobia
treatise.. 11. ichthyology
worship.. 12. ichthyolatry
young brood.. 3. fry
fisherman... 6. angler 8. piscator
fishery... 7. piscary
fishing... 4. chug (through ice)
8. snelling 9. halieutic, piscation
fishing vessel... 5. smack 6. seiner
7. trawler
fishy... 4. dull 6. vacant 8. fishlike
9. deceptive, dishonest
10. improbable, lusterless, suspicious,
unreliable 11. extravagant
14. expressionless
fissure... 3. gap 4. leak, lode, open,
rent, rift, rima, seam, slit, vein
5. break, chasm, chine, chink, cleft,
crack, sever, split 7. crevice
fissured... 5. cleft 6. rimate, rimose
fist... 4. duke, hand (closed) 5. nieve
6. clench 8. tightwad
11. handwriting
fit... 3. due, fay, pat 4. able, gear,
meet, mesh, ripe, suit, whim
5. adapt, equip, fancy, ready, spasm,
train 6. attack, enmesh, frenzy,
proper, stroke, suited 7. adapted,
caprice, conform, healthy, prepare,
tantrum 8. disposed, dovetail,
eligible, outbreak, suitable
9. competent, qualified
11. accommodate, appropriate
fit (pert to)...
an arrow (archery).. 4. nock
fury.. 4. rage
groove (Arch).. 4. dado
resentment.. 4. huff, mood 5. pique
7. tantrum
to eat.. 6. edible

to till.. 6. arable
fitchew... 5. skink, zoril 7. foumart,
polecat
fitful... 8. restless, unstable, variable
9. impulsive, irregular, orderless,
spasmodic 10. capricious, convulsive
12. intermittent
fitly... 4. duly 5. right 6. timely
8. properly, suitably 10. decorously
fitness... 7. decorum 9. congruity
10. expedience, timeliness
11. eligibility, suitability
12. preparedness
fitting... 3. apt, pat 4. just, meet
6. proper, seemly, timely
8. adapting, suitable 9. expedient
11. appropriate
five (pert to)...
Books of Moses.. 10. Pentateuch
children (born at once)..
11. quintuplets
Civilized Tribes (Ind).. 5. Creek
7. Choctaw 8. Cherokee, Seminole
9. Chickasaw
comb form.. 5. penta
cornered.. 11. pentagonous
divided by.. 11. quinquesect
dollar bill.. 1. V 3. fin 5. fiver
feet.. 10. pentameter
five–year period.. 6. pentad 7. lustrum
(census) 12. quinquennial
fold.. 9. quintuple
group.. 6. pentad 8. fivesome
lines (nonsense).. 8. limerick
Nations (Ind Confed).. 7. Cayugas,
Mohawks, Oneidas, Senecas
9. Onondagas
trump card (auction pitch).. 5. pedro
fix... 3. peg, pin, set 4. mend, moor,
nail 5. amend, brace, bribe, imbed,
limit, stamp 6. adjust, anchor,
cement, define, fasten, ossify, punish,
repair, settle 7. arrange, confirm,
delimit, dilemma, prepare, rectify
8. organize, solidify 9. condition,
establish, stabilize, stipulate
10. prearrange
fixed... 3. set 4. firm 5. rigid
6. formal, intent, nailed, static
7. assured, limited, settled, special
8. arranged, habitual 9. immovable,
permanent, unwinking
11. established, prearranged,
traditional
fixed (pert to)...
allowance.. 4. diet 6. ration
7. stipend 10. remittance
beforehand.. 13. predetermined
by choice.. 8. elective
manner.. 9. immovably
star.. 4. Veda
time.. 3. era 4. date, fast
fizgig... 9. fireworks, whirligig
flabellate... 9. fan–shaped
flabrum... 3. fan 9. flabellum
flaccid... 4. limp, weak 6. flabby
8. yielding
flag... 3. sag 4. fail, fane, iris, pave,
pine, sign, weak, wilt 5. Roger
(pirate) 6. banner, burgee, colors,
cornet, ensign, fanion, flower, guidon,
pennon, signal 7. bunting, calamus,

decline, pennant 8. gonfalon,
masthead, standard, streamer,
vexillum 9. banderole 16. Quincunx
of Heaven

flagging . . . 4. weak 7. languid
8. pavement 10. flagstones, spiritless
11. languishing

flagging in energy . . . 9. lassitude

flagitious . . . 6. wicked 7. corrupt,
heinous 8. criminal, flagrant
10. scandalous, villainous

flagon . . . 3. jug 4. ewer 5. stoup
6. bottle, carafe 7. canteen
8. demijohn

flagpole standard . . . 7. bracket
9. bracciale

flagrant . . . 4. rank 5. great 6. absurd,
wanton, wicked 7. glaring, hateful,
heinous, obvious, scarlet, violent
8. infamous, terrible 9. abandoned,
atrocious, monstrous, nefarious
10. profligate, villainous

flail . . . 4. beat, flag, whip 6. thrash,
weapon (anc) 7. swingle

flam . . . 4. hoax 5. cheat, spoof, trick
6. cajole 7. pretext 8. drumbeat,
flimflam 9. deception, falsehood

flambeau . . . 5. torch (flaming)
7. cresset 11. candlestick

flamboyant . . . 4. wavy (Arch) 6. florid,
ornate 8. brilliant, flamelike
11. resplendent

flame . . . 3. arc 4. beam, burn, fire,
glow, leye (obs), love, zeal 5. ardor,
blaze, flare, flash, glare, ingle, light,
lover 6. redden 7. scarlet
8. flammule (small) 10. brightness,
sweetheart

flamen . . . 6. priest (anc)

flamenco . . . 5. dance (gypsy)

Flaminian Way . . . 4. Rome

Flanders, Belgium . . .
brick . . 4. Bath
capital . . 5. Ghent (East) 6. Bruges
(West)
city . . 5. Alost 6. Ostend 7. Dixmude
(Dixmuide)
people (anc) . . 5. Celts 6. Franks
11. Burgundians
poppy . . 9. corn poppy

flap . . . 3. tab 4. blow, slap, sway,
wave 5. skirt 6. dangle, lappet,
stroke 7. flapper, flutter
9. appendage

flare . . . 5. blaze, flame, flash, fusee,
glare, light 6. signal, spread
7. display, flicker 8. outburst
10. illuminate

flaring . . . 5. gaudy 6. spread
7. burning, glaring 8. dazzling,
flashing

flash . . . 4. show 5. blaze, burst, gleam,
glint, shine, spark 6. glance, signal
7. display, glimmer, glisten, glitter,
instant, shimmer, sparkle 8. dispatch
9. telegraph

flashing . . . 5. showy 6. flashy
8. meteoric, snapping 9. transient

flashy . . . 3. gay 5. fiery, gaudy, showy
6. frothy, garish, sporty 7. raffish
8. vehement 9. flaunting, impetuous
13. grandiloquent

flask . . . 4. ewer, olpe 5. betty
6. flagon 7. ampulla, canteen
9. aryballus (aryballas, anc)

flask-shaped . . . 10. lageniform

flat . . . 3. low 4. palm 5. banal, blunt,
level, molle, plain, plane, prone,
stale, suite, tract, vapid 6. boring,
dreary, wholly 7. insipid, uniform
8. tenement, unbroken 10. horizontal

flat (pert to) . . .
boat . . 3. ark 4. punt, scow 5. barge
breastbone . . 6. ratite
canopy . . 6. tester
flatfoot . . 9. pes planus 13. talipes
planus
iron . . 7. sadiron
nosed . . 6. simous
piece . . 4. slab
surface . . 4. area 6. pagina 7. tabular
worm . . 9. planarian, trematode

flatfish . . . 3. dab 4. sole 5. brill, fluke
6. acedia, turbot 7. halibut
8. flounder

flatten . . . 4. even 5. level 6. deject,
smooth 7. depress 8. dispirit
9. prostrate 10. discourage,
dishearten

flattened . . . 6. evened, oblate
7. leveled 8. smoothed 9. applanate

flatter . . . 3. oil 4. coax, palp 5. charm,
float 6. cajole, caress, please, praise,
smooge, soothe 7. adulate, beguile,
blarney, flutter 8. blandish
9. encourage 10. compliment,
ingratiate

flatterer . . . 6. flunky, glozer 7. Jenkins
8. adulator, courtier, parasite
9. sycophant

flattering . . . 9. adulatory, gnathonic,
insincere 10. obsequious
13. complimentary

flattery . . . 5. gloze, taffy 6. praise
7. blarney, eyewash, fawning, palaver
8. cajolery 9. adulation
10. compliment, sycophancy
14. obsequiousness

flaunt . . . 4. wave 5. boast, vaunt
6. parade 7. display, flutter
8. brandish

**Flavian, House of Flavius,
Emperors** . . . 5. Titus 8. Domitian
9. Vespasian

Flavian Amphitheater . . . 9. Colosseum
(Rome)

flavor . . . 4. gust, odor, tang, zest
5. aroma, imbue, sapid, sapor,
sauce, savor, scent, taste 6. season
7. perfume 8. piquancy 9. flavoring
14. characteristic

flaw . . . 3. gap, mar 4. rase, rift
5. cleft, fault 6. breach, defect
7. blemish, fissure, sophism
8. fracture 12. imperfection

flax . . . 3. lin, tow 5. linen

flax (pert to) . . .
capsule . . 4. boll
dust . . 5. pouce
filaments . . 4. harl
process plant . . 7. rettery
refuse . . 4. pob, tow 5. hurds
seed . . 7. linseed
soak . . 3. ret

weed.. 8. toadflax
flaxweed... 8. toadflax
flay... 4. peel, skin 6. fleece
  7. censure, reprove, scarify
  9. criticize, excoriate
flea... 4. puce 5. pulex 6. beetle,
  chigoe 7. chigger, cyclops
  8. reminder 13. Ctenocephalus
fleam... 6. lancet, stream
  10. millstream
fleck... 4. flea, mark, spot 5. flake
  6. blotch, dapple, streak, stripe
  7. freckle, speckle, stipple 8. particle
  9. variegate
flection, flexion... 7. bending, turning
flee... 3. fly, run 4. shun 5. avoid,
  elope, evade, speed 6. vanish
  7. abandon, forsake 9. disappear
fleece... 3. abb, nap 4. flay, pile, skin,
  wool 5. fleck, mulct, sheer, strip
  6. divest 7. despoil, swindle
  10. overcharge
fleer... 4. gibe, jeer, mock 5. flout,
  scoff, sheer, taunt
fleet... 4. fast, flit, flow, navy, sail,
  swim 5. drift, group, quick, rapid,
  swift 6. armada, hasten, nimble,
  speedy 9. transient 10. evanescent,
  transitory
fleeting... 7. passing 9. transient
  10. evanescent, transitory
Fleet Street... 5. Fleta (book written
  in prison) 6. prison (London)
  11. London press
Flemish painter... 5. David 6. Rubens
  7. Van Dyke
flesh... 3. kin 4. body, meat, pink,
  pulp, race (human) 6. family, fatten,
  muscle 7. kindred, kinsmen, mankind
  8. humanity 9. mortality
  10. sensuality
flesh (pert to)...
  eating.. 8. omophagy (raw)
    9. omophagia 10. omophagous
    zoophagous 11. carnivorous,
    creophagous
  fond of.. 12. sarcophilous
  like.. 7. carnose
  lust for.. 9. carnality
  resembling.. 7. sarcoid
  slain animals.. 7. carnage
fleshpots... 6. plenty, wealth 10. high
  living, prosperity 12. fat of the land
fleshy... 3. fat 5. beefy, human,
  obese, plump, pulpy, stout 6. carnal
  7. adipose, carnose 9. corpulent
fleshy fruit... 4. pear, pome 5. bacca,
  berry, drupe
fleur-de-lis... 3. lis (Her) 4. iris, lily,
  luce 6. emblem
flew... see *fly*
flexible... 4. limp 5. lithe 6. limber,
  pliant, supple 7. elastic, lissome
flexion, flection... 9. anaclasis
flexure... 4. genu 5. crook 7. bending
flicker... 4. burn, flit 5. blaze, glare,
  waver 7. flutter, high–hoe
  10. woodpecker
flickering... 7. burning, lambent
  8. flickery 9. irregular
flier, flyer... 3. ace 4. bird 5. pilot,

train 6. airman, gamble, insect
  7. aviator, speeder, sunfish, venture
  11. speculation
flight... 3. hop 4. rout 5. arrow
  (volley), flock, skein (wild fowl), speed
  6. exodus, fletch (arrows), flying,
  hegira, perron, stairs, throng
  7. soaring 8. escapism, mounting,
  stampede, swarming 9. excursion,
  formation, migration 10. volitation
flighty... 5. barmy, swift 6. fickle, fitful
  7. foolish 8. fanciful, freakish, volatile
  9. frivolous 10. capricious
flimflam... 5. freak, hocus, trick
  6. humbug 7. caprice, swindle
  8. nonsense, trifling 9. deception,
  deceptive 11. nonsensical
flimmer... 7. flicker, glimmer
flimsy... 4. limp, rare, thin, vain, weak
  5. frail 6. feeble, paltry, sleazy,
  slimsy 7. flaccid, shallow, trivial
  9. illogical 11. superficial
  13. unsubstantial
flinch... 4. game 5. quail, start, wince,
  wonde 6. blench, cringe, falter,
  flense, recoil, shrink, swerve
fling... 3. shy 4. dart, dash, gibe,
  hurl, toss 5. cheat, dance, flock
  (sandpipers), revel, sling, sneer, throw
  6. baffle, spirit 7. cast off, sarcasm
  9. prostrate
flint... 5. chert, clint, silex 6. quartz
  7. lighter 8. hardness 9. firestone,
  skinflint
flip... 3. hop, tap 4. flap, glib, snap,
  toss 5. drink (spiced), flick, flirt,
  throw 6. fillip 8. flippant, turn over
  10. somersault 11. impertinent
flippant... 4. flip, glib, pert 5. cocky
  6. chatty, fluent 8. impudent
  10. persiflate 11. impertinent
flipper... 3. arm, fin, paw 4. hand
  5. panel 8. flapjack
flirt... 3. toy 4. dart, fike, flip, jerk,
  jilt, mash, play, toss 5. dally
  6. coquet, fillip, masher, trifle
  7. trifler 8. coquette 11. philanderer
flirtation... 5. dance 8. coquetry,
  trifling 10. love affair
flit... 3. fly 4. dart 5. glide, hover
  6. nimble 7. flicker, flutter, migrate
flitter... 3. rag 5. hover, piece
  6. tatter 7. flicker, flutter, fritter
  8. fragment
flittermouse... 3. bat
float... 4. buoy, cork, hove, lure, raft,
  ride, sail, soar, swim, waft 5. balsa,
  drift, hover, ladle 6. launch
  7. support 8. navigate, undulate
  9. transport 10. inaugurate
floating... 4. free 5. awash, loose
  6. adrift, natant 7. buoyant,
  movable, rumored 8. changing,
  drifting, shifting 9. launching,
  wandering
floating herb... 7. frogbit
  16. Hydrocharitaceae
flock... 4. bevy, fold, herd, pack, raft
  6. flight, hirsel 7. company
  9. multitude 10. assemblage,
  collection 11. aggregation
flock (pert to)...

bees.. 4. hive 5. swarm 6. colony
cattle.. 4. herd
fish.. 5. shoal
geese.. 5. skein 6. gaggle
herons.. 5. sedge
insects.. 5. swarm
like.. 6. gregal
lions.. 5. pride
partridge.. 5. covey
pheasants.. 4. nide (nid)
sandpipers.. 5. fling
walrus.. 3. pod
flocks, god of... 3. Pan
floe... 3. ice 4. berg
flog... 3. cat, tan 4. beat, cane, goad,
  lash, wale, welt, whip 6. larrup,
  punish, strike, thrash 8. chastise
flogging... 4. toco (toko) 7. beating
  8. whipping 9. thrashing
  10. punishment 12. chastisement
flood... 3. sea 5. eagre, spate
  6. deluge, drench, excess 7. freshet,
  torrent 8. cataract, inundate, overflow
  9. cataclysm 10. oversupply
  14. superabundance
flood (pert to)...
disaster.. 9. Galveston (1900),
  Johnstown (1889)
gate.. 4. gool, lock, slow 6. sluice
  8. penstock
lights.. 5. klieg
tidal.. 5. eagre
floor... 4. base, pave, sill 5. chess
  (pontoon), story 6. baffle, bottom,
  defeat 7. coaming, silence
  9. overthrow 10. substratum
floor leader... 4. whip
flora... 6. plants 11. florilegium
flora and fauna... 5. biota
Florence gallery... 5. Pitti 6. Uffizi
Florentine (pert to)...
color.. 7. scarlet
family (famed).. 6. Medici
lily.. 6. giglio
school.. 6. Tuscan
sculptor.. 8. Ammanati, Ghiberti
florid... 3. red 5. ruddy 6. ornate,
  rococo 7. flowery, flushed
  8. enriched, rubicund 10. figurative,
  melismatic, rhetorical 11. embellished
  13. grandiloquent
Florida...
capital.. 11. Tallahassee
city.. 5. Miami, Tampa 7. Key West
  8. Sarasota 9. Pensacola 11. St
  Augustine (1565) 12. St Petersburg
discoverer.. 11. Ponce de Leon
  (1513)
fish.. 6. mullet, shrimp, tarpon, testar,
  tetard 8. blue crab
flower.. 13. orange blossom
Indian.. 8. Seminole
lake.. 10. Okeechobee
museum.. 10. Circus Hall (Ringling)
plant.. 7. coontie
river.. 8. Suwannee
State admission.. 13. twenty–seventh
State motto.. 22. Liberty and
  Independence
State nickname.. 8. Sunshine
swamp, park.. 10. Everglades
trail.. 7. Tamiami

flounce... 4. flap, fold, jerk, trim
  5. caper, frill, twist 6. edging, frolic
  8. flounder, struggle
flounder... 4. roll 6. bungle, muddle,
  welter 7. stumble 8. struggle
  9. fluctuate
flounder (fish)... 3. dab 5. fluke
  6. plaice, turbot 8. flatfish
flour... 4. bran, meal 6. farina, pinole,
  powder 9. middlings, pulverize
flour (pert to)...
diabetic.. 9. aleuronat
gravy.. 4. roux
maker.. 6. miller
pudding.. 4. duff
flourish... 4. grow, show, wave
  5. vaunt 6. flaunt, paraph (signature),
  thrive 7. display, fanfare, prosper,
  roulade 8. arpeggio, brandish,
  ornament 9. embellish, luxuriate
  11. ostentation
flout... 4. defy, gibe, jeer, mock
  5. fleer, scoff, scout, sneer, taunt
  6. insult 8. ridicule
flow... 3. jet, run 4. bore, flow, flux,
  gush, ooze, pour, roll, teem 5. glide,
  issue, river, spout 6. abound, afflux,
  course, stream 7. current, fluency,
  flutter 9. streaming 10. outpouring
flow (pert to)...
along.. 4. lave
back.. 7. redound
jet.. 4. gush 5. spurt
out.. 5. exude, issue, spill
over.. 5. slosh, spill 6. deluge, engulf
  8. inundate 9. overwhelm
tide.. 3. ebb 4. flow, neap
flower... 3. bud 4. best, blow
  5. bloom 6. unfold 7. blossom,
  develop, essence, produce
  8. choicest, ornament 11. Four
  Hundred (Society)
flower (types of)... 3. gul (rose) 4. iris,
  ixia, lily, pink, rose 5. aster, calla,
  canna, daisy, pansy, peony, phlox,
  poppy, stock, tulip 6. azalea,
  cosmos, crocus, dahlia, lupine,
  maypop, orchid, oxalis, violet, zinnia
  7. arbutus, begonia, fuchsia, gentian,
  passion, petunia, rhodora, verbena
  8. amaranth, arethusa, camomile,
  cyclamen, daffodil, geranium,
  hepatica, hyacinth, larkspur, magnolia,
  marigold, Mariposa (lily), primrose,
  sweet pea 9. amaryllis, calendula,
  carnation, edelweiss, gladiolus,
  hollyhock, mayflower, narcissus, water
  lily 10. cornflower, delphinium,
  fleur–de–lis, marguerite, mignonette,
  nasturtium, periwinkle, poinsettia,
  snapdragon 11. forget–me–not,
  strawflower 13. chrysanthemum
  15. lily of the valley
flower (pert to)...
arranging.. 7. ikebana
bed, garden.. 8. floretum, parterre
bloom (full).. 8. anthesis
bud (sauce).. 5. caper
bunch.. 4. posy 7. bouquet, corsage,
  nosegay
bursting into.. 12. efflorescent
cluster, clustered.. 4. cyme 5. umbel

8. racemose 9. glomerule
10. paniculate
largest.. 9. rafflesia (3–ft diameter)
like.. 7. anthoid
meadow–grown.. 6. pratal
part.. 4. stem 5. bract, calyx, petal,
sepal, torus 6. carpel, pistil
7. corolla, petiole 8. epicalyx,
peduncle, perianth
poet's.. 8. asphodel 9. narcissus
sacred.. 5. lotus
seed.. 5. ovule
shaped.. 7. fleuron
small.. 7. fleuret
stand.. 7. epergne
flower, shrub... 5. lilac 6. azalea,
laurel 7. dogwood, heather, jasmine,
spiraea, syringa 8. bayberry,
hawthorn 9. jessamine, mistletoe,
sagebrush 10. bitterroot
12. rhododendron
flower, vine... 8. clematis, wisteria
11. honeysuckle 12. morning glory
flower, wild... 5. bluet, daisy
6. cactus, clover, myrtle, pasque
7. anemone, cowslip 8. bluebell,
camellia 9. buttercup, goldenrod,
mayflower, sunflower 10. bluebonnet
12. lady's–slipper
flowering again... 9. remontant
flowers... 9. flowerage
flowers, goddess of... 5. Flora (Rom)
Flowery Kingdom... 5. China
flowing... 5. fluid 6. afflux, fluent
7. copious, cursive, emanant, fluxing
8. coursing, eloquent 9. streaming
10. transitive
flowing (pert to)...
from source.. 6. rising 9. emanating
together.. 9. confluent
veil.. 5. colet (anc)
well.. 6. gusher
fluctuate... 4. roll, vary, veer 5. waver
7. vibrate 8. intermit, undulate,
unsteady 9. oscillate, vacillate
10. irresolute 12. undetermined
flue... 4. barb 5. fluke 6. funnel,
tunnel 7. chimney
fluent... 4. glib 5. fluid, ready
6. facile, smooth, solute 7. copious,
elegant, flowing, gliding, verbose,
voluble 8. eloquent 9. talkative
10. loquacious
fluff... 4. down, girl, lint, yarn 5. floss
6. bungle 8. softness 9. lightness
fluffy... 4. soft 5. downy, drunk, fuzzy,
linty 8. feathery 9. forgetful
12. undependable
fluid... 3. gas, ink, oil 4. bile, milk
5. ichor, serum, water 6. fluent,
liquid, plasma, watery 7. flowing
8. floating, nonsolid
fluke... 3. fish, worm 5. blade (whale)
8. accident, flatfish, flounder
flume... 5. shoot 6. raving, sluice
7. channel, conduit
flunk... 4. fail, miss, slip 5. shirk
7. flinch 7. back out
flunky, flunkey... 5. snob 5. toady
6. cookee, lackey 7. footman,
servant 8. henchman 9. stagehand
flurry... 3. ado 4. fret, gust 5. haste,

hurry 6. bustle, squall 7. bluster,
fluster, flutter 8. snowfall
9. agitation, commotion, confusion
10. excitement
flush... 3. hot, jet 4. full, glow, gush,
rush 5. blush, cards, color, drunk,
fever, rinse, ruddy 6. drench, lavish,
redden, thrill 7. healthy, wealthy
8. abundant, affluent, prodigal,
rosiness, squarely, unbroken
10. prosperous
flushed... 3. hot, red 4. ruby
5. aglow, drunk 6. elated, florid
7. excited, fervent 8. blushing,
exultant, feverish, reddened
fluster... 4. move 5. shake 6. bustle,
excite, flurry, pother 8. distract
10. excitement 11. distraction
flute... 5. crimp, twill 6. furrow,
groove 7. magadis 9. organ stop,
wineglass 10. instrument
flute (pert to)...
bagpipe part.. 7. chanter
nose.. 3. bin 5. pungi
player.. 6. aulete 7. tootler
shrill.. 7. piccolo
stop.. 7. ventage
transverse.. 4. fife
fluting... 5. strix 7. gadroon, shading
10. decoration
flutter... 4. flap, flit, wave 5. float,
haste, hover, waver 6. bustle, ruffle
7. agitate, pitapat 8. disorder
9. agitation, confusion, palpitate
flux... 4. flow, fuse, melt 5. flood,
purge, resin, rosin, smalt, smear
6. course 7. flowing, liquefy, outflow,
solvent
fly... 3. hop 4. flee, flit, leap, melt,
soar, wave, whir, wing 5. alate,
float, glide, speed 6. aviate, elapse,
escape, insect, spring, vanish
7. avigate, avolate 8. fishhook
9. cease to be, disappear
fly (types of)... 3. bot 4. gnat
5. cadew, horse, house, midge
6. Asilus, caddis, gadfly, punkie,
tsetse 7. Diptera, nosee–um
8. dipteron, lacewing, mosquito
11. caterpillar
fly (pert to)...
African.. 4. zimb (zebub) 6. tsetse
agaric.. 8. mushroom (poisonous)
artificial.. 4. harl 5. alder, sedge
6. Cahill, claret 7. grannom
blow.. 4. eggs 5. larva
catcher.. 4. tody 6. peewee (pewit),
phoebe 8. kingbird
flying... 5. a–wing, brief, hasty, yarak
(falcon) 6. volant, waving 7. fleeing
8. fleeting, floating 9. temporary,
transient 12. aeronautical
flying (pert to)...
adder.. 9. dragonfly
boat.. 8. airplane, seaplane
9. amphibian
cat.. 5. lemur 6. marmot
Dutchman.. 7. opera 7. mariner
(fabled) 8. wanderer
fox.. 3. bat 6. kalong
island.. 7. Laputa (Gulliver's Travels)
machine.. 9. gyroplane, orthopter

foal... 4. colt 5. filly 8. Equuleus (Astron) 9. youngling

foam... 4. barm, boil, fume, rage, scum, suds 5. froth, spume, yeast 6. trivia 7. bubbles

foaming... 7. spumous 8. bubbling 10. fermenting, infuriated 11. overwrought

fob... 4. sham 5. cheat, trick 6. impose, pocket 7. palm off 8. ornament

focal point... 8. omphalos

focus... 6. center 8. converge, omphalos 10. adjustment 11. concentrate

fodder... 3. hay 4. corn, feed 5. straw, vetch 6. forage, silage, stover 7. stubble 8. ensilage 9. pasturage, provender

fodder (pert to)...
pit.. 4. silo
storage.. 6. haymow
store.. 6. ensile
stored.. 6. silage

foe... 4. army 5. enemy, rival 8. opponent 9. ill-wisher

fog... 4. blur, daze, haar, haze, mist, roke, smog 5. brume, cloud, vapor 6. nebula, opaque, stupor 7. aerosol, confuse, pogonip (Sierras) 9. confusion

fogdog... 5. stubb 8. fogeater

foggy... 3. dim 4. dull, hazy, roky 5. dense, misty, vague 6. cloudy, opaque 7. muddled, obscure 8. confused, nubilous 9. beclouded, uncertain 10. indistinct 12. muddleheaded

foghorn... 5. siren, voice (hoarse) 6. signal

fogle... 12. handkerchief (thieves')

fogy... 4. dull, slow 6. dotard, fogram, Hunker 8. mossback 10. Barnburner 12. conservative, old-fashioned 16. overconservative

foible... 5. blade (part), fault 7. failing, frailty 8. weakness 9. infirmity 12. imperfection

foil... 4. balk 5. actor, metal, sheet, stump, sword 6. defeat, offset, outwit, stooge, thwart, weapon 7. failure, repulse 9. frustrate 10. disappoint 11. frustration

Foism... 8. Buddhism

foist... 4. palm 5. cheat 7. intrude 9. interpose 11. interpolate

fold... 3. end, lap, pen, ply 4. coil (serpent), fail, furl, loop, pile, reef, ruga, sile, tuck, wrap 5. clasp, close, crimp, drape, laity, plait, pleat, plica 6. crease, dewlap, double, infold, lamina, lappet, rimple, suffix 7. entwine, envelop, plicate (fanlike) 8. collapse 9. plicature 10. go bankrupt

folded, not... 8. explicate

folder... 7. booklet, leaflet 8. pamphlet 13. advertisement

foliage... 5. spray 6. leaves, ramage 7. bouquet, leafage, umbrage 8. ornament (Arch)

folio... 4. case, leaf 5. paper (folded)

6. folder, number (serial)

folk... 4. race 5. tribe 6. nation, people 8. servants 9. followers, relatives, retainers 11. aggregation

folk (pert to)...
learned.. 7. pedants
lore.. 6. legend 9. mythology, tradition 12. superstition
song.. 4. fado, lied 7. art song, lullaby 9. Kunstlied, Volkslied
tale.. 4. myth, saga 5. fable, Nancy 6. legend, mythos, mythus 7. fantasy, parable

follow... 3. dog, tag 4. heed, heel, next, nose, obey, seek, tail 5. after, ensue, trace, trail 6. pursue, result, shadow 7. conform, draggle, emulate, imitate, observe, replace, succeed 8. come next, practice, supplant 9. persevere, supervene 10. understand

follower... 3. fan, ist (suff), ite (suff), son 4. aper 5. lover (of) 6. copier, ensuer, votary, zealot 7. devotee, pursuer, sequent 8. adherent, believer, disciple, henchman, partisan 9. Christian, dependent, satellite 10. enthusiast 11. cuadrillero

follower of...
Arius.. 5. Arian
Buddha.. 8. Buddhist
Confucius.. 9. Confucian
Falstaff.. 3. Nym
Mohammed.. 6. Moslem 8. Islamite

following... 4. next, sect 5. suant 7. ensuing, pursuit, sequent 8. trailing 9. resultant 10. subsequent, succeeding, successive 13. accompaniment

following (pert to)...
exact words.. 7. literal
one's death.. 10. posthumous
stories.. 6. sequel, series

folly... 3. sin 5. crime 6. levity, lunacy 7. blunder, foolery, madness 8. lewdness, unwisdom 9. silliness 10. desipience, imprudence, wantonness 11. foolishness 12. indiscretion

foment... 3. egg 4. abet, brew, spur 5. bathe, rouse 6. arouse, excite, incite 7. agitate, cherish 9. encourage, instigate

fomentation... 6. lotion, stupes 10. excitement 11. instigation 13. encouragement

Fomoriana (Celt Myth)... 10. sea robbers (race of)

fonda... 3. inn 5. hotel 8. fonduk

fondle... 3. pet 4. neck 5. ingle 6. caress, coddle, cosset, foster, pamper 7. cherish 8. blandish

fondling... 3. pet 4. fool 5. ninny 9. caressing, simpleton 10. love-making

fondly... 6. dearly 8. tenderly 14. affectionately

fondness... 3. gra 4. love 6. desire, doting, liking, relish 8. appetite 9. affection 10. attachment, propensity

fond of...

drink.. 8. bibulous
hunting.. 7. venatic
sea.. 15. thalassophilous
wife (overly).. 8. uxorious
font... 3. jet 4. fons, lava 5. stoup
　6. source, spring 7. piscina
　8. fountain 9. reservoir
Fontinalia... 19. Festival of Fountains
　(Rome)
food... 3. cud, pap 4. cate, chow,
　diet, eats, fare, grub, meat 5. bread,
　manna, scran 6. cereal, gluten,
　viands 7. aliment, cuisine, edibles,
　tapioca 8. victuals 9. nutriment,
　nutrition, provender 10. sustenance
　11. comestibles, nourishment
food (pert to)...
animal.. 6. forage 9. provender
Arctic.. 8. pemmican (pemican)
bit.. 6. morsel
devotee.. 7. epicure, gourmet
digestant.. 5. chyle
digested (partly).. 5. chyme
dislike of.. 9. sitomania
　10. cibophobia
element.. 7. vitamin
fasting (Lenten).. 9. xerophagy
gods, The.. 6. amrita 8. ambrosia
Hawaiian.. 3. poi
heavenly.. 5. manna
impure.. 4. tref
provide.. 5. cater, scaff 6. tucker
room.. 5. ambry 6. pantry, spence
　7. butlery, pantler
Southern.. 4. okra 5. gumbo
　7. hoecake 9. corn bread
　12. chitterlings
fool... 3. ass, toy 4. butt, dolt, dupe,
　nizy, raca (Bib), simp 5. clown, idiot,
　moron, ninny 6. dotard, jester,
　noodle, trifle 7. buffoon, deceive,
　fathead 9. ignoramus, simpleton
foolhardy... 4. rash 7. Icarian
　8. reckless 11. adventurous
fool hen... 6. grouse
foolish... 3. mad 4. daft, raca, rash,
　zany 5. inane, inept, palty, silly
　6. absurd, harish, simple, stupid,
　unwise 7. asinine, fatuous, idiotic,
　puerile, witless 9. brainless,
　desipient, imprudent, ludicrous,
　senseless 10. ill-advised, irrational,
　ridiculous 12. preposterous
　13. insignificant
foolish fancy... 7. chimera (chimaera)
foolishness... 5. folly 6. levity
　9. absurdity, stupidity 10. triviality
fool's bauble... 7. marotte
fool's gold... 6. pyrite
fool's paradise... 5. limbo
foot... 3. pad, paw, pes (pref)
　4. base, hoof, inch (part), sole, step,
　walk 5. sum up, tread 6. reckon
　7. residue 9. calculate, extremity
foot (pert to)...
bone.. 6. tarsus 10. metatarsus
care of.. 8. pedicure 9. chiropody
　11. chiropodist
horse.. 4. hoof 7. fetlock, pastern
lever.. 5. pedal 7. treadle
like.. 8. pediform
measure.. 4. inch

part.. 3. toe 4. arch, heel, sole
prefix.. 4. pedi
race course (anc).. 7. diaulos
reference to.. 5. pedal, podal
rest.. 4. rail 7. cricket, hassock,
　ottoman, support 8. footrail
　9. footstool
sole.. 7. plantar
study of.. 8. podiatry
unstressed part (Pros).. 5. arsis
foot, feet (metric)... 4. iamb, mora,
　unit 6. dactyl, dipody, iambus
　7. anapest, dimeter, pyrrhic,
　spondee, tripody 8. trimeter
　9. hexameter 10. heptameter,
　pentameter
footed... 5. biped 7. bipedal, megapod
　(large), metered
footing... 4. lace, rank 5. basis,
　dance, tread 6. status 7. support
　8. foothold, progress, standing
　9. condition 11. calculation
footman... 6. varlet, walker 7. servant
　9. attendant 10. pedestrian
footprint mold... 7. moulage
footway... 7. catwalk (Naut)
fop... 3. nob 4. Adon, buck, dude
　5. dandy, puppy, sport, swell
　6. Adonis, masher 7. coxcomb,
　gallant 9. exquisite, pretender
　12. boulevardier
foppish... 6. dapper, spruce 7. finical,
　foplike 8. dandyish 9. conceited,
　dandified
for... 2. to 3. pro 5. spite
　7. because, instead 8. behalf of
　9. intending 10. indicating
　11. preparation
for (pert to)...
each.. 3. per
example.. 2. as, eg 4. vide
　13. exempli gratia
fear.. 4. lest
most part.. 6. mostly 7. chiefly,
　usually 9. generally
nothing.. 6. gratis, naught
　9. lagniappe (lagnappe)
this reason.. 4. ergo 5. hence
forage... 4. food, mast, raid 5. spoil
　6. browse, ravage 7. plunder
　9. pasturage
foramen... 4. pore 7. opening, orifice,
　passage 8. fenestra
foray... 4. raid 6. ravage 7. pillage
　9. incursion
forbade... see *forbid*
forbear... 4. lose, shun 5. avoid
　6. desist, endure 7. abstain, decline,
　refrain 8. part with 9. be patient
forbearance... 5. mercy 6. disuse,
　lenity 8. leniency, mildness, patience
　9. tolerance 10. abstinence,
　temperance 11. forgiveness,
　placability
forbid... 3. ban 4. deny, tabu, veto
　5. debar, taboo 6. disbar, hinder,
　impede, oppose 7. exclude, inhibit,
　prevent 8. disallow, preclude, prohibit
　9. interdict, proscribe
　11. countermand
forbiddance... 3. ban 4. veto
　11. unallowable 12. disallowance,

interdiction, proscription
forbidden city... 5. Lhasa (Tibet), Pekin (walled, now Peiping)
forbidden food (Bib)... 4. tref 8. terephah
forbidding... 4. grim, ugly 5. plain, stern 6. fierce, odious 9. offensive, revolting 10. prevention, unpleasant 11. displeasing, prohibitive
force... 3. vim, vis 4. dint, make, urge 5. drive, impel, power, press, repel, staff, vigor 6. coerce, compel, effect, energy, extort, hasten, strain 7. impetus, meaning 8. eloquent, momentum, pressure, validity, violence 9. constrain, influence, puissance 10. compulsion, constraint 11. necessitate
force (pert to)...
alleged.. 2. od
armed.. 4. army 5. posse
by seizure.. 5. usurp
down.. 7. detrude
full.. 5. amain
substance.. 8. catalyst
unit.. 4. dyne 5. staff, tonal 7. poundal
forced... 7. labored 9. reluctant, unwilling 10. artificial, compulsory, farfetched 11. constrained
forced feeding... 6. gavage
forceful... 5. valid 6. mighty, potent, strong 7. dynamic 8. eloquent, emphatic, vigorous 9. effective, energetic 10. compulsory
forces... 4. army 5. armed 6. troops
forcible... 6. cogent, mighty, potent 7. violent, weighty 8. eloquent, emphatic, positive, puissant 9. energetic 10. compulsory, impressive 11. influential
forcible entry... 10. effraction
forciform... 6. forked 7. furcate 11. forficulate 14. scissors–shaped
ford... 4. wade 5. cross 6. stream
fore... 3. way 5. front, prior, track 6. former 7. journey
forebear... 4. sire 5. elder 6. parent 8. ancestor 10. antecedent, forefather, progenitor
forebode... 5. augur 7. betoken, portend, predict, presage 8. foretell 15. prognostication
foreboding... 6. augury 8. croaking, sinister 11. pessimistic, presagement 12. apprehension, presentiment
forecast... 4. bode, plan 6. scheme 7. foresee, fortune, predict 8. foretell, prophecy 9. calculate, foresight, foretoken 10. foreordain, prediction 12. presentiment
forecaster... 4. seer 5. vates 6. oracle 7. diviner, palmist, prophet 8. dopester, presager 10. astrologer, soothsayer 11. Nostradamus 13. meteorologist 14. prognosticator
foreclose... 5. debar 6. hinder 7. prevent, shut out 8. preclude 10. dispossess
foredoom... 4. doom 7. predict 12. predestinate

foredoomed... 3. fey 5. fatal 8. accursed
forefather... 4. sire 5. elder 6. parent 8. ancestor, forebear 10. progenitor
forefinger... 5. index
foregather... 4. meet 7. convene 8. assemble 9. encounter
forego, forgo... 6. pass by 7. neglect, precede 8. renounce
foregoing... 4. past 5. above 6. former, prefix 7. leading 10. antecedent
foregone... 4. past 8. previous 11. predestined, preordained, preresolved 13. predetermined
foregone conclusion... 9. certainty
forehead... 4. brow 8. calvaria, glabella, sinciput 9. assurance 10. effrontery
forehead, divination by...
11. metopomancy
forehead, frontal... 7. metopic
foreign... 4. xeno (comb form) 5. alien, fremd 6. exotic, remote 7. distant, outside (of country), strange 8. excluded 9. extrinsic, peregrine, unrelated 10. extraneous, outlandish 11. incongruous 12. adventitious
foreign (pert to)...
accent.. 4. burr 6. brogue, patois 7. dialect
crystals (Geol).. 7. epigene
disease.. 7. ecdemic
insertion.. 13. interpolation
place.. 6. forane
quarter.. 4. Para 5. Latin 6. French 7. enclave
service residence.. 9. consulate
foreigner... 5. alien 6. gringo 8. outsider, stranger 9. outlander, uitlander 10. tramontane 12. ultramontane
foreland... 8. headland 10. promontory
forelock... 4. bang 7. cowlick, fetlock 8. linchpin 9. cotter pin, fastening (armor)
foreman... 4. boss 5. chief 6. leader 7. juryman, overman 10. supervisor 14. superintendent
foremost... 5. chief, first, front 7. leading, supreme 8. headmost 13. most important
forensic... 10. rhetorical 13. argumentative
foreordain... 7. destine 9. predicate, preordain 12. foreordinate, predestinate, predetermine
forerun... 6. herald 7. advance, prelude, presage 8. announce, antecede 9. forestall, introduce, prefigure 10. anticipate, foreshadow
forerunner... 4. omen, sign 6. augury, herald 8. ancestor 9. harbinger, messenger, precursor 10. forefather, foreganger, progenitor, prognostic 11. predecessor
foreshadow... 6. shadow (beforehand) 7. presage 9. adumbrate, prefigure
foresight... 8. sagacity 9. prevision 10. precaution, prediction, prescience, prevoyance, providence

11. omniscience 13. foreknowledge

forest... 4. wold, wood 5. grove,
woods 6. jungle, timber 8. woodland
9. greenwood 10. timberland,
wilderness

forest (pert to)...
deity.. 3. Pan 7. Aegipan
fire.. 5. crown, stand 6. ground
7. surface
fire–finding instrument.. 7. alidade
glade.. 6. camass (camas, cammas)
love of, lover of.. 9. nemophile,
nemophily
regarding.. 6. sylvan 7. nemoral
tilled.. 7. thwaite
warden.. 6. ranger

forestall... 6. hinder 7. exclude, head
off, prevent 9. intercept
10. anticipate, monopolize

foretell... 4. bode, spae 5. augur,
insee 7. portend, predict, presage
8. forebode, forecast, prophesy
10. vaticinate 13. prognosticate

foretelling... 6. augury 7. fatidic
9. fatidical, prophetic 10. vaticinant

forethought... 8. prepense, prudence
9. foresight, provident 10. deliberate,
precaution 12. aforethought,
anticipation 13. premeditation

foretoken... 4. omen 7. presage
8. foreshow, indicant 10. presignify
13. preindication, prognosticate

foretooth... 5. biter 6. cutter
7. incisor 9. milk tooth

forever... 3. ake (Maori), aye (ay)
4. olam, ever 6. always, eterne
7. endless 8. infinity 9. continual,
perpetual 10. constantly, invariably
11. ceaselessly, continually,
incessantly, perpetually, unceasingly
12. interminably, unchangeably
13. everlastingly

forewarning... 4. omen 7. caution,
portent 9. informing 10. admonition,
foreboding

foreword... 5. proem 7. preface,
prelude 8. exordium, preamble,
prologue 12. introduction

forfeit... 4. fine, lose, loss 5. forgo,
mulct 6. forego, pledge 7. deodand,
penalty

forfeiture... 4. fine, loss 5. dédit,
mulct 7. penalty 10. amercement

forfend... 5. avert 6. forbid 7. prevent,
protect 8. preserve, prohibit

forfex... 6. shears

forgather... 4. meet 7. consort,
convene 8. assemble 9. encounter
10. fraternize

forge... 4. coin, form, mint 5. feign
6. create, smithy, stithy, swinge
7. falsify, imitate 8. bloomery,
smithery 11. counterfeit

forgery... 4. sham 7. fiction
9. falsehood, invention
11. counterfeit, fabrication
13. falsification

forget... 4. omit 5. lapse, remit
6. slight 7. neglect 9. disregard
11. disremember

forgetfulness... 5. Lethe (Myth), lotus
(legend) 7. amnesia, amnesty

8. Manasseh, oblivion
12. carelessness, heedlessness
13. obliviousness

forgive... 5. remit, spare 6. acquit,
excuse, pardon 7. condone

forgiveness... 6. pardon 9. remission
10. absolution 11. condonation,
exoneration, magnanimity

forgiving... 6. humane 8. merciful,
placable 9. remissive
11. magnanimous

forgo... 4. quit 5. leave, waive 6. give
up, resign 7. abstain, forbear, forfeit,
forsake, neglect, refrain 8. overlook,
renounce 9. do without
10. relinquish

forhoo... 7. abandon, despise

fork... 4. tine 5. prong 6. expend, pay
out 7. dilemma, diverge
10. divaricate, divergence
headstream 11. bifurcation

fork (pert to)...
garden.. 5. graip
pickle.. 13. runcible spoon
table.. 5. salad 6. dinner, oyster
7. dessert 8. ice–cream

forked... 5. bifid 6. horned, ramous
7. divided, furcate 8. branched,
crotched 9. ambiguous, equivocal
10. bifurcated, branchlike

forlorn... 4. reft 5. alone 6. abject,
bereft 8. deserted, desolate, forsaken,
helpless, pitiable 9. abandoned,
destitute, miserable 10. friendless
12. disconsolate

form... 4. body, cast, idea, mold, rite
5. build, guise, model, shape
6. beauty, create, figure, invent,
ritual 7. compose, contour, formula,
outline, pattern, profile, species,
variety 8. ceremony, conceive,
document 9. establish, formality
10. appearance 11. arrangement
12. conformation 13. configuration,
questionnaire 15. conventionality

form (pert to)...
bust.. 6. taille
chainlike.. 8. catenate
deceptive.. 5. ghost 7. specter
8. phantasm
display.. 4. rack
good.. 4. chic 6. fettle
government.. 6. polity
hollow.. 5. shell
into fabric.. 4. knit, spin 5. weave
primitive.. 9. prototype
spiral.. 5. helix
suffix.. 5. shape 10. resembling

formal... 4. prim 5. exact, stiff
6. solemn 7. orderly, outward,
precise, regular, stilted 8. affected,
apparent, starched 9. formative
10. ceremonial, methodical
11. pharisaical, ritualistic, superficial
12. conventional

formal introduction... 5. debut
12. presentation

formalities... 5. rites 9. etiquette
10. ceremonies

formal warning... 5. alarm 6. caveat
12. caveat emptor

format... 4. size 5. shape, style

formation... 4. form 5. order
9. structure 11. arrangement,
composition 12. construction
formation (pert to)...
chain (twisted).. 9. torquated
geologic.. 7. terrain, terrane
military.. 4. line 5. herse 7. echelon
sand.. 4. dene, dune
formed... 4. made 6. built 7. created,
decided, matured, settled 8. arranged
9. fashioned, organized
11. constructed
formed (pert to)...
by law.. 9. corporate
by lips.. 6. labial
mountain foot.. 8. piedmont
on earth's surface.. 7. epigene
plates (two).. 11. bilamellate
formed into...
chain.. 8. catenate 9. torquated
fabric.. 4. spun 5. woven 7. knitted
mass (hard).. 4. iced 5. caked
6. frozen 9. congealed
mosaic.. 9. tessellar 11. tessellated
former... 2. ex 3. old 4. erst, late,
once, past 5. front, prior 6. passed,
whilom 7. ancient, earlier 8. previous
9. foregoing, preceding
10. antecedent
former days... 3. eld, old 4. yore
formerly... 3. nee 4. erst, once, then
6. before, whilom 7. one–time
8. sometime 9. aforetime, erstwhile
10. heretofore, previously
formicary... 7. anthill 8. ant's nest
formicid... 3. ant 5. emmet
7. Formica
formidable... 7. fearful 8. alarming,
dreadful, menacing, terrible
9. difficult 11. redoubtable,
threatening
formless... 5. arupa 7. anidian, chaotic
9. amorphous, shapeless
13. indeterminate
Formosa, Taiwan...
capital.. 6. Taipei
city.. 6. Tainan 7. Hualien, Keelung
9. Kaohsiung
group.. 6. Penghu (64 Isls)
island.. 5. Matsu 6. Quemoy
formula... 3. law 4. form, rule
5. axiom, creed, lurry, maxim, model
6. method, recipe, ritual
12. prescription
forsake... 4. deny, quit, shun 5. avoid,
leave 6. depart, desert, refuse, reject
7. abandon 8. renounce, withdraw
9. surrender
forsaken... 4. lorn 6. vacant 7. forlorn
8. deserted, lovelorn, rejected
9. abandoned
forspeak... 5. curse 6. forbid
7. asperse, bewitch 8. renounce
9. relinquish
fort... 5. redan, tower 6. abatis,
castle, escarp, glacis (bank of)
7. bastion, bulwark, castlet
8. bastille, fastness, fortress
10. stronghold 13. fortification,
propugnaculum
Fort (Fr Ind War)... 9. Necessity
forth... 3. out 4. away 6. abroad,

onward 7. forward, outward
forthright... 5. ahead 7. frankly
8. forwards 9. downright
11. immediately, straightway
13. straightforth
forthwith... 3. now 6. pronto
8. promptly 9. summarily
11. immediately, straightway
fortification... 4. wall 5. redan
6. abatis 7. bastion, citadel, defense,
parados, ravelin, redoubt 8. barbette
(part), fortress 10. stronghold
13. corroboration, strengthening
fortify... 3. arm, man 4. gird 5. add
to, spike, stank 6. defend, secure
7. confirm, refresh 8. embattle
10. adulterate (drink), invigorate,
strengthen, vitaminize 11. corroborate
fortitude... 6. virtue 7. bravery,
courage 8. strength 9. endurance
10. resolution 12. resoluteness
14. impregnability
fortress... see **fort**
fortuitous... 3. hap 6. chance
10. accidental 12. unexpectedly
fortunate... 5. happy, lucky 6. timely
7. favored 10. auspicious,
prosperous, successful
12. providential
fortune... 3. hap, lot 4. doom, fate,
luck 6. chance, estate, riches, wealth
7. destiny, success 8. accident
10. prosperity 13. circumstances
fortune (pert to)...
gypsy.. 4. bahi
ill.. 9. mischance
planet (Astrol).. 5. Venus 7. Jupiter
teller.. 4. seer 5. sibyl, Tyche
6. oracle 7. spaeman
forward... 2. on, to 3. aid 4. abet,
bold, fore, help, pert, send, ship,
vain 5. ahead, along, eager, front,
impel, ready, relay, saucy, ultra
6. active, bright, hasten, onward
7. deliver, earnest, extreme, further,
radical, willing 8. advanced,
immodest, impudent, transmit
9. audacious, encourage
10. precocious 11. progressive
12. presumptuous
forward moving (Zool)... 5. proal
(digestion) 11. mastication
fosse, foss... 3. pit 4. moat 5. canal,
ditch, fossa, grave 6. cavity, trench
10. depression
fossil, fossils... 5. relic, stone
7. antique, remains
fossil (pert to)...
egg.. 7. ovulite
footprint.. 7. ichnite
resin.. 5. amber
shell.. 6. dolite 8. ammonite
site.. 8. Badlands (Dakota, Nebraska)
study of.. 12. paleontology
toothlike.. 8. conodont
worm track.. 7. nereite
foster... 4. rear 5. breed, nurse
7. cherish, gratify, indulge, promote
9. cultivate
fosterage... 7. nurture
11. development
foster child... 4. dalt 5. norry (nurry)

7. stepson 8. nursling
12. stepdaughter

fought... see *fight*

foul... 3. bad 4. olid, ugly 5. dirty,
fetid, grimy, nasty, reeky, spoil, sully
6. defame, filthy, malign, odious,
putrid, rotten, thwart, unfair
7. abusive, confuse, noisome,
obscene, profane, unclean
8. entangle, indecent, infamous,
shameful, stagnant, stinking
9. dishonest, obnoxious
10. complicate, malodorous,
scurrilous 11. contaminate,
ill-smelling, unfavorable
12. inauspicious, unpropitious

foul play... 6. murder, unfair (play)
7. perfidy 8. violence 9. deception,
treachery 10. unfairness

found... 3. fix 4. base, cast 5. endow,
set up 6. attach, create 9. establish,
institute, originate

foundation... 3. bed 4. base, plot, sill
5. basal, basis 6. legacy, riprap
7. bedding, charity, premise, support
8. cosmetic, creation, donation,
pedestal 9. placement
11. corporation 13. justification

found by chance (thing)...
11. serendipity

founded on...
base.. 10. predicated
evidence.. 10. evidential
experience.. 7. empiric 9. empirical
imagination.. 7. Utopian

founder... 4. fail, fall, sink 6. author
7. capsize, creator, stumble
8. miscarry 9. break down, organizer
10. originator

foundling... 3. oaf 4. waif 5. child
(unclaimed) 6. orphan 8. derelict,
nursling

fountain... 3. jet, spa 4. font, head,
well 6. spring 9. reservoir
11. scuttlebutt (ship's)
12. fountainhead

fountain (pert to)...
god of.. 4. Fons
Muse (Gr).. 8. Aganippe
nymph.. 5. naiad 6. Egeria
of Lions.. 8. Alhambra (Granada, Sp)

four (pert to)...
bits.. 7. quarter (silver)
Books.. 8. Classics (Chin)
footed.. 8. tetrapod
genii, of Amenti.. 13. Horus' children
group.. 6. tetrad
Hundred.. 5. elect, elite 7. society
letters, word of.. 9. tetragram
seas.. 13. Great Britain's
senses (Bib).. 15. interpretations

four-flusher... 5. cheat, fraud
7. bluffer 8. impostor 9. pretender

fourth (pert to)...
Caliph.. 3. Ali
century martyr.. 8. St Blaise
estate.. 5. press 10. newspapers
part.. 6. fardel 7. quarter
stomach (cow).. 8. abomasum

fowl... 3. hen 6. bantam, Gallus
7. Blue Hen, broiler, chicken,
Dorking, leghorn, Minorca, poultry,

rooster, seafowl 8. pheasant
9. guinea hen, waterfowl
11. chanticleer

fox... 3. cub, tod 4. stag 5. vixen

fox (pert to)...
African.. 4. asse
Asian.. 5. adive 6. corsac
female.. 5. vixen
genus.. 6. Vulpes
hedge (hunter's).. 4. oxer
foot.. 3. pad
Indian.. 10. Algonquian
Russian.. 6. corsac 7. karagan

foxglove... 9. digitalis

foxy... 3. sly 6. artful, crafty
7. cunning

foyer... 5. lobby 8. anteroom, entrance
9. greenroom

fracas... 3. row 5. brawl, melee,
set-to 6. uproar 7. quarrel
9. commotion 11. disturbance

fraction... 3. bit 4. part 5. piece,
scrap 6. sector 7. element, ruction
8. division, fragment 9. commotion

fractious... 4. ugly 5. cross 6. unruly
7. peevish, waspish 8. perverse,
snappish 9. irritable 10. ill-humored
11. disobedient

fracture... 4. rend 5. break, cleft,
crack 6. breach, injury 7. rupture

fragile... 4. weak 5. brash, frail
6. frough (obs), infirm, slight
7. brittle 8. delicate, slattery
9. frangible

fragment... 3. bit, ort 4. chip, grot,
part, snip 5. groat, piece, relic,
scrap, shard, sherd, shred, torso (art)
6. morsel, sippet 7. flinder
8. fraction

fragments... 3. ana 6. fardel, groats,
rubble 8. buttings, excerpts, flinders
10. miscellany 11. smithereens

fragrance... 4. odor 5. aroma, elemi,
smell 7. incense, perfume
9. redolence

fragrant... 4. nard 5. balmy, olent,
spicy, sweet 7. odorous 8. aromatic,
redolent 9. ambrosial 11. odoriferous
12. sweet-scented
13. sweet-smelling

frail... 4. girl, thin, weak 5. woman
6. basket (fig), feeble, sickly, slimsy
7. brittle, fragile 8. strumpet,
unchaste 10. weak-willed
12. destructible

frailty... 5. fault 6. defect 7. failing
8. thinness, weakness 9. fragility,
infirmity 12. imperfection

frame... 4. body, make, plan, rack,
sess, sill 5. build, easel, grate,
herse, knape 6. abacus, border,
charge (falsely), direct, tenter
7. carcass, chassis, cresset (torch),
fashion, prepare, setting, taboret
8. conceive, skeleton 9. construct
10. prearrange

framework... 4. rack, sill 5. cadre,
shell 6. cradle 7. trestle 8. skeleton
11. scaffolding

France... see also *French*
anc name.. 4. Gaul 6. Gallia
Bay.. 6. Biscay

Botanical Gardens.. 16. Jardin des Plantes
capital.. 5. Paris
city.. 4. Nice 5. Lyons 7. LeHavre 8. Bordeaux, Toulouse 9. Marseille 10. Strasbourg
dread of.. 11. Gallophobia
island.. 6. Comoro (Afr), Tahiti 7. Corsica, Réunion 10. Guadeloupe (Leeward), Martinique (Windward) 12. New Caledonia
lover of.. 10. Gallophile
mountain.. 4. Alps, Jura 5. Pelat 8. Pyrenees 9. Mont Blanc 11. Pic Montcalm
port.. 4. Caen 5. Brest, Havre 6. Calais, Toulon 8. Bordeaux 9. Dunkerque (Dunkirk)
resort.. 3. Pau 5. Vichy 6. Cannes, Menton (Mentone) 7. Riviera 11. Aix–les–Bains (anc)
river.. 3. Lys 4. Yser 5. Aisne, Eiser, Loire, Meuse, Rhône, Seine
Southern.. 4. Midi
Verdun battle site.. 4. Vaux
franchise... 4. vote 5. right 6. patent 7. freedom, license 8. immunity, suffrage 9. exemption
frank... 4. free, mail, open 5. blunt, naive, plain 6. candid, direct, honest 7. artless, liberal, sincere 8. generous 9. ingenuous, outspoken 10. unreserved 11. frankfurter 15. straightforward, unsophisticated
frankincense... 4. thus 8. gum resin, olibanum 9. fragrance
Frankish (pert to)...
dynasty.. 11. Carolingian, Merovingian
king.. 5. Pepin 6. Clovis
law.. 5. Salic
site.. 4. Gaul
tribe (anc).. 6. Salian
Franklin, Benjamin... 11. Poor Richard
frantic... 3. mad 4. mang 5. moved, rabid 7. furious 8. frenetic, frenzied 9. delirious, desperate, turbulent 10. distracted, distraught 11. overwrought
frappé... 3. ice 5. chill 6. freeze 7. dessert, mixture (sweet) 8. beverage
fraternal... 4. kind 5. order, twins 7. society 8. friendly 9. brotherly
fraud... 4. fake, sham, wile 5. cheat, covin, craft, guile 6. deceit, ringer 7. defraud, roguery 8. artifice, cozenage, impostor, subtlety, swindler, trickery 9. deception, imposture, stratagem 10. imposition 13. circumvention
fraudulence... 9. improbity 10. subreption
fraudulent... 4. fake, wily 5. snide 6. crafty, quacky 7. cunning, knavish 8. cheating, guileful, spurious 9. deceitful, deceiving, deceptive, designing, dishonest, insidious 10. fallacious 11. counterfeit, treacherous
fraught... 4. lade, load 5. cargo, equip, laden 6. burden, filled

7. freight 9. freighted, transport
fray... 4. fret (cloth), wear 5. broil, dread, melee, panic, ravel 6. affray, combat, fright, hassle, terror, tumult 7. contest, frazzle, ruction 9. commotion 12. apprehension
freak... 4. flam, lune, whim 5. fancy, prank, sport 6. streak, vagary 7. caprice, checker, crochet, monster 9. eccentric, variegate 11. monstrosity 12. whimsicality
freakish... 7. curious 9. eccentric, fantastic, whimsical 10. capricious, changeable
freck... 4. bold, hale 5. eager, frack, lusty, ready, stout 6. strong 7. forward 8. desirous
freckle... 4. mark, spot 7. blemish, ephelis, lentigo, speckle 10. ferntickle
free... 3. rid 4. easy, open 5. clear, frank, loose 6. acquit, candid, exempt, gratis, immune, vacant 7. absolve, inexact, manumit, not busy, release, relieve, unbound 8. liberate 9. extricate, footloose, voluntary 10. autonomous, gratuitous, unconfined, unhampered 11. emancipated 12. uncontrolled, unrestrained, unrestricted
free (pert to)...
bacteria.. 7. aseptic, sterile
difficulty.. 9. extricate
doubt.. 7. resolve
flesh (dietary).. 6. maigre
knots.. 7. enodate, unravel
reproach.. 9. blameless
slavery.. 7. manumit 10. emancipate
suspicion.. 5. clear, purge 6. acquit 7. absolve 9. exculpate, exonerate
sweetness.. 5. sec
freebooter... 5. rover 6. pirate 8. pillager 9. plunderer 10. filibuster
freed... 3. rid 6. loosed, spared, untied 8. released 9. delivered, liberated 10. manumitted 11. emancipated
freedom... 6. candor 7. leisure, liberty, license 8. latitude 9. exemption, privilege 11. manumission 12. emancipation, independence
freedom (pert to)...
abused.. 7. liberty (excess), license
from doubt.. 9. assurance, certitude
from sepsis.. 7. asepsis
Freedom Our Rock (motto)... 7. Tammany (1789)
free enterprise... 6. policy 8. commerce 10. capitalism 15. noninterference
freely... 6. gratis 7. largely, readily 9. bountiful, copiously, liberally, willingly 10. abundantly, generously 11. bounteously, plenteously, plentifully, voluntarily 12. gratuitously
freeze... 3. ice 5. be–ice, chill 6. steeve 7. congeal, terrify 8. preserve, solidify 9. stabilize 11. anesthetize, refrigerate
freezing, science of... 10. cyrogenics
freight... 4. load, ship 5. cargo, laden, train 6. burden, charge, lading 7. fraught, rattler 8. shipment

9. transport 14. transportation
freight boat... 5. barge 9. freighter
freit, freet... 4. omen 5. charm
fremd (obs)... 5. alien 7. foreign,
hostile 9. unrelated
French (people)...
artist, painter.. 4. Doré 5. Corot,
David, Monet 6. Gervex, Greuze,
Renoir 7. Gauguin, Lemoine, Matisse
8. Daubigny, Rousseau
author.. 4. Hugo, Loti, Zola
5. Dumas, Renan, Verne (Jules)
6. Balzac, Proust
caricaturist.. 7. Gavarni
chemist.. 7. Gautier, Holbach, Pasteur
composer.. 4. Lalo 5. Bizet, Ravel
6. Gounod 7. Debussy
conqueror (anc).. 6. Clovis
crusader.. 7. Godfrey (of Bouillon)
dramatist.. 6. Favart 8. Quinault
dynasty.. 5. Caput 6. Valois
Foreign Legion creator, 1831..
8. Philippe (Louis)
impressionist.. 5. Monet 8. Pissarro
marshal.. 3. Ney 4. Foch, Niel, Saxe
5. Murat
naturalist.. 8. Audebert
navigator.. 9. Freycinet
pantomimist.. 7. Pierrot
patron saint.. 5. Denis 6. Martin
philosopher.. 5. Bayle, Camus
6. Pascal 7. Abelard 8. Rousseau
9. Descartes
physician.. 7. Laveran
physicist.. 5. Binet 6. Ampere
poet.. 6. Villon 7. Gilbert, Mistral
8. Rousseau 9. Deschamps
radical.. 7. Jacobin
scientist.. 5. Curie 7. Pasteur
sculptor.. 4. Etex 5. Barye, Rodin
6. Gerome, Millet
statesman.. 4. Coty 5. Laine, Laval,
Morny 6. Carnot 7. Briande, Herriot
8. DeGaulle
therapist.. 4. Coué
French (pert to)...
academic rank.. 6. agrégé
Academy.. 12. The Institute
and.. 2. et
annuity.. 5. rente
anthem.. 12. Marseillaise
article.. 2. la, le, un 3. les, une
beast:.. 4. bête
calender (Rev).. 6. Nivose 7. Ventose
champagne.. 2. Ay
cheese.. 4. Brie 6. Chevre
9. Camembert
chorus (male).. 7. orpheon
coach.. 6. fiacre
coat-of-arms.. 10. fleur-de-lis
coffee (black).. 8. café noir
company (Bus).. 3. cie
crown (gold coin).. 3. ecu
cult (art).. 7. Dadaism
daisy.. 10. marguerite
dance.. 3. bal 5. gavot 6. cancan
decree, edict.. 5. arrêt
dialect.. 6. patois
dugout.. 4. abri
father.. 4. père
fortification.. 7. parados
fugitive.. 6. émigré

God.. 4. Dieu
hairdresser.. 7. friseur
hat.. 5. beret 7. chapeau
here.. 3. ici
inn.. 6. hostel
lace.. 5. Cluny
language (Provence).. 9. Provençal
laugh.. 3. ris
liquor.. 8. absinthe (banned 1915)
mask.. 4. loup
morning.. 5. matin
mountain peak.. 3. pic
narcissus.. 10. polyanthus
native.. 8. Gallican
nursemaid.. 5. bonne
ornaments (set of).. 6. parure
outcast.. 5. Agote, Cagot 6. pariah
pancake.. 5. crepe
parliament.. 5. Sénat
pastry.. 7. dariole, galette
plane.. 5. avion
poem, poetry.. 3. dit 6. aubade,
rondel
police.. 6. Sûreté 8. gendarme
political club.. 7. Jacobin
porcelain.. 6. Sèvres 7. Limoges
priest.. 4. abbe, pere
racecourse.. 7. Auteuil
restaurant.. 4. café 6. bistro
sauce.. 8. ravigote 9. allemande
school.. 5. école, lycée
school of painting.. 8. Barbizon
securities.. 6. rentes
smoking room.. 9. estaminet
soldier.. 5. poilu 6. Zouave
stable.. 6. écurie
stock exchange.. 6. Bourse
storm.. 5. orage
street.. 3. rue
summer.. 3. été
theater.. 16. Comédie Française
verse.. 3. lai 4. alba 6. rondel
7. ballade, virelay
wall.. 3. mur
water.. 3. eau
wind.. 7. mistral
wine.. 5. Medoc 6. Barsac, brandy,
claret, Cognac, masdeu 8. Bordeaux,
Burgundy, sauterne 10. Beaujolais
world.. 5. monde
Frenchman... 4. frog, Gaul 6. froggy,
Picard (of Picardy) 8. Parisian
9. frogeater
Frenchy.. 6. Gallic
frenzied... 4. amok 5. rabid
7. enraged, frantic, madding
8. maddened 9. turbulent
11. overwrought
frenzy... 3. mad 5. furor, mania
7. frantic, madness 8. delirium
9. agitation 10. excitement,
turbulence
frequent... 3. oft 5. haunt, often,
usual 6. common 7. current
8. familiar, habitual, intimate (with)
9. recurrent 10. persistent
frequenter... 7. habitué, visitor
8. attender
frère... 5. friar 7. brother
fresh... 3. new 4. good, lush 5. relay,
ruddy, sound, sweet 6. florid, lively,
strong, unused 7. healthy, unfaded,

untried 8. impudent, original
10. additional, refreshing, unimpaired
13. inexperienced
freshen... 4. cool 5. renew 6. revive
7. refresh, sweeten
freshet... 4. gush 5. flood, spate
6. stream 7. outflow, torrent
10. inundation (sudden)
freshman... 5. frosh 6. novice
7. student
freshness... 7. newness, novelty
8. verdancy 9. impudence
11. originality
freshwater fish... 2. id (ide) 4. chub,
dace, inid (porpoise) 6. anabas
7. herring 8. drumfish
fret... 3. eat, nag, orp, rub, vex
4. fray, fume, gall, gnaw, stew
5. adorn, annoy, chafe, grate, tease,
worry 6. abrade, grieve, harass,
plague, strait 7. agitate, consume,
disturb, network, roughen
8. diminish, irritate, ornament
fretful... 5. angry 6. repine 7. peevish,
pettish 8. captious, petulant
9. impatient, irascible, irritable,
plaintive, querulous 10. ill-humored,
ill-natured
friable... 5. crisp, frail, mealy, short
7. brittle 8. fragible
friar... 3. fra 4. fish (small), monk
5. abbot, Minor 6. lister (obs)
7. brother 8. cenobite, Minorite,
Teresian (anc) 9. Carmelite,
Dominican 10. Franciscan
11. Augustinian
friction... 7. erasure, rubbing
8. clashing 9. attrition, disaccord
10. resistance 12. disagreement
13. counteraction
friend... 3. ami, pal 4. ally, amie,
chum, kith, sect 5. amigo, crony
7. comrade 8. promoter
9. associate, attendant, companion,
supporter 10. benefactor, sweetheart,
well-wisher
Friend... 6. Quaker
friendless... 5. alone 7. forlorn
8. helpless 9. destitute (friends)
friendly... 3. sib 4. kind 7. affable
8. amicable, homelike, sociable
9. favorable 10. harmonious,
hospitable 11. comfortable
Friendly Islands... 5. Tonga
friendship... 4. kelt 5. amity
7. harmony 8. good will, relation
9. affection, right hand
10. attachment 12. friendliness
frieze... 4. band (sculptured) 5. adorn,
chase 6. taenia (Doric) 8. ornament,
trimming 10. decoration, embroidery
Frigga, Norse Myth (pert to)...
goddess.. 3. sky
maid.. 5. Fulla
named for.. 6. Friday
wife of.. 4. Odin
fright... 3. awe 4. fear, ogre 5. alarm,
panic, scare, shock 6. terror
7. eyesore 13. consternation
frighten... 3. cow 5. alarm, appal,
scare 7. startle, terrify 10. intimidate
frightened... 3. mad 5. eerie, timid

6. afraid 8. skittish
frightful... 5. awful, great 6. horrid
7. hideous 8. alarming, dreadful,
horrible, shocking, terrible, terrific
11. frightening
frightfulness... 13. atrociousness
15. Schrecklichkeit
frigid... 3. icy 4. cold 5. stiff
6. formal 8. freezing, impotent,
reserved
frijol, frijole... 4. bean
frill... 4. purl 5. jabot, ruche (rouche)
6. border, edging, ruffle 8. furbelow
9. frillback (pigeon) 11. superfluity
fringe... 4. lace, loma, tuft 5. thrum
6. border, edging, margin 8. ciliella,
trimming
frisk... 4. skip 5. brisk, caper 6. frolic,
gambol, lively, search 7. disport,
rejoice
frisky... 3. gay 6. lively 7. playful
8. sportive 10. frolicsome
frisson... 5. chill 6. quiver, shiver, thrill
7. shudder 10. excitement
frivolous... 5. giddy, petty 6. fickle,
slight 7. fatuous, trivial 9. worthless
13. shallow-witted
frock... 4. gown, wrap 5. dress, tunic
6. jersey, kirtle (anc) 8. mantle
7. garment, soutane
frog... 3. pad (horse's) 4. Rana, toad
5. Anura 6. peeper 7. croaker,
paddock, tadpole 8. Amphibia,
pollywog 9. Batrachia, Frenchman,
Salientia 10. hoarseness
froglike... 6. ranine
frogman... 5. diver 6. seaman
7. swimmer 9. Frenchman
frog pond... 8. ranarium
frolic... 3. fun 4. lark, ogle, play,
ramp, romp 5. binge, caper, frisk,
prank, spree, trick 6. gambol, shindy
7. disport, marlock, shindig, wassail
8. carousal
frolicsome... 3. gay 5. merry 6. frisky
7. playful, waggish 8. sportive
from... 2. at, de (pref), of 3. apo
(pref) 4. away 5. above, out of
6. source 8. away from, downward
from (pert to)...
beginning to end.. 4. over 7. through
egg to apple.. 16. ab ovo usque ad
mala
head to foot.. 7. cap-a-pie
slang.. 10. soup to nuts 11. stem to
stern
front... 3. bow, van 4. face, fore
5. aface, afore, blind (false), forne
(obs) 6. before, façade 9. obverse
8. confront, mediator 9. forefront
10. appearance, figurehead
11. affectation 12. intermediary
frontier defense... 11. arcifinious
frontiersman... 5. Boone 6. Carson
(Kit)
frost... 3. ice, mat 4. cold, foam, rime
5. chill 6. freeze, whiten 7. failure
8. severity (manner)
14. unfriendliness
frosty... 3. icy 4. cold, gray, rimy
5. chill, hoary, white 6. frigid
8. freezing, inimical 10. unfriendly

froth... 4. foam, scum, suds 5. spume, yeast 6. lather 7. bubbles

frothy... 5. foamy, light, sudsy 7. spumous 8. sillabub

frow... 4. froe (tool), wife 5. woman 6. maenad 8. slattern

froward... 5. cross 7. peevish, wayward 8. perverse, petulant, scolding, shrewish, untoward 9. obstinate 10. refractory, unyielding 11. disobedient 12. ungovernable

frowl... 9. guillemot

frown... 5. gloom, lower, scowl 6. glower

frowsey, frowzy... 5. musty 7. unkempt 8. slovenly 9. offensive 10. discordant, disordered

frozen... 4. cold 5. frore (anc), froze, gelid, glacé 6. chilly, mousse 7. chilled 9. congealed, terrified, unfeeling, unmovable 10. unyielding 11. coldhearted 12. refrigerated 13. unsympathetic

frugal... 5. chary 6. meager, saving 7. careful, sparing, thrifty 9. provident 10. economical, unwasteful 11. inexpensive 12. parsimonious

frugality... 6. thrift 7. economy 9. parsimony

fruit (types of)... 3. fig 4. lime, pear, plum, pome 5. apple, berry, drupe, grape, guava, lemon, mango, melon, olive, peach, pomum 6. banana, cherry, orange, papaya, pawpaw, pomelo 7. apricot, azarole, genipap 8. shaddock 9. persimmon, tangerine 10. grapefruit

fruit... 4. diet, food 5. yield, young 7. benefit, product 9. offspring, outgrowth, posterity 11. consequence

fruit (pert to)...
aggregate.. 7. etaerio
astringent.. 4. sloe
basket.. 6. pottle
buttercup.. 6. achene 8. achenium
class.. 6. simple 9. aggregate 10. collective
cordial.. 7. ratafia (ratafee)
decay.. 4. blet
dried.. 6. raisin
drink.. 6. nectar
goddess.. 6. Pomona
gourd.. 4. pepo
grapefruit.. 6. pomelo
imperfect.. 6. nubbin
jelly substance.. 6. pectin
Jove's.. 9. persimmon
part.. 7. epicarp 8. mesocarp, pericarp 9. sarcocarp
preserve.. 7. compote
pulpy.. 3. uva
rose.. 3. hip
study of.. 9. carpology
tree.. 4. date, nuts 5. regma 6. camato, samara (winged)
tropical.. 3. fig 4. date 5. guava, mango, papaw (pawpaw) 6. papaya

fruitful... 7. fertile, uberous 8. abundant, prolific 9. plenteous

fruitfulness, goddess of... 7. Demeter

fruitless... 4. vain 6. barren 7. sterile, useless 10. profitless 11. ineffectual 12. unprofitable, unsuccessful

frump... 3. vex 4. mock, snub 5. crone, flout, shrew 6. gossip, insult 7. provoke 8. irritate

frustrate... 4. balk, bilk, foil 5. block, cross, elude 6. baffle, blight, defeat, outwit, thwart 7. nullify 8. confound 9. checkmate 10. circumvent, disappoint, disconcert

frustrater... 7. marplot 8. thwarter

frustration... 4. balk 6. defeat, fiasco 13. circumvention 14. disappointment 15. disillusionment

fry... 4. cook 5. brood (fish), group, sauté, young 8. offspring

frying pan... 6. spider 7. skillet

fubsy... 5. plump, short 6. chubby, stuffy

fuddle... 4. bout (drinking) 5. drink (strong), spree 6. muddle, tipple 7. confuse 9. confusion, inebriate

fuddler... 8. drunkard

fudge... 4. fake 5. candy, cheat 6. bungle, humbug 7. trump up 8. nonsense 9. makeshift 10. substitute 11. counterfeit

Fuegian... 3. Ona 5. tribe 6. Indian, Yakgan 8. Alikuluf 14. Tierra del Fuego (pert to)

fuel... 3. gas, log, oil 4. coal, coke, peat 6. elding 7. nuclear 9. petroleum 11. combustible

fugie... 4. cock (nonfighter) 6. coward

fugient... 7. fleeing 9. retiring

fugitive... 5. exile 6. outlaw, roving 7. fleeing, refugee, roaming, runaway 8. fleeting, unstable, vagabond, volatile 9. fugacious, strolling, uncertain 10. evanescent

fugue... 5. theme, tonal 7. amnesia, stretto (stretta) 9. psychosis, ricercare

fulcrum... 4. axis, bait, prop 5. pivot, scale (fish), thole 7. support

fulfill... 4. meet 6. finish, redeem 7. execute, satisfy 8. complete 10. accomplish, effectuate

fulfillment... 8. fruition 9. execution, flowering 10. completion 11. performance 14. accomplishment

full... 3. fat 4. fill 5. drunk, sated 6. entire, filled, rotund 7. perfect, plenary, replete, satiety 8. abundant, adequate, complete, occupied, resonant, satiated, thorough 9. satisfied

full (pert to)...
blooded.. 6. virile 8. rubicund 12. thoroughbred
bloom.. 8. anthesis, blooming, maturity
control.. 7. mastery
force.. 5. amain
house.. 3. SRO

full of...
cracks.. 6. rimose
hollows.. 8. lacunose
love.. 7. amative
meaning.. 5. pithy
openings (tiny).. 6. porous
sand.. 7. arenose
substance.. 5. meaty

suffix.. 3. ose
thorns.. 6. briary
vigor.. 5. lusty
fulness, fullness... 4. much
7. orotund, pleroma, satiety, surfeit
9. abundance, greatness, plenitude,
repletion, resonance 10. perfection
12. completeness
fulsome... 3. bad, .fat 4. base, foul,
full 5. nasty, plump, suave
7. copious, overfed 8. abundant
9. offensive, overgrown, repulsive
10. disgusting
Fulton's Folly... 8. Clermont
fumble... 5. grope 6. bungle, huddle,
mumble 7. confuse
fume... 4. odor, rage, rant, reek
5. anger, smoke, steam, vapor
8. outburst 10. excitement,
exhalation
fun... 4. gell, jest, joke, play 5. chaff,
sport 9. amusement, merriment
function... 3. act, use 4. duty, rite,
role, work 5. party 6. office
7. calling, operate, purpose, service
8. ceremony, province
10. providence
function (pert to)...
math.. 5. sine 6. cosine
mind.. 8. ideation
social.. 3. tea
functional... 8. official 9. operative
11. ceremonious, utilitarian
fund... 5. basis, money 6. bottom,
supply 7. capital, provide, revenue
10. foundation, groundwork
fundamental... 4. tone 5. basal, basic,
vital 7. basilar, organic, primary,
radical 8. original, rudiment
9. elemental, essential, principle
10. elementary
Fundamental Orders (US Hist)...
8. document (1639) 12. Constitution
(first, 1639 Conn)
funds... 5. means 6. assets, moneys
8. finances
funeral... 5. rites 6. burial 8. exequies
9. obsequies 10. procession
funeral (pert to)...
bell.. 5. knell
ceremony.. 6. exequy
hymn, song.. 5. dirge, éloge, elogy
7. requiem 8. threnody
oration, poem.. 5. elegy
pile.. 4. pyre
procession.. 6. exequy 7. cortege
vase.. 3. urn
funereal... 3. sad 4. dark 6. dismal,
solemn 8. exequial, mournful
9. dirgelike
fungi... 5. rusts, Uredo 6. mildew
7. Boletus
fungoid... 6. fungal, fungus
fungus... 4. bunt, mold, rust, smut
5. ergot, morel, uredo 6. agaric,
mildew 7. aminita, blewits, boletus,
geaster, truffle 8. mushroom, puffball
9. toadstool
fungus, edible... 5. morel 7. truffle
8. mushroom
funguslike... 6. agaric
funk... 4. kick, odor, rage 5. panic,

smell (bad), smoke, spark 6. flinch,
fright, shrink, terror 8. frighten
9. cowardice, touchwood
funnel... 4. cone, flue, pipe, tube
6. hopper 7. channel
funnel-shaped... 8. choanoid
funny... 3. odd 5. comic, droll, queer,
witty 7. comical, rowboat (Eng),
strange 8. humorous 9. eccentric,
laughable
fur... 3. fox 4. mink, pelt, seal, vair
5. coypu, fitch, genet, otter, sable,
skunk 6. badger, ermine, martin,
nutria 7. miniver (anc) 8. squirrel
10. chinchilla
fur (pert to)...
collective.. 6. peltry
cover.. 4. pelt 6. pelage
garment.. 4. robe 5. stole 6. tippet
7. pelisse
tippet.. 8. palatine
furbish... 3. rub 4. vamp 5. clean,
scour 6. polish 7. burnish, touch up
8. renovate 9. embellish
Furies... 5. Dirae 6. Alecto, ghosts,
Semnae 7. Erinyes (Erinys), Magaera,
spirits (avenging) 9. Eumenides,
Tisiphone
Furies, The Three... 6. Alecto
7. Magaera 9. Tisiphone
furious... 5. angry, hasty 6. fierce
7. frantic, violent 8. frenzied,
vehement 9. impetuous, turbulent
10. boisterous, passionate,
tumultuous 11. overwrought
furl... 4. roll, wrap 6. bundle, inroll
furlough... 5. leave 14. leave of
absence
furnace... 4. etna, kiln, oven 5. forge,
stove 7. caldron, reactor, rotator,
smelter
furnish... 3. fit 4. bear, give, lend
5. adorn, cater, endow, equip, indue
6. afford, fit out, render, supply
7. appoint, provide
furnishing... 7. fitting 8. fixtures,
ornament 9. adornment, apparatus,
furniture, provision 10. enrichment
furnish with...
funds.. 5. endow
meals.. 5. board, cater
Mil equipment.. 8. accoutre
tapestry.. 5. arras
wings.. 3. imp
furniture... 5. goods 6. Empire, graith,
outfit 7. Regency (Regence)
8. hardware, Sheraton, supplies
9. equipment 10. decoration,
housewares 11. Chippendale,
Renaissance
furor... 4. fury, rage 5. anger, craze
6. fervor, flurry, frenzy, furore, tumult
7. madness 10. excitement,
turbulence
furrow... 3. rut 4. plow 6. groove,
gutter, trench 7. channel, wrinkle
furrowed... 5. rutty 6. rivose
7. grooved
further... 3. aid, and, new, yet
4. abet, more 7. advance, develop,
improve, promote, remoter, thither
10. additional

furtherance... 3. aid 4. help 6. relief, succor 8. progress 9. promotion 11. advancement, development, improvement
furtherer... 7. abettor 8. promoter
furthermore... 3. and, yet 4. then 5. again 7. au reste, besides 8. moreover 10. in addition 12. additionally
furtive... 3. sly 4. wary 6. covert, secret, sneaky, stolen 8. skulking, stealthy 9. deceitful 11. clandestine
fury... 3. ire 4. rage 5. anger, wrath 6. frenzy 7. madness 8. violence 10. excitement, turbulence 13. desperateness
Fury... 6. Erinys, Spirit (avenging) 7. Atropos
furze... 4. Ulex, whin 5. gorse, shrub
fuse... 4. flux, frit (partly), melt 5. blend, smelt, unite 6. anneal, mingle, solder 7. combine, liquefy 8. dissolve 9. detonator
fusee... 5. flair, torch 6. signal
fusion... 5. alloy, blend 7. melting,

mixture 8. fluidity 9. coalition 12. liquefaction 14. good–for–nothing
fuss... 3. ado 4. spat, to–do 5. busle 6. bother, bustle, pother, tumult 7. bombast, dispute, quarrel, trouble 9. confusion
fussy... 7. finical 8. overnice 9. fastidious, meticulous
fustian... 4. rant 5. cloth, tumid 7. bombast, pompous 8. claptrap, inflated 9. bombastic, worthless
fustic... 3. dye 5. amber, morin 7. dyewood
futile... 4. idle, vain 6. otiose 7. trivial 8. hopeless 11. ineffectual
futility... 8. nugacity 10. invalidity 11. uselessness
future... 3. yet 4. to be 5. later, still, tense 6. fiancé 8. expected, intended 9. hereafter 11. prospective
fuzzy... 5. downy, hairy 6. fluffy 7. blurred, frizzly 9. imperfect 10. indistinct
fyke... 3. net 6. bag net
fylfot... 8. swastika 9. gammadion

G

G... 4. tone (scale) 6. letter (7th)
Ga... 7. Negroes (Gold Coast)
gab... 3. lie 4. mock, talk 5. boast, mouth, prate, scoff, taste 6. tongue 7. chatter, deceive 9. utterance
gabardine... 6. cotton, woolen
gabble... 4. chat 6. babble, gabble, jabber, mumble 7. chatter 8. nonsense
gabelle... 3. tax 5. likin (imports) 6. excise, impost
gaberdine... 4. gown 5. frock 6. mantle 7. garment (loose) 8. covering, pinafore 9. gabardine
gable... 6. roof (part) 7. aileron (half) 8. pediment
gablock... 4. gaff, spur 5. spear 6. gaffle 7. crowbar 8. gavelock
Gabriel (pert to)...
 astrology.. 10. moon spirit
 New Test.. 6. herald 11. good tidings
 Old Test.. 5. angel
 tradition.. 9. archangel (one of seven), messenger
gaby... 4. fool 9. simpleton
gad... 3. bar, God (oath), rod 4. goad, roam, rove, whip 5. ingot, spear, staff 6. billet, chisel, wander 7. on the go, run wild, traipse (trapes) 8. gadabout 9. gallivant
Gad (pert to)...
 Bib.. 7. prophet
 deity (Bib).. 7. Fortune
 father.. 5. Jacob
 tribe.. 6. Gadite, Israel (one of seven)

gadabout... 3. gad 6. roving 7. dogcart, gadding, on the go, traipse (trapes)
Gaddang, Gaddan... 7. Malayan 8. language (Indonesia)
gadfly... 6. botfly, insect 8. horsefly
gadget... 6. device, jigger 7. gimmick 8. gimcrack 11. contrivance, thingumajig
Gadsden Purchase (1853)... 5. tract 7. Arizona 9. New Mexico (parts of each State)
gadwell... 4. duck
Gaea, Gaia... 12. Earth goddess
Gael... 4. Celt, Kelt, Manx, Scot 10. Highlander
Gaelic (pert to)...
 for John.. 3. Ian
 hero.. 6. Ossian
 language.. 4. Erse
 native.. 4. Erse 5. Irish 6. Celtic, Keltic, Scotch
 pagan god.. 5. Dagda (harpist)
 sea god.. 3. Ler
 spirit.. 7. banshee
 warriors.. 7. Fenians
gaff... 4. hoax, hook, spar, spur, talk 5. fraud, spear, trick 6. deceit, fleece, gamble 7. chatter, prating 8. trickery 9. spearhead
gag... 4. hoax, joke 5. choke, retch 7. closure, prevent, shackle 8. obstruct, restrain, silencer 9. imposture 10. instrument 13. interpolation

gage, gauge... 4. rule, test 5. scale
  6. device, pledge 7. measure
  8. capacity, defiance, diameter
  (firearm), mortgage, security
  9. challenge 11. measurement
gaggle... 5. flock (geese), group
  (women) 6. cackle
gaiety, gayety... 4. gala, glee, show
  5. mirth 6. finery 7. begonia, jollity
  8. vivacity 9. festivity, merriment,
  showiness 10. liveliness
  12. colorfulness, conviviality
  13. sprightliness
gain... 3. get, net, win 4. earn, pelf,
  reap 5. booty, clear, lucre, reach
  6. attain, come by, obtain, profit,
  secure, trover 7. acquire, benefit,
  procure, realize 8. addition, arrive at,
  increase 9. advantage 11. acquisition
  12. accumulation 13. amplification
gainsay... 4. deny 6. forbid, impugn,
  oppose, refute 7. dispute
  10. contradict, controvert
gait... 3. run, way 4. lope, pace, trip,
  trot, walk 5. amble, order, strut,
  tread 6. canter, gallop 8. slowness,
  velocity
gaiter... 4. boot, spat 5. strad
  6. puttee 7. legging 8. overshoe
  11. galligaskin
gala... 4. fete, pomp 5. festal, fiesta,
  gaiety 8. festival 9. festivity
  11. celebration
Galago... 5. lemur
Galatea... 7. heroine 8. sea nymph
  9. sculpture (Pygmalion)
  11. shepherdess
galaxy... 6. throng 8. Milky Way
  10. assemblage 11. celebrities
gale... 4. gust, wind 5. storm
  8. outburst 9. hurricane
galea... 6. helmet
galeate... 8. helmeted
  12. helmet–shaped
Galen (Gr)... 9. physician
Galilean (pert to)...
  astronomer.. 7. Galileo
  province.. 9. Palestine
  religion.. 9. Christian
  town.. 4. Cana (1st miracle)
  8. Tiberias
gall... 3. vex 4. bile, fret 5. annoy,
  chafe, grate, spite 6. bitter, harass,
  rancor 8. irritate 9. impudence,
  secretion, virulence
gallant... 4. hero 5. dandy, lover,
  noble, spark, swain 6. escort, suitor
  7. stately 8. cavalier, cicisbeo
  9. attentive, courteous
  10. chivalrous, courageous
  16. cavalier servente
gallantry... 7. bravery, courage, display
  8. courtesy 9. courtship
  11. intrepidity
galleon... 6. vessel (sailing)
gallery... 3. poy 4. hall 5. salon
  6. dedans, loggia, museum
  7. passage, veranda 8. audience,
  corridor, platform 9. promenade
  10. ambulatory 11. observatory
galley... 4. boat, tray 6. vessel
  7. caboose, caravel (caravelle),

  dromond, kitchen 8. cookroom
galley, Roman...
  one–bank oared.. 7. unireme
  three–bank oared.. 7. trireme
  two–bank oared.. 6. bireme
  six–bank oared.. 7. hexeris
  slave.. 5. rower 6. drudge
Gallic... 4. Gaul 6. French 7. Frenchy
Gallic chariot... 5. essed
gallimaufry... 4. hash, olio, stew
  6. medley, ragout 9. potpourri
  10. hodgepodge
gallipot... 6. vessel (Medit) 8. druggist
gallo... 7. rooster 12. fighting cock
gallop... 3. run 4. lope, ride 6. canter
  7. tantivy
gallopade... 5. dance, galop 6. curvet
  (manège)
gam... 3. leg 4. herd 5. visit
  6. school
gambit... 4. move 7. comment,
  opening (chess) 8. maneuver
  9. launching 10. concession
gamble... 3. bet 4. dice, game, risk
  5. stake, wager 6. chance, hazard,
  plunge 9. speculate 11. uncertainty
gambler... 5. shill 7. sharper
gambol... 3. hop 5. bound, caper,
  prank 6. cavort, curvet, frolic
Gambrinus (King)... 6. brewer (1st)
game... 4. lark, play, prey 5. brave,
  dodge, prank, sport 6. frolic, gamble,
  gritty, plucky, quarry 7. contest,
  pastime 8. resolute 9. amusement,
  diversion 10. courageous
game, ball... 4. golf, polo, pool
  5. Rugby 6. hockey, pelota, soccer,
  squash, tennis 7. cricket, croquet
  8. baseball, football
game, beans... 6. fan–tan 8. beanbags
game, board... 4. keno 5. bingo,
  chess, lotto 7. pachisi (parchesi)
  8. checkers, cribbage
  10. backgammon
game, card... 3. gin, pam 4. bank,
  faro, skat 5. pitch, poker, rummy,
  whist 6. bridge, écarté, flinch, hearts
  7. bezique, canasta, cassino, old
  maid, seven–up
game, club... 4. golf 6. hockey
  7. cricket
game, court... 6. pelota, squash,
  tennis 7. jai alai 9. badminton
game, ring... 6. quoits
game, parlor... 5. jacks 7. marbles
  8. charades, dominoes
  11. tiddlywinks
gamin... 3. tad 4. serf 6. urchin
  7. mudlark
gamut... 5. orbit, range 6. extent
  7. compass
gamy... 4. game 7. lustful 8. sporting
  12. high–flavored
gander... 5. goose 6. stroll
  9. simpleton
Gandhi (Hind)... 6. leader 7. Mahatma
  (Mohandus)
gang... 3. mob, set 4. band, crew,
  pack, team, walk (cattle) 5. group,
  horde, sheet (Print), shift 6. clique
  7. company 9. pasturage
Ganges dolphin... 4. susu

gangling... 5. lanky 9. spindling
gangrene... 5. decay 6. slough
   8. necrosis 9. sphacelus
   13. mortification
gangster... 4. thug 5. thief 6. bandit
   7. mobster 8. criminal, hireling
   9. racketeer
gannet... 4. ibis, Sula 5. booby,
   goose, solan 6. gander
gap... 3. col 4. hole, pass 5. break,
   chasm, cleft, fault, meuse, shard,
   space, split 6. breach, hiatus,
   lacuna, lacune, ravine 7. opening
gaping... 5. agape 6. chappy
   7. ringent, yawning 9. expectant
garb... 5. array, dress, habit, style
   6. clothe 7. apparel, costume,
   fashion, raiment, uniform 8. clothing
   10. appearance, habiliment
garbed... 5. clad 7. attired, dressed,
   habited
garble... 5. alloy 6. mangle 7. distort,
   falsify, pervert 8. mutilate
   12. misinterpret, misrepresent,
   sophisticate
garden... 3. bed 4. yard 5. hardy,
   patch 6. jardin, verger 7. topiary
   8. outfield 9. arboretum, cultivate,
   enclosure, herbarium
garden (pert to)...
   Berlin.. 10. Tiergarten
   Bible.. 4. Eden
   city.. 4. Kent 6. Sicily 7. Chicago
      8. Touraine
   colony.. 5. Natal
   Colorado.. 9. of the Gods
   Kansas.. 9. of the West
   kind of.. 5. truck 8. kaleyard
      9. botanical 10. zoological
   State.. 9. New Jersey
garden implement... 3. hoe 4. fork,
   rake 5. graip, mower 6. scythe,
   sickle, trowel, weeder
Garfield's death site... 7. Elberon
   (NJ)
Gargantua (pert to)...
   character.. 4. King (Rabelais romance)
   son.. 10. Pantagruel (giant)
gargantuan... 4. huge 7. titanic
garish... 5. gaudy, showy 7. flighty,
   glaring 8. dazzling
garland... 3. lei 6. anadem, circle,
   corona, fillet, rosary, trophy, wreath
   7. chaplet, coronal, festoon
   8. headband 9. anthology
   11. compilation
garlic... 4. herb, moly 5. clove
   6. ramson
garment... 4. cape, coat, gown, robe,
   suit, vest, wrap 5. cloak, dress,
   frock, shift, simar, smock, stole, tunic
   6. coatee, duster 7. pelisse, raiment,
   surcoat, topcoat 8. overcoat,
   vestment
garment (pert to)...
   African.. 6. kaross
   ancient.. 5. burel
   Arab.. 3. aba
   clerical.. 3. alb 5. amice 6. chimer
      7. cassock, zimarra 8. surplice
   cover.. 5. apron 8. overalls, pinafore
      9. coveralls

Eskimo.. 5. parka
Jewish.. 5. ephod
knight's.. 6. tabard
patchwork.. 5. cento
thin.. 8. gossamer
garner... 4. reap 5. amass, store
   6. gather 7. collect 10. accumulate
garnet... 3. gem, red 5. color
   6. aplome, pyrope 7. olivine (green)
   8. cinnamon (stone), essonite
   (yellow), melanite (black)
   9. almandine (almandite, dark red),
   uvarovite (green)
garnish... 4. trim 5. adorn 6. attach,
   bedeck 7. fetters 8. decorate,
   ornament
garnishment... 4. lien 7. summons
   8. ornament 10. attachment,
   decoration
garret... 4. loft 5. attic 6. turret
   8. cockloft 10. watchtower
garrot... 5. goldeneye (duck)
   10. tourniquet
garrote, garrotte... 8. strangle
   9. execution 10. throttling
   13. strangulation
garrulous... 5. gabby, wordy 6. chatty
   7. diffuse 9. talkative 10. loquacious
gas... 4. brag, talk 5. vapor 6. poison
   7. chatter 8. gasoline, nonsense
   10. anesthesia, asphyxiate, illuminant
   11. anesthetize
gas... 3. air 4. neon 5. argon, ether,
   ozone, radon, xenon 6. arsine,
   butane, ethane, helium, ketene,
   nebula (luminous), oxygen 7. methane
   8. chlorine, cyanogen, etherion,
   hydrogen, nitrogen 9. butadiene
gascon... 7. boaster 8. braggart
   11. braggadocio 12. swashbuckler
gasconade... 4. brag 5. boast
   7. bluster, bravado 11. fanfaronade,
   rodomontade
gaseous... 4. smog, thin 5. smoke
   7. tenuous 8. vaporous
   13. unsubstantial
gash... 3. cut 5. cleft, notch, sever,
   slash 6. furrow, gossip, injury, tattle
   8. incision
gasp... 3. say 4. pant, yawn 5. utter
   7. breathe
gasping... 5. agasp 7. panting
gastropod... 4. slug 5. Harpa, Murex,
   Oliva, snail, whelk 6. Nerita, volute
   7. abalone, mollusk 8. sea snail
gat... 3. gun, rod 7. channel, passage
   8. revolver
gate... 3. dar 4. door, hole, pass
   5. start (racing), toran, valve
   6. defile, portal 7. barrier, opening,
   postern 8. Lion–Gate 9. floodgate,
   turnstile 10. Needle's Eye
   (Jerusalem), portcullis
gateau... 4. cake
gather... 4. bale, brew, fold, meet,
   reap 5. amass, glean, pleat, rally,
   shirr 6. bundle, deduce, garner,
   muster, pucker 7. acquire, collect,
   compile, convene, convoke, harvest,
   procure, suppose 8. assemble
   10. accumulate
gatherer, collector of...

coins.. 11. numismatist
money.. 5. miser
news.. 8. reporter 10. journalist
stamps.. 11. philatelist
gathering... 3. sum 4. stag 5. crowd,
party, troop 6. galaxy, smoker
7. abscess, meeting 8. swelling
10. assemblage, harvesting
11. contraction 12. accumulation,
congregation 14. conglomeration
gaucho... 6. cowboy (pampas)
8. herdsman, horseman
gaucho weapon... 4. bola
gaud... 4. jest, joke 5. adorn, fraud,
paint, sport, trick 6. finery, flashy,
gewgaw 7. trinket 8. artifice,
ornament
gaudy... 4. fine, loud 5. cheap, feast,
showy 6. flashy, flimsy, garish,
tawdry, tinsel 7. glaring, trinket
9. flaunting 11. pretentious
12. meretricious, ostentatious
13. overdeveloped
gaufre... 4. iron (waffle) 6. waffle
gauge, gage... 4. norm, rate, rule, size
5. judge, scale, value 6. assess
7. measure 8. estimate
gauge (pert to)...
airplane.. 10. tachometer
distance.. 10. micrometer
miles.. 8. odometer
pointer.. 3. arm
rain.. 8. udometer
velocity.. 11. speedometer
wind.. 10. anemometer
Gaul... 5. Aedui 6. France, Gallia
9. Frenchman
Gauls... 4. Remi 5. Celts, Cymry
gaunt... 4. bony, lank, lean, thin, ugly
5. spare 7. haggard 8. desolate
gauntlet... 4. cuff 5. armor (part),
glove 7. bandage
gaur... 5. gayal 7. buffalo
gauss... 4. unit (Elec)
Gauss... 13. mathematician
gauze... 4. haze, leno 5. crape, lisse,
marli (marly) 6. barege, filter, tissue
8. dressing
gauze film on wine... 8. beeswing
gavage... 7. feeding
gave... see *give*
Gavia... 5. loon
gavial... 11. crocodilian
gaw... 4. gape 5. drain 6. trench
gawk... 4. dolt, gowk, left, lout
5. booby, stare 9. simpleton
gawky... 6. clumsy, cuckoo, stupid
7. awkward, foolish 8. clownish
gay... 4. airy, glad 5. drunk, gaudy,
jolly, merry, riant, showy 6. blithe,
cheery, jovial, joyful, joyous, lively
7. dashing, festive, gleeful
8. cheerful, colorful, rory–tory,
sportive 9. convivial, sprightly,
vivacious 10. frolicsome, profligate
12. lighthearted
gay time... 4. lark 5. spree
8. jamboree
gazabo, gazebo... 4. cony 6. rabbit,
turret 7. balcony, blunder, whopper
11. summerhouse
gaze... 3. con, eye 4. gape, look,

moon, peer, pore, scan 5. glare,
gloat, stare 6. glower, regard
gazelle... 3. ahu, goa 4. admi, cora,
dama, kudu, mohr, oryx 5. ariel,
brown, korin 7. chikara (4–horn),
corinne, dibatag 8. antelope
9. springbok
gazette... 7. journal, publish
8. announce 9. newspaper
15. Arkansas Gazette (1819)
gazetteer... 7. newsman 9. newspaper
10. dictionary
gear... 3. cam, rig 5. equip, goods,
tools, wheel 6. things 7. baggage,
conform, harness, rigging 8. adjust
to, clothing, cogwheel, garments
9. equipment, mechanism, trappings,
vestments 10. appliances, implements
gecko... 6. lizard 7. tarente
geese... 5. brant, quink, solan
geese (pert to)...
fat.. 6. axunge
flock.. 4. raft 6. gaggle
genus.. 4. Chen 5. Anser 6. Branta
Gekko... 6. lizard
gelatin, gelatine... 4. agar, food, jell
5. jelly 6. collin 7. protein
8. agar–agar
gelid... 3. icy 4. cold 6. frozen
gem... 4. jade, onyx, opal, ruby, sard,
type 5. agate, beryl, jewel, pearl,
stone, topaz 6. garnet, ligure, spinel,
zircon 7. cat's–eye, diamond,
emerald, jacinth 8. amethyst,
hawk's–eye, sapphire 9. carnelian,
moonstone 10. aquamarine
11. alexandrite, lapis lazuli 12. star
sapphire
gem (pert to)...
artificial.. 5. paste
carver.. 8. lapidary
Egyptian.. 6. scarab
flaw.. 8. gendarme
food.. 6. muffin
imperfect.. 5. loupe
semiprecious.. 5. cameo 8. intaglio
six rays.. 7. asteria
surface.. 5. bezel, facet
weight.. 5. carat
gemel... 4. bars (Her), twin 6. paired
7. coupled, doubled
gemsbok... 4. goat, oryx 7. chamois
Gem State... 5. Idaho
gendarme... 4. blue, flaw (gem)
5. guard 6. police 7. soldier, trooper
9. policeman 10. cavalryman
gender... 3. sex 5. breed, genus
7. grammar (term) 8. engender
genealogy... 4. tree 5. order (of
descent) 6. family 7. account,
history, lineage, peerage, progeny
8. pedigree, register 9. offspring
genealogy of the gods... 8. theogony
gener... 8. son–in–law
general... 5. gross, usual, vague,
whole 6. common, public 7. officer
8. catholic, communal 9. extensive,
prevalent, universal, well–known
10. encyclical, indefinite
11. approximate
general (pert to)...
agreement.. 5. chief, court

aspect.. 6. facies
chief.. 6. Führer, Il Duce 9. president
  10. Grand Mogul 13. Generalissimo
court.. 5. Synod
direction.. 5. tenor, trend 6. course
favor.. 7. popular 10. popularity
feature.. 5. motif
group.. 8. ensemble
orders.. 7. routine
rule.. 5. canon
summary.. 8. synopsis
type.. 7. average
generalize... 5. widen 6. extend,
  reason, spread 7. broaden
  12. universalize
General Sherman (pert to)...
  Civil War march.. 15. Atlanta to the
  Sea
  giant trees.. 8. sequoias
  tree.. 10. eucalyptus
generate... 5. beget, breed, cause
  6. create 7. develop, produce
  8. engender 9. originate, procreate,
  propagate
generation... 3. age 7. descent
  8. lifetime 9. epigonous (later),
  formation, genealogy 10. production
  11. abiogenesis, procreation
generosity... 10. liberality
  11. hospitality, magnanimity,
  munificence
generous... 4. free 5. large 7. liberal
  8. tolerant 9. indulgent, plentiful,
  unstinted 10. hospitable
  11. magnanimous
genesis... 4. Book 5. birth 6. origin
  (of races) 8. nascency 9. beginning,
  ethnology, etymology, inception
  10. generation
genet... 3. fur 5. civet
genethliac... 5. stars (influence)
  9. birthdays
Geneva Cross... 8. Red Cross
genial... 4. warm 5. bland 6. jovial,
  kindly 7. amiable, festive, nuptial
  8. cheerful, friendly, pleasant
  9. expansive 10. enlivening
geniculate... 5. kneel
genie... 4. jinn 6. genius
genius... 5. deity, jinni 6. talent
  7. ability, prodigy 9. endowment
  (supreme) 11. inspiration
  12. intelligence
Genoa lace... 4. tape 6. bobbin
  7. macramé 13. gold and silver
genos... 4. clan, gens, race
genre... 3. art (style) 4. kind, sort
  5. genus 6. gender 7. species
  8. category
genteel... 6. polite 7. refined
  8. wellborn, well-bred
Gentiles... 6. goyims 10. Christians,
  non-Moslems
  14. non-Mohammedans
gentle... 4. calm, easy, meek, mild,
  soft, tame 5. bland, suave 6. docile,
  humane, kindly, tender 7. amabile
  (Mus), clement, genteel, refined,
  subdued 8. moderate, peaceful,
  soothing, tranquil, wellborn
  9. courteous, honorable, temperate,
  tractable 10. chivalrous

  11. considerate 13. compassionate
gentleman... 3. sir 6. knight
  7. esquire, shoneen (would-be),
  younker 8. nobleman
gentleness... 6. lenity 8. elegance,
  leniency, meekness, softness
  9. lightness 10. kindliness,
  moderation 11. genteelness
genuflect... 5. kneel 6. curtsy
genuine... 4. pure, real, true 5. frank,
  pucka (pukka) 7. germane, sincere
  8. existent 9. authentic, simon-pure,
  unalloyed, veritable 10. unaffected
  13. unadulterated
genus... 4. kind, sort 5. class, order
genus, animal life...
  animals (one-celled).. 6. Amoeba
  8. Protozoa 9. Rhizopoda
  ants.. 6. Eciton
  apes.. 5. Simia
  armadillos.. 9. Glyptodon
  auks.. 4. Alle
  bears.. 5. Ursus
  bees (honey).. 4. Apis
  beetles.. 10. Coleoptera
  birds.. 7. Ratitae
  bivalve mollusks.. 6. Anomia
  8. Estheria
  bugs (long-legged).. 5. Emesa
  cats.. 5. Felis
  cattle.. 3. Bos
  crabs.. 4. Maia
  dogs.. 5. Canis
  ducks.. 3. Aix 4. Anas 7. Harelda
  8. Clangula
  elks.. 5. Alces
  fish.. 6. Cybium, Remora 7. Girella,
  Muraena
  flies.. 6. Asilus 8. Glossina (tsetse)
  frogs.. 4. Rana 5. Anura 8. Amphibia
  9. Batrachia
  geese.. 4. Chen 5. Anser
  goats.. 5. Capra
  gulls.. 4. Xema
  herons.. 7. Egretta
  hogs.. 3. Sus
  horses.. 5. Equus
  insects.. 10. Coleoptera
  lemurs.. 6. Galago
  lizards.. 3. Uta 5. Agama
  mammals.. 4. Homo
  Man.. 11. Homo sapiens
  marten.. 7. Mustela
  mice.. 3. Mus
  monkeys (spider).. 6. Ateles
  moose.. 5. Alces
  moths.. 5. Tinea
  oysters.. 6. Ostrea
  peacocks.. 4. Pavo
  pigeons (crowned).. 5. Goura
  porcupines.. 7. Hystrix
  porpoise.. 4. Inia
  rats.. 6. Spalax
  roadrunners.. 9. Geococcyx
  scorpions.. 4. Nepa
  seabirds.. 4. Sula
  sloths.. 11. Megatherium
  slugs.. 5. Arion
  snails.. 5. Mitra 6. Nerita, Triton
  8. Geophila
  snakes.. 4. Eryx (sand) 7. Ophidia
  spiders.. 7. Agalena

squirrels.. 7. Sciurus
swans.. 4. Olar 6. Cygnus
ticks.. 6. Ixodes
tortoises.. 4. Emys
turkeys.. 4. Meleagris
wasps.. 5. Vespa
whales.. 4. Orca 5. Areta
   9. Sibbaldus (blue)
genus, plant life..
algae (blue–green).. 10. Gloeocapsa
apple trees.. 5. Malus
cabbage.. 3. Cos
currant.. 5. Ribes
elms.. 5. Ulmus
evergreen, heaths.. 5. Erica
fern.. 6. Anemia
fungi.. 7. Boletus 10. geoglossum
grasses.. 3. Poa (blue) 5. Avena
   6. Elymus 7. Setaria
herbs.. 4. Arum 6. Asarum, Asitis
   (mustard), Cassia, Seseli
   7. Hedeoma, Linaria 8. Solidago
holly.. 4. Ilex
ipecac.. 5. Evea
ivy.. 11. Hedera helix
lily.. 7. Bessera
maples.. 4. Acer
olives.. 4. Olea
orchids.. 5. Vanda 7. Listera
palms.. 5. Areca, Assai 6. Bacaba
poplar.. 5. Alamo
rhubarb.. 5. Rheum
vines (woody).. 6. Hedera
geode... 3. vug (vugg, vugh, voog)
   5. druse 6. nodule
geological (pert to)...
division.. 3. eon, era
era.. 6. Eocene 7. Miocene
   8. Cenozoic, Mesozoic 9. Paleozoic
   11. Archaeozoic
period.. 4. Dyas, Lias 5. Trias
prelife.. 5. Azoic
zone (fossil).. 6. assise
geologist... 6. Strabo (anc Gr)
   8. geognost 12. mineralogist
geometric (pert to)...
angle.. 9. incidence
axis.. 8. abscissa
contact.. 10. osculation
curve.. 6. spiral 7. evolute
pottery.. 7. Dipylon (anc)
geometric figure... 4. cone, cube,
   lune 5. prism 6. gnomon, oblong,
   square 7. hexagon, octagon, polygon,
   rhombus 8. heptagon, pentagon,
   triangle 9. rectangle, trapezoid
   10. quadrangle 13. parallelogram
geometric proposition (pert to)...
ratio.. 2. pi (3.1416)
surface.. 4. tore 5. nappe
term.. 4. sine 5. locus 6. secant
   7. tangent 11. asses' bridge
geometry (pert to)...
figure.. 6. conoid 9. ellipsoid
   10. paraboloid
mathematician.. 6. Euclid, Pascal
proposition.. 6. porism
geoponic.. 5. rural 6. rustic
Georgia...
capital.. 7. Atlanta
city.. 5. Macon 7. Augusta

   8. Columbus, Marietta, Savannah
   9. Brunswick
holiday.. 10. Georgia Day (Feb 12)
memorial.. 11. Warm Springs
   16. Little White House (FDR)
mountain.. 7. Lookout 9. Blue Ridge
   11. Alleghenies
peak.. 9. High Point 13. Brasstown
   Bald
river.. 8. Savannah, Suwannee
settler (1st).. 10. Oglethorpe
State admission.. 6. Fourth
State nickname.. 5. Peach 7. Cracker
   16. Empire of the South
swamp.. 10. Okefenokee
Georgian of the Caucasus... 4. Svan
georgic.. 4. poem (rural)
geosphere... 5. earth
Geraint, Sir.. 6. Knight (Round Table)
germ... 3. bud 4. ovum, seed
   5. spore 6. embryo, origin
   7. microbe 8. bacteria (pl)
   9. bacterium 13. microorganism
germ (free)... 7. aseptic 10. antiseptic
German... 3. Hun 5. Boche, jerry
   6. Almain (Alman), Teuton
   9. Deutscher
German (pert to)... see also Germany
air force.. 9. Luftwaffe
airplane.. 5. Gotha, Stuka 7. Dornier,
   Heinkel, Junkers 13. Messerschmitt
article.. 3. das, der, ein
battleship.. 8. Graf Spee (1939)
beverage.. 5. lager
cake.. 5. torte
castle.. 7. schloss
Christmas.. 11. Weihnachten
dance.. 9. allemande
drinking salute.. 6. prosit
folklore.. 5. gnome 6. kobold
gun.. 6. Bertha (Big)
hail.. 4. heil
highway.. 8. autobahn
knight.. 6. Ritter (title)
language.. 7. Deutsch
law.. 5. Salic
league.. 4. Bund 6. Verein
   9. Hanseatic 10. Turnverein
letter.. 4. rune
lyric poems.. 6. lieder
mister.. 4. Herr
ox (wild).. 4. urus
parliament.. 9. Bundestag, Reichstag
people.. 5. Quadi 6. Franks, Saxons
   7. Teutons, Vandals 8. Lombards
   9. Prussians 10. Herminones
police.. 7. Gestapo
prison.. 6. stalag
society.. see league (above)
song.. 4. lied
student set.. 7. Kommers
teacher.. 6. docent 12. privatdocent
title.. 3. Von 4. Graf, Herr 6. Ritter
tribal group.. 3. gau
union.. 7. Auschluss
vowel change.. 6. umlaut
wheat.. 5. spelt
wine.. 4. wein 5. Rhine 7. Moselle
woman.. 4. frau 8. fraulein
yes.. 2. ja
germane... 4. akin 6. allied 7. kindred
   8. relevant 11. appropriate

German people (famed)...
actor.. 8. Jannings (Emil)
astrologer.. 5. Faust
astronomer.. 5. Galle 6. Kepler
author.. 4. Dahn 5. Ebers
   8. Brentano
bacteriologist.. 4. Koch (Nobel Prize, 1905)
biographer.. 6. Ludwig
chemist.. 6. Bunsen
composer.. 3. Abt 4. Bach 5. Hasse
   6. Handel, Wagner
deity.. 5. Donar (thunder)
educator.. 5. Grimm 6. Beneke
   7. Francke
Egyptologist.. 5. Ebers
general.. 6. Rommel
geographer.. 6. Ritter
Gestapo chief.. 7. Himmler
goldsmith (anc).. 5. Faust
historian.. 4. Dahn 5. Moser
   7. Neander (Eccl)
inventor.. 6. Diesel
metaphysician.. 4. Kant 5. Lange
mystic.. 7. Eckhart
naturalist.. 9. Ehrenberg
neurologist.. 5. Ebing 6. Krafft
painter.. 5. Durer 7. Lessing
pathologist.. 6. Eberth
philologist.. 5. Grimm, Heyne
philosopher.. 4. Elze 5. Groos, Hegel, Weber 6. Ritter 8. Spengler
   9. Feuerbach
physician.. 8. Hufeland
physicist.. 3. Ohm 5. Weber
   6. Franck 7. Doppler 10. Fahrenheit
pianist.. 5. Bauer
poet.. 4. Elze 5. Heine 6. Goethe, Uhland 7. Lessing 8. Schiller
president (first).. 5. Ebert
sculptor.. 5. Begas
Socialist.. 10. Liebknecht
theologian.. 5. Bauer 6. Spener (Pietist) 7. Francke

Germany...
capital.. 4. Bonn 6. Berlin
cathedral town.. 5. Essen
city.. 3. Ulm 4. Bonn, Gera
   5. Baden, Emden, Essen, Gotha
   6. Munich
coal region.. 4. Ruhr, Saar 6. Aachen
East.. 10. Third Reich
empire.. 14. Deutsches Reich
kingdom.. 6. Saxony 7. Bavaria, Hanover
lake.. 9. Constance
leader.. 6. Hitler (Fuehrer), Kaiser
   13. von Hindenburg
mountain.. 4. Harz
port.. 5. Emden
river.. 3. Aar 4. Elbe, Iser, Oder, Ruhr 5. Rhine, Saale
steel region.. 5. Essen
West.. 15. Federal Republic
wine (white).. 4. hock

germicide... 6. iodine (iodin), phenol
   10. antiseptic 12. disinfectant
germinate... 3. bud 4. grow 5. beget
   6. sprout 7. develop 8. vegetate
   10. effloresce
Geronimo... 6. Apache (Chief)
gerrymander (Polit)... 6. divide (unfairly)

10. manipulate
gesticulation... 6. motion 7. gesture
gesture... 3. act 4. gest (geste), sign
   5. sanna 6. beckon, behave, motion
   7. perform, pretext 8. carriage (body)
   11. gesticulate 13. gesticulation
get... 3. pen, win 4. earn, hear, pain, take, trap 5. beget, fetch, incur, learn 6. attain, become, derive, induce, obtain, profit, secure
   7. achieve, acquire, capture, prepare, procure, receive 8. contract, contrive, discover 9. ascertain, determine
   10. understand
get along... 3. age 5. hurry
   6. begone, depart, manage, move on
   7. advance, prosper
get around... 5. evade 6. cajole, outwit, spread 7. deceive 9. circulate
   10. circumvent
get off... 5. start, utter 6. alight, depart, escape, go free 8. dismount
get out... 4. exit 5. scram 6. elicit, escape, reveal 7. draw out, leak out, publish 8. evacuate 9. extricate
get over... 4. move 5. cover
   6. bridge, finish 7. recover
   8. surmount 9. make clear
Ghana, capital of... 5. Accra (Gold Coast)
ghastly... 3. wan 4. grim, pale
   5. lurid 6. dismal, grisly, pallid
   7. deathly, hideous 8. gruesome, horrible, shocking, terrible
   9. deathlike, frightful 10. cadaverous
ghost... 3. Ker 5. larva (Rom Relig), lemur, shade, spook 6. daemon, spirit, wraith 7. banshee (banshie), eidolon, phantom, specter
   8. phantasm, revenant
   10. apparition, glimmering, substitute
   11. ghostwriter, poltergeist
ghostly... 5. eerie (eery) 8. spectral
   9. spiritual
giant... 4. huge, ogre 5. Titan
   6. afreet, nozzle, thurse 7. monster
   8. colossus 9. monstrous
   10. gargantuan, prodigious, tremendous
giant (pert to)...
Biblical.. 7. Goliath, Rephaim
classic.. 5. Atlas
crafty.. 5. Cacus
Greek.. 5. Mimas
hundred–armed.. 9. Enceladus
land, country.. 9. Utgarthar
   10. Jotunnheim 11. Brobdingnag
Norse.. 4. Ymir (Ymer) 5. Mimir
   6. Jotunn (Jotun) 12. Utgartha–Loki
one–eyed.. 5. Arges 7. Brontes,
   Cyclops 10. Polyphemus
primeval.. 4. Ymir 5. Titan
   12. Utgartha–Loki
rock.. 9. Gibraltar 13. Stone Mountain
   (Atlanta)
sea god.. 5. Aegir
seer.. 5. Mimir
strong.. 6. Samson, Targan
   7. Antaeus 8. Hercules
Teutonic.. 4. Wade 5. Aegir
thousand–armed.. 4. Bana
three–hundred handed, many–handed..

8. Briareus

giantess (Teut Myth)... 4. Norn

gibbed... 9. castrated (cat)

gibber... 4. chat, hump, talk (rapid)
5. stone (loose) 6. mumble
7. boulder, chatter 8. swelling

gibberish... 4. talk 5. lingo 6. jargon,
patois, patter 8. nonsense

gibbet... 3. jib 4. hang 7. gallows
9. execution

gibbon... 3. ape, lar 6. wou–wou
7. hoolock, siamang 10. anthropoid

gibe... 4. jape, jeer, jibe, quip 5. fleer,
flirt, flout, scoff, sneer, taunt
6. heckle

Gibraltar...
named for (legend).. 5. Gobir
ruled by.. 12. Great Britain
site.. 5. Spain (coast)

giddy... 4. reel 5. dizzy, tipsy, whirl
6. fickle 7. flighty 8. gyratory,
heedless 9. delirious
14. scatterbrained

gift... 4. alms, bent, boon, dole, free
5. bribe, grant, knack, token
6. legacy, talent 7. aptness, faculty,
largess (largesse), present
8. aptitude, blessing, donation,
gratuity 9. endowment, lagniappe
(lagnappe), readiness 11. serendipity
12. contribution

gifted... 7. endowed 8. talented

gigantic... 4. huge 5. giant, large,
titan 7. immense, mammoth
8. colossal, enormous 9. colossean,
monstrous 10. prodigious

giggle... 5. laugh (silly), te–hee
6. tee–hee, titter 7. chuckle, snicker,
snigger

Gila monster... 4. Gila 6. lizard

gild... 4. coat, lure 5. adorn, paint,
tempt 7. aureate, falsify 8. brighten
9. embellish

gilding... 4. gilt, gold 6. ormolu
7. coating 8. ornament, painting

gill... 5. brook, leach, organ, penny
6. tipple, valley, wattle 7. measure
10. sweetheart

gimcrackle... 3. fob, toy 5. showy
6. bauble, gewgaw, paltry, trifle
7. trinket 8. trumpery, whimwham
15. Jack–of–all–trades

gimlet... 3. awl 4. tool 5. drink
(mixed) 6. wimble

gimp... 5. orris (upholstery) 6. fabric,
thread, galloon 8. fishline,
trimming

gin... 4. game, sloe, tool, trap, whim
5. snare, trick 6. device, liquor,
scheme, thresh 7. machine
8. artifice, schnapps 11. contrivance

ginger... 3. pep 5. color 6. Asarum,
energy, lively, mettle, spirit
8. pungency, Zingiber 10. rootstalk

gingerbread... 4. cake 5. money
6. flimsy, frills, wealth 8. ornament
(tawdry) 11. superfluity

gingerly... 6. warily 7. charily
9. carefully, finically, guardedly
10. cautiously 12. fastidiously

gingham... 5. cloth 8. umbrella
(cheap)

gipsy... see *gypsy*

giraffe... 5. okapi 6. mammal, spinet
10. cameloopard 13. constellation

girasol, girasole... 4. opal
9. artichoke, sunflower

gird... 4. belt, bind, gibe, girt, sill
5. brace, equip, scoff, sneer
6. fasten, girdle, secure 7. enclose,
environ 8. surround 10. strengthen

girder... 4. beam 5. truss 6. timber
7. support

girdle... 3. obi 4. band, belt, cest,
ring, sash 6. cestus, cingle, circle,
corset 8. cincture, encircle
10. cummerbund

girdle bone... 12. sphenethmoid

Girdle of Venus (pert to)...
bridal.. 11. power of love
palmistry line.. 8. hysteria
11. nervousness

girl... 3. sis 4. bint, chit, dame, lass,
minx, miss 5. filly, sissy, skirt
6. damsel, female, giglet, hoyden
(hoiden), lassie, maiden, shiver, thrill,
tomboy 7. colleen, damosel, fillock,
ingénue, roebuck 10. sweetheart
11. maidservant

girlish... 4. pert 5. sissy 7. artless
8. immature, maidenly 10. flapperish

girt... 4. band 6. fasten, saddle
7. besiege 8. encircled

girth... 4. band, hoop, size 5. brace,
strap 6. girdle, saddle 7. measure
8. encircle 13. circumference

gist... 3. nub 4. core, crux, meat, pith
5. point (main) 7. essence, meaning

give... 3. gie 4. hand 5. endow,
grant, yield 6. accord, afford,
bestow, confer, devote, donate,
impart, remise, render, supply
7. present, proffer, provide
9. attribute, vouchsafe
10. administer, elasticity

give (pert to)...
and take.. 11. reciprocity
authority.. 7. empower
away.. 5. break, grant, marry, yield
6. bestow, betray 7. discard, divulge,
succumb 8. disclose 9. sacrifice
10. relinquish
back.. 4. echo 5. remit 6. recede,
remand, remise, retire, return
7. replace, restore, retreat
birth to.. 4. foal 5. calve 6. farrow,
mother 9. originate
expectation.. 7. promise
forth.. 4. emit 5. blaze 6. afford,
exhale 7. publish
information.. 4. tell 6. inform, report
7. divulge, publish 8. disclose
9. advertise
out.. 4. deal, emit 5. exude, issue,
print, utter (publicly) 6. report,
weaken 7. declare, publish, release
8. announce 9. apportion, circulate
prominence.. 4. star 7. feature
8. headline
up.. 4. cede, emit, fail, quit 5. demit,
waive, yield 6. betray, disuse, resign,
vacate 7. abandon, despair, succumb
8. abdicate, part with, renounce,
swear off 9. sacrifice, surrender

    10. relinquish

given... 5. dated, datum, fixed
    6. stated 7. assumed, granted
    8. accorded, addicted, bestowed,
    inclined, set forth 10. determined,
    disposed to

given (pert to)...
    by word of mouth.. 4. oral 5. parol
    name.. 7. surname
    particularly.. 9. specified

given (to)...
    experiment.. 7. empiric
    expression.. 13. demonstrative
    meditation.. 13. contemplative
    suspicion.. 9. querulent

giving... 6. ceding 7. largess (largesse)
    8. bestowing 10. conferring, liberality
    12. philanthropy, presentation
    13. administering

giving name to a country...
    8. eponymic

giving up... 8. yielding
    10. abandoning, despairing
    11. sacrificing 12. surrendering
    13. relinquishing

glacial (pert to)...
    deposit.. 6. placer 7. moraine
    direction.. 5. stoss (opp to lee)
    drift.. 8. diluvium
    dust.. 10. kryokonite
    erosion wall.. 6. cirque
    mill.. 6. moulin
    ridge.. 4. kame (Scot) 5. esker (eskar)
    snow.. 4. neve

glaciarium... 4. rink (skating)

glacis... 5. slope 7. incline
    13. fortification

glack... 4. fork (road) 6. defile, ravine,
    valley

glad... 3. gay 4. fain 5. merry
    6. elated, joyful, joyous 8. animated,
    cheering, pleasing 9. animating,
    beautiful, delighted, gratified
    11. exhilarated, well–pleased
    12. exhilarating

gladden... 5. cheer, elate 6. please
    7. gratify

gladdy... 12. yellowhammer

glade... 4. dell, nemo (comb form),
    vale 5. laund 6. valley 8. clearing
    9. everglade, open space

gladiator... 6. fencer 7. lanista

gladiator's arena... 4. ludi

gladly... 4. fain, lief 5. fitly 6. freely
    7. eagerly, readily 8. joyfully, properly
    9. willingly 10. cheerfully, preferably

gladsome... 4. glad 6. blithe, joyful
    7. festive, jocular, pleased
    8. cheerful

Gladstone... 3. bag (travel) 4. wine
    7. Liberal (Party) 8. carriage,
    Irishman 11. portmanteau

glad tidings... 3. joy 6. gospel
    7. evangel

glamorous... 8. alluring, charming
    10. bewitching 11. fascinating

glance... 3. eye 4. hint, leer, look,
    ogle, scry, skew 5. flash, gleam,
    glint, touch 6. allude, signal
    7. glimpse

gland... 5. gonad, liver, lymph, ovary
    6. spleen, thymus 7. adrenal,

    carotid, parotid, thyroid 8. pancreas,
    salivary 9. pituitary 10. suprarenal

gland (pert to)...
    enlargement.. 6. ademia
    full of.. 7. adenose
    glandlike.. 7. adenoid 9. glandular
    inflammation.. 8. adenitis
    secretion.. 7. hormone
    tumor.. 7. adenoma

glaring... 5. clear, plain 6. bright,
    garish 7. evident, flaring, obvious,
    staring, visible, vividly 8. apparent,
    distinct, flagrant, manifest
    9. barefaced 11. conspicuous

glass... 4. lens, pony 5. glaze, purex
    6. goblet, liquor, mirror, seidel
    7. binocle, crystal, reflect, tumbler
    9. barometer, binocular, hourglass,
    telescope 10. microscope, opera
    glass 11. stactometer, thermometer

glass (pert to)...
    blue.. 5. smalt
    device.. 7. ironman
    flask.. 7. matrass (mattrass)
    French for.. 5. verre
    furnace, oven.. 4. lehr (leer) 5. bocca,
    siege, tisar 7. drosser (part)
    like.. 6. vitric 8. vitreous
    material.. 4. frit (fritt)
    mineral.. 7. hyalite 8. feldspar
    molten.. 7. parison
    mosaic.. 7. tessera
    paste (jewelry).. 6. strass
    red.. 7. schmelz (schmelze)
    refuse.. 4. calx
    rod.. 5. punty (pontil)
    sheet.. 4. pane 5. slide 7. platten
    showcase.. 7. vitrine
    volcanic.. 6. pumice 8. obsidian
    worker.. 7. glazier

glass (type of)... 3. cut 4. milk
    6. safety 7. hobnail, Lalique, plastic,
    stained, Swedish 8. Fostoria,
    Sandwich, Venetian 9. Fiberglas,
    Plexiglas, Vitaglass

glass blowing (pert to)...
    annealing term.. 4. fuse, heat
    glass content.. 4. sand, zinc
    6. potash, temper 7. soda ash
    oven.. 4. lehr (leer)
    rod.. 5. punty (pontil)

glazier's diamond... 5. emery (emeril)

glazing machine... 8. calender

gleam... 3. ray 4. glow 5. flash, glint,
    gloze, light 7. glimmer, shimmer
    8. radiance 9. coruscate
    10. brightness

glean... 4. reap 5. sheaf (of hemp)
    6. bundle, deduce, gather 7. collect,
    harvest, procure

glee... 3. joy 4. club, song 5. mirth
    7. delight 8. pleasure 9. merriment
    12. cheerfulness

glen... 4. dale, dell, vale 6. dingle,
    ravine, valley 10. depression

glib... 4. easy, oily 5. suave 6. facile,
    fluent, smooth 8. castrate, flippant,
    slippery 9. talkative 10. loquacious

glide... 4. sail, skid, slip, soar
    5. coast, slide

gliding over... 7. lambent
    10. slithering

glimmer... 3. bit 4. hint, leam
5. blink, flash, gleam, glint
7. glimpse, glitter 10. perception
(slight)

glimpse... 4. view (quick) 5. flash,
tinge, trace 6. glance, luster
7. glimmer, inkling

glisten... 5. flash, shine 7. glister,
sparkle 9. coruscate

glitter... 5. glare, gleam, shine
7. glimmer, glisten, sparkle
9. coruscate, showiness
14. attractiveness

gloaming... 4. dusk 8. twilight
9. darkening 11. candlelight

globe... 3. map, orb 4. ball, moon
5. earth 6. sphere 10. hemisphere
(half)

Globe, The... 7. Theater (London, first
to play Shakespeare)

globular... 5. beady 7. globose
9. orbicular, spherical 10. orbiculate
11. globe-shaped

globule... 4. bead, blob, drop, pill,
tear 5. minim 6. bubble 8. spherule

glochis... 4. hair (barbed) 7. bristle

glockenspiel... 4. lyra, stop (organ)
8. carillon 10. instrument

gloom... 5. cloud, frown, scowl
7. dimness, sadness 8. darkness
9. dejection, heaviness, obscurity
10. cloudiness, depression,
melancholy, sullen look

gloomy... 3. dim, sad, wan 4. dark,
dour, glum 5. drear, eerie, lurid,
moody, murky 6. cloudy, droopy,
lowery, morose 7. obscure
8. darkling, dejected, dolesome,
downcast 9. darkening, depressed,
tenebrous 10. depressing, foreboding,
tenebrific 11. pessimistic
12. disheartened

Gloomy Dean... 4. Inge

gloomy person... 7. killjoy

Gloria... 4. rite 8. doxology

glorification... 6. praise 7. worship
8. doxology, honoring 9. festivity
10. apotheosis 13. jollification
14. sanctification

glorify... 4. laud 5. adore, bless, exalt,
extol, honor 6. praise 7. elevate,
worship 8. beautify, sanctify
9. celebrate

glorious... 3. sri 5. grand, noble
6. elated, superb 7. eminent, radiant
8. ecstatic, renowned, splendid
9. beautiful, hilarious 10. celebrated,
delightful 11. illustrious, magnificent,
resplendent 12. praiseworthy

glory... 4. fame, halo 5. bliss
(celestial), boast, éclat, honor
6. heaven, nimbus (cloud of), praise,
renown 8. grandeur 10. admiration,
brilliancy, effulgence 11. distinction
13. glorification

gloss... 4. glow 5. color, sheen, shine
6. enamel, luster, polish, remark
7. burnish, pretext 8. glossary,
palliate 9. extenuate 10. brightness,
commentary 14. interpretation

gloss over... 4. fard (obs), wink
5. blink, color 6. excuse 8. palliate

glossy... 5. glacé, nitid, shiny, sleek
6. luster, sheeny, smooth 7. radiant,
shining 8. lustrous, polished
10. reflecting

glove... 3. mit 4. mitt 5. trank
(shaped) 6. boxing, ceatus, mitten
7. gantlet 8. gauntlet
12. mousquetaire

glow... 4. burn 5. ardor, flame, flush,
glean, shine 6. beauty, redden
7. redness 8. eloquence
10. luminosity 13. incandescence

glower... 4. gaze 5. glare, scowl, stare

glowing... 3. red 4. warm 5. drunk
6. ardent, cadent 7. burning,
excited, fervent, flushed 8. eloquent,
luminous 9. beautiful 12. enthusiastic

glucose... 5. rutin, sugar 8. dextrose

glue... 3. fix 4. join 5. paste, stick
6. adhere, cement, fasten, sizing
7. gelatin 8. adhesive, fastener
9. viscosity

glum... 3. sad 5. moody 6. dismal,
gloomy, sullen 8. frowning

glut... 4. cloy, fill, sate 5. gorge, stuff
6. pamper 7. engorge, satiate,
satisfy, surfeit 8. overfill, overload,
plethora, saturate

gluten... 3. gum 4. glue 6. fibrin
7. gliadin 8. adhesive

glutinous... 4. sizy 5. gluey 6. viscid
8. adhesive

glutton... 6. rascal, wretch 7. epicure
8. gourmand 9. cormorant,
scoundrel, wolverine 11. gormandizer,
greedy eater

gluttony... 5. greed 7. edacity
8. voracity 12. intemperance
13. voraciousness

glycerine machine man... 8. effetman

gnar, gnarr (of dogs)... 5. growl, snarl

gnarl... 4. knot 5. growl, snarl, twist
6. tangle 7. contort, distort, roughen
10. contortion 12. protuberance
(tree)

gnarled... 5. rough 6. knotty, rugged
7. complex, knotted, twisted
12. cross-grained

gnash... 4. bite 5. grate, grind (teeth)

gnat... 3. fly 5. nidge 6. insect
8. mosquito

gnaw... 3. eat 4. bite, chew 5. grind,
waste 6. rankle 7. corrode 8. wear
away

gnede... 6. scanty 7. lacking, miserly,
sparing

gnib... 5. ready, sharp 6. clever

gnome... 3. elf, imp, saw 5. bodie,
bogey, dwarf, maxim, nisse
6. goblin, kobold, sprite 8. aphorism

gnomic... 8. didactic 10. aphoristic

gnomic poets (Gr)... 5. Solon
8. Theognis (of Megara)
10. Phocylides (of Miletus)

gnostic... 4. wise 6. shrewd
7. knowing 9. sagacious

Gnostic... 6. Ophite 7. Abraxas
(Abrasax), Sethite

gnu... 6. kokoon 8. antelope

go... 3. act, die, gae, run 4. fail, fare,
game, move, pass, turn, walk, wane,
wend, work 5. leave, sally 6. betake,

decamp, depart, elapse, embark,
energy, extend, result, retire, travel,
weaken 7. advance, entrain, journey,
proceed 8. continue, diminish,
withdraw 9. eventuate, harmonize

go (pert to)...
around.. 6. detour 7. circuit
8. surround
ashore.. 4. land 9. disembark
astray.. 3. err
at.. 6. attack 9. undertake
away.. 4. exit, scat, shoo 5. scoot,
scram 6. begone, depart
9. disappear
back.. 3. ebb 6. recede, repass,
retire, return, revert 7. regress,
retrace
before.. 7. precede 8. antecede
11. participate
down, under.. 4. fail, sink 7. capsize,
descend, founder, succumb, undergo
8. submerge 14. deteriorate
easily.. 4. lope 5. amble
furtively.. 5. steal 6. tiptoe
over.. 5. renew 6. revise 7. retrace
8. rehearse, traverse 9. backtrack,
re-examine
through.. 4. pass 5. spend 6. suffer
7. exhaust (fortune), persist, undergo
9. persevere 10. experience
up.. 4. fail, rise 5. arise, raise
6. ascend
with.. 4. suit 5. agree, court
6. accord 7. coincide 9. accompany
10. understand
goa.. 5. Tribe (Queensland) 6. mugger
7. gazelle
goad... 3. egg 4. poke, prod, prog,
spur, urge 5. ankus (elephant),
decoy, impel, prick, sting, thorn,
valet (manège) 6. incite 7. inflame
8. irritate, stimulus 9. incentive
goal.. 3. aim, end 4. base, fate,
home, mark 5. bourn (bourne),
Mecca, reach, score, Thule (Myth)
6. object 7. purpose 9. objective
11. destination
goanna.. 6. iguana, lizard 7. monitor
goat... 4. buck, dupe 5. brown
6. engine, lecher 9. scapegoat
13. laughingstock
goat (pert to)...
astronomy.. 9. Capricorn
fig.. 8. caprifig
fish.. 6. mullet
get one's.. 3. irk, vex 4. rile 5. pique
6. nettle
god.. 3. Pan
haircloth.. 3. Tibet (Thibet) 6. camlet
hair cord (Bedouin).. 4. agal
goat (type of)... 3. kid, ram, tur, zac
4. ibex, tahr, urus 5. Capra, goral,
pasan (pasang), serow, takin
6. Alpine, Angora, chamal, Jemlah,
mammal 7. aurochs, markhor
8. Cashmere, ruminant
goatsucker... 4. bird 7. dorhawk,
grinder 9. nighthawk
12. whippoorwill
gob... 4. lump, mass 5. choke, mouth
6. sailor 8. mouthful, quantity
goby... 4. fish, mapo

go–by... 4. snub 7. evasion, passing
13. circumvention
god (Myth, Relig)...
Babylonian.. 2. Zu 3. Anu, Sin
4. Adad, Enzu, Nama, Nebo (Nebu)
5. Aruru, Cirru, Dagan, Nintu
8. Ningirsu 10. Ninkhursag
11. Ningishzida
Celtic.. 6. Aengus
Cymric.. 4. Lleu (Llew)
Egyptian.. 2. Ra 3. Bes, Dis, Geb
(Keb), Min, Seb 4. Amen, Amon,
Ptah 5. Horus, Thoth 6. Dhouti,
Osiris
false.. 4. Baal, idol 5. Mammon
Greek.. 4. Ares, Zeus 5. Comus,
Hymen, Momus, Pluto 6. Hermes,
Somnus 7. Bacchus 8. Dionysus
Hebrew.. 3. Jah 7. Jehovah
Hindu.. 4. Agni, Deva, Kama, Siva
(Shiva) 6. Varuna
household.. 3. Lar 5. Lares 6. Penate
Irish.. 5. Dagda (pagan)
love of, for.. 5. piety 6. bhakti
9. theophile
Norse.. 2. Er, Ve 3. Tyr, Ull, Van
4. Loki, Odin, Thor, Ymir 5. Aesir,
Donar, Vanir, Wodin
Roman.. 4. Jove 5. Comus, Janus,
Orcus 7. Bacchus, Mercury 8. Dis
pater
Semitic.. 5. Hadad 6. Nergal
Supreme.. 3. Dei, Deo, Dio 4. Deus,
Soul, Zeus 6. Elohim, Spirit
12. Infinite Mind, Supreme Being
Teutonic.. 3. Tiu 4. Hoth
god (of)...
agriculture.. 4. Nebo 6. Faunus
beauty.. 6. Aengus (Oengus)
beginnings, creation.. 4. Ptah, Zeus
5. Janus 6. Varuna
commerce.. 5. Vanir 7. Mercury
darkness, evil.. 3. Set, Sin 6. Nergal
day.. 5. Horus
dead.. 5. Orcus 6. Osiris
discord.. 4. Loki
earth.. 3. Geb (Keb), Seb 5. Dagan
east wind.. 5. Eurus
evil.. 2. Zu 3. Set, Sin 6. Nergal
fate.. 5. Moira (Moera)
fire.. 4. Agni 5. Girru 6. Vulcan
flocks.. 3. Pan
January.. 5. Janus
joy.. 5. Comus
justice.. 7. Forseti (Forsete)
law.. 4. Zeus
lightning.. 4. Agni
love.. 4. Amor, Ares, Eros, Kama
5. Bhaga, Cupid 6. Aengus (Oengus)
March.. 4. Mars
marriage.. 5. Hymen
medicine.. 11. Ningishzida
mountains.. 5. Atlas 7. Olympus
music.. 6. Apollo
Northmen.. 5. Aesir
oceans.. 7. Oceanus
poetry.. 5. Bragi
ridicule.. 5. Momus
sea.. 7. Neptune, Proteus
sky.. 3. Anu
sleep, dreams.. 6. Somnus
8. Morpheus

storm.. 2. Zu 6. Teshup
sun.. 2. Ra (Re) 6. Apollo, Nergal
thunder.. 4. Thor 7. Jupiter
Thursday.. 4. Thor
Tuesday.. 3. Tiu, Tyr
underworld.. 3. Dis 5. Pluto 6. Osiris
    7. Serapis 8. Dis pater
    11. Ningishzida
war.. 3. Ira, Tyr 4. Mars 5. Woden
    8. Ningirau
wealth.. 5. Bhaga 6. Plutus
Wednesday.. 5. Woden
wind.. 4. Adad 5. Eolus, Eurus,
    Hadad 6. Aeolus, zephyr 8. Favonius
wine.. 7. Bacchus 8. Dionysus
wisdom.. 4. Nebo 5. Thoth 6. Dhouti
woods.. 7. Silenus
youth.. 6. Apollo
goddess... 3. Ate, Dea, Eir, Eos, Nox,
    Nyx, Ops, Pax, Uni 4. Apet, Eris,
    Fury, Gaea, Hera, Isis, Leda, Maat,
    Nike, Nina, Sati 5. Aruru, Damia,
    Diana, Doris, Epona, Freya, Hygea,
    Irene, Pakht, Salus, Venus, Vesta
    6. Allatu, Athena, Aurora, Cybele,
    Hecate, Hestia, Ningal, Pietho,
    Selene, Semele, Tellus, Vacuna
    7. Artemis, Demeter, Minerva, Parvati
    9. Aphrodite, Eumenides, Mnemosyne
    10. Persephone, Proserpina
goddess of...
agriculture.. 3. Ops 7. Demeter
arts.. 6. Athena, Pallas
beauty.. 3. Sri 5. Freya, Venus
    7. Lakshmi
dawn.. 3. Eos 5. Ushas 6. Aurora,
    Matuta
destiny.. 4. Fate 5. Moira, Parca
discord.. 3. Ate 4. Eris
earth.. 4. Gaea 5. Aruru 6. Ishtar,
    Tellus
Eskimos.. 5. Sedna
fertility.. 7. Demeter
fire.. 6. Hestia
fortune.. 5. Tyche
freedom.. 7. Feronia
fruit.. 6. Pomona
grain, harvest.. 3. Ops 5. Ceres
Hawaiians.. 4. Pele
healing.. 3. Eir 4. Gula
health.. 5. Damia, Hygea, Salus
hearth.. 5. Vesta
history.. 4. Saga
horses.. 5. Epona
hunt.. 5. Diana 6. Vacuna
infatuation.. 3. Ate
justice.. 7. Nemesis
light.. 6. Lucina
love.. 5. Venus 6. Ishtar 9. Aphrodite
magic, witchcraft.. 6. Hecate
marriage.. 5. Hera
maternity.. 4. Apet
mischief.. 3. Ate 4. Eris
moon.. 4. Luna 5. Diana 6. Phoebe,
    Selene (Selena)
mother of the gods.. 4. Rhea
nature.. 4. Rhea 5. Nymph 6. Cybele
night.. 3. Nox, Nyx
peace.. 3. Pax 5. Irene 6. Athena
poetry.. 5. Erato
rainbows.. 4. Iris

sea.. 5. Doris
seasons.. 5. Horae
summer.. 5. Aestus
sun.. 5. Pakht (Pacht)
trees.. 6. Pomona
truth.. 4. Maat
underworld.. 4. Fury 6. Allatu
    10. Persephone, Proserpina
vengeance.. 3. Ara, Ate 7. Nemesis
victory.. 4. Nike
virtue.. 5. Fides
war.. 5. Anath, Bella
wealth.. 3. Sri 7. Lakshmi
wisdom.. 6. Athena 7. Minerva
youth.. 4. Hebe
Godforsaken... 6. vacant 7. forlorn
    8. desolate, wretched 9. neglected
godly... 5. pious 6. devout, divine
    7. saintly 9. religious, righteous
godmother... 6. cummer (kimmer)
    7. sponsor
God's...
abode.. 7. Olympus
acre.. 10. churchyard
board.. 14. communion table
country.. 4. home 8. homeland
    9. Vaterland 10. fatherland
cupbearer.. 8. Ganymede
fluid (vein).. 5. ichor (icor)
food.. 8. ambrosia
gods, The (pert to)...
death of.. 9. theoktony
marriage of.. 8. theogamy
messenger of.. 6. Hermes
mother of.. 4. Rhea
Twilight of.. 8. Ragnarok
worship of.. 9. theolatry
Goetae... 7. wizards (anc) 9. sorcerers
    14. thaumaturgists
Goethe (pert to)...
home.. 6. Weimer (Ger)
masterpiece.. 5. Faust
talent.. 4. poet 8. novelist
    9. dramatist
goffer, gauffer... 5. crimp, flute, plait
    (lace, paper)
gog... 3. bog 4. stir 9. agitation
Gog (Bib)... 5. Ruler (of Magog), tribe
goggle... 3. eye 4. roll 5. state
    6. squint 11. roll the eyes
goggler... 4. fish (oceanic)
goggles... 6. screen 7. glasses
    8. blinkers, eyeshade 10. spectacles
going... 6. moving, travel 7. current,
    working 9. departure 10. obtainable
    11. in operation
gola... 7. granary 9. storeroom
    11. Indian caste
golach, goloch... 6. beetle, earwig
    9. centipede
Golconda... 6. wealth 8. rich mine
gold... 2. Au 3. oro 4. gelt, gilt
    5. aurum, color, lucre, metal, money
    6. riches, wealth 7. bullion
gold (pert to)...
alloy.. 4. asem 6. oroide
artificial.. 8. Mannheim
assayer cup.. 5. cupel
bar.. 5. ingot
braid, lace.. 6. orris
brick.. 7. swindle
coin (US).. 5. eagle

compound.. 6. auride
containing.. 4. doré
discoverer (US).. 6. Sutter (1849)
field (Bib).. 5. Ophir
fish.. 9. shubunkin
fool's.. 6. pyrite
gilding.. 6. ormolu 9. imitation
Heraldry.. 2. or
King (Myth).. 5. Midas
land of (Bib).. 5. Ophir
like.. 5. auric 7. aureate
measure.. 5. carat
Rush.. 8. Klondike (1897)
   10. California (1849)
seekers (Calif.).. 9. Argonauts (1849)
   11. Forty–Niners
symbol.. 2. Au
vein.. 4. lode
washing pan.. 5. cupel
gold and silver.. 11. noble metals
golden... 4. gilt 5. auric, blest
   6. blonde, yellow 7. aureate,
   aureous, halcyon 8. metallic,
   precious, valuable 9. Pactolian
   10. auspicious 11. flourishing
golden (pert to)...
Age.. 9. Saturnian, siècle d'or
apple.. 3. bel 4. Eris (goddess)
   5. Paris (giver) 6. tomato
bird.. 6. oriole
bough.. 9. mistletoe
Fleece seeker.. 5. Jason 8. Argonaut
Fleece ship.. 5. Argos
rod.. 8. solidago
goldenrod (pert to)...
genus.. 8. Solidago
State Flower of.. 7. Alabama
   8. Kentucky, Nebraska
goldfish... 4. carp 9. shubunkin
Goldfish (Astron)... 6. Dorado
golf (pert to)...
club.. 4. iron 5. baffy, spoon
   6. driver, mashie, putter 7. brassie,
   midiron, niblick
hazard.. 4. trap 5. stymy 6. bunker
   11. restriction
score.. 3. par 4. bogy (bogie)
   5. eagle 6. birdie
stroke.. 4. baff, chip, hook, loft, putt
   5. drive, slice
term.. 3. ace, par, tee 4. baff, fore
   5. bogey, divot, eagle, green, slice
   6. birdie, dormie, sclaff, stymie
   (stimy) 7. gallery
Golgotha... 7. Calvary 8. cemetery
goliath... 4. frog 5. crane, giant,
   heron
Goliath (pert to)...
Bib.. 5. giant (Philistine)
death site.. 4. Elah
home.. 4. Gath
slayer.. 5. David
Gomorrah (Bib)... 5. Sodom
   13. wicked country
Gomuti palm... 5. areng
gondola race (Venice)... 7. regatta
gone... 3. ago, off 4. dead, left, lost,
   past, yore 5. since 6. absent,
   passed, ruined 8. departed, past
   hope, vanished 9. forgotten
   10. infatuated
goober... 6. peanut

good... 2. eu (pref) 3. bon, fit 4. able,
   full, gain, just, kind 5. ample, godly,
   moral, nifty, pious, sound, valid
   6. benign, devout, expert, profit,
   savory 7. genuine, helpful, liberal,
   trained, upright 8. decorous, interest,
   pleasing, salutary, suitable, virtuous
   9. admirable, competent, enjoyable,
   estimable, excellent, favorable,
   honorable, indulgent, reputable
   10. auspicious, beneficial,
   courageous, gratifying, profitable,
   sufficient 11. commendable,
   well–behaved 12. considerable,
   satisfactory, stouthearted
good (pert to)...
bye.. 4. ta–ta 5. adieu, adios, ciaou
   6. so long 7. cheerio 8. farewell
for nothing.. 4. mean 5. idler
   6. wretch 7. useless 8. indolent
   9. worthless 11. rapscallion
health.. 5. skoal 6. prosit
management.. 6. eutaxy
mighty.. 7. skookum
ordinarily.. 8. mediocre
spirit.. 6. daemon 8. Eudaemon
   12. agathodaemon
tidings.. 6. gospel 7. evangel
will.. 5. favor 9. affection, readiness
   11. benevolence 12. friendliness
goodness... 5. piety 6. virtue
   8. kindness, validity 9. godliness,
   propriety 10. excellence, generosity,
   savoriness
goods... 5. wares 7. ability 8. chattels,
   property 11. information, merchandise
goods cast overboard, sunk...
   5. lagan (lagend) 6. jetsam
   7. flotsam 10. contraband
goose... 4. bean, dupe, fool, gull, iron,
   snow, tule 5. Anser, brant, solan
   6. Canada, gander, gannet, goslet
   7. gosling, graylag (greylag)
   8. barnacle 12. white–fringed
goose (pert to)...
grease.. 6. axunge
pygmy.. 6. goslet
relating to.. 8. anserine
story character.. 5. ganza
gooseberry... 5. fabes (color)
   6. escort, groser (groset), thapes
   8. chaperon, feaberry
gopher... 5. snake 6. rodent 7. burglar
   8. squirrel, tortoise 10. salamander
Gopher State... 9. Minnesota
gore... 3. mud 4. dirt, dung, stab
   5. blood, cloth (triang), filth, slime
   6. pierce 8. heraldry 9. bloodshed,
   penetrate
gorge... 3. eat 4. bolt, glut, sate
   5. chasm, gully 6. canyon, coulee,
   defile, nullah, ravine, valley 7. choke
   up, overeat, pitcher, satiate 8. overfill
gorgeous... 5. grand, showy
   8. colorful, dazzling 9. beautiful
   10. delightful 11. magnificent,
   resplendent
gorgon... 4. ogre, ugly 7. Jezebel
   (Bib), monster
Gorgons (Gr Myth)... 6. Medusa,
   Stheno 7. Euryale 9. sentinels
gorilla... 3. ape 4. thug 5. brute

6. monkey 8. assassin
gorilla man... 9. Du Chaillu (brought ape from Africa)
gormandizer... 9. chowhound 11. trencherman
gorse... 5. furze 7. juniper
goshawk... 5. Astur 6. tercel
gospel... 5. faith, truth 6. belief 7. epistle, evangel 8. doctrine 9. orthodoxy, selection (Bib) 10. revelation 11. glad tidings 12. proclamation
Gospels (Four)... 11. diatessaron
gossip... 3. cat, eme, gup 4. chat, news, talk 5. on--dit 6. claver, gabble, norate, report, tattle 7. clatter 8. idle talk, quidnunc 9. chatterer 10. newsmonger, talebearer
gossoon... 3. boy, lad (serving) 5. youth 6. garçon
got... see *get*
Gotham... 9. Newcastle (Eng) 11. New York City
Gothamite... 9. New Yorker
Gothic (pert to)...
alphabet.. 11. Moeso--Gothic
architecture.. 6. French
design.. 7. writing 12. architecture
era.. 10. Middle Ages
people.. 4. rude 5. Goths 6. fierce 7. Teutons
printing type.. 5. Doric 9. square--cut
gouge... 4. tool 5. cheat 6. chisel, groove 7. defraud, swindle 8. impostor 10. imposition
Gounod's opera... 5. Faust
gourd... 4. pepo 5. color, flask, melon 6. squash 8. calabash, cucurbit 9. Cucurbita 11. calabazella
gourmand... 5. eater (luxurious) 6. taster 7. epicure, glutton, gourmet 10. fastidious, gluttonous, voluptuary 11. connoisseur
gourmet... 7. epicure 8. gourmand 11. connoisseur
gout... 4. clot, drop 6. blotch 7. disease 9. arthritis
govern... 3. run 4. curb, lead, rein, rule 5. reign 6. bridle, direct, manage 7. conduct, control, preside 8. dominate, regulate, restrain 9. influence, supervise
governess... 4. ayah 5. nurse 6. abbess, duenna 8. guardian 12. instructress
government... 4. rule, sway 6. polity 7. control, regimen 10. management 12. jurisdiction 14. administration
government (pert to)...
agent.. see *representative* below
centralized.. 12. totalitarian
church.. 9. hierarchy 10. hierocracy
foe.. 3. Red 9. anarchist, mercenary, terrorist
form.. 6. polity
grant.. 6. patent
in exile.. 7. de facto
lands.. 5. amani
levy.. 3. tax 6. impost
official.. 10. bureaucrat
representative.. 6. consul 8. diplomat,

minister 10. ambassador
science of.. 8. politics
strong.. 5. power
system.. 6. regime
vicarious.. 7. regency
without.. 6. acracy
government by...
church.. 9. hierarchy 10. hierocracy
few.. 9. oligarchy
God.. 8. theonomy
holy body.. 9. hagiarchy 10. hagiocracy
inner control.. 8. endarchy
law.. 9. nomocracy
men.. 9. andocracy
mob.. 10. ochlocracy
no one.. 6. acracy
rich.. 10. plutocracy
seven.. 9. heptarchy
six.. 12. sextumvirate
slaves.. 10. doulocracy
ten.. 8. decarchy (dekarchy)
three.. 8. triarchy 11. triumvirate
women.. 11. gynecocracy
worst men.. 12. kakistocracy
governor... 4. woon 5. chief, nabob, ruler 6. dynast, regent 7. alcalde, decarch (of 10 men), viceroy 8. decurion, director 9. mechanism 10. magistrate
gown... 4. robe, toga 5. cloak, dress, frock 6. chiton, clothe, cyclas, invest, kimono, mantle 7. cassock, college, garment, matinee, soutane (Eccl), sultane 8. negligee, peignoir 9. nightgown
gozell, gozill... 10. gooseberry
gozzard... 9. gooseherd
gra... 4. love 5. agrah 6. liking 8. fondness 10. sweetheart
grab... 3. nab 4. game (cards), take 5. grasp, seize 6. arrest, clutch, snatch, vessel
grabble... 4. feel 5. grope 6. grovel, sprawl 7. harvest 11. appropriate
grace... 4. fate, luck, note, tact 5. adorn, charm, favor, honor, mercy, title 6. beauty, become, bedeck, polish, prayer, virtue 7. dignify, enhance 8. clemency, easiness, elegance, kindness, reprieve 10. comeliness, refinement, seemliness 12. graciousness, thanksgiving
graceful... 4. airy, easy, feat 6. comely, seemly 7. elegant, fitting, tactful 8. charming, debonair 9. beautiful, courteous, sylphlike 11. appropriate
Graces, The Three (Gr Myth)...
5. Aegle (Mother) 6. Aglaia (Brilliance), Thalia (Bloom) 10. Euphrosyne (Joy)
gracile... 4. slim, thin 6. slight 7. slender
gracious... 4. kind 5. suave 6. benign, urbane 7. affable 8. generous 9. courteous, favorable
grackle... 3. daw 4. bird, myna 7. jackdaw 9. blackbird
gradation... 4. step 5. scale, steps 6. ablaut, nuance, series, stages

7. degrees **10.** graduation, succession

grade... **4.** even, rank, rate, size, sort, step **5.** level, order **6.** assort, degree, school, smooth **7.** arrange, incline **8.** classify, gradient, graduate

gradual... **4.** easy, slow **6.** gentle **9.** leisurely

graduate... **4.** pass, size **5.** grade, taper **6.** alumna **7.** alumnus, promote, student **8.** shade off

graffito (scratched crudely)... **7.** drawing **10.** scratching **11.** inscription

Graf Spee blown up... **7.** Uruguay (1939)

graft... **3.** dig **4.** cion (scion), join, toil, work **5.** ditch, fraud, labor, spade, unite **6.** boodle, fasten, inarch, trench **7.** bribery, implant, joining

grafted (Her)... **4.** enté

Grail... see *Holy Grail*

grain... **3.** jot, rye **4.** atom, bran, corn, dram, food, grit, iota, malt, meal, mite, oats, rice, whit **5.** fiber, maize, scrap, spark, trace, wheat **6.** barley, millet, sesame **8.** particle

grain (pert to)...
Bible.. **4.** ador
bundle.. **5.** sheaf **7.** sheaves
chaff.. **4.** bran, grit
cracked.. **6.** groats
ear of.. **4.** spike **6.** ressum (rizzom)
exchange (Finan).. **3.** pit
feeding on.. **11.** granivorous
fungus, disease.. **4.** rust, smut **5.** ergot **6.** mildew
goddess of.. **5.** Ceres
ground.. **4.** meal **5.** flour, grist
husks.. **4.** bran **5.** straw
measure.. **6.** thrave
mill.. **5.** quern
mixture.. **6.** fodder **7.** farrage **9.** bullimong
small.. **7.** granule
spike.. **3.** ear **6.** rizzom
stack.. **4.** rick
storage, warehouse.. **3.** mow **4.** silo **5.** hutch **8.** elevator

grammar (pert to)... **5.** parse **6.** gender, simile, syntax **7.** diction, parsing, prosody, synesis, wordage **8.** enallage, language, metaphor, paradigm **9.** accidence, etymology, phonology **10.** conformity, declension, inflection **11.** conjugation

grammatical case... **6.** dative **8.** ablative, genitive, vocative **9.** objective **10.** accusative, nominative

grampus... **3.** arc **4.** orca **5.** whale **6.** killer **7.** dolphin **8.** cetacean

granada... **11.** pomegranate

Granada Moorish Castle site... **8.** Alhambra (Sp)

granary... **3.** bin **6.** grange **8.** cornloft **10.** repository, storehouse (grain)

grand... **4.** epic **5.** great, large, lofty, money, noble, piano **6.** august, epical, famous, superb, swanky **7.** eminent, sublime **8.** gorgeous,

majestic, splendid, thousand **9.** dignified, grandiose, important, sumptuous **11.** illustrious, magnificent

Grand Canyon State... **7.** Arizona

grandchild... **2.** oe, oy

grandchild, great... **5.** ieroe

grandee... **7.** magnate **8.** nobleman **10.** clarissimo

grandeur... **5.** glory **7.** dignity, majesty **8.** elegance, eminence, vastness **9.** greatness, immensity, sublimity **10.** augustness **11.** stateliness

grandeval... **4.** aged **7.** ancient

grandfather... **4.** aiel (obs), avus **6.** atavus **8.** gudesire

grandiloquent... **5.** grand, lofty **6.** turgid **7.** pompous **9.** bombastic **12.** magniloquent

grandiose... **4.** epic **5.** grand **6.** turgid **8.** imposing **9.** bombastic, flaunting **12.** ostentatious

Grandma Moses... **17.** Anna Mary Robertson

grandmother... **6.** beldam (beldame), granny, gudame **7.** grandam (grandame), grandma **8.** babushka

grandparent (pert to)... **4.** aval

grandson... **6.** nepote

Grand Teton peak... **7.** Wyoming

grange... **4.** farm **7.** granary **9.** farmhouse **11.** association (1867) **18.** Patrons of Husbandry

granite... **4.** rock **5.** stone **6.** aplite, marble, quartz **8.** feldspar **9.** pegmatite

Gran Quivira... **5.** ruins (mission) **16.** National Monument (N M)

grant... **4.** cede, deed, enam, gift, give, lend, loan, mise **5.** admit, allow, bonus, jagir (jaghar), spare **6.** accord, bestow, confer, demise, permit, remise **7.** appease, concede, confess, subsidy **8.** appanage, sanction, transfer **10.** conveyance **11.** acknowledge

granulated... **5.** rough **6.** coarse **7.** grained **8.** granular, hardened **12.** crystallized

grape... **3.** fox, uva **5.** Tokay **6.** Malaga, Muscat **7.** Catawba, Concord, Hamburg, Mission, Niagara **8.** Delaware, grenache, Isabella, Thompson **9.** Chasselas, muscadine **10.** sweetwater **11.** scuppernong

grape (pert to)...
cluster.. **6.** raceme
color.. **7.** blue–red **9.** cathedral
conserve.. **5.** uvate
cultivation.. **11.** viticulture
dried.. **4.** pasa **6.** raisin
family, genus.. **5.** Vitus **8.** Vitaceae
juice.. **4.** dibs, must, sapa, stum
military.. **4.** shot
pomace.. **4.** marc, rape
preserve.. **7.** raisine
residue.. **4.** marc, rape **6.** pomace
seed.. **6.** acinus
sugar.. **7.** maltose **8.** dextrose

grapefruit... **6.** pomelo **8.** shaddock **12.** Citrus Maxima

grapevine... **4.** caro **5.** rumor **6.** canard, report **8.** maneuver

(wrestling), pipeline 9. dance step
11. information, underground

graph... 5. chart 7. contour, diagram,
drawing

graphic... 5. clear, drawn, vivid
7. written 8. engraved 9. pictorial
11. descriptive, picturesque,
significant 12. diagrammatic

grasp... 4. grip, hent (obs), hold, take
5. catch, clasp, gripe, seize
6. clinch, clutch, gowpen (gowpin)
7. control 8. handgrip 9. apprehend
10. comprehend, understand

grasping... 4. avid 5. close 6. greedy
7. holding, miserly 8. covetous
9. rapacious 10. avaricious,
prehensive 11. acquisitive
13. comprehending, understanding

grass... 3. eel, hay, Poa, rye 4. cane,
Coix, crab, gama, herb, oats, reed,
rice, rush, tare, wire 5. ankee,
Avena, Briza, brome, chess, goose,
grain, grama, hedge, otate, spart,
spear 6. bamboo, barley, darnel,
fescue, marram, millet, redtop,
sesame, switch 7. alfalfa, Bermuda,
buffalo, esparto, Hordeum, Poeceae,
timothy 8. mesquite 9. blue–grass,
Boutelous

grasshopper... 4. grig 6. cicada, locust
7. katydid

grassland... 3. lea, sod 4. mead, veld
(veldt) 5. llano, range, sward
7. pasture, prairie, savanna
(savannah)

grate... 3. rub 4. fret, grid, grit, rasp
5. annoy, chafe, grind 6. abrade,
scrape 7. network 8. irritate

grateful... 7. cumshaw (beggar's
phrase), welcome 8. pleasing,
thankful 9. gratifying
12. appreciative

gratification... 6. relish, reward
8. gratuity, pleasure 10. indulgence,
recompense

gratified... 4. glad 7. pleased

gratify... 5. favor, grace, humor
6. arride, foster, pamper, please
7. appease, delight, flatter, indulge,
requite, satisfy 10. remunerate

grating... 4. grid 5. grate, grill, harsh,
raspy 6. grille 7. lattice, network
8. strident 9. partition 10. irritating
11. latticework 12. nerve–racking

gratis... 4. free 6. freely 9. on the
cuff 10. for nothing, gratuitous, on
the house 12. gratuitously

gratitude... 5. grace 6. praise, thanks
12. appreciation, gratefulness,
thankfulness

gratuitous... 4. free 5. given 6. gratis,
wanton 7. assumed 8. baseless,
needless 9. voluntary 10. groundless
11. superfluous, unwarranted

gratuity... 3. fee, tip 4. dole, gift,
give, vail 5. bonus, bribe 6. bounty
7. cumshaw, pension, present
9. baksheesh (bakshish), buonamano,
lagniappe (lagnappe), pourboire

grave... 3. pit, urn 4. bier, tomb
5. fosse (foss), sober, staid
6. sedate, solemn, trench 7. earnest,

engrave, serious 8. sermonic
9. important, momentous, ponderous,
sculpture, sepulcher

grave (pert to)...

cloth.. 6. shroud 8. cerement
9. cerecloth

coffin.. 4. pall

comb form.. 5. serio

mound (anc).. 6. barrow 7. hillock,
tumulus

person.. 10. sobersides

robber.. 5. ghoul

gravel... 7. geest, grain, stone
6. baffle, defeat, refute 7. calculi,
erratic (boulder), pebbles
10. meerschaum (color)

graven... 6. etched 7. infixed
8. engraved 10. sculptured

gravestone... 5. stele (stela) 6. cippus,
marker, pillar 8. monument
9. tombstone 11. sarcophagus

gravitation... 7. descent, gravity
10. attraction

gravity... 6. weight 7. dignity, sadness
8. enormity, grimness, sobriety
9. formality, solemnity 10. attraction,
importance 11. earnestness,
seriousness, weightiness
12. significance 13. momentousness

gravity law, discoverer... 6. Newton

gray, grey... 3. dim, old, sad 4. aged,
dark, dull, gris, obex 5. dingy, hoary,
polio (comb form), sober 6. animal
(gray), dismal, somber 7. hueless,
neutral, silvery 9. cheerless
10. achromatic

gray, grey (color)... 3. ash, bat, dun
4. ashy, dove, iron, lead, mole, zinc
5. acier, ashen, dusty, mouse, pearl,
slate, smoke, steel, taupe 6. French,
Oxford, Quaker, reseda, silver
7. cesious, dappled, grizzle
8. charcoal, cinereal, gunmetal
10. battleship, dapple–gray
13. pepper–and–salt

graze... 3. eat, rub 4. drab, rase, skim
5. brush, shave 6. browse, feed on,
scrape 7. scratch

grease... 3. fat, oil, tip 4. daub, lard,
mort, saim, soil 5. bribe, smear,
suint 6. axunge 7. fatness, fawning,
lanolin 8. flattery 9. lubricate

greasy... 4. oily 5. dirty, gross, thick
6. smooth 8. slippery, unctuous
10. indelicate

great... 3. big 4. good, huge, vast
5. ample, chief, large, major, stout,
whole 6. famous, grande 7. drastic,
eminent, extreme 8. intimate,
numerous 9. elaborate, important
11. magnanimous 12. considerable
13. distinguished

great (comb form)... 5. macro, megal

Great (pert to)...

Barrier (NZ).. 4. Otea (Isl) 9. coral
reef

Beyond.. 5. grave 9. afterlife,
hereafter 10. after world, The
Unknown 11. eternal home
14. beyond the grave

Cham of Literature.. 13. Samuel
Johnson (Dr)

Circle sailing.. **10.** orthodromy
Commoner.. **4.** Clay, Pitt **7.** Stevens
   (Thaddeus) **9.** Gladstone
Divide.. **7.** Rockies **8.** Rocky Mts
   9. watershed (US) **14.** Rocky
   Mountains **17.** Continental Divide
Fire.. **6.** London (1666) **7.** Chicago
   (1871)
Lakes.. **4.** Erie **5.** Huron **7.** Ontario
   8. Michigan, Superior
Mogul.. **5.** Akbar (Hind) **7.** diamond
   (787 carats)
Names.. **6.** Hector **8.** Hercules,
   Lysander **9.** Alexander
Pyramid.. **6.** Cheops
Spirit (Ind).. **4.** Mana, Zemi **5.** Wakan
   6. Manito (orenda), Pokunt
White Way.. **8.** Broadway (NY)
Great Britain... **5.** Wales **7.** England
   8. Scotland **12.** Commonwealth
   13. United Kingdom **15.** Northern
   Ireland
greatest... **6.** utmost **7.** extreme,
   noblest
greatness... **9.** largeness
   10. famousness, importance
   11. magnanimity
Grecian... see *Greek*
Greco, Graeco (comb form)... **5.** Greek
   7. Grecian
Greece... see also *Greek*
ancient.. **4.** Elis **5.** Argos, Doris, Ionia
   6. Attica, Epirus, Hellas **7.** Argolis,
   Boeotia
cape.. **5.** Melea **7.** Matapan
capital.. **4.** Elis (anc) **6.** Athens
citadel.. **9.** Acropolis
city.. **6.** Patras, Sparta **7.** Corinth,
   Piraeus **8.** Salonika, Thessaly
island.. **5.** Chios, Corfu, Crete, Samor
   6. Lesbos **10.** Dodecanese,
   Samothrace
mountain.. **3.** Ida **5.** Athos **6.** Peleon,
   Pindus **7.** Olympus **9.** Parnassus
peninsula.. **6.** Balkan
river.. **4.** Arta **7.** Hellada **9.** Archelous
sea.. **6.** Aegean, Ionian
seaport.. **4.** Enor, Volo **5.** Corpu,
   Pylos **8.** Salonika **9.** Gallipoli
Greek (pert to)...
abbess.. **4.** amma
alphabet.. see *Greek alphabet*
altar.. **7.** eschara
architecture.. **5.** Doric, Ionic **6.** xystus
   (part) **10.** Corinthian
assembly.. **4.** pynx **5.** agora
avenging spirit.. **3.** Ate, Ker **6.** Erinys
boat.. **6.** caique
bowl (golden).. **5.** depas
breath.. **6.** pneuma
chariot.. **4.** biga
church section.. **6.** andron, bemata
citadel.. **9.** Acropolis
city (Greek for).. **5.** polis
commander (anc).. **7.** navarch
commune.. **4.** deme, nome
contest.. **4.** agon (anc) **6.** Delian
   7. Pythian
courtesan (Athen).. **5.** Thais
cup, bowl.. **5.** depas **6.** cotula
cupid.. **4.** Eros
dance (anc).. **6.** hormos **7.** pyrrhic,

strophe, **9.** dithyramb
department.. **8.** nomarchy
epic.. **5.** Iliad **7.** Odyssey
female worshipper.. **5.** orant
game.. see *contest* above
garment.. **5.** tunic **6.** chiton, peplos
gravestone.. **5.** stele
horse (talking).. **5.** Arion
hospitality.. **5.** zenia
judge.. **6.** dicast
language.. **6.** Romaic
lawgiver.. **5.** Minos, Solon
magistrate.. **6.** archon, eparch
   7. nomarch
mistress.. **7.** hetaera (hetaira)
monster.. **8.** Typhoeus (100–headed)
note.. **4.** nete **5.** neume **6.** pneuma
   9. hexachord **10.** tetrachord
Old Testament.. **10.** Septuagint
platform.. **4.** bema **7.** logeion
poem.. **5.** Iliad **7.** Odyssey
portico.. **4.** stoa, xyst
sacred enclosure.. **5.** sekos
sacred object.. **6.** sacrum
sacrificial offering.. **5.** hiera
   8. sphagion
school.. **7.** Eleatic
serpent.. **4.** seps **6.** Python
slave.. **5.** Baubo, helot, iambe
   6. penest
soldier.. **7.** hoplite
song.. **5.** melos
sorceress.. **5.** Circe
spirit.. **5.** Momus (evil)
temple.. **4.** naos **5.** cella (part)
theater.. **5.** odeon
war cry.. **5.** alala
youth (would–be citizen).. **7.** ephebus
Greek alphabet... **2.** Mu, Nu, Pi, Xi
   3. Chi, Eta, Phi, Psi, Rho, Tau
   4. Beta, Iota, Zeta **5.** Alpha, Delta,
   Gamma, Kappa, Omega, Sigma,
   Theta **6.** Lambda **7.** Digamma (obs),
   Epsilon, Omicron, Upsilon
Greek Furies... **5.** Alecto, Erinys
   7. Magaero **9.** Tisiphone
Greek god of...
atmosphere.. **5.** Hadad
chief.. **4.** Zeus
dreams.. **8.** Morpheus
fire.. **6.** Vulcan
flocks.. **3.** Pan
heavens.. **6.** Uranus
love.. **4.** Eros
lower world.. **5.** Hades
ridicule.. **5.** Momus
river.. **8.** Eridanus
sea.. **6.** Nereus
storm.. **7.** Teshup **7.** Hittite
sun.. **6.** Apollo, Helios **7.** Phoebus
vegetation.. **8.** Dionysus
war.. **4.** Ares **8.** Enyalius
winds.. **5.** Eurus **6.** Aeolus
youth.. **6.** Apollo, Pothos (winged)
Greek goddess of...
agriculture.. **7.** Artemis, Demeter
beauty.. **9.** Aphrodite
chase.. **7.** Artemis
clouds.. **5.** Niobe
dawn.. **3.** Eos **7.** Alcmene, Ariadne
discord.. **4.** Eris
earth.. **2.** Ge **4.** Gaea

fate.. 5. Moira
fortune.. 5. Tyche
heaven.. 4. Hera
infatuation.. 3. Ate
magic.. 6. Hecate (3-headed)
memory.. 9. Mnemosyne
moon.. 2. Io 5. Diana 6. Selene
nature.. 7. Artemis
night.. 3. Nyx 4. Leto 6. Hecate
peace.. 5. Irene
phallus.. 5. Baubo
retribution.. 7. Nemesis
underworld.. 6. Hecate (Hekate)
vengeance.. 3. Ara 7. Nemesis
victory.. 4. Nike
wisdom.. 6. Pallas 7. Minerva
youth.. 4. Hebe
Greek Myth...
  character.. 5. Niobe, Sinon 6. Adonis,
    Gorgon, Rhesus 7. Calchus, Icarius,
    Pandora, Phrixos 8. Atalanta,
    Endymion, Meleager, Tantalus
    12. Erichthonius
  deity.. 5. Satyr, Titan 6. Cronus
  enchantress.. 5. Circe, Medea
  giant.. 7. Antaeus 8. Enceladus
    (100-armed)
  huntress.. 8. Atalanta
  monster.. 8. Typhoeus (100-headed)
  nymph.. 5. Oread 6. Nereid
  serpent.. 6. Python
  spirit (evil).. 5. Momus
Greek personalities...
  astronomer.. 12. Eratosthenes
  author.. 6. Lucian
  biographer.. 8. Plutarch
  counselor.. 6. Nestor
  dramatist.. 9. Aeschylus (Poet),
    Euripedes, Sophocles
    12. Aristophanes
  fabulist.. 5. Aesop
  geographer.. 6. Strabo
  hero.. 4. Ajax 5. Talos 6. Nestor,
    Thesus 7. Cecrops 10. Hippolytus
  historian.. 8. Xenophon 9. Dionysius,
    Herodotus 10. Thucydides
  mathematician.. 6. Euclid
    10. Archimedes
  painter.. 7. Apelles, El Greco
  patriarch.. 5. Arius
  philosopher.. 5. Galen, Plato, Timon
    6. Nestor 8. Diogenes 9. Aristotle
    10. Heraclitus, Parmenides,
    Pythagorus, Xenophanes
    11. Anaximander
  physician.. 5. Galen
  poet.. 5. Arion, Homer 6. Pindar
    7. Thespis 8. Anacreon 9. Aeschylus
  poetess.. 6. Erinna, Sappho
    7. Corinna
  sage.. 6. Thales
  sculptor.. 5. Myron 7. Phidias
  statesman.. 8. Pericles 9. Aristides
green... 3. raw 4. vert 5. fresh, mossy
  6. callow, praseo (comb form),
  unripe 7. emerald, verdant
  9. malachite, unskilled, untrained
  11. flourishing 13. inexperienced
  15. unsophisticated
green (pert to)...
  back.. 4. frog 11. legal tender (US)
  blue.. 4. cyan, saxe 7. sistine

  comb form.. 6. praseo
  eyed.. 7. jealous
  famous.. 6. Gretna (Scot)
  film.. 6. patina
  gray.. 5. olive 6. reseda
  pale.. 7. celadon
  pigment.. 10. terre-verte
  quartz.. 5. prase
  sickness.. 9. chlorosis
  tea.. 5. Hyson
green-back herring... 5. cisco
Greenland...
  Bay.. 6. Baffin
  capital.. 8. Godthaab
  Danish word.. 8. Crönland
  explorer.. 9. Frobisher (1576)
    10. Eric the Red
  natives.. 6. Eskimo (mostly)
  settlement.. 4. Etah
  strait.. 5. Davis
  whale.. 5. right
Green Mt Boys' leader... 10. Ethan
  Allen (1775)
Green Mt State... 7. Vermont
greenness... 5. color 8. sourness
  9. ignorance 10. immaturity
  11. gullibility 12. inexperience
Greenwich time (London)...
  8. absolute, standard 16. Royal
  Observatory
Greenwich Village... 9. Manhattan
  11. New York City
greeting... 3. ave, how 4. hail 5. hallo
  6. accoil, halloa, salute 7. address,
  welcome 8. saluting 9. reception
  10. compliment, salutation
  14. correspondence
gregarious... 6. common, social
  7. affable 8. sociable
  12. social-minded 13. communicative
grego... 5. cloak 6. jacket 9. greatcoat
Gregory... 4. Code (Rom law), Pope,
  year 5. chant, staff (Mus) 6. church
  8. calendar
grenier.. 5. attic
grey... see *gray*
grid... 5. grill 7. grating, griddle,
  network 8. gridiron 13. football field
grief... 3. rue, woe 4. care, pain, ruth
  5. abuse, dolor, trial 6. mishap,
  sorrow 7. anguish, offense, remorse,
  sadness 8. disaster, distress,
  document 9. grievance, suffering
  10. affliction 11. bereavement,
  lamentation
grieve... 3. cry, rue 4. erme, pain
  5. mourn, wound 6. lament, sorrow
  7. afflict 8. complain, distress
  10. discomfort
grievous... 4. sore 6. bitter, severe
  7. hateful, heinous, intense
  8. terrible 9. sorrowful
  10. disastrous, oppressive
  11. distressing, gravaminous
griff... 4. claw, glen 6. griffe, ravine
griffe... 4. spur (Arch) 7. mulatto
griffin, griffon... 6. charge (Her)
  7. monster 10. decoration
grig... 3. eel 5. annoy, dwarf
  7. cricket, heather 8. irritate
  9. tantalize 11. grasshopper
grill... 4. cook 5. broil 7. griddle,

network, torture 8. gridiron
10. restaurant 11. interrogate
12. cross–examine

grille ... 6. window (ticket) 7. grating,
network

grilse ... 6. salmon 7. botcher

grim ... 4. dour, sour 5. gaunt, harsh,
stern 6. grisly, horrid, savage, sullen
7. ghastly, hideous 8. horrible,
pitiless, ruthless, sinister 9. ferocious,
frightful, merciless, repellent
10. forbidding, inexorable, relentless,
unyielding

grimace ... 3. mop, mow, mug 4. face,
mock, moue, pout, sham 8. pretense
10. distortion 11. affectation

grimalkin ... 3. cat 5. vixen 6. feline
8. old woman

grime ... 4. dirt, smut, soot 5. sully
9. blackness

grin ... 5. fleer, smile, smirk

grind ... 3. dig, rub, vex 4. bray, grit,
mull, whet 5. crush, gnash, grate,
study 6. abrade, drudge, harass,
polish, powder, satire, school, squash
7. operate, routine, sharpen
8. drudgery 9. comminute, masticate,
pulverize, triturate

grinder ... 5. molar, tooth, tutor
8. sideshow 9. announcer
10. flycatcher, goatsucker

grinding ... 6. boning 7. grating
9. attrition 10. burdensome,
irritating, tyrannical 12. excruciating

grinding (pert to) ...
  mental .. 6. boning 8. cramming,
  studying
  stone .. 4. mano 6. metate, muller
  9. millstone
  substance .. 5. emery 8. abrasive

gringo ... 5. alien 8. American
9. foreigner 10. Englishman

grip ... 3. bag 4. hold 5. clasp, cleat,
ditch, drain, grasp, seize, spasm
6. clench, clutch, furrow, grippe,
handle, obsess, trench, valise
7. control, illness 8. gripsack,
handfast

gripe ... 4. grip, hold, pain 5. annoy,
brake, colic, grasp, pinch, spasm
6. clutch, harass 7. afflict, control,
mastery, vulture 8. complain, distress
9. complaint 10. affliction,
oppression

griskin ... 4. chop, loin 5. steak

grisly ... 4. grim 5. harsh 7. ghastly,
hideous 8. gruesome, terrible
9. deathlike 10. forbidding

grist ... 3. lot 4. malt 5. grain, grind
8. quantity (bees)

grit ... 4. sand 5. nerve, pluck
6. gravel 7. bravery, courage, Liberal
9. sandstone 11. persistence
12. perseverance

grivet ... 4. tota, waag 6. monkey

grizzly bear ... 7. Ephraim (hunter's)
15. Ursus horribilis

groats ... 5. grain, wheat (cracked)
6. cereal

grog ... 3. rum 5. rumbo 8. beverage
9. firewater

groggy ... 5. dazed, drunk, shaky, tipsy

8. unsteady, wavering 9. tottering

groin ... 4. lisk 6. inguen

groom ... 4. syce, tidy 5. brush, curry,
dress, preen, train 7. hostler,
servant, shopboy 9. assistant,
stableman 10. bridegroom,
manservant

groove ... 3. rut 4. dado 5. chase,
croze, flute, scarf, stria, track
6. furrow, rabbet, raggle, scrobe,
sulcus 7. channel, rifling, routine
8. philtrum 10. excavation
11. canaliculus

grooved ... 6. fluted 7. striate, sulcate
11. canalicular 12. canaliculate

grope ... 4. feel 5. fumble, search
7. grabble, grubble

groper ... 4. fish 7. grouper

grosbeak ... 5. finch 8. hawfinch

gros point ... 4. lace (Venetian)
6. stitch (Aubusson) 8. tapestry
(Gobelin) 11. cross–stitch

gross ... 3. fat 5. obese 6. brutal,
coarse, earthy, greasy, impure, vulgar
7. brutish, massive, obscene,
sensual, witless 8. flagrant, indecent,
receipts 9. aggregate, unrefined
10. indefinite, indelicate, scurrilous

grotesque ... 3. odd 5. antic, clown,
freak 6. unique 7. awkward, baroque,
bizarre 8. deformed, fanciful
9. fantastic 11. incongruous

grotesque figure (Chin) ... 5. magot

grotto ... 3. den 4. blue, cave, grot
5. crypt, speos, vault 6. cavern,
recess 9. catacomb

ground ... 3. bog 4. acre, area, base,
clay, clod, farm, land, moor, park,
plot, root, soil 5. basis, cause, earth,
field, hurst, marsh, ridge, solum,
swale, train 6. belief, bottom, milled,
region 7. country, gritted, opinion,
premise, terrain (terrane) 8. initiate,
instruct 9. establish, territory,
viewpoint 10. background,
foundation, substratum

ground (pert to) ...
  beetles .. 5. Amara
  berry .. 9. cranberry 12. checkerberry
  grain .. 4. bran, meal 5. flour, grist
  nut .. 5. chufa, gobbe 6. goober,
  peanut
  squirrel .. 5. Xerus 6. gopher, hackee,
  rodent 8. chipmunk 11. spermophile

groundhog (pert to) ...
  American .. 5. marmot
  day .. 9. Candlemas (Feb 2)
  home .. 8. Puxatori
  termed .. 6. marmot, rodent
  8. aardvark, whistler 9. woodchuck
  10. whistlepig

groundless ... 4. idle 5. false
8. baseless 9. unfounded
11. unwarranted 13. unsubstantial

grounds ... 4. lees, park 5. basis,
dregs 7. residue 8. scruples

group ... 3. set 4. band, bevy, clan,
crew, gang, herd, pack, sect, sept,
team, unit 5. batch, bunch, class,
clump, corps, flock, genus, order,
panel, shift, tribe 6. legion, troupe
7. arrange, bracket, cluster,

company, species **8.** assemble,
category, classify, division
10. assemblage **11.** aggregation
group (pert to)...
actors.. **6.** troupe
animals.. **3.** gam, nid, nye, pod
4. herd, nide **5.** covey, drove, pride
(lions)
birds.. **4.** Pici (woodpeckers)
brilliant.. **6.** galaxy
far out.. **6.** hippie **7.** hipster
laymen.. **5.** laity
political.. **4.** bloc, ring **5.** party
7. machine
singer.. **4.** duet **5.** choir, octet
6. chorus **7.** chanter, quartet
(quartette)
students (graduate).. **7.** seminar
trees.. **4.** tope **5.** copse, grove,
woods **7.** alameda, orchard, pinetum
(pines)
group (quota of)...
eight.. **5.** octad, octet (octette)
five.. **6.** pentad
four.. **6.** tetrad **7.** quartet (quartette)
nine.. **6.** ennead
seven.. **6.** heptad, septet (septette)
six.. **6.** sextet (sextette)
ten.. **5.** decad **6.** decade
three.. **4.** trio **5.** triad, trine **7.** Trinity
two vowels.. **6.** digram **7.** digraph
9. diphthong
grouped... **7.** classed **8.** agminate,
arranged, gathered **9.** assembled,
collected, organized **10.** classified
grouper... **4.** fish **5.** guasa **6.** groper
8. rock hind
grouse... **4.** bird **6.** repine **7.** grumble
8. complain **9.** ptarmigan
12. capercaillie
grouse (pert to)...
courtship.. **3.** lak
red.. **7.** Lagopus
ruffed.. **6.** Bonasa
grouty... **5.** cross, sulky **6.** crabby,
grumpy **7.** grouchy
grove (pert to)...
living in.. **7.** nemoral
mango.. **4.** tope
pine.. **7.** pinetum
poplar.. **7.** alameda
sacred.. **5.** Altis (Gr), Nemus (to
Diana)
small trees.. **5.** copse
grovel... **4.** fawn, roll **5.** crawl, creep
6. cringe, crouch, shrink, tumble,
wallow, welter **7.** debauch, truckle
8. flounder
groveling, grovelling... **6.** abject
7. fawning **9.** prostrate, truckling
11. bootlicking
grow... **3.** bud, wax **4.** come **5.** raise
6. accrue, expand, mature, thrive
7. augment, develop, enlarge,
improve, produce **8.** increase,
vegetate **9.** cultivate
grow (pert to)...
dark.. **6.** darkle
dim.. **5.** blear
intense, profound.. **6.** deepen
thin.. **8.** emaciate
tiresome.. **4.** bore, pall

together.. **7.** accrete
worse.. **7.** deteriorate
growing (pert to)...
angry.. **8.** irascent
from without.. **9.** ectogenic
10. ectogenous
in.. **6.** linose
on trees.. **10.** epidendral, epidendric
11. xylophilous (fungus)
out from.. **3.** bud **4.** stem **5.** enate
6. sprout
spontaneously.. **9.** adventive
together.. **7.** accrete, joining
8. adhering
growing in...
clusters.. **8.** racemose
fields.. **8.** agrestal **9.** agrestial
10. campestral
ground.. **9.** geogenous
mud.. **9.** uliginose
pairs.. **6.** binate
rubbish.. **7.** ruderal
snow.. **5.** nival
water.. **7.** aquatic
growl... **4.** girn, gnar, rome **5.** snarl
6. mutter **7.** grumble **8.** complain
growler... **3.** cab, can **4.** bass (black)
7. iceberg, pitcher **8.** clarence
growth... **3.** bud, wen **4.** rise **5.** felon,
shoot, tumor **6.** effect, result
7. increase, swelling **9.** expansion
10. vegetation **11.** consequence,
development, enlargement
12. augmentation
growth (pert to)...
from within.. **8.** endogeny
from without.. **9.** ectogenic
10. ectogenous
fungus.. **4.** mold, moss **6.** mildew
marine.. **7.** seaweed
of wood.. **5.** copse **7.** coppice
9. brushwood
premature.. **9.** precocity
process of.. **8.** nascency
retarding.. **9.** paratonic
grub... **3.** dig **4.** food, plod, root,
spud **5.** larva, mathe, slave, stump
6. assart, drudge, maggot, search
7. plodder **8.** victuals
grubby... **5.** dirty, grimy, small
8. dwarfish, infested, slovenly,
toadfish
grudge... **4.** envy **5.** covet, spite
6. hatred **7.** grumble **8.** begrudge
10. resentment
grudging spender... **8.** tightwad
gruel... **4.** diet **6.** cereal, liquid
7. disable **8.** porridge
grueling, gruelling... **6.** trying
9. demanding, punishing, weakening
10. exhausting
gruesome... **4.** ugly **6.** grisly, horrid,
sordid **7.** ghastly, hideous, macabre
9. deathlike
gruff... **4.** deep, rude, sour **5.** bluff,
harsh, surly **6.** clumsy, hoarse,
morose, severe **7.** austere, bearish,
brusque
grum... **4.** glum, sour **6.** sullen
8. gutteral **13.** harsh–sounding
grumble... **4.** fret, hone, kick **5.** growl,
snarl **6.** grouse, mumble, mutter,

repine, rumble **7.** maunder
8. complain
guacharo . . . **6.** owlish **7.** oilbird
10. goatsucker
Guam . . .
capital . . **5.** Agana
discoverer . . **8.** Magellan (1521)
idol, fetish . . **5.** anito
island . . **7.** Mariana
mountain peak . . **6.** Lamlam
port . . **4.** Apra
guanaco . . . **5.** llama (like) **6.** alpaca
guarantee . . . **6.** avouch, ensure, insure,
surety **7.** endorse, promise, warrant
8. guaranty, security, warranty
9. agreement
guaranty . . . **4.** bond **6.** pledge
8. security, warranty **9.** agreement,
assurance, guarantee
guarapucu . . . **5.** wahoo
guard . . . **3.** van **4.** care, curb, keep,
tend, tile **5.** tiler, watch **6.** bantay,
bridle, convoy, defend, escort, fender,
gaoler, jailer, keeper, patrol, picket,
police, shield, warden **7.** defense,
protect **8.** restrain, sentinel,
watchman **9.** attention, protector
10. cowcatcher, precaution,
protection
guarded . . . **4.** wary **7.** careful
8. cautious, defended, discreet,
vigilant, watchful **9.** protected
10. restrained **11.** circumspect,
sentinelled
guardhouse . . . **4.** brig
guardian . . . **5.** angel, tutor **6.** helper,
keeper, patron, warden **7.** trustee
8. defender, tutelary **9.** custodian,
protector **10.** mystagogue (Church
relics)
guardian (Gr) . . . **5.** Argus (100–eyed)
8. Cerberus (3–headed)
guardianship . . . **4.** care **5.** charge
7. custody, tuition **8.** guidance,
tutelage **13.** protectorship
Guatemala . . .
ant . . **5.** kelep
bird (sacred) . . **7.** quetzal (quezal)
capital . . **13.** Guatemala City
coin (gold) . . **7.** quetzal
fruit (avocadolike) . . **4.** anay
Indian tribe . . **4.** Inca
port . . **7.** San José **10.** Champerico
13. Puerto Barrios
ruins . . **5.** Mayan
volcano . . **4.** Agua **5.** Fuego
gudgeon . . . **4.** bait, dupe, goby
9. killifish **10.** allurement
gue . . . **5.** rogue **7.** sharper
guenon . . . **6.** monkey (long–tailed)
guerdon . . . **5.** crown, prize **6.** reward
8. requital **10.** recompense
guereza . . . **6.** monkey
Guernsey . . . **6.** brandy, cattle, Island
(Channel) **7.** garment
guess . . . **5.** fancy, think **6.** divine
7. imagine, presume, surmise,
suspect **8.** estimate **10.** conjecture
guest . . . **6.** caller, inmate, lodger,
patron **7.** visitor **9.** inquiline (insect)
Guiana . . .
British capital . . **10.** Georgetown

Dutch (Surinam) capital . .
10. Paramaribo
French capital . . **7.** Cayenne
guide . . . **3.** con, key **4.** clew, clue,
lead, rein, sign, sley **5.** order, pilot,
steer, teach, tutor, usher **6.** advise,
direct, dirigo, govern, guidon
7. adviser, conduct, courier, marshal
8. Baedeker (book), cicerone,
director, polestar, regulate
9. regulator
Guido (scale) . . . **2.** ut **3.** alt, A re, B
mi, E la (highest) **5.** E la mi, gamut
7. alamire
guild . . . **5.** hanse **7.** society
10. fellowship **11.** association,
brotherhood
Guildhall statue (London) . . . **3.** Gog
5. Magog (1708)
guile . . . **5.** craft **6.** deceit **9.** duplicity,
falseness, treachery **11.** furtiveness
guileless . . . **5.** naive **6.** simple
7. artless, natural, sincere
8. innocent
guillemot . . . **3.** auk **4.** coot **5.** murre
guilt . . . **3.** sin **4.** sake **5.** culpa
8. iniquity, peccancy **10.** guiltiness,
wickedness **11.** criminality, culpability
14. impeachability
guilty . . . **6.** nocent **8.** culpable
Guinea, W Afr . . .
capital . . **7.** Conakry (Konakri)
city . . **4.** Boke, Labe
export . . **7.** bananas **10.** pineapples
government . . **8.** republic
mineral . . **4.** gold **7.** bauxite
8. diamonds
tree . . **4.** akee
tribe . . **6.** Fullah **7.** Malinke, Soussou
guinea fowl . . . **3.** hen **4.** keet
6. turkey **7.** pintado **8.** pheasant
guinea pig . . . **4.** boar, cavy **5.** Cavia
8. capybara
guise . . . **3.** way **4.** form, garb, mask,
mien, mode **5.** cloak, cover
6. aspect, custom **7.** fashion, pretext
8. behavior **9.** semblance
10. appearance
guitar (pert to) . . .
Hindu . . **4.** vina
like . . **4.** lute **7.** bandore
octaves . . **5.** three
Oriental . . **5.** sitar
pitch (term) . . **5.** dital
ridge . . **7.** samisen
small . . **7.** ukulele
strings, number . . **3.** six
gula . . . **4.** cyma, neck, ogee **6.** gullet
7. cavetto, molding
gulch . . . **5.** cleft, gorge **6.** arroyo,
coulee, ravine
gulf . . . **3.** bay, pit, sea (landlocked)
4. eddy **5.** abyss, basin, chasm,
cleft, inlet **6.** vorago **7.** opening
9. whirlpool **10.** separation (wide)
gull . . . **4.** dupe, fool, gray **5.** brick,
cheat, cully, fraud **7.** cheater,
deceive, defraud, mislead **8.** impostor
gull (bird) . . . **3.** cob (cobb), mew
4. Lari, pirr, skua, tern, Xema
5. pewit (laughing) **7.** Larinae
8. seedbird **9.** kittiwake

gullet... 3. maw 4. tube 5. gully
6. throat 7. channel, harness (part)
9. esophagus

Gulliver, Lemuel (pert to) ..
brutes.. 6. Yahoos (race of)
character, story by.. 5. Swift
romance.. 16. Gulliver's Travels
voyage.. 6. Laputa 8. Lilliput
9. Houyhnhnm 11. Brobdingnag

gully... 3. gut 4. wadi (wady) 5. drain,
gorge, gulch 6. arroyo, gutter, ravine
7. couloir 11. watercourse

gum... 3. ase 4. chew, lerp (larp,
laarp) 5. eiemi, myrrh, xylan
6. acacia, arabic, chicle, conima,
thwart, tupelo 7. camphor, deceive,
elastic, gingiva 8. bdellium (Bib),
mucilage 12. frankincense

gum (pert to)...
Africa.. 4. kino 7. catechy
Asia.. 4. Stora 8. galbabum
Australia.. 5. tuart
Central America.. 6. chicle
Egypt.. 5. kikar
India.. 5. amrad
Philippines.. 8. galagala
United States.. 5. Nyssa 6. tupelo

gumbo... 3. mud 4. okra (ocra), sail,
soup 6. patois

gumboil... 7. abscess, parulia

gummy... 5. lumpy 6. viscid
7. viscous 8. adhesive, resinous

gumption... 8. sagacity 10. enterprise,
initiative, shrewdness

gums... 3. ula 6. resins 8. gingivae

gun... 3. gat, rod 4. iron, pump, roer
5. Maxim, rifle, thief, tommy
6. ack–ack, Archie, barker, Bertha,
cannon, mortar, pistol, Rodman
7. bazooka, carbine, firearm, Gatling,
machine, shotgun 8. amusette,
ordnance, revolver

gun (pert to)...
blow.. 8. sumpitan
caliber.. 4. bore
case (leather).. 7. holster
chamber.. 5. gomer
cleaner.. 6. ramrod
cotton.. 5. nitro 9. explosive, pyroxylin
mount.. 6. turret
platform.. 11. emplacement

gunfire... 5. salvo 6. strafe 8. enfilade

gunner... 10. bombardier
12. artilleryman

guppy... 6. minnow 8. Lebistes
9. killifish

gurnard... 4. fish 6. rochet, Trigla
8. dragonet, sea robin

guru (Ind)... 7. teacher

gush... 3. jet 4. flow, pour 5. emote,
spurt 7. chatter 10. outpouring
14. sentimentalize

gushing... 7. flowing 8. diffused,

effusive, spurting 9. exuberant
11. sentimental 13. demonstrative

gusset... 4. gore 7. bracket
9. abatement (Her)

gust... 4. blow, gale, scud, wind
5. berry, blast, storm 6. flurry, squall
8. outburst 10. excitement

gusto... 4. élan, zest 5. savor, taste
6. fervor, liking, relish 9. eagerness
12. appreciation

gut... 3. sac (silkworm) 5. gully
6. bowels, catgut, defile, strait
7. destroy, plunder 8. entrails
9. intestine 10. disembowel,
eviscerate

guts... 5. belly, force, pluck 6. vitals
7. courage, insides, stamina,
stomach 8. backbone, gluttony
10. intestines

gutta... 4. drop, spot 5. latex
7. campana, marking 8. ornament

guttate... 7. spotted 8. droplike

gutter... 4. rone 5. brook, ditch, drain,
eaves, gully, siver 6. cullis, groove
7. channel, conduit, scupper
11. watercourse

gutteral... 3. dry 4. burr 5. husky,
velar 6. hoarse 7. rasping, throaty

guttersnipe... 4. Arab 5. gamin
6. poster 9. ragpicker, sandpiper,
vulgarian

guy... 3. rod 4. flee, rope, stay, vang
5. chaff, chain, guide 6. banter,
decamp, effigy (Guy Fawkes), fellow,
person

Guy Fawkes Day... 13. Gunpowder
Plot (Eng, Nov 5,1605)

guzzle... 3. tun 4. tope 5. drain,
drink, spree 6. gutter, liquor, throat,
tipple 7. debauch, swallow

gymnast... 7. acrobat, athlete, teacher

gymnastics... 9. exercises
10. acrobatics 12. calisthenics

gypsy (pert to)...
book.. 3. lil
devil.. 5. theng
Dutch.. 8. Heidenen
horse.. 3. gri (gry)
Hungarian.. 7. Czigany
husband.. 3. rom
India.. 7. Bazigar
language.. 6. Romany
man.. 4. chal
sea.. 6. Selung
Spanish.. 6. gitano 7. Zincalo
Syrian.. 5. Aptal
term.. 4. calo 5. nomad
woman.. 4. chai (chi)

gyrate... 4. spin 5. twirl, whirl
6. rotate 7. revolve

gyre... 5. demon, whirl 10. revolution

gyves... 5. irons 6. chains 7. fetters
8. shackles

H

H... 5. aitch, zygal (shaped) 6. letter
(8th), symbol 8. aspirate
haab... 8. calendar (Mayan)
haar... 3. fog
haba... 4. bean 8. lima bean
Habakkuk... 4. Book (Old Test)
7. prophet
habble... 5. brawl 6. gabble, hobble,
uproar 9. confusion 8. difficulty
habeas corpus... 4. writ 7. summons
(you have the body)
habile... 3. apt, fit 4. able 6. adroit,
clever, expert 8. skillful (skilful),
suitable 9. dexterous
habiliment... 4. garb 5. dress, habit
6. attire 7. apparel, costume,
raiment 8. clothing, vestment
11. furnishings
habilitate... 5. dress, equip 6. clothe,
fit out 7. entitle, qualify (for teaching)
habit... 3. rut, use 4. garb, suit, vice,
wont 5. array, dress, haunt, usage
6. attire, clothe, custom, joseph
(riding), nature 7. costume
8. clothing, habitude, practice
9. mannerism 10. deportment,
habiliment
habitat... 4. home 5. abode, house,
hovel 6. harbor, reside 7. exhibit
(museum), lodging, station
habitation... 4. ecad, home 5. hovel
6. ghetto, warren (rabbit) 7. lodging
8. domicile, dwelling, tenement
9. occupancy, residence
habitual... 5. usual 6. common,
wonted 7. orderly, regular
9. customary 10. accustomed,
inveterate
habituate... 5. enure, inure 6. addict,
inborn, season, settle 8. accustom,
frequent, inherent 9. acclimate
11. acclimatize, familiarize
habitué... 8. attender 10. frequenter
hacendero... 6. farmer 10. proprietor
hache... 2. ax 7. hatchet
hacienda... 4. farm 5. abode, croft
6. estate 7. revenue
13. establishment
hack... 3. cut, hew 4. chop, jade, rent
5. coach, cough, devil, horse
(rented), sever 6. drudge, mangle,
writer 8. carriage, mutilate
9. mercenary 11. chronometer
hackberry... 6. Celtis 8. hapberry,
oneberry 10. sugarberry
hackee... 8. chipmunk
hackle... 3. fly (angling) 4. comb, hack
6. shiner, temper 7. feather, hatchel,
plumage 11. stickleback
hackneyed... 3. saw 5. banal, corny,

trite 6. cliché 8. timeworn
10. threadbare 11. commonplace,
stereotyped 13. platitudinous
Hades... 3. pit 4. hell 5. abyss, limbo
7. inferno 9. perdition 10. lower
world, underworld 11. netherworld
Hades (pert to)...
  Babylonian.. 5. Aralu
  capital.. 11. Pandemonium
  god.. 5. Pluto
  Greek.. 8. Tartarus
  Hebrew.. 5. Sheol 7. Abaddon,
  Gehenna 8. Apollyon
  Hindu.. 6. Naraka
  mother.. 4. Rhea
  river.. 4. Styx 5. Lethe 7. Acheron
  Roman.. 3. Dis 5. Orcus
hadj... 10. pilgrimage
haft... 4. ansa, grip, hold 6. handle
8. dwelling
hag... 4. Fury, goad 5. crone, ghost,
Harpy, vixen, witch 6. beldam
(beldame), goblin 8. harridan, old
woman 9. hobgoblin
hageen, hagein... 9. dromedary
hagfish... 5. borer 6. Mysine
7. lamprey (lowest existing craniate
vertebrate)
haggard... 4. bony, lank, lean, pale,
thin, wild 5. gaunt, spare 6. wanton
7. anxious, untamed 8. harrowed,
unchaste, wild–eyed 9. deathlike,
suffering, untrained 10. cadaverous
11. intractable, overwrought
haggle... 3. cut, hew 4. hack, prig
5. cavil 6. chisel, dicker, higgle,
palter 7. bargain, chaffer, stickle,
wrangle
Hague, The... 7. capital (Neth)
Haida (pert to)...
  famed for.. 6. totems 7. carving
  10. seamanship
  Indian.. 15. British Columbia
  tribe.. 11. Skittagetan
hail... 3. ave, ice 4. ahoy, call
5. avast, greet, skoal 6. accost,
health, signal 7. acclaim, address,
graupel, pellets
hair... 3. cue, fur, mop 4. lock, mane,
seta, shag 5. pilus, plume, tress
6. thread 7. bristle 8. filament
10. narrowness
hair (pert to)...
  accessory.. 3. net, pin 8. barrette
  Angora.. 6. mohair
  band.. 5. snood 6. fillet
  braid.. 3. cue 4. fall 5. queue
  7. pigtail
  cell.. 12. Organ of Corti
  cloth.. 3. aba 5. shirt 6. cilice

247

comb form.. 4. pilo
curly.. 10. cymotrichy
disease.. 8. dandruff, psilosis
dresser.. 7. friseur (Fr)
dryness.. 7. xerasia
falling out.. 7. pilosis
flaxen.. 5. linus
horse's foot.. 7. fetlock
intestinal.. 6. villus
lock.. 5. tress 7. earlock, ringlet
  8. lovelock
loss of.. 8. alopecia, baldness
of the.. 6. crinal
remover.. 9. decalvant, epilatory
  10. depilatory
straight.. 10. leiotrichy
style.. 4. tete 7. chignon 8. coiffure
tuft.. 4. coma 5. beard 6. goatee
  7. cirrose, Galways, Vandyke
  8. whiskers 9. sideburns
wave.. 6. marcel
wig.. 6. peruke 7. periwig
wooly.. 9. ulotrichy
hairiness... 7. villous 9. villosity
hairless.. 4. bald 5. acoma
  7. acomous, epilose 8. depilous,
  glabrous
hairpin.. 6. bodkin 8. bobby pin
hairsplitting... 9. quibbling
  11. distinction 13. hypercritical
  14. hypercriticism, overparticular
hairy... 4. noil 6. pilar 6. comate,
  comoid, comose, crinal, pilose,
  shaggy 7. bristly, crinose, hirsute
  8. trichoid
Haiti, Haitian...
bandit.. 4. caco
capital.. 12. Port–au–Prince
discoverer.. 8. Columbus (1492)
evil spirit.. 4. baka (boko)
island.. 10. Hispaniola 15. Greater
  Antilles
language.. 6. Creole, French, patois
liberator.. 9. Toussaint
product.. 6. coffee
sweet potato.. 6. batata
hake.. 4. fish 5. idler, tramp 6. loiter
  7. handgun 8. kingfish
halberd.. 4. bill 5. frame (flogging)
  6. glaive, weapon (Mil)
halcyon... 4. bird, calm 8. peaceful,
  tranquil 10. auspicious, kingfisher
Halcyone (pert to)...
changed to.. 10. kingfisher
daughter of.. 6. Aeolus
wife of.. 4. Ceyx (Gr)
hale.. 3. tug 4. drag, draw, haul,
  pull, well 6. hearty, robust, strong
  7. healthy 8. vigorous
half... 4. demi, hemi, part, semi, term
  5. share 6. moiety 7. divided, partial
  8. division, semester 9. equal part
  11. imperfectly
half (pert to)...
and half.. 5. equal, mixed 6. halved
  7. neutral
boot.. 3. pac (pack) 6. buskin
breed.. 5. metis 6. mustee (mestee)
  7. mestizo, metisse, mulatto
  10. crossbreed, Republican (1881)
man, half bull.. 8. minotaur
man, half horse.. 7. centaur

mask.. 6. domino
moon–shaped.. 8. semilune
  10. semilunate
nelson (wrestling).. 4. hold
stem to stern.. 8. midships
turn (manège).. 8. caracole (caracol)
wit.. 4. dolt 5. dunce 9. blockhead
Half Moon ship (pert to)...
captain.. 11. Henry Hudson
country.. 11. Netherlands
first to sail.. 11. Hudson River (1609)
Halicarnassus, famed for...
Historians (Gr).. 9. Dionysius,
  Herodotus
monument.. 9. Mausoleum (Tomb of
  Mausolus, 325 BC)
hall... 4. aula, room, sala 5. entry,
  foyer, odeum (odeon) 6. atrium,
  lyceum 7. hallway, passage, theater
  8. corridor 10. auditorium,
  passageway
hallow... 5. bless 8. dedicate, sanctify,
  venerate 9. celebrate 10. consecrate
hallowed place... 4. fane, holy
  5. altar 6. bethel, church, shrine,
  temple 9. cathedral, synagogue
hallucination... 6. mirage 7. chimera,
  fantasy 8. delusion 9. nightmare
hallux... 3. toe 5. digit
halo... 3. arc 4. aura, glow, nimb,
  ring 5. glory, light 6. areola, brough,
  circle, corona, nimbus 7. aureole
  (aureola) 8. encircle
halt... 3. end 4. camp, lame, limp,
  stop 5. cease, stand 6. arrest, hold
  up, maimed 7. limping 8. crippled,
  lameness 9. mutilated 10. stand still
halter... 4. hang, rope 5. noose, strap
  6. hamper 7. shackle 8. cavesson,
  restrain
halting... 4. lame 6. maimed
  7. limping 8. spavined
  10. hesitating, stammering
  11. vacillating
halting place... 4. camp 5. étape
  10. encampment
halved... 9. dimidiate
Hamburg...
city of.. 7. Germany
color.. 5. white 6. yellow 7. carmine
  11. carmine lake
fowl.. 11. Leghornlike
fruit.. 5. grape
lace.. 6. edging
root (edible).. 7. parsley
steak.. 4. beef
hamiform... 6. curved, hooked
  7. hamulus 8. aquiline
  10. hook–shaped
Hamilton (pert to)...
dynamics.. 8. equation
famed as.. 9. statesman
  11. philosopher 13. mathematician
math.. 10. quaternion
Hamite (N Afr)... 5. Fulah 6. Berber,
  Somali (Somal)
hamlet... 4. dorp, vill 5. aldea (aldee)
  casal (casale), thorp (thorpe)
  7. grouper (fish), village
Hamlet (pert to)...
character.. 11. Shakespeare
country.. 7. Denmark

friend.. **7.** Horatio
site.. **8.** Elsinore
hammer... **4.** beat, claw, jack, maul,
  peen, tack, tamp **5.** gavel, kevel,
  madge, pound **6.** beetle, martel,
  oliver, sledge, strike, swinge
  7. belabor **8.** malleate
hammer (pert to)...
  bird.. **8.** umbrette
  blacksmith's.. **5.** fuller, oliver
  bricklayer's.. **6.** scutch
  end.. **4.** poll
  face.. **4.** trip
  head.. **4.** peen **5.** shark
  medical.. **6.** plexor **7.** plessor
  out.. **5.** anvil, forge
  smite.. **5.** skite
  stone.. **5.** kevel, spall
hamper... **3.** ped **4.** clog, curb, load,
  slow **5.** cramp, crate, maund
  6. basket, burden, fetter, hinder,
  hopple, impede, seroon **7.** confine,
  hanaper, manacle, shackle, trammel
  8. encumber, restrain, restrict
  9. container, embarrass
  10. impediment
Ham's son.. **4.** Cush
hamster... **6.** rodent **8.** Cricetus
hamus.. **3.** hook **7.** process (Zool)
hanaper... **6.** basket, hamper
hand... **3.** paw **4.** fist, give, mano,
  palm, part, pass, side, till **5.** claut,
  grasp, index, manus, power, share,
  skill **6.** agency, worker **7.** ability,
  pointer, workman **8.** applause,
  tendency, transmit **9.** craftsman,
  handiwork, signature **10.** metacarpus
  11. handwriting, performance
  15. instrumentality
hand (pert to)...
  back of.. **10.** opisthenar
  bag.. **4.** etui, grip **5.** cabas, purse
  8. reticule
  book.. **4.** tome **5.** codex **6.** manual
  9. vade mecum
  cuffs.. **7.** darbies **8.** manacles
  9. bracelets
  handful.. **4.** kirn **6.** gowpen
  7. maniple **8.** quantity
  measure.. **8.** fistmele
  me–down.. **4.** used, worn **5.** cheap
  9. ready–made **10.** secondhand
  of the.. **6.** chiral, manual
  palm.. **4.** loof **6.** thenar
  picked.. **5.** eleme **6.** choice
  8. selected
  script.. **6.** Neshki (Neski)
  stone (grinding).. **4.** mano
  without.. **7.** amanous
  writing.. **11.** chirography
  writing on walls.. **4.** doom, mene
  (Bib), omen **8.** graffito
handicap... **4.** lisp, race **6.** burden,
  hamper, hinder, impede
  8. encumber, equalize, penalize
  9. advantage **10.** impediment,
  stuttering **11.** encumbrance
  12. disadvantage
handicraftsman... **7.** artisan
handkerchief... **7.** malabar
  8. mouchoir **9.** neckcloth
  11. neckerchief

handle... **3.** ear, paw, ply, use
  4. ansa, bail, deal, feel, haft, hilt,
  knob, maul, name, toat, tote
  5. helve, pilot, snath, swipe, title,
  touch, treat, wield **6.** deal in, direct,
  manage, rounce, second, sneath,
  tiller **7.** control, operate
handle (pert to)...
  awkwardly.. **6.** fumble, mumble
  carelessly.. **6.** cajole **7.** tweedle
  roughly.. **4.** maul **6.** bruise, injure,
  mangle
  shaped.. **6.** ansate
  skillfully.. **6.** manage **7.** control
  10. manipulate
hands (pert to)...
  nautical.. **4.** crew, gang
  off.. **4.** don't, quit, stop **5.** taboo
  6. desist **9.** interdict
  on hips.. **6.** akimbo
  without.. **7.** amanous
handsome... **5.** ample **6.** comely,
  heppen (dial) **7.** elegant, gallant,
  liberal **8.** generous, gracious,
  pleasing, suitable **9.** agreeable,
  beautiful **10.** jimpricute
  11. appropriate, magnanimous
  12. considerable
handwriting on the wall... **4.** mene
  (Bib) **8.** graffito, upharsin
handy... **4.** deft **5.** adept, ready
  6. adroit, heppen, nearby, wieldy
  8. skillful (skilful) **9.** dexterous,
  versatile **10.** accessible, convenient
hang... **3.** sag **4.** pend, rest, sway
  5. cling, drape, droop, hover, knack
  6. cleave, dangle, depend
  7. execute, meaning, suspend
hang (pert to)...
  around.. **4.** loaf, wait **6.** loiter
  8. frequent
  back.. **3.** lag **5.** demur, loath **6.** falter
  9. reluctant
  down.. **3.** lop **4.** lave **5.** droop
  6. depend
  loosely.. **3.** lop **4.** flag, loll **6.** bangle,
  dangle
  on, onto.. **5.** cling **6.** adhere, depend
  9. persevere
  over.. **6.** impend
  together.. **4.** loin **6.** cohere
  9. co-operate
hanger–on... **3.** bur **5.** toady **6.** heeler
  8. follower, loiterer, parasite
  9. appendage, dependent, sycophant,
  toadeater (menial) **10.** blackguard
hanging... **5.** arras, drape, loose
  7. curtain, pendant (pendent),
  pensile, valance **8.** downcast,
  pendency **9.** execution, suspended
hanging (pert to)...
  Eccl.. **6.** dorsal, dossal (dossel)
  Gardens of Babylon, builder..
  14. Nebuchadnezzar (Nebuchadrezzar)
  ornament.. **6.** bangle **7.** pendant
  stage.. **7.** scenery
hangman... **8.** carnifex **9.** Jack Ketch
  11. executioner
hangman's noose... **4.** rope
  6. hempen
hangnail... **6.** agnail **7.** whitlow
hangout... **5.** joint **10.** rendezvous

hank... 3. ran (twine) 4. coil 5. skein
hanker after... 5. crave, yearn
  6. aspire, desire, hunger 7. long for
Hannibal (pert to)...
  accomplishment.. 8. Punic War (2nd)
  father.. 13. Hamilcar Barca
  native of.. 8. Carthage
  rank.. 7. General (genius)
  victory at.. 6. Cannae
Hanover, House of... 8. Victoria
Hanukkah, Hanukka... 7. holiday
  (Jew) 16. Festival of Lights (Bib)
  17. Feast of Dedication (Jew)
haphazard... 6. chance, random
  8. accident, careless 9. orderless
haply... 9. perchance
happen... 4. come, fall, fare 5. evene
  (obs), occur 6. arrive, befall, betide,
  chance, mayhap 8. eventuate,
  transpire
happening... 4. fact 5. event (chance)
  6. tiding 7. episode 8. incident,
  periodic, sporadic 10. occurrence
happily... 5. fitly, haply 6. gladly
  9. tactfully, willingly 10. blissfully,
  cheerfully, gracefully 11. contentedly,
  opportunely 12. auspiciously,
  felicitously, prosperously, successfully
  13. appropriately
happiness, science of...
  11. eudaemonics
happy... 3. apt 4. cosh, glad 5. blest,
  faust, lucky, ready, seely, sunny
  6. joyful, timely 7. blessed, content,
  fitting 8. cheerful 9. contented,
  fortunate, pertinent 10. auspicious,
  felicitous, propitious, prosperous
Happy Valley... 8. paradise (of
  Rasselas, Andrew Jackson)
hara–kiri (Jap)... 7. seppuku, suicide
harangue... 3. nag 4. rant 5. orate,
  spiel, spout 6. screed, speech, tirade
  7. address, declaim, expound,
  lecture, oration
harass... 3. din, fag, nag, try, vex
  4. bait, fret, gall, haze, jade, raid,
  tire 5. annoy, beset, bully, chafe,
  grind, harry, tease, weary, worry
  6. badger, bother, heckle, hector,
  molest, pester, plague 7. agitate,
  disturb, hagride, perplex, provoke,
  torment, trouble 8. distress, irritate
  9. persecute, tantalize
harbinger... 4. host, omen 5. usher
  6. herald 7. presage, shelter
  8. fourrier, harborer 9. informant,
  messenger, precursor 10. forerunner
harbinger of Spring... 5. robin
  6. crocus
harbor, harbour... 3. bay 4. cave,
  port 5. haven 6. covert, foster,
  refuge 7. lodging, outport, retreat,
  shelter
hard... 3. fit 4. cold, dour, firm, iron,
  mean 5. close, harsh, rigid, stern,
  stony 6. knotty, robust, steely, stingy,
  strict, strong 7. callous, onerous
  8. diligent, rigorous, toilsome
  9. difficult, harsh, intricate,
  strenuous, stringent, wearisome
  10. inflexible, relentless, unyielding
  12. impenetrable, incorrigible

  13. unsympathetic
hard (pert to)...
  boiled.. 4. hard 5. tough 6. strict
  7. callous 8. hardened 10. solidified
  13. sophisticated
  coal.. 10. anthracite
  money.. 6. silver 8. metallic
  prefix.. 3. dys
  question.. 5. poser
  rubber.. 7. ebonite 9. vulcanite
  shell.. 7. lorica
  stone.. 7. adamant (diamond)
  wood.. 4. mabi, teak 5. maple
  6. walnut 8. mahogany
harden... 3. gel, set 4. cake, kern
  5. enure, inure, steel 6. freeze,
  ossify, temper 7. toughen
  8. indurate, solidify 9. habituate
  10. strengthen
hardened... 4. hard 5. caked
  6. frozen, wicked 7. callous, steeled
  8. indurate, obdurate, ossified
  9. heartless, reprobate, unfeeling
  10. impenitent, impervious,
  inveterate, solidified 12. impenetrable
hardening of the arteries...
  16. arteriosclerosis
hardening of the eyeball...
  8. glaucoma
hardheaded... 5. boche (Boche)
  6. German, shrewd, strict
  9. obstinate, sagacious
hardhearted... 4. mean 5. cruel
  7. callous 8. pitiless 9. unfeeling
  13. unsympathetic
hardship... 5. rigor 6. injury 7. trouble
  8. hardness 9. adversity, privation
hardtack... 5. bread 7. galette
  10. sea biscuit
hardwood... 3. ash, oak 4. ipil, mabi,
  teak 5. maple 6. walnut
  8. mahogany
hardy... 4. bold, hale, rash 5. brave,
  lusty, stout 6. daring, strong
  7. healthy, spartan 8. intrepid,
  resolute 9. audacious, confident
  10. courageous
hare... 3. doe, wat (watt) 4. buck,
  cony, pika (tailless) 5. lapin, Lepus
  6. rabbit, rodent, tapeti 7. leveret
hare (pert to)...
  constellation.. 5. Lepus
  harelike.. 6. agouti 8. leporine
  tail.. 4. scut
  track.. 4. slot
  type.. 10. cottontail, jack rabbit
harem... 5. serai 6. purdah, zenana
  8. seraglio 9. gynaeceum
harem room... 3. oda (odah)
harem slave... 9. odalisque (odalisk)
hark... 4. heed, hist 6. listen
  7. hearken, whisper 9. attention
harkened... 5. heard 6. heeded
  8. listened 9. hearkened
harlequin... 4. duck (sea) 5. clown,
  color 7. buffoon 9. fantastic, trickster
  11. masquerader 12. multi–colored,
  parti–colored
Harlequin (comedy)... 11. pantomimist
harm... 3. mar 4. bane, dere, evil,
  hurt, pain 5. grief, wrong
  6. damage, impair, injure, injury,

scathe (scath), sorrow
10. misfortune, wickedness
12. disadvantage

harmful... 3. bad 4. evil, upas
6. nocent 7. baneful, hurtful, malefic,
noisome, noxious 8. damaging,
sinister 9. injurious 10. pernicious
11. deleterious, detrimental
12. insalubrious

harmless... 5. seely 6. unhurt
8. dehorned, unharmed
9. innocuous, undamaged, uninjured
11. unoffending

harmonious... 6. syntax 7. harmony,
musical, orderly, spheral, tuneful
9. accordant, agreeable, congruous,
consonant, eurythmic (eurhythmic),
melodious 10. compatible,
concordant, euphonious
11. conformable, symmetrical

harmonize... 2. go 3. gee 4. tone
5. agree, blend, chime 6. attune
7. conform, consist 8. reconcile
10. correspond, symmetrize,
sympathize

harmony... 4. tone, tune 5. music,
order, triad, unity 6. accord, cosmos,
melody, unison 7. concord, euphony
8. symmetry 9. agreement,
harmonics 10. conformity,
consonance

harness... 4. gear 5. armor, equip
6. graith, tackle 7. uniform
8. accouter, ornament 9. caparison,
parachute

harness part... 3. tug 4. hame, rein
5. trace 6. collar, halter, terret
7. apparel 9. hackamore
10. breastband, martingale

harp... 4. arpa, koto, lyre, Lyra (Astron)
5. nanga 8. Irishman 11. clairschach

harp (pert to)...
key.. 5. C Flat
octaves (number).. 11. six and a half
pedals.. 5. seven
star.. 12. Harp of Arthur
strings.. 8. forty-six

harping... 7. humdrum, tedious
9. iterating, repeating 11. repetitious

harpoon... 5. spear 7. javelin 11. lily
iron

harpsichord... 6. spinet 8. clavecin
9. lyrichord 12. clavicembalo

harpy... 3. bat 5. eagle, fiend
9. plunderer 12. extortionist

Harpy (Myth)... 5. Aello, ghoul
7. Celaeno, monster (part bird,
woman), Ocypete, Podarge (The Iliad)

harridan... 3. hag 5. vixen, witch
6. virago 7. Jezebel 8. strumpet
9. termagant

harrier... 3. dog 4. hawk 5. bully,
hound 7. heckler 8. badgerer
9. tormentor

harrow... 4. dish, pain 5. harry, herse
(Hist), wound 7. oppress, torment,
torture 8. distress, lacerate
9. cultivate, formation (geese),
implement

harrowing... 7. painful, racking, tilling
9. agonizing, torturous

11. cultivating, distressing
12. heart-rending

harry... 3. vex 4. sack 5. annoy,
hound, worry 6. harass, hector,
plague, ravage, ravish 7. agitate,
besiege, pillage, plunder, violate
8. lay waste 9. persecute

Harry... 5. Devil (Shak)

harsh... 3. raw 4. dure, grim
5. acerb, acrid, asper, crude, gruff,
raspy, stern, stiff 6. bitter, coarse,
severe, unkind 7. drastic, painful,
pungent, rasping 8. clashing,
guttural, jangling, rigorous, strident
9. inclement, offensive, repellent
10. discordant, relentless
11. acrimonious, disagreeing

harshness... 5. rigor 7. raucity
8. acrimony, pungency, severity
9. gruffness 11. raucousness

hart... 4. deer, stag 5. spade

hartebeest... 4. asse, tora 5. caama
(kaama) 6. lecama 7. bubalis
8. antelope 10. Alcelaphus

Harvard College honor... 4. book
5. detur 12. let it be given

harvest... 4. crop, gain, rabi, reap
5. fruit, yield 6. autumn, gather,
reward 7. acquire, produce

harvest (pert to)...
god.. 6. Cronus, Saturn
goddess.. 3. Ops 5. Ceres
home.. 4. kirn, mell 6. hockey
moon.. 4. full 15. autumnal equinox
second.. 7. aftermath
tick.. 6. acarid

hash... 4. food 5. mince 6. jumble,
medley, ragout 7. mixture
10. hodgepodge 11. gallimaufry, olla
podrida

hashish... 4. hemp 5. bhang (bang)
8. cannabis, narcotic

hassle... 4. fray 5. brawl, melee

hasten... 3. hie 4. scud, urge
5. amain, apace, hurry, scamp,
speed 7. further 8. expedite
10. accelerate 11. precipitate

hastened... 3. ran 4. hied, sped
5. raced 6. rushed 7. hurried,
scooted 8. galloped 9. expedited
11. accelerated 12. precipitated

hasty... 4. fast, rash 5. brash, eager,
fleet, quick, swift 6. speedy, sudden,
urgent 7. cursory, hurried 8. reckless
9. impetuous, impulsive, premature
11. expeditious, precipitate

hasty pudding... 4. mush 9. stirabout

hat... 3. fez, tam, top 4. felt, hood,
silk 5. beret, derby, gibus, opera,
straw, terai, toque 6. bonnet, cloche,
cocked, fedora, Panama, sailor,
topper, turban 7. chapeau, picture,
pillbox, porkpie, tricorn 8. sombrero
9. headdress, sou'wester, stovepipe,
ten-gallon 11. mortarboard
13. three-cornered

hat (pert to)...
antique.. 7. bycoket (bycocket),
petasos (petasus)
covering.. 8. havelock
crown.. 4. poll
defensive.. 4. coif

Eccl .. 7. biretta 9. Cardinal's
military .. 5. shako
opera .. 4. tile 5. gibus 6. topper
pass (the hat) .. 10. collection
slang .. 4. plug 5. dicer
stovepipe .. 8. caroline
under one's .. 6. secret 9. to oneself
hatch ... 4. door, gate, line (art), plot
5. breed 6. invent 7. concoct,
produce 8. contrive, hatchway,
incubate 9. floodgate, originate
10. bring forth, sluice gate
hatchet ... 2. ax (axe) 3. adz (adze)
4. mogo 8. tomahawk
hate ... 4. miso (comb form) 5. abhor,
odium 6. detest, hatred, loathe,
rancor 7. despise, dislike
9. abominate, antipathy
hateful ... 6. odious 7. heinous
8. terrible 9. abhorrent, execrable,
invidious, loathsome, malicious,
obnoxious, offensive, revolting
10. abominable, detestable,
disgusting 11. distasteful
12. disagreeable
hater of ...
children .. 10. misopedist
mankind .. 11. misanthrope
marriage .. 10. misogynist
mathematics .. 8. misomath
newness .. 9. misoneist
sights .. 11. misoscopist
strangers .. 8. misoxene
work .. 11. ergophobiac
hatred ... 5. odium 6. enmity, rancor
8. aversion 9. animosity, malignity
10. abhorrence, repugnance
11. detestation, malevolence
hatred of ...
argument .. 8. misology
change .. 9. misoneism
children .. 9. misopedia
God, gods .. 10. misotheism
mankind .. 11. misanthropy
marriage .. 8. misogamy
strangers .. 8. misoxeny
10. xenophobia
war .. 9. polemical 11. misopolemic
wisdom .. 8. misosophy
women .. 8. misogyny
hauberk ... 5. armor 9. habergeon
haughty ... 4. airy, bold, high 5. lofty,
noble, proud 6. snooty 7. fatuous,
stately 8. arrogant, cavalier, orgulous,
scornful 10. disdainful, hoity–toity
11. domineering, highfalutin
12. contemptuous, supercilious
haul ... 3. lug, tow, tug 4. cart, drag,
draw, pull 5. booty, bouse, catch,
check, shift 9. reprimand, transport
haul down a flag ... 6. strike
haunch ... 3. hip 4. huck 10. leg and
loin 12. hindquarters
haunch bone ... 10. innominate
haunt ... 3. den 4. dive, nest 5. ghost,
habit 6. infect, obsess, resort
7. torment 8. frequent, practice
hautboy ... 4. oboe
have ... 3. get, hae, own 4. hold,
keep, know 5. beget, trick 6. accept,
effect, retain 7. cherish, perform,
possess, swindle 10. experience,

understand, suffer from
have (pert to) ...
ambition .. 6. aspire
charge .. 4. tend
on .. 4. wear
thoughts of .. 6. ideate
to do with .. 4. deal
weight .. 8. militate
haven ... 3. bay 4. port 5. hithe
(small), inlet 6. asylum, harbor,
recess, refuge 7. shelter 9. sanctuary
havier ... 4. deer
having (pert to) ...
blind end .. 6. caecal
branches .. 6. ramose
clamp, pincers .. 7. chelate
dignity .. 8. majestic
equal sides .. 9. isosceles
eyes .. 7. oculate
faith .. 8. trusting
featherlike petals .. 7. pinnate
feelers .. 9. antennae
fingers .. 8. digitate
foreknowledge .. 9. prescient
four feet .. 11. quadrupedal
harmful quality .. 9. innocuous
leaves .. 6. foliar 7. foliate
limits .. 6. finite
local designation .. 7. topical
lumps .. 7. noduled
more than one mate .. 9. polyandry
no angles .. 6. agonic
no interest .. 6. supine
no teeth .. 7. edental 8. edentate
nothing to do .. 6. otiose
one foot .. 6. uniped
pits, depressions .. 7. foveate
9. foveolate
plane surfaces .. 7. faceted
pointed end .. 6. peaked 7. cuspate
8. aristate
power over fire .. 10. ignipotent
power to believe .. 9. creditive
reflecting surface .. 8. specular
same ending .. 11. conterminal
same parents .. 7. germane
sawlike edge .. 7. serrate
scales .. 8. perulate
scalloped edge .. 7. crenate
taste .. 5. sapid
thorns .. 7. spinate
three broods yearly .. 11. trigoneutic
two feet .. 5. biped 7. bipedal
two horns .. 6. bicorn
two meanings .. 9. ambiguous
unequal sides .. 7. scalene
web feet .. 8. pinniped
wings .. 4. alar
having a ...
backbone .. 10. vertebrate
beak .. 8. rostrate
beard .. 8. aristate
handle .. 6. ansate
large nose .. 6. nasute
shield .. 9. clypeated
stem .. 9. petiolate
tail .. 7. caudate
tuft .. 6. comose
veil .. 6. velate
will .. 7. testate
havoc ... 4. harm 5. botch, waste
7. destroy 11. destruction,

devastation 12. annihilation
haw... 4. sloe 5. fence, hedge
6. eyelid (3rd) 7. stammer
8. hawthorn, messuage, turn left
9. enclosure 11. exclamation
Hawaii... see also *Hawaiian*
capital.. 8. Honolulu
city.. 4. Hilo 7. Wailuku
crater.. 7. Kilauea 9. Haleakala
district.. 7. Lahaina
explorer.. 4. Cook (Capt)
harbor.. 5. Pearl (bombed 12/7/41)
islands (major).. 4. Maui, Oahu
5. Kauai, Lanai 6. Hawaii, Niihau
7. Molokai 8. Kahoolawe
lake.. 5. Waiau
native.. 10. Polynesian
old name.. 15. Sandwich Islands
peak.. 8. Mauna Kea, Mauna Loa
9. Waialeale
resort.. 7. Waikiki
Southernmost point (US).. 5. Ka Lae
State admission.. 8. Fiftieth
State flower.. 8. hibiscus
State nickname.. 5. Aloha
20. Paradise of the Pacific
volcano.. 8. Mauna Loa (largest
active)
Hawaiian... 6. Kanaka 10. Melanesian,
Polynesian 16. South Sea islander
Hawaiian (pert to)...
banquet, feast.. 7. ahaaina
basket.. 2. ie
beverage.. 4. kava 8. kavakava
bird.. 2. io, o-o 3. iwa 4. iiwi,
mamo (ext), noio, o-o-a-a 6. olomao
(thrush) 8. drepanis
canoe.. 5. waapa
chant.. 4. mele
cloth, clothes.. 4. kapa, tapa
coffee.. 4. kona
dance.. 4. hula
fern.. 4. pulu
fiber (pine).. 2. ie
fish.. 3. awa 4. ulua 5. akule, lania
flower wreath, garland.. 3. lei
food.. 3. poi 4. kalo, taro
garment.. 6. holoku, muumuu
god.. 5. Wakea 7. Kanaloa (Pantheon)
goddess.. 4. Pele (volcanoes, fire)
gooseberry.. 4. poha
grass.. 6. emoloa
greeting.. 5. aloha
herb.. 3. pia (starch root)
king (first).. 10. Kamehameha
lava.. 2. aa 8. pahoehoe
loincloth, girdle.. 4. malo
musical instrument.. 7. ukulele
pepper.. 3. ava 4. kava 8. kavakava
precipice.. 4. pali
Queen.. 8. Kamamalu
royalty.. 4. alii
seaweed (edible).. 4. limu
shampoo, massage.. 8. lomi-lomi
shrub.. 3. pia 4. akia, pulu 5. olona
temple.. 5. heiau
tern.. 4. noio
veranda.. 5. lanai
windstorm.. 4. kona
woman.. 5. haole
yam.. 3. hoi
hawfinch... 8. grosbeak

hawk... 3. cry 4. hunt, sell, vend
6. peddle 7. canvass 9. plunderer
hawk (bird)... 2. io 3. hen 4. eyas,
kahu, kite, nyas, seel (blind)
5. Astur, Buteo 6. falcon, osprey,
tercel 7. buzzard, Cooper's, goshawk,
harrier, kestrel, puttock, sparrow
8. caracara 9. Accipiter, red-tailed
hawker of fruit (Eng)... 6. coster
12. costermonger
hawk-eyed deity... 2. Ra
Hawkeye State... 4. Iowa
hawking... 7. hunting, vending
8. falconry
hawk moth... 6. sphinx 8. sphingid
10. Sphingidae
hawksbill... 4. pawl 6. turtle
8. tortoise
hawkshaw... 6. sleuth 9. detective
11. sleuthhound
hawk's nest... 5. aerie (aery)
hawser... 4. line, rope
hawser post... 4. bitt 7. ballard
hawthorn... 3. may 5. hazel (fruit)
6. red haw 7. haw tree
9. mayflower
Hawthorne, Nathaniel... 6. author
8. novelist
hay... 6. fodder 7. timothy
hay (pert to)...
bird.. 7. hay jack 8. black cap
9. sandpiper (pectoral)
bundle.. 3. mow 4. bale, rick
5. stack
fork.. 5. pikel (pikle), pitch
herb.. 8. sainfoin
mown.. 5. swath
second cutting.. 5. rowen
stack.. 4. rick 7. hayrick
storage site.. 3. mow 4. barn, loft,
silo
hazard... 3. fog 4. dare, game, jump,
risk 5. peril 6. gamble, sanger,
stroke 7. imperil, jeopard, presume,
venture 8. cabstand, casualty,
endanger, jeopardy 11. restriction
hazardous... 5. jumpy, risky 6. chancy,
queasy, unsafe 7. unsound
8. perilous 9. uncertain, venturous
10. fortuitous 11. speculative,
venturesome
haze... 3. fog 4. beat, film, glin (at
sea), mist, smog 5. scold, smoke,
vapor 7. dimness, drizzle 9. frighten
hazy... 3. dim 5. filmy, foggy, misty,
smoky, thick, vague 6. cloudy,
opaque, stupid 7. muddled, nebular,
obscure 9. invisible, uncertain
10. indistinct
he... 2. il 3. man 4. ipsi, male 6. any
one, letter 7. pronoun
he remains (stage direction)..
5. manet
head... 3. aim, nob 4. lead, pate, poll,
tete 5. caput, chief, skull 6. noggin,
source 7. cranium
head (pert to)...
abbey.. 5. abbot 6. abbess
back of.. 7. occiput
bald.. 9. pilgarlic
bone.. 8. parietal 9. occipital
Gorgon.. 6. Medusa (Myth)

hard.. 5. boche
of hair.. 5. crine
pert to.. 8. cephalic
proportion.. 14. mesitacephalic
shaven.. 7. tonsure
shrunken.. 7. tsentsa
headache... 6. megrim 8. migraine
11. cephalalgia
head covering... 3. cap, hat, tam, wig
4. hair, hood, veil 5. beret, miter,
scalp 6. bonnet, peruke, toupee,
wimple 7. biretta 8. sombrero
10. fascinator
headdress... 3. wig 4. pouf, tête
5. busby, miter, shako, tiara
6. coiffe, diadem, hennin, peruke,
pinner 7. bandore, buzz wig, coronet,
periwig 8. coiffure, headtire
headdress (Egypt)... 6. uraeus (with
sacred asp)
headhunters (Luzon)... 7. Igorots
heading... 3. top 5. front, title, topic
6. pillow 7. bolster, caption
8. headline 9. direction
12. decapitation
headland... 4. cape, mull, ness
5. morro, ridge 10. promontory
headless... 6. stupid 7. acephal,
topless 9. acephalus (monster)
10. acephalous
headline... 6. banner 7. caption,
display, heading
headliner... 4. star 7. feature
8. composer
headlong... 4. rash 5. hasty, steep
6. head–on, sudden 8. reckless
9. headfirst, impetuous, impulsive
10. recklessly 11. impulsively,
precipitate, precipitous
headpiece... 3. cap, hat, top 4. atef
5. crown 6. halter, helmet, lintel
7. fitting 8. covering, ornament, skull
cap 9. headboard, headdress,
headstall
head–shaped... 8. capitate
headstrong... 4. rash 6. entêté, unruly
7. violent, wayward 9. obstinate
11. intractable, opinionated
12. contumacious, ungovernable
heal... 4. cure, knit, mend 6. doctor,
pacify, remedy, repair 7. correct,
restore 8. cicatrize
healing (pert to)...
agent.. 6. balsam
compound.. 4. balm
goddess.. 3. Eir
magic.. 6. powwow
process.. 4. scar 8. cicatrix
remedy.. 8. curative, sanative
science.. 9. iatrology
suffix.. 7. iatrics
health (pert to)...
care.. 7. welfare
comb form.. 4. sani
conditions.. 8. sanitary
goddess.. 5. Salus 6. Hygeia
7. Minerva
Latin.. 5. salus
neurotic.. 13. hypochondriac
resort.. 3. spa 7. springs
symbol.. 5. pansy

healthful... 7. healthy 8. curative,
salutary, sanatory 9. medicinal
10. salubrious
healthy... 4. hale, sane, well
6. hearty, robust 8. salutary,
vigorous 9. healthful, wholesome
10. salubrious
heap... 3. cop 4. dess, load, lump,
pile, pyre, raff, raft 5. amass, cairn,
crowd, stack 6. plenty, sorite, throng
7. cumulus 9. multitude
10. accumulate
heaped... 5. piled 7. stacked
8. acervate 9. collected
hear... 3. see 4. feel, heed, oyez
(oyes) 5. favor, judge, learn
6. attend, listen 7. hearken (harken)
8. listen to, perceive 9. attention
10. adjudicate
hearer... 7. audient, auditor
8. disciple, listener 9. hearkener
(harkener) 12. eavesdropper
hearing (pert to)... 3. act, aid, ear
4. otic, oyer 5. aural, sense
(special), sound, trial 6. otosis, tryout
7. earshot 8. audience, audition,
auditory 9. attention, auricular,
interview, knowledge
hearken, harken... 4. hear, heed
6. attend, listen 7. give ear, inquire
hearsay... 4. talk 5. bruit, rumor
6. gossip, report 8. evidence
heart... 3. cor 4. card, core, gist, life,
love, mood, soul 5. cheer, organ
6. center, depths, kardia, middle,
spirit, vitals 7. courage, emotion,
essence, feeling 9. affection,
substance 10. conscience
11. temperament
heart (pert to)...
ache.. 5. grief 6. sorrow 7. anguish
active.. 7. sthenic
beat.. 5. pulse, throb 7. systole
8. diastole 9. pulsation
10. palmoscopy
bleeding (flower).. 8. dicentra
burn.. 4. envy 6. enmity 7. burning,
pyrosia 8. jealousy 10. cardialgia,
discontent, heartscald (heart–scaud)
cavity.. 6. atrium
chamber.. 6. atrium 7. auricle
9. ventricle 11. ventriculum
contraction.. 7. systole
disease.. 14. angina pectoris
Egypt.. 2. Ab 4. hati
expansion.. 8. diastole
felt.. 4. dear, deep, real, true
7. genuine, sincere
shaped.. 7. cordate
valve.. 6. mitral 8. bicuspid
9. tricuspid
hearten... 5. cheer 7. comfort
8. embolden, inspirit, reassure
9. encourage
hearth... 4. home 5. ingle 6. astrer
(pert to) 8. fireside 9. fireplace
hearth goddess... 5. Vesta 6. Hestia
hearty... 4. hale, rich, warm
5. heavy, lusty 6. active, robust,
stanch 7. cordial, earnest, fervent
8. friendly, vigorous 9. convivial,
energetic, unfeigned 10. nourishing

11. substantial
heat... 4. fire, race, warm, zeal
5. ardor, calor, cauma, fever, tepor
6. degree, warmth 7. inflame,
passion 10. excitement
11. temperature
heat (pert to)...
heating.. 9. calorific
measure.. 5. therm (therme) 7. calorie
(calory) 10. centigrade, Fahrenheit
pert to.. 7. thermic
plaster.. 4. mull 7. steatin
principle.. 7. caloric
white.. 13. incandescence
heater... 4. etna, kiln, oven 5. forge,
stove, tisar 6. boiler, retort
7. brazier, furnace 8. annealer,
register 12. electron tube
heath... 4. moor 5. Erica, plain, savin,
waste 8. tamarisk 10. underbrush
heathen... 5. pagan 6. ethnic, paynim
7. gentile, godless, infidel
10. unbeliever 11. irreligious
13. unenlightened
heathen deity... 4. idol 5. image
6. symbol
heather... 5. color, Erica, plant
9. crowberry 12. poverty plant
heaume... 6. helmet (armor)
heave... 4. cast, draw, hurl, lift, toss
5. fling, hoist, pitch, raise, retch,
scena, throw 11. rise and fall
heaven... 3. sky 4. ciel, Eden 5. ether
6. utopia, welkin 7. arcadia, Elysium,
Nirvana 8. empyrean, Paradise,
Valhalla (Valhall) 9. firmament
heavenly... 5. godly 6. divine, sacred
7. angelic, blessed, uranian
8. supernal 9. beautiful, celestial
10. delightful
heavenly (pert to)...
being.. 5. angel, saint 6. cherub,
seraph 7. Madonna 8. cherubim, Dei
Mater, seraphim
belt.. 6. galaxy, zodiac
body.. 3. sun 4. luna, moon, star
5. comet 6. planet 8. luminary
city.. 4. Zion 12. New Jerusalem
path.. 5. orbit
solar apparatus.. 6. orrery
sphere.. 8. empyrean
twins (Gemini).. 6. Castor, Pollux
heavens... see **heaven**
heaves... 6. emphysema
heavy... 3. sad 4. deep, dull, hard,
role 5. actor, dense, grave, great,
inert, massy 6. coarse, gloomy,
leaden, sleepy, strong, viscid
7. doleful, onerous, serious, villain,
violent, weighty 8. burdened,
grievous, overcast, pregnant, profound
9. difficult, ponderous 10. afflictive,
burdensome, encumbered, oppressive
11. substantial 13. consequential
heavy (pert to)...
handed.. 6. clumsy 7. awkward,
unhandy 8. bungling 9. maladroit
10. oppressive
headed.. 4. dull, logy 6. drowsy,
stupid
hearted.. 3. sad 10. despondent,

melancholy
laden.. 6. loaded 8. careworn
9. oppressed 12. weighted down
with moisture.. 6. sodden
Hebrew... 3. Jew 4. Zion 6. Habiri,
Habiru, Semite 7. Semitic
Hebrew (pert to)...
abode of the dead.. 5. Sheol
acrostic.. 4. agla
amulet.. 4. agla
demon.. 8. Asmodeus
eternity.. 4. Olam 8. Olam haba
excommunication form.. 5. herem
festival.. 5. Purim, Seder 8. Passover
flute (Bib).. 8. nehiloth
forbidden.. 4. tref
God.. 2. El 5. Eloah 6. Adonai,
Elohim 7. Jehovah
grammar.. 7. stative
greeting.. 6. Shalom
instrument (lyrelike).. 4. asor
kinsman.. 4. goel
law book.. 5. Torah (Tora) 6. Talmud
7. Mishnah (Mishna) 8. Tosephta
10. Pentateuch
lesson (Nebiim).. 9. haphtarah
marriage custom.. 6. levirate
month (Spring).. 4. Abib 5. Nisan
Order (Cenobite).. 6. Essene
plural ending.. 2. im
prayer shawl.. 7. tallith
proselyte.. 3. ger
psalm of praise.. 6. hallel
quarters.. 6. ghetto
rabbis, teachers.. 6. sabora
7. amoraim, tannaim 8. saboraim
sacred objects.. 4. Urim 7. Thummin
school.. 5. heder (cheder)
spice (anc).. 6. stacte
town.. 6. Mizpah (Mizpeh)
trumpet.. 7. shophar (shofar)
underworld.. 5. Sheol
Hebrew alphabet... 2. he, pe
3. mem, nun, sin, tav, vau 4. ayin,
beth, caph, koph, resh, shin, yodh
5. aleph, cheth, gimel, sadhe, zayin
6. daleth, lamedh, samekh
Hebrides, New...
administrators.. 6. French 7. British
church.. 6. Celtic (early)
islands.. 4. Iona, Skye 5. Banks
6. Torres
people.. 10. Melanesian
type rule.. 11. Condominium
hecatomb... 9. sacrifice 11. hundred
oxen
hecco... 8. hickwall 10. woodpecker
heckle... 6. gibe 6. badger, hackle,
harass
hectic... 5. fever, flush 7. excited
8. feverish, restless 9. reddening
11. consumptive
hector... 5. bully, worry 6. harass
7. bluster, swagger 8. browbeat
9. roisterer 10. intimidate
Hector (pert to)...
character in.. 5. (The) Iliad
companion.. 8. Diomedes
father.. 5. Priam
mother.. 6. Hecuba
slain by.. 8. Achilles
wife.. 10. Andromache

heddle... 4. loom 5. blade (with eyelet) 7. weaving
hedge... 3. bar, haw, hem, pen 4. boma 5. fence 6. hinder, raddle 7. barrier, enclose, quibble 8. boundary, obstruct, sidestep, surround
hedgehog... 6. animal, tenrec, urchin 7. dredger, echidna, echinus, pudding (fruit) 8. herisson, hurcheon 9. porcupine 11. transformer
hedge trimmer... 7. plasher, topiary
hedonism (pert to)...
  advocate.. 8. Cyrenaic 9. Epicurean
  doctrine of.. 8. pleasure
  fulfillment.. 15. pleasure–seeking
heed... 3. ear 4. care, hear, mind, note, obey 6. attend, listen, notice, regard 7. caution, observe 8. consider 9. attention, be careful, diligence 10. cognizance, solicitude 11. observation
heedful... 4. wary 6. attent 7. careful, mindful 8. cautious, vigilant 9. advertent, attentive 11. considerate
heedless... 6. remiss 8. careless 9. desperate, impulsive, negligent 10. insouciant, regardless 11. improvident, inadvertent, inattentive, thoughtless, unobservant, without heed 13. inconsiderate
heel... 3. cad, tip 4. cant, foot (part), knob, tilt 5. stern 6. career, follow 7. bounder, deviate, incline 9. scoundrel 12. protuberance
Heidi author... 12. Johanna Spyri
heifer... 3. cow 4. quey 5. stirk, woman 6. bovine 8. terrapin (fem) 10. colpindach
height... 3. alt, top 5. pitch 6. summit 7. stature 8. altitude, eminence, highness 9. elevation 10. The Heavens
heighten... 5. raise 7. augment, elevate 8. increase 9. aggravate, intensify 10. exaggerate
height of action, drama... 10. catastasis
heimlich... 10. reticently 12. mysteriously
Heimweh... 9. nostalgia 12. homesickness
heinous... 3. bad 6. odious, wicked 7. hateful 8. flagrant, infamous, terrible 9. atrocious, malicious 10. outrageous
heir... 5. scion 7. heritor, legatee 8. atheling (apparent), parcener (joint) 9. firstborn, inheritor, successor 11. beneficiary
Hejaz...
  city.. 5. Islam, Mecca 6. Medina
  monument.. 14. Tomb of Mohammed (Mosque of the Prophet)
  province of.. 11. Saudi Arabia
  shrine.. 5. Kaaba
helcos... 5. ulcer
helcos (pert to)...
  repair.. 11. helcoplasty
  science.. 9. helcology
  ulceration.. 8. helcosis

held... see hold
Helen of Troy (pert to)...
  abductor.. 5. Paris
  brother–in–law.. 9. Agamemnon
  famed for.. 6. beauty
  husband.. 8. Menelaus (King)
  lover.. 5. Paris
  mother.. 4. Leda
  sister of.. 11. The Dioscuri
helical... 5. helix (formed) 6. spiral
helical year... 6. Sothic
helicoid... 6. curved, ear rim (like) 10. snail shell (like)
helicon... 4. tuba
helicopter developer... 8. Sikorski
heliophobia... 14. fear of sunlight 16. sensitivity to sun
Heliopolis... 12. City of the Sun (Egypt)
Helios... 3. Sol 6. sun god 16. Colossus of Rhodes
Helix... 5. snail
hell... 5. grave, Hades, limbo 7. dungeon, inferno 9. perdition, purgatory 10. underworld
hell (pert to)...
  bottomless pit.. 9. barathrum (barathron)
  capital of.. 11. Pandemonium
  Hebrew.. 5. Sheol
  Hindu.. 6. Naraka
  Iliad.. 8. Tartarus
  Jewish.. 6. Tophet 7. Gehenna
  Norse.. 7. Niflhel (Neflheim)
  Queen.. 3. Hel
hellbent... 7. dead set, like mad 8. full tilt, reckless 10. determined, recklessly 12. determinedly
Hellene... 5. Greek
Hellenistic school (Sculp)... 9. Pergamene
Hellespont, Turkey...
  ancient name.. 11. Dardanelles (The) 17. Strait of Gallipoli
  city.. 6. Abydos (legend), Sestos
  heroine.. 4. Hero
  legend.. 14. Hero and Leander
  swimmer.. 7. Leander
helm... 5. wheel 6. helmet, rudder, summit, tiller 7. control 10. management 12. steering gear
helmet... 5. armet, armor, galea, topee (topi) 6. casque, heaume, morion, sallet, sconce 8. basinet
helmet (pert to)...
  flap.. 8. aventail
  lower part.. 6. beaver
  nose guard.. 5. nasal
  opening.. 3. vue
  part.. 4. bell 5. crest 7. ventail 8. aventail
  shaped.. 7. galeate
  upper piece.. 5. visor (vizor)
  wreathe.. 4. orle
helmet of Hades... 5. magic 8. Tarnhelm 9. invisible, Tarnkappe
helminth... 4. worm
helmsman... 5. pilot 6. conner, guider 8. coxswain 9. steersman
helot... 4. esne, serf 5. slave 6. thrall, vassal 7. servant
help... 3. aid 4. abet, back, cure

5. avail, boost, serve, stead
6. assist, relief, remedy, succor
7. benefit, forward, further, improve, prevent, relieve, servant, serving, subsidy, support, sustain
helper... **5.** aider **8.** teammate
 9. assistant **10.** apprentice, benefactor
helpful... **6.** useful **7.** helping
 8. salutary **10.** beneficial, tiding over
 12. instrumental
helpless... **4.** limp, weak **7.** forlorn
 8. impotent, unaiding **9.** destitute, powerless, spineless **10.** bewildered, unsupplied **11.** defenseless, unprotected **12.** irremediable
helpmate... **4.** wife **6.** helper
 8. helpmeet **9.** assistant, companion
helter-skelter... **5.** haste, hurry
 7. hastily **8.** disorder **9.** confusion
 10. carelessly, recklessly
helve... **5.** lever **6.** handle
hem, hem in... **3.** pen **4.** edge
 5. beset **6.** border, margin
 7. environ, stammer **8.** hesitate, surround **9.** hem and haw
 11. exclamation
hemal, haemal (pert to)... **5.** blood
 12. blood vessels
hemeralopia... (opp of nyctalopia)
 12. day blindness
hemi... **4.** half, semi (pref)
hemiplegia... **9.** paralysis (body half)
hemlock... **3.** kex **5.** Tsuga **6.** conium
 (fruit) **9.** evergreen, poisoning
hemophilia... **8.** bleeding
 10. hemorrhage (uncontrollable)
hemp... **3.** ife, kef **4.** flax, keef, kief, rine, sunn **5.** abaca, bhang, istle, sisal (sizal) **6.** fennel, Manila
 7. hashish, lhiamba (liamba)
 8. cannabis
hemp (pert to)...
 bagasse.. **6.** linaga
 cannabis.. **5.** ganja (smoking)
 fabric.. **6.** burlap
 filament.. **4.** harl
 leaves.. **5.** sabzi
 like.. **9.** cannabine
 loose.. **5.** oakum
 resin (narcotic).. **6.** charas
 seed.. **5.** rogue, scamp
 short.. **3.** tow
hen... **4.** fowl, wife **6.** pullet
hen (pert to)...
 Chaucer character.. **7.** Partlet
 clam.. **4.** surf **5.** pismo
 hawk.. **7.** buzzard, harrier
 heath.. **4.** gray **6.** grouse (black)
 poison.. **7.** hebenon, henbane
 water.. **9.** gallinule
hence... **2.** so **4.** away, ergo **8.** away from **9.** therefore
henchman... **4.** page **5.** groom
 6. gillie, squire **8.** follower, hanger–on **9.** attendant, supporter
 12. right–hand man
hend, hende... **4.** fair, kind, near
 5. civil **6.** clever, comely, gentle, kindly **8.** gracious, pleasant, skillful (skilful) **9.** dexterous **10.** convenient
heortology, science of... **14.** liturgical

year
hepar... **5.** liver **8.** compound (Chem)
hepatitis... **12.** liver disease
Hephaestus (Gr Relig)... **9.** god of Fire
Hepplewhite... **9.** furniture
heptad... **5.** seven (group of)
Hera (pert to)...
 husband.. **4.** Zeus
 mother of.. **4.** Ares, Rhea
 rival.. **2.** Io **4.** Leto
herald... **5.** crier **6.** tabard **7.** presage, usher in **8.** announce, proclaim
 9. harbinger, messenger
 10. forerunner
heraldic (pert to)...
 balls.. **5.** palle (6 balls of Medici)
 band.. **3.** bar **6.** fess, fill
 barnacle.. **4.** brey
 bearing.. **4.** ente, gore, orle **5.** pheon
 6. charge **8.** tressure
 boss.. **5.** rumbo
 charge.. **5.** fusil, gyron **7.** bearing, humetty (humettee)
 circle (gold).. **6.** bezant
 cross.. **4.** paty, urde **6.** cleche, pattée (patté), raguly **7.** patonce, saltier (saltire)
 decoration.. **4.** seme **5.** crest
 design (fur).. **4.** pean, vair
 division.. **4.** ente, paly **5.** barry
 6. canton **7.** compone
 11. counterpaly
 embattled.. **8.** bretessé
 end (metal).. **7.** boterol (boteroll)
 large.. **5.** pavis
 lozenge (voided).. **6.** mascle
 opening.. **6.** rustre
 panel.. **9.** hatchment (death)
 sardonyx.. **8.** sanguine
 scalloped, edged.. **8.** invected
 segment.. **6.** flanch
 ship.. **7.** lymphad
 star.. **6.** mullet **7.** estoile
 stripe.. **4.** pale
 swallow.. **10.** hirondelle
 winged.. **4.** aile
 wreath.. **5.** torse **7.** chaplet, garland
heraldic (pet to animals)...
 animal's head.. **8.** caboshed (caboched)
 bear.. **5.** grise
 beast, running.. **7.** courant
 beast, sitting.. **5.** assis **6.** sejant
 beasts.. **6.** enurny
 beast's leg.. **4.** gamb (gambe)
 bird.. **7.** issuant (half visible), martlet
 9. half eagle
 duck (footless).. **6.** cannet
 fish, swimming.. **6.** naiant
 headless.. **5.** etête
heraldic (pert to color)...
 black.. **5.** sable
 blue.. **5.** azure
 brown.. **5.** tenne
 gold, yellow.. **2.** or
 green.. **4.** vert
 purple.. **7.** purpure
 red.. **5.** gules
heraldic shield (pert to)...
 back.. **8.** aversant
 back–to–back.. **8.** addorsed
 bent.. **9.** debruised

broken.. 5. rompu
Danes.. 5. raven
England.. 14. lilies of France
facing each other.. 8. affronté
savages.. 6. tattoo
toward spectator.. 4. gaze 7. gardant
tribe of Judah.. 4. lion
herb... 3. pia, rue 4. aloe, anet, balm,
  dill, hemp, mint, moly, sage, woad,
  yamp 5. anise, basil, nondo, sedge,
  senna, tansy, thyme 6. arnica,
  borage, catnip, cicely, clover, endive,
  fennel, hyssop, jacoby, madder,
  yarrow 7. boneset, caraway, chervil,
  chicory, figwort, gentian, ginseng,
  henbane, parsley, ragwort
  8. abelmosk, licorice, marjoram,
  rosemary, samphire, tarragon
  9. coriander, digitalis, spikenard
  10. elecampane, pennyroyal,
  turtlehead
herb (pert to)...
bitter.. 3. rue 4. aloe 5. tansy
  7. boneset 8. centaury 9. snakehead
  10. turtlehead
dill.. 4. anet
genus.. 3. Iva 4. Arum, Ruta
  5. Galax, Inula, Lemna, Rubia
  6. Cassia, Mentha, Oxalis, Sagina
  7. Alpenia, Anemone, Freesia,
  Hedeoma, Tellima, Tovaria
  8. Hepatica, Psorales 9. Grundelia
living on.. 11. herbivorous
  12. phytophagous
mythical.. 4. moly
narcotic.. 4. hemp
onionlike.. 5. chive
poisonous.. 4. loco 6. conium
  7. hemlock, henbane 9. hellebore
salad.. 6. endive 7. chicory
  10. watercress
Hercules (pert to)...
father.. 4. Zeus
hero of.. 8. strength 12. twelve
  labors
mother.. 7. Alcmene
statue.. 7. Farnese
stone.. 9. loadstone
sweetheart.. 4. Iole
wife.. 4. Hebe
herd... 3. mob 5. crowd, drive, drove,
  flock, guard 6. gregis, rabble
  7. shelter 11. aggregation
herd's grass... 7. timothy
herdsman... 4. senn 5. drover
  7. vaquero (vaciero) 8. Damoetas,
  ranchero, wrangler
herdsman's god... 5. Pales
here... 3. ici, now 6. hereat, hither
  7. present 8. vicinity 9. this place
  11. in this place
here and now... 8. thisness
  9. haecceity 11. specificity
here and there... 5. about 6. passim
  10. everywhere
hereditary... 6. inborn, innate, lineal
  8. heirship 9. ancestral, descended,
  lineality 11. inheritable, inheritance,
  patrimonial
heredity... 4. gene 5. birth 7. atavism
  8. heritage 10. Mendel's law
  11. inheritance

heretic... 9. dissenter, sectarian
  10. schismatic 13. nonconformist
heretofore... 6. erenow 7. prior to
  8. formerly, hitherto, previous
heritage... 3. lot 9. cleronomy
  10. birthright 11. inheritance
heritrix, heretrix... 7. heiress
herl, harl... 3. fly (angling) 4. barb
hermeneutics... 14. interpretation
  (Scriptures)
Hermes (pert to)...
birthplace.. 7. Cyllene
character.. 6. herald 9. messenger
father.. 4. Zeus
god of.. 5. youth 7. science
  9. eloquence, invention
mother.. 4. Maia
Roman equivalent.. 7. Mercury
shoes (winged).. 7. talaria
hermetic... 6. closed, sealed
  7. magical 8. airtight 10. alchemical
hermetic art... 7. alchemy
hermit... 4. monk 5. cooky 7. ascetic,
  eremite, recluse, stylite (Hist)
  8. headsman 9. anchorite, pillarist
  11. hummingbird
hermitary... 3. hut 4. cell
hern, herne... 4. hers, hook 5. heron
  6. corner
hero... 4. idol, star 5. model
  7. demigod, warrior 8. champion
  9. celebrity, conqueror
  11. protagonist
hero (pert to)...
American.. 5. Allen (Ethan), Bowie
  6. Bonham, Travis 8. Crockett
Babylonian.. 5. Etana
deified.. 7. demigod
genealogy.. 8. heroogony
Greek.. 3. Ion 4. Ajax
legendary.. 6. Amadis, Roland
  7. Paladin, Tancred
lore.. 9. heroology
Persian.. 5. Rustam (Rustum)
romantic.. 4. Erec 6. Amadis
  7. Leander
Russian.. 4. Igor
heroic... 4. bold, epic, huge 5. brave,
  great, noble 6. epical, poetic, viking
  7. extreme, gallant, valiant
  8. fearless, intrepid, powerful
  10. courageous 11. magnanimous,
  venturesome
heroic poem, story... 4. epic, epos
  6. epopee
heroine... 4. Tess 5. actor 6. Esther,
  Europa 8. Atalanta 9. celebrity
  11. demigoddess
heroism... 5. valor 7. bravery, courage
  9. fortitude 11. magnanimity
  13. unselfishness
heron... 5. Ardea, crane, egret, herle
  7. Bittern 8. Ardeidae, heronsew
  9. Great Blue 10. Great White, Little
  Blue
heron flock... 5. sedge
herpes... 6. eczema 8. cold sore,
  shingles
herring... 3. cob 4. alec, brit, raun
  (fem), sile 5. cisco, matie, sprat
  7. alewife, anchovy, shadine
  8. scuddawn

herring (pert to)...
　barrel.. 4. cade, cran
　bone.. 7. pattern 11. arrangement
　fry.. 4. sile
　herringlike.. 5. cisco 7. anchovy
　young.. 4. brit 5. sprat (sprot)
Herse (Gr)... 7. goddess (dew)
Hershef (Egypt)... 5. deity (tutelary)
hesitate... 3. haw, hem 4. wait
　5. delay, demur, pause, stall
　6. falter, loiter 7. stammer
　13. procrastinate
hesitation... 5. doubt, pause, waltz
　9. faltering, hesitancy 10. reluctance,
　stammering 11. uncertainty,
　vacillation 15. procrastination
hesped (Heb)... 6. eulogy 7. funeral
Hesperides (pert to)...
　group name.. 10. Atlantides
　guards of.. 12. golden apples (Hera)
　nymph.. 5. Aegle 6. Hestia
　7. Hespera 8. Arethusa, Erytheia
Hesperus... 4. poem (Wreck of the
　Hesperus) 5. Venus 6. Hesper
　11. evening star
Hessian... 3. fly 5. boots, Hesse
　6. German 9. mercenary
　10. adventurer
hest... 6. behest 7. command,
　precept, promise 10. injunction
Hestia (pert to)...
　goddess of.. 6. hearth
　guard of.. 12. golden apples
　mother.. 4. Rhea
hetaera, hetaira (Gr)... 4. Lais
　6. Phryne 8. mistress, paramour
hetaerocracy, governed by...
　8. hetaerae 10. college men
Heterodontus... 5. shark
heterodox... 9. heretical
　10. unorthodox 11. nonorthodox
heterogeneous... (opposed to
　homogeneous) 5. mixed 6. unlike
　7. diverse 9. different 10. dissimilar
　11. diversified 13. miscellaneous
hew... 3. cut 4. chop, fell, hack
　5. carve, sever
hex... 3. hag, six 4. jinx 5. lamia,
　spell 7. bewitch 9. sorceress,
　witchwife
hexad... 3. six 6. sestet
hexameter verse...
　meter.. 6. six feet
　terms.. 4. iams 8. dipodies, trochees
　9. anapaests
hexapod... 7. six feet 9. six-footed
hexarchy... 9. six States (group)
hexastich, poem or stanza... 8. six
　lines 9. six verses
heyday... 3. joy 4. acme 8. wildness
　11. high spirits 12. highest vigor
　14. frolicsomeness
heyrat... 7. kinkajou (obs)
Hezekiah (pert to)...
　Biblical.. 4. King (12th)
　kingdom.. 5. Judah
　mother.. 3. Abi
hiatus... 3. col, gap 5. break, chasm,
　pause, space 6. lacuna 7. fissure,
　opening 8. interval 12. interruption
Hiawatha (pert to)...
　character, poem by.. 10. Longfellow

　grandmother.. 7. Nokomis
　mother.. 7. Wenonah
　tribe (Ind).. 8. Iroquois
hibernate... 6. hole up (summer in
　torpor), winter 8. estivate
　10. latibulize
Hibernia... 4. Erin 7. Ireland
Hibernian (pert to)...
　color.. 5. green
　native.. 8. Irishman
　secret society (US 1832)..
　24. Ancient Order of Hibernians
hickory... 4. cane 5. Carya, pecan
　6. switch 8. kiskatom 9. shellbark
hidalgo... 5. title 8. nobleman (lower
　class)
hidden... 4. dern, lurk 5. inner, perdu
　6. arcane, buried, cached, closed,
　covert, latent, masked, occult, secret
　7. covered, cryptic, obscure,
　unknown 8. abstruse, screened,
　secluded, secreted 9. concealed,
　latescent 10. mysterious
　11. clandestine
hide... 3. kip 4. bury, cyst, dern
　(derne), lurk, mask, pelt, skin, veil
　5. cache, cloak, cover, skulk
　6. screen, shroud 7. conceal,
　eelskin, rawhide, secrete 8. carucate,
　disguise, ensconce, suppress
　9. dissemble 10. camouflage
hidebound... 5. bound, pervy 6. little,
　narrow 7. bigoted 9. barkbound
　10. restrained (opinion)
　11. strait-laced 12. conventional,
　narrow-minded 13. hyperorthodox
hideous... 4. grim, ugly 6. grisly,
　horrid, odious 7. ghastly 8. scabrous,
　terrible 9. frightful, revolting
　10. detestable, terrifying
hiding place... 3. mew 4. lair
　5. cache 9. latibulism
hi-fi devotee... 10. audiophile
high... 3. alt, dry, ela (note) 4. tall
　5. aloft, drunk, great, noble, steep
　6. costly, shrill 7. eminent, haughty
　8. elevated, foremost, stranded,
　towering 9. excessive, expensive
high (pert to)...
　and mighty.. 8. arrogant 9. imperious
　brow.. 4. snob 7. Brahmin, egghead,
　high-hat, learned 12. intellectual
　14. intelligentsia
　flown diction.. 8. euphuism
　flying.. 7. Icarian 9. visionary
　11. extravagant, pretentious
　12. ostentatious 13. grandiloquent
　handed.. 9. arbitrary 10. autocratic,
　imperative 11. domineering,
　overbearing
　hat.. 8. snobbish 12. aristocratic
　priest.. 3. Eli (Israel) 11. Melchezedek
　(Mormon)
　sounding.. 4. loud 7. fustian
　9. high-toned 13. grandiloquent
　spirited.. 4. edgy 5. fiery 6. lively
　9. excitable 10. mettlesome
　11. high-mettled
　strung.. 4. taut 5. tense 7. nervous
　9. excitable
　time.. 3. fun 5. binge, spree
　8. carousal 11. opportunity

toned.. 5. tense 7. stylish 8. elevated
9. dignified 11. fashionable

highest... 3. top 4. best 6. utmost
7. maximum, supreme, topmost
8. bunemost 9. nth degree,
uppermost

highest (pert to)...
comb form.. 4. acro
dice number.. 3. six 4. sise (sice)
point.. 3. top 4. acme, apex
6. apogee, climax, summit, vertex,
zenith 7. ceiling, noonday
8. meridian, noontide, pinnacle
11. ne plus ultra

highway... 3. via, way 4. iter, path,
pike, road, toby 6. artery, course,
street 7. freeway, parkway 8. arterial,
turnpike 9. boulevard, concourse
10. expressway 12. thoroughfare

highwayman... 5. thief 6. bandit,
robber 7. brigand, footpad, ladrone
8. hijacker 9. bandolero
10. bushranger, highjacker

hike... 4. jerk, toss, walk 5. hitch,
march, raise, throw, tramp
8. increase

hilarious... 3. mad 5. merry, noisy
7. festive 8. mirthful 9. ludicrous

hilarity... 4. glee 5. mirth 6. gaiety,
levity 7. jollity, whoopee 8. laughter
9. joviality 10. jocularity, joyousness
12. cheerfulness, exhilaration

hill... 3. kop, tor 4. dene, dune, heap,
holt, kame, knob, loma, mesa, paha,
rath 5. bargh, butte, esker, morra,
mound 6. barrow, summit
9. acclivity, elevation, monadnock

hill myna... 8. starling

hillside... 4. bank, brae, hill, knop,
ramp 5. cleve (cleeve), cliff, knoll,
scarp, slope 6. glacia

hilt... 4. haft 6. handle

hilum... 3. eye (bean) 5. hilar, notch
7. opening (kidney)

Himalaya (pert to)...
antelope.. 5. goral, serow
bear.. 5. bhalu
bearcat.. 5. panda
bird.. 5. monal (pheasant) 6. chough
(crow)
cat.. 5. ounce
cedar.. 6. deodar
dweller.. 8. Nepalese
formations.. 7. Siwalik
goat.. 4. ibex, kail, tahe
kingdom.. 5. Hunza
mountain peak.. 3. Api 7. Everest,
The Hump
pass.. 7. Nathula
plant.. 4. nard (Med)
sheep (wild).. 6. bharal, nahoor
swamp.. 5. Terai
tree.. 3. fir (silver) 5. Neoza (pine)
6. Bhutan

himself... 4. ipse

hind... 3. doe 4. back, deer, rear,
stag 5. haunch, rustic 7. peasant,
servant 8. domestic 9. posterior
11. hindquarter

hind (red fish)... 7. grouper 8. cabrilla

hinder... 3. bar 5. block, check,
cramp, debar, delay, deter, embar

6. cumber, hamper, impede, retard
7. prevent 8. restrain 9. posterior

hindrance... 3. bar, rub 4. clog, snag,
stop 5. check, delay 8. obstacle
9. deterrent, restraint
10. impediment 11. obstruction
12. interruption

Hindu, Hindoo... 4. Koli, Sikh
5. Tamil 6. Indian 9. Hindustan

Hindu (pert to)...
alphabet.. 6. Sarada
apartment.. 5. mahal
ascetic.. 4. yati, yogi 5. sadhu
atheist.. 7. Nastika
author of law.. 4. Manu (Code)
bird.. 5. Munia 6. garuda
Buddha's mother.. 4. Maya
caravansary.. 8. choultry
carriage.. 6. gharry (gharri)
caste.. 4. Bhil 5. Palli, Sudra, Tamil
7. Brahman
ceremony.. 7. sradha
city (sacred).. 5. Mecca 7. Benares
9. Allahabad
coin.. 5. anna
cymbals.. 3. tal
dancing girl.. 8. bayadere
darkness (spiritual).. 5. tamas
deity.. 4. Deva, Siva (Shiva), Yama
5. Ahura, Asura 6. Brahma, Vishnu
7. Krishna 8. Trimurti
deity consort.. 5. sakti
dialect.. 5. Tamil
division.. 5. Patti, Taraf 6. zillah
7. Pargana
Dravidian.. 5. Tamil
drink (sacrificial).. 4. soma
evil spirit.. 4. Mara 5. Asura
6. yaksha
festival.. 4. Holi, tali 6. Dewali
9. Dashahara
first mortal to die.. 4. Yama
flute.. 3. bin 5. pungi
garment.. 4. sari (saree)
Gautama's wife.. 6. Ahalya
gentleman (Mr).. 5. baboo (babu),
sahib
giant.. 4. Bana (thousand–armed)
government.. 6. sircar
guitar.. 4. vina 5. sitar
hero.. 4. Nala
incarnation.. 4. Rama 5. asura
6. yaksha
jackal.. 4. kola
king.. 5. Rajah
language (oldest).. 5. Tamil
language (sacred).. 4. Pali
loincloth.. 5. dhoti
magic.. 4. jadu (jadoo), maya
magician.. 4. yogi 5. fakir
meal (wheat).. 4. atta (ata)
mendicant.. 4. naga 8. sannyasi
merchant.. 6. banian (banya)
7. goladar
mind.. 5. manas
monkey god.. 7. Hanuman
mountain.. 4. Meru
mystic.. 4. yogi
nursemaid.. 4. ayah
paradise.. 7. Nirvana
patriarch.. 5. Pitri
peasant.. 4. ryot

philosophy.. 4. yoga, Yuga 5. tamas
physicist.. 5. Raman (Nobel 1930)
pillar.. 3. lat
poet.. 5. rishi 6. Tagore (Nobel 1913)
reign.. 3. raj
sage.. 5. rishi 6. Dharma 7. Gautama, Mahatma
savant.. 5. swami
scarf.. 4. sari (saree)
serpent (semi-human).. 4. Naga
servant.. 5. hamal
slave.. 4. dasi (fem)
soldier.. 4. sikh 5. sepoy
supernatural being.. 6. Garuda
swan.. 5. hansa
syllable of assent.. 2. om
Taraf ruler.. 8. tarafdar
title.. 3. Sri 4. Raja, Rana, Rani 5. Rajah, Ranee 6. sirdar 8. maharaja (maharajah)
tree (sacred).. 4. pipal 6. bo tree
tribesman.. 4. Naga
tunic.. 4. jama (jamah)
underworld (series).. 6. Patala
village.. 5. abadi
virtue.. 6. sharma
widow (cremation).. 6. suttee
woman (first).. 6. Ahalya

Hindu Ages, Yoga...
1st.. 5. Krita
2nd.. 5. Treta
3rd.. 7. Dvapara
4th.. 4. Kali
end.. 7. Pralaya
total.. 4. Maha 10. Manvantara

Hindu goddess... 3. Sri, Uma 4. Devi, Kali 5. Durga, Gauri 6. Chandi, Shakti 7. Lakshmi, Parvati 9. Haimavati (Durga)

Hindu god of...
ancestors.. 5. Pitri
dead.. 4. Yama
fire.. 4. Agni
love.. 4. Kama
spirit.. 5. Asura
unknown.. 2. Ka
wisdom (elephant-headed).. 6. Ganesa (Ganesha)

Hindu religion...
abode of gods.. 4. Meru
call to prayer.. 4. azan (adan)
ceremony, rite.. 7. araddha
congregation.. 5. samaj
convert (to Islam).. 6. shaikh
creator.. 6. Brahma
cremation.. 4. sati 6. suttee
doctrine, destiny.. 5. karma
first human to die (deified).. 4. Yama
hell.. 6. Naraka
Hinduism.. 5. Agama 6. Tantra 7. Jainism 8. Buddhism 10. Brahmanism
holy man.. 5. Sadhu (Sadh)
image worship.. 5. arati
incarnation.. 4. Rama 6. avatar 11. Ramachandra
literature (sacred).. 4. Veda 7. Shastra
lord of the world.. 9. Jagannath (Jagannatha)
monastery.. 4. math
philosophy (life).. 5. artha, atman,

prana 6. tattva
prayer, call to.. 4. azan (adan)
prayer rug.. 5. asana, Melas
religion.. 5. Agama 6. Tantra 7. Jainism 8. Buddhism 10. Brahmanism
scripture.. 4. Veda 5. Agama 6. Tantra 7. Shastra
sect.. 4. Jain (Jaina), Sikh 6. tantra
Shastra (4 parts).. 5. aruti 6. purana, smriti, tantra
Siva worshiper.. 5. Saiva
Supreme Spirit.. 5. atman 7. jivatma
teacher.. 4. guru 5. swami
Trimurti (Triad).. 4. Siva 6. Brahma, Vishnu
trinity, triad.. 8. Trimurti (Siva, Brahma, Vishnu)
unorthodox.. 7. Jainism
widow (cremation).. 6. suttee

Hindustan (pert to)...
dialect.. 4. Urdu 10. Hindustani
people.. 9. Dravidian
poet.. 5. Siraj (Beng)
rice.. 7. aghanee
tribesman.. 4. toda

hinge... 3. pan (part) 4. axis, axle, hang, knee, turn 5. joint, pivot, stand 6. depend, fasten, lamina, pintle

hint... 3. cue 5. imply, refer, tinge, trace 6. allude, glance 7. eyewink, inkling, suggest 8. allusion, innuendo, intimate, reminder 9. insinuate 10. intimation, suggestion 11. insinuation, supposition

hip... 3. hop, pod 4. coxa, limp, miss, skip 6. haunch 8. greeting

hip, hips (pert to)...
bone.. 4. coxa 5. ilium 7. os coxae 10. innominate
muscle.. 9. iliopsoas
nerve.. 7. sciatic (largest)
rose fruit.. 10. pseudocarp

Hippocrates (pert to)...
drug.. 5. mecon (possibly opium)
famed as.. 9. physician (Gr)
oath.. 11. Hippocratic

hippopotamus.. 5. hippo 6. seacow, zeekoe 8. behemoth (Bib)

hippopotamus, thong of hide... 7. chicote

Hiram... 9. most noble 10. King of Tyre (Bib)

hire... 3. let, use 4. hack, rent 5. bribe, lease, price, wages 6. employ, engage, reward, salary 7. charter, stipend 9. allowance 12. compensation

hireling... 4. esne, serf 5. slave, venal 8. employee 9. mercenary

hirmos... 4. hymn 8. canticle 9. troparion

hirondelle (Her)... 7. swallow

hirsel... 4. herd 5. flock 7. pasture

hirsute... 5. hairy, rough 6. coarse, shaggy 7. boorish, bristly, uncouth

Hispania (anc)... 16. Spain and Portugal

hispid... 5. rough 7. grooved 8. strigose

hiss... 3. boo, tst 4. fizz 7. condemn

8. derision, sibilate 10. effervesce, sibilation

historian... 5. actor 6. writer
8. annalist 10. chronicler

history... 5. drama 6. events, memoir
7. account 8. relation, treatise
9. chronicle, narrative

history (pert to)...
development.. 8. ontogeny
Father of.. 9. Herodotus
muse of (Gr Myth).. 4. Clio
period.. 3. era
personal.. 7. memoirs 9. biography, genealogy 13. autobiography
study, knowledge of.. 10. historical 12. historiology

histrio... 5. actor

histrion... 5. actor

histrionics... 6. acting, actors
9. theatrics 11. theatricals

hit... 3. bop, lob, rap, tap 4. blow, bunt, slam, slap, slog, suit, swat
5. flick, knock, shoot, smite
6. buffet, larrup, please, strike
7. succeed, success 9. collision

hitch... 3. hop, tie, tug 4. halt, jerk, knot, limp, pull, yoke 5. catch, cling, crick, marry, unite 6. enlist, fasten, hobble 8. obstacle 9. hindrance
10. enlistment

hitherto... 3. ago, yet 5. as yet
7. prior to 8. formerly, until now

hit or miss... 6. casual 8. at random, by chance, careless 9. haphazard

Hittite (pert to)...
ancestor (Bib).. 4. Heth
city.. 6. Hamath, Pteria (ruins)
country.. 6. Khatti (Asia Minor)
people (anc).. 8. Hittites
10. aborigines
storm god.. 6. Teshup (Teshub)

hoar... 4. aged, gray, rime 5. hoary, white 7. ancient 9. hoarfrost, venerable

hoard... 5. amass, lay up, store
6. garner, supply 7. husband
8. treasure, treasury 10. accumulate, collection

hoarder... 5. miser 6. storer
7. treasurer

hoarfrost... 3. rag 4. hoar, rime
7. needles (ice) 9. Jack Frost

hoarse... 3. old 4. aged, gray
6. remote (in time) 7. ancient
9. canescent

hoatzin, hoactzin... 4. anna 5. hanna
8. pheasant 9. stinkbird
11. Opisthocomi (group)

hoax... 3. bam 4. bilk, ruse, sham
5. bluff, cheat, trick 6. canard
7. deceive 8. artifice 9. deception

hob... 3. elf, hub, peg, pin 4. game, mark 5. clown, fairy, havoc 6. ferret, rustic, sprite 7. hobnail 8. mischief
9. fireplace, hobgoblin

hobble... 4. clog, gait (unequal), halt, limp 5. dance 6. fetter, tether, wabble 7. dilemma, pastern, shackle
11. predicament

hobbledehoy... 4. gawk 5. youth

hobbler... 5. pilot 7. boatman, hoveler, laborer, soldier 8. retainer

hobby... 3. fad, nag 5. dolly, horse
6. falcon 7. bicycle, pastime
9. avocation, plaything
10. hobbyhorse 12. rocking horse

hobgoblin... 3. elf, imp 4. bogy, pixy, Puck 5. scrat 6. sprite 7. bugaboo
9. coltpixie 10. apparition 15. Robin Goodfellow

hobnob... 9. associate (with), drink with, hit or miss

hobo... 3. bum 5. tramp 6. beggar
7. vagrant 8. vagabond

hock... 3. ham 4. pawn 5. ankle, joint, thigh (man) 6. pledge
7. disable 9. hamstring

hockey (pert to)...
ball, disk.. 3. nur 4. knur, puck
cup.. 7. Stanley (prize)
goal.. 4. cage
stick.. 6. shinny 7. cammock
team number.. 5. seven

hocus... 4. drug 5. cheat 6. liquor (drugged) 7. deceive, falsify
8. cheating, trickery 10. adulterate

hocus–pocus... 5. cheat, trick
6. bunkum, humbug 7. juggler
8. flimflam, nonsense, quackery
9. deception, trickster 11. incantation
12. charlatanism 13. sleight of hand
15. juggler's formula

hod... 3. tub 4. hide 6. barrow, trough 7. scuttle

hodgepodge... 4. mess, olio, stew
5. cento 6. medley 7. mélange, mixture 10. miscellany
11. gallimaufry, olla–podrida

hog... 3. pig, sow, Sus 4. bene, boar, galt, gilt 5. sheep (unshorn), shoat, swine 6. barrow 8. babirusa (babiroussa), javelina 9. boschvark, razorback

hog... 6. corner (the market) 7. glutton
8. slattern 9. take it all
10. locomotive, monopolist

hog (pert to)...
breed.. 5. Essex 9. Hampshire
food.. 4. mast
ground.. 6. marmot
hoglike.. 7. porcine
salted side.. 5. bacon 6. flitch
shears (snout).. 7. snouter
thigh (cured).. 3. ham

hogfish... 7. capitan, pigfish
8. scorpene

hoggerel... 5. sheep 6. hogger

hoggery... 4. hogs 5. greed
11. beastliness 14. hoggish manners

hoggish... 6. filthy, greedy 7. porcine, selfish, swinish 10. gluttonous

hogshead... 4. cask 6. barrel
7. measure

hogwash... 5. swill, waste

hoi polloi... 3. mob 5. herde
6. masses, rabble 7. the many
8. populace 9. multitude

hoist... 4. lift, sail 5. boost, heave, hoise, raise 7. elevate 8. elevator

hoisting device... 3. gin 4. jack
5. crane, davit, lewis 7. capstan, derrick 8. elevator, windlass
9. parbuckle

hoity–toity... 5. giddy, proud 6. snooty

7. flighty, haughty 8. arrogant
11. exclamation, harum–scarum,
patronizing, thoughtless
13. irresponsible

hold... 3. own 4. bind, have, keep,
lien, seat, stow 5. avast, cling,
delay, grasp, judge 6. adhere, arrest,
cleave, clench, defend, detain,
endure, harbor, regard, retain
7. contain, control, custody
8. consider, foothold, maintain,
thurrock (ship's), treasury
9. anchorage, constrain, entertain,
prosecute 11. compartment

hold (pert to)...
back.. 3. dam 4. last, stem 5. delay,
deter, stint 6. detain, hinder, refuse,
retard 7. abstain, inhibit, repress
8. restrain
belief.. 7. suppose
dear.. 7. cherish
fast.. 5. cling 6. adhere 9. persevere
forth.. 5. offer, speak 7. declaim,
descant, exhibit, expound
8. continue, maintain, propound
off.. 5. avert, delay 7. repulse, ward
off 9. stay aloof, temporize
on.. 4. stop, wait 6. endure, retain
7. forbear 8. continue
opinion.. 4. deem
out.. 4. last 6. endure, refuse, resist
7. exclude 8. continue
session.. 3. sit 7. convene
8. assemble
together.. 6. adhere, cohere 8. be
joined 9. co–operate
up.. 3. rob 4. buoy, halt, lift, rein
5. check, delay, raise 6. hinder,
resist, retard 7. display, exhibit,
pillory (to scorn), robbery, support,
sustain
water.. 5. sound 10. consistent

holder.. 3. cop (yarn) 4. file
5. owner, payee 6. bearer, binder,
lienor, tenant 7. trustee 8. endorsee
9. mortgagor, possessor, recipient
10. receptacle

hold in...
check.. 4. curb, rein 6. arrest, bridle
7. control 8. restrain
custody.. 4. jail 6. detain, intern
hand.. 6. assure 7. control, promise,
toy with
mind.. 6. harbor 7. cherish
9. entertain

holding... 5. asset, claim, stake, tenet,
title, trust 6. belief, equity, estate,
tenure 8. interest, property
9. retention 10. possessing,
possession, supporting

holding fast... 9. tenacious
10. persistent

holding sway... 7. regnant
8. dominant, reigning

hole... 3. den, pit 4. bore, cave, cove,
dive, flaw, gulf, lair, nook, slot, vent
5. abyss, chasm, fault, hovel, place,
shaft 6. burrow, cavern, cavity,
celiar, hollow, prison 7. impasse,
opening, orifice, ostiole
10. excavation 11. predicament

hole (pert to)...

bowling ball.. 4. grip
cable (ship's).. 5. hawse
enlarger.. 6. reamer
implement.. 3. awl, eye 4. bore
5. drill 8. stiletto
metal mold.. 5. sprue
mud.. 6. wallow
wall.. 5. niche
water.. 5. oasis
whirlpool.. 5. gourd (obs)

Holi (or **Hoolee**)... 8. festival (Hind)

holia... 8. salmon (humpback)

holiday... 4. fete 5. feria, merry
6. fiesta, jovial, outing 7. festive,
playday 8. festival, vacation
9. convivial, festivity 10. recreation

holiness... 5. piety, title (Pope)
8. sanctity 9. godliness
10. sacredness 11. saintliness
13. righteousness

Holland... 11. Netherlands (which see)

Holland...
capital.. 8. The Hague (Court)
9. Amsterdam
city.. 3. Ede 5. Doorn 6. Leyden
9. Amsterdam, Rotterdam
government.. 8. monarchy
liquor.. 3. gin 8. schnapps
oddity.. 5. dikes 6. canals, tulips
painter.. 6. Rubens 7. Van Eyck
people.. 5. Dutch
port.. 4. Edam
pottery.. 5. delft (delf)
province.. 4. Edam 7. Drenthe,
Zeeland
river.. 3. Ems, Lek 5. Meuse, Rhine
7. Scheldt (Schelde)
sea.. 5. North
village.. 3. Ede

hollow... 3. den, pit 4. thin, void
5. bight, empty, false, gaunt, sinus
6. cavern, cavity, cirque, corrie,
groove, hungry, socket, sunken,
vacant 7. concave, unsound
8. capsular, specious 9. cavernous,
depressed, faithless, insincere,
worthless 10. sepulchral
12. unsatisfying

hollowed... 6. cavate 7. concave,
glenoid

holly... 4. holm, hull, ilex 5. yapon
6. hulver, laurel 8. Eryngium
9. blackjack, Ilicaceae 10. Sapindales

hollyhock... 5. color 7. Althaea,
blue–red 9. perennial

holm... 3. oak 5. holly, islet, marsh
7. bottoms, low land

holobaptist... 12. immersionist

holocaust... 9. sacrifice (by fire)
11. destruction 13. burnt offering

holy... 5. godly, pious 6. chaste,
devout, sacred 7. epithet (Relig),
sainted 8. hallowed 9. venerated

Holy, holy (pert to)...
carpet.. 5. kiswa (kiswah)
comb form.. 5. hagio
Joe.. 8. sky pilot 9. clergyman
oil.. 6. chrism 7. unction
Ones.. 9. Innocents (slain by Herod)
pilgrim.. 6. palmer
receptacle.. 5. cruet, stoup
Rood.. 5. cross 8. crucifix

water sprinkler.. 11. aspergillum
Holy Grail (pert to)...
  castle.. 9. Monsalvat (Mt)
  guardian.. 8. Amfortas
  knight.. 7. Galahad
  legend.. 8. Sangraal (Sangreal)
  quest by.. 4. Bors 7. Galahad
    9. Percivale
  terms.. 7. platter, wine cup
homage... 5. dulia, honor, liege
    6. fealty, latria 7. loyalty, ovation,
    respect, worship 9. deference,
    obeisance, reverence 10. allegiance
    12. commendation
homard... 7. Homarus, lobster
hombre... 3. man 4. homo, male
    6. fellow
home... 4. care, goal (games), kern
    (kirn), nest 5. abode, astre, grave,
    heart 6. asylum, estate, hearth
    7. habitat, village 8. domicile,
    dwelling 9. residence 10. fatherland,
    habitation
home (pert to)...
  base.. 3. den 5. plate
  dislike.. 9. ecophobia
  Home Sweet Home author.. 5. Payne
    (John Howard 1823)
  Irish King's.. 4. Tara
  of the gods.. 7. Olympus
  of the Golden Fleece.. 7. Colchis
homely... 4. ugly 5. plain 6. humble,
    kindly, simple 7. plainly 8. domestic,
    homelike, informal, plebeian,
    uncomely 9. unsightly 10. intimately
    11. comfortable 13. unpretentious
homemade... 5. plain 6. simple
    8. domestic, handmade, homespun
Homer (pert to)...
  birthplace.. 5. Chios (claimed)
  book.. 5. Iliad 7. Odyssey
  burial place.. 3. Ios (Isl)
  hero.. 6. Aeneas
Homer's poems (pert to)...
  rhapsodists.. 9. Homeridae
  student, reciter of.. 7. Homerid
    8. Homerist
  study of.. 10. Homerology
  style.. 7. Homeric
homesickness... 7. Heimweh 9. mal
    du pays, nostalgia
homespun... 5. cloth, plain, rough
    6. coarse, russet 8. domestic,
    homemade 10. not elegant,
    unpolished (person)
homicide... 5. morth 6. murder
    7. killing 12. manslaughter
homily... 5. adage 6. sermon
    8. assembly, converse
    9. communion, discourse
homing pigeon... 13. carrier pigeon
hominy... 4. samp 5. maize 10. hulled
    corn
Homo sapiens... 3. man 4. homo
    9. anthropos
Honduras...
  capital.. 11. Tegucigalpa
  city.. 4. Tela 6. Roatan 8. Trujillo
    12. Puerto Cortes
  discoverer.. 8. Columbus
  gulf.. 7. Fonseca
  Indian tribe.. 5. Lenca

language.. 7. Spanish
  people.. 6. Indian 7. Spanish
  river.. 4. Ulua 5. Negro 6. Patuca
hone... 4. long, pine 5. delay, dress,
    stone (sharpening), strop, yearn
    6. lament 7. grumble, sharpen
    8. oilstone 9. whetstone
honest... 4. open 5. frank 6. candid,
    chaste 7. genuine, up and up,
    upright 8. faithful, suitable, virtuous
    9. guileless, honorable, ingenuous,
    integrity 10. creditable
    13. unadulterated 15. straightforward
honesty... 5. honor 6. equity
    7. justice 8. fairness 9. integrity,
    rectitude 11. genuineness,
    uprightness 12. truthfulness
    15. trustworthiness
honey... 3. mel 5. melli (comb form),
    sweet 6. nectar 7. sweeten
    10. endearment
honey (pert to)...
  bear (sloth).. 8. Melursus
  bearing.. 11. melliferous
  bee.. 4. Apis 6. dingar 7. deseret
    9. mellifera
  bird.. 3. iao 6. manuao 10. honey
    eater
  buzzard.. 4. kite, pern
  comb.. 4. raat 5. favus 8. alveolus
  drink.. 4. mead 5. morat
  flowing.. 11. mellifluent, mellifluous
  pert to.. 8. melissic
  sucking.. 11. mellisugent, mellivorous
  yellow.. 6. dorado 10. melichrous
Hong Kong...
  capital.. 8. Victoria
  government.. 11. Crown Colony
  island.. 12. Stonecutters
  peninsula.. 7. Kowloon
Honolulu...
  capital of.. 6. Hawaii
  island site.. 4. Oahu
  port.. 11. Pearl Harbor
  suburb.. 3. Ewa
honorable, honourable... 5. moral,
    title 7. upright 8. honorary
    9. estimable, reputable, venerable
    10. creditable 11. commendable,
    illustrious, meritorious, respectable
honorably... 5. nobly 6. fairly, justly
    8. worthily 9. equitably, reputably,
    uprightly
honorarium... 7. douceur
honored... 5. famed, feted 6. graced
    7. awarded, revered 8. knighted
    9. accoladed
hood... 4. corf, cowl, hide, mail
    (armor) 5. amice, blind, cloak
    6. bonnet, camail, capote
    7. capuche (capouch) 8. babushka,
    burnoose (burnous), capsheaf,
    covering, liripipe, mozzetta, tapadera
    12. strong–arm man
hood (suff)... 9. condition
hooded... 9. cucullate
hooded seal... 11. bladdernose
hoodwink... 4. dupe, fool, hide, wile
    5. blear, blind, cheat, cover, cozen
    6. befool, delude 7. deceive, mislead
    9. blindfold
hooey... 4. blah, bunk 5. tripe

7. baloney, hogwash 8. buncombe,
malarkey, nonsense 13. horsefeathers
hoof... 4. clee, frog, walk 5. cloof
(clufe, cluve) 6. ungula 7. pastern
(part) 8. periople (part), pododerm
hoof–paring tool... 8. butteris
hoof–shaped... 8. ungulate
hoof track... 5. piste
hook... 4. gaff, lure 5. catch, chape,
cleek, crome, curve, hamus, snare,
steal 6. anchor, clevis, fasten,
hangle, tenter 7. hamulus
hookah, hooka... 4. pipe 8. narghile
hooked... 6. curved, hamate
7. angular, cleeked 8. aduncous
(adunc), anchoral, aquiline, uncinate
Hooker (Thomas)... 9. clergyman
18. Luther of New England
hooks (group)... 5. Party (Neth)
9. pulldevil, scrodgill 10. Kabbeljaws
(Nobles)
hookworm... 7. Necator 9. Uncinaria
hooligan... 4. tyke 6. gorilla,
hoodlum, ruffian 8. larrikin
hoop... 4. bail, band, ring 5. clasp
6. circle, wicket 7. circlet
8. surround
hoop skirt... 9. crinoline
11. farthingale
Hoosier poet... 5. Riley (J Whitcomb)
Hoosier State... 7. Indiana
hop... 3. fly 4. drug, halt, jump, leap,
limp, trip, vine 5. bound, caper,
dance, frisk, opium 6. flight, gambol,
spring 8. narcotic
hope... 3. bay 4. opal, spes, Spes
(Goddess) 5. haven, inlet, trust
6. aspire, desire, expect 7. cherish,
promise 8. optimism, reliance
11. expectation 12. anticipation
hoped for... 7. sperate
hopeful... 8. probable, sanguine
9. confident, expectant 10. propitious
hopeless... 4. vain 6. futile 7. forlorn,
useless 8. downcast 9. desperate,
incurable 10. despairing, despondent
11. ineffectual 12. disconsolate,
irremediable 13. irrecoverable,
irretrievable
hopelessness... 7. despair 8. futility
13. impossibility
hop kiln... 4. oast (ost)
hoplite... 7. soldier
hopper... 3. box 5. chute 6. dancer,
jumper, leaper 7. penguin (rock)
10. receptacle 11. grasshopper
hopscotch... 6. pebble, peever
7. pallall
Horace... 4. poet 10. Ars Poetica
Horae (Gr Relig)... 4. dike (justice)
6. Eirene (peace) 7. Eunomia
(wisdom) 9. goddesses 11. Book of
Hours
horal... 6. hourly
horde... 4. army, camp, clan, pack
5. crowd, swarm, tribe, troop
Horde, Golden... 6. Tatars (Mongol)
Horde, Great (Anthrop)... 5. Kazak
7. Kirghiz
horizon... 4. blue 5. limit, range
6. circle, sea rim 7. azimuth, sea
line, sky line 8. junction (earth and

sky), boundary
horizon glass... 7. sextant
horizontal... 4. flat 5. level 8. parallel
(to horizon)
hormone... 8. estrogen 9. cortisone
horn... 4. Cape, cusp, gore, peak,
tuba 5. alarm, bugle, cornu, keras,
siren 6. antler, beaker, cornet, vessel
7. buccina, process (animal), trumpet
8. tentacle 9. appendage
horn (pert to)...
blare.. 4. toot 7. fanfare, tantara
9. tantarara
comb form.. 5. kerat 6. kerato
crescent moon.. 4. cusp
drinking (anc).. 6. rhyton
insect's.. 7. antenna
Jewish.. 7. shophar (shofar)
player.. 6. bugler 9. cornetist,
trumpeter
producing.. 11. keratogenic
trumpet.. 6. kerana (kerrana)
unbranched (antler).. 3. dag 7. pricket
hornbill... 4. bird, tock 6. homrai,
toucan 7. Buceros
horned animal (Myth)... 7. Unicorn
9. Monoceros
horned rattlesnake... 3. asp 5. viper
8. cerastes 10. sidewinder
horned toad... 6. lizard 9. Iguanidae
hornet... 4. wasp 5. Vespa 6. crabro
horny tissue... 7. keratin 8. keratoid
(ceratoid), keratose (ceratose)
horologe... 4. dial 5. clock, watch
horoscope... 3. map 5. chart
6. scheme 7. diagram
horrendous... 7. fearful 8. horrible
horrible... 4. dire, grim 6. grisly,
horrid, odious 7. ghastly, hideous
8. dreadful, shocking, terrible
9. atrocious, frightful, revolting
10. detestable, horrendous
horror... 3. awe 4. fear 5. dread
6. aghast, terror 8. aversion, distress
10. abhorrence 11. abomination,
detestation 13. consternation
hors d'oeuvre... 6. canapé, relish
8. aperitif 9. antipasto, appetizer
horse... 3. cob, nag 4. colt, foal,
mare, mule, plug, pony, prad, race,
stud 5. beast, burro, draft, filly,
genet (jennet), hobby, mount, pacer,
steed 6. bronco (broncho), cheval,
dobbin, donkey, equine, garran,
hippos, maiden, pelter, rouncy
7. caballo, cavalry, charger, courser,
Equidae, gelding, hackney, harness,
mustang, prancer, quarter, stepper,
trotter 8. roadster, stallion, trotting
9. broomtail
horse (pert to)...
ankle.. 4. hock
arena.. 10. hippodrome
Australian.. 5. dingo, myall
8. warragal, yarraman
breastplate.. 7. poitrel (peytrel)
broken–down.. 6. garran, gleyde
buyer (of nags).. 6. coper 7. knacker
calico.. 5. pinto
collar.. 7. bargham
comb form.. 4. hipp 5. hippo
6. hippus

command.. 3. gee, haw, hup
   4. whoa 6. giddap
covering.. 9. caparison
cry.. 5. neigh 6. whinny
dealer.. 7. chanter, scorser
disease.. 5. surra (surrah) 6. heaves,
   lampas, spavin 7. founder, lampers
draft.. 9. Percheron
family.. 7. Equidae 9. Miohippus,
   Orohippus
fast.. 6. pelter
feed box.. 6. manger
female.. 4. mare, yaud 5. filly
fly.. 4. cleg (clegg) 6. botfly
foot.. 4. frog, hoof 7. fetlock, pastern
forehead.. 8. chanfrin
gait.. 3. run 4. lope, pace, trot, walk
   6. canter, gallop
genus.. 5. Equus
giant (Norse).. 7. Goldfax
goddess.. 5. Epona
gray.. 8. schimmel
hide.. 8. cordovan
hired.. 4. hack
hoof (part).. 7. caltrop 8. periople
laugh.. 5. snort 6. guffaw, heehaw
leap.. 6. curvet, hurdle 9. ballotade
lover.. 10. hippophile
mackerel.. 5. atule, tunny 6. bonita
male.. 4. stud 7. gelding 8. stallion
manège term.. 5. longe, mount
   6. pesade 7. piaffer, saccade
   8. caracole 9. estrapage
measure.. 4. hand
miracle (Myth).. 5. Arion
monster (fabled).. 11. Hippocampus
old.. 4. jade, yaud 5. skate
   8. harridan, old paint
opera.. 7. Western
pace.. 4. lope, trot 5. amble
   6. canter
pack.. 7. sumpter
pair.. 4. span, team
pasturage right.. 9. horsegate
piebald.. 5. pinto
pole.. 5. poler, wheel
prehistoric.. 8. Eohippus
   10. Mesohippus, Pliohippus
   13. Protorohippus
racer.. 4. pony 6. mudder, plater,
   staker
ref to.. 6. equine, equoid, hippic
   9. caballine
relay (remounts).. 6. remuda
riding.. 3. cob
rope.. 5. longe 6. halter
roundup.. 5. rodeo
saddle.. 3. cob 5. mount 7. palfrey
shoer.. 7. farrier 10. blacksmith
slang.. 3. nag 4. hack, plug
   6. dobbin 8. bangtail
small.. 3. cob, tit 4. pony 5. bidet,
   genet (jennet) 8. Galloway, Shetland
sorrel.. 4. roan 8. chestnut
spirited.. 4. Arab 5. steed 6. rearer
   7. courser
stable.. 6. string
study of.. 9. hippology
swift.. 6. pelter 7. Pacolet
talking (Myth).. 5. Arion
three (harnessed).. 6. tandem

   7. unicorn
track, arena.. 10. hippodrome
trappings.. 5. manta 6. tackle
   7. harness 9. caparison
trotting.. 6. Morgan
turn.. 7. passade
war.. 5. steed 7. charger 8. destrier
   (anc)
white-streaked face.. 4. shim
wild.. 6. bronco, tarpan 7. mustang
   8. warragal (warrigal)
winged.. 7. Pegasus
horse, breed... 4. Arab, Barb 5. Shire,
   Waler 6. Cayuse, Morgan 7. Arabian,
   Belgian, Hackney, Mustang, Suffolk
   8. Galloway, Normandy, Palomino,
   Shetland 9. Appaloosa, Miohippus,
   Percheron 10. Clydesdale
horse, color... 3. bay, tan 4. pied,
   roan 5. cream, pinto 6. calico, sorrel
   7. brindle, dappled, piebald
   8. chestnut, palomino, schimmel,
   skewbald 10. flea-bitten
horse, famed (and rider)... 4. Tony
   (Tom Mix) 5. Grani (Sigurd)
   6. Bayard (Rinaldo), Rienzi (Gen
   Sherman), Silver (Lone Ranger),
   Trojan (legend), Whitey (Zachary
   Taylor) 7. Alborak (Mohammed),
   Morengo (Napoleon), Pegasus (Gr
   Myth), Trigger (Roy Rogers), Xanthus
   (Achilles) 8. Comanche (Gen Custer),
   Sleipnir 8-legged (Odin), Soapsuds
   (Will Rogers) 9. Black Bess (Dick
   Turpin), Houyhnhnm (Gulliver's
   Travels), Incitatus (Caligula), Rosinante
   (Don Quixote), Traveller (Gen Robt E
   Lee) 10. Bootlegger (Will Rogers),
   Bucephalus (Alexander the Great),
   Cincinnati (Gen Grant), Copenhagen
   (Wellington at Waterloo), King Philip
   (Gen Forrest) 11. Black Beauty
   (legend), Vegliantino (Orlando)
   12. Little Sorrel (Stonewall Jackson)
horseman... 5. rider 6. cowboy
   7. centaur, vaquero 8. buckaroo
   10. cavalryman, equestrian
   12. broncobuster
horsemanship... 6. manège
horseradish tree... 3. ben (oil)
   5. behen (behn) 7. Moringa
Horus (pert to)...
bird.. 6. falcon
father.. 6. Osiris
hawk-headed god of.. 3. day
mother.. 4. Isis
slayer of.. 4. Seth
hospice... 3. inn 6. asylum, imaret
   9. hospitium, infirmary
hospitable... 6. kindly 7. cordial
   8. friendly, gracious 9. receptive,
   welcoming 10. neighborly
hospital... 6. crèche, refuge
   9. ambulance (mobile), infirmary
   10. nosocomium, sanatorium,
   sanitarium 11. institution,
   xenodochium 12. ambulatorium
hospitality... 7. accueil, welcome
   8. open door 9. open house,
   xenodochy 10. cordiality
   13. receptiveness
host... 3. sum (obs) 4. army 5. swarm

6. legion, throng 8. assemble,
landlord 9. multitude, sacrifice
11. entertainer
hostel... 3. inn 5. hotel, motel
6. tavern 8. lodgings 9. residence
(student)
hostelry... 3. inn 5. hotel 6. hostel,
tavern 11. caravansary
hostile... 5. enemy 7. adverse (law),
opposed 8. contrary, inimical
10. malevolent, unfriendly
11. belligerent 12. antagonistic
13. unsympathetic
hostilities... 3. war 5. feuds, raids
hostility... 5. anger 6. animus, enmity,
hatred, rancor 7. ill will, warfare
8. opponent 9. animosity, antipathy
10. antagonism, bitterness,
opposition, resentment 11. contrariety
13. antisocialism 14. unfriendliness,
vindictiveness
hostler... 5. groom 7. equerry
9. innkeeper, stableboy, stableman
Host vessel... 3. Pyx 5. paten
hot... 3. red 5. calid, eager, fiery
6. fervid, raging, recent, torrid,
urgent 7. burning, calidus, excited,
fervent, glowing, peppery, violent
8. feverish, sizzling, vehement
10. hot-blooded, passionate
hot cakes... 8. kneepads (army sl)
hotel... 3. inn 5. lodge 6. hostel,
tavern 7. albergo 11. caravansary
hot-tempered... 5. angry, breth, fiery
7. enraged, iracund 8. choleric,
wrathful 10. hot-blooded
Hottentot, S Africa (pert to)...
cloak.. 6. kaross
hut.. 5. kraal
mixed native.. 6. Griqua
musical instrument.. 4. gora (gorah)
nickname.. 9. Khoi-Khoin (Koi-Koin)
(men of men)
purest tribe.. 5. Namas 7. Namaqua
race.. 6. Bantus 7. Bushmen
tribe.. 6. Damara, Herero
9. Ovahehero
hound... 4. hunt 5. chase, track
6. follow, pursue 7. devotee
9. scoundrel
hound (animal)... 4. alan 6. Afghan,
basset, beagle, setter 7. harrier,
skirter 8. Cerberus (Myth), elkhound,
foxhound 9. boarhound, dachshund,
deerhound, greyhound, staghound,
wolfhound 10. bloodhound,
otterhound
hounds, relay of... 8. avantlay
hour (pert to)...
astrology.. 7. inequal 9. planetary
by the.. 5. horal 6. horary
Eccl.. 4. sext 9. canonical
Latin.. 4. hora 5. Horae (Book of
Hours)
measure.. 9. hourglass
term.. 4. time 6. period 7. measure
8. interval
houri... 5. nymph (Moham)
Hours, Book of... 5. Horae
house... 3. eco (comb form) 4. casa,
firm, home 5. abode, cover, lodge,
tribe 6. billet, family 7. cottage,

enclose, lineage, mansion, quarter,
shelter, theater 8. audience,
bungalow, Congress, domicile,
dwelling 9. playhouse, residence,
workhouse 10. habitation, Parliament
house (pert to)...
astrology.. 7. mansion, mundane
9. planetary
boarding.. 3. inn 5. hotel 6. tavern
9. dormitory
comb form.. 3. eco 4. oeco, oiko
correction.. 9. Bridewell (Eng)
11. reformatory
dog.. 6. kennel
government.. 5. Lords 7. Commons
15. Representatives
ranch.. 4. casa 6. casita 8. hacienda
roof.. 9. penthouse
small.. 3. hut 4. nest 5. cabin, shack
stately.. 5. villa 6. palace 7. mansion
summer.. 6. casino, gazebo
9. belvedere
warming.. 6. infare
household (pert to)...
deity.. 5. Lares 7. Penates
domestic.. 6. family, menage
fairy.. 4. Puck
linen.. 6. napery
housekeeping... 8. oikology
10. management 11. hospitality
House of... 4. Keys (Isle of Man)
5. David, Lords, Peers 7. Bishops,
Commons, Windsor 11. Seven
Gables
housewarming... 6. infare
11. merrymaking
Houston, Texas...
capital.. 8. Republic (Texas, 1837)
college.. 4. Rice
named for.. 10. Sam Houston (Gen)
nickname.. 12. Space City USA
site.. 11. Ship Channel
site of.. 4. NASA
hovel... 3. den, hut 4. shed 5. cabin,
hutch, shack 6. dugout 7. shelter
hover... 4. flit, soar 5. brood, drift,
float 6. linger 7. shelter 9. hang
about 12. be irresolute
however... 3. but, how, tho, yet
6. anyhow, though 7. at least
8. although 11. at all events
12. nevertheless 15. notwithstanding
howl... 3. bay, cry 4. wail, yell, yowl
6. lament 7. ululate
howling monkey... 5. araba
hoyden, hoiden... 4. rude 5. a romp
6. tomboy 7. ill-bred
Hoyle (Edmond)... 6. writer
12. encyclopedia (of games)
hub... 3. hut 4. axle, nave 6. center
(centre) 7. hummock
12. protuberance (rough)
Hub (The)... 6. Boston
hubbub... 3. ado, din 4. game (US
Ind), stir 6. bustle, clamor, outcry,
racket, rumpus, tumult, uproar
8. rowdy-dow 9. agitation,
commotion, confusion 10. turbulence
hubristic... 8. arrogant, insolent
12. contemptuous
hubshi... 5. Negro
huck... 3. hip 4. hook, howk

6. haunch, higgle, hollow 7. bargain
huckleberry... 5. bacca 9. blueberry
12. Vacciniaceae
huckleberry endocarp... 6. pyrene
huckster... 6. broker, hawker, vendor
7. peddler 8. pitchman, retailer
9. middleman
huddle... 3. hug 5. crowd 6. bustle,
confer, jumble, mingle 7. confuse
8. assemble, disorder, grouping
(football) 9. confusion, skinflint
10. conference 14. conglomeration
Hudson (pert to)...
boat.. 8. Half Moon (Henry Hudson's)
explorer.. 11. Henry Hudson
River School.. 8. Painters (19th Cent)
River seal.. 7. muskrat
hue... 4. form, tint, tone 5. color,
guise, shade, shout, swart, tinge
6. outcry 7. swarthy 8. shouting
10. complexion
huff... 4. puff 5. anger, bully, swell
6. offend 7. inflate
hug... 3. hold 5. clasp, seize
6. adhere 7. embrace, welcome
8. greeting
huge... 3. big 4. vast 5. giant, great,
large 7. immense, mammoth,
massive, monster, titanic 8. colossal,
enormous, gigantic 9. monstrous
10. gargantuan
Huguenot... 10. Protestant
Huguenot leader... 6. Adrets (Baron)
hui (Chin)... 4. firm 5. guild 7. society
(secret) 11. partnership
huisache... 4. wabe (wabi) 5. shrub
7. popinac
huissier... 5. usher 7. bailiff, sheriff
10. doorkeeper
huitre... 6. oyster
hulky... 5. bulky, large 6. clumsy
7. hulking, loutish
hull... 3. pod 4. free, husk 5. calyx,
frame (ship), shell, shoot, strip
8. covering
hullabaloo... 3. din 6. clamor
(clamour), hubbub, outcry, racket,
tumult, uproar 9. confusion
hulled corn... 4. samp 5. maize
6. hominy
hulver... 5. holly
hum... 4. buzz, sing (with closed lips)
5. croon, drone 6. murmur
7. deceive
human... 3. man 4. homo, kind
6. humane, mortal 7. Adamite
8. merciful
human (pert to)...
being.. 3. man 6. mortal, person
7. Adamite 8. creature
bondage.. 7. slavery
race.. 3. man 7. mankind
skull.. 10. death's-head
structure.. 7. anatomy
trunk.. 5. torso
humble... 3. low 4. mean, meek, mild,
poor 5. abase, abash, demit, lower,
lowly, plain 6. modest, simple,
subdue 7. degrade, mortify
8. chastise, deferent, disgrace,
plebeian, reverent 9. humiliate
10. unassuming 12. unpretending

humbug... 4. bosh, fake, flam, guff,
hoax, sham 5. cheat, fraud, guile,
trick 7. deceive, mislead 8. pretense
9. deception, imposture, stratagem
humid... 4. damp, dank 5. moist
6. sultry 8. vaporous
humiliate... 5. abase, abash, shame
6. humble, nither 7. affront, degrade,
mortify 8. disgrace
humiliation... 7. subdual 9. abasement
11. disgraceful 13. mortification
humility... 6. humble (spirit)
7. modesty 8. meekness, mildness
9. lowliness (mind) 10. humbleness
hummingbird... 3. ava 4. star
5. sylph, topaz 6. rufous, Sappho
7. colibri, Lucifer 8. calliope
9. sheartail, thornbill, thorntail
10. rackettail 11. Trochilidae
humor, humour... 3. fun, wit 4. baby,
mood, whim 5. blood, cater, fancy,
fluid, freak, quirk 6. comedy, levity,
nature, please 7. caprice, gratify,
indulge 8. drollery 10. comicality
11. inclination, temperament
humorist... 3. wag 5. comic, droll
8. comedian 11. entertainer
humorous... 5. funny, humid, moist,
witty 6. jocose 7. amusing, jocular
9. facetious, laughable, whimsical
10. capricious
hump... 4. arch, hunk, lump 5. bulge,
exert, hurry, mound, sulks
7. hummock 8. shoulder
12. protuberance
humpbacked... 6. humped, kyphos
8. deformed, kyphosis 9. camel back
11. hunchbacked
humpbacked fish... 5. whale
6. salmon, sucker 9. whitefish
humus... 4. mold, soil 5. humin,
mulch
Hun... 6. Attila, vandal 7. soldier
9. barbarian 10. Ephthalite
hunch... 4. bend, hump, lump
5. crook, fudge, shove 6. chilly,
crouch, frosty, thrust 9. intuition
12. protuberance
Hunchback of Notre Dame (pert to)..
character.. 9. Esmeralda (gypsy),
Quasimodo (The Hunchback)
French name.. 16. Notre Dame de
Paris
literature (famed).. 5. novel
hunched... 7. gibbous
hundred (pert to)...
comb form.. 5. centi, hecto
7. hecaton
eyed being.. 5. Argus
fold.. 8. centuple 12. centuplicate
historian (of centuries)..
11. centuriator
Latin.. 6. centum
men, soldiers.. 7. century
12. centumvirate
number.. 7. ten tens 9. five score
symbol.. 1. C
victim sacrifice.. 8. hecatomb
weight.. 6. cental 7. centner
years.. 7. century 9. centenary,
centurial
Hundred Days (pert to)... 8. Napoleon,

Waterloo (Battle 1815)
hundred percent... 5. quite 8. entirely
10. altogether 14. unquestionable
hundredth of a right angle... 4. grad
Hundred Years War... 5. Crecy
(Cressy)

hung... see *hang*

Hungarian (pert to)... see also *Hungary*
army.. 6. Honvéd 9. Honvédség
cavalryman.. 6. Hussar
dance.. 7. czardas
gypsy.. 7. tzigane
hash.. 7. goulash
legislature.. 8. Felsohaz
measure.. 5. antal, itcze
partridge.. 6. Perdix
physicist.. 6. Teller
poet.. 5. Arany
Pretender to the throne.. 4. Otto
racial unit.. 3. Hun 6. Magyar
surgeon.. 6. Schick
turnip.. 8. kohlrabi
wine.. 5. Tokay

Hungary (People's Republic of)...
capital.. 8. Budapest (Budapesth)
city.. 6. Szeged (Szegedin)
8. Debrecen 9. Kecskemet
government.. 9. Communism
lake.. 7. Balaton 10. Neusiedler
mountain.. 5. Tatra 11. Carpathians
Plain (fertile).. 6. Alfold
port.. 5. Fiume
river.. 4. Raab 5. Drava (Drave)
6. Danube, Theiss 7. Vistula

hunger... 4. long, want 6. acoria,
desire, famine, thirst 7. craving
8. appetite, coveting, voracity
9. esurience

hungry... 4. avid, poor 5. eager
6. barren, hollow, jejune 7. starved
8. esurient, famished, indigent
10. avaricious

Hung Society (secret)... 5. Triad (Man,
Earth, Heaven) 6. Deluge

hunt... 3. dig 4. seek 5. chase, delve,
hound, probe, quest, track, trail
6. ferret, follow, pursue, search,
shikar

hunter... 3. dog 5. green, horse,
jager, Jason, Orion 6. cuckoo,
Nimrod 7. shikari (shikaree), stalker,
trapper, venerer 8. huntsman

hunting (pert to)...
act of.. 6. venery 7. pursuit
10. cynegetics
coyotes.. 7. wolfing
dog.. 5. dhole 6. basset, beagle,
setter 7. pointer
Dogs (Astron).. 13. Canes Venatici
expedition.. 6. safari
fond of.. 7. venatic
horn.. 5. bugle
leopard.. 7. cheetah

hurdy–gurdy... 4. lire, rota 5. organ
(street) 7. sambuke 10. instrument
(lutelike), waterwheel

hurl... 4. cast, pelt, rush, toss
5. fling, pitch, sling, throw 6. elance
(dart), hurtle 8. overthrow

hurlbarrow... 11. wheelbarrow

hurled... 4. cast, sent 5. flung, slung,

threw 6. pelted, tossed 7. hurtled,
twisted 8. betossed

hurly–burly... 5. storm 6. tumult,
uproar 9. agitation, confusion
10. excitement

huron... 6. grison (animal) 9. black
bass

Huron... 4. lake 6. Indian 9. Iroquoian

hurrah... 3. joy 4. viva 5. cheer,
huzza, shout 7. triumph 8. applause
10. hallelujah 11. exclamation
13. encouragement

hurricane... 5. storm 6. baguio
7. cyclone, Hurakan (god), tornado,
typhoon (in China Sea)

hurry... 3. hie 4. rush, scud 5. chase,
haste, impel, sessa, speed 6. hasten,
scurry, tumult, urge on 7. quicken
8. dispatch, expedite 9. agitation,
commotion 10. expedition
11. disturbance, precipitate

hurst... 4. hill, wood 5. copse, grove,
knoll 7. hillock (wooded)

hurt... 4. harm, maim, pain 5. lesed,
parry 6. damage, grieve, impair,
injure, injury, offend 8. distress,
mischief 9. detriment 10. impairment

hurtful... 6. malign, nocent 7. baneful,
harmful, malefic, nocuous, noisome,
noxious, painful 9. injurious
10. pernicious 11. destructive,
detrimental, prejudicial
15. disadvantageous

hurtle... 4. dash, push 5. clash, fling
6. assail, jostle 7. collide, resound
8. brandish

husband... 3. eke 4. mate, save
5. marry, store 6. direct (frugally),
farmer, spouse, tiller 7. espouse,
granger, manager, steward
8. conserve 9. cultivate, economize
10. husbandman

husbandry... 6. thrift 7. economy,
farming, tillage 10. management
(domestic) 11. agriculture, cultivation

husband's brother... 5. levir

hush... 3. tut 4. calm, hist, lull
5. allay, quiet, still 6. soothe
7. appease, silence 10. keep secret

husk... 4. bran, leam, rind 5. shood,
shuck, straw

husky... 3. dry 5. burly, harsh
6. hoarse, strong 7. raucous
8. powerful

Husky... 3. dog 6. Eskimo
8. Malemute

huss... 7. dogfish

hussar... 4. fish (banded) 6. dolman
(jacket) 10. cavalryman, skirmisher

hussy... 4. girl, jade 8. strumpet
9. housewife

hustings... 5. court 8. platform
(Guildhall)

hut... 3. cot 4. cote, isba, shed, skeo
(fisherman's) 5. cabin, hogan, hovel,
igloo, jacal, scale 6. lean–to, shanty,
wigwam

hutch... 3. bin, box, car, hut, pen
4. coop 5. chest, hoard, hovel
6. coffer, humped, shanty, warren

hyacinth (pert to)...
color.. 5. tenne 7. blue–red

genus.. 10. Hyacinthus
mineral.. 6. zircon
myth.. 4. iris, lily (Turk's cap)
of Peru.. 9. Cuban lily
precious stone.. 8. sapphire (legend)
wild.. 6. camass
hybrid... 7. mongrel 9. half–breed
hybrid (pert to)...
buffalo.. 7. cattalo
dog.. 5. Husky 7. mongrel
fruit.. 7. plumcot, tangelo 8. citrange
horse.. 4. mule 5. hinny, jenny
vegetable.. 6. pomato
zebra.. 7. zebrass, zebrula 8. zebrinny
hydra... 4. evil 6. polyps
11. thermometer
Hydra (Gr)... 6. island 7. serpent
13. constellation
hydraulic (pert to)...
brake.. 8. cataract
element.. 5. water
engine.. 3. ram 6. tremie
product.. 5. power
hydria... 3. jar 6. kalpis
hydrocarbon... 7. tolan (tolane)
6. ethane, octane, pinene, pyrene,
tolane, toluol 7. benzene, methane,
terpene 9. acetylene
hydrocarbon radical... 4. amyl
6. pentyl
hydrocyanic acid... 7. cyanide, prussic
8. fumigant
hydrogen... 1. H 3. gas 7. element
(univalent)
hydroid... 9. polyplike
hydrophobia... 5. lyssa 6. rabies
Hydrus... 12. water serpent (fabled)
13. constellation
hyena... 6. mammal 8. aardwolf
9. earthwolf 13. Tasmanian wolf
hygienic... 7. sterile 8. sanitary
9. healthful 10. uninfected
12. prophylactic
hylophagous... 10. wood–eating
hymenopter, hymenopteron... 3. ant,
bee, fly 4. wasp 9. ichneumon
hymn... 3. ode 4. song (of praise)
5. dirge, music, paean (pean)
6. anthem, hirmos, Te Deum
7. chorale 8. doxology 9. Trisagion
11. recessional

hymn (pert to)...
book.. 6. hymnal
composer.. 7. hymnist
12. hymnographer
science of.. 9. hymnology
singing of.. 7. hymnody
victory.. 9. epinicion
hypnotic... 6. opiate, sleepy
8. mesmeric, narcotic, sedative
9. soporific 12. somnifacient
13. sleep–inducing
hypnotist... 6. Mesmer 9. mesmerist
10. hypnotizer
hypnotize... 5. charm 6. dazzle
8. entrance 9. fascinate, mesmerize,
spellbind
hypochondriac... 4. hypo 6. insane
7. invalid (imaginary) 8. dejected,
neurotic 9. depressed, psychotic
10. nosomaniac
hypocrisy... 4. cant 6. deceit
8. feigning 9. falseness
10. sanctimony, simulation
11. outward show
hypocrite... 4. fake 5. cheat 7. tartufe
(tartuffe) 8. deceiver 10. dissembler
hypocritical... 5. false 8. specious
9. insincere 11. pharisaical
13. sanctimonious, self–righteous
hypodermic glass vessel...
7. ampoule (ampule)
hypodermic injection... 4. shot
11. inoculation
hypothesis... 3. ism 6. theory
7. premise, theorem 8. proposal
9. condition, postulate
10. assumption 11. proposition,
supposition
hypothetical... 8. academic
11. conditional, conjectural,
speculative, theoretical
hypothetical (pert to)...
being.. 3. ens 5. entia (pl) 6. entity
biological unit.. 2. id
force.. 2. od
medium.. 5. ether
hyrax... 8. procavia
hyssop... 4. mint 11. aspergillum
hysteria... 7. anxiety 12. emotionalism
hysterical... 7. frantic 8. frenzied,
wild–eyed 9. emotional
12. uncontrolled

I

I... 2. me 3. eye 4. iota (Gr), self 6. letter (9th), myself 7. pronoun

I (pert to)...
big.. 3. ego
excessive.. 8. iotacism
love.. 3. amo

Iago... 7. villain (Othello)

iambus.. 4. foot, iamb

iatrics (comb form)... 11. treatment of

iatrology... 7. healing 8. treatise

Iberia... 5. Spain 7. Georgia (anc)

Iberian Madonna (now in Moscow)... 4. icon (Mt Athos)

ibex... 3. tur, zac 4. kail (kyl) 6. sakeen 8. antelope

ibid... 6. lizard 7. monitor

ibidem... 4. ibid 9. same place

ibis... 5. guara, stork 9. gourdhead

Ibsen (pert to)...
famed as.. 4. poet 9. dramatist
native of.. 6. Norway
story character.. 3. Ase 4. Gynt, Nora

ice... 4. rime 5. frost, glacé, glaze 6. freeze 7. congeal, diamond, jewelry 11. refrigerant, refrigerate

ice (pert to)...
cream dish.. 4. cone, soda 6. frappé, mousse, sundae 7. parfait
dessert.. 5. glacé 6. frappé 7. sherbet
fine, slushy.. 4. grue, hail, sish, snow 5. flake, frost, sleet
fishing.. 4. chug
glacier.. 4. neve 5. serac
mass.. 4. berg, calf, floe 5. serac 6. icecap 7. glacier, growler
pendent.. 6. icicle
sea.. 6. sludge

Iceland...
airport.. 8. Keflavik
assembly.. 7. Althing
bird.. 4. gull 6. falcon 10. gyrofalcon
capital.. 9. Reykjavik
city.. 8. Akureyri
dramatist.. 12. Sigurjonsson
epic.. 4. Edda
first discoverer.. 8. Norseman (about 870)
giant.. 4. Atli
god (Norse).. 3. Tyr 4. Odin (Othin), Thor, Vali, Ymir 5. Aesir 6. Balder 7. Forseti 8. Heimdall, Valkyrie
government.. 8. republic (1944)
legends.. 5. Eddas, Sagas 12. Volsunga Saga
mountain.. 5. Jokul 10. Orafa-jokul
Parliament.. 7. Althing (world's oldest)
product.. 7. herring
sculptor.. 9. Sveinsson
volcano.. 5. Askja, Hekla, Katla

ichneumon... 3. fly 8. mongoose 9. Herpestes 12. hymenopteron

ichor... 5. fluid (of the gods)

ichthus... 4. fish 6. amulet, symbol 8. talisman

ichthyophagy... 10. fish eating

icicle... 7. shoggle 10. stalactite, stalagmite

icing... 8. frosting, meringue

icterus... 6. oriole 7. disease 8. jaundice 10. yellowness

ictus... 4. beat (rhythm), blow 6. accent, stress, stroke

icy... 4. cold 5. algid, gelid 6. frigid, frosty, frozen 7. glacial 8. chilling

id... 4. idem, unit 5. idant 6. libido, psyche, suffix 7. the same

Idaean (pert to)...
dweller of.. 5. Mt Ida
goddess.. 4. Rhea (Crete) 6. Cybele (Asia Minor)
nature goddess.. 6. Cybele 11. Great Mother

Idaho...
capital.. 5. Boise
city.. 7. Orofino 9. Pocatello 10. Idaho Falls 11. Coeur d'Alene
crop (famed).. 8. potatoes
dam.. 5. Oxbow 8. Brownlee
famed citizen.. 5. Borah (Sen)
monument.. 16. Craters of the Moon
mountain.. 8. Sawtooth 11. Bitterroots
river.. 5. Snake
salmon (landlocked).. 7. kokanee
State admission.. 10. Forty-third
State motto.. 11. Live Forever 12. Esto Perpetua
State nickname.. 8. Gem State

ide (id)... 3. orf (orfe) 4. fish 7. the same

idea... 4. clue, idée, ideo (comb form) 5. ethic, motif 6. belief, notion 7. concept, meaning, opinion, wrinkle 10. impression 11. supposition

ideal... 4. type 5. dream, model, Thule (Myth) 6. unreal 7. paragon, pattern, perfect, typical, Utopian 8. complete, exemplar, fanciful 9. faultless, imaginary, visionary 10. conceptual, consummate, idealistic 11. mental image, theoretical 12. intellectual

idealist... 7. dreamer 8. romancer 9. visionary 11. illusionist

idealistic... 9. fictional, visionary 13. philosophical

ideate... 5. think 6. invent 8. conceive 9. prefigure

identical... 4. same, self, twin 5. alike, equal 10. equivalent, tantamount

identification... 3. tag 4. disk, sign

5. badge, brand 6. naming
7. earmark 11. recognition,
unification
identify... 4. name 5. place, prove
8. coalesce 9. designate, establish
13. associate with
identity... 5. unity 7. oneness
8. equality, sameness 9. exactness
11. homogeneity 13. individuality
ideologist... 7. dreamer 8. theorist
9. visionary
idiocy... 7. amentia, anoesia, fatuity,
idiotry 10. deficiency (mental)
11. foolishness
idiograph... 9. trademark
idiom... 6. phrase 7. diction
8. language 11. peculiarity
idiosyncrasy... 9. mannerism
11. peculiarity 12. eccentricity
14. characteristic
idiot... 3. oaf 4. dolt, fool 5. booby,
dunce, moron 6. cretin, nitwit
7. dullard, half–wit 8. imbecile
9. blockhead, simpleton
idiotic... 4. daft 5. crazy 7. foolish
9. senseless 12. feeble–minded
idle... 4. laze, lazy, loaf, sorn, vain
5. drone, empty, inert 6. loiter,
otiose, tiffle, truant, unused, vacant
7. leisure, loafing, trivial, useless
8. baseless, inactive, indolent,
slothful, trifling 9. unfounded,
worthless 10. groundless,
unemployed, unoccupied
11. ineffectual, unwarranted
idleness... 5. folly, sloth 6. vanity
7. inertia 8. delirium, faniente,
laziness 9. silliness 11. inactivity,
triviality 15. lightheadedness
idler... 4. hobo 5. drone 6. loafer
7. dawdler, lounger 8. loiterer
idol... 3. god (sacred) 4. Baal, icon,
zemi 5. afgod, deity (heathen), eikon,
satyr 6. effigy, fetish, idolum, statue
7. darling, fallacy, phantom, picture
8. impostor 9. pretender
idolater... 5. pagan 6. adorer
7. admirer, Baalist, Baalite, heathen
8. idolizer 9. worshiper
idolize... 5. adore 6. esteem, revere
7. worship 10. idolatrize
idyl, idyll... 4. poem 5. image
7. bucolic, eclogue, picture
8. pastoral
i. e.... 5. id est 6. that is
if... 2. si 3. gif 8. granting, provided
9. supposing
if ever... 4. once
if not... 4. else, nisi (law) 6. unless
igneous rock... 4. boss, dike, trap
5. magma 6. basalt 7. peridot
10. granophyre 11. molten magma
ignis... 4. fire
ignite... 4. burn, fire, heat 5. light
6. kindle 7. blaze up, flare up 9. set
fire to
ignoble... 3. low 4. base, mean, vile
6. menial 8. plebeian, shameful
11. disgraceful 12. dishonorable,
disreputable
ignoramus... 4. dolt, fool 5. dunce
6. nitwit, no bill (law)

11. know–nothing
ignorance... 5. tamas (Hind)
9. nescience 12. inexperience
ignorant... 7. unaware 8. nescient
9. unknowing, untutored
10. illiterate, unlettered
13. inexperienced, unintelligent
ignore... 3. cut 4. omit, snub
7. condone, disobey, neglect
8. overlook 9. disregard, eliminate
Igorot... 6. Bontok 7. Nabaloi
8. Kankanai 10. Indonesian
iguana... 6. goanna (goana), lizard
7. monitor, tuatara 9. Iguanidae
10. lace lizard
I Have Found It... 6. Eureka (Calif
motto)
ihi (Maori)... 7. skipper 8. halfbeak
10. stitchbird
IHS... 5. Jesus 6. symbol 10. In hoc
signo
iiwi... 4. bird
ikbal... 7. arrival 8. prestige
10. prosperity
Iknaton... 9. Amenhotep, Amenophis
(IV)
ikona... 9. greenhorn, simpleton
ileum... 9. intestine (small)
ilex... 5. holly 7. holm oak
11. Paraguay tea
Iliad (pert to)...
founder (anc).. 4. Troy 5. Ilium
poem author.. 5. Homer
poem character.. 4. Ajax 6. Hector
7. Stentor 8. Achilles, Brisseis
9. Agamemnon, Cassandra
ilium... 4. bone (pelvic)
Ilium... 4. Troy (anc)
ill... 3. bad, mal (comb form) 4. evil,
hard, poor, rude, sick 5. badly,
wrong 6. ailing, malice, poorly,
savage, unkind 7. noxious, painful,
unlucky 9. dangerous, difficult
10. disastrous, indisposed, iniquitous,
malevolent, unpolished, unskillful
11. unfavorable, unfortunate,
unwholesome 12. disagreeable,
inauspicious
ill (pert to)...
at ease.. 7. awkward 9. graceless,
maladroit
bred.. 4. rude 7. uncivil 8. impolite
9. bourgeois
hap.. 10. misfortune
humored.. 5. cross, moody
natured.. 4. dour 5. cross, moody,
surly 6. morose, sullen 7. crabbed
10. crosspatch
tempered.. 7. bilious 8. choleric
timed.. 5. inapt 8. untimely
9. premature 10. malapropos
11. inexpedient, inopportune
will.. 6. enmity, malice
11. malevolence
illegal... 4. foul 7. illicit 8. outlawry,
unlawful, wrongful 10. contraband,
unofficial 12. illegitimate,
unauthorized
illegal entry... 6. ringer
illimitable... 4. vast 8. infinite
9. boundless 11. measureless
12. immeasurable, unrestricted

Illinois...
airport.. 5. O'Hare
capital.. 8. Vandalia (first)
   11. Springfield
city.. 5. Elgin 6. Peoria 7. Chicago,
   Decatur 8. Evanston, Waukegan
   9. Centralia
lake.. 8. Michigan
slogan.. 13. Land of Lincoln
State admission.. 11. Twenty–first
State nickname.. 7. Prairie

illiterate... 6. unread 8. ignorant,
   untaught 9. inerudite, unlearned,
   unrefined, untutored, unwritten
illness... 6. malady 8. cachexia,
   sickness 9. complaint, distemper
   10. affliction 13. indisposition
illuminant... 3. gas 4. lamp
   9. petroleum 10. Kleig light
illuminate... 5. adorn, color, light
   6. illume 7. explain, lighten, miniate
   8. emblazen, illumine 9. elucidate,
   enlighten, irradiate, rubricate
   10. illustrate
illumination, unit of... 3. lux 4. phot
illusion... 5. fancy 6. mirage
   7. chimera, fallacy, mockery,
   phantom 8. delusion, phantasy
   9. deception, false show
   10. apparition 13. hallucination,
   misconception
illusive... 5. false 6. unreal 8. spectral
   9. deceitful, deceptive, imaginary
   10. phantasmal, transitory
illusory... 5. false 8. delusory, illusive
   9. deceptive, erroneous, imaginary,
   unfounded 10. fallacious
illustrate... 4. cite, draw 5. adorn
   7. explain, picture 8. beautify
   9. elucidate, exemplify, represent
   10. illuminate
illustrious... 5. noble, noted
   6. famous, heroic 7. eminent,
   exalted, radiant 8. glorious, luminous,
   renowned, splendid 9. brilliant,
   honorable 10. celebrated
image... 3. god 4. copy, icon, idea,
   idol, ikon, type 6. alraun, aspect,
   effigy, idolon, mirror, recept, sphinx,
   statue, typify 7. eidolon, phantom,
   picture, portray 8. illusion, likeness,
   phantasm 9. semblance
   10. apparition, conception,
   simulacrum 11. counterpart
   12. reproduction
imaginary... 5. ideal 7. fancied
   8. fanciful, illusory, mythical
   10. fictitious
imaginary disease... 9. nosomania
imagination... 5. dream, fancy
   8. phantasy, poetical
imagine... 5. dream, fancy, opine,
   think 6. ideate 7. suppose
   8. conceive 9. conjecture
imam... 6. caliph, priest (Moham)
imbecile... 4. dolt, weak 5. anile,
   idiot, inane, moron 6. cretin, dotard,
   feeble, stupid, witlet 7. fatuous,
   idiotic, witling 9. driveling
   10. half–witted 12. feeble–minded
imbed... 5. embed, inset 6. cement
   9. establish

imberbe... 9. beardless
imbibe... 4. soak 5. drink, imbue,
   learn 6. absorb, inhale 8. saturate
   10. assimilate
imbroglio... 5. brawl 11. embroilment,
   predicament 16. misunderstanding
imbrue... 3. fig, wet 4. soak 5. color,
   stain (with blood), steep 6. defile,
   drench 7. moisten 8. saturate
imbue... 3. dye 5. steep, teach, tinge
   6. infuse, leaven 7. ingrain, inspire
   8. permeate, saturate, tincture
   9. inculcate 10. impregnate
imitant... 9. imitation 11. counterfeit
imitate... 3. ape 4. copy, mime, mock
   5. mimic 6. borrow 7. emulate
   8. pastiche, resemble, simulate
   9. dissemble, reproduce
imitation... 4. copy, echo, sham
   5. apery, apism, paste 6. ectype,
   olivet (pearl), parody 7. mimesis,
   mimicry 8. travesty 9. burlesque
   10. caricature, simulation
   12. onomatopoeia
imitative... 5. apish 8. apatetic
   9. emulative, imitation 10. simulative
   11. counterfeit
immaculate... 4. pure 5. clean
   6. chaste 8. spotless, unsoiled
   9. faultless, undefiled, unstained,
   unsullied
immanence... 7. inbeing 9. inherence
   10. indwelling, innateness
immanent... 5. inner 6. inward
   8. internal 9. intrinsic 10. indwelling
immaterial... 6. slight 8. trifling
   9. spiritual 10. impalpable, intangible
   11. disembodied, incorporeal,
   unimportant 12. supernatural
   13. insignificant, unsubstantial
immature... 5. crude, green 6. callow,
   unripe 7. untried 8. untimely,
   youthful 9. premature 10. unfinished
   11. undeveloped
immeasurable... 7. endless 8. infinite
   9. boundless, unlimited 10. indefinite
   11. illimitable, innumerable
   12. immensurable, incalculable,
   unfathomable 13. indeterminate
   16. incomprehensible
immediacy... 9. awareness, closeness
   10. directness 11. punctuality
immediate... 4. next 6. direct, prompt
   7. instant, nearest, present
   10. continuous, succeeding
immediately... 3. now 4. anon
   7. closely 8. directly, promptly
   9. instantly, therewith 11. straightway
   12. without delay
immemorial... 3. old 7. ageless,
   ancient 8. dateless 9. out of mind
   11. prehistoric, traditional
immense... 4. huge, vast 5. grand,
   great 6. superb 7. mammoth, titanic
   8. enormous, infinite 9. monstrous
   10. prodigious, unmeasured
immerge... 3. dip 4. sink 5. merge
   6. engulf, plunge 7. immerse
   8. inundate, submerge
immerse... 3. dip 4. bury, dunk, sink
   5. douse, souse 6. absorb, plunge
   7. baptize, engross 9. overwhelm

imminent... 7. nearing 8. menacing, upcoming 9. impending 10. near at hand 11. approaching, forthcoming, overhanging, threatening

immobile... 3. set 5. fixed, inert 6. stable 8. moveless 9. immovable, obstinate, unfeeling 10. inflexible, motionless, stationary

immoderate... 5. ultra, undue 7. extreme 9. excessive 10. exorbitant, inordinate 11. extravagant, intemperate 12. unreasonable

immolation... 8. oblation, offering 9. sacrifice

immoral... 3. bad 6. wicked 7. corrupt, vicious 8. depraved, indecent 9. dissolute 10. licentious, misconduct

immortal... 6. divine 7. abiding, endless, eternal, godlike, undying 8. enduring 9. ambrosial, ceaseless, celebrity, perpetual 10. superhuman 11. amaranthine, everlasting 12. imperishable 13. incorruptible

Immortal (Taoism)... 8. Chang Kuo

immortality... 4. fame 6. amrita (conferring) 9. anathasia 11. lasting fame 13. deathlessness 15. everlastingness

immovable... 3. pat 4. fast, firm 5. fixed, rigid 6. stable 7. adamant 8. immobile, obdurate 9. obstinate, unfeeling 10. inflexible, stationary

immunity... 7. freedom 8. impunity 9. exemption 10. resistance (power of) 11. unrestraint

immure... 4. wall 6. entomb 7. confine 8. imprison, surround 9. encompass 11. incarcerate

immutable... 4. firm 6. stable 7. eternal 8. constant 9. obstinate 10. inflexible, invariable 12. unchangeable 13. unadulterated

imp... 3. bud, elf, fay 4. brat, cion, pixy, slip 5. child, demon, devil, fairy, graft, rogue, scion, shoot, youth 6. repair (falconry), spirit, sprite 7. progeny 9. offspring

impact... 4. pack, slam 5. brunt, force, shock, wedge 6. effect, stroke 7. contact, impulse, meaning 8. striking 9. collision, fix firmly, impinging

impair... 3. mar 4. harm, hurt, ruin, rust, wear 5. break, spoil 6. damage, debase, injure, lessen, reduce, weaken 7. vitiate 8. decrease, enfeeble 11. deteriorate

impairment of...
capital.. 4. loss 7. deficit
character.. 6. injury 10. defamation 11. degradation 13. deterioration
nerve (a).. 11. anerethisia

impale... 4. edge, gore, join (Her), spit, stab 5. hem in, spike 6. border, pierce, punish 7. confine, torture 8. encircle, surround

impalement... 5. calyx 8. stabbing 10. punishment 11. coats of arms (united)

impalpable... 4. fine 10. immaterial, intangible 13. infinitesimal

impart... 3. say 4. give, lend, tell 5. grant, share, yield 6. confer, convey, inform, reveal 7. divulge 8. disclose, discover 9. partake of 10. distribute 11. communicate

impartial... 4. even, fair, just 7. neutral 8. unbiased 9. equitable 12. unprejudiced 13. disinterested, dispassionate

impartiality... 7. justice 8. fairness 10. neutrality 11. unprejudice 17. disinterestedness

impassable... 6. stolid 9. impassive 10. impervious, unpassable 11. impermeable, unnavigable 12. impenetrable

impasse... 8. cul-de-sac 9. stalemate 10. blind alley

impassible... 9. impassive, unfeeling

impassioned... 6. ardent 7. amorous, zealous 8. eloquent, vehement 10. passionate

impassive... 4. calm 6. serene 7. passive 8. apathetic 10. impassable 12. invulnerable 13. insusceptible

impatient... 5. eager, testy 6. uneasy 7. anxious, fretful, itching, peevish, restive 8. choleric, petulant, restless 9. impetuous, irascible, irritable 10. intolerant

impavid... 8. fearless

impeach... 4. harm 6. accuse, charge, hinder, impair, impede, indict 7. arraign, censure, prevent 9. challenge, criminate, discredit, disparage

impeccable... 8. flawless, innocent 9. faultless 10. immaculate

impede... 3. bar, let 4. clog 5. block, debar, estop 6. hamper, hinder, retard, stymie (stimy) 8. encumber, obstruct, restrict

impediment... 3. bar, rub 4. snag 5. hitch 6. defect, malady 7. baggage, barrier 8. obstacle 9. hindrance 10. difficulty 11. encumbrance, obstruction

impel... 3. put 4. move, urge 5. drive, force, forge 6. compel, incite, induce, obsess, prompt, propel 7. actuate 9. constrain, influence

impel a boat... 3. oar, row 4. pole 5. scull

impelling force... 7. impetus 8. momentum

impending... 7. nearing 8. awaiting, imminent, menacing 9. hindering 11. overhanging, threatening

impenetrable... 5. dense 10. impervious 11. impregnable, inscrutable 12. inaccessible, unfathomable 13. unimpressible 14. unintelligible

impenitent... 8. obdurate 10. uncontrite 11. unrepentant, unrepenting

imperative... 4. mood (Gram) 6. needed, urgent 7. binding 8. pressing 9. directive, imperious, mandatory, necessary

10. compulsory, obligatory, peremptory 13. authoritative

imperceptible ... 6. subtle 9. invisible 10. insensible 13. inappreciable, indiscernible, infinitesimal 14. unintelligible

imperfect ... 3. mal (pref) 4. cull 5. frail 6. faulty, second 7. errable 8. fallible, immature, impaired 9. blemished, defective 10. inadequate, incomplete

imperfection ... 4. flaw, vice 5. fault 6. defect 7. blemish, failing 8. fraility, weakness 10. deficiency 11. shortcoming 14. incompleteness

imperfectly ... 8. slightly 12. inadequately

imperial ... 5. regal, royal 6. kingly, lordly, purple 8. majestic 9. imperious, masterful, monarchal, sovereign

imperial (pert to) ...
　Academy .. 6. Han–lin (Chin)
　blue .. 5. smalt
　cap .. 5. crown
　city (anc) .. 4. Rome
　domain .. 6. empire
　legislature .. 4. Diet (Jap)
　officer .. 8. palatine

imperil ... 4. risk 6. expose 8. endanger 10. jeopardize

imperious ... 6. lordly 7. haughty 8. arrogant, despotic, dominant, pressing 10. commanding, compelling, tyrannical 11. dictatorial, domineering, overbearing

imperishable ... 7. eternal, undying 8. enduring, immortal 11. everlasting 14. indestructible

impermanent ... 8. fleeting, temporal, unstable 9. ephemeral, momentary, temporary, transient 10. evanescent, short–lived

impersonate ... 3. ape 4. pose 6. pose as, typify 7. portray 9. exemplify, personate (law), personify, represent, symbolize

impertinence ... 4. sass 9. impudence, insolence, unfitness 10. incivility 11. impropriety, irrelevance

impertinent ... 4. rude 6. saucy 7. ill–bred 8. impudent, insolent 9. frivolous, officious 10. inapposite, irrelevant 12. inapplicable, inconsequent 13. disrespectful

imperturbability ... 8. ataraxia (ataraxy), serenity

imperturbable ... 4. calm, cool 6. placid, serene, steady 8. tranquil 9. impassive 10. phlegmatic 13. dispassionate

impervious ... 5. tight 6. opaque 7. callous 10. impassable 12. impenetrable, inaccessible

impetuosity ... 5. ardor 6. fougue 8. rashness

impetuous ... 3. hot 4. rash 5. eager, hasty, heady, sharp 6. ardent, bensel (motion), fervid, sudden 7. furious, violent 8. forcible, headlong, reckless, vehement 9. impulsive 10. passionate 11. precipitate

impetus ... 4. birr 7. impulse 8. momentum, stimulus 9. incentive

impi (Zulu) ... 8. armed men, warriors

impignorate ... 4. pawn 6. pledge 8. mortgage

impious ... 7. godless, profane 9. nefandous, undutiful 10. irreverent 11. irreligious

impish ... 5. elvan 6. elfish 7. puckish 9. malignant 11. mischievous

implacable ... 6. enmity 11. immitigable 12. unappeasable 14. uncompromising

implant ... 4. root 5. infix, inset, plant 6. enroot, infuse, insert 7. enforce, engraft, impress, inspire, instill 9. establish, inculcate, inoculate, insinuate, introduce

implement ... 3. kit 4. peel, tool 5. dolly, knife, means, scoop, tongs 6. pestle, petard 7. fulfill, utensil 8. carry out, complete, material, scissors 9. equipment 10. accomplish, instrument

implement (pert to) ...
　ancient .. 4. celt 6. eolith 9. paleolith (stone)
　cleaning .. 3. mop 5. broom, brush 6. vacuum 7. sweeper
　hide flesher .. 6. slater
　holding .. 5. tongs 6. pliers 8. tweezers
　lifting .. 3. pry 5. crane, lever, tongs
　lumbering .. 4. tode 6. peavey (peavy)
　nap .. 6. teasel
　printing .. 5. biron, press 6. brayer
　reaping .. 5. mower 6. reaper, scythe, shears, sickle
　surgical .. 7. scalpel 9. tenaculum
　threshing .. 5. flail

implicate ... 5. imply 7. embroil, entwine, involve 8. entangle 10. interweave 11. incriminate

implicit ... 5. tacit 7. implied, virtual 8. complete, inherent 9. entangled, potential 11. unqualified 12. constructive 13. unquestioning

implied ... 5. tacit 11. inferential 12. not expressed

implore ... 3. ask, beg 4. pray 5. crave 7. beseech, entreat, solicit 8. petition 10. supplicate

imply ... 4. hint, mean 5. argue 6. infold 7. connote, involve, suggest, suppose 9. predicate

impolite ... 4. rude 5. crude, rough 7. uncivil 10. ill–behaved, mannerless, ungracious, unmannerly, unpolished 12. discourteous 13. disrespectful

impolitic ... 6. unwise 9. untactful 10. indiscreet 11. inexpedient 12. undiplomatic

import ... 5. drift, sense, value 6. denote, weight 7. betoken, meaning, signify 8. commerce, indicate 9. introduce, of concern 10. importance 11. consequence, implication, importation, merchandise

importance ... 6. moment, stress, weight 8. prestige 9. influence 10. famousness 11. consequence,

importunity **12.** solicitation
important... **5.** grave **6.** famous,
urgent **7.** pompous, weighty
8. material **9.** momentous
11. considerate, influential,
significant, substantial
12. considerable, ostentatious
13. consequential
import tax... **4.** duty **6.** tariff
importune... **3.** beg, ply, tax, woo
4. coax, push, urge **5.** beset, impel,
plead, press **6.** appeal, cajole
7. entreat, press on
importunity... **11.** importunate,
pertinacity **12.** solicitation
impose... **3.** tax **4.** duty, levy
6. burden, entail **7.** command,
confirm (Eccl) exploit, inflict, intrude,
obtrude, penalty, presume
10. discommode
imposing... **5.** noble, regal **6.** august
7. stately **9.** dignified, grandiose
10. commanding, impressive
11. ceremonious **13.** grandiloquent
impossible... **6.** absurd **8.** hopeless,
terrible **9.** insoluble **10.** outlandish
11. unthinkable **12.** unimaginable
13. contradictory, impracticable
impost... **3.** tax **4.** levy, task, toll
5. abwab **6.** custom, excise, surtax,
tariff, weight **7.** tribute **8.** handicap
impostor... **5.** fake **6.** fraud, phony,
quack **6.** humbug **7.** empiric
9. charlatan, pretender
10. mountebank
imposture... **5.** fraud, trick **8.** delusion,
quackery **9.** deception **10.** imposition
impotent... **4.** weak **6.** barren
7. cripple, sterile **9.** deficient,
incapable, powerless **13.** uninfluential
impound... **5.** pen in, seize, store
6. freeze **7.** collect **8.** imprison
9. reservoir **10.** confiscate
11. appropriate
impoverish... **4.** ruin **6.** beggar
7. despoil, exhaust **8.** bankrupt,
make poor **11.** make sterile
imprecation... **4.** oath **8.** anathema
10. execration **11.** malediction
impregnable... **4.** hard **10.** inviolable
12. inexpugnable, invulnerable
13. unconquerable
impregnate... **5.** imbue **6.** infuse
8. fructify **9.** fertilize, inculcate
impresa... **5.** maxim, motto **6.** device,
emblem
impresario... **7.** manager **9.** conductor,
projector (opera) **12.** entrepreneur
impress... **3.** awe, fix **4.** bite, dent,
levy, mark, seal **5.** press, print,
stamp **6.** affect, effect, enlist, indent
7. engrave, imprint **8.** printing,
shanghai **9.** conscript, engraving,
inculcate **10.** commandeer,
impression **11.** indentation
14. characteristic
impressed... **4.** awed **7.** infixed,
stamped **8.** affected, engraved
9. imprinted
impression... **4.** form, idea, mark
5. hunch, print, stamp **6.** macule,
signet **7.** emotion, opinion **8.** printing

9. engraving, sensation
10. appearance **11.** inculcation,
indentation, supposition
impressionable... **7.** pliant **7.** plastic
9. sensitive, teachable **10.** responsive
11. suggestible, susceptible
impressive... **6.** solemn **8.** dramatic,
eloquent **9.** arresting, grandiose
10. convincing
imprint... **3.** fix **4.** dint **5.** infix, press,
stamp **6.** indent **7.** edition, engrave
8. printing **9.** engraving
imprison... **4.** bond, cage, gaol, jail
5. limit **6.** arrest, detain, immure,
intern, lock up **7.** confine, impound
8. restrain **11.** incarcerate
imprisonment... **4.** band **6.** duress
8. coercion **9.** restraint
10. constraint, immurement,
internment **11.** confinement,
impoundment **13.** incarceration
impromptu... **6.** extemp **7.** offhand
11. extemporary **13.** improvisation
14. extemporaneous
15. autoschediastic
improper... **3.** ill, pah **4.** evil **5.** amiss,
wrong **6.** vulgar **7.** illegal, naughty
8. indecent, unseemly, unsuited,
untoward **9.** incorrect, inelegant
10. inaccurate, indecorous, indelicate,
unbecoming, unsuitable
impropriety... **5.** wrong **8.** solecism
9. indecency, vulgarity
11. malapropism, misbehavior
improve... **4.** mend **5.** amend, edify,
emend, moise, train **6.** better,
employ, uplift **7.** advance, augment,
correct, enhance, perfect, promote,
recover, rectify, upgrade **9.** cultivate,
get better, intensify, meliorate
10. ameliorate, recuperate
improvident... **4.** rash **8.** prodigal,
wasteful **9.** negligent **10.** thriftless
11. thoughtless
improvise... **5.** ad lib **6.** invent **7.** ad
libit **9.** ad libitum **11.** extemporize
13. autoschediaze
imprudence... **5.** brass **8.** rashness
9. hardihood **12.** indiscretion,
recklessness
impudence... **5.** cheek **8.** rudeness
9. flippancy, indecency, insolence
10. brazenness, disrespect
12. impertinence **13.** shamelessness
impudent... **4.** bold, pert, rude
5. brash, saucy **6.** brazen
8. flippant, insolent, malapert
9. audacious, shameless
11. impertinent **13.** disrespectful
impugn... **4.** deny **5.** blame **6.** assail
(by words), oppose, refute
7. asperse, censure, gainsay
impulse... **3.** ate **4.** rush, urge
5. force **6.** motive **7.** impetus
8. instinct **9.** incentive
11. instigation
impulsive... **5.** hasty, quick **6.** moving
9. impellent, impetuous
10. motivating **11.** instinctive
13. ill-considered
impure... **4.** foul, lewd **5.** dirty, mixed
6. filthy, unholy **7.** bastard, defiled,

obscene, unclean 8. unchaste
10. inaccurate, unhallowed
11. adulterated, unwholesome
impure metal... 5. alloy, matte
6. speiss
impure rock... 5. chert 9. flintlike
imputation... 7. censure 8. charging
9. aspersion, criticism
10. accusation, ascription
11. attribution, insinuation
impute... 6. accuse, charge, credit,
impart, reckon, regard 7. arraign,
ascribe 8. consider 9. attribute
impy... 11. mischievous
in... 2. at 4. amid, into 5. among
6. at home, inside, within
in (pert to)...
abundance.. 5. store 6. galore
accordance.. 8. pursuant
addition.. 3. too, yet 4. also, more,
plus 11. furthermore
all directions.. 8. everyway
12. everywhither
an undertone.. 9. sotto voce
as much as.. 5. for 5. since
6. seeing 7. because, insofar
back.. 3. aft 5. arear 6. astern
7. postern
behalf of.. 3. for, pro 7. favor of
camera.. 9. in private 10. in
chambers
common.. 4. same 5. alike
concert.. 8. together
contact.. 8. touching 9. attingent
current style.. 3. a la 7. alamode,
popular
existence.. 6. extant
fact.. 5. truly 6. indeed 7. de facto
favor of.. 3. aye, pro, yea
good health.. 3. fit 4. hale 7. healthy
love.. 7. smitten 9. enamoured
need.. 7. straits 8. distress
open air.. 7. outdoor 8. al fresco
passing.. 9. en passant
place of.. 3. for 5. stead 7. instead
possession.. 5. title 6. seizin
private.. 8. in camera
regard to.. 5. anent
rows.. 4. arow 6. serial 7. aligned
(alined)
so far as.. 3. qua
spite of.. 6. mauger 7. despite,
however 11. nonetheless
standing position.. 7. statant
store.. 5. ready 7. waiting 8. awaiting
straight lines.. 8. e regione
succession.. 6. series 8. serially,
seriatim
the future.. 5. hence, later 6. mañana
12. subsequently
the know.. 3. hep
the same place.. 4. ibid 6. ibidem
the year of.. 4. anno
truth.. 6. certes, indeed, verily
8. forsooth
what way.. 3. how 7. quo modo
inability... 9. impotence
10. inadequacy, incapacity
12. incapability, incompetence
inability to...
articulate.. 7. inaudia
chew.. 8. amasesis

comprehend.. 11. acatalepsia
move.. 7. apraxia
name objects.. 9. paranomia
read.. 6. alexia
stand erect.. 7. astasia
swallow.. 7. aphagia
inaccessible... 8. reserved
10. unsociable 11. out-of-the-way
12. unattainable 14. unapproachable
inaccurate... 5. loose 6. faulty
7. inexact 9. defective, erroneous,
imperfect, incorrect
13. ungrammatical
inaction... 6. torpor 7. inertia
8. abeyance, idleness 9. inertness
10. suspension
inactive... 4. idle 5. inert 7. abeyant,
neutral, not busy 8. sluggish
9. sedentary 10. indisposed
inadequacy... 9. inability
10. deficiency, inequality
11. inferiority 12. incompetence
13. insufficiency 14. incompleteness
inadvertence... 5. error 7. neglect
11. inattention 12. carelessness,
heedlessness 15. thoughtlessness
inadvertent... 9. negligent, unwitting
11. inattentive
inadvertently... 10. heedlessly
11. unwittingly 12. neglectfully
inane... 4. vain, void 5. empty, inept,
silly 6. famous 7. fatuous, foolish,
puerile, trivial 8. trifling 9. frivolous
11. ineffectual, thoughtless
13. characterless
inappropriate... 5. inept,-undue
8. untimely 10. irrelevant, unsuitable
11. inexpedient
inapt... 5. inept 10. unsuitable
inattentive... 3. lax 6. absent, remiss
8. careless, heedless 9. negligent,
unheeding, unmindful 10. distracted,
regardless 11. inadvertent
inaugurate... 5. admit, begin, start
6. induct 7. install, instate, usher in
8. initiate 9. auspicate, institute,
introduce 10. consecrate
inauspicious... 7. adverse, ominous,
unlucky 8. sinister, untimely
9. ill-omened 12. unpropitious
inborn... 6. allied, inbred, innate,
native 7. cognate, natural 8. inherent
10. connatural
inbred... 6. inborn, innate
9. endogamic 10. bred within 15. to
the manner born
Inca (pert to)...
descent.. 6. the sun
empire.. 4. Peru (11th cent)
government.. 11. communistic
king.. 9. Atahualpa (15th cent)
prince.. 7. Huascar (16th cent)
incalculable... 8. infinite 9. boundless,
uncertain, very great 11. illimitable
12. immeasurable 13. unforeseeable
incandescent... 5. clear, light, white
7. glowing, shining
incantation... 5. magic, spell
6. powwow 7. sorcery 8. exorcism
10. hocus-pocus, mumbo jumbo
incapable... 6. unable 8. impotent
11. incompetent, inefficient,

unqualified 12. disqualified
incapacitate... 7. cripple, disable,
invalid 10. disqualify 11. render unfit
incapacitated... 8. crippled, disabled
9. hamstrung, paralyzed
11. invalidated 12. disqualified
13. superannuated (retired)
incarcerate... 5. hem in 6. immure,
intern, lock up, retire 7. confine,
impound 8. imprison 10. disqualify
incarnate... 4. rosy 6. embody
9. enshrined 11. incorporate,
personified 12. impersonated
incarnation... 6. avatar, Christ
10. embodiment
Incarnation of Vishnu (eight)...
4. Apis, Rama 7. Krishna (8th)
incase... 3. box, can 4. pack 5. box
up, cover, crate 6. carton
7. enclose, package 8. surround
incaution... 4. rash 6. unwary
8. careless, heedless, reckless
9. impolitic, imprudent 10. indiscreet
incendiarism... 5. arson 9. pyromania
incendiary... 5. firer 7. exciter
8. agitator, arsonist, incitive
9. seditious 10. instigator
12. inflammatory
incense... 3. ire 5. anger 6. arouse,
enrage, incite 7. inflame, provoke
8. irritate 9. instigate
incense (pert to)...
burner.. 6. censer 8. thurible
9. incensory
carrier.. 8. thurifer
Hebrew for.. 7. keturah
pert to.. 5. aroma, spice 7. perfume
9. fragrance, redolence
product.. 5. matti, myrrh 6. storax
7. linaloa 8. gum resin, olibanum,
pastille, thurible 9. lignaloes,
tacamahac 12. frankincense
sacrifice.. 8. oblation
spice.. 6. balsam, stacte
tree bearing.. 7. linaloa 8. agalloch,
calambac 9. Boswellia
vessel.. 6. censer 7. navette
incensed... 3. mad 5. angry, irate,
vexed, wroth 6. peeved, piqued
7. angered, enraged, nettled
8. wrathful 11. exasperated
incentive... 4. brod, call, goad, spur,
urge, whet 5. spark 6. motive
7. impulse, rousing 8. inciting,
stimulus 9. influence 10. incitement,
inducement 11. provocation,
stimulative 13. encouragement
inception... 6. origin, source
9. reception 10. inchoation, initiation
12. commencement
15. intussusception
inceptive... 9. beginning 10. inchoative
incessant... 7. endless 8. constant
9. ceaseless, continual, perpetual
10. continuous 11. unremitting
13. unintermitted
inch (pert to)...
barometric.. 6. degree
forward.. 4. edge 7. crowhop
inch by inch.. 9. gradually, piecemeal
meal.. 9. gradually
three parts.. 11. barleycorns (anc)

twelve parts.. 5. lines
twelve seconds.. 6. a prime (anc)
verb.. 5. creep 7. measure
inches... 4. hand (4), nail (2 1/4),
span (9)
inchoate... 6. partly 8. initiate, recently
9. beginning, incipient
10. incomplete
inchpin... 10. sweetbread
incident... 5. event 7. episode, subject
8. accident, casualty 9. befalling,
happening 10. incidental, occurrence
11. contingency 12. circumstance,
slight matter
incidental... 3. bye 6. casual, chance,
liable 8. episodic 9. accessory,
extrinsic 10. accidental, contingent,
fortuitous, occasional 11. subordinate
12. nonessential 13. parenthetical
incidentally... 6. obiter 8. by chance,
by the way 9. en passant, in passing
incinerate... 4. burn 7. consume,
cremate
incipient... 4. seat 6. induct 7. initial
8. inchoate 9. beginning, embryonic
10. commencing, inaugurate
11. rudimentary
incise... 3. cut 4. open 5. carve,
lance, sever 6. furrow 7. engrave
incised... 6. carved 7. notched
8. engraved, furrowed 9. laciniate
10. laciniated
incision... 3. cut 4. gash, slit 5. cleft
6. furrow, injury 7. cutting
9. engraving 10. laceration,
separation 11. penetration
incite... 3. egg, tew 4. abet, fire,
goad, prod, spur, urge 5. impel,
sting 6. arouse, foment, stir up,
suborn 7. agitate, animate, inflame,
provoke 9. encourage, stimulate
inclemency... 4. cold 5. rigor
8. coldness, severity, violence
9. bleakness, frigidity, harshness
13. mercilessness
inclination... 3. dip, nod 4. bent,
bias, love, urge 5. fancy, grade,
slant, slope, taste, trend 6. animus,
bowing, desire, liking, nature
8. aptitude, penchant, tendency
9. affection, attention, deviation,
direction, intention, obeisance,
proneness 10. attachment, proclivity,
propensity 11. disposition
12. predilection 13. prepossession
incline... 3. dip, tip 4. bend, cant,
heel, lean, tend, tilt 5. alist, bevel,
grade, slant, slide, slope, trend 9. be
willing, gravitate
inclined... 3. apt, dip 4. wont
5. prone 6. sloped 7. leaning,
pronate, willing 8. disposed
11. predisposed
inclined (pert to)...
plane.. 4. ramp 7. oblique
to believe.. 9. credulous
to droop.. 3. sag
to sin.. 13. transgressive
inclose... see also *enclose* 3. hem,
pen, pin 4. case, mure 5. embar
6. encase, encave, incase
7. enclose, environ

inclosure... 3. pen, ree, sty 4. cage, cote, sept 5. hutch, kraal 6. corral 8. sepiment 9. enclosure 10. impalement

include... 6. shut up 7. confine, contain, embrace, enclose, inclose, involve 8. comprise 9. encompass

including... 8. covering 10. comprising, containing 12. encompassing 13. comprehensive

incognito... 6. veiled 7. feigned 8. disguise, not known 10. camouflage

incoherent... 5. loose 6. broken 8. detached, inchoate 9. delirious, illogical 11. incongruous 12. disconnected, inconsequent, inconsistent

income... 4. gain 5. rente, wages 6. profit, return, usance 7. annuity, pension, produce, revenue, tontine 8. interest, proceeds, receipts 9. emolument

incommensurate... 7. unequal 12. insufficient 14. unsatisfactory 16. disproportionate

incommode... 3. vex 5. annoy 6. molest, plague, put out 7. disturb, trouble 8. disquiet 13. inconvenience

incomparable... 7. eminent, unalike 8. peerless 9. matchless, unrivaled 10. surpassing 11. superlative 12. transcendent, without equal

incompatible... 9. differing 10. intclerant 11. disagreeing 12. inconsistent, inharmonious 13. contradictory, unsympathetic 14. irreconcilable

incompetence... 9. inability, unfitness 10. disability, inadequacy 13. insufficiency 15. unqualification

incompetent... 5. inept, unfit 7. wanting 8. impotent 9. incapable 10. unskillful 11. inefficient 12. disqualified, insufficient 14. incommensurate

incomplete... 5. crude 6. undone 7. lacking 8. immature, inchoate 9. defective, deficient, imperfect, partially 10. unfinished

incomprehensible... 8. infinite 9. wonderful 10. miraculous, mysterious, unreadable 11. unthinkable 12. unfathomable, unimaginable 13. inconceivable, unconceivable 14. unintelligible

incongruity... 9. inharmony 10. dissonance 11. incoherence 12. disagreement, inexpedience 13. inconsistency 14. unsuitableness

incongruous... 5. alien 6. absurd, motley 8. off–color 9. differing, illogical 10. solecistic, unsuitable 12. disagreeable, inconsistent, inharmonious 13. inappropriate

inconsequent... 7. invalid 8. unproved 9. illogical 10. irrelevant 11. impertinent, unimportant 12. inconsistent 13. inconsecutive

inconsiderate... 4. rash 5. hasty 6. unkind 8. careless, heedless 9. imprudent, impulsive 10. ill–advised, incautious, indiscreet, neglectful 11. improvident, injudicious, thoughtless

inconsistent... 9. differing, dissonant, fanatical, illogical 10. discordant, discrepant, incoherent, inconstant 11. incongruous 12. incompatible, inharmonious 13. contradictory 14. irreconcilable

inconspicuous... 9. unseeable 10. out of sight, unapparent 12. not prominent 13. imperceptible, indiscernible

incontestable... 7. certain 10. undeniable 11. indubitable, irrefutable 13. unimpeachable 14. unquestionable

inconvenience... 6. bother 8. disquiet 9. incommode 10. uneasiness 11. awkwardness, disturbance 12. disadvantage, untimeliness, unwieldiness

inconvenient... 5. unfit 7. unhandy 8. annoying, improper, unwieldy 10. unsuitable 11. inexpedient, inopportune, troublesome 12. unreasonable 15. disadvantageous

incorporate... 3. mix 4. fuse 5. blend, merge, unite 6. embody 7. combine, include 8. embodied 10. assimilate

incorporation... 5. union 9. inclusion 10. embodiment 11. affiliation, association, combination, composition, incarnation 12. assimilation

incorporeal... 7. phantom 8. bodiless 9. spiritual 10. immaterial 13. unsubstantial

incorrect... 5. wrong 6. faulty 8. improper 9. erroneous, inelegant 10. inaccurate, solecistic, unbecoming 13. ungrammatical

incorrect naming of objects... 9. paranomia

incorruptible... 4. just 7. upright 8. immortal 11. trustworthy 14. indestructible

increase... 3. add, eke, wax 4. gain, grow, rise 5. add to, amass, raise, swell 6. accrue, dilate, enrich, expand, extend 7. accrete, advance, augment, enhance (inhance), inflate, promote, upswing 8. heighten, multiply 9. accession, aggravate, crescendo, expansion, extension, increment, intensify 10. accelerate 11. aggravation, enlargement 13. amplification 15. intensification

incredible... 8. fabulous, unlikely 9. fantastic, marvelous, wonderful 10. improbable, remarkable 12. unbelievable

increment... 6. growth 8. addition, increase 11. enlargement 12. augmentation

incriminate... 6. accuse 7. involve 9. implicate, inculpate

incubator... 8. couveuse, isolette

incubus... 4. ogre 5. demon, dream 6. burden 9. nightmare 10. evil spirit 13. hallucination

inculcate... 5. imbue, infix 7. implant, impress, instill (instil) 12. indoctrinate

incumbent... 5. vicar 6. rector 8. resident 9. clergyman, impending, overlying 10. burdensome, obligatory (upon) 11. threatening 12. superimposed

incumbents... 3. ins

incunabula... 7. infancy 10. beginnings

incur... 5. bring 6. accrue, entail 7. bring on 8. be liable, contract, fall into 10. be involved

incurable... 8. hopeless 9. apathetic 11. inattentive, indifferent, unconcerned, uninquiring 12. uninterested 13. uninquisitive

incur hostility... 10. antagonize 11. contend with

incursion... 4. raid 5. foray 6. attack, influx, inroad 8. invasion 9. intrusion

incus... 4. bone (ear) 5. anvil 6. hammer

indecency... 8. impurity 9. immodesty, indecorum, obscenity, vulgarity 10. indelicacy, unchastity

indecent... 5. gross 6. impure, vulgar 7. obscene 8. immodest, improper, uncomely 9. offensive 10. ill–looking, indecorous, indelicate 11. inexpedient

indecision... 5. doubt 10. hesitation 11. uncertainty, vacillation 12. irresolution

indecisive... 7. dubious 8. formless 9. uncertain 10. hesitating, indefinite, indistinct, irresolute 11. unsupported, vacillating 12. inconclusive

indecorous... 4. rude 5. wrong 6. coarse, vulgar 7. uncivil 8. impolite, improper, indecent, unseemly 9. inelegant 10. out of place, unbecoming 11. inexpedient

indefatigable... 6. active 8. sedulous, tireless, untiring 9. unwearied, weariless 10. unwearying 11. persevering

indefinite... 5. loose, vague 7. general, inexact, neutral 8. formless 9. ambiguous, equivocal, uncertain 10. inexplicit, unmeasured 12. undetermined 13. indeterminate

indefinite amount... 3. any 4. some 5. about 10. more or less

indehiscent (pert to)...
fruit.. 3. uva 4. pepo (gourd) 5. apple, grape 6. orange, samara 9. sunflower
legume.. 3. pea 4. bean 6. loment
vegetable.. 5. melon 6. squash, tomato 7. pumpkin 8. cucumber

indelible... 4. fast 5. fixed 8. deepfelt 9. permanent 10. inerasable 12. ineffaceable, ineradicable, inexpungible 13. unforgettable

indelicate... 5. gross 6. coarse, vulgar 7. fulsome 8. impolite, improper, indecent, unseemly 9. offensive, unrefined 10. indecorous, unbecoming

indemnification... 9. atonement 10. recompense 11. restitution 12. compensation 13. reimbursement

indemnify... 3. pay 6. recoup, secure 8. make good 9. reimburse 10. compensate, recompense

indent... 3. cut, jag 4. dent 5. inlay, notch, press, stamp, tooth 6. emboss, furrow, recess, zigzag 7. impress, imprint, press in 8. contract, covenant, draw upon 9. indenture 11. requisition

indentation... 3. jab 4. dint, nick 5. choil, notch 6. crenel, furrow, hollow, recess 7. imprint 8. crenelet 10. depression, impression

indented... 6. dented, jagged, milled 7. notched, sinuous 8. serrated (Her) 9. impressed 10. undulating

indenture... 4. dent 5. notch 8. contract, document 9. agreement 10. depression 11. indentation

independence... 7. freedom 9. exemption 10. competency, neutralism, Urania blue 13. unrelatedness 14. nonpartisanism 15. self–subsistence

independent... 4. free 5. Party (Polit) 7. neutral, wealthy 8. separate 9. competent, exclusive, free–lance, isolative, sovereign, uncoerced, unrelated 12. irrespective, uncontrolled, unrestricted 13. self–governing

independent land... 7. alodium (law)

indescribably... 9. ineffably 11. wonderfully

indeterminate... 5. vague 7. apeiron, general, neutral, obscure 8. formless, infinite

index... 4. face, file, fist, list 5. guide, ratio, table 6. gnomon 7. pointer 8. exponent 9. indicator 10. forefinger, indication

India... see also *Indian*
anc.. 9. Hindustan
Bay.. 6. Bengal
Cape.. 7. Comorin
capital.. 4. Agra (anc) 5. Simla (summer) 8. New Delhi
city.. 4. Agra, Gaya 5. Dacca, Delhi, Poona, Surat 6. Bombay, Jaipur, Lahore, Madras, Madura, Nagpur, Nysore 8. Calcutta, Kolhapur, Mandalay, Mirzapur, Shahpura 10. Darjeeling
city, sacred.. 5. Nasik 7. Benares
kingdom.. 5. Asoka, Nepal
mountain.. 5. Ghats 8. Sulaiman (Throne of Solomon) 9. Himalayas, Hindu Kush 12. Vindhya Hills
Persian name (anc).. 9. Hindustan
region.. 3. Goa 5. Assam, Surat 6. Baroda 7. Benares, Kashmir
relics (famed).. 8. Taj Mahal (Agra) 10. Kutab Minar 11. Ajanta Caves
river.. 6. Kistna
State.. 4. Rewa 5. Delhi 6. Baroda, Indore, Jaipur, Madras, Marwar, Punjab, Rampur, Sakkim 7. Manipur

Indian (pert to)...
aeon.. 5. kalpa
animal.. 4. zebu 5. sasin 6. nilgai
apartment.. 6. zenana
army officer.. 4. naik (naig)

7. jemadar
attorney.. 6. muktar
bandit.. 6. dacoit
bard.. 4. bhat
bird.. 4. baya, kala, koel, kyak
   5. sarus, shama 6. seesee, shahin
   8. amadavat
boat.. 5. dhoni (doni)
book (sacred).. 6. Avesta
bracelet.. 6. sankha
bread (unleavened).. 8. chapatty
breakfast.. 5. hazri
buffalo.. 4. arna (arnee)
carpet.. 4. Agra
carriage.. 4. ekka 5. tonga 6. gharry
   (gharri)
caste.. 3. Jat, Meo 4. Ahir 5. Sudra,
   Varna 6. Lohana, Rajput, Vaisya
   7. Brahman (Brahmin) 9. Kahatriya
cavalryman.. 5. sowar 7. ressala
charm.. 6. mantra
chief.. 4. Raja 5. Rajah 6. sirdar
   7. Gaekwar
cigarette (cheap).. 4. biri
claim (legal).. 3. hak (hakh)
college (Sanskrit).. 3. tol
Court, Supreme.. 6. Sudder
crocodile.. 6. gavial, mugger (muggar,
   muggur)
cymbal.. 3. tal
dagger.. 5. katar
dam.. 6. anicut (annicut)
dancer (fem).. 8. bayadere
dancing girls.. 6. nautch
deer.. 4. axis 5. kakar 6. sambur
deity.. 4. Deva
demon.. 4. bhut 5. asura 6. daitya
devil's tree.. 4. dita
dialect.. 4. Urdu 5. Hindi, Tamil
   7. Prakrit
disciple.. 5. chela
dog.. 5. dhole 6. pariah
drama.. 6. nataka
drink.. 4. soma 5. bhang (bang)
   6. arrack
dust storm.. 7. peesash, shaitan
   (sheitan)
elephant.. 6. hathi
elephant driver.. 6. mahout
elephant trappings.. 5. jhool
epic.. 8. Ramayana 11. Mahabharata
falcon.. 6. shahin (shaheen)
father.. 4. babu
festival.. 4. Holi, Mela 6. Dewali
   10. Rathayatra
fig tree (sacred).. 5. pipal 6. banian,
   banyan
garment.. 4. sari 7. luhinga
gateway.. 5. toran
ghost.. 4. bhut
god.. 4. Deva, Yama 5. Shiva
goddess.. 4. Amma
governor.. 5. nazim
grove.. 5. Sarna
guard.. 7. daloyet
hall.. 6. durbar
handkerchief.. 7. malabar
harem.. 5. serai 6. zenana 8. seraglio
heiress.. 5. Begum
herb.. 6. sesame 7. curcuma,
   tumeric, zeodary

holy.. 3. sri (shri)
holy powder.. 4. abir (perfumed)
hunt.. 6. shikar
intoxicant.. 4. soma
jungle.. 5. shola
king.. 4. Shah
king of serpents (Myth).. 6. Shesha
   (Sesha)
king's son.. 8. shahzada
knife.. 3. dah 5. kukri
lady.. 7. sahibah
language.. 4. Urdu 5. Hindu, Tamil
   8. Sanskrit (anc)
leader.. 13. Mahatma Gandhi
legal claim.. 3. hak (hakh)
leopard.. 7. cheetah
licorice.. 9. jequirity (bean)
loincloth.. 5. dhoti
lover of.. 9. Indophile
mahogany.. 4. toon
mail.. 3. dak (dawk)
medicine man.. 6. Shaman
mendicant.. 5. fakir
merchant.. 8. soudagar
midwife.. 4. dhai
Minister of Finance.. 5. Dewan
mountain pass.. 4. ghat
musical instrument.. 5. ruana
narcotic.. 4. bang 5. bhang
   7. hashish
native.. 5. Hindu, Sepoy, Tamil
   8. Assamese 10. Hindustani
Negro.. 6. hubshi
palanquin (conveyance).. 6. palkee
   (palhi)
palm.. 7. Calamus, malacca
peasant.. 4. ryot
pheasant.. 5. monal (monaul)
philosopher.. 4. Yogi
pillar.. 3. lat
pipe.. 6. hookah
police.. 4. peon 5. sepoy
police station.. 5. thana
priest.. 5. mobed 6. shaman
prince.. 4. rana
princess.. 4. rani (ranee) 5. Begum
queen.. 4. rani (ranee) 8. maharani
religious body.. 5. samaj 7. ajivika
   (anc)
resort.. 3. Abu 5. Mt Abu
rope dancer.. 3. nat
rubber.. 10. caoutchouc
ruler.. 4. rana 5. nabob, nawab,
   nizam
sage.. 6. pundit
sailor.. 6. lascar
sarsaparilla root.. 7. nunnari
servant.. 3. par 4. amah, maty
sheep.. 5. urial 6. nahoor
shrine.. 6. dagoba
silkworm.. 3. eri
snake.. 5. krait 6. bongar, katuka
soldier.. 4. peon 5. sepoy, singh
split pea.. 3. dal
study of.. 8. Indology
sugar (crude).. 3. gur 9. tabasheer
   (bamboo)
Supreme Court.. 6. Sudder
sword (short).. 5. kukri
syllable of assent.. 2. om
tapir.. 8. saladang

tariff.. 6. zabeta
teacher.. 6. mullah (mulla)
temple.. 4. rath 12. Seven Pagodas
(of Madras)
title of respect.. 3. sri (shri) 4. mian
tower.. 5. minar, sikar 7. sikhara
10. Kutab Minar (Delhi)
tree.. 3. saj 4. dita, teak 5. dhava
6. banyan, sissoo
umbrella.. 6. chatta
water carrier.. 7. bheesty (bheestie)
wheat.. 4. suji
wildcat.. 4. balu
wine.. 5. shrab
yellow (color).. 5. piuri 7. majagua
Indian, American (pert to)...
chief.. 6. Joseph, Philip, sachem
7. Cochise, Pontiac 8. Geronimo,
Red Cloud, Tecumseh 9. Massasoit
10. Crazy Horse 11. Sitting Bull,
Spotted Tail
dance.. 7. cantico
festival.. 8. potlatch
half–breed.. 5. sambo (zambo)
hatchet.. 8. tomahawk
hero.. 4. Rama (S Am)
largest tribe.. 6. Navaho (Navajo)
lodge.. 5. hogan, igloo, tepee
6. wigwam
married.. 5. squaw (fem) 6. sannup
(male)
Mexico.. 4. Maya 5. Aztec
7. Tehueco
money.. 6. sewan (beads) 6. wampum
Newfoundland.. 6. Micmac
pipe (peace).. 7. calumet
pony.. 6. cayuse
richest tribe.. 5. Osage
S America.. 3. Ona 4. Cara (anc),
Inca, Peru, Tupi 5. Carib 6. Arawak,
Aymara 7. Quechua
Spirit, Great.. 6. Manito 7. Manitou
12. Gitchi Manito
squaw.. 6. mahala
symbol.. 5. totem
tax, impost.. 5. abwab
village.. 6. pueblo
water lily.. 5. wokas (wocas)
Indian tribes... 3. Fox, Oto (Otoe),
Ree, Sac, Ute 4. Cree, Crow, Erie,
Hopi, Iowa, Maya, Mono, Sauk,
Yuma, Zuni 5. Aleut, Cadoo, Carib,
Coree, Creek, Huron, Miami, Moqui,
Omaha, Osage, Piute, Ponca, Sioux,
Sooke, Teton, Yazoo 6. Ahtena
(Alaska), Apache, Biloxi, Dakota,
Eskimo, Isleta, Lenape, Mohawk,
Mojave, Navaho, Nootka, Oneida,
Paiute (Piute), Pawnee, Seneca,
Siwash 7. Amerind, Bannock,
Catawba, Chinook, Ojibway, Yavapai
8. Arapahoe, Cherokee, Chippewa,
Comanche, Iroquois, Kickapoo, Nez
Percé, Onondaga, Sagamore,
Seminole, Shoshone 9. Algonquin,
Athabasca, Blackfoot, Chickasaw,
Winnebago 10. Muskhogean
12. Narragansett
Indiana...
capital.. 12. Indianapolis
city.. 4. Gary 6. Muncie 7. Hammond
9. Fort Wayne, Vincennes 10. Terre

Haute 11. Bloomington
industrial region.. 7. Calumet
monument (Hist).. 7. Lincoln
12. Indian Mounds 13. Wyandotte
Cave
New Harmony founder.. 4. Owen
Postoffice (famed).. 10. Santa Claus
resort.. 10. French Lick
river.. 6. Maumee, Wabash
10. Tippecanoe
State admission.. 10. Nineteenth
State motto.. 19. Crossroads of
America
State nickname.. 7. Hoosier
indicate... 4. cite, hint, mark, mean,
show 5. point 6. denote, evince,
reveal, sketch 7. bespeak, betoken,
connote, declare, display, signify,
specify 8. disclose, evidence,
intimate, manifest, point out, register
9. designate, foretoken
indicated... 6. marked, signed
7. denoted, implied 8. presumed
9. betokened, portended, suggested
indicating succession... 7. ordinal
indication... 4. clue, hint, mark, note,
omen, sign 5. proof, token, trace
6. signal 7. reading (a) 8. evidence
10. suggestion 13. manifestation
indicative... 7. ominous 10. evidential,
indication, meaningful, suggestive
13. significative
indicator... 4. dial, hand, sign, vane
5. arrow, gauge, index, level
6. gnomon 7. indices (pl), pointer
9. grape fern (belief) 10. instrument
11. annunciator, thermometer
15. telethermometer
indicia (sing **indicium**)... 5. marks,
signs 6. tokens 8. markings (PO)
11. appearances, indications, metered
mail
indict... 6. charge, decree 7. arraign,
impeach 8. proclaim
indictive... 8. declared 9. appointed
10. proclaimed
indictment... 6. charge 10. accusation,
imputation 11. arraignment
indifference... 5. shrug 6. apathy
7. inertia 8. coldness 9. unconcern
10. mediocrity, negligence, neutrality
12. carelessness, heedlessness,
unimportance 13. insensibility
14. insignificance
indifferent... 3. ill 4. cold, cool, sick
5. blasé 6. casual, poorly 7. neutral,
stoical, uneager 8. careless,
heedless, listless, mediocre
9. apathetic 10. nonchalant,
regardless 11. adiaphorous,
unimportant 12. nonessential,
uninterested, unprejudiced
indigence... 4. lack, need, want
6. penury 7. poverty 10. deficiency
indigene... 6. native 9. primitive
10. autochthon
indigenous... 6. inborn, innate, native
7. edaphic, endemic, natural
8. endemism, inherent
13. autochthonous
indigent... 4. free, poor, void 5. needy
6. bereft 7. lacking, wanting

8. beggarly 9. destitute, penniless
10. pauperized 11. impecunious,
necessitous 15. poverty–stricken
indigestion... 8. disorder, phthisis
9. dyspepsia 10. immaturity
indignant... 3. hot 5. angry, irate,
wroth 7. annoyed 8. incensed,
wrathful 9. resentful 11. exasperated
indignation... 3. ire 4. base, fury
5. anger, wrath 7. disdain
8. contempt
indignity... 7. affront, dudgeon
10. uncivility
indigo... 3. dye 4. anil, blue
indigo (pert to)...
  bale of.. 6. seroon
  compound.. 6. isatin
  plant.. 4. anil
  source.. 7. indican 9. indigotin
  wild.. 8. Baptisia
indirect... 7. devious, oblique
9. deceitful, dishonest 10. circuitous,
contingent, misleading, roundabout
indirect expense... 8. overhead
indiscreet... 4. rash 5. hasty, silly
6. unwise 7. foolish, witless
8. careless, heedless 9. imprudent
10. incautious 11. injudicious
12. undiscerning 13. inconsiderate
indiscriminate... 5. mixed 7. mingled
9. extensive, haphazard, orderless,
wholesale 13. heterogeneous
indispensable... 5. basic, vital
6. needed 7. exigent 8. integral
9. essential, requisite, right–hand
10. imperative 13. irreplaceable
indisposed... 3. ill 4. sick 6. averse
9. unwilling 10. disordered, unfriendly
11. disinclined
indisposition... 7. ailment, illness,
malaise 10. averseness, reluctance
13. unwillingness
indisputable... 4. sure 7. certain,
evident 8. positive 10. undeniable
11. inbubitable 12. irrefragable
13. incontestable
indistinct... 3. dim 4. hazy 5. vague
7. blurred, obscure, unclear
8. confused 9. ambiguous, undefined
10. indefinite 16. undiscriminating
17. indistinguishable
indite... 3. pen 5. write 6. phrase
7. compose 8. describe, inscribe
individual... 3. man, one 4. bion, idio
(comb form), self, sole, unit, zoon
6. egoist, person, single 7. special
8. organism, selfsame 9. identical
11. inseparable, personality
individuality... 5. being, seity
6. nature 7. oneness 8. ethology,
identity, selfness
individually... 9. severally
10. personally 12. each by itself
14. distributively
Indo–Aryan (pert to)...
  deity.. 5. Indra
  native of.. 5. India
  speech.. 5. Aryan
  type.. 4. Jats 7. khatris, Rajputs
Indo–Chinese (pert to)...
  language.. 3. Tai (Thai)
  mammal.. 4. zebu

  river.. 6. Mekong
  State (former French).. 4. Laos
  7. Vietnam 8. Cambodia
indoctrinate... 5. coach, edify, imbue,
teach 8. instruct 12. rehabilitate
indolence... 5. scorn, sloth 7. inertia,
languor 8. inaction, laziness
10. ergophobia 11. lotus–eating,
spring fever 13. indisposition
indolent... 4. idle, lazy 5. inert
6. otiose 8. inactive, slothful,
sluggish 10. unemployed
indomitable... 10. invincible
11. intractable, "never say die"
13. unconquerable
Indonesia...
  capital.. 7. Jakarta (Djakarta)
  formation.. 11. archipelago (once
  world's largest)
  former name.. 7. Batavia 15. Dutch
  East Indies
  government.. 8. Republic (1950)
  islands (3,000 in all).. 4. Bali, Java
  7. Sumatra 8. Sulawesi (Celebes)
  9. New Guinea (W half)
  10. Kalimantan (W Borneo)
  president.. 7. Sukarno
  race.. 5. Dyaks (Dayaks) 7. Battaks
  (Bataks), Igorots 8. Balinese,
  Javanese
  religion.. 6. Moslem
  shrine.. 6. dagoba
indorse, endorse... see *endorse*
indorsement, endorsement... 4. visa,
visé (passport)
Indra (Hindu)... 3. God 5. Deity, Sakra
(Sakka)
indubitable... 4. fact, sure 7. evident
10. infallible, undeniable
11. irrefutable 12. irrefragable,
unanswerable 13. incontestable
14. unquestionable
16. incontrovertible
induce... 4. lead, move, urge
5. cause, impel, infer 6. allure, elicit,
entice, incite 8. persuade
9. influence, instigate, prevail on
inducement... 6. motive, reason
8. stimulus 9. incentive, influence
10. persuasion 13. consideration
induct... 6. enroll 9. install
8. initiate 9. conscript, introduce
inductance unit... 5. henry
inductile... 10. inflexible, unyielding
induction... 5. logic 7. causing
8. entrance 9. accession, beginning,
deduction 10. conclusion, initiation,
production 12. commencement,
conscription, installation, introduction
indue... 5. endow 6. assume, clothe,
draw on, invest, supply (spiritual)
7. furnish
indulge... 3. pet 5. grant, humor, yield
6. pamper 7. cherish, gratify
indulgences... 8. excesses
10. tolerances
indulgent... 4. easy 7. lenient, patient
8. tolerant, yielding 9. compliant
10. permissive 11. considerate,
intemperate
indurate... 6. harden 7. callous
10. solidified

indurated... 3. set 5. fixed
9. calloused 10. solidified
industrial magnate... 6. shogun,
tycoon
industrious... 4. busy 6. active
7. zealous 8. diligent, sedulous
9. assiduous 11. intentional,
painstaking 13. indefatigable
industry... 4. toil, work 5. labor, trade
7. concern 8. commerce 9. diligence
12. perseverance, sedulousness
indweller... 6. native 7. denizen
8. indigene
indwelling... 7. inbeing 8. immanent,
inherent 9. immanence, inherence
10. inhabiting
inearth... 5. inter 6. inhume
inebriacy... 11. drunkenness
12. intemperance
inebriate... 3. sot 5. addle, drunk,
toper 7. stupefy, tippler 8. drunkard
10. exhilarate (by liquor), intoxicate
ineffable... 4. surd 6. sacred
9. wonderful 11. unspeakable,
unutterable 13. indescribable,
inexpressible 15. unpronounceable
ineffaceable... 9. indelible
10. inerasable 12. ineradicable
ineffectual... 4. vain, weak 6. futile
7. useless 9. fruitless 10. unavailing
11. inefficient 12. unsuccessful
13. inefficacious, uninfluential
inefficient... 6. unable 10. indisposed
11. incompetent 12. unproficient
inelegant... 6. clumsy, vulgar
8. indecent 9. deficient (in beauty)
11. unbeautiful
inept... 4. null, void 5. silly, unfit
6. absurd 7. foolish 8. unsuited
10. out of place, unbecoming,
unskillful, unsuitable 11. inexpedient
inequality... 9. disparity, diversity
10. inadequacy, unevenness
12. disagreement, variableness
13. disproportion
ineradicable... 7. lasting 9. indelible,
permanent 12. ineffaceable
inerrant... 8. unerring 10. infallible
inert... 4. dead, lazy 6. latent, stupid,
supine, torpid 7. passive 8. inactive,
lifeless, listless, slothful, sluggish
9. apathetic, inanimate, lethargic
10. motionless, phlegmatic
inertia... 9. indolence, inertness
10. immobility
inesculant (rare)... 9. indelible
inestimable... 9. priceless
10. invaluable 12. incalculable
inevitable... 3. due 5. fated
7. nemesis 9. necessary
11. unavoidable
inexorability... 5. rigor 9. obstinacy
10. strictness
inexorable... 6. strict 9. obstinate
10. inflexible, relentless, unyielding
inexpedience, inexpedient... 6. unwise
8. untimely 9. ignorance, impolitic,
imprudent, unfitting 10. indiscreet
unwiseness 11. inadvisable
15. disadvantageous
inexperience... 6. unwise 9. ignorance,
imprudent 10. immaturity, indiscreet

11. inadvisable 12. unprofitable
14. unskillfulness
15. disadvantageous
inexperienced... 3. raw 4. naif
5. green, naive 6. callow
8. ignorant, immature, prentice
9. unskilled 10. amateurish
11. unpracticed
inexplicable... 11. undefinable
12. supernatural 13. preternatural,
unaccountable, unexplainable
inextricable... 4. mazy 5. stuck
8. involved 9. intricate 10. insolvable
infallible... 4. sure, true 6. gospel
7. certain 8. inerrant, unerring
9. inerrable 11. indubitable
infamous... 4. base 6. odious, wicked
8. shameful, terrible 9. nefarious
10. detestable 11. ignominious
12. contemptible, disreputable
infamy... 5. shame 8. disgrace,
dishonor, ignominy, reproach
9. disrepute 10. opprobrium
11. abomination
infancy... 8. babyhood, minority
9. beginning
infant... 4. babe, baby 5. child, minor
6. novice 8. bantling 9. foundling
infantryman... 6. Zouave 7. dog–face
8. chasseur 9. musketeer
11. footslogger, foot soldier
14. gravel agitator
infatuated... 7. foolish, smitten
8. enamored, obsessed 9. bewitched
10. captivated, enraptured
12. enthusiastic
infatuation... 3. ate, mad 4. love
5. craze, folly 10. enthusiasm
11. foolishness
infeasible... 8. unlikely 10. improbable,
unsuitable 13. impracticable
infect... 5. taint 6. defile, excite,
poison 7. corrupt, deprave, pollute
11. contaminate
infection... 7. disease 8. epidemic
9. pollution 11. implication (law),
inspiration 13. contamination
infelicity... 6. misery 9. inaptness
10. misfortune 11. unhappiness
12. inexpedience, untimeliness,
wretchedness
infer... 4. hint 5. drive, guess, imply
6. deduce 7. presume, suppose,
surmise 8. conclude, construe
inference... 5. truth 8. illation
9. corollary, deduction
10. assumption, conclusion
11. implication, proposition
inferential... 8. illative 9. deductive,
inducible 10. deductible, suggestive
15. inconsequential
inferior... 3. bad 4. less, poor
5. baser, lower, minor, petit, petty
6. lesser, menial, nether 7. humbler,
unequal 8. anterior, mediocre
10. inadequate, low–blooded
11. subordinate
inferior lawyer... 9. leguleian
11. pettifogger
infernal... 6. cursed, plaguy, wicked
7. hellish, satanic 8. damnable,
devilish 9. chthonian, execrable,

malignant, Tartarean 10. demoniacal, detestable, outrageous

inferno (pert to)...
  Bib.. 4. Hell 5. abyss, limbo
  Buddah.. 6. Naraka
  Egypt.. 6. Amenti
  ferry to.. 4. Styx
  Hebrew.. 5. Sheol 7. Abaddon, Gehenna
  myth.. 5. Aralu, Hades, Orcus
    7. Acheron, Niflhel 8. Tartarus

infest... 3. vex 5. annoy, beset
    6. assail, molest, plague 7. overrun, torment 8. frequent

infidel... 5. deist, pagan 6. Kaffir
    7. atheist, Saracen, skeptic
    8. agnostic 10. unbeliever
    11. freethinker 12. non–Christian
    13. non–Mohammedan

infidelity... 6. deceit 7. perfidy
    8. unbelief 9. misbelief, treachery
    10. disloyalty 11. incredulity
    13. faithlessness

infinite... 4. vast 5. vague 6. divine
    7. endless, eternal, immense, perfect
    9. boundless, limitless, unlimited
    10. indefinite 11. illimitable, interminate, omnipresent, The Absolute 12. all–embracing, interminable, undetermined
    13. inexhaustible, The Omnipotent
    16. all–comprehensive

Infinite Being... 3. God

Infinite knowledge... 11. omniscience

infinitesimal... 5. small 7. minimum
    9. invisible, molecular 10. evanescent
    11. microscopic

infirm... 4. weak 5. anile, frail
    6. senile 7. fragile 8. decrepit
    9. doddering 10. irresolute
    11. vacillating

infirmity... 6. defect, foible, malady, old age 7. disease, failing, frailty, illness 8. debility, weakness
    10. feebleness

inflame... 4. burn, fire 5. anger
    6. arouse, enrage, excite, ignite, kindle, madden, rankle, redden
    7. incense 8. irritate 10. exasperate

inflammable... 5. fiery 6. tinder
    7. piceous, burnable 9. excitable, irascible, irritable 10. accendible
    11. combustible

inflammable substance... 6. ethane, tinder 7. acetone, bitumen

inflammation... 8. ignition, soreness
    10. congestion, excitement, incitement

inflammation (pert to)...
  bladder.. 8. cystitis
  bone.. 7. rickets 8. osteitis
    13. osteomyelitis
  ear.. 6. otitis
  eye.. 6. iritis 7. uveitis
  joints.. 4. gout 9. arthritis
    10. rheumatism
  spinal cord.. 13. poliomyelitis
  stomach.. 9. gastritis
  suffix.. 4. itis
  vein.. 9. phlebitis

inflect... 3. bow 4. bend 5. curve
    7. decline, deflect 8. modulate

inflection, inflexion... 4. tone
    5. angle, curve 7. bending
    8. paradigm 9. accidence
    10. modulation

inflexible... 4. iron 5. rigid, stiff
    6. strict 8. obdurate, rigorous
    9. immovable, immutable, obstinate, unbending 10. implacable, inexorable, relentless, unyielding 11. unalterable
    14. uncompromising

inflict... 3. add 4. deal 5. wreak
    6. impose, punish

inflorescence... 4. cyme 5. whorl
    6. cymose 7. budding, flowers
    8. racemose 9. flowerage, flowering
    10. unfoldment 13. efflorescence

inflow... 6. influx 9. inpouring
    11. inspiration

influence... 3. win 4. lead, move, pull, sway 5. aegis (egis), bribe, force, impel, lobby 6. affect, effect, induce, influx, leaven, obsess 7. control, inspire, mastery 8. dominate, effusion, persuade, prestige
    9. authority, determine

influence (world–wide)... 8. ecumenic

influenced... 6. biased 7. induced, pliable (easily) 8. affected
    10. prejudiced

influential... 6. potent, strong
    7. weighty 8. momentus, powerful
    9. effective 13. authoritative

influx... 4. tide 5. firth, mouth (river)
    6. import, inflow 7. estuary, illapse
    9. influence, inpouring
    11. debouchment

infold... see *enfold*

inform... 4. tell 5. teach, train
    6. advise, notify, report 7. animate, apprise, inspire 8. instruct
    9. enlighten

informal... 7. offhand 9. irregular

information... 3. air, tip 4. data, lore, news 5. aviso, datum, facts
    6. digest 7. advices, tidings
    9. knowledge 10. annotation
    11. instruction 12. intelligence

informed... 2. up 3. hep 4. up on, wise 6. posted 8. apprised, educated, versed in 10. instructed
    11. enlightened

informer... 3. spy 4. tout 6. gossip, snitch, teller 7. delator 8. affirmer, betrayer, mouchard, reporter, telltale
    9. informant, spokesman
    10. talebearer, tattletale

informer (sl)... 4. fink, nark 6. canary, snitch 7. stoolie 8. snitcher, squealer
    9. blabberer 11. stool pigeon
    12. blabbermouth

infraction... 6. breach 7. fracture, trespass 9. intrusion, violation
    12. encroachment, infringement, overstepping 13. transgression

infrequency... 6. rarity 7. fewness
    8. rareness, solitude 9. isolation
    12. uncommonness

infrequent... 4. rare 6. scarce, seldom, sparse 8. uncommon
    9. spasmodic 10. occasional

infrequently... 6. rarely, seldom 8. not often, sparsely

infringe... 6. defeat, refute 7. confute, destroy, violate 8. encroach, overstep, trespass 9. frustrate

infringement... 6. breach, piracy (copyright) 9. intrusion, violation 10. infraction 12. overstepping 14. nonfulfillment

infundibulum... 4. cone, lura 10. gray matter (brain)

infuriate... 5. anger 6. enrage, incite, madden 8. irritate 10. antagonize

infuscate... 7. darken 8. obscure

infuse... 4. fill, shed 5. steep 6. drench 7. implant, instill 9. insinuate, introduce

infusion... 3. tea 4. wort 8. affusion, tincture 9. admixture, decoction, inpouring 12. instillation

ingang... 5. porch 8. entrance 10. intestines

ingenious... 5. sharp, smart, witty 6. adroit, clever, daedal, gifted, shrewd, subtle 8. skillful, talented 9. Daedalian, deviceful 11. intelligent, resourceful

ingenuity... 5. skill 6. candor, genius 10. adroitness 11. originality 13. inventiveness

ingenuous... 4. naif, open 5. frank, naive, noble, plain 6. candid, innate 7. artless, sincere 8. freeborn, innocent 9. guileless 10. unreserved 15. unsophisticated

ingest... 3. eat 5. learn 6. take in 7. consume, swallow

ingot... 3. gad, pig 4. mold 5. metal 7. bullion

ingratiate... 4. fawn 7. commend, flatter 9. insinuate, introduce

ingredient... 6. factor 7. element 9. component 11. constituent

ingress... 4. go in 5. entry 6. access, portal 8. entrance 9. reception 11. entranceway

ingrowing nail... 7. acronyx

inhabitant... 3. cit 6. inmate, people, tenant 7. citizen, denizen 8. resident

inhabitant (pert to)...
Alaska.. 9. sourdough
desert.. 4. Arab 5. nomad
earliest.. 9. aborigine
foreign.. 5. alien
Maine.. 10. down–easter
moon.. 8. selenite
northern.. 6. Yankee 11. Septentrion (Lowell)

inhabitants, equator's other side...
8. antiscii 10. antiscians

inhabited... 5. lived 7. dwelled, peopled 8. occupied, tenanted 9. populated

inhabiting (pert to)...
caves.. 8. spelaean (spelean) 10. troglodyte
ground.. 9. terricole 11. terricolous
groves.. 7. nemoral 10. nemoricole
islands.. 7. nesiote
lakes.. 9. lacustral
sea.. 7. pelagic 15. thalassophilous
seashore.. 8. littoral

inhale... 4. suck 5. smell, smoke, sniff 7. breathe, inspire, respire

inharmonious... 7. jarring 9. differing, dissonant, unmusical 10. discordant 11. conflicting, disagreeing

inherent... 6. inborn, innate 7. infixed 8. immanent 9. immanence, intrinsic 10. indwelling, subsistent 11. instinctive 13. indispensable

inheritance... 6. legacy 7. bequest, legitim 8. heirship, heredity, heritage, Salic law 9. cleronomy 10. birthright

inheritance diminisher... 6. abator

inheritor... 4. heir 6. coheir 7. heiress, legatee 10. coparcener 11. beneficiary

inhibit... 5. check 6. forbid, hinder 8. prohibit, restrain 9. interdict

inhibition... 3. ban, bar 4. writ 6. embargo 8. checking 9. hindrance, restraint 10. impediment 11. prohibition 12. interdiction

inhuman... 4. fell 5. cruel 6. brutal, savage 7. bestial, brutish 8. devilish, nonhuman 9. barbarous, ferocious 10. demoniacal, diabolical

inhumation... 6. burial 9. arenation, interment

inhume... 4. bury 5. inter, inurn 7. deposit, inearth

inimical... 7. adverse, hostile, opposed 8. contrary 10. unfriendly 11. belligerent, unfavorable

iniquity... 3. sin 4. evil, vice 5. crime 7. misdeed 8. injustice 10. immorality, wickedness

initial... 6. paraph 9. incipient 11. large letter 12. commencement

initiate... 4. open 5. admit, begin, epopt (anc) 6. induct 7. install, instate 8. inchoate 10. inaugurate 11. preinstruct

initiation... 8. ceremony 9. admission 10. admittance 12. inauguration, introduction

injection... 4. hypo 5. enema 7. clyster 9. immission

injudicious... 4. rash 6. unwise 9. impolitic, imprudent 11. inexpedient

injunction... 3. ado 4. writ 5. order, union 6. behest 7. mandate, precept 9. direction 11. prohibition

injure... 3. mar 4. harm, hurt, lame, maim 5. wound, wrong 6. assail, damage, grieve, impair, scathe 7. affront, slander, tarnish

injurious... 3. bad 4. evil 7. abusive, harmful, hurtful, noxious 10. defamatory, slanderous 11. detrimental, mischievous

injury... 3. ill, mar 4. dere (obs), evil, harm, hurt, loss, pain, tort 5. wound, wrong 6. damage, lesion, mayhem, trauma 7. slander 9. detriment, indignity, injustice 10. impairment

injustice... 5. wrong 6. injury 7. umbrage 8. hardship, inequity, iniquity 10. imposition, unfairness

ink... 3. jet 5. black 7. blacken 8. atrament, blacking

ink (pert to)...

bag.. 3. sac (fish)
berry.. 5. holly 6. indigo
black.. 10. atramental
    11. atramentous
cap.. 8. mushroom
fish.. 5. squid 6. cuttle
pad.. 7. tompion (tampion)
ref to.. 10. atramental
source.. 7. inkweed, oak gall
    8. inkstone, pokeweed 9. gallberry
spreader.. 6. brayer
inkle... 4. hint, tape, yarn 5. braid,
twist 6. thread 8. intimate
inkling... 4. hint 5. rumor 6. desire,
report 10. intimation 11. supposition
inlaid... 6. mosaic 7. adorned, set into
9. champleve, decorated
inlay... 4. buhl, line 5. inset 6. insert,
mosaic, niello, tarsia 7. filling,
implant 8. buhlwork, intarsia
9. champleve
inlet... 3. bay, ria, voe 4. cove, slew,
sump 5. admit, bayou, bight, creek,
fiord (fjord), firth, inlay 6. estero,
recess, strait 7. estuary, orifice
8. entrance, waterway
inn... 3. pub 4. khan 5. abode, fonda,
hotel, motel, serai 6. hostel, imaret,
posada, tavern 7. albergo, cabaret,
hospice, locanda, osteria, pension,
shelter 8. alehouse, hostelry
9. roadhouse 11. caravansary
innate... 4. born 6. inborn, inbred,
native 7. natural 9. ingrained,
inherited, intrinsic 10. congenital,
hereditary, inveterate 11. instinctive
14. constitutional
innate ability... 6. genius, talent
innate idea (Philos)... 11. immortality
inn courts... 11. Inner Temple
inner... 4. ento (comb form) 5. ental
6. inside, inward, secret 7. obscure
8. esoteric, interior, internal
9. intestine 10. indistinct
14. intramolecular
inner circle... 3. set 4. clan, club,
ring 5. group, junta, junto 6. clique
inner man... 4. mind, self, soul
6. psyche 7. stomach
innermost coating... 6. intima
Inner Temple... 11. Inns of Court
Innisfail... 4. Eire, Erin 7. Ireland
15. Island of Destiny
innocence... 6. purity 7. diamond
11. sinlessness 12. harmlessness
13. guiltlessness, innocuousness
innocent... 4. Holy, pure 5. idiot,
naive, seely 6. benign, lawful
7. artless, sinless, upright 8. spotless
9. destitute, guiltless, ingenuous,
permitted, simpleton, stainless,
unsullied 11. unblamable
12. simple–minded 13. free from
guilt
innocuous... 8. harmless, hurtless,
innocent 9. innoxious 11. inoffensive,
unoffending
innovation... 3. new 6. change
7. novelty 13. prolification
innuendo... 4. hint, slur 6. change
7. meaning 9. aspersion
10. intimation 11. implication,

indirection, insinuation
Innuit... 4. Yuit (Eskimo)
innumerable... 6. legion, myriad
8. infinite, numerous 9. countless
10. numberless
inodorous... 8. odorless 9. scentless
inopportune... 8. ill-timed, untimely
10. malapropos, unsuitable
11. contretemps, inexpedient
12. embarrassing, unseasonable
inordinate... 5. undue 9. excessive,
fanatical 10. disordered, disorderly,
exorbitant, immoderate
11. unregulated 12. unrestrained
inorganic... 7. mineral 9. inanimate
13. nonbiological
inquest... 4. jury 5. quest, trial
6. assize, search 7. inquiry
11. examination 13. investigation
inquire... 3. ask 4. seek 5. query
7. examine 8. question
11. interrogate, investigate
inquirer... 6. seeker 7. querier,
student, zetetic 8. searcher
inquiry... 5. query 6. examen, tracer
7. examine, seeking 8. question,
research 11. examination
13. investigation
inquisition... 5. trial 6. search
7. inquiry 8. tribunal 11. examination
13. investigation
Inquisition... 6. French (1772)
7. Spanish (1480–1834)
inquisitive... 4. nosy 5. peery
6. prying 7. curious 8. meddling
10. meddlesome
inquisitor... 6. tracer 7. coroner,
sheriff 8. examiner
in re... 10. concerning 13. in the
matter of
inroad... 4. raid 5. foray 8. invasion,
trespass 9. incursion, intrusion,
irruption 12. overstepping
13. transgression
insane... 3. mad 4. daft, loco, luny
5. batty, crazy, loony 6. crazed
7. cracked, foolish, frantic, rammish,
touched, witless 8. demented,
deranged 9. non compos 15. non
compos mentis
insane urge to steal...
11. kleptomania
insanity... 5. mania 6. frenzy, lunacy,
trance 7. madness 8. delirium,
dementia 10. alienation
11. derangement 16. mental
deficiency
inscribe... 4. draw, etch 5. infix,
stamp, write 6. blazon, enroll
7. address, engrave, impress
8. dedicate, depencil
inscribed... 5. runed 7. written
8. engraved, recorded 10. registered,
rupestrian (on rocks)
inscription... 4. text 5. motto, title
6. legend 7. epitaph, writing
8. colophon, epigraph, graffito
9. lettering, sgraffito 10. dedication
14. superscription
inscrutable... 6. secret 8. abstruse
10. mysterious 12. impenetrable,
inexplorable, unfathomable

16. incomprehensible

insect... 3. ant, bee, bug, dor, fly
4. flea, gnat, lerp, lice, mite, moth,
tick, wasp 5. aphid, borer, cadew,
emmet, leech, louse, roach, Vespa
6. acarid, beetle, cicada, earwig,
hornet, locust, mantis, sawfly, scarab,
spider 7. ant lion, chigger, firefly,
gallfly, katydid, ladybug, pismire,
termite 8. bullhead, glowworm,
mosquito, stinkbug, turicata
9. bumblebee, butterfly, caddis fly,
centipede, cockroach, dragonfly,
ichneumon, tsetse fly, tumblebug
10. silverfish 11. caterpillar,
grasshopper 12. yellow jacket

insect (pert to)...
adult.. 5. imago
aquatic.. 7. Ranatra
arboreal.. 7. katydid
back.. 5. notum
Bible.. 7. ant lion
butterfly.. 11. Lepidoptera
egg.. 3. nit
eyes.. 6. ocelli 7. stemmas
feelers.. 5. palps 8. antennas
9. tentacles
fly.. 7. Diptera
hymenopterous.. 3. ant, bee 4. wasp
6. sawfly 7. gallfly
immature.. 3. grub, pupa 5. larva
6. maggot 9. chrysalis
immature covering.. 6. cocoon
leg.. 6. proleg
like.. 8. entomoid
long-legged.. 5. emesa
mature.. 5. imago
molting.. 6. instar 7. ecdysis
parasitic.. 4. lice 5. louse
plant.. 5. aphid, aphis, borer, thrip
plate.. 6. scutum
praying.. 6. mantis
reference to.. 11. entomologic
relationship to host.. 7. metochy
science.. 10. entomology
sound.. 5. chirr 6. stridor
stage.. 4. pupa 5. imago, larva
6. instar 9. chrysalis
stinging.. 3. ant, bee 4. wasp
6. hornet 7. sciniph (Bib) 12. yellow
jacket
wingless.. 4. flea 6. aptera
wing vein.. 5. media

Insectivora (mammals)... 5. moles
6. shrews 7. desmans, tenrecs
9. hedgehogs

insecure... 5. risky, shaky 6. infirm,
unsafe, unsure 7. dubious, rickety
8. unstable 9. dangerous, hazardous
10. precarious

insensate... 5. blind, harsh 6. brutal,
unwise 7. fatuous, foolish 8. lifeless
9. inanimate, unfeeling, untouched
10. insensible, insentient
11. insensitive 13. unintelligent

insensibility... 4. coma 8. neurosis
9. analgesia 13. lack of feeling

insensible... 4. slow 7. gradual,
unaware 9. apathetic, inanimate,
insensate, senseless 11. indifferent,
insensitive, unconscious
13. inappreciable

insert... 4. gore 5. foist, graft, immit,
inset, panel, wedge 7. ingraft
8. ornament 9. interpose, introduce
11. intercalate, interpolate

insertion... 5. inset 9. injection
10. embroidery, needlework

insertion (pert to)...
cords in cloth.. 5. shirr
day in calendar.. 13. intercalation
newspaper.. 2. ad 13. advertisement
phrases, words.. 11. parenthesis
sound in a word.. 9. anaptyxis
10. epenthesis

inset... 5. panel 6. inflow, influx
10. phenocryst

inside out, turning... 5. evert
8. aversion 9. evertible

insidious... 4. deep, wily 8. guileful
9. deceitful, dishonest 11. full of
plots, treacherous

insight... 3. ken 6. acumen
9. intuition 11. discernment,
penetration 12. clairvoyance
13. understanding

insignia... 3. bar 4. ankh, flag
5. badge, cross, crown 6. banner,
emblem, symbol 7. chevron, regalia,
scepter 8. caduceus, swastika
15. hammer and sickle

insignificance... 8. trifling 9. smallness
10. slightness 12. unimportance

insignificant... 4. puny 5. minor, petit,
petty, small 6. paltry 7. trivial
8. inferior 9. senseless
11. meaningless, unimportant
12. contemptible 13. inconsiderate

insignificant object... 8. molehill

insincere... 5. false 8. affected
9. deceptive, imperfect
12. hypocritical

insinuate... 4. hint 5. enter, imply
6. allude, infuse 7. instill, intrude,
suggest 8. intimate 9. penetrate
10. ingratiate

insinuation... 4. hint 5. sneer
8. innuendo 9. aspersion, insertion,
intrusion 10. intimation
11. insinuation 12. ingratiation,
interjection

insipid... 3. dry 4. dead, dull, flat,
tame 5. heavy, prosy, stale, vapid
6. jejune 7. prosaic 8. lifeless,
mediocre 9. tasteless
10. monotonous, namby-pamby,
spiritless, unanimated, wishy-washy
11. indifferent 13. uninteresting

insisted... 5. urged 6. held to
7. pressed 8. demanded 9. persisted
10. maintained, stipulated

insolence... 5. serve 6. insult
8. defiance 9. arrogance, contumely,
impudence 11. haughtiness

insolent... 4. pert, rude 7. abusive,
defiant 8. arrogant, impudent
9. insulting 10. disdainful
11. extravagant, overbearing
12. contemptuous, contumelious
13. disrespectful

insouciant... 8. carefree
11. indifferent, unconcerned

inspect... 3. pry, spy 4. view 5. grade
7. examine 10. scrutinize

inspector... 4. ager 6. conner, grader, police, sealer, tester 8. examiner, overseer
inspiration... 6. sprite 8. afflatus, hiccough 9. influence, intuition 10. exhalation, inhalation, motivation
inspire... 4. fire 5. cheer, exalt 6. infuse, inhale 7. animate, breathe, enliven 8. motivate 9. encourage, infatuate 11. communicate (to the spirit)
inspired power.. 7. entheos
inspiring... 8. cheering, eloquent 11. provocative
inspiring (pert to)...
awe.. 4. fear 5. awful, eerie
confidence.. 11. encouraging
favor.. 13. prepossessing
horror.. 6. grisly
inspirit... 5. cheer, elate, rouse 7. animate, enliven, hearten, inspire, quicken 9. encourage 10. ingratiate, invigorate
instability... 8. weakness 10. changeable, insecurity, mutability, unsafeness 11. inconstancy 12. irresolution, unsteadiness 13. changeability, unreliability
install... 4. seat 6. induct, ordain 7. instate 8. initiate 9. establish 10. inaugurate
instance... 4. case, suit 6. motive 7. example, request, urgency 8. occasion 10. suggestion 11. instigation
instant... 3. pop 4. time, urge 5. flash, trice 6. direct, minute, moment, second, urgent 7. current, solicit 8. pressing 9. immediate, importune 11. importunate
instantly... 3. now 8. directly, in a flash, in a trice
instate... 5. admit, endow 6. invest 7. install 9. establish
instead of... 4. else 5. stead 6. in lieu, rather 10. equivalent, substitute
instigate... 3. egg 4. abet, goad, move, prod, spur, urge 5. impel 6. foment, incite, suborn 7. provoke 8. motivate 9. stimulate
instigator... 5. urger 7. abettor, exciter, inciter 8. agitator, fomenter, inflamer, provoker 10. ringleader
instill, instil... 5. imbue 6. impart, infuse, pour in 7. pervade 9. inculcate, insinuate
instinct... 5. knack 6. libido, talent 7. impulse 8. aptitude 11. instigation, orientation
instinctive... 6. innate 7. natural 8. inherent, original 9. automatic, intuitive 11. involuntary, spontaneous
institute... 5. erect, found 6. create, ordain, school 7. academy, college, precept, society 8. initiate, organize, seminary 9. originate, principle 10. inaugurate 12. organization
Institute (The)... 5. Gaius 6. France 8. Politics 10. Technology
institute a suit... 3. sue 7. go to law 8. litigate 9. prosecute
Institution, International (maritime)...

7. Veritas 13. Bureau Veritas
instruct... 5. show 5. coach, edify, order, teach, train 6. advise, direct, inform 7. command, confirm, educate, nurture 9. enlighten 10. discipline 12. indoctrinate
instruction... 3. act 4. lore, news 6. lesson, report 7. precept, tuition 8. pedagogy, teaching, tutorage 9. paideutic 11. information 13. propaedeutics
instructive... 8. didactic, sermonic 10. commanding, preceptive 11. educational, informative 12. propaedeutic
instructor... 5. tutor 6. mentor 7. adviser, teacher, trainer 8. lecturer 9. preceptor, professor
instrument... 4. barb, bill, deed, tool, writ 5. agent, means 6. medium 7. utensil, writing 8. document 9. implement 11. contrivance
instrument, musical (pert to)...
ancient.. 4. asor, lyre 5. rebab, rocta, shawn 7. cithern, theorbo 8. penorcon, psaltery
brass.. 4. horn 6. cornet 7. helicon
keyboard.. 5. organ, piano 6. spinet 10. clavichord 11. harpsichord
percussion.. 4. drum, gong 5. bells 6. chimes 7. cymbals, marimba 8. carillon 9. castanets, xylophone 10. vibraphone 12. glockenspiel
sacred (Mormon).. 4. Urim 7. Thummim
stringed.. 4. asor, harp, lute, lyre, rota 5. banjo, cello, ribec (ribeck), viola 6. fiddle, guitar, violin 7. ukulele 8. dulcimer, mandolin 10. hurdy-gurdy
stringed (anc).. 7. bandora
supplementary.. 7. ripieno
wind.. 3. sax 4. horn, oboe, reed, tuba 5. flute, organ 6. cornet 7. althorn, bassoon, ocarina, piccolo, trumpet 8. clarinet, trombone 9. accordion, flageolet, harmonica, saxophone
instrument, others (pert to)...
astronomical.. 5. armil
Biblical.. 4. Urim
butcher's.. 5. steel 7. cleaver
communication.. 9. telegraph, telephone 10. hydrophone
cooking (eggs).. 7. oometer
cutting.. 5. knife, razor 6. scythe, shears, sickle 7. cutlery 8. scissors, strickle
drawing.. 10. pantograph
gripping.. 4. vise 5. clamp, tongs 7. pincers 8. tweezers
legal.. 4. deed, writ 6. escrow
mathematics.. 6. abacus 8. mesolabe
measure.. 7. ammeter 8. odometer, otoscope, rheostat 9. barometer, koniscope, rheometer 11. pyronometer
medical.. 6. trocar (trochar) 7. dilator, levator, ligator, scalpel 8. trephine
mining.. 6. jumper
music.. 4. bell 9. ergograph, metronome

navigating.. 7. pelorus, sextant
optical.. 7. alidade (alidad)
   9. periscope, telescope
pointed.. 3. awl 6. stylet, stylus
   8. stiletto
time.. 11. chronometer, chronoscope
two—pronged.. 6. bident
instrumental... 6. useful 7. helpful
   9. conducive, promoting, symphonic
   10. orchestral 11. implemental,
   serviceable
instrumental (pert to)...
composition.. 5. fugue, rondo
   6. sonata 7. cantata 8. symphony
grammar.. 4. case
introduction.. 7. intrada
instrumentality... 5. means 6. agency,
   medium 7. organon 9. mechanism
insubordinate... 8. mutinous
   10. unresigned 11. disobedient
   12. contumacious, unsubmissive
insubstantial... 5. frail 6. flimsy
   9. illogical 10. unreliable
   12. apparitional
insufficient... 5. short 6. scanty,
   scarce 7. unequal, wanting
   9. deficient 10. inadequate
   14. incommensurate, unsatisfactory
insular... 5. alone 6. narrow
   7. nesiote 8. detached, islander,
   isolated, secluded 9. illiberal,
   insulated, sclerosis, separated,
   unrelated 10. contracted 12. Island
   of Reil (Anat)
insulated... 5. isled, taped 8. isolated
   9. separated 10. segregated
insulating material... 4. tape 5. kapok
   6. balata, Kerite 7. okonite 10. fiber
   glass 12. friction tape
insult... 3. cag 4. mock, slur 5. flout
   6. offend, revile 7. affront, assault,
   offense, outrage 8. contempt
   9. contumely, indignity
insulting... 8. arrogant, insolent
   9. offensive 10. affrontive
   13. disrespectful
insurance... 4. risk 7. annuity, promise
   8. guaranty, security, warranty
   9. assurance 10. protection
insurance group... 7. tontine
insurance personnel... 5. agent
   6. broker 7. actuary 8. adjuster
insurgent... 5. rebel 8. agitator,
   mutineer, revolter 10. rebellious
   13. insubordinate
insurmountable... 10. impassable,
   invincible 11. insuperable 13. beyond
   control
insurrection... 4. riot 6. mutiny, revolt
   8. sedition, uprising 9. rebellion
   10. insurgence, revolution
intact... 5. sound, whole
   9. unchanged, undefiled, undivided,
   uninjured, untouched 10. unimpaired
intaglio... 3. die, gem 6. relief
   7. carving 9. engraving
intangible... 5. vague 7. phantom
   10. immaterial, impalpable
   13. imperceptible, insubstantial,
   unsubstantial
integer... 3. one 5. whole 6. entity,
   number 8. integral

integral... 3. all 5. inner, whole
   8. totality 9. component, essential
integration... 5. whole 10. adjustment
   11. unification 12. coordination,
   equalization 13. accommodation
integrity... 5. unity 6. purity, virtue
   7. honesty, probity 8. innocence,
   soundness 12. completeness
integument... 4. aril, coat, derm, skin
   5. testa 8. covering, envelope
   10. investment
intellect... 3. wit 4. mind, nous
   5. inwit, mahat 6. genius, noesis,
   reason 7. noetics, wise man
   9. mentality 12. intelligence
   13. understanding
intellectual... 6. brainy, mental, noetic,
   sophic 7. egghead, learned
   8. highbrow 11. intelligent
intelligence... 4. mind, news 5. sense,
   spies 6. acumen, spirit 8. capacity
   9. intellect, knowledge
   11. information 13. understanding
intelligent... 3. apt 4. sane 5. acute,
   aware, smart 6. astute, bright,
   versed 7. knowing, skilled 8. rational,
   sensible 9. cognizant
   13. understanding
intelligentsia... 8. literati 10. illuminati
   11. the educated 13. intellectuals
intelligible... 5. clear, plain
   8. knowable 10. cognizable,
   conceptual, explicable, fathomable
   11. perspicuous 13. suprasensuous
   14. comprehensible, understandable
intelligibly... 6. simply 7. clearly,
   lucidly, plainly 13. unequivocally
   14. comprehendingly, understandably
intemerate... 4. pure 9. inviolate,
   undefiled
intemperance... 6. excess 8. bibacity,
   gluttony, severity, tippling
   10. debauchery, inclemency
   11. drunkenness 12. inabstinence,
   incontinence
intemperate... 6. Frigid (Zone), severe,
   Torrid (Zone) 7. extreme 8. addicted,
   bibulous 9. excessive, inclement,
   indulgent 10. gluttonous,
   immoderate, inordinate
   12. ungovernable, unrestrained
intend... 3. aim 4. mean, plan
   5. serve 6. design, direct, expect,
   regard, set out, strive 7. proceed,
   propose 8. aspire to, attend to,
   consider
intended... 5. meant 8. designed,
   purposed, remedial 9. affianced,
   betrothed, meditated 10. calculated,
   considered 11. deliberated, intentional
   12. contemplated
intense... 4. deep 5. great, vivid
   6. strong 7. violent 8. powerful
   9. energetic 10. high degree
intensely... 4. very 5. quite 7. acutely
intensify... 6. deepen 7. enhance
   8. condense, heighten, increase
   9. aggravate
intensity... 5. depth 6. deepen,
   degree, energy 7. density
   8. loudness, softness, strength
   9. greatness, vehemence

12. colorfulness

intent... 4. rapt 5. eager, tense
6. design 7. earnest, meaning,
purpose 9. intention

intention... 3. aim, end 4. will
6. animus, design, motive, object
7. concept, healing, meaning,
purpose 8. intentio 13. determination

intentional... 5. aimed, meant
7. knowing 8. designed, intended
9. voluntary 10. calculated, deliberate
12. contemplated

intently... 7. eagerly, fixedly
9. earnestly, zealously 10. diligently,
sedulously 11. attentively, steadfastly

inter (pref)... 5. among, intra
6. mutual, within 7. between
10. reciprocal

inter (verb)... 4. bury 5. inurn
6. entomb, inhume 7. inearth

intercalary month... 6. Veadar 8. leap
year 10. bissextile

intercalate... 6. insert 11. interpolate

intercede... 6. umpire 7. bargain,
mediate, referee 9. arbitrate, go
between, interpose, intervene

intercessor... 5. agent, front
6. bishop, Christ 8. mediator
9. middleman 10. interceder
11. internuncio

interchange... 5. trade 6. barter
7. permute 8. commerce, exchange
9. alternate 10. transposal
11. alternation, reciprocate, retaliation

intercourse... 7. dealing 8. commerce
10. connection, fellowship
12. conversation 13. communication

interdependence... 9. mutuality
13. interrelation 16. interaffiliation

interdict... 3. ban 4. veto 5. debar,
taboo (tabu) 6. forbid 7. inhibit
8. prohibit 9. proscribe

interest... 4. hold, weal 5. savor,
share, usury 6. behalf, engage
7. attract, concern 9. entertain

interested... 4. rapt 7. partial 8. a
party to, involved, partisan
9. attentive 10. prejudiced

interesting... 8. exciting 10. attractive
11. provocative

interfere... 5. clash 6. hinder, meddle,
molest, tamper 7. intrude
9. interpose, intervene
11. intermeddle

interim... 7. respite 8. interval,
meantime 9. interlude, meanwhile
12. intermission

interior... 5. inner 6. center, inland,
inside, secret 8. internal 9. enclosure

interjection... 2. eh, lo 3. bah
4. ahem, alas, egad, haha, whew
7. heavens 11. ejaculation,
exclamation

interlace... 3. mix 5. braid, unite
9. alternate, interlink 10. intertwine,
interweave 11. interpolate, intersperse

interlock... 4. knit, mesh 5. unite,
weave 6. device, engage 7. connect
9. interjoin, interlace 11. interrelate

interlope... 6. insert 7. intrude,
obtrude 9. interfere, intervene
11. intermeddle, interpolate

interloper... 8. intruder 10. trespasser
11. gate crasher

interlude... 5. farce, pause, truce
6. verset 7. interim, respite
8. entr'acte, overture, versicle
10. intermezzo 11. performance
13. entertainment

intermediary... 5. agent 6. medium,
middle 8. mediator 9. go-between
10. interagent 11. intervening,
mediatorial

intermediate... 5. mesne 6. grades,
medial, medium, middle 7. aniline
(dye), mediate 8. mediator
9. naphthols 11. interjacent,
intervening 12. intermediary

interminable... 4. aeon, long
7. endless, eternal 8. infinite,
unending 9. boundless, limitless,
perpetual, unlimited 10. continuous,
protracted

intermission... 4. rest 5. pause
6. recess 7. respite 8. entr'acte,
interval 9. cessation 10. suspension
12. interruption

intermit... 4. stop 5. cease, recur
7. suspend 9. interpose, interrupt
11. discontinue

intermittent... 6. broken, fitful
8. periodic 9. irregular, recurrent,
spasmodic 11. alternating

internal... 5. inner 6. inside, inward,
mental, within 7. revenue
8. domestic, esoteric, interior
9. intrinsic, spiritual

internal organs... 6. vitals 7. viscera

international (pert to)...
agreement... 4. pact 6. accord, treaty
7. entente 8. suzerain
business combine.. 6. cartel
fixed calendar.. 9. Cotsworth
language... 2. Ro 3. Ido 5. Arulo
7. Volapük 9. Esperanto
10. Occidental 11. Interlingua

interpolate... 5. alter 6. insert
7. corrupt, implant 11. intercalate

interpose... 7. intrude, mediate
9. intercede, interfere, interject,
intervene, introduce

interpret... 4. read, rede, scan
6. define 7. explain, expound
8. construe, diagnose, exegesis
9. elucidate, translate

interpretation... 5. sense 8. solution
9. rendering 10. definition
11. explanation, translation

interpretation, science of...
7. anagoge (Bib) 8. exegesis
9. dittology 12. hermeneutics

interpreter... 5. ulema 6. gnomon
7. exegete, latiner 8. dragoman,
exponent 9. catechist, exegetist,
explainer, go-between, hermeneut
12. oneirocritic (dreams)

interrogate... 3. ask 4. pump, quiz,
test 5. query 7. examine, inquire
9. question 10. catechize

interrogation... 7. eroteme (question
mark) 8. erotisis, question, quizzing
11. examination, questioning

interrupt... 4. stop 5. break, check
6. arrest, hinder, thwart 7. break in,

intrude 8. obstruct 9. intercept
11. interpolate

interrupter (electric)... 8. rheotome

interruption... 3. gap 5. pause
6. hiatus 7. interim 8. interval
9. cessation, hindrance
10. suspension 11. obstruction
12. intermission, intervention
13. interposition

intersect... 3. cut 4. meet 5. cross
6. divide, pierce 9. decussate
10. intercross

intersperse... 6. insert, thread
7. scatter 9. diversify

interstice... 4. mesh, pore 5. chink,
crack, space 6. areola 7. crevice
8. interval 10. interspace

intertwine... 5. unite, weave
8. entangle 9. interknit, interlace
10. intertwist

interval... 3. gap 4. rest 5. break,
lapse, pitch, space 6. degree, period,
recess 7. diastem, interim, respite
8. diastema, distance, half step
10. interspace 12. intermission,
interruption

intervals, at... 8. brokenly, fitfully
11. haphazardly, irregularly
12. occasionally 14. intermittently
15. longo intervallo

intervene... 7. intrude, mediate
9. interlude, interpose 10. lie
between 11. come between

intervening (pert to)...
between, among.. 11. interjacent
law.. 5. mesne
space.. 8. distance
time.. 7. interim 9. interlude

interweave... 3. mat 4. plat 5. braid,
plait, plash 6. enlace, raddle, splice,
wattle 8. intermix 9. interlace
13. twist together

intestinal... 7. enteric 8. visceral

intestine (pert to)...
coating.. 4. caul
comb form.. 6. entero
part.. 5. colon, ilium, large, small
6. caecum, rectum 7. jejunum
8. appendix, duodenum
15. alimentary canal

intestines... 4. guts 6. bowels
8. entrails

intimacy... 9. closeness
10. connection, friendship
11. association, familiarity, sociability

intimate... 3. sib 4. hint, near
6. friend, united 8. familiar, friendly,
informal, personal, sociable
9. confidant, innermost
12. confidential

intimation... 3. cue 4. clue, hint
5. trace 7. inkling 9. reference
10. foreboding, indication, suggestion
11. supposition 12. announcement,
notification

intimidate... 3. awe, cow 5. abash,
bully, daunt, deter 7. overawe, terrify
8. browbeat, frighten, threaten

intolerance... 7. bigotry 9. dogmatism,
prejudice 10. impatience, narrowness
12. illiberality

intolerant... 6. narrow 7. bigoted

8. dogmatic 9. impatient
10. prejudiced 11. not enduring

intolerant person... 5. bigot 7. fanatic

intone... 4. sing 5. chant, croon,
sound 7. introit

intoxicated... 3. lit, sot 4. tosy
5. drunk, heady, tipsy 6. boiled
7. fervent, fuddled, maudlin
8. besotted, temulent 9. befuddled
10. inebriated

intractable... 5. tough 6. sullen, unruly
7. restive, willful (wilful) 8. indocile,
perverse, stubborn 9. obstinate,
unbending, unpliable 10. headstrong,
inflexible, refractory 11. unteachable
12. ungovernable

intransitive... 6. neuter, verbal
8. confined 10. in transitu

intrenchment... 2. pa (pah) 4. fort
7. defense, parapet 8. stockade
12. encroachment, infringement

intrepid... 4. bold 5. brave 6. heroic
7. doughty, valiant 8. fearless,
resolute 9. dauntless, undaunted
10. courageous

intrepidity... 5. nerve, valor
7. courage, prowess 8. boldness,
valiancy 9. gallantry

intricacy... 9. sinuosity 10. complexity,
involution, perplexity 11. complexness
12. complication, entanglement

intrigue... 4. plot 5. amour, cabal
6. brigue, scheme 8. artifice,
cheating 9. fascinate 10. conspiracy
11. machination

intrinsic... 4. real, true 5. inner
6. inborn, inbred, inward, native
7. genuine, natural 8. immanent,
implicit, inherent 9. essential,
necessary 11. inseparable
13. indispensable

intrinsically... 5. truly 6. really
10. internally 11. essentially

intrinsic being... 7. essence

introduce... 5. immit, start, usher
6. broach, herald, infuse, insert,
submit 7. bring in, preface, present,
sponsor 8. acquaint, approach,
initiate, innovate 10. inaugurate
11. preinstruct

introduced from foreign country...
6. exotic 10. extraneous

introduced serum... 10. inoculated

introduction... 5. debut, guide, proem
7. introit, isagoge, preface
8. exordium, foreword, preamble
9. insertion 10. innovation
11. instruction, preparation
12. inauguration, presentation

introduction (pert to)...
Biblical.. 9. isagogics
drama (anc).. 8. protasis
new words.. 7. neology
spurious matter.. 13. interpolation

introductory... 9. prefatory, prelusive
11. preliminary

introit... 4. hymn, rite 5. psalm
8. entrance 12. introduction

introrse... (opp of extrorse) 12. facing
inward

introversion... (opp of extroversion)
9. inversion, reticence

intrude... 5. enter 6. invade, meddle
8. encroach, infringe, overstep,
trespass 9. interfere, interlope
intruder... 7. invader 8. outsider
9. buttinsky 10. interloper, trespasser
intrust, entrust... 6. commit
7. confide, consign 8. delegate
10. commission
intuition... 5. hunch 6. noesis, regard
7. insight 9. knowledge, reference
13. contemplation
intuitive... 6. noetic, seeing 7. sensing
10. perceiving 11. instinctive
inulase... 6. enzyme
inunction... 7. unguent 8. inunctum,
ointment
inundate... 3. dip 4. dunk 5. douse,
drunk, flood 6. deluge, engulf
7. baptize, immerse 8. overflow,
submerge 9. overwhelm
10. oversupply
inure... 6. harden, season 7. benefit,
callous, toughen 8. accustom
9. habituate
inurn... 4. bury 5. inter 6. entomb
invade... 4. raid 5. enter (foeman),
usurp 6. attack, infest 7. intrude,
overrun, violate 8. encroach, trespass
invader... 4. Pict 8. attacker, intruder
9. aggressor, assailant 10. trespasser
invalid... 4. null, sick, void, weak
5. frail 6. feeble, infirm, sickly
8. nugatory 11. ineffectual
14. valetudinarian
invalidate... 4. undo 5. annul, quash
7. abolish, nullify, vitiate 8. disprove
10. disqualify, neutralize
invalidism... 13. indisposition
17. valetudinarianism
invaluable... 6. useful 8. precious
9. priceless, worthless
11. inestimable
invariable... 7. uniform 8. constant
10. unchanging 12. unchangeable
invasion... 4. raid 5. foray 6. attack,
breach, inroad 8. entrance (hostile)
9. incursion, intrusion, irruption
10. infraction 11. infestation
invective... 5. abuse, curse 6. tirade
7. inveigh, railing 8. diatribe
10. revilement 11. malediction
12. vituperation
inveigle... 4. lure, rope 5. snare
6. allure, entice, entrap, seduce
7. deceive, wheedle 10. lead astray
invent... 4. coin 5. frame 6. create,
design, devise 7. concoct 8. discover
9. fabricate (mentally), originate
inventive... 6. adroit 7. fertile
8. creative, original 9. ingenious
inventor... 7. creator 8. imaginer
10. discoverer, originator
inventor, discoverer of...
airplane.. 6. Fokker, Wright (Bros)
baseball.. 9. Doubleday
brake (safety).. 4. Otis
cotton gin.. 7. Whitney
dynamite.. 5. Nobel
electric light.. 6. Edison
elevator.. 4. Otis
gun.. 4. Colt 5. Maxim 9. Remington
harp (Bib).. 5. Jubal

lamp (safety).. 4. Davy
phonograph.. 6. Edison
printing.. 9. Gutenberg
radio.. 8. De Forest
sewing machine.. 4. Howe
steamboat.. 5. Fitch 6. Fulton
steam engine.. 4. Watt
telegraph.. 5. Morse
wireless.. 7. Marconi
X-ray.. 8. Roentgen
inventory... 4. list 5. index 7. account
8. register 9. catalogue (catalog)
10. tally sheet
inverse... 8. inverted, opposite,
reversed
inversely club-shaped... 9. obclavate
inversely oval... 7. obovate
inversion... 8. overturn, reversal
9. overthrow, reversion
10. conversion 12. introversion
invert... 7. capsize, convert, pervert
(obs), reverse, tip over 8. overturn
9. transpose 10. turn turtle
invertebrate... 5. polyp 6. insect,
sponge 7. mollusk 9. spineless
10. weak-willed
invest... 4. don 4. vest, wrap
5. array, dress, endow, indue, spend
6. clothe 7. empower, envelop,
instate 8. surround
invest (pert to)...
  authority.. 8. accredit, sanction
  ministry.. 6. ordain
  sovereignty.. 8. enthrone
investigate... 3. pry 4. sift 5. probe,
study, track 6. excuse, search
7. discuss, explore 8. indagate
9. scrutinize
investigation... 6. examen 7. inquiry,
zetetic 8. research 9. discovery,
heuristic 10. discussion
11. examination
investiture... 7. clothes, vesture
8. clothing, covering 9. induction
10. holy orders, investment (money),
ordination 11. instatement
12. installation 15. enfranchisement
investment... 5. siege 7. finance,
garment 8. blockade, clothing,
covering, purchase, vestment
9. endowment 11. empowerment
investment list... 9. portfolio
inveterate... 3. old 6. rooted
7. chronic 8. habitual, hardened
9. confirmed, ingrained
10. deep-rooted 11. established,
traditional 15. long-established
invidious... 6. odious, ornery
7. envious, hateful 9. malignant
14. discriminating (unjustly)
invigorate... 3. pep 5. brace, cheer,
nerve, renew 6. vivify 7. animate,
enliven, fortify, refresh 8. energize
9. stimulate 10. exhilarate,
strengthen
invigorating... 4. cool 5. tonic
8. cheering 9. energizing,
life-giving, refreshing 11. stimulating
invincible... 10. unbeatable
11. indomitable 13. unconquerable
inviolate... 6. sacred, secret
8. faithful, unbroken 9. unchanged,

undefiled, unstained 10. inviolable, unimpaired, unprofound 13. incorruptible

invisible... 3. hid 6. hidden 10. indistinct, unapparent 13. infinitesimal, undiscernible, unperceivable

Invisible, The... 3. God 11. Rosicrucian 16. German Protestant

invisible emanation... 4. aura

invitation... 3. bid 4. call 7. bidding, summons 10. allurement, inducement 12. solicitation

invite... 3. ask, beg, bid, try 4. bade 5. court, order, tempt 6. allure, entice, induce 7. request, solicit 9. encourage

invocation... 4. call, plea, rite 6. appeal, prayer, sermon 7. summons 8. entreaty 11. conjuration, incantation 12. supplication

invoice... 4. bill 7. account (written) 8. manifest 9. reckoning 12. bill of lading

invoke... 3. beg 4. pray 6. appeal 7. address, conjure, entreat, implore, solicit 8. draw down 10. supplicate

involuntary... 9. not willed, reluctant, unwilling, unwitting 11. instinctive, spontaneous 13. unintentional

involve... 3. lap 4. coil, wind, wrap 5. imply 6. employ, entail, evolve, infold 7. concern, ensnare, entwine, envelop, include 8. interest 9. embarrass, implicate 10. complicate 11. incriminate

involved... 7. complex, implied 8. involute, tortuous 9. engrossed 10. implicated

involving punishment... 8. punitive

invulnerable... 10. invincible 11. impregnable, insuperable 12. impenetrable, unassailable

inward... 4. into 5. entad, inner 6. inside 7. ingoing, muffled 8. interior, internal 9. spiritual 10. internally

inwards... 8. entrails 10. intestines

Io... 7. goddess (Gr) 9. butterfly, satellite (of Jupiter)

iodine, iodin (pert to)...
comb form.. 3. iod 4. iodo
compound.. 6. iodide
containing.. 5. iodic 6. iodous
poisoning.. 6. iodism 9. iododerma
source.. 4. kelp 8. sea water 9. salt peter 12. thryoid gland
standard.. 9. idiometry
substitute.. 7. Aristol

ion... 5. anion 6. cation (kation) 8. electron, particle (Elec)

Ionian (pert to)...
city.. 4. Teos (birthplace of Anacreon)
islands.. 5. Greek 9. Asia Minor
mode (Mus).. 6. Lydian

Ionic (pert to)...
architecture.. 5. Order
dialect.. 5. Greek
poetry.. 4. foot 5. meter
printing.. 4. type

iota... 3. ace, jot 4. atom, mite, star (9th brightest), whit 6. letter (Gr), tittle 8. particle

Iowa...
capital.. 9. Des Moines
city.. 4. Ames 8. Waterloo 9. Davenport, Fort Dodge, Marquette, Sioux City 10. West Branch 11. Cedar Rapids
famed attractions.. 10. Hoover home 12. Effigy Mounds 17. Little Brown Church
famed first.. 12. apple orchard (1799)
famed names.. 6. Joliet 7. Dubuque 9. Marquette
flower.. 8. wild rose
locale.. 8. farm belt (Midwest)
river.. 8. Missouri 11. Mississippi
State admission.. 11. twenty–ninth (1846)
State nickname.. 7. Hawkeye

ipecac... 4. evea 6. emetic 7. emetive 9. purgative

irade... 6. decree (Turk)

Iran... see also *Iranian*
capital.. 7. Teheran (Tehran)
city.. 6. Abadan, Shiraz 7. Isfahan
conqueror.. 6. Darius 9. Alexander
founder.. 5. Cyrus (the Great)
lake.. 7. Rezaieh
mountain.. 6. Elburz, Zagros 8. Damavand (peak)
parliament.. 6. Majlis (Mejlis)
people.. 3. Tat 7. Indians
ruins.. 10. Persepolis (Shiraz)

Iranian (pert to)...
almond.. 5. badam
books.. 5. Koran, Yasma 6. Avesta
country.. 4. Elam 5. Media
demigod.. 4. Yima
demon.. 7. Ahriman
diadem.. 3. taj
dynasty.. 6. Safavi, Seljuk 10. Sassanidae
fire worshiper.. 5. Parsi (Parsee)
god.. 6. Ormazd (Supreme) 7. Mithras
Koran student.. 5. hafiz
poet.. 4. Omar 5. Saadi
Relig founder.. 9. Zoroaster
tapestry.. 7. susanee
tentmaker.. 4. Omar

Iraq, Mesopotamia...
capital.. 6. Bagdad (Baghdad)
culture (anc).. 8. Sumerian
historic city.. 2. Ur 5. Eridu 7. Babylon, Nineveh
historic Valley.. 15. Tigris–Euphrates
port.. 5. Basra (Busrah)
product.. 3. oil 4. date 5. sheep
river.. 6. Tigris 9. Euphrates

irascibility... 3. ire 6. choler 9. crossness, testiness 10. perversity 11. waspishness 12. churlishness, irritability

irate... 3. hot 5. angry, wroth 7. enraged 8. incensed 9. irascible

ire... 5. anger, wrath 7. madness 8. vexation 9. vehemence 10. enragement, resentment 12. exasperation

ireful... 5. angry, wroth 7. iracund 9. irascible 10. passionate

Ireland... 4. Eire, Erin 5. Irena 6. Old
Sod, Ulster 8. Hibernia 9. Innisfail
11. Emerald Isle, Erin go brath
14. Ireland Forever
Ireland (pert to)... see also *Irish*
Bay.. 6. Bantry, Dingle, Galway
7. Donegal
capital.. 4. Tara (old) 6. Dublin
channel.. 5. North 9. St George's
city.. 4. Cobh (Queenstown), Cork,
Tara 6. Galway, Tralee, Ulster
7. Belfast, Donegal, Kildare, Wexford
8. Kilkenny, Limerick 9. Tipperary
island.. 4. Aran
legislature.. 4. Dail
mountain.. 7. Errigal 13. Carrantuohill
river.. 3. Lee 4. Erne, Suir 6. Liffey
7. Shannon
sea.. 5. Irish
seaport.. 4. Cobh 6. Tralee
seat of archbishops.. 6. Armagh
irenic... 7. henotic 8. peaceful
11. harmonizing 12. conciliatory
iridescent... 7. opaline 9. prismatic
10. opalescent
iris.. 4. flag 6. flower 7. rainbow
iris (pert to)...
astronomy.. 8. asteroid (7th)
color.. 11. reddish–blue
eye part.. 4. uvea 5. irian
Florentine.. 5. orris (orrice)
inflammation.. 6. iritis
mineral.. 7. quartz (iridescent)
Iris, goddess... 7. rainbow
Irish (pert to)...
alphabet (early).. 4. ogam (ogham)
battle cry.. 3. abu (aboo) 9. To
Victory 11. Erin go brath
cattle.. 5. Kerry
churchman.. 7. erenach (herenach)
club, cudgel.. 10. shillalagh (shillalah)
convention (anc).. 4. Feis 10. Feis of
Tara
cordial.. 10. usquebaugh
dagger (anc).. 5. skean
dance.. 3. jig 4. rink 10. rinkafadda
emblem.. 8. shamrock
exclamation.. 3. aru 5. arrah
fairy, spirit.. 4. shee (sidhe)
7. banshee (banshie) 10. leprechaun
festival.. 4. feis
goblin.. 5. pooka
god.. 3. Ler (sea)
goddess.. 4. Dana
king's home.. 4. Tara
landholding.. 7. rundale
legislature.. 10. Oireachtas (House)
11. Dail Eireann (Chamber)
13. Seanad Eireann (Senate)
liquor house (illegal).. 7. shebeen
love, sweetheart.. 3. gra
moss.. 9. carrageen
peasant.. 4. kern (lerne)
pig.. 5. bonav
policeman.. 8. spalpeen
potato city.. 7. Youghal
queen (folklore).. 4. Medb
Society (secret).. 6. Fenian
soldier.. 4. kern (kerne) 10. galloglass
tenant.. 4. saer
tribal lord.. 6. tanist
verse.. 4. rann

whisky, whiskey (illegal).. 6. poteen
(potheen)
Irish (people)...
ancestor (fabled).. 3. Mil 6. Miledh
author.. 4. Shaw 5. Wilde
chemist.. 5. Boyle
composer.. 7. Herbert
Irishman.. 4. Aire, Celt, Gael
6. Teague 8. Milesian 9. Hibernian,
Orangeman 10. Eireannach
lawyer.. 6. brehon
Nuns (Order).. 15. Ladies of Loretto
patriot.. 5. Emmet, Tandy 6. Oakboy
poet.. 5. Colum, Moore, Wilde, Yeats
7. Russell (George)
refugee.. 7. fuidhir
saint (patron).. 7. Patrick
Saxon.. 8. Sasanach
sea robbers (Myth).. 9. Fomorians
surgeon.. 6. Colles
tribe (family).. 4. sept 5. cinel
irk... 3. vex 4. bore, tire 5. annoy,
weary 6. nettle 7. disgust, trouble
10. exasperate
irksome... 5. vexed, weary 7. operose,
painful, tedious 8. annoying
9. fatiguing, vexatious, wearisome
10. burdensome, exhausting,
monotonous 12. disagreeable
iron... 2. Fe (symbol) 5. harsh, metal,
power, press 6. ferrum, fetter,
mangle, pistol, severe 7. firearm,
manacle, shackle, sideros
8. firmness, handcuff, hardness,
strength 10. inflexible, unyielding
11. unrelenting
iron (pert to)...
casting.. 5. mitis
comb form.. 5. ferro 6. sidero
compound.. 5. steel
containing.. 6. ferric
dog.. 7. firedog
dross.. 6. sinter
herb.. 8. Vernonia 9. ironweeds
lump.. 3. pig
magnet.. 8. armature
meteoric.. 8. siderite
ore.. 7. turgite 8. hematite, siderite
11. sesquioxide
ref to.. 6. ferric 7. ferrous
8. siderous
rod.. 5. punty (puntee)
salts of.. 10. chalybeate
sand.. 7. iserine
science of.. 10. siderology
symbol.. 2. Fe
tailor's.. 5. goose
tool.. 6. lifter
vessel, basket.. 7. cresset
ironclad... 6. severe 7. armored,
Monitor (ship) 8. exacting, rigorous
9. stringent
ironic, ironical... 3. dry 7. cynical,
satiric 9. sarcastic 10. figurative
11. Rabelaisian
irons... 5. gyves 6. chains 7. fetters
8. manacles, shackles 9. handcuffs
Ironsides... 7. cavalry (Cromwell's)
8. Cromwell
ironwood... 4. acle 5. olive 6. colima
7. breakax 8. hornbeam
9. stavewood

irony... 6. banter, satire 7. lampoon, sarcasm 8. ridicule

Iroquoian Indian... 4. Erie 5. Huron 6. Cayuga, Mohawk, Oneida, Seneca 7. Wyandot 8. Cherokee, Onondaga 9. Conestoga, Tuscarora

Iroquois (pert to)...
famed.. 11. Five Nations
native of.. 7. New York 9. Wisconsin
tribes (Five).. 6. Cayuga, Mohawk, Oneida, Seneca 8. Onondaga

irrational... 6. stupid 9. fanatical, illogical, senseless 10. ridiculous 11. impractical 12. preposterous, unreasonable 13. unintelligent

irregular... 4. wild 5. erose, rough 6. fitful, rugged, uneven 7. atactic, crooked, devious, erratic, mutable, styptic, unequal 8. aberrent, abnormal, atypical, informal, variable 9. anomalous, desultory, distorted, eccentric, haphazard, orderless, unsettled 10. changeable, immoderate, inconstant 11. intemperate 12. unsystematic

irregularity... 6. ataxia (muscular) 7. anomaly 8. disorder 9. deviation 10. distortion 11. abnormality, informality 12. eccentricity

irrelevant... 7. foreign 9. unrelated 10. extraneous 11. impertinent, unessential 12. inconsequent 13. insignificant

irreligious... 5. pagan 7. godless, impious, profane 11. unreligious

irreparable... 4. gone, lost 5. ruined 11. irrevocable 12. incorrigible, irremediable 13. irrecoverable, irretrievable

irrepressible... 7. Homeric (laughter) 12. ungovernable, unrestrained

irrepressible conflict... 8. civil war

irreproachable... 7. perfect 9. blameless 10. impeccable, inculpable

irresolute... 6. fickle, unsure 8. doubtful, unstable 9. uncertain, undecided 10. capricious, changeable, inconstant 12. undetermined

irresolution... 10. fickleness, indecision 11. fluctuation, uncertainty, vacillation 14. capriciousness

irresponsible... 6. fickle 7. lawless 8. carefree 9. insolvent 12. independable 13. unaccountable, untrustworthy

irretrievable... 8. hopeless 9. incurable 11. irreparable 12. irremediable, unchangeable 13. irrecoverable

irreverence... 7. impiety 8. dishonor 9. profanity 10. disrespect

irrevocable... 3. end 4. past 5. final 10. inevitable, past recall 11. unalterable 9. beyond recall, unchangeable

irrigate... 3. wet 5. water 6. dilute, sluice 7. moisten, refresh

irritable... 4. edgy 5. cross, techy, testy 6. cranky, ornery, touchy 7. fretful, iracund, peevish, tempery,

twitchy 8. snappish

irritate... 3. irk, nag, vex 4. fret, gall, rasp, rile 5. anger, annoy, chafe, cross, grate, peeve, pique, rouse, sting, tease 6. excite, incite, madden, needle, nettle, rankle 7. incense, provoke 10. exacerbate, exasperate 14. rub the wrong way

irritated... 4. sore 5. afret, testy 6. peeved 7. annoyed, nettled, rankled 8. provoked

irritation... 4. itch 5. pique 6. temper 9. annoyance 10. resentment 12. exasperation

irruption... 5. foray 6. inroad 8. invasion 9. incursion

Irving pseudonym... 13. Knickerbocker (Diedrich)

is... 6. exists 10. represents 11. personifies

Isaac (pert to)...
Bib.. 9. patriarch (Heb)
father of.. 4. Esau 5. Jacob
grandfather of.. 4. Edom
husband of.. 7. Rebekah
son of.. 5. Sarah 7. Abraham

Ishmael (pert to)...
ancestor.. 11. Ishmaelites
Bib.. 6. pariah 7. outcast
father of.. 8. Nebaioth
son of.. 5. Hagar 7. Abraham

isinglass... 4. huso, mica 7. gelatin 8. agar–agar

Isis (pert to)...
daughter of.. 3. Geb, Nut
goddess of.. 9. fertility 10. motherhood
identified with.. 7. Dog Star
mother of.. 4. Sept (Horus)
represented (at times).. 9. cow–headed
shrine of.. 5. Iseum (Iseium)
wife of.. 6. Osiris

Islam, religion (pert to)...
founder.. 7. Mahomet
God.. 5. Allah
people.. 7. Moslems
prophet.. 8. Mohammed

Islamic (pert to)...
convert.. 5. ansar
holy city.. 5. Mecca 6. Medina
mosque.. 6. masjid
pilgrimage.. 5. Kaaba (Caaba) 10. Supreme Stone
Supreme Being.. 5. Allah
teacher.. 4. alim 5. ulema 6. mullah (mulla)

island... 3. ait, cay, ile, key 4. calf, cayo, eyot, holm, isle, reef 5. atoll, islet 7. isolate 8. insulate

island (pert to)...
city.. 8. Montreal
coral.. 5. atoll 8. Zanzibar
enchanted.. 4. Bali
fabled.. 4. Meru 6. Avalon, Bimini 8. Atlantis
fabulous.. 7. Zangbar
group.. 8. Antilles, Marshall 11. archipelago
inhabitant, native.. 7. nesiote 8. islander
universe (Astron).. 6. galaxy

Island of...
 Langerhans.. 8. pancreas
 Odysseus.. 6. Ithaca
 Reil.. 5. brain
 Saints.. 4. Erin
 Seven Cities (imaginary).. 7. Antilia
Isle of Man...
 Celtic name.. 4. Manx
 city.. 4. Peel 6. Ramsey 7. Douglas
 division.. 5. Treen
 judge.. 8. deemster (dempster)
 legislature.. 7. Tynwald
 mountain peak.. 8. Snaefell
 Northern point.. 4. Ayre
 site.. 8. Irish Sea
Isle of Wight...
 Queen's summer home.. 12. Osborne
    House
 site.. 10. English Sea
 sport (famed).. 9. yacht race
 town.. 7. Newport
 watering place.. 4. Ryde
Isles of Galway Bay... 4. Aran
ism... 4. cult 5. dogma, ideal, tenet
    6. belief, school, system 8. doctrine,
    practice 11. abnormality
isochromatic... 9. same color
isochronal... 9. equal time 11. uniform
    time
isocracy... 9. equal rule 10. equal
    power
isodont (Zool)... 10. alike teeth
isogonal... 11. equal angles
isolate... 4. isle 6. enisle 7. seclude
    8. insulate, separate 9. segregate,
    sequester 10. quarantine
isolation... 8. escapism, solitude
    9. seclusion 10. insulation,
    loneliness, separation 11. segregation
isomer... 7. metamer 8. compound
    (Chem)
isonomy... 11. equal rights
isonym... 7. paronym 8. same name
isosceles... 10. equal sides (triangle)
Israel (Bib)... 4. Jews 5. Jacob, Zions
    13. Hebrew Kingdom
Israel (pert to)... see also *Israelite*
 appellation.. 8. Jeshurun
 capital.. 9. Jerusalem
 city.. 5. Haifa, Jaffa 7. Galilee,
    Jericho, Tel Aviv
 desert.. 5. Negev
 dust storm.. 7. khamsin
 lawgiver.. 5. Moses
 Plain of.. 6. Sharon
 priest.. 3. Eli
 river.. 6. Jordan
 sea.. 4. Dead 7. Galilee
 song (Zionist).. 8. Hatikvah
Israelite (pert to)...
 hero.. 6. Gideon
 judge.. 4. Elon 8. Jephthah
 king.. 4. Ahab, Jehu, Saul (1st)
    5. David (2nd) 7. Solomon
 lawgiver.. 5. Moses
 priest.. 3. Eli
 tribe.. 3. Dan 5. Asher 6. Reuben
 tribe, priestly.. 4. Levi
issue... 3. son 4. come, emit, flow,
    gush 5. arise, child, sally, spout,
    stock, topic, utter 6. effect, emerge,
    escape, sortie, source, upshot
    7. edition, emanate, proceed,
    product, progeny 8. question
    9. emergence, offspring, posterity
    11. publication
Istanbul (Constantinople)...
 capital of.. 6. Turkey (to 1923)
 foreign quarter.. 4. Pera
 Greek quarter.. 5. Fanar
 site.. 8. Bosporus 10. Golden Horn
isthmus (pert to)...
 American.. 6. Panama
 anatomy.. 6. fauces
 Greek (anc).. 7. Corinth
 Siam.. 3. Kra
it... 5. charm, thing 6. itself, person
    7. egotist, pronoun
Ita... 4. Acta 7. Negrito
Italian (pert to)... see also *Italy*
 card game.. 5. tarot
 carriage.. 7. vettura
 cathedral.. 5. duomo
 cheese.. 6. Romano 8. Parmesan
 condiment.. 6. tamara (tamarind)
 deity.. 4. faun
 dome, peak.. 4. cima
 dough.. 5. pasta
 entertainment.. 7. ridotto
 festival.. 5. festa
 grape.. 6. verdea
 hamlet.. 5. casal
 house.. 4. casa 6. casino (summer)
 inlay.. 6. tarsia
 inn.. 7. locanda
 innkeeper.. 7. padrone
 lady.. 5. donna 7. signora
 law.. 6. Latium 8. Jus Latii
 lover.. 7. amoroso
 magistrate (anc).. 8. podestra
 marble (statuary).. 4. Neri 7. carrara,
    cipolin
 marsh.. 7. maremma
 opera house.. 7. La Scala (1778)
 pastry.. 7. lasagne, ravioli
 peasant.. 9. contadino
 policeman.. 6. sbirro
 political faction.. 7. Bianchi
    10. Ghibelline
 pottery.. 8. majolica
 secret society.. 6. Maffia (Mafia)
    7. Camorra
 sheep.. 6. merino
 vessel.. 9. trabacolo
 wind (hot).. 7. sirocco
 wine.. 4. Asti 5. Capri 7. Chianti,
    Orvieto 12. Asti Spumante
Italian (people)...
 anti-Fascist.. 6. Sforza
 architect.. 8. Bramante
 astronomer.. 6. Secchi 7. Galileo
 author.. 5. Dante
 deity.. 6. Faunus
 dictator.. 9. Mussolini
 educator.. 10. Montessori
 explorer.. 8. Columbus, Vespucci
    9. Marco Polo
 family (princely).. 4. Este 5. Doria
    6. Medici
 family (violin).. 5. Amati
 friend (outside).. 10. Italophile
 geographer.. 8. Amoretti
 goddess.. 3. Ops 4. Juno 5. Diana
 hero.. 7. Orlando

historian.. 4. Dion 5. Cantu
king.. 7. Umberto
musician.. 5. Guido, Verdi 7. Puccini,
   Rossini 9. Scarlatti
naturalist.. 4. Poli
noblewoman.. 8. Marchesa
   11. Marchioness
painter.. 5. Lippi 6. Giotti 7. da
   Vinci, Raphael 10. Botticelli
   11. Della Robbia 12. Michelangelo
patriot.. 7. Foscolo 9. Garibaldi
people.. 7. Italici 8. Umbrians
   9. Etruscans, Ligurians
philosopher.. 7. Rosmini
physician.. 5. Abano 9. Eustachio
physicist.. 5. Volta 7. Galvani,
   Marconi
poet.. 4. Redi 5. Dante, Tasso
   7. Manzoni 8. Annunzio, Casanova,
   Petrarch 9. Boccaccio
saint.. 4. Neri 7. Aquinas (Thomas)
sculptor.. 5. Dupre, Leoni
   8. Ammanati 12. Michelangelo
singer.. 5. Patti 6. Caruso
statesman.. 5. Rossi 8. Gioberti
   11. Machiavelli
theologian.. 7. Peronne
tribe (anc).. 5. Aequi
Italy...
  Alps.. 5. Cozie 6. Carnac, Julian
   7. Atesine, Letiche, Pennine
   8. Maritime 9. Lepontine
  capital.. 4. Rome
  city.. 4. Lodi, Pisa 5. Anona, Fiume,
   Genoa, Milan, Padua, Pavia, Trent,
   Turin 6. Mantua, Modena, Naples,
   Spezia, Venice, Verona 7. Messina,
   Palermo, Pompeii, Ravenna, Trieste
   8. Brandisi, Florence, Sorrento
  commune.. 6. Rivoli (Hist) 7. Trieste
  country (anc).. 7. Etruria, Lucania,
   Tuscany
  gulf.. 7. Salerno
  historical site.. 10. Blue Grotto
   18. Leaning Tower of Pisa
  island.. 4. Elba 5. Capri, Leros
   6. Eschia, Sicily 8. Sardinia
  lake.. 4. Como 6. Albano, Lugano
   8. Maggiore
  mountain.. 4. Alps, Rosa 5. Blanc
   12. Gran Paradiso
  port (fishing).. 4. Amalfi
  resort.. 4. Lido 5. Capri 6. Agnone
   7. Riviera
  river.. 2. Po 4. Arno 5. Tiber
  sea.. 6. Ionian 8. Apennine

   10. Tyrrhenian
  strait.. 7. Messina, Obranto
  volcano.. 4. Etna 8. Vesuvius
   9. Stromboli
itch... 4. reef, riff 5. mange, psora
   6. desire, eczema 7. scabies, sycosis
   9. cacoethes, hankering, psoriasis,
   sensation 10. irritation
ite... 8. adherent, disciple, follower
item... 3. bit 4. news 5. asset, entry,
   scrap, topic 6. detail 7. article,
   integer 9. commodity
   10. memorandum 11. information
iter... 4. eyre, road (Rom) 7. circuit
iterate... 6. recite, repeat, retell,
   review 7. recount 8. rehearse
iteration... 5. recap 10. repetition
   11. restatement
ithand... 8. constant, diligent
   14. unintermittent
itinerant... 5. mover, nomad 6. roamer
   7. nomadic 8. gadabout 9. traveling,
   unsettled, wandering, wayfaring
itinerary... 4. gest (royal), plan
   5. route 6. prayer, record
   8. register, roadbook 9. directory,
   guidebook
Ivanhoe (pert to)...
  author.. 5. Scott
  character.. 5. Boeuf 6. Cedric,
   Rowena, Ulrica
  hero.. 7. Ivanhoe
ivories (pert to)...
  anatomy.. 5. teeth
  game.. 4. dice
  piano.. 4. keys
ivory (pert to)...
  anatomy.. 5. tooth 7. dentine
  block.. 4. dice 7. tessera
  carving.. 9. toreutics
  color.. 5. white (off)
  Latin.. 4. ebur
  mixture (dust, cement).. 7. eburine
  plum.. 11. wintergreen
  tower.. 7. retreat
ivy... 5. Rheus, sumac 11. Hedera
  helix
iwa... 11. frigate bird
IWW... 6. sab–cat (emblem), wabbly
  (Chin), wobbly
Izaac Walton... 9. fisherman
izar (Hind)... 4. star 7. garment 9. loin
  cloth
izle... 4. root 5. ember, spark
Izmir... 6. Smyrna
izzat... 5. honor 6. credit 8. prestige
   10. reputation

J

J... 3. Jay 6. letter (10th)
ja (Ger)... 3. yes
jaal goat... 4. ibex 5. beden
jab... 3. dig, hit, jag 4. poke, prod, stab 5. punch 6. strike, thrust
jabber... 4. chat 5. prate 6. babble, gabble, jargon 7. chatter, twaddle 8. nonsense 9. gibberish
Jabberwock... 6. Jubjub 7. monster (Through the Looking Glass)
Jabberwocky... 4. poem 6. prolix 8. nonsense 9. rigmarole 10. double talk
jabble... 6. splash 7. dashing 8. rippling 9. agitation, confusion, splashing
jabiru... 5. stork
jack... 3. can, jug, man 4. card, coat, flag, male, pump 5. knave, money 6. lifter, sailor 7. mariner 8. nickname
jackal... 3. dog (wild) 4. dieb, kola, Thos 7. cat's-paw 8. henchman
jackass... 3. ass 4. deer (mule), dolt, fool, hare 6..clover, donkey, rabbit 7. morwong, penguin, witling 9. blockhead
jackdaw... 3. daw, kae 4. crow 7. grackle
jacket... 4. coat, Eton, pelt 5. cover (book) 6. blouse, bolero, casing, jerkin, jumper, reefer 7. garment, Mae West, wrapper 8. penelope
jacket (pert to)...
Arctic.. 6. anorak
armor.. 5. acton
Eskimo.. 6. temiak
knitted.. 6. jersey, sontag 7. sweater 8. cardigan
Levant.. 5. grego
Scottish.. 4. jupe
Spanish.. 8. chaqueta
Jack Ketch... 7. hangman (Eng) 11. executioner (public)
jackknife... 6. barlow 11. toadstabber, toadsticker
jackstones... 4. dibs, game 7. pebbles
Jacob... 6. Israel 9. patriarch
Jacob (pert to)...
brother.. 4. Edom, Esau
daughter.. 5. Dinah
father-in-law.. 5. Laban
parents.. 5. Isaac 7. Rebekah
retreat.. 5. Haran
son.. 3. Gad, San 4. Levi 5. Asher, Judah 6. Reuben (oldest)
wife.. 5. Leah 6. Rachel
Jacobin... 4. Club 5. Friar (Dominican) 7. plotter, radical, Society 8. Democrat (Fr 1789)

Jacob's ladder... 4. herb 8. hyacinth 10. belladonna 11. bittersweet 12. Solomon's seal
jade... 4. bore, tire 5. green, horse, stone, wench 7. fatigue 8. strumpet
jaded... 8. fatigued, shopworn 10. bedraggled
jaeger (jager)... 4. gull (like), skua 6. teaser
jager... 6. hunter 7. diamond 8. huntsman, rifleman
jagged... 5. erose, rough, sharp 6. barbed, pinked, ragged, rugged 7. cutting, notched, pointed, slashed 8. serrated
jagua... 4. palm 7. genipap
jaguar... 3. cat 4. puma 5. ounce 6. cougar 7. panther 11. snow leopard
Jah (Heb)... 3. God 7. Jehovah
jai alai... 4. game 5. cesta 6. pelota 7. fronton
jail... 3. jug 4. brig, gaol 5. clink 6. cooler, lockup 8. hoosegow 9. Bridewell (London), calaboose 11. incarcerate
jailer, jailor... 5. guard 6. gaoler, keeper, warden 7. alcaide, turnkey
jail sentence... 3. rap
jalousie... 5. blind 7. shutter
Jamaica...
beverage.. 3. rum 4. jake
capital.. 8. Kingston
cucumber.. 7. gherkin
ebony.. 10. crocuswood
island.. 10. West Indies
pepper.. 8. allspice
tree (drug).. 7. quassia
jangle... 5. brawl, chide, noise, prate 6. babble, gossip 7. chatter, grate on, quarrel, ringing, whimper
Janizary (anc)... 5. slave 7. soldier
Janus (Rom)... 3. god (two-faced)
Japan... 5. Jipun (Chin), Nihon, Nisei 6. Nippon 7. Cipango (of Marco Polo)
Japan... see also *Japanese*
capital.. 4. Nara (anc) 5. Kyoto (anc), Tokyo
capital, Department.. 5. Kyoto, Osaka, Tokyo
city.. 4. Kobe 5. Osaka 6. Yawata 8. Kumamoto, Nagasaki, Yokohama, Yokosuka 9. Hiroshima
current.. 8. Kuroshio
islands.. 6. Honshu, Kyushu 7. Shikoku 9. Haikkaido (Yezo)
mountain.. 6. Kunlun 8. Fujiyama
naval base.. 8. Yokosuka
port.. 4. Kobe 5. Osaka 6. Nagoya

299

8. Yokohama
protectorate.. 9. Manchukuo
river.. 4. Yalu (Annock)
shrine.. 7. Toshogu (at Nikko)
spring (hot).. 6. Hakone
volcano.. 9. Asamayama
Japanese (pert to)...
airplane.. 4. Zero
annals, chronicles.. 7. Nihongi
apricot.. 3. ume
army (conscription).. 6. geneki
army officer.. 7. samurai
art of self–defense.. 4. judo 7. jujitsu
  (jujutsu, jiujutsu)
badge (family).. 3. mon
banjo.. 7. samisen
battle cry.. 6. banzai
brazier.. 7. hibachi
button (carved).. 7. netsuke
cape.. 4. mino
cedar.. 4. sugi
chess.. 5. shogi
church (Buddhist).. 4. tera
circle, ship (suffix).. 4. maru
deer.. 4. sika
dog.. 6. tanate
drama.. 2. no 6. no–gaku
drink.. 4. sake
entertainer.. 6. geisha
festival.. 3. Bon 15. Feast of Lanterns
fish.. 3. ayu, tai 4. fugu
flower arranging.. 7. ikebano
flower design.. 10. Shin, Soe, Tai
  (Heaven, Man, Earth)
game (forfeits).. 3. ken
gateway.. 5. torii
girdle.. 5. obi
girdle box.. 4. inro
greeting.. 6. banzai
herb (edible).. 3. udo
legislature.. 4. Diet
litter (covered).. 7. norimon
news agency.. 5. domei
newspaper (Tokyo).. 12. Asahi
  Shimbun
outlaw.. 5. ronin
pagoda.. 3. taa
painting school.. 4. Kano
palanquin, litter.. 4. pago 7. norimon
persimmon.. 4. kaki
plant.. 3. udo (edible) 6. sugamo
porgy.. 3. tai (fish)
pottery.. 7. Satsuma
prefecture.. 2. fu
radish.. 4. daikon
religion.. 6. Shinto 8. Buddhism
  9. Shintoism
robe.. 6. kimono
salmon.. 4. masu
screen (partition).. 5. shoji
seaweed.. 4. nori
self–defense, art of.. 4. judo 7. jujitsu
  (jujutsu, jiujutsu)
ship suffix.. 4. maru
shout (greeting).. 6. banzai
shrine.. 7. Toshogu (at Nikko)
silk.. 7. habutai 8. chirimen (crepe)
silkworm.. 4. eria 7. yamamai
sock (separate big toe).. 4. tabi
song.. 4. uta
suicide.. 7. seppuku 8. hara–kiri
  (hari–kari)

tree.. 5. akeki, kiaki 7. camphor,
  hinooki
verse.. 5. hokku, tanka 6. haikai
wrestling.. 4. sumo
Japanese people...
aborigine.. 4. Ainu (Aino)
admiral.. 3. Ito 4. Togo
admirer.. 11. Japanophile
American–born.. 5. Issei, Nisei
army officer.. 7. samurai
baron.. 6. daimio
Buddha, Great.. 8. Daibutsu
caste (nobility).. 7. kwazoku
clan.. 7. Satsuma 8. Fujiwara,
  Minamoto
deity.. 5. Amita (Amida) 8. Amitabba
Emperor.. 8. Hirohito
Emperor, founder.. 5. Jimmu (660
  BC)
Emperor, title.. 5. Tenno 6. Mikado
God of Happiness.. 7. Jurojin
  10. Fuku–roku ju
nobility (caste).. 7. kwazoku
outlaw.. 5. ronin
paradise (of Amita).. 4. Jodo
race.. 4. Ainu
jape.. 4. fool, jeer, jest, jipe, mock
  5. fraud, trick 6. banter, deride
japery.. 4. jest, joke 7. jesting
  8. trickery 10. buffoonery
jar... 3. jolt 5. grate, shake 6. incase,
  rattle 7. startle, vibrate 8. preserve
  9. vibration
jar... 3. jug, urn 4. ewer, lute
  (rubber), olla 5. cadus (anc), crock,
  cruse 6. dolium, goglet, hydria
  7. amphora, terrine 10. jardiniere
jararaca... 7. serpent 10. fer–de–lance
  11. jararacussu
jardiniere... 3. jar, jug, urn 4. vase
  5. stand (plant) 9. flowerpot
jargon... 4. cant 5. argot, idiom, lingo,
  slang 6. drivel, patois, patter, zircon
  7. Chinook, Yiddish 8. nonsense
  9. gibberish 10. vocabulary (secret)
jasmine, jasmin... 4. bela 5. color,
  papaw 7. jessamy 9. jessamine
Jason (pert to)...
friend, sweetheart.. 5. Medea
heroes.. 9. Argonauts
quest.. 12. Golden Fleece
ship.. 4. Argo
son.. 4. Aeson
uncle.. 6. Pelias
jaundice... 7. disease, icterus
  8. jealousy 9. prejudice
  10. yellowness
jaunt... 4. ride, trip 6. ramble
  7. journey 9. excursion
jaunty... 4. airy 5. perky, showy, smart
  6. dapper, rakish 7. finical, stylish
  12. lighthearted
Java... see also *Javanese*
city.. 7. Batavia, Jakarta (Djakarta)
  8. Samarang, Surabaya 9. Surakarta
island group.. 10. East Indies
Java Man (anc).. 15. Pithecanthropus
  (erectus)
location.. 7. equator 16. Malay
  Archipelago
Javanese (pert to)...
arrow poison.. 4. upas

badger.. 5. ratel 6. teledu
carriage.. 4. sado (sadoo)
cotton.. 5. kapok
dancers.. 6. bedoyo
dog (wild).. 5. adjag
ox (wild).. 7. banteng
pantomime.. 6. topeng
plum.. 5. jambo (jambul) 6. lomboy
puppet show.. 6. wajang (wayang)
rice field.. 5. sawah
squirrel.. 8. jelerang
temple.. 6. chandi (candi)
tree.. 4. upas 5. ligas 7. gondang
javelin... 3. bat 4. dart, pike 5. lance,
　spear 6. jereed (jirid) 7. assagai
　(assegai)
javelina... 4. boar 5. peccary
jaw... 3. maw 4. chop 5. scold
　6. berate, splash 7. chatter, orifice
　8. scolding
jaw (pert to)...
angle of.. 6. gonion
bone.. 7. maxilla 8. mandible
comb form.. 6. gnatho
disease.. 7. lump jaw
　13. actinomycosis
formation.. 8. gnathism
Greek for.. 7. gnathos
muscle.. 8. masseter
ref to.. 5. malar 7. gnathic
without.. 8. agnathic
jawab... 5. reply 6. answer, mosque
　(false Arch)
jay... 3. gae 4. bird, blue, dupe
　9. chatterer
jayhawker... 6. Kansan, spider
　7. soldier 8. guerilla
Jayhawker State... 6. Kansas
jazz... 4. jive 5. dance, music, swing
　9. syncopate 11. syncopation
jealous... 7. envious, zealous
　8. doubtful, grudging, vigilant,
　watchful 9. jaundiced 10. solicitous
　11. distrustful 12. apprehensive
jealousy... 4. envy 5. doubt 7. rivalry
　8. distrust, jaundice, mistrust
　12. covetousness
jeans... 7. overalls, trousers
jeer... 4. gibe, hoot, jape, taunt 6. deride
　5. flout, scoff, sneer, taunt 6. deride
　8. ridicule
Jehovah... 3. God, Jah 4. Lord
　6. Yahweh (Yahwe) 8. Almighty (The)
　12. Supreme Being
Jehovah's comfort... 8. Nehemiah
jehu (humorous)... 8. coachman
　10. fast driver
Jehu's father (Bib)... 11. Jehoshaphat
jejune... 3. dry 4. arid 5. banal,
　empty, stale, trite 6. barren, hungry,
　meager 7. insipid 8. foodless
　12. unproductive
jelly... 3. jam, rob (rhob) 4. food,
　sapa 5. aspic 6. pectin 7. gelatin
　8. gelatine, Kei Apple 10. semiliquid
jellyfish... 5. quarl 6. coward, medusa
　7. acaleph 8. weakling 9. Acalephae
jellyfish (pert to)...
class.. 9. Acalephae
group.. 10. discophora
part.. 8. pileus 8. umbrella
　10. exumbrella

stinging.. 9. sea nettle
swim organ.. 5. stene
jemmy... 4. boot (riding) 5. jimmy,
　lever 7. crowbar 9. greatcoat
Jena (Ger).. 5. glass 6. battle (1806)
jenna... 8. Paradise (Moham)
jennet... 3. ass 5. horse 6. donkey
jenny... 3. ass 5. crane (moving)
　6. female 8. airplane 13. spinning
　wheel
jenny (pert to)...
billiards.. 6. hazard
folklore.. 4. wren
howlet.. 3. owl 5. owlet
machine.. 13. spinning wheel
spinner.. 3. fly (angling)
jeopardize... 4. risk 6. expose, hazard
　7. imperil 8. endanger
jeopardy... 4. risk 5. peril 6. hazard,
　menace
jeremiad... 3. woe 6. lament, plaint,
　tirade 9. complaint
jerk... 3. tic 4. flip, jolt, push, yank
　5. shake, tweak 6. chorea, thrust,
　twitch 7. charqui
jerkin... 4. coat 6. jacket, salmon
　9. gyrfalcon, waistcoat
jeroboam... 4. bowl 6. battle, goblet
Jeroboam... 4. King (of Israel)
jerry... 5. aware 6. flimsy, Geremy,
　German 7. knowing 9. beer house,
　conscious
jersey... 5. cloth 6. cattle, jacket
Jersey Red... 5. swine
　11. Duroc–Jersey
Jersey tea... 11. wintergreen
　12. checkerberry
Jerusalem... 5. Ariel, Salem 8. Holy
　City 11. City of David
Jerusalem (pert to)...
artichoke.. 7. girasol 10. topinambou
capital of.. 6. Israel
corn.. 5. durra
Garden.. 10. Gethsemane
haddock.. 4. opah
hill.. 6. Olivet 13. Mount of Olives
historic site.. 11. Wailing Wall
　12. Mosque of Omar 13. Mount of
　Olives (Olivet) 18. Garden of
　Gethsemane
mosque.. 4. Omar
pool.. 6. Siloam 8. Bethesda
region.. 5. Perea 6. Gilead
Relig.. 7. Judaism 12. Christianity
　13. Mohammedanism
spring.. 5. Gihon 6. Siloam
star.. 7. salsify
Sunday.. 11. Refreshment
thorn.. 7. catechu 12. Christ's-thorn
willow.. 8. oleaster
jess... 5. strap (hawk's leg) 6. ribbon
jessamy... 3. fop 5. dandy 7. jasmine
jessant (Her)... 7. issuing 9. lying over
jessur... 5. viper (Russell's)
jest... 3. fun, mot, wit 4. fool, jape,
　jeer, joke, quip 5. droll, prank, sport,
　taunt, trick 6. banter, rail at, trifle
　8. ridicule
jester... 4. fool, mime 5. clown
　7. buffoon, goliard 8. humorist
　11. merry–andrew
jester's cap... 7. coxcomb

Jesuit... 5. Order 7. casuist, sectary
8. explorer 9. intriguer
10. missionary 14. Society of Jesus
(S J)
jet... 3. jut 4. gush, spew 5. black,
ebony, ladle, raven, spout, spray,
spurt 6. burner, nozzle, stream
7. mineral, outpour 8. spouting
9. black onyx
jet coal... 6. cannel
jetty... 4. mole, pier 5. wharf
8. buttress
Jew... 6. Essene, Hebrew, Semite
9. Israelite
jewel... 3. gem 4. naif, opal, ruby
5. beryl, stone 6. garnet 7. bearing,
diamond, emerald 8. ornament
9. bespangle, brilliant 10. rhinestone
13. precious stone, precious thing
jewel cutter... 10. lapidarist
jeweler's glass... 5. loupe
jeweler's weight... 4. tola 5. carat
(karat, kerat)
jewelry... 3. ice 4. ring 5. paste
6. parure, strass 7. costume
10. bijouterie
Jewish... 6. Hebrew 7. Yiddish
9. Israelite
Jewish (pert to)...
academy (Talmudic).. 8. Yeshinah
adherent.. 7. Zionist
benediction.. 5. Shema
Bible.. 5. Torah (Tora) 6. Gemara,
Talmud 7. Haggada, Halakah
10. Pentateuch
calendar.. 4. Adar, Ahab, Elul, Iyar
5. Nisan, Sivan, Tebet 6. Kislev,
Shebat, Tammuz, Tishri, Veadar (leap
year) 7. Heshvan
Day of Atonement.. 9. Yom Kippur
Dispersion.. 8. Diaspora
divorce.. 3. get (gett)
doctrine.. 7. Mishnah (Mishna)
enemy (Bib).. 5. Haman
faction.. 7. Zealots
father, patriarch.. 7. Abraham
festival.. 5. Purim, Seder (Sedar)
7. Sukkoth
greeting, peace.. 6. Shalom
high priest.. 3. Eli 4. Ezra 5. Aaron,
Annas 8. Caiaphas
high priest costume.. 4. urim
5. abnet 7. petalon, tallith, yamilke
historian.. 8. Josephus
holiday.. 7. Sukkoth 8. Hanukkah
(Hannukka), Tishabov 11. Rosh
Hashana (Rosh Hashonoh)
horn.. 7. shophar (shofar)
lawgiver.. 5. Moses
leader.. 8. Nehemiah
liturgy.. 6. minhah (PM) 9. shaharith
(AM)
loaves (unleavened).. 9. shewbread
(showbread)
mystical writing.. 6. atbash
patriots.. 9. Maccabees
prayer book.. 6. siddur
prophet.. 6. Elijah
psalms of praise.. 6. hallel
quarter (living).. 6. ghetto
ram's horn.. 7. shophar (shofar)
slaughter (Relig).. 8. shehitah

song (Zionist anthem).. 8. Hatikvah
(Hattikvah)
jew's harp... 8. guimbard
9. crembalum
Jezebel (pert to)...
epithet.. 5. vixen 6. virago
8. strumpet
father.. 7. Ethbaal
husband.. 4. Ahab (King)
murdered (caused to be).. 6. Naboth
jib... 3. gib, jaw 4. balk, boom, sail,
spar, tack 5. crane, shift 6. fleece
8. underlip
jibe... 3. fit 4. gibe 5. agree, shift
9. harmonize
jiff, jiffy... 5. trice 6. moment
7. instant, quickly 9. instantly,
twinkling
jig... 4. jerk, jolt 5. dance 6. ballad,
twitch 8. fishhook
jigger... 4. club, dram
jiggle... 5. sauce, shake
jimmy... 3. pry 5. handy, smart
6. spruce 7. coal car, crowbar, pry
open 10. sheep's head
jimson weed... 6. dature
10. stramonium, thorn apple
11. apple of Peru
jingle... 4. poem, rime 5. clink, rhyme
6. tinkle 13. two-wheeled car
jinn, jinnee... 5. demon, Eblis, genie
6. afreet 8. jenniyeh
jinx... 3. hex 5. Jonah 6. hoodoo,
whammy
jitters... 6. nerves 7. dithers, fidgets
8. trembles
jittery... 4. edgy 5. jumpy 7. nervous
jivatma (Hind)... 4. soul 9. life force
10. life energy 11. human spirit
Joan of Arc's appellation...
7. pucelle 13. Maid of Orleans
job... 3. act 4. hire, task 5. chare,
chore, stint 6. position, sinecure
Job (pert to)...
Book.. 9. patriarch 12. Old Testament
friend.. 6. Zophar
home.. 2. Uz
literally.. 9. afflicted 10. persecuted
jockey... 3. pad 5. cheat, racer, rider
6. outwit 7. cushion 8. cavalier,
horseman, minstrel, vagabond 9. Earl
Sande (famed)
jocose... 3. dry 5. droll, lepid, merry
7. jocular 8. humorous 9. facetious
jocular... 3. gay 4. airy, loco 5. droll,
funny, merry, witty 6. elated, jocund,
lively, ribald 7. comical, festive,
gleeful, jesting, playful, waggish
8. animated, mirthful 9. convivial,
facetious, hilarious, laughable,
vivacious 10. frolicsome
jocund... 3. gay 4. airy 5. merry
6. lively 7. jocular 8. cheerful,
sportive
jog... 4. gait, jolt, lope, plod, push,
trot, walk 6. canter, notify, remind,
trudge 8. slow pace 9. suggest to
John... 3. Ian 4. Ivan, Jack, Juan
8. Chinaman, Johannes 9. policeman
John (pert to)...
Bull.. 10. Englishman
Company.. 9. East India

Crow.. 7. buzzard (turkey)
Doe (law).. 7. a nobody 9. false
name
Hancock.. 9. autograph, signature
Q Public.. 6. people 8. populace
johnnycake... 4. pone 7. hoecake
9. corn bread
join... 3. add, mix, pin, tie, wed
4. ally, fuse, link, lock, meet, pair,
seam, team, weld, yoke 5. annex,
blend, enter, graft, group, hitch,
marry, merge, unite 6. adjoin, attach,
cement, concur, couple, engage,
enlist, fasten, mingle, solder, splice,
suture, syzygy 7. combine, conjoin,
connect 8. assemble, coalesce,
compound 9. associate
11. incorporate
joint... 3. ell, hip 4. knee, node, seam
5. alula, elbow, hinge, tenon, wrist
6. rabbet, resort 7. hangout, pastern
12. articulation
joint (pert to)...
cavity.. 5. bursa
firs.. 7. ephedra
fluid.. 7. synovia 8. synovial
grass stem.. 4. culm
pert to.. 5. nodal 9. articular
put out of.. 6. lucate 9. dislocate
without.. 10. acondylous
joke... 3. fun, gag, pun 4. fool, hoax,
jape, jest, quip 5. prank, rally, sport
6. banter, humbug 7. bromide
8. chestnut
joker... 3. dor, wag, wit 4. card
7. buffoon, farceur 8. humorist
9. mistigris
jollity... 4. jest 5. mirth 6. gaiety
8. hilarity 9. enjoyment, festivity,
joviality, merriment 12. conviviality
jolly... 6. banter, jovial, joyful, mellow
7. flatter, jocular 9. make merry
Jolly Roger... 5. Roger 10. pirate flag
jolt... 3. jar, jig, jut 4. blow, butt
5. shake, shock 6. jostle, jounce
7. startle 8. jail term (thieves')
Jonah (pert to)...
Bib.. 7. prophet (Heb)
Book.. 12. Old Testament
slang.. 4. jinx
swallowed by.. 5. whale
Jordan...
capital.. 5. Amman
city.. 7. Jericho, Samaria
9. Bethlehem
historic trove.. 14. Dead Sea Scrolls
people (anc).. 7. Essenes
region.. 5. Perea 6. Basham
river.. 6. Jordan
Jorth (pert to)...
goddess.. 5. Earth
husband.. 4. Odin
named also.. 6. Forgyn
son.. 4. Thor
Joseph (pert to)...
Bib.. 9. patriarch
buyer of.. 8. Potiphar
called also.. 17. Joseph of Arimathea
coat of.. 10. many colors
councilor of.. 10. Arimathaea
father.. 5. Jacob
mother.. 6. Rachel

son.. 5. Jesus 7. Ephraim
wife.. 4. Mary
josh... 3. guy, kid 5. chaff, spoof,
tease 6. banter
Joshi (Ind)... 10. astrologer,
astronomer
Joshua (pert to)...
associate.. 5. Caleb
Book.. 12. Old Testament
burial place.. 5. Gaash
successor to.. 5. Moses
tree.. 5. yucca
jostle... 4. jolt, push, rush 5. crowd,
elbow, joust, shake, shove 6. hustle,
thrust
jot... 3. ace, bit 4. atom, iota, item,
mite, whit 5. minim, point 6. tittle
8. particle
jouk... 4. dart, duck, fawn, hide
5. cheat, dodge, evade, perch, roost,
skulk 6. cringe 9. obeisance
Joule, James P... 9. physicist
journal... 3. log 5. diary, paper
6. record 7. daybook, diurnal,
logbook, support 8. magazine,
register 9. chronicle 10. periodical
11. account book
journalist... 6. editor, legman
7. newsman 8. reporter
9. columnist, gazetteer
11. interviewer 13. correspondent
journey... 3. run 4. fare, iter, ride,
tour, trek, trip, wend 5. jaunt
6. travel, voyage 7. odyssey
8. traverse 9. excursion
10. expedition, pilgrimage
13. peregrination
journey (pert to)... 4. eyre (circuit)
6. viatic 8. anabasis (upward)
9. itineracy, itinerary, traveling
10. travelling
joust... 4. bout, spar, tilt 6. combat
10. tournament
Jove... 7. Jupiter
jovial... 5. jolly, merry 6. elated,
joyous 7. festive, jocular 8. Jovelike
9. convivial, hilarious
14. mirth-inspiring
jowl... 3. jaw 4. chop 5. cheek
6. dewlap, wattle 7. jawbone
joy... 4. glee 5. bliss, exult, gelid
6. gaiety 7. delight, ecstasy, rapture,
rejoice 8. felicity, gladness, hilarity,
pleasure 9. beatitude, happiness,
merriment, transport 10. exultation
joyous... 3. gay 4. glad 5. happy,
merry 6. blithe, elated, festal, joyful
7. festive, jocular 8. cheerful,
mirthful
joy powder... 8. morphine
jubilant... 6. elated 8. exultant,
exulting 9. overjoyed, rejoicing
10. triumphant
Judah (pert to)...
ancestry.. 12. tribe of Judah
brother.. 4. Levi 6. Reuben, Simeon
father.. 5. Jacob
kingdom.. 9. Palestine
son.. 2. Er 6. Shelah
translation (Heb).. 10. celebrated
Judas (pert to)...
Bible.. 7. apostle, traitor 8. betrayer,

deceiver, disciple
called.. 8. Iscariot
historic.. 13. Paschal candle
kiss.. 8. betrayal 11. double–cross,
   treacherous
priest.. 4. oath
suicide site.. 8. Aceldama
Judea (pert to)...
governor.. 6. Pilate
king.. 3. Asa 5. Herod 7. Jehoram
   11. Jehoshaphat
location.. 5. Berea
people.. 4. Jews
province of.. 9. Palestine
judge.. 3. try 4. deem, rate 5. opine,
   think 6. critic, puisne 7. arbiter,
   referee, suppose 8. deemster,
   estimate, mediator, sentence
   9. arbitrate, criticize 10. adjudicate,
   magistrate 11. connoisseur
judge (pert to)...
bench.. 4. banc (bancus)
chamber.. 6. camera
circuit.. 4. iter
gavel.. 4. mace
group.. 5. bench 9. judiciary
of the dead.. 6. Osiris
opinion.. 12. obiter dictum
sittings.. 7. assizes
summary.. 6. postea
judgment.. 4. doom 5. arrêt, award,
   sense, taste 7. censure, opinion
   8. decision, judicium, sentence
   9. criticism 10. conclusion,
   discretion, persuasion (Relig),
   punishment 11. arbitration, sensibility
judgment (pert to)...
creditor.. 13. quasi contract
day.. 7. last day 8. Dies Irae,
   doomsday
left to one's.. 13. discretionary
note.. 10. promissory
seat.. 3. bar 5. mercy 8. tribunal,
   woolsack
judicial.. 5. legal 8. critical
   9. judicious 10. judicatory
judicial (pert to)...
council.. 5. cabal, junta, junto
   7. coterie
hearing.. 5. trial
order.. 4. writ 6. elegit, venire
   7. precept
security.. 7. custody
judicious.. 4. wise 7. politic, prudent
   8. cautious, discreet 9. sagacious
   10. discerning 11. circumspect,
   well–advised
jug.. 4. ewer, jail, olpe, toby
   5. askos, buire, cruse, gotch
   6. flagon, gomlah, lockup, prison,
   tinaja, urceus 7. pitcher
   13. Schnabelkanne
Juggernaut.. 6. Vishnu (Hind)
juggler.. 5. cheat, trick 7. buffoon
   8. deceiver 13. sleight of hand
   14. legerdemainist
Jugoslavia, Yugoslavia...
area.. 6. Kosovo 8. Dalmatia
brandy.. 5. rakia 9. slivovitz
capital.. 8. Belgrade
language.. 7. Slovene
   10. Macedonian, Serbo–Croat

leader.. 4. Tito
monarch.. 5. Peter
money.. 5. dinar
organization.. 9. Comitadji
people.. 4. Cerb 5. Croat 7. Slovene
juice.. 3. rob, sap 4. milk (plant),
   must, stum 5. fluid, latex, syrup
   (sirup) 7. essence, hebenon, moisten
   10. succulence 11. electricity
jujitsu, jiujitsu.. 11. self–defense
juju... 5. charm, magic 6. amulet,
   belief, fetish, voodoo
jujube.. 3. ber 5. fruit, jelly
   7. lozenge 8. Zizyphus
Jules Verne's captain... 4. Nemo (the
   Nautilus)
Julian Emperors (first Five).. 4. Nero
   8. Augustus, Caligula, Claudius,
   Tiberius
jumble... 2. pi 3. mix 4. cake, hash,
   heap, mess, raff, stir 5. blend,
   botch, chaos, shake 6. medley,
   muddle 7. agitate, confuse, mixture
   8. disorder, riffraff
jumble type... 3. pie (pi)
jump... 3. hop, lep 4. leap, move
   (checkers) 5. bound, caper, halma,
   salto, scold, start, vault 6. chorea,
   escape, hurdle, spring, twitch
   7. saltary, saltate 8. increase
   9. advantage 10. transition
jumping (pert to)...
adjective.. 7. saltant
Frog, tale by.. 9. Mark Twain
music.. 7. saltato
rodent.. 5. mouse 6. jerboa
   11. kangaroo rat
stick.. 4. pogo, pole
junction... 4. axil, seam 5. union
   6. suture 7. joining, meeting
   11. combination, concurrence
juncture... 4. pass 5. joint, pinch
   6. crisis, strait 8. exigency, quandary
   9. emergency 10. connection
   11. conjuncture, predicament
   12. articulation
June bug... 3. dor 6. beetle, May bug
   8. figeater
jungle... 4. camp 7. thicket
   8. woodland 11. dense growth
   12. complication
jungle (pert to)...
dweller.. 5. beast 6. savage
fever.. 7. malaria
grass.. 3. poa
ox.. 4. gaur 5. gayal 7. timarau
sheep.. 7. muntjac
junior... 5. cadet, petty 6. puisne
   recent 7. student, younger 8. inferior
   9. unskilled
juniper... 4. cade, puny 5. cedar,
   gorse, retem (raetem), savin
junket... 4. dish (milk), food, meal
   5. feast 7. banquet 8. festival
   9. excursion, sweetmeat
Juno (pert to)...
consort.. 7. Jupiter
goddess (Rom).. 3. sky 5. light
identified with.. 4. Hera
messenger.. 4. Iris
junta, junto... 5. cabal 6. circle,
   clique 7. coterie, council, faction

8. intrigue 11. combination
jupe... 4. coat 5. jupon, shirt, skirt,
　　tunic 6. bodice, jacket
Jupiter (pert to)...
　angel.. 7. Zadkiel
　astronomy.. 6. planet (largest)
　daughter.. 4. Bura
　deity.. 4. Jove 9. Father Sky
　festival.. 14. Vinalis sustica
　god of.. 7. Heavens
　heraldry.. 5. azure
　lover.. 2. Io
　son.. 6. Castor, Pollux
　triad.. 7. Juno 7. Minerva
　wife.. 4. Juno
Jupiter, god of...
　law.. 6. Fidius 10. Dius Fidius
　lightning.. 6. Fulgur
　rain.. 7. Pluvius
　thunder.. 6. Tonans
jurat... 3. juror 8. recorder
　　10. magistrate (Channel Isls)
jure... 3. jus (ius), law 5. right
　　13. jurisprudence
jurisprudence... 3. law, soc 4. soke
　　5. power (legal) 6. charge, sphere
　　7. control, custody, emirate
　　8. authority, consulate
　　10. government, judicature, patriarchy
juror... 5. dicast 7. assizer, juryman
　　9. venireman
jury... 5. panel, tales (additions)
　　6. venire
jus... 3. law 5. gravy, juice 10. legal
　　power, legal right
just... 4. fair, tilt 5. equal, exact, valid
　　7. logical, upright 8. provided,
　　unbiased 9. equitable, righteous
　　10. legitimate

just begun... 8. inchoate
justice... 4. doom 5. right 6. equity,
　　virtue 8. fairness, fair play, justness
　　9. rectitude 10. judicature 11. give
　　and take 12. rightfulness
justice of the peace... 6. squire
　　10. magistrate
justification... 7. apology, defense
　　11. vindication
justify... 5. clear 6. defend, excuse
　　7. absolve, support, warrant
　　8. maintain, sanction, underpin
　　9. authorize, exculpate, vindicate
　　12. substantiate
justly... 5. truly 6. fairly 7. equally
　　8. honestly 9. equitably
　　10. deservedly
justness... 7. fitness, justice
　　8. accuracy, validity 9. exactness
　　11. correctness
Justus... 4. just
jute... 5. fiber, gunny 6. burlap
　　7. sacking
Jute... 4. Dane 9. Jutlander
jutty... 4. mole, pier 5. jetty
　　7. project 8. buttress, protrude
juvenile... 5. actor, young, youth
　　8. immature, youthful 9. youngling,
　　youthlike 11. undeveloped
juvia... 9. Brazil nut
juxta... 4. near 6. nearby
juxtaposition... 5. touch 7. contact
　　8. nearness 9. proximity
　　10. contiguity, side by side
jynx... 5. charm, spell 7. wryneck
　　10. woodpecker
Jynx... 11. woodpeckers
J'y suis, j'y reste... 18. I am here
　　here I remain

K

K... 5. kappa (Gr) 6. letter (11th)
Ka... 3. God (Hind)
Kaaba, Caaba (pert to)...
　content.. 10. Black Stone (of Mecca)
　location.. 11. Great Mosque (Mecca)
　pilgrimage.. 7. Islamic
　praying direction.. 6. Kiblah
　shape.. 7. cubical
kaama... 10. hartebeest
Kaddish... 8. Doxology
Kadiak, Kodiak, bear... 5. brown
　　7. Alaskan
Kaffir (pert to)...
　club weapon.. 10. knobkerrie
　country.. 11. South Africa
　creed.. 11. unbeliever
　　13. non–Mohammedan
　race.. 5. Bantu
　servant.. 6. umfaan
　tribes (world's tallest).. 4. Xosa, Zulu
　　5. Pondo, Temby

　warriors.. 4. impi
　weapon.. 4. keri 10. knobkerrie
Kaiser brown... 6. ginger
Kaiser's residence... 5. Doorn
kaka... 6. parrot
kakapo... 6. parrot 9. owl parrot
kakar... 7. muntjac
kakariki... 6. lizard
kaki... 5. stilt (bird) 9. persimmon
kakkak... 5. heron 7. bittern
kakke... 8. beriberi
kala... 6. bulbul (bird)
kale... 4. cole 5. money 7. cabbage,
　　collard 8. colewort, corecole
kaleidoscopic... 7. varying
　　10. changeable, variegated
Kali (pert to)...
　Hindu.. 10. evil genius
　Persian.. 6. carpet
　Vedic Myth.. 12. tongue of Agni
　　(fire–god)

kallah... 5. bride (Jew)
kamavachara... 6. heaven (Buddh)
Kamchatka...
  capital.. 13. Petropavlovsk
  peninsula.. 7. Siberia
  people.. 7. Russian 9. Mongolian
  sea.. 6. Bering 7. Okhotsk
Kamehameha Day... 7. holiday (Haw)
Kamerad... 7. comrade 9. surrender
kamik... 12. sealskin boot
Kammerspiel... 5. drama 7. theater
Kanaka... 3. man 8. Hawaiian
  10. Melanesian, Polynesian
  16. South Sea islander
Kanaloa... 3. God (Pantheon)
kangaroo (pert to)...
  class.. 9. marsupial
  family.. 12. Macropodidae
  female.. 3. doe, gin, 'roo
  giant.. 8. forester
  leaping.. 6. jeroba 7. bettong
    (bettonga)
  male.. 5. bilby (bilbi)
  rat.. 7. pototoo
  reference to.. 7. wallaby
    11. macropodine
  small.. 7. wallaby
  young.. 4. joey
kangaroo court... 9. mock court, moot
  court 14. irregular court
Kansas...
  capital.. 6. Topeka
  city.. 5. Dodge 7. Abilene, Wichita
    10. Hutchinson, Kansas City
    11. Leavenworth
  Eisenhower home.. 7. Abilene
  military post.. 9. Fort Riley
  penitentiary.. 11. Leavenworth
  State admission.. 12. Thirty-fourth
  State motto.. 16. Ad Astra per
    Aspera (To the Stars Through
    Difficulties)
  State nickname.. 9. Sunflower
kapok tree... 7. God tree 9. Ceiba
  tree 10. silk-cotton
kappa... 1. K (Gr) 4. star 6. letter
  (10th)
karakul, karakule... 5. sheep
  9. astrakhan, broadtail
karma... 4. fate 7. destiny 8. casualty
Kartvelian people... 4. Svan (Svane)
  9. Georgians 10. Imeritians,
  Svanetians
kasha... 4. mush (Russ)
Kashmir, India...
  alphabet.. 6. Sarada
  capital.. 8. Srinagar
  deer.. 6. hangul
  official.. 6. pundit
Kashyapa (Vedic Myth)... 8. tortoise
Kaskaskia... 5. epoch 6. Indian
  10. Algonquian
kat... 5. shrub 8. narcotic
katar... 6. dagger
katchung... 6. peanut
katogle... 8. eagle owl
kava, kavakava... 6. Kawaka, pepper
kayak... 5. canoe
kea... 6. parrot
Keat's poem... 8. Endymion, Hyperion
keek... 3. spy (of rival fashions)
  6. peeper

keel... 4. cool, seel, ship, skeg, tilt
  6. careen, ruddle, timber (ship's)
  7. capsize 8. overturn, red ocher,
  turn over 10. guinea fowl
keelbill, keelbird... 3. ani
keeling... 7. codfish
keel-shaped... 6. carina 7. carinal
keen... 4. avid, cute, gare, good, nice,
  tart 5. acute, alert, eager, sharp,
  smart, snell, vivid, witty 6. astute,
  bitter, clever, shrewd, shrill
  7. caustic, fervent 9. sensitive,
  trenchant 11. acrimonious,
  penetrating
keenness... 4. edge 5. acies (of sight),
  nifty 6. acumen 8. acrimony,
  pungency 9. acuteness, eagerness,
  sharpness, smartness, wittiness
keep... 4. save 6. detain, retain
  7. confine, custody, fulfill, husband,
  reserve 8. conserve, maintain,
  preserve, restrain, withhold
  14. accommodations
keep (pert to)...
  account.. 5. score
  afloat.. 4. buoy
  apart.. 7. seclude 8. separate
  back, out.. 3. bar, dam 4. save
    5. debar, delay 6. detain, except,
    hinder, retard 7. exclude, reserve
    8. restrain, withhold
  from.. 5. avoid, delay 7. abstain,
    boycott, prevent
  hidden.. 7. secrete
  in.. 6. retain
  off.. 4. fend 7. prevent, repulse, ward
    off
  on.. 6. endure 9. persevere
keeper... 5. guard 6. warden
  9. constable, custodian, possessor
  10. maintainer
keeper of...
  birds.. 8. aviarist
  borders.. 8. margrave
  door.. 5. tiler
  elephant.. 6. mahout
  golden apples (Myth).. 6. Ithunn
    (Ithun)
  parks.. 6. ranger
  prison.. 6. gaoler, jailer, jailor, warden
    7. turnkey
keeping... 4. care 5. board, guard,
  trust 7. custody 8. tutelage
  9. retention 10. caretaking,
  conformity, possession, preserving,
  protection 11. maintenance
  12. guardianship
keeve... 3. tub 4. tuft 5. knoll, plume
  8. haystack
kef... 6. dreamy 7. languor
  12. tranquillity (tranquility)
keg... 3. tun, vat 4. cade, cask
  6. firkin
kelly... 5. derby, killy (fish)
kelp... 4. game 5. sight, wrack
  7. insight, seaweed 9. water lily
ken... 4. lore 9. recognize
  10. cognizance, prescience
  13. understanding
Kentish freedman... 4. laet
Kentucky...
  bluegrass.. 3. poa

capital.. 9. Frankfort
city.. 7. Paducah 9. Lexington
  10. Louisville 12. Bowling Green
famed road.. 15. Wilderness Trail
famed sights.. 7. Obelisk (J Davis)
  8. Fort Knox, Log Cabin (Lincoln)
  11. Federal Hill (My Old Ky Home),
  Mammoth Cave
famed sport.. 13. Kentucky Derby
  (Churchill Downs)
mountain.. 4. Pine 10. Cumberland
pioneer.. 11. Daniel Boone
river.. 4. Ohio 10. Cumberland
State admission.. 9. Fifteenth
State name meaning (Indian)..
  8. tomorrow
State nickname.. 9. Bluegrass
Kenya, E Africa...
capital.. 7. Nairobi
product.. 3. tea
tribe.. 4. Embu
kept... see *keep*
Ker (Gr)... 4. doom, fate 5. ghost
  6. spirit
kermis, kermess... 4. fair 8. festival
kernel... 3. nut 4. core, gist, meat,
  pith, seed 5. grain, heart 6. acinus,
  nutmeg 7. nucleus
ketch... 4. Jack, saic, ship 6. vessel
ketone... 5. irone 6. carone
  7. acetone, camphor 8. deguelin
kettle... 3. pot 4. drum, pail 6. kibble
  7. caldron 8. cauldron 9. teakettle
  10. kettledrum
kettledrum... 4. drum 5. naker, tabor
  6. atabal 7. anacara 8. tympanon
key... 4. clue, crib, isle, quay, reef,
  tone 5. islet, pitch, tasto 6. clavis,
  cotter, fasten, island, opener, switch,
  tapper 7. digital 8. mainstay, solution
  11. explanation, fundamental,
  translation
keyed up... 4. agog 5. eager, fired
  7. aroused, stirred 8. hopped up,
  worked up 10. stimulated
Keys, House of... 9. Isle of Man,
  officials
Keystone State... 12. Pennsylvania
khan... 3. inn 4. lord 6. prince
  9. resthouse 11. caravansary
kiang... 5. diver 6. onager 7. wild ass
kick... 4. blow, boot, funk, punt
  6. energy, object, thrill 7. grumble,
  protest 8. complain, pungency,
  sixpence 9. complaint 10. calcitrate,
  enthusiasm
Kickapoo... 6. Indian 10. Algonquian
kickshaw... 3. toy 6. trifle 7. trinket
  8. delicacy
kid... 3. guy 4. fool, goat, hoax, joke,
  josh, twit 5. child, jolly, suede
  6. banter, humbug 8. antelope
  (young), yeanling 9. youngling
kidang... 4. deer 7. muntjac
kidney... 4. neer 5. gland, reins
  7. nephros
kidney (pert to)...
comb form.. 6. nephro
disease.. 7. nephria 9. nephritis
pyramid.. 9. reniculus
reference to.. 4. reni 5. renal
  6. vitals 7. nephric

shaped.. 8. reniform
stone.. 6. pebble 8. nephrite
kiki... 14. castor oil plant
kill... 4. slay, veto 5. blast, creek
  6. defeat, murder 7. channel,
  destroy, execute, silence 8. dispatch,
  immolate, lapidate, massacre,
  overbeat 9. slaughter
  11. assassinate, exterminate
killer... 4. Cain 6. gunman, slayer
  7. butcher 8. cannibal, man–eater,
  mongoose, murderer 9. cutthroat
  12. assassinator
killer whale... 3. orc 4. orca
  7. grampus
killing... 5. fatal 6. deadly, murder
  7. amusing, carnage, cleanup
  (speculation), garrote 8. homicide
  9. execution 10. euthanasia
  11. captivating 12. overpowering
killing of...
brother.. 10. fratricide
cats.. 8. felicide
father.. 9. patricide
man.. 8. homicide
mother.. 9. matricide
old men (tribal).. 8. senicide
self.. 7. suicide 9. martyrdom
sister.. 10. sororicide
wolf.. 8. lupicide
kiln... 4. oast, oven 5. clamp, stove,
  tiler 7. furnace
kilo (pref).. 8. thousand
kind... 3. ilk 4. good, race, sort, type
  5. class, genre, genus, order, seely,
  style 6. benign, gender, humane,
  loving, strain 7. kindred, lenient,
  species 8. gracious 9. benignant
  10. benevolent 11. sympathetic
  12. well–disposed
kindle... 4. burn, fire 5. brood, light,
  rouse, young 6. excite, ignite, incite,
  litter 7. animate, inflame, provoke
kindly... 4. mild 6. benign, blithe,
  genial, humane 7. natural
  8. benignly, heartily 9. agreeably,
  benignant, indulgent 10. beneficent,
  legitimate, pleasantly 11. sympathetic
kindness... 5. favor 8. clemency,
  goodness, humanity, mildness
  9. benignity 10. compassion,
  generosity, gentleness, indulgency,
  tenderness
kindred... 3. sib, tie 4. akin, clan, kith
  5. blood 6. allied, family 7. cognate,
  descent, kinship, kinsmen, related
  8. kinsfolk 9. relations
  12. relationship 14. consanguineous
kine... 4. cows 5. cattle
kinetic... 6. active, moving
king... 3. rex, rey, roi 4. rank 5. chief,
  ruler 6. master 7. regulus
  8. chessman 9. potentate, sovereign
king (pert to)...
beasts.. 4. lion
birds.. 5. eagle
chamber.. 9. camarilla
cheeses.. 4. Brie
child.. 6. prince 8. princess
dwarfs.. 8. Alberich (Ger)
fairies.. 6. Oberon
family.. 7. dynasty

gods.. **7.** Jupiter
heaven.. **3.** God **6.** Christ
herrings.. **4.** opah **7.** oarfish
  8. chimaera
mackerel.. **4.** cero
March (The).. **5.** Sousa
metals.. **4.** gold
monkeys.. **7.** guereza
murder of.. **8.** regicide
myth.. **4.** Atli **5.** Midas
myth (classical).. **4.** Zeus **7.** Jupiter
rivers.. **6.** Amazon
serpents (race of).. **6.** Shesha (Sesha)
symbol.. **7.** scepter (sceptre)
vultures.. **4.** papa
waters.. **7.** Neptune, Pacific
Woods (The).. **13.** Rex Nemorensis
King Arthur (pert to)...
abode.. **6.** Avalon **7.** Camelot
battleground (fatal).. **6.** Camlan
home.. **8.** Caerleon (on the Usk)
Knights of the Round Table..
  6. Gawain **7.** Galahad **8.** Lancelot,
  Tristran, Percivale
Queen.. **9.** Guinevere
quest of.. **9.** Holy Grail (The)
shield.. **7.** Pridwin
sword.. **9.** Excalibur
kingdom.. **5.** realm **6.** empire, estate
  8. dominion, kingship, monarchy
kingdom (pert to)...
ancient.. **4.** Elam, Moab
Asia.. **5.** Nepal
between Spain, France.. **7.** Navarra
  (Navarre)
confusion.. **5.** Babel
divisions.. **6.** animal **7.** mineral
  9. vegetable
Indo–China.. **5.** Annam (Anam)
kingfish.. **4.** cero, haku, opah
  7. kingpin, pintado **8.** big wheel
  9. threadfin
kingly.. **5.** grand, noble, regal, royal
  6. august **7.** leonine **8.** imperial,
  majestic, princely **9.** dignified,
  sovereign **11.** monarchical
King of...
Albania.. **3.** Zog
Bashan.. **2.** Og
Bulgaria.. **5.** Boris
Greece (anc).. **9.** Agamemnon
Israel.. **4.** Ahab, Jehu, Saul **5.** David
  7. Solomon **8.** Jeroboam
Judea.. **3.** Asa
Kings.. **3.** God **6.** Christ
Men.. **4.** Odin, Zeus **7.** Jupiter
Oriental.. **11.** King of Kings
Persia (Iran).. **5.** Cyrus **6.** Xerxes
Troy.. **5.** Priam
Tyre.. **5.** Hiram
Visigoths.. **6.** Alaric
Kipling, Rudyard (pert to)...
award.. **10.** Nobel Prize (1907)
birthplace.. **6.** Bombay
poem (for Queen Victoria)..
  11. Recessional
kissing, science... **13.** philematology
knee (pert to)...
bend.. **9.** genuflect
bent.. **10.** geniculate
bone.. **6.** rotula **7.** kneepan, patella
britches.. **6.** smalls **8.** knickers

on bended.. **7.** humbled **8.** obeisant
  10. submissive, worshipful
  12. supplicatory
kneeling desk... **8.** prie–dieu
knew... see *know*
Knickerbocker, Father... **9.** New
  Yorker (Hist)
knickknack... **4.** toy **6.** bauble,
  gewgaw, trifle **7.** trinket **8.** gimcrack
knife.. **4.** bolo, snee, stab **5.** corer,
  prune **6.** cutter, weapon
knife (pert to)...
Burmese.. **3.** dah
Hindu.. **5.** kukri
Irish.. **5.** skean **8.** skean dhu
Malay.. **4.** kris **6.** barong, creese
New Zealand.. **4.** patu
one–bladed.. **6.** barlow
Scottish.. **4.** dirk
Spanish.. **7.** machete
surgical.. **7.** scalpel **10.** greffotome
Turkish.. **8.** yataghan (yatagan)
US Navy.. **7.** cutlass
knife maker... **6.** cutler
knife-throwing game...
  11. mumbletypeg
  12. mumble–the–peg
knight (pert to)...
adventure.. **8.** errantry
adventurer.. **8.** cavalier **9.** caballero,
  chevalier
cloak.. **6.** tabard
combat.. **5.** joust
ensign.. **8.** gonfalon, gonfanon
errant.. **7.** Paladin
hero.. **7.** Paladin
servant.. **4.** page **6.** varlet
title.. **3.** Sir **8.** banneret
wife.. **4.** Dame, Lady
wreath (with crest).. **4.** orle
Knight of the Round Table... **3.** Kay
  6. Gawain **7.** Galahad, Paladin
  8. Lancelot, Tristram **9.** Percivale
Knight of the Rueful Countenance...
  10. Don Quixote
knit... **4.** bind, heal, join, seam
  5. plait, unite, woven **6.** cement,
  couple, fasten **7.** conjoin, connect,
  wrinkle **8.** contract **9.** interlace
  11. consolidate
knitting machine guide... **4.** sley
knitting stitch... **4.** knit, purl
knob... **3.** nub **4.** boss, head, hill,
  lump, node, stud, umbo **5.** bulge,
  knurl **6.** croche (antler), pommel
  8. tubercle **12.** protuberance
knobkerrie... **4.** club, kiri **5.** stick
knock... **3.** hit, rap, tap **4.** bang,
  bash, beat, bump, dash, glow, hill,
  pass, slay, snop **5.** pound, thump
  6. hammer, jostle, strike **7.** collide
  9. criticism, criticize, disparage
  12. faultfinding
knock (pert to)...
about.. **6.** travel, wander
down.. **4.** fell, raze **6.** deject, strike
  8. vanquish
off.. **3.** die **6.** deduct, recess
  9. improvise
out.. **2.** KO **4.** kayo
knocking... **6.** rat-tat **7.** rapping,
  tapping **9.** rat–tat-tat

knock–knee... 6. in–knee
knoll... 4. bank, clod, hill, knap, knob,
lump 5. bunch, hurst, knell, mound
7. hillock
knot... 3. bow, nep, tie 4. burl, knar,
knob, knur, lump, node, noil, snag
5. gnarl, noose 6. clique, nodule,
tangle 7. dilemma, lanyard, problem,
rosette 9. sandpiper 10. sheepshank
12. complication, protuberance
knotted... 5. nep 5. noded, nowed
(Her) 6. knotty 7. clotted, complex,
gnarled, knitted, nodated 8. abstruse,
puzzling 9. difficult, entangled
knotty... 5. nodal, rough 7. gnarled,
knarred, knobbed, knurled, nodular
9. difficult, entangled, intricate
10. perplexing
know... 3. ken, wis, wot 5. sense
6. regard, reveal 8. perceive
9. apprehend, be certain, recognize
11. be cognizant, distinguish
knowing... 3. hep 6. artful, crafty,
scient, shrewd 7. cunning
8. informed 9. cognitive, conscious,
wide–awake 10. perceptive
11. intelligent, intentional 12. familiar
with 13. comprehension
know–it–all... 6. gossip 8. quidnunc,
wiseacre
knowledge... 3. ken 4. kith, lore
5. ology 6. wisdom 7. science
8. learning, scientia 9. erudition
11. familiarity, information, instruction
12. acquaintance
knowledge (pert to)...
acquisition of.. 7. organon
ancestral.. 9. tradition
epithet of Muses.. 7. Pierian
exhibition of.. 6. pedant
instrument.. 7. organon
lack of.. 9. ignorance, nescience
object of.. 7. scibile
pert to.. 7. gnostic 8. instinct
9. epistemic, intuition, sciential
12. epistemology
pretender to.. 7. aeolist (eolist)
8. sciolist
seeker of.. 10. philonoist
slight.. 7. inkling, smatter
10. smattering
summarized.. 12. encyclopedia
(encyclopaedia)
superficial.. 9. sociology
system.. 7. science
universal.. 9. pantology
without.. 8. atechnic
know–nothing... 5. dunce 8. agnostic
9. ignoramus
kobird... 6. cuckoo
kobold... 3. elf, imp 5. gnome
8. folklore 9. hobgoblin
Kodiak, Kadiak bear... 7. Alaskan
Kohinoor... 7. diamond (700 carats)
kohl... 5. horse 8. antimony, cosmetic
kola... 3. nut 6. jackal
kooky... 7. offbeat
kopje... 5. mound 7. hillock
Koran, Alcoran (pert to)...
author.. 8. Mohammed
division.. 4. Sura (chapter)
learned man.. 5. ulema
recording angel.. 6. sijill (sijil)
scriptures.. 10. Mohammedan
teacher.. 5. ulema 7. alfaqui (alfaquin)
Korea...
capital.. 5. Keijo, Seoul
city.. 6. Gensan
mountain peak.. 6. Paekdu
old name.. 6. Chosen 13. Hermit
Kingdom
peninsula.. 6. Ongjin
province.. 5. Fusan (Fuzan)
river.. 4. Yalu 5. Tuman 7. Naktong
kosher... 5. clean 8. kashruth
10. sanctioned
kra... 3. ape (long–tailed)
krimmer... 8. lambskin
Krishna (Hind)... 5. deity (of Vishnu)
6. avatar (8th), Goloka
Krupp steel works, site... 5. Essen
(Ger)
kudu... 8. antelope 9. gray–brown
kusimansel... 6. mangue 8. mongoose
Kwantung capital... 6. Dairen
kwazoku (Jap)... 8. nobility (modern)
kyah... 9. partridge
kyaung... 9. monastery
kymatology, science of... 5. waves
10. wave motion
kyphosis... 8. humpback 9. hunchback
15. spinal curvature
kyte... 5. belly 7. stomach
Kyushu (Jap)... 6. Island
(southernmost)

L

L... 5. fifty (Rom num) 6. lambda, letter (12th) 7. lammedh
laager, lager... 4. camp
laagte... 6. bottom, valley 8. riverbed
Laban (pert to)...
  daughter.. 4. Leah 6. Rachel
  father.. 7. Bethuel
  son–in–law.. 5. Jacob
label... 3. tab, tag 4. band, name 6. fillet, lappet, tassel, ticket 8. insignia 9. designate
labellum... 3. lip 6. labium, labrum
labia... 4. lips
labial stop... 9. organ stop
labial teeth... 6. canine 7. incisor
labile... 8. shifting, unstable
labium... 3. lip
La Boheme... 4. Mimi 7. Puccini
labor, labour... 4. moil, task, toil, work 5. sweat 6. strive 7. travail, work for 8. drudgery, endeavor, exertion, industry
labored... 6. heavy 6. forced, strove 7. not easy, operose 8. strained 9. difficult, elaborate, laborious 11. painstaking
laborer... 4. hind, peon, toty 5. navvy 6. coolie, toiler, worker 7. bracero, wetback, workman
laborious... 4. hard 7. arduous, operose 8. toilsome 9. difficult 11. hard working, industrious, painstaking
labor leader... 5. Hoffa, Lewis, Meany 7. Gompers (1st), Reuther 8. Petrillo
Labrador (pert to)...
  Arctic flow.. 7. Current
  dog.. 9. retriever 12. Newfoundland
  missionary.. 8. Grenfell (Dr)
  part.. 12. Newfoundland
  tea.. 5. Ledum 8. gowiddie
labyrinth... 4. maze 7. circuit, cochlea 10. perplexity 12. complication
labyrinthe... 7. complex 8. involved 9. intricate 10. circuitous 11. complicated
lac... 4. milk 5. resin 7. lacquer, shellac
lace... 3. net, tat, tie, web 4. band, beat, cord, flog, lash, line, trim 5. braid, filet, lacis, snare 6. fasten, string, tissue 7. network 9. embroider 10. intertwine, shoestring 13. dash of spirits
lace (pert to)...
  Antwerp.. 7. pot lace
  bobbin.. 3. val 12. Valenciennes
  cape, scarf.. 8. mantilla
  edge.. 7. picot
  Flemish.. 7. malines, Mechlin

French.. 5. filet 7. guipure
frill.. 5. ruche
front.. 5. jabot
gold, silver.. 5. orris
make.. 3. tat 5. weave 7. crochet, entwine
needlepoint.. 7. Alençon
opening.. 6. eyelet
patterned.. 7. guipure
lacerate... 3. cut, rip 4. pain, rend, tear 6. harrow, injure, mangle 7. afflict, torture
lachryma... 4. tear 5. fluid 8. teardrop
lachrymal, lachrymose... 5. teary, weepy 7. tearful 8. tearlike
lack... 4. need, want 6. dearth 7. absence, lacking, missing, require 8. have need, scarcity 9. fall short, neediness 10. deficiency
lack (pert to)...
  blood cells (red).. 6. anemia
  correspondence.. 13. nonconformity
  energy.. 5. atony, tepid 6. energy 7. aimless, sapless
  feeling.. 10. insensible 13. insensibility
  firmness.. 4. limp 8. boneless 9. spineless
  interest.. 6. apathy 9. apathetic
  knowledge.. 9. ignorance, nescience
  melody.. 6. atonic 9. atonality
  preparation.. 8. unfitted
  reasoning.. 7. idiotic
  refinement.. 5. gross 9. grossness, inelegant 10. inelegance
  vigilance.. 6. unwary
lackadaisical... 7. languid 8. listless 10. spiritless
Laconia (anc)...
  capital.. 6. Sparta
  clan.. 3. obe
  inhabitant.. 5. Lacon
  location.. 5. Peloponnesus
  race.. 6. Dorian
laconic... 5. brief, pithy, short, terse 7. concise, pointed, summary 8. succinct, taciturn
lacquer... 3. lac, red (color) 5. japan, resin 6. enamel 7. shellac, varnish
lacrimando... 9. lamenting, plaintive
lactarium... 5. dairy
lacteal... 5. milky
lacune, lacuna... 3. gap, pit 5. break 6. hiatus 7. opening (small) 10. depression
ladder... 3. run, sty 5. scale 7. scalade 8. escalade 10. stepladder
lade... 3. dip 4. bail, draw, fill, load, ship 5. drain, ladle 6. burden
laden... 6. loaded 8. burdened

310

9. freighted

lading... 4. load 5. cargo 6. burden
7. freight

ladle... 3. dip 4. bowl 5. scoop,
spoon 6. dipper

lady... 4. burd (anc), dame 5. donna
6. domina, female, senora 7. signora
8. ladylove 13. harlequin duck

lady (pert to)...
  bird.. 6. beetle 7. Vedalia
  fish.. 6. wrasse
  killer.. 4. wolf 5. shiek 7. Don Juan
    8. Casanova
  like.. 6. female, polite 7. genteel
    8. feminine

Lady Godiva's town... 8. Coventry

Lady of the Lake character
  (legend)... 6. Merlin, Vivian

Lady's Book author... 5. Godey

lady's-slipper... 6. balsam, orchid
8. Noah's ark 9. nerveroot

lady's-thumb... 9. peachwort, persicary

lag... 4. slow 5. delay, tardy
6. dawdle, linger, loiter 7. belated
10. dillydally, fall behind

lagarto... 9. alligator 10. lizard fish

laggard... 4. slow 5. idler 7. lagging
8. backward, dilatory, indolent,
loiterer, sluggish 9. loitering, straggler

La Gioconda... 8. Mona Lisa

lagniappe, lagnappe... 5. pilon
7. largess (largesse), present (trifling)
8. gratuity

lagoon... 4. lake, pond, pool 5. atoll

laic... 3. lay 5. civil 6. layman
7. secular 8. temporal

lair... 3. bed, den, pen 4. cave, shed,
trap 5. abode, couch 6. cavern
7. retreat

Lais (Gr)... 7. hetaera (of Corinth)
8. mistress 14. beautiful woman

laissez faire, laisser faire... 5. let go
7. let pass 8. inaction, inactive
9. do–nothing, passivism, unconcern
12. indifference 15. noninterference

Laius' son... 7. Oedipus (of Thebes)

lake... 4. loch, mere, pond, pool, tarn
5. lacus 6. lagoon 7. carmine (color)

lake (pert to)...
  bass.. 4. rock 6. calico
  deposit.. 5. trona
  duck.. 5. scaup 6. mallard
  dweller.. 10. lacustrian
  dwelling.. 7. crannog
  growing in.. 10. lacustrine
  Hades (of).. 7. Avernus
  highest.. 9. Titicaca
  pert to.. 9. lacustral
  poet (Eng).. 6. lakist 7. Southey
    9. Coleridge 10. Wordsworth
  State.. 8. Michigan

lama... 4. monk 5. Dalai

Lamaism... 8. Buddhism

Lamaism, Buddhism (pert to)...
  convent.. 7. lamasery
  dignitary.. 8. hutukhtu
  palace site.. 5. Lhasa
  priest, monk.. 4. lama 6. Getsul
    9. Dalai Lama, Grand Lama
  reliquary, stupa.. 7. chorten

lamb... 3. ean, ewe 4. cade, yean
5. gigot, sheep 6. cosset 7. eanling,

lambkin 8. yearling 9. youngling
10. endearment

Lamb, Charles... 4. Elia (pen name)

lambaste... 4. beat, whip 6. thrash
7. reprove

lambent... 7. glowing, radiant
8. wavering 10. flickering 11. gliding
over

Lambeth (London)... 6. palace (of
Archbishops) 15. religious center

Lamb of God... 7. paschal 8. Agnus
Dei

lame... 4. halt 5. halting, limping
8. crippled, disabled, hobbling
9. defective 11. inefficient

lame (pert to)...
  brains.. 9. balminess, daffiness,
    goofiness, wackiness
  duck.. 7. session 9. insolvent
    10. politician, speculator

Lamech (pert to)...
  descendant of.. 4. Cain
  father of.. 5. Jabal, Jubal
    9. Tubal–cain

lament... 3. rue 4. keen, moan, sigh,
wail, weep 5. mourn 6. bemoan,
bewail, grieve, plaint, regret, repine,
yammer 7. condole, deplore, elegize,
weeping 8. jeremiad

lamentation... 3. cry, woe 5. dolor,
grief, tears 6. sorrow 7. anguish,
wailing

Lamentations... 4. Book (Old Test)

lamia... 5. witch 7. monster, vampire
(Myth) 8. cub shark 9. sorceress

lamina... 4. obex (brain) 5. blade,
flake, hinge, layer

lamp... 4. davy, etna 5. light, torch
6. crusie 7. lantern, lucigen
9. veilleuse

lamp (pert to)...
  black.. 4. soot
  holder.. 11. candelabrum
  lighter.. 5. spill
  safety.. 4. davy 7. Geordie
  slang.. 6. look at
  waving of.. 5. arati

lampadedromy (Gr)... 8. foot race
(with torch)

lampoon... 4. skit 5. squib 6. iambic
8. ridicule, satirize 10. pasquinade

lampoon writer... 8. satirist

lamprey... 3. eel 6. ramper

Lamps of the Lord... 5. yucca
(blooms)

Lancashire (Eng)... 6. Eccles

lance... 3. cut 4. dart, hurl, stab
5. blade, spear 6. incise, launch,
pierce, weapon 7. javelin

lance (pert to)...
  battle.. 5. joust
  head.. 5. morne
  knight.. 10. lansquenet (Hist)
  officer.. 3. Jack
  surgical.. 6. lancet

Lancelot... 6. Knight 13. Lancelot du
Lac

Lancelot's beloved... 6. Elaine

lancer... 5. uhlan 6. Hussar
7. cossack, soldier, spearer

land... 3. lot 4. acre, farm 5. arada,
downs, field, range, tilth 6. alight,

debark, ground, region 7. country,
pasture 9. disembark
land (pert to)...
absolute ppty.. 4. alod 7. alodium
alluvial.. 5. delta
ancestral.. 5. ethel
assessor.. 8. cadastre (cadaster)
church.. 5. glebe
heritable.. 4. odal, udal
holding.. 6. tenure 9. leasehold
leasehold.. 5. feoff
locked in.. 13. mediterranean
mythical.. 4. Eden 6. Utopia
9. Shangri–La
northernmost.. 5. Thule (Greenland)
open.. 4. moor, wold 5. heath
pile.. 5. cairn
prefix.. 4. agro
reversion.. 7. escheat
sandy.. 4. dene
surveyor.. 9. arpenteur
Sussex tract (Eng).. 5. laine
treeless.. 5. llano 6. steppe 7. prairie
verb.. 3. win 4. gain 5. catch
6. secure 7. capture
waste.. 5. heath
landed estate... 5. manor 7. demesne
landing place... 4. deck, dock, pier,
quay 5. field, levee, strip, wharf
7. airport 8. platform 9. staircase
landmark... 4. copa, tree 5. senal
Land of (the)...
bondage.. 5. Egypt
Cush.. 8. Ethiopia
Eden (East of).. 3. Nod
Enchantment.. 9. New Mexico
Leal.. 6. Heaven
Little Sticks (Canada).. 19. Barren
Islands border
Midnight Sun.. 6. Alaska, Norway
O'Cakes.. 8. Scotland
Opportunity.. 8. Arkansas
Plenty.. 6. Goshen
Promise.. 6. Canaan
Regrets.. 5. India
Rising Sun.. 5. Japan
Rose.. 7. England
Shamrock.. 4. Eire 7. Ireland
sleep.. 3. Nod
Steady Habits.. 11. Connecticut
Thistle.. 8. Scotland
Thousand Lakes.. 7. Finland
White Elephant.. 4. Siam
landscape... 7. paysage, scenery,
topiary
landslide... 9. avalanche
10. éboulement
Landsmaal, Landsmal... 8. language
(Norway)
Landstag... 4. Diet 8. assembly
11. legislature
lane... 4. path, road 5. alley, route,
track 6. airway, course, gullet, throat
7. channel, red land 8. footpath
10. passageway
language... 6. langue, speech, tongue
7. dialect, diction 8. parlance
9. utterance 11. linguistics
language (pert to)...
acquiring.. 12. chrestomathy
ancient.. 4. Pali 5. Aryan, Greek,
Latin 6. Hebrew 7. Chinese

8. Sanskrit
artificial.. 2. Od, Ro 3. Ido
7. Volapük 9. Esperanto
classical.. 5. Greek, Latin
conversant in.. 9. pantoglot
dead.. 4. Pali
deaf–mute.. 11. dactylology
expression, peculiar.. 5. idiom, lingo
6. jargon 7. dialect 13. colloquialism
international.. 2. Od, Ro 3. Ido
7. Volapük 9. Esperanto
pert to.. 8. semantic
pretentious.. 7. bombast
11. highfalutin'
Romance.. 5. Latin 6. French
7. Catalan, Italian, Spanish
9. Provençal 10. Portuguese
sacred.. 4. Pali
sign.. 11. dactylology
thieves'.. 5. argot
languid... 4. slow, weak 5. faint, inert,
weary 6. dreamy, feeble, sickly,
supine, torpid 7. passive 8. careless,
drooping, flagging, heedless, indolent,
sluggish 9. apathetic 10. spiritless
languish... 3. die 4. fade, fail, flag,
pine, wilt 5. droop, faint 6. repine,
sicken, weaken, wither 7. decline
languor... 3. kef (kief) 7. fatigue
8. dullness, weakness 9. indolence,
lassitude 10. dreaminess, drowsiness,
stagnation 12. listlessness,
sluggishness
lanky... 4. lean, tall, thin 5. gaunt,
spare 12. loose–jointed
lanner... 6. falcon
Lanterns, Feast of (Jap)...·3. Bon
Laodicean... 8. lukewarm 9. apathetic
11. indifferent
Laos...
aborigine.. 3. Kah
capital.. 9. Vientiane 12. Luang
Prabang
native.. 7. Chinese
14. Thai–Indonesian
religion.. 8. Buddhism
river.. 6. Mekong
tribesman.. 3. Yun
lap... 3. sip 4. fold, lick, wrap 5. drink
6. ripple, tipple 7. circuit
lapel... 4. fold 5. rever 6. facing,
lappet
lapicide... 11. stonecutter
lapidate... 4. kill (by stoning), pelt
5. stone
lapin... 6. rabbit
lapis lazuli... 4. blue 5. stone
8. lazurite, sapphire 10. azure stone
Lapland...
people.. 5. Lapps 10. Laplanders
11. Ural–Altaics 12. tent–dwellers
sledge (traveling).. 5. pulka (pukk)
sledge puller.. 8. reindeer
town.. 6. Kiruna
waterfalls.. 11. Harspranget
lappet... 4. flap, fold, lobe 5. lapel
6. wattle 9. appendage
lapse... 3. err 4. fall, slip 5. error,
fault, pause 6. expiry 7. decline,
misstep, relapse 8. apostasy
9. reversion
lapsus... 4. slip 5. error

12. inadvertence

lapsus calami . . . 10. lipography
12. slip of the pen

lapsus linguae . . . 15. slip of the tongue

lapwing . . . 4. gull 5. pewee, pewit 6. plover

larceny . . . 5. theft 7. robbery 8. burglary, stealage 10. scrounging

larch . . . 5. Larix 8. tamarack

lard . . . 3. fat 4. line, pork 5. adeps, bacon, baste, enarm 6. axunge, cerate, enrich, fatten, grease 7. garnish 8. saindoux 9. lubricate

larder . . . 6. pantry 7. buttery 8. cupboard 12. commissariat

lares (Rom) . . . 4. gods (household) 7. spirits

large . . . 3. big, nth 4. bold, huge, much, vast 5. ample, bulky, burly, giant, great, loose, scads 7. copious, immense, leonine, liberal, massive, titanic, weighty 8. colossal, enormous, gigantic, spacious 9. excessive, extensive, plentiful 11. exaggerated 12. considerable 13. comprehensive

large (pert to) . . .
artery . . 5. aorta
comb form . . 5. macro
fish . . 4. opah, tuna 9. swordfish
intestine . . 5. colon 6. caecum, rectum
knife . . 4. bolo, snee
lettered . . 6. uncial
number . . 4. slew 6. myriad
pulpit . . 4. ambo
volume . . 4. tome

largess, largesse . . . 4. gift 6. bounty 7. charity, present 10. generosity, liberality 11. beneficence

largest bird . . . 6. condor 7. ostrich 13. whooping crane

largest fish (freshwater) . . . 8. arapaima

larghetto . . . 9. slow tempo

larghissimo . . . 8. very slow

lariat . . . 4. rope 5. honda (part), lasso, noose, reata, riata

lark . . . 5. ghost (anc), prank, revel 6. frolic 7. skylark, titlark 8. songbird 9. adventure, Alaudidae, parchment (color)

larrigan . . . 8. moccasin

larrikin . . . 5. rough, rowdy 6. loafer 10. street Arab

larrup . . . 3. hit 4. beat, blow, flog, whip

larva . . . 3. bot (bott) 4. grub, pupa 5. redia 6. embryo, maggot 7. atrocha 8. cercaria 9. chrysalis, doodlebug 11. caterpillar

lascivious . . . 4. lewd 5. bawdy 6. erotic, wanton 7. lustful, sensual 9. lecherous, salacious 10. libidinous, licentious

laser . . . 9. light beam

lash . . . 3. tie 4. beat, bind, flag, whip 5. scold, smite 6. splice, strike 7. scourge

lass . . . 4. girl 6. lassie, maiden 7. colleen 11. maidservant

lassitude . . . 7. languor 8. debility, lethargy, weakness 9. weariness

lasso . . . 4. lash, rope 5. noose, reata (riata), snare 6. lariat 8. cabestro

last . . . 3. end 5. final, omega 6. endure, latest, lowest, newest, penult, ultima, utmost 7. extreme, supreme 8. eventual, rearmost, terminal, ultimate 9. penultima 10. antepenult, conclusive, most recent

last (pert to) . . .
at last . . 6. Eureka
but one . . 6. penult
cry . . 10. dernier cri
evening . . 9. yesterday
long . . 7. outwear, perdure 9. perendure
month . . 3. ult 6. ultimo
offer . . 9. ultimatum
person in contest . . 4. mell
shoe . . 5. block
syllable but one . . 6. penult
syllable but two . . 10. antepenult

Last (pert to) . . .
Assize . . 11. Last Inquest 12. Last Judgment
Days of Pompeii character . . 4. Ione 5. Nydia 7. Glaucus
Gospel . . 4. Mass
of the Gothic Kings . . 8. Roderick
of the Mohicans . . 5. Uncas (Chief)
Supper . . 6. Christ 9. disciples

lasting . . . 4. long 6. stable 7. abiding, durable, eternal 8. constant 9. continual, lingering, permanent, steadfast 11. substantial, unforgotten

lasting briefly . . . 9. ephemeral, temporary

lat . . . 6. column, pillar

latchet . . . 3. tap 4. lace (leather) 5. strap, thong 9. fastening

late . . . 3. neo (comb form), new 4. sero 5. tardy 6. former, recent 7. belated, overdue 8. neoteric 10. behindhand

latent . . . 5. inert 6. hidden 7. dormant 9. disguised, potential, quiescent, suspended 10. underlying

later . . . 4. anon, soon 5. after 6. future, mañana, puisne 9. posterior, presently 12. subsequently

lateral . . . 5. flank, raphe 8. indirect, sideward

lath . . . 4. slat 9. wood strip

lathe . . . 4. tool 7. mandrel

lather . . . 4. foam, suds 5. froth

Latin (pert to) . . .
alphabet letters . . 9. twenty—one
and . . 2. et
bath . . 7. balneum
behold . . 4. ecce
booth . . 7. taberna
bowl . . 6. patina
bronze . . 3. aes
church . . 8. Catholic
couch . . 9. accibutum
country . . 6. French 7. Italian, Spanish
dish . . 4. lanx 6. patina
foot . . 3. pes
God . . 3. Dei, Deo 4. Deus 7. Mercury

goddess . . 3. Dea
grammar (case) . . 6. dative 8. ablative,
genitive, vocative 10. accusative,
nominative
historian . . 6. Justin
holidays . . 5. feria
hymn . . 13. Adesti Fideles
javelin . . 5. aclys, pilum
land . . 4. ager
law . . 6. Latium
life . . 4. vita
people . . 6. Romans
poet . . 4. Ovid 6. Horace
pronoun . . 2. tu 3. ego, hic 4. ille,
ipse, iste
quarter (section) . . 5. Paris 10. New
Orleans
ram . . 5. aries
rite . . 4. orgy 5. sacra
seat . . 5. sella
trumpet . . 4. tuba 7. buccina
Way . . 9. Via Latina
latite . . . 4. lava
latitude . . . 4. zone 5. scope, width
6. extent 7. breadth, freedom
8. distance 10. liberality
latrant . . . 7. barking
latter . . . 4. last 5. final 6. latest
7. foregoing 10. more recent
Latter–day Saint . . . 6. Mormon
lattice . . . 6. grille 7. trellis 8. cancelli
9. crossbars, framework 12. crossed
slats
latticelike . . . 7. grating 8. espalier
9. clathrate 10. cancellate
Latvia . . .
capital . . 4. Riga
city . . 6. Dvinsk, Libava (Libau)
money unit . . 3. lat (gold)
people . . 5. Letts
river . . 2. Aa
laud . . . 4. sing 5. extol 6. praise
7. applaud, commend, glorify,
magnify 8. eulogize
laudable . . . 9. admirable, estimable
11. commendable, meritorious
12. praiseworthy
laudatory . . . 9. panegyric 10. flattering
11. approbatory, encomiastic
12. commendatory
laugh . . . 4. roar 5. fleer, smile, snort
6. cackle, deride, giggle, guffaw,
hawhaw, tee–hee 7. chortle, chuckle
8. ridicule 10. cachinnate
laughable . . . 3. odd 5. droll, funny,
merry, queer, witty 7. amusing,
comical, jocular, risible, strange,
waggish 8. humorous, sportive
9. burlesque, diverting, facetious,
ludicrous 10. ridiculous
laughing . . . 3. gay 5. merry, riant
6. rident
laughing (pert to) . . .
bird . . 4. loon 10. woodpecker
falcon . . 4. hawk
gas . . 12. nitrous oxide
jackass . . 10. kingfisher, kookaburra
pert to . . 8. gelastic
laughter . . . 4. gelo (comb form)
5. gelos, mirth, risus 6. guffaw
12. cachinnation
launch . . . 4. hurl 5. begin, float, lance,

shove, start, throw 6. plunge
7. descant 9. undertake
10. inaugurate
laureate . . . 4. poet 6. decked (with
laurel) 7. drowned, honored
13. distinguished
laurel . . . 3. bay, ivy, oak, oil
6. daphne, Kalmia, salmon
8. magnolia 9. sassafras, spoonwood
laurel wreath . . . 7. Iresine
lava . . . 2. aa, oo 3. ash 5. ashes
6. coulee, latite, scoria 8. lapillus,
pahoehoe
lava field . . . 8. pedregal
lavaliere, lavalier . . . 7. pendant
8. ornament
lavatory . . . 5. basin 7. piscina
8. washroom 9. washbasin
lave . . . 4. lade, pour, wash 5. bathe,
rinse 6. drench 8. absterge
lavender . . . 4. mint 6. purple
7. blue–red, perfume 9. fragrance
laver . . . 4. bowl 5. basin 6. trough,
vessel 7. cistern, seaweed
Lavinia (pert to) . . .
father . . 7. Latinus
husband . . 6. Aeneas
mother . . 5. Amata
myth . . 5. Roman
lavish . . . 4. free, lush, rank, wild
5. spend 7. profuse 8. abundant,
generous, prodigal, reckless, squander
9. bountiful, exuberant, impetuous,
luxuriant, plentiful, unstinted
10. immoderate 11. extravagant
12. unrestrained 13. superabundant
law . . . 3. act, jus, lex 4. bill, code,
jure, nisi, rule 5. axiom, canon,
droit, edict, mercy, mesne 6. decree,
equity, Latium, police 7. justice,
precept, statute 9. enactment
12. constitution 13. jurisprudence
law (pert to) . . .
action . . 3. res 4. suit 5. actus
6. trover 7. impeach, implead
8. gravamen, replevin 9. ademption
Bible . . 6. Mosaic 12. Old Testament
claim . . 4. lien
code . . 9. Hammurabi 10. codex juris
16. Codex Justinianus
decree . . 4. nisi 5. edict
degree . . 3. LLD
divine . . 11. commandment
document . . 4. deed, writ 6. capias,
eligit
drafting . . 10. nomography
evidence . . 7. constat
expert (US) . . 5. Moore (John B)
for fourth offender (NY) . . 6. Baumes
German Franks . . 5. Salic
goddess . . 4. Maat (Egypt)
heredity . . 8. Gresham's
Manu . . 5. sutra
mathematics . . 7. formula
morals . . 7. conduct
Moses . . 5. Torah (Tora)
10. Pentateuch
offender . . 5. felon 6. sinner
8. criminal 9. wrongdoer
offense . . 4. tort 5. crime, malum
6. delict
pert to . . 3. res 9. judiciary

philology.. **6.** Grimm's
science.. **8.** nomology
   13. jurisprudence
student.. **8.** stagiary
thought.. **7.** noetics
warning.. **6.** caveat
within the.. **5.** licit **8.** judicial
wrong.. **4.** tort
lawful... **3.** due **5.** legal, licit, valid
   9. permitted **10.** legitimate
   11. permissible
lawgiver... **5.** Moses
lawless... **4.** lewd **6.** unruly **7.** illegal
   10. anarchical, disorderly
lawlessness... **4.** riot **6.** mutiny
   7. anarchy, license **12.** disobedience
lawmaker... **5.** solon **7.** senator
   10. legislator **11.** congressman
lawn... **5.** green **7.** batiste **9.** grassplot
   12. village green
lawyer... **5.** agent **6.** jurist, legist
   7. abogado, shyster **8.** advocate,
   attorney, lawgiver **9.** barrister,
   counselor (counsellor), leguleian,
   solicitor **11.** intercessor, pettifogger
lax... **4.** dull, free, limp, open, slow
   5. loose, slack, tardy **6.** remiss
   7. lenient **8.** backward, dilatory,
   inactive, indolent, not tense
   9. dissolute, scattered **10.** licentious,
   unconfined **12.** unrestrained
lay... **3.** bet, put **4.** lair, pave, poem,
   song **5.** allay, ditty, place, quiet,
   stake, still **6.** ballad, hazard, impose,
   impute, pacify **7.** appease, ascribe,
   deposit, relieve, store up **9.** direction
   10. profession
lay (pert to)...
aside.. **5.** table **6.** remove, shelve
   7. dismiss, reserve **8.** postpone
   9. segregate
away.. **4.** heap, hive **5.** amass,
   cache, hoard, store **7.** husband
   8. treasure **10.** accumulate
bare.. **5.** strip **6.** denude, expose,
   reveal **7.** uncover
down.. **3.** bet, set **5.** level **6.** give up
   7. declare, deposit **8.** postulate,
   prescribe, stipulate, surrender
off.. **4.** don't, stop **5.** cease
   6. recess **7.** dismiss, measure
out.. **4.** plan **5.** set up **6.** design
   7. pattern
waste.. **6.** ravage **7.** destroy
   8. desolate **9.** depredate, devastate
layer... **3.** bed **4.** coat, derm, tier,
   uvea **5.** sloam (earth) **6.** lamina
   7. stratum (strata, pl)
   10. substratum
lazar... **5.** leper **9.** loathsome
lazaretto, lazaret... **8.** hospital **9.** pest
   house **10.** lazar house
laziness... **7.** inertia **8.** oisivity,
   vagrancy **9.** indolence
   10. ergophobia, remissness
   12. slothfulness **13.** shiftlessness
lazy... **3.** lax **4.** idle, slow **5.** slack
   6. otiose, remiss **7.** dronish, laggard
   8. dilatory, inactive, indolent, slothful,
   sluggish **9.** shiftless **13.** lackadaisical
lazy man... **3.** bum **4.** lusk **5.** drone,
   idler **6.** rotter **9.** lazybones

   11. Weary Willie
lea... **4.** mead **5.** haugh **6.** meadow
   7. pasture **9.** grassland
leach... **3.** wet **7.** moisten **9.** lixiviate,
   percolate
lead... **3.** cue, key, van **4.** cart, clue,
   head, lode **5.** begin, guide, pilot,
   plumb, usher **6.** direct, entice,
   escort, govern, induce **7.** conduct,
   pioneer, precede **8.** antecede,
   guidance **9.** direction, influence,
   precedent **10.** precedence
lead (mineral)... **4.** came (rod), gray,
   shot **6.** ceruse, fother, galena,
   leaden, strass (glass) **7.** bullets,
   plummet **8.** graphite, litharge,
   plumbago
lead astray... **4.** lure, mang **6.** allure,
   delude, entice, induce **7.** deceive,
   pervert **8.** inveigle
leader... **4.** head **5.** chief, guide,
   sinew **6.** cantor, tendon **7.** special
   8. choragus, director **9.** chieftain,
   conductor **10.** forerunner
leader (Eccl)... **3.** fra **4.** pope **5.** rabbi
   6. bishop, priest **8.** cardinal,
   minister, preacher **10.** evangelist
leading... **5.** chief, first **6.** ruling
   7. guiding **8.** foremost, in the van
   9. directing, governing
   11. controlling
leaf... **3.** ola **4.** gear, page **5.** blade,
   frond, petal, sepal **6.** areola, ligula,
   spathe **7.** tendril
leaf (pert to)...
book.. **5.** folio
bud.. **5.** gemma
curvature.. **8.** epinasty (down)
   9. hyponasty (upward)
floating.. **3.** pad
green.. **11.** chlorophyll
heart-shaped.. **9.** obcordate
mold.. **5.** humus
network.. **6.** areola
part.. **5.** bract, costa, stoma
   6. pagina, stipel **7.** petiole
   9. petiolule
point, pointed.. **5.** mucro
   9. mucronate **13.** mucroniferous
pore.. **8.** lenticel
secretion.. **4.** lerp
stalk.. **7.** petiole **8.** petiolus
vein.. **3.** rib **5.** costa
leafless... **9.** aphyllous
leaflet... **5.** pinna, tract **6.** folder
   7. booklet **8.** pamphlet
   13. advertisement
league... **4.** band, Bund **5.** Hanse,
   union **7.** combine **8.** alliance
   9. coalition **10.** federation
   11. affiliation, combination
   13. confederation
League of Nations site... **5.** Paris
   (1920) **6.** Geneva (Secretariat)
League of the Iroquois... **11.** Five
   Nations
Leah's sister... **6.** Rachel
leak... **4.** drip, hole, seep **5.** crack
   6. escape, run out **7.** crevice, fissure
   10. be revealed
leal... **4.** just, real, true **5.** legal, loyal
   6. lawful **7.** correct, genuine

8. accurate, faithful

lean... 4. bare, cant, lank, poor, rely, slim, tend 5. gaunt, slope, spare 6. barren, meager 7. scraggy, slender 8. not plump 9. deficient, gravitate

lean (pert to)...
animal, person.. 4. ribe (Scot)
emaciated.. 6. marcid
make.. 8. macerate
towards.. 6. prefer

Leander's love... 4. Hero

leaning... 5. slope 6. desire 7. pronate, tending 8. aptitude, enclitic, penchant, tendency 9. prejudice 10. partiality

Leaning Tower... 4. Pisa 6. Venice 7. Bologna 8. Zaragoza

lean-to... 4. roof, shed, wing 5. shack 9. extension (bldg)

leap... 4. dive, jump, ramp, skip 5. bound, caper, lunge, salto, spang, vault 6. spring 7. saltary 8. capriole

leaping... 7. jumping, salient, saltant 8. bounding, salience 9. saltation

learn... 4. lere (anc) 6. master 8. memorize 9. ascertain, determine

learned... 3. wot 4. read, sage 6. legist 7. erudite 8. lettered, literate, schooled 9. scholarly 12. well-informed

learned man... 6. pundit 7. scholar, teacher 8. mastered 9. professor

learning... 3. art, ken, wit 4. lore 7. culture 8. pedantry 9. education, erudition, knowledge, philology (love of), philomath 11. scholarship

lease... 3. let 4. hire, rent 5. weave 6. demise, remise, tenure 8. contract

leasehold... 6. rental, tenure

leash... 4. bind, cord, lash, lune (hawking) 5. reins, three 6. fasten, string, tierce 9. restraint 11. subjugation

leash hound... 5. limer

least... 5. grain 6. little, lowest, merest 7. minimum 8. minority, shortest, simplest, smallest 9. slightest

leather... 4. hide, skin 5. aluta, leder (old spelling) 6. vellum 7. canepin 8. cheveril (cheverel) 9. toughness

leather (kinds)... 3. kid, kip 4. calf, napa, vici 5. Mocha, suede 6. patent, saddle, skiver 7. chamois, Morocco 8. cordovan 9. sheepskin

leather (pert to)...
artificial.. 7. keratol
bookbinding.. 4. roan 6. levant
bottle.. 4. olpe 6. matara
cuirass.. 6. lorica
glove.. 5. suede, trank 8. capeskin
pare.. 5. skive
patch.. 5. clout
piece of.. 5. strap, thong 6. latigo
pouch (Highlander's).. 7. sporran
process.. 3. tan, taw
strap.. 5. thong 6. latigo
term.. 8. efflower
tool.. 6. skiver
worker.. 6. chamar, tanner 8. chuckler

leatherneck... 6. marine

leave... 2. go 4. quit 6. depart, retire, vacate 7. liberty 9. allowance 10. permission

leave (pert to)...
desolate.. 7. bereave
empty.. 6. vacate
isolated.. 6. desert, maroon
of absence.. 4. exeat 8. furlough
off.. 4. don't, stay 5. cease 6. desist
out.. 4. omit, skip 8. pass over
taking.. 5. adieu 6. congee 7. vamoose 9. departure

leaven... 4. barm 5. imbue, yeast 6. enzyme 7. corrupt (implied), ferment, pervade 10. impregnate

leaves... 5. pages, shaws 6. sepals 7. foliage

leaves, feeding on... 13. phyllophagous

leavings... 4. left, orts, rest 5. culls, dregs, dross, waste 6. refuse 7. remains, residue 8. remnants

leban, lebban... 5. drink 8. beverage, sour milk

Lebanon capital... 6. Beirut

Lebanon city... 7. Tripoli

lech (anc)... 4. slab 8. capstone, monument

lecher... 7. glutton 8. gourmand, parasite 9. debauchee, libertine

lectern... 4. ambo, desk 6. pulpit 10. escritoire

lecture... 4. jobe, rate 5. scold 6. lesson 7. declaim, expound, lection, reproof, reprove 8. instruct, scolding 9. discourse 10. admonition

lecturer... 6. docent, reader 7. teacher 9. prelector

Leda (pert to)...
geology.. 4. clay (marine)
husband.. 4. Zeus
mother of.. 6. Castor, Pollux
   11. Helen of Troy
zoology.. 7. mollusk

ledge... 4. berm, edge, lode, reef, sill 5. shelf 7. retable, stratum

leechlike... 8. bdelloid

lees... 5. draff, dregs 8. sediment

leeward... (opp of windward) 9. protected, sheltered

Leeward Islands... 5. Nevis 7. Antigua, Barbuda, Redonda 8. Anguilla, Sombrero 10. Montserrat 13. St Christopher

Leeward Islands group... 6. Virgin 7. Society

leeway... 10. enough rope

left... see also *leave* 3. haw, kay 8. departed, larboard 9. abandoned, remaining

left (pert to)...
aground.. 6. neaped 8. beneaped
animal (motherless).. 4. cade 5. dogie
comb form.. 8. sinistro
hand (Mus).. 8. sinistra
hand page.. 5. verso
hand pitcher.. 8. southpaw
out.. 7. omitted 8. excluded 10. eliminated
spirally.. 11. sinistrally
to one's judgment.. 13. discretionary
toward the.. 5. aport 9. sinistrad,

sinistral 12. levorotatory (Chem)

left–handed... 6. clumsy, gauche
7. oblique 8. southpaw 9. insincere, insulting 14. sinistromanual
16. counterclockwise

left–handed marriage...
10. morganatic

leftist... 7. liberal, radical
10. left–winger, liberalist
11. progressive

leg (pert to)...
armor.. 4. jamb 6. greave 7. jambeau
bone.. 4. shin 5. tibia 6. fibula
calf.. 5. sural
insect.. 4. coxa
joint.. 4. hock, knee 5. thigh
longest bone.. 5. femur
of lamb (cooked).. 5. gigot
term.. 4. crus 5. jambe 6. crural

legacy... 4. gift, will 6. devise
7. bequest, codicil 9. testament
10. bequeathal

legal... 4. leal 5. licit, valid 6. lawful
10. authorized, legitimate

legal (pert to)...
abstract.. 6. précis
act, thing.. 5. actus
action.. 3. res 4. case 7. detinet, lawsuit, summons
case, postponed.. 7. remanet
claim.. 4. lien
confirmation.. 10. validation
contestant.. 6. suitor 8. litigant
9. plaintiff
critic.. 6. censor
decree, divorce.. 10. decree nisi
defense.. 5. alibi
delay.. 4. mora
denial, stoppage.. 8. estoppel
extract.. 7. estreat
order.. 4. writ
paper.. 4. deed, writ 5. lease
6. escrow
possession.. 6. seizin (seisin)
power (to take).. 7. prender (prendre)
process.. 6. caveat 7. detinet
right, by.. 6. ex jure
security.. 4. bond
surrender.. 6. remise

legally competent... 5. capax

legate... 8. envoy 8. bequeath, delegate 10. ambassador, diplomatic

legend... 4. Edda, myth, saga, tale
5. fable 7. history 9. narrative, tradition 11. inscription

legendary... 8. fabulous 9. imaginary, narrative 11. traditional
12. mythological

legendary (pert to)...
goddess (slave).. 5. Baube, lambe
primate.. 6. Dubric
water sprite.. 6. undine

legendry... 7. legends (collectively)

leggings... 5. chaps, spats 6. strads
7. gaiters, greaves, puttees
8. gamashes, gambados
12. galligaskins

legislate... 3. act 5. elect, enact
8. pass laws 10. put through

legislative (pert to)...
agent.. 8. lobbyist
assembly.. 4. diet 8. assize, senate

8. congress 10. parliament
group.. 4. bloc

legislator... 5. solon 7. senator
8. lawgiver, lawmaker 9. statesman
11. congressman 14. representative

legislature... 4. Diet 5. House
6. Senate 8. Congress 9. bicameral
(2 branches)

legitimate... 4. real, true 5. legal, licit, valid 6. cogent, lawful 7. genuine
9. permitted 11. efficacious, justifiable

legman... 8. newshawk

legume... 3. pea, pod, uva 4. bean, soya 6. clover, lentil, loment
7. alfalfa

leisure... 4. ease, time, toom 5. otium
6. otiose 7. freedom 9. spare time
11. convenience, opportunity

lemming... 4. maki, vari 5. mouse
6. rodent

lemur... 5. indri, loris, makis, potto
6. anguid, aye–aye, colugo, galago, macaco, monkey 7. tarsier
8. Anguidae, mongoose
10. angwantibo

Lenape... 6. Indian (Del)

lend... 4. loan 5. grant 6. devote (to)
7. advance

length (pert to)...
measure.. 4. area 5. gauge 6. linear, volume
ten meters.. 9. decameter
three–quarters inch.. 5. digit
time.. 3. age, eon, era 6. moment, period
two and 1/4 inches.. 4. nail
unit.. 6. micron, parsec (Astron)

lengthen out... 7. prolong, stretch
8. continue, elongate, protract

lengthwise... 5. along 12. horizontally
14. longitudinally

lenient... 3. lax 4. easy, mild
7. clement, patient 8. merciful, relaxing, tolerant 9. assuasive, emollient, softening

Lenin (pert to)...
birthplace.. 9. Ulyanovsk
famed as.. 8. Dictator (Russ)
real name.. 7. Ulianov

Leningrad (Russ)... 9. Petrograd
12. St Petersburg 15. Window on the West

lenis... 4. soft 6. gentle, smooth

lenitive... 4. mild 6. gentle
8. mitigant, ointment, remedial
9. assuasive, emollient, mitigator, relieving, softening 10. palliative, qualifying

lens... 5. toric 7. bifocal, lentoid
8. meniscus, sunglass 9. lenticula
10. anastigmat 13. apochromatism

Lent... 6. carême 9. Forty days, Great
Fast 12. Quadragesima

lentamento... 6. slowly

lentando... 9. retarding 14. becoming slower

lenticula... 7. freckle, lentigo (freckly)

lento... 4. slow

Leo constellation star... 7. Regulus, the Lion

leopard... 4. pard 5. ounce 6. jaguar,

ocelot 7. cheetah, panther
leper... 5. lazar, mesel 6. Naaman
(Bib)
Lepontine Alps... 10. Monte Leone
(peak)
lepra... 7. leprosy 14. Hansen's
disease
Lesbos... 5. Assos (Aristotle's)
6. Island (Sappho's) 8. Mytilene
Les Miserables author... 4. Hugo
(Victor)
lessen... 4. bate, wane 5. abate,
lower, peter, relax 6. impair, minify,
narrow, reduce, shrink, weaken
7. cut down, relieve 8. decrease,
diminish, mitigate, moderate, palliate
11. deteriorate
lesser... 4. less 5. minor (Mus)
7. smaller 8. inferior
Lesser Bear (Astron)... 9. Ursa Minor
Lesser Dog (Astron)... 10. Canis Minor
Lesser Lion (Astron)... 8. Leo Minor
let... 4. hire, rent 5. allow, lease,
leave 6. hinder, impede, permit
7. prevent
let (pert to)...
down.. 5. lower 8. comedown,
drawback, relaxing 10. slackening
14. disappointment
fall.. 4. drop, slip 5. spill 7. mention
in.. 5. admit, enter 6. insert
it be given.. 6. detur
it stand.. 3. sta (Mus) 4. stet
up.. 4. rest 5. cease, pause, relax
6. slow up 7. slacken 8. decrease
lethal... 5. fatal, feral 6. deadly, mortal
7. deathly, killing 11. destructive
12. death–dealing
lethargic... 4. dull 5. heavy, inert
6. drowsy, sleepy, torpid
8. comatose, listless 9. apathetic
lethargy... 4. coma 5. sleep, sopor
6. apathy, stupor, torpor 7. languor
8. hebetude, neurosis 9. lassitude
10. drowsiness (morbid)
Lethe... 5. abyss, Hades, river
8. oblivion 13. forgetfulness
lethiferous... 6. deadly 11. destructive
Leto (pert to)...
mother of.. 6. Apollo 7. Artemis
Roman name.. 6. Latona
wife of.. 4. Zeus
letter... 4. note, type 7. epistle,
message 9. character
13. communication
letter (pert to)...
bright star.. 4. Beta
carrier.. 6. correo 7. mailman,
postman
cross stroke.. 5. serif
first.. 7. initial
letter for letter.. 9. literatim
marks.. 5. breve
of advice.. 11. lettre d'avis
of challenge.. 6. cartel
representation.. 10. literation
short.. 4. line, note 6. billet
sloping.. 6. italic
sound loss (last).. 7. apocope
two letters (one sound).. 7. digraph
9. diphthong

writer.. 13. correspondent
letters (pert to)...
decorate with.. 7. miniate
10. illuminate
man of.. 9. literatus
ref to.. 8. literary
lettuce... 3. cos 4. head 7. Lactuca,
romaine
leukocyte... 9. corpuscle (white)
Levant... 4. East 6. Orient 7. leather
(Morocco) 8. East wind
Levantine (pert to)...
country.. 13. Mediterranean
garment.. 6. caftan
herb.. 6. madder
ketch.. 3. bum 4. jerm, saic 5. xebec
6. settee 8. levanter
valley.. 4. wadi (wady)
wind.. 7. Morocco
levee... 4. bank, dike, pier, quay
5. ridge 6. durbar, trench
8. assembly 9. reception
10. embankment
level... 4. even, fell, flat, just, raze
5. equal, grade, plane, plani (comb
form), point 6. peavey (peavy),
smooth, steady, topple 7. flatten,
terrace, uniform 8. demolish,
equalize, parterre 12. well–balanced
lever... 3. bar, lam, pry 5. crank,
jimmy, pedal, prise 6. peavey
(peavy), tappet, tiller 7. crowbar,
treadle
leviathan (pert to)...
animal (Bib).. 5. whale 6. dragon
9. crocodile
embroidery.. 6. canvas
11. cross–stitch
political.. 12. (the) commonwealth
size.. 4. huge 7. titanic
10. formidable
Levi's father (Bib)... 5. Jacob
Levite... 5. tribe 10. descendant
Levitical... 7. Aaronic 9. Aaronical
10. priesthood (Mormon)
Leviticus... 10. Pentateuch
levity... 6. gaiety 8. buoyancy
9. frivolity, lightness 10. triviality,
volatility
levy... 3. tax 4. fine, wage (war)
5. rally, stent 6. assess, impose
7. collect, estreat 9. recruital
lex... 3. law 7. statute
lexicon... 4. book (of words)
10. dictionary, vocabulary
lex loci... 13. law of the place
lex non scripta... 12. unwritten law
liability... 4. debt 5. debit 6. cessavit
9. proneness 10. likelihood,
obligation 11. possibility
14. responsibility
liable... 3. apt 5. bound 6. likely
7. exposed, subject 10. answerable,
chargeable 11. responsible
liable (pert to)...
likely to.. 3. apt 5. prone
11. predisposed
not liable.. 6. exempt
to objection.. 13. exceptionable
to penalty.. 6. guilty
Lia Fail... 12. Stone of Scone
15. Coronation Stone (Ir)

liaison... 4. link 7. joining 8. intimacy, intrigue 11. co–operation 18. intercommunication

liana... 4. cipo 5. vines (woody) 9. wild grape

liar... 5. cheat 6. fibber 7. Ananias, wernard (obs) 8. deceiver, fabulist, perjurer 12. prevaricator

Lias system... 8. Jurassic

libation... 5. drink 8. oblation, offering, potation

libel... 4. bill 6. defame 7. lampoon, request, slander 8. circular (obs), handbill, roorback 10. defamation 11. certificate, declaration 12. supplication

liberal... 4. free, Whig 5. ample, frank 7. copious, profuse 8. eclectic, generous 9. bountiful, extensive, plentiful 10. hospitable, munificent 11. broad–minded, magnanimous 12. uncontrolled

liberate... 4. flee, free 5. loose 6. redeem 7. deliver, manumit, release 8. separate, unfetter 9. disengage 10. emancipate

Liberia...
capital.. 8. Monrovia
city.. 8. Buchanan 10. Greenville
gulf.. 5. Sidra
language.. 3. Kru 7. English
people.. 3. Vai (Vei) 5. Negro

liberty... 4. ease, free 5. leave 7. freedom, license 9. exemption, privilege 10. permission 11. opportunity

librarian... 7. bookman 10. bibliosoph, bibliothec 13. bibliothecary

Libya, Africa...
astronomy.. 4. Mars (portion)
capital.. 7. Tripoli 8. Benghazi
district.. 6. Fezzan 9. Cyrenaica 12. Tripolitania
language.. 7. Hamitic
oasis (saline).. 6. Sebkha (Sebka)
people.. 5. Arabs
sea.. 13. Mediterranean

Libya, Gr (pert to)...
children.. 5. Belus 6. Agenor
heroine of.. 5. Libya
husband.. 8. Poseidon

license... 5. right 6. bandon, permit 7. dismiss, freedom, liberty 8. sanction 9. approbate, authority, authorize, privilege 10. permission 11. lawlessness 13. authorization

licentious... 3. lax 4. lewd 5. loose 7. immoral, lawless 9. debauched, dissolute 10. lascivious, profligate 12. uncontrolled, unrestrained

licet... 6. lawful 7. granted 12. it is conceded

lichens (pert to)...
abounding in.. 9. lichenose
derivative.. 4. moss 5. usnic 6. litmus
genus.. 5. Usnea 7. Evernia
study of.. 11. lichenology

licit... 3. sue 4. just 5. legal 6. lawful 9. permitted

lick... 3. lap, win 4. flog, whip 5. lap up, taste 6. baffle, defeat, thrash

7. conquer 8. overcome, vanquish

licorice... 5. abrin 9. jequirity

lid... 3. cap, hat 4. bred, case, roof 5. cover 6. eyelid 7. stopper 9. operculum

lid, put on the... 3. end 6. hush up 7. license 8. complete, suppress

lie... 3. fib 4. rest 7. falsify, falsity, recline, untruth 8. deception, falsehood, mendacity 10. equivocate 13. prevarication

lie (pert to)...
at ease.. 4. loll 5. droop 6. dangle
face down.. 7. pronate
hidden, in ambush.. 4. lurk, plot 6. in wait 9. insidiate 11. concealment
in warmth.. 4. bask 9. luxuriate
low.. 6. abased 9. prostrate
prostrate.. 4. flat 5. creep 6. grovel

Liebestraum composer... 5. Liszt

Liechtenstein, Europe...
capital.. 5. Vaduz
government.. 12. principality
language.. 6. German
religion.. 8. Catholic

lief (anc)... 4. dear, fain, glad 7. willing 8. disposed 9. agreeably, favorably

lieutenant... 6. deputy 10. substitute 11. locum tenens

life... 3. vie 4. bios 5. being 6. always, energy, spirit 8. vitality, vivacity 9. animation, existence

life (pert to)...
after death.. 8. Olam–haba
animal.. 4. bios 5. biota (flora, fauna)
biology.. 4. bios
comb form.. 3. bio
giving.. 9. animative 11. procreative
god of.. 6. Faunus
insurance.. 7. tontine
jacket (sl).. 7. Mae West
later, older.. 8. autumnal
lifelike.. 5. alike, vital 6. biotic 9. realistic
plant.. 4. bios 5. biota
principle.. 5. atman, prana, tenet 6. spirit
prolonger.. 6. elixir
science of.. 7. anatomy, biology, zoology 12. paleontology
sea.. 5. coral 8. plankton
staff of.. 5. bread
without.. 4. dead 5. azoic 8. lifeless 9. inanimate

lifeless... 4. abio (comb form), dead, dull, flat 5. amort, azoic, heavy, inert, vapid 6. jejune, torpid 8. inactive, listless 9. bloodless, exanimate, inanimate, powerless, tasteless 10. lackluster, spiritless, unanimated

lifetime... 3. age, day, eon (aeon) 6. always 8. duration 10. generation

lift... 3. aid, pry 4. jack, perk 5. boost, exalt, heave, hoist, raise, steal, theft 6. puff up, thrill 7. derrick, elevate, improve, inspire 8. elevator 11. inspiration

lifting device... 4. jack, pump

5. crane, davit, lever, tongs
7. capstan, derrick, erector
8. elevator, heighten, windlass
lifting muscle... 7. erector, levator
ligament... 4. bond, cord 6. tendon
7. bandage
ligan, lagan... 6. debris, jetsam
7. flotsam
ligature... 3. tie 4. band, bond, cord,
note 6. amulet, binder, taenia
7. bandage
light... 3. arc, gay, sun 4. dawn,
easy, glim, lamp, lume, mild, pale,
soft 5. flare, flood, klieg, taper
6. alight, aspect, blonde, bright,
candle, gentle, ignite, illume,
medium, window 7. cresset, fragile,
glimmer, glowing, trivial 8. buoyancy,
daylight, delicate, illumine, radiance,
trifling 9. effulgent 10. brightness,
weightless 11. information
12. incandescent
light (pert to)...
apparatus.. 9. holophote
circle.. 4. halo, nimb 6. nimbus
7. aureola, aureole
cloud.. 6. nimbus
coating.. 4. film
footed.. 4. fast 5. agile
globe.. 4. bulb
god.. 6. Balder (Baldr)
handed.. 4. deft
headed.. 5. dizzy 6. fickle
9. beeheaded
image.. 8. spectrum
leading.. 8. luminary
reflector.. 4. lens 6. mirror
refractor.. 5. prism
science.. 6. optics
source.. 3. sun
touch.. 3. dab
unit.. 3. lux, pyr 5. lumen 6. carcel,
Hefner
without.. 4. dark 7. aphotic, obscure
8. starless 9. pitch–dark
10. caliginous
yellow.. 5. amber
light and airy... 7. tenuous
8. delicate, ethereal
light and quick... 6. nimble, volent
light dress fabric... 6. merino
8. cashmere 9. bombazine,
paramatta (Chin)
lighten... 4. ease 5. allay, cheer, clear
6. reduce 7. gladden, relieve
8. brighten, illumine, jettison
9. alleviate, disburden 10. illuminate
lighter... see also *light* 4. scow
5. barge 7. gabbard, pontoon
8. chopboat (Chin)
lighthearted... 3. gay 8. carefree,
cheerful 9. vivacious
Light Horse Harry... 3. Lee (Gen
Henry Lee)
lighthouse... 5. tower 6. beacon,
pharos 7. seamark 10. watchtower
lightness... 6. gaiety, levity 8. airiness,
buoyancy, sobriety 9. flippancy,
frivolity, giddiness 10. fickleness,
triviality, volatility, wantonness
11. flightiness, inconstancy, instability
12. unsteadiness 14. weightlessness

15. thoughtlessness
lightning... 4. lait 5. flash, levin
8. flashing 9. discharge
lightning (pert to)...
bug.. 6. beetle 7. firefly
discharge.. 4. bolt 11. thunderbolt
reference to.. 8. fulgural
rod.. 8. arrester
stone.. 9. fulgurite
war.. 10. blitzkrieg
Light of the World... 11. Jesus
Christ
lightsome... 3. gay 4. airy 5. agile,
clear, light, lucid, merry 6. fickle,
nimble 7. lighted 8. cheerful,
cheering, graceful, luminous, unsteady
9. frivolous 12. lighthearted
lights out... 4. taps
Light That Failed, author... 7. Kipling
ligneous... 5. woody 6. wooden, xyloid
8. firewood
lignite... 4. coal
like... 2. as 4. copy, love 5. enjoy,
equal, liken, savor 6. admire, desire
7. similar 11. counterpart,
homogeneous
like (pert to)...
bore.. 6. osteal
fern.. 6. frondose, frondous
gland.. 7. adenose
gold.. 7. aureate
house, dome.. 5. domal
kneecap.. 7. rotular 10. rotuliform
sea lion.. 7. otarian, otarine
suffix.. 2. ar, ic 3. ine, oid, ose
likeable, likable... 6. genial
8. charming, pleasant
likelihood... 8. prospect 10. good
chance 11. probability 14. apparently
true
likely... 3. apt, fit 5. prone 6. comely
8. credible, feasible, probable,
suitable 9. promising 11. verisimilar
likeness... 4. copy, icon, twin
5. guise, image 6. effigy, statue
7. parable, picture, replica
8. parallel, portrait 9. imitation,
semblance 10. comparison,
photograph, similarity 11. counterfeit
12. reproduction 14. representation
likewise... 3. too 4. also 5. ditto
8. moreover
liking... 4. like, love, lust 5. fancy
6. comely 7. delight 8. pleasing
12. predilection
lilac... 5. lilas, mauve 6. purple
7. syringa
lilac throat... 11. hummingbird
Lilliputian... 4. tiny 5. dwarf, minim
6. midget 7. dwarfed 10. diminutive
lilt... 3. air 4. song, tune 5. swing
6. poetic, rhythm 7. rejoice
lily... 2. ti 3. lis 4. aloe, ixia, sego
5. calla, lotus, onion, water, wokas
(wocas), yucca 6. Allium, Nuphar
8. daffodil, mariposa, martagon,
soaproot 9. narcissus
lily (pert to)...
family, genus.. 4. Aloe 6. Tulipa
7. Bessera 9. Liliaceae
10. Hyacinthus
grass.. 10. cuckoopint

iron.. 7. harpoon
of France.. 10. fleur–de–lis
shaped.. 7. crinoid 9. crinoidal
water.. 8. Castalia, Nymphaea
lily of the valley (pert to)...
bud.. 3. pip
Cape Cod.. 13. barney–clapper
English.. 6. mugget
family.. 15. Convallariaceae
liliaceous plant.. 5. yucca
shrub.. 10. fetterbush
tree.. 6. sorrel
lima bean disease... 6. mildew
    9. yeast spot
liman... 5. marsh 6. lagoon
limb... 3. arm, fin, imp, leg 4. wing
    5. bough, scamp 6. branch, member
    7. flipper 9. anaclasis
limber... 4. limp, weak 5. agile, lithe,
    loose 6. flabby, pliant, supple
    7. flaccid, lissome 8. flexible, yielding
limbo... 4. hell, jail 6. prison
    9. purgatory
limbs, absence of... 6. amelia
    7. acolous
lime... 4. calx 5. color, fruit
    8. chlorine, fumigant 9. deodorant,
    quicklime 11. green–yellow
    12. linden yellow
limen... 9. threshold
limestone... 4. calp, malm 5. chalk
    6. marble, oolite 8. pisolite
lime tree... 6. linden, tupelo
limey... 6. sailor 7. soldier
limit... 3. end, fix, ori (comb form)
    4. term 5. allot, bourn 6. summit
    7. confine 8. boundary, capacity,
    restrain, restrict, terminal
    11. restriction, termination
    12. consummation
limited... 3. few 5. local, scant
    6. finite, narrow, scanty 7. bounded,
    topical 8. confined, reserved
    9. astricted, parochial 10. restricted
    11. conditional, topopolitan
    13. circumscribed
limiting... 7. hedging 10. qualifying,
    relational 11. restraining, restricting,
    restrictive
limn... 4. draw 5. paint 6. depict
    7. portray 8. decorate 9. delineate
    10. illuminate
limp... 3. hop, lax 4. halt, soft, thin,
    weak 5. loose 6. flabby, limber
    7. flaccid 8. drooping, flexible
    9. inelastic 13. unsubstantial
limpid... 4. pure 5. lucid 6. bright
    7. crystal 8. pellucid 11. translucent,
    transparent 12. intelligible
Lincoln, Abraham (pert to)...
assassin.. 15. John Wilkes Booth
birthplace.. 8. Kentucky (1809)
debater.. 7. Douglas (Stephen A)
dog.. 4. Fido
mother.. 10. Nancy Hanks
Secy of State.. 6. Seward
Secy of War.. 7. Stanton
son.. 10. Robert Todd
wife.. 8. Mary Todd
Lincoln (pert to)...
color.. 9. Carthamus 11. yellow–green
sheep (breed).. 7. English

Lindbergh, Charles A (pert to)...
birthplace.. 7. Detroit (1902)
flight field.. 9. Roosevelt (LI)
flight to (1927).. 5. Paris (1st)
retreat.. 10. Illiec Isle (Fr)
wife.. 10. Anne Morrow
linden... 3. lin 4. lime, teil 5. Tilia
line... 3. row 4. arow, axis, cant, ceil,
    clew, cord, face, mark, race, rail,
    rein, rule, seam, side 5. angle,
    align, raphe, ridge, route, stria, track
    6. crease, isobar, policy, series,
    streak, stripe 7. engrave, outline
    8. boundary, vocation, wainscot
    9. delineate
line (pert to)...
adjusting.. 9. alinement
central.. 4. axis
comb form.. 4. lino
conceptual, geological.. 6. agonic,
    isotac, tropic 7. equator 8. isothere,
    isotherm, latitude, meridian
    9. longitude
equidistant.. 8. parallel
fine (type).. 5. leger, serif
fishing.. 5. snell 7. ratline (ratlin)
imaginary.. 7. equator, Maginot
mathematics.. 4. sine 5. agone
    6. secant 7. tangent
measure.. 3. gry 4. rule
meteoric.. 6. isobar
nautical.. 6. earing 7. halyard,
    hawsing
poetic.. 5. stich, verse
racing.. 4. wire
raised.. 4. weal, welt 5. ridge
selling.. 11. merchandise
soldiers.. 4. file, rank 6. cordon
transport.. 5. stage 7. carrier
    8. carriage
type.. 5. agate, serif
up, lineup.. 4. plan 5. align
    6. muster 7. arrange 8. schedule
    9. formation 11. arrangement,
    parallelize
lineage... 3. kin 4. race 5. birth,
    blood, stock, tribe 6. family, strain
    7. descent 8. pedigree 9. offspring
    10. extraction, progenitor
lineal... 6. racial 10. continuous,
    delineated 12. genealogical
lineman... 3. end 5. guard 6. center,
    tackle 7. wireman 11. electrician
linen... 4. crea, duck, lawn, lint
    5. crash, gulix, inkle (tape), toile
    6. barras, damask, dowlas, napery,
    sheets 7. cambric, Holland, lockram
ling... 4. fish, hake 5. heath 6. burbot
    7. eelpout, Gidadae, heather
    8. chestnut
linger... 3. lag 4. drag, idle, wait
    5. dally, defer, delay, dwell, hover,
    tarry 6. dawdle, go slow, loiter,
    remain 8. continue, hesitate
    13. procrastinate
lingerie... 9. underwear 10. underlinen
    11. underthings 14. unmentionables
lingering... 5. delay 7. chronic
    8. dilatory, slowness 10. protracted
lingo... 4. cant 6. jargon, lingua,
    patois, patter, tongue 8. language
lingua... 5. lingo 6. jargon, tongue

11. hypopharynx
lingual... 7. glossal 9. lingulate
10. linguiform, tonguelike
linguistics... 6. syntax 7. grammar
8. language 9. phonology, semantics
10. lexicology
link... 3. tie 4. bond, join, loop, yoke
5. annex, nexus, torch, unite
6. couple, member, relate
7. connect, liaison, passage
8. catenate 12. intermediary
linkage... 5. tie–up, union 6. hookup
7. joinder, joining 8. junction
11. conjunction
linking... 7. liaison 9. anrœtent
links in a chain... 7. hundred
lion... 3. cat, cub, leo 4. puma
5. simba 6. cougar, Lionel, lionet
8. Felis leo 9. celebrity 12. King of
Beasts
Lion (pert to)...
  England.. 8. heraldry
  God.. 3. Ali
  Lucerne.. 11. Switzerland (Sculpture)
  St Mark.. 6. Venice (winged)
  the North.. 6. Sweden (King
    Adolphus)
lionlike... 6. feline 7. catlike, leonine
lip... 3. jib, rim 4. edge, kiss, talk
5. cheil, words 6. flange, labium,
labrum, speech 7. cheilos
8. labellum 10. mouthpiece
12. impertinence
lip (pert to)...
  comb form.. 5. chilo, labio
  formed.. 6. labial
  inflammation.. 9. cheilitis
  ornament.. 6. labret
  service.. 9. hypocrisy 10. sanctimony
    12. unctuousness
  surgery.. 9. chilotomy 11. chiloplasty
  tumor.. 7. chiloma
lipped... 6. labial 7. labiate
liquefy... 4. fuse, melt, thaw
6. reduce 8. dissolve, fluidify
10. deliquesce
liqueur... 5. crème, noyau, sirup
6. cognac, genepi, kummel
7. cordial, curaçao, ratafia
8. absinthe, anisette 9. Cointreau
11. Benedictine
liquid... 5. clear, fluid 6. watery
7. flowing 8. beverage, manifest, not
solid
liquid (pert to)...
  assets.. 4. cash 5. money
    9. resources
  chemical.. 7. acetone 8. furfural
  inflammable.. 3. gas 5. ether
    7. alcohol 8. gasoline
  oily.. 5. olein 7. aniline, picamar
  soap.. 6. napalm
  thick.. 3. tar 4. dope 5. syrup (sirup)
  weak.. 5. blash
liquidate... 4. kill 6. depose, pay off,
settle 8. amortize 9. discharge
11. exterminate
liquor... 3. ale, dew, gin, rum, rye
4. beer, brew, grog, lush, sake, wine
5. hooch, kefir, punch, stout, vodka
6. arrack (arak), arrope, elixir, whisky
(whiskey) 8. cocktail, highball

9. applejack, moonshine
10. chasse–café
liquor container... 3. keg 5. flask
6. barrel, bottle 8. cellaret, decanter
liquor maker... 6. abkari (Ind), brewer
7. vintner 9. distiller
liquor server... 6. barman 7. barmaid,
skinker (anc), tapster
liquor shop... 3. bar 6. saloon, tavern
7. barroom, cabaret, shebeen (Scot),
taproom 8. alehouse 9. groghouse,
honky–tonk 11. rathskeller (ratskeller)
liripipe, liripoop (Hist)... 4. hood
5. scarf 6. dotard, tippet
lissom... 5. layer 7. stratum
8. platform 12. strand of rope
lissome... 5. agile, lithe 6. limber,
nimble, supple 7. willowy 8. flexible
list... 3. tip 4. edge, file, roll, rota,
rote 5. index, limit, panel, table
6. careen, edging, enlist, record,
roster, stripe 7. catalog, incline
8. calendar, classify, manifest,
register, schedule, tabulate
9. catalogue, enclosure, inventory,
repertory 10. repertoire
11. enumeration
list (pert to)...
  actors.. 4. cast
  competitors.. 5. entry, slate
  foods.. 4. menu 5. carte
  investments.. 9. portfolio
  memoranda.. 5. scrip
  officers.. 6. roster
  references.. 5. index
listen... 3. ear 4. hear, heed 6. attend
7. give ear, hearken (harken)
8. overhear 9. eavesdrop
listening... 7. audient 9. attentive
listing... 4. list 6. strips 7. selvage
10. enlistment, enrollment
listless... 4. dull 6. abject, drowsy,
moping, supine 7. languid
8. careless, heedless, sluggish
9. apathetic 10. spiritless
11. unconcerned 13. uninteresting
litchi nut... 8. rambutan
literary... 6. versed 8. lettered
9. classical 11. book–learned
literary (pert to)...
  composition.. 5. cento, essay, opera
    8. rhetoric
  criticism.. 9. epicrisis
  drudge.. 4. grub, hack
  extracts.. 9. anthology
  fragments.. 3. ana 5. notes
    8. analecta, analects
  laws.. 9. copyright
  piracy.. 10. plagiarism
  selection.. 7. excerpt
  style.. 5. prose 6. purism 8. pedantic
literature... 4. book, epic, Veda
5. drama, lyric, novel 6. ballad,
poetry 7. fiction, writing
10. nonfiction 13. belles–lettres
lithe... 4. slim 6. limber, supple, svelte
7. lissome, slender 8. flexible
Lithuania...
  capital.. 5. Vilna (Vilnius) 6. Kaunas
    (Kovno)
  Jew.. 6. Litvak
  people.. 5. Balts, Letts 6. Aestii

port.. 8. Klaipeda (Memel)
river.. 6. Niemen
litigant... 6. suitor 9. defendant,
   disputant, litigator, plaintiff
litigation... 4. suit 7. contest, dispute,
   lawsuit 10. contention, discussion
litigious... 10. disputable
   11. belligerent, contentious
litten... 7. lighted 8. cemetery
   10. churchyard
litter... 3. bed, hay 4. bier, mess
   5. couch, dooly (doolie), mulch,
   straw, young 6. coffin, jumble
   7. clutter, rubbish 9. palanquin,
   stretcher
litter of pigs... 6. farrow
little... 3. sma, wee 4. puny, tiny,
   weak 5. brief, petit, petty, scant,
   short, small 6. dapper, petite, slight
   7. not much 8. trifling 9. niggardly
   11. unimportant 12. narrow–minded
   14. inconsiderable
little (pert to)...
   bethel.. 6. chapel (seaman's), church
   by little.. 6. slowly 7. peu à peu
   9. piecemeal, poco a poco
   comb form.. 5. steno
   devil.. 3. imp 4. minx 5. rogue
   7. ruffian 13. mischief–maker
   fellow.. 6. shaver
   finger, toe.. 7. minimus
   flag.. 9. banderole
   music term.. 4. poco
   ring.. 7. annulet
Little Rhody... 11. Rhode Island
Little Women, author... 6. Alcott
   (Louisa)
littoral... 4. zone (marine) 5. shore
   7. coastal 9. bordering
liturgical... 10. ceremonial
   11. ritualistic
liturgy... 4. rite 6. ritual 8. ceremony
   14. consuetudinary
live... 5. dwell, exist 6. reside
   7. breathe 8. continue, have life
live (pert to)...
   by sponging.. 5. cadge
   by stratagems.. 5. shark
   by wits.. 5. cheat 7. deceive, falsify
   13. Machiavellize
   earlier.. 8. pre–exist
   in.. 7. inhabit
   in tents.. 5. nomad 7. scenite
   in the country.. 9. rusticate
live... 5. alert, alive, vital, vivid
   6. bright, lively, living, virgin (mineral)
   7. charged, not dead 8. vigorous
   9. energetic 11. electrified
lively... 3. gay, vif 4. airy, grig, keen,
   pert, spry, yare 6. active, blithe,
   bright, snappy 7. animate, buoyant,
   pungent, tittupy (tittuppy) 8. spirited
   9. energetic, sprightly, vivacious
   10. enlivening, rebounding
   11. interesting 12. effervescent
liver (pert to)...
   comb form.. 6. hepato
   disease.. 5. cirrhosis, hepatitis
   duct.. 4. bile
   pert to.. 5. hepar 7. hepatic
   resembling.. 8. hepatoid
Liverpool native... 12. Liverpudlian

liverwort... 6. Riccia 8. agrimony,
   hepatica 9. bryophyte
living... 4. life 5. alive, being, quick
   6. extant 7. animate, organic, topical
   8. benefice, existent, lifelike
   10. livelihood 11. subsistence
living (in, on, near)...
   currents.. 5. lotic
   ground.. 7. epigeal
   holes.. 11. latebricole
   leaves.. 13. phyllophagous
   oxygen.. 7. aerobic
   plane (same).. 8. coplanar
   poverty.. 11. necessitous
   river bank.. 9. riparious
   rivers, streams.. 9. rheophile
   seas (deep).. 8. bathybic
   shores.. 8. littoral
   solitude, seclusion.. 10. eremitical
   11. eremiticism
   tents.. 7. scenite
   together.. 11. contubernal
living (pert to)...
   again.. 6. Buddha 7. revived
   8. Hutukhtu 9. redivivus
   being.. 5. wight 6. animal
   8. organism
   capable of.. 6. viable
   dull.. 10. vegetation
   individual.. 4. bion
   near the ground.. 7. epigeal
   together.. 8. intimate 11. contubernal
   (contubernial)
lixivium... 3. lye 6. bleach 8. cleanser
lizard... 3. dab, eft 4. adda, gila,
   newt, seps, uran 5. agama, anoli,
   gecko, skink, varan 6. dragon,
   hardim, iguana, moloch 7. monitor,
   saurian, tuatera 8. basilisk
   9. chameleon 10. chuckwalla,
   salamander
llama... 6. alpaca, vicuna 7. guanaco
load... 3. jag 4. fill, lade, onus
   5. cargo 6. burden, charge, weight
   7. fraught, freight, oppress, prepare
   8. contents, encumber 10. imposition
   11. encumbrance
loaded... 5. drunk, flush, laden, ready
   7. charged, fraught 8. burdened,
   weighted 10. in the chips
loader of vessels... 9. stevedore
loadstone, lodestone... 6. magnet
   8. terrella 9. magnetite
loaf... 4. idle, lump 5. bread 6. loiter,
   lounge 9. Eucharist
loafer... 5. idler 6. beggar 7. lounger
   8. vagabond
loam... 3. rab 4. clay, lime, silt, soil
   5. chalk, loess, slepur
loan... 4. lend 6. borrow 7. advance
   10. provisions 13. accommodation
loath... 6. averse 7. hostile
   9. disliking, reluctant, unwilling
loathe... 4. hate 5. abhor 6. detest
   7. despise, dislike 9. abominate
loathsome... 4. foul, vile 5. nasty
   6. odious 7. cloying, hateful
   9. abhorrent, offensive, repellant
   10. abominable, disgusting
lob... 3. box, cop 4. step, till, toss,
   vein 5. stair, throw 7. lugworm,
   pollack 9. chandelle

lobby... 4. hall, room 5. foyer
8. anteroom, corridor, coulisse
9. enclosure, vestibule 10. wirepuller
13. pressure group

lobe... 5. alula 6. earlap, lappet, lobule
7. pendant

lobster (pert to)...
claw.. 5. chela 6. nipper, pincer
eggs.. 3. roe 5. coral
French.. 6. homard
genus.. 7. Homarus, Macrura
8. Nephrops
part.. 6. thorax
tail.. 6. telson
trap.. 3. pot 4. corf 5. creel 6. bow
net

local... 7. edaphic, topical 8. regional
9. parochial 10. epichorial (epichoric)
13. autochthonous

local court... 5. gemot (gemote)

locale... 4. site 5. place, scene, venue

locality... 4. area, spot 5. place, situs
7. endemic, habitat 8. position

locate... 4. find, spot 6. settle
7. situate 9. establish

locatio... 7. leasing, letting

location... 4. seat, site, spot 5. locus,
place, situs 6. ubiety 7. habitat
8. district 9. situation
12. neighborhood

locator of forest fires... 7. alidade

loch... 3. bay 4. lake, pond 5. inlet,
lough

lock... 4. bolt, hasp, hold 5. Gatun,
latch 6. cotter, detent, fasten, fetter
8. fastener 9. floodgate

lockjaw... 7. tetanus, trismus
11. ankylostoma

lockman... 8. summoner (Isle of Man)
11. executioner

lock of hair... 4. curl 5. tress
6. berger 7. daglock, ringlet
8. lovelock, spit curl

lockup... 3. jug 4. jail 5. clink
6. cooler 8. hoosegow (hoosgow)
9. calaboose

loco... 3. mad 4. daft 5. craze, crazy
6. crazed 7. disease 10. moonstruck
15. non compos mentis

locomotion... 6. lation (Astrol), moving,
travel 7. transit 8. progress

locomotive... 3. hog 5. dolly, mogul
6. diesel, dinkey, engine, mikado
9. iron horse

locomotive cowcatcher... 5. pilot

locus... 4. area, drug, site 5. place
8. locality

locus (pert to)...
in quo.. 5. where 12. place in which
sigilli.. 14. place of the seal

locust... 4. weta 6. beetle, cicada,
cicala, kowhai 7. Locusta
9. wetapunga 11. grasshopper

locust (pert to)...
berry.. 5. drupe 9. glamberry
bird.. 4. dial 7. grackle 8. starling
10. white stork
like.. 6. mantis
plant.. 5. senna
sound.. 7. stridor 10. stridulate
tree.. 5. carob, honey 6. acacia

lode... 3. vug (vugg) 4. path, road,
vein 5. canal, drain, ledge 6. course
7. deposit 8. waterway

lodestar... 8. cynosure, polestar
11. guiding star

lodestone, loadstone... 6. magnet
8. terrella 9. magnetite

lodge... 3. hut, lie 4. camp, tent
5. cabin, hovel 6. billet, encamp,
reside 7. deposit, quarter
11. brotherhood

lodge doorkeeper... 5. tiler

lodging... 3. inn 4. gite, room
5. abode, hotel, roost 6. billet,
harbor (harbour), tavern 8. barracks,
dwelling, hostelry, quarters
9. dormitory, harborage (harbourage)
10. habitation

loess... 4. loam, silt, soil

lof... 6. praise 7. measure

loft... 3. bin 4. balk 5. attic

loftiness... 6. height 7. dignity
8. eminence 9. eloquence
11. distinction, magnanimity

lofty... 4. high, tall 5. proud 6. aerial,
Alpine, Andean 7. eminent, exalted,
haughty, stately, sublime 8. arrogant,
elevated, eloquent, majestic, towering
9. dignified 11. magisterial,
magnanimous 13. distinguished

lofty place... 4. peak 5. aerie, eyrie
(eyry) 6. summit 8. eminence,
pinnacle

log... 4. birl, slab 5. diary 6. record
8. firewood, mountain, puncheon,
register 11. speedometer

log (pert to)...
cock.. 10. woodpecker
gin.. 6. jammer
hauler (sled).. 4. tode
implement.. 6. nigger, peavey (peavy),
rosser
measure.. 7. scalage
noser.. 6. sniper
rolling.. 7. birling
section.. 6. spalt
support.. 3. nog

logarithmic terms... 3. bel 5. curve
6. spiral 7. ellipse, tangent
9. decrement

logarithm inventor... 6. Napier

loge... 3. box 5. booth, stall

loggerhead... 4. tool 6. turtle
7. fathead 8. bonehead, numskull
9. blockhead 10. thickskull

loggia... 7. gallery

logging (pert to)...
boots.. 4. pacs
rock.. 6. loggan
sled.. 4. tode 8. travois (travoise)
wheels.. 7. katydid

logic... 9. reasoning 13. argumentation

logic (pert to)...
fallacy.. 6. idolum
induction.. 7. epagoge
proposition.. 5. lemma 7. ferison
9. enthymeme, obvertend
specious.. 7. sophism
term.. 5. Darii, Ferio 8. Celarent

logical... 4. sane 5. sound, valid
8. coherent, credible, rational
9. plausible 10. consistent,
reasonable

logician... 8. reasoner
logogriph... 5. rebus 6. riddle
  7. anagram 8. logogram
logy... 4. dull 6. drowsy 8. sluggish
Lohengrin (pert to)...
  character.. 4. Elsa 8. Parsifal
  composer.. 6. Wagner (1850)
  Knight.. 15. Knight of the Swan
loin (pert to)...
  beef.. 10. tenderloin
  mutton.. 4. rack 5. chump
  pork.. 7. griskin
loincloth... 5. dhoti, pagne 7. G–string
  11. breechcloth
loir... 8. dormouse
Loire, France...
  Dept capital.. 12. Saint Etienne
  river's old name.. 5. Liger
  town.. 6. Nantes
  tributary.. 5. Indre
loiter... 3. lag 5. dally, delay, tarry
  6. dawdle, linger 7. saunter
loiterer... 4. slug 5. drone, idler
  6. lagger 7. dawdler, laggard
  8. sluggard
Loki (pert to)...
  god.. 7. Discord 8. Mischief
  wife.. 5. Sigyn
loll... 4. hang 5. droop 6. dangle,
  frowst (froust), lounge, repose, sprawl
  7. recline
loma, lomita... 4. hill
Lombard (pert to)...
  ancient.. 6. cannon
  historic.. 4. bank, loan
  Italy.. 5. tribe
  King.. 6. Alboin (legend)
  school.. 11. Renaissance
  street.. 6. London
Lombardy province... 4. Como
lomboy... 8. Java plum
lomilomi (Haw)... 3. rub 7. massage,
  shampoo
London, England...
  art gallery.. 4. Tate
  bank.. 27. Old Lady of Threadneedle
    Street
  borough.. 6. Ealing
  bridge.. 6. Thames
  bridle path.. 6. Rotten Row
  brown.. 9. carbuncle
  clock.. 6. Big Ben
  club (Whigs).. 6. Kit–Kat
  district.. 4. Soho 7. Alsatia, Lambeth,
    Mayfair (fashion) 9. Wimbledon
    10. Marylebone
  hawker.. 6. coster
  monument (Guildhall).. 3. Gog
    5. Magog
  Opera Company.. 12. Sadler's Wells
  porter.. 6. George
  prison.. 7. Newgate 8. Bridewell
  quarter.. 8. Vauxhall
  roisterer (Hist).. 3. mum
  Roman name.. 6. Agusta
  stables.. 4. mews
  stock exchange.. 17. Throgmorton
    Street
  street.. 9. Cheapside, Whitehall
    10. Piccadilly 11. Throgmorton
    12. Threadneedle
Londoner... 7. Cockney

Londres... 5. cigar
lone... 3. one 5. alone 6. lonely,
  single 7. forlorn 8. solitary
  9. unmarried 12. unfrequented
loneliness... 8. loneness, solitude
  9. aloneness, dejection, isolation
  10. depression, desolation
  12. lonesomeness
lonely... 4. lorn 6. dreary 8. desolate,
  lonesome, secluded, solitary
  10. friendless 11. sequestered
  12. unfrequented
Lone Star State... 5. Texas
long... 3. yen 4. pine 5. crave, wordy,
  yearn 6. aspire, prolix, thirst
  7. lengthy, tedious 8. tiresome
  9. prolonged, wearisome
  10. protracted
long (pert to)...
  ago, since.. 3. eld 4. yore
  beard.. 9. graybeard 10. bellarmine
    (jug)
  discourse, speech.. 6. screed, tirade
    7. descant 9. philippic, rigmarole
  dog.. 9. dachshund, greyhound
  dozen.. 8. thirteen
  established.. 8. habitual 10. inveterate
    11. traditional
  for.. 4. hope, pine 5. covet, crave
  horn.. 6. cattle (Tex)
  inlet.. 3. ria
  journey.. 4. trek 7. odyssey
  jump.. 5. halmo
  letters.. 7. screeds
  life.. 9. longevity
  limbed.. 5. rangy
  lived.. 9. macrobian
  periods.. 4. ages, eons
  scarf.. 4. sari
  suffering.. 7. patient 10. forbearing
  Tom.. 3. gun 8. titmouse
  windedness.. 9. garrulity, prolixity
    13. longiloquence
longing... 5. yen 6. desire, pining
  7. craving, wistful 8. yearning
  9. hankering, nostalgia
longitudinal... 10. euthytatic (stress),
  lengthwise
longshoreman... 6. docker, loader,
  lumper, stower 9. stevedore
  10. roustabout
loo... 3. pam 4. game
look... 3. con, ken, pry, see 4. haze,
  heed, leer, peep, scry, seek, seem
  5. point, stare, watch 6. appear,
  expect 7. examine, inspect, observe
  8. indicate, perceive 9. search for
look (pert to)...
  after.. 4. tend 5. serve 6. follow
    7. care for 9. keep vigil, supervise
  at.. 3. eye 4. face, scan, upon
    6. regard 7. examine
  back.. 6. recall 7. retrace
    8. remember 9. recollect 10. call to
    mind
  down upon.. 4. leer, snub 5. fleer,
    gloat 7. askance, despise
  forward to.. 5. await 6. expect
    7. foresee 10. anticipate
  like.. 8. resemble
  obliquely.. 4. skew
  slyly.. 4. leer, ogle, peer

sullen.. 5. frown, lower 6. glower
toward.. 4. face
upon.. 2. at 4. deem 6. behold
 11. contemplate
lookout... 4. view 5. guard, watch
 6. conner 7. outlook 9. vigilance
looks... 4. cons, face, kens, sees
 5. peers, pores, pries, seeks, seems
 6. visage 8. features 9. resembles
 10. appearance 11. countenance
loom... 3. auk 4. loon, tool 6. appear,
 puffin, vessel, weaver 7. machine
 9. guillemot, implement
 10. receptacle
loom part... 3. lam 4. caam, leaf, sley
 5. easer, lathe, lever 6. heddle
loon... 5. diver (great Northern), Gavia,
 grebe, wabby 10. Gavia immer
loon... 4. dolt 6. menial (anc), rascal
 7. lunatic
loop... 3. eye, tab 4. ansa, clew, kink
 5. bight, bride, honda, noose, picot,
 sling, wootz (iron) 6. becket
 7. folding 8. doubling
loophole... 4. hole, plea 5. mense,
 oilet 6. escape, eyelet, outlet
 7. opening, pretext 8. aperture
loop–shaped... 9. fundiform
 11. sling–shaped
loose... 3. lax 4. free, limp 5. slack
 6. detach, remiss, unlash, wanton,
 wobbly 7. escaped, immoral,
 movable, relaxed, slacken, unbound,
 unleash 8. insecure, unstable
 9. discharge (gun, arrow)
 10. unconfined 11. improvident
 12. loose–moraled
 14. unconventional
loose (pert to)...
 ends.. 4. dags 5. slack 7. tagrags
 8. restless
 garment.. 5. simar 6. banion, chimar,
 kimono 7. zimarra 8. peignoir
 jointed.. 5. lanky, rangy 6. wobbly
 7. rickety 10. ramshackle
loosely dressed... 8. discinct
loosen... 4. ease, free, undo 5. pried,
 relax 6. soften 7. slacken
looseness... 7. laxness 8. limpness
 9. slackness, vagueness
 10. remissness, wantonness
loot... 3. rob 4. gelt, haul, sack, swag
 5. booty 6. spoils 7. pillage,
 plunder, seizure 10. contraband
looter... 6. rifler, sacker 7. ravager,
 spoiler 8. marauder, pillager
lop (off)... 3. bob, cut 4. oche, sned,
 trim 5. droop, prune 6. cut off,
 snathe 8. truncate
lopsided... 4. alop 7. leaning
 8. top–heavy 10. unbalanced
 13. unsymmetrical
loquacious... 4. glib 6. chatty
 7. voluble 9. garrulous, talkative
 10. chattering
loquacity... 7. fluency, leresis
 8. glibness 9. gabbiness, garrulity
 12. effusiveness
lord... 3. aga (agha), bey, God 4. earl,
 peer, rule, tsar 5. liege, ruler, title
 6. master, prince 7. Jehovah,
 marquis, Saviour 8. governor,

 nobleman, seignior, suzerain, viscount
 10. proprietor 11. Jesus Christ
Lord (pert to)...
 Buddhism.. 6. Buddha
 Jacobite.. 3. Mar
 of Heaven.. 7. Tien Chu (Chin)
 of Lords.. 8. Demiurge (Plato)
 11. King of Kings 13. Prince of
 Peace
 of Wisdom.. 5. Mazda 6. Ormazd
Lord have mercy upon us...
 12. Kyrie eleison 14. Christe eleison
lordly... 6. uppish 8. arrogant,
 despotic 9. dignified, masterful
 10. tyrannical 11. domineering,
 overbearing
Lord's Prayer... 11. Pater Noster
lore... 4. lear 6. advice, wisdom
 7. counsel 8. learning 9. erudition,
 mythology, tradition 12. superstition
lorgnette... 7. lorgnon 8. eyeglass
 10. opera glass
lorica... 5. shell 7. cuirass
 11. Breastplate (St Patrick's)
lorikeet... 6. lories, parrot
loris... 5. lemur
lorn... 6. bereft 7. forlorn 8. deserted,
 desolate, forsaken 9. abandoned
 11. Godforsaken
loro... 10. monk parrot, parrot fish
lose... 4. fail, miss, omit 5. leese
 (obs), spill, waste 6. forget, mislay,
 perish 7. forfeit, let slip 8. estrange,
 squander 9. incur loss 10. wander
 from
lose (pert to)...
 balance.. 4. trip 7. stumble
 courage.. 7. despair, despond
 flesh.. 8. emaciate
 freshness.. 4. fade, wilt 6. wither
 ground.. 7. regress 8. slow down
 9. fall short 10. fall behind
 luster.. 7. tarnish
 vigor.. 3. fag, sag 4. fail, flag, pine
 6. weaken 7. decline
loser... 6. victim 7. also ran
 8. defeatee, underdog
loss... 4. ruin, weak 6. damage, injury
 9. decrement, detriment, privation
 10. forfeiture 11. bereavement,
 destruction
loss of...
 commodities.. 6. ullage
 eyebrows, lashes.. 9. madarosis
 feeling.. 7. agnosia 10. anesthesia
 (anaesthesia)
 hair.. 8. alopecia
 loved one.. 11. bereavement
 memory.. 7. amnesia
 reason.. 7. amentia
 smell.. 7. anosmia
 speech.. 4. mute 6. alalia 7. aphasia
 10. laloplegia
 voice.. 7. aphonia
 willpower.. 6. abulia
lost... 4. asea, gone, lorn 5. unwon
 6. hidden, ruined, sinful, wasted
 7. mislaid 8. absorbed, confused,
 defeated, obscured, vanished
 9. abandoned, forfeited, forgotten,
 perplexed, reprobate, subverted
 10. abstracted, bewildered,

dissipated, overthrown, parted with
11. preoccupied 13. irreclaimable,
irretrievable

lost (pert to)...
cause.. 8. Civil War
color.. 5. faded, paled
consciousness.. 7. fainted, swooned
life fluid.. 4. bled
to view.. 5. perdu
tribes (ten).. 10. Israelites

lot... 3. tax 4. doom, fate, luck,
much, plat 5. share 6. chance,
hazard, studio 7. destiny, fortune,
portion 9. allotment, great deal
13. apportionment

Lot (pert to)...
father.. 5. Haran
penalty.. 12. pillar of salt
sister.. 6. Milcah
son.. 4. Moab
uncle.. 7. Abraham

lots, divination by... 9. sortilege
lottery... 4. game 5. bingo, lotto
6. chance, raffle 7. Genoese, grab
bag 11. sweepstakes
lottery prize... 4. tern (from three
numbers)
lotus... 7. nelumbo 10. chinquapin
lotus (pert to)...
bird.. 6. jacana
eaters.. 9. indolents, Lotophagi
11. daydreamers
tree.. 4. sadr 6. jujube, nettle
9. persimmon
loud... 5. crass, gaudy, noisy, showy
6. coarse, flashy, garish, vulgar
7. blatant, booming 8. vehement
9. clamorous, turbulent, unrefined
10. blustering, boisterous,
tumultuous, vociferous
11. stentorious 12. thersitical
loudmouthed... 10. scurrilous,
stentorian 11. thersitical
Louise de la Ramée (novelist)...
5. Ouida (pen name)
Louisiana...
bird.. 7. pelican
capital.. 10. Baton Rouge
city.. 10. New Orleans, Shreveport
county.. 6. parish
dialect.. 6. Creole
dish (cooked).. 9. jumbalaya
flower.. 8. magnolia
hero.. 6. De Soto, de Vaca, Pineda
7. La Salle
native.. 5. Cajun 6. Creole, French
7. Acadian, Spanish
purchased from.. 8. Napoleon (1803)
river.. 5. Pearl 6. Sabine
11. Mississippi
State admission.. 10. Eighteenth
State motto.. 22. Union, Justice,
Confidence
State nickname.. 7. Pelican
tradition.. 10. pirate lore
Louis Viaud (author)... 10. Pierre Loti
(pen name)
lounge... 4. loaf, loll, sofa 5. divan
6. frowst, repose 7. recline
louse... 5. aphis 6. cootie, insect,
slater 8. Anoplura, arachnid
9. Hemiptera, scoundrel

lout... 3. oaf 4. boor, clod, dolt
6. lubber, rustic 7. bumpkin
loutish... 4. rude 7. awkward, boorish,
ill-bred 9. clownish 11. countrified
lovable... 7. amiable 8. adorable,
charming 9. desirable, endearing
love... 3. amo, gra, woo 4. like
5. adore, amore, fancy 6. liking
7. charity 8. fondness, good will
9. affection 10. endearment,
sweetheart
love (pert to)...
affair.. 7. liaison, romance
10. flirtation
apple.. 6. tomato
bird.. 6. parrot
call.. 3. coo
feast.. 5. agape
flower.. 4. lily
full of.. 5. dote 6. doting, erotic
7. amative 9. idolizing
god of.. 4. Amor, Ares, Eros, Kama
5. Bhaga, Cupid
goddess of.. 5. Athor, Freya (Freyja),
Venus 6. Ishtar 9. Aphrodite
intrigue.. 5. amour
knot, token of.. 6. amoret
meeting.. 5. tryst 10. rendezvous
of.. 5. phile (comb form)
parental.. 7. storge
potion.. 7. philter
science.. 9. erotology
song.. 6. serena (evening) 8. madrigal
lover... 4. beau 5. amant, Romeo
6. minion 7. amorist, Don Juan
8. paramour 9. enamorato
10. sweetheart
lover of... see also *craze for*
animals.. 10. zoophilist
beauty.. 8. aesthete (esthete)
wealth.. 9. plutocrat
work.. 9. ergophile
Lover's Leap... 10. Cape Ducato
Lovers' Quarrels... 12. amantium Irae
loving... 4. fond 5. phile (comb form)
6. ardent, erotic 7. adoring, amative,
amatory, amorous, devoted
8. charming, enamored, romantic
11. sentimental 12. affectionate
loving cup... 3. tyg (tig)
low... 3. bas, moo 4. base, deep,
neap, orra 5. faint 6. humble,
menial, sneaky, vulgar, wicked
8. dejected, indecent, infamous,
inferior, plebeian 9. inelegant
11. unfavorable
low (pert to)...
born.. 4. rude 5. lowly 6. common
7. lowbred 8. plebeian
bred.. 5. crude 6. coarse, vulgar
brow.. 9. ignoramus
church.. 11. evangelical
comedy.. 8. travesty
country.. 7. Belgium, Holland
9. Luxemburg 11. Netherlands
German.. 5. Saxon 8. Frankish
12. Plattdeutsch
in spirits.. 4. blue 6. megrim
8. dejected, downcast 10. dispirited,
melancholy 11. crestfallen
Roman wall.. 5. spina
shrubs, plants.. 4. moss 5. Erica

syllable (Mus).. 2. ut
tide.. 3. ebb 4. neap 8. low water
lower.. 3. dip 4. vail, vase 5. abase,
demit, frown, neath 6. bemean,
debase, deepen, demean, demote,
humble, lessen, meaner, nether,
reduce 7. cheapen, degrade, depress,
descent 8. diminish, inferior
10. depreciate
lower (pert to)...
case letter.. 5. small
Empire.. 9. Byzantine
geology.. 5. Chalk (Eng) 6. strata
7. stratum
most.. 6. bottom, lowest 7. bedrock
10. nethermost
world.. 4. hell 5. earth, Hades, limbo,
orcus, Sheol 7. Abaddon, Gehenna
8. Cerberus 9. perdition, purgatory
lowering.. 4. dark 6. gloomy, sullen
7. ominous 8. frowning 9. deepening
10. cheapening 11. threatening
lowery.. 6. cloudy, gloomy 9. lowering
lowest (pert to)...
animal life.. 6. amoeba (ameba)
deck.. 5. orlop
least.. 5. minim 6. bottom
7. minimum
pedestal member (Arch).. 6. plinth,
quadra
peer (ranking).. 5. baron
point.. 5. depth, nadir 6. bottom
10. nethermost
point, planet.. 7. perigee
lowing.. 6. mooing 7. mugient
9. bellowing
lowland.. 4. flat, holm, spit 5. plain,
terai 6. bottom 8. molehill
lowly.. 4. mean, meek 6. humble,
humbly, meekly, menial, modest
8. inferior, modestly, plebeian
12. unpretending
loxia.. 7. wryneck 9. crossbill
loy.. 5. slick (tool), spade
loyal.. 4. feal, leal, true 5. liege
6. stanch 7. staunch 8. constant,
faithful, obedient
loyalty.. 5. faith 6. fealty, homage
8. devotion, fidelity 9. constancy
10. allegiance, stanchness
(staunchness) 12. faithfulness
13. steadfastness
Loyolite.. 7. Jesuit
lozenge.. 5. candy, facet 6. jujube,
tablet, troche 7. diamond, molding
8. pastille (pastil, pastile)
11. perforation
lubber.. 4. boor, dolt, gawk, lout
5. churl, drone, idler, thick 6. sailor
8. landsman 11. grasshopper
lubricity.. 8. lewdness
10. smoothness 12. slipperiness
lubricous.. 4. lewd 6. tricky, wanton
7. elusive 8. unstable 10. lascivious
lucban.. 8. shaddock
luce.. 4. pike 10. fleur–de–lis
lucent.. 5. clear 6. bright 7. shining
11. translucent, transparent
lucern.. 3. dog 4. lynx
lucerne.. 4. herb 6. fodder 7. alfalfa
11. purple medic
lucet, luce... 4. pike (fish)

Lucia's home... 10. Lammermoor
lucid... 4. sane 5. clear, vivid
6. bright, lucent 7. shining
8. luminous, pellucid 11. translucent
12. intelligible
luck... 3. hap 4. cess 5. deuce
6. chance 7. ambsace 8. fortuity
11. good fortune
lucky... 5. canny, happy 6. timely
9. fortunate 10. auspicious 11. good
fortune
lucky animal... 6. mascot
lucky token... 4. mojo 5. charm
6. amulet 7. periapt 8. talisman
9. alectoria 10. rabbit foot
12. antiganting
lucrative... 3. fat 6. paying 7. gainful
10. productive, profitable, worthwhile
12. remunerative
lucre... 4. gain, pelf 6. profit, riches
9. emolument 11. acquisition
lucubrate... 18. burn the midnight oil
ludicrous... 5. antic, comic, droll,
funny 6. absurd 7. amusing, comical,
jesting, risible 9. burlesque, laughable
10. ridiculous
Ludolphian... 2. pi (3.14159)
14. Ludolph's number
Luftpost... 7. airmail, air post
lug... 3. box, ear, hug 4. drag, hale,
haul, loop, pull, tote 5. carry
6. basket 7. container
lugs... 4. airs 7. clothes (showy),
tobacco 10. affections
lugubrious... 3. sad 6. woeful
7. doleful 8. grievous, mournful
9. plaintive 10. lamentable
lugworm... 3. lob 7. annelid
9. Arenicola
luhinga... 9. petticoat
lukewarm... 4. cool 5. tepid 6. tepefy
8. tepidity 9. not ardent
10. irresolute 11. indifferent
lumber... 4. wood 5. bungle, litter,
refuse, rumble, timber, trudge
7. lombard 9. rough wood
10. pawnbroker 11. impedimenta
lumberman... 6. logger, sawyer, scorer
9. timberman 10. lumberjack,
woodcutter
lumberman's half boot... 3. pac
lumberman's sled... 4. tode
7. go-devil, travois (travoise)
luminary... 3. sun 4. fire, star 5. light
7. wise man 9. celebrity
12. illumination, leading light
luminescence... 7. foxfire
12. fluorescence
15. phosphorescence
luminous... 5. clear, lucid 6. bright
7. shining 9. brilliant
11. enlightened, illuminated,
intelligent, transparent
14. phosphorescent
luminous circle... 4. halo
luminous impression... 9. phosphene
10. afterimage
lummox... 4. boor, dolt, lout 5. yahoo
7. bumpkin, bungler 12. clumsy
fellow
lump... 3. gob, lob, wad 4. beat,
blob, clot, hunk, loaf, mass 5. bulge

6. nodule, nubble, nugget, thresh
7. cluster 8. swelling
12. protuberance

lump (pert to)...
butter.. 3. pat
clay.. 4. clag, clod
metal.. 3. pig 5. ingot

lumpish... 4. dull 5. bulky, inert
6. clumsy, stolid, stupid 7. boorish
8. sluggish 9. heaviness, inertness,
ponderous 11. countrified
13. shapelessness

lumpy... 5. drunk, rough 6. choppy
7. nodular

lumpy jaw... 6. big jaw
13. actinomycosis

luna... 6. silver 11. moon goddess

lunacy... 4. moon 5. mania
7. madness 8. insanity 9. craziness
11. derangement, foolishness

lunar... 5. orbed 6. lunate 8. crescent,
moonlike 9. celestial, satellite
10. moon–shaped

lunar (pert to)...
appulse.. 7. eclipse
bone.. 7. lunatum
cycle.. 7. Metonic 9. Callippic
deity.. 6. Selene (Selena)
halo.. 6. corona, nimbus 7. aureola

lunatic... 3. mad 5. crazy, idiot
6. insane, madman 8. demoniac
10. moonstruck

lunatic asylum... 9. Bethlehem
(London)

lunch... 5. snack 6. repast, tiffin
8. luncheon, nuncheon 9. collation
11. refreshment 12. luncheonette

lunchroom... 6. eatery 10. coffee
shop, restaurant

lundyfoot... 5. snuff (by Lundy Foot)

lunge... 3. cut, jab 4. grab, pass, stab
5. feint, swing 6. thrust

lungs (pert to)...
ailment.. 9. emphysema 10. chalicosis
12. tuberculosis
having.. 9. pulmonate
part.. 5. lobes 6. lights 7. bronchi,
trachea
sound.. 4. rale 6. rattle

lurch... 4. joll, roll, sway 5. lunge
6. careen, topple 7. deceive
8. flounder 10. disappoint

lure... 4. bait, trap 5. decoy, snare,
tempt 6. allure, entice, invite
7. attract, trumpet, tweedle
10. enticement

lurid... 3. wan 4. dark, pale 5. color,
vivid 6. dismal, gloomy 7. ghastly,
obscene 9. deathlike 11. sensational

lurk... 4. hide, lote (obs) 5. creep,
prowl, skulk, slink, sneak 9. lie in
wait, pussyfoot

luscious... 4. rich 5. sweet 6. creamy,
wanton 7. cloying, honeyed
8. sensuous 9. delicious
10. lascivious, voluptuous

lush... 4. soft 5. drink, drunk, juicy
6. lavish, limber, liquor, mellow
8. flexible 9. luxuriant, succulent
11. intoxicated

lusory... 7. playful 8. sportive

lust... 5. greed 6. desire, libido

7. longing, passion 8. virility
14. lasciviousness

luster, lustre... 4. naif 5. glory, gloss,
sheen, shine 6. beauty, polish
7. glitter, lustrum 8. radiance,
schiller, splendor 10. brightness
11. distinction, iridescence

lusterless... 3. dim, mat 4. dead, dull
14. expressionless

lustful... 4. lewd 9. lecherous
10. lascivious

lustrous... 4. naif 5. nitid 6. bright
7. radiant, shining 11. illustrious,
transparent

lustrous mineral... 4. spar

lustrum (Roman)... 6. census, luster
12. purification (5 yrs), quinquennium

lusty... 6. active, robust, strong, sturdy
7. healthy 9. corpulent

lute... 4. clay, ring (rubber), seal
6. cement

lute, lutelike... 4. asor 6. guitar
7. bandore, pandore, theorbo, ukulele
8. archlute (archilute)

lute tablature... 7. lyraway

lutjanoid fish... 4. sesi 7. snapper

Luxemburg, Luxembourg...
capital.. 10. Luxembourg
government.. 8. monarchy 10. Grand
Duchy
language.. 6. French, German
13. Letzeburgesch
river.. 7. Moselle

luxuriant... 4. lush, rank, rich
6. ornate, uberty 7. fertile, opulent,
profuse, teeming 8. abundant, prolific
9. Sybaritic

luxuriate... 4. bask 5. revel 8. flourish

luxurious... 5. plush 6. ornate, superb
8. imposing 9. expensive, grandiose,
sumptuous 10. impressive
11. extravagant

luxury... 4. lust 7. lechery
8. elegance, pleasure, richness
10. prosperity, sensuality
11. superfluity 12. extravagance
13. gratification, sumptuousness
14. voluptuousness

luxury lover... 8. Sybarite

Luzon...
dialect.. 6. Itaves
mountain.. 3. Iba 6. Pagsan (Sicapoo)
people.. 3. Malay 7. Tagalog
8. Tinggian (Tinguian)
savage.. 6. Igorot (Igorrote)
seaport.. 5. Vigan 6. Aparri, Cavite
volcano.. 5. Mayon

lyam... 5. leash (Her) 10. bloodhound

lycanthrope... 8. werewolf
9. loup–garou

Lycia (pert to)...
citizen.. 6. Lycian
city.. 4. Myra
district of.. 9. Asia Minor
language.. 5. Greek 6. Lycian

Lydia...
capital.. 6. Sardis
conqueror.. 13. Cyrus the Great
dynasty of.. 5. Gyges 7. Croesus
13. Cyrus the Great
name, later.. 6. Persia
name, old.. 5. Ionia

queen.. 7. Omphale
river.. 8. Pactolus
ruins.. 6. temple
lye... 4. buck 6. bleach, potash
    8. lixivium
lying... 5. false 6. deceit 7. fudging
    9. decumbent, mendacity, reclining,
    recumbent 10. untruthful
lying (pert to)...
across.. 10. transverse
at mountain base.. 8. piedmont
hidden.. 6. latent 11. delitescent
in.. 12. accouchement
near earth's axis.. 5. polar
on the back.. 5. prone 6. supine
    7. passive
lymph... 3. sap 5. chyle, fluid, serum,
    water 6. plasma 7. cassein
lynch... 4. hang 6. murder, punish
    (lawlessly) 7. execute
lynx... 6. bobcat, lucern 7. caracal,
    wildcat 8. carcajou 13. constellation

lynx–eyed... 7. oxyopia
lyre... 4. asor, harp 6. kissar, sabeca,
    trigon, zither 7. cithara, cittern,
    testudo 8. phorminx
lyre (pert to)...
bird.. 6. Menura 8. lyretail, pheasant
shaped.. 6. lyrate
tree.. 5. tulip
turtle.. 11. leatherback
lyric (pert to)...
Arabic.. 5. gazel
Muse.. 5. Erato 10. Polyhymnia
music, poetry.. 3. lay, ode 4. epic,
    poem 5. epode, melic, rhyme (rime),
    verse, vocal 6. epopee, poetic
    7. canzone, musical, rondeau
    8. operatic, palinode 9. dithyramb
poet.. 5. odist
lyrical... 6. epodic
lyrichord... 11. harpsichord
lyssa... 6. rabies 11. hydrophobia
lyssophobia... 17. fear of hydrophobia

M

M... 2. Mu (Gr) 6. letter (13th)
    8. thousand
Ma (Ma Bellona)... 7. goddess
    (fertility)
maarib (Jew)... 7. liturgy
Maat (Egypt)... 7. goddess (justice)
Mab (Queen Mab)... 4. poem 10. fairy
    queen
mabolo... 4. plum 7. camagon
macabre... 4. grim 5. lurid, weird
    6. grisly 7. ghastly 8. gruesome
    12. Dance of Death
macaco... 5. lemur 6. Macaca
    7. macaque 10. Barbary ape
macan... 4. rice
macao... 4. game (gambling)
Macao... 6. Island 7. seaport
macaque... 6. machin, monkey
Macassar... 7. seaport (Celebes)
macaw... 3. ara 6. arara 8. parrot
    7. maracan 8. aracanga (blue and
    red), ararauna (blue and yellow)
Macbeth (pert to)...
author.. 11. Shakespeare (1605)
character.. 4. Duff, Ross 5. Angus
    6. Hecate, Lennox 7. Macduff
murder victim.. 6. Duncan
play type.. 7. tragedy
rival.. 7. Macduff
McBurney's Point (Med)...
    13. abdominal wall
Maccabees... 11. Hasmonaeans
    14. fraternal order, Jewish patriots
maccaboy... 5. snuff
mace... 4. maul 5. baton, gavel, spice
    (nutmeg), staff 6. ensign, mallet
    7. scepter (sceptre)
mace bearer... 5. macer 6. beadle

Macedonia, Balkans...
capital (anc).. 5. Pella
city.. 5. Berea 6. Edessa 8. Salonika
people.. 6. Greeks 8. Serbians
    9. Albanians 10. Bulgarians
ruler.. 6. Philip 9. Alexander (the
    Great)
site.. 15. Balkan Peninsula
macerate... 3. ret, vex 4. soak
    5. steep 6. soften 7. mortify,
    oppress, torture 8. emaciate
    9. waste away
machete... 4. bolo, fish 5. knife
    6. guitar 11. cutlass fish
Machiavellian, Machiavelian... 4. wily
    6. crafty 7. cunning 8. guileful,
    scheming 9. deceitful
    12. falsehearted
machila... 7. hammock
machin... 6. monkey 7. macaque
machinate... 4. plan, plot 6. scheme
    8. contrive, maneuver
machination... 6. design, device,
    scheme 7. machine 8. intrigue
    9. stratagem 10. conspiracy
machine... 3. car 4. auto 6. device,
    engine 7. vehicle 9. apparatus,
    automaton 10. automobile
    11. association, standardize
machine (pert to)...
cloth maturing.. 4. ager
cloth stretching.. 6. tenter
cotton.. 3. gin 4. mule 5. baler
glazing.. 8. calender
hay.. 5. baler 6. tedder
hoisting.. 3. gin, pry 4. pump
    5. crane, davit, lever, tongs
    7. derrick
hummeling.. 5. awner

hydraulic.. 9. telemotor
imitating.. 9. automaton
military.. 3. ram 6. onager
mixing.. 9. malaxator
ore.. 6. vanner
planing.. 8. surfacer
planting.. 6. seeder
political.. 5. party 6. system
    7. faction
reckoning.. 6. abacus 8. tabulator
    10. calculator
rubber shaping.. 8. extruder
stage effect.. 13. deus ex machina
tool.. 5. drill, lathe
machine gun... 4. nest (hidden place)
    5. Maxim 6. cannon 7. Gatling
    9. Hotchkiss 10. chatterbox
machine–made... 11. stereotyped
machine power, energy... 5. input
    6. output
machinist... 7. artisan 8. mechanic
mackerel... 5. atule, spike, tunny
    6. sierra, tinker
mackerel (pert to)...
bait.. 9. jellyfish
bird.. 7. wryneck 9. kittiwake
genus.. 7. Scomber
goose.. 9. phalarope
like.. 4. cero 6. bonito 7. escolar
net.. 7. spiller
shark.. 9. porbeagle
sky.. 6. clouds 9. striation
small (allowable size).. 5. spike
    6. tinker 7. blinker
mackle... 4. blur, spot 6. blotch,
    macule
macrobiotic... 9. long–lived
mad... 4. vain, wild 5. angry, crazy,
    irate, rabid, vexed 6. insane, maniac
    7. enraged, foolish, frantic, furious
    8. demented, frenetic, maniacal,
    reckless 9. hilarious, turbulent
    10. distraught, infatuated, infuriated
    12. arreptitious
Madagascar, Malagasy...
animal.. 5. indri, lemur 6. aye–aye,
    tenrec (tendrac) 9. babacoote
capital.. 10. Tananarive
cattle.. 4. zebu (humped)
city.. 7. Majanga 8. Tamatave
civet.. 7. fossane
govenment.. 8. Republic (1960)
language.. 16. Malayo–Polynesian
native.. 4. Hova 8. Sakalava
palm.. 6. raffia
religion.. 7. Animist 9. Christian
Madam... 3. Mrs 4. Frau, lady,
    Ma'am 5. donna, hussy 6. Madame,
    Señora 8. goodwife, mistress
    9. courtesan
madcap... 3. wag 4. rash, wild
    5. blood 6. madman 7. hotspur,
    violent 8. reckless 9. daredevil,
    foolhardy
madden... 3. vex 5. craze 6. enrage,
    incite 8. incense 9. infuriate
    10. antagonize
madder... 2. al 3. aal, red 4. herb,
    rose (color) 5. brown, Rubia
    6. orange, violet, yellow 7. crimson,
    xanthin 9. turkey–red
made... 5. built 7. created, trained

    8. invented, prepared, produced,
    rendered 10. artificial, successful
    11. constructed 12. enfranchised,
    manufactured
made (pert to)...
accurate.. 5. trued
believe.. 7. feigned 9. pretended,
    simulated
blind.. 6. seeled
clear.. 9. explained 10. elucidated
destitute.. 6. bereft
fun of.. 6. jeered, mocked 7. derided
    9. ridiculed
hard, obdurate.. 7. steeled
light of.. 7. dwarfed 9. belittled
    10. disparaged
over.. 8. reformed, revamped
    9. remodeled
plain.. 9. evidenced, exhibited
    10. manifested
public.. 5. aired 7. accused, delated
    8. reported
scalloped edges.. 6. pinked
sound.. 7. bleated, rumbled, swished
tart.. 7. euchred
up.. 9. composite 10. artificial,
    fabricated 12. manufactured
up mind.. 7. decided
valid.. 6. proved 9. confirmed
    13. authenticated
whole again.. 7. renewed
    10. reconciled 13. redintegrated,
    re–established
Madeira Islands...
capital.. 7. Funchal
embroidery.. 6. eyelet
nut.. 6. walnut
owner of Islands.. 8. Portugal
wind.. 5. leste
wine.. 4. bual 5. tinta (red)
    7. malmsey, sercial 8. verdelho
wood.. 8. ironwood (white), mahogany
madhouse... 5. chaos 6. asylum,
    bedlam 8. nuthouse
madman... 3. nut 4. coot, loon
    6. maniac 7. lunatic 9. phrenetic
madness... 3. ire 4. fury, rage
    5. anger, mania 6. frenzy, lunacy
    8. insanity 9. agitation, theomania
    (Relig) 11. foolishness, inspiration
Mad Parliament (1258)...
    18. Provisions of Oxford
Madras, India...
capital.. 6. Madras
city.. 5. Adoni, Arcot 7. Calicut
export.. 4. lace 7. fabrics 9. kerchiefs
    (for turbans)
government.. 10. presidency
madrepore... 5. coral 6. fossil, marble
    8. Acropora 12. Madreporaria
Madrid, Spain...
architecture.. 7. Moorish
boulevard.. 5. Prado 12. Salon de
    Prado
noted buildings.. 7. Armeria
    11. Prado Museum, Royal Palace
madrigal... 3. ode 4. glee, poem
    5. lyric, music 6. verses
maduro... 5. cigar 6. mature
    11. dark–colored
maelstrom... 5. churn 6. foment
    7. turmoil 9. whirlpool (Norway)

maestro... 6. master 7. teacher
8. composer, musician 9. conductor
13. Kapellmeister
maestro–di–cappela... 11. choirmaster
Mae West... 8. life belt
Maffia... 7. syndicate 10. underworld
12. organization (Sicilian)
maffle... 6. muddle, mumble
7. confuse, stammer 8. squander
mafoo, mafu (Chin)... 5. groom
9. stable boy
mag... 6. magpie 7. chatter
8. titmouse 9. halfpenny
magadis... 5. flute 9. monochord
magazine... 4. shop 5. depot, store
6. review 7. arsenal, chamber (gun),
tabloid 8. ephemeris, reservoir,
warehouse 9. periodical, repository,
storehouse
magazine rifle... 6. Mauser
8. repeater
mage... 5. Magus 6. Merlin 7. Houdini
8. conjurer, magician
magenta... 3. dye 7. fuchsia
maggot... 4. grub, mawk 5. larva,
mathe 6. notion 7. caprice, Diptera
12. eccentricity
Magi (Three Wise Men)... 6. Gaspar
8. Melchior 9. Balthasar
magic... 3. art 4. juju, mana, maya,
rune, show 5. charm, fairy, spell
6. voodoo 10. necromancy
11. conjuration, enchantment,
legerdemain
magic (pert to)...
art (black).. 7. demonry 9. diablerie,
diabolism
art (white).. 5. turgy 7. theurgy
ejaculation.. 2. om (um) 6. sesame
goddess.. 5. Circe 6. Hecate
image.. 5. sigil 8. sigillum
lantern.. 11. epidiascope
12. stereopticon
lantern slide.. 6. tinter
staff, wand.. 6. rhabdo 8. caduceus
symbol.. 5. charm 6. caract, fetish
8. pentacle 9. pentalpha
word.. 2. om (um) 6. presto, sesame
10. abacadabra
magical... 6. goetic (goety)
8. charming
magician... 4. mage 5. magus
6. Merlin, wizard 7. Houdini, juggler
8. conjurer, mandrake, sorcerer
9. archimage, charlatan, enchanter
11. entertainer, necromancer,
thaumaturge 13. thaumaturgist
15. prestidigitator
magician (pert to)...
attendant.. 7. famulus
command.. 6. presto 11. abracadabra
manual.. 8. grimoire
magirics... 7. cookery
magirist... 4. cook
magisterial... 5. lofty, proud
6. august, lordly 7. haughty, stately
8. arrogant, dogmatic, judicial, official
9. dignified, imperious, masterful
10. commanding 11. dictatorial,
domineering, overbearing
13. authoritative
magistrate... 4. doge 5. ephor, judge

6. aedile (edile), archon, bailli,
puisne, syndic 7. alcalde (alcaid),
alcalde, bailiff
magistrate's orders... 4. acta
magma... 5. dregs 8. sediment
10. molten rock, suspension (Pharm)
magna cum laude... 14. with great
honor
magnanimous... 4. free 5. lofty, noble
7. exalted, liberal 8. generous
9. honorable, unselfish, unstinted
10. high–minded 11. great of mind
13. disinterested
magnate... 4. lord 5. baron, mogul,
noble 6. bashaw, bigwig, tycoon
7. grandee, richman 9. personage
11. millionaire
magnesium (pert to)...
limestone.. 8. dolomite
nitrate.. 9. saltpeter
silicate.. 4. talc
sulphate.. 10. Epsom salts
magnet... 7. terella 8. solenoid
9. loadstone, lodestone
magnet (type)... 3. bar 9. horseshoe
10. artificial
magnetic... 10. attractive, electrical
14. attractiveness
magnetism... 5. oomph 8. polarity
magnificence... 5. glory 8. grandeur,
splendor 15. superexcellence
magnificent... 5. grand, regal
6. lavish, superb 7. exalted,
pompous, sublime 8. imposing,
palatial, splendid, striking 9. brilliant,
grandiose, sumptuous 10. munificent
magnify... 4. laud 5. exalt, extol
6. expand, praise 7. enlarge, glorify,
worship 8. increase 9. intensify,
overstate 10. exaggerate
magnitude... 4. size 6. extent
7. bigness 8. grandeur, nobility
9. extension, greatness
Magnolia State... 11. Mississippi
magnum... 4. bone (wrist) 6. bottle
9. capitatum
magnum opus... 9. great work
11. achievement
magpie... 3. daw, mag, pie 4. Pica,
piet (pyet) 5. madge, scold
6. pigeon, talker 9. chatterer
10. chattermag
magpie type...
diver.. 4. smew
shrike.. 7. tanager
maguari... 5. stork
magus... 8. magician 9. one of Magi
Magyar... 3. Hun 9. Hungarian
Mah (Persian)... 9. moon angel
maha... 10. sambar deer
Mahabharata (blind king, Hind)...
13. Dhritarashtra
mahajan, mahajun (Ind)... 8. great
man 11. moneylender
mahal... 8. Taj Mahal 9. residence
(summer) 10. apartments, Natal
brown
mahala... 5. squaw
maharaja, maharajah... 5. ruler
6. prince
maharani, maharanee... 5. queen
mahatma... 4. sage 7. wise man

9. great soul, occultist 21. Great
White Brotherhood (member)
mahogany... 3. roe (burl) 4. toon,
wood 5. brown 6. totara 7. ratteen
maholi... 5. lemur
Mahomet... see *Mohammedan*
Mahound... 5. Devil 8. Mohammed
mahout... 6. driver (elephant), keeper
Mah to Mahi... 10. Fish to Moon
Maia (pert to)...
  mountain nymph.. 7. Arcadia
  son.. 6. Hermes
  star.. 8. Pleiades
maid... 4. girl, lass 5. bonne, woman
6. damsel, maiden, virgin 7. abigail,
servant 8. spinster 9. tirewoman
Maid (of)...
  Astolat.. 6. Elaine
  Athens.. 12. Theresa Macri
  Lydia.. 7. Arachne (changed to a
    spider)
  Orléans.. 9. Joan of Arc
  Zeus.. 2. Io (changed to heifer)
maidenhair... 4. fern 8. Adiantum
10. Venus's hair
maidenhair tree... 6. gingko
maidenly... 6. gentle, modest 7. girlish
9. unmarried
maigre... 4. diet, fish
mail... 3. dak (dawk) 4. post 5. armor
7. consign, letters, plumage
8. dispatch
mail, coat of... 5. armor 6. byrnie
(brinie) 7. broigne, cuirass (part),
hauberk, panoply
mail boat... 6. packet
maim... 6. injure, mangle, mayhem
7. disable 8. mutilate 9. tear apart
main... 3. sea 4. duct 5. chief, first,
great, prime, sheer, utter 6. mighty,
potent 7. chiefly, conduit, leading
8. foremost 9. conductor, essential,
principal 10. on the whole
11. essentially 13. most important
main (pert to)...
  act (drama).. 8. epitasis
  beam.. 6. girder 7. walking
  part.. 4. body
  point.. 3. jet, nub 4. crux, gist, pith
  post.. 9. sternpost
  sea (poet).. 11. Spanish Main
    (Caribbean Sea)
Maine...
  bay.. 5. Casco 13. Passamaquoddy
  capital.. 7. Augusta
  city.. 4. Saco 5. Hiram, Orono
    6. Bangor 8. Lewiston, Portland
    11. Millinocket
  college.. 5. Bates, Colby 7. Bowdoin
  Easternmost city.. 8. Eastport
  Easternmost point.. 19. West Quoddy
    Head Light
  Easternmost town.. 5. Lubec
  lake.. 6. Sebago 9. Moosehead
  mountain.. 5. Kineo 8. Cadillac,
    Katahdin
  resort.. 9. Bar Harbor
  resort island.. 8. Mt Desert
  river.. 8. Kennebec 9. Penobscot
  State admission.. 11. Twenty–third
  State motto.. 6. Dirigo 7. I Direct
  State nickname.. 8. Pine Tree

  trout.. 7. oquassa
Maine, The... 10. battleship (Sp–Am
War)
maintain... 4. aver, hold, keep
5. claim 6. affirm, allege, assert,
avouch, defend, endure, insist, retain
7. justify, support, sustain
8. continue, preserve
maintainable... 7. tenable
maintenance... 3. aid 6. upkeep
7. alimony, defense, support
9. retention 10. livelihood,
sustenance 11. continuance
12. conservation, preservation,
sustentation
maison... 5. house
Maison Carrée... 12. Norman Temple
(Nîmes)
maison de santé... 6. asylum
8. hospital 10. sanatorium
maître d'hôtel (famed)... 5. Oscar
maize... 3. Zea 4. corn 7. mealies
maja, majo... 5. belle, dandy
majestic... 5. grand, great, lofty,
noble, regal, royal 6. august, kingly
7. stately, sublime 8. elevated,
eloquent, imperial, splendid
9. dignified, grandiose
11. ceremonious, magnificent
majesty... 5. title 7. crowned (Her),
dignity 8. grandeur 9. eloquence,
greatness, loftiness, sceptered (Her)
major... 3. dur (Mus) 6. course
(study), ditone 7. greater, officer
8. legal age, majority
major–domo... 6. butler 7. bailiff,
steward 9. seneschal
majority... 3. age 4. most 6. quorum
7. greater 8. maturity 9. majorship,
plurality, seniority 12. more than half
make... 2. do 4. earn, form, gain,
kind 5. shape 6. compel, create,
induce, render 7. compose, execute,
produce 8. contrive, generate
9. structure 10. accomplish
11. composition, manufacture
make (pert to)...
  affidavit.. 4. affy
  allowance.. 5. abate, admit
    7. concede
  allusion to.. 7. mention
  amends.. 5. atone 7. redress
  as if.. 7. pretend 8. as though
  bare.. 5. strip 6. balden, denude
  believe.. 4. sham 5. feign 7. pretend
    8. pretense
  better.. 5. widen 6. soften
    7. broaden, improve 9. meliorate
    10. ameliorate
  book.. 10. record bets
  buoyant.. 8. levitate
  calm.. 5. allay, quiet 6. serene
    7. appease, compose
  certain.. 5. assure, ensure
  cheerful.. 6. solace 7. comfort,
    console
  choice.. 3. opt 4. cull 6. choose,
    select 7. pick out
  clean breast of.. 7. confess
    8. disclose
  clear.. 7. explain 9. elucidate
  coins.. 4. mint

counumbercharge.. 11. recriminate
crisp.. 9. embrittle
deduction.. 6. rebate
desolate.. 5. strip 7. bereave
diminutive.. 9. bantamize
do.. 3. eke 5. get by 8. piece out
  9. improvise
eccentric.. 8. decenter
edging.. 3. tat 7. crochet
effective.. 6. compel 7. enforce
enduring.. 6. anneal, temper
equal.. 6. equate
evident.. 6. evince
familiar.. 8. accustom
famous.. 8. eternize 11. immortalize
fast.. 4. snub 5. belay 6. batten,
  secure
faulty.. 6. impair 7. vitiate
  11. contaminate
firm.. 3. fix 5. brace 6. cement
fit.. 4. suit 5. adapt 6. adjust
  7. conform
foolish, stupid.. 4. daff 8. stultify
  10. ridiculous
fun of.. 3. rib 5. scoff 8. ridicule
glass.. 7. platten
good.. 7. absolve, justify, succeed
  9. indemnify, vindicate
happy.. 5. elate 7. beatify 8. felicity
  (obs)
hard, harsh.. 5. steel 6. freeze
  7. roughen
harmonious.. 6. attune
headway.. 4. gain 7. advance
  8. progress
holy.. 5. bless 6. hallow
  10. consecrate
honorable.. 5. exalt 6. uplift
  7. ennoble
ineffective.. 4. void 5. annul
insensible to pain.. 11. anesthetize
  (anaesthetize)
into law.. 5. enact 8. legislate
known.. 6. impart, reveal 7. divulge,
  publish, uncover 8. disclose,
  discover, proclaim
lace.. 3. tat 7. crochet
less dense.. 4. thin 6. rarefy
less smooth.. 7. roughen
level.. 4. true
light.. 6. jetsam 8. illumine, jettison
lively.. 8. energize
love.. 5. coo, woo 5. court
merry.. 5. laugh 6. banter 7. disport
mild.. 6. mitigate, modulate
moral.. 8. ethicize
much of.. 6. praise 7. enthuse, lionize
  10. exaggerate
muddy.. 4. roil
notes.. 8. annotate
out.. 4. know 5. solve 6. decode,
  draw up 7. analyze, discern
  8. contrive, decipher 10. understand
over.. 4. redo 6. revamp 7. convert
  9. refashion, reproduce
pale, sickly.. 8. etiolate
possible.. 6. enable
pottery.. 7. spattle
precious.. 6. endear
pretentious.. 7. buckram
public.. 3. air 5. bruit, noise
  6. delate 7. publish 9. divulgate

  11. acknowledge
ready.. 4. gear 5. coach, prime
  7. prepare
reparation.. 5. atone
resistance.. 5. rebel 6. mutiny, revolt
secure.. 3. fix, pin 4. nail, snub
  5. belay 6. batten, fasten
shift.. 9. temporary
short work of.. 6. hasten 7. destroy
  10. accomplish
shrill noise.. 10. stridulate
smooth.. 4. buff, iron 5. sleek, slick
  6. scrape
spruce.. 4. perk 7. smarten
strong.. 7. stouten
thin.. 9. attenuate
three-cornered.. 11. triangulate
unhappy.. 8. embitter 10. exacerbate
up.. 5. atone, build 6. invent, settle
  7. compose, concoct, prepare
  8. assemble, cosmetic 9. construct,
  improvise, reconcile 10. compensate
use of.. 5. apply 6. borrow, employ
  7. utilize 11. appropriate
waste (law).. 7. estrepe
watertight.. 4. calk, seal
white.. 6. blanch, bleach
worse.. 9. aggravate
zealous.. 7. enthuse

maker of...
arrows.. 8. fletcher
barrels.. 6. cooper
bundles.. 5. baler
infusion.. 7. steeper
knives.. 6. cutler
pottery.. 6. potter 8. ceramist

makeshift... 7. stopgap
maki... 5. lemur
mal (comb form)... 3. bad, ill 5. badly
  7. disease 8. sickness
Malabar (pert to)...
bark.. 5. ochna
nutmeg.. 10. Bombay mace
palm.. 7. talipot
rat.. 9. bandicoot
Malacca... 7. seaport (Malaya)
Malachi... 4. Book (Old Test)
  7. prophet
malachite... 4. bice 5. green
  6. copper 7. pigment
maladroit... 6. clumsy 7. awkward,
  unhandy 8. bungling 9. all thumbs,
  graceless 10. blundering, left-handed,
  ungraceful
maladventure... 6. mishap
  8. escapade 12. ill adventure
malady... 5. amok 7. ailment, disease,
  illness 8. disorder, sickness
  9. complaint, distemper
  13. indisposition
mala fide... 10. in bad faith
Malaga... 5. city (Sp), wine
  10. oxblood red
Malagasy lemur... 6. aye-aye
Malagasy region... 10. Madagascar
malaise... 4. pain 10. discomfort,
  uneasiness
malapert... 4. bold, pert 5. saucy
  8. impudent
malaria... 5. miasm 6. miasma
  10. strophulus
malaxation... 7. massage 9. softening

Malay Archipelago...
animal.. 4. mias 5. tapir, tsine
   6. gibbon, taguan 7. banteng
apparel.. 5. banju 6. sarong
buffalo.. 4. gaur 7. carabao, seldang
canoe.. 4. proa 5. prahu
chief (tribal).. 4. dato (datto)
crane.. 5. sarus
dagger, knife.. 6. creese (kris), parong
disease (jumping).. 4. lata (latah)
garment.. 6. sarong
gentlemen.. 3. sir 4. tuan
island.. 4. Bali, Java 5. Timor
   7. Celebes, Sumatra 9. New Guinea
   11. Philippines
isthmus.. 3. Kra
jacket.. 4. baju
language.. 7. Tagalog
native.. 5. Bajau 6. Ifugao 9. Samal
   Laut 10. sea gypsies
palm.. 6. Arenga, gomuti (gomuto)
   8. Saguerus
pygmy.. 4. Aeta
rice field.. 5. sawah
seaport.. 7. Malacca
State.. 5. Kedah, Perak 6. Jahore
tree.. 4. upas 5. kapur, niepa, terap
   6. durian (fruit)
vessel.. 4. toup 6. lugger

malcontent... 5. rebel 6. Fenian,
   uneasy 7. repiner 8. agitator,
   grumbler 10. rebellious
   12. discontented
mal du pays... 12. homesickness
male... 2. he 3. cob, him, tom
   4. bull, galt, jack, stud 5. andro
   (comb form), manly 6. tercel, virile
   7. rooster 8. stallion 9. masculine
male (pert to)...
column (Arch).. 7. telamon 8. atlantes
One Hundred eyes.. 5. Argus
malediction... 5. curse 6. threat
   7. malison, slander 8. anathema
   11. imprecation 12. denunciation
malefaction... 5. crime 7. offense
   9. malum in se 15. malum
   prohibitum
malefactor... 5. felon 7. culprit
   8. criminal, evildoer 9. wrongdoer
malevolence... 4. hate 5. pique, spite
   6. grudge, malice, rancor 7. ill will
   8. inimical 9. animosity, malignity
   10. bitterness
malevolent... 4. evil 6. hating
   7. envious, hateful 8. spiteful
   9. malicious, rancorous
   11. ill-disposed
malfeasance... 7. misrule 8. impolicy
   10. wrongdoing 11. evil conduct,
   illegal deed
malfeasant... 8. criminal, evildoer
malgré... 9. in spite of
   15. notwithstanding
malheur... 10. misfortune
malice... 4. envy, evil 5. malum,
   pique, spite, wrong 6. rancor 7. ill
   will 9. animosity, malignity, malintent
   10. bitterness 11. malevolence
malicious... 4. evil, mean 6. bitter,
   malign, ornery 7. hateful 8. sinister,
   spiteful 9. rancorous, resentful,
   vitriolic 11. ill-disposed

   12. cantankerous, unpropitious
malicious (pert to)...
destruction.. 5. arson 8. sabotage
   9. vandalism
gossip.. 4. dirt 7. scandal, slander
intention.. 6. animus
maliform... 11. apple-shaped
malign... 4. evil 5. abuse, libel
   6. deadly, defame, revile, vilify
   7. asperse, baleful, harmful, slander,
   traduce 8. virulent 10. calumniate
   12. unpropitious
malignancy... 6. malice 9. virulence
   10. deadliness 11. harmfulness,
   noxiousness
malignant... 3. ill 4. evil 5. felon
   6. deadly, wicked 7. harmful,
   heinous, vicious 8. spiteful, virulent
   9. felonious, invidious, malicious,
   poisonous, rancorous 10. rebellious
   11. deleterious
maligner... 8. libelist
malignity... 4. evil, hate 5. spite,
   venom 11. harmfulness, heinousness
malines, maline... 3. net 11. Mechlin
   lace
malingerer... 6. truant 7. quitter,
   shirker, slacker, welsher
malison... 5. curse 11. malediction
malkin... 3. cat, mop 4. drab, hare
   6. sponge 8. slattern 9. scarecrow
mall... 4. gull, walk 5. alley, prado
   6. mallet 7. alameda 8. assembly
   9. esplanade, promenade
mallangong... 8. duckbill
mallard... 4. Anas, duck 5. drake
malleable... 4. soft 6. pliant 7. ductile
   9. teachable
mallemuck... 6. fulmar, petrel
   9. albatross
mallet... 3. tup 4. club, mace, maul
   5. gavel, madge 6. beater, beetle,
   driver, hammer
malm... 4. marl 5. chalk 9. limestone,
   White Jura
malmsey... 4. wine
malodorous... 4. rank 5. fetid
   6. rotten 7. noisome, odorous
   11. ill-smelling, odoriferous
malt (pert to)...
froth.. 4. barm
ground.. 5. grist
infusion.. 4. wort 9. sweetwort
liquor.. 4. beer, suds 6. swipes
material.. 5. grain 6. barley
mixture.. 6. zythum 7. maltate
vinegar.. 4. wort 6. alegar
Malta, Mediterranean Isle...
capital.. 8. Valletta
famed marker.. 15. Neolithic Temple
fever.. 8. undulent
group island.. 4. Gozo 6. Comino
honor.. 11. George Cross (1942)
maltreat... 5. abuse 6. misuse 8. ill
   treat 9. do wrong by
malty... 5. drunk
malum... 4. evil 5. wrong 7. offense
malversation... 9. extortion (in office)
   10. corruption 11. evil conduct,
   fraudulence, misbehavior
mammal... 3. ape, man 4. homo
   10. vertebrate

mammal . . 2. ai, ox 3. ape, bat, cat, cow, dog, hog, orc, pig, rat, yak 4. bear, bull, deer, lion, mink, mole, paca, seal, tait, zebu 5. camel, coati, daman, koala, lemur, llama, moose, mouse, okapi, otter, ounce, panda, ratel, rhino, sable, shark, sheep, swine, tapir, tayra, whale 6. alpaca, badger, desman, dugong, marten, monkey, ocelot, rytina (ext), tenrec (tendrac), walrus, weasel 7. dolphin, manatee, opossum, peccary, raccoon 8. aardvark, anteater, antelope, elephant, kangaroo, mongoose, reindeer 10. chevrotain, rhinoceros 12. hippopotamus

mammal (pert to) . . .
coat.. 4. hide, skin 6. pelage
cud–chewing.. 8. ruminant
edentate.. 8. anteater, pangolin, tamandua (anteater)
extinct.. 6. rytina 8. mastodon 9. Glyptodon
flying.. 3. bat
largest.. 5. whale
man.. 6. Bimana (group)
meat–eating.. 7. carnivore
nipple.. 4. teat 8. mammilla
omnivorous.. 3. hog, pig 5. swine
Order.. 7. Cetacea 8. Edentata, Rodentia
Order, highest.. 7. Primata 8. Mammalia
Order, lowest.. 9. Marsupial
plantigrade.. 7. raccoon
primate (except Man).. 10. Quadrumana
scaled.. 8. pangolin
shelled.. 9. armadillo
smallest.. 5. shrew
snake–eating.. 8. mongoose
toothless.. 8. edentate
web–footed.. 6. aliped
wing–footed.. 6. aliped
zebralike.. 6. quagga

mammock.. 4. tear 5. break, scrap 8. fragment
mammon... 5. money 6. riches, wealth 11. fallen angel (Bib) 15. demon of cupidity
mammoth... 5. giant, large (very) 7. titanic 8. behemoth, elephant, gigantic, mastodon 9. pachyderm 11. Dinotherium 12. hippopotamus
man...3. arm, fit, rig 4. homo, male 5. adult, equip, fit up, human, staff 6. outfit, person 7. fortify, furnish, mankind, prepare, someone 9. human race 10. human being

man (of)...
all work.. 4. mozo 6. Friday 8. factotum 9. assistant
Blood and Iron.. 8. Bismarck
Destiny.. 9. Bonaparte (Napoleon)
Galilee.. 11. Jesus Christ
God.. 5. saint 6. priest 9. clergyman 12. ecclesiastic
law.. 6. lawyer 7. counsel 8. attorney 9. counselor (counsellor)
learning.. 6. pundit, savant 7. scholar 9. literatus 11. litterateur
quackery.. 7. buffoon 9. trickster

10. mountebank
the sea.. 3. tar 6. merman, sailor
the signs.. 12. homo signorum
the woods.. 6. rustic 8. silvanus, woodsman 9. orangutan
the world.. 7. layman 11. cosmopolite 12. sophisticate
war.. 7. frigate, soldier, warrior

man (pert to)...
aged.. 3. vet 9. patriarch 12. octogenarian
bachelor.. 4. stag 8. celibate
bald.. 9. pilgarlic
conceited.. 7. coxcomb
cunning.. 5. rogue 6. rascal 7. shyster 10. mountebank
dissolute.. 4. roué
eccentric, elderly.. 4. sire 5. uncle 6. codger, gaffer 11. grandfather
effeminate.. 9. androgyne
entire (soul and body).. 3. ego
fashionable.. 3. fop 4. dude 5. dandy 11. Beau Brummel 12. boulevardier
fungus.. 9. earthstar (the)
handsome.. 6. Adonis
hardheaded.. 5. Boche
hard–pressed.. 3. Job
important.. 4. hero, lion 5. chief, nabob 6. tycoon 7. mugwump
Isle of, capital.. 7. Douglas
lady's.. 4. beau 6. fiancé
lawless.. 7. ruffian
learned.. 6. pundit, savant 7. erudite, scholar 9. literatus 11. philologist
like.. 7. android 10. anthropoid
little.. 6. mankin, shrimp, squirt 10. homunculus
loud–voiced.. 7. stentor
lowbred.. 4. serf 5. churl 6. rustic 7. peasant 8. plebeian
medicine, magic.. 6. shaman
millionaire.. 7. Croesus 10. capitalist, Corinthian
newspaper.. 6. editor 8. reporter 10. journalist
old.. 5. elder 7. veteran 12. octogenarian
prehistoric.. 4. cave 6. Ice Age 8. eolithic, Grimaldi, Piltdown 9. neolithic 11. paleolithic
red.. 6. Indian
strong.. 6. Samson 8. ironside
wise.. 4. sage, seer 5. solon 6. nestor 7. Solomon
without a country.. 5. Nolan (Philip)

manacle... 4. gyve, iron 5. chain 6. fetter 7. shackle 8. handcuff 9. restraint
manada... 4. herd 5. drove, flock
manage... 3. man, run 4. boss, head, lead, tend 5. cater, dight, guide, pilot, wield 6. direct, govern 7. control, husband, operate 8. contrive, engineer 10. administer, manipulate
manageable... 4. easy, tame, yare 6. docile, wieldy 7. ductile 9. compliant, tractable 10. governable 12. controllable
management... 4. care 6. charge, menage 7. conduct, control, gestion 9. direction 10. government

11. negotiation
manager ... 4. boss 6. gerent
7. steward 8. director, governor,
operator, overseer 9. economist
12. entrepreneur 13. administrator
managery ... 7. cunning 8. artifice
9. frugality, husbandry
10. management 12. manipulation
14. administration
mañana ... 8. tomorrow 10. before
long
manas (Hind) ... 3. ego 4. mind
Manasseh ... 5. tribe (Israel) 11. King
of Judah
Manchuria ...
capital .. 6. Mukden (old)
9. Changchun
government .. 9. Communist (Chin)
Japanese name .. 9. Manchukuo
native .. 9. Mongolian
river .. 4. Amur, Liao, Yalu
manciple ... 5. slave 7. servant,
steward 8. purveyor
mandarin (pert to) ...
bird .. 4. duck
city .. 9. Chungking
color .. 3. red
dialect .. 7. Chinese
figure in Chiness dress, seated ..
9. grotesque
fruit .. 6. orange 9. tangerine
official .. 8. governor 10. bureaucrat
residence .. 5. yamen
ware .. 9. porcelain
mandate ... 5. edict, order 6. behest,
charge, decree, mandat 7. bidding,
command, precept 9. direction
10. injunction, referendum
mandatory ... 10. imperative, obligatory,
preceptive
mandible ... 3. jaw 4. beak 5. chops,
molar (part) 9. chelicera
mandrel, mandril ... 3. hob 4. axle,
pick (miner's) 5. arbor 7. spindle
mandriarch ... 9. monk ruler
mandrill ... 6. baboon
mane ... 4. hair, juba, shag 6. thatch
manege ... 6. school (riding)
7. academy (riding) 8. cavesson
(halter)
manes (Rom) ... 4. gods (lower world)
7. spirits
maneuver, manoeuvre ... 4. ruse
5. trick 6. device, jockey, scheme,
tactic 7. operate 8. artifice, intrigue,
strategy 9. stratagem 10. manipulate
13. Immelmann turn
mangabey ... 6. monkey
manger ... 3. bin 4. crib, meal, rack
6. bunker, trough 7. banquet
mangle ... 3. cut, mar 4. hack
5. press 6. bruise, injure, ironer
8. calender, demolish, lacerate,
mutilate 9. dismember
mango (pert to) ...
bird .. 6. oriole 11. hummingbird
fish .. 9. threadfin
fruit .. 5. amini, bauno, drupe, melon
9. muskmelon
grove .. 4. tope
mangy ... 3. mean 6. itchy, seedy

6. ronyon, scurvy, shabby 7. squalid
12. contemptible
manhandle ... 4. maul 5. abuse
7. rough up 8. maltreat, mistreat
mania ... 4. rage 5. craze, furor
6. frenzy, furore, lunacy 7. madness,
passion 8. delirium 10. alienation
11. fascination, infatuation
mania (for) ...
buying .. 9. oniomania
drink .. 9. potomania 10. dipsomania
foreign customs .. 9. xenomania
narcotics .. 10. narcomania
religion .. 9. theomania
stealing .. 10. erotomania
11. kleptomania
wandering .. 9. dromomania
work .. 9. ergomania
manifest ... 4. list, open, show
5. clear, index, overt 6. evince,
liquet, patent 7. declare, evident,
express, obvious, visible 8. apparent,
disclose 11. indubitable
12. indisputable, unmistakable
manifestation ... 4. aura 5. phase
7. display 8. evidence
10. appearance, disclosure,
exhibition, indication, revelation
13. demonstration
manifestation of ...
deity .. 4. Apis 7. serapis
divinity .. 6. Christ 8. Epiphany
Vishnu .. 6. avatar
manifesto ... 5. edict 6. decree
8. evidence, rescript 11. declaration
(public) 12. announcement
13. demonstration
manikin ... 5. dwarf, model, pygmy
6. figure 7. phantom 9. mannequin
Manila ...
boat .. 6. bilalo
capital of .. 11. Philippines
hemp .. 5. abaca
hero .. 5. Dewey (Adm)
island site .. 5. Luzon
native .. 7. Chinese, Tagalog
9. Filipinos
maniple ... 5. fanon, orale 7. handful,
phalanx, platoon
manipulate ... 3. rig, use 4. work
5. pilot, treat, wield 6. handle,
manage 7. operate
manipulation ... 5. using 8. handling,
intrigue 9. operation, stratagem
10. management, use of hands
Manitoba, Canada ...
capital .. 8. Winnipeg
Indian .. 4. Cree
lake .. 8. Manitoba
river .. 3. Red
mankind ... 3. man 4. Adam, folk
7. menfolk 8. humanity 9. human
race
mankind (pert to) ...
division .. 4. race 5. tribe
group (kindred) .. 6. ethnos, socius
hater .. 11. misanthrope
science .. 9. ethnogeny, ethnology
12. anthropology
manly ... 4. bold 5. adult, brave, hardy,
noble 6. daring 8. resolute
9. honorable, masculine, undaunted

10. courageous

manna... 4. food (miracle), lerp (laap, laarp) 7. godsend 10. gazangabin

manner... 3. air, way 4. kind, mien, mode, sort 5. guise, style 6. aspect, custom, method 7. fashion 8. behavior 10. appearance, deportment

manner (pert to)...
frenzied.. 4. amok 5. amuck, huffy 7. haughty
law.. 5. modus
like.. 4. thus 6. in kind 8. parallel
meddlesome.. 9. officious
meditative.. 13. contemplative
rough.. 7. brusque 10. irreverent

mannerism... 4. mode 8. elegance 11. affectation

mannerly... 4. nice 5. moral, suave 6. seemly 8. decorous, politely 9. courteous 10. well-spoken 12. ingratiating

manner of...
making something.. 7. facture
pronouncing.. 6. accent, brogue
speaking.. 7. grammar

manners... 5. mores 8. behavior 9. amenities, etiquette

Mannheim gold... 5. brass

mano (comb form)... 4. hand

manoc... 4. fowl (jungle) 7. chicken, rooster

manor... 4. hall 5. abode 6. estate 7. demesne, mansion

manred... 6. homage 9. vassalage 10. leadership (in war)

mansion... 4. seat 5. house, manor, manse 8. dwelling 9. astrology

manta... 3. ray (fish) 4. wrap 5. cloak, cloth 7. blanket 8. mantelet (mantlet) 9. devilfish

mantilla... 4. cape, veil 5. cloak

mantis... 4. Cagn (deity) 6. insect 7. mantoid 9. rearhorse

mantis crab... 7. squilla

mantle... 4. cape, cope, robe 5. cloak, cover 6. capote, kittel 7. garment 8. filament, insignia, mantelet, mantling (Her), vestment 10. witzchoura 11. mantelletta

manto... 3. ore 4. gown 5. cloak 6. mantle, mantua

mantoid... 6. mantis

Mantua (pert to)...
birthplace of.. 6. Vergil (Virgil)
capital.. 7. Mantova
walled by.. 11. Charlemagne

Manu (Myth)...
laws.. 8. creation, religion
progenitors of.. 3. Man
Seventh Age, author of.. 10. Code of Manu (Hind laws)

manual... 4. book 7. clavier (Mus), didache 8. exercise, handbook 14. consuetudinary

manual (pert to)...
alphabet (deaf).. 11. dactylology
arts.. 6. crafts
crafts.. 5. sloyd (sloid, slojd) 10. handicraft
digit.. 3. toe 5. thumb 6. finger 8. dactylar

ritual.. 7. rituale 8. breviary 9. formulary

manufacture... 4. make 6. invent 7. produce, trump up 9. fabricate

manufacturer of drugs, liquors... 6. abkari (abkary)

manumission... 7. freeing 10. liberation (slave) 12. emancipation

manumit... 4. free 5. let go 6. unhand 7. dismiss, release 8. liberate

manuscript (Ms, Mss).. 4. copy (author's), opus 5. codex, folio 7. writing 8. document 11. composition, handwriting 13. written by hand

manuscript (pert to)...
back.. 5. dorso
blank space.. 6. lacuna
copier.. 6. scribe
mark (old).. 6. obelus

many... 6. divers 7. diverse, several, various 8. frequent, manifold, numerous 9. different, multitude 10. multiplied

many (pert to)...
footed.. 8. multiped
prefix.. 4. poly, vari 5. multi
sided.. 9. versatile 12. multilateral
times.. 5. often 10. frequently

manyplies... 12. third stomach (ruminant)

mao... 7. peacock

Maori (pert to)...
Adam, ancestor.. 4. Tiki
bird.. 3. tui 4. weka (flightless)
canoe, raft.. 4. moki, waka
charm (grotesque).. 7. heitiki
compensation.. 3. utu
fish.. 4. hiku 7. rainbow 9. trumpeter
hero.. 4. Maui
people.. 9. cannibals (anc) 10. aborigines
priest.. 7. tuhunga
sect.. 7. Ringatu
tatooing.. 4. moko
tree.. 5. mapau
tribe.. 3. Ati 4. Hapu
village.. 4. kaik (kaika)
weapon.. 4. mere, patu, rata 6. marree

Maoriland... 10. New Zealand

map... 4. plat 5. chart, image 6. charte, design, isobar (weather line), sketch, survey 7. diagram, epitome, explore, picture 9. delineate 10. embodiment 14. representation

maple (pert to)...
bowl.. 5. mazer, rogan (sap)
flowering.. 8. abutilon
genus.. 4. Acer 9. Aceraceae
insect scale.. 10. pulvinaria
seed.. 6. samara
sugar tube.. 5. stile
tree.. 8. box elder 9. moosewood

map maker... 4. Eric (Father) 7. charter 8. Mercator 12. cartographer

mapo... 4. goby (fish)

mar... 3. ruin, scar 5. botch, spoil 6. damage, deface, impair, mangle

7. blemish 8. mutilate 9. disfigure
Mar... 4. Lord (Jacobite)
marabou, marabout... 5. stork
6. argala, covert 8. adjutant
maracan... 5. macaw
maranon... 6. cashew
marasca, maraschino... 6. cherry
marasma... 5. waste 7. disease
10. emaciation 12. malnutrition
maraud... 3. rob 4. loot, raid, rove,
sack 6. forage 7. brigand, cateran,
pillage, plunder 10. plundering
marble... 3. mib, mig, taw 4. cold,
hard 5. agate, white 6. basalt,
marmor 7. pattern (mottled)
8. dolomite 9. limestone, sculpture,
unfeeling
marble (pert to)...
Belgian.. 5. rance
Catalonia.. 8. brocatel (brocatelle)
cork (tree).. 9. tambookie
famous.. 6. Parian 7. Carrara
8. Pentelec
game.. 3. taw 5. alley
group (famed).. 5. Elgin (Marbles)
made of.. 9. marmoreal
mosaic.. 7. tessera
Roman.. 7. cipolin
slab.. 5. dalle
marbled... 9. marmorate
Marbles... 5. Elgin 7. Arundel
marc... 6. refuse, spirit 7. residue
14. eau de vie de marc
marcato (Mus)... 6. marked
8. accented, emphatic
march... 4. fill, hike, step, trek
5. troop 6. border, parade
7. advance, proceed 8. boundary,
drumbeat, frontier, lockstep,
movement, progress, smallage
9. cavalcade, quickstep
March King... 5. Sousa (John Philip)
marcid... 4. weak 7. decayed, tabetic
8. withered 9. exhausted
10. emaciating
Marcobrunner... 4. wine (White Rhine)
Mardi Gras... 8. carnival 10. fat
Tuesday (literal) 13. Shrove Tuesday
Mardi Gras King... 3. Rex
mare... 4. yaud 5. filly, horse
6. goblin, grasni (gypsy) 7. incubus,
specter, trestle 8. the blues
9. nightmare 10. blue devils,
melancholy
marge, margent... 3. rim 4. brim,
edge, side 5. brink, shore 6. border,
fringe, margin 8. marginal
margin... 3. rim 4. brim, edge, rand,
room, side 5. brink, limit 6. amount,
border, reward 10. collateral
margin (pert to)...
business.. 5. gross
notched.. 5. erose
note.. 7. apostil 8. scholium
10. annotation
scalloped.. 7. crenate
set in.. 6. indent
straighten (to).. 5. align
marginal note... 4. kere (kri, keri)
7. apostil 8. scholium 10. annotation
marigold... 5. aster, boots, caper,
finch 6. orange (cadmium)

7. cowslip, Tagetes
marijuana... 3. hay 4. hemp 6. reefer
7. tobacco (wild) 8. locoweed
9. cigarette
marikina... 7. tamarin 8. marmoset
marimba... 9. xylophone
marina... 4. dock 5. basin
9. esplanade, promenade (seaside)
marinal... 6. marine, sailor, saline
marine... 3. tar 5. jolly, naval
7. mariner, oceanic, pelagic
8. maritime, nautical 11. leatherneck
marine (pert to)...
animal.. 3. orc 4. brit, seal 5. coral,
polyp 6. dugong, Otaria, teredo,
walrus 7. manatee, mollusk, octopus
clam.. 8. shipworm
crustacean.. 4. brit 8. barnacle
fauna, flora.. 7. benthos
fish.. 5. shark 8. menhaden
gastropod.. 5. conus (snail), murex
7. terebra
growth.. 4. kelp 5. algae 6. enalid
7. seaweed 10. ditch grass
individual.. 6. merman 7. mermaid
skeleton.. 5. coral
slogan.. 6. gung-ho
mariner... 3. gob, tar 4. salt 5. Jacky
6. sailor, seaman 8. waterman
mariner's card... 5. chart
mariner's compass points...
6. rhumba
marionette... 4. doll, duck 6. figure,
puppet
maritime... 5. naval 6. marine
7. oceanic 8. nautical
marjoram... 3. dot 4. mint 6. origin
8. origanum 9. flavoring
mark... 3. aim, tee 4. heed, line,
note, rist, seal, sign 5. brand, label,
notch, score, stain, stamp, trait
6. denote, symbol, target
7. betoken, blemish, earmark,
engrave, impress, imprint, insigne
8. evidence, identify, insignia,
landmark 9. emphasize, objective,
punctuate, signature, trademark
10. indication 11. distinction,
distinguish 14. characteristic
mark (pert to)...
bad.. 7. demerit
bounds.. 7. delimit 9. demarcate
contest (in a).. 5. bogey (bogie)
critical.. 6. obelus
diacritical.. 5. tilde 6. tittle 7. cedilla
disgrace.. 7. stigma
fingerprint.. 5. whorl
logic.. 11. differentia
misconduct.. 7. demerit
off.. 4. plot 6. assign 7. measure
12. characterize, circumscribe
of homage.. 7. ovation
of whip.. 4. wale, welt
out.. 6. cancel 10. obliterate
possessive.. 10. apostrophe
printing.. 4. dele, stet 5. caret
6. dagger, diesis, obelus 7. obelisk
10. apostrophe
pronunciation.. 5. breve 6. macron
proofreading.. 4. dele 5. caret
prosody.. 7. caesura, triseme
9. diaeresis, tetraseme

punctuation.. 4. dash 5. colon,
comma 6. period 9. diaeresis
(dieresis), semicolon 10. apostrophe
question.. 7. eroteme (erotema)
reference.. 4. star 6. dagger, diesis
8. asterisk
with bars.. 5. grill
with dots, spots.. 6. dapple 7. stipple
with pointed instrument.. 6. scrive
with ridges.. 3. rib
marked by...
dispute.. 13. controversial
maneuvering.. 8. tactical
nicety.. 7. elegant
small areas.. 9. areolated
time.. 5. dated
marked with...
colors.. 7. mottled 10. variegated
11. psychedelic
depressions.. 7. dimpled
furrows.. 6. rivose
grooves.. 6. lirate
lines.. 5. ruled 6. linear, notate
sables (Her).. 8. pelleted
spots.. 6. notate 7. mottled
stripes.. 7. lineate
zones.. 6. zonate
marker.. 4. buoy 5. pylon 6. scorer,
signal 7. brander, counter, monitor
8. bookmark, marksman, monument,
recorder 9. indicator
market.. 4. mart, sale, sell, shop
5. forum, trade 6. rialto, square
9. clientele
market (pert to)...
bonds.. 5. float
day (Rom).. 7. nundine
French.. 8. débouché
place.. sook 5. agora, plaza, store
6. bazaar, rialto 8. emporium,
exchange
marketable... 6. staple 7. salable
8. in demand, vendible
12. merchantable
markhor... 4. goat
marking (crescent)... 6. lunula, lunule
7. lunulet 9. engraving
markings... 7. rasceta
marksman... 4. shot 6. gunner, sniper
7. shooter 9. Orangeman
Mark Twain (pert to)...
category.. 8. humorist
character.. 7. Tom Sawyer
15. Huckleberry Finn
name.. 13. Samuel Clemens
tale.. 9. Gilded Age 10. Roughing It
15. Innocents Abroad
marl... 4. malm 5. earth, fiber
6. manure 7. deposit (earthy), marlite
9. greensand 10. fertilizer,
overspread
marli... 4. lace 5. gauze, tulle
6. border (raised on dish)
marlin... 6. curlew, godwit 8. sailfish
9. spearfish
marlinspike... 3. fid 4. bird, tool
6. jaeger 8. skua gull
marmalade... 3. jam 6. Achras, sapote
8. plum tree, preserve 12. mammee
sapota
marmit... 6. kettle 7. soup pot
marmite (Mil)... 4. bomb (soup kettle)

5. shell
marmor... 6. marble
marmoset... 4. mico (black–tailed)
6. monkey, sagoin 7. tamarin
marmot... 5. bobac 6. rodent
7. Marmota 8. Arctomys, whistler
9. ground hog, woodchuck
maroon... 5. slave 7. abandon, cast
off, forsake, isolate 8. chestnut
13. leave helpless
marquee... 4. tent 6. canopy
marriage... 5. union 7. wedding,
wedlock 9. matrimony 10. nuptiality
11. espousement
marriage (pert to)...
absence of.. 5. agamy
age.. 6. mature, nubile
broker.. 9. schatchen 10. matchmaker
forswearer.. 8. celibate
god.. 5. Hymen
goddess.. 4. Hera
hater.. 10. misogamist
intermarriage.. 13. miscegenation
late in life.. 8. opsigamy
more than one.. 6. bigamy, digamy
8. polygamy 9. polyandry, tetragamy
(4th) 11. deuterogamy
notice.. 5. banns
of the gods.. 8. theogamy
outside the tribe.. 7. exogamy
pert to.. 7. marital, spousal
8. hymeneal 9. connubial, endogamic
portion.. 3. dot 5. dotal, dowry
promise.. 7. betroth 8. affiance
secret.. 9. elopement
married... 5. wived 6. wedded
8. espoused 9. connubial
married (pert to)...
more than once at a time..
9. polyandry (woman)
once at a time.. 8. monandry
person.. 4. wife 6. spouse
7. husband 8. benedict
twice.. 6. bigamy, digamy
11. deuterogamy
marrow... 4. pith 6. center
7. essence, medulla 9. substance
Mars... 3. god (of War) 4. Ares
6. planet, war–god
Mars (pert to)...
altar.. 13. Campus Martius (field of
Mars)
constellation.. 3. Ara
festival.. 5. March 7. October
pert to.. 5. Arean 7. Martian
priests.. 5. Salii
red.. 5. totem
satellites.. 6. Deimos, Phobos
ship.. 8. moon ship 9. spaceship
sons (twin).. 5. Remus 7. Romulus
spot.. 5. oasis
Marseillaise... 4. song (1792)
Marseille, France...
capital of Dept.. 14. Bouches du
Rhone
church.. 9. Notre Dame
fort.. 11. Rue Noailles 13. Rue
Cannebière
old name.. 8. Massilia
seaport site.. 13. Mediterranean
marsh... 3. bog, fen 4. meer, mire,
moor, slue 5. liman, swale, swamp

6. morass, saline, slough
7. maremma
marsh (pert to)...
bird.. 4. sora 5. snipe, stilt
crocodile.. 3. goa
elder.. 3. Iva
fever.. 7. helodes
gas.. 7. methane 8. firedamp
grass.. 5. sedge, spart
hawk.. 5. harpy 7. harrier
hen.. 4. rail
inhabiting.. 12. limnophilous
mallow.. 5. altea
marigold.. 5. boots, calla 7. cowslip
pert to.. 8. paludine
shrub.. 4. reed 5. sedge 7. bulrush,
cattail 8. moorwort 12. pickerelweed
marshal... 3. Ney (Fr) 4. lead 5. align,
aline, array, groom, guide, range,
usher 6. direct, parade 7. farrier,
officer 8. official
Marshall Islands...
chains (two).. 6. Ralick (eleven isls)
7. Rattach (13 isls)
government.. 11. trusteeship
WWII scene.. 6. Bikini 8. Eniwetok
9. Kwajalein
marshberry, marshwort... 9. cranberry
marshy... 3. wet 5. boggy, fenny,
liman 7. moorish 8. morassey,
paludine
marsupial... 4. frog, tait 5. kaola
6. wombat 7. opossum, wallaby
8. kangaroo 9. bandicoot, phalanger,
tapoatafa 10. Diprotodon
11. Marsupialia
marsupium... 5. pouch
martel (Hist)... 6. hammer
martel–de–fer... 6. weapon
12. hammer of iron
marten... 3. fur 4. pelt 5. sable
6. mammal 7. Mustela
martial... 4. Mars (pert to) 5. brave
7. warlike 8. fighting, militant,
military
Martinique...
capital.. 8. St Pierre (former) 12. Fort
de France
formation.. 8. volcanic
mountain peak.. 9. Mont Pelée
martyr... 4. kill 5. title 7. Stephen
(Christian), torture 8. sufferer
marvel... 4. gape 6. wonder
7. miracle, portent, prodigy
8. astonish
marvelous... 6. superb 7. strange
9. wonderful 10. improbable,
incredible, remarkable 11. astonishing
13. extraordinary
Maryland...
bay.. 10. Chesapeake
capital.. 9. Annapolis
city.. 9. Baltimore
Hist site.. 8. Antietam 10. State
House (nation's oldest) 11. Fort Mc
Henry
mountain.. 8. Backbone, Piedmont
11. Appalachian
race (famed).. 9. Preakness
12. Steeplechase
race track.. 5. Bowie 6. Butler, Laurel
7. Pimlico

school.. 9. Annapolis (Acad)
12. Johns Hopkins
settler.. 7. Calvert (Leonard)
State admission.. 7. Seventh
State motto.. 22. Manly Deeds,
Womanly Words
State nickname.. 4. Free 7. Old Line
mash... 4. feed, ogle, pulp 5. crush,
flirt, press, smash, steep 6. jumble,
soften 7. mixture 9. pulverize
11. infatuation
mashal... 7. parable, proverb
masher... 5. dandy, flirt, ricer
7. utensil 10. pulverizer
11. philanderer
masjid... 6. mosque
mask... 4. ball, loup, veil 5. cloak,
cover, dance, drama, onkos
6. domino, screen 7. conceal,
pretext 8. disguise 10. subterfuge
masked... 6. comedy, cowled, hidden,
veiled 7. larvate, obscure
8. shrouded 9. concealed, disguised
masker... 5. mimer 6. mummer
11. masquerader
maslin... 5. brass 6. kettle 7. mixture
(grain) 9. potpourri
Masonic doorkeeper... 5. tiler
masonry... 6. ashlar 9. revetment
mass... 3. cob, dab, gob, mop, pat,
wad 4. blob, body, bulk, load, loaf,
lump, roll, size 5. solid 8. quantity
9. large part, magnitude 11. large
amount 12. accumulation,
congregation
mass (pert to)...
book.. 6. missal
collection.. 9. aggregate
directory (RCCh).. 4. ordo
for dead.. 7. requiem
matter.. 5. molar
molten glass.. 7. parison
nerve tissue.. 8. ganglion
tangled.. 3. mop 4. shag
vestment (Eccl).. 5. amice
Massachusetts...
capital.. 6. Boston (1630)
city.. 5. Salem 7. Concord
8. Plymouth 9. Cambridge, Lexington
10. Gloucester, New Bedford
12. Provincetown
college (oldest, US).. 7. Harvard
explorer.. 5. Cabot 7. Gosnold
9. Capt Smith (John)
hero.. 10. Paul Revere
island.. 9. Nantucket 15. Martha's
Vineyard
mountain.. 3. Tom 8. Greylock
10. Berkshires
river.. 10. Housatonic 11. Connecticut
school (first free).. 6. Dedham (1649)
settlers.. 8. Pilgrims, Puritans
State admission.. 5. Sixth
State nickname.. 8. Bay State 9. Old
Colony
massacre... 5. havoc 6. pogrom
7. carnage 8. butchery, decimate,
genocide 9. slaughter
massage... 3. rub 5. knead 6. stroke
7. therapy
massive... 3. big 4. bold 5. bulky,
large, massy 7. weighty 8. imposing

9. ponderous 10. impressive
11. substantial
mast... 3. cue, fid 4. pole, spar
5. stick, stuff (oneself)
master... 3. man, rab 4. lord, mian,
rule 5. chief, judge, rabbi, tutor
6. expert, humble, subdue
7. captain, conquer, maestro,
padrone, subject, teacher
8. dominate, overcome, regulate,
surmount, vanquish 9. commander,
conqueror, craftsman, preceptor,
subjugate
master (pert to)...
African.. 5. bwana
Eton.. 4. beak
fencing.. 7. lanista
hard.. 6. despot
Indian.. 5. sahib
music.. 7. maestro
of a house.. 13. paterfamilias
of ceremonies.. 2. M C 5. emcee
of Heaven.. 16. Celestial Teacher
of the horse.. 7. equerry
stroke.. 4. coup
masterful... 6. lordly 7. haughty
8. arrogant, skillful 9. arbitrary,
imperious 10. commanding
11. dictatorial, domineering,
magisterial, overbearing
13. authoritative
mastery... 4. gree 5. power, skill
7. control, victory 8. dominion
10. ascendancy 11. proficiency
12. vanquishment
mastic... 3. asa, gum 5. resin
6. liquor 8. adhesive 9. red–yellow
masticate... 4. chew 5. crush, grind
8. macerate
mastiff... 3. dog 5. burly, matin
7. massive
mastodon... 5. giant 6. animal,
Mammut 7. mammoth 8. behemoth
9. dinothere 10. Dinotheres,
Mammutidae 11. Dinotherium
mat... 3. rug 4. dull (finish) 5. doily,
platt, twist 7. webbing 8. entangle,
material 11. interweave, lusterless
matador (pert to)...
garment.. 4. cape
staff.. 6. muleta (with red flag)
sword.. 7. estoque
matagasse... 11. butcherbird
match... 3. pit 4. copy, game, mate,
pair, peer, sort 5. equal, fusee,
marry, tally, vesta 6. compare,
contest, lighter, lucifer 8. coincide,
marriage, parallel 10. correspond
11. counterpart
matched... 5. mated 6. paired, pitted,
teamed 7. equaled (equalled)
matchless... 5. alone 6. unlike
7. unequal 8. peerless 9. unequaled
10. inimitable 12. incomparable
matchlock... 3. gun 7. gunlock
mate... 4. pair, wife 5. equal, marry,
match 6. seaman, spouse
7. comrade, husband, mariner,
partner 9. companion
11. confederate, counterpart
matelassé... 6. fabric 8. quilting
(imitation) 13. ornamentation

material, materiel... 4. data 5. goods,
stuff 6. fabric, matter, plasma,
staple, swatch 7. weighty
8. relevant, supplies, tangible
9. apparatus, corporeal, equipment,
essential 11. substantial
12. nonspiritual 13. materialistic
material (pert to)...
building.. 4. frit, lime, tile, wood
5. adobe, brick, rabat, tapia
6. cement, thatch 7. plywood
8. asbestos, Masonite 9. wallboard
discard.. 4. slag 5. scrap 6. refuse
7. rubbish
dress.. 4. silk, wool 5. crepe, linen,
satin, surah, tulle, tweed 6. baleen,
faille, sennit, tricot, velvet
8. corduroy
household.. 5. scrim 6. carpet,
damask, lampas, mohair, napery
7. drapery 8. tapestry
needlework.. 4. lace, yarn 6. thread
8. arrasene, chenille
paper.. 3. wax 4. bond, news, note,
rice 6. letter, tissue, vellum
7. drawing, writing 8. wrapping
9. cardboard, onionskin, parchment
11. papier–mâché
polishing.. 11. rottenstone
materia medica... 7. acology
10. leechcraft
maternal... 7. enation 8. motherly
10. motherlike
math... 6. mowing 9. aftermath,
monastery
mathematician... 6. Euclid 7. actuary
9. physicist, Whitehead
mathematics (pert to)...
abbreviation.. 3. QED
arbitrary.. 5. radix 9. parameter
deduction.. 8. analysis
diagram.. 5. graph
element.. 4. cube, root 6. factor
7. decimal, divisor, formula, minuend
8. dividend, fraction, quotient,
repetend 10. multiplier, subtrahend
12. multiplicand
equation.. 2. pi 4. cosh, sine, surd
6. cosine
factor.. 10. quaternion
instrument.. 6. sector 7. compass
8. arbalest
number.. 5. digit
operation, operator.. 5. nabla
6. scalar 7. operand 10. quaternion
proposition.. 7. theorem
quantity.. 6. addend, augend, scalar
sheets of.. 4. cone 5. nappe
symbol.. 5. digit 7. facient, operand
12. multiplicand
type.. 4. pure 6. higher 7. algebra,
physics 8. abstract, calculus,
geometry 10. arithmetic, elementary,
quadratics 12. trigonometry
mathemeg... 7. catfish
matie... 7. herring
matin... 6. aubade (song) 7. morning,
service 8. watchdog 11. morning
song 13. morning prayer
matinee... 5. levee, party, salon
6. soiree 8. negligee 9. reception
13. conversazione, entertainment

matipo... 4. wood (fuel) 5. napau
matka, matkab... 4. seal
matlow... 6. sailor
matrass... 4. tube 5. flask 6. bottle,
carafe 8. bolthead
matriculate... 4. list 5. admit, adopt,
enter 6. enroll 8. register
10. naturalize
matrimonial... 7. marital, nuptial,
spousal 8. conjugal, hymeneal
9. connubial
matrimony... 7. wedlock 8. marriage
matrix... 3. bed 4. cast, form, mold,
womb 5. cutis 6. gangue
10. foundation, impression
matron... 4. dame, wife 5. widow
11. housekeeper
matter... 3. gas, pus 4. body, gear,
malm, pith 5. atoms, fluid, vapor
6. affair, amount, solids 7. problem,
trouble 8. business, elements,
material 10. importance
11. constituent 12. circumstance
matter (pert to)...
alluvial.. 5. geest
celestial.. 6. nebula
coloring.. 5. eosin 10. endochrome
fatty.. 5. sebum
noxious.. 6. miasma
of doubt.. 7. dubiety
of fact.. 7. literal, prosaic 9. practical,
pragmatic
of law.. 3. res
of note.. 8. notandum
particle.. 4. atom
perfume.. 7. essence
spinal cord.. 4. alba
uniform (physics).. 7. inertia
volcanic.. 2. aa, oo 4. lava
mature... 3. age, due, old 4. ripe
5. adult, grown, ripen 6. digest,
mellow, season 7. develop, fall due,
grow old, perfect 8. complete
9. full-grown, perfected, ratheripe
maturity... 8. ripeness 9. adulthood,
readiness 10. falling due
11. development
matutinal... 5. early, matin 7. morning
12. antemeridian
maty... 7. servant
maud... 3. rug 5. plaid, shawl
maudlin... 5. beery, drunk, silly, tipsy
7. tearful, weeping 10. lachrymose
11. sentimental (overly)
maul, mall... 4. beat, bung, club,
mace, mall, moth 5. abuse, gavel,
staff 6. beetle, bruise, mallet
maumet... 3. god (false), guy 4. doll,
idol 5. image 6. puppet
9. scarecrow
maund, maun... 3. beg 6. basket,
hamper 7. begging, measure
Maundy... 4. alms 8. ceremony
10. Last Supper
Maundy Thursday (Bib)... 8. Holy
Week 13. washing of feet
Mauritius, Ile de France...
capital.. 9. Port Louis
government.. 7. British
product.. 5. coral, sugar
site.. 11. Indian Ocean
Mauser... 5. rifle 7. firearm

mauve... 5. lilac 6. mallow, purple,
violet 10. atmosphere (color)
maverick... 4. calf (orphan) 5. dogie
6. animal 8. newcomer
13. nonconformist
mavis, mavie... 6. thrush
maw... 4. craw, crop 6. gullet, mallow
7. gizzard, stomach
mawk... 6. maggot
mawkish... 5. vapid 6. sickly
8. nauseous 9. squeamish
10. disgusting 11. sentimental
maxilla... 7. jawbone
maxim... 3. saw 4. dict, rule
5. adage, axiom, gnome, motto,
tenet, truth 6. saying 7. precept,
proverb 8. aphorism, apothegm
10. apophthegm
maxims... 5. logia 9. moralisms
maximum... 4. most 5. limit
7. highest, supreme 8. greatest
12. consummation
maximus... 7. largest
may... 3. can 6. be able 9. be
allowed 11. in one's power,
opportunity
May (pert to)...
apple.. 8. mandrake
bird.. 6. thrush
cock.. 5. melon 6. plover
curlew.. 8. whimbrel
Duke.. 6. cherry
festival.. 7. Beltane (anc)
First.. 7. Beltane 14. May-day festival
fish.. 9. killifish
flower.. 7. arbutus 8. hawthorn,
marigold 9. calla lily 10. stitchwort
12. cuckooflower
fly.. 3. dun 7. shad fly 9. ephemerid
goddess.. 4. Maia
gowan.. 5. daisy
Maya... 3. Mam (tribe) 6. Indian
8. Pokonchi
Mayan calendar...
five added days.. 5. uayeb
no leap year.. 5. solar
twenty-day month.. 5. uinal
year.. 4. haab
Mayan underworld... 7. xibalba
maybe... 2. if 7. perhaps 8. possibly
9. perchance 11. conceivably,
possibility, uncertainty
Mayfair... 6. London (fashionable)
Mayflower (pert to)...
boat of.. 8. Pilgrims (1620)
Compact.. 7. agreement (1620)
sister ship.. 9. Speedwell
mayhap... 7. perhaps 12. peradventure
mayor... 5. maire 7. alcalde
10. magistrate 11. burgomaster
mazarine... 4. blue (color from Cardinal
Mazari)
maze... 5. fancy 7. stupefy
8. confound, delirium, delusion
9. confusion, deception, labyrinth
12. bewilderment, complication
mazed... 4. lost 7. in a maze
9. stupefied 10. bewildered
mazuma... 5. money
mead... 5. drink 6. meadow
8. hydromel 9. metheglin
meadow... 3. lea 4. mead 5. field,

haugh, pampa, swale **7**. pasture,
savanna (savannah) **9**. grassland
10. agostadero
meadow (pert to) . . .
chicken . . **8**. sora rail
crocus . . **7**. saffron
crowfoot . . **9**. buttercup
hen . . **4**. coot, rail **7**. bittern
mouse . . **4**. vole **8**. arvicole
part . . **5**. swale
sage . . **6**. salvia
saxifrage . . **6**. seseli
sweet . . **7**. Spiraea
meager, meagre . . . **4**. arid, bare, lank,
poor, slim **5**. gaunt, scant, spare
6. barren, jejune, lenten, narrow,
sparse **7**. starved, sterile, trivial
9. emaciated **10**. inadequate
meal . . . **3**. tub **4**. bran, dune, mess
5. feast, grout, salep, snack
6. bucket, fodder, powder, ration,
repast, tiffin **7**. banquet **8**. sandbank
9. collation, pulverize
mealy . . . **4**. pale **7**. friable, powdery
10. soft-spoken **11**. farinaceous
12. mealymouthed
mealy (pert to) . . .
Amazon . . **6**. parrot
back . . **6**. cicada
bird, duck . . **5**. squaw
bug . . **4**. pest **5**. scale **10**. pear blight
mouth . . **7**. warbler
tree . . **9**. arrowwood, wayfaring
mealy-mouthed . . . **7**. suave
10. flattering **12**. hypocritical
13. sanctimonious
mean . . . **3**. low **4**. base **5**. petty,
small, snide, solar (time), sorry
6. common, denote, design, humble,
intend, medium, menial, middle,
midway, paltry, shabby, sordid, stingy
7. average, ignoble, purport, purpose,
servile, squalid **8**. beggarly, ordinary,
plebeian, shameful, wretched
9. difficult, malicious, niggardly,
penurious **10**. despicable,
ill-humored, spiritless **11**. closefisted,
disgraceful **12**. contemptible,
dishonorable, narrow-minded,
parsimonious
mean clef (Mus) . . . **5**. C clef
meaning . . . **4**. null (without) **5**. sense
6. import, intent, spirit **7**. purport
8. semantic **9**. intending, intention,
knowledge **10**. understand
12. significance **13**. signification
14. interpretation
meaningless . . . **4**. rote **5**. banal, derry
7. aimless **9**. senseless
10. designless **11**. purposeless
13. insignificant
meanness . . . **6**. infamy, malice
8. baseness, ill-humor **9**. servility
10. humbleness, paltriness,
sordidness, stinginess **11**. inferiority
means . . . **5**. funds **7**. capital
8. averages **9**. resources
11. wherewithal
means of . . .
access . . **4**. adit **5**. inlet **7**. ingress
8. aperture
communication . . **4**. note **5**. flags,

phone, radio, smoke **6**. letter, postal,
tom-tom **8**. telegram **9**. telegraph,
telephone
livelihood . . **4**. work **5**. labor, trade
8. vocation **10**. profession
outlet . . **4**. door, exit **6**. egress
8. aperture
support . . **5**. funds **6**. assets
7. aliment **11**. maintenance
meantime . . . **5**. while **7**. interim
8. interval, same time **9**. meanwhile
measles . . . **7**. rubella, rubeola
8. morbilli
measure (pert to) . . .
area . . **2**. ar **3**. are, rod **4**. acre, area,
mile, rood **6**. square **7**. geodesy,
hectare, section **8**. township
Bible . . **3**. cab (kab), kor, log **4**. epha
5. cubit, homer
gauge . . **3**. erg, lea (yarn) **5**. ergon,
level, plumb, scale, stone **6**. denier,
square **7**. calorie (calory), compass,
sextant **8**. calipers, quadrant
length . . **3**. ell, mil, rod **4**. foot, hand,
inch, knot, mile, nail, pace, rule,
tape, yard **5**. chain, cubit, meter
6. league **7**. furlong **8**. kilometer,
yardstick **10**. centimeter, micrometer,
millimeter
nautical . . **4**. knot **6**. fathom, league
paper . . **4**. page, ream **5**. quire, sheet
poetry . . **6**. dipody, iambic, rhythm,
sestet **7**. anapest, couplet, distich,
tripody **8**. quatrain **9**. hexameter
10. ottava rima, pentastich,
tetrameter, tetrastich **11**. Alexandrine
printer . . **2**. em, en **4**. pica **5**. agate
volume, weight . . **3**. ton, tun (wine)
4. bale, butt, cord **5**. carat, liter,
minim, ounce, pound, quart
6. barrel, bushel, finger, gallon,
magnum, pottle **8**. hogshead,
teaspoon **9**. kiloliter **10**. tablespoon
measurement . . . **4**. size **6**. amount,
alnage, extent, metage **7**. azimuth
8. abscissa, capacity, quantity
9. substance **11**. calculation,
mensuration
measuring instrument . . . **6**. stadia
7. alidade, caliper **8**. odometer
12. perambulator (surveyor)
meat . . . **4**. beef, fish, food, lamb, pork
5. flesh **6**. fillet, kernel, mutton,
quarry **7**. brisket **9**. aitchbone
(icebone), spareribs
meat (pert to) . . .
ball . . **7**. rissole **9**. croquette,
hamburger
cured, dried . . **3**. ham **5**. bacon
6. flitch, jerked **7**. biltong (biltongue)
8. pemmican
jellied . . **5**. aspic
minced, roll . . **7**. rissole
roasted . . **5**. cabob (kabob)
9. barbecued
slaughterhouse . . **8**. abattoir
smoking place . . **6**. buccan (bucan)
stew . . **8**. mulligan **9**. lobscouse
meatus . . . **4**. burr (ear) **5**. canal
7. opening, passage
meaty . . . **5**. pithy, solid **11**. substantial
Mecca, Arabia . . . **8**. Holy City **16**. City

of the Prophet
Mecca (pert to)...
birthplace of.. 8. Mohammed
capital.. 5. Hejaz
color.. 11. Tuscan brown
famed for.. 5. Kaaba (Caaba, Kaabeth)
  10. Black Stone 11. Great Mosque
governor.. 6. sherif (shereef)
pilgrimage.. 4. hadj
pilgrim's dress.. 5. ihram
rug.. 6. Shiraz
mechanic... 7. artisan, workman
  8. operator 9. artificer, craftsman,
  machinist, operative
mechanical... 8. machinal
  9. automatic, practical, technical
  11. involuntary, stereotyped
mechanical (pert to)...
adjustment.. 9. tentation
drawing.. 8. drafting
law, motion.. 8. dynamics, kinetics
lever.. 6. tappet
part.. 5. rotor 6. stator
mechanics... 9. technique
  11. mechanology
mechanism.. 4. gear, tool 5. means
  6. tackle 7. control, rigging
  9. apparatus, machinery, technique
medal... 4. coin, disk (disc) 5. badge
  6. plaque 8. medallion
  10. decoration
medallion... 4. coin 5. cameo, medal,
  panel 6. tablet 8. ornament
meddle... 3. pry 4. nose 6. dabble,
  tamper 8. obtrude 9. interfere
meddler... 8. busybody 9. pragmatic
meddlesome... 7. Paul Fry 8. meddling
  9. officious 11. inquisitive,
  pragmatical
Mede... 6. Median 7. Persian
medial, median... 4. mean 5. mesne,
  raphe (valve) 6. medium, middle
  7. average 11. intervening
  12. intermediate
Median... 4. Magi, Mede 5. Medic
mediate... 5. opine 9. intercede,
  interpose, reconcile
mediator... 5. muser 7. arbiter
  9. go-between 10. interagent
  11. intercessor
medic.. 3. doc 6. clover, doctor,
  median, medico 9. physician
medical (pert to)...
comb form.. 3. oma 4. itis 6. iatric
  7. iatrics
compound.. 5. hepar
fluid.. 5. blood, lymph, serum
man.. 5. medic 6. shaman, voodoo
monster.. 5. teras
officer.. 7. coroner
practitioner.. 2. MD 6. doctor, intern
  (interne) 7. surgeon 8. sawbones
system.. 7. therapy 9. allopathy
  10. homeopathy, psychiatry
term.. 5. curative 9. medicinal
medical terms...
chicken pox.. 9. varicella
flat feet.. 9. pes planus
headache.. 11. cephalalgia
heartburn.. 7. pyrosis
hives.. 9. urticaria
measles.. 7. rubella, rubeola

mumps.. 9. parotitis
whooping cough.. 9. pertussis
medicinal (pert to)...
agent.. 3 tea 6. tisane 9. decoction
bark.. 6. cartex
dropper.. 7. pipette
equal parts.. 3. ana
herb, plant.. 3. rue 4. aloe 5. ergot,
  jalap, orris, senna, tansy 6. arnica,
  cohosh, ipecac 7. boneset, chirata,
  comfrey 8. licorice, valerian
pain allaying.. 7. anodyne 8. sedative
  9. goofballs, paregoric
  11. barbiturate
patent.. 7. nostrum
remedy.. 5. drops, salve 6. elixir,
  iodine 7. panacea 8. antidote,
  ointment
science.. 7. biology 10. physiology,
  psychology
tablet.. 4. pill 6. troche 7. lozenge
term.. 4. drug 11. therapeutic
mediety... 6. loiety 10. moderation,
  temperance
medieval, mediaeval... 7. archaic
  10. Middle Ages
medieval (pert to)...
galley (ship's).. 3. nef 5. xebec
  6. bireme, galiot (galliot) 7. dromone
  (dromon), trireme, unireme
garment.. 6. tabard
headdress.. 6.' abacot
helmet.. 5. armet
instrument (stringed).. 5. rebec
  (rebeck)
money of account.. 3. ora
monster.. 5. golem 9. automaton
  12. Frankenstein
shield.. 3. ecu 6. scutum
title, teacher.. 8. magister
weapon, club.. 4. mace 5. oncin
Medina, Saudi Arabia (pert to)...
anc name.. 9. Lathrippa
Mohammed supporters.. 6. ansars
sacred city of.. 5. Islam
tombs.. 4. Omar 6. Fatima
  8. Mohammed
mediocre... 4. mean, so–so 6. medium
  7. average 8. middling, ordinary,
  passable 9. tolerable 11. indifferent
meditate... 4. muse, plan, pore
  5. brood, study, watch, weigh
  6. ponder 7. purpose, reflect, revolve
  8. cogitate, consider 11. contemplate
meditation... 4. yoga 7. thought
  8. devotion 10. rumination
  11. thanatopsis 13. contemplation
  14. omphaloskepsis
mediterranean... 6. inland 7. midland
  10. landlocked
Mediterranean (pert to)...
boat.. 3. nef 4. saic 5. xebec (zebec)
  6. galiot (galliot), mistic (mistico),
  settee (setee) 7. felucca, hexeris
cat.. 5. genet
coast.. 7. Riviera
falcon.. 6. lanner
fish.. 6. remora
fowl.. 5. leghorn
fruit.. 5. olive 7. azarole
gulf.. 5. Tunis
herb.. 4. Ammi

inland.. 3. sea
island.. 4. Elba, Gozo 5. Crete, Malta
   6. Candia, Cyprus, Ebusis, Sicily
   7. Majorca 8. Belearic (group),
   Sardinia
island, volcanic.. 6. Lipari, Salina
   7. Vulcano 9. Stromboli
port.. 5. Tunis 7. Tunisia
storm.. 7. borasca (borasco, borasque)
tree.. 5. carob 7. azarole
wind.. 6. solano 7. etesian, gregale,
   mistral, sirocco 8. levanter
   10. euroclyden
medium... 4. agar (cultured), doer,
   mean 5. color, organ 6. degree,
   medial, oracle 7. average, psychic
   8. mediator, mediocre
   10. instrument, interagent
   11. environment 12. intermediary,
   spiritualist
medley.. 4. olio 5. relay 6. jumble
   7. ferrago, mélange, mixture
   8. fantasia, mingling 9. potpourri
   10. hodgepodge, salmagundi
medrick... 4. gull (Bonaparte's), tern
   (Wilson's)
medulla... 4. pith 6. marrow
   7. summary 9. oblongata
   10. compendium
Medusa (Myth)... 6. Gorgon, Stheno
   (sister) 9. gorgoneum
Medusa's head (pert to)...
constellation (cluster).. 7. Perseus
star.. 5. Algol
vegetable.. 8. mushroom
Zool.. 10. basket fish
meed... 5. bribe, merit, repay, share
   6. desert, reward 7. bribery
   10. recompense
meek... 4. mild 6. docile, gentle,
   humble, modest 7. pacific, patient
   8. moderate, yielding 10. spiritless,
   submissive
meerkat... 6. monkey
meerschaum... 4. pipe 6. gravel
   (color) 7. seafoam 9. sepiolite
meet... 3. fit 4. face, game, join
   5. equal, match, touch 6. battle,
   combat, concur 7. collide, conform,
   contact, contest, convene, fulfill,
   satisfy 8. assemble, confront
   9. encounter 10. congregate,
   experience, rendezvous
meet halfway... 7. mediate
   10. compromise
meeting... 4. mall, race 5. court,
   gemot (gemote), joint, synod, tryst,
   union 6. caucus, powwow, séance
   7. contact, joining 8. assembly,
   conclave, junction 9. encounter,
   gathering, in contact 10. conference,
   convention, converging, rendezvous
   11. convergence 12. congregation,
   intersection
mega, meg (comb form)... 5. great
   6. mighty
megalith... 5. stone (huge) 6. dolman
   7. boulder 8. monument (Prehist)
megapode, megapod... 6. leipoa
   9. mound bird 10. jungle fowl
   11. brush turkey
megascope... 12. magic lantern

megaseism... 10. earthquake
megrim, megrims... 4. whim 5. fancy,
   freak, humor 8. headache
   9. dizziness 12. hypochondria
Mehitabel, Mehetabel... 3. cat
Mekong River tribe... 3. Moi (Asian)
mel... 5. honey
melancholia... 7. sadness 8. neurosis
   9. nostalgia, psychosis
   10. depression
melancholy... 3. sad 4. blue, dark,
   glum 5. drear, gloom 6. sombre,
   sorrow 7. doleful, sadness
   8. atrabile, liverish, tristful
   9. dejection 10. depressing,
   depression, dispirited, lamentable
   11. despondency, downhearted,
   pensiveness 12. hypochondria,
   mournfulness
Melanesia... 14. Pacific Islands
Melanesian (pert to)...
island.. 4. Fiji 7. Solomon 11. New
   Hebrides
native.. 4. Fiji 6. Papuan
   10. Polynesian
superbeing.. 5. adaro
mélange... 4. olio 6. jumble, medley
   7. mixture 8. pasticcio
   10. miscellany 14. conglomeration
melee... 3. row 4. fray 5. fight
   6. affray 7. contest, diamond (small
   cut) 8. skirmish 9. commotion
melicocca... 5. genip 9. soapberry
melicratum... 4. mead 8. beverage,
   hydromel
melilotus... 6. clover
meliorate... 6. soften 7. improve
   10. ameliorate
melisma... 6. melody 7. cadenza
Melissa... 4. balm 12. Old World mint
mell... 3. mix 4. maul 5. grain (last
   cut), honey 6. beetle, hammer,
   mallet, meddle, mingle
mellow... 4. rich, ripe, soft 5. drunk
   6. genial, jovial, mature, tender
   7. amiable, matured 9. melodious
melodic... 6. ariose 7. cadenza,
   melisma 9. melodious
melodious... 6. ariose, arioso, dulcet
   7. musical, tunable, tuneful
   10. harmonious
melodist... 6. singer 8. composer,
   musician 9. harmonist
melodramatic... 8. dramatic, romantic
   11. sensational
melody... 3. air 4. aria, tune 5. canto,
   charm, dirge, melos, music
   6. rhythm, strain 7. harmony,
   melisma, rosalia 9. cantilena,
   cantilene 11. tunefulness
melon... 4. musk, pepo 6. casaba
   7. Persian 8. honeydew
   9. muskmelon, red-yellow
   10. cantaloupe, paddymelon,
   watermelon
melon (pert to)...
financial.. 4. plum 8. dividend
like.. 5. gourd
pear.. 6. pepino
political.. 5. graft 6. spoils
melongena... 7. brinjal (brinjaul)
   8. eggplant

melos... 4. song 6. melody
melt... 3. run 4. frit, fuse, thaw
  5. smelt, swale 6. render, soften
  7. liquefy 8. diminish, dissolve
  9. disappear 12. disintegrate
member... 4. limb, part 5. organ
  6. branch, fellow, joiner 7. section
  8. belonger, district, enlistee, enroller
  9. associate
member (pert to)...
  boy's club.. 3. cub 5. scout
  Caliph dynasty.. 6. Omniad
  chapter (Eccl).. 9. capitular
  crew.. 4. hand
  diplomatic staff.. 6. consul 7. attaché
    8. minister 10. ambassador
  Jewish brotherhood.. 6. Essene
  laity.. 6. layman
  literary club.. 9. academist
    11. academician
  oldest.. 4. dean
  regiment.. 8. legioner 9. grenadier,
    legionary 11. legionnaire
  religious sect.. 5. Amish 6. Quaker,
    Shaker
  Roman Catholic society.. 6. Jesuit
  State.. 7. citizen
  swing band.. 6. hepcat 7. swinger
membrane... 4. caul, skin, tela
  5. lemma 6. lamina 8. ectoderm,
  striffin
membrane (pert to)...
  brain.. 13. meninges mater
  diffusion.. 7. osmosis
  ear.. 7. eardrum
  fold.. 5. plica
  optical.. 6. retina
  weblike.. 4. tela
memento... 5. relic, token 6. trophy
  8. keepsake, memorial, souvenir
  11. remembrance
Memnon (pert to)...
  famed statue.. 11. vocal Memnon
  father.. 8. Tithonus
  Greek name.. 9. Amenhotep
  king of.. 8. Ethiopia
  mother.. 3. Eos (Aurora)
  war hero.. 7. Trojan
memoir... 4. hint, note 5. éloge, essay
  6. record, report 7. account, history
  9. biography, narrative, reminding
  10. memorandum 12. dissertation
  13. autobiography
memorabilia... 3. ana 5. notes
  6. record 7. memoirs 8. memories
memorable... 7. namable, notable
  9. reminding 11. reminiscent
memorandum... 4. chit, note 5. diary
  6. minute, record 7. tickler
  8. protocol, reminder
memoria... 4. tomb 6. chapel, church,
  shrine 8. monument 9. reliquary
memorial... 6. memoir, memory,
  record, trophy 8. mnemonic,
  monument 10. memorandum
  11. celebrative, remembrance
  12. recollection 13. commemorative
memorial mound... 5. cairn (stone),
  totem (carved)
memory... 4. mind 6. recall
  9. retention 11. remembrance
  12. recollection, reminiscence

  13. commemoration
memory (pert to)...
  aid.. 10. anamnestic
  book.. 5. diary 9. scrapbook
  jog.. 6. remind
  loss of.. 5. lethe 7. amnesia, aphasia
    (partial) 13. forgetfulness
  term.. 6. mnesic 8. mnemonic
Memphis, Egypt (pert to)...
  deity.. 2. Ra (Re) 3. Shu, Tem
  dynasty.. 3. Memphite
  god, chief.. 4. Ptah
men (pert to)...
  armed body.. 5. posse
  gymnasts.. 8. acrobats
  learned.. 6. erudites, literati
  mechanical.. 6. robots
  of same tongue.. 6. langue
  old.. 7. gaffers 10. patriarchs
  party of.. 4. stag 6. smoker
  section, Gr Church.. 6. andron
  single.. 5. stags 9. bachelors,
    celibates
  slang.. 6. blokes
  Three Wise.. 4. Magi (Gaspar,
    Melchior, Balthazar)
  wild.. 7. savages 9. cannibals
menace... 6. threat 8. forebode,
  threaten 10. intimidate
  11. fulmination
menacing... 7. ominous 8. imminent
  11. threatening
menage... 4. club 7. society
  9. homestead, household, husbandry
  10. management 12. housekeeping
menagerie... 3. zoo 10. collection,
  Tiergarten
menald (said of horses)... 8. speckled
  10. variegated
Menaspis... 5. shark (crescent–shaped)
mend... 3. fix, sew 4. cure, darn,
  heal, knit 5. alter, amend, botch,
  emend, moise, patch 6. better,
  cobble, reform, repair 7. correct,
  improve 9. reconcile 10. ameliorate
mendacious... 5. false, lying 6. untrue
  7. in error 9. truthless 10. fallacious
mendacity... 3. lie 5. lying 6. deceit
  7. falsity, fibbery, untruth
mendicant... 5. fakir 6. beggar
  7. begging
mendicant order... 10. Carmelites,
  Dominicans 11. Franciscans
  12. Augustinians
mendole... 4. fish 8. cackerel
Menelaus' wife... 11. Helen of Troy
menhaden... 4. pogy 7. sardine
  8. bonyfish 10. mossbunker
menhir... 5. stone (standing)
  8. monolith
menial... 6. flunky, varlet 7. servant,
  servile, serving, slavish
meninges membrane... 8. pia mater
  9. arachnoid, dura mater
meniscus... 4. lens 8. crescent
  12. crescent moon
Mennonite leader... 11. Menno
  Simons
Mennonite sect... 5. Amish
meno... 4. less 5. month (comb form)
menology (Eccl)... 8. calendar, register
Menominee, Menomini... 5. Falls

(Wis), river 6. Indian 9. whitefish
Menorah... 11. candelabrum (Jew)
12. organization
mensk... 5. adorn, favor, grace, honor
6. credit 8. ornament 9. reverence
12. graciousness
mental... 7. phrenic 9. of the mind,
psychotic 11. intelligent
12. intellectual
mental (pert to)...
alienation.. 8. insanity
deficiency, deficient.. 5. ament, idiot,
moron 6. idiocy 8. imbecile
discipline.. 8. mathesis
disorder.. 7. aphasia 8. insanity,
neurosis, paranoia 9. psychosis
11. megalomania 12. hypochondria
13. forgetfulness, schizophrenia
faculties.. 4. mind, wits
feeling.. 7. emotion
image, picture.. 4. idea 6. idolus
8. phantasm 10. conception
peculiarity.. 12. idiosyncracy
science, study.. 10. New Thought,
psychiatry
state.. 6. morale 7. doldrum
(doldrums) 8. euphoria
strain.. 7. tension
mentality... 4. mind 5. sense
6. acumen, sanity 7. endowment,
intellect 11. mental power
12. intelligence
mention... 4. cite, mind, name
5. refer, speak, trace 6. denote,
notice, record, remark 7. specify,
vestige 8. citation, indicate 9. make
known, statement 10. indication
mentor... 7. adviser, teacher, wise
man 10. instructor
mentum... 4. chin
menu... 4. card, list 5. carte
8. schedule 10. bill of fare
Mephistopheles... 5. devil, Faust,
Satan
mephitis... 4. odor 5. skunk, smell
6. stench 7. polecat 10. exhilation
(earth)
mercantile... 5. trade 7. trading
10. commercial, industrial
mercenary... 4. hack 5. hired, venal
6. sordid 7. Hessian 8. hireling,
salaried, vendible
merchandise... 4. ware 5. goods,
wares 7. effects 9. vendibles
10. emporeutic (pert to)
11. commodities 12. stock in trade
merchant... 5. buyer 6. trader
7. vintner 10. shopkeeper, trafficker
11. storekeeper
merchant (pert to)...
group.. 5. guild, hanse 6. cartel
Indian.. 4. seth
League.. 9. Hanseatic
ship.. 6. argosy 8. Indiaman
wine.. 7. vintner
Merchant of Bagdad... 7. Sindbad
Merchant of Venice character...
6. Portia 7. Antonio, Shylock
merci... 7. thanks
merciful... 4. kind, mild 6. humane,
tender 7. clement, lenient
9. benignant 10. charitable

13. compassionate
merciless... 5. cruel 8. pitiless
9. unsparing 10. relentless
13. unsympathetic
mercurial (pert to God Mercury)...
4. fast 5. swift 6. active, clever,
fickle 8. metallic 9. saturnine
11. money-making
mercurous chloride... 7. calomel
mercury... 5. azoth, guide, metal
7. chibrit, element 9. barometer
11. quicksilver, temperature,
thermometer
Mercury (pert to)...
astronomy.. 6. planet (smallest)
god of.. 8. commerce
Greek name.. 6. Hermes
staff.. 8. caduceus
statue, image.. 5. herma
winged cap.. 7. petasos (petasus)
winged shoes.. 7. talaria
mercy... 4. pity, ruth 5. grace
6. blithe, lenity 7. charity
8. clemency, lenience, leniency
9. tolerance 10. compassion,
indulgence 11. forbearance
mercy killing... 10. euthanasia
mercy seat... 5. bench 11. golden
plate (on the Ark), Throne of God
12. judgment seat 13. seat of
justice
mere... 3. sea 4. bare, lake, only,
pool, sole, such, wisp 5. bound,
limit, sheer, small 6. divide, simple
8. absolute, boundary, landmark, only
this
mère... 6. mother
merely... 4. also, just, only 5. quite
6. barely, purely, simply, singly,
solely 7. utterly, entirely, scarcely
9. unmixedly 10. absolutely
mere show... 4. airs 5. front
8. pretense 9. formality
10. pretension 11. affectation
mere taste... 3. nip, sip 4. gulp
7. draught
merganser... 3. nun 4. duck, smee,
smew 5. Mergus 7. bec-scie
8. Merginae 9. goosander
merge... 4. sink 5. blend, unite
6. mingle 7. combine, immerse
8. coalesce 11. consolidate
merger... 4. pool 5. union 6. cartel,
fusion 7. monopoly 10. absorption
12. amalgamation
meridian... 3. top 4. apex, noon
5. plane 6. midday, summit, zenith
8. latitude, southern 9. celestial
11. culmination 12. highest point
meringue... 5. icing 8. egg white,
frosting
Merino... 4. wool, yarn 5. sheep
merit... 4. earn, meed 5. worth
6. desert, reward 7. deserve
10. excellence
merited... 3. fit 4. just 6. worthy
8. adequate, deserved, suitable
9. warranted
meritorious... 5. valid 6. worthy
7. merited 9. deserving, honorable
12. praiseworthy
merlin... 6. falcon

Merlin... 7. prophet, romance
   8. magician
mermaid... 5. siren 6. merrow
   7. Oceanid, swimmer 8. sea nymph
   9. sea spirit 14. marine creature
mermaid's hair... 4. alga
mero... 4. fish 5. guasa 7. grouper
   8. rock hind
merogenesis... 12. segmentation
meropia... 9. blindness (partial)
meros... 5. thigh 10. meropodite
merriment... 3. fun 4. glee 5. mirth
   6. gaiety (gayety) 8. laughter
   9. amusement, diversion
   11. merrymaking
merrow... 7. mermaid
merry... 3. gai, gay 4. glad 5. funny,
   happy 6. blithe, bonnie, jocose,
   jovial, joyous 7. comical, festive,
   gleeful, jocular 8. cheerful, mirthful,
   sportive 9. favorable, hilarious,
   sprightly 13. sweet-sounding
merry-andrew... 4. mime, zany
   5. antic, clown, joker 6. jester
   7. buffoon 8. merryman
merry-go-round... 9. carrousel
   (carousel) 17. revolving platform
merrymaking... 4. reel 5. momus,
   revel 7. festive, wassail 9. festivity,
   merriment 12. conviviality
merrythought... 8. wishbone
merrytrotter... 5. swing 6. seesaw
merrywing... 4. duck 9. goldeneye
   10. bufflehead
merse... 3. dip 5. marsh 6. plunge
   7. immerse
merycism... 7. chewing 10. rumination
mesa... 7. mesilla, oakwood (color),
   terrace 14. flat-topped hill
mesel... 5. leper
mesh... 3. net, web 5. catch 6. areola
   7. complex, ensnare, netting, network
   10. crisscross 11. interaction
mesial plane... 6. meson (Zool)
   6. median, middle
mesmeric... 11. fascinating, hypnotizing
   12. irresistible, spellbinding
mesmeric force... 2. od
Mesopotamia...
   ancient city.. 2. Ur 5. Eridu
     7. Babylon, Ninevah
   city.. 5. Basra, Mosul 6. Edessa
   colloquialism.. 6. Mespot
   culture.. 8. Sumerian
   export.. 3. oil
   language.. 6. Arabic
   people (anc).. 8. Aramaean (Aramean)
   river.. 6. Tigris 9. Euphrates
   wind.. 6. shamal
Mesopotamian... 5. Iraqi
Mesozoic era... 7. reptile 8. dinosaur
   10. evergreens, ganoid fish
mesquin... 4. mean 6. shabby, sordid
mesquita... 6. mosque
mesquite... 5. pacay 7. thicket
   8. Prosopis 9. algarroba
mesquite bean flour... 6. pinole
mess... 3. meal 5. batch, share, spoil
   6. bungle, jumble, litter 7. eyesore,
   failure, mixture 8. disorder
   9. confusion 11. predicament
   12. kettle of fish

mess (up)... 5. botch, spoil 6. muss
   up 7. clutter, derange, shuffle
   10. disarrange
message... 4. news, note, wire, word
   5. cable 6. brevet, letter, notice
   7. epistle, evangel, tidings
   8. dispatch, telegram
   10. communiqué 13. communication
message medium... 5. Ouija
messenger... 4. Iris, page, sand, toty
   5. angel, envoy 6. herald, nuncio,
   Revere (Paul) 7. apostle, carrier,
   courier, prophet, totyman
   8. delegate, minister 9. estafette
   (estafet) 10. forerunner
messenger bird... 9. secretary
Messenger of the Gods... 6. Hermes
   (Gr) 7. Mercury (Rom)
Messiah... 6. Christ 7. Saviour (Savior)
   8. Oratorio (Handel) 9. deliverer
Messina Rock... 6. Scylla
messy... 5. dirty 6. untidy 7. jumbled
   8. slovenly 10. disordered
mestive... 8. mournful
mesto... 3. sad 7. pensive
met... 3. sat 7. equaled, measure
   11. measurement (see also *meet*)
metabolism... 9. anabolism
   10. catabolism 12. assimilation
   13. dissimilation, metamorphosis
   14. transformation
metacarpus... 4. bone
metad... 3. rat
metagnomy... 10. divination
metagnostic... 10. unknowable
metal... 3. tin 4. gold, iron, lead, zinc
   5. steel 6. cobalt, copper, erbium,
   nickel, radium, silver, sodium
   7. cadmium, calcium, element,
   gallium, iridium, lithium, mercury,
   terbium 8. cast iron 9. potassium
   11. quicksilver
metal... 6. mettle, spirit 8. material
   9. substance
metal (pert to)...
   bar.. 3. gad 5. ingot
   cake.. 4. slag
   casting.. 3. pig
   cement.. 6. solder
   clippings.. 7. scissil
   coarse.. 5. matte
   coat.. 6. patina
   color.. 10. pearl blue
   content.. 3. ory
   crude.. 5. matte
   deposit.. 4. lode
   disc.. 5. paten
   dross.. 5. slag
   electric.. 6. magnet
   filings.. 5. lemel
   forging term.. 5. sprue
   goldlike.. 6. oroide
   impurity.. 7. regulus
   layer.. 4. seam, vein 5. stope
   lightest.. 7. lithium
   lump.. 3. pig 4. slug 6. nugget
   patch.. 6. solder
   plate.. 4. foil, shim
   rare.. 6. erbium 7. iridium, terbium,
     yttrium 8. platinum
   refuse.. 4. slag 5. dross 6. scoria
   rock.. 3. ore

science of.. 10. metallurgy
tag.. 5. aglet (aiglet)
test.. 5. assay
tool.. 5. swage 7. stemmer
ware.. 4. tole 6. Revere
worker.. 6. welder 7. riveter
    9. goldsmith 11. silversmith
metamerism... 12. segmentation (Zool)
metamorphosis... 6. change
    9. oxidation 10. hydrolysis
    12. degeneration, ossification
    14. transformation
metaphor... 5. trope 6. simile
    10. comparison 11. tralalition
metaphysics... 5. being 6. nature
    8. ontology, theology 9. cosmology
    10. psychology
mete... 4. give, goal 5. award
    7. measure 8. boundary 9. apportion
    10. distribute
meteor... 5. bolis 6. Bielid, bolide,
    Leonid, Lyraid 7. Arietid, Perseid
    8. fireball 9. Andromede
meteorite (pert to)...
iron.. 10. siderolite
shower.. 6. Leonid 9. Andromede
    (Andromedid)
stony.. 8. aerolite
meteor mark... 6. crater
meteorology... 9. astronomy
    10. atmosphere 11. climatology
meter, metre... 5. gauge 6. rhythm
    7. cadence, measure 8. measurer
meter (pert to)...
cubic.. 5. stere
measure.. 5. litre
millionth.. 6. micron
prosody.. 4. mora
square.. 7. centare
ton.. 5. tonne
unit term.. 3. are 6. decare
    9. decameter, decastere
weight.. 4. gram
methane... 8. paraffin
metheglin... 4. mead 8. beverage
mether... 3. cup
method... 3. way 4. mode, plan, rule
    5. means, order, usage 6. course,
    manner, system 7. fashion, process
    9. procedure 11. arrangement
    14. classification
methodic, methodical... 6. formal
    7. orderly, regular 10. systematic
Methuselah (pert to)...
Bib.. 7. aged man 9. Patriarch
father.. 5. Enoch
metic... 5. alien 7. settler
    9. immigrant
meticulous... 4. nice, prim 5. fussy
    7. careful, fearful, precise 8. exacting
    9. selective 10. fastidious, scrupulous
    14. discriminating
métier... 4. line 7. calling 8. business
    10. occupation, profession
metis, metisse... 7. mulatto
    8. octoroon 9. half-breed
Metis... 6. asteroid 9. Zeus's wife
metrical... 8. measured, poetical,
    rhythmic
metrical composition... 4. poem
    5. poesy 6. poetry

metrical foot... 4. iamb 6. iambus
    7. anapest, spondee, trochee
    8. choriamb
metrical stress... 4. scan 5. arsis,
    ictus 6. thesis
metronome (Maelzel's)... 5. timer
metropolis... 4. city, seat, town
    6. center 8. district 9. metropole
metropolitan... 5. chief, urban
    6. bishop, center 7. leading
    9. principal
mettle... 5. ardor, honor, nerve, pluck,
    spunk 6. spirit 7. courage
    9. fortitude 11. temperament
meuse, muse... 3. gap 4. hole
    7. opening 8. loophole
Meuse River... 4. Maas
mew... 3. cob, den 4. cage, cast,
    coop, gull, molt, shed 5. miaow,
    miaul 6. change 7. seagull, stables
    8. spicknel 11. concealment,
    confinement
mewl... 3. cry, mew 6. squall
    7. whimper
Mexican (pert to)... see also *Mexico*
agave.. 5. datil 6. zapupe
    8. henequen
almond.. 7. Malabar
American.. 6. gringo
ancient.. 4. Maya 5. Aztec, Nahua
    6. Mixtec, Toltec 7. Zapotec
antelope.. 9. pronghorn
asphalt.. 9. chapapote
bean.. 6. frijol 7. frijole
bedbug.. 8. conenose
beverage (alcoholic).. 6. mescal,
    pulque 7. tepache
bird.. 6. jacana, towhee 7. jacamar,
    tinamou 8. zopilote
blanket.. 6. serape
brigand.. 7. ladrone
bull.. 4. toro
cactus.. 6. chaute, mescal
cape.. 6. serape
cat.. 6. margay
cherry tree.. 7. capulin
chief.. 4. jefe 12. jefe politico
cloak.. 5. manta
cockroach.. 9. cucaracha
common land (law).. 6. ejidos
coral drops (lily).. 7. Bessera
cottonwood.. 5. alamo
dance (solo).. 8. guaracha
dish.. 5. atole, chili (chile), tacos
    6. tamale 8. frijoles, tortilla
    9. enchilada 13. chili con carne
dog.. 9. Chihuahua
dollar.. 4. peso 5. adobe
dove.. 4. Inca
drug.. 7. damiana
elm.. 6. mezcal 8. Ulmaceae
estate, farm.. 8. hacienda
fever.. 10. tabardillo
fish (food).. 6. salema 7. totuava
game (card).. 4. frog
grass.. 3. mat 5. otate 6. petate
    8. henequen
herdsman.. 8. ranchero
hog.. 7. peccary
hut, house.. 5. jacal
insect.. 8. turicata
labor system.. 7. peonage

landmark.. 5. senal
masonry.. 5. adobe
moon god (Aztec).. 6. Meztli
mullet.. 4. bobo
musical instrument.. 6. clarin (anc)
   7. maracas
Noah.. 6. Coxcox
onyx.. 6. tecali
orange.. 7. Choisya
peasant.. 4. peon
persimmon.. 7. chapote
phlox.. 6. cobaea
plant, shrub.. 4. pita 5. agave,
   amole, datil, istle, sisal, sotol, yucca
   6. maguey 8. ocotillo
   10. candlewood, Dasylirion
rose.. 9. portulaca
saloon.. 7. cantina
sandal.. 8. huaracho (huarache)
sauce.. 7. Tabasco
scarf.. 6. tapalo
shawl.. 6. serape
stirrup.. 7. estribo
stirrup hood.. 8. tapadera (tapadero)
sugar.. 7. panocha
tea.. 6. basote 7. apasote
thong.. 5. romal
throwing stick.. 6. atlatl
tree.. 3. ule 5. alamo, ocote
   6. colima, poplar 7. capulin
   10. cottonwood
war god.. 7. Mexitli
yucca.. 5. izote (isote)
Mexican people...
composer.. 6. Chavez
conqueror.. 6. Cortez
Dictator.. 4. Diaz
historian.. 6. Orozco
painter.. 6. Rivera
Mexico...
battleground.. 6. Puebla
capital.. 10. Mexico City
city.. 6. Merida, Puebla 7. Durango,
   Tampico 8. Mazatlan, Monterey, Vera
   Cruz 11. Guadalajara
conqueror.. 6. Cortes (Cortez)
hero.. 6. Juarez 11. Poncho Villa
lake.. 7. Chapala
mountain.. 12. Popocatepetl
peninsula.. 4. Baja 7. Yucatan
people.. 5. Mayas 6. Aztecs
   7. Toltecs 10. Cuitlateco
river.. 9. Rio Grande
volcano.. 6. Colima 7. Jorullo, Orizaba
   12. Ixtaccihuatl, Popocatepetl
mezzanine... 8. entresol, low story
miaow, miaou... 3. mew
mias... 9. orangutan
miasma... 4. fume 6. poison
   7. malaria, malodor 9. contagion
mib... 7. a marble
mica... 4. talc 5. glist 7. biotite
   8. chlorite, silicate 9. damourite,
   hydromica, isinglass, muscovite
   10. lepidolite
Micah... 4. Book (Old Test) 7. prophet
mice... 3. Mus 5. voles 7. rodents
miche... 5. skulk, sneak 6. lie hid
   7. conceal
micher... 5. sneak, thief 6. truant
Michigan...
capital.. 7. Lansing

city.. 5. Flint 7. Detroit, Lansing
   8. Ann Arbor 9. Marquette
explorer.. 7. Jolliet, Nicolet
   9. Marquette 13. Sault Ste Marie
river.. 4. Cass 5. Huron
State admission.. 11. Twenty–sixth
State motto.. 6. Tuebor 11. I Will
   Defend
State nickname.. 9. Wolverine
mickey finn... 5. drink 8. narcotic
Micky... 8. Irishman
mico... 6. monkey 8. marmoset
micraner... 3. ant (small)
micro (comb form)... 4. moth 5. petty,
   small
microbe... 4. germ 5. virus
   8. organism 9. bacterium
   13. microorganism
microcosm... 4. body (humerous)
   5. world (small) 8. universe
microscopic (pert to)...
algae.. 6. amoeba, diatom
anatomy.. 7. histology
size.. 5. small 6. minute 9. very
   small 13. infinitesimal
microspores... 6. pollen
Midas (Gr)... 13. King of Phrygia
midday... 4. noon 7. noonday
   8. meridian, noontide
midday nap... 6. siesta
middle... 5. mesne, midst 6. center,
   centry, median, medium, mesial
   7. central 8. interior 11. intervening
   13. intermediator
middle (pert to)...
Age.. 8. Medieval
class.. 9. bourgeois 11. proletarian
comb form.. 3. mes 4. medi, meso
finger.. 6. medius 10. third digit
ground.. 4. mean 7. average
   9. mid–course
man.. 5. agent 6. broker, medium
   8. mediator 9. go–between
   11. intercessor 12. intermediary
middling... 4. fair 6. medium, middle
   7. average, between, midland
   8. mediocre, moderate, ordinary
   10. middle–aged
midge... 3. fly 4. gnat 6. midget,
   punkie 7. minutia
Midi... 8. The South (France)
Midian king... 3. Evi 4. Reba
Midian priest... 6. Jethro
midriff... 9. diaphragm
midshipman... 5. cadet 6. reefer
   8. toadfish
Midsummer Night's Dream (play)...
   4. Puck, Snug 6. Bottom, Oberon
   7. Titania
midwife... 4. baba, dhai 6. cummer
   (kimmer) 11. accoucheuse
mien... 3. air, eye 4. look 5. guise
   6. aspect, manner, ostent
   7. bearing, posture 8. behavior,
   carriage, demeanor 10. appearance,
   deportment
miff... 3. vix 4. tiff 5. anger 6. offend
   7. dudgeon, quarrel 9. displease,
   sulkiness 10. sullenness
mig... 4. duck 7. a marble
might... 3. arm 5. force, power
   7. ability 8. efficacy, strength

9. greatness

mighty... 4. huge, vast, very
6. potent, strong 7. eminent, violent
8. enormous, forcible, powerful,
puissant 9. extremely 10. omnipotent
11. efficacious 13. authoritative

migniard... 6. dainty, minion
7. mincing 8. delicate, mistress

mignon... 5. small 6. dainty, petite
7. blue–red 8. delicate, graceful

mignonette (pert to)...
color.. 5. green 6. reseda
emblem of.. 6. Saxony
herb.. 6. reseda
tree.. 5. henna
vine.. 7. Madeira, tarweed

migraine... 6. megrim 8. headache
10. hemicrania

migrate... 4. move, trek 8. transfer
12. transmigrate

migration... 4. trek 5. exode
6. exodus 7. passage 8. shifting
(Chem)

migratory... 6. moving, roving
7. nomadic 9. peregrine, wandering

migratory (pert to)...
ant.. 6. driver
cell.. 9. leucocyte
thrush.. 5. robin

mihrab... 4. slab 5. niche 7. chamber
(mosque)

Mikado... 5. dairi, opera, title
9. red–yellow, sovereign

Mikado character... 4. Ko–Ko
6. Yum–Yum 7. Pooh–Bah

Mikania... 7. dogbane, thistle
11. Willugbaeya (Willugheia)
12. Ancylocladus

mike... 4. loaf 6. loiter
10. microphone

mil... 5. mille 8. thousand

milady... 5. woman 10. noblewoman
11. gentlewoman

Milan (pert to)...
hat.. 5. straw
opera house.. 5. Scala
point.. 10. bobbin lace 12. point de
Milan

mild... 4. calm, kind, meek, soft, warm
5. bland 6. benign, gentle
7. clement, insipid, lenient
8. benedict, gracious, lenitive,
moderate, soothing, tranquil
9. assuasive, indulgent, temperate
10. mollifying 11. considerate

mildew... 4. mold, must, rust, smut
6. blight, fungus 8. honeydew

mild expression... 9. euphemism

mild offense... 6. delict

mile... 3. sea 7. statute 8. nautical
9. Admiralty 12. geographical

Miledh... 8. ancestor (fabled)

Milesian... 4. Celt 8. Irishman
10. Miledh's son

milestone... 5. stele 8. landmark,
milepost

milfoil... 4. herb 6. yarrow

milieu... 8. ambience 11. environment
12. surroundings

militant... 7. warlike 8. battling,
fighting 9. combating, combative

11. contentious

military... 7. martial 8. soldiers

military (pert to)...
advance.. 8. anabasis
aide.. 7. attaché
automobile.. 4. jeep
base.. 4. camp 5. depot, field
7. billets 8. barracks, quarters
10. encampment
call.. 6. tattoo 8. reveille
cap.. 4. kepi 5. busby, shako
cap, hat cover.. 8. havelock
cloak.. 5. sagum (anc)
commission.. 6. brevet
defense.. 4. fort 6. abatis
depot.. 4. base
division.. 4. unit 5. corps, squad
7. company, platoon 8. regiment
engine.. 6. onager 7. robinet
expedition to Holy Land.. 7. Crusade
force.. 4. army 5. troop 6. legion
7. reserve
guard.. 6. patrol
horsemen.. 7. cavalry, hussars
inspection.. 5. drill 6. parade, review
instrument.. 7. althorn
landing point.. 9. beachhead
maneuver.. 6. tactic
messenger.. 7. estafet
night attack.. 8. camisade
obstruction.. 6. abatis
officer.. 5. major 7. captain, colonel,
general 8. corporal, sergeant
9. brigadier, subaltern 10. lieutenant
operations.. 8. campaign, strategy
order.. 7. command
organization.. 5. cadre
pit.. 10. trou–de–loup
police.. 2. MP 9. gendarmes
12. constabulary
punishment.. 9. strappado
quarters.. 4. camp 7. billets
8. barracks
salute (artillery).. 5. salvo
science.. 3. war 8. warcraft
9. logistics
service stripes.. 9. hashmarks
signal.. 7. chamade (anc)
staff.. 5. cadre
storehouse.. 5. étape 7. arsenal
supplies.. 8. materiel, ordnance
survey.. 11. reconnoiter
testament, will.. 11. nuncupative
tool (hook–shaped).. 4. croc (anc)
truck (cannon).. 6. camion
vehicle.. 4. jeep, tank 6. camion
7. caisson

militate... 5. fight 6. debate
7. contend 8. conflict

milk... 3. lac 5. drain, fluid 6. elicit,
suckle 7. despoil, draw out, exploit,
extract 9. beverage

milk (pert to)...
beverage.. 4. whig 10. buttermilk
coagulator.. 4. ruen 6. rennet
curd.. 5. zeiga 6. casein
curdled.. 6. yogurt 7. clabber
fermented.. 5. kefir 6. kumiss
(koumiss) 8. matzoon
fish.. 3. awa 6. Chanos, sabalo
food (fasting).. 10. lacticinia
glass.. 7. opaline 8. cryolite

mouse.. 6. spurge
pail.. 5. bowie, eshin
pert to.. 6. lactic 7. lactary, lacteal
product.. 6. cheese, yogurt
sap.. 5. latex
sop.. 5. sissy 11. mollycoddle
sour.. 4. curd, whey, whig 6. blinky
store.. 5. dairy 9. lactarium
strainer.. 6. milsey (milsie)
sugar.. 7. lactose
watery part.. 4. whey
with (milk).. 6. au lait
milkweed.. 6. spurge 7. dogbane
    10. sow thistle 14. Asclepiadaceae
milkwood.. 8. Moraceae 9. paperbark
milky.. 4. mild, tame, weak 5. timid,
    white 6. gentle, liquid 7. lacteal
    8. emulsion,/ emulsive, lactesce (to
    become), timorous 10. effeminate
Milky Way.. 6. Galaxy 9. Via Lactea
    14. galactic circle
Milky Way black spaces...
    9. Coalsacks
mill... 3. box 4. beat, coin (to)
    5. crush, dress, fight, grind, knurl,
    quern, shape 6. finish, powder,
    thrash 7. factory, machine, serrate
    8. arrastra, snuffbox, vanquish,
    workshop 9. comminute, pulverize,
    transform 10. move around
    12. housebreaker
mill (pert to)...
beetle.. 9. cockroach
bill.. 3. adz
clapper.. 10. chatterbox
course.. 4. lade 8. millrace, tailrace
end.. 7. remnant
run of.. 7. average 8. millrace,
    ordinary
millefleurs... 7. perfume
millenarian... 8. chiliast
millennium... 6. period, utopia
    9. millenary 13. thousand years
millepede... 6. insect 8. myriapod
millepore... 5. coral 9. madrepore
miller... 3. ray 4. moth 5. boxer
    7. harrier 8. pugilist 10. flycatcher
miller's thumb... 4. bird, fish
    7. warbler 8. titmouse (long–tailed)
    9. goldcrest
millesimal... 10. thousandth
millet... 4. moha 5. bajra, grass,
    hirse, milly 8. cenchrus
    9. broomcorn 10. hirse grass
    14. non–Moslem group
millimeter... 6. micron 14. thousandth
    part
millions, one thousand... 7. billion
millions of millions... 9. trillions
Mills grenade... 4. bomb
milo.. 5. durra 12. grain sorghum
Milvus... 4. kite
Milwaukee... 21. German Athens of
    America
mime... 3. ape 4. aper, copy 5. actor,
    clown, mimic 6. jester, mummer
    7. buffoon, imitate
mimesis... 7. mimicry 9. imitation
mimic... 3. ape 4. aper, copy, mime,
    mimo, mock 5. actor 6. mummer,
    parrot 7. buffoon, copying, imitate,
    mimetic 8. imitator 9. imitative

    11. counterfeit
mimicry... 5. apery, apism 7. mimesis,
    mockery 8. parrotry
mimic thrush... 11. mockingbird
Mimidae, Miminae... 7. catbird
    8. thrasher 11. mockingbird
Mimir... 5. giant
mimsey... 4. prim 7. prudish
min... 5. ruler 6. memory, prince,
    remind 8. remember
    11. remembrance
Min (Egypt)... 3. god (procreation)
    5. deity
Minar... 4. myna 5. Kutab (Delhi),
    tower
minaret... 4. lamp 5. tower
    10. lighthouse
minaway... 6. minuet
mince... 3. cut 4.- chop, dice, hash
    5. slash 8. diminish, prim step
    9. subdivide 10. short steps
minced meat... 7. rissole
minced oath... 4. drat, egad
minchen... 3. nun
minchery... 7. nunnery
minchiate... 5. tarot
mind... 4. care, heed, mens, obey,
    reck, tend, will 6. desire, memory,
    psyche 7. opinion 9. intellect,
    intention 11. remembrance
    12. intelligence
mind (pert to)...
development.. 13. psychogenesis
jubilant.. 7. elation
peace of.. 8. ataraxia, calmness
    16. imperturbability
pert to.. 6. mental 7. phrenic
picture.. 4. idea 5. image
split.. 13. schizophrenic
Mindanao...
language.. 3. Ata
site.. 11. Philippines
town.. 4. Dapa 5. Davao
    9. Zamboanga
tribe.. 3. Ata 4. Moro 5. Lutao
    6. Bagobo, Illano
volcano.. 3. Apo 9. Malindany
mindful... 8. disposed 9. observant,
    regardful 11. remembering
mine... 2. my 3. bal, dig, mio, pit,
    sap 4. meum 5. stope 6. cavity,
    quarry 7. gallery, passage
    10. excavation 12. entrenchment
mine (pert to)...
basket, tub.. 4. corf
ceiling.. 5. astel
coal.. 3. rob
deviation (lode).. 4. hade
device (sweeper).. 4. gad 8. paravane
entrance, passage.. 4. adit 5. stulm
excavation.. 5. stope
floor.. 4. sill
guardian (Myth).. 5. gnome
holes.. 7. gophers
prop.. 5. sprag, stull
reservoir.. 4. sump 8. standage
shack.. 3. doe
shaft.. 4. sump 6. upcast
signalman.. 5. cager 7. cageman
step.. 7. stemple (stempel)
surface.. 6. placer
thrower.. 6. minnie 11. minenwerfer

tunnel.. 5. stulm
vein.. 4. lode
waste.. 3. gob 4. goaf
worker.. 5. cager, miner 8. onsetter
miner (pert to)...
disease.. 8. phthisis
instrument.. 4. dial
lamp.. 4. davy
pick.. 3. gad 7. mandrel
sieve.. 6. dillue
worm.. 8. hookworm
mineral... 3. ore, tin 4. alum, iron
5. pitch 6. barite, egeran, gangue,
iolite, pinite, quartz 7. apatite,
asphalt, ataxite, bullion, epidote,
felsite, felspar 8. danalite, edentite,
misenite 9. uraninite
mineral (ore)...
black.. 3. jet 6. cerine, yenite (Elba)
7. niobite 8. graphite 10. minguetite
blue–green.. 5. beryl
brittle.. 7. euclase
brown.. 6. cerine, egeran, rutile
9. elaterite
calcium, plus.. 7. calcite 8. calespar,
diopside
crosslike.. 10. staurolite
dark.. 7. minette
fibrous.. 8. asbestos (abeston)
flaky.. 4. mica
gray white.. 5. trona
green.. 7. alalite, erinite 9. malachite
gunpowder.. 5. niter 7. thorite
hard.. 4. ruby 6. spinel (spinelle)
7. adamant
jelly.. 8. vaseline
jewelry.. 8. diopside
lustrous.. 4. spar 7. blendes
magnetic.. 9. lodestone (loadstone)
nonmetallic.. 5. boron 6. iodine
plaster of Paris.. 6. gypsum
rare, brittle.. 7. euclase, thorite
red.. 4. ruby 6. garnet
soft.. 4. talc
waxlike.. 9. ozocerite 11. hatchettine
white, colorless.. 6. barite, gypsum
yellow.. 5. topaz 6. pyrite 7. epidote
mineral (pert to)...
cavity.. 3. vug (vugg, vugh, voog)
dark spot.. 7. macle
deposit.. 4. lode 6. placer
greasy.. 7. atopite
oil.. 5. colza
pitch.. 7. asphalt
pocket.. 4. nest
salt.. 4. alum
spring.. 3. spa 4. well
tallow, wax.. 9. ozocerite
11. hatchettine
tar.. 6. maltha
water.. 6. lithia 7. Seltzer 8. alkaline
Minerva (pert to)...
feast.. 11. Quinquatrus
flower, plant.. 6. azalea
goddess of.. 5. civic 6. health
11. handicrafts
shield.. 5. aegis (egis)
temple site.. 8. Aventine (Rome)
ming... 6. remind 7. mention, recount
8. remember
Ming (Chin)... 7. dynasty
mingle... 3. mix 4. fuse, meld

5. admix, blend, merge, unite
7. combine, concoct 8. coalesce,
intermix 9. associate 10. amalgamate
11. consolidate
mingle–mangle... 6. jumble, medley
7. mixture 8. potpourri
10. hodgepodge, miscellany
minhag (Jew)... 6. custom, manner
7. liturgy
miniate... 5. paint 8. decorate,
luminate 9. rubricate
minikin... 4. type 5. baize 6. dainty
7. elegant, mincing 8. affected,
delicate 10. diminutive
minim... 3. jot 4. drop 5. Order
(RCCh) 6. minute 8. smallest
11. small amount
minimize... 6. reduce 7. detract
8. belittle 9. disparage
10. depreciate 13. underestimate
minimum... 3. jot 5. least 6. lowest
minion, minionette... 4. idol, neat
5. lover 6. dainty, pretty 7. darling,
elegant 8. delicate, favorite, ladylove,
mistress, paramour
minister... 4. tend 5. angel, cater,
serve 6. afford, attend, curate,
parson, pastor, priest, supply
7. furnish 8. diplomat, executor,
preacher 9. clergyman, officiate
ministerial... 7. serving 9. executive
12. instrumental 14. administrative,
ecclesiastical
minister's home... 5. manse
9. parsonage
Minnesota...
capital.. 6. St Paul
city.. 6. Duluth 11. Minneapolis
hero.. 14. Father Hennepin
lake.. 3. Red 10. Minnewaska
land of.. 16. Ten Thousand Lakes
mountain.. 6. Cayuna, Mesabe
9. Vermilion
river.. 3. Red 10. St Lawrence
11. Mississippi
State admission.. 12. Thirty–second
State motto.. 13. L'Etoile du Nord
14. Star of the North
State nickname.. 6. Gopher 9. North
Star
Minoan... 6. Cretan 7. culture (Prehist)
8. language
minor... 3. key 4. less, mode 5. friar
(Franciscan), petit, petty, scale, youth
6. course, infant, league, lesser
7. smaller 8. inferior, interval,
underage 9. youngling
minority... 3. few 6. nonage
7. smaller 8. underage
10. immaturity 11. inferiority
Minos (pert to)...
daughter.. 7. Ariadne
father.. 4. Zeus
king of.. 5. Crete
mother.. 6. Europa
Minotaur (Gr)... 7. monster (half man,
half bull)
minster... 6. church 9. monastery
minstrel... 3. lay 4. bard, poet, show
6. end man, troupe 7. gleeman,
goliard 8. jongleur, musician
9. troubador 11. entertainer

minstrel show (pert to)...
end man.. 5. bones
middleman.. 12. interlocutor
part.. 4. olio
mint... 3. aim 4. blow, coin, sage
5. basil, feint, money 6. hyssop,
intend, invent, mentha, ramona
7. attempt, purpose, venture
8. endeavor 9. fabricate
mint (pert to)...
charge, levy.. 8. brassage
11. seigniorage
drink.. 5. julep
family.. 5. basil 6. catnip 8. calamint
9. Lamiaceae
genus.. 6. Ramona 7. Melissa
geranium.. 8. costmary
hog.. 8. shilling
sauce.. 5. money
minuet... 5. dance 7. scherzo
minus... 4. lack, less 6. absent, bereft,
defect 7. short of, without
8. subtract 10. deficiency
minuscule... 4. type 5. petty, small
6. letter (lower case) 10. diminutive
minute... 3. jot, wee 4. mite, note,
tiny 5. draft, petty, small 6. atomic,
little, moment, period, record, slight,
tittle 7. instant 8. atomical, trifling
10. memorandum 11. unimportant
12. sixty seconds 14. circumstantial
minute (pert to)...
animal.. 10. animalcule
details.. 11. particulars
difference.. 5. shade
glass.. 9. hourglass
Jack.. 10. timeserver
opening.. 4. pore 5. stoma
organism.. 5. monad, spore
8. zoospore
part.. 6. tittle
particle.. 4. atom, iota, mote
record.. 8. protocol
minutely... 9. continual, unceasing
11. every minute
minutes... 4. acta 6. record
minutia... 6. detail, minute 11. minor
detail, petty matter
minx... 4. brat, doll, miss 6. pet dog
7. colleen 8. pert girl 9. saucy girl,
saucy jade 13. mischief–maker
minyan... 6. quorum 7. pottery
Miohippus... 5. horse
miqra... 9. Bible text (Heb)
mir (Pers)... 4. head 5. chief, title
9. president
miracle... 4. feat, play 5. anomy
6. marvel, wonder 10. occurrence,
phenomenon 17. supernatural event
miracle scene... 4. Cana
miracle wheat... 7. poulard
miracle worker... 8. magician
11. thermaturge
miraculous... 9. marvelous, wonderful
12. supernatural 13. wonder–working
mirador... 5. brown, oriel 6. loggia,
turret 7. balcony 9. bay window
10. watchtower
mirage... 5. serab 7. chimera, reflect
8. illusion 10. phenomenon
mire... 3. bog, mud, wet 4. glar, moil,
ooze, slud 5. addle, dirty, marsh,

slush, stall 7. sludder
mirror... 5. glass 7. crystal, paragon,
pattern, reflect 8. exemplar,
speculum 9. reflector 11. image
worker 12. looking glass
mirror iron... 12. spiegeleisen
mirth... 3. fun, joy 4. glee 6. gaiety
(gayety), levity, spleen 7. delight,
jollity 8. gladness, hilarity
9. happiness, merriment, rejoicing
10. joyousness 12. cheerfulness
mirthful... 3. gay 5. happy, jolly
miry... 4. oozy 5. boggy, muddy, slimy
6. filthy, lutose
mis (comb form)... 5. amiss, wrong
misadventure... 6. mishap 8. accident,
calamity, casualty, disaster
9. mischance 10. misfortune
misandry (opp of misogyny)...
12. dislike of man (by woman)
misanthrope... 5. cynic, Timon (Shak)
8. man hater 9. pessimist
12. mankind hater
misapply... 5. misdo 6. misuse
12. misinterpret
misapprehend... 7. mistake
8. misapply 11. misconceive
13. misunderstand
misbegotten... 8. deformed
12. illegitimate
miscalculate... 3. err 8. misjudge
9. misreckon, overshoot
miscall... 5. abuse 6. revile
7. misname 9. read amiss
12. mispronounce
miscarriage... 5. lapse 6. mishap
7. failure, misdeed, mistake
8. abortion 9. mischance
11. misdemeanor
13. mismanagement 14. premature
birth
miscegenation... 8. marriage
13. interbreeding, intermarriage
miscellaneous... 5. mixed 6. medley,
varied 7. blended, diverse, mingled
8. combined 12. conglomerate
13. heterogeneous 14. indiscriminate
miscellany... 6. medley 7. mixture
8. excerpts 9. anthology
10. collection 11. odds and ends
mischance... 6. mishap 8. calamity,
disaster 10. misfortune
12. misadventure
mischief... 3. ill 4. evil, harm
5. wrack 6. damage 7. trouble
mischief (pert to)...
god.. 4. Loki
goddess.. 3. Ate 4. Eris
maker.. 8. agitator 12. troublemaker
mischievous... 4. arch 6. elfish
(elvish), impish 7. harmful, mocking,
naughty, parlous, roguish, waggish
8. sportive
misconduct... 7. offense
10. wrongdoing 11. delinquency,
misbehavior, misdemeanor
13. mismanagement
miscreant... 6. rascal, wretch
7. heretic, villain 8. polisson
9. reprobate 10. unbeliever, villainous
11. fallen angel, misbeliever
12. unscrupulous

miscue... 3. err 4. miss, slip 5. error
6. bungle 7. mistake
misdeed... 5. crime, wrong 7. offense
8. wrongful 11. misdemeanor
misdemeanor... 3. sin 4. tort 5. crime
7. misdeed, offense 10. illegality,
wrongdoing 11. misbehavior
mise... 4. levy 5. grant 6. layout,
treaty 8. expenses (law), immunity
9. privilege
miser... 5. hunks, Nabal (Bib)
6. nipper, wretch 7. boarder, niggard
miserable... 3. sad 6. abject, paltry
7. forlorn, pitiful, unhappy
12. disconsolate, disreputable
13. commiserative
misericord, misericorde... 4. hall, pity
5. mercy 6. dagger 9. refectory
10. compassion 12. dispensation
miserly... 4. mean 5. close, tight
6. stingy 7. churlish, covetous
9. niggardly, penurious 10. avaricious
12. parsimonious
misery... 3. woe 5. grief 7. anguish,
avarice, poverty, sadness 8. calamity,
distress 9. heartache, privation
10. affliction, misfortune
11. despondency, Pandora's box,
unhappiness 12. covetousness,
wretchedness 13. niggardliness
misfeasance... 5. wrong 8. trespass
10. wrongdoing
misfortune... 3. ill 4. evil, harm
6. mishap 7. bad luck, reverse
8. calamity, disaster 9. adversity,
holocaust, mischance 11. catastrophe
12. misadventure
misgiving... 5. doubt, qualm 7. anxiety
10. foreboding 12. apprehension
mishap... 4. slip 8. accident, casualty
10. misfortune 11. contretemps,
miscarriage 12. misadventure
Mishnah, Mishna... 4. Moed 5. tenet
6. Nashim 7. Nezikim 8. doctrine,
Halakoth, Kodashim, Tohoroth
9. tradition
misinterpret... 3. err 4. warp
7. distort 8. misjudge
misjudge... 3. err 11. misconstrue
12. miscalculate
misky... 5. foggy, misty
mislay... 4. lose 8. displace, misplace
misle... 4. mist, rain 6. mizzle
7. drizzle
mislead... 4. fool 5. blear 6. delude,
seduce 7. deceive 8. misguide
9. deception, misbehave, misinform,
mismanage
misleading... 5. false 7. crooked
8. illusory 9. deceptive
10. fallacious, fraudulent
12. misinforming 14. misinformation
mislippen... 6. delude 7. neglect,
suspect 10. disappoint
mismanage... 5. blunk, misdo
6. bungle, misuse 8. mishandle
misogynist... 8. celibate 10. woman
hater
misplace... 4. lose 6. mislay, misset
8. displace 9. mislocate
11. anachronism
misplay... 3. err 5. error 6. renege

7. mismove 9. wrong play
misprise, misprize... 5. scorn 6. slight
7. despise, disdain, mistake
8. contempt 9. underrate
10. misprision, undervalue
13. underestimate
misprision... 5. scorn 7. mistake
8. contempt, misprize
10. misconduct 11. misdemeanor
12. depreciation
16. misunderstanding
mispronunciation... 8. cacology
10. bad diction
misrepresent... 5. belie 7. deceive,
distort, falsify 8. disserve
miss... 3. err 4. chit, fail, girl, lack,
lose, omit, skip 5. evade, lapse, title
7. failure, mistake 8. mistress 9. fall
short 10. prostitute
12. mademoiselle
missal... 4. book (Eccl)
missel... 9. mistletoe
misshapen... 4. ugly 8. deformed
9. distorted, monstrous, unshapely
missile... 4. Nike, Thor 5. Atlas,
Snark, Titan 7. grenade, matador
8. Redstone 9. Minuteman
missing... 3. out 4. lost 6. absent
7. lacking, wanting 8. vanished
11. nonexistent
mission... 3. job 4. body, duty, task
5. Alamo 6. charge, church, errand
7. calling, embassy 8. legation
10. assignment, commission,
delegation, deputation, missionary
missionary... 7. apostle 8. emissary
10. evangelist
Missionary Ridge... 11. Chattanooga
(Tenn)
Mississippi...
Bubble (Polit).. 10. Law's Scheme
capital.. 7. Jackson
city.. 6. Biloxi 7. Natchez 8. Gulfport
9. Vicksburg 13. Pass Christian
explorer, colonizer.. 6. DeSoto
9. Iberville
festival.. 9. Mardi gras (Biloxi)
king crop.. 6. cotton
kite (bird).. 9. everglade
mountain.. 6. Woodal
river.. 5. Yazoo 11. Mississippi
State admission.. 9. Twentieth
State motto.. 14. Virtute et Armis (By
Valor and Arms)
State nickname.. 5. Bayou
8. Magnolia
Mississippian (Geol)...
15. Eocarboniferous (system)
Mississippi River head... 10. Lake
Itasca (Minn)
Mississippi River nickname...
10. Great River 14. Father of Waters
missive... 4. note 6. billet, letter
7. message, missile 8. document
Missouri...
capital.. 13. Jefferson City
city.. 7. Sedalia, St Louis
8. Hannibal, St Joseph
12. Independence
Compromise.. 17. Kansas–Nebraska
Act
famed native.. 6. Carver (G W),

Truman (Pres) 9. Mark Twain
10. Jesse James
gourd.. 11. calabazilla
mountain.. 8. Ozarks
river.. 8. Big Muddy, Missouri
11. Mississippi
skylark.. 13. Sprague's pipit
State admission.. 12. Twenty–fourth
State nickname.. 6. Show Me
sucker (fish).. 10. black horse
misspelling... 10. cacography
misspend... 4. lose 5. waste
8. squander 10. spend amiss
miss poignantly... 6. regret
misstep... 4. slip, trip 7. faux pas
mist... 3. dim, fog 4. blur, film, gray,
haze, rain, smur 5. bedim, brume,
cloud 7. droplet 9. obscurity
11. uncertainty
mistake... 3. err 4. bull, slip 5. boner,
error, fault, folly 7. blunder, erratum,
violate 8. miscount, solecism
11. anachronism 12. inadvertence
13. misconception
15. misapprehension
16. misunderstanding
mistaken... 5. wrong 9. erroneous
12. misconceived 13. misunderstood
14. judging wrongly
mistletoe... 6. emblem (Okla), missel,
Viscum 8. Loranthus
12. Loranthaceae
mistonusk... 6. badger
mistress... 4. bibi (beebee) 5. title,
woman 6. matron 7. control, teacher
8. Dulcinia, ladylove 9. concubine,
governess, patroness 10. proprietor,
sweetheart
Mistress of...
Adriatic.. 6. Venice
Charles II.. 4. Nell
Seas.. 12. Great Britain
World.. 4. Rome (anc)
misty... 3. dim 4. hazy, roky 5. foggy,
rouky, vague 6. blurry, cloudy, hoarse
7. obscure, shadowy 10. indistinct
13. unenlightened, unillumined
14. unintelligible
misuse... 5. abuse 6. revile 7. pervert
8. maltreat, misapply, wrong use
9. misemploy 12. misrepresent
misuse of words in speech...
11. heterophemy
mite... 3. bit, jot 4. atom, coin, mote
5. child, speck 6. acarus, insect
7. bdellid, chigger, smidgen (smidge)
8. acaridan, particle
miter, mitre... 4. belt 5. frank, joint,
tiara 6. fillet, girdle, gusset, tavern
7. petalon (Eccl) 8. dovetail,
headband, insignia 9. headdress
mithridate... 8. antidote 9. electuary
12. alexipharmic
mitigate... 4. ease, tone 5. abate,
allay, mease, relax, remit, slake
6. lessen, reduce, soften, temper
7. appease, mollify, qualify, relieve
8. diminish, lenitive, moderate,
palliate 9. alleviate, extenuate,
meliorate
mitigation... 6. relief 9. abatement
10. diminution, moderation

11. extenuation 13. mollification
mix... 3. pug (clay) 4. ease, join,
meng, stir 5. addle, blend, cross,
knead, unite 6. jumble, mingle,
muddle 7. combine, fluster
8. coalesce 9. associate
10. complicate
mixable... 8. miscible
mixed (pert to)...
blood.. 5. metis 7. mestizo
breed.. 7. mongrel 8. quadroon
type.. 2. pi
with water.. 6. slaked
with yeast.. 6. barmed, frothy
mixture... 4. hash, mash, olio
5. blend, chaos, mixed 6. batter,
medley, miscue 7. amalgam, mélange
8. compound, solution 9. admixture,
potpourri 11. combination,
preparation
mixture (pert to)...
beverage.. 5. clary 10. shandygaff
cement.. 5. putty
medicinal.. 5. hepar 6. potion
12. prescription
metallic.. 6. speiss
sand and clay.. 4. loam
mix–up... 5. melee 6. muddle, tangle
8. conflict 9. confusion
Mizar... 4. Zeta (Great Dipper)
mizmaze... 9. confusion
12. bewilderment
mizzenmast... 9. aftermast, third mast
mizzle... 4. mist, rain 5. misle
6. decamp 9. slink away
mizzy... 3. bog 8. quagmire
Mnenosyne (pert to)...
ancestor.. 5. Titan
goddess.. 6. memory
mother of.. 8. The Muses
moa... 6. ratite (flightless) 8. Dinornis
moab... 3. hat (anc)
Moabite (pert to)...
dwelling (Bib).. 7. Dead Sea
language.. 7. Semitic
mountain.. 4. Nebo
people.. 4. Emim
stone (Bib).. 11. black basalt
moan... 3. cry 4. suum, wail 5. groan,
sough 6. bemoan, bewail, grieve,
lament, suffer 9. complaint
11. lamentation
moat... 4. foss (fosse) 5. ditch
6. trench 13. fortification
mob... 3. set 4. gang, herd, mass
5. crowd, drove, flock, group, taunt
6. clique, rabble, throng 7. company
8. canaille, populace, ridicule
10. faex populi, miscellany
mobile... 7. movable 8. not fixed
9. versatile 10. automobile,
changeable
Mobile Bay hero... 8. Farragut (Adm)
mob member... 6. rioter 8. criminal,
mobocrat 9. roisterer
mobocracy... 7. mob rule
Moby Dick (pert to)...
author.. 8. Melville (Herman)
character.. 4. Ahab 5. Peleg
theme.. 7. whaling 10. White Whale
moccasin... 3. pac 4. shoe 5. snake
6. Flower (Minn State), orchid

8. larrigan 10. argus brown
11. cottonmouth
moch... 4. moth
mocha... 4. bark, town (Arab)
6. coffee, dollar 7. leather 9. moss
agate
mock... 3. ape 4. defy, gibe, jape,
jibe, sham 5. feign, fleer, flout,
mimic, scoff, sneer, taunt 6. delude,
deride 7. imitate, mockery, pretend
8. ridicule 10. disappoint
11. counterfeit
mock (pert to)...
brawn.. 10. headcheese
cucumber.. 11. balsam apple
duck.. 4. meat 8. pork chop
hero.. 5. comic
jewelry.. 5. logie, paste 9. imitation
lead, ore.. 10. sphalerite
moon.. 10. paraselene
nightingale.. 7. warbler 8. blackcap
olive.. 9. axbreaker 12. cherry laurel
orange.. 7. syringa (seringa)
plane.. 8. sycamore
sun.. 9. parhelion
turtle.. 9. calf's head
mockage... 7. mimicry, mockery
9. imitation
mocker... 5. mimic 7. scoffer
8. deceiver 11. mockingbird
mockernut... 7. hickory
mockery... 5. farce 6. satire
7. mimicry, sarcasm 8. derision
9. imitation 11. counterfeit
mockingbird... 5. Mimus
mode... 3. fad, way 4. form 5. flair,
style, vogue 6. manner, method
7. fashion, variety
mode (pert to)...
expression.. 10. vernacular
government.. 6. regime, system
logic.. 7. Ferison (3rd figure)
procedure.. 5. order 6. system
speech.. 8. parlance 11. phraseology
standing.. 4. pose 6. stance
7. posture 8. position
model... 3. act 4. form, idea, mold,
norm, plan, plat, pose 6. ideal,
image, shape 7. example, manikin,
measure, paragon, pattern, templet
8. ensample, paradigm, standard,
template 9. archetype, mannequin,
precedent 11. meritorious
12. reproduction
model (of)...
a word.. 8. paradigm
a work.. 9. archetype
excellence.. 7. paragon 8. exemplar
solar system.. 6. orrery
11. planetarium
moderate... 4. bate, ease, slow, some
5. abate, lower, slake 6. frugal,
lessen, soften, temper 7. control,
lenient, mediate, modesto
8. mediocre, modulate, slow down
9. temperate 10. reasonable
11. inexpensive 12. conservative
14. inconsiderable
moderation... 7. control 9. abatement,
restraint 10. diminution, governance,
limitation, mitigation 11. restriction
13. temperateness

moderator... 5. judge 6. umpire
7. arbiter 8. mediator 10. arbitrator,
controller
modern... 3. neo (pref), new 4. late
6. latter 7. present 8. neoteric
modernize... 6. update 10. streamline
Modern School of Art... 4. Dada
7. Dadaism (1920)
modern Syriac script... 5. serta
8. peshitta
modest... 3. coy, mim, shy 6. chaste,
demure, humble, seemly 8. reserved,
retiring, virtuous 9. diffident
11. well-behaved 13. unpretentious
14. inconsiderable
modesty... 7. decency, reserve,
shyness 8. chastity, humility, pudicity
10. diffidence, humbleness
11. self-control
modicum... 3. bit 4. drop 5. minim,
share 6. little 11. small amount
12. small portion
modification... 4. tone 6. change,
umlaut 9. variation 10. adaptation,
alteration, limitation 13. qualification
15. differentiation
modify... 4. vary 5. alter, limit
6. change, master, temper
7. assuage, qualify 8. attemper,
mitigate, moderate, quantify
9. influence 13. differentiate
modish... 4. chic, trim 5. smart 7. in
vogue, stylish 8. vogueish (voguish)
11. fashionable
modiste... 8. milliner 9. couturier
10. couturière, dressmaker
modulated... 5. toned 6. merged
7. adapted, attuned, changed,
intoned 8. softened, tempered
9. inflected, regulated
modulation... 4. tone 6. change
8. shifting 9. tempering
10. alteration, inflection, moderation
moggan... 8. stocking 10. knit sleeve
moggy... 3. cat, cow 4. calf 7. pet
name 8. slattern 9. scarecrow
mogo... 7. hatchet
mogul... 4. lord 5. nabob 6. tycoon
7. magnate 8. autocrat 9. dignitary
10. locomotive, panjandrum
14. great personage
Mogul... 6. Empire, Mongol 7. dynasty
9. Mongolian
Mohammed (pert to)...
birthplace.. 5. Mecca
daughter.. 6. Fatima
flight to Mecca.. 6. hegira
horse.. 5. Fadda (white mule)
7. Alborak
names.. 7. Mahomet, Mahound
son-in-law.. 3. Ali
Mohammedan (pert to)...
angel of death.. 6. Azrael
ascetic.. 4. Sufi 5. fakir (fakeer)
8. Marabout
caliph.. 3. Ali 4. Omar 6. Othman
7. Abu Bekr
chief.. 3. aga (agha) 4. dato (datto)
5. sayid 6. Caliph
crier (for prayer).. 7. muezzin
crusader's enemy (Moslem)..
7. Saracen

deity.. 5. Allah 9. Termagant
demon.. 5. afrit, eblis, jinni (jinnee)
   7. Shaitan (Sheitan)
Malay (Javanese).. 6. Sassak
Moslem.. 5. hanif 9. Mussulman
noble.. 4. amir (ameer), emir
nymph.. 5. houri
officer.. 3. aga 5. diwan 6. vizier
   (vizir)
princess, queen.. 5. begum
saint.. 3. pir 6. santon
scholars, body of.. 5. ulema
sect.. 6. Wahabi (Wahabee, Wahhabi)
student (Theol).. 5. softa
successor.. 6. Caliph (Calif)
teacher.. 5. mufti 6. mullah (mollah)
unbeliever.. 6. Kaffir (Kafir)
Mohammedanism (pert to)...
   Bible, book.. 5. Koran 7. Alcoran
bier, tomb.. 5. tabut
cap.. 3. taj
caravansary.. 6. imaret
crusade.. 5. jihad (jehad)
custom, tradition.. 6. sunnah
divorce.. 5. talak 7. mubarat
dome, over tomb.. 6. turbeh
Easter.. 3. Eed
Fast (annual).. 7. Ramadan
festival.. 6. Bairam
garment.. 4. izar 6. jubbah
house (men's part).. 8. selamlik
instrument.. 5. rebab
marriage custom.. 5. iddat
marriage settlement.. 4. mahr
Messiah, priest.. 4. Imam (Imaum)
   5. Mahdi
monastery.. 5. ribat
platform, porch.. 7. mastaba
prayer.. 4. azan (adan) 5. namaz
property (law).. 6. mushaa
religion.. 8. Moslem 8. Islamism
saber.. 8. yataghan (yatagan)
salutation.. 6. salaam (salam)
shrine (Mecca).. 5. Kaaba (Caaba,
   Kaabeh) 10. Black Stone
veil.. 7. yashmak (yashmac)
war (Relig).. 5. jihad (jehad)
moho... 4. rail 9. gallinule 10. honey
   eater
mohr... 7. gazelle
moider... 4. toil 5. crowd, worry
   6. wander 7. smother 8. bewilder,
   encumber
moiety... 4. half, part (small)
   7. portion
moil... 4. spot, tire, toil 5. labor, taint
   6. seethe 7. torment, trouble,
   turmoil 8. drudgery 9. confusion
   10. defilement
moiré... 7. clouded, watered
moist... 3. wet 4. damp, dank, dewy,
   uvid 5. humid, rainy 7. tearful
moisten... 3. wet 4. hose, moil
   5. bedew, spray 6. anoint, dampen,
   sparge 8. humidify, sprinkle
moisture... 3. dew, fog 5. vapor,
   water 6. liquid 8. dampness,
   dankness, dewdrops, humidity
moisture (pert to)...
   body.. 6. humors 9. exudation
condensed.. 4. drip, drop
excess, swelling.. 5. edema

expose to.. 3. ret
remove.. 4. wipe 5. wring
mojo... 4. Moxo 5. charm (voodoo)
   6. amulet 7. majagua
moke... 4. dolt, mesh 5. horse
   6. donkey 7. network 8. minstrel
   9. performer
moki... 4. raft
moko... 9. tattooing
moky... 5. foggy, misty
molar... 5. tooth 6. molary
   7. chopper, grinder 8. grinding
molarimeter... 11. thermometer
molasses... 5. sirup 7. treacle
   8. theriaca
mold, mould... 3. die 4. cast, form,
   must 5. humus, knead, nowel,
   plasm, sprue 6. blight, growth
   (fungus), matrix, mildew 7. moulage
   9. sculpture 12. reproduction
Moldavia, Rumania...
   balm.. 4. mint
capital.. 5. Balta 8. Tiraspol
govt.. 9. Socialist
molding... 3. ess 4. bead, beak,
   cyma, ogee, reed, tori 5. conge,
   gulla, ovolo, splay, torus 6. fascia,
   fillet, listel, reglet, scotia 7. cavetto,
   cornice, reeding, shaping 8. astragal,
   bezantee 12. reproduction
molding (pert to)...
   convex.. 5. torus
decoration.. 4. dado
egg and dart.. 9. arrowhead
series.. 7. surbase
suit of.. 8. ledgment (ledgement)
moldy, mouldy... 5. fusty, mucid,
   musty, stale 8. mildewed
mole (rat)... 4. gray 5. fault, nevus
   (naevus), shrew, snake, Talpa, taupe
   6. rodent 7. blemish, Nesokia
   9. birthmark 12. imperfection
molecule... 3. ion 4. atom, unit
   6. steric 8. particle
molest... 4. harm 5. annoy, tease
   6. bother, harass, pester 7. disturb
   8. mistreat 9. incommode
   13. interfere with
Molière (pert to)...
   author of.. 5. drama, plays
   6. comedy, L'Avare, satire 8. Tartuffe
character (story).. 5. Damis 6. Eraste,
   Scapin 7. Dorante
mollify... 4. calm 5. allay, relax, sleek
   6. pacify, relent, soften, temper
   7. appease, lighten, qualify, relieve
   9. alleviate 10. conciliate
mollitious... 8. sensuous 9. luxurious,
   softening
mollusk... 3. asi 4. clam, pipi, slug,
   spat 5. chama, snail, squid, whelk
   6. cockle, limpet, mussel, oyster
   7. abalone, bivalve, octopus, scallop,
   veliger 8. univalve 10. cuttlefish
mollusk... 5. Anoma, Chama, Murex
   6. Chiton 7. Astarte, Etheria
   8. Buccinum, Mollusca, Nautilus
mollusk (pert to)...
   bait.. 6. limpet
eight-armed.. 7. octopus
freshwater.. 7. etheria
marine.. 7. abalone, scallop

8. nautilus
shell.. 4. test 5. testa 6. cockle, cowrie (cowry)
shell, without.. 4. slug
shell concretion.. 5. pearl
teeth.. 6. radula
ten–armed.. 5. squid
young.. 5. spat
mollycoddle... 6. coddle, pamper
8. weakling 12. spoiled child
13. effeminate boy
Moloch (pert to)...
Bible.. 5. deity
doctrine.. 4. evil
zoology.. 6. agamid, lizard
Molotov cocktail... 4. bomb
molt, moult... 3. mew 4. cast, mute, shed 7. ecdysis 8. exuviate
molten rock... 2. aa
Moluccas, Spice Islands...
capital.. 7. Amboina
island.. 5. Banda
product.. 5. spice
site.. 9. Indonesia
moly... 4. herb (fabled) 6. garlic
momble... 6. jumble, tangle
mome (anc)... 4. fool 7. buffoon
9. blockhead
moment... 4. time 5. avail, flash, nonce, point, trice, value 6. crisis, minute, second, weight 7. impetus, instant 9. influence, twinkling
10. importance 11. consequence
13. consideration, signification
momentary... 9. ephemeral, transient
10. transitory 13. instantaneous
momentous... 7. weighty 8. eventful
9. important 11. influential
13. authoritative
momo... 3. owl
Momus (Gr)... 3. god (of ridicule)
6. critic 11. faultfinder
mon (anc)... 5. badge (imperial) 7. kikumon
13. chrysanthemum
monachal... 8. celibate, monastic
9. claustral
monad... 3. one 4. atom, unit
5. deity, monas 8. particle
10. individual 12. Supreme Being
monadnock... 4. hill 8. mountain (NH)
Mona Lisa (pert to)...
famed for.. 5. smile (subtle)
named also.. 10. La Gioconda
painter.. 7. da Vinci
site (of picture).. 6. Louvre (The)
monandry... 10. one husband (at a time)
monarch... 4. czar, king, shah
5. chief, queen, ruler 6. dynast, kaiser, sultan 7. czarina, emperor
9. potentate, sovereign 13. royal highness
monarch... 9. butterfly
13. constellation
monastery... 5. abbey 6. friary, priory
7. convent, hospice, nunnery
8. cloister
monastery (pert to)...
head.. 3. dom 5. abbot
Pavia.. 10. Carthusian
room.. 4. cell
Tibet.. 8. lamasery

monastic... 4. monk 5. friar
7. monkish 8. celibate 9. claustral
monde... 5. globe, world (fashion)
6. circle (fashion) 7. coterie, société, society 9. beau monde
monetary... 7. coinage 8. currency
9. financial, pecuniary
money... 3. wad 4. cash, coin, grig, mina, pelf 5. frank, funds, lucre, maneh, uhllo (ullo) 6. mazuma, talent, wampum, wealth 8. currency
10. spondulics (spondulix) 11. legal tender
money (pert to)...
ancient.. 3. aes
bank (Eur).. 5. banco
box, chest.. 4. arca, safe, till, tray
5. chest 6. drawer 7. brazier
8. register
changer.. 6. banker, broker, shroff (saraf), usurer 7. cambist
coinage.. 4. mint
English slang.. 7. ooftish (oof)
found.. 5. trove
gamblers'.. 6. barato
gift.. 4. alms 7. bequest
9. endowment
lender.. 6. banker, usurer 7. Shylock
10. pawnbroker
luck.. 6. barato 7. handsel
maker.. 6. coiner, minter
13. counterfeiter
manual.. 7. cambist
matters.. 6. fiscal 9. economics
of account.. 3. ora
paper.. 4. bill, kale 7. lettuce
pledge.. 5. arles
premium.. 4. agio
roll (coins).. 7. rouleau
shell.. 5. uhllo (ullo) 6. cowrie (cowry)
slang.. 4. gilt, jack, lour 5. rhino
6. boodle, wampum
spinner.. 6. usurer 10. speculator
to coin.. 4. mint
wildcat.. 9. yellow dog
worthless.. 4. pelf
moneyed... 4. rich 5. flush 7. opulent, wealthy 8. affluent, well–to–do
10. prosperous, well–heeled
monger... 6. dealer, mercer, trader, vendor 7. peddler 8. merchant
9. tradesman
mongler... 9. sandpiper
Mongol... see also *Mongolian*
5. Asian, Tatar 9. yellow man
Mongolian (pert to)...
ass (wild).. 8. chigetai
capital.. 4. Urga
conjurer.. 6. shaman
conqueror.. 9. Tamerlane
desert.. 4. Gobi
dynasty.. 4. Yuan
monk, priest.. 4. lama
religion.. 9. Shamanism, Shintoism
12. Confucianism
river.. 3. Pei 4. Onon
tribe.. 3. Lai 4. Lapp 5. Ordos
7. Khalkas, Tsaktar 9. Ouryantai
mongoose... 4. urva 5. lemur
9. ichneumon
mongrel... 3. cur 5. mixed 6. hybrid
10. crossbreed 14. stilt sandpiper

mongrel fish... 5. skate (angelfish)
8. tullibee (whitefish)
monial... 3. nun
moniker... 4. name 8. nickname
monition... 6. advice, notice
7. summons, warning
10. admonition, dissuasion, intimation
11. forewarning
monitor... 4. ship (Civil War), uran
5. varan 6. lizard, manual, mentor,
nozzle 7. adviser, student, warning
8. conenose (bug), director, recorder,
reminder 9. informant
monk... 3. fra 4. bede, lama, saki
5. fakir, friar, padre 6. ferret,
monkey 7. ascetic, caloyer, dervish
8. anchoret, capuchin, celibate,
cenobite 9. anchorite, bullfinch,
touchwood
monkey (pert to)...
African.. 4. waag 5. potto 6. grivet,
vernet
American.. 4. saki 5. acari 7. ouakari
8. marmoset 9. beelzebub
bearded.. 8. entellus
bonnet.. 4. zati 5. toque
bread.. 6. baobab
chimpanzee.. 6. nchega
crying.. 4. kaha
cups.. 9. nepenthes 12. pitcher plant
family.. 10. Catarrhina
flower.. 7. mimulus (herb)
genus.. 5. Cebus 6. Ateles
7. Colobus, Saimiri, Tarsius
8. Alouatta
handsome.. 4. mona
house.. 5. apery
howling.. 4. mono 5. araba 7. stentor
8. alouatte
large.. 5. sajou
Madagascar.. 8. mangabey (mangaby)
organ grinder.. 5. Cebus 8. capuchin
Oriental.. 7. macaque
puzzle.. 6. piñon
small.. 8. marmoset
South American.. 4. titi 6. grison
9. beelzebub
spider.. 7. sapajou
squirrel.. 7. saimiri
tailless.. 3. ape
wrench.. 7. spanner
monk's hood.. 6. cowl
monkshood... 4. atis 7. aconite
9. dandelion
monoceros... 4. fish (one-horned)
7. sawfish, Unicorn 9. swordfish
13. Constellation
monochord... 7. concord, harmony
9. sonometer 10. clavichord,
instrument
monocle... 8. eyeglass
monocleid, monocleide... 4. desk (one
key) 7. cabinet
monocracy... 9. autocracy
13. undivided rule
Monodelphia... 7. mammals
8. Eutheria
monody... 3. ode 4. poem (lament),
song 5. dirge 6. melody
9. homophony
monogamy... 11. one marriage
monogram... 6. cipher, sketch

7. outline 8. initials 9. character
monolith... 5. stone 6. menhir, pillar,
statue 8. monument
monologue... 6. speech 9. soliloquy
monomachy... 4. duel 6. combat
monopoly... 5. grant, right, trust
6. corner 7. charter, control
9. privilege, syndicate 10. possession
(exclusive)
monotonous... 4. dead, drab, dull
5. drone, thrum 6. dreary, samely
7. humdrum, tedious 8. singsong
9. wearisome 11. repetitious
monotony... 6. tedium 8. sameness
9. wearisome 10. sameliness,
uniformity 15. repetitiousness
monoxylon, monoxyle... 4. boat
5. canoe
monseigneur... 5. title 6. My Lord
monster... 4. ogre 5. fiend, harpy,
teras 6. dragon, ellops, geryon,
gorgon, sphinx 8. behemoth,
Cerberus 11. monstrosity
monster (pert to)...
classic.. 8. minotaur
comb form.. 6. terato
eight-headed.. 6. Scylla
fabled.. 5. harpy 6. kraken, sphinx
7. centaur 9. bucentaur
flame-breathing.. 7. chimera
(chimaera)
half man, half bull.. 8. minotaur
headless.. 9. acephalus
like.. 8. teratoid
man-eating.. 4. ogre 5. lamia
medical.. 5. teras
three-bodied.. 6. Geryon (slain by
Hercules)
twin.. 10. xiphopagus
two-bodied.. 7. disomus
two-headed.. 10. dicephalus,
opodidymus
winged.. 5. harpy
monstrous... 4. huge, ugly, vast
5. enorm (anc) 6. absurd, wicked
7. strange, titanic 8. deformed,
gigantic, infamous 9. fantastic,
monstrous, unnatural 10. prodigious,
stupendous 12. overpowering,
overwhelming 13. extraordinary
Montana...
capital.. 6. Helena
city.. 5. Butte 8. Anaconda, Billings
10. Great Falls
Historic site.. 14. Custer Cemetery
lake.. 8. Flathead
mountain.. 7. Rockies 17. Continental
Divide
park.. 7. Glacier 11. Yellowstone
peak.. 7. Granite
reservation (Ind).. 4. Cree, Crow
5. Sioux 8. Cheyenne, Chippewa
9. Blackfeet
State admission.. 10. Forty-first
State motto.. 13. Gold and Silver
State nickname.. 8. Treasure
montanto... 6. rising 10. broadsword
Monte Cristo, Count of (pert to)...
author.. 5. Dumas (Alexandre)
hero.. 6. Dantès
Montenegro... 10. Yugoslavia
montero... 3. cap (hunter's) 6. ranger

8. forester, huntsman, mountain
Montezuma (pert to)...
　Chief of.. 6. Aztecs
　cypress.. 9. ahuehuete
　hero of.. 6. Mexico
　prisoner of.. 6. Cortez
　ruins, site of.. 6. Pueblo
month (pert to)...
　astronomy.. 5. lunar, solar
　half.. 9. fortnight
　revolution.. 8. sidereal 9. synodical
　term.. 5. epact 6. ultimo 7. proximo
　twelfth part.. 8. calendar
monticule... 4. cone (volcano)
　5. mount 7. hillock 10. prominence
　(small)
montilla... 6. sherry
Montmorency... 6. cherry
monture... 5. frame, horse (saddle),
　mount
monument... 4. tomb 5. cairn, stele
　(stela), tower, vault 6. bilith, dolmen
　7. obelisk 8. cenotaph, cromlech,
　monolith 9. sepulcher 10. gravestone
　11. commemorate, remembrance
monumental... 4. high 5. great
　7. mammoth, massive, notable
　8. colossal 10. impressive, sculptural,
　stupendous
Monumental City... 9. Baltimore
moo... 3. low (of a cow) 6. lowing
mooch... 4. loaf 5. skulk, sneak, steal
　6. loiter, pilfer 7. vagrant
moocha... 6. girdle 9. loincloth
mood... 3. tid 4. tone, vein, whim
　5. freak, humor 6. nature 7. caprice
　11. disposition
moody... 3. sad 4. glum 5. sulky
　6. gloomy, sullen 7. pensive
　9. whimsical 10. capricious
mool... 4. bury, mold, soil 5. earth,
　grave 6. mingle 7. crumble
mools... 10. chilblains
moon... 4. idle, Luna 5. Diana
　6. Phoebe, wander 7. Cynthia
　8. crescent 9. satellite 13. celestial
　body
moon (pert to)...
　age (first of year).. 5. epact
　area.. 4. mare
　Astrol.. 6. Cancer (mansion), planet
　autumn.. 7. harvest
　beam.. 4. ray 9. pearl blue
　bird.. 11. goldencrest
　blindness.. 10. nyctalopia
　calf.. 4. dolt 7. monster 8. born fool,
　imbecile
　comb form.. 5. selen
　fern.. 8. moonwort
　festival.. 8. neomenia
　fish.. 4. opah 6. minnow 7. sunfish
　9. spadefish
　flower.. 10. oxeye daisy
　gazing.. 16. absent-mindedness
　geographer.. 13. selenographer
　god.. 3. Sin 6. Nannar
　heraldry.. 6. argent
　inhabitant.. 8. Selenite
　instrument.. 11. selenoscope
　lighter.. 9. serenader 10. moonshiner
　11. night worker
　lily.. 10. moonflower

mad.. 7. lunatic
mock.. 10. paraselene
month.. 5. lunar
new.. 6. phasis
phase.. 7. gibbous, horning
picture of.. 11. selenograph
point.. 4. cusp, horn 5. apsis
　6. apogee 7. perigee
position.. 6. octant
raker.. 10. stupid lout
　12. woolgatherer
stone.. 3. gem 8. feldspar
　10. hecatolite
struck.. 7. lunatic 8. obsessed
Uranus's.. 5. Ariel
valley.. 4. rill (rille) 5. cleft
moon goddess...
Greek.. 6. Hecate, Phoebe 7. Artemis,
　Cynthia
Italian.. 5. Diana
Phoenician.. 6. Tanith (Tanit)
　7. Astarte
Roman.. 3. Dea 5. Virgo 9. Caelestis
moonish... 7. flighty 10. capricious
moonshine... 5. empty 6. liquor,
　poteen, whisky (whiskey) 7. bootleg
　8. egg sauce, nonsense
　10. balsamweed
moony... 5. round 6. dreamy
　9. moonlight 10. abstracted
　14. crescent-shaped
moor... 3. bog, fen 4. hill, root
　5. heath, marsh, swale 6. anchor,
　fasten, secure 9. fix firmly
Moor... 6. Berber, Moslem
　7. Moorman, Saracen 8. goldfish
　(black), Moroccan
moor (pert to)...
berry.. 9. cranberry
bird.. 6. grouse
blackbird.. 5. ouzel
buzzard.. 5. harpy 7. harrier
cock.. 9. blackcock
dance.. 7. morisco
grass.. 5. heath 6. sundew
hen.. 4. coot 9. gallinule
monkey.. 7. macaque
stone.. 7. granite
Moorish... 6. Moslem 8. Moresque
Moorish (pert to)...
garment.. 5. jupon
horse.. 4. barb (Barbary)
judge.. 4. cadi
kettledrum.. 5. tabor 6. atabal
Order.. 7. Alcazar 8. Alhambra
　9. horseshoe, Saracenic
palace.. 7. Alcazar
moose... 3. elk 4. alce 5. eland
　7. society (Loyal Order)
moose bird... 9. Canada jay
moot... 4. pose 5. argue, plead, speak
　6. debate 7. discuss, propose
mop... 4. swab, wipe 5. scrub
　6. merkin 7. drink up, grimace
　9. blindfold, implement
mope... 4. sulk 5. dumps, idler
　6. grieve
moppet... 3. tot 4. baby, doll, tike
　7. darling, toddler 8. youngster
mora... 4. tree (Trinidad) 5. delay,
　stool 7. default 8. syllable
　9. footstool 11. Spartan army

12. postponement
moral... 4. good, pure 5. maxim
  6. lesson 7. epimyth, ethical,
  upright, virtual 8. likeness, virtuous
  9. righteous
moral (pert to)...
  excellence.. 6. virtue
  fault.. 4. vice
  law.. 9. Decalogue
  obligation.. 4. duty
  poem.. 3. dit
  principle.. 7. precept
  story.. 5. fable 7. parable
  8. apologue
morale... 4. hope, zeal 6. morals,
  spirit 8. morality 10. confidence
moralist... 4. prig 7. teacher
  9. moralizer 10. sermonizer
morality... 6. amoral, ethics, virtue
  13. righteousness
morals... 8. morality 10. ethography
morass... 3. bog, fen 4. moor
  5. marsh, swamp 6. slough
  8. quagmire 9. everglade
moratorium... 5. delay 10. suspension
Moravia, capital... 5. Brünn (Brno)
Moravian... 9. Christian 10. Herrnhuter
  13. Unitas Fratrum 19. Church of
  the Brethren
moray... 3. eel 6. hamlet 7. Muraena
  8. food fish 10. Muraenidae
morbid... 4. sick 6. gloomy 7. ghastly,
  unsound 8. diseased 9. unhealthy
  11. unwholesome
morbid (pert to)...
  appetite.. 10. adephagous
  complex.. 11. inferiority
  condition.. 8. ochlesis
  desire for music.. 9. melomania
  displacement.. 7. ectopia
morbus... 7. disease, illness
morceau... 3. bit (Mus) 6. morsel
mordant... 4. acid, keen 6. biting
  7. burning, caustic, pungent
  8. scathing 9. corrosive, sarcastic
  11. acrimonious
more... 3. yea 4. also, mair, plus,
  some 5. again, extra 6. plural
  7. greater 10. additional
  13. approximately
more (pert to)...
  cunning.. 5. slyer 6. tricky
  difficult.. 6. harder
  distant.. 8. ulterior
  mature.. 5. older, riper
  miserly.. 5. closer, meaner, nearer
  not any.. 4. dead, past 8. vanished
  11. nonexistent
  or less.. 4. some 8. somewhat
  13. approximately
  over.. 3. and 4. also, else
  7. besides, further, thereto
  precious.. 6. dearer
  relative.. 11. comparative
  severe.. 7. sterner
  so.. 3. yea
  than.. 4. over 5. above 6. beyond
  9. exceeding 10. in excess of
  than enough.. 3. too
  than one.. 4. many 6. plural
  7. several
  than this.. 3. yes

  unusual.. 5. rarer
  vapid.. 6. staler
morel... 6. fungus 8. mushroom
morello... 4. ruru 6. cherry
  7. boobook 8. morepork, mulberry
  (color)
morena... 8. brunette
mores... 7. customs, manners
  9. etiquette 11. conventions
Moreton Bay... 9. Australia
Morgan... 5. horse 10. sea dweller
morganatic marriage...
  10. left–handed (royal)
morgay... 7. dogfish
morglay... 5. sword
morgue... 8. mortuary 9. deadhouse,
  stolidity 11. haughtiness, impassivity
Morgue (The)... 17. Library of
  Congress
moribund... 4. sick 5. dying 9. near
  death
moriform... 14. mulberry–shaped
morindin dye... 2. al
morion... 6. helmet, quartz 8. cabasset
Mormon Church (pert to)...
  Band (Polit).. 6. Danite (1837)
  cricket.. 11. grasshopper
  emblem.. 3. bee
  Indian.. 8. Lamanite
  instrument.. 4. Urim 7. Thummin
  officer.. 5. Elder
  official name.. 36. Church of Jesus
  Christ of Latter Day Saints
  patriarch.. 11. Joseph Smith
  12. Brigham Young
  prophet.. 6. Moroni
  State.. 4. Utah
  tea plant.. 7. Brigham
  tree.. 11. black poplar
morning (pert to)...
  clouds.. 4. velo
  coat.. 7. cutaway
  concert.. 6. aubade
  glory.. 3. nil 7. ipomoea
  14. Convolvulaceae
  goddess.. 3. Eos
  performance.. 7. matinee
  prayer.. 5. matin
  reception.. 5. levee
  star.. 4. Mars 5. Venus 6. Saturn
  7. Daystar, Jupiter, Lucifer, Mercury
  8. Phosphor
  term.. 4. dawn 5. matin, wight
  6. Aurora 7. sunrise 9. matutinal
moro... 5. finch
moro (comb form)... 6. stupid
Moro... 6. Moslem
Morocco...
  capital.. 5. Rabat
  city.. 7. Tangier 10. Casablanca
  color.. 3. red
  enclave.. 4. Ifni
  famed site.. 5. Casba
  hat.. 3. fez
  island.. 7. Madeira
  Jewish quarter.. 8. El Millah
  language.. 6. Arabic
  leather imitation.. 4. roan
  military expedition.. 5. harka
  millet.. 12. Johnson grass
  people.. 4. Arab, Moor 6. Berber
  plateau.. 6. mesata

ruler.. 4. king 5. malek 6. sultan
soldier.. 5. askar
morology... 5. folly 8. nonsense
moron... 4. dull 5. ament, idiot, zombi
6. nitwit, stupid 8. imbecile, sluggish
12. stupid person
morose... 4. blue, dour, glum, grum,
sour 5. moody, surly 6. crusty,
gloomy, sullen 7. crabbed, unhappy
9. splenetic 10. embittered
Morpheus (Gr)... 10. god of Sleep
11. god of Dreams
morphine... 6. heroin 8. hypnotic
9. analgesic, calmative
morphology... 7. anatomy 8. cytology
9. histology 10. embryology
12. organography
morris... 4. game 5. chair, dance
morro... 4. hill 6. Castle (Havana)
7. hillock 11. point of land
Mors (Rom)... 5. Death, deity
Morse... 4. code, lamp 8. alphabet
morsel... 3. ort 4. bite, chip 5. piece,
scran (sl), scrap, snack 6. tidbit,
titbit 7. morceau 8. delicacy,
fragment 11. small amount
mort... 4. dead, lard 5. dead, fatal
6. deadly, grease, salmon
9. abundance
mortacious... 4. very 9. extremely
mortal... 5. fatal, human 6. deadly,
lethal 10. perishable
mortally... 5. amort 6. deadly 7. à la
mort, deathly, fatally 9. extremely
10. grievously
mortar... 3. rab 4. bowl 5. putty
6. cannon 7. mortier 10. night light
(Hist)
mortarboard... 3. cap (Acad)
mortgage... 4. bond, pawn 6. pledge
mortician... 8. embalmer
10. undertaker 15. funeral director
mortification... 5. decay, shame
7. chagrin 8. gangrene, vexation
11. humiliation
mortify... 5. abase, abash, abuse,
shame, spite 6. ashame, deaden,
humble 7. chagrin 9. embarrass,
humiliate
mortis causa... 15. by reason of
death
mortise, mortice... 6. cavity, insert
8. amortize 10. foundation
mortuary... 4. gift (burial) 6. morgue
7. funeral 8. funeral 9. deadhouse,
sepulcher 10. cinerarium
12. corsepresent (offering, Hist)
mosaic... 5. virus 6. design
7. ceramic, picture 10. decoration,
variegated 11. tessellated
mosaic (pert to)...
apply.. 7. incrust
gold.. 6. ormolu
law.. 5. Torah (Moses)
piece.. 7. tessera
Moscow...
capital of.. 6. Russia
citadel.. 7. Kremlin
river.. 6. Moskva
shrine.. 9. Lenin Tomb, Red Square
Third Internat.. 9. Comintern
Moselle... 4. Saar, wine 5. river,

Ruwer 9. Rhine wine
Moses (pert to)...
Bible.. 7. prophet 8. lawgiver
brother.. 5. Aaron
emissary.. 5. Caleb
father.. 5. Amram
father–in–law.. 6. Jethro
law.. 5. Torah (Tora) 10. Pentateuch
mother.. 8. Jochebed
mountain.. 4. Nebo
sister.. 6. Miriam
successor.. 6. Joshua
wife.. 8. Zipporah
mosey... 6. depart, stroll 7. shuffle
Moslem... 5. Hanif, Islam, Salar
7. Saracen 9. Mussulman
10. Mohammedan
Moslem (pert to)...
ablution.. 4. wudu (widu, wuzu)
cap.. 3. fez, taj
capturer of Jerusalem.. 4. Omar
caste.. 5. mopla (moplah)
chief.. 4. dato (datto), rais
city (holy).. 5. Mecca
college, school.. 8. madrasah
(madrasa, madrasseh)
dagger.. 7. khanjar
deity.. 5. Allah, Eblis
devil.. 5. Eblis
devotee.. 6. santon 7. dervish
Easter.. 3. Eed
guide (spiritual).. 3. pir
interpreter.. 5. ulema
invocation.. 9. bismillah
javelin.. 6. jereed
judge.. 4. cadi
lawyer.. 5. mufti
market, booth.. 4. sook
monastery.. 5. ribat 7. khankah
mosque.. 6. masjid
noble.. 4. amir (ameer), emir
officer.. 5. dewan (diwan)
pilgrimage to Mecca.. 4. hadj
prayer.. 4. azan (adan)
priest.. 4. imam (imaum)
saint.. 3. pir 6. santon 8. Marabout
sect.. 6. Senusi (Senousi, Senussite)
shrine, Mecca.. 5. Kaaba (Caaba,
Kaabeh)
teacher.. 4. Alim 8. mujtahid
title.. 3. Sid 5. Sayid (Said)
tradition.. 7. Al Sirat (Bridge to
Paradise)
tribesman.. 4. Moro
Turkish.. 5. Salar
university.. 8. madrasah (madrasa)
viceroy.. 7. Saracen
mosque... 4. Omar 5. Kaaba (Caaba)
6. masjid 11. Great Mosque
mosque tower... 7. minaret
mosque warden... 5. nazir
mosquito (pert to)...
bite preventive.. 10. culicifuge
coast.. 8. Honduras 9. Nicaragua
comb form.. 6. culici
destroyer.. 8. culicide
disease.. 7. malaria 11. yellow fever
family.. 9. Culicidae
fish.. 8. gambusia
genus.. 5. Aedes, Culex 7. Diptera
8. Mansonia 9. Anopheles, Culicidae
10. Psorophora

hawk.. 9. dragonfly, nighthawk
Indian drink.. 6. mushla
larvae.. 8. wigglers
plant.. 4. mint 10. pennyroyal
shaped.. 10. culiciform
State (nickname).. 9. New Jersey
term.. 7. culicid 11. gallinipper
moss.. 3. bog, rag 4. agar 5. Maium,
money, Musci, swamp 6. lichen,
morass 7. skeeter 8. agar–agar
9. treebeard
moss (pert to)...
back.. 4. fogy (fogey) 9. old turtle
10. Southerner (1861)
12. conservative
berry.. 9. cranberry
capsule.. 9. operculum
color.. 5. green
coral.. 8. bryozoan
duck.. 7. mallard 8. moss–head
9. merganser
fish.. 8. menhaden 10. mossbunker
grown.. 10. antiquated
kind.. 4. peat 7. Spanish
like.. 6. mnioid
mossy.. 4. dull 5. boggy, downy
6. marshy, stupid 9. crumbling,
overgrown
most.. 7. highest, maximum
8. greatest, main part, majority
9. nearly all
most favorable... 7. optimum
Most High... 3. God 12. Supreme
Being
most northerly land... 5. Thule
mot... 5. maxim, motto 7. opinion
9. witticism
mote... 4. atom, hill, iota 5. match,
speck, squib 6. barrow, height, trifle
7. tumulus 8. eminence, particle
mote nut... 5. carap
motet... 4. hymn 6. anthem, choral
7. chorale
moth... 2. io 5. egger, tinea
6. lappet, miller 7. noctuid, Tineina
8. forester (8–spotted), Tineidae
9. Tineoidea 11. Lepidoptera
moth (pert to)...
hawk.. 10. goatsucker
kind.. 5. gypsy 6. carpet 9. browntail
larva.. 11. caterpillar
spot (Med).. 8. chloasma
spot (wing).. 8. fenestra
mother... 2. ma 3. dam 4. amma
5. adopt, mamma, mater 6. abbess,
parent 7. care for, creator
8. ancestor, begetter, genetrix,
producer 10. procreator
mother (pert to)...
church.. 9. cathedral 16. Christian
Science
goddess.. 6. matris 7. Shaktis
10. sapta–matri (7 mothers)
goddess of motherhood (Egypt)..
4. Isis
godmother.. 4. Rhea 6. cummer
(kimmer) 9. Brigantia
Goose character.. 5. Simon, Sprat
6. Bo–peep
Govt.. 10. matriarchy, metrocracy
house.. 7. convent 9. monastery
Hubbard.. 4. gown 5. dress

Maid.. 10. Virgin Mary
Mother Carey's chickens.. 7. petrels
(stormy)
Myth (Gr).. 5. Niobe
related.. 6. enatic
spiritual.. 4. amma
Tagalog.. 3. Ina
motherly... 8. maternal
mother of...
Castor.. 4. Leda
gods.. 4. Rhea 9. Brigantia
Graces.. 5. Aegle
Nature.. 6. Cybele
Night.. 3. Nox, Nyx
pearl.. 5. nacre 7. abalone
presidents.. 8. Virginia
States.. 8. Virginia
the month.. 4. Moon
motif... 5. theme, topic 6. edging
motion... 3. bob 4. lipe, move
5. impel, trend 6. seesaw, travel,
tremor, unrest 7. gesture, propose,
request, suggest 8. kinetics,
movement, petition
motionless... 5. inert, rigid, still
6. static 8. immobile, stagnant
10. stock–still
motion picture... 5. movie 6. cinema
motion picture arc light... 5. klieg
motivate... 4. move 5. force, impel
6. compel, incite, induce, propel
7. actuate, animate, promote
9. stimulate
motive... 4. sake, spur 5. cause,
motif, topic 6. reason 7. pretext
8. stimulus 9. incentive, influence,
intention 10. incitement, inducement
11. instigation 13. consideration
motley... 5. mixed 6. fabric 7. diverse,
mixture, mottled 9. checkered,
diversity 10. variegated
12. parti–colored 13. heterogeneous
motor... 5. mover, rotor 6. Diesel,
dynamo, engine 7. turbine 8. motor
car 9. locomotor 10. automobile
motor speed control... 8. rheocrat
mottled... 3. roe 4. pied 5. pinto
6. calico 7. dappled, marbled,
piebald, spotted 13. pepper–and–salt
mottled soap... 7. castile 8. Eschwego
(Eschweg)
motto... 3. mot 5. adage, axiom,
gnome, maxim 6. advice 7. empresa
(impresa), precept 8. aphorism
9. principle 11. inscription
motto of...
Boy Scouts.. 10. Be Prepared
Coast Guard.. 11. Always Ready
13. Semper paratus
Order of the Garter.. 20. Honi soit
qui mal y pense
Queen Elizabeth.. 11. Semper Eadem
13. Always the Same
mouche... 5. patch (black)
mouchoir... 12. handkerchief
mouflon, moufflon... 5. sheep
mould, mold... 5. knead 6. matrix
moulrush... 7. pollack (food fish)
mound... 3. dam, dun, tee 4. bank,
dene, doon, dune, heap, hill, terp,
tomb, tump 5. knoll 6. bounds
7. barrier, bulwark, rampart, tumulus

8. boundary 9. elevation
10. embankment 13. fortification
mound (pert to)...
bird.. 8. megapode
City.. 7. St Louis
lily.. 5. yucca
memorial.. 5. cairn
of light.. 8. Kohinoor (diamond)
Polynesian.. 3. ahu
prehistoric.. 5. matte
Scottish.. 5. toman
mount... 3. fly, set (jewel) 4. glue,
hill, lift, pony (polo), rise 5. arise,
climb, horse, paste 6. ascent
7. elevate 8. increase, mountain
10. promontory
Mount (pert to)...
Etna city.. 7. Catania
Everest peak.. 6. Lhotse
Parnassus fountain, spring.. 8. Castalia
mountain...
Africa.. 11. Kilimanjaro
Alaska.. 8. McKinley
Asia.. 7. Everest
Babylonia.. 6. Ararat
California.. 6. Shasta 7. Whitney
Crete.. 3. Ida
Europe.. 4. Ural 8. Pyrenees
fabled.. 4. Meru
Greek (Myth).. 7. Helicon
Japan.. 8. Fujiyama
legendary.. 3. Kaf, Qaf (Moslem)
4. Meru
Mexico.. 12. Popocatepetl
Montana.. 6. Tetons
Switzerland.. 4. Alps 10. Matterhorn
Thessaly.. 4. Ossa 6. Pelion
U S Chain.. 5. Rocky 7. Sawback,
Sierras 8. Blue Ridge
11. Appalachian
Yukon.. 5. Logan
mountain (pert to)...
ash.. 5. rowan
badger.. 6. marmot
balsam.. 3. fit
banana.. 3. fei
barometer.. 8. orometer
beaver.. 8. sewellel
blackbird.. 5. ouzel
cat.. 4. lynx 6. bobcat, cougar
10. cacomistle
comb form.. 3. oro
cowslip.. 8. auricula
crest, spur.. 5. arête
curassow (pheasant).. 10. oreophasis
defile.. 3. gap 4. gate, ghat (ghaut),
pass 5. gorge
depression.. 3. col
dew.. 6. whisky
eagle.. 6. golden
goat.. 4. ibex
highest.. 7. Everest
ice.. 4. berg 7. glacier
ivy.. 6. laurel
lake.. 4. tarn
lion.. 4. puma 6. cougar
lodge.. 4. gite
low.. 5. butte
nymph.. 5. oread
oak.. 8. chestnut
peak.. 3. tor
raspberry.. 10. cloudberry

rose.. 6. laurel
sheep.. 7. bighorn 13. Rocky
Mountain
shrub.. 10. fetterbush
sickness.. 7. soroche
State.. 7. Montana
sunset.. 9. alpenglow
Tatars.. 5. Tauli
witch.. 9. quail dove
mountaineer... 7. climber
11. backsettler
mountains, science of... 7. orology
9. orography
mountant... 6. raised, rising
8. mounting 9. ascendant
mountebank... 4. gull 5. cheat, quack
7. buffoon, empiric 8. impostor
9. charlatan, pretender 11. quack
doctor
mounted men... 7. knights
mounting... 6. ascent 7. rimbase,
seating, setting 9. adjusting,
equipment 13. embellishment
mourn... 3. rue 4. erme, long, sigh,
wail, weep 6. bemoan, bewail,
grieve, lament, murmur, repine,
sorrow 7. deplore
mourner... 6. keener, wailer 7. griever
8. lamenter
mournful... 3. sad 6. repine 7. elegiac
8. grievous 9. elegiacal, plaintive,
saddening, sorrowful, threnodic,
woebegone
mournful poem... 5. elegy
mourning... 3. sad 4. garb 5. crape,
weeds (dress) 6. lament, sorrow
7. drapery 9. sorrowing 10. black
badge 11. lamentation
mourning dress... 5. weeds 6. sables
mouse... 3. erd, Mus 4. buck, vole
5. prowl, shrew 6. jerboa, migale
7. harvest, toy with
mouse (pert to)...
bird.. 4. coly 6. shrike
color.. 4. gray
deer.. 7. plandok 10. chevrotain
ear.. 8. hawkweed 9. bloodwort,
chickweed 11. forget–me–not
fish.. 9. sargassum
hare.. 4. pika
hound.. 6. weasel
kind.. 6. pocket 7. harvest, jumping
leaping.. 6. jerboa
milk.. 6. spurge
mouselike.. 6. murine
web.. 6. cobweb, phlegm
8. gossamer
mousse... 7. dessert 9. moss green
12. gelatine dish
moutan... 5. peony
mouth... 2. os 3. mow, mun 4. boca,
dupe, lade, lick 5. inlet, stoma
6. cavity, rictus 7. declaim, opening,
orifice 8. aperture, lorriker
9. impudence
mouth (pert to)...
away from.. 6. aboral
deformity.. 7. harelip
disease.. 6. canker 10. stomatitis
furnace.. 5. bocca
glands.. 8. salivary
muscle.. 7. caninus

organ.. 4. harp 7. Pandean
8. jew's-harp 9. crembalum,
harmonica
part.. 3. lip 5. uvula 6. palate
7. pharynx
pert to.. 4. oral 6. rictal, stomal
8. stomatic
piece (Mus).. 10. embouchure
through the.. 7. peroral
tissue.. 3. gum
toward.. 4. orad
wide, gaping.. 6. rictus
mouthed, loud... 11. thersitical
mouton... 5. sheep 9. prison spy
movable... 6. mobile 10. changeable
12. transferable
movable property... 8. chattels
move... 3. act, gee, mog, say
4. goad, sell, spur, stir 5. budge,
cause, impel, rouse, shift 6. excite,
incite, induce, kindle, motion,
prompt, travel 7. actuate, advance,
animate, propose, provoke
9. instigate, recommend, stimulate
move (pert to)...
about.. 8. locomote
along.. 5. mosey, scram 7. maunder
back.. 3. ebb 6. recede, retire, revert
7. retreat 10. retrogress
back and forth.. 6. teeter, wigwag
7. shuttle 9. oscillate
clumsily.. 4. joll
false.. 4. balk 5. feint
forward.. 4. edge, scud 5. drive
7. advance 8. progress
furtively.. 5. slink, sneak
heavily.. 3. lug 6. fidget, lumber,
trudge
in circles.. 4. purl
place to place.. 7. migrate
8. emigrate
quickly.. 3. ply 4. dart, dash, scud,
shot 5. scoot, spank 6. bustle,
gallop, hurtle
restlessly.. 6. kelter
rhythmically.. 5. dance
sideways, sidewise.. 4. slue 5. sidle
slowly.. 3. jog, lag 4. edge, inch,
pant
smoothly.. 4. slip 5. glide, skate,
slide
spasmodically.. 6. twitch
to and fro.. 3. wag 4. flap, sway
together.. 5. unite 8. converge
towards each other.. 8. converge
towards the east.. 9. orientate
unsteadily.. 4. reel 6. wabble
7. stagger
up and down.. 3. bob 6. teeter
with exertion.. 5. heave
with measured tread.. 5. march
moved by entreaty... 8. exorable
moved easily... 5. loped 6. mobile
8. affected 9. emotional
movement... 5. cause, trend 6. action,
motion, rhythm, travel 7. emotion,
gesture, impulse 8. activity,
maneuver, progress
movement (pert to)...
backwards.. 13. retrogression
dance step.. 4. lilt 6. chassé
9. pirouette

music.. 4. moto 7. con moto
of ships.. 5. heave, pitch, scend
of waves.. 4. roll, toss 5. surge
6. tumble, welter
vibratory.. 6. tremor
moving... 6. active, motile 7. nomadic
8. eloquent, exciting, pathetic
9. affecting, impelling, traveling
10. motivating
moving stairway... 9. escalator
mow... 3. cut, lay, mew 4. dess, fell,
heap, mass, math, mock, raze, stow
5. mouth, stack 6. garner, smooth
7. cut down, grimace, harvest,
shorten 9. cornfield
mowana... 6. baobab
mowing... 7. cutting, mockery
8. derision 9. grimacing
10. harvesting, meadowland
mowing machine... 5. mower
6. scythe, sickle
moxieberry... 9. snowberry
moy... 4. mild 6. demure, gentle
8. affected
moyen... 3. way 5. means 6. agency,
course 8. property 9. influence
Mozambique...
Bay.. 8. Mossuril
capital.. 15. Lourenco Marques
native.. 3. Yao
port.. 10. Mozambique
mozo... 10. manservant
Mrs... 5. madam 8. goodwife, Mistress
mucaro... 3. owl
much... 3. lot 4. high, many 5. great
7. greatly 8. abundant, uncommon
9. great deal 10. indefinite
12. considerable
muchacha... 4. girl, lass
muchacho... 3. boy, lad 7. servant
mucid... 5. musty, slimy 6. clammy,
mucous 8. muculent
mucilage... 3. gum 5. paste
6. mucago 8. adhesive 9. lubricant
mucilaginous... 5. moist 6. sticky,
viscid
muckender... 12. handkerchief
mucker... 4. fall (from a horse), mess
6. muddle, wretch 8. disorder
9. confusion, vulgarian
muckle... 4. club, fret 6. bother,
putter
muckraker... 7. defamer 8. vilifier
9. slanderer
mud... 4. mire, muck, silt, slop
5. abuse, gumbo, limus, shine
6. gobbet, sludge 12. offscourings
14. abusive charges
mud (pert to)...
bath.. 10. illutation
dab.. 8. flounder
dauber.. 4. wasp
devil.. 10. hellbender
eel.. 5. siren
hole.. 6. puddle 8. quagmire
lark.. 5. gamin, horse 6. magpie,
urchin
like.. 7. luteous
living in.. 10. limicolous
peep.. 9. sandpiper 11. meadow pipit
pike.. 5. saury
puppy.. 10. hellbender, salamander

rake.. **5**. claut
shoveler.. **13**. spoonbill duck
snipe.. **8**. woodcock
sunfish.. **4**. bass **8**. warmouth
teal.. **9**. greenwing
volcano.. **5**. salse
Mudcat State... **11**. Mississippi
muddle... **3**. mix **4**. daze, mess, soss,
stir **5**. addle **6**. bemuse, jumble
7. confuse, perplex, stupefy
8. befuddle, bewilder, confound,
disorder, squander **10**. intoxicate
11. predicament
muddled... **3**. ree **5**. drunk, muzzy,
tipsy **7**. burbled, fuddled **8**. confused
9. befuddled, entangled
muddlehead... **4**. dolt **9**. blockhead
muddy... **4**. base, miry **5**. dingy, dirty,
roily, slaky **6**. lutose, opaque, slushy,
turbid **7**. clouded, obscure
8. confused **9**. besmeared
muddy places... **7**. wallows
muezzin... **4**. azan (adan) **5**. crier
(Moham)
muff... **5**. beard, cover **6**. bungle
7. bungler, failure **8**. feathers
11. mollycoddle, whitethroat
muffed... **5**. vexed **7**. crested
9. irritated
muffet... **11**. whitethroat
muffetee... **7**. muffler **8**. wristlet
muffin... **3**. cob, gem (bread)
5. bread, hazel, plate **7**. biscuit,
crumpet, popover
muffle... **3**. gag **4**. damp, dull, mute,
wrap **5**. deaden, mumble, shroud,
stifle **7**. conceal **8**. decorate,
envelope **9**. blindfold
muffler... **3**. gag **4**. mute **5**. scarf
6. muzzle, tippet **8**. silencer
10. suppressor
mufflin... **8**. titmouse
mufti... **5**. dress (civilian)
mufti (Moham)... **4**. alim **5**. judge
6. priest **8**. assessor, official
mug... **3**. cup **4**. cram, dupe, face,
fool, Toby **5**. mungo, pulse, sheep,
study **6**. noggin **7**. drizzle, grimace
8. quantity **10**. photograph
muga... **4**. moth, silk **11**. caterpillar
mugger... **3**. goa **6**. tinker **7**. peddler
9. crocodile
mugget... **8**. woodruff **15**. lily of the
valley
muggins (game)... **5**. cards **7**. penalty
8. dominoes
muggy... **4**. damp, warm **5**. humid,
moist, moldy **6**. sticky, stuffy, sultry
11. whitethroat
mug house... **6**. tavern **7**. barroom
8. alehouse, pothouse
mugient... **6**. lowing **9**. bellowing
mugwump... **5**. chief **8**. apostate,
objector **11**. independent, nonpartisan
16. Republican bolter
Muhammed... see *Mohammed*
muir... **4**. wall
muirfowl... **9**. red grouse
muishond... **5**. zoril **6**. weasel
mujer... **4**. wife **5**. woman
mulatto... **5**. metis **8**. quadroon
mulberry... **2**. al **5**. Morus **6**. murrey

10. blackberry **12**. thimbleberry
mulberry (pert to)...
bark (paper).. **4**. tapa (tappa)
beverage.. **5**. morat
bird.. **8**. starling
dye.. **3**. aal **8**. morindin
fig.. **8**. sycamore
purple.. **7**. blue–red **8**. camerier
tree.. **5**. Morus
wild.. **7**. yawweed
mulch... **5**. straw **6**. ground, leaves
7. sawdust
mulct... **4**. fine, scot **6**. amerce,
defect, punish **7**. blemish, deceive,
penalty, swindle **10**. amercement
mulcter... **7**. amercer
mule... **4**. mewl, mool, mute **5**. coble,
hinny, jenny **6**. acemia, hybrid
7. slipper, tractor **9**. chilblain
10. crossbreed, locomotive
15. obstinate person
mule (pert to)...
chair.. **7**. cacolet
driver.. **7**. skinner **8**. muleteer
drove.. **5**. atajo
killer.. **6**. mantis
leading.. **8**. cencerro
skinner.. **6**. driver
untrained.. **9**. shavetail
muleteer... **4**. peon **6**. driver
mulga... **6**. acacia, shield, wattle
muliebria... **8**. feminine
muliebriety... **9**. womanhood
10. effeminacy, femininity
11. womanliness
mulier... **4**. wife **5**. woman **6**. mother
mulish... **6**. hybrid, sullen **7**. asinine,
sterile **8**. stubborn **9**. obstinate
mull... **3**. cow **4**. crag, dust, heat,
mess, mold **5**. crush, grind, snout,
spice **6**. fumble, muddle, muslin,
muzzle, ponder **7**. failure, rubbish,
squeeze, steatin, sweeten **8**. cogitate,
ointment, snuffbox **9**. pulverize
10. promontory
mullah... **6**. priest **7**. teacher (Moham)
mullet... **4**. bobo, fish, star **6**. puffin
mullet hawk... **6**. osprey
mulligan... **4**. stew
mulligatawny... **4**. soup
mulligrubs... **5**. blues, colic, sulks
mullock... **5**. spoil, waste **6**. refuse
(mine) **7**. rubbish
mulloway... **7**. jewfish
multi (comb form)... **4**. many
multifarious... **8**. manifold **9**. multifold,
multiplex **10**. multiphase
multifold... **7**. diverse **8**. manifold,
multiple, numerous
multilingual... **8**. polyglot
multiped... **10**. many–footed
multiplier... **6**. bulbil **7**. facient
8. operator
multiply... **5**. breed **6**. spread
7. amplify, magnify **8**. increase
9. calculate, pluralize, procreate
multitude... **3**. mob **4**. host, many,
mass, much **5**. crowd, horde, shoal,
swarm **6**. legion, throng **8**. populace
12. numerousness
multitudinous... **6**. myriad
mum... **3**. ale **4**. mute **6**. silent

8. taciturn 11. not speaking
mumble... 4. chew, mump 6. chavel,
   fumble, mutter, patter
mumbo jumbo... 6. genius
   7. bugaboo 12. superstition
   13. awesome person
mummer... 5. actor 6. guiser
   7. buffoon 9. performer
mummy... 5. brown, Congo (color),
   relic 6. corpse, mother 7. cadaver,
   carcass
mummy apple... 6. papaya
mump... 3. beg 5. cheat, sulks
   6. mumble, sponge 7. deceive,
   grimace 10. impose upon
mumpish... 4. dull, glum 5. sulky
   8. sullen
mumruffin... 8. titmouse
mundane... 6. cosmic 7. earthly,
   horizon, secular, terrene, worldly
   8. temporal 11. unspiritual
mundatory... 9. cleansing
   11. purificator
mundil... 6. turban (embroidered)
mungo... 4. herb, wool (reclaimed)
   8. mongoose, mung bean
   13. mongoose plant
municipal... 5. civic, urban 7. oppidan
   9. political 10. municipium
munificence... 6. bounty 7. largess
   (largesse) 9. generosity, liberality
   13. bounteousness, unselfishness
muniment... 6. record 7. defense
   8. evidence, writings 9. valuables
   10. furnishing 13. fortification
munity... see *immunity* 11. privilege
munshi (Hind)... 6. writer 7. teacher
   9. secretary 11. interpreter
muntjac, muntjak... 5. kakar, ratwa
   6. kidang
mura (Jap)... 7. village 9. community
Mura... 6. Indian
mural... 4. wall (pert to) 5. crown
   8. painting
murder... 4. kill, slay 7. carnage
   8. homicide 9. slaughter
   11. assassinate 12. manslaughter
murder of...
  brother.. 10. fratricide
  father.. 9. patricide
  king.. 8. regicide
  mother.. 9. matricide
  own child.. 9. prolicide
  parent.. 9. parricide
  prophet.. 8. vaticide
  sister.. 10. sororicide
  spouse (by the other).. 10. mariticide
  wife.. 9. uxoricide
  woman.. 8. femicide
murderous... 4. gory 5. cruel
   6. bloody, deadly, savage 7. killing
   10. sanguinary 12. bloodthirsty
mure... 4. meek, soft, wall 6. gentle,
   immure, modest 8. imprison
murk, mirk... 3. fog 4. dark, mist
   5. gloom 6. opaque 7. blacken
   8. darkness 9. dark color
   11. dark-colored
murky, mirky... 4. dark 5. dense,
   foggy, thick 6. gloomy, opaque
   7. obscure, stained 11. dark-colored
   12. impenetrable

murmur... 3. coo, hum 4. blow, curr,
   fret, purl 6. babble, mutter, repine
   7. trickle, whisper 8. complain
muscle... 4. beef, thew 5. brawn,
   sinew, teres 6. flexor, lacert, tensor
   8. lacertus, retentor
muscle (pert to)...
  affection.. 5. crick 6. ataxia
  bending.. 6. flexor
  chemistry.. 6. inosic 8. inosinic
  column.. 10. sarcostyle
  contracting.. 7. agonist
  expander.. 7. dilator
  extending.. 8. extensor
  eyeball.. 6. rectus
  lifting.. 7. levator
  loin, tenderloin.. 5. psoas
  lower.. 9. depressor
  raising.. 7. deltoid, erector, levator
  recording.. 8. ergogram 9. ergograph
  round.. 5. teres
  segment.. 8. myocomma
  sense.. 11. kinesthesia
  separating.. 11. divaricator
  spasm.. 5. tonus
  stretching.. 6. tensor
  sugar.. 8. inositol
  trapezius.. 10. cucullaris
  triangular.. 7. deltoid
  turning.. 7. evertor, rotator
  two-headed.. 7. biceps
muscovite... 4. mica 11. yellow-green
Muscovite... 7. Russian
muscular... 4. wiry 5. beefy, thewy
   6. brawny, mighty, sinewy, strong,
   torose 8. athletic, stalwart, vigorous
muscular (pert to)...
  contraction (involuntary).. 3. tic
   5. spasm
  co-ordination.. 7. synergy
  in-co-ordination.. 6. ataxia
   15. locomotor ataxia
  non-co-ordination in walking..
   6. abasia
  spasm.. 5. tonus
  stomach.. 7. gizzard
muse... 4. mull, poet, rune 5. dream
   6. ponder 7. bagpipe, reverie
   8. cogitate, consider, meditate,
   ruminate
Muse of...
  astronomy.. 6. Urania
  choral song.. 11. Terpsichore
  comedy.. 6. Thalia
  dancing.. 11. Terpsichore
  eloquence.. 8. Calliope
  history.. 4. Clio
  joy.. 4. Tara
  music.. 7. Euterpe
  poetry.. 5. Erato (lyric) 6. Thalia
   (bucolic) 8. Calliope (heroic)
  tragedy.. 9. Melpomene
Muses... 4. Clio 5. Erato 6. Thalia,
   Urania 7. Euterpe 8. Calliope,
   Polymnia (Polyhymnia) 9. Melpomene
   11. Terpsichore
Muses (pert to)...
  epithet.. 7. Pierian
  fountain.. 9. Aganippe (near Thebes)
  mother of.. 9. Mnemosyne
  mountain.. 6. Pierus 7. Helicon
   9. Parnassus

number.. 4. nine
sacred place.. 5. Aonia (Boeotia)
spring.. 7. Pierian
The Muses (Gr).. 8. Pierides
musette... 3. air, bag 4. oboe
    7. bagpipe, gavotte
museum... 6. Louvre 7. gallery
    8. Ptolemy I 10. Pinakothek
    11. glyptotheca, pinakotheke
    14. Madame Tussaud's
museum keeper.. 7. curator
    9. custodian
mush... 3. cut 4. call, face, pulp
    5. atole, march (over snow), notch
    6. cereal, indent, sepawn 8. flattery,
    umbrella 12. hasty pudding
    14. sentimentality
mushroom... 5. morel, plant 6. agaric,
    anchor, fungus 7. parvenu, upstart
    8. umbrella 11. beaver brown
mushroom (pert to)...
   disease.. 5. flock
   edible.. 5. morel 11. chanterelle
   poisoning.. 8. mycetism
   poisonous.. 7. amanita 9. toadstool
   stem.. 5. stipe
   umbrella top.. 6. pileus
music (pert to)...
   abridgment.. 7. ridotto
   accompaniment.. 9. obbligato
   aftersong.. 5. epode
   all voices.. 5. tutti
   as written.. 3. sta
   chapel.. 9. a cappella
   character.. 3. bar, key 4. clef, rest,
     slur 5. cleft, neume, segno
   chord.. 8. arpeggio
   clear-cut.. 8. staccato
   closing measure.. 4. coda
   comic.. 6. bouffe
   do.. 2. ut
   drama.. 5. opera
   duet.. 3. duo
   encore.. 3. bis
   flourish.. 7. cadenza
   half note.. 5. minim
   half tone.. 8. semitone
   impassioned, emotional..
     12. appassionato
   interlude.. 6. verset
   interval.. 6. octave 7. tritone
   introduction.. 7. prelude
   it proceeds.. 2. va
   knowledge.. 10. musicology
   lead cue.. 5. presa
   left-handed.. 8. sinistra
   light notes.. 6. ottava
   low pitch.. 5. grave
   lutelike.. 10. hurdy-gurdy
   major.. 3. dur
   major third.. 6. ditone
   melodious.. 6. arioso
   melody.. 5. melos
   nine-piece composition.. 5. nonet
   one performer (choral).. 4. soli
   opera (comic).. 6. bouffe
   organization.. 4. band 5. Ascap, choir
     6. chorus 8. symphony 9. orchestra
   organ stop.. 6. dulcet, tromba
     7. celesta
   performance.. 7. recital
   phrase.. 9. leitmotiv (leitmotif)

pick.. 8. plectrum
pitch C.. 2. du
pompous.. 7. orotund
refrain.. 5. epode 8. repetend
repetition.. 5. rondo
scale.. 5. gamut
sestet.. 7. sestuor
sextuplet.. 7. sestole (sestolet)
soprano part.. 5. canto
speaking part.. 8. parlando
study.. 5. étude
tenor part.. 5. canto (original)
theme.. 4. tema
third.. 6. tierce
three-chord note.. 5. triad
thrice.. 3. ter
time.. 4. temp 6. giusto
timing device.. 9. metronome
twice.. 3. bis
variations, set of.. 7. partita
whimsical.. 8. bizzarro 9. capriccio
musical direction (pert to)...
   accented.. 8. sforzato 9. sforzando
   bold.. 6. audace
   brisk.. 5. tanto 9. animato
   detached.. 8. spiccato, staccato
   dying away.. 7. calendo
   emphatic.. 7. marcato
   evenly.. 10. egualmente
   fantastic.. 11. carpiccioso
   fast.. 4. vivo 5. tosto 6. presto,
     vivace 10. tostamente
   faster.. 7. stretto
   fluctuating.. 6. rubato
   gay.. 7. giocoso 10. brilliante
   gentle.. 5. dolce
   half.. 5. mezzo
   held firmly.. 6. tenuto
   high.. 3. alt
   hurried.. 7. agitato
   less.. 4. meno
   let it stand.. 3. sta
   lightly.. 10. con agilita
   little by little.. 9. poco a poco
   lively.. 6. vivace 7. allegro, animato
   loud.. 5. forte 10. fortissimo
   louder.. 9. crescendo
   lutelike.. 10. hurdy-gurdy
   more rapid.. 7. stretto (stretta)
   movement (with).. 7. con moto
   muted.. 5. sorda, sordo
   narrating.. 8. narrante
   one by one.. 7. uno a uno
   quick.. 6. presto
   quickening.. 11. affrettando
   quicker than.. 7. andante 9. andantino
   repeat.. 3. bis 5. da capo 7. ripresa
   sadly.. 7. dolente 8. doloroso
   shake.. 5. trill
   silent.. 5. tacet
   sliding.. 9. glissando
   slow.. 5. largo, lento, molto, tardo
     6. adagio 7. andante
   slow (very).. 5. molto
   slowing.. 9. allentato 10. ritardando
     11. rallentando
   smooth.. 6. legato
   soft.. 5. dolce, piano
   softer.. 10. diminuendo
   spirited.. 7. con moto
   strict tempo.. 6. giusto
   sustained.. 6. tenuto 9. sustenuto

tenderly.. **10.** affettuoso, con affetto
turn.. **5.** verte **9.** gruppetto
vivacious.. **7.** con brio
musical form... **3.** jig, ode **4.** aria,
jazz, olio, opus, song **5.** derry, dirge,
elegy, fugue, melos, motet, opera
6. arioso, ballad, medley, melody,
minuet, sonata **7.** ragtime, toccata
8. carillon (bells), hornpipe, operetta,
oratorio, serenade, symphony
9. barcarole, interlude, polonaise
11. rock and roll **12.** boogie woogie
musical instruments... **3.** sax **4.** asor,
drum, fife, harp, horn, lute, lyre,
oboe, pipe, reed, tuba, viol **5.** banjo,
bugle, cello, flute, organ, piano,
rebec (rebeck), rocta, tabor, viola
6. atabal, cither, citole, cornet,
fiddle, guitar, spinet, tabret, violin,
zither **7.** althorn, bagpipe, bandore,
bassoon, celesta, clarion, clavier,
gittern, helicon, marimba, musette,
ocarina, pandora, theorbo, trumpet,
ukulele **8.** castanet, clarinet,
dulcimer, mandolin, trombone
9. flageolet, saxophone
10. concertina, sousaphone (tuba),
tambourine **11.** harpsichord,
violoncello
musical instruments (foreign)...
Africa.. **5.** nanga **7.** sistrum
China.. **3.** kin
E Indies.. **4.** bina
Egypt.. **7.** sistrum
Greece.. **7.** cithara (anc)
Hindu.. **4.** vina (anc)
India.. **5.** ruana
Italy.. **6.** tromba
Java.. **8.** gamelang (gamelan)
Mexico.. **6.** clarin **7.** maracas
Spain.. **6.** atabal **9.** castanets
musician... **4.** bard **5.** piper
6. hepcat, lyrist, singer **7.** chorist,
crooner, drummer, fiddler, flutist,
pianist, yodeler **8.** bandsman,
composer, minstrel, organist
9. conductor, serenader, troubador,
violinist **10.** prima donna, trombonist
11. clarinetist, minnesinger,
saxophonist **12.** interlocutor
13. Kapellmeister
musicians' group... **4.** band, duet, trio
5. nonet **6.** septet, sextet
7. nonetto, quartet **8.** ensemble,
septette, sextette, symphony
9. orchestra, quartette
musicians' patron saint... **7.** Cecelia
musk... **4.** deer **7.** perfume
musk (pert to)...
beaver.. **7.** muskrat
cat.. **5.** civet
cattle.. **4.** oxen
cucumber.. **11.** cassabanana
deer.. **10.** chevrotain
duck.. **7.** Muscovy
hog.. **7.** peccary
melon.. **10.** cantaloupe
okra.. **8.** abelmosk
shrew.. **6.** desman
weasel.. **5.** civet
muskellunge... **4.** fish, pike
musket... **4.** hawk **5.** rifle **7.** firearm

9. flintlock
Musketeers, Three... **5.** Athos
6. Aramis **7.** Porthos **9.** D'Artagnan
muskmelon... **6.** atimon, casaba
10. cantaloupe
muskrat... **5.** shrew **6.** desman
7. ondatra
muslin... **3.** ban, cap **4.** mull **5.** doria
(dorea), shela **6.** canvas, gurrah
7. organdy **8.** nainsook, sheeting,
tarlatan **9.** womanhood **10.** femininity
muss... **4.** mess, soil **5.** chaos, dirty
6. bitter, muddle, rumple, tousle
7. confuse, wrinkle **8.** dishevel,
scramble, squabble **10.** disarrange
mussel... **4.** food, naid, unio **5.** horse,
naiad **6.** byssus, mucket, nerita
7. mollusk, Mytilus
Musselman... **6.** Moslem **7.** Saracen
10. Mohammedan
must... **4.** mold, musk, sapa, stum
5. juice, ought, shall **6.** blight,
mildew, refuse **7.** malodor
9. necessity **10.** obligation
mustang... **5.** horse, pinto **6.** bronco,
sphinx
mustard... **5.** nigra, senvy **7.** sinapis
8. charlock
mustard (pert to)...
chemistry.. **8.** sinapine
gas.. **7.** yperite
genus.. **7.** Sinapis **8.** Brassica
plaster.. **8.** sinapism
mustee... **8.** octaroon **9.** half–breed
Mustelidae... **5.** minks **7.** badgers,
martens, weasels
muster... **4.** levy **5.** erect **6.** gather,
summon **7.** collect, marshal
8. assemble, comprise
10. assemblage
muster out... **7.** disband
musty... **3.** bad, old **4.** damp, hoar,
rank **5.** fetid, fusty, moist, moldy,
rafty, stale, trite **6.** rancid
7. pungent
mutable... **6.** fickle **7.** erratic
8. variable **9.** alterable, changeful
11. vacillating
mute... **3.** mum **4.** dumb, lene, surd
6. muffle, silent **8.** deadener,
silencer, taciturn **9.** voiceless
10. speechless
mutilate... **3.** mar **4.** geld, hack, maim
6. deface, deform, garble, injure,
mangle **7.** cripple, destroy
8. castrate, demolish **9.** dismember,
tear apart
mutinous... **6.** unruly **9.** seditious,
turbulent **10.** rebellious, refractory
11. intractable
mutiny... **6.** Putsch (Swiss), revolt,
strife, tumult **9.** commotion, rebellion
12. insurrection **15.** insubordination
mutter... **5.** growl **6.** murmur, patter,
plaint **7.** grumble, maunder
8. complain **9.** mussitate
mutton... **4.** meat **5.** cabob (kabob),
gigot, sheep **8.** candle
muttonfish... **4.** sama **5.** pargo
7. abalone, eelpout, mojarra, snapper
mutton–legger... **4.** sail
mutual... **4.** plan **5.** joint **6.** common

8. intimate 9. symbiotic
10. reciprocal, responsive
15. interchangeable

mutual understanding... 9. agreement, unanimity 12. consentience, co-ordination 13. interrelation 17. interrelationship

mux... 4. mess 5. batch

muy... 4. very 7. greatly

muzhik, muzjik... 7. peasant

muzzle... 3. gag 4. cope, maul, nose 5. mouth, snout 6. clevis, thrash 7. shackle, sheathe, silence 8. restrain 10. respirator

my... 3. mes, mon 4. mine 7. due to me 11. exclamation

myall... 4. wild, wood (fragrant) 6. acacia 11. uncivilized

mycoderma... 5. fungi 6. mother (formed on wine) 8. membrane (ferment)

mycophagy... 11. eating fungi 15. eating mushrooms

myna, mynah... 4. bird 7. grackle 8. starling

Mynheer... 8. Dutchman

myo (comb form)... 6. muscle

myomancy, divination by... 14. muscle movement

myopic... 11. nearsighted

myriad... 11. innumerable, ten thousand 13. multitudinous

myriapod... 9. centipede

myrmicid... 3. ant

myrtle... 8. ramarama 10. periwinkle 11. candleberry

mysterious... 4. dark 6. arcane, mystic, occult, secret 7. cryptic 8. abstruse, esoteric 9. recondite, sphinxian 10. cabalistic 12. inexplicable, unfathomable

mystery... 4. cult, rune 6. arcane, cabala, enigma, puzzle, secret 7. arcanum, esotery, miracle 8. whodunit 9. sacrament 13. inexplainable 16. incomprehensibility

mystic... 4. seer, yogi 5. magic, runic 6. occult, orphic, secret 7. cryptic,

Mahatma 8. cabalist, esoteric, symbolic 9. enigmatic, recondite 10. cabalistic, mysterious

mystic (pert to)...
cry.. 4. evoe
doctrine.. 5. cabal 7. esotery 8. esoteric
initiate.. 5. epopt (Gr Antiq)
ocean isle.. 6. Avalon
theosophy.. 6. cabala
word.. 2. om 7. abraxas 11. abracadabra

mystical... 6. muddle, puzzle 7. confuse, cryptic, furtive, obscure 9. enigmatic, obfuscate

mystical (pert to)...
character (Teut Myth).. 8. Eckehart
meaning.. 7. anagoge
word.. 11. abracadabra

mystify... 5. befog 6. muddle, puzzle 7. becloud, confuse, perplex 8. befuddle, bewilder 9. bamboozle, obfuscate

myth... 4. tale 5. fable, fancy, story 6. legend 7. figment, parable 9. apocrypha, falsehood

mythical... 7. fancied 8. fabulous 9. fictional, imaginary, legendary 10. fictitious 12. mythological

mythical (pert to)...
being.. 6. Garuda, Icarus 7. centaur, griffin
bird.. 3. roc
deity.. 6. Moloch (tyrant)
demon.. 4. Rahu (tail called Kehu)
hero.. 4. Ajax 8. Achilles
heroine.. 4. Leda 6. Europa 8. Atalanta
hunter.. 5. Orion
island.. 8. Atlantis
king (Hind).. 4. Nala
monster.. 4. ogre 7. chimera
mother.. 5. Niobe
river.. 4. Styx
serpent.. 5. Apepi
winged creature.. 7. Alborak
woman.. 6. Gorgon, Medusa, Stheno 7. Euryale

mythogony, science of... 5. myths

mythologist... 9. mythmaker

N

N... 2. en, Nu 8. nitrogen (symbol)

nab... 4. grab 5. catch, seize 6. arrest, nibble, snatch 7. capture 9. apprehend

Nabal's wife (Bib)... 7. Abigail

nabob... 5. nawab 6. bigwig, tycoon 7. viceroy 8. governor 9. plutocrat 10. viceregent

nacelle... 4. boat 7. shelter

nacket... 3. boy 4. cake 5. lunch

6. caddie 8. saucy boy

nacre... 9. shellfish 10. conchiolin 13. mother-of-pearl

Nadab (Bib)... 12. King of Israel

nadir... 4. pole 11. lowest point (opp zenith)

nag... 4. pony, twit 5. annoy, cobra, horse, scold, snake, tease 6. heckle, hector, peck on, pester, plague 7. henpeck 8. harangue

nagor... 8. antelope, reedbuck
nahoor... 5. sheep 6. bharal
naiad... 5. nymph 6. mussel, Nereid
   7. limniad, Oceanid
nail... 3. cut, hob 4. brad, claw, spad,
   stud, tack, wire 5. clout, spike,
   sprig, talon 6. fasten, secure, unguis,
   ungula 7. capture, measure
   8. sparable 9. finishing, intercept
   12. upholstering
nail (pert to)...
   headless.. 5. sprig
   ingrowing.. 7. acronyx
   marking, fingernail.. 6. lunule
   size.. 8. tenpenny
   slanted.. 4. toed
naissance... 5. birth 6. origin
naive... 5. frank 6. simple 7. artless,
   ingenue 8. childish, gullible, untaught
   9. guileless, ingenuous, unworldly
   10. simplicity 13. unphilosophic
   15. unsophisticated
naked... 4. bald, bare, mere, nude,
   open 5. clear, plain 6. barren,
   meager 7. exposed, literal, obvious
   8. manifest, stripped 9. unadorned,
   uncovered 11. defenseless,
   unprotected, unsupported
nakoo... 6. gavial 9. crocodile
namaycush... 5. togue, trout
namby–pamby... 5. inane, silly, vapid
   7. insipid 10. wishy–washy
   15. sentimental
name... 3. dub, nom 4. call, cite,
   term 5. clepe, nomen, style, title
   6. y–clepe 7. appoint, entitle,
   mention 8. cognomen, identify
   9. celebrity, enumerate, personage
   10. denominate, reputation
   11. appellation, designation
   12. denomination
name (pert to)...
   added.. 7. agnomen
   assumed.. 3. pen 5. alias 7. John
   Doe 9. incognito, pseudonym,
   sobriquet 10. nom de plume
   bad.. 7. caconym
   binomial.. 7. teutonym
   by location.. 7. toponym
   derivation.. 7. eponymy
   family (father's).. 7. eponymy
   9. patronymy
   fictitious.. 9. pseudonym
   first.. 9. baptismal, Christian,
   praenomen
   Japanese.. 4. maru
   known.. 9. onomatous
   nickname.. 7. moniker (monicker)
   8. cognomen
   nominate.. 9. designate
   secret.. 9. cryptonym
   spelled backwards (real name)..
   6. ananym
   surname.. 7. eponymy
   technical.. 4. onym
   unknown.. 9. anonymous
   wrong.. 8. misnomer
name as agent... 6. depute
named... 5. cited 6. called, y–clept
   (y–cleped)
named for a god... 10. theophorous

nameless... 7. bastard, obscure 8. not
   known 9. aforesaid, anonymous,
   unnamable 10. unrenowned
   12. illegitimate 13. indescribable,
   inexpressible 15. undistinguished
namelessness... 9. anonymity
namely... 5. to wit 9. expressly,
   nominally, videlicet (viz)
names, divination by... 8. onomancy
names, science of... 11. onomatology
namesake... 6. eponym 7. homonym
nanga... 7. harp
nanism... 12. dwarfishness (opp of
   gigantism)
Nanking...
   capital.. 5. China (1932–1937)
   color.. 12. Naples yellow
   province.. 7. Kiangsu
   river site.. 7. Yangtze
nanoid... 8. dwarfish
nanpie... 6. magpie
naos... 5. cella 6. shrine, temple
Naos... 4. star
nap... 3. nod 4. doze, pile, shag, wink
   5. fluff, grasp, seize, sleep, steal
   6. duffel, siesta, snooze
nape... 5. nucha, nuque, scrag
   6. scruff, turnip 7. niddick
   9. auchenium
napellus... 9. monkshood
napery... 5. linen (table)
napiform... 12. turnip–shaped
napkin... 5. doily, towel 6. diaper
   8. kerchief 9. serviette
   11. neckerchief
Naples...
   biscuit.. 10. ladyfinger
   famed building.. 9. Cathedral (Gothic,
   1272)
   red.. 5. ochre 6. Indian
   site.. 11. Bay of Naples
napoleon... 4. game 6. pastry 7. top
   boot 11. reddish–blue, sweet cherry
   13. crimson clover
Napoleon I (pert to)...
   birthplace.. 7. Ajaccio (Corsica)
   brother–in–law.. 5. Murat
   death site.. 8. St Helena
   exiled to.. 4. Elba
   father.. 7. Charles
   island.. 5. Capri
   marshal.. 3. Ney (executed)
   title.. 7. Emperor (of France)
   warfare site.. 5. Ligny, Malta
   7. Marengo 8. Waterloo
   10. Alexandria
napped (short)... 3. ras
nappy... 3. ale 4. dish 5. downy,
   heady, wooly 6. liquor, shaggy,
   sleepy 7. foaming 10. inebriated
napu... 10. chevrotain
Naraka (Hind)... 4. hell
Narcissus (Gr)... 6. egoist 14. beautiful
   youth
narcosis... 5. sleep 10. drowsiness
narcotic... 4. dope, drug, hemp, junk
   5. bhang (bang), ether, opium
   6. heroin 7. anodyne, cocaine,
   hashish 8. hypnotic, mandrake,
   morphine 9. soporific 10. belladonna,
   hyoscyamus, stramonium
narcotic (pert to)...

dose.. 3. fix 5. locus
package.. 6. bindle
seller.. 6. pusher 7. peddler
user (group).. 6. love–in 9. snow
party
nard... 6. anoint 8. matgrass,
ointment, rhizomes
nardoo, nardu... 6. clover
nares... 8. nostrils
narghile, nargile, nargileh... 4. pipe
6. hookah
nargil... 7. coconut
nark... 3. spy 5. annoy 8. informer
11. stool pigeon
Narragansett... 3. Bay 5. horse
6. Indian, turkey
narrate... 4. tell 6. detail, recite, relate
7. recount 8. describe
narration... 4. tale 5. drama (acted),
story 6. detail 7. account, recital
8. relation 9. discourse, narrative,
rehearsal
narrative... 4. epic, epos, myth, poem,
saga, tale 5. conte, drama, fable,
story 6. legend 7. account, episode,
history, parable 8. allegory, anecdote
9. narration, statement
narrator... 9. raconteur 11. storyteller
narrow... 4. mean, poor 5. inlet,
scant, taper 6. linear, strait
7. closely, slender 8. strictly
9. confining, illiberal, niggardly
10. restricted, straighten
11. reactionary 12. parsimonious
13. circumscribed
narrow (pert to)...
comb form.. 4. sten 5. steno
leather strip.. 5. thong
minded.. 6. petty 7. biased
7. bigoted 10. intolerant, prejudiced
opening.. 4. rima, slot 9. stenopaic
souled.. 10. ungenerous
narrowly incised... 9. laciniate
narrows... 5. sound 6. strait
narthex... 7. portico 9. asafetida
(asafoetida)
narwhal, narwal... 5. whale
8. cetacean
nasab (Moham Law)... 7. kinship
13. consanguinity
nasal... 4. nose 5. sound 6. narine,
rhinal, twangy 11. inspiratory
nascency... 5. birth 6. origin
7. genesis 8. beginning
naseberry... 9. sapodilla
Nasi... 6. prince 8. Gamaliel
9. patriarch
Nasicornia... 7. rhinoceros
nasology... 9. nose study
Nassau..
capital.. 7. Bahamas
hamlet.. 7. grouper
sports.. 4. golf
nastika... 7. atheist
nasty... 4. foul, mean 5. dirty 6. filthy,
odious 7. obscene 8. indecent,
unsavory 9. offensive
12. disagreeable, dishonorable
Nasua... 5. coati 6. coatis
nasute... 10. large–nosed
nasutiform... 8. noselike
natal... 6. inborn, native 7. gluteal,

nascent 9. from birth
Natal... 7. seaport (Braz) 8. Province
(S Afr)
natator... 7. swimmer
natatorium... 4. pool 6. plunge
12. swimming hole
natchbone... 9. aitchbone
Natchez... 4. city (La) 6. Indian
nation... 4. host, race 5. caste, class,
state 6. people, polity 7. country
9. community, multitude
national... 4. blue 6. racial 7. citizen,
federal
nationality... 4. race 6. nation
8. nativity 9. statehood
11. nationalism
national salute... 13. Twenty–one
guns
native... 3. ite, son 5. natal 6. innate,
normal, simple 7. genuine, natural,
primary 8. inherent, original, primeval
9. unbranded 10. aboriginal,
indigenous, unaffected 11. not
acquired
native (pert to)...
agent.. 9. comprador (compradore)
bear.. 5. koala
cat.. 7. dasyure
dog.. 5. dingo
Indian.. 4. Arab
juniper.. 9. blueberry
Madagascan.. 4. Hova
naturalized person.. 7. denizen
plant, animal.. 8. indigene
salt.. 6. halite
nativity... 5. birth 9. beginning,
horoscope, sculpture
Nativity, The.. 8. festival
9. Christmas 13. birth of Christ
natterjack... 4. toad
natty... 4. chic, neat, tidy, trim
6. spruce 10. fastidious
Natty Bumppo's alias... 7. Hawkeye
15. Leatherstocking
natural... 3. raw 4. born 5. flesh,
usual 6. common, cretin, expert,
inborn, inbred, innate, normal
7. genuine, regular, typical
8. informal, inherent, lifelike, ordinary
9. character (Mus), dice throw,
unassumed, unfeigned 10. unaffected
10. artificial
natural (pert to)...
capacity.. 9. endowment
condition.. 4. norm
group.. 4. race 6. ethnic, family
location, position.. 4. site 5. situs
not (natural).. 5. alien 8. acquired
10. artificial
philosophy.. 7. physics
science.. 10. physiology
voice (Mus).. 7. dipetto
naturalist... 4. Muir (John) 7. animist,
Burbank (Luther) 9. biologist, scientist
11. taxidermist
naturalize... 5. adapt 8. accustom
9. acclimate 11. domesticate,
familiarize
nature... 4. kind, self, sort, soul, type
6. cosmos 7. essence 8. tendency,
universe 11. naturalness,
temperament 14. characteristic
nature (pert to)...

concealed.. 7. latency
divinity of.. 5. dryad, naiad, nymph
god.. 3. Pan
goddess.. 6. Cybele 7. Artemis
in the raw.. 6. nudity
of the case.. 9. ipso facto
worship.. 11. physiolatry
natus... 4. born
nausea... 4. pall 5. qualm 8. loathing,
   mal de mer 10. queasiness
   11. seasickness
nauseous... 7. fulsome, mawkish
   9. loathsome, offensive, sickening,
   squeamish 10. disgusting
nautical... 5. naval 6. marine
   7. oceanic 8. maritime
nautical (pert to)...
almanac.. 9. ephemeris
direction.. 5. avast, belay
hail.. 4. ahoy
instrument.. 3. aba 7. compass,
   pelorus, sextant
measure.. 3. ton 4. knot 6. fathom
   7. sea mile
nautilus... 7. mollusk 8. argonaut
   9. submarine 10. diving bell
Navaho, Navajo... 5. hogan 6. Indian
   7. blanket 9. red–yellow
naval... 6. marine 8. nautical
naval (pert to)...
brigade.. 7. militia
commander.. 7. navarch
depot.. 4. base
device.. 6. dolter
officer.. 5. bosun 6. ensign, yeoman
   7. admiral, captain 9. boatswain
   (bosun), commander 10. lieutenant
nave... 3. hob, hub, nef 4. apse, fist
   5. nieve 7. apsidal
navel... 6. middle, orange 8. omphalos
   9. umbilicus 10. depression
navigate... 4. keel, sail 7. avigate
   11. ship science
navigator... 5. navvy 12. third
   command (or 4th)
navy (fleet)... 7. tankers 8. cruisers,
   flattops, gunboats 10. destroyers,
   submarines 11. battleships 12. mine
   sweepers 13. hospital ships
   16. aircraft carriers
navy (pert to)...
bean.. 6. kidney
coffee.. 3. mud
color.. 4. blue 10. marine blue
drinking fountain.. 11. scuttlebutt
fleet.. 6. armada 13. combat vessels
plug.. 7. tobacco
ships, collectively.. 5. fleet 6. armada
song.. 13. Anchors Aweigh
training camp.. 8. boot camp
underwear.. 8. skivvies
nawab, nabob... 5. ruler, title
   7. viceroy
nay... 2. no 4. deny 5. flute, never
   6. denial, naysay, refuse 7. refusal
   8. negative 11. prohibition
nayaur... 5. sheep
nayword... 6. byword 7. proverb (of
   reproach) 9. watchword
Nazarene (pert to)...
artist.. 8. Overbeck (of Rome)
disciple.. 9. Christian

native.. 11. Jesus Christ
native of.. 8. Nazareth
Nazi... 9. Hitlerite
Nazi emblem... 6. fylfot 8. swastika
nchega... 6. monkey 10. chimpanzee
neanic... 8. immature, youthful
neap... 4. tide 6. tongue (vehicle)
   7. low tide 8. low water
Neapolitan (pert to)...
dance.. 10. tarantella
fever.. 8. undulent
Italian.. 6. Naples
medlar.. 5. fruit 7. azarole
music.. 5. chord (6th)
ointment.. 6. mercurial
yellow.. 6. Naples
near... 2. at 4. nigh 5. about, close,
   handy 6. around, within 7. closely,
   related 8. adjacent, approach,
   imminent, intimate 11. approximate
   13. propinquitous
nearby, near–by... 3. gin 4. nigh
   5. anent, handy 6. beside, nearly
   7. close by, close to, vicinal
   8. adjacent 9. adjoining
   10. convenient
Nearctic... 9. Greenland, Holarctic
   11. Palaearctic 13. Arctic America
Near East... 7. Balkans 12. Balkan
   States
Near East valley... 4. wadi (wady)
   5. oasis 6. ravine
nearest... 4. next 7. closest
   9. proximate
nearly... 5. about 6. almost 7. closely
   8. narrowly 10. similarity
   13. approximately
nearness... 8. affinity, intimacy,
   likeness, relation 9. closeness
   11. propinquity
near of kin... 7. germane
nearsighted... 6. myopic 8. purblind
   12. narrow–minded, shortsighted,
   undiscerning
neat... 3. pat 4. prim, smug, snod,
   tidy, trig, trim 5. natty 6. adroit,
   dapper, spruce 7. orderly, perjink,
   precise 9. shipshape 10. meticulous,
   perjinkety 12. spick–and–span
neatherd... 7. cowherd 8. herdsman
neathmost... 6. lowest
neb... 3. tip 4. beak, bill, face, kiss,
   nose 5. point, snout
Nebo, Nebu... 8. mountain (Bib)
   11. god of wisdom
Nebraska...
capital.. 7. Lincoln
city.. 5. Omaha 8. Hastings
   11. Scottsbluff
Indian.. 4. Otoe 5. Omaha 6. Pawnee
meaning.. 11. water valley
railroad (1865).. 12. Union Pacific
river.. 6. Nemaha, Platte 8. Missouri
State admission.. 13. Thirty–seventh
State motto.. 20. Equality Before the
   Law
State nickname.. 4. Beef
   10. Cornhusker
nebula... 3. sky 4. mist 5. cloud,
   vapor 10. atmosphere
Nebula of... 4. Lyra 5. Orion
   9. Andromeda

nebulous... 4. hazy 5. misty, vague
6. cloudy 7. clouded, nebular
8. nebulose

nebulous envelope... 4. coma
9. chevelure

necessarily... 8. perforce
11. unavoidably 12. consequently
13. indispensably

necessary... 5. vital 7. needful
9. essential, mandatory, requisite
11. requirement, unavoidable
13. indispensable

necessitate... 5. force, impel
6. compel, entail, oblige 7. require
9. constrain

necessity... 4. food, need, want
5. drink 7. aliment, poverty, urgency
9. neediness 10. constraint
14. inevitableness

neck... 4. hals (halse) 5. crane, scrag,
swire 6. cervix, fondle, strait
7. channel, embrace, isthmus

neck (pert to)...
armor.. 6. gorget 8. gorgerin
artery.. 7. carotid
back of.. 4. nape 5. nucha, nuque
6. scruff
frill.. 5. jabot, ruche 6. wimple
land.. 6. strake 9. peninsula
muscle.. 8. scalenus
pendant.. 6. locket 9. lavaliere
piece.. 3. boa 5. amice, rabat, scarf,
stole 6. collar
water.. 6. strait
zoology.. 4. gula 6. wattle 7. withers

neckcloth... 6. cravat 7. muffler
9. barcelona 11. neckerchief

neckerchief... 7. belcher 8. kerchief
12. handkerchief

necklace... 5. beads 6. torque
7. baldric, chaplet, rivière
11. shark's-teeth

neckpiece... 3. boa 5. ascot, rabat,
scarf, stole 6. collar 8. kerchief

necktie... 3. tie 4. band 5. ascot,
scarf 6. cravat 10. four-in-hand

necrology... 9. death roll 13. death
register 14. obituary notice

necromancy... 5. goety, magic
7. sorcery 9. sortilege
11. conjuration, enchantment

necropolis... 8. cemetery

necropsy... 7. autopsy
10. post-mortem

nectar... 3. red 5. drink, honey
8. beverage

nectar of the gods... 8. ambrosia

neddy... 6. donkey 13. life preserver

need... 4. lack, poor, thar, want
7. poverty, require, urgency
8. exigency 9. extremity, necessity
10. compulsion, deficiency
11. requirement

needle... 3. sew 4. acus, goad, sail
5. tease, thorn 6. bodkin, pierce
7. darning, obelisk 9. astatizer
10. upholstery

needle (pert to)...
bath.. 3. jet 9. sprinkler
bird.. 9. phalarope 10. needlebill
bug.. 4. Nepa 7. Ranatra
case.. 4. etui (etwee)
fish.. 3. gar 8. pipefish
gun.. 11. Dreyse rifle
kind.. 5. blunt, sharp 7. between,
crochet, darning 8. knitting
long-eyed.. 10. embroidery
medical.. 10. hypodermic
needlelike body.. 7. spicule
needlework.. 7. crochet, sampler
8. knitting 10. embroidery
record.. 10. phonograph
shaped.. 6. acuate 7. acerose
8. acicular
under the skin.. 5. seton

needy... 4. poor 7. almoner
8. indigent 9. necessary, penniless,
requisite 10. distressed

neel-bhunder... 8. wanderoo 10. blue
monkey

neep... 6. turnip

ne'er-do-well... 5. idler 6. wretch
8. poltroon 9. schlemiel
14. good-for-nothing

nef... 4. nave 5. clock (ship-shaped)

nefarious... 6. wicked 7. heinous,
impious 8. horrible, infamous, terrible
9. atrocious 10. detestable,
iniquitous, villainous

nefas... 6. sinful

negate... 4. deny 6. refuse, refute
7. nullify 8. disprove 10. counteract

negative... 2. ir, ne, no 3. nay, non,
nor, not 4. deny, film, veto 5. minus
6. refuse 7. neutral 8. disprove,
negation 9. privative
13. contradiction

negative (pert to)...
electrode, pole.. 7. cathode (kathode)
eyepiece.. 8. Campani's 9. Huygenian
ion.. 5. anion
sign.. 5. minus

neglect... 4. fail, omit, slip, snub
5. shirk, slight 7. failure
8. omission 9. disregard, negligent,
pretermit 11. inattention

negligee... 4. gown, robe 6. attire
8. peignoir

negligence... 7. laxness 9. oversight,
unconcern 10. remissness
11. inattention 12. carelessness,
inadvertence

negligent... 3. lax 4. lash 6. remiss,
supine 8. careless, heedless
10. neglectful 11. unconcerned

negotiate... 4. deal, pass 5. treat
6. manage, treaty 7. bargain,
mediate 8. transact

Negrito (pert to)...
African.. 4. Akka 5. Batwa, Pygmy
7. Bambute, Bushman
Dutch New Guinea.. 6. Tapiro
Indonesian.. 3. Ata 4. Aeta (Ita)
Malay.. 6. Semang

Negro (pert to)...
dance.. 4. juba
dish.. 9. jambalaya
Egyptian.. 6. Nubian
friend of.. 10. negrophile
magic (anc).. 6. voodoo
spiritual.. 8. Swing Low

neigh... 4. akin 5. whinny 7. whicker

neighborhood... 7. purlieu 8. environs,
vicinity 9. proximity 10. thereabout

neighborhood law... 5. venue
neither masculine nor feminine...
  6. neuter 7. sexless
neither right nor wrong...
  11. adiaphorous, indifferent
Nemesis... 7. avenger, goddess,
  penalty
nemoral... 6. sylvan 14. living in a
  grove
neology... 8. new words 9. neologism
  11. new doctrine 14. new
  expressions
neonatus... 7. new baby, newborn
neophobia *(fear of)*... 6. the new
neophyte... 4. tyro 6. novice
  7. convert 8. beginner 9. proselyte
  10. catechumen
neosology *(study of)*... 10. young birds
neoteric... 3. new 4. late 6. modern,
  recent
nep... 6. catnip
Nepal...
  aborigines.. 10. Mongolians
  capital.. 8. Katmandu
  district.. 7. Mustang
  mountain.. 7. Everest 9. Himalayas
  ruler.. 9. Maharajah
nepesh... 4. soul 10. animal soul
  12. divine breath
nephew... 6. neve 6. nepote
nephrite... 4. jade 7. mineral
  11. kidney stone
nephroid... 8. reniform
  12. kidney–shaped
nephros... 6. kidney
nepote... 6. nephew 8. grandson
nepotism... 9. patronage
  10. favoritism, preference
Neptune... 3. sea 5. ocean 6. sea
  god
Neptune *(pert to)*...
  Astron.. 6. planet (3rd largest)
  Celtic.. 3. Ler
  consort.. 7. Salacia
  emblem.. 7. trident
  Greek.. 8. Poseidon
  Roman.. 6. sea god
  son.. 6. Triton
  wife.. 6. Medusa
Nereid *(Gr)*... 8. sea nymph
Nero *(pert to)*...
  excesses.. 7. cruelty 13. burning of
    Rome (64 AD)
  mother.. 9. Agrippina
  Roman title.. 7. Emperor
  wife.. 6. Sabina 7. Octavia
nerve... 4. pulp 5. cheek, fiber, pluck,
  sinew 6. aplomb, energy, tendon,
  tissue 7. courage, nervure
  8. audacity, coolness, strength
  10. resolution
nerve *(pert to)*...
  action.. 9. neurergic
  cell.. 4. axon 6. neuron
  center.. 8. ganglion
  comb form.. 5. neuro
  fiber.. 5. motor 7. sensory
  8. afferent, efferent
  force.. 7. neurism
  gray matter.. 7. cinerea
  inflammation, medical.. 8. neuritis,

    neurosis 9. neurotomy
  10. neurectasy, neurolysis, neuropathy
  11. neurologist 13. tic douloureux
  network.. 4. rete 6. plexus
  of Wrisberg.. 6. facial
  operation.. 10. neurolysis
  passage.. 4. rete 5. hilum 8. ganglion
  ref to.. 6. neural, neuric 7. neuroid
    8. neurotic
  root.. 5. radix
  science.. 9. neurology
  sheath.. 9. medullary
  tissue.. 7. cinerea, neurine
    9. neuroglia
  tumor.. 6. glioma 7. neuroma
nerveless... 4. dead 5. inert
  9. foolhardy, powerless
  10. courageous
nervous... 5. tense, timid 6. neural,
  touchy 7. fearful, jittery 8. eloquent,
  neurotic, timorous 9. excitable,
  sensitive 10. high–strung
  12. apprehensive
nervous *(pert to)*...
  affliction.. 3. tic 6. ataxia, chorea
    7. aphasia 8. neurosis
  energy deficiency.. 7. aneuria
  seizure.. 4. amok (amuck)
  system, center.. 5. brain, spine
  system, description.. 11. neurography
  system, name.. 9. neuronymy
  system, science.. 9. neurology
  system, specialist.. 12. neuropathist,
    psychiatrist
  tissue tumor.. 11. neurocytoma
ness... 4. cape 8. headland
  10. promontory
nest... 3. bed, den, nye, web 4. inro
  5. abode, aerie, eyrie, group, haunt,
  nidus 6. cuddle, series (graduated)
  7. lodging, retreat 9. residence
  10. nidificate 13. breeding place
nest *(pert to)*...
  boxes.. 4. inro
  eagle's.. 5. aerie, eyrie (eyry)
  pheasant's.. 4. nide
  spider's.. 3. web
  squirrel's.. 4. dray (drey)
  swallow's.. 9. nidus avis
  to build.. 6. nidify
nestle... 3. pet 4. nest 6. cuddle,
  pettle, settle 7. protect, shelter,
  snuggle
nestling... 4. bird 5. child 9. fledgling,
  youngling
Nestor *(pert to)*...
  famed for.. 6. wisdom
  King of.. 5. Pylos
  known as.. 4. sage 7. adviser 8. The
    Elder 9. Patriarch
net... 3. gin, web 4. mesh, toil, trap,
  weir 5. clear, lacis, score, seine,
  snare, weave 6. profit 7. enclose,
  network, trammel 8. receipts
  9. reticulum
net *(pert to)*...
  fishing.. 4. fyke 5. seine, trawl
    7. trammel
  hair.. 5. snood
  lacemaking.. 5. lacis
  silk.. 5. tulle 6. maline
  winged (lacy).. 12. neuropteroid

Netherlands... see also *Dutch, Holland*
  capital.. 9 Amsterdam
  cheese.. 4. Edam
  city.. 5. Delft 7. Utrecht
    9. Eindhoven, Rotterdam
  gin.. 8. schnapps
  government.. 8. monarchy
  government seat.. 8. The Hague
  inhabitant.. 5. Dutch 7. Flemish
  lake.. 7. Haarlem
  legislative body.. 4. Raad
  low land.. 6. polder
  port.. 9. Rotterdam
  possession.. 7. Surinam (Dutch
    Guiana) 8. Antilles (W Ind)
  river.. 3. Eem 5. Meuse, Rhine
    6. Ijssel (Yssel), Kromme
  sea (inland).. 9. Wadden Sea, Zuider
    Zee 10. Ijssel Lake, Ijsselmeer
nettle... 3. vex 4. fret, herb, line,
    whip 5. anger, annoy, pique, rouse
    6. incite, Urtica 7. provoke 8. irritate
    10. Parietaria, Urticaceae
nettle (pert to)...
  bird.. 11. whitethroat
  geranium.. 6. coleus
  rash.. 6. hives, uredo 9. urticaria
  sea.. 5. cnida
network... 3. web 4. caul, fret, kell,
    lace, mesh, moke, rete 5. chain
    6. cobweb, plexus, reseau, sagene
    7. webwork
neume... 5. neuma 6. pneuma
neurad... 12. to neural side
neural... 6. dorsal, nerval 7. ventral
    9. posterial
neuralgia... 3. tic 4. pain 8. face
    ague 13. tic douloureux
neuter... 6. gender 7. neither, neutral,
    sexless 9. impartial
neutral... 7. antacid 8. mediocre,
    middling, negative, unbiased
    10. achromatic 11. indifferent,
    nonpartisan 12. noncombatant,
    noncommittal
neutral equilibrium... 7. astatic
neutralize... 5. annul 6. offset
    7. nullify, vitiate 9. frustrate
    10. counteract 11. countervail
    14. counterbalance
Nevada...
  capital.. 10. Carson City
  city.. 3. Ely 4. Elko 6. Sparks
    7. Boulder 8. Las Vegas
  lake.. 4. Mead 6. Mohave 7. Pyramid
  mine (famed).. 12. Comstock Lode
    (1859)
  mountain.. 7. Rockies, Wasatch
    13. Sierra Nevadas
  native Indian.. 6. Digger
  resort.. 4. Reno 8. Las Vegas (The
    Meadows) 9. Lake Tahoe
  State admission.. 11. Thirty-sixth
  State motto.. 16. All For Our Country
  State nickname.. 6. Silver
    9. Sagebrush
neve... 4. firn, snow 6. nephew
    7. glacier
nevel, nevell... 9. fisticuff
never... 4. nary 6. nowise 7. not ever
    8. at no time, not at all 9. by no

means, nevermore
nevertheless... 3. but, yet 5. still
    6. anyhow 7. however
    15. notwithstanding
nevus... 4. mark, mole 5. tumor
    7. blemish 9. birthmark
new... 3. neo (pref) 4. anew, late,
    nova (star) 5. fresh, novel 6. growth,
    modern, recent 8. neoteric, original,
    untested 9. recreated, renovated
    12. unaccustomed 13. inexperienced
New Brunswick...
  capital.. 11. Fredericton
  city.. 8. St John
  gulf.. 10. St Lawrence
new but yet old... 10. novantique
New England (pert to)...
  book.. 6. Primer
  explorer.. 13. Capt John Smith
  native.. 6. Yankee
  theology.. 9. Calvinism
Newfoundland...
  city.. 7. St John's 9. Grand Bank
  discoverer.. 9. John Cabot (1497)
  gulf.. 10. St Lawrence
New Guinea, Papua Island..
  capital.. 6. Rabaul
  hog (wild).. 4. bene
  island size (world).. 5. third
  native.. 6. Papuan
  parrot.. 4. lory
  port.. 4. Daru 7. Moresby
  region.. 10. Melanesian
  river.. 3. Fly
New Hampshire...
  capital.. 7. Concord
  city.. 6. Durham 7. Hanover
    8. Merrimac 10. Manchester,
    Portsmouth
  cog rail (first).. 12. Mt Washington
  lake.. 13. Winnipesaukee
  mountains.. 5. White
  Our Town.. 13. Grover's Corner
  park.. 13. Crawford Notch, Dixville
    Notch
  range.. 12. Presidential
  river.. 8. Merrimac 11. Connecticut
  sculpture.. 14. Great Stone Face
    (Profile Peak)
  State admission.. 5. Ninth
  State motto.. 13. Live Free or Die
  State nickname.. 7. Granite
New Jersey...
  capital.. 7. Trenton
  city.. 6. Camden, Newark 7. Raritan
    9. Montclair 12. Fort Monmouth,
    New Brunswick
  college.. 9. Princeton (1746)
  inventor.. 6. Edison
  naval air station.. 9. Lakehurst
  poet.. 11. Walt Whitman
  resort.. 7. Cape May 8. Wildwood
    9. Ocean City 10. Asbury Park
    12. Atlantic City
  river.. 7. Raritan
  State admission.. 5. Third
  State motto.. 20. Liberty and
    Prosperity
  State nickname.. 6. Garden
New Mexico...
  capital.. 7. Santa Fe
  city.. 4. Taos 7. Roswell

11. Albuquerque
Fort.. 5. Tejon
Indian Reservation.. 5. Acoma (Sky City) 11. Chaco Canyon
peak.. 7. Wheeler
river.. 4. Gila 5. Pecos 8. Canadian 9. Rio Grande
space center.. 6. Sandia 8. Holloman, Kirtland 9. Los Alamos 10. White Sands
State admission.. 12. Forty–seventh
State motto.. 12. Crescit Eundo 15. It Grows as It Goes
State nickname.. 17. Land of Enchantment
State wonder.. 15. Carlsbad Caverns
new moon festival... 8. neomenia
news... 5. flash, scoop 6. report 7. courier, evangel, tidings
news agency... 2. AP, UP 3. DNB 4. Tass 5. Aneta, Domei 7. Reuters 9. syndicate
newspaper (pert to)...
editor.. 7. reviser 8. redactor
file.. 6. morgue
flag.. 8. masthead
writer.. 8. reporter 9. columnist 10. newscaster 13. correspondent
news stand... 5. booth, kiosk, stall
new star... 4. nova
newt... 3. eft 6. lizard, triton 10. salamander
New Testament... 6. Gospel 8. Epistles 15. Pauline Epistles
new wine... 4. must
new word, usage... 7. neology 9. neologism, neoterism
New York...
borough.. 5. Bronx 6. Queens 8. Brooklyn, Richmond 9. Manhattan
buyer (for $24).. 11. Peter Minuit
capital.. 6. Albany
city.. 5. Utica 7. Buffalo, New York 8. Saratoga 9. Rochester 11. Schenectady 12. Poughkeepsie
college.. 7. Colgate, Cornell 8. Columbia 9. West Point
Falls.. 7. Niagara
monument.. 7. Obelisk 10. Grant's Tomb 15. Statue of Liberty
Indian.. 6. Oneida, Seneca 8. Iroquois
Irving's home.. 9. Tarrytown
island.. 6. Staten 9. Manhattan 10. Long Island
mountain.. 9. Catskills
name, old.. 12. New Amsterdam
nickname.. 6. Gotham
river.. 4. East 6. Harlem, Hudson
river channel.. 8. Hellgate
section (famed).. 16. Greenwich Village
State admission.. 8. Eleventh
State motto.. 9. Excelsior 10. Ever Upward
State nickname.. 6. Empire
New Yorker... 8. Dutchman 9. Gothamite 13. Knickerbocker
New Zealand...
capital.. 10. Wellington
city.. 7. Dunedin 8. Auckland, Hamilton 12. Christchurch
discoverer.. 6. Tasman

explorer.. 4. Cook (James)
location.. 12. South Pacific
native.. 5. Maori 10. Polynesian
peak.. 6. Mt Cook
sect.. 7. Ringatu
soldier.. 5. Anzac
tribe.. 3. Ati 5. Maori
volcano.. 7. Ruapehu
New Zealand (pert to)...
bird.. 3. kea, moa, poe 4. titi, weka 7. apteryx, boobook, wrybill, Xenicus
caterpillar.. 5. aweto
club, weapon.. 4. mere
mahogany.. 6. totara
mollusc.. 4. pipi
morepork.. 4. peho, ruru
myrtle.. 8. ramarama
palm.. 5. nikau
parrot.. 6. kakapo 9. owl parrot
pigeon.. 4. kuku
reptile.. 7. tuatara
white pine.. 5. kauri (kaury)
next... 4. then 5. aware, neist 7. closest, nearest, proximo 9. adjoining, immediate 10. contiguous, succeeding
next to... 6. almost, beside, nearly 8. adjacent
next to last syllable... 6. penult 11. penultimate
nexus... 3. tie 4. bond, link 5. group 6. series 10. connection 15. interconnection
Nez Percé... 6. Indian 11. pierced nose
niagara... 5. flood, grape (green)
Niagara Falls (pert to)...
cataract.. 8. American, Canadian 9. Horseshoe
division between.. 10. Bridal Veil, Goat Island
point of interest.. 14. Cave of the Winds
nib... 3. end 4. beak, bill 5. point (pen), prong 6. tongue
nibble... 3. eat, nab, nip 4. gnaw, peck 5. champ, munch 6. browse
Nicaragua...
capital.. 7. Managua
city.. 7. Granada
lake.. 7. Managua
mountain range.. 10. Cordillera
river.. 4. Coco, Tuma 7. San Juan
nice... 4. fine, good, kind, neat 6. dainty, proper, queasy, subtle, tickle 7. elegant, finical, genteel, prudish, refined 8. exacting, pleasant, pleasing, suitable 9. agreeable, squeamish 10. appetizing, delightful, fastidious, particular, scrupulous 11. considerate, punctilious, well–behaved 13. hypercritical 14. discriminating, discriminative
Nicene Creed... 10. Confession (325 AD)
nicety... 7. finesse, modesty 8. accuracy, delicacy 9. precision 11. preciseness 13. squeamishness 14. fastidiousness
niche... 4. apse, nook 5. space (recessed) 6. alcove, covert, recess 7. retreat, secrete 10. tabernacle

nick... 3. gap 4. dent, dint, slit
  5. notch, steal 7. swindle
  11. opportunely
nickel (pert to)...
  alloy.. 5. Invar
  bronze.. 11. cupranickel
  coin.. 13. five–cent piece
  color.. 4. gray 5. nimbus
  compound.. 8. argenton
  11. maillechort
  silver.. 6. German
  symbol.. 2. Ni
nickelodeon... 4. juke 7. jukebox,
  theater (5–cent)
nickname... 3. pun 6. agname,
  monica 7. misname, moniker
  (monicker) 8. cognomen, misapply
  10. soubriquet
nicknaming pun... 12. prosonomasia
nictate... 4. wink 7. twinkle
  9. nictitate
nid... 3. nod 10. bend and bob
nide... 4. nest 5. brood
nidge... 3. nig 5. shake 6. quiver
nidificant... 12. nestbuilding
nidology, science... 10. birds' nests
nidor... 5. aroma, scent
nidus... 4. nest 5. abode 7. nucleus
  13. breeding place
Nietzsche... 11. philosopher
nieve... 4. fist, hand
niffer... 7. bargain 8. exchange
niffy–naffy... 7. finical 8. trifling
Niflheim, Nifelheim (Norse Myth)...
  8. Universe (division of) 10. Nine
  Worlds
nifty... 5. smart 7. stylish 8. very
  good
Nigeria...
  capital.. 5. Lagos
  city.. 3. Ede 5. Ibadan
  export.. 5. cocoa
  tribe.. 4. Eboe 5. Benin
nigh... 2. at 3. nei 4. left, near
  5. about, anear, close 6. almost,
  direct, nearly 8. adjacent
  10. contiguous 11. neighboring
night... 4. nuit 5. death 7. evening
  8. darkness 9. adversity, nightfall
  11. concealment
night (pert to)...
  bird.. 5. potoo 8. nightjar
  9. nighthawk 10. goatsucker,
  nightchurr, owl swallow, shearwater
  11. nightingale
  blindness.. 10. nyctalopia
  cap.. 6. biggin
  club.. 7. cabaret
  goddess.. 3. Nox, Nyx
  jasmine.. 10. hursinghar
  Norse.. 4. Nott
  sight (only).. 11. hemeralopia
  wandering.. 11. noctivagant
nightfall, at... 6. sunset 9. acronical
  (achronal) (opp of cosmical)
nightingale... 6. thrush 8. philomel
  9. bed jacket
nightjar... 5. potoo 10. goatsucker
nightmare... 3. alp 4. Mara, ogre

  5. dream 7. incubus 9. cauchemar
  13. hallucination
nightshade... 5. morel (moril)
  7. henbane 10. belladonna
  11. bittersweet
nigrescent... 8. blackish
nihil... 7. nothing, no value
nihil debet... 13. he owes nothing
nihil ex nihilo... 18. nothing (comes)
  from nothing
Nihilist... 9. anarchist, Socialist
Nile (pert to)...
  bird.. 4. ibis 7. wryneck
  boat.. 5. baris 6. nuggar 8. dahabeah
  city.. 7. Rosetta
  color.. 3. boa 5. green
  dam.. 5. Aswan
  Falls.. 5. Ripon
  fish.. 5. bagre 8. mormyrid (sacred)
  god.. 4. Hapi
  headstream.. 6. Kagera
  houseboat.. 8. dahabeah
  island.. 4. Roda (Rhoda)
  star.. 6. Sirius 7. Dog Star
  waste.. 4. sudd
nilgai... 8. antelope
nimble... 4. deft, fast, flit, gleg, lish,
  spry 5. agile, alert, brisk, fleet,
  quick, smart, swift 6. active, adroit,
  clever, lively, prompt, volant
  9. sensitive
nimbose... 6. cloudy, stormy
  7. clouded 8. nebulous, nubilous,
  overcast
nimbus... 4. disk, halo 5. cloud, vapor
  6. fabric, gloria, nickel 7. aureole
  10. atmosphere
nimiety... 6. excess 10. redundancy
niminy–piminy... 7. mincing, refined
  10. effeminate
nimmer... 5. thief
Nimrod (Bib)... 5. ruler 6. hunter
  8. Cush's son
nimshi... 4. fool 7. half–wit 11. silly
  person
Nimshi's son (Bib)... 11. Jehoshaphat
nine (pert to)...
  angles.. 7. nonagon
  banded armadillo.. 4. peba
  based on.. 8. novenary
  Books of nine chapters.. 7. Enneads
  comb form.. 6. ennead
  composition for nine.. 5. nonet
  days' devotion.. 6. novena
  eyes.. 7. lamprey
  gems.. 7. Vikrama
  gods.. 9. Etruscans
  group.. 6. ennead, nonary 18. Ennead
  of Heliopolis
  headed monster.. 5. Hydra
  inches.. 4. span
  number.. 5. ennea, nueve
  pert to.. 8. enneadic
  players.. 8. baseball
  poetic.. 8. ninefold
Nineteenth amendment...
  14. Woman's Suffrage
Nineveh (Bib)...
  capital.. 7. Assyria
  famed for.. 11. excavations (1814)
Nine Worlds (Norse)... 3. Hel
  6. Asgard 7. Alfheim, Midgard

8. Niflheim, Vanaheim
10. Jotunnheim 12. Muspellsheim
13. Svartalfaheim

Nine Worthies... 5. David, Judas
6. Arthur, Caesar, Hector, Joshua
7. Godfrey 9. Alexander
11. Charlemagne

ninny... 4. dolt, fool 9. blockhead,
simpleton

ninth... 5. nones (day before Ides)
8. enneatic, ninefold
11. ennea–eteric (year)

Ninth of Ab (Jew)... 7. fast day

ninut... 6. magpie

Niobe (pert to)...
changed by Zeus to.. 5. stone
father.. 8. Tantalus
husband.. 12. King of Thebes

nip... 3. bit, cut, sip 4. bite, clip,
dram, peck 5. blast, cheat, check,
chill, clamp, draft, drink, hurry, pinch,
seize, sever, steal, thief 6. benumb,
blight, catnip, cut off, freeze, snatch,
tipple 7. shorten, squeeze
8. compress 10. pickpocket

nipa (pert to)...
drink.. 9. alcoholic
genus.. 4. palm
mat.. 6. thatch
palm.. 4. atap
palm sap.. 6. sugar 7. alcohol

nipcheese... 5. miser 6. purser

nipper... 3. boy, lad 4. claw, grab
5. biter, drink, miser, thief
6. cunner, mitten, urchin 7. gripper,
incisor, pincers 12. costermonger

nippers... 6. pliers 7. pincers 8. leg
irons, pince–nez 9. handcuffs
10. eyeglasses

nipple... 3. pap 4. teat 7. mamelon,
papilla 8. mammilla 10. projection
12. protuberance

nippy... 4. cold 5. brisk 6. active,
biting 7. nipping, pungent
8. grasping, vigorous

Nirvana... 4. rags 6. heaven
8. oblivion 12. emancipation

Nisan (Jew calendar)... 10. first month
(Mar–Apr)

nisi... 5. if not 6. unless

nissen... 6. goblin, kobold 7. brownie

nisus... 7. impulse 8. endeavor,
striving

nit... 3. egg 4. mite 8. parasite

nitency... 6. luster 10. brightness

niter, nitre... 6. natron 9. saltpeter
13. sodium nitrate 16. potassium
nitrate

nither... 5. blast 6. debase, shiver
7. oppress, tremble 9. humiliate

nithing (anc)... 6. coward 7. dastard,
niggard

nitid... 3. gay 6. bright 8. lustrous

nitric acid... 10. aqua fortis

nitrogen... 3. azo (comb form), gas
5. azote 7. element 10. atmosphere

nitrogen compound... 7. ammonia

nitroglycerin, nitroglycerine...
8. dynamite (1846) 9. explosive,
guncotton

nitrous oxide... 3. gas 10. anesthetic
11. laughing gas

niveau... 5. level

niveous... 5. snowy, white (shining)

nix... 2. no 5. no one 6. nobody,
sprite 7. nothing

Njorth, Njord (Norse)... 3. god
(fertility) 5. Vanir

Njorth's daughter... 5. Freya (Freyja)
7. goddess (love and beauty)

Njorth's son... 3. god (fertility, crops,
peace) 4. Frey

no... 3. naw, nay, nit 4. baal, dead,
gone, none 5. not so 6. denial,
no–gaki, not any 8. not at all

Noah (Bib) (pert to)...
boat.. 3. Ark
dove.. 7. Columba
father.. 6. Lamech
flood.. 6. Deluge
Genesis.. 9. patriarch
grandson.. 4. Aram
landing, the Ark.. 6. Ararat
raven.. 6. Corvus
son.. 3. Ham 6. Shem 7. Japheth
wine cup.. 6. crater

nob... 4. head, nave 6. hobnob
8. nobleman 9. personage

nobby... 5. smart 7. stylish 11. fishing
boat

Nobel powder... 10. Ballistite

noble... 4. epic, fine, peer 5. ducal,
grand, lofty, manly 6. epical
7. eminent, grandee, liberal, stately,
sublime 8. elevated, generous,
imposing, renowned, splendid
9. dignified, high birth, honorable
10. impressive 11. illustrious,
magnanimous, magnificent
12. aristocratic

nobleman... 3. sir 4. duke, earl, lord,
peer 5. baron 6. barony, flaith,
thakur 7. baronet, grandee, marquis
8. margrave, optimate, viscount
9. blueblood, patrician 10. aristocrat,
chess piece

nobleness of birth... 6. eugeny

noblewoman... 4. lady 7. duchess,
peeress 8. baroness, countess,
marquise 11. marchioness

nobody... 4. none 5. no one 8. no
person 9. jackstraw, nonentity
10. not anybody

nocent... 6. guilty 7. harmful, hurtful
8. criminal (opp of innocent)

nocturnal... 5. night 7. nightly
8. darkness, nocturne

nocturnal (pert to)...
animal.. 3. bat 4. coon 5. lemur,
ratel 6. possum 7. opossum
astronomy.. 9. astrolabe
bird.. 3. owl
signs.. 8. zodiacal

nocturne... 7. lullaby 8. serenade
10. night scene (art)

nocuous... 7. hurtful, noxious

nod... 3. bow 4. beck, bend, tend,
wink 6. beckon, signal 7. bidding
8. greeting

Nod (Bib)... 9. Land of Nod 10. East
of Eden

nodding... 6. nutant 7. annuent,
weeping (as a willow) 8. cernuous,
drooping

noddy... 3. auk 4. fool 6. drowsy, fulmar, noodle, sleepy 7. foolish, hackney 9. simpleton
node... 4. knob,. knot, knur, plot 5. joint, nodus 7. dilemma 8. swelling 10. difficulty 12. complication, protuberance
nodule... 4. auge, bump, knot, lump, mass 5. geode 7. granule, nablock 8. tubercle 12. complication
nodus... 4. knot, node 10. difficulty 12. complication
noel... 5. carol (Xmas), shout 9. sign of joy
Noel... 6. Natale 9. Christmas
noeud... 3. bow 4. knot
nog... 3. peg, pin 5. block 6. eggnog, noggin 8. treenail 9. brickwork
nogada... 10. pecan candy
nogal... 5. pecan
noggin... 3. cup, mug 4. head, pate
noise... 3. din, pop, rap 4. bang, boom, klop, roar, rout 5. blare, blast, bruit, chang, clang, click, rumor, sound 6. clamor, outcry, racket, report, strife, uproar 7. brattle, chortle, discord, quarrel, rapping 9. shoutings
noise (pert to)...
ghost.. 11. poltergeist
harsh.. 4. bray 7. stridor 9. caterwaul
respiration.. 4. rale
rustling.. 5. swish
Scotch.. 5. chang
water.. 5. plash 6. ripple, splash
whirring.. 4. burr
noised... 6. dinned 7. rumored 8. reported
noisemaker... 4. horn 5. siren 6. rattle 7. clacker, whistle 8. whiz-bang
noisome... 3. bad 4. foul 5. fetid, nasty 7. harmful, noxious 8. stinking 9. offensive 10. malodorous, pernicious 11. destructive, unwholesome 12. insalubrious
noisy... 4. loud 7. blatant 8. brawling, clattery 9. clamorous, turbulent 10. blustering, boisterous, vociferous 12. obstreperous, rattley-bang
nom... 4. name
nomad... 4. arab 5. gypsy 6. roamer, Romany 7. Bedouin, Saracen, scenite, zingaro 8. wanderer
nomadic... 9. itinerant
nomarchy (Gr)... 4. nome 8. province 10. department
nom de plume... 7. pen name 9. pseudonym
nomen... 4. gens, name 7. agnomen 8. cognomen 9. praenomen
nomenclature... 4. name 5. onymy 8. glossary, onymatic, register 10. dictionary, Latin names, vocabulary 11. designation, terminology
nominal... 3. par 6. unreal 7. not real, titular, topical 8. so-called
nominal recognizance (law)... 3. Doe
nonage... 6. neanic 8. immature, minority, pupilage, youthful
nonary... 9. nine group 10. base of

nine 11. group of nine
nonbeliever... 5. pagan 7. atheist, heathen, infidel 8. agnostic 11. disbeliever 12. non-Christian
nonce... 3. now 8. meantime 11. temporarily
nonchalant... 4. cool 6. casual 8. careless 10. insouciant 11. indifferent, unconcerned 13. imperturbable
noncompliance... 7. refusal 12. disobedience 13. recalcitrance
non compos mentis... 7. unsound 8. demented, deranged 11. disoriented
nonconformist... 7. heretic, sectary 8. objector, recusant 9. dissenter, protester
nondescript... 11. exceptional 13. indescribable 14. indeterminable
none... 2. no 4. nary 5. nones, no one 6. nobody, not any, not one 10. nobody else
nonentity... 7. a nobody. nullity 8. nihility, nonbeing 9. res nihili 11. nothingness 12. nonexistence
nonessential... 8. needless 9. extrinsic 10. adiaphoron, incidental, irrelevant 11. superfluous 12. adventitious
non licit... 8. unlawful
non-Mahometan... 5. Kafir 6. giaour 9. non-Moslem
nonmetallic... 4. spar 5. argon, boron 6. carbon, helium, iodine, oxygen 7. bromine 8. chlorine, nitrogen
nonpareil... 4. type 7. paragon 8. nonesuch, peerless 9. unrivaled 11. unsurpassed 14. painted bunting
nonplus... 4. stop 5. blank, stump 6. baffle, puzzle, thwart 9. mystify, perplex 8. quandary
nonproductive... 6. barren 7. sterile 9. fruitless
nonprofessional... 3. ham, lay 4. laic 5. laity 7. amateur 10. apprentice
nonsense... 2. bah 4. bosh, bunk, tosh 5. folly, stite 6. drivel, humbug, jargon 7. blarney, foolery, trifles, twaddle 8. falderal, flimflam, trumpery 9. absurdity, frivolity, poppycock, senseless, silliness 10. balderdash, tomfoolery, triviality 11. monkeyshine 12. fiddle-dee-dee
nonsense verse... 9. amphigory (amphigouri), rigmarole
non tanto (Mus)... 9. non troppo, not as much
noodle... 4. fool, head 5. brain, ninny 9. blockhead, simpleton 12. stupid person
nook... 4. cant, cove 5. angle, herne, niche 6. corner, cranny, recess 7. crevice 10. promontory
noon... 6. midday, summit 8. meridian, noontide 9. ninth hour 11. noon of night (poet)
noonday rest... 6. siesta
noose... 3. tie 4. bond, hang, loop 5. snare 6. circle, halter 7. laniard (lanyard) 12. hangman's rope
Nootka... 3. Aht, dog 6. Indian
norati... 5. noise 6. gossip

Norbertine... 12. Premonstrant
Nordic... 8. Germanic 12. Scandinavian
norie... 9. cormorant
norm... 4. rule, type 5. model, norma
7. average, measure, pattern
8. standard, template
norma... 4. rule 5. gauge, model
6. square 7. pattern 8. standard,
template 13. constellation
normal... 3. par 4. just, mean, sane
5. usual 6. common 7. average,
logical, natural, orderly, regular,
typical 8. everyday, ordinary
9. customary
Norman... 6. French 7. crimson
8. Northman 10. Romanesque
17. conquest of England (1066)
Normandy...
beach.. 5. Omaha
capital.. 4. Caen 5. Rouen (old)
city.. 5. Havre 6. Dieppe 7. Alençon
9. Cherbourg
conqueror.. 5. Rollo 8. William I
governed by.. 6. France (1940)
Viking duke (anc).. 5. Rollo
Norn (Teut Myth)... 4. Urth, Wyrd
5. Skuld 9. Verthandi
Norse... 9. Norwegian
12. Scandinavian
Norse (pert to)...
abode of gods.. 6. Asgard
alphabet.. 6. runics
ash tree, universe.. 10. Yggdrasill
bard.. 5. scald (skald) 7. sagaman
collected songs, myths.. 4. Edda
deity.. 4. Odin, Thor
demon (fire).. 4. Surt (Surtr)
earth.. 7. Midgard
epic.. 4. saga
explorer.. 11. Leif Ericson
first man.. 4. Askr
giant.. 4. Loki, Ymir (Ymer) 5. Jotun
6. Fafnir
horse.. 8. Brimfaxi 9. Skinfaksi
horse (Odin's).. 10. Yggdrasill
king.. 4. Atli
language (old).. 9. Icelandic
man.. 8. Northman
monster.. 6. kraken 7. Midgard
patron saint.. 4. Olaf
poem.. 4. rune
toast.. 5. skoal
warrior.. 8. beserker
watchdog (Hel's).. 4. Garm (Garmr)
wolf.. 6. Fenrir
Norse goddess of...
death.. 3. Hel, Ran
fate.. 4. Norn, Urth, Wyrd
flowers.. 4. Nott
giantess.. 4. Nott
love, beauty.. 5. Freya
peace, healing.. 3. Eir
sky.. 5. Frigg (Frigga)
underworld.. 3. Hel
Norse god of...
day.. 3. Dag
evil.. 4. Loki
fertility.. 4. Frey (Freyr) 6. Njorth
(Njord)
giants.. 4. Ymir
justice.. 4. Frey 7. Forseti

light.. 6. Balder
night.. 4. Nott
poetry.. 4. Odin 5. Bragi
primeval (the world).. 4. Ymir (Ymer)
sea.. 5. Aegir
thunder.. 4. Thor
war.. 4. Odin (Wodin)
watchfulness.. 8. Heimdall
wisdom.. 4. Odin (Wodin)
Norse gods, chief... 3. Tyr (Tiu)
4. Frey, Jarl, Loki, Odin (Wodin),
Thos (Donar), Ymir 6. Balder, Njorth
7. Asynjur (group), Forseti
8. Heimdall
North (far)... 6. Arctic
North Africa... see also *Africa*
country.. 7. Algeria, Tunisia
fruit.. 3. fig 4. date
people.. 4. Moor 6. Berber, Hamite,
Libyan
port.. 4. Sfax
North America... see also *America*
Indian blanket.. 6. stroud
mountain, highest.. 8. McKinley
orchid.. 8. arethusa
owl.. 7. wapacut
rail.. 4. sora
reindeer.. 7. caribou
river, longest.. 5. Yukon 8. Missouri
11. Mississippi
snake.. 5. adder
North Atlantic (pert to)...
cape.. 5. Sable
island.. 7. Britain, Iceland, Ireland
9. Greenland, Manhattan
sea gull.. 4. skua
North Carolina...
cape.. 4. Fear 7. Lookout 8. Hatteras
capital.. 7. Raleigh
city.. 6. Durham 9. Asheville,
Charlotte 12. Winston–Salem
explorer.. 6. De Soto 9. Verrazano
famed person.. 12. Virginia Dare
16. Sir Walter Raleigh
mountain.. 9. Blue Ridge 10. Great
Smoky, Mt Mitchell
pine.. 8. loblolly
river.. 3. Tar 5. Neuse 6. Peedee
(Yadkin)
State admission.. 7. Twelfth
State motto.. 14. Esse Quam Videri
20. To Be, Rather Than To Seem
State nickname.. 7. Tarheel 8. Old
North
North Dakota...
capital.. 8. Bismarck
city.. 5. Fargo, Minot
fort.. 6. Mandan 7. Lincoln
11. Abercrombie
historic site.. 24. International Peace
Garden
mountain.. 10. White Butte
reservoir.. 8. Garrison
State admission.. 8. Fortieth (or
Thirty–ninth)
State nickname.. 5. Sioux
11. Flickertail
northeaster... 4. gale, wind 5. storm
Northern... 6. boreal 11. hyperborean
13. septentrional
Northern Bear... 6. Russia
Northern constellation... 3. Cor

9. Andromeda
northernmost world (inhabitable)...
    5. Thule 9. Trondheim
North Pole... 10. boreal pole
North Sea.. 6. Baltic, German
North Sea arm... 8. Kattegat
    9. Skagerrak (Skager–Rak)
North Sea canal... 4. Kiel
North Star... 7. Polaris 8. Cynosure,
    lodestar (loadstar), polestar
north wind... 6. Boreas
    10. tramontane
Norway... see also *Norwegian*
    capital.. 4. Oslo 11. Christiania (old)
    city.. 6. Bergen 7. Drammen
      9. Trondheim
    county.. 5. fylke
    inlet.. 5. fiord (fjord)
    mountain.. 6. Kjolen
    parliament.. 8. Storting (Storthing)
    patron saint.. 5. Olaf (Olaus)
    phenomenon.. 11. midnight sun
      14. Northern Lights
    plateau.. 5. fjeld
    river.. 2. Oi 4. Tana 7. Glommen
Norwegian (pert to)...
    bird.. 4. rype 9. ptarmigan
    cart.. 11. stolkjaerre
    dance.. 7. halling
    duck.. 7. widgeon
    embroidery.. 9. hardanger
    goblin.. 5. Nisse 6. kobold
    guardian spirit.. 6. fylgja 8. hamingja
    haddock.. 8. rosefish
    language.. 5. Norse 8. Rigsmaal
      9. Landsmaal
    liquor.. 7. akevitt
    sea monster.. 6. kraken
    tales.. 4. Edda
Norwegian people...
    author, explorer.. 8. Sverdrup
    composer.. 5. Grieg
    dramatist.. 5. Ibsen
    explorer.. 6. Nansen (Nobel Prize)
    king.. 6. Harold (The Fairhaired)
      15. Harold Hardraade
    philologist.. 5. Assen
    raiders.. 7. Vikings
    saint.. 4. Olaf (Olaus)
    violinist.. 7. Ole Bull
    zoologist.. 4. Sars
nose... 3. neb, pry 4. conk, prow
    5. nasus, scent, smell, snout
    6. meddle, muzzle, nuzzle 8. olfactor
    9. detective, proboscis
    11. investigate
nose (pert to)...
    ailment.. 6. coryza 8. rhinitis
    bees, birds.. 4. lore 5. lorum
    bleeding.. 9. epistaxis
    cartilage.. 6. septum
    glasses.. 8. pince–nez
    large.. 6. nasute
    muscle.. 7. nasalis
    opening.. 5. naris (nares, pl) 7. nostril
    partition.. 5. vomer
    plug.. 12. rhineurynter
    relating to.. 5. nasal 6. narial, rhinal
    snub.. 6. simous
    surgery.. 11. rhinoplasty
noseband (bridle)... 6. misrol
nosegay... 4. posy 7. bouquet,

perfume 9. fragrance 10. frangipani
    (tree)
nosocomium... 8. hospital
nosography, nosology (*science of*)...
    7. disease
nostalgia... 8. yearning 11. wistfulness
    12. homesickness 14. sentimentality
nostology (*study of*)... 8. senility
    10. geriatrics 11. gerontology
Nostradamus... 4. seer 7. prophet
    10. astrologer
nostril... 5. naris (nares, pl) 6. narial
    9. olfactory
nostril–shaped... 8. nariform
nosy... 5. nasal 6. prying 7. curious
    8. fragrant 10. malodorous
    11. inquisitive
Nosy, Old (nickname)... 16. Duke of
    Wellington
not (pert to)...
    any.. 2. no 4. nane, nary, none
      7. no trace
    at all.. 5. nohow 6. nowise
    easy.. 7. labored
    either.. 7. neither
    feral.. 4. tame
    harmed.. 9. unscathed
    having a will.. 9. intestate
    hollow.. 5. solid
    in motion.. 5. fixed 6. stable, static
      7. stabile 10. stationary
    in the least.. 6. nowith
    moral.. 6. amoral 7. immoral
    open (fruit).. 11. indehiscent
    prefix.. 2. il, im, in, ir, un 3. non
    professional.. 4. laic 7. amateur
    qualified.. 5. unfit
    running (stream).. 8. stagnant
    separable.. 11. indivisible
    settled.. 4. moot
    subjugated.. 7. unbowed
    suitable.. 5. inept
    the same.. 5. other 9. different
    to know.. 5. unken 10. unfamiliar
notable... 6. famous 8. historic
    9. celebrity, important, memorable,
    notorious 10. noteworthy, remarkable
    13. distinguished, extraordinary
notandum... 4. note 5. entry
    10. memorandum
notary... 5. notar 8. attestor,
    notebook, official 9. scrivener
    12. notary public, stenographer
notation... 4. memo, note 5. entry
    7. comment, marking 9. etymology
    10. annotation
notator... 5. noter 8. recorder
    9. annotator
notch... 3. gap, jap 4. dent, dint,
    kerf, nick, nock 5. cleft, crena, score
    6. defile, dentil (Her), indent
    7. passage 8. undercut 9. indenture
    11. indentation
notched bar (door)... 4. risp
notched opening (Anat)... 5. hilum
note... 2. ut 3. jot 4. chit, heed,
    mark, memo, sign, sole, song, tone,
    tune 5. breve, gloss, sound, token
    6. billet, notice, postil, record,
    remark, report 7. apostil (apostille),
    comment, epistle 8. dispatch,
    eminence, indicate, marginal,

scholium 9. character 10. annotation, importance, indication, memorandum, reputation 11. certificate, observation

note (pert to)...
death sound.. 4. mort
explanatory.. 5. gloss 8. scholium
half.. 5. minim
high.. 3. alt, E la
marginal.. 6. postil 7. apostil (apostille)
musical.. 5. breve 6. ecbole 7. punctus
stem of.. 5. filum

notebook... 6. street 7. estreat 8. ratebook 10. adversaria, memorandum

noted... 4. seen 5. famed 6. famous, marked 7. eminent, notable 8. far-famed, renowned 9. distingué, prominent, well-known 10. celebrated

notes... 5. duole 6. strain 7. tiralee 11. solmization

nothing... 3. nil, nox 4. luke, rien, void, zero 5. nihil 6. naught, nichil, nought, trifle 7. a nobody 9. nonentity 11. empty-handed 12. nonexistence

nothing doing... 4. calm 6. hushed, no dice, no soap, placid 7. I refuse 9. by no means, God forbid, quiescent

notice... 2. ad 3. see 4. heed, idea, mark, mind, news, note, sign 5. blurb, edict, quote 6. advice, espial, notion, regard, remark 7. affiche, mention, observe, warning 8. bulletin, citation 9. attention 10. commentary 11. information, observation 12. announcement, intelligence 13. advertisement

notice (pert to)...
advance.. 8. ballyhoo
death.. 4. obit 8. obituary
marriage.. 4. bans 5. banns

notify... 4. cite, page, tell, warn 6. inform, remind 7. apprise, declare, publish 8. announce

notion... 4. idea, view, whim 5. freit 6. belief, theory, vagary 7. caprice, impulse, opinion 9. intention 10. conception, denotation, knickknack 11. supposition

notionable... 8. fanciful 9. whimsical

notional... 6. unreal 9. imaginary, visionary, whimsical

notions... 5. goods, wares 11. commodities, merchandise

notoriety... 4. fame, plug 5. éclat 8. ballyhoo 9. limelight, publicity, spotlight

notorious... 5. known, noted 6. arrant, famous, notour 8. flagrant, infamous, talked of 10. recognized 11. conspicuous

notorious character... 5. James (Jesse) 7. Cochise, Younger 8. Geronimo, Jennings, Murietta 9. Jack Ketch, Wyatt Earp 11. Billy the Kid, Poncho Villa, Sitting Bull 12. Calamity Jane 13. John Dillinger 14. Wild Bill Hickok

notum... 4. back

notus... 4. back (comb form)

notwithstanding... 3. but, yet 5. still 6. mauger (maugre), though 7. despite, however 8. although 9. in spite of 12. nevertheless

nought, naught... 3. bad, nil 4. zero 5. wrong 7. nothing, useless 9. worthless

noughty... 3. bad 9. worthless

noumenal... 4. real 5. ontal (opp of phenomenal)

noun... 7. subject

noun (pert to)...
gender, common.. 7. epicene
indeclinable.. 6. aptote
irregular.. 5. pecus 11. heteroclite
suffix.. 2. et, ia 3. ent, ery, ier, ion, ior, ist, ite 4. ence
verbal.. 6. gerund

nourish... 4. feed, grow 5. nurse 6. foster, suckle, supply 7. support, sustain 9. cultivate 13. promote growth

nourishing... 6. alible 8. nutrient 9. nutritive 10. alimentary

nourishment... 3. aid 4. food 5. manna, meats 7. aliment, pabulum 9. nutriment, nutrition 10. sustenance 13. nutritiveness 14. nutritiousness

nous... 4. mind 8. ready wit 9. intellect 11. world spirit

Nova... 4. star

Nova Scotia...
bay.. 5. Fundy 10. Chedabucto
cape.. 5. Canso
capital.. 7. Halifax
greens.. 11. sea plantain
island.. 10. Cape Breton
lake, salt.. 7. Bras d'Or
native.. 7. Acadian 8. Bluenose
poetic name.. 6. Acadia (Acadie)
settlement, first.. 9. Port Royal

novel... 3. new 4. book, rare 5. fresh, story 7. fiction, romance, strange, unusual 8. original

novelty... 3. fad 7. newness 9. freshness 10. innovation, recentness 11. originality

novice... 3. nun 4. puny, tyro (tiro) 5. chela, rooky 6. tyrone 7. amateur, convert, learner 8. beginner, freshman, initiate, neophyte, newcomer 9. fledgling, greenhorn, postulant 10. apprentice, catechumen 11. abecedarian 13. alphabetarian

novitiate... 6. novice 9. probation 14. apprenticeship

now... 3. noo 4. here 6. at once 7. present 9. at present, forthwith, instantly 10. very lately 12. at this moment

nowhere... 5. limbo 6. absent 7. no place 8. oblivion 9. nowhither 11. nonexistent, not anywhere, nullibicity

nowhere else... 5. there

nowise... 8. not at all

Nox (pert to)...
brother.. 6. Erebus
daughter.. 10. Hesperides
goddess (Rom).. 5. Night

husband.. 5. Chaos
noxious... 4. evil 5. nasty 6. nocent,
odious 7. baneful, harmful, hurtful,
noisome 9. injurious, miasmatic
10. corruptive, pernicious
11. destructive, unwholesome
12. insalubrious
nozzle... 3. tew 4. nose, vent
5. giant, snout 6. nuzzle, outlet,
tuyère 7. conduit
nuance... 5. shade 9. gradation,
variation
nub... 4. gist, knob, knot, knub, lump,
neck, snag 9. main point
12. protuberance
nubia... 4. wrap 5. cloud
Nubia (pert to)...
afterglow.. 14. second twilight
animal.. 4. goat 5. horse
autonym.. 6. Berber 7. Barabra
harp.. 5. nanga
tribe.. 4. Nuba
nucha... 4. nape, neck
nuclear complex... 7. Oedipus
nuclear network fiber... 5. linin
nucleus... 4. core 5. cadre, focus,
umbra 6. center, kernel 8. rudiment
nude... 4. bare 5. color, naked
6. Seasan (color) 7. denuded
8. stripped, undraped 9. unadorned,
unclothed, undressed
nudge... 3. jog, nog 4. knub, lump,
poke, prod, push 5. block, elbow
6. remind, signal
nudibranch... 7. mollusk
nugatory... 4. vain 7. invalid, trivial
8. trifling 9. worthless 11. ineffectual
nuisance... 4. bane, bore, harm, hurt,
pest 6. injury 9. annoyance
nuit... 5. night
null... 4. void 6. vacant 7. invalid
8. nugatory 11. nonexistent
13. insignificant
nullifidian... 7. skeptic 9. nullibist,
skeptical 10. unbeliever
11. disbeliever
nullify... 4. undo, void 5. annul
6. cancel, negate 7. abolish, destroy
8. abrogate 10. counteract, neutralize
numb... 6. clumsy, freeze, stupid,
torpid 8. benumbed, deadened,
helpless 9. apathetic, incapable,
rigescent 10. insensible
12. anesthetized
number... 3. sum 5. count, digit, limit
7. integer, numeral 8. quantity
9. aggregate, enumerate
10. complement 11. information
number (pert to)...
added.. 6. encore
again.. 10. renumerate
by tens.. 7. decimal
cardinal.. 7. primary (one, two)
consecutively.. 5. folio
copies (printed).. 7. edition
describable.. 6. scalar
four.. 6. tetrad
irrational.. 4. surd
least whole.. 4. unit
lucky.. 5. seven
many.. 4. herd 6. myriad 7. several
9. multitude 12. considerable

nine.. 6. ennead, nonare
ordinal.. 5. first 6. second (etc)
third power.. 4. cube
votes.. 4. poll
whole.. 7. integer
numbles, nombles... 6. umbles
7. inwards 8. entrails
numbness... 6. torpor 10. rigescence
numeral... 5. Roman 6. Arabic, figure
9. character
numerous... 4. lots, many 7. copious,
crowded 8. abundant, measured,
thronged 9. plentiful
Numidia (pert to)...
city.. 5. Hippo
crane.. 10. demoiselle
language (written).. 5. Punic
6. Tuareg 7. Hamitic
modern kingdom.. 7. Algeria
people (anc).. 8. Numidian
numskull... 4. dolt 5. dunce
10. loggerhead
nun... 4. moth, smew 5. Clare
(Franciscan), Vesta 6. monial, pigeon,
sister 8. titmouse, votaress
9. priestess 11. Lady of Loretto
nun bird... 6. Monasa 8. puffbird
nunciate... 9. announcer, messenger
11. internuncio
nuncio... 7. legate 8. delegate
9. messenger 11. internuncio
nuncupate... 7. declare 8. dedicate,
inscribe, proclaim 9. designate
nuncupative... 4. oral 9. unwritten
(will) 11. designative
nun headdress... 6. wimple
nunnari root... 12. sarsaparilla
nunnery... 5. abbey 7. convent
8. cloister
nunnery head... 6. abbess
nunni... 7. blesbok (blesbuck)
8. antelope
Nuphar... 12. spatterdocks 16. yellow
pond lilies
nuptial... 6. bridal 7. marital
9. connubial 11. matrimonial
nurse... 4. amah, ayah, feed, rear,
tend 5. bonne, mammy 6. caress,
suckle 8. care for, cherish, nourish,
nurture, nutrice 9. nursemaid
nursed... 3. fed 6. tended 7. cradled,
suckled 8. nurtured 9. nourished
nursery... 6. crèche, school
nurse shark... 4. gata
nurture... 3. aid 4. feed, rear 5. nurse
6. foster 7. care for, cherish
8. breeding, training 9. education,
encourage, nutriment
nut... 4. anta, kola (cola) 5. acorn,
betel, pecan, piñon 6. almond, Brazil,
cashew, litchi, peanut, walnut
7. filbert, hickory, maranon
8. beechnut, chestnut 9. butternut
nut (pert to)...
bearing.. 10. nuciferous
brown.. 5. hazel 6. walnut
8. chestnut
cake.. 8. doughnut
coal.. 10. anthracite
collectively.. 4. food 5. shack
9. beechnuts
confection.. 8. marzipan 9. marchpane

cracker.. 4. crow
eating.. 10. nucivorous
   11. nuciphagous
edible part.. 6. kernel
grass.. 5. sedge
Med.. 4. kola 5. bichy 9. gourounut
odd.. 9. eccentric
palm.. 5. betel, lichi 7. coconut
ref to.. 5. nucal
shell.. 4. case, hull 6. trifle
Nut (pert to)...
consort of.. 3. Geb
daughter.. 4. Isis 8. Nephthys
goddess of.. 5. earth
son.. 2. Ra
nutation... 3. nod 7. nodding
nuthatch... 4. bird 5. sitta 6. xenops
   8. titmouse 9. nutpecker
nutmeg.. 4. mace 5. drupe 6. beaver
   (color)
nutmeg (pert to)...
bird, finch.. 5. cowry 10. weaverbird
family.. 13. Myristicaceae
tree.. 6. camara
Nutmeg State... 11. Connecticut
nutpecker... 8. nuthatch
nut quad... 6. en quad
nutria... 3. fur 5. grège 10. beaverlike
nutria fur bearer... 5. coypu
nutrice... 5. nurse
nutriment... 4. food 7. aliment,
   pabulum 9. nutrition 11. nourishment
nutritious... 9. alimental
   10. alimentary, nourishing
nuts... 4. food, mast 5. shack
   9. beechnuts
nutty... 4. gaga, zest 5. queer, smart,
   spicy 7. amorous, piquant
   10. unbalanced 11. fascinating
   14. cracker–brained
nuzzle... 5. nurse 6. burrow, cuddle,
   foster, nestle 7. cherish 8. make
   snug
nyctalopia... 14. night blindness

nye... 4. eyas, nest, nide 5. brood
nymph... 4. nais 5. deity, dryad,
   naiad, oread, siren, sylph 6. Nereid
   7. Oceanid 9. hamadryad
nymph (pert to)...
Arcadian.. 6. Syrinx
beloved of Narcissus.. 4. Echo
color.. 4. pink
Cretan.. 8. Cynosura
fountain, river.. 4. nais 5. naiad
   6. Egeria
German legend.. 7. Lorelei
Greek.. 4. Echo 6. Daphne
   8. Arethusa
Hesperides (one of).. 5. Aegle
   7. Hespera
hills, mountain.. 5. oread
laurel tree.. 6. Daphne
Messina Strait.. 6. Scylla
Mohamm paradise.. 5. houri
monster.. 6. Scylla
Mt Ida.. 6. Oenone
ocean.. 5. siren 6. Nereid 7. Galatea,
   Oceanid 10. Callirrhoe
pursued by Apollo.. 6. Daphne, Syrinx
   8. Arethusa
Queen.. 3. Mab
sea bird.. 6. Scylla
tree.. 5. Dryad 9. Hamadryad
water.. 5. Naiad 6. Undine 7. Hydriad
woods.. 5. Dryad 8. Arethusa
   9. Hamadryad
young.. 7. nymphet
Nymphaea... 8. Castalia 11. water
   lilies
nymphs... 10. Atlantides, Hesperides
nystagmus... 14. eyeball disease
Nyx, Nox (pert to)...
daughter.. 4. Eris
father.. 5. Chaos
goddess of.. 5. Night
mother of.. 11. Day and Night
Nzambi... 7. goddess (Afr) 11. earth
   mother

O

O (pert to)...
interjection.. 11. exclamation
letter.. 5. tenth
mathematics.. 4. zero 6. cipher
pref (family).. 5. Irish
oaf... 4. boor, dolt, lout 5. idiot,
   ouphe, yokel 9. blockhead, simpleton
   10. changeling
oafish... 6. simple, stupid
oak... 4. club 5. brave, color, oaken,
   stout 6. strong 7. Quercus
   8. hardness, strength 13. artificial fly
oak (pert to)...
apple.. 4. gall 10. she–oak cone
beauty.. 4. moth
California.. 5. roble 6. encina

comb form.. 6. querci
evergreen.. 4. holm, ilex 5. holly
family.. 8. Fagaceae
fern.. 8. polypody
fruit.. 5. acorn 6. camata
fungus.. 10. armillaria
gall.. 8. oak apple
Jerusalem.. 7. ambrose
kinds.. 3. bur, red 5. black, white
   6. ground, poison, willow
   8. chestnut 10. canyon live
plantation.. 9. quercetum
resembling.. 9. roboreous
tannin.. 7. quercic 9. quercinic
thicket.. 9. chaparral
Turkey.. 6. cerris

web.. 10. cockchafer
young.. 8. flittern
oam... 5. steam 7. warm air
Oannes (Bab)... 5. deity (part man, part fish)
oar... 3. row 5. blade, remus, rower, scull 6. paddle, propel 7. oarsman
oar (pert to)...
blade.. 4. palm, peel
feather.. 5. remex
fulcrum, lock.. 5. pivot, thole
lop.. 6. rabbit
shaft.. 4. loom
shaped.. 7. remiped 8. remiform
oars (pert to)...
collective.. 6. oarage, sculls
one bank.. 7. unireme
reverse.. 6. sheave
three banks.. 7. trireme
two banks.. 6. bireme
oasis... 3. ojo 4. wadi (wady) 5. Gafsa 6. Dakhla 11. fertile spot
oast... 4. kiln, oven
oat (pert to)...
cake.. 5. caper
ear (Old World).. 4. bird 7. wagtail
fowl.. 11. snow bunting
genus.. 5. Avena 6. oathay
grass.. 4. ulla 9. chaparral
husks.. 5. shood (shude)
like.. 10. avenaceous
rent (paid as).. 7. avenage
oath... 3. God, aith, drat, egad 5. bedad, curse 6. pledge 7. serment 8. affidavit, holy smoke, profanity 10. deposition 11. affirmation
Obadiah (Bib)... 6. Quaker 7. prophet
obbligato... 8. required 13. accompaniment, indispensable
obduction... 7. autopsy 8. covering
obdurate... 4. firm, hard 5. rough, stony 6. mulish, rugged 7. adamant, callous 8. stubborn 9. heartless, obstinate, unbending, unfeeling 10. impenitent, inflexible, insensible, unyielding 11. hardhearted, intractable
obedient... 6. docile 7. duteous, dutiful, orderly 8. amenable, yielding 9. attentive, compliant 10. submissive 11. conformable
obeisance... 3. bow 5. binge, congé 6. curtsy, fealty, homage 9. deference 10. respectful 14. obsequiousness
obeisance, to make... 3. bow 6. congee, curtsy, salaam
obelisk... 5. pylon 6. guglia (guglio), needle, obelus, pillar 16. Cleopatra's Needle
Oberon (pert to)...
Astron.. 9. satellite
character of.. 11. Shakespeare
classic.. 4. poem 5. opera
husband of.. 7. Titania
Myth.. 13. King of Fairies
obese... 3. fat 5. puffy, pursy, squab, stout 6. fleshy, turgid 8. liparous 9. corpulent
obey... 3. ear 4. hear, mind 5. yield 6. comply, submit

obfuscate... 3. dim 6. darken, opaque 7. confuse, perplex 8. bewilder
obi... 4. sash 6. girdle
obit... 4. rest 5. death 6. notice 7. decease, release 8. obituary 9. obsequies 10. necrologue 11. Requiem Mass 12. mortuary roll
obiter... 9. in passing 12. incidentally
obiter dictum... 7. opinion (of judge)
object... 3. aim, end 4. goal, hulk 5. cavil, demur, scoff, thing 6. appose, expose, motive, oppose 7. article, grammar, protest, purpose 9. intention
object (pert to)...
bulky.. 4. hulk
circular.. 7. trundle
cloudlike.. 6. nebula
illustrative.. 6. realia (pl)
rare.. 5. curio 7. antique
rational.. 8. noumenon
sacred.. 4. Urim 7. Thummim
small.. 4. mite
object for...
devotion, worship.. 4. icon, idol 5. totem 6. fetish
dread.. 5. bogey (bogie) 6. goblin 8. the Devil
going and coming.. 6. errand
greed.. 5. lucre, money 6. wealth
knowledge.. 7. scibile
objection... 3. bar 5. cavil 7. protest, quarrel 8. demurrer, obstacle 9. exception 11. disapproval
objectionable... 9. offensive 11. exceptional, inexpedient 13. uncommendable
objective... 3. aim, end 4. goal 6. motive, target 7. purpose
objector, conscientious... 6. conchy
objects (Bib)... 4. Urim 7. Thummim
objects (floating)... 7. flotsam
objurgate... 5. abuse, chide, scold 6. rebuke 7. reprove, upbraid 9. reprimand
oblate... 5. oblat 7. devoted 9. dedicated, flattened (opp of prolate)
obligated... 5. bound 6. in debt 7. obliged 8. beholden 9. obstringe
obligation... 3. tie, vow 4. bond, debt, duty, oath, onus 7. promise 8. civility, contract 9. agreement, necessity 10. compulsion 11. obstriction
obligatory... 7. binding 8. imposing, required 9. mandatory, necessary 10. compulsory
oblige... 4. bind, pawn 5. favor 6. compel, engage 7. gratify 8. obligate 9. constrain, obstringe 11. accommodate
obliged... 7. favored 8. beholden, grateful 9. duty bound
obliging... 4. kind 5. helpful 9. agreeable, courteous, indulgent 11. complaisant, considerate 13. accommodating
oblique... 4. cant, skew 5. bevel, slant, slope 7. obscure, scalene 8. inclined, perverse, sidelong, sidewise, sinister, slanting

9. underhand 10. circuitous,
collateral, transverse 12. disingenuous
oblique angle... 5. acute 6. obtuse
obliquely... 4. skew 6. aslant
7. askance 8. sideways, sidewise
9. on the bias 10. slantingly
obliterate... 4. blot, dele 5. erase
6. cancel, delete, efface, sponge
7. expunge
obliteration... 6. rasure 7. erasure
8. deletion 10. extinction
oblivion... 7. nirvana, silence
9. unfeeling 13. forgetfulness
15. unconsciousness
oblivion, producing... 8. nepenthe
oblivion, river of... 5. Lethe
oblivious... 6. asleep 8. heedless
9. forgetful, unfeeling 10. abstracted
11. unconscious
oblong... 8. elliptic 9. elongated
11. rectangular 12. quadrangular
obloquy... 5. abuse 6. infamy
7. calumny 9. criticism
11. malediction 12. reprehension
obnoxious... 4. vile 5. nasty
6. odious, rancid 7. hateful
8. amenable, infamous, terrible
9. offensive 13. objectionable
oboe... 4. reed 5. shawm (anc)
7. hautboy, musette 8. schalmei
(schalmey) 9. chalumeau
obscuration... 7. eclipse 9. darkening,
vagueness
obscure... 3. dim, fog 4. dark, hazy,
slur 5. bedim, blind, mirky, misty,
murky 6. cloudy, darken, delude,
mystic, opaque, remote 7. becloud,
conceal, eclipse, shadowy, unknown
8. darkling, formless, nameless,
nubilous, obstruse, oversile (obs)
9. enigmatic, undefined
10. indistinct, unrenowned
obscurity... 3. fog 5. gloom
7. dimness, opacity, unknown
8. darkness 9. nonentity, vagueness
12. formlessness 13. imperspicuous
14. insignificancy, uncomprehended
obsecrate... 7. beseech, entreat
10. supplicate
obsequies... 5. wakes 8. funerals
9. last rites
obsequious... 5. slick 6. abject
7. devoted, dutiful, fawning, servile,
slavish 8. cringing, funereal,
obedient, toadying 9. attentive,
compliant 11. subservient
observance... 3. act 4. form, rite
6. custom 8. behavior, ceremony,
practice 9. attention, deference,
sacrament, vigilance 10. conformity
11. celebration
observant... 7. careful, heedful, mindful
8. faithful, vigilant, watchful
9. attentive, regardant, regardful
observation... 4. idea 6. espial, remark
7. opinion 9. attention
observatory... 4. Lick 6. Yerkes
7. lookout, Palomar 8. Mt Wilson
11. planetarium
observe... 2. lo! 3. eye, see, spy
4. espy, heed, keep, nark, note,
obey, tout 6. behold, notice, remark

7. conform, examine, witness
8. preserve 9. celebrate, solemnize
observed, to be... 8. notandum
10. memorandum
observer... 4. eyer, nark 7. aviator,
student, witness 8. beholder,
informer, looker-on, onlooker
9. spectator 11. stool pigeon
obsess... 5. beset, haunt 6. harass
7. bewitch, possess 8. demonize
9. influence, preoccupy
obsession... 5. mania 8. impelled
11. bewitchment 13. spirit control
obsignate... 4. seal 5. stamp 6. ratify
obsolete... 3. old 5. passé 6. effete
7. archaic, disused, effaced, outworn,
worn out 9. out of date
10. antiquated 12. old-fashioned
obstacle... 3. dam 4. snag 6. hurdle
9. hindrance 10. difficulty,
impediment 11. obstruction
obstetrician... 6. doctor
10. accoucheur
obstetrix... 7. midwife
obstinate... 3. set 5. balky, tough
6. dogged, mulish, sullen 7. willful
8. perverse, stubborn 9. pigheaded
10. determined, headstrong,
self-willed 11. opinionated
obstreperous... 5. noisy 6. unruly
7. blatant 9. clamorous, turbulent
10. vociferous 11. disobedient
12. ungovernable
obstruct... 3. bar, dam, dit 4. clog,
ditt, stop 5. beset, block, check,
choke, delay 6. arrest, hamper,
oppose, stop up 7. occlude
9. barricade, embarrass, interfere,
interrupt
obstruction... 3. ban, dam 4. clog,
reef, snag 7. barrier 8. obstacle
9. hindrance 10. difficulty, filibuster,
impediment 11. retardation
obtain... 3. buy, eke, get, win
4. earn, fang, gain 5. fetch, reach
6. attain, derive, elicit, secure
7. achieve, acquire, capture, prevail,
procure, receive
obtain (pert to)...
by intimidation.. 9. blackmail
by threats.. 6. extort
control of.. 6. corner 8. overcome
equivalent.. 6. recoup
obtest... 6. beg for 7. beseech
10. supplicate
obtrude... 5. eject, expel 6. impose
7. intrude
obtrusive... 7. forward, pushing
9. intrusive, officious
obtund... 4. dull 5. blunt, quell
6. deaden 8. moderate
obtuse... 4. dull 5. blunt, crass, dense
6. stupid 9. unfeeling 11. insensitive
obvelation... 7. veiling 10. concealing
obverse... 5. front 8. converse
10. complement 11. counterpart
obviate... 7. head off, rule out
8. preclude 9. forestall 10. anticipate
obvious... 5. clear, gross, plain
7. evident, patient 8. apparent,
distinct, manifest, palpable
11. conspicuous, open and shut

obvolute... 7. twisted 9. contorted, convolute 11. overlapping

occasion... 4. sele, time 5. cause, event, nonce 6. excuse, motive 7. pretext 8. ceremony, exigency, function, incident 9. condition, happening 11. opportunity 12. circumstance

occasional... 3. odd 4. orra 5. stray 6. casual 10. contingent, incidental, infrequent

occasionally... 7. at times 9. sometimes 10. now and then 11. at intervals

occasive... 8. westward 10. setting sun

Occident... 4. West 6. sunset 17. Western Hemisphere (opp of Orient)

Occidental... 6. ponent 7. The West, Western 9. Hesperian

occiput... 10. back of head 11. back of skull

occlude... 3. dam 4. shut 5. close 6. shut up 8. obstruct

occult... 5. magic 6. hidden, mystic 7. alchemy, cryptic 8. esoteric 9. concealed, recondite 10. mysterious, necromancy 11. supernormal 12. supernatural 13. imperceptible

occultation... 4. gone, lost 7. eclipse 11. concealment

occultism... 6. cabala 7. mystery

occult science... 9. esoterics

occupant... 6. inmate, tenant 10. inhabitant

occupation... 3. job 4. call, note, work 5. hobby, trade 6. career, tenure 7. calling, pursuit 8. business, vocation 9. avocation 10. employment, habitation, possession, profession 11. engrossment

occupied... 3. sat 4. busy, held 6. filled 7. engaged 8. employed, pervaded 9. engrossed, inhabited

occupy... 3. use 4. fill, hold 6. employ, engage, expend, invest 7. engross, inhabit, oversit, pervade, possess 8. interest

occur... 4. come, fall, meet 5. clash 6. appear, befall, betide, happen

occurrence... 3. hap 5. event 8. incident, presence 9. existence, happening 10. appearance 11. eventuality 12. circumstance

occurring (pert to)...
after death.. 10. posthumous
at nightfall.. 9. acronical
every eighth day.. 5. octan
every fifth year.. 10. penteteric (modern, 4th year)
every third day.. 7. tertian
occasionally.. 8. sporadic
often.. 8. frequent 10. frequently

ocean... 3. sea 4. brim, deep, main 5. brine 6. depths, pelago 8. great sea

ocean (pert to)...
approach.. 7. sea gate
bottom.. 3. bed

deep.. 7. bathyal
deepest.. 7. bathybic
deepest, lowest.. 12. bathypelagic
division.. 6. Arctic, Indian 7. Pacific 8. Atlantic 9. Antarctic
floating matter.. 5. algae 7. flotsam
geography.. 12. oceanography
mammal.. 4. seal 5. whale
on (the ocean).. 4. asea
periodic motion.. 4. tide
ref to.. 7. pelagic 9. Neptunian
route.. 4. lane
sealing.. 7. pelagic

Oceania, Oceanica... 9. Melanesia, Polynesia 10. Micronesia 12. Pacific lands

Oceanids (Gr Myth, pert to)...
father.. 7. Oceanus
mother.. 6. Tethys
nymphs.. 13. three thousand

Oceanus (Gr Myth, pert to)...
children.. 5. Doris 8. Eurynome (goddess), Oceanids
god of.. 6. rivers
wife.. 6. Tethys

ocellus... 3. eye 6. stemma 7. eyespot

ocelot... 3. cat 7. leopard

ocher, ochre (pert to)...
red.. 5. tiver 7. almagra 8. hematite 9. faded rose
yellow.. 3. sil 7. Chinese 8. limonite 9. ochrolite

ochlocracy... 7. mob rule

ochlophobia *(fear of)*... 6. crowds

ocotillo... 5. shrub 10. candlewood

ocracy... 9. group rule

octad... 5. eight (group)

octaemeron... 12. eight-day fast

octagon... 8. octangle 11. eight angles

octahedron... 10. eight faces

octameter... 8. octapody 9. eight feet

octan... 9. eighth day (every)

octarchy... 11. rule by eight

octastich... 6. octave 10. eight lines 11. eight verses

Octateuch (Old Test)... 10. Eight Books (1st)

octave... 4. utas 5. eight 6. eighth 8. wine cask 10. eight notes

Octavia (pert to)...
sister of.. 8. Augustus
wife of.. 10. Mark Antony

Octavian... 7. Library (Rome's 1st) 16. committee of eight (one of)

octet, octette... 7. huitain 12. group of eight

October (pert to)...
bird.. 8. bobolink
birthstone.. 4. opal 5. beryl
Club.. 9. political
drink.. 3. ale
month.. 5. tenth

octogenarian... 13. eighty-year-old

octopod... 9. eight arms, eight legs

Octopoda... 8. mollusks (8-armed) 9. argonauts, octopuses

octopus... 5. poulp (poulpe)

octroi, octroy... 3. tax 9. privilege 10. concession

ocular... 3. eye (pert to) 5. optic, sight 6. visual 10. ophthalmic

oculus... 3. eye 14. Corona Borealis

odd... **4.** orra, rare **5.** droll, extra,
outré, queer **6.** uneven, unique
7. azygous, bizarre, strange, unequal,
unusual **8.** unpaired **9.** eccentric,
remaining, unmatched **10.** occasional
oddity... **9.** queerness **11.** peculiarity,
singularity **12.** eccentricity,
idiosyncrasy
odds... **6.** gamble **7.** dispute, quarrel
8. gambling, variance **9.** advantage
10. difference, dissension, inequality
11. probability **12.** disagreement
13. probabilities
odds and ends... **4.** orts **6.** refuse,
scraps **7.** mixture, remains
8. remnants **10.** miscellany
ode... **4.** like (suff), poem **5.** psalm
8. canticle, serenata
ode (type)... **7.** Lesbian, regular
8. Horatian, Pindaric **9.** irregular
odeon... **4.** hall **7.** gallery, theater
Odin (pert to)...
  attendants.. **9.** Valkyries
  god of.. **3.** war **6.** poetry, wisdom
  hall.. **8.** Valhalla
  horse.. **8.** Sleipner
  son.. **4.** Tyre, Vali **6.** Balder
  Teutonic name.. **5.** Woden
  wife.. **5.** Frigg
odious... **4.** foul, vile **5.** nasty
7. hateful **8.** infamous, terrible
odium... **6.** hatred, infamy **9.** antipathy
10. abhorrence, opprobrium
11. detestation
odontist... **7.** dentist
odontology *(science of)*... **5.** teeth
9. dentistry
odor, odour... **4.** fume, funk, nose
5. aroma, fetor, nidor, scent, smell
6. flavor **7.** essence, malodor,
perfume **9.** fragrance, redolence
odor, meat cooking... **5.** fumet
(fumette)
odorous... **8.** aromatic, fragrant,
redolent, smelling
Odysseus (pert to)...
  chieftain.. **9.** Trojan War
  dog.. **5.** Argos
  father.. **7.** Laertes
  hero of.. **10.** The Odyssey (Homer)
  king of.. **6.** Ithaca (Gr)
  magic herb.. **4.** moly
  modern name.. **7.** Ulysses
  wife.. **8.** Penelope
oecist... **9.** colonizer
oecodomic... **13.** architectural
Oedipus (pert to)...
  daughter.. **8.** Antigone
  father.. **5.** Laius (King of Thebes)
  mother.. **7.** Jocasta
oeno (comb form)... **4.** wine
oenomancy... **12.** wine prophecy
oenophilist... **9.** wine lover
oenopoetic... **10.** wine making
oestrus... **4.** fury **5.** sting **6.** desire,
frenzy **7.** impulse **8.** stimulus
of... **2.** in, on **4.** over, upon, with
5. about, avent **10.** indication
of (pert to)...
  a chamber.. **7.** cameral
  a class (related).. **7.** generic
  a father.. **6.** agnate

a flock.. **6.** gregal
a forefather.. **9.** ancestral
a grandfather.. **4.** aval
all.. **3.** ava
a mother.. **7.** cognate
an epoch.. **4.** eral
an order.. **7.** ordinal
a wife.. **7.** uxorial
common gender.. **7.** epicene
each.. **3.** ana
earth.. **4.** geal
equal value.. **10.** comparable
French.. **2.** du **3.** des
great importance.. **7.** capital
9. momentous
high standing.. **8.** sterling
little importance.. **5.** petty **7.** trivial
morning.. **5.** matin **7.** matinal
New Stone Age.. **9.** Neolithic
no avail.. **6.** futile
nostrils.. **6.** narine
old age.. **8.** gerontal
planet's path.. **7.** orbital
recent times.. **6.** lately **9.** latter-day
reign.. **6.** regnal
river banks.. **8.** riparian
same family.. **7.** cognate, germane
sound.. **5.** tonal
summer.. **7.** estival
tears.. **8.** lacrimal
the country.. **5.** rural
the mouth.. **4.** oral
the third degree.. **7.** cubical
the throat.. **5.** gular
the tongue.. **7.** glossal
the wrist.. **6.** carpal
this day.. **9.** hodiernal
thread color.. **7.** ficelle
winter.. **6.** hiemal
yore.. **5.** olden
off... **3.** ill **4.** agee, away, doff
5. aside **6.** begone, insane, remote
7. distant, tainted **9.** dissonant,
erroneous, imperfect, right-hand
10. unemployed
offal... **5.** filth **6.** ordure, refuse
7. carrion, garbage, rubbish
offbeat... **14.** unconventional
off-color... **6.** risqué **7.** dubious
8. inferior
offend... **3.** cag, sin, vex **4.** miff
5. anger, annoy, pique, wound
6. assail, insult, revolt **7.** affront, do
wrong, mortify **9.** displease
offender... **6.** sinner **8.** criminal
9. wrongdoer **10.** malefactor
12. transgressor
offense... **3.** sin **5.** crime, delit, fault,
grief, malum **6.** delict, felony, insult
7. outrage, umbrage **8.** trespass
9. indignity **10.** resentment
11. delinquency, misdemeanor,
stellionate
offensive... **4.** foul, ugly **6.** attack,
odious, ribald, vulgar **7.** abusive,
eyesore, fulsome, harmful, obscene
8. invading, shocking **9.** assailant,
attacking, insulting, obnoxious,
repugnant, revolting **10.** aggressive,
malodorous, scurrilous
11. approbrious, displeasing,
distasteful **12.** disagreeable

13. transgressive

offer... 3. bid 6. adduce, tender
7. proffer, propine, propose
8. immolate, overture 9. ultimatum

offered for sale... 6. vended
9. auctioned

offering... 4. gift 6. corban
8. deodate, present 8. oblation
9. sacrifice

offering resistance... 8. renitent

offhand... 8. careless, informal,
slapdash 9. extempore, impromptu
10. carelessly, nonchalant
11. extemporary 12. nonchalantly
15. autoschediastic

office... 4. duty, post, rite, wike (obs)
5. place, trust 7. station
8. ceremony, function, position
9. situation 11. appointment

office (pert to)...
chief.. 7. manager
divine.. 9. akoluthia
for the dead.. 7. trental
holder.. 8. placeman
of a datary (Roman Curia).. 7 dataria
of a ruler.. 7. regency
relinquish (to).. 5. demit
third hour.. 7. tierce

officer... 6. tindal 7. bailiff, command,
conduct, general, manager, marshal,
sheriff 8. adjutant, avigator, director
9. constable, policeman, president

officer (pert to)...
assistant.. 4. aide
Brit Royal Guard.. 4. exon
chief executive.. 3. dey 4. czar
5. mayor 7. emperor, monarch,
premier 8. governor 9. president
10. chancellor
church.. 5. elder 6. sexton
civil law.. 5. notary, police 7. bailiff,
marshal, sheriff 9. constable,
policeman 10. magistrate
club.. 7. steward
corrupt.. 7. grafter
despotic.. 6. satrap
diplomatic.. 7. attaché
Jewish Relig.. 6. parnas
King's stables.. 6. avener
monastic.. 5. prior
naval.. 6. ensign, yeoman
parish.. 6. beadle, bedral
ship's.. 9. boatswain (boson)
weights, measures.. 6. sealer

official... 6. formal 9. authentic
10. functional 13. authoritative

official (pert to)...
command.. 5. edict
despotic.. 6. satrap
game.. 5. judge 6. umpire 7. referee
government.. 10. bureaucrat
insurance.. 7. actuary 8. adjuster
itinerant (Hist).. 6. missus
mark.. 5. stamp
order (RCCh).. 8. rescript
proclamation.. 5. ukase 6. decree
record.. 5. actum
state.. 8. governor 9. secretary

officious... 4. cool, pert 5. saucy
6. formal 8. arrogant, impudent,
official 9. pragmatic 10. meddlesome
11. efficacious, impertinent,

pragmatical 12. contemptuous

officiousness... 10. pragmatism

offing... 10. background

offshoot... 3. rod 5. scion 6. branch,
member 8. addition 9. by–product
10. descendant 12. organization

offspring... 3. son 4. brat, seed
5. child, fruit, issue, sprig 6. origin,
result 7. produce, product, progeny
8. fountain 9. posterity
10. descendant

oficina... 5. works 6. office 7. factory
10. laboratory

often... 3. oft 9. many times
10. frequently, repeatedly 11. over
and over 13. time after time

ogdoad... 5. eight 10. eight group

ogee... 4. gula 5. talon 7. molding
9. cyma recta 11. cyma reversa

ogle... 3. eye 4. gaze, leer 5. stare
7. examine

Ogpu... 8. Gay–Pay–Oo (Russ secret
service)

O Henry... 6. Porter (Wm Sydney)

Ohio...
capital.. 8. Columbus
city.. 5. Akron 6. Dayton, Toledo
9. Cleveland 10. Cincinnati
first settlement.. 8. Marietta
hero.. 12. Anthony Wayne (Gen)
lake.. 4. Erie
name meaning (Indian).. 14. Beautiful
River
State admission.. 11. Seventeenth
State motto.. 27. With God All Things
are Possible
State nickname.. 7. Buckeye

oil... 3. ben, fat 4. balm, ghee
5. bribe, oleum 6. aceite, anoint,
asarum, grease, olanin 8. flattery,
medicate, painting 9. lubricant,
lubricate, petroleum 10. illuminant

oil (pert to)...
beetle.. 5. meloe
berry.. 5. olive
bird.. 8. guachare
cask.. 4. rier
class.. 5. fatty, fixed 6. animal
7. mineral 8. volatile 9. essential,
vegetable
cloth.. 8. linoleum
coal.. 8. photogen
comb form.. 2. ol 3. ole
fish.. 7. escolar
flask.. 4. olpe
gauge.. 9. oleometer
glands (birds).. 9. uropygial
11. elaeodochon
lamp.. 7. lucigen
mineral.. 7. naphtha
plant.. 6. sesame 9. castor–oil
prefix.. 2. ol
rock.. 5. shale 9. limestone
seed.. 3. til (teel) 6. sesame
7. linseed 8. rapeseed 10. castor
bean, cottonseed
skin.. 5. sebum
stone.. 4. hone 9. whetstone
term.. 5. oleic
tree.. 4. eboe (ebo), tung 5. mahua
6. illupi 7. oil palm 9. candlenut,
castor–oil

tube.. 5. vitta
whale.. 5. sperm
oil of...
  cloves.. 7. eugenol
  myrcia.. 6. bay oil
  orange blossoms.. 6. neroil
  roses.. 4. otto 5. attar (atar)
  salt.. 7. bittern
oils... 10. elaeoptene (elaeopten) (opp
  of stearoptene)
oily... 3. fat 4. glib 5. bland, oleic,
  suave 6. olease, supple 8. unctuous
  9. compliant, plausible 10. flattering,
  oleaginous 11. insinuating,
  subservient 12. hypocritical
oily liquids... 3. tar 6. cresol, octane
  7. aniline, picamar
oily tissue... 3. fat
ointment... 4. balm, cere, lard, nard
  5. salve 6. balsam, carron, cerate,
  ceroma, grease 7. pomatum, unguent
  8. liniment 9. spikenard, xeromyron
  10. petrolatum 11. embrocation
Oise (France)... 5. Aisne (tributary),
  river 10. department
Ojibway secret order... 4. mide
  (meda) 9. midewiwin
ojo... 5. oasis
OK... 6. righto 7. correct
Okinawa...
  capital.. 4. Naha
  island group (64).. 6. Ryukyu
  prefecture of.. 5. Japan
Oklahoma...
  capital.. 12. Oklahoma City
  city.. 3. Ada 4. Enid 5. Tulsa
  6. Lawton 8. Muskogee
  9. Claremore 12. Bartlesville
  Five Civilized Tribes.. 5. Creek
  7. Choctaw 8. Cherokee, Seminole
  9. Chickasaw
  lake.. 6. Texoma
  mountain.. 5. Ozark 6. Boston
  8. Ouachita 9. Black Mesa
  museum.. 6. Indian 8. Woolaroc
  native son (famed).. 10. Will Rogers
  old name.. 15. Indian Territory
  State admission.. 11. Thirty–third
  State flower.. 9. mistletoe
  State motto.. 16. Labor Conquers All,
  Labor Omnia Vincit (Labor Conquers
  All Things)
  State nickname.. 6. Sooner
okra... 5. bendy, gumbo 6. mallow
old... 3. ald, eld 4. aged 5. anile
  6. infirm, senile 7. ancient, antique,
  archaic 8. obsolete 9. doddering,
  senescent, venerable 10. antiquated
old (pert to)...
  age.. 6. senile 7. geratic 8. gerontic,
  senility 10. geriatrics (Med),
  senescence
  ancient (very).. 7. Ogygian
  billy, granny.. 5. squaw
  fashioned.. 4. fogy 7. antique
  9. primitive 12. conservative
  hat.. 5. trite 9. out-of-date
  maid.. 5. prude 10. fussbudget
  man.. 5. elder, timer 6. gaffer,
  geezer, Nestor 8. kangaroo
  10. fuddy–duddy
  sailor.. 4. salt

saying.. 3. saw 5. adage, maxim
time.. 3. eld 4. syne
woman.. 3. hag 4. fogy 5. crone
  6. dotard, gammer
womanish.. 5. anile 6. senile
  10. effeminate
Old (pert to)...
  Bailey.. 12. English court
  Bay State.. 13. Massachusetts
  Dominion.. 8. Virginia
  Empire.. 4. Maya
  English alphabet.. 10. Anglo–Saxon
  Faithful.. 6. geyser
  Franklin State.. 9. Tennessee
  Gentleman Harry.. 5. Devil
  Gooseberry.. 5. Devil, Satan
  Glory.. 15. Stars and Stripes
  Guard (Waterloo).. 9. Napoleon's
  Hickory.. 13. Andrew Jackson
  Ironsides.. 15. USS Constitution
  Kingdom.. 7. Memphis (Egypt)
  Lady of Threadneedle Street..
  13. Bank of England
  Line State.. 8. Maryland
  Man of the Mountain.. 7. Profile (The)
  Noll.. 14. Oliver Cromwell
  North Church.. 12. Christ Church
  North State.. 13. North Carolina
  Rough and Ready.. 13. (Gen) Zachary
  Taylor
  Serpent.. 5. Satan
  Sod.. 4. Erin 7. Ireland
  Sol.. 3. sun
  Stone Age.. 11. Paleolithic
  Three Stars.. 5. (Gen) Grant
  World.. 7. Eastern
olden... 6. bygone
older... 5. elder 6. senior 8. ancestor
oldest... 4. dean 6. eldest 7. stalest
Old Testament (pert to)...
  Books (number).. 10. Thirty–nine
  Elohim.. 3. God (The Hexateuch)
  Hexateuch.. 13. first Six Books
  Land of riches.. 5. Ophir
  objects (sacred).. 4. Urim
  7. Thummim
  Pentateuch.. 11. Law of Moses
  14. first Five Books
  writer.. 7. Elohist (The Hexateuch)
Old World (pert to)...
  ape.. 7. Primate 10. Catarrhina,
  catarrhine
  carnivore.. 5. genet
  falcon.. 5. saker
  herb.. 5. tansy
  lizard.. 5. Agama
  shrub.. 4. Olax
oleaginous... 4. oily 5. oleic
  8. unctuous
oleander... 6. Nerium 11. rhododaphne
  12. rhododendron
oleoresin... 5. anime, elemi 6. balsam
  7. copaiba
oleum... 3. oil
olfaction... 7. osmesis 8. smelling
  12. sense of smell
olfactory organ... 4. nose 8. olfactor
olid... 4. foul 5. fetid 6. rancid, smelly
  10. malodorous 11. strong smell
oligarchy... 10. rule by a few
olinda bug... 6. weevil
olio... 4. olla, stem 6. medley

7. mixture 8. chowchow
9. burlesque, potpourri
10. collection, hodgepodge
11. olla–podrida

oliphant... 8. elephant 9. ivory horn

oliprance... 4. romp, show 7. jollity
11. merrymaking, ostentation

olive (pert to)...
branch.. 5. child, peace 6. symbol (peace)
color.. 11. yellow–green
dun.. 3. fly (fishing)
enzyme.. 6. olease
family.. 8. Oleaceae
fly.. 3. dun 4. gnat 5. quill
gray.. 10. Scotch gray
gum.. 6. olivil
overripe.. 5. drupe
stuffed.. 6. pimola
true.. 4. Olea
wild.. 8. oleaster
yard.. 6. olivet
yellow.. 9. moss green 10. chartreuse

olla... 3. jug, pot 4. olio 8. palm leaf (palmyra) 11. olla–podrida

olla–podrida... 4. hash, olio 6. medley 10. hodgepodge

oloroso... 6. sherry

olpe... 5. flask 8. oenochoë 11. wine pitcher

olycook, olykoek... 7. cruller
8. doughnut

Olympia... 4. ship 7. capital (Wash)
8. heavenly 9. sanctuary (anc)

Olympiad... 14. four–year period

Olympian god... 4. Ares, Zeus
6. Apollo, Hermes 8. Dionysus, Hercules, Poseidon 10. Hephaestus

Olympian goddess... 4. Hera
6. Athena, Hestia 7. Artemis, Demeter 9. Aphrodite

Olympic cupbearer... 8. Ganymede

Olympic Games (pert to)...
honor of.. 4. Zeus
period.. 14. four years apart
revival site.. 6. Athens (1896)
site (first).. 4. Elis 7. Olympia
time of games.. 8. four days

Olympieion, Olympium... 6. temple (Athens)

Olympus (Gr)... 3. sky 5. Mount
6. heaven 8. mountain

Olympus (Hind)... 4. Meru

Omaha... 4. city (Neb) 5. Sioux
6. Indian

Omar Khayyam (pert to)...
country.. 4. Iran 6. Persia
fish (fabled).. 3. mah
poem.. 8. Rubaiyat

omasum... 9. manyplies 10. psalterium
12. third stomach

ombro (comb form)... 4. rain

ombrometer... 9. rain gauge

omega... 3. end 4. last 5. final
6. letter (Gr)

omen... 4. bode, sign 5. abode, knell, token 6. augury 7. auspice, portent, presage 8. forebode, foreshow
9. abodement 10. divination
15. prognostication

omer... 3. ephah, sheaf 9. fifty days (Passover to Pentecost)

ominous... 4. dour, trim 8. sinister
9. ferocious 10. inexorable, portentous 12. inauspicious

omission... 4. want 5. caret, error
7. neglect 9. oversight
10. deficiency, leaving out
13. nonobservance

omission of end syllables...
7. apocope

omission of words... 8. ellipsis

omit... 4. dele, pass, skip 5. elide
6. delete, ignore 7. exclude
11. leave undone

omitting... 7. elision 9. excepting, excluding 10. precluding

omneity... 7. allness
16. all–comprehensive

omnipotent... 6. divine 8. almighty
9. unequaled, unlimited
11. all–powerful

omniscient... 4. wise 6. divine
7. learned 10. all–knowing

omnitude... 7. allness 8. totality
12. universality

omnivorous... 6. greedy 9. all–eating
10. gluttonous

omoplate... 7. scapula

omphalos... 3. hut 4. knob 5. altar, navel 6. center 9. umbilicus

on... 2. at 4. atop, upon 5. above, ahead, along 6. toward 7. against, forward 10. concerning
13. juxtaposition

On (Bib)... 7. Baalbek 8. holy city
10. Heliopolis (Egypt) 12. City of the Sun

on (pert to)...
account of.. 3. for
all sides.. 5. about 6. around
and on.. 7. forever, tedious
9. tediously
behalf of.. 3. for
dit.. 5. rumor 6. report
going.. 7. forward 10. proceeding
grand scale.. 4. epic
hand.. 4. here 7. present 9. available
high.. 5. aloft
other side.. 4. over 6. across
sheltered side.. 4. alee
this side.. 3. cis (pref) 9. cisalpine
10. cismontane, cispontine
windward side.. 8. aweather

onager... 3. ass 5. kiang 8. catapult

once in a while... 7. erstwhile
10. now and then 12. occasionally

once upon a time... 6. one day
7. the past, time was 8. formerly
10. the long ago

Oncorhynchus... 6. salmon

ondoyant... 4. wavy (art)

one... 2. an, un 3. ace, ain, ein
4. unit 5. alone, unity, whole
6. person, single 9. unmarried
10. individual

one (pert to)...
after the other.. 8. serially, seriatim
12. successfully
bearing heraldic arms.. 7. armiger
behind the other.. 6. tandem
born in serfdom.. 4. neif
bringing good luck.. 6. mascot
by one.. 6. apiece, singly 10. one at

a time 12. individually
comb form .. 3. uni 4. mono
curious .. 6. gossip 8. quidnunc
despondent in views .. 9. pessimist
fond of women .. 11. philogynist
footed .. 6. uniped
frantic for freedom ..
    15. eleutheromaniac
gigantic in size .. 5. giant, titan
happy in views .. 7. optimist
horse .. 5. petty 6. little 8. inferior
    10. second-rate 13. insignificant
in a thousand .. 6. oddity 7. paragon,
    prodigy
in second childhood .. 6. dotard
instructed in secret system .. 5. epopt
    8. initiate
living on another .. 8. parasite
moving stealthily .. 7. prowler
sided .. 5. askew 7. partial
    10. prejudiced, unilateral
thousand .. 3. mil
time .. 7. quondam 8. formerly
undergoing change .. 6. mutant
oneberry ... 9. hackberry
    14. partridgeberry
one devoted to ...
deviltry .. 7. hellion
fast driving .. 4. jehu 7. speeder
indolence .. 10. daydreamer,
    lotus-eater
own opinion .. 5. bigot
physical feats .. 7. athlete
pursuit .. 3. ist (suff)
table delicacies .. 7. epicure
onefold ... 6. simple, single 7. sincere
    9. guileless
onegite ... 8. amethyst
Oneida ... 6. Indian 8. Iroquois
    9. Community (NY)
oneiros .. 5. dream
oneirotic ... 6. dreams (pert to)
oneism ... 6. egoism, monism
oneness ... 5. union, unity 7. concord
    8. identity, sameness 9. agreement,
    aloneness, constancy 10. loneliness,
    singleness, uniformity, uniqueness
    11. singularity 13. undividedness
one of ...
ancient race .. 4. Mede 7. Iberian
Buddhist precepts .. 6. nidana
Persian dynasty .. 8. Sassanid
religious sect .. 10. Anabaptist
the Bears .. 4. Ursa
the Greek Wise Men .. 6. Thales
the initiated .. 5. epopt
twins .. 5. gemel (Her)
onerous ... 4. load 5. heavy 6. burden
    7. onerose 9. difficult, laborious,
    ponderous 10. burdensome,
    oppressive 12. impedimental
one versed in ...
children's diseases .. 12. pediatrician
law .. 6. legist
literature .. 6. savant 9. literatus
memory .. 9. mnemonist
politics .. 9. statesman
religious law .. 8. canonist
resources, wealth .. 9. economist
one who ...
absconds .. 6. eloper 8. decamper,

    deserter
appropriates .. 9. pre-emptor
attacks .. 9. aggressor
believes in all religions .. 6. omnist
believes in personal God .. 5. deist
believes in self .. 9. solipsist
beseeches .. 7. pleader
brings meat to royal table .. 7. dapifer,
    steward
cherishes .. 8. fosterer
collects voluntary taxes .. 6. tither
conveys property .. 7. alienor
dies for a cause .. 6. martyr
differs .. 4. anti 9. dissenter, dissident
disowns .. 10. repudiator
displays learning .. 6. pedant
disposes by will .. 7. devisor
edits .. 7. reviser
feigns illness .. 10. malingerer
fights for cause .. 8. crusader
forsakes faith principles .. 8. apostate
frustrates a plan .. 7. marplot
gives up .. 9. abnegator
grants by deed .. 7. remiser
hates argument .. 10. misologist
hates people .. 11. misanthrope
holds office .. 2. in 9. incumbent
inculcates .. 7. infuser 9. instiller
inflicts retribution .. 7. nemesis
misuses authority .. 6. satrap
plunders .. 6. sacker 8. pillager
practises palmistry .. 11. chiromancer
prevents entrance .. 5. hajib
quarrels .. 7. rowdy
removes nuisance .. 6. abator
rules, manages .. 6. gerent
sells provisions to troops .. 6. sutler
shoots from ambush .. 6. sniper
sponges .. 6. cadger 8. parasite
stays .. 5. bider
summons spirits .. 8. evocator
testifies .. 8. deponent
transfers property .. 7. alienor
ongall ... 5. onset 6. attack
onion ... 3. set (bulbs) 4. boll, bulb,
    cepa, leek 5. chive, cibol, pearl,
    reeve 6. Allium 7. Bermuda, onionet,
    shallot 8. eschalot, rareripe, scallion
onkos (Gr) ... 7. topknot
only ... 4. just, lone, mere, sole
    5. chief 6. lonely, merely, simple,
    simply, single, singly, solely
    8. uniquely 11. exclusively
    13. companionless 14. above all
    others
onocentaur ... 3. ape 5. demon
    (fabled)
onomasticon ... 7. lexicon
    10. dictionary, vocabulary (Gr)
onomatology *(science of)* ... 5. names
    11. terminology
onomatopoeic ... 6. echoic 9. imitative
    (of natural sound)
onset, onslaught ... 6. attack
    7. assault 11. rushing upon, setting
    upon
Ontario ...
Bay .. 6. Hudson
capital .. 7. Toronto
city .. 6. Ottawa 7. Timmins
    8. Hamilton
lake .. 9. Great Lake (one of five)

province.. **6**. Canada
river.. **6**. Ottawa, Thames **7**. Niagara **10**. St Lawrence
ontogeny... **9**. evolution
ontology *(science of)*... **5**. being **7**. reality
onus... **4**. duty, load **6**. burden, charge **10**. impediment, imposition, obligation
onus probandi... **13**. burden of proof
onward, onwards... **5**. ahead, forth **6**. future, moving **7**. forward **8**. forwards, progress **9**. in advance
onychauxis... **14**. nail overgrowth
onyx... **6**. nicolo (niccolo), tecali
ooid... **9**. egg-shaped
oology *(science of)*... **8**. bird eggs
oomancy *(divination by)*... **4**. eggs
oont... **5**. camel **13**. beast of burden
oop... **4**. join **5**. unite
oopak, oopack... **3**. tea (black)
oorial... **3**. sha **5**. sheep, urial
ooze... **3**. bog **4**. drip, leak, seep, sipe, soak **5**. exude, marsh **6**. be damp **7**. leather **8**. transude **9**. percolate
oozy... **4**. miry **5**. muddy, slimy
opah... **4**. fish, soko **8**. kingfish **9**. Lampridae
opal... **3**. gem **4**. blue **5**. stone **7**. hyalite **10**. pearliness
opal, variety of... **4**. wood **5**. black, noble, pitch, resin **6**. common **7**. girasol, hyalite **8**. menilite, precious **9**. cacholong, geyserite, harlequin **10**. chalcedony
opalescent... **6**. pearly **7**. opaline **8**. irisated **10**. iridescent
opaque... **4**. dark **6**. obtuse, stupid **7**. obscure **8**. eyeshade **10**. not shining **13**. unilluminated **14**. not transparent
open... **3**. ope **4**. ajar, bare, free, undo **5**. agape, begin, clear, frank, overt, plain, start, untie **6**. candid, honest, patent, public, reveal, unbolt, unfold, unfurl, unlock, unseal, unstop, vacant **7**. artless, evident, exposed, natural, obvious, sincere, unbosom, unclose **8**. apparent, commence, disclose, expanded, initiate, patulous, revealed, unclosed, unfasten **9**. spreading, uncertain, uncovered, unfeigned **10**. accessible, unreserved **11**. unprotected **12**. questionable
open *(pert to)*...
acknowledgment.. **6**. avowal
air.. **8**. alfresco
and shut.. **7**. assured, obvious **11**. prearranged
bursting.. **10**. dehiscence
cabinet.. **7**. étagère
country.. **5**. veldt, weald
court.. **4**. area **5**. patio
door.. **6**. policy **11**. hospitality
eyed.. **7**. curious **8**. vigilant **9**. attentive, expectant
for discussion.. **4**. moot
fully.. **4**. wide **9**. dehiscent, full-blown
land.. **4**. moor **5**. heath **6**. desert, plains
out.. **6**. deploy (Mil)

partly.. **3**. mid **4**. ajar
passage in forests.. **5**. glade
to scorn.. **9**. derisible
to view.. **5**. overt
opening... **2**. os **3**. bay, gap **4**. door, gate, hole, loop, pore, rift, slot, vent **5**. cleft, mouth, sinus, start **6**. breach, eyelet, hiatus, outlet, portal **7**. display, foramen, initial, orifice, vacancy **8**. aperture, fenestra, position **9**. admission, beginning **10**. passageway, unfoldment **11**. entranceway, opportunity
opening *(pert to)*...
chess.. **6**. gambit
ear.. **4**. burr
enlarge.. **4**. ream
from 3rd ventricle (Anat).. **4**. pila
having.. **10**. fenestrate
in a mold.. **6**. ingate
minute.. **5**. stoma
narrow.. **4**. rima, slot **7**. crevice **9**. stenopaic
nasal.. **4**. nare
small.. **4**. pore **5**. chink **6**. cranny, eyelet, lacuna **7**. foramen, orifice, pinhole
wide (Bot).. **9**. dehiscent
openings... **3**. ora **7**. stomata
openwork... **6**. eyelet **7**. Madeira, tracery **10**. decoration
opera *(pert to)*...
comic (singer).. **5**. buffa, buffo **7**. buffoon
glass.. **7**. binocle **9**. binocular, lorgnette
hat.. **5**. crush, gibus **6**. topper
kind.. **4**. soap **5**. horse **8**. burletta
singer.. **4**. bass, diva **5**. buffa, buffo, tenor **7**. buffoon, soprano **10**. basso buffo, coloratura
solo.. **4**. aria **5**. scena
star.. **4**. diva **10**. prima donna
text.. **8**. libretto
opera, composer... **5**. Bizet, Gluck, Verdi **6**. Glinka, Gounod, Handel, Hayden, Mozart, Wagner **7**. Puccini, Rossini **9**. Donizetti **11**. Deems Taylor **14**. Rimski-Korsakov (Korsakoff)
opera, drama... **4**. Aïda **5**. Boris, Faust, Orfeo, Thaïs, Tosca **6**. Bohême, Carmen, Coq d'or, Daphne, Isolde **7**. Alceste **9**. Lohengrin, Pagliacci, Rigoletto **10**. Magic Flute, Prince Igor, Tannhäuser **11**. Don Giovanni, Il Travatore **13**. Peter Ibbetson **14**. Tales of Hoffman **15**. Hansel and Gretel, Madame Butterfly **16**. Marriage of Figaro
operation... **6**. action, agency **7**. surgery **8**. creation **9**. influence **11**. functioning, transaction
operation, surgical... **5**. major, minor **6**. trepan **8**. excision **9**. resection **10**. amputation, castration **11**. exploratory **12**. appendectomy, hysterectomy **13**. tonsillectomy
operative... **6**. worker **7**. artisan, working **8**. mechanic **9**. detective
operative, become... **5**. inure (enure)
operator... **5**. agent, quack **6**. dealer,

worker 7. creator, handler, surgeon
10. mountebank, speculator
operculum (Bot)... 3. cap, lid
7. stopper 8. covering
operose... 4. busy 8. diligent
9. difficult, laborious 11. painstaking
Ophidia... 6. snakes 8. reptiles,
serpents 9. Serpentes
ophidian... 5. snake, viper 7. serpent
ophiolatry... 12. snake worship
ophthalmic... 6. ocular 7. optical
9. eye region
ophthalmology, science... 6. the eye
opiate... 4. drug, hemp, snow
5. opium 6. heroin 7. anodyne,
cocaine, hashish (hasheesh), soother
8. narcotic 9. analgesic, paregoric
11. somniferous 12. somnifacient
opine... 4. deem 5. judge, think
6. remark 7. opinion, suppose
10. conjecture
opinion... 4. idea, view 6. belief,
esteem, notion, report 7. feeling
8. judgment 9. sentiment
10. estimation, impression, ober
dictum, reputation
opinion (pert to)...
expert.. 9. expertise
expression, common.. 5. theme
expression, formal.. 4. vote
religious, unorthodox.. 6. heresy
opinions (pert to)...
collection.. 9. anthology, symposium
professed.. 6. credo
opium... 4. drug 9. narcotic
10. intoxicant
opium (pert to)...
concentrate.. 6. heroin
derivative (Chem).. 7. meconic
Egyptian.. 8. thebaine
extract.. 7. chandoo (chandu), codeine
8. morphine 9. narcotine
10. papaverine
overuse.. 8. opiumism
poppy seed.. 3. maw
source.. 5. poppy
tincture.. 9. paregoric
variety.. 6. Indian, Smyrna, Turkey
7. Chinese, Persian
opodeldoc... 7. plaster 8. liniment
opodidymus... 7. monster (two-headed)
opossum... 7. Marmosa 9. didelphid,
marsupial, phalanger
opossum (pert to)...
S America.. 5. quica 7. sarigue
variety.. 5. mouse, water, wooly
water.. 5. yapok (yapock)
wood.. 10. silver bell
opponent... 3. foe 4. anti 5. enemy,
rival 7. adverse 8. opposite
9. adversary, combatant
10. antagonist
opportune... 3. fit, pat 5. ready
6. timely 7. apropos 8. suitable
9. expedient, well-timed
10. convenient 11. appropriate
opportunist... 10. politician, vacillator
opportunity... 4. turn 6. chance
7. opening 8. occasion
12. circumstance 16. suitable
occasion
oppose... 3. pit 4. deny, face 5. fight,

rebel 6. expose, oppugn, refute,
resist 7. contest, exhibit, gainsay
8. confront 10. antagonize,
contradict, contravene, counteract
opposed... 3. met 4. anti, vied
5. coped 6. averse, pitted
7. adverse, fronted 8. contrary,
renitent, resisted 9. contested,
withstood 12. oppositional
opposed (pert to)...
against.. 6. pitted
lee.. 5. stoss
to change.. 7. die-hard
11. reactionary 12. conservative
to entad (inward).. 5. ectad
zenith.. 5. nadir
opposite... 5. polar 6. facing
7. adverse, antonym, hostile,
opposed, reverse 8. contrary,
converse 9. different, repugnant
10. opposition 12. antagonistic
13. contradictory 14. contrapositive
opposite (pert to)...
directly.. 10. antipodean
exact.. 8. antipode
in action, in nature.. 5. polar
7. inverse
prefix.. 6. contra
science.. 3. art
to spring tide.. 4. neap
opposition... 9. hostility, opponency
10. antagonism, antithesis, refutation,
resistance 11. contrariety, disapproval
13. contradiction
oppress... 4. rape 5. crush 6. burden,
harass, nither (Scot), ravish
7. depress, swelter 8. distress,
macerate, suppress 9. overpower,
overwhelm, persecute, tyrannize
10. extinguish
oppressive... 5. harsh 6. severe,
stuffy, sultry 7. onerous 8. rigorous
9. ponderous 10. burdensome,
depressing, tyrannical
oppressor... 4. czar (tsar), Nero
6. despot, tyrant 8. autocrat,
burdener 11. Simon Legree
opprobrious... 7. abusive 8. despised,
infamous 9. insulting, offensive
10. scurrilous 11. disgraceful
12. contumelious
opprobrium... 5. odium 6. infamy
8. disgrace 11. malediction
oppugn... 6. assail, oppose
10. controvert, counteract
oppugnant... 7. hostile, opposed
8. contrary 12. antagonistic
13. counteractive
Ops (pert to)...
called also.. 10. Ops Consiva
consort of.. 6. Consus, Saturn
Festival.. 6. Opalia
Greek counterpart.. 4. Rhea
Roman goddess of.. 7. Harvest
opsigamy... 14. old-age marriage
opt... 4. pick 5. elect 6. choose
11. make a choice
optic... 6. ocular, visual 11. optological
optical (pert to)...
device.. 9. stenopaic
glass.. 4. lens
illusion.. 6. mirage

instrument.. 5. prism 7. alidade,
reticle 8. eriometer, optometer
10. microscope
membrane.. 6. retina
organ.. 3. eye
optic defect... 6. myopia
optimistic... 4. rosy 7. hopeful,
roseate 8. cheerful, sanguine
9. expectant 10. auspicious
optimum... 4. best 7. maximum
13. most favorable
option... 6. choice, future (Finan)
7. refusal 8. free will 11. alternative
13. right to choose
optional... 8. elective 9. voluntary
10. permissive 13. not compulsory
opulence... 6. plenty, riches, wealth
9. abundance, affluence, amplitude,
profusion
opulent... 4. rich 6. lavish 7. profuse,
wealthy 8. abundant, affluent
9. luxuriant
opulus... 11. guelder-rose
13. cranberry tree
opus... 4. work 5. étude
10. embroidery, needlework
11. composition
oquassa... 5. trout
oracle... 4. seer 5. sibyl 6. Dodona,
medium, mentor 7. prophet, wise
man 8. Delphian (Delphic)
10. revelation
oracular... 4. wise 5. vatic (vatical)
9. prophetic 10. predictive
11. forecasting
orage... 5. storm 7. tempest
oral... 5. parol, vocal 6. spoken, verbal
10. not written 11. nuncupative
orang... 9. orangutan (orangutang)
orange (pert to)...
Bowl site.. 5. Miami
bird.. 7. tanager
color.. 5. ocher, peach 6. carrot
7. apricot 8. mandarin
flower oil.. 6. meroli
genus.. 6. Citrus
heraldry.. 5. tenné
kind.. 4. mock 5. hedge, navel,
Osage 6. bergamot, mandarin,
Valencia 9. tangerine
leaf.. 6. karamu
marigold.. 9. tangerine
membrane.. 4. zest
mock.. 7. seringa
seed.. 3. pip
Orangeman... 14. North Irelander
orangutan... 4. mias 5. orang, Pongo,
satyr, Simia
orate... 5. plead, speak, spiel
8. harangue
oration... 5. éloge 6. eulogy, prayer,
sermon, speech 7. lecture
8. encomium, petition 9. discourse
orator... 6. rhetor 7. speaker
9. perorator 10. petitioner
11. rhetorician, spellbinder
orator, famed... 5. Bryan (Wm
Jennings) 6. Cicero 9. Churchill
11. Demosthenes
oratory... 6. chapel 7. chantry
9. elocution, eloquence
orb... 3. eye, sun 4. ball, moon, star

5. earth, globe, world 6. bereft,
circle, planet, sphere 7. enclose
8. encircle, insignia, surround
orbed... 5. lunar, round
orbit... 4. path 5. globe, route
6. sphere 7. circuit 10. trajectory
orbit (pert to)...
cavity.. 9. eye socket
curve.. 10. trajectory
of a planet.. 7. ellipse
point.. 5. apsis
point, farthest.. 6. apogee
orc, Orca... 5. whale 7. grampus
orchestra (pert to)...
bells.. 12. glockenspiel
circle.. 7. parquet 8. parterre
small.. 11. symphonette
orchestra instrument group...
brass.. 4. horn, tuba 6. cornet
7. trumpet 8. trombone
percussion.. 4. drum 7. cymbals,
timpani (tympani) 8. triangle
strings.. 5. cello, viola 6. violin
10. contrabass 11. violoncello
wind.. 4. oboe 5. flute 7. bassoon
8. clarinet
orchid... 4. Disa 5. vanda 6. Ophrys
7. Listera, lycaste, pogonia
8. arethusa, Cattleya, Oncidium
9. cymbidium, puttyroot 10. letterleaf
orchid (pert to)...
appendage.. 8. caudicle
handsomest.. 4. Disa
largest.. 10. letterleaf
meal.. 5. salep
petal.. 8. labellum
tuber, root.. 5. salep 7. cullion
Orcus... 3. God (Rom) 5. Hades, Pluto
(Gr) 10. lower world
ordain... 4. plan 5. allot, enact, equip
6. decree 7. appoint, arrange,
command, destine, install 8. canonize
9. institute 10. predestine
ordeal... 4. gaff, test 5. trial
7. sorcery 8. judgment
10. experience (painful)
order... 3. bid 4. fiat, ordo, rank, rule,
sect, will 5. array, class, edict,
genus, money 6. cosmos, decree,
direct, enjoin, genera (pl), manage,
system 7. arrange, command,
dispose, mandate, prepare, verdict
8. regulate, sequence 9. condition,
procedure 10. injunction
11. arrangement
order (pert to)...
back.. 6. remand
connecting.. 6. in turn 8. seriatim
cosmic.. 3. tao 4. rita
for writ.. 7. precipe
good.. 6. eutaxy
grammar.. 5. taxis
judicial.. 4. fiat, writ 7. summons
proper.. 6. kilter
written.. 6. billet
Order, architecture... 5. Doric, Ionic
6. Tuscan 8. Etruscan 10. Corinthian
Order, association... 4. Club 5. Guild
7. DeMolay, Society, St Clare
8. Sodality, Sorority 9. The Garter,
Trappists 10. Fellowship, Fraternity,
Sisterhood 11. Brotherhood, Eastern

Star, Purple Heart 12. The Rising
Sun
ordered... 4. bade, trim 7. regular
8. arranged, measured, ordained
9. regulated
orderly... 4. neat, tidy, trim 7. regular,
uniform 8. obedient, peaceful
9. attendant, regularly, shipshape
10. methodical, systematic
order of...
amphibians.. 5. Anura
aquatic animals.. 7. Cetacea
holy beings.. 9. hierarchy
insects.. 7. Diptera
mammals.. 8. Edentata, Primates
mites.. 6. acarid
the day.. 8. schedule 12. instructions
whales.. 4. Cete
ordinal... 6. number, ritual, serial
10. succession 11. Book of Rules
(Eccl), categorical
ordinance... 3. law 4. rite 5. bylaw,
edict 6. assize, decree 7. control,
statute 8. decretum 9. allotment,
direction, enactment, sacrament
10. management, regulation
ordinarily... 7. plainly, usually
8. commonly 9. generally, naturally
11. customarily
ordinary... 4. ruck, so–so 5. judge,
nomic, plain, prosy, usual
6. common, normal, tavern
7. average, natural, prosaic, vulgate
8. everyday, habitual, mediocre,
plebeian, workaday 9. of the Mass
10. table d'hôte
ordinate... 6. ordain 7. appoint,
orderly, regular 8. moderate
9. harmonize 10. co–ordinate
ordination... 5. order 11. appointment,
arrangement, disposition
12. organization
ordnance... 4. guns 5. armor, orgue
7. petards, rabinet, weapons
8. armament, firearms, supplies
9. artillery, torpedoes
10. ammunition 14. apparatus belli
ordo... 5. order 11. publication
ore... 3. tin 4. gold, iron, lead, paco
5. brass, metal, ochre 6. copper,
silver, speiss 7. mercury, mineral,
seaweed, uranium 8. cinnabar,
tungsten 9. loadstone (lodestone)
11. quicksilver
ore (pert to)...
box.. 6. sluice
deposit.. 4. lode, mine 7. bonanza
fuser.. 7. smelter
horizontal layer.. 5. stope
impure.. 6. speiss
iron.. 5. ocher 8. hematite
9. magnetite
lead.. 6. galena
loading platform.. 4. plat
machine separator.. 6. vanner
refuse.. 6. scoria 8. tailings
roller.. 9. edgestone
silver.. 5. noble (metal)
sluice.. 5. trunk
stirrer.. 5. dolly
tin.. 5. scove
trough.. 6. strake

vein.. 4. lode 5. scrin, stope
worthless.. 5. matte
oread... 5. nymph 7. seamaid
Oregon...
capital.. 5. Salem
caves.. 11. Marble Halls
city.. 6. Eugene 7. Astoria, Medford
8. Portland 12. Klamath Falls
crab apple.. 7. powitch
emigrant route.. 11. Oregon Trail
famed persons.. 4. Gray (Capt)
5. Astor, Clark, Lewis
Indian.. 5. Modoc 7. Chinook,
Klamath 8. Nez Percé
mountain.. 4. Hood 5. Coast
8. Cascades
native nickname.. 7. webfoot
river.. 5. Rogue 7. Klamath
8. Columbia 10. Willamette
State admission.. 11. Thirty–third
State motto.. 8. The Union
State nickname.. 6. Beaver
13. Sawdust Empire
wind.. 7. chinook
oremus... 9. let us pray
Oreortyx... 5. quail
Orestes (pert to)...
father.. 9. Agamemnon
friend.. 7. Pylades
mother.. 12. Clytemnestra
sister.. 7. Electra
wife.. 8. Hermione
orf, orfe... 3. ide 4. fish
orfevrerie... 7. jewelry 9. gold plate
organ (pert to)...
anatomy.. 3. ear, eye 4. lung, nose
5. brain, heart, liver 6. kidney,
syrinx, tongue, tonsil 7. viscera (pl)
bristlelike.. 4. seta
desk.. 7. console
fish.. 8. drumfish
honey–secreting.. 7. nectary
plant.. 5. stoma 7. tendril
motion.. 6. muscle
respiratory.. 4. lung
secretion.. 5. gland
spider's spinner.. 9. spinneret
stop (music).. 8. register
tactile.. 6. feeler 8. tentacle
organic... 5. state, vital 6. innate
8. inherent 9. organized
10. structural 11. fundamental
14. constitutional
organic (pert to)...
compound.. 5. amine 6. enzyme,
ketone
disease.. 11. organopathy
memory.. 5. mneme
radical.. 5. ethyl
remains.. 5. azoic
soil.. 5. humus
organism (pert to)...
bacterial.. 4. germ 7. microbe
body of.. 4. soma
elementary.. 5. monad
minute.. 5. spore 6. amoeba
pelagic.. 6. nekton
plant.. 5. spore
potential.. 7. idorgan
sea.. 6. nekton 7. benthos
8. plankton
type.. 5. plant 6. animal 9. vegetable

vegetable.. 4. tree 5. plant
organization... 4. bloc, sect, unit
   5. cadre, guild, party, setup
   6. empire 11. association,
   corporation 12. constitution
   13. establishment 14. classification
organized body... 5. corps, posse
organized matter... 5. fauna, flora
   6. living, nekton 7. animate, benthos
   8. plankton
organology, science... 10. phrenology
   13. splanchnology
organoscopy... 10. phrenology
orgueil... 5. pride 11. haughtiness
orgy... 4. lark, romp 5. binge, revel,
   rites (anc), spree 6. frolic, ritual,
   shindy 7. debauch, revelry, shindig,
   wassail 8. carousal 11. celebration,
   merrymaking
oribi... 7. bleebok, Ourebia 8. antelope
oriel... 3. bay 6. recess, window
   7. balcony, gallery, portion
   8. corridor 10. moucharaby
   11. meshrabiyeh (Moham)
orient... 4. dawn 7. eastern, shining,
   sunrise 8. oriental, pellucid
   11. resplendent
Orient... 4. Asia, East 6. Levant
oriental (pert to)...
   abode, gateway.. 3. dar
   animal.. 4. zebu
   archangel.. 5. Uriel
   beverage.. 6. arrack
   building.. 6. pagoda
   burden bearer.. 5. hamal
   cap (sheepskin).. 6. calpac (calpack)
   caravansary.. 4. khan 5. serai
   6. imaret
   carpet.. 4. kali
   carriage.. 10. jinrikisha (jinricksha)
   cart, wagon.. 5. araba
   chief.. 4. Khan 6. Mikado
   Christian.. 5. Uniat
   corn.. 4. para
   cosmetic.. 4. kohl
   council.. 5. Divan
   cymbals.. 5. zels
   deity.. 3. Bel
   destiny.. 6. Kismet
   disease.. 8. beriberi
   dish.. 4. rice 5. pilau (pilaw) 6. pilaff
   8. chop suey, chow mein
   drug.. 4. opium 6. heroin 7. hashish
   (hasheesh)
   drum.. 6. tom–tom
   dulcimer.. 6. santir
   fan.. 3. ogi
   food.. 4. rice 5. salep
   garment.. 3. aba 6. sarong
   guitar.. 5. sitar
   head cover.. 6. turban
   hospice.. 6. imaret
   inn.. 5. serai
   instrument (Mus).. 7. samisen
   laborer.. 6. coolie (cooly)
   leader.. 4. amir (ameer)
   liquor.. 4. sake, saki
   litter.. 5. dooly (doolie) 9. palanquin
   lute.. 3. tar
   maid.. 4. amah, ayah, eyah
   manservant.. 5. hamal 6. coolie
   marketplace.. 6. bazaar

   monkey.. 7. macaque
   nurse.. 4. amah, ayah (governess)
   obeisance.. 6. salaam (salam)
   pagoda.. 3. taa
   people.. 4. Sere (anc) 5. Asian, Malay
   6. Indian 7. Chinese, Eastern, Tartars
   (Tatars) 8. Japanese
   10. Mohammedan
   pipe.. 8. narghile
   rice paste.. 3. ame
   rug.. 8. sedjadeh 11. Baluchistan
   ruler.. 4. Khan, Shah 5. sahib (saheb)
   6. caliph (calif), sultan
   sabre.. 8. scimitar
   sailor.. 6. lascar
   sash.. 3. obi
   tambourine.. 5. daira
   taxi.. 7. ricksha (rickshaw)
   10. jinrickisha
   trousers (women).. 9. shaksheer
   vessel (sailing).. 4. dhow, saic
   wagon.. 5. araba
   warehouse.. 6. godown
   wind.. 7. monsoon
   worker.. 6. coolie (cooly)
orifice.. 4. hole, lura, pore, vent
   5. inlet, mouth, porus, stoma
   6. outlet, ostium 7. chimney,
   opening, ostiole 8. aperture,
   bunghole, spiracle
origin... 3. nee 4. rise, root, seed
   5. alpha, birth, cause, start
   6. nature, parent, source 7. genesis
   9. beginning, etymology, inception,
   parentage 10. inconabula, provenance
   11. provenience 12. commencement,
   fountainhead
original... 3. new 5. basic, first, novel
   6. fontal, native, primal, primer,
   unused 7. genuine, pattern, primary
   8. pristine 9. aborigine, beginning,
   inventive, primitive 10. inimitable
   11. fundamental, origination
   12. commencement
original copy... 6. ectype
originate... 4. coin, open, rise, stem
   5. arise, begin, breed, start
   6. author, create, derive, invent
   7. emanate, produce 8. generate,
   initiate 11. etymologize
originator... 5. cause, maker
   7. creator 8. inventor, producer
   9. contriver 10. discoverer
oriole... 5. pirol 6. golden, hooded,
   loriot, Mimeta 7. orchard
   8. Bullock's 9. Baltimore, Icteridae
Orion (pert to)...
   Astron.. 7. Dog Star 10. Canis Major
   11. Orion's Hound 13. constellation
   color.. 11. Holland blue
   Gr Myth.. 6. hunter
   Jacob's Staff.. 10. Yard and Ell
   13. Golden Yardarm
   slain by.. 7. Artemis
   star.. 5. Rigel
orison... 6. prayer
Orkney Islands, Scotland...
   capital.. 8. Kirkwall
   Firth.. 8. Pentland
   fishing grounds.. 4. haaf
   island, largest.. 6. Pomona
   President, Supreme Court.. 4. foud

stone tower (Prehist).. 5. broch
orle (Her).. 6. border, fillet, wreath
7. bearing, chaplet 10. escutcheon
(voided)
Orloff.. 5. horse 7. diamond (Russ,
194 3/4 carats)
orlop.. 4. deck (lowest)
Ormazd (Pers)... 5. deity (supreme)
ormer... 7. abalone 8. ear shell
ornament... 4. ouch, semé 5. adorn,
decor, gutta, honor 6. amulet,
brooch, emboss, finery, sequin
7. antefix 8. appliqué, decorate
9. embellish 10. decoration
13. embellishment
ornament (pert to)...
apex.. 6. finial
ball.. 6. pompon
bell–shaped.. 9. clochette
Bible.. 4. Urim
boat–shaped.. 3. nef
brilliant.. 4. gaud 5. spang 6. sequin,
tinsel 8. spangle
circular.. 7. rosette
delicate.. 7. tracery
diamond–shaped.. 11. epigonation
dress.. 5. jabot 8. stomacher
10. embroidery
egg–shaped.. 3. ove
hair, head.. 4. comb 5. tiara
8. barrette
indented.. 5. chase
Japanese girdle.. 4. inro
leaves and grapes.. 6. pampre
magical.. 6. amulet
mantel.. 7. bibelot, trinket
pendant.. 6. bangle, tassel 7. earring
9. lavaliere (lavalier)
pretentious.. 6. rococo
protuberant.. 4. boss
raised design.. 7. brocade
scroll–like.. 6. volute
set of.. 6. parure
setting in.. 5. inlay 7. emblema
silverware.. 7. gadroon
spiral.. 5. helix
terminal.. 6. finial
wall.. 6. plaque, sconce
ornamental (pert to)...
bottle.. 8. decanter
button.. 4. stud
description.. 5. fancy 10. decorative
lace edge.. 5. picot 7. tatting
metal.. 6. niello
raised.. 7. brocade
stand.. 7. étagère
vase.. 3. urn
ornamented... 6. chased, etched,
tooled 8. engraved
ornate... 4. gay 5. fancy 6. florid,
tawdry 7. adorned 9. decorated
ornery... 8. perverse, stubborn
9. malicious 11. ill–tempered
ornithoid... 8. birdlike
ornithology (study of)... 5. birds
ornithon... 6. aviary
oro... 4. gold 5. money
Oro... 3. God (Tahiti)
oro (comb form)... 5. month, serum
8. mountain
orology (science of)... 9. mountains
orotund... 7. pompous 9. bombastic

orp... 4. fret, weep
Orpheus (pert to)...
astronomy.. 6. Cygnus
eighteenth century.. 6. Handel
father.. 6. Apollo
mother.. 8. Calliope
poet.. 8. Thracian
reference.. 6. Orphic
river.. 6. Hebrus
wife.. 8. Eurydice
Orphic... 3. egg (Creation's) 5. hymns
7. tablets (gold) 13. Book of the
Dead (rites)
orphrey... 10. embroidery (gold)
orpit (Scot)... 7. fretful
orra... 3. odd 5. oddly 10. not
matched, occasional, unemployed
13. miscellaneous
ort... 3. end 4. bits 5. scrap
6. refuse, scraps 7. remnant
8. leavings, leftover
orthodox... 7. Trinity 8. accepted,
approved, believer, standard
9. canonical, customary
12. conventional
Orthodox Moslem... 5. hanif
orthography... 8. spelling
ortolan... 7. bunting 8. bobolink, sora
rail, wheatear
Oryx... 5. beisa 7. gazelle, gemsbok
8. antelope, leucoryx
os... 4. bone 5. mouth, osker (Geol)
7. opening
Osage... 5. river 6. Indian (Sioux)
10. orange tree
Osaka, Japan... 7. capital
10. prefecture
oscillate... 3. wag 4. rock, sway, vary
5. swing, waver, weave 7. vibrate
9. fluctuate
Oscines... 12. singing birds
oscitancy... 6. gaping 7. yawning
8. dullness, lethargy 10. drowsiness
oscitant... 4. dull 6. drowsy, gaping,
sleepy 7. yawning 8. careless,
sluggish 9. apathetic
osculate... 4. buss, kiss
osculation... 4. kiss 7. contact, kissing
osier... 3. rod 4. wand 6. sallow,
willow 7. dogwood
Osiris, Egypt (pert to)...
brother.. 3. Set (Seth)
crown.. 4. atef
enemy.. 3. Set 7. brother
father.. 3. Geb
god.. 9. fertility 10. underworld
god (Gr).. 8. Dionysus
husband of.. 4. Isis
king of.. 5. Egypt
mother.. 3. Nut
seat.. 6. Abydos
son.. 5. Horus 6. Anubis
Osmanli... 4. Turk 8. language
osmesis... 8. smelling 9. olfaction
osmosis... 10. absorption
12. infiltration
osprey... 4. hawk 7. feather (hat)
8. fish hawk 9. ossifrage
10. breakbones
ossature... 8. skeleton 9. framework
(Arch)
osse... 4. dare 7. attempt, presage,

promise 8. prophecy

osseous... 4. bony, hard 10. ossiferous

ossifrage... 5. eagle 6. osprey
11. lammergeier

ossuary... 3. urn 4. tomb
10. depository 12. charnel house
13. burial chamber

ostend... 6. reveal 7. exhibit
8. manifest 11. demonstrate

ostensible... 5. shown 6. avowed
7. alleged, seeming 8. apparent,
declared, specious 9. exhibited,
plausible, professed

ostent... 3. air 4. mien 5. token
7. portent 10. appearance

ostentatious... 4. arty, vain 5. dashy
6. sporty 7. pompous
11. conspicuous, pretentious

ostiole... 4. pore 5. stoma 7. orifice
8. aperture

ostler... 7. hostler 9. stableman

ostracize... 5. exile, expel 6. banish,
deport 7. cast out, exclude
9. extradite 10. expatriate

ostrich... 3. emu 4. Rhea 5. nandu
8. Struthio 9. cassowary

ostrichlike... 11. struthiform

ostrich tail feather... 3. boo

Otaheite... 6. Tahiti

otalgia... 7. earache

Othello (pert to)...
 opera by.. 5. Verdi
 tragedy by.. 11. Shakespeare
 villain.. 4. Iago
 wife.. 9. Desdemona

other... 2. or 5. alter, ither 6. either,
second 8. one of two 9. different
10. additional

others... 7. the rest 9. remaining

otherwise... 2. or 5. alias, ossia, other
6. or else 9. different 10. contrarily
11. differently

Othman... 4. Turk 5. Osman 6. sultan
7. Osmanli, Ottoman, Turkish

Othman's successor... 3. Ali

otiant... 4. idle 8. in repose
10. unemployed

otiose... 4. idle 6. at ease, futile
7. sterile, useless 8. indolent
12. functionless

otium... 7. leisure

otkon... 4. okee (oki) 5. demon
(Iroquois)

otologist... 6. aurist 9. ear doctor

ottava... 6. eighth, octave

ottava rima... 15. eight-line stanza

ottavino... 7. piccolo

ottoman... 4. seat 5. couch, stool
7. cricket 9. footstool

Ottoman (pert to)... see also *Othman*
 color.. 9. vermilion
 court.. 5. Porte 12. Sublime Porte
 Empire.. 7. Turkish
 fabric.. 6 ribbed 10. corded silk
 governor.. 3. bey, dey 5. pasha
 leader.. 5. Osman
 native.. 4. Turk
 poetry (couplet).. 4. beyt
 province.. 6. eyalet (former) 7. vilayet
 Turkish.. 7. Osmanli

oubliette... 7. dungeon (top opening)

ouch... 5. bezel, clasp, jewel
6. brooch 8. ornament
11. exclamation

ought... 4. duty, must, zero 5. at all,
aught, owned 6. cipher, should
7. behoove, nothing 8. anything, in
need of 9. possessed 10. obligation

Ouija board... 10. planchette

ouk... 4. week

ouphe... 3. elf 6. goblin

Our (pert to)...
 Father.. 11. Lord's Prayer
 French.. 5. notre
 Lady.. 10. Virgin Mary
 Lady's-mint.. 9. spearmint
 Lady's Wand (Astron).. 10. Orion's
 Belt
 Lady's Way.. 6. Zodiac

ourie... 4. cold 5. dingy 6. dreary

ousia... 6. nature 7. essence
9. substance, true being

oust... 3. bar 5. eject, evict
6. depose, remove 7. turn out

out... 3. odd 4. away 5. drunk
6. absent, beyond, excuse, issued,
outlet 9. published 10. dislocated,
extinguish 11. unconscious
12. extinguished, not available

out and out... 8. absolute, complete,
outright, thorough 9. downright
13. thoroughgoing

outbreak... 4. rash, riot 5. burst, spurt
6. emeute, tumult 7. outcrop,
ruction 8. eruption, hysteria, outburst
12. insurrection 13. recrudescence

outburst... 4. gale 5. blast, flare, flash
8. ejection, eruption 9. explosion
10. ebullition

outcast... 5. exile, leper, ronin
6. pariah 7. quarrel 8. castaway,
derelict, vagabond 10. expatriate

outclass... 5. excel, outdo 6. outvie
7. outrank, surpass 8. outshine
10. outperform

outcome... 5. issue 6. effect, outlet,
result, sequel, upshot 7. emanate,
product 8. solution 10. denouement
11. consequence

outcry... 4. wail, yell 5. alarm, shout
6. clamor, plaint 7. suction
8. proclaim 11. exclamation

outdo... 5. excel 6. defeat, exceed,
outwit

outdoor game... 4. polo 6. hockey,
tennis 7. cricket, croquet

outer... 5. ectad, ectal 7. outside,
outward 8. exterior, external
9. objective 10. extraneous

outer (pert to)...
 boundary.. 9. perimeter
 coat.. 4. coat, hull 5. testa 6. extine,
 jacket 8. tegument
 garment.. 4. suit, wrap 5. cloak,
 dress 7. paletot, sweater
 8. mackinaw, mantilla, overcoat,
 raincoat
 layer of roots.. 7. exoderm
 opposed to.. 5. ental
 shell.. 4. test
 skin.. 9. epidermis

Outer Mongolia...
 capital.. 4. Urga 14. Ulan Bator

Khoto
desert.. 4. Gobi
outermost... 6. utmost 7. extreme,
outmost 8. farthest
outfit... 3. kit, rig 4. gear, suit, unit
5. equip, group 7. company,
costume 8. wardrobe
12. organization 13. paraphernalia
outflow... 4. gush, teem 6. deluge,
efflux 7. freshet, outflux, outpour
10. ebullience
outgate... 4. exit, vent 6. egress,
outlet 7. outcome
outknee... 6. bowleg
outlander... 5. alien 8. stranger
9. foreigner, Uitlander
outlandish... 3. odd 6. remote
7. bizarre, foreign, strange, uncouth
9. barbarous, inelegant, unrelated
10. extraneous, impossible,
tramontane
outlaw... 5. horse, ronin 6. bandit,
banish 7. outcast 8. criminal, fugitive
9. ostracize, proscribe
outlet... 4. exit, vent 5. bayou
6. stream 7. opening, outcast,
passage
outline... 3. map 5. chart, draft,
frame, shape 6. sketch 7. contour,
drawing, summary 8. scenario
9. adumbrate, delineate, lineament,
perimeter, summarize
10. compendium 11. delineation
13. configuration
outlook... 5. scope, vista, watch
7. purview 8. frontage, prospect
9. viewpoint 10. perception
11. probability 12. watchfulness
outmoded... 5. passé 7. offbeat
8. outdated
outmost... 5. final, utter 6. remote,
utmost 8. farthest 9. extremest,
outermost, uttermost 15. farthest
outward
out of...
agreement.. 6. dehors
danger.. 4. safe
date, style.. 3. old 5. passé
10. antiquated
place.. 5. inept
prefix.. 2. ec
sorts.. 5. nohow 7. peevish
the ordinary.. 7. unusual
the question.. 10. impossible
the way.. 5. aside 6. afield
outpeer... 5. excel 7. surpass
output... 3. cut 5. expel, power, yield
6. amount, energy 7. turnout
10. production
outraged... 6. abused, harmed
8. insulted, offended 9. affronted
10. mistreated
outrageous... 6. absurd 7. furious,
heinous, obscene 8. flagrant
9. atrocious, excessive, monstrous
10. exorbitant, scandalous
11. disgraceful, unwarranted
outré... 3. odd 6. absurd 7. bizarre
10. immoderate 11. extravagant
Outre-Mer... 13. Book of Travels
(Longfellow, 1835)
outremer... 12. beyond the sea,

foreign parts
outrigger... 4. proa, spar 5. canoe
outright... 8. thorough 10. completely
11. unqualified 12. unreservedly
outrival... 5. excel 6. outvie
7. eclipse, outrank 8. outclass,
outshine, outstrip
outside... 3. exo (pref) 4. ecto (comb
form) 6. exterior, external, outdoors
10. extraneous 11. superficial
outside the body... 12. heterogenous
(opp of autogenous)
outspoken... 4. free 5. blunt, frank
6. candid 10. unreserved
13. communicative
outstanding... 3. due 5. famed, noted
6. famous, unpaid 7. eminent,
obvious 8. exterior 9. important,
principal, prominent 10. projecting
11. conspicuous, uncollected
outstrip... 4. best, lead 5. excel
7. surpass 8. outrival
outward... 5. ectad, evert, outer, overt
6. formal, spiral 8. apparent,
exterior, external 9. extrinsic
11. superficial
outwit... 4. balk, best, foil 5. block,
check, cross 6. baffle, thwart
9. checkmate, frustrate
10. circumvent, disappoint
outwork (Fort)... 7. ravelin 8. tenaille
(tenail)
ouvrage... 4. work
ouzel, ousel... 4. piet 6. thrush
8. whistler 9. blackbird
oval... 6. circle 7. ellipse 10. elliptical
11. ellipsoidal
ovale... 3. egg
ovate... 4. bard, oval 7. obovate
(inversely)
oven... 3. umu 4. kiln, oast (oste)
7. furnace 8. hot place 12. brick
chamber
oven (pert to)...
glass annealing.. 4. lehr (leer)
hop drying.. 4. oast
mop.. 5. scovel
Polynesian.. 3. umu
over... 3. o'er, too 4. also, anew
5. above, again, ended, super, supra
8. finished
overact... 3. haw 5. emote, spout
overalls... 5. chaps 8. trousers
10. chaparajos
overbearing... 7. haughty 8. arrogant,
cavalier, snobbish, subduing
10. highhanded 11. domineering
12. overpowering
overcast... 3. dim 4. dark 6. cloudy,
darken, gloomy 10. overturned (Geol)
overcoat... 5. benny 6. capote, raglan,
slip-on, ulster 7. paletot, surtout,
topcoat 9. greatcoat, inverness
(sleeveless)
overcome... 3. awe, win 4. beat
5. crush 6. beaten, defeat, exceed
7. conquer 8. outstrip, overbear,
overturn, persuade, surmount,
unnerved, vanquish 9. overpower,
overthrow, overwhelm, prostrate
overcrowded... 9. congested
overdue... 4. late 5. tardy 7. belated

8. mistimed

overfeed... 4. glut 6. agrote, pamper
7. satiate, surfeit 8. overfill
9. crapulate, overstuff

overflow... 4. teem 5. spate
6. abound, deluge, outlet 7. copious,
overrun 8. inundate, opulence,
overload, plethora, teem with
9. abundance, pour forth
10. ebullience

overfond of... 4. dote 5. silly

overfull... 4. inflated, satiated
9. plethoric 10. overloaded

overhang... 3. jut 6. beetle 7. project,
suspend 9. advantage 11. over and
over

overlapping... 8. obvolute 9. imbricate,
syphering

overloaded... 6. turgic 8. inflated,
overfill 9. bombastic, plethoric

overlook... 4. face, miss, scan, skip,
snub 6. acquit, excuse, ignore,
slight, survey 7. absolve, condone,
forgive, neglect, overtop 9. disregard,
oversight, rise above, supervise

overlord... 6. master 8. domineer,
governor 9. tyrannize

overly... 3. too 8. careless
9. negligent 11. overbearing,
superficial 12. supercilious

overmodest... 7. prudish 8. priggish
11. puritanical, strait-laced

overnice... 5. fussy 6. purist
7. elegant, finicky 8. affected
9. fastidious

overpower... 3. awe 4. rout, stun
5. crush 6. dazzle, defeat, master,
subdue 7. conquer 8. overbear,
overcome, vanquish 9. overthrow,
overwhelm

overpowering... 6. fierce 8. exciting
12. overwhelming

overreach... 4. dupe 5. cheat
6. exceed, nobble, outwit, overgo,
strain 7. deceive 10. circumvent

overrun... 5. crush, swarm 6. abound,
desert, exceed, infest, outrun, ravage,
spread 7. destroy, pervade, run over,
trample 8. overflow 9. overwhelm
11. superabound

overscrupulous... 7. prudish
9. overexact 10. overstrict
14. overfastidious

overshadow... 5. excel 6. darken
7. eclipse, obscure, shelter
8. dominate 9. overcloud

overshoe... 3. gum 6. arctic, galosh
(galoshe)

oversight... 4. care 5. error, lapse,
watch 6. charge 7. control, neglect
8. omission 9. direction
10. inspection 11. supervision
12. guardianship, surveillance
13. nonobservance

overskirt... 7. pannier (anc) 10. upper
skirt

oversleeve... 6. armlet

overspread... 5. cover 6. infest
7. overrun, pervade 8. disperse,
suffused

overt... 4. open 6. patent, public
7. obvious 8. apparent, manifest

10. open to view

overtake... 5. catch, reach, seize
6. detect, rejoin 7. ensnare
9. apprehend, captivate

overthrow... 4. down, rout, ruin
5. worst 6. defeat, depose, refute,
unseat 7. conquer, deposal, destroy,
ruinate, unhorse 8. demolish,
disprove, overcome, overturn,
vanquish 9. prostrate 10. revolution

overthrown... 6. fallen, ruined
8. defeated 9. disproved

overtones... 5. tones 8. partials
9. harmonics

overtop... 5. dwarf, excel 7. obscure,
surpass 8. go beyond, overhead,
override 9. transcend 10. tower
above

overture... 5. offer, proem 7. opening,
prelude 8. aperture, proposal
11. composition, proposition
13. peace offering

overturn... 3. tip 4. tilt 5. throw,
upset 6. topple 7. capsize, conquer,
destroy, overset, reverse, subvert
9. overthrow, overwhelm

overweight... 7. obesity
11. overbalance 13. preponderance

overwhelm... 4. bury, rout 5. crush
6. defeat, deluge, engulf 7. confute,
conquer, engross, immerse, oppress
8. overturn, submerge 9. overpower,
overthrow

Ovidae, Ovinae... 5. goats, sheep

oviparous... 11. ovoviparous 12. egg
producing (opp of viviparous)

ovoid, ovoidal... 7. egglike
9. egg-shaped

ovule... 3. egg 4. seed 6. embryo,
ovulum

ovum... 3. egg 4. seed 5. spore
6. gamete 8. germ cell

owe... 3. due, own 7. possess 9. be
obliged 10. be indebted

ower... 6. debtor

owl (pert to)...
barn.. 4. lulu 5. padge
breed.. 6. pigeon
eagle.. 7. katogle 14. Tiger of the
Wood
eye.. 4. disc
family.. 9. Strigidae
female.. 3. hen
genus.. 4. Bubo 5. Ninox, Strix
7. Syrnium
horned.. 4. Bubo 6. aziola (small)
8. Hush-wing
light.. 4. dusk
like.. 4. owly 8. strigine
parrot.. 6. kakapo
Puerto Rican.. 6. mucaro
short-eared.. 8. marsh owl
tawny.. 8. billywix
term.. 4. hoot 11. bird of night
13. bird of Minerva
white.. 7. wapacut
young.. 4. utum 5. owlet

own... 4. have 5. admit 7. confess,
possess 11. acknowledge

owner... 6. master 7. planter
(plantation) 8. landlady, landlord
10. proprietor

ownership... 4. oadl (anc law)
5. claim 7. tenancy 8. dominium,
interest, property 10. possession
11. seigniorage 12. seignioralty
14. proprietorship
ox... 5. beeve, steer 6. bovine
8. strength 13. beast of burden
ox (pert to)...
Celebes.. 4. anoa
genus.. 3. Bos
harness.. 4. yoke
horned.. 4. reem
India.. 4. gaur
like.. 5. bison 6. bovine 7. taurine
stall.. 5. boose
Tibetan.. 3. yak
type.. 4. zebu
wild.. 4. urus 7. banteng
working.. 4. aver
yoke.. 4. span
oxeye... 4. boce (fish) 5. daisy
6. dunlin, plover
oxford... 4. gray, shoe 5. cloth
Oxford (pert to)...
college accts.. 6. battel
color.. 4. blue, gray

Marbles.. 7. Arundel
Museum.. 9. Ashmolean (1683)
officer.. 6. beadle (bedel at Oxford)
(bedell at Cambridge)
scholarship.. 6. Rhodes
school.. 10. University (1570)
sheep (hornless).. 4. Down
oxide of iron... 4. rust
oxide of sodium... 4. soda
oxidize... 4. rust 5. erode 9. sulphuret
(Philat)
oxter... 3. arm 6. armpit 7. embrace
oxtongue... 5. plant 7. biltong,
bugloss
oxwort... 9. butterbur
oxygen... 3. gas 5. oxide, ozone
7. element
oxyopia... 10. extra sight
oyster... 6. huitre 7. bivalve, mollusk
oyster (pert to)...
gatherer.. 7. tongman
rake.. 5. tongs
shell.. 4. husk, test 5. shuck
spawn.. 6. cultch
young.. 4. spat
Ozark State... 8. Missouri
ozone... 3. air 6. oxygen

P

P... 2. Pi 6. letter (16th)
pa... 4. Papa 6. father
pa, pah... 4. fort 7. village
10. settlement (fortified)
paauw... 7. bustard
pabulum... 4. food, fuel 7. aliment,
support 9. nutriment 10. sustenance
11. nourishment
pac, pack... 8. half boot, moccasin
paca... 6. rodent 9. Cuniculus
pace... 3. run 4. gait, lope, rate, step,
trot, walk 5. speed 7. measure
8. movement, velocity
pace (L)... 5. peace
Pace... 5. Pasch 6. Easter
pachyderm... 8. elephant
10. rhinoceros 12. hippopotamus,
Pachydermata
pachydermous... 11. thick-walled
12. thick-skinned
pacific... 4. calm 6. irenic, serene
8. irenical, peaceful, tranquil
9. peaceable, quiescent
12. conciliatory
Pacific (pert to)...
Coast tree.. 7. madrona 8. knob pine
Highway.. 10. Camino Real
island bird.. 4. kagu
island shark.. 4. mako 11. blue
pointer
island tree.. 4. ipil
islands.. 4. Guam, Wake 5. Samos
7. Oceania 8. Caroline, Tasmania

9. Melanesia, Polynesia
10. Micronesia
shrub.. 5. salal
States.. 6. Oregon 10. California,
Washington
stepping stones.. 9. Aleutians (Russia
to America)
Pacific Ocean discoverer... 6. Balboa
pacifier... 3. sop 4. ring (baby's)
6. nipple 7. soother 8. sedative
10. peacemaker
pacify... 4. calm, ease, lull 5. abate,
allay 6. soften, soothe 7. appease,
assuage, mollify, placate 8. mitigate,
palliate 9. alleviate 10. conciliate,
propitiate 11. tranquilize (tranquillize)
pack... 3. ram, set, wad 4. cram, fill,
load, stow, tamp 5. carry, flock,
horde, steve, truss 6. bundle, embale
8. assemble, encumber, quantity,
send away
pack (pert to)...
animal.. 3. ass 5. burro, camel, llama
6. donkey
back.. 8. knapsack
horse.. 7. sumpter
horse bag.. 5. kyack 7. pannier
of hounds.. 6. kennel
package... 3. pad 4. bale 5. fadge
6. bundle, packet, parcel, robbin
(peppers), seroon 11. combination
packing... 4. lute, seal 7. stowage
9. packaging 10. rubber ring

paco... 3. ore 6. alpaca
Pacolet... 10. swift horse
pact... 6. pactum 7. bargain
   8. contract 9. agreement
Pactolian... 6. golden
Pactolus, Myth (pert to)...
   famed for.. 5. Midas 11. gold–bearing
   river (Asia Minor).. 5. Lydia
pad... 3. mat, paw 4. fill, foot, frog,
   line, path, walk 5. quilt, stuff, track,
   tramp 6. tablet, trudge 7. bedding,
   bolster, cushion, footpad
   8. notebook, protract, saturate
   9. footprint, pulvillus 10. highwayman
pad (pert to)...
   cloth.. 7. housing 11. saddlecloth
   hair.. 3. rat
   harness, part.. 5. panel 6. terret
     7. housing 10. horsecloth
   perfume.. 6. sachet
padding... 6. lining 7. wadding
   8. softness, stuffing 11. superfluity
paddle... 3. oar, row 4. beat, stir,
   wade, whip 5. blade, board, scull,
   spank, spoon 6. dabble, propel
   7. flipper 8. lumpfish
paddle (pert to)...
   English.. 7. trample 8. lumpfish
     9. tread upon 10. paddlecock
   Scotch.. 3. hoe 4. spud
paddock (pert to)...
   paddockstool.. 9. toadstool
   piper.. 9. horsetail
   stone.. 10. greenstone
paddy... 4. rice, soft 7. padlike
   8. cushiony 9. rice field 10. hod
   carrier
Paddy... 7. Patrick 8. Irishman
paddymelon... 7. wallaby
Paddy's hurricane (Naut)... 4. calm
paddywhack... 4. beat, blow
   6. temper 9. ruddy duck, thrashing
padge... 7. barn owl
padmasana... 11. cross–legged
   (Buddha style), lotus–shaped
padre... 4. monk 6. Father, priest
   8. chaplain, minister
padrona... 8. landlady, mistress
padrone... 6. master, patron
   8. landlord 9. innkeeper
paedarchy... 14. rule by children
pagan... 6. ethnic, paynim 7. heathen
   10. heathenism, idolatrous, unbeliever
   11. irreligious
Paganalia... 8. festival (Rom)
pagan god... 4. idol
page... 3. boy 4. leaf 5. child, folio
   6. summon 9. attendant, messenger
page (pert to)...
   beginning.. 7. flyleaf
   book.. 5. folio 6. cahier, sheets
   lady's.. 7. esquire 8. escudero
   left–hand.. 5. verso
   number.. 5. folio
   right–hand.. 5. recto
   title.. 5. unwan 6. rubric
     12. frontispiece
pageant... 4. pomp, show 5. drama
   6. parade, tableau 8. aquacade
   9. spectacle 10. exhibition
   11. ostentation
pages... 7. paginal 8. paginate

Pagliacci... 5. opera 9. character
pagne... 9. loincloth, petticoat
pagoda... 2. ta 3. taa 4. idol
   5. booth 6. temple
   11. summerhouse
pagoda (pert to)...
   finial.. 3. tee
   sleeve.. 12. funnel–shaped
   stone.. 12. Agalmatolite
   tree.. 6. banyan 10. frangipani
paha... 4. hill 5. ridge (glacial)
pahi... 4. ship 5. canoe (seagoing)
pahmi... 5. bobac 6. marmot
paho... 7. pahutan 11. prayer stick
pahutan... 5. mango
paid... 5. hired 6. cashed 7. content,
   settled, yielded 9. satisfied
   10. discharged
paideutics... 8. pedagogy, teaching
paid office (without work)...
   8. sinecure
paid out... 5. spent 8. expended
   9. disbursed
paigle... 7. cowslip 8. crowfoot
   10. stitchwort 12. cuckooflower
pail... 3. can, pan 4. beat 6. bucket,
   harass, situla, thrash, vessel
   8. cannikin
paillasse, pailliasse... 3. bed (masonry)
   8. mattress (straw)
pailles... 6. straws (cookery)
paillou, pailoo... 7. archway
   (memorial)
pain... 3. ail 4. ache, agra, pang
   5. agony, labor, thraw, throb, wound
   6. grieve, stitch 7. afflict, ailment,
   gnawing, torture, trouble 8. disquiet,
   distress 9. suffering 10. affliction,
   punishment
painful... 4. sore 7. careful 8. diligent
   9. difficult, laborious 10. afflictive,
   unpleasant 11. industrious,
   painstaking
painkiller... 7. anodyne 8. medicine,
   sedative 9. analgesic, calmative
   10. depressant
painstaking... 5. fussy 7. careful,
   labored 8. diligent, thorough
   9. assiduity, assiduous, laborious
paint... 4. coat, draw, limn 5. adorn,
   color, rouge, stain 6. depict, parget,
   sketch 7. picture, pigment, portray
   8. cosmetic, describe 9. delineate,
   embellish 11. application (Med)
paint (pert to)...
   blue, green.. 4. bice
   comb form.. 5. picto
   face.. 4. fard
   glossy.. 6. enamel
   Latin.. 6. pinxit
   spreader.. 7. spatula
   through pattern.. 7. stencil
   with vermilion.. 7. miniate
paintbrush... 8. hawkweed 10. painted
   cup 11. St John's wort
painted... 6. coated 7. colored,
   feigned 8. disguised, portrayed
   10. artificial, variegated
painted (pert to)...
   bat.. 11. Vespertilio
   beauty.. 9. butterfly
   bunting.. 5. finch

duck.. 8. mandarin 9. harlequin
enamel.. 7. Limoges
hyena.. 14. Cape hunting dog
lady.. 7. thistle 8. sweet pea
   9. butterfly
process.. 7. scumble
trillium.. 9. wake–robin
turtle.. 8. carapace
painter... 4. puma 6. cougar
   7. panther
painter... 4. Dali 5. Monet 6. Millet,
   Rubens 7. da Vinci, El Greco,
   Picasso, van Gogh 8. Reynolds,
   Whistler 9. Rembrandt
   12. Gainsborough, Grandma Moses,
   Michelangelo
Painter's Easel... 6. Pictor
   (constellation)
painting... 3. oil 5. genre, mural, Pietà
   (sacred), secco 6. fresco, marine
   7. impasto, tempera 8. encaustic,
   grisaille, landscape 10. cerography
   11. portraiture 12. illustration
pair... 3. duo, two 4. dyad, mate,
   span, team, yoke 5. brace, unite
   6. couple
paired... 5. gemel (Her) 7. coupled,
   leagued
pairs, growing in... 6. binate, double
paisano... 7. peasant 10. countryman,
   road runner
pal... 4. chum, pard 5. buddy, crony
   6. cobber 7. partner 9. companion
   10. accomplice
palace... 5. court, Doges, house
   (Astrol) 6. palais 7. palazzo
   10. praetorium (pretorium)
paladin... 4. hero 6. knight (Round
   Table)
Paladins of France... 9. The Twelve
palais... 6. palace 10. courthouse
Palamedes... 4. hero (Trojan War)
palampore... 7. hanging (cotton)
   8. bedcover
palanquin, palankeen... 4. kago
   5. dooly (doolie), palki 6. litter,
   palkee 10. conveyance
palanquin bearer... 5. hamal 6. sirdar
palas... 4. dhak, tree (yellow dye)
palatable... 5. sapid, tasty 6. savory
   8. pleading, seasoned 10. acceptable
palate... 4. cion 5. taste, uvula, velum
   6. relish 10. epipharynx
palatine... 4. bone 6. artery, county
   8. palatial
Palatine Confession... 10. Heidelberg
palaver... 4. talk 6. confer 7. chatter
   8. converse, flattery 10. conference
   12. conversation
pale... 3. dim, wan 4. ashy, fade, lily
   5. ashen, fence, lurid, pasty, stake,
   white 6. blanch, bounds, paling,
   pallid, pallor, sallow, sickly, sphere
   7. haggard, obscure, whitish
   8. palisade 9. deathlike 10. indistinct
palea, palet... 4. fold 5. bract, scale
   6. dewlap 8. ramentum
paleo (comb form)... 3. old 7. ancient
paleolithic culture... 8. Stone Age
Paleozoic... 10. Appalachia
Palestine (pert to)...
   ancient name.. 6. Canaan

animal.. 4. cony (Bib) 5. daman
conqueror.. 5. David, Turks
   11. Constantine
country (anc).. 4. Edom 5. Endor
   (Indur) 8. Nazareth 9. Philistia
lake.. 7. Dead Sea, Galilee
language.. 7. Aramaic
mountain (Bib).. 4. Zion 6. Carmel,
   Gilead, Hermon 13. Mount of Olives
plain, steppe.. 5. Negeb 6. Sharon
river.. 6. Jordan
town, district.. 4. Gaza 5. Haifa
   7. Samaria 9. Jerusalem
paletot... 4. coat 8. overcoat
pali... 9. precipice 10. steep slope
pali (comb form)... 5. again
   8. backward
Pali... 7. dialect (anc) 12. dead
   language
palimpsest... 9. parchment, rewritten
   10. re–engraved 15. codex rescriptus
palindrome (same backward, forward)...
   8. wordplay 9. inversion
paling... 5. fence, limit, palis, stake
   6. fading, picket 8. fencing
   9. enclosure
palisade... 5. cliff, fence, stake
   6. picket 7. defense, enclose, fortify
   8. espalier, palisado, surround
   9. precipice 10. impalement
   13. fortification
pall... 4. pale 5. cloak, cover, faint,
   qualm 6. coffin, mantle, nausea
   7. secrecy 12. graveclothes
pallall... 9. hopscotch
palle... 5. balls 6. six balls (Medici)
pallet... 3. bed 4. pate 5. quilt
   7. blanket 8. mattress 9. headpiece,
   paillasse
palliard... 6. beggar, lecher, rascal
   8. vagabond
palliate... 4. hide 5. abate, cloak,
   cover, gloss 6. excuse, lessen, soften
   7. conceal, qualify, relieve, shelter
   8. disguise, mitigate, moderate
   9. alleviate, extenuate
pallid... 3. wan 4. gray, pale 5. pasty,
   white 6. anemic, sallow
Pallu... 10. Reuben's son (Bib)
palm... 4. hand (part) 5. areca, bribe,
   steal 6. bacaba, handle, rattan,
   stroke, trophy
palm (pert to)...
   civet.. 6. musang
   cockatoo.. 5. arara
   down.. 6. pronate
   drink.. 5. assai
   drink (alcoholic).. 4. beno, nipa
   hand.. 6. palmus, thenar
   handlike.. 7. palmate
   house.. 8. palmetum
   lily.. 2. ti
   mat.. 6. petate
   off.. 5. foist
   ref to.. 10. palmaceous
   sap (fermented).. 5. toddy
   starch.. 4. sago
   sugar.. 7. jaggery
   thatch.. 6. nipa
palm (tree)...
   African.. 7. palmyra (sugar, wine)
   Arab.. 4. doum (doom)

Asiatic.. 4. atap, nipa
betel.. 5. areca, bonga 6. pinang
book.. 4. tara 7. taliera
Brazil.. 7. urucuri (urucury)
bussu, thatching.. 7. troolie (trooly)
cabbage.. 5. Sabal 8. palmetto
Ceylon.. 4. tala 7. talipot (fanleaf)
climbing, flexible.. 6. rattan
dwarf.. 5. Sabal
E Indies.. 4. atap, nipa 7. jaggery
     (sugar), tokopat (hat)
fan.. 7. talipot 8. palmetto
fiber.. 3. tal 6. raffia 8. piassava
     (piassaba)
Florida.. 5. royal
gingerbread tasting.. 4. doum (doom)
leaf.. 3. tal 4. olla (ola)
     12. chiquichiqui
Malayan, feather.. 4. irok 6. gomuti
palmyra.. 4. brab, olla 6. ronier
Philippine (coconut).. 4. niog
pinnate.. 5. assai, nikau 7. calamus,
     feather
S America.. 5. bussu, datil 6. tooroo
     12. chiquichiqui
spiny.. 6. grugru
palmate... 6. antler, webbed
     10. hand–shaped
palmer... 6. ferule 7. pilgrim (Holy
     Land) 8. date palm
     15. prestidigitator
Palmetto State... 13. South Carolina
palmistry... 10. chirognomy,
     chiromancy
palmodic (Med)... 5. jerky
palp... 6. feeler, palpus 8. tentacle
palpable... 5. plain 6. patent
     8. manifest, tangible 9. touchable
     10. noticeable, ponderable
palpebra... 6. eyelid
palpebrate... 4. wink
palpitate... 4. beat, drum 5. throb
     7. flutter, pulsate
palpitation... 7. flutter, tremble
     9. pulsation, quivering, throbbing
     10. excitement
palsied... 5. shaky 9. paralyzed,
     tottering
palter... 5. shift 6. babble, haggle,
     mumble, parley 7. bargain, chatter,
     quibble 9. vacillate 10. equivocate
     11. prevaricate
paltry... 4. mean, vile 5. petty, trash
     6. trashy 7. pitiful, rubbish
     8. picayune, trifling 9. worthless
     10. despicable 12. contemptible
pampas... 5. Pampa 6. plains (treeless)
pamper... 3. pet 4. cram, glut
     5. humor, spoil 6. caress, coddle,
     cosset, cuddle, dandle, posset
     7. gratify, indulge 11. mollycoddle
pamphagous... 10. omnivorous
pamphlet... 5. tract 6. folder
     7. booklet, leaflet 8. brochure
pan... 3. tab 4. part, tina (mining),
     wash 5. basin, roast, title (nobility)
     6. frying, lappet, spider, vessel
     7. cranium, hardpan, portion, skillet,
     subsoil 8. ridicule, saucepan
     9. criticize 10. acetabulum
pan (comb form)... 3. all 5. every

Pan (pert to)...
animal.. 3. ape 10. chimpanzee
god (Gr).. 6. flocks
instrument.. 4. pipe, reed
music.. 9. Pan's pipes
Pipes of.. 6. syrinx 8. Panpipes
Roman identity.. 6. Faunus
seat of worship.. 7. Arcadia
son.. 7. Silenus
panacea... 4. cure 6. elixir, remedy
     7. allheal (plant), cure–all
     8. nepenthe 10. catholicon
     11. panchreston
panache... 4. tuft (feathered) 5. plume
     7. swagger
Panama...
bay.. 5. Limon
capital.. 10. Panama City
city.. 5. Colon 6. Balboa 9. Cristobal
engineer.. 8. Goethals
gulf.. 6. Darien
Indian.. 4. Cuna
isthmus of.. 6. Darien (old name),
     Panama 7. San Blas
redwood.. 5. quira
river.. 7. Chagres
Panama Canal Lock... 5. Gatun
     10. Miraflores
panarchy... 13. universal rule
panaris... 5. felon 7. whitlow
     10. paronychia
panary... 5. bread 11. breadmaking
panatela... 5. cigar
pancake... 6. froise (fraise) 7. fritter
     11. griddlecake
Pancake Day... 13. Shrove Tuesday
pancreas... 5. gland 10. sweetbread
     16. Isle of Langerhans
panda... 7. bearcat
pandemonium... 4. hell 5. noise
     6. tumult, uproar
Pandemonium (pert to)...
abode of.. 6. demons
capital of.. 4. Hell
palace of.. 6. Satan
pert to.. 15. infernal regions
pander... 4. bawd, pimp 5. cater,
     serve 7. toady to 12. administer to
pandle... 7. a shrimp
Pandora's Box... 6. plague 9. human
     ills
Pandora's husband... 10. Epimetheus
panegyric... 5. éloge, elogy 6. eulogy
     7. oration, writing 8. encomium
     9. discourse, laudation
pang... 3. fit 4. pain 5. throe
     6. twinge 9. paroxysm
pangolin... 5. Manis 8. anteater
     9. Pholidota
panhandle... 3. beg
Panhellenic... 5. games (Isthmian)
     6. Greece 10. fraternity (Greek–letter)
panic... 4. fear, fray 5. alarm, chaos,
     scare 6. fright 8. stampede
pannier... 6. basket, dosser (dorser)
     7. corbeit 9. overskirt
panoply... 7. defense 11. suit of
     armor
panorama... 4. view 5. scene
     7. picture, scenery 9. cyclorama
pant... 4. beat, gasp 6. heave, throb
     7. breathe, pulsate 11. palpitation

Pantagruel (pert to)...
character (romantic).. 5. giant
companion.. 7. Panurge
father.. 9. Gargantua
pantaloon, pantaloons... 5. pants
6. dotard, old man 8. breeches,
trousers 11. Patron Saint (Venice)
Pantheon (pert to)...
aggregate.. 4. gods 7. deities
builder.. 7. Hadrian (120 AD)
building.. 6. shrine, temple 10. le
Pantheon (Paris) 16. Westminster
Abbey
Rome.. 15. Temple of the Gods
panther, painter... 4. pard, puma
6. cougar, jaguar, ocelot 7. leopard
pantler... 6. butler 7. servant
pantry... 5. ambry 6. larder 7. buttery,
pannier, pantler 8. cupboard
pants... 5. chaps 7. drawers
8. trousers 10. chaparajos
(chaparejos), pantaloons
panuelo... 6. collar 8. kerchief
9. neckcloth
pap... 4. teat 6. nipple 8. mammilla,
soft diet
papa... 3. dad 4. clay, Pope
6. baboon, father, potato, priest
7. vulture
papal... 9. apostolic 10. pontifical
papal (pert to)...
book of decrees.. 8. decretal
chancery.. 6. datary
Court.. 3. See 5. Curia
envoy.. 8. ablegate
letter.. 4. bull
reformer.. 7. Gregory
seal.. 5. bulla
vestment.. 5. fanon, orale
paper (pert to)...
absorbent.. 7. blotter
broken.. 5. casse
brown.. 6. manila
coated.. 6. charta
collection.. 7. dossier
copy.. 6. carbon
crinkled.. 5. crepe
crisp.. 6. pelure
currency.. 5. scrip
cutlet wrap.. 8. papilote
damaged.. 5. casse, salle 6. retree
design.. 9. watermark
fine.. 5. linen 6. vellum 9. parchment
flower.. 11. strawflower
folded.. 5. folio
for pounding gold sheets.. 7. cutches
gummed.. 5. label, stamp 7. plaster,
sticker
legal.. 4. writ 5. title
measure.. 4. page, ream 5. quire,
sheet
nautilus.. 8. argonaut
official.. 5. targe 8. document
pad.. 6. tablet
postage stamp.. 6. pelure
size.. 3. cap 4. copy, demy, pott,
quad 5. atlas, crown, folio, legal
6. octavo 8. foolscap, imperial
9. colombier
small piece.. 5. scrip
thin.. 4. rice 6. pelure, tissue
9. onionskin

transfer.. 12. decalcomania
untrimmed.. 6. deckle (deckel)
10. deckle edge 11. deckle-edged
writing size.. 3. cap
paper chase... 13. hare and hounds
papilla... 6. nipple 10. projection
papule... 6. papula, pimple
papyra (comb form)... 5. paper
papyrus... 4. pith, reed 5. paper,
sedge 6. scroll
par... 2. by 5. value 7. average, by
way of, strokes, through 8. equality,
superior
parable... 4. myth, tale 5. fable, story
8. allegory, apologue
10. comparison, similitude
parabola... 5. curve
parade... 4. pomp, show 5. march
6. flaunt 8. flourish, grandeur,
splendor 9. pageantry, promenade,
spectacle 10. pretension, procession
11. ostentation 12. magnificence
13. formal display
paradigm... 5. model 7. example,
pattern
paradisaic... 6. Edenic
Paradise... 4. Eden 5. Jenna
6. Aidenn, heaven, Utopia 7. Elysium
Paradise (pert to)...
apple.. 5. dwarf
Arabic form.. 6. Aidenn
Buddhist, Western.. 4. Jodo
fool's.. 5. limbo
grosbeak.. 9. cutthroat (bird)
Mohammedan.. 5. Jenna
plumage.. 14. bird of paradise
poem (Milton).. 12. Paradise Lost
16. Paradise Regained
river.. 5. Gihon (Bib)
tree.. 9. China tree
paragon... 4. type 5. ideal, match,
model 7. diamond (100 carats),
paladin, pattern 8. parallel
9. nonpareil
paragram... 3. pun
Paraguay...
capital.. 8. Asunción
city.. 9. Paraguari 10. Concepcion,
Villarrica
language.. 7. Guarani, Spanish
river.. 6. Paraná 8. Paraguay
tea.. 4. maté 5. yerba 11. yerba de
maté
parakeet... 5. green 6. parrot, puffin
11. budgereegah (budgerygah)
paralysis... 5. palsy 7. paresis
10. hemiplegia, paraplegia 11. loss
of power
paralyze... 5. scram 6. benumb,
deaden 7. astound, terrify, unnerve
paramount... 3. top 5. chief, liege
6. ruling 7. supreme 8. dominant,
superior 9. principal 10. preeminent
13. most important
paramour... 5. amour, leman, lover,
wooer 8. mistress 9. gallantry
10. sweetheart
paranoia... 9. catatonia, monomania,
nosomania
parapet... 5. redan 7. barrier, bulwark,
rampart
parasite... 3. bur, sug 5. drone, toady

6. Gnatho, insect, sponge 7. entozoa
8. hanger–on 9. entophyte,
sycophant
parasite (pert to)...
animal.. 6. cuckoo 7. cowbird,
entozoa
external.. 12. ectoparasite
internal.. 7. entozoa
marine.. 6. remora, sponge
plant.. 9. entophyte
slang.. 6. flunky
trout.. 3. sug
parasitic (pert to)...
fish.. 6. remora
fungus.. 4. rust 6. lichen
worm.. 8. trichina (larva)
parcel... 3. lot 4. mete, part 5. piece,
solum (law) 6. bundle, packet
7. package, portion 8. fragment
parch... 3. dry 4. burn 5. dry up,
roast, toast 6. scorch 7. shrivel,
torrefy
parched... 4. sere 5. burnt, dried
7. thirsty 8. withered
parchment (pert to)...
bookcover.. 5. forel (forrel)
fine.. 6. vellum
manuscript.. 10. palimpsest
roll.. 4. pell 6. scroll
school.. 7. diploma
pard... 4. chum 5. tiger 7. comrade,
leopard, panther, partner
10. camelopard 11. confederate
pardesi (Hind)... 9. foreigner, outlander
pardie, parde, pardi (anc)... 4. oath
6. indeed, surely, verily 9. certainly
pardon... 5. mercy, remit, spare
6. acquit, excuse 7. absolve,
amnesty, condone, forgive 8. tolerate
9. acquittal, remission
10. absolution, indulgence (Eccl)
11. forgiveness
pardonable... 6. venial 8. expiable
9. excusable 10. forgivable
pardon chair, stall... 12. confessional
pare... 3. cut 4. peel, skin 5. shave
6. cut off, remove, resect
parent... 3. dad 4. sire 5. pater
6. father, mother, source 7. genitor
8. begetter 10. progenitor
parental affection (animal)... 6. storge
parget... 4. coat 5. paint 7. plaster
8. decorate, ornament 9. whitewash
parhelion... 3. sun (mock)
pariah... 3. dog (half–wild) 7. outcast
8. commoner, low caste
parian... 6. marble, market
Parian... 5. Paros 6. marble
(sculptural) 9. porcelain
parimutuel machine... 9. totalizer
11. totalizator
Paris (pert to)...
blue.. 6. cobalt 8. Prussian
daisy.. 10. marguerite
Garden (London).. 10. bear garden
green.. 11. insecticide
Paris, France...
anc name.. 7. Lutetia (Lutice)
capital of.. 6. France
criminal.. 6. apache
famed sites.. 6. Louvre 8. Pantheon
9. Notre Dame 10. Montmartre
11. Eiffel Tower 13. Champs Elysées,
Napoleon's Tomb
native.. 8. Parisian
patron saint.. 5. Denis (Denys)
racecourse.. 7. Auteuil
river.. 5. Seine
subway.. 5. Metro
Paris, Gr legend...
brought about.. 9. Trojan War
10. Fall of Troy
father.. 5. Priam (King of Troy)
killer of.. 8. Achilles
mother.. 6. Hecuba
wife.. 6. Oenone
parish... 5. laity 7. diocese 8. district
9. parochial
paristhmion... 6. tonsil
park... 4. area (enclosed) 5. place,
tract 6. claire, common, settle
7. pasture (Eng) 8. woodland
9. grassland, pleasance
10. playground 11. reservation, set
and leave
Park, Highway...
Avenue.. 9. Manhattan
Lane.. 6. London
Row.. 9. Manhattan
Park, Historical... 6. Shiloh 8. Pea
Ridge, Saratoga 9. Minute Man
10. Gettysburg, Morristown
12. Harper's Ferry, Independence
Park, US... 4. Zion 7. Glacier,
Olympic (rain forests) 8. Sequoyah
(Sequoja), Yosemite 9. Haleakala,
Mesa Verde 10. Everglades, Mt
McKinley, Shenandoah 11. Grand
Canyon, Kings Canyon, Yellowstone
12. Harper's Ferry 15. Petrified
Forest
parlay, parley... 4. chat 5. parle, treat
6. confer 7. discuss 8. converse
10. conference, discussion
11. arbitration
parliament... 4. Diet 8. Congress
11. legislature
parlous... 4. keen 5. risky 6. shrewd
7. cunning 8. shocking 9. dangerous
Parnassian... 4. muse, poet
9. butterfly 10. Parnassius
Parnassus, Greece...
mountain.. 6. Phocis
site of.. 6. Delphi 8. Castalia
(fountain) 13. Delphic Apollo
symbol of.. 6. poetry
parody... 5. farce 6. satire 7. mockery,
take–off 9. burlesque, imitation
10. caricature
paroemia... 7. proverb
parol, parole... 4. oral, word
6. speech 7. freedom, promise,
release 8. pleading 11. word of
mouth
paronomasia... 3. pun 7. punning
8. wordplay 9. assonance
12. agnomination
paroxysm... 3. fit 4. pang 5. throe
6. access, attack, frenzy 7. illness
9. agitation 10. fit of anger
12. exacerbation
paroxysm of grief... 5. agony
parricide (murder of)... 7. kinsman
parrot... 3. ara, hia, kea 4. jako, kaka,

loro, lory 5. arara, cagit, macaw,
polly 6. kakapo, tiriba 7. corella,
lorilet 8. cockatoo, lorikeet, lovebird,
parakeet 9. Psittacus (Old World)
14. Psittaciformes
parrot (pert to)...
  disease.. 11. psittacosis ·
  genus.. 6. Nestor 9. Psittacus
  gray.. 4. jako
  green.. 5. cagit
  hawk.. 3. hia
  long–tailed.. 5. macaw
  monk.. 4. loro
  New Zealand.. 4. kaka
  owl.. 6. kakapo
  parrot fish.. 4. loro, scar 5. lauia
    6. scarid 7. labroid 8. Labridae,
    Scaridae
  parrotlike (tongued).. 12. anthropoglot
  sheep–killing.. 3. kea
  short–tailed.. 7. lorilet
parry... 4. fend, ward 5. avert, avoid,
  elude, evade, shift 6. refute, thwart
pars... 4. part
Parsee Bible... 6. Avesta 10. Zend
  Avesta
Parsei, Parsi... 6. Gheber (Ghebre)
  11. Zoroastrian 13. fire worshiper
Parsifal (pert to)...
  character.. 6. Knight
  healer of.. 8. Amfortas
  son.. 9. Lohengrin
parsimonious... 4. near 5. close
  6. frugal, meager, skimpy, sordid,
  stingy 7. miserly, sparing
  8. covetous, grasping 9. illiberal,
  mercenary, penurious 10. avaricious
parsley... 4. herb 5. cumin 7. garnish
  9. Ammiaceae, flavoring
parsley camphor... 6. apiole
parson... 6. rector 8. minister,
  preacher 9. clergyman, guidepost
parsonage... 5. gleve, manse, tithe
  7. rectory 8. benefice, vicarage
  9. pastorate 10. presbytery
parson bird... 3. tui
parson–in–the–pulpit... 10. cuckoopint
part... 3. cut, die 4. open, role, twin
  5. allot, break, piece, sever, share
  6. depart, divide, member, sunder
  7. analyze, disband, disjoin, divorce,
  portion, section, segment 8. dissever,
  disunite, division, fragment, function,
  separate 9. component
  12. discriminate
part (pert to)...
  basic.. 4. core, pith 7. essence,
    nucleus
  choice.. 5. cream, elite 6. marrow
  coarse.. 7. dregs
  composite.. 7. section
  corresponding.. 7. isomere
  essential.. 4. core, gist, pith 5. heart
  extra.. 5. spare
  greater.. 4. bulk
  hardest.. 5. brunt
  infinitesimal.. 4. atom, mite
  insignificant.. 3. bit 4. iota 6. trifle
  kept.. 6. retent
  main.. 4. body 5. trunk
  narrow.. 4. neck
  proportional.. 5. quota

rootlike.. 7. radicle
sawlike.. 5. serra
segment.. 5. tmema
small.. 3. bit, jot 4. iota 6. detail
  7. snippet
smallest.. 4. whit 5. minim
solo accompaniment.. 9. obbligato
tenth.. 5. tithe
unpaid.. 6. arrear 9. arrearage
uppermost.. 3. top 4. peak 6. upside
  7. topside
winglike.. 3. ala
with.. 7. discard 10. relinquish
partage... 4. part 5. share 7. portion
  8. division
partake... 3. eat 5. share
  11. participate
partan... 4. crab
parted... 5. cleft 6. cloven 7. divided,
  severed 9. separated 11. apportioned
parterre... 10. level space 12. theater
  boxes, theater space 17. ornamental
  gardens
parthogenesis... 7. apogamy
  10. thelyotoky 12. reproduction
partial... 6. biased, unfair, unjust
  7. limited 8. not total, one-sided,
  partisan 9. imperfect 10. fractional,
  incomplete, prejudiced
  11. predisposed 13. foolishly fond
partiality... 4. bias 6. desire
  9. injustice, prejudice 10. preference
  11. inclination, partisanism
  12. partisanship, predilection
participant... 6. sharer 7. entrant
  8. partaker 9. accessory
  12. participator
particle... 3. ace, bit, ion, jot
  4. atom, drop, iota, mite, mote, whit
  5. grain, piece, shred, spark 6. tittle
  7. globule, granule
particle (pert to)...
  electric.. 3. ion 5. anion 6. proton
  least possible.. 5. minim
  minute.. 3. jot, ray 4. atom, iota
    5. grain, speck 7. granule
  negative.. 3. nor, not
parti–colored... 4. pied, roan 5. pinto
  6. motley 7. piebald 9. harlequin
  10. variegated
particular... 4. item, nice, part, sole
  5. event, fussy 6. detail 7. precise,
  special, topical 8. detailed, especial,
  peculiar, separate, specific
  9. attentive 10. fastidious, individual,
  overminute 12. circumstance,
  technicality
partisan, partizan... 4. pike 5. staff
  6. zealot 7. partial 8. adherent,
  advocate, follower 9. supporter
  10. fractional, prejudiced
partition... 4. wall 5. allot 6. divide,
  screen, septum 7. scantle 8. set
  apart 9. apportion, severance
  10. distribute, separation
  13. apportionment
partitioned... 7. septate
partly... 6. in part 9. partially
partly illuminated... 6. shaded
  8. penumbra
partly open... 4. ajar
partner... 3. pal 4. ally, mate, wife

6. sharer, spouse 7. comrade, husband 9. associate, coadjutor, colleague 10. accomplice 11. confederate, participant

partnership... 4. firm 7. cahoots, co-mated 8. business, contract 10. fellowship 11. affiliation 13. participation

part of...
anchor.. 4. palm
bird wing.. 5. alula
cannon.. 5. chase
church.. 4. apse, nave 5. altar 7. chancel 8. transept
circle.. 3. arc 6. degree 7. segment
compass.. 6. needle
ear.. 4. lobe 5. pinna 6. tragus 8. tympanum 9. labyrinth
eye.. 4. iris, uvea 5. pupil 6. cornea, retina
flower.. 4. stem 5. calyx, petal, sepal
foot lever.. 5. pedal 7. treadle
fort.. 5. redan 7. bastion
head.. 4. pate 5. scalp, skull 7. cranium
minstrel show.. 4. olio 5. bones 6. end man 12. interlocutor
newspaper.. 3. ear 4. item, page 6. by-line 9. editorial
optical measure.. 7. alidade
printing press.. 6. platen
rifle (anc).. 4. tige
ship.. 3. bow 4. brig, deck, helm, keel, mast 5. stern, wheel 6. anchor, bridge, rudder 8. steerage
step.. 5. riser, tread 6. nosing
theater.. 3. box 4. loge 5. foyer, stage 7. balcony, curtain, gallery, parquet 8. parterre 9. orchestra
turtle.. 7. calipee 8. calipash

partridge... 4. hill, snow, yutu 5. covey (flock) 6. bamboo, chukar (chukor), Perdix, seesee 7. cinerea, tinamou 8. raw umber 9. francolin 11. Francolinus 12. ruffed grouse

party... 3. tea 4. ball, drum, sect, side 6. clique, fiesta, person 7. company, faction 8. sociable 9. reception 10. detachment 11. association, combination 12. participator

party (pert to)...
deserter.. 6. bolter
evening.. 6. soiree
lawn.. 4. fete
man.. 8. partisan
member.. 8. Democrat, Federate 9. Communist, Dixiecrat, Greenback (Hist), Socialist 10. Republican 11. Independent
men's.. 4. stag 6. smoker

Parvati (pert to)...
consort.. 4. Siva
father.. 7. Himavat
goddess.. 8. mountain

parvenu... 4. snob 7. upstart 12. nouveau riche

Pasch, pasch... 4. lamb, moon 6. candle, Easter, supper 8. Passover 10. Good Friday 11. candlestick, celebration

pascual... 8. pascuage, pastures

pasear... 4. walk 6. parade, stroll 9. promenade 11. perambulate

pasha, pacha... 3. dey 4. emir 5. title 6. bashaw (early) 8. nobleman 10. magistrate

pashalik (pashalic)... 9. territory (pasha's) 12. jurisdiction

pashm... 6. fleece (Tibetan goat)

pasigraphy... 6. system (Universal) 7. symbols 8. language

Pasiphae (pert to)...
mother of.. 7. Ariadne
son.. 8. minotaur (monster)
wife of.. 5. Minos

pasquinade... 5. squib 6. satire 7. lampoon, pasquil

pass... 2. go 3. die, end, gap 4. ghat, hand, lane, pace, step 5. canto, enact, gorge, lapse, occur, relay, spend, throw 6. convey, crisis, defile, elapse, exceed, happen, passus, perish, permit, ratify, ticket 7. excrete, passage 8. hand over, passport, surmount, transfer 10. permission 11. Annie Oakley 13. complimentary

pass (pert to)...
Alpine.. 3. col
around.. 4. skirt 6. detour
as genuine.. 5. cheat, foist 11. interpolate
away.. 3. die, end 6. perish, vanish 9. cease to be, disappear, obsolesce
by.. 4. cote, omit, skip, snub 6. elapse, forego, ignore 7. proceed 8. overlook 9. disregard
hurriedly.. 7. scamper, skitter 9. skim along
into.. 5. glide, merge 6. become 7. get to be 9. penetrate
judgment.. 4. rule 6. decree, ordain 8. sentence
on.. 3. die 6. confer, ratify 7. advance 8. bequeath, continue
out.. 3. die 4. exit 5. faint 7. be dazed 9. disappear 11. be dead drunk 13. be unconscious
over.. 4. omit, skip 5. cross 6. elapse, excuse, exempt, ignore, slight 7. condone, exclude, neglect 8. overlook, transfer, traverse
sudden.. 5. lunge
through.. 5. cross, reeve (cringle) 6. pierce 7. pervade, undergo 8. traverse 9. penetrate 10. comprehend, experience
up.. 4. snub 5. evade 6. reject 7. decline 9. disregard
without touching.. 5. clear

passable... 4. so-so 7. current 8. mediocre, moderate, traveled 9. navigable, tolerable, traversed 10. acceptable, accessible, admissible 12. satisfactory

passado (fencing)... 6. thrust

passage... 4. adit, exit, flue, ford, gang, hall, iter 5. aisle, allay, allée, canal, death 6. atrium, avenue, egress, travel, voyage 7. channel, excerpt, journey, transit 8. corridor, incident, progress, sanction 9. enactment, migration

10. transition 11. altercation,
negotiation, preterition
12. thoroughfare
passage (pert to)...
  book.. 7. excerpt
  brain.. 4. iter
  closed end.. 7. impasse 8. cul–de–sac
  covered.. 4. pawn
  history.. 5. alure
  mine.. 5. stope
  mine floor.. 4. sill
  narrow.. 3. gut 5. aisle, alley, gully,
    slype 6. defile, strait
  river.. 7. estuary
passageway... 4. hall, lane, ramp, slip
  5. aisle, alley, lumen 6. access,
  arcade, avenue, defile, outlet, strait,
  tunnel 7. gangway 8. corridor
passant... 7. cursory, walking (Her)
  8. passer–by 9. ephemeral, excelling
  10. surpassing, transitory
passé... 4. aged, past, worn 5. faded
  6. gone by 8. obsolete
  10. antiquated 13. superannuated
passed (pert to)...
  by.. 6. bygone, former 8. preterit
    (preterite)
  into use.. 6. enured (inured)
  over swiftly.. 7. fleeted 11. preterition
    (Theol)
  through pores.. 7. osmosed
    8. dialyzed 9. permeated, transuded
passenger... 4. fare 6. pigeon, trekku
  7. pilgrim, tourist 8. commuter,
  traveler, wayfarer 9. sightseer,
  transient
passerine bird... 5. finch 7. sparrow
  8. songbird
passing... 7. cursory 8. elapsing,
  fleeting 9. departing, enactment,
  ephemeral, exceeding, happening,
  transient, vanishing 10. surpassing,
  transitory 11. preterition
passion... 3. ire, yen 4. love, lust,
  rage, zeal 5. anger, craze, wrath
  6. desire 7. emotion, feeling
  9. eloquence, martyrdom
  10. enthusiasm, excitement
passion (pert to)...
  cross.. 5. Latin
  flower.. 6. maypop 11. passionwort
  flower Family.. 10. Passiflora
  for doing great things..
    11. megalomania
  for music.. 9. melomania (melomane)
  music.. 8. oratorio
  Play.. 14. Christ's Passion
    (Oberammergau)
  Week.. 8. Holy Week
passionate... 3. sad 5. angry
  6. ardent 7. amorous, excited,
  fervent, pitiful, violent 8. agitated,
  eloquent, vehement 9. emotional,
  irascible 10. passionato
  11. hot–tempered, impassioned
passionless... 4. calm 8. painless
  9. heartless, unfeeling 10. spiritless
  11. unemotional 13. dispassionate
passive... 5. inert, quiet, stoic
  6. stolid 7. languid, patient
  8. inactive 9. apathetic
  10. submissive 11. acquiescent,

indifferent, unresisting
Passover (pert to)...
  festival.. 5. Seder 6. Jewish
  pert to.. 7. paschal
  psalm.. 6. hallel 14. Egyptian Hallel
  sacrifice.. 11. paschal lamb
  The (Passover).. 5. Pasch
passport... 4. pass, visa (vise)
  5. congé 6. congee, permit
  8. document 11. safe conduct
passus... 5. canto
password... 9. watchword 10. mot de
  passé, open sesame 11. countersign
past... 2. by 3. ago 4. date, dead,
  gone, over, yore 5. after, since
  6. beyond, ultimo 7. elapsed,
  outworn 9. foregoing, yesterday
paste... 3. pap, poi 4. glue, sham
  5. dough, stick 6. mastic, strass
  8. adhesive, frippery, mucilage
  10. confection 13. stick together
pastel... 5. light 6. crayon, sketch
  9. pale color
pastille... 6. troche 8. lozenge
  9. fireworks
pastime... 4. game 5. hobby, sport
  9. amusement, diversion
  10. recreation 13. entertainment
pastor... 5. rabbi 6. curate, divine,
  keeper, parson, priest, rector
  8. chaplain, guardian, minister,
  Reverend, shepherd
pastoral... 4. poem 5. drama, rural
  6. poetic 7. romance
  14. ecclesiastical
pastoral (pert to)...
  cantata.. 8. serenata
  crook, staff.. 5. pedum 7. crosier
  god.. 3. Pan
  oboe.. 7. musette
  pert to.. 6. rustic 8. agrestic,
    herdsman, shepherd
  pipe.. 3. oat 4. reed
  poem.. 4. idyl 7. bucolic, eclogue
pastry... 3. pie 4. tart 6. éclair
  7. dariole, strudel 8. napoleon,
  pandowdy, turnover 9. cream puff,
  shortcake 10. pâtisserie
past tense... 8. preterit (preterite)
pasturage, right of... 9. horsegate
pasture... 3. ham, lea 4. feed, food
  5. agist, grama, grass, graze
  6. meadow 9. grassland
  10. agostadero
pasture bird... 6. plover 7. sparrow
pat... 3. dab, fit, paw, tap 4. blow,
  lump 5. fixed, impel, known, throw
  6. caress, smooth, stroke 7. flatten
  9. immovable 10. seasonable
Patagonia...
  city.. 10. Magellanes (S Am)
  deity.. 7. Setebos
  Indian tribe.. 9. Tehuelche
    10. aboriginal
  race (said of).. 6. giants 7. Big Feet,
    tallest 9. Patagones
  rodent.. 4. cavy 8. capybara, Caviidae
patamar (pattamar).. 6. vessel (Naut)
  7. courier 8. messenger
patata... 6. potato 11. sweet potato
patch... 4. mend, vamp 5. bodge,
  botch, clump, cover, field 6. blotch,

cobble, parcel 8. addition
9. reconcile
patch (pert to)...
  cloth .. 5. clout
  imprinting .. 5. friar
  metal .. 6. solder
  of trees .. 4. mott
patcher (humorous)... 6. sartor
patchwork... 5. quilt 6. jumble, pillow, scraps 7. mixture 9. checkered, fancywork, fragments
  10. hodgepodge
pate... 3. pie, top 4. head 5. brain, crown, pasty, patty 6. badger
pâté de foie gras... 5. patty (goose liver and truffles)
patella... 3. pan 4. bone, dish, vase 7. kneecap, kneepan
paten... 4. disc, dish, disk 5. plate 7. patener (bearer of)
patent... 4. open 5. berat (Turk), right 7. license, warrant 8. document, manifest 9. available, copyright, privilege, trademark 10. accessible, protection, university
  12. unobstructed
pater... 6. father, priest
Pater Noster... 11. Lord's Prayer
Paternoster Row... 6. street (London)
Pater Patriae... 18. Father of his country (Cicero, Marius, Trajan, Washington, etc)
path... 3. way 4. lane, line 5. piste, route, swath, track, trail 6. course 7. footway
path (pert to)...
  along a slope .. 4. berm (berme)
  animal .. 5. piste, spoor 6. roddin 7. rodding
  of energy .. 7. ergodic
  of moving parts .. 5. locus
  of planets .. 5. orbit
  Spanish .. 6. camino, comino
pathetic... 3. sad 5. teary 8. dolorous, grievous, stirring 9. affecting
  10. lamentable
pathological... 6. morbid 9. unhealthy
pathological reaction... 7. allergy
patience... 9. endurance, fortitude, solitaire, tolerance 10. submission, sufferance 11. forbearance, resignation 12. acquiescence, perseverance
patient... 4. calm, meek 6. client 8. tolerant 9. unsettled
  11. persevering 13. long-suffering
patio... 5. court 9. courtyard
patriarch... 4. Noah, sire 5. elder, pater 6. bishop, father 7. aged man, veteran 9. churchman
  10. Methuselah 13. paterfamilias
patrimonial... 9. inherited
  10. hereditary
patrimony... 8. heritage 10. birthright
  11. ancient rite, inheritance
patriot... 4. Cato (Rom), Otis (Am) 5. jingo 7. chauvin 9. flag–waver
  10. chauvinist, countryman
patriotism... 10. chauvinism
  11. nationalism 13. love of country
patrol... 5. guard 7. protect
  8. traverse 9. keep guard

13. perambulation
patron... 5. buyer, guest 6. backer, seller, trader 8. customer, guardian 9. financier, protector, supporter
  10. benefactor
patronage... 5. aegis (egis), favor 6. defend 7. support 8. auspices 9. clientele, fosterage 10. assistance
  13. condescension, encouragement
patronizing... 8. deigning 9. financing, revealing 10. sponsoring
  13. condescending
patrons (group)... 7. backers, masters 9. clientele, customers
Patron Saint of...
  beggars .. 5. Giles
  boys .. 8. Nicholas
  England .. 4. Anne 6. George
  fishermen .. 5. Peter
  France .. 5. Denis
  Ireland .. 7. Patrick
  lawyers .. 4. Ives
  motherhood .. 6. Gerard
  musicians .. 7. Cecilia
  Pueblo Indians .. 7. Stephen
  sailors .. 4. Elmo
  Scotland .. 6. Andrew
  shoemakers .. 7. Crispin
  swineherds .. 7. Anthony
  Venice .. 4. Mark 9. Pantalone
  Wales .. 5. David
patten... 4. clog 5. skate 8. footgear, overshoe, snowshoe
pattern... 4. norm, seme 5. habit, model 6. design, format 7. diagram, paragon 8. paradigm, parterre, template
pavilion... 4. tent 5. cover, kiosk 6. canopy 8. covering 9. gloriette
  10. tabernacle
pavis... 5. cover 6. screen, shield 7. protect
paw... 3. pad, pud 4. foot, hand 5. patté, pedal 6. handle, stroke 7. foreleg (Her) 8. forefoot
  10. manipulate
pawl... 4. bolt, sear, trip 5. click 6. detent, pallet, tongue 7. ratchet 9. mechanism
pawn... 4. gage, hock, tool 6. pledge 7. counter, peacock 8. chessman, guaranty, hockshop 9. put in pawn
  10. pawnbroker
Pawnee... 6. Indian
pawnie... 7. peacock
pay... 3. aby (abye), fee, tip 4. ante, meet, wage 5. remit, repay 6. defray, reward, salary, suffer 7. requite, satisfy 9. indemnify, reimburse, retaliate 10. compensate, punishment, recompense, remunerate
  11. retribution 12. compensation
pay (pert to)...
  attention .. 4. heed 6. listen
  back .. 6. rebate, refund 9. reimburse, retaliate
  dirt .. 3. ore
  envelope .. 5. wages 6. salary 7. stipend
  extra .. 5. bonus 8. kickback
  for .. 3. aby (abye) 5. atone 6. suffer
  off .. 6. punish 7. requite 9. pay in

full, retribute 10. compensate
out.. 5. spend 6. expend, settle
  7. hand out 8. disburse
  10. distribute 12. exorbitantly
  14. through the nose
up.. 4. ante 5. settle 9. liquidate
paymaster... 6. burser, purser
  7. cashier
payment... 3. cro, fee 4. dues, mail
  6. return 8. defrayal, requital
  10. punishment, recompense
  12. chastisement, compensation
payment (pert to)...
  for homicide, murder.. 3. cro 4. eric
  (Brehon Law) 7. galanas (Welsh),
  wergild (weregild)
  immediate.. 4. cash
  upon delivery.. 3. COD 14. cash on
  delivery
paynim... 5. pagan 7. heathen, infidel
  8. Pagandom 10. Mohammedan
payong... 8. umbrella (pert to)
paysage... 7. picture (landscape)
  9. landscape
pea (pert to)...
  bird.. 6. oriole
  chick.. 4. gram 5. Cicer
  everlasting (Bib).. 9. vetchling
  family.. 8. Fabaceae
  flour (seasoned).. 9. Erbswurst
  heath.. 7. carmele
  pigeon.. 3. dal 5. arhar
  sausage.. 9. Erbswurst
  shaped.. 8. pisiform
  soup.. 3. fog (dull yellow)
  split.. 3. dal
  tree.. 8. laburnum
  tropical.. 4. dove 7. Zenaida
  12. mourning dove
  vine.. 8. earthpea
peace... 4. pax 5. amity, quiet, truce
  6. accord, repose 7. harmony,
  Nirvana, silence 8. ataraxia (ataraxy),
  serenity 9. stillness 10. quiescence
  11. tranquility
peaceable... 5. quiet, still 6. irenic,
  silent 7. henotic, pacific 8. amicable,
  tranquil 9. quiescent 10. concordant,
  harmonious 11. undisturbed
peaceful... 4. calm 5. irene 6. irenic,
  placid, serene 7. halcyon, pacific
  8. tranquil 11. comfortable
peace pipe... 7. calumet
peach... 5. fruit 6. accuse, betray,
  brandy, indict, inform 7. impeach
  8. quandong 9. red-yellow
peach (pert to)...
  cordial.. 7. persico 8. persicot
  family.. 12. Amygdalaceae
  French.. 8. persicot
  grafted (quince).. 9. melocoton
  like.. 6. almond
  origin.. 5. China
  stone.. 7. putamen
  variety.. 7. Elberta 8. Crawford
  9. freestone, nectarine 10. clingstone
peacock... 3. mao 4. Pavo (Astron),
  pawn, pose 5. strut 9. swaggerer
peacock (pert to)...
  blue (color).. 4. paon
  butterfly.. 2. io
  fan.. 9. flabellum

feather part.. 4. marl
female.. 6. peahen
fish.. 6. wrasse
flower.. 9. poinciana
heron.. 7. bittern
ref to.. 7. peafowl 8. pavonine
tail spot.. 3. eye
peak... 3. alp, epi, pic, top, tor
  4. acme, apex, cone, crag, cusp,
  dent, dolt 5. crown, piton, slink,
  sneak, steal 6. finial, shrink, summit
  8. headland, mountain 9. simpleton
  10. promontory
Peak... 5. Borah, Logan 7. Everest, St
  Elias 8. McKinley 9. Mont Blanc
  10. Matterhorn 11. Kilimanjaro
  12. Popocatepetl
peal... 4. boom, clap, echo, ring, toll
  6. appeal, shovel 7. resound,
  summons, thunder 8. carillon
peanut... 5. pinda (pindal, pindar)
  6. goober, trifle 8. earthnut,
  earthpea, katchung
pear (pert to)...
  alligator.. 7. avocado
  cider.. 5. perry
  Latin.. 5. pirum
  prickly.. 4. tuna 5. nopal 7. Opuntia
  shaped.. 8. pyriform
  shaped vessel.. 6. aludel
  squash.. 7. chayote
  type.. 4. Bosc 8. Bartlett
pearl... 3. gem 4. drop 5. nacre,
  tooth, white 9. margarite
pearl (pert to)...
  bird.. 10. guinea fowl
  color.. 4. blue 13. mother-of-pearl
  eye.. 8. cataract
  imitation.. 6. olivet
  of great luster.. 6. orient
  opal.. 9. cacholong (opaque)
  oyster.. 7. Avicula
  seed.. 7. aliofar (obs)
  vegetable.. 6. onion
pearly... 5. milky, quick, smart
  7. opaline, whitish 8. pellucid
  10. opalescent 11. flourishing
Pearly Gates (Bib)... 6. heaven, twelve
peasant... 4. boor, hind, peon, serf
  5. clown, knave, swain 6. carlot,
  cotman, cottar, rascal, rustic
  10. countryman
peasant (pert to)...
  Arab, Syria.. 6. fellah
  cropsharer.. 7. metayer
  English.. 4. hind 5. churl
  Indian.. 4. ryot
  Irish.. 4. kern (kerne) 7. cottier
  like.. 4. base, rude 8. clownish
  Russian.. 5. kulak (rich)
  Scottish.. 4. tyke (tike) 6. cotter
  (cottar)
pease... 5. quiet 6. pacify 7. appease
  9. reconcile
peasecrow... 4. tern
peat... 3. bog, pet 4. coal, fuel, moor,
  moss, turf 6. minion 7. darling
  8. favorite 11. combustible
peat (pert to)...
  cutter.. 5. piner
  moss.. 8. sphagnum
  turf spade.. 5. slave

wood.. 11. loosestrife
peau... 4. skin (silks) 6. fabric
peba... 9. armadillo
pebble... 5. scree, stone, talus
6. quartz 7. chuckie (chucky), crystal,
psephos 11. gravelstone, pebblestone
peccadillo... 4. slip 5. error, fault,
lapse 12. indiscretion
peccant... 3. bad 5. wrong 6. guilty,
morbid, wicked 7. corrupt, sinning,
spoiled 9. incorrect, unhealthy
12. insalubrious
peccary... 6. mammal (piglike)
7. Tagassu, Tayassu 8. javelina
pech... 4. pant 11. breathe hard
pecht (Scot)... 5. fairy, gnome, pygmy
peck... 3. dab, dot, eat, nag 4. food,
hole, jerk, kiss 5. pitch, prick, throw
6. peggle, stroke 7. measure
8. quantity 11. large amount
peck at... 3. nag 4. carp, twit
5. tease 6. attack, harass
pectase... 6. enzyme
peculiar... 3. odd 4. idio (comb form)
5. queer 6. oddish, unique
7. curious, special, strange, typical
8. distinct, separate, singular
9. different, eccentric 10. particular
14. characteristic
peculiar expression... 5. idiom
peculiarity... 4. kink 5. quirk, trait
6. oddity 7. oddness 8. mannerism
10. partiality 11. singularity
12. eccentricity 14. characteristic
peculiar to a district... 7. endemic
pecuniary... 6. fiscal 8. monetary
9. financial
pedagogue... 5. tutor 6. pedant
7. teacher 12. schoolmaster
pedal... 4. foot 5. lever 6. driver
7. treadle 9. propeller
pedant... 4. prig 5. tutor 6. dorbel,
purist 7. formalist, pedagogue
10. conformist 12. bluestocking,
precisionist, schoolmaster
peddle... 4. hawk, sell, vend 6. piddle,
retail 11. disseminate
peddler, pedlar... 6. cadger, coster,
hawker, mugger, sutler 7. chapman
8. huckster 9. vivandier
12. costermonger
peddler's French... 6. jargon (thieves')
9. gibberish
pedestal... 7. support 10. foundation
pedestal part... 3. die 4. base, dado
5. socle 6. plinth, quadra
pedestrian... 3. ped 4. dull, slow
5. hiker 6. hoofer, walker
11. commonplace 12. foot traveler
13. unimaginative
pedicel... 3. ray (of an umbel) 4. stem
5. stalk 8. peduncle
pediculosis... 9. lousiness
Pediculus... 4. lice
pedigree... 6. stemma 7. descent,
lineage 8. ancestry, register
9. genealogy 10. family tree
pedio (comb form)... 4. sole 6. instep
pedology... 9. soil study 10. child
study
pedometer... 5. watch 8. odograph
10. instrument, passometer

pedregal... 9. lava field
pedum... 5. crook, staff (pastoral)
peduncle... 4. stem 5. scape, stalk
7. pedicel, pedicle, sessile
peek... 3. pry 4. peep 5. chirp, flash
6. glance 7. glimpse 9. look slyly
peekaboo... 4. game 6. bopeep
peel... 4. bark, pare, rind, skin
5. slipe, stake, strip 6. cut off,
lamina, shovel 8. car blade, palisade,
stockade
peel (off)... 4. harl, pare, tear 7. come
off 8. get loose 11. decorticate
peeler... 4. crab (shedding), yarn
5. corer 7. hustler 8. pillager
9. policeman
peep... 3. pry 4. peek, peer, pule,
skeg 5. cheep, chirp, pipit, sight
(firearms) 6. glance, squeak
7. crevice 8. peephole 9. sandpiper
peephole... 4. hole 6. eyelet
8. aperture 9. sighthole
peer... 4. duke, earl, fere, gaze, mate
5. baron, equal, match, noble, stare,
stime (styme) 7. marquis
8. nobleman, superior, viscount
Peer Gynt (pert to)...
drama, poem by.. 5. Ibsen
mother.. 3. Ase
music suite by.. 5. Grieg
peerless... 9. matchless, nonpareil,
paper size, unequaled, unmatched
10. unexcelled 11. ne plus ultra,
superlative
peesweep, peesweep... 7. lapwing
10. greenfinch
peetweep... 9. sandpiper (spotted)
peeved... 4. sore 7. annoyed, nettled
9. irritated
peevish... 3. coy 4. sour 5. cross,
sulky, techy, testy 6. crusty, morose,
touchy 7. fretful, pettish, spleeny,
waspish 8. captious, choleric,
contrary, perverse, petulant, snappish
9. irascible, irritable, querulous,
splenetic
peg... 3. hob, leg, nob, nog, pin
4. dram, skeg 5. drink, stake, tooth
6. drudge, fasten, reason 7. pretext,
support 9. persevere, recognize
peg (pert to)...
cribbage... 4. game
iron.. 5. piton
out.. 7. croquet
shoe.. 5. cleat
wood.. 5. spill, thole 8. treenail
pega... 5. shark 6. remora
Pegasus... 5. horse (winged), steed
13. constellation
Pegasus's rider... 11. Bellerophon
pegomancy, divination by...
7. springs 9. fountains
peho... 8. morepork
peignoir... 8. negligee 12. dressing
gown, dressing sack
pejorative... 11. disparaging
12. depreciatory
Peking, Pekin... 4. blue, city, duck
7. spaniel
pelagic... 6. marine 7. oceanic
9. underseas
pelagic organism... 6. nekton

7. benthos 8. plankton
Pele... 7. goddess (volcanoes)
pêle-mêle... 8. pellmell
Peleus (pert to)...
    father.. 6. Aeacus
    King of.. 9. Myrmidons
    son.. 8. Achilles
    wife.. 6. Thetis
pelf... 3. fur, rob 4. gain 5. booty,
    lucre, money, spoil, trash 6. pilfer,
    profit, refuse, riches, wealth
    7. rubbish 10. ne'er-do-well
Pelias (pert to)...
    daughter.. 5. Medes
    King of.. 6. Iolcus
    nephew.. 5. Jason
    son.. 7. Acastus
pelican (pert to)...
    heraldry.. 10. in her piety
    symbolic of.. 6. Christ 7. charity
Pelican State... 9. Louisiana
pell... 3. fur 4. hide, pelt, skin
    5. hurry 6. hasten 13. parchment
    roll
pellagra... 5. zeism
pellar, peller... 6. wizard 8. conjurer
pellet... 4. ball, pill 6. bullet
    7. granule, missile, pallion
pellicle... 4. film, scum 6. lamina
    7. coating 8. membrane
pell-mell, pellmell... 10. vehemently
    12. furious taste 13. helter-skelter
pellock... 8. porpoise
pellucid... 5. clear 6. bright, limpid
    8. luminous 11. translucent,
    transparent 12. intelligible
pelmet... 7. valance (short)
Peloponnesus...
    capital.. 7. Corinth
    city.. 7. Argolis
    League.. 11. Confederacy
    peninsula (Gr).. 5. Morea
        12. Peloponnesos (old), Peloponnesus
        (modern)
    race (anc).. 6. Dorian 7. Spartan
    School.. 6. Dorian 9. Sculpture
    War.. 12. Athens-Sparta (BC)
Pelops (pert to)...
    father.. 8. Tantalus
    son.. 6. Atreus 8. Thyestes
    wife.. 10. Hippodamia
pelota... 4. ball, game 5. cesta
    7. fronton, jai alai
pelt... 3. fur 4. blow, fell, hide, push,
    skin 5. stone 6. hurl at, pelage,
    refuse, strike, thrust 7. apparel (of
    skins), rubbish 8. woolfell
peltry... 4. furs, pelt 5. skins
peludo... 9. armadillo (six-banded)
pelvic bone... 5. ilium 7. ischium
    8. seat bone
pelvic-shaped... 11. basin-shaped
pemmican... 4. meat (dried) 7. buffalo,
    venison
pen... 3. cot, sty 4. bolt, coop, gaol
    5. abode, hutch, quill, write
    6. fasten, indite 7. confine
    9. enclosure 12. penitentiary
pen (pert to)...
    like.. 7. styloid
    name.. 6. anonym 9. pseudonym
        10. nom de plume

point.. 3. neb, nib 4. stub
text.. 5. ronde
penalize... 4. fine 5. mulct 6. punish
    8. handicap
penalty... 4. fine, loss 7. forfeit
    8. handicap, hardship
    10. punishment, repentance
Penang Islands capital...
    10. Georgetown
penchant... 4. bent 6. desire, liking
    7. leaning 8. tendency 10. attraction
    11. inclination 12. decided taste
pendant... 3. bob, tag 4. tail 5. aglet
    (aiglet), queue 6. tassel 7. eardrop,
    earring, hanging 8. appendix,
    pendulum 9. lavaliere 10. chandelier
pendent... 3. lop 4. pend 7. hanging
    8. appended 9. impending,
    pendulous 11. jutting over,
    overhanging
pendent cone (limestone)...
    10. stalactite
pendulous fold, skin... 6. dewlap
Penelope (pert to)...
    father.. 7. Icarius
    husband.. 7. Ulysses 8. Odysseus
    island.. 6. Ithaca
    suitor.. 7. Agelaus
penetrate... 4. bore, gore, stab
    5. delve, elbow, enter 6. pierce
    7. pervade 8. permeate 9. perforate
    10. move deeply
penetrating... 4. cold, deep 5. acute,
    sharp 6. shrill, subtle 7. caustic,
    odorous 8. incisive 9. pervading,
    sagacious, searching
penetration... 6. acumen 7. ingress,
    insight 9. acuteness, sharpness
    11. discernment, perforation
    14. discrimination
Peneus (pert to)...
    father of.. 6. Daphne
    genus of.. 6. prawns
    god of.. 11. Peneus River (Thessalia)
penguin... 3. auk 6. Johnny 10. rock
    hopper
penguin (pert to)...
    aviation.. 13. training plane
    duck.. 12. Indian Runner (duck)
    genus.. 8. Eudyptes
    nest.. 7. rookery 10. penguinery
    type.. 4. king 6. Adelie 7. emperor,
        jackass
peninsula... 4. neck 6. penile
    10. chersonese
Peninsula...
    Asia.. 5. Malay
    Cimbrian, Cimbric.. 7. Jutland
    Iberia.. 5. Spain
    Seward.. 6. Alaska
    Tauric.. 6. Crimea
    Thracian.. 9. Gallipoli
penitent... 5. sorry 8. contrite
    9. repentant
penitential discipline... 7. penance
penitential period... 4. Lent
pennant... 4. fane, flag, whip
    6. banner, burgee (yacht), ensign,
    pennon, pinion 9. banderole
pennant fish... 11. cobblerfish
pennate... 6. winged 7. pinnate
    9. feathered, penniform

pennon... 4. flag, wing 6. banner, pinion 8. streamer

Pennsylvania...
capital.. 10. Harrisburg
city.. 4. Erie 7. Reading 8. Scranton 10. Pittsburgh 12. Philadelphia
famed site.. 10. Gettysburg 11. Liberty Bell, Valley Forge 16. Independence Hall
founder.. 11. William Penn
mountain.. 5. Davis 11. Alleghenies
named, first.. 10. Penn's Woods
river.. 4. Ohio 8. Delaware 10. Schuylkill 11. Susquehanna
State admission.. 6. second
State motto.. 28. Virtue, Liberty and Independence
State nickname.. 8. Keystone

penny... 4. cent, coin 5. pence 6. copper, stiver 8. denarius (Bib)

penologist, famed.. 5. Lawes

penology, study of... 11. criminology 18. punishment for crime

pensive... 3. sad 5. mesto, sober 6. dreamy, musing 7. wistful 10. meditative, melancholy, reflective, thoughtful 13. contemplative

pentastich... 4. poem 6. stanza 7. strophe 10. five verses

Pentateuch... 5. Torah (Tora) 10. Law of Moses 14. First Five Books (Old Test) 16. Five Books of Moses

Pentecost... 8. festival 10. Whitsunday

Pentheus (pert to)...
grandson of.. 6. Cadmus
King of.. 6. Thebes
mother.. 5. Agave

penthouse... 6. lean-to 7. leaning, pentice 9. apartment (roof) 11. overhanging

penury... 4. want 7. poverty 9. indigence, privation 10. scantiness 11. destitution, miserliness

peon... 4. pawn (chess), serf 7. laborer, peasant, soldier 9. attendant, constable, messenger, policeman

peony... 4. piny 6. moutan 7. Paeonia 11. Burmese ruby

people... 3. kin, men 4. folk, ones, race, Rais 5. demos, laity 6. family, nation, public 7. kinsmen, persons 8. populace, subjects 9. citizenry 10. population

people (pert to)...
Am Indian, Eskimo.. 7. Amerind
ancient.. 5. Medes 6. Greeks, Romans 7. Sabines 9. Egyptians, Etruscans
class, lowest.. 8. canaille
common.. 6. vulgar 7. tilikum (tilicum)
headless (Myth).. 8. Acephali
old-fashioned.. 6. prudes 7. squares 13. antediluvians
ref to.. 4. laic 6. ethnic 7. demotic
Spanish.. 5. gente
wild young.. 10. rantipoles

people (of)...
culture (earliest).. 8. Grecians
gentle birth.. 6. gentry
one government.. 6. nation
rank.. 11. aristocracy, aristocrats

the people.. 6. ethnic

peopled... 5. abadi (Ind village) 8. occupied, populous 9. populated

pep... 2. go 3. vim 4. dash 6. energy 7. quicken 9. stimulate 10. initiative, liveliness

pepper... 4. pelt 5. shoot 6. energy 7. bombard 8. sprinkle 9. condiment

pepper (pert to)...
betel.. 4. siri (sirih)
black.. 11. Piper nigrum
box.. 5. tower 8. spitfire
Capsicum, source of.. 7. cayenne, chilies (chili), paprika
climbing.. 5. betel 6. nigrum
condiment.. 7. cayenne, paprika
dulse.. 7. seaweed (red)
genus.. 8. Capsicum
grass.. 5. crass 8. pillwort
sauce.. 7. Tabasco
turnip.. 15. jack-in-the-pulpit

pepper (pert to country)...
Australia.. 4. kava (cava) 8. kavakava
Borneo.. 4. kava (cava)
Guinea.. 5. chili 8. Capsicum
Malay.. 4. siri (sirih)
Spain.. 7. paprika, pimento 8. allspice, pimiento

pepper-and-salt... 4. gray 17. harbinger-of-spring

peppermint... 3. oil 4. herb 6. spirit 7. essence, gum tree, lozenge, menthol (camphor)

peppery... 5. fiery 7. piquant, pungent 8. choleric, spirited, stinging 10. passionate 11. hot-tempered

per... 2. by 7. for each, through 9. by means of 11. according to

peradventure... 3. hap 5. doubt 7. it may be 8. possibly 11. uncertainty

perambulate... 4. walk 6. ramble, stroll 8. traverse 9. promenade, walk about

perceive... 3. see 4. hear, know, note 5. sense 6. behold, descry, detect, divine, notice, remark 7. discern, observe, sensate 9. apprehend 10. comprehend, understand 11. distinguish 12. discriminate

perceptible... 5. faint 7. tactile, visible 8. knowable, manifest, tangible 10. cognizable 11. appreciable, discernible, perceivable

perception... 3. ear 4. tact 5. sense, taste 6. acumen, seeing 8. sagacity 9. awareness, sensation 10. cognizance 11. discernment 13. consciousness 14. discrimination

perceptive... 7. knowing 8. sensible 9. sagacious 14. discriminative

perch... 3. bar, peg, rod, sit 4. fish, pole 5. aerie, barse, roost, sit on, staff 6. alight, aviary, sauger, settle, weapon 7. measure 9. trumpeter

Percheron... 5. horse 15. Percheron Norman

perchers... 5. birds 7. candles 8. Passeres 10. Insessores

percolate... 4. ooze, seep, sift, silt, sipe 5. exude, leach, steep 6. filter, strain 7. trickle 8. permeate, transude

percussion... **9.** collision
10. concussion, detonation
percussion instrument... **4.** drum,
gong **5.** bells, bones, traps
6. Becken, chimes, tom–tom
7. celesta, cymbals, marimba, potlids
8. carillon, clappers, triangle
9. castanets, xylophone
10. tambourine, vibraphone
12. glockenspiel
perdition... **4.** hell, loss (soul), ruin
5. wreck **6.** damnation
11. destruction
peregrinate... **6.** travel, wander **7.** go
about, sojourn
peregrine... **5.** alien **6.** exotic, falcon
7. foreign, pilgrim, strange
9. foreigner
perempt... **5.** quash **6.** defeat
7. destroy
peremptory... **5.** final **7.** express
8. absolute, arrogant, decisive,
dogmatic, positive, resolute
9. arbitrary, mandatory
10. compulsory, conclusive,
imperative, obligatory **11.** dictatorial
13. authoritative **16.** incontrovertible
perennial... **7.** lasting **8.** constant,
enduring **9.** continual, evergreen,
permanent, perpetual, unceasing
10. continuous **12.** never–failing
perennial (pert to)...
climbing.. **5.** liana (liane)
grass.. **4.** lyme **6.** Elymus (genus)
7. wild rye
herb.. **4.** Geum **5.** avens
weed.. **8.** toadflax
perfect... **4.** holy, pure, sole **5.** ideal,
model, teleo (comb form), whole
6. entire **7.** correct, develop, improve
8. finished **9.** blameless, faultless,
inviolate, righteous **10.** consummate,
satisfying **11.** unqualified
perfection... **4.** acme **5.** ideal
7. paragon **8.** accuracy, maturity
10. completion, excellence
13. faultlessness
perfectly... **5.** quite **7.** ideally, rightly,
utterly **9.** correctly **10.** absolutely,
accurately, altogether, completely,
flawlessly, thoroughly
perfecto... **5.** cigar (tapering)
perficient... **6.** actual **9.** effective,
effectual
perfidious... **6.** shifty **8.** disloyal
9. faithless **11.** disaffected,
treacherous **12.** falsehearted
perfidy... **7.** treason **8.** apostasy
9. duplicity, treachery **10.** disloyalty
13. faithlessness
perforate... **4.** bore, dock **5.** drill,
punch **6.** pierce, pounce, riddle
9. penetrate **10.** umbilicate
perforated...
block.. **3.** nut
initials (Philat).. **10.** stamp marks
nozzle.. **4.** rose
space.. **5.** brain
sphere.. **4.** bead
perforation... **4.** bore, hole **6.** eyelet
8. aperture, piercing, punching
perform... **2.** do **3.** act **4.** play

5. enact, exert **6.** effect **7.** execute,
fulfill, produce **8.** complete, transact
9. officiate **10.** accomplish, bring
about, perpetrate
performance... **3.** act **4.** test, work
6. action **7.** exploit **8.** ceremony
9. operation **10.** completion,
exhibition, observance, production
12. consummation
14. accomplishment
performance (pert to)...
clumsy.. **6.** bungle
daytime.. **7.** matinee
for one.. **4.** solo
notable.. **4.** feat
of duty.. **8.** feasance
performer... **4.** doer **5.** actor
6. dancer, worker **6.** magician,
musician, thespian **9.** pretender
15. prestidigitator
perfume... **4.** balm, odor **5.** aroma,
attar, orris, savor, scent, smell
7. bouquet, cologne, essence, rose
oil **9.** fragrance, redolence
10. frangipani
perfume (pert to)...
base.. **4.** musk **9.** ambergris
cherry.. **7.** mahaleb
essence.. **8.** bergamot
medicated.. **8.** pastille (pastil)
musky.. **5.** civet
oriental.. **5.** myrrh **7.** incense
12. frankincense
scent.. **7.** jasmine **8.** lavender
10. heliotrope
toilet.. **6.** bay rum **12.** eau de
Cologne
unguent.. **6.** pomade
violet.. **5.** irone
pergola... **5.** arbor, bower, kiosk
6. pandal **7.** balcony, trellis
9. colonnade **11.** summerhouse
perhaps... **5.** maybe **6.** ablins (Scot),
belike, mayhap **8.** doubtful, possibly,
probably **9.** perchance **10.** contingent
peri... **3.** elf **5.** about (pref), fairy
6. beauty
periapt... **5.** charm **6.** amulet
pericarp... **3.** pod **5.** berry, shell
8. seedcase
Pericles (Gr)... **9.** statesman
periculum (Rom law)... **4.** risk **5.** peril
6. danger
perigee (Astron)... **12.** nearest earth
(opp of apogee)
peril... **4.** risk **6.** danger, hazard,
menace **8.** jeopardy
perilously high... **7.** Icarian (flying)
perimeter... **5.** ambit **6.** border
7. outline **8.** boundary **9.** periphery
period... **3.** age, day, dot, end, eon,
era, eve **4.** stop, term, time, year
5. cycle, epoch, limit, spell
6. degree, moment, season
8. duration, sentence **10.** conclusion
11. termination
period (pert to)...
historical.. **4.** eral **6.** Eocene
7. Neocene
penitential.. **4.** Lent
statutory.. **10.** limitation
Tertiary.. **6.** Eocene **7.** Miocene,

Neocene 8. Pliocene
periodic... 4. eral 6. annual 7. etesian
8. seasonal 9. recurrent
10. rhythmical 12. intermittent
periodic (pert to)...
sea motion.. 4. tide
wind.. 2. oe 7. chinook, etesian,
monsoon
windstorm.. 2. oe 7. tornado
9. whirlwind
periodical... 5. paper 6. review
7. etesian, journal 8. magazine
9. recurring 11. publication
periodical cicada... 6. locust (17 yrs)
period of...
delay.. 7. moratorium
dryness.. 7. drought
evolution.. 6. hemera
fifty days.. 13. quinquagesima
five years.. 6. pentad
holding.. 6. tenure
instruction.. 7. session
possession.. 6. lease
probation.. 6. parole
prosperity.. 4. boom 6. golden
recovery.. 13. convalescence
14. reconstruction
sleep.. 11. hibernation
ten years.. 6. decade
time.. 3. age, day, eon 4. span
work.. 4. turn 5. shift, spell, watch
youth.. 6. nonage
peripatetic... 7. walking 8. rambling
Peripatetic (pert to Aristotle)...
6. school 8. disciple 10. Philosophy
peripheral... 6. distal 8. outmost
8. external 9. outlinear 10. round
about
periphery... 3. lip, rim 4. brim
5. ambit 6. areola, border
8. confines 9. perimeter
10. borderland 13. circumference
periqua... 7. tobacco (strong) 10. otter
brown
perish... 3. die, rot 4. fade 5. decay,
waste 8. pass away, squander
9. cease to be, disappear 11. be
destroyed
perissodactyl... 15. odd-numbered
toes
peristyle... 7. columns (range of)
8. corridor 9. colonnade
10. peripteral
peritoneum fold... 7. omentum
periwig... 3. wig 6. frizzy, peruke
9. shellfish 10. periwinkle
periwinkle... 4. blue 5. snail
6. mussel, myrtle 9. evergreen
perjink... 4. neat, nice 7. precise
perjure... 7. violate 8. forswear
perjury... 9. violation 12. breech of
oath 13. false swearing
perk... 5. preen, prink 7. smarten
9. percolate 10. perquisite
perkin... 5. cider
perk up... 7. cheer up, improve, raise
up, refresh 10. recuperate
permanent... 5. fixed 6. innate, stable
7. abiding, durable, lasting
8. constant, enduring, inherent
9. perpetual 10. changeless,
continuing 12. unchangeable

permeate... 5. imbue 7. pervade
8. saturate
permission... 5. grace, leave
7. consent, license 9. allowance
10. sufferance 13. authorization
permissive... 8. optional 9. allowable,
permitted, tolerated 10. consenting,
permitting 13. power of choice
permit... 3. let 4. leve 5. allow, grant,
leave 6. suffer 7. consent, license,
warrant 8. tolerate 9. authorize
10. permission
permit to live... 5. spare 8. reprieve
permutate... 6. change 9. rearrange
11. interchange
permutation... 6. barter
11. interchange 13. transmutation
14. transformation
pern... 6. Pernis 7. buzzard (honey)
pernicious... 4. bane 5. fatal
6. anemia, deadly, malign, wicked
7. baleful, baneful, harmful, hurtful,
noisome, noxious, ruinous, vicious
10. villainous 11. deleterious
pernio... 9. chilblain
perorate... 5. speak (at length)
7. declaim 8. harangue 9. expatiate
perpendicular... 4. sine 5. erect,
plumb, sheer, steep 7. apothem,
upright 8. binormal, vertical
9. rectitude 10. standing up
11. precipitous
perpetrate... 6. commit 7. perform
12. carry through
perpetual... 7. endless, eternal
8. constant, unending 9. continual,
perennial, permanent, unceasing
10. continuous 11. everlasting
perpetually... 9. endlessly, eternally
11. ceaselessly 12. interminably
perpetuity... 7. annuity 8. eternity
11. endless time
perplex... 3. vex 4. cark 5. amaze
6. puzzle, riddle 7. confuse
8. bewilder, entangle 9. obfuscate
10. complicate
perplexity... 3. fog 6. tangle
7. anxiety, dilemma, problem
8. question 9. confusion, situation
10. complexity 11. distraction
12. bewilderment, complication
perquisite... 3. tip 4. gain 6. boodle
8. appanage, gratuity
perquod... 7. whereby
per se... 6. itself 8. directly
11. essentially 13. intrinsically
perse... 4. blue
persecute... 5. annoy, harry, hound
6. harass 7. afflict, oppress, torment
8. hunt down 9. martyrize
persecution... 9. treatment
10. harassment, oppression
12. mistreatment
Persephone (pert to)...
abductor.. 5. Hades
Attica, name.. 4. Kore (Cora)
deity of.. 11. agriculture
father.. 4. Zeus
Greek name.. 11. Persephassa
mother.. 7. Demeter
Orphic literary name.. 8. Despoina
queen of.. 15. infernal regions

Roman name.. 10. Proserpine
(Proserpina)
Perseus (pert to)...
Astron.. 13. Constellation
father.. 4. Zeus
mother.. 5. Danae
slayer of.. 6. Medusa
perseverance... 8. patience
9. constancy 10. resolution,
steadiness 11. persistence, pertinacity
13. steadfastness
persevere... 5. abide 6. endure, insist,
keep on 7. carry on, persist
8. continue
Persia (Iran, Irani)... see also *Persian*
capital.. 7. Teheran (Tehran)
city.. 5. Niriz 6. Abadan, Shiraz,
Tabriz 7. Hamadan, Ispahan
country (anc).. 4. Elam 7. Chaldea
gulf.. 4. Oman 7. Persian
gulf port.. 7. Bushire 9. Mohamerah
gulf province.. 6. Kuwait
gulf wind.. 6. shamal
lake.. 7. Rezaieh, Urumidh (Salt)
mountain.. 6. Ararat, Elburz, Zagros
9. Hindu Kush
pert to.. 6. Persic
river.. 5. Safid 9. Euphrates
ruins.. 10. Persepolis (Shiraz)
Persian (pert to)... see also *Iranian*
blue.. 10. regimental
calendar reformer.. 9. Jalalaean
(Jalalian)
carpet, rug.. 4. kali 5. Herat (Herati),
Senna 6. Kerman, Tabriz
11. Baluchistan
cushion.. 6. musnud
diadem.. 4. taj
door.. 3. dar
evergreen.. 4. olax
grass.. 6. millet
gum.. 10. tragacanth
hat.. 3. fez 6. turban
idiom.. 7. persism
javelin.. 6. jereed (jerid)
rose.. 3. gul
rug.. see *carpet* (above)
screen.. 6. purdah
Persian animals, birds, fruit...
apple.. 6. citron
bird.. 6. bulbul
cat.. 6. Angora
deer.. 5. maral 6. fallow
gazelle.. 4. cora
lamb.. 9. astrakhan, broadtail
lynx.. 7. caracul
tick (venomous).. 8. Miana bug
Persian Myth, Religion...
angel.. 3. Mah
deity.. 6. Ormazd (Supreme)
demigod, hero.. 4. Yima
demon.. 7. Apaosha
fairy.. 3. elf, fay 4. peri
fire worshiper.. 5. Parsi (Parsee)
god of light.. 7. Mithras
mystic.. 4. sufi
nymph.. 5. houri
religion founder.. 9. Zoroaster
religious doctrine.. 6. Babism
(Babiism)
sacred books (Zoroastrian).. 6. Avesta

scriptures (Moham).. 5. Koran
spirit.. 7. Ahriman
Persian people, government...
assembly (1906).. 6. Majlis (Mejlis)
caste (priestly).. 4. Magi 7. Wise Men
chief.. 3. mir 4. Shah
chief's wife, lady.. 4. bibi
civil officer.. 4. khan
dynasty.. 5. Kajar 7. Arsacid
8. Selencid 10. Sassanidae
(Sassanid)
governor (anc).. 6. satrap
King.. 4. Shah 5. Cyrus 6. Darius,
Xerxes
language (anc).. 4. Zend 7. Pahlavi
(Pahlevi)
natives.. 5. Kurds, Medes, Mukri,
Perse 6. Aryans
New Year's Day.. 7. Nowroze
people.. 7. Hadjemi, Iranics
8. Iranians
poet.. 4. Omar 5. Hafiz, Saadi
ruler.. 4. Shah 6. atabeg (atabek),
Sultan
student (Koran).. 5. hafiz
trader.. 4. Sart
tribe.. 4. Leks, Lurs 5. Arabs, Kurds,
Turks 7. Gypsies 8. Baluchis
Wise Men.. 4. Magi
persiflage... 6. banter 8. raillery
persimmon... 4. kaki 7. chapote
persist... 4. last, urge 6. endure
7. prevail 9. persevere
persistent... 7. durable 8. constant,
habitual 10. determined, inveterate
11. persevering 13. indefatigable
persistently opposed... 8. renitent
9. obstinate 12. recalcitrant
person... 3. one 4. body, soul
5. being, wight 6. figure 8. creature
9. character 10. individual
person (pert to)...
accuser, challenger.. 9. appellant
acting for another.. 5. proxy
9. alternate
baptized (anc).. 11. illuminatus
base.. 7. caitiff, hangdog
bringing bad luck.. 4. jinx 5. Jonah
bringing good luck.. 6. mascot
canonized.. 5. saint
careless.. 7. trifler 11. pococurante
charged with high mission.. 7. apostle
charitable.. 9. samaritan
cheerful.. 8. optimist
clumsy.. 3. oaf 5. staup 6. lummox
7. bungler
common.. 3. lay 8. roturier
conceited.. 4. prig
contemptible.. 3. cad 4. heel, toad
7. bauchle (Scot)
crazed.. 6. maniac 10. monomaniac,
psychopath
credulous.. 5. Simon
cruel.. 5. fiend
dishonorable.. 6. rotter
dissolute.. 4. roué
drunken.. 4. lush
dull.. 4. dolt 5. dunce, moron, stock
6. dorbel 9. blockhead
dwarf.. 5. shurf
educated.. 6. pedant, pundit, savant
7. erudite, learned, student

8. cultured, highbrow 9. literatus
12. intellectual
emitting smoke.. 7. whiffer
enterprising.. 8. go-getter
fabulously rich.. 5. Midas
foolish.. 3. sop 4. zany 5. clown,
idiot 6. dotard 7. buffoon
9. simpleton
gigantic.. 5. giant, titan 7. monster
gloomy.. 7. killjoy 10. crosspatch
good luck.. 6. mascot
grotesque.. 9. golliwogg
guilty.. 7. culprit
held as pledge.. 7. hostage
image of.. 4. doll, idol 6. poppet,
puppet
impatient.. 6. fidget 7. hotspur
important.. 5. mogul 7. magnate,
notable 9. personage
indifferent.. 5. stoic
inexperienced.. 9. greenhorn
insignificant.. 5. sprat 6. little, nobody
lacking in common sense..
9. simpleton
lazy.. 5. drone 8. sluggard
learned.. see *educated* (above)
left-handed.. 6. clumsy 8. sinister
9. portsider
loud-voiced.. 7. stentor
low-bred.. 3. cad
miserly.. 9. skinflint 10. curmudgeon
non-Jewish.. 5. Aryan 7. Gentile
overmodest.. 5. prude
perfidious.. 5. snake 7. traitor
9. faithless
rapacious.. 4. wolf 5. harpy
representing another.. 5. proxy
9. alternate
respondent to appeal.. 8. appellee
rich.. 7. wealthy 9. plutocrat
10. capitalist 11. millionaire
rude, ill-mannered.. 4. boor 5. yahoo
scatterbrained.. 6. madcap
self-centered.. 6. egoist 7. egotist
8. extrovert, introvert
self-righteous.. 8. pharisee
sharp-eyed.. 5. Argus
sick.. 9. aegrotant
skilled.. 6. artist, master 7. artisan
8. mechanic
slipshod, untidy.. 6. sloven
staff (Mil).. 10. aide-de-camp
stupid.. 3. ass 4. dolt, gump
5. moron, stock
supercilious.. 4. snob 9. concerted
thankless.. 7. ingrate
unclassified.. 11. nondescript
unique.. 4. oner
unknown.. 7. inconnu 8. inconnue
unmarried.. 6. maiden 8. bachelor,
celibate, spinster
valorous.. 4. hero
violent-tempered.. 6. tartar
wealthy.. 5. nabob, pluto (comb form)
10. capitalist 11. millionaire
who reads, writes.. 8. literate
witty.. 3. wag 7. punster
8. comedian 10. comedienne
worthless.. 5. lorel, losel
writ serving.. 6. elisor
young.. 9. stripling
14. whippersnapper

personage... 5. image, mogul
7. bearing, stature 8. great man,
one's body, portrait
13. impersonation
persona grata... 13. welcome person
16. acceptable person
personal (pert to)...
appearance.. 8. presence
comb form.. 4. idio
history.. 6. memoir
ornament.. 6. parure
ownership, land.. 6. estate
7. demesne 8. chattels, property
personality... 3. ego 5. being
6. person 8. identity 13. individuality
15. distinctiveness
persona non grata... 18. unacceptable
person
personate... 5. enact 7. feigned
9. represent 10. personated
11. counterfeit
personification... 3. Una (truth)
10. embodiment 11. attribution
14. representation
person of...
age.. 5. major
courage.. 7. Spartan
eighty years.. 12. octogenarian
encyclopedic learning.. 10. polyhistor
fifty years.. 15. quinquagenarian
forty years.. 14. quadragenarian
great intellect.. 6. genius
nervous disorders.. 8. neurotic
ninety years.. 12. nonagenarian
one hundred years.. 11. centenarian
seventy years.. 14. septuagenarian
sixty years.. 12. sexagenarian
skill.. 6. master, talent 7. magnate
two races.. 9. half-caste
persons of...
a familiar set.. 7. coterie
a family tree.. 6. stirps
groups.. 4. army, band, team
6. chorus, troupe 7. company
8. assembly 9. orchestra
organized bodies.. 6. corps, posse
perspicacity... 6. acumen, vision
8. sagacity 9. acuteness
11. discernment, penetration
perspicuity... 6. lucidity, sagacity
12. translucency, transparency
perspiration... 5. sudor, sweat
7. sudoric 8. hard work
11. evaporation, saline fluid
13. transpiration
persuade... 4. coax, sway, urge
6. entice, induce, reason 7. convert,
suasion 8. convince, inveigle
9. influence, plead with
persuasible... 6. pliant 11. persuadable
14. open-mindedness
persuasive... 8. eloquent 9. impelling
10. convincing, persuading
pert... 3. gay 4. bold, keen 5. brash,
sassy, saucy 6. clever, comely,
dapper, daring, lively, nimble
7. forward 8. handsome, skillful
9. exquisite, officious, sprightly
11. impertinent 12. presumptuous
pert (girl)... 4. chit, minx
pertain... 5. belie 6. belong, relate
7. adjunct 8. function, peculiar

9. accessory, appendage, appertain, attribute

pertaining to...

act of rising.. 6. ortive 7. eastern
agriculture.. 7. georgic
ancestral type.. 9. ataristic
ancient Egyptian capital.. 4. Sais
ancient Greeks.. 9. classical
ancient Nile City.. 4. Sais (Saite)
ancient Troy.. 5. Iliac
anything remote.. 6. forane
apostles.. 7. petrine
Asiatic (old).. 8. Chaldean
Asiatic mountain.. 6. Altaic
Athens.. 5. Attic
authorized doctrine.. 8. dogmatic
    10. dogmatical
birthmark.. 6. nevoid (naevoid)
body.. 5. somal
body of land.. 11. continental
book description.. 13. bibliographic
both ears.. 8. binaural
both sexes.. 7. epicene
breadmaking.. 6. panary
breastbone.. 7. sternal
bristles.. 5. setal
brown race.. 7. Malayan
bunch.. 5. comal
canonical hours.. 7. matinal
carving.. 6. glypic 7. glyptic
cheek.. 5. malar
church, part.. 7. apsidal
city.. 5. civic, urban
cod family.. 6. gadoid
coins.. 12. numismatical
colors.. 9. chromatic
common people.. 7. demotic
construction.. 8. tectonic
cork.. 7. suberic
cough.. 7. tussine
court.. 5. aulic 9. judiciary
crown.. 7. coronal
dance.. 6. gestic 13. terpsichorean
daughter.. 6. filial
dawn.. 4. eoan
day (ordinary).. 6. ferial
desert wastes.. 6. eremic
diaphragm.. 7. phrenic
dogma.. 9. levitical
doves.. 9. columbine
downward air.. 9. katabatic
downy.. 5. dotal
dreams.. 7. oneiric 9. oneirotic
ducks.. 7. anatine
early church.. 9. patristic
early culture.. 8. eolithic
early school of Philos.. 7. Eleatic
earth.. 4. geal 5. terra 7. teluric
    9. planetary
earthquake.. 7. seismic
east.. 4. eoan
elms.. 9. ulmaceous
engraving.. 7. glyptic
essence.. 5. basic
fallow deer.. 6. damine
fashion.. 5. modal
fats.. 6. adipic, sebaic
feet.. 5. pedal
fields.. 8. agrarian
fine arts.. 9. aesthetic (esthetic)
fingers.. 7. digital
first principles.. 9. elemental

fissure.. 5. rimal
flood.. 8. diluvian
forehead.. 7. metopic
frogs.. 6. anuran, ranine
funeral music.. 10. threnodial
funerals.. 8. exequial
gold.. 5. auric
gospel.. 9. evangelic
gulls.. 6. larine
gums (Anat).. 8. gingival
hair.. 5. pilar
hands.. 6. chiral, manual
head.. 8. cephalic
holiday.. 6. ferial (Eccl)
honey.. 10. melaginous
horse.. 6. equine
house.. 5. domal
hypothetical force.. 4. odic
infernal regions.. 7. avernal
ink.. 10. atramental
insects.. 11. entomologic
intellect.. 6. noetic
iron.. 6. ferric
islands.. 7. insular
jaw.. 5. malar
kidney.. 5. renal
knots.. 5. nodal
land.. 8. praedial (predial)
language meaning.. 8. semantic
laughter.. 8. risorial
leg.. 6. crural 7. fibular
lips.. 6. labial
liver.. 7. hepatic
living organism.. 13. parasitologic
lockjaw.. 7. tetanic
love.. 6. erotic 7. amatory 8. erotical
male line.. 7. agnatic
marriage.. 7. marital 8. hymeneal
marsh.. 8. paludine
meaning, in language.. 8. semantic
medicine.. 6. iatric 8. iatrical
medulla oblongata (brain).. 6. bulbar
memory.. 6. mnesic 7. mnestic
    8. mnemonic
midday.. 8. meridian
milk.. 7. lactary, lacteal
mind.. 6. mental 7. phrenic
money matters.. 8. economic
morning.. 5. matin, sunup 7. matinal
    9. matutinal
motion.. 7. kinetic
mouth.. 4. oral 7. oscular, palatal
    8. stomatic
mustard family.. 11. cruciferous
nephew.. 7. nepotal
north wind.. 6. boreal
nose.. 5. nasal 6. narial, rhinal
nut.. 5. nucal
ocean.. 7. pelagic
old age.. 6. senile 7. geratic
    8. gerontic
Old World.. 13. gerontogenous
peacock.. 8. pavonine
people.. 4. laic 7. demotic
pigs.. 7. porcine
pleasure.. 7. hedonic
priests.. 10. sacerdotal
prophecy.. 9. vaticinal
public.. 7. cameral
public prayer.. 8. liturgic 10. liturgical
punishment.. 5. penal 8. punitive
queen.. 7. reginal

rainbow.. **6.** iridal
reason.. **6.** noetic
region without earthquakes..
   11. peneseismic
rhubarb.. **7.** rheumic
river.. **5.** amnic
river bank.. **8.** riparian
rock.. **7.** petrean
royal court.. **5.** aulic
salvation.. **8.** soterial **9.** soterical
sarcasm.. **8.** ironical
school of philosophy.. **7.** Eleatic
sea.. **6.** marine **7.** oceanic, pelagic
   9. thelassic
seacoast.. **8.** littoral
sense of taste.. **9.** gustatory
sepulchral mound.. **7.** tumular
shin, shinbone.. **7.** cnemial
ship's sails.. **5.** velic
singing birds.. **6.** oscine
skull.. **5.** inial
sole of foot.. **7.** plantar
spring.. **6.** vernal
stars.. **6.** astral **7.** stellar **8.** sidereal
state affairs.. **9.** pragmatic
stepmothers.. **8.** novercal
storks.. **7.** pelagic
summer.. **7.** estival (aestival)
   8. festival
sun.. **5.** solar **6.** heliac
tail.. **6.** caudal
teaching.. **9.** pedagogic
tears.. **8.** lacrimal
tempo.. **6.** agogic
the plague.. **7.** loimic
the skin.. **5.** deric **6.** dermic
thread.. **5.** filar
tile.. **7.** tegular
time.. **7.** chronic
tin.. **7.** stranic
tissue.. **5.** telar
tongue.. **7.** glossal, lingual
tortoises.. **9.** chelonian
touch.. **7.** tactile
travel.. **7.** viatic
trees.. **8.** arboreal
verse stress.. **5.** ictic
walls.. **5.** mural **8.** parietal
wax.. **5.** ceral
weight.. **5.** baric **8.** ponderal
whales.. **5.** rotal
wife.. **5.** uxorial
wine.. **5.** vinic
wine making.. **10.** oenopoetic
wings.. **5.** alary
winter.. **6.** hiemal
womanhood.. **9.** muliebral
woods.. **6.** sylvan
wrist.. **6.** carpal
pertaining to country...
Asiatic.. **8.** Chaldean
Asiatic mountain.. **6.** Altaic
Athens.. **5.** Attic
Carthage.. **5.** Punic
Celts.. **4.** Erse
Cretan language.. **6.** Minoan
Dissenters' meeting house.. **7.** pantile
   (from the roofing)
England.. **8.** Anglican
Ethiopian religion.. **6.** Coptic
France.. **6.** Gallic
Franks.. **5.** Salic

Gentiles.. **6.** ethnic
German State.. **8.** Bavarian
Greek epic.. **9.** Homerical
Greek philosophy.. **7.** Eleatic
   8. Platonic
Greek race (anc).. **6.** Aeolic
Greek valley.. **6.** Nemean **8.** Argolian
Hindu books, writing.. **5.** Vedic
   7. Tantric
Hindu philosophy, inertia.. **5.** tamas
Irish.. **6.** Celtic, Gaelic
Isle of Man.. **4.** Manx
Mars.. **5.** Arean
Mediterranean.. **6.** Levant
Moses.. **6.** Mosaic
Nile city (anc).. **4.** Sais (Saite)
Norse poem.. **5.** runic
Passover.. **7.** Paschal
Red Sea colony.. **8.** Eritrean
Rhine.. **7.** Rhenish
Scotch Highlander.. **6.** Gaelic
Spice Islands.. **7.** Molucca
Troy (anc).. **5.** Iliac **6.** Trojan
Vulcan.. **11.** Mulcibirian
West Indies.. **9.** Antillean
pertenencia... **10.** concession
   11. mining claim
Perth... **6.** Atholl (Athole) **7.** Ontario
   9. Australia
pertinacious... **4.** firm **8.** adhering,
   resolute **9.** tenacious **10.** determined,
   inflexible, persistent, unyielding
   11. persevering
pertinacity... **9.** obstinacy
   11. persistency
pertinence... **7.** fitness **9.** relevancy
   10. timeliness **12.** appositeness
perturb... **5.** alarm **6.** excite
   7. agitate, derange, disturb, fluster,
   trouble **8.** bewilder, disorder, distress
   9. confusion
perturbation... **5.** alarm **7.** anxiety,
   fluster **9.** agitation, confusion
   10. excitement **11.** fearfulness
   12. bewilderment, irregularity
pertusion... **8.** piercing, punching
   11. perforation, punched hole
pertussis... **5.** cough **13.** whooping
   cough
Peru... see also *Peruvian*
capital.. **4.** Lima **5.** Cuzco (Inca)
   14. City of the Kings
hero.. **7.** Bolivar, Pizarro
lake.. **8.** Titicaca
mountain.. **5.** Andes **10.** Cordillera
port.. **6.** Callao **7.** Iquitos
   8. Mollendo
river.. **4.** Sama **5.** Santa **6.** Amazon
   7. Maranon, Ucayali **8.** Urubamba
ruins.. **4.** Inca **5.** huaco (relics)
Peruvian (pert to)...
animal.. **4.** paco **5.** llama **6.** alpaca
bark.. **8.** cinchona
goddess of fertility.. **4.** Mama
inn, tavern.. **5.** tambo
king (petty).. **7.** cacique
plant.. **3.** oca
rodent.. **10.** chinchilla
tinamou.. **4.** yutu
tree.. **8.** cinchona
university.. **9.** San Marcos
volcano.. **7.** El Misti

wind (cold).. 4. puna
pervade... 4. fill 5. imbue 6. extend
   8. permeate, traverse 9. penetrate
pervading... 9. prevalent, universal
perverse... 3. awk 4. awry, wogh
   5. wrong 6. cranky, erring
   7. corrupt, forward, froward,
   wayward, willful (wilful) 8. contrary,
   petulant 9. obstinate 10. ill-humored
perversion... 5. error 6. misuse
   8. apostasy 9. sophistry
   10. corruption, distortion
   13. falsification 17. misinterpretation,
   misrepresentation
perversion of taste... 7. malacia
pervert... 4. ruin 5. upset 6. divert,
   misuse 7. corrupt, distort, falsify,
   heretic 8. apostate, overturn,
   renegade 9. turn aside
   10. degenerate, lead astray
   12. misinterpret, misrepresent
pervulgate... 7. publish
Pesach, Pesah... 8. Passover (Feast)
pesante... 5. heavy 10. impressive
peshkash... 3. tax 7. present, tribute
   8. offering
peskar... 5. agent 7. steward
   8. minister 10. accountant
pesky... 6. plaguy 7. teasing
   9. harassing 10. tormenting
pes planus... 8. flatfoot 13. talipes
   planus
pess... 7. hassock (church)
pessimist... 5. cynic 6. malist
   9. defeatist, worrywart
pessimistic... 6. gloomy 7. cynical
   8. cowardly, hopeless 10. despairing,
   foreboding, uncheerful
pest... 3. nag 4. bane 6. plague
   7. ragweed 8. epidemic, nuisance
   9. annoyance 10. pestilence
pester... 3. nag, rib 5. annoy, tease,
   worry 6. badger, harass, impede,
   infest 7. torment 8. entangle
   9. importune 10. overburden
pestilence... 4. bane 5. disease,
   scourge 8. epidemic 13. bubonic
   plague
pestilent... 6. deadly 7. noxious
   8. annoying 9. pestering, poisonous
   10. contagious, infectious, pernicious
   11. mischievous, troublesome
pestle... 4. club 6. muller 7. crusher,
   pounder
pes valgus... 9. bowlegged 13. talipes
   valgus
pet... 4. dear, tiff 5. humor 6. caress,
   coddle, cosset, dandle, fondle,
   pamper 7. darling, dudgeon, indulge
   8. cade lamb, favorite
   10. endearment
petals (pert to)...
   flower.. 7. corolla
   having.. 8. petalous
   orchid.. 8. labellum
   ref to.. 5. whorl 8. petaline, petaloid
   without.. 9. apetalous
petard... 9. explosive 11. firecracker
peteman (thieves' sl)... 5. thief
   7. burglar 8. peterman
   9. cracksman, fisherman (Hist)
   10. safeblower

Peter (pert to)...
   Bell.. 4. poem
   Bible.. 5. Simon (also called)
      7. epistle (New Test)
   Ibbetson.. 5. novel
   Pan.. 3. boy 4. play
   Pan dog.. 4. Nana
   the Great.. 4. Czar
   the Great's father.. 6. Alexis
   the Hermit.. 8. Crusader (1st)
peter out... 4. fade, fail, tire, wane
   6. weaken 7. dwindle 9. cease to
   be
petiole... 4. stem 5. stalk 8. peduncle
   9. leafstalk 10. mesopodium
petit... 4. mean 5. petty, small
   6. little 13. insignificant
petite... 5. small 6. demure, little
petite (pert to)...
   bourse.. 5. Market (Finan)
   marmite.. 4. soup
   noblesse.. 8. nobility (lesser)
petition... 3. ask, beg, sue 4. plea,
   pray 5. apply, plead 6. prayer
   7. entreat, relator, request, solicit
   8. entreaty 10. supplicate
peto... 5. wahoo
petrified... 8. hardened 9. terrified
   15. carved from stone
petrified body... 6. fossil
petrify... 4. numb 6. deaden, harden
   7. astound, stupefy 8. paralyze
   11. become stone
petroglyph... 11. rock carving 15. rock
   inscription
Petrograd... 9. Leningrad
petroleum product... 6. butane, diesel
   7. naphtha, propane 8. gasoline
petrology *(science of)*... 5. rocks
petrosal... 4. bone 5. sinus, stony
   7. petrous 8. ganglion
petticoat... 4. girl, kilt 5. jupon,
   pagne, woman 6. kirtle 8. basquine
   9. undercoat, waistcoat
   10. fustanella, underskirt
petticoat tails... 7. teacake
   9. shortcake
pettifogger... 4. tyro 5. quack
   6. lawyer 7. shyster 8. attorney
pettish... 7. fretful, peevish 9. irritable
pettle... 6. cuddle, nestle, potter
   7. cherish
petto... 12. in one's breast 15. in
   contemplation
petty... 4. mean, orra 5. minor, small
   6. paltry 7. trivial 8. childish,
   inferior, nugatory, trifling 9. miniscule
   10. diminutive 11. small-minded,
   subordinate, unimportant
   12. narrow-minded 13. insignificant
   14. inconsiderable
petty (pert to)...
   captain.. 9. centurion
   fault.. 10. peccadillo
   larceny.. 10. scrounging
   mullein.. 7. cowslip
   objection.. 5. cavil
   prince.. 6. satrap
petulance... 8. ill humor, pertness
   9. insolence, sauciness
   10. wantonness 11. peevishness,
   pettishness

petulant... 4. pert 5. cross, huffy, saucy, testy 6. wanton 7. forward, fretful, peevish, wayward, willful 8. contrary, immodest, insolent 9. querulous

peu à peu... 9. by degrees 14. little by little

pewee... 5. pewit 6. phoebe 8. woodcock 10. flycatcher

pewit... 5. pewee 7. lapwing 12. laughing gull

Pfefferkuchen... 11. gingerbread

Phaëthon, Class Myth (pert to)...
bird.. 4. swan
car.. 3. sun
father.. 6. Helios
sun god.. 6. Helios

phagomania... 8. insanity 16. insatiable hunger

Phalacrocorax... 5. coots 10. cormorants

phalacrosis... 8. alopecia, baldness

phalanger... 5. tapoa 9. marsupial

phalanx... 4. bone 5. pawns 6. troops 7. company (Mil) 8. infantry

phalera... 4. boss 5. cameo

phantasm... 5. dream, fancy, ghost 6. idolum, spirit 7. eidolon, fantasy, phantom, specter (spectre) 8. delusion, illusion 10. apparition

phantasy, fantasy... 5. fancy, image 6. autism 8. daydream 11. imagination

phantom... 5. fairy, ghost 7. eidolon, specter (spectre) 10. simulacrum

Pharaoh (Bib).. 4. faro, king

Pharaoh (pert to)...
ancestor.. 2. Ra
chicken, hen.. 7. vulture (Egypt)
fig.. 8. sycamore
mouse.. 9. ichneumon

phare... 6. beacon, pharos 10. lighthouse

pharisee... 7. pietist 9. hypocrite

pharmacology... 5. drugs 13. materia medica

pharos... 5. cloak 6. beacon 10. chandelier (Eccl), lighthouse, watchtower

phase... 4. facet, stage 6. aspect 7. caprice, chapter, horning (moon)

phases, having many... 11. Hydra-headed

phasm... 6. meteor 7. phantom

pheasant... 5. cheer, monal 6. pukras 7. kallege 8. tragopan 12. ruffed grouse

pheasant (pert to)...
brood.. 3. nye 4. nide (nid) 5. flock
cuckoo.. 6. coucal
duck.. 7. pintail 9. merganser
finch.. 7. waxbill
genus.. 10. Oreophasis
wren.. 7. emu wren

pheasant species... 5. argus, blood 6. golden, silver 7. kallege 8. curassow 9. Mongolian 10. ring-necked 12. Lady Amherst's

phenomenal... 7. unusual 8. eventful, sensible 9. objective, wonderful 13. extraordinary

phenomenon... 4. fact 5. event

(unusual) 7. prodigy

phial... 3. cup 4. bowl, vial 6. bottle, vessel

phiale... 5. laver 6. vessel 8. fountain (Eccl)

Phi Beta Kappa (pert to)...
badge.. 8. watch key
founding.. 21. William and Mary College (1776)
meaning.. 24. Philosophy the guide of life
society.. 11. Greek-letter (oldest)

philabeg (filibeg)... 4. kilt

Philadelphia...
city.. 12. Pennsylvania
fleabane.. 7. skevish
lawyer.. 6. shrewd
meaning.. 13. brother-loving
ref to.. 12. Philadelphus (Ptolemy II)

philander... 5. flirt, lover 7. opossum 10. flirtation, love-making, lover of men

philanthropic... 6. humane 10. benevolent 12. eleemosynary

philanthropist... 5. donor 8. altruist, do-gooder 9. Robin Hood 10. benefactor, benevolist, Montefiore, Rothschild 12. humanitarian

philanthropy... 7. charity 8. good will 10. almsgiving 11. beneficence, benevolence (opp of misanthropy)

Philippic... 6. screed, tirade 7. oration 8. diatribe 9. Philippus

Philippine, Philippines...
archipelago.. 4. Sulu 5. Malay
bay.. 6. Manila
capital.. 6. Baguio (summer), Manila 10. Quezon City
city.. 5. Albay, Davao 6. Cavite 7. Dagupan
district.. 7. Lepanto
fort.. 4. Gota 10. Corregidor
island.. 4. Cebu 5. Leyte, Luzon, Panay, Samar, Ticao 6. Negros 7. Palawan, Paragua 8. Mindanao
mountain.. 3. Apo, Iba 5. Mayon
river.. 4. Abra, Agno 5. Pasig 8. Mindanao, Pampanga
university.. 10. Santo Tomas (1611)
volcano.. 3. Apo 5. Mayon

Philippine (pert to)...
animal.. 5. civet, lemur
ant, termite.. 4. anay (anai)
barracks.. 7. cuartel
boat, canoe, raft.. 5. balsa, banca
breadfruit.. 7. camansi
buffalo.. 7. carabao, timarau (timerau)
chair (on poles).. 7. talabon
dagger.. 4. itac
drink.. 4. beno 5. bubud
fabric.. 4. pina 9. pineapple
fetish, idol.. 5. anito
food.. 3. poi 4. Musa, saba, taro
hemp.. 5. abaca 6. Manila
house.. 5. bahay
knife.. 4. bolo
litter, pole chair.. 7. talabon
lizard.. 4. ibid (monitor)
mango.. 5. bauno 7. pahutan
market day.. 7. tiangue
melon.. 6. atimon

mudfish.. 5. dalag
palm.. 4. nipa 6. anahau (anahao)
parrot (green).. 5. cagit
reptile.. 6. python
rice.. 4. paga 5. macan
rice field bank.. 7. pilapil
river.. 4. ilog
shrub.. 4. alem
sweetsop.. 4. ates
town.. 4. agoa
tree.. 3. tui 4. ipil (ypil) 5. asana,
    ligas, narra, yacal 6. molave
    7. Eugenia, tindalo 8. macaasim
turnip.. 7. cincoma
vehicle (public).. 9. carromata
water jar.. 5. banga
wood.. 4. teak 5. ebony 6. sandal
    8. mahogany
Philippine people (pert to)...
discoverer.. 8. Magellan (1521)
farmer.. 3. tao
headman.. 4. datu
language.. 4. Moro 7. Tagalog (Tagal)
    8. Filipino
Luzon savage.. 4. Aeta 6. Igorot
    (Igorrote)
Moham, Moslem.. 4. Moro
native.. 3. tao 4. Moro, Sulu
native race.. 3. Lao 4. Aeta (dwarf)
    7. Tagalog, Visayan
native worker.. 7. polista
Negrito.. 3. Ati 4. Aeta
patriot.. 5. rizal
peasant.. 3. tao
priest (Moro).. 7. pandita
servant.. 4. bata 5. alila
tribe (Chr).. 5. Bikol (Bico, Vicol)
tribe (pagan).. 6. Italon
Philistine.. 5. enemy 7. prosaic
    9. philister 10. conformist,
    uncultured 11. antagonistic
    13. prosaic person, unenlightened
Philistine (pert to)...
anc name.. 9. Palestine, Philistia
assimilated by.. 7. Semites
city.. 4. Gaza 5. Ekron (Bib)
god.. 4. Baal 5. Dagon
philo (comb form)... 6. fond of, loving
philogeant... 12. lover of earth
philogyny... 11. love of women
philology... 11. linguistics 14. love of
    learning
Philomela (pert to)...
father.. 7. Pandion (King of Athens)
sister.. 6. Procne
turned into.. 7. swallow
    11. nightingale
philosopher...
American.. 9. Santayana
Chinese.. 9. Confucius
Dutch.. 7. Spinoza
English.. 5. Bacon
French.. 5. Renan 8. Rousseau,
    Voltaire
German.. 4. Kant 9. Nietzsche
    12. Schopenhauer
Greek.. 4. Zeno
Scottish.. 4. Hume
Seven Sages (7 Wise Men of
    Greece).. 4. Bias 5. Solon
    6. Chilon, Thales 8. Pittacus
    9. Cleobulus 10. Epimenides (or

    Periander)
Philosopher of...
Farney.. 8. Voltaire
Malmesbury.. 6. Hobbes
Sans Souci.. 17. Frederick the Great
Syracuse.. 4. Dion
Wimbledon.. 14. John Horne Tooke
philosopher's school... 7. Eleatic
philosophical.. 4. wise 7. erudite,
    logical, sapient 8. rational
    9. temperate, unruffled
philosophical being... 6. entity 9. real
    being
philosophy (pert to)...
choice of.. 11. eclecticism
of law.. 13. jurisprudence
of pantheists.. 5. Stoic
sublimated.. 17. Transcendentalism.
theory.. 4. yoga 9. pantheism,
    Platonism, solipsism 12. epistemology
phlegmatic.. 4. calm, dull, slow
    5. inert 6. mucous, watery
    7. viscous 8. sluggish 9. apathetic
phlogistic.. 5. fiery 6. heated
    7. burning 11. impassioned
    12. inflammatory
Phoebad... 7. seeress 9. priestess
    (Delphian) 10. prophetess
Phoebe (pert to)...
daughter.. 4. Leto
epithet of.. 7. Artemis
mother.. 4. Gaea (earth goddess)
poetic.. 4. moon
phoebe.. 4. fish 5. craps, pewit
    6. peewee 7. satellite (Saturn)
    10. flycatcher
Phoebus... 3. Sol 6. sun god
Phoenicia...
capital city.. 4. Tyre 5. Sidon
Colony.. 5. Hippo 8. Carthage
deity.. 4. Baal
famed for.. 9. purple dye
    10. navigation
goddess of fertility.. 6. Baltis
    7. Astarte
god of healing.. 6. Eshmun (Eshmoun)
king.. 6. Agenor
region.. 5. Syria
Phoenix... 4. bird (fabled), palm
    7. capital (Ariz)
phonetic (pert to)...
science.. 9. phonology
sound.. 7. phoneme
stop.. 9. occlusive
system.. 5. romic
phonic.. 6. spoken, voiced 7. sounded
    8. auditory 9. accoustic, vibration
phony (comb form)... 5. sound, voice
phony... 4. fake 5. faked
    11. counterfeit
photograph... 4. film 5. image, photo
    7. picture 8. likeness, portrait
    9. ferrotype, pictorial, portrayal
    10. heliograph 12. photogravure
photographic bath... 5. toner
    7. reducer 9. developer
photography, science of... 5. light
    6. optics 7. photics
photography inventors... 6. Niepce,
    Talbot
photometric unit... 3. pyr, rad
phrase... 5. idiom 6. remark, saying,

slogan 7. diction, epigram, epithet, passage 8. flattery 9. catchword 10. expression 11. phraseology

phraseology... 5. style 6. jargon 7. diction, wording 8. parlance

phratry (Hist).. 4. clan 5. group

phrenetic... 3. mad 5. crazy 6. madman 7. fanatic, frantic, violent 9. delirious 10. passionate

phrenology, science of... 5. skull 10. craniology

Phrygia, Asia Minor...
cap (comical).. 10. liberty cap
deity.. 5. Attis
Eccl Hist.. 9. Montanist
founder.. 7. Gordius (800 BC)
King.. 5. Midas
marble (anc).. 9. pavonazzo (pavonazzetto)
music.. 4. mode
river.. 7. Meander

phylactery (Eccl)... 4. case 5. charm, chest, miter 6. amulet, infula, record, scroll

phylarchy... 12. rule by tribes

phyletic... 6. racial 7. descent, species 12. phylogenetic

phyllophagous... 15. feeding on leaves

physical... 6. bodily 7. natural, somatic 8. material 9. corporeal

physical force... 10. attraction

physical unit... 3. erg

physician... 5. medic 6. doctor, healer, intern 7. coroner 8. restorer

physician (pert to)...
ancient.. 5. Galen
comb form.. 5. iatro
French Nobel Prize.. 7. Laveran
Greek (anc).. 5. Galen 11. Asclepiades
quack.. 10. medicaster
symbol.. 8. caduceus

physicist... 7. Faraday, Galvani, Marconi 10. naturalist

physiognomy... 3. mug 4. face 11. countenance 14. external aspect, interpretation

physique... 4. body 6. figure

physis (Gr)... 5. nature

phytology, science of... 6. botany, plants

piacle... 3. sin 5. crime, guilt 7. offense 15. sacrificial rite 17. expiatory offering

pian... 5. tumor 9. frambesia

piano (pert to)...
direction.. 10. pianissimo (softly)
duet, upper part.. 5. primo
dumb keyboard.. 10. digitorium
early.. 6. spinet
Italian.. 10. Cristofori
keyboard.. 7. clavier 8. pedalier
pedal.. 7. celeste
pianolike.. 7. celesta
player.. 7. pianola
slang.. 11. eighty–eight
small.. 8. pianette

piatti... 7. cymbals

piazza... 5. campo, porch 6. square 7. gallery, portico, veranda

pic... 4. peak 8. picayune

picacho... 4. hill 5. butte

picador... 3. wit 6. jester 7. debater 8. horseman (with lance), toreador 11. bullfighter

picaro... 5. knave, rogue 7. sharper 8. vagabond 10. picaresque

picaroon... 5. rogue, thief 6. pirate, rascal 7. brigand, corsair 8. prey upon

pick... 4. cull, gaff, peck, sort 5. elect, pluck, strum 6. assort, choose, indent, pickax, pierce, select 7. diamond (card), harvest, the best 8. plectrum, the elite 9. toothpick

pick (pert to)...
flaws.. 5. cavil
out.. 6. pilfer, select 7. acquire, procure, specify 9. eliminate, segregate 11. distinguish
pick–me–up.. 5. tonic 6. bracer 9. kittiwake, stimulate 11. restorative
up.. 4. tidy 6. arrest 7. improve 9. stimulant 10. recuperate

picked... 4. trim 5. piked, spiny 6. choice, chosen, culled, dainty, peaked, spruce 7. adorned, plucked, pointed 8. stripped 10. fastidious

pickerel... 4. fish, pike 9. Esox niger 12. walleyed pike

picket... 3. peg 4. pale, post, tern 5. fence, guard, stake 6. bullet, fasten, paling, sentry, tether 7. enclose, fortify, shackle 8. sentinel 10. go on strike

pickle... 4. alec, peck 5. achar, brine 6. dawdle, nibble, piddle, pilfer, trifle 7. chutney, vitrial

pickled... 5. drunk 6. soused 9. marinated

pickled pig's feet... 5. souse

pickle fork... 8. runcible

pickle–herring... 7. buffoon 11. merry–andrew 12. Pickelhering

pickpocket... 4. wire 5. thief 6. bulker

picnic... 3. fun 4. camp, play 6. junket, outing 9. festivity

Pict (anc)... 4. Scot 5. Aryan 9. aborigine

Pictland... 8. Scotland

pictorial... 8. painting 11. illustrated, picturesque

Pict's house (Archaeol)... 8. dwelling (subterranean)

picture... 3. oil 4. copy, draw, icon 5. image, print, scene 6. chromo, depict, pastel 7. diorama, etching, portray, porture, tableau 8. describe, likeness, painting, portrait 9. engraving, paintings, represent, visualize 10. photograph 11. description 14. representation

picture (pert to)...
mounting, border.. 3. mat 5. frame 8. kakemono, makimono (scroll)
moving.. 4. film 5. movie 6. cinema
positive.. 5. print
puzzle.. 5. rebus
small.. 5. cameo 9. miniature
stand.. 5. easel
viewer.. 11. alethoscope, stereoscope 12. magic lantern, stereopticon

picturesque... 5. vivid 6. scenic 7. graphic 9. pictorial

picuda... 9. barracuda (great), picudilla (small)
picudo... 6. weevil 10. boll weevil
piddle... 3. toy 4. pick, play 6. putter, trifle 9. waste time
pie... 4. food, mess 5. chaos, patty 6. jumble, magpie, pastry 7. cobbler, dessert, measure 9. confusion
piebald... 4. pied 5. mixed, pinto 6. motley 7. mongrel, mottled, pintado 10. variegated 13. heterogeneous
piece... 3. bit 4. join, part, role 5. crumb, drama, piece, scrap, shred 6. sample 7. measure, portion, writing 8. chessman, fragment, specimen, treatise
piece (pert to)...
armor.. 5. tasse (tace) 8. corselet
de résistance.. 6. entrée 8. main dish
door, jamb.. 6. lintel
eccentric.. 3. cam
fastening.. 3. gib
fitted.. 4. shim 5. tenon
flat.. 4. slab, slat 5. flake, strip
meal.. 8. by degrees, fragments 12. piece by piece 14. little by little
metal.. 3. sow
neck.. 3. boa 5. rabat, scarf, stole 8. kerchief
of one's mind.. 6. rebuke 7. reproof 13. candid opinion
out.. 3. eke 6. cantle
preventing slippage.. 5. cleat
short.. 4. skit
side.. 3. rib 5. stave
split off.. 6. sliver, splint 8. splinter
tapering.. 4. gore 6. gusset
work (art).. 4. pavé 6. mosaic, niello
pieces of...
eight.. 6. dollar, escudo
meat.. 5. cabob
silk waste.. 4. noil
pied... 4. foot 5. pinto 7. colored (2 or more colors), dappled, piebald 10. variegated 12. parti–colored
pied (pert to)...
blackbird.. 6. thrush
brant.. 5. goose
diver.. 4. smew
duck.. 8. Labrador
Friar (Eccl Hist).. 9. mendicant
monk.. 10. Bernardine, Cistercian
Piper of Hamelin.. 8. musician 10. rat charmer
widgeon.. 8. garganey 9. goldeneye
Piedmont, Italy... 7. capital (Turin)
pieplant... 7. rhubarb
pier... 4. anta, dock, mole, quay 5. groin, wharf 6. pillar 7. landing 8. buttress, gatepost 9. promenade 10. breakwater
pierce... 3. bore, cold, gore, pain, tart 5. enter, gride, lance, probe, spear, spike, sting, wound 6. riddle, tunnel 7. discern 8. puncture 9. penetrate, perforate 10. comprehend
piercing... 4. keen, loud 5. acute 6. shrill 7. caustic, clearly, painful, piteous, pungent, sharply, shrilly, spiking, violent 8. deep–felt, poignant, spearing, stabbing

9. searching
Pieria, Macedonia (pert to)...
epithet of.. 5. Muses
native.. 7. Pierian
reference to.. 6. poetry 9. knowledge
seat of.. 5. Muses
piet... 5. ouzel 6. magpie 7. piebald 10. chatterbox, chattering 11. saucy person
Pietà (It)... 9. sculpture 10. Virgin Mary
pietose (Mus)... 11. sympathetic 13. compassionate
piety... 4. pity, zeal (worship) 6. filial 8. devotion, holiness, religion 9. reverence 10. compassion, devoutness, sanctimony 11. dutifulness
pig... 3. car (RR), ham, hog, sow 4. boar, pork 5. bacon, crosk, flask, swine 6. farrow 7. casting, dogboat, glutton 8. pressman, sixpence, slattern 9. policeman 11. stoolpigeon
pig (pert to)...
bed.. 3. pen, sty 5. reeve 6. pigsty
female.. 3. sow 4. gilt
guinea.. 4. cavy
headed.. 6. stupid 9. obstinate
iron.. 5. ingot
iron, ballast (Naut).. 9. kentledge
iron, cast.. 9. kentledge (Mil)
last of litter.. 4. runt
lead, weight.. 6. fother
litter.. 6. farrow
piglike.. 7. hoglike, porcine, suiform
piglike animal.. 7. peccary 8. babirusa
potato.. 7. cowbane
rat.. 9. bandicoot
skin.. 6. saddle 8. football
yoke.. 7. sextant 8. quadrant
young.. 5. grice, shoat 6. farrow, piglet 9. gruntling
pigdan... 8. spittoon
pigeon... 3. nun 4. barb, dove, dupe, fowl, girl, gull, ruff 5. heart, piper, pluck, sweet 6. coward, fleece, pouter, roller, turbit 7. fantail, jacobin, pintail, tumbler 9. trumpeter
pigeon, pidgin (pert to)...
Australia.. 5. wonga 10. wonga–wonga
berry.. 7. dogwood 9. Juneberry, wild elder
blood.. 6. garnet
carrier.. 5. homer 6. homing 10. scandaroon
extinct.. 4. dodo
food.. 7. saltcat
genus.. 5. Goura 7. Columba
hawk.. 6. falcon, merlin
house.. 7. dovecot 9. columbary
ref to.. 12. peristeronic
short–beaked.. 4. barb
wood.. 6. cushat 8. ringdove
young.. 5. piper
pigment... 3. red 4. blue, gray, pink 5. black, brown, color, green, ocher (ochre), paint, white 6. orange, purple, yellow 8. colorant
pigment (pert to)...
arsenic, yellow.. 8. orpiment
black.. 3. tar 5. sepia 7. melanin

blue.. 5. smalt
blue–green.. 4. bice
brown.. 5. sepia, umber 6. bister
(bistre), sienna (burnt) 7. cypress
brownish yellow.. 6. sienna
calico yellow.. 7. canarin (canarine)
coal tar.. 7. aniline
cuttlefish.. 5. sepia
madder root.. 7. rubiate
orange red.. 7. realgar
oxide of lead.. 8. massicot
red.. 7. turacin
yellow.. 5. ocher (ochre) 7. etiolin
pigmy... see *pygmy*
pignus... 4. pawn 6. pledge
pig's feet... 9. pettitoes
pigtail.. 5. braid, queue 7. tobacco
(rolled) 8. rope's end (Naut)
pika... 7. rodent
pike... 3. ged (gedd) 4. fish, luce, pick
6. beacon, pickax
pike (pert to)...
North American.. 11. muskellunge
perch.. 6. sauger
pikelike.. 3. gar 4. luce 5. lucet
6. robalo 8. robalito 9. barracuda
walleyed.. 4. doré
pikel, pikle.. 7. hayfork 9. pitchfork
pikelet.. 7. crumpet
piker... 5. thief, tramp 6. coward
7. gambler, quitter, shirker, vagrant
8. tightwad
pilar... 5. downy, hairy
pilaster... 4. anta 6. alette (part),
column
Pilate (Bib)... 10. procurator (Judean)
pilchard... 7. sardine
pile... 3. awn, mow, nap 4. heap,
load, mole, pier, rick, shag
5. amass, slack, spile, stake 6. heap
up, pillar, wealth 7. fortune, store
up, texture
pile (pert to)...
burning.. 4. pyre
defense.. 8. estacade
driver.. 7. fistuca
of hay.. 3. mow 4. dess, rick
5. stack
up.. 4. heap 7. smashup, store up
9. shipwreck 10. exaggerate
pilfer... 3. rob 4. lift, loot 5. filch,
steal, swipe 6. rustle (cattle), snitch
7. purloin
pilgrim... 5. exile (Relig) 6. palmer
8. crusader, newcomer, traveler,
wanderer, wayfarer 9. immigrant,
sojourner 10. tenderfoot
12. peregrinator
Pilgrim (pert to)...
father.. 9. John Alden
Fathers.. 11. Separatists (1620)
garment.. 5. ihram (Mecca)
landing.. 12. Plymouth Rock (1620)
Scotch.. 6. palmer
ship.. 9. Mayflower, Speedwell
pilgrimage to Mecca... 4. hadj
Pilgrim's bottle... 7. ampulla, costrel
Pilgrim's Progress... 8. allegory
(Bunyan)
pill... 3. rob 4. ball, bore, pare, pell,
pool 5. bolus, creek 6. bullet, pellet,
pilule 8. medicine 9. cigarette

11. decorticate
pillage... 4. flay, loot, prey, sack
5. booty, harry, spoil, strip 6. rapine,
ravage 7. despoil, plunder, robbery
9. depredate, extortion 10. spoliation
pillar... 4. post, slab 5. shaft, stele
(stela), tower 6. column 7. support
8. mainstay, monument, pedestal
pillar (pert to)...
airfield.. 5. pylon
Buddhist.. 3. lat
carved.. 9. totem pole
little.. 8. pillaret
of society.. 9. personage
pillarlike.. 6. stelar
saint.. 7. recluse, stylite
tall, slender.. 7. obelisk
with front figure.. 7. osiride
Pillars of Hercules site... 5. Abila,
Calpe 17. Strait of Gibralter
pillbox... 3. cap, hat 8. brougham,
fortress 13. fortification
pillory... 4. yoke 5. stock, trone
6. cangue, punish
pillow... 3. pad 5. block 7. cushion,
support
pillow (pert to)...
case, cover.. 4. sham, slip
long.. 7. bolster
stuffing.. 5. kapok 8. feathers
pilose... 5. hairy 6. pilous
pilot... 4. lead 5. flyer, guide, steer
6. aviate, direct, leader 8. director,
helmsman, preacher 9. clergyman,
navigator 10. cowcatcher
pilot (pert to)...
bird.. 6. plover
expert.. 3. ace
fish.. 6. remora 9. amberfish,
whitefish
house.. 10. wheelhouse
jacket.. 9. pea jacket
sky.. 8. preacher 9. clergyman
snake.. 10. copperhead
weed.. 9. rosinweed
whale.. 9. blackfish
Piltdown, England (pert to)...
Hist yield.. 7. Dawn Man, fossils
Prehist station.. 6. Sussex
piltock.. 8. coalfish
pilum... 6. pestle 7. javelin
pilus... 4. hair
Pima... 5. Opata 11. Indian tribe
pimento... 6. pepper 7. paprika
8. allspice, pimiento
pin... 3. hob, peg, pen 4. axle, bolt,
coak (coag), join 5. affix, badge,
dowel, rivet, thole 6. brooch, cotter,
fasten, secure, trifle 7. confine,
enclose, gudgeon, jewelry, spindle
stopper, trenail 8. linchpin, ornament,
transfix 10. chatelaine
pin (pert to)...
axle.. 8. linchpin
dial.. 5. style
fish.. 11. stickleback
game.. 7. skittle
grass.. 9. alfilaria (forage)
jackstraw (game).. 8. spilikin (spillikin)
meat fastener.. 6. skewer
quoits.. 3. hob
sailmaker's.. 3. fid

small.. 3. peg 4. lill
with looped head.. 7. eyebolt
pinafore... 5. apron, smock 7. tablier
  8. sun dress
Pinafore... 5. opera (Gilbert & Sullivan)
pinag... 4. lake (rain season)
piñata... 5. globe (swinging, with gifts)
pinax... 4. dish 5. table 6. plaque,
  scheme, tablet 7. picture
  9. catalogue
pinbone... 7. hipbone
pince–nez... 7. glasses, nippers
  10. eyeglasses
pincers... 3. tew 5. chela, tongs
  6. pliers 7. forceps, pinette
pinch... 3. nip, rob 4. pain, raid
  5. cramp, gripe, pugil (anc), steal,
  stint, tweak 6. arrest, crisis, extort,
  scrimp, snatch, snitch, strait, twinge
  7. afflict, confine, squeeze, urgency
  8. compress, contract, exigency,
  straiten
pinchbeck... 4. sham 5. alloy (cheap
  jewelry) 8. frippery, spurious
  11. counterfeit
pinched... 4. poor, thin 8. squeezed
  10. compressed, contracted,
  distressed, straitened
pinchem... 8. titmouse
pinda... 6. peanut
Pindar... 4. poet (lyric)
pindaric... 3. ode 9. irregular
  12. unrestrained
pine... 4. flag 5. waste, yearn
  6. grieve, lament, needle, repine,
  sicken, weaken, wither 8. languish
  11. deteriorate
pine (pert to)...
  Brazil.. 6. paraná
  chemical.. 5. pinic
  exudation.. 5. resin, rosin
  family.. 3. fir 5. larch, piñon
    6. spruce
  finch.. 6. siskin
  fir.. 6. balsam 12. Balm of Gilead
  fruit.. 4. cone
  genus.. 5. Pinus
  gum.. 8. sandarac
  knot.. 7. dovekie
  leaf.. 6. needle
  low–growing.. 5. piñon
  mahogany.. 6. totara
  New Zealand.. 5. kauri (kaury)
  Pacific coast.. 8. knobpine
  Philippine.. 7. Amboina 8. galagala
  screw.. 3. ara 6. pandan
  tar extract.. 6. retene
  tulip.. 10. pipsissewa
pineal... 5. brain, gland 8. pine cone
pineapple... 4. bomb, pina 5. fiber,
  fruit 6. ananas 8. pine cone
  12. Bromeliaceae
pineapple (pert to)...
  cheese.. 7. Cheddar
  cloth.. 4. pina
  segment.. 3. pip
  weed.. 8. marigold
Pine Tree State... 5. Maine
pinguescent... 9. fattening
pinguid... 3. fat 4. oily, rich 5. fatty
  8. unctuous
pinguitude... 7. fatness, obesity

  8. oiliness 10. greasiness
pink... 3. cut, Red 4. deck, rose, stab
  5. adorn, blink, color, coral, smart,
  wound 6. flower, indent, minnow,
  pierce, salmon, vessel 7. radical,
  serrate 8. decorate, grayling
  9. carnation 11. fashionable
pink (pert to)...
  coat.. 10. foxhunter's
  eye.. 4. duck 14. conjunctivitis
  family.. 7. Campion 9. Carnation
    15. Caryophyllaceae
  fish.. 8. gobylike
  genus.. 6. Silene
  lady.. 3. fly (fishing) 8. cocktail
  needle.. 9. alfilaria
  Pearl.. 6. azalea
  pill.. 7. cure–all
  root.. 8. wormroot
pinkeen... 6. minnow 19. insignificant
  person
pinna... 3. fin 4. wing 7. auricle,
  feather, leaflet
pinnace... 4. boat 5. woman 6. tender
  (Naut) 9. procuress 10. prostitute
pinnacle... 3. epi, tee, tor 4. acme,
  apex, peak 5. crest, crown, serac,
  spire 6. finial, needle, summit
pinnate... 11. featherlike
pinniped... 4. seal 6. walrus
pinochle term... 3. dix 4. meld
piñon... 4. pine, seed 8. pignolia
  12. monkey puzzle
pintado... 4. cero, fish, sier (fish)
  5. pinto 6. chintz, pigeon, sierra
pintail (pert to)...
  duck.. 4. smee 5. river, ruddy
  grouse.. 4. sand 11. sharp–tailed
pinto (horse)... 4. pied 6. calico
  7. mottled, painted, piebald, spotted
Pinto... 6. Indian (Pakawa tribe)
pinwing... 7. penguin
pioneer... 4. lead 5. guide, miner
  6. digger, open up 7. settler
  8. colonist, explorer 9. excavator
  10. forerunner
Pioneer's Day... 4. Utah (July 24)
  5. Idaho (June 15)
pious... 5. godly, loyal 6. devout,
  worthy 9. excellent, religious
  11. reverential 13. sanctimonious
pip... 3. ace 4. paip, peep, roup,
  seed, spot, trey 7. disease
  12. officer's star
pipe... 2. TD 3. see, tee 4. blow,
  clay, duct, reed, tube 5. spout, voice
  6. convey, dudeen, hookah (hooka),
  outlet 7. channel 9. brierwood
pipe (pert to)...
  connection.. 3. ell, tee 5. cross,
    elbow
  dream.. 8. illusion 10. bemusement
  end.. 4. taft 6. nozzle
  line.. 9. grapevine
  Oriental.. 8. narghile (nargile)
  pastoral, shepherd's.. 3. oat 4. reed
    7. larigot 9. flageolet
  peace.. 7. calumet
  player.. 5. fifer 8. shepherd
  short.. 6. dudeen
  smoke.. 5. tewel
  steam.. 5. riser

tobacco.. 10. meerschaum
wood.. 5. brier (briar) 9. brierwood
wrench.. 8. Stillson
pipette... 6. taster, tubule 7. dripper
pipit... 7. titlark
piquancy... 4. zest 5. spice
  8. pungency, raciness, tartness
  11. conciseness
piquant... 4. racy, tart 5. salty, sharp,
  spicy, zesty 7. concise, cutting,
  pungent 11. interesting, provocative
pique... 4. dive, fret, goad 5. anger,
  annoy, sting, tempt 6. grudge, incite,
  nettle, offend 7. dudgeon, offense,
  provoke, umbrage 8. irritate
  9. displease 10. irritation, resentment
  11. displeasure
pir (Moham)... 4. tomb 5. guide, saint
pirate... 6. robber 7. corsair, mariner
  8. marauder, picaroon 9. buccaneer
  10. freebooter 11. appropriate
pirate (famed)... 4. Kidd 6. Morgan
  7. Lafitte 10. Blackbeard (Capt
  Teach)
pirate (pert to)...
  bird.. 10. jaeger gull
  flag.. 5. Roger
  gallows.. 7. yardarm
  perch.. 8. Xenarchi
  weapon.. 5. snee
piraya... 6. caribe (fish) 7. piranha
pirogue... 5. canoe 7. piragua
pirol... 6. oriole
Pisa, Italy...
  capital of.. 7. Tuscany
  famed for.. 9. campanile 12. Leaning
  Tower
  river.. 4. Arno
pis aller... 10. last resort
piscary... 7. fishery 12. fishing place
  13. fishing rights
piscatology (*science of*)... 7. angling,
  fishing 10. halieutics
Pisces... 4. fish 6. fishes
  13. constellation
piscina... 4. tank 5. basin (Eccl)
  8. fishpond 9. reservoir
Piscis Volans... 10. flying fish
  13. constellation
Pisgah (pert to)...
  site.. 4. Nebo 8. mountain (top)
  view.. 12. Land of Canaan 13. Land
  of Promise
  viewer.. 5. Moses
pismire... 3. ant 5. emmet
pistachio... 3. nut 5. green
piste... 4. path 5. spoor, track, trail
  10. racecourse
pisteology, pistiology... 5. faith
  6. belief
pistil... 5. ovary 6. carpel
  9. gynoecium
pistol... 3. dag 7. firearm 9. derringer
pistol (pert to)...
  case.. 7. holster
  lock.. 5. rowet
  slang.. 3. gat, rod 6. barker, cannon,
  heater
pistology (Theol)... 5. faith
piston... 7. plunger
pit... 4. cave, hole, mine, pool, sump,
  tomb, trap, well 5. abyss, arena,

grave, sluig, snare 6. cavity, slough
  7. alveola, cockpit, dungeon
  8. audience 9. waterhole
  10. excavation 13. Stock Exchange
pit (pert to)...
  anatomy.. 5. fossa, fovea
  botany.. 7. alveola, pitamen
  8. endocarp
  bottomless.. 7. Abaddon
  fodder.. 4. silo
  Hades.. 4. hell
  Hawaiian.. 3. imu
  theater.. 7. parquet
  viper.. 9. Viperidae 11. rattlesnake
pitch... 3. key, tar 4. camp, hurl, tilt,
  tone, toss 5. black, color, erect,
  fling, heave, lurch, resin, sense,
  slope, throw 6. degree, encamp,
  plunge, settle, topple 7. incline
  8. flounder 9. sales talk
pitch (pert to)...
  high.. 6. shrill
  identity.. 6. unison
  inflammable.. 7. piceous
  mineral.. 7. asphalt, bitumen
  music.. 4. flat 6. accent, stress
  8. paranete 9. tonometer
pitchlike... 7. piceous
pitchblende... 6. radium 7. uranium
pitched ball, curving away...
  8. outshoot
pitcher... 3. jug 4. ewer, olla, olpe,
  toby 5. gorge 8. cruisken (cruiskeen),
  oenochoe (wine), southpaw
  (left-handed)
pitcher (pert to)...
  plant, genus.. 9. Nepenthes
  10. Cephalotus, Sarracenia
  plus catcher.. 7. battery
  shaped.. 9. urceolate
  shaped vessel.. 8. aiguière
piteous... 5. pious 6. devout, paltry,
  tender 7. pitiful, pitying 8. pitiable
  13. compassionate
pitfall... 3. pit 4. lure, trap 5. decoy,
  snare 6. danger 10. difficulty
pith... 3. jet, nub 4. gist, meat, pulp
  6. center, kernel, marrow
  7. essence, meaning, nucleus
  9. substance
pith helmet... 3. cap, hat 5. topee
  (topi)
pith tree (Nile)... 7. ambatch (ambash)
pithy... 4. soft 5. crisp, meaty, pulpy,
  terse 7. laconic 10. meaningful
  12. epigrammatic
pithy (pert to)...
  expression.. 7. epigram
  saying.. 3. mot
  sentence.. 5. motto
pitiable... 3. sad 6. woeful 7. piteous
  8. grievous, terrible 9. miserable,
  sorrowful 10. lamentable
pitiful... 4. mean 6. paltry 7. piteous
  8. pathetic, shameful 10. despicable
  12. contemptible 13. compassionate,
  tenderhearted
pitiless... 5. cruel 8. ruthless
  9. merciless 10. relentless
  13. unsympathetic
pitpit... 8. guitguit 12. honey creeper
Pitri, Hindu (pert to)...

ancestor of.. 4. gods 6. demons
  10. four castes
Prajapatis, one of.. 10. progenitor
  (human race)
semidivine.. 6. father 9. patriarch
  10. forefather
pittance... 4. alms, dole, gift, scat
  7. bequest 8. donation 9. allowance
  11. small amount
pity... 4. ruth 5. mercy, yearn
  7. remorse 8. clemency, sympathy
  10. compassion, condolence,
  repentance 13. commiseration
pivot... 3. toe 4. slew, slue, turn
  5. hinge 6. pintle, swivel
pivotal... 4. crux 5. polar 7. turning
pixy, pixie... 3. elf, imp 5. fairy
  6. goblin, sprite 13. mischief-maker
Pizarro (pert to)...
  adventurer.. 7. Spanish
  conqueror of.. 6. Peru
  founder of.. 4. Lima (capital)
placable... 8. peaceful 9. agreeable,
  forgiving, peaceable 10. appeasable
placard... 4. bill, post 5. edict
  6. notice, poster 7. affiché
  9. manifesto, stomacher
  12. proclamation
placate... 5. calm 6. pacify, soothe
  7. appease 10. conciliate
  11. tranquilize
place... 3. put 4. lieu, site, spot
  5. abode, locus, posit, situs, stead
  6. locale, locate, region, street
  7. arrange, demesne, deposit
  8. classify, location, position
  9. recognize, situation
place (of)...
  amusement.. 4. park 6. casino,
  midway
  bliss.. 4. Eden 8. paradise
  confinement.. 3. pen 4. brig, cage,
  coop, gaol, jail, stir 6. asylum,
  corral, prison 7. dungeon
  9. calaboose 12. penitentiary
  confusion.. 5. Babel
  content.. 7. Arcadia
  darkness.. 6. Erebus
  exit.. 6. egress
  honor.. 9. right hand
  origin.. 6. cradle, source
  refuge.. 3. ark 4. port 5. haven
  resort.. 7. purlieu
  rest.. 3. bed, den 4. lair, nook
  5. chair, couch, grave, niche
  sleep.. 3. bed 4. doss 5. berth,
  couch 6. pallet 7. hammock
  suffering.. 10. Armageddon,
  Gethsemane
  trial.. 5. venue
place (pert to)...
  apart.. 6. enisle 7. isolate
  9. sequester
  beneath.. 9. infrapose
  between.. 9. interpose
  burial.. 5. grave 8. catacomb,
  cemetery 9. graveyard 10. necropolis
  by itself.. 7. isolate
  camping.. 5. étape
  confidence in.. 7. entrust
  different.. 10. otherwhere
  for boats.. 7. portage

for candles.. 9. chandlery
forest (open).. 5. glade
for keeping animals.. 3. zoo 4. barn
  7. pasture 9. menagerie
frequented.. 4. dive 5. haunt
  6. resort
from which jury is taken.. 5. venue
hallowed.. see *sacred* below
hiding.. 3. mew 4. lair 5. niche
high.. 7. eminent 8. eminence
horse training.. 4. ring 5. longe
in a row.. 5. align, aline
in bondage.. 7. enslave
in order.. 7. arrange 11. systematize
in statu quo.. 7. put back, replace,
  restore
interpretation on.. 8. construe
landing.. 4. dock, pier 5. wharf
  7. airport
market.. 4. mart 5. agora 6. rialto
meeting.. 5. tryst
of.. 4. lieu 5. stead
on mound.. 3. tee
opposite.. 6. appose
over.. 11. superimpose
sacred.. 4. fane 5. altar 6. chapel,
  church, shrine, temple 9. synagogue
  10. tabernacle
side-by-side.. 9. collocate, juxtapose
sleeping.. 3. bed 4. bunk 5. berth,
  couch 6. pallet 7. hammock
under.. 9. infrapose
under restraint.. 6. arrest, intern
value upon.. 5. price 6. assess
  8. appraise, estimate
wet.. 4. slew 5. marsh 6. slough
wrestling.. 5. arena 9. palaestra
  (palestra)
placed... 3. put 7. located
  8. arranged, situated 10. classified
placed in lodgings... 6. roomed
  8. billeted
placid... 4. calm 5. quiet, suant
  6. demure, gentle, serene
  8. composed, peaceful 9. agreeable,
  quiescent, unruffled 11. undisturbed
pladaroma... 5. tumor (eyelid)
plafond... 7. ceiling 14. contract
  bridge
plage... 5. beach
plagiarism... 6. piracy 8. cribbing,
  stealing 10. purloining
  13. appropriation
plague... 3. dun, vex 4. bane, pest,
  twit 5. harry, tease, worry 6. harass,
  hector, infest 7. scourge, torment
  8. epidemic, nuisance 10. Black
  Death, pestilence 11. infestation
plaguy... 6. vexing 8. annoying
  9. difficult, harassing 10. tormenting
  11. troublesome
plaice... 8. flatfish, flounder
plaid... 4. maud 6. tartan
plain... 3. lea 4. chol, mesa, moor,
  wold 5. blunt, camas, clear, frank,
  heath 6. lenten 7. artless, evident,
  genuine, legible, obvious, prairie
  8. apparent, distinct, explicit, ordinary
  9. downright, primitive, unadorned
  10. unaffected
plain (pert to)...
  clothes.. 10. unofficial

dealing.. 4. open 5. frank
knitting.. 12. garter stitch
of Mars.. 9. palmistry
spoken.. 15. straightforward
Plains (pert to)...
Arctic.. 6. tundra
Europe.. 6. steppe
Florida.. 7. savanna (savannah)
Italy.. 8. campagna
Russia.. 6. steppe, tundra
S African.. 6. pampas
Sp American.. 4. vega 5. llano
6. salada (salt–covered)
Plains Indians... 6. Kiowan, Siouan
7. Caddoan 10. Algonquian,
Athapascan, Uto–Aztecan
plainsman... 6. cowboy 7. llanero
8. herdsman
Plains of Abraham... 10. Quebec City
plaint... 6. bewail, lament 9. complaint
11. lamentation
plaintiff... 4. suer 6. orator 7. accuser
8. claimant, libelant (libellant)
10. complainer 11. complainant
plaintive... 3. sad 5. cross 7. elegiac,
fretful, peevish, pettish, wailful,
wistful 8. mournful, petulant, repining
9. lamenting, sorrowful
10. melancholy 11. complaining
12. discontented
plait... 4. fold, hair, knit, lace, plat
5. braid, pleat, weave 6. pleach,
wimple 9. corrugate, interlace
10. interweave
plaited... 5. Milan (straw) 6. folded,
kilted, sennit (palm leaves)
8. pleached 10. interlaced
11. intertwined
plan... 3. map, way 4. form, idea,
line, plat, plot 5. chart, draft, ettle,
frame, setup 6. design, devise,
intend, layout, method, scheme
7. arrange, diagram, outline, pattern,
project 8. engineer, strategy
9. calculate, procedure
11. arrangement, contemplate,
preconceive, premeditate
plan (pert to)...
architecture.. 5. draft, épure
frustrator of.. 7. marplot
preliminary.. 4. idea 6. map out
8. proposal
secretly.. 4. plot 7. connive
8. conspire
planate... 5. plane 9. flattened
plancher... 3. bed 5. board (occult),
floor, plank 6. pallet 8. planking,
platform
plancier... 6. soffit 7. cornice
plandok... 9. mouse deer
plane... 3. fly 4. even, flat, ramp,
scar, tool 5. level 6. degree, smooth
7. jointer, surface 8. airplane
10. smoothness
plane (pert to)...
block.. 5. stock
boundary.. 9. perimeter
four–angled.. 6. square 7. rhombus
8. tetragon 10. quadrangle
handle.. 4. tote (bench plane)
inclined.. 4. ramp 5. chute
iron.. 5. blade

kind.. 3. mig 5. stuka 6. router
measure.. 10. planimeter
smoothing, chamfering.. 5. howel
tree.. 6. chinar (Orient) 8. Platanus
type.. 5. bench, block, stock
6. trowel 7. jointer, routing
planet... 4. Mars, star 5. Earth, Pluto,
Venus 6. Saturn, Uranus 7. Jupiter,
Mercury, Neptune 8. wanderer
planet (pert to)...
astrology.. 9. alfridary
brightest.. 5. Venus
cone.. 8. strobile
course.. 5. orbit
minor.. 9. satellite
nearest sun.. 7. Mercury
orbit.. 7. ellipse
red.. 4. Mars
remotest.. 5. Pluto (1930)
resembling.. 8. asteroid
ringed.. 6. Saturn
satellite.. 4. moon
shadow.. 5. umbra
small.. 8. asteroid
sphere.. 6. oblate
planet (solar system) *by size*...
7. Jupiter 6. Saturn 7. Neptune
6. Uranus 5. Earth, Venus, Pluto
4. Mars 7. Mercury
planetarium... 5. Zeiss 6. orrery
planetary... 7. earthly, erratic
9. celestial, wandering, worldwide
planetology (study of)... 7. planets
10. satellites
plangor... 4. wail 11. lamentation
planisphere... 7. sextant 9. astrolabe
plank... 3. sny 4. deal, slab 5. board,
shole, stone 6. timber 7. pay down
8. planking 10. gravestone
plank down... 3. pay 7. advance,
deposit
planner... 8. designer, engineer,
gardener 9. architect, projector
plant... 3. fix, sow, spy 4. ache, bury,
herb, seed, trap 5. cache, decoy,
shrub 6. clover 7. falsify 8. colonize,
workshop 9. deception, detective,
equipment, vegetable
plant (pert to)...
abnormal environs.. 4. ecad
adjustment.. 6. ecesis
air.. 8. epiphyte
appendage.. 7. stipula
biggest.. 10. Aspidistra
body.. 6. cormus 7. thallus
bud.. 4. cion 5. scion
climbing.. 4. vine 5. liana
coloring matter.. 11. chlorophyll
crossbred.. 6. hybrid
cross–fertilization.. 9. phytogamy
disease.. 4. gall, rust, smut 5. ergot
7. blister 8. ramentum
embryo.. 8. plantule
enchantment–proof.. 7. haemony
(Milton's Comus)
flowerless.. 4. fern 6. lichen
9. cryptogam 11. Cryptogamia (opp
of phanerogam)
growing on rock.. 6. lichen
growing on sea bottom.. 6. enalid
growing wild.. 9. agrestial
history.. 12. phytogenesis

legendary, forgetfulness.. 5. lotus
male.. 3. mas
mosslike.. 6. orpine
mushroom type.. 6. fungus
native.. 8. indigene
orifice.. 5. stoma
pigment lacking.. 6. albino
poisonous.. 4. atis 6. datura
   7. amanita 8. oleander
poisonous to cattle.. 4. loco
   8. locoweed
pore.. 8. lenticel
round–leaved.. 9. pennywort
science of.. 6. botany
seedless.. 6. agamic
stem, stalk.. 4. bine 5. haulm
   6. caulis
tequila–yielding.. 5. agave
tissue.. 7. tapetum
without chlorophyll.. 6. albino
without petals.. 9. apetulous
woody.. 6. xyloid
plant (type of)...
aconite.. 5. bikh
agave, century plant.. 4. aloe, pita
   9. amaryllis
ammoniac.. 5. oshac
anise.. 4. dill
aquatic.. 6. sugamo 7. frogbit
   8. plankton
aromatic.. 4. mint, nard 5. basil,
   tansy, thyme 8. tarragon
arum.. 4. sago 6. starch 9. arrowroot
aster family.. 5. daisy 8. fleabane
bitter.. 3. rue
bitter vetch.. 3. ers
box.. 5. Buxus 7. boxwood
broom.. 5. spart 6. Canary 7. genista
bryophytic.. 4. moss
burdock.. 5. elite 8. Xanthium
burning bush.. 5. wahoo
butter–and–eggs.. 8. ranstead
cactus.. 6. dildo 6. cereus, chaute,
   mescal 7. saguaro 9. xerophyte
century.. 4. aloe 5. agave 6. maguey
dill.. 4. anet
evergreen.. 3. ivy 5. holly 6. laurel
   8. conifers 9. mistletoe
everlasting.. 6. orpine 11. live–forever
furze.. 4. ulex 5. gorse
garlic (wild).. 4. moly
leguminous.. 3. pea 4. bean
   6. Cassia, clover, lentil
lilaceous.. 4. aloe, iris, leek 5. lotus,
   onion, tulip, yucca
linen.. 4. flax
medicinal.. 4. alem, aloe 5. anise,
   wahoo 6. arnica, cacoon, catnip,
   ipecac 7. aconite, boneset, gentian,
   lobelia, rhatany 8. camomile
pea family.. 7. Cytisus
perennial.. 4. Geum 5. avens
   10. sneezewort
poisonous.. 6. datura 8. oleander
poisonous to cattle.. 8. locoweed
poisonous to fowl.. 7. henbane
prickly, thorny.. 5. brier 6. cactus,
   nettle, teasel 7. thistle
satinpod (transparent).. 7. honesty
soap.. 5. amole
tapioca.. 7. cassava
thorny.. see *prickly* 6. fatsia

trifoliate.. 6. clover 8. shamrock
plant, typical of...
Africa.. 5. argel (arghel)
Alps.. 9. edelweiss
Arabia.. 3. kat (stimulant)
Australia.. 5. Hakes, lilac 6. Correa
   7. columba, fuchsia 8. Rutaceae
China.. 5. ramie
Egypt.. 5. anise, cumin 7. aniseed
   8. nepenthe
Hawaii.. 5. olona
Japan.. 3. tea 5. acuba 6. quince
   7. cydonia 8. japonica
Japan (vine).. 8. Bignonia 14. trumpet
   creeper
Mexico.. 4. chia 5. datil 6. salvia
   9. sabadilla
Peru.. 3. oca 7. rhatany
Philippines.. 4. alem (Med) 6. agamid
Spain.. 3. aji 6. pepper 8. Capsicum
Syria.. 5. cumin
tropical vine.. 8. redwithe
   10. tillandsia
tropics.. 4. arum, palm, taro
   5. agave, zamia 7. dasheen, hamelia
   8. mangrove
plantain... 6. banana
plantation pines... 7. pinetum
plantation trees... 4. holt 6. forest
   7. nopalry (cactus), orchard
planters, Govt of... 11. plantocracy
plantigrade mammal... 5. panda
plaque... 5. medal, patch 6. brooch,
   tablet 8. ornament, platelet (Anat)
plash.. 4. plop, pool 5. swash
   6. puddle, ripple, splash
plasm... 4. mold 6. matrix
plasma... 4. cell, whey 5. blood (fluid)
   10. protoplasm
plaster... 4. teer 5. gesso, grout, salve
   6. gypsum, parget, stucco
   8. adhesive, poultice 9. inebriate
plastered... 5. drunk 7. crocked,
   smeared 8. mortared
plasterer... 5. mason
plaster of Paris... 5. gesso
   6. gypsum 15. calcium sulphate
plastic... 3. pug 5. gesso, vinyl
   6. slurry 7. ductile, fictile, pliable,
   viscose 8. creative 9. compliant,
   formative, teachable
   14. impressionable
plastic, commercial... 6. Lucite
   7. Formica 8. Bakelite, Vinylite
   9. Plexiglas
plasty (pert to)...
comb form.. 7. molding
eyelid.. 14. blepharoplasty
face lift.. 13. rhytidoplasty
nose.. 11. rhinoplasty
plat... 3. map 4. flat, plan, plot
   5. braid, chart, field, level, plain,
   plait, pleat 6. flatly, scheme
   7. outline, plateau 8. absolute,
   directly, straight 9. tableland
   10. interweave 15. straightforward
platanist... 4. fish, susu
plate... 3. gib 4. disc, dish, shoe
   (horse) 5. paten 6. lamina, patera
   7. coating, denture, overlay
   9. bookplate, engraving
   10. receptacle

plate (pert to)...
armor.. 6. cuisse (cuish)
battery.. 4. grid
bone (Anat).. 7. scapula
cooking.. 4. grid
culture.. 8. bacteria
Eccl.. 5. paten 6. patina
graduated.. 4. dial
holder.. 8. cassette
horny.. 5. scute
horse.. 6. plater
insect (bony).. 6. scutum
mark.. 8. hallmark 9. engraving
numbered.. 4. disc
of glass.. 5. slide
perforated metal.. 3. dod
ship-shaped.. 3. nef
plateau... 4. dish, mesa, puna 5. plain
    6. plaque, salver 9. tableland
platform... 3. map 4. dais, deck,
    k'ang, plan 5. arena, chart, plank,
    stage 6. lissom, lyceum, podium,
    policy, pulpit, scheme 7. estrade,
    outline, rostrum, soapbox, tribune
    8. hustings 9. bandstand 14. public
    speaking
platform (pert to)...
fort.. 8. barbette
gun.. 11. emplacement
mining.. 6. sollar (soller)
nautical.. 7. foretop, maintop
    9. gangplank
scaffold (funeral).. 10. catafalque
wheeled.. 5. float
platic (Astrol)... 8. not exact
    9. imperfect
plating... 5. armor 6. lamina
    7. shoeing
platinum wire... 4. oese
platitude... 6. cliché, old hat, truism
    7. bromide 8. banality 9. staleness,
    triteness 11. commonplace
    15. commonplaceness
Plato (pert to)...
famed for.. 9. Dialogues
    10. philosophy
founder of.. 7. Academe, academy
name, real.. 10. Aristocles
pupil of.. 8. Socrates
platoid... 4. flat 5. broad
Platonic (pert to)...
idea.. 5. eidos
love.. 4. pure 5. ideal 6. chaste
    8. virtuous 10. idealistic
    11. comradeship
philosophy.. 8. idealism 9. Platonism
    11. theoretical
solids.. 10. hexahedron, octahedron
    11. icosahedron, tetrahedron
    12. dodecahedron
platoon... 3. set 4. unit 5. squad
    7. company, coterie 11. subdivision
platoon school... 4. Gary (Ind)
platter... 4. dish, lanx 5. grail, plate
    6. record 9. scutellum
platter-shaped... 10. scutellate
platyfish... 8. moonfish
platypus... 8. duckbill
plaudit... 5. cheer, éclat 6. encore
    8. applause, approval, clapping,
    encomium 10. plaudation
    11. acclamation, approbation

plausible... 8. credible, probable,
    specious 10. applausive, believable,
    ostensible, plauditory, reasonable
    11. conceivable
plausible excuse... 5. alibi
play... 3. act, fun, toy 4. game, jest,
    romp 5. dally, drama, enact, feign,
    sport, wager 6. affect, frolic
    7. disport, operate, pretend
    9. amusement, diversion, melodrama,
    pantomime 10. recreation
    11. impersonate 13. entertainment
play (pert to)...
exhibit a.. 5. stage
for time.. 5. stall
house.. 5. movie 6. cinema
    7. theater 9. dollhouse
musical.. 5. opera 8. burletta,
    operetta
outline.. 8. scenario
part.. 4. role 7. prelude 8. epilogue,
    epitasis, prologue
pranks.. 4. haze
silent.. 9. pantomime
story.. 8. scenario
stupid.. 5. boner
the bagpipe.. 5. skirl 6. doodle
the buffoon.. 5. droll
the coquette.. 5. flirt
tricks.. 4. hoax, shab
truant.. 5. miche
unskillfully.. 5. strum
upon words.. 3. pun 11. paronomasia
playa... 5. beach, shore 7. salt pan
playboy... 4. fool 5. clown, cutup
    7. buffoon, reveler 8. carouser
    10. merrymaker 12. Jack of Trumps
    (Spoilfive)
player... 3. dub 4. star 5. actor, idler,
    piper 7. gambler, trifler 8. gamester,
    musician, stroller, thespian
    9. frolicker, performer
    11. barnstormer
player on words... 7. punster
playful... 3. gay 6. lusory 7. jocular
    8. humorous, playsome, sportive
    9. facetious, kittenish
    11. mischievous
playing cards... 4. deck, pack
    6. tarots
playlet... 4. skit 9. short play
plaything... 3. die, toy 4. dupe
    6. bauble 7. cat's-paw
plea... 4. suit 5. claim 6. abater,
    appeal, excuse, prayer 7. apology,
    defense, pretext 8. argument,
    entreaty, pretense 10. advocation,
    allegation 13. nolo contendre
plead... 3. beg, sue 5. argue
    6. adduce, allege 7. entreat, implore
plead (for)... 7. entreat, justify, solicit
    10. supplicate
pleader... 4. suer 6. lawyer
    8. advocate 9. entreater, justifier
    11. intercessor
pleading... 4. oyer 8. advocacy,
    demurrer, entreaty 9. imploring,
    objection 11. litigation
    12. intercession, supplication
pleasant... 3. fun, gay 4. nice
    5. merry, sweet 6. genial 7. affable,
    amusing, leesome, winsome

8. cheerful, friendly, humorous, pleasing, sportive 9. agreeable, diverting, laughable, sprightly

pleasant (pert to)...
manners.. 9. amenities
sound.. 6. dulcet 8. euphonic
  9. melodious 10. harmonious
to peruse.. 8. readable
weather.. 4. fair, fine 6. bright
  8. rainless 9. cloudless

please... 4. like, suit 5. fancy 6. arride
  7. appease, content, delight, gratify, indulge, placate, satisfy 9. vouchsafe

pleased... 4. fain, game, glad
  5. happy 9. contented, gratified

pleasing... 4. cool, lief, nice 5. sooth
  6. comely, eesome, savory
  7. amiable, roseate, welcome
  8. pleasant 9. agreeable, desirable
  10. delectable 11. pleasureful

pleasurable... 7. hedonic 8. pleasant
  10. gratifying

pleasure... 3. joy 4. gree, will, wish
  5. mirth, sport 6. choice, gaiety
  7. delight, purpose 8. gladness, hedonism, hilarity 9. amusement, diversion, enjoyment, happiness, merriment 11. delectation
  12. satisfaction 13. gratification

pleasure (pert to)...
god.. 3. Bes
ground.. 4. park 9. pleasance
pert to.. 7. hedonic
philosophy.. 8. Hedonism
seeker.. 5. sport 7. epicure, playboy
  8. hedonist

pleat... 4. fold 5. braid, plait

pleater... 8. plicator

plebeian... 4. pleb (Rom) 6. common, vulgar 7. ignoble, ill-bred, lowborn
  8. ordinary

plebiscite... 4. vote 6. decree
  10. referendum

pleck... 4. plot (ground), spot
  5. speck, stain 9. enclosure

plectrum... 4. pick 5. uvula 6. tongue
  7. malleus 8. plectron

pledge... 3. bet, vas, vow 4. bond, gage, gate, oath, pawn, seal, wage
  5. swear, toast, troth 6. engage, parole, plight 7. chattel, earnest, promise 8. guaranty, mortgage, obligate, security 9. assurance
  10. collateral 11. impignorate

pledget... 4. swab 8. compress

Pleiad (pert to)...
Alexandria.. 10. Seven Poets
French.. 10. The Pléiade
lost Pleiad.. 6. Merope 7. Electra
philosophical (Gr).. 12. Seven Wise Men

Pleiades (pert to)...
Seven Daughters of Atlas..
  10. Atlantides
star.. 4. Maia 7. Sterope 8. Asterope
star cluster.. 8. in Taurus (Constellation)

plenary... 4. full 5. great 6. entire
  7. perfect 8. absolute, complete
  9. unlimited 11. unqualified

plenipotentiary... 5. envoy
  8. diplomat, minister 10. ambassador

plenteous... 6. plenty 7. copious, fertile, liberal 8. abundant, fruitful, generous 9. bounteous, bountiful, plentiful 10. productive

plentiful... 4. full, rich, rife 5. ample
  6. lavish 7. copious, fertile, liberal, opulent, profuse 9. abounding, bounteous, bountiful
  13. superabundant

plentifully... 6. galore 9. abounding, abundance

plenty... 4. enow 6. enough, galore, uberty 8. fullness 9. abundance, plenitude 10. perfection
  11. copiousness 12. completeness, considerable 14. superabundance

plenum... 5. space 8. assembly, fullness (of space) (opp of vacuum)

pleon... 6. telson 7. abdomen

pleonasm... 8. fullness 10. redundancy
  11. diffuseness, reiteration

plethora... 4. glut 6. excess
  9. repletion 14. superabundance

plethoric... 6. turgid 8. inflated, overfull 9. bombastic 10. overloaded

plexiform... 4. rete 7. network
  11. complicated

plexus... 4. rete 5. solar 7. network

pliable... 4. limp 6. limber, pliant, supple 7. plastic 8. flexible, suitable
  9. compliant, teachable

pliant... 7. bending, pliable, tensile, willowy 8. flexible, workable, yielding
  9. adaptable, compliant

plicate... 4. fold 5. pleat 6. folded
  7. plaited

plight... 4. fold 5. braid, plait
  6. status 7. embrace, promise
  8. position 9. condition, situation
  (bad) 11. predicament

plinth... 4. orlo 7. subbase

Pliosaurus (extinct)... 7. reptile

plod... 3. dig, mog 4. slog, toil, tore
  6. drudge, trudge

plodder... 3. fag 4. grub, hack
  5. slave 6. drudge

plot... 3. lot, map 4. acre, area, brew, burn, pack, plan, plat 5. cabal, frame, tract, trick 6. design, scheme, scorch, secret 7. diagram, project
  8. conspire, intrigue 10. conspiracy, prearrange 11. machination

plot (of ground)... 3. lot 4. acre, area, plat 5. grave, tract 7. terrain

Plotinus... 11. philosopher (Alexandrian School)

plotted... 7. charted, hatched
  8. lineated 9. conspired
  10. delineated 11. prearranged

plotter... 5. Haman 7. Jacobin, planner, schemer 8. agitator
  9. contriver 11. conspirator

ploughshare (plowshare) part...
  6. colter (coulter)

plover... 4. dupe 5. piper, sandy
  7. lapwing 9. courtesan, sandpiper, shorebird

plover (pert to)...
crab.. 5. drome
crested.. 7. lapwing
egg.. 11. darning ball
genus.. 12. Charadriidae

Old World.. 8. dotterel, killdeer
page.. 6. dunlin 9. sandpiper
quail.. 13. plain wanderer
ring.. 5. pandy

plow... 4. rove, till 5. break, miner, scaut 6. furrow, turn up 7. break up 8. reinvest 9. cultivate

plow (pert to)...
fish.. 3. ray
gang.. 6. oxgang 7. measure
light.. 10. Plow Monday 13. hoggler's light
man.. 6. rustic 10. countryman, husbandman
part.. 4. buck, chip, hale 5. share, slade, stilt 6. clevis, colter
type.. 5. sulky 8. mole plow

plowed land... 5. arada, arado

pluck... 3. pug, rob, tug 4. grab, jerk, pick, pull 5. nerve, spunk, steal, strip, strum 6. avulse, divest, fleece, gather, twitch 7. courage, harvest, pick off, plunder, strip of, swindle 10. resolution, straighten (wool)

plucky... 4. game 5. brave, nervy 6. spunky, sticky 8. adhesive, resolute, spirited 10. courageous

plug... 3. peg, tap, top 4. blow, bung 5. horse, knock, punch, shoot, spile, wedge 7. commend, hydrant, stopper, stopple, tobacco 9. persevere, publicity, publicize 12. commendation

plug (pert to)...
board.. 11. switchboard
cannon muzzle.. 7. tampion (tampeon, tampoon)
dentristy.. 7. filling
hat.. 4. tile 5. gibus 6. topper
medical.. 4. clot 6. fibrin, tampon 7. embolus
slender.. 5. spill
up.. 4. calk (caulk)

plum... 5. drupe, money, prune 6. Prunus 8. dividend 9. good thing, sugarplum

plum (pert to)...
beetle.. 8. curculio
bitter.. 4. sloe
California (wild).. 5. islay
coco.. 5. icaco
England.. 6. damson
Europe.. 7. bullace
hybrid.. 7. plumcot
India.. 7. hog plum
Java.. 7. jambool (jambul) 8. jambolan
type.. 4. gage 6. damson 9. greengage, wild-goose 11. Reine Claude

plumage... 4. down 6. hackle 7. floccus (first down) 8. feathers, ornament

plumb... 4. seal, true 5. delve, gauge, sound, utter 6. adjust, fathom, sinker, weight (lead) 7. examine, measure, plummet 8. absolute, complete, vertical 9. downright 13. perpendicular

plumbage... 8. leadwork

plumbog... 9. raspberry (dwarf)

plumcot... 6. hybrid 11. plum apricot

plume... 5. crest, egret, preen, pride 6. plumet 7. feather, panache 8. decorate, plumelet

plummet... 4. dive, drop, fall, lead, plop, test 5. pitch, sound, swoop 6. fathom, plunge, weight 9. criterion

plump... 3. fat 4. drop, dull, fall, plop, rude, sink, tidy 5. blunt, buxom, flock, fubsy, obese 6. chubby, dilate, fatten, flatly 7. distend 8. blurt out, straight 9. corpulent, filled out 10. vertically 11. well-rounded

plumpness of person... 9. stoutness 10. embonpoint

plunder... 3. rob 4. boot, loot, pelf, prey, raid, rape, sack 5. booty, poach, raven, reave, rifle, strip 6. boodle, fleece, maraud, profit, rapine, ravage, spoils 7. despoil, pillage 8. spoliate 9. depredate

plundered... 4. reft 6. looted, robbed

plunderer... 5. thief 6. looter, pirate, preyer, raider, robber 7. spoiler, stealer 8. pillager 10. freebooter

plunge... 3. bet, dip 4. dash, dive, fall, pool, risk, sink 5. douse, drive, lunge, plumb, souse 6. gamble, thrust 7. baptize, immerse 8. flounder 9. gravitate, overwhelm, speculate

plunge (into)... 4. clap, dive 5. begin 7. immerge, immerse 9. set to work, undertake

plunger... 5. diver 6. risker 7. gambler 10. speculator

plunk... 4. blow, drop, pull, push, sink, thud 5. drive, plump, strum, throw 7. a dollar 10. play truant

plurality... 8. majority 9. multitude 11. greater part, large number

plural marriage... 8. polygamy

Plutarch (Gr)... 10. biographer

Pluto (pert to)...
Astron.. 6. planet (most remote)
god of.. 10. lower world
Greek name.. 5. Hades
kingdom.. 5. Hades
Roman name.. 3. Dis 5. Orcus
wife.. 10. Proserpina

plutocracy... 13. rule by wealthy 17. dominion of the rich

Plutus (pert to)...
god of.. 6. wealth
son of.. 6. Iasion 7. Demeter

pluvia... 4. rain 9. pluviosus

pluviometer, pluvioscope... 9. rain gauge

pluvious... 5. rainy 7. pluvial

ply... 4. bend, fold, mold, sail, urge 5. exert, plait, wield 6. employ, handle, lamina 8. navigate 9. importune, thickness

pneuma... 4. soul 5. neume 6. breath, spirit 9. breathing, life force, vital soul

pneumology (science of)... 5. lungs 17. respiratory organs

poach... 3. mix, ram 4. poke, push, sock, stir 5. drive, force, shirr (egg), steal 6. thrust 7. trample 8. encroach, trespass

poacher ... 7. lurcher, stalker, widgeon
Poblacht ... 8. Republic
Pocahontas (pert to) ...
  father.. 8. Powhatan (Chief)
  husband.. 9. John Rolfe
  Indian title.. 8. Princess
  name.. 12. Rebecca Rolfe
  rescuer of.. 9. John Smith (Capt)
pocket ... 3. bag, bin, cly, fob, sac
  4. poke, sack, take 5. money,
  pouch, purse 6. cavity, hollow
  7. conceal, confine, enclose
  8. envelope
pocketbook ... 3. bag, lil 5. pouch,
  purse 6. income, wallet 8. notebook
  9. resources
pod ... 3. bag, kid, sac 4. aril, boll
  5. belly, carob, chili, pouch, shuck
  6. legume
poem ... 3. dit, lay, ode 4. Edda, epic,
  epos, hymn, rune, saga 5. elegy,
  epode, idyll, psalm, verse 6. ballad
  (ballade), jingle, rondel (roundelle),
  sonnet 7. eclogue, erotics, rondeau
  8. limerick, rondelet 9. dithyramb
  10. villanelle 11. acatalectic
poem (pert to) ...
  division.. 5. canto, epode, verse
    6. stanza 7. refrain
  eight lines.. 7. triolet
  famed.. 6. Iliad 7. Odyssey
  foot.. 6. iambic 7. anapest, pyrrhic
  imitation.. 6. parody
  line.. 5. stich 6. octave, septet,
    sestet, tercet 7. couplet, triplet
    8. cinquain, quatrain
  meter.. 6. iambic 8. spondaic,
    trochaic 9. dactyllic, hexameter
    10. anaepestic (anapestic),
    pentameter
  ref to.. 5. meter, rhyme, verse
    7. cadence, helicon 8. feminine,
    scansion 9. masculine
  religious.. 4. hymn 5. psalm
  rhythmic break.. 7. caesura
  satirical.. 3. dit 6. parody
poem, famed..
  Homer.. 5. Iliad 7. Odyssey
  Khayyám.. 8. Rubáiyát
  Milton.. 12. Paradise Lost
  Ovid.. 13. Metamorphoses
  Poe.. 8. The Raven
  Poem in Marble.. 8. Taj Mahal
  poem of declaration.. 8. Invictus
  Shakespeare.. 7. Macbeth
  Spenser.. 12. Faerie Queene
poems ... 5. poesy, sylva 6. poetry
poet ... 4. bard 5. odist, rimer 6. lyrist
  7. dreamer 8. laureate 9. poetaster,
  rhymester, versifier
poet (famed) ...
  German.. 5. Heine
  mythology.. 6. Ossian
  Negro.. 11. Braithwaite
  Persian.. 7. Khayyám
  Sierra.. 13. Joaquin Miller
Poet Laureate (a few) ... 6. Dryden
  7. Spenser 8. Tennyson 9. Ben
  Jonson, Masefield 10. Wordsworth
poetry (pert to) ...
  Muse of.. 5. Erato 6. Thalia
    8. Calliope

Norse god of.. 5. Bragi
School of (anc).. 9. Parnassus
type.. 4. epic 5. lyric 6. ballad
  8. didactic 9. free verse, narrative
  10. blank verse
pogoniate ... 7. bearded
pogonip ... 3. fog (Sierras)
pogonology (study of) ... 6. beards
pogrom ... 8. massacre
poi ... 4. food, taro, then (Mus)
poignant ... 4. keen 5. acute 6. biting,
  bitter 7. cutting, pungent
point ... 3. aim, dot, jab, jot, neb, nib,
  pin 4. apex, barb, cape, gaff, gist,
  node, peak, stop, tack 5. focus,
  prong, quill, spike 6. bodkin, direct,
  needle, period, summit, zenith
  7. apicula, punctum 10. breakwater,
  promontory
point (pert to) ...
  antler, branch.. 4. snag
  astronomy.. 5. apsis 6. syzygy
  central, pivotal.. 4. crux
  farthest from earth.. 6. apogee
  focal.. 9. epicenter
  geometry.. 6. acnode 7. crunode
  highest.. 4. acme, apex, peak
    6. summit, zenith 8. meridian,
    pinnacle
  lace.. 10. petit point 11. needlepoint
  law.. 3. res 5. locus
  lowest.. 5. nadir 6. bottom
  mathematics.. 5. unode
  nearest earth.. 7. perigee
  of contact.. 5. focus
  of debate.. 5. issue, topic
  of honor.. 7. scruple
  of view.. 5. angle, slant 8. attitude
  opposite zenith.. 5. nadir
  reference to.. 6. apical
  salient.. 7. feature
  starting, golf.. 3. tee
  strong.. 5. forte
  utmost.. 7. extreme
  weak.. 4. flaw 5. fault 6. foible
pointed ... 5. aimed, noded, piked,
  sharp, terse 6. acuate, marked,
  peaked 7. angular, concise, conical
  8. aculeate, piercing, poignant,
  spicated, stinging 9. acuminate,
  pertinate, spiculate 10. emphasized
  11. conspicuous, significant
  12. epigrammatic
pointed (pert to) ...
  architecture.. 5. ogive 6. Gothic
  end.. 4. cusp
  fox.. 3. red
  instrument.. 3. awl, gad 4. prod
    6. gimlet, stylet
  rod.. 4. goad
pointer ... 3. arm, dog, tip 4. sign
  5. index 6. fescue, gnomon
pointless ... 4. dull 5. blunt, inane,
  silly, vapid 6. stupid 7. insipid,
  witless
poise ... 6. aplomb 7. balance, ballast
  8. carriage 9. composure, equipoise,
  stability
poison (pert to) ...
  arrow.. 4. inee, upas 5. urari
    6. curare (curari)
  deadly.. 4. bane, upas 5. arrow

7. arsenic, cyanide, hemlock
10. strychnine
study of.. 10. toxicology
poissarde... 8. fishwife, low woman
poisson.. 4. fish
poisson bleu... 7. catfish 8. bluefish, grayling
poitrel.. 5. armor, plate 9. stomacher
11. breastplate
poke.. 3. bag, jab, jog, pry 4. bore, goad, prod, root, sack 5. grope, nudge, probe, purse 6. dawdle, potter, search, thrust, wallet
7. project, tobacco
poker... 3. rod 6. beadle 7. bugbear, pochard 9. hobgoblin
poker (pert to)...
face.. 8. immobile
form of.. 4. draw, stud
painting.. 10. pyrography
picture.. 11. pyrogravure
stake.. 3. pot 4. ante 6. roodle
poky, pokey... 4. dull, mean, slow
5. dowdy, small 6. bonnet, narrow, shabby 7. cramped, tedious
Poland... see also *Polish*
ancestors.. 5. Lakha, Slavs
ancient name.. 7. Polonia
capital.. 6. Warsaw
city.. 4. Lodz 6. Gdynia, Krakow, Lublin
river.. 7. Dnieper, Vistula
Poland China... 5. swine
polar... 5. curve 6. Arctic 7. guiding
8. opposite 9. Antarctic, magnetism
Polar base (exploration)... 4. Etah
Polaris... 5. Alpha 9. North Star
11. guiding star
pole... 3. bar, oar, pew, poy, rod, xat
4. axle, beam, mast, prop, spar
5. shaft, sprit, staff, stool, totem
pole (pert to)...
bad end.. 7. raw deal
burn.. 7. disease (tobacco)
cat.. 5. skunk, zoril 6. ferret, musang
7. fitchew 8. Putorius 9. scoundrel
cat weed.. 12. skunk cabbage
electric.. 5. anode, pitch 7. cathode
8. magnetic 9. electrode
Gaelic.. 5. caber
head.. 7. tadpole
Spanish.. 4. pale, palo
star.. 5. guide 7. polaris 8. lodestar
9. North Star 13. l'Etoile du Nord
vehicle.. 4. cope, crab 5. thill
well.. 5. sweep
polemic.. 9. disputant 11. contentious
13. argumentative, controversial
polenta... 8. porridge
poles of cold... 7. Siberia (Verkhoyansk) 12. Grinnell Land (Fort Conger)
police (pert to)...
badge.. 6. buzzer, shield
club.. 8. spontoon
man.. 3. cop 5. guard 6. bobbie, copper, peeler, Ranger 7. officer, sheriff, trooper 10. constable, detective, N W Mounted
11. carabinière (carabineer)
station.. 5. thana 6. lockup
8. bargello

policy... 3. wit 4. plan 6. wisdom
8. regulate, sagacity 9. insurance
10. government, management, shrewdness 11. contrivance
13. judiciousness 14. administration
policy of segregation... 9. apartheid
polish... 3. rub 4. buff 5. glaze, gloss, rabat, scour, shine 6. finish, luster, smooth 7. burnish, culture, furbish
8. brighten, civilize, elegance, lapidate, levigate, urbanity
10. refinement
Polish (pert to)...
Bull.. 13. Constellation
cake.. 4. baba
carriage.. 7. britska
composer, pianist.. 6. Chopin
10. Paderewski
dance.. 7. mazurka 9. polonaise
11. cracovienne (krakowiak)
nobleman.. 7. starost
premier.. 10. Paderewski (pianist)
president (1st).. 10. Philsudski
scientist.. 5. Curie (Madame)
polishing material... 5. emery, rabat, rouge 6. pumice 11. rottenstone
polite... 4. neat, tidy 5. civil, suave, urban 6. gentle, smooth, urbane
7. gallant, genteel, refined
8. polished 9. courteous, debonaire (debonair, debonnaire) 10. cultivated
11. complaisant
politesse... 10. politeness (formal)
11. cleanliness, courtliness
12. decorousness
politic... 4. wary 7. cunning, tactful
8. cautious, discreet 9. judicious, political, politique, provident
10. diplomatic
political (pert to)...
boss.. 7. cacique
district.. 4. city, ward 5. State
6. canton, county, parish 7. borough
10. palatinate
economy.. 9. economics
faction.. 4. bloc, ring 5. junta, party
7. machine
hanger-on.. 6. heeler 10. ward heeler
influence.. 5. lobby, rally 6. caucus
party (old).. 4. Tory, Whig 9. Politique
politician... 7. schemer 9. intriguer, statesman 11. gerrymander
12. politicaster
politics... 7. cunning 8. scheming
10. government, profession
15. partisan rivalry 16. political affairs
Polizei... 9. the police
poll... 3. cut, tax 4. clip, head, roll, vote 5. shear, skull 6. fleece, survey
7. despoil 8. election, schedule
pollan... 9. whitefish
polled... 5. shorn 6. shaved
8. hornless
pollen... 4. seed 6. anther 8. fine dust 11. microspores 13. fertilization
pollen brush (bee's)... 5. scopa
pollenization... 5. xenia 13. fertilization
pollent... 6. strong 8. powerful
poller... 5. voter 6. barber
9. plunderer 11. extortioner, taxgatherer

pollex... 5. thumb 11. bastard wing (bird) 13. dactylopodite
pollex impression... 10. thumbprint
polliwog... 7. tadpole
pollute... 4. soil 5. taint 6. befoul, defile, ravish 7. corrupt, debauch, profane 9. desecrate, inebriate 11. contaminate
pollution... 8. impurity 9. infection 10. corruption, defilement 13. contamination
Pollux (pert to)...
  brother (twin).. 6. Castor
  father.. 4. Zeus
  mother.. 4. Leda
  protector of.. 7. sailors
  star.. 13. Beta Geminorum
Polonius... 8. courtier (Shak)
polony... 7. sausage
poltergeist (folklore)... 5. ghost 6. spirit
poltfoot... 8. clubfoot
poltroon... 4. idle, lazy 6. coward, craven, wretch 7. buffoon, dastard 8. cowardly 9. dastardly 10. ne'er-do-well, scaramouch
polverine... 6. potash (of Levant) 8. pearlash
polyandrium (Gr)... 8. cemetery
polyandry... 8. polygamy 14. plural husbands (Tibet)
polychromatic... 10. variegated
polyglot... 6. jargon 9. languages (confusion of) 10. dictionary 11. philologist 12. Complutensian Polyglot (Bib)
polygon... 6. isagon 7. decagon, hexagon, nonagon, octagon 8. heptagon 9. dodecagon
polygyny... 8. polygamy 11. plural wives
polyhedron... 5. solid 6. figure 14. trisoctahedron 17. triakisoctahedron
polymny... 10. sacred song
Polynesia...
  native.. 5. Maori 6. Kanaka 8. Hawaiian 10. Melanesian
  ocean.. 7. Pacific
  origin (probable).. 7. Savaiki (Isl)
  South Sea Island group.. 5. Samoa 6. Hawaii, Tahiti 7. Savaiki 10. New Zealand
Polynesian (pert to)...
  butterfly.. 2. io
  chestnut.. 4. rata
  cloth.. 4. tapa
  demon.. 4. atua
  dragon.. 3. ati
  goddess of volcanoes.. 4. Pele
  god of forests.. 4. Tane
  hero.. 4. Maui
  homeland (fabled).. 7. Havaiki
  loincloth.. 5. pareu
  memorial.. 4. ahu
  oven.. 3. umu
  social tradition.. 6. tattoo
  tribe.. 3. Ati
  wages, reward.. 4. utu
polyp... 5. coral, Hydra, tumor 10. sea anemone 12. invertebrate
polyphone... 4. lute

polytropic... 9. versatile
pomade... 6. anoint 7. pomatum, unguent 8. ointment
pome... 4. pear 5. apple, fruit 6. quince 11. pomegranate
pomelo... 8. shaddock 10. grapefruit
Pomerania (pert to)...
  animal.. 3. dog
  capital.. 7. Stettin
  formerly.. 5. duchy (Prussia)
  river.. 4. Oder
pomme de terre... 6. potato
Pomona... 4. city (Calif) 7. college, goddess (of fruit)
pomp... 5. pride, state 6. parade 7. cortege, display, pageant 8. grandeur 9. pageantry, spectacle 10. ceremonial 11. ostentation 12. magnificence
pompano... 7. alewife
Pompeii, Italy (pert to)...
  10. earthquake, excavation, Mt Vesuvius (site)
pompous... 5. budge 6. august, stilty 7. Podsnap (Dickens), stilted 8. bombastic, grandiose 11. ceremonious 12. high-sounding, ostentatious, stuffed shirt
Ponce de Leon (pert to)...
  discoverer of.. 7. Florida 15. Fountain of Youth
  famed as.. 8. explorer
  landing site, America.. 11. St Augustine
pond... 4. pool 5. ocean (humorous) 6. lagoon 7. lakelet
pond (pert to)...
  apple.. 9. evergreen
  crow, hen.. 4. coot
  dogwood.. 10. buttonbush
  duck.. 7. mallard
  fish.. 7. sunfish
  frog.. 8. ranarium
  glass.. 8. aquarium
ponder... 4. mull, muse, pore 5. brood, opine, weigh 7. perpend, reflect 8. appraise, cogitate, consider, evaluate, meditate, ruminate
ponderous... 4. dull, huge 5. bulky, heavy 7. weighty 8. ungainly 9. important, momentous 11. elephantine
pongee... 4. silk 6. tussah 8. shantung
poniard... 4. dirk, kill 5. sword 6. dagger, pierce
ponica... 8. gardener
pont... 5. ferry, float 6. bridge 7. caisson, pontoon 9. ferryboat
Pontiac... 4. city (Mich) 5. Chief (Ottawa Indian) 6. Indian
pontiff... 4. pope 6. bishop 8. pontifex
pony... 3. cab, nag 4. crib 5. glass, horse, pinto 6. bronco 7. Express (mail, 1860), piebald 8. Shetland 11. translation
pooch... 3. dog 5. pouch
pooka... 6. goblin 7. specter
pool... 3. lin, pot 4. carr, fund, game, linn, mere, pond, tank, tarn 5. kitty, stake 6. cartel, lagoon, league, puddle

7. alberca, plashet 9. billiards, reservoir, resources 10. natatorium 11. aggregation

pool ball... 3. cue 4. spot 6. ringer

poon tree... 5. domba, keena

poor... 3. bad 4. mean, thin 5. needy 6. feeble, humble, meager, paltry, shabby, sickly 7. hapless, unlucky 8. indigent, inferior 9. destitute, illogical, imperfect, infertile 10. unskillful (unskilful) 11. impecunious, unfavorable, unfortunate 12. impoverished, inauspicious, insufficient 14. unsatisfactory

poor (pert to)...
creature.. 9. pilgarlic
joe.. 5. heron
John.. 3. cod 4. hake 8. mean fare
man's remedy.. 8. valerian
Richard.. 8. Saunders (Richard)
section of city.. 4. slum 6. ghetto 7. skid row 10. shantytown
soldier.. 9. friarbird

poorly... 3. ill 5. badly 8. abjectly, meagerly, shabbily 10. indisposed 11. defectively 13. disparagingly

pop... 4. bang, snap, soda 5. bulge, burst, crack 6. bubble 7. concert 8. beverage

popadam... 5. wafer (fried) 10. popper cake

popdock... 8. foxglove

pope... 3. fin 4. ruff 6. bishop, puffin, shrike, weevil 8. beverage 9. bullfinch 14. painted bunting

Pope (pert to)...
cathedral.. 7. Lateran
collar.. 5. orale
court officer.. 6. datary
crown.. 5. tiara 6. triple
first.. 5. Peter
headdress.. 5. miter (mitre)
name.. 4. Pius 5. Ratti 7. Gregory
palace.. 7. Vatican
poetry.. 10. Essay on Man
scarf.. 5. fanon

popeler... 7. sea gull 9. spoonbill

popinac... 8. huisache

popinjay... 6. parrot

poplar... 5. abele, alamo, aspen, bahan, white 10. cottonwood 12. balm of Gilead

poplar (pert to)...
Arabic.. 5. bahan, garab
balsam.. 9. tacamahac
Fr black.. 4. liar 10. cottonwood
N American.. 7. Populus 8. Lombardy
white.. 5. abele, bolle

poppy... 3. maw 7. Papaver (opium), ponceau 8. foxglove

poppycock... 3. rot 4. bosh 8. nonsense

populace... 3. mob 4. mass 5. demos, plebs 6. people 11. inhabitants 12. common people

popular... 3. lay, pop 5. cheap, liked, usual 6. famous, simple, vulgar 7. crowded, demotic, secular 8. accepted, epidemic, favorite, populous 9. prevalent, well-known, well-liked 11. fashionable, proletarian

12. nontechnical

popular belief... 4. lore 7. opinion 9. tradition 12. old wives' tale, superstition

popularity... 4. fame 5. vogue 10. reputation 15. fashionableness

popular success... 3. hit

population study... 10. larithmics

porcelain... 4. frit 5. china 6. kaolin 7. ramekin (mold)

porcelain (kind)... 5. Spode 6. Sèvres 7. celadon, Dresden, Limoges 8. Haviland

porch... 4. door, stoa 5. stoop 6. harbor, loggia 7. galilee, gallery, portico, veranda 8. entrance 9. colonnade

porcine animal... 3. hog, pig, sow 5. shoat, swine 6. porker 7. peccary 8. babirusa (babiroussa) 9. razorback

porcupine (pert to)...
anteater.. 7. echidna
Canada.. 8. urson 7. cawquaw
disease.. 10. ichthyosis
grass.. 5. stipa
species.. 6. rodent, tenrec (tendrac) 8. hedgehog, quill pig

pore... 3. con 4. duct, gaze, vent 5. stare, stoma, study 6. ponder 7. eporose (without), opening, orifice, ostiole 8. lenticel

porgy... 4. fish, scup 5. bream, pargo 6. pagrus, red tai

pork (pert to)...
barrel.. 4. fund (Polit) 6. boodle
chop.. 7. griskin
fish.. 4. sisi

porker... 3. hog, pig 5. swine, sword (obs)

porpoise... 4. Inia 6. seahog 7. dolphin, pellock 8. cetacean, Phocaena

porr... 4. cram, kick, poke, push, stir 5. poker 6. thrust

porrect... 6. tender 7. present

porridge... 3. pob 4. pobs, samp 6. cereal 7. oatmeal, polenta, pottage 9. stirabout

port... 4. gate, left, mien, wine 5. armor, haven 6. harbor, portal 7. airport, bearing, opening, posture 8. carriage, demeanor, larboard, porthole, portside 10. deportment 11. destruction

portable... 6. mobile 7. movable

portable altar... 10. altar stone, superaltar (Hist)

portal... 4. door, gate 5. porch 7. gateway 8. entrance 9. vestibule 12. porte-cochere

portcullis... 3. bar 4. shut 5. herse 7. barrier, grating, lattice (Her) 13. fortification

Porte... 12. Ottoman court (anc), Sublime Porte

porte-bonheur... 5. charm 6. amulet

porte-cochere... 5. porch (carriage) 7. gateway

portefeuille... 9. portfolio

portend... 4. bode 5. augur 7. betoken, predict, presage

8. forebode, foreshow, foretell,
prophecy 9. foretoken

portent... 4. omen, sign 6. marvel,
ostent 7. prodigy 11. forewarning

portentous... 4. dire 5. fatal, grave
6. solemn 7. fateful, ominous
8. sinister 9. monstrous, wonderful
10. impressive 13. extraordinary

porter... 3. ale 4. beer 5. hamal
(hammal), stout (drink) 6. bearer
7. carrier, janitor 9. attendant
10. doorkeeper

Porter's pseudonym... 6. O Henry

Portia (pert to)...
  character (Merchant of Venice)..
    7. heiress
  husband.. 8. Bassanio
  husband's friend.. 7. Antonio
  maid.. 9. Nerissa

portico... 4. stoa 6. atrium, xystus
(xyst) 7. pteroma, veranda
9. colonnade, peristyle, vestibule

portion... 3. bit, cut, dab, lot 4. dole,
dose, dunt, fate, half, mete, part,
some 5. piece, share, whack
6. moiety, parcel 7. section,
segment 8. quantity 9. allotment,
apportion, partition

portion (pert to)...
  curve.. 3. arc 7. segment
  detached.. 6. coupon
  inheritance.. 7. legitim 9. dead's part
  marriage.. 5. dowry
  sectional.. 5. curve
  widow's.. 5. dower

Portland (pert to)...
  arrowroot, sago.. 4. arum
  beds (Eng).. 11. Upper Oolite
    13. Upper Jurassic
  city of.. 5. Maine 6. Oregon
  stone.. 6. cement 8. concrete
  vase.. 9. Barberini (Rom palace)
    10. cameo glass

portmanteau... 3. bag 4. word
(blended) 5. cloak 6. mantle, valise
7. gunwale 8. portlass

portoise... 7. gunwale 8. portlass

Porto Rico... see *Puerto Rico*

portrait... 4. copy 5. image 7. picture
8. likeness, painting 10. similitude
11. description, portraiture
12. lifelikeness 14. representation

portrait on dollars...
  fifty.. 5. Grant
  five.. 7. Lincoln
  five hundred.. 8. McKinley
  five thousand.. 7. Madison
  one.. 10. Washington
  one hundred.. 8. Franklin
  one hundred thousand.. 6. Wilson
  one thousand.. 9. Cleveland
  ten.. 8. Hamilton
  ten thousand.. 5. Chase
  twenty.. 7. Jackson
  two.. 9. Jefferson

portray... 3. act 4. draw, form, limn
5. enact, frame, image, paint
6. depict 7. fashion, picture
8. describe 9. delineate, represent

portrayal... 3. act 5. drama
7. process 8. portrait 9. depiction
11. delineation, description

portreeve... 5. mayor 7. bailiff

Port Royal... 15. Cistercian abbey
(Versailles)

Portugal... see also *Portuguese*
  bridge.. 7. Salazar
  capital.. 6. Lisbon
  city.. 5. Braga 6. Aveiro, Guarda,
    Oporto 7. Granada
  island.. 6. Azores 7. Madeira
    8. Principe
  mountain.. 15. Serra da Estrella
  peninsula.. 7. Iberian
  port.. 6. Aveiro
  province.. 3. Goa 5. Macao, Timor
    9. Cape Verde 10. Mozambique
  resort.. 7. Estoril
  river.. 5. Tagus (Tajo)

Portuguese (pert to)...
  author.. 9. de Lobeira
  bird, fish.. 8. man–of–war
  ceremonial (Inquisition).. 8. auto de fe
  coin (gold).. 6. escudo 7. milreis (old)
  lady.. 4. dona
  legislature.. 6. Cortes 12. Cortes
    Geraes
  money of account.. 4. reis
  navigator.. 6. da Gama 8. Magellan
  wine.. 5. porto

Portunus (Rom Relig)... 10. god of
gates

posada... 3. inn 5. hotel

Posaune... 8. trombone 9. organ stop

posca... 5. drink (Hist)

pose... 3. put, sit 5. model 6. baffle,
puzzle, stance 7. nonplus, posture,
pretend, propose 8. attitude,
position, pretense, propound
9. postulate 11. affectation,
impersonate

Poseidon (pert to)...
  attributes.. 5. horse 7. dolphin,
    trident
  cult site.. 7. Corinth
  father.. 6. Cronus
  god of.. 3. sea 6. waters
  mother.. 4. Rhea
  wife.. 9. Amphitrite

poser... 5. facer 6. puzzle 7. problem,
sticker 14. attitudinarian

posh... 5. smart 6. spruce 7. elegant
9. luxurious

position... 3. job, lie 4. pose, rank,
seat, site 5. coign (coigne), place,
situs, stand, state 6. manner, stance,
ubiety 7. opinion, posture, premise
8. attitude, location, prestige,
proposal 9. viewpoint 11. affirmation,
supposition

position (pert to)...
  anchorlike.. 5. apeak
  fencing.. 7. septime
  finder (gun).. 13. triangulation
  golf.. 6. stance
  inescapable.. 7. impasse
  of affairs.. 6. status
  relative.. 8. standing
  secure.. 7. footing
  with no responsibility.. 8. sinecure

positive... 4. plus, sure 5. exact
6. actual, thetic 7. certain
8. dogmatic, emphatic 9. assertive,
convinced, downright 11. dictatorial

positive (pert to)...

charge (Elec).. **8.** positron
evidence.. **7.** constat
pole.. **5.** anode
saying.. **6.** dictum
school, criminology.. **10.** Lombrosian (by Lombroso)
positivism... **7.** Comtism **9.** certainty, dogmatism **10.** confidence **11.** materialism
positure... **7.** posture **11.** arrangement, disposition **13.** configuration
posnet... **3.** pot (3-footed) **8.** saucepan
poss... **4.** beat, dash, push **5.** drive, knock, pound, stamp **6.** thrust
posse... **5.** crowd **6.** throng **7.** company **9.** armed band **10.** detachment (police)
possess... **3.** own **4.** have, know, take **5.** haunt **6.** inform, occupy **7.** bewitch, inhabit **8.** convince, demonize, persuade
possessed... **5.** hadst, owned **6.** insane **7.** haunted **8.** demoniac, obsessed **9.** bewitched
possessing (pert to)...
feeling.. **6.** souled
flavor.. **5.** sapid, tasty
land.. **5.** acred
pincer claws.. **8.** chelated
power.. **11.** plenipotent
sensation.. **8.** sentient
special ability.. **6.** gifted **8.** talented
possession... **4.** hold **5.** asset **6.** taking, wealth **7.** control, country, mastery **8.** dominion, property **9.** obsession, ownership **10.** equanimity **11.** bewitchment
possession (pert to)...
again.. **6.** revest
law.. **6.** seizin (seisin)
not in (possession).. **6.** devoid
suffix.. **3.** ose
possessions... **6.** assets, estate, wealth **7.** effects **8.** property
posset... **4.** turn **5.** curdle, pamper **8.** beverage, infusion **9.** coagulate
possibility... **4.** bare **5.** latency **9.** liability, potential **10.** good chance, likelihood **11.** contingency **13.** improbability **16.** prospective value
possible... **6.** latent, liable, likely **8.** feasible **9.** plausible, potential **11.** practicable
possibly... **5.** maybe **7.** perhaps **9.** perchance **11.** conceivably
post... **3.** bet, dak (dawk), xat **4.** bitt, fort, list, mail, trot **5.** enter, newel, opium, place, stake, totem **6.** admit, assign, hasten, inform, marker, office, pillar, pledge **7.** bollard, placard, station, upright **8.** dispatch, position **9.** messenger, sternpost **12.** enter account
post (pert to)...
adverb.. **5.** after, later **9.** afterward
boat.. **4.** mail **5.** stage **6.** packet
boy.. **7.** courier **9.** postilion (postillion)
dance (army sl).. **8.** struggle
goal (anc).. **4.** meta
Indian memorial.. **3.** xat **5.** totem

meridian.. **9.** afternoon
mortem.. **7.** autopsy **8.** necropsy **10.** after death
office.. **6.** correo
prefix.. **5.** after **6.** behind **10.** subsequent
stair.. **5.** newel
postage stamp paper (pert to)...
design.. **8.** spandrel
paper.. **6.** pelure
pattern.. **6.** burele **8.** burelage
poster... **4.** bill, card **7.** placard, sticker **8.** bulletin **9.** messenger **10.** billposter
posthumous... **5.** after **10.** after death, post-mortem
postiche... **9.** false hair **10.** artificial **11.** counterfeit
postilion... **5.** guide **7.** postboy **9.** postrider
postimpressionist... **6.** cubist, Derain **7.** Cezanne, Matisse
postpone... **4.** wait **5.** defer, delay, remit, table **6.** put off, shelve **7.** adjourn, reserve, suspend **8.** hold over, prorogue **10.** pigeonhole **11.** subordinate **13.** procrastinate
postponement... **7.** remanet, respite **8.** deferral, reprieve **9.** deferment **11.** prorogation
postprandial... **11.** after dinner
postulate... **6.** assume **7.** prelude, premise **9.** condition, predicate, stipulate **10.** hypothesis **11.** stipulation, supposition
posture... **4.** pose **6.** stance **8.** attitude, position, pretense **9.** viewpoint **11.** frame of mind
pot... **3.** jug, pan **4.** olla **5.** belly, crock, cruse **6.** aludel, kettle, liquor, teapot **7.** amphora (anc), caldron **9.** flowerpot **10.** jardiniere
potash... **6.** potass, saline **7.** potassa **8.** pearlash **18.** potassium carbonate
potassium (pert to)...
bitartrate.. **13.** cream of tartar
bromide.. **8.** sedative
carbonate.. **6.** potash
compound.. **4.** alum
dichromatic.. **6.** chrome
iodide.. **8.** medicine
nitrate.. **5.** niter **9.** saltpeter
permanganate.. **8.** oxidizer **12.** disinfectant
sulphate.. **4.** alum
potate... **9.** liquefied
potation... **5.** draft, drink **6.** liquor **8.** beverage, tippling **12.** drinking bout
potato... **3.** oca, yam **4.** papa, spud **5.** tuber
potato (pert to)...
beetle.. **8.** hardback
bogle.. **9.** scarecrow
French.. **12.** pomme de terre
French style.. **9.** lyonnaise
genus.. **10.** Solanaceae
Indian.. **4.** yamp
moss.. **9.** pondgrass
S Am.. **7.** Uruguay
sweet.. **6.** patata
potator... **5.** poter **7.** tippler

potboiler... 4. book 6. writer
8. painting (for quick money)
9. potwaller
potdar... 7. assayer, cashier, weigher
potence, potency... 3. vis 4. élan
5. cross, power 6. energy, gibbet
7. gallows 8. virility 9. authority,
influence
potent... 4. able 6. cogent, mighty,
strong, virile 7. dynamic, warrant
(Mil) 8. forcible, heraldry, powerful,
puissant, virulent 9. effective, efficient
11. efficacious, influential
13. authoritative
potentate... 4. amir (ameer), emir
(emeer) 5. mogul, ruler 6. dynast,
prince 7. emperor, monarch
8. syzerain 9. sovereign
potential... 4. mood (Gram) 5. ergal
6. latent, mighty 8. possible
11. influential, in the making,
possibility, undeveloped
potentiality... 5. power 7. latency
11. possibility
poter... 5. toper 7. drinker
potgun... 5. rumor 6. cannon, mortar,
pistol 8. braggart
pothead... 7. dullard 8. terminal (Elec)
9. blackfish
pother... 3. ado, row 4. fuss, stir
5. worry 6. bother, bustle, harass
7. fluster, perplex, trouble
9. commotion 10. excitement,
perplexity 11. disturbance
12. perturbation
potherb... 4. mint 6. greens
7. spinach
pothook... 3. rod 4. hook (S–shaped)
5. crook 6. scrawl, stroke (S–like)
9. pot lifter 10. iron collar (penalty)
pothouse... 3. bar, low 6. saloon,
tavern, vulgar 7. barroom
8. alehouse, grogshop, mughouse
11. public house
potiche... 4. vase 7. ceramic
potion... 4. dose, dram, drug 5. draft,
drink 7. draught, philter 8. nepenthe
potlatch... 4. gift 5. feast 8. Festival
potomania... 10. dipsomania
15. delirium tremens
potong... 5. crown 6. wreath 9. head
cloth
potoroo... 11. rat kangaroo
potpourri... 4. olio, stew 5. medley
7. mixture, perfume 9. anthology
11. olla–podrida, salamagundi
potrero... 4. farm 7. pasture
10. cattle farm
pottage... 4. soup 6. brewis
8. porridge
pottah... 5. lease 6. tenure 9. title
deed
potter... 3. pry 4. mess, poke, push
6. dawdle, doodle, meddle, putter,
tamper, trifle 7. saunter 8. ceramist
potter's clay, earth... 4. slip 5. argil
5. galena, kaolin 8. alquifou
10. terra cotta
potter's wheel... 4. disk 5. lathe,
throw 6. jigger, pallet (palet)
pottery... 5. Delft 6. Samian
7. celadon (Chin), keramos (Gr)

8. Arretine (It), ceramics, Majolica (It)
9. delftware (Holland), keramikos (Gr)
11. earthenware 14. terra sigillata
(anc)
pottery (pert to)...
  black.. 6. basalt
  broken.. 5. shard (sherd)
  decorate.. 6. stamps 9. sigillate
  decoration.. 11. sigillation
  firing box.. 6. sagger
  glasslike.. 8. vitreous
  glaze.. 6. enamel
  mineral.. 8. feldspar
  paste.. 9. barbotine
  red.. 7. aretine
pottle... 3. pot 6. basket, vessel
7. tankard
potty... 3. pot 5. crazy 7. foolish,
haughty 8. trifling 12. supercilious
13. insignificant
pot–valiant... 10. courageous (when
drunk)
pouch... 3. bag, pod, sac 4. cyst,
poke, sack 5. bulge, bursa, purse
6. gipser (Hist), pocket 7. bladder,
mailbag, silicle, sporran (sporan)
10. pocketbook
pouch bone... 9. marsupial
pouched (pert to)...
  dog.. 9. thylacine 13. Tasmanian wolf
  frog.. 9. marsupial
  gopher.. 6. pocket
  mouse.. 9. marsupial
  rat.. 8. kangaroo
  rodent (cheek–pouched)..
    11. spermophile
  stork.. 8. adjutant
poultry... 4. fowl, hens 5. cocks,
ducks, geese 6. capons 7. Bantams,
peahens, pigeons, turkeys
8. chickens, peacocks, roosters,
volaille 9. cockerels, pheasants
10. guinea fowl
poultry (breeds)... 6. Ancona, Bantam,
Brahma 7. Cornish, Dorking,
Hamburg, Leghorn, Minorca
9. Wyandotte 12. Plymouth Rock
14. Rhode Island Red
poultry (pert to)...
  disease.. 3. pip 4. roup, tick
  dish.. 9. galantine
  farm.. 7. hennery
pounamu... 4. jade 6. weapon
8. nephrite 10. greenstone
pound... 3. hit, ram 4. beat, ding,
drum, maul, pond, tamp 5. money,
pen up, thump 6. bruise, hammer,
kennel, prison 7. impound
9. enclosure, pulverize
pounding instrument... 6. hammer,
pestle
pounds (100)... 6. cental
13. hundredweight
pour... 4. flow, gush, rain, teem, vent,
well 5. flood 6. abound, effuse,
stream 7. niagara, radiate, torrent
8. downpour 9. discharge
11. extravasate
pour (pert to)...
  molten glass.. 7. dagrade
  molten steel.. 4. teem
  off.. 5. drain 6. decant

oil upon.. 6. anoint, pacify
out.. 11. extravasate
sacrificial liquid.. 6. libate
pouring hole (mold)... 5. sprue
pout... 3. bib, mop 4. fish, moue, sulk
   5. pique 7. catfish, eelpout, grimace
   9. sulkiness
poverty... 4. lack, need, want 5. illth
   (opp of wealth) 6. dearth, penury
   8. leanness, poorness, scarcity
   9. indigence, pearlweed
   11. destitution
powder... 4. dust, talc 5. boral
   6. pollen, yttria 7. crumble
   8. cosmetic, sprinkle 9. explosive,
   pulverize
powder (pert to)...
antiseptic.. 6. formin 7. aristol
bag.. 6. sachet
festival (Ind).. 4. abir (perfumed)
goa.. 7. araroba
heater, melter.. 6. sinter
insecticide.. 9. hellebore
medical.. 8. tannigen
perfumed.. 6. empasm
polishing.. 5. emery 7. tripoli
smokeless.. 6. poudre 8. amberite
stamping.. 6. pounce
powdered (Her)... 4. semé
power... 3. arm, art, can, jet, vis
   4. dint, gift, iron, sway, will
   5. force, magic, might, steam, vigor
   6. degree, energy 7. control, faculty,
   magnate, potency 8. capacity,
   efficacy, strength 9. authority,
   eloquence, influence, magnetism,
   puissance 10. efficiency, government
   11. mathematics (term)
power (pert to)...
creative.. 6. Shakti
device.. 9. telemotor
hammer.. 4. trip
inherent.. 6. energy
of attorney.. 5. agent 10. procurator
of feeling.. 7. sensate
of mind.. 4. wits
of resistance.. 7. stamina
persuasive.. 8. rhetoric 9. political
sovereign.. 6. throne
spiritual.. 8. divinity
superior.. 10. prepotency
under one's.. 10. subjugated
unit.. 3. erg 4. dyne 8. kilowatt
powerful... 4. loud 5. great 6. cogent,
   mighty, potent, strong 7. drastic,
   intense, leonine, skookum
   8. eloquent, forcible, puissant
   9. effective, effectual, efficient
   10. armipotent, convincing
   11. efficacious, influential
   13. authoritative
powerful force... 6. libido
powerful man, businessman...
   5. titan 6. tycoon 7. magnate
powerless... 4. weak 8. impotent
pownie... 7. peacock
powwow... 6. frolic, priest 7. meeting
   8. assembly, ceremony, congress,
   conjurer 9. gathering 10. conference,
   convention
poyou... 9. armadillo
prabble... 7. chatter, quarrel

   8. squabble
practic... 6. artful, shrews 7. cunning,
   skilled 9. difficult, practical, practiced
   11. experienced
practicable, practical... 5. utile
   6. usable, useful 7. virtual, working
   8. feasible, possible, workable
   9. available, expedient, operative,
   pragmatic, realistic 11. pragmatical,
   utilitarian
practical (pert to)...
Christianity.. 10. New Thought
example.. 6. praxis
joke.. 4. hoax 5. trick 6. humbug
judgment.. 7. ethical (Kant)
practically... 9. virtually 11. essentially
   13. approximately
practice, practise... 2. do 3. ply, ure,
   use 4. plot, rite 5. drill, habit, train,
   usage 6. action, addict, custom,
   scheme, tryout 7. perform
   8. ceremony, exercise, intrigue,
   rehearse, training, vocation
   9. procedure 10. experience,
   experiment, observance
practice (pert to)...
corrupt.. 5. abuse
established.. 5. canon 6. custom
fraud.. 5. cheat, shark 8. trickery
specific.. 6. praxis
voice.. 8. intonate
witchcraft.. 3. hex
practicer of evasions...
   13. tergiversator
practicer of palmistry...
   11. chiromancer
prad... 5. horse
pragmatic... 7. meddler, skilled
   8. busybody, dogmatic, meddling
   9. conceited, officious, practical
   10. systematic 11. opinionated
pragmatical... 8. dogmatic 9. officious,
   practical 10. meddlesome
   11. commonplace
Prague, Praha...
capital of.. 14. Czechoslovakia
famed bldg.. 10. University (1st in
   Cent Eur, 1348)
famed teachers (anc).. 4. Huss
   6. Jerome
founder.. 14. Duchess Libussa (722)
prairie... 3. bay 5. llano, plain
   6. camass (camas, cammas),
   meadow, steppe 7. quamash
   (camass) 9. grassland 10. prairillon
prairie (pert to)...
anemone, crocus.. 12. pasque flower
antelope.. 9. pronghorn
apple.. 9. breadroot
artichoke.. 9. sunflower
berry.. 9. trompillo
chicken.. 6. grouse
dog.. 6. marmot
mud.. 5. gumbo
pigeon.. 6. plover 9. sandpiper
rose.. 14. Baltimore belle
schooner.. 12. covered wagon
squirrel.. 11. spermophile
tree (clump).. 5. motte
weed.. 10. cinquefoil
wolf.. 6. coyote
Prairie State... 8. Illinois

praise... 4. laud 5. bless, extol, honor, kudos 6. eulogy 7. acclaim, applaud, commend, glorify, magnify, plaudit 8. applause, encomium, eulogize, macarize 9. adulation, celebrate, panegyric 11. approbation 12. commendation

praise (pert to)...
continual.. 5. chant
high... 5. extol 8. encomium
hymn of.. 8. doxology
insincere.. 4. bull 7. flatter 8. flattery
of another's blessing.. 8. macarism 9. Beatitude
to God.. 7. Laus Deo
Ye The Lord.. 8. Alleluia (Alleluiah) 10. Hallelujah (Halleluiah)

praiseworthy... 8. laudable 11. commendable, meritorious

prana (Hind)... 6. spirit 9. life force 10. life breath

prance... 4. gait 5. caper, dance 6. cavort, spring 7. swagger

prank... 3. jig 4. fold, joke, prat 5. antic, caper, pleat, shine, trick 6. frolic, prance 7. caprice, dress up 8. escapade 11. monkeyshine

prankish... 9. facetious 10. frolicsome 11. mischievous

prate... 3. gab 4. chat, talk 6. gossip 7. chatter, twaddle 8. nonsense

prattle... 3. gab 4. chat, talk 5. clack, prate 6. babble 7. blather 12. impudent talk, trifling talk

prawn... 6. shrimp 10. crustacean, shrimp pink

pray... 3. ask, beg, sue 7. entreat, implore, request, worship 8. devotion 10. supplicate

praya... 4. bund, road 5. beach 6. strand

prayer... 3. ave 4. bead, bene, plea, suit 5. credo, grace, matin 6. litany, orison, vesper 7. request, worship 8. petition 12. intercession, supplication

prayer (pert to)...
book.. 4. ordo 6. missal 7. portass (portas) 8. breviary
call (Moham).. 4. azan (adan)
call tower.. 7. minaret
cloak.. 6. zizith (fringed) 7. tallith
evening.. 7. complin (compline) 9. night song
figure.. 5. orant
Incarnation.. 7. Angelus 11. Angelus Bell
liturgical.. 6. litany 7. complin
Lord's (prayer).. 11. Paternoster
morning.. 5. matin
nine days' devotional.. 6. novena
response.. 7. antiphon
short.. 5. grace
stick.. 4. paho

praying... 8. entreaty 9. precation 12. supplication

praying cricket... 6. mantis

praying figure... 5. orant

preach... 6. exhort 7. expound, lecture 8. advocate, homilize 9. discourse, sermonize

preacher... 6. parson, rector

preaching... 6. sermon 7. kerygma (kerugma) 10. preachment 11. exhortation

preaching friar... 9. Dominican

Preaching of Peter... 9. Apocrypha

preamble... 5. proem 7. preface, prelude 11. preliminary 12. introduction

prebellum... 7. antewar 12. before the war

prebend... 7. stipend 8. benefice 9. allowance

precarious... 7. assumed, dubious 8. insecure, unstable 9. hazardous, uncertain, unsettled 10. unreliable

preceded... 3. led 8. prefaced, was prior 9. anteceded, antedated 10. introduced, went before 13. had precedence, occurred first

precedence... 3. pas 4. lead, rank 8. priority 12. anteposition

precedent... 4. sign 5. model, usage 7. example, leading 8. anterior, decision, standard 10. antecedent, forerunner 11. going before

preceding others... 5. first 7. leading, ternary (by threes) 10. antecedent

precept... 4. rule, writ 5. adage, axiom, maxim, order, sutra (sutta), torah (tora) 6. belief 7. command 8. doctrine 9. direction 11. commandment, instruction

preceptor... 4. guru 5. guide, tutor 6. master, mentor, mullah, pundit 7. teacher 8. educator 10. instructor

precinct... 5. ambit, space 6. region 8. boundary, district, environs

precious... 4. dear, rare 5. great 6. costly, valued 7. beloved, elegant, perfect 8. complete, esteemed, overnice, valuable 9. downright 10. beloved one, fastidious, particular

precious (pert to)...
Blood (RCCh).. 5. Feast (July 1)
garnet.. 6. pyrope
stone.. 3. gem 4. opal, ruby 5. pearl, topaz 6. garnet, ligure 7. diamond, emerald, jacinth (Bib) 8. hyacinth, sapphire
stone, sometimes.. 7. cat's-eye 11. alexandrite

precipice... 4. crag, linn, pali 5. bluff, cliff 9. declivity

precipitancy... 5. haste 8. rashness

precipitation... 3. gel 4. fall, hail, mist, rain, snow 5. haste, sleet 8. downpour 9. hastening 11. prematurity 12. acceleration, condensation, recklessness

precipitous... 4. rash 5. hasty, steep 6. abrupt, sudden 7. rushing (headlong) 9. very rapid 11. precipitate

précis... 5. sketch 7. epitome, pandect, summary 8. abstract, synopsis 9. summarize

precise... 4. prim 5. exact 7. correct, literal, special 8. accurate, definite, detailed, overnice 10. meticulous,

overminute, particular, scrupulous
11. ceremonious, punctilious
preciseness... 9. exactness
10. strictness 12. definiteness
14. fastidiousness
precision... 6. nicety 8. accuracy
9. exactness, formality
11. preciseness 12. definiteness
preclude... 3. bar 4. omit, stop
5. avert, debar, estop 6. hinder,
impede 7. head off, prevent, shut
out 8. prohibit
precocious... 7. forward 8. advanced
9. premature
preconceive... 6. ideate, precox
7. presume 8. foreknow, prejudge
9. predecide 10. presuppose
predatory... 7. looting 9. marauding,
pillaging, piratical 10. plundering,
predaceous (predacious)
11. destructive
predatory bird... 3. owl 4. hawk, kite
6. falcon
predatory raid... 5. foray
predestine... 4. doom, fate 6. decree,
ordain 7. appoint 9. determine,
foretoken 10. foreordain
predetermine... 4. bias 7. destine
8. prejudge 9. prejudice, preordain
10. prepossess 11. premeditate
predicament... 3. fix 4. pass 5. state
6. plight, scrape 7. dilemma,
impasse 8. quandary 9. condition,
situation
predicator... 4. seer 5. friar
7. prophet 8. preacher 9. predicter
predict... 4. bode, dope, omen
7. foresee, portend, presage
8. forecast, foretell, prophecy
13. prognosticate
prediction... 6. augury 8. prophecy
9. foresight 10. foreboding
11. foretelling 15. prognostication
predilection... 4. bias 6. desire
8. tendency 9. prejudice
10. favoritism, partiality, preference,
propensity 11. disposition
13. preconception 14. predisposition
predominant... 5. chief 6. ruling
8. reigning, superior 9. hegemonic
11. controlling, influential,
outstanding
predominate... 5. excel 7. prevail
8. dominate 10. be superior
12. preponderate
pre-eminent... 3. top 4. only, star
5. chief 7. palmary, ranking
8. superior 9. excellent, principal
11. outstanding
pre-emption... 8. monopoly, purchase
10. prior right 13. appropriation
preen... 3. pin, sew 4. perk 5. clasp,
dress, groom, plume, primp
6. bodkin, brooch, stitch 9. make
sleek
preface... 5. front, proem 6. herald,
prayer 7. prelude, problem
8. exordium, foreword, preamble,
prologue 10. paraphrase
12. introduction
prefect, praefect... 4. dean (Jesuit)
6. chih fu 7. monitor, officer

8. director, minister, official
9. president 10. magistrate
prefecture... 7. eparchy
prefer... 5. elect, offer 6. choose,
select 7. outrank, present, proffer,
promote 8. be partial 12. give
priority
preference... 6. choice 8. favorite,
priority 9. advantage 10. favoritism
11. alternative, prior choice
12. predilection
prefiguration... 4. omen 9. foretoken,
prototype 12. typification
13. preindication
prefigure... 7. imagine, suggest
8. foretell 10. foreshadow
prefix for...
about.. 3. amb 4. peri
above.. 3. epi, sur 5. hyper, super,
supra
across.. 3. dia 4. tran 5. trans
again.. 2. re
against.. 4. anti
ahead.. 3. pre
all.. 4. omni
alongside.. 3. par 4. para
an.. 2. al
apart.. 2. se 3. dia, dis
appearing to.. 5. quasi
around.. 4. peri
away.. 3. aph, apo
back.. 2. re 3. ana
backward.. 5. retro
bad.. 3. dys, mal
badly.. 3. mis
beauty.. 5. calli (kalli)
before.. 2. ob 3. pre, pro 4. ante,
prae
beside.. 3. par 4. para
between.. 3. dia 4. meta 5. inter
black.. 4. atra
blood.. 4. haem, hemo
bone.. 4. oste 5. osteo
both.. 4. ambi
Chinese.. 4. sino 5. chino
clear.. 4. delo
dawn.. 2. eo
difficult.. 3. dys
distant.. 3. tel 4. tele
double.. 2. di
down.. 2. de 4. cata
earnest.. 5. serio
earth.. 3. geo
eight.. 3. oct 4. octa, octo
equal.. 3. iso
equally.. 4. equi
evil.. 3. mal
far.. 3. tel 4. tele
faulty.. 3. mis
fictitious.. 6. pseudo
fire.. 3. pyr
for.. 3. pro
former.. 2. ex
four.. 5. tetra
from.. 2. ab, de, ec
from away.. 3. apo
gas.. 4. aero
good.. 2. eu
half.. 4. demi, hemi, semi
hard.. 3. dys 6. stereo
ill.. 3. mal, mis
in, into.. 2. en

lizard.. 5. saura, sauro
many.. 4. mult, poly 5. multi
modern.. 3. neo
mountain.. 3. oro
nail.. 4. helo
negative.. 2. il, ir, un 3. mon
new.. 3. neo
not.. 2. il, im, ir, un 3. non
numerical.. 3. uni
one.. 3. uni 4. mono
out of, outer.. 2. ec, ex 3. ect, exo 4. ecto
over.. 3. epi, sur 5. super, supra
possession.. 3. ose
pray.. 3. ora
priority.. 3. pre
recent.. 3. neo
release.. 2. un
reversed.. 2. di
same, equal.. 3. iso 4. equi, homo
separation.. 2. di 3. dis
shoulder.. 6. humero
single.. 3. mono
son of.. 3. Mac
ten.. 3. dec 4. deca
this side of.. 3. cis
three, thrice.. 3. ter, tri 4. tris
through.. 3. dia, per
to.. 2. ap
together.. 3. com, con, cor, syn
toward.. 2. ob, oc
turning.. 4. roto
twice.. 2. bi, di
twofold.. 2. bi, di 3. dua
under.. 3. sub
upon.. 2. ep 3. epi
upward.. 3. ana, ano
very much.. 3. eri
well.. 2. eu
with.. 3. col, com, pro, syl, syn
within.. 3. eso 4. endo 5. intra
without.. 2. se 3. ect 4. ecto
wood.. 4. xylo
wrong.. 3. mis
pregnancy... 6. cyesis 10. cyesiology
prehistoric (pert to)...
animal.. 6. reptile 8. dinosaur, mastodon 9. phytosaur
continent.. 8. Atlantis (Atlantis)
man.. 4. cave, Dawn 11. lake dweller
ref to.. 9. primitive
tool.. 6. eolith
prejudiced... 6. biased 7. partial 8. partisan 11. opinionated 12. prepossessed
prejudicial... 9. injurious 11. detrimental 15. disadvantageous
prelate... 4. head, pope 5. abbot, chief 6. bishop, priest 7. primate, red–blue 8. minister, superior 9. Monsignor (Monsignore)
prelector, praelector... 6. reader 7. teacher 9. lecturer 12. professor
preliminary... 5. prior 7. preface, prelude 8. entrance, previous, proemial 9. precedent, prefatory, threshold 10. antecedent 11. preparatory 12. introduction, introductory
preliminary memo... 8. protocol
preliminary plan... 4. idea
prelude... 5. proem 6. verset

7. preface 8. overture, ritornel (ritornelle)
premature... 6. infant 8. too early, untimely 10. precocious
premier... 3. bet (gambling) 5. chief 7. leading 8. earliest 9. principal 13. prime minister
premiere... 4. show 10. first night 12. presentation 16. first performance
premium... 4. agio 5. bonus, prize, stake 6. reward 8. gratuity, interest 10. recompense
premonition... 5. hunch 6. notice 7. warning 8. forecast 10. foreboding 11. forewarning, information 12. presentiment
preoccupied... 4. lost 6. absent, filled 8. absorbed, observed 9. engrossed 10. abstracted, pre–engaged 13. lost in thought
preparation... 8. training 9. equipment, study hour 10. groundwork 11. making ready 12. introduction
preparation (pert to)...
of a dress.. 7. fitting
place.. 10. laboratory, paratorium
sugar, for candy.. 7. fondant
without.. 5. ad lib 9. impromptu
prepare... 3. fit, fix, get 4. cook, gird, make, pave, yark 5. adapt, equip, ready, train 6. adjust 7. arrange
prepare (pert to)...
by boiling.. 6. decoct
for golf game.. 3. tee
for melting glass.. 4. frit
for publication.. 4. edit
for seasoning.. 8. marinate
skins.. 3. taw
prepared... 5. armed, ready 7. adapted, groomed, skilled, trained 8. equipped, provided
prepared instruction... 13. propaedeutics
preponderance... 6. weight 8. dominion, majority 9. influence 11. outweighing, superiority
prepose... 6. prefix 7. preface 11. place before
preposition... 2. at, by, ex, in, of, on, to, up 3. off, out, tae 4. into, onto, over, unto, upon, with
prepossession... 4. bent, bias 9. obsession, prejudice 10. preference 11. inclination 12. predilection 13. appropriation, preconception 14. predisposition
presage... 4. bode, omen, osse, sign 5. token 6. augury, betide, divine 7. portend, predict 8. forebode, foretell 10. prediction, prognostic 11. preindicate 13. foreknowledge
presager... 7. prophet 9. foreboder
presbytery... 6. church, clergy 7. council 8. ministry 9. parsonage 10. presbyters
prescribe... 3. set 5. allot, guide, limit, order 6. advise, bestow, direct, ordain 7. control, dictate 9. designate
presence... 4. mien, port 7. bearing, posture, specter 8. phantasm

9. existence, proximity 10. apparition, appearance, attendance
11. personality
present... 3. now 4. boon, gift, give
5. grant, nonce, offer 6. bestow, bounty, donate 7. largess (largesse)
8. donation, gratuity 9. introduce
11. benefaction
present (pert to)...
for acceptance.. 6. tender
pupil to teacher.. 8. minerval
time.. 3. now 5. nonce, today
7. current
to customers.. 6. trifle 9. lagniappe (lagnappe)
to foreign ambassador.. 6. xenium
presentation... 4. gift, plan 5. debut, offer 7. present 8. bestowal, donation, offering 10. appearance, exhibition 12. introduction
14. representation
presently... 4. anon, soon 6. at once
7. shortly 9. forthwith 10. before long 11. immediately
preservation... 6. saving 9. retention, safeguard 10. protection
11. maintenance, safekeeping
12. conservation, perpetuation
preservative... 4. salt 5. spice
7. alcohol, vinegar 10. protective
14. sodium benzoate
preserve... 3. can, jam, tin 4. corn, cure, keep, salt, save 5. guard, jelly, spare, store 6. defend, pickle, retain, secure, shield, uphold 7. compote, protect, sustain 8. conserve, maintain
9. safeguard
preserve (pert to)...
by drying.. 9. desiccate
fruit.. 7. compote
grape.. 5. uvate (conserve)
in brine.. 4. corn, cure, salt
in oil.. 8. marinate
president... 4. head 5. ruler
8. governor 9. sovereign
President (US)... 4. Ford, Polk, Taft
5. Adams (John), Adams (John Q), Grant, Hayes, Nixon, Tyler 6. Arthur (Chester), Hoover, Monroe, Pierce, Taylor, Truman, Wilson 7. Harding, Jackson, Johnson (Andrew), Johnson (L B), Kennedy, Lincoln, Madison
8. Buchanan, Coolidge, Fillmore, Garfield, Harrison (Benj), Harrison (Wm Henry), McKinley, Van Buren
9. Cleveland, Jefferson, Roosevelt (Theo), Roosevelt (F D)
10. Eisenhower, Washington
presidente... 5. mayor 7. headman
press... 3. dun 4. cram, iron, urge
5. crowd, force, wedge 6. compel, hasten, smooth, throng, thrust
7. impress, squeeze 8. compress, condense, insist on 9. extractor, importune 10. compulsion, journalism
12. conscription
press (pert to)...
ancient.. 6. Aldine
bookbinder.. 7. smasher
corrector.. 11. proofreader
critic.. 6. censor

forward.. 5. drive
ranks.. 5. serry
pressed (pert to)...
amber.. 8. amberoid
cheese.. 7. cheddar
grapes, residue.. 4. marc (mark)
into a mass.. 7. kneaded
together.. 5. dense 6. mashed
7. compact, crowded, serried
pressing... 6. urgent, urging 7. exigent
9. insistent 10. compelling, extraction, motivating 11. importunity
pressing need... 8. exigency
pressure... 4. urge 5. force 6. compel, stress, weight 7. squeeze, urgency
8. exigency, instancy 9. authority, influence 10. compulsion, constraint
11. compression
pressure (pert to)...
barometer.. 7. mesobar
boiler, cooker.. 9. autoclave
instrument (for liquids).. 9. manometer
10. piezometer 11. Bourdon tube
of necessity.. 7. urgency
resisting.. 8. renitent
unit.. 5. barad
yard.. 16. Old Newgate Prison (London)
prestidigitation... 8. juggling
11. legerdemain 13. sleight of hand
prestige... 4. bias, face, sway 5. éclat
6. renown, repute 7. sorcery
8. illusion 9. authority, deception, influence 10. importance
11. superiority
presto... 5. magic 7. command, passing, quickly 8. suddenly
9. instantly 10. rapid tempo
11. immediately 13. instantaneous
presumably... 7. no doubt 8. probably
10. ostensibly, supposedly
presume... 4. dare, hope 5. imply, judge, think 6. assure, impose
7. suppose, venture 10. presuppose
11. preconceive 14. take for granted
presumption... 4. hope 6. daring
7. opinion 8. audacity 9. arrogance, impudence, insolence 10. effrontery
11. implication, probability, supposition
presumptive... 5. brash 7. assumed, Icarian 8. arrogant, probable
10. evidential
presumptuous... 5. undue 7. forward, haughty 8. arrogant, insolent
9. foolhardy 11. venturesome
pretend... 3. act, aim 4. fake, sham
5. claim, feign, feint 6. affect, allege, assume, pose as 7. presume, pretext, profess 8. disguise, simulate
11. impersonate, make believe
pretended... 4. sham 7. alleged
8. affected, intended, proposed, so-called 10. ostensible
pretended omission (Rhet)...
9. apophasis 11. paraleipsis (paralepsis)
pretender... 4. idol, snob 5. cowan, quack 6. seemer 7. Aeolist (Eolist)
8. claimant, impostor 9. charlatan
10. mountebank 11. four-flusher
pretense, pretence... 3. act 4. flam,

ruse, sham, show 5. claim, cloak,
cover, feint, horse, study 6. excuse,
tinsel 7. pretext 8. artifice, stalking
10. appearance, masquerade,
subterfuge 11. affectation, fabrication,
ostentation

pretentious... 4. arty 5. showy
6. rococo 7. elegant, pompous
8. affected, boastful 9. high–flown
12. ostentatious 13. grandiloquent

pretentious words, use of...
9. bombastic 10. lexiphanic

pretermit... 4. omit 6. pass by
7. neglect, suspend 8. intermit, pass
over 9. interrupt

pretext... 4. flam, plea 5. cloak, cover,
trick 6. excuse 8. pretense (pretence)
9. deception, semblance

pretty... 3. toy 4. cute, fair, joli, very
5. bonny (bonnie) 6. clever, comely,
lovely, rather 7. dollish, finical,
foppish 8. handsome 9. ingenious,
tolerably 10. attractive, knickknack
11. good–looking, interesting
15. pulchritudinous

prevail... 3. win 5. exist 6. induce,
subdue 7. succeed, triumph
8. dominate, frequent 9. prevalent
11. predominate

prevailed... 3. got, won 5. urged
9. succeeded, triumphed

prevailing... 4. rife 5. chief, usual
6. common 7. current, general
8. abundant, dominant 9. prevalent
10. widespread 11. predominant

prevail upon... 4. urge 6. induce
8. persuade

prevalent... 4. rife 6. potent
7. current 8. dominant, powerful
9. extensive 10. prevailing,
successful, victorious, widespread
11. efficacious, influential

prevaricate... 3. lie 5. evade
7. deviate, quibble, shuffle

prevene... 7. prevent 9. forestall
10. anticipate

prevent... 4. warn 5. avert, debar,
deter, estop 7. ward off 8. preclude
9. forestall, frustrate 10. circumvent

preventative, preventive... 8. antidote
9. deterrent 12. prophylactic

previous... 4. past 5. prior 6. before,
former 7. earlier 8. untimely
9. foregoing, preceding, premature
11. unwarranted

previously... 4. erst 6. before
7. earlier 8. formerly 9. aforesaid
10. heretofore

prey... 3. rob 5. booty, spoil
6. quarry, victim 7. plunder

prey (to seize)... 9. raptorial

prey upon... 3. eat 4. feed 5. ravin
(raven) 7. plunder, torment
9. predacity

Priam (pert to)...
daughter.. 8. Polyxena 9. Cassandra
grandfather.. 4. Ilus
King of.. 4. Troy
servant.. 7. Agelaus
son.. 5. Paris 6. Hector 7. Troilus
wife.. 6. Hecuba

price... 3. sum 4. cost, fare, odds,

rate 5. offer, value, worth 6. charge
7. expense 10. estimation,
excellence, recompense
12. preciousness

priceless... 7. amusing 8. precious
10. high–priced, invaluable, not
salable

prick... 4. goad, pain, pang 5. sting,
wound 6. pierce 7. prickle, remorse
8. distress

pricked... 6. dotted, pinked 7. pointed
9. punctured

prickle... 4. burr, prod, seta 5. spike,
thorn 6. pierce, tingle 7. acantha
8. stinging

prickly... 6. tingly 7. pointed
8. echinate

prickly (pert to)...
flower.. 4. burr
pear.. 4. tuna 5. nopal 6. cactus
7. Opuntia
plant.. 3. ash 5. briar, elder 6. teasel
7. juniper, lettuce, thistle
12. Hercules'–club

pride... 6. vanity 7. conceit, egotism
9. arrogance, proudness
11. self–respect

priest... 3. Eli, fra 4. abbé, curé,
lama, père 5. clerk, druid, padre
6. cleric, father 7. prester
9. oratorian

priest (pert to)...
assistant.. 7. acolyte
Brit order (anc).. 5. Druid
cap.. 5. miter (mitre) 7. biretta
collar.. 5. amice, stole
fish.. 8. rockfish
mantle.. 4. cope
newly ordained.. 9. priesteen
priest–in–the–pulpit.. 10. cuckoopint
relating to.. 10. sacerdotal
tribe (Israel).. 4. Levi
vestment.. 3. alb 5. ephod
8. scapular

priestly caste... 4. Magi 7. wise men

prig... 3. beg, fog, pan 4. buck, snob
5. dandy, filch, plead, prink, prude,
steal, thief 6. haggle, pilfer, purist,
tinker 7. bargain, entreat, pitcher
8. pilferer

priggish, prim... 7. prudish
8. snobbish, thievish

prim... 4. fish, neat, smug 5. primp,
smelt 6. demure, formal 7. precise,
prudish 8. decorous

prima donna... 4. diva 6. singer

prima facie... 7. at sight 9. first view
10. apparently

primal... 5. basic, chief, first
7. primary 8. original 9. elemental,
primitive

primary... 5. basic, color, first
6. primal 7. initial 8. election,
primeval, pristine 9. elemental,
essential, firsthand, primitive, principal
10. elementary 11. fundamental

primary (pert to)...
armament.. 6. cannon
circles.. 7. equator, horizon
8. ecliptic, galactic
colors.. 3. red 4. blue 6. yellow

primate, bishop... 10. Archbishop

Primates (Order of)... 3. ape, man
5. lemur 6. mammal, monkey
8. marmoset 9. orangutan
(orangoutang)
prime... 4. best, dawn 5. first, paint
7. primary, the best 8. original,
primeval 9. primitive
prime minister... 7. premier
primer... 5. paint 8. hornbook,
textbook, type size 9. detonator
10. battledore
primeval... 6. primal 7. primary
8. original, pristine
primeval deity... 5. Titan
primitive... 5. basic, first 6. embryo,
native, quaint 7. ancient, priscan
8. pristine 10. aboriginal, antiquated
11. fundamental
primitive (pert to)...
area.. 5. Idaho 8. Colorado
art objects.. 9. artifacts
group.. 6. ethnos
self.. 2. id 8. instinct
primness... 8. neatness, niceness
9. stiffness 11. preciseness
primo... 5. chief, first 12. leading
tenor
primordial... 7. primary 8. original
9. elemental, primitive 10. prototypal
11. rudimentary 12. first created
primrose (pert to)...
called.. 10. an innocent 13. flower of
youth
color.. 6. yellow 10. snapdragon
genus.. 7. Primula 11. Primulaceae
green.. 5. color
League.. 13. Conservatives (Eng)
path.. 7. sensual
prince... 4. knez 5. prinz 7. dynasty,
monarch 8. archduke 9. potentate,
princekin, sovereign 10. princeling
prince (pert to)...
Albert.. 9. frock coat
allowance.. 8. appenage
petty.. 6. satrap
princely... 5. noble, regal, royal
6. kingly 10. munificent
11. magnificent
princely Italian family... 4. Este
Prince of...
Afghanistan.. 4. amir
apostate angels.. 5. Eblis
Apostles.. 6. St Paul 7. St Peter
darkness.. 5. devil, Satan 7. Ahriman
demons.. 5. devil 9. Beelzebub
destruction.. 9. Tamerlane
evil spirits.. 7. Sammael
liars.. 5. Pinto
Peace.. 7. Messiah 11. Jesus Christ
Spanish poetry.. 4. Vega
the Church.. 8. cardinal
the ode.. 7. Ronsard
the sonnet.. 6. Bellay 15. Joachim du
Bellay
this world (Bib).. 5. Satan
Tunis.. 3. bey
princess (pert to)...
literally.. 5. Sarah
loved by Cupid.. 6. Psyche
loved by Zeus.. 6. Europa
Mohammed.. 5. begum
mythical.. 5. Danae 8. Atalanta

royal.. 14. eldest daughter
Tyrian.. 4. Dido (Elissa)
principal... 3. top 4. arch, head, main
5. chief, major, prime 6. Führer,
leader, master, origin, source
7. captain, leading, palmary, primary
8. foremost 9. important, organ
stop, preceptor 10. capital sum
11. outstanding
principality... 6. Monaco
principal meal (Rom)... 4. cena
principle... 4. rule 5. axiom, canon,
prana, tenet 6. dictum 7. precept,
theorem 9. essential 10. foundation
principle (pert to)...
active in tobacco.. 8. nicotine
distance.. 11. perspective
Hindu.. 5. Sakti
life, theosophy.. 5. prana, tenet
musical.. 8. tonality
vital.. 4. soul 5. anima
principles... 5. creed 9. generalia
10. essentials 12. generalities
princox, princock... 7. coxcomb
9. pert youth
prink... 4. deck, wink 5. adorn, preen,
primp 6. bedeck, glance 7. dress up
print... 5. stamp 7. edition, engrave,
impress, picture, publish
11. indentation
printed (pert to)...
defamation.. 5. libel
fabric.. 4. silk 6. calico 7. percale
sheets.. 8. pamphlet
printer... 8. pressman 9. publisher
11. typographer 12. lithographer
printer (pert to)...
aid.. 5. devil 10. apprentice
dauber.. 5. biron
direction.. 4. stet
hand ink roller.. 6. brayer
ink pad.. 6. dabber
manuscript.. 4. copy
mark.. 4. dash, stet 5. caret, serif,
tilde 8. asterisk
measure.. 2. em, en 4. pica
type, mixed.. 3. pie (pi)
printing (pert to)...
blur.. 6. mackle, macule
cylinder.. 6. rounce
error.. 7. erratum
form.. 3. die
for the blind.. 7. braille
mark.. 4. dele 6. diesis 8. ellipsis
measure.. 2. em, en 5. agate
metal block.. 4. quad
press part.. 6. platen, rounce
7. frisket
prion... 6. petrel 7. sea bird
prior... 3. ere 4. fore, past 6. before,
former 8. previous, priorate
9. preceding 10. antecedent
priority... 10. precedence 11. order of
time
priory... 5. abbey 8. cloister
priscan... 9. primitive
Priscian... 7. grammar 10. grammarian
Priscilla (pert to)...
Bib.. 16. Christian convert
color.. 7. fog blue
Hist.. 7. Puritan
husband.. 9. John Alden

tale.. 24. Courtship of Miles Standish
prism (optical device)... 5. Porro
prismatic... 10. iridescent, variegated
prison... 3. jug 4. brig, gaol, jail,
keep, quod 5. clink 6. carcer
10. guardhouse 12. penitentiary
prison (pert to)...
courtyard.. 4. quad
English (old).. 7. Newgate 9. Bridewell
French.. 8. Bastille
German university.. 6. Carcer
guarded.. 10. panopticon
keeper.. 5. guard 6. gaoler, jailer,
keeper, warden 7. turnkey
slang.. 3. jug 4. quod, rock 5. clink,
limbo 6. cooler 8. big house,
hoosegow
spy.. 6. mouton
Prisoner of...
Chillon.. 16. François Bonivard
Vatican.. 4. Pope
Zenda.. 5. novel (by Anthony Hope)
prisoner's release... 6. parole
pristine... 7. primary 8. original
9. primitive
prittle–prattle... 7. chatter, prattle
8. chitchat 9. chatterer, empty talk
privacy... 7. privity, retreat, secrecy
8. solitude 9. seclusion
private... 5. privy 6. covert, secret
7. one's own 8. esoteric, personal,
secluded, separate, solitary
11. sequestered 12. confidential
15. uncommunicative
privateer... 4. Kidd (Capt) 5. caper
6. pirate 7. corsair, soldier (not
enlisted)
privately... 5. aside 6. secret 8. in
secret 10. personally, unofficial
12. unofficially
privation... 4. loss, want 6. misery
7. poverty 8. hardship
10. divestment 11. destitution
privilege... 3. soc, use 5. favor, right
7. charter 8. easement 9. advantage
10. concession
privileged... 6. exempt 8. licensed
prix... 5. prize
prize... 3. cup 5. award, booty, Detur
(Harvard), medal, plate, price, purse,
stake, value 6. assess, esteem,
trophy 7. premium, respect
8. treasure
prizefight... 2. go 4. bout, spar
6. boxing 7. contest 8. pugilism
10. fisticuffs
pro... 3. aye, for 6. before 8. behalf
of 9. in front of 12. professional
probability... 4. odds 6. chance
7. vantage 9. liability 10. conclusion,
good chance, likelihood, likeliness
11. credibility
probe... 3. dig 4. prod, tent 5. sound
6. feeler, pierce, search, stylet
7. examine, explore, feel out, inquiry
10. instrument, scrutinize
11. probationer
probity... 6. virtue 7. honesty
9. integrity, rectitude 11. uprightness
problem... 3. nut 4. crux, knot
6. enigma, riddle 7. theorem
8. question 9. situation

pro bono publico... 16. for the public
good
proboscis... 4. nose 5. snout, trunk
proboscis monkey... 7. nose ape
procaccia... 4. cart (carrier's) 7. carrier
procacious... 4. pert 8. insolent,
petulant
procacity... 8. pertness 9. insolence,
petulance
Procavis... 4. cony 5. hyrax 6. rabbit
procedure... 4. step 5. order
6. custom, method, policy, system
7. process 8. behavior
11. continuance
proceed... 2. go 4. fare, move, pass,
wend 5. arise, issue 6. derive
7. emanate 8. continue, progress
9. originate
proceed (pert to)...
hastily.. 5. speed
leisurely.. 5. mosey (mosy)
on one's way.. 4. wend
rapidly.. 6. gallop
proceeding... 4. step 5. actum
6. course 7. conduct, measure,
process 8. activity, behavior
9. procedure 11. transaction
proceeding (pert to)...
by threes.. 7. ternary
from earth.. 8. telluric
from the sun.. 5. polar
proceedings... 4. acta 5. trial
6. doings 7. affairs, lawsuit, minutes
8. activity
proceeds... 4. gain, goes 6. income
7. marches, profits, returns
procerity... 6. height 8. tallness
process... 4. cook, writ 5. lapse (of
time), order 6. course, notice
7. advance, mandate, summons
8. progress 9. emanation, operation,
outgrowth, procedure, sterilize
process (pert to)...
beak (small).. 9. rostrulum
electroplating, steeling.. 8. acierage
fabric coloring.. 5. batik
fish (winglike).. 3. fin
growth food.. 9. nutrition
in organisms.. 6. miosis
of development.. 7. nascent
pointed.. 3. awn
steel–making.. 8. Bessemer
11. cementation
surveying.. 13. triangulation
transferring pictures..
12. decalcomania
procession... 4. file 5. train 6. parade
7. cortege 8. sequence 9. formation
prochein, prochain... 4. next
7. nearest
proclaim... 4. tout 5. blaze, voice
6. herald 7. declare, enounce,
presage, publish 8. announce
10. promulgate
proclamation... 5. bando, banns
(bans), blaze, edict, ukase 6. decree,
notice 12. announcement,
promulgation
proclivity... 4. bent 6. desire
7. leaning 8. tendency
10. propensity 11. disposition,
inclination

procrastinate... 5. defer, delay, stall
    7. soldier 8. postpone
procrastination... 5. delay, stall
    7. laxness 10. hesitation
    11. vacillation 12. dilatoriness
procrastinator... 7. delayer, trifler
    8. deferrer
procreant... 8. fruitful 9. producing
    10. generating 11. propagative
Procrustes (Gr legend)...
    10. highwayman (Attica)
    14. Procrustean bed
procurator... 5. agent 6. lawyer
    7. proctor, steward
procure... 3. get 4. gain 5. bring,
    fetch 6. effect, elicit, induce, obtain
    7. acquire 8. contrive, purchase
prod... 3. egg, jab 4. goad, poke,
    urge 6. thrust
prodigal... 4. cloy 6. lavish 7. spender
    9. plentiful 10. squanderer
    11. extravagant, intemperate,
    spendthrift, squandering
prodigality... 5. waste 9. abundance
    12. extravagance, intemperance
    13. superabundant
prodigious... 4. huge 5. great
    7. amazing, immense 8. enormous
    9. marvelous, monstrous, wonderful
    10. miraculous, portentous,
    tremendous 11. astonishing
    13. extraordinary
prodigy... 4. omen, sign 6. genius,
    marvel, oddity, wonder 7. miracle
prodition... 7. treason 8. betrayal
produce... 2. do 4. bear, make, show,
    wage 5. carry, cause, stage, yield
    6. author, create, effect 7. exhibit,
    product 8. engender, generate,
    receipts 10. originate 10. accomplish
    11. merchandise
produce (pert to)...
    copy of.. 4. type
    effect.. 3. act
    ideas.. 6. ideate
    noise.. 5. sound
produced... 8. extended 9. elongated,
    prolonged
produced (pert to)...
    by heat.. 7. igneous 8. volcanic
    by kitchen gardens.. 7. olitory
    8. potherbs
    by wind.. 7. aeolian
    regularly.. 6. staple
producer... 4. doer 6. farmer, parent
    7. creator 10. theaterman
    12. manufacturer
producing (pert to)...
    cold.. 7. algific
    fire.. 8. sparking
    illusions.. 15. phantasmagorial
    poison.. 6. septic
product... 3. sum 4. crop 5. fruit
    6. result 7. hormone 8. artifact,
    creation 9. commodity, outgrowth
production... 3. hit 4. book, work
    5. fruit 7. produce 8. creation
    9. execution, extension
    14. accomplishment
productive... 4. rich 7. fertile, gainful
    8. creative, fruitful 9. inventive
    10. generative

proem... 7. preface, prelude
    8. foreword, preamble
    12. introduction
profane... 6. misuse, unholy, wicked
    7. godless, impious, ungodly, worldly
    8. temporal 9. desecrate
    10. unhallowed 11. blasphemous,
    unspiritual 12. unsanctified
profess... 4. avow 5. claim, feign
    6. affirm, allege 7. declare
    11. acknowledge
profession... 5. claim, faith, trade
    6. avowal, career, metier 7. calling,
    pretext 8. vocation 9. testimony
    10. occupation 11. affirmation
    14. acknowledgment
professional... 4. paid 5. hired
    6. expert 7. skilled, trained
    8. finished
professional, non... 3. lay 4. laic
    7. amateur 9. unskilled
proffer... 3. bid 4. give 5. offer
    6. tender
proficient... 3. apt 5. adept 6. expert,
    versed 7. skilled 12. accomplished
profile... 4. draw, form 7. contour,
    diagram, outline, picture 9. biography
    14. representation
profit... 3. net 4. boot, gain, good,
    mend 5. avail 6. return 7. benefit,
    rake–off, results 8. interest
    9. advantage 11. share of gain
    12. remuneration
profitable... 6. paying, useful
    7. helpful 8. repaying 9. expedient,
    lucrative 10. beneficial
    12. remunerative
profligate... 6. wicked 7. corrupt,
    spender, vicious 8. depraved,
    prodigal, wasteful 9. abandoned,
    dissolute, reprobate 10. overthrown
    11. extravagant
profound... 4. deep, wise 5. heavy
    7. abysmal, intense, learned
    8. abstruse, complete, deep–felt,
    poignant 9. downright, recondite,
    sagacious 11. far–reaching
    12. encompassing, unfathomable
    13. thoroughgoing
profundity... 5. depth 6. wisdom
    9. deepness 12. abstruseness
profuse... 6. galore, lavish 7. diffuse,
    liberal, palaver 8. abundant,
    generous, numerous, prodigal,
    wasteful 9. bountiful 10. munificent
    11. extravagant, overflowing
profusion... 6. plenty 9. abundance
    11. diffuseness, prodigality
    12. extravagance, lavish supply
progenitor... 4. sire 6. parent
    8. ancestor 9. precursor
    10. forefather
progenitor of giants (Norse Myth)...
    4. Ymir 8. rime–cold
progeny... 3. son 4. race 5. issue
    6. family 7. outcome 8. children,
    daughter, outbirth 9. offspring,
    parentage, resultant 11. descendants
prognosis... 7. outlook 8. forecast
    9. diagnosis 10. prediction
    14. interpretation
prognosticate... 4. bode, omen

7. betoken, predict, presage
8. forebode, foreshow, foretell,
prophecy 9. foretoken

program, programme... 4. bill
(printed), card, plan 5. edict
6. notice, policy 7. outline
8. bulletin, platform, schedule,
syllabus 9. broadcast, catalogue,
programma 10. prospectus
12. proclamation, prolegomenon
13. advertisement

programma... 5. edict 6. decree,
notice 7. preface 12. prolegomenon

progress... 4. fare, tour, wend
5. march 6. course, travel
7. advance, journey 10. expedition
11. progression

progress (pert to)...
chart.. 5. Gantt
clumsily.. 8. scramble
intelligently.. 6. egress 7. telesis
(telesia)
laborious.. 4. plod, wade
outward.. 6. egress
weakly.. 6. feebly

progressive... 6. modern, onward
7. forward, gradual, liberal
9. advancing, improving
11. consecutive 12. enterprising

prohibit... 3. ban, bar, bid 5. debar,
estop, taboo (tabu) 6. enjoin, forbid,
hinder 7. prevent 9. interdict

prohibited... 7. illegal, illicit
8. unlawful

prohibition... 3. ban 7. embargo
8. estoppel 9. exclusion
10. prevention, temperance
11. forbiddance 12. interdicting

project... 3. jet, jut 4. abut, cast,
idea, plan 5. shoot 6. beetle,
design, device, scheme 7. pattern,
problem 8. contrive, proposal,
protrude 9. intention 10. conception
11. undertaking

projectile... 4. bomb 5. shell 6. bullet,
rocket 7. missile, torpedo
8. parabola 9. cartridge

projection... 3. arm, ear, fin, jag, toe
4. barb, cape, lobe, ness, prop,
snag 5. apsis, bulge, ledge, prong,
redan, socle, tenon 6. lobule, tappet
8. headland

projet... 4. plan 6. design

prolific... 6. fecund 7. fertile, teeming
8. fruitful 9. inventive 10. generative
11. propagative 12. reproductive

prolix... 5. wordy 7. diffuse, verbose
8. tiresome 9. prolonged, rigmarole,
wearisome 10. long–winded,
pleonastic, protracted

prolocutor... 6. orator 7. speaker,
teacher 8. chairman 9. spokesman
10. mouthpiece 11. Lord Speaker
(Eng)

prolong... 4. spin 7. draw out
8. continue, lengthen, postpone,
protract

prolonged... 7. chronic, delayed
8. extended 9. continued, postponed
10. lengthened, protracted

promenade... 4. mall, walk 6. airing,
marina, pasear 7. alameda, gallery

Prometheus (pert to)...
famed as.. 5. Titan (a)
poem (Shelley).. 17. Prometheus
Unbound
tale, tragedy.. 15. Prometheus Bound
16. Prometheus Loosed
24. Prometheus the Fire Bringer

prominence... 4. cusp 6. height
8. eminence, prestige, salience
9. greatness 10. famousness,
importance 11. distinction,
obviousness, prosiliency
12. distinctness, protuberance

prominent... 4. high, star 5. great
6. famous, marked 7. obvious,
salient 8. distinct, manifest
9. important 10. celebrated,
noticeable, prosilient, protruding
11. conspicuous, distinctive,
outstanding 13. distinguished

promiscuous... 5. mixed 8. careless
9. haphazard, orderless
14. indiscriminate

promise... 3. vow 4. hope, oath
5. swear 6. engage, parole, pledge,
plight, votive (by vow) 7. betroth,
predict 8. affiance, contract, give
hope 9. assurance, ray of hope
11. declaration

Promised Land... 6. heaven, utopia
8. Paradise 9. millenium, Shangri–La
11. Happy Valley 13. Celestial City

promontory... 3. tor 4. cape, naze
(nase), ness, scaw 5. mount, point
8. headland 10. projection

promote... 4. help 5. exalt, nurse
6. extend, prefer 7. actuate,
advance, dignify, elevate, finance,
further, improve 8. increase
9. advertise, encourage, patronize

promoter... 5. agent 6. backer
7. planner 8. lobbyist 9. financier,
publicist

promotion... 6. brevet 7. advance
10. preferment 11. advertising,
furtherance, improvement

prompt... 3. cue 4. easy, hint, soon,
tell, yare (anc) 5. alert, early, quick,
ready 6. advise, remind 7. animate,
suggest 8. punctual 11. expeditious

prompter... 3. aid 4. cuer 6. pit man,
reader 7. inducer, reciter 8. reminder

promptly... 4. tite (anc) 6. at once
7. quickly 9. willingly

promulgate... 7. declare, publish
8. proclaim 9. make known

prone... 3. apt 4. bent, flat 5. apish
6. supine 7. willing 8. downward
9. prostrate, recumbent
13. ventricumbent

prone to sin... 8. peccable

prong... 3. nib, peg 4. fang, fork, tine
5. spike, tooth 6. branch

pronghorn... 6. cabree (cabrie)
9. prong buck, springbok

prong key... 7. spanner

pronoun... 2. he, it, me, my, us, we,
ye 3. her, him, one, she, thy, who,
you 4. that, thee, them, they, thou,
what, your 5. these, those 6. itself,
myself 7. herself, himself, oneself,
ourself 8. one's self, yourself

9. ourselves 10. themselves
pronoun (possessive)... 2. my 3. her,
his, its, our 4. hers, mine, one's,
ours, your 5. their, yours 6. theirs
pronounce... 3. say 5. bless (holy),
speak, utter 6. affirm, assert
7. adjudge, declare, deliver
8. announce 9. enunciate
10. adjudicate, articulate, assibilate
pronouncement... 6. decree
8. judgment 9. manifesto
11. affirmation, declaration
12. announcement
pronto... 5. quick 7. quickly
8. promptly 11. immediately
pronunciation... 4. burr 8. orthoepy
9. utterance (clear) 11. enunciation
pronunciation mark... 5. tilde
7. cedilla 8. dieresis
proof... 4. test 5. trial 6. result
7. outcome 8. evidence 9. testimony
11. galley proof 12. confirmation,
verification 13. certification
proofreader's mark... 4. dele, stet
5. caret, space
prop... 3. beg, gib, nog 5. brace,
shore, sprag, staff, stell 6. shorer
7. fulcrum, support 9. stanchion
propagate... 5. breed 6. extend,
spread 7. diffuse, publish
8. disperse, engender, generate,
increase, multiply, transmit
propel... 3. row 4. pole, push, urge
5. drive, impel 7. project
propeller... 3. fan, gun, oar 4. vane
5. screw 6. driver 9. plane part
propensity... 4. bent 6. desire
7. leaning 8. aptitude, tendency
9. proneness 10. proclivity
11. disposition, inclination
proper... 3. fit 4. fine, just, meet,
prim, smug 5. exact, right 6. chaste,
decent, goodly, honest, kilter
7. correct 8. decorous, inherent,
orthodox, suitable 9. excellent,
expedient 11. appropriate,
grammatical, respectable
12. conventional
properly... 5. fitly 7. rightly, utterly
8. decently, strictly, suitably
9. correctly 11. expediently
14. conventionally
proper sense of worth... 5. pride
property... 3. res 4. bona, gear
5. asset, goods, trait 6. estate,
nature, realty, wealth 8. holdings
9. attribute, copyright, ownership
10. real estate 11. peculiarity,
possessions 14. characteristic
property (pert to)...
act to regain.. 8. replevin (repleven)
destruction of.. 8. sabotage
9. vandalism
landed property.. 9. cadastral
light without heat..
15. phosphorescence
movable.. 4. gear 8. chattels
no private ownership..
11. aspheterism
of matter.. 7. inertia
one's own.. 7. alodium
right.. 4. lien

stolen.. 4. loot, pelf 5. lucre, spoil
suit for recovery.. 6. trover
transferrer.. 7. alienor, grantor
wife to husband.. 3. dos
woman's (Hindu).. 9. stridhana
(stridhan)
prophecy... 6. oracle 9. utterance
10. prediction 11. foretelling
prophesy... 4. osse 5. augur
7. predict, presage 8. forecast,
foreshow, foretell 10. vaticinate
11. preindicate 13. prognosticate
prophet... 4. seer 6. medium, oracle
7. psychic 8. Mohammed, preacher,
presager 9. John Smith, predictor
10. soothsayer 11. Joseph Smith
(Mormon)
prophet (Bib)... 4. Amos 5. Cyrus,
Hosea 6. Elijah (Elias) 7. Malachi,
Obadiah
prophet, murder of... 8. vaticide
prophetess... 5. sibyl 7. seeress
9. Cassandra (of evil)
prophetic, prophetical... 5. vatic
6. mantic 7. fateful, vatical
8. oracular 9. vaticinal
10. divinatory, presageful
11. predicative
propinquity... 7. kinship 8. nearness
9. proximity 12. neighborhood,
relationship 13. consanguinity
propitiate... 5. atone 6. pacify
8. atone for 10. conciliate
propitiation... 9. atonement, expiation
12. pacification, satisfaction
14. reconciliation
propitious... 4. rosy 5. happy, lucky
6. benign, timely 7. helpful
9. favorable, opportune, promising
10. auspicious, benevolent,
prosperous 12. advantageous,
well-disposed
proponent... 8. advocate
10. propounder
proportion... 4. part, rate 5. quota,
ratio, share 6. adjust, extent
7. analogy, compare, euphony,
prorate 8. equalize, symmetry
9. apportion
proportional... 4. rate 8. relative
10. comparable, respective
11. dimensional
proportionate... 5. equal 8. adequate,
relative 9. analogous 10. respective
11. comparative 13. corresponding
proposal... 3. bid 4. plan 5. offer
6. feeler, motion 8. marriage
9. intention 10. nomination,
suggestion 11. proposition,
supposition
propose... 5. image, offer, state, toast
6. intend, submit 7. purpose
8. nominate, propound 9. postulate
proposed (pert to)...
for consideration.. 9. suggested
for debate.. 6. mooted
international language.. 2. Ro 3. Ido
9. Esperanto
proposition... 4. plan 5. axiom, lemma
6. porism, thesis 7. project
8. empirema, proposal 9. corollary
•11. supposition, undertaking

proposition, proof of... 18. reductio ad absurdum

propound... 6. submit 7. propose 8. set forth 9. postulate

proprietary... 5. owner, title 8. interest, medicine (secret) 9. ownership 10. proprietor 12. landed estate

propriety... 7. decency, decorum, fitness 8. standard 9. ownership 10. convention, expedience, properness 11. correctness, suitability 12. tastefulness 13. possessorship

propugnaculum... 7. bulwark, defense 8. fortress

prorogue... 5. defer 6. extend 7. adjourn, prolong 8. postpone, protract

prosaic... 4. drab, dull, flat 5. plain, prosy 6. prolix, stupid 7. humdrum, insipid, tedious 8. ordinary, tiresome 10. unexciting 11. commonplace 12. matter–of–fact 13. unimaginative

proscribe... 3. ban 6. forbid, outlaw 7. condemn (to death) 8. prohibit, restrain 9. interdict, ostracize

proscription... 5. exile 8. outlawry 11. prohibition 12. interdiction

prosecute... 3. sue 4. urge 5. chase 6. intend (law), pursue 7. carry on, enforce, execute

prosecutor... 6. lawyer 7. accuser, relator 8. attorney

proselyte... 3. ger (to Judaism) 7. convert

proseuche, proseucha... 7. oratory 9. synagogue 13. place of prayer

prosody... 13. versification

prospect... 4. view 5. buyer, scene, vista 6. survey 7. explore, foresee, outlook 8. customer 9. applicant, candidate, foresight, intention 10. contestant 11. probability 12. anticipation

prosper... 4. fare 5. cheve, speed 6. thrive 7. succeed 8. flourish

prosperity... 3. hap, ups 4. boom, weal 6. thrift 7. success, welfare 9. well–being 11. good fortune

Prospero (pert to)...
character.. 9. Ferdinand
daughter.. 7. Miranda
servant.. 5. Ariel
slave.. 7. Caliban
The Tempest.. 11. Duke of Milan

prosperous... 4. weal 5. lucky, palmy, sonsy (sonsie) 7. wealthy 8. thriving 9. favorable, fortunate 10. auspicious, successful 11. flourishing

prostitute... 4. drab 5. venal 6. harlot 7. corrupt 8. infamous 12. street walker

prostrate... 4. flat, raze 5. abase, prone 6. fallen, grieve, supine 7. exhaust 8. helpless, supinate 9. flattened, recumbent 10. obsequious, submissive

prosy... 3. dry 4. dull 6. jejune 7. prosaic, tedious 11. commonplace 13. plain–speaking

protagonist... 4. hero, lead (theater) 5. actor 6. leader 8. advocate, champion, defender 9. contender, principal, spokesman 11. participant

Protagorus (Gr)... 7. Sophist, teacher 11. philosopher

protasis... 5. maxim 9. drama part 11. proposition 12. introduction

protect... 3. arm 4. save 5. guard 6. defend, insure, police, screen, sheath, shield 7. cherish, shelter 8. enshield, preserve 9. safeguard

protected... 5. armed 6. shaded 7. aproned, guarded 8. shielded 12. invulnerable

protection... 3. bib, lee 4. coat, fort, moat 5. aegis (egis), apron, armor, guard, shade, shell, smock 6. glacis, refuge, safety 7. defense, parapet, shelter 8. havelock, passport, security 11. safekeeping 12. preservation

protector... 6. patron, regent 8. defender, guardian 10. safekeeper

protector of vineyards (Gr)... 7. Priapus

protégé... 4. ward 6. charge 9. dependent

Proteida... 7. Proteus 10. amphibians 11. salamanders

protein... 6. casein 7. albumin, mucedin, peptone 8. globulin, lecithin, nutrient 9. protamine 11. chlorophyll

protein (pert to)...
blood.. 6. fibrin 8. globulin
castor oil bean.. 5. ricin (poison)
egg.. 7. albumin
milk.. 6. casein
muscles.. 8. creatine
seeds.. 8. edestin 8. aleurone, prolamin

Proteles... 7. aardwolf

protest... 4. aver, beef, deny 6. assert 7. declare 9. objection, stipulate 10. asseverate 11. expostulate 13. expostulation

protestation... 6. avowal (public) 7. protest 11. affirmation, obtestation 12. asseveration, supplication

Proteus (pert to)...
biology.. 3. olm 6. amoeba 8. bacteria 10. salamander
Gr Myth.. 6. sea god
Shakespeare.. 17. Gentleman of Verona

protocol... 5. rules (official) 7. compact 8. schedule 9. agreement, etiquette 10. memorandum (diplomatic) 12. original copy

protograph... 9. holograph 12. illustration (of species)

protoplasm... 5. spore 7. nucleus 9. archetype, cytoplasm 10. primordium 11. basis of life

protoplasmic (pert to)...
body.. 8. ectosark 9. ectoplasm, endoplasm
cell.. 6. amoeba (ameba)
cell contents.. 9. metaplasm
substance.. 8. gel

Protozoa... 6. amoeba (ameba), Lobosa, phylum 11. unicellular

protract... 4. spin 5. defer, delay

6. extend 7. prolong, stretch
8. continue, elongate, lengthen,
postpone, protrude 9. expatiate
protrude... 3. jut 5. bulge 6. exsert
7. project 9. thrust out
protuberance... 3. jag, nub, wen
4. boss, bump, cere, hump, knob,
knot, lobe, lump, node, snag, wart
5. bulge, caput, inion, knurl, torus
8. eminence, swelling 9. extrusion
10. projection
proud... 4. vain 5. grand, lofty, noble
6. elated, lordly 7. haughty, pleased,
stately, valiant 8. arrogant, boastful,
imposing, splendid 9. conceited,
gratified 10. impressive
11. independent, magisterial,
magnificent 12. presumptuous,
supercilious
prove... 3. try 4. test 5. check, nurse
6. evince, try out, verify 7. confirm,
justify, probate 8. identify, manifest
9. ascertain, establish
11. corroborate, demonstrate
prove false... 6. refute
Provençal dialect... 9. langue d'oc
provender... 3. hay 4. food 5. grain
6. fodder 8. ensilage
proverb... 3. saw 5. adage, axiom
6. byword, enigma, saying
8. aphorism, link verb, paroemia
proverbial... 10. aphoristic
11. sententious 12. epigrammatic
provide... 4. give 5. cater, endow,
endue, equip, stock, treat, yield
6. afford, ration, supply 7. care for,
finance 9. make ready 10. contribute
provided... 2. if, so 5. boden
6. sobeit 8. afforded, equipped,
prepared, supplied 11. on condition
13. conditionally
Providence founder... 13. Roger
Williams (1636)
provident... 4. wise 6. frugal, saving
7. prudent, thrifty 9. judicious
10. economical 11. precautious,
preparatory
providential... 5. lucky 7. prudent
9. opportune, provident
10. miraculous 11. foresighted
province... 4. area, beat, nome
5. arena, range, shire, tract
6. colony, domain, empire, eparch,
region, sphere 7. circuit, diocese,
kingdom 8. district 9. territory
10. palatinate (royal) 12. jurisdiction
provincial... 4. rude 5. crude, local,
rural 6. narrow 7. insular, limited
8. suburban 10. restricted,
uncultured 11. countrified
12. narrow-minded
15. unsophisticated
provincialism (diction)... 6. patois
10. patavinity
provision... 4. fare, food 5. board,
stock, store 6. vivres 7. proviso
9. condition 11. preparation
provisional... 9. makeshift, temporary,
tentative 10. promissory, substitute
11. conditional, preparatory
12. experimental 14. circumstantial
provision seller (Mil)... 6. sutler

proviso... 5. salvo 6. clause
provocative... 9. desirable, provoking
10. appetizing, stirring up, suggestive
11. interesting
provoke... 3. ire, vex 4. bate, goad,
move, rile, spur, stir 5. anger,
annoy, start 6. arouse, incite, induce,
invite, invoke, nettle, offend, stir up,
summon 7. incense 8. irritate
9. challenge 10. antagonize,
exasperate
provoking... 8. annoying, exciting
10. suggestive 11. interesting
12. antagonizing
provoking laughter... 7. risible
prow... 3. bow 4. beak, duty, good,
proa, stem 5. brave, honor, prore
6. steven 7. courage, gallant, gun
deck
prowess... 5. valor 9. gallantry
proximal... 9. immediate (opp of distal)
proximate... 4. next 6. direct
7. closest, nearest 9. immediate
10. succeeding
proximity... 8. nearness, nighness,
relation, vicinity 9. adjacence,
closeness 11. propinquity
proxy... 5. agent, power 6. agency,
ballot, deputy 7. proctor 9. authority
10. procurator, substitute
prudence... 6. virtue, wisdom
7. caution, economy 8. sagacity
9. foresight 11. calculation,
forethought 13. judiciousness
14. circumspection
prudent... 4. wary, wise 5. canny
6. frugal 8. cautious, discreet
9. judicious, penny-wise, provident
10. economical 11. circumspect,
considerate
prudish... 4. prim 8. priggish
prune... 3. cut, lop 4. clip, food, frog,
plum, trim, weed 5. dress, plume,
preen, purge, shape 6. anoint 7. cut
down, tonsure 9. simpleton
prunelike fruit... 9. myrobalan
pruning knife... 8. serpette
prurient... 7. itching, longing, lustful
10. lascivious
Prussia...
bay.. 4. Kiel 6. Danzig
10. Pomeranian
cathedral city.. 5. Essen 7. Cologne
10. Düsseldorf
city.. 6. Aachen
color.. 4. blue 12. gold pheasant
Knight.. 8. Noachite
lagoon.. 4. haff 12. Frisches Haff
lancer.. 5. Uhlan
land aristocracy.. 6. Junker
legislature.. 7. Landtag
mountain.. 4. Harz
resort.. 3. Ems
river.. 3. Ems 4. Elbe, Oder, Saar
seaport.. 4. Kiel 5. Emden 7. Stettin
State.. 6. German
pry... 4. nose, peek 5. lever, mouse,
snoop 6. meddle, search
prying... 7. curious, peeking, peeping,
peering 8. snooping 9. searching
10. meddlesome 11. inquisitive
psalm (pert to)...

book.. **7.** Psalter
Fiftieth, Vulgate.. **8.** Miserere
Mass opening.. **7.** introit
Ninety–fourth, Vulgate.. **6.** Venite
Psalms (Old Test)... **7.** Psalter
psalterium... **4.** lyra **6.** omasum
   7. stomach **9.** manyplies
psammite... **4.** rock **9.** sandstone
psephology... **7.** pebbles (study of)
psephomancy... **19.** divination by
   pebbles
pseudatoll... **9.** coral reef
pseudo... **4.** sham **5.** bogus, false
   6. untrue **7.** feigned **8.** spurious
   9. deceptive, imitation, pretender
pseudologist... **4.** liar (humorous)
pseudology... **5.** lying **9.** falsehood
pseudonym... **5.** alias **6.** anonym
   7. pen name **10.** nom de plume
pseudonym (famed)...
  C L Dodgson.. **12.** Lewis Carroll
  Mary Ann Evans.. **11.** George Eliot
  Samuel Clemens.. **9.** Mark Twain
  W S Porter.. **6.** O Henry
psychagogic... **9.** inspiring
   10. attractive, persuasive
psyche... **4.** mind, self, soul **6.** spirit
psychic... **6.** mental **9.** spiritual
   10. Gnosticism **11.** incorporeal
   12. spiritualist, supernatural
   13. psychological
psychic (pert to)...
  emanation.. **4.** aura
  devotion.. **6.** autism
  monism.. **10.** one reality
psychotic... **3.** mad **6.** insane
   8. neurotic **12.** psychopathic
Ptah (pert to)...
  Egypt Relig.. **8.** chief god (of
   Memphis)
  father of.. **3.** men **4.** gods
  representation.. **5.** mummy
  symbolic of.. **4.** life **8.** strength
ptarmigan... **4.** rype **6.** grouse
pterodactyl... **7.** reptile (extinct)
   9. pterosaur **11.** ornithosaur
pterography (description of)...
   8. feathers
pteroid... **8.** fernlike, winglike
pteropod... **6.** Clione (Arctic)
   7. mollusk
ptilosis... **7.** plumage **9.** madarosis
   10. loss of hair **15.** loss of
   eyelashes
ptisan... **3.** tea **5.** drink **6.** coddle
   9. decoction
Ptolemy (pert to)...
  author of.. **8.** Almagest
  birthplace.. **5.** Egypt (130 AD)
  famed as.. **10.** astronomer,
   geographer
public... **3.** inn **4.** open **5.** state
   6. people, vulgar **8.** communal
   9. clientele, community
public (pert to)...
  assembly.. **4.** Diet
  conveyance.. **3.** bus, cab, car **4.** taxi,
   tram **5.** train **10.** jinrikisha (jinricksha)
  display.. **10.** exhibition
   13. exhibitionism
  edict.. **3.** ban **12.** proclamation

entertainment.. **7.** ridotto
hangman (Eng).. **9.** Jack Ketch
lands.. **4.** ager (Hist) **6.** domain
official.. **6.** notary
position.. **8.** official
storehouse.. **5.** étape
walk.. **4.** mall **7.** alameda
   9. esplanade, promenade
publication... **4.** book **8.** pamphlet,
   printing **12.** notification, proclamation,
   promulgation
publication (pert to)...
  article.. **7.** feature
  condensed.. **7.** tabloid
  make–up.. **6.** format
  prelim.. **9.** prodromus
publicist... **5.** solon **6.** Gallup, lawyer,
   writer **10.** journalist, publicizer
   11. commentator
publish... **4.** edit, vent **5.** issue, print
   6. blazon, delate **7.** divulge
   8. proclaim **10.** promulgate
   11. disseminate
publish (pert to)...
  abroad.. **8.** promulge
  after death.. **10.** posthumous
  banns.. **7.** betroth **8.** marriage
  far and wide.. **6.** blazon
  without authority.. **6.** pirate
   10. plagiarize
publisher's description (book)...
   5. blurb **13.** advertisement
publisher's inscription (book)...
   5. facts **8.** colophon
Puccini heroine... **4.** Mimi
pucker... **4.** fold **5.** bulge, purse
   6. crease **7.** anxiety, fluster, wrinkle
   8. contract
puckered... **7.** bullate **8.** wrinkled
   10. contracted
puckish... **6.** impish **8.** Pucklike
   10. mysterious **11.** mischievous
pud... **3.** paw **4.** hand **8.** forefoot
pudding... **4.** duff, mush, plum, sago
   6. junket **7.** custard, dessert, tapioca
   8. roly–poly, softness, stuffing (game)
   9. Yorkshire
puddle... **3.** mud **4.** mess, pond, pool
   5. plash, swamp **6.** muddle
   7. plashet, pollute
puddle duck... **7.** mallard
puddock... **4.** kite, toad **7.** buzzard
   9. enclosure (paddock)
pueblo... **4.** town **7.** village
Pueblo (pert to)...
  ceremonial chamber.. **4.** kiva
  Indian (American).. **4.** Hopi, Piro,
   Tano, Zuni **5.** Acoma **7.** Keresan
   12. cliff dweller
  water jar.. **4.** olla
puerile... **4.** weak **5.** young
   7. babyish, trivial **8.** childish,
   juvenile, youthful **12.** simple–minded
Puerto Rican (pert to)...
  bark, beverage.. **4.** mabi
  dove.. **4.** rola
  fish.. **4.** sama, sisi **8.** porkfish
Puerto Rico... see also *Puerto Rican*
  capital.. **7.** San Juan
  city.. **5.** Ponce **7.** Arecibo
  discoverer.. **8.** Columbus
  first settlement.. **7.** Caparra

government.. 12. Commonwealth
Indian name.. 9. Borinquen
island (off shore).. 4. Mona
7. Culebra
island group.. 15. Greater Antilles
politically.. 12. Commonwealth
program (Polit).. 18. Operation
Bootstrap
sea.. 9. Caribbean
puff... 4. blow, blub, chug, flam, pant, pegh (Scot), pouf, waff 5. elate
7. efflate
puffbird... 6. barbet 8. barbacou
pug... 3. dog, elf 4. moth, puck, snub
5. chaff, dwarf 6. harlot, refuse (grain), sprite 8. bargeman, mistress, pugilist 9. footprint, hobgoblin
pugging... 8. grasping, thieving
pugilistic... 6. fistic 10. pugnacious
pugnacious... 9. combative
11. belligerent, quarrelsome
pugnacious man... 12. fighting cock
pug−nosed... 5. camus (camuse)
puisne... 4. puny 5. judge, later, petty 6. feeble, junior 9. associate, unskilled 10. law student, subsequent
11. subordinate
puissance... 5. force, might, power
8. strength 9. authority
puissant... 6. mighty, potent
7. mastery 8. forcible, powerful
13. authoritative
pulchritude... 5. grace 6. beauty
10. comeliness, loveliness
pule... 5. peep, whine
7. ululate, whimper
pulicat... 8. bandanna (bandana)
puling... 6. sickly 7. babyish, howling, whining 8. childish, delicate
Pulitzer prizes... 6. awards
10. journalism, literature
pull... 3. pu 3. lug, tow, tug 4. drag, draw, haul, yank 5. bouse, drink, tweak 6. effort, strain 7. attract, extract 9. influence 10. attraction
pull (pert to)...
apart.. 4. rend, tear 7. destroy
8. demolish, enfeeble, separate
back.. 5. demur 6. recoil 7. retract
8. withdraw
down.. 4. fell, raze 9. dismantle
off.. 3. pug 6. avulse, commit
8. carry out 10. accomplish
one's leg.. 4. hoax, joke 7. deceive, flatter 8. hoodwink 9. make fun of
out.. 5. leave 6. secede 7. extract
9. eradicate
up.. 4. stop 5. elate 6. aviate
7. arraign, extract
pullet... 4. fowl 5. child 7. bivalve
8. poullard
pulley (pert to)...
groove.. 5. gorge
grooved.. 5. fusee (fuzee)
part.. 4. arse
wheel.. 6. sheave (grooved)
pulp... 3. pap 4. marc, mash, mass
5. chyme 9. magazine 10. fleshy part
pulpit... 4. ambo, bema, dais, desk
5. stage 6. clergy 7. rostrum
8. platform, scaffold

pulpy... 5. mushy 7. squashy
pulpy (pert to)...
dregs.. 5. magma
fruit.. 3. uva 4. pome 6. sidder (siddow)
state.. 4. mash, soft 6. fleshy
pulsate... 4. beat, drum 5. throb
7. vibrate
pulsation... 5. ictus 6. moving, rhythm
7. impulse, systole 8. acrotism (failure), vitality 9. throbbing, vibrating
pulsatory... 8. rhythmic, systolic
9. throbbing
pulse... 3. dal (split) 5. seeds (edible), throb 6. rhythm 7. beating
8. resonate 9. pulsation, throbbing
pulse family... 3. pea 8. Fabaceae
pulverize... 4. bray, mull 5. crush, grind 6. abrade, powder 7. atomize
8. levigate 9. triturate
12. disintegrate
pulverulent... 5. dusty 7. crumbly
8. powdered
puma... 6. cougar 7. Quechua (Kochua)
pummel... 4. beat, maul 5. thump
6. batter, buffet, hammer, pommel, strike
pump... 3. gin, ram 4. draw, emit, quiz 5. eject 6. elicit, propel
7. extract 10. pulsometer
11. interrogate
pumpernickel... 5. bread (Westphalian)
pump handle... 5. sweep, swipe
pumpkin (pert to)...
head.. 4. dolt 7. Puritan
9. blockhead, Roundhead
seed.. 7. sunfish 8. sailboat
yam.. 11. sweet potato
pun... 4. yoke 8. paragram
9. assonance, equivoque (equivoke), witticism 11. paronomasia
punch... 3. die 4. blow, poke, prod, tool 5. douse, drink, negus, paste
6. liquor, pierce 8. mattoir (etcher's)
8. beverage, puncture 9. perforate
11. punch cattle
Punch and Judy dog... 4. Toby
Punch Bowl... 6. crater 9. graveyard (Honolulu), hot spring (Yellowstone)
puncheon... 3. die 4. cask 5. punch, stamp 6. dagger
puncher... 6. cowboy 10. cowpuncher, perforator
punching... 8. piercing 9. pertusion
punctilious... 4. nice 5. exact
6. formal, strict 7. correct, precise
8. exacting 9. observant
10. meticulous, scrupulous
punctuation mark... 3. dot 4. dash, star 5. brace, breve, colon, comma, tilde 6. dagger, hyphen, period, tittle, umlaut 8. brackets, ellipsis
9. ampersand, semicolon
10. apostrophe, circumflex
11. exclamation 12. question mark
pundit... 6. nestor, savant 7. Brahmin, scholar, teacher 10. learned man
pung... 4. sled 6. sleigh
pungent... 4. keen, racy, sour, tart
5. acrid, acute, sharp, smart, snell
6. biting, bitter 7. caustic, odorous,

painful, peppery, piquant 8. piercing,
poignant, stabbing 11. stimulating
pungent herb .. 6. Asarum
punish .. 4. fine 5. mulct, spank,
wreak 6. amerce 7. chasten, correct
8. chastise, penalize 9. castigate
10. discipline
punishment (pert to) ..
  Brehon law .. 4. eric
  by torture .. 9. strappado
  church .. 15. excommunication
  condign .. 11. retributive
  law .. 5. peine
  term .. 5. penal 7. penalty, revenge
  8. punitive
  Turk, Chin .. 9. bastinade
  Welsh law (anc) .. 3. cro 7. galanas
punitive .. 5. penal 10. revengeful,
vindictive 11. castigatory
Punjab, India ..
  capital .. 6. Lahore (West) 8. Amritsar
  (East)
  language .. 7. Panjabi
  name meaning .. 10. Five Rivers
  soldier .. 4. Sikh
  summer capital .. 5. Simla
punk .. 3. bad 5. child 6. amadou
7. lighter 8. inferior 9. touchwood
punto .. 3. hit 5. joint (fencing)
6. stitch (needle)
puny .. 4. weak 5. frail, petty 6. little,
meager, puisne, sickly 8. delicate
14. inconsiderable
pupa .. 5. shell 9. chrysalis
pupil .. 3. eye, son 4. tyro 5. élève,
youth 7. écolier, learner, scholar
8. disciple, neophyte
puppet .. 3. guy 4. doll 5. image
6. maumet 9. miniature, nonentity
10. figurehead, marionette
puppeteer, famed .. 4. Sarg
puppy .. 3. dog, fop 5. shark, whelp
purblind .. 10. dim-sighted 11. partly
blind 12. narrow-minded,
undiscerning
purchasable .. 5. venal 8. bribable,
hireling 9. mercenary 11. corruptible
purchase .. 3. buy, win 4. earn, hold
5. bribe 6. buying, obtain
7. acquire, bribery, procure
8. barratry, foothold, leverage
purchaser .. 5. buyer 6. patron,
vendee 8. customer 9. acquéreur
13. adjudicataire
purdah (Ind) .. 4. veil 6. screen
7. curtain
pure .. 4. neat, real 5. clean, fresh,
godly, sheer, utter 6. candid, chaste,
simple, vestal 7. genuine, perfect,
refined, unmixed 8. absolute, filtered,
innocent 9. downright, faultless,
inviolate, stainless, undefiled, unsullied
11. pure-blooded, uncorrupted,
unqualified 13. unadulterated
purga (Russ) .. 8. blizzard
9. snowstorm
purgative .. 5. jalap 6. physic
8. absterge 9. catharsis, cathartic,
cleansing
purgatory .. 4. hell 5. limbo 6. erebus
7. torment
purified .. 10. elutriated

purified wool fat .. 7. lanolin (lanoline)
purify .. 5. clean, purge 6. filter,
refine, spurge 7. cleanse, epurate
8. lustrate, renovate, sanctify
9. elutriate
purifying .. 7. smectic 8. depurant
9. cathartic, cleansing 10. distilling
Purim .. 7. holiday 8. festival (Jew)
11. Feast of Lots
puritan .. 5. prude 7. ascetic
9. precisian 10. Separatist
puritan clergyman .. 10. Cartwright
puritanical .. 6. strict 7. ascetic
11. strait-laced 13. hyperorthodox
purity .. 8. chastity 9. innocence
purl .. 4. eddy 5. frill 6. murmur,
ripple 7. trickle
purloin .. 5. filch, steal, swipe
6. finger 11. appropriate
purple .. 4. bice, lake, plum, puce
5. lilac, mauve, pansy, regal, showy
6. damson, orchid, ornate, Tyrian,
violet 7. Cassius, magenta, mollusk,
pigment 8. amaranth, Burgundy,
imperial, mulberry 9. brilliant,
cathedral 11. sovereignty
purple (pert to) ..
  bottle .. 4. moss
  cactus .. 8. Missouri
  death adder .. 10. black snake
  emperor .. 9. butterfly
  Forbidden City .. 5. Lhasa
  granadilla .. 13. passion flower
  haw .. 7. capulin (Mex) 8. bluewood
  Heart, Order of .. 5. medal (Mil) (est
  by Washington, re-est.1932)
  laurel .. 12. rhododendron
  lily .. 8. Turk's cap
  martin .. 7. swallow
  navy .. 10. marine blue
  nightshade .. 9. trompillo
purport .. 4. feck, gist, mean
5. sense, tenor 6. allege, import,
intent 7. meaning 9. substance
purpose .. 3. aim, end 4. goal, idly,
main, plan, sake 5. avail 6. design,
intend, intent, motive 7. meaning,
resolve 8. function 9. determine,
discourse, intention, objective,
predesign
purposive .. 5. telic
purse .. 3. bag, cly 5. pouch
6. pucker, wallet 7. wrinkle
8. crumenal (obs) 10. pocketbook
12. porte-monnaie
purser .. 5. clerk (ship's) 6. bursar
7. boucher, cashier 9. paymaster
purse rat .. 12. pocket gopher
pursue .. 3. run 4. hunt, seek, tack
5. chase, court 6. follow 7. carry
on, proceed 9. persecute
10. specialize
pursuit .. 5. chase, quest, scent
9. objective 10. occupation
purvey .. 5. cater 6. supply 7. foresee,
provide
purveyor of untruth (Bib) ..
  7. Ananias
purview .. 4. body (statute) 5. field
(law), range, scope 7. compass
8. province
push .. 2. go 4. bunt, butt, gang,

ping, pole, prod, urge 5. crowd, elbow, impel, nudge, press, shove
6. attack, energy, propel, thrust
9. importune, offensive (Mil)
10. forge ahead, propulsion
12. press forward

pusillanimous... 4. base, weak
5. timid 6. craven 8. cowardly
12. fainthearted, mean–spirited

put... 3. set 4. butt, dupe, fool, sail
5. place, throw 6. impose, option, phrase, repose, rustic 7. deposit
8. invest in 9. attribute

put (pert to)...
an end to.. 5. quash (law)
away.. 4. kill 5. store 6. murder
back.. 6. demote 7. replace, restore
before.. 6. appose
down.. 6. humble 7. degrade, deposit, depress 8. suppress
forth.. 5. exert 7. propose 9. circulate
off.. 4. doff, haft, sail 5. defer, delay, evade 8. postpone
on alert.. 5. alarm 6. alarum
out.. 3. vex 4. oust 5. eject
9. ostracize 10. expatriate
over.. 4. bilk 5. cheat, trick
7. deceive

put in, into...
action.. 6. excite
holy place.. 8. enshrine
motion.. 6. arouse
opposition.. 3. pit
order.. 4. trim 5. mense 6. settle
7. arrange 8. organize
11. systematize
rapture.. 8. entrance
relation to.. 9. correlate
10. coordinate, co–ordinate
rhythm.. 5. meter
scabbard.. 7. sheathe

putrefaction... 3. rot 5. decay
13. decomposition 14. disintegration

puttee... 6. gaiter 7. legging

put to...
flight.. 4. rout
strain.. 3. tax
trouble.. 10. discommode
use.. 5. apply
wrong use.. 8. misapply

put up... 3. pay 4. ante, hang
5. build, offer 6. pledge 7. install
8. nominate 9. construct

put up with... 4. bear 5. stand
6. endure, permit 7. stomach
8. tolerate

puzzle... 3. cap 4. crux, pose 5. griph (griphus), poser, rebus 6. enigma, riddle 7. anagram, confuse, mystify, nonplus, paradox, perplex, problem
8. entangle 9. conundrum
10. complicate, disconcert

puzzle (pert to)...
monkey.. 5. piñon
picture.. 5. rebus
word.. 7. charade 9. crossword
10. anacrostic

puzzling... 6. knotty 10. perplexing
11. enigmatical, paradoxical

pygarg, pygargus... 5. addax 8. sea eagle 9. quadruped (Bib)

Pygmalion (pert to)...

color.. 5. brown
endowed with life.. 7. Galatea (statue)
king of.. 6. Cyprus
sister.. 4. Dido
talented as.. 8. sculptor

pygmy, pigmy... 3. elf 4. Akka, Doko, pixy 5. atomy, Batwa, dwarf, gnome, minim, short 6. Abongo, Achuas
7. manikin 9. dandiprat

pygmy (pert to)...
hog.. 7. Porcula
musk deer.. 10. chevrotain
owl.. 8. gnome owl
rattlesnake.. 10. massasauga
squirrel (smallest known).. 9. Sciuridae

pyic... 8. purulent, virulent

pyknic... 3. fat 5. round, stout

pylon... 4. post 5. tower 6. marker
7. gateway 14. monumental mass

pyosis... 3. pus 4. boil
11. suppuration

pyramid... 4. cone, heap, pile, tomb
5. tower 8. monument 9. speculate

pyramid (pert to)...
builder, largest.. 6. Cheops (khufu)
Egypt.. 9. The Sphinx 12. Great Pyramid, Tomb of Cheops
group.. 5. Gizeh 7. Menkare
8. Chephren 9. Mycerinus
kidney (Anat).. 7. Perrein
10. Malpighian
Mexico.. 7. Benares
site of Cheops.. 4. Giza (Gizeh)
texts.. 12. inscriptions 13. Book of the Dead
world wonder.. 12. Great Pyramid, Tomb of Cheops

pyramidal... 4. huge 7. angular, conical 8. enormous, imposing

pyre... 4. bier, heap, pile
9. cremation, death fire

Pyrenees (pert to)...
bandit.. 8. Miquelet
mountain chain.. 11. France–Spain
peak.. 9. Pic d'Aneto 11. Pic de Méthou
resort.. 3. Pau
State.. 7. Andorra (Fr)

pyriform... 10. pear–shaped

pyrology (study of)... 4. heat

pyromaniac... 7. firebug 8. arsonist
10. incendiary

pyrope... 3. red 6. garnet 7. mineral

pyrophobia... 11. dread of fire

pyrotechnics... 7. oratory, science
9. fireworks

pyrrhic... 4. foot (Pros) 5. dance

Pyrrhic victory... 11. at great cost

pyrrho (comb form)... 3. red 5. tawny

Pyrrho (Gr)... 7. teacher (Pyrrhonism)

pyrrhotist... 7. redhead

Pyrrhulexia... 5. finch 8. grosbeak

Pythagorus (Gr)...
birthplace.. 5. Samos
daughter.. 4. Camo
famed as.. 11. philosopher
friend.. 5. Damon
teacher of.. 8. theorems 18. influence of numbers

Pythian (pert to)...
contests.. 6. Delphi
Festival.. 11. Panhellenic

patron.. 6. Apollo
term.. 8. ecstatic 9. phrenetic
python... 3. boa 8. anaconda
Python (pert to)...
  home.. 11. Mt Parnassus
  myth.. 14. monster serpent
  slaver.. 6. Apollo
  survivor of.. 10. muddy earth (anc)
pythonic... 4. huge 6. Pythia (Delphi),

python 8. oracular 9. monstrous
pythonism, art of... 8. prophecy
  10. divination
pyx, pix... 3. box 4. test, veil
  5. chest 6. coffer, vessel (Eccl)
  8. binnacle, ciborium 10. tabernacle
pyxie... 5. shrub 9. evergreen
pyxis... 3. box 4. Argo (Astron), vase
  9. jewel case

Q

Q... 5. queue 6. letter (17th)
QED... 21. Quod Erat Demonstrandum
Q–ship (Eng)... 11. mystery ship
qua, quabird... 10. night heron
quachil... 12. pocket gopher
quack... 3. cry (duck) 5. faker
  7. empiric 8. impostor 9. charlatan,
  pretender 10. medicaster,
  mountebank
quack medicine... 6. patent
  7. nostrum
quad (pert to)...
  printing.. 5. crown 7. quadrat
  school.. 4. yard 6. campus
  10. quadrangle
  slang (Brit).. 5. horse
quadra... 6. fillet, listel, plinth
quadragenarian... 12. forty–year–old
  (person)
Quadragesima... 4. Fast, Lent
  6. Sunday (1st in Lent) 7. Holy Day
  9. Forty Days
quadrangle... 5. plane (four–angles)
  6. square 7. rhombus 8. tetragon
quadrant... 4. gill 6. fourth
  7. measure, quarter 8. farthing, six
  hours 10. instrument, semicircle
quadrate... 4. suit 5. adapt, agree,
  ideal 6. square 7. conform, perfect,
  squared 8. balanced 10. correspond
  13. correspondent
quadriga... 3. car 7. chariot (4–horse)
  10. four horses
quadrumane... 3. ape 6. mammal
  7. gorilla, Primate (except Man)
  10. chimpanzee 13. feetlike hands
quadruped... 3. ass, cat, cow, dog
  5. bull, calf, colt, foal, lion, mule
  5. burro, horse, jenny, panda, tiger
  6. badger, donkey, mammal
  7. bullock 10. four–footed
quaff... 5. draft, drink 6. tipple
quag... 5. quake 6. quiver 8. quagmire
quagga... 5. zebra 7. wild ass
quaggy... 5. boggy, fenny 6. spongy
  7. queachy 8. yielding
quagmire... 3. bay, fen 4. lair
  5. marsh, swamp 6. morass
  11. predicament
quahog... 4. clam
quail... 3. cow 4. bird 5. colin, cower,

quake, shake 6. blench, curdle,
  flinch, shrink, tremor, Turnix
  7. massena, tremble 8. bobwhite,
  Coturnix 9. coagulate, courtesan,
  eddish hen
quail (pert to)...
  button.. 6. Turnix
  call.. 4. pipe
  color.. 9. hair brown
  flock.. 4. bevy
  French.. 6. caille
  hawk.. 6. falcon
  quailhead.. 11. lark sparrow
  snipe.. 9. dowitcher
quaint... 3. odd 4. wise 5. proud
  6. expert, pretty, proper 7. curious,
  prudent, refined, strange, uncouth
  8. fanciful, peculiar
quake... 5. shake 6. quiver, shiver,
  tremor 7. shudder, tremble, vibrate
  10. earthquake
Quaker (pert to)...
  bird.. 9. albatross (sooty)
  city.. 12. Philadelphia
  colonizer.. 4. Penn (Wm)
  color.. 4. drab, gray 5. acier
  poet.. 6. Barton 8. Whittier
  sect.. 16. Society of Friends
  sect founder.. 9. George Fox
  State.. 12. Pennsylvania
qualified... 3. fit 4. able 6. fitted
  7. adapted, capable, enabled, limited
  8. eligible, entitled, equipped,
  modified, prepared, tempered
  9. competent 10. restrained,
  restricted 11. conditional
qualify... 3. fit 4. name 5. abate,
  adapt, be fit, equip, limit, train
  6. enable, modify, soften, temper
  7. assuage, prepare 8. diminish,
  mitigate, modulate, quantify, regulate,
  restrain, restrict
quality... 5. prime, trait, value
  6. nature, pathos, strain 7. caliber,
  texture 8. accident, capacity, inferior,
  nobility, property 9. attribute,
  character, specialty 10. difference,
  excellence 14. characteristic
quality of heredity... 9. lineality
qualm... 4. pall 5. demur, doubt,
  spasm 6. nausea, regret 7. scruple

9. faintness, misgiving
11. compunction 12. apprehension
quandary... 3. fix 6. pickle, strait
7. dilemma 10. perplexity
11. predicament
quandy... 9. squaw duck
quant... 11. punting pole
quantity... 3. ace, any, gob, lot, sea,
sum 4. bulk, dose, drop, mass,
much, raff, raft, scad, size, some
5. batch, scads, store 6. amount,
cupful, degree, extent, hatful,
number, oceans 7. handful
quantity (pert to)...
fixed.. 8. constant
mathematics.. 4. surd 5. graph
6. scalar, vector
minute.. 4. atom, dram, iota, mill
standard.. 4. unit
time unit.. 4. rate
quantum... 4. body 5. share
6. amount, energy, theory
7. atomics, portion 8. quantity
quap... 5. heave, throb 6. quaver
9. palpitate
Quapaw... 5. Sioux 8. Arkansas
11. Indian tribe
quarantine... 7. confine, isolate
8. pratique (marine) 9. forty days
(law), isolation, segregate
11. confinement
quarantine flag... 6. yellow 7. warning
10. yellow jack
quarenden... 5. apple (deep red)
quarentene... 4. rood 7. furlong
quark... 3. caw 5. croak, quawk
quarl, quarle... 4. sour, tile 5. brick
6. curdle, medusa 9. jellyfish
quarred... 6. soured 7. curdled (beer)
quarrel... 3. row 4. spat, tiff, tile
5. arrow, brawl, broil, cavil, flite
(flyte), gnarr, scene, scrap 6. affray,
bicker, chisel 7. diamond, wrangle
8. argument, squabble 9. complaint
10. accusation, Donnybrook,
free-for-all 11. altercation
12. disagreement
16. misunderstanding
quarrel (pert to)...
hereditary.. 4. feud
noisy.. 6. fracas, jangle
over.. 6. bicker 7. dispute, wrangle
8. squabble
petty.. 4. miff, spat, tiff
quarrelsome... 8. choleric, petulant
9. irascible, irritable, litigious
10. discordant, pugnacious
11. belliferent, contentious
13. argumentative
quarry... 4. delf, game, heap, mine,
prey 8. entrails, excavate 12. object
hunted
quart... 5. gills (eight) 6. fourth
7. measure 8. schooner
quarter... 4. coin, side 5. house
6. fourth, region 7. measure
8. insignia, semester 9. direction,
dismember 10. quadrature (Astron),
quadrisect
quarter (pert to)...
acre.. 4. rood
animal.. 5. horse

astronomy.. 10. quadrature
fathom.. 6. fourth
military.. 8. clemency (to enemy)
music.. 4. note 8. crotchet
nautical.. 4. deck, lift 6. galley
pint.. 4. gill
sports.. 4. back 11. quarterback
quartered... 8. billeted
12. quartersawed (wood)
quarters (living)... 4. camp, room
7. housing, lodging, shelter
8. barracks, diggings, lodgings,
lodgment 9. dormitory
Quartodeciman... 10. paschalist (Jew)
quartz... 4. onyx, sard 5. flint 6. silica
7. mineral
quartz (pert to)...
banded, spotted.. 4. onyx 5. agate
6. jasper 8. sardonyx
blue–red.. 10. bloodstone, heliotrope
brown.. 5. smoky 9. cairngorm
brownish–red.. 7. sinople
chalcedony.. 4. sard 9. carnelian
11. chrysoprase
flint.. 9. hornstone 10. touchstone
glass.. 6. silica
green.. 5. prase (dull) 6. plasma
(bright) 11. chrysoprase
hard.. 5. flint
opaque.. 6. jasper
purple.. 8. amethyst
red.. 4. sard 9. carnelian
ruby–red.. 7. rubasse
silica.. 5. silex
transparent.. 11. rock crystal
violet.. 8. amethyst
yellow.. 5. topaz (false) 7. citrine
quash... 4. cass, void 5. abate, annul,
crush, quell, shake 6. hush up,
subdue 7. shatter 8. suppress
9. overthrow 10. extinguish
quasi... 4. as if 8. as it were, as
though 9. seemingly
Quasimodo... 9. Low Sunday (1st after
Easter)
quatern... 4. fourfold 10. quadrangle
12. four quarters (having)
quaver... 5. shake, trill 6. quiver
7. tremble, tremolo, vibrate
11. trepidation
quawk... 3. caw 5. heron (night)
7. screech 8. quagmire
quay, key... 4. pier 5. levee, wharf
7. landing
queachy... 4. boggy, bushy, fenny
6. marshy, swampy
quean... 4. girl, jade, slut 5. wench
6. harlot
queasy... 4. sick 8. delicate, qualmish,
ticklish, troubled 9. hazardous, ill at
ease, nauseated, squeamish,
uncertain, unsettled
Quebec...
battle site.. 15. Plains of Abraham
capital.. 6. Quebec (province)
city.. 6. Verdun 8. Montreal
11. Three Rivers
founder.. 9. Champlain (1608)
river.. 10. St Lawrence
vehicle.. 7. calèche (2–wheeled)
quebrada... 3. gap 5. brook, gorge
7. fissure

qued, quede... **3.** bad **4.** evil **8.** The
Devil
queen... **3.** ant, bee, cat **7.** empress,
goddess, monarch **8.** chessman,
honeybee **9.** sovereign **10.** chess
piece **11.** playing card
queen (pert to)...
bee.. **8.** honeybee
cactus.. **7.** Mexican **10.** ornamental
conch.. **5.** shell
fern.. **5.** royal
pigeon.. **7.** crowned
Queen (pert to)...
Bernice's Hair (Astron).. **13.** Coma
Berenices
City of the Lakes.. **7.** Buffalo
City of the West.. **10.** Cincinnati
Mab.. **11.** Fairie Queen (Rom/Juliet)
Victoria.. **14.** Widow of Windsor
(nickname by Kipling)
Queen Anne's...
lace.. **6.** carrot (wild)
melon.. **6.** dudaim
War... **17.** Spanish Succession
War treaty.. **14.** Peace of Utrecht
queen of...
chess.. **4.** fers
fairies.. **5.** Mab **7.** Titania **8.** Gloriana
gods.. **4.** Hera (Gr), Juno (Rom)
Hearts.. **9.** Elizabeth
heaven.. **10.** Virgin Mary
Isles (Brit).. **6.** Albion
night.. **4.** moon
Sheba.. **6.** Balkis (Koran)
Spades (solo).. **5.** basta
the Adriatic.. **6.** Venice
the Antilles.. **4.** Cuba
the East.. **7.** Antioch (Syria), Batavia
(Java), Zenobia
the tides.. **7.** the moon
the underworld.. **3.** Hel
queen's (pert to)...
arm.. **6.** musket
flower.. **9.** bloodwood
hub.. **7.** tobacco
July flower.. **8.** damewort
ware.. **9.** Wedgewood
Queensland (Austral)...
animal.. **8.** kangaroo **9.** koala bear
(teddy bear)
bean.. **8.** snuffbox
capital.. **8.** Brisbane
fire tree.. **5.** tulip
fish.. **9.** trumpeter
hemp.. **4.** sida **6.** lucern **9.** jellyleaf
11. paddy lucern
plum.. **8.** Burdekin
tree (timber).. **3.** box **4.** pine
5. beech, ebony **10.** sandalwood
12. Dundathu pine
queer... **3.** odd, rum **4.** sham **5.** false,
funny **6.** insane, thwart **7.** strange
8. peculiar, singular, spurious
9. eccentric, fantastic, interfere
10. disconcert, suspicious
11. counterfeit **12.** questionable
queer fellow... **4.** coot, goop
6. galoot, geezer **9.** character
queersome... **3.** odd **7.** strange
8. abnormal
Queer Street... **9.** imaginary
queest... **8.** ringdove

queet... **4.** coot **5.** ankle
quell... **3.** end **4.** calm **5.** allay, crush,
quash, quiet **6.** pacify, reduce,
soothe, stifle, subdue **7.** destroy,
repress **8.** suppress **9.** overpower
10. extinguish
quench... **4.** cool, damp, sate **5.** allay,
check, slake, still **6.** stifle, subdue
7. assuage, gratify **8.** suppress
10. discourage, extinguish **11.** clamp
down on
quenelle... **8.** meatball
Quercus... **4.** oaks
queriman... **4.** fish **6.** mullet
quern... **4.** mill (grain)
quernal... **5.** crown (oak leaves)
querulous... **7.** fretful, peevish
9. plaintive **11.** complaining
12. faultfinding
query... **5.** doubt **6.** murmur
7. inquire, inquiry, whining
8. question
quest... **3.** bay (dog's) **4.** hunt, seek
6. desire, pursue, search **7.** inquest,
request **8.** seek alms **9.** adventure
12. solicitation
question... **3.** ask **4.** quiz **5.** cavil,
doubt, grill, poser, query, scout,
topic **6.** riddle **7.** dispute, inquire,
inquiry, problem **8.** erotesis
9. catechize (catechise)
11. interrogate, uncertainty
12. interpellate (formally)
13. interrogation
question, out of the... **6.** absurd
7. refused **8.** hopeless, rejected
10. impossible, prohibited
11. unthinkable
questionable... **4.** moot **7.** dubious
8. doubtful **9.** debatable, dishonest,
uncertain **10.** disputable, improbable
12. unbelievable **13.** problematical
questioning (prolonged)...
11. inquisition
question mark... **7.** erotema, eroteme
quet... **3.** auk **5.** murre **9.** guillemot
quethe... **3.** say **4.** call, tell, will
5. quoth, speak **6.** clamor
8. bequeath **9.** testament
quetzal, quezal... **6.** trogon
14. national emblem (Guatemala)
Quetzalcoatl... **10.** god of winds
(Aztec)
queue... **4.** cue **6.** hair, line (waiting),
tail **7.** pigtail **9.** lance rest
quey... **6.** heifer
quia-quia... **9.** cigarfish
quib, quibble... **3.** pun **4.** carp, quip
5. argue, cavil, cheta, evade
7. shuffle
Quiche, Indian... **5.** Mayan
quick... **3.** apt **4.** deft, fast, yare
5. agile, alert, brisk, fiery, fleet,
hasty, rapid, ready, smart, swift
6. lively, nimble, presto, prompt,
pronto, speedy, sudden **7.** animate
9. dexterous, impatient, impulsive,
sprightly, vital part **10.** passionate
11. expeditious, hot-tempered
quicken... **5.** hurry, rouse, speed
6. excite, hasten, incite, revive, vivify
7. animate, further, refresh, sharpen

8. energize, expedite 9. stimulate
10. accelerate 11. resuscitate
12. reinvigorate

quickly... 4. cito, fast, soon 5. apace
6. presto, pronto 7. briefly, hastily,
rapidly 8. promptly, speedily, vigorous

quickness... 4. nous (humor) 5. haste
6. acumen 7. acidity, agility
8. alacrity, celerity, dispatch,
pungency, rapidity 9. acuteness,
briskness, fleetness, sharpness,
smartness 10. expedition, promptness
13. impulsiveness

quicksand... 3. bog 4. syrt 6. Syrtis

quickset... 5. hedge 7. thicket
8. hawthorn

quicksilver... 5. metal 7. mercury

quid... 3. cud, fid 6. guinea
7. essence, tobacco 9. sovereign

quidam... 8. somebody 10. one
unknown

quidnunc... 6. gossip 7. what now
11. inquisitive

quid pro quo... 9. tit for tat
10. equivalent, substitute
11. interchange

quiescent... 5. quiet, still 6. at rest,
latent, silent, static 8. sleeping
10. motionless

quiet... 2. sh 3. pet 4. calm, ease,
hush, lull, mild 5. peace, sober, still
6. gentle, hushed, modest, placid,
smooth, soothe 7. halcyon, restful,
silence 8. peaceful, tranquil
9. contented, peaceable, quiescent,
reposeful, unruffled 10. unmolested
11. undisturbed

quietist... 6. mystic (Quietism)

quietive... 8. sedative

quietly... 6. calmly, gently, simply
8. modestly, silently 9. patiently,
peaceably, privately 10. composedly
11. noiselessly 16. unostentatiously

quietude... 4. rest 5. peace 6. repose
7. silence 10. quiescence
12. tranquillity (tranquility)

quietus... 4. mort, obit 5. death
6. defeat 7. release 9. acquittal,
deathblow, discharge (of debt)

quiff... 4. coif, puff 5. whiff

quilkin... 4. frog, toad

quill... 3. cop, pen 5. remex
6. bobbin 7. spindle

quilt... 3. pad 4. flog, gulp 5. duvet
6. caddow 7. swallow 8. coverlet
9. patchwork 11. comfortable,
counterpane

quin... 7. scallop

quincentenary... 11. anniversary
13. commemoration 16. five hundred
years

quindecemvir (Rom)... 10. custodians
(Sibylline Books), fifteen men

quink... 5. brant, goose

quinoa... 6. cereal 7. pigweed

Quinquagesima Sunday... 10. before
Lent 12. Shrove Sunday

quinque (comb form)... 4. five

quinsy... 10. sore throat 11. tonsillitis

quint... 3. tax (one 5th) 7. E string
8. interval, schooner (5–masted)
9. organ stop

quintal... 13. hundredweight

quintessence... 3. col 5. elite 6. elixir
7. essence, the best 10. perfection

quip... 3. mot 4. gibe, jest 5. sally,
taunt 6. oddity 7. caprice, quibble
8. gimcrack 9. witticism
12. equivocation

quires, twenty... 4. ream 6. sheets
(20)

quirk... 3. quip, turn 5. clock, shift,
twist 7. caprice, evasion, quibble
8. flourish 9. deviation, mannerism,
witticism 12. eccentricity

quirt... 4. whip 5. romal

quis... 8. woodcock

quisby... 5. idler, queer 8. bankrupt
10. down and out

quit... 3. rid 4. free, stop 5. cease,
clear, leave, pay up, repay, yield
6. depart, resign 7. abandon,
discard, forsake, release, relieve,
requite 8. abdicate, liberate,
renounce 9. surrender 10. relinquish
11. discontinue

quitclaim... 6. acquit 7. release
12. convey a claim 13. deed of
release 14. relinquishment

quite... 3. all, yes 4. very 5. stark,
truly 6. really, wholly 7. totally
8. entirely, somewhat 10. absolutely,
completely, positively

quite so... 8. that is so, very true,
very well

quite some... 12. considerable

quittance... 5. repay 6. return
7. requite 8. reprisal, requital
9. atonement, departure, repayment
10. recompense 11. acquittance

quitter... 5. piker 6. coward, truant
7. shirker, welsher

quiver... 4. case 5. quake, shake
6. quaver, sheath, shiver, tremor
7. flicker, tremble, tremolo, vibrate
11. trepidation

quiver leaf... 5. aspen

Quivira (pert to)...
   famous for.. 5. wealth
   sought by.. 8. Coronado (1541)
   town site.. 6. Kansas

Quivira, Gran... 12. mission ruins
16. National Monument (N Mex)

qui vive... 5. alert 7. excited
9. challenge 12. who goes there

quixotic... 7. utopian 9. visionary
10. Don Quixote (like)
11. impractical

quiz... 4. hoax, jest, joke, mock
5. coach 6. banter 8. ridicule
11. examination, inquisitive,
interrogate, questioning

quizzical... 3. odd 7. amusing, teasing
9. bantering, eccentric, inquiring,
perplexed

quizzing... 6. banter 11. questioning

quizzing glass... 7. monocle
8. eyeglass

quod... 3. jug 6. prison 8. imprison

quoddies... 7. herring

quod erat demonstrandum... 3. QED
24. which was to be demonstrated

quodlibet... 6. medley 8. fantasia,
subtlety 13. what you please

quoit... 4. disc 6. discus
quoit pin... 3. hob
quoits... 4. game 8. cromlech
  10. stone cover
quo modo... 5. means 6. manner,
  method
quondam... 6. former 8. formerly,
  sometime
quorum... 7. council 8. majority
  10. select body
quota... 4. part 5. share 6. ration
  10. proportion
quotable... 7. citable
quotation... 5. chria, cital, motto,
  price, stock 7. passage 8. citation

  10. memorandum, repetition
quotation mark... 9. guillemet
quote... 4. cite, name 5. price
  6. adduce, repeat 7. extract
  9. quotation, reference
quoth... 4. said 5. spoke
quotha... 6. indeed 8. forsooth
quotidian... 5. daily 8. day by day,
  every day, ordinary 9. recurring
  11. commonplace
quotient... 6. number, result
quotity... 5. group, quota 7. integer
  10. collection
quotum... 5. quota, ratio
quo vadis... 16. whither goest thou
Quo Vadis tyrant... 4. Nero

R

R... 3. rho (Gr) 6. letter (18th)
Ra, Egypt Relig (pert to)...
  atmosphere.. 3. Shu
  god of.. 3. sun
  morning sun.. 7. Chepera, Khepera
  night sun.. 7. Sokaris
  representation.. 3. cat 4. lion
    5. Bacis (bull) 6. falcon 9. solar disk
  rising sun.. 5. Horus 9. Marmachis
  setting sun.. 3. Tem
  solar disk.. 4. Aten
  son.. 6. Khonsu
  son of.. 5. Nut (the sky)
  wife.. 3. Mut
raad... 15. electric catfish
raad... 7. council (S Afr) 9. volksraad
raadzaal... 11. council hall (S Afr)
rab... 5. mixer (mortar) 6. beater
Rab... 4. title 6. master, rabban
  7. teacher 8. Gamaliel
rabato, rebato... 4. ruff 6. collar
  9. piccadill
rabbet... 4. weld 5. miter 6. groove,
  recess 7. channel 8. dovetail
rabbi... 4. lord 5. rabat, title
  6. master 7. teacher 9. clergyman
  11. breastpiece
rabbi (pert to)...
  examiners.. 8. sabaraim (saboraim)
  interpreters.. 7. amoraim
  teachers.. 7. tannaim
rabbit... 4. cony (coney), hare, tyro
  5. bunny, lapin 6. animal, novice,
  rodent 10. cottontail 11. Belgian
  hare
rabbit (pert to)...
  breeding ground.. 6. warren
    8. rabbitry
  ear.. 7. antenna 8. toadflax
  female.. 3. doe
  fever.. 9. tularemia
  fiction.. 6. Harvey
  fish.. 8. chimaera 9. globefish,
    porcupine

  foot.. 5. charm 8. talisman
  fur.. 4. cony (coney) 5. lapin
  genus.. 5. Lepus
  male.. 4. buck
  mouthed.. 10. harelipped
  rat.. 9. bandicoot
  S America.. 6. tapeti
  shelter.. 5. hutch
  stew.. 12. hasenpfeffer
  tail.. 3. fud 4. scut
rabbitry... 5. hutch 6. warren
rabble... 3. mob 4. herd, raff, rout,
  skim, stir 5. crowd 6. ragtag, tumult
  7. bobtail 8. canaille, riffraff
  9. confusion, rigmarole, the masses
  12. accumulation (chaotic)
rabble rouser... 6. ragtag
Rabelais (Fr)... 6. author 8. satirist
  9. Gargantua (1st work)
rabid... 3. mad 6. raging 7. frantic,
  furious, rampant, violent 8. frenzied
  9. fanatical 10. infuriated
rabies... 5. lyssa 11. hydrophobia
raccoon, ally of... 5. coati, panda
race... 3. cut, hie, run 4. flow, lane,
  line, rush, slit, sort, stem 5. breed,
  caste, flume, relay, speed 6. course,
  family, nation, people, strain
  7. contest, regatta, running, scratch
  10. passageway 11. competition,
  watercourse
race (pert to ethnos)...
  ancient.. 4. Mede 6. Belgae, Sabine
    7. Hittite, Iberian, Walloon
  comb form.. 4. geno
  family.. 3. ilk 6. stirpo
  human.. 3. Man
  mythical.. 7. centaur
  prehistoric.. 5. Aryan, Brunn
  rule by.. 10. ethnocracy
  science of.. 9. ethnology
  undivided.. 9. holethnos
  wandering.. 5. gypsy (gipsy)
race (pert to horses)...

chariot.. 13. Circus Maximus
gait.. 4. lope, pace
horse.. 4. pony 5. racer 6. maiden,
mantis, plater 8. bangtail
11. steamer duck
horse race.. 6. impost
mill.. 4. lade (Scot)
open.. 10. Donnybrook, free-for-all
water.. 5. flume 6. arroyo 7. channel
racecourse, racetrack... 3. lap
4. heat, oval, tout, turf 5. track
6. circus (anc), colors 7. raceway,
tipster 8. dopester
Rachel (pert to)...
daughter of.. 5. Labab
mother of.. 6. Joseph 8. Benjamin
sister of.. 4. Leah
wife of.. 5. Jacob
racing colors... 5. silks
rack... 3. gin 4. gait, gear, pain, ruin
5. agony, frame 6. punish, strain,
wrench 7. agonize, support, torment,
torture 9. framework 10. excruciate
rack (pert to)...
barrel.. 3. job
comb.. 9. toothcomb
corn.. 4. crib
floating.. 5. vapor
plate.. 5. creel
skin of.. 6. rabbit
racket... 3. bat, din 5. fraud, noise,
revel 6. bustle, clamor, crosse,
outcry, scheme 8. vocation
9. commotion 15. illicit business
rackety... 5. noisy 8. clattery, exciting
9. turbulent 10. boisterous
racy... 5. brisk, fresh, naive, smart,
spicy 6. lively, risqué 7. piquant,
pungent, zestful 8. eloquent, spirited,
stirring 11. interesting
12. exhilarating, full-flavored
rad... 5. eager, quick, ready 6. afraid,
elated 11. exhilarated
radar (pert to)...
beacon.. 4. buoy 5. racon 6. ramark
navigation.. 5. navar
range (Navig).. 5. loran 6. shoran
sight.. 6. radome
signal.. 3. pip 4. beam, blip
television.. 7. teleran
raddle... 3. rod 4. beat, twig
5. cheat, color, fence, hedge
6. branch, hurdle, ruddle, thrash
7. wheedle 10. interweave
radeau... 4. raft 5. gloat 15. floating
battery
radial... 3. ray 8. quadrant
9. diverging
radiance... 5. beamy, glare, light,
nitor, sheen 6. beauty, luster
7. beaming, glitter, glowing, lambent,
shining 8. splendor 9. brilliant,
radiation 10. brilliancy, effulgence
12. cheerfulness
radiant... 5. aglow, beamy, sheen
7. beaming, glowing, lambent,
shining 8. glorious 9. beautiful,
diverging, effulgent 11. resplendent
radiate... 4. beam, emit, shed
5. gleam, shine 7. diffuse, diverge,
emanate 9. irradiate 10. illuminate
radiation... 5. light, polar (point)

10. divergence 12. illumination
13. radiant energy
radiation unit... 8. roentgen
radical... 3. red 4. atom, left, root,
surd 5. basic, radix, ultra, vital
7. capital, drastic, extreme
8. cardinal, reformer 9. extremist
10. foundation 11. fundamental
radicated... 6. rooted 11. established
radicle... 4. root 5. radix 6. etymon
7. rootlet
radio (pert to)...
activity.. 7. fallout 9. radiation
antenna.. 6. aerial
detector.. 5. radar
frequency.. 5. audio
interference.. 6. static
operator.. 3. ham (amateur)
11. dit-da-artist
rating.. 6. Hooper
rays.. 5. beams
receiver, interfering.. 7. blooper
tube.. 4. grid 5. diode
radium (pert to)...
discoverer.. 5. Curie (1898)
emanation.. 5. niton, radon
paint.. 8. luminous
source of.. 7. uranite 9. carnotite
radius... 4. area, bone 5. spoke
6. circle, extent 8. diameter
radix... 4. root 6. etymon, source
7. radical, radicle
raff... 4. heap, rake, scum 5. sweep,
trash 6. jumble, litter 7. rubbish
8. leavings, riffraff
raffia... 4. palm 5. fiber 10. jupati
palm
raffish... 3. low 6. common, flashy,
frowsy 7. unkempt 9. worthless
12. disreputable
raffle... 6. chance, rabble, tangle
7. confuse, crumple, lottery, perplex,
serrate 8. entangle, plucking, riffraff
9. stripping 10. plundering
raft... 3. lot 4. spar 5. balsa, float
6. rafter 7. to flock 10. collection
(large)
raft-breasted (Ornith)... 6. ratite
raft duck... 5. scaup 7. redhead
8. bluebill
rag... 3. fog 4. mist, sail 5. cloth,
scold, shred 6. berate, catkin, lichen,
tatter 7. ragtime, remnant 8. farthing
9. hoarfrost 11. syncopation
rag (pert to)...
bag.. 10. depository
doll.. 3. toy 6. moppet, puppet
10. marionette
fish.. 10. lcosteidae
rag picker.. 5. tramp
weed.. 3. lva
wool.. 5. mungo 6. shoddy
ragamuffin... 8. titmouse 9. ragged
boy 14. tatterdemalion
rage... 3. fad 4. fume, fury, gret,
ramp, rant, tear 5. anger, chafe,
craze, furor (furore), storm, wrath
6. fervor, frenzy 7. bluster, passion
8. violence 9. vehemence
10. excitement
ragged... 5. harsh, rough 6. jagged,
raguly (Her), scoury, shabby, uneven

7. shreddy 9. defective, dissonant, irregular 10. straggling
   11. dilapidated

raging... 4. grim 5. rabid 7. acharne
   8. storming 9. ferocious, turbulent
   10. blustering, infuriated
   11. overwrought

raglan... 8. overcoat 11. sleeve style

Ragnarok, Norse (pert to)...
  leader.. 4. Loki
  meaning.. 16. world destruction
  repeopler of the world.. 3. Lif
   10. Lifthrasir

ragout... 4. beef 5. civet, salmi
   6. mutton 7. goulash, haricot

rahdar... 14. tollroad keeper

raid... 4. tata 5. foray, seize 6. inroad
   8. invasion 9. incursion

rail... 3. bar, jaw 4. coot, jest, rant,
   sora 5. cloak, crake, dress, scoff,
   scold 6. banter, revile, septum (altar)
   7. courlan, garment, inveigh, limpkin,
   ortolan 8. reproach

railbird... 4. bird, weka 5. crake
   7. clocker, wood hen 9. spectator
   12. horse watcher

railing... 5. fence, rails 7. barrier,
   parapet 10. balustrade

raillery... 5. chaff, sport 6. banter
   7. asteism (Rhet) 8. badinage,
   ridicule 10. persiflage

railroad (pert to)...
  flare.. 5. fusee
  signal.. 9. semaphore
  sleeper.. 3. tie 7. pullman
  switch.. 4. frog
  torpedo.. 9. detonator
  worker.. 6. dinger 8. strapper
   11. gandy dancer

Rail Splitter... 14. Abraham Lincoln

raiment... 4. garb 5. amice, dress
   7. apparel, clothes, vesture
   8. clothing, garments

rain (pert to)...
  cloud.. 6. nimbus
  coat.. 4. mino 6. poncho 7. slicker
  comb form.. 5. hyeto, ombro
   6. pluvio
  fine.. 4. mist 6. serein
  fowl.. 6. cuckoo 10. woodpecker
   11. channelbill
  gauge.. 8. udometer 10. hyetometer
  glass.. 9. barometer
  icy.. 4. hail 5. sleet
  protection.. 9. ombrifuge
  short.. 6. shower
  storm.. 5. spate 13. precipitation
  study.. 9. hyetology, ombrology
  sudden.. 5. plash, spate 6. deluge
   7. torrent 8. downpour

rainbow... 3. arc 4. arch, iris, omen

rainbow (pert to)...
  bridge (Norse Myth).. 7. Bifrost (to
   Asgarth)
  chaser.. 9. visionary 11. doctrinaire
  flower.. 4. iris
  goddess.. 4. Iris
  term.. 6. iridal
  tree.. 6. saman 8. genisaro
  unit.. 4. inch
  worm.. 8. nematode 9. earthworm

rainy... 3. wet 7. showery

---

rais, reis (Moslem)... 5. chief, title
   7. captain (ship's)

Rais... 10. Mongoloids

raise... 3. end 4. grow, levy, lift, rear,
   stir 5. boost, breed, erect, exalt,
   heave, hoist, rouse 6. awaken,
   excite, gather, leaven, muster,
   remove, uplift 7. collect, elevate,
   enhance, lighten, present, produce,
   provoke, recruit 8. heighten, increase
   9. construct, cultivate, promotion,
   propagate 10. aggrandize

raise (pert to)...
  a nap.. 5. tease 6. teasel
  Cain.. 3. Ned 4. hell 5. cut up 7. be
   noisy 10. vociferate
  the dead.. 13. lift the anchor
  vegetables.. 12. olericulture

raised... 4. bred, hove 6. buoyed,
   enlève, hefted, lifted, reared
   7. hoisted 8. elevated, leavened,
   produced, promoted

raised (pert to)...
  spirits.. 6. elated
  to 3rd power.. 5. cubed
  troops.. 6. levied 7. drafted
   11. conscripted
  type.. 7. braille
  uproar.. 6. rioted
  with a bar.. 7. levered

raisin... 4. pasa 5. grape, lexia

raja, rajah... 4. king, rana 5. title
   6. prince 9. dignitary

raja's consort... 4. rani (ranee)
   8. princess

Rajmahal hemp... 5. fiber 9. jiti fiber

Rajput... 5. caste 9. Kshatriya

rake... 3. rut 4. comb, path, raff, roué
   5. slope, teeth, track 6. lecher
   7. debauch, seducer 8. enfilade,
   Lothario 9. cultivate, implement,
   libertine

rakehell... 4. free, rake 9. debauched,
   debauchee, dissolute 10. dissipated,
   licentious, profligate

rakh... 3. hay 8. hayfield 9. grassland

raki, rakee... 7. spirits (distilled)

rale... 6. rattle 8. rhonchus
   11. morbid sound

rallentando... 9. direction (Mus)
   10. ritardando, slackening

Rallidae... 5. birds, coots, rails, wekas
   6. crakes 10. gallinules

rally... 6. banter 7. recover, reunite
   8. assemble, recovery, ridicule
   10. assemblage, call to arms

rallying cry... 4. call 6. slogan
   9. battle cry, bugle call

ralph... 5. raven

ram... 3. hit, pun, tup 4. buck, butt,
   tamp 5. Aries, crash, sheep
   6. rancid, wether 7. collide

Rama... 11. Ramachandra (7th of
   fame) 19. incarnation of Vishnu

ramada... 5. arbor 7. pergola

Ramadan (Moham)... 7. fasting
   10. ninth month (for fasting)

ramage... 4. wild 5. rough 6. branch
   (tree), unruly 7. untamed 8. frenzied

ramage hawk... 8. brancher

ramass... 6. gather 7. collect

ramberge... 6. galley (swift)

ramble... 3. gad 4. roam, rove, walk
5. jaunt, prowl, range 6. stroll,
wander 7. deviate, digress, saunter
8. straggle

rambling... 7. devious 9. desultory,
deviation, deviative, wandering
10. circuitous, discursive, distracted
14. discursiveness

rambunctious... 4. wild 6. unruly
10. rampageous 12. obstreperous
14. uncontrollable

ramentum... 5. palea (palet) 6. scales
8. a shaving, particle (minute)

Rameses Dynasties (pert to)...
famed for.. 5. ruins 7. papyrus
kings.. 6. twelve
site.. 5. Egypt

ramex... 6. hernia 10. varicocele

ram-headed goat... 5. Ammon

ramie... 4. hemp, rhea 5. plant (fiber)
7. garment 9. Boehmeria 10. China
grass

ramification... 3. arm 5. ramus
6. branch 8. offshoot 9. branching
10. divergence 12. embranchment

rammack... 4. gawk, romp 5. scamp

rammel... 4. hard 6. coarse 7. new
milk, raw milk 9. brushwood
11. undergrowth

Ramona (pert to)...
heroine.. 9. half-breed (Ind)
novel by.. 7. Jackson (Helen Hunt)
shrub.. 4. mint

ramp... 3. rob 4. rage, romp, walk
5. bound, climb, crawl, creep, storm
6. dupery, unruly 7. incline,
rampage, swindle 8. gradient,
platform 9. helicline, impetuous
10. cuckoopint

rampant... 6. fierce, unruly, vallum
(anc) 7. ramping 8. abundant, reared
up (Her) 9. exuberant, prevalent,
unchecked 10. rampageous
12. high-spirited, unrestrained
13. perpendicular

rampart... 4. wall 5. agger, mound,
redan 6. escarp 7. barrier, bulwark,
defense, parapet, ravelin 8. buttress
9. earthwork 10. embankment
13. fortification

ram's horn (Heb)... 7. shophar (shofar)

ran... 4. fled, sped 6. flowed
7. coursed, managed, trotted
8. operated

ran (pert to)...
aground.. 8. decamped, levanted,
stranded
away.. 4. fled 6. eloped
9. absconded
out.. 5. spilt 7. petered, spilled

rana (Ind)... 5. title 6. prince

Rana... 5. frogs 10. amphibians
(tailless)

ranarium... 8. frog pond

rance... 4. prop 6. marble 7. support

ranch... 4. casa, farm 6. estate
8. estancia, hacienda

ranchero... 6. cowman 7. vaquero
8. herdsman 9. cattleman

rancid... 4. rank 5. musty, stale
6. reechy 9. obnoxious, offensive
10. unpleasant

rancor, rancour... 3. ire 4. gall
5. spite 6. enmity, hatred, malice,
rankle 7. ill will 9. animosity
10. resentment

rand... 4. edge, rant 5. ridge, storm
6. border, margin

random... 5. stray 6. casual, chance
7. aimless 8. casually 9. at liberty,
haphazard, orderless 10. accidental,
fortuitous 11. haphazardly

randy... 4. wild 5. revel, spree
6. beggar, coarse, frolic, virago
7. canvass 8. carousal 9. festivity
10. disorderly 11. ill-mannered
12. unmanageable

rang (pert to)... see also *ring*
loudly.. 7. clanged
mournfully.. 6. tolled 7. knelled
slowly.. 6. tolled

range... 3. row 4. ally, area, line,
rank, roam, size 5. align, gamut,
orbit, scope 6. limits, ramble, region,
series, wander 7. arrange, compass,
earshot, habitat, pasture 8. classify,
mountain 9. cookstove

range (pert to)...
finder.. 9. mekometer, telemeter
10. trekometer
man.. 5. rider 6. warden
of hills.. 5. ridge
of knowledge.. 3. ken
of stables.. 4. mews

rangle... 5. stray 6. wander
8. entangle, straggle

rani, ranee (Hind)... 4. wife 5. queen
7. empress 9. princess

rani (Romany)... 4. lady, wife

Ranier, Mt... 10. Washington (State)

ranine... 5. frogs 7. Raninae 8. mink
frog

rank... 3. bad, row 4. file, foul, line,
rate, size, tier 5. caste, class, grade,
gross, order, range 6. degree,
estate, rancid, status, wicked
7. arrange, glaring, tainted
8. absolute, abundant, classify,
eminence, flagrant, indecent,
infamous, nobility, palpable, position,
prestige, unsavory 9. downright,
formation, luxuriant, plentiful
10. malodorous 11. distinction

rank (pert to)...
and file.. 4. army 8. regulars
10. commonalty 11. third estate
celestial.. 9. hierarchy
exalted.. 8. eminence
military (old).. 8. banneret
noble.. 10. patriciate
rider.. 8. reckless 10. highwayman
social.. 5. caste

rankle... 5. chafe 6. fester 7. putrefy
8. make sore 9. suppurate 10. be
inflamed

rann... 5. verse 6. stanza, strain

ransack... 4. rake, sack 5. rifle
6. search 7. plunder, rummage

ransom... 4. fine 6. redeem, rescue
7. expiate 8. recovery

ranstead... 8. toadflax (yellow)
13. butter-and-eggs

rant... 4. rage, rail, rave 5. boast

6. steven 7. bluster, bombast, declaim 9. gay frolic 10. get excited
rantipole... 4. wild 6. rakish, unruly 9. termagant
ranula... 4. cyst
Ranunculaceae... 7. anemone 8. aconitum, clematis, crowfoot 10. delphinium, ranunculus
rap... 3. bop, hit 4. bang, blow, gibe, grab, knap, tirl 5. knock, steal 6. rascal, snatch, trifle 8. betrayal, sentence (prison) 9. criticism, reprimand 11. punishment 11. skein of yarn
rapacious... 6. greedy, rapine 8. grasping, ravenous 9. devouring, voracious 10. avaricious, predacious
rapacity... 5. greed, ravin (raven) 6. rapine 8. appetite 9. predacity
rapid... 4. fast 5. fleet, quick, swift 7. stretto (stretta)
rapidity... 5. haste, speed 8. celerity, velocity 9. fleetness, quickness
rapidly... 5. amain, apace 7. quickly, swiftly 8. snappily
rapids... 5. rifts 6. dalles
rapier... 5. bilbo, sword 6. verdun 7. ricasso (part)
rapine... 7. pillage, plunder 8. spoiling 10. ravishment, spoliation
rapport... 6. accord 7. empathy, harmony 8. relation 9. agreement 11. co-operation (hypnotism)
rapt... 8. absorbed, ecstatic 10. enraptured, interested 11. preoccupied, transported
rapture... 3. joy 4. love 5. bliss 6. trance 7. delight, ecstasy 8. rhapsody 9. transport 10. exultation
rapturous... 8. ecstatic
rare... 3. odd, raw 4. thin 6. scarce, seldom, sparse 7. notable, unusual 8. rarefied, uncommon 10. infrequent 11. undercooked
rare (pert to)...
bird.. 8. rara avis
earth.. 6. cerium 7. terbium, yttrium
metallic element.. 7. yttrium
object.. 5. curio 6. oddity 7. antique
Rare Ben, inscription... 15. tomb of Ben Jonson (Westminster Abbey)
rarebit... 10. cheese dish 11. Welsh rabbit
rarefy... 4. thin 6. dilute, expand 9. attenuate
rarely... 6. finely, seldom 8. not often, scarcely 9. extremely, unusually 11. beautifully 12. infrequently
rarity... 6. oddity 7. fewness, tenuity 8. scarcity, thinness 11. infrequency
ras... 4. cape 6. prince 11. -short-napped 13. Fascist leader
rasa... 3. sap (tree) 5. fluid, taste 6. amrita, flavor 7. essence 11. living water
rascal... 3. cad, imp 5. knave, rogue, scamp 6. varlet 9. miscreant
rascally... 4. mean 6. impish 7. knavish, roguish 8. scampish 11. mischievous
rase... 3. cut, rub 4. tear 5. graze,

level 6. scrape 7. scratch
rash... 3. mad 4. wild 5. giddy, hasty, heady, hives, scamp 6. unwary, wanton 7. Icarian 8. careless, eruption, heedless 9. desperate, exanthema, impetuous 10. headstrong, incautious, indiscreet 11. temerarious, thoughtless
rasher... 5. piece, slice 7. portion 9. thin slice
rashness... 6. acrisy 7. acrisia 8. temerity 9. hastiness
rasion... 6. filing 7. erasing, rasping, shaving 8. scraping
Rasores... 4. fowl 5. birds 6. quails 7. turkeys 8. Columbae, Gallinae 9. pheasants 10. partridges
rasp... 3. rub 4. file 5. belch, chafe, erupt, grate 6. abrade, offend, scrape 8. irritate 9. raspberry
raspberry... 3. red 5. apple, Rubus 6. raspis 7. plumbog 8. blackcap
rasping... 5. harsh 6. chafing, grating, raucous 8. grinding, scraping, very fast 9. offensive 10. irritating
raspings... 6. refuse 7. filings, remains
rasse... 5. civet
rasure... 3. cut 5. shave 7. erasure, polling, scratch, tonsure 8. scraping 12. obliteration
rat... 3. rut 4. scab, snob, wart 5. track 6. desert, ratton, rodent 7. scratch, traitor 8. deserter 9. hairpiece, scoundrel
rat (pert to)...
fish.. 8. chimaera
goose.. 11. common brant
hare.. 4. pika
kangaroo.. 7. Potorus 9. marsupial
pineapple.. 7. pinguin
poison.. 8. ratsbane
ratlike.. 4. vole
rhyme.. 6. jargon 13. doggerel verse
ratafia... 7. biscuit (almond), curacao, liqueur (Danzig)
ratchet... 4. pawl 5. click 6. bobbin, detent
rate... 4. fare, pace 5. price, ratio, style, tempo, value 6. assess, berate, charge, reckon, regard 7. account, deserve, premium, reprove 8. appraise, classify, estimate, evaluate, interest
rate (of exchange)... 4. agio 5. batta
rath (anc)... 4. hill, home (walled)
rath, ratha... 3. car 6. temple (Seven Pagodas, Madras) 7. chariot
Rathaus... 8. town hall
rathe, rath... 4. soon 5. eager, quick, speed 7. betimes, quickly 8. speedily
rather... 3. ere, yes 6. before 7. earlier, however, instead 8. somewhat 9. more truly, tolerably 10. especially, preferably 11. immediately 14. on the other hand
ratification... 4. amen 5. logic 8. sanction 9. reasoning 11. endorsement 12. confirmation
ratify... 4. amen, pass, seal 6. enseal, verify 7. approve, confirm, consent, endorse 8. roborate, sanction

9. authorize

ratio... 2. pi 4. rate, sine 5. share
6. cosine, ration 7. portion
10. proportion

ratiocination... 5. logic 7. thought
9. reasoning

ration... 5. share 6. budget 8. relation
9. allotment, allowance, provision
11. calculation

rational... 4. sane, wise 5. sober
7. logical 8. sensible 9. reasoning
10. reasonable 11. philosophic

rationale... 6. reason 11. explanation
12. the how and why

ratio scripta... 13. written reason

ratite... (opp of carinate) 7. Ratitae
8. unkeeled 14. flat breastbone

ratite bird... 3. emu (emeu), moa
7. ostrich 9. cassowary

ratoon... 5. shoot, stalk 6. spring,
sprout

rattan, ratan... 4. cane, palm, sega,
whip 6. switch 7. calamus

ratteen... 8. mahogany

rattle... 3. toy 4. herb, rale, rick, tirl
5. annoy, clack 6. assail, prison
(Nav), racket, uproar 7. agitate,
chatter, clapper, clatter, confuse,
fluster, maracas, prattle 8. nonsense
9. chatterer, rapid talk
10. disconcert, noisemaker

rattle (pert to)...
bones.. 8. clappers, snappers
9. castanets
headed.. 8. confused
11. empty—headed 13. rattlebrained
mouse.. 3. bat
nut.. 10. chinquapin
pate.. 3. ass
root.. 7. bugbane

rattlesnake... 7. rattler 8. belltail,
Crotalus, pit viper 9. Sistrurus

rattlesnake (pert to)...
bean.. 6. cedron
bite.. 9. meadow rue
fern.. 9. chain fern, sporangia
flag (Maine).. 13. Don't Tread on Me
(Hist)
herb.. 9. baneberry
leaf.. 8. plantain
pilot.. 10. copperhead
plantain.. 6. orchid
variety.. 3. red 6. banded, timber
7. prairie 11. diamondback
venom.. 8. crotalus

rattletrap... 6. gewgaw 7. rickety
8. claptrap, the mouth
10. knickknack, ramshackle

ratton... 3. rat

ratwa... 7. muntjac

raucous... 3. dry 4. bray, loud
5. harsh, noisy 6. hoarse, raucid,
rauque 8. strident 11. cacophonous

rauk, roke... 4. poke, stir 5. vapor
7. scratch

raun... 3. roe 4. fish 5. spawn

ravage... 4. loot, ruin, sack 5. havoc,
spoil, waste 6. damage, infest
7. debauch, destroy, overrun, pillage,
plunder 9. devastate 10. desolation
11. despoilment, devastation,
infestation

ravages of time... 13. deterioration
14. disintegration

rave... 4. rage, rant 5. crush, storm
7. bluster, declaim, enthuse 8. be
insane, harangue

ravel... 4. fray 6. runner, slough,
unwind 7. involve, unravel, untwist,
unweave 8. entangle, separate
11. disentangle, loose thread

ravelin... 7. railing 8. demilune,
half—moon 13. fortification

raven... 4. bird, crow 6. Corvus
8. standard (vikings) 10. raven—black
11. Corvus corax

Raven (The)... 4. poem (Edgar Allen
Poe)

ravening... 3. mad 5. rabid 6. greedy,
prying 8. desirous 9. rapacious,
turbulent

ravenous... 6. greedy 8. edacious
9. rapacious, voracious
10. gluttonous 11. catawampous

ravine... 3. gap 4. dell, linn (lin), wadi
(wady) 5. chine, gorge, gulch, slade,
strid 6. arroyo, clough, gulley, nullah
8. barranca

ravish... 3. rob 4. rape 5. seize
7. corrupt, debauch, delight, despoil,
plunder, violate 8. deflower, entrance
9. enrapture, transport

raw... 4. cold, sore 5. bleak, crude,
naked 6. chilly, unripe, vulgar
7. natural, not spun, untried
8. immature, indecent, uncooked
9. inclement, unskilled, wind—swept
10. unprepared 11. undeveloped,
unprocessed 13. inexperienced

rawboned... 4. lank 5. gaunt
7. angular 8. skeletal

rawbones... 5. Death 8. skeleton

raw—flesh—eating... 9. omophagia

rawhide... 4. skin (untanned), whip

rawhide whip... 5. knout, quirt, thong
7. sjambok

raw sugar... 9. cassonade

rax... 5. reach 6. become, strain
7. stretch

ray... 4. beam, dorn, soil, X—ray
5. array, dress, gamma, order, skate
(fish) 6. defile, radius, stripe, vision
7. besmear, raiment 8. particle,
radiance, stingray 11. arrangement,
irradiation

raya... 9. broadbill

rayless... 4. dark 5. blind

rayon... 3. ray 5. fiber 6. radius
14. postal district (Switz)

raze, rase... 3. cut 4. fell, ruin
5. erase, graze, level, shave
6. efface, scrape 7. destroy
8. demolish 9. dismantle, prostrate
10. obliterate

razee... 3. cut (Naut) 5. prune
7. abridge

razor (pert to)...
back.. 3. hog 4. boar 5. ridge
10. roustabout (circus)
bill.. 3. auk 7. skimmer
billed auk.. 4. falk 5. murre, noddy
clam.. 5. Solen 11. chopa blanca
grinder.. 10. goatsucker
sharpen.. 4. hone 5. strop

stone.. 9. whetstone 10. novaculite
strap.. 5. strop
type.. 5. safety 7. rattler
razz... 5. chaff, tease 6. banter, deride
8. ridicule 9. raspberry
razzle–dazzle.. 5. cinch (game), spree
6. dazzle 7. confuse 8. bewilder
9. commotion 10. noisemaker
re... 4. back (pref) 5. about, again,
anent, tone D (Mus) 8. syllable
(Mus) 10. concerning
Re.. 2. Ra (Egypt) see also *Ra*
reach... 4. come, gain, hawk, ryke,
spar, spit 5. equal, retch 6. advene,
arrive, attain, extend, length
7. achieve, compass, earshot,
expanse, possess, stretch
8. distance, overtake 9. influence
10. understand
reach (pert to)...
across.. 4. span
for applause.. 9. captation
high point.. 9. culminate
out.. 6. extend 7. stretch
under.. 7. subtend
up.. 6. aspire
reaction... 4. kick 6. change (Chem)
7. tropism 8. response 9. influence
10. opposition
reactionary... 4. Tory 10. malcontent
12. conservative, recalcitrant
read... 3. con 4. pore, scan, skim, tell
5. guess, solve 6. advise, browse,
peruse, recite, relate 7. counsel,
declare, discern, foresee, prelect
(praelect), stomach 8. decipher,
describe, foretell 9. interpret
10. understand
readable... 7. legible 12. decipherable
reader... 6. lector, lister, primer
(McGuffey) 7. browser, license,
reciter, speaker, teacher 8. anagnost
(anagnostes), literate, textbook
9. churchman, prelector (praelector)
10. pocketbook 11. proofreader
12. elocutionist
readily... 6. at once, easily 7. quickly
8. probably 9. willingly 10. very
likely
readjust... 7. readapt, restore
9. rearrange 11. reconstruct
12. rehabilitate
ready... 3. apt, fit, fix 4. bain, free,
here, ripe, yare 5. alert, apert,
eager, handy, point, quick 6. facile,
fitted, prompt 7. willing 8. cheerful,
disposed, inclined, prepared, skillful
9. dexterous 12. unhesitating
ready acceptance... 11. embracement
ready for... 6. awaits 8. liable to
10. in store for 11. prepared for
ready–to–wear... 12. haute couture
real... 4. true, very 5. pucka (pukka)
6. actual 7. factual, genuine, sincere
8. absolute, existent, handmade,
tangible 9. authentic, veritable
10. unaffected 11. substantial
real (pert to)...
being.. 6. entity
estate.. 5. lands 6. domain, houses,
realty 7. demesne 8. easement,

freehold, property 9. tenements
13. hereditaments
map.. 4. plot
name (backwards).. 6. ananym
school.. 10. Realschule
realistic... 5. vivid 8. lifelike
9. practical 11. descriptive
reality... 5. truth 7. realism
11. genuineness
reality, non–existent... 8. nihilism
realize... 3. get, win 4. gain, know
5. sense 7. convert 8. conceive
10. accomplish
realm... 6. domain, empire, region,
sphere 7. country, demesne, kingdom
8. division, province 10. department
12. jurisdiction
realm (of)...
darkness (Myth).. 2. po
Jamshid.. 7. Persia
perfection.. 6. Utopia
ream... 4. bore, foam, scum 5. widen
6. bundle 7. enlarge 8. bevel out
11. countersink 14. enormous
amount
reanimate... 5. rally 6. revive
7. refresh 9. resuscitate
12. reinvigorate
rear... 3. aft 4. back, grow, lift, loom,
rise, rump 5. breed, build, erect,
raise, stern, train 6. behind, foster
7. arriere, educate, elevate, produce
8. instruct 9. construct, establish,
posterior 10. background
rear (pert to)...
admiral.. 7. two bars (silver)
commodore, yacht club.. 7. officer
end.. 6. breech 7. hind end
9. afterpart, posterior
horse (insect).. 6. mantis
most.. 4. last
toward.. 3. aft 5. abaft 6. astern
8. backward, rearward
rearing up (horse)... 5. stend
6. pesade
rearrange... 4. sort 8. readjust
10. reordinate, reorganize
reason... 5. argue, logic, sense,
think 6. deduce, ground, motive,
sanity 7. discuss 8. argument,
conclude, judgment, question,
solution 9. discourse, intellect
11. explanation, ratiocinate, rationalize
13. justification, understanding
reason (pert to)...
discursively.. 11. ratiocinate
doctrine of, author.. 10. Anaxagoras
higher.. 4. mind, nous 5. logic
Latin.. 5. causa
ostensible.. 7. pretext
proof of.. 8. argument
want of.. 7. amentia
why.. 5. cause 6. motive
reasonable... 4. fair, just, sane
6. proper 7. logical 8. rational
9. equitable, plausible, practical
10. fair–minded 11. inexpensive,
intelligent, justifiable
reasoning (pert to)...
basis of.. 7. premise
delusive.. 7. fallacy

exact.. 5. logic
harmonize.. 11. rationalize
plausible.. 8. specious
reassure... 6. assure, solace
7. comfort, console, hearten
8. embolden, give hope
reata... 4. rope 5. lasso, riata 6. lariat
reave... 3. rob 4. rend, tear 5. break,
burst, seize, split 7. plunder
reb... 5. rebel
rebate... 3. check 6. reduce, weaken
8. diminish, discount 9. abatement,
deduction, remission
rebato (Hist)... 4. ruff 6. collar, rabato
9. piccadill
Rebekah (pert to)...
husband.. 5. Isaac
sister.. 5. Laban
son.. 4. Esau 5. Jacob
rebel... 3. reb 4. rise 6. resist, revolt
8. renounce, turncoat 9. insurgent
13. revolutionist
rebellion... 5. Great (Eng 1642–49)
6. mutiny, revolt 8. American (Civil
War 1861–65) 10. resistance,
revolution 12. insurrection,
renunciation
rebellious... 8. mutinous 9. insurgent
10. refractory 12. contumacious
13. insubordinate, revolutionary
rebirth... 7. revival 9. salvation
10. conversion 11. renaissance
13. reincarnation
rebound... 4. stot 5. carom
6. bounce, recoil, re-echo, spring
7. resound 8. rebounce, ricochet
11. reverberate
rebuff... 4. slap, snub 5. chide, scold
6. defeat, lesson, recoil, refuse,
reject, resist 7. censure, refusal
(brusque), reprove, repulse
9. reprimand
rebuke... 3. nip 4. slap 5. check,
chide, rebuff 7. repress, reproof,
reprove 8. admonish, reproach,
restrain 9. criticize, reprehend,
reprimand 11. comeuppance
recalcitrant... 5. rebel 8. renitent
9. obstinate, recoiling, resistant
10. rebellious, refractory
11. disobedient 12. ungovernable
recall... 5. annul 6. encore, recant,
remind, repeal, revoke, summon
7. retract 8. remember, withdraw
9. recollect, reminisce
11. recantation 12. recollection
recant... 6. abjure, revoke 7. disavow,
retract 8. renounce, withdraw
9. repudiate 10. contradict
recapitulate... 5. essay, sum up
6. repeat, review 7. restate
8. argument 9. reiterate, summarize
recapture... 6. recall, regain, retake
7. recover
recede... 3. ebb 4. wane 6. depart,
retire 7. deviate, regress, retreat
8. withdraw 10. retrograde
receipt... 5. axiom 6. acquit, answer,
recipe 7. formula 12. prescription
14. acknowledgment
receipts... 7. the take

receive... 3. get 4. hold, take
5. admit, greet, learn, reset
6. accept, assent, derive, obtain,
take in 7. acquire, contain, procure
9. apprehend
receive (pert to)...
a confession.. 6. shrive
a reward.. 4. reap
stolen property.. 5. reset
receiver... 5. donee, fence 7. catcher
8. believer 9. recipient, treasurer
10. receptacle
receiver (pert to)...
fixed income.. 7. rentier
profits (law).. 6. pernor
property in trust.. 6. bailee
stolen property.. 5. fence
recension... 6. review 8. revising,
revision 9. reviewing
11. enumeration, examination
recent... 3. new 4. late, past 5. fresh
6. former, modern 7. current,
newborn 8. neonatal, neoteric
receptacle... 3. bag, bin, box, can,
cup, pan 4. case, cask, cyst (anc),
etui, pail, tank, tray, vase 5. basin,
crock 6. basket, bottle, bucket,
carton, holder, hopper 7. compote,
hanaper, platter 8. canister, catchall
9. container 10. repository
receptacle (pert to)...
assayer's, stonecutter's.. 7. sebilla
botany.. 5. torus
coal.. 3. bin
corporal (RCCh).. 5. burse
grain.. 3. bin 8. elevator
holy water.. 5. stoup
vote.. 5. situla
reception... 3. tea 5. levee, salon
6. infare, soiree 7. accueil, ovation,
receipt, welcome 8. ceremony,
sociable 9. admission, interview,
intuition 12. housewarming
13. entertainment
reception hall, room... 5. salon
6. atrium, parlor 9. vestibule
receptionist... 4. host 7. hostess
8. landlord
receptive... 6. pliant 8. sensible
9. acceptant, admissive, teachable
10. hospitable, open–minded
11. persuasive
receptor... 5. basin 8. receiver
10. dispositor (Astron), sense organ
recess... 3. ala, bay, pan (leaf)
4. apse, nook, rest 5. crypt, niche,
pause, sinus, space 7. adjourn,
respite, retreat 9. recession, seclusion
11. indentation 12. intermission
recipe... 5. axiom 7. formula, receipt
12. prescription
recipient... 4. heir 5. donee 7. legatee
8. receiver
reciprocal... 5. joint 6. mutual, shared
8. exchange 9. alternate
11. convertible, correlative, retaliatory
15. interchangeable
reciprocate... 5. bandy 6. accord,
concur 8. exchange 9. alternate,
retaliate 10. correspond
11. interchange
recision... 6. repeal 7. pruning

9. canceling (cancelling)
10. rescinding

recital... 4. tale 5. story 6. lesson, speech 7. account, concert (exhibition) 8. musicale 9. narration, narrative, rehearsal 10. recitation, repetition 11. enumeration, reiteration

recitation... 6. lesson, speech 7. reading 10. exhibition

recite... 4. tell 5. quote, speak, state 6. relate, repeat 7. declaim, narrate, recount 8. rehearse, tell over 9. enumerate, pronounce 12. recapitulate

recite (pert to)...
in monotone.. 6. intone
metrically.. 4. scan
rhetorically.. 7. declaim
to music.. 5. chant 10. cantillate

reciter... 4. book (of extracts) 5. roter 7. relator, speaker 8. narrator

reck... 4. care, deem, heed, mind 6. regard 7. concern 8. estimate

reckless... 4. rash 5. perdu (perdue) 6. madcap 7. hotspur 8. careless, heedless 9. desperate, hotheaded, imprudent 10. neglectful, regardless 11. indifferent, thoughtless, unconcerned 13. inconsiderate

reckon... 4. aret (arette), date, deem, tell 5. class, count, judge, tally, think 6. impute, number, regard, repute 7. account, compute, include, suppose 8. consider, estimate, evaluate 9. calculate, enumerate

reckon in... 7. contain, embrace, include 8. comprise

reckoning... 3. sum 4. bill, shot 5. score, tally 6. esteem 7. account, verdict 8. counting 9. summation 10. estimation 11. calculation

reckoning instrument... 6. abacus 9. tabulator 10. calculator

reclaim... 4. tame 5. renew, train 6. ransom, recall, redeem, revoke 7. convert, recover, restore 8. civilize 10. regenerate 12. rehabilitate

recline... 3. lay, lie, sit 4. lean, loll, rest 6. repose 7. incline, lie down

reclining... 4. flat 5. prone 6. supine 7. lolling 8. couchant, reposing 9. prostrate, recumbent, sprawling

recluse... 3. fra, nun 4. monk 6. hermit, hidden, secret, shut up 7. ascetic, eremite, retired (from world) 8. anchoret, solitary 9. anchorite 10. cloistered 11. sequestered

recognition... 4. fame 6. recall 9. detection 10. cognizance 11. discernment 14. acknowledgment

recognize... 3. see 4. know 5. admit 6. detect 7. consent 8. perceive 10. appreciate, recognosce 11. acknowledge

recoil... 3. shy 4. funk 6. resile, shrink 7. rebound, retreat 8. reaction, withdraw

recollect... 6. recall, revive 7. think of 8. remember 10. call to mind

recollection... 4. mind 6. memory 9. anamnesis 11. remembrance

12. reminiscence

recommence... 4. zoom 5. renew 6. resume 8. return to 9. begin anew

recommend... 4. tout, urge 6. advise, commit, denote, praise 7. commend, consign, entrust 8. advocate

recompense... 3. fee, pay 4. meed 5. repay 6. reward 7. guerdon, premium, requite 8. requital 9. indemnify, reimburse 10. compensate, remunerate 11. reciprocate

recompense (pert to)...
Brehon Law.. 4. eric
Germanic law.. 7. wergild
Scot law.. 3. cro
Welsh law.. 7. galanas

reconcile... 4. suit, wean 5. atone 6. adjust, pacify, settle 7. cleanse (Eccl), conform, reunite 9. harmonize 10. conciliate, propitiate

reconciliation... 7. harmony, reunion 10. adjustment, conformity 12. pacification 13. reconcilement

reconciliator... 10. reconciler 13. intermediator

recondite... 4. dark, deep 6. hidden, mystic, occult 7. cryptic 8. abstract, abstruse, esoteric 9. concealed

reconnaissance... 6. survey 8. scouting 11. examination

reconnoiter... 5. scout 6. survey 7. examine

reconstruct... 6. recast, remake 7. rebuild, remodel 9. reproduce 11. re-establish

record... 3. log, tab 4. disc, file, list, memo 5. annal, diary, enter, entry, score 6. agenda, legend, memoir, postea 7. archive, estreat, history 8. memorial, register 9. chronicle 10. chronology, transcribe, transcript

record (pert to)...
criminal investigation.. 7. dossier
document.. 8. protocol
earth tremor.. 11. seismograph
formal.. 8. register
historic.. 6. annals 7. rotulet
keeper.. 9. registrar 10. chartulary
of events.. 5. annal, fasti 7. history
official.. 8. actum
pictorial.. 5. graph
ship's voyage.. 3. log
year's.. 8. calendar

recount... 3. min 4. tell 5. sum up 6. reckon, relate, repeat, retail 7. narrate 8. rehearse 9. enumerate, reiterate

recoup... 4. gain 7. recover 9. indemnity, reimburse 10. compensate

recourse... 3. use 5. recur 6. access, betake, refuge, resort, return, revert 7. retreat

recover... 3. get 4. cure, gain, heal 5. rally, reach, upset 6. obtain, recoup, redeem, regain, rescue, resume 7. get well, reclaim, recruit 8. overcome, retrieve 9. repossess 10. recuperate

recovery... 6. return 7. salvage

9. retrieval 11. reclamation, reformation, restoration
recreant... 6. coward, wretch
7. dastard, knavish 8. apostate, betrayer, cowardly, deserter
9. reprobate 10. unfaithful
recreation... 4. food, game, meal, play
5. sport 7. holiday, renewal
8. vacation 9. amusement, diversion
11. refreshment 12. reproduction
14. reconstruction
recrement... 5. dross 6. refuse, scoria
recruit... 5. raise 6. enlist, gather, muster, novice, revive, rookie
7. recover, refresh, restore
8. assemble, inductee, newcomer
9. conscript, reinforce, replenish
12. reinvigorate
rectangle... 10. quadrangle
13. parallelogram
rectangular... 6. oblong
12. quadrangular
rectify... 5. amend, emend, right
6. adjust, better, reform, remedy
7. correct, justify 8. emendate, regulate, set right 10. straighten
rector... 5. chief 6. leader, master (Oxford), pastor 8. director, governor
9. churchman, clergyman
10. headmaster
rectory... 8. benefice 9. personage
recumbent... 4. idle 5. lying, prone
7. leaning, resting 8. inactive, reposing 9. reclining
recuperate... 4. rest 6. recoup, regain
7. improve, recover, restore 9. get better, reimburse
recur... 5. again 6. repeat, return
7. persist, reoccur 8. reappear
recurrent... 10. repetitive
recurring (pert to)...
continually.. 8. constant
10. habitually, repeatedly
ninth day.. 5. nonan
seventh day.. 6. septan
third day.. 7. tertian
red... 4. rosy 5. color, ruddy 7. radical
8. blushing, inflamed, rutilant, sanguine 9. bloodshot
12. bloodstained 13. revolutionary
red (color)... 4. fire, lake, pink, puce, rose, ruby, tile, wine 5. blood, brick, canna, coral, flame, flesh, henna, poppy 6. auburn, cerise, cherry, claret, damask, maroon, minium, raddle, salmon, titian, Turkey
7. anemone, annatto, carmine, Chinese, crimson, lobster, magenta, nacarat, scarlet, stammel 8. cardinal, cinnabar 9. carnation, carnelian, vermilion
red (pert to)...
cap (Turk).. 8. tarboosh
cell.. 11. erythrocite
corpuscle.. 10. hemoglobin (source of)
dog.. 4. game 8. banknote
dye.. 3. aal, lac 4. chay (choy)
5. aurin (aurine), eosin (eosine)
6. morindin
gum.. 10. strophulus
hair.. 6. titian
herring.. 4. ruse 9. diversion

minded.. 7. radical
planet.. 4. Mars
race.. 7. Indians
robbin.. 14. scarlet tanager
truffle.. 12. melanogaster
viper.. 10. copperhead
Red (pert to)...
Book.. 7. Austria 13. Royal Kalendar
Crescent.. 8. Red Cross (Turk)
Cross.. 9. St George's (Eng)
Friar.. 13. Knight Templar
Guard.. 4. Army 7. Russian
Hand.. 13. Badge of Ulster
Horse.. 10. Kentuckian
Planet.. 4. Mars
Polled.. 6. cattle (hornless)
Prince.. 7. Russian (Frederick Charles)
Ribbon.. 14. Order of the Bath
Rose.. 16. House of Lancaster
Russian.. 9. Bolshevik
Sea.. 14. Erythraean main
Sea city.. 9. Leningrad
Sea colony.. 7. Eritrea
Sea gulf.. 5. Aqaba
Square.. 6. Moscow
The Red.. 4. Eric (Scand)
Triangle.. 4. YMCA (symbol)
redact... 4. edit 5. draft, frame
6. revise
redactor... 6. editor 7. reviser
9. redacteur
reddish (pert to)...
blue.. 5. smalt 9. damascene
brown.. 3. bay 4. roan 5. henna
6. auburn, russet, sorrel 8. chestnut
dye.. 7. annatto
yellow.. 5. amber 6. orange
rede... 6. advice, relate 7. counsel, explain, predict 9. interpret
redeem... 3. pay 6. ransom, regain, rescue 7. convert, fulfill, reclaim, recover 8. liberate 10. repurchase, substitute
redeemer... 4. goel (Heb) 7. saviour (savior) 9. deliverer, liberator
11. emancipator
Redeemer, The... 8. Son of God
10. The Messiah, The Saviour
11. Jesus Christ
redintegrate... 5. renew, unite
7. restore 9. reconcile
11. re-establish
redness... 4. glow 8. blushing
10. erubescent, rubescence
redolence... 4. odor 5. aroma, scent
9. fragrance, sweetness
redolent... 5. balmy 7. odorous, scented 8. aromatic, fragrant
11. impregnated, reminiscent
redouble... 6. re-echo, repeat
7. reflect, reprise (fencing)
9. intensify 10. ingeminate, repetition
11. reduplicate
redoubt... 4. fear 5. doubt 6. reduit
7. defense, ravelin
redound... 5. surge 6. abound, return
7. conduce, resound 8. flow back, overflow 10. contribute (to)
11. reverberate
redpoll... 5. finch 6. linnet 7. warbler
Red Polled cattle... 8. hornless
redress... 4. help 5. amend, emend

6. reform, remedy 7. correct, relieve
8. atone for, reprisal 9. atonement
10. correction, recompense,
reparation 11. reformation, restitution

reduce... 3. cut 4. bant, bate, pare,
thin 5. abase, abate, lower, razee
6. demote, derate, humble, lessen,
subdue, weaken 7. abridge, analyze,
cheapen, conquer, curtail, deplete,
qualify, relieve, shorten 8. decrease,
diminish, discount, minimize,
moderate 9. subjugate
10. impoverish, slenderize

reduce in flesh... 8. emaciate

reduce in rank... 6. demote

reduce to...
ashes.. 7. cremate
average.. 4. mean 6. equate
bondage.. 7. enslave
common measure.. 12. commensurate
half.. 9. dimidiate
lower grade.. 6. demote 7. degrade
mean time.. 6. equate
spray.. 7. atomize

reduction... 6. rebate 7. subdual
8. decrease, demotion, discount,
lowering 9. weakening
10. abridgment, cheapening,
conversion, moderation

reduction (pert to)...
in value.. 12. depreciation
to absurdity.. 18. reductio ad
absurdum
to common level.. 15. standardization
to compactness.. 12. condensation
to standard.. 15. standardization

redundancy... 6. excess 7. profuse
8. pleonasm, verbiage 9. prolixity,
talkative, tautology, verbosity
10. repetition 11. periphrasis
13. diffusiveness 14. circumlocution

redundant... 6. lavish 7. copious,
diffuse, verbose 9. excessive,
exuberant, plethoric 10. pleonastic
11. overflowing, repetitious,
superfluous 13. superabundant

ree... 3. dam 4. sift, wild 5. crazy,
drunk, river 6. harbor, riddle
7. channel, fuddled 8. coalyard
9. enclosure, sheepfold

re-echo... 7. resound 11. reverberate

reechy... 5. fetid 6. rancid

reed... 4. stem, tube 5. arrow, straw
6. thatch 10. instrument

reed (pert to)...
bird.. 4. wren 7. babbler, warbler
8. bobolink
buck.. 6. bohor, nagar 8. antelope
bunting.. 7. sparrow 8. reedling
loom.. 4. sley
mace.. 7. cattail, matreed
measure. *(Jew)*.. 9. six cubits
pipe.. 5. kazoo 8. mirliton

reef... 3. bar, cay (cayo), key (quay)
4. itch, lode, sail, vein 5. islet,
mange, shoal 6. island 7. shorten
8. eruption

reef (pert to)...
coral.. 3. key
knot.. 6. square
mining.. 4. lode, vein
nautical.. 5. sails

sand.. 3. bar

reefer... 5. miner 6. jacket, oyster
9. cigarette 10. midshipman

reek... 3. fug, rig 4. fume 5. equip,
exude, smell, smoke, steam
7. malodor, seaweed 8. fetid air,
smell bad, vaporize 10. exhalation

reel... 4. eddy, pirn, rock, sail, sway,
wind 5. dance, lurch, spool, swift
(yarn), swing, waver, wince 6. tatter
7. scrieve, stagger 8. flounder,
titubate, windlass 9. Virginia reel

reeling... 5. drunk 7. swaying, winding
8. rotating

reem (Bib)... 6. animal (horned), wild
ox 7. unicorn

re-embody... 7. combine, reshape
10. reorganize 11. reincarnate
13. reincorporate

reeve... 3. pen 4. ruff 5. strip
6. thread 8. official (Eng Hist)
9. enclosure, sheepfold

refect... 7. refresh, restore

refectory... 6. frater (monastery)
8. mess hall 10. dining hall

refer... 4. cite 5. apply, recur
6. allude, appeal, charge, impute,
relate, return 7. ascribe 9. appertain,
attribute

refer (to)... 4. harp 6. advert
7. consult, mention

referee... 5. judge 6. umpire 7. arbiter
8. attorney 9. moderator
10. arbitrator

reference... 6. regard 7. respect
8. allusion, relation 9. character,
relevance 10. connection, pertinence
14. recommendation

reference (pert to)...
book.. 5. atlas 8. handbook, syllabus
9. thesaurus 10. dictionary
12. encyclopedia

referendum... 4. vote 7. mandate
8. politics 10. plebiscite

refine... 5. smelt 6. rarefy 7. clarify,
elevate, improve, sublime
9. elaborate, sensitize, sublimate

refined... 4. fine, nice, pure, rare
5. urban 6. chaste 7. elegant,
smelted 8. cleansed, highbred,
purified, well-bred 9. clarified,
courteous, perfected 10. cultivated,
fastidious, meticulous

refined spirit... 5. grace 6. elixir

refinement... 5. taste 6. polish
7. finesse 8. delicacy, elegance,
fineness 9. gentility 11. cultivation,
rarefaction 13. clarification

refinery (ore)... 7. smelter

refining cup... 5. cupel

reflect... 3. say 4. muse, pore
5. radar, think 6. divert, mirror,
ponder 7. deflect 8. cogitate,
consider, meditate, ruminate, turn
back 9. reproduce 11. reverberate

reflecting... 6. musing 9. judicious
10. reflective, ruminating, thoughtful
11. insinuating 13. reverberatory
15. casting reproach

reflection... 4. idea 5. image, light
6. musing 7. bending, thought
8. reaction, thinking 10. cogitation,

meditation, rumination
12. afterthought, recollection
13. consideration, contemplation

reflex... 4. bent 6. turned 8. allusion,
reaction, reversed 9. duplicate,
reflected 13. introspection

reflux... 3. ebb 6. ebbing, reflow
8. backflow, reaction 9. refluence,
returning

reform... 4. mend 5. amend, emend,
renew 6. better, remake, remass,
repair 7. convert, rebuild, reclaim,
rectify, restore 8. amendment
10. regenerate 11. reformation

reformation... 7. rebirth
10. conversion, emendation
12. regeneration, reproduction
15. re-establishment

Reformation leaders (Hist)... 4. Knox
6. Calvin, Luther, Ridley 7. Cranmer,
Latimer, Zwingli 8. Campbell
11. Melanchthon

reformer... 7. amender, reviser
9. reformado, reformist 10. politician

refraction... 7. rebound 9. dioptrics
11. deflection, dispersion
11. anaclastics

refractor... 5. prism 9. telescope

refractory... 7. restive 8. indocile,
stubborn 11. disobedient
12. ungovernable

refrain... 4. curb, shun 5. avoid,
cease, derry, epode 6. chorus,
govern 7. abstain, forbear
8. response, restrain

refrain from using... 5. spare
7. boycott

refresco... 4. food 5. drink
11. refreshment

refresh... 3. air, dew 4. cool 5. cheer,
renew, slake 6. repose, revive
7. freshen, relieve 8. recreate,
renovate 9. reanimate, replenish
10. invigorate, strengthen
11. refreshment 12. reinvigorate

refreshing... 5. balmy 7. bracing
8. regaling 10. heartening
11. stimulating 12. exhilarating

refrigerant... 3. ice 6. cooler
7. ammonia, coolant, cryogen

refrigeration... 7. cooling 8. cryogeny
10. anesthetic, cryogenics
12. preservation

refuge... 3. ark 4. plea 5. haven
6. asylum, covert, excuse 7. retreat,
shelter 8. hospital, recourse, resource
9. sanctuary 10. protection, safety
zone

refugee... 5. exile, fleer 6. émigré
7. escapee, evacuee 8. fugitive,
renegade

refulgence... 6. luster 8. radiance,
splendor 10. brilliancy

refund... 5. repay 6. rebate
9. reimburse

refurbish... 4. vamp 5. renew
8. brighten, renovate 11. recondition

refusal... 3. nay 6. denial 9. rejection
11. declination

refuse... 3. cot (wool), ort 4. balk,
coom (coomb), culm, deny, junk,
marc, scum 5. attle, chaff, dregs,

dross, repel, scrap, trash, waste,
weeds 6. debris, give up, litter,
midden, naysay, reject, renege,
scoria, scraps 7. abandon, bagasse,
cast off, decline, garbage, hogwash,
repulse 8. disclaim, leavings,
oddments, renounce, withhold
9. excrement, repudiate 11. odds
and ends

refuse to...
accept.. 6. reject
acknowledge.. 7. disavow 9. repudiate
comply.. 12. recalcitrant
proceed.. 4. balk

refutation... 6. answer 8. disproof,
elenchus, rebuttal 11. confutation

refute... 4. deny, meet 5. rebut, refel
6. assoil 8. disprove, elenctic,
redargue 9. overthrow 10. contradict

regain... 6. recoup 7. get back,
recover 8. retrieve 9. get back to
10. reach again

regal... 5. royal 6. groove, kingly
7. channel, stately 8. imperial,
majestic, splendid 9. dignified,
sovereign

regale... 4. dine, fete 5. amuse, feast,
treat 7. gratify, refresh 9. entertain
11. refreshment

regalia... 6. finery 7. costume,
emblems, symbols 8. insignia
11. decorations 12. special dress
13. paraphernalia

regard... 3. air, awe 4. care, deem,
gaze, heed, hold, look, love, mind,
obey (law), rate, sake, view 5. honor,
judge, think, treat 6. aspect, behold,
esteem, remark, repute 8. attitude,
consider, estimate, hold dear, listen
to 9. attention, relevance, viewpoint
10. appearance, estimation
11. contemplate, observation
13. consideration

regard (pert to)...
for others... 8. altruism
for other's wish.. 9. deference
highly.. 6. admire 7. lionize
with approval.. 6. admire
with deference.. 5. honor 7. respect
with veneration.. 7. revere

regardful... 7. careful, mindful
8. cautious 9. attentive, observant
10. altruistic, respectful, thoughtful
11. considerate

regarding... 2. re 5. anent
10. concerning, respecting

regardless... 6. anyhow 8. careless,
heedless, slighted 9. negligent
10. neglectful 11. inattentive,
indifferent, unconcerned, unobservant
15. notwithstanding

regards... 8. respects 9. greetings
11. compliments

regatta cup... 5. Platt 8. Carnegie,
Grimoldi

regency... 4. rule 8. dominion
10. government

regenerate... 5. shape 6. redeem,
reform, revive 7. convert, restore
8. re-create 9. reproduce
11. fashion anew

regeneration... 7. renewal, revival

9. reversion **10.** re-creation
11. reformation **12.** reproduction
14. divine function
regent... **5.** ruler **6.** deputy, ruling
7. regnant **8.** governor
Regent diamond, 137 carats (pert
to)...
   included in.. **11.** State jewels (France)
   named for.. **14.** Regent of France
   placed in.. **6.** Louvre
   sold (1717) to.. **4.** Pitt (Gov of
    Madras, Ind)
regime, regimen... **4.** diet, rule
6. system **7.** therapy
10. government, regulation
14. administration
regiment... **4.** unit, wing **6.** outfit
8. organize **11.** systematize
regiment, framework of... **5.** cadre
regina... **5.** queen
region... **4.** area, belt, zone **5.** clime,
place, realm, space, tract **6.** sphere
7. climate, cockpit, country,
demesne, kingdom, section
8. district, province
region (pert to)...
   beyond Jordan.. **5.** Perea **6.** Basham
   blissful.. **4.** Eden
   comb form.. **5.** nesia
   desert.. **3.** erg **5.** waste
   indefinite.. **5.** tract
   infernal.. **7.** Avernal **8.** Tartarus
   meteorological.. **6.** pleion
   wooded.. **4.** wold
   woodless.. **5.** weald
region of...
   contentment.. **6.** Arcady
   dead (Egypt Myth).. **6.** Amenti
   fabled wealth.. **8.** Eldorado
   nether darkness.. **6.** Erebus
   opposite side earth.. **9.** Antipodes
   Solomon's gold (Bib).. **5.** Ophir
register... **3.** act **4.** list, roll **5.** annal,
entry, index **6.** docket, enlist, enroll,
record **7.** rotulet **8.** archives,
recorder, schedule **9.** catalogue,
chronicle, necrology, registrar
11. account book, matriculate
registrar... **8.** recorder **9.** accounter
regius... **5.** royal **13.** professorship
regret... **3.** rue **4.** ruth **5.** grief, sorry
6. repent, repine, sorrow **7.** deplore,
remorse **9.** penitence **10.** repentance
11. compunction **12.** self-reproach
regretful... **5.** sorry **8.** repining
9. repentant
regular... **4.** even **5.** usual **6.** formal,
normal, smooth, stated **7.** correct,
orderly, typical, uniform **8.** constant,
habitual, ordinary, ordinate, rhythmic,
standard **9.** isometric **10.** systematic
regularity... **7.** order **8.** symmetry
9. constancy **10.** smoothness,
uniformity
regularly... **6.** always **7.** usually
8. properly, smoothly **9.** correctly
10. constantly, habitually
12. methodically, periodically
13. symmetrically
regulate... **3.** set **4.** rule **6.** adjust,
direct, govern, manage, ordain,
remedy **7.** arrange, control, dispose

8. organize **9.** influence, methodize
11. standardize
regulation... **3.** law **4.** rule **5.** bylaw,
order **6.** system **7.** control, precept
9. direction, principle
regulator... **7.** control **8.** governor,
rheostat **9.** rheometer
Regulus... **4.** king, star **5.** Alpha
8. warblers **9.** Cor Leonis (star)
rehabilitate... **7.** restore **9.** reeducate,
reinstall
rehash... **7.** restate **9.** réchauffé
rehearse... **3.** say **4.** tell **5.** speak,
sum up, train **6.** detail, recite, relate,
repeat, try out **7.** mention, narrate,
recount **8.** describe **9.** enumerate,
reiterate **12.** recapitulate
rehoboam... **3.** hat **4.** bowl **6.** flagon
8. jeroboam
Rehoboam (Bib)... **11.** King of Judah
(1st) **12.** King of Israel (last)
reif... **7.** plunder, robbery
reign... **3.** raj **4.** rule, sway **5.** guide,
realm **6.** empire **7.** kingdom, prevail
8. dominion, flourish **11.** sovereignty
12. supreme power
Reign of Terror (Fr Hist)... **7.** anarchy
9. bloodshed, despotism
12. confiscation
reimburse... **3.** pay **5.** repay **6.** refund
7. pay back, replace **9.** indemnify
10. recompense
Reims, Rheims (pert to)...
   capital (anc).. **4.** Remi
   famed building.. **9.** Cathedral (Gothic)
   famed site.. **15.** crowning of kings
    (Fr)
rein... **4.** curb, stop **5.** check, leash
6. direct, retard **7.** control
8. reindeer, restrain **9.** hindrance
10. bridle part
reina... **8.** rockfish
reindeer... **6.** tarand **7.** caribou
13. constellation
reindeer (pert to)...
   age, epoch.. **11.** Paleolithic
   flower.. **9.** buttercup (white)
   genus.. **8.** Rangifer
reinforce... **4.** back **5.** add to, brace,
reman **7.** restore, support
9. intensify, replenish **10.** strengthen
reinforcement... **7.** adjunct, support
8. addition **13.** replenishment,
strengthening
reins... **5.** loins **7.** harness, kidneys
9. restraint
reis... **6.** escudo **7.** milreis **14.** money
of account
reit... **5.** sedge **7.** seaweed
reiterate... **4.** drum, harp **6.** repeat
8. rehearse **12.** recapitulate
reject... **5.** repel, spurn **6.** disown,
recuse (law), refuse **7.** decline,
discard, dismiss **8.** athetize, disallow
9. repudiate
rejectamenta... **6.** wrack **6.** refuse,
reject **7.** rubbish **9.** excrement
rejection... **6.** heresy **7.** discard,
refusal **8.** ejection **9.** exclusion,
objection **11.** disapproval, repudiation
rejoice... **5.** cheer, elate **7.** delight,
gladden **8.** jubilate

rejoinder... 5. reply (law) 6. answer, retort, return 8. comeback

rejuvenate... 6. revive 7. restore 9. stimulate 12. reinvigorate

relâche... 10. relaxation 12. intermission 13. no performance (Theat)

relapse... 4. sink 5. lapse 7. subside 8. slip back 9. backslide, reversion 10. recurrence 11. falling back 12. recidivation

relate... 4. tell 5. state 6. assert, detail, recite, report 7. narrate, pertain, recount 8. describe, rehearse 9. appertain, associate

related (pert to)...
  by blood.. 3. sib 4. akin 7. cognate
  on father's side.. 6. agnate 8. agnation
  on mother's side.. 5. enate 6. enatic 7. cognate, enation 9. umbilical
  to land.. 8. praedial (predial)

relating to...
  bread.. 6. panary
  Chinese.. 7. Sinitic
  dancing.. 6. gestic
  fruit jelly.. 7. pectous
  grandparents.. 4. aval
  Hindu literature.. 5. Vedic
  holly.. 4. Ilex
  life.. 6. vital
  morn.. 7. matinal
  motion.. 9. kinematic
  realities.. 7. factual
  soft palate.. 5. velar
  stars.. 6. astral
  vascular fluid.. 5. hemic

relation... 3. kin 4. mode, tale 6. status, ubiety 7. account, analogy, kinship, kinsman, recital, telling 8. relative 9. character, narration, reference, rehearsal, rishtadar (Hind law) 10. connection 13. consanguinity

relationship... 4. outs 7. kinship, kinsman, metochy 8. affinity, relative 13. consanguinity

relative... 3. eme, kin, sib, son 4. aunt 5. niece, uncle 6. allied, cousin, father, mother, nephew, sister 7. brother, kindred 8. apposite, daughter, kinsfolk 9. pertinent 11. comparative, correlative 13. corresponding, proportionate

relative (pert to)...
  favor to.. 8. nepotism
  on father's side.. 6. agnate 7. cognate
  on mother's side.. 5. enate
  rank.. 6. degree
  to.. 7. apropos 12. in proportion

relax... 4. ease, open, rest 5. abate, loose, remit 6. divert, loosen, soften, unbend 7. detente, slacken 8. mitigate, slow down

relay... 3. dak (dawk) 4. race 5. shift 6. remuda 7. relieve 8. avantlay 10. television (station)

release... 4. drop, free, trip, undo 5. death, let go, loose, undam, unpen, untie 6. acquit, escape, exempt, loosen, parole, remise 7. deliver, freedom, manumit, receipt, relieve, unleash, unloose 8. liberate 9. discharge 10. liberation, relinquish 11. acquittance, deliverance

relegate... 5. exile, refer 6. assign, banish, commit, deport, remove 7. consign, discard, dismiss, exclude 8. delegate

relent... 5. abate, yield 6. regret, soften, submit 7. slacken

relentless... 6. strict 9. merciless 10. inflexible, unyielding 11. persevering, unremitting

relevant... 7. germane 9. pertinent 10. sufficient 11. referential

reliable... 4. safe, sure 5. tried 6. stable, trusty 7. solvent 11. trustworthy

reliance... 4. hope 5. trust 6. belief 8. mainstay 10. confidence, dependence

relic... 5. curio, huaca, huaco, ruins 7. antique, memento, remains 8. fragment, memorial, souvenir, survival 9. antiquity

relic cabinet... 7. étagère, whatnot

relict... 5. widow 7. widower 8. survivor

relied... 6. banked 7. counted, reposed, trusted 8. confided, depended, reckoned

relief... 3. aid 4. bote (bot), dole, ease, fret (Arch), help 5. spell 6. remedy, succor 7. comfort, outline, redress, relieve, welfare 8. easement 10. assistance, embossment, mitigation, substitute, sustenance 11. alleviation, deliverance 15. indemnification

relieve... 3. aid 4. cure, ease, free, help 5. abate, allay, clear, raise, spell 6. assist, remedy, remove, succor 7. assuage, lighten, redress, refresh, support, sustain, unloose 8. diminish 10. substitute

religion (pert to)... 4. sect 5. creed, deism, faith, piety, trust 6. belief, hermit, schism, theism, voodoo 8. monastic, theology 9. solipsism 10. conformity, persuasion

religion, type... 6. Mormon, Taoism, Yogism 7. Jainism, Judaism 8. Buddhism, Hinduism, Islamite 9. Moslemism, Shintoism 11. Anglicanism, Catholicism 12. Christianity, Confucianism 13. Mohammedanism, Protestantism

religious... 4. holy 5. exact, godly, pious, rigid 6. devout, sacred 7. devoted, fervent, zealous 9. pharasaic, spiritual 10. devotional, meticulous, scrupulous 11. theological 13. conscientious

religious (pert to)...
  assembly.. 12. congregation
  belief.. 5. deism 6. omnist
  brotherhood.. 8. sodality
  center.. 7. Lambeth (Eng)
  composition.. 5. motet
  cult, sect.. 5. fakir 6. Shaker, Shinto 7. Dadaism, Pietism, Sikhism 8. cenobite 9. anchorite

devotee . . 5. fakir
devotion . . 6. novena
division . . 6. schism
expedition (Mil) . . 7. crusade
fasting . . 4. Lent 9. Ember Days
   10. Ember Weeks
festival . . 4. mela (Ind) 5. Purim (Jew)
madness, mania . . 9. theomania
metaphysics . . 7. gnostic
musical . . 6. anthem
offering . . 7. deodate 8. oblation
Order member . . 6. Marist 7. Templar
poem . . 5. psalm
primitive . . 6. voodoo
psalm . . 4. hymn, poem, song
publication (RCch) . . 4. ordo
relinquish . . . 3. let 4. cede, quit
   5. forgo, leave, waive, yield
   6. desert, desist, forego, give up,
   remise, resign 7. abandon, forsake,
   release 8. abdicate, renounce
   9. surrender 11. leave behind
   12. withdraw from
relinquishment . . . 9. surrender
   11. abandonment 12. renunciation
reliquary, reliquiae (pl) . . . 3. box
   4. arca, tomb 5. chest 6. casket,
   chasse, shrine 8. monument
relish . . . 4. gust, tang, zest 5. achar,
   enjoy, gusto, sauce, taste 6. canape,
   caviar, degust, flavor, liking
   8. pleasure 9. condiment, degustate,
   enjoyment, flavoring, seasoning
   11. hors d'oeuvre 13. gratification
relucent . . . 5. lucid 6. lucent
   7. radiant, shining 8. lightish
   9. refulgent
reluctance . . . 8. aversion
   10. repugnance 13. indisposition,
   unwillingness 14. disinclination
reluctance unit (Elec) . . . 3. rel
reluctant . . . 5. chary, loath 6. averse
   8. hesitant, not ready 9. resisting,
   unwilling 11. disinclined
reluctate . . . 5. repel 6. oppose
   9. repudiate
rely . . . 4. hold, lean, rest 5. count,
   trust 6. cleave, depend, reckon,
   repose 7. confide
rely on, upon . . . 4. hope 5. trust
   6. depend, lippen 7. believe
remain . . . 3. lie 4. bide, last, rest, stay
   5. abide, tarry 6. endure, reside
   8. continue
remainder . . . 4. rest, stub 5. relic,
   stump 6. estate 7. balance, remnant,
   residue, surplus 8. fragment,
   leavings, residual, residuum
remaining . . . 4. left, over 6. ledger
   (leger) 7. durable, remnant, staying,
   surplus 8. residual 9. permanent
remaining stationary . . . 6. static
   7. waiting 8. awaiting
remains . . . 5. ashes, ruins, stays
   6. corpse, relics 7. cadaver, fossils
   9. remainder
remanent . . . 4. left 7. further, lasting,
   remains, remnant, residue
   8. enduring, leftover, residual
   9. permanent, remainder
   10. additional 13. supplementary
remark . . . 3. say, see 4. heed, note

   5. gloss, state 6. notice, regard
   7. comment, observe 8. perceive,
   point out 9. statement
   10. annotation, commentary,
   indication 11. observation
   12. interjection
remark (pert to) . . .
amusing, witty . . 3. gag 4. quip
clever . . 3. mot
commonplace . . 9. platitude
smarting . . 7. sarcasm, stinger
upon . . 7. explain
witless . . 5. boner
remarkable . . . 5. great 7. notable,
   strange, unusual 8. uncommon
   9. wonderful 10. noteworthy,
   noticeable, observable
   11. conspicuous 13. extraordinary
Rembrandt (pert to) . . .
birthplace . . 6. Leyden (Neth)
color . . 5. brown
famed as . . 6. etcher (Dutch)
   7. painter
style . . 14. Rembrandtesque
remedial . . . 6. remedy (pert to)
   7. healing 9. curative, panacean
   10. corrective 11. therapeutic
remedy . . . 3. aid, fix 4. bote (bot),
   cure, gain, help 5. amend 6. doctor,
   relief 8. antidote, medicine
   10. assistance, reparation
remedy (pert to) . . .
cure–all . . 6. elixir
mysterious (of Paracelsus) . .
   7. arcanum
quack . . 7. nostrum
soothing . . 4. balm 6. balsam
universal . . 7. panacea
remember . . . 3. min 9. recollect,
   reminisce 10. keep in mind
remembrance . . . 4. fame 5. token
   6. memory, Minnie, trophy
   7. memento 8. allusion, memorial,
   reminder, souvenir 12. recollection
   13. commemoration
remex . . . 12. quill feather
remind . . . 6. prompt, recall
   8. remember 13. call attention
reminder . . . 4. memo, twit 7. memento
   8. souvenir 10. memorandum
   11. remembrance
reminiscence . . . 3. act 4. fact
   5. power 6. memory 8. anecdote
   10. experience 11. memorabilia
   12. recollection
remise . . . 6. giving, return 7. release,
   replace, respite 8. granting
   9. remission, surrender
remiss . . . 3. lax 5. slack 7. lenient
   8. careless, dilatory, heedless
   9. negligent 10. neglectful
   11. inattentive, thoughtless
remissness . . . 7. neglect 9. indolence
   10. negligence 12. improvidence
remit . . . 3. pay 5. relax 6. acquit,
   assign, cancel, excuse, pardon,
   reduce, resign 7. absolve, forgive,
   release, restore, suspend 8. abrogate,
   liberate, mitigate, recommit
   9. surrender
remnant . . . 3. ash, end, ort, rag
   4. dreg, left, rest, stub 5. piece,

relic, scrap, shred, trace 7. oddment, remains, yet left 8. fragment 9. remainder, remaining 10. suggestion

remolade... 5. sauce 8. dressing, ointment

remonstrate... 5. plead 7. protest 8. point out 11. expostulate

remontant... 7. flowering again

remora... 4. fish, pega (pegora)

remord... 5. taint 6. ponder, rebuke 7. afflict, censure, remorse

remorse... 4. pity 6. regret, sorrow 8. distress 9. penitence, repentent 10. compassion 11. compunction

remorseful... 5. sorry 7. pitiful 8. contrite, merciful, penitent, pitiable 9. regretful 13. compassionate

remorseless... 8. pitiless 9. merciless, unpitying 10. implacable, inflexible, relentless, unmerciful 11. unregretful

remote... 3. far, off 5. alien, vague 6. elenge, forane, ultima 7. distant, foreign 8. abstruse, reserved, secluded, ulterior 10. farfetched, unsociable 11. out–of–the–way

remote control... 10. pushbutton, tele–action

remote region... 5. Thule (Greenland)

remotest... 7. endmost, very end 8. farthest 14. ghost of a chance

removal... 8. ejection 9. deduction 10. divestment, evacuation, extraction 11. elimination 12. transference

remove... 3. rid 4. dele, doff, move, void, weed 5. erase, evict, expel, strip 6. change, debunk, delete, depose, divest, eloign (law) 7. dismiss, extract, relieve 8. abstract, displace, evacuate, put aside, transfer 9. eliminate, eradicate, translate 11. assassinate

remove (pert to)...
cover.. 5. uncap
from office.. 4. oust 6. depose, recall
moisture.. 3. dry 5. wring 9. dehydrate
point of origin.. 6. distal
seed from flax.. 6. ribble
seeds.. 3. gin, pit
stalk.. 5. strig
to another place.. 8. transfer 9. translate
whole blubber.. 6. flense

removed... 4. took 5. apart 6. betook, remote 7. distant, far away 8. reserved, secluded 9. separated, unrelated 10. unsociable

remover... 6. porter 7. carrier, drayman, solvent 9. scavenger 10. contractor, eradicator

remunerate... 3. pay 5. repay 6. reward 7. requite, satisfy 9. reimburse 10. compensate, recompense

remuneration... 3. pay 6. reward 7. payment 8. pittance, requital 9. emolument 10. recompense 12. compensation, satisfaction 13. reimbursement

Remus (pert to)...
brother.. 7. Romulus

father.. 4. Mars
legendary founder of.. 4. Rome (with brother)
slayer.. 7. Romulus

renable... 4. glib 5. ready 6. fluent 8. eloquent

renaissance... 7. rebirth, revival

Renaissance (pert to)...
Archit.. 12. Roman classic
art.. 10. neoclassic
associated with.. 8. Petrarch
furniture.. 6. carved 7. English, Flemish
Italian reference.. 12. Resorgimento (new arising)
lace.. 10. Battenburg

renal... 6. kidney 7. nephric

renascence... 7. rebirth, revival 14. The Renaissance

rencounter... 4. duel 5. clash 6. action, combat, flight 7. contest, meeting 8. conflict 9. collision

rend... 3. rip 4. rive, tear 5. break, burst, sever, split, wrest 7. extract, rupture 8. fracture

render... 3. pay, put 4. give, make, melt 6. return 7. clarify, convert, deliver, execute, extract, narrate, present, requite 8. transmit 9. translate 10. understand 11. communicate

render (pert to)...
accessible.. 4. open
agreeable.. 7. dulcify
angry, choleric.. 6. enrage
conformable to Eng.. 7. Anglify 9. Anglicize
divine.. 5. deify
dull.. 8. hebetate
enduring.. 6. anneal
fat.. 3. try 6. try out
fertile.. 6. enrich
free from bacteria.. 9. sterilize
ineffective.. 4. void 5. annul 10. invalidate
intelligible.. 9. elucidate
less pliant.. 7. stiffen
muddy, turgid.. 4. roil
oblique.. 5. splay
obscure.. 6. darkle 9. obfuscate
sharp.. 9. acuminate
unconscious.. 4. stun

rendezvous... 5. tryst 6. refuge 7. meeting, retreat 11. appointment

rendition... 7. account 8. delivery 9. surrender 10. extraction 11. performance, translation 14. interpretation

renegade... 3. rat 5. rebel 7. pervert, traitor 8. apostate, deserter, fugitive, turncoat

renege... 4. deny 6. desert, revoke 7. decline 8. renounce

renew... 6. resume, revamp, revive 7. convert, refresh, restore 8. renovate 10. invigorate, regenerate 12. redintegrate

renewal... 10. conversion, renovation, resumption 11. restoration

renitent... 7. opposed 9. reluctant, resistant 12. recalcitrant

rennet... 3. lab 5. apple 6. curdle,

rennin 7. extract 9. coagulate

rennin... 6. enzyme

renommé... 8. renowned
10. celebrated

Renommist... 8. braggart, renowner
9. swaggerer

renounce... 4. cede, deny 5. forgo
(forego), waive 6. abjure, desert,
disown, recant, reject, renege, resign
7. abandon, forsake, retract
8. abnegate, forswear, swear off
9. repudiate, surrender 10. relinquish
12. abrenunciate

renouncement... 9. rejection
10. temperance 11. abandonment,
recantation

renovate... 5. renew 6. repair, resume,
revive 7. restore 10. regenerate

renown... 4. fame, note 5. éclat, glory
10. reputation

renowned... 5. famed, noted
6. famous 10. celebrated
11. illustrious 13. distinguished

rent... 3. let, pay 4. dues, hire, hole,
slit, tear, toll, tore, torn 5. break,
cleft, lease, share, split 6. reward
7. revenue, rupture, slitted, tribute
8. tattered

rent (pert to)...
asunder.. 5. rived
harvest.. 7. onstand
in oats.. 7. avenage
paid.. 3. tac

renter... 6. lessee, lodger, tenant

renunciation... 6. denial 9. disavowal,
rejection, surrender 10. abjuration,
disclaimer, temperance
11. abandonment, recantation
14. relinquishment

repaid in kind... 10. retaliated

repair... 3. fix 4. darn, heal, mend
5. amend, patch, renew 6. doctor,
remedy, resort 7. correct, rebuild,
restore 8. atone for 9. condition
13. betake oneself

reparation... 6. amende, amends,
remedy, repair, reward 7. damages,
redress 8. reprisal, requital
9. atonement, indemnity
10. recompense 11. restitution
12. compensation, satisfaction

repartee... 3. wit 5. reply 6. retort
7. riposte

repast... 3. tea 4. feed, meal 5. feast,
lunch, treat 6. tiffin 8. mealtime, .
prandial 9. collation

repatriate... 5. exile 6. banish
10. expatriate

repay... 4. meed 6. answer, avenge,
refund, return 7. requite, restore
9. reimburse, retaliate
10. compensate, recompense,
remunerate

repeal... 5. annul, emend, forgo
(forego) 6. appeal, cancel, recall
7. abandon, abolish, rescind, retract,
reverse 8. abrogate, renounce,
withdraw

repeat... 4. copy, echo, rame 5. recur
7. iterate, restate 8. remember
9. duplicate, reiterate

repeat (pert to)...

mathematics.. 8. repetend

mechanically.. 6. parrot

noisily.. 3. din

performance.. 8. encore

twice (pref).. 3. bis

repeating... 4. rote 10. repetitive
11. repetitious

repel... 5. avert, check 6. offend,
oppose, rebuff, refuse, reject, resist,
revolt 7. disgust, repulse 9. drive
back, force back

repellent... 5. harsh 6. odious
9. repulsive, resistant, revolting

repent... 3. rue 5. reform, regret
9. do penance

repentance... 4. ruth 5. shame
6. regret 9. penitence 10. contrition
11. compunction

repercussion... 4. blow 6. impact
9. afterclap, aftermath 10. reflection

repertory... 5. list 6. index, store
8. calendar, magazine, treasure
9. catalogue 10. collection,
repertoire, storehouse

repetition... 4. rote 5. troll 6. encore
8. iterance, iteration 11. reiteration
14. recapitulation

repetition (pert to)...
biology.. 6. merism
music.. 5. rondo 7. tremolo
rhetoric.. 8. anaphora 9. tautology
sound.. 4. echo
sounds (slight).. 6. patter

repetitive... 8. habitual 9. redundant
11. repetitious

repine... 4. fret 6. lament, regret
7. grumble 8. complain

replace... 4. stet 5. reset, stead
6. repone 7. restore 8. supplant
9. discharge, supersede
10. substitute

replaceable... 10. expendable

replenish... 4. feed, fill 5. store
6. refill 7. perfect, provide
8. complete

replete... 3. fat 4. full 5. sated
6. filled, gorged 7. bloated
8. abundant 9. surfeited

replevin... 4. bail, writ 8. recovery

replica... 3. bis 4. copy 6. repeat
9. duplicate, facsimile

reply... 4. echo 5. rebut 6. answer,
oracle, rejoin, retort 7. defense,
epistle, respond 8. reaction, repartee,
response 9. rejoinder 11. retaliation

report... 3. cry, pop 4. bang, note
5. bruit, rumor, sound, state, story
6. delate, recite, relate, repute
7. account, hearsay, recital, verdict
8. describe 9. narration, narrative,
statement 10. accounting,
commentary, responsory
11. information, publication

report (pert to)...
common.. 6. gossip
false, absurd.. 5. rumor 6. canard
7. slander
following lightning.. 7. thunder
for duty.. 14. present oneself
official.. 7. hansard
of proceedings.. 6. cahier

reporter... 3. cub 6. legman, pistol

7. newsman 8. newshawk
9. informant 12. newspaperman
reporter's rounds... 8. newsbeat
reporter's sign off... 6. thirty
repose... 3. lie, sit 4. ease, rely, rest
5. peace, place, sleep 7. deposit,
recline 8. quiescent, quietness
10. quiescence, relaxation
repository... 3. ark 4. file 5. vault
6. chapel (RCCh), museum
8. treasury 9. confidant, sepulcher
10. depository, storehouse
11. auction room
reposoir... 5. altar
repoussé... 7. art work
reprehensible... 8. blamable, culpable
9. accusable, obnoxious
10. censurable, reprovable
11. blameworthy
reprehension... 5. blame 7. censure,
reproof 9. reprimand 11. reprobation
12. condemnation, denunciation
represent... 4. enact 6. denote,
depict, typify 7. betoken, exhibit,
portray, produce 8. describe
9. delineate
representation... 3. art 4. copy, icon,
idea, idol, show 5. drama 6. avowal,
symbol 7. picture 9. depiction,
enactment, portrayal, spectacle
10. exhibition, profession
11. delineation, description,
portraiture 12. reproduction
representation (pert to)...
by characters (Mus).. 8. notation
graphic.. 5. chart
Medusa's head.. 9. gorgoneum
mental.. 5. image 7. eidolon,
phantom
of scene.. 7. tableau
of solar system.. 6. orrery
of star.. 7. estoile
small.. 5. model 9. miniature
representative... 4. heir, type
5. agent, envoy 6. deputy, legate
7. example, tribune, typical
8. delegate, exponent, symbolic
9. successor 10. ambassador,
legislator, lieutenant, substitute
12. illustrative
repress... 4. curb, rein, stop 5. check,
crush, quell 6. hush up, muffle, stifle
7. put down 8. restrain, suppress
9. overpower
reprieve... 5. delay 6. pardon, relief
7. relieve, respite 8. postpone
reprimand... 5. chide, scold, slate
6. rebuke 7. censure, reprove
reprisal... 7. revenge, revenue
8. requital 11. retaliation
reproach... 4. taca, twit 5. abuse,
blame, chide, shend, taunt
6. accuse, revile, vilify 7. censure,
condemn, reproof, sarcasm, upbraid
8. disgrace, dishonor 9. disrepute,
invective 10. accusation, opprobrium
12. vilification
reproach, free of... 9. blameless
reprobate... 6. disown, reject, wicked
7. abandon, corrupt, knavish, vicious
8. depraved, hardened, recreant
9. condemned, miscreant, reprehend,

scoundrel 10. black sheep
12. unprincipled 13. reprehensible
reproduce... 4. copy 6. recite, remake,
repeat 8. multiply 9. duplicate,
propagate
reproduction... 4. copy 6. ectype,
recall 7. picture, replica 8. likeness
10. repetition 11. counterpart,
duplication 14. representation
reproductive... 5. gamic, spore
10. recreative 12. regenerative
reproof... 5. roast 6. rebuke
7. chiding 8. disgrace, reproach
9. reprimand 10. admonition,
censurable, refutation
11. blameworthy, confutation
12. reprehension 13. reprehensible
reprove... 4. rate 5. blame, chide,
scold 6. berate, rebuke 7. censure,
correct, upbraid 8. admonish,
reproach 9. objurgate, reprehend,
reprimand
reproving... 10. admonitive
reptile... 4. toad, worm 5. snake,
viper 6. dragon, iguana, lizard, turtle
7. monitor, serpent 8. creeping,
Reptilia 9. scoundrel
reptile (pert to)...
class.. 8. Reptilia
crocodile.. 6. mugger
extinct.. 9. pterosaur 10. diplodocus
11. pterodactyl, Pterosauria
group.. 6. Sauria
hard–shelled.. 6. iguana, turtle
8. terrapin, tortoise
iguanalike.. 7. tuatara
large.. 3. boa 9. alligator, crocodile
10. salamander
lizard.. 3. eft 4. adda, newt, seps
5. skink (scink) 6. Anolis, iguana,
moloch 7. monitor 9. chameleon
10. chuckwalla 11. Gila monster
Mesozoic.. 8. dinosaur
myth.. 6. dragon 8. basilisk
10. cockatrice, salamander
oldest.. 9. sea turtle
salamander.. 3. eft 4. newt
scale.. 5. scute
snake.. 3. asp 5. adder, cobra, krait
6. garter, python 8. anaconda,
Squamata 10. copperhead
reptilian... 7. saurian
Reptilian Age... 8. Mesozoic
Republic... 5. State 6. France
7. Andorra (Andorre) 9. San Marino
10. commonweal, government
12. United States
Republican Party... 3. GOP
7. mugwump (bolter 1884)
Republic of Plato... 4. Book (famed)
8. dialogue 10. ideal State
repudiate... 4. deny 6. abjure, disown,
recant, reject 7. disavow, discard,
exclude 8. renounce
repugnance... 4. hate 5. odium
7. nausea 8. disgust, opposed
8. aversion, loathing 9. antipathy,
hostility 10. abhorrence, antagonism,
opposition, reluctance
12. disagreement
repugnant... 6. odious 7. adverse,
hostile, opposed 8. inimical

9. offensive, repellent, repulsive
10. refractory 11. distasteful
12. incompatible 14. irreconcilable

repulse... 5. repel 6. denial, rebuff
7. refusal 9. rejection

repulsive... 4. ugly, vile 5. nasty
6. odious, fulsome 9. offensive,
repellent, resistant, revolting
10. disgusting, forbidding,
malodorous

repurchase... 6. redeem

reputable... 6. worthy 9. estimable,
honorable 10. creditable
11. respectable

reputation... 4. fame, name, note
5. glory, honor 9. celebrity, notoriety
11. distinction 13. consideration

repute... 4. hold, word 5. éclat, honor
6. credit, esteem, regard, report,
revere 8. prestige 9. reputable
10. popularity, reputation

reputed... 6. deemed 7. assumed
8. accepted, presumed, putative,
supposed 10. understood

request... 3. ask, beg 4. plea, pray,
suit 6. appeal, behest, demand
7. entreat, solicit 8. entreaty,
petition, rogation 12. supplication

requiescat in pace... 11. rest in
peace

requiescence... 6. repose

requin... 5. shark 6. man–eater

require... 3. ask 4. need 5. claim,
exact, force 6. charge, compel,
demand, enjoin, entail, oblige
8. obligate 11. necessitate

requisition... 5. order 6. demand
11. application, requirement

requital... 7. payment, revenge
8. reprisal 10. recompense
11. retaliation, retribution
12. compensation

requite... 3. pay 5. atone, repay
6. avenge, return, reward
7. revenge, satisfy 9. retaliate
10. compensate, recompense
11. interchange

reredos... 4. wall 6. screen
9. back–plate (armor), partition

reremouse... 3. bat

res... 5. point, thing 6. matter

rescind... 5. annul 6. cancel, recall,
recant, repeal, revoke 7. abolish
8. abrogate

rescue... 3. aid 4. free, save
6. ransom, redeem, regain 7. deliver,
reclaim, recover, release 8. delivery,
liberate 9. extricate 11. deliverance

rese... 4. rage, rush 5. hurry, onset,
quake, shake 7. impulse, tremble
8. rashness

resemblance... 6. ringer 7. analogy
8. affinity, likeness 9. agreement,
semblance 10. similarity, similitude

resembling (pert to)...
bark.. 11. corticiform
comb.. 8. pectinal
goose.. 8. anserine
gypsum.. 11. alabastrine
horse.. 6. equoid
man.. 7. android
minute animals.. 11. animalcular

rind.. 8. cortical
salt.. 6. haloid
seed.. 6. ovular
snakes.. 7. elapine 8. viperine
star.. 7. stellar 8. stellate 9. stellated
turf.. 5. soddy
wall.. 5. mural

resentment... 3. ire 5. pique, spite
6. choler, enmity, hatred, malice,
rancor 7. dudgeon, umbrage
9. animosity, malignity
11. displeasure, indignation

reservation... 5. tract 8. preserve
9. reticence 10. engagement,
limitation 11. withholding
13. qualification

reserve... 4. bank, fund, keep, save
5. allot, spare, stock, store
6. engage, refuge 7. backlog,
modesty, shyness 8. coldness,
distance, postpone, withhold
9. exception, restraint, retention,
reticence, sanctuary 10. constraint,
diffidence, limitation, substitute
11. self–control, taciturnity

reserved... 3. coy 4. cool, kept, unco
5. aloof, saved, staid, taken
6. modest, sedate 7. distant
8. reticent 15. uncommunicative

reservoir... 4. font, pool, sump
5. store 6. cavity, cenote, supply
7. piscina, reserve 8. fountain

reservoir of Pecquet (Anat)...
12. lymph channel 13. cisterna chyli

res gestae... 5. deeds, facts
8. exploits 10. things done

resiant... 7. present 8. resident

reside... 4. bide, live, room, stay
5. abide, dwell, lodge 6. remain
7. sojourn 8. habitate

residence... 4. home, seat, stay
5. abode 6. palace 7. deanery
8. domicile, dwelling 9. consulate,
residency 10. habitation

residencia... 5. court, trial

resident... 3. cit 6. intern, tenant
7. burgess, citizen 8. diplomat,
occupant 10. inhabitant

residual... 7. remnant 8. residuum
9. remainder

residue... 3. ash, ort 4. coke, dreg,
marc, rest, silt, slag 5. ashes
6. pomace, relics 7. balance,
remains, remnant 8. leavings,
sediment 9. remainder

residuum... 7. residue 8. hangover,
leavings 9. remainder

resign... 4. cede, quit 5. demit, waive,
yield 6. give up, submit 7. abandon,
consign 8. abdicate, renounce
9. surrender 10. relinquish

resignation... 5. demit 8. patience
9. demission, endurance
10. abdication, submission
12. renunciation 14. relinquishment

resigned... 9. contented
10. submissive 11. acquiescent
13. uncomplaining

resilient... 7. buoyant, elastic
8. cheerful 9. recoiling
10. rebounding 11. returning to
12. recuperative

resin... 3. gum, lac 4. aloe, tolu
　5. amber, anime, copal, jalap, rosin
　6. dammar, mastic
resin (pert to)...
　aromatic.. 4. balm 5. elemi, myrrh
　　6. balsam 7. acouchi, camphor,
　　copaiba 8. sandarac 12. frankincense
　Bib.. 8. bdellium
　bitter.. 8. labdanum (ladanum)
　brown (mineral).. 9. elaterite
　Chian turpentine.. 3. alk
　fossil.. 5. amber 8. retinite
　gum.. 5. gugal (googul)
　hard.. 5. rosin
　medicinal.. 7. aroeira 9. asafetida
　　(asafoetida)
　narcotic.. 6. charas
　pine.. 7. galipot
　soft.. 5. animé, copal, elemi
　translucent.. 8. sandarac
　tropical.. 5. copal
　varnish ingredient.. 6. dammar
　yellowish.. 5. amber 7. gamboge
resinous substance... 3. gum, lac
　5. copal 8. shellac
resist... 4. fend, stem 5. rebel, repel
　6. defeat, oppose 7. prevent, ward
　off 8. outstand 9. withstand
　10. counteract
resistance... 6. rebuff 7. defense
　8. rheostat 9. hostility 10. opposition
resistant... 5. tough 8. obdurate
　9. resisting 10. unyielding
　13. counteractive
resisting... 7. hostile 8. opposing
　9. oppugnant, tenacious
　12. antagonistic
resisting (pert to)...
　description.. 11. indefinable
　power.. 4. wiry
　pressure.. 8. renitent
　pressure bar.. 5. strut
resolute... 4. bold, firm 5. fixed, stern
　6. gritty, steady 7. decided
　8. constant, positive, resolved,
　unshaken 9. desperado, obstinate,
　steadfast 10. determined, inflexible,
　unyielding 11. perseverant,
　persevering
resolution... 4. firm 5. nerve
　6. motion, steady 7. courage,
　purpose, resolve, verdict 8. analysis,
　decision, resolved, strength
　9. assurance, constancy, fortitude
　10. conversion, conviction, relaxation,
　separation 11. persevering
　12. perseverance 13. determination,
　steadfastness 15. disentanglement
resolve... 4. melt 5. lapse (law),
　parse, relax, solve 6. assure, decide,
　dispel, inform, reduce, settle
　7. analyze, explain, purpose, unravel
　8. convince, dissolve, separate
　9. determine, transform
　11. disentangle
resonance... 8. sonority, vibrance
　10. resounding
resonant... 7. echoing, ringing, vibrant
　8. sonorous, sounding
　10. resounding 11. reverberant
resort... 3. spa 4. dive 5. haunt
　6. betake, casino, refuge 7. finagle,

purlieu 8. frequent, recourse,
resource 9. expedient, fainaigue,
honky-tonk
resound... 4. echo, peal, ring 6. be
　loud, re-echo 8. proclaim
　11. reverberate
resounding... 4. loud 13. reverberating
resource... 5. means, skill 6. refuge,
　resort, supply 9. expedient
　10. capability 11. contrivance
resourceful... 5. sharp 9. Daedalian,
　ingenious
resources... 5. funds, means, money
　6. assets, supply 7. resorts
　10. expedients 12. contrivances
respect... 3. awe 4. heed 5. defer,
　favor, honor 6. aspect, detail,
　esteem, homage, regard, repute,
　revere 7. concern, observe, regards
　8. attitude, venerate 9. attention,
　deference, relevance, reverence,
　viewpoint 10. politeness
　13. consideration
respectable... 6. decent 9. estimable,
　honorable, reputable, tolerable
　11. presentable
respectful... 5. civil 6. polite
　7. careful, duteous, heedful
　8. reverent 11. deferential
respective... 6. mutual 7. careful,
　heedful, several, special 9. attentive,
　regardful 10. particular
　12. distributive
respiration... 4. rale, sigh 7. eupnoea
　9. breathing
respire... 7. breathe
respite... 4. rest 5. delay, frist, pause
　6. breath 7. leisure 8. postpone,
　reprieve 9. extension (time)
　10. suspension 11. opportunity,
　short shrift 12. intermission
resplendent... 5. grand 7. aureate,
　radiant, shining 8. lustrous, splendid
　9. beautiful, brilliant, refulgent
　10. epiphanous 11. illustrious
respond... 4. echo 5. react, reply
　6. accord, answer, retort 8. response
　10. correspond 11. reciprocate
response... 4. echo 5. reply
　6. answer, anthem, chorus
　7. rapport, refrain 8. antiphon (Mus),
　reaction
responsibility... 4. care, duty, onus
　6. charge 8. solvency 11. reliability
　14. accountability 15. trustworthiness
responsible... 6. liable 7. solvent
　8. amenable, reliable 10. answerable
　11. accountable, respectable,
　trustworthy
responsive... 6. pliant 7. elastic
　8. reactive 9. answering, sensitive,
　teachable 10. open-minded
　11. persuasible, sympathetic
res publica... 5. state 8. republic
　10. commonweal 12. commonwealth
rest... 3. lay, set, sit 4. base, calm,
　ease, lair, lean, prop, seat, slip, stay,
　stop 5. cease, death, found, pause,
　peace, quiet, relax, renew 6. depend,
　desist, ground, repose, settle
　7. balance, leisure, recline, refresh,
　remains, remnant, reposal, respite,

silence, support, surplus 8. at
anchor, interval, lodgment
9. cessation, quietness, remainder,
stillness 10. quiescence, remain idle
12. intermission, peacefulness,
tranquillity

rest (pert to)...
assured.. 9. be certain, believe me
at rest.. 4. abed, dead 6. otiose
    11. comfortable
day.. 7. Sabbath
foot.. 4. rail 7. hassock
house (Orient).. 5. serai
musket.. 6. gaffle
reading.. 7. caesura (cesura)

restaurant... 4. café 5. diner
7. automat, tearoom 9. cafeteria
10. coffee shop 11. eating house

resting... 4. abed 7. dormant
9. quiescent

resting place... 4. tomb 5. roost
6. hearth 7. lairage, landing, support
8. quarters

restitution... 6. return 9. atonement,
repayment 10. recompense
reparation 12. compensation
13. reinstatement

restless... 6. roving, uneasy 7. agitato,
fidgety, inquiet, restive, wakeful
8. agitated 9. impatient, sleepless,
unceasing, unrestful, unsettled,
wandering 10. changeable, reposeless
12. discontented

restoration... 6. repair, return
7. renewal, revival 8. recovery
10. renovation, reparation
11. improvement, restitution
14. redintegration
15. re-establishment

restorative... 6. acopon 7. anodyne
8. remedial 10. reparative

restore... 4. cure, heal 5. renew,
repay 6. redeem, refund, repone,
revive 7. rebuild, recover, replace
8. renovate 9. reinstate
11. reconstruct, re-establish
12. redintegrate, rehabilitate

restore (pert to)...
after cancelling.. 4. stet
certainty, confidence.. 8. reassure
to former position.. 9. reinstate
to proper position.. 5. right

restrain... 3. dam 4. bate, bind, curb,
rein, stay 5. check, cramp, deter,
limit, stint 6. arrest, bridle, fetter,
halter, hinder, tether 7. abridge,
confine, control, inhibit, overawe,
qualify, repress 8. restrict, suppress,
withhold 9. constrain, detention

restraint... 3. bit 4. curb, stop
5. check, force 7. durance, modesty,
reserve 9. condition, hindrance,
reticence 10. abridgment, constraint,
inhibition, limitation, moderation,
repression, temperance
11. confinement, deprivation,
self-control 12. tastefulness

restraint, lack of... 9. looseness

restrict... 3. tie 4. bind, curb
5. bound, cramp, limit, scant, stint
6. censor, coerce, modify 7. confine,
qualify, repress 8. specialize

12. circumscribe

restricted... 5. local 6. narrow
7. limited, topical 10. restrained
11. specialized

restriction... 5. stint 9. restraint
10. limitation, narrowness, regulation,
tightening 11. reservation
12. constriction 13. qualification

resty... 5. quiet 6. rancid, reasty
7. restive 8. sluggish, stubborn
11. disobedient

result... 3. end, sum 4. rise 5. arise,
ensue, event, fruit, issue, total
6. accrue, answer, effect, follow,
sequel, spring 7. proceed, product
8. solution 9. aftermath, deduction,
eventuate, terminate 10. conclusion
11. achievement, consequence,
termination

resulting from luck... 8. aleatory

resume... 5. recur, renew 6. reopen
7. recover 8. reoccupy 9. epitomize,
reiterate, summarize 10. recommence

résumé... 8. abstract 10. compendium
11. reiteration

resurrection... 6. rising 7. revival
10. apotheosis 11. restoration

resuscitate... 6. revive 7. restore
8. revivify

ret... 3. rot 4. soak 5. steep
6. expose, impute 7. ascribe

retable... 5. ledge, shelf 6. gradin
(gradine) 8. predella

retail... 4. sale, sell 6. repeat
8. dispense, disperse

retain... 4. hold, keep, save, stet
6. employ 8. maintain, preserve,
remember 9. recollect

retainer... 3. fee 4. cage 6. menial,
minion, vassal, yeoman 7. servant
9. bodyguard

retaining wall... 9. revetment

retaliate... 5. repay 6. avenge
7. requite 12. make requital

retaliation... 8. talion (Mosaic law, eye
for eye, tooth for tooth) 7. revenge
8. reprisal, requital 10. punishment
11. retribution

retard... 4. clog, drag, slow 5. defer,
delay, laten 6. belate, deaden,
detain, hinder, impede 8. keep back,
obstruct, postpone, slow down

retardant... 4. clog, drag 6. remora
8. obstacle

retardate... 6. impede 8. retarded

retch... 3. gag 4. hawk, spit 5. reach,
vomit 6. expand, extend, strain
7. stretch

rete... 3. net 6. plexus 7. network

retention... 6. memory 7. holding,
keeping 8. tenacity 11. maintenance,
self-control

retentive... 6. memory 7. keeping
9. tenacious 12. recollective

retenue... 7. reserve 10. discretion
11. self-control 13. self-restraint

rethe... 5. cruel 6. ardent, fierce,
severe

retiary... 6. spider 7. netlike
9. gladiator, retiarius

reticence... 7. reserve, silence
9. restraint 13. secretiveness

reticulated... 3. web 6. meshed, netted 7. network 12. intercrossed

reticule... 3. bag 4. etui 5. cabas (caba) 7. handbag, reticle, workbag

reticulum... 7. network, stomach (2nd) 9. neuroglia

retinue... 4. crew 5. harem, suite, train 6. escort 7. cortege, service 8. equipage 9. entourage, retainers 10. attendants

retire... 6. depart, depose, pay off, recede, vanish 7. go to bed, retreat 8. withdraw 9. disappear, discharge

retired... 4. abed, left, lone, paid 7. receded 8. departed, emeritus, recessed, resigned, secluded, solitary, vanished, withdrew 9. pensioned 10. disengaged 11. disappeared, sequestered

retirement... 7. deposal, payment, privacy, retreat 8. solitude 9. departure, recession, reticence 10. withdrawal 11. resignation 13. disemployment

retiring... 3. shy 6. modest 8. reserved, reticent 9. diffident 10. not forward, retreating 11. unobtrusive

retort... 3. mot 4. quip 5. reply 6. answer 7. riposte (ripost) 8. repartee 9. retaliate 11. retaliation

retract... 6. abjure, disown, draw in, recent, repeal 7. disavow, rescind, swallow 8. take back 9. repudiate

retraction... 6. repeal 8. palinode 10. revocation, withdrawal 11. recantation

retrad... 8. backward 11. posteriorly

retral... 8. backward 9. posterior 10. retrograde

retreat... 3. den 4. abri, lair, nest, nook, rout 6. asylum, recede, recoil, refuge, retire 7. privacy, retiral, sanctum, shelter 8. fallback, solitude 9. departure, katabasis, seclusion 10. retirement, withdrawal

retrench... 6. cut off, excise, lessen, reduce 7. abridge, curtail, cut down 8. decrease, diminish 9. economize, intercept

retrenchment... 3. cut 8. excision 9. lessening, reduction 10. abridgment 11. curtailment, economizing

retribution... 3. pay 6. return, reward 7. nemesis 8. reprisal, requital 9. vengeance 10. punishment 11. restitution 12. Last Judgment

retrieve... 5. fetch 6. redeem, regain, rescue, revive 8. make good

retrograde... 4. slow 6. recede, retral, revert 7. regress 8. backward, decadent, rearward 10. regressive 11. deteriorate 12. reversionary

retroussé... 6. pugged (nose) 8. turned up

retund... 4. beat, dull 5. blunt 6. refute, subdue 9. attenuate, drive back 10. render weak

return... 5. recur, repay, reply 6. answer, render, repeat, report, revert 7. regress, relapse, requiet,

respond, restore 9. repayment 11. restitution, retaliation

return (pert to)...
day.. 12. answer to writ
evil for evil.. 7. revenge 9. retaliate
tennis term.. 5. lob
thrust (fencing).. 7. riposte (ripost)
to.. 6. resume 7. relapse, revisit
to 1st theme (Mus).. 7. reprise

returns... 5. gains, polls 8. receipts

reune... 4. join 7. reunite 10. reassemble

reunion... 7. joining 8. sociable 14. reconciliation

re–up... 8. re–enlist

reus... 9. defendant

Reuter's News Agency... 6. London

reveal... 3. bid 4. bare, jamb, open, tell, wray 6. impart, unveil 7. divulge, exhibit, uncover 8. disclose, discover, evidence, indicate, manifest 11. communicate

reveal (in trust)... 7. confide

reveal intentionally... 4. tell 6. betray, expose 7. divulge, mislead

reveille... 4. call 5. levet 6. signal (sunrise)

revel... 3. joy 4. orgy, riot, wake 5. feast, spree, watch 6. frolic 7. carouse, delight, rejoice, revelry, wassail 8. carousal, festival 11. celebration, merrymaking 12. conviviality

revelant... 5. clear 8. manifest 12. intelligible

revelation... 6. oracle, vision 8. The Bible 9. discovery 10. appearance, disclosure 13. communication, manifestation

Revelation (Bib)... 10. Apocalypse

revelry... 3. joy 4. evoe, orgy, riot 6. revels 8. carnival, carousal 9. revelment, revelrout 11. merrymaking

revenant... 5. ghost 7. eidolon, specter (spectre) 9. recurring 10. apparition

revendicate... 7. reclaim, recover 10. real action

revenge... 6. avenge 7. requite 8. reprisal, requital 9. retaliate, vengeance 10. punishment 11. retribution

revenue... 3. tax 5. yield 6. income, profit 7. annates

reverberate... 4. echo, ring 5. repel, reply 6. return 7. rebound, reflect, resound

reverberation... 4. echo 9. reboation 10. reflection, resounding

revere... 4. love 5. adore, honor 6. esteem, regard, repute 7. respect, worship 8. venerate

reverence... 3. awe 5. dread, honor, piety 7. respect, worship 8. venerate 9. adoration, deference 10. veneration

reverent... 5. pious 6. devout 7. dutiful 10. respectful, worshipful

reverie... 4. muse 5. dream 6. notion, trance, vision 7. fantasy

reversal... 6. defeat, repeal

9. inversion, reversion
14. tergiversation

reverse... 4. back 5. upset 6. back
up, defeat, invert, repeal, revert,
revoke 7. relapse 8. contrary,
converse, opposite, overturn
9. transpose 10. misfortune

reversion... 6. estate 7. revival
8. transfer 9. inversion
10. regression 11. inheritance

reversion (pert to)...
ancestral.. 7. atavism 9. atavistic
insurance.. 7. annuity
land.. 7. escheat

revert... 5. react, recur 6. advert,
return 7. regress, relapse
11. antistrophe

revest... 4. robe 5. dress 6. attire,
clothe 8. reinvest 9. reinstate

review... 4. edit 6. parade, relate,
survey 8. critique, remember
9. criticism, criticize, re–examine
10. certiorati, commentary,
compendium, discussion, inspection,
periodical, reconsider
11. examination, reiteration
12. recollection 15. reconsideration

reviewer... 6. critic, writer
11. commentator

revile... 4. rail 5. abuse, curse
6. berate, debase, vilify 7. asperse
8. reproach, ridicule

revise... 4. edit 5. amend, emend
6. redact 7. correct, rewrite
8. readjust

revision... 7. revisal 10. correction,
emendation 11. rebeholding
13. re–examination

revival... 7. rebirth, renewal
10. quickening 11. reanimation,
renaissance, restoration
12. resurrection

revive... 4. stum (wine) 5. rally,
renew, rouse 6. come to 7. enliven,
recover, refresh, respire, restore
8. rekindle, remember 11. resuscitate

revocate... 6. recall, revoke 7. repress

revocation... 6. repeal 8. reversal
10. retraction, withdrawal
11. recantation

revoke... 5. adeem, annul 6. abjure,
cancel, recall, recant, renege, repeal,
revive 7. abolish, retract 8. abrogate
9. fainaigue 11. countermand

revolt... 5. rebel 6. mutiny, offend,
strike 8. nauseate, sedition, uprising
9. rebellion 10. revolution
12. insurrection

revolting... 4. ugly 7. hideous
8. shocking 9. offensive, repellent
10. disgusting, nauseating

revolution... 3. gyre, turn 5. cycle,
epoch, round 6. revolt 7. circuit
8. disorder, rotation 9. rebellion

revolutionary... 3. new 7. radical
12. catastrophic 15. insurrectionary

Revolutionary hero... 5. Allen (Ethan),
Gates 6. Revere 8. Burgoyne
10. Cornwallis, Washington
15. Lighthorse Harry (Gen Lee)

revolve... 4. pirl, roll, spin, turn
5. recur, wheel, whirl 6. circle,

gyrate, ponder, rotate 7. trundle
8. meditate 9. circulate
10. deliberate

revolver... 3. gat, gun, rod 6. pistol
7. firearm 10. six–shooter

revolving... 3. orb 4. cowl (metal cap)
6. rotary

revolving (pert to)...
in thought.. 8. perusing
light.. 10. lighthouse
part.. 3. cam 5. rotor
storm.. 7. cyclone

revue... 6. medley, review 9. burlesque
13. musical comedy

reward... 3. pay, utu 4. meed
5. award, bonus, merit, Oscar, yield
6. hallow (to hounds) 7. guerdon
8. reprisal 10. recompense,
remunerate 11. retribution
12. compensation, remuneration

reword... 5. alter 7. restate
8. rephrase 9. reiterate
10. paraphrase

rex... 4. king

rey... 4. king

Reynard... 3. fox (epic character)

rezai... 8. coverlet (quilted)

rhamn... 7. Rhamnus 9. buckthorn

rhapontic... 7. rhubarb 8. knapweed,
pieplant

rhapsodic... 6. poetic 8. ecstatic

rhapsodist... 4. poet 8. minstrel
9. visionary 10. enthusiast

rhapsody... 6. jumble, medley
9. utterance (ecstatic) 10. recitation
11. composition

rhea... 3. emu (emeu) 5. nandu
7. ostrich

Rhea (pert to)...
called.. 15. Mother of the Gods
father.. 6. Uranus
home.. 5. Mt Ida (Crete)
mother.. 4. Gaea
mother of.. 4. Hera, Zeus 5. Hades
8. Poseidon
wife of.. 6. Cronus

rhebok... 5. peele 8. antelope

Rheims... see *Reims*

rhema... 4. term, verb, word

rheophile... 15. living in streams

rhetoric... 7. diction, oratory
9. eloquence 11. composition

rhetorical term... 6. aporia, simile
10. antithesis, oratorical
11. catachresis

rhetoric digression... 6. ecbole

rheumatism root... 7. wild yam

rheumatism weed... 10. Indian hemp,
pepsissewa

rhexis... 7. rupture

rhinal... 5. nasal 6. narial

rhine... 5. ditch, drain 6. runnel

Rhine (pert to)...
breed.. 7. rabbits
native.. 11. Rhinelander
nymph.. 7. Lorelei
ref to.. 7. Rhenish
tributary.. 4. Ruhr 6. Neckar
wine.. 7. Moselle

rhino... 3. cash, nose (comb form)
5. money 10. rhinoceros

rhinoceros (pert to)...

Bib.. 4. reem
bird.. 8. hornbill 9. beefeater
black.. 6. borele 7. keitlos
Malay.. 5. abada
viper.. 5. snake (poisonous)
rhizopod... 6. amoeba 8. Protozoa
Rhoda... 4. rose
Rhode Island...
bay.. 12. Narragansett
capital.. 10. Providence
city.. 7. Newport 9. Pawtucket
10. Woonsocket
famed cotton mill.. 6. Slater
founder.. 13. Roger Williams (1636)
Rebellion.. 5. Dorr's (1842)
resort.. 7. Newport 11. Block Island
river.. 9. Pawtucket 10. Blackstone
settlers.. 8. Puritans
State admission.. 10. Thirteenth
State motto.. 4. Hope
State nickname.. 11. Little Rhody
Rhode Island Red... 4. fowl
Rhodesia...
capital.. 9. Salisbury
Falls.. 8. Victoria
Falls discoverer.. 11. Livingstone
(1855)
river.. 7. Zambezi (Zambesi)
tribe.. 5. Bantu
rhododaphne... 8. oleander
Rhoeadales... 5. poppy
11. Papaverales
rhomb... 7. rhombus 10. magic wheel
11. spinning top
rhomboid... 13. parallelogram
rhombus... 5. rhomb 13. parallelogram
(equilateral)
Rhone tributary... 5. Isere
rhubarb... 5. Rheum 6. hassle
7. citrine, yawweed 8. argument,
pieplant 9. rhapontic 10. discussion
Rhus... 5. sumac 7. wax tree
rhyme, rime... 4. poem 5. poetry,
rhythm 7. measure 9. assonance
rhythm... 4. beat, lilt 5. meter, pulse,
swing, tempo 6. poetry 7. cadence,
euphony 8. rhythmus, symmetry
rhythmical break... 7. caesura
ria... 5. creek, inlet
rial... 4. coin, king 5. great, noble,
royal 6. prince 8. splendid
9. excellent, stag's horn
11. magnificent
rialto... 4. mart 6. Bridge (Venice),
market 7. theater 8. exchange
riant... 3. gay 6. blithe, bright
7. smiling 8. laughing
riata... 4. rope 5. lasso 6. lariat
rib... 4. bone, meat, vein 5. costa,
ridge 6. lierne
ribald... 3. low 6. coarse, harlot,
vulgar 7. obscene 10. scurrilous
11. blasphemous 12. ribble–rabble
riband... 6. ribbon
ribbed... 3. rep 5. piqué 6. corded,
ridged 7. costate
ribble–rabble... 6. gabble, rabble,
ribald 7. chatter 10. incoherent
ribbon... 3. bow 5. strip 6. fillet
10. decoration
ribbon (pert to)...
badge.. 6. cordon

band.. 5. corse 9. banderole
fish.. 7. oarfish 8. dealfish
inked.. 10. typewriter
knot.. 7. rosette
ribbonlike.. 8. taenioid
snake.. 6. garter
Society.. 7. Ireland
worm.. 8. tapeworm 9. nemertine
ribwort... 8. plantain
rice (pert to)...
bird.. 4. rail, sora 8. bobolink
dish.. 5. pilau (pilaw) 7. risotto
8. kedgeree 9. jambalaya, ricetable
drink.. 5. bubud
feeding on.. 11. oryzivorous
field.. 5. paddy
hen.. 9. gallinule
inferior.. 4. chit, pago
paste.. 3. ame
rat.. 8. Oryzomys
refuse.. 5. shood (shud)
Spanish.. 5. arroz
wild.. 4. reed
wine.. 4. sake
rich... 3. fat 5. opime 6. creamy,
fecund, fruity, mighty, ornate, potent
7. copious, fertile, moneyed, opulent,
wealthy 8. abundant, affluent,
colorful, powerful, resonant, valuable
9. bountiful, expensive, luxuriant,
sumptuous 10. in the chips
13. grandiloquent
rich (pert to)...
English slang.. 4. oofy 6. oofier
man.. 5. Dives (Bib), Midas, nabob
7. Croesus 9. plutocrat 10. capitalist
11. millionaire
musically.. 7. orotund
richard... 9. plutocrat
riches... 5. lucre, means 6. mammon
(Bib), wealth 8. opulence 9. affluence
riches, demon of... 6. Mammon
rick... 4. heap, pile 5. noise, scold,
stack, twist 6. pile up, rattle, sprain,
wrench 7. chatter
rickets... 7. disease 8. rachitis
rickety... 4. weak 5. crazy, shaky
6. senile 7. unsound 8. unstable,
unsteady 9. tottering 10. ramshackle
rickle... 4. heap, pile, rick 5. stack
6. jingle, rattle
rickrack... 5. braid 6. edging
9. insertion
ricksha, rickshaw... 10. jinrikisha
ricochet... 5. carom 7. rebound
10. bounce back
rid... 4. doff, free, kill 5. clear, empty
6. remove, rescue 7. deliver, destroy,
discard 9. dispose of, drive away,
eliminate 11. disencumber
riddance... 6. escape 7. discard
11. elimination 14. relinquishment
riddle... 3. ree 4. crux, sift 5. rebus,
sieve 6. enigma, pierce 7. perplex
8. separate 9. conundrum, perforate
ride... 4. twit 5. drive, float 6. pester,
travel 7. be borne, journey, overlap
8. domineer, ridicule 9. carrousel
(carousel), cavalcade, excursion
10. forest road 12. merry–go–round
13. roller coaster
ride (pert to)...

herd.. 9. guard over
off.. 4. polo (term)
roughshod over.. 9. tyrannize
shank's mare.. 4. walk
to hog, pig.. 11. boar hunting
to line.. 4. herd
rident... 5. riant 7. smiling 8. laughing
rider... 5. ryder 6. clause, knight
    7. allonge, codicil 8. addition,
    horseman 9. performer
    10. freebooter, highwayman
    11. endorsement, mosstrooper
Rider Haggard's novel... 3. She
ridge... 3. aas, rib 4. hill, rand, wale,
    weal, welt 5. arête, bulge, chine,
    crest 7. wrinkle
ridge (pert to)...
anatomy.. 4. ruga 6. carina
barrier.. 5. parma
between furrows.. 7. porcate
    8. porcated
coral.. 4. reef
glacial.. 2. os 5. esker (eskar)
military.. 6. rideau
mountain.. 4. loma 5. arête 6. sierra
narrow, raised.. 4. wale
oak.. 9. blackjack
raised by stroke.. 5. wheal, whelk
short.. 4. kame
sloping.. 6. cuesta
steep.. 7. hogback
stony.. 4. rand
zoology term.. 5. varix
ridicule... 3. guy, pan 4. butt, gibe,
    jeer, mock, quiz, twit 5. chaff, irony,
    sneer, taunt 6. banter, deride, satire
    7. asteism, mockery, sarcasm
    8. derision, raillery 9. burlesque
ridiculous... 5. funny 6. absurd
    7. amusing 8. farcical 9. grotesque,
    laughable, ludicrous 10. impossible,
    outrageous 12. preposterous,
    unbelievable
ridiculous failure... 6. fiasco
riding (pert to)...
bitts.. 11. anchor cable
breeches.. 8. jodhpurs
dress, costume.. 5. habit
knot.. 8. slipknot
rhyme.. 7. couplet
school.. 6. manège
whip.. 4. crop 5. quirt
rife... 7. replete, rumored 8. abundant
    9. abounding, plentiful, prevalent
    10. prevailing, widespread
riff... 6. rapids, riffle, ripple 7. midriff
    9. diaphragm 13. improvisation
riffle... 7. shallow, shuffle, wavelet
riffraff... 3. mob 4. mean 5. offal
    6. rabble, refuse, trashy 7. rubbish
    9. sweepings
rifle... 3. rob 5. reeve, steal, strip
    6. Mauser, search, snider 7. carbine,
    despoil, firearm, pillage, plunder,
    ransack
rifle (pert to)...
accessory.. 6. ramrod
ball.. 5. Minié 6. bullet
bird.. 14. bird of paradise
bomb.. 7. grenade
French.. 9. chassepot
old form.. 4. tige

rifler... 4. hawk 6. robber
rift... 3. gap, lag 4. rima, rive
    5. break, cleft, split 6. cleave, divide
    10. falling out
rig... 3. fit 4. gear, suit 5. dress,
    equip 6. lateen 7. bedizen, costume,
    rigging, vehicle 9. Bermudian (Naut)
Riga (pert to)...
balsam.. 5. resin (Swiss pine)
capital of.. 6. Latvia
native.. 4. Lett 7. Latvian
rine.. 4. hemp
rigging (ship)... 4. gear, rope, spar
    6. tackle 9. equipment
right... 3. fit, pat 4. fair, true
    6. adjust, dexter, proper, remedy
    7. correct, justice, upright
    8. becoming, suitable 9. equitable,
    faultless, franchise, privilege, propriety
    10. put in order 11. appropriate,
    prerogative 13. justification
right (pert to)...
angled.. 10. orthogonal
comb form.. 6. dextro
exclusive.. 6. patent 10. concession
hand.. 6. dexter
hand page.. 5. recto
law.. 5. droit
neither right nor wrong..
    11. adiaphorous
of belligerent (Naut).. 6. angary
of ownership.. 5. title
of procedure.. 3. pas
real estate.. 8. easement
royal.. 7. regalia
time.. 3. tid
to choice.. 6. option
to pasture.. 6. eatage
turn.. 3. gee
righteous... 4. holy, just 5. godly,
    moral, pious 6. worthy 7. upright
    8. virtuous 9. believers, blameless,
    equitable, guiltless
righteousness... 6. equity, virtue
    8. holiness 9. godliness, rectitude
    11. uprightness
rightful... 4. just, true 5. legal, right
    6. honest, lawful, proper 7. fitting,
    genuine 9. equitable 11. appropriate
rigid... 3. set 4. firm, hard 5. exact,
    stern, stiff, tense 6. formal, narrow,
    not lax, severe, strict 7. ascetic,
    austere 8. rigorous 9. obstinate,
    stringent, unbending 10. inflexible,
    meticulous, unyielding
rigidity... 7. tensity 8. hardness,
    severity 9. exactness, obstinacy,
    stiffness
rigol... 4. ring 6. circle, groove
    7. channel
Rigoletto... 5. dance, opera (Verdi)
rigor, rigour... 4. cold, fury 7. cruelty
    8. asperity, rigidity, severity, violence
    9. exactness, harshness, rigidness
    10. shuddering, strictness
    13. inflexibility
rigor mortis... 10. stiffening (death)
    12. rigor of death
rigorous... 4. cold 5. exact, harsh,
    rigid, stern, stiff 6. severe, strict
    7. austere, drastic, violent
    8. accurate 9. inclement, obstinate,

puritanic 10. inexorable, inflexible, relentless

rikk... 10. tambourine

rile... 3. vex 4. roil 5. anger, muddy 6. offend 7. agitate 8. irritate 9. turbidity

rill... 5. brook 6. course, runnel 7. rillock, rivulet 9. streamlet

rim... 3. lip, web 4. band, brim, edge, orle, tire 5. bezel, brink, felly (felloe), verge 6. border, flange, margin, shield 7. enclose, horizon, rimrock 8. boundary 9. perimeter

rima... 5. cleft 7. fissure 8. aperture 10. breadfruit

rima oris... 16. space between lips

rim ash... 9. hackberry

rimate... 8. fissured

rime... 4. hoar, poem, rent 5. chink, cleft, crack, frost, rhyme 6. poetry 7. fissure 8. aperture 9. assonance, hoarfrost 10. ladder step

rime-cold giant (Norse)... 4. Ymir (Ymer)

rimple... 4. fold 6. ripple, rumple 7. wrinkle

rimption... 3. lot 9. abundance

Rinaldo's steed... 6. Bayard

rind... 4. bark, husk, peel, skin 5. crust 6. cortex 7. epicarp 9. hoarfrost

rindle... 5. brook 6. runnel 7. rivulet

ring... 3. rim, set 4. band, halo, hoop, peal, toll 5. arena, bague, chime, group, knell 6. circle, clique, collar 7. annulus, circlet, coterie, resound 8. encircle, insignia, ornament, surround 9. encompass 11. association

ring (pert to)...
around.. 7. environ
around the sun.. 6. corona
barrel.. 4. hoop
bill.. 4. duck
bird.. 11. reed bunting
comb form.. 4. gyro
dove.. 6. cushat
finger.. 5. third
fruit jar.. 4. lute
gem crown.. 5. bezel
gem setting.. 6. chaton
gun carriage.. 7. lunette (lunet)
harness part.. 7. terret
horse training.. 5. longe
Latin.. 7. annulus
leader.. 6. rouser 9. demagogue 12. rabble-rouser
little.. 7. annulet, circlet
ornament (metal).. 3. bee (angling)
ouzel.. 6. thrush
rope.. 7. grommet
sail.. 4. hank 6. ringtail
tail.. 3. cat 4. coon 5. lemur 6. godwit, marlin 10. cacomistle 11. golden eagle (young)

ringed boa... 5. aboma

ringed worm... 7. annelid

ringhals... 5. snake (spitting)

ringing... 7. clangor, orotund, pealing, tolling 8. clanging, resonant 10. resounding

ringle-eye... 7. walleye

ringlet... 4. curl, lock 5. tress 6. circle 7. circlet 9. fairy ring

ringworm... 5. tinea 6. tetter 7. disease, serpigo 9. millepede

rink... 4. hero, race, ring 6. circle, course 7. warrior 8. encircle, ice sheet (skating) 9. encounter

rinse... 4. lave, sind, wash 5. flush 6. sluice 7. cleanse 8. absterge

rinthereout, rintherout (Scot)... 5. tramp 7. vagrant 8. vagabond

rio... 5. river 6. coffee, stream

Rio de Janeiro... 7. capital (old, Braz)

Rio Grande... 5. river 7. disease (lettuce)

riot... 3. din 5. brawl, melee 6. clamor, excess, pogrom, revolt, tumult, uproar 7. dispute, quarrel, revelry 8. carousal, disorder, violence 9. commotion

riotous... 4. raid 5. aroar 6. wanton 7. violent 9. dissolute, luxuriant, seditious 10. profligate, tumultuous 12. unrestrained

riotous jollity... 9. dissolute 11. saturnalian

rip... 3. cut 4. rend, rent, tear 5. break, horse (old) 7. riptide 9. debauchee, libertine, reprobate 10. fish basket, laceration

ripe... 3. fit 5. ready, rifle 6. mature, mellow 7. plunder 8. finished, prepared, rareripe 9. developed, full-grown, perfected 10. consummate

ripen... 3. age 5. addle 6. digest, mellow, nature 7. develop, perfect, prepare 8. complete, grow ripe

riposte, ripost... 5. reply 6. answer, retort, thrust 8. repartee

ripping... 5. bully, grand, swell 9. admirable, hunky-dory 12. fine and dandy

rippit... 9. fist fight

ripple... 3. cut, lap 4. fret, purl, riff, tear, wave 5. acker, eagre, graze 6. dimple, murmur 7. crinkle, disturb, scratch, trickle, wavelet 11. corrugation

ripple grass plantain... 7. ribwort

ris de veau... 10. sweetbread

rise... 4. grow, soar, well 5. arise, begin, climb, get up, mount, raise, reach, rebel, start, surge, tower 6. ascend, ascent, attain, be high, emerge, growth, height, revolt, spring, thrive 7. succeed 8. eminence, flourish, increase, levitate, reaction 9. acclivity, ascension, beginning, elevation, originate 11. development

rise (pert to)...
above.. 4. loom 8. surmount 11. triumph over
again.. 7. resurge 11. resurrected
and fall of the sea.. 5. scend, tidal 6. welter
by buoyancy.. 8. levitate
gradually.. 4. loom
hawk's.. 6. mounty
high.. 5. tower

risible... 5. funny 6. absurd

9. laughable

rising... 6. ascent, ortive, revolt
  7. growing, montant, sloping, surgent
  8. elevated, emergent, gradient (by
  degrees), swelling 9. acclivity,
  advancing, ascending, ascension
rising and falling... 5. tidal 7. surging
  8. undulant
risk... 4. dare 5. peril 6. chance,
  danger, expose, gamble, hazard,
  injury, plight 7. venture 8. endanger
  10. investment 12. disadvantage
risky... 6. risqué 9. hazardous
  11. venturesome
risp... 3. rub 4. file, rasp, tirl 5. stalk
  7. bulrush, scratch
risper... 11. caterpillar
risqué... 4. racy 5. risky, salty
  8. off-color 9. hazardous
  10. suggestive
rissle... 4. pole 5. staff, stick
risus... 5. laugh 8. laughter
rit (rare)... 3. cut, rip 4. slit, tear
  5. split 6. pierce 7. scratch
ritardando... 9. direction, retarding
  10. slackening 11. rallentando
rite... 4. cult, form 5. ritual, sacrum
  7. formula, liturgy, tonsure
  8. ceremony 9. solemnity
  10. ceremonial, initiation, observance
  12. patriarchate
ritratto... 7. picture 8. portrait
Ritter... 6. knight
ritual... 4. book, code, cult, form, rite
  5. feast, salat 6. novena, prayer
  7. liturgy 8. ceremony
  10. ceremonial
ritus... 5. usage 6. custom
ritzy... 5. smart (vulgarly), swank
  6. swanky 11. pretentious
  16. ultra-fashionable
rivage... 4. bank, duty 5. coast, green,
  shore
rival... 3. foe, vie 4. even, peer
  5. excel, match 7. compete, emulate
  8. emulator, opponent
  10. antagonist, competitor
  11. compete with
rivalry... 4. feud 9. emulation
  11. competition
rive... 3. rip 4. bank, open, rent, rift,
  tear 5. cleft, sever, shore, split
  6. cleave 8. lacerate
rive droite... 9. Right Bank (Seine)
rive gauche... 8. Left Bank (Seine,
  Paris, including Latin Qtr)
rivel... 6. shrink 7. shrivel, wrinkle
river... 2. ea 3. ria, rio, run 4. ilog
  5. amnis, brook, creek 6. stream
  7. rivulet, torrent 8. riverlet
  9. streamlet
river (pert to)...
  arm (of sea).. 7. estuary
  bank.. 4. ripa 5. levee
  bank, pert to.. 8. riparian
  bed.. 6. holm 16. alveus, bottom
    7. channel
  bend.. 5. oxbow
  boat.. 3. ark
  delta branch.. 5. bayou
  dog.. 10. hellbender
  dragon.. 9. crocodile

  duck.. 4. teal
  fish (spawning, from sea)..
    10. anadromous
  horse.. 5. hippo 12. hippopotamus
  inlet.. 4. slew 5. fiord (fjord)
    6. slough
  islet.. 3. ait 4. holm
  mouth.. 4. lade 5. delta 7. estuary
  mussel.. 4. unio
  Near East.. 4. wadi (wady)
  Nile measure.. 9. Nilometer
  nymph.. 4. nais 5. naiad
  rat.. 5. thief
  ref to.. 5. amnic
  region (near).. 8. riverine
  siren.. 7. Lorelei
  thief.. 3. rat 6. ackman
  winding.. 3. ess
river in...
  Africa.. 4. Nile, Tana 5. Niger
  Austria.. 4. Iser 5. Drava
  Bavaria.. 4. Eger, Isar
  Belgium.. 4. Yser
  Bohemia.. 4. Elbe, Iser
  Brazil.. 3. Rio
  Bulgaria.. 5. Mesta
  China.. 3. Wei 6. Yellow 7. Hwang
    Ho
  England.. 4. Isis 6. Thames
  France.. 5. Seine
  Germany.. 6. Danube
  Italy.. 4. Arno 5. Tiber
  Netherlands.. 3. Eem 4. Maas
    (Meuse)
  S America.. 6. Amazon
  Siberia.. 2. Ob 4. Lena
  Switzerland.. 3. Aar 5. Reuss
river of...
  Annie Laurie.. 4. Nith
  Caesar.. 7. Rubicon
  lower regions.. 4. Styx 5. Lethe
    7. Acheron
  woe.. 7. Acheron
rixy... 4. tern
road... 3. via, way 4. iter, path, raid
  5. agger 7. estrada, highway,
  journey, passage 8. pavement
  9. incursion, roadstead
  10. expedition
road (pert to)...
  block.. 3. dam 4. weir
  goose.. 5. brant
  hog.. 8. motorist 10. monopolist
  horse.. 6. saddle (horse)
  impassable.. 7. impasse
  man.. 7. drummer, peddler
    8. salesman 9. canvasser
  map.. 5. chart, globe 9. directory
  master.. 10. supervisor
    11. trackmaster
  nautical.. 9. roadstead
  no outlet.. 8. cul-de-sac
  paving.. 6. Tarmac 7. ballast,
    macadam
  runner.. 6. cuckoo
  scraper.. 4. harl
  weed.. 8. plantain
roam... 2. go 3. err, gad 4. rove
  5. prowl, range 6. ramble, stroll,
  wander 7. meander 9. gallivant
roan... 5. horse (bay, gray, chestnut)
  8. antelope 9. sheepskin, yellow-red

roanoke... 6. wampum
Roanoke...
  city.. 8. Virginia
  famed as.. 11. First Colony (1584)
  famed for.. 12. Virginia Dare (1st
    white child, 1587)
  settler.. 16. Sir Walter Raleigh
    19. Sir Richard Grenville
roar... 4. bell, blow, boom, rote (surf)
  5. brool, laugh, shout 6. bellow,
  steven 7. ululate 8. cry aloud
  9. loud sound
roaring... 5. aroar, great 7. booming,
  riotous 10. disorderly
Roaring (pert to)...
  Forties.. 8. Broadway (NYC)
  game.. 7. curling (Scot)
  Twenties.. 14. Golden Twenties
    16. Age of Red Hot Mamas
roast... 4. beef, cook 5. cabob, parch
  6. assate, banter 7. torrefy
  8. ridicule 9. criticize
roasting (pert to)...
  ear.. 4. corn
  jack.. 9. smokejack
  stick.. 4. spit
rob... 4. loot, pelf 5. pinch (sl), reave,
  rifle, steal, touch 6. pilfer, ravish,
  snatch, snitch 7. despoil, pillage,
  plunder 10. plagiarize
robbed... 5. stole 6. rubato (Mus)
  8. snatched, snitched
robber... 4. yegg 5. crook (sl), thief
  6. bandit, reaver, rifler 7. brigand,
  burglar, yeggman 8. pillager
  9. despoiler, embezzler, larcenist,
  peculator 10. depredator,
  highwayman, shoplifter
robber (pert to)...
  grave.. 5. ghoul
  high seas.. 6. pirate 7. corsair
    9. privateer
  highway.. 7. footpad, ladrone
  Indian.. 6. dacoit
robbery... 5. reif 5. theft 6. burgle,
  piracy 7. larceny, pillage, plunder
  8. burglary 10. spoliation
  11. depredation
robe... 5. array, cover, dress, tunic
  6. invest, mantle 7. costume,
  garment 8. clerical, vestment
robe (pert to)...
  bishop's.. 6. chimer
  camel's hair.. 3. aba
  long.. 5. talar
  loose.. 5. cymar (symar)
  royal.. 6. ermine, purple
robin... 4. bird, lout, tody 6. thrush
  7. bumpkin 8. trimming 9. redbreast
  10. toxalbumin
robin (pert to)...
  dipper.. 14. bufflehead duck
  runaway.. 7. dewdrop
  sandpiper.. 4. knot 5. snipe
    9. dowitcher
  songbird.. 8. accentor
Robin Bluestring... 13. Robert
  Walpole
robinet... 6. cannon 9. chaffinch
Robin Goodfellow... 4. Puck 6. sprite
  9. hobgoblin
Robin Hood (pert to)...

famed as.. 6. archer, outlaw, yeoman
followers.. 9. Friar Tuck 10. Little
  John, Maid Marian
forest.. 8. Sherwood (Eng)
habit.. 11. robbing rich (for the poor)
Robinson Crusoe's man... 6. Friday
roborant... 4. drug 5. tonic 6. bracer
  8. pick-me-up 9. stimulant
roborean... 5. oaken, stout 6. strong
robot... 9. automaton
Rob Roy... 5. canoe 6. outlaw (Scot)
  15. Robert MacGregor
robust... 4. hale 5. hardy, lusty,
  rough, sound, stout, wally 6. hearty,
  sinewy, strong, sturdy 7. healthy
  8. muscular, vigorous
roc... 4. bird (Arabian Nights)
  7. simurgh (simurg)
rocca... 4. hold 6. donjon 8. fortress
rock... 3. orc 4. lull, peak, sway, trap,
  tufa, tuff 5. agate, chert, cliff, quiet,
  shake, slate, stone 6. basalt, egeran,
  gneiss, refuge, schist, teeter
  7. diamond, missile 8. dolomite,
  porphyry, strength 9. whinstone
  10. promontory
rock (pert to)...
  black.. 6. basalt
  brittle.. 5. shale
  broken.. 4. sand 5. attle
  cavity.. 5. druse
  chain.. 4. reef
  coarse.. 8. psammite, psephite
  crystal.. 6. silica
  crystalline.. 6. gneiss, schist
  decomposed.. 6. gossan
  fluid.. 4. lava
  fragments.. 5. scree 8. detritus,
    xenolith
  geyser deposit.. 6. sinter
  glacial.. 7. moraine
  granitelike.. 6. gneiss
  granular.. 6. oolite, quartz 7. diorite
    10. rockallite
  gray.. 5. slate 8. andesite
  igneous.. 4. boss, trap 6. basalt
    7. peridot
  jutting.. 3. tor 4. crag
  nodule.. 5. geode
  pinnacle.. 4. scar 6. needle
  porous.. 4. tufa, tuff
  rounded.. 6. rognon
  science.. 9. petrology
  Sicilian.. 6. Scylla (opp Charybdis)
  stratified.. 5. shale
  suffix.. 3. ite, yte
  volcanic.. 4. tufa 6. basalt, domite,
    latite
rock, animal...
  badger.. 4. cony
  cavy.. 6. rodent
  dassie.. 6. rabbit
  goat.. 4. ibex
  kangaroo.. 7. wallaby
  squirrel.. 11. spermophile
rock, bird...
  blackbird.. 9. ring ouzel
  dove.. 9. guillemot 10. rockpigeon
  duck.. 9. harlequin
  goose.. 9. kelp goose
  grouse.. 9. ptarmigan
  hawk.. 6. falcon, merlin

hopper.. 7. penguin
lark.. 5. pipit
pigeon.. 10. sand grouse
sandpiper.. 5. pipit, snipe
shrike.. 10. rock thrush
starling.. 5. ouzel
swallow.. 10. rock martin
rock, fish...
bass.. 5. black 7. striped
clam.. 5. borer
cod.. 7. grouper
cook.. 6. wrasse 7. whiting
eel.. 6. gunnel
gurnet.. 9. fortescue
hind.. 7. grouper (spotted)
lobster.. 8. crayfish
salmon.. 7. codfish 9. amberfish
sucker.. 7. lamprey
trout.. 9. greenling
rock, flora...
bell.. 9. columbine
brake.. 8. polypody
candytuft.. 8. gold–dust
cedar.. 7. juniper
cranberry.. 8. mountain
elm.. 11. slippery elm
garden.. 6. alpine
geranium.. 8. alumroot
hair.. 6. lichen
lily.. 9. columbine 12. pasqueflower
maple.. 5. sugar
melon.. 10. cantaloupe
shrub.. 8. buckthorn
rocket... 5. lance 8. ascend, ascent,
     fire at 8. aircraft, firework
     9. skyrocket, spaceship
rocket (famed)... 5. Titan 6. Apollo,
     Gemini, Saturn 7. Jupiter, Mercury
     8. Redstone
Rock of Chickamauga... 6. Thomas
     (Gen), (Civil War)
rocks... 5. money
rocks, on the... 7. aground
     8. bankrupt, stranded 10. saxicoline
rocky... 4. hard 5. stony 6. rugged
     7. sickish 8. obdurate, unsteady
     9. unfeeling
Rocky Ford... 9. muskmelon
Rocky Mountain...
group.. 5. Coast 8. Cascades
     12. Sierra Nevada
park.. 6. Estes
peak.. 6. Elbert 8. McKinley
popular name.. 7. Rockies
range.. 5. Teton, Uinta
rococo... 6. florid 7. baroque, bizarre
     9. fantastic, grotesque
     13. ornamentation
rod... 3. gat, gun 4. pole, wand, whip
     5. baton, perch, power, scion, staff
     7. measure, scepter
rod (pert to)...
comb form.. 5. rhabd 6. rhabdo
fibrous.. 5. lytta
flat.. 6. ferula, ferule
grooved.. 4. came (stained glass)
knitting.. 6. needle
meat–holding.. 4. spit
mechanical.. 6. piston
metal.. 7. stemmer
mixing.. 3. rab
pointed.. 4. goat, spit

rodlike.. 9. vergiform
rotating.. 7. spindle
short.. 6. toggle
spinning.. 7. spindle
rodd... 8. crossbow, stonebow
rodent... 4. cony, hare, paca 5. hutia
     (jutia), mouse, stoat 6. agouti
     (agouty), beaver, gerbil, gopher,
     marmot, murine 7. lemming, leveret
     8. chipmunk, hedgehog, mongoose,
     squirrel 9. guinea pig, porcupine
rodent (pert to)...
Andes.. 8. abrocome
aquatic.. 6. beaver 7. muskrat
Belgian.. 8. leporide
burrowing.. 6. marmot 8. sewellel
disease.. 9. tularemia
European.. 4. cony 5. lerot
fur–bearing.. 6. beaver
genus.. 3. Mus 5. Lepus
gnawing.. 3. rat 4. mole
hare.. 6. rabbit
jumping.. 6. jerboa
largest.. 8. capybara (capibara)
migrating.. 7. lemming
Mongoloid.. 3. rat 6. gopher
     12. pocket gopher
mouselike.. 4. vole
rabbitlike.. 4. pika
reference to.. 7. gnawing 8. rosorial
S American.. 4. degu 5. coypu
     6. agouti 8. capybara 10. chinchilla
spiny.. 9. porcupine
rodeo... 4. show 7. roundup
     9. spectacle 11. performance (public)
rodomontade... 4. brag, rant 5. boast
     7. bluster 8. boastful, boasting,
     braggart, bragging
roe... 2. ra 3. doe 4. deer, hind, raun
     5. coral (lobster) 8. fish eggs
Roentgen, Röntgen (Wilhelm)...
famed as.. 9. physicist
famed for.. 5. X–rays 10. Nobel Prize
     (1901) 12. Roentgen rays
rogan... 4. bowl (wooden)
     10. receptacle (maple sap)
Roger's plane (Will)... 9. Winnie May
rogue... 3. imp, wag 4. kite 5. cheat,
     knave, scamp, shark, tramp
     6. beggar, pirate, rascal 7. corsair,
     vagrant, villain 8. elephant, picaroon,
     vagabond 13. mischief–maker
roguish... 3. sly 4. arch 5. pawky
     7. knavish 8. espiegle, rascally
     10. frolicsome, picaresque
     11. mischievous
roguishly... 5. slyly 8. impishly, trickily
     10. prankishly
roid... 5. rough 6. severe 7. riotous
     10. frolicsome 12. unmanageable
roil... 3. vex 4. foul, roam, romp
     5. anger, annoy, horse (Flemish),
     muddy 6. fidget, ruffle, wander
     7. agitate, disturb 8. irritate
roister... 4. brag, rude 5. bully
     7. bluster, boorish, swagger, violent
     9. gilravage
roisterer (Hist)... 3. mun
rojo... 3. Red 6. Indian (Mex)
     7. Redskin
roke... 3. fog 4. stir 5. moist, smoke,
     steam, vapor 8. moisture

roker... 3. ray 8. rockling 9. thornback

roky... 4. damp 5. foggy, misty, smoky 6. hoarse

role... 4. duty, part 6. office 8. capacity, function 9. character 13. impersonation

roll... 3. bun, rob 4. coil, film, food, furl, list, pell, rota, sway, wind, wrap 5. trill, troll 6. billow, bundle, rotate, rumble, scroll 8. bankroll, cylinder, rotation

roll (pert to)...
along.. 7. trundle
back.. 6. reduce 8. retrench
bread.. 3. bap
butter.. 3. pat
cloth.. 4. bolt
coins.. 7. rouleau
fish.. 7. rissole
hair.. 3. rat 7. chignon
military.. 5. cadre 6. roster
the bones.. 4. dice 10. shoot craps
tobacco.. 5. cigar
to one side.. 5. lurch
up.. 4. furl 6. bundle 10. accumulate

roller... 4. wave 5. inker, skate, towel 6. canary, caster, fillet, pigeon, platen 7. bandage, rotator, sirgang 8. cylinder 10. Holy Roller, pulverizer

rolling (pert to)...
movement.. 6. welter
pin.. 6. roller 8. cylinder
stock.. 7. coaches, engines 8. cabooses, Pullmans 9. motor cars 11. locomotives
stone.. 8. wanderer
weed.. 10. tumbleweed

rollix... 4. play 6. frolic 7. rollick

romaine... 10. cos lettuce

romal... 5. quirt, thong

Roman... 5. brave, Latin 6. frugal, honest, simple 7. Italian

Roman (pert to)... see also *Rome*
afterpiece (theater).. 5. exode, farce 8. travesty
alcove.. 8. tablinum
apostle (Bib).. 4. Neri
assembly.. 5. forum 7. comitia
augur.. 6. auspex
awning.. 8. velarium
barrack, hut.. 6. canaba (cannaba)
basilica.. 7. Lateran
booth, shelter.. 7. taberna
bowl.. 6. patina
boxing glove.. 6. cestus
breastplate.. 6. lorica
bronze.. 3. aes
building.. 5. aedes (worship)
case.. 5. bulla (for amulets)
cathedral.. 7. Lateran
chariot.. 5. essed (esseda)
chest.. 4. cist
circus post.. 4. meta
circus wall.. 5. spina
cistern.. 9. impluvium
citadel.. 3. arx
citizen (nonvoting).. 8. aerarian
clan.. 4. gens
cloak.. 5. sagum (Mil) 6. abolla 7. planeta
concert hall.. 5. odeum
court (Pope's).. 5. Curia

cuirass.. 6. lorica
Curia office.. 6. datary 7. dataria
date.. 4. ides 5. nones 7. calends
dish.. 6. patera
division (Polit).. 5. curia
earthwork (Mil).. 5. agger
Empire district.. 5. Pagus
era.. 5. Varro
farce.. 5. exode
festival days.. 5. feria 10. feriae Jovi (festivals of Jupiter)
fish sauce.. 4. alec 5. garum
foot coverage, sock.. 3. udo
galley.. 6. bireme 7. trireme
garment.. 4. toga 5. palla, stole, tunic
general's cloak.. 12. paludamentum (paludament)
Govt of two men.. 10. duumvirate
Hades.. 5. Orcus 10. lower world
hairpin.. 4. acus
hall (concert).. 5. odeum
helmet.. 5. galea
highway.. 3. via 4. iter
highway, famed.. 9. Appian Way
hills.. 7. Viminal 8. Aventine, Palatine, Quirinal 9. Esquiline 10. Capitoline
javelin.. 5. pilum
land (public).. 4. ager
language.. 5. Latin
law.. 3. jus 4. cern
law, divine.. 3. fas
market day.. 7. nundine
marriage.. 13. confarreation
matron's garment.. 5. stola, stole
meal (chief).. 4. cena (coena)
military cloak.. 5. sagum
military machine.. 7. terebra
military unit.. 6. legion 7. maniple
money.. 3. aes
ornament (neck).. 5. bulla
palace.. 7. Lateran
peace.. 3. pax
provisions (free).. 6. annona
ram (battery).. 5. aries
religious law.. 3. fas
religious rite.. 5. sacra
road.. 4. iter 6. Appian (paved)
robe.. 4. toga
room.. 3. ala 6. atrium 8. tablinum
seat.. 5. sella
shelter, shop.. 7. taberna
shield.. 6. scutum
soldier's protection.. 7. testudo
spirits (group).. 5. manes 7. lemures
tablet (writing).. 7. diptych
temple.. 4. naos 5. cella
tent.. 7. taberna
theater.. 5. odeum
travesty.. 5. exode
vase.. 7. amphora (wine) 8. murrhine
warship.. 6. bireme 7. trireme
Way (famed).. 6. Appian
wine shop.. 7. taberna

romance... 5. fancy, novel, story 7. fantasy, fiction, romanza, romaunt 8. idealize 9. falsehood, sentiment 11. imagination

romance (pert to)...
language.. 6. French 7. Catalan, Italian, Spanish 9. Provençal 10. Portuguese

ref to.. **8.** knightly **10.** chivalrous
verse.. **7.** sestina
Roman god (of)...
chief.. **4.** Jove **7.** Jupiter
dead.. **5.** Orcus
fire.. **6.** Vulcan
Hades.. **3.** Dis **5.** Pluto **8.** Dispater
households.. **5.** Lares **7.** Penates
husbandry, animals.. **6.** Faunus
love.. **4.** Amor **5.** Cupid
mirth.. **5.** Comus
sun.. **3.** Sol
Supreme.. **4.** Jove **7.** Jupiter
two–faced.. **5.** Janus
underworld.. **3.** Dis **5.** Pluto
8. Dispater
war.. **4.** Mars **8.** Quirinus
Roman goddess (of)...
agriculture.. **3.** Ops **5.** Ceres
beauty.. **5.** Venus
burials.. **8.** Libitina
childbirth.. **6.** Lucina
crops.. **6.** Annona
dawn.. **6.** Aurora
earth.. **6.** Tellus
fertility.. **6.** Annona
handicrafts.. **7.** Minerva
harvests.. **3.** Ops
health.. **7.** Minerva
hearth.. **5.** Vesta
horses.. **5.** Epona
love.. **5.** Venus
moon.. **4.** Luna **7.** Phoebus
mothers, nursing.. **6.** Rumina
night.. **3.** Nox
peace.. **3.** Pax **5.** Irene
religion.. **4.** Maia
strife.. **9.** Discordia
victory (war).. **6.** Vacuna
womanhood.. **4.** Juno
Roman people...
author.. **5.** Pliny, Varro
biographer.. **5.** Nepos
Bishop.. **4.** Pope
boy (free birth).. **8.** camillus
Catholic priest.. **8.** sacerdos
Catholic Society.. **6.** Jesuit
consul.. **6.** Scipio
Cupid.. **4.** Eros
deity.. **4.** faun
Diana.. **7.** Artemis
dictator.. **5.** Sulla **11.** Cincinnatus
diviner.. **5.** augur **6.** auspex
divinity (chief).. **4.** Jove
Emperor.. **4.** Nero, Otto **5.** Titus
7. Maximus **8.** Tiberius
11. Constantine **12.** Heliogabalus
Eros.. **5.** Cupid
farmer.. **7.** colonus
Fates.. **4.** Nona **5.** Morta **6.** Decuma
General.. **5.** Sulla, Titus **6.** Antony,
Marius, Scipio
ghosts.. **7.** lemures
gladiator.. **7.** Samnite **9.** retiarius
gladiator trainer.. **7.** lanista
governor.. **9.** proconsul
guard.. **6.** lictor
historian.. **4.** Livy **5.** Nepos **7.** Sallust
8. Appianus (Appian)
judge.. **6.** aedile (edile)
king (1st).. **7.** Romulus
king's adviser (Myth).. **6.** Egeria

magistrate, official.. **5.** augur **6.** aedile
(edile), censor, consul **7.** praetor
(pretor), tribune
maiden, betrayer to Sabrines..
7. Tarpeia
military officer.. **9.** proconsul
Naturalist.. **5.** Pliny
nun.. **6.** vestal
nymph (fountain).. **6.** Egeria
officer.. **6.** lictor **8.** triumvir (one of
three)
official of public games.. **7.** Asiarch
orator.. **5.** Pliny **6.** Cicero
palace officer.. **8.** palatine
patriot.. **4.** Cato
people (anc).. **7.** Sabines **8.** Samnites
9. plebeians **10.** patricians
philosopher.. **4.** Cato **6.** Seneca
7. Rosmini
physician.. **11.** Aesculapius
poet.. **4.** Ovid **5.** Lucan **6.** Horace,
Vergil **7.** Juvenal (satirical)
politician, courtier.. **7.** Sejanus
priest.. **5.** epulo **8.** tresviri (10 in all)
9. decemviri **10.** septemviri
priest, serving a god.. **6.** flamen
priestess.. **6.** vestal
priests of Faunus.. **7.** Luperci
race (conquered).. **6.** Sabine
saint.. **4.** Neri
scholar.. **5.** Varro
serf.. **6.** colona (fem) **7.** colonus
(male)
slave (befriended lion).. **9.** Androcles
soldiers (body of).. **6.** cohort
statesman.. **4.** Cato **6.** Caesar, Cicero,
Seneca
Tarquin rulers.. **9.** Etruscans
tenant farmer.. **7.** colonus
triumvirate, first.. **6.** Caesar, Pompey
7. Crassus
triumvirate, second.. **6.** Antony
7. Lepidus **8.** Octavius
troops.. **6.** alares
tyrant.. **4.** Nero
virgin.. **6.** vestal
writer (comic).. **7.** Terence
Romany, Rommany... **5.** gypsy
10. mascot blue
Rome...
cathedral (world's largest).. **8.** St
Peter's
churches.. **7.** Lateran **8.** Castello,
Gandolfo
conqueror.. **6.** Alaric
founder (legendary).. **7.** Romulus
hills.. **5.** Seven **6.** Sabine **7.** Viminal
8. Aventine, Palatine, Quirinal
lake.. **4.** Nemi
original city.. **12.** Roma Quadrata
palace (world's largest).. **7.** Vatican
peak (Capitoline).. **8.** Tarpeian
port (anc).. **5.** Ostia
prairie.. **8.** Campagna
river.. **5.** Tiber
seat of.. **7.** Holy See **11.** Vatican City
site, ancient.. **13.** Campus Martius
site, founding.. **12.** Palatine Hill
street (famed).. **5.** Corso
Romulus (pert to)...
brother.. **5.** Remus
city site.. **12.** Palatine Hill

father . . 4. Mars
founder (Myth) . . 4. Rome
king (1st) . . 4. Rome
mother . . 6. Sylvia
rescued from . . 5. Tiber
suckled by . . 7. she–wolf
ronde . . . 6. script (heavy) 9. round
hand
rondeau . . . 4. game, poem 5. rondo
6. rondel
rondel, rondelle . . 4. poem 5. tower
(Fort) 8. round gem
rondure . . . 9. plumpness, roundness
ronier . . 7. palmyra
ronin . . . 6. outlaw 7. outcast, samurai
rood . . . 5. cross (holy), goose
7. measure 8. crucifix
roodebok . . . 6. impala 9. duikerbok
roof . . . 3. hip 4. dome, eave, flat,
nave, tile 5. cover, gable, slate, spire
6. cupola, lean–to 7. chopper,
gambrel, mansard, pitched, shingle
8. housetop, thatched 9. penthouse
10. jerkinhead
roof (pert to) . . .
boards (thin) . . 4. sark
brain cover . . 4. tela 14. telachorioidea
frame (raised) . . 7. coaming
material . . 3. tin 4. tile 5. paper, slate
6. copper, shakes 7. roofage
8. shingles
mouth . . 6. palate
ornament . . 3. epi
tile . . 7. pantile
timber . . 6. rafter
tin (coating) . . 5. terne
tool . . 3. zax
Roof of the World, Asia . . . 6. Pamirs
(The) 7. Bam i Dunya
rook . . . 4. bird, crow, dupe 5. cheat
6. castle 7. defraud, sharper
8. chessman 9. ruddy duck
rookery . . . 4. slum 9. confusion
13. breeding place (rooks, herons,
penguins) 14. breeding ground (seals)
rookie, rooky . . . 6. novice 7. recruit
8. beginner, newcomer
rooky . . . 4. roky 5. foggy
room . . . 3. ala (anc), den 4. aula, cell,
hall, sala, seat, shed 5. attic, lodge,
place, salon, scope, space 6. cellar,
leeway, pantry, parlor, reside
7. chamber, drawing, laundry,
nursery, quarter 8. capacity
9. apartment, storeroom
11. opportunity
room (pert to) . . .
church (bishop's) . . 4. apse
convent . . 9. parlatory
dining . . 7. cenacle, dinette
9. refectory
harem . . 3. oda
household . . 5. ewery
inner . . 3. ben
large . . 4. aula, hall 7. rotunda,
theater 10. auditorium
monastery . . 4. cell
outer . . 3. but
pantry . . 6. larder 8. cupboard
prayer . . 7. oratory
Pueblo Ind ceremonial . . 4. kiva
Roman . . 6. atrium

ship's . . 4. brig 5. cabin, salon
sleeping . . 5. lodge 6. dormer
7. barrack, bedroom, chamber
9. dormitory
tower (bell) . . 6. belfry
roomy . . . 4. airy 5. ample 8. spacious
9. capacious, expansive
10. commodious 11. large–framed
roon . . . 5. shred 6. border 7. darling
8. treasure
roorback, roorbach . . . 3. lie 6. canard
7. lampoon 9. falsehood
roose . . . 5. boast, vaunt 6. praise
Roosevelt . . .
president, 26th . . 8. Theodore
president, 32nd . . 8. Franklin
roost . . . 3. bed, sit 4. jouk, pole, rest
5. perch 6. settle 7. lodging,
support
rooster . . . 4. cock, male (animal)
5. gallo 7. percher 11. chanticleer
12. fighting cock
root . . . 4. bulb, word 5. cheer, plant,
radix, tuber 6. source 7. radical
8. take root 9. establish
root (pert to) . . .
aromatic . . 9. sassafras
edible . . 3. oca, yam 4. beet, eddo,
taro 6. carrot, potato, radish, turnip
7. parsnip 8. rutabaga
food (Maori) . . 3. roi
medicinal . . 4. atis 5. jalep 6. ipecac,
senega 7. Senegal
out . . 4. seek 7. extract 9. eliminate,
eradicate
perfume . . 5. orris
pungent . . 6. ginger
starch . . 7. cassava
stock . . 7. rhizome
stringy . . 5. watap (watape)
taro . . 4. eddo
word . . 4. etym 6. etymon
rooted . . . 8. habitual 9. implanted
10. deep–seated 11. established,
traditional
rootlet . . . 7. radicel, rhizoid, taproot
rope . . . 3. tew, tie, tye 4. bind, cord,
line, rood 5. cable, cigar, lasso,
longe, noose, reata, wanty 6. fasten,
halter, hawser, lariat, string, tether
7. cordage, lanyard, measure
8. hangman's, inveigle
rope (pert to) . . .
boat's . . 4. rode 6. hawser 7. painter
chain . . 3. tye 9. stern fast
dancer, walker . . 8. balancer
11. equilibrist, funambulist
flag raising . . 7. halyard
gun carriage . . 8. prolonge
guy . . 4. stay, vang
nautical . . 3. tye 4. vang, wapp
6. parrel (parral) 7. snotter
of onions . . 5. reeve
security device . . 4. butt 5. cleat
ship's . . 3. tye 4. stay, vang
6. hawser, shroud 7. painter, ratline,
snotter
splicer's tool . . 3. fid
straw, twisted . . 5. sugan (soogan)
two strand . . 7. marline
walker . . 11. funambulist
ropery . . . 6. banter 7. roguery

roral... 4. dewy, rory 5. roric
rorqual... 5. whale 7. finback
Ros... 10. Slav rulers (Russ),
Varangians
rosary... 4. aves 5. beads (prayer)
7. chaplet (of roses), garland
8. devotion
rose... 3. cut (jewelry) 5. color, flush,
Rhoda 6. emblem, flower, nozzle,
symbol, window 7. fixture
rose (pert to)...
apple.. 4. plum 6. cherry 7. jambool
8. poma rosa
beetle.. 6. chafer, weevil
City.. 8. Portland (Oreg)
colored.. 8. alluring 10. auspicious,
optimistic
cross.. 6. symbol 11. Rosicrucian
14. cross in a circle
genus.. 4. Rosa 6. Acaena
8. Rosaceae
hiller.. 7. rosella 8. parakeet
moss.. 9. portulaca
of Sharon.. 6. Althea
petal oil.. 4. otto 5. attar
rash.. 7. roseola
under the rose.. 6. secret 7. sub
rosa
wild.. 9. eglantine
Rosetta Stone (pert to)...
decipherer.. 11. Champollion
famed for.. 11. inscription
13. hieroglyphics
site found.. 4. Nile (1799)
type.. 11. black basalt
roster... 4. list, roll, rota 5. slate
8. schedule
rostrum... 4. beak, dais, prow
5. snout, stage 6. pulpit 8. platform
9. proboscis
rosy... 3. red 4. pink 7. flushed,
roseate 8. blooming, blushing
9. rosaceous 10. auspicious,
optimistic
rot... 3. die 5. decay, spoil 6. blight
7. corrupt, disease, putrefy
8. nonsense 9. decompose
10. degenerate 12. putrefaction
13. decomposition
rota... 4. Club (Eng), list, roll 5. court,
round (Mus) 6. roster 15. Sacra
Romana Rota
rotate... 4. roll, spin, turn, whiz
5. recur, wheel 6. gyrate 7. rabatte,
revolve, trundle 8. rotiform
rotation... 4. spin, turn 5. round
7. turning 8. sequence
10. revolution, succession
rotator... 5. rotor 6. muscle 7. whirler
9. carrousel 12. merry-go-round
rotche, rotch... 5. goose, rotge
7. dovekie
rote... 6. course, custom, system
7. by heart, routine 8. par coeur,
practice 9. condition
roti... 5. roast 7. roasted
rotor... 5. wheel 6. roller, stator
7. rotator, turbine 8. impeller
rotten... 3. bad 4. foul, punk
5. doted, fetid 6. putrid, wicked
7. decayed, tainted, unsound
8. depraved, unstable 9. dishonest,

offensive, putrefied 10. putrescent,
undermined 13. disintegrated
Rotten Row (Hyde Park, London)...
12. thoroughfare (equestrian)
rottenstone... 6. polish 7. tripoli
rotter... 3. cad 7. bounder, shirker,
slacker 10. blackguard
rottgoose... 5. brant
rotund... 5. plump, round, stout
6. chubby 7. rounded 8. roly-poly
9. corpulent, spherical
Rotwelsch... 5. argot, slang 6. jargon
14. secret language
roué... 4. rake, wolf 7. rounder
9. debauchee, libertine
rouge... 5. blush, flush 6. polish,
redden 7. radical 8. cosmetic
rough... 4. hard, rude 5. crude, draft,
harsh, raspy, rowdy, seamy, stern
6. broken, choppy, coarse, hoarse,
rugged, severe, shaggy 7. boorish,
inexact, jarring, jolting, ruffled
8. scabrous, unsmooth 9. imperfect,
turbulent 10. incomplete, tumultuous,
unfinished 11. approximate
rough (pert to)...
avens.. 6. bennet (herb)
cloth.. 5. terry
footed (bird).. 9. feathered
hair.. 4. shag
hewn.. 6. brutal 10. unpolished
12. uncultivated
house.. 5. cut up 9. rowdiness
10. disorderly, noisy sport
jest (Mus).. 9. charivari
neck.. 4. boor 5. rowdy, tough
rider.. 9. Roosevelt (Teddy)
10. cavalryman
rock.. 4. crag
shod (to ride).. 7. trample
8. dominate 9. tyrannize
rough and...
hoarse.. 7. raucous
lean.. 6. craggy
ready.. 4. rude 10. unpolished
Ready.. 6. Taylor (Gen Zachary)
roughen... 4. chap, shag 8. asperate
roughly... 6. rudely 7. harshly
8. coarsely, severely, unevenly,
vulgarly 9. brusquely 10. unsmoothly
13. approximately
roughness... 6. lipper (of the sea)
8. acrimony, asperity, pungency,
unfinish 9. gruffness, harshness,
vulgarity 10. hoarseness
roughsome... 5. rough 6. rustic
7. uncouth
roulade... 3. run 8. arpeggio, division,
flourish 13. vocal flourish
roulette... 3. bas (bet) 4. disk, game
5. wheel 6. roller 8. wagering
rounceval... 5. giant, large 6. strong,
virago 9. termagant
round... 4. beat, bout, rota, rung, turn
5. cycle, orbed, rondo 6. circle,
curved, rotate, rotund, series, sphere
7. circuit, routine 8. circular, globular
9. in a circle, spherical
11. cylindrical
round (pert to)...
bone.. 3. hip
building.. 7. rotunda

clam.. 6. quahog
fish.. 9. whitefish
head.. 5. Swede 7. Puritan
house.. 5. cabin, coach 6. lockup,
  prison 10. watch house
of applause.. 7. plaudit
regular.. 5. beat
robin.. 6. angler, letter 7. pancake,
  request 9. cigarfish
worm.. 4. nema 7. ascarid, Ascaris,
  eelworm
roundabout... 5. about, dance
  6. detour, jacket 7. ambient, devious
  8. indirect 10. circuitous
  13. approximately 14. circumlocution
rounded (pert to)...
heap of stone.. 5. cairn
irregularly.. 7. gibbous
leaf.. 6. retuse
molding.. 5. ovolo
projection.. 4. lobe 5. tooth
scalloped.. 7. crenate
Round Table (pert to)...
knight.. 7. Galahad 8. Lancelot
seating.. 7. knights (King Arthur's)
site.. 7. Camelot
type.. 6. marble
roundup... 5. rodeo
roup... 4. cold 6. clamor 7. auction
  8. shouting 10. hoarseness
rouse... 3. hie 4. stir, wake 5. alarm,
  raise, start, upset, waken 6. awaken,
  bestir, elicit, excite, kindle 7. disturb
  9. stimulate
rouser... 7. stirrer 8. surprise
  9. demagogue (demagog)
  10. instigator
roussette... 5. shark 7. dogfish 8. fruit
  bat
roust... 4. roar, stir 5. rouse
  6. bellow, tumult 7. current (tidal),
  roaring 9. bellowing
roustabout... 6. lumper 7. laborer
  8. handy man 12. longshoreman
rout... 3. low, mob 4. bray, roar
  5. crowd, snort 6. bellow, defeat,
  rabble 7. debacle, scatter
  8. disperse, stampede, vanquish
  9. agitation, discomfit, overpower,
  overthrow 11. put to flight
route... 3. way 4. line, path 5. march
  6. detour 7. circuit
routh... 6. plenty 8. abundant
  9. abundance, plentiful
routier... 6. robber 7. brigand 9. free
  lance, plunderer
routine... 3. rut 5. grind, habit, order,
  round, troll 6. course, system
  7. regular 8. everyday 9. treadmill
rove... 3. gad 4. flit, part, roam
  5. range, stray 6. maraud, ramble,
  stroll, swerve, wander, washer
  7. deviate 8. straggle
rover... 5. nomad 6. bandit, pirate,
  viking 7. corsair, pilgrim, vagrant
  8. marauder, wanderer
roving... 8. errantry 9. desultory,
  deviative 10. discursive
row... 3. air, oar 4. file, fuss, live,
  spat, tier 5. align, brawl, broil
  6. lineup, paddle, propel, series
  7. quarrel, ruction 9. commotion

rowboat... 3. cog, gig 4. dory
  5. canoe, coble, skiff 6. randan
rowdy... 5. cutup, rough, tough
  7. boorish, ruffian 8. larrikin,
  plug-ugly 10. boisterous, disorderly
rowdy contention... 10. donnybrook
rowel... 4. spur 5. wheel
rowen... 4. crop (secondary) 5. field
  7. stubble 9. aftermath
rowing... 5. sport 6. randan 7. regatta
  8. sculling
rox... 3. rot 5. decay
royal... 4. real, rial, stag, true 5. basil,
  noble, regal 6. august, kingly
  7. stately 8. imperial, majestic,
  princely, splendid 9. dignified,
  sovereign 11. magnificent
royal (pert to)...
agaric.. 8. mushroom
bay.. 6. laurel
color.. 4. blue 5. smalt
court.. 5. aulic 6. ermine
crest.. 10. fleur–de–lis (Fr)
deer's antler.. 8. tres–tine
fur.. 6. ermine
mace.. 7. scepter (sceptre)
martyr.. 8. Charles I (Eng. 1649)
maundy.. 4. alms
officer.. 7. naperer
rights.. 7. regalia
rock snake.. 6. python
stables.. 4. mews
stars (Astrol).. 7. Antares, Regulus
  9. Aldebaran, Fomalhaut
Royal (pert to)...
Academy.. 4. Arts (1768)
Arcanum.. 7. Society (1877)
Canadian Mounted Police..
  8. Mounties 16. Northwest Mounted
Castle.. 8. Balmoral
Crown.. 5. tiara
Highlanders.. 10. Black Watch
Highness.. 5. title 6. prince
  8. princess
House.. 5. Tudor 6. Stuart, Valois
  7. Bourbon, Hanover, Windsor
Oak (Eng Hist).. 7. lottery
  10. Shropshire
Psalmist.. 9. King David
Scot.. 16. Lothian Regiments
royet... 4. wild 6. unruly 7. romping
  11. mischievous
rub... 4. crux, fret, wipe 6. abrade,
  polish, scrape, smooth, stroke
  7. burnish, massage 8. friction,
  irritate 9. hindrance, triturate
rub (pert to)...
away.. 6. abrade
down.. 4. comb 5. curry, groom
  7. massage
elbows.. 9. associate 10. fraternize
off.. 5. erase 6. abrade, remove
  10. obliterate
out.. 4. kill 5. erase 6. cancel,
  efface, excise 7. expunge, wipe out
  10. obliterate
wrong way.. 6. ruffle 8. irritate
  9. displease 10. antagonize
rub-a-dub... 6. clamor 7. clatter,
  pit-a-pat, rat-a-tat 8. rattatoo
  9. drumbeats
Rubáiyát (pert to)...

author.. 11. Omar Khayyám
stanza form.. 8. quatrain
translator.. 10. Fitzgerald (1859)
rubber... 4. para 5. stare 6. eraser
7. ebonite, elastic 8. massager,
sight–see 10. caoutchouc
rubber (pert to)...
city.. 5. Akron
hard.. 7. ebonite
India (pure).. 10. caoutchouc
plant.. 5. Ficus
ring.. 4. lute 6. gasket
sap.. 5. latex
shoe.. 6. galosh (galoshe)
tree.. 5. ule 7. guayule
wild.. 5. Ceara 6. caucho
rubbish... 4. junk, ross 5. attle, dross,
stent, trash, waste 6. debris, refuse,
rubble, trashy 8. nonsense, riffraff,
trumpery 9. worthless
rubble... 5. brash, chalk, stone, trash
7. rubbish 8. nonsense
11. foolishness
rube... 4. dolt 6. rustic 7. hayseed
rubedity... 7. redness 9. ruddiness
rubella... 7. measles, rubeola
rubescent... 3. red 8. flushing
9. reddening 10. erubescent
rubiator... 4. rake 5. bully 6. rascal
Rubicon... 5. river (Caesar's)
9. Fiumicino (modern)
rubicund... 3. red 4. ruby 5. ruddy
6. florid 7. redness
rubric... 3. rod 6. paraph, ritual
8. category, red chalk 14. title page
in red
rubrics (book of)... 4. ordo
ruby (pert to)...
bird.. 11. hummingbird
heraldry.. 5. gules
stained quartz (red).. 6. Ancona
7. rubasse 9. Mont Blanc
stone.. 3. gem 5. balas 6. spinel
type.. 4. size
ruck... 3. rut, sit (on eggs) 4. heap,
pile, rick 5. cower, crowd, squat,
stack 6. crease, crouch, furrow,
horses (race), pucker 7. wrinkle
9. multitude 10. generality
ruckus... 3. ado, row 5. fight
6. rumpus, uproar 7. quarrel, ruction
8. outbreak 9. commotion
rudd... 3. hue 4. carp, fish 6. redden
7. azurine, redness 10. complexion
rudder... 4. helm 5. guide
rudder part... 8. bearding 9. whipstaff
rude... 3. raw 4. curt 5. rough, rowdy
6. clumsy, coarse, rugged, simple,
vulgar 7. boorish, uncouth
8. ignorant, insolent 9. barbarous,
inclement, makeshift, turbulent,
unlearned, unskilled, untrained
10. boisterous, unpolished
11. impertinent, uncivilized
12. discourteous
rudeness... 6. ferity 8. curtness
9. impudence, insolence, vulgarity
11. raucousness 12. impertinence
rudiment... 5. first 6. anlage, embryo,
origin 7. element 9. first step
rudimentary... 5. basic 7. initial

8. original 9. beginning, elemental,
embryonic, vestigial 11. undeveloped
rudimentary digit... 7. dewclaw
rue... 3. rake, Ruta 6. grieve, regret,
repent, sorrow 7. afflict, deplore
10. bitterness, compassion,
repentance 14. disappointment
ruff... 3. ree 5. pride, reeve, ruche,
trump 6. collar, fringe, rebato
7. sunfish 8. drumbeat 9. sandpiper,
vainglory
ruffian... 4. fish, pimp, thug 5. rowdy,
tough 6. brutal, cuttle, pander
8. assassin, paramour, the Devil
9. cutthroat, desperado, murderous,
vulgarian
ruffle... 3. vex 4. fret, roil 5. anger,
annoy, frill, jabot 6. edging, muddle,
nettle, rumple, tousle 7. agitate,
disturb, flounce, fluster, shuffle
8. dishevel, disorder, drumbeat,
irritate 9. balayeuse 10. disarrange,
discompose
ruffler... 5. bully 7. boaster, ruffian
8. braggart 9. swaggerer
10. attachment (sewing)
rug... 3. mat 4. maud, shag
5. Senna, throw 6. carpet, hooked,
petate 7. Chinese, drugget, steamer
8. coverlet, Oriental 9. Samarkand
ruga... 4. fold 7. wrinkle 8. membrane
Rugby... 5. Fives 6. Rugger, school
(Eng) 8. football
Rugby term... 9. scrum half,
scrummage
rugged... 4. rude 5. asper, hardy,
harsh, rough, surly 6. craggy, fierce,
robust, seamed, shaggy, strong,
sturdy 7. austere, crabbed, healthy,
uncivil 8. vigorous, wrinkled
9. irregular, not smooth, turbulent
11. substantial
rugged mountain crest... 5. arête
ruin... 4. bane, doom, fate, loss
5. blast, havoc, spoil, wrack, wreck
6. defeat 7. debauch, destroy,
subvert 8. bankrupt, demolish,
downfall 9. perdition 10. desolation,
subversion 11. destruction,
devastation
ruined... 4. gone 7. spoiled, wrecked
8. bankrupt, defeated 9. destroyed
11. dilapidated 12. irremediable
ruinous... 6. deadly 7. baneful,
decayed 10. demolished, disastrous,
pernicious, submersive, tumbledown
11. destructive
ruins... 5. relic, wreck 7. remains
rukh... 6. forest, jungle
rule... 3. law 4. norm, sway 5. axiom,
guide, habit, order, regle, reign
6. decree, govern, manage, method,
regime, screed 7. counsel, measure,
precept, prevail, regency, regimen
8. dominate, persuade, standard
9. criterion, direction, influence,
principle 12. jurisdiction
15. totalitarianism
rule by...
children.. 9. paedarchy
ecclesiasts.. 9. hierarchy
one.. 8. monarchy

race.. 10. ethnocracy
ten.. 8. decarchy
the mob.. 9. mobocracy
the people.. 9. democracy
tribes.. 9. phylarchy

rule out...
6. cancel, excise 7. obviate

ruler... 3. min 4. amir (ameer), czar,
emir, lord 5. queen 6. despot,
dynast, ferule, gerent, prince, regent,
satrap, sultan, tyrant 7. emperor,
monarch 8. autocrat, governor,
hierarch, measurer 9. potentate

ruling... 3. law 6. decree 7. average,
regnant, statute, verdict 8. decision,
reigning 9. governing, prevalent
11. predominant 12. drawing lines

rullion... 4. shoe 6. sandal

rum... 3. dye (blue), odd 4. good
5. queer, tafia (taffia) 6. liquor
8. Demon rum

rumal... 6. fabric 8. kerchief (man's)

Rumania...
capital.. 9. Bucharest
city.. 4. Cluj, Iasi 7. Ploesti
king.. 5. Carol (former)
mountains.. 10. Carpathian
port.. 6. Galati (Galatz)
privileged class.. 5. boyar (boyard)
river.. 6. Danube

rumble... 4. boom, seat (back)
5. rumor 6. murmur, ripple, stir up
9. complaint 11. rolling tone

rumen... 3. cud 5. tripe 6. gullet,
paunch 7. stomach (1st)

ruminant... 2. ox 3. cow, yak 4. bull,
deer, gaur, goat, oryx, zebu
5. bison, camel, eland, gayal, llama,
moose, okapi, sheep, steer
6. alpaca, nilgai, vicuna, wapiti
7. banteng, buffalo, caribou,
chamois, gemsbok, giraffe
8. antelope, elephant, reindeer,
seladang 9. dromedary, nannygoat,
pronghorn 10. cud-chewing,
hartebeest, meditative, rhinoceros,
thoughtful

ruminant (pert to)...
division.. 8. Ungulata 10. Ruminantia
first stomach.. 5. rumen 6. paunch
fourth stomach.. 8. abomasum
9. rennet bag
second stomach.. 9. reticulum
third stomach.. 6. omasum
9. manyplies 10. psalterium

ruminate... 4. chew, muse 6. ponder
7. reflect 8. consider, meditate

rummage... 4. junk 6. litter, search
7. collect (by search), ransack

rumor, rumour... 4. Fama, talk
5. bruit, noise, story 6. norate,
report 7. hearsay, tidings
11. scuttlebutt

rump... 3. bone 6. breech, sacrum
7. meat cut 8. bankrupt, buttocks
9. remainder

rumpade... 3. rob 6. hold up

rumple... 4. muss 5. touse 6. crease,
ruffle, tousle 7. crinkle, crumple,
wrinkle 8. dishevel 10. disarrange

rumpus... 3. row 6. fracas, hubbub,
uproar 8. commotion, confusion
11. disturbance

rumtytoo... 8. ordinary
11. commonplace

run... 2. go 3. fly, gad, hie 4. dart,
flee, flow, lope, melt, race, scud,
tend, trot 5. blend, hurry, speed,
trend 6. charge, course, elapse,
endure, extend, manage, pursue,
sprint, stream 7. average, liquefy,
operate, proceed, roulade, routine,
smuggle, stretch, trickle 8. continue
9. discharge, suppurate

run (pert to)...
about.. 5. wagon 6. gadder
8. roadster, runagate, vagabond
after.. 5. chase, fleet, toady
6. pursue 7. lionize
aground.. 6. strand 7. founder
along the edge.. 5. skirt
away.. 4. bolt, flee 5. elope
6. decamp, escape 8. stampede
before the wind.. 4. scud
between ports.. 3. ply
down.. 3. hit 4. find 5. trace 7. run
over 9. exhausted 11. dilapidated
12. deteriorated
out.. 3. end 5. lapse, waste
6. elapse, emerge, escape
7. exhaust 8. squander
over.. 6. browse, exceed, ponder
7. trample 8. overflow 9. reiterate
quickly, swiftly.. 4. dart, race, scud
5. scoot 6. gallop, sprint 7. scuttle
stocking.. 6. ladder
through.. 4. stab 6. pierce 7. inspect,
pervade 8. rehearse, squander,
transfix 11. superabound
up against.. 4. find 9. encounter,
stumble on 10. experience

runagate... 7. runaway 8. apostate,
fugitive, renegade, vagabond,
wanderer

rundle... 4. ball, coil, rung, step
5. round 6. circle, roller, sphere,
stream

rune... 5. magic 6. secret, symbol
7. mystery 9. character (anc)

rung... 4. step 5. round, spoke, stair,
tread 6. degree, rundle 7. girdled,
ratline

runic... 5. verse 6. poetic 7. writing
8. alphabet (anc), Norsemen

runner... 3. ski (skee) 4. sled 5. miler,
racer, stolo 6. stolon 7. tendril
8. operator, procurer, salesman,
smuggler, sprinter 9. messenger,
solicitor

running... 7. current, cursive, fleeing,
flowing, melting 9. advancing,
prevalent, smuggling 10. continuous

running knot... 5. noose

running race... 5. relay 6. sprint

running toad... 10. natterjack

runt... 3. elf 4. chit (letter), wrig
5. dwarf, pygmy 6. pigeon
10. diminutive

runway... 4. file, ramp 8. airstrip

rupa... 4. body, form (visual)

rupee... 4. anna, coin 14. money of
account

rupestrian... 14. composed of rock
15. inscribed on rock

ruption... 7. ruction, rupture

8. bursting

rupture ... 4. rent 5. break, burst
6. hernia, injury, rhexis 7. quarrel
8. hostility 10. disruption, falling out,
separating

rural ... 6. rustic 7. bucolic 8. agrestic,
pastoral 12. agricultural

rural (pert to) ...
deity .. 3. Pan 6. Faunus
genus .. 6. potato
life .. 8. pastoral
poem .. 7. eclogue, georgic
Spanish .. 9. policeman
term .. 8. agrestic

Rusa ... 4. deer 6. sambar

ruse ... 4. fall, slip, wile 5. fraud, trick
6. deceit 8. artifice 9. stratagem
10. subterfuge

rush ... 3. jet 4. dart, dash, flow, scud
5. brook, haste, hurry, plant, press,
scoot, spate, speed, surge 6. charge,
course, defeat, demand, hasten,
runlet, sortie 7. cattail, repulse
8. outburst, reed mace, stampede
9. attention, thronging

rush (pert to) ...
forth .. 5. sally
hour .. 4. peak
light .. 6. candle, feeble
nut .. 5. chufa
Scot .. 5. sprat (herb) 6. Juncus
toad .. 10. natterjack
wheat .. 10. couch grass

rusk ... 5. bread 7. biscuit

rusma ... 9. quicklime 10. depilatory

Russia ... see also *Russian*
capital .. 6. Moscow 9. Petrograd (old)
citadel .. 7. Kremlin
city .. 4. Baku, Kiev, Omsk 5. Minsk
6. Rostov 7. Kharkov 8. Smolensk
9. Leningrad (St Petersburg),
Petrograd 10. Sevastopol (Sebastopol)
11. Vladivostok
coal fields .. 6. Donets (Ukraine)
fleet base .. 10. Sevastopol, Stalingrad
former name .. 7. Muscovy
founder .. 4. Ivan 15. Ivan the Terrible
gulf .. 4. Azov
isthmus .. 7. Karelia
lake .. 6. Onega 6. Baykal 7. Aral Sea
10. Caspian Sea
mountains .. 4. Ural 8. Caucasus
peninsula .. 4. Kola 6. Crimea
resort .. 5. Yalta 6. Crimea
river .. 2. Ob 4. Amur, Lena, Neva,
Ural 5. Volga 6. Donets 7. Dneiper,
Yenisei
sea .. 4. Azov 5. Black, White
6. Baltic 7. Caspian
strait .. 6. Bering

Russian (pert to) ...
antelope .. 5. saiga
aristocratic order .. 4. knez 5. Boyar
assembly .. 4. duma, rada 7. zemstoo
association, guild .. 5. artel
bank .. 4. game
beer, beverage .. 5. kvass, vodka
boat .. 6. baidak (baydak)
braid (trim) .. 8. soutache
calendar (to 1918) .. 6. Julian
cap (peasant) .. 4. aska
carriage .. 6. drosky, troika

9. tarantass (tarantas)
cart, wagon .. 6. telega
cathedral .. 5. sober
cloak (fur) .. 5. shuba
council .. 4. duma, rada 6. soviet
dance (rustic) .. 7. ziganka
decree .. 5. ukase
dog (wolfhound) .. 6. borzoi
7. owtchah
dress (peasant) .. 7. sarafan
duke, prince .. 4. knez (kniaz)
edict .. 5. ukase
fur (lamb) .. 7. karakul (karakule)
9. astrakhan
guild .. 5. artel
hemp .. 4. rine
hut .. 4. isba
leather .. 5. jufti (jufts) 6. Bulgar
8. shagreen
marsh, lagoon .. 5. liman
massacre .. 6. pogrom
musical instrument .. 5. gudok, gusla
9. balalaika
naval academy .. 6. Frunze
news agency .. 4. Tass
parliament .. 4. duma
peasant .. 4. Slav 5. kulak 6. muzhik
(muzjik)
plain (treeless) .. 6. steppe, tundra
police (secret) .. 5. Cheka
pound .. 4. pood
prince, duke .. 4. knez (kniaz)
satellite .. 7. sputnik
soup (cabbage) .. 5. stchi (shchi)
6. borsch
stockade .. 5. etape
synod .. 5. sobor
tea urn .. 7. samovar
turnip .. 8. rutabaga
villa .. 5. dacha
wagon (springless) .. 6. telega
wheat .. 5. emmer
whip .. 4. plet (plete) 5. knout
wolfhound .. 6. borzoi
yes .. 2. da

Russian people ...
chess champ (1892) .. 8. Alekhine
composer .. 3. Cui 10. Rubenstein,
Stravinsky 12. Tschaikovsky
14. Rimsky–Korsakov
conqueror .. 6. Tatars 7. Mongols
Cossack .. 5. Tatar
czar .. 4. Ivan 13. Peter the Great
duke .. 5. kniaz (knez, knyoz)
empress .. 7. Czarina, Tsarina
General .. 10. Timoshenko
grand duke .. 8. Nicholas
language deviser .. 8. Zamenhof
9. Esperanto (pseudonym)
leader .. 5. Lenin 6. Stalin 7. Molotov
8. Brezhnev
little Russian .. 7. Russene (Ruthene)
monk .. 8. Rasputin
novelist .. 7. Tolstoy
people .. 4. Lett, Slav 7. Cossack
8. Russniak 9. Muscovite, Ruthenian
poet .. 7. Pushkin, Yesenin
9. Pasternak
premier .. 5. Lenin 7. Kosygin,
Molotov 8. Bulganin 10. Kruschchev
saint .. 4. Olga
teacher, monk .. 7. starets

Youth Union.. 8. Comsomol
rust... 3. eat 5. erode 6. aerugo,
   patina 7. erosion, oxidize
   9. corrosion
rustic... 4. boor, carl, rube, rude
   5. churl, clown, Damon, rough, rural,
   swain, yokel 6. coarse, simple,
   sturdy, sylvan 7. artless, awkward,
   boorish, bucolic, Corydon, plowboy
   8. agrestic, pastoral 9. agrestian
   10. clodhopper, countryman,
   unpolished
rustic (pert to)...
   lover.. 5. swain
   maiden.. 9. Thestylis
   peasant.. 4. boor
   pipe.. 4. reed
   poetic.. 4. carl
   verse.. 4. idyl (idyll)

rustle... 4. flow 5. steal, swish, whisk
   7. crinkle 11. sound softly
rut... 5. ditch, track 6. furrow, groove,
   strake 7. routine, wrinkle
Ruth (pert to)...
   Book.. 12. Old Testament
   country.. 4. Moab
   husband.. 4. Boaz
   mother–in–law.. 5. Naomi
ruthless... 5. cruel 8. pitiless
   9. merciless 10. ironfisted
rye... 5. bread, grain, grass 6. cereal,
   whisky 9. gentleman (gypsy)
rye bread... 5. black 10. knackebrod
   12. pumpernickel
ryot... 6. farmer, tenant 7. peasant
Rytina... 6. dugong, sea cow
   7. manatee 12. Hydrodamalis
   14. Steller's sea cow
Ryukyu Islands... 7. Okinawa

S

S (pert to)...
   curve.. 4. ogee
   letter.. 10. nineteenth
   shaped.. 7. sigmate, sigmoid
   suffix.. 6. plural
Saal... 4. hall, room (large)
sabalo... 6. tarpon 8. milkfish
sabana... 5. plain 7. plateau, savanna
   (savannah)
sabbat... 8. assembly (demons), festival
   (orgies)
Sabbatarian... 9. ritualist 11. Russian
   sect
Sabbath... 6. Sunday 7. holy day
sabbatical year... 7. seventh
   8. vacation 14. leave of absence
sabbatism... 4. rest 9. ritualism
   12. intermission (labor)
Sabbatist (pert to)...
   devotee of.. 4. cult (Oriental)
   member.. 6. Semite
   named for.. 5. Sabbe (goddess)
   8. Sambathe
saber, sabre (pert to)...
   bean.. 4. jack
   bill.. 6. curlew
   fish.. 7. cutlass
   knot.. 8. military
   legged (horse).. 12. sickle–hocked
   Mohammedan.. 8. yataghan (yatagan)
   oriental.. 8. scimitar
   toothed.. 3. cat 5. tiger
   12. machairodont
   wing.. 11. hummingbird
sabino... 9. ahuehuete, rock cedar
sabio... 4. sage 6. priest 7. wise man
sable... 4. ebon, pelt 5. black, brush
   6. mammal, marten 8. antelope
   10. mysterious, Russia iron
sabotage... 6. damage, mayhem

   9. undermine 11. destruction
   (malicious)
Sabrina... 10. river nymph 11. River
   Severn
sabuline, sabulous... 5. sandy
   6. gritty 8. psammous
   10. arenaceous
sabutan... 5. fibre, straw
sac... 3. bag 4. cyst, sack 5. ascus,
   bursa, pouch, purse, theca 6. cavity,
   pocket, saccus 7. saccule, vesicle
   8. sacculus
Sac, Sauk... 11. Indian tribe
sacalait... 7. crappie 8. warmouth
   9. killifish
saccadic... 5. jerky 9. twitching
   11. eye movement
saccharine... 5. sweet 7. honeyed
   10. sweetening
saccos... 7. tunicle 8. vestment
sacerdocy... 10. priesthood 13. priestly
   order
sacerdos... 6. priest
sachem... 5. chief (Indian) 8. governor
   (Tammany)
sachet... 3. bag 5. pouch 6. powder
   7. perfume 8. reticule 11. perfumed
   pad
sack... 3. bag 4. loot, poke, wine
   5. ascus, bursa, catch, pouch, purse
   6. defeat, ravage, secure 7. pillage,
   plunder 8. desolate 9. discharge,
   dismissal
sack (pert to)...
   baseball.. 3. bag 4. base
   Bible.. 8. mourning
   but.. 4. butt, cask 8. trombone (anc)
   cloth.. 7. penance, sacking 15. garb
   of penitence
   dress.. 4. robe 6. jacket, sacque

sacrament... 3. act 4. oath 5. token
   6. pledge, symbol 7. mystery
   8. ceremony, covenant, practice
   9. communion, Eucharist
   10. intinction (to administer)
Sacramento (pert to)...
   capital, river.. 10. California
   cat.. 10. horned pout
   pike.. 9. squawfish
   salmon.. 7. quinnat
sacrarium (anc)... 6. chapel, shrine
   7. oratory 8. sacristy 9. sanctuary,
   synsacrum
sacred... 4. holy 6. divine 7. blessed
   8. hallowed, reverend 9. dedicated,
   inviolate, religious, venerable
   10. inviolable, sacrosanct
   11. consecrated 13. sanctimonious
sacred (pert to)...
   bark.. 7. cascara 14. cascara sagrada
   bean.. 11. Indian lotus
   beetle.. 10. scarabaeus
   bird.. 4. ibis
   book.. 5. Bible, Koran
   bo tree.. 3. fig 5. pipal
   bull.. 4. apis, zebu
   chest.. 4. arca 8. reliquary
   comb form.. 5. hagio, hiero
   dialect (Buddh writings).. 4. Pali
   grove.. 5. Altis (Olympia)
   image.. 4. icon (ikon) 5. Pietà
   instrument.. 4. Urim 7. Thummim
   malady.. 5. epilepsy
   monkey.. 6. baboon, rhesus
   8. entellus
   most.. 10. sacrosanct
   music.. 4. hymn 5. chant, motet
   8. oratorio
   river (Ind).. 6. Ganges (Ganga)
   room.. 8. sacristy
   traffic (in sacred things).. 6. simony
   weed.. 7. vervain
   wine vessel.. 3. ama
   writ.. 10. Scriptures
sacrifice... 4. lose, loss 5. offer
   6. give up, victim 8. chiliomb
   (1,000 oxen), hecatomb (100 oxen),
   immolate, libation, oblation, offering
   9. atonement, holocaust, martyrdom,
   privation, surrender 11. crucifixion,
   destruction
sacrificer... 6. martyr
sacrificial fire... 5. ignis
sacrilege... 7. robbery (church)
   9. blasphemy 11. desecration,
   profanation
sacrilegious... 7. impious
   10. irreverent 11. blasphemous,
   irreligious
sacrosanct... 4. holy 6. sacred
   8. ironical, most holy
sad... 3. bad 4. blue, dark, dire, dull
   5. dusky, sorry 6. solemn, somber,
   triste, wicked 7. doleful, pensive,
   unhappy 8. dejected, downcast,
   grievous, pathetic, shameful, terrible
   9. cheerless, depressed, sorrowful
   10. calamitous, deplorable,
   depressing, melancholy
   11. distressing, unfortunate
saddle... 4. meat (cut of), ride, seat
   5. ridge 6. burden 7. harness (part)

   8. encumber, straddle
saddle (pert to)...
   back.. 4. hill 5. ridge
   bag.. 7. alforja, pannier
   blanket.. 6. corona, tilpah
   boot.. 7. gambado
   cloth.. 5. cover 7. housing
   8. shabrack 9. appendage
   10. horsecloth
   elephant.. 6. howdah
   girth.. 5. cinch
   horse.. 5. mount 6. remuda 7. palfrey
   light.. 5. pilch 7. pillion
   pack.. 7. aparejo
   part.. 6. cantle, crutch, pommel
   8. tapadera (tapadero) 9. saddlebow
   place behind.. 5. croup
   rock.. 6. oyster
   strap.. 5. girth 6. latigo
saddler... 4. seal 5. horse 6. cozier
   7. cobbler, lorimer 8. merchant
   9. shoemaker
sadness... 5. dolor 6. pathos, sorrow
   9. dejection 10. gloominess,
   melancholy 11. unhappiness
   13. sorrowfulness
sad tree... 10. hursinghar (dye yield)
safari... 4. tour, trip 6. junket
   7. caravan, journey 10. expedition,
   pilgrimage
safe... 4. pete (thieves' sl), sane, sure
   5. chest, vault 6. closet, secure,
   unhurt 8. cautious, cupboard,
   unharmed 9. protected, strongbox
   11. trustworthy
safeblower... 7. burglar, peteman
   8. peterman
safe conduct... 4. pass 5. cowle,
   guard 6. convoy, escort 8. passport
   10. precaution, protection
safekeeping... 4. care 7. custody,
   storage 10. protection
   12. preservation
safety lamp (miner's)... 4. Davy
safety rail... 9. guardrail
saffron... 6. crocus, yellow
   10. colchicine
sag... 4. bend, hang, reed, rush, sink,
   wilt 5. drift, droop, sedge, slump
   6. weaken 10. depreciate
saga... 4. Edda, epic, tale 5. story,
   witch 6. legend 7. recital, sagaman
   9. narrative
Saga... 7. goddess, seeress
sagacious... 5. sage, wise 5. aware,
   witty 6. argute, astute, shrewd
   7. politic, sapient 9. judicious
   10. discerning, farsighted
   11. penetrative 13. perspicacious
sagacity... 3. ken 6. acumen, wisdom
   9. acuteness, quickness
   10. shrewdness 11. discernment,
   penetration 13. judiciousness
sage... 4. mint, wise 5. solon
   6. astute, Salvia, shrewd 7. sapient
   9. counselor, judicious, sagebrush
   10. discerning 11. philosopher
Sage (of)...
   Chelsea.. 7. Carlyle (Thomas)
   Concord.. 7. Emerson (Ralph W)
   Emporia.. 5. White (Wm Allen)
   Ferney.. 8. Voltaire

Monticello.. 9. Jefferson (Thomas)
Pylos.. 6. Nestor
sage (pert to)...
Bethlehem.. 9. spearmint
cheese.. 7. Cheddar
chippy.. 14. Brewer's sparrow
cock, hen.. 6. grouse
rose.. 5. alder (yellow)
tea.. 5. tonic
Sagebrush State... 6. Nevada
sagene... 5. seine 7. measure, network
sagitta... 7. otolith 8. keystone (Arch),
   The Arrow
sagittarius... 6. archer, bowman
Sagittarius... 9. The Archer
   13. constellation
sago (pert to)...
palm.. 6. gebang, gomuti
plant.. 10. cuckoopint
product.. 6. starch
tree.. 7. coontie
sagoin... 8. marmoset
saguaro... 6. cactus, flower
saguing... 6. banana
Sahara... 5. cocoa (color), leste (wind)
   6. desert
sahib... 5. title 6. master
   9. gentleman
sai... 6. monkey 8. capuchin
said... 6. stated 7. uttered 9. aforesaid
   15. before–mentioned
said to be... 7. reputed, rumored
   8. reported
saiga... 8. antelope
Saigon nickname... 14. Paris of the
   East
sail... 3. jib, lug 4. luff, tack 5. craft,
   float 6. vessel, voyage 8. navigate
sail (pert to)...
around.. 14. circumnavigate
close to wind.. 4. luff
end.. 7. yardarm
fast.. 4. scud
fish.. 12. basking shark 15. quillback
   sucker
fore and aft.. 7. spanker
foresail.. 9. spinnaker
line.. 6. earing
part.. 4. clew, yard 5. leech
poetic.. 4. keel
rope.. 5. sheet
secure, lash.. 7. trice up
strings.. 10. reef points
type.. 3. jib, lug, top, try 4. main,
   reef, stay 6. lateen, mizzen, square
   7. topsail 9. mainsail
sailboat... 4. yawl 5. ketch, skiff,
   sloop, yacht 7. caravel (caravelle)
sailing term... 3. leg, run 4. asea,
   beat, jibe, tack 5. point, reach
   7. gliding
sailing vessel... 4. bark (barque), brig,
   saic, yawl 5. sloop 7. frigate
   8. schooner 10. barkentine
   (barquentine)
sailor... 3. gob, tar 4. salt, wave
   5. middy 6. lascar, matlow
   7. mariner, voyager 8. seafarer
   10. bluejacket, lobscouser (sl)
sailor (pert to)...
associate at meals.. 8. messmate
kit.. 8. ditty bag 9. housewife

knot.. 8. geranium
mess tub.. 3. kid
patron saint.. 4. Elmo
song.. 7. chantey 9. barcarole
tobacco.. 7. mugwort
Saimiri... 4. titi 6. monkey 8. squirrel
sain doux... 4. lard 6. grease
saint... 3. Ste 5. angel 7. apostle,
   pietist 8. canonize, enshrine, sanctify
   10. holy person 11. godly person
Saint (pert to)...
Anthony's fire.. 10. erysipelas
Buddhist.. 5. arhat
Elmo's fire (or light).. 6. Helena
   9. corposant
Esprit.. 9. holy ghost
Francis of Assisi.. 11. il Poverello
   13. little poor man
Gaudens.. 8. sculptor
George's flag.. 14. national emblem
Helena's hemlock.. 7. jellica
John Lateran.. 12. Mother Church
John's bread.. 5. carob 9. algarroba
Leger (Eng).. 9. horse race
Luke's summer.. 12. Indian summer
Martin.. 13. Bishop of Tours
Martin's feast.. 9. Martinmas
Mary–le–Bow.. 15. Cheapside Church
   (Cockney area)
Mohammedan.. 3. pir
Patrick's breastplate.. 6. lorica
Paul.. 5. Saul of Tarsus
Paul's Church (London) designer..
   18. Sir Christopher Wren
Peter's dome architect..
   12. Michelangelo
Vitus' dance.. 6. chorea
Saint, patron...
children's.. 8. Nicholas (Santa Claus)
English.. 6. George
French.. 5. Denis
hospitals.. 9. John of God 10. Juan
   Ciudad
Irish.. 7. Patrick
Italian.. 7. Anthony
lawyer's.. 4. Ives
lover's.. 9. Valentine
sailor's.. 4. Elmo
Scottish.. 6. Andrew
Spanish.. 5. James
Welsh.. 5. David
saints (pert to)...
biography.. 9. hagiology
   11. hagiography
catalogue.. 7. diptich 9. hagiology
tomb.. 6. shrine
worship of.. 10. hagiolatry
sajou... 6. monkey 7. sapajou
sake... 4. beer 6. motive, reason
   7. purpose 8. beverage (rice)
salacious... 4. lewd 7. lustful, obscene
   8. unchaste 9. lecherous
salad plant, vegetable... 5. cress
   6. celery, endive 7. cabbage, lettuce,
   romaine 10. watercress
salamander... 3. eft 4. newt 5. poker
   6. triton 7. axolotl, Caudata, Urodela
   9. fire–eater 10. hellbender
   12. pocket gopher
salary... 3. fee, pay 4. hire, wage
   5. wages 6. reward 7. stipend
   8. pittance 9. allowance, emolument,

salt money (anc) 10. honorarium
12. compensation, remuneration
salat... 6. prayer (facing Mecca)
sale... 4. deal, vend 6. barter,
demand, market 7. auction, handsel
(1st in morning) 8. contract
11. black market
salesman... 5. agent 6. vendor
7. drummer 9. solicitor
14. representative 18. commercial
traveler
salient... 4. bold 6. trench 7. eminent,
jetting, jumping, leaping, obvious
8. bounding, extended 9. prominent
10. noticeable, protruding
11. conspicuous
salient angle... 5. arris, Doric
Salientia... 5. Anura, frogs, toads
8. Amphibia (tailless)
salient point... 7. feature (detail)
saline... 5. salty 6. salina 8. solution
10. saliferous
saliva... 7. spittle 8. digester, ptyalism
salivary gland... 8. racemose
sallow... 3. wan 4. gray, pale
5. muddy, pasty 6. pallid
9. yellowish
sally... 4. jest, leap, trip 5. issue,
jaunt, start 6. sortie 7. journey
8. escapade, outburst 9. witticism
salmagundi... 4. hash, olio, stew
6. medley 7. mixture 9. potpourri
10. periodical (old)
salmon... 4. fish 5. color 6. orlean,
sauqui 7. annatto, saumont
salmon (pert to)...
  adult.. 7. gilling
  after spawning.. 4. kelt
  cured.. 6. kipper
  dog.. 4. keta
  family.. 10. Salmonidae
  female.. 4. raun 6. baggit
  genus.. 12. Oncorhynchus
  herring.. 8. milkfish
  humpbacked.. 5. haddo, holia
  kind.. 7. quinnat
  landlocked.. 7. kokanee
  male.. 3. gib 6. kipper
  newly hatched.. 4. pink
  second year.. 6. hepper
  silver.. 4. coho
  small.. 4. peal 6. grilse
  third year.. 4. mort
  trout.. 5. sewen
  young.. 3. fog 4. parr 5. smolt
    6. grilse, samlet 7. essling
Salome (pert to)...
  Bib.. 6. dancer
  father.. 8. Herodias
  grandfather.. 5. Herod
  opera, by.. 7. Strauss
salon... 7. gallery 8. New Salon
(Paris), Old Salon 9. reception
10. assemblage, exhibition
11. drawing room
Salon del Prado (Madrid)...
9. promenade
saloon... 3. bar 4. deck 6. tavern
7. barroom, cantina, gallery
8. dramshop, groggery 11. drawing
room
saloop... 8. hot drink 9. sassafras

salt... 3. sal 4. cure 5. brine, taste
6. flavor, halite, sailor, saline
8. piquancy 9. seasoning
10. antiseptic, corrective 14. sodium
chloride
salt (pert to)...
  acetic acid.. 7. acetate
  alkaline.. 5. borax
  astringent.. 4. alum
  block, rock.. 3. pig
  boric acid.. 6. borate
  cat.. 4. lump 10. pigeon food
  comb form.. 4. sali
  cracker.. 7. saltine
  dish for.. 10. saltcellar
  ethereal.. 5. ester
  flat.. 5. playa
  lake.. 5. shott (chott)
  marsh, pond.. 6. salina
  native.. 6. halite
  nature of, like.. 6. haloid
  of the earth.. 7. the best
    10. commonalty
  peter, petre.. 5. niter
  rock, block.. 3. pig
  spring.. 4. lick
  tax.. 7. gabelle
  tree.. 4. atle (atlee) 5. cedar
    7. tamarix 8. tamarisk
  working.. 7. halurgy
  works.. 7. saltern, saltery 9. salthouse
saltant... 7. dancing, jumping, leaping
8. bouncing, bounding
salted... 5. briny, cured 6. corned
7. treated 8. brackish, hardened,
seasoned 11. experienced
salty... 3. reh 5. briny, salic, witty
6. risqué, saline
salubrious... 4. good 8. salutary
9. healthful, wholesome
10. beneficial
salutary... 7. healthy 8. curative
9. medicinal 10. salubrious
11. restorative
salutation... 2. hi 3. ave 4. hail
5. aloha, hello, howdy, skoal
6. curtsy, homage, kowtow, Mizpah
(Mizpeh), prosit, salaam (salam)
7. Dear Sir 8. greeting, serenade
salute... 4. hail, kiss 5. greet
6. homage, signal 7. address
salvage... 4. save 6. redeem, rescue
10. redemption 11. reclamation
salvation... 8. soterial 10. liberation,
redemption 11. deliverance,
soteriology 12. preservation
salve... 3. tip 4. balm, cure 5. allay,
quiet 6. anoint, cerate 7. assuage,
relieve 8. flattery, medicate, ointment
9. gloss over, lubricate, mitigator
10. medication
salver... 4. tray 9. flatterer 11. serving
dish
salvo... 6. excuse 7. gunfire, pretext,
proviso, quibble, rockets 8. applause
9. discharge, exception
11. projectiles, reservation
Samaria (pert to)...
  capital (anc).. 6. Israel
  deity.. 6. Nibhaz
  destroyer.. 6. Romans
  founder.. 4. Omri (925 BC)

people.. 9. Assyrians
province of.. 9. Palestine
rebuilder.. 5. Herod (the Great)
Samaritan, good.. 5. aider 6. helper
　　10. befriender, benefactor
　　11. helping hand
Sambal (Zambal) language... 4. Tino
sambar (sambur)... 4. deer, maha,
　　rusa
same... 2. id 3. ilk, one 4. ibid, idem,
　　self 5. alike, ditto 7. cognate, identic
　　8. selfsame 9. identical
　　10. equivalent
sameness... 6. parity, tedium
　　7. analogy, oneness 8. identity,
　　monotony 9. alikeness 10. similarity,
　　uniformity 11. equivalence
　　14. correspondence
Samian (pert to)...
　　island.. 5. Samos
　　Sage.. 10. Pythagoras
　　sea.. 6. Aegean
　　ware.. 8. Arretine
samlet... 4. parr 6. salmon (young)
Samoa...
　　capital.. 4. Apia
　　councilor.. 7. faipule
　　islands.. 8. American
　　islands, main.. 5. Manua, Upolu
　　　6. Savaii 7. Tutuila
　　natives.. 10. Polynesian
　　owl (barn).. 4. lulu
　　political council.. 4. fono
　　town.. 8. Pago Pago
　　warrior.. 4. toa
samovar... 3. urn 6. teapot
Samoyed, Samoyede... 3. dog (Arctic)
　　8. Siberian
sample... 4. test 5. model, taste
　　6. swatch 7. example, pattern
　　8. specimen
sampler... 8. original 9. archetype
　　10. needlework
Samson (pert to)...
　　Bib.. 5. judge (Israelite)
　　death site.. 4. Gaza (Syria)
　　famed as.. 9. strong man
　　opera.. 16. Samson and Delilah
　　tribe.. 3. Dan
　　wife.. 7. Delilah (betrayer)
Samuel... 4. Book (Old Test) 5. judge
　　7. prophet
samurai... 6. vassal 7. officer
Sana native... 8. Yemenite
San Andreas rift... 15. earthquake
　　fault (Calif)
San Antonio mission... 5. Alamo
sanative... 7. healing 8. curative,
　　sanatory
Sancta Sanctis... 20. Holy things for
　　the holy
sanctify... 5. honor 6. hallow
　　10. consecrate 11. free from sin
sanctimonious... 4. holy 6. sacred
　　7. saintly 8. affected 12. hypocritical
sanction... 4. abet, amen, fiat
　　6. assent, permit, ratify 7. approve,
　　endorse, support 8. approval
　　9. approbate, authority, authorize
　　11. countenance, endorsement
　　12. ratification 13. authorization
sanctity... 8. holiness 9. godliness,

solemnity 10. sacredness
　　11. saintliness 13. inviolability
sanctuary... 4. bema, fane, holy, naos
　　5. abbey, bamah, cella, haven
　　6. priory, refuge, temple 7. Alsatia,
　　convent, retreat, shelter 8. cloister
　　9. monastery 10. penetralia
sanctum... 3. den 5. study 6. adytum,
　　office 7. retreat
sand... 4. grit 5. arena, nerve, pluck,
　　stone
sand (pert to)...
　　applied to body.. 9. arenation
　　bog.. 4. syrt 9. quicksand
　　eel.. 4. grig 6. launce
　　flea.. 6. chigoe, red bug 7. chigger,
　　　sandboy
　　fluke.. 7. sand dab 8. flounder
　　hill, mound.. 4. dene, dune
　　hog.. 7. laborer (in compressed air)
　　　8. tunneler (tunneller)
　　inhabiting.. 11. arenicolous
　　like (sand).. 9. arenulous
　　　10. arenaceous
　　man.. 5. genie
　　mixture (clay).. 4. loam 9. sandstone
　　pear.. 5. Pyrus
　　submerged bank.. 3. bar 5. hurst,
　　　shoal
　　sugar.. 5. niter
　　widgeon.. 7. gadwall
sandal... 4. boat, shoe, sock 7. talaria
sandpiper... 3. ree 4. knot, pume,
　　ruff, stib 5. stint (long-toed)
　　6. dunlin 8. pectoral, triddler
sandstone... 7. sarsens 8. ganister
Sandwich Islands... 6. Hawaii
　　8. Hawaiian
sandy... 6. desert, gritty 7. arenose
　　8. granular, sabulous, Scotsman
　　9. sandpiper 10. arenaceous, ring
　　plover
sane... 5. lucid, sound 7. logical
　　8. rational, sensible 9. practical
　　10. reasonable
San Francisco Mil Post... 8. Presidio
sang... 5. blood, sheng 7. chanted,
　　ginseng, Society
sang-froid... 8. coolness 9. cold
　　blood, composure 11. insouciance
sanguinary... 3. ant (slave) 4. gory
　　5. cruel 6. bloody, yarrow
　　8. sanguine 9. bloodroot, murderous
　　12. bloodthirsty
sanguine... 4. warm 5. ruddy
　　6. ardent 7. hopeful 8. blood-red
　　9. confident 10. optimistic
　　12. bloodthirsty
sanity... 6. reason 8. lucidity, saneness
　　9. soundness 13. wholesomeness
San Juan Hill... 4. Cuba (Battle,
　　1898)
San Juan Indian... 4. Tewa
San Kuo... 13. Three Kingdoms (Shu,
　　Wei, Wu)
San Marino, Europe (pert to)...
　　famed as.. 11. oldest State (Eur)
　　government.. 8. Republic (smallest)
　　mountains.. 8. Appenine
　　site.. 8. Mt Titano
sannup... 6. Indian (married male) (opp
　　of squaw)

Sanskrit (pert to)...
college.. 3. tol
dialect.. 4. Pali
drama.. 9. Sakuntala (Shakuntala)
epic.. 8. Ramayana
god.. 4. Kama (Cupid), Vayu (wind)
  5. Indra (Great) 6. Aditya
goddess.. 3. Uma (Splendor) 4. Devi
  (Mother) 5. Aditi, Gauri
human spirit.. 7. jivatma
literature.. 5. sruti (shruti)
period.. 5. Vedic
Phonet (sounds).. 6. sandhi
poem (epic).. 11. Race of Raghu,
  Raghuvamsha
poet.. 8. Kalidasa
sacred books.. 4. Veda
soul.. 5. atman
treatise.. 9. Upanishad
Santo Domingo... 7. capital
  (Dominican Republic)
sap... 3. gum 4. dupe, fool, mine,
  seve, upas 5. drain, fluid, lymph,
  sapor 6. juices, trench, weaken
  7. essence 8. unsettle 9. simpleton,
  undermine
sapid... 5. tasty 7. zestful 8. flavored
  9. palatable, toothsome
sapient... 4. sage, wise 6. shrewd
  7. knowing 8. sagacious
  10. discerning
sapiutan... 4. anoa 6. wild ox
sapodilla... 5. chico 6. chicle, zapote
  7. nispero 8. naseberry
sapor... 5. savor, taste 6. flavor, relish
sapper... 5. miner 6. digger
  9. excavator
Saracen... 4. Arab 5. nomad, pagan
  6. Moslem 7. heathen, infidel,
  ragwort 9. Moor's head (Her)
  12. architecture
Saracen Knight... 8. Ruggiero
Sarah (pert to)...
bird.. 9. wake–robin
husband.. 7. Abraham
mother of.. 5. Isaac
slave of.. 5. Hagar
sarcasm... 4. gibe 5. irony, taunt
  6. satire 8. ironical, ridicule
  10. causticity
sarcastic... 3. dry 6. biting, ironic
  7. caustic, cutting, satiric 8. ironical,
  sardonic 9. malicious 10. mordacious
sarcophagic... 10. sarcophagy
  11. flesh–eating 13. sarcophageous
sarcophagus... 5. chest 6. coffin
  9. limestone 11. Assian stone, lapis
  Assius
sardine... 4. bang 7. alewife, anchovy,
  herring (young) 8. pilchard
Sardinia, Italy...
capital.. 8. Cagliari
island.. 13. Mediterranean
sheep.. 7. mouflon (moufflon)
town (Prehist).. 7. nuraghe (nuragh)
sardonic... 3. dry 6. ironic, morose
  7. cynical, satiric 8. derisive
  9. sarcastic 11. Rabelaisian
sartor... 6. tailor
sash... 3. obi 4. band, belt, benn,
  tobe 6. girdle 8. casement
  10. cummerbund

sash pulley weight... 5. mouse
Saskatchewan, Canada...
capital.. 6. Regina
city.. 8. Moose Jaw 9. Saskatoon
  12. Prince Albert
river.. 12. Saskatchewan
sassaby... 8. antelope
sassafras (pert to)...
nut.. 8. pichurim
oil of (part).. 6. safrol
tea.. 6. saloop
tree.. 4. ague
Satan... 5. Demon, Devil, Eblis, fiend
  6. Belial 7. Lucifer, Tempter
  9. archfiend 14. Mephistopheles
  16. Prince of Darkness
Satan (pert to)...
angel (bottomless pit).. 8. Apollyon
associate.. 6. Azazel 9. Beelzebub
before his fall.. 7. Lucifer
Jewish.. 8. Asmodeus
Scottish.. 4. deil
son.. 3. Imp (jocular)
satanic... 5. cruel 6. wicked
  8. devilish, infernal 10. diabolical
satchel... 3. bag 4. case, etui, sack
  5. cabas 6. valise
sate... 4. cloy, glut 5. gorge
  7. gratify, satiate, satisfy, surfeit
  8. saturate
sated... 4. full 5. blasé 6. gorged
satellite... 4. Echo, luna, moon
  6. planet 7. Sputnik 8. follower
  9. companion, dependent
satellite of Jupiter... 2. Io (1st)
  6. Europa (2nd) 8. Callisto,
  Ganymede
satellite of Saturn... 4. Rhea
  5. Dione, Mimas, Titan 6. Phoebe,
  Tethys 8. Hyperion 9. Enceladus
satellite of Uranus... 5. Ariel
  6. Oberon 7. Titania, Umbriel
satellite's path... 5. orbit
Sati (Egypt)... 5. Queen
satiate... 4. cloy, glut, pall, sate
  5. gorge 7. gratify, satisfy, surfeit
satin... 4. silk 6. étoile, fabric, sateen,
  satiny 7. satinette 10. smoothness
satinette... 6. pigeon (frilled)
satire... 3. wit 5. irony, verse
  6. parody 7. lampoon
satiric, satirical... 3. dry 6. bitter,
  ironic 7. abusive, caustic, cutting
  8. ironical, poignant 9. burlesque,
  sarcastic 11. reproachful
satisfaction... 3. cro 4. duel
  6. amends 7. comfort, content,
  payment, satiety 8. adequacy,
  pleasure, reprisal 9. atonement
  10. recompense, reparation
  11. contentment, fulfillment
  12. compensation, propitiation,
  remuneration 13. gratification
  15. indemnification
satisfied... 5. proud, sated 7. content,
  pleased 8. satiated 9. contented,
  convinced, gratified 10. paid in full
satisfy... 2. do 3. pay 4. fill, sate,
  suit 5. atone, solve 6. pay off,
  please, supply 7. assuage, content,
  fulfill, gratify, indulge, requite, satiate
  8. atone for, convince

satrap (anc)... 5. ruler 6. despot, prince 8. governor, overlord

saturate... 3. ret, sop, wet 4. fill, soak 5. imbue, souse, steep 6. drench, seethe 7. satiate 8. overfill, permeate 10. impregnate

saturated... 4. full 6. soaked, sodden 8. overfull

Saturday... 6. Samedi 9. sabbatine 13. Jewish Sabbath

Saturn (pert to)...
Astron.. 6. planet
consort.. 3. Ops
god of.. 4. seed
Latin.. 8. Saturnus
rings.. 7. moonlet 9. particles
rings, part.. 4. ansa
satellite.. 4. Rhea 5. Dione, Titan 7. Iapetus 8. Hyperion
Temple treasury (State).. 8. aerarium

saturnalia... 4. orgy 7. debauch 8. Festival (of Saturn) 11. pandemonium

saturnine... 6. dismal, gloomy, somber 8. funereal

satyr... 4. faun 5. deity 7. demigod, silenus 8. butterfly, capripede, orangutan

sauce... 3. soy 4. alec, pulp 5. caper, curry, garum, gravy 6. gansel 7. catchup (catsup), soubise, Tabasco, veloute 8. dressing 9. espagnole, insolence, seasoning 12. impertinence

saucy... 4. bold, pert, vain 5. brash, cocky, smart 7. forward 8. impudent, malapert 9. officious 11. impertinent 13. disrespectful

Saudi Arabia...
city.. 5. Islam
founder.. 7. Ibn Saud (1913)
gulf.. 7. Persian
Mohammed's tomb.. 6. Medina
mosque.. 5. Kaaba
peninsula.. 7. Arabian
provinces.. 4. Asir, Nejd 5. Hejaz 6. El Hasa
sea.. 3. Red
sect.. 6. Wahabi (Wahabee, Wahhabi)

Sauerbraten... 8. pot roast

sauger... 9. pike perch

Saul (pert to)...
concubine.. 6. Rizpah
daughter.. 6. Michal
father.. 4. Kish
herdsman.. 4. Doeg
of Tarsus.. 4. Paul
uncle.. 3. Ner
wife.. 7. Ahinoam
witch of.. 5. Endor

Sault Ste Marie... 3. Soo 6. rapids 9. ship canal

saumont... 6. salmon

saunter... 3. jog, lag, mog 4. roam, rove, walk 5. range, stray 6. dawdle, loiter, lounge, potter, ramble, stroll, wander 8. ruminate

sauqui... 6. salmon

saurian... 6. lizard, Sauria 7. reptile 9. crocodile

sausage... 6. salame 7. bologna, botulus, saveloy 8. rolliche (rollejee,

rollichie) 10. knackwurst

sausage-shaped... 9. allantoid 10. botuliform

savage... 3. att 4. rude, wild 5. brute, cruel, feral, yahoo 6. ferine, fierce, Indian 7. brutish, howling 8. cannibal, pitiless 9. atrocious, barbarian, ferocious, merciless, primitive 11. uncivilized 12. uncultivated

Savage Island...
language.. 4. Niue
native.. 5. Niuan
ocean.. 7. Pacific
other name.. 4. Niue

savanna, savannah... 5. plain 9. grassland 11. level region

savant... 4. sage 6. pundit 7. scholar 9. scientist 10. classicist 12. man of letters

save... 3. but 4. keep 5. catch, hoard, lay by 6. except, redeem, rescue, scrimp 7. prevent, protect, reserve, salvage 8. conserve 9. economize, excepting, safeguard 10. accumulate

savin, savine... 5. cedar 7. juniper 9. evergreen

savior, Saviour... 8. Redeemer 9. deliverer, liberator 11. emancipator, Jesus Christ

savoir-faire... 4. tact 10. cleverness, experience 12. ease of manner, mannerliness

savor, savour... 4. odor, zest 5. nidor, sapor, scent, smack, smell, taste 6. flavor, relish 9. degustate

savory, savoury... 5. sapid, tasty 7. piquant 8. gustable 9. agreeable 10. appetizing, delightful

saw... 3. cut 4. dict 5. adage, maxim 6. cliché, saying 7. noticed, proverb 9. platitude, serration

saw (kind)... 3. jig, rip 4. band, buzz, hack, whip 5. crown, power 8. crosscut

saw (pert to)...
back.. 6. sierra
bill.. 6. motmot 9. merganser
buck.. 8. sawhorse 13. ten-dollar bill
crosscut.. 5. briar
fish.. 3. ray
grass.. 5. sedge
horse.. 4. buck, rack 7. sawbuck
log.. 5. edger
of sawfish.. 5. serra
surgeon's.. 6. trepan (trephine)
teeth.. 5. tines
two-bladed.. 6. stadda

sawmill gate... 4. sash

saw-whet... 10. Acadian owl

saxhorn... 4. tuba 7. althorn 8. bass tuba 9. saxcornet

saxifrage... 6. Seseli

Saxon (pert to)...
color.. 5. smalt 8. Saxe blue 10. Bremen blue 13. indigo carmine
king.. 6. Egbert 8. Ethelred 14. Alfred the Great
language.. 10. Anglo-Saxon 12. Plattdeutsch
people.. 7. English 9. Sassenach 10. Anglo-Saxon 11. Lowland Scot

serf.. 4. esne
swineherd.. 5. Gurth (Ivanhoe)
warrior.. 5. thane
Saxony capital... 7. Dresden
    10. Wittenburg (anc)
say... 4. aver, cite, tell 5. gnome,
    speak, state, utter 6. affirm, answer,
    assert, assume, recite, remark,
    speech 9. authority 11. declaration
    12. conversation
say (pert to)...
    a blessing.. 5. bensh
    again.. 6. repeat 7. restate
      9. reiterate
    further.. 3. add
    no (to).. 6. negate, refuse 8. prohibit
      10. disapprove
    one thing, mean another.. 6. palter
      7. falsity 9. fluctuate 10. equivocate
      12. be capricious
    uncle.. 4. cede 9. surrender
      10. capitulate 15. throw in the
      towel
saying... 3. dit, mot, saw 4. quip
    5. adage, axiom, maxim 6. byword,
    enigma, phrase, remark 7. proverb
    8. aphorism, apothegm
    11. declaration
saying, sayings (pert to)...
    collection of.. 9. gnomology
    criterion, party cry.. 10. shibboleth
    dogmatic.. 6. dictum
    religious.. 5. logia
scab... 3. rat 4. sore 5. crust, mange
    6. rotter 7. blemish 8. deserter
    9. scoundrel 12. incrustation
    13. strikebreaker
scabbard... 6. sheath 7. holster,
    pilcher 13. emblem of peace
scabbard fish... 7. cutlass 9. frostfish
scaddle... 5. cruel, timid 6. fierce
    7. nervous 8. skittish, thievish
    11. mischievous
scads... 4. gobs, wads 5. heaps,
    money, piles 6. oodles 11. great
    number 12. considerable
scaffold, scaffolding... 5. easel, stage
    7. staging, support 8. platform
    9. grain loft
scalawag, scallawag... 5. scamp
    6. rascal 7. sculpin 10. scapegrace
scale... 3. hut 4. husk, peel, rate,
    shed, size 5. climb, crust, flake,
    gamut, rustre (anc armor), series,
    lamina, rustre (anc armor), series,
    weight 7. compare, measure
    12. incrustation
scale (pert to)...
    botany.. 5. palea
    color.. 10. tintometer
    comb form.. 4. cten 5. cteno, lepis
    duck.. 9. merganser, sheldrake
    fish.. 6. ganoid 8. scabbard
    grand.. 4. epic
    music.. 3. E la (highest note)
      5. gamut, minor 9. chromatic,
      hexachord 10. tetrachord
    slide.. 7. vernier
    tail.. 6. rodent
    Zool.. 6. scutum
scallop... 4. quin 5. crena, notch
    7. mollusk 9. serration, shellfish

    12. summer squash
scalloped... 6. cooked 7. notched
    8. invected (Her) 9. crenulate
scalpel... 5. knife 6. lancet 7. dissect
    8. bistoury
scaly... 5. flaky 6. crusty, scabby,
    scurfy 7. leprose 8. squamous
scamp... 3. imp 5. cheat, knave,
    rogue 6. rascal, slight 7. bacalao,
    codfish 8. scalawag, spalpeen
    9. scoundrel 15. worthless fellow
scamper... 3. hie, run 4. dash, race,
    scud 5. haste 6. hasten 7. brattle
    9. hasten off, skedaddle 11. hasty
    flight
scan... 3. eye 6. browse, peruse
    7. examine 10. scrutinize
    11. contemplate 16. recite metrically
scance... 5. blame, shine 6. glance
    7. comment, glitter
scandal... 5. odium, shame 6. gossip
    7. calumny, offense, slander
    8. disgrace, ignominy
    10. defamation, detraction,
    opprobrium 11. abomination
scandalous... 6. wicked 8. libelous,
    terrible 10. defamatory, slanderous
    11. disgraceful, opprobrious
Scandinavia, countries... see also
    Scandinavian 6. Norway, Sweden
    7. Denmark, Iceland
Scandinavian (pert to)...
    alphabetical character.. 4. rune
    ash tree.. 10. Yggdrasill
    author.. 8. Andersen (Hans C)
    bay.. 5. fjord
    explorer.. 4. Eric
    goblin, brownie.. 5. nisse 6. kobold
    god.. 4. Lake, Thor
    goose.. 5. nisse
    hall of Odin (heroes' souls)..
      8. Valhalla
    legend.. 4. Edda, saga
    maiden of Odin.. 8. Valkyrie
    navigator.. 4. Eric
    people.. 4. Dane, Lapp 5. Swede
      8. Norseman 9. Norwegian
    people, type.. 8. Teutonic
    pert to.. 5. runic
    plateau.. 5. fjeld
    rulers.. 10. Varangians
    saga narrator.. 7. sagaman
    sea monster (fabled).. 6. kraken
    supernatural being (dwarf or giant)..
      5. troll
scant... 3. few 5. chary 6. meager,
    narrow, scarce, slight, sparse
    7. slender, sparing 12. parsimonious
scanty... 4. rare 6. meager (meagre),
    narrow, scarce, sparse 7. scrimpy
    12. insufficient 14. inconsiderable
scapegoat... 4. goat (Bib) 9. sacrifice
    10. substitute
scapegrace... 5. scamp 8. scalawag
    (scallawag) 9. reprobate
    10. profligate 12. incorrigible
scar... 3. arr, shy 4. seam, sear
    5. cliff, mound 7. blemish 8. cicatrix
scarce... 4. rare 5. short 6. scanty
    7. sparing 8. uncommon 9. deficient
    10. infrequent
scarcely... 6. barely, hardly 7. but just

12. infrequently

scarcity... 4. lack, want 6. dearth, famine, rarity 7. paucity 8. rareness 11. infrequency 13. insufficiency

scare... 3. cow 5. alarm, panic 7. startle, terrify 8. affright, frighten

scarecrow... 4. ogre 5. bogle 6. effigy, goblin, malkin, shewel (sewel) 9. jackstraw 10. frightener 11. hide-and-seek

scarf... 3. boa, tie 4. sash 5. ascot, cloud, nubia 6. tippet 7. muffler 9. rigolette 10. fascinator

scarf (pert to)...
bird.. 9. cormorant
broad.. 5. shawl
clerical.. 5. fanon, orale, rabat, stole
feather.. 5. boa
head.. 10. fascinator
Hindu.. 4. sari
India.. 7. dopatta
Mexico.. 6. tapalo
skin.. 7. cuticle 9. epidermis

Scarlet Letter... 5. novel (Hawthorne)

Scarlet O'Hara's home... 4. Tara

scarp... 5. cliff, pitch 7. descent, incline 9. declivity

scary... 5. eerie, timid, weird 7. ghostly, uncanny 8. alarming 12. easily scared

scat... 4. hiss 5. burst, smash 6. buffet 7. scatter

scat, scatt (Orkney Isls)... 3. tax 7. tribute

scathe... 4. flay, harm, hurt 6. assail, damage, injury, scorch 7. scarify 9. excoriate 10. misfortune

scatter... 3. sow, ted 4. deal, rout 5. spray, strew 6. dispel, litter, shower, splash, spread 7. bestrew, diffuse, radiate 8. disperse, separate, squander 9. circulate, dissipate 10. disarrange, strew about

scattered... 4. semé 5. dealt 6. sparse, strewn 8. confused, sparsile, sporadic 9. broadcast, dispersed, separated, sprinkled 10. widespread 11. distributed

scattering... 3. few 8. Diaspora 10. dispersion, separating 13. dissemination

scatty... 7. showery

scaup... 4. duck 8. bluebill 9. blackhead, broadbill

scavenger... 4. bird 8. organism 10. saprophyte 16. garbage collector

scaw... 8. headland 10. promontory

scene... 4. site, view 5. anger, sight, vista 6. locale 7. diorama, picture, tableau

scene (pert to)...
behind the.. 8. secretly 9. backstage, invisible
inside.. 7. neorama
last.. 6. finale
of action.. 5. arena, stage 6. sphere
of confusion.. 5. babel
of miracle (Bib).. 4. Cana
opera.. 5. scena
wright.. 6. artist 8. designer (scenery), stageman

scenic... 8. dramatic 9. panoramic

11. picturesque

scenic (pert to)...
enigma.. 7. charade
pert to.. 5. stage 7. episode, scenery
representation.. 7. diorama
13. motion picture

scent... 4. aura, clue, nose, odor 5. aroma, flair, nairn, nidar, smell, spoor 6. detect 7. perfume 9. fragrance

scented... 5. olent 6. odored 8. perfumed, smelling 11. odoriferous

scepter, sceptre... 3. rod 4. mace 5. baton, staff 6. emblem (royal) 8. insignia 11. sovereignty

schedule... 4. card, list 5. slate 7. program 8. calendar, document 9. catalogue, inventory

scheme... 3. aim 4. lark, plan, plot 5. cabal 6. device, devise, racket, system 7. complot, concoct, diagram, epitome, outline, project, purpose 8. artifice, contrive 9. boomerang 10. conspiracy, enterprise 11. machination

schemer... 7. plotter 8. conniver, finalger 9. intriguer

schism... 4. rent, sect 5. split 6. breach 7. dissent, faction 8. division 10. falling-out, separation

schismatic... 7. heretic, sectary 8. apostate 9. dissenter, sectarian 10. factionist

schist... 4. mica, rock 5. slate 10. hornblende

scholar... 6. pedant, savant 7. learner, student 8. disciple 11. philologist

scholarly... 7. erudite, learned 8. academic, studious 9. philomath 10. scholastic

scholarship... 5. burse 8. learning 9. education, erudition, knowledge 10. foundation 11. instruction

school... 4. cult, sect 5. class, drill, flock, order, teach, train 7. convent, educate, seminar 8. instruct, seminary 9. institute

school (pert to)...
book.. 6. primer, reader 7. speller
English.. 4. Eton 6. Oxford 9. Cambridge
French.. 5. école, lycée
German.. 6. schule
head, inspector.. 9. scholarch
master.. 7. dominie 9. pedagogue (pedagog)
ref to.. 10. scholastic
riding.. 10. manège
teacher.. 4. marm
term.. 8. semester
wrestling.. 9. gymnasium, palaestra (palestra)

school of...
art.. 4. Dada
Fine Arts.. 9. Wagnerian
fishes.. 5. shoal
philosophers.. 7. Eleatic
philosophy.. 7. Gnostic
seals.. 3. pod
thieves.. 4. gang
whales.. 3. gam, pod

schooner... 4. boat, brig, tern 5. glass

6. vessel 7. measure, prairie (Hist)
schuit, schuyt... 5. sloop 6. vessel
  7. eelboat
science... 3. art 5. ology, skill
  9. knowledge 11. proficiency
science of...
agriculture.. 8. agronomy
better living.. 9. euthenics
breeding.. 8. eugenics
character.. 8. ethology
children's diseases.. 10. pediatrics
  (paediatrics)
controversy.. 8. polemics
creatures.. 8. entomology
dining.. 10. aristology
doctrines.. 9. esoterics
ears.. 7. otology
family symbols.. 8. heraldry
forest trees.. 7. silvics (sylvics)
good.. 6. ethics 9. euthenics
  10. agathology
government.. 8. politics
happiness.. 9. eudaemonics
healing.. 9. iatrology
health.. 7. hygiene
kissing.. 13. philematology
language.. 9. philology, semantics
  11. linguistics
life.. 7. biology 10. entomology
light.. 6. optics
mind.. 10. psychology
moral conduct.. 6. ethics
organism behavior.. 7. ecology
  (oecology) 9. bionomics
philosophy.. 6. noesia
reality.. 10. philosophy
reasoning.. 5. logic
rocks.. 9. petrology
sea (the).. 12. oceanography
self-defense.. 4. judo 7. jujitsu
sound.. 9. acoustics
theology interpretation.. 8. exegesis
  12. hermeneutics
verse.. 7. prosody
virtue.. 8. aretaics
words.. 9. semantics
scientific... 5. exact 9. realistic,
  technical 16. precise knowledge
scimitar, scimiter... 4. snee 5. saber
  8. billhook
scintilla... 4. atom, iota, whit
  5. spark, trace 7. modicum
scintillate... 5. flash, gleam, spark
  7. be witty, glitter, twinkle
  9. coruscate 10. be eloquent
scion, cion... 3. son 4. slip 5. graft,
  shoot 10. descendant
scold... 3. jaw, nag 4. carp, rail, rate
  5. chide, shrew 6. berate, chider,
  rebuke 7. reprove, upbraid
  8. admonish 11. reprimand
scolding... 7. froward 8. reproach,
  shrewish 10. upbraiding
  12. admonishment, reprimanding
sconce... 3. top 4. head 5. brain,
  mulct, skull 6. screen 7. bulwark,
  lantern, redoubt, skelter
  11. candlestick, counterfort
scoop... 4. bail, beat, lade, news
  5. empty, ladle, spoon 6. bucket,
  hollow, shovel 8. excavate, gather in

scoop out... 3. dig 5. gouge
  6. chisel, hollow 7. fashion
scope... 4. area, room 5. ambit,
  arena, range, reach 6. degree,
  domain 7. compass, freedom, liberty
  8. latitude 9. gyroscope, intention,
  periscope, telescope 10. microscope
  11. stethoscope 12. kaleidoscope,
  spectroscope
scorch... 4. burn, char, sear, sere
  5. parch, singe, speed 7. shrivel
  9. criticize
scordato... 9. out of tune 14. made
  discordant
score... 3. peg, run, sum, tab 4. debt,
  gain, goal, rate 5. corge, judge,
  notch, scold, slash, tally 6. berate,
  furrow, groove, points, reason, twenty
  7. account, arrange, scratch
  8. incision 9. calculate, tally mark
  10. obligation 11. arrangement,
  composition, orchestrate
  12. indebtedness
scoria (volcano)... 4. lava, slag
  5. dross 6. refuse 7. residue
scorn... 4. defy, geck, mock 5. spurn
  6. deride, reject 7. contemn,
  despise, disdain 8. contempt,
  derision, disgrace 9. contumely
scornful... 8. derisive, insolent
  10. disdainful 12. contemptuous,
  contumelious
Scorpio (pert to)...
constellation in.. 8. Milky Way
genus.. 8. Scorpius
night mansion of.. 4. Mars
pictured as.. 8. scorpion
star (brightest).. 7. Antares
zodiac sign.. 8. eighth
scorpion... 4. nepa 7. alacran, scourge
  (Bib) 8. arachnid, catapult 10. pine
  lizard, vinaigrier 11. vinegarroon
  (vinagron) 15. blue-tailed skink
Scot... 3. Mac 4. Celt, Gael 5. Saxon
  6. Sawney 7. bluecap 8. Scotsman
  10. Caledonian, Highlander
Scotland... see also *Scottish*
capital.. 7. Edinburgh
city.. 3. Ayr 5. Perth 6. Atholl
  (Athole), Dundee 7. Glasgow
  (largest), Renfrew 8. Aberdeen
  9. Inverness
congress (musical).. 3. Mod
district.. 6. Argyll, Atholl
  10. Midlothian
famed site.. 9. Trossachs (Lady of the
  Lake) 10. Loch Lomond 11. Loch
  Katrine
firth.. 3. Tay 4. Loch 5. Clyde, Forth,
  Moray, Tweed
islands.. 6. Orkney 8. Hebrides,
  Shetland
Latin name (anc).. 9. Caledonia
moors.. 10. Lochar Moss
mountain.. 9. Grampians
poetic name.. 6. Scotia 9. Caledonia
resort.. 4. Oban
river.. 3. Ayr, Dee, Tay 5. Afton,
  Clyde, North, Tweed 6. Teviot
  7. Deveron
seaport.. 4. Leth 6. Dundee
Scotland Yard headquarters...

6. London 18. Metropolitan Police
Scott, Sir Walter (pert to)...
estate.. 10. Abbotsford (Scot)
famed as.. 4. poet 8. novelist
novel.. 7. Ivanhoe
poem.. 13. Lady of the Lake
Scottish (pert to)...
accent.. 4. birr
alder.. 3. arn
attendant (hunter's).. 6. gillie (gilly)
bagpipe music.. 7. pibroch
beret.. 3. tam 11. tam-o'-shanter
bird.. 3. gae (blue) 6. grouse
  7. snabbie (snabby) 9. swinepipe
blessing.. 6. rebuke 8. scolding
blood money.. 3. cro 7. galanas
blue.. 6. homage 8. infernal
  11. reddish-blue
bluebell.. 8. harebell
boat.. 4. zulu 7. coracle, skaffie
bonnets.. 8. mushroom
brandy.. 6. Athole
breeches.. 5. trews
brier, briar.. 4. rose
broth.. 5. brose
bull, ox.. 4. stot
cake (tea).. 5. scone
cap.. 3. tam 8. Balmoral 9. Glengarry
  11. tam-o'-shanter
carpet.. 13. Kidderminster
cattle.. 8. Aberdeen 9. Ayrshire
celebration.. 4. kirn (harvest)
child.. 5. bairn 6. scuddy (naked)
church.. 4. kirk
cloth.. 4. kelt 6. tartan
coalfish.. 7. glashan, sillock
court officer.. 5. macer
cup.. 4. tass
dagger (anc).. 4. dirk
dagger, knife.. 8. skean dhu
dance.. 4. reel 5. fling 9. ecossaise
  10. strathspey 13. Highland fling
devil.. 4. deil 6. Hornie
dirge.. 8. coronach (as on bagpipes)
duck.. 4. coot 6. scoter
earth.. 4. eard
elder.. 7. tobacco
elm.. 7. wych-elm
excuse.. 6. sunyie
eye.. 2. ee
family (same).. 3. ilk
festival.. 3. Mod 7. uphelya (Epiphany)
fish.. 4. sile 7. sillock 8. spalding
fog.. 4. haar
Gaelic.. 4. Erse
ghost.. 6. taisch
girl.. 4. lass 6. lassie, towdie
  7. winklot
goblin.. 8. barghest
godmother.. 6. cummer (kimmer)
grandchild.. 2. oy (oye)
grandfather.. 8. gudesire
hill, hillside.. 4. brae 6. strone
icicle.. 7. shoggle
kilt.. 7. filibeg
kiss (stolen).. 8. smoorich
lake.. 4. loch
language.. 4. Erse 6. Lallan (Lalland)
liquor.. 5. scour 6. Athole 7. whitter
lovage.. 10. sea parsley
money, silver.. 6. siller
nephew.. 6. nepote

New Year's Day.. 7. Cake Day
  8. hogmanay
nightingale.. 7. warbler
ox, bullock.. 4. nowt
plaid.. 4. maud 6. tartan
porridge.. 5. brose
pouch, purse (kilt front).. 7. sporran
pudding.. 6. haggis
reel (fishing).. 4. pirn
rod, over the door.. 10. willow wand
sausage.. 9. whitehass (whitehawse)
schoolmaster.. 3. dux
shawl (plaid).. 4. maud
stream, brook.. 4. sike
sweetheart.. 2. jo
sword.. 8. claymore
toad.. 3. ted 4. taed
tobacco.. 5. elder
topaz.. 9. cairngorm
townhall.. 8. tolbooth (tollbooth)
uncle.. 3. eme
village.. 3. rew
waistcoat (under).. 6. fecket
whirlpool.. 7. swilkie
whisky.. 9. Glenlivet (Glenlivat)
  10. usquebaugh
window.. 7. winnock
youth.. 6. chield (chiel) 7. callant
  (callan)
scoundrel... 3. cad 5. cheat, knave,
  scamp 6. varlet 7. villain
  8. scalawag 9. miscreant
  10. blackguard 11. rapscallion
scoup.. 3. run 4. leap, skip
  7. scamper
scourge... 4. bane, flog, lash, whip
  6. punish, swinge, switch 8. chastise
  10. affliction, infliction, punishment
Scourge of God... 6. Attila (King of
  Huns)
Scourge of Princes... 7. Aretino (It
  satirist)
scout... 3. spy 5. flout, scoff
  7. lookout, servant 8. emissary,
  watchman 9. guillemot
  11. reconnoiter 14. razor-billed auk
scow... 4. acon 6. garvey 7. lighter
scowl... 5. frown, lower 6. aspect
  (gloomy), glower 7. wrinkle (brow)
  10. sullen look
scraggly... 5. rough 6. ragged
  7. unkempt 9. irregular
scraggy... 4. bony 5. rough
  6. meager, rugged, skinny
  7. knotted, scrawny, stunted
scram... 6. begone, benumb, decamp
  7. vamoose
scramble... 4. push 5. climb, crowd,
  crush 6. jostle, strive 7. clamber,
  scatter 8. struggle
scrap... 3. bit, end, ort, rag 4. chip,
  junk 5. fight, melee, piece, waste
  6. morsel, refuse 7. cutting, discard,
  excerpt, extract, quarrel, remnant
  8. fragment, ramentum
scrape... 3. row, rub 4. rake, rasp
  5. grate, graze, shave 6. abrade, eke
  out, injure, sclaff 7. collect, scratch
  9. economize, obeisance 10. difficulty
  11. predicament
scraper... 4. harl (wool), tool
  6. barber, rasper 7. abrader, fiddler,

strigil 8. grattoir

scrappy . . . 9. irregular 10. pugnacious 11. contentious, fragmentary, quarrelsome

scratch . . . 3. mar, rit, rub 4. claw, draw, itch, mark, rake, rist, tear 5. erase 6. cancel, injury, scrape 7. blemish, roughen, scarify 8. scribble, withdraw

scrawl . . . 6. doodle 7. scratch 8. scribble

scrawny . . . 4. lean, poor, thin 5. spare 6. skinny 7. scranny 8. rawboned

scream . . . 3. cry 4. wail, yell 6. shriek, squeal 7. screech

screamer . . . 5. swift (bird) 7. blunder 8. headline

scree . . . 5. stone, talus 6. debris, pebble

screech . . . 3. cry, say 6. outcry, scream, shriek, squeal 7. ululate

screech (pert to) . . .
    hawk . . 10. goatsucker
    martin . . 5. swift
    owl . . 4. barn 5. Scops

screed . . . 4. list, rend, tear 5. shred 6. tirade 7. lecture 8. fragment 12. dissertation

screen . . . 3. net 4. hide, laun, mask, sift, sort, veil 5. arras, blind, cloak, pavis, shade, sieve, spier 6. defend, grille, riddle, sifter, sorter 7. conceal, curtain, protect, reredos, shelter 8. parclose 9. partition, safeguard 10. protection 12. discriminate

screw . . . 3. key 4. coil, turn 5. horse, twist 6. fasten, gimlet, rotate, spend 7. contort, distort, tighten, turnkey 9. bargainer, propeller, skinflint 10. contortion, thumbscrew

screwlike . . . 6. spiral 7. spiroid

scribble . . . 6. doodle, scrawl 7. scratch 8. scrabble

scribe . . . 5. clerk 6. author, jurist, lawyer, penman, writer 8. recorder 10. amanuensis, cuttlefish, journalist 13. bibliographer

scriggle . . . 5. twist 6. squirm 7. wriggle 8. curlicue

scrimmage . . . 3. row 5. fight 6. tussle 8. football (term), practice, skirmish, struggle

scrimp . . . 4. save 5. scant, stint 6. scanty, scrape, sparse 7. sparing 9. economize

scrip . . . 3. bag 4. list 5. money 6. wallet 7. writing 8. document, schedule

script . . . 5. ronde 6. letter 7. writing 8. scenario 10. manuscript, typescript 11. handwriting

scriptural . . . 7. written 8. Biblical, orthodox

scriptural interpreter . . . 7. exegete

scripture . . . 4. writ 5. motto, truth 7. passage, writing 8. document 10. manuscript 11. inscription 13. sacred writing

Scripture, Scriptures . . . 4. text 5. Bible 6. lesson 7. Oracles, passage, Vulgate

Scripture interpretation . . . 8. exegesis

12. hermeneutics

scrivello . . . 4. tusk (elephant's)

scrivener . . . 6. notary, scribe, writer 8. recorder 10. amanuensis

scroll . . . 4. list, roll 5. draft 6. record, spiral, volute 7. engross, writing 8. document, inscribe, schedule, streamer 9. parchment

scroll roll . . . 8. makimono

scrub . . . 3. mop, rub 4. mean, runt, tree, wash 5. clean, dwarf, scour 6. drudge, paltry 7. cleanse 8. inferior 10. undersized

scrubby . . . 4. base 6. paltry, shabby, stubby 7. bristly, shrubby, stunted 10. underbrush 13. insignificant

scruff . . . 4. nape, scum, slur 5. crust, dross, scuff 6. refuse 7. surface 8. dandruff

scruple . . . 4. coin 5. demur, qualm 6. object, weight 9. small part 10. hesitation 13. unwillingness

scrupulous . . . 4. nice 5. exact 6. formal, proper, strict 8. qualmish 10. fastidious, meticulous 11. punctilious 13. conscientious

scrutinize . . . 3. eye, pry 4. scan 5. probe 7. examine, inspect, observe

scud . . . 4. dash, foam, gust, rain, sail, skim 5. speed 6. clouds, shower

scuffle . . . 4. fray 5. melee 6. strive, tussle 7. contend, shamble, shuffle 8. struggle

sculduddery . . . 9. grossness, obscenity

scull . . . 3. oar 4. gull 5. shoal, skate 6. basket, paddle, propel 7. rowboat

scullion . . . 4. base 6. menial 7. servant 10. dishwasher, kitchenman

scullog, scullogue . . . 6. farmer, rustic 7. laborer

sculp . . . 5. carve 7. engrave 8. seal skin 9. engraving, sculpture

sculptor . . . 6. artist, carver, imager, molder 8. chiseler 13. constellation 19. Apparatus Sculptoris (constellation)

sculptor (famed) . . . 5. Rodin 7. Cellini, Phidias 10. Praxiteles 12. Michelangelo, Saint Gaudens

sculptor's tool . . . 6. chisel, graver 9. ébauchoir

sculpture . . . 4. form 5. carve, model 6. figure, statue 9. engraving 11. alto-relievo

scum . . . 4. film, foam 5. cover, dross, froth, scurf, spume 6. refuse, scoria 7. coating 9. riffraff 10. impurities

scup . . . 5. bream, porgy

scurrility . . . 5. abuse 9. indignity, obscenity

scurrilous . . . 3. low 4. vile 5. gross 6. vulgar 7. abusive 8. indecent, scurrile 9. insulting 11. foulmouthed, opprobrious

scurry . . . 3. hie 4. dash 5. scoot, speed 6. flurry, hasten 7. scamper, scuttle 9. skedaddle

scurvy . . . 4. base, mean 7. disease 12. contemptible, discourteous

scuttle . . . 3. hod, run 4. dish, sink

5. haste, scoot 6. basket, hasten, scurry, shovel 7. octopus, platter 8. hatchway 10. cuttlefish

scutum... 5. scute 6. shield 13. constellation (Milky Way) 15. Scutum Sobieskii

Scylla (pert to)...
father.. 5. Nisus
home.. 4. rock (coast of Italy)
lover.. 5. Minos
menace to.. 9. seafarers
Myth.. 7. monster
transformed to.. 7. sea bird

scythe.. 2. sy (sye) 5. swath

scythe handle... 5. snath, snead

sea... 3. Red 4. Aral, Azov, Ross, wave 5. Black, brine, China, ocean, swell, water 6. aequor 7. Caspian 8. seashore 9. Caribbean

sea (pert to)...
adder.. 5. pipefish 11. stickleback
anemone.. 5. polyp
Antarctic.. 4. Ross
arm.. 4. gulf, meer, mere 5. bayou, firth 7. estuary
bird.. 3. auk 4. erne (ern), gull, smew, tern 5. booby, cahow, solan 6. gannet, petrel, puffin 9. albatross 10. shearwater
comb form.. 3. mer
cow.. 6. dugong, rytina (Steller's), walrus 7. manatee 8. sirenian 12. hippopotamus
cucumber.. 7. trepang
devil.. 9. angelfish, devilfish
dog.. 4. seal (Her) 6. fogdog, sailor
dragon.. 8. dragonet, sea horse
dread of.. 14. thalassophobia
duck.. 5. eider, scaup 6. scoter
eagle.. 4. erne (ern) 6. osprey
ear.. 7. abalone
eel.. 6. conger
farer.. 3. tar 6. sailor, seaman 7. mariner
foam.. 5. froth 9. sepiolite 10. meerschaum
fowl.. 3. auk 4. gull, tern 6. gannet, petrel
fox.. 5. shark
god, deity.. 3. Lar 5. Aegir 6. Triton 7. Neptune, Phorcus, Proteus 8. Poseidon
goddess.. 4. Nina 5. Doris 10. Amphitrite
gull.. 3. cob, mew 9. kittiwake
hare.. 7. mollusk
hen.. 4. skua 9. guillemot
hog.. 8. porpoise
holly root.. 6. eryngo (eringo)
ladder.. 6. Jacob's
lion.. 4. seal
mammal.. 4. seal 5. whale 6. dugong 7. manatee 10. bladdernose
mouse.. 4. duck (harlequin) 6. dunlin 7. annelid
nymph.. 5. naiad, siren 6. nereid 7. oceanid
onion.. 6. squill
otter.. 5. kalan
owl.. 6. puffin 8. lumpfish
pig.. 6. dugong 7. dolphin

8. porpoise
pumpkin.. 8. cucumber
quail.. 6. auklet 9. turnstone
raven.. 7. sculpin 9. cormorant 10. squaretail
reference to.. 5. naval 6. marine 7. oceanic, pelagic 8. maritime 9. Neptunian, thalassic
robber.. 6. jaeger, pirate 7. corsair 9. buccaneer, privateer
serpent.. 5. Hydra 8. snake eel
shell.. 5. conch
sickness.. 8. mal de mer 9. naupathia
spider.. 10. spider crab
turtle.. 5. green 9. hawksbill 10. loggerhead, thalassian 11. leatherback
unicorn.. 7. narwhal
urchin.. 5. heart 10. echinoderm, Spatangina 13. cushionflower
wolf.. 4. seal 6. pirate 9. privateer, submarine

sea king... 3. Ler 5. chief 6. pirate, Viking 7. Neptune

seal (pert to)...
bearded.. 5. ursuk 6. makluk
breeding ground.. 7. rookery
eared.. 5. otary
flock.. 3. pod
fur (fem).. 5. matka (matkah)
harp (male).. 7. saddler
leather.. 3. pin
limb.. 7. flipper
skin.. 5. sculp
type.. 3. fur 7. sea lion 8. elephant, pinniped
young.. 3. pup

sealed instrument... 6. escrow

seam... 4. line, load, scar 5. joint, ridge, strip 6. burden, groove, stitch, streak, suture 7. crevice, stratum 9. horseload 10. interstice, packsaddle

seaman... 3. gob, tar 6. sailor, Seabee 7. mariner

seaman's chapel... 6. bethel, church

seamark... 6. beacon 10. lighthouse

seamy... 5. rough 8. wrinkled 12. disreputable

séance... 7. session, sitting 9. treatment

séance holder... 6. medium

sear, sere... 3. dry 4. burn, cook 5. parch 6. braise, scorch, wither 7. dried up, shrivel 8. deadened, withered 9. cauterize 10. threadbare 11. deteriorate

search... 4. comb, fish, hunt, look, seek 5. frisk, ghoom, grope, probe, quest 6. ferret, forage, survey 7. inquire, ransack, rummage, zetetic 9. expiscate 10. scrutinize 11. investigate

searchlight... 4. beam 10. flashlight

seashell... 4. clam 5. conch, snail 7. scallop

season... 3. age 4. fall, salt, tide, time 5. devil, inure, spice 6. flavor, mature 7. qualify 8. accustom, preserve 11. acclimatize

season (pert to)...

Astron.. 5. Aries, Libra 6. Cancer
    11. Capricornus
Eccl.. 4. Lent 6. Advent, Easter
    7. Trinity 8. Epiphany 9. Christmas
    11. Whitsuntide
Lent.. 6. carême
Scot.. 4. sele
yearly.. 6. Autumn, Spring, Summer,
    Winter
seasonable... 6. timely 7. apropos
seasoning... 4. sage, salt 5. spice,
    thyme 6. cloves, garlic, pepper
    7. mustard, paprika 8. allspice,
    estragon, marjoram, rosemary,
    turmeric 9. condiment
Seasons, goddesses of...
justice.. 4. Dike
order (Universe).. 5. Horae
peace.. 6. Eirene
wise laws.. 7. Eunomia
seat... 3. pew 4. root, site 5. bench,
    chair, embed, sella, stool 6. settee,
    settle 7. install 9. establish
seat (pert to)...
church.. 3. pew 6. sedile
of justice.. 4. banc
of self.. 3. ego
on elephant.. 6. howdah
outdoor.. 6. exedra
privileged.. 6. curule
series (one of).. 6. gradin (gradine)
seaweed... 4. kelp 5. algae, dulse,
    laver, varec, wrack 6. Alaria
    8. agar–agar
secco... 3. dry
secern... 7. secrete 8. separate
    11. distinguish 12. discriminate
Secessionist (S Carolina)... 5. Rhett
secluded... 5. aloof, apart 6. hidden,
    lonely, remote, secret 7. private,
    retired 8. debarred, expelled, isolated,
    recessed, retiring, screened, solitary
    9. cloistral, concealed
seclusion... 7. privacy, retreat
    8. solitude 9. aloofness, exclusion
    10. quarantine, retirement, separation
second... 3. aid 4. abet, back, echo,
    time 5. jiffy, trice 6. assist, attend,
    backer, double, moment 7. instant,
    support, sustain 8. inferior
    9. assistant, encourage, imperfect,
    prototype, reinforce 11. corroborate,
    subordinate
second (pert to)...
childhood.. 6. dotage, dotard
    8. senility
crop.. 5. rowen
lieutenant.. 7. shavetail
number.. 6. addend
rate.. 8. inferior, mediocre
Republic.. 6. French (1848–52)
sight.. 6. myopia 7. psychic
    9. intuition 12. clairvoyance
team.. 5. scrub 9. Yannigans
thought.. 6. sequel 12. afterthought
    15. reconsideration
secondary... 4. less 5. minor
    6. deputy 8. inferior, offshoot
    9. auxiliary, dependent, satellite
    10. contingent, derivative,
    second–rate, subsequent, substitute
    11. subordinate, unessential

12. nonessential, quill feather
secondary color... 5. green 6. orange,
    purple
secondary school... 4. prep 5. lycée
    7. academy 10. Realschule
secrecy... 4. tile 6. hiding 7. mystery,
    privacy, privity 8. velation
    9. reticence, seclusion
    10. confidence 11. concealment
secret... 3. key 4. dern 5. close,
    inner, privy 6. arcane, covert, hidden,
    mystic, occult 7. arcanum, cryptic,
    mystery, private, unknown 8. esoteric,
    intimate (armor), reticent, secluded,
    skullcap 9. concealed, recondite,
    secretive, underhand 10. confidence,
    mysterious 11. clandestine
    12. confidential 13. surreptitious
secret (pert to)...
agent.. 3. spy 5. scout 6. espier
    7. spotter 8. emissary
    13. undercover man
council.. 5. by–end, junto 7. purpose
language.. 5. argot 7. dialect
meeting.. 5. tryst
movement.. 7. stealth
name.. 9. cryptonym
place.. 5. cache 6. adytum
    7. sanctum 9. sanctuary
society.. 5. hui (Chin) 4. tong
    7. Camorra (It)
secretary... 4. bird, desk 5. agent
    6. scribe 7. officer 8. recorder
    9. confidant 10. amanuensis,
    escritoire
secrete... 4. bury, hide, stow 5. exude
    7. conceal
secretion (pert to)...
gland.. 7. hormone
inflammation.. 3. pus
liver.. 4. bile
mammal gland.. 9. lactation
mouth.. 6. saliva
nasal.. 10. secernment
scale, insect.. 3. lac
shrubs.. 4. lerp
whale.. 9. ambergris
secretly... 5. aside, slyly 7. sub rosa
    8. covertly 9. not openly
    13. clandestinely
sect... 4. clan, cult, part 5. Alogi
    (Hist), class, group, order, party
    6. essene, school, Yezidi (Kurdish)
    9. following, Mennonite
    10. shibboleth (Bib)
    12. denomination
sectarian... 7. heretic 8. partisan
    9. dissenter, heterodox
    13. nonconformist
    14. denominational
section... 4. area, part, plot 5. panel,
    piece, slice, tmema, torso 6. region
    7. portion, segment, ternion
    8. parabola, surgical 9. paragraph,
    signature 11. subdivision
secular... 3. lay 4. laic 5. civil
    6. laical 7. earthly, profane, worldly
    8. temporal 9. centuried, temporary
secure... 3. fix, get, pin 4. bind, easy,
    fast, firm, moor, nail, safe, tape
    5. fetch, spike, trice (sail) 6. elicit,
    ensure, fasten, obtain, stable

7. acquire, assured, certain, procure, receive 8. make fast 9. confident, guarantee 10. dependable 11. undisturbed

security... 4. bail, gage 5. guard 6. pledge, safety, vadium 7. defense, shelter 8. guaranty 9. guarantee, insurance, stability 10. protection

sedate... 4. calm 5. douce, quiet, sober, staid 6. demure, proper, serene, solemn 7. serious, settled 8. composed, decorous 9. dignified, unruffled 11. unobtrusive 13. contemplative, dispassionate

sedative... 6. remedy 7. anodyne, bromide, chloral, veronal 8. atropine, barbital, lenitive, soothing 9. palliative, mitigator, paregoric 10. palliative, phenacetin 12. tranquilizer (tranquillizer) 13. phenobarbital

sedent... 7. sitting (statue)

sediment... 4. lees, silt 5. dregs 7. deposit, grounds, siltage 9. settlings

sedition... 6. revolt, strife, tumult 7. treason 9. commotion 10. dissension, turbulence

seditious... 7. riotous 8. factious 9. turbulent 11. treasonable 15. insurrectionary

seduce... 4. lure 5. decoy, tempt 6. allure, enamor, entice 7. corrupt, mislead 8. inveigle

seducer... 7. enticer, tempter 8. Lothario 9. debaucher

seduction... 5. charm 10. allurement, corruption, temptation 11. debauchment

sedulous... 4. busy 6. steady 8. diligent, untiring 9. assiduous, laborious, unwearied 10. persistent 11. persevering, unremitting

see... 3. spy 4. espy, heed, know, look, scry, seat, view 5. visit 6. behold, descry, detect 7. diocese, discern, witness 8. discover, perceive 9. apprehend, interview, visualize 10. comprehend, understand 11. contemplate

seed... 3. egg, pip, pit, sow 4. germ 5. grain, ovule, plant, sperm, spore 6. kernel, origin 7. lineage, progeny 8. rudiment 9. beginning 11. descendants

seed (pert to)...
apple.. 3. pip
aromatic.. 5. anise 7. aniseed, caraway
coat.. 3. pod 4. aril, burr, husk 5. testa 6. carpel 8. pericarp
container, envelope.. 3. bur (burr), pod 6. loment, vessel 7. capsule
edible.. 3. pea 4. bean 5. grain 6. lentil
enclosing soft fruit.. 5. drupe
flower.. 6. pistil
immature.. 5. ovule
lemon, orange, apple.. 3. pip
licorice.. 9. jequerity
medicinal.. 8. flaxseed
Moringa, tropical.. 3. ben

naked (one-seeded fruit).. 6. achene (akene)
oak.. 5. acorn
one-celled.. 6. carpel
part.. 6. tunica
poppy, opium.. 3. maw
underground.. 6. peanut
winged.. 6. samara

seeds (pert to)...
cocoa.. 5. cacao
feeding on.. 11. granivorous
perfume.. 8. abelmosk
rudiments.. 3. ova 4. eggs, pips, pits 6. ovules, sperms

seedy... 5. dingy, lousy, tacky 6. shabby 7. worn out 8. slovenly 10. spiritless 11. spawn-filled 12. bearing seeds

seek... 3. beg 4. hunt 5. essay 6. pursue, search 7. explore, solicit 8. endeavor 9. neologize (new words) 11. investigate

seeker... 6. prober, tracer 7. pursuer, zetetic 8. aspirant, searcher 9. applicant 10. petitioner

seeker of...
knowledge.. 10. philonoist
new words.. 9. neologist
pleasure.. 7. epicure 8. hedonist

seem... 4. look 6. appear 7. pretend 8. resemble

seeming... 5. guise, quasi 8. apparent, illusion, illusory, pretense, specious 9. befitting

seeming contradiction... 7. paradox

seeming truth... 14. verisimilitude

seemly... 3. fit 4. meet 6. comely, decent, proper, suited 7. elegant, fitting 8. decorous, tasteful 9. expedient

seep... 4. leak, ooze 5. exude 6. filter 8. transude 9. percolate

seer, seeress... 5. sibyl 6. oracle, scryer 7. Phoebad, prophet 9. predictor, visionary 10. forecaster, prophetess, soothsayer 11. Nostradamus 14. prognosticator

seesaw... 6. teeter, tilter 7. pastime 9. alternate, crossruff, fluctuate, vacillate 11. oscillation 12. teeter-totter

seethe... 4. boil, stew, teem 5. be hot, steep 6. bubble 7. be angry

segment... 3. pip 4. part 5. tmema 6. cantle 7. portion, section 8. fragment 12. cross section

segment (pert to)...
botany.. 5. tmema 7. lacinia
corresponding part.. 7. isomere
curve.. 3. arc
shaped.. 5. toric
Zool.. 6. somite, telson 8. metamere, somatome

seine... 3. net 5. trawl 6. sagene 7. dragnet, network

seism... 10. earthquake

seize... 3. bag, cly, cop, nab, net 4. bind, bite, grab, grip, take, trap 5. annex, catch, grasp, ravin, reave, usurp, wrest 6. arrest, clutch, collar, fasten, ravish, snatch 7. capture, embargo, grapple 8. distrain

9. apprehend, lay hold of
10. confiscate, understand
11. appropriate
seizin... 9. occupancy 10. possession
seizing... 4. cord 7. lashing
9. arresting, raptorial
seizure... 3. fit 4. grip, hold 5. spasm
6. arrest, attack, frenzy, seizin
9. ownership 10. occupation
11. manucapture
seladang... 4. gaur 7. buffalo
selah (Bib)... 4. sign 5. pause
select... 4. cull, name, pick, take
5. elect, elite 6. choice, choose,
picked 7. appoint, pick out, specify
9. exclusive, segregate 10. registrate
11. outstanding
selection... 5. piece 6. choice
7. analect, excerpt, passage
10. collection 11. appointment
selective... 5. draft 8. eclectic
9. exclusive 10. particular
14. discriminative
self... 3. ego, own 4. same 5. being
6. person, psyche 7. oneself
10. individual 11. personality
self (pert to)...
acting.. 9. automatic, voluntary
assertion.. 8. egoism, vanity
centered.. 7. selfish 9. egotistic
10. egocentric 11. independent
12. self-absorbed
comb form.. 4. auto
complacent.. 13. self-satisfied
confidence.. 5. poise 6. aplomb
9. assurance 11. self-reliant
contained.. 8. reserved 10. controlled,
sufficient (in itself) 11. independent
15. uncommunicative
control.. 8. stoicism 9. restraint
10. automation, equanimity,
temperance
determination.. 8. autonomy
12. independence
enjoyment.. 13. gratification
esteem.. 5. pride 6. vanity 7. concept
evident.. 5. axiom, clear 6. truism
9. axiomatic
examination.. 13. introspection,
introspective
French.. 3. soi
love of.. 6. egoism
ref to.. 8. personal
reproach.. 7. remorse
righteous.. 5. pious 13. sanctimonious
14. holier-than-thou
same.. 9. identical
satisfied.. 4. smug 6. jaunty
Scottish.. 3. sel (sell)
worship.. 8. idolatry 9. autolatry
selfish... 11. egotistical, self-seeking
12. self-centered
sell... 4. vend 5. scalp, trade
6. barter, market, retail 7. auction,
bargain 8. convince, exchange,
persuade 9. negotiate
sell (out)... 6. betray, desert 8. inform
on
seller... 6. dealer, vender, vendor
7. peddler 8. salesman 9. tradesman
10. saleswoman

semantics... 8. meanings
11. semasiology
semblable... 4. like 5. alike
7. seeming, similar 8. apparent,
suitable 10. ostensible, resembling
11. conformable
semblance... 4. copy, face, form
5. guise, image 6. aspect, figure
7. pretext, umbrage 8. illusion
10. appearance, similarity
11. countenance, presumption,
resemblance
semeiology, semeiotics... 5. signs
(signalling) 11. diagnostics
14. interpretation, symptomatology
semester... 4. term 6. course, period
Seminole chief... 7. Osceola
(1804-38)
Semitic (pert to)...
deity.. 4. Baal
dialect.. 4. Geez
god (evil).. 6. Moloch
language.. 6. Iraqui, Syrian
7. Arabian, Aramaic 8. Egyptian
11. Palestinian
people.. 6. Harari 8. Moabites
tribe (nomadic).. 6. Shagia (Shaikiyeh)
semper eadem... 13. always the same
(motto of Queen Elizabeth)
semper fidelis... 14. always faithful
semper idem... 13. always the same
semper paratus... 11. always ready
senate... 5. boule 7. council (Rom)
8. assembly 11. legislature
18. administrative body
send... 4. mail, ship 5. drive, grant,
issue, speed 6. bestow, convey,
export, launch, propel 7. forward
8. dispatch, transmit 10. commission
send (pert to)...
back.. 5. remit 6. remand, return
11. reverberate
by different person.. 5. relay
off.. 5. start 6. launch 7. impulse
8. dispatch 11. consignment
13. demonstration
out.. 4. emit, spew 5. shoot
out rays.. 7. radiate
payment.. 5. remit
to an address.. 7. deliver
to obscurity.. 8. relegate
Seneca... 6. Indian 9. Iroquoian
Senegal...
capital.. 5. Dakar
ebony.. 9. blackwood
gazelle.. 5. korin
gum.. 9. gum arabic
mahogany.. 9. cailcedra
native.. 10. Senegalese
river, in.. 6. Africa
senescence... 5. aging 10. growing
old
senicide... 13. killing old men (tribal)
senility... 6. dotage, old age
8. caducity, dementia 10. feebleness
senior... 5. aine, dean 6. chief, elder
7. ancient, student 8. superior
sensation... 5. sense 6. benumb, thrill,
wonder 7. emotion 8. rhigosis (cold)
12. great success
sensational... 5. lurid 6. superb

8. dramatic, exciting 9. emotional
12. melodramatic

sense... 4. feel, mind, sane 5. flair,
sight, smell 7. feeling, meaning
8. sapience 9. awareness, intuition,
sensation, sentience 10. perception,
understand 11. discernment,
recognition 12. intelligence

senseless... 5. inept 6. insane, stupid,
unwise 7. fatuous, foolish, idiotic,
inanity 9. illogical, inanimate,
insensate, unfeeling 10. irrational
11. meaningless, purposeless,
unconscious 12. unreasonable
13. unintelligent

sense of...
  beauty.. 8. aesthete (esthete), tasteful
    9. aesthetic
  dignity.. 5. pride
  distance.. 11. telesthetic
  hearing.. 8. audition 12. auscultation
  humor.. 10. risibility
  sight.. 6. vision
  smell.. 7. osmatic 9. olfaction
  taste.. 6. palate

sense organ... 3. ear, eye 4. nose,
skin 6. tongue 8. receptor, sensilla

senses... 4. wits 6. sanity 7. sensory
9. sensation

sensible... 4. sane 5. aware, privy,
sound 7. logical, prudent 8. rational
9. cognizant, practical, sensitive
10. reasonable, responsive
11. intelligent, susceptible

sensitive... 4. nice, sore 5. acute
6. pliant, tender, touchy 7. sensory
8. sensible 9. receptive
10. responsive 11. susceptible
14. discriminating, impressionable

sensitivity... 9. emotional, hebetated
(blunted) 11. sensibility 12. irritability
14. discrimination

sentence... 4. doom 5. maxim, motto
6. phrase, remark, saying
7. condemn, passage, thought,
verdict 8. decision, judgment,
proposal 9. statement
12. condemnation

sentence (pert to)...
  balance.. 7. parison
  clause (concluding).. 8. apodosis
  concluding.. 8. epilogue (epilog)
  construction.. 6. syntax
  difficult articulation.. 13. tongue
    twister
  introductory.. 8. protasis
  judicial.. 5. futwa
  pithy.. 5. motto 8. aphorism
  punishment.. 11. year and a day
  subordinate part.. 6. clause, phrase

sententious... 5. pithy, terse
7. concise, laconic 10. aphoristic
13. grandiloquent

sentient... 4. mind 5. aware 7. feeling
8. sensible 9. conscious, sensitive
10. perceptive 13. consciousness

sentiment... 5. toast 7. emotion,
feeling, opinion 8. attitude
10. perception, sentimento
11. sensibility 14. sentimentality

sentimental... 6. loving 7. maudlin,
mawkish 8. romantic 9. emotional

13. lackadaisical

sentimental song... 11. strephonade

sentinel... 5. guard 6. picket, sentry
7. vedette (mounted) 8. watchman
10. lookout man, watchtower

sepad... 5. think 7. believe, suppose

sepal... 4. leaf 5. petal

separate... 4. open, part, shed, sift,
sort 5. alone, apart, sever, space
6. cleave, detach, divide, secern,
single, sleave, sunder, winnow
7. disband, diverge, diverse, divided,
divorce, isolate 8. alienate, discrete,
distinct, peculiar, secluded
9. disjoined, partition, segregate,
sequester, unrelated 10. dissociate,
particular, respective
11. disembodied, unconnected

separate (pert to)...
  Chem.. 11. fractionate
  from others.. 5. aloof 8. isolated
  metal from ore.. 5. smelt
  thread.. 6. sleave

separation... 6. tmesis 7. divorce
8. autotomy 9. partition, secession,
seclusion 10. alienation
11. disjunction, separating
13. sequestration 14. discontinuance,
discrimination

separatist... 7. heretic, seceder
8. apostate 9. dissenter
12. secessionist 13. nonconformist

sepia... 3. dun, ink 5. color
7. pigment 10. cuttlebone, cuttlefish

sepiment... 5. hedge 7. defense
9. enclosure

Sepiola... 10. cuttlefish

sepiolite... 10. meerschaum

sepoy... 7. soldier 9. policeman

seps... 6. lizard 7. serpent

sept... 4. clan 5. class, seven, tribe
7. lineage

septic... 6. morbid, pyemia (pyaemia)
8. diseased, infected, poisoned
9. gangrened, mortified, poisonous
10. septicemia (blood poison)

sepulcher, sepulchre... 4. bury, tomb
5. crypt, grave, vault 6. entomb
9. sepulture 10. repository

sepulchral... 5. urnal 6. gloomy,
hollow 7. charnel 8. funereal
9. deep-toned

sepulchral (pert to)...
  chest.. 4. cist
  mound.. 7. tumulus
  vault.. 6. burial 8. catacomb,
    monument 9. interview

sequel... 5. issue 6. effect, series,
upshot 7. outcome 8. follow up,
sequence, sequitur 9. posterity
10. succession

sequela... 7. disease (resulting)
8. adherent 9. inference
10. conclusion 11. concomitant,
consequence 15. morbid condition

sequence... 5. gamut 6. course
(usual), series, tierce (three cards)
8. straight 10. succession

sequential... 9. deducible, resultant
10. continuous, succeeding
11. consecutive

sequestered.. 6. lonely, secret

7. private, recluse, retired
8. isolated, secluded, solitary,
withdrawn 9. concealed, separated
12. unfrequented

sequitur... 9. inference, influence, it
follows 14. natural sequent

sequoia, Sequoia... 4. Park (Calif)
6. Indian (famed for alphabet) 7. big
tree, conifer, redwood

seraglio... 5. harem, serai 6. zenana
9. enclosure

serape... 5. shawl 7. blanket

seraph... 5. angel 6. cherub

seraphic... 7. angelic, sublime
8. cherubic 9. unworldly

Serb... 4. Slav 7. Serbian (Servian)

Serbia, Yugoslavia...
church.. 8. Orthodox
conqueror.. 5. Turks
hero.. 6. Dushan, Nemaya (1159)
queen.. 7. Natalie
Revolutionary.. 7. Chetnik

sere... 4. claw, sear, worn 5. talon
6. effete, yellow 8. withered
10. desiccated

serenade... 4. sing 5. music
8. serenata 9. charivari,' entertain
10. callithump 11. celebration

serene... 4. calm, cool 5. clear, quiet
6. placid 8. peaceful, serenity,
tranquil 9. collected, unruffled
11. undisturbed 12. tranquillity
(tranquility)

serenity... 5. peace 6. repose
8. calmness, coolness 9. composure
10. quiescence

serf... 4. esne, neif (fem), peon
5. helot, slave 6. thrall, vassal
7. captive, villein

series... 3. set 4. nest 5. class,
gamut, group 8. sequence
9. seriation 10. succession

series, connected... 5. chain, suite
6. catena

series of...
discussions.. 9. symposium
heroic events.. 4. epos
meetings.. 7. session
pictures.. 8. panorama
races.. 7. regatta
rings.. 4. coil
six.. 5. hexad
steps.. 5. scale
syllogisms.. 7. sorites
travels.. 7. odyssey

serious... 4. keen 5. grave, serio
(comb form), sober, staid 6. demure,
sedate, solemn 7. capital, earnest,
weighty, zealous 8. resolute
9. important 10. thoughtful

seriousness... 4. zeal 7. gravity
10. importance 11. earnestness

sermon... 4. talk, text 5. psalm
6. homily, lesson, preach 7. address,
lecture, reproof 8. harangue
9. discourse, preaching
10. admonition

seron... 5. crate 6. hamper
7. boxwood, spanner

serotine... 3. bat 4. adda 9. late
bloom

serpent... 3. asp 4. seps (anc)

5. cobra, krait, racer, snake

serpent (pert to)...
deity, of good.. 12. agathodaemon
13. agathos daemon
fabulous.. 5. Hydra 6. dragon
8. basilisk 11. amphisbaena
large.. 3. boa 5. aboma 6. python
8. jararaca
monster.. 6. ellops
Old.. 5. Satan
semihuman (Hind Myth).. 4. Naga
sky (Vedic Myth).. 3. Ahi
worshipers (Gnostic).. 7. Ophites

serpentine... 4. wily 5. snaky
6. subtle, zigzag 7. sinuous, winding
8. diabolic, tempting 9. snakelike
10. circuitous, meandering

serpigo... 8. ringworm 11. skin disease

serrano... 12. squirrelfish

serrate... 7. notched, toothed
8. indented 10. saw-toothed

serried... 5. dense 7. compact,
concise, crowded

serum... 4. whey 5. blood, fluid
6. serous 9. antitoxin

servant... 3. gyp 4. bata, cook, maid,
maty, mozo, serf, syce 5. agent,
boots, chela, nurse, slave, valet
6. bildar, butler, flunky, garçon, gillie
(gilly), menial, servus, vassal, wallah
(walla) 7. equerry (nobleman's)
8. coistrel, domestic, handmaid
9. assistant 11. chamberlain

servant of God... 6. bishop

serve... 2. do 3. act, aid 4. deal,
help, wait 5. avail, cater 6. assist,
succor 7. advance, bestead, forward,
further, suffice, work for 8. bear
arms, fight for 9. officiate
10. administer, distribute

serve (pert to)...
as accomplice.. 4. abet
as escort.. 6. squire
food.. 4. wait 5. cater 7. dish out
religion.. 4. obey 7. worship
tennis.. 7. deliver

server... 4. tray 6. player, salver
7. acolyte

Servia... see Serbia

service... 3. aid, use 4. help, mail,
Mass, rite 5. favor, matin 6. employ,
ritual 7. benefit, nocturn, utility
8. ceremony, evensong, kindness,
ministry 9. servitude 10. attendance,
employment 12. ministration

service tree... 4. sorb 6. rowan

servile... 4. mean 6. abject, menial,
minion 7. fawning, slavish
8. cringing, faithful 9. dependent,
parasitic, truckling 10. obsequious,
submissive 11. subservient,
sycophantic

Servite... 9. mendicant 13. Order of
Friars (1233)

servitude... 7. bondage, serfdom,
service, slavery 8. servitus
9. vassalage 14. apprenticeship

sesame... 3. oil 4. herb 5. benne
7. gingili (seed), teel oil 8. ajonjoli,
sesamine

Sesame, Open... 10. magical key
12. magic command (Arab Nights)

sess... 4. heap, pile 9. soap frame

session... 5. court 6. séance
8. assembly 11. legislature

set... 3. lay 4. form, heal, laid, pose,
post 5. brood, class, fixed, group,
place, posit, ready, staid, stand
6. adjust, clique, define, fasten,
formal, ossify, series, settle
7. confirm, congeal, coterie, station,
stiffen 8. regulate, solidify
9. coagulate, designate, direction,
obstinate, stabilize 10. collection,
determined, solidified 11. established,
prepared for

set (pert to)...
afloat.. 6. launch
against.. 6. oppose 10. antagonize
apart.. 5. allot, taboo
6. exempt 7. isolate, reserve,
seclude 8. allocate, separate
9. segregate, sequester
11. distinguish 13. differentiate
aside.. 4. void 5. annul 6. except,
reject 7. abolish, discard, dismiss,
earmark, exclude 8. overrule,
postpone
at an angle.. 4. cant
back.. 4. loss 5. check 6. demote,
hinder, recess 7. relapse 8. restrain,
slow down
exclusive.. 5. elect, taboo 6. clique
fire to.. 6. ignite, kindle 7. emblaze,
inflame 8. irritate
firmly.. 5. embed, plant, posit
6. cement, ossify
forth.. 5. adorn 6. depart, expose, lay
out 7. arrange, commend, display,
enounce, exhibit, explain, expound,
present, promote, propone, publish
8. announce, decorate, indicate,
manifest 9. translate 10. promulgate
11. demonstrate
free.. 6. acquit 7. absolve, release,
unloose 8. liberate 10. emancipate
11. disillusion
off.. 6. incite, offset 7. measure
8. beautify, detonate 9. demarcate,
embellish 11. distinguish
on firm basis.. 9. establish
out.. 4. plot 5. allot, begin
7. arrange
right.. 5. teach 6. adjust, direct,
remedy 11. disillusion
up.. 3. rig 4. plan 5. build, cause,
erect, exalt, hoist, print, raise
7. elevate, finance, install
9. construct, establish
10. inaugurate, prearrange

set (pert to in)...
a groove.. 5. dadoe
a row.. 4. tier 5. align, aline, range
columns.. 7. tabular 8. tabulate
from margin.. 6. indent
operation.. 4. move 5. start 6. launch
opposition.. 3. pit
order.. 5. align 6. adjust 7. arrange

set (pert to of)...
eight.. 6. ogdoad
friends.. 7. coterie
jeweled ornaments.. 6. parure
laws.. 4. code 8. statutes
on end.. 5. upend 10. topsy–turvy

opinions.. 5. credo

organ pipes.. 5. stops

rules.. 4. code

sheets (paper).. 5. quire

seta... 4. hair 5. spine 7. bristle,
feather

Seth (pert to)...
brother.. 4. Abel, Cain
father.. 4. Adam
son.. 4. Enos
wife.. 8. Nephthys

setting... 5. scene 6. locale
8. mounting, planting
10. background

settle... 3. fix, pay 4. nest, root, seat,
sink 5. agree, clear, lodge, order,
prove, quiet, solve 6. assign, assure,
decide, locate, pay off, purify, secure,
soothe 7. arrange, clarify, confirm,
mediate, resolve 8. colonize,
ensconce, regulate 9. designate,
determine, establish, reconcile
10. strengthen 11. tranquilize

settled... 4. paid 5. ended, fixed
6. proved, sedate 7. assured,
decided, located 9. steadfast
10. unchanging 11. established

settled in advance...
13. predetermined

settled in mind... 10. equanimity

settlement... 3. dos 4. camp
6. colony, hamlet 7. payment
8. fixation, sediment, showdown
9. community, endowment
10. adjustment 12. colonization,
conciliation, satisfaction
13. determination, establishment

Settlement House... 9. Hull House
(Chicago) 10. University (NY)
11. Toynbee Hall (London)

settler... 6. Sooner (Okla) 7. pioneer,
planter, Puritan 8. colonist
9. immigrant

settlings... 4. lees 5. dregs
8. sediment 10. settlement
12. precipitates

seven (pert to)...
angles.. 8. heptagon 9. septangle
arts.. 5. logic, music 7. grammar
8. geometry, rhetoric 9. astronomy
10. arithmetic
comb form.. 5. hepta, septi
days and nights.. 8. sennight
fold.. 8. septuple
gods of happiness.. 5. Ebisu, Hotei
6. Benten 7. Daikoku, Jurojin
8. Bishamon 10. Fuku–roku–ju
group.. 6. heptad, septet 8. septuple
12. septemvirate
Hills.. 4. Rome
languages.. 9. heptaglot
Latin.. 6. septum
number.. 8. hebdomad 9. septenary
Old Test Books (1st seven)..
10. Heptateuch
Seas.. 11. world oceans
Stars.. 8. Pleiades
tones.. 10. heptachord, heptatonic

seventy... 12. septuagenary

seventy–day period...
12. septuagesima

seventy–year–old... 14. septuagenarian

sever... 3. cut, lop 4. part, rend 5. break 6. behead, cleave, detach, divide, except, exempt 7. disjoin 8. accurate, disunite, separate 9. interpose, segregate 10. decapitate, disconnect, dissociate 12. disassociate

several... 4. many 6. divers, sundry 7. diverse, various 8. distinct 9. different 10. respective

severe... 3. bad 4. dure, hard, keen, sore, tart 5. acute, cruel, exact, grave, harsh, rigid, snell, sober, stern 6. biting, bitter, chaste, sedate, simple, solemn, strict, taxing, trying 7. arduous, austere, condign, drastic, extreme, intense, painful, serious, violent 8. accurate, rigorous 9. draconian, strenuous, stringent 10. censorious, restrained

severe critic (of Alexandria)... 9. Aristarch

severity... 5. rigor 7. cruelty 8. hardness, pungency, violence 9. austerity, exactness, gruffness, harshness, solemnity, sternness, stiffness 10. bitterness, difficulty, inclemency, simplicity, strictness 12. rigorousness

Seville cathedral tower... 7. Giralda

Seville orange... 9. red–yellow 12. bitter orange

Sèvres blue... 5. color 9. bleu de roi, porcelain 11. bleu céleste

sew... 4. mend 5. baste, unite 6. fasten, needle, secure, stitch

sewan... 5. beads, money 6. wampum

sewing... 6. sutile 8. suturing 9. stitching 10. needlework

sewing case... 4. etui

sewing machine inventor... 9. Elias Howe

sex... 4. male 6. female, gender

sexagenarian... 13. a sixty–year–old

sexagesimal... 5. sixty

sexes, common to both... 7. epicene

sexless... 6. neuter 7. epicene 10. effeminate

sextet, sextette... 6. sestet 8. six parts 10. group of six 13. six–line stanza

sexton... 6. beetle 7. sacrist 9. sacristan 12. underofficer (church)

sextuplet... 7. sestole (sestolet) 8. six notes

sha... 5. sheep, urial (oorial)

shabbash... 5. bravo 8. well done

Shabbath... 7. Sabbath (Jew)

shabbiness... 8. baseness, slovenry 9. seediness

shabby... 4. base, mean, worn 5. dowdy, faded, ratty, seedy, tacky 6. paltry, ragged, scurvy 7. outworn, shab–rag, squalid 10. despicable, ragamuffin, threadbare 12. contemptible

shack... 3. coe, hut 4. husk, plug 5. chase, tramp 6. shanty 7. stubble 8. vagabond 9. hibernate

shackle... 3. tie 4. band, bind, bond, gyve, iron, ring 5. chain 6. fetter, hobble, impede, pinion 7. manacle, trammel 8. restrain

shackled... 4. tied 5. bound, gyved 6. curbed, ironed 7. hobbled 8. fettered, hampered, hindered, manacled 10. restrained

shad... 4. fish 5. Alosa 7. crappie, mojarra

shade... 3. hue 4. dull, roof, tint, tone, veil 5. tinge, visor 6. awning, canopy, darken, degree, follow, nuance, screen, shadow, shield, sprite 7. eclipse, foliage, parasol, protect, shelter, umbrage 10. overshadow, protection 11. adumbration

shade, affording... 9. umbratile

shadow... 3. dim, dog 4. hide, tail 5. cloud, image, umbra 6. attend, screen 7. blacken, conceal, protect, remains 8. follower, hanger–on, illusion, penumbra 9. adumbrate 10. protection

shadow fighting... 9. sciamachy

shadowless... 6. ascian

Shadrach (pert to)...
enemy.. 14. Nebuchadnezzar
name once.. 7. Ananias 9. Hannaniah
one of three Hebrew youths..
7. Meshach 8. Abednago, Shadrach

shady... 4. dark 5. faint, fishy 7. shadowy 9. deceitful, dishonest, underhand 10. indistinct, unreliable 12. questionable

shaft... 3. pit, rod 4. axle, fust, mine, orlo (part), stem, tige, tole 5. arrow, scape, shank, spire, stalk, thill, tower, trunk 6. column, tongue 7. feather, missile, obelisk 8. monument 9. flagstaff

shag... 3. nap 4. hair, mane, pile 5. chase 6. follow, rascal 7. tobacco 9. cormorant, make rough 10. blackguard

shaggy... 5. bushy, furry, nappy, rough 6. ragged 7. hirsute, unkempt, villous 8. confused (of thought), uncombed 10. unpolished

shagrag... 6. ragged, tagrag 7. unkempt 8. rascally

shake... 3. jar, jog, wag 4. jolt, rock, stir, sway, toze 5. swing, trill 6. dither, dodder, quiver, shimmy, shiner, weaken 7. agitate, flutter, shingle, shudder, tremble, tremolo 8. enfeeble 10. earthquake

Shakespeare (pert to)...
actor.. 4. Ward 7. Sothern 8. Modjeska
called.. 10. Bard of Avon
character, female.. 6. Juliet, Portia 7. Ophelia 9. Cleopatra
character, male.. 5. Romeo, Timon 6. Antony, Hamlet 7. Macbeth, Othello
forest.. 5. Arden
river.. 4. Avon
site.. 6. Verona 8. Elsinore
villain.. 4. Iago
wife.. 12. Anne Hathaway

shaky... 6. infirm, wabbly, wobbly 7. fearful, nervous, unsound

8. agitated, unsecure 9. tottering, trembling, uncertain, unsettled 10. precarious, unreliable 12. questionable

shale... 4. rock 5. flake, scale 8. dandruff

Shalimar Gardens... 6. Lahore

shallow... 5. shoal 6. lagoon (lagune) 7. cursory, trivial 9. depthless, frivolous, insincere 11. superficial

sham... 3. ape 4. fake, hoax, mock 5. dummy, false, fraud, trick 6. deceit, humbug 7. feigned 8. pretense 9. imitation, imposture, pretended

Shamash (pert to)...
centers of worship.. 5. Larsa 6. Sippar
consort.. 3. Aya (Ai)
deity (Babylon).. 6. sun god
messenger.. 6. Bunene
Sumerian equivalent.. 3. Utu (Utug) 6. Babbar

shame... 5. abash 7. mortify 8. disgrace, dishonor 9. humiliate 11. abomination, humiliation, impropriety

shameful... 4. mean, vile 5. gross 6. wicked 8. flagrant, improper, indecent, infamous, terrible 9. degrading 10. outrageous, scandalous 11. disgraceful, ignominious 12. dishonorable, disreputable, vituperative

shameless... 6. arrant, brazen 8. immodest, impudent 9. audacious 10. unblushing 11. brazenfaced

shammer... 8. impostor

shanghai... 6. abduct, to drug 9. slingshot

shank... 3. leg 4. crus, gamb (gambe) 7. meat cut 12. travel on foot

shape... 4. bend, form, mold (mould), plan 5. frame, model 6. adjust, create, cut out, design, devise, figure 7. arrange, conform, contour, develop, fashion, incline 8. phantasm 10. appearance, figuration 11. arrangement

shaped like a...
comb.. 9. pectinate
shield.. 7. peltate, scutate
strap, thong.. 6. lorate
urn.. 9. urceolate

shapeless... 7. lumpish 8. deformed, formless 9. amorphous, contorted, distorted, unshapely

shapely... 3. fit 4. neat, trim 6. comely, gainly 10. well-formed 11. symmetrical 16. well-proportioned

share... 3. cut, lot 4. dole, part 5. enter, quota 6. ration 7. partake, portion 8. take part 9. allowance, apportion 11. co-operative, participate

sharecropper... 7. metayer

shark... 5. fraud 6. lawyer 8. parasite, swindler 9. trickster

shark (fish)... 4. gata, mako, tope

5. lamia (cub), Rhina 6. Galeos, Galeus, requin 7. dogfish, tiburon 8. man-eater, Mustelus, Selachii, sharklet, Squatina 9. porbeagle 10. Carcharias, hammerhead 11. Carcharodon, Galeorhinus

shark-clinger... 4. pega 6. remora

sharp... 4. acid, curt, edgy, keen, tart 5. acerb, acrid, acute, alert, brisk, crisp, edged, harsh, quick, smart, steep, witty 6. abrupt, astute, bitter, crafty, shrill 7. angular, caustic, cutting, nipping, painful, pointed, pungent, sharper 8. incisive, poignant 9. penetrant, sagacious, sarcastic, trenchant 10. discerning, proficient 11. acrimonious, penetrating, well-dressed

sharp (pert to)...
answer.. 6. retort
blow.. 4. slap
cornered.. 7. angular
edged.. 5. arris
flavor.. 4. tang
make.. 10. cacuminate
pointed.. 5. acute
saw.. 8. titmouse
Scot.. 5. snell 6. snelly
sighted.. 4. keen 6. astute 7. lyncean
sound.. 4. ping
Tuesday.. 13. Shrove Tuesday
witted.. 6. shrewd 10. discerning 11. intelligent

sharpen... 3. nib, ted 4. edge, hone, whet 5. grind, point, strop 6. acuate 7. enhance, quicken 9. intensify 10. cacuminate

sharper... 5. cheat, knave, rogue 6. keener 8. deceiver, swindler 9. trickster

shatter... 5. blast, break, crash, smash, split 8. splinter

shave... 3. cut 4. pare 5. cheat, strip 6. cut off 7. swindle, tonsure 9. cut prices, thin slice

shaver... 3. boy, lad 4. tool 5. cheat 6. barber 8. swindler 9. youngster 11. extortioner

shavetail... 4. mule 6. ensign 10. lieutenant

shawl... 5. manta 6. serape 7. paisley 8. cashmere

Shawnee (pert to)...
chief.. 7. Tecumseh
Indian tribe.. 9. Algonquin
location (present).. 8. Oklahoma

sheaf... 4. kern, omer 6. bundle 7. cluster 11. hyperpencil

shear... 3. cut 4. clip, snip, trim 5. sever 6. fleece, remove 7. scissor, whittle

shears... 5. lewis 6. forfex 8. secateur

sheatfish... 4. wels 7. catfish

sheath... 4. case 5. forel (book), glove, ocrea, theca 6. sleeve, spathe 7. stipule 8. scabbard

sheathe... 4. wrap 5. cover, drape 6. encase 7. envelop 8. enshroud

sheave... 5. wheel 6. pulley 9. back water, eccentric

shebang... 6. affair, boodle, outfit 7. concern 11. contrivance

13. establishment 14. kit and
caboodle

she—cat... 4. elle 9. grimalkin

shed... 3. hut 4. abri, cote, lair, molt
5. scale, spill 6. effuse, hangar,
lean—to, slough 7. cottage, diffuse,
radiate, shelter

shed (light)... 4. glow 7. explain
10. illuminate

shedding... 7. ecdysis (Zool), molting

sheen... 5. glint, gloss, shine 6. luster
7. glitter 8. splendor 9. shininess
10. brightness

sheep... 3. ewe, ram, sha, teg, tup
4. buck, lamb, Ovis, zenu 5. bidet,
dumba, oudad 6. argali, cosset,
gimmer, hogget, mutton, sheder,
wether 8. ruminant, shearhog,
yeanling 9. blackface

sheep (pert to)...
cry.. 3. baa 5. bleat
disease.. 3. doe, gid, rot 4. bane
5. braxy 7. anthrax
faced.. 3. shy 7. bashful 8. sheepish
female.. 3. ewe, teg 6. sheder
flock leader.. 10. bellwether
fold.. 3. ree 4. cote 5. kraal, reeve,
stell 6. church
head.. 3. jimmy 8. powsowdy
headed.. 5. silly 6. stupid
12. simple—minded
kidney extract.. 5. renes
laurel.. 6. Kalmia
leg wool.. 4. gare
male.. 3. ram, tup 4. buck 5. heder
6. wether
owner's mark.. 4. smit 6. ruddle
pet.. 6. cosset
sheeplike.. 5. ovine
skin, leather.. 4. pelt, roan 5. basil
7. chamois, diploma 8. woolfell
stealing.. 7. abigest
symbol.. 3. ram
tick.. 3. ked
wild.. 3. sha 4. Ovis 5. urial
6. aoudad, argali, bharal, nayaur
7. mouflon (moufflon) 9. Thian Shan
(Marco Polo's)

sheep, breeds... 6. Merino, Romney
7. Cheviot, Delaine, Dishley, Karakul,
Suffolk, Targhee 8. Cotswold,
Dartmoor 9. Kerry Hill, Leicester,
Southdown, Teeswater 10. Corriedale,
Dorset Horn, Oxford Down,
Shropshire 13. Hampshire Down

sheer... 4. mere, pure, thin, turn
5. brant, steep, utter 6. abrupt,
swerve 7. deviate, unmixed
8. absolute 9. deviation, downright,
undiluted 10. completely, diaphonous
11. transparent 13. perpendicular

sheet... 4. leaf, rope, sail 5. paper
6. shroud 9. cover with, duodecimo
(12—fold), newspaper

sheik, sheikh... 4. Arab 5. chief
6. prince

shelf... 4. berm (berme), reef, sell
5. ledge, shoal 6. mantel 7. stratum
8. postpone, put aside

shell... 3. pod 4. boat, bomb, husk
5. conch, crust, shard, shuck
6. cowrie (cowry) 7. bombard,

capsule, grenade, missile
8. carapace, exterior 9. cartridge
10. projectile

shell (pert to)...
button source.. 5. troca 6. lorica,
mucket
cone.. 7. admiral
ear.. 7. abalone
explosive.. 3. dud 4. bomb
7. grenade
fish.. 4. clam, pipi 6. cockle, limpet,
mussel, oyster 7. abalone, lobster,
mollusk, scallop 8. barnacle
9. trunkfish
fossil.. 8. ammonite
game.. 10. thimblerig 13. sleight of
hand
marine.. 6. cowrie (cowry)
money.. 5. hawok, sewan, uhllo (ulo)
6. cowrie, wampum
out.. 4. give 6. expend, pay out
protective.. 6. lorica
ridge.. 4. lira 5. varix
seaweed.. 8. frustule
spiral.. 5. chank, whelk 8. caracole
trumpet (Triton's).. 5. conch

Shelley's sonnet hero...
10. Ozymandias

shelter... 3. lee 4. abri, camp, cote,
port, roof, shed, skug, tent 5. cover,
haven, house, hutch, shack, shade
6. asylum, burrow, dugout, hangar,
harbor, refuge, screen, shield
7. defense, hospice, pillbox, protect,
retreat 8. mantelet (mantlet),
quarters, security 9. coverture,
sanctuary 10. protection

sheltered side... 3. lee 4. alee
7. leeward

shelve... 5. slope, table 6. retire
7. dismiss, incline 8. postpone, put
aside 10. pigeonhole

Shem (pert to)...
brother.. 3. Ham
descendant.. 6. Semite
son.. 3. Lud 4. Aram, Elam

shenanigan... 7. evasion, foolery
8. trickery 11. monkeyshine

shend... 3. mar 4. harm, ruin 5. spoil
6. injure, revile 7. destroy, stupefy
8. confound, disgrace, reproach

Sheol... 4. Hell 5. Aralu, grave, Hades
6. the pit, Toppet 7. Abaddon,
Gehenna 10. underworld 11. nether
world 14. abode of the dead

shepherd... 5. guide 6. direct, escort,
feeder, herder, pastor, shadow
9. clergyman

shepherd, shepherds (pert to)...
band of.. 10. pastoureau
dog.. 5. sheep 6. collie
flute.. 7. musette 9. flageolet
god.. 3. Pan
pipe.. 3. oat 4. reed 7. larigot
spider.. 13. daddy—long—legs
staff.. 4. Kent 5. crook

sheriff (pert to)...
aide.. 5. posse
deputy.. 6. elisor 7. bailiff
jurisdiction.. 9. bailiwick
sheriffdom.. 10. shrievalty

Sherlock Holmes' housekeeper...

9. Mrs Hudson

sherry... 5. jerez, Xeres 7. oloroso
8. montilla

Shetland Islands (pert to)...
fishing grounds (deep-sea).. 4. haaf
kingdom of.. 8. Scotland
land, fee simple.. 4. udal
promontory.. 4. noup
Supreme Court Pres.. 4. foud
viol.. 3. gue

shewbread, showbread (Bib)...
6. ritual 10. unleavened

shibboleth (Bib)... 4. mode 5. habit
6. saying, slogan 9. criterion,
watchword 11. peculiarity (speech)

shield... 3. écu 4. boss, umbo
5. aegis (egis), armor, cover, pavis,
pelta, scute, shade, shell, targe (anc)
6. defend, scutum, target
7. defense, protect, shelter
8. insignia 9. protector
10. escutcheon, protection

shield (pert to)...
Athena's.. 5. aegis (egis)
bearer.. 8. escudero
border.. 4. orle 7. bordure
emblem.. 7. impresa
French (anc).. 8. rondache
heraldry.. 4. enté 6. points
part.. 4. enté, orle, umbo
Roman.. 6. scutum
sacred.. 6. ancile (Rom)
shaped.. 7. peltate, scutate
8. aspidate

shift... 4. eddy, fend, jibe, move, ruse,
stir, tack, veer 5. shunt, smock, trick
6. baffle, change, device, rustle
7. deviate, pretext, quibble
8. artifice, mutation, transfer
9. deviation, expedient, fluctuate,
vacillate 10. conversion, subterfuge
12. redistribute 13. transposition

shifty... 6. crafty, tricky 7. devious,
evasive, furtive 9. deceitful, makeshift
10. changeable 11. treacherous

shill, shillaber (circus term)...
5. decoy 8. employer, hanger-on
10. accomplice

shillalagh, shillalah... 4. club
6. cudgel 7. sapling

shilly-shally... 8. hesitate 9. vacillate
10. hesitation, indecision
11. vacillation

Shiloh... 4. town (anc) 6. Seilun
(modern) 9. sanctuary (the ark)
10. battle site (Tenn)

shimmy... 5. quake 6. quiver
7. chemise, tremble, vibrate 9. jazz
dance, vibration

shin... 5. climb, tibia 6. cnemis
7. foreleg

shindy... 3. row 4. lark, orgy, riot,
romp 5. dance, party, revel, spree,
wince 6. frolic, uproar 7. wassail
8. carousal 9. commotion, festivity
11. merrymaking

shine... 3. ray 4. beam, beek, star
5. excel, gloss, prank 6. polish
7. furbish, glisten, glister, glitter,
radiate, splurge 8. rutilate 9. irradiate

shiner... 6. bruise 8. black eye
9. bootblack 10. dollarfish

shingle... 4. sign, wood 6. hairdo
7. haircut, overlap 8. chastise,
coiffure, detritus 9. signboard

shingles... 7. disease 12. herpes
zoster

shining... 5. aglow, lucid, nitid, shiny
6. glossy, lucent 7. beaming,
glowing, radiant 8. luminous,
lustrous, nitidous, rutilant, splendid
9. refulgent 10. glistening, glittering
11. illustrious, irradiating, resplendent

Shinto (pert to)...
adherent.. 8. Japanese 9. Shintoist
cult.. 8. Japanese
deity.. 8. Hachiman
temple.. 3. sha 5. jinja (jinsha)
7. yashiro
temple deity.. 5. Jinja (Jinsha)
temple gateway.. 5. torii

shiny... 5. nitid, sleek 6. bright
7. radiant, shining 8. luminous,
nitidous 9. unclouded

ship... 3. ark 4. lade, load, send
5. liner, tramp 6. argosy, vessel
7. freight, steamer 9. freighter,
transport 10. watercraft

ship (pert to)...
abandoned.. 8. derelict
Argonaut's.. 4. Argo
armored.. 7. carrack, cruiser
9. destroyer, submarine
attendant.. 7. steward
auxiliary.. 4. dory, life 6. dinghy
(dingy), tender
biscuit.. 8. hardtack 10. pilot bread
cabin.. 6. saloon 9. stateroom
crane.. 5. davit
deck.. 4. main, poop 5. orlop, upper
deck, cut down.. 5. razee
deserter.. 3. rat
duck shooting.. 4. skag
flat bottom.. 4. keel 5. barge
fleet.. 6. armada
invoice.. 8. manifest
jail.. 4. brig
kitchen.. 6. galley 7. caboose
Levantine.. 4. saic
loader.. 9. stevedore
Mediterranean.. 5. xebec 6. galiot
(galliot) 7. polacre
officer.. 4. mate 6. purser 7. steward
9. boatswain (bosun)
one-masted.. 5. sloop
part.. 4. brig, keel, skeg 5. stern,
waist 6. bridge, rudder 8. binnacle,
taffrail
permit to enter.. 8. pratique
platform (boarding).. 9. gangplank
privateer.. 8. brigantine
prow.. 5. prore (Poet)
quarters.. 8. steerage 10. forecastle
(fo'c's'le)
record.. 3. log
rope.. 4. line 6. hawser 7. halyard,
lanyard, painter, ratline
sailing.. 4. bark (barque), dhow, proa,
saic 5. ketch, sloop, xebec
6. caique, cutter, galley, lugger
7. Geordie, pinnace, polacre
side.. 3. lee 4. port 9. starboard
station.. 5. berth
three-oar bank.. 7. trireme

twin–hulled.. 9. catamaran
two–oar bank.. 6. bireme
Venetian.. 9. frigatoon
voyage record.. 3. log
war.. 3. sub 7. cruiser, flattop
   9. destroyer, submarine
   11. dreadnaught
window.. 4. port 8. porthole
worm.. 5. borer 6. teredo
ship, famed... 4. Nina 5. Maine, Pinta
   6. Bounty 7. Monitor, Titanic
   8. Clermont, Half Moon, Merrimac
   9. Mayflower 10. Golden Hind, Santa
   Maria 12. Constitution (Old Ironsides)
   15. Bonhomme Richard
shipment... 5. cargo 7. carload
shippage.. 3. fee 4. levy 8. shipping
shipshape... 3. nef (clock) 4. neat,
   tidy, trim 7. orderly
shipwreck, cargo overboard...
   6. jetsam 7. flotsam
shire... 5. horse 6. county 8. district,
   province 11. subdivision
shirk... 4. duck, pike 5. avoid, dodge,
   evade, slink 7. goof off 9. fainaigue
   (finagle)
shirker... 5. piker 6. truant 7. quitter,
   slacker 8. embusqué 10. malingerer
shirt... 4. polo, sark 6. blouse,
   camisa, cilice, skivvy, T–shirt
   8. pullover
shiver... 5. quake, shake 6. be cold
   7. shatter, shudder, tremble, vibrate
   8. fragment 11. trepidation
shivering... 4. cold 6. creepy
   7. nervous, shaking 8. fragment
   9. agitation, twitching 10. chilliness
shoal... 3. bar 4. bank, reef, spit
   5. crowd, flock 6. throng 8. sand
   bank (shallow) 9. multitude
shock... 3. jar 4. blow, heap (grain),
   jolt, stun 5. appal, brunt, bushy
   (hair), shake, stack, start 6. appall,
   impact, offend, stroke, trauma
   7. disgust, horrify, startle, terrify
   8. calamity, frighten, paralyze
   9. collision, electrify 10. concussion
shock absorber... 7. cushion, snubber
shocking... 3. bad 5. awful, lurid
   6. horrid 7. ghastly, hideous
   8. horrible, terrible 9. appalling,
   frightful, offensive, revolting, startling
   10. abominable
shoe (pert to)... 4. boot, clog, geta,
   mule, pump 5. horse, moyle, sabot,
   scuff 6. ballet, bootee, brogan,
   buskin, gillie, loafer, Oxford, patten,
   planch (planche), sandal, secque
   7. chopine, rullion, slipper, sneaker,
   talaria 8. moccasin, sabotine, solleret
   10. clodhopper
shoe (pert to)...
   form.. 4. last, tree
   grip.. 5. cleat
   lace.. 3. tie 5. aglet (aiglet), lacet
   6. lacing 7. latchet 8. bootlace
   10. shoestring
   maker.. 5. sutor 7. cobbler, Crispin
   (patron saint) 8. zapatero
   part.. 3. cap 4. rand, vamp, welt
   6. insole 7. counter 9. inner sole
shoebill, shoebird... 5. stork

shoemaker's patron saint... 7. Crispin
shogun... 5. chief, title (Jap) 6. tycoon
   7. shikken
shoneen... 4. snob 5. toady
shoot... 3. rod 4. bine, dart, film, fine,
   hunt, kill, plug, twig, weft 5. bough,
   craps, eject, gemma, plant, scion,
   snipe, spear, sprig, throw, tuber,
   vimen 6. branch, sprout, stolon
   7. execute, project 9. discharge
   10. descendant, photograph
shooting (pert to)...
   fish.. 10. archer fish
   iron.. 6. pistol 7. firearm 8. revolver
   match.. 3. tir 5. skeet
   objective.. 6. target
   star.. 5. comet 6. meteor 7. cowslip
shop... 4. mart 5. burse, store
   6. market, saloon 7. atelier
   8. boutique, emporium
shopping mania... 9. oniomania
shore... 4. bank, prop 5. beach, coast,
   marge, playa 6. rivage, strand
   7. support 9. foreshore, waterside
   10. run aground, waterfront
shore (pert to)...
   bird.. 3. ree 5. snipe 6. avocet,
   curlew, plover, wading 9. Limicolae
   inhabiting.. 8. littoral
   pine.. 4. sand 8. tamarack
   9. lodgepole 10. hack–me–tack
   recess.. 3. bay 4. cove 5. bayou,
   inlet
short... 4. curt, rude 5. brief, brusk,
   scant, terse 6. abrupt, scanty
   7. curtate, friable, summary
   8. abridged, succinct 12. insufficient
short (pert to)...
   and pointed.. 5. terse
   and stout.. 5. dumpy 6. stocky,
   stodgy 8. roly–poly, thickset
   essay.. 5. tract
   legged.. 8. breviped
   letter.. 4. chit
   lived.. 9. ephemeral
   stop.. 5. delay, pause 7. respite
   8. interval 9. cessation
shortage... 4. want 6. ullage
   10. deficiency 13. insufficiency
shorten... 3. bob, cut, lop 4. clip,
   dele, dock 5. elide 6. lessen,
   reduce, reef in 7. abridge, curtail
   8. condense, contract, decrease, hold
   back 9. decurtate 10. abbreviate
shortening a syllable... 7. systole
shorthand... 3. Gregg 6. Pitman
   8. Tironian (Rom) 11. stenography
   12. brachygraphy, speed writing
shortly... 4. soon 6. curtly, not far
   7. harshly, quickly 8. abruptly
   9. presently
shortsighted... 4. dull 6. myopic,
   obtuse 8. purblind 11. nearsighted
Shoshone Indian... 3. Ute 4. Hopi
   5. Piute 7. Bannock 8. Comanche
shot... 4. dram 5. carom, speed
   6. birdie, bullet, gamble, pellet,
   ruined 7. gunfire, missile, worn out
   8. marksman, unnerved 9. discharge
   10. detonation, photograph, projectile
   11. dilapidated, vaccination
shoulder... 5. carry, shelf 6. épaule

7. meat cut, scapula, support
8. buttress, omoplate

shoulder (pert to)...
armor.. 9. épaulière
badge, ornament.. 7. epaulet
blade.. 7. scapula 8. omoplate
comb form.. 3. omo 6. humero
inflammation.. 6. omitis 7. omalgia
of a road.. 4. berm (berme)
reference.. 7. humeral 8. scapular

shout... 3. cry 4. call, hoop, hoot,
root, yell 5. cheer 7. acclaim
8. applause, laughter

shouting... 6. clamor, crying 7. calling,
hooting, yelling 9. bellowing

shove... 4. push 5. drive, eject, elbow
6. propel, thrust

shovel... 4. peel, spud 5. scoop,
skeet, spade 7. scooper 8. strockle
10. antler part

show... 4. lead 5. movie, prove, revue,
teach 6. cinema, escort, evince,
reveal 7. betoken, display, divulge,
exhibit 8. evidence, indicate,. instruct,
manifest 11. demonstrate
13. demonstration

show (pert to)...
case (glass).. 7. vitrine
deference.. 3. bow 6. salaam
disapproval.. 3. boo 4. hiss, pout
house.. 4. hall 5. odeum, opera
6. circus 8. coliseum, showboat
musical.. 5. revue
off.. 6. flaunt 10. grandstand
of learning.. 6. pedant
pompous.. 6. parade 7. display,
pageant 9. cavalcade 10. exhibition
to a seat.. 5. guide, usher 6. escort
7. conduct
up.. 6. appear, arrive, attend, expose

shower... 4. bath, give, rain 6. abound
8. sprinkle

shower of meteorites... 6. Leonid
(from Leo) 9. Andromede

showing...
animal remains.. 6. zootic
care.. 9. attentive, regardful
11. considerate
display.. 10. exhibition
12. presentation
envy.. 9. invidious
first.. 8. premiere
good judgment.. 6. astute 8. sensible

showy... 3. gay 4. arty, loud 5. gaudy
6. flashy, garish, sporty, tinsel
7. pompous 8. gorgeous, splendid,
striking 9. sumptuous
12. ostentatious 13. grandiloquent

shred... 3. rag 4. snip 5. piece, strip
6. sliver, tatter 7. vestige
8. fragment, particle

shrew... 3. erd 4. tana 5. satan,
scold, Sorex, vixen 6. mammal,
migale, tartar 7. Blarina, outcast,
villain 9. scoundrel, termagant,
Xanthippe

shrewd... 3. sly 4. cagy, foxy, sage,
wily 5. acute, canny, harsh, sharp,
smart, stern 6. artful, astute, biting,
clever, crafty 7. cunning, knowing,
practic, sapient, subtile 8. shrewish

9. sagacious 10. discerning
11. penetrating, sharp—witted
13. perspicacious

shrewdness... 6. acumen 9. smartness
10. craftiness

shriek... 3. cry, yip 4. yell 5. laugh
6. holler, outcry, scream 7. screech

shrievalty... 7. sheriff (office of)

shrill... 4. keen, pipy 5. acute, clear,
sharp 6. biting, squeak 7. screech
8. piercing, strident
11. high—pitched, penetrating

shrimp... 4. pink 5. dwarf, prawn
7. artemia 8. crevette
10. crustacean

shrine... 3. box 4. case, tomb
5. altar, chest 6. chapel, temple
8. monument 9. holy place, reliquary
10. receptacle

shrine (pert to)...
ancient.. 4. naos
Buddhist.. 4. tope 5. stupa
9. Amaravati
India.. 6. dagoba (dagaba) 7. chaitya
Mecca.. 5. Kaaba (Caaba) 11. Great
Mosque
secret, of goddesses.. 9. anaktoron

shrink... 5. cower, parch, quail, rivel,
wince 6. blench, cringe, flinch,
huddle, recoil 7. dwindle, shrivel
8. contract, draw back 9. constrict
10. depreciate

shrinking... 3. coy, shy 5. timid
6. afraid 7. recoiling, sensitive
10. withdrawal 11. contraction

shrivel... 3. age, dry 5. parch, wizen
6. shrink, wither 11. deteriorate

shroud... 4. cowl, hide, mask, veil,
wrap 5. cloak, cover, sheet
6. clothe, screen 7. conceal, curtain,
foliage, protect 8. cerement
9. cerecloth 12. graveclothes

Shrove (pert to)...
cake.. 7. pancake
Sunday.. 13. Quinquagesima
tide.. 9. pre—Lenten (3 days)
Tuesday.. 9. Mardi gras 10. Pancake
Day

shrub... 4. bush 5. plant (woody)
6. frutex 8. beverage

shrub (pert to)...
Adam's needle.. 5. yucca 9. lady's
comb
Arabian tea, narcotic.. 3. kat
aromatic.. 3. tea 4. mint, sage
5. thyme 6. Aralia 7. jasmine
(jasmin) 8. lavender, rosemary
Asian.. 5. musky 8. abelmosk
cherry.. 6. Prunus 7. Cerasus
12. laurocerasus
Chinese.. 6. Kerria
climbing.. 5. grape, liana, Vitis
8. Bignonia, clematis 14. trumpet
creeper
creeping.. 5. pyxie
dogwood.. 6. aucuba, Cornus
evergreen.. 3. box, yew 4. ilex, moss,
titi 5. erica, heath, pyxie, salal, savin
6. laurel, myrtle 7. jasmine, juniper
8. camellia, oleander 9. mistletoe
flowering.. 5. lilac 6. azalea, laurel
7. spiraea, syringa 10. mignonette

fragrant.. see *aromatic* (above)
Hawaiian.. **5**. akala
Mexican.. **7**. guayule
New Zealand.. **4**. tutu **6**. myrtle
   8. ramarama
ornamental.. **8**. hawthorn
parasitic.. **9**. mistletoe
pea.. **5**. broom
pepper.. **4**. kava **8**. kavakava
poisonous.. **4**. tutu **5**. sumac
prickly.. **5**. Rubus **6**. smilax
   8. dewberry **9**. raspberry
   10. blackberry
S America.. **5**. ceibo
tropical.. **4**. sida **5**. henna **7**. lantana
   8. Oacaceae **10**. frangipani
   (frangipane)
shrunken... **4**. lank, thin **5**. dried
   6. shrunk, wasted **7**. atrophied,
   shriveled
shudder... **4**. grue **5**. abhor, dread,
   quake **6**. agrise, loathe, quiver,
   shiver, tremor **7**. frisson, tremble
shuffle... **3**. mix **5**. scuff, shift
   6. huddle, juggle, riffle **7**. confuse,
   evasion, quibble, scuffle
   10. equivocate **12**. walk slovenly
shuffle off... **5**. evade, shirk **6**. put off
   7. push off
shun... **5**. avoid, evade, evite
   6. eschew **10**. escape from
   11. keep clear of
shut... **3**. bar **4**. stop **5**. close
   7. close in, exclude **8**. prohibit
shut (pert to)...
   in.. **3**. hem **5**. embar **6**. fenced,
   hemmed **7**. bottled, confine,
   impound, invalid, reclude **8**. confined,
   enclosed **10**. surrounded
   out.. **3**. ban, bar **6**. defeat
   7. exclude, lockout, occlude
   8. obstruct, preclude, prohibit
   up.. **3**. dam, end **4**. cage, pent
   5. close, mewed, pen in **6**. refute
   7. confine, enclose **8**. conclude,
   imprison **9**. terminate
shutter... **3**. lid **4**. gate **5**. blind
   6. screen **7**. seclude **8**. jalousie
   9. diaphragm
shuttle... **5**. train **6**. looper, weaver
   7. type bar **9**. vacillate **10**. oscillator
   11. money drawer
shy... **3**. coy, mim **4**. wary **5**. aloof,
   dodge, throw, timid **6**. demure,
   modest, recoil, shrink **7**. bashful,
   evasive, fearful, quibble, rabbity
   8. hesitant, reserved, retiring,
   secluded, sheepish, skittish
   9. diffident, reluctant, shrinking
   10. shamefaced, unassuming
   11. distrustful, unobtrusive
Shylock (pert to)...
   character in.. **16**. Merchant of Venice
   coin.. **5**. ducat
   daughter.. **7**. Jessica
   famed as.. **6**. usurer **11**. money
   lender **12**. extortionist
   friend.. **5**. Tubal
shyness... **7**. coyness, reserve
   8. timidity **10**. diffidence
   11. bashfulness
Siam... **8**. Thailand

Siamese (pert to)...
   group.. **3**. Kui, Lao
   temple.. **3**. wat
   twins.. **9**. pygopagus (joined at spine)
   11. Chang and Eng
sib... **4**. akin **6**. allied **7**. kinsman,
   related (by blood)
Siberia... see also *Siberian*
   capital.. **7**. Irkutsk (E) **11**. Novosibirsk
   (W)
   conqueror.. **9**. Timafeyev **11**. Genghis
   Khan
   government.. **7**. Russian
   gulf.. **2**. Ob (Arctic)
   Mongoloid.. **6**. Tartar
   mountains.. **4**. Ural **5**. Altai
   people.. **5**. Yakut **6**. Tartar (Tatar)
   9. Mongolian
   plain.. **6**. steppe, tundra
   river.. **2**. Ob, Om **4**. Lena **5**. Vitim
   6. Abakan **7**. Yenisei
   squirrel.. **7**. miniver
   storm.. **5**. buran
Siberian (pert to)...
   antelope.. **5**. saiga
   hunters, fishers (tribe).. **6**. Giliak
   (Gilyak)
   mammal.. **5**. sable
   squirrel fur.. **7**. calaber (calabar)
   swamp.. **5**. urman
   tent.. **4**. yurt (yurta)
   windstorm.. **5**. buran (bura)
sibilate... **4**. hiss, lisp **8**. aspirate
sibling... **5**. child
Sibyl (Gr)... **6**. oracle **7**. seeress
   10. prophetess **13**. fortuneteller
Sibylline Books (3)... **7**. oracles
   16. prophetic sayings (BC)
sic... **4**. thus
siccity... **7**. aridity, drought, dryness
sice... **3**. six (dice) **8**. sixpence
Sicilian Vespers (pert to)...
   Bull (anc).. **8**. Phalaris
   massacre of.. **6**. French (1282)
   saffron.. **6**. crocus
   secret society.. **5**. Mafia
Sicily...
   aborigines.. **6**. Sicani
   anc name.. **9**. Trinacria
   capital.. **7**. Palermo **8**. Syracuse (anc)
   composer.. **7**. Bellini
   harbor.. **7**. Palermo
   island.. **6**. Lipari (group)
   11. Pantelleria
   river.. **4**. Acis
   volcano.. **4**. Etna **7**. Vulcano
   9. Stromboli
   whirlpool.. **9**. Charybdis
sick... **3**. ill, sad, wan **4**. pale
   5. weary **6**. sickly, unwell
   9. disgusted, nauseated
   10. indisposed
sick (pert to)...
   bay.. **9**. infirmary **10**. dispensary
   be.. **3**. ail
   flag.. **6**. yellow **10**. quarantine
   headache.. **8**. migraine
   Man of the East.. **13**. Turkish Sultan
   of.. **7**. tired of **8**. satiated
   9. disgusted
   person.. **7**. patient **9**. aegrotant
   unto death.. **5**. amort **7**. à la mort

worker.. 5. nurse 11. nursekeeper
sicken... 4. tire 5. weary 6. impair,
    weaken 7. afflict, depress, surfeit
    8. languish 10. impoverish
sickly... 4. pale, sick, weak 5. faint
    6. ailing, feeble, infirm, weakly
    7. languid, mawkish 8. diseased
    9. unhealthy
Siddhartha, Siddhattha... 6. Buddha
side... 4. face, team, wall 6. behalf,
    border, region 7. faction, lateral,
    support, surface 9. declivity
side (pert to)...
   board.. 5. table 6. buffet 8. dressoir,
    whiskers
   by side.. 8. parallel
   ditch.. 6. escarp
   drum.. 5. snare
   hog (salted).. 6. flitch
   kick.. 3. pal 7. comrade, partner
    9. assistant 11. confederate
   left.. 4. port 5. larboard
   long.. 7. lateral, oblique, sloping
    8. indirect, slanting
   meat.. 5. bacon 8. salt pork
   of head.. 6. temple
   of triangle.. 3. leg
   on the side.. 5. apart
   sheltered.. 3. lee 4. alee 8. windless
   sidewalk salesman.. 8. pitchman
   step.. 4. duck 5. dodge, evade,
    hedge 6. astral, starry 7. quibble
   view.. 7. profile
   ways, wise.. 7. athwart, lateral
    9. laterally, obliquely
   whiskers.. 9. sideburns 10. sideboards
   windy.. 4. port 9. starboard
sidereal... 6. astral, starry 7. stellar
    9. celestial
sidero (comb form)... 4. iron
siderography... 14. steel engraving
siderology (science of)... 4. iron
sides, unequal... 7. scalene
sidle... 4. cant, edge, skew, tilt
    7. advance (furtive)
siècle... 3. age 7. century
siècle d'or... 9. Golden Age
siege... 7. besiege 8. assièger
    9. besetting 11. besiegement
    12. wearying time 13. beleaguerment
Siegfried (pert to)...
   hero of.. 5. opera (Wagner's)
   slayer.. 5. Hagen
   sword.. 7. Balmung
   wife.. 9. Kriemhild
Sierra Nevada fog... 7. pogonip
Sierra poet... 13. Joaquin Miller
siesta... 3. nap 4. lull, rest 5. cat
    nap, midday, snooze 10. forty winks
sieve... 3. lue 4. bolt, sift, sile
    5. purée 6. bolter, filter, riddle,
    semmet, sifter, sorter, strain
    7. dilluer 8. strainer 9. segregate,
    separator
sievelike... 8. cribrate
Sif (Norse), (pert to)...
   goddess of.. 4. home
   wife of.. 4. Thor
sift... 3. lue 4. bolt 5. sieve
    6. dredge, filter, riddle, screen,
    sorter, winnow 7. refiner 8. cribrate
sigh... 3. sob 5. mourn, sithe, yearn

    6. bemoan, bewail, exhale, grieve,
    lament 7. deplore 10. lament over
    11. suspiration
sight... 3. see 4. espy, gaze, view
    5. scene, sense 6. behold, descry,
    vision 7. discern, display 8. aperture
    10. exhibition 11. observation
sight (pert to)...
   acuteness of.. 7. oxyopia
   come into.. 4. loom 5. issue
   disorder.. 7. anopsia 8. paropsis
   imaginary.. 6. vision
   offensive.. 7. eyesore
   out of.. 5. range 6. absent
    8. vanished 9. invisible
    10. exorbitant 11. disappeared
   second.. 3. ESP 7. psychic
sigil... 4. seal 5. image (magic), stamp
    8. sigillum 9. signature
    11. endorsement
sigmoid... 3. ess 5. curve 9. intestine
sign... 3. cue, nod 4. code, hire,
    mark, neon, omen 5. token, trace
    6. emblem, engage, intone, motion,
    notice, signal, symbol 7. endorse,
    execute, insigne, portent, presage,
    symptom, vestige, warning
    8. evidence, password 9. semaphore,
    subscribe, watchword 10. forerunner,
    indication, underwrite 11. countersign
    13. advertisement, constellation
sign (pert to)...
   astrological.. 5. Aries 6. Gemini,
    Pisces, Taurus 8. Aquarius
    9. Capricorn 11. Sagittarius
   briefly.. 7. initial
   by the same.. 8. likewise, moreover
    11. accordingly
   diacritical.. 5. tilde 7. cedilla
   language.. 11. dactylology
   music.. 5. presa
   off.. 8. withdraw 10. Yours truly
    11. discontinue
   ref to.. 5. semic 7. semeion
   representing a word.. 8. logogram
   spiritual.. 9. sacrament
   up.. 4. join 6. enlist
   zodiac.. see *astrological* (above)
signal... 3. cue 4. code, fire, flag,
    sign 5. alarm, flare, token
    6. beacon, emblem, notify, wigwag
    7. eminent, lantern, notable, warning
    8. striking 9. memorable, prominent,
    semaphore, watchword
    10. lighthouse, remarkable
    11. communicate, conspicuous
    13. extraordinary
signal (pert to)...
   aviator's.. 5. roger
   danger, warning.. 4. bell 5. alert,
    fusee
   flag.. 6. ensign, wigwag
   night.. 6. beacon, curlew, pharos
    10. lighthouse
   preceding taps.. 6. tattoo
   railroad.. 5. fusee 9. semaphore
signature... 4. mark, sign, visa (vise)
    5. prima, sigil, stamp 6. signum
    9. autograph 11. endorsement
signed by writer... 9. onomatous (opp
   of anonymous)
signet... 4. mark, seal 5. sigil, stamp

9. signature 10. impression
11. endorsement
significance... 6. import, moment,
weight 7. anagoge, meaning
significant... 4. sign 5. token
6. symbol 7. ominous 8. sinister
9. important, momentous
10. expressive, indicative, meaningful,
portentous, suggestive
13. consequential
signification... 6. import 7. meaning
10. indication 11. consequence
12. notification 13. comprehension,
specification
signify... 4. hint, mean, sign 5. imply,
utter 6. denote, import, matter,
signal 7. betoken, connote, declare,
specify 8. announce, evidence,
foreshow, indicate, intimate, manifest
11. communicate
signum... 4. bell (tower), mark, sign
5. cross 9. signature
sika... 4. deer
sike... 4. rill 5. brook, ditch, gully
6. ravine, stream, trench
sikhara, sikhra... 5. tower (pyramidal)
silage... 4. feed 6. fodder
8. pasturage, provender
Silas (pert to)...
Bib.. 7. prophet 8. Silvanus
character.. 4. Wegg
companion of.. 4. Paul (Bib)
novel.. 11. Silas Marner
sile... 3. fry 4. beam, drip, drop, fall,
flow, pass, pour, sink, skim 5. cheat,
cover, glide, sieve, spawn 6. betray,
filter, strain, stream 7. conceal,
deceive, herring (young), subside
8. strainer
silence... 3. gag 4. hush, kill, lull,
mute, rest 5. quiet, shush, still,
tacet 6. defeat, muffle 7. confute,
repress, secrecy 8. oblivion, preclude,
restrain, suppress 9. eliminate,
stillness 10. silentness 11. taciturnity
13. noiselessness, tacit omission
silent... 3. mum 4. mute, tace
5. quiet, still, tacet, tacit
8. reserved, reticent, taciturn
9. soundless 10. speechless
11. unexpressed
15. uncommunicative
silhouette... 6. shadow 7. contour,
outline, picture, profile 9. delineate,
hourglass
silica... 4. opal 5. silex
silicate... 4. mica 8. calamine, wellsite
silk (pert to)...
ancient.. 6. Mantua, sendal
artificial.. 5. nylon, rayon
Assam.. 4. eria
black.. 5. crape (mourning), crepe
brown.. 4. muga 6. tussah
corded.. 6. faille 7. Ottoman
embroidery thread.. 5. floss
8. arrasene
fiber.. 5. floss
gland.. 9. serictery
gland of.. 7. spiders 9. silkworms
11. insect larva 12. caterpillars
gold.. 4. tash 6. samite 7. brocade
heavy.. 4. crin

kind of.. 5. China, crepe, moiré,
ninon, satin, surah, tabby, tulle
6. pongee, tobine, tussah 7. taffeta
lining.. 8. sarcenet (sarsenet)
muslin.. 16. mousseline de soie
raw.. 8. marabout
rustle of.. 6. scroop
source.. 6. cocoon
thin, glossy.. 7. alamode
thread (for velvets).. 4. tram (trame)
unspun.. 6. sleave
upholstery.. 7. tabaret
waste.. 4. noil 6. strass
watered.. 5. moiré
yarn.. 4. tram 5. schappe
yarn size.. 6. denier
silken... 5. seric, silby, sleek, suave
6. gentle, smooth, tender 7. elegant
8. delicate, lustrous, silklike
9. luxurious 10. effeminate
12. ingratiating
silkworm (pert to)...
Assam.. 3. eri 4. eria
China.. 6. pernyi 9. Ailanthus
cocoon.. 4. clew
disease.. 7. pebrine
genus (moth).. 6. Bombyx
India.. 6. tussah
Japan.. 7. yamamai
silky... 4. soft 5. quiet 6. glossy,
smooth 8. delicate 9. sericeous
11. filamentary 12. ingratiating
silky fabric... 6. barège
sill... 4. base, beam, seat, sile
5. basis 6. timber 8. threshold
10. foundation
silly... 3. mad 4. daft, fond 5. anile,
apish, dazed, dense, inane 6. dottle,
simple 7. asinine, fatuous, foolish,
shallow, trivial 9. brainless
10. indiscreet 12. simple–minded
silver... 2. Ag 4. gray 5. metal,
money, plate, white 6. argent
7. bullion 8. argentum, eloquent,
metallic, sterling
silver (pert to)...
alchemy.. 4. luna 6. occamy
alloy.. 6. billon
ball.. 4. pome
coin.. 6. tester
containing.. 5. lunar
German.. 6. albata
gilded.. 7. vermeil
ingots.. 5. sycee
jackal.. 9. silver fox
lace (with gold).. 5. orris 8. filigree
leaf.. 4. foil 8. hardhack
9. hydrangea, jewelweed 12. buffalo
berry
oak.. 11. flannelbush
tongued.. 7. musical 8. eloquent
uncoined.. 7. bullion
silversides... 5. smelt 6. minnow
12. silver salmon
Silver State... 6. Nevada
silverware... 5. vases 6. dishes
8. flatware 9. ornaments, tableware
silvery... 7. frosted, musical
8. lustrous, metallic 9. argentine
simian... 3. ape 4. monkey 7. apelike
similar... 4. akin, like, such 5. alike
7. uniform 8. analogic 9. analogous

11. homogeneous
similarity... 7. analogy 8. likeness
11. homogeneity, resemblance
13. approximation
simile... 8. allegory, metaphor
simper... 5. smirk 10. silly smile
13. affected smile
simple... 4. easy, mere 5. naive
6. dorian, oafish 7. artless
8. innocent 9. ingenuous
10. elementary 11. open and shut
15. unsophisticated
simpleton... 3. ass, daw, oaf 4. boob,
dolt, dupe, fool, gaby, gawk, gump,
simp, zang 5. dunce, goose, idiot,
ikona, moron, Simon, yokel, zombi
6. dawkin, gander, nitwit 7. half-wit
8. Abderite 9. greenhorn
10. nincompoop 11. Simple Simon
simplicity... 6. purity 7. modesty,
naiveté 9. clearness, ignorance,
innocence, plainness, rusticity
10. homeliness, humbleness,
simpleness 11. gullibility, informality
13. ingenuousness
14. unaffectedness
simplify... 7. clarify, explain, expound
9. elucidate, interpret
simply... 5. alone, truly 6. barely,
easily, merely, purely, really, solely
7. plainly 10. informally
simulate... 3. act, ape 4. sham
5. feign 6. affect, assume 7. imitate
11. counterfeit
simulated... 4. aped, sham 5. acted
7. assumed, feigned, shammed
9. pretended 10. fictitious
simurgh, simug (Myth)... 3. roc
12. gigantic bird
sin... 3. err 4. evil, vice 5. crime,
error, guilt, wrong 6. felony, heresy
7. offense 8. iniquity, peccancy
9. deviation 10. immorality,
wickedness 11. misdemeanor
13. transgression
Sinai (pert to)...
famed for.. 5. Moses 15. Ten
Commandments
location.. 6. Red Sea 11. Gulf of
Aqaba (Akaba)
mountain (Bib)... 5. Horeb 6. Serbal
9. Catharine, Umm Shomer
sinapis... 7. mustard
sinawa... 10. Ceylon hemp
sinay bean... 8. rice bean
since... 2. as 3. ago, for 4. ergo,
gone, past, syne 5. hence, later
7. already, because, whereas
8. inasmuch, until now 9. therefore,
thereupon 10. seeing that
11. considering 12. subsequently
sincere... 4. open, pure 5. frank
6. candid 7. correct, earnest,
genuine, intense, unmixed, upright,
zealous 9. authentic, unfeigned,
veracious 10. unaffected
11. unvarnished 13. unadulterated
15. straightforward
sincerity... 4. zeal 6. candor
7. honesty 10. heartiness
11. genuineness, sincereness
sincerity symbol... 8. amethyst

sind... 5. rinse 6. drench, quench
7. rinsing
Sind (Ind)...
capital.. 7. Karachi
ibex.. 8. wild goat
prince.. 5. ameer
Sindbad's bird... 3. roc
Sindbad the Sailor... 9. character
(Arabian Nights)
sindico... 7. trustee 8. assignee,
receiver
sine... 7. without
sinew... 4. thew 5. nerve, power
6. muscle, string, tendon
sinewy... 4. firm, wiry 5. thewy, tough
6. brawny, strong 7. fibrose, stringy
8. powerful, vigorous
sinful... 3. bad 4. evil 5. wrong
6. wicked 7. vicious 10. iniquitous
11. unrighteous
sing... 3. hum, say 4. hymn, lilt
5. carol, chant, croon, yodel
6. intone, warble 7. rejoice
8. proclaim, vocalize 9. celebrate
sing (pert to)...
exultantly.. 4. lilt 7. chortle
10. cheerfully
jovially.. 5. troll
off key.. 4. flat
or whistle.. 7. tweedle
shrilly.. 4. pipe
softly.. 5. croon
sorrowfully.. 7. despond 8. complain
Swisslike.. 5. yodel
with trills.. 6. warble 7. roulade
singe... 4. burn, sear 6. scorch
8. discolor
singer... 4. bard, bird, diva, poet
5. blues, siren, tenor, torch
6. cantor, hymner 7. caroler,
crooner, warbler, yodeler 8. minstrel,
songster, vocalist 9. chanteuse,
descanter 10. cantatrice, prima
donna 11. minnesinger
Singhalese tree... 4. poon 5. domba
singing (pert to)...
birds.. 5. Oscine
canary.. 10. white whale
fish.. 8. toadfish
group.. 5. choir 6. chorus
Memnon.. 9. Amenhotep (statue)
ref to.. 5. melic
single... 3. ace, odd, one 4. lone,
only, sole, unit 6. simple, unique
8. sporadic 9. unmarried
single (pert to)...
algebra.. 6. nomial
comb form.. 3. uni
odd.. 7. azygous
racing term.. 4. heat
tones (one of two).. 10. monotonous
singleness... 5. unity 8. celibacy
9. sincerity, unmarried
singly... 4. once, only, solo 5. alone,
apart 6. simply 8. uniquely
9. severally 12. individually,
particularly, single-handed
singular... 3. odd 4. each, rare, sole,
unit 5. queer 6. unique 7. eminent,
special, strange, unusual 8. peculiar,
separate, uncommon 9. eccentric,
fantastic, whimsical 10. individual,

remarkable, unexampled
11. exceptional 12. unparalleled
13. extraordinary, unprecedented
14. characteristic

singularity... 6. oddity 7. oddness,
oneness 8. peculiar 11. peculiarity
12. eccentricity 13. individuality
15. distinctiveness

Sinic... 7. Chinese, Sinitic

sinister... 4. evil, grim, left 7. adverse,
corrupt, ominous 9. dishonest,
injurious, malicious, underhand
10. disastrous, portentous
11. unfortunate

sinistral... 7. baneful 10. left-handed
12. illegitimate, inauspicious (opp of
dextral)

sink... 3. age, bog, dip, ebb, sag
4. cave, drop, fall, mire, sump
5. drain, droop, lapse, lower, quail
6. cavity, deject, engulf, go down,
recede, settle, sicken, weaken
7. decline, depress, descend,
despond 8. decrease, diminish,
submerge 10. degenerate

sinuous... 4. wavy 7. winding
9. deviating, intricate 10. circuitous

Sioux (pert to)...
division.. 5. Teton 6. Santee
famed as.. 8. warriors
tribe.. 3. Oto (Otoe) 4. Crow, Iowa
5. Omaha, Osage 6. Dakota, Plains
9. Winnebago

sip... 3. lap, sup 4. gulp 5. drink,
quaff, taste 6. tipple

sircar... 5. ruler 6. master 7. servant
8. province (Mogul) 10. government

siren... 5. alarm, Circe, deity, lurer,
vixen 7. charmer, enticer, foghorn,
Lorelei, mermaid 9. bewitcher,
Cleopatra, temptress

Sirenia... 6. dugong, mammal
7. manatee 14. Steller's sea cow

siriasis... 9. sunstroke

Sirius... 4. star 7. Dog Star 10. Canis
Major, dog of Orion (Gr Myth)

sissy... 5. softy 6. prissy, sister
10. effeminate, pantywaist
11. mollycoddle

sister... 3. kin, nun, sib 5. nurse,
soror

sisterhood... 4. nuns 8. sorority

Sistrurus... 11. rattlesnake

sit... 3. fit 4. isle, loll, pose, rest
5. brood, perch, press, roost, squat
6. repose 7. convene 8. incubate

site... 4. ruin, seat 5. place, scene,
venue 6. locale, locate 8. location,
position

site of Taj Mahal... 4. Agra (Ind)

sitting... 4. seat 6. séance, sedent
7. posture, sessile, session
10. incubation 11. convocation

situated... 3. lie, set 4. case, seat
5. fixed 6. clutch, placed, plight
9. ensconced, stationed
11. established

situated (pert to)...
at back.. 6. astern 7. postern
9. posterior
at base.. 5. basal
between folds.. 11. interplical

in middle.. 6. medial, median
on left hand.. 9. sinistrad
on right hand.. 6. dexter

situation... 3. job 4. case, post
5. place, situs, state 6. office, plight
7. station 8. locality, location,
position 9. condition, placement

situation (pert to)...
approximate.. 11. whereabouts
difficult.. 6. scrape 7. dilemma
8. quandary 9. imbroglio
11. predicament 12. circumstance
doomed.. 7. rattrap
favorable.. 7. vantage
Latin.. 5. situs
perplexing.. 6. strait
three choices.. 8. trilemma

Siva, Shiva (pert to)...
consort.. 3. Uma 4. Devi
dancer.. 8. Natajara
god, deity.. 8. Hinduism 9. Destroyer
title.. 8. Mahadeva
trident.. 6. trisul (trisula)

six (pert to)...
balls (Medici).. 5. palle
dice number.. 4. sice
eyed.. 8. senocular
feet of earth.. 5. grave
fold.. 8. sextuple
footed.. 7. hexaped 9. hexapodal
group.. 5. hexad
lines.. 6. sestet 7. sextain
pence.. 6. bender 7. fiddler
pert to.. 6. senary
pointed figure.. 4. star
square.. 9. hexagonal

sixty, sixties... 5. cycle, saros
7. numeral

size... 3. cap 4. area, bulk, pica,
pope, pott 5. agate, grade 6. adjust
7. arrange, measure, portion
8. classify 9. magnitude
10. gargantuan 11. measurement

sizzle... 3. fry 4. hiss 5. speed 7. be
angry 10. effervesce

sjambok... 4. flog, whip

skate... 3. jag, ray (fish) 4. plug, skim
5. glide, horse, scull, spree

skean... 4. dirk 6. dagger

skedaddle... 4. bolt, flee, flit 6. scurry
7. run away, scamper

skein... 3. rap (120 yds), web
4. hank, yarn 6. thread 7. spireme
12. flight of fowl

skelder... 5. cheat 7. vagrant
9. panhandle

skeleton... 4. cage 5. bones, frame,
mummy 6. sketch 7. contour,
diagram, outline 8. thinness
9. framework

skeleton (pert to)...
at the feast.. 7. kill-joy 10. wet
blanket 11. crapehanger
English dialect.. 4. reme
framework.. 5. cadre
in the closet.. 4. evil 6. secret
13. mortification
key.. 6. master
marine animal.. 6. sponge
polyp.. 5. coral

skeptic, sceptic... 7. doubter, infidel
8. aporetic 10. Pyrrhonist, unbeliever

11. freethinker, irreligious, nullifidian

skeptical, sceptical... 8. doubtful, doubting 11. incredulous, unbelieving

sketch... 3. jap, jot 4. draw, idea, limn, plan, skit 5. draft, trace 6. aperçu, design 7. diagram, drawing, outline 8. esquisse, treatise 9. delineate 11. delineation, description

sketchy... 5. rough, vague 10. unfinished

skewer... 3. pin, rod 5. truss 6. fasten, pierce 9. brochette

skid... 4. clog, shoe, slip, trig 5. brake, check, slide 7. travois 8. sideslip

skiff... 4. boat, skim 5. canoe, glide, graze 6. caique 7. rowboat 11. slight touch

skill... 3. art 5. craft, knack 6. gifted, talent 7. ability, address, aptness, cunning, finesse, mastery 8. aptitude, deftness, facility 9. adeptness, dexterity, expertise, readiness, smartness 10. adroitness, cleverness, proficient 11. proficiency

skilled... 5. adept 6. expert 7. endowed, trained 8. talented 10. conversant, proficient

skilled (pert to)...
in government.. 9. statesman
in mechanics.. 5. sloyd
in strategy.. 7. finesse

skillful, skilful... 3. apt 4. able, deft, fine 6. adroit, clever, crafty, daedal, expert 7. capable 8. artistic, dextrous, tactical 9. daedalian, dexterous, ingenious 10. proficient, well-versed 12. accomplished

skim... 4. flit, sail, scan, scud 5. glice, graze, scoon, skirr 6. slight 8. pass over

skin... 4. bark, derm, fell, flay, hide, pare, peel, pelt, rind, scum 5. cheat, cutis, derma, fraud, scalp 6. fleece, lamina, scrape 7. callous, cuticle, defraud, swindle 8. covering, tegument 9. epidermis 10. integument 11. decorticate

skin (pert to)...
animal.. 4. coat, hide, pelt 7. pellage
animal's neck fold.. 6. dewlap
beaver.. 4. plew
comb form.. 4. derm 5. derma
decoration.. 6. tattoo
destitute of.. 8. apellous
disease.. 4. acne 5. hives, mange, uredo 6. eczema, herpes, tetter 8. ringworm 9. urticaria
drying frame.. 5. herse
dryness.. 7. xerosis
fawnskin (of Dionysus).. 6. nebris
fold.. 5. plica 6. dewlap
fruit.. 7. epicarp
gobbler's throat.. 3. tar
layer.. 5. cutis, derma
layer, outer.. 7. epicarp
opening.. 4. pore
pert to.. 6. dermal 7. dermoid
piece.. 5. blype
pigment, excess.. 8. melanism
protuberance.. 4. mole, wart

salting bin.. 5. kench
squirrel.. 4. vair
tan.. 3. taw
tanned.. 5. suede
unsheared.. 8. woolfell

skinflint... 5. cheat, miser 9. bargainer

skink... 4. adda 6. lizard

skinned... 6. bested 7. euchred, fleeced

skinned (pert to)...
dark.. 7. melanic, swarthy
pert to.. 5. bared 7. denuded 8. stripped
slang.. 7. euchred, fleeced
thick.. 9. pachyderm 11. pachydermic

skinny... 4. lean, thin 5. scant 6. stingy 8. skinlike 9. emaciated, niggardly

skip... 3. dap 4. gait, jump, leap, omit 5. bound, caper, elide, frisk, salto, vault 6. gambol, lackey, spring 7. abscond 8. ricochet

skipjack... 3. fop 4. pike 5. saury 6. bonito 7. bounder, parvenu, upstart 8. bluefish, sailboat 9. stripling (conceited) 10. butterfish 14. snapping beetle

skipper... 5. saury 6. locust, maggot, master, serang 8. skipjack 9. butterfly 11. grasshopper

ski race (obstacle)... 6. slalom

skirling... 5. trout 6. salmon

skirmish... 4. fray 5. brush, clash, melee 6. combat 8. conflict, flourish 9. encounter 10. velitation

skirt... 5. dress, evade, woman 6. border, edging, fringe 9. appendage, baseboard, periphery, petticoat 10. pass around, saddle part

skirt (pert to)...
armor.. 5. tasse (tace) 7. lamboys
attached to blouse.. 6. peplum
chaser.. 9. libertine 11. philanderer
dance.. 6. ballet
short.. 4. kilt

skit... 3. joke, play 5. caper 6. parody, shower, sketch

skittish... 3. coy, shy 5. jumpy 6. fickle, frisky, tricky 7. bashful 8. unstable, volatile 9. excitable 10. capricious 13. irresponsible

skittles... 4. game, play 8. ninepins 9. enjoyment (not all beer and skittles)

skoal... 5. toast 10. salutation 11. exclamation 14. pledge of health

skulk... 4. lurk 5. cower, dodge, hedge, sneak 8. malinger

skull... 4. bean, head, mind 5. brain 7. cranium, harnpan 8. brain box

skull (pert to)...
cap.. 6. beanie 7. calotte 9. zucchetto 10. berrettino
cavity.. 5. fossa
measure.. 11. craniometer
monk's.. 6. pileus
operation.. 6. trepan
part.. 5. inion 6. bregma 7. calotte, occiput
ref to.. 5. inial 6. cranic 7. cranial
science of.. 10. craniology

skull and crossbones... 5. death (symb) 10. danger sign

skunk... 5. zoril 6. defeat 7. fitchew, polecat, stinker 8. conepate (conepati), zorrillo 9. scoundrel

sky... 4. blue 5. ether, vault 6. caelum, canopy, heaven, welkin 7. heavens, the blue 8. empyrean 9. firmament 10. blue yonder

sky (pert to)...
color.. 4. blue 5. azure 7. celeste 8. cerulean
god.. 3. Anu
lark.. 5. pipit 6. Alauda, frolic 7. titlark
light.. 6. window 8. abatjour
lure.. 7. horizon
parlor.. 5. attic 6. garret
pilot.. 8. chaplain 9. clergyman 10. missionary
serpent.. 3. Ahi

slab... 3. mud 4. tile 5. board, dalle, plank, slime 6. lamina, ledger, pillar (stone), puddle 7. portion 8. monument 9. flagstone

slab (pert to)...
grave.. 5. stele (stela)
marble.. 5. dalle 6. tablet
slablike.. 6. stelar

slack... 3. lax 4. lull, slow 5. chaff, inert, let up, loose, shirk, tardy 6. abated, remiss 7. relaxed 8. careless, dilatory, inactive, indolent, sluggish 9. reluctant, secondary 10. diminished, inadequate 11. inattentive

slacken... 5. abate, delay, relax 6. loosen, reduce, repose, retard 7. let down, relieve 8. hold back

slackening of strained relations... 7. detente (Internat)

slag... 4. lava 5. dross 6. cinder, scoria 7. residue 9. recrement 11. agglomerate

slain... 4. dead 6. fallen, killed 8. murdered 12. assassinated

slake... 4. cool, sate 5. abate, allay, slack 6. quench 7. assuage, crumble, hydrate, refresh, relieve, satisfy, slacken 8. decrease, mitigate, moderate 10. extinguish 12. disintegrate

slam... 4. bang, blow, give, shut, vole 5. abuse, score 6. impact 9. criticism, criticize

slander... 5. belie, libel 6. defame, malign, vilify 7. asperse, blacken, distort, traduce 8. derogate, disgrace, reproach 10. defamation, scandalize 12. misrepresent

slang... 4. cant 5. argot 6. jargon, patois 7. hep talk 10. vernacular

slant... 4. bend, cant, skew 5. angle, bevel, slope 6. aslant, aspect, biased, glance 7. incline, opinion 8. attitude, occasion 9. obliquely, viewpoint 10. hypotenuse 11. inclination, opportunity

slap... 3. hit 4. blow, clap, cuff, snub 5. crack, skelp, sound, twank 6. buffet, rebuff, slight, strike 8. chastise 12. chastisement

slash... 3. cut 4. gash, lash, slit 5. marsh, sever 6. attack, reduce, stripe 7. censure, scourge 8. price cut 9. criticize, reduction

slate... 4. list, rock 5. color, scold, sculp 6. ballot, enroll, record, roster, tablet, thrash 7. censure, roofing, writing 8. register, schedule, slattern 9. criticize, reprimand

slate (pert to)...
ax.. 7. mattock
black.. 4. gray
blue.. 9. Swiss blue
gray.. 7. Russian 9. red–yellow 10. sandy beige 13. oriental pearl
roof.. 3. rag
tool.. 3. zax 7. scantle

slater... 6. critic 7. hellier

slattern... 4. slut 5. frump, idler, mopsy 6. sloppy 7. trifler, trollop 8. careless, slovenly 9. litterbug

slaughter... 4. kill, slay 6. battue, murder, pogrom 7. butcher, carnage, killing 8. butchery, hecatomb, massacre, occision 9. bloodshed 10. butchering 11. destruction

slaughterhouse... 8. abattoir, Aceldama, butchery, matadero, shambles 9. stockyard 12. field of blood

Slav... 4. Pole, Slav, Sorb, Wend 5. Croat, Czech 6. Slovak 7. Russian, Serbian, Servian 8. Bohemian, Croatian, Moravian 9. Bulgarian

slave... 4. boor, esne, peon, serf 5. chela, helot, thane 6. drudge, lascar, minion, thrall, vassal 7. bondman, captive, chattel, enslave, odalisk, servant 8. slave ant 9. bondslave

slave (pert to)...
block (selling).. 7. catasta
born.. 4. neif
comedy (stock name).. 5. Davus
dealer.. 5. bichy, mango (obs)
Eleusinian (Gr Relig).. 5. Baubo, lambe
female.. 9. concubine, odalisque (odalisk)
free.. 5. thane (thegn)
fugitive.. 8. marooner
Indian.. 10. Athapascan
The Tempest.. 7. Caliban

slavery... 4. bond 7. bondage, service 8. drudgery 9. captivity, servitude, thralldom, vassalage 11. enslavement 12. enthrallment

Slave States... 5. Texas 7. Alabama, Florida, Georgia 8. Arkansas, Delaware, Kentucky, Maryland, Missouri, Virginia 9. Louisiana, Tennessee 11. Mississippi 13. North Carolina, South Carolina

slay... 4. kill 5. amuse, burke, knock, lynch, smite 6. murder, strike 7. butcher, destroy 9. slaughter 10. annihilate 11. assassinate, destroy life, exterminate

slayer... 6. killer 8. criminal, murderer, regicide, vaticide 9. matricide, patricide 10. fratricide, sororicide

sleave... 4. sley 5. floss 6. tangle
  8. separate 9. floss silk
  11. disentangle 13. untwisted silk
sled... 4. pung 6. sledge, sleigh,
  travoy, troika 8. toboggan
sledge... 4. sled 6. hammer, sleigh,
  strike 7. seven–up (game), vehicle
sleep... 3. nap, nod 4. dorm, doss,
  doze, wink 5. death, sopor
  6. drowse, snooze, somnus
  7. slumber 10. narcolepsy,
  somnipathy 11. hibernation
sleep (pert to)...
  comb form.. 5. somni
  deep.. 6. stupor 8. lethargy
  10. narcolepsy
  hypnotic.. 10. somnipathy
  inducing.. 5. dwale 6. opiate, potion
  8. sedative 9. soporific
  10. anesthesia, belladonna
  insensible.. 4. coma
  midday.. 6. siesta
  prolonged.. 5. sopor
  upon.. 8. consider, postpone
sleeper... 3. tie 4. beam 6. rafter,
  rester, timber 7. Pullman, reposer,
  support 8. dormouse 9. slumberer
  10. slow seller 11. sleeping car
sleeping... 4. dead 5. inert 6. asleep,
  latent 7. dormant 8. dormient,
  inactive 9. quiescent 10. quiescence
  11. inattentive
sleeping (pert to)...
  pill.. 9. soporific
  place.. 3. bed, cot 4. bunk, doss
  5. berth, couch 6. pallet 7. cubicle
  9. dormitory
  sickness.. 6. nagana, tsetse
  9. lethargus
sleepwalking... 8. neurosis
  12. nightwalking, somnambulism
sleepy... 4. dull 5. tired 6. drowsy
  8. soporose 9. lethargic, somnolent
  11. somniferous
sleeve... 3. arm 5. gigot
  (leg–o'–mutton) 10. copper tube
  14. British channel
sleigh... 4. pung 6. cutter
sleight of hand performer... 4. mage
  8. magician 14. legerdemainist
  15. prestidigitator
slender... 4. lank, lean, slim, thin
  5. gaunt, lanky, leger, reedy
  6. lissom, narrow, svelte 7. gracile,
  tenuous, trivial, willowy 9. elongated
slender pinnacle... 3. epi
sleuth... 6. tracer 8. hawkshaw
  9. detective, sleuthdog
  11. sleuthhound 12. investigator
slice... 3. cut, saw 4. gash, slab
  5. piece, share, shave 6. rasher,
  sliver, stroke 7. portion 8. golf term,
  splinter 12. cross section
slick... 4. neat, tidy 5. alert, sleek,
  smart 6. clever, smooth 8. slippery,
  unctuous 9. first–rate, lubricate
  10. glistening 12. accomplished
slide... 3. ski 4. rule, skid, slip, slue
  5. chute, clasp, glide, plane
  (sloping), scoot, skate 6. elapse
  7. lantern, slither 8. toboggan
  9. avalanche 11. deteriorate

slight... 3. cut 4. defy, rare, snub,
  thin 5. faint, frail, leger, minor, oligo
  (comb form), scorn, small 6. flimsy,
  ignore, little, meager 7. disdain,
  fragile, neglect, nominal, scantly,
  shallow, trivial 8. contempt, delicate
  9. disregard, indignity 10. immaterial
  11. unimportant 13. imperceptible,
  unsubstantial 14. inconsiderable
slight (pert to)...
  convexity.. 6. camber
  sound.. 4. peep
  variation.. 6. nuance 7. shading
slightest... 5. least 6. barest
slightly (pert to)...
  damaged paper.. 6. retree
  sour.. 8. acescent
  tapering.. 7. terete
slim... 3. sly 4. lean, mean, thin
  5. small, spare 6. adroit, scanty,
  sparse, svelte 7. slender, tenuous
  9. worthless
slime... 3. mud 4. ooze 5. filth, gleet
  6. mucous
slip... 3. err, pew, sin 4. dock, fail,
  pier, skid, slue 5. boner, cover,
  error, fault, glide, lapse, slide, strip
  6. bungle, elapse 7. blunder, cutting,
  failure, faux pas, misdeed, mistake,
  slither, youngling 10. pillowslip
  12. undergarment 13. transgression
slipknot... 5. noose
slipper... 4. mule, neap, shoe
  5. apron, moyle, Romeo 6. pinson,
  sandal 7. scuffer 8. babouche
  (baboosh), covering
slippery... 3. sly 4. eely, glib 5. slick
  6. crafty, fickle, shifty, tricky, wanton
  7. cunning, elusive, evasive
  8. unctuous, unstable 9. deceitful,
  uncertain 10. intangible, precarious,
  unreliable 11. treacherous
  13. untrustworthy
slit... 4. kerf 5. cleft, slash, split
  6. furrow 7. severed
slither... 5. crawl, glide, sidle, slide
sliver... 3. cut 5. shred, slice, split
  8. fragment, splinter
sloe... 3. haw 4. plum
sloe (pert to)...
  berry.. 7. juniper
  bush.. 10. blackthorn
  color.. 9. blue–black
  fruit (blackthorn).. 3. haw 4. sloe
  gin.. 12. sloe–flavored
slogan... 3. cry 5. motto 6. phrase
  9. catchword, watchword
  10. shibboleth (Bib)
sloop... 5. yacht 6. cutter, schuit
  (schuyt) 7. eelboat
slope... 3. dip, lie 4. bank, hade,
  ramp 5. bevel, scarp, slant, talus
  6. calade, decamp, escarp, glacis
  7. terrace 9. declivity 10. declension
  11. inclination
sloping bank... 4. brae 7. terrace
sloth... 2. ai 4. pack (bears), pazy,
  unau 6. acedia, mammal 7. inertia
  8. idleness, slowness 9. indolence
slothful... 4. lazy 8. inactive, indolent,
  sluggish
sloth monkey... 5. lemur, loris

slough... 3. bog 4. husk, mire, molt, shed, skin 5. bayou, swamp 7. channel, discard

sloughing... 7. ecdysis, molting 8. shedding 10. discarding

slovenly... 5. dowdy, messy 6. frowzy, sloppy, untidy 8. careless, slattern, slipshod 9. negligent 10. disorderly, slatternly 13. ungrammatical

slow... 4. dull, late, poky 5. delay, inert, relax 6. boring, hinder, retard, stupid 7. slacken 8. boresome, dilatory, inactive, moderate 9. lingering 10. inch by inch, phlegmatic 13. unprogressive

slow (pert to)...
  action.. 6. dawdle 10. deliberate
  adverb.. 10. behindhand
  down.. 4. idle 6. retard
    10. decelerate
  music.. 5. largo, lento, molto, tardo 6. adagio 7. andante 8. lentando 10. lentamente
  poke.. 5. snail 7. dawdler
  up.. 3. lag 6. retard 7. decline
  witted.. 4. dull 6. stupid

sludge... 3. mud 4. mire, ooze 5. slime 8. sediment

slug... 3. hit 4. blow, dose 5. Arion, drink, drone, idler, Limax, space, token 6. bullet, loiter, nugget 7. trepang 8. sluggard 9. gastropod

sluggish... 4. logy, slow 5. dopey, inert 6. drowsy, stupid, supine 7. dronish, languid 8. dilatory, inactive, indolent, listless, stagnant 9. stagnancy, stupidity, torpidity

sluice... 4. race 5. flush 6. drench, stream 7. channel 9. floodgate

slumber... 4. doze 5. sleep 6. drowse, repose, somnus 14. arms of Morpheus

slump... 4. drop, fall 7. decline, descend, dessert, sinkage 9. fall short 10. depreciate, depression

slur... 4. blur 5. elide 6. defame, insult, mackle, slight, stigma 7. calumny, traduce 8. disgrace, innuendo, reproach, skim over 9. aspersion, disparage 10. calumniate, stigmatize

slush... 3. mud 4. mire, snow 5. slime 14. sentimentality

sly... 4. arch, foxy, wary, wily, wink 5. cagey, catty, snaky 6. covert, crafty, feline, shrewd, sneaky, subtle 7. cunning, furtive 8. craftily 9. underhand 11. mischievous, underhanded 15. surreptitiously

smack... 3. bit 4. bang, buss, glow, kiss, tang 5. taste 6. strike, vessel 8. chastise, sailboat 12. chastisement

smacking... 5. brisk 6. lively 7. dashing 8. spanking, vigorous 9. energetic

small... 3. tot, wee 4. thin, tiny, wisp 5. dwarf, petty 6. humble, little, meager, minute, modest, petite 7. faintly, trivial 8. picayune, trifling 9. miniature, miniscule, thumbnail 10. undersized 11. unimportant

small (pert to)...
  amount.. 4. dram 5. minim 6. morsel 7. modicum 8. pittance
  anvil.. 5. teest
  area.. 6. areola
  armadillo.. 4. peba
  arms.. 3. bow 5. rifle, sword 6. pistol 7. carbine, grenade
  attractive.. 4. cute
  bomb.. 6. petard
  bottle.. 4. vial 5. phial
  case, handbag.. 4. etui
  comb form.. 5. lepto, micro
  dab.. 3. pat, wad 5. chunk
  deer.. 4. napu
  delicately.. 6. mignon
  distance.. 4. step
  drink.. 4. pony
  drum.. 5. tabor
  field.. 5. croft
  fish.. 3. ide
  flag.. 6. fanion
  fruits.. 10. low growing
  fry.. 4. fish, kids, tots 8. children 10. youngsters
  insect.. 5. midge
  island.. 3. ait 4. isle
  lake.. 4. mere, pond
  law.. 5. petit
  minded.. 4. mean 5. petty 10. prejudiced, vindictive
  neat.. 6. dapper
  number.. 7. paucity
  opening.. 4. pore 5. stoma 7. orifice
  ox.. 4. anoa
  part.. 4. iota 6. detail 7. snippet
  particle.. 4. atom, mote 8. molecule
  people.. 6. common 5. fairies
  piece.. 3. mot 4. chip, tate 5. speck 7. driblet, morceau
  post.. 9. paper size
  quantity.. 4. drop, mite 5. trace 7. handful
  rope (Naut).. 7. marline (marling)
  Scot.. 3. sma, wee
  shield.. 3. écu 9. scutellum
  stream.. 3. run 4. rill 6. rillet
  surface.. 5. facet
  talk.. 4. babble 7. prattle 8. chitchat
  task.. 5. chore
  things.. 3. fry
  tower.. 6. turret 7. minaret
  very.. 3. wee 8. picayune 11. Lilliputian
  world.. 9. microcosm

smallest nation... 5. Nauru

smallpox... 7. variola

smaragd... 7. emerald

smart... 3. apt 4. chic, perk, posh, trig, trim, wise 5. acute, alert, natty, nifty, quick, sting 6. astute, clever, shrewd, spruce 7. dashing, painful, pungent, stylish 8. impudent, poignant, pricking 9. competent 10. precocious 11. fashionable, intelligent

smash... 4. blow, mash, pulp, ruin 5. break, crush, drink (spirits), stave, wreck 6. defeat 7. collide, debacle, destroy, failure, shatter, success

8. accident, beverage 9. collision, pulverize

smear... 3. dab, rub 4. daub, gaum 5. slake, stain, sully 6. anoint, bedaub, defame, defile, grease, malign, smirch, smudge 7. besmear, plaster, pollute, slander 8. besmirch

smear with...
egg white.. 5. glair 8. meringue
mud.. 5. slime
ointment.. 6. anoint

smell... 4. odor, olid, reek 5. aroma, fetor, scent, sense, sniff, stink 6. detect 7. perfume 9. fragrance, redolence 10. atmosphere

smell (pert to)...
acute.. 8. oxyrhine
loss of sense of.. 7. anosmia
offensive.. 3. bad 4. foul, olid 5. fetor 8. stench
sense of.. 6. osmics 7. osmesis 9. olfaction

smelling salts... 9. hartshorn 17. ammonium carbonate

smelt... 4. fish, fuse, melt 6. tomcod 7. scorify 10. silverside

smilax... 8. catbrier 10. greenbrier

smile... 4. grin 5. laugh, smirk, sneer 6. simper 8. greeting

smiling... 5. agrin, merry, riant 6. rident 8. gleaming, grinning

smirch... 4. blot 5. smear, stain, sully, taint 6. blotch, smutch, stigma, vilify 7. begrime, blacken, blemish, tarnish 8. discolor 10. blackening

smirk... 4. grin, leer 6. simper

smite... 4. kill, slap 6. lay low, strike 7. chasten, impress, inflict, trouble 8. chastise

smithy... 6. forger, stithy 7. farrier 8. smithery 10. blacksmith

smock... 5. kamis, shift, tunic, woman (obs) 7. chemise 9. philander 11. overgarment

smoke... 4. burn, cure, floc, fume, pipe 5. cigar, cloud, cubeb, flume, smook, vapor 6. smudge 7. incense, tobacco 8. fumigate, preserve 9. cigarette

smokestack... 6. funnel 7. chimney 8. fumiduct

smoking apparatus (Orient)...
7. tabagie 8. narghile (nargile)

smolder, smoulder... 4. burn 5. choke, smoke 6. smudge 7. smother 9. suffocate

smooth... 4. comb, ease, even, iron, lene, pave 5. bland, clear, level, plane, press, sleek, slick, suave 6. glossy, mangle, pacify, urbane 7. uniform 8. hairless, unctuous 10. facilitate, flattering 12. frictionless, ingratiating

smooth (pert to)...
breathing.. 13. spiritus lenis
comb form.. 3. lio
feathers, hair.. 5. preen
hard, transparent.. 6. glassy
phonetically.. 4. lene
tare.. 12. slender vetch
tongued.. 4. glib 5. suave 12. hypocritical

smooth and...
soft.. 5. furry, silky, soapy 7. velvety
soothing.. 5. bland
sweet.. 11. mellifluent
white.. 11. alabastrine

smother... 4. daub, kill 5. befog, choke, cover 6. deaden, hush up, muffle, stifle, welter 7. overlie, smolder 8. suppress 9. suffocate, to blanket 11. exterminate

smudge... 4. blot, smut, soil, spot 5. smear, smoke, stain 6. smutch 7. begrime, smolder

smug... 4. neat, tidy, trim 5. smart, suave 6. pilfer 7. correct 9. confident 10. complacent 13. self-satisfied

smuggler... 6. runner 9. rumrunner 13. contrabandist

smur... 4. mist 5. cloud, smurr 7. drizzle

Smyrna... 5. Izmir (present name)

Smyrna fig... 5. eleme (elemi)

Smyrna melon... 6. casaba

snail... 4. slug 5. drone, Helix, Mitra, whelk 6. Nerita, Triton 7. mollusk 9. gastropod 10. periwinkle

snake... 3. asp, ess 4. tree, worm 5. adder, cobra, coral, racer, viper 6. garter, gopher 7. hognose, rattler, reptile 8. Micrurus, moccasin 9. Heterodon 10. bushmaster, copperhead, sidewinder 11. cottonmouth, diamondback, rattlesnake 12. schaapsteker

snake (pert to)...
African.. 5. mamba
bird.. 6. darter
black.. 5. racer
cobra.. 3. nag (naga)
comb form.. 5. ophio, ophis 6. herpes
crusher.. 6. python 8. anaconda 14. boa constrictor
dance.. 4. Hopi 6. ophism
division (serpents).. 7. Ophidia 9. Serpentes
expert.. 13. herpetologist
fear of.. 13. herpetophobia
Florida.. 8. moccasin
front-fanged.. 5. cobra, mamba 6. elapid 8. Elapinne
garter.. 5. Elaps
genus.. 7. Ophidia
heraldic.. 5. bisse
horned.. 8. cerastes
India.. 5. krait 6. bongar
killer.. 8. mongoose
like.. 7. ophioid 9. colubrine
mouth.. 6. orchid
movement.. 4. coil, drag, wind 5. crawl, sneak, twist
mythical.. 6. Python (on Mt Parnassus)
nonpoisonous.. 4. king 6. garter, gopher 9. Colubrina
pert to.. 5. ophic 7. anguine 8. viperine 9. colubrine, scoundrel
poisonous.. 3. asp 5. adder, coral 7. rattler 8. moccasin 10. copperhead 11. cottonmouth 13. thanatophidia

python.. 8. anaconda
python deity.. 5. zombi (zombie)
reptilelike.. 9. herpetoid
Russell's viper.. 6. daboia, jessur
sacred.. 6. Shesha
S America.. 5. aboma
sand snake.. 4. Eryx
semihuman, race of.. 4. Naga
shaped.. 9. anguiform
skin.. 6. exuvia
spitting.. 8. ringhals
snaky... 3. sly 4. wavy 7. anguine,
sinuous, wriggly 8. spiteful, twisting,
venomous 9. snakelike 10. perfidious,
serpentine 11. treacherous
snaky sisters... 6. Erinys
17. snaky-haired Furies
snap... 3. bit 4. bite, flip 5. break,
crack, flick, quick, snarl, thump
6. energy, fasten, fillip (fingers)
7. bargain, crackle 8. easy task,
handcuff, snapshot 9. crispness,
fastening, smartness 10. gingersnap,
photograph, resilience 11. sharp
retort
snapper... 4. bean, sesi 5. error,
pargo 6. beetle, bonbon, tamure,
turtle 7. cracker, grouper 8. fastener,
rosefish 9. countfish 10. stitchwort,
stringbean, woodpecker
11. firecracker
snappy... 4. cold, fast 5. quick
6. lively, sudden 7. pungent
8. snappish 9. crackling, energetic
snare... 3. beg, gin, net, web 4. lure,
mesh, trap 5. benet, catch, noose,
steal 6. entoil, trepan 7. pitfall
9. deception
snark... 3. nag 5. snort 6. boojum
8. creature (fabled)
snarl... 4. gnar, knot 5. gnarr, growl,
scold, snare 6. tangle 7. confuse,
ensnare, grumble, quarrel
8. complain, entangle 9. confusion
10. complicate 12. complication
snatch... 4. grab, jerk, take 5. catch,
erept, grasp, gripe, pluck, seize,
steal, wrest 6. clutch, kidnap, rescue
7. seizure
sneak... 4. lead (game), lurk 5. cower,
creep, knave, slink, snoop 6. coward,
cringe, tattle 7. smuggle 11. furtive
move
sneaking... 3. sly 4. mean, poor
6. craven, hidden, paltry, secret
7. furtive 8. cowardly, stealthy
9. dastardly, niggardly, underhand
12. contemptible 13. surreptitious
sneer... 4. gibe, jeer, mock 5. fleer,
flout, laugh, scoff, scorn
sneer, expressive... 8. sardonic
snell... 4. keen 5. acute, eager, quick,
sharp, snood, swift 6. active, biting,
severe 7. caustic, pungent
8. piercing
snicker... 5. laugh, neigh, sneer
6. giggle, nicker, tittle, whinny
7. snigger 8. laughter
sniff... 4. nose 5. scent, smell, snuff
6. detect, inhale 7. sniffle 8. sibilate,
smell out 14. show of contempt
snifter... 3. nip 4. dram, good

5. drink, sniff, snort 6. snivel
9. excellent
snip... 3. bit, cut 4. clip, snap
5. notch, piece, shred 8. fragment,
particle
snipe (pert to)...
eel.. 6. thread
flock.. 4. wisp
game.. 6. godwit
hawk.. 7. harrier
verb.. 7. shoot at 10. sharpshoot
snippy... 4. curt, tart 5. brief, sharp
8. snippety, snobbish
11. fragmentary 12. supercilious
snirl... 5. gnarl, snare 6. tangle
7. wrinkle
snitch... 5. pinch, steal 6. betray,
inform, pilfer, snatch, tattle
8. informer, particle
snob... 4. prig 7. cobbler, parvenu
8. bluenose, commoner, courtier
9. sycophant
snobby, snobbish... 5. proud
6. uppish 7. haughty 8. arrogant
9. exclusive 11. overbearing
snood... 5. snell 6. fillet 7. hairnet
snook... 4. fish 5. smell 6. robalo,
search 9. barracuda
snoop... 3. pry 4. nose 5. prowl,
sneak 6. meddle 7. meddler
8. busybody 10. sneak thief
snooze... 3. nap 4. doze 5. sleep
6. cuddle, nuzzle, siesta 7. snoozle,
snuggle
snore, snoring... 4. rale 5. sleep
7. stertor 8. rhonchus, sibilate
10. sibilation, stertorous 15. hoarse
breathing
snort... 5. drink, grunt, laugh, snore
snotty... 5. dirty, nasty 6. offish,
snooty 7. high-hat 9. offensive
12. contemptible, supercilious
snow... 4. firn, neve 5. opium
8. narcotic 12. interference
snow (pert to)...
bunting.. 5. finch 9. snowflake
glacial.. 4. firn, neve
grouse, quail.. 9. ptarmigan
house.. 5. igloo
leopard.. 5. ounce
lily.. 6. violet (white)
living in.. 5. nival
mouse.. 4. vole 7. lemming
ref to.. 5. nival
ridges.. 8. sastrugi (zastrugi)
runner.. 3. ski 4. sled
shoe.. 3. pac 7. webfoot
sliding.. 9. avalanche
slope.. 8. glissade
snub... 3. cut 5. check, quell, scold
6. cut off, ignore, rebuff, rebuke,
slight 7. neglect, shorten 8. restrain
9. reprimand 10. inhalation
snuff... 5. scent, smell, sniff 6. draw
in, inhale, snoose 7. tobacco
(pulverized), umbrage 10. extinguish,
inhalation
snuff (pert to)...
a candle.. 4. snot
box.. 4. mull 9. tabatière
color.. 10. mummy brown
type.. 6. rappee 8. Maccaboy

10. Copenhagen

snug... 4. cozy, neat, safe, trim
5. close, tight 6. secure 7. compact
8. homelike, reticent 9. concealed,
secretive 10. prosperous
11. comfortable

snuggle... 6. cuddle, nestle

sny (shipbuilding)... 5. curve (of plank)

so... 2. as 3. how 4. ergo, thus, very
5. hence 6. if only 7. because
8. likewise, provided 9. therefore
11. accordingly, in order that
12. consequently

so (pert to)...
far.. 3. yet 7. thus far 8. until now
Latin.. 3. sic
so be it.. 4. Amen
to speak.. 8. as it were
12. figuratively

soak... 3. dip, sog, sop, wet 4. sock
5. souse, steep 6. drench, imbrue,
strike, tipple 7. extract, immerse
8. drunkard, macerate, marinate,
permeate, saturate 9. percolate
10. overcharge

soap... 4. sapo, suds, wash 5. bribe
6. lather 7. bribery 8. cleanser,
flattery 9. slush fund

soap (pert to)...
box.. 4. dais 5. stage 8. platform
convert to.. 8. saponify
fish.. 10. lizard fish
frame bar.. 4. sess
ingredient.. 3. lye
liniment (camphorated).. 9. opodeldoc
making.. 14. saponification
mottled.. 8. Eschwege (Eschweg)
opera.. 6. serial 9. broadcast
13. network serial
plant.. 5. amole
soft.. 8. flattery

soar... 3. fly 4. flit, rise, wing 5. float,
plane 6. ascend, aspire, be high
9. transcend

soaring... 6. flight 7. gliding, planing,
winging 8. essorant 9. skyriding
10. ballooning

sob... 3. cry 4. bawl, weep
6. boohoo, simper 7. whimper
9. shed tears

sobeit... 4. amen 8. provided

sober... 4. calm, cool, dark, sane
5. grave, quiet, staid 6. gentle,
sedate, solemn, somber, subdue,
temper 7. chasten, earnest, regular,
serious 8. composed, moderate,
sensible 9. abstinent, collected,
dignified, temperate 10. abstemious,
thoughtful 11. impassioned
13. unintoxicated

sobriety... 6. sanity 9. composure,
restraint, soberness 10. abstinence,
moderation, temperance
11. seriousness

sobriquet... 5. alias, title 6. byname
7. epithet 8. cognomen, nickname
11. appellation

sociable... 5. party 7. affable
8. familiar, friendly, informal
9. reception 10. accessible,
gregarious 13. communicative,
companionable

social... 3. tea 5. party 6. smoker
9. convivial, gathering
13. companionable

social (pert to)...
career.. 5. debut
class.. 4. clan, sept 5. caste
6. estate
ethics.. 6. morals 9. standards
10. principles
function.. 3. bee, tea 4. ball 5. party
6. soiree 7. reunion 9. reception
gathering, men.. 4. stag 6. smoker
group.. 4. sept 5. tribe 6. ethnos
8. smart set 10. upper crust
11. cafe society 13. kaffeeklatsch
insect.. 3. ant, bee
outcast.. 5. leper 6. pariah
standing.. 6. estate
system.. 6. regime

socialist... 3. Red 8. Nihilist
9. anarchist, communist
10. Bolshevist 12. collectivist

society... 5. union 7. company
8. alliance, populace 9. community
10. fellowship 11. association,
partnership 13. companionship,
confederation, participation

society (pert to)...
bud.. 3. deb
Chinese.. 4. Tong
German.. 6. Verein
high.. 5. elite 10. upper crust
Italian.. 6. maffia (mafia)
of Friends.. 7. Quakers
secret.. 5. lodge, Order

Society Islands...
capital.. 7. Papeete
chief island.. 6. Tahiti
site.. 12. South Pacific

Socrates (pert to)...
birthplace.. 6. Athens
disciple of.. 5. Plato
famed as.. 7. teacher 11. Grecian
sage
wife.. 9. Xanthippe (Xantippe)

sod... 4. soil, turf 5. divot, glebe,
sward 7. stratum 10. greensward

soda... 3. sal 8. beverage 9. saleratus,
saltpeter

sodden... 5. drunk, moist, soggy
6. soaked, stewed, stupid
7. drunken, steeped 9. saturated
11. intoxicated

sodium (pert to)...
carbonate.. 4. soda 5. borax, trona
7. sal soda, saltcat
chloride.. 3. sal, tar 4. NaCl, salt
nitrate.. 5. niter
salicylate.. 8. medicine
symbol.. 2. Na

sofa... 5. couch, divan 6. lounge,
settee 7. dos-à-dos 8. causeuse,
love seat 9. davenport, tête-à-tête
12. chesterfield

soft... 4. easy, limp, weak 5. bland,
downy, mushy, pulpy 6. dreamy,
gentle, placid, silken, supple, tender
7. clement, ductile, lenient, lightly,
quietly, squashy, velvety 8. flexible,
gullible, merciful, tranquil
9. temperate, tractable
10. effeminate, peacefully

11. comfortable, sentimental,
sympathetic 13. compassionate
soft (pert to)...
cancer.. 11. encephaloma
coal.. 10. bituminous
food.. 3. pap
head.. 9. simpleton
job.. 4. snap 8. sinecure
mass.. 4. pulp
music.. 5. dulce, piano
palate.. 4. cion 5. uvula, velum
pedal.. 3. ban 4. curb 6. subdue
8. tone down
soap.. 7. blarney 8. blandish, flattery
9. wheedling
spoken.. 4. mild 5. suave
soften... 4. melt, thaw 5. allay, malax,
relax 6. affect, lenify, pacify, relent,
soothe, temper, weaken 7. appease,
assuage, cushion, mollify, relieve
8. emoliate, enervate, enfeeble,
macerate, mitigate, modulate
9. alleviate, meliorate 11. tranquilize
soften (pert to)...
by kneading.. 5. malax
by soaking.. 8. macerate
leather.. 5. sammy (sam)
skins.. 3. taw
temper.. 6. relent
softening... 7. lenient 8. emulsive
9. relenting, relieving, tempering
10. lightening, mitigating
softening of the brain... 8. dementia
softhearted... 4. kind 6. tender
8. merciful
softly... 3. low 5. sotto 6. easily,
gently 10. delicately
13. unobtrusively
soggy... 3. wet 4. damp 5. heavy
6. soaked, sodden, watery
9. saturated
soil... 4. clay, daub, dirt, land, loam,
sand, spot 5. adobe, dirty, earth,
glebe, gumbo, humus, stain, sully
6. bedaub, bemire, ground, region,
smirch, vilify 7. begrime, besmear,
corrupt, debauch, pollute, tarnish
8. alluvium 9. bedraggle, bespatter
11. contaminate 12. fuller's earth
soil (pert to)...
barren.. 4. arid, gall 8. lifeless
goddess of.. 7. Demeter
kind of.. 4. clay, lair, loam, malm
5. adobe, humus
oneself.. 4. moil
poetic.. 5. glebe
sojourn... 4. bide, stay, stop 5. abide
6. reside 8. abidance, stop over
11. peregrinate
solace... 5. allay, amuse, cheer
6. soothe 7. assuage, comfort,
console 9. alleviate, entertain
10. relaxation 11. consolation
solan... 5. goose 6. gannet
solar (pert to)...
deity.. 2. Ra 3. Shu (Su) 6. Helios
disk.. 4. aten
exposure.. 9. sunstroke 10. heatstroke
halo.. 6. nimbus 7. aureole
12. vesica piscis
plexus.. 10. stomach pit
system.. 6. bodies, planet

15. celestial bodies
system apparatus.. 6. orrery
year.. 5. epact
soldier... 3. ant 5. cadet, poilu
6. galoot 7. fighter, private, regular,
trooper, veteran, warrior
8. gendarme, servitor 9. combatant,
grenadier, musketeer 11. enlisted
man
soldier (pert to)...
Algeria.. 6. Zouave
cavalryman.. 6. lancer 7. dragoon,
trooper
Croatian.. 5. Croat
field worker.. 6. sapper
flask.. 7. canteen
French.. 5. poilu
Gaelic.. 4. Kern
girl.. 3. WAC (Army)
Gr Myth.. 8. Myrmidon
hireling.. 9. mercenary
Ind (Brit).. 5. sepoy
Ind (Brit), with own horse.. 8. silladar
Moroccan.. 5. askar
of fortune.. 7. Hessian 10. adventurer
Prussian.. 5. uhlan
slang.. 6. galoot 7. chicken
8. shackman
soldiers, soldier's...
body of.. 5. troop 6. cohort
7. brigade, company, platoon
captured, wounded.. 6. losses
flask.. 7. canteen
Maryland (Rev War).. 10. macaronies
overcoat.. 6. capote
quarters.. 7. billets 8. barracks
Three.. 5. tales (by Kipling)
vacation.. 4. pass 5. leave
8. furlough
sole... 3. one 4. base, fish, only
5. alone, slade 6. entire, lonely,
single, unique 8. desolate, isolated,
solitary, unshared 9. exclusive,
unmarried, unmatched
10. underframe
sole (pert to)...
cookery.. 8. Marguéry
foot.. 4. vola 6. planta
hand (palm).. 4. vola
pert to.. 7. plantar
plow.. 5. slade
toward the sole.. 7. plantad
solecism... 5. error 7. blunder
9. barbarism, deviation
11. impropriety
solemn... 3. sad 5. grave, pious,
sober 6. august, devout, formal,
gloomy, ritual, silent 7. earnest,
serious, stately, sublime 8. funereal
9. dignified 10. ceremonial,
devotional 11. ceremonious,
reverential 12. awe-inspiring
solemnity... 4. pomp 7. dignity,
sadness 8. ceremony 9. formality
10. importance
solicit... 3. ask, beg 4. lure, seek,
tout 5. claim, court, crave, plead
6. accost, demand, invite, obtain
7. beseech, canvass, entreat,
implore, request 8. campaign,
petition 9. challenge, importune,
panhandle, prosecute 10. supplicate

solicitor... 6. barker, lawyer 8. attorney
9. canvasser
solicitude... 4. care, coda, heed
7. anxiety, caution, concern
9. attention 11. carefulness
12. apprehension
15. considerateness
solid... 4. cone, cube, firm, full, good,
hard 5. dense, level, sound, stiff
6. stable, strong 7. uniform
8. complete, resolute, sensible,
sterling 9. estimable, unanimous
10. dependable, inflexible
11. homogeneous, responsible,
substantial, trustworthy
solid (pert to)...
comb form.. 6. stereo
geometrical.. 5. prism
seven–faced.. 11. heptahedron
six–faced.. 4. cube
tapering.. 6. cone 7. pyramid
solidarity... 5. unity 10. correality
11. nationality 12. completeness
solidity... 5. unity 6. volume
7. density 8. firmness, hardness,
solvency, strength 9. solidness,
stability 11. compactness
12. completeness 13. dependability
14. substantiality
solidum... 4. dado 9. entire sum
soliloquy... 4. poem 9. discourse,
monologue 16. talking to oneself
solitaire... 8. Canfield
solitary... 3. one 4. lone, only, sole
5. alone, eremo (comb form)
6. hermit, lonely, single 7. recluse
8. desolate, lonesome 10. individual
12. unfrequented
solitude... 6. desert 7. privacy, retreat
9. aloneness, isolation, seclusion
10. loneliness, wilderness
solo accompaniment... 9. obbligato
Solomon (pert to)...
author of (reputed).. 8. Proverbs
9. Canticles 12. Ecclesiastes
15. Wisdom of Solomon
called also.. 8. Koheleth 11. The
Preacher
famed as.. 4. sage 7. wise man
12. King of Israel
father.. 5. David
literally.. 9. peaceable
mother.. 9. Bathsheba
Solomon Islands site... 9. South Seas
solon... 4. sage 8. lawmaker
9. statesman
solstice... 5. limit 13. farthest point
(from equator)
solution... 3. key 6. answer 7. solving
8. analysis 10. denouement,
resolution 11. explanation
15. disentanglement
solution (pert to)...
alkaline.. 3. lye
antiseptic.. 5. eusol
saline.. 5. brine
strength.. 5. titer (titre)
Somaliland...
capital.. 7. Berbera
desert.. 4. Aror
people.. 6. Somali 7. Hamitic
port.. 5. Zeila 6. Bulhar

Relig.. 10. Mohammedan
somber, sombre... 3. sad 4. dark
5. grave 6. solemn 7. austere
9. depressed 10. depressing,
foreboding, lackluster, melancholy
11. dark–colored
some... 3. any, one 5. about 6. plural,
suffix 9. several 10. indefinite, more
or less 13. approximately
somebody... 6. person 7. big name
8. luminary 9. celebrity, personage
somersault... 4. flip, leap 8. somerset
9. cartwheel 10. end over end
something... 6. object 8. somewhat
9. personage 12. in some degree
something (pert to)...
abnormal.. 5. freak 11. monstrosity
12. malformation
else.. 10. irrelevant
extra.. 5. bonus 6. bounty
7. premium 9. lagniappe
found.. 5. trove 11. serendipity
13. treasure–trove
frightening.. 7. bugbear
heavy.. 4. onus 9. ponderant
illogical.. 7. alogism
imagined.. 5. story 7. figment
inserted.. 4. gore 5. inset, wedge
like.. 7. related, similar 8. somewhat
poisonous.. 4. upas 5. snake
similar.. 8. analogue
small.. 3. dot, jot 4. atom, iota, whit
6. tittle
soothing.. 7. unction
superfluous.. 5. luxus 6. luxury
unexplained.. 7. mystery
unfinished.. 4. quab
somewhat... 4. part 6. little, partly,
rather 12. in some degree
somnifacient... 4. drug 8. hypnotic,
sedative 9. soporific
somniloquy... 12. sleep talking
somnolence... 10. drowsiness,
sleepiness
somnus... 5. sleep
Somnus (pert to)...
brother.. 4. Mors (Death)
known also as.. 6. Hypnos
son of.. 3. Nox (Night)
son, son of (pert to)...
a gun.. 5. rogue 6. fellow, wretch
Anak.. 5. giant
a Scot.. 3. Mac
God.. 11. Jesus Christ
Heaven (China).. 7. Emperor
in–law.. 5. gener
in Trinity.. 6. second (person)
Jacob.. 4. Levi
Man.. 4. male 6. mortal
Odin.. 2. Ve
Odysseus.. 9. Telegonus
Priam.. 5. Paris
reference to.. 3. ben 4. fils 5. scion
6. filial 9. offspring 10. descendant
Seth.. 4. Enos
the soil.. 6. farmer 7. peasant
youngest.. 5. cadet
sonance... 4. tune 5. sound
7. sonancy
sonant... 5. sound, tonic, vocal
6. voiced 8. sounding 9. intonated
song... 3. air, lay, ode 4. aria, leed,

lilt, noel, poem, tune 5. carol, chant,
ditty, melos, troll, verse 6. ballad,
melody, strain, trifle 7. chantey
(chanty), descant 8. canticle, pittance
9. cabaletta
song (pert to)...
 after.. 5. epode
 Bib.. 8. canticle 11. Song of Songs
  13. Song of Solomon
 boat, gondolier.. 7. chantey (chanty)
 choral Muse.. 11. Terpsichore
 collection.. 9. anthology
  10. cancionero
 college.. 4. glee
 depressing.. 5. blues
 evening.. 6. vesper 8. evensong,
  serenade
 French.. 7. chanson
 funeral.. 5. dirge, elegy 6. lament
  8. threnody 9. epicedium
 gay.. 4. lilt
 German.. 4. lied 9. Kunstlied
 gypsy.. 10. zingaresca
 Italian.. 7. canzone
 lament.. 8. threnody
 love.. 5. lyric 6. ballad 8. madrigal,
  serenade
 merry.. 4. lilt
 morning.. 5. matin
 mountaineer.. 5. yodel
 pert to.. 5. melic
 praise.. 5. carol, paean (pean)
 sacred.. 4. hymn 5. chant, motet,
  psalm 6. anthem
 sailor's.. 7. chantey (chanty)
  9. barcarole
 short.. 7. arietta
 simple.. 6. ballad
 words.. 6. lyrics
songbird... 4. lark 5. mavis, robin,
 veery 6. canary, oriole, thrush
 8. throstle 11. mockingbird
sonic recorder... 9. echograph
sonnet... 4. poem, song 5. verse
sonnet (pert to)...
 first eight lines.. 5. octet
 last six lines.. 6. sestet
 two quatrains.. 10. Petrarchan
sonorous... 4. loud 6. tonous
 7. ringing 8. resonant 9. melodious
 10. impressive, resounding
sonsy, sonsie... 5. buxom, happy
 6. comely 11. good-natured
sontag... 4. cape 6. jacket
soon... 3. ere 4. anon 5. early, later
 6. at once 7. betimes, erelong,
 quickly, readily, shortly 8. promptly,
 speedily 9. certainly, presently
 11. immediately
Sooner State... 8. Oklahoma
sooner than... 3. ere 6. before
soot... 5. smut, stup 5. black, grime,
 smoke 6. carbon, smudge 7. residue
 9. lampblack
soothe... 3. pet 4. calm, lull 5. allay,
 quiet 6. pacify, please, solace
 7. assuage, compose, mollify, relieve,
 satisfy 8. mitigate, palliate
 9. alleviate 11. tranquilize
soother... 4. balm 6. luller
 7. anodyne, placebo 8. lenitive,
 pacifier, sedative 9. flatterer

soothing... 5. balmy, sirup (syrup)
 6. dulcet, gentle 7. calming
 8. lenitive, sedative 9. appeasing,
 demulcent 13. tranquilizing
soothsayer... 4. seer 5. augur, vatis
 6. mantis 7. diviner, prophet
 8. Chaldean, haruspex 9. Cassandra
 13. praying insect 14. prognosticator
sooty (pert to)...
 brown.. 6. bister 8. teakwood
 color.. 5. black
 mangabey.. 6. monkey
 pert to.. 9. albatross 10. fuliginous
 petrel.. 7. skimmer 10. shearwater
sophistical... 8. captious 9. deceptive,
 sophistic
sophistication... 9. sophistry
 10. corruption, experience
 11. worldliness 13. ungullibility
soporific... 4. drug 6. drowsy, opiate
 7. anodyne 8. hypnotic, narcotic,
 sedative 11. somniferous 12. sleep
 inducer, somnifacient
soprano (operatic)... 4. Alda, Bori,
 Lind, Pons 5. Calvé, Eames
 6. Callas, Steber
sora... 4. rail 5. crake
sorcerer... 4. mage 5. Magus
 6. wizard 7. diviner 8. conjurer,
 magician 11. necromancer
sorceress... 3. hex 5. Circe, lamia,
 Medea, witch 6. Gorgon 7. vampire
 12. Witch of Endor
sorcery... 5. magic, obeah, spell
 6. voodoo 8. pishogue 9. diablerie,
 diabolism 10. black magic,
 necromancy, witchcraft
sordid... 3. low 4. base, mean, vile
 5. gross 6. filthy, menial 7. ignoble,
 servile, squalid 8. sluttish, wretched
 10. despicable, slatternly
 12. contemptible
sore... 4. pain, sair 5. angry, vexed,
 wound 6. tender 7. painful
 8. abrasion, inflamed, offended
 9. irritated, vexatious 11. distressing
 12. inflammation
soreness... 4. ache 5. anger
 8. vexation 10. bitterness, tenderness
 11. painfulness 12. irritability
sorghum... 4. milo 5. durra (dari),
 grain, sorgo 6. imphee, shallu
 8. feterita
sorority... 4. club 7. society
 10. fellowship, sisterhood
sorrel... 3. oca 4. buck, herb 5. color
 (horse), Rumex 7. roselle
Sorrento, Italy (pert to)...
 anc name.. 9. Sorrentum
 famed as.. 6. resort
 famed for.. 9. cathedral
 site.. 11. Bay of Naples
sorrow... 3. rue, woe 4. sigh, teen,
 weal 5. dolor, grief, mourn 6. grieve,
 lament, misery, repent 7. remorse,
 trouble 8. calamity, distress,
 egrimony, mourning 9. adversity,
 penitence 10. affliction, contrition
 11. lamentation, tribulation
 12. disconsolate, wretchedness
sorrowful... 3. sad 4. blue 5. drear,
 sadly 6. dismal, dolent, dreary, rueful

7. doleful, grieved, tearful, unhappy
8. mournful 9. plaintive 10. afflictive,
melancholy 11. distressing
12. disconsolate

sorry... 3. sad 4. hurt 5. vexed
6. dismal, gloomy, regret 7. chagrin,
painful, pitiful, unhappy 8. contrite,
grievous, mournful, penitent,
shameful, wretched 9. afflicted,
mortified, regretful, worthless
10. displeased, melancholy
12. disappointed

sort... 3. ilk, way 4. cull, kind, rank
5. blend, class, grade, group
6. assort, manner, nature, strain
7. quality, species, variety 8. classify,
separate 9. character 11. description

sortie... 4. raid 5. foray, sally
6. attack

sottish... 4. dull 6. stupid 7. doltish,
drunken, foolish 8. bibulous
9. senseless

sotto (It)... 5. below, under

sotto voce... 5. aside 8. secretly
9. privately, undertone 14. under the
breath

soubrette... 9. lady's maid
10. intrigante 11. maidservant

soudagur... 8. merchant
10. shopkeeper

soul... 2. ba, ka 3. ego, God 4. life
5. anima 6. pneuma, spirit
7. essence 8. inspirer 9. substance
10. embodiment 15. exemplification,
personification

soul (pert to)...
beatified.. 5. saint
destiny of.. 8. theodicy
dwelling place.. 2. po
Egypt.. 2. Ba
Hindu.. 5. atman 7. jivatma
lost.. 9. âme damnée, the damned
maligners.. 7. Harpies
of mud.. 9. âme de boue
personified.. 6. Psyche
transmigration.. 7. rebirth
13. reincarnation

sound... 3. bam, cry, hum 4. bong,
hale, honk, rale, ring, sane, test,
tone, toot 5. drone, noise, plumb,
probe, snore, valid, whole 6. intact,
jingle, report, robust, stable, sturdy
7. feel out, perfect, resound
8. flawless, reliable, susurrus
9. undamaged 10. scrutinize
11. trustworthy

sound (pert to)...
addition to word end.. 8. paragoge
adventitious.. 4. rote
atonic.. 4. surd
dashing.. 5. swash
discordant.. 6. jangle 9. cacophony
drum, beating.. 8. rataplan
explosion.. 6. report
fixed.. 5. toned
flogging.. 6. larrup
harsh.. 3. caw 4. bray 5. creak,
twang 7. stridor 9. cacophony
insect's.. 5. chirr
loud.. 4. peal 5. blare, clang
low.. 3. hum 4. moan 5. drone

metallic.. 4. ping, ting 5. clank, clink,
twank 6. tinkle
pert to.. 5. tonal 6. sonant
10. acoustical
prosody.. 4. rime (rhyme)
reflected.. 4. echo
sharp.. 3. pop 7. rat–a–tat, tapping
shrill.. 5. reedy
sibilant.. 4. hiss
similar.. 8. assonant
small.. 4. peep 6. rustle
surf.. 4. rote 5. swish
throwing.. 8. abat–sons
trumpet.. 7. clarion
warning.. 5. alarm, siren 6. tocsin
whispering.. 8. susurrus
without.. 8. assonant
with rhythm.. 5. music

sounding... 5. depth 6. sonant
7. ringing 8. sonation
10. resounding

soundness... 5. truth 6. sanity
8. solidity, solvency, strength
9. integrity, rectitude, stability
10. heartiness 11. healthiness

soup... 3. fog 5. broth, purée
6. bisque, potage 7. pottage
8. consommé 10. oyster stew
12. mulligatawny

soupçon... 5. taste 7. portion
9. suspicion 10. suggestion

soup dish... 6. tureen

sour... 3. wry 4. acid, tart 5. acerb,
acrid 6. acetic, bitter, morose, off
key, rancid 7. acetose, acidify,
crabbed, pungent, tainted
8. acescent, embitter 9. acidulous
10. astringent, unpleasant

sour (pert to)...
aspect.. 4. dour, hard 6. sullen
berry.. 4. cranberry
bread.. 8. leavened
cherry.. 7. morello
stomach.. 4. acor
turn sour.. 5. prill 6. bleeze

source... 4. font, germ, mine, rise,
root, seed 5. cause, fount 6. origin,
parent, quarry 8. fountain
9. beginning 10. wellspring
12. fountainhead

source (pert to)...
income.. 7. revenue
insecticides.. 9. sabadilla
iodine.. 4. kelp
ipecac.. 4. evea
metal.. 3. ore
opium.. 5. poppy
rubber.. 3. ule

South Africa... see also *South African*
capital.. 8. Cape Town, Pretoria
city.. 6. Durban 9. Germiston
division.. 5. Natal 9. Transvaal
14. Cape of Good Hope 15. Orange
Free State
exports.. 4. gold 8. diamonds
legislature seat location.. 8. Cape
Town
people.. 5. Boers 7. British, Kaffirs
10. Hottentots 11. Afrikänders
(Dutch)
river.. 4. Vaal 6. Orange

South African (pert to)...

antelope.. 3. gnu 5. eland, oribi,
peele.. 6. rhebok 7. sassaby
armadillo.. 4. para
ass (wild).. 6. quagga
bird.. 4. taha
camp.. 6. laager
Cape ash.. 9. essenhout
cocktail.. 9. sundowner
cony.. 3. das
council.. 4. Raad
dialect.. 4. Taal 9. Afrikaans
diamond (blue–white).. 5. jager
fox.. 4. asse 5. caama
grass hut.. 8. rondawel (rondavel)
grassland.. 4. veld (veldt) 8. bushveld
mountain, hill.. 3. kop
snake.. 8. eggeater
tableland.. 5. karoo
tree (dogwood).. 7. assagai (assegai)
tribe.. 4. Zulu 5. Bantu
village.. 5. kraal
war.. 4. Boer
warrior.. 4. impi
weaverbird.. 4. taha
whip.. 7. sjambok
South American (pert to)...
aborigine.. 6. Arawak
animal.. 2. ai 4. paca 5. llama, sloth,
tapir 6. jaguar 8. anteater
9. armadillo
armadillo.. 4. apar (apara)
10. pichiciago (burrowing)
arrow poison.. 6. curare (curari)
balsam.. 4. tolu
bellbird.. 8. arapunga 9. campanero
bird.. 4. rara, taha 5. agami, arara,
chaja, macaw 6. barbet 7. oilbird,
seriema, tinamou 8. bellbird, boatbill,
caracara, guacharo, puffbird
blanket.. 6. serape
cloth.. 4. crea
dog (wild).. 7. agouara
drink.. 5. assai
fiber.. 6. yachan
fish.. 4. paru 7. scalare 8. arapaima
hare, rabbit.. 6. tapeti
Indian.. 2. Ge (Gesan) 3. Ona 4. Inca
5. Carib 6. Tapuya (50 tribes)
knife.. 7. machete
leader.. 6. Franco 7. Pizarro
liberator.. 7. Bolivar
mammal.. 5. llama, tapir 6. alpaca
8. kinkajou
marmoset.. 7. tamarin
monkey.. 3. sai 4. saki, titi 5. araba
8. orabassu 9. barrigudo
mountain.. 5. Andes
native.. 5. Carib
ostrich.. 4. rhea
palm.. 5. assai 12. chiquichiqui
parrot.. 5. macaw
plains.. 6. llanos, pampas
plainsman.. 7. llanero
plant.. 6. ipecac 11. ipecacuanha
poison.. 6. curare
rabbit.. 6. tapeti
river.. 3. Apa 4. Acre, Pará 5. Plata
6. Paraná
rodent.. 5. coypu 6. agouti (agouty)
8. capibara, viscacha, vizcacha
10. chinchilla
snake.. 4. lora 5. aboma 8. anaconda

10. bushmaster
stork.. 7. maguari
tinamou.. 7. tataupa
toucan.. 7. aracari
trumpeter.. 5. agami
tuber.. 3. oca
vulture.. 6. condor
weapon.. 4. bola
wild cat.. 4. eyra
wind.. 7. pampero
South Carolina
capital.. 8. Columbia
city.. 8. Beaufort 10. Charleston
11. Spartanburg
monument.. 10. Fort Sumter
mountain.. 9. Blue Ridge, Sassafras
resort.. 11. Myrtle Beach
State admission.. 6. Eighth
State motto.. 13. Dum Spiro, Spero
(While I Breathe, I Hope)
State nickname.. 8. Palmetto
State secession.. 5. First (1860)
South Dakota...
capital.. 6. Pierre
city.. 5. Huron 8. Deadwood 9. Rapid
City 10. Sioux Falls
Indians.. 5. Brule, Sioux
mine (US largest).. 9. Homestake
monument.. 10. Mt Rushmore
mountain.. 10. Black Hills, Harney
Peak
pheasant capital.. 5. Huron
river.. 5. White 8. Cheyenne, Missouri
State admission.. 8. Fortieth (or
Thirty–ninth)
State flower.. 12. pasqueflower
State motto.. 21. Under God the
People Rule
State nickname.. 6. Coyote
8. Sunshine
topography.. 8. Bad Lands 10. Black
Hills
southeast wind... 5. Eurus
southern... 7. austral
Southern (pert to)...
Buddhism.. 8. Hinayana
Chariot.. 13. Southern Cross
Cross.. 4. Crux 12. Stars and Bars
Crown.. 15. Corona Australis
dish.. 4. pone 7. catfish, hoecake
11. hush puppies
shrub.. 8. magnolia, oleander
States.. 5. Dixie
Southenmost city... 12. Puerto Arenas
(Chile)
South Pole bird... 4. skua 7. penguin
South Pole constellation... 4. Pavo
South Sea... 12. Pacific Ocean
South Sea Bubble... 6. scheme
(1720) 10. stock fraud (Eng)
South Wales people... 7. Silures
southwest wind... 4. afer
south wind... 5. Notus
souvenir... 5. relic, token 6. memory,
trophy 7. memento 8. keepsake,
memorial, reminder 11. remembrance
12. recollection, remembrancer
sovereign... 5. chief, liege, regal, ruler
6. divine, prince, ruling 7. empress,
monarch, supreme 8. princely,
superior, suzerain 9. effectual, gold
piece, paramount, potentate

11. controlling, independent
sovereign (pert to)...
claim.. 11. seigniorage
coin.. 4. skiv
decree.. 5. arrêt
pardon.. 7. amnesty
petty.. 8. tetrarch
power.. 6. throne
sovereignty... 5. realm 6. diadem,
empery, empire 7. dynasty, scepter
(sceptre) 8. dominion 9. supremacy
Soviet, Russian (pert to)...
committee.. 9. presidium
farm.. 7. sovkhoz (sovkhose)
government.. 9. Communism,
Sovietism 10. Bolshevism
hero.. 5. Lenin 6. Stalin
newspaper.. 6. Pravda 8. Izvestia
police, secret service.. 4. Ogpu
8. Gay–Pay–Oo
sow... 3. pig 4. gilt, seed 5. plant
7. implant, scatter 8. disperse,
squander 9. broadcast
10. salamander 11. disseminate
sow bug... 6. slater
sow thistle... 7. Sonchus
soybean... 4. Soja 8. soya bean
soybean enzyme... 5. urase 6. urease
spa... 3. Ems 4. Bath 5. Baden
6. Bilina (Bilin)
space... 3. gap 4. area, rank, room,
time, void 5. blank, inane, niche,
place, range 6. areola, areole,
degree, extent, vacuum 7. arrange,
expanse 8. capacity, distance, interval
9. concourse
space (pert to)...
architectural.. 6. metope 8. pediment
around a house.. 5. ambit
blank.. 7. hiatus, lacuna
botany (leaves).. 6. areola
larynx.. 7. glottis
man.. 9. astronaut, cosmonaut,
rocketman
occupied.. 6. volume
postage stamp triangle.. 8. spandrel
ref to.. 7. areal 8. lacunal, spatial
ship.. 6. rocket
storage.. 4. shed 5. attic, depot
6. cellar, garage 9. storeroom,
warehouse
theory.. 7. plenism
time.. 8. interval
void.. 5. chasm 7. inanity
wall.. 5. niche
zoology.. 4. lore (birds) 5. lorum
(bees)
spacious... 5. ample, broad, roomy
9. capacious, expansive, extensive
10. commodious, far and wide,
widespread 13. comprehensive
spadassin... 5. bravo 7. duelist
9. swordsman
spade... 3. dig, loy 4. spud, stag
(3–yr old), suit (cards) 5. slade
6. shovel 11. playing card
spade (pert to)...
bone.. 13. shoulder blade
fish.. 5. porgy 10. paddlefish
foot.. 4. toad
grass.. 4. rush
Irish.. 5. slane

money.. 7. Chinese (early)
peat.. 5. slade
triangular.. 5. didle
spae... 6. divine 8. foretell
Spain... see also *Spanish*
cape.. 9. Trafalgar
capital.. 6. Madrid
city.. 4. Irun 5. Cadiz 6. Malaga
7. Cordoba, Granada, Seville
8. Valencia
city cathedral.. 9. Saragossa
islands.. 5. Ceuta 6. Canary 7. Melilla
8. Balearic
mountain.. 8. Asturias, Pyrenees
old name.. 6. Iberia
palace.. 8. Escorial
river.. 4. Ebro, Muga 5. Tagus
8. Guadiana 12. Guadalquivir
span... 3. two 4. arch, join, pair, team
6. bridge, extend, length, period
(time) 7. breadth, measure, stretch
8. overarch 9. encompass
spangle... 6. aiglet, sequin 7. glitter,
sparkle 8. ornament, zecchino
spaniel... 5. trasy 8. springer
Spanish (pert to)...
arbor.. 6. ramada
battle.. 6. Armada (1588)
bayonet.. 5. yucca
boat.. 5. aviso 7. galleon (ship)
brandy.. 11. aguardiente
Christmas.. 7. Navidad
cloak.. 4. capa 5. manta 6. mantle
7. zamarra (zamarro)
corral.. 5. atajo
dance.. 5. tango 6. bolero, gitano
8. fandango, saraband
dollar.. 4. duro
fabric.. 4. crea (cotton) 5. tiraz (silk)
fortress chief.. 4. caid 7. alcaide
friend.. 5. amigo
fruit.. 8. pimiento
game.. 6. pelota 7. jai alai
garment.. 6. serape 8. mantilla
gift bag.. 6. piñata
gold.. 3. oro 8. El Dorado
governor.. 10. gobernador
grass.. 5. spart 7. esparto
gruel.. 5. atole
gypsy.. 7. zincalo
holiday.. 6. fiesta
horse.. 5. genet 6. jennet 7. caballo
hotel.. 6. posada
house.. 4. casa 6. casita
jar.. 4. olla, tina 6. tinaja
knight.. 8. cavalier 9. caballero
language.. 6. Basque 7. Catalan,
Spanish 8. Galician 9. Castilian
mausoleum.. 8. Escorial
musical instrument.. 6. atabel
8. castanet
plant.. 3. aji 8. capsicum
porridge.. 5. atole
promenade.. 5. paseo
raisin.. 4. pasa
river.. 3. ria, rio
road.. 7. camino
room.. 4. sala
shawl.. 5. manta 6. serape
sheep.. 6. merino
sherry.. 5. Xeres 7. oloroso
slaughterhouse.. 8. matadero

sorcerer.. **5.** brujo
street.. **5.** calle
three.. **4.** tres
title.. **3.** don **5.** señor **6.** señora
   7. hidalgo **8.** señorita
trail.. **6.** camino
vehicle.. **7.** tartana
watch.. **5.** reloj
watchtower.. **7.** atalaya
watchword.. **6.** alerta
watercourse.. **6.** arroyo
wind.. **6.** solano
window.. **7.** ventana
witchcraft.. **8.** brujeria
year.. **3.** ano

Spanish people ...
   chaperone.. **6.** duenna
   conqueror.. **7.** Pizarro
   dramatist.. **9.** Echegaray (Nobel Prize
     1904)
   explorer.. **7.** Mendoza
   gentleman.. **5.** señor **8.** cavalier
   9. caballero
   God.. **4.** Dios
   herdsman.. **7.** llanero **8.** ranchero
   hero.. **3.** Cid
   justice of the peace.. **7.** entrada
   king.. **6.** Aragon **8.** Alphonso
   lady.. **4.** doña **6.** señora **8.** señorita
   letter carrier.. **6.** correo
   man.. **3.** don **6.** hombre
   monk.. **5.** padre
   painter.. **4.** Dali, Goya **9.** Velasquez
   peasant.. **7.** paisano
   people.. **5.** genta
   pianist.. **6.** Iturbi
   soldier.. **8.** miquelet
   soprano.. **4.** Bori (Lucrezia)

spar... **3.** box **4.** beam, boom, gaff,
   mast, rung, yard **5.** sprit, steve
   6. timber **7.** dispute, quarrel,
   topmast, yardarm
spare... **4.** lean, thin **5.** chary, lanky
   6. afford, exempt, frugal, meager,
   scanty **7.** sparing, surplus
   8. preserve **9.** duplicate, parsimony
   10. economical, occasional
   11. superfluous **12.** parsimonious
spare time... **7.** leisure
sparing... **5.** chary **6.** frugal, meager,
   saving, scanty **7.** scrimpy, thrifty
   8. merciful, reticent, stinting
   9. scrimping **12.** parsimonious
spark... **4.** beau, fire, funk **5.** aizle,
   court, dandy, lover **6.** incite
   7. diamond, gallant, glitter, modicum,
   sparkle **8.** humorist **10.** sweetheart
   11. scintillate
sparkle... **5.** flash, gleam, glint, shine,
   trace **7.** be smart, be witty, glisten,
   glister, glitter, radiate, reflect,
   spangle, twinkle **8.** be lively
   9. coruscate **10.** effervesce,
   illuminate **11.** scintillate
   13. scintillation
sparkling... **4.** dewy **5.** crisp, witty
   6. bright, starry **7.** shining
   8. cheerful, eloquent, glittery,
   gorgeous, mousseux (wine)
   9. twinkling **10.** glittering, reflecting
   12. effervescent
sparoid fish... **4.** scup **5.** porgy

   8. sea bream **10.** sheepshead
Sparta, Greece... see also *Spartan*
   capital.. **7.** Laconia (anc)
   kingdom.. **12.** Peloponnesus
   river.. **7.** Eurotas
spartan... **5.** hardy, stoic
   10. courageous **13.** uncomplaining
Spartan (pert to)...
   army division.. **4.** mora **6.** lochus
   cipher writing.. **7.** scytale
   class (anc).. **8.** perioeci
   commander.. **7.** lochage
   dog.. **10.** bloodhound
   festival.. **6.** Carnea **7.** Carneia
   king.. **8.** Leonidas, Menelaus
   lawgiver.. **8.** Lycurgus
   magistrate.. **5.** ephor
   native.. **8.** Laconian **9.** Spartiate
   serf.. **5.** helot
spasmodic... **6.** fitful **7.** snatchy
   9. excitable, irregular **10.** convulsive
   12. intermittent **13.** highly wrought
spasmodic (pert to)...
   disease.. **5.** croup **7.** tetanus
   inspiration.. **8.** hiccough
   twitch.. **3.** tic
spat... **3.** row **4.** slap, tiff **5.** spawn
   6. gaiter, oyster, strike **7.** dispute,
   legging, quarrel **10.** oysterseed
spate... **4.** gush **5.** flood **7.** freshet,
   torrent **9.** overwhelm, rainstorm
   10. waterspout
spatial... **5.** areal **8.** sterical
   11. dimensional
spatter... **3.** wet **4.** soil, spot **5.** spurt
   6. dabble, splash **7.** sputter
   8. splutter, sprinkle
spawn... **3.** ova, roe **4.** eggs, germ,
   seed **7.** lay eggs **8.** generate
   13. numerous issue
speak... **3.** say **4.** chat, lisp, talk, tell
   5. orate, utter **6.** reveal **7.** address,
   chatter, declaim, sputter **8.** converse,
   proclaim **9.** discourse, pronounce
   10. articulate **11.** tell in words
speak (pert to)...
   affectedly.. **4.** mime **5.** mince
   against.. **6.** oppose
   boastfully.. **4.** brag **5.** vaunt
   7. enlarge **10.** exaggerate
   from memory.. **6.** recite
   ill of.. **5.** decry **8.** backbite
   9. disparage
   noisily.. **4.** rant, rime **8.** harangue
   offhand.. **11.** extemporize
   slowly.. **5.** drawl
   softly.. **7.** whisper
   under breath.. **5.** mouth **6.** mumble,
   murmur, mutter **7.** grumble
speaker... **5.** sayer **6.** lisper, orator,
   proser **8.** lecturer **9.** demagogue
   10. mouthpiece, prolocutor
   11. spellbinder
speaker of languages... **8.** linguist,
   polyglot
speaking (pert to)...
   generally.. **7.** as a rule, roughly
   12. in the long run
   13. approximately
   of.. **7.** apropos **12.** incidentally
   offhand.. **13.** extemporizing
   privately.. **7.** whisper **9.** in one's ear

11. into one's ear
publicly.. 7. oratory 11. declamation
style.. 8. fluently
spear.. 4. dart, pike, stab 5. catch,
lance 6. pierce, weapon 7. javelin,
missile 9. penetrate

spear (pert to)..
anc Teutons.. 6. framea (fram)
fish.. 3. gig 4. gaff
iron–tipped.. 7. assagai
shaped.. 7. hastate
three–pronged.. 7. trident
two–pronged.. 6. bident
spearfish.. 5. marlin 9. quillback
special... 4. rare 5. extra 6. unique
7. notable, unusual 8. concrete,
detailed, favorite, specific, uncommon
10. individual, noteworthy, particular,
restricted 11. distinctive, exceptional
13. extraordinary

special (pert to)..
ability.. 5. forte 6. talent 7. charism
8. charisma
commodity.. 6. leader 7. feature
10. best seller
edition.. 5. extra
favor.. 9. influence, privilege
train.. 5. flier 7. express
10. cannonball
specialist (pert to)...
atomic.. 9. physicist
ear.. 6. aurist 9. otologist
eye.. 7. oculist 15. ophthalmologist
medical.. 6. doctor 7. surgeon
money.. 9. economist
specialty.. 5. skill 8. aptitude,
contract 13. particularity
14. characteristic
specie.. 4. cash, coin 5. money (hard)
species... 4. kind, sort, type 5. class,
genre, genus, group 7. general,
isotope, mankind, variety 8. category,
humanity 11. Homo sapiens
12. nomenclature
specific... 5. exact, virus 6. remedy
7. limited, precise, special
8. definite, detailed, explicit, peculiar
specificity... 9. haecceity
specify... 4. name 5. limit, state
6. define, detail 8. indicate 9. be
precise, designate, enumerate,
stipulate
specimen... 4. copy 5. model, piece,
taste, token 6. person, sample,
swatch 7. example, pattern
14. representative
specious... 4. fair 5. showy 7. alleged
8. illusory, pleasing 9. plausible
10. ostensible 12. hypocritical
speck... 3. bit, dot, jot, nit 4. blot,
iota, mark, mite, mote, spot, whit
5. fleck, stain 7. blemish 8. particle
10. sand darter
speckled... 6. menald 7. mottled
9. sprinkled 10. variegated
spectacle... 4. show, view 5. scene,
sight 6. wonder 7. diorama, display,
pageant 8. panorama, spyglass
10. exhibition 14. representation
spectacles... 7. glasses
spectator... 6. espier, viewer
7. watcher, witness 8. audience,

beholder, kibitzer, looker–on, observer,
onlooker 9. bystander
specter, spectre... 4. bogy (bogey,
bogie) 5. ghost, shade, spook
6. idolum, spirit, wraith 7. eidolon,
phantom 8. illusion, phantasm,
revenant 9. apparition
spectral... 5. eerie (eery) 6. ghosty,
spooky 7. ghostly, phantom
12. apparitional
speculate... 5. guess, think 6. gamble,
ponder, wonder 8. consider,
meditate, ruminate, theorize
10. deliberate, doctrinize, philosophy
11. contemplate
speculative... 5. risky 9. uncertain
10. thoughtful 11. inquisitive,
theoretical 12. experimental
13. contemplative
speculator... 7. lookout, scalper
8. explorer, observer, theorist
12. investigator
speculum... 7. diopter 9. reflector
sped... 4. hied 5. raced 6. darted,
dashed, let fly 8. galloped, hastened
10. discharged
speech... 5. spiel 6. dilogy, orison
7. address, chatter, diction, oration
8. colloquy, harangue, language
9. elocution, utterance
12. conversation

speech (pert to)..
abusive.. 6. tirade
blunder.. 8. improper, solecism
comb form.. 4. logo
conclusion.. 10. peroration
conversational.. 13. colloquialism
defective.. 10. disphrasia
difficulty.. 9. baryphony
10. baryphonia
famous.. 9. Philippic (Demosthenes)
goddess.. 3. Vac
hasty.. 7. stammer, stumble, stutter
impediment.. 4. lisp 8. betacism,
mytacism
intemperate.. 6. tirade
loss of.. 6. alalia 7. aphasia
movements.. 9. vocimotor
parts.. 4. verb 6. adverb 9. adjective
11. conjunction, preposition
12. interjection
pompous.. 12. magniloquent
provincial.. 6. patois 7. dialect
set speech (drama).. 6. rhesis
term.. 6. zeugma 9. syllepsis
understatement.. 7. litotes
vitriolic.. 6. tirade
voiceless.. 7. spirate
without.. 4. mute 6. alogia
world.. 7. Volapük 9. Esperanto
speechless... 4. dumb, mute 6. silent
7. aphasic 8. taciturn 9. voiceless
speed... 3. fly, hie, run 4. flit, race,
zoom 5. haste, hurry, spurt 6. assist,
go fast, hasten 8. celerity, dispatch,
expedite, promptly, rapidity, velocity
9. posthaste, quickness, swiftness
10. accelerate, expedition, facilitate
12. precipitance
speedily... 4. soon 5. apace 6. presto
7. betimes, quickly, rapidly, swiftly
8. promptly 13. expeditiously

speedy ... 4. fast 5. apace, fleet, hasty,
   quick, rapid, swift 6. prompt, racing,
   sudden

spell ... 4. bout, mean, snap, tell, turn
   5. charm, magic, relay, shift
   6. glamor, relate, relief, trance
   7. explain, relieve, sorcery, syncope
   9. take turns 11. abracadabra
   12. entrancement 13. substitute for

spell (pert to) ...
   binder .. 6. orator 7. charmer, spieler
   bound .. 10. astonished, interested
     11. under a spell
   brief .. 4. snap
   in another alphabet .. 13. transliterate
   out .. 7. explain, itemize
   pretended .. 11. abracadabra
   under a spell .. 9. in a trance
     10. hypnotized, mesmerized
   with loss of letter .. 7. syncope

spend ... 3. use 4. pass 5. waste
   6. employ, expend, lavish, weaken
   7. consume, exhaust 8. disburse,
   squander 9. dissipate, sacrifice
   10. distribute

spend the summer ... 8. estivate
   (aestivate)

spendthrift ... 4. daft 6. waster
   7. spender, wastrel 8. prodigal
   10. profligate, squanderer

Spenser, Edmund (pert to) ...
   character .. 3. Una
   famed as .. 4. poet
   famed work .. 12. Faerie Queene
   poetic stanza .. 10. Spenserian

Spenser's Ireland personified ...
   5. Irene

spent ... 4. paid 5. weary 6. effete,
   used up, wasted 7. worn out
   8. consumed, lavished, tired out
   9. exhausted 10. squandered

speos ... 4. cave, tomb 6. grotto

sphenoid ... 11. wedge-shaped

sphere ... 3. orb 4. ball, star 5. arena,
   earth, field, glove, orbit, realm, scope
   6. extent, planet 7. circuit, heavens
   8. terrible 10. atmosphere
   12. jurisdiction

sphere of ...
   action .. 6. domain
   life .. 5. world
   making .. 7. orbific

spherical (pert to) ...
   aberration, free from .. 9. aplanatic
   geometry .. 10. magnitudes
   lune .. 7. portion
   magnet .. 8. terrella (terella)
   nearly .. 8. obrotund
   reference to .. 6. rotund 7. globose
     9. orbicular 15. celestial bodies
   ungula .. 5. wedge

sphericity ... 9. globosity, rotundity,
   roundness

sphinx (pert to) ...
   builder (Great Sphinx) .. 6. Khafre (IV
     Dynasty)
   Great Sphinx site .. 4. Gaza (Egypt)
   Greek myth .. 7. monster (sphinxlike)
   reference to .. 8. enigmatic
     11. inscrutable
   Zool .. 8. hawk moth

spice ... 4. dill, herb, mace, sage

5. chili, clove 6. cassia, nutmeg,
   pepper, season, stacte 7. mustard
   8. marjoram, pungency
   9. condiment, flavoring, fragrance,
   seasoning

spicy ... 3. hot 4. keen, racy, sexy
   5. balmy, natty, smart 6. risque
   7. gingery, peppery, piquant, pungent
   8. aromatic, fragrant, spirited

spider ... 3. cob, pan 5. arain
   6. Epeira, katipo, tripod, trivet
   7. pokomoo, retiary, skillet, spinner
   8. arachnid, attercop, telarian
   9. tarantula 10. black widow

spider (pert to) ...
   comb form .. 7. arachno
   crab .. 4. Maia (genus)
   fly .. 4. tick
   genus .. 4. Maia 6. Aranea
     7. Agalena, Attidae, Pholcus
     9. Drassidae
   Gr Myth .. 7. Arachne (Lydian girl)
   Latin .. 6. aranea
   leaping .. 10. saltigrade
   monkey .. 6. ateles, coaita
   nest .. 5. nidus
   scorpion .. 8. pedipalp
   scorpion appendage .. 10. pedipalpus
   study of .. 10. araneology
   web (anc) .. 8. attercop
   weblike .. 9. arachnoid
   web-spinning organ .. 9. spinneret

spieler ... 5. crier 6. barker, talker
   7. sharper, speaker 8. lecturer
   9. solicitor 10. ballyhooer

spiffy ... 4. fine, neat 5. smart
   8. splendid 9. excellent

spigot ... 3. peg, tap 5. spile, spout
   6. dossil, faucet 7. stopper

spike ... 3. cob, ear 4. brob, stab,
   tine, umbo 5. ament, prong, thorn
   6. antler, flower, pierce, spadix
   7. amentum, disable, spinule, trenail
   10. adulterate 12. tenpenny nail

spikenard ... 3. phu (Cretan) 4. herb,
   nard 8. ointment

spile ... 3. pin, rod 4. plug, tube
   5. spill, spout, stake 6. Aralia, spigot

spill ... 4. blab, fall, shed, slop
   5. flosh, waste 6. let out, splash,
   tumble 7. divulge, scatter
   8. downpour, overflow, overture
   11. tell secrets

spin ... 4. birl, fish, reel, ride, turn
   5. swirl, twirl, twist, whirl 6. extend,
   gyrate, rotate 7. prolong, revolve

spinach (wrinkled) ... 5. savoy

spinal (pert to) ...
   column .. 9. vertebrae
   cord .. 4. alba 6. myelon (marrow)
     16. medulla oblongata
   disease .. 8. myelitis 10. meningitis
   muscle (attached) .. 5. psoas

spindle ... 3. pin, rod 4. axis, axle,
   hasp 5. pivot, xeres 6. swivel
   7. mandrel

spindle-legged ... 4. lean 5. lanky
   14. spindle-shanked

spindling ... 4. long 5. gawky, leggy
   6. skinny 7. slender 11. ineffectual

spine ... 3. awn 4. axis, seta 5. chine,
   ridge, thorn 6. spirit 7. acicula,

courage, process 8. backbone,
spiculum 9. scoliosis (curvature)
12. spinal column

spinel... 5. balas (ruby) 7. mineral
8. spinelle

spineless... 4. limp, weak 5. frail
10. weak-willed 12. invertebrate

spinet... 5. piano 7. giraffe 8. virginal
10. clavichord 11. couched harp,
harpsichord

spinnaker... 4. sail

spinner... 3. top 4. liar 6. spider,
weaver 8. narrator 9. nighthawk
10. goatsucker 11. storyteller
12. whippoorwill

spinning... 6. rotary 7. strobic
8. telarian, whirling 9. revolving

spinning device... 5. jenny 7. distaff,
spindle 8. throstle

spiracle... 4. pore, vent 7. orifice
8. aperture, blowhole

spiral... 4. coil, curl 5. helix 6. galaxy,
volute 7. helical, winding 8. circling,
helicoid 9. corkscrew

spire... 4. coil, surl 5. tower, twist,
whorl 6. ascend, finial, summit
7. steeple

spire finial... 3. épi

spirit... 3. imp, pep, vim 4. dash,
élan, fire, life, mood, pixy, soul
5. demon, devil, fairy, genie, ghost,
heart, metal, pluck, Satan, shade,
spook, verve 6. animus, breath,
energy, fervor, goblin, intent, morale,
pneuma, sprite 7. bravery, courage,
essence, extract, gremlin, specter
8. spiritus 9. animation
10. enterprise, individual 11. real
meaning 12. cheerfulness
13. consciousness

spirit, spirit of (pert to)...
avarice.. 6. Mammon
bad.. 6. afreet 7. Amaimon
(Amaymon)
Egypt.. 2. ba, ka 3. akh
English folklore.. 2. po
evil.. 4. jinn 5. Aecto, jinni (jinnel)
6. Azazel, Belial, Erinys 7. Tempter
(The) 9. Beelzebub
female.. 6. undine 7. banshee
good.. 8. Eudaemon
household.. 5. Lares 15. Lares and
Penates
infatuation.. 3. Ate
knights.. 8. errantry
malignant.. 3. Ker
mockery.. 5. Momus
people.. 5. ethos
refined.. 6. elixir
tapping (theory).. 9. typtology
the air.. 5. Ariel
the sea.. 5. siren 6. Triton
7. mermaid, Neptune 9. Davy Jones

spirited... 3. gay 4. gamy, racy
5. brisk, eager, fiery 6. lively, plucky,
spunky 7. dashing, fervent
8. eloquent, generous, vigorous
9. audacious, energetic, spiritoso,
sprightly 10. mettlesome

spiritless... 4. dead, dull, meek
5. amort, vapid 6. gloomy
8. dejected, lifeless, listless

9. depressed, heartless
10. despondent, dispirited

spirits (pert to)...
Babylonian.. 5. Igigi
dwelling.. 2. po 5. Hades 7. Elysium
low.. 5. blues, dumps, gloom
8. doldrums
of the dead.. 5. Manes (Rom)
7. lemures 9. chthonian (Gr)

spiritual... 4. holy, pure, song
5. pious 6. devout, divine, sacred
7. psychic 8. churchly, internal,
platonic, spectral 9. unworldly
10. immaterial 11. disembodied,
incorporeal 12. supernatural
14. ecclesiastical, heavenly minded

spiritual (pert to)...
affinity.. 8. soul mate
apathy.. 6. acedia
being.. 3. ens 5. angel 6. seraph
darkness.. 4. Hell 5. tamas
director.. 7. confessor
meaning of words.. 7. anagoge
meeting.. 6. séance
shrine.. 7. adytum 7. sanctum

spirt... 3. jet 4. gush 5. flare, spurt
6. squirt

spit... 3. rod 4. rain 5. eject, image,
stick 6. impale, pierce, saliva,
skewer, sputum 7. hissing, spindle,
sputter 8. likeness, sprinkle, turnspit
9. exsputory 11. expectorate

spite... 3. vex 4. hate 5. pique,
shame, venom 6. enmity, malice,
offend, thwart 7. dislike, ill will
8. disgrace, dishonor 9. animosity,
cattiness, humiliate 10. resentment
11. malevolence 12. spitefulness

spiteful... 4. mean 5. catty 7. cattish
8. annoying 9. malicious, malignant
10. irritating, vindictive

spittoon... 6. pigdan 8. crachoir,
cuspidor

splash... 3. lap, wet 4. spot 5. spray,
swash 6. blotch, flouse (floush),
ripple 7. scatter, spatter, splurge
8. cut a dash, splatter 9. dashingly
14. ostentatiously

splashboard... 4. gate (false) 5. plank
6. fender, screen 9. dashboard
10. flashboard, flushboard

splay... 3. hem 4. turn 5. adorn,
carve, slant, slope 6. clumsy,
expand, spread 7. awkward, display
9. dislocate, displayed, expansion

spleen... 3. fit 4. fire, mood, whim
5. anger, ardor, freak, gland
6. malice, temper 7. impulse 8. ill
humor 10. low spirits, melancholy,
resentment 11. impetuosity

spleen (pert to)...
amarinth.. 4. weed
excision.. 13. splenectomize
reference to.. 6. lienal 7. splenic

splendid... 4. braw, fine 5. grand,
regal, showy 6. costly, superb
7. gallant, shining, sublime
8. glorious, gorgeous 9. beautiful,
brilliant, excellent, sumptuous
10. brilliance, effulgence
11. illustrious, magnificent

splendor... 4. gite, pomp 5. éclat,

glory 6. beauty, luster 7. display
8. grandeur, radiance, richness
9. pageantry, showiness
10. brilliance 12. gorgeousness,
magnificence, resplendence

splint... 4. scob, tace 5. brace, plate,
strip 6. fasten, tasset 7. confine
8. splinter

splinter... 4. chip 5. break, broom
6. shiver, sliver 7. shatter
8. fragment 9. matchwood

split... 3. cut, rit 4. chap, open, rend,
rent, rive, tear 5. break, burst, cleft,
crack, laugh, riven, wedge 6. bisect,
cleave, cloven, divide, sunder
7. dispart, divided, rupture, shatter
8. separate 9. apportion, partition
10. separation

split (pert to)...
hairs.. 7. quibble 12. discriminate
13. differentiate
into two parts.. 5. bifid 6. cloven
pea.. 3. dal 5. dahll
the divisions.. 5. share 7. average
10. compromise
up.. 5. cleft 7. disband, divorce
8. separate 9. apportion, partition

spoil... 3. mar, rot 4. loot, prey, ruin,
sack 5. botch, decay, harry
6. impair, injure, pamper 7. destroy,
estrepe, pillage, plunder, vitiate
9. frustrate

spoilation... 6. rapine 7. pillage
10. plundering, spoliation

spoiled... 3. bad 5. moldy, musty
6. addled, marred, molded, preyed,
wasted 7. botched, decayed, tainted
8. pampered, pillaged 9. plundered
12. deteriorated

spoiler... 6. robber 7. marplot
8. pillager 9. despoiler, plunderer

spoils... 4. loot, prey, swag 5. booty

spoilsport... 7. marplot 10. wet
blanket

spoke... 3. bar, pin, ray, rod 4. rung,
said 5. check, round, spake, stake
6. radius, speech 7. uttered
9. hindrance 10. impediment

spoke monotonously... 6. droned

spoken... 4. oral 5. parol
9. declaimed, ideophone (word)

spoliation... 6. rapine 7. pillage
10. spoilation

sponge... 3. dry, wet 4. bath, swab
5. erase, mooch 6. absorb, animal,
efface, eraser, extort 7. badiaga,
cleanse, sponger, zimocca
8. drunkard, parasite 9. absorbent,
sycophant 10. obliterate, porousness

sponge (pert to)...
Europe.. 7. badiaga
fruit.. 5. luffa (loofah)
Mediterranean.. 7. zimocca
opening.. 7. apopyle
orifice.. 7. osculum
young.. 5. ascon 6. rhagon

sponger... 4. sorn 6. cadger
8. parasite 10. freeloader

sponsor... 5. angel 6. backer, patron
7. finance 9. financier, guarantee,
guarantor, patronize

sponsorship... 5. aegis (egis)

8. auspices

spontaneous... 4. free 6. native
8. untaught 9. automatic, voluntary
10. self–acting 11. instinctive,
involuntary

spontoon... 4. club, pike 7. halberd,
pantoon 9. espanton, espontoon,
truncheon

spoof... 3. guy 4. fool, hoax, joke
5. trick 7. deceive, swindle
8. nonsense 9. deception

spook... 5. ghost 6. spirit 7. specter
9. hobgoblin 10. apparition

spooky... 5. eerie, weird 7. ghostly,
haunted, uncanny 8. spectral

spool... 4. reel, wind 6. bobbin
7. spindle 8. cylinder

spoon... 4. club 5. labis, ladle, lover,
ninny 6. shovel 7. fish for
8. cochlear, make love, runcible
9. simpleton

spoonbill... 5. ajaja (ayaya)
9. sandpiper

Spoon River poet... 7. Masters (E L)

spoon–shaped... 8. cochlear

spore (pert to)...
capsule, sac.. 5. ascus, theca
10. sporangium
cluster.. 5. sorus
formation.. 6. tetrad
fruit.. 7. asocarp

sport... 3. fun, toy 4. game, hunt,
jest, joke, play, romp, wear
5. dandy, mirth 6. banter, flaunt,
frolic, gamble, racing, skiing
7. contest, gambler, jesting, mockery,
pastime 8. raillery 9. amusement,
bon vivant, diversion, good loser,
plaything, sportsman 10. pleasantry,
recreation 13. entertainment

sport (pert to)...
art of (contests).. 10. agonistics
cheap.. 5. piker
of kings.. 6. racing 7. the turf

sportive... 3. gay 5. merry 7. jocular,
playful 8. frolicky, playsome
9. facetious 10. frolicsome

sports... 5. Rugby, track 6. soccer
8. baseball, football 9. athletics,
palaestra 10. acrobatics, gymnastics

sports attendance... 4. gate

sports official... 5. coach, judge
6. umpire 7. referee 8. linesman
10. timekeeper

sporty... 5. rorty, showy 6. dressy,
flashy

spot... 3. dot 4. blet, blot, flaw, mark,
site, soil 5. fleck, place, point,
speck, stain, taint 6. detect, locate,
macula, macule, stigma 7. asperse,
blemish, freckle, speckle, splotch
8. discolor, disgrace, locality,
location, position 9. bespatter,
limelight, recognize 11. predicament,
small amount

spot (pert to)...
bird.. 6. pigeon 7. red drum
8. drumfish
cards.. 3. pip
fertile.. 5. oasis
fish.. 7. pinfish
mineral.. 5. macle

on the spot.. **3.** now **4.** here
7. imperil, present **8.** promptly
payment.. **4.** cash
secluded.. **6.** alcove
sun.. **6.** lucule **7.** granule
wood.. **3.** wem
spotless... **4.** pure **5.** clean **6.** chaste
8. innocent **9.** blameless, faultless,
unsullied **10.** immaculate
11. unblemished, untarnished
14. irreproachable
spotted... **6.** espied, marked, soiled
7. dappled, guttate (droplike),
mottled, stained, sullied **8.** speckled
9. blemished, sprinkled, tarnished
11. diversified
spouse... **4.** mate, wife **5.** bride
7. consort, partner **9.** companion
10. better half
spout... **3.** jet, jut, lip **4.** dale, gush,
pawn, rant, spew **5.** erupt, spile,
spurt **6.** pledge, recite, spigot, squirt,
trough **7.** chatter, conduit, declaim
8. downpour, gargoyle (carved)
9. discharge, waterfall
10. waterspout
spouter... **5.** whale **6.** geyser **7.** oil
well, speaker **9.** declaimer
11. speechifier
sprat... **6.** garvie **7.** herring
8. sixpence
spray... **3.** jet **4.** foam **5.** stour, water
6. squirt **7.** atomize, flowers, gunfire
8. perfumer, sprinkle **9.** spindrift
10. spoondrift
spread... **3.** ted **4.** meal **5.** bruit,
feast, flare, strew, widen **6.** expand,
extent, sprawl, unfurl **8.** divulge,
radiate, scatter **8.** disperse
9. broadcast **11.** disseminate
13. advertisement
spread (pert to)...
by defamation.. **5.** libel
by report.. **6.** norate
by rumor.. **5.** noise
eagle.. **8.** boastful, insignia
9. patriotic **12.** exaggeration
out.. **3.** fan **4.** open, span **5.** flare
6. deploy
over.. **5.** cover, smear
thickly.. **7.** slather
thin.. **4.** bray
spree... **4.** lark, orgy, romp **5.** binge,
revel **6.** bender, frolic, shindy
7. wassail **8.** carousal
sprig... **4.** trim, twig **5.** scion, shoot,
smart **6.** active, spruce **8.** ornament
9. youngling
sprightly... **3.** gay **4.** airy, pert
5. alive, brisk, peart **6.** blithe, lively
7. briskly, ghostly **8.** vigorous
10. enlivening, spiritedly
11. incorporeal
spring... **3.** fly, hop, spa **4.** dart, font,
jump, leap, well **5.** shoot, spurt,
vault, young **6.** bounce, energy,
geyser, origin, season, source
9. saltation **10.** elasticity, resilience
spring (pert to)...
back.. **6.** recoil, resile **7.** rebound
of the Muses.. **7.** Pierian
ref to.. **6.** vernal

up.. **4.** grow **5.** arise, occur
6. appear, ascend **9.** originate
springing into being... **9.** renascent
springs... **4.** spas **5.** baths, fonts
6. resort (health) **7.** thermae
sprinkle... **3.** deg, dot, wet **4.** rain
5. bedew, spray, strew, water
6. bedrop, sparge, spreng **7.** baptize,
scatter **9.** bespatter
sprinkler... **11.** aspergillum (Eccl)
sprinkle with...
flour.. **6.** dredge
grit.. **4.** sand
heraldic.. **4.** semé
powder.. **4.** dust
water.. **3.** deg
sprint... **3.** run **4.** dash, race
sprite... **3.** elf, fay, hob, imp, nix
4. peri **5.** fairy, ghost, gnome, pixie,
sylph **6.** goblin, spirit **7.** brownie
9. hobgoblin **10.** apparition
sprite (pert to)...
fiction.. **5.** Ariel
Irish.. **10.** leprechaun
mischievous.. **4.** Puck
ref to.. **6.** elfish
sprocket... **5.** tooth, wheel **8.** cylinder
(toothed) **10.** projection
sprout... **3.** bud, son **4.** cion, grow
5. scion, shoot, spire, sprit
6. branch, ratoon, tiller **7.** burgeon,
upstart **8.** offshoot **9.** germinate
10. descendant
spruce... **4.** chic, neat, posh, smug,
tree, trig, trim **5.** adorn, natty, smart
6. dapper **7.** finical, smarten
8. titivate
spruce (pert to)...
beverage.. **4.** beer
black.. **7.** yew pine
fir.. **6.** Norway
genus.. **5.** Abies, Picea
Japanese.. **8.** Alcock
type.. **7.** Douglas, hemlock
white.. **8.** épinette
sprue... **5.** dross, waste **6.** thrush
7. disease **8.** psilosis **9.** asparagus
spry... **5.** agile, brisk, quick, smart
6. active, nimble **8.** vigorous
9. sprightly
spud... **5.** drill, knife, spade **6.** dagger,
paddle, potato, reamer, shovel
spume... **4.** foam, scum **5.** froth
spunky... **4.** game **5.** quick **6.** plucky,
touchy **8.** spirited **10.** courageous,
mettlesome **13.** quick-tempered
spur... **3.** egg **4.** goad, move, urge
5. drive, press, ridge, rowel, spine
6. calcar, excite, griffe, incite, needle
7. provoke **8.** stimulus **9.** instigate,
stimulate **10.** incitement
spur (pert to)...
badge.. **10.** knighthood
fowl.. **5.** quail **9.** partridge
gamecock's.. **4.** gaff **7.** gablock
mountain.. **5.** arête
pert to.. **7.** spicate
railroad.. **5.** track
wheel.. **5.** rowel
spurious... **4.** fake, sham **5.** false
6. pseudo **7.** bastard **10.** adulterate,
apocryphal, artificial, fictitious,

fraudulent 11. counterfeit
12. illegitimate 14. supposititious
spurious (pert to)...
  fruit.. 10. pseudocarp
  olive.. 9. heartwood
  rainbow.. 8. faint arc
  wing.. 7. bastard
spurn... 4. defy 5. scorn 6. reject,
  strike 7. contemn, disdain
spurt... 3. jet, jut 4. dash, gush, spew
  5. burst, spout 7. outpour, upsurge
  8. outbreak
spy... 3. pry, see 4. espy, note, tout
  5. scout, sneak, snoop, watch
  6. behold, descry, detect, search
  7. examine, snooper 8. discover,
  emissary, informer, perceive
  10. scrutinize 11. reconnoiter
spy (pert to)...
  city.. 7. Belgium
  in clothing circles.. 4. keek
  Man of.. 14. paleolithic man
  prison.. 6. mouton
squab... 3. fat 4. fowl, sofa 5. piper,
  plump 6. fat man, pigeon 7. cushion
  8. nestling 9. fledgling
squabble... 5. brawl 6. bicker, jangle
  7. contend, quarrel, wrangle
  10. disarrange (Print)
  13. collieshangie
squad... 4. team, unit 5. posse
  7. company
squalid... 4. foul, mean, poor 5. dirty
  6. filthy, sordid 7. unclean
  8. slovenly 9. repellent, repulsive
  11. squalidness 15. poverty-stricken
squall... 3. cry, row 4. blow, gale,
  gust, wail, wind, yell 6. squawk,
  squeal 9. commotion 11. disturbance
squalor... 4. dirt, mire 5. filth
  8. slovenry 9. dirtiness 10. filthiness
  11. squalidness 16. unkempt
  condition
squander... 5. waste 6. lavish
  7. scatter 8. disperse, misspend
  9. dissipate, throw away 10. run
  through
squanderer... 5. loser 7. wastrel
square... 4. even, meal 5. bribe, plaza
  6. common, honest, settle 7. exactly,
  obelisk, old fogy 8. absolute, cube
  face, directly, equalize, quadrate
  9. city block, divergent
  11. unequivocal 13. parallelogram
  14. unsophisticate
  15. straightforward
squash... 4. mash, pepo, pulp
  5. crush, gourd, press 6. cushaw,
  refute, simlin, simnel, soften
  7. cymling (cymbling), Hubbard,
  squeeze 8. pattypan, suppress
  9. crookneck 10. extinguish
  11. calabazilla
squat... 3. low 5. dumpy, pudgy,
  quash, stoop 6. crouch, hunker,
  settle, stubby 7. sit down
  8. squatter, thickset
squatter... 6. nester (illegal) 7. pioneer
  9. sandpiper 11. homesteader
Squatter State... 6. Kansas
squaw... 6. coween, Indian, mahala
  (mahaly)

squeal... 6. betray, inform 7. protest,
  quarrel
squealer... 4. fink 6. grouse, pigeon,
  plover 7. traitor 8. informer
squeamish... 4. nice 5. dizzy
  6. dainty, queasy 7. prudish
  8. overnice, qualmish 9. nauseated
  10. fastidious, scrupulous
squeeze... 3. hug, jam, nip 4. cram,
  crux 5. crowd, crush, pinch, press,
  wring 6. crisis, extort 7. embrace
  8. compress 9. constrict, influence
  10. constraint 11. compression
squeezer, fruit... 6. juicer, reamer
squelch... 5. crush, quash, quell
  6. rebuke, refute, subdue 7. repress,
  silence 8. suppress 10. disconcert
squib... 4. bomb, fuse, pipe, skit, tube
  6. speech, squirt 7. explode,
  lampoon, writing 9. bespatter
  10. pasquinade 11. firecracker
squire... 4. beau 5. court, lover
  6. escort 7. gallant 8. henchman,
  nobleman 9. attendant, gentleman,
  landowner
squirm... 5. twist 6. wiggle, writhe
  7. wriggle
squirrel (pert to)...
  African.. 5. xerus
  American.. 5. bunny 7. assapan
    8. chipmunk 9. chickaree
  American, flying.. 7. assapan
  Asian.. 5. sisel 6. suslik
  Austral, flying.. 9. phalanger
  burrowing.. 6. gopher
  cage.. 8. treadmill
  color.. 4. lead
  E Ind, flying.. 6. taguan
  fish.. 7. serrano
  fur (Her).. 4. vair
  genus.. 6. Tamias 7. Sciurus
  Java.. 8. jelerang
  like.. 8. sciuroid
  nest.. 4. dray, drey
  shrew.. 4. tana 6. Tupaia
  skin.. 4. vair
  Spanish.. 7. ardilla
squirrellike mammal... 8. banxring,
  dormouse
stab... 4. gore, pang, pink 5. knife,
  knive, lunge, wound 6. attack, injury,
  pierce, thrust 7. poniard, slander
  8. puncture, stoccado
stability... 5. poise 7. balance
  8. firmness, strength 9. constancy
  10. permanence, stableness,
  steadiness 11. reliability
  12. immovability, immutability
  13. steadfastness
stabilize... 3. set 5. poise 6. steady
  7. ballast 8. regulate
stable... 3. mew (Royal) 4. barn, byre,
  firm, safe 5. fixed, solid, sound, stall
  6. steady, strong 7. durable, lasting,
  paddock, support 8. constant, reliable
  9. confirmed, permanent, steadfast
  10. stationary, unwavering
  11. established, trustworthy
stableman... 5. groom 7. hostler
  (ostler)
staccato... 7. détaché 8. ricochet
  12. disconnected

stack... 4. heap, load, pile, rick
5. mound, shock 6. pile up
7. chimney, conduit 8. quantity
stacked... 11. accumulated,
prearranged
stacked pack, cards... 8. cold deck
stadium... 5. stage 6. course, dromos
8. foot race (anc)
stadium race, start... 7. aphesis
staff... 4. rod 5. club, mace, pole
6. baton, music, stave 7. scepter,
support 8. caduceus, insignia,
pastoral 9. personnel 10. assistants,
associates
staff (pert to)...
Bacchus.. 7. thyrsus
bearer.. 5. macer
magician's.. 7. rhabdos
marshal's.. 5. baton
member, officer.. 4. aide 7. attaché
mountain climbing.. 10. alpenstock
pastoral.. 5. pedum 7. baculus,
crosier (crozier)
shepherd's.. 5. crook, pedum
sovereign's.. 7. scepter (sceptre)
stag... 4. colt, deer (red), hart
5. party, royal, spade 7. male fox,
pollard 8. gamecock, informer
stage... 4. dais, tier 5. arena, phase,
scene 6. degree 7. display, estrade,
perform, rostrum 8. platform, scaffold
9. dramatize, gradation
10. proscenium, stagecoach
stage (pert to)...
call (trumpet).. 6. sennet
direction.. 5. aside, manet 6. sennet
of disease.. 9. catabasis
of insects.. 5. imago, larva
part.. 5. stair 8. dutchman (patch)
10. proscenium
scene (side).. 8. coulisse
scenery.. 3. set
stagger... 4. reel, stot, stun, sway,
walk 5. lurch 6. excite, totter, zigzag
7. be drunk, tremble, vibrate
8. astonish, flounder, frighten,
titubate, unsettle 9. alternate,
fluctuate
staggering... 5. areel 9. startling
10. astounding 11. the staggers
12. unbelievable
Stagirite, The... 9. Aristotle
stagnant... 4. dull, foul 5. inert, stale,
still 8. inactive, sluggish, standing
10. motionless, not flowing
13. unprogressive
stagnate... 3. rot 4. dull 5. inert
8. stagnant, vegetate 10. motionless
staid... 5. grave, sober 6. demure,
sedate, solemn 7. serious, settled
8. composed, decorous, sensible
9. steadfast
stain... 3. dye 4. blot, soil, spot, tint
5. color, paint, smear, sully
6. infamy, smudge, stigma
7. blemish, corrupt, pigment, tarnish
8. discolor, disgrace, dishonor,
maculate 9. pollution 10. stigmatize
11. contaminate 13. discoloration
stained by decay... 4. doty
stained glass rod (lead)... 4. came
stair... 4. step 5. riser, stage, tread

6. degree, flight (series)
staircase (pert to)...
French.. 8. escalier
moving.. 9. escalator
outdoor.. 6. perron
post.. 5. newel
ship's.. 12. companionway
spiral.. 8. caracole
stairs to bath (Ind)... 4. ghat (ghaut)
stake... 3. bet, peg, pel, pin 4. ante,
pale, pile, post, risk, spit 5. sowel,
teest, wager 6. chance, estate,
gamble, hazard, picket, pledge
7. finance, venture
stale... 3. old 5. banal, fusty, trite,
vapid 7. insipid, spoiled
9. hackneyed, tasteless 10. flavorless
11. commonplace
stalemate... 6. corner 7. impasse
8. cul-de-sac, deadlock 10. blind
alley, standstill
stalk... 4. axis, hunt, risp, stem, walk
6. pursue, stride 7. pedicel
8. peduncle 11. reconnoiter
stalk (pert to)...
cotton, sugar cane.. 6. ratoon
dry.. 3. hay, kex 5. haulm (halm)
flower.. 7. petiole
grain, grass.. 4. culm 5. straw
6. ressum
strawberry.. 4. risp
stalkless... 7. sessile
stall... 3. cot, pew 4. crib, fail, loge,
mire, stop 5. booth, check, choir,
stick 6. hinder, manger, stable
7. disgust 9. temporize 10. dillydally
11. compartment 12. parking space
13. procrastinate
stalwart... 5. brave, stout 6. strong,
sturdy 7. valiant 8. partisan, resolute
9. corpulent 10. courageous,
unyielding
stamina... 5. pluck, vigor 7. courage
8. backbone, strength 9. endurance,
fortitude 12. staying power
stammer... 3. haw, hem 4. mant
6. falter 7. stumble, stutter
8. hesitate
stammering... 8. psellism
stamp... 3. die 4. date, dink, form,
mark, seal, sign, tool 5. brand, infix,
label 6. signet 7. engrave, impress,
imprint, postage, trading 8. tressure
(tressour) 11. endorsement
14. characteristic
stamp (pert to)...
border.. 8. tressure (tressour)
collecting.. 9. philately
collector.. 11. philatelist
madness.. 11. timbromania
paper.. 6. pelure
postage.. 6. timbre
space.. 8. spandrel
stampede... 3. run 4. rout, rush
5. panic 6. flight 7. debacle
11. wild scamper
stance... 4. pose 7. posture, station
8. position
stanch... 5. allay, check, quell
6. steady, strong 7. zealous
8. faithful 9. steadfast 10. extinguish
11. substantial

stanchion... 3. bar 4. post, prop
   5. brace, piton 6. secure 7. support,
   upright
stand... 4. bear, bier, halt, rack, stop,
   zarf 5. abide, arise, booth, easel,
   store, table 6. endure, tripod
   7. coaster, étagère, footing, impasse,
   sustain, taboret 8. attitude, foothold,
   pedestal, position, tolerate
   9. withstand 10. standstill
stand (pert to)...
   against.. 4. resist
   by.. 3. aid 6. defend 7. support
      9. be present
   cost of.. 5. treat
   Eccl.. 4. ambo
   for.. 6. permit, typify 9. represent,
      symbolize
   for candles.. 7. epergne
      10. candelabra
   in.. 6. deputy 10. substitute
   it.. 4. bear 5. brook 6. suffer
   offish.. 4. cold 5. aloof 8. reserved
      10. not cordial
   opposite.. 4. face
   three–legged.. 6. teapoy, tripod, trivot
   up to.. 5. brave 6. resist
standard... 3. par 4. flag, norm
   5. grade, model, usual 6. ensign
   7. average, classic, paragon, precept
   8. orthodox 9. customary, principle
      13. authoritative
standard (pert to)...
   battle.. 9. oriflamme (oriflamb)
   bearer.. 6. leader 7. officer
      10. politician
   chem test.. 5. titer (titre)
   ensign.. 8. gonfalon, gonfanon
   flag (Rom).. 8. vexillum
   of excellence.. 4. idea
   of intelligence.. 5. Binet
   of light.. 6. carcel
   of quantity.. 4. unit
   Ottoman Emp.. 4. alem
standardize... 9. calibrate, normalize
standing... 4. rank 5. fixed, state
   6. at rest, status 7. footing, settled,
   station, upright 8. duration, prestige
   9. permanent 10. durability,
   reputation
standing (pert to)...
   long.. 7. durable 8. duration
      11. traditional
   mode of.. 6. stance
   out.. 7. eminent, salient
   room only.. 3. SRO
   social.. 6. estate, status 8. prestige
   upright.. 11. orthostatic
stannum... 2. Sn 3. tin
stanza... 4. rann, unit 5. stave, verse
   6. octave, sestet 7. strophe, triolet
   (8–lined)
stanza scheme... 6. ballad 10. Gray's
   Elegy, Spenserian
star... 3. sun 4. hero, lead 5. actor,
   shine 6. étoile 7. destiny, fortune
   8. asterisk, insignia, ornament
   9. emphasize, principal
   11. hummingbird 12. heavenly body,
   luminous body
star (pert to)... see also *Stars*
   brightest.. 3. Cor, sun 5. Deneb
      6. Altair, Lucida, Sirius
   Bull's Eye.. 9. Aldebaran
   divination.. 9. astrology
   Dog.. 4. Sept 6. Sirius 8. Canicula
      12. Canis Majoris
   evening.. 5. Venus 6. Hesper, Vesper
      7. evestar 8. Hesperus
   feather.. 9. comatulid
   five–pointed.. 9. pentagram, pentalpha
   French.. 6. étoile
   gazer.. 4. fish 10. astronomer
   giant.. 10. Betelgeuse (Betelgeux)
   group (fixed).. 13. constellation
   guiding.. 5. Alpha, North 7. Polaris
      8. Cynosure, loadstar, lodestar,
      polestar
   large.. 5. Rigel
   morning.. 4. Mars 5. Venus 6. Saturn
      7. daystar, Jupiter, Mercury
      8. Phosphor
   new.. 4. Nova
   North.. 7. Polaris 8. loadstar, lodestar
   of Africa.. 15. Cullinan diamond
   of Bethlehem (Bib).. 11. guide of
      Magi
   of the sea.. 11. Maris Stella (Stella
      Maris)
   ornament.. 4. semé
   path.. 5. orbit
   ref to.. 6. astral, starry 7. sideral,
      stellar 8. sidereal 9. planatoid
   representation.. 6. étoile
   shooting.. 5. comet 6. Leonid, meteor
starch... 3. vim 4. sago 5. hilum,
   vigor 6. amidin, energy, farina, fecula
   7. cassava 8. glycogen 9. arrowroot,
   formality, stiffness
starchy... 5. stiff 6. formal, viscid
   7. amyloid, precise 9. unbending
stare... 4. gape, gawk, gaze, look,
   ogle, peer 5. glare 6. glower,
   goggle, wonder
starfish... 7. asteria 10. echinoderm
stark... 4. bare, mere 5. rigid, tense
   6. barren, wholly 7. violent
   8. absolute, complete, entirely
   9. downright, unadorned
   10. absolutely
starling... 4. myna, sali 6. pastor
Stars (pert to)...
   and Bars.. 15. Confederate flag
   belt, tract (luminous).. 6. Galaxy
      8. Milky Way
   circumpolar group.. 5. Draco
      6. Dragon
   four (famed).. 4. Crux 13. Southern
      Cross
   North Pole group.. 9. Great Bear
      10. Little Bear 11. Septentrion
   Ursa Major.. 9. Big Dipper, Great
      Bear
   Ursa Minor.. 10. Little Bear 12. Little
      Dipper
start... 4. dart, dash, jerk, rush
   5. begin, enter, sally 6. broach,
   origin, twitch 7. get away, startle
   8. commence 9. advantage,
   beginning, departure, originate
   10. inaugurate
starting point... 4. text (sermon)
   7. scratch 9. departure
startle... 5. alarm, rouse, scare, shock

6. excite, fright 8. astonish
9. electrify
starve . . 3. die 4. kill 5. crave
6. famish, perish, scrimp 7. atrophy,
destroy 10. be indigent
starved . . 4. thin 5. empty 6. frozen,
hungry 8. famished, ravenous
starwort . . 5. aster 9. colicroot
stash . . 5. cache, plant, store 7. lay
away 8. hide away
state . . 3. say 4. aver, case, état,
mode, tell 5. utter 6. affirm, allege,
assert, plight, recite, remark, report
7. country, declare, expound,
express, narrate 8. announce,
propound 9. condition, enunciate,
postulate, pronounce, territory
10. government, possession
11. body politic 12. circumstance,
commonwealth
state (pert to) . . .
a fact . . 4. aver 5. posit 6. avouch
7. declare
agitated . . 9. disturbed, perturbed
disordered . . 9. cluttered
formally . . 8. propound 9. enunciate,
pronounce
French . . 4. état
hypnotic . . 6. trance
ideal . . 6. Utopia
office . . 8. governor 11. secretariat
on oath . . 6. depose
police . . 7. trooper
reference . . 6. statal
secret . . 7. arcanum
specifically . . 6. define 7. itemize
13. particularize
treasury . . 4. fisc 6. fiscus
ultimate . . 3. end
under foreign control . .
12. protectorate
without proof . . 6. allege
stately . . 5. grand, largo, lofty, regal,
royal 6. august, coldly, kingly
7. haughty, queenly, togated
8. eloquent, imperial, imposing,
majestic 9. dignified, grandiose
11. magnificent
statement . . 4. bill, list 5. audit, dixit
6. dictum, remark, report, resumé
7. account, invoice, premise
8. abstract, proposal, schedule
9. affidavit, assertion, manifesto
10. accounting, expression, recitation
11. declaration 12. announcement,
presentation
statement (pert to) . . .
abridged . . 6. précis, resumé
7. summary 10. abridgment
11. abridgement
assumed true . . 7. premise
contradictory . . 7. paradox
defamatory . . 5. libel
detailed . . 8. schedule
dogmatic . . 6. dictum
introductory . . 5. proem 7. preface,
prelude 8. foreword, prologue
legal . . 11. declaration
mathematical . . 7. theorem
of belief . . 5. credo, creed
of introduction . . 8. prologue
-ise . . 8. aphorism

self–evident . . 6. truism
sworn . . 9. affidavit
State nicknames . . .
Alabama . . 6. Cotton 12. Heart of
Dixie, Yellowhammer
Alaska . . (no official)
Arizona . . 11. Grand Canyon
Arkansas . . 10. Land of Opportunity
California . . 6. Golden
Colorado . . 10. Centennial
Connecticut . . 6. Nutmeg
Delaware . . 5. First
Florida . . 8. Sunshine
Georgia . . 5. Peach
Hawaii . . 5. Aloha
Idaho . . 3. Gem
Illinois . . 7. Prairie
Indiana . . 7. Hoosier
Iowa . . 7. Hawkeye
Kansas . . 9. Sunflower
Kentucky . . 9. Bluegrass
Louisiana . . 7. Pelican
Maine . . 8. Pine Tree
Maryland . . 4. Free 7. Old Line
Massachusetts . . 3. Bay 9. Old Colony
Michigan . . 9. Wolverine
Minnesota . . 6. Gopher 9. North Star
Mississippi . . 8. Magnolia
Missouri . . 6. Show Me
Montana . . 8. Treasure
Nebraska . . 4. Beef 10. Cornhusker
Nevada . . 6. Silver 9. Sagebrush
New Hampshire . . 7. Granite
New Jersey . . 6. Garden
New Mexico . . 17. Land of
Enchantment
New York . . 6. Empire
North Carolina . . 7. Tarheel 8. Old
North
North Dakota . . 5. Sioux 11. Flickertail
Ohio . . 7. Buckeye
Oklahoma . . 6. Sooner
Oregon . . 6. Beaver
Pennsylvania . . 8. Keystone
Rhode Island . . 11. Little Rhody
South Carolina . . 8. Palmetto
South Dakota . . 6. Coyote 8. Sunshine
Tennessee . . 9. Volunteer
Texas . . 8. Lone Star
Utah . . 7. Beehive
Vermont . . 13. Green Mountain
Virginia . . 11. Old Dominion
Washington . . 9. Evergreen
West Virginia . . 8. Mountain
Wisconsin . . 6. Badger
Wyoming . . 8. Equality
state of . . .
dissension . . 8. scission
disuse . . 9. desuetude
ecstasy . . 6. trance 7. rapture
8. paradise
hostility . . 6. feudal
mind . . 4. mood 5. humor 6. morale
8. attitude
unconsciousness . . 4. coma 5. faint
state of being . . .
a layman . . 9. laicality
artless . . 7. naiveté
a son . . 7. sonship
a woman . . 10. muliebrity
behindhand . . 9. in arrears
beyond natural laws . . 12. supernatural

complete.. 9. plenitude
confined.. 10. internment
free from error.. 9. inerrancy
married twice, illegally.. 6. bigamy
married twice, legally.. 6. digamy
overfull.. 8. plethora
passive.. 9. stolidity
poison.. 7. toxic 8. toxicity
voiced.. 7. sonancy
worse.. 8. pejority
wrong.. 7. errancy
static... 5. inert, noise 6. stable
7. resting 8. electric, inactive
9. quiescent 10. stationary
12. atmospherics, interference
station... 4. fire, post, rank, seat, stop
5. berth, depot, place, radio, serai
6. health, police 7. calling, dignity
8. location, position, prestige
9. situation 11. institution
stationary... 3. set 5. fixed, still
6. stable, static, stator 8. immobile
9. immovable 10. motionless,
unchanging
stationery... 3. pen 5. paper 6. pencil
9. onionskin, papeterie 12. writing
paper
statue... 4. bust 5. image 8. acrolith,
figurine, monument 9. sculpture,
statuette
statue (pert to)...
at Thebes.. 6. Memnon
gigantic.. 8. Colossus
Guildhall (London).. 3. Gog 5. Magog
holy.. 4. icon (ikon)
male figure (support).. 7. telamon
part.. 5. socle, trunk 6. plinth
primitive.. 6. xoanon
Pygmalion's.. 7. Galatea
world wonder.. 6. Helios (Rhodes)
status... 4. rank 5. class, state
7. station 8. position, prestige,
standing
status symbol... 11. swivel chair
statute... 3. act, jus, law, lex
5. bylaw, canon, edict, title
6. decree, rubric, treaty 8. statutum
9. enactment, ordinance
10. regulation 11. legislation
staunch, stanch... 4. firm, true
6. hearty 7. devoted 8. faithful,
resolute 9. steadfast 10. dependable
11. trustworthy
stave... 3. bar, leg 4. fend, pole,
rung, slat 5. staff, stick 6. cudgel,
lathee, letter, stanza 7. baculus,
support, ward off 8. overcome
11. set of verses
stave off... 4. fend 7. prevent
8. postpone
staves, bundle of... 5. shook
stay... 3. guy, leg, rib 4. prop, rely,
stop, wait 5. abide, brace, cease,
check, pause, tarry 6. adhere, arrest,
linger, remain, retard, status
7. prevent, respite 8. postpone,
restrain 9. cessation, hindrance
10. impediment 12. postponement
stead... 4. help, lieu 5. place
6. assist, behalf 7. replace, service,
support 9. advantage, farmstead,
homestead

steadfast... 4. firm, true 5. fixed
6. stable 7. durable, staunch
8. constant, faithful, reliable
9. unwinking 10. unchanging,
unswerving 11. unalterable
steadiness... 5. nerve 7. balance
9. constancy, stability 10. uniformity
11. reliability
steady... 4. firm 5. fixed, grave, sober,
staid 6. stable, sturdy 7. assured,
equable, regular, uniform 8. constant,
resolute 9. incessant, steadfast
10. invariable, unswerving
11. unfaltering, unmitigated
13. uninterrupted
steal... 3. cly, cop, gyp, nim, rap, rob
4. crib, lift, loot 5. filch, pinch,
poach, swipe 6. finger, kidnap, pilfer,
snitch 7. purloin 8. embezzle,
peculate 10. plagiarize
11. appropriate
steal (pert to)...
a march on.. 5. evade 7. precede
10. anticipate 13. gain advantage
away.. 5. creep, slink, sneak
cattle.. 6. rustle
feloniously.. 6. ratten
game.. 5. poach 8. trespass
insane desire to.. 11. kleptomania
nautical.. 7. manavel
stealer... 5. crook, thief 6. lifter, pirate
7. abactor, abigens, filcher, rustler
8. pilferer 9. embezzler, peculator,
purloiner 10. pickpocket, plagiarist
11. biblioklept 12. kleptomaniac
stealthy... 3. sly 6. artful, feline,
secret 7. catlike, cunning, furtive
11. clandestine
steam... 4. boil, fume, heat, mist, reek
5. force, power, smoke, stufa, vapor
6. energy, pother (puther) 8. vaporize
9. evaporate
steam (pert to)...
boat.. 5. liner 7. steamer
9. steamship 11. side-wheeler
jet of.. 5. stufa 8. suffione
organ.. 8. calliope
steamboat cabin (officer's)... 5. texas
steamy... 5. misty 7. excited
8. vaporous 9. steamed up
steatite... 4. talc 9. soapstone
steed... 3. nag 5. horse 7. charger,
courser, Pegasus (winged)
steel... 5. inure 6. harden, smooth
10. strengthen
steel (pert to)...
armor plate.. 4. tace 5. tasse
color.. 4. gray 9. steel blue
12. Prussian blue
conversion to.. 10. acieration
India.. 5. wootz 10. wootz steel
metallurgy of.. 9. siderurgy
process.. 8. Bessemer
11. cementation
type.. 6. damask, Toledo
8. Damascus
steep... 3. ret, sop 4. brae, buck,
high, soak, stew, tall 5. cleve
(cleeve), hilly, lofty, scarp, sharp,
sheer 6. abrupt, clifty, escarp,
imbrue, infuse, seethe 7. extract,
extreme 8. elevated, headlong,

macerate 9. difficult, excessive, expensive, precipice 10. exorbitant 11. precipitous 13. perpendicular

steeple... 5. spire, tower 6. flèche 7. minaret 8. pinnacle

steer... 2. ox 3. cow, ply, yaw 4. helm, luff, stot 5. guide, pilot 6. bovina, direct, govern, manage 7. bullock, control, operate

steer clear of... 4. snub 5. avert, avoid 9. sidetrack, step aside 14. be inhospitable

steer close to wind... 4. luff

steeve... 4. lade, pack, spar (a) 5. store, stuff 6. freeze

stein... 3. mug 4. Toby

stellar... 6. astral, starry 7. leading, starlit 8. starlike, stellate 10. theatrical

Steller's sea cow... 6. Rytina

stem... 3. dam 4. axis, base, cion, corm, prow, root, stop, tige 5. check, shaft, stalk, tuber 6. branch, breast, oppose, scapel, stanch 7. lineage, petiole 8. ancestry, peduncle 9. originate

stem (pert to)...
bulblike.. 4. corm, drub
cylinder.. 4. stele
grass.. 4. culm
joint.. 4. cane, node
mushroom... 5. stipe
plant.. 4. bine
seedling.. 7. tigella (tigelle) 9. hypocotyl
strawberry.. 4. risp
twining.. 7. tendril
underground... 5. tuber

stemless herb (evergreen)... 5. Galax 11. acaulescent

stench... 4. odor 5. fetor, smell, stink

stenographer of Cicero... 4. Tiro

step... 3. pas, way 4. gait, pace, rung 5. dance, grise, phase, riser, stair, stalk, strut, tread 6. degree, stride 7. advance, imprint, measure, process 8. distance, footstep 9. footprint, gradation 10. stepladder

step (pert to)...
arrangement of troops.. 7. echelon
clumsy.. 5. stamp
dance.. 3. pas 6. chassé
mincingly.. 6. sashay
mother.. 7. noverca
stately.. 5. stalk
up.. 8. approach 9. intensify 10. accelerate

steppe... 5. plain 9. grassland

steps (outdoor flight)... 6. perron

stereotyped... 5. banal, corny, trite 6. common, old hat 9. hackneyed 11. cut and dried

sterile... 4. arid 6. barren 7. useless 8. impotent 9. fruitless 10. unfruitful 11. ineffective, ineffectual 12. unproductive

stern... 4. dour, grim, hard, rear, rump 5. harsh 6. gloomy, severe, strict, sullen, unkind 7. austere 8. buttocks, hind part, rigorous 9. harshness, unfeeling 10. strictness, unyielding hardhearted 14. uncompromising

sternutation... 8. sneezing

sternutative... 7. errhine

stertorous... 7. snoring 15. hoarse breathing

stevedore... 5. lader 6. loader, stower 7. carrier 8. unloader 12. longshoreman

stew... 3. pot 4. boil, cook, food, fret, fume, mess, olio, olla 5. anger, imbue, steep, worry 6. bustle, ragout, seethe, simmer 7. haricot, swelter 8. meat dish 9. Brunswick 10. excitement, hodgepodge 11. predicament

steward... 5. agent, reeve 6. seaman, waiter 7. dapifer, erenach, foreman, granger, manager, servant 8. manciple 9. custodian, major–domo, seneschal, treasurer 10. magistrate 11. chamberlain, fiscal agent

Stewart, Stuart sovereigns (last)... 4. Anne 5. Henry

stewed fruit... 7. compote

stick... 3. bar, bat, bow, gad, gum, rod 4. cane, dolt, glue, mast, pogo, ship, stab, wand, wood 5. baton, cling, fagot, paste, shaft, staff, stall, stave, stilt 6. adhere, baffle, ballow, cleave, cohere, mallet, pierce, puzzle, thrust 7. defraud 8. chatwood, revolver, transfix 9. drumstick, persevere 10. matchstick, overcharge 13. stick–in–the–mud

stick (pert to)...
bamboo.. 6. lathee (lathi)
bundle.. 5. fagot 6. fasces
crooked.. 5. caman 7. cammock, gambrel
insects.. 5. Emesa
mountain climbing.. 10. alpenstock

sticker... 4. burr 5. label, poser, thorn 6. poster, puzzle, weapon 7. bramble 8. adherent

sticky... 3. goo 5. gluey, humid, moist, woody 6. clammy, slushy, viscid 7. viscous 8. adhesive 9. difficult, glutinous, tenacious 10. saccharine

stiff... 4. dead, hard, hobo, limp, taut 5. harsh, horse, idler, rigid, stark, tense 6. corpse, formal, proper, severe, strict 7. awkward, cadaver, starchy 8. resolute, rigorous, starched 9. dead–drunk, obstinate, unbending 14. uncompromising

stiff–necked... 8. stubborn 9. ankylotic, obstinate 11. strait–laced 12. contumacious

stiffness... 8. rigidity 9. formality, toughness 10. strictness 11. starchiness

stifle... 3. gag 4. stop 5. choke 6. deaden, muffle, quench 7. repress, smother 8. strangle, throttle 9. suffocate 10. extinguish

stigma... 4. blot, mark, scar, slur 5. brand, odium, stain, stamp, taint 6. defect 7. blemish 8. disgrace, reproach

stigmatism... 7. blemish 10. refraction (eye)

stigmatize... 5. brand 6. defame
8. denounce
still... 3. but, mum, yet 4. calm,
even, lull, moot 5. allay, check, inert,
quiet 6. always, hushed, pacify,
silent, soothe, subdue 7. silence,
subdued 8. inactive, restrain,
suppress, tranquil, until now
9. quiescent 10. distillery,
motionless, photograph
11. continually 12. nevertheless
15. notwithstanding
still water... 4. pond, pool 6. lagoon
stilt... 6. crutch 7. yeguita
(black–necked)
stilted... 6. formal 7. pompous
8. elevated, inflated, on stilts
9. bombastic, inelegant
stimulant... 3. tea 5. salts, tonic
6. bracer, coffee 7. alcohol
8. caffeine, stimulus 9. digitalis,
sassafras 10. adrenaline, strychnine
11. epinephrine
stimulate... 4. jog, pep 4. goad, stir,
urge, whet 5. elate, impel, rouse,
sting 6. excite, fillip (filip), incite,
spur on 7. animate, enliven, quicken,
refresh. 8. energize, motivate
9. encourage, instigate, sensitize
10. exhilarate, invigorate
stimulating... 4. cool 7. piquant
8. exciting 10. energizing, refreshing
stimulus... 4. spur 5. sting 6. motive
7. impetus 8. incentive, stimulant
sting... 4. bite, pain 5. smart
6. offend, tingle 8. irritate
sting of conscience... 5. pangs, voice
6. qualms, twinge 11. compunction
sting organ... 10. nematocyst
stingy... 4. dree, mean, near 5. close
6. scanty 7. miserly, selfish
8. covetous 9. niggardly
10. avaricious 11. closefisted
12. parsimonious
stinkbird... 7. hoatzin
stint... 4. duty, task 5. limit 6. scrimp
7. confine 8. be frugal, restrict
9. be sparing
stipend... 3. ann, fee, pay 5. annat,
wages 6. salary 7. annates, pension,
subsidy 9. allowance
12. compensation, remuneration
stipulate... 5. agree 6. demand
7. bargain, specify 8. contract,
indicate 9. designate, guarantee,
postulate
stipulation... 4. bond 6. clause,
demand, detail 7. compact, proviso
8. contract, covenant 9. agreement,
condition 11. arrangement
13. specification
stir... 3. ado, mix 4. fuss, jail, move,
poke, roil, to–do 5. budge, churn,
rally, rouse, shake, stoke, waken
6. arouse, awaken, bestir, bustle,
excite, flurry, hubbub, pother, prison,
rustle, tumult 7. agitate, animate,
disturb, inflame, provoke 8. activity,
movement 9. commotion
12. penitentiary
stir (pert to)...
  colors (calico).. 4. teer

fire.. 5. stoke
together.. 3. mix 6. stodge
up.. 3. mix 4. rile, roil 5. anger,
awake, rouse 6. arouse, foment,
incite
stirring... 6. moving 7. rousing
8. bustling, eventful, exciting
9. animating, inspiring
11. stimulating
stirrup... 4. ring 5. strap 6. saddle
(part), stapes 7. support 8. footrest,
tapadera
stitch... 3. bit, hem, sew 4. mend,
pain 5. baste, piece, ridge 6. suture,
tailor 8. particle 9. embroider
stitch (type)... 3. hem 5. chain, coral,
cross 6. carpet, damask, suture
7. glover's 11. needlepoint,
over–and–over
stitchbird... 3. ihi 10. honey eater
stithy... 5. anvil, forge 6. smithy
8. smithery
stoa... 7. portico 9. colonnade
stoat... 6. ermine, weasel
stob... 4. post, stab, stub 5. stake
6. gibbet, pierce
stoccado, stoccata... 4. stab 6. thrust
(rapier)
stock... 4. fund, line, race, stem
5. breed, broth, hoard, store, trunk
6. assets, cravat, pillar, strain, supply
7. capital, lineage, provide, rhizome
8. credence, original 9. livestock,
provision, replenish 10. progenitor
stock (pert to)...
  book.. 6. ledger
  breeding.. 5. brood
  certificate.. 5. scrip 8. document
  flower.. 11. gillyflower
  hawk.. 15. peregrine falcon
  in trade.. 6. assets, supply
    11. merchandise
  market.. 6. Bourse 8. Exchange
    10. Wall Street
  of goods.. 4. line
  owl.. 8. eagle owl
  pile.. 7. reserve 12. accumulation
  theater.. 5. plays
stockade... 3. pen 5. étape, pound
6. corral, kennel, laager 7. barrier,
bulwark, parapet, rampart, redoubt
8. palisade 9. barricade, earthwork,
enclosure
stocking... 4. hose, sock 6. anklet,
argyle 7. bandage, fortune, hosiery
8. seamless 9. livestock
12. bluestocking 15. Leatherstocking
(Natty Bumppo)
stocks... 7. pillory, shackle
10. securities
stoic, stoical... 7. passive, Spartan
8. enduring 9. impassive
11. unflinching
Stoic School founder... 4. Zeno
stoker... 5. firer 6. seaman, teaser
7. fireman, greaser 8. trainman
stolen (pert to)...
  goods receiver.. 5. fence 7. smasher,
    swagman
  property.. 4. pelf 5. booty, spoil
stolid... 4. dull, slow 5. beefy
6. stupid 7. adamant, passive

9. impassive, inanimate
11. inexcitable, unexcitable

stoma.. 4. pore 5. mouth 7. opening, orifice

stomach... 3. gut, maw 4. craw, crop, vell 5. belly, rumen, taste 6. desire, endure, gaster, paunch 7. abdomen, gizzard 8. tolerate 10. resentment

stomach (pert to)...
ache.. 5. colic, cramp 7. gullion
8. rumbling 11. borborygmus
acidity.. 4. acor
animal.. 3. maw
bird.. 4. craw, crop
comb form.. 6. gaster 7. gastero
ref to.. 7. gastric, pyloric
ruminant.. 5. rumen 6. omasum
8. abomasum, roddikin 9. manyplies,
reticulum 10. psalterium

stone... 3. gem, pit 4. kill, pelt, rock, seed 5. agate, block, geode, jewel, lapis, shale, slate, spall 6. attack, pebble 7. diamond, peridot, sharpen 8. monument, pavement 9. hailstone, sculpture, whetstone 10. gravestone, grindstone 12. philosopher's

stone (pert to)...
abrasive.. 5. emery
Age.. 8. Eolithic 9. Neolithic
11. Paleolithic
alchemy.. 4. carmot 12. philosopher's
arch (top stone).. 8. keystone
Bib.. 4. ezel
broke.. 4. flat 8. strapped
broken.. 6. rubble
carved.. 5. cameo 8. intaglio
chisel.. 4. celt
cutters' disease.. 9. silicosis
10. chalicosis
famed.. 4. Hope, Pitt 5. Mogul, Sancy 6. Jonker, Orloff, Regent 7. Blarney, Rosetta 8. Cullinan, Kohinoor (Kohinur) 9. Excelsior 10. Great Mogul 12. Plymouth Rock, Star of Africa
flat.. 4. flag, slab 5. slate
fruit.. 3. pip 4. paip, seed 5. cling 7. putamen 8. endocarp
gem.. 4. jade, opal, ruby, sard 5. agate, pearl, topaz 6. garnet, ligure, spinel 7. diamond, emerald, peridot 8. amethyst, sapphire 9. turquoise 11. alexandrite
gem cutting.. 6. adamas
hammer.. 5. kevel
hard.. 7. adamant 9. chatoyant (cat's-eye)
heap.. 5. cairn
instrument.. 8. lapideon
masonry.. 6. ashlar
medical.. 4. gall 5. renal 7. biliary, otolith 8. calculus
oil.. 4. hone
ornamental.. 9. scagliola
pert to.. 7. lithoid
pillar.. 8. monolith
pyramid.. 6. benben
quarry.. 6. latomy
small.. 6. pebble 8. lapillus
special.. 3. key, lap, oil, rub 4. curb, flag, head, lime, lode, mile, tomb, whet 5. birth, flint, grave, grind

6. cobble, corner 8. stepping
statue (part wood).. 8. acrolith
to dress.. 3. nig
uncut.. 4. naif
woman turned to stone by Zeus..
5. Niobe

stonecutter (pert to)...
disease of.. 9. silicosis 10. chalicosis
receptacle.. 7. sebilla
tool.. 6. eolith
type.. 6. jadder 7. jeweler 8. lapidary
worker.. 5. mason

stonecutting art... 10. stereotomy

stoning, death by... 10. lapidation

stony... 4. cold, hard 5. rigid, rocky
6. rugged 7. adamant 8. lapidose, obdurate, pitiless 9. petrified
10. inflexible, relentless, unyielding
15. uncompassionate

stooge... 4. foil 5. toady 6. flunky
7. cat's-paw 8. henchman

stool... 4. seat 5. bench 6. pigeon, tripod 7. taboret 8. informer

stop... 2. ho 3. bar, dam, end
4. balk, foil, halt, kill, quit, stay, stem, whoa 5. avast, block, cease, check, choke, close, delay 6. arrest, desist, detain 7. impasse, prevent, silence 8. preclude, swear off
10. standstill 11. discontinue, obstruction, punctuation 12. lower the boom

stop (pert to)...
close.. 8. obturate
debate.. 7. cloture
fermentation.. 4. stum
gap.. 7. stopper 9. expedient, makeshift
momentarily.. 5. pause
nautical.. 5. avast
organ.. 5. viola 7. gemsbok
8. dulsiana
seams (boat).. 4. calk
short.. 5. pause 7. respite 8. interval
12. intermission
unintentional.. 5. stall
watch.. 5. timer
with clay.. 3. pug

stopper... 4. bung, cork, plug 5. spile
7. bouchon

storage (pert to)...
bin.. 3. mow 4. loft, shed, silo
7. granary 8. elevator
fodder (in silo).. 6. ensile
hidden.. 5. cache
place.. 3. bin 4. barn 8. attic, depot, étape 6. cellar, closet 7. arsenal, granary 8. cupboard, elevator, magazine 10. promptuary, repository

stork... 4. ibis 6. jabiru 7. Maguari, marabou 8. adjutant

storklike... 8. pelargic

storm... 4. blow, fume, fury, rage, rain, rave, snow, wind 5. orage
6. attack, shower, simoom (simoon), tumult 7. bluster, disturb, tempest, trouble 8. calamity, eruption, outbreak, upheaval, violence
9. agitation 11. disturbance

storm (pert to)...
cold.. 11. northeaster
evil storm god.. 2. Zu 9. blackbird

(symb), Hlorrithi
extreme.. 4. gale 7. cyclone, monsoon, tempest, tornado 9. hurricane
occidental.. 6. wester
recorder (thunder).. 11. brontometer
sand.. 6. tebbad
snow.. 5. buran

stormy... 5. rainy 7. furious, riotous, violent 8. agitated 9. inclement, turbulent 10. tumultuous 11. tempestuous

story... 3. fib, lie 4. hoax, joke, lore, saga, tale, tier, yarn 5. fable, floor 6. gossip, legend, serial 7. mystery, narrate, parable, romance 8. anecdote 9. chronicle, falsehood, tradition

story (pert to)...
absurd.. 4. hoax, yarn 6. canard
doleful.. 8. jeremiad
exclusive.. 4. beat, news 5. scoop
part.. 6. serial
short.. 5. conte 7. novella

storyteller... 4. liar 5. Aesop 6. fibber 7. relater 9. raconteur

stot... 2. ox 4. bull 5. steer 6. bounce 7. paunchy, stammer, stumble, stutter

stout... 3. fat 4. bold 5. brave, bulky, burly, hardy, obese, plump 6. fleshy, rotund, stocky, strong 7. haughty, violent 8. forcible, powerful, resolute, thickset 9. corpulent, undaunted 10. courageous, persistent

stoutness... 7. courage 8. strength 10. corpulence, embonpoint

stove... 4. etna, kiln, oven 5. grate, plate, range 6. heater 7. Coleman, furnace, smelter

stove part... 4. oven, pipe 6. burner 7. firebox, griddle

stow... 4. cram, hide, mass, pack 5. crowd, lodge, store, stuff 6. steeve 7. arrange, secrete

straddle... 5. salvo 6. option 7. astride 8. bestride 9. be neutral, go halfway

straggle... 4. rove 6. wander 7. deviate, meander

straight... 5. cards, erect, exact, rigid, stern 6. candid, direct, honest 7. correct, exactly, unmixed 8. directly, reliable, sequence, unbroken, vertical 9. authentic 10. horizontal, racing term 11. straightway, undeviating 13. uninterrupted 15. straightforward

straight (pert to)...
baseball.. 5. liner
course.. 7. beeline
edge.. 5. ruler
line.. 6. secant 8. enfilade 9. asymptote
Math.. 8. vinculum
out.. 6. candid 9. downright 11. unqualified 13. thoroughgoing 14. uncompromising
shooter.. 11. on the square
way.. 4. anon 8. directly 9. forthwith 11. immediately

straighten... 5. align, aline, level,

order, plumb 6. tidy up 7. rectify, unravel 11. disentangle

straightforward... 5. frank 6. candid, direct, honest 7. sincere 8. outright 9. outspoken 10. forthright 11. undeviating

straightway... 4. anon 8. directly 9. downright, forthwith 10. forthright 11. immediately

strain... 3. sye, tax, try, tug 4. bend, dash, kind, mood, ooze, race, sort, tone, vein 5. breed, shade, stock, tense, touch 6. filter, melody, overdo, poetry, refine, sprain, streak, stress, strive 7. descent, fatigue, lineage, progeny, stretch, tension, variety 8. ancestry, endeavor, exertion 9. constrain, overheave, percolate 10. generation

strained... 4. taut 5. tense 6. forced 7. intense, labored 8. wrenched 9. stretched 10. farfetched

strainer... 4. sile 5. sieve, tamis 6. filter, screen, sifter 8. colander, filterer 17. Hippocrates' sleeve

strait... 3. gut 4. neck, need 5. inlet 6. angust, narrow, strict 7. channel, limited 8. rigorous 9. difficult 10. restricted, scrupulous 11. distressful, predicament

Strait... 6. Bering 7. Surigao 8. Bosporus 9. Belleisle

Strait of Gibraltar... 17. Pillars of Hercules

Straits Settlements...
capital, Penang.. 10. Georgetown
capital, Singapore.. 9. Singapore
city.. 7. Malacca
peninsula.. 5. Malay
port.. 4. Prai

strand... 3. sea 4. bank, quay 5. beach, shore 6. maroon, thread 7. channel, current 8. filament

strange... 3. coy, new, odd, shy 4. rare, xeno (comb form) 5. alien, eerie, novel, queer, timid 6. exotic, quaint 7. curious, erratic, unknown, unusual 8. peculiar, singular, uncommon 9. eccentric, unrelated 10. extraneous, outlandish, tramontane, unfamiliar 12. unaccustomed, unacquainted 13. extraordinary, preternatural

stranger... 3. ger 5. alien, guest 7. visitor 8. intruder 9. foreigner, outlander

strangle... 5. choke 6. stifle 7. execute, garrote, repress, squeeze 8. suppress, throttle 9. suffocate

strap... 3. tie 4. belt, bind, hang, jess, rein, riem, whip 5. leash, strop, thong 6. enarme, latigo, oxreim 7. lanyard (laniard) 8. chastise

strap–shaped... 6. lorate 8. ligulate

strass... 5. glass, paste 10. silk refuse

strata... 6. layers 7. classes 10. formations

stratagem... 4. coup, ruse, trap, wile 5. trick 6. device 7. finesse 8. artifice

strategy... 7. tactics 8. artifice, intrigue, maneuver

stratum... 3. bed 4. coat 5. layer
straw... 4. stem 5. mulch 6. fodder,
sennit, trifle 7. remains, sabutan
straw (pert to)...
bid.. 5. fraud 7. auction 9. worthless
coat (Jap peasant).. 4. mino
color.. 6. flaxen
flower.. 11. everlasting
hat.. 4. baku 5. milan 6. panama
like.. 6. chaffy 11. stramineous
vote.. 5. Roper 6. Gallup
stray... 3. err, gad, sin 4. cavy, roam,
rove, waif 5. range 6. swerve,
wander 7. deviate, digress
8. aberrant, aberrate, go astray
9. wandering 10. occasional
streak... 3. roe 4. line, seam, vein
5. fleck, layer, stria 6. groove, strain,
strake, stripe
streaked... 4. liny 6. banded
7. brindle, striped 8. brindled,
striated
stream... 3. run 4. burn, flow, rill, sike
(syke) 5. brook, creek, river
6. abound, course, rillet, runlet,
runnel, throng 7. current, rivulet,
torrent 9. streamlet 11. watercourse
stream (pert to)...
dry.. 6. arroyo, spruit
gold.. 6. placer
of consciousness.. 8. thoughts
10. psychology 11. abstraction
of forgetfulness.. 5. Lethe
underground.. 3. aar
street... 4. road 5. calle 6. avenue
7. highway, roadway 8. chaussée
9. boulevard 12. thoroughfare
street (pert to)...
car.. 4. tram
famed.. 4. Beal, Main, Wall 5. Canal
6. Beacon 7. Downing 8. Broadway
9. Peachtree 12. Threadneedle
French.. 3. rue
narrow.. 4. lane 5. alley
show.. 4. peep 5. raree
Spanish.. 5. calle
urchin.. 4. Arab 5. gamin 7. outcast
8. vagabond 11. guttersnipe
Street called Straight (Bib)...
8. Damascus
strength... 3. vis 4. iron, thew
5. brawn, force, might, nerve, power,
rally, sinew, titer, vigor 6. energy,
health 7. potency, stamina, sthenia,
support 8. firmness 9. endurance,
lustiness, stoutness, toughness,
vehemence, willpower 10. robustness,
stronghold
strengthen... 4. grow, prop 5. brace,
nerve 6. deepen 7. confirm, fortify,
nourish, toughen 8. increase,
roborate 10. encourage, intensify,
reinforce 10. invigorate
11. consolidate
strengthening... 7. bracing 8. roborant
12. invigorating, invigoration
strenuous... 6. ardent, severe
7. zealous 8. vigorous 9. difficult,
energetic, laborious 11. industrious
repent... 4. loud 5. noisy
erous... 4. loud 5. harsh
oisily 9. turbulent 10. boisterous

strepor... 5. noise
stress... 5. arsis, ictus, labor
6. accent, insist, strain, weight
7. urgency 8. emphasis, exigency,
pressure 9. emphasize 10. elasticity,
exaggerate 12. exaggeration
stretcher... 3. bar, lie 6. litter, racker
9. falsehood
stretch out... 6. be long, extend
9. expatiate
strew... 3. ted 6. spread 7. diffuse,
overlay, scatter 8. disperse
10. distribute 11. disseminate
strewn... 4. semé 8. littered
9. scattered 12. disseminated
stria... 4. line 5. ridge, strip 6. fillet,
furrow, groove, hollow, streak, stripe
7. channel 9. striation
stricken... 7. smitten, worn out,
wounded 8. unnerved
13. incapacitated
strickle... 5. rifle 7. pattern
8. template 10. sweepboard
13. striking board
strict... 4. hard 5. exact, harsh, rigid,
stern 6. severe 7. ascetic, austere,
precise 8. accurate, rigorous
9. puritanic, stringent 10. forbidding,
inexorable, inflexible, meticulous,
relentless, scrupulous
11. strait-laced, undeviating
13. conscientious
14. uncompromising
strict disciplinarian... 8. martinet
strict discipline... 13. regimentation
stricture... 7. binding, censure
9. criticism, narrowing
11. contraction 12. constriction
stride... 4. gait, pace, step, walk
8. bestride, progress, straddle,
velocity
strident... 6. shrill 7. grating, raucous
11. cacophonous
strife... 3. war 4. feud 5. fight
6. battle, combat, stasis 7. contest,
quarrel 8. conflict, exertion, struggle
9. logomachy 11. altercation
strike... 3. hit, pat, rap 4. bump,
bunt, slap, swat 5. clout, labor,
smite, whack 6. attack, revolt
7. impinge 9. discovery
strike (pert to)...
a balance.. 5. weigh 7. average
8. equalize 10. compromise
against.. 7. collide 8. illision
and rebound.. 5. carom (carrom)
9. carambole
breaker.. 4. fink, scab
dumb.. 4. stun
heavily.. 3. lam, ram 4. bash, slam,
slog, sock, wham 5. punch, smite
obliquely.. 5. carom 6. glance
out.. 3. fan 4. dele 5. elide, erase
6. cancel, delete 9. eliminate
to and fro.. 5. bandy
with beak.. 4. peck
with fist.. 5. pound, punch
with head.. 4. butt
with weapon.. 5. crunt
with wonder.. 4. awe 7. astound
striking... 7. salient 8. dramatic,
eloquent, exciting 9. arresting,

wonderful 10. noticeable, remarkable, surprising
striking effect... 5. éclat
striking part... 7. clapper
string... 3. ran, set 4. bind, cord 5. lacet, snare, twine 6. fasten, series, thread 10. succession
string (pert to)...
alphabet.. 5. knots (for blind)
of beads.. 6. rosary 8. necklace
of horses.. 6. stable
out.. 6. line up 8. lengthen 9. expatiate
pottery.. 13. Schnurkeramik (neolithic)
stringed instrument... 4. harp, lute, lyre 5. banjo, piano, recta, viola 6. fiddle, guitar, violin, zither 7. bandore, mandore, ukulele 8. mandolin, psaltery 9. mandolute 11. harpsichord
stringed instrument bridge... 5. magas
stringent... 4. ropy 5. rigid, tight 6. cogent, severe, strict 10. convincing 11. acrimonious, restrictive
stringy... 4. ropy 5. gluey, tough 6. sinewy, viscid 7. fibrous 10. threadlike 11. filamentous
strip... 4. bare, belt, lone, pare, peel, skin, slat 5. cleat, shred, unrig 6. denude, divest, remove, strake 7. deprive, plunder, pull off, uncloak, uncover, undress 9. dismantle 10. dispossess, impoverish 11. decorticate
strip (pert to)...
blubber.. 6. flense
curved.. 5. stave
lead (stained glass).. 4. came
leather.. 4. welt 5. thong 6. latido 7. belting
narrow.. 4. lath, slat, tape, welt 5. reeve, stave, strap
off skin.. 4. flay
of possessions.. 4. milk 5. bleed, bunko (bunco), shear 6. fleece 7. despoil, swindle 10. dispossess
raised.. 5. ridge
tease dancer.. 8. stripper 9. ecdysiast
wood.. 5. stave 6. reglet, spline
stripe... 3. bar, pin 4. band, beat, line, mark, sort, type, wale, weal, welt, whip 5. chalk, strip, vitta 6. streak 7. chevron 8. insignia 9. striation
striped (pert to)...
alder.. 11. winterberry
antelope.. 5. bongo
gillyflower.. 9. carnation
longitudinally.. 7. vittate
stripling... 3. boy, lad 5. youth 8. juvenile 9. youngster
strive... 3. aim, try, tug 4. toil 5. labor 6. battle, buffet, strain 7. compete, contend, emulate 8. endeavor, struggle
strive (pert to)...
for.. 3. aim 4. seek
to equal.. 5. rival 6. strain 7. emulate
to overtake.. 5. ensue

with.. 3. vie 7. compete
strobile... 4. cone 8. pine cone
strockle... 6. shovel
stroke... 3. fit, pat, pet, rub 4. beat, blow, coup, flip, line, putt, shot 5. ictus, serif, spasm, trait, whisk 6. caress, fondle 7. illness, solidus
stroll... 4. roam, walk 5. range, stray 6. go slow, ramble, wander 7. meander, saunter 8. ambulate 9. promenade 11. perambulate
stroller... 5. actor, tramp 6. beggar 7. peddler, vagrant 8. wanderer 9. saunterer 12. perambulator
strolling... 7. nomadic 8. rambling 10. meandering 13. perambulation
strong... 3. fit, hot 4. able, firm, hale, hard, wiry 5. fetid, hardy, lusty, solid, sound, stout, tough 6. potent, robust, sinewy, stable, sturdy, virile 7. healthy, intense, odorous, tainted 8. accented, forceful, forcible, muscular, resonant, stalwart, vigorous 9. effective, energetic 10. outrageous, persuasive, pronounced, remarkable 11. substantial 12. concentrated
strong (pert to)...
drink.. 6. liquor 7. spirits 9. distilled
flavor.. 4. racy 5. acrid 7. pungent
hold.. 4. fort 7. citadel 8. fastness, Fort Knox, fortress, muniment, treasury
man.. 5. Atlas 6. Samson (Sampson)
muscles.. 5. brawn, thewy
music.. 4. loud 5. forte 7. saccade
willed.. 8. resolute 9. obstinate 10. determined
wind.. 7. pampero
stroygood... 7. wastrel 11. spendthrift
strubbly... 6. untidy 7. unkempt
struck... 4. smit 5. smote 7. smitten, swatted 8. shutdown (see also *strike*)
struck (pert to)...
an attitude.. 5. posed
out.. 5. deled 6. elided, erased, fanned 7. deleted
with fear.. 6. aghast 7. alarmed
with missiles.. 6. pelted
structure... 3. dam 4. dais, form, pier 5. frame, house, jetty, kiosk, stage, tower 6. bridge, make–up, pagoda 7. edifice 8. building, platform 9. formation 10. tabernacle 11. composition 12. constitution, construction
structure (pert to)...
calcareous.. 5. coral
conical.. 7. pyramid
crownlike.. 6. corona
filamentous.. 4. hair
human.. 8. physique
monumental.. 5. pylon
roof.. 6. cupola, dormer
tall.. 5. tower 7. steeple 8. campanile
tentlike.. 10. tabernacle
struggle... 3. tug, vie 4. cope, wade 5. labor 6. effort, Peniel (Bib) strife, strike, strive, tussle 7. contend, contest, scuffle, wrestle 8. endeavor, flounder, scramble 10. contention, difficulty

strumpet... 5. belie 6. harlot
  7. debauch, slander 8. harridan
  10. prostitute
stub... 3. end 4. dolt, tail 5. squat,
  stump 6. coupon, stocky 7. remnant
  8. thickset 11. counterfoil
stubble... 4. beard, stump 6. arrish
  7. bristle 8. eelgrass
stubborn... 3. set 4. rude 5. fixed,
  hardy, rough, tough 6. coarse,
  mulish, sturdy 7. restive 8. perverse,
  resolute, starkish, vigorous
  9. obstinate, pigheaded
  10. determined, headstrong,
  inflexible, refractory, unyielding
  11. intractable
stuck... 4. fast 7. baffled, cohered
  8. coherent, stranded (see also *stick*)
stuck-up... 4. vain 8. arrogant
  9. conceited 12. supercilious
  13. self-important
stud... 3. dot, pin 4. boss, knob
  5. haras 6. enstar 7. hobnail
  8. ornament, stallion 9. studhorse
student... 4. co-ed 5. cadet, élève,
  plebe, pupil 6. tosher 7. learner,
  scholar 8. disciple
student of...
  behavior (human).. 12. psychologist
  birds.. 13. ornithologist
  birds' eggs.. 8. oologist
  Eton.. 7. Etonian
  law.. 8. stagiary
  medical.. 6. intern (interne)
  military.. 5. cadet, plebe
  natural history.. 10. naturalist
  navy.. 5. cadet 10. midshipman
  Oxford.. 8. commoner
  proverbs.. 14. paroemiologist
  punishment.. 10. penologist
  reptiles.. 13. herpetologist
  spiders.. 13. arachnologist
students, advanced group...
  7. seminar
studied... 5. boned, pored 6. formal
  7. learned, planned, weighed
  8. designed, measured, reasoned
  10. well-versed 11. intentional
  12. premeditated
studio... 4. shop 7. atelier, bottega
  8. workshop 11. working room
study... 3. con, den 4. bone, muse,
  pore, scan 5. étude, grind, learn,
  weigh 6. peruse, ponder 7. analyze,
  discuss, examine, reverie, science,
  subject, thought 8. endeavor,
  learning, treatise 10. discussion,
  inspection 11. contemplate
  13. contemplation
study of...
  animals.. 7. zoology 9. zoography
  bees.. 8. apiology
  birds' eggs.. 8. oology
  disease.. 8. nosology
  fingerprints.. 13. dactylography
  handwriting.. 10. graphology
  insects.. 10. entomology
  man.. 15. anthropogenesis
  mountains.. 7. orology
  organisms (senile).. 9. nostology
  population.. 10. larithmics
  punishment.. 8. penology

sacred images.. 9. iconology
temples.. 7. naology
words.. 9. etymology
stuff... 3. goo, pad, ram, wad
  4. cram, fill, stow 5. gorge, trash
  6. fabric, matter, potion 7. content,
  element, rubbish, satiate 8. marinate,
  material, nonsense, overfill, trumpery
  9. principle, substance 10. gluttonize
stuffiness... 7. prudery 8. dullness
  9. obstinacy 10. sullenness,
  sultriness 11. pompousness
  15. straitlacedness
stuffing... 6. lining 7. padding
  8. contents, dressing 9. forcemeat
stuffy... 3. fat 4. dill, prim 5. close,
  stout 6. stodgy, sullen, sultry
  7. airless, pompous, prudish
  8. resolute 9. bombastic, obstinate
  10. old-fogyish 11. strait-laced
  12. conservative 13. ill-ventilated
stulm... 4. adit 7. passage 8. entrance
stumble... 3. err 4. fall, trip 5. lurch
  6. boggle, bungle, chance, falter,
  happen 7. blunder, perplex, stagger,
  stammer 8. confound, flounder
stump... 4. butt, dare, skeg, snag,
  stab, stub 5. clump, scrab 6. baffle,
  trudge 7. declaim, nonplus
  8. platform 9. challenge, remainder,
  tortillon 11. electioneer
stun... 4. bowl, daze 5. amaze, daunt
  6. benumb, bruise, deaden
  7. astound, stupefy, terrify
  8. astonish, bewilder 9. overpower,
  overwhelm
stunning... 8. striking 9. beautiful
  10. astounding, stupefying, terrifying
stunt... 4. feat 5. blunt, check, cramp,
  crowl, dwarf, whale (2-yr) 6. hinder
  7. curtail, exploit, shorten
  9. undersize
stunted... 7. blunted, checked, dwarfed
  9. curtailed, shortened
  10. undersized
stupa... 4. tomb 5. mound, tower
  6. shrine 8. monument
stupefied... 5. doped 6. aghast, sotted
  7. drugged, shocked, stunned
  8. benumbed 9. petrified
stupefy... 4. daze, dope, drug, numb,
  pall, stun 5. besot, blunt, shock
  6. bedaze, bemuse, muddle
  7. astound, confuse, petrify, terrify
  8. bewilder, confound 10. incrassate,
  make stupid
stupid... 4. clod, dull, dumb 5. blunt,
  crass, dense, inane 6. oafish, obtuse,
  simple, stolid 7. asinine, doltish,
  foolish, witless 8. blockish, Boeotian,
  gullible 9. brainless, senseless
  11. heavy-witted 13. unintelligent
stupid (pert to)...
  grossly.. 7. asinine
  people.. 5. geese
  person.. 3. ass, oaf 4. clod, coot,
  dolt, loon, lout 5. goose, stirk
  7. tomfool 11. gillygaupus
  render.. 8. hebetate
stupidity... 7. fatuity 8. dullness,
  hebetude 11. foolishness
  12. indifference 13. foolish remark

stupor... 4. coma 5. sleep, sopor
6. apathy, torpor, trance 8. lethargy,
neurosis, numbness
15. unconsciousness

sturdy... 4. firm 5. burly, hardy, lusty,
stout 6. robust, stable, steady,
strong 8. resolute, stalwart, stubborn,
vigorous 10. courageous, determined,
unyielding 11. substantial

sturgeon... 6. beluga, caviar 7. sterlet
9. Acipenser 10. hackleback

stutter... 7. stammer

sty... 3. pen 4. boil 5. hovel, stair,
steps, stile 6. ladder, pimple
7. pustule 8. swelling 9. enclosure

style... 3. air, pen, way 4. form, kind,
mode, name 5. get-up, gusto, vogue
6. gnomon, graver, phrase, stylus
7. alamode, diction, fashion
8. elegance 9. execution
10. appearance 12. characterize,
presentation

style (pert to)...
architecture.. 5. Doric, Greek, Ionic,
Roman 6. Gothic, Norman 7. Italian
8. Colonial, Georgian 9. Byzantine
10. Corinthian, Romanesque
11. Renaissance
expression.. 4. epic 7. archaic,
Byronic, Italian
painting.. 5. genre 11. Renaissance
type.. 5. Ionic, runic 6. italic

styled... 5. named 6. called, termed,
y-clept (y-cleped) 7. phrased

stylet... 5. probe 6. trocar 7. poniard
8. stiletto 9. specillum

stylish... 4. chic, tony 5. nifty, smart
6. dressy, jaunty, modish 7. alamode
8. vogueish 11. fashionable

styptic... 4. alum 10. astringent,
tannic acid 12. constringent

Styx (pert to)...
ferryman.. 6. Charon
pert to.. 5. nymph
river (lower world).. 7. Arcadia

suant... 4. even 6. demure, smooth,
steady 7. equable, regular

suave... 4. oily, smug 5. bland
6. urbane 7. fulsome 8. unctuous
9. agreeable 12. ingratiating,
mealy-mouthed

suavity... 7. amenity 8. civility,
courtesy, urbanity 10. gentleness

subdue... 3. cow 4. calm, tame
5. allay, crush, lower, quash, quell,
sober 6. disarm, muffle, reduce,
soften 7. conquer, repress, squelch
8. mitigate, overcome, suppress,
surmount, vanquish 9. overpower,
subjugate 11. subordinate

subdued... 4. meek, soft 7. muffled,
quelled 8. disarmed, relieved,
tempered 9. conquered, toned down
10. made gentle, subjugated
11. soft-colored

subject... 4. text, word 5. cause,
prone, theme, topic 6. matter,
motive, submit, vassal 7. citizen,
servant 8. inferior 9. subjugate,
substance 10. predispose
11. subordinate 12. part of speech

subjective... 6. mental 7. topical

8. fanciful, illusory 9. of the mind
10. nominative 11. introverted

subject of...
discourse.. 5. theme
disease.. 4. case 7. patient
lawsuit.. 3. res
sentence.. 4. noun

subject to...
abuse.. 6. revile
analysis.. 7. titrate
argument.. 4. moot
change.. 7. mutable 8. amenable
choice.. 5. elective
control.. 7. rulable
death.. 6. mortal
depression.. 5. moody
dislike.. 8. aversion
mistakes.. 7. erratic
tension.. 8. strained
vassalage.. 5. feoff

sublimation... 9. underling
12. underscoring

sublime... 4. high 5. grand, great,
lofty, noble, proud 6. refine
7. exalted, haughty 8. elevated,
eloquent, empyreal, majestic,
splendid, upraised, vaporize
9. beautiful, expletive
11. magnanimous

Sublime Porte... 12. Ottoman Court
17. Turkish government

sublimity... 4. acme 6. beauty
7. majesty 8. grandeur 9. greatness
10. excellence 11. distinction
12. magnificence

submarine... 3. sub 4. boat, ship
8. Nautilus, Scorpion, Thresher
11. submersible

submarine eye... 9. periscope

submission... 5. kneel 8. fatalism,
meekness, patience, yielding
9. deference, obedience, surrender
10. compliance, confession
11. resignation 13. nonresistance

submissive... 4. meek, tame
6. humble 7. dutiful, patient
8. obedient, resigned, uxorious (to
wife), yielding 9. compliant
11. acquiescent, conformable

submit... 3. bow 4. obey 5. defer,
remit, stoop, yield 6. soften, temper
7. succumb 8. moderate
9. acquiesce, postulate, surrender
10. condescend

submit to... 4. obey 6. endure
11. acknowledge

subordinate... 4. exon 5. minor
6. subdue 7. servant, subject
8. inferior, parergon 9. appendage,
assistant, dependent, secondary
10. collateral, incidental, submissive
11. subservient

subsequent... 5. later 7. ensuing
9. following, postnatal
10. succeeding

subservient... 6. vassal 7. servile,
subject 9. assistant, truckling
10. submissive 11. subordinate
12. instrumental

subside... 3. ebb 4. bate, fall, lull,
sink, wane 5. abate 6. settle
7. descend, relapse 8. decrease,

languish 9. gravitate 11. deteriorate
subsidiary... 8. inferior 9. assistant,
auxiliary, extrinsic, tributary
10. collateral 11. stipendiary
12. nonessential 13. supplementary
subsist... 2. be 4. live 5. abide, exist
6. endure, remain 7. prevail, survive
8. continue
subsist on prey... 9. rapacious
substance... 3. sum 4. gist, meat
5. stuff 6. import, matter, wealth
7. aliment, element, essence,
meaning, purport, summary
8. hardness, material 9. actuality,
affluence, solidness 11. consistency
substance (pert to)...
absorbent.. 5. fomes
aeriform.. 3. gas 5. argon
amorphous.. 7. ferrite
antitoxic.. 5. serum
aromatic.. 5. myrrh, spice 6. balsam
basic.. 7. element
bitter.. 5. aloes, aloin, linin
7. amarine, emetine 8. elaterin
brittle.. 5. glass
cleansing, purifying.. 8. depurant
10. abstergent, clarifiant
corrosive.. 4. acid 7. caustic
dissolved.. 6. solute
dissolving.. 9. resolvent
electrical.. 3. ion
elemental.. 5. metal
expanding.. 8. dilatant
fatty.. 5. lipin, suint
ferment.. 9. activator
flocculent.. 4. wool
food.. 7. protein
fruit jellying.. 6. pectin
gelatinous.. 4. agar
hard.. 4. bone 5. ivory 7. adamant
hypnotic.. 4. ural
inflammable.. 6. tinder 7. bitumen
inorganic.. 7. mineral
ipecac root.. 7. emetine
light.. 4. cork
milk curdling.. 6. rennet
moss (Ceylon).. 4. agar 8. agar–agar
neutralizing.. 6. alkali
resinous.. 3. gum, lac 5. copal
7. shellac
rubberlike.. 5. gutta
soapmaking.. 3. lye
stabilizing.. 7. ballast
sulphur.. 5. hepar
tar.. 6. cresol
unctuous.. 3. fat, oil 7. pinguid
vegetable.. 5. resin, rosin
wax, waxy.. 5. cerin 7. suberin
8. paraffin
whale (perfume).. 9. ambergris
wood ash.. 6. potash
substantial... 4. firm, real, true
5. pucka (pukka), solid, stout
6. actual, bodily, hearty, stable,
strong, sturdy 7. genuine
8. abundant, tangible 9. corporeal,
essential, important 10. nourishing
12. considerable
substantiate... 8. embody, verify
7. confirm, justify 8. underpin
9. establish 11. corroborate
substantive... 4. firm, noun 5. sound

6. actual, entity 7. pronoun
9. essential 11. substantial
13. self–contained
substitute... 5. proxy, vicar 6. deputy,
ersatz 7. apology, replace
8. exchange, nominate 9. alternate,
surrogate 10. understudy, viceregent
11. replacement
subterfuge... 4. ruse 5. blind, trick
6. refuge 7. evasion, pretext
8. artifice, pretense 9. expedient
13. prevarication
subterranean... 6. hidden, secret
8. hypogeal, plutonic 10. in the
earth 11. underground
subtile... 3. sly 4. rare, wily 6. crafty,
subtle 7. cunning, elusive
9. beguiling
subtle... 3. sly 4. fine, nice, rare, thin
6. artful, clever, crafty, shrewd
7. cunning, refined, subtile
8. analytic, delicate 9. beguiling,
designing, ingenious 10. mysterious
14. discriminating
subtle (pert to)...
emanation (invisible).. 4. aura
10. atmosphere
sarcasm.. 5. irony
variation.. 6. nuance
subtlety... 5. guile 7. cunning, finesse,
slyness 8. delicacy, fineness
9. quodlibet 10. shrewdness
subtraction, terms... 7. minuend
9. deduction 10. difference,
subtrahend
subversion (utter)...
9. overthrow 10. corruption,
revolution 11. destruction
subvert... 4. ruin 5. evert, upset
6. refute, uproot 7. corrupt, destroy,
pervert 8. alienate, overturn
9. overthrow, undermine
subvertive... 8. eversive
subway... 4. tube 5. train 6. tunnel
11. underground 18. underground
railway
succade... 8. preserve 10. confection
succeed... 5. ensue, occur 6. attain,
follow, thrive 7. achieve, devolve,
prosper, replace, triumph 8. come
next, flourish, supplant
10. accomplish
succeeding... 4. next 7. ensuing,
sequent 9. following 10. subsequent,
successful 11. in the wake of
success... 2. go 3. hit 4. luck
5. elate 7. fortune, outcome
8. accolade, smash hit 10. prosperity
11. consequence
successful... 5. lucky 8. thriving
9. fortunate 10. prosperous,
succeeding, triumphant
11. flourishing
succession... 3. row, run 5. music
(rhythmic) 6. series 7. dynasty,
lineage 8. sequence 9. posterity
succin... 5. amber
succinct... 4. curt 5. brief, hasty,
short, terse 7. compact, concise,
laconic, summary 10. compressed
11. compendious, sententious
succor, succour... 3. aid 4. abet, help

6. brandy (Alpine), relief, rescue
7. comfort, deliver, relieve, sustain
8. befriend, mitigate 10. assistance
succulent... 3. uva 4. lush 5. juicy,
pappy, tasty 6. cactus, tender
succumb... 3. die 5. faint, yield
6. perish, submit 7. give way 8. get
tired
such (as)... 3. sic 4. like 7. certain,
similar 8. analogue 9. analogous
suction (as in clicks of Bantu)...
9. implosive
Sudan, Africa...
capital.. 8. Khartoum
desert.. 6. Libyan, Nubian
export.. 9. gum arabic
gazelle.. 4. dama
gum forests.. 8. Kordofan
lake.. 4. Chad
language.. 2. Ga 6. Arabic
people.. 4. Arab, Sere 5. Fulah
(Fula), Negro 6. Nubian
Plain.. 6. Gezira
river.. 8. Blue Nile 9. White Nile
town.. 5. Segou
sudden... 4. rash 5. hasty, swift
6. abrupt, prompt, speedy 7. violent
8. headlong 9. impetuous,
impromptu, impulsive
10. unexpected, unforeseen
11. precipitate, precipitous
sudden (pert to)...
all of a.. 5. short 6. presto
8. suddenly
and brilliant.. 8. meteoric
fear.. 13. consternation
sally.. 6. sortie
shock.. 4. jolt
stroke.. 4. coup, dash
thrust.. 3. jab 5. lunge
sudor... 5. sweat 8. sudation
9. exudation 12. perspiration
Sudra caste... 3. mal (low) 5. palli
sue... 3. beg, woo 4. plea, urge
5. court, plead 6. appeal, pursue
7. entreat, request 8. continue,
petition 9. prosecute, seek after
suet... 6. tallow 8. leaf lard
Suez Canal builder... 9. de Lesseps
(Ferdinand)
suffer... 3. let 4. bear, dree 5. admit,
allow 6. endure, permit, submit
7. undergo 8. tolerate
10. experience
suffer (pert to)...
distress.. 5. gripe, groan, smart
6. starve
from heat.. 7. swelter
remorse.. 3. rue
ruin.. 5. wreck
sufferance... 4. pain 6. misery
9. endurance, passivity
10. permission 11. forbearance
suffering, scene of... 10. Gethsemane
suffice... 2. do 5. avail, serve
6. answer 7. appease, content,
satisfy 11. sufficiency
sufficiency... 4. fill 7. ability, conceit
8. adequacy, capacity, validity
9. abundance 10. competency
14. self-confidence
sufficient... 3. due, fit 4. enow, full,

good 5. ample, valid 6. enough,
plenty 7. suffice 8. adequate
9. qualified 11. responsible
12. satisfactory
suffix, for or denoting...
abounding in.. 5. ulent
abundant.. 3. ose
act of.. 3. ure 4. ance, tion
advocate.. 3. ite
alcohol.. 2. ol
being.. 3. ure
capable of.. 3. ile
chemical.. 2. ac 3. ane, ene, ile, ine,
iol, ole, ose 4. alic, idin, itol
diminutive.. 2. el 3. cle, ole, ule
4. ette
disease.. 4. itis
doer.. 4. ator
enzyme.. 3. ase
feminine.. 3. ess
follower.. 3. ist, ite
full of.. 3. ose
geological age.. 4. cene
inflammation.. 4. itis
inhabitants of.. 3. ese 4. ites
jurisdiction.. 3. ric
law.. 2. ee
medicine.. 2. ia 3. oma 4. itis
profession.. 3. eer
suffocate... 5. burke, choke 6. stifle
7. smother 8. strangle, suppress,
throttle 10. asphyxiate, extinguish
12. deprive of air
suffrage... 4. vote 5. voice 6. assent,
ballot, prayer 7. witness 8. petition
9. franchise 10. assistance 11. right
to vote 12. intercession, supplication
sugar... 4. cane 5. biose, bribe,
candy, maple, money 6. doctor,
season 7. sucrose, sweeten
9. sugarcoat 10. endearment,
saccharose, sweetening
12. carbohydrate 13. dissaccharide
14. monosaccharide
sugar (pert to)...
and molasses.. 6. melada
burnt.. 7. caramel
chemical.. 6. acrose 7. osamine,
sucrose 8. fructose 10. saccharose
crude.. 3. gur 5. maple
10. massecuite, piloncillo
fruit, honey.. 8. levulose
plant.. 7. sorghum
raw.. 9. cassonade, muscovado
sand.. 5. niter
simple.. 6. ketose, triose 7. glucide
substitute.. 5. honey
syrup.. 7. treacle 8. molasses
tree.. 5. maple
without.. 3. sec
wood.. 6. xylose
sugar cane (pert to)...
disease.. 5. sereh
pulp, refuse.. 4. marc 7. bagasse
stalk.. 6. ratoon
sugared... 5. sweet 7. honeyed
9. sweetened 11. mellifluous,
sugarcoated
suggest... 4. hint, mean, move
5. imply 6. advise, allude, prompt
7. connote, inspire, propose
8. indicate, intimate 9. insinuate

suggestion... 4. clue, hint, idea, plan
5. tinge, trace 6. advice, symbol
7. soupçon 8. proposal 9. hypnotism
10. indication, intimation 11. small
amount, supposition
Suidae... 5. swine
suit... 3. fit 4. plea 5. befit, cards,
dress, habit, match, serve, tally
6. adjust, answer, attire, become,
prayer, wooing 7. clothes, comport,
conform, costume, lawsuit, retinue
8. petition, sequence 9. courtship
10. litigation 11. accommodate
suit (pert to)...
at law.. 10. litigation
for property.. 6. trover
maker.. 6. sartor, tailor
starter.. 7. relator
the occasion.. 6. timely
suitability... 7. fitness 9. propriety
10. expedience, timeliness
11. eligibility 13. qualification
suitable... 3. apt, due, fit, pat
4. meet 6. proper, timely
8. adequate, apposite, eligible,
idoneous 9. accordant, agreeable,
competent, congruent, congruous,
consonant, expedient 10. compatible,
consistent 11. appropriate
12. commensurate 13. correspondent
suitably proportioned...
13. commensurable
suite... 3. set 5. music, staff
7. retinue 8. sequence 9. apartment
10. attendance, succession
11. consequence
suitor... 5. swain, wooer 7. amoroso
10. petitioner 12. party to a suit
sulk... 3. pet 4. mope, plow, pout
6. furrow
sulky... 3. gig 4. dull, glum, plow
5. moody, pouty, surly 6. gloomy,
go-cart, sullen 8. carriage
9. obstinate
sullen... 4. dour, glum, grim, sour
5. cross, gruff, harsh, moody, pouty,
sulky, surly 6. crusty, gloomy,
morose 7. austere, cynical, fretful,
peevish, pettish 8. chumpish,
churlish, petulant, spiteful
9. obstinate, saturnine
sully... 4. foul 5. dirty, smear, stain,
taint 6. defile, smirch, vilify
7. blemish, corrupt, debauch,
disdain, pollute 9. bespatter,
denigrate 10. stigmatize
11. contaminate
sulphur (pert to)...
alchemy.. 7. chibrit
alloy.. 6. niello
butterfly.. 7. clouded 9. cloudless
color.. 6. yellow
comb form.. 5. thion
element.. 11. nonmetallic
reference to.. 7. thionic 9. brimstone
sultan (pert to)...
decree.. 5. irade
fowls.. 5. breed
home.. 5. serai
Mohammedan State.. 5. ruler
6. prince 9. sovereign
Turkish ruler.. 6. Caliph 8. Padishah

13. Grand Seignior
wife.. 7. sultana
sultana... 4. roll (dessert), wife
5. grape 8. mistress 9. gallinule
sultry... 3. hot 5. humid, lurid
6. torrid 7. dog days, sensual
10. oppressive, sweltering
sum... 3. add, tot 4. loot 5. count,
gross, total, whole 6. amount,
number, result 7. summary
8. addition, quantity 9. aggregate,
summarize, summation
12. recapitulate
sum (pert to)...
forfeited.. 5. dédit
of money.. 6. budget
total.. 8. entirety
unexpended.. 7. savings
up.. 3. tot 5. count 8. perorate
sumac... 5. Rheus 7. dogwood
8. shadbush 9. squawbush
13. Toxicodendron 14. buckthorn
brown
Sumatra...
harbor.. 6. Padang 9. Palembang
island of.. 16. Malay Archipelago
kingdom.. 5. Achin, Jambi
mountain.. 12. Bukit Barisan
raft (bamboo).. 5. rakit
river.. 4. Musi 5. Jambi, Rokan
6. Asahan
squirrel shrew.. 4. tana
wildcat.. 4. balu
sumless... 11. inestimable
12. incalculable 13. unaccountable
summary... 5. brief, short 6. digest,
prompt, resume 7. epitome
8. abstract 10. compendium
11. abridgement, enumeration,
reiteration 14. recapitulation
summary (pert to)...
book.. 5. blurb
concise.. 6. précis
of facts.. 7. roundup
of knowledge.. 12. encyclopedia
(encyclopaedia)
of principles.. 5. creed
of speech.. 5. notes
summer... 3. été 6. season
summer (pert to)...
bird.. 7. cuckold, sparrow, tanager,
wryneck
coot.. 9. gallinule
house.. 6. gazebo 9. belvedere
lilac.. 8. damewort
pert to.. 7. estival
rash.. 9. prickly heat
resort.. 4. camp
squash.. 7. cymling, scallop
9. crookneck
summit... 3. top 4. acme, apex, knap,
peak 5. crest, crown, knoll, spire
6. height 7. Everest 8. pinnacle
9. fastigium 10. perfection
11. culmination, mountaintop
summon... 4. call, cite, page, sist
5. evoke 6. call up, demand, elicit,
invite, muster 7. conjure, evocate
8. remember 9. conscript
sumpter... 4. mule 9. pack horse
sun... 3. orb, Sol 4. bask 6. Helios
7. Phoebus 12. heavenly body

13. celestial body

sun (pert to)...
clock.. 6. gnomon (part) 7. sundial
comb form.. 5. helio
crossing the equator.. 7. equinox
disk.. 4. aten
down.. 3. eve 8. twilight
farthest from.. 8. aphelion
fish.. 4. mola, opah 5. bream
god.. 2. Ra 4. Amen, Baal, Lier
  (Llew) 7. Apollo, Helios 7. Khepera
  (Chepera), Shamash, Sokaris
  8. Hyperion
mock.. 9. parhelion
nearest to.. 10. perihelion
outer layer.. 6. corona
over the equator.. 7. equinox
path.. 4. halo 6. circle 8. ecliptic
pert to.. 5. solar 6. heliac
  9. heliology
poetic.. 5. glory, power 6. sunset
  7. daystar, sunrise 8. splendor
satellite.. 6. planet
spot.. 6. facula 7. freckle
squall.. 6. jellyfish
stroke.. 8. siriasis 9. calenture
sundang.. 4. bolo 5. knife
sunder... 4. part, rend, rive 5. sever,
  split 6. cleave, divide 7. divorce
  8. dissever, disunite, sejugate
sundry... 6. divers 7. several, various
  8. frequent, manifold, numerous
  9. different 10. multiplied
  12. multifarious 13. miscellaneous
sunflower... 8. marigold, rockrose
  10. heliotrope
Sunflower State... 6. Kansas
sunk... 4. turf 7. baffled, concave,
  lowered 8. dejected, overcome
  9. depressed (see also *sink*)
sunk fence... 4. ha-ha (haw-haw)
sunny... 4. warm 5. clear, merry
  6. bright, sunlit 8. cheerful
  9. sparkling, vivacious
sunrise... 4. dawn
sunset... 3. eve 4. dusk 7. evening,
  sundown 8. twilight
Sunset State... 6. Oregon 7. Arizona
Sunshine State... 9. New Mexico
  11. South Dakota
supawn... 4. mush 12. hasty pudding
superabundance... 5. flood 6. excess,
  plenty 7. surplus 8. plethora
  10. exuberance 11. superfluity
superabundant... 4. rank 6. lavish
  7. profuse 9. excessive, exuberant,
  luxuriant, plentiful 11. overflowing
  14. oversufficient
superannuate... 6. retire 9. antiquate
  10. pension off 13. prove obsolete
superb... 4. rich 5. grand, noble
  6. lordly 7. elegant, stately
  8. majestic, splendid 9. sumptuous
  11. magnificent 13. extraordinary
  14. superexcellent
supercilious... 5. proud 7. haughty
  8. arrogant 9. arbitrary
  11. overbearing 12. contemptuous
  13. hypercritical
supercilious person... 4. snob
superficial... 4. glib 6. slight, square
  7. cursory, shallow, smatter, surface,

trivial 8. apparent, external
  9. frivolous, insincere
superfluity... 6. excess, luxury, wealth
  7. overset 8. frippery 10. redundancy
  11. prodigality 14. superabundance
superfluous... 4. over 5. luxus, spare
  6. excess 7. surplus, useless
  8. needless, wasteful 9. redundant
  10. inordinate 11. extravagant
  12. nonessential 13. superabundant
  14. supererogatory
superhuman... 6. divine 9. Herculean
  12. supernatural 13. extraordinary
superimposed... 4. over, upon
  5. above 7. covered, layered
  8. overlaid 9. overlying
superintend... 4. boss 5. guide
  6. direct, manage 7. oversee
  8. overlook 9. look after, supervise
  10. administer, have charge
superintendent... 4. boss 7. curator,
  manager 8. director, overseer
  9. inspector, straw boss
  10. supervisor 11. chamberlain
superior... 4. over, peer 5. above,
  chief, upper 6. higher, senior
  7. exalted, mastery, ranking
  8. goodness, priority 9. advantage,
  paramount, seniority 10. ascendancy,
  excellence, pre-eminent, surpassing
  11. pre-eminence 12. predominancy
superlative... 4. acme, best, peak
  6. utmost 7. elative, extreme,
  supreme, the best 8. peerless
  9. hyperbole 12. exaggeration
supernatural... 5. eerie, magic
  6. divine 10. miraculous,
  superhuman 13. hyperphysical,
  preternatural
supernatural (pert to)...
being.. 3. God 4. atua 5. jinni
  (jinnee) 7. banshee (banshie), specter
  (spectre)
event.. 7. miracle
power.. 4. ngai 6. fetish 8. talisman
  11. incantation
superscribe... 6. direct 7. address (a
  letter), engrave 9. inscribe
supersede... 4. omit 7. replace,
  succeed 8. displace, make void,
  supplant
superstition... 6. notion, voodoo
  8. folklore, idolatry 9. tradition
  10. Aberglaube 12. old wives' tale
superstitious... 6. goetic 7. magical
  10. idolatrous 11. fetishistic
  (fetichistic)
supervene... 5. occur 6. accrue,
  happen 7. be added 12. be
  subsequent
supervise... 4. boss, read, scan
  5. check 6. direct, govern, peruse,
  revise 7. inspect, oversee
  11. superintend
supervisor... 4. boss 7. foreman,
  proctor 9. inspector, straw boss
supine... 5. inert, prone 6. abject,
  drowsy 7. servile, unalert 8. careless,
  inclined, indolent, listless, sluggish
  9. apathetic, lethargic, recumbent
  11. inattentive, indifferent,
  thoughtless

supplant... 5. upset, usurp 6. remove, uproot 7. replace 8. displace, drive out 9. eradicate, extirpate, overthrow, supersede

supple... 3. sly 4. bent 5. agile, lithe 6. limber, nimble, pliant 7. fawning, lissome 8. flexible, yielding 9. compliant, resilient 10. obsequious, responsive 11. complaisant

supplement... 3. add, eke 5. add to 6. sequel 7. ripieno 8. addition, appendix, complete 9. accessory 10. complement 12. nonessential 13. reinforcement

supplementary, music... 7. ripieno

supplicate... 3. beg 4. pray 5. crave, plead 6. appeal, obtest 7. beseech, conjure, entreat, implore, solicit 8. petition, importune, obsecrate

supplication... 4. plea 6. litany, prayer 7. craving 8. entreaty, petition, rogative 11. obtestation 12. solicitation

supplies... 6. hoards, relays, stocks, stores 8. estovers, ordnance 9. provender

supply... 4. fund, give 5. cache, cater, hoard, relay, stock, store, yield 6. purvey, remuda 7. provide, reserve 9. provision, reservoir 10. administer, contribute

supply (pert to)...
food.. 4. feed 5. cater 9. alimental
fuel.. 5. stoke
funds.. 5. endow
horses.. 5. relay
provisions.. 6. purvey

support... 3. aid, arm, fid, guy, leg, peg, rib 4. abet, ally, back, base, buoy, limb, mast, prop 5. brace, cleat, shore, spile, stell, strut, tenon 6. backer, pillar, second, uphold 7. bolster, fulcrum, trestle 8. buttress, underlie 9. auxiliary, encourage, reinforce, stanchion 10. assistance, foundation 11. corroborate 12. substantiate 13. corroboration

support (pert to)...
anatomy.. 3. rib 5. spine
cannon.. 8. trunnion
coffin.. 4. bier
mast.. 4. bibb
resilient.. 6. spring
three–legged.. 5. easel 6. tripod, trivot
upright.. 8. baluster 9. stanchion
wedge–shaped.. 5. cleat

supporters... 6. allies, braces 7. backers, bracers, garters 10. suspenders 11. ministerialists

suppose... 3. wis 4. deem, trow 5. allow, imply, judge, opine, think 6. assume, expect, repute 7. presume 8. conclude, consider 9. apprehend, intention 10. conjecture 11. supposition

supposed... 8. putative

supposition... 2. if 6. theory 7. surmise 8. supposed 9. postulate 10. assumption, conjecture,

hypothesis 11. connotation, implication

suppress... 4. kill, stop 5. check, crush, elide, quash, quell 6. hush up, muffle, retard, stifle 7. abolish, exclude, oppress, smother 8. hold back, prohibit, restrain, withhold 9. interdict, overpower 10. extinguish

suppression... 6. hush up 7. reserve 8. hush–hush 9. overthrow, restraint 10. inhibition

supremacy... 5. power 7. control, mastery, primacy 8. dominion 9. influence 10. ascendancy, domination, first place 11. sovereignty 12. championship

supreme... 3. top 4. last 5. chief, final 6. divine, ruling 7. crucial, highest 8. foremost, greatest, peerless 9. paramount 10. preeminent

supreme being... 3. God 4. Lord 5. Allah, Deity, monad 6. Brahma, Buddha 7. Creator, Jehovah 8. autocrat

surcease... 3. end 4. rest, stop 5. defer, delay 6. desist, relief 7. respite 8. drop work, postpone 9. cessation

surd... 4. deaf, mute 7. aphonic, radical 9. voiceless

sure... 3. yes 4. fast, firm, safe, true 5. bound 6. indeed, secure, stable, steady, strong 7. assured, certain 8. positive, reliable 9. confident, steadfast, unfailing 10. guaranteed, inevitable, infallible 11. trustworthy 12. indisputable 13. incontestable 14. unquestionable

surety... 4. bail, bond, fact 6. backer, pledge, safety 7. sponsor 8. security, sureness 9. certainty 10. confidence, engagement

surf... 4. foam, rote, wave 5. bathe, spray, surge, swell 7. breaker

surface... 4. area, face, orlo, pave, plat, skin 5. facet, meros 6. facing, patina 7. outside 8. exterior 9. periphery

surface (pert to)...
artificial.. 4. rink
front (coin).. 7. obverse
gem.. 5. facet
geometric.. 6. toroid
medical.. 7. acrotic
toward.. 5. ectad
under.. 6. latent 10. internally
water.. 4. ryme

surfeit... 4. cloy, feed, glut, jade, sate 6. excess 7. replete, satiate, satisfy 9. satiation 11. overindulge, superfluity

surge... 4. eddy, flow, rush, wave 5. swarm, swell, whirl 6. billow, thrill 7. estuate 9. gurgitate 11. rise and fall

surgeon (pert to)...
ancient.. 10. chirurgeon
case (instrument).. 6. tweeze (tweese)
slang.. 8. sawbones

surgery... 7. aciurgy 8. medicine 9. operation, resection

surgery (pert to)...
chin.. 11. mentoplasty
ears.. 9. otoplasty
face lift.. 13. rhytidoplasty
   14. blepharoplasty (eyelids)
Father of (Fr).. 4. Paré (1517–90)
fractures.. 10. agmatology
mouth, lip.. 11. chiloplasty
nose.. 11. rhinoplasty
vein.. 10. phlebotomy
surgical (pert to)...
appliance.. 4. X–ray 6. splint 8. iron
   lung 10. respirator, tourniquet
   11. stethoscope 12. resuscitator
compress.. 4. swab 5. stupe
counterirritant.. 5. seton
hook.. 9. tenaculum
instrument.. 3. saw 5. fleam, lance,
   probe 6. catlin, lancet, stylet, trepan,
   xyster 7. forceps 8. hemostat,
   keratome, speculum, tweezers
knife.. 7. scalpel
plug.. 6. tampon
puncture.. 8. centesis
saw.. 6. trepan
stitch.. 5. seton 6. suture
Surinam (pert to)...
called also.. 11. Dutch Guiana
capital.. 10. Paramaribo
disease.. 6. Panama (plant)
kingdom of.. 11. Netherlands
mountain.. 10. Tumuc–Humac
toad.. 4. pipa
surly... 4. glum, grum, rude 5. gruff
   6. abrupt, grumpy, morose, sullen
   7. crabbed 8. arrogant, growling
   10. ill–natured 11. intractable
surmise... 4. deem, fancy, guess,
   judge, opine, think 7. imagine,
   presume 8. mistrust 9. suspicion
   10. assumption, conclusion,
   conjecture 11. supposition
surmount... 3. top 4. pass, rise
   5. climb, excel, mount 6. subdue
   7. conquer, surpass 8. overcome
   9. transcend
surname... 6. eponym, family, maiden
   7. agnomen 8. cognomen
   10. patronymic 11. appellation
surpass... 3. cap, top 4. best
   5. excel, outdo 6. better, exceed,
   outvie, outwit 7. outrank, outride
   8. go beyond, outrange, outreach,
   outshine, outstrip, surmount
   9. transcend
surpassing... 12. transcendent
surplice... 3. fee 5. cotta, ephod
   6. collar 7. pelisse
surplus... 4. over, rest 5. epact
   6. excess 7. overage, reserve
   8. overplus 9. remaining
   10. additional, redundancy
   11. superfluous
surprise... 3. awe 5. alarm, amaze,
   seize, shock 6. wonder 7. astound,
   capture, perplex, startle 8. astonish,
   bewilder, confound, dumfound
   9. amazement, dumbfound,
   overwhelm, surprisal 10. wonderment
   11. flabbergast 12. astonishment
surprising... 7. amazing 8. striking
   9. startling 10. unexpected

   11. astonishing, unlooked for
   13. extraordinary
surrender... 4. cede, give 5. yield
   6. give up, remise, resign
   7. abandon, cession, deliver
   8. dedition, remittal 9. extradite
   10. relinquish, submission
   11. abandonment, divestiture,
   extradition 12. cancellation
   14. relinquishment
surreptitious... 3. sly 6. hidden, secret
   8. stealthy 9. concealed, deceitful
   10. fraudulent 11. clandestine
surround... 4. gird, isle, wrap
   5. beset, hem in, inarm 6. circle,
   encase, incase, invest 7. besiege,
   enclave, enclose, envelop, environ
   8. encircle, inundate, overflow
   9. encompass 12. circumscribe
   14. circumnavigate
surrounding... 5. about, beset, midst
   7. ambient, setting 9. hemming in,
   perioptic 10. encircling, enveloping
   11. circumpolar 12. circumjacent
survey... 4. plan, poll, scan 5. study,
   vista 6. regard, review 7. examine,
   inspect, oversee 8. traverse
   9. delineate, determine 10. scrutinize
   11. examination, reconnoiter,
   superintend 14. reconnaissance
surveying (pert to)...
instrument.. 7. alidade (alidad), transit
   9. stadia rod 10. throdolite
mathematics.. 7. geodesy
process.. 13. triangulation
surveyor (pert to)...
helper.. 6. rodman 7. lineman,
   poleman
land.. 8. measurer, overseer
   9. arpenteur
measure.. 5. chain
mine.. 6. dialer
survival... 5. relic 9. outliving
   10. durability
survivor... 6. relict 8. outliver,
   remainer, survival 11. joint tenant
susceptibility... 5. sense 7. emotion,
   feeling, pliancy 11. sensibility
   12. teachability 13. affectibility
   14. sentimentality
susceptible... 4. easy 6. liable, pliant
   7. exposed, subject 8. sensible
   9. receptive, sensitive, teachable
   10. responsive, vulnerable
   11. softhearted 13. tenderhearted
   14. impressionable
suslik... 5. sisel 8. squirrel
   11. spermophile
suspect... 4. fear 5. doubt, fancy,
   guess 7. imagine, presume, suppose
   8. distrust, mistrust 9. discredit
   10. disbelieve, suspicious
suspecting... 4. wary 8. doubtful,
   doubting 11. incredulous, mistrusting
suspend... 4. hang, oust, stay, stop
   5. cease, debar, defer, expel, remit
   6. dangle, depose, recess
   7. adjourn, pensile 8. intermit,
   postpone, set aside, withhold
   9. pretermit
suspended... 4. hung 5. inert
   6. barred, latent 7. abeyant, pendent

8. inactive 9. pendulous
11. inoperative, interrupted
suspenders... 4. pegs 5. belts, hooks,
rings 6. braces, straps 7. gallows,
garters 8. galluses 9. bretelles
10. supporters 11. clothespins
suspense... 5. pause 7. anxiety
10. expectancy 11. uncertainty
12. apprehension, irresolution
14. indecisiveness
suspension... 4. stop 5. delay
7. deposal, failure, hanging, respite
8. abeyance, buoyancy
11. withholding 12. intermission,
interruption
suspicious... 4. fear, hint 5. doubt,
hunch, trace 7. askance, inkling,
soupçon 8. distrust, jealousy,
mistrust, wariness 9. mere trace,
misgiving 10. diffidence, intimation,
skepticism, suggestion 11. incredulity,
supposition 12. apprehension
Sussex (pert to)...
breed (Eng).. 4. fowl 6. cattle
kingdom (anc).. 7. English
land measure.. 4. wist
land tract (Downs).. 5. laine
man.. 8. Piltdown (Prehist)
spaniel.. 6. gun dog
sustain... 4. bear, buoy, feed, prop
5. abide, carry 6. endure, foster,
keep up, uphold 7. confirm, justify,
nourish, prolong, support, undergo
8. continue, maintain, preserve
9. encourage, establish
10. strengthen 11. corroborate
sustained... 6. tenuto, upheld
9. permanent, prolonged, supported
10. unflagging
Susu... 5. tribe (Afr)
suttee... 5. widow 9. cremation,
sacrifice 14. self–immolation
suture... 5. unite 6. stitch 7. pterion
12. synarthrosis
swagger... 3. brag, gait, walk 5. bluff,
boast, bully, strut, swell 6. prance
7. bluster, dashing, roister, stagger,
stylish 8. domineer 11. braggadocio,
ostentation 16. ultrafashionable
swain... 3. boy, lad 4. beau 5. lover
6. suitor 7. admirer, gallant, peasant
8. shepherd 10. countryman
swallow... 3. sip 4. gulp 5. drink
6. absorb, englut, engulf, imbibe,
ingest, recant 7. consume, engorge,
retract 8. tolerate 10. bear meekly
swallow (pert to)...
chimney.. 5. swift
European.. 6. martin
hawk.. 4. kite
plover.. 10. pratincole
sea.. 4. tern
tail.. 4. coat 9. butterfly
the anchor.. 10. quit the sea
swamp... 3. bog, fen 4. mire, muck,
sink, slue, sump 5. flood, marsh
6. deluge, engulf, morass, slough
7. cienaga, pocosin 8. quagmire,
submerge 9. everglade, overwhelm
swamp (pert to)...
boggy.. 7. queachy 8. muskeggy
earth.. 4. muck

gas.. 6. miasma
grass.. 5. sedge
marsh.. 5. slash 8. paludine
tract.. 10. Everglades
swan... 3. cob, pen 4. Olor 5. swear
6. cygnet, cygnus 7. declare
9. trumpeter
swan (pert to)...
astronomy.. 6. Cygnus
flower.. 6. orchid
goose.. 7. Bewick's, Chinese
myth (Hind).. 5. hansa
poem.. 12. Swan of Thames (Pope)
15. Sweet Swan of Avon (Jonson)
star (brightest).. 5. Deneb
trumpeter.. 4. wild
type.. 4. mute 5. black 8. whooping
11. black–necked
swap... 4. beat 5. trade 6. barter,
thrash 8. exchange
11. give–and–take
sward... 3. sod 4. lawn, turf 5. grass
10. greensward
swarm... 3. fry 5. crowd, flock, horde
6. abound, infest, throng 7. pervade
9. migration, multitude
10. congregate 11. aggregation
swarthy... 3. dun 4. dark 5. dusky
8. bistered (bistred), blackish
swashbuckler... 5. bravo 6. gascon
7. ruffian 8. Almanzor 9. blusterer,
daredevil, swaggerer 10. Drawcansir
swastika (swastica).. 6. fylfot, symbol
(since 1918) 9. gammadion
10. hakenkreuz
swat... 3. bat, hit 5. clout 6. strike
7. hit hard
swathe... 4. band, bind, wrap
6. enfold 7. envelop, swaddle
sway... 4. bend, bias, rock, rule, veer,
wave 5. lurch, power, shake, swing,
waver, wield 6. direct, empire,
govern, induce, totter, waddle
7. command, control, deflect, incline
8. flounder 9. fluctuate, influence,
oscillate, vacillate 10. ascendancy
11. fluctuation
swayback... 8. lordosis
swaying... 7. pensile, sagging
8. swinging, waddling 11. influential,
oscillating
swear... 3. vow 4. oath 5. curse,
vouch 6. adjure, pledge (sacred)
7. confirm, declare, promise
10. asseverate, deposition 11. bear
witness
swear (pert to)...
at.. 5. clash (colors), curse
8. disagree
by.. 5. bet on 7. count on 8. take
oath
falsely.. 7. perjure
off.. 4. stop 6. eschew, give up
7. abandon 8. renounce
sweat... 4. work 5. exude, grill, sudor
6. drudge 7. excrete, ferment
8. perspire, transude 9. exudation
10. impatience 11. nervousness
Sweden... see also *Swedish*
capital.. 9. Stockholm
city.. 7. Uppsala (Upsala)
dynasty (1st).. 8. Ynglings

gulf.. 7. Bothnia
lake.. 6. Wenner
mountain.. 5. Kölen (Kjölen)
parliament.. 7. Riksdag
peninsula.. 11. Scandinavia
port.. 8. Göteborg 9. Stockholm
river.. 3. Ume 4. Klar 6. Tornes
    7. Götaalv
sea.. 6. Baltic
university (oldest).. 7. Uppsula
    (Upsula, 1477)
Swedish (pert to)...
artist.. 4. Zorn
bread.. 10. knäckebröd
clover.. 6. alsike
dance.. 6. polska
explorer.. 5. Hedin
fir.. 10. Scotch pine
idiom.. 7. Suecism
manual training.. 5. sloyd (slojd)
novelist.. 8. Lagerlöf (Pulitzer Prize,
    1909)
philosopher.. 10. Swedenborg
religion (State).. 8. Lutheran
soprano.. 10. Jennie Lind
    18. Swedish Nightingale
turnip.. 8. rutabaga
sweep... 3. oar 4. scan 5. clean,
    clear, cover, curve, glide, strip,
    surge, swish, trail 6. course, vision
    7. contour 8. traverse
sweeping... 8. complete, thorough
    9. extensive 12. all–embracing
    13. comprehensive
sweet... 5. bonny, candy, dolce,
    douce, fresh, spicy 6. dulcet, gentle,
    sugary, syrupy 7. caramel, honeyed,
    lovable 8. aromatic, fragrant,
    luscious, pleasant, preserve
    9. agreeable, ambrosial, melodious,
    nectarine 10. confection, saccharine
    11. mellifluous, mellisonant
sweet (pert to)...
and fair.. 5. bonny
bread.. 4. food 6. thymus
    8. pancreas 9. ris de veau
brier.. 4. rose 9. eglantine
drink.. 6. nectar
meat.. 4. cake 5. candy 6. comfit,
    éclair, pastry 7. caramel, dessert
    8. marzipan 10. confection
potato.. 3. yam 6. batata
potato, musical.. 7. ocarina
sop.. 4. ates, atta 6. Annone
    14. Annona squamosa
sounding.. 11. mellisonant
wine.. 5. Lunel
sweetheart... 2. jo 3. gra 4. beau,
    lass 5. flame, leman, lover, spark,
    swain 7. darling 8. dowsabel,
    ladylove 9. Amaryllis, inamorata,
    valentine
swell... 3. fob, nob 4. grow, rise,
    surf, wave 5. bulge, dandy, grand,
    heave, mound, surge 6. billow,
    dilate, expand, growth, puff up,
    tiptop 7. distend, inflate, stylish
    8. increase, protrude 9. sumptuous
    10. aristocrat, prominence
    11. enlargement 12. augmentation
swell (pert to)...

bell–shaped.. 5. tulip
ocean.. 4. surf 6. billow, expand,
    roller
rolling.. 7. seagate
slang.. 3. nob 5. dandy, grand
    9. first–rate
swelled (pert to)...
head.. 3. ego 7. conceit 9. cockiness
    14. self–importance
out.. 4. lump, node 5. tumid
    6. bulged, podded, turgid
    9. grandiose
swelling... 4. sore 5. bulge, edema
    6. dropsy 9. bombastic
    10. distention, increasing
    12. protuberance
swelter... 4. fret 5. exude, roast,
    sweat 8. perspire 10. sultry heat
swerve... 4. veer 5. dodge, sheer,
    shift 6. recoil 7. deflect, deviate
    9. deviation, turn aside
swift... 4. bird, fast, racy, reel
    5. alert, fleet, quick, rapid, ready
    6. lizard, prompt, speedy, sudden,
    winged
swift (pert to)...
astronomer.. 5. Lewis (Swift)
bird.. 4. crin 7. chimney
boat.. 7. flyboat 9. canalboat
footed.. 5. ariel (gazelle) 7. Mercury
satirist.. 8. Jonathan (Swift)
swiftness... 5. haste, speed 8. celerity,
    velocity 9. quickness 10. promptness
swimmer... 5. diver 6. bather
    7. Cloelia (Tiber Riv), Leander
    (Hellespont), natator
swimming... 6. natant 7. vertigo
    9. dizziness
swimming (pert to)...
birds.. 9. natatores
bladder.. 10. air bladder (fish)
pert to.. 5. dizzy 7. aquatic
    8. natatory
pool.. 4. hole, tank 10. natatorium
sandpiper.. 9. phalarope
swindle... 3. con, gyp 4. dupe, fake,
    sell 5. bunco, cheat 6. trepan
    7. defraud 8. flimflam 10. gold brick
swindler... 3. gyp 5. biter, cheat,
    crook, knave, rogue, shark 6. gypper
    7. sharper 9. defrauder
swindling... 6. estafa
swine... 3. hog, pig, sow, Sus 4. boar
    7. Anthony (smallest), peccary
    8. slattern 9. scoundrel
swine, breed of... 8. Cheshire,
    Tamworth 9. Berkshire, Hampshire,
    razorback, Yorkshire
    11. Duroc–Jersey, Poland China
    12. Chester–White
swineherd (pert to)...
patron saint.. 7. Anthony
reference to.. 7. sybotic
swinelike... 7. porcine
swing... 4. hang, jazz, jive, lilt, sway
    5. shake, trend, waver, wield
    6. dangle, manage, rhythm, totter
    7. suspend, trapeze, vibrate
    8. pendulum, undulate 9. fluctuate,
    oscillate
swingtree... 11. whippletree
swinish... 5. gross 6. carnal, filthy,

greedy 7. beastly, porcine, sensual
8. gluttony
swipe... 4. gulp 5. draft, drink, lever,
steal, swape, swath, sweep
6. handle, pilfer, snatch 7. purloin
swipes... 4. beer (Eng sl)
swirl... 4. curl, eddy 5. curve, gurge,
surge, twist, whirl, whorl
swirly... 7. knotted, tangled, twisted
Swiss (pert to)... see also *Switzerland*
ax (ice).. 5. piolet
bell.. 9. alpenhorn (alphorn)
cabin.. 6. chalet
composer.. 4. Raff
flower, emblem.. 9. edelweiss
herdsman.. 4. senn
hero.. 11. William Tell
language.. 6. French, German
7. Italian 8. Romansch
legislature.. 9. Bundesrat (Bundesrath),
Grosse Rat (Grossrat)
mathematician.. 5. Euler
pine.. 6. arolla
scientist.. 6. Haller (von)
surgeon.. 6. Kocher (Nobel Prize)
theologian.. 5. Vinet
warble.. 5. yodel
warbler.. 7. yodeler (yodeller)
wind.. 4. bise
wine.. 7. Dezaley
Switzerland (pert to)...
ancient.. 8. Helvetia
canton.. 5. Aarau
capital.. 5. Berne (Bern)
city.. 5. Basel 6. Geneva, Zurich
7. Locarno, Lucerne 8. Lausanne
9. Constance
famed for.. 5. banks (Finan)
lake.. 3. Uri 6. Brienz, Geneva, Zurich
7. Lucerne 8. Maggiore
9. Constance, Neuchâtel
10. Stattersee
mountain.. 4. Alps, Jura 5. Blanc
8. Jungfrau 9. Monte Rosa (peak)
10. Matterhorn
resort.. 7. Urseren, Yverdon
river.. 3. Aar 5. Reuss, Rhine, Rhone
tunnel.. 5. Cenis 7. Gothard, Simplon
11. Loetschberg
university (oldest).. 5. Basel
valley.. 3. Aar
swollen... 5. pursy, tumid 6. turgid
7. bloated, bulbous, bulging,
pompous 8. enlarged, inflated, puffed
up, varicose 9. bombastic, distended,
plethoric, tumescent 11. protuberant
swoon... 3. fit 5. faint, spell
7. ecstasy, syncope 8. languish
10. heavy sleep
swoop... 5. seize, sweep 6. attack,
pounce 7. descend
sword (pert to)...
ancient.. 5. estoc 6. glaive
cavalry.. 5. saber (sabre)
curved.. 7. cutlass, Ferrara
8. Claymore, scimitar
fencing.. 4. foil, epee 6. rapier
fine.. 6. Toledo 8. Damascus
handle.. 4. haft, hilt
India.. 5. kukri
like.. 7. xiphoid

Mohammedan's.. 8. scimitar
part.. 5. forte, talon 6. foible
practice.. 5. fence
scabbard tip.. 7. crampit
Scot Highlander's.. 4. dirk
seaman's.. 6. hanger
shaped.. 6. ensate 7. xiphoid
(xyphoid) 8. ensiform, gladiate
sheik's.. 4. pata
Siegfried's.. 4. Gram 7. Balmung
Sir Bevis'.. 7. Morglay
Spanish.. 5. bilbo
support.. 7. baldric
two—handed.. 7. espadon
type.. 4. epee, pata 5. blade, degen,
estoc, gully, saber 6. barong, creese,
parang, rapier 7. cutlass 9. gladiolus
swordfish... 6. dorado, Dorado
(constellation), espada 7. espadon,
Xiphias 9. broadbill
sword of...
Damocles.. 12. fateful thing
God.. 6. Khaled (Moslem hero)
mercy.. 7. Curtana (pointless)
Sir Bevis.. 7. Morglay (death)
St George.. 7. Askelon
the Cid.. 7. Colada
swordsman... 6. fencer 7. duelist,
epeeist, saberer, sabreur 9. gladiator
11. Beau Sabreur
sworn statement... 9. affidavit
sworn to secrecy... 5. tiled
sybarite... 7. epicure 10. voluptuary
11. luxury lover
sybil (sibil)... 4. seer 5. witch
7. seeress 10. prophetess
13. fortuneteller
syce... 5. groom
sycophant... 5. toady 7. fawning,
spaniel 8. hanger—on, informer,
parasite 9. charlatan, flatterer,
toadeater 10. talebearer
sycophantic... 7. fawning, servile,
slavish 8. obedient, toadying
10. obsequious 11. bootlicking
syllable...
accented.. 5. arsis
by syllable.. 11. syllabation
charm.. 2. om 6. mantra
last.. 6. ultima
last, omission of.. 7. apocope
last but one.. 6. penult
last but two.. 10. antepenult
lengthening of.. 7. ectasis
ref to.. 5. affix 6. prefix, suffix
8. dactylic, syllabic
short.. 4. mora
shortening.. 7. systole
stress.. 5. ictus
table.. 9. syllabary
unaccented.. 4. lene 6. thesis
syllabled, three... 7. triseme (3
moras) 11. trisyllabic
syllabus... 6. aperçu, digest
8. abstract, synopsis
10. compendium, conspectus
syllogism... 7. premise, sorites
9. deduction, reasoning
11. epicheirema (epichirema)
18. deductive reasoning
sylvan, silvan... 5. woody 6. groved,
rustic, wooded 8. forested

10. forestlike
sylvan deity... 3. Pan 4. faun
  5. Satyr, Vidar 6. Faunus
symbol... 2. om 4. icon, palm, sign,
  type 5. badge, crest, cross, image,
  token, totem 6. emblem, ensign,
  figure, letter, number 9. character
  (graphic), prototype, trademark
  12. abbreviation
symbol (pert to)...
  authority.. 4. mace
  bondage.. 4. yoke
  ecclesiastic.. 4. ring
  England.. 4. lion
  France.. 4. lily
  mathematics.. 7. operand
  military.. 3. bar 4. star 5. eagle,
    wings 6. stripe 7. chevron, epaulet
    (epaulette) 8. caduceus
  peace.. 4. dove
  power.. 4. mace
  prayer figure (anc).. 5. orant
  royal.. 3. rod 5. crown, tiara
    6. corona 7. scepter (sceptre)
  Tammany Hall.. 5. tiger
  tribal.. 5. totem (pole)
  victory.. 4. palm
symbol for...
  arsenic.. 2. As
  calcium.. 2. Ca
  chromium.. 2. Cr
  copper.. 2. Cu
  gold.. 2. Au
  iron.. 2. Fe
  lead.. 2. Pb
  neon.. 2. Ne
  nickel.. 2. Ni
  radium.. 2. Ra
  silver.. 2. Ag, Ar
  sodium.. 2. Na
  tin.. 2. Sn
symbolic, symbolical... 7. typical
  9. imagerial 10. figurative, relational
  11. allegorical, significant
  12. emblematical 14. representative
symbolism... 7. mystery, writing
  9. mysticism, ritualism, symbolics
  10. figuration 11. hieroglyphy
  14. representation
symmetric, symmetrical... 7. orderly,
  regular, spheral, uniform 8. balanced
  10. euphonious
symmetry... 5. order 7. balance,
  euphony, harmony 8. equality
  9. congruity 10. conformity,
  proportion 11. consistency
sympathetic... 4. kind 6. humane,
  tender 7. empathy, pitying
  8. dewy-eyed 10. responsive
  13. compassionate, understanding
sympathy... 4. pity 5. favor
  7. consent, harmony, support
  8. affinity, interest 9. agreeable,
  agreement, tolerance 11. sensitivity
  13. commiseration, understanding
sympathy, lack of... 8. dyspathy
  9. antipathy
symphony... 6. accord 7. concert,
  harmony 8. ritornel 9. orchestra
  10. consonance 11. composition
symposium... 4. book, talk 7. banquet
  8. dialogue, tippling 10. collection,

  discussion 11. compotation
symptom... 4. mark, note, omen, sign
  5. alarm, token 7. warning
  10. indication
synagogue... 6. temple 10. tabernacle
  12. congregation
synagogue (pert to)...
  founder (anc).. 4. Ezra
  platform.. 7. almemar
  singer.. 6. cantor, chazan (chazzan)
synchronize... 5. agree 6. concur
  8. coincide 9. harmonize
  12. contemporize
syncopation... 5. tempo 7. ragtime,
  syncope
syncope... 5. faint, swoon 7. elision
  8. fainting, swooning 9. haplology
  11. contraction, hyphaeresis
syndicate... 5. chain (journalistic),
  group, trust 6. cartel, school
  7. combine, council 9. committee
  10. underworld 11. association
  12. organization
synonym... 7. antonym, homonym,
  metonym 8. identity 9. heteronym
synonymous... 4. like 5. alike
  7. similar 10. equivalent,
  homonymous
synopsis... 6. digest, manual
  7. epitome, summary 8. abstract,
  syllabus 9. statement 10. abridgment
  (abridgement), compendium,
  conspectus, tabulation
synthesis... 5. logic 11. combination,
  composition 13. incorporation
  14. identification
Syracuse (pert to)...
  ancient name.. 8. Siracusa
  city of.. 6. Sicily
  famed for.. 6. battle (BC)
  founded by.. 6. Greeks
  tyrant of.. 9. Dionysius
Syria, Arab Republic... see also
  Syrian
  ancient name.. 4. Aram
  capital.. 8. Damascus
  city.. 4. Hama, Homs 6. Aleppo,
    Beirut 7. Antioch, Latakia
    8. Damascus
  language.. 6. Arabic
  organization, party.. 5. Baath
  river.. 6. Barada, Jordan 7. Orontes
    9. Euphrates
Syrian (pert to)...
  antiquarian.. 11. Syriologist
  deity.. 2. El 4. Baal 6. Mammon
    7. Resheph
  goat.. 6. Angora
  grass.. 7. Johnson
  mallow.. 4. okra
  script.. 8. Peshitta (Peshito)
    10. estrangelo 11. Syro-Chaldee
  sect.. 5. Druse
  tribe.. 7. Ansarie (Ansarieh)
  wind (hot).. 6. simoom (simoon)
syrinx... 4. larynx 7. Panpipe
  10. mouthpiece (anc lute)
  13. Arcadian nymph
syrup, sirup... 4. Karo, sapa 5. maple
  6. orgeat 7. dhebbus, glucose,
  sorghum, treacle 8. molasses
  9. grenadine

system... 3. ism, way 4. code, plan
  5. order 6. regime, theory
  8. religion, universe 9. procedure
  10. hypothesis, regularity
  11. arrangement, orderliness
system (pert to)...
  conduct.. 4. code
  eating.. 4. diet 7. dietary
  geological.. 5. Trias
  management.. 6. regime
  manual training.. 5. sloyd
  mystic.. 6. cabala
  numbering.. 7. decimal
  pitch (Mus).. 5. neume
  religious.. 4. cult 6. cultus
  solar.. 6. planet
  weights.. 4. long, troy 5. cubic
    6. liquid 11. avoirdupois
    12. apothecaries'
systematic... 4. neat 6. formal
  7. orderly, regular 9. organized,

  schematic 10. methodical
systematics... 8. taxonomy
  14. classification
systematize... 4. code 6. codify
  7. arrange 8. classify, organize,
  regiment 9. catalogue (catalog),
  formulate
systematized knowledge... 7. science
systole (pert to)...
  correlative.. 8. diastole
  medical.. 11. contraction (heart)
    14. coming and going
  rhyme.. 10. shortening (syllable)
syzygy (pert to)...
  astronomy.. 7. appulse
    11. conjunction
  Gnosticism.. 5. aeons (pair)
  rhyme.. 11. coupled feet (group)
  zoology.. 5. union 7. segment
szlachta... 8. nobility (Poland)
szopelka... 4. oboe (Russ)

T

T... 3. tau (Gr) 6. letter (20th)
taa... 6. pagoda
Taal... 8. language 9. Afrikaans
taar... 10. tambourine
Taaroa... 3. God
tab... pan, tag 4. bill, cost, flap,
  loop 5. aglet (aiglet), label, strip
  6. eartab, record 7. account, latchet,
  pendant (pendent) 9. afterpart,
  appendage, reckoning 10. accounting
tabac... 5. brown, snuff 7. tobacco
tabard... 4. cape 5. cloak 6. chimer,
  jacket, mantle
Tabard... 3. Inn (Canterbury Tales)
tabatière... 8. snuffbox
tabby... 3. cat 4. gown, silk 5. dress
  6. fabric, gossip 7. old maid, taffeta
tabernacle... 4. tent 5. abode, niche
  6. church, temple 7. shelter, support
  8. enshrine 9. sanctuary
  10. habitation
table... 4. fare, list, slab 5. board,
  panel, plate, stand 6. lamina, repast,
  tablet, teapoy 7. console, plateau,
  weights 8. postpone, put aside,
  synopsis, tabulate 9. reference
  10. collection 14. multiplication
table (pert to)...
  calculating.. 7. abacus
  centerpiece.. 7. epergne
  communion.. 5. altar 8. credence,
    credenza
  contents.. 5. index
  cover.. 5. baize, tapis
  dish.. 6. tureen
  land.. 4. mesa 6. karroo (karoo),
    plains 7. plateau
  linen.. 6. napery
  philosophy.. 13. deipnosophism

  talk (versed in).. 13. deipnosophist
  type.. 3. tea 4. turn 6. coffee,
    gaming 7. dinette, dresser, gate-leg,
    kitchen, taboret 8. captain's,
    drop-leaf
tableau... 5. drama, scene 7. picture
  8. schedule 14. representation
tablet... 3. pad 4. pill, slab 5. facia,
  slate, stele 6. troche 7. lozenge
  8. monument, notebook
taboo, tabu... 3. ban 4. deny
  5. debar 6. forbid 7. embargo
  8. disallow, prohibit 9. forbidden,
  interdict, proscribe 11. prohibition
  12. interdiction
tabulate... 4. list 6. record 7. tabular
  8. classify, schedule
tabulation... 7. listing 8. calendar,
  paradigm 12. registration
taccada... 9. fanflower
tacit... 6. silent 7. implied
  8. unspoken, wordless 9. indicated,
  noiseless 10. understood
taciturn... 6. silent 8. reserved,
  reticent 9. saturnine
tack... 4. brad, gear, jibe, join, rope,
  sail, trip 5. baste, lease, route
  6. course, fasten, secure, staple,
  tackle 7. clothes 9. fastening
  10. supplement
tackle... 3. cat, rig 4. gear, tack
  5. davit, seize 6. burton, collar,
  garnet 7. cordage, grapple, harness,
  rigging 8. football (term)
  9. encounter, equipment, undertake
tacky... 5. crude, dowdy, seedy
  6. shabby, sticky, untidy 8. adhesive,
  slovenly
tact... 5. grace, poise, taste

7. address, finesse 8. delicacy
9. diplomacy 10. adroitness,
cleverness, discretion
11. discernment, savoir-faire
14. discrimination

tadpole... 4. frog, toad 8. polliwog,
porwigle 9. youngling

tag... 3. add, end, rag, tab 4. flap,
game, loop, name 5. aglet (aiglet),
label, sheep, strip 6. fasten, follow
7. frazzle, pendant, taglock
9. appendage 11. aiguillette
(ornamental)

Tagalog, Tagal (pert to)...
child, servant.. 4. anac, bata
deity.. 6. Batala
game (gambling).. 10. panguingui
native of.. 5. Luzon 11. Philippines
peasant.. 3. tao
race.. 4. Aeta (dwarf) 7. Malayan

Tahiti...
arrowroot.. 3. pia
boat.. 4. pahi
capital.. 7. Papeete (of all Society
Isles)
food plant.. 4. taro
god.. 6. Taaroa (Supreme)
old name.. 8. Otaheite
robe (coronation).. 4. malo
woman.. 6. wahine (vahine)

Tai, Thai tribes... 4. Laos, Shan
7. Siamese

tail... 3. bun, cue, end 4. arse, back,
hair, last, rear 5. cauda, stern
6. follow, shadow 7. pendant
8. entailed, streamer 9. afterpart,
appendage, extremity

tail (pert to)...
aircraft's.. 9. empennage
boar's.. 6. wreath
dog's.. 5. plume, stern, twist
having a.. 7. caudate
peacock's.. 5. train
pert to.. 6. caudal 9. coccygeal
rabbit's.. 4. scut
rudimentary.. 6. coccyx
tailrace.. 5. flume 7. channel

tailing... 5. chaff, waste 6. refuse

tailless... 6. tenrec (mammal)
7. acaudal, anurous, Ranidae
8. acaudate, ecaudate

tailor... 3. cut, fit 4. form 6. darzee,
draper, sartor 8. tailleur 13. cut and
fashion

tailor (pert to)...
goose.. 4. iron 12. pressing iron
made.. 6. fitted 9. fashioned
reference to.. 9. sartorial
twist.. 10. silk thread (stout)

taint... 3. due, hue 5. color, imbue,
spoil, stain, sully, tinge 6. defile,
infect, poison, stigma 7. blemish,
corrupt, deprave, pollute, vitiate
8. disgrace 9. infection
10. corruption, stigmatize
11. contaminate

tainted... 3. bad 6. soiled 7. stained
8. diseased 9. corrupted

taintless... 4. good 5. clean 6. chaste
8. flawless, innocent

Taj Mahal (pert to)...
architecture.. 9. Saracenic
builder.. 9. Shah-Jahan
mausoleum site.. 4. Agra
named for.. 4. wife

take... 2. go 3. get, win 4. deem,
doff, gain, shut 5. atone, booty,
carry, catch, seize, snare, steal,
usurp 6. accept, borrow, deduce,
endure, obtain 7. capture, conduct,
control, detract, receive 8. proceeds,
receipts, subtract, tolerate
9. apprehend 11. appropriate

take (pert to)...
a chair.. 3. sit
a direction.. 5. steer
advantage of.. 5. abuse 6. misuse
apart.. 5. demolish 11. disassemble
as one's own.. 5. adopt 6. borrow
away.. 5. adeem, clear, reave, steal,
wrest 6. adempt, deduct, remove
7. deprive, detract, retract
8. derogate, subtract, withdraw
11. expropriate
back.. 6. recant, repeal, return
by storm.. 5. seize 6. attack
by stratagem.. 4. trap
care of.. 4. mind 5. guard, nurse,
serve, watch 6. beware 10. provide
for
charge of.. 8. attend to 9. look after
down.. 4. fell, raze 5. lower, write
6. humble, record 7. reprove,
swallow 8. emaciate
first.. 7. pre-empt
for granted.. 5. infer 6. assume,
expect 7. believe, presume, suppose
in.. 3. eat, see 4. hear 5. admit,
annex, learn 6. absorb, attend
7. embrace, include, involve, receive,
shorten 9. encompass
notice.. 2. NB 3. see
out.. 4. dele 5. elide 6. delete, efface
7. expunge
out of earth.. 5. exter
place of.. 8. supplant 9. supersede
the floor.. 5. speak 7. address
9. legislate
to flight.. 4. flee 7. run away,
scamper 9. skedaddle
up.. 4. fill, lift 5. adopt, begin, raise
6. absorb, assume, gather, occupy
8. engage in 9. undertake
without authority.. 5. usurp

taker of profits... 6. pernor

talapoin... 6. monkey (guenon)
8. poonghie 12. Buddhist monk

talc... 6. powder, talcum 7. agalite
8. steatite 9. soapstone

tale... 3. lai, lay, lie 4. myth, saga,
yarn 5. conte, fable, story 6. gossip,
legend 7. romance 8. anecdote
9. discourse, falsehood, narration,
narrative 11. declaration
12. conversation

tale (pert to)...
adventure.. 4. gest
bearer.. 6. gossip 7. blabber, tattler
8. informer 13. scandalmonger
chivalry.. 7. romance
doleful.. 8. jeremiad
fatality.. 5. drama 7. tragedy
symbolic.. 8. allegory
traditional.. 4. saga

talent... 4. gift 5. dower, flair, forte, money (anc), skill 6. genius 7. ability, faculty 8. aptitude, artistry 9. attribute 11. disposition 14. accomplishment
talesman... 5. juror 8. narrator
talisman... 4. juju, mojo, tara 5. charm, karma 6. amulet, fetish, grigri (greegree), scarab 7. periapt 12. antinganting
talk... 3. gab, yap 4. blab, blat, chin, harp, rant, rave 5. lingo, orate, parle, prate, rumor, speak, spiel 6. babble, confab, confer, gabble, gossip, jargon, lesson, speech 7. address, blabber, chatter, declaim, discuss 8. causerie, chitchat, colloquy, converse, language, parlance 9. dalliance, discourse 11. communicate 12. conversation
talk (pert to)...
  about.. 6. gossip
  affected, pretentious.. 4. cant, rant
  ancient.. 5. parle
  back.. 4. sass 6. retort 7. riposte 8. repartee
  flattering.. 7. palaver
  fluent.. 7. verbose, voluble
  idiotically.. 6. drivel
  long.. 8. gibberish, rigmarole
  loud.. 5. blate
  running.. 6. patter
  silly.. 5. drool 6. drivel, footle 7. blather, prattle, twaddle
  slang.. 3. gab, gas 4. sass 5. spiel
  slowly.. 6. drawl
  small.. 3. gab 4. chat, chin 7. prattle 8. chitchat
  Spanish.. 7. palabra
  wildly.. 4. rave
talkative... 4. glib 6. fluent 7. verbose, voluble 9. garrulous 10. loquacious 13. communicative
talker... 6. gasser, proser, ranter 7. speaker, spieler 10. chatterbox 17. conversationalist
tall... 4. high, long 5. lofty 6. seemly 7. procere, sky-high 8. towering, yielding 10. incredible 11. exaggerated
tall (pert to)...
  order.. 9. falsehood 10. difficulty
  person.. 9. hypermeter
  structure.. 7. steeple
  talk.. 4. brag 12. exaggeration 14. grandiloquence
tallest known race... 10. Patagonian
tally... 3. run, sum, tab 4. goal, list, mark 5. agree, check, count, match, notch, score 6. accord, reckon, record 7. account, compare, count up 8. coincide, estimate 9. reckoning 10. correspond
Talmud... 9. Jewish law
Talmud (pert to)...
  academy.. 8. Yeshivah (Yeshiva)
  commentary.. 6. Gemara
  student.. 5. bahur
  text.. 7. Mishnah
talon... 3. paw 4. claw, fang, nail 6. clutch, finger, pincer
talus... 5. ankle 8. clubfoot

tamarisk... 4. atle (atlee) 8. salt tree
tambo... 3. inn 6. corral, stable, tavern 10. tambourine
tambor... 6. puffer 8. rockfish
tambour... 4. desk, drum, lace 5. frame 6. stitch 7. drummer 8. ornament, stockade 9. embroider
tambourine... 4. dove, drum, taar 5. daira 7. timbrel 8. minstrel
tambourine effect (Mus)... 7. travale
tambreet... 8. duckbill
tamburone... 4. drum 8. bass drum
tame... 4. dull, meek, mild 5. inert 6. docile, gentle, humble, subdue 7. crushed, insipid, subdued 8. tone down 9. tractable 10. cultivated 11. domesticate 12. domesticated
Tamil... 5. Hindu 8. language (oldest Dravidian) 9. Dravidian
tamis... 5. sieve, tammy 8. strainer
Tammany (pert to)...
  Hall.. 14. Democratic Club
  man.. 10. politician
  officer.. 8. Wiskinky (Wiskinkie)
  scandal.. 9. Tweed Ring
  Society site.. 11. New York City (1789)
  symbol.. 5. tiger
tamper with... 4. plot 5. alter, bribe 6. meddle, scheme, tinker 7. falsify 9. influence, interfere
tampion, tampon... 4. plug 6. tympan 7. stopper, turnpin 9. rhynobyon
tan... 3. dun, taw 4. buff, ecru, tent, whip 5. beige, brown, color, tawny 6. rabbit, suntan, thrash 8. sunburn
tanager... 5. lindo 7. Piranga
tanbark... 3. oak 7. hemlock
Tancred... 6. leader (1st crusade)
Tanganyika, Tanzania...
  capital.. 11. Dar es Salaam (Haven of Peace)
  famed Mt... 11. Kilimanjaro
  famed plains.. 9. Serengeti
  famed town.. 5. Ujiji (Stanley found Livingston, 1871)
  lake.. 10. Tanganyika
  language.. 7. Swahili
  natives.. 5. Bantu
  ocean.. 6. Indian
  river.. 5. Congo
tangible... 4. real 7. tactile 8. palpable 9. objective, touchable 11. substantial
tangle... 3. mat, mop 4. kink, shag 5. ravel, snare, snarl, weave 6. entrap, medley, muddle, sleave 7. ensnare, involve 8. quandary 9. interlock 10. complicate, interweave
tank... 3. vat 4. lake, pond, pool 5. basin 7. cistern, stomach 9. reservoir 11. hard drinker
tanker... 4. ship 5. oiler 8. fuel ship
tanning shrub... 5. alder, sumac (sumach)
tantalize... 3. vex 5. taunt, tease 6. harass, plague 7. torment
tantalum symbol... 2. Ta
Tantalus (pert to)...
  father.. 4. Zeus
  father of.. 5. Niobe 6. Pelops

genus of.. 4. ibis
king (rich).. 6. Greece
tantamount... 5. equal 9. identical
  10. equivalent 13. corresponding
tantara... 7. fanfare 9. tantarara
  12. trumpet blare
tantrum... 3. fit 4. rage 7. caprice
  8. tirrivee (tirrivie) 10. conniption
Tanzania... see *Tanganyika*
Taoism, names... 6. Kwanti, Laotze
  7. Yu Hwang
tap... 3. dum, hit, hob, rap 4. plug,
  tamp 5. sound, spile 6. faucet,
  liquor, siphon, spigot, strike
  7. censure, reprove
tape... 3. gin, tie 4. band, wick
  5. strip 6. fillet, ribbon, secure
  7. bandage, measure 9. recording
taper... 4. ream, wick 5. point, snape,
  spire 6. candle, cierge 7. conical
  8. decrease, diminish 9. acuminate
  11. pyramidical
tapering (pert to)...
  blades.. 6. spires
  pert to.. 6. spired, terete 7. conical,
    pointed 8. fusiform 9. narrowing
  piece.. 4. gore 5. miter 6. gusset
  pillar.. 7. obelisk
  solid.. 4. cone
tapestry... 5. arras, tapis 6. Bayeux,
  dosser 7. Gobelin
tapeworm... 6. Taenia 7. disease,
  measles
tapeworm (pert to)...
  embryonic.. 10. oncosphere
  like.. 8. taenioid
  segment.. 8. strobila
tapioca, source... 5. salep 7. cassava
  (casava)
Tapirus... 6. tapirs
tapster... 7. barmaid, skinker
tar... 3. gob 4. brea, pave, salt
  5. black, pitch 6. cresol, maltha,
  sailor, seaman 7. mariner
  8. telegram 10. bluejacket
tarantula... 6. spider 7. mygalid
  10. wolf spider
tarboosh... 3. fez 6. red cap
tardy... 3. lag, lax 4. late, slow
  5. slack 6. remiss 7. belated,
  lagging, overdue 8. dilatory
  10. behindhand 11. cunctatious
tare... 4. weed (Bib) 5. vetch
  8. discount 9. allowance, deduction
target... 3. aim, tee 4. butt, goal,
  goat, mark 5. sight 6. object, shield,
  tassel 8. bull's-eye, ridicule
  9. objective
tariff... 4. duty, list, rate 6. charge
  7. tribute 8. schedule
tariffist... 8. advocate 13. protectionist
tarnish... 3. dim 4. dull, soil, spot
  5. cloud, stain, sully, taint 6. smirch,
  stigma, vilify 7. blemish, destroy,
  obscure 8. besmirch, discolor
  10. lose luster, stigmatize
taro... 3. poi 4. eddo, food, gabi
  (gabe) 5. cocco, tania (tanier)
  12. elephant's-ear
tarried... 6. waited 7. dallied
  8. lingered, remained
tarry... 3. lag 4. bide, stay, wait

  5. abide, await, dally, delay, pause
  6. dawdle, linger, loiter, retard
  7. outstay
tarsus... 5. ankle 7. segment
tart... 4. acid, sour 5. acrid, sharp
  6. pastry, severe 7. caustic, pungent
  8. poignant, turnover 10. astringent
  11. acrimonious
tartan... 4. wool 5. plaid 7. pattern
  (plaid) 10. Highlander
tartar... 5. argol (argal), shrew, valet
  12. incrustation
Tartar, Tatar... 4. Turk 6. Mongol
Tartar, Tatar (pert to)...
  domain.. 7. Khanate
  horseman.. 6. Cossack
  lancer.. 5. uhlan
  nobleman.. 5. murza
  people of.. 6. Turkey 8. Mongolia
  republic capital.. 5. Kazan
  title.. 4. Khan
  tribe.. 2. Hu 3. Hun 6. Mongol
tartarean... 5. cruel 7. hellish
  8. infernal
Tartarus (Myth)... 4. hell 5. Hades
  15. infernal regions (Iliad)
task... 3. job 4. duty, snap, test, toil
  5. chore, labor, stent, stint
  6. burden, dargue, impost, strain
  10. assignment, employment
  11. undertaking
Tasmania (pert to)...
  animal (burrowing).. 6. wombat
  discoverer.. 6. Tasman (1642)
  marsupial (savage).. 7. Daysure
    9. phalanger
  mountain.. 6. Cradle 9. Ben Lomond
  strait.. 4. Bass
taste... 3. sip, sup 4. tang 5. flair,
  sapor, savor, sense, smack, style
  6. liking, palate, relish, sample
  7. soupçon 8. delicacy, elegance,
  fondness, judgment 9. gustation
  10. experience 14. discrimination
  15. aesthetic liking
taste (pert to)...
  bite.. 5. snack
  decided.. 8. fondness, penchant
  French.. 7. soupçon
  fundamental,: 4. acid, salt 5. sweet
    6. bitter
  lacking.. 4. rude 10. unpolished
  ref to.. 7. palatal 9. gustatory
  sharp.. 4. acid, tang
tasteless... 4. dull, flat 5. vapid
  6. vulgar, watery 7. insipid 8. lifeless
  9. savorless 10. inartistic
tasty... 6. savory 8. saporous, tasteful
  9. palatable, toothsome
Tatar... see *Tartar*
tatouay... 9. armadillo
tatter... 3. rag 4. tags, tear 5. patch,
  piece, shred 6. ribbon
tatterdemalion... 5. gamin 9. ragpicker
  10. ragamuffin
tattle... 4. blab, tell 5. prate 6. gossip
  7. chatter, divulge, prattle 8. idle
  talk, inform on
tattler... 6. gossip, willet 8. quidnunc,
  redshank, telltale 10. alarm clock,
  talebearer, yellowlegs
tattoo... 4. call (drum, bugle), pony, .

scar 13. entertainment
tau... 4. ankh, crux, rood 5. cross
6. letter (Gr) 7. T-shaped
tau cross... 4. ankh 6. symbol
8. crucifix, insignia 10. St Anthony's
taunt... 4. gibe, jeer, mock, twit
5. sneer, tease 6. deride 7. provoke
8. reproach, ridicule 9. aggravate
Taurus... 4. bull 8. Pleiades
13. constellation
taut... 4. firm, snug, tidy 5. tense,
tight 6. severe, strict 7. nervous
9. distended
tautology... 8. pleonasm
10. redundancy, repetition
tavern... 3. inn, pub 5. hotel
7. barroom, cabaret, Gasthof, taberna
8. alehouse, Gasthaus, hostelry
taw... 4. game, whip 5. marble
7. tanning
tawdry... 4. loud 5. cheap, gaudy,
showy 6. garish 7. blatant
tawny, tawney... 3. tan 5. dusky,
olive, tenne 6. tanned 7. jacinth
8. brindled 9. bullfinch
tax... 4. cess, duty, geld, levy, scat
(scatt), task, toll 5. stent 6. assess,
burden, custom, excise, impose,
income, octroi, strain 7. doomage,
license, tribute 8. exaction, overtire
9. prescribe 10. assessment
tax (pert to)...
ancient.. 3. cro 4. geld 7. galanas
assessment.. 4. rate 5. ratal
7. doomage
church.. 5. tithe
commodity.. 6. octroi
French history.. 6. taille
kind.. 5. tithe 6. excise, surtax, taille
7. boscage 8. auxilium, carucage
9. surcharge
liquor.. 6. abkari (abkary)
pasturage (Shetland Isls).. 4. scat
(scatt)
tea... 5. dance, party, shrub 6. supper
8. beverage, function, sociable
9. collation, reception
tea (pert to)...
chemical content.. 6. tannin, theine
(thein) 8. caffeine
Chinese.. 5. black, hyson
Formosa.. 6. oolong
Ind Ceylon.. 5. pekoe
infusion.. 6. ptisan, tisane
Labrador.. 5. Ledum 8. gowiddie
Paraguay.. 5. yerba
receptacle.. 5. caddy 8. canister
table.. 6. teapoy (tepoy)
type.. 3. cha 4. tsia 5. Assam, black,
green, hyson, Ledum, oopak, pekoe
6. oolong 8. cambric 9. gowiddie
urn.. 3. pot 7. samovar
weak.. 7. cambric
teach... 4. show 5. coach, drill, edify,
guide, prime, train, tutor 6. direct,
impart, preach, school 7. educate,
show how 8. instruct 9. enlighten
11. demonstrate
teacher... 5. coach, guide, rabbi, tutor
6. doctor, mentor, pastor, pedant,
priest, pundit, reader, regent, rhetor,
scribe 7. edifier, starets 8. educator,

preacher 9. pedagogue, preceptor
10. instructor
teacher (pert to)...
Alexandrian.. 6. Origen
Indian.. 4. guru
Jewish.. 5. rabbi
Mohammedan.. 3. pir 4. imam
6. mullah
of the deaf.. 7. oralist
Russian.. 7. starets
teaching... 5. moral 6. docent
7. precept 8. doctrine 11. instruction
Teaching of the Twelve... 10. The
Didache
team... 3. two 4. haul, join, pain,
span, yoke 5. brood, chain, wagon
7. vehicle 8. carriage 9. yannigans
teamster... 6. carter, driver 7. carrier
Teapot Dome (pert to)...
known as.. 8. Scandals (Teapot
Dome)
leased by.. 4. Fall (Sec'y of Interior)
lease of.. 8. oil field
site.. 8. Elk Hills (Wyo)
tear... 3. rip 4. rend, rent, rive
5. revel, sever, speed, split, spree
6. cleave, hasten 7. destroy, shatter,
torment 8. lacerate, separate
10. dilacerate
tear (pert to)...
apart.. 7. disjoin 8. demolish
asunder.. 10. dilacerate
down.. 4. rase, raze
limb from limb.. 6. punish
9. dismember
to shreds.. 6. tatter
_up_.. 3. rip 6. damage
up the roots.. 6. arache
teardrop lace design... 5. larme
tearful... 3. sad 7. maudlin, weeping
9. lachrymal (lacrimal)
tears... 5. drops (lachrymal), grief,
rheum 6. lament 9. teardrops
tease... 3. guy, nag, rag, vex 4. twit
5. annoy, devil, taunt 6. bother,
harass, heckle, needle, pester, plague
7. provoke, torment 8. irritate
9. aggravate, tantalize
teaser... 4. gull 6. carder, curler,
sniper, stoker 7. curtain, fireman,
problem 8. pesterer, willower
9. tormentor 13. advertisement
technical... 7. skilled, trained
8. specific 11. specialized
12. professional
technocracy... 12. organization
17. rule by technicians
technology... 3. art 7. science
9. technique 10. agrotechny,
virtuosity 11. terminology
12. nomenclature 13. ethnotechnics
techy... 6. touchy, vexing 7. fretful,
peevish 9. irascible, irritable, sensitive
tedious... 3. dry 4. dull 5. bored,
prosy 6. boring, prolix 7. irksome,
noxious 11. displeasing, repetitious
13. uninteresting
tedium... 5. ennui 7. boredom
10. melancholy 11. tediousness
teeming... 4. full 6. aswarm
7. pouring, replete 8. crowding,
numerous, prolific 9. abounding

10. productive 11. overflowing

teeny... 3. wee 4. tiny 5. small
6. minute 10. teeny–weeny

teer... 4. daub 6. stir up 7. plaster

teeter... 4. rock 5. waver 6. jiggle,
seesaw 9. alternate, fluctuate,
sandpiper, vacillate 12. teeter–totter

teeth... 5. bucks, fangs 6. molars,
tushes 7. canines, ivories
8. grinders, incisors

teeth (pert to)...
all alike.. 7. isodont
covering.. 6. enamel
crustation.. 6. tartar
destitute of.. 5. morné (Her)
8. edentate 10. edentulous
elephant's.. 9. scrivello 11. scrivelloes
false.. 8. dentures
few.. 12. oligodontous
large.. 8. megadont 9. macrodont
like.. 8. odontoid
long pointed.. 5. fangs, tusks
6. tushes
ref to.. 4. pulp 5. molar 6. dental
7. dentine
science.. 10. odontology
without.. 8. edentate

teething... 6. growth 9. dentition,
odontosis 10. odontogeny,
odontotomy

teetotaller... 3. dry 7. non–user
9. nephalist, Rechabite (Bib)
11. teetotalist

teg, tag... 3. doe 5. sheep (young),
woman 6. fleece (sheep's)

teguexin... 4. teju 6. lizard

tegument... 4. bark, coat, skin
5. cover 6. cortex 10. integument

tekke... 3. rug 6. carpet 8. convent
9. monastery

tela... 6. tissue 8. membrane

telamon... 7. support (caryatid)
10. male figure

Telamon (pert to)...
brother.. 6. Peleus
companion.. 8. Hercules
expedition.. 8. boar hunt
10. Argonautic
son.. 4. Ajax 6. Teucer

telegraph (pert to)...
cable.. 4. wire
code.. 5. Morse
inventor.. 5. Morse (Samuel F)
key.. 6. tapper
service.. 8. dispatch

telephone (pert to)...
inventor.. 4. Bell (Alexander)
receiver.. 8. cymaphen
term.. 3. PBX 4. buzz, call, dial, ring,
toll 6. call up 8. exchange
11. switchboard

telescope... 4. Lick 6. Yerkes
7. Palomar 8. Galilean (1609)
9. Gregorian (Scot 1663)

telescopic... 9. farseeing

telescopic object (faint)...
11. debilissima

tell... 3. say 4. talk 5. count, peach,
utter 6. assail, impart, inform, recite,
reckon, relate, repeat, report, reveal
7. divulge, narrate, recount
8. acquaint, disclose, rehearse

9. recognize 11. communicate

teller... 6. banker 8. informer, narrator
9. describer, informant

telling... 6. cogent, potent 8. forceful,
striking 9. affective, narration,
pertinent 11. influential, significant

telltale... 4. blab, clue, hint 6. bearer,
device, gossip 7. tattler 8. informer
9. indicator, informing 10. indication,
talebearer

Tell the truth and... 13. shame the
Devil

tellurian... 2. Te 7. earthly
11. terrestrial 12. earth dweller

temeritous, temerarious... 4. rash
8. heedless, reckless 10. headstrong

temerity... 4. gall 5. cheek, nerve
8. audacity, rashness 10. effrontery
12. recklessness
15. venturesomeness

temper... 4. mood 5. humor 6. adjust,
animus, anneal, attune, dander,
harden, nature, season, soften
7. assuage, mollify, tantrum
8. hardness, mitigate, moderate
9. composure 10. equanimity,
irritation 11. disposition, temperament

temper (pert to)...
bad.. 5. angry, rabid 6. fuming,
savage 7. furious, ranting
clay.. 6. puddle
even.. 4. calm 5. staid 6. sedate
heat of.. 6. choler
in a.. 4. huff, rage, stew 5. tizzy
metal.. 6. anneal, harden 7. toughen

temperament... 4. mood 6. crasis,
nature 8. artistic 11. disposition

temperance... 6. virtue 8. calmness,
sobriety 10. abstinence, moderation
11. self–control 13. self–restraint
14. abstemiousness

temperate... 4. calm, cool 5. sober
8. moderate 10. abstemious,
restrained 14. self–controlled

tempered... 5. angry 6. sedate
8. annealed, disposed, moderate
9. moderated, mollified, qualified

tempest... 4. gale, wind 5. blast,
orage, storm 6. tumult 7. turmoil
9. agitation, commotion, windstorm
10. excitement 12. thunderstorm

Tempest (pert to)...
Cuban.. 6. bayamo
in a teapot.. 10. triviality
12. exaggeration
spirit.. 5. Ariel
The (character).. 7. Caliban, Miranda
8. Prospero

tempestuous... 5. windy 6. stormy
7. excited, violent 9. turbulent

temple... 4. fane, naos 5. cella, ratha,
speos 6. aedile, church, pagoda
7. edifice

temple (pert to)...
Anglo–Ind.. 5. kovil (covil)
approach.. 6. toran (torana)
Aztec site.. 12. Tenochtitlan
basin.. 5. laver
Chinese.. 6. pagoda
Hawaiian.. 5. heiau
Mexico.. 8. teocalli
Mohammedan.. 6. mosque

part.. 4. naos 5. cella 6. adytum
   7. narthex, sanctum 10. penetralia
ref to.. 6. hieron
sanctuary.. 10. penetralia
Shinto.. 3. Sha 5. jinja (jinsha)
   7. yashiro
Temple Bar (London)... 7. gateway
Temple Butte site... 11. Grand
   Canyon
Temple of Heaven... 7. Peiping
Temple of Onias... 5. Egypt
Temple of Reason... 9. Notre Dame
Temple of the Sphinx... 5. Egypt
tempo... 4. pace, time 5. grave, largo,
   speed 6. adagio, presto, rhythm
   7. allegro, andante 8. moderato
   11. synchronism
temporal... 4. bene, laic 5. civil
   7. earthly, secular, worldly
   9. ephemeral, temporary
   10. transitory 11. present time
   13. chronological
temporize... 5. delay 6. demand,
   parley 9. negotiate 13. procrastinate
tempt... 4. lead, lure 5. decoy
   6. allure, entice, induce, seduce
   7. attract 8. persuade 9. seduction
   10. inducement
Tempter, The... 5. Devil, Satan 7. Evil
   One 10. Evil Spirit, Old Serpent
   14. Prince of Devils
temptress... 5. siren 7. Delilah (Bib),
   mermaid 11. enchantress
ten (pert to)...
ace.. 10. bridge game
Commandments.. 9. Decalogue
dollars.. 7. sawbuck
fold.. 6. denary 7. decuple
footed.. 7. decapod
gallon hat.. 7. Stetson 8. sombrero
geometric figure.. 7. decagon
   10. decahedron
measure.. 4. acre, bath 6. decare
number.. 5. decad 7. several
physics.. 3. bel
poetic.. 9. decameter (decametre)
prefix.. 4. deca (deka)
stringed.. 9. decachord
thousand.. 6. myriad
year period.. 6. decade 9. decenniad
   decennium
tenable... 10. defensible
   12. maintainable
tenacious... 5. tough 6. dogged, viscid
   7. viscous 8. adhesive, cohesive,
   sticking, stubborn 9. glutinous,
   obstinate, retentive 10. persistent
   12. pertinacious
tenant... 4. saer 5. ceile, dreng
   (drengh) 6. holder, leaser, lessee,
   renter, vassal 7. cottier, dweller,
   villein 8. occupant 10. inhabitant
tenant's tribute... 4. cens
tend... 4. care, heed, lean, mind, wait
   5. nurse, offer, serve, watch
   6. attend, manage 7. incline, oversee
   8. converge, minister 9. cultivate,
   gravitate, look after
tendency... 4. bent, bias, tide 5. drift,
   drive, trend 6. course, object
   7. bearing, leaning 8. aptitude,
   relation 9. direction, proneness

   10. proclivity, propensity
   11. disposition, inclination
tender... 3. bed, pay 4. boat, fond,
   gift, give, kind, soft, sore 5. offer,
   young 6. extend, gentle, humane,
   waiter 7. pitiful, present, rail car
   8. delicate, merciful 9. attendant,
   sensitive 10. effeminate
   11. softhearted, sympathetic,
   warmhearted 12. affectionate
   13. compassionate
tender (pert to)...
animal.. 6. cowboy, herder
farm.. 10. husbandman
feeling.. 9. sentiment
foot.. 4. dude 6. novice 8. newcomer
   10. raw recruit
hearted.. 4. kind 8. merciful
horse.. 5. groom 6. ostler 7. hostler
regard.. 4. love 6. tendre
ship.. 7. pinnace
style.. 7. amoroso
tenderloin... 4. meat 7. brothel
   12. city district, vice district
tenderness... 4. love, pity 8. sympathy
   9. affection 10. compassion,
   gentleness
tending to...
arouse.. 7. emotive
assist memory.. 8. mnemonic
check.. 10. repressive
clear of guilt.. 11. exculpatory
control.. 10. regulating
drive away.. 9. repellant
evade.. 7. elusory
lateness.. 7. tardive
separate.. 9. divisive
tear.. 10. lacerative
wear away.. 8. abrasive
tendon... 4. cord, thew 5. sinew
   8. ligament 11. aponeurosis
tendril... 4. coil, curl 5. shoot, sprig
   6. branch, cirrus 7. stipule
   8. filament
tenet... 3. ism 4. rule 5. canon,
   creed, dogma, maxim 6. belief
   7. precept 8. doctrine 9. principle
tenne... 5. brown, color
Tennessee...
battle.. 11. Chattanooga 14. Above
   the Clouds
capital.. 9. Nashville (Athens of the
   South)
city.. 7. Memphis 8. Oak Ridge
   9. Knoxville 11. Chattanooga
first State.. 8. Franklin
Mts.. 7. Lookout 10. Cumberland,
   Great Smoky 13. Clingman's Dome
museum.. 9. Hermitage, Parthenon
   12. Atomic Energy (Oak Ridge)
   13. Ancestral Home (Pres Polk)
park.. 6. Shiloh
river.. 9. Tennessee
State admission.. 9. Sixteenth
State motto.. 16. America At Its Best
State nickname.. 9. Volunteer
tennis (pert to)...
four persons.. 7. doubles
player.. 6. netman
score.. 3. ace 4. love 5. deuce
series.. 3. set
site.. 5. court

stroke . . 3. cut, lob
term . . 3. ace, lob, net, set 5. serve
  6. hazard 7. receive
two persons . . 7. singles
tenon . . . 3. cog 4. tusk 5. tooth
  7. mortise
tenor . . . 4. alto (violin), copy, mode,
  tone 5. drift, trend 6. course, intent,
  singer 7. meaning, purport
  8. tenoreno 9. male voice, procedure
  10. transcript
tense . . . 4. rapt, taut 5. rigid, tight
  6. intent 7. intense, nervous, stretch
  8. strained 9. stretched
  10. breathless
tense (grammar) . . . 4. past 6. future
  7. perfect, present 9. preterite
  10. pluperfect 11. past perfect,
  progressive
tensile . . 6. pliant 7. ductile
  8. tensible
tension . . . 6. strain, stress 7. detente,
  nervous 9. disaccord, stiffness
tent . . . 3. hut 4. camp, show 5. cover,
  lodge 6. dossil 7. marquee
  8. pavilion
tent (pert to) . . .
  covering . . 4. tilt
  Eskimo . . 5. tubik (skin)
  general's . . 10. praetorium (pretorium)
  India . . 4. pawl
  Indian . . 5. tepee 6. teepee, wigwam
  occupant . . 5. nomad 6. camper
    7. tourist
  Russian . . 7. kibitka
  Scottish . . 6. pulpit
  surgical . . 6. screen
  tribe (Arab) . . 5. Kedar
  type . . 3. fly, pup 4. bell, wall
    6. Sibley 8. pavilion
tentacle . . . 4. hair, palp 6. feeler
  7. tendril
tentative . . . 7. feeling, testing
  9. makeshift, temporary
  10. substitute 11. making trial,
  provisional 12. experimental
tenterhooks . . . 6. strain 8. suspense
  10. uneasiness
tenth . . . 5. decim, tithe 6. decima
  9. organ stop
tenth Muse . . . 6. Sappho
Tent Maker . . . 4. Omar
tenuity . . . 6. rarity 7. poverty
  8. delicacy, subtlety, thinness
  9. indigence, unreality
tenuous . . . 4. rare, thin 7. slender,
  subtile 8. delicate, ethereal
  13. unsubstantial
tenure . . . 4. term 5. lease 6. socage
  7. holding 10. possession
tepee, teepee . . . 4. tent 6. wigwam
tepid . . . 4. mild, warm 8. lukewarm
tequila . . . 6. liquor 12. century plant
teraphim . . . 5. idols 6. images
teras . . . 7. monster
tergiversate . . . 3. lie 5. evade, shift
  10. apostasize, equivocate
term . . . 3. age, end, era 4. date,
  name, time, word 5. epoch, limit,
  style 6. estate, period, tenure
  7. premise 8. duration, semester,
  terminus 12. nomenclature

term (pert to) . . .
  connotation . . 6. intent 11. designation
  death . . 4. doom, mort
  for years . . 10. real estate
  glacial . . 5. stoss
  golf . . 4. hook 5. bogey (bogie), divot,
    eagle, slice 6. birdie
  grammar . . 6. phrase, syntax
    11. phraseology
  logic . . 4. mode 5. major, minor
  of life . . 3. age 5. sands (hourglass)
  Rugby . . 5. scrum
  sea . . 4. ahoy 5. avast, belay
  tennis . . 4. love 5. deuce, serve
termagant . . . 5. scold, shrew, vixen
  6. Amazon, virigo 7. furious
  8. scolding 9. turbulent
  10. boisterous, tumultuous
  11. quarrelsome
Termagant . . . 5. deity 14. imaginary
  being
terminal . . . 3. end 4. goal 5. anode,
  depot, final, limit 6. finish 7. limital,
  station 8. desinent, terminus,
  ultimate 9. end of life, extremity
  10. concluding 11. desinential,
  destination, termination
terminal (pert to) . . .
  battery . . 5. anode 7. cathode
    9. electrode
  leaf . . 8. apiculus
  ornament . . 6. finial
  town (end of line) . . 8. terminus
terminate . . . 3. end 4. halt 5. cease,
  close, limit 6. expire, result 7. end
  with 8. complete, conclude .
termination . . . 3. end 4. amen
  5. close, limit 6. ending, result
  7. outcome 8. terminus 9. desinence
  10. completion, conclusion, expiration
termite . . . 3. ant (white) 4. anay (anai)
  8. Isoptera (Order)
tern . . . 4. darr (black), gull 6. Sterna
  (genus) 8. schooner (Naut)
  9. threefold 10. sea swallow
ternary . . . 5. three, triad 6. tercet
  (Poet), triple 7. ternion, trinity
  9. threefold
ternate . . . 4. tern 9. threefold
  12. trifoliolate
terpsichore . . . 5. dance 6. dancer
  7. dancing
Terpsichore (Myth) . . . 13. Muse of
  dancing
terra . . . 5. earth 10. terra firma
terrace . . . 4. flaw (marble), mesa, step
  7. balcony, gallery, plateau, portico
  8. platform (earth) 9. colonnade
terrain, terrane . . . 4. land 5. tract
  6. region 11. environment
terrapin . . . 4. Emys 6. turtle
  8. Chelonia, Emydinae, tortoise
  9. cheloniid
terrapin, turtle (pert to) . . .
  color . . 9. grapenuts
  type . . 6. potter, slider 10. red–bellied
    11. diamondback 13. yellow–bellied
  War . . 14. Eighteen Twelve (1812)
terrene, terrestrial . . . 4. land 5. earth,
  realm 6. earthy, mortal 7. earthly,
  mundane, worldly
terrestrial planets . . . 4. Mars 5. Venus

7. Mercury

terrible... 3. bad 4. dire 5. awful
6. tragic 7. fearful, ghastly, hideous,
painful 8. dreadful, horrible, terrific
9. appalling, frightful 10. formidable,
terrifying, unpleasant

Terrible, The... 4. Ivan (Russ Czar)

terrier... 3. fox 4. bull, Skye 5. Cairn,
Irish, Welsh 6. Boston 8. Airedale,
Scottish, Sealyham 9. Kerry blue,
schnauzer 10. Bedlington, Clydesdale
13. Dandie Dinmont

terrific... 5. great 6. superb
7. extreme 8. dreadful, exciting,
terrible 9. appalling, excessive,
frightful 10. tremendous

terrify... 3. awe, cow 4. stun
5. alarm, appal, haunt, scare, shock
6. appall, freeze 7. horrify, petrify
8. affright, frighten

territory... 4. area, land 5. banat, field
6. canton, region 7. country
8. district, environs, Pashalic
(Pasha's), province 10. palatinate

terror... 3. awe 4. fear 5. alarm,
dread, panic 6. fright, horror
7. hellion, Reign of (Hist)
13. consternation

terrorism... 11. subjugation
12. intimidation

terse... 4. curt, neat 5. pithy
6. smooth 7. compact, concise,
laconic, pointed, refined 8. succinct
11. sententious 12. accomplished,
epigrammatic

Tertiary period... 6. Eocene
7. Miocene 8. Pliocene 9. Oligocene
12. Age of Mammals

tertium quid... 12. third someone
13. third somewhat

tertulia... 4. club 5. party 7. meeting

tessellated... 6. mosaic 9. checkered

tessera... 3. die 4. cube, tile 5. token
6. marble, ticket 8. password
11. certificate

test... 3. try 4. exam, feel 5. assay,
proof, prove, taste, tempt, trial
6. ordeal, sample 7. examine,
witness 8. evidence, standard
9. criterion, testimony
10. experience, experiment
11. examination, performance
12. authenticate

test (pert to)...
fineness.. 3. pyx
orally.. 7. examine
ore, value.. 5. assay
pot.. 8. crucible
severe.. 6. ordeal

testa... 7. coating 8. covering,
tegument

testament... 3. New, Old 4. will
8. covenant

testator... 7. legator, witness
9. testatrix

tester... 6. canopy, helmet, prover,
taster 7. assayer, candler, sampler

testify... 4. avow 6. affirm, depone,
depose 7. declare, profess, protest
8. indicate, manifest 11. bear
witness

testimonial... 5. token 7. tribute,

warrant 8. evidence 9. reference
10. compliment 11. certificate

testimony... 7. witness 8. evidence
10. Scriptures 11. affirmation,
attestation, declaration

testy, tetchy... 6. touchy 7. fretful,
peevish 8. petulant, snappish
9. irascible, obstinate 10. headstrong

tetched in the head... 9. pixilated

tetrad... 4. four 7. quartet (quartette),
quatern 8. foursome 10. quaternion

tetragon... 4. four 6. square
7. rhombus 9. courtyard
10. quadrangle

Tetragrammaton... 7. Jehovah
12. Supreme Being 14. four
consonants (unpronounced)

Teuton... 4. Goth 6. German

Teutonic (pert to)...
alphabet character.. 4. rune
deity.. 2. Er 3. Tiu (Tiwaz), Tyr
4. Frea, Odin, Thor 5. Aesir, Bragi,
Wodin 6. Balder, Frigga 7. Forseti
8. Heimdall
demon.. 3. alp
giantess.. 4. Norn 11. demigoddess
goddess.. 3. Eir, Hel, Ran 4. Norn,
Urth (Urthr), Wyrd
homicide (tribal).. 5. morth
land.. 4. odal
law.. 5. Salic
nymph (water).. 3. nis
race.. 5. Goths, Jutes 6. Franks,
Saxons 7. Vandals 8. Lombards
10. Norwegians 13. Scandinavians
supernatural being.. 5. troll

Teutonic goddess of...
death.. 3. Hel, Ran
healing.. 3. Eir
peace.. 7. Nerthus

Teutonic god of...
justice.. 7. Forseti (Forsete)
pantheon.. 5. Aesir (group)
peace.. 6. Balder
sea.. 5. Aegir
skill.. 3. Ull (Ullr)
sky.. 2. Er 3. Tiu (Tiwaz), Tyr
thunder.. 4. Thor 5. Donar
war.. 3. Tiu (Tiwaz), Tyr

Texas...
birthplace of Pres.. 10. Eisenhower
capital.. 6. Austin
cattle.. 8. longhorn
city.. 4. Waco 6. Dallas, El Paso
7. Abilene, Denison, Houston 9. Fort
Worth, Galveston 10. San Antonio
flags (six).. 5. Spain 6. France,
Mexico 8. Republic (of Texas)
11. Confederate 12. United States
flower.. 10. bluebonnet, yellow rose
Indian tribe.. 5. Caddo
monument (Battle).. 10. San Jacinto
police.. 7. Rangers
river.. 3. Red 5. Pecos 9. Rio Grande
shrine, mission.. 5. Alamo
State admission.. 12. Twenty-eighth
State motto.. 5. Tejas 10. Friendship
State nickname.. 8. Lone Star

text... 4. book 5. topic, verse
7. passage 8. libretto, textbook
11. letterpress

textile screw pine... 3. ara

textile shop... 7. mercery
texture... 3. web 4. wale, warp, wooz
   5. grain, weave 6. cobweb, fabric
   7. textile 9. roughness, structure
   10. smoothness
Thailand (Siam), capital... 7. Bangkok
Thames River town... 4. Eton
thana... 13. police station
thanador... 7. officer (Hind)
thanatology doctrine... 5. death
thane... 5. baron (anc) 7. servant,
   warrior 8. Scots peer
thankless... 7. ingrate 10. ungrateful
   13. unappreciated
thanks... 5. grace 6. prayer
   8. gramercy 9. gratitude
   12. appreciation 14. acknowledgment
Thanks to God... 10. Deo gratias
that (pert to)...
   is.. 2. ie 5. id est
   is to say.. 3. viz 5. to wit 6. namely
   9. videlicit
   pronoun.. 3. who 4. what
thatch (pert to)...
   grass.. 4. rope 6. slough
   hair.. 3. mop 4. crop, mane
   palm.. 5. Sabal 7. Thrinax
   roofing.. 5. reeds, straw 6. rushes
   support.. 6. wattle
thatcher... 7. hellier
thaumaturgy... 5. magic 7. sorcery
   8. wizardry 11. legerdemain
the (pert to)...
   end.. 5. omega 6. thirty
   French.. 2. la, le 3. les
   German.. 3. das, der, die
   Italian.. 2. il, la, le 4. ella
   same.. 4. idem 5. ditto
   Spanish.. 2. el, la 3. las, los
theater, theatre... 5. arena, drama,
   odeum, stage 6. lyceum 8. coliseum
   9. playhouse 12. amphitheater
theater (pert to)...
   actress.. 7. heroine, ingénue
   box.. 4. loge
   curtain.. 4. drop 6. teaser
   district.. 6. Rialto 8. Broadway
   floor (lower).. 7. parquet
   full house.. 3. SRO
   Greek.. 5. odeum (odeon)
   part.. 3. box, pit 4. loge 5. foyer,
   stage 7. balcony, gallery, parquet
   8. parterre 9. orchestra
   10. proscenium
theatrical... 5. showy, stagy
   8. affected, dramatic 10. artificial,
   histrionic 12. melodramatic
theatrical (pert to)...
   art.. 10. histrionic
   company.. 6. troupe
   machine.. 9. eccyclema
   spectacle.. 5. revue 7. pageant
   star.. 4. hero, lead 7. heroine
Theban (pert to)...
   bard.. 6. Pindar
   deity.. 4. Amon (Amon) 6. Amen–Ra
   god.. 5. Ammon (Zeus)
   king.. 5. Laius 7. Amphion, Oedipus
   8. Pentheus
   queen.. 5. Niobe 7. Jocasta
   soothsayer (blind).. 8. Tiresias
   triad.. 3. Mut 6. Amen–Ra, Khonsu

Thebes...
   capital of.. 10. Upper Egypt (anc)
   famed avenue.. 8. Sphinxes
   famed for.. 5. ruins
   location.. 4. Nile
   ruined temple.. 5. Ammon 6. Karnak
   Seven against (one of).. 6. Tydeus
theca... 3. pod 4. case, cell
   7. capsule
theft... 6. holdup, piracy 7. larceny,
   robbery 8. burglary, stealing
   10. plagiarism 12. embezzlement
theftlike... 7. piratic 9. piratical
theme... 4. text 5. essay, lemma,
   motif, thema, topic 6. matter, thesis
   7. subject 9. discourse, leitmotiv
then... 3. poi (Mus) 4. also, next,
   when 5. hence 7. besides
   8. formerly 9. therefore
   12. subsequently
thence... 4. away 5. hence 9. after
   that, elsewhere, therefore
   10. henceforth, thereafter
theogamy... 14. marriage of gods
theologian... 5. Arius (Bib) 6. Luther
   7. a divine 8. canonist
theology... 7. irenics 8. canonics,
   religion 9. depositum 10. doctrinism
theorem... 3. law 4. rule 5. axiom,
   topic 7. premise 9. principle,
   statement 11. proposition
theoretical... 5. ideal 8. academic,
   platonic 11. conjectural, impractical,
   speculative 12. hypothetical, not
   practical
theorize... 6. reason 9. postulate,
   speculate
theory... 3. ism 4. plan 6. scheme
   7. formula, opinion 8. analysis,
   doctrine 10. hypothesis
   11. speculation, supposition
   13. contemplation
theory of...
   evolution.. 9. Darwinism
   10. Lamarckism 13. Spencerianism
   knowledge.. 12. epistemology
   language.. 6. bowwow 8. ding–dong,
   pooh–pooh
   philosophy.. 13. phenomenalism
   relativity.. 8. Einstein
theosophist... 7. Mahatma
theosophy... 4. yoga 6. cabala
   7. Nirvana 8. kamarupa (Kama)
therapeutic... 7. healing 8. curative,
   remedies
therapy... 4. cure 5. faith 9. dietetics,
   medicines, treatment
   12. hydrotherapy, therapeutics
   13. psychotherapy
there... 3. yon 5. ready 6. yonder
   7. thereat, thither 11. at that place
therefore... 2. as, so 4. ergo
   5. hence, since 7. thence
   9. thereupon, to that end, wherefore
   11. accordingly 12. consequently
thermometer... 5. Hydra 7. Reaumur
   10. Centigrade, Fahrenheit
Thesaurus compiler... 5. Roget
thesis... 5. essay, theme, topic
   6. accent 7. premise 8. treatise
   9. postulate 10. assumption
   11. affirmation 12. dissertation

thespian... 3. art 5. actor 6. player, tragic 7. actress, Thespis (founder) 8. dramatic

Thessaly, Greece...
ancient name.. 9. Thessalia
famed for.. 8. horses 8. horsemen
mountain.. 4. Ossa 6. Pelion
native.. 5. Greek 10. Thessalian
town.. 7. Larissa

thew... 5. brawn, sinew 6. manner, muscle, virtue 8. strength

they go out... 6. exeunt

thick... 4. burr, dull, hazy 5. broad, bushy, close, crass, dense, gross, husky, plump, solid, squat 6. coarse, espeso, stodgy, stupid 7. crowded, grumous, muffled 8. familiar, friendly, intimate, numerous, thickset 9. luxuriant 10. indistinct 11. inspissate 12. impenetrable

thicken... 3. gel 4. clot, curd 5. cloud, flock 6. curdle, deepen, harden 7. congeal, stiffen 8. increase, solidify 9. intensify 10. incrassate, inspissate, strengthen

thicket... 4. bosk, rone 5. copse, grove, hedge, shola 6. bosket (bosquet) 7. boscage, coppice, spinney 9. brushwood, chaparral 10. underbrush

thickheaded... 4. dull 5. dense 6. stupid 7. doltish

thickness... 3. ply 5. layer 7. density 8. diameter, intimacy 9. luxuriant 10. opaqueness 11. consistency, measurement

thickset... 5. squat, stout 6. stocky, stodgy, stubby 14. closely planted

thick-skinned... 7. callous 11. hardhearted, insensitive, pachydermic 14. pachydermatous

thick soup... 5. purée

thief... 5. scamp 6. ackman, bandit, looter, pirate, rascal, robber 7. burglar, filcher, rustler, stealer 8. gangster, larcener 9. larcenist, scoundrel 10. freebooter, pickpocket, plagiarist

thieves (famed)... 5. Fagin 9. Robin Hood 10. Dick Turpin, Jesse James 11. Claude Duval 12. Jonathan Wild 13. Thief of Bagdad

thieves' Latin... 4. cant 5. slang 12. secret jargon

thigh (pert to)...
animal's.. 3. ham 4. hock 5. flank
armor plate.. 6. cuisse (cuish)
bone.. 5. femur, ilium
ref to.. 5. groin, meros (merus) 6. crural

thimble... 3. cap 4. ring 5. cover, watch

thimble (pert to)...
berry.. 9. raspberry 10. blackberry
eye.. 12. chub mackerel
flower.. 8. foxglove
rig.. 5. cheat 7. swindle 13. sleight of hand
weed.. 6. clover

thin... 4. bony, lank, lean, poor, rare, slim, weak 5. gaunt, lanky, lathy, reedy, sheer, spare, washy 6. dilute,

meager, rarefy, shrill, sleazy, slinky, sparse, watery 7. haggard, insipid, scraggy, scrawny, slender 8. araneous, rarefied 10. attenuated, diaphanous 11. transparent

thin (pert to)...
air.. 5. smoke, vapor 6. bubble
and delicate.. 8. araneous 10. diaphanous
and haggard.. 5. gaunt
and withered.. 7. wizened 9. shriveled
fabric.. 8. gossamer
out.. 5. peter
plate, bone.. 6. tegmen
plate, metal.. 4. leaf
plate, Zool.. 6. lamina 7. lamella
skinned.. 6. gentle, tender, touchy
Thin Man's dog.. 4. Asta

thine... 4. tuum

thing... 3. act, res 4. deed, fact, idea, unit 5. being, event 6. affair, entity, gadget, object 7. article, reality 8. anything, creature 9. happening, situation, something

thing (pert to)...
added.. 6. insert 8. addendum 9. insertion 10. supplement
assumed.. 7. premise 11. implication
complete.. 4. unit
cursed.. 8. anathema
done.. 5. actum
following.. 6. sequel
found.. 5. trove
hard to classify.. 11. nondescript
huge.. 7. monster
indefinite.. 7. so-and-so 10. thingumbob (thingumabob) 12. what's-its-name
nonexisting.. 9. nonentity
of little worth.. 6. stiver, trifle 7. trinket
the (thing).. 7. the rage
unique.. 4. sole

things (pert to)...
added.. 7. addenda 11. additaments
brought into being.. 9. creations
found, surprise.. 11. serendipity
intricate.. 9. involutes
little.. 16. inconsequentials
moving to and fro.. 7. wigwags
of like nature.. 8. cognates
suitable to eat.. 9. esculents
theoretical.. 7. noumena
to be done.. 6. agenda
to be learned.. 7. lessons
to follow.. 7. sequels 8. sequelae
to sharpen.. 10. whetstones
widely separated.. 8. extremes

think... 3. wis 4. deem, muse, trow 5. opine 6. reason 7. believe, imagine, reflect, suppose 8. cogitate, conceive, meditate 11. contemplate

think (pert to)...
better of.. 6. repent 10. reconsider
bring to mind.. 6. recall 7. imagine 10. conjecture
logically.. 6. reason
of.. 5. judge 6. intend, recall 8. consider, remember 9. recollect 10. call to mind
over.. 3. wis 4. mull, muse 5. brood 6. ponder 8. meditate

up.. 6. devise, scheme 7. concoct
thinker, Relig freedom...
    14. latitudinarian
thinness... 6. rarity 7. tenuity
    8. rareness 11. slenderness
third (pert to)...
    comb form.. 3. tri 4. trit
    day (Quakers).. 7. Tuesday
    estate.. 6. people
    figure.. 7. ferison
    in number.. 8. tertiary
    music.. 6. tierce
    ordinal of.. 5. three
    person.. 6. escort 7. grammar
        8. chaperon
    power.. 4. cube
    Republic.. 6. French (1871)
thirst... 6. desire, hunger 7. craving,
    dryness, longing
this... 4. near 9. the nearer
Thisbe's lover (Bab)... 7. Paramus
thisness... 9. haecceity
thistle (pert to)...
    bird.. 9. goldfinch
    color.. 6. violet (cobalt)
    emblem.. 8. Scotland
    genus.. 6. Arnica, Cosmos 7. Carlina
    star.. 7. caltrop (caltrap)
thistledown... 6. pappus
    12. thistlebeard
thither... 3. yon 5. hence 6. yonder
thong... 4. lash, riem, whip 5. knout,
    lorum, quirt, romal, strap 6. lorate
    7. amentum, lanyard (laniard)
Thor (pert to)...
    father.. 4. Odin
    German.. 5. Donar
    god of.. 7. thunder
    other name.. 9. Hlorrithi
    stepson.. 3. Ull (Ullr)
    wife.. 3. Sif
thorax... 5. chest 6. cavity 7. cuirass
    8. pectoral 11. breastplate
thorn... 4. bane 5. briar (brier), spine
    7. acantha, bramble, prickle
thorn (pert to)...
    apple.. 3. haw 6. Datura
    back.. 3. ray 4. dorn 5. skate
        10. spider crab 11. stickleback
    bill.. 11. hummingbird
    comb form.. 5. spini
    full of.. 6. briary
    letters.. 2. th 3. edh
    lizard.. 6. moloch
    pert to.. 6. spinal
    small.. 7. spinule
thornless... 5. inerm 8. inermous
thorny... 5. sharp, spiny 7. brambly,
    prickly 9. acanthoid, bristling, difficult
thorough... 4. full 8. absolute,
    complete 9. downright, intensive
    10. exhaustive 11. painstaking
thoroughfare... 4. road 6. artery,
    street 7. highway, parkway, passage,
    roadway, thruway 8. arterial,
    autobahn, highroad, pent road,
    turnpike, waterway 9. boulevard,
    concourse 10. autostrada
thoroughgoing... 4. zeal 7. extreme
    9. downright 11. painstaking
thoroughly... 3. all 9. intensive,
    out-and-out 11. intensively

    13. letter-perfect
thorp, thorpe... 4. dorp, town
    6. hamlet 7. village
those (pert to)...
    adept at table talk..
        14. deipnosophists
    brought to terms.. 11. transigents
    in office.. 3. ins
    in the stock market.. 5. bears, bulls
        7. traders 9. investors
    of a habit.. 7. addicts
    of the same goal.. 6. rivals
    outside a profession.. 5. laity
those who...
    read and write.. 9. literates
    ridicule.. 8. deriders
    verify.. 13. corroborators
    work together.. 13. collaborators
thou... 3. tha 7. pronoun 8. thousand
thought... 4. care, heed, idea, view
    5. logic 6. deemed, opined
    7. anxiety, opinion 9. attention,
    cogitated, reasoning 10. cogitation,
    meditation, reflection 11. cerebration
    12. deliberation, recollection
    13. consideration, ratiocination
thought (pert to)...
    continuous.. 10. meditation
    deep in.. 10. cogitabund
    form.. 6. ideate
    laws of.. 7. noetics
    reader.. 11. telepathist
thoughtful... 4. kind 5. moody
    7. mindful, museful, pensive,
    prudent, serious 9. attentive
    10. cogitative, meditative, reflective,
    ruminative, solicitous
    11. circumspect, considerate
    13. contemplative
thoughtless... 4. rash 6. stupid
    7. foolish 8. careless, heedless,
    reckless 9. brainless, impulsive
    11. harum-scarum, inattentive,
    thought-free 12. unreflecting
    13. inconsiderate
thousand... 3. mil 5. mille 7. chiliad
    10. ten hundred
Thousand and One Nights...
    13. Arabian Nights
thousand men, command of...
    11. chiliarchia
thousandth... 9. chiliadal
    10. millesimal
thousand years... 7. chiliad
    9. millenary 10. millennium
thrall... 4. esne, serf 5. slave
    7. bondage, bondman, captive,
    slavery 9. thralldom 10. oppression
thrash... 3. lam, tan 4. beat, cave,
    drub, flog, whip 5. flail, pound, twist
    6. defeat, punish, strike, swinge,
    thresh 7. belabor, trounce
    8. urticate, vanquish 9. pulverize,
    toss about
thrashing... 7. beating, milling
    8. drubbing, flogging, whipping
    10. punishment
thread... 4. flax, jute, line, silk, vein,
    wire, yarn 5. fiber, floss, linen, lisle,
    rayon 6. cotton, dacron, sleave
    8. arrasene, filament
thread (pert to)...

ancient.. 4. byss
a needle.. 5. reeve
ball.. 4. clew (clue)
cell.. 5. cnida
coiled.. 3. cop
comb form.. 3. nem 4. nema
    5. nemat 6. nemato
fish.. 7. cutlass 9. threadfin
    11. cobblerfish
herring.. 11. gizzard shad
like.. 5. filar 6. filose
loose.. 4. lint 5. raveled
medical.. 5. seton
metal.. 4. wire
mystery lead.. 4. clue
shoemaker's (obs).. 6. lingel (lingle)
silk.. 5. floss 9. filoselle
tangle.. 6. sleave
tape, braid (thread).. 5. inkle
tester.. 9. serimeter
weaving term.. 4. warp, weft, woof
    5. leash
threadbare... 4. sere, worn 5. trite
    6. shabby
threaten... 4. warn 5. curse
    6. menace 7. portend 8. forebode
    9. comminate 10. intimidate
    12. anathematize
threatening... 4. dark 7. ominous
    8. imminent, lowering, menacing
three (pert to)...
banded armadillo.. 4. apar 5. apara
comb form.. 3. ter
dimensional.. 5. bruit, cubic
    12. stereoscopic
fold.. 4. tern 6. ternal, treble, triple
    7. ternate
group of.. 4. trio 5. triad 7. triplet
    8. triplets
hundredth anniversary..
    13. tercentennial
in one.. 6. triune 7. trinity 10. The
    Godhead
legged stand.. 6. teapoy, tripod, trivet
lined.. 9. trilinear
masted vessel.. 5. xebec 7. frigate
    8. schooner
math term.. 2. pi (3.1416)
prefix.. 3. tri
R's.. 7. reading, writing
    10. arithmetic
seeded.. 11. trispermous
sided figure.. 7. trigon 8. triangle
spot.. 4. trey
styled.. 10. trystylous
toed sloth.. 2. ai
Three Kingdoms (Chin)... 2. Wu
    3. Shu, Wei
Three Kings of Cologne... 6. Gaspar
    8. Melchior 9. Balthasar 12. Three
    Wise Men
Three Musketeers... 5. Athos
    6. Aramis 7. Porthos 9. D'Artagnan
    (friend)
Three Sisters (Myth)... 5. Fates
    6. Clotho 7. Atropos 8. Lachesis
Three Wise Men (Kings of Cologne)...
    6. Gaspar 8. Melchior 9. Balthasar
threnody... 5. dirge 7. requiem
    8. coronach
threshold... 3. eve 4. gate, sill
    5. limen 6. portal 8. doorsill

threw... see also *throw* 4. cast
    5. flung, slung 6. bunged, heaved,
    hurled, pelted, tossed 7. pitched
thrice... 3. ter, tri 5. fully 6. highly
    10. repeatedly, three times
thrift... 7. economy 8. prudence
    9. husbandry 10. providence
    11. thriftiness
thriftless... 6. lavish 8. prodigal,
    wasteful 11. extravagant, improvident
thrifty... 6. frugal, saving 7. careful,
    prudent, sparing 9. provident
    10. economical, forehanded,
    prosperous 11. flourishing
thrill... 4. tirl 6. dindle, thrush, tingle,
    tremor 7. delight 9. electrify
    10. excitement
thrive... 4. grow 5. moise (Eng)
    6. batten 7. prosper, succeed
    8. flourish, increase
throat... 3. maw 4. crop, neck
    5. gular, halse, mouth, voice
    6. groove, gullet, larynx, mutter
    7. channel, glottis, jugular, orifice,
    pharynx, trachea 9. esophagus
    10. passageway 12. constriction
throb... 4. ache, beat, drum, pant
    5. pulse 7. pulsate, vibrate
    9. palpitate
throe... 4. pang 5. agony 7. anguish
    8. struggle
Throgmorton Street... 13. Stock
Exchange (London)
throne... 3. see 4. apse 5. exalt
    8. enthrone 9. royal seat
    11. sovereignty, supreme rank
    12. Chair of State
throng... 4. crew, host, push
    5. crowd, horde, press, swarm
    6. bustle, stress 7. hurried
    9. confusion, multitude
throttle... 5. choke, lever, seize
    6. throat 7. garrote 8. strangle,
    suppress, windpipe
through... 2. by 3. dia, per 4. into,
    thru 5. ended 7. perpend 8. finished
    9. because of, by means of,
    completed
throughout... 5. about 6. during
    8. thorough 10. completely,
    everywhere
throw... 3. cob, don, lob, peg, shy
    4. bear, cast, hurl, kist, pelt, toss,
    yerk 5. chuck, fling, heave, pitch,
    sling, twist, whirl 6. baffle, strike,
    thwart 8. discard, project
    9. prostrate
throw (pert to)...
a scare.. 7. terrify
away.. 7. discard 8. handbill,
    squander
back.. 5. repel 6. reject, revert
dice (term).. 4. sise 7. ambsace
in the towel.. 4. cede, quit
    9. surrender
into confusion.. 7. disturb, perturb,
    trouble 8. stampede 10. demoralize
into ecstasy.. 9. enrapture
into shade.. 7. eclipse
off.. 4. cast, shed 6. derail, reject
    7. abandon, discard
out.. 4. emit, lade 5. egest, eject,

expel 6. bounce 7. discard, project
9. eliminate
over.. 4. jilt 5. build 6. give up,
refute 7. abandon, discard
9. eliminate
overboard.. 8. jettison
water upon.. 5. douse
throwback... 7. setback 9. reversion
10. misfortune, regression
throwing (pert to)...
rope.. 5. lasso, reata, riata 6. lariat
science.. 10. ballistics
stick (anc).. 6. womera (woomera)
thrum... 3. bit, hum 4. drum, tuft
5. strum 6. fringe, repeat
thrush... 5. brown, mavis, robin, veery
7. disease 8. shagbark, songbird
9. blackbird
thrush (pert to)...
American.. 5. robin, veery 12. hermit
thrush
European.. 5. ouzel (ousel) 6. missel
7. redwing 11. nightingale
golden.. 6. oriole
Hawaiian.. 4. omao
Ind.. 5. shama
Scot.. 8. throstle
thrust... 3. dig, jab 4. gird, poke,
push, stab 5. lunge 6. obtrude,
pierce 7. intrude, obtrude, riposte
8. protrude 9. interject, interpose
thrust (pert to)...
aside.. 5. shove 7. dismiss 8. brush
off
down.. 7. detrude
fencing term.. 5. lunge 7. allonge,
riposte 8. estocade
one's self in.. 5. enter 7. intrude
out.. 5. eject 6. extend 8. protrude
thug... 4. goon, yegg 6. cuttle,
gunman 7. ruffian 8. assassin
9. cutthroat, roughneck
thumb... 6. pollex, thenar
thumb (pert to)...
a ride.. 9. hitchhike
bird.. 9. goldcrest
lady's (herb).. 9. peachwort, persicary
mark.. 4. soil 10. impression
11. fingerprint 14. identification
nail.. 5. small 8. complete
over.. 4. skim 6. browse
part.. 6. thenar
thump... 4. bang, beat, blow, drum,
thud, whip, yerk 5. knock, pound
6. hammer, pummel, strike, thrash
8. chastise 10. pound along
thunder... 4. boom, peal, roar
5. storm 6. fulminate
thunder (pert to)...
bolt.. 5. speed 6. Caesar 8. surprise
9. lightning 11. fulmination
fish.. 4. raad 5. loach 7. catfish
(electric)
god.. 4. Thor 6. Manito
of applause.. 5. cheer 7. ovation
peal.. 4. clap 5. crash
smitten goddess.. 6. Semele
8. Keraunia
thurible... 6. censer
thurifer... 12. censer bearer
Thursday... 4. Thor 8. fifth day
12. god of thunder

thus... 2. so 3. sic 5. hence 7. this
way 9. therefore 11. for instance
12. consequently
thwack... 3. rap 4. bang, blow, club
5. crush, knock, whack 6. defeat,
pommel, strike, thrash 7. belabor
thwart... 4. balk, foil 5. block, clash,
cross, parry, spite 6. defeat, gaffle,
oppose, outwit 7. oblique, prevent
8. obstruct, stubborn 9. frustrate,
interpose 10. across from, disappoint
thymus... 5. gland 10. sweetbread
(lambs, calves)
tiara... 5. crown 6. diadem 7. coronet
8. ornament
Tibbett opera... 12. Emperor Jones
(1932)
tibert... 3. cat
Tibet, Asia... see also *Tibetan*
animal.. 3. goa, sus 5. panda
capital.. 5. Lhasa
dialect.. 9. Bhutanese
kingdom.. 5. Nepal
Mts.. 8. Himalaya 9. Karakoram
religion.. 7. Lamaism
river.. 5. Hwang, Indus 7. Yangtze
11. Brahmaputra
ruler.. 9. Dalai Lama
Tibetan (pert to)...
beer (barley).. 5. chang
deer.. 4. shou
food (barley).. 6. tsamba
gazelle.. 3. goa
monk, priest.. 4. lama
ox.. 3. yak
sheep.. 3. sha 5. urial 6. bharal,
nahoor, nayaur
wild ass.. 5. kiang
wildcat.. 5. manul
tibia... 4. bone, shin 5. flute
6. cnemis
Tibur (anc)... 6. Tivoli
tiburon... 5. shark
Tiburtine... 12. Sibyl of Tibur
tick... 3. ked, tap 4. beat, mark, mite,
pest 5. Argas 6. acarid, Ixodes
7. instant 8. carapato, function,
ticktock 10. pajahuello (pajaroello)
ticket... 3. tag 4. note, pass, slip
5. check, ducat, label, token
6. ballot, billet, permit, record
7. license, voucher 8. document
11. certificate
ticket dealer... 7. scalper
tickle... 5. amuse 6. thrill, tingle
7. delight 9. titillate, vellicate
ticklish... 5. risky 6. fickle, queasy,
touchy 7. comical 8. unstable,
unsteady 9. uncertain 10. precarious,
unreliable
tidal (pert to)...
creek.. 6. estero 7. estuary
current.. 8. tiderace
flood.. 5. eagre
flow.. 3. ebb 4. bore, neap 5. surge
tidbit, titbit... 5. goody 6. morsel
7. saynete 8. delicacy
tide... 3. ebb, rip 4. high, neap, time
5. drift 6. period, stream 7. current
8. low water 9. be carried
tide (pert to)...
gate.. 9. floodgate

go with.. 5. drift, float 7. proceed
13. be fashionable
out with.. 3. ebb 6. recede
8. diminish, fade away
over.. 6. endure 8. surmount 11. live
through

tidings.. 4. news, word 6. gospel,
report, rumors 7. message
10. evangelist 11. information

tidy... 4. neat, trig, trim 5. groom,
natty, plump 6. spruce 7. orderly
9. shipshape 10. put in order
12. antimacassar, considerable

tie... 4. bind, bond, draw, even, knot,
lash, link 5. ascot, equal, nexus,
noose, trice, truss 6. cravat, enlace,
fasten, relate, tether 7. confine,
necktie, sleeper 8. equality, fastener,
restrain, shoelace 10. allegiance,
obligation

tie (pert to)...
off.. 5. belay
ornament.. 3. pin
ready—made.. 4. teck
securely.. 7. trammel
sports.. 8. dead heat
uniting.. 4. bond 5. tache
up.. 4. bind, wrap 5. truss 6. fasten
8. restrain

tier... 3. row 5. grade, layer 6. series

Tiergarten... 4. park 16. Zoological
Garden

tiff... 3. sip 4. huff, spat 5. drink
7. dudgeon, quarrel 8. outburst
10. fit of anger

tiffin... 3. tea 5. brown, lunch
6. repast 8. luncheon

tiger... 5. bully 6. emblem, savage
9. swaggerer

tiger (pert to)...
American.. 6. jaguar
bird.. 5. finch 8. amadavat
family.. 3. cat 6. mammal 11. Felis
tigris
hunting dog.. 5. dhole
S African.. 7. leopard
Tasmania.. 9. thylacine 13. Tasmanian
wolf
wolf.. 5. hyena
young.. 3. cub

tight... 4. fast, snug, taut, trim
5. alert, close, drunk, tense
6. narrow, stingy 7. exactly, shapely
9. condensed 11. closefisted
12. close–fitting, parsimonious

tight (pert to)...
fisted.. 6. stingy 12. parsimonious
lipped.. 5. terse 9. secretive
wad.. 5. miser 10. curmudgeon

tighten... 4. frap, lace 5. brace, tense
6. fasten, tauten 7. squeeze
9. constrict

Tigris River city of ruins...
7. Nineveh (anc)

til... 4. tree 6. sesame

tilde... 4. dash, mark, sign 6. accent,
tittle 15. diacritical mark

tile... 3. red 5. slate 6. domino,
mosaic, pament (pamment), tegula
7. ceramic, pantile, tessera
8. pavement

tiler... 5. thief 6. slater 7. hellier

10. doorkeeper

till... 3. box 4. farm, plow, tray, when
5. labor, while 6. before, casket,
drawer, whilst 7. develop 9. cultivate

tillable... 6. arable

tiller... 4. helm 5. stalk 6. farmer,
sprout 7. plowman, rancher
8. harrower 10. cultivator,
husbandman

tilt... 3. tip 4. cant, heel, list 5. joust,
pitch, slant, slope 6. careen, oliver
(hammer), seesaw, unload 7. incline
8. log house 10. tournament
11. altercation

timber... 3. log 4. beam, tree, wood
6. forest, lumber 7. support
9. underpier

timber (pert to)...
bend.. 3. sny
building.. 4. sill, stud 5. joist
6. purlin, rafter 8. stringer
convex.. 6. camber
cribs (logging).. 4. dram
cut.. 6. lumber 7. fallage
decay.. 4. doty (doaty)
end.. 5. tenon
hard, heartwood.. 7. duramen
Naut.. 3. rib 4. bitt, keel, mast, spar,
wale 8. sternson
support.. 6. corbel
upright.. 8. puncheon
wolf.. 5. lobo

timbre... 4. tone 5. clang, crest (Her),
miter 7. coronet 9. resonance, tone
color

timbrel... 4. drum 5. tabor 7. sistrum
10. tambourine

time... 3. age, day, eon, era 4. aeon,
date, hour, term, turn, week, year
5. clock, epoch, shift, tempo
6. decade, minute, moment, period,
season, second 7. century
8. duration, occasion, schedule
9. fortnight

time (pert to)...
accurate.. 10. isochronon
equal.. 10. isochronal
Fast.. 4. Lent
geologic.. 5. azoic
granted.. 4. stay 5. delay 8. reprieve
legal.. 6. usance 11. year and a day
long ago.. 4. once, yore 8. formerly
medical.. 3. tid 8. ter in die (three
times a day)
of vigor.. 6. heyday
one.. 4. once
present.. 5. nonce 12. contemporary
prior.. 9. antedated 11. retroactive
right.. 3. tid
same.. 7. however 9. meanwhile
10. concurrent 11. synchronous
14. simultaneously
spare.. 7. leisure
waste.. 4. idle, loaf 5. dally 6. loiter
wrong.. 11. anachronism
13. anachronistic

timeless... 7. ageless, eternal, undated
8. dateless, unending, untimely
9. premature 11. everlasting
12. interminable

timely... 3. apt, pat 4. soon 5. early
6. prompt 9. opportune

10. seasonably 11. opportunity
timepiece... 4. dial 5. clock, watch
  6. gnomon 8. egg glass, horologe
  9. clepsydra, hourglass, metronome
  10. isochronon, wristwatch
  11. chronometer
times... 3. ago, eld 4. yore 5. often
  10. frequently, yesterdays 11. ups
  and downs
timid... 3. shy 5. eerie, henny, mousy,
  pavid, scary 6. afraid, trepid
  7. bashful, fearful, nervous, not bold
  8. cowardly, retiring, timorous
  9. diffident, shrinking 12. fainthearted
  13. pusillanimous
timocracy (pert to)...
  defined by.. 5. Plato
  principle.. 11. love of honor
  State.. 6. Sparta (anc)
Timon of Athens... 5. Cynic (The)
  11. misanthrope
timorous... 5. timid 6. afraid
  7. bashful, fearful 8. hesitant
  9. shrinking
Timothy (pert to)...
  Bib.. 7. convert 8. Epistles
  grass.. 3. hay 10. herd's grass
timpani... 11. kettledrums
tin... 3. can, pan 5. money, plate
  7. element, stannum 8. preserve
  10. not genuine
tin (pert to)...
  alloy (copper).. 6. pewter
  box.. 7. trummel
  coat with.. 5. terne 10. terneplate
  comb form.. 6. stanni
  extract.. 8. prillion
  foil, plate.. 4. tain
  mine.. 8. stannary
  ref to.. 7. stannic
  sheet.. 6. latten
  symbol.. 2. Sn
tinamou... 4. yutu 7. tataupa
  9. partridge
tincture... 4. dash 5. color, imbue,
  myrrh, tinge, trace 6. iodine
  7. extract, vestige 8. solution
  9. paregoric, suspicion 10. extraction
tinder... 4. punk 5. spunk 6. amadou
  9. touchwood
tine... 3. nib 5. prong, spike, tooth
tinea... 7. sycosis 8. ringworm
tinge... 3. dye 4. tint 5. color, imbue,
  shade, stain, taint 6. flavor
  8. coloring, tincture 10. suggestion
tingle... 4. ring 5. sting 6. dingle,
  thrill 8. prickle 9. sensation,
  stimulate
tinkle... 5. clink 6. dingle, tingle
tint... 3. due, hue 4. tone 5. blush,
  color, tinge 6. nuance
tintinnabulum... 4. bell 6. tinkle
  9. rhymester
tintype... 9. ferrotype
  12. old-fashioned
tiny... 3. wee 5. small, teeny
  6. atomic, infant, minute, petite
  9. miniature 10. diminutive
  13. infinitesimal
tip... 3. cue, end, fee, neb, top
  4. apex, cant, heel, hint, lean, list,
  tilt 5. crown, point, slant, spire,

upset 6. careen, inform, summit,
  tiptop 7. cumshaw, incline
  8. bonamano, gratuity, overturn
  9. extremity, overthrow
tip (pert to)...
  end.. 3. neb
  French.. 9. pourboire
  Italian.. 8. bonamano
  near.. 6. apical
  Near East.. 9. baksheesh (bakshish)
  scabbard.. 5. chape 7. crampet
    (crampette)
  slender.. 6. arista
  to one side.. 4. list, tile 5. alist
    6. careen
  up and over.. 4. cant
tippet... 4. cape, hood 5. amice, scarf
  6. almuce 7. muffler 8. liripipe,
  palatine 9. comforter
tipple... 3. bib, nip, pot, sip 4. suck
  5. drink, quaff 6. fuddle, guzzle,
  liquor, tumble 7. spirits 8. beverage,
  overturn
tippler... 3. sot 5. souse, toper
  7. drinker 9. draftsman
tipster... 4. tout 8. dopester
  9. informant, predictor
  10. forecaster, speculator
tipsy... 4. awry 5. drunk, shaky
  6. groggy 7. fuddled, muddled
  10. staggering 11. intoxicated
tiptoe... 5. alert 6. warily 7. eagerly,
  quietly 8. cautious, stealthy
  10. cautiously
tirade... 6. screed, speech 8. berating
  9. philippic
tire... 3. fag, lag, rim 4. bore, jade
  5. dress, weary 6. attire 7. exhaust,
  fatigue
tired... 5. bored, jaded, spent, weary
  6. aweary
tireless... 8. untiring 9. unwearied
  10. unwearying 13. indefatigable
tiresome... 3. dry 4. dull, tame
  6. boring, prolix 7. irksome, tedious
  8. annoying 9. fatiguing, vexatious,
  wearisome 10. irritating
tissue... 3. web 4. bast, tela 5. fiber,
  paper 6. fabric 7. culture
  8. meshwork
tissue (pert to)...
  Biol.. 4. bone 5. nerve 6. muscle
    8. ganglion 10. epithelium
  cell.. 8. meristem
  cellular.. 10. epithelium
  connecting.. 6. stroma, tendon
    8. ligament
  decay.. 6. caries
  fatty.. 3. fat 4. suet
  hardening of.. 9. sclerosis
  horny.. 7. keratin
  layer.. 7. stratum
  lymphoid.. 7. tonsils
  nerve.. 8. ganglion
  ref to.. 4. tela 5. telar
  spinal.. 4. alba
  vegetable.. 4. bast 7. endarch
    8. meristem
  wood.. 6. lignin, lignum
Titan... 4. Rhea, Thea 5. Coeus,
  Creus, deity, Dione, giant, Theia
  6. Phoebe, Tethys, Themis

7. Cronius, Iapetus, Oceanus
8. Hyperion 9. Mnemosyne

titanic... 4. huge 5. great 7. immense
8. colossal, enormous, gigantic

Titan War (Thessaly)...
11. Titanomachy

tithe... 3. tax 4. part 5. teind, tenth
11. frank pledge

titi... 6. monkey 7. sea bird
8. ironwood 9. buckwheat

Titian... 3. red 6. artist 7. red hair
9. red-haired

titillate... 5. amuse 6. thrill, tickle
7. delight 8. interest

titlark... 5. pipit

title... 3. sir 4. dame, deed, earl, lord,
name, sire, term, type 5. claim, right
6. knight, madame, squire
7. caption, epithet, esquire, heading
8. muniment 9. designate
11. appellation, designation

titled member, Stock Exchange...
6. orchid (sl)

titmouse... 3. mag, tit 4. wren
5. Parus 6. parine, tomtit 7. jacksaw
9. mumruffin

titter... 5. laugh, te-hee 6. giggle,
tee-hee 7. snicker

tittle... 3. dot, jot 4. iota, mark, whit
5. tilde 6. gossip, tattle 8. particle

tittle-tattle... 6. gossip 8. idle talk
16. scandalmongering

tittupy... 3. gay 5. shaky 6. lively
8. prancing, unsteady

titubate... 4. reel 6. totter 7. stagger,
stammer

titular... 7. nominal 9. incumbent (of a
title)

Tlingit... 6. Indian (Alaska)

TNT... 6. trotol 9. explosive
15. trinitrotoluene

to... 2. at 4. into, till, unto 5. until
6. toward 7. as far as, thither
11. preposition

to (pert to)...
to be.. 4. esse, être
to-do.. 3. ado 4. fuss, stir 6. bustle
commotion
to each his own.. 10. suum cuique
to which.. 7. whereto
to wit.. 3. viz 6. namely 8. scilicet
9. videlicet

toad... 4. agua, Bufo, frog, pipa
6. anuran, peeper 7. crapaud
9. amphibian, Batrachia, spadefoot
10. natterjack

toad (pert to)...
eater.. 5. toady 8. hanger-on,
parasite
fish.. 6. puffer, slimer 8. frogfish
head.. 6. plover (golden)
lily.. 9. waterlily
stabber.. 9. jackknife
tree.. 4. Hyla

toadflax... 8. flaxweed, ranstead
13. butter-and-eggs

toadstool... 5. morel 6. fungus
8. mushroom, puffball

toady... 4. ugly 8. parasite, truckler
9. repulsive, sycophant, toadeater

toast... 3. tan 4. cook, leep 5. bread,
brede, brown, parch, roast, skoal

6. pledge, sippet 7. drink to
8. cinnamon

tobacco (pert to)...
ash.. 6. dottle (dottel)
Cuban.. 4. capa 6. Vuelta (leaf)
disease.. 6. calico, mosaic 7. walloon
English.. 8. bird's-eye
epithet.. 12. Lady Nicotine
French.. 7. caporal
Greek.. 7. Knaster
hookah smoking.. 7. goracco
Indian.. 7. uppowoc
introduced by.. 7. Raleigh (Sir Walter)
Kentucky.. 6. Burley
kind.. 4. capa, shag 5. tabac
6. Burley, Vuelta 7. caporal,
henbane, Latakia, perique, Turkish
8. Virginia 9. salvadora
paste.. 7. goracco
Persian.. 6. tumbak (tumbaki)
pipe.. 7. calumet, chibouk (chibouque)
principle (active).. 8. nicotine
receptacle.. 4. pipe 7. humidor
S American.. 8. canaster
small cut.. 3. cud 4. plug, quid
6. dottle (dottel) 7. carotte
Turkish.. 7. Latakia
wrapping.. 9. broadleaf

toboggan... 4. sled 5. coast, glide
7. coaster 12. sharp decline
14. downhill course

toby... 3. dog (Punch's), jug, mug, rob
5. cigar 7. highway, pitcher

tocsin... 5. alarm 9. alarm bell
13. warning signal

toe... 3. tae, tip 5. digit 6. dactyl,
hallux 7. minimus

toehold... 7. footing 8. foothold,
purchase

toes, odd-numbered...
13. perissodactyl

together... 3. com, con, syn 4. mass,
with 5. union 10. conjointly
11. unanimously 12. coincidently,
concurrently, continuously

toggery... 3. set 4. garb, togs
5. dress 7. clothes, harness
9. trappings 12. haberdashery

tolerable... 4. so-so 8. bearable,
passable 9. endurable
10. acceptable, fairly well, sufferable
11. supportable

tolerance... 8. patience
10. indulgence, permission

tolerant... 7. lenient, patient
9. indulgent 10. forbearing,
permissive

tolerate... 4. bear, bide 5. abide,
allow, brook, stand 6. endure,
permit, suffer 9. put up with

toll... 3. due, tax 4. call, duty, peal,
ring 5. knell 6. allure, charge,
custom, entice, impost, invite, strike
7. ringing 8. exaction
10. assessment 12. compensation

Tolypeutes... 4. apar 9. armadillo

Tom, Dick and Harry... 8. everyone,
humanity 15. persons at random

tomahawk... 3. axe 4. kill 6. attack
7. hatchet

tomb... 4. cist, lair 5. crypt, grave,
speos, vault 6. shrine 7. mastaba

(mastaba), orruary, tritaph
8. catacomb, cenotaph
9. mausoleum, sepulcher
tombé... 4. drum
tomboy... 3. meg 4. romp 5. rowdy
6. hoyden (hoiden), tomrig
tomcat... 3. gib
tomcod... 8. bocaccio
tome... 4. book, opus 5. atlas
6. volume 11. papal letter,
publication
tomorrow... 5. later 6. mañana 9. the
morrow
tonant... 7. blatant 10. thundering
tone... 4. mode, mood, note, tang,
tune 5. pitch, reedy, sound, trend,
twang, vigor 6. accent, energy,
melody, nuance, timbre 7. cadence
8. modulate, monotone, tonology
9. harmonize 10. inflection,
intonation, modulation
tone (pert to)...
down.. 3. dim 6. mellow, modify,
soften 8. moderate
lacking.. 5. atony 6. atonal
quality, color.. 6. timbre
series.. 5. scale
single.. 8. monotone
succession.. 5. melos
thin.. 7. sfogato
vibrant.. 5. twang
toneless... 4. weal 5. stony 6. silent
9. colorless
tonga... 7. vehicle (2–wheeled)
Tonga... 15. Friendly Islands
tongue... 3. gab 4. meat 5. lingo,
speak 6. speech 7. clapper, lingula
8. language, lorriker, parlance
9. utterance
tongue (pert to)...
classical.. 5. Greek, Latin 6. Hebrew
fish.. 4. sole
Jesus.. 7. Aramaic
lash.. 5. scold 8. scolding
pivoted.. 4. pawl
reference to.. 7. glossal, lingual
sacred.. 4. Pali
shaped.. 9. lingulate
tied.. 4. mute 8. taciturn
wagon.. 4. neap, pole
tongueless... 4. dumb, mute
10. speechless
tonic... 6. bracer, catnip, liquor
7. bracing 8. medicine, remedial,
roborant 9. stimulant 10. refreshing
11. corroborant 12. invigorating
tonsil... 8. amygdala
tonsorialist... 6. barber
tonsured... 4. bald 5. shorn 6. shaven
7. clipped 10. baldheaded
too... 3. and 4. also, over, very
6. overly 7. besides 8. likewise
9. extremely 11. excessively
12. additionally
too (pert to)...
bad.. 4. alas
much.. 4. trop 6. excess 7. nimiety
small.. 13. unappreciable
soon.. 9. premature
tool... 3. axe, saw 4. dupe, file
5. agent 6. device, gadget, puppet
7. engrave, gimmick, utensil, utility

9. appliance 11. contrivance
tool (type)... 2. ax (axe) 3. adz (adze),
awl, bit, hob, hoe, saw, sax, tap
4. file, jack, pick, tong, vise
5. brush, burin, drill, knife, lathe,
level, plane, punch, razor, spade
6. chisel, gimlet, hammer, lifter,
peavey (peavy), pliers, reamer, shears,
slater, slicer, square, trepan, wrench
7. cleaver, mattock, mattoir, scalpel,
spatula 11. screwdriver
tools (pert to)...
category.. 5. power, speed 7. cutlery,
machine, medical 9. precision
11. labor–saving 12. straightedge
prehistoric.. 4. celt 6. eolith
9. paleolith
stone.. 6. banner
theft of.. 6. ratten
toosh... 4. gown (short), robe
9. nightgown
toot... 3. pry, spy 4. fool, gaze, peep
5. blare, drink, revel, shout, spree
6. sprout 7. whistle 8. carousal,
eminence, proclaim 9. blow a horn,
elevation
tooth... 3. cog 4. dent, fang, snag,
tine, tusk 5. ivory, molar, point,
prong, taste 6. canine, cuspid,
wisdom 7. grinder, incisor
8. bicuspid, eyetooth 10. projection
tooth, teeth (pert to)...
ache.. 8. dentagra 9. dentalgia
comb form.. 5. denti, odont
6. odonto 7. odontia
cutting of.. 8. teething 9. dentition
decay.. 6. caries, cavity
11. saprodontia
destitute of.. 8. edentate
irregularity.. 11. odontoloxia
molar.. 4. wang
ref to.. 6. dental 7. odontic
science.. 10. odontology
Scot.. 3. gam
socket.. 8. alveolus
toothlike.. 8. odontoid 9. dentiform
toothless... 8. decrepid, edentate
toothsome... 5. tasty 9. delicious,
palatable
top... 3. cap, fid, lid, tip, toy
4. acme, apex, pate, roof 5. crest,
criss, crown, excel, mensa, outdo,
ridge, scalp 6. finial, summit, vertex,
zenith 7. highest, supreme, surpass,
topmost 8. dominate, pinnacle,
teetotum 9. uppermost
topaz... 3. gem 5. color 7. mineral
11. hummingbird 13. precious stone
tope... 4. tomb, wren 5. drink, grove,
shark, stupa, tower 6. guzzle, shrine
7. dogfish
toper... 3. sot 4. tope 5. shark
6. barfly, boozer 7. guzzler, tippler,
tosspot 8. drunkard 9. alcoholic,
inebriate 12. bacchanalian
tophet, topheth... 4. hell 5. chaos
8. darkness
topi, topee... 3. cap, hat 8. antelope
topiary... 6. garden 9. gardening
topic... 4. plot, text 5. theme
6. reason, remedy 7. subject
8. argument 11. application

topical... 5. local 9. temporary 10. thematical

topknot... 5. crest, onkos 6. pigeon 8. flounder 9. headdress

topmost... 6. apical 7. highest, supreme 8. foremost 9. uppermost

topnotcher... 3. ace 4. hero, star 6. tiptop 7. supreme 9. first-rate 11. unsurpassed

topography... 7. mapping 8. location 9. surveying 11. description 15. regional anatomy

topple... 3. tip 4. fall, tilt 5. pitch, upset 6. totter, tumble 8. overturn 9. overthrow 10. somersault

topsail... 5. raffe (raffee)

topsy-turvy... 8. confused 10. contrarily, disordered 11. withershins

toque... 3. hat 6. monkey (bonnet) 9. headdress

tor... 4. crag, peak 5. mound 8. pinnacle

torah, tora... 3. law 7. precept 10. Law of Moses, Pentateuch, revelation

torch... 4. lamp 5. blaze, flare, fusee (fuzee), light 7. lighter, lucigen 8. flambeau 9. flashlight

torero... 11. bullfighter

torment... 3. rib, vex 4. bait, pain, rack 5. agony, devil, harry, tease, worry 6. badger, harass, harrow, hector, pester, plague, stir up 7. afflict, anguish, bedevil, torture 8. distress, vexation 9. suffering, tantalize 10. punishment 11. persecution

torn... 4. rent 5. riven, split 6. ripped 7. severed 8. tattered 9. alienated, lacerated (see also *tear*)

tornado... 4. wind 5. cyclone, twister 8. blizzard, outburst 9. hurricane, whirlwind, windstorm 12. thunderstorm

toro... 4. bull 7. cavalla, cowfish

torpedo... 3. ray 4. boat, mine 5. shoot 6. attack, gunman 7. explode 8. fire upon, firework, numbfish 9. crampfish, detonator, submarine

torpid... 4. dull, numb 5. inert 6. stupid 7. dormant 8. benumbed, inactive, lifeless, listless, sluggish 9. apathetic, lethargic

torpor... 4. coma 6. acedia, apathy, stupor 7. languor 8. dormancy, lethargy 9. inertness 10. inactivity 12. sluggishness 13. insensibility

torque... 5. chain 6. collar 7. torsion 8. necklace, ornament

torrefy... 5. parch, roast 6. scorch

torrent... 5. flood, spate 6. stream 7. current, roaring 8. downpour, outburst

torrential... 12. overwhelming

torrid... 3. hot 4. arid 7. burning, parched 8. scorched, tropical 10. oppressive, passionate

tortilla cooking dish... 5. comal

tortoise... 4. emydd, Emys 6. gopher, turtle 7. hicatee 8. Chelonia,

matamata 9. ellachick

tortuous... 6. spiral 7. devious, sinuous, winding 8. twisting 10. circuitous, roundabout 12. labyrinthine

torture... 4. flay, pain, rack 5. agony, twist 6. impale, punish, wrench 7. crucify, distort, torment 10. punishment

tory, Tory... 6. bandit, outlaw, Papist 8. loyalist, marauder, partisan, Royalist 11. reactionary 12. Conservative

toss... 3. lob 4. cast, flip, hurl 5. bandy, chuck, fling, flirt, heave, pitch, throw 6. billow, thrash 7. disturb 8. flounder, scramble 9. commotion 10. excitement

toss (pert to)...
a coin.. 4. flip
and turn.. 6. thrash 8. flounder 9. vacillate
off.. 5. drink 6. tipple 9. dispose of, improvise
out.. 5. eject 8. trick out
together.. 8. scramble

tosspot... 3. sot 5. drunk, toper 6. flagon 8. drunkard

tossup... 6. gamble 10. even chance 11. uncertainty

tota... 6. grivet, monkey

total... 3. add, all, sum, tot 5. gross, utter, whole 6. amount, entire 7. perfect, summary 8. absolute, complete, entirety 9. aggregate

totally... 5. quite 6. wholly 8. entirely 10. completely

totem... 4. pole, post 6. fetish, pillar, symbol

totem pole... 3. xat

toto... 3. all 4. baby 5. totum

totter... 4. reel, rock, sway 5. pitch, shake, waver 6. falter, seesaw 7. stagger 8. titubate 9. fluctuate, vacillate

toucan... 4. toco 7. aracari 8. hornbill 13. constellation (opp Southern Cross)

touch... 3. dab, tag, tap, tig 4. abut, feel, meet 5. taste, trait 6. adjoin, border 7. contact 9. acuteness

touch (pert to)...
acuteness of.. 8. oxyaphia
bound.. 4. abut
closely.. 7. impinge 8. osculate
examine.. 7. palpate
light, lightly.. 3. pat 5. brush 7. attinge, lambent
off.. 4. fire 6. incite
ref to.. 7. tactile, tactual
stone.. 8. basanite 9. criterion 11. Lydian stone
wood.. 4. punk 6. amadou, tinder

touching... 6. moving 7. contact, feeling, tangent 8. pathetic 9. affecting, attingent 10. concerning 11. interesting

touchy... 4. sore 5. cross, testy 7. peevish 8. ticklish 9. irascible, irritable, sensitive 10. precarious 13. oversensitive

tough... 4. hard, wiry 5. hardy, rowdy,

stiff 6. robust, sinewy, strong
7. ruffian 8. adhesive, hardened, leathery, stubborn 9. difficult, obstinate, resistant, tenacious
10. unyielding

toupee... 3. wig 6. peruke 7. periwig
9. false hair

tour... 4. trip 5. shift 6. travel
7. circuit, journey 9. barnstorm, excursion

tourmaline... 3. gem 6. schorl
9. rubellite 10. indicolite

tournament... 3. tilt 5. games, joust, trial 6. battle 7. contest, regatta, tourney 8. Olympics 9. encounter
11. Turnierfest

tourniquet... 6. binder, garrot
7. bandage

tousle, tousel... 4. pull, tear
6. rumple, tussle 8. dishevel

tout... 3. spy 5. scout, watch
6. praise 7. canvass, lookout, tipster
8. give a tip, informer, smuggler
9. predictor, solicitor

tow... 3. tew, tug 4. drag, draw, haul, pull, rope 5. chain 6. hawser
8. cordelle

toward... 2. ad, at, to 4. near
5. anent 6. facing 7. forward, towards, willing 8. imminent
9. compliant, headed for
11. approaching

blood vessels.. 5. hemad (haemad)
center.. 5. entad 6. inward
direction.. 7. leeward, seaward
8. homeward, landward, windward
9. earthward 10. heavenward
exterior.. 5. ectad
front.. 8. anterior
left.. 3. haw 5. aport 9. sinistrad, sinistral
mouth.. 4. orad
right.. 7. dextrad 9. dextrally
stern.. 3. aft 5. abaft 6. astern

towards... 7. ynesche

tower...3. tor 4. boom, silo, soar
5. exalt, pylon, spire, stupa 6. belfry, height, turret, uplift 7. bulwark, defense, elevate, steeple, surpass
8. domineer, fortress 9. campanile
10. stronghold, watchtower

tower (pert to)...
astrology.. 7. mansion 14. planetary house
bell.. 9. campanile
chess.. 6. castle
church.. 5. spire 6. belfry, cupola
glacial.. 7. serac
India.. 5. minar 7. sikhara
marker.. 5. pylon
of.. 4. Pisa 5. Babel, Minar 6. Eiffel, Hunger, London 7. silence (dakhma)
10. Kutab Minar
Oriental.. 7. minaret
watch.. 7. mirador

towering... 4. high, huge, tall
5. great, lofty 6. Alpine 7. eminent, soaring 11. overweening

towhee... 5. finch 7. bunting, chewink

town... 4. burg, deme 6. ciudad, hamlet, Podunk, suburb 7. borough,

commune, village 8. boom town, township 9. ghost town

townsman... 3. cit 7. citizen, oppidan (Eton student) 8. resident
9. selectman

toxic... 7. noxious 8. poisoned, venomous, virulent 9. poisonous

toxicology *(science of)*... 7. poisons
9. antidotes

toxology... 7. archery

toxophilite... 6. archer

toy... 3. pet, top 4. doll, hoop, play, whim 5. dally, fancy, flirt 6. bauble, gewgaw, hoople, rattle, trifle 7. cat's paw, trinket 8. flirting 9. plaything
10. knickknack

trace... 4. clew (clue), copy, find, hint, mark, nose, seek, sign 5. refer, shade, tinge, track, trail 6. deduce, derive, detect, follow, sketch
7. glimpse, outline, thought, vestige
8. evidence, traverse 9. delineate, footprint 11. investigate, small amount

trachea... 4. duct 8. windpipe

tracing... 4. copy 6. record
8. ergogram 10. cardiogram
12. reproduction

track... 3. rut, way 4. path, rail, slot, spur, wake 5. route, spoor, trail, tread 6. follow, pursue 7. nereite (worm), vestige 8. traverse
9. footprint, spectacle

tract... 4. area, plot, zone 5. essay, range 6. estate, region 7. booklet, country, expanse, leaflet, quarter, stretch 8. brochure, district, pamphlet, treatise 9. territory
10. exposition 11. subdivision
12. dissertation

tract (pert to)...
arid.. 4. dene 6. desert
boggy, swampy.. 6. morass
10. Everglades
grassland.. 7. prairie
lava.. 8. pedregal
treeless.. 5. llano 6. steppe 7. prairie

tractable... 4. easy 6. docile, gentle, pliant 7. ductile 8. amenable, flexible
9. adaptable, compliant, malleable
10. governable 11. conformable

trade... 3. buy 4. deal, sell, swap, wind 5. craft 6. barter, merger, metier 7. bargain, calling, dealing, pursuit, traffic 8. business, commerce, exchange, practice, purchase, vocation 10. handicraft, occupation 11. intercourse

trade–mark, trademark... 5. brand, label

trader... 6. dealer, monger, sutler
8. merchant 9. tradesman
10. shopkeeper

trading association... 5. hanse (hansa)

trading station (Mil)... 2. PX 4. fort, post

tradition... 4. lore, myth 5. usage
6. custom, legend 7. culture
8. folklore 10. convention (established) 12. superstition

traditional... 3. old 9. legendary
10. historical 12. conventional,

long-standing 15. long-established
traditional tale... 4. saga 6. legend
traduce... 3. slur 5. abuse, belie
6. debase, defame, malign, vilify
7. asperse, pervert, slander
8. disgrace 10. calumniate
traffic... 3. buy 4. sell 5. trade
6. barter, simony (sacred)
8. business, carriage, commerce,
dealings 11. familiarity, intercourse
tragedy... 6. misery 8. calamity,
disaster 10. misfortune
tragic... 3. sad 4. dire 5. fatal
8. dramatic, pathetic 10. calamitous,
disastrous, fatal event
tragopan... 8. pheasant
trail... 3. lag 4. drag, hunt, path, slot,
spur 5. blaze, piste, route, scent,
spoor, trace, track 6. camino, follow
7. draggle 8. be behind, footpath
9. lag behind
Trail (famed)... 6. Mormon, Oregon
7. Santa Fe, Spanish 8. Chisholm, El
Camino, Heritage 10. Lewis–Clark,
Wilderness 11. Appalachian
12. Natchez Trace, Pacific Crest
trail (pert to)...
blazer.. 7. pioneer
deer.. 5. slot
mark a.. 5. blaze
marker.. 5. cairn
mountain.. 4. pass
Spanish.. 6. camino
train... 2. el 4. line, load, tail
5. breed, chain, coach, drill, flier,
focus, shape, suite 6. direct, school,
series 7. caravan, cortege, educate,
retinue 8. accustom, instruct,
railroad, rehearse 9. afterpart,
entourage, following 10. attendants,
conveyance, discipline, line of cars,
procession 11. progression,
streamliner 13. accommodation
trained mechanic... 7. artisan
trainee... 6. rookie 7. recruit, student
8. enrollee
traipse... 3. gad 5. trail, tramp
6. trudge, wander 8. gadabout
trait... 5. habit, touch 6. streak
7. feature, quality 9. lineament,
mannerism 11. peculiarity
13. individuality 14. characteristic
traitor... 3. rat 8. informer, Quisling,
turncoat 10. treasonist
13. double–crosser, Judas Iscariot
14. Benedict Arnold
traject... 3. way 4. sage 5. ferry,
route 6. course 7. passage
8. crossing
trajectory... 5. route 6. rocket
9. celestial 10. fixed orbit
tram... 3. car 4. limb 5. wagon
7. carrier, railway, tramcar, trolley,
vehicle 9. streetcar 10. conveyance
tramontane... 5. alien 8. polestar
9. foreigner, North Star
11. transalpine
tramp... 3. bum 4. hike, hobo, hoof,
step, walk 5. jaunt, nomad, tread
6. beggar, trudge, wander
7. sponger, traipse, trample, vagrant
8. vagabond 9. sundowner

10. landlouper (landloper), pedestrian
11. bindle stiff 12. foot traveler
trample... 5. crush, tread 6. bruise,
subdue 7. conquer, destroy, run over
9. press down
trance... 4. coma, doze 5. dream,
spell, swoon 6. raptus, stupor
7. amentia, ecstasy, rapture
8. hypnosis 9. catalepsy, enrapture,
hypnotize, spellbind
tranchant... 5. sharp 7. cutting
9. trenchant
tranquil... 4. calm, cool, easy, mild
5. quiet, still 6. gentle, placid,
serene 8. pacific, restful
8. composed, peaceful 9. quiescent
11. undisturbed 13. imperturbable
tranquility... 3. keg 5. peace, quiet
8. calmness, serenity 9. composure
10. quiescence 12. peacefulness
tranquilize... 4. calm, lull 5. allay,
quiet, still 6. pacify, settle, soothe
7. appease, assuage, compose
transaction... 4. deal, sale 6. action,
affair 7. bargain 8. business
9. discharge, execution
10. proceeding 11. negotiation,
performance, proposition 16. buying
and selling
transcend... 3. cap 5. excel, mount
6. ascend, exceed 7. surpass 8. go
beyond, outstrip, surmount
transcendent... 5. above 8. ethereal,
heavenly, superior 9. recondite
10. superhuman, surpassing
12. metaphysical, supernatural,
transmundane 13. extraordinary
14. transcendental 15. beyond
knowledge
transcribe... 4. copy 5. write
6. record 9. reproduce, translate
10. paraphrase
transcript... 4. copy 6. record
8. apograph 9. duplicate, imitation
12. reproduction
transfer... 4. cede, deed, pass, sale
5. grant, shift 6. assign, attorn,
change, convey, depute, remove
7. removal 8. alienate, delivery
9. transport 10. conveyance,
transcript
transfer (pert to)...
conveyance (estate).. 5. lease
6. demise
crown to successor.. 6. demise
design.. 5. decal 12. decalcomania
medical.. 10. transplant
of ownership.. 8. attorn
10. abalienate, alienation, conveyance
of property.. 8. disposal
transfigure... 5. exalt 6. change
7. glorify 8. idealize 9. irradiate,
transform, transmute
12. metamorphose
transfix... 3. pin 4. hold 5. spear
6. fasten, impale, pierce 9. hold
fixed 11. transpierce 14. hold
motionless
transform... 4. turn 5. alter
6. change, revamp 7. convert
9. transmute 10. assimilate
11. transfigure 12. metamorphose,

transmogrify 16. transubstantiate

transformation... 3. wig 6. change
8. mutation 10. conversion, false
front 13. metamorphosis,
transmutation 17. anthropomorphosis

transgress... 3. err, sin 5. cross
6. exceed, offend, thwart 7. disobey,
infract, violate 8. overstep, trespass
9. break a law

transgression... 3. sin 5. crime, fault
7. misdeed, offense 8. trespass
9. violation 10. effrontery, infraction
11. lawbreaking 12. infringement
13. nonconformity

transgressor... 6. sinner 8. offender
9. wrongdoer 10. delinquent,
malefactor

transient... 5. brief 6. lodger 7. flighty
8. fleeting, fugitive, traveler
9. ephemeral, migratory, momentary
10. evanescent, short-lived, transitory

transit... 6. travel 7. passage
9. metabasis 10. conveyance
12. transference

transition... 5. shift 7. passage
9. anabolism, evolution, metabasis
10. catabolism (katabolism),
conversion, metabolism, modulation
11. transfusion

transitory... 5. brief, fleet 8. fleeting,
temporal 9. ephemeral, temporary,
transient 10. evanescent 11. not
enduring

transitory things... 8. ephemera

translate... 4. read, rede 6. decode,
render 7. convert 8. construe,
transfer 9. interpret 10. paraphrase

translation... 4. pony, trot 7. version
9. rendition 10. paraphrase
12. transference 14. interpretation
15. transliteration

translucent... 6. limpid 8. luminous
11. transparent 14. shining through

transmit... 4. send 6. convey, render
7. devolve, forward 8. bequeath,
hand down, transfer
11. communicate

transmutation... 9. evolution

transmute... 6. change 7. convert,
resolve 9. transform 11. transfigure
12. metamorphose
16. transubstantiate

transparent... 4. open 5. clear, gauzy,
lucid, sheer 6. bright, candid, glassy,
lucent 7. crystal, pelucid, shining
8. luminous, lustrous 9. guileless
10. diaphanous 11. crystalline,
perspicuous, translucent, unconcealed

transparent thing... 4. mica, silk, veil
5. beryl, water 6. quartz, tissue
7. crystal, diamond 8. gossamer
9. isinglass

transport... dak 4. boat, move, raft,
send, ship 5. bring, carry, truck
6. banish, convey, deport, vessel
7. ecstasy, freight, passion, rapture,
smuggle 8. carriage, emigrate,
entrance, palander, transfer
9. enrapture, troopship

transpose... 5. shift 6. change,
convey, invert 7. convert, reverse
8. transfer 9. rearrange, translate,

transmute 11. interchange

transposition of sounds, words...
10. metathesis, spoonerism

Transvaal (pert to)...
capital.. 8. Pretoria
city.. 12. Johannesburg
daisy.. 7. gerbera
discovery.. 4. gold, Rand (The)
famed emigration.. 9. great trek
(1836)
legislature.. 4. raad
policeman.. 4. zarp
settlers.. 5. Boers
War.. 4. Boer (1899–1902)

transverse... 6. across 7. oblique,
transom 8. diagonal 9. crosswise
10. crosspiece

trap... 3. gin, net, pat, web 4. cage,
door, lure, rock, tipe, tree, weir
5. catch, creel, mouth, snare
6. ambush, corner, device, eelpot,
enmesh, recess 7. dragnet, ensnare,
pitfall, springe 8. carriage, deadfall,
trapping, trickery 9. caparison, road
block, stratagem

trapper... 5. lurer 6. hunter, netter,
snarer 7. decoyer

trappings... 4. gear, tack 5. props
7. scenery 8. wardrobe 9. apparatus,
caparison, ornaments 10. horse cloth
13. paraphernalia

trash... 4. bosh, dirt, junk 5. waste
6. debris, refuse, rubble 7. rubbish
8. nonsense, riffraff, trumpery
10. balderdash

trashy... 5. cheap, toshy 6. paltry
7. useless 8. rubbishy 9. worthless
11. nonsensical

trauma... 5. shock, wound 6. injury

travail... 4. pain, toil 5. agony, labor
7. journey, trouble 9. suffering
11. parturition

trave... 9. crossbeam

travel... 2. go 4. fare, move, mush,
post, ride, taxi, tour, trek, wend
5. coast 6. motion 7. commute,
journey, migrate, sojourn 8. progress,
traverse 9. gallivant 11. peregrinate

travel (pert to)...
equipment.. 7. baggage 9. viaticals
expense.. 9. viaticum
group.. 7. caravan
over obstacles.. 9. roughshod
pert to.. 6. viatic
place to place.. 9. itinerate

traveler, travelers... 5. farer 6. viator
7. caravan, tourist 8. salesman,
wayfarer 9. journeyer

travels... 7. odyssey 8. journeys
14. peregrinations

traverse... 4. deny, pass 5. cross
6. refute, thwart 7. athwart, oblique,
parados 8. navigate 10. counteract

travesty... 5. drama 6. parody, satire
7. lampoon 8. disguise 9. burlesque
10. caricature 11. incongruity

tray... 6. salver, server 7. ashtray,
coaster

treacherous... 5. false, Judas, punic,
snaky 8. disloyal, plotting, unstable
9. deceitful, faithless, insidious
10. perfidious, traitorous, unreliable

11. disaffected 13. Machiavellian (Machiavelian), untrustworthy

treachery... 5. guile 6. deceit
7. perfidy, treason 8. betrayal
10. disloyalty

treacle... 4. cure 6. remedy
7. claggum, sweeten 8. molasses
10. sweetening

treacle water... 7. cordial

tread... 3. rut 4. gait, mark, pace, step, volt, walk 5. crush, stair
6. course 7. conquer, set foot, trample 8. footstep, shoe sole
9. footprint

treadle... 5. lever, pedal 7. chalaza

tread underfoot... 5. crush 6. subdue
7. oppress, run over 8. domineer
9. tyrannize

treason... 7. perfidy 8. betrayal, sedition 9. treachery

treasonable, treasonous...
10. perfidious, traitorous
11. treacherous

treasure... 4. fisc (fisk), fund, roon
5. cache, chest, hoard, prize, purse, store, trove, value 6. coffer, fiscus, riches, wealth 7. cherish 8. hold dear 9. exchequer, thesaurus
10. appreciate, depository, repository, storehouse

treasurer... 6. bursar, purser
7. cashier, curator, officer 8. receiver
9. paymaster 11. chamberlain

Treasure State... 7. Montana

treasure-trove... 5. money (hidden)
7. bullion 9. discovery 14. buried treasure

treat... 4. dose 5. Dutch, feast
6. doctor, handle, regale, repast
7. delight, discuss, process
8. consider 9. discourse, entertain, negotiate 10. manipulate

treat (pert to)...
improperly.. 4. snub 5. flout, spite
6. insult, misuse, offend 9. humiliate
maliciously.. 5. frame, spite
of morals.. 6. ethics
royally.. 6. regale 9. with honor
silk (for rustle).. 6. scroop
snobbishly.. 7. high hat, high-hat
surgically.. 7. operate
tenderly.. 6. coddle, pamper
with contempt.. 5. flout, scorn, scout, spurn 7. contemn
with deference.. 7. respect

treatise... 5. essay, study, tract
6. thesis 7. article 9. discourse
10. discussion 12. dissertation

treatise on...
forests.. 5. silva
fruit trees.. 6. pomona
language.. 7. grammar
pines.. 7. pinetum

treatment (pert to)...
application (Med).. 5. stupe
compassionate.. 5. mercy
harsh.. 5. abuse 8. misusage, severity
ill.. 5. abuse
preparatory.. 8. training 10. ground work, processing
term.. 5. usage 8. addition (to soil), handling

treaty... 4. mise, pact 6. cartel
7. compact, entente 8. contract
9. agreement 10. convention
11. arrangement, negotiation
12. capitulation 13. understanding

treaty (pert to)...
bound nations.. 6. allies
Elm.. 12. Philadelphia (1682)
first draft.. 8. protocol
peace.. 5. truce 6. Pax Dei
9. armistice 10. pax in bella
secret.. 13. the Engagement (1647)

treble... 5. three, voice 6. latten, triple
7. soprano 9. threefold
11. high-pitched

treble clef... 3. Gee 5. G clef, staff
(G clef)

tree... 5. plant 6. corner, timber
7. gallows 9. genealogy

tree (pert to)... see also **trees**
antidote for snakebite.. 6. cedron
aromatic.. 9. sassafras
bear.. 7. raccoon
cactus.. 7. saguaro
camphor.. 5. kapur
cat.. 9. palm civet
cobra.. 6. mambra
cone-bearing.. 3. fir, yew 5. alder, cedar, larch 7. conifer
evergreen fruit.. 5. lemon 6. orange
exudation.. 3. gum, lac, sap
India.. 4. dita 10. devil's tree
lotus.. 4. sadr
mineral (formed on).. 8. dendrite
of Buddha.. 2. bo
of chastity.. 11. agnus castus
of life.. 10. arbor vitae
of strength.. 3. oak
rain.. 5. saman (zaman) 8. genisaro
resin.. 3. fir 4. pine 6. balsam
sacred (Bib).. 7. asherah
salt.. 4. atle (atlee) 8. tamarisk
snake.. 4. gimp, lora
sprout.. 5. copse, sprig 7. coppice
sugar.. 5. maple
Texas.. 5. alamo 6. poplar
tiger.. 7. leopard
toad.. 4. hyla
trunk.. 4. bole 5. caber, stock
umbrella.. 5. wahoo
victor's crown.. 6. laurel
worshiper.. 5. dryad, nymph (wood)

trees (pert to)...
grove.. 5. copse
plantation.. 6. forest 7. orchard, pinetum
poem.. 6. Kilmer (Joyce)
ref to.. 8. arboreal 9. cacuminal
science.. 7. silvics 12. silviculture
service (rowan).. 5. sorbs

trefoil... 6. clover 8. shamrock
10. black medic, clover leaf (Her)

tregetour (anc)... 7. juggler
8. magician

trek... 6. travel 7. journey, migrate
10. expedition

trellis... 5. arbor 7. lattice, pergola
8. espalier 11. latticework

tremble... 5. quake, shake 6. doddle, falter, quaver, quiver, shiver, tatter, thrill, tremor 7. shudder, tremolo, twitter, vibrate 8. be afraid 9. be

excited, trepidate
trembling... 5. aspen 6. dither, trepid
   7. fearful, nervous, quaking, quavery,
   shaking 9. vibrating
tremendous... 3. big 4. huge
   5. awful, giant, great 6. superb
   8. horrible, powerful, terrific
   9. frightful, momentous, monstrous
   10. terrifying 13. extraordinary
tremolo... 6. quaver 10. fluttering
tremor... 5. palsy, quake, shake
   6. quiver, thrill 7. tremble
   9. vibration
tremulous... 5. aspen, quaky, timid
   7. excited, fearful, nervous, palsied,
   shaking, shivery 9. quavering,
   sensitive, trembling, vibratory
   11. palpitating
trench... 3. gaw 4. bury, gash, leat,
   moat 5. canal, carve, ditch, drain,
   fosse 6. furrow, groove, gutter
   7. acequia, intrude 8. aqueduct,
   encroach, entrench, infringe, trespass
   10. excavation 12. entrenchment
trenchant... 4. keen 5. acute, sharp
   6. biting 7. cutting 8. clear–cut,
   incisive 11. penetrating
trencherman... 6. eater 7. sponger
   8. gourmand 9. chowhound
   11. gormandizer
trend... 4. tone, turn, vein 5. drift,
   skirt, swing, tenor 6. strike
   7. deviate, revolve 8. movement,
   tendency 9. direction 11. inclination
trepan... 3. saw 4. lure, tool 5. snare,
   trick 6. entrap 7. deceive, swindle
   8. deceiver, trephine 9. stratagem,
   trickster
trepang... 10. bêche–de–mer 11. sea
   cucumber 14. sea caterpillar
trepid... 7. quaking 8. timorous
   9. trembling
trepidation... 4. fear 5. alarm
   6. dismay 7. quaking 8. agitation,
   confusion 10. excitement
   11. disturbance, oscillation
   12. perturbation 13. consternation
trespass... 3. sin 4. tort 5. poach
   6. breach, invade, trench 7. intrude,
   offense 8. encroach, entrench,
   infringe, overstep 10. infraction,
   transgress 11. misfeasance
   12. infringement 13. transgression
tress... 4. curl, hair 5. braid, plait
   7. ringlet 10. lock of hair
tressure... 4. band 6. border, fillet,
   ribbon 9. headdress
trestle... 5. bench 7. support, viaduct
tret... 9. allowance
triad... 5. chord, three, trine 7. trinary,
   trinity 9. trivalent 12. ternary group
trial... 2. go 4. bout, case, test
   7. venue 6. assize, ordeal
   7. attempt, contest, empiric
   8. evidence, hardship 9. prolusion,
   trying out 10. experiment
   11. examination, tribulation
triangle... 6. trigon 8. virginal
   13. constellation
triangle (pert to)...
connection.. 5. delta

draw circle within.. 7. escribe
military.. 10. punishment
music instrument.. 10. percussion,
   triquetrum (anc)
side.. 3. leg
three acute angles.. 6. oxygon
two equal sides.. 9. isosceles
unequal sides.. 7. scalene
triangular (pert to)...
decoration.. 8. pediment, triqueta
muscle.. 7. deltoid
pert to.. 10. trilateral
piece.. 4. gore 5. miter, wedge
   6. gusset
sail.. 6. lateen 9. spinnaker
shaped.. 7. deltoid 8. oxygonal
tribal custom... 7. couvade (childbirth)
tribal symbol... 5. totem 9. totem
   pole
tribe... 4. clan, kind, race, sept
   5. class, group 6. family 7. company
   11. aggregation 14. classification
tribe (pert to)...
birds.. 5. flock
head of.. 5. chief 6. sachem
   9. patriarch
Israel.. 3. Dan 4. Levi 6. Reuben
migrated.. 5. Aryan
New Zealand.. 3. ati
of Ben.. 5. poets (Ben Jonson)
Tribes, Five Civilized... 5. Creek
   7. Choctaw 8. Cherokee, Seminole
   9. Chickasaw
Tribes, Five Nations (Iroquois)...
   6. Cayuga, Mohawk, Oneida, Seneca
   8. Onondaga
tribulation... 5. trial 6. ordeal, sorrow
   8. distress 9. suffering
tribunal... 3. bar 4. banc, seat
   5. bench, court, curia, forum
   9. Areopagus (anc)
tributary... 4. fork, vein 6. branch,
   feeder 8. affluent, effluent, influent
   9. auxiliary 11. subordinate
   12. contributary
tribute... 3. fee, pay, tax 4. cain,
   duty, levy, scat 5. allow, grant
   6. assign, bestow, homage, impost,
   praise, rental 7. chevage (Hist),
   ovation, payment, pension, respect
   8. encomium 9. attribute, gratitude
   10. allegiance, contribute, obligation
   11. retribution
tricar... 8. tricycle 10. motorcycle (with
   extra car)
trice... 5. jiffy 6. moment 7. instant
   9. twinkling
trick... 3. fob, gag 4. dido, dupe,
   feat, flam, gull, jest, ruse, wile
   5. cheat, child, dodge, fraud, guile,
   knack, prank, shift, stunt 6. deceit,
   delude 7. deceive, defraud, finesse,
   pretext 8. artifice, delusion, flimflam,
   illusion 9. chicanery, deception,
   imposture 10. subterfuge
   11. contrivance, legerdemain
trickery... 5. fraud, hocus 6. deceit
   7. roguery 8. artifice, cheating,
   trumpery 9. chicanery, deception,
   duplicity 10. hanky–panky
   11. amenability, legerdemain
trickle... 4. drip, drop, flow, leak

7. distill (distil), dribble, dripple, leakage

tricks... 4. shab 5. ruses 7. roguery 10. deceptions

trickster... 3. fox 5. cheat, rogue 6. rascal 7. slicker 8. deceiver 12. Artful Dodger

tricky... 3. sly 5. snide 6. artful, clever, crafty, shrewd 7. cunning, devious 8. rascally 9. deceitful 13. Machiavellian

trident... 5. curve, spear 6. symbol 7. leister

tried... 4. true 6. proved, tested 8. devoted 8. faithful, reliable 11. trustworthy

tries... 5. tests 6. assays 8. attempts, contests

trifle... 3. ace, bit, fig, toy 4. doit, fico, fool, jest 5. dally, fable, straw 6. bauble, dabble, dawdle, doodle, fiddle, gewgaw, palter, pewter, potter, wanton 7. dessert, nothing, traneen 8. flimflam, gimcrack, make love 9. bagatelle 10. knickknack, peccadillo, triviality 11. small amount 12. treat lightly

trifler... 7. dallier, flaneur 8. palterer, putterer 10. dilettante

trifles... 4. toys 6. trivia 7. gewgaws, palters 8. minutiae, trumpery

trifling... 4. idle, mere 5. inane, petty 6. little 7. trivial 8. badinage, frippery 9. nugacious 10. immaterial 13. insignificant

trifolium... 6. clover 8. shamrock

trig... 3. chic, neat, prim, tidy, trim 5. natty, smart 6. lively, spruce 7. precise 10. methodical

trigo... 5. wheat

trigon... 4. game, harp, lyre (anc) 8. triangle

trigonometry term... 4. sine 6. cosine, secant 7. tangent 8. spherics 10. goniometry

trihoral... 11. three–hourly 15. every three hours

trill... 4. move, sing 5. shake, twirl 6. quaver, ripple, warble 7. mordent, tremolo, trickle, vibrate 8. grupetto 12. pralltriller

trillion... 5. trega (comb form) 14. million million

trim... 3. bob, cut, lop 4. chic, clip, crop, neat, perk, snod, tidy, whip 5. adorn, natty, nifty, panel, preen, prune, shear, shrag 6. border, dapper, defeat, punish, reduce 7. compact, orderly 8. decorate, ornament 9. embellish, shipshape 10. decoration

trimming... 4. gimp, lace 5. braid, jabot, ruche 6. edging, frieze, fringe, piping 7. falbala, ruching 8. furbelow, ornament 9. chicanery, garniture 10. decoration 11. accessories 13. passementerie

trinity... 5. three, triad 6. triune

Trinity (Eccl)... 7. Godhead (Father, Son, Holy Ghost) 8. Trimurti

trinket... 3. toy 4. gaud, tali (tahli) 5. bijou, jewel 6. bangle, gewgaw,

trifle 7. bibelot 8. ornament 10. knickknack

trip... 3. err, run 4. halt, skip, slip, trap 5. caper, dance, jaunt, speed 6. bungle, cruise, errand, flight, frolic, voyage 7. journey, misstep, stumble 8. obstruct 9. excursion 10. expedition

triple... 3. tri 5. trine 6. tercet, treble 9. intensify, threefold 12. three–base hit

triple crown... 5. tiara (Pope's)

triplet (one of)... 4. trin

tripletail... 4. fish, sama 9. berrugate, spadefish

tripod... 3. cat (6–legged) 5. easel, stand, three 6. trivet

Tripoli, Libya...
  capital of.. 12. Tripolitania
  caravan route to.. 5. Wadai 8. Lake Chad, Timbuktu
  famed arch to.. 14. Marcus Aurelius
  people.. 4. Arab, Turk 5. Negro 6. Berber
  ruler.. 3. bey, dey

triptych... 5. volet (part) 10. altarpiece, writing pad 13. writing tablet (3–part)

trismus... 7. lockjaw, tetanus 16. gnashing the teeth

trist... see *tryst*

Tristan and Isolde... 5. opera (Wagner)

triste... 3. sad 4. full 6. dismal 10. depressing

tristful... 3. sad 10. melancholy

tristich group... 10. three lines 11. three verses (stanza)

Tristram & Iseult... 4. poem (Arnold)

trite... 5. banal, corny, petty, stale, vapid 6. betide, cliché, common, jejune 7. bromide 9. hackneyed, well–known 10. threadbare, unoriginal 11. commonplace, stereotyped 13. platitudinous

triton... 3. eft 4. newt 5. shell, snail 10. salamander

Triton (pert to)...
  art figure.. 7. demigod
  Gr Myth.. 10. sea demigod
  symbol.. 7. trumpet

triumph... 3. win 5. exult, glory 6. defeat 7. ceremony (anc), conquest 10. exultation 11. achievement

trivia... 5. trash 7. trifles 8. trumpery

trivial... 5. banal, petty, small, trite 6. common, paltry, slight 7. nominal, piperly, shallow 8. doggerel, ordinary, trifling 9. frivolous, nugacious 11. commonplace, unimportant 13. insignificant

triviality... 3. toy 6. bauble, gewgaw, trifle 8. falderal, nugacity 9. bagatelle, frivolity 10. knickknack 14. insignificance

troche... 4. pill 6. button, rotula, tablet 7. lozenge 8. pastille (pastil) 9. cough drop 10. deer's tines

trochee... 4. foot (2–syllable) 5. meter 7. choreus

trod... see *tread*

trogger... 7. peddler, vagrant
trogon... 7. quetzal
Troilus (pert to)...
  butterfly genus.. 7. Papilio
  legendary hero of.. 7. Chaucer
  son of.. 5. Priam
Trojan (pert to)...
  astronomy.. 9. asteroids
  epic.. 5. Iliad 6. Aeneid 7. Odyssey
  expedition hero.. 4. Ajax 8. Achilles
  founder of.. 4. Troy
  hero.. 5. Paris 6. Hector
    9. Palamedes
  horse.. 6. wooden
  horse builder.. 5. Epeus
  king.. 5. Priam
  native.. 6. Dardan
  soothsayer.. 7. Helenus
  war cause.. 5. Helen (of Troy)
  war leader.. 9. Agamemnon
  warrior.. 6. Agenor
troll (Myth)... 5. dwarf, giant, gnome
troll... 4. bowl, fish, roll, sing 5. angle
  (fishing), rondo 6. allure, entice,
  propel 7. revolve, trundle 9. circulate
trolley... 4. cart, tram 5. truck
  6. barrow, sledge 7. tramcar
  8. handcart 9. streetcar
trolley, off his... 4. nuts 5. balmy,
  batty, daffy, dippy, dotty, goofy
  6. cuckoo
trollop... 5. slump 6. slouch
  8. slattern
trombone (pert to)...
  ancient.. 7. sackbut, sambuke
  instrument.. 5. brass
  mouthpiece.. 5. bocal
  popular size.. 5. tenor
troop... 4. army, band, unit 5. crowd
  7. company, march on, ressala
  8. quantity, soldiers 9. go forward
  10. armed force
troop (pert to)...
  arrangement.. 7. echelon
  encampment.. 5. étape
  formation.. 4. line
  one of.. 7. peltast 8. chasseur
  ship.. 9. transport
troops (pert to)...
  assemble.. 6. muster
  German.. 6. Panzer
  hidden.. 6. ambush
  Hungary.. 7. Hussars
  mounted.. 7. cavalry
  sally.. 6. sortie
  term for.. 4. army 5. squad 6. forces
  7. battery, militia, phalanx
  11. commandos 11. armed forces
trophy... 3. cup 4. palm 5. award,
  medal, Oscar, prize 6. reward
  7. laurels, memento 8. memorial
tropical (pert to)...
  animal.. 4. eyra 5. araba, coati, potto
  6. agouti 7. peccary
  bird.. 3. ani 4. tody 5. jalap
  6. motmot 7. jacamar
  dolphin.. 4. inia
  fish.. 4. toro 6. remora, salema
  fruit.. 3. fig 4. date 5. guava,
  mango, papaw 6. banana, papaya
  lizard.. 5. agama
  rodent.. 6. agouti

tree.. 4. coco, palm 5. balsa, seron
  6. sapota 8. tamarind
vine.. 7. cowhage, lantana
  14. trumpet creeper
trot... 3. jog, run 4. gait, pony
  5. hurry 7. routine 11. translation
trotting horse... 6. Morgan
  7. Hackney 12. Hambletonian
trottoir (rare)... 8. footpath, pavement,
  sidewalk
troubadour... 4. bard, poet
  8. jongleur, minstrel, musician
  9. trovatore
trouble... 3. ado, ail, irk 4. fuss,
  harm, stir 5. annoy, grief, worry
  6. bother, effort, grieve, harass,
  pester, plague, sorrow 7. agitate,
  anxiety, concern, disturb, perturb,
  torment 8. calamity, disorder,
  disquiet, distress, mischief
  9. adversity, annoyance, commotion
  10. affliction, difficulty, misfortune
  11. disturbance 13. inconvenience,
  interfere with
troubled... 6. queasy 7. annoyed,
  anxious 8. agitated 9. disturbed
  10. distressed
troublemaker... 8. agitator, gossiper
  13. mischief-maker
troublesome... 5. pesky 8. annoying,
  perverse 9. difficult, laborious,
  turbulent, vexatious, wearisome
  10. bothersome, burdensome,
  disturbing, oppressing 11. distressing
  12. inconvenient
trough... 3. bin 4. bosh, bowl, dale,
  tank 5. basin, chute, drain, toper
  6. coffin, gutter, manger, sluice,
  trench 7. channel, conduit
trounce... 4. beat, flog 5. scald
  6. indict, punish, thrash 7. censure,
  journey
trout... 4. char, peal 7. oquassa
  9. namaycush 11. Dolly Varden
trout (pert to)...
  genus.. 5. Salmo 9. Trutta
  lake.. 9. namaycush
  Maine.. 7. oquassa
  parasite (external).. 3. sug
  ref to.. 11. truttaceous
  type.. 3. sea 4. rock 5. brook,
  brown, river 7. oquassa, rainbow
  8. speckled 9. cutthroat
trovatore... 10. troubadour
trove... 4. find 8. treasure (buried)
  9. discovery 10. thing found
  13. treasure-trove
trow... 4. boat, hope 5. barge, think,
  trust 6. expect 7. believe, suppose
  9. catamaran
trowing... 5. creed 6. belief 7. opinion
Troy, or Ilium...
  capital of.. 5. Troad (anc)
  defender.. 6. Aeneas
  famed for.. 5. ruins
  founder (Myth).. 4. Ilus (son of Tros),
  Tros
  king.. 5. Priam 9. Agamemnon
  king's wife.. 5. Helen
  mountain.. 3. Ida
  name, present.. 9. Hissarlik
  pert to.. 5. Iliac 6. Trojan

site.. 9. Asia Minor
troy weight... 5. grain, ounce, pound
11. pennyweight
truant... 4. idle 7. shirker, trivant, vagrant, absentee
truant, to play... 5. miche
truce... 5. pause, peace, trêve
9. armistice, cessation 10. brief quiet 12. intermission
truck... 3. van 4. deal, dray, haul
5. bogie, dance, lorry, trade
6. barter, peddle 7. flatcar, traffic
8. commerce, exchange, nonsense
9. groceries
truckle... 4. fawn 5. toady 6. cringe, submit 7. knuckle
truculent... 4. base, mean 5. cruel
6. fierce, savage 8. ruthless, scathing 9. barbarous, ferocious
11. destructive
trudge... 4. pace, plod, slog, walk
5. tramp 6. go slow 7. traipse
true... 2. so 4. fact, leal, pure, real
6. gospel, honest, lawful 7. certain, devoted, germane, precise, sincere, upright 8. faithful, orthodox, reliable, straight, unerring 9. authentic, steadfast, veracious, veritable
10. legitimate 11. trustworthy, unfaltering
true (pert to)...
blue.. 5. loyal 8. faithful, orthodox
10. man of honor
copy.. 7. estreat
not.. 5. false 10. figurative
poetic.. 4. leal
skin.. 4. derm (suff) 5. derma
to fact.. 7. literal
to life.. 8. lifelike 11. descriptive
truffle... 5. fungi, tuber 8. earthnut
10. ascus fruit
truism... 5. axiom, truth 9. platitude
11. commonplace
trull... 4. girl, lass 5. demon, fiend, giant, wench 7. trollop 8. strumpet
truly... 3. yea 4. amen 5. sooth
6. indeed, justly, verily 7. exactly, rightly 8. properly 9. certainly
10. accurately, positively, truthfully
trump... 3. pam 4. card, ruff (cards), suit 7. surpass 10. good fellow
12. masterstroke
trumpery... 5. fraud, trash 6. deceit
7. rubbish 8. nonsense
trumpet... 4. horn 5. blare
6. summon 7. clarion 8. proclaim
9. organ stop 12. elephant's cry
14. wind instrument
trumpet (pert to)...
blare.. 7. fanfare, tantara
call (stage).. 6. sennet
creeper.. 6. tecoma
fish.. 7. bellows 10. flutemouth
lily.. 5. calla 7. Bermuda
trumpeter... 4. bird, fish, swan
5. agami, perch 6. pigeon 7. whiting
8. musician 9. messenger
truncheon... 4. club 5. baton, staff
6. cudgel 8. splinter
trunk... 3. box, log 4. body, bole, pool, soma, tank 5. chest, stalk, torso 6. coffer 7. railway 8. main

stem 9. proboscis 10. lobster pot
trunkfish... 4. toro 7. cowfish
truss... 3. tie 4. bind, gird, pack
6. bundle, fasten 7. support
10. strengthen
trust... 4. hope, rely, task 5. faith
6. belief, commit, credit, dartle, depend, estate 7. believe, confide, consign, custody, entrust, loyalty
8. credence, reliance, security
9. assurance, syndicate
10. confidence, dependence, give credit, investment 12. organization
trustee... 6. bailee 7. sindico
9. fiduciary, treasurer 10. depository
13. administrator
trustful... 5. liege 7. reliant 8. trusting
9. confiding, credulous
13. unquestioning
trustworthiness... 9. axiopisty
12. trustability 13. dependability
trustworthy... 4. safe 5. solid
6. honest 7. certain 8. reliable
9. authentic 10. dependable
trusty... 7. convict 8. faithful, prisoner
10. dependable 11. trustworthy
truth... 3. tao 4. fact, real 5. sooth (anc) 6. verity 7. honesty, reality
8. fidelity, veracity 9. constancy, exactness, orthodoxy, sincerity
11. correctness 14. verisimilitude
truth (pert to)...
ancient term.. 5. sooth 6. certes
Chinese Philos.. 3. tao
goddess.. 4. Maat
personified.. 3. Una 4. Maat
ref to.. 6. verily 11. verisimilar
14. verisimilitude
self-evident.. 5. axiom 6. truism
truthful... 6. honest 7. veridic
9. veracious, veridical
truthfulness... 5. truth 7. honesty
8. accuracy, veracity
13. veraciousness
try... 2. do 3. say 4. test 5. annoy, assay, ettle, prove, taste, trial
6. purify, refine, render, sample, strive 7. attempt, contest, torment
8. audition, endeavor, irritate
9. prosecute, undertake
10. experiment 11. demonstrate, investigate
trying... 7. irksome, painful, tasting
8. annoying, sampling 10. attempting
12. exasperating 13. experimenting
tryst... 6. invite, market 7. beguile, meeting 9. agreement, betrothal
10. engagement, rendezvous
11. appointment 12. meeting place
tsamba... 5. flour 6. barley
tsar... 4. czar, tzar 6. despot
8. autocrat
tsetse, tsetse fly... 4. kivu
8. Glossina, parasite
tsetse fly disease... 6. nagana
16. sleeping sickness
T-shaped... 3. tau
tsine... 6. wild ox 7. banteng
tuatara, tuatera... 7. reptile (iguanalike)
tub... 3. hod, keg, kid, soe, tun, vat
4. cask, ship, wash 5. barge, bathe,

bowie, keeve 6. barrel, firkin, piggin,
vessel 7. bathtub, cistern, washtub
9. container, fat person
tuba... 6. liquor (palm) 7. helicon,
trumpet (anc) 9. bombardon
10. contrabass 11. bass saxhorn
12. mythical tree
Tubal–cain's father... 6. Lamech
Tubal's father... 7. Japheth
tube... 3. cop 4. bulb, duct, hose,
pipe 5. auget, chute, diode
6. siphon, tunnel 7. burette, cannula,
conduit, fistula, matrass, railway,
salpinx 8. cylinder, electron, stenosis
9. spaghetti, telescope
tuber... 3. oca, yam 4. beet, bulb,
eddo, root, taro 5. jalap, salep
6. potato 12. protuberance
tubular... 4. pipy 5. round 6. tubate
8. cannular, fistular, tubiform
11. cylindrical
tuck... 3. eat, nip 4. cram, fold, poke
5. feast, pinch, pleat, press
7. shorten, tighten 9. appendage
tucker... 3. bib 4. food, meal
5. board 6. ration
Tuesday (pert to)...
French.. 5. Mardi
Norse god.. 3. Tyr (Tiu)
Shrove.. 9. Mardi gras
Teutonic.. 10. Martis dies
tufa... 4. rock, toph, tuff 5. trass
tuft... 4. coma, doss, hair 5. beard,
bunch, clump, crest 6. button,
goatee, pompon, tassel 7. cluster,
fetlock 8. aigrette, feathers
tug... 3. tow 4. drag, draw, haul, pull,
toil 5. labor 6. drudge, effort, strain,
tussle 7. contend, contest, wrestle
8. struggle
tulip (pert to)...
center (World).. 7. Holland
color.. 6. auburn 9. tulipwood
genus.. 6. Tulipa
Mexican.. 6. orchid
military slang.. 9. explosive
tree.. 6. timber 7. majagua, waratah
type.. 6. Darwin, parrot 7. breeder,
cottage
tumble... 4. fall, flop, trip, veer
5. pitch, spill 6. jumble, rumple,
topple, tousle, wallow 7. stumble
8. collapse, disorder, flounder, roll
over 9. break down, confusing
10. handspring, somersault
11. precipitate
tumbler... 3. dog 4. cart, drum
5. glass 6. Dunker, pigeon, vessel
7. acrobat, gymnast, tippler, tumbrel
8. lock part 13. contortionist
tumbleweed... 6. indigo 7. bugseed,
pigweed, thistle 10. amaranthus
tumbrel, tumbril... 4. cart 5. wagon
8. dumpcart 12. cucking stool (Hist)
tumescent, tumid... 6. turgid
7. bloated, bulging, pompous
8. inflated 9. bombastic, disturbed,
plethoric 11. protuberant
tumor... 3. wen 4. cyst, wart
6. cancer, goiter, growth, lipoma,
struma 7. adenoma, sarcoma
8. ganglion, swelling 11. excrescence

12. protuberance
tumor, eyelid... 9. pladaroma
tumult... 3. din, mob 4. fray, riot
5. Babel, brawl, noise 6. affray,
babble, bustle, émeute, hubbub,
uproar 7. bluster, ferment, turmoil
8. disorder, outbreak, uprising
9. agitation, commotion, confusion
10. excitement, turbulence
11. disturbance
tumultuous... 4. wild 5. noisy, rough
7. lawless, riotous, violent
8. agitated, confused 9. disturbed,
turbulent 10. boisterous, disorderly,
hurly–burly
tumulus... 5. mound, stump 6. barrow
7. hillock
tun... 3. cup (anc), jar, tub, vat
4. cask, year (Mayan, 360–day)
5. drink 6. guzzle, vessel 7. measure
tuna... 5. tunny 8. albacore
tune... 3. air, key 4. aria, lilt, port,
song 5. pitch 6. adjust, melody
7. chorale, harmony, sonance
9. harmonize 10. adjustment,
intonation
tune (pert to)...
correctly.. 3. key
down.. 6. reduce, soften 8. moderate
musical instrument.. 6. string
out of.. 9. dissonant 11. inaccordant
12. unconforming
tungsten... 7. wolfram
Tunisia...
cape.. 3. Bon
capital.. 5. Tunis
famed ruins.. 8. Carthage
gulf.. 5. Gabes
oasis.. 5. Gafsa
people.. 5. Arabs 7. Berbers
resort island.. 6. Djerba
river.. 8. Medjerda
ruler.. 3. dey 5. pasha
seaport.. 4. Sfax 7. Bizerte
tunnel... 4. adit, bore, cave, tube
5. drift 6. burrow, dig out, funnel,
subway 10. excavation, smokestack
tunny... 4. tuna 8. albacore
tup... 3. ram 4. beat, butt 5. sheep
6. mallet 7. cuckold
turban... 6. entrée, fillet, Moslem,
mundil, squash 8. bandanna,
seerband 9. headdress
turbid... 4. dark, dull 5. dense,
muddy, roily 6. cloudy, impure,
opaque 7. clouded, muddled
8. confused, feculent, polluted
turbot... 5. brill 8. flatfish
turbulence... 4. fury 6. tumult, uproar
7. bluster, rioting, turmoil
9. agitation, commotion
10. excitement, unruliness
11. disturbance, impetuosity
14. tumultuousness
turbulent... 4. loud, wild 5. noisy,
rough 6. stormy 7. excited, furious
8. virulent 10. tumultuous
turf... 3. sod 4. peat, slab 5. divot,
glebe, grass, sward, track 10. race
course
turgid... 5. tumid 7. bloated,
pompous, swollen 8. inflated

9. bombastic, distended, grandiose, redundant 12. magniloquent, ostentatious 13. grandiloquent

Turk... 5. Tatar 6. Tartar 7. Osmanli, Ottoman 9. Kizilbash

Turkestan people.. 5. Uzbek (Uzbeg)

turkey.. 4. fowl 5. poult 7. bustard, gobbler, vulture

Turkey... see also *Turkish*
capital.. 6. Angora (anc), Ankara
city.. 5. Adana, Izmir (Smyrna)
6. Edessa, Samsun 7. Scutari
8. Istanbul (Constantinople)
10. Adrianople
founder.. 6. Othman
mountain.. 6. Ararat
peninsula.. 9. Anatolian
river.. 5. Mesta 6. Seyhan

Turkish (pert to)...
army corps.. 4. ordu 8. seraglio
commander, ruler.. 3. aga (agha), bey
4. wali 5. pasha 6. atabeg (atabek)
court (Ottoman).. 5. Porte
12. Sublime Porte
dignitary.. 5. pasha
dish (food).. 5. cabob 6. pilaff (pilau)
drink.. 4. boza (bozah), raki 5. airan
6. mastic 9. lion's milk
dynasty.. 6. seljuk
emblem.. 8. crescent
Empire.. 7. Ottoman
flag.. 4. alem, toug (former)
harem girl.. 6. kadein (kadine)
hat, cap.. 3. fez 6. calpac (calpack)
hospice, inn.. 6. imaret
infidel.. 6. giaour
javelin.. 6. jereed (jerid)
judge.. 4. cadi (kadi)
minister of state.. 6. vizier
money of account.. 5. asper
mosque.. 4. jami
music.. 8. janizary
native.. 6. Edesan (anc)
palace.. 5. serai
pavilion.. 5. kiosk
pipe (long-stemmed).. 7. chibouk (chibouque)
regiment.. 4. alai
religious war.. 5. jihad (jehad)
rug.. 5. Melas, Tekke, Yomud, Yuruk
6. Afghan 8. Turkoman 9. Kurdistan
ruler.. 3. bey, dey 4. khan 6. sultan
7. chambul
sailing vessel.. 4. saic 6. mahone
sailor.. 9. galiongee (galionji)
soldier.. 5. nizan, redif 6. Arnaut
(Arnaout) 8. Janizary
11. bashi-bazouk
statute.. 8. Tanzimat (1839)
sultan.. 5. Ahmed, Selim 7. Ilderim,
Saladin
sultan's title.. 6. caliph (calif)
sword.. 8. yataghan (yatagan)
tambourine.. 5. daira
tax (from Christians).. 6. avania
title.. 3. aga (agha), ali 4. amir
(ameer)
tobacco.. 7. chibouk (chibouque),
Latakia
tribe.. 5. Ersar, Tatar 7. Bashkir,
Viddhal
Turkoman.. 11. tribal group

veil (double).. 7. yashmak (yashmac)
vest.. 6. jelick
whip, lash.. 7. kurbash

turmeric... 3. rea 4. ango, herb
5. olena 8. curcumin

turmoil... 3. ado, din 5. upset, worry
6. tumult, unrest 7. ferment,
tempest, trouble 8. disquiet
9. agitation, commotion, confusion
10. excitement, turbulence
12. perturbation

turn... 3. bow, lap 4. bend, deed,
gyre, roll, slew, slue, spin, tour,
veer, vert 5. curve, lathe, pivot,
quirk, round, shift, spell, wheel,
whirl, whorl 6. abvert, change, crisis,
gyrate, rotate, swivel, zigzag
7. deflect, deviate, reverse, revolve
8. aptitude, circuity, maneuver,
persuade, rotation, tendency
9. deviation, pirouette, reversion
11. convolution 12. metamorphose

turn (pert to)...
about.. 9. alternate
aside, away.. 4. slew, slue 5. avert,
deter, repel, shunt 6. divert, swerve
7. deflect, deviate, digress, diverge
back.. 5. repel 6. coward, revert
7. evolute, head off, reflect
coat.. 7. traitor 8. apostate, deserter,
renegade
comb form.. 5. tropo
down.. 4. veto 5. refuse, reject
7. decline
gate.. 5. stile 9. turnstile
inside out.. 5. evert 6. invert
7. ransack
inward.. 8. introrse 9. introvert
left.. 3. haw 4. port
of duty.. 5. spell, trick
off.. 5. shunt 7. dismiss, execute
10. extinguish
on axis.. 6. obvert, rotate
one's back upon.. 4. flee, snub
5. avoid 6. ignore, oppose, refuse,
reject
on pivot.. 6. swivel
out.. 4. fare, oust 5. array, evert,
expel, track 6. detour, output, siding
7. dismiss 8. assemble, clearing
9. eventuate, gathering
10. accomplish, extinguish
outward.. 5. evert, splay 8. extrorse
9. extrovert
over.. 3. pie 4. keel, tart 5. sales,
shift, spill 6. assign, pastry
7. capsize 8. hand over, overturn
over a new leaf.. 6. change, reform
over pages.. 4. leaf 6. thumb
over to others.. 4. farm 7. farm out
to left.. 3. haw 4. port
to right.. 3. gee 9. starboard
up.. 4. find, keel 5. occur 6. appear,
arrive 7. be found
upside down.. 4. roll 6. invert, whelve
7. ransack 8. overturn

turned up (nose).. 9. retroussé

turning... 6. rotary 7. bending,
crooked, winding 8. rotation,
twisting, whirling 9. deviating,
deviation 10. circuitous, revolution
11. convolution, sinistrorse

turning (pert to)...
  left to right.. 9. dextrorse
  machine.. 5. lathe
  point.. 6. crisis 8. decision, landmark
    11. climacteric 13. crucial period
  right to left.. 11. sinistrorse
turnip... 4. neep, rape, root
  8. rutabaga
turnip (pert to)...
  large.. 7. Russian, Swedish
  8. rutabaga
  shaped.. 8. napiform
  wild.. 5. navew
Turnix... 4. bird (3–toed) 5. quail
  10. Hemipodius
Turpentine State... 13. North Carolina
turpentine tree... 4. pine 6. tarata
  9. terebinth
turpid... 3. low 4. base, vile
  8. cowardly
turpitude... 6. fedity 8. baseness,
  vileness 9. decadence, depravity
  10. corruption
turquoise... 3. gem 4. blue
  7. mineral, Turkish
turret... 4. loom, soar 5. tower
  6. cupola (revolving), height
  9. structure 10. stronghold,
  watchtower
turtle (pert to)...
  edible.. 8. terrapin
  freshwater.. 4. emyd 8. tortoise
  genus.. 4. Emys
  hawklike.. 5. carat 9. hawk's–bill
  large.. 5. arrau 6. jurara, mamata
  largest.. 11. leatherback
  ref to.. 9. chelonian
  sea.. 10. thalassian
  shell.. 8. carapace
  snapping.. 6. cooter 8. shagtail
Tuscany...
  birthplace of.. 7. Galileo (Astronomer)
  capital.. 8. Florence
  city.. 4. Pisa 7. Leghorn
  color.. 9. colcothar
  famed tower.. 4. Pisa (1174)
  island.. 4. Elba (1st exile, Napoleon)
  native.. 6. Tuscan
  marble.. 7. Carrara
  province.. 4. Pisa
  river.. 4. Arno 6. Cecina 7. Ombrone
  wine.. 7. chianti
tusk... 4. fang 5. ivory, tooth
  6. canine 7. incisor 9. scrivello
  (elephant's)
Tussaud, Madame's London district...
  8. Waxworks (Museum)
  10. Marylebone
tussis... 5. cough
tussle... 7. contend, contest, scuffle,
  wrestle 8. struggle
tutelage... 7. nurture 8. teaching,
  tutorage 9. oversight, tutorship
  11. instruction 12. guardianship
tutelary gods (Rom)... 5. lares
  7. penates
tutor... 5. coach, teach 6. docent,
  ground, mentor, school 7. teacher
  8. instruct 9. pedagogue (pedagog),
  preceptor
twaddle... 3. rot 6. drivel, gabble
  7. chatter, fustian, prattle

  8. claptrap, nonsense 9. absurdity,
  silly talk 10. flapdoodle 16. trash
  and nonsense
twang... 4. tang 5. strum 6. accent
  7. dialect 8. pungency
tweak... 4. jerk, pain 5. pinch
  6. snatch, twitch
tweeg... 10. hellbender, salamander
tweezers... 7. pincers 10. instrument
twelfth... 5. twait, uncia 8. duodenal
  9. duodenary
Twelfth Night character... 5. Viola
  6. Olivia, Orsino 7. Sir Toby
  8. Malvolio 12. Sir Toby Belch
Twelfthtide... 8. Epiphany
  10. Twelfth–day
twelve (pert to)...
  amount.. 5. dozen
  angles.. 9. dodecagon
  prefix.. 5. dodec 6. dodeca
  rule of.. 9. dodecarch
  series.. 8. dodecade
Twelve, The... 8. Apostles
twenty (pert to)...
  Anglo–Ind.. 5. carge, score
  comb form.. 4. icos 5. icosa, icosi
  faces.. 11. icosahedron
  pert to.. 7. icosian 8. vicenary
  quires.. 4. ream
  symbol.. 2. XX
  years.. 9. vicennial
twenty–fourth part (gold alloy)...
  5. carat (karat)
twibil (twibill)... 2. ax (axe) 6. pickax
  (pickaxe) 7. mattock 8. battle–ax
  (battle–axe)
twice... 2. bi, di 6. doubly 7. twofold
  8. two times
twig... 4. reis 5. besom, birch, bough
  6. branch, sallow, switch, twitch,
  wattle
twigs, bundle of... 5. fagot 6. barsom
  (sacred)
twilight... 3. dim 4. blue, dusk
  6. shaded 7. obscure 8. foredawn,
  gloaming 9. cocklight 10. crepuscule
Twilight of the Gods... 9. Ragnarok
twill... 3. rib 5. flute, weave 6. fabric
  9. tricotine
twilled... 3. rep 5. reedy, ridgy, sedgy,
  serge 6. corded, fluted
twin... 3. two 4. dual, mate, pair
  5. gemel, macle 6. couple, double
  7. didymus, Siamese 8. didymous,
  matching 9. duplicate, identical
  11. counterpart 12. accompanying
Twin Cities (Minn)... 6. St Paul
  11. Minneapolis
twine... 4. bend, coil, turn, wind, wrap
  5. braid, snarl, twist, weave
  6. enfold, enlace, tangle 7. embrace,
  enclasp, entwine, wreathe
  8. convolve, encircle 9. interlace
  10. intertwine, interweave
  11. intermingle
twine (pert to)...
  color.. 4. dune 7. anamite
  hank of.. 3. ran
  left to right.. 9. dextrorse
  right to left.. 11. sinistrorse
  Scot.. 4. part
twinge... 4. ache, pain, pang

5. pinch, qualm 6. twitch

twin stars... 6. Castor, Pollux

twin stock... 4. bees 7. beehive (two colonies)

twirl... 4. coil, eddy, gyre, spin 5. pitch, querl, twist, whirl 6. gyrate, writhe 7. revolve 8. flourish, rotation 11. convolution

twist... 3. cue, ply 4. coil, curl, slew, slub, slue, spin, turn, warp, wind 5. braid, quirk, tweak, wrest 7. contort, deflect, distort, falsify, meander, pervert, wreathe, wriggle 8. convolve 9. insinuate, interlace, prejudice 11. distortion 12. eccentricity, misrepresent

twisted... 3. wry 4. awry, cued 5. askew, kinky, torse, wrung 6. warped 7. complex, torqued, tortile, wrested, writhed

twisted cord... 7. torsade

twister... 3. lie 7. cruller, tornado 8. doughnut 9. dust whirl 10. sand column, somersault, waterspout

twit... 4. gibe, josh 5. blame, taunt, tease, tweet 6. banter 7. upbraid 8. reproach, ridicule

twitch... 3. nip, tic, tug 4. hurt, jerk, yank 5. pluck, shake, tweak 6. snatch 9. be excited, quick pull, vellicate 11. contraction

twitter... 3. chirp 6. giggle, titter 7. chatter, tremble 9. agitation

two (pert to)...
chambered.. 9. bicameral
colored.. 9. dichromic
edged.. 9. ancipital
faced.. 5. false 6. double 9. deceitful 11. treacherous 12. falsehearted
fisted.. 6. virile
fold.. 4. dual, twin 6. binary, double, duplex 8. didymous
forked.. 6. bident 9. bifurcate 11. dichotomous
handed.. 7. bimanal 8. bimanous 10. secondhand 12. ambidextrous
headed.. 9. ancipital 11. dicephalous
masted ship.. 4. yawl, zulu
parts.. 3. duo 4. duad, dyad 7. duality
poetic.. 5. twain
prefix.. 2. bi, di
Scot.. 3. twa
Spanish.. 3. dos
spot.. 5. deuce
time.. 7. deceive
wheeled carriage, chariot.. 3. gig 6. esseda 10. jinrikisha (jinriksha)

Tyche... 7. Fortuna 16. goddess of Fortune

tycoon... 6. shogun 7. magnate 9. financier 13. industrialist

tylopod... 5. camel

tympanum... 7. eardrum 9. middle ear 10. water wheel

tympany... 6. tympan 7. bombast 9. inflation 10. distention

typal... 7. typical 8. symbolic

type... 2. pi 4. font, form, kind, norm, sign, sort 5. genre, genus, model, print, Roman, token 6. emblem, italic, minion, symbol 7. measure,

pattern, species 8. boldface, classify, standard 9. archetype, character 10. transcribe 11. Baskerville 14. characteristic, representative

type (pert to)...
assortment.. 4. font, kern
block of.. 4. quad 7. quadrat
bold style.. 4. text
bridge.. 7. bascule
classic.. 5. Roman 6. italic 11. black letter (Gothic)
line.. 4. slug
measure.. 2. em, en
mixed.. 2. pi
mold.. 6. matrix
perfection.. 7. paragon
set.. 7. compose
setter.. 8. linotype, monotype 10. compositor
size.. 4. norm, pica, ruby 5. agate, canon, pearl 6. minion 7. diamond
stroke.. 5. serif
tray.. 6. galley

typewriter (pert to)...
bar.. 6. spacer
cylinder.. 6. platen, spacer
type.. 4. pica 5. elite
type of.. 6. ticker 8. teletype 9. stenotype

typhoon... 4. wind 5. storm 7. cyclone

typhus fever... 10. tabardillo

typical... 4. norm 5. typal 6. normal 7. regular 10. conforming, emblematic, figurative 11. precedental 14. characteristic, representative

typify... 6. embody 9. prefigure, represent, symbolize

Tyr (Norse)... 3. Tiu 6. sky–god, war–god

tyrannical... 5. cruel 6. lordly 8. despotic 9. imperious 10. oppressive 11. domineering

tyrannize... 7. oppress 8. domineer

tyranny... 8. severity 9. despotism

tyrant... 4. czar, Ivan, Nero, tsar, tzar 6. despot 7. monarch

Tyre... see also *Tyrian*
capital of.. 9. Phoenicia (anc)
famed for.. 9. purple dye
seaport of.. 7. Lebanon
site.. 9. peninsula 13. Mediterranean

Tyrian (pert to)...
alphabet.. 7. Moabite
Cynosure.. 9. Ursa Minor
god (Teut).. 2. Er
king.. 5. Hiram
princess.. 4. Dido (Elissa)

tyro, tiro... 5. pupil 6. novice 7. amateur 8. beginner, neophyte 9. commencer, fledgling, greenhorn 10. apprentice 11. abecedarian

Tyrol...
capital.. 9. Innsbruck
dialect.. 5. Ladin
district.. 8. Trentino
mountain.. 4. Alps 9. Dolomites
province of.. 7. Austria
river.. 4. Isar

tzar, tsar, czar... 4. king 5. ruler 6. tyrant

tzigane... 5. gypsy

U

U... 6. letter (21st)
uang... 6. beetle
uberous... 7. copious 8. abundant, fruitful 9. plentiful
uberty... 6. plenty 12. fruitfulness
ubiety... 8. location, position, relation 9. whereness
ubiquity... 8. doctrine (Luther) 10. everywhere 12. omnipresence
U–boat... 3. sub 9. submarine
base.. 4. Kiel
Uca... 11. fiddler crab
Uchean Indian... 5. Yuchi (Uchee)
udometer... 9. rain gauge
Uffizi Gallery... 8. Florence
Uganda (pert to)...
capital.. 7. Kampala
Falls.. 4. Owen 9. Murchison
lake.. 8. Victoria
lake explorer.. 7. Stanley
mountain.. 9. Ruwenzori
18. Mountains of the Moon
tribe.. 5. pygmy
ugly... 5. cross, surly 6. cranky, homely 7. crabbed, hideous, vicious 8. gruesome, uncomely, unlovely 9. frightful, loathsome, offensive, repulsive, unsightly 10. ill-favored, ill-natured, unpleasant 11. ill-tempered, quarrelsome 12. disagreeable
uhlan... 6. lancer 7. militia, soldier 10. cavalryman
uhllo... 6. wampum 8. currency (shell)
uitlander... 9. foreigner, outlander
ukase... 5. edict, order 12. proclamation
Ukraine (pert to)...
capital.. 4. Kiev 7. Kharkov
legislature.. 4. rada
official name.. 12. Ukrainian SSR
Relig.. 9. Ruthenian 13. Little Russian
scientist.. 10. Bogomolets
sea.. 5. Black
seaport.. 6. Odessa
statesman.. 7. Mazeppa
writer.. 6. Franko
ullage... 5. dregs 7. deficit, wantage 8. shortage 9. shrinkage 10. deficiency
Ulmas... 3. elm
ulna... 4. bone 5. elbow 7. cubitus
ulster... 8. overcoat
ulterior... 6. future 7. further, remoter, thither 10. additional, extraneous, subsequent, succeeding 11. undisclosed
ultima... 4. last 5. final 8. farthest 10. most remote 12. last syllable
ultimate... 3. end 4. dire, last

5. final, telus 6. future, latest, result 7. extreme, maximum 8. eventful, eventual, farthest, terminal 9. elemental 10. conclusive, end product
ultimatum... 5. offer 6. demand 13. ultimate point 14. final objective
ultimo... 3. ult 9. past month (opp of proximo)
ultra... 6. beyond 7. extreme, radical 9. excessive, extremist, fanatical 11. extravagant 14. uncompromising
ultramarine... 11. blue pigment, lapis lazuli 12. beyond the sea
ultramontane... 5. alien 6. beyond 9. foreigner 10. tramontane 13. beyond the Alps, Roman Catholic
ulu (Esk)... 5. knife
ululate... 4. hoot, howl, wail, yelp 6. bellow, lament
Ulysses (pert to)...
antagonist.. 4. Irus
dog.. 5. Argos
enchantress.. 5. Circe
father.. 7. Laertes
Greek name.. 8. Odysseus
hero.. 7. Odyssey (Homer's)
literally.. 5. hater
son.. 9. Telegonus
wife.. 8. Penelope
umber... 3. raw 5. brown, burnt 6. shadow, Turkey 8. grayling, umbrette 10. brown earth
umbilicus (pert to)...
anatomy.. 5. navel
botany.. 5. hilum
geometry.. 5. focus
paleology.. 5. stick (papyrus)
zoology.. 3. pit 10. depression
umbra... 4. fish 5. ghost, shade 6. shadow 7. phantom, vestige
umbrage... 5. doubt, pique, shade, trace 6. offend, resent 7. foliage, offense, shelter 8. disfavor 9. semblance, suspicion 10. overshadow, resentment 11. displeasure
umbrella... 4. gamp 5. cover, guard, shade 6. chatta, payong, pileus (of a jellyfish) 7. parasol, shelter 9. parachute, sea anchor 11. bumbershoot
umbrella tree... 5. bendy 7. dogwood, ginseng 8. magnolia
umbrette... 4. bird, fish 5. omber (ombre) 9. hammerkop
umpire... 5. judge 7. arbiter, referee 8. mediator 9. moderator 10. arbitrator, negotiator
Umpqua... 6. Indian 10. Athapascan

unable... 6. cannot 8. helpless, impotent 9. incapable 11. incompetent, inefficient, unqualified 13. incapacitated
Una boat... 7. catboat
unabridged... 8. complete 11. uncondensed
unaccented... 4. lene 6. atonic
unaccountable... 7. lawless, strange 9. fantastic 10. mysterious 12. inexplicable, unfathomable 13. irresponsible, unpredictable
unacknowledged... 9. anonymous, forgotten, unthanked 10. unrewarded
unadorned... 4. bald, bare, form 5. grace, naked, stark 7. austere 13. plain–speaking
unadulterated... 4. pure 5. naked 6. honest 7. unmixed 9. unalloyed, undiluted 11. uncorrupted
unaffected... 4. naif, real 5. naive, plain 6. simple 7. artless, genuine, natural, sincere 8. informal 9. unaltered, untouched 12. uninfluenced 13. plain–speaking
Unalaska... 5. Aleut, tribe 9. Eskimauan
unanimous... 5. solid 6. agreed, mutual, united 8. agreeing 9. of one mind 10. concordant 11. consentient 12. with one voice
unanimously... 7. una voce 12. with one voice
unapproachable... 8. reserved 10. unsociable 12. inaccessible
unapt... 4. dull, slow 5. inapt 8. backward 10. unskillful, unsuitable 13. inappropriate
unaroused... 6. latent 7. dormant 8. inactive 9. unstirred
unaspirated... 4. lene 6. smooth
unassuming... 3. shy 6. modest 7. genuine, natural 8. informal, retiring 9. diffident 11. undeceptive 14. unostentatious
unau... 5. sloth (2–toed)
unavailing... 6. futile 8. gainless
unbalanced... 6. insane, uneven, unjust 7. unequal 8. deranged, lopsided, one–sided 9. off center 10. disordered
unbecoming... 4. rude 5. inept 8. unseemly 10. indecorous, unsuitable 12. unattractive
unbelievable... 9. fantastic, untenable 10. incredible, unreliable 11. implausible, unthinkable 13. inconceivable
unbeliever... 5. pagan 6. Kaffir (Kafir) 7. atheist, doubter, heretic, infidel, skeptic 8. agnostic
unbend... 4. rest, thaw 5. frese, relax, yield 6. loosen 7. slacken 8. be pliant, unfasten 10. condescend, straighten
unbending... 5. rigid, stern, stiff 8. resolute 10. inexorable, inflexible, unyielding
unbiased... 4. fair, just 9. impartial 12. free from bias, unprejudiced
unbind... 4. free, undo 5. loose, untie 6. loosen 7. absolve, deliver, release

8. dissolve, unfasten
unbound... 4. free 5. loose 10. unconfined
unbounded... 8. infinite 9. limitless, unchecked, unlimited 10. unconfined 11. measureless 12. uncontrolled, unrestrained
unbridled... 4. free 5. loose 7. lawless, violent 10. licentious 12. uncontrolled, unrestrained
unbroken... 4. even 5. undug, whole 6. direct, entire, intact, smooth 7. untamed 8. constant, straight, unplowed 10. continuous 13. uninterrupted
uncanny... 5. eerie (eery), weird 6. spooky 7. ghostly, strange 8. careless 9. unnatural 10. mysterious
unceasing... 6. eterne 7. endless, eternal 9. continual, incessant 11. everlasting
unceremonious... 4. curt 5. blunt 6. abrupt, casual 7. offhand 8. informal 14. unconventional
uncertain... 4. hazy 5. vague 6. chancy, fickle, fitful, shifty, unsure 7. dubious 8. doubtful, unsteady, variable 9. ambiguous, irregular, undecided 10. changeable, indefinite, irresolute, precarious 11. unequivocal 12. questionable 13. indeterminate, problematical, untrustworthy
uncertainty... 5. doubt 6. wonder 7. dubiety 8. suspense 9. dubiosity 10. fickleness, skepticism 12. irresolution 14. precariousness
unchanging... 7. eternal, settled, uniform 8. immutable, unvarying 10. invariable, stationary
unchaste... 4. lewd 5. bawdy 6. impure 7. obscene 8. immodest
unchecked... 4. free 5. loose 7. rampant 8. permanent, unbridled
unchristian... 5. pagan 7. heathen, infidel, ungodly 8. barbarous, excessive 11. irreligious, uncivilized
uncivil... 4. rude 6. savage 7. ill–bred 8. impolite 9. barbarous 10. indecorous, ungracious 11. ill–mannered, uncivilized 12. discourteous 13. disrespectful
uncivilized... 4. rude, wild 5. feral 6. brutal, ferine, savage 8. barbaric 9. primitive, unrefined
uncle... 3. eme (yeme), oom
unclean... 4. foul, tref, vile 5. dirty 6. filthy, immund, impure 8. polluted, unchaste 11. unwholesome
Uncle Tom's Cabin (pert to)...
author.. 5. Stowe (Harriet Beecher)
character... 5. Topsy 6. Legree 8. Uncle Tom 9. Little Eva
subject.. 7. slavery
unclose... 3. ope 4. open 6. reveal 7. expound 8. disclose
uncolored... 7. genuine 9. colorless 10. achromatic
uncommon... 3. odd 4. nice, rare 5. novel 6. scarce, unique 7. special, strange, unusual

8. unwonted 10. infrequent, remarkable 11. exceptional 12. unaccustomed 13. extraordinary

uncommunicative... 6. silent 8. reserved, reticent 9. secretive 10. unsociable

uncomplaining... 5. stoic 7. stoical

uncompromising... 4. firm 5. rigid 6. strict 9. obstinate, unbending 10. inflexible, unyielding 12. conservative, intransigent

unconcerned... 4. cool, free 8. careless 9. apathetic 10. insouciant 11. indifferent, not involved 13. disinterested

unconditional... 4. free 8. absolute, explicit 10. unreserved

unconfined... 5. loose 9. boundless, limitless, unlimited 12. unrestrained

unconscious... 3. out 6. asleep 7. unaware, heedless, ignorant, mindless 8. inanimate, senseless, unfeeling 10. abstracted, insensible 11. involuntary 12. subconscious

unconstrained... 4. easy, free 6. candid 7. natural 8. informal 11. spontaneous 12. unrestrained

uncontrolled... 4. free, wild 5. loose 7. lawless 8. impulsive, irregular, unmanaged 10. capricious, changeable, licentious, ungoverned 11. not governed, unregulated 12. unrestrained

unconventional... 4. easy 5. outré 6. casual 7. devious, offbeat 8. Bohemian, informal 10. unorthodox 13. unceremonious

uncorrupted... 8. pristine

uncouth... 3. odd 4. rude 5. crude 6. clumsy, rustic 7. awkward, boorish, strange 9. inelegant, unrefined, untrained 10. outlandish, uncultured, unpolished

uncover... 4. bare, open 6. detect, divest, expose, remove, reveal, unveil 7. divulge, lay bare, take off, undrape 8. disclose, discover

uncovered... 4. bald, bare, nude, open 7. exposed 8. divested, revealed, stripped, unveiled 9. décolleté 10. bareheaded 11. unprotected

unction... 4. balm, rite 6. fervor 7. lanolin, unguent 8. flattery, function (divine), ointment 10. anointing

unctuous... 4. oily, smug 5. bland, fatty, salvy, suave 6. fervid, greasy 7. gushing, pinguid, plastic 10. flattering, oleaginous 12. hypocritical 13. sanctimonious

uncultured... 7. artless, boorish, uncouth 8. Bohemian 9. unlearned, unrefined 10. Philistine 11. countrified, undeveloped

undaunted... 4. bold 5. brave 7. Spartan, untamed 8. fearless, intrepid, unafraid 9. confident, dauntless 10. courageous, undismayed 11. persevering, unconquered

undecided... 4. moot 7. pending 8. doubtful, wavering 9. uncertain,

unsettled 10. inconstant, irresolute, unresolved 13. problematical

undependable... 6. fickle 7. erratic 9. uncertain 13. irresponsible, untrustworthy

under... 3. sub 4. alow 5. below, least, neath, sotto 6. nether 7. beneath 8. guidance 9. lower than 10. subjection, underneath 11. subordinate

undercover... 6. secret 7. furtive 11. clandestine, underground 13. surreptitious

underestimate... 8. belittle, minimize 9. set too low, underrate 10. undervalue

underfong... 6. entrap 7. ensnare, receive, sustain 9. undertake 10. circumvent

undergo... 4. bear, dree, pass 5. shirt 6. endure, suffer 7. sustain 9. undermine 10. experience

underhanded... 3. sly 4. dern, mean 5. shady 6. covert, crafty, secret, sneaky 8. sneaking, unfairly 9. deceitful, dishonest 10. fraudulent 11. clandestine, short-handed 13. unobtrusively 15. surreptitiously

underling... 6. menial, minion 7. servant 8. inferior 11. subordinate

underlying... 5. basic 8. cardinal 11. fundamental

undermine... 3. sap 4. ruin 5. drain, erode 6. weaken 7. subvert 8. enfeeble, excavate

understand... 3. ken, see 4. know 5. grasp, infer, savvy, sense 6. follow, reason 7. discern, explain, realize, signify 8. conceive, perceive 9. apprehend, interpret 10. comprehend

understandable... 5. clear, lucid 12. intelligible

understanding... 5. amity, sense 6. accord, reason, treaty 7. compact, concept, entente, knowing 8. sympathy, Verstand 9. agreement, intellect, knowledge, tolerance, unanimity 10. acceptance, accordance, perception 11. discernment, penetration 12. intelligence 13. comprehension

understatement... 7. litotes

understood... 5. clear, known, lucid, tacit 7. assumed, implied, settled 8. implicit 11. traditional

undertake... 3. try 4. dare 6. accept, assume, pledge 7. attempt, promise, reprove 8. contract, covenant, endeavor, engage in, set about 9. guarantee, underfong

undertaker... 5. cerer 6. surety 7. manager, rebuker, sponsor 8. embalmer 9. godfather, mortician 12. entrepreneur

undertaking... 3. act 4. task 6. cautio 7. calling, project, promise, venture 8. business 9. adventure, guarantee 10. enterprise

undertone... 4. tone (low) 5. aside 6. murmur 12. subdued color

undertow... 7. riptide

underworld... 3. Dis 4. hell 5. Hades, limbo, Mafia, Orcus, Sheol 6. Erebus, Tophet 7. Abaddon, Xibalba 8. Dis pater, gangland 9. Black Hand, chthonian, perdition, purgatory

underwrite... 6. assure, insure 7. finance, sponsor 8. submit to

underwriter... 7. insurer 8. endorser 9. financier 10. underclerk 13. Stock Exchange 14. Lloyd's of London

undesirable condition... 6. malady

undetermined... 5. vague 7. dubious 8. not fixed, unproved 9. uncertain, undecided 10. irresolute

undeveloped... 5. crude 6. embryo, latent 8. immature 10. unprepared 11. rudimentary

undignified... 6. vulgar 8. informal, infra dig, unworthy 9. inelegant

undine... 3. nix 5. gnome, sylph 6. vessel (glass) 9. planetoid 10. salamander

undivided... 3. one 5. total, whole 6. entire, intact, joined 7. unitary 8. unbroken 9. not shared 10. continuous

undo... 4. open 5. annul, loose 6. cancel, defeat, foredo, unlash, unwrap 7. destroy, disjoin, nullify, release, uncover, unravel 8. unfasten 10. disconnect, invalidate

undoing... 4. ruin 6. defeat 8. downfall 9. annulment, overthrow 11. destruction, disassembly

undomesticated... 4. wild 5. feral 6. ferine

undone... 3. raw 9. neglected 10. defeasible

undue... 5. wrong 6. unjust 7. extreme 8. improper, not owing 9. excessive 10. exorbitant, immoderate, inordinate, undeserved, unsuitable 11. unwarranted 13. inappropriate

undulating... 4. wavy 6. waving 7. aripple, rolling 8. rippling 11. fluctuating 16. rising and falling

undulation... 4. beat, wave 5. heave, surge, swell 6. motion, waving 7. tremolo, vibrato 8. waviness 9. pulsation 11. convolution

undying... 6. eterne 7. ageless, endless, eternal 8. immortal, unending 9. deathless 11. amaranthin 12. imperishable 14. indestructible

unearth... 4. find 5. dig up 6. exhume, expose 7. uncover 8. disclose, discover, disinter 12. bring to light

unearthly... 5. eerie (eery), godly, weird 7. awesome, ghostly, strange, uncanny 8. heavenly, terrific 9. appalling, deathlike 10. mysterious, outlandish 12. preposterous, supernatural 13. preternatural

uneasiness... 5. worry 6. unrest 7. anxiety, malaise 8. disquiet 10. impatience 11. displeasure, disquietude, disturbance

12. apprehension

uneasy... 5. stiff 7. anxious, awkward, inquiet, restive, worried 8. agitated, cramping, restless 9. difficult, impatient, perturbed 10. disquieted, distressed 11. constrained, troublesome

unemotional... 4. cold 5. stoic 7. stoical 10. phlegmatic

unemployed... 4. idle, lazy 6. otiose, unused 7. not used 8. inactive, leisured 11. not invested

unencumbered... 4. free

unending... 7. endless, eternal 8. termless, timeless 9. boundless, perpetual 10. continuous 12. interminable

unequal... 3. odd 4. odds 5. aniso (comb form) 6. uneven, unfair, unjust 8. variable 9. disparate, irregular 11. fluctuating, not adequate 12. asymmetrical 16. disproportionate

unequaled... 7. supreme 8. peerless 9. matchless, nonpareil, unmatched, unrivaled 10. inimitable, surpassing, unbeatable, unexcelled 12. unparalleled

unequivocal... 5. clear, plain 6. candid 7. sincere 8. explicit 9. downright 11. categorical, indubitable

unerring... 4. sure, true 5. exact 7. certain 8. accurate, virtuous 9. unfailing 10. infallible

unessential... 8. needless 9. extrinsic 10. irrelevant 11. superfluous, unimportant 13. insignificant, void of essence

unethical... 6. amoral

uneven... 3. odd 5. erose, rough 6. rugged, unfair, unjust 7. erratic, unequal, varying 8. not level 10. ill-matched 11. fluctuating

unexamined... 7. a priori

unexampled... 8. peerless 10. unimitated 12. unparalleled 13. extraordinary, unprecedented

unexpected... 6. abrupt, sudden 7. unusual 9. inopinate 10. unforeseen 14. not anticipated

unfair... 4. foul 5. wrong 6. biased, uneven, unjust 8. unseemly 9. dishonest, unethical 10. not cricket, unsporting 11. inequitable, unfavorable 12. disingenuous, not equitable

unfaithful... 6. betray 7. infidel, traitor 8. apostate, recreant, turncoat 9. faithless 10. inaccurate 12. nonobservant 13. untrustworthy

unfamiliar... 3. new 7. strange, unknown 8. not known 12. unaccustomed, unconversant

unfasten... 4. free, open, undo 5. unbar, unfix, unpin, untie 6. detach, loosen, unhook, unlock 7. unloose 8. unbutton 9. disengage

unfavorable... 3. bad, ill 6. averse 7. adverse, opposed 8. contrary, untimely 9. repulsive 12. inauspicious

unfeeling... 4. dull 5. cruel, stoic, stony 6. brutal, steely, stolid, unkind 7. callous 8. numbness, obdurate

9. apathetic, bloodless, heartless, inanimate, insensate 10. insensible 11. hardhearted 13. unsusceptible 16. unimpressionable

unfeigned... 4. real 7. genuine, natural, sincere 11. undeceptive 14. not counterfeit 15. not hypocritical

unfermented grape juice... 4. stum

unfertile... 4. arid 6. barren

unfettered... 4. free 5. broad 9. liberated, unchained 10. unshackled

unfinished... 5. crude, rough 7. sketchy 9. imperfect 10. incomplete 11. uncompleted

unfit... 5. inept 6. faulty, not fit, unable 8. disabled 9. untenable 11. handicapped, incompetent, unqualified 12. disqualified

unfledged... 4. eyas 5. green 6. callow 8. immature 11. undeveloped 12. not feathered

unflinching... 7. staunch 8. resolute, unafraid 9. steadfast 10. unwavering, unyielding 12. not shrinking

unfold... 3. ope 4. open 6. evolve, expand, flower, reveal, spread, unfurl 7. develop, display, divulge, evolute, explain, release 8. disclose

unfortunate... 3. ill 4. poor 6. wretch 7. hapless, unlucky 8. luckless, untimely 10. calamitous 12. inauspicious, unsuccessful

unfounded... 4. idle, vain 8. baseless 9. untenable 10. chimerical 11. unsupported, unwarranted

unfriendly... 3. icy 4. cool 7. asocial, hostile, not kind, opposed 8. inimical, unsocial 10. unsociable 12. inhospitable

unfruitful... 6. barren, wasted 7. sterile, useless 9. fruitless, infertile 12. unproductive, unprofitable 13. not productive

unfurl... 4. open 6. expand, spread, unfold, unroll

ungainly... 5. gawky, lanky 6. clumsy, gauche 7. awkward, uncouth 8. bungling 10. cumbersome, ungraceful

ungenteel... 6. vulgar 7. ill–bred 8. plebeian 9. inelegant 10. unmannerly

ungentle... 4. rude 5. harsh, rough 7. ill–bred 12. discourteous

ungodly... 6. sinful, wicked 7. impious 9. atheistic 11. unbelieving

ungovernable... 4. wild 6. unruly 9. unbridled 10. disorderly, licentious, rebellious, refractory 12. incorrigible, obstreperous, recalcitrant 13. irrepressible 14. uncontrollable

unguent... 4. balm 5. salve 6. cerate, chrism, pomade 7. unction 8. ointment 9. lubricant, unguentum

ungula... 4. claw, hoof, nail 6. unguis

ungulate... 3. pig 4. deer 5. horse, swine, tapir 6. hoofed 8. elephant, Ungulata 10. rhinoceros 15. hoofed quadruped

unhallowed... 6. unholy, wicked 10. desecrated

unhappy... 3. sad 6. dismal, woeful 8. dejected, ill–fated, wretched 9. miserable, sorrowful 10. calamitous, displeased 11. melancholic, unfortunate 12. discontented, unsuccessful

unhealthy... 3. ill 4. sick 6. sickly, unsafe 11. unwholesome

unhesitating... 4. sure 5. ready 8. implicit, resolute 10. undoubting

unholy... 6. wicked 7. impious, profane 8. shocking 10. scandalous, unhallowed

unicorn... 4. reem (Bib), unie 7. monster 8. narwhale 9. monoceros, spike team 10. pursuivant (Her), rhinoceros (one–horned)

uniform... 4. even 5. equal 6. livery, outfit, simple, smooth 7. equable, orderly, regular 8. constant, equiform 9. unvarying 10. consistent, invariable, unchanging 11. symmetrical

uniformity... 5. order 8. equality, evenness, sameness, symmetry 10. compliance, conformity, smoothness 11. consistency, homogeneity 13. invariability

unify... 5. merge, unite 7. combine, make one 8. coalesce 9. integrate 11. consolidate

unimaginative... 4. dull 7. literal, prosaic 10. unfanciful

unimpaired... 4. free 6. entire, intact 8. unmarred 9. undamaged, unspoiled

unimpressed... 6. unawed 7. unmoved 9. unstirred 10. unaffected, uninspired

uninformed... 8. ignorant, nescient 9. unknowing 10. unapprized 13. unenlightened, unintelligent

uninhabited... 5. empty 6. vacant 8. deserted, desolate, forsaken 9. abandoned, unpeopled 10. unoccupied, untenanted

uninspired... 4. dull 6. stodgy 9. uninhaled

unintelligent... 4. dumb 5. brute 6. stupid, unwise 7. foolish 8. ignorant 9. senseless

unintentional... 7. unmeant 9. unwitting 10. accidental, unintended 11. inadvertent, involuntary, unmeditated 14. unpremeditated

uninterested... 5. bored 9. apathetic, impartial, incurious 11. unconcerned 13. disinterested

uninteresting... 3. dry 4. arid, drab, dull 6. boring, prolix, stupid 7. humdrum, insipid, prosaic, tedious 8. tiresome 9. colorless 10. unexciting

union... 3. one 4. bond 5. joint, unity 6. accord, fusion, league, merger 7. amalgam, entente, liaison, oneness 8. alliance, junction, marriage 9. coalition 10. federation

11. affiliation, association, combination, concurrence, confederacy, conjunction
13. juxtaposition
Union (pert to) . . .
ensign, British.. 12. three crosses (St Andrew, St George, St Patrick)
General.. 7. Sherman (Civil War)
of States.. 6. Empire 12. United States
of workers.. 5. artel, guild
Union of So Africa . . .
capital.. 8. Cape Town (Legis), Pretoria (Admin)
city.. 6. Durban 9. Germiston 12. Johannesburg
famed Park.. 6. Kruger
Union of Soviet Socialist Republics... see also *Russia*
anc citadel.. 7. Kremlin
capital.. 6. Moscow
city.. 9. Leningrad
Republics (number).. 7. fifteen
resort.. 5. Yalta 6. Crimea
river.. 2. Ob 3. Don 4. Lena, Neva, Ural 5. Volga 7. Dnieper
sea.. 4. Aral, Azov 5. Black, White 6. Baltic 7. Caspian
strait.. 6. Bering
unique... 3. odd, one 4. rare, sole 5. alone, novel 6. single 7. notable, special, unusual 8. original, peculiar, peerless, singular 9. matchless 12. single–valued 13. extraordinary
unison... 5. union 6. accord, assent 7. concord, harmony 8. agreement, unanimity 10. concordant, consonance
unit... 3. ace, ane, one 4. item, word 5. digit, group 6. entity 7. measure 8. syllable
unit (pert to) . . .
astronomy.. 6. parsec
biology.. 5. idant
electrical.. 3. amp, mho, ohm, rel 4. volt, watt 5. farad, henry, joule 6. ampere, proton 7. coulomb
energy.. 3. erg, rad 5. ergon 6. kilerg 7. quantum
fluidity.. 3. rhe
force.. 4. dyne 5. tonal 7. kinetic
heat.. 5. therm (therme) 7. calorie (calory)
induction.. 5. henry
light.. 3. lux, pyr, rad 5. lumen 6. Hefner
linear.. 3. ell 4. foot, inch, mile, yard 7. furlong
magnetic.. 5. gauss, weber 7. maxwell, oersted
matter.. 5. monad
measure.. 3. are, rod 4. pint 5. maund, meter, stere
military.. 7. brigade, platoon 8. regiment
power.. 2. HP 3. bel 5. dynam, horse
pressure.. 5. barad, barie
reluctance.. 3. rel
resistance.. 3. ohm
speed.. 4. velo

telegraphic.. 4. baud
thermal.. 7. calorie (calory)
velocity.. 4. velo
volume.. 3. ton 4. cord, peck, pint 5. ounce, pound 6. barrel, bushel, gallon 8. hogshead
weight.. 3. ton 5. carat (karat), ounce, pound
wire.. 3. mil
work.. 3. erg 5. ergon, joule 6. kilerg
yarn.. 6. denier
unite... 3. fay, tie, wed 4. ally, bind, fuse, join, knit, link, meld, weld 5. annex, graft, marry, merge 6. adhere, cement, concur, mingle, solder 7. combine, connect 8. coalesce, condense, converge, federate, side with 9. affiliate, associate 10. amalgamate, federalize 11. consolidate, incorporate
unite (pert to) . . .
by freezing.. 8. regelate
by interweaving.. 5. plash 6. pleach, splice
by joints.. 10. articulate
closely.. 11. concentrate
in concordance.. 9. harmonize
timbers.. 6. rabbet
united... 3. one, wed 4. knit, tied 5. added 6. allied, banded, joined, linked, merged, welded 7. cohered, grafted, rallied, spliced 8. cemented, clannish 9. concerted, corporate 10. concurrent, corporated
United Provinces... 11. (The) Netherlands 14. Dutch Republic
United States... 9. Etats–Unis
United States... see also *American*
artist.. 4. Pyle, Wood 5. Flagg, Moses (Grandma), Peale, Ryder, Sloan 6. Eakins, Stuart
author.. 3. Ade, Poe 4. Pyle, Ward 5. Alger, Barth, Beach, Davis, Field, Harte, James, Lewis, Stowe 6. Alcott, Bryant, Cooper, Ferber, Hersey, Holmes, Irving, London, Lowell, O'Henry, Porter 7. Clemens, Dreiser, Emerson, Stewart, Thoreau, Whitman 8. Faulkner, Sinclair, Whittier 9. Hawthorne, Hemingway 10. Longfellow, Tarkington
canal.. 4. Erie 6. Panama
capital.. see separate States
composer.. 4. Kern 5. Foote, Nevin 6. Berlin, Foster 7. Rodgers 8. Gershwin 9. Bernstein
emblem.. 5. eagle
explorer.. 4. Byrd, Long, Pike 5. Boone, Clark, Lewis, Logan, Perry
Falls.. 7. Niagara 8. Yosemite 9. Multnomah
Indian.. see under *Indian (Am)*
inventor.. 3. Hoe 4. Bell, Howe 5. Fiske, Fitch, Morse 6. Edison, Fulton 7. Whitney
mountain.. 4. Hood 6. Elbert, Helena, Shasta 7. Rainier, Whitney 8. Katahdin, McKinley
naturalist.. 4. Muir 5. Beebe, Seton 7. Thoreau
ornithologist.. 7. Audubon

philosopher.. 5. James
pirate.. 4. Kidd
poet.. 3. Poe 4. Nash 5. Benét,
Field, Moore, Wylie 6. Bryant,
Holmes, Kilmer, Lanier, Lowell, Millay
7. Whitman 8. Whittier
10. Longfellow
unity... 3. one 5. union 6. accord
7. concord, harmony, oneness
8. alliance 9. agreement
10. singleness, uniformity
11. conjunction, unification
12. completeness
universal... 3. all 5. local, total, usual,
whole 6. cosmic, entire, public
7. general 8. catholic 9. prevalent,
unlimited, well-known 11. widely
known
universal (pert to)...
knowledge.. 9. pantology
language.. 2. Ro 3. Ido 9. Esperanto
language, written.. 10. pasigraphy
remedy.. 7. panacea
solvent.. 8. alkahest
successor, heir.. 5. heres (haeres)
universe... 4. olam 5. world
6. cosmos, system 9. macrocosm
10. Great World
universe, controlling principle...
5. logos
unkempt... 5. messy, rough 6. frowsy,
shaggy, untidy 7. ruffled, squalid,
tousled, uncouth 9. unrefined
10. disarrayed, disheveled, unpolished
unkind... 3. ill 5. cruel, harsh, stern
6. brutal, severe 8. ungenial
9. inclement 10. ungracious,
ungrateful 13. unsympathetic
15. uncompassionate
unknowable... 6. mystic 8. mystical,
noumenon 9. enigmatic
13. indiscernible 14. unintelligible
15. absolute reality (Kant), ultimate
reality (Spencer)
unknowable object... 3. God 7. the
soul 8. noumenon
unknown... 7. inconnu, strange
8. stranger 9. anonymous, hereafter,
incognito, unheard of 10. unfamiliar,
unrenowned 12. incalculable
unlawful... 7. bastard, illegal, illicit,
lawless 9. irregular 10. contraband
11. unwarranted 12. illegitimate,
unauthorized
unlearned... 4. lewd 5. gross
8. ignorant, untaught 10. illiterate,
uneducated 11. instinctive
unleashed... 4. free 5. loose 6. untied
8. released 10. unfettered,
unshackled, untethered
unleavened... 7. azymous
unleavened bread... 4. azym 5. azyme
7. matzoth
unless... 4. nisi, save 6. except
7. without 9. except for, excepting
10. except that
unlettered... 8. ignorant 10. illiterate,
uneducated
unlike... 6. sundry, uneven 7. dislike,
diverse 9. different, irregular
10. dissimilar, improbable
11. unpromising 12. disagreeable

13. heterogeneous
unlikelihood... 11. small chance
13. improbability
unlikeness... 8. contrast
13. dissimilarity
unlimited... 4. vast 9. boundless,
unbounded, universal 10. unconfined
11. illimitable 12. immeasurable,
unrestricted 13. indeterminate
unload... 3. rid 4. dump, sell
5. empty 7. discard, lighten
9. disburden, discharge, liquidate
unlucky... 3. bad, fey, ill 7. infaust
8. ill-fated, untimely 9. ill-omened
11. unfortunate 12. inauspicious, not
favorable
unmannerly... 4. rude 7. boorish,
uncivil 8. impolite 10. mannerless
12. discourteous
unmelodious... 9. dissonant
11. cacophonous
unmerciful... 5. cruel 6. unkind
7. extreme, inhuman 8. pitiless,
ruthless 9. heartless, merciless
10. relentless
unmistakable... 4. open 5. clear, plain
6. patent 7. certain, evident, obvious
8. apparent, distinct, manifest
11. unqualified
unmitigated... 5. mere 6. sheer
6. arrant 8. clear-cut, thorough
9. downright 11. not softened,
unqualified
unmoved... 4. calm, dead, firm
5. inert 6. serene 8. obdurate,
unshaken 9. apathetic
unnatural... 5. eerie (eery) 7. labored,
strange, uncanny 8. abnormal,
affected 9. eccentric, irregular
10. artificial, factitious
unnecessary... 4. fuss 7. useless
8. needless 11. not required,
superfluous, uncalled-for
12. nonessential
unobtrusive... 6. modest 8. retiring
11. clandestine
unoccupied... 4. idle, void 5. empty
7. not busy 8. deserted
10. unemployed, untenanted
11. empty-headed, uninhabited
unorthodox... 9. heretical
10. fallacious, left-handed
14. unconventional
unostentatious... 5. quiet 6. lenten,
modest 10. restrained
unparalleled... 5. alone 6. unique
8. peerless 9. matchless, unequaled,
unmatched 10. inimitable
13. extraordinary
unpleasant... 8. unsavory 9. offensive
10. not amiable, ungracious
11. displeasing, distasteful
12. disagreeable
unpolished... 5. bruit, crude, rough
6. coarse, rugged 7. uncouth
8. agrestic, unpolite 9. inelegant
10. agrestical 11. countrified
unprecedented... 3. new 5. novel
10. unexampled, unimitated
13. extraordinary
unprejudiced... 4. fair 7. neutral
8. unbiased 9. impartial

10. impersonal 13. dispassionate
unprepared... 3. raw 5. unfit
6. unwary 7. unready 9. premature, unskilled
unprepossessing... 4. grim, ugly
9. grim-faced 10. ill-looking
unpretentious... 6. humble, modest, simple 7. natural 10. unaffected
11. in good taste
unprincipled... 7. corrupt 9. dishonest
10. fraudulent, perfidious
12. dishonorable, unscrupulous
unprofessional... 3. lay 6. laical
7. amateur 9. unskilled
10. amateurish 14. unbusinesslike
unprofitable... 6. barren 7. useless
8. gainless 9. fruitless 10. unfruitful
unpropitious... 7. adverse, ominous, opposed 8. untimely 10. disastrous
12. inauspicious
unqualified... 5. unfit 6. unable
7. genuine, plenary 8. absolute, complete, unfitted 9. incapable
10. ineligible 11. incompetent
12. not qualified 13. unconditional
unquestionable... 7. certain, decided, evident 8. positive 10. undeniable
11. indubitable, irrefutable
12. indisputable 13. unimpeachable
unravel... 4. undo 5. feaze, solve
6. unfold, unlace 8. separate
9. disengage 10. disinvolve
11. disentangle
unreal... 5. false, ideal 7. fancied
8. fanciful, illusory, spurious
9. fantastic, imaginary, visionary
10. artificial, fictitious 11. imaginative
13. unsubstantial
unreasonable... 3. mad 6. absurd, unwise 9. excessive, fanatical, illogical, senseless 10. capricious, exorbitant, immoderate, irrational
11. extravagant, impractical
12. unjustifiable
unrecognizable... 3. dim 5. vague
7. blurred, obscure, unclear
9. undefined 10. indistinct
14. unintelligible
unrecognized... 6. unsung 7. unknown
13. unappreciated
unrefined... 3. raw 4. loud, rude
5. crass, crude, gross, rough
6. coarse, common, earthy, vulgar
7. uncouth 9. inelegant
11. countrified 12. uncultivated
unrefuted... 4. true 6. proved
8. undenied 10. unanswered
unrelaxed... 4. taut 5. rigid, tense
7. nervous
unrelenting... 4. grim, hard, iron
5. stern 6. severe, strict 8. rigorous
9. merciless 10. inexorable, relentless, unyielding
unreliable... 6. fickle, unsafe
9. uncertain 10. capricious, changeable 12. undependable
13. irresponsible, untrustworthy
14. tergiversating
unremitting... 4. busy 8. constant
9. continual, incessant, perpetual
10. continuous, persistent
11. persevering

unrequited... 6. unpaid 9. forgotten, unthanked 10. ungrateful, unrewarded
unreserved, unreservedly... 4. free, open 5. frank 6. openly 7. frankly
8. candidly, outright, thorough
9. outspoken 12. unrestricted
unrest... 7. bustle 8. disquiet
9. commotion 12. restlessness
unrestrained... 3. lax 4. free, wild
5. loose 6. candid, wanton
7. lawless, riotous 9. unbridled, unlimited 10. capricious
unrestricted... 4. free, open
9. unlimited 11. extravagant
12. undiminished 13. communicative
unruffled... 4. calm, cool 5. still
6. placid, poised, sedate, serene, smooth 9. quiescent, unexcited
10. unaffected 11. undisturbed
unruly... 7. lawless 9. fractious, obstinate, turbulent 10. disorderly, licentious, refractory 11. disobedient
12. recalcitrant, ungovernable, unmanageable
unsafe... 7. dubious, exposed, unsound
8. insecure, perilous 9. dangerous
10. unreliable 12. undependable
unsatisfactory... 8. inferior
10. inadequate, unbearable
11. intolerable 12. insufficient, ungratiating 13. disheartening, unsupportable
unsavory... 7. insipid 9. offensive, tasteless 10. unpleasant
11. unpalatable 12. disagreeable
unscrupulous... 7. devious
9. dishonest 12. unparticular, unprincipled 12. untrustworthy
16. indiscriminating
unseasonable... 8. untimely
9. premature 11. inopportune
unseemly... 5. inapt, wrong 6. vulgar
8. improper, indecent 9. inelegant
10. indecorous, solecistic, unbecoming 11. undignified
13. ungrammatical
unseen... 6. hidden 8. unheeded, viewless 9. invisible, unnoticed
12. undiscovered
unsettled... 4. moot 6. fickle, queasy
8. confused, deranged, restless, unplaced, unproved, unstable
9. ambiguous, disturbed, irregular, uncertain, unquieted 10. irresolute, unoccupied, up in the air
11. unpopulated
unshorn... 5. hairy, whole 6. shaggy
unshorn sheep (2nd year)... 3. tag, teg
unsightly... 4. ugly 8. uncomely, unlovely 9. inelegant, not comely
12. unattractive
unskilled... 5. green 6. puisne
8. ignorant, malapert
unskillful... 5. inept 7. artless, awkward 9. maladroit
12. unproficient 13. inexperienced
unsophisticated... 4. naif, pure, soft
5. green, naive 6. simple 7. artless, genuine 8. gullible, innocent
9. ingenuous 11. uncorrupted
unsound... 4. weak 5. crazy, dotty,

risky, shaky 6. addled, fickle
8. impaired, insecure 9. defective,
imperfect
unspoken... 5. tacit 6. silent
7. implied 9. ineffable, unuttered
unstable... 4. weak 6. fickle, fitful,
labile, scanty 7. astatic, erratic,
flighty, plastic 8. insecure, not solid,
ticklish, unsteady 9. ephemeral,
irregular, unsettled 10. inconstant,
precarious, unreliable 11. fluctuating,
vacillating
unsteady... 5. dizzy, shaky 6. groggy,
wobbly 7. quavery, rickety, unsound
8. titubate, unstable, wavering
9. irregular, uncertain 10. capricious,
changeable, flickering, inconstant,
precarious 11. fluctuating,
ill-balanced, lightheaded, vacillating
unsubstantial... 5. airy, rare, slim
5. filmy, light 6. aerial, flimsy,
papery 8. illusory 9. illogical,
visionary 10. immaterial, intangible,
unreliable
unsuitable... 5. inept, undue, unfit
8. untimely 10. unbecoming
11. inexpedient 13. inappropriate
14. unsatisfactory
unsullied... 4. pure 5. clean 6. chaste
8. innocent, spotless, virginal
10. immaculate
unsure... 4. weak 5. timid 6. infirm
8. doubtful 10. precarious
11. vacillating
unsweetened... 3. dry, sec 4. sour,
tart 10. unpleasant
unsympathetic... 6. unkind 7. hostile
8. pitiless 9. heartless 10. intolerant
11. hardhearted 12. unresponsive
untamed... 4. wild 5. feral 6. savage
9. unsubdued 11. uncivilized
untangle... 4. free 5. loose, solve
6. sleave 9. extricate 11. disentangle
untenable... 10. incredible
11. implausible 12. unbelievable,
unreasonable 15. inconceivable
unthinking... 4. rash 5. puerile
8. careless, heedless 9. impetuous,
impulsive 11. injudicious, instinctive,
involuntary, thoughtless
13. inconsiderate
untidy... 5. dowdy, messy 6. frowzy,
shabby 8. careless, frumpish,
slipshod, slovenly, unsuited, untimely
10. disheveled
untie... 4. free 5. loose 6. loosen,
unbind, unknot, unlash 8. unfasten
9. disengage
until now... 8. hitherto
untiring... 8. sedulous, tireless
9. unwearied 10. unflagging
13. indefatigable
untold... 4. vast 8. infinite
9. boundless, countless
10. uninformed, unrevealed
11. innumerable, unexpressed
12. immeasurable, incalculable,
undetermined
untouched... 4. new 5. pure 6. intact,
unused 8. pristine, virginal
10. impenitent, unaffected
untoward... 6. unruly 7. unlucky

8. perverse, stubborn, unseemly
10. indecorous, ungraceful
11. unfavorable, unfortunate
12. unpropitious
untrained... 4. soft, wild 5. green
8. indocile 9. unskilled, untutored
10. amateurish 11. unpracticed
14. unaccomplished
untrammeled... 4. free 5. loose 8. not
bound 9. unimpeded, unlimited
10. unfettered, unhampered,
unhindered
untransferable... 11. inalienable
untried... 3. new 5. fresh, green
8. unproved 9. unhandled
13. inexperienced
untrue... 5. false, wrong 8. disloyal
9. dishonest, erroneous, incorrect,
not honest 10. fallacious, unfaithful
untrustworthy... 6. tricky, unsafe
8. slippery 9. deceitful, dishonest,
uncertain 10. perfidious
untruth... 3. lie 5. error, fable
7. falsity 9. falsehood, treachery
10. disloyalty 11. fabrication
13. faithlessness
unusual... 3. odd 4. rare 5. novel,
queer 6. exotic, quaint, unique
7. strange 8. terrific, uncommon
9. anomalous 10. infrequent,
remarkable 11. exceptional
13. extraordinary
unutterable... 6. sacred, secret
9. ineffable, wonderful
11. unspeakable 13. inexpressible
unvarnished... 5. plain 6. simple
7. genuine 8. unadorned, unglossed
11. undeceptive 13. unembellished
unvarying... 7. uniform 8. constant
9. permanent 10. monotonous
unwarranted... 4. idle, vain 5. undue
7. illegal 8. baseless 9. excessive,
unfounded, untenable 10. exorbitant,
unentitled 11. unjustified
unwary... 4. rash 7. unaware
8. heedless, off guard 9. unguarded
10. unwatchful
unwavering... 4. firm, sure 5. solid
8. constant 9. steadfast
10. unweakened 11. not yielding,
persevering
unwelcome... 8. non grata, unwanted
9. intrusive, uninvited
unwholesome... 6. evil, sick 6. impure
7. corrupt, immoral, noisome,
noxious 9. unhealthy 12. insalubrious
unwieldy... 5. bulky 6. clumsy
7. awkward, restive 8. ungainly
9. ponderous 10. cumbersome
12. unmanageable 13. insubordinate
unwilling... 5. loath (loth) 6. averse
9. reluctant 11. disinclined,
involuntary
unwilling to prosecute... 7. nol-pros
13. nolle prosequi
unwise... 7. foolish 9. impolitic,
imprudent, senseless 10. irrational
11. inexpedient, injudicious
unwonted... 4. rare 6. unused
7. unusual 8. uncommon 9. not
wonted 10. infrequent
12. unaccustomed

unworldly... 5. eerie (eery), godly, naive, weird 8. heavenly 9. spiritual, unearthly 10. immaterial 12. supernatural

unyielding... 3. set 4. firm, hard, iron 5. rigid, stern, stiff 6. strict 7. adamant 8. obdurate, stubborn 9. immovable, obstinate 10. adamantine, determined, inexorable, inflexible 14. uncompromising

up (pert to)...
and coming.. 7. go-ahead 8. hustling
and down.. 6. seesaw, uneven 8. vertical 10. undulating 13. perpendicular
in arms.. 6. at odds 8. prepared 9. resistant
ref to.. 10. at the plate (game)
to.. 4. able, till, unto 5. until 9. cognizant, competent
to date.. 3. new 6. modern 7. stylish 11. fashionable

upas tree, arrow poison... 6. antiar

upbraid... 4. twit 5. blame, chide, scold, score 6. rebuke 7. reprove 8. admonish, reproach 9. reprimand 10. put to shame

upheaval... 5. storm 6. revolt 9. agitation, cataclysm, elevation 10. convulsion

upheld... 5. aided 6. backed 7. abetted 8. defended 9. supported, sustained 10. encouraged, maintained

uphill... 6. upward 7. upgrade 9. ascending, difficult, laborious 10. slantingly

uphold... 3. aid 4. abet, back, buoy 5. favor, raise 6. defend 7. confirm, support, sustain 8. maintain, preserve 9. encourage 11. corroborate, countenance, lend support

upkeep... 4. cost 6. repair 7. support 11. maintenance

upland... 4. wold 5. weald 6. coteau, inland 7. country, plateau 8. highland

uplands... 7. country 9. highlands 10. the country

uplift... 5. elate, erect, raise 7. elevate, ennoble, glorify, improve 8. upheaval 9. elevation 11. inspiration

upon... 2. up 3. on 4. atop, onto 5. about, above 7. against 9. by means of 10. after which

upon (pert to)...
law.. 3. sur
prefix.. 3. epi, sur
that.. 7. whereat 9. whereupon
which.. 7. whereat

upper... 6. higher 8. superior

upper (pert to)...
bed.. 4. bunk
crust.. 7. society 11. aristocracy 13. highest circle
end.. 3. tip 4. apex, head
hand.. 7. mastery 8. dominion 9. advantage, influence 10. preference
House of Congress.. 6. Senate
shoe part.. 4. vamp

uppermost... 3. top 6. upmost

7. highest, supreme, topmost 8. farthest, foremost 9. outermost

uppish... 5. drunk, proud 6. uppity 7. haughty, peevish, stuck-up 8. arrogant, assuming, snobbish 9. high-flown

upright... 4. good, just, true 5. erect, moral, piano 6. honest, square 7. endwise, sincere 8. vertical, virtuous 9. equitable, honorable, righteous 13. perpendicular

upright (pert to)...
chair part.. 4. slat
comb form.. 5. ortho
posture.. 8. orthotic 11. orthostatic
slab.. 5. stela
timber.. 4. jamb, stud

uprising... 4. riot 5. ascent, mutiny, revolt 7. sloping 9. acclivity, ascending, rebellion 12. insurrection

uproar... 3. din 4. riot, rout 5. noise 6. bedlam, bustle, clamor, fracas, hubbub, outcry, tumult 7. turmoil 8. outbreak 9. commotion, confusion 10. donnybrook, hurly-burly, tintamarre, turbulence 11. pandemonium 12. insurrection

upset... 3. irk 4. rile, ruin, stir 6. defeat, refute, topple 7. agitate, capsize, confuse, disturb, fluster, startle, subvert, unnerve 8. distress, overturn, startled, unnerved 9. embarrass, overthrow 10. discompose, disconcert, distressed, frustrated, overturned, refutation, revolution 11. frustration, overwrought

upshot... 3. end 5. fruit, issue 6. result, sequel 7. outcome 10. conclusion 11. consequence, eventuality, termination 12. consummation

upside down... 8. confused, disorder 9. confusion 10. resupinate, topsy-turvy

upsilon (Gr)... 5. hyoid, vowel 7. Y-shaped

upstart... 4. snob 7. bounder, parvenu 13. social climber

up-to-date... 6. modern 7. alamode, topical 8. informed 11. fashionable

upward... 2. up 3. ano (comb form) 4. over 5. above, aloft 6. onward 7. skyward 8. upstream 9. ascending

upward movement of vessels... 5. scend

uraeus (Egypt Relig)... 3. asp 6. symbol 8. symbolic

Ural... 5. river 9. mountains

Urania (pert to)...
blue.. 12. independence
epithet of.. 9. Aphrodite
genus of.. 5. moths
Gr Myth.. 4. Muse (Astron)

uranology (study of)... 7. heavens 15. celestial bodies

Uranus (pert to)...
astronomy.. 6. planet
daughter.. 4. Rhea
father of.. 9. The Titans (12)
personification of.. 6. heaven
satellite.. 5. Ariel 6. Oberon

7. Titania, Umbriel
son.. 6. Cronus
urare, urari... 6. curare
urban... 5. civic 6. ghetto, polite,
uptown 7. oppidan, refined
8. downtown, polished 9. courteous,
municipal 12. metropolitan
13. sophisticated
urbane... 5. civil, suave 6. polish,
polite 7. affable 8. gracious
9. courteous 11. deferential
urbanity... 7. amenity 8. civility,
courtesy 9. deference
urchin... 3. boy, elf, imp, tad 4. arab,
brat 5. gamin 6. elfish 8. hedgehog
9. dandiprat, sea urchin, youngster
urge... 3. dun, egg, hie, ply, yen
4. abet, coax, goad, prod, push,
spur 5. drive, egg on, impel, press
6. advise, compel, dehort, desire,
exhort, fillip, hasten, incite, induce
7. animate, entreat, solicit
8. persuade 9. constrain, importune,
influence, instigate 10. inducement
urgent... 3. hot 5. grave 7. clamant,
exigent, instant 8. critical, pressing
9. impelling, important, insistent,
necessary 11. importunate
urial... 3. sha 5. sheep 6. oorial
Uriel... 9. archangel 10. flame of God
(Bib)
Urim and Thummim (Bib)...
11. instruments 12. interpreters
(Mormon)
urn... 3. jar 4. ewer, urna (anc), vase
5. grave, steen 6. vessel 7. pitcher,
samovar, vaselet 10. jardiniere
urn–shaped... 8. urceolus 9. urceolate
Ursa... 9. bear 9. Ursa Major (Great
Bear), Ursa Minor (Little Bear)
ursal... 7. fur seal
ursuk... 11. bearded seal
Ursula... 5. Saint 7. she–bear
9. butterfly 15. British princess
(legend)
urubu... 7. vulture
Uruguay...
capital.. 10. Montevideo
city.. 4. Melo 5. Minar 9. Maldonado
estuary.. 5. Plata 12. Rio de la Plata
lake.. 5. Merim
river.. 7. Uruguay
settler.. 7. Cabot (Sebastian, 1527)
university.. 10. Montevideo (1849)
windstorm.. 7. pampero
urus... 2. ox 3. tur 7. aurochs
usable... 3. fit 9. practical
10. functional 11. serviceable,
utilitarian
usage... 3. use 4. wont 5. habit, ritus
6. custom, method 7. utility
8. behavior, practice 9. treatment
10. convention
use... 3. try 5. apply, avail, exert,
spend, treat, wield 6. employ,
expend, occupy 7. consume, exploit,
utilize 8. function 10. manipulate
11. consumption, utilization
use (pert to)...
abusive language.. 4. rail
divining rod.. 5. dowse
frugally.. 5. stint

pert to words.. 7. neology, verbose
8. enallage, pleonasm 9. verbosity
poetry.. 4. vail
refrain from.. 7. boycott
subterfuge.. 7. chicane
up.. 3. eat 7. consume, deplete,
exhaust, fatigue
useful... 4. good 5. utile 7. helpful
9. practical 10. beneficial,
commodious 11. serviceable,
subservient 12. advantageous,
instrumental
usefulness... 5. avail, value 6. profit
7. utility 15. conduciveness
useless... 4. idle, null, vain 6. futile,
otiose 7. of no use 8. bootless,
hopeless 9. fruitless, worthless
10. fifth wheel 11. ineffectual,
superfluous 12. unprofitable
13. unserviceable 14. good for
nothing
uselessness... 8. futility 9. inutility
10. inefficacy
usher... 4. lead, page 5. guide
6. escort 7. chobdar, teacher
9. attendant, harbinger, precursor
10. doorkeeper, forerunner,
inaugurate
usquebaugh... 6. whisky 7. cordial
ustion... 7. burning 13. cauterization
ustulate... 8. scorched 10. discolored
usual... 7. average, typical, usitate
8. everyday, frequent 11. status in
quo
usuer... 5. shark 6. loaner 7. Shylock
11. moneylender
usurp... 4. take 5. seize 6. assume
8. arrogate 11. appropriate
Utah...
capital.. 12. Salt Lake City
city.. 5. Logan, Ogden, Provo
7. Bingham
dam.. 10. Glen Canyon 12. Flaming
Gorge
lake.. 6. Powell 9. Great Salt
mountain.. 5. Uinta 7. Wasatch
9. King's Peak
name desired.. 7. Deseret
natural wonder.. 4. Zion 5. Bryce
13. Rainbow Bridge
settled by.. 7. Mormons 12. Brigham
Young 15. Latter–day Saints
State admission.. 10. Forty–fifth
State motto.. 8. Industry
State nickname.. 7. Beehive
utensil... 3. mop, pan, pot 4. tool
5. broom, brush 6. device, ramrod
7. skillet, sweeper 9. apparatus,
appliance, implement 10. instrument
utilitarian... 5. plain 6. useful
8. economic 9. practical
10. functional 12. matter–of–fact
utility... 3. use 4. tool 5. avail
6. profit 7. benefit, service
9. appliance, happiness, implement
10. usefulness
utmost... 4. best, last 5. final
7. extreme, maximum, supreme
8. farthest, greatest 9. uttermost
11. most distant
Utopia... 4. Eden 6. heaven, island
(imaginary) 7. Erewhon 8. paradise

9. fairyland, Shangri-La
10. millennium
utopian... 5. ideal 6. Edenic
8. Quixotic, romantic 9. visionary
10. chimerical, idealistic, millennial
utter... 3. say 4. emit, pass, tell, vent
5. issue, sheer, speak, total, voice
6. assert, entire, mumble, reveal
7. deliver, divulge, express, extreme,
publish, unusual 8. abnormal,
absolute, complete, disclose,
disperse, intonate 9. downright,
enunciate, out-and-out, pronounce
10. peremptory 11. unqualified
13. unconditional
utter (pert to)...
harshly.. 3. rap 4. bray
heedlessly.. 4. blat
in devotion.. 4. pray
in slow tone.. 5. drawl
musically.. 6. warble
publicly.. 4. tell 5. voice 7. enounce
softly.. 6. murmur 7. whisper
want.. 9. indigency 11. destitution

with effort.. 5. heave
with impulse.. 9. ejaculate
without voice.. 4. surd 7. spirate
utterance (pert to)...
dogmatic.. 6. dictum
gushing.. 8. effusion
rhythmic.. 7. cadence
voice.. 8. phonesis, speaking
9. phonation 12. articulation
wise.. 6. oracle
utterer of pithy remarks... 8. aphorist
utterly... 5. fully, stark 7. totally
8. entirely 10. absolutely, completely
17. straightforwardly
uttermost... 5. final 6. utmost
7. extreme
utu... 6. reward 12. compensation,
satisfaction
uva... 5. fruit, grape
uvate... 8. conserve (grape)
uvea... 4. iris
uxor... 4. wife
uxoricide... 10. wife murder
Uz (Bib)... 8. Job's home
Uzziel... 5. angel (Paradise Lost)

V

V... 5. notch 6. letter (22nd), symbol
14. five-dollar bill
vaagmer... 8. dealfish (mare of the
sea)
Vac (Hind)... 7. goddess (of speech)
vacant... 4. free, idle, void 5. blank,
empty, inane 6. barren, devoid
7. leisure, vacuous 8. unfilled
10. disengaged, untenanted
11. thoughtless 12. unencumbered
14. expressionless
vacate... 4. free, quit, void 5. annul,
empty, leave 6. depart 7. abandon
8. abdicate, abrogate, evacuate,
withdraw
vacation... 4. rest 5. leave 6. outing,
recess, repeal 7. nonterm, respite
8. furlough, justitum 10. recreation
12. intermission 14. leave of
absence
vacation place... 3. spa 4. lake, park
5. beach 6. forest, resort
9. mountains
vaccination... 11. inoculation
vaccine (pert to)...
discoverer.. 4. Salk 6. Jenner
protection for.. 5. virus 6. cowpox
term.. 5. lymph, serum, virus
vacillate... 4. sway 5. waver 6. dacker
(daiker), seesaw, teeter, totter
7. flutter, stagger 8. hesitate,
titubate 9. fluctuate, oscillate
13. procrastinate
vacillation... 5. doubt 8. wavering
9. faltering, hesitancy 10. fickleness,

indecision, titubation 11. oscillation,
uncertainty 12. irresolution
14. changeableness
15. procrastination
vacuate... 5. empty 8. evacuate
vacuous... 4. dull, void 5. blank,
empty 6. stupid 8. unfilled
9. senseless 11. empty-headed,
thoughtless 13. unintelligent
vacuum... 3. gap 4. void 9. emptiness
11. rarefaction
vagabond... 3. bum, vag 4. hobo
5. lorel, scamp, tramp 6. beggar,
picaro, rascal, rodney 7. vagrant,
wastrel 8. Bohemian, brodyaga,
wanderer 10. ne'er-do-well
vagary... 4. whim 5. caper, fancy,
jaunt, prank, trick 6. notion, ramble
7. caprice, whimsey (whimsy)
9. excursion, wandering
10. digression 13. manifestation
vagrant... 3. bum 4. hobo 5. rogue,
tramp 6. roving, truant 7. nomadic,
prowler, wayward 8. brodyaga,
vagabond, wanderer 9. desultory,
deviative, itinerant 10. capricious
vague... 3. dim 4. dark, hazy 5. loose,
misty 6. dreamy 7. obscure,
shadowy, unfixed 8. confused,
formless, nebulous, not clear
9. ambiguous, unsettled, wandering
10. indefinite, indistinct, intangible
13. indeterminate
vail... 3. tip 4. doff (a hat), dole
5. avail, bribe, yield 6. humble,

submit 7. descend 8. gratuity
10. beneficial 12. advantageous

vain... 4. idle 5. empty, proud
6. devoid, futile, otiose, snooty
7. foolish, trivial, useless 8. arrogant,
boastful, nugatory 9. conceited,
fruitless, worthless 10. unavailing,
unrewarded 11. empty–headed,
overweening, unimportant
12. vainglorious

vain boasting... 11. fanfaronade

vainglorious... 4. vain 7. heroics
8. boastful 9. gasconade

vair... 3. fur

vajra (Buddh)... 7. diamond, trident
(Indra's) 10. adamantine
11. thunderbolt

valance... 5. drape 6. border, pelmet,
ruffle 7. curtain, drapery, hanging

vale... 4. dale, dell, glen 5. earth,
glade, world 6. valley

valediction... 5. adieu 7. address
8. farewell 11. valedictory

valedictory... 7. address, oration
10. apopemptic 11. leave–taking,
valediction

Valentine (pert to)...
romance.. 5. Orson 8. love song
Saint.. 6. martyr (Rom) 7. holiday
8. feast day
State.. 7. Arizona (adm 2/14/1912)
sweetheart.. 11. one's beloved

valerian... 4. drug 5. plant 7. panacea

valet... 3. man 7. Crispin
9. attendant, cameriere, chamberere
10. manservant 11. body servant
14. valet de chambre

valetudinarian... 6. infirm, shut–in,
sickly, weakly 7. invalid
11. languishing

Valhalla (Valhall)... 8. Pantheon
(Bavaria) 10. hall of Odin (Norse
Myth)

valiant... 4. bold, fine 5. brave
6. heroic, strong, sturdy 7. doughty
8. intrepid, stalwart, vigorous,
virtuous 9. steadfast 10. chivalrous,
courageous 11. meritorious
12. stouthearted

valid... 4. good, just, true 5. legal,
sound 6. cogent, lawful, proved
7. binding, weighty 9. authentic,
effective 10. sufficient 11. efficacious
12. well–grounded

validate... 6. affirm, attest 7. confirm
8. legalize 12. substantiate

validity... 5. force 7. cogency
9. authority, soundness
14. substantiality

Valjean (pert to)...
discoverer.. 6. Javert
friend.. 7. Marius
hero of.. 13. Les Miserables (Victor
Hugo)
protégé.. 7. Cosette

valley... 4. dale, dell, dene, glen, vale,
wady 5. glade, gully 6. coulee,
dingle, ravine, trough 10. depression

valley (pert to)...
anatomy.. 9. vallecula
circular.. 6. rincon
deep.. 6. canyon

geology.. 5. atrio
India.. 5. dhoon
Jerusalem (near).. 6. Hinnom
7. Gehenna, Rephaim
moon.. 5. rille
open.. 6. canada
where David killed Goliath.. 4. Elah
(Bib)

valonia oak... 6. camata (fruit)
9. evergreen

valor... 5. merit, worth 6. virtue
7. bravery, courage, heroism,
prowess 8. boldness, chivalry
9. gallantry 11. distinction
12. fearlessness

valuable... 4. dear 5. asset 6. prized,
useful, worthy 8. precious
9. estimable, treasured
10. worthwhile

value... 3. par, use 4. rate 5. price,
prize, worth 6. assess, esteem,
parity, status 7. apprize (apprise),
cherish, compute, meaning, respect,
utility 8. appraise, estimate, evaluate
9. valuation 10. estimation,
excellence, importance

value (pert to)...
equal.. 6. parity
least possible.. 5. plack
nominal.. 3. par
reduction.. 12. depreciation

valueless... 4. baff 9. worthless
10. threepenny 14. good–for–nothing

valve... 3. tap 4. cock, door, gate
6. faucet, piston, spigot 7. petcock

vamoose... 2. go 4. blow, scat
5. leave, scram 6. beat it, decamp
7. skiddoo 9. skedaddle

vamp... 4. hose, sock 5. flirt, patch,
upper 6. recoct, repair, seduce
7. beguile, bewitch, concoct, touch
up 9. improvise, temptress, transform

vampire... 3. bat 5. fiend, ghost,
lamia, witch 6. Alukah 9. bewitcher,
sorceress, temptress 11. bloodsucker,
extortioner 12. extortionist

van... 3. lead, wing 5. front, wagon
6. shovel, summit, winnow 7. vehicle
9. forefront 10. baggage car
12. advance guard

vandal... 3. Hun 7. wrecker
9. destroyer, mutilator, plunderer
10. iconoclast

vandalize... 3. mar 5. wreck 6. deface

Vandyke... 5. beard, brown 6. artist,
collar 7. picture

vane... 4. cock 11. weathercock,
weathervane

vanish... 3. die 4. fade, flee, melt,
pass 6. perish 8. evanesce 9. cease
to be, disappear

vanity... 5. pride 6. egoism
7. conceit, egotism, falsity 8. futility
9. arrogance, emptiness, vainglory
10. hollowness 11. fatuousness,
self–conceit 12. boastfulness
13. dressing table

vanity case... 4. etui 6. make–up
7. compact 9. cosmetics

vanquish... 3. win 4. beat, best, rout
5. expel 6. defeat, subdue
7. conquer 8. confound, overcome,

suppress, surmount 9. overthrow
vantage... 4. gain 9. advantage
    10. perquisite 11. opportunity,
    superiority
vapid... 3. dry 4. dead, dull, flat
    5. inane, stale 7. insipid, prosaic
    8. lifeless 9. pointless, tasteless
    10. spiritless, unanimated
    11. indifferent 13. uninteresting
vapor... 3. air, fog, gas 4. fume, haze,
    mist 5. brume, cloud, fancy, humor,
    smoke, steam 6. breath, bubble
    7. halitus 8. humidity, illusion,
    phantasm 9. evaporate 10. exhalation
vaporous... 4. vain 5. foggy, misty
    6. cloudy, steamy 7. gaseous
    8. ethereal, fanciful, fleeting
    13. unsubstantial
variable... 6. fickle, fitful, mobile
    7. protean, unequal 8. shifting,
    unstable, unsteady 10. capricious,
    changeable, inconstant
variance... 3. out 7. dissent
    9. deviation, disaccord
    10. contention, difference
    11. discrepancy 12. disagreement
varied... 5. mixed 6. daedal, motley
    7. changed, dappled, diverse,
    mottled, piebald, several, various
    8. speckled 9. different
    10. variegated 11. diversified
variegated... 5. pinto 6. daedal,
    motley, varied 7. dappled, diverse,
    mottled, painted 9. different
    11. diversified, many-colored
variegation... 7. variety 9. diversity
    10. multicolor
variety... 4. kind, mode, sort 5. class
    6. change 7. species 9. diversity,
    variation 10. assortment, difference
    13. entertainment
variola... 6. cowpox 8. smallpox
various... 4. many 6. divers, sundry
    7. diverse, several 8. manifold,
    variable 9. different, many-sided,
    uncertain 10. changeable, inconstant,
    variegated 11. diversified
varnish... 4. spar 5. adorn, gloss,
    japan, paint 7. distort, falsify, furbish,
    lacquer, pretext 8. coat over
    9. embellish
Varuna (pert to)...
    art consorts.. 5. Jumna 6. Ganges
    deity.. 6. cosmic (supreme)
    god.. 3. sea
    Vedic equiv.. 13. Avestan Ormazd
    Vedic Relig.. 5. Aditi (fem deity)
vary... 5. alter, range, shift 6. change,
    differ, modify 7. deviate, dissent,
    diverge 8. disagree 9. alternate,
    diversify, fluctuate, vacillate, variegate
    13. differentiate
vas... 4. duct 6. pledge, surety, vessel
vascular (pert to)... 5. hemic (haemic)
    6. vessel (blood, lymph) 7. tubular
    9. vesicular 10. hot-blooded
vase... 3. jar, urn 4. bowl 5. ascus
    6. vessel 8. ornament
    10. cassolette, jardiniere
vase (pert to)...
    covered.. 7. potiche
    Etruscan.. 7. canopic

Greek.. 5. askos, diota 6. deinos
    (dinos) 7. amphora
Roman.. 8. murrhine
vassal... 3. man 4. esne, serf
    5. helot, liege, slave 6. varlet
    7. bondman, servant, servile, subject
    9. dependent, feudatory
    11. subordinate, subservient
    12. feudal tenant
vassalage... 5. valor 6. fealty
    7. courage, enfeoff, prowess, slavery
    8. dominion 9. servitude
    10. subjection
vast... 4. huge 5. broad, great, large
    6. cosmic, mighty, untold
    7. immense, mammoth 8. colossal,
    enormous, gigantic, spacious
    9. cyclopean, extensive
    11. far-reaching
vast (pert to)...
    expanse.. 5. ocean 6. desert, empire,
    region
    numbers.. 6. myriad
    period.. 3. eon, era 5. cycle
    space.. 5. waste 9. boundless,
    immensity, limitless
vastness... 6. extent 7. expanse
    9. greatness, magnitude
vat... 3. bac, pit, tub, tun 4. cask,
    gyle, kier, tank 6. barrel, vessel
    7. caldron (cauldron), chessel,
    cistern, measure, salt pit 8. chessart
Vatican (pert to)...
    chapel.. 7. Sistine
    church.. 8. St Peter's
    city.. 10. Papal State (Rome)
    palace of.. 4. Pope
    statuary group.. 7. Laocoon
vaticination... 8. prophecy
    10. prediction 11. prophesying
vault... 3. sky 4. arch, dome, leap,
    over, tomb 5. bound, crypt, enbow,
    groin 6. canopy (of heaven), coffer,
    curvet, grotto, welkin 10. depository
    11. testudinate
vaunt... 4. brag 5. boast
Vauxhall... 6. resort 13. London
    Quarter (Thames) 14. Lambeth
    Gardens
Veda (pert to)...
    hymns.. 8. Sama-Veda
    language.. 13. Vedic Sanskrit
    literature.. 6. sacred (most anc)
    oldest.. 7. Rig-Veda
    prose, poetry (popular)..
    11. Atharva-Veda
    ritualistic.. 9. Yajur-Veda
Vedic (pert to)...
    cosmic order.. 4. Rita
    dialect.. 4. Pali
    god.. 4. Agni 5. Dyaus 6. Aditya,
    Varuna 7. Savitar
    goddess.. 5. Aditi
    hymn.. 6. mantra
    language.. 4. Pali 8. Sanskrit
    sky serpent.. 3. Ahi
    text, treatise.. 6. shakha (sakha)
    9. Upanishad
veer... 3. shy, yaw 4. slue, sway, turn
    5. alter, shift, sidle 6. careen,
    change, swerve 7. deviate, digress
    9. fluctuate

veery... 6. thrush 13. Wilson's thrush

vegetable... 3. pea, yam 4. bean, beet, corn, leek, okra 5. onion 6. carrot, celery, lentil, potato, radish, squash, tomato, turnip 7. cabbage, lettuce, parsnip, rhubarb, shallot, spinach (spinage) 8. broccoli, eggplant, rutabaga, scallion 9. artichoke 11. cauliflower

vegetable (pert to)...
and meat dish.. 4. stew 6. ragout
caterpillar.. 5. aweto
dealer.. 8. huckster 11. greengrocer 12. costermonger
floating matter.. 4. sudd
green.. 5. sabzi
herb.. 7. salsify
leafy.. 5. chard 6. endive 7. lettuce, romaine
oil.. 8. macassar
pear.. 7. chayote
poison.. 5. abrin
salad.. 5. chard 6. endive 7. lettuce, romaine
sugar-yielding.. 4. beet

vegetate... 4. grow 5. exist
vegetation, goddess of... 5. Ceres
vehemence... 3. ire 4. fire, fury, rage, zeal 5. anger, ardor 8. violence 9. eloquence 11. impetuosity

vehement... 3. hot 5. angry, eager, fiery 6. ardent, fervid, heated 7. animose, furious, intense, violent, zealous 8. forceful, vigorous 9. impetuous 10. boisterous, passionate

vehicle... 3. ark, bus, cab, car, van, wag 4. auto, cart, dray, hack, jeep, shay, sled, tank 5. buggy, coach, lorry, sulky, tonga, truck, wagon 6. go-cart, hansom, landau, sleigh, travoy, troika 7. calèche, caravan, chariot, kibitka, minibus, omnibus, phaeton, scooter 8. brougham, carriage 9. buckboard 10. automobile, conveyance, jinrikisha (jinriksha)

vehicle for oil colors... 6. megilp (meguilp)

veil... 3. dim 4. caul, film, mask 5. cloak, cover, orale, shade, velum, volet 6. fannel, masque, screen, shroud, soften 7. conceal, curtain, garment, pretext, secrecy 8. disguise 9. incognito 11. superimpose

veiled... 5. vague 6. masked, shaded, velate 7. covered 8. shrouded 9. curtained

veiling... 5. tulle, voile 7. curtain 8. covering 10. obvelation

vein... 3. rib 4. dash, hilo, lode, mood, tang, vena, wave 5. costa, shade, smack, spice, tinge, touch 6. cavity, streak 7. bonanza, channel, crevice, fissure, mineral, stratum

vein (pert to)...
arrangement.. 9. neuration
inflammation.. 9. phlebitis
leaf.. 3. rib
of wealth.. 7. bonanza
ref to.. 5. veiny 6. veinal, venous 7. marbled 8. venulose

small.. 6. venule 7. veinlet
stone.. 6. gangue, matrix 9. lodestuff
without a.. 7. avenous

velar... 7. palatal, throaty 8. gutteral
veld, veldt... 6. meadow 8. bushveld 9. grassland, grassveld
velleity... 4. hope 6. desire 8. volition 9. faint hope 10. slight wish
vellicate... 3. nip 5. pinch 6. tickle, twitch 9. titillate
vellum... 9. parchment 10. manuscript (on parchment)
velocity... 4. pace 5. speed 8. celerity, rapidity 9. quickness, swiftness 10. speediness
velocity measure... 4. velo
velum... 6. palate (soft) 8. membrane
velvet (pert to)...
breast.. 9. merganser
cotton.. 9. velveteen
fabric.. 5. panne 6. velure
Japanese.. 6. birodo
knife.. 6. trevet
leaf.. 6. mallow 7. mullein
seed.. 14. seven-year apple
texture.. 4. soft 5. nappy 6. smooth
venal... 5. hired 6. venous 7. corrupt, salable (saleable), vedible 8. hireling, vendible 9. mercenary 11. corruptible
vend... 3. hawk, sell 5. trade 6. market, peddle 8. dispense 13. publish abroad
vender, vendor... 6. seller 7. alienor
vendetta... 4. feud
vendue... 4. sale 7. auction
venerable... 3. old 4. aged, hoar, sage 5. hoary, olden, title 6. august, sacred 7. ancient, antique, classic, elderly, revered 9. dignified 11. reverential
venerate... 4. love 5. adore 6. revere 7. respect, worship
veneration... 3. awe 4. fear 5. dulia, piety 6. esteem, latria 7. respect, worship 8. devotion 9. adoration, reverence
Venetian (pert to)...
barge.. 9. bucentaur
beach, resort.. 4. Lido
boat.. 7. gondola
bridge (famed).. 6. Rialto
magistrate.. 4. doge 7. podesta
medal (New Year's).. 5. osela (osella)
painter.. 6. Titian 7. Bellini (family), Vecchio 10. Tintoretto
school of.. 8. painting
song.. 9. barcarole
window (Arch).. 9. Palladian
Venezuela...
anc name.. 12. Little Venice
capital.. 7. Caracas
city.. 8. La Guaira, Valencia 9. Maracaibo 12. Cuidad Guyana 13. Cuidad Bolivar
copper center.. 4. Aroa
Falls (world's tallest).. 5. Angel (found 1937)
hero, liberator.. 7. Bolivar
lake.. 9. Maracaibo, Tacarigua
Mt.. 5. Andes 6. Concha, Parima, Sierra 9. Pacaraima
plains.. 6. llanos

river.. 6. Caroni 7. Orinoco
sea.. 9. Caribbean
snake.. 4. Iora
vengeance... 4. harm 7. revenge
8. reprisal, requital 10. avengement,
punishment 11. retaliation, retribution
Vengeance, goddess of (Gr)... 3. Ara,
Ate 7. Nemesis
Vengeance, god of (Gr)... 6. Erinys
7. Alastor
veni, vidi, vici... 19. I came, I saw, I
conquered (Caesar)
venial... 7. trivial 9. excusable,
tolerable 10. pardonable
13. insignificant
Venice... see also *Venetian*
beach.. 4. Lido
bridge.. 6. Rialto
canal.. 5. Grand 8. Merceria, San
Marco
capital of.. 7. Venetia (province)
color.. 4. blue
island.. 6. Rialto
landmark.. 9. Campanile 12. Doges'
Palaces 13. Bridge of Sighs
of the North.. 9. Stockholm
river.. 6. Brenta
venison... 8. pemmican (pemican)
vennel... 4. lane 5. alley, sewer
6. gutter
venom... 4. gall 5. spite, virus
6. malice, poison 9. animosity,
malignity, virulence
venomous... 5. toxic 6. deadly
7. baneful, noxious 8. spiteful,
virulent 9. envenomed, malicious,
malignant, poisonous, rancorous
vent... 3. say 4. exit, hole, slit
5. eject, utter 6. egress, escape,
outlet 7. air hole, fissure, opening,
publish, release, ventage, volcano
8. aperture, let loose
10. escapement
venta... 3. inn
ventilate... 3. air, fan 5. utter
6. aerate 7. discuss, publish, refresh
9. oxygenate
ventose... 5. windy 9. flatulent
12. cupping glass
ventral... 7. sternal 9. abdominal
venture... 3. hap, try 4. dare, risk,
wage 5. brave, guess, stake 6. be
bold, chance, danger, gamble, hazard
7. attempt, presume 8. run a risk
9. adventure, haphazard, speculate
10. enterprise, investment
11. speculation, undertaking
venturesome... 4. bold, rash 5. brave,
risky 6. daring, heroic 8. fearless,
reckless 9. dangerous, foolhardy,
venturous 11. adventurous,
temerarious 12. enterprising
venturous... 4. bold, rash 5. hardy,
risky 6. daring 8. fearless
9. dangerous, hazardous
11. temerarious, venturesome
venue... 4. bout, site 5. match, onset
6. thrust 7. arrival, assault
9. encounter
Venus (pert to)...
astronomy.. 6. planet
church.. 11. Verticordia

goddess.. 7. Victrix 9. Aphrodite
goddess of (Rom).. 6. Beauty
son.. 5. Cupid
sweetheart.. 6. Adonis
zoology.. 7. mollusk
Venus statue (marble)...
Florence.. 8. de Medici
Louvre.. 7. of Arles 8. Genetrix
Melos.. 6. de Milo
Naples.. 7. of Capua
Rome.. 8. Borghese 12. of the
Capitol
veracity... 5. truth 7. honesty
8. accuracy, trueness 11. correctness
12. truthfulness
veranda, verandah... 4. pyal, stoa
5. lanai, porch, stoep 6. loggia,
piazza 7. gallery, portico
verb (Gram)... 5. rhema 6. action
verbal... 4. oral 5. wordy 7. literal,
verbose 8. verbatim 9. talkative,
vocabular
verbal noun... 6. gerund
verbatim... 6. orally 7. literal
8. verbally 11. word for word
verbiage... 4. talk 7. chatter, diction,
fustian, wording 8. claptrap
9. prolixity, verbosity, wordiness
10. redundancy
verbose... 5. wordy 6. prolix 7. diffuse
9. redundant
verbosity... 10. redundancy
verboten... 5. taboo (tabu)
9. forbidden 10. prohibited
verdant... 3. raw 5. color, green
6. unripe 9. evergreen
13. inexperienced 15. unsophisticated
verdelho... 4. wine (white)
verdict... 4. word 7. finding, opinion
8. decision, judgment
13. consideration
verdigris... 4. drug 5. green 6. aerugo
7. deposit (on copper)
verecund... 6. modest 7. bashful
verge... 3. lip, rim, top 4. edge, tend,
wand 5. brink, limit, marge, range,
scope 6. border, emblem, extend,
margin 7. incline 9. extremity
10. contiguous 13. circumference
Vergil (pert to)...
birthplace.. 6. Mantua (It)
called.. 10. Roman Homer
famed as.. 4. poet
friend.. 8. Maecenas
name (last).. 4. Maro
poem.. 6. Aeneid 8. Eclogues,
Georgics
poetic form.. 4. epic 15. heroic
hexameter (Aeneid)
verification... 4. oath, test
8. averment 9. collation
12. confirmation 13. ascertainment
verify... 4. back, test 5. check, prove
6. affirm, attest, second 7. confirm,
support 8. maintain 12. authenticate,
substantiate
verily... 3. yea 4. amen 5. truly
6. certes, indeed, in fact, really
9. certainly 10. positively
11. confidently
verisimilitude... 5. truth 10. likelihood
11. probability, verisimilar

veritable... 4. real, true 6. actual, gospel, honest 7. genuine 9. authentic

verity... 4. fact 5. truth 7. honesty, reality 8. veracity

vermilion... 3. dye, red 7. pigment, vermeil 8. cinnabar

vermin... 4. lice, mice, rats 5. filth, fleas, flies, moths, worms 7. bedbugs, beetles, insects, spiders, weasels, weevils 8. riffraff, termites 9. parasites 10. centipedes, mosquitoes 11. cockroaches

Vermont...
capital.. 10. Montpelier
city.. 5. Barre 7. Rutland 10. Burlington 11. Brattleboro
first town.. 10. Fort Dummer
hero.. 10. Ethan Allen
historic group.. 17. Green Mountain Boys
lake.. 9. Champlain
mountain.. 5. Green 7. Taconic 9. Mansfield
museum.. 9. Shelburne 10. Bennington
product.. 6. marble 10. maple sugar
river.. 5. Otter 11. Connecticut
State admission.. 10. Fourteenth
State motto.. 15. Freedom and Unity
State nickname.. 13. Green Mountain

vernacular... 5. lingo, local 6. common, jargon, native, patois, vulgar 7. dialect 10. colloquial, indigenous

vernal... 4. mild, warm 5. fresh 10. springlike

verse... 4. epic, poem, rime 5. canto, lyric, rhyme, stave, stich 6. poetry, rondel, sonnet, stanza 7. measure, strophe, triolet, trochee 8. limerick

verse (pert to)...
art.. 10. orthometry
book of.. 5. poesy 9. anthology
devotion.. 8. antiphon
form.. 7. virelay 10. villanelle
Homeric.. 4. epic 6. epopee
Irish.. 4. rann
pause.. 6. cesura 9. diaeresis (dieresis)
romantic.. 7. sestina
satiric.. 6. iambic
scripture.. 4. text
stress.. 5. ictus
term.. 5. ictic, meter 6. accent, poetic, rhythm, scheme 7. cadence 8. eye rhyme, scansion 10. synaeresis (syneresis) 12. alliteration
trivial.. 6. jingle 8. doggerel, limerick

verse (pert to feet)...
eight.. 9. octameter
four.. 10. tetrameter
one.. 9. monometer
three.. 7. tripody
two.. 7. dimeter

versed... 4. adept 7. erudite, learned, skilled 8. familiar 9. practiced 10. acquainted, conversant, proficient

versification... 7. prosody 10. orthometry

versifier... 4. bard, muse, poet

5. rimer 6. rhymer 7. poetess 8. ballader, eulogist 9. poetaster, rhymester

version... 7. edition 9. rendition 10. paraphrase 11. translation

version, Bible... 5. Douay, Greek, Latin 6. Coptic, Geneva, Gothic, Italic (Itala) 7. Aramaic, Bishops', Luther's, Revised, Targums, Vulgate 8. Cranmer's, Georgian, Matthew's, Peshitta, Slavonic 9. Apocrypha, King James, Serampore 10. Pentateuch, Septuagint 11. Alexandrian

vers libra... 9. free verse

verso (opp of recto)... 7. reverse 9. back cover 12. left–hand side

versus... 3. con 7. against 8. contrast, opposite 11. alternative

vertebra, vertebrae... 4. axis 8. backbone 12. spinal column

vertebrate... 6. linked 8. well–knit 9. backboned

vertebrates (pert to)...
division.. 6. somite 10. Vertebrata
feathered.. 5. birds
group.. 4. Aves 7. Amniota

vertex... 3. top 4. apex 6. summit 11. culmination

vertical... 5. apeak, erect, plumb, sheer 6. height 7. upright 10. upstanding 13. perpendicular

vertical panel... 5. stile

verticil... 5. whorl 6. circle

vertigo... 5. dinus 6. megrim 9. confusion, dizziness, giddiness 11. disturbance 12. bewilderment

verve... 3. pep 4. dash, élan 5. vigor 6. energy, fervor, spirit 8. vivacity 9. animation 10. liveliness

vervet... 6. monkey

very... 3. eri (comb form) 4. much, real, très, true 5. truly, utter 6. actual, in fact, really 7. exactly, genuine 8. absolute, especial, peculiar, truthful 9. extremely, precisely, veracious, veritable 10. legitimate 11. exceedingly

Very light... 5. flare 6. signal (Very system)

vesica... 7. bladder

vesicate... 7. blister

vesicle... 3. sac 4. cyst 5. bulla 6. bubble, cavity, vessel 7. bladder, blemish, blister

Vespa... 4. wasp 6. hornet

vespers... 6. prayer 7. service 8. ceremony, evensong

vessel... 3. ark, can, cup, jar, jug, mug, pod, pot, tub, urn, vas, vat 4. boat, bowl, dhow, drum, duct, ewer, junk, olla, olpe, proa, said, seed, ship, tank, vase, yawl 5. bocal, craft, crock, cupel, glass, gourd, jorum, ketch, stein 6. aftaba, aludel, ampule, barrel, bottle, bucket, caster, cutter, dipper, firkin, goblet, kettle, picard, retort, trader, trough 7. catboat, cistern, coracle, cruiser, frigate, pitcher, psykter, steamer, tankard, utensil 8. aiguière, ciborium, decanter, demijohn, hogshead, schooner 9. alcarraza, catamaran,

privateer, washbasin 10. receptacle
11. earthenware
vessel (pert to)...
  anc.. 3. nef 5. yanky 6. bireme
    7. caravel, galleon, trireme
  Arab.. 4. dhow
  baptismal.. 4. font 7. piscina
  chemist.. 4. etna 6. aludel, beaker,
    retort
  Columbus.. 7. caravel
  cooking.. 9. autoclave
  druggist.. 4. vial 5. phial 8. gallipot
  Dutch.. 4. koff 5. yanky 6. galiot
    (galliot)
  Eccl.. 3. ama, pyx 4. wine 5. amula
    7. stamnos
  Hebrides.. 7. birlinn (birling)
  heraldry.. 7. lymphad
  India.. 6. shibar
  Mediterranean.. 5. xebec 6. settee
    (setee) 7. tartan 7. polacre
  merchant.. 6. argosy 7. baggala
  Nile houseboat.. 8. dahabeah
  oil-burning.. 7. cresset
  part.. 4. deck, keel, prow, skeg
    5. brail 8. steerage
  sacred.. 3. ama
  Scottish.. 6. pourie
  Thames (fishing).. 6. bawley
  Venice.. 9. bucentaur
  war.. 3. sub 5. Maine 6. corvet
    7. carrier, cruiser, felucca, flattop,
    Monitor 11. dreadnaught 12. Old Ironsides
vessel (sailing)... 3. hoy 4. bark, brig,
    koff, proa, saic, ship, yawl 5. ketch,
    sloop, smack, xebec
vest... 4. robe 5. endow, gilet
    6. invest, jerkin, linder, weskit
    7. furnish, garment 9. waistcoat
vesta... 5. match
Vesta (Rom)... 7. goddess (Hearth)
    8. asteroid
vestal... 4. pure 6. chaste 8. virginal
vestige... 4. mark, sign 5. relic, shred,
    tinge, trace, track 7. remains
    8. footstep 9. vestigium
vestiture... 4. garb 5. dress
    8. clothing, covering
vestment... 3. alb 4. cope, garb,
    gown, hood, robe 5. amice, cotta,
    dress, ephod, miter, orale, tunic
    6. saccos, tippet 7. cassock,
    garment, maniple 8. chasuble,
    crucifix, dalmatic, scapular, surplice
    10. habiliment, omophorion
vestry... 4. room 5. group (Eccl)
    8. sacristy, wardrobe 10. repository
Vesuvius (pert to)...
  Great Eruption (79 AD).. 6. buried
  city.. 7. Pompeii 11. Herculaneum
  mountain.. 8. volcanic
  site.. 6. Naples
veteran... 4. long 7. old hand, soldier
    8. seasoned 9. practiced
    11. experienced
veterinarian... 7. farrier, surgeon
veto... 6. forbid 8. negative, prohibit
    10. disapprove 12. interdiction
vex... 3. irk 4. cark, fret, fuss, gall,
    miff, rile, roil 5. anger, annoy, harry,
    spite, tease, worry 6. bother, harass,

nettle, plague, pother, ruffle
    7. agitate, chagrin, despite, dispute,
    disturb, pervert, provoke, torment
    8. disquiet, irritate 9. displease
vexation... 7. anxiety, chagrin, fatigue,
    trouble 8. disquiet, irritate
    9. annoyance, weariness
    10. affliction, foreboding, harassment,
    irritation 11. disturbance
    13. mortification
vexatious... 5. pesky 6. thorny
    7. irksome 8. annoying 9. disturbed,
    pestilent, provoking, worrisome
    10. afflictive 11. troublesome
vexillum... 3. web 4. flag 5. cross
    6. banner, colors, ensign 7. labarum,
    pennant 8. standard 10. Jolly Roger
via... 2. by 3. way 4. away, road
    6. begone 7. by way of, passage,
    through
viaduct... 4. span 6. bridge 7. trestle
vial... 5. cruet, phial 6. bottle, caster,
    castor, vessel 7. ampoule (ampul),
    ampulla 9. container
viameter... 7. measure 8. odometer
    12. perambulator
viander... 4. host 6. vendor
viands... 4. cate, fare, food 7. viandry
    8. victuals 10. provisions
viaticum... 5. money 8. supplies
    9. allowance, last rites 10. provisions
    14. Extreme Unction
viator... 8. traveler, wayfarer
vibrant... 5. alive 7. pulsing, travale
    8. resonant, sonorous, vigorous
    9. energetic, thrilling, vibrating
    10. resounding
vibrate... 4. beat, rock, tirl, whir
    5. pulse, quake, swing, throb, waver
    6. dindle, quaver, quiver, shimmy,
    shiver, thrill 7. agitate, resound,
    tremble 8. brandish, flichter, resonate
    9. fluctuate, oscillate
vibration... 6. quiver, thrill, tremor
    7. flutter, pulsing 9. resonance,
    throbbing 11. oscillation
vibration, music... 5. trill 7. sonance,
    tremolo, vibrato
vibration measure... 9. tonometer
vicar... 5. proxy 6. curate, deputy,
    priest 9. churchman, clergyman
    10. substitute, vicegerent
vice... 3. sin 4. evil 5. crime, fault,
    taint 6. defect 7. blemish, stopper
    8. iniquity 9. depravity, in place of,
    instead of 10. corruption, substitute,
    succeeding, wickedness, wrongdoing
    11. viciousness
viceroy... 5. nabob 6. satrap
    8. governor 9. butterfly
vicinity... 6. region 9. proximity
    11. propinquity 12. neighborhood
vicious... 3. bad, ill 4. evil, foul, lewd,
    mean, ugly, vile 5. faulty, impure,
    wicked 7. corrupt, immoral, noxious
    8. depraved, spiteful 9. dangerous,
    malicious, nefarious, obstinate,
    perverted 10. iniquitous, profligate
    11. ill-tempered
vicissitude... 6. change 8. mutation,
    shifting 9. variation 10. revolution
    11. fluctuation

victim... 4. dupe, gull, prey 5. cully
6. sucker 7. patient 8. sufferer
victor... 6. captor, master, winner
8. unbeaten 9. conqueror
10. vanquisher
victor fish... 3. aku 6. bonito
Victoria, victoria... 4. plum 5. cross
(Maltese) 7. goddess 8. asteroid,
carriage 10. automobile
Victorian... 3. era 4. prim 6. stuffy
7. antique, archaic, prudish
10. antiquated 11. puritanical,
strait-laced
victorious... 7. winning 8. unbeaten
9. defeating 10. conquering,
triumphant
victory... 7. mastery, success, triumph
8. conquest 9. supremacy
victory (pert to)...
  at too great cost.. 7. Pyrrhic
  Day.. 9. Armistice
  goddess.. 4. Nike
  hymn.. 9. epinicion (epinikion)
  memorial.. 6. trophy
  symbol.. 4. palm
Victrola dog (symbol)... 6. Nipper
victuals... 4. food, grub 6. viands
8. supplies 11. nourishment
videlicet... 3. viz 5. to wit 6. namely
8. scilicet
vie... 3. bet 4. cope, life 5. bandy,
stake, wager 6. endure, oppose,
strive 7. compare, compete, contend,
contest, emulate 8. struggle
9. challenge
Vienna...
  artist.. 4. Lieb, Pilz 6. Makart, Zauner
    7. Kisling
  boulevard (famed).. 11. Ringstrasse
  capital of.. 7. Austria
  Ger name.. 4. Wien
  musician.. 5. Gluck, Haydn 6. Czerny,
    Mozart 7. Strauss 8. Schubert,
    Schumann 9. Beethoven
  palace.. 10. Schönbrunn
  park.. 6. Prater
  river.. 6. Danube
Vietnam road... 14. Ho Chi Minh Trail
view... 3. aim, end, eye, ken, see
4. look, scan 5. scene, vista
6. aperçu, aspect, object, regard,
survey 7. examine, glimpse, opinion,
outlook, picture 8. attitude,
judgment, panorama, prospect
9. intention 10. appearance,
perception, scrutinize
11. contemplate, expectation
13. contemplation
vigil... 3. eve 4. wake 5. guard,
watch 6. patrol 8. watchman
9. keep guard 11. wakefulness
13. sleeplessness
vigilant... 4. agog, wary 5. alert,
awake, aware 6. awatch 7. wakeful
8. cautious, open-eyed, watchful
9. attentive, observant, sleepless
11. circumspect
vigilantes... 5. posse 9. committee
(vigilance)
vigor, vigour... 3. pep, vim, vir
4. life, zeal 5. force, power, verve
6. energy, health 7. potency,

stamina, sthenia 8. strength, validity,
virility 9. animation, fraîcheur,
vehemence 10. liveliness
vigorous... 4. able, hale, racy, spry
5. eager, frank, fresh, hardy, lusty,
tough 6. potent, robust, strong
7. healthy, zealous 8. athletic,
forceful, spirited, vehement
9. effective, energetic, sprightly,
strenuous 11. efficacious, flourishing
Viking... 4. Eric 5. rover 6. pirate
8. Norseman, Northman, sea rover
9. plunderer 12. Scandinavian
vile... 3. bad 4. base, evil, foul, mean
5. cheap, lowly, nasty 6. coarse,
filthy, impure, odious, sinful, sordid,
wicked 7. corrupt, debased, ignoble,
obscene, unclean, vicious
8. depraved, infamous 9. degrading,
loathsome, nefarious, repulsive
10. abominable, disgusting
12. contaminated
vilify... 5. abuse, curse, libel
6. debase, defame, malign, revile
7. asperse, cheapen, degrade,
slander, traduce 8. belittle, disgrace,
reproach, vilipend 9. blaspheme,
disparage 10. calumniate, stigmatize
vilipend... 6. slight 7. despise
8. belittle 9. disparage
10. depreciate, slanderous
12. calumniatory
villa... 5. aldea, dacha 9. residence,
villaette 10. villanette
village... 3. mir 4. dorp, stad 5. thorp
(thorpe), tract 6. aldeia, castle,
hamlet, pueblo
Village Blacksmith author...
10. Longfellow
villain... 4. boor, lout, ogre, serf
5. demon, heavy, knave, rogue
6. rascal 7. caitiff 9. miscreant,
scoundrel
villainous... 3. bad, low 4. base, evil,
mean, vile 6. vulgar, wicked
7. boorish, knavish 8. criminal,
rascally, terrible, wretched
9. dastardly 10. detestable, iniquitous
11. scoundrelly 13. objectionable
villous... 5. nappy 6. napped, shaggy
vim... 3. pep, zip 4. dash, élan, fire,
gimp, kick 5. drive, force, verve,
vigor 6. energy, esprit, spirit
8. strength
vinaigre... 7. vinegar
vindicate... 4. free 5. claim, clear
6. acquit, assert, avenge, defend,
excuse, uphold 7. absolve, justify,
support, sustain 8. maintain
9. exculpate, exonerate
vindication... 7. defense
vindictive... 7. hostile 8. punitive,
spiteful, vengeful 10. revengeful
11. retaliatory, retributive
vine... 3. hop, ivy 4. bine, odal
5. betel, grape, liana (liane), Vitis
7. cupseed, trailer 8. clematis,
wisteria 9. grapevine 10. chilicothe
11. honeysuckle 12. morning glory
vinegar... 4. acid, sour 6. acetum,
alegar 8. vinaigre
vinegar (pert to)...

acid.. 6. acetic
comb form.. 5. aceto
dregs.. 6. mother
eel.. 4. worm
ester.. 7. acetate
fly.. 5. fruit
preserve in.. 6. pickle 8. marinate
salt.. 7. acetate
spice.. 8. tarragon
tree.. 13. staghorn sumac
Vinegar Joe (Army) ... 9. Stillwell (Gen)
vinegarroon ... 8. scorpion, vinagron
vinegary ... 4. sour, tart 7. acetose,
crabbed, pungent 9. unamiable
vineyard ... 3. cru 7. Priapus (god of)
10. plantation
vinology *(science of)* ... 5. vines
10. grapevines
vinous ... 4. winy 5. color
vintner ... 8. merchant (wine)
viol ... 3. gue 4. rope 5. rebec, ruana
6. vielle 7. quinton, sarinda 9. organ
stop
viola ... 5. gamba 7. sarangi 9. organ
stop 11. tenor violin
violate ... 5. abuse, break, wrong
6. defile, invade, ravage, ravish
7. debauch, outrage, pollute, profane
8. deflower, dishonor, mistreat
9. desecrate 10. transgress
violation ... 7. offense 10. infraction
11. anacoluthon, disturbance,
profanation 12. infringement,
interruption 13. nonobservance,
transgression
violence ... 5. anger, force 6. unjust
7. assault, cruelty, outrage
8. coercion 9. vehemence
10. roughhouse 11. profanation
12. infringement
violent ... 4. loud 5. acute, great,
rabid, sharp, vivid 6. fierce, savage,
stormy 7. extreme, furious, intense
8. coercive, vehement 9. turbulent
10. passionate 11. tempestuous
violent (pert to) ...
Norse folklore.. 8. warriors
9. beserkers
outbreak.. 4. riot 6. tumult, uproar
8. eruption
pain.. 4. pang 5. throe 6. fierce
violet (pert to) ...
color.. 5. mauve 6. purple
7. blue–red
dye.. 6. archil (orchil)
emblem of.. 7. gravity 8. chastity
genus.. 9. Violaceae
perfume.. 5. irone 6. ionone
9. orrisroot
tip.. 9. butterfly
violin (pert to) ...
ancient.. 5. rebab, rebec, rocta
12. viola de gamba
bar.. 4. fret
bass.. 11. violoncello
bow.. 5. arcus
city (famed).. 7. Cremona (It)
make.. 5. Amati 7. Cremona
10. Guarnerius 12. Stradivarius
maker.. 5. Amati 9. Guarnieri
10. Stradivari
reference to.. 4. pins 5. belly

Scot.. 6. fiddle
small.. 3. kit
tenor.. 4. alto
violinist (famed) ... 5. Elman, Stern
7. Heifitz, Menuhin
violinist, first ... 13. concertmaster
viper ... 3. asp 5. adder, Echis, snake
6. kupper 7. serpent 8. cerastes,
ophidian 9. scoundrel
10. bushmaster
vir ... 5. vigor
virage ... 5. scold, shrew, vixen, woman
7. beldame, rullion 9. termagant
Virgil ... see *Vergil*
virgin ... 3. new 4. maid, pure
6. chaste, maiden, vestal 8. spinster
9. undefiled, unsullied, untouched
13. unadulterated
virginal ... 3. new 5. piano (spinet)
6. chaste, ritual 7. natural
8. maidenly 9. unmarried, unsullied
Virginia ...
bay.. 10. Chesapeake
capital.. 8. Richmond
city.. 7. Norfolk, Roanoke
9. Arlington, Lexington, Lynchburg
11. Newport News 12. Hampton
Roads
famed sites.. 8. Mt Vernon
10. Monticello 12. Williamsburg
13. Stratford Hall
first white child born.. 12. Virginia
Dare
historic town.. 8. Yorktown
9. Jamestown 10. Appomattox
Indian sachem.. 7. Powhatan
mountain.. 9. Blue Ridge
11. Alleghenies
resort.. 13. Virginia Beach
river.. 4. York 5. James 7. Potomac,
Rapidan 12. Rappahannock
settlement (first).. 9. Jamestown
State admission.. 5. Tenth
State motto.. 17. Sic Semper
Tyrannis 19. Thus Always to Tyrants
State nickname.. 11. Old Dominion
Virgin Islands, British ...
capital.. 8. Road Town
crop.. 9. sugar cane
group.. 7. Leeward
number islands.. 6. thirty
Virgin Islands, United States ...
capital.. 8. St Thomas 15. Charlotte
Amalia (former)
discoverer.. 8. Columbus (1493)
largest.. 6. St John 7. St Croix 8. St
Thomas
virginity ... 8. celibacy, chastity
10. maidenhood 12. spinsterhood
Virgin Mary ... 5. Pietà (image) 7. Our
Lady 11. Maris Stella, Mother of
God 12. Star of the Sea 13. Mother
of Jesus
viridity ... 5. youth 7. verdure
9. freshness, greenness 10. grass
color
virile ... 4. male 5. manly 8. forceful,
powerful, vigorous 9. masculine,
masterful
virose ... 5. fetid 8. virulent
9. poisonous 10. malodorous
virtu ... 5. curio 7. antique 8. artistry

12. love of curios 15. artistic quality, study of fine arts
virtual... 9. essential, potential 10. energizing 12. constructive
virtually... 7. morally 11. potentially, practically
virtue... 5. valor, value, worth 6. energy, purity 7. potency, probity 8. chastity, efficacy, goodness, morality 9. godliness, innocence, integrity, rectitude 11. uprightness 13. righteousness
virtue, logic... 8. aretaics
virtues, cardinal... 4. hope 5. faith 7. charity
virtuoso... 6. expert 7. scholar 11. connoisseur, philosopher
virtuous... 4. good, pure 5. brave, godly, moral 6. chaste, honest, potent 7. upright, valiant 8. valorous 9. righteous 11. efficacious
virulent... 5. acrid, rabid 6. deadly, potent 7. noxious 8. venomous 9. animosity, malignant, poisonous 10. infectious, resentment 11. acrimonious
visa, visé... 7. endorse 9. signature 11. certificate, endorsement (passport)
visage... 4. face, look 5. image 11. countenance 14. visible surface
vis-à-vis... 4. seat, sofa 8. carriage, opposite 9. encounter 10. face to face
viscera... 4. guts 6. bowels, vitals 7. insides 8. entrails 10. intestines 11. inside parts
visceral... 7. enteric 10. intestinal, splanchnic
viscid... 4. ropy, waxy 5. slimy 6. sticky 7. viscous 8. adhering, adhesive 9. glutinous
viscosity... 8. tenacity 10. stickiness
viscous... 4. ropy, sizy 5. gluey, gummy, tarry 6. mucous, sticky, viscid 7. stringy 9. glutinous 10. stickiness
vise... 3. jaw 4. tool 5. clamp, winch 6. device 7. squeeze
Vishnu (pert to)...
consort.. 3. Sri 7. Lakshim
deity (supreme).. 6. bhakti
9. preserver
eighth.. 7. Krishna
epithet.. 8. bhagavat
seventh.. 4. Rama
tenth, last incarnation.. 5. Kalki
vehicle.. 6. Garuda
visible... 4. open, seen 5. clear 6. extant, in view 7. evident, in sight, obvious 8. apparent, manifest 10. noticeable 11. discernible, perceivable, perceptible
Visigoth king... 6. Alaric
vision... 3. eye 5. dream, fancy, image, sight 6. glance, mirage 7. glimpse, imagine, specter 8. eyesight 10. apparition
vision (pert to)...
comb form.. 4. opto
daylight.. 8. photopia
defect.. 6. anopia, myopia

double.. 8. diplopia
illusory.. 5. image
lacking.. 8. purblind
measure.. 9. optometer
night.. 8. scotopia
science of.. 9. optometry
term.. 8. optic 6. ocular 9. binocular, monocular
visionary... 4. aery, airy, seer, wild 5. ideal 6. dreamy, unreal 7. dreamer, Laputan, utopian 8. delusive, idealist, quixotic, romantic 9. fantastic, imaginary 10. chimerical, rhapsodist 11. imaginative, impractical
visit... 3. see, vis 4. call, chat, go to, slum 5. haunt 6. attend, call on 10. inspection, visitation 12. conversation
visitor... 5. guest 6. caller 7. company 8. visitant
visne... 5. venue 8. neighbor, vicinage
vison... 4. mink
visor, vizor... 4. mask 6. vizard 8. disguise 10. camouflage
vista... 4. view 5. scene, visto 7. outlook 8. corridor, panorama, prospect
visual... 5. optic 6. ocular 11. perceptible
visualize... 7. imagine, picture 8. envisage, envision 9. objectify
vital... 4. live 5. basic 6. living, mortal, viable 7. animate, exigent, needful, organic 8. inherent, vigorous 9. essential, important, necessary, requisite 10. imperative 11. fundamental 13. indispensable
vital (pert to)...
air.. 6. oxygen
force.. 6. energy, spirit 7. neurism 8. bathmism, phrenism 9. theosophy
impulse.. 6. libido 8. instinct
organs.. 6. vitals 7. viscera
records.. 10. demography, statistics
strength.. 7. stamina
vitality... 3. sap, vim 4. life 5. vigor 8. strength 9. animation, lustiness 10. liveliness
vitals... 7. insides, viscera 9. internals 11. vital organs (heart, liver, lungs, brain)
vitamin... 6. biotin, niacin 7. carotin, thiamin 10. riboflavin 11. lactoflavin 12. ascorbic acid
vitellus... 4. yolk 7. egg yolk
vitiate... 5. spoil, taint 6. debase, impair, poison, weaken 7. corrupt, deprave, pervert, pollute 10. adulterate, demoralize, invalidate 11. contaminate
vitiated... 5. pical 6. wicked 7. corrupt, debased, spoiled 9. defective 11. ineffective, invalidated
vitiosity... 4. vice 6. defect 9. depravity 11. viciousness
vitium... 5. fault 6. defect
vitric... 9. glasslike
vitrics... 9. glassware, glasswork
vitrify... 5. glaze 13. make into glass
vitriolic... 4. acid 5. sharp 6. biting,

bitter **7.** caustic **8.** scathing, virulent
11. acrimonious
vituperate... **5.** abuse, curse, scold
6. berate, revile **7.** censure
vituperative... **7.** abusive, railing
8. reviling, scolding **10.** scurrilous
11. maledictory, opprobrious
vivacious... **3.** gay **4.** airy **5.** merry
6. active, lively **8.** animated,
gamesome, spirited, sportive
9. energetic **12.** lighthearted
vivacity... **4.** dash, élan, fire, keen,
zeal, zest **5.** ardor, verve, vigor
6. energy, gaiety (gayety)
9. animation **10.** liveliness
Viverra... **6.** civets **9.** civet cats
vivers... **4.** food **8.** victuals
vix... **8.** scarcely
vixen... **3.** cat, fox **5.** scold, shrew,
witch **6.** virago **9.** termagant
12. female animal
viz... **5.** to wit **6.** namely **9.** videlicet
vizard... **4.** mask **5.** guise, visor
8. disguise
vlei (vley)... **5.** creek, marsh, swamp
voar... **6.** spring (of the year)
vocabulary... **5.** words **6.** jargon
7. diction, lexicon **8.** glossary,
wordbook **10.** dictionary
vocabulist... **6.** writer
13. lexicographer
vocal (pert to)...
chink.. **7.** glottis
composition.. **4.** aria, song **5.** motet
7. cantata
expression.. **4.** oral **9.** utterance
flourish.. **7.** roulade
handicap.. **4.** lisp **7.** stutter
sound.. **5.** vowel **6.** sonant
statue.. **6.** Memnon
vocalist... **4.** alto **5.** basso, tenor
6. artist, cantor, singer **7.** caroler,
crooner, soprano, yodeler **8.** songster
10. coloratura, prima donna,
songstress
vocalization... **11.** melismatics
vocalize... **4.** sing **5.** sound, utter
6. phrase
vocation... **4.** call **5.** trade **6.** career
7. calling **8.** business
10. employment, occupation,
profession
vociferous... **4.** loud **5.** noisy
7. blatant **8.** brawling, strident
9. clamorous, turbulent
11. loudmouthed **12.** obstreperous
vogue... **3.** ton **4.** mode **5.** style
6. custom **7.** fashion **8.** practice
10. popularity
voice... **3.** say, vox **4.** alto, bass,
tone, vote, wish **5.** rumor, tenor,
utter **7.** divulge, opinion, soprano
8. announce, falsetto **9.** utterance
10. expression **12.** articulation
voice (pert to)...
box.. **6.** larynx
Greek.. **9.** phthongos
handicap.. **4.** lisp **7.** stammer, stutter
loss of.. **7.** anaudia, aphonia
loud.. **12.** megalophonic
phonetics.. **9.** affricate

quality.. **6.** timbre (timber)
quiet.. **5.** sotto
raise.. **6.** insist **10.** supplicate
raise against.. **5.** decry **6.** accuse,
object
singing, above natural.. **8.** falsetto
singing, natural.. **7.** dipetto
stress.. **5.** arsis
with one.. **9.** unanimous
12. concurrently
voiced... **6.** sonant, spoken **7.** sounded
9. phthongal **11.** articulated
voiceless... **4.** dumb, mute, surd
6. atonic, silent **7.** spirate **9.** not
voiced **12.** not expressed
void... **4.** idle, lack, null, want
5. abyss, annul, egest, empty
6. devoid, hollow, vacant, vacuum
7. abolish, nothing, nullify, useless
8. evacuate **9.** destitute, emptiness
10. unoccupied **11.** ineffectual,
nonexistent
void of...
interest.. **6.** jejune **7.** insipid
sense.. **5.** inane, silly
space.. **5.** blank **6.** vacuum
volaille... **4.** fowl **7.** poultry
volant... **5.** agile, light, quick **6.** flying,
nimble **7.** current **8.** volatile, volitant
volatile... **4.** airy **5.** light **6.** fickle,
flying, lively, volant **7.** alcohol,
ammonia, buoyant, flighty, gaseous
8. fleeting, vaporous **9.** ephemeral,
mercurial **10.** capricious, changeable,
transitory **11.** vaporizable
12. lighthearted
volatile (pert to)...
alkali.. **7.** ammonia
flux.. **5.** smear
liquid.. **5.** ether **7.** alcohol
oil.. **7.** essence, perfume
volcanic (pert to)...
glass.. **6.** pumice **7.** perlite
8. obsidian
matter.. **2.** aa **4.** lava, slag, tufa
5. trass **6.** pumice **8.** lapillus,
pahoehoe
mud.. **5.** salse
orifice of gas issue.. **8.** fumarole
ref to.. **9.** excitable, explosive
11. hot-tempered
rock.. **5.** trass **6.** dacite **8.** tephrite
saucer.. **6.** crater
volcano (pert to)...
Africa.. **11.** Kilimanjaro
Alaska.. **6.** Katmai **8.** Wrangell
Chile.. **6.** Lascar
Ecuador.. **8.** Cotopaxi
goddess.. **4.** Pele (Hawaii)
Guatemala.. **5.** Fuego **7.** Atitlan
Hawaii.. **8.** Mauna Loa
Iceland.. **5.** Askja, Hekla
Italy.. **4.** Etna **8.** Vesuvius
9. Stromboli
Japan.. **4.** Fuji **9.** Asamayama
Java.. **4.** Gede
Mexico.. **12.** Popocatepetl
Philippines.. **3.** Apo (Mindanao)
Sumatra.. **6.** Merapi
United States (mainland).. **6.** Lassen,
Shasta **7.** Rainier
West Indies.. **5.** Pelée

vole... 6. craber, rodent 8. water rat
  10. field mouse 11. meadow mouse
volée... 6. flight, volley
volery (volary)... 6. aviary 8. bird
  cage
volition... 4. will 6. choice
  11. voluntarily 13. determination
volley... 4. fire 5. blast, salvo, shots
Voltaire... 11. philosopher (of Ferney)
voluble... 4. glib 6. fluent 8. rotating,
  unstable 9. garrulous, revolving,
  talkative 10. loquacious
volume... 4. book, bulk, mass, size,
  tome 6. amount 7. compass
  8. capacity, fullness (fulness)
  9. aggregate, Decameron
  10. crassitude 14. fullness of tone
voluntary... 4. free 7. prelude, willing
  8. elective, intended, purposed
  9. volunteer, willingly 10. deliberate,
  volitional 11. intentional, spontaneous
  13. not accidental
volunteer... 5. offer 6. enlist 7. proffer
  9. be willing, voluntary 11. be of
  service
Volunteer State... 9. Tennessee
volute... 4. turn 5. whorl 6. cilery
  (cillery) 8. rolled up 10. scroll-like
voodoo... 5. magic, obeah 6. fetish
  8. sorcerer
voracious... 6. greedy, hungry
  8. edacious, esurient, ravening,
  ravenous 9. devouring, rapacious
  10. gluttonous, immoderate,
  insatiable
voracity... 5. greed 7. edacity
  8. gluttony, rapacity 9. esurience
vorago... 4. gulf 5. abyss
vortex... 4. apex, eddy 5. whirl
  7. tornado 8. flatworm 9. whirlpool,
  whirlwind 10. waterspout
votary... 6. zealot 7. devotee
  8. adherent, aesthete, follower
  9. supporter 10. enthusiast
vote... 3. vow 5. elect, straw
  6. ballot, choice, ticket 7. declare
  8. suffrage 9. designate
  10. plebescite, referendum
vote (pert to)...
  group.. 4. bloc
  in.. 5. elect
  of assent.. 6. placet
  plump.. 14. straight ticket
  receptacle.. 6. situla
voter... 6. poller 7. elector 8. balloter
  11. constituent
voters... 10. electorate
votive... 7. devoted 11. consecrated
vouch... 4. back 6. affirm, attest,
  depose 7. confirm, declare, promise,
  sponsor, support 8. accredit
  9. assertion 11. attestation, bear
  witness
vouchsafe... 4. give 5. deign
  6. accept, assure, bestow, permit
  7. concede 8. guarantee
  10. condescend
voussoir... 8. keystone
vow... 3. vum 4. oath 5. swear,
  vouch 6. behest, devote, pledge
  7. declare, promise 8. dedicate

  9. assertion 10. consecrate,
  obligation 11. asseveration
  12. supplication
vowel (pert to)...
  change of.. 6. umlaut
  contradiction.. 6. crasis 7. digraph
    9. diphthong
  loss of.. 7. aphesis
  mark.. 6. macron
  point (Heb).. 4. sere (tsere)
  separate syllables.. 9. diaeresis
    (dieresis)
  short.. 5. breve
  two, contracted.. 6. crasis
  two, group.. 6. digram 7. digraph
    9. diphthong (dipthong)
  unaspirated.. 4. lene
vowels, none... 6. syzygy
vowels in sequence... 8. caesious
vox (pert to)...
  clandestina.. 7. whisper
  Dei.. 10. Voice of God
  Latin for.. 5. voice
  populi.. 16. voice of the people
voyage... 4. trip 6. cruise, travel
  7. journey, passage, passing (sea)
  9. excursion 10. expedition,
  pilgrimage 11. undertaking
Vulcan (pert to)...
  consort.. 4. Maia
  epithet.. 8. Mulciber
  feast of.. 10. Vulcanalia
  god of.. 4. fire
  Greek.. 10. Hephaestus
  work site.. 4. Etna
vulcanite... 7. ebonite
vulcanize... 9. rubberize
vulgar... 3. low 4. lewd 5. crude,
  gross 6. coarse, common, garish,
  public, ribald 7. boorish, general,
  obscene, profane 8. indecent,
  ordinary, plebeian 9. inelegant,
  offensive, unrefined 10. boisterous, in
  bad taste, rowdydowdy
vulgarian... 4. snob 9. pretender
Vulgate... 10. Scriptures
vulnerable... 6. liable 7. exposed
  8. beatable 9. pregnable, subject to
  10. expungable 11. conquerable,
  defenseless, susceptible
vulpine... 4. foxy 6. artful, crafty,
  tricky 7. cunning, foxlike 9. alopecoid
  10. vulpecular
vult... 4. mien 6. aspect
  10. expression 11. countenance
vulture (pert to)...
  African.. 8. aasvogel
  American.. 4. aura 5. urubu
    6. condor 13. turkey buzzard
  European.. 7. griffin 11. lammergeier
    (lammergeir)
  king.. 4. papa
  large.. 6. condor 11. lammergeier
  Mexican.. 8. zopilote
  raven.. 9. Corvultur
  Spanish.. 9. gallinazo
  term.. 5. harpy 6. raptorial 10. bird
    of prey, predacious
vulturous... 6. lupine 7. wolfish
  8. ravenous 9. rapacious
vying... 7. emulous 8. rivaling
  9. competing 11. competitive

W

W... **6.** letter (23rd) **7.** double U
WAAC... **24.** Women's Auxiliary Army
Corps
waag... **6.** grivet, monkey
waapa... **5.** canoe
wabber... **4.** cony **5.** daman
wabble... see *wobble*
wabby... **4.** loon (red–throated)
wabe, wabi... **5.** shrub **8.** huisache
wachna... **7.** codfish
wad... **3.** pad, ram **4.** cram, lump,
mass, plug, roll, tuft **5.** money, stuff,
track **6.** bundle, pledge, wealth
7. stopper **8.** bankroll
wadding... **4.** wads **6.** lining
7. padding **8.** compress, stopping,
stuffing
waddle... **4.** sway **5.** mince **6.** toddle,
wabble, wamble, wobble **10.** clumsy
gait
waddy, waddie... **3.** peg **4.** beat, club
5. stick **6.** attack, cowboy
wade... **4.** ford, pass **5.** study
6. attack, drudge, paddle, plodge
8. struggle
wader... **4.** coot, ibis, rail **5.** crane,
heron, snipe, stork **6.** jaçana
9. sandpiper, shore bird
11. Grallatores
wadi, wady... **5.** oasis, river **6.** ravine,
valley **7.** channel **11.** watercourse
waeg... **9.** kittiwake
wafer... **4.** cake, disk, ring, seal, snap
5. bread **7.** biscuit, cracker **10.** altar
bread
waff... **3.** wag **4.** flap, wave **5.** ghost
7. lowborn, vagrant **8.** inferior
9. worthless **12.** disreputable
waft... **4.** gust, puff, wave **5.** carry,
float, whiff **6.** beckon, convey,
convoy, signal **7.** glimpse, pennant
9. beckoning, transport
wag... **3.** wit **4.** card, wave **5.** joker,
rogue, shake **6.** signal, waddle,
wiggle **7.** farceur, vibrate
8. humorist, jokester **9.** oscillate
wagang... **5.** death **9.** departure
11. leave–taking
wage, wages... **3.** bet, fee, pay, utu
4. hire, levy, pawn, risk **5.** fight,
incur, stake, yield **6.** employ, engage,
pledge, reward, salary **7.** attempt,
contend, hire out, stipend, venture
9. emolument **10.** recompense
12. compensation, remuneration
wage insurance... **7.** chômage
wager... **3.** bet, bid, vie **4.** risk
5. sport, stake **6.** gamble, hazard,
parlay, pledge **7.** venture
waggish... **5.** droll, merry **7.** jesting,

jocular, parlous, roguish
8. humorous, sportive **9.** facetious
10. frolicsome **11.** mischievous
Wagnerian opera... **6.** Rienzi
8. Parsifal **9.** Lohengrin
10. Tannhauser
15. Gotterdammerung
wagon... **3.** car, van **4.** cart, dray,
tram, wain **5.** araba, coach, lorry,
tonga **6.** telega **7.** caisson, chariot,
vehicle **8.** carryall, schooner (prairie)
12. perambulator
wagon (pert to)...
canvas–covered.. **15.** prairie schooner
lit.. **7.** Pullman **11.** sleeping car
load.. **6.** fother
maker.. **10.** wagonsmith, wainwright
on the (wagon).. **8.** sworn off, teetotal
part.. **4.** neap **5.** blade, thill
police.. **3.** van **10.** Black Maria
sideless.. **6.** rolley
wah... **5.** panda
wahine... **4.** wife **5.** woman
8. mistress **10.** sweetheart
wahoo... **4.** bark, fish, peto **5.** shrub
7. rock elm **8.** nonsense, tommyrot
9. buckthorn, guarapucu
12. umbrella tree
waif... **4.** Arab, flag **5.** gamin, stray
7. vagrant, wastrel **8.** castaway,
homeless, wanderer **9.** lost sheep
wail... **3.** cry, sob **4.** howl, moan,
weep **5.** mourn **6.** bemoan, grieve,
lament **7.** deplore, screech, ululate
11. lamentation **14.** mournful outcry
wainscot... **4.** base, ceil, line **5.** panel
6. lining **8.** paneling (panelling)
9. partition
waist... **4.** wasp **5.** shirt **6.** basque,
blouse, bodice, dickey, middle, taille
7. corsage, garment **9.** garibaldi
12. undergarment
waistcoat... **4.** vest **5.** benjy **6.** jacket,
jerkin, weskit
wait... **4.** bide, rest, stay, stop
5. dally, defer, delay, hover, serve,
tarry, watch **6.** attend, expect, linger,
remain **7.** observe **8.** hesitate,
postpone **11.** expectation
12. watchfulness
waiter... **4.** tray **6.** garçon, salver,
server **7.** messboy, messman,
servant, steward **8.** servitor
9. attendant
wait on... **4.** help **5.** await, cater,
serve **6.** escort **7.** toady to
9. accompany
waive... **5.** defer, forgo (forego)
6. desert, give up, reject, vacate
7. abandon, cast off, forsake

630

8. postpone 9. disregard
10. condescend, relinquish
waka... 5. canoe
Wakashan Indian... 6. Nootka
    8. Kwakiutl
wake... 4. call, stir 5. rouse, track,
    vigil, waken, watch 6. arouse,
    awaken, excite, revive 10. death
    watch
wakeful... 5. alert 8. restless, vigilant,
    watchful 9. sleepless, wide–awake
Wake Island... 6. Ottori (Jap name)
wake–robin... 4. Arum 8. Trillium
    9. Anthurium 10. cuckoopint
    12. philodendron
wale... 3. rib 4. welt 5. ridge, wheal
    6. stripe
Wales... see also *Welsh*
    anc.. 7. Cambria
    city.. 7. Rhondda, Swansea
      8. Hereford, Pembroke 9. Carnarvon
    congress of literati.. 10. eisteddfod
    deity.. 4. Bran
    emblem (floral).. 4. leek
    language.. 7. Cymraeg
    mountain.. 7. Snowdon
    native.. 5. Cymry (Kymry)
    patron saint.. 5. David
    port.. 7. Cardiff
    river.. 3. Dee, Wye 6. Severn
    sea.. 5. Irish
walk... 3. mog, pad 4. foot, gait,
    hike, hoof, pace, path, plod, ramp,
    step 5. allee, amble, scuff, strut,
    tramp, tread 6. ramble, sphere,
    stride, stroll, toddle, travel, trudge
    7. conduct, shuffle, traipse
    8. ambulate, behavior, frescade,
    province, sidewalk 9. esplanade,
    promenade, wandering
    10. passageway 11. base on balls,
    perambulate 13. peregrination
walk (pert to)...
    a beat.. 6. patrol
    about.. 11. perambulate
    clumsily.. 5. mince 6. lumber, totter
    health.. 14. constitutional
    lime–bordered.. 9. tilicetum
    proudly.. 5. strut 6. prance
    public.. 4. mall 6. arcade 7. alameda
      9. esplanade, promenade
    wearily.. 4. limp, plod 5. tramp
      6. hobble, trudge
    with speed.. 10. heel and toe
walking (pert to)...
    about.. 7. passant (Her)
      11. peripatetic
    bearlike.. 11. plantigrade
    meter.. 9. pedometer
    papers.. 7. deposal, the sack
      8. mittimus, pink slip 9. discharge,
      dismissal 10. retirement
wall... 4. dado, dike, ha–ha, mure,
    pier 5. fence, levee, panel, redan
    6. escarp, hinder, immure, paries,
    podium, septum, shut in 7. barrier,
    defense, enclose, fortify, parapet,
    rampart 8. espalier, palisade, restrain,
    stockade 9. barricade, enclosure,
    encompass, partition, precipice,
    revetment 13. fortification
wall (pert to)...

bracket.. 6. corbel, sconce
creeper.. 4. bird
go to the (wall).. 4. fail 10. go
    bankrupt
lining.. 8. wainscot
lizard.. 4. newt 5. gecko
masonry.. 9. revetment
pert to.. 5. mural 8. parietal
recess.. 5. niche 6. alcove
Street.. 9. Manhattan 11. money
    market, stock market
up.. 6. immure
wallaby... 8. kangaroo, Macropus,
    wallaroo 10. paddymelon
wallah, walla... 5. agent 6. master,
    person 7. servant
waller... 4. wels 9. saltmaker,
    sheatfish
wallet... 3. bag 4. pack, poke, sack
    5. purse 8. billfold, knapsack
    10. pocketbook 12. porte–monnaie
walleye... 9. exotropia 10. strabismus
wallow... 4. fade, sail 5. surge
    6. grovel, welter, wither 7. debauch,
    founder, insipid 8. flounder,
    kommetje, nauseous 9. tasteless
walnut... 6. bannut
walrus... 3. pod (group) 5. morse
    6. mammal, sea cat 8. pinniped
    9. rosmarine (fable) 10. pinnipedia
Waltonian... 6. angler 16. disciple of
    Walton (Izaak)
wamble... 5. twist 6. quiver, ramble,
    rumble, totter, writhe 7. revolve,
    stagger, wriggle
wame... 4. room, womb 5. belly
    7. stomach
wampum... 4. peag 5. beads, money,
    uhllo 6. shells 7. jewelry, roanoke
    8. ornament 10. wampumpeag
wan... 3. dim, sad 4. ashy, dark, pale,
    sick 5. ashen, black, dusky, faint,
    lurid 6. dismal, gloomy, pallid, sickly
    7. ghastly, languid 8. deathlike,
    sorrowful 10. lusterless
    11. lead–colored
wand... 3. rod 4. mace, pole
    5. baton, osier, staff, stick (magic)
    6. switch, wattle 7. pointer, rhabdos
    (magic), scepter (sceptre)
    8. caduceus 9. horsewhip
wander... 3. err, gad 4. moon, rave,
    roam, rove 5. drift, prowl, range,
    stray 5. cruise, depart, ramble, stroll,
    travel 7. digress, meander, saunter,
    traipse 8. divagate, traverse
    9. circulate, itinerate, scamander
    11. peregrinate
wanderer... 4. Arab, waif 5. gypsy,
    nomad, rover 6. ranger, roamer,
    truant 7. migrant, pilgrim, vagrant
    9. butterfly, itinerant, straggler
    10. covenanter 12. peregrinator
wandering... 5. vague 6. astray,
    errant, roving, vagary 8. aberrant,
    delirium, straying 9. delirious,
    deviating, deviation, itinerant
    10. circuitous, discursive, journeying
    11. noctivigant, perambulant
    13. peregrination
wandering (pert to)...
    bird.. 9. albatross

long.. 7. odyssey
minstrel.. 4. bard 10. troubadour
stars.. 12. seven planets
tattler.. 9. shore bird
votary.. 6. palmer
wanderoo... 6. langur, monkey
7. macaque
wand–shaped... 7. virgate
wane... 3. age, ebb 4. fail, sink, want
5. abate, peter 6. defect, lessen,
recede, repine 7. decline, grow dim,
subside 8. decrease, diminish
10. deteriorate 13. deterioration
wanga... 5. charm, spell 6. voodoo
7. philter, sorcery
wangle... 4. fake, plot 6. adjust,
juggle, obtain, totter, wiggle
7. finagle (finaigue), wriggle
8. contrive, maneuver (manoeuvre)
9. extricate 10. manipulate
want... 4. lack, miss, need, wish
5. crave 6. dearth, desire, hunger,
penury 7. absence, craving, lacking,
poverty 8. scarcity, shortage
9. deficient, indigence, privation
10. inadequacy 11. destitution,
requirement
want (of)...
appetite.. 6. asitia
desire.. 11. inappetence
lacking.. 4. sans 5. out of 7. empty
of, scant of, short of 8. bereft of
10. deprived of
power.. 5. atony
sense (good).. 5. folly
wanting... 4. void 5. minus, needy
6. absent, bereft, devoid 7. lacking,
missing, short of, without
9. deficient, destitute, imperfect
wanting (pert to)...
be found.. 9. fall short 10. be inferior
confidence.. 11. distrustful
in energy.. 6. atonic
in firmness.. 7. flaccid
in intelligence.. 12. feebleminded
wanton... 3. gay 4. lewd 5. merry
6. frisky, harlot, unruly 7. immoral,
lustful, wayward 8. flagrant, insolent,
sportive, unchaste 9. dissolute,
merciless 10. capricious, frolicsome,
licentious 11. extravagant
13. undisciplined
wapiti... 3. elk 4. deer, stag
war... 5. fight 6. attack, battle
8. conflict
war (pert to)...
agreement.. 6. cartel
cause of.. 10. casus belli
club.. 4. mace
fleet.. 6. armada
gas.. 8. adamsite
German.. 5. krieg 10. blitzkrieg
god.. 3. Ira, Tyr 4. Ares
goddess.. 5. Bella 6. Ishtar
hating.. 13. misopolemical
hawk.. 5. jingo 7. bailiff
horse.. 5. steed 7. charger
8. partisan 10. campaigner, politician
of words.. 9. logomachy
religious.. 5. jihad (jehad)
vessel, ship.. 3. sub 7. cruiser, frigate
8. corvette (corvet) 9. destroyer,

submarine 11. dreadnought
(dreadnaught)
war bird... 7. aviator, tanager (scarlet)
warble... 4. sing 5. carol, trill, yodel
6. quaver 7. twitter, vibrate
warbler... 4. wren 6. singer
8. blackcap, grosbeak, redstart,
songster 9. beccafico 10. bluethroat
11. whitethroat
ward... 4. jail, part, rule 5. watch
6. govern, prison 7. custody, keeping
8. district, garrison, guardian,
watchman 9. dependent
10. stronghold 12. guardianship
ward (pert to)...
division.. 4. army, jail 6. forest
8. hospital
French.. 14. arrondissement
heeler.. 8. henchman 10. politician
off.. 4. fend 5. fence, parry, repel,
stave 7. expiate, forfend, prevent
warden... 5. guard, nazir 6. dizdar
(disdar), jailer, keeper, ranger, sexton
7. alcaide (alcaid), turnkey
8. director, guardian, official,
watchman 9. concierge, custodian
10. gatekeeper
warder... 6. warden 7. turnkey
wardrobe... 4. room 6. closet
7. almirah, apparel, cabinet, clothes
8. costumes 12. clothespress
ware... 4. sage, wary, wise 5. aware,
china, goods, spend 6. shrewd
7. careful, heedful, pottery, prudent,
seaweed 8. cautious, vigilant
9. cognizant, commodity, conscious,
porcelain 11. commodities,
earthenware, merchandise
warehouse... 4. silo 5. depot, étape
6. fonduk (fondouk), godown
7. storage 8. entrepôt
warfare... 7. contest 8. conflict,
struggle 11. hostilities 12. armed
contest
wariness... 7. stealth 8. distrust
9. chariness, suspicion
warlock... 6. wizard 7. monster (Myth)
8. conjuror, magician, sorcerer
warm... 3. red 4. heat, keen, mild
5. angry, calid, eager, humid,
muggy, tepid, toast 6. ardent, excite,
genial, hearty, heated, torrid
7. clement, cordial, fervent
8. friendly, generous 10. responsive
11. sympathetic 12. affectionate,
enthusiastic 13. near discovery, near
the object (see also *hot*)
warm (pert to)...
bath.. 5. therm
growing.. 9. calescent
hearted.. 4. kind 6. hearty, kindly,
tender 7. cordial 8. friendly,
generous 11. sympathetic
12. affectionate
pert to.. 7. thermal
praise.. 8. encomium
room.. 10. tepidarium
springs (Rom).. 7. thermae
warmblooded... 6. ardent 9. irascible
13. homoiothermic, quick–tempered
14. haematothermal (hematothermal)
warmed over... 5. stale, trite

8. rehashed, reheated 9. rechauffé, twice-told

warmth... 4. élan, glow, heat, zeal 5. ardor 7. ardency, thermal 8. fervency 9. animation, eloquency, geniality, vehemence 10. enthusiasm, excitement 11. calefaction, earnestness

warn... 4. flag 5. alarm, alert 6. advise, exhort, inform, notify, remind, signal 7. apprise (apprize), caution, counsel, previse 8. admonish, forebode, threaten 9. reprehend

warning... 4. bell, omen 5. alarm, alert, radar, siren 6. alarum, beacon, beware, caveat, signal, threat, tocsin 7. blinker, sematic, summons 10. admonition, admonitive 12. caveat emptor

warp... 4. bend, bias, hurl, sway, turn, woof 5. fling, throw, twist, weave 6. buckle, swerve 7. contort, deflect, distort, pervert 9. fabricate 10. aberration, distortion 12. misinterpret

warp (pert to)...
cross threads.. 4. woof
threads.. 5. lease 6. stamen
yarn.. 3. abb

warragal, warrigal... 5. dingo, horse, myall

warrant... 4. earn, writ 5. order 6. attest, ensure, permit, secure 7. defense, justify, precept, promise, voucher 8. document, guaranty, sanction, security 9. authorize, guarantee, safeguard 10. credential, instrument, protection 11. acknowledge, certificate 13. authorization

warranty... 4. writ 5. proof 7. promise, warrant 8. guaranty, sanction, security 13. authorization

warrior... 4. hero, impi 5. brave 6. Amazon 7. fighter, martial, soldier 10. halberdier

warrior (pert to)...
Bib.. 4. Ehud
female.. 6. Amazon
Indian.. 6. sannup
Roman.. 9. gladiator
Trojan.. 6. Agenor, Hector
Zulu.. 4. impi 7. Kaffirs

Warsaw (pert to)...
capital.. 6. Poland
river.. 7. Vistula
suburb.. 5. Praga

wary... 3. shy 5. alert, canny, chary, leery 7. careful, guarded, prudent 8. cautious, discreet, watchful 10. economical 11. circumspect

wash... 3. lap, pan 4. lave 5. bathe, clean, elute, flush, leach, marsh, paint, purge, rinse, slosh, swash 6. debris, drench, dry bed (river), purify, splash 7. cleanse, immerse, launder, overlay, shampoo 8. ablution 9. lixiviate

wash (pert to)...
basin.. 4. bowl 6. lavabo
bear.. 7. raccoon

dish.. 11. pied wagtail
for gold.. 3. pan
one's hands of.. 6. give up, refuse 10. relinquish
out.. 4. fade 5. elute, flunk 7. failure, freshet
sale (finance).. 10. fictitious

washing... 7. coating 8. ablution 9. drenching

Washington, DC (famed sites)... 7. Capitol (Bldg), The Mall 8. Pentagon, Treasury 10. Blair House, White House 11. Mount Vernon 12. Ford's Theater (Lincoln Museum), Supreme Court 14. cherry blossoms 15. Iwo Jima Monument, Lincoln Memorial 16. National Archives, Naval Observatory 17. Jefferson Memorial, Library of Congress 18. Walter Reed Hospital, Washington Monument 19. Unknown Soldier's Tomb 22. Smithsonian Institution 25. Arlington National Cemetery

Washington (State of)...
capital.. 7. Olympia
city.. 6. Tacoma, Yakima 7. Everett, Seattle, Spokane 10. Bellingham, Walla Walla
dam.. 10. Bonneville 11. Grand Coulee
discoverer.. 4. Gray 9. Vancouver
explorer.. 5. Clark, Lewis 6. Wilkes 7. Fremont
Falls.. 10. Snoqualmie
Fort.. 5. Lewis
lake.. 5. Union 6. Chelan 8. Crescent
mountain.. 7. Rainier 8. Cascades, Olympics
river.. 5. Snake, White 7. Spokane 8. Columbia
Sound.. 5. Puget 7. Rosario
State admission.. 14. Forty-second
State motto.. 4. Al–Ki (By and By)
State nickname.. 9. Evergreen
wind (SW).. 7. chinook

wasp... 5. Sphex, vespa, whamp 6. dauber, hornet, Tiphia, vespid 8. Vespidae 12. Hymenopteron, yellow jacket

waspish... 4. mean 5. cross, testy 6. cranky 7. bearish, peevish, slender 8. choleric, churlish, petulant, snappish, spiteful 9. fractious, irascible, irritable 12. cantankerous

wasp's nest... 8. vespiary

wassail... 4. lark, orgy, romp 5. toast 6. frolic, shindy 7. carouse 8. beverage, carousal 9. festivity 10. salutation 11. celebration 12. drinking bout

waste... 3. eat 4. idle, junk, loss, rind, ross, sack, slag, vain, wear, wild 5. chaff, chips, dross, havoc, spill, trash 6. barren, desert, expend, lavish, ravage, refuse 7. atrophy, exhaust, fritter, rubbish 8. clinkers, demolish, desolate, squander 9. dissipate 10. desolation, diminution 11. destruction, devastation, dissipation, prodigality, uninhabited 12. uncultivated,

unproductive 13. unserviceable
waste (pert to)...
allowance.. 4. tret
away.. 3. age 6. shrink, sicken
  7. decline 8. marasmus
  11. deteriorate
lay waste.. 4. sack 6. ravage
  7. destroy 8. decimate
matter.. 3. ort 4. slag 5. dross
  7. clinker
mine.. 3. gob
silk.. 4. knob, noil 6. frison
time.. 4. idle, lazy 5. dally 6. daddle,
  footle, loiter 10. dillydally
wasted... 7. haggard 8. phthisic
wasteful... 6. lavish 10. thriftless
  11. extravagant, improvident
wasteland... 5. heath, marsh, swamp
  6. desert, morass 8. badlands
  10. barren land, everglades
wasting... 5. aging 6. awaste
  8. marasmic 10. enfeebling
  11. consumption, devastating
  13. deteriorating
wastrel... 4. waif 5. idler 8. vagabond
  10. profligate 11. spendthrift
watch... 3. eye, spy 4. espy, heed,
  mark, mind, tend, time, wake
  (funeral) 5. guard, vigil 6. ambush,
  patrol, police, sentry 7. bivouac,
  lookout, observe 8. horologe, sentinel
  9. ambuscade, timepiece, vigilance
  11. chronometer, observation,
  wakefulness
watch (pert to)...
chain.. 3. fob 6. Albert
face.. 5. bezel
maker.. 10. horologist
military.. 5. perdu (perdue) 6. sentry
  7. vedette
stop.. 5. timer
tower.. 6. beacon 7. atalaya, mirador
  10. lighthouse
word.. 6. signal 10. shibboleth (Bib)
  11. countersign
works.. 10. escapement
watchful... 3. Ira (Heb) 4. wary
  5. alert, aware 7. careful, heedful
  8. cautious, open–eyed, vigilant
  9. observant, regardful
  11. circumspect
watchman... 5. guard 6. sentry,
  warder 8. sentinel, watchdog
  10. gatekeeper
watchword... 4. hint, word 6. signal
  8. party cry 10. intimation,
  shibboleth (Bib) 11. countersign
watchworks... 10. escapement
water... 3. eau, ice, wet 4. aqua, rain
  5. fluid, flume, spray 6. dilute,
  lagoon, liquid 7. moisten
  8. beverage, calendar, irrigate,
  sprinkle 10. adulterate
water (pert to)...
baptismal.. 5. laver
bath.. 7. balneum
bird.. 4. coot, loon 5. diver, ouzel
  6. dipper 7. pintail, swimmer
  9. merganser
bottle.. 4. olla 6. carafe
buffalo.. 2. ox 7. carabao
channel.. 5. canal, flume 6. strait

  8. tailrace
chart.. 10. hydrograph
color (art).. 9. aquarelle
comb form.. 5. hydro 6. hydato
congealed.. 3. ice 4. snow 5. glacé
  6. icicle
course.. 4. clow 5. bayou, gorge,
  gully 6. nullah, ravine, sluice
  9. watergate
cow.. 6. sea cow 7. buffalo, manatee
cure.. 10. hydropathy
  12. hydrotherapy
deer.. 10. chevrotain
destitute of.. 9. anhydrous
divination by.. 10. hydromancy
eagle.. 6. osprey
element.. 6. oxygen 8. hydrogen
elephant.. 12. hippopotamus
exhibition.. 8. aquacade
fowl.. 7. pelican
gauge (rain).. 8. udometer
goddess.. 4. Nina 7. Anahita, Anaitis
hare.. 11. swamp rabbit
heater.. 4. etna
history.. 10. hydrognosy
hog.. 8. capybara
hole.. 5. oasis 6. tinaja 7. alberca
jug.. 4. lota (lotah), olla 5. banga
  6. hydria, kalpis
lava.. 12. hellgrammite
lily.. 5. lotus 6. Nuphar 7. Nelumbo
  8. Nymphaea, Victoria
  11. spatterdock
measure.. 10. hydrometer
meter.. 7. Venturi
mineral.. 5. Vichy 6. Shasta
  7. Seltzer
monster.. 6. nicker (fabled)
nymph.. 5. naiad 6. undine
  7. Oceanid
of oblivion.. 5. Lethe 12. river of
  Hades
opossum.. 5. yapok (yapock)
pert to.. 7. aqueous 8. hydatoid
plug.. 3. tap 4. cock, cork 6. faucet,
  spigot 7. hydrant
pocket.. 6. tinaja
rat.. 4. vole 8. vagabond
reddish (with iron).. 6. riddam
reservoir (underground).. 6. cenote
rough.. 4. eddy 5. ocean 6. rapids
  7. riptide 8. undertow
sapphire.. 6. iolite 10. saphir d'eau
scorpion.. 4. Nepa 7. Ranatra
search for.. 5. dowse
sheet of.. 5. nappe
spirit.. 3. Nix 5. Ariel, Nixie 6. kelpie,
  nicker, sprite
spout.. 5. spate 8. gargoyle
sprite.. 3. Nix 5. Nixie
stratum.. 7. aquifer
study, science of.. 9. hydrology
  11. hydrography
surface.. 4. ryme
swelling.. 5. edema
turkey.. 9. snakebird
vessel.. 3. jug 4. ewer, lota (lotah),
  pail 5. cruse, flask 6. bottle, bucket,
  tinaja 7. pitcher, stamnos
  8. decanter
wheel.. 5. noria 6. sakieh (sakiyeh)
  7. turbine 8. tympanum

without.. 9. anhydrous
watery... 8. ichorous
Watling Street (London)... 6. Galaxy
  8. Milky Way 9. Roman road
wattle... 3. rod 4. beat, flog, plat,
  wand 5. fence, twist, weave, withe
  6. barbel, dewlap, hurdle, lappet
  8. caruncle 9. boobyalla, loose flap
  10. intertwine, interweave 11. skin
  process 12. native willow
wattlebird... 4. crow 10. honey eater
  11. brush turkey
Wattle Day... 7. holiday
wave... 3. ola, sea, wag 4. flap, tide
  5. crest, eagre, flood, ridge, surge,
  swell, tilde 6. beckon, billow,
  comber, flaunt, hairdo, marcel, ripple,
  roller, signal 7. breaker, decuman,
  flutter, tsunami, vibrate 8. brandish,
  coiffure, flourish, greeting, undulate
  9. fluctuate, vibration 10. undulation
waver... 4. reel, sway, veer 5. demur,
  quake 6. falter, quiver, totter
  7. flicker, flutter, stagger, tremble,
  vibrate 8. hesitate 9. fluctuate,
  oscillate, vacillate 12. be indecisive
wavering... 6. fickle 8. doubtful,
  unsteady 9. desultory 10. irresolute
wavy... 4. onde, undé (undee)
  5. curly, snaky 6. repand, undate
  7. billowy, rolling, sinuous
  8. undulant 9. undulated
  10. undulatory
wax... 4. cere, grow 6. candle, cerate,
  polish 7. beeswax, cerumen
  8. increase, paraffin 9. lubricant,
  lubricate 12. zietrisikite (mineral)
wax (pert to)...
  beeswax cells.. 9. honeycomb
  beeswax substitute.. 7. ceresin
  candle.. 6. cierge
  chemical.. 9. adipocere
  Chinese.. 4. pela
  molded in.. 7. fictile 9. ceroplast
  ref to.. 5. ceral
  substance.. 5. cerin
way... 3. via 4. lane, mode, path,
  plan, ramp, road 5. alley, habit,
  means, Milky, route, track 6. avenue,
  course, manner, method, street
  7. highway, passage 8. causeway,
  distance, sidewalk 9. banquette,
  direction, procedure
way (pert to)...
  astronomy.. 6. Galaxy 8. Milky Way
  give.. 5. break, yield 6. weaken
    7. despair 10. depreciate
  god of.. 6. Hermes
  in.. 7. ingress 8. entrance
  in a way.. 8. as it were, somewhat
    13. theoretically
  inclined.. 4. ramp
  out.. 4. exit 6. egress, escape
  roundabout.. 6. detour
waylay... 3. rob 5. await, seize
  6. ambush, lay for 8. surprise
  9. ambuscade
wayward... 6. unruly 7. erratic, willful
  8. perverse, stubborn, untoward
  10. capricious, headstrong, refractory
  11. disobedient, intractable
weak... 3. dim, lax, wan 4. pale,

puny, thin, worn 5. faint, frail, washy
  6. dotish, feeble, infirm, sickly,
  simple, unwise, watery 7. flaccid,
  foolish, fragile, insipid 9. cowardly,
  decrepit, fatigued, impotent, wavering
  9. enfeebled, exhausted, nerveless,
  powerless 10. effeminate
  11. debilitated, ineffective
  12. unconvincing
weak (pert to)...
  fish.. 7. totuava 9. gray trout
    10. squeteague
  hearted.. 6. afraid 7. fearful
    12. fainthearted
  kneed.. 6. cowardly, yielding
    10. irresolute
  sister.. 6. coward 8. weakling
    11. mollycoddle
weaken... 3. sap 4. tire 5. break
  6. dilute, impair, lessen, reduce
  7. cripple, disable, exhaust, unnerve
  8. enervate 9. undermine
  10. debilitate
weakness... 4. flaw 5. atony, fault
  6. defect, foible, liking 7. failing,
  fatigue, frailty 8. asthenia, debility
  9. cowardice, impotence, infirmity
  10. feebleness, infirmness
  11. decrepitude 12. imperfection
  13. powerlessness
weal... 4. mark, wale, welt 5. ridge,
  wheal 6. riches, wealth 7. welfare
  9. happiness, well-being
  10. commonweal
wealth... 4. good, weal 5. money
  6. assets, mammon, riches
  7. capital, fortune, welfare
  8. opulence, property, treasure
  9. abundance, affluence, well-being
  10. prosperity 11. possessions
wealth (pert to)...
  god of.. 6. Plutus
  person of.. 6. monied 7. magnate,
    opulent 9. plutocrat
  pursuit of.. 10. plutomania
  study of.. 9. economics, plutology
  worship of.. 10. plutolatry
wealthy... 4. rich 5. ample
  8. abundant, affluent
wealthy (pert to)...
  English slang.. 4. oofy
  man.. 5. nabob 10. capitalist
  rule by.. 9. plutocracy
wean... 6. detach 8. alienate, estrange
  9. reconcile
weapon... 3. arm, gat, gun 4. bola,
  bolo, celt, club, dart, epee, snee
  5. arrow, knife, lance, rifle, saber
  (sabre), spear, sword 6. dagger,
  musket, pistol, poleax (poleaxe),
  rapier 7. bayonet, bazooka, carbine,
  gisarme, halberd, machete, trident
  8. battle-ax (battle-axe), catapult,
  crossbow, revolver, stiletto, tomahawk
  9. derringer, Excalibur
  11. blunderbuss
wear... 3. use 4. bear, fray, fret, show
  5. chafe, weary 7. fatigue
  12. disintegrate
wear (pert to)...
  away.. 3. eat, end 5. erode
    6. abrade 7. corrode, decline

down.. **4.** tire **8.** persuade
9. influence
out.. **4.** tire **5.** waste **7.** fatigue
weariness... **5.** ennui **6.** tedium
7. boredom, fatigue **9.** lassitude
wearisome... **4.** hard **6.** boring,
dismal, dreary, tiring **7.** irksome,
tedious **8.** tiresome, toilsome
9. fatiguing, laborious, vexatious
10. monotonous
weary... **3.** fag, irk, sad **4.** bore, jade,
pall, tire, weak **5.** bored, spent, tired
6. plague **7.** fatigue, languid
9. forjesket
weasel... **4.** stot, vare **5.** ratel, stoat
6. ermine, ferret
weasellike... **4.** mink **5.** otter, tayra
9. musteline, musteloid
weather (pert to)...
cock.. **4.** vane
glass.. **9.** barometer, baroscope
man.. **13.** meteorologist
map.. **6.** isobar
weave... **3.** mat **4.** knit, lace, reel,
spin, sway **5.** plait, unite **6.** devise,
wattle **7.** canelle, entwine, fashion
8. contrive **9.** fabricate, interlace,
interwind **10.** intertwine, intertwist
11. push one's way
weaver bird... **4.** baya, maya, taha
5. Munia
weaving (pert to)...
art of.. **4.** loom
fabric (rich).. **3.** web **7.** brocade,
webbing
French.. **5.** lisse **8.** Jacquard
material.. **5.** reeds, twigs **6.** raffia
term.. **4.** beam, dent, loom, sley
7. shuttle
together.. **7.** plexure
weazen (wizen)... **6.** shrink, wither
7. shrivel
web... **3.** net, ply **4.** caul, tela, trap,
veil, warp **5.** snare **6.** tissue
7. network, texture **8.** filament,
gossamer, membrane, vexillum
12. entanglement
web (pert to)...
footed.. **7.** palmate
like.. **4.** lacy **5.** telar **7.** spidery
spinning.. **6.** telary **7.** retiary
term.. **5.** telar
toed.. **11.** totipalmate
winged.. **3.** bat
work.. **4.** maze, mesh **6.** tangle
11. Gordian knot
wed... **4.** join, mate **5.** marry, mated,
unite **6.** joined **7.** espouse, pledged,
spliced **13.** give in wedlock
wedding... **8.** ceremony, espousal,
marriage, nuptials
wedding (anniversary)...
1st.. **5.** paper
2nd.. **5.** straw
3rd.. **5.** candy
4th.. **7.** leather
5th.. **6.** wooden
7th.. **6.** floral
10th.. **3.** tin
12th.. **5.** linen
13th.. **4.** lace
15th.. **7.** crystal

20th.. **5.** china
25th.. **6.** silver
30th.. **5.** pearl
35th.. **5.** coral
40th.. **7.** emerald
45th.. **4.** ruby
50th.. **6.** golden
75th.. **7.** diamond
wedding (pert to)...
flower.. **13.** orange blossom
proclamation.. **5.** banns (bans)
snow.. **4.** rice
term.. **7.** marital, wedlock
8. marriage, nuptials **9.** matrimony
11. espousement
wedge... **3.** jam **4.** club, shoe
5. cleat, ingot, split **6.** sector,
wedgie **7.** niblick **8.** triangle, voussoir
9. machinery
wedge-shaped... **7.** cuneate
9. cuneiform (cuniform)
Wednesday... **5.** Woden (wise god)
9. fourth day, Woden's Day
wee... **3.** bit **4.** dock, fine, tiny
5. small, teeny **6.** little, minute
10. diminutive, teeny-weeny
weed... **3.** bur (burr), hoe, rag **4.** loco,
milk, sida, tare **5.** cigar, flesh, vetch
6. darnel, excise, Jimson, knawel,
spurge, tumble **7.** allseed, mallows,
mustard, ragweed, tobacco
8. plantain, purslane, toadflax
9. cultivate, dandelion
11. undergrowth
weeds... **8.** garments (mourning)
week... **8.** hebdomad **9.** seven days
week (pert to)...
day.. **6.** ferial
Eccl.. **4.** Holy **7.** Passion
of Sundays.. **5.** seven **8.** hebdomad
of years.. **5.** seven
past.. **10.** yesterweek
weekly... **5.** aweek **10.** hebdomadal,
periodical **11.** publication
weeks, two... **9.** fortnight
weel... **4.** pool, trap **6.** basket **8.** fish
trap
ween... **5.** think **6.** expect **7.** believe,
imagine, suppose **8.** conceive
weep... **3.** cry, orp, sob **4.** drip, rain,
wail **5.** exude, mourn **7.** blubber,
lapwing **9.** percolate, shed tears
weeping... **6.** crying **7.** sobbing
9. festering
weeping (pert to)...
monkey.. **8.** capuchin
queen.. **5.** Niobe
tree.. **5.** cedar **6.** spruce, willow
Weeping Philosopher (anc)...
10. Heraclitus
weevil (pert to)...
cotton.. **4.** boll
malt.. **4.** boud
snout.. **8.** curculio
type (other).. **3.** pea **4.** palm, pine,
rice, seed **5.** flour
weigh... **4.** tare, test **5.** hoist, poise,
scale **6.** ponder, regard **7.** balance,
be heavy, compare, measure
8. consider, encumber, estimate,
ruminate **9.** apportion, press hard
weigh down... **4.** lade, load

6. burden, hamper 7. ballast, depress, oppress 11. overbalance

weight... 4. load, mass 5. force, power 6. burden, import, moment 7. gravity, tonnage 8. encumber, pressure 9. authority, heaviness, influence 10. importance 11. consequence 12. significance

weight (pert to)...
allowance.. 4. tare, tret 7. scalage
comb form.. 4. baro
gem.. 5. carat (karat)
light.. 6. suttle
system.. 3. net 4. troy 6. metric 10. apothecary 11. avoirdupois
total.. 5. gross

weighty... 3. fat 5. bulky, heavy, hefty, large, obese 6. solemn 7. massive, onerous, serious 8. forcible, powerful 9. corpulent, important, momentous, ponderous 10. burdensome, cumbersome, impressive, oppressive 11. influential 13. authoritative

weir... 3. dam, net 4. bank 5. fence, levee, seine 7. barrier, milldam 9. floodgate

weird... 3. odd 4. omen, wild 5. eerie (eery), queer, scary 6. creepy, spooky 7. awesome, curious, ghostly, macabre, strange, uncanny 8. eldritch 9. deathlike, frightful 10. mysterious, prediction

Weird Sisters (Scot)... 5. Fates

welcome... 4. hail 5. adopt, greet 7. acclaim, accueil 8. grateful, greeting, pleasing 9. agreeable, bienvenue, desirable 10. acceptable, salutation

weld... 5. unite 11. consolidate

welfare... 4. good, weal 5. Salus (goddess) 9. good cheer 10. prosperity 14. material plenty

welkin... 3. air, sky 6. heaven 10. atmosphere

well... 3. fit, gay, pit 4. gush, hale, pool 5. aweel, fount, fully 6. easily, gusher, hearty, justly, kindly, source 7. cistern, closely 8. artesian, expertly, fountain, friendly 10. full degree, intimately 11. excellently 12. satisfactory

well (pert to)...
being.. 4. weal 7. comfort 8. eucrasia 9. happiness
Bib.. 4. Esek
born.. 5. noble 7. eugenic
bred.. 5. polite 7. genteel, refined 8. cultured, wellborn 9. pedigreed 10. cultivated 11. gentlemanly 12. thoroughbred
comb form.. 4. mene
defined.. 8. distinct 11. distinctive
groomed.. 4. neat 5. sleek 6. soigné (soignée)
grounded.. 5. valid 7. logical 9. plausible 11. established, substantial 12. well-informed
gushing.. 8. artesian
heeled.. 4. rich 5. armed 7. moneyed, wealthy, well-off 8. well-to-do
known.. 6. famous 7. eminent

12. acknowledged
land drain.. 4. sump
lining.. 5. steen
off.. 5. lucky 10. prosperous
oil.. 6. gusher
pole.. 5. sweep
prefix.. 2. eu
timed.. 6. timely 8. opportune
versed.. 7. erudite
watered.. 9. irrigated, irriguous

welsh (welch)... 5. cheat 6. not pay, renege 7. swindle 10. shirk out of

Welsh (pert to)... see also *Wales*
boat.. 7. coracle
congress of literati.. 10. eisteddfod
fine, for murder.. 7. galanas
god, underworld.. 4. Bran
instrument (reed).. 7. pibcorn
man.. 5. Taffy 8. Cambrian
onion.. 5. cibal
population.. 6. Cymric
rabbit.. 7. ramekin (ramequin), rarebit
romance collection.. 10. Mabinogion (Mabinogi)

welt... 4. mark, wale 5. ridge 6. stripe, thrash

welter... 4. reel, roll, sail, toss 6. grovel, tumble, wallow 7. stagger 8. flounder, overturn 9. confusion

wen... 4. cyst, rune 5. tumor 7. blemish 11. excrescence 12. protuberance

wench... 4. doxy, gill, girl 5. child, squaw, trull, woman 6. damsel, maiden 7. consort, servant 8. strumpet 11. maidservant

wend... 2. go 4. fare, pass 6. depart, direct, travel 7. circuit, proceed 8. progress

went (pert to)... see also *go*
astray.. 6. failed 10. miscarried
away.. 4. left 8. departed
before.. 3. led 8. preceded 9. antecded
swiftly.. 3. ran 4. sped 6. darted 7. scooted, scudded 8. decamped

wenzel... 4. jack (card game) 5. knave

werewolf... 6. jaguar 8. uturuncu, werefolk 11. lycanthrope

wergild... 3. cro 4. eric 7. galanas 9. Brehon Law

Wesleyan... 9. Methodist 14. Wesley follower

West African (pert to)...
baboon.. 5. drill 8. mandrill
city.. 5. Accra, Dakar
gazelle.. 4. kudu, mohr (mhorr), oryx
lemur.. 5. potto 8. kinkajou
monkey.. 4. mona 6. guenon
native.. 5. Ashanti (Ashantee)
pepper.. 5. cubeb
tree.. 5. iroko, odoom
tribe.. 5. Igara

West End, London... 7. Mayfair 9. Belgravia 11. fashionable 12. aristocratic

Western... 9. Hesperian 10. Occidental

Westernmost US... 9. Aleutians 11. Attu Islands 12. Cape Wrangell

West Indies...
bird.. 4. tody 6. mucaro
boat.. 7. drogher (droger)

chief.. 7. cacique
clingfish.. 6. testar
crop.. 5. sugar 7. bananas
ebony.. 9. cocuswood
fish.. 4. cero, paru, sesi 6. testar
flea.. 6. chigoe
fruit.. 5. papaw (pawpaw)
islands.. 4. Cuba 5. Haiti 6. Cayman,
Virgin 7. Antigua, Bahamas, Leeward
8. Antilles, Windward
liquor.. 5. mobby (mobbie), tafia
(taffia)
lizard.. 6. arbalo
magic.. 6. obeah
music.. 7. calypso
owl.. 6. mucaro
resident.. 9. Antillean
rodent.. 6. agouti (agouty)
snuff.. 8. Maccaboy
tea.. 8. goatweed
tortoise.. 7. hicatee
tree.. 4. ausu 5. ebony, papaw
6. bonduc 8. bayberry 9. sapodilla,
satinwood
volcano.. 5. Pelée
wood.. 9. cocuswood, sapodilla
10. granadilla
Westminster clock (London)... 6. Big
Ben
West Pointer... 5. cadet, plebe
8. yearling
West Point motto... 16. Duty, Honor,
Country
West Virginia...
capital.. 10. Charleston
city.. 5. Logan 8. Wheeling
11. Parkersburg
crop.. 4. coal
mountain.. 10. Spruce Knob
11. Alleghenies
park (famed).. 12. Harpers Ferry
river.. 4. Ohio 7. Kanawha
11. Monongahela
Springs (resort).. 8. Berkeley
12. White Sulphur
State admission.. 11. Thirty-fifth
State motto.. 19. Montani Semper
Liberi 22. Mountaineers Always Free
State nickname.. 8. Mountain
West wind... 8. Favonius, Zephyrus
wet... 4. asop, damp, dank, dewy, rain
5. foggy, humid, leach, misty, moist,
mushy, rainy, soggy, soppy
6. dampen, drench, soaked, sodden,
watery 7. moisten 8. sprinkle
wet blanket... 7. kill-joy 8. deadhead
10. discourage, spoilsport
whale... 3. orc 4. cete, lash, whip
5. whack 6. beluga, blower, thrash
7. grampus, ripsack 8. hardhead
9. zeuglodon 13. sulphur–bottom
whale (pert to)...
Arctic.. 7. narwhal
bird.. 4. gull 6. petrel 9. phalarope
blubber pot.. 6. try-pot
blue.. 9. Sibbaldus
bone.. 6. baleen
carcass.. 5. kreng
constellation.. 5. Cetus
fat.. 7. blubber
food.. 4. brit
gray.. 7. ripsack 8. hardhead

killer.. 4. orca
killer of.. 8. ceticide
legendary.. 9. Mysticeti
monster.. 4. Cete
mustache (legend).. 9. Mysticeti
Order.. 7. Cetacea
ref to.. 5. cetic, sperm 6. baleen
7. blubber 8. cetacean
school of.. 3. gam, pod
secretion (perfume).. 9. ambergris
small.. 7. grampus
sperm type.. 8. cachalot
study of.. 8. cetology
toothed.. 10. odontocete, zeuglodont
type.. 3. orc 4. blue, orca 5. right,
sperm 6. killer 7. dolphin, rorqual
8. cachalot, humpback, porpoise
9. whalebone
wax.. 10. spermaceti
whalebone.. 6. baleen 10. stiffening
young.. 4. calf 9. shorthead
wharf... 4. dock, pier, quay 5. jetty
6. staith 7. landing
wharf (pert to)...
fish.. 6. cunner
master.. 10. wharfinger
worker.. 9. stevedore
whatnot... 5. thing 6. object
(nondescript) 7. étagère
10. miscellany
what's what... 4. fact 5. truth
7. reality 10. what's right
what wonders has God wrought
(Arabic exclamation)... 9. mashallah
whaup... 6. curlew, outcry
9. scoundrel
wheal... 4. wale, weal, welt 5. whelk
6. stripe 7. pustule
wheat (pert to)...
beard.. 3. awn
beverage.. 6. zythem
bird.. 4. lark 8. wheatear 9. chaffinch
chaff.. 4. bran
duck.. 7. widgeon 8. baldpate
Europe.. 5. emmer, spelt (speltz)
flour.. 4. atta 5. Hovis
hard.. 5. durum
India.. 4. suji 8. semolina
storage bin.. 4. silo 8. elevator
wheedle... 4. coax, gain 5. tease
6. banter, cajole, entice 7. blarney,
flatter 8. blandish, inveigle, persuade
9. influence
wheel... 3. cam, cog 4. bike, disc,
helm, ride, roll, rota 5. drive, pivot,
rotor, rowel, whirl 6. caster, roller,
rotate 7. bicycle, revolve, rotator,
torture, vehicle 8. tricycle 10. water
wheel
wheel (pert to)...
gem-grinding.. 5. skive
hub.. 4. nave
man.. 5. pilot 7. cyclist 8. helmsman,
pedalist 9. bicyclist
monkey.. 3. gin
part.. 3. rim 5. felly (felloe), spoke
6. hubcap
pulley.. 6. sheave
shaped.. 8. circular, rotiform
spoke.. 6. radius
spur.. 5. rowel
stopper.. 4. grig 5. sprag

swiveled . . 6. caster
toothed . . 3. cog 4. gear 6. pinion
turbine . . 5. rotor
type . . 3. cog, fly, pin 4. cart, mill, spur 5. wagon 6. Ferris, paddle 7. balance, potter's 9. of fortune
water . . 5. noria 6. sakieh (sakiyeh)
wheels, logging . . . 7. katydid
wheen . . . 3. few 5. group 7. several 8. division, quantity
wheerikins . . . 10. posteriors
wheetle . . . 5. chirp 7. whistle
wheeze . . . 3. gag 4. joke 5. hoose (hooze) 6. cliché, saying 7. breathe 8. sibilate 9. witticism 10. sibilation
whelk . . . 4. acne 5. snail 6. papule, pimple 7. pustule
whelp . . . 3. boy, cub, pup 5. child, puppy, tiger, youth 8. give birth, youngling
when . . . 2. as 3. tho 5. until 6. though 7. how soon, whereas 8. although, whenever 10. how long ago 11. at which time
where . . . 4. here, spot 5. place, there 7. whither 10. inasmuch as 11. at what place, whereabouts
whereas . . . 5. since
whereby . . . 7. perquod
whereness . . . 6. ubiety
whereupon . . . 5. when 7. on which 9. upon which 10. after which
wherewithal . . . 5. means, money 9. resources
whet . . . 4. hone 5. grind, point, rouse 6. excite 7. quicken, sharpen 9. intensify, stimulate
whether . . . 2. if 6. either
whey . . . 4. curd 5. serum
whiff . . . 4. blow, fish, gust, odor, puff, waft 6. breath, exhale, stanch 7. puff out 8. blow away 10. inhalation
while . . . 2. as 3. yet 4. time 5. until 7. beguile, interim, whereas 11. space of time
whilom . . . 4. erst, once 5. of old 6. former 8. sometime 9. erstwhile
whim . . . 3. fad, pun, toy 4. idea 5. fancy, freak, megrim, notion, vagary 7. boutade, caprice, whimsey (whimsy), widgeon 8. migraine
whimper . . . 3. cry, sob 4. mewl, moan, pule, weep 5. whine 7. sniffle
whimsey, whimsy . . . 3. wit 4. whim 5. craze, fancy, freak 7. caprice
whimsical . . . 3. fad, odd 4. dish 5. droll, queer, witty 7. amusing 8. fanciful, freakish, notional 9. crotchety, eccentric, fantastic, grotesque 10. capricious
whine . . . 4. moan, pule, wail 6. snivel 7. screech, ululate, whimper 8. complain 12. moaning sound
whinny . . . 4. bray 5. neigh, whine
whip . . . 3. cat, tan 4. beat, crop, flag, flog, goad, lace, lash, wale 5. birch, froth, quirt, seize, spank, strap 6. defeat, incite, punish, strike, swinge, thrash 7. agitate, chabouk (chabuk), conquer, scourge 8. emulsify, lambaste 9. bullwhack

10. discipline 11. congressman
whip (pert to) . . .
hand . . 8. dominion 9. advantage, influence
mark . . 4. wale, weal, welt
political . . 5. party 11. floor leader
riding . . 4. crop 5. quirt
Russian . . 4. plet (plete) 5. knout
sewing . . 8. overcast
socket . . 5. snead
whir . . . 3. fly 4. burr, buzz, whiz 5. hurry, swirl, whizz 6. hurtle 7. revolve, vibrate 9. commotion
whirl . . . 4. eddy, reel, spin, tirl, turn 5. twirl 6. circle, gyrate, rotate 7. revelry, revolve 9. commotion, pirouette, turn about 10. excitement
whirlpool . . . 4. eddy 6. gurges (Her), vortex 7. sea puss (sea purse) 9. maelstrom
whirlwind . . . 2. oe (Faroes) 7. cyclone, tornado, twister, typhoon 9. hurricane, maelstrom 10. willy-willy
whisk . . . 4. tuft, whip, wist 5. froth, sweep, swish 6. convey 7. agitate
whiskers . . . 4. chin 5. beard 8. vibrissa 9. sideburns
whisky, whiskey . . . 3. rye 4. corn 6. poteen, redeye 9. moonshine 10. usquebaugh
whisky (pert to) . . .
base . . 3. rye 5. wheat 6. barley
drink . . 4. soda, sour 5. punch, smash 7. stinger
Insurrection . . 12. Pennsylvania (1794)
Ring . . 10. Conspiracy (1875)
term . . 6. lively 7. flighty
whisper . . . 3. tip 4. blow, buzz 5. rumor 6. breeze, murmur 7. divulge 14. vox clandestina
whist, game . . . 9. Cavendish 10. Yarborough
whistle . . . 4. hiss, pipe, sing, toot 5. alarm 6. rustle, warble, wheeze 12. interference
whistle (pert to) . . .
duck . . 9. goldeneye
fish . . 8. rockling
pig . . 9. woodchuck
stop . . 12. one-horse town
tree (for boys' whistles) . . 5. maple 6. willow
Whistler painting . . . 15. Little White Girl, Whistler's Mother
whistling (pert to) . . .
coot . . 6. scoter
dick . . 6. thrush
duck . . 6. scoter 9. goldeneye
hawk . . 5. eagle
snipe . . 8. woodcock
sound . . 7. stridor
teal . . 6. scoter 8. tree duck
whit . . . 3. bit, jot 4. atom, iota 5. bodle, speck 8. particle
white . . . 3. wan 4. milk, pale, snow 5. ashen, chalk, color, happy, ivory, snowy 6. albino, chalky, chaste, honest, pallid 7. ivorine, silvery 8. innocent, platinum 9. alabaster, albescent, Caucasian, favorable, fortunate, honorable

11. snow-covered
white (pert to)..
admiral.. 9. butterfly
ant.. 4. anay (anai) 7. termite
belly.. 6. pigeon 7. widgeon
  14. prairie chicken
cat.. 7. catfish
cell.. 9. leucocyte
chub.. 10. spawneater
cloud.. 6. cirrus 7. tendril
coal.. 10. water power
crow.. 7. vulture
curlew.. 4. ibis
devil.. 7. nailrod
elephant.. 6. burden 8. Oriental
ensign.. 7. British naval
fish.. 5. cisco 6. atinga, beluga
  8. menhaden 9. Coregonus
  10. white whale
grouse.. 9. ptarmigan
growing (hoary).. 9. canescent
head.. 6. pigeon 9. blue goose
  10. surf scoter
heat.. 6. anger 13. incandescence
livered.. 6. feeble 8. cowardly
  13. pusillanimous
matter (nerve).. 4. alba
merganser.. 4. smew
miller.. 11. clothes moth
monk.. 10. Cistercian
mule.. 3. gin 6. whisky (illicit)
  9. moonshine
oak.. 5. roble
of egg.. 5. glair
partridge.. 9. ptarmigan
plague.. 7. disease 8. phthisis
  11. consumption 12. tuberculosis
plantain.. 8. pussytoe
poplar.. 5. aspen
pot.. 7. pudding
pudding.. 7. sausage 9. whitehass
pyrite.. 9. marcasite
shark.. 8. man-eater
throat.. 6. muffet (Eng) 7. warbler
whale.. 8. beluga
White (pert to)...
Chapel (Jewish).. 13. London Quarter
Holland.. 6. turkey
Horse.. 6. emblem (Saxons) 7. carving
House designer.. 5. Hoban
Relig.. 6. Friars 7. Fathers, Sisters
  8. Brethren
Rose (Eng).. 6. emblem (House of
  York)
Sands (N Mex).. 13. proving ground
Squadron.. 4. Navy (US Navy 1883)
Tower.. 13. Tower of London
whiten.. 6. blanch, bleach 8. etiolate
  9. whitewash
whitewash... 5. paint 6. defeat,
  whiten 7. conceal 8. disinfect,
  exculpate, gloss over
whither... 5. where 7. whereto 11. to
  what place, whereabouts
whiting... 4. fish 5. chalk 6. tomcod
  10. butterfish
whitish... 4. pale 5. white
  9. albescent
whitlow... 4. herb, sore 5. felon
  6. agnail, fetlow 8. hangnail
  9. saxifrage 10. paronychia
  12. inflammation

Whitsunday... 9. Pentacost
Whittington, Dick... 9. Lord Mayor
  (London)
whittle... 3. cut, hew 4. gash, hack,
  pare, trim 5. knife 6. reduce
  7. blanket
whiz, whizz... 3. hum 4. buzz, hiss,
  pirr, whir, zizz 5. whirr 6. corker,
  rotate 8. sibilate 10. speed along
  12. clever person
who... 3. wer, wha 5. which
  6. person 7. one that, pronoun
whole... 3. all, sum 4. pure, sole, unit
  5. gross, total, uncut, unity
  6. entire, intact, mostly, system
  7. healthy, perfect 8. absolute,
  complete, entirety, totality
  9. aggregate, generally, unanimous,
  undivided
whole (pert to)...
comb form.. 4. toti, toto
footed.. 5. frank 8. intimate
  9. ingenuous 10. flat-footed
hearted.. 7. devoted, earnest, sincere
  8. complete 10. unreserved
  11. unmitigated
hog.. 8. whole way 12. all or nothing
note.. 9. semibreve
number.. 7. integer
skinned.. 6. unhurt 9. unscathed
souled.. 5. noble 7. devoted, sincere,
  zealous 11. noble-minded
  12. wholehearted
wholesome... 4. sane 5. sound
  6. hearty, robust 7. healthy
  8. salutary, vigorous 9. favorable,
  healthful 10. beneficial, propitious,
  salubrious
wholly... 3. all 4. toto (comb form)
  5. fully, quite 6. solely 7. totally
  8. entirely, entirety 9. perfectly
  10. altogether, completely, thoroughly
  11. exclusively
whoop... 4. call, hoot, urge, yell
  5. cheer, shout 6. halloo, hoopee
  10. enthusiasm
whooping cough... 9. pertussis
whoop it up... 7. be noisy 8. energize
  9. make merry 12. create gaiety
whop... 4. bang, beat, bump, fall,
  flop, whip 5. knock 6. strike, stroke
whopper... 3. lie (monstrous) 6. story
  (false)
whorl... 4. curl 5. helix, spire
  8. flywheel, verticil, volution (shell)
  11. fingerprint
wicked... 3. bad, ill 4. evil, vile
  6. guilty, sinful, unjust 7. heinous,
  hellish, profane, roguish, ungodly,
  vicious 8. criminal, depraved, devilish,
  diabolic, flagrant 9. abandoned,
  atrocious, malicious, nefarious,
  perverted 10. diabolical, flagitious,
  iniquitous, villainous 11. irreligious,
  mischievous, unrighteous
wickedness... 3. sin 4. evil 6. Belial
  (Bib) 7. badness 8. baseness, iniquity
  10. sinfulness 13. maliciousness
wicked one... 5. Demon, Satan 7. Evil
  One 8. The Devil
wicker (pert to)...
basket.. 5. cesta 6. hamper, kipsey

7. pannier
cradle.. 8. bassinet
material.. 5. twigs 6. osiers, willow,
withes
ware.. 8. basketry, plaiting
wicket... 4. arch, door, gate, hoop
6. grille, window 7. grating, guichet,
lattice 8. loophole 12. grated
window, ticket window
wickiup, wikiup... 3. hut 7. shelter
Widal's, Widal reaction... 16. typhoid
fever test
widbin... 7. dogwood 8. woodbine
11. honeysuckle
widdy... 4. rope (twig) 5. noose,
widow, withy 6. halter 7. gallows
11. gallows bird
wide... 5. ample, broad, large, loose,
roomy 6. opened 7. liberal
8. expanded, spacious 9. capacious,
distended 13. comprehensive
wide–awake... 3. hat 4. keen, tern
(sooty) 5. alert 7. knowing
8. watchful
widemouthed... 4. loud 5. noisy
6. greedy 7. barking 9. devouring
widen... 4. ream 6. dilate, expand,
extend, spread 7. amplify, broaden,
enlarge
widespread... 4. rife 5. broad
7. diffuse, general 8. not local,
sweeping 9. dispersed, extensive,
prevalent, scattered, universal
13. comprehensive
widgeon... 4. duck, smee 5. goose
6. Mareca, zuisin 7. poacher
8. baldpate 9. simpleton
widow... 6. relict 7. bereave, dowager,
viduate
widow (pert to)...
bird.. 5. finch, Vidua 6. whidah
cremated.. 6. suttee
fish.. 5. viuva
monkey.. 4. titi
suicide.. 6. suttee
widower... 6. relict
widow's (pert to)...
lock.. 8. hairline 10. widow's peak
mite.. 4. coin 6. lepton
portion.. 5. dower
right.. 5. terce
weeds.. 8. mourning 9. black veil,
widowhood
width... 5. girth 7. breadth
8. diameter, latitude, wideness
wield... 3. ply, use 4. cope, deal, rule
5. power, swing 6. direct, employ,
handle, manage 7. control
8. brandish 10. manipulate
wife... 4. frau, mate, rani, uxor
5. bride, mujer 6. matron, spouse
7. consort 8. gudewife (guidwife),
helpmate, helpmeet 10. better half
12. married woman
wife (pert to)...
French.. 5. femme
killing.. 9. uxoricide
of a rajah.. 4. Rani (Ranee)
one.. 8. monogamy
pert to.. 8. uxorial
slave's.. 9. broadwife
wig... 4. tête 5. jasey 6. peruke,

toupee 7. censure, periwig 8. seal
hood 9. dignitary
wight... 3. man 4. loud 5. brave,
fairy, swift, witch 6. active, nimble
7. valiant 8. creature, powerful
11. living being
wigwag... 6. signal 8. to and fro
11. oscillation
wigwam... 4. tent 5. hogan, tepee
6. teepee
wild... 3. mad 5. feral, myall, waste,
weird 6. ferine, savage, stormy,
unruly 7. bestial, howling, riotous
8. aberrant, desolate, dramatic,
frenetic, reckless, untilled, wildwood
9. barbarian, barbarous, ferocious,
imprudent, primitive, unbridled,
uncertain 10. boisterous, chimerical,
irrational, profligate, tumultuous,
unexplored, wilderness
11. harum–scarum, uncivilized,
uninhabited 12. obstreperous,
uncontrolled, uncultivated
14. uncontrollable
wild (pert to)...
alder.. 8. goutweed
animal.. 3. gnu 4. bear, deer, lion,
lynx 5. kiang, moose, tiger
6. dragon, onager 7. polecat
8. antelope 10. wildebeest
banana.. 5. papaw (pawpaw)
beasts.. 4. ziim
buffalo.. 4. arna 5. arnee
carrot.. 8. hilltrot
cat.. 4. balm, eyra 6. ocelot
7. panther
coffee.. 9. feverroot
crocus.. 12. pasqueflower
fancy.. 6. vagary
fowl.. 4. duck 5. goose, quail
8. pheasant 9. partridge
garlic.. 4. moly
goat.. 3. tur 4. tahr 7. markhor
(markhoor)
gourd.. 7. pumpkin 11. calabazilla
growing.. 8. agrarian
hog.. 4. boar 9. razorback
10. babiroussa
hop.. 6. bryony
horse.. 6. tarpan
ibex.. 5. Capra
Irishman (shrub).. 10. tumatakuru
jalap.. 8. mayapple
mustard.. 8. charlock
ox.. 3. yak 4. anoa
pieplant.. 7. rhubarb
pineapple.. 7. pinguin
plum.. 4. sloe 5. islay
sheep.. 3. sha 5. urial (oorial)
6. argali
sweet potato.. 7. manroot
West show.. 5. rodeo
wildebeest... 3. gnu
wilderness... 5. waste, wilds 6. forest
8. wildwood 9. confusion
12. complication
wile... 3. art, toy 4. lure, ruse
5. fraud, guile, trick 6. deceit
7. cunning 8. artifice, trickery
9. stratagem
will... 4. wish 6. behest, choice,
decree, demise, desire 7. bequest,

command 8. volition 9. intention,
testament 10. resolution
11. disposition, inclination
13. determination

will (pert to)...
appendix.. 7. codicil
convey.. 6. demise 7. bequest
having made.. 7. testate
maker of.. 8. testator
power.. 7. purpose 10. resolution
13. determination 14. strength of
mind
proof of.. 7. probate
to live (Buddh).. 5. tanha

willful, wilful... 3. mad 4. rash
5. heady 7. wayward 8. perverse,
stubborn 9. impetuous, obstinate,
voluntary 11. intentional
14. self-determined

willing... 4. free 5. prone, ready
6. minded 8. desirous, disposed,
unforced 9. agreeable, voluntary
10. consenting, deliberate, ready to
act, volitional 11. intentional
12. well-disposed

willingly... 4. fain, lief 6. freely, gladly
7. happily, readily 10. cheerfully
12. with pleasure

willow... 3. iva 4. itea 5. osier, salix
6. sallow, teaser

willow (pert to)...
basket.. 7. prickle
genus.. 5. Salix
green.. 6. reseda
lark.. 12. sedge warbler
pattern.. 7. Nanking 11. earthenware
twig.. 5. withe 6. sallow
wren.. 10. chiffchaff

willowy... 5. lithe 6. pliant, supple,
svelte 7. slender 8. flexible, graceful
15. tall and graceful

Will Rogers' plane... 9. Winnie May

wilsome... 4. wild 6. astray, dreary
7. violent, willful (wilful) 8. desolate
10. bewildered

wilt... 3. sag 4. flag, tire 5. droop,
quail 6. sicken, wither 8. languish
11. deteriorate, lose courage, make
flaccid

Wilton... 3. rug 6. carpet

wily... 3. sly 4. foxy 5. canny, smart
6. artful, astute, crafty, shrews,
subtle 7. cunning 9. cautelous

wimble... 3. awl 4. bore 5. auger,
brace, scoop, twist 6. gimlet, pierce
9. sprightly, whimsical

wimick... 3. cry 7. whimper

wimple... 4. fold, veil 7. meander
8. covering (head)

win... 3. get 4. earn, gain 5. to get
6. attain, defeat, obtain, secure
7. achieve, acquire, succeed, triumph
8. be victor, endeavor, vanquish
9. captivate 10. accomplish

win (pert to)...
all tricks (game).. 4. slam
by guile.. 8. inveigle
one's spurs.. 10. knighthood
over.. 7. convert 8. convince
persuade.. 10. conciliate

wince... 4. reel 5. start 6. cringe,
flinch, recoil, shrink 8. draw back,

windlass 10. shrink from

wind... 2. oe 3. air 4. bora, coil,
gale, gust, talk, turn, wrap 5. blast,
buran, crank, trade 6. boreal, breath,
breeze, simoom, zephyr 7. chinook,
conceit, cyclone, deviate, etesian,
meander, monsoon, sinuate, sirocco,
tempest, tornado, typhoon
8. convolve, williwaw 9. hurricane,
idle words, windstorm 10. instrument

wind (pert to)...
action on land.. 8. eolation
around.. 6. master 8. dominate
9. influence 13. lead by the nose
cloud.. 4. scud
comb form.. 5. anemo
fall.. 7. godsend 8. buckshee, gratuity
flower.. 7. anemone
gauge.. 4. vane 10. anemometer
god.. 4. Adad 6. Aeolus
god of north wind.. 6. Boreas
god of SE wind.. 5. Eurus
instrument.. 3. sax 4. fife, horn
5. flute, organ 6. cornet 7. bassoon,
hautboy, helicon, ocarina 8. clarinet
9. harmonica, saxophone
in the (wind).. 5. drunk 7. sailing
8. imminent 9. happening
into a ball.. 11. agglomerate
personified.. 6. Caurus 7. Caecias
8. Favonius, Zephyrus
ref to.. 7. Aeolian (Eolian)
rose.. 5. poppy
science.. 9. anemology
storm.. 4. gale 7. cyclone, typhoon
9. hurricane
up.. 3. end 7. prepare 8. complete,
conclude
yarn.. 6. windle

wind (type)...
Adriatic (cold).. 4. bora
cold.. 4. bise, bora, puna 7. mistral
8. williwaw
desert.. 6. simoom 7. sirocco
dry.. 9. harmattan
East.. 8. levanter
Egypt.. 7. khamsin (kamsin)
equator.. 5. trade
fierce.. 4. gale 6. buster, squall
7. monsoon 8. blizzard 9. hurricane
gentle.. 4. aura 6. zephyr
Malta (cold).. 7. gregale
Mediterranean.. 6. solano 7. etesian
8. levanter
North.. 6. Boreas
Northwest.. 6. Caurus 7. etesian
Oriental.. 7. monsoon
Peru.. 4. puna
S America.. 4. puna 7. pampero
South.. 6. Auster
Southeast.. 5. Eurus
Southwest.. 7. chinook
Spain.. 6. solano
West (personified).. 8. Favonius
whirl.. 2. oe

windiness... 7. conceit
12. boastfulness

winding... 5. curve, snaky 6. spiral
7. sinuous, twining 8. rambling,
tortuous 9. deviative, meandrous
10. circuitous

windjammer... 6. bugler, talker, vessel

(sailing) 8. bandsman 9. trumpeter
windlass... 4. reel 5. winch 6. windle
    7. capstan, machine (hoisting)
windle... 4. reel 5. winch 6. basket
    7. measure, redwing
window (pert to)...
    arrangement.. 8. fanlight
    12. fenestration
    bay.. 5. oriel
    dormer, roof.. 5. gable 7. lucarne
    8. skylight
    frame.. 4. sash
    Latin.. 8. fenestra
    leading.. 4. came
    nautical.. 8. porthole
    oval.. 5. oxeye
    part.. 4. pane, sash, sill 5. glass
    7. shutter
    recess.. 6. exedra 9. embrasure
    ship's.. 4. port 8. porthole
    ticket.. 6. wicket 7. guichet
    type.. 4. port 5. gable, oriel
    7. eucarne 8. casement, skylight
windpipe... 6. gullet, throat
    7. trachea, weasand
windrow... 5. swath (swathe) 6. furrow
Winds, Father of (Gr)... 8. Astraeus
windward... 5. aloof 8. aweather
    9. weatherly
Windy City... 7. Chicago
wine (pert to)...
    and honey.. 5. clary, mulse
    7. oenomel
    Baden.. 8. Ruländer
    bag.. 8. wineskin
    bibber.. 3. sot 5. toper 7. tippler
    8. drunkard
    Bordeaux.. 6. claret
    bottle.. 6. magnum 8. decanter
    cask.. 3. tun
    cellar.. 6. bodega
    comb form.. 4. oeno
    cruet.. 7. burette
    cup.. 3. ama 6. goblet 7. chalice
    divination by.. 9. oenomancy
    dry.. 3. sec
    film.. 8. beeswing
    French.. 6. Masden, Pontac (Pontacq)
    8. muscatel 9. Hermitage
    10. Montrachet 12. Saint–Emilion,
    Saint–Estèphe
    glass.. 6. rummer (Rom)
    grower.. 8. vigneron
    hater of.. 11. oenophobist
    Italian.. 7. Orvieto 8. muscatel
    kind.. 4. port 5. Medoc, Rhine, tinta,
    Tokay 6. canary, claret, Malaga,
    sherry 7. Chablis, Madeira
    8. Burgundy, muscatel, sauterne,
    vermouth 9. champagne
    lover of.. 11. oenophilist
    maker.. 6. abkari (abkary)
    making.. 10. oenopoetic
    merchant.. 5. abkar
    miracle scene.. 4. Cana (Bib)
    palm.. 5. taree
    Persian.. 6. Shiraz
    pitcher.. 4. olpe 8. oenochoe
    reference to.. 5. vinic
    residue.. 4. marc
    sherry.. 5. Xeres 7. Catawba, Moselle,
    oloroso

shop.. 3. bar 6. bistro, bodega
    Spain.. 6. Malaga
    sparkling.. 8. mousseux
    study of.. 8. oenology
    sweet.. 5. lunel
    taster.. 10. oenologist
    Tuscan.. 7. Chianti
    white.. 6. Malaga 8. Riesling,
    sauterne, verdelho 12. Marcobrunner
    year.. 7. vintage
wing... 3. ala, arm, fly 6. convey,
    flight, member, pinion 7. faction
    8. addition, dispatch
wing (pert to)...
    anterior.. 7. elytron
    comb form.. 7. pterygo
    false.. 5. alula
    fish.. 8. sea robin
    footed.. 6. aliped
    Greek.. 6. pteryx
    quill.. 7. remiges
    shaped.. 7. aliform
    tip.. 7. aileron
    winglike.. 4. alar 7. pteroid
    9. pterygoid
winged... 4. aile (Her), fast 5. alate,
    lofty, rapid, swift 7. pennate, sublime
    9. aliferous, aligerous
winged (pert to)...
    boots (of Hermes).. 7. talaria
    child.. 6. cherub
    fruit.. 6. samara
    monster.. 5. harpy
Winged Horse (Gr Myth)... 7. Pegasus
Winged Victory... 4. Nike
wingless... 7. apteral, Apteryx, exalate
    8. dealated (dealate)
wink... 3. nap, nod 4. hint 5. blink,
    flash 6. glance, signal, twitch
    7. flicker, instant, nictate, twinkle
    9. nictation, nictitate, twinkling
    10. palpebrate, periwinkle
winker... 3. eye 7. blinker, eyelash
    8. blinkard
winking... 13. blepharospasm
winks, forty... 3. nap 6. catnap
    10. light sleep
winner... 3. ace 6. earner, reaper,
    victor 7. sleeper 8. bangster
    9. conqueror 11. breadwinner
winning... 7. gaining, lovable, victory,
    winsome 8. alluring, charming
    10. attractive, successful, victorious
    11. acquisition, captivating
winninish, winnonish... 6. salmon
    (landlocked) 10. ouananiche
winnock... 6. window
winnow... 3. fan 4. sift, stir 6. assort,
    select, thresh 8. disperse, separate
    9. eliminate
winsome... 3. gay 5. bonny, merry
    7. lovable, winning 8. alluring,
    charming, cheerful, pleasant
    10. attractive 11. captivating
    12. lighthearted
winter... 4. bise, snow 5. hiems
    6. old age, season 8. coldness
winter (pert to)...
    beer.. 6. Schenk
    berry.. 4. Ilex 5. holly
    bloom.. 6. azalea 10. witch hazel
    bonnet.. 4. gull

duck.. 7. pintail 8. old squaw
fever.. 9. pneumonia
god.. 5. Hiems
lettuce.. 6. endive
mew.. 4. gull
pert to.. 6. brumal, hiemal
quarters.. 10. hibernacle
   12. hibernaculum
sleep.. 11. hibernation
teal.. 9. greenwing
Winter Palace (Leningrad)...
   6. museum
wipe... 3. dry, mop, rub 5. cheat,
   clean, erase 6. cancel, remove
   7. abolish, defraud 10. obliterate
   11. exterminate
wire... 4. coil, cord, line, whip
   5. cable, snare 6. thread 7. fencing,
   lametta (gold), netting, reticle
   8. telegram, wirework 9. cablegram,
   telegraph 10. pickpocket 14. knitting
   needle
wirepuller... 10. influencer, machinator,
   politician, strategist
wiry... 4. lean 5. hardy, stiff, tough
   6. sinewy, strong 7. stringy
   8. enduring, muscular
wis... 5. think 7. imagine, suppose
Wisconsin...
capital.. 7. Madison
city.. 7. Racine 8. Kenosha, Oshkosh
   8. Green Bay 9. Fond du Lac,
   Milwaukee
famed as.. 17. America's Dairyland
first white man.. 7. Nicolet (Jean)
lake.. 8. Michigan, Superior
   9. Winnebago
river.. 7. St Croix 11. Mississippi
State admission.. 9. Thirtieth
State motto.. 7. Forward
State nickname.. 6. Badger
wisdom... 5. logos 6. judgment,
   learning, sagacity, sapience
   9. erudition, knowledge
   10. discretion, profundity
wisdom god... 4. Nebo (Nabu)
   6. Ganesa (Ganesha)
wisdom goddess... 6. Athena
   7. Minerva (Gr)
wise... 3. hep 4. sage, sane, wary
   5. aware 6. shrewd, subtle, versed
   7. erudite, knowing, learned, politic,
   sapient 8. discreet, informed,
   profound 9. cognizant, expedient,
   judicious, provident 10. omniscient
   11. circumspect, enlightened,
   philosophic 13. sophisticated
wise (pert to)...
councilor.. 6. mentor, nestor
man.. 4. sage 5. solon, witan
   6. nestor, wizard 7. Solomon
saying.. 4. rede 5. adage
Wise Men (three)... 6. Gaspar
   8. Melchior 9. Balthasar
Wise Men of Greece... 5. Seven
Wise Men of the East... 19. Three
   Kings of Cologne
wish... 4. care, hope, will, wuss
   5. yearn 6. aspire, desire, invoke
   7. longing, request 8. optative,
   petition 10. aspiration
   11. imprecation

wishbone... 7. furcula 8. furculum
   10. fourchette 12. merry thought
wisp... 4. floc 5. brush, flock, shred
   6. bundle 7. handful 8. fragment
wistful... 7. longing, pensive
   8. desirous, yearning 9. nostalgic
   10. melancholy
wit... 3. pun, wag 5. humor, sense
   6. acumen, esprit, satire, wisdom
   7. punster 8. comedian, humorist,
   repartee 9. alertness 11. philosopher,
   savoir-faire 12. intelligence
   13. understanding
wit (to)... 3. viz 5. truly 6. indeed,
   namely, that is 8. scilicet 9. videlicet
witch... 3. hag, hex 4. baba 5. Circe,
   crone, lamia, shrew, vixen
   6. cummer, Hecate (Hekate), Lilith
   (Lilis), wizard 7. warlock 8. old
   woman 9. grimalkin, sorceress
   11. witch doctor 12. ugly old
   woman
witchcraft... 5. charm, magic, wanga
   7. cunning, hexerei, sorcery
   8. brujeria 9. sortilege, voodooism
   10. bewitchery, black magic
   11. enchantment 12. invultuation
witch doctor... 3. hex 6. shaman
   9. voodooist, wangateur
witchery... 5. charm, spell 7. sorcery
   8. wizardry 10. allurement,
   necromancy 11. enchantment,
   fascination
with (pref)... 2. co 3. com, con, cum,
   mit, syn 4. avec
with... 5. among 7. jointly 8. together
   9. alongside, including 10. hand in
   hand 11. association
   12. concurrently 13. co-operatively
withal... 5. still 9. thereupon 10. for
   all that
withdraw... 4. absent, deduct, recall,
   recant, recede, remove, repeal, retire,
   secede 7. abandon, detract, disavow,
   forsake, refrain, regress, retract,
   retreat, subside 8. alienate, evacuate,
   renounce 9. disengage 10. relinquish
withdrawal... 6. repeal 7. regress,
   retiral, retreat 8. escapism
   9. departure, recession, seclusion
   10. detachment, extraction,
   retraction, separation
   11. abandonment, recantation,
   resignation
withdrawn... 7. ingrown 8. detached,
   secluded
withe... 4. band, rope 5. snare
   6. halter, wattle, willow
wither... 3. age, die, dry 4. fade,
   sear, sere, wilt 5. decay, droop, dry
   up, wizen 6. blight, shrink 7. shrivel,
   wrinkle 8. languish 11. deteriorate
withered... 4. sere 8. shrunken
   9. shriveled
withering... 7. caustic 9. shrinking
   10. marcescent 12. contemptuous
   13. deteriorating
withhold... 4. curb, deny 5. check
   6. detain, refuse, retain 7. abstain,
   prevent, refrain, repress, reserve
   8. hold back, postpone, restrain
within... 6. at home, during, inside

7. indoors 8. inside of, inwardly
9. inner side
without... 4. sans, sine 5. minus
6. beyond, except, lack of, unless
7. lacking, not with 9. absence of,
outwardly 10. externally, out–of–doors
without (pert to)... see also *absence of*
action.. 8. deedless
animation.. 5. amort
appointment (of day).. 7. sine die
beginning, or end.. 7. eternal
cause.. 10. unprovoked
connections.. 7. tieless
delay.. 9. summarily
doubt.. 9. sine dubio
ethics.. 6. amoral
exception.. 11. universally
feet.. 8. apod 9. apodal
foliage.. 8. aphylous
friends.. 4. lorn 7. forlorn 8. forsaken
knowledge.. 8. ignorant
mate.. 3. odd
prefix.. 4. ecto
rule.. 8. anarchic
substance.. 5. inane
support.. 7. legless 9. dependent
teeth.. 8. edentate 9. toothless
this.. 7. sine hoc
warning.. 12. out of the blue
wings.. 7. apteral
withstand... 4. bear, bide, defy, last
5. abide 6. endure, oppose, resist
8. confront 10. contradict
witless... 3. mad 5. crazy, dazed
6. stupid 7. foolish, unaware
8. heedless 9. brainless, unknowing
10. indiscreet 13. unintelligent
witness... 3. eye, see 4. know
5. swear, teste, vouch 6. attend,
attest, beheld, behold, testor
7. observe, testify 8. beholder,
deponent, evidence, observer,
onlooker 9. informant, spectator,
subscribe, testimony 11. attestation
witticism... 3. mot, pun 4. jest, joke,
quip 5. droll, sally, slent 8. repartee
9. wisecrack 10. pleasantry
11. gauloiserie, witty saying
wittingly... 8. by design 9. knowingly
13. intentionally
witty... 4. wise 5. comic, droll, sharp
6. clever, facete, jocose, jocund
7. amusing, comical, jocular, knowing
8. humorous 9. facetious, whimsical
wivern, wyvern (Her)... 6. dragon
(2–legged)
wizard... 4. mage, sage 6. expert,
genius, Merlin, pellar, shaman
7. magical, prodigy 8. conjurer,
magician, sorcerer 10. Wizard of Oz
11. necromancer, thaumaturge, witch
doctor 13. thaumaturgist
Wizard of the North... 14. Sir Walter
Scott
wizen... 3. age, dry 4. thin 6. gullet,
shrink, weazen, wither 7. shrivel
8. windpipe 11. deteriorate
wlo (obs)... 3. hem 6. fringe
woad... 3. dye 4. herb 5. tinge
8. dyestuff 10. pastel blue
wobble, wabble... 4. walk 5. shake,

waver 7. stagger, tremble
8. hobbling 9. fluctuate, oscillate,
vacillate
Woden, Wodan (Myth)... 3. god
(chief) 4. Odin 9. Wednesday (named
for Woden)
woe... 4. bale, bane 5. grief
6. misery, sorrow 7. anguish, trouble
8. anathema, calamity 10. affliction,
melancholy, misfortune
woebegone... 3. sad 6. woeful
7. unhappy 8. dejected, desolate
10. dispirited, melancholy
woeful... 3. sad 6. paltry 7. direful,
pitiful 8. grievous, mournful, wretched
9. afflicted, miserable, sorrowful,
woebegone 10. deplorable
12. disconsolate
wold... 3. lea 4. wood 5. downs,
plain, weald 6. forest, meadow
7. low hill
wolf... 4. lobo 5. lupus 6. coyote,
mammal 7. Isegrim 8. werewolf
9. libertine 11. philanderer
wolf fish... 6. blenny
wolfhound... 6. borzoi
wolflike... 6. lupine, thooid
wolverine... 4. Gulo 11. Michigander,
Michiganite
Wolverine State... 8. Michigan
woman... 4. dame, girl, lady, rani, wife
5. adult, begum, gentry, madam,
squaw 6. female 7. distaff
8. feminine, paramour, senorita
9. weaker sex, womankind
10. sweetheart
woman (pert to)...
adviser.. 6. Egeria (Rom Myth)
apartment of.. 3. oda (harem)
8. thalamus
beautiful.. 4. doll 5. filly, pin–up,
siren, sylph, Venus 7. charmer,
Zenobia 8. Musidora
bewitching.. 4. peri 5. siren, vixen
7. charmer
celibate.. 7. agapeta
chaser.. 9. libertine 11. philanderer
club (of women).. 7. sorosis
8. sorority
comb form.. 3. gyn
dignified, elderly.. 7. dowager
dowdy.. 5. frump 6. untidy 8. slattern
gossipy.. 3. cat 15. flibbertigibbet
graceful.. 5. sylph 7. slender
gypsy.. 5. romni
hater.. 10. misogynist
hatred of.. 8. misogyny
kept.. 8. mistress 9. concubine
12. demimondaine
killer.. 8. femicide
learned.. 12. bluestocking
loose.. 4. drab 5. whore 6. harlot
7. trollop 9. prostitute
12. streetwalker
lover of.. 11. philogynist
modest (affectedly).. 5. prude
mythical (ugly).. 6. Gorgon
noisy.. 9. termagant
of rank.. 4. dame
old.. 5. crone, frump 6. granny
7. carline, dowager 8. grandame
9. cailleach

ruler.. 9. matriarch
scolding.. 5. shrew 6. virago
socialite.. 3. deb 6. subdeb
  9. debutante 13. fashion leader
stately.. 4. lady 6. matron
suffragist.. 8. feminist
vixenish.. 5. shrew 6. virago
  8. harridan
weeping.. 5. Niobe
will maker.. 9. testatrix
young, unmarried.. 4. lass 6. damsel
  8. spinster 10. demoiselle
womanhood... 4. Emer 10. femininity
woman's property (free)...
  10. parapherna
wonder... 3. awe 6. marvel, rarity
  7. miracle, prodigy 8. surprise
  9. amazement 10. admiration,
  wonderment 12. astonishment
wonderful... 6. superb, unique
  7. amazing, corking, mirific, strange
  8. wondrous 9. admirable,
  marvelous, mirifical 10. remarkable,
  surprising 11. astonishing
  13. extraordinary
wont... 3. use 5. habit, usage
  6. custom
woo... 3. sue 6. invite 7. beseech,
  entreat, solicit
wood... 4. tree 5. xylon 6. lignum,
  lumber, timber 8. firewood
wood (pert to)...
  aromatic.. 5. aloes, cedar 8. agalloch
  ash.. 6. potash
  black.. 5. ebony
  block.. 3. nog 4. dook
  boring (of insects).. 8. xylotomy
  bundles.. 6. fagots
  carving.. 10. xyloglyphy
  clearing.. 5. glade
  color.. 7. biscuit
  comb form.. 4. hylo, xylo 5. ligni,
  ligno, xylon
  core.. 3. ame
  curved strip.. 5. stave
  dealer.. 10. xylopolist
  deity.. 3. Pan 4. faun 5. Diana, Satyr
  7. Silenus 8. Silvanus
  eating.. 11. xylophagous
  goddess.. 5. Diana
  growing on.. 6. fungus
  11. xylophilous
  growth.. 7. boscage, coppice, thicket
  hard.. 3. ash, elm 4. rate, teak
  5. ebony, maple 6. walnut
  8. mahogany
  inlay.. 9. marquetry
  nymph.. 4. moth 5. dryad
  overlay.. 6. veneer
  resembling.. 6. xyloid
  stork.. 4. ibis
  strip.. 4. lath, slat 5. sprag, stave
  6. batten
  touch.. 4. punk 5. spunk (sponk)
  9. touchwood
  tough, elastic.. 3. ash
  tract.. 5. grove 6. forest
woodchuck... 6. marmot 9. ground
  hog
Woodchuck Day... 9. Candlemas
woodcock... 5. pewee 6. peewee,
  shrups 10. woodpecker

wooden (pert to)...
  container.. 3. box 4. case 6. barrel
  horse.. 6. Trojan
  Indian.. 15. cigar-store brave
  joint.. 5. tenon
  made of.. 5. treen
  pert to.. 4. dull 6. clumsy, stolid,
  stupid 8. lifeless 14. expressionless
  pin.. 3. fid, nog, peg 5. dowel, spile
  pole.. 4. palo
  shoe.. 5. sabot 6. patten
  stand.. 5. criss
  tub.. 3. soe
woodpecker... 4. chab 5. Picus
  6. yaffle, yukkel (yuckle) 7. flicker,
  wryneck 8. hickwall 9. sapsucker
  10. carpintero, pickerwood
  11. woodknacker
woods (pert to)...
  inhabiting.. 7. nemoral
  lover of.. 11. nemophilist
  pert to.. 6. sylvan (silvan)
  10. sylvestral
  sacred (grove).. 10. Nemorensis
woodwind... 4. oboe 5. flute
  7. bassoon, piccolo 8. clarinet
  9. saxophone
woody... 6. sylvan, xyloid 8. ligneous
woof... 3. abb 4. weft 6. fabric
  7. filling, texture
wool... 3. fur 4. down, hair 5. cloth,
  llama, sheep 6. fleece 8. barragan
  (barragon)
wool (pert to)...
  card.. 3. tum 4. comb 5. tease
  clean.. 7. garnett
  cloth.. 5. serge, tweed, yerga
  6. angora, duffel, kersey, satara,
  tartan, tricot, vicuña 7. doeskin,
  flannel, ratteen 8. cashmere
  10. broadcloth
  comb form.. 4. lani
  dead sheep's.. 8. mortling
  dryer.. 5. fugal
  fat.. 7. lanolin (lanoline)
  fatty substance.. 5. suint
  garment.. 6. alpaca, linder
  implement.. 6. carder, shears, teaser
  7. distaff, spindle
  inferior, dirty.. 7. cleamer
  kind.. 6. alpaca, angora, merino
  8. picklock
  leg.. 4. gare
  reclaimed.. 5. mungo 6. shoddy
  reference to.. 5. wooly 6. lanate,
  lanose 10. flocculent
  spun.. 4. yarn
  tuft.. 8. floccule 9. flocculus
  undyed, natural.. 5. beige
  waste.. 3. fud 4. noil
  yarn.. 3. abb 7. eis wool
wooly (woolly)... 5. downy, fuzzy
  6. fleecy, lanate 7. blurred
  8. confused, floccose, peronate
word... 4. news, oath 5. adage,
  maxim, parol 6. avowal, remark,
  report 7. command, dispute,
  message, promise, tidings, vocable
  8. acrostic, password 9. discourse,
  statement 11. declaration, information
  13. communication
word, words (pert to)...

action.. 4. verb
battle of.. 9. logomachy
blindness.. 6. alexia
book.. 6. Gradus 7. lexicon, speller
    8. glossary 9. thesaurus
    10. dictionary
contraction.. 9. haplology
deletion at end.. 7. apocope
derivation.. 6. etymon 9. etymology
distinguishing (Bib).. 10. shibboleth
divine.. 5. Logos
excessive interest.. 10. verbomania
figurative use.. 5. trope
figure of speech.. 7. metonym,
    paronym
first on walls (Bib).. 21. mene, mene,
    tekel, upharsin
for word.. 8. verbatim 9. literally
hard to pronounce.. 10. jawbreaker
imitating natural sounds..
    9. onomatope 12. onomatopoeia
inventor of.. 6. coiner 9. neologist
last syllable.. 6. ultima
last syllable but one.. 6. penult
last syllable omitted.. 7. apocope
law.. 7. by parol 11. word of mouth
legislator.. 9. logogogue
letter.. 8. logogram 9. logograph
    11. grammalogue
longest in dictionary..
    28. antidisestablishmentarianism
loss from middle.. 7. syncope
magical.. 6. sesame
meaning.. 9. semantics
misuse.. 11. catachresis, heterophemy,
    malapropism
mysterious (Bib).. 5. selah
new.. 9. neologism
new usage.. 7. neology
of different name for same thing..
    9. heteronym
of honor.. 6. parole 7. promise
of opposite meaning.. 7. antonym
of same derivation.. 7. paronym
of same meaning.. 7. synonym
of same sound.. 7. homonym
of imitation.. 8. echoic 9. onomatope
    12. onomatopoeia
pretentious use.. 10. lexiphanic
puzzle.. 5. rebus 7. anagram
    8. acrostic 9. crossword
repetition.. 7. ploce
root.. 6. etymon
same back to front.. 10. palindrome
science.. 10. lexicology
scrambled.. 7. anagram
song hits.. 6. lyrics
substitution.. 5. trope 7. metonym
theory.. 6. bowwow 8. pooh–pooh
The Word (Bib).. 5. Logos
unnecessary use.. 8. pleonasm
with loss of vowel at beginning..
    7. aphasia 10. aphaeresis (apheresis)
without vowels.. 6. rhythm, syzygy
with vowels (all).. 7. eulogia, miaoued,
    sequoia 12. ambidextrous
with vowels in sequence.. 8. caesious
wordiness... 8. pleonasm, verbiage
    9. prolixity, verbacity 10. redundance
wording... 8. phrasing 10. expression
wordless... 5. tacit 6. silent

wordy... 6. prolix 7. verbose
    9. garrulous 10. long–winded
    12. long–drawn–out
work... 3. job, mix 4. book, deed,
    duty, make, opus, plan, task, to–do,
    toil 5. chore, ergon, labor, solve,
    trade 6. action, Arbeit, create, effect,
    effort 7. ferment, operate, perform,
    product, travail 8. business, drudgery,
    endeavor, function, industry, struggle
    10. accomplish, employment,
    management, occupation, profession
    11. achievement, performance,
    undertaking
work (pert to)...
agreement.. 4. code, pact 8. contract
aversion to.. 10. ergophobia
bag.. 8. reticule
carelessly.. 5. scamp
clothes.. 8. overalls 9. coveralls,
    dungarees
comb form.. 3. erg 4. ergo
disposed to.. 7. ergasia
divine.. 7. miracle, theurgy 9. occult
    art
hard.. 3. peg, tew 4. char, moil,
    plug, toil 5. labor, sweat 6. drudge
    7. travail 9. lucubrate 18. burn the
    midnight oil
hate of.. 10. ergophobia
horse.. 2. ox 4. mule 5. burro
household.. 4. char 5. chare
incomplete art.. 7. ébauche
inlay.. 6. mosaic, niello
lover of.. 9. ergophile
measure of.. 9. ergometer
of excellence.. 7. classic
out.. 5. solve 7. arrange, develop
    9. calculate
over.. 6. recast, rehash, revamp
    9. brainwash, influence
shift.. 5. swing 9. graveyard,
    moonlight
slowly.. 6. potter, putter 7. ca'canny
study of.. 8. ergology
together.. 4. team 9. cooperate
    11. collaborate
unit of.. 3. erg 5. ergon, joule
up.. 4. plan 5. rouse 6. excite, incite
    7. advance, agitate, develop
    10. manipulate
workable... 6. pliant 7. operant
    8. feasible, operable, solvable
    9. practical 11. practicable
worker... 5. diver, mason, miner
    6. barman, cooper, slater, smithy,
    tanner, warper, wright 7. analyst,
    cobbler, glazier, plumber, riveter,
    sandhog, servant, spinner
    8. honeybee, mechanic, strapper
    9. carpenter, clinician, machinist,
    stevedore 11. breadwinner
worker (pert to)...
fellow.. 5. buddy 8. confrere
group.. 4. crew, gang, team
    5. corps, staff 9. personnel
hard.. 6. beaver, drudge, fagger
head.. 4. boss 7. foreman
    8. employer, overseer
    14. superintendent
indifferent.. 4. scab 11. scissorbill
migrant.. 4. hobo 6. boomer

7. floater, wetback

workhouse... 6. prison 9. almshouse, poorhouse

workman... 4. peon 6. coolie, earner 7. artisan, laborer 8. operator, opificer 9. artificer, craftsman, performer

workshop... 3. lab 4. mill 5. plant 6. studio 7. atelier, factory 10. laboratory 11. ergasterion

world... 5. globe, realm 6. cosmos, domain 7. kingdom, society 8. creation, humanity, universe 9. multitude, the public

world (pert to)...
external.. 6. nonego
great.. 9. macrocosm
lower.. 5. Hades, Orcus
miniature.. 9. microcosm
of fairies.. 6. faerie (faery)
precreation.. 10. premundane 11. antemundane
reference to.. 7. mundane 11. terrestrial

worldly... 7. earthly, mundane, secular, terrene 11. terrestrial 13. materialistic, sophisticated

world's oldest city, still inhabited... 8. Damascus

world's speech... 7. Volapuk 9. universal

worm... 3. ess 4. coil, grub, wind 5. borer, tinea 6. blight, insect, maggot, vermin, wretch 8. helminth 9. trematode, vermicule 10. Nemertinea (Nemertina)

worm (pert to)...
Africa.. 3. loa 6. Guinea
aquatic, marine.. 7. eunicid, lugworm 8. flatworm 9. planarian 13. platyhelminth
arrow.. 7. sagitta
bait.. 9. angleworm, earthworm
bloodsucking.. 5. leech
caddie.. 5. cadew
cotton.. 8. bollworm 10. boll weevil
edible.. 6. palolo
eye–infecting.. 3. loa
genus.. 6. Virmes 7. Ascaris, Filaria 8. Annelida 10. Nemertinea (Nemertina)
grublike.. 5. larva
killer.. 9. vermicide
larva.. 4. army, slug 5. cadew 6. caddis, looper 8. wireworm 11. caterpillar
luminous.. 8. glowworm
marine.. 7. eunicid
measuring.. 6. looper 8. inchworm
parasitic.. 7. Ascaris, Filaria 8. trichina, woodworm 9. trematode 10. Guinea worm 12. enthelmintha
ref to.. 8. annelid 9. nemertean, nemertine, nemertoid, trematoid
ring.. 5. tinea 7. annelid
round.. 7. ascarid, Ascaris
segmented.. 8. Annelida
ship.. 5. borer 6. teredo
silk.. 4. eria
soft.. 4. grub
study of.. 10. vermeology 13. helminthology

tape.. 6. taenia
track.. 7. nereite 11. helminthite
wire.. 4. lava 9. millepede

worm (type)... 3. cut, dew, lug, pin 4. army, boll, eria, flat, glow, inch, ring, ship, silk, slug, tape, wire, wood 5. angle, earth, larva, leech, round, tinea 6. marine 9. measuring, parasitic

wormlike... 7. vermian 11. helminthoid

wormy... 6. earthy, humble, rotten 8. crawling 9. groveling

worn... 3. old 4. sere, used 5. stale, trite 7. abraded, haggard 8. attrited, tattered, weakened 9. exhausted, hackneyed 10. secondhand 11. commonplace

worn–out... 4. used 5. jaded, passé, seedy, spent, trite 6. shabby, used up 7. haggard 8. consumed, fatigued, impaired, tired out 9. enfeebled, exhausted 10. threadbare

worried... 5. cared, fazed 6. stewed 7. annoyed, anxious, fearful, fretted 8. troubled 9. perturbed

worry... 3. nag, rux, vex 4. care, cark, faze, fret, stew 5. annoy, brood, harry 6. bother, harass, pester, plague, pother 7. anxiety, bedevil, concern, perturb, torment, trouble 8. distress 9. annoyance 10. harassment, uneasiness

worship... 5. adore, honor, serve 6. bhakti, homage, revere 7. idolize, liturgy, respect 8. blessing, devotion, idolatry, venerate 9. adoration, deference, reverence 10. veneration

worship (pert to)...
form of.. 6. preces, ritual 7. liturgy
house of.. 6. chapel, church, mosque, shrine 9. cathedral, synagogue 10. tabernacle
object of.. 4. icon, idol 5. totem 6. fetish
place of.. 5. altar
system of.. 4. cult 6. cultus, fetish, ritual 8. doctrine

worshiper... 6. adorer, bhakti, votary 8. disciple, idolater 10. ignicolist 12. iconomachist

worshipful... 6. devout 7. notable 8. esteemed 9. honorable, venerable 13. distinguished

worship of...
a god.. 9. theolatry
angels.. 5. dulia
genii.. 10. geniolatry
god.. 6. latria (RCCh)
idols.. 8. idolatry
images.. 10. iconolatry
nature.. 11. physiolatry
one god.. 9. monolatry
snakes.. 10. ophiolatry
soul.. 7. animism
sun.. 10. heliolatry
the mob.. 9. mobolatry

worst... 3. bad 4. beat, evil 6. defeat, wicked 7. harmful 8. inferior 10. calamitous, pernicious, unpleasant 12. disagreeable

worsted... 4. yarn 6. crewel

7. genappe

worth... 5. merit, price, value
6. desert, repute, riches, stiver,
wealth 8. eminence, meriting,
property 9. deserving 10. excellence,
importance, usefulness

worthless... 3. bad, ort 4. base, evil,
mean, raca (Bib), vile 6. futile,
nought (naught), paltry 7. fustian,
useless 8. nugatory, rubbishy,
unworthy 9. valueless
11. undeserving
14. good–for–nothing

worthwhile... 6. useful 7. gainful
9. expedient, well–spent
10. invaluable, profitable

worthy... 3. fit 7. merited 8. eligible,
valuable 9. celebrity, competent,
deserving, estimable, excellent,
honorable, qualified, reputable
11. meritorious

worthy of... 8. credible, meriting
9. deserving 10. entitled to

wound... 3. cut 4. gore, harm, hurt,
pain, rist, scar, sore, stab 5. sting
6. breach, damage, grieve, injury,
lesion, offend, trauma 8. distress
9. detriment

wound (pert to)...
  discharge.. 5. ichor 6. sanies
  dressing.. 7. bandage, pledget
  mark.. 4. scab, scar, welt 7. blister

woven... 3. spun 10. fabricated

wow... 4. howl, rave, wail 5. whine

wrack... 4. kelp, rack, ruin 5. tease,
trash, weeds, wreck 6. refuse
7. seaweed 8. eelgrass, wreckage
9. shipwreck 11. destruction

wraith... 4. food 5. ghost, spook
8. illusion 10. apparition
12. Doppelgänger, doubleganger

wrangle... 4. herd, spar 5. argue,
brawl 6. bicker, debate 7. contend,
dispute, quarrel 8. haggling
9. altercate, bickering 11. altercation,
controversy 12. disagreement

wrangler... 6. cowboy 7. debater,
student (Cambridge, Eng)
8. herdsman, opponent
9. combatant, disputant
10. antagonist

wrangling... 11. belligerent,
contentious

wrap... 3. rug 4. cape, cere, furl, roll,
wind 5. cloak, gange 6. afghan,
encowl, enfold, swathe 7. blanket,
conceal, package 8. covering,
enshroud, enswathe, envelope
9. encompass

wrapped up... 7. bound up, selfish
8. absorbed, included, involved
9. dependent, devoted to, engrossed
11. inseparable

wrapper... 4. gown 5. cerer 6. fardel,
kimono, tillot 7. garment, pelisse
8. envelope, peignoir

wrapping... 6. charta 7. wrapper
8. cerement, covering 9. parchment

wrasse... 4. fish 6. ballan, cunner,
Labrus 7. seawife 11. peacock fish

wrath... 3. ire 4. fury, grim, rage
5. anger 6. choler 7. passion

8. violence 10. turbulence
11. indignation 12. exasperation

wrathful... 3. mad 5. angry, irate
6. ireful, raging 7. angered
8. incensed 9. indignant, malignant
10. passionate

wreak... 4. do to 6. avenge 7. gratify,
indulge, inflict 13. bring down upon

wreath... 3. lei 4. band, orle
5. crown, torse (Her), whorl
6. anadem, circle, corona, laurel,
trophy 7. coronet, festoon, garland,
Iresine 8. encircle

wreathe... 4. coil, wind 5. crown,
twine, twist 6. entwine 8. decorate,
encircle 9. interlace 10. twist about

wreck... 4. raze, ruin, undo 5. crash,
smash 6. jalopy 7. destroy, disable
8. accident, demolish, derelict
9. shipwreck 10. broken form
11. disassemble, The Hesperus

wreckage... 5. ruins 6. jetsam
7. flotsam 8. driftage

wrench... 4. jerk, pipe, pull, tear
5. twist, wrest 6. sprain, twinge
7. distort 8. crescent, distress

wrench, type of... 3. box, pin
5. wramp 6. monkey 7. spanner
8. carriage, Stillson 9. alligator

wrest... 4. rend, turn 5. exact, force,
seize, twist, wring 6. elicit, extort,
wrench 7. distort, extract, pervert,
wrestle 8. misapply

wrestle... 3. tug 6. squirm, tussle
7. contend, grapple, scuffle, wriggle
8. struggle 9. throw down 10. twist
about 11. come to grips

wrestling school... 9. palaestra
(palestra)

wretch... 3. dog 5. miser, ronin
6. outlaw, pariah 7. caitiff, cullion,
outcast 8. derelict, sufferer
9. miscreant 10. base person
11. offscouring, rapscallion
14. good–for–nothing 16. pitiable
creature

wretched... 3. sad 4. base, mean
6. dismal, paltry, woeful 7. baleful,
forlorn, squalid, unhappy, very bad
8. grievous 9. execrable, miserable
10. despicable, distressed
12. contemptible, disreputable

wretchedness... 6. misery 8. distress,
meanness, poorness 10. paltriness
11. unhappiness 13. penuriousness

wriggle... 5. twist 6. squirm, writhe
7. meander

wriggle out of... 4. turn, wind
5. dodge, snake, twist 6. squirm,
writhe 8. slip away 10. crawl out of
11. squirm out of 13. find a
loophole

wring... 5. twist, wrest 6. extort,
wrench 7. extract, torture, wrestle
8. compress, convolve 9. cause pain
10. contortion, extraction

wrinkle... 3. fad 4. fold, idea, ruga,
seam 5. crimp, knack, ridge, rivel
6. crease, furrow, pucker, rimple,
ripple, rumple 7. crinkle, novelty
8. contract 9. corrugate
11. corrugation 12. clever notion

wrinkled... 4. aged 5. savoy
6. rugate, rugose, rugous 7. creased
8. crinkled, crumpled, furrowed,
puckered, rugulose 9. shriveled
10. contracted, corrugated

wrinkles... 5. rugae

wrist... 5. joint 6. carpal, carpus
8. os magnum 9. capitatum

writ... 5. breve, tales 6. capias, elegit,
venire 7. process 8. detainer,
document, mittimus, replevin,
subpoena 10. certiorari, instrument
11. fieri facias

writ (pert to)...
common law.. 11. fieri facias
court.. 7. summons 8. subpoena
execution.. 6. elegit
jury.. 5. tales 6. venire
law.. 4. capo, pone 5. breve, error
6. capias, elegit 7. mandate,
process, warrant 8. citation
10. certiorari

write... 3. pen 5. draft, trace
6. decree, depict, draw up, enroll,
indite, record, scrive 7. compose,
scriven 8. inscribe, scribble
11. communicate

write (pert to)...
carelessly.. 6. scrawl 8. scrabble,
scribble
in large hand.. 7. engross
off.. 4. drop 6. cancel, deduct, repeal
out.. 6. record 8. spill out 12. put in
writing
poetry.. 7. versify
up.. 6. record, report 7. article
9. publicize 11. press report

writer... 4. hack, poet 6. author,
penman, penner, scribe 7. elegist,
glosser, hymnist 8. annalist,
composer, lyricist, novelist, parodist,
scriptor 9. annotator, columnist,
scrivener 10. chronicler, journalist
13. correspondent

writer's afterthoughts... 7. addenda

writhe... 4. bend, coil, curl, wind
5. twist, wring 6. squirm 7. contort,
distort, wriggle

writing... 4. book, poem 6. script
7. article, epistle 8. covenant,
document, makimono 10. expression,
penmanship, profession
11. chirography, composition,
handwriting, inscription, publication

writing (pert to)...
alternate.. 13. boustrophedon
ancient characters.. 9. cuneiform
ancient manuscript.. 6. uncial
cipher.. 12. cryptography
instrument.. 3. pen 5. quill 6. stylus
italic.. 7. cursive
mania for.. 11. graphomania
material.. 3. pad 5. paper, slate
6. tablet 9. parchment 10. stationery
omission of a letter.. 8. lipogram
10. lipography
pert to.. 7. scribal
record.. 3. log 5. album, diary
script.. 5. ronde
scroll.. 8. makimono
scroll hanging.. 8. kakemono
secret.. 4. code 10. cryptogram

12. cryptography

unrhymed.. 5. prose

writings, sacred... 5. Bible, Koran
6. Psalms, Talmud 9. Testament
(Old, New) 10. Scriptures

written (pert to)...
agreement.. 6. cartel
characters.. 6. script
it is.. 8. it must be 10. in the
books, in the cards 12. the die is
cast
law.. 10. legislated
law, unwritten.. 6. common
memo.. 5. scrip

wrong... 3. bad, off, out, sin 4. awry,
evil, harm, side, tort, vice 5. amiss,
cheat, crime, false, malum, unfit
6. faulty, injure, injury, seduce,
sinful, unjust, wicked 7. defraud,
immoral, misdeed, offense
8. improper, iniquity, mistaken
9. erroneous, incorrect, injustice,
violation 10. inaccurate, iniquitous
11. impropriety, inexpedient,
malfeasance, misfeasance
12. illegitimate

wrong (pert to)...
go (wrong).. 3. err 4. fail 5. lapse
8. go astray, go to ruin 9. backslide
10. misbelieve 11. go to the dogs
in the.. 6. guilty 7. at fault, in error
8. mistaken 9. violation
law.. 4. tort 5. crime, malum
name.. 8. misnomer
nor right (neither).. 7. neutral
11. adiaphorous
prefix.. 3. mis
side of.. 5. shady
way.. 5. amiss 6. astray 10. out of
place

wrongdoer... 6. sinner 8. criminal,
evildoer, violator 10. malefactor,
trespasser 12. transgressor

wroth... 3. mad 5. angry, irate
7. violent, incensed, wrathful
9. turbulent, wrought up
11. exasperated

wrought... 4. made 6. formed,
shaped, worked 9. decorated,
fashioned, processed 10. elaborated,
ornamented 11. embroidered
12. manufactured

wrought up... 4. agog 5. angry, eager
7. excited 9. disturbed, stirred up

wry... 4. awry 6. biased, swerve,
turned 7. crooked, twisted
9. contorted

wryneck... 4. Jynx, weet 5. loxia
9. snakebird 11. torticollis

Württemberg, Germany...
capital.. 9. Stuttgart
city.. 3. Ulm 9. Esslingen, Heilbronn,
Hohenheim
lake.. 9. Constance
river.. 6. Danube, Neckar

Wyandot... 6. Indian (Iroquois)

Wyandotte... 4. cave, city, fowl

Wycliff (Wyclif), John (pert to)...
birthplace.. 9. Yorkshire (Eng)
disciple.. 4. Huss
remains cast into.. 10. Swift River
translator of.. 5. Bible

Wyoming...
capital.. 8. Cheyenne
city.. 4. Cody 6. Casper 7. Big Horn,
   Laramie 8. Cheyenne, Sheridan
historic site.. 11. Fort Laramie
   17. Buffalo Bill Center
mountain.. 6. Tetons 7. Rockies
   11. Gannett Peak
park.. 10. Grand Teton

   11. Yellowstone
river.. 4. Wind 6. Platte 7. Big Horn
river source.. 8. Colorado, Columbia,
   Missouri
State admission.. 11. Forty–fourth
State motto.. 11. Equal Rights
State nickname.. 8. Equality
Woman Suffrage.. 10. first State
   (1869)

X

X... 3. ten 5. error 6. letter (24th),
   symbol
xanthic... 6. cyanic, yellow
Xanthippe, wife of... 8. Socrates
xanthoderm... 17. yellow–skinned race
xanthoma... 9. xanthosis 11. skin
   disease 13. yellow patches
xanthos... 6. yellow 15. unknown
   quantity
Xanthus (pert to)...
ancient site.. 7. marbles (Xanthian)
placed now.. 13. British Museum
xebec... 6. vessel 7. corsair
xen, xeno (comb form)... 7. foreign
   8. stranger
xenium... 4. gift 7. present (official)
Xenocrates (Gr)... 11. philosopher
xenogamy... 18. cross–fertilization
xenomania (*craze for*)... 14. foreign
   customs 15. foreign fashions
Xenophon's historic tale...
   8. Anabasis
xenophthalmia... 11. foreign body
   (eye) 14. conjunctivitis
Xenopus... 5. toads
Xenorhynchus... 6. storks
Xenurus... 7. tatouay 10. armadillos
Xeres... 5. jerez 6. sherry
xero (comb form)... 3. dry
xerophagy, xerophagia... 4 Fast
   (Lenten)
xerotes... 7. dryness (body)
Xerus... 9. squirrels

Xerxes (pert to)...
crossing of.. 10. Hellespont
destroyer of.. 6. Athens (BC)
king of.. 6. Persia
xibalba... 10. underworld 14. abode of
   the dead
Xinca... 6. Indian, Jincan
Xipe, Xipe–totec... 11. god of sowing
Xiphias... 5. comet (sword–shaped)
   6. Dorado (constellation) 9. swordfish
xiphoid... 4. bone 8. ensiform
   9. swordlike 12. xiphisternum
Xiphopagus... 7. monster (twinlike)
Xiphosura... 8. king crab
Xiuhtocutli... 7. fire god (Aztec)
Xmas... 9. Christmas
X–ray (pert to)...
inventor.. 8. Roentgen
measure.. 11. quantimeter
named.. 12. Roentgen rays
xylo, xyl (comb form)... 4. wood
xyloglyphy... 11. wood carving (art)
xylography... 13. wood engraving
xyloid... 5. woody 8. ligneous,
   woodlike
xylomancy, divination by... 4. wood
   10. wood pieces
xylophone... 5. saron 7. gambang,
   marimba 8. gamelang (gamelan),
   gigelira, sticcado
xyrid... 4. iris 5. Xyris
xystus, xyst (Gr)... 7. portico
   9. colonnade

Y

Y... 4. tube 5. curve, track 6. letter
   (25th), prefix, suffix
yabber... 4. talk 6. jabber 8. language
yabby, yabbie... 8. crayfish
yaboa... 10. night heron
yabu, yaboo... 4. pony
yacht... 4. boat, race, sail, ship
   9. raceabout 10. knockabout
yaffle... 6. armful 7. handful

   10. woodpecker
yahoo... 4. lout 7. bumpkin 9. poor
   white
Yahoo (pert to)...
race of.. 6. brutes
represented by.. 10. Houyhnhnms
   (horses of reason)
tale.. 16. Gulliver's Travels
Yahweh, Yahwe... 7. Jehovah (Bib)
yak... 2. ox 6. sarlak (sarlyk)

yakalo, yakattalo... 8. creature
10. crossbreed (yak, cattle)
yakka... 4. work 5. labor
yaksha... 4. ogre 5. demon, dryad,
fairy, gnome, jinni 6. Kubera (Chief),
spirit 7. tree-god 13. guardian angel
Yale (pert to)...
college.. 8. New Haven
color.. 4. blue 7. Rameses
founded at.. 8. Saybrook
founder.. 9. Elihu Yale
graduate.. 9. Yalensian
Yalta Conference... 6. Crimea (1945)
yam (pert to)...
Fiji.. 6. uviyam 8. white yam
Hawaiian.. 3. hoi
reference to.. 5. tuber 6. igname
Scot.. 6. potato
tropical.. 8. cush-cush
US.. 11. sweet potato
yamstchik... 7. postboy 8. coachman
9. postilion
yang... 4. good, male 6. bright (opp
of yin)
yang-kin... 8. dulcimer
yank... 4. jerk, pull 6. Yankee
Yankee... 12. New Englander
Yannigans... 9. scrub team (baseball)
Yao... 6. Indian 9. aborigine
yap... 3. cur, dog, gab 4. bark, talk,
yell, yelp 6. jabber 7. bumpkin,
hoodlum 8. easy mark 9. greenhorn
yapok, yapock... 6. monkey
7. opossum
yapp... 11. bookbinding
yapster... 3. dog
Yaqui... 6. Indian
yard... 3. rae (sail) 4. lawn, spar,
wand 5. garth, stick, verge
6. campus 7. confine, enclose,
measure 9. courtyard, curtilage,
enclosure, yardstick 10. playground
yarn... 3. abb, cop 4. hank, joke, tale
5. fiber, skein, story 6. caddis,
crewel, spinel, thread 7. genappe
9. falsehood
yarn (pert to)...
clew.. 4. ball
holder.. 3. cop
measure.. 4. hank, hasp 5. skein
7. spangle
size.. 6. denier
winder.. 10. yarnwindle
yashiro... 3. sha 6. temple (Shinto)
yashmak... 4. veil (double)
yati... 7. ascetic, devotee
yaw... 4. sail, tack 5. steer, tumor
7. deviate 9. deviation
yawl... 4. boat, howl, wail, yell, yowl
5. ketch 9. jolly boat
yawn... 3. gap 4. gape 5. chasm,
mouth 7. opening, stretch 8. open
wide, oscitate 12. seek greedily
yaws... 9. frambesia
yawweed... 5. shrub 7. rhubarb
12. wild mulberry
Yazoo (pert to)...
Fraud.. 9. land grant (1795)
Indian.. 11. Mississippi
river.. 11. Mississippi
yclept, ycleped.. 5. named 6. called,
styled

year (pert to)...
after year.. 10. constantly, repeatedly
11. over and over
book.. 7. almanac
division of.. 6. season 8. semester
9. trimester
Latin.. 5. annus
of mourning.. 11. annus luctus
of our Lord.. 10. Anno Domini
11. annus Domini, year of grace
of thirteen months (384 days)..
10. embolismic
of travel.. 10. sabbatical, Wanderjahr
14. leave of absence
old (Zool).. 10. annotinous
pert to.. 5. epact
quarter.. 5. raith
record.. 5. annal 8. calendar
yearly (pert to)...
church income.. 7. annates
payment.. 4. cens
recurring.. 6. annual 7. etesian
8. annually
yearn for... 3. yen 4. ache, hope,
itch, long, pine, sigh, wish 6. desire,
hanker
yearning... 3. yen 4. wish 5. eager
7. anxious, longing 9. hankering,
nostalgia 10. tenderness
11. languishing 12. homesickness
years (pert to)...
adolescent.. 4. teen
ago.. 4. ages 9. long since 10. days
of yore, yesteryear
eight.. 9. octennial
fifteen.. 9. indiction
five.. 6. pentad 7. lustrum
hundred.. 9. centenary 10. centennial
ten.. 6. decade 9. decennary
thousand.. 7. chiliad 10. millennium
two.. 8. biennial, biennium
yeast... 4. barm, foam, koji 5. froth
6. leaven 7. anamite, ferment
9. agitation
yeasty... 5. foamy, light, spumy
6. frothy 8. restless 9. frivolous,
leavening
yegg... 5. thief, tramp 6. robber
7. burglar, yeggman 8. criminal
10. safeblower 11. safebreaker,
safecracker
yell... 3. cry 4. howl, roar, wail, yowl
5. cheer, shout 6. outcry, scream,
shriek
yelling... 7. bawling 8. shouting,
strident 9. clamorous 11. full of yells
yellow... 3. dun, sil 4. buff, cuir,
deer, ecru, flax, gull, mean, nude,
yolk 5. amber, beige, color, cream,
grège, jaune, lemon, maize, ocher
(ochre), straw, taupe, topaz, twine
6. bisque, butter, canary, Cassel,
chrome, citron, creamy, flaxen,
golden, mimosa, sallow, Seasan
7. anamite, annatto, aureate, egg
yolk, envious, etiolin, jealous, jonquil,
saffron, sulphur, xanthic, xanthin
8. cowardly, ocherous, primrose,
recreant 9. champagne, dandelion,
flavicant, goldenrod, jaundiced,
lutescent, sunflower 10. flavescent,
melancholy 11. treacherous

yellow (pert to)...
  brown.. 3. dun 5. straw 6. manila
  coloring.. 7. xanthic 8. xanthine
  comb form.. 5. luteo
  dyestuff.. 5. morin 7. annatto
    8. luteolin
  golden.. 2. or (Her) 4. gild, gilt
  green.. 5. olive 8. tarragon
    10. chartreuse, serpentine
  herb.. 3. iva
  jacket.. 4. wasp
  medical.. 7. icterus 8. jaundice
    11. xanthoderma
  mustard.. 8. charlock
  ocher, ochre.. 3. sil
  pert to.. 7. xanthic
  pigment.. 7. etiolin 8. orpiment
  race.. 9. Mongolian
  red.. 4. roan 5. aloma, sandy
    6. bisque, dorado, orange
    7. annatto, nacarat
  sensational.. 5. press 7. journal
yellow fever mosquito... 12. Aëdes
    aegypti
yellowhammer... 4. yite 5. ammer,
    finch, skite 6. gladdy 7. flicker
    10. woodpecker 13. yellow bunting
Yellowhammer State... 7. Alabama
yellow jacket... 4. wasp 8. eucalypt
Yellowstone Park geyser... 11. Old
    Faithful
yelp... 3. cry, yip 4. bark, yell
    5. shout 6. outcry, shriek, squeal
    7. ululate 8. complain 9. criticize
yelper... 8. redshank 10. yellowlegs
    11. hunting call
yeme... 4. heed 5. guard 6. govern,
    regard
Yemen (pert to)...
  archeology site.. 4. Sana 5. Marib
  Bib kingdom.. 5. Sheba (Saba)
  capital.. 4. Sana
  citadel.. 5. Damar
  division of.. 6. Arabia
  plateau.. 7. El Jebel
  port.. 5. Mocha 7. Hodeida, Loheiya
  ruler.. 4. Imam
  sea.. 3. Red
yemochik... see *yamstchik*
yen... 4. coin, urge 5. yearn 6. desire,
    hanker 7. longing
yeoman... 4. exon 5. clerk 6. butler,
    seaman 8. retainer 9. assistant,
    attendant 10. freeholder
    11. subordinate 12. petty officer
yep... 3. yes 4. bold 5. alert, smart
    6. active 8. vigorous
yerba... 4. herb, maté 5. plant
    11. Paraguay tea
yes...
  English.. 3. aye, yea, yep 5. uh–huh
    6. assent 11. affirmation
  French.. 3. oui
  German.. 2. ja
  Italian, Spanish.. 2. si
  Russian.. 2. da
yesterday... 6. yester 7. the past
    10. days gone by, heretofore,
    yesteryear 11. bygone times
yet... 3. but 5. still 6. algate
    7. besides, however 10. eventually

    11. nonetheless 15. notwithstanding
yew... 5. green, Taxus 7. conifer,
    hemlock 9. evergreen
Yiddish... 6. Jewish
    12. Judaeo–German (Judeo–German)
yield... 3. bow, net 4. bear, bend,
    cede, crop, give, lose, obey, vail
    5. admit, allow, defer, grant, stoop,
    waive 6. accede, afford, comply, give
    up, relent, render, reward, soften,
    submit 7. concede, consent,
    produce, provide, requite, revenue,
    succumb 9. acquiesce, surrender
    10. capitulate, relinquish
    11. acknowledge
yielding... 4. meek, soft 6. pliant,
    supple 7. bearing 8. flexible
    9. compliant, deference, producing,
    tractable 10. compliance,
    manageable, submissive
Yigdal... 4. poem (Jew Relig)
yill-caup... 6. ale cup
yin... 4. dark, evil (opp of yang)
Ymir, Ymer (pert to)...
  blood of.. 3. sea
  bones of.. 9. mountains
  brains of.. 7. clouds
  flesh of.. 5. earth
  killed by.. 2. Ve 4. Odin, Vili
  Norse Myth.. 3. God 13. rime–cold
    giant (body–shaped world)
yodel, yodle... 4. call, sing (falsetto)
    5. carol, shout 6. warble
yoga (pert to)...
  follower of.. 4. yogi (yogin) 5. fakir
    7. ascetic 9. occultist
  objective.. 16. mental discipline
  stages.. 5. jnana, karma 6. bhakti
  trance.. 6. dhyana 7. dharana,
    samadhi
yoke... 3. two 4. join, link, pair, span,
    team 5. frame, marry 6. cangue,
    couple, inspan 7. bondage, enclave,
    harness, oppress, pillory, shackle,
    slavery 9. associate, servitude
yoked... 6. united 7. coupled
    9. conjugate
yokel... 3. oaf 4. boor, clod, hick,
    lout, rube 6. rustic 7. bumpkin,
    hayseed, plowboy 8. Abderite (anc),
    gullible 9. simpleton 10. countryman,
    slow–witted
yokemate... 4. mate 6. fellow, spouse
    7. partner 9. companion
yolked (egg)... 6. yellow 8. lecithal,
    vitellus
Yom Kippur (Jew)... 7. fast day
    14. Day of Atonement
Yom Teruah (Jew)... 15. Feast of
    Trumpets
Yom Tob, or Tov (Jew)... 8. festival
yon, yonder... 4. away 6. beyond
    7. distant, thither 11. at a distance
yore... 5. of old, olden 6. before 9. in
    old time, long since
young... 3. fry, new 4. tyro 5. brood,
    fresh, green 6. litter, novice, tender
    7. pliable 8. childish, immature,
    juvenile, youthful 9. offspring,
    succulent 13. inexperienced
young (pert to)...
  bear, fox.. 3. cub

birds.. 5. brood
calf (motherless).. 5. dogie
hare.. 7. leveret
herring.. 4. brit
horse.. 4. colt, foal
oyster.. 4. spat
pigeon.. 5. piper
youngling... 5. youth 6. novice
  8. beginner, neophyte
youngster... 3. boy, kid, lad, pup, tod
  4. baby, lass, tike 5. child, youth
  6. filius, shaver, urchin 7. Aladdin
  (Arab Nights) 8. teenager
  9. fledgling, stripling
younker... 5. child, youth 6. knight
  7. gallant 8. nobleman 9. gentleman,
  stripling
youth goddess... 4. Hebe
yo–yo... 3. top, toy
Ypres, Belgium...
  famed for.. 7. battles (WWI)
  lace.. 12. Valenciennes
  province of.. 8. Flanders
  ruins rebuilt.. 9. Cloth Hall 15. Gothic
  Cathedral (St Martin)
ypsiliform *(shape of)*... 7. letter T (Gr)
yu (Chin)... 4. jade
Yucatan, Cent America...
  anc domain of.. 5. Mayas
  capital.. 6. Mérida
  city.. 5. Sisal
  peninsula of.. 6. Mexico
yucca (pert to)...
  called.. 11. Adam's needle
  family.. 9. Liliaceae
  native of.. 7. America
  species.. 9. bear grass

State flower of.. 9. New Mexico
Yugoslavia...
  capital.. 8. Belgrade
  city.. 5. Senta 7. Skoplje
  leader.. 4. Tito (Communist)
  lead works (among world's largest)..
    6. Trepca
  natives.. 5. Serbs 6. Croats
    8. Slovenes
  river.. 5. Drava, Drina 6. Danube,
    Morava, Vardar
  sea.. 8. Adriatic
  seaport.. 6. Rijeka
yukkel... 7. flicker 10. woodpecker
Yukon...
  famed for.. 4. gold (mining)
  ocean.. 6. Arctic
  river.. 5. Lewes, Yukon
  territory of.. 6. Canada
  town.. 10. Whitehorse
Yule (pert to)...
  ancient.. 9. Christmas
    13. Christmastide 18. Feast of the
    Nativity
  popular use.. 6. poetic
  related to.. 5. holly 8. yuletide
    9. Christmas, mistletoe 11. wassail
    bowl
Yuma (Ariz)... 4. city 9. Tulkepaia
  (Indian)
yun... 9. Laos tribe (tatooed)
Yunca... 6. Indian (Peru)
Yurok... 6. Indian (Calif)
Yurma... 6. Indian (Brazil)
yurt, yurta... 4. tent (Siberia)
Yuruk... 10. Turkish rug
yutu... 7. tinamou
Yuzen birodo... 6. velvet (designed)

Z

Z... 3. end, zed, zee 5. omega
  6. izzard, letter (26th)
zac... 4. ibex
zacate... 7. herbage 9. rice grass
Zacchaeus (Zaccheus)... 4. pure
  8. innocent, publican (Bib)
Zachariah, Zacharias (Bib)...
  father.. 9. Barachias
  father of.. 14. John the Baptist
  literally.. 21. Jehovah hath
    remembered
Zadkiel (Jew)... 5. angel (of planet
  Jupiter)
Zagreus... 3. god 8. Dionysus
  (identified with)
zakuska... 11. hors d'oeuvre
zaman, zamang... 8. rain tree
Zambia, Africa...
  capital.. 6. Lusaka
  former.. 16. Northern Rhodesia
  wealth.. 6. copper (3rd largest)
Zamenhof *(inventor of)*... 9. Esperanto
zampogna... 7. bagpipe, panpipe

zanja... 5. canal, gully 6. arroyo
zany... 3. wag, wit 4. dolt, fool
  5. clown, crazy, nutty 6. madcap,
  sawney 7. acrobat, buffoon, idiotic
  8. clownish 9. simpleton
  10. lieutenant, mountebank
  11. merry–andrew
Zanzibar, now Tanzania...
  attractions (anc).. 7. gardens, palaces
  capital.. 11. Dar es Salaam (Haven of
    Peace)
  nickname.. 12. Isle of Cloves
  population.. 6. Moslem
zapatero... 7. boxwood, cobbler,
  dogwood
zarp... 9. policeman
zati... 6. monkey (bonnet)
zeal... 5. ardor, piety 6. desire, fervor
  7. passion 8. devotion 9. eagerness
  10. enthusiasm, fanaticism
zealot... 4. sect 5. bigot 6. votary
  7. devotee, faddist, fanatic, pietist
  8. partisan 10. enthusiast
zealous... 5. eager, pious 6. ardent,

fervid 7. devoted, fervent
9. phrenetic 11. industrious
zebra (pert to) . . .
  ally.. 6. quagga
  Burchell's.. 4. dauw (nonstriped legs)
  hybrid.. 8. zebrinny
  insect.. 9. butterfly
  ref to.. 7. zebrine, zebroid
zebrawood... 5. shrub 7. araroba
  10. marblewood
zebu... 2. ox 5. zebus (group)
  6. cattle 12. Brahmany bull (sacred)
  13. beast of burden
zecchino... 6. sequin (chequeen)
Zechariah (Bib)... 7. prophet 12. King
  of Israel
zeekoe... 12. hippopotamus
zeism... 8. pellagra 11. morbid state
zemi... 4. holy (Peru) 5. huaca (huaco)
  6. fetish, sacred, spirit (magic)
Zemzem... 10. sacred well (Mecca)
Zen... 12. Buddhist sect
zenana... 5. harem, serai 7. mission
  8. seraglio
Zenda, Prisoner of.. 9. Ruritania
Zend–Avesta... 10. sacred text
  (Zoroastrian)
zenith... 3. top 4. acme, apex, blue,
  peak 6. apogee, climax, summit,
  vertex 11. culmination 14. greatest
  height (opp of nadir)
Zeno... 5. Stoic 11. philosopher (Gr)
zenography (*study of*)... 7. Jupiter
  (planet)
zenu... 5. sheep
zephyr... 5. shawl 6. breath, breeze
zero... 3. nil 4. hour 6. cipher, nought
  (naught) 7. nothing, nullity
  11. temperature
zest... 4. tang 5. gusto, savor
  6. flavor, relish 8. membrane (fruit),
  piquancy, pungency 9. eagerness
  10. enthusiasm
Zeus (pert to) . . .
  attendant.. 4. Nike
  consort.. 6. Europa
  brother of.. 5. Hades 8. Poseidon
  deity.. 7. supreme 12. father of gods
  father.. 6. Cronus
  games in his honor.. 6. Nemean
  8. Olympian
  messenger.. 4. Iris 6. Hermes
  mother.. 5. Rhea
  oracle.. 6. Dodona
  Roman.. 7. Jupiter
  sister.. 4. Hera
  son.. 4. Ares 5. Argus 6. Apollo,
  Hermes 7. Perseus 8. Dionysus,
  Hercules, Tantalus
  temple (Athens).. 10. Olympieion
  (Olympium)
ziara, ziarat... 4. tomb (Moslem saint)
  6. shrine
zibet, zibeth... 5. civet
ziganka... 5. dance (rustic)
zigeuner... 5. gypsy 7. czigany,
  Zincalo, zingaro
ziggurat... 11. temple tower
  12. Tower of Babel (Bib)
zigzag... 5. turns 6. angles 7. stagger
  8. flexuous, wavering 9. alternate
zimb... 3. fly

zimmis... 4. dish (food)
zinc (pert to) . . .
  alloy.. 5. bidri 7. paktong
  alloy with copper.. 6. oroide
  crude.. 7. tutenag (tutenague)
  slabs.. 6. solder 7. spelter
  symbol.. 2. Zn
zing... 3. pep, vim, zip 5. vigor
  6. energy, spirit, thrill
  10. enthusiasm
zingaresca (gypsy)... 4. song 5. dance
  11. composition
zingaro... 5. gypsy
Zion (pert to)... 4. hill (Jerusalem)
  10. Israelites 12. chosen people, the
  theocracy
zip... 4. zing 5. close, speed 6. energy
  8. pungency 10. sibilation
zizith... 7. fringes (Bib), tassels
zoanthropy... 9. monomania
  15. changed to animal (belief)
zobo... 6. hybrid 7. mongrel (yak and
  cow) 10. zebu and yak
zodiac... 4. belt, zone 5. stars
  7. circuit
zodiac signs (twelve)... 3. Leo
  5. Aries, Libra, Virgo 6. Cancer,
  Gemini, Pisces, Taurus 7. Scorpio
  8. Aquarius 9. Capricorn
  11. Capricornus, Sagittarius
zoetic... 5. vital 6. living 7. organic
zone... 4. area, band, belt, isle, path
  5. Canal, clime, girth, tract
  6. assise, circle, course, Frigid,
  region, Torrid 7. stratum 8. cincture,
  latitude 9. Temperate
zoo... 9. menagerie 10. collection
  12. animal garden
zoo, zo (comb form)... 6. animal
zoologist... 9. biologist, scientist
zoology (*science of*)... 7. animals
zoology, term... 8. ditakous (two eggs
  at a time), (two young at a time)
zoology branches... 8. taxonomy
  9. bionomics, phylogeny
  10. embryology, entomology
  11. herpetology, ornithology
zoopathology (*science of*)... 8. diseases
  (animal) 11. zoonosology
zoophilist... 11. animal lover
zoophobia... 13. fear of animals
zoophyte... 5. coral 6. sponge
  10. sea anemone
zootheism (*belief in*)... 10. animal gods
zootomy... 13. animal anatomy
  16. animal dissection
zootrophy... 13. animal rearing
zoril... 7. polecat, zorilla
Zoroaster, Zarathustra... 7. Persian
  8. reformer (Relig)
Zoroastrianism (pert to) . . .
  adherence to.. 5. Parse (Parsee)
  demon.. 4. deva
  doctrine.. 7. dualism 11. good and
  evil
  evil spirit.. 7. Ahriman
  fire worshiper.. 6. Gheber
  founder.. 9. Zoroaster
  literature.. 6. Avesta
  lord of creation.. 6. Ormazd
  religion of.. 6. Persia (anc)
zorrillo... 5. skunk

zoster... 4. zona 6. girdle 8. shingles
(Med) 12. herpes zoster
Zouave... 4. Zu–Zu 8. chasseur
11. infantryman
Zu (Bab Myth)... 8. storm god (evil)
9. blackbird (symbol)
Zuider Zee (pert to)...
  gulf.. 8. North Sea
  Netherlands.. 4. dike 7. highway
  present name.. 9. Ijsel Lake, Ijselmeer
zuisin... 7. widgeon
Zulu (pert to)...
  army.. 4. impi 7. Kaffirs
  boy.. 6. umfaan
  conference.. 6. indaba
  marauders.. 4. Viti
  people.. 6. Santus 7. Kaffirs
  spear.. 7. assagai (assegai)

Zululand capital... 6. Eshowe
Zuñi (pert to)...
  famed for.. 19. Seven Cities of Cibola
  (Myth)
  Indian.. 4. Hopi 6. Ashivi
  kingdom of Cibola.. 16. gold–paved
  streets (Myth)
zwieback... 4. rusk 7. biscuit (toasted)
Zwinger... 6. palace (Dresden)
zygal... 7. H–shaped
zygodactyl (zygodactyle)...
  8. yoke–toed 10. paired toes
zygon... 5. bench 6. thwart 9. brain
part
zygous... 5. yoked 6. paired
zymology *(science of)*...
  12. fermentation
zymosis... 12. fermentation
zythum... 4. beer (anc Egypt)

?????

___ 49891   THE QUICK AND EASY WAY TO
                EFFECTIVE SPEAKING $3.50

___ 44739   SHORT CUTS TO EFFECTIVE ENGLISH,
                Harry Shefter $2.95

___ 53087   6 MINUTES A DAY TO PERFECT SPELLING,
                Harry Shefter $3.50

___ 47761   6 WEEKS TO WORDS OF POWER,
                Wilfred Funk $3.50

___ 53031   30 DAYS TO A MORE
                POWERFUL VOCABULARY $3.50

___ 44294   THE WASHINGTON SQUARE PRESS
                HANDBOOK OF GOOD ENGLISH
                Edward D. Johnson $4.95

___ 53154   WORDS MOST OFTEN MISSPELLED AND
                MISPRONOUNCED,
                Gleeson & Colvin $3.50